VISUAL C#® 2005

HOW TO PROGRAM

SECOND EDITION

Deitel® Ser

How To Program Series

Advanced Java™ 2 Platform How to Program

C How to Program, 4/e

C++ How to Program, 5/e—Including Cyber Classroom

e-Business and e-Commerce How to Program

Internet and World Wide Web How to Program, 3/e

Java™ How to Program, 6/e—Including Cyber Classroom

Perl How to Program

Python How to Program

Small C++ How to Program, 5/e – Including Cyber Classroom

Small Java™ How to Program, 6/e– Including Cyber Classroom

Visual C++® .NET How to Program

Visual C#® 2005 How to Program, 2/e

Visual Basic® 2005 How to Program, 3/e

Wireless Internet & Mobile Business How to Program

XML How to Program

ies Page

Simply Series

Simply C++: An Application-Driven Tutorial Approach

Simply C#: An Application-Driven Tutorial Approach

Simply Java™ Programming: An Application-Driven Tutorial Approach

Simply Visual Basic® .NET: An Application-Driven Tutorial Approach (Visual Studio .NET 2002 Edition)

Simply Visual Basic® .NET 2003: An Application-Driven Tutorial Approach

Computer Science Series

Operating Systems, 3/e

Also Available

SafariX Web Books
www.SafariX.com

To follow the Deitel publishing program, please register at:

    www.deitel.com/newsletter/subscribe.html

for the free *Deitel® Buzz Online* e-mail newsletter.

To communicate with the authors, send e-mail to:

    deitel@deitel.com

For information on corporate on-site seminars offered by Deitel & Associates, Inc. worldwide, visit:

    www.deitel.com

or write to

    deitel@deitel.com

For continuing updates on Prentice Hall/Deitel publications visit:

    www.deitel.com,
    www.prenhall.com/deitel or
    www.InformIT.com/deitel

Library of Congress Cataloging-in-Publication Data
On file

Vice President and Editorial Director, ECS: *Marcia J. Horton*
Associate Editor: *Jennifer Cappello*
Assistant Editor: *Carole Snyder*
Executive Managing Editor: *Vince O'Brien*
Managing Editor: *Bob Engelhardt*
Production Editors: *Donna M. Crilly, Marta Samsel*
Director of Creative Services: *Paul Belfanti*
A/V Production Editor: *Xiaohong Zhu*
Art Studio: *Artworks, York, PA*
Creative Director: *Juan López*
Art Director: *Kristine Carney*
Cover Design: *Abbey S. Deitel, Harvey M. Deitel, Bob Depew, Kristine Carney*
Interior Design: *Harvey M. Deitel, Kristine Carney*
Manufacturing Manager: *Alexis Heydt-Long*
Manufacturing Buyer: *Lisa McDowell*
Executive Marketing Manager: *Robin O'Brien*
Marketing Assistant: *Barrie Reinhold*

© 2006 by Pearson Education, Inc.
Upper Saddle River, New Jersey 07458

10 9 8 7 6 5 4 3 2 1

ISBN 0-13-152523-9

Pearson Education Ltd., *London*
Pearson Education Australia Pty. Ltd., *Sydney*
Pearson Education Singapore, Pte. Ltd.
Pearson Education North Asia Ltd., *Hong Kong*
Pearson Education Canada, Inc., *Toronto*
Pearson Educacion de Mexico, S.A. de C.V.
Pearson Education–Japan, *Tokyo*
Pearson Education Malaysia, Pte. Ltd.
Pearson Education, Inc., *Upper Saddle River, New Jersey*

VISUAL C#® 2005

HOW TO PROGRAM

SECOND EDITION

H. M. Deitel

Deitel & Associates, Inc.

P. J. Deitel

Deitel & Associates, Inc.

Upper Saddle River, New Jersey 07458

Trademarks

To José Antonio González Seco:

It's a privilege for us to work with such an extraordinary and unselfish reviewer. Extraordinary with regard to the depth and breadth of your C# knowledge—and unselfish with regard to the remarkable amount of time you devoted to helping us "get it right."

Harvey M. Deitel and Paul J. Deitel

Contents

6   Control Statements: Part 2   223

7   Methods: A Deeper Look   272

11 Polymorphism, Interfaces & Operator Overloading   **508**

15   Multithreading   719

16   Strings, Characters and Regular Expressions   765

Preface

"Live in fragments no longer, only connect."
—Edgar Morgan Foster

Welcome to C# and the world of Windows, Internet and Web programming with Visual Studio 2005 and the .NET 2.0 platform! This book presents leading-edge computing technologies for computer science students, software developers and IT professionals.

At Deitel & Associates, we write computer science textbooks for college students and professional books for software developers. We also teach this material in industry seminars at organizations worldwide.

This book was a joy to create. To start, we put the previous edition under the microscope:

- We audited our C# presentation against the most recent Ecma and Microsoft C# Language Specifications, which can be found at `www.ecma-international.org/publications/standards/Ecma-334.html` and `msdn.microsoft.com/vcsharp/programming/language/`, respectively.

- All of the chapters have been significantly updated and upgraded.

- We changed to an early classes and objects pedagogy. Now readers build reusable classes starting in Chapter 4.

- We updated our object-oriented presentation to use the latest version of the *UML (Unified Modeling Language)—UML™ 2.0*—the industry-standard graphical language for modeling object-oriented systems.

- We added an optional OOD/UML automated teller machine (ATM) case study in Chapters 1, 3–9 and 11. The case study includes a complete C# code implementation of the ATM in Appendix J.

- We added several multi-section object-oriented programming case studies.

- We incorporated key new features of Microsoft's latest release of C#—Visual C# 2005—and added discussions on generics, .NET remoting and debugging.

- We significantly enhanced our treatment of XML, ADO.NET, ASP.NET and Web services.

All of this has been carefully scrutinized by a substantial team of academics, .NET industry developers and members of the Microsoft C# development team.

We believe that this book and its support materials have everything instructors and students need for an informative, interesting, challenging and entertaining C# educational experience. In this Preface, we overview various conventions used in the book, such as syntax shading the code examples and code highlighting. We also discuss the book's comprehensive suite of ancillary materials that help instructors maximize their students' learning experience, including the Prentice Hall *Instructor's Resource Center*, PowerPoint® Slide lecture notes, companion Web site, SafariX (Pearson Education's WebBook publications) and more.

Visual C# 2005 How to Program, 2/e presents 230 complete, working C# programs and depicts their inputs and outputs in actual screen shots of running programs. This is our signature "live-code" approach—we present concepts in the context of complete working programs.

As you read this book, if you have questions, send an e-mail to deitel@deitel.com; we will respond promptly. For updates on this book and the status of C# software, and for the latest news on all Deitel publications and services, visit www.deitel.com regularly and be sure to sign up for the free *Deitel® Buzz Online* e-mail newsletter at www.deitel.com/newsletter/subscribe.html.

Before You Begin

Downloading Microsoft Visual C# 2005 Express Edition Software

On November 7, 2005 Microsoft released its Visual Studio 2005 development tools, including the Visual C# 2005 Express Edition. Per Microsoft's Web site, Microsoft Express Editions are "lightweight, easy-to-use and easy-to-learn tools for the hobbyist, novice and student developer." This product is available free for download through November 6, 2006. After this date, if you have already downloaded the software, it will still work. However, if you need to download the software after this one-year period, Microsoft may charge a fee for the download.

You may use this software to compile and execute the example programs in the book. You can download Visual C# 2005 Express Edition at:

> msdn.microsoft.com/vstudio/express/

Microsoft provides a dedicated forum for help using the Express Edition:

> forums.microsoft.com/msdn/ShowForum.aspx?ForumID=24

Visual C# 2005 How to Program, 2/e Code Examples

The book's source code is available free for download at **www.deitel.com/books/csharphtp2/**. We assume that you are using Microsoft Windows. If you are running a different operating system and have questions about copying the example files to your computer, please see your instructor.

Once you download the complete examples.zip file, extract the files to the C:\ folder on your computer. This will create an examples folder that contains subfolders for each chapter (e.g., ch01, ch02, etc.).

Additional Software Downloads

For the examples in Chapter 17, Graphics and Multimedia, we use Microsoft Agent. If students use the examples in a lab environment, more than likely this software will have to be installed as part of the lab setup.

> www.microsoft.com/msagent/downloads/default.asp

For Chapter 20, you will need SQL Server 2005 Express Edition (also available as part of the Visual C# 2005 Express Edition download) msdn.microsoft.com/vstudio/express/sql/

For Chapters 21 and 22, you will need Visual Web Developer 2005 Express Edition

msdn.microsoft.com/vstudio/express/vwd/

We provide updates on the status of this software at www.deitel.com and in our free e-mail newsletter www.deitel.com/newsletter/subscribe.html.

Features in *Visual C# 2005 How to Program, 2/e*

This new edition contains many new and enhanced features.

Updated for Visual Studio 2005, C# 2.0 and .NET 2.0

We updated the entire text to reflect Microsoft's latest release of Visual C# 2005. New items include:

- Screenshots updated to the Visual Studio 2005 IDE.
- Property accessors with different access modifiers.
- Viewing exception data with the Exception Assistant (a new feature of the Visual Studio 2005 Debugger).
- Using drag-and-drop techniques to create data-bound windows forms in ADO.NET 2.0.
- Using the IDE's **Data Sources** window to create application-wide data connections.
- Using a BindingSource to simplify the process of binding controls to an underlying data source in ADO.NET 2.0.
- Using a BindingNavigator to enable simple navigation, insertion, deletion and editing of database data on a Windows Form.
- Using the **Master Page Designer** to create a common look and feel for ASP.NET Web pages.
- Using Visual Studio 2005 smart tag menus to perform many of the most common programming tasks when new controls are dragged onto a Windows Form or ASP.NET Web page.
- Using Visual Web Developer's built-in Web server to test ASP.NET 2.0 applications and Web services.
- Using an XmlDataSource to bind XML data sources to a control.
- Using a SqlDataSource to bind a SQL Server database to a control or set of controls.
- Using an ObjectDataSource to bind a control to an object that serves as a data source.
- Using the ASP.NET 2.0 "login" and "create new user" controls to personalize access to Web applications.

- Using generics and generic collections to create general models of methods and classes that can be declared once, but used with many types of data.
- Using generic collections from the `Systems.Collections.Generic` namespace.

New Interior Design

Working with the creative services team at Prentice Hall, we redesigned the interior styles for our *How to Program Series* books. In response to reader requests, we now place the key terms and the index's page reference for each defining occurrence in ***bold italic*** text for easier reference. We emphasize on-screen components in the **bold Helvetica** font (e.g., the **File** menu) and emphasize C# program text in the `Lucida` font (for example, `int x = 5`).

Syntax Shading

We syntax shade all the C# code, similar to the way most C# integrated-development environments and code editors syntax color code. This greatly improves code readability—an especially important goal, given that this book contains 17,500+ lines of code. Our syntax-shading conventions are as follows:

```
comments appear in italic
keywords appear in bold, italic
errors and JSP scriptlet delimiters appear in bold, black
constants and literal values appear in bold, gray
all other code appears in plain, black
```

Code Highlighting

Extensive code highlighting makes it easy for readers to spot each program's featured code segments—we place white rectangles around the key code.

Early Classes and Objects Approach

We still introduce basic object-technology concepts and terminology in Chapter 1. In the previous edition, we developed custom classes in Chapter 9, but in this edition, we start doing that in the completely new Chapter 4. Chapters 5–8 have been carefully rewritten with an "early classes and objects approach."

Carefully Tuned Treatment of Object-Oriented Programming in Chapters 9–11

We performed a high-precision upgrade of *Visual C# 2005 How to Program, 2/e*. This edition is clearer and more accessible—especially if you are new to object-oriented programming (OOP). We completely rewrote the OOP chapters, integrating an employee payroll class hierarchy case study and motivating interfaces with an accounts payable hierarchy.

Case Studies

We include many case studies, some spanning multiple sections and chapters:

- The `GradeBook` class in Chapters 4, 5, 6 and 8.
- The optional, OOD/UML ATM system in the Software Engineering sections of Chapters 1, 3–9 and 11.
- The `Time` class in several sections of Chapter 9.
- The `Employee` payroll application in Chapters 10 and 11.
- The `GuestBook` ASP.NET application in Chapter 21.

- The secure book database ASP.NET application in Chapter 21.
- The airline reservation Web service in Chapter 22.

Integrated GradeBook Case Study

To reinforce our early classes presentation, we present an integrated case study using classes and objects in Chapters 4–6 and 8. We incrementally build a GradeBook class that represents an instructor's grade book and performs various calculations based on a set of student grades—finding the average, finding the maximum and minimum, and printing a bar chart. Our goal is to familiarize you with the important concepts of objects and classes through a real-world example of a substantial class. We develop this class from the ground up, constructing methods from control statements and carefully developed algorithms, and adding instance variables and arrays as needed to enhance the functionality of the class.

The Unified Modeling Language (UML)—Using the UML 2.0 to Develop an Object-Oriented Design of an ATM

The Unified Modeling Language™ (UML™) has become the preferred graphical modeling language for designing object-oriented systems. All the UML diagrams in the book comply with the UML 2.0 specification. We use UML class diagrams to visually represent classes and their inheritance relationships, and we use UML activity diagrams to demonstrate the flow of control in each of C#'s control statements.

This *Second Edition* includes a new, optional (but highly recommended) case study on object-oriented design using the UML. The case study was reviewed by a distinguished team of OOD/UML academic and industry professionals, including leaders in the field from Rational (the creators of the UML and now a division of IBM) and the Object Management Group (responsible for maintaining and evolving the UML). In the case study, we design and fully implement the software for a simple automated teller machine (ATM). The Software Engineering Case Study sections at the ends of Chapters 1, 3–9 and 11 present a carefully paced introduction to object-oriented design using the UML. We introduce a concise, simplified subset of the UML 2.0, then guide the reader through a first design experience intended for the novice object-oriented designer/programmer. The case study is not an exercise; rather, it is an end-to-end learning experience that concludes with a detailed walkthrough of the complete C# code. The Software Engineering Case Study sections help readers develop an object-oriented design to complement the object-oriented programming concepts they begin learning in Chapter 1 and implementing in Chapter 4. In the first of these sections at the end of Chapter 1, we introduce basic OOD concepts and terminology. In the optional Software Engineering Case Study sections at the ends of Chapters 3–6, we consider more substantial issues, as we undertake a challenging problem with the techniques of OOD. We analyze a typical requirements document that specifies the system to be built, determine the classes needed to implement that system, determine the attributes the classes need to have, determine the behaviors the classes need to exhibit and specify how the classes must interact with one another to meet the system requirements. In Appendix J, we include a complete C# implementation of the object-oriented system that we design in the earlier chapters. We employ a carefully developed, incremental object-oriented design process to produce a UML model for our ATM system. From this design, we produce a substantial working C# implementation using key programming notions, including classes, objects, encapsulation, visibility, composition, inheritance and polymorphism.

Web Forms, Web Controls and ASP.NET 2.0

The .NET platform enables developers to create robust, scalable Web-based applications. Microsoft's .NET server-side technology, Active Server Pages (ASP) .NET, allows programmers to build Web documents that respond to client requests. To enable interactive Web pages, server-side programs process information users input into HTML forms. ASP .NET provides enhanced visual programming capabilities, similar to those used in building Windows forms for desktop programs. Programmers can create Web pages visually, by dragging and dropping Web controls onto Web forms. Chapter 21, ASP.NET, Web Forms and Web Controls, introduces these powerful technologies.

Web Services and ASP.NET 2.0

Microsoft's .NET strategy embraces the Internet and Web as integral to software development and deployment. Web services technology enables information sharing, e-commerce and other interactions using standard Internet protocols and technologies, such as Hypertext Transfer Protocol (HTTP), Extensible Markup Language (XML) and Simple Object Access Protocol (SOAP). Web services enable programmers to package application functionality in a manner that turns the Web into a library of reusable software components. In Chapter 22, we present a Web service that allows users to manipulate huge integers—integers too large to be represented with C#'s built-in data types. In this example, a user enters two huge integers and presses buttons to invoke Web services that add, subtract and compare the two integers. We also present a Blackjack Web service and a database-driven airline reservation system.

Object-Oriented Programming

Object-oriented programming is the most widely employed technique for developing robust, reusable software. This text offers a rich treatment of C#'s object-oriented programming features. Chapter 4 introduces how to create classes and objects. These concepts are extended in Chapter 9. Chapter 10 discusses how to create powerful new classes quickly by using inheritance to "absorb" the capabilities of existing classes. Chapter 11 familiarizes the reader with the crucial concepts of polymorphism, abstract classes, concrete classes and interfaces, which facilitate powerful manipulations among objects belonging to an inheritance hierarchy.

XML

Use of the Extensible Markup Language (XML) is exploding in the software-development industry and in the e-business community, and is pervasive throughout the .NET platform. Because XML is a platform-independent technology for describing data and for creating markup languages, XML's data portability integrates well with C#-based portable applications and services. Chapter 19 introduces XML, XML markup and the technologies, such as DTDs and Schema, which are used to validate XML documents' contents. We also explain how to manipulate XML documents programmatically using the Document Object Model (DOM™) and how to transform XML documents into other types of documents via Extensible Stylesheet Language Transformation (XSLT) technology.

ADO.NET 2.0

Databases store vast amounts of information that individuals and organizations must access to conduct business. As an evolution of Microsoft's ActiveX Data Objects (ADO) technology, ADO.NET represents a new approach for building applications that interact with databases. ADO.NET uses XML and an enhanced object model to provide developers with the tools they need to access and manipulate databases for large-scale, extensible, mission-critical multi-tier applications. Chapter 20 introduces the capabilities of ADO.NET and the Structured Query Language (SQL) to manipulate databases.

Visual Studio 2005 Debugger

In Appendix C we explain how to use key debugger features, such as setting "breakpoints" and "watches," stepping into and out of methods, and examining the method call stack.

Teaching Approach

Visual C# 2005 How to Program, 2/e contains a rich collection of examples that have been tested on Windows 2000 and Windows XP. The book concentrates on the principles of good software engineering and stresses program clarity. We avoid arcane terminology and syntax specifications in favor of teaching by example. We are educators who teach leading-edge topics in industry classrooms worldwide. Dr. Harvey M. Deitel has 20 years of college teaching experience and 15 years of industry teaching experience. Paul Deitel has 12 years of industry teaching experience—he has taught courses at all levels to government, industry, military and academic clients of Deitel & Associates.

Learning C# via the Live-Code Approach

Visual C# 2005 How to Program, 2/e is loaded with live-code examples—each new concept is presented in the context of a complete working C# application that is immediately followed by one or more sample executions showing the program's inputs and outputs. This style exemplifies the way we teach and write about programming. We call this method of teaching and writing the "live-code" approach.

World Wide Web Access

All of the source-code examples for *Visual C# 2005 How to Program, 2/e,* (and for our other publications) are available for download from:

```
www.deitel.com/books/csharphtp2/
www.prenhall.com/deitel
```

Registration is quick and easy, and the downloads are free. Download all the examples, then run each program as you read the corresponding text discussions. Making changes to the examples and immediately seeing the effects of those changes is a great way to enhance your C# learning experience.

Objectives

Each chapter begins with a statement of objectives. This lets students know what to expect and gives them an opportunity, after reading the chapter, to determine if they have met these objectives.

Quotations

The learning objectives are followed by quotations. Some are humorous, philosophical or offer interesting insights. We hope that you will enjoy relating the quotations to the chapter material. Many of the quotations are worth a second look after reading the chapter.

Outline

The chapter outline helps students approach the material in a top-down fashion, so they can anticipate what is to come, and set a comfortable and effective learning pace.

17,544 Lines of Code in 230 Example Programs (with Program Outputs)

Our live-code programs range in size from just a few lines of code to substantial examples containing hundreds of lines of code (e.g., our ATM system implementation contains 655 lines of code). Each program is followed by a window containing the outputs produced when the program is run, so you can confirm that the programs run as expected. Our programs demonstrate the diverse features of C#. The code is syntax shaded, with C# keywords, comments and other program text emphasized with variations of bold, italic and gray text. This facilitates reading the code, especially when you're reading the larger programs.

725 Illustrations/Figures

An abundance of charts, tables, line drawings, programs and program outputs is included. We model the flow of control in control statements with UML activity diagrams. UML class diagrams model the fields, constructors and methods of classes. We use additional types of UML diagrams throughout our optional OOD/UML ATM case study.

317 Programming Tips

We include programming tips to help students focus on important aspects of program development. We highlight these tips in the form of *Good Programming Practices, Common Programming Errors, Error-Prevention Tips, Look-and-Feel Observations, Performance Tips, Portability Tips* and *Software Engineering Observations*. These tips and practices represent the best we have gleaned from a combined six decades of programming and teaching experience. One of our students—a mathematics major—told us that she feels this approach is like the highlighting of axioms, theorems and corollaries in mathematics books; it provides a basis on which to build good software.

Good Programming Practice 3.1

Good Programming Practices call attention to techniques that will help you produce programs that are clearer, more understandable and more maintainable.

Common Programming Error 3.1

Students learning a language tend to make certain kinds of errors frequently. Pointing out these Common Programming Errors reduces the likelihood that readers will make the same mistakes.

Error-Prevention Tip 3.1

When we first designed this tip type, we thought the tips would contain suggestions for exposing bugs and removing them from programs. In fact, many of the tips describe aspects of C# that prevent bugs from getting into programs in the first place, thus simplifying the testing and debugging processes.

Look-and-Feel Observation 3.1

We provide Look-and-Feel Observations *to highlight graphical-user-interface conventions. These observations help you design attractive, user-friendly graphical user interfaces that conform to industry norms.*

Performance Tip 3.1

Students like to "turbo charge" their programs. We include Performance Tips *that highlight opportunities for improving program performance—making programs run faster or minimizing the amount of memory that they occupy.*

Portability Tip 3.1

We include Portability Tips *to help you write portable code and to explain how C# achieves its high degree of portability.*

Software Engineering Observation 3.1

The object-oriented programming paradigm necessitates a complete rethinking of the way we build software systems. C# is an effective language for achieving good software engineering. The Software Engineering Observations *highlight architectural and design issues that affect the construction of software systems, especially large-scale systems.*

Wrap-Up Section

Each chapter ends with a brief "wrap-up" section that recaps the chapter content and transitions to the next chapter.

Summary Bullets

Each chapter ends with additional pedagogical devices. We present a thorough, bullet-list-style summary of the chapter. This helps the students review and reinforce key concepts.

Terminology

We include an alphabetized list of the important terms defined in each chapter—again, for further reinforcement. Each term also appears in the index, and the defining occurrence of each term is highlighted in the index with a ***bold, italic*** page number so the student can locate the definitions of terms quickly.

Self-Review Exercises and Answers

Extensive self-review exercises and answers are included for self-study. This gives you a chance to build confidence with the material and prepare for the regular exercises. We encourage students to do all the self-review exercises and check their answers.

Exercises

Each chapter concludes with a set of exercises, including simple recall of important terminology and concepts; writing individual C# statements; writing small portions of C# methods and classes; writing complete C# methods, classes and applications; and writing major term projects. The large number of exercises across a wide variety of areas enables instructors to tailor their courses to the unique needs of their classes and to vary course assignments each semester. Instructors can use these exercises to form homework assignments, short quizzes and/or major examinations. The solutions for the vast majority of the exercises are included in the Prentice Hall *Instructor's Resource Center,* which is *available only to instructors* through their Prentice Hall representatives. [**NOTE: Please do not write to us requesting access to the Prentice Hall Instructor's Resource Center. Access is limited strictly to college instructors teaching from the book. Instructors may obtain access only through their Prentice Hall representatives.**]

Approximately 5500 Index Entries

We have included an extensive index which is especially useful to developers who use the book as a reference.

"Double Indexing" of C# Live-Code Examples

Visual C# 2005 How to Program, 2/e has 230 live-code examples, which we have double indexed. For every source-code program in the book, we indexed the figure caption both alphabetically and as a subindex item under "Examples." This makes it easier to find examples using particular features.

A Tour of the Optional Case Study on Object-Oriented Design with the UML

In this section we tour the book's optional case study on object-oriented design with the UML. This tour previews the contents of the Software Engineering Case Study sections (in Chapters 1, 3–9, 11 and Appendix J). After completing this case study, you will be thoroughly familiar with an object-oriented design and implementation for a significant C# application.

The design presented in the ATM case study was developed at Deitel & Associates, Inc. and scrutinized by academic and industry professionals. Our primary goal was to create a simple design that would be clear to OOD and UML novices, while still demonstrating key OOD concepts and the related UML modeling techniques.

Section 1.17—(Only Required Section of the Case Study) **Software Engineering Case Study: Introduction to Object Technology and the UML**—introduces the object-oriented design case study with the UML. The section presents basic concepts and terminology of object technology, including classes, objects, encapsulation, inheritance and polymorphism. We discuss the history of the UML. This is the only required section of the case study.

Section 3.10—(Optional) **Software Engineering Case Study: Examining the ATM Requirements Document**—discusses a *requirements document* that specifies the requirements for a system that we will design and implement—the software for a simple automated teller machine (ATM). We investigate the structure and behavior of object-oriented systems in general. We discuss how the UML will facilitate the design process in subsequent Software Engineering Case Study sections by providing several additional types of diagrams to model our system. We include a list of URLs and book references on object-oriented design with the UML. We discuss the interaction between the ATM system and its user. Specifically, we investigate the scenarios that may occur between the user and the system itself—these are called *use cases*. We model these interactions, using UML *use case diagrams*.

Section 4.11—(Optional) **Software Engineering Case Study: Identifying the Classes in the ATM Requirements Documents**—begins to design the ATM system. We identify its classes by extracting the nouns and noun phrases from the requirements document. We arrange these classes into a UML class diagram that describes the class structure of our simulation. The class diagram also describes relationships, known as *associations*, among classes.

Section 5.12—(Optional) Software Engineering Case Study: Identifying Class Attributes in the ATM System—focuses on the attributes of the classes discussed in Section 3.10. A class contains both *attributes* (data) and *operations* (behaviors). As we see in later sections, changes in an object's attributes often affect the object's behavior. To determine the attributes for the classes in our case study, we extract the adjectives describing the nouns and noun phrases (which defined our classes) from the requirements document, then place the attributes in the class diagram we created in Section 3.10.

Section 6.10—(Optional) Software Engineering Case Study: Identifying Objects' States and Activities in the ATM System—discusses how an object, at any given time, occupies a specific condition called a *state*. A *state transition* occurs when the object receives a message to change state. The UML provides the *state machine diagram*, which identifies the set of possible states that an object may occupy and models that object's state transitions. An object also has an *activity*—the work it performs in its lifetime. The UML provides the *activity diagram*—a flowchart that models an object's activity. In this section, we use both types of diagrams to begin modeling specific behavioral aspects of our ATM system, such as how the ATM carries out a withdrawal transaction and how the ATM responds when the user is authenticated.

Section 7.15—(Optional) Software Engineering Case Study: Identifying Class Operations in the ATM System—identifies the operations, or services, of our classes. We extract from the requirements document the verbs and verb phrases that specify the operations for each class. We then modify the class diagram of Section 3.10 to include each operation with its associated class. At this point in the case study, we will have gathered all information possible from the requirements document. As future chapters introduce such topics as inheritance, we will modify our classes and diagrams.

Section 8.14—(Optional) Software Engineering Case Study: Collaboration Among Objects in the ATM System—provides a "rough sketch" of the model for our ATM system. In this section, we see how it works. We investigate the behavior of the simulation by discussing *collaborations*—messages that objects send to each other to communicate. The class operations that we discovered in Section 6.10 turn out to be the collaborations among the objects in our system. We determine the collaborations, then collect them into a *communication diagram*—the UML diagram for modeling collaborations. This diagram reveals which objects collaborate and when. We present a communication diagram of the collaborations among objects to perform an ATM balance inquiry. We then present the UML *sequence diagram* for modeling interactions in a system. This diagram emphasizes the chronological ordering of messages. A sequence diagram models how objects in the system interact to carry out withdrawal and deposit transactions.

Section 9.17—(Optional) Software Engineering Case Study: Starting to Program the Classes of the ATM System—takes a break from designing the behavior of our system. We begin the implementation process to emphasize the material discussed in Chapter 8. Using the UML class diagram of Section 3.10 and the attributes and operations discussed in Section 4.11 and Section 6.10, we show how to implement a class in C# from a design. We do not implement all classes—because we have not completed the design process. Working from our UML diagrams, we create code for the `Withdrawal` class.

Section 11.9—(Optional) Software Engineering Case Study: Incorporating Inheritance and Polymorphism into the ATM System—continues our discussion of object-oriented programming. We consider inheritance—classes sharing common characteristics may inherit attributes and operations from a "base" class. In this section, we investigate how our ATM system can benefit from using inheritance. We document our discoveries in a class diagram that models inheritance relationships—the UML refers to these relationships as *generalizations*. We modify the class diagram of Section 3.10 by using inheritance to group classes with similar characteristics. This section concludes the design of the model portion of our simulation. We implement this model in C# in Appendix J.

Appendix J—ATM Case Study Code—The majority of the case study involves designing the model (i.e., the data and logic) of the ATM system. In this appendix, we fully implement that model in C#, using all the UML diagrams we created. We apply the concepts of object-oriented design with the UML and object-oriented programming in C# that you learned in the chapters. By the end of this appendix, you will have completed the design and implementation of a real-world system, and should feel confident tackling larger systems, such as those that professional software engineers build.

Appendix K—UML 2: Additional Diagrams Types—Overviews the UML 2 diagram types not discussed the OOD/UML Case Study.

Teaching Resources for *Visual C# 2005 How to Program, 2/e*

Visual C# 2005 How to Program, 2/e, has extensive instructor resources. The Prentice Hall *Instructor's Resource Center* contains the *Solutions Manual* with solutions to the vast majority of the end-of-chapter exercises, a *Test Item File* of multiple-choice questions (approximately two per book section) and PowerPoint slides containing all the code and figures in the text, plus bulleted items that summarize the key points in the text. Instructors can customize the slides. If you are not already a registered faculty member, contact your Prentice Hall representative or visit `vig.prenhall.com/replocator/`.

Deitel® *Buzz Online* Free E-mail Newsletter

Our free e-mail newsletter, the *Deitel*® *Buzz Online*, includes commentary on industry trends and developments, links to free articles and resources from our published books and upcoming publications, product-release schedules, errata, challenges, anecdotes, information on our corporate instructor-led training courses and more. It's also a good way for you to keep posted about issues related to *Visual C# 2005 How to Program, 2/e*. To subscribe, visit

```
www.deitel.com/newsletter/subscribe.html
```

Acknowledgments

It is a great pleasure to acknowledge the efforts of many people whose names may not appear on the cover, but whose hard work, cooperation, friendship and understanding were crucial to the production of the book. Many people at Deitel & Associates, Inc. devoted long hours to this project.

- Andrew B. Goldberg is a Computer Science graduate of Amherst College. Andrew updated Chapters 19–22. He co-designed and co-authored the new, optional OOD/UML ATM case study. He also co-authored Appendices J and K.

- Su Zhang holds B.Sc. and a M.Sc. degrees in Computer Science from McGill University. Su contributed to Chapters 26 and 27 as well as Appendix J.

- Cheryl Yaeger graduated from Boston University with a bachelor's degree in Computer Science. Cheryl helped update Chapters 3–14.

- Barbara Deitel, Chief Financial Officer at Deitel & Associates, Inc. applied copyedits to the book.

- Abbey Deitel, President of Deitel & Associates, Inc., and an Industrial Management graduate of Carnegie Mellon University, co-authored Chapter 1.

- Christi Kelsey, a graduate of Purdue University with a degree in business and a minor in information systems, co-authored Chapter 2, the Preface and Appendix C. She edited the Index and paged the entire manuscript. She also worked closely with the production team at Prentice Hall coordinating virtually every aspect of the production of the book.

We would also like to thank three participants of our Honors Internship and Co-op programs who contributed to this publication—Nick Santos, a Computer Science major at Dartmouth College; Jeffrey Peng, a Computer Science student at Cornell University and William Chen, a Computer Science student at Cornell University.

We are fortunate to have worked on this project with the talented and dedicated team of publishing professionals at Prentice Hall. We especially appreciate the extraordinary efforts of Marcia Horton, Editorial Director of Prentice Hall's Engineering and Computer Science Division. Jennifer Cappello and Dolores Mars did an extraordinary job recruiting the review team for this book and managing the review process. Bob Depew and Kristine Carney did a wonderful job updating the book's cover. Vince O'Brien, Bob Engelhardt, Donna Crilly and Marta Samsel did a marvelous job managing the production of the book.

We'd like to give special thanks to Dan Fernandez, C# Product Manager, and Janie Schwark, Senior Business Manager, Division of Developer Marketing, both of Microsoft for their special effort in working with us on this project. And thanks to the many other members of the Microsoft team who answered our questions throughout this process:

Anders Hejlsburg, Technical Fellow (C#)
Brad Abrams, Lead Program Manager (.NET Framework)
Jim Miller, Software Architect (.NET Framework)
Joe Duffy, Program Manager (.NET Framework)
Joe Stegman, Lead Program Manager (Windows Forms)
Kit George, Program Manager (.NET Framework)
Luca Bolognese, Lead Program Manager (C#)
Luke Hoban, Program Manager (C#)
Mads Torgersen, Program Manager (C#)
Peter Hallam, Software Design Engineer (C#)
Scott Nonnenberg, Program Manager (C#)
Shamez Rajan, Program Manager (Visual Basic)

We wish to acknowledge the efforts of our reviewers. Adhering to a tight time schedule, they scrutinized the text and the programs, providing countless suggestions for improving the accuracy and completeness of the presentation.

Microsoft Reviewers
George Bullock, Program Manager at Microsoft, `Microsoft.com` Community Team
Dharmesh Chauhan, Microsoft
Shon Katzenberger, Microsoft
Matteo Taveggia, Microsoft
Matt Tavis, Microsoft

Industry Reviewers
Alex Bondarev, Investor's Bank and Trust
Peter Bromberg, Senior Architect Merrill Lynch and C# MVP
Vijay Cinnakonda, TrueCommerce, Inc.
Jay Cook, Alcon Laboratories
Jeff Cowan, Magenic, Inc.
Ken Cox, Independent Consultant, Writer and Developer and ASP.NET MVP
Stochio Goutsev, Independent Consultant, writer and developer and C# MVP
James Huddleston, Independent Consultant
Rex Jaeschke, Independent Consultant and Editor of the *C# Standard ECMA-334, 2005*, produced by committee Ecma TC39/TG2.
Saurabh Nandu, AksTech Solutions Pvt. Ltd.
Simon North, Quintiq BV
Mike O'Brien, State of California Employment Development Department
José Antonio González Seco, Andalucia's Parliamient
Devan Shepard, XMaLpha Technologies
Pavel Tsekov, Caesar BSC
John Varghese, UBS
Stacey Yasenka, Software Developer at Hyland Software and C# MVP

Academic Reviewers
Rekha Bhowmik, California Lutheran University
Ayad Boudiab, Georgia Perimiter College
Harlan Brewer, University of Cincinnati
Sam Gill, San Francisco State University
Gavin Osborne, Saskatchewan Institute of Applied Science and Technology
Catherine Wyman, DeVry-Phoenix

Well, there you have it! C# is a powerful programming language that will help you write programs quickly and effectively. C# scales nicely into the realm of enterprise-systems development to help organizations build their business-critical and mission-critical information systems. As you read the book, we would sincerely appreciate your comments, criticisms, corrections and suggestions for improvement. Please address all correspondence to:

deitel@deitel.com

We will respond promptly, and we will post corrections and clarifications on our Web site:

www.deitel.com

We hope you enjoy reading *Visual C# 2005 How to Program, Second Edition* as much as we enjoyed writing it!

Dr. Harvey M. Deitel
Paul J. Deitel

About the Authors

Dr. Harvey M. Deitel, Chairman and Chief Strategy Officer of Deitel & Associates, Inc., has 44 years of academic and industry experience in the computer field. Dr. Deitel earned B.S. and M.S. degrees from the Massachusetts Institute of Technology and a Ph.D. from Boston University. He has 20 years of college teaching experience, including earning tenure and serving as the Chairman of the Computer Science Department at Boston College before founding Deitel & Associates, Inc., with his son, Paul J. Deitel. He and Paul are the co-authors of several dozen books and multimedia packages and they are writing many more. With translations published in Japanese, German, Russian, Spanish, Traditional Chinese, Simplified Chinese, Korean, French, Polish, Italian, Portuguese, Greek, Urdu and Turkish, the Deitels' texts have earned international recognition. Dr. Deitel has delivered hundreds of professional seminars to major corporations, academic institutions, government organizations and the military.

Paul J. Deitel, CEO and Chief Technical Officer of Deitel & Associates, Inc., is a graduate of the MIT's Sloan School of Management, where he studied Information Technology. Through Deitel & Associates, Inc., he has delivered Java, C and C++ courses to industry clients, including IBM, Sun Microsystems, Dell, Lucent Technologies, Fidelity, NASA at the Kennedy Space Center, the National Severe Storm Laboratory, White Sands Missile Range, Rogue Wave Software, Boeing, Stratus, Cambridge Technology Partners, Open Environment Corporation, One Wave, Hyperion Software, Adra Systems, Entergy, CableData Systems and many more. Paul is one of the world's most experienced Java trainers, having taught about 100 professional Java courses. He has also lectured on C++ and Java for the Boston Chapter of the Association for Computing Machinery. He and his father, Dr. Harvey M. Deitel, are the world's best-selling programming language textbook authors.

About Deitel & Associates, Inc.

Deitel & Associates, Inc., is an internationally recognized corporate training and content-creation organization specializing in computer programming languages, Internet and World Wide Web software technology, object technology education and Internet business development. The company provides instructor-led courses on major programming languages and platforms, such as Java, Advanced Java, C, C++, C#, Visual C++, Visual Basic, XML, Perl, Python, object technology, and Internet and World Wide Web programming. The founders of Deitel & Associates, Inc., are Dr. Harvey M. Deitel and Paul J. Deitel. The company's clients include many of the world's largest computer companies, government agencies, branches of the military and business organizations. Through its 29-year publishing partnership with Prentice Hall, Deitel & Associates, Inc. publishes leading-edge programming textbooks, professional books, interactive multimedia *Cyber Classrooms*, *Complete Training Courses*, Web-based training courses and e-content for popular course management systems such as WebCT, Blackboard and Pearson's CourseCompass. Deitel & Associates, Inc., and the authors can be reached via e-mail at:

> deitel@deitel.com

To learn more about Deitel & Associates, Inc., its publications and its worldwide *DIVE INTO*™ Series Corporate Training curriculum, see the last few pages of this book or visit:

> www.deitel.com

and subscribe to the free *Deitel*® *Buzz Online* e-mail newsletter at:

> www.deitel.com/newsletter/subscribe.html

Individuals wishing to purchase Deitel books, Cyber Classrooms, Complete Training Courses and Web-based training courses can do so through:

> www.deitel.com/books/index.html

Bulk orders by corporations and academic institutions should be placed directly with Prentice Hall.

1

Introduction to Computers, the Internet and Visual C#

The chief merit of language is clearness.

——Galen

High thoughts must have high language.

—Aristophanes

Our life is frittered away with detail. . . . Simplify, simplify.

—Henry David Thoreau

My object all sublime I shall achieve in time.

—W. S. Gilbert

Man is still the most extraordinary computer of all.

——John F. Kennedy

OBJECTIVES

In this chapter you will learn:

- Basic hardware and software concepts.
- The different types of programming languages.
- Which programming languages are most widely used.
- The history of the Visual C# programming language.
- Some basics of object technology.
- The history of the UML—the industry-standard object-oriented system modeling language.
- The history of the Internet and the World Wide Web.
- The motivation behind and an overview of the Microsoft's .NET initiative, which involves the Internet in developing and using software systems.
- To test-drive a Visual C# 2005 application that enables you to draw on the screen.

1.1 Introduction

Welcome to Visual C# (pronounced "C-Sharp") 2005! We have worked hard to provide you with accurate and complete information regarding this powerful computer programming language, which from this point forward, we shall generally refer to simply as C#. C# is appropriate for technically oriented people with little or no programming experience and for experienced programmers for use in building substantial information systems. *Visual C# 2005 How to Program, Second Edition* is an effective learning tool for each of these audiences. We hope that working with this book will be an informative, challenging and entertaining learning experience for you.

How can one book appeal to both novices and skilled programmers? The core of this book emphasizes achieving program clarity through the proven techniques of object-oriented programming (OOP) and event-driven programming. Nonprogrammers learn basic skills that underlie good programming; experienced developers receive a rigorous explanation of the language and may improve their programming styles. Perhaps most important, the book presents hundreds of complete, working C# programs and depicts their inputs and outputs. We call this the *live-code approach*. All of the book's examples may be downloaded from www.deitel.com/books/csharphtp2/index.html and www.prenhall.com/deitel.

Computer use is increasing in almost every field of endeavor. Computing costs have been decreasing dramatically due to rapid developments in both hardware and software technologies. Computers that might have filled large rooms and cost millions of dollars a few decades ago can now be inscribed on silicon chips smaller than a fingernail, costing a few dollars each. Fortunately, silicon is one of the most abundant materials on earth—it's an ingredient in common sand. Silicon chip technology has made computing so economical that about a billion general-purpose computers are in use worldwide, helping people in business, industry and government, and in their personal lives.

We hope that you will enjoy learning with *Visual C# 2005 How to Program, Second Edition*. You are embarking on a challenging and rewarding path. If you have any questions as you proceed, please send e-mail to

```
deitel@deitel.com
```

To keep current with C# developments at Deitel & Associates and to receive updates to this book, please register for our free e-mail newsletter, the *Deitel® Buzz Online,* at

```
www.deitel.com/newsletter/subscribe.html
```

1.2 What Is a Computer?

A *computer* is an electronic device capable of performing computations and making logical decisions at speeds millions, billions and even trillions of times faster than human being. For example, many of today's personal computers can perform a billion additions per second. A person operating a desk calculator could spend an entire lifetime performing calculations and still not complete as many calculations as even today's more modest personal computers can perform in one second. (Points to ponder: How would you know whether the person added the numbers correctly? How would you know whether the computer added the numbers correctly?) The most powerful computers are called *supercomputers*; some of these are already performing trillions of additions per second!

Computers process *data* under the control of sets of instructions called *computer programs*. These programs guide computers through orderly sets of actions that are specified by people known as *computer programmers*.

A computer consists of various devices referred to as *hardware* (e.g., the keyboard, screen, mouse, hard drive, memory, DVDs and processing units). The programs that run on a computer are referred to as *software* (e.g., word processing programs, e-mail and games). Hardware costs have been declining dramatically in recent years, to the point that personal computers have become a commodity. Historically, however, software development costs have risen steadily as programmers develop ever more powerful and complex applications without being able to significantly improve the software development process. In this book, you will learn object-oriented programming—a technology that is dramatically reducing software development costs.

1.3 Computer Organization

Regardless of differences in physical appearance, virtually every computer may be envisioned as being divided into six *logical units* or sections:

1. *Input unit.* This is the "receiving" section of the computer. It obtains information (data and computer programs) from *input devices* (e.g., the keyboard and the mouse) and places this information at the disposal of the other units so that it can be processed. Information also can be entered in many other ways, including by speaking to your computer, scanning images and having your computer receive information from a network, such as the Internet.

2. *Output unit.* This is the "shipping" section of the computer. It takes information that the computer has processed and places it on various *output devices* to make the information available for use outside the computer. Most information output from computers today is displayed on screens, printed on paper or used to control other devices. Computers also can output their information to networks, such as the Internet.

3. *Memory unit.* This is the rapid-access, relatively low-capacity "warehouse" section of the computer. The memory unit retains information entered through the input unit so that it will be immediately available for processing when needed. The memory unit also retains processed information until it can be placed on output devices by the output unit. Information in the memory unit is typically lost when the computer's power is turned off. The memory unit is often called either *memory* or *primary memory.* (Historically, this unit has been called "core memory," but that term is fading from use today.)

4. *Arithmetic and logic unit (ALU).* This is the "manufacturing" section of the computer. It is responsible for performing calculations, such as addition, subtraction, multiplication and division. It contains the decision mechanisms that allow the computer, for example, to compare two items from the memory unit to determine whether they are equal.

5. *Central processing unit (CPU).* This is the "administrative" section of the computer. It coordinates and supervises the operation of the other sections. The CPU tells the input unit when information should be read into the memory unit, tells the ALU when information from the memory unit should be used in calculations and tells the output unit when to send information from the memory unit to certain output devices. Many of today's computers have multiple CPUs and thus can perform many operations simultaneously—such computers are called *multiprocessors*.

6. *Secondary storage unit.* This is the long-term, high-capacity "warehousing" section of the computer. Programs or data not actively being used by the other units normally are placed on secondary storage devices, such as your hard drive, until they are again needed, hours, days, months or even years later. Information in secondary storage takes much longer to access than information in primary memory, but the cost per unit of secondary storage is much less than that of primary memory. Other secondary storage devices include CDs and DVDs, which can hold up to hundreds of millions of characters and billions of characters, respectively.

1.4 Early Operating Systems

Computers of the 1950s could perform only one *job* or *task* at a time. This is often called single-user *batch processing*. The computer runs one program at a time while processing data in groups or batches. In these early systems, users generally submitted their jobs to a computer center on decks of punched cards and often had to wait hours or even days before printouts were returned to their desks. Computers were very large (often filling entire rooms) and expensive (often costing millions of dollars). Personal computers did not exist; people did not have computers at their desks and in their homes.

Software systems called *operating systems* were developed to make using computers more convenient. Early operating systems smoothed and speeded up the transition between jobs, increasing the amount of work, or *throughput*, computers could process.

As computers became more powerful, it became evident that single-user batch processing was inefficient, because so much time was spent waiting for slow input/output devices to complete their tasks. It was thought that many jobs or tasks could share the resources of the computer to achieve better utilization. This is achieved by *multiprogramming*—the simultaneous operation of many jobs that are competing to share the computer's resources. With early multiprogramming operating systems, users still submitted jobs on decks of punched cards and waited hours or days for results.

In the 1960s, several groups in industry and the universities pioneered *timesharing* operating systems. Timesharing is a special case of multiprogramming in which users access the computer through terminals, typically devices with keyboards and screens. Dozens, or even hundreds, of users share the computer at once. The computer actually does not run the users' jobs simultaneously. Rather, it runs a small portion of one user's job, then moves on to service the next user, perhaps providing service to each user several times per second. Thus, the users' programs *appear* to be running simultaneously. An advantage of timesharing is that user requests receive almost immediate responses.

1.5 Personal Computing, Distributed Computing and Client/Server Computing

In the early years of computing, computer systems were too large and too expensive for individuals to own. In the 1970s, silicon chip technology appeared, making it possible for computers to be much smaller and so economical that individuals and small organizations could own the machines. In 1977, Apple Computer—creator of today's popular Macintosh personal computers and iPod digital music players—popularized *personal computing*. In 1981, IBM, the world's largest computer vendor, introduced the IBM Personal Computer, legitimizing personal computing in business, industry and government organizations.

These computers were "stand-alone" units—people transported disks back and forth between computers to share information (creating what was often called "sneakernet"). Although early personal computers were not powerful enough to timeshare several users, these machines could be linked together in computer networks, sometimes over telephone lines and sometimes in *local area networks* (*LANs*) within an organization. This led to the phenomenon of *distributed computing*, in which an organization's computing, instead of being performed only at some central computer installation, is distributed over networks to the geographically dispersed sites where the organization's work is performed. Personal computers were powerful enough to handle the computing requirements of individual users as well as the basic communications tasks of passing information between computers electronically.

Today's personal computers are as powerful as the million-dollar machines of just a few decades ago; complete personal computer systems often sell for as little as $500–1000. The most powerful desktop machines provide individual users with enormous capabilities. Information is shared easily across computer networks, where computers called *file servers* offer a common data store that may be used by *client* computers distributed throughout the network—hence the term *client/server computing*. In Chapters 19–22, you'll learn how to build Internet- and Web-based applications; we'll talk about Web servers (computers that distribute content over the Web) and Web clients (computers that request and receive the content offered up by Web servers).

1.6 Hardware Trends

Every year, people generally expect to pay at least a little more for most products and services. The opposite has been the case in the computer and communications fields, especially with regard to the costs of the hardware supporting these technologies. For many decades, hardware costs have fallen rapidly, if not precipitously. Every year or two, the capacities of computers have approximately doubled without any increase in price. This often is called *Moore's Law*, named after the person who first identified and explained the trend, Gordon Moore, co-founder of Intel—the company that manufactures the vast majority of the processors in today's personal computers. Moore's Law is especially true in relation to the amount of memory that computers have for programs, the amount of secondary storage (such as disk storage) they have to hold programs and data over longer periods of time, and their processor speeds—the speeds at which computers execute their programs (i.e., do their work). Similar growth has occurred in the communications field, in which costs have plummeted as enormous demand for communications bandwidth has attracted intense competition. We know of no other fields in which technology improves so quickly and costs fall so rapidly. Such phenomenal improvement in the computing and communications fields is truly fostering the so-called Information Revolution.

When computer use exploded in the 1960s and 1970s, many people discussed the dramatic improvements in human productivity that computing and communications would cause, but these improvements did not materialize. Organizations were spending vast sums of money on these technologies, but without realizing the expected productivity gains. The invention of microprocessor chip technology and its wide deployment in the late 1970s and 1980s laid the groundwork for the productivity improvements that individuals and businesses have achieved in recent years.

1.7 Microsoft's Windows® Operating System

Microsoft Corporation became the dominant software company in the 1980s and 1990s. In 1981, Microsoft released the first version of its DOS operating system for the IBM personal computer. In the mid-1980s, Microsoft developed the *Windows operating system*, a graphical user interface built on top of DOS. Microsoft released Windows 3.0 in 1990; this new version featured a user-friendly interface and rich functionality. The Windows operating system became incredibly popular after the 1992 release of Windows 3.1, whose successors, Windows 95 and Windows 98, virtually cornered the desktop operating systems market by the late 1990s. These operating systems, which borrowed many concepts (such as icons, menus and windows) popularized by early Apple Macintosh operating systems, enabled users to navigate multiple applications simultaneously. Microsoft entered the corporate operating systems market with the 1993 release of Windows NT®. Windows XP, which is based on the Windows NT operating system, was released in 2001 and combines Microsoft's corporate and consumer operating system lines. Windows is by far the world's most widely used operating system.

The biggest competitor to the Windows operating system is Linux. The name Linux derives from Linus (after Linus Torvalds, who developed Linux) and UNIX—the operating system upon which Linux is based; UNIX was developed at Bell Laboratories and was written in the C programming language. Linux is a free, *open source* operating system, unlike Windows, which is proprietary (owned and controlled by Microsoft)—the source code for Linux is freely available to users, and they can modify it to fit their needs.

1.8 Machine Languages, Assembly Languages and High-Level Languages

Programmers write instructions in various programming languages, some directly understandable by computers and others requiring intermediate *translation* steps. Hundreds of computer languages are in use today. These may be divided into three general types:

1. Machine languages

2. Assembly languages

3. High-level languages

Machine Languages

Any computer can directly understand only its own *machine language*—the "natural language" of a computer that is defined by its hardware design. Machine languages generally consist of strings of numbers (ultimately reduced to 1s and 0s) that instruct computers to perform their most elementary operations one at a time. Machine languages are *machine dependent* (i.e., any given machine language can be used on only one type of computer). Such languages are cumbersome for humans, as illustrated by the following section of an early machine-language program that adds overtime pay to base pay and stores the result in gross pay:

```
+1300042774
+1400593419
+1200274027
```

Assembly Languages

Machine-language programming was simply too slow and tedious for most programmers. Instead of using the strings of numbers that computers could directly understand, programmers began using English-like abbreviations to represent the elementary machine operations. These abbreviations formed the basis of *assembly languages. Translator programs* called *assemblers* were developed to convert early assembly-language programs to machine language at computer speeds. The following section of an assembly-language program also adds overtime pay to base pay and stores the result in gross pay:

```
load    basepay
add     overpay
store   grosspay
```

Although such code is clearer to humans, it is incomprehensible to computers until translated to machine language.

High-Level Languages

Computer usage increased rapidly with the advent of assembly languages, but programmers still had to use many instructions to accomplish even the simplest tasks. To speed the programming process, *high-level languages* were developed in which single statements could be written to accomplish substantial tasks. Translator programs called *compilers* convert high-level language programs into machine language. High-level languages allow programmers to write instructions that look almost like everyday English and contain commonly used mathematical notations. A payroll program written in a high-level language might contain a statement such as

```
grossPay = basePay + overTimePay
```

From the programmer's standpoint, obviously, high-level languages are preferable to machine and assembly languages. Microsoft's Visual Studio languages (e.g., Visual C#, Visual C++ and Visual Basic) and other languages such as C, C++ and Java are among the most widely used high-level programming languages. Figure 1.1 compares machine, assembly and high-level languages.

The process of compiling a high-level language program into machine language can take a considerable amount of computer time. *Interpreter* programs were developed to execute high-level language programs directly, although much more slowly. Interpreters are popular in program development environments in which new features are being added

	Sample code	Translator	From the programmer's perspective	From the computer's perspective
Machine language	+1300042774 +1400593419 +1200274027	None	Slow, tedious, error prone	Natural language of a computer; the only language the computer can understand directly
Assembly language	LOAD BASEPAY ADD OVERPAY STORE GROSSPAY	Assembler	English-like abbreviations, easier to understand	Assemblers convert assembly language into machine language so the computer can understand
High-level language	grossPay = basePay + overTimePay	Compiler	Instructions resemble everyday English; single statements accomplish substantial tasks	Compilers convert high-level languages into machine language so the computer can understand

Fig. 1.1 | Comparing machine, assembly and high-level languages.

and errors corrected. Once a program is fully developed, a compiled version can be produced to run most efficiently. Interpreters are also popular with so-called scripting languages on the Web. We'll study the development of Web-based applications in Chapters 19–22.

1.9 C#

The advancement of programming tools and consumer-electronic devices (e.g., cell phones and PDAs) created problems and new requirements. The integration of software components from various languages proved difficult, and installation problems were common because new versions of shared components were incompatible with old software. Developers also discovered they needed Web-based applications that could be accessed and used via the Internet. As a result of the popularity of mobile electronic devices, software developers realized that their clients were no longer restricted to desktop computers. Developers recognized the need for software that was accessible to anyone and available via almost any type of device. To address these needs, in 2000, Microsoft announced the *C#* programming language. C#, developed at Microsoft by a team led by Anders Hejlsberg and Scott Wiltamuth, was designed specifically for the .NET platform (which is discussed in Section 1.14) as a language that would enable programmers to migrate easily to .NET. It has roots in C, C++ and Java, adapting the best features of each and adding new features of its own. C# is object oriented and contains a powerful *class library* of prebuilt components, enabling programmers to develop applications quickly—C# and Visual Basic share the Framework Class Library (FCL), which is discussed in Section 1.14. C# is appropriate for demanding application development tasks, especially for building today's popular Web-based applications.

The *.NET platform* is one over which Web-based applications can be distributed to a great variety of devices (even cell phones) and to desktop computers. The platform offers a new software-development model that allows applications created in disparate programming languages to communicate with each other.

C# is an event-driven, visual programming language in which programs are created using an *Integrated Development Environment* (*IDE*). With the IDE, a programmer can create, run, test and debug C# programs conveniently, thereby reducing the time it takes to produce a working program to a fraction of the time it would have taken without using the IDE. The .NET platform enables language interoperability: Software components from different languages can interact as never before. Developers can package even old software to work with new C# programs. Also, C# applications can interact via the Internet, using industry standards such as XML, which we discuss in Chapter 19, and the XML-based Simple Object Access Protocol (SOAP), which we discuss in Chapter 22, Web Services.

The original C# programming language was standardized by Ecma International (www.ecma-international.org) in December, 2002 as *Standard ECMA-334: C# Language Specification* (located at www.ecma-international.org/publications/standards/Ecma-334.htm). Since that time, Microsoft proposed several language extensions that have been adopted as part of the revised Ecma C# standard. Microsoft refers to the complete C# language (including the adopted extensions) as *C# 2.0*.

[*Note:* Throughout this book, we provide references to specific sections of the *C# Language Specification*. We use the section numbers specified in Microsoft's version of the specification, which is composed of two documents—the *C# Language Specification 1.2* and the *C# Language Specification 2.0* (an extension of the 1.2 document that contains the C# 2.0 language enhancements). Both documents are located at: msdn.microsoft.com/vcsharp/programming/language/.]

1.10 C, C++, Java and Visual Basic

C

The *C* programming language was developed by Dennis Ritchie at Bell Laboratories in 1973. C first gained widespread recognition as the development language of the UNIX operating system. C is a hardware-independent language, and with careful design, it is possible to write C programs that are portable to most computers.

C++

C++ was developed by Bjarne Stroustrup in the early 1980s at Bell Laboratories. C++ provides a number of features that "spruce up" the C language, but more important, it provides capabilities for *object-oriented programming* (*OOP*). Many of today's major operating systems are written in C or C++. At a time when the demand for new and more powerful software is soaring, the ability to build software quickly, correctly and economically remains an elusive goal. This problem can be addressed in part through the use of *objects*, reusable software *components* that model items in the real world (we discuss object technology in Section 1.17). A modular, object-oriented approach to design and implementation can make software development groups much more productive than is possible using earlier programming techniques. Furthermore, object-oriented programs are often easier to understand, correct and modify.

Java

Microprocessors are having a profound impact in intelligent consumer electronic devices. Recognizing this, Sun Microsystems in 1991 funded an internal corporate research project that resulted in the development of a C++-based language. When a group of Sun people visited a local coffee shop, the name *Java* was suggested and it stuck. As the World Wide Web exploded in popularity in 1993, Sun saw the possibility of using Java to add *dynamic content* (e.g., interactivity, animations and the like) to Web pages. Sun formally announced the language in 1995. This generated immediate interest in the business community because of the commercial potential of the Web. Java is now used to develop large-scale enterprise applications, to enhance the functionality of Web servers (the computers that provide the content we see in our Web browsers), to provide applications for consumer devices (such as cell phones, pagers and personal digital assistants) and for many other purposes. Visual C# is similar in capability to Java. Current versions of C++, such as Microsoft's Visual C++ and Borland's C++Builder, also have similar capabilities.

Visual Basic

Visual Basic evolved from BASIC (Beginner's All-Purpose Symbolic Instruction Code), developed in the mid-1960s by Professors John Kemeny and Thomas Kurtz of Dartmouth College as a language for writing simple programs. BASIC's primary purpose was to familiarize novices with programming techniques.

The widespread use of BASIC on various types of computers (sometimes called *hardware platforms*) led to many language enhancements. When Bill Gates co-founded

Microsoft, he implemented BASIC on several early personal computers. With the development of the Microsoft Windows graphical user interface (GUI) in the late 1980s and early 1990s, the natural evolution of BASIC was Visual Basic, introduced by Microsoft in 1991. Visual Basic makes the development of Windows applications convenient.

Until the first version of Visual Basic appeared in 1991, developing Microsoft Windows-based applications was a difficult and cumbersome process. Although Visual Basic is derived from the BASIC programming language, it is a distinctly different language that offers such powerful features as graphical user interfaces, event handling, object-oriented programming, and exception handling. Visual Basic is an event-driven language (i.e., the programs respond to user-initiated events such as mouse clicks and keystrokes) and a visual programming language in which programs are created using an Integrated Development Environment (IDE).

1.11 Other High-Level Languages

Although hundreds of high-level languages have been developed, only a few have achieved broad acceptance other than those we've discussed.

Fortran

IBM Corporation developed *Fortran* (FORmula TRANslator) in the mid-1950s to create scientific and engineering applications that require complex mathematical computations. Fortran is still widely used.

COBOL

COBOL (COmmon Business Oriented Language) was developed in 1959 by a group of computer manufacturers in conjunction with government and industrial computer users. COBOL is used primarily for commercial applications that require the precise and efficient manipulation of large amounts of data. Much of today's business software is still programmed in COBOL.

Pascal

During the 1960s, many large software-development efforts encountered severe difficulties. People began to realize that software development was a far more complex activity than they had imagined. Research activity resulted in the evolution of *structured programming*—a disciplined approach to creating programs that are clear, demonstrably correct and easy to modify. One of the results of this research was the development of the *Pascal* programming language by Professor Niklaus Wirth in 1971. Pascal, named after the mathematician and philosopher Blaise Pascal, was designed for teaching structured programming in academic environments and rapidly became the preferred introductory programming language in most colleges. Unfortunately, the language lacked many features needed to make it useful in commercial, industrial and government applications. By contrast, C, which also arose from research on structured programming, did not have the limitations of Pascal, and programmers quickly adopted it instead.

Ada

The *Ada* programming language was developed under the sponsorship of the U. S. Department of Defense (DOD) through the early 1980s. DOD wanted a single language that would meet its needs. The language was named after Lady Ada Lovelace, daughter of the poet Lord Byron. Lady Lovelace is generally credited with writing the world's first computer program, in the early 1800s (for the Analytical Engine mechanical computing device designed by Charles Babbage). An important capability of Ada is *multitasking*, which allows programmers to specify that many activities are to occur in parallel. As we will see in Chapter 15, C# offers a similar capability, called *multithreading*.

1.12 The Internet and the World Wide Web

The *Internet*—a global network of computers—was initiated almost four decades ago with funding supplied by the U.S. Department of Defense. Originally designed to connect the main computer systems of about a dozen universities and research organizations, its chief benefit proved early on to be the capability for quick and easy communication via what came to be known as *electronic mail* (*e-mail*). This is true even on today's Internet, with e-mail, instant messaging and file transfer facilitating communications among hundreds of millions of people worldwide. The Internet has exploded into one of the world's premier communication mechanisms and continues to grow rapidly.

The *World Wide Web* allows computer users to locate and view multimedia-based documents on almost any subject over the Internet. Even though the Internet was developed decades ago, the introduction of the Web was a relatively recent event. In 1989, Tim Berners-Lee of CERN (the European Organization for Nuclear Research) began to develop a technology for sharing information via hyperlinked text documents. Berners-Lee called his invention the *HyperText Markup Language* (*HTML*). He also wrote communication protocols to form the backbone of his new information system, which he referred to as the World Wide Web.

In the past, most computer applications ran on computers that were not connected to one another. Today's applications can be written to communicate among the world's computers. The Internet mixes computing and communications technologies, making our work easier. It makes information instantly and conveniently accessible worldwide, and enables individuals and small businesses to get worldwide exposure. It is changing the way business is done. People can search for the best prices on virtually any product or service, while special-interest communities can stay in touch with one another, and researchers can be made instantly aware of the latest breakthroughs. The Internet and the World Wide Web are surely among humankind's most profound creations. In Chapters 19–22, you will learn how to build Internet- and Web-based applications.

In 1994, Tim Berners-Lee founded an organization, called the *World Wide Web Consortium* (*W3C*), that is devoted to developing nonproprietary, interoperable technologies for the World Wide Web. One of the W3C's primary goals is to make the Web universally accessible—regardless of disabilities, language or culture.

The W3C (www.w3.org) is also a standardization organization. Web technologies standardized by the W3C are called Recommendations. Current W3C Recommendations include the *Extensible Markup Language* (*XML*). We introduce XML in Section 1.13 and present it in detail in Chapter 19, Extensible Markup Language (XML). It is the key technology underlying the next version of the Word Wide Web, sometimes called the "semantic Web." It is also one of the key technologies that underlies Web services, which we discuss in Chapter 22.

1.13 Extensible Markup Language (XML)

As the popularity of the Web exploded, HTML's limitations became apparent. HTML's lack of *extensibility* (the ability to change or add features) frustrated developers, and its ambiguous definition allowed erroneous HTML to proliferate. The need for a standardized, fully extensible and structurally strict language was apparent. As a result, XML was developed by the W3C.

Data independence, the separation of content from its presentation, is the essential characteristic of XML. Because XML documents describe data in a machine independent manner, any application conceivably can process them. Software developers are integrating XML into their applications to improve Web functionality and interoperability.

XML is not limited to Web applications. For example, it is increasingly being employed in databases—the structure of an XML document enables it to be integrated easily with database applications. As applications become more Web enabled, it is likely that XML will become the universal technology for data representation. All applications employing XML would be able to communicate with one another, provided they can understand their respective XML markup schemes, called *vocabularies*.

The *Simple Object Access Protocol* (*SOAP*) is a technology for the transmission of objects (marked up as XML) over the Internet. Microsoft's .NET technologies (discussed in the next two sections) use XML and SOAP to mark up and transfer data over the Internet. XML and SOAP are at the core of .NET—they allow software components to interoperate (i.e., communicate easily with one another). Since SOAP's foundations are in XML and *HTTP* (*Hypertext Transfer Protocol*—the key communication protocol of the Web), it is supported on most types of computer systems. We discuss XML in Chapter 19, Extensible Markup Language (XML), and SOAP in Chapter 22, Web Services.

1.14 Microsoft's .NET

In 2000, Microsoft announced its *.NET initiative* (www.microsoft.com/net), a new vision for embracing the Internet and the Web in the development and use of software. One key aspect of .NET is its independence from a specific language or platform. Rather than being forced to use a single programming language, developers can create a .NET application in any .NET-compatible language. Programmers can contribute to the same software project, writing code in the .NET languages (such as Microsoft's Visual C#, Visual C++, Visual Basic and many others) in which they are most competent. Part of the initiative includes Microsoft's *ASP.NET* technology, which allows programmers to create applications for the Web. We discuss ASP.NET in Chapter 21, ASP.NET 2.0, Web Forms and Web Controls. We use ASP.NET technology in Chapter 22 to build applications that use Web services.

The .NET architecture can exist on multiple platforms, not just Microsoft Windows–based systems, further extending the portability of .NET programs. One example is Mono (www.mono-project.com/Main_Page), an open-source project by Novell. Another is DotGNU Portable .NET (www.dotgnu.org).

A key component of the .NET architecture is *Web services*, which are reusable application software components that can be used over the Internet. Clients and other applications can use Web services as reusable building blocks. One example of a Web service is Dollar Rent a Car's reservation system (www.microsoft.com/resources/casestudies/

`CaseStudy.asp?CaseStudyID=11626`). An airline partner wanted to enable customers to make rental-car reservations from the airline's Web site. To do so, the airline needed to access Dollar's reservation system. In response, Dollar created a Web service that allowed the airline to access Dollar's database and make reservations. Web services enable computers at the two companies to communicate over the Web, even though the airline uses UNIX systems and Dollar uses Microsoft Windows. Dollar could have created a one-time solution for that particular airline, but it would not have been able to reuse such a customized system. Dollar's Web service enables many airlines, hotels and travel companies to use its reservation system without creating a custom program for each relationship.

The .NET strategy extends the concept of software reuse to the Internet, allowing programmers and companies to concentrate on their specialties without having to implement every component of every application. Instead, companies can buy Web services and devote their resources to developing their own products. For example, a single application using Web services from various companies could manage bill payments, tax refunds, loans and investments. An online merchant could buy Web services for online credit-card payments, user authentication, network security and inventory databases to create an e-commerce Web site.

1.15 The .NET Framework and the Common Language Runtime

The Microsoft *.NET Framework* is at the heart of the .NET strategy. This framework manages and executes applications and Web services, contains a class library (called the .NET Framework Class Library, or FCL), enforces security and provides many other programming capabilities. The details of the .NET Framework are found in the *Common Language Infrastructure (CLI)*, which contains information about the storage of data types (i.e., data that has predefined characteristics such as a date, percentage or currency amount), objects and so on. The CLI has been standardized by Ecma International (originally known as the European Computer Manufacturers Association), making it easier to create the .NET Framework for other platforms. This is like publishing the blueprints of the framework—anyone can build it by following the specifications.

The *Common Language Runtime (CLR)* is another central part of the .NET Framework—it executes .NET programs. Programs are compiled into machine-specific instructions in two steps. First, the program is compiled into *Microsoft Intermediate Language (MSIL)*, which defines instructions for the CLR. Code converted into MSIL from other languages and sources can be woven together by the CLR. The MSIL for an application's components is placed into the application's executable file (known as an *assembly*). When the application executes, another compiler (known as the *just-in-time compiler* or *JIT compiler*) in the CLR translates the MSIL in the executable file into machine-language code (for a particular platform), then the machine-language code executes on that platform. [*Note:* MSIL is Microsoft's name for what the C# language specification refers to as *Common Intermediate Language* (*CIL*).]

If the .NET Framework exists (and is installed) for a platform, that platform can run any .NET program. The ability of a program to run (without modification) across multiple platforms is known as *platform independence*. Code written once can be used on another type of computer without modification, saving both time and money. In addition, software can target a wider audience—previously, companies had to decide whether converting their programs to different platforms (sometimes called *porting*) was worth the cost. With .NET, porting programs is no longer an issue (once .NET itself has been made available on the platforms).

The .NET Framework also provides a high level of *language interoperability*. Programs written in different languages are all compiled into MSIL—the different parts can be combined to create a single unified program. MSIL allows the .NET Framework to be *language independent*, because .NET programs are not tied to a particular programming language. Any language that can be compiled into MSIL is called a *.NET-compliant language*. Figure 1.2 lists many of the programming languages that are available for the .NET platform (msdn.microsoft.com/netframework/technologyinfo/overview/default.aspx).

Language interoperability offers many benefits to software companies. For example, C#, Visual Basic and Visual C++ developers can work side by side on the same project without having to learn another programming language—all of their code compiles into MSIL and links together to form one program.

The .NET Framework Class Library (FCL) can be used by any .NET language. The FCL contains a variety of reusable components, saving programmers the trouble of creating new components. This book explains how to develop .NET software with C#.

1.16 Test-Driving a C# Application

In this section, you will "test-drive" a C# application that enables you to draw on the screen using the mouse. You will run and interact with a working application. You will build a similar application in Chapter 13, Graphical User Interface Concepts: Part 1.

.NET programming languages	
APL	Mondrian
C#	Oberon
COBOL	Oz
Component Pascal	Pascal
Curriculum	Perl
Eiffel	Python
Forth	RPG
Fortran	Scheme
Haskell	Smalltalk
Java	Standard ML
JScript	Visual Basic
Mercury	Visual C++

Fig. 1.2 | .NET programming languages.

The **Drawing** application allows you to draw with different brush sizes and colors. The elements and functionality you see in this application are typical of what you will learn to program in this text. We use fonts to distinguish between IDE features (such as menu names and menu items) and other elements that appear in the IDE. Our convention is to emphasize IDE features (such as the **File** menu) in a bold sans-serif Helvetica font and to emphasize other elements, such as file names (e.g., Form1.cs), in a sans-serif Lucida font. The following steps show you how to test-drive the application.

1. *Checking your setup.* Confirm that you have installed Visual C# 2005 Express or Visual Studio 2005 as discussed in the *Preface.*

2. *Locating the application directory.* Open Windows Explorer and navigate to the C:\examples\Ch01\Drawing directory.

3. *Running the* **Drawing** *application.* Now that you are in the correct directory, double click the file name Drawing.exe to run the application.

   In Fig. 1.3, several graphical elements—called *controls*—are labeled. The controls include two GroupBoxes (in this case, **Color** and **Size**), seven RadioButtons and a Panel (these controls will be discussed in depth later in the text). The **Drawing** application allows you to draw with a red, blue, green or black brush of small, medium or large size. You will explore these options in this test-drive.

   You can use existing controls—which are objects—to get powerful applications running in C# much faster than if you had to write all of the code yourself. In this text, you will learn how to use many preexisting controls, as well as how to write your own program code to customize your applications.

   The brush's properties, selected in the RadioButtons (the small circles where you select an option by clicking the mouse) labeled **Black** and **Small**, are default settings, which are the initial settings you see when you first run the application. Programmers include default settings to provide reasonable choices that the application will use if the user chooses not to change the settings. You will now choose your own settings.

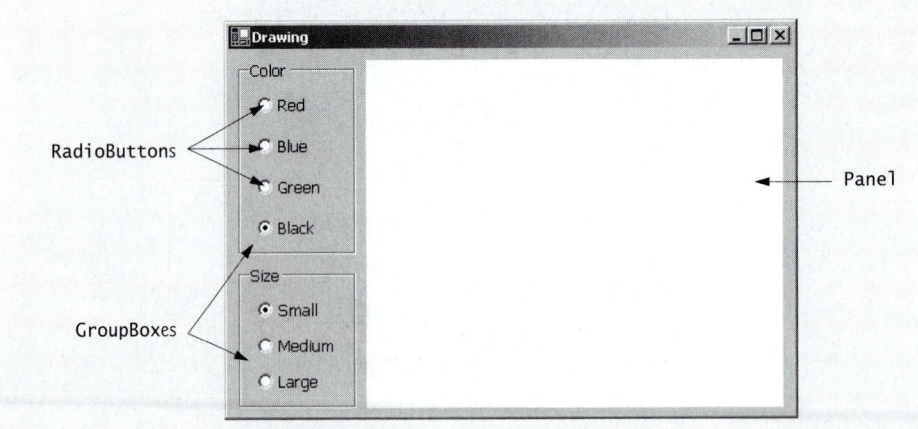

Fig. 1.3 | Visual C# **Drawing** application.

4. *Changing the brush color.* Click the RadioButton labeled **Red** to change the color of the brush. Hold the mouse button down with the mouse pointer positioned anywhere on the Panel, then drag the mouse to draw with the brush. Draw flower petals as shown in Fig. 1.4. Then click the RadioButton labeled **Green** to change the color of the brush again.

5. *Changing the brush size.* Click the RadioButton labeled **Large** to change the size of the brush. Draw grass and a flower stem as shown in Fig. 1.5.

6. *Finishing the drawing.* Click the RadioButton labeled **Blue**. Then click the RadioButton labeled **Medium**. Draw raindrops as shown in Fig. 1.6 to complete the drawing.

7. *Closing the application.* Click the ***close box***, ☒, to close your running application.

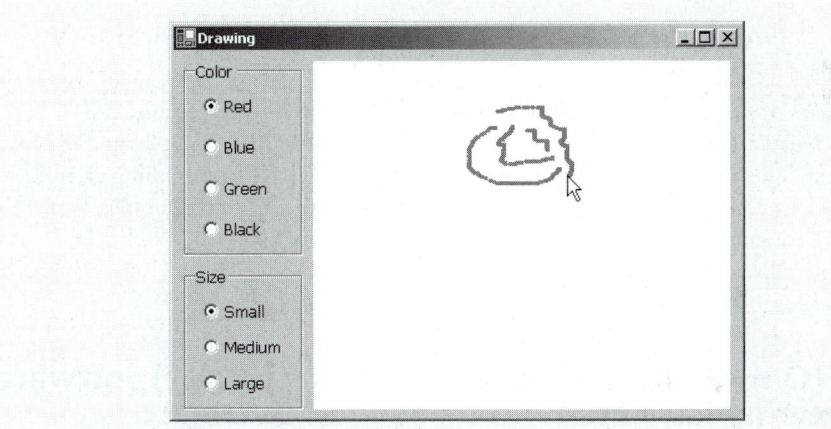

Fig. 1.4 | Drawing with a new brush color.

Fig. 1.5 | Drawing with a new brush size.

Fig. 1.6 | Finishing the drawing.

Additional Applications Found in **Visual C# 2005 How to Program, 2/e**

Figure 1.7 lists a few of the hundreds of applications found in the examples and exercises in this text. These programs introduce some of the powerful and entertaining capabilities of C#. We encourage you to practice running some of them. The examples folder for Chapter 1 contains all of the files required to run each application listed in Fig. 1.7. Simply double click the file names for any application you would like to run. [*Note:* The Garage.exe application assumes that the user inputs a value from 0 to 24.]

1.17 (Only Required Section of the Case Study) Software Engineering Case Study: Introduction to Object Technology and the UML

Now we begin our early introduction to object orientation, a natural way of thinking about the world and writing computer programs. Chapter 1, 3–9 and 11 each end with a brief "Software Engineering Case Study" section in which we present a carefully paced introduction to object orientation. Our goal here is to help you develop an object-oriented

Application name	Chapter location	File to execute
Parking Fees	Chapter 7	Garage.exe
Tic Tac Toe	Chapter 9	TicTacToe.exe
Drawing Stars	Chapter 17	DrawStars.exe
Drawing Shapes	Chapter 17	DrawShapes.exe
Drawing Polygons	Chapter 17	DrawPolygons.exe

Fig. 1.7 | Examples of C# programs found in *Visual C# 2005 How to Program, 2/e.*

way of thinking and to introduce you to the *Unified Modeling Language*™ (*UML*™)—a graphical language that allows people who design object-oriented software systems to use an industry-standard notation to represent them.

In this, the only required section of the case study, we introduce basic object-oriented concepts and terminology. The optional sections in Chapters 3–9 and 11 present an object-oriented design and implementation of the software for a simple automated teller machine (ATM) system. The "Software Engineering Case Study" sections at the ends of Chapters 3–9

- analyze a typical requirements document that describes a software system (the ATM) to be built.

- determine the objects required to implement the system.

- determine the attributes the objects will have.

- determine the behaviors the objects will exhibit.

- specify how the objects will interact with one another to meet the system requirements.

The "Software Engineering Case Study" sections at the ends of Chapters 9 and 11 modify and enhance the design presented in Chapters 3–8. Appendix J contains a complete, working C# implementation of the object-oriented ATM system.

Although our case study is a scaled-down version of an industry-level problem, we nevertheless cover many common industry practices. You will experience a solid introduction to object-oriented design with the UML. Also, you will sharpen your code-reading skills by touring a complete, straightforward and well-documented C# implementation of the ATM.

Basic Object Technology Concepts

We begin our introduction to object orientation with some key terminology. Everywhere you look in the real world you see *objects*—people, animals, plants, cars, planes, buildings, computers and so on. Humans think in terms of objects. Telephones, houses, traffic lights, microwave ovens and water coolers are just a few more objects we see around us every day.

We sometimes divide objects into two categories: animate and inanimate. Animate objects are "alive" in some sense—they move around and do things. Inanimate objects do not move on their own. Objects of both types, however, have some things in common. They all have *attributes* (e.g., size, shape, color and weight), and they all exhibit *behaviors* (e.g., a ball rolls, bounces, inflates and deflates; a baby cries, sleeps, crawls, walks and blinks; a car accelerates, brakes and turns; a towel absorbs water). We will study the kinds of attributes and behaviors that software objects have.

Humans learn about objects by studying their attributes and observing their behaviors. Different objects can have similar attributes and can exhibit similar behaviors. Comparisons can be made, for example, between babies and adults and between humans and chimpanzees.

Object-oriented design (*OOD*) models software in terms similar to those that people use to describe real-world objects. It takes advantage of class relationships, where objects of a certain class, such as a class of vehicles, have the same characteristics—cars, trucks, little red wagons and roller skates have much in common. OOD takes advantage of *inheritance* relationships, where new classes of objects are derived by absorbing characteristics of existing classes and adding unique characteristics of their own. An object of "convertible" class certainly has the characteristics of the more general class "automobile," but more specifically, the roof goes up and down.

Object-oriented design provides a natural and intuitive way to view the software design process—namely, modeling objects by their attributes, behaviors and interrelationships, just as we describe real-world objects. OOD also models communication between objects. Just as people send messages to one another (e.g., a sergeant commands a soldier to stand at attention, or a teenager text messages a friend to meet at the movies), objects also communicate via messages. A bank account object may receive a message to decrease its balance by a certain amount because the customer has withdrawn that amount of money.

OOD *encapsulates* (i.e., wraps) attributes and *operations* (behaviors) into objects— an object's attributes and operations are intimately tied together. Objects have the property of *information hiding*. This means that objects may know how to communicate with one another across well-defined *interfaces*, but normally they are not allowed to know how other objects are implemented—implementation details are hidden within the objects themselves. You can drive a car effectively, for instance, without knowing the details of how engines, transmissions, brakes and exhaust systems work internally—as long as you know how to use the accelerator pedal, the brake pedal, the steering wheel and so on. Information hiding, as you will see, is crucial to good software engineering.

Languages like C# are *object oriented*. Programming in such a language is called *object-oriented programming* (*OOP*), and it allows computer programmers to conveniently implement an object-oriented design as a working software system. Languages like C, on the other hand, are *procedural*, so programming tends to be *action oriented*. In C, the unit of programming is the *function*. In C#, the unit of programming is the *class*, from which objects are eventually *instantiated* (an OOP term for "created"). C# classes contain *methods* (C#'s equivalent of C's functions) that implement operations, and data that implements attributes.

Classes, Data Members and Methods

C# programmers concentrate on creating their own *user-defined types* called classes. Each class contains data as well as the set of methods that manipulate the data and provide services to *clients* (i.e., other classes that use the class). The data components of a class are called attributes, or *fields*. For example, a bank account class might include an account number and a balance. The operation components of a class are called methods. For example, a bank account class might include methods to make a deposit (increase the balance), make a withdrawal (decrease the balance) and inquire what the current balance is. The programmer uses built-in types (and other user-defined types) as the "building blocks" for constructing new user-defined types (classes). The *nouns in a system specification* help the C# programmer determine the set of classes from which objects are created that work together to implement the system.

Classes are to objects as blueprints are to houses—a class is a "plan" for building objects of the class. Just as we can build many houses from one blueprint, we can instantiate (create) many objects from one class. You cannot cook meals in the kitchen of a blueprint, but you can cook meals in the kitchen of a house. You cannot sleep in the bedroom of a blueprint, but you can sleep in the bedroom of a house.

Classes can have relationships with other classes. For example, in an object-oriented design of a bank, the "bank teller" class needs to relate to other classes, such as the "customer" class, the "cash drawer" class, the "safe" class and so on. These relationships are called *associations*.

Packaging software as classes makes it possible for future software systems to *reuse* the classes. Groups of related classes often are packaged as reusable *components*. Just as realtors often say that the three most important factors affecting the price of real estate are "location, location and location," some people in the software development community often say that the three most important factors affecting the future of software development are "reuse, reuse and reuse."

Software Engineering Observation 1.1

Reuse of existing classes when building new classes and programs saves time, money and effort. Reuse also helps programmers build more reliable and effective systems, because existing classes and components often have gone through extensive testing, debugging and performance tuning.

Indeed, with object technology, you can build much of the new software you will need by combining existing classes, just as automobile manufacturers combine interchangeable parts. Each new class you create will have the potential to become a valuable software asset that you and other programmers can reuse to speed and enhance the quality of future software development efforts.

Introduction to Object-Oriented Analysis and Design (OOAD)

Soon you will be writing programs in C#. How will you create the code for your programs? Perhaps, like many beginning programmers, you will simply turn on your computer and start typing. This approach may work for small programs (like the ones we present in the early chapters of the book), but what if you were asked to create a software system to control thousands of automated teller machines for a major bank? Or what if you were asked to work as part of a team of 1,000 software developers building the next generation of the U.S. air traffic control system? For projects so large and complex, you could not simply sit down and start writing programs.

To create the best solutions, you should follow a detailed process for *analyzing* your project's *requirements* (i.e., determining *what* your system is supposed to do) and developing a *design* that satisfies them (i.e., deciding *how* your system should do it). Ideally, you would go through this process and carefully review the design (and have your design reviewed by other software professionals) before writing any code. If this process involves analyzing and designing your system from an object-oriented point of view, it is called *object-oriented analysis and design* (*OOAD*). Experienced programmers know that proper analysis and design can save many hours by helping avoid an ill-planned system development approach that has to be abandoned partway through its implementation, possibly wasting considerable time, money and effort.

OOAD is the generic term for the process of analyzing a problem and developing an approach for solving it. Small problems like the ones discussed in the first few chapters of this book do not require an exhaustive OOAD process. It may be sufficient, before we begin writing C# code, to write *pseudocode*—an informal text-based means of expressing program logic. It is not actually a programming language, but you can use it as a kind of outline to guide you as you write your code. We introduce pseudocode in Chapter 5.

As problems and the groups of people solving them increase in size, OOAD quickly becomes more appropriate than pseudocode. Ideally, a group should agree on a strictly defined process for solving its problem and a uniform way of communicating the results of that process to one another. Although many different OOAD processes exist, a single graphical language for communicating the results of *any* OOAD process has come into wide use. This language, known as the Unified Modeling Language (UML), was developed in the mid-1990s under the initial direction of three software methodologists: Grady Booch, James Rumbaugh and Ivar Jacobson.

History of the UML

In the 1980s, increasing numbers of organizations began using OOP to build their applications, and a need developed for a standard OOAD process. Many methodologists—including Grady Booch, James Rumbaugh and Ivar Jacobson—individually produced and promoted separate processes to satisfy this need. Each process had its own notation, or "language" (in the form of graphical diagrams), to convey the results of analysis (i.e., determining *what* a proposed system is supposed to do) and design (i.e., determining *how* a proposed system should be implemented to do what it is supposed to do).

By the early 1990s, different organizations were using their own unique processes and notations. At the same time, these organizations also wanted to use software tools that would support their particular processes. Software vendors found it difficult to provide tools for so many processes. A standard notation and standard process were needed.

In 1994, James Rumbaugh joined Grady Booch at Rational Software Corporation (now a division of IBM), and the two began working to unify their popular processes. They soon were joined by Ivar Jacobson. In 1996, the group released early versions of the UML to the software engineering community and requested feedback. Around the same time, an organization known as the Object Management Group™ (OMG™) invited submissions for a common modeling language. The OMG (www.omg.org) is a nonprofit organization that promotes the standardization of object-oriented technologies by issuing guidelines and specifications, such as the UML. Several corporations—among them HP, IBM, Microsoft, Oracle and Rational Software—had already recognized the need for a common modeling language. In response to the OMG's request for proposals, these companies formed the UML Partners—the consortium that developed the UML version 1.1 and submitted it to the OMG. The OMG accepted the proposal and, in 1997, assumed responsibility for the continuing maintenance and revision of the UML. We present the recently adopted UML 2 terminology and notation throughout this book.

What is the UML?

The *Unified Modeling Language* (*UML*) is the most widely used graphical representation scheme for modeling object-oriented systems. It has indeed unified the various popular notational schemes. Those who design systems use the language (in the form of diagrams, many of which we discuss throughout our ATM case study) to model their systems. We use several popular types of UML diagrams in this book.

An attractive feature of the UML is its flexibility. The UML is *extensible* (i.e., capable of being enhanced with new features) and is independent of any particular OOAD process. UML modelers are free to use various processes in designing systems, but all developers can now express their designs with one standard set of graphical notations.

The UML is a feature-rich graphical language. In our subsequent (and optional) "Software Engineering Case Study" sections on developing the software for an automated teller machine (ATM), we present a simple, concise subset of these features. We then use this subset to guide you through a first design experience with the UML. We will use some C# notations in our UML diagrams to avoid confusion and improve clarity. In industry practice, especially with UML tools that automatically generate code (a nice feature of many UML tools), you would probably adhere more closely to UML keywords and UML naming conventions for attributes and operations.

This case study was carefully developed under the guidance of distinguished academic and professional reviewers. We sincerely hope you enjoy working through it. If you have any questions, please communicate with us at `deitel@deitel.com`. We will respond promptly.

Internet and Web UML Resources

For more information about the UML, refer to the following Web sites. For additional UML sites, please refer to the Internet and Web resources listed at the end of Section 3.10.

`www.uml.org`

This UML resource site from the Object Management Group (OMG) provides specification documents for the UML and other object-oriented technologies.

`www.ibm.com/software/rational/uml`

This is the UML resource page for IBM Rational—the successor to the Rational Software Corporation (the company that created the UML).

Recommended Readings

Many books on the UML have been published. The following recommended books provide information about object-oriented design with the UML.

- Arlow, J., and I. Neustadt. *UML and the Unified Process: Practical Object-Oriented Analysis and Design, Second Edition*. London: Addison-Wesley, 2005.

- Fowler, M. *UML Distilled, Third Edition: Applying the Standard Object Modeling Language*. Boston: Addison-Wesley, 2004.

- Rumbaugh, J., I. Jacobson, and G. Booch. *The Unified Modeling Language User Guide, Second Edition*. Upper Saddle River, NJ: Addison-Wesley, 2005.

For additional books on the UML, please refer to the recommended readings listed at the end of Section 3.10, or visit `www.amazon.com`, `www.bn.com` and `www.informIT.com`. IBM Rational, formerly Rational Software Corporation, also provides a recommended-reading list for UML books at `www.ibm.com/software/rational/info/technical/books.jsp`.

Section 1.17 Self-Review Exercises

1.1 List three examples of real-world objects that we did not mention. For each object, list several attributes and behaviors.

1.2 Pseudocode is _____.
    a) another term for OOAD
    b) a programming language used to display UML diagrams
    c) an informal means of expressing program logic
    d) a graphical representation scheme for modeling object-oriented systems

1.3   The UML is used primarily to _____.
   a) test object-oriented systems
   b) design object-oriented systems
   c) implement object-oriented systems
   d) Both a and b

Answers to Section 1.17 Self-Review Exercises

1.1   [*Note:* Answers may vary.] a) A television's attributes include the size of the screen, the number of colors it can display, and its current channel and volume. A television turns on and off, changes channels, displays video and plays sounds. b) A coffee maker's attributes include the maximum volume of water it can hold, the time required to brew a pot of coffee and the temperature of the heating plate under the coffee pot. A coffee maker turns on and off, brews coffee and heats coffee. c) A turtle's attributes include its age, the size of its shell and its weight. A turtle crawls, retreats into its shell, emerges from its shell and eats vegetation.

1.2   c.

1.3   b.

1.18 Wrap-Up

This chapter introduced basic hardware and software concepts and basic object technology concepts, including classes, objects, attributes and behaviors. We discussed the different types of programming languages and which languages are most widely used. We presented a brief history of operating systems, including Microsoft's Windows operating system. We discussed the history of the Internet- and the Web. We presented the history of C# programming and Microsoft's .NET initiative, which allows you to program Internet and Web-based applications using C# (and other languages). You learned the steps for executing a C# application. You test-drove a sample C# application similar to the types of applications you will learn to program in this book. You learned about the history and purpose of the UML—the industry-standard graphical language for modeling software systems. We launched our early objects and classes presentation with the first of our "Software Engineering Case Study" sections (and the only one which is required). The remaining (all optional) sections of the case study use object-oriented design and the UML to design the software for our simplified automated teller machine system. We present the complete C# code implementation of the ATM system in Appendix J.

   In the next chapter, you will use the Visual Studio IDE (Integrated Development Environment) to create your first C# application using the techniques of visual programming. You will also learn about Visual Studio's help features.

1.19 Web Resources

Deitel & Associates Web Sites

www.deitel.com/books/csharphtp2/index.html
The Deitel & Associates site for *Visual C# 2005 How to Program, Second Edition* includes links to the book's examples and other resources.

www.deitel.com
Please check this site for updates, corrections and additional resources for all Deitel publications.

`www.deitel.com/newsletter/subscribe.html`

Please visit this site to subscribe to the free *Deitel® Buzz Online* e-mail newsletter to follow the Deitel & Associates publishing program and to receive updates on C# and this book.

`www.prenhall.com/deitel`

Prentice Hall's site for Deitel publications. Includes detailed product information, sample chapters and *Companion Web Sites* containing book- and chapter-specific resources for students and instructors.

Microsoft Web Sites

`msdn.microsoft.com/vstudio/express/visualcsharp/`

The Microsoft Visual C# Developer Center site includes product information, downloads, tutorials, chat groups and more. Includes case studies on companies using C# in their businesses.

`msdn.microsoft.com/vcsharp/programming/language/`

Microsoft's C# Language specifications and reference page.

`msdn.microsoft.com/vstudio/default.aspx`

Visit this site to learn more about Microsoft's Visual Studio products and resources.

`www.gotdotnet.com/`

This is the site for the Microsoft .NET Framework Community. It includes message boards, a resource center, sample programs and more.

`www.thespoke.net`

Students can chat, post their code, rate other students' code, create hubs and post questions at this site.

Resources

`www.ecma-international.org/publications/standards/Ecma-334.html`

The Ecma International page for the C# Language Specification.

`www.w3.org`

The World Wide Web Consortium (W3C) develops technologies for the Internet and the Web. This site includes links to W3C technologies, news and frequently asked questions (FAQs).

`www.error-bank.com/`

The Error Bank is a collection of .NET errors, exceptions and solutions.

`www.csharp-station.com/`

This site provides news, links, tutorials, help and other C# resources.

`www.csharphelp.com/`

This site includes a C# help board, tutorials and articles.

`www.codeproject.com/index.asp?cat=3`

This resource page includes C# code, articles, news and tutorials.

`www.dotnetpowered.com/languages.aspx`

This site provides a list of languages implemented in .NET.

UML Resources

`www.uml.org`

This UML resource page from the Object Management Group (OMG) provides specification documents for the UML and other object-oriented technologies.

`www.ibm.com/software/rational/uml`

This is the UML resource page for IBM Rational—the successor to the Rational Software Corporation (the company that created the UML).

C# Games

www.c-sharpcorner.com/Games.asp
Visit this site for numerous games developed using C#. You can also submit your own games to be posted to the site.
www.gamespp.com/cgi-bin/index.cgi?csharpsourcecode
This resource site includes C# games, source code and tutorials.

Summary

Section 1.1 Introduction
- Computers that might have filled large rooms and cost millions of dollars a few decades ago can now be inscribed on silicon chips smaller than a fingernail, costing a few dollars each.
- Silicon chip technology has made computing so economical that about a billion general-purpose computers are in use worldwide, helping people in business, industry and government, and in their personal lives.

Section 1.2 What Is a Computer?
- Computers process data under the control of sets of instructions called computer programs. These programs guide the computer through sets of actions specified by computer programmers.
- A computer consists of various devices referred to as hardware (e.g., the keyboard, screen, disk drives, memory and processing units).
- The computer programs that run on a computer are referred to as software.
- A computer is a device capable of performing computations and making logical decisions at speeds millions, billions and even trillions of times faster than humans.

Section 1.3 Computer Organization
- The input unit is the "receiving" section of the computer. It obtains information from input devices and places it at the disposal of the other units for processing.
- The output unit is the "shipping" section of the computer. It takes information processed by the computer and places it on output devices to make it available for use outside the computer.
- The memory unit is the rapid-access, relatively low-capacity "warehouse" section of the computer. It retains information that has been entered through the input unit, making it immediately available for processing when needed, and retains information that has already been processed until it can be placed on output devices by the output unit.
- The arithmetic and logic unit (ALU) is the "manufacturing" section of the computer. It is responsible for performing calculations and making decisions.
- The central processing unit (CPU) is the "administrative" section of the computer. It coordinates and supervises the operation of the other sections.
- The secondary storage unit is the long-term, high-capacity "warehousing" section of the computer. Programs or data not being used by the other units are normally placed on secondary storage devices (e.g., disks) until they are needed, hours, days, months or even years later.

Section 1.4 Early Operating Systems
- Software systems called operating systems were developed to help make using computers more convenient.
- Multiprogramming involves the simultaneous operation of many jobs that are competing to share the computer's resources.

Section 1.5 Personal Computing, Distributed Computing and Client/Server Computing
- With distributed computing, an organization's computing is distributed over networks to the sites where the work of the organization is performed.
- The most powerful desktop machines provide individual users with enormous capabilities. Information is shared easily across computer networks, where computers called file servers offer a common data store that may be used by client computers distributed throughout the network—hence the term client/server computing.

Section 1.6 Hardware Trends
- Every year or two, the capacities of computers approximately double while their prices remain relatively constant. This often is called Moore's Law, named after the person who first observed the trend, Gordon Moore, co-founder of Intel.
- The invention of microprocessor chip technology and its wide deployment in the late 1970s and 1980s laid the groundwork for the productivity improvements that individuals and businesses have achieved in recent years.

Section 1.7 Microsoft's Windows® Operating System
- In the mid-1980s, Microsoft developed the Windows operating system, a graphical user interface built on top of the DOS operating system.
- The Windows operating system became incredibly popular after the 1993 release of Windows 3.1, whose successors, Windows 95 and Windows 98, virtually cornered the desktop operating systems market by the late 1990s.
- These operating systems, which borrowed many concepts (such as icons, menus and windows) popularized by early Apple Macintosh operating systems, enabled users to navigate multiple applications simultaneously.
- Windows XP, which is based on the Windows NT operating system, was released in 2001 and combines Microsoft's corporate and consumer operating system lines. Windows is by far the most widely used operating system.
- The biggest competitor to the Windows operating system is Linux. Linux is a free, open-source operating system.

Section 1.8 Machine Languages, Assembly Languages and High-Level Languages
- Any computer can directly understand only its own machine language. Machine languages generally consist of strings of numbers (ultimately reduced to 1s and 0s) that instruct computers to perform their most elementary operations one at a time.
- English-like abbreviations form the basis of assembly languages. Translator programs called assemblers convert assembly-language programs to machine language.
- Compilers translate high-level language programs into machine-language programs. High-level languages (like C#) contain English words and conventional mathematical notations.
- Interpreter programs execute high-level language programs directly, although much more slowly. Once a program is fully developed, a compiled version can be produced to run efficiently.

Section 1.9 C#
- C# is object oriented and contains a powerful class library of prebuilt components, enabling programmers to develop applications quickly—C# shares the Framework Class Library (FCL) with the other .NET languages.
- The .NET platform is one over which Web-based applications can be distributed to a great variety of devices (even cell phones) and to desktop computers.

- The C# programming language, developed at Microsoft by a team led by Anders Hejlsberg and Scott Wiltamuth, was designed specifically for the .NET platform as a language that would enable programmers to migrate easily to .NET.

- C# is an event-driven, fully object-oriented, visual programming language in which programs are created using an Integrated Development Environment (IDE).

Section 1.10 C, C++, Java and Visual Basic

- The C programming language was developed by Dennis Ritchie at Bell Laboratories in 1973. C first gained widespread recognition as the development language of the UNIX operating system.

- C++ was developed by Bjarne Stroustrup in the early 1980s at Bell Laboratories. C++ provides a number of features that "spruce up" the C language, but more important, it provides capabilities for object-oriented programming (OOP).

- Objects are reusable software components that model items in the real world. A modular, object-oriented approach to design and implementation can make software development groups much more productive than is possible using only earlier programming techniques, such as structured programming. Object-oriented programs are often easier to understand, correct and modify.

- Java is now used to develop large-scale enterprise applications, to enhance the functionality of Web servers, to provide applications for consumer devices and for many other purposes.

- Visual Basic offers powerful features including graphical user interfaces, event handling, object-oriented programming and exception handling.

- Visual Basic is an event-driven language (i.e., the programs respond to user-initiated events such as mouse clicks and keystrokes) and a visual programming language in which programs are created using an Integrated Development Environment (IDE).

Section 1.11 Other High-Level Languages

- Fortran (FORmula TRANslator) was developed by IBM Corporation in the mid-1950s for scientific and engineering applications that require complex mathematical computations.

- Pascal, named after the mathematician and philosopher Blaise Pascal, was designed for teaching structured programming in academic environments.

- COBOL (COmmon Business Oriented Language) was developed in the late 1950s. COBOL is used primarily for commercial applications that require precise and efficient data manipulation.

- Ada was developed under the sponsorship of the U. S. Department of Defense through the early 1980s. An important capability of Ada is multitasking, which allows programmers to specify that many activities are to occur in parallel.

- The language was named after Lady Ada Lovelace, daughter of the poet Lord Byron. She is generally credited with writing the world's first computer program, in the early 1800s.

Section 1.12 The Internet and the World Wide Web

- The Internet—a global network of computers—was initiated almost four decades ago with funding supplied by the U.S. Department of Defense. Originally designed to connect the main computer systems of about a dozen universities and research organizations, the Internet today is accessible by hundreds of millions of computers worldwide.

- The World Wide Web allows computer users to locate and view multimedia-based documents on almost any subject over the Internet.

- In 1989, Tim Berners-Lee of CERN (the European Organization for Nuclear Research) began to develop a technology for sharing information via hyperlinked text documents. Berners-Lee called his invention the HyperText Markup Language (HTML).

- The World Wide Web Consortium (W3C) is devoted to developing nonproprietary, interoperable technologies for the World Wide Web. One of the W3C's primary goals is to make the Web universally accessible—regardless of disabilities, language or culture.

Section 1.13 Extensible Markup Language (XML)

- XML is a standardized, fully extensible and structurally strict language for describing data.

- Data independence, the separation of content from its presentation, is the essential characteristic of XML. Because XML documents describe data, any conceivable application can process them.

- The Simple Object Access Protocol (SOAP) is a technology for the transmission of objects (marked up as XML) over the Internet.

- Microsoft's .NET uses XML and SOAP to mark up and transfer data over the Internet. XML and SOAP are at the core of .NET—they allow software components to interoperate (i.e., communicate easily with one another).

Section 1.14 Microsoft's .NET

- In 2000, Microsoft announced its .NET initiative, a new vision for embracing the Internet and the Web in the development and use of software. One key aspect of .NET is its independence from a specific language or platform. Rather than being forced to use a single programming language, developers can create a .NET application in any .NET-compatible language.

- Microsoft's ASP.NET technology allows programmers to create applications for the Web.

- A key component of the .NET architecture is Web services, which are reusable application components that can be used over the Internet. Clients and other applications can use these Web services as reusable building blocks.

- The .NET strategy extends the concept of software reuse to the Internet, allowing programmers and companies to concentrate on their specialties without having to implement every component of every application. Instead, companies can buy Web services and devote their resources to developing their own products.

Section 1.15 The .NET Framework and the Common Language Runtime

- Microsoft's .NET Framework manages and executes applications and Web services, contains a class library called the Framework Class Library (FCL), enforces security and provides many other programming capabilities.

- The details of the .NET Framework are found in the Common Language Infrastructure (CLI), which contains information about the storage of data types, objects and so on.

- The Common Language Runtime (CLR) executes .NET programs.

- Programs are compiled into machine-specific instructions in two steps. First, the program is compiled into Microsoft Intermediate Language (MSIL), which defines instructions for the CLR. When an application executes, another compiler (known as the just-in-time compiler or JIT compiler) in the CLR translates the MSIL in the executable file into machine-language code (for a particular platform), then the machine-language code executes on that platform. This second compilation phase is known as just-in-time compilation.

- The Framework Class Library (FCL) can be used by any .NET language. It contains reusable components, saving programmers the trouble of creating new components.

Section 1.16 Test-Driving a C# Application

- You can use existing controls—which are objects—to get powerful applications running in C# much faster than if you had to write all of the code yourself.

- The default settings for controls are the initial settings you see when you first run the application. Programmers include default settings to provide reasonable choices that the application will use if the user chooses not to change the settings.

Section 1.17 (Only Required Section of the Case Study) Software Engineering Case Study: Section Introduction to Object Technology and the UML

- The Unified Modeling Language (UML) is a graphical language that allows people who build systems to represent their object-oriented designs in a common notation.

- Object-oriented design (OOD) models software components in terms of real-world objects. It takes advantage of class relationships, where objects of a certain class have the same characteristics. It also takes advantage of inheritance relationships, where newly created classes of objects are derived by absorbing characteristics of existing classes and adding unique characteristics of their own. OOD encapsulates data (attributes) and functions (behavior) into objects—the data and functions of an object are intimately tied together.

- Objects have the property of information hiding—objects of one class are normally not allowed to know how objects of other classes are implemented.

- Object-oriented programming (OOP) allows programmers to implement object-oriented designs as working systems.

- C# programmers concentrate on creating their own user-defined types called classes. Each class contains data as well as the set of methods that manipulate that data and provide services to clients (i.e., other classes or methods that use the class).

- The data components of a class are called attributes or fields. The operation components of a class are called methods.

- Classes can have relationships with other classes. These relationships are called associations.

- Packaging software as classes makes it possible for future software systems to reuse the classes. Groups of related classes are often packaged as reusable components.

- An instance of a class is called an object.

- With object technology, programmers can build much of the software they will need by combining standardized, interchangeable parts called classes.

- The process of analyzing and designing a system from an object-oriented point of view is called object-oriented analysis and design (OOAD).

Terminology

action	behavior of an object
action oriented	C programming language
Ada programming language	C# programming language
"administrative" section of the computer	C# 2.0 programming language
arithmetic and logic unit (ALU)	C++ programming language
ASP.NET	central processing unit (CPU)
assembler	class
assembly language	class library
association	client
attribute of an object	client of a class
batch processing	client/server computing

close box
COBOL programming language
Common Intermediate Language (CIL)
Common Language Infrastructure (CLI)
Common Language Runtime (CLR)
compiler
component
computer
computer program
computer programmer
control
data
data independence
design
distributed computing
dynamic content
e-mail (electronic mail)
encapsulate
extensible
field of a class
file server
Fortran programming language
Framework Class Library (FCL)
function
hardware
hardware platform
high-level language
HTML (HyperText Markup Language)
HTTP (Hypertext Transfer Protocol)
information hiding
inheritance
input device
input unit
instantiate an object of a class
Integrated Development Environment (IDE)
interface
Internet
interpreter
Java programming language
job
just-in-time (JIT) compiler
language independence
language interoperability in .NET
live-code approach
local area network (LAN)
logical unit
machine dependent
machine language
"manufacturing" section of the computer
member function

memory
memory unit
method
Microsoft .NET
Microsoft Intermediate Language (MSIL)
Moore's Law
multiprocessor
multiprogramming
multitasking
multithreading
.NET Framework
.NET initiative
.NET-compliant language
nouns in a system specification
object
object oriented
object-oriented analysis and design (OOAD)
object-oriented design (OOD)
object-oriented programming (OOP)
operating system
operation of an object
output device
output unit
Pascal programming language
personal computer
personal computing
platform independence
portability
primary memory
procedural programming
pseudocode
"receiving" section of the computer
reusable software component
secondary storage unit
"shipping" section of the computer
SOAP (Simple Object Access Protocol)
software
software reuse
structured programming
supercomputer
task
throughput
timesharing
translation
translator program
UML (Unified Modeling Language)
user-defined type
Visual Basic programming language
Visual C# programming language
visual programming

W3C (World Wide Web Consortium)
Web service
Windows operating system

World Wide Web (WWW)
XML (Extensible Markup Language)
XML vocabulary

Self-Review Exercises

1.1 Fill in the blanks in each of the following statements:
a) Computers can directly understand only their native _____ language, which is composed only of 1s and 0s.
b) Computers process data under the control of sets of instructions called computer _____.
c) The _____ is the long-term, high-capacity "warehousing" section of the computer.
d) The three types of languages discussed in the chapter are machine languages, _____ and _____.
e) Programs that translate high-level language programs into machine language are called _____.
f) Visual Studio is a(n) _____ in which C# programs are developed.
g) C is widely known as the development language of the _____ operating system.
h) Microsoft's _____ provides a large programming library for the .NET languages.
i) The Department of Defense developed the Ada language with a capability called _____, which allows programmers to specify activities that can proceed in parallel. C# offers a similar capability called multithreading.
j) Web services use _____ and _____ to mark up and send information over the Internet, respectively.

1.2 State whether each of the following is *true* or *false*. If *false*, explain why.
a) The UML is used primarily to implement object-oriented systems.
b) C# is an object-oriented language.
c) To use a control in C#, you must write all of the code. This process can be time consuming.
d) C# is the only language available for programming .NET applications.
e) Procedural programming models the world more naturally than object-oriented programming.
f) Computers can directly understand high-level languages.
g) MSIL is the common intermediate format to which all .NET programs compile, regardless of their original .NET language.
h) The .NET Framework is portable to non-Windows platforms.
i) Compiled programs run faster than their corresponding interpreted programs.
j) Multiprogramming involves the simultaneous operation of many jobs that are competing to share the computer's resources.

Answers to Self-Review Exercises

1.1 a) machine. b) programs. c) secondary storage unit. d) assembly languages, high-level languages. e) compilers. f) Integrated Development Environment (IDE). g) UNIX. h) Framework Class Library (FCL). i) multitasking. j) XML, SOAP.

1.2 a) False. The UML is used primarily to design object-oriented systems. b) True. c) False. C# allows you to use existing controls to get powerful applications running faster than if you had to write all of the code yourself. d) False. C# is one of many .NET languages (others are Visual Basic and Visual C++). e) False. Object-oriented programming (because it focuses on *things*) is a more natural way to model the world than procedural programming. f) False. Computers can directly understand only their own machine languages. g) True. h) True. i) True. j) True.

Exercises

1.3 Categorize each of the following items as either hardware or software:
    a) CPU.
    b) Compiler.
    c) Input unit.
    d) A word-processor program.
    e) A C# program.

1.4 Translator programs, such as assemblers and compilers, convert programs from one language (referred to as the source language) to another language (referred to as the target language). Determine which of the following statements are *true* and which are *false*:
    a) A compiler translates high-level language programs into target-language programs.
    b) An assembler translates source-language programs into machine-language programs.
    c) A compiler converts source-language programs into target-language programs.
    d) High-level languages are generally machine dependent.
    e) A machine-language program requires translation before it can be run on a computer.
    f) The C# compiler translates high-level language programs into SMIL.

1.5 What are the basic requirements of a .NET language? What is needed to run a .NET program on a new type of computer (machine)?

1.6 Expand each of the following acronyms:
    a) W3C.
    b) XML.
    c) SOAP.
    d) OOP.
    e) CLR.
    f) CLI.
    g) FCL.
    h) MSIL.
    i) UML.
    j) OMG.
    k) IDE.

1.7 What are the key benefits of the .NET Framework and the CLR? What are the drawbacks?

1.8 What are the advantages to using object-oriented techniques?

1.9 You are probably wearing on your wrist one of the world's most common types of objects—a watch. Discuss how each of the following terms and concepts applies to the notion of a watch: object, attributes and behaviors.

1.10 What was the key reason that C# was developed?

1.11 What is the key accomplishment of the UML?

1.12 What did the chief benefit of the early Internet prove to be?

1.13 What is the key capability of the Web?

1.14 What is the key vision of Microsoft's .NET initiative?

1.15 How does the FCL facilitate the development of .NET applications?

1.16 What are Web services and why are they so crucial to Microsoft's .NET strategy?

1.17 What is the key advantage of standardizing .NET's CLI (Common Language Infrastructure) with Ecma?

1.18   Why is programming in an object-oriented language such as C# more "natural" than programming in a procedural programming language such as C?

1.19   Despite the obvious benefits of reuse made possible by OOP, what do many organizations report as the key benefit of OOP?

1.20   Why is C# said to be an event-driven language?

1.21   Why is XML so crucial to the development of future software systems?

2

Seeing is believing.
—Proverb

Form ever follows function.
—Louis Henri Sullivan

Intelligence ... is the faculty of making artificial objects, especially tools to make tools.
—Henri-Louis Bergson

Introduction to the Visual C# 2005 Express Edition IDE

OBJECTIVES

In this chapter, you will learn:

- The basics of the Visual Studio Integrated Development Environment (IDE) that assists you in writing, running and debugging your Visual C# programs.

- Visual Studio's help features.

- Key commands contained in the IDE's menus and toolbars.

- The purpose of the various kinds of windows in the Visual Studio 2005 IDE.

- What visual programming is and how it simplifies and speeds program development.

- To create, compile and execute a simple Visual C# program that displays text and an image using the Visual Studio IDE and the technique of visual programming.

2.1 Introduction

Visual Studio® 2005 is Microsoft's Integrated Development Environment (IDE) for creating, running and debugging programs (also called *applications*) written in a variety of .NET programming languages. In this chapter, we provide an overview of the Visual Studio 2005 IDE and demonstrate how to create a simple Visual C# program by dragging and dropping predefined building blocks into place—a technique called *visual programming*. This chapter is specific to Visual C#—Microsoft's implementation of Ecma standard C#.

2.2 Overview of the Visual Studio 2005 IDE

There are many versions of Visual Studio available. For this book, we used the *Microsoft Visual C# 2005 Express Edition*, which supports only the Visual C# programming language. Microsoft also offers a full version of Visual Studio 2005, which includes support for other languages in addition to Visual C#, such as Visual Basic and Visual C++. Our screen captures and discussions focus on the IDE of the Visual C# 2005 Express Edition. We assume that you have some familiarity with Windows.

Again, we use fonts to distinguish between IDE features (such as menu names and menu items) and other elements that appear in the IDE. We emphasize IDE features in a sans-serif bold **Helvetica** font (e.g., **File** menu) and emphasize other elements, such as file names (e.g., `Form1.cs`) and property names (discussed in Section 2.4), in a sans-serif `Lucida` font.

Introduction to Microsoft Visual C# 2005 Express Edition
To start Microsoft Visual C# 2005 Express Edition in Windows XP, select **Start > All Programs > Visual C# 2005 Express Edition**. For Windows 2000 users, select **Start > Programs > Visual C# 2005 Express Edition**. Once the Express Edition begins execution, the ***Start Page*** displays (Fig. 2.1). Depending on your version of Visual Studio, your **Start Page** may look different. For new programmers unfamiliar with Visual C#, the **Start Page** contains a list of links to resources in the Visual Studio 2005 IDE and on the Internet.

From this point forward, we will refer to the Visual Studio 2005 IDE simply as "Visual Studio" or "the IDE." For experienced developers, this page provides links to the latest developments in Visual C# (such as updates and bug fixes) and to information on advanced programming topics. Once you start exploring the IDE, you can return to the **Start Page** by selecting the page from the location bar drop-down menu (Fig. 2.2), by selecting **View > Other Windows > Start Page** or by clicking the **Start Page** icon from the IDE's **Toolbar** (Fig. 2.9). We discuss the **Toolbar** and its various icons in Section 2.3. We use the **>** character to indicate the selection of a menu command from a menu. For example, we use the notation **File > Open File** to indicate that you should select the **Open File** command from the **File** menu.

Links on the Start Page
The **Start Page** links are organized into sections—**Recent Projects, Getting Started, Visual C# Express Headlines** and **MSDN: Visual Studio 2005**—that contain links to helpful pro-

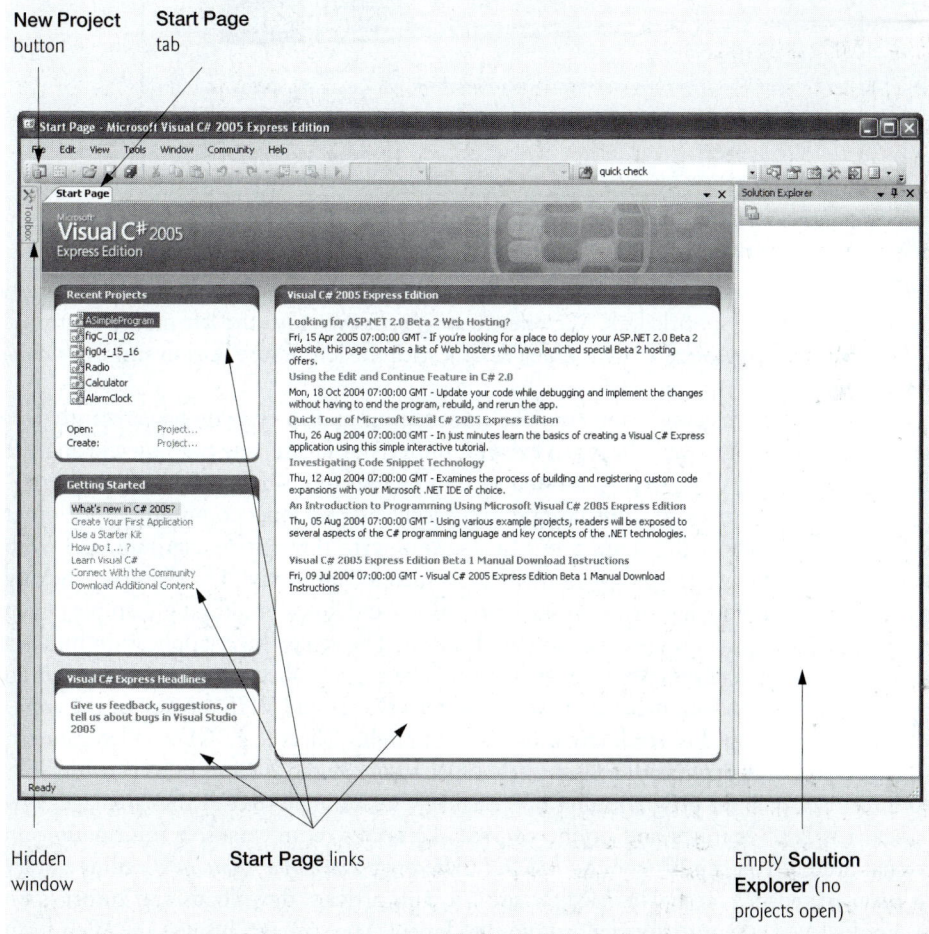

Fig. 2.1 | **Start Page** in Visual C# 2005 Express Edition.

Requested Web page
(URL in location bar
drop-down menu)   Selected tab for requested Web page

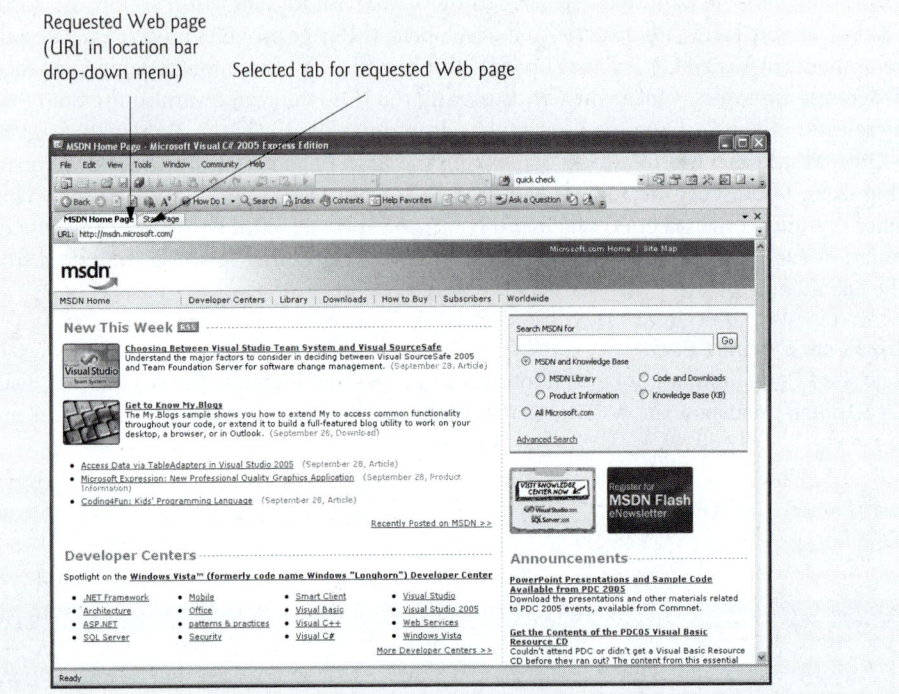

Fig. 2.2 | Displaying a Web page in Visual Studio.

gramming resources. Clicking any link on the **Start Page** displays the relevant information associated with the specific link. We refer to *single clicking* with the left mouse button as *selecting* or *clicking*; we refer to double clicking with the left mouse button simply as *double clicking*.

The **Recent Projects** section contains information on projects you have recently created or modified. You can also open existing projects or create new ones by clicking the links in the section. The **Getting Started** section focuses on using the IDE to create programs, learning Visual C#, connecting to the Visual C# developer community (i.e., other software developers with whom you can communicate through newsgroups and Web sites) and providing various development tools such as starter kits. For example, clicking the link **Use a Starter Kit** provides you with resources and links for building a simple screen saver application or a movie collection application. The screen saver application builds a screen saver that displays current news articles. The movie collection starter kit builds an application that lets you maintain a catalog of your DVDs and VHS movies, or the application can be changed to track anything else you might collect (e.g., CDs, video games).

The **Visual C# Express Headlines** and **MSDN: Visual Studio 2005** sections provide links to information about programming in Visual C#, including a tour of the language, new Visual C# 2005 features and online courses. To access more extensive information on Visual Studio, you can browse the *MSDN (Microsoft Developer Network)* online library at msdn.microsoft.com. The MSDN site contains articles, downloads and tutorials on technologies of interest to Visual Studio developers. You can also browse the Web from the IDE using Internet Explorer. To request a Web page, type its URL into the location bar (Fig. 2.2) and press the *Enter* key—your computer, of course, must be connected to the Internet. (If the location bar is not already present in the IDE, select **View > Other Windows > Show Browser.**) The Web page that you wish to view will appear as another *tab*, which you can select, inside the Visual Studio IDE (Fig. 2.2).

Customizing the IDE and Creating a New Project

To begin programming in Visual C#, you must create a new project or open an existing one. There are two ways to create a new project or open an existing project. You can select either **File > New Project...** or **File > Open Project...** from the **File** menu, which creates a new project or opens an existing project, respectively. From the **Start Page**, under the **Recent Projects** section, you can also click the links **Create: Project** or **Open: Project/Solution.** A *project* is a group of related files, such as the Visual C# code and any images that might make up a program. Visual Studio 2005 organizes programs into projects and *solutions*, which contain one or more projects. Multiple-project solutions are used to create large-scale programs. Each of the programs we create in this book consists of a single project.

Select **File > New Project...** or the **Create: Project...** link on the **Start Page** to display the ***New Project*** *dialog* (Fig. 2.3). *Dialogs* are windows that facilitate user-computer communication. We will discuss the detailed process of creating new projects momentarily.

Visual Studio provides templates for several project types (Fig. 2.3). *Templates* are the project types users can create in Visual C#—Windows applications, console applications and others (you will primarily use Windows applications and console applications in this textbook). Users can also use or create custom application templates. In this chapter,

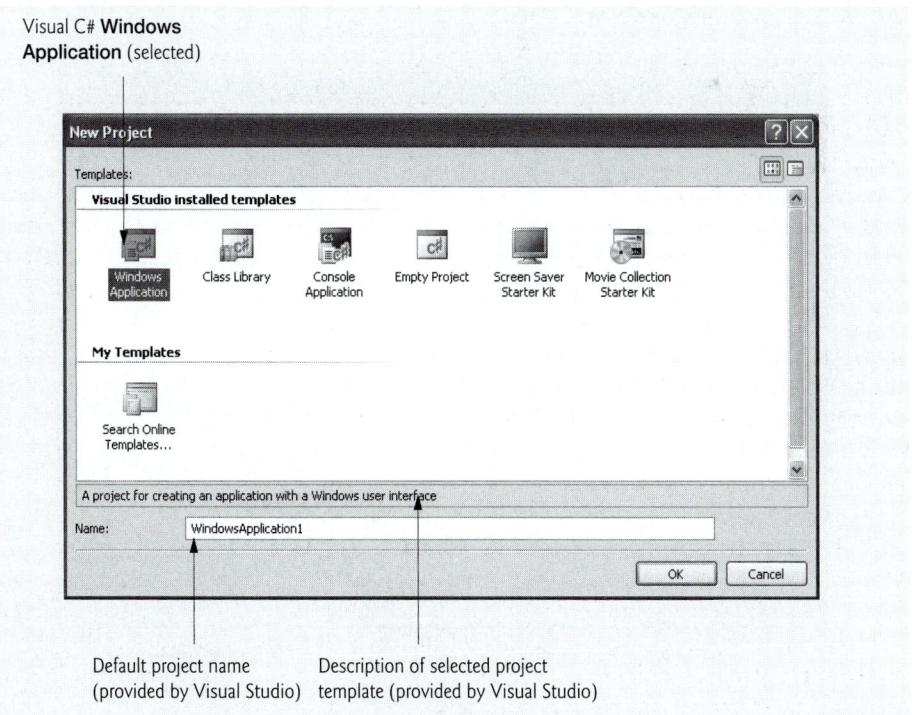

Visual C# **Windows Application** (selected)

Default project name (provided by Visual Studio)

Description of selected project template (provided by Visual Studio)

Fig. 2.3 | **New Project** dialog.

we focus on Windows applications. We discuss the **Console Application** template in Chapter 3, Introduction to C# Applications. A *Windows application* is a program that executes within a Windows operating system (e.g., Windows 2000 or Windows XP) and typically has a *graphical user interface* (*GUI*)—the visual part of the program with which the user interacts. Windows applications include Microsoft software products like Microsoft Word, Internet Explorer and Visual Studio; software products created by other vendors; and customized software that you and other programmers create. You will create many Windows applications in this text. [*Note:* Novell sponsors an open source project called *Mono* that enables developers to create .NET applications for Linux, Windows and Mac OS X. Mono is based on the Ecma standards for C# and the Common Language Infrastructure (CLI). For more information on Mono, visit www.mono-project.com.]

By default, Visual Studio assigns the name **WindowsApplication1** to the new project and solution (Fig. 2.3). Soon you will change the name of the project and the location where it is saved. Click **OK** to display the IDE in *design view* (Fig. 2.4), which contains all the features necessary for you to begin creating programs. The design view portion of the IDE is also known as the *Windows Form Designer*.

The gray rectangle titled **Form1** (called a *Form*) represents the main window of the Windows application that you are creating. C# applications can have multiple Forms (windows); however, most of the applications you will create in this text use only one Form. Later in the chapter, you will learn how to customize the Form by adding controls (i.e.,

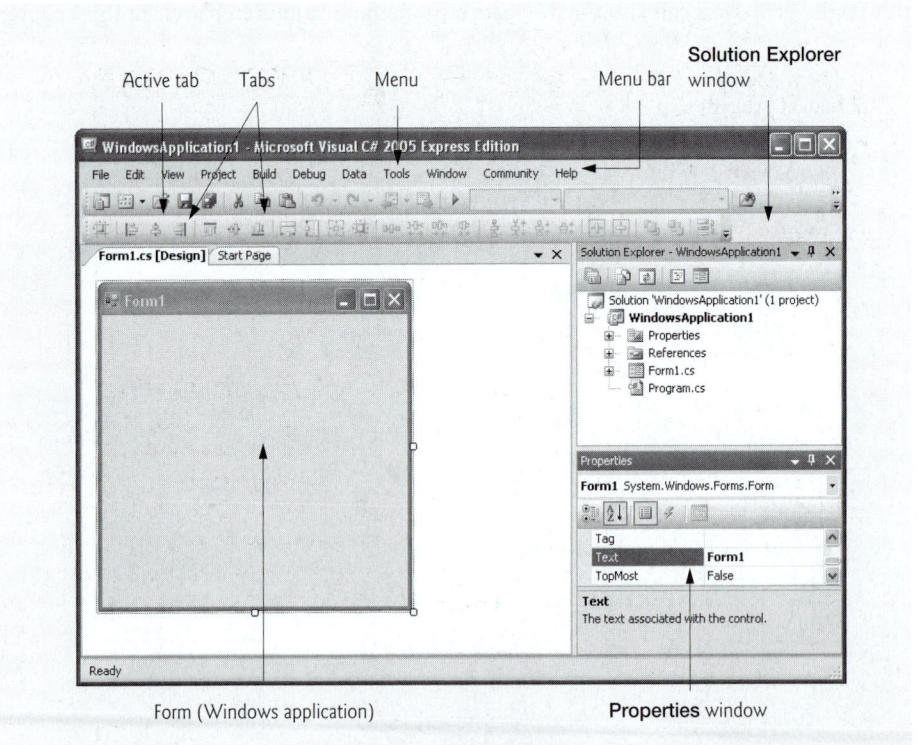

Fig. 2.4 | **Design** view of the IDE.

reusable components) to a program—in this case, a Label and a PictureBox (as you will see in Fig. 2.27). A *Label* typically contains descriptive text (e.g., "Welcome to Visual C#!"), and a *PictureBox* displays images, such as the Deitel bug mascot. Visual Studio has over 65 preexisting controls you can use to build and customize your programs. Many of these controls are defined and used throughout this book. In addition to the controls provided with Visual C# 2005 Express or Visual Studio 2005, there are many other controls available from third parties. You can download several third party controls from msdn.microsoft.com/vcsharp/downloads/components/default.aspx.

As you begin programming, you will work with controls that are not necessarily part of your program, but rather are part of the FCL. As you place controls on the form, you can modify their properties (discussed in detail in Section 2.4) by entering alternative text in a text box (Fig. 2.5) or selecting options then pressing a button, such as **OK** or **Cancel**, as shown in Fig. 2.6.

Collectively, the Form and controls constitute the program's GUI. Users enter data (*input*) into the program in a variety of ways, including typing at the keyboard, clicking the mouse buttons and typing into GUI controls, such as TextBoxes. Programs use the GUI to display instructions and other information (*output*) for users to read. For example, the **New Project** dialog in Fig. 2.3 presents a GUI where the user clicks the mouse button to select a project template, then inputs a project name from the keyboard (note that the figure is still showing the default project name **WindowsApplication1** supplied by Visual Studio).

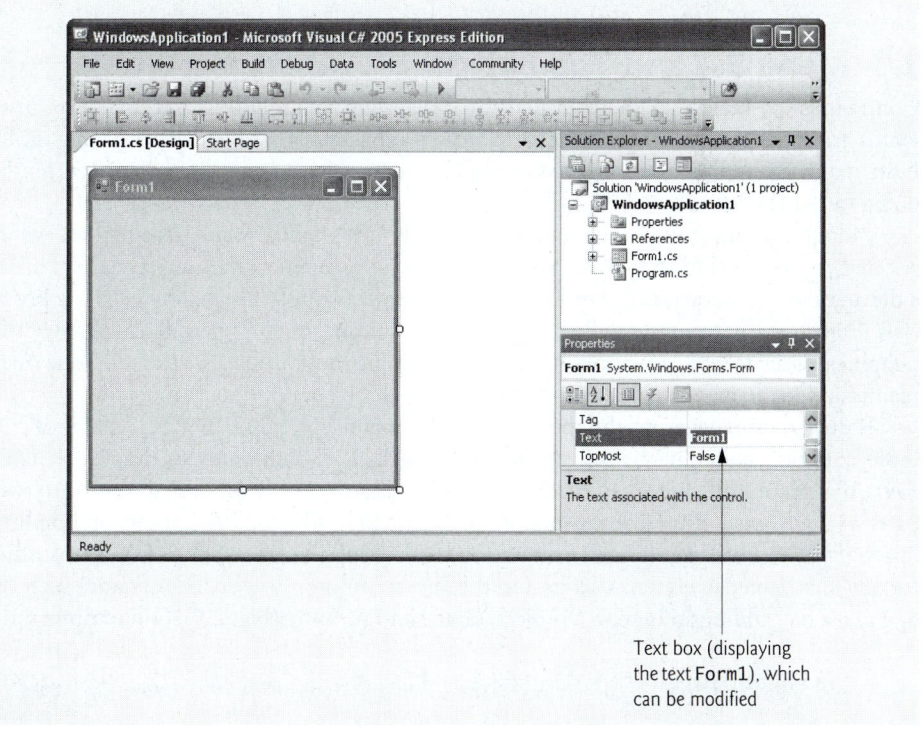

Text box (displaying
the text Form1), which
can be modified

Fig. 2.5 | Example of a text box control in the Visual Studio IDE.

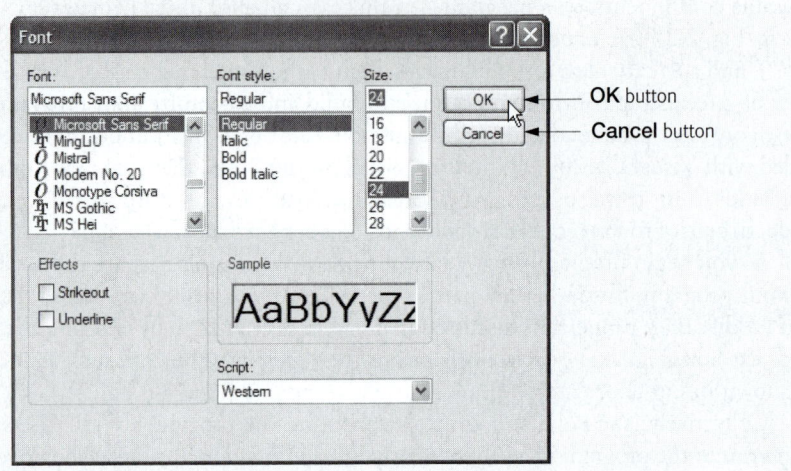

Fig. 2.6 | Examples of buttons in the Visual Studio IDE.

The name of each open document is listed on a tab—in Fig. 2.4, the open documents are **Form1.cs [Design]** and the **Start Page**. To view a document, click its tab. Tabs facilitate easy access to multiple open documents. The *active tab* (the tab of the document currently displayed in the IDE) is displayed in bold text (e.g., **Form1.cs [Design]** in Fig. 2.4) and is positioned in front of all the other tabs.

2.3 Menu Bar and Toolbar

Commands for managing the IDE and for developing, maintaining and executing programs are contained in *menus*, which are located on the *menu bar* of the IDE (Fig. 2.7). Note that the set of menus displayed in Fig. 2.7 changes based on what you are currently doing in the IDE.

Menus contain groups of related commands (also called *menu items*) that, when selected, cause the IDE to perform specific actions (e.g., open a window, save a file, print a file and execute a program). For example, new projects can be created by selecting **File > New Project....** The menus depicted in Fig. 2.7 are summarized in Fig. 2.8. In Chapter 14, Graphical User Interface Concepts: Part 2, we discuss how to create and add your own menus and menu items to your programs.

Rather than navigating the menus from the menu bar, you can access many of the more common commands from the *toolbar* (Fig. 2.9), which contains graphics, called *icons*, that graphically represent commands. [*Note:* Figure 2.9 divides the toolbar into two parts so that we can illustrate the graphics more clearly—the toolbar appears on one line inside the IDE.] By default, the standard toolbar is displayed when you run Visual Studio for the first time; it contains icons for the most commonly used commands, such as opening a file, adding an item to a project, saving and running (Fig. 2.9). Some commands

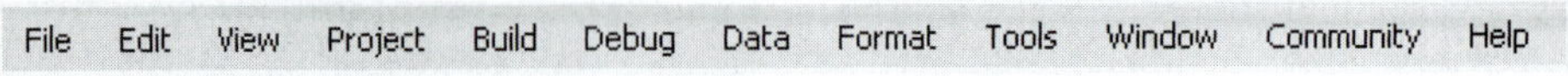

File   Edit   View   Project   Build   Debug   Data   Format   Tools   Window   Community   Help

Fig. 2.7 | Visual Studio menu bar.

Menu	Description
File	Contains commands for opening, closing, adding and saving projects, as well as printing project data and exiting Visual Studio.
Edit	Contains commands for editing programs, such as cut, copy, paste, undo, redo, delete, find and select.
View	Contains commands for displaying windows (e.g., **Solution Explorer**, **Toolbox**, **Properties** window) and for adding toolbars to the IDE.
Project	Contains commands for managing projects and their files.
Build	Contains commands for compiling a program.
Debug	Contains commands for debugging (i.e., identifying and correcting problems in a program) and running a program. Debugging is discussed in detail in Appendix C.
Data	Contains commands for interacting with databases (i.e., organized collections of data stored on computers), which we discuss in Chapter 20, Database, SQL and ADO.NET).
Format	Contains commands for arranging and modifying a form's controls. Note that the **Format** menu appears only when a GUI component is selected in **Design** view.
Tools	Contains commands for accessing additional IDE tools (e.g., the **Toolbox**) and options that enable you to customize the IDE.
Window	Contains commands for arranging and displaying windows.
Community	Contains commands for sending questions directly to Microsoft, checking question status, sending feedback on Visual C# and searching the CodeZone developer center and the Microsoft developers community site.
Help	Contains commands for accessing the IDE's help features.

Fig. 2.8 | Summary of Visual Studio 2005 IDE menus.

are initially disabled (i.e., unavailable to use). These commands, which are initially grayed out, are enabled by Visual Studio only when they are necessary. For example, Visual Studio enables the command for saving a file once you begin editing the file.

You can customize the IDE by adding more toolbars. Select **View** > **Toolbars** (Fig. 2.10). Each toolbar you select will be displayed with the other toolbars at the top of the Visual Studio window (Fig. 2.10). Another way in which you can add toolbars to your IDE (which we do not show in this chapter) is through selecting **Tools > Customize**. Then, under the **Toolbars** tab, select the additional toolbars you would like to have appear in the IDE.

To execute a command via the toolbar, click its icon. Some icons contain a down arrow that, when clicked, displays a related command or commands, as shown in Fig. 2.11.

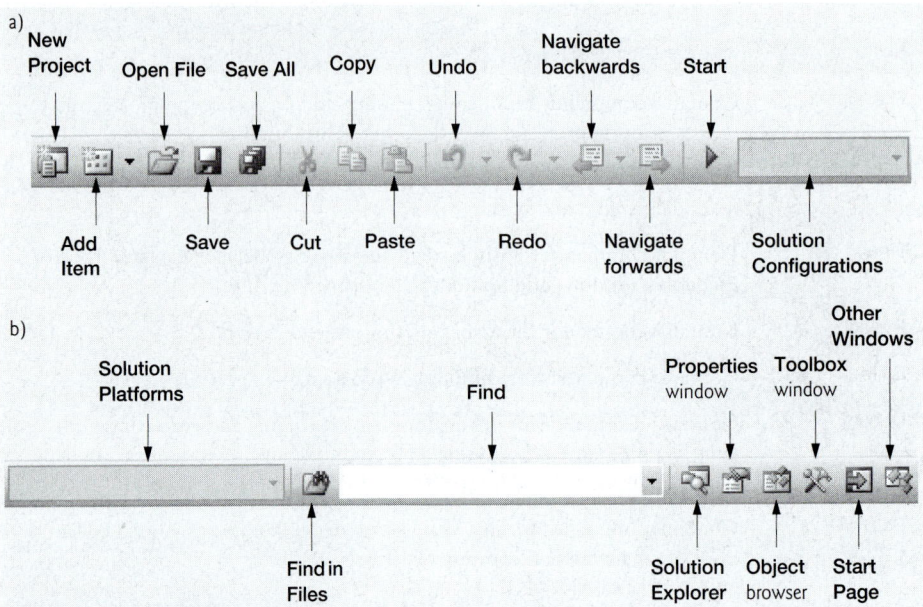

Fig. 2.9 | Standard toolbar in Visual Studio.

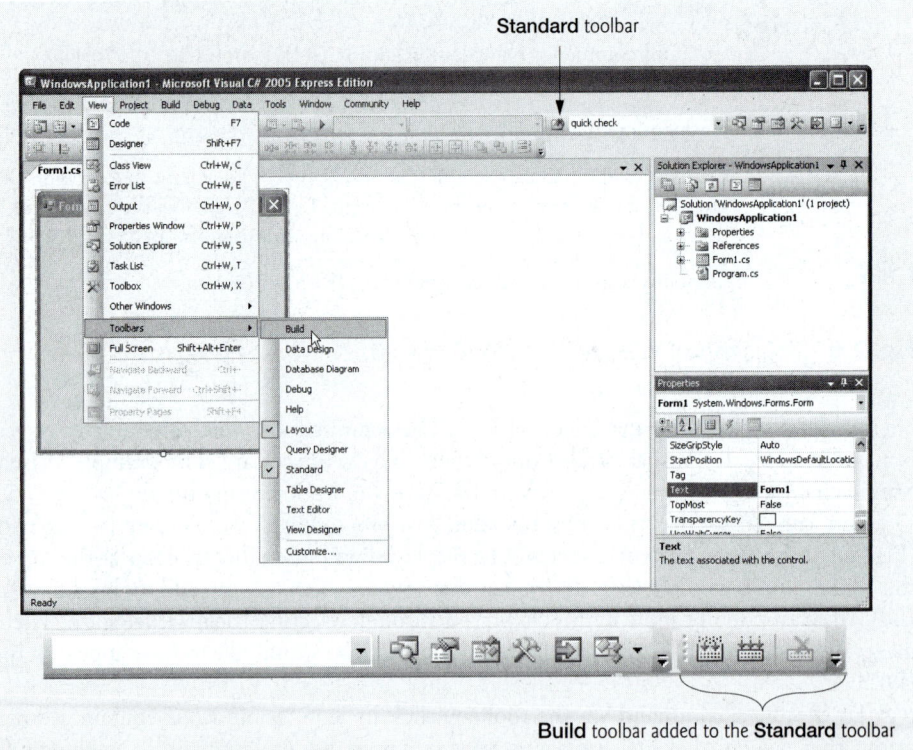

Fig. 2.10 | Adding the **Build** toolbar to the IDE.

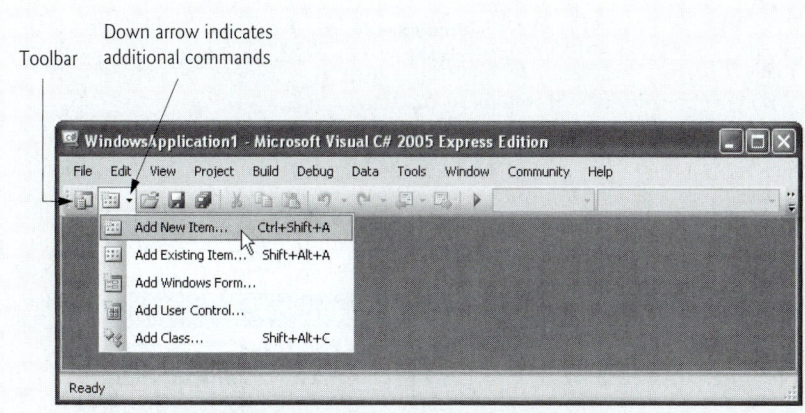

Fig. 2.11 | IDE toolbar icon showing additional commands.

It is difficult to remember what each of the icons on the toolbar represents. Positioning the mouse pointer over an icon highlights it and, after a brief delay, displays a description of the icon called a *tool tip* (Fig. 2.12). Tool tips help novice programmers become familiar with the IDE's features and serve as useful reminders of each toolbar icon's functionality.

2.4 Navigating the Visual Studio 2005 IDE

The IDE provides windows for accessing project files and customizing controls. In this section, we introduce several windows that you will use frequently when developing Visual C# programs. These windows can be accessed via toolbar icons (Fig. 2.13) or by selecting the name of the desired window in the **View** menu.

Visual Studio provides a space-saving feature called *auto-hide*. When auto-hide is enabled, a tab appears along either the left or right edge of the IDE window (Fig. 2.14). This tab contains one or more icons, each of which identifies a hidden window. Placing

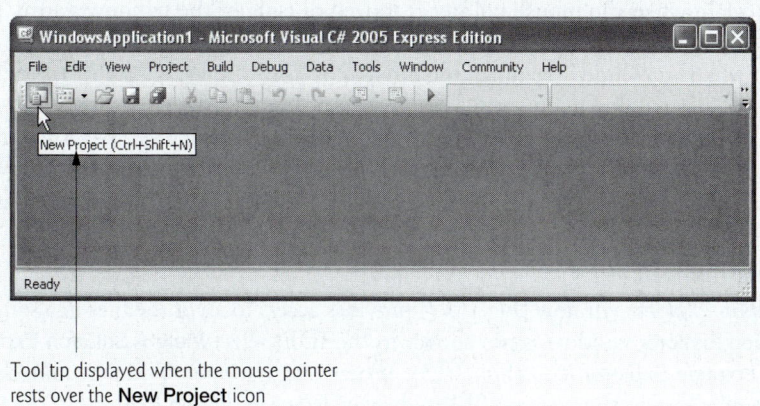

Fig. 2.12 | Tool tip demonstration.

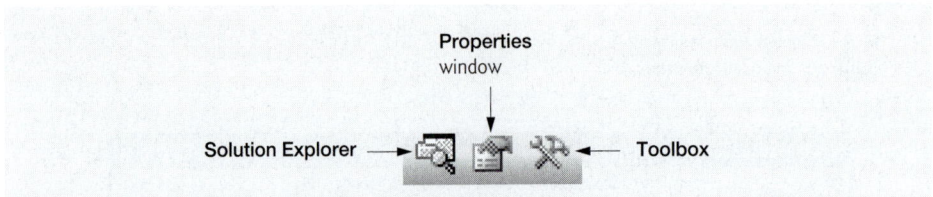

Fig. 2.13 | Toolbar icons for three Visual Studio windows.

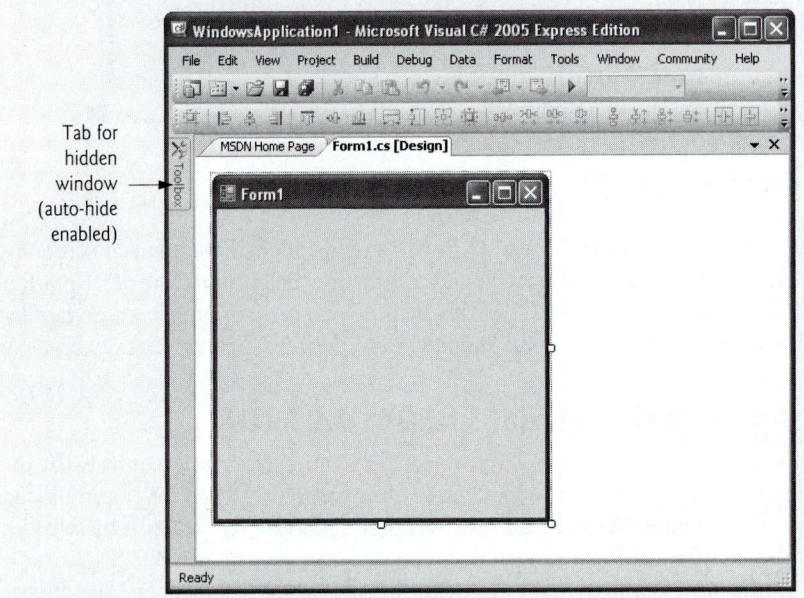

Fig. 2.14 | Auto-hide feature demonstration.

the mouse pointer over one of these icons displays that window (Fig. 2.15). The window is hidden again when the mouse pointer is moved outside of the window's area. To "pin down" a window (i.e., to disable auto-hide and keep the window open), click the pin icon. Note that when auto-hide is enabled, the pin icon is horizontal (Fig. 2.15), whereas when a window is "pinned down," the pin icon is vertical (Fig. 2.16).

The next few sections overview three of the main windows used in Visual Studio—the **Solution Explorer**, the **Toolbox** and the **Properties** window. These windows show information about the project and include tools that will help you build your programs.

2.4.1 Solution Explorer

The *Solution Explorer* window (Fig. 2.17) provides access to all of the files in a solution. If the **Solution Explorer** window is not shown in the IDE, select **View > Solution Explorer** or click the **Solution Explorer** icon (Fig. 2.13). When you first open Visual Studio, the **Solution Explorer** is empty; there are no files to display. Once you open a solution, the **Solution Explorer** displays the contents of the solution and its projects or when you create a new project, its contents are displayed.

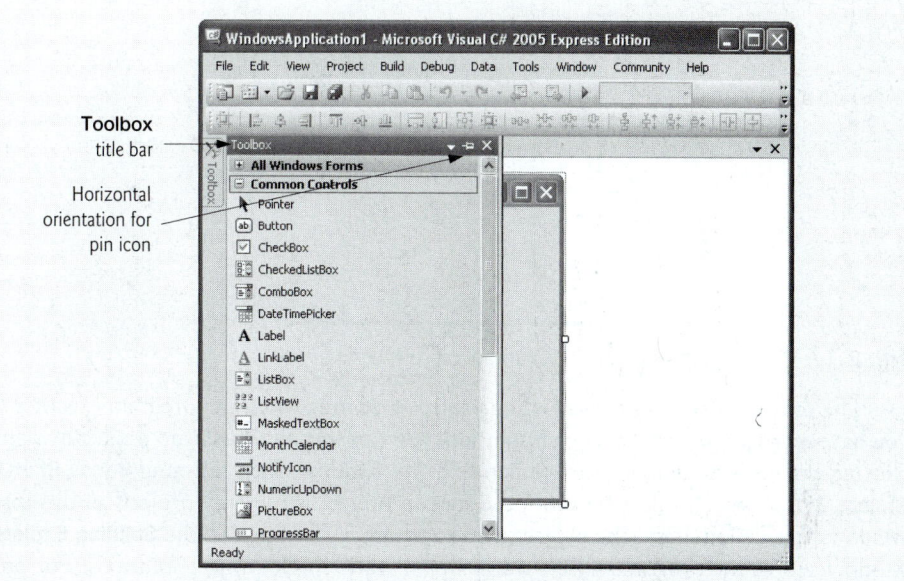

Fig. 2.15 | Displaying a hidden window when auto-hide is enabled.

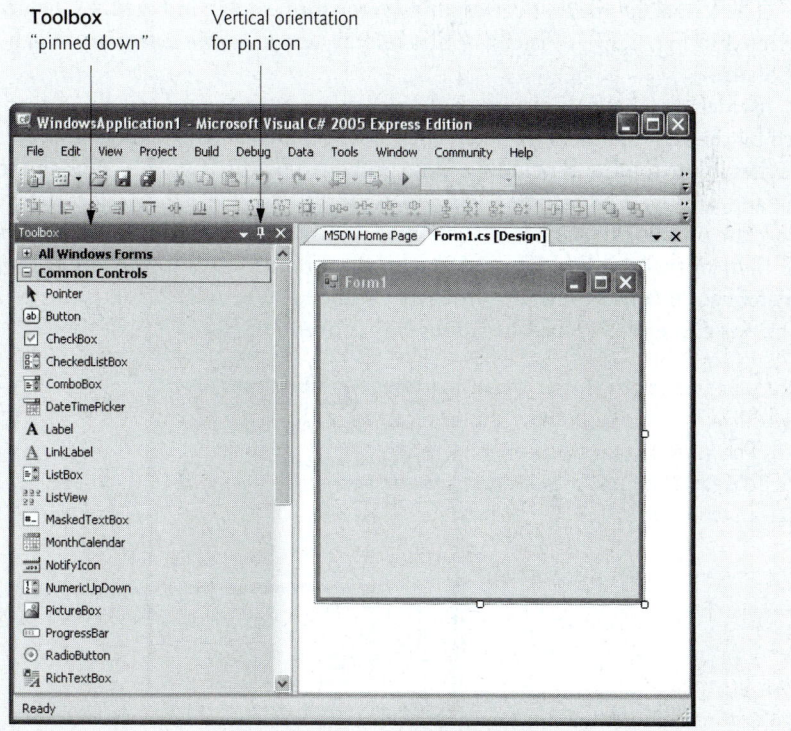

Fig. 2.16 | Disabling auto-hide ("pinning down" a window).

Show all files icon

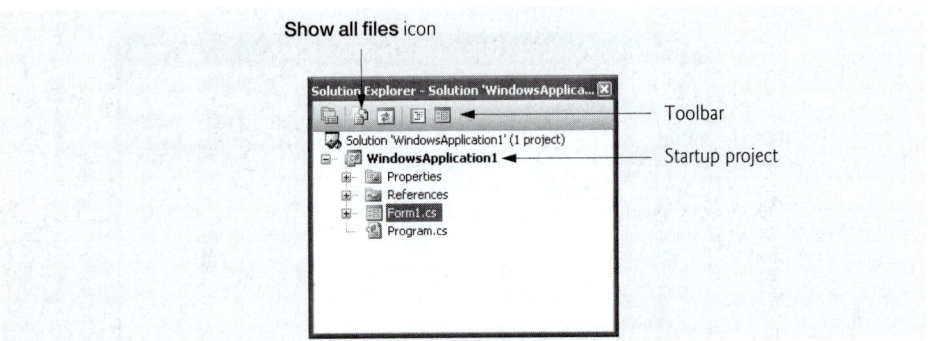

Fig. 2.17 | **Solution Explorer** with an open project.

The solution's *startup project* is the project that runs when the program executes. If you have multiple projects in a given solution, you can specify the startup project by right-clicking the project name in the **Solution Explorer** window, then selecting **Set as StartUp Project**. For a single-project solution, the startup project is the only project (in this case, **WindowsApplication1**) and the project name appears in bold text in the **Solution Explorer** window. All of the programs discussed in this text are single-project solutions. For programmers using Visual Studio for the first time, the **Solution Explorer** window lists only the **Properties, References, Form1.cs** and **Program.cs** files (Fig. 2.17). The **Solution Explorer** window includes a toolbar that contains several icons.

The Visual C# file that corresponds to the form shown in Fig. 2.4 is named Form1.cs (selected in Fig. 2.17). (Visual C# files use the *.cs filename extension*, which is short for "C Sharp.")

By default, the IDE displays only files that you may need to edit—other files generated by the IDE are hidden. When clicked, the *Show all files icon* (Fig. 2.17) displays all the files in the solution, including those generated by the IDE. The plus and minus boxes that appear (Fig. 2.18) can be clicked to expand and collapse the project tree, respectively. Click the plus box to the left of **Properties** to display items grouped under the heading to the right of the plus box (Fig. 2.19); click the minus boxes to the left of **Properties** and **References** to collapse the tree from its expanded state (Fig. 2.20). Other Visual Studio windows also use this plus-box/minus-box convention.

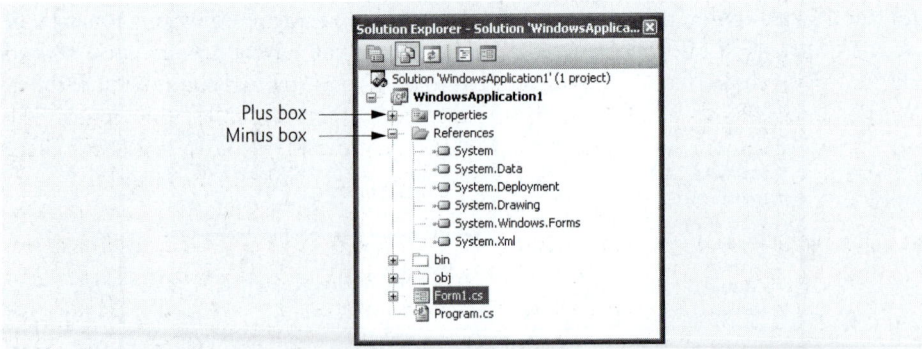

Fig. 2.18 | **Solution Explorer** showing plus boxes and minus boxes for expanding and collapsing the tree to show or hide project files.

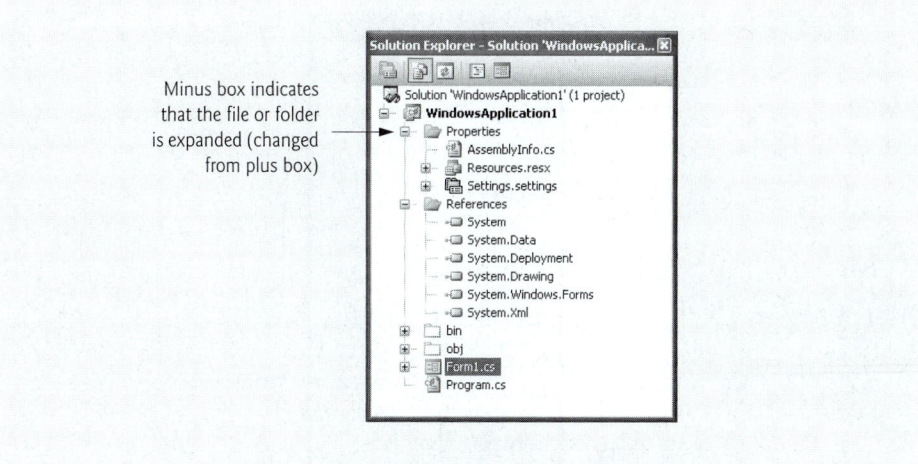

Minus box indicates that the file or folder is expanded (changed from plus box)

Fig. 2.19 | **Solution Explorer** expanding the **Properties** file after clicking its plus box.

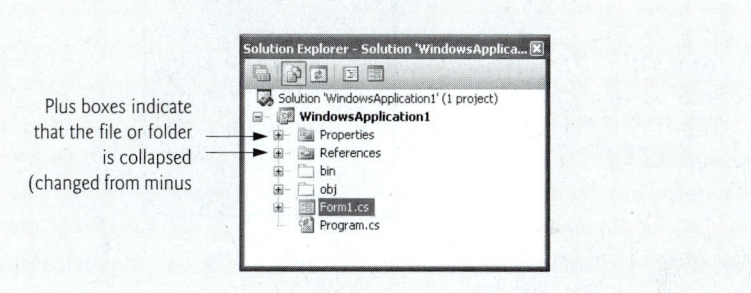

Plus boxes indicate that the file or folder is collapsed (changed from minus

Fig. 2.20 | **Solution Explorer** collapsing all files after clicking any minus boxes.

2.4.2 Toolbox

The **Toolbox** contains icons representing controls used to customize forms (Fig. 2.21). Using visual programming, you can "drag and drop" controls onto the form, which is faster and simpler than building them by writing GUI code (we introduce writing this type of code in Chapter 5, Control Statements: Part 1). Just as you do not need to know how to build an engine to drive a car, you do not need to know how to build controls to use them. Reusing pre-existing controls saves time and money when you develop programs. The wide variety of controls contained in the **Toolbox** is a powerful feature of the .NET FCL. You will use the **Toolbox** when you create your first program later in the chapter.

The **Toolbox** contains groups of related controls. Examples of these groups, **All Windows Forms, Common Controls, Containers, Menus & Toolbars, Data, Components, Printing, Dialogs** and **General**, are listed in Fig. 2.21. Again, note the use of plus and minus boxes to expand or collapse a group of controls. The **Toolbox** contains over 65 prebuilt controls for use in Visual Studio, so you may need to scroll through the **Toolbox** to view additional controls other than the ones shown in Fig. 2.21. We discuss many of the **Toolbox**'s controls and their functionality throughout the book.

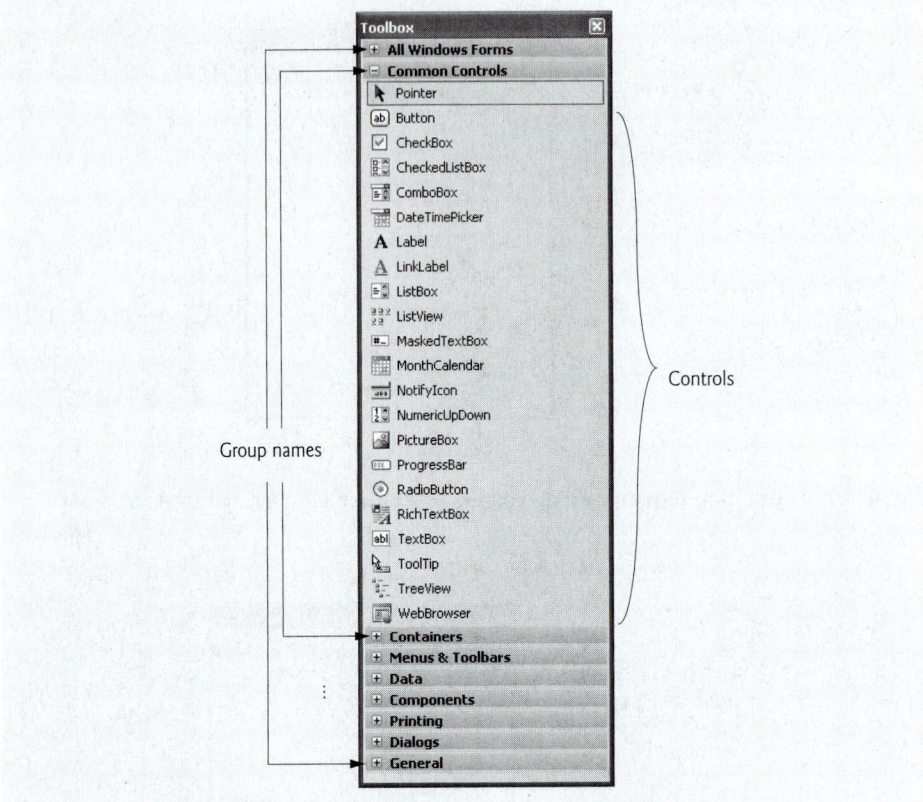

Fig. 2.21 | **Toolbox** window displaying controls for the **Common Controls** group.

2.4.3 Properties **Window**

To display the **Properties** window if it is not visible, you can select **View > Properties Window**, click the **Properties** window icon shown in Fig. 2.13 or you can press the *F4* key. The *Properties window* displays the properties for the currently selected Form (Fig. 2.22), control or file in design view. *Properties* specify information about the form or control, such as its size, color and position. Each form or control has its own set of properties; a property's description is displayed at the bottom of the **Properties** window whenever that property is selected.

Figure 2.22 shows the form's **Properties** window. The left column lists the Form's properties; the right column displays the current value of each property. Icons on the toolbar sort the properties either alphabetically by clicking the *Alphabetical* icon or categorically by clicking the *Categorized* icon. You can sort the properties alphabetically in ascending or descending order—clicking the **Alphabetical** icon repeatedly toggles between sorting the properties from A–Z and Z–A. Sorting by category groups the properties according to their use (i.e., **Appearance**, **Behavior**, **Design**). Depending on the size of the **Properties** window, some of the properties may be hidden from view on the screen, in which case, users can scroll through the list of properties. We show how to set individual properties later in this chapter.

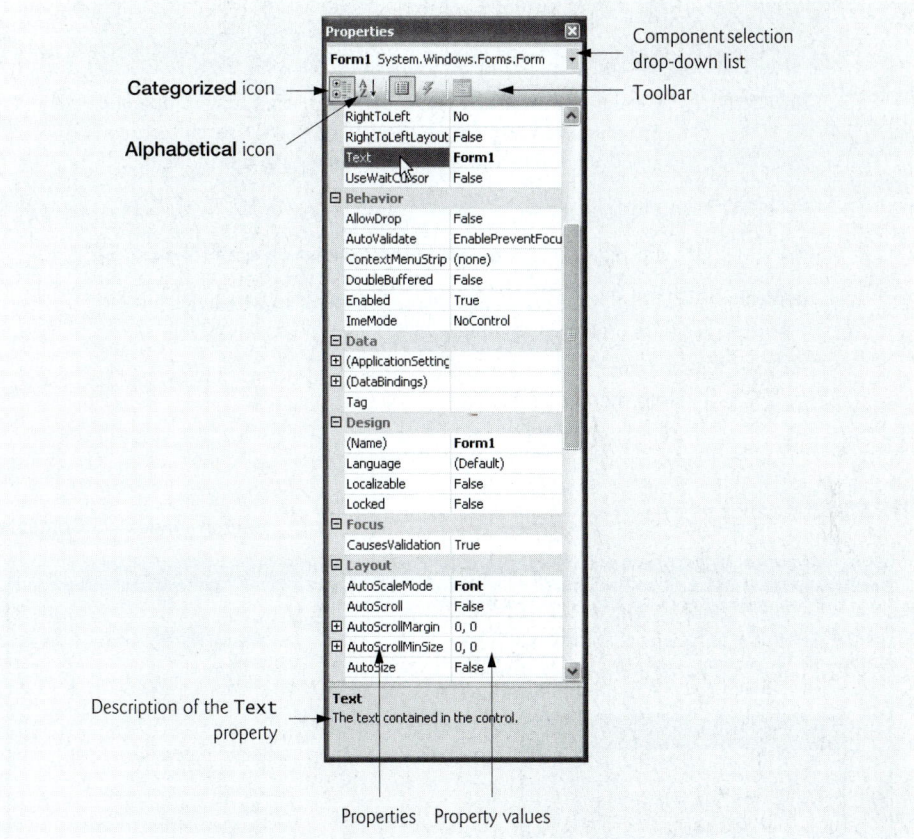

Categorized icon

Alphabetical icon

Component selection drop-down list

Toolbar

Description of the Text property

Properties   Property values

Fig. 2.22 | **Properties** window displaying the Text property of the Form.

The **Properties** window is crucial to visual programming; it allows you to modify a control's properties visually, without writing code. You can see which properties are available for modification and, where appropriate, can learn the range of acceptable values for a given property. The **Properties** window displays a brief description of the selected property, helping you understand its purpose. A property can be set quickly using this window—usually, only one click is required, and no code needs to be written.

At the top of the **Properties** window is the *component selection drop-down list*, which allows you to select the form or control whose properties you wish to display in the **Properties** window (Fig. 2.22). Using the component selection drop-down list is an alternative way to display properties without selecting the actual form or control in the GUI.

2.5 Using Help

Visual Studio provides extensive help features. The *Help menu* commands are summarized in Fig. 2.23.

Dynamic help (Fig. 2.24) is an excellent way to get information quickly about the IDE and its features. It provides a list of articles pertaining to the "current content" (i.e., the selected items). To open the *Dynamic Help window*, select **Help > Dynamic Help**.

Command	Description
How Do I	Contains links to relevant topics, including how to upgrade programs and learn more about Web services, architecture and design, files and I/O, data, debugging and more.
Search	Finds help articles based on search keywords.
Index	Displays an alphabetized list of topics you can browse.
Contents	Displays a categorized table of contents in which help articles are organized by topic.

Fig. 2.23 | **Help** menu commands.

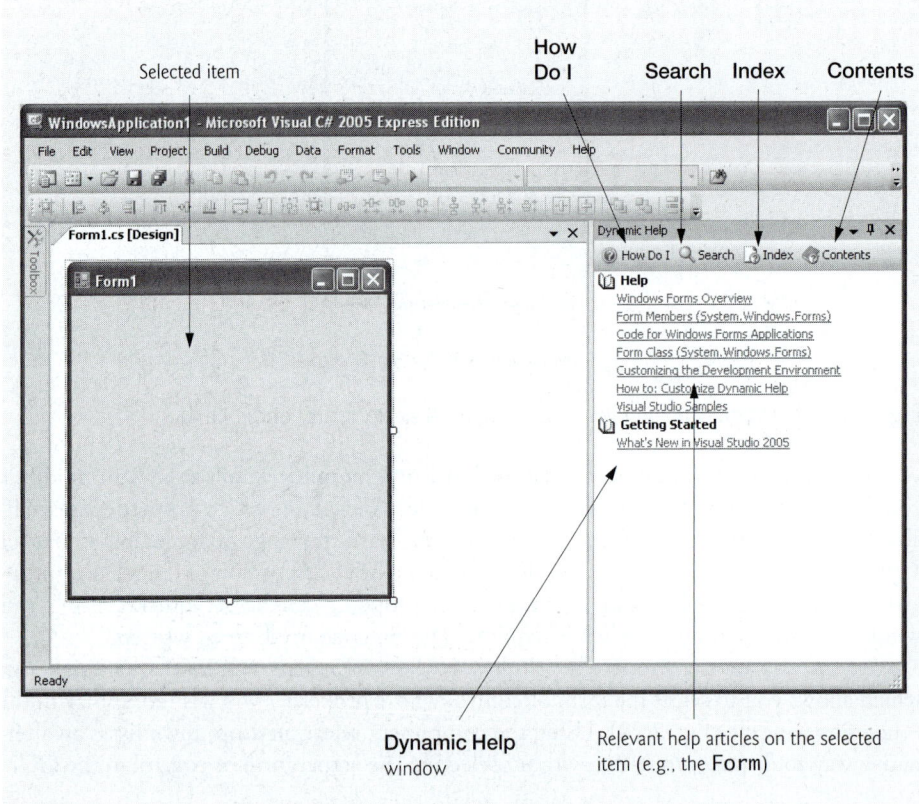

Fig. 2.24 | **Dynamic Help** window.

Then, when you click a word or component (such as a form or control), links to help articles appear in the **Dynamic Help** window. The window lists help topics, code samples and other relevant information. There is also a toolbar that provides access to the **How Do I**, **Search**, **Index** and **Contents** help features.

Visual Studio also provides *context-sensitive help*, which is similar to dynamic help, except that it immediately displays a relevant help article rather than presenting a list of articles. To use context-sensitive help, click an item, such as the form, and press the *F1* key. Figure 2.25 displays help articles related to a form.

The **Help** options can be set in the **Options** dialog (accessed by selecting **Tools > Options...**). To display all the settings that you can modify (including the settings for the **Help** options), make sure that the **Show all settings** checkbox in the lower-left corner of the dialog is checked (Fig. 2.26). To change whether the **Help** is displayed internally or externally, select **Help** on the left, then locate the **Show Help using:** drop-down list on the right. Depending on your preference, selecting **External Help Viewer** displays a relevant help article in a separate window outside the IDE (some programmers like to view Web pages separately from the project on which they are working in the IDE). Selecting **Integrated Help Viewer** displays a help article as a tabbed window inside the IDE

2.6 Using Visual Programming to Create a Simple Program Displaying Text and an Image

In this section, we create a program that displays the text `"Welcome to Visual C#!"` and an image of the Deitel & Associates bug mascot. The program consists of a single form that uses a `Label` and a `PictureBox`. Figure 2.27 shows the results of the program as it executes. The program and the bug image are available with this chapter's examples. You can download the examples from `www.deitel.com/books/csharphtp2/index.html`.

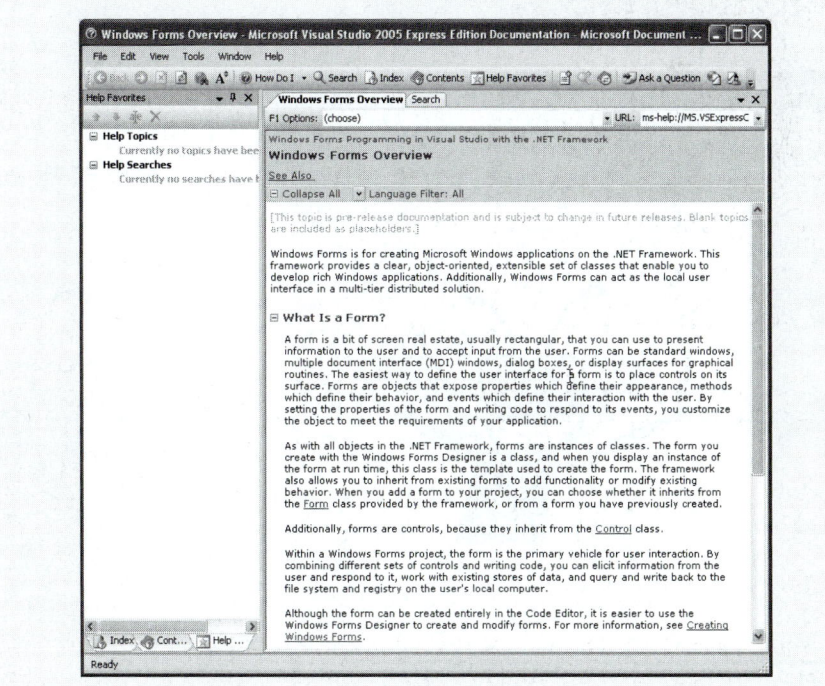

Fig. 2.25 | Using context-sensitive help.

Help options selected   **Show Help using:** box

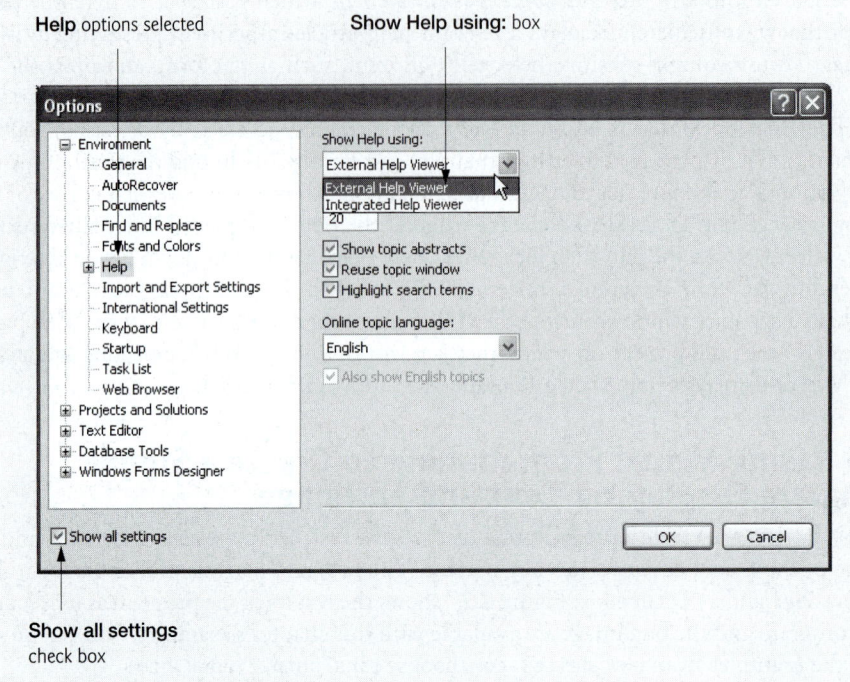

Show all settings
check box

Fig. 2.26 | **Options** dialog displaying **Help** settings.

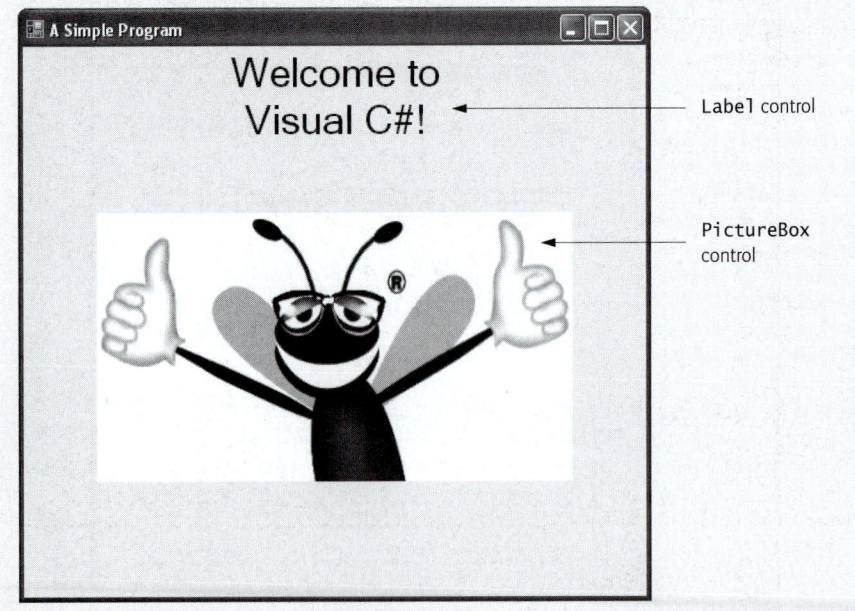

Label control

PictureBox
control

Fig. 2.27 | Simple program executing.

To create the program whose output is shown in Fig. 2.27, you will not write a single line of program code. Instead, you will use visual programming techniques. Visual Studio processes your actions (such as mouse clicking, dragging and dropping) to generate program code. Chapter 3 begins our discussion of how to write program code. Throughout the book, you produce increasingly substantial programs that often include a combination of code written by you and code generated by Visual Studio. The generated code can be difficult for novices to understand—fortunately, you rarely need to look at this code.

Visual programming is useful for building GUI-intensive programs that require a significant amount of user interaction. Visual programming cannot be used to create programs that do not have GUIs—you must write such code directly.

To create, run and terminate this first program, perform the following 13 steps:

1. *Create the new project.* If a project is already open, close it by selecting **File > Close Solution**. A dialog asking whether to save the current project might appear. Click **Save** to save any changes. To create a new Windows application for our program, select **File > New Project...** to display the **New Project** dialog (Fig. 2.28). From the template options, select **Windows Application**. Name the project **ASimpleProgram** and click **OK**. [*Note:* File names must conform to certain rules. For example, file names cannot contain symbols (e.g., ?, :, *, <, >, # and %) or Unicode® control characters (Unicode is a special character set described in Appendix E). Also, file names cannot be system reserved names, such as "CON", "PRN", "AUX" and "COM1" or "." and "..", and cannot be longer than 256 characters in length.]

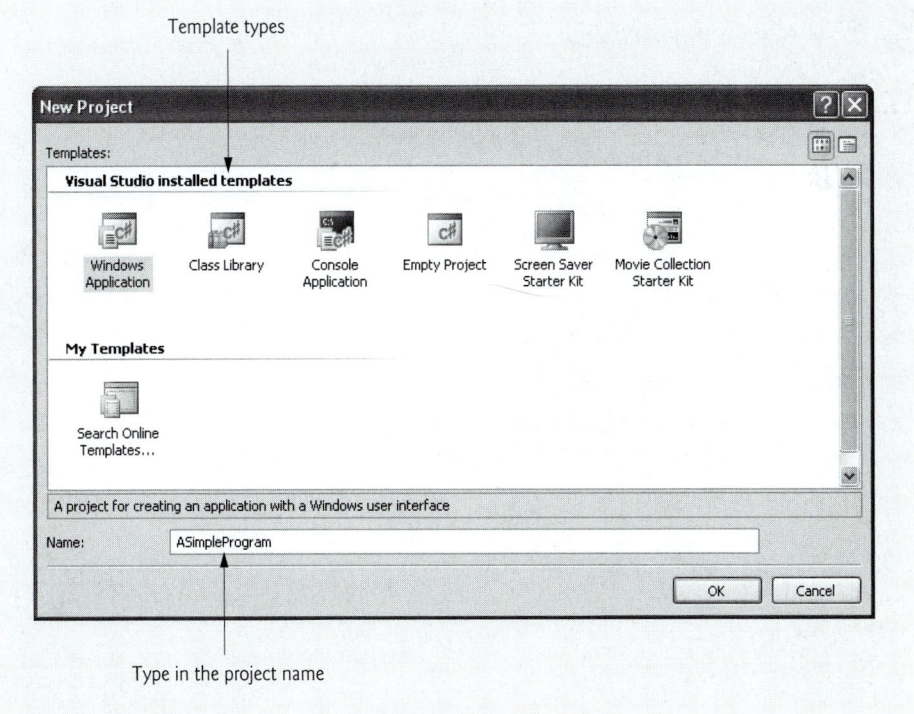

Fig. 2.28 | **New Project** dialog.

We mentioned earlier in this chapter that you must set the directory in which the project will be saved. In the complete Visual Studio, you do this in the **New Project** dialog. To specify the directory in Visual C# Express, select **File > Save All** to display the ***Save Project dialog*** (Fig. 2.29). To set the project location, click the **Browse...** button, which opens the ***Project Location dialog*** (Fig. 2.30). Navigate through the directories, select one in which to place the project (in our example, we use a directory named **MyProjects**) and click **OK** to close the dialog. Make sure the **Create directory for Solution** checkbox is selected (Fig. 2.29). Click **Save** to close the **Save Project** dialog.

When you first begin working in the IDE, it is in ***design mode*** (i.e., the program is being designed and is not executing). While the IDE is in design mode, you have access to all the environment windows (e.g., **Toolbox**, **Properties**), menus and toolbars, as you will see shortly.

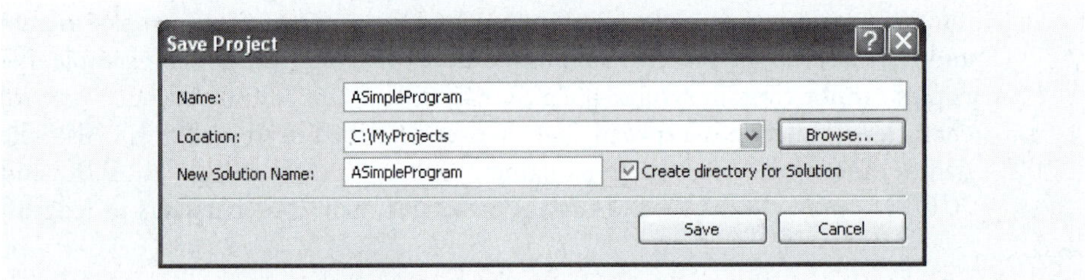

Fig. 2.29 | **Save Project** dialog.

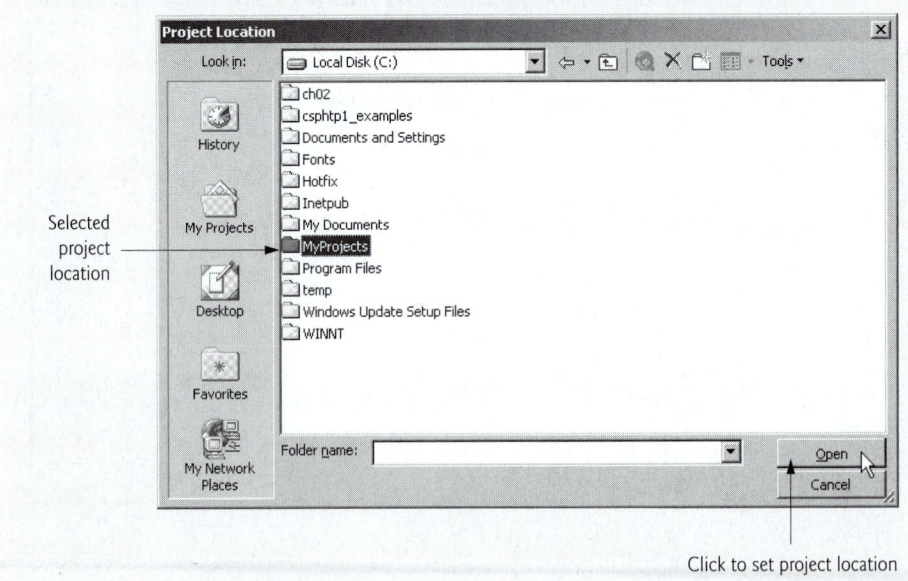

Fig. 2.30 | Setting the project location in the **Project Location** dialog.

2. *Set the text in the form's title bar.* The text in the form's ***title bar*** is the value of the form's ***Text property*** (Fig. 2.31). If the **Properties** window is not open, click the properties icon in the toolbar or select **View > Properties Window**. Click anywhere in the form to display the form's properties in the **Properties** window. Click in the textbox to the right of the Text property box and type "A Simple Program", as in Fig. 2.31. Press the *Enter* key when finished; the form's title bar is updated immediately (Fig. 2.32).

3. *Resize the form.* Click and drag one of the form's ***enabled sizing handles*** (the small white squares that appear around the form, as shown in Fig. 2.32). Using the mouse, select and drag the sizing handle to resize the form (Fig. 2.33).

4. *Change the form's background color.* The ***BackColor property*** specifies a form's or control's background color. Clicking BackColor in the **Properties** window causes a down-arrow button to appear next to the value of the property (Fig. 2.34). When clicked, the down-arrow button displays a set of other options, which vary depending on the property. In this case, the arrow displays tabs for **Custom**, **Web** and **System** (the default). Click the ***Custom tab*** to display the ***palette*** (a grid of colors). Select the box that represents light blue. Once you select the color, the palette closes and the form's background color changes to light blue (Fig. 2.35).

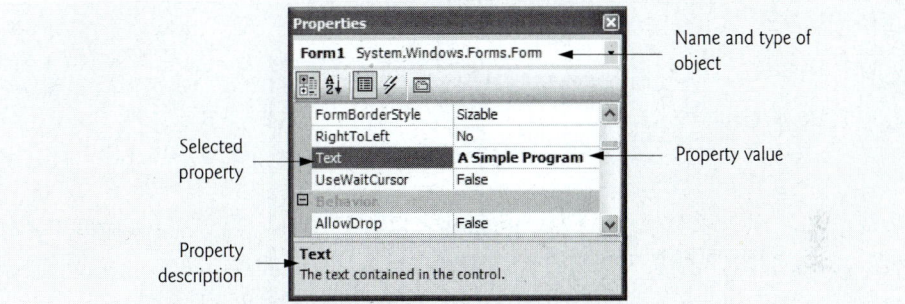

Fig. 2.31 | Setting the form's Text property in the **Properties** window.

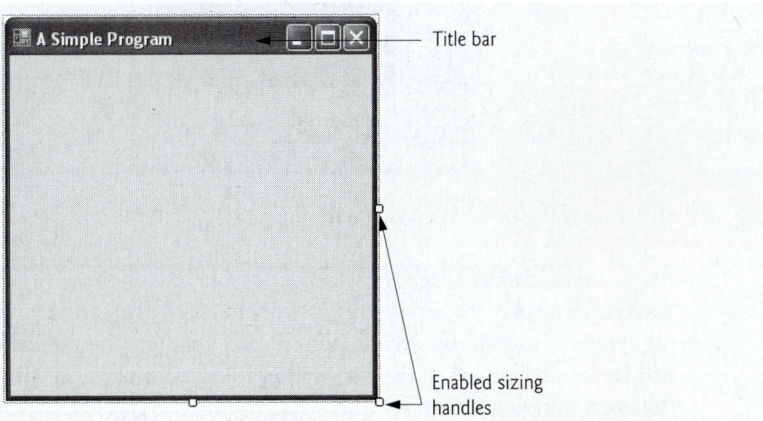

Fig. 2.32 | Form with enabled sizing handles.

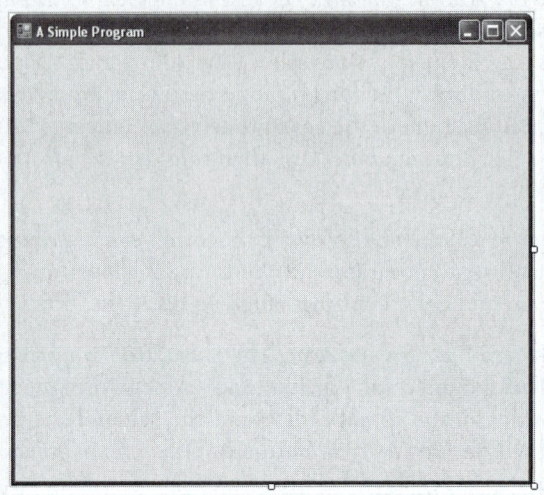

Fig. 2.33 | Resized form.

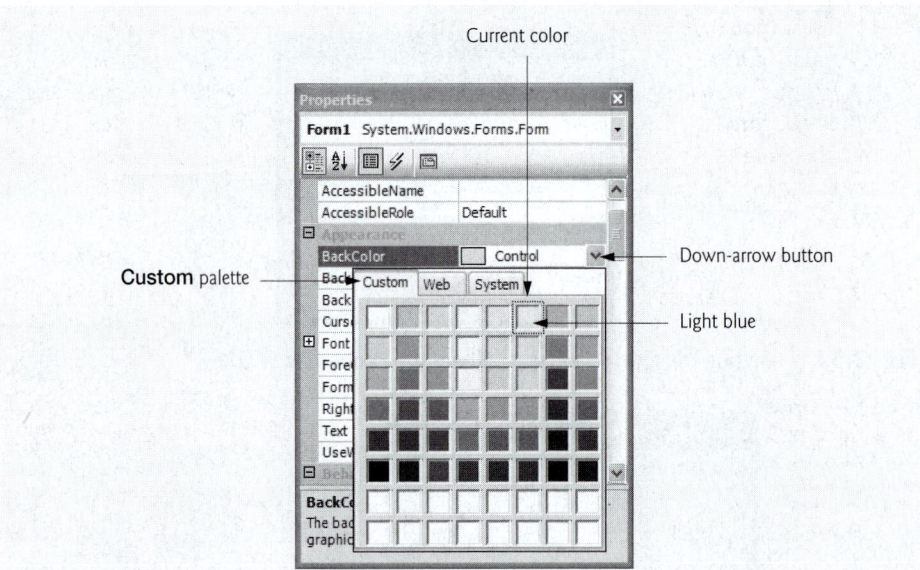

Fig. 2.34 | Changing the form's `BackColor` property.

5. *Add a Label control to the Form.* If the **Toolbox** is not already open, select **View > Toolbox** to display the set of controls you will use for creating your programs. For the type of program we are creating in this chapter, the typical controls we use will be located in either the **All Windows Forms** category of the **Toolbox** or the **Common Controls** group. If either group name is collapsed, expand it by clicking the plus sign (the **All Windows Forms** and **Common Controls** groups are shown near the top of Fig. 2.21). Next, double click the Label control in the **Toolbox**.

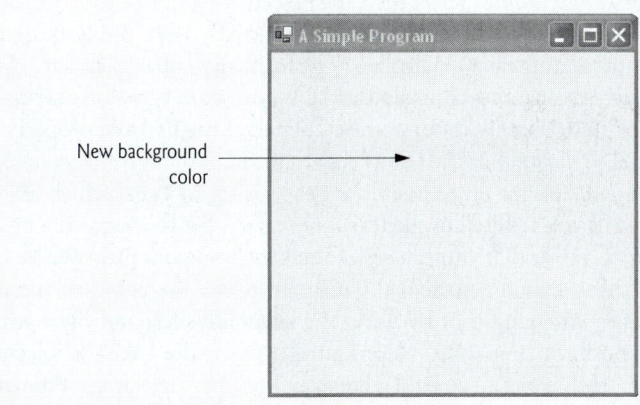

New background color

Fig. 2.35 | Form with new `BackColor` property applied.

This action causes a `Label` to appear in the upper-left corner of the form (Fig. 2.36). [*Note:* If the `Form` is behind the **Toolbox**, you may need to close the **Toolbox** to see the `Label`.] Although double clicking any **Toolbox** control places the control on the form, you also can "drag" controls from the **Toolbox** to the form (you may prefer dragging the control because you can position it wherever you want). Our `Label` displays the text **label1** by default. Note that our `Label`'s background color is the same as the form's background color. When a control is added to the form, its `BackColor` property is set to the form's `BackColor`. You can change the `Label`'s background color to a different color than the form by changing its `BackColor` property.

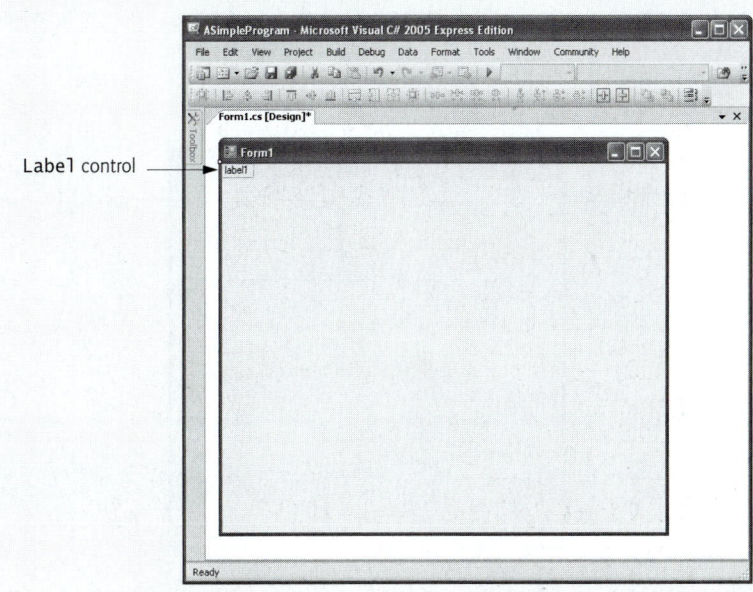

Label control

Fig. 2.36 | Adding a `Label` to the form.

6. *Customize the Label's appearance.* Select the Label by clicking it. Its properties now appear in the **Properties** window (Fig. 2.37). The Label's Text property determines the text (if any) that the Label displays. The form and Label each have their own Text property—forms and controls can have the same types of properties (such as BackColor and Text) without conflict. Set the Label's Text property to **Welcome to Visual C#!**. Note that the Label resizes to fit all the typed text on one line. By default, the *AutoSize property* of the Label is set to True, which allows the Label to adjust its size to fit all of the text if necessary. Set the AutoSize property to False (Fig. 2.37) so that you can resize the Label on your own. Resize the Label (using the sizing handles) so that the text fits. Move the Label to the top center of the form by dragging it or by using the keyboard's left and right arrow keys to adjust its position (Fig. 2.38). Alternatively, when the Label is selected, you can center the Label control horizontally by selecting **Format > Center In Form > Horizontally**.

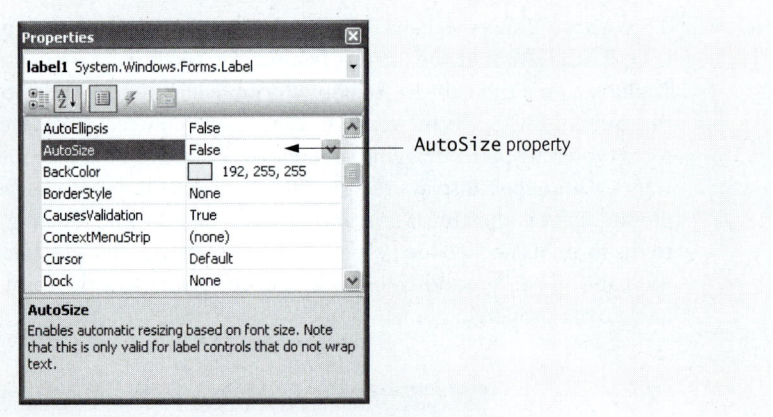

Fig. 2.37 | Changing the Label's AutoSize property to False.

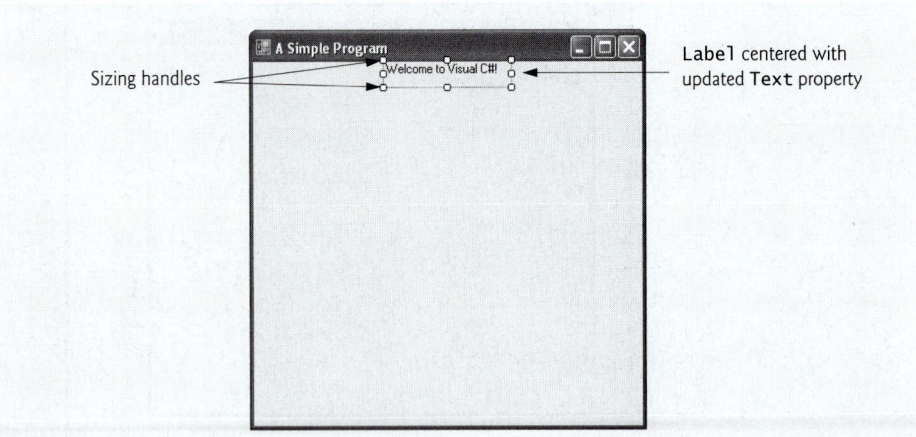

Fig. 2.38 | GUI after the form and Label have been customized.

7. *Set the Label's font size.* To change the font type and appearance of the Label's text, select the value of the ***Font property***, which causes an ***ellipsis button*** (📖) to appear next to the value (Fig. 2.39). When the ellipsis button is clicked, a dialog that provides additional values—in this case, the ***Font dialog*** (Fig. 2.40)— is displayed. You can select the font name (e.g., **Microsoft Sans Serif, MingLiU, Mistral, Modern No. 20**—the font options may vary, depending on your system), font style (**Regular, Italic, Bold**, etc.) and font size (**16, 18, 20**, etc.) in this dialog. The **Sample** area shows sample text with the selected font settings. Under **Size**, select **24** points and click **OK**. If the Label's text does not fit on a single line, it wraps to the next line. Resize the Label vertically if it's not large enough to hold the text.

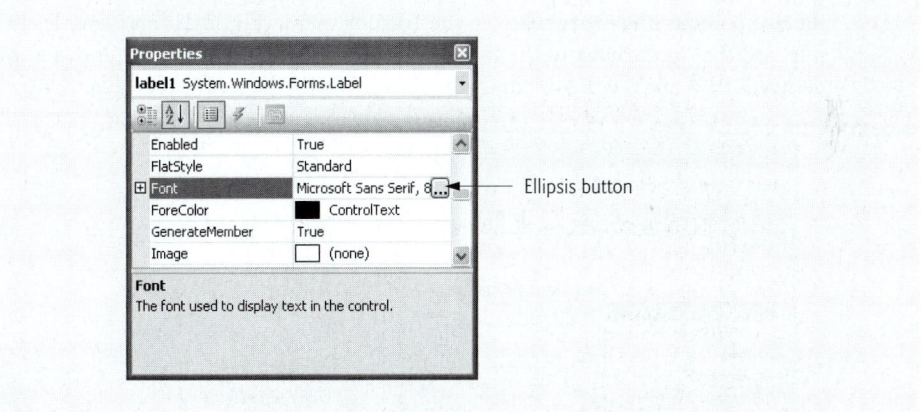

Fig. 2.39 | **Properties** window displaying the Label's properties.

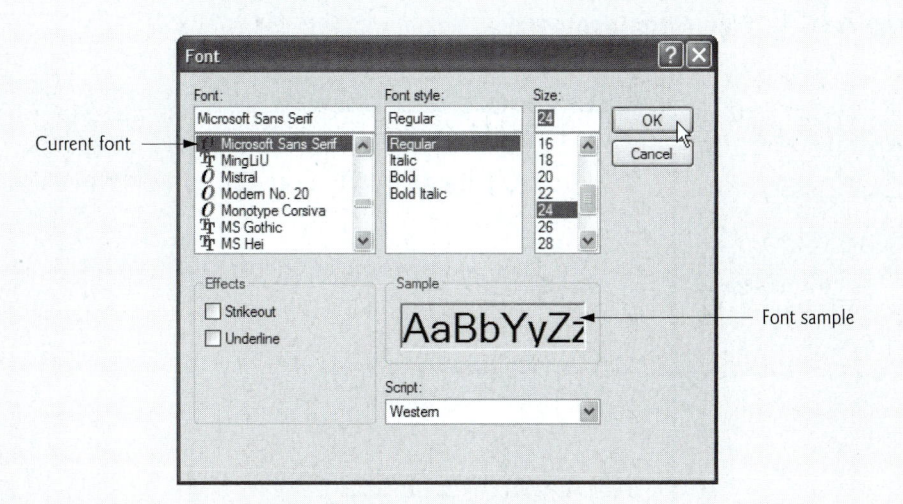

Fig. 2.40 | **Font** dialog for selecting fonts, styles and sizes.

8. *Align the Label's text.* Select the Label's ***TextAlign*** property, which determines how the text is aligned within the Label. A three-by-three grid of buttons representing alignment choices is displayed (Fig. 2.41). The position of each button corresponds to where the text appears in the Label. For this program, set the TextAlign property to MiddleCenter in the three-by-three grid; this selection causes the text to appear centered in the middle of the Label, with equal spacing from the text to all sides of the Label. The other TextAlign values, such as TopLeft, TopRight and BottomCenter, can be used to position the text anywhere within a Label. Certain alignment values may require that you resize the Label larger or smaller to better fit the text.

9. *Add a PictureBox to the form.* The PictureBox control displays images. The process involved in this step is similar to that of *Step 5*, in which we added a Label to the form. Locate the PictureBox in the **Toolbox** menu (Fig. 2.21) and double click it to add the PictureBox to the form. When the PictureBox appears, move it underneath the Label, either by dragging it or by using the arrow keys (Fig. 2.42).

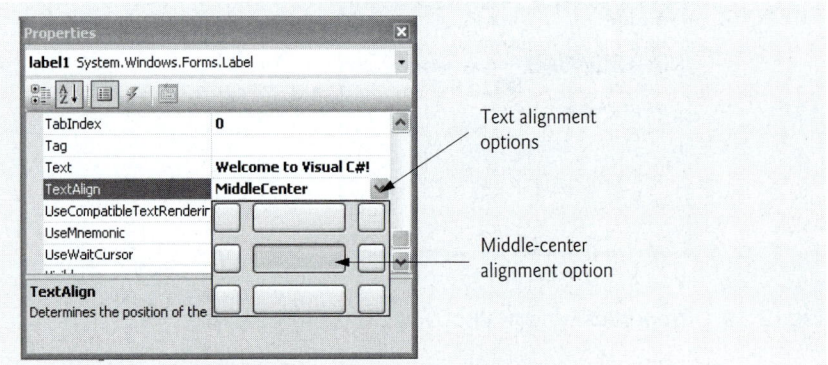

Fig. 2.41 | Centering the Label's text.

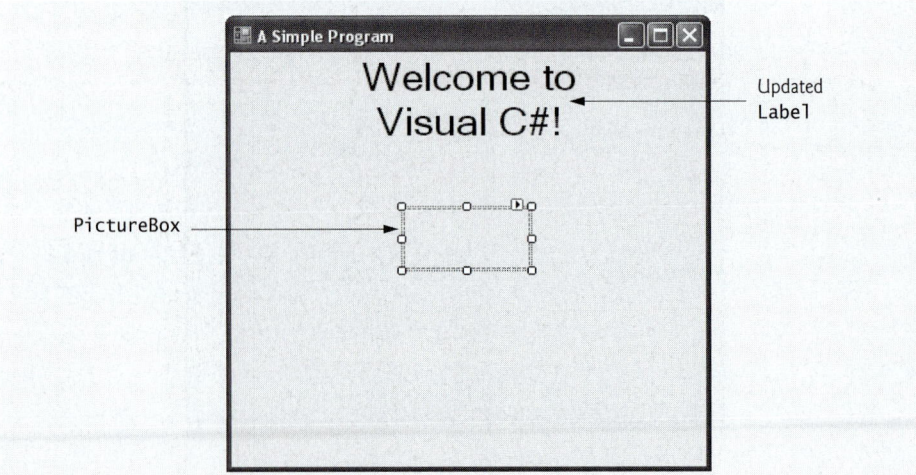

Fig. 2.42 | Inserting and aligning a PictureBox.

10. *Insert an image.* Click the PictureBox to display its properties in the **Properties** window (Fig. 2.43). Locate the ***Image** property*, which displays a preview of the image, if one exists. No picture has been assigned, so the value of the Image property displays **(none)**. Click the ellipsis button to display the **Select Resource dialog** (Fig. 2.44). This dialog is used to import files, such as images, to any program. Click the **Import...** button to browse for an image to insert. In our case, the picture is bug.png. In the dialog that appears (Fig. 2.45), click the image with the mouse and click **OK**. The image is previewed in the **Select Resource** dialog (Fig. 2.45). Click **OK** to place the image in your program. Supported image formats include PNG (Portable Network Graphics), GIF (Graphics Interchange Format), JPEG (Joint Photographic Experts Group) and BMP (Windows bitmap). Creating a new image requires image-editing software, such as Jasc® Paint Shop Pro™ (www.jasc.com), Adobe® Photoshop™ Elements (www.adobe.com) or Microsoft Paint (provided with Windows). To size the image to the PictureBox, change the ***SizeMode** property* to ***StretchImage*** (Fig. 2.46), which scales the image to the size of the PictureBox. Resize the PictureBox, making it larger (Fig. 2.47).

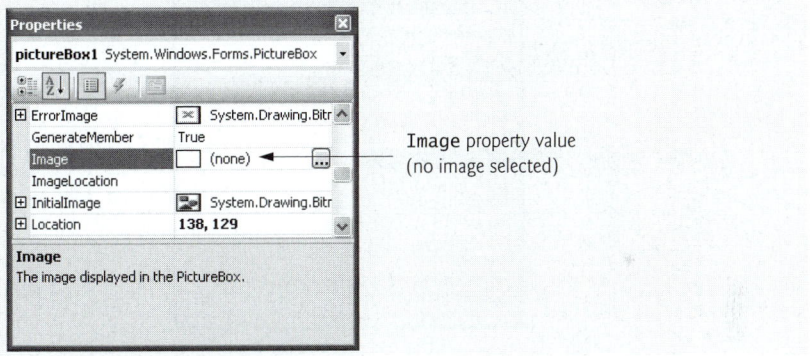

Image property value
(no image selected)

Fig. 2.43 | Image property of the PictureBox.

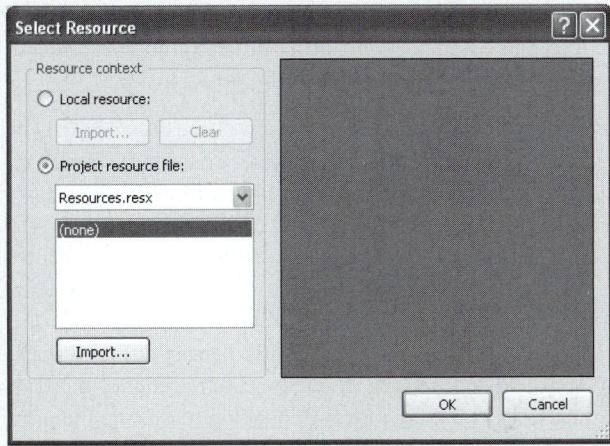

Fig. 2.44 | **Select Resource** dialog to select an image for the PictureBox.

Fig. 2.45 | **Select Resource** dialog displaying a preview of selected image.

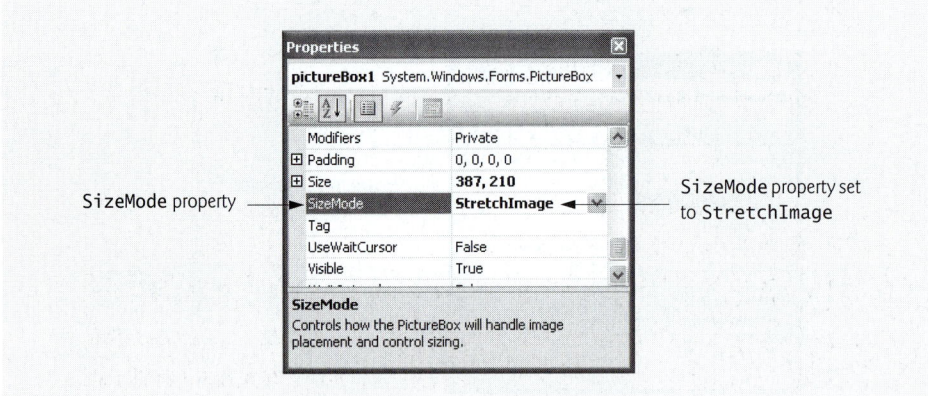

Fig. 2.46 | Scaling an image to the size of the `PictureBox`.

11. *Save the project.* Select **File > Save All** to save the entire solution. The solution file contains the name and location of its project, and the project file contains the names and locations of all the files in the project.

12. *Run the project.* Recall that up to this point we have been working in the IDE's design mode (i.e., the program being created is not executing). In *run mode*, the program is executing, and you can interact with only a few IDE features—features that are not available are disabled (grayed out). The text **Form1.cs [Design]** in the tab (Fig. 2.48) means that we are designing the form visually rather than programmatically. If we had been writing code, the tab would have contained only the text **Form1.cs.** To run the program you must first build the solution. Select **Build > Build Solution** to compile the project (Fig. 2.48). Once you build the solution (the IDE will display "**Build succeeded**" in the lower-left corner of the IDE—also known as the status bar), select **Debug > Start Debugging** to execute the program. Figure 2.49 shows the IDE in run mode. Note that many toolbar icons and menus are disabled. The running program will appear in a separate window outside the IDE (Fig. 2.49).

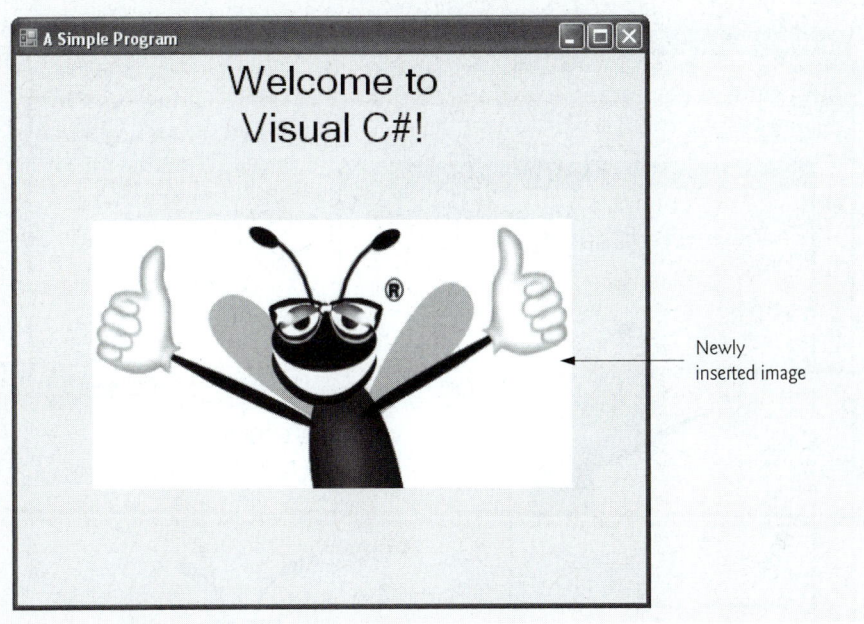

Newly inserted image

Fig. 2.47 | PictureBox displaying an image.

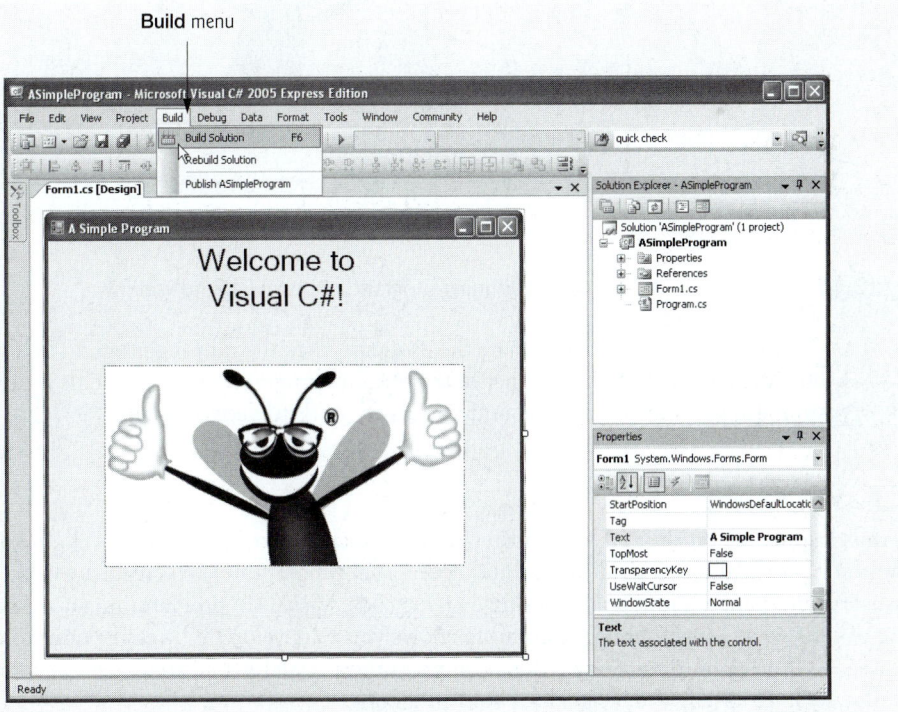

Build menu

Fig. 2.48 | Building a solution.

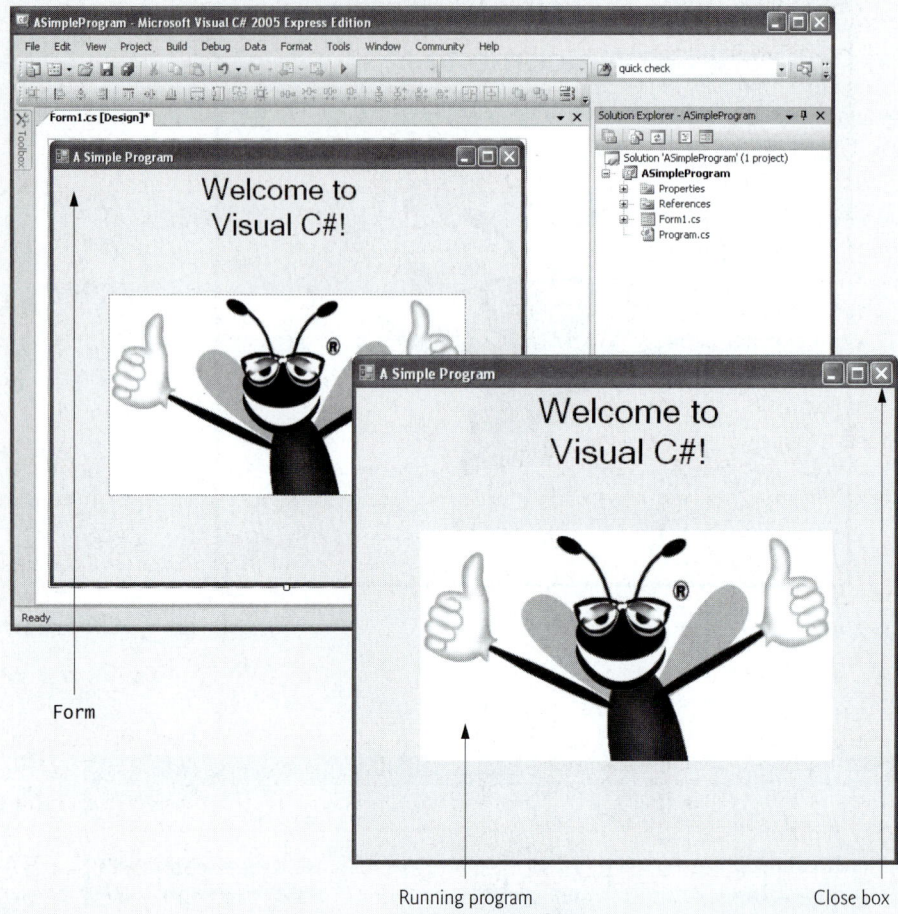

Form

Running program   Close box

Fig. 2.49 | IDE in run mode, with the running program in the foreground window.

13. *Terminate execution.* To terminate the program, click the running program's close box (the **X** in the top-right corner of the running program's window). This action stops the program's execution and returns the IDE to design mode.

2.7 Wrap-Up

In this chapter, we introduced key features of the Visual Studio Integrated Development Environment (IDE). You used the technique of visual programming to create a working Visual C# program without writing a single line of code. Visual C# programming is a mixture of the two styles—visual programming allows you to develop GUIs easily and avoid tedious GUI programming; conventional programming (which we introduce in Chapter 3) allows you to specify the behavior of your programs.

You created a Visual C# Windows application with one form. You worked with the **Solution Explorer**, **Toolbox** and **Properties** windows, which are essential to developing

Visual C# programs. The **Solution Explorer** window allows you to manage your solution's files visually. The **Toolbox** window contains a rich collection of controls for creating GUIs. The **Properties** window allows you to set the attributes of a form and controls.

You explored Visual Studio's help features, including the **Dynamic Help** window and the **Help** menu. The **Dynamic Help** window displays links related to the item that you click with the mouse. You learned how to set **Help** options to display and use help resources. We also demonstrated how to use context-sensitive help.

You used visual programming to design the GUI portions of a program quickly and easily, by dragging and dropping controls (a Label and a PictureBox) onto a Form or by double clicking controls in the **Toolbox**.

In creating the **ASimpleProgram** program, you used the **Properties** window to set the Text and BackColor properties of the form. You learned that Label controls display text and that PictureBoxes display images. You displayed text in a Label and added an image to a PictureBox. You also worked with the AutoSize, TextAlign and SizeMode properties of a label.

In the next chapter, we discuss "nonvisual," or "conventional," programming—you will create your first programs that contain Visual C# code that you write, instead of having Visual Studio write the code. You will study console applications (programs that display text to the screen without using a GUI). You will also learn memory concepts, arithmetic, decision making and how to use a dialog to display a message.

2.8 Web Resources

msdn.microsoft.com/vstudio/default.aspx
Microsoft's Visual Studio site provides news, documentation, downloads and other resources.

lab.msdn.microsoft.com/vs2005/
This site provides information on the newest release of Visual Studio, including downloads, community information and resources.

www.worldofdotnet.net
This site offers Visual Studio news and links to newsgroups and other resources.

www.c-sharpcorner.com
This site contains articles, reviews of books and software, documentation, downloads, links and searchable information on C#.

www.devx.com/dotnet
This site has a dedicated zone for .NET developers that contains articles, opinions, newsgroups, code, tips and other resources discussing Visual Studio 2005.

www.csharp-station.com
This site provides articles on Visual C#, especially 2005 updates. The site also includes tutorials, downloads and other resources.

Summary

Section 2.1 Introduction
- Visual Studio is Microsoft's Integrated Development Environment (IDE) for creating, running and debugging programs written in a variety of .NET programming languages.
- Creating simple programs by dragging and dropping predefined building blocks into place is called visual programming.

Section 2.2 Overview of the Visual Studio 2005 IDE

- The **Start Page** contains a list of links to resources either within the Visual Studio 2005 IDE or on the Internet.
- A project is a group of related files, such as the Visual C# code and any images that might make up a program.
- The Visual Studio 2005 IDE organizes programs into projects and solutions; a solution may contain one or more projects.
- Dialogs are windows that facilitate user-computer communication.
- Visual Studio provides templates for the project types available for users to create in Visual C#, including Windows applications and console applications.
- The **Form** represents the main window of the Windows application that you are creating.
- Collectively, the form and controls constitute the program's graphical user interface (GUI), which is the visual part of the program with which the user interacts.

Section 2.3 Menu Bar and Toolbar

- Commands for managing the IDE and for developing, maintaining and executing programs are contained in the menus, which are located on the menu bar.
- Menus contain groups of commands (menu items) that, when selected, cause the IDE to perform actions (e.g., open a window, save a file, print a file and execute a program).
- Tool tips help you become familiar with the IDE's features.

Section 2.4 Navigating the Visual Studio 2005 IDE

- The **Solution Explorer** window lists all the files in the solution.
- The **Toolbox** contains controls for customizing forms.
- By using visual programming, you can place predefined controls onto the form instead of writing the code yourself.
- Moving the mouse pointer over a hidden window's icon opens that window. When the mouse pointer leaves the area of the window, the window is hidden. This feature is known as auto-hide. To "pin down" a window (i.e., to disable auto-hide), click the pin icon into the vertical position.
- The **Properties** window displays the properties for a form or control (in design mode). Properties are information about a form or control, such as size, color and position. The **Properties** window allows you to modify controls visually, without writing code.
- Each control has its own set of properties. The left column of the **Properties** window shows the properties of the control; the right column displays property values. This window's toolbar contains options for organizing properties either alphabetically when the **Alphabetic** icon is clicked or categorically (e.g., **Appearance**, **Behavior**, **Design**) when the **Categorized** icon is clicked. Clicking the **Alphabetic** icon repeatedly toggles between sorting the properties from A–Z and Z–A.

Section 2.5 Using Help

- The **Help** menu contains a variety of options: The **How Do I** menu provides specific resources to help users accomplish a given task, such as converting programs and participating in community discussions. The **Contents** menu displays a categorized table of contents; the **Index** menu displays an alphabetical index that you can browse; the **Search** menu allows you to find particular help articles, by entering search keywords.
- **Dynamic Help** provides a list of articles based on the current content (i.e., the items in the vicinity of the mouse pointer).
- Context-sensitive help is similar to dynamic help, except that it immediately brings up a relevant help article instead of a list of articles. To use context-sensitive help, click an item and press the *F1* key.

Section 2.6 Using Visual Programming to Create a Simple Program Displaying Text and an Image

- Visual C# programming usually involves a combination of writing a portion of the program code yourself and having the Visual Studio generate the remaining code.
- The text that appears at the top of the form (the title bar) is specified in the form's Text property.
- To resize the form, click and drag one of the form's enabled sizing handles (the small square or squares around the form). Enabled sizing handles appear as white boxes.
- The BackColor property specifies the background color of a form. The form's background color is the default background color for any controls added to the form.
- Double clicking any **Toolbox** control icon places a control of that type on the form. Alternatively, you can drag and drop controls from the **Toolbox** to the form.
- The Label's Text property determines the text (if any) that the Label displays. The form and Label each have their own Text property.
- A property's ellipsis button, when clicked, displays a dialog containing additional options.
- In the **Font** dialog, you can select the font for a form's or Label's text.
- The TextAlign property determines how the text is aligned within the Label's boundaries.
- The PictureBox control displays an image. The Image property specifies the image to display.
- Select **File > Save All** to save the entire solution.
- A program that is in design mode is not executing.
- In run mode, the program is executing; you can interact with only a few IDE features.
- When designing a program visually, the name of the Visual C# file appears in the project tab, followed by **[Design]**.
- Terminate execution by clicking the close box.

Terminology

active tab
Alphabetical icon
application
auto-hide
AutoSize property of TextBox
BackColor property of Form
background color
BMP (Windows bitmap) image
Categorized icon
clicking
close a project
collapse a tree
component selection drop-down list
context-sensitive help
.cs filename extension
Custom tab
customize a form
Data menu
debug a program
Debug menu
design mode

design view
dialog
double clicking
down arrow
dragging
dynamic help
Dynamic Help window
Edit menu
ellipsis button
expand a tree
external help
F1 help key
File menu
Font property of Label
font name
font size
font style
Font dialog
form
Format menu
form's background color

form's title bar

GIF (Graphics Interchange Format) image

GUI (graphical user interface)

Help menu

icon

IDE (Integrated Development Environment)

Image property of `PictureBox`

input

integrated help

JPEG (Joint Photographic Experts Group) image

`Label`

menu

menu item

menu bar in Visual Studio

Microsoft Visual C# 2005 Express Edition

mouse pointer

MSDN (Microsoft Developers Network)

New Project dialog

opening a project

output

palette

`PictureBox`

pin a window

PNG (Portable Network Graphics) image

project

Project menu

Project Location dialog

Properties window

property of a form or control

run mode

Save Project dialog

Select Resource dialog

selecting

Show all files icon

single clicking

`SizeMode` property of `PictureBox`

sizing handle

solution

Solution Explorer in Visual Studio

Start Page

startup project

`StretchImage` value

tabbed window

template

Text property of a control

`TextAlign` property of `Label`

title bar

tool tip

toolbar

toolbar icon

Toolbox

Tools menu

View menu

visual programming

Visual Studio

Windows application

Windows Form Designer

Windows menu

Self-Review Exercises

2.1 Fill in the blanks in each of the following statements:

a) The technique of _____ allows you to create GUIs without writing any code.

b) A(n) _____ is a group of one or more projects that collectively form a Visual C# program.

c) The _____ feature hides a window when the mouse pointer is moved outside the window's area.

d) A(n) _____ appears when the mouse pointer hovers over an icon.

e) The _____ window allows you to browse solution files.

f) A plus box indicates that the tree in the **Solution Explorer** can _____.

g) The properties in the **Properties** window's can be sorted _____ or _____.

h) A form's _____ property specifies the text displayed in the form's title bar.

i) The _____ allows you to add controls to the form in a visual manner.

j) Using _____ displays relevant help articles, based on the current context.

k) The _____ property specifies how text is aligned within a `Label`'s boundaries.

2.2 State whether each of the following is *true* or *false*. If *false*, explain why.

a) The title bar displays the IDE's mode.

b) The **X** box toggles auto-hide.

c) The toolbar icons represent various menu commands.

d) The toolbar contains icons that represent controls.

e) Both forms and `Labels` have a title bar.

f) Control properties can be modified only by writing code.

g) `PictureBoxes` typically display images.

h) Visual C# files use the filename extension `.csharp`.

i) A form's background color is set using the `BackColor` property.

Answers to Self-Review Exercises

2.1   a) visual programming. b) solution. c) auto-hide. d) tool tip. e) **Solution Explorer.** f) expand. g) alphabetically, categorically. h) `Text`. i) **Toolbox.** j) **Dynamic Help.** k) `TextAlign`.

2.2   a) True. b) False. The pin icon toggles auto-hide. The **X** box closes a window. c) True. d) False. The **Toolbox** contains icons that represent controls. e) False. Forms have a title bar but `Labels` do not (although they do have `Label` text). f) False. Control properties can be modified using the **Properties** window. g) True. h) False. Visual C# files use the filename extension `.cs`. i) True.

Exercises

2.3   Fill in the blanks in each of the following statements:

a) When an ellipsis button is clicked, a(n) _____ is displayed.

b) To save every file in a solution, select _____.

c) Using _____help immediately displays a relevant help article. It can be accessed using the _____ key.

d) GUI is an acronym for _____.

2.4   State whether each of the following is *true* or *false*. If *false*, explain why.

a) A control can be added to a form by double clicking its control icon in the **Toolbox**.

b) The form, `Label` and `PictureBox` have identical properties.

c) If your machine is connected to the Internet, you can browse the Internet from the Visual Studio 2005 IDE.

d) Visual C# programmers usually create complex programs without writing any code.

e) Sizing handles are visible during execution.

2.5   Some features that appear throughout Visual Studio perform similar actions in different contexts. Explain and give examples of how the plus and minus boxes, ellipsis buttons, down-arrow buttons and tool tips act in this manner. Why do you think the Visual Studio 2005 IDE was designed this way?

2.6   Fill in the blanks in each of the following statements:

a) The _____ property specifies which image a `PictureBox` displays.

b) The _____ menu contains commands for arranging and displaying windows.

c) The _____ property determines a form's or control's background color.

2.7   Briefly describe each of the following terms:

a) toolbar

b) menu bar

c) **Toolbox**

d) control

e) form

f) solution

[*Note:* In the following exercises, you are asked to create GUIs using controls that we have not yet discussed in this book. The exercises will give you practice with visual programming only—the programs will not perform any actions. You will be placing controls from the **Toolbox** on a form to familiarize yourself with what each control looks like. We have provided step-by-step instructions for you. If you follow these, you should be able to replicate the screen images we provide.]

2.8 *(Notepad GUI)* Create the GUI for the notepad as shown in Fig. 2.50.

    a) *Manipulating the Form's properties.* Change the Text property of the Form to My Notepad.

    b) *Adding a MenuStrip to the Form.* After inserting the MenuStrip, add items by clicking the **Type Here** section, typing a menu name (e.g., **File**, **Edit**, **View** and **About**), then pressing *Enter.*

    c) *Adding a RichTextBox to the Form.* Change the Size property to 267, 220 or use the sizing handles to resize the RichTextBox to the correct size. Change the Text property to Enter Text Here. Finally, set the Location property to 13, 34.

2.9 *(Calendar and Appointments GUI)* Create the GUI for the calendar and appointments as shown in Fig. 2.51.

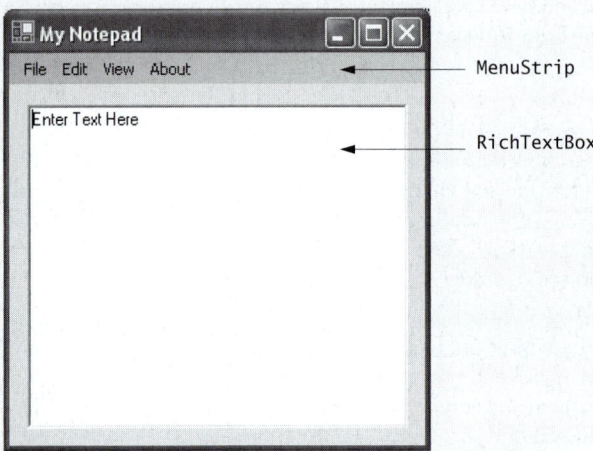

Fig. 2.50 | Notepad GUI.

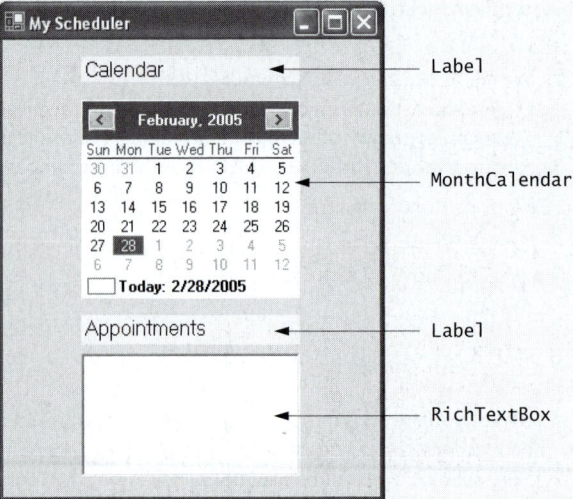

Fig. 2.51 | Calendar and Appointments GUI.

a) *Manipulating the Form's properties.* Change the Text property of the Form to My Scheduler. Set the Form's Size property to 332, 470.

b) *Adding Labels to the Form.* Add two Labels to the Form. Set the Labels' AutoSize properties to False. Both should be of equal size (178, 21) and should be centered in the Form horizontally, as shown. Set the Label's Text properties to match the figure as shown, using 12-point font size. Also set the BackColor property to Yellow.

c) *Adding a MonthCalendar control to the Form.* Add this control to the Form and center it horizontally in the appropriate place between the two Labels.

d) *Adding a RichTextBox control to the Form.* Add a RichTextBox control to the Form and center it below the second Label. Resize the RichTextBox accordingly.

2.10 *(Calculator GUI)* Create the GUI for the calculator as shown in Fig. 2.52.

a) *Manipulating the Form's properties.* Change the Size property of the Form to 272, 192. Change the Text property of the Form to Calculator.

b) *Adding a TextBox to the Form.* Set the TextBox's Text property in the **Properties** window to 0. Change the Size property to 240, 20. Set the TextAlign property to Right; this right aligns text displayed in the TextBox. Finally, set the TextBox's Location property to 8, 16.

c) *Adding the first Panel to the Form.* Panel controls are used to group other controls. Change the Panel's BorderStyle property to Fixed3D to make the inside of the Panel appear recessed. Change the Size property to 88, 108. Finally, set the Location property to 8, 48. This Panel contains the calculator's numeric keys.

d) *Adding the second Panel to the Form.* Change the Panel's BorderStyle property to Fixed3D. Change the Size property to 72, 108. Finally, set the Location property to 112, 48. This Panel contains the calculator's operator keys.

e) *Adding the third (and last) Panel to the Form.* Change the Panel's BorderStyle property to Fixed3D. Change the Size property to 48, 72. Finally, set the Location property to 200, 48. This Panel contains the calculator's **C** (clear) and **C/A** (clear all) keys.

f) *Adding Buttons to the Form.* There are 20 Buttons on the calculator. Add a Button to the Panel by dragging and dropping it on the Panel. Change the Text property of each Button to the calculator key it represents. The value you enter in the Text property will appear on the face of the Button. Finally, resize the Buttons, using their Size properties. The Buttons labeled 0–9, x, /, -, = and . should have a size of 24, 24. The **00** and **OFF** Buttons are sized 48, 24. The **+** Button is sized 24, 64. The **C** (clear) and **C/A** (clear all) Buttons are sized 32, 24.

2.11 *(Alarm Clock GUI)* Create the GUI for the alarm clock as shown in Fig. 2.53.

a) *Manipulating the Form's properties.* Change the Size property of the Form to 256, 176. Change the Form's Text property to Alarm Clock.

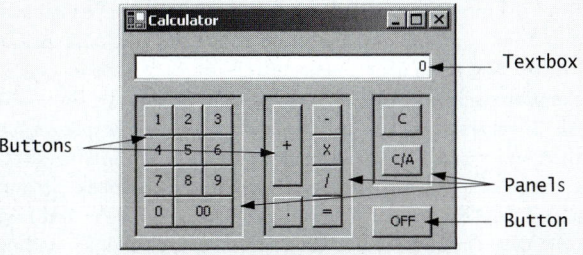

Fig. 2.52 | Calculator GUI.

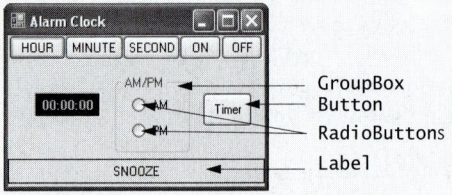

Fig. 2.53 | Alarm clock GUI.

   b) *Adding Buttons to the Form.* Add six Buttons to the Form. Change the Text property of each Button to the appropriate text. Change the Size properties of the **Hour, Minute** and **Second** Buttons to 56, 23. The **ON** and **OFF** Buttons are sized 40, 23. The **Timer** Button is sized 48, 32. Align the Buttons as shown.

   c) *Adding a Label to the Form.* Add a Label to the Form. Change the Text property to Snooze and set the AutoSize property to False. Set its Size to 248, 23. Set the Label's TextAlign property to MiddleCenter. Finally, to draw a border around the edge of the **Snooze** Label, change the BorderStyle property of the **Snooze** Label to FixedSingle.

   d) *Adding a GroupBox to the Form.* GroupBoxes are like Panels, except that GroupBoxes can display a title. Change the Text property to AM/PM, and set the Size property to 72, 72. To place the GroupBox in the correct location on the Form, set the Location property to 104, 38.

   e) *Adding* **AM/PM** *RadioButtons to the GroupBox.* Change the Text property of one RadioButton to AM and the other to PM, then set the AutoSize property of each RadioButton to False. Then place the RadioButtons as shown by setting the Location of the **AM** RadioButton to 16, 16 and that of the **PM** RadioButton to 16, 40. Set their Size properties to 48, 24.

   f) *Adding the time Label to the Form.* Add a Label to the Form and change its Text property to 00:00:00. Change the BorderStyle property to Fixed3D and the BackColor to Black. Set the AutoSize property to False, then set the Size property to 64, 23. Use the Font property to make the time bold. Change the ForeColor to Silver (located in the **Web** tab) to make the time stand out against the black background. Set TextAlign to MiddleCenter to center the text in the Label. Position the Label as shown.

2.12   *(Radio GUI)* Create the GUI for the radio as shown in Fig. 2.54. [*Note:* All colors used in this exercise are from the **Web** palette, and the image can be found in the examples folder for Chapter 2.]

   a) *Manipulating the Form's properties.* Change the Form's Text property to Radio and the Size to 576, 240. Set BackColor to PeachPuff.

   b) *Adding the* **Pre-set** *Stations GroupBox and Buttons.* Set the GroupBox's Size to 232, 64, its Text to Pre-set Stations, its ForeColor to Black and its BackColor to RosyBrown. Change its Font to bold. Finally, set its Location to 24, 16. Add six Buttons to the GroupBox. Set each BackColor to PeachPuff and each Size to 24, 23. Change the Buttons' Text properties to 1, 2, 3, 4, 5 and 6, respectively.

   c) *Adding the* **Speakers** *GroupBox and CheckBoxes.* Set the GroupBox's AutoSize property to False, then set its Size to 160, 72, its Text to Speakers and its ForeColor to Black. Set its Location to 280, 16. Add two CheckBoxes to the GroupBox. Set each CheckBox's Size to 56, 24. Set the Text properties for the CheckBoxes to Rear and Front.

   d) *Adding the* **Power On/Off** *Button.* Add a Button to the Form. Set its Text to Power On/Off, its BackColor to RosyBrown, its ForeColor to Black and its Size to 72, 64. Change its Font style to Bold.

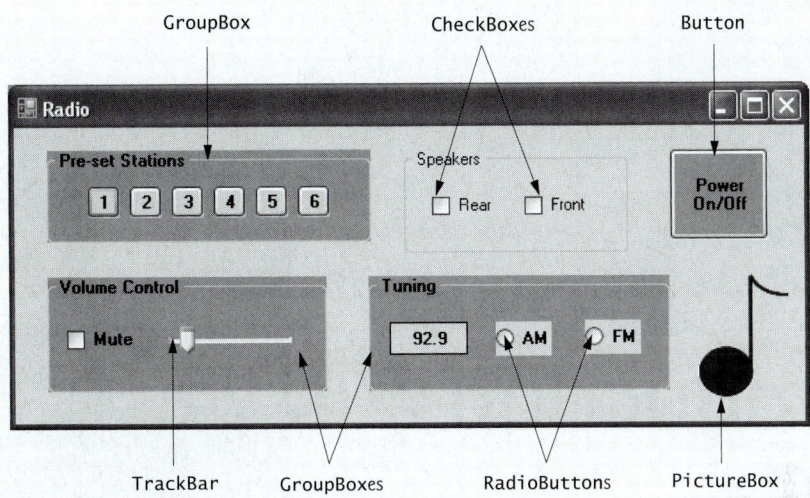

Fig. 2.54 | Radio GUI.

e) *Adding the* **Volume Control** *GroupBox, the* **Mute** *CheckBox and the* **Volume** *TrackBar.* Add a GroupBox to the Form. Set its Text to Volume Control, its BackColor to RosyBrown, its ForeColor to Black and its Size to 200, 80. Set its Font style to Bold. Add a CheckBox to the GroupBox. Set its Text to Mute, its AutoSize property to False and its Size to 56, 24. Add a TrackBar to the GroupBox.

f) *Adding the* **Tuning** *GroupBox, the radio station* Label *and the* **AM/FM** *RadioButtons.* Add a GroupBox to the Form. Set its Text to Tuning, its ForeColor to Black and its BackColor to RosyBrown. Set its Font style to Bold and its Size to 216, 80. Add a Label to the GroupBox. Set its BackColor to PeachPuff, its ForeColor to Black, its BorderStyle to FixedSingle, its Font style to Bold, its TextAlign to MiddleCenter, its AutoSize to False and its Size to 56, 23. Set its Text to 92.9. Place the Label as shown in the figure. Add two RadioButtons to the GroupBox. Change the BackColor to PeachPuff, set the AutoSize to False and change the Size to 40,24. Set the Text of one to AM and the other's to FM.

g) *Adding the image.* Add a PictureBox to the Form. Set its BackColor to Transparent, its SizeMode to StretchImage and its Size to 66, 85. Set the Image property to Music-Note.gif (located in the examples folder for Chapter 2).

3

Introduction to C# Applications

OBJECTIVES

In this chapter you will learn:

■ To write simple C# applications using code rather than visual programming.

■ To write statements that input and output data to the screen.

■ To declare and use data of various types.

■ To store and retrieve data from memory.

■ To use arithmetic operators.

■ To determine the order in which operators are applied.

■ To write decision-making statements.

■ To use relational and equality operators.

■ To use message dialogs to display messages.

3.1 Introduction

We now introduce C# application programming, which facilitates a disciplined approach to application design. Most of the C# applications you will study in this book process information and display results. In this chapter, we introduce *console applications*—these input and output text in a *console window*. In Microsoft Windows 95/98/ME, the console window is the *MS-DOS prompt*. In other versions of Microsoft Windows, the console window is the *Command Prompt.*

We begin with several examples that simply display messages on the screen. We then demonstrate an application that obtains two numbers from a user, calculates their sum and displays the result. You will learn how to perform various arithmetic calculations and save the results for later use. Many applications contain logic that requires the application to make decisions—the last example in this chapter demonstrates decision-making fundamentals by showing you how to compare numbers and display messages based on the comparison results. For example, the application displays a message indicating that two numbers are equal only if they have the same value. We carefully analyze each example one line at a time. We provide many fun and challenging problems in the chapter's exercises.

3.2 A Simple C# Application: Displaying a Line of Text

Every time you use a computer, you execute various applications that perform tasks for you. For example, your e-mail application helps you send and receive e-mail, and your Web browser lets you view Web pages from Web sites around the world. Computer programmers create these applications.

Let us consider a simple application that displays a line of text. (Later in this section, we discuss how to compile and run an application.) The application and its output are shown in Fig. 3.1. The application illustrates several important C# language features. C# uses notations that may look strange to nonprogrammers. For your convenience, each program we present in this book includes line numbers, which are not part of actual C# code. In Section 3.3, we show how to display line numbers for your C# code in the IDE. We will soon see that line 10 does the real work of the application—namely, displaying the phrase

```
 1    // Fig. 3.1: Welcome1.cs
 2    // Text-printing application.
 3    using System;
 4
 5    public class Welcome1
 6    {
 7       // Main method begins execution of C# application
 8       public static void Main( string[] args )
 9       {
10          Console.WriteLine( "Welcome to C# Programming!" );
11       } // end method Main
12    } // end class Welcome1
```

```
Welcome to C# Programming!
```

Fig. 3.1 | Text-printing application.

Welcome to C# Programming! on the screen. We now consider each line of the application—this is called a *code walkthrough*.

Line 1

```
// Fig. 3.1: Welcome1.cs
```

begins with //, indicating that the remainder of the line is a *comment*. Programmers insert comments to document applications and improve their readability. This helps people to read and understand applications. The C# compiler ignores comments, so they do not cause the computer to perform any action when the application is run. We begin every application with a comment indicating the figure number and the name of the file in which the application is stored.

A comment that begins with // is called a *single-line comment*, because it terminates at the end of the line on which it appears. A // comment also can begin in the middle of a line and continue until the end of that line (as in lines 7, 11 and 12).

Delimited comments such as

```
/* This is a delimited
   comment. It can be
   split over many lines */
```

can be spread over several lines. This type of comment begins with the delimiter /* and ends with the delimiter */. All text between the delimiters is ignored by the compiler. C# incorporated delimited comments and single-line comments from the C and C++ programming languages, respectively. In this book, we use only single-line comments in our programs.

Common Programming Error 3.1

*Forgetting one of the delimiters of a delimited comment is a syntax error. The **syntax** of a programming language specifies the rules for creating a proper application in that language. A **syntax error** occurs when the compiler encounters code that violates C#'s language rules. In this case, the compiler does not produce an executable file. Instead, the compiler issues one or more error messages to help you identify and fix the incorrect code. Syntax errors are also called **compiler errors, compile-time errors** or **compilation errors**, because the compiler detects them during the compilation phase. You will be unable to execute your application until you correct all the syntax errors in it.*

Line 2

```
// Text-printing application.
```

is a single-line comment that describes the purpose of the application.

Line 3

```
using System;
```

is a ***using directive*** that helps the compiler locate a class that is used in this application. A great strength of C# is its rich set of predefined classes that you can reuse rather than "reinventing the wheel." These classes are organized under ***namespaces***—named collections of related classes. Collectively, .NET's namespaces are referred to as the *.NET Framework Class Library* (*FCL*). Each using directive identifies predefined classes that a C# application should be able to use. The using directive in line 3 indicates that this example uses classes from the System namespace, which contains the predefined Console class (discussed shortly) used in Line 10, and many other useful classes.

Common Programming Error 3.2

All using *directives must appear before any other code (except comments) in a C# source code file; otherwise a compilation error occurs.*

Error-Prevention Tip 3.1

Forgetting to include a using *directive for a class used in your application typically results in a compilation error containing a message such as "*The name 'Console' does not exist in the current context.*" When this occurs, check that you provided the proper* using *directives and that the names in the* using *directives are spelled correctly, including proper use of uppercase and lowercase letters.*

For each new .NET class we use, we indicate the namespace in which it is located. This information is important because it helps you locate descriptions of each class in the *.NET documentation.* A Web-based version of this documentation can be found at

msdn2.microsoft.com/en-us/library/ms229335

This can also be found in the Visual C# Express documentation under the **Help** menu. You can also place the cursor on the name of any .NET class or method, then press the *F1* key to get more information.

Line 4 is simply a blank line. Programmers use blank lines and space characters to make applications easier to read. Together, blank lines, space characters and tab characters are known as ***whitespace***. (Space characters and tabs are known specifically as ***whitespace characters***.) Whitespace is ignored by the compiler. In this and the next several chapters, we discuss conventions for using whitespace to enhance application readability.

Line 5

```
public class Welcome1
```

begins a *class declaration* for the class Welcome1. Every application consists of at least one class declaration that is defined by you—the programmer. These are known as ***user-defined classes***. The ***class keyword*** introduces a class declaration and is immediately followed by the *class name* (Welcome1). Keywords (sometimes called *reserved words*) are reserved for use by C# and are always spelled with all lowercase letters. The complete list of C# keywords is shown in Fig. 3.2.

By convention, all class names begin with a capital letter and capitalize the first letter of each word they include (e.g., SampleClassName). This is frequently referred to as *Pascal casing*. A class name is an *identifier*—a series of characters consisting of letters, digits and underscores (_) that does not begin with a digit and does not contain spaces. Some valid identifiers are Welcome1, identifier, _value and m_inputField1. The name 7button is not a valid identifier because it begins with a digit, and the name input field is not a valid identifier because it contains a space. Normally, an identifier that does not begin with a capital letter is not the name of a class. C# is *case sensitive*—that is, uppercase and lowercase letters are distinct, so a1 and A1 are different (but both valid) identifiers. Identifiers may also be preceded by the @ character. This indicates that a word should be interpreted as an identifier, even if it is a keyword (e.g. @int). This allows C# code to use code written in other .NET languages where an identifier might have the same name as a C# keyword.

Good Programming Practice 3.1

By convention, always begin a class name's identifier with a capital letter and start each subsequent word in the identifier with a capital letter.

C# Keywords				
abstract	as	base	bool	break
byte	case	catch	char	checked
class	const	continue	decimal	default
delegate	do	double	else	enum
event	explicit	extern	false	finally
fixed	float	for	foreach	goto
if	implicit	in	int	interface
internal	is	lock	long	namespace
new	null	object	operator	out
override	params	private	protected	public
readonly	ref	return	sbyte	sealed
short	sizeof	stackalloc	static	string
struct	switch	this	throw	true
try	typeof	uint	ulong	unchecked
unsafe	ushort	using	virtual	void
volatile	while			

Fig. 3.2 | C# keywords.

Common Programming Error 3.3

C# is case sensitive. Not using the proper uppercase and lowercase letters for an identifier normally causes a compilation error.

In Chapters 3–8, every class we define begins with the keyword ***public***. For now, we will simply require this keyword. You will learn more about public and non-public classes in Chapter 9. When you save your public class declaration in a file, the file name is usually the class name followed by the .cs filename extension. For our application, the file name is Welcome1.cs.

Good Programming Practice 3.2

By convention, a file that contains a single public class should have a name that is identical to the class name (plus the .cs extension) in terms of both spelling and capitalization. Naming your files in this way makes it easier for other programmers (and you) to determine where the classes of an application are located.

A *left brace* (in line 6 in Fig. 3.1), {, begins the *body* of every class declaration. A corresponding *right brace* (in line 12), }, must end each class declaration. Note that lines 7–11 are indented. This indentation is one of the spacing conventions mentioned earlier. We define each spacing convention as a *Good Programming Practice*.

Error-Prevention Tip 3.2

Whenever you type an opening left brace, {, in your application, immediately type the closing right brace, }, then reposition the cursor between the braces and indent to begin typing the body. This practice helps prevent errors due to missing braces.

Good Programming Practice 3.3

Indent the entire body of each class declaration one "level" of indentation between the left and right braces that delimit the body of the class. This format emphasizes the class declaration's structure and makes it easier to read. You can let the IDE format your code by selecting Edit > Advanced > Format Document.

Good Programming Practice 3.4

*Set a convention for the indent size you prefer, then uniformly apply that convention. The **Tab** key may be used to create indents, but tab stops vary among text editors. We recommend using three spaces to form each level of indentation. We show how to do this in Section 3.3.*

Common Programming Error 3.4

It is a syntax error if braces do not occur in matching pairs.

Line 7

```
// Main method begins execution of C# application
```

is a comment indicating the purpose of lines 8–11 of the application. Line 8

```
public static void Main( string[] args )
```

is the starting point of every application. The *parentheses* after the identifier Main indicate that it is an application building block called a method. Class declarations normally contain one or more methods. Method names usually follow the same Pascal casing capitalization conventions used for class names. For each application, exactly one of the methods in a class must be called `Main` (which is typically defined as shown in line 8); otherwise, the application will not execute. Methods are able to perform tasks and return information when they complete their tasks. Keyword ***void*** (line 8) indicates that this method will not return any information after it completes its task. Later, we will see that many methods do return information. You will learn more about methods in Chapters 4 and 7. For now, simply mimic `Main`'s first line in your applications.

The left brace in line 9 begins the ***body of the method declaration***. A corresponding right brace must end the method's body (line 11 of Fig. 3.1). Note that line 10 in the body of the method is indented between the braces.

Good Programming Practice 3.5

As with class declarations, indent the entire body of each method declaration one "level" of indentation between the left and right braces that define the method body. This format makes the structure of the method stand out and makes the method declaration easier to read.

Line 10

```
Console.WriteLine( "Welcome to C# Programming!" );
```

instructs the computer to ***perform an action***—namely, to print (i.e., display on the screen) the ***string*** of characters contained between the double quotation marks. A string is sometimes called a ***character string***, a ***message*** or a ***string literal***. We refer to characters between double quotation marks simply as ***strings***. Whitespace characters in strings are not ignored by the compiler.

Class ***Console*** provides ***standard input/output*** capabilities that enable applications to read and display text in the console window from which the application executes. The ***Console.WriteLine method*** displays (or prints) a line of text in the console window. The string in the parentheses in line 10 is the ***argument*** to the method. Method `Console.WriteLine` performs its task by displaying (also called outputting) its argument in the console window. When `Console.WriteLine` completes its task, it positions the ***screen cursor*** (the blinking symbol indicating where the next character will be displayed) at the beginning of the next line in the console window. (This movement of the cursor is similar to what happens when a user presses the *Enter* key while typing in a text editor—the cursor moves to the beginning of the next line in the file.)

The entire line 10, including `Console.WriteLine`, the parentheses, the argument `"Welcome to C# Programming!"` in the parentheses and the ***semicolon*** (`;`), is called a ***statement***. Each statement ends with a semicolon. When the statement in line 10 executes, it displays the message `Welcome to C# Programming!` in the console window. A method is typically composed of one or more statements that perform the method's task.

Common Programming Error 3.5

Omitting the semicolon at the end of a statement is a syntax error.

Error-Prevention Tip 3.3

When learning how to program, sometimes it is helpful to "break" a working application so you can familiarize yourself with the compiler's syntax-error messages. Try removing a semicolon or brace from the code of Fig. 3.1, then recompiling the application to see the error messages generated by the omission.

Error-Prevention Tip 3.4

When the compiler reports a syntax error, the error may not be in the line indicated by the error message. First, check the line for which the error was reported. If that line does not contain syntax errors, check several preceding lines.

Some programmers find it difficult when reading or writing an application to match the left and right braces ({ and }) that delimit the body of a class declaration or a method declaration. For this reason, some programmers include a comment after each closing right brace (}) that ends a method declaration and after each closing right brace that ends a class declaration. For example, line 11

```
} // end method Main
```

specifies the closing right brace of method `Main`, and line 12

```
} // end class Welcome1
```

specifies the closing right brace of class `Welcome1`. Each of these comments indicates the method or class that the right brace terminates. Visual Studio can help you locate matching braces in your code. Simply place the cursor next to one brace and Visual Studio will highlight the other.

Good Programming Practice 3.6

Following the closing right brace of a method body or class declaration with a comment indicating the method or class declaration to which the brace belongs improves application readability.

3.3 Creating Your Simple Application in Visual C# Express

Now that we have presented our first console application (Fig. 3.1), we provide a step-by-step explanation of how to compile and execute it using Visual C# Express.

Creating the Console Application

After opening Visual C# 2005 Express, select **File > New Project...** to display the **New Project** dialog (Fig. 3.3), then select the **Console Application** template. In the dialog's **Name** field, type `Welcome1`. Click **OK** to create the project. The IDE now contains the open console application, as shown in Fig. 3.4. Note that the editor window already contains some code provided by the IDE. Some of this code is similar to that of Fig. 3.1. Some is not, and uses features that we have not yet discussed. The IDE inserts this extra code to help organize the application and to provide access to some common classes in the .NET Framework Class Library—at this point in the book, this code is neither required nor relevant to the discussion of this application; delete all of it.

The code coloring scheme used by the IDE is called *syntax-color highlighting* and helps you visually differentiate application elements. Keywords appear in blue, and other text is black. When present, comments are green. In this book, we syntax shade our code similarly—bold italic for keywords, italic for comments, bold gray for literals and constants, and black for other text. One example of a literal is the string passed to `Console.WriteLine` in line 10 of Fig. 3.1. You can customize the colors shown in the code editor by selecting **Tools > Options...**. This displays the **Options** dialog (Fig. 3.5). Then click the plus sign, +, next to **Environment** and select **Fonts and Colors**. Here you can change the colors for various code elements.

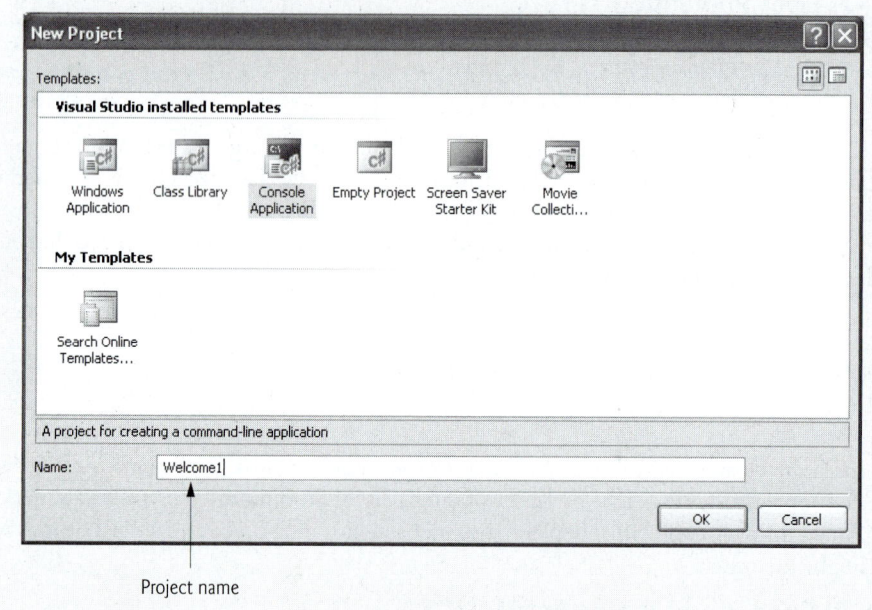

Project name

Fig. 3.3 | Creating a **Console Application** with the **New Project** dialog.

Editor window

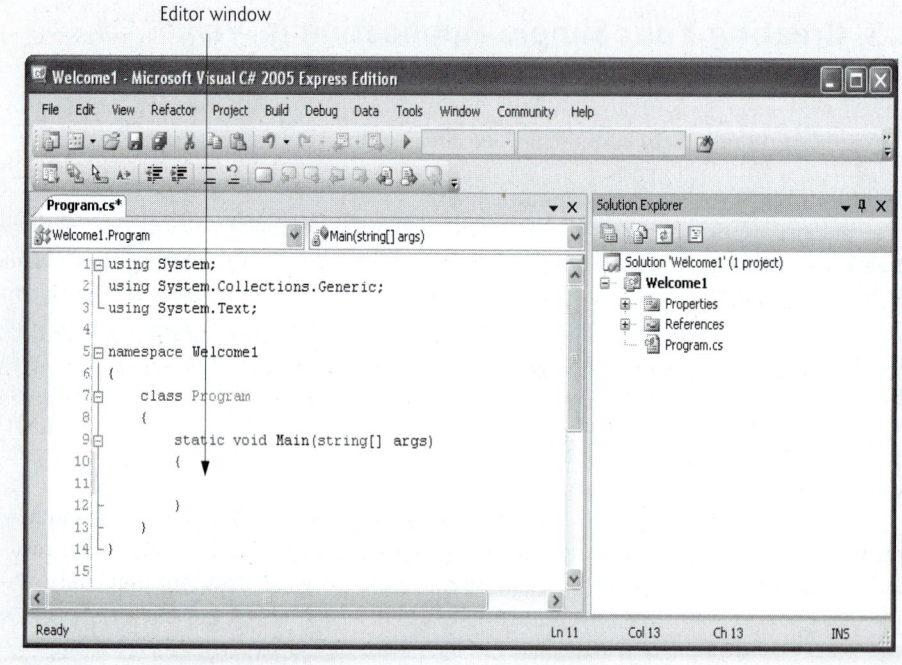

Fig. 3.4 | IDE with an open console application.

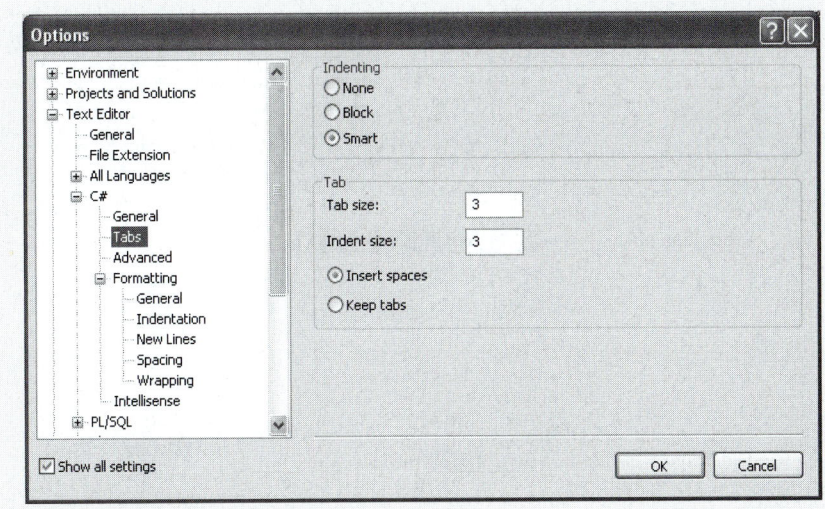

Fig. 3.5 | Modifying the IDE settings.

Modifying the Editor Settings to Display Line Numbers

Visual C# Express provides many ways to personalize your coding experience. In this step, you will change the settings so that your code matches that of this book. To have the IDE display line numbers, select **Tools > Options…**. In the dialog that appears, click the **Show all settings** checkbox on the lower left of the dialog, then click the plus sign next to **Text Editor** in the left pane and select **All Languages**. On the right, check the **Line Numbers** check box. Keep the **Options** dialog open.

Setting Code Indentation to Three Spaces per Indent

In the **Options** dialog that you opened in the previous step (Fig. 3.5), click on the plus sign next to C# in the left pane and select **Tabs**. Enter **3** for both the **Tab Size** and **Indent Size** fields. Any new code you add will now use three spaces for each level of indentation. Click **OK** to save your settings, close the dialog and return to the editor window.

Changing the Name of the Application File

For applications we create in this book, we change the default name of the application file (i.e., `Program.cs`) to a more descriptive name. To rename the file, click `Program.cs` in the **Solution Explorer** window. This displays the application file's properties in the **Properties** window (Fig. 3.6). Change the *File Name property* to `Welcome1.cs`.

Writing Code

In the editor window (Fig. 3.4), type the code from Fig. 3.1. After you type (in line 10) the class name and a dot (i.e., `Console.`), a window containing a scrollbar is displayed (Fig. 3.7). This IDE feature, called *IntelliSense*, lists a class's *members*, which include method names. As you type characters, Visual C# Express highlights the first member that matches all the characters typed, then displays a tool tip containing a description of that member. You can either type the complete member name (e.g., `WriteLine`), double click the member name in the member list or press the *Tab* key to complete the name. Once the complete name is provided, the *IntelliSense* window closes.

Solution Explorer

Click **Program.cs** to display its properties

Properties window

Type **Welcome1.cs** here to rename the file

File Name property

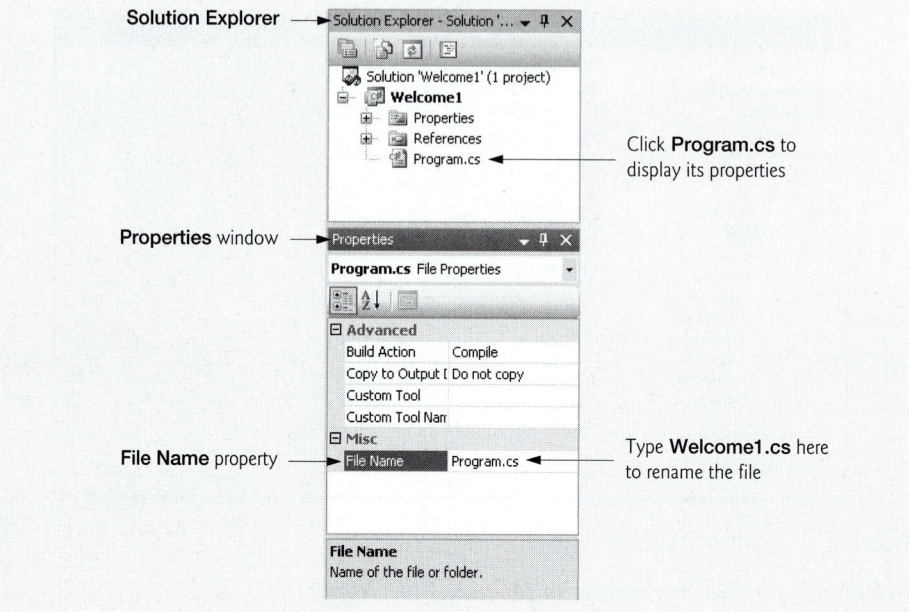

Fig. 3.6 | Renaming the program file in the **Properties** window.

Partially-typed member

Member list

Highlighted member

Tool tip describes highlighted member

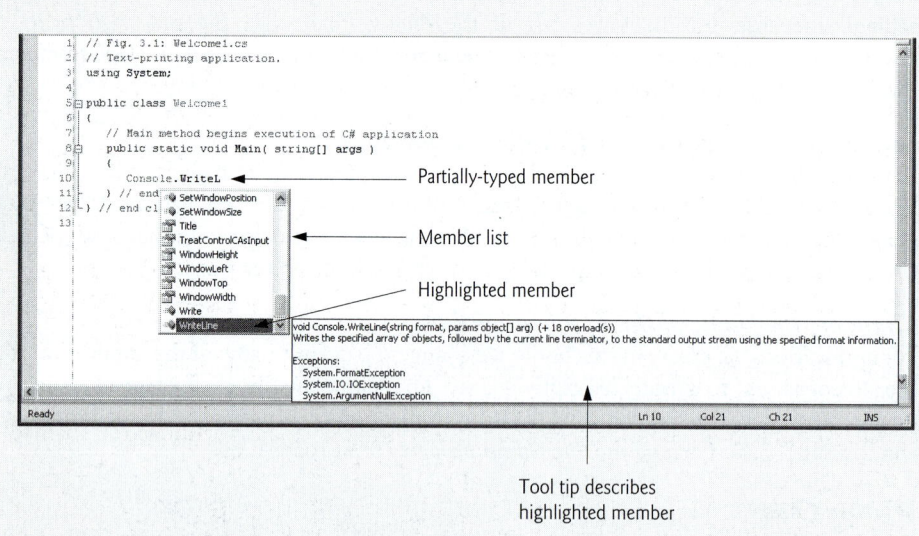

Fig. 3.7 | *IntelliSense* feature of Visual C# Express.

When you type the open parenthesis character, (, after Console.WriteLine, the *Parameter Info* window is displayed (Fig. 3.8). This window contains information about the method's parameters. As you will learn in Chapter 7, there can be several versions of a method—that is, a class can define several methods that have the same name as long as they have different numbers and/or types of parameters. These methods normally all perform

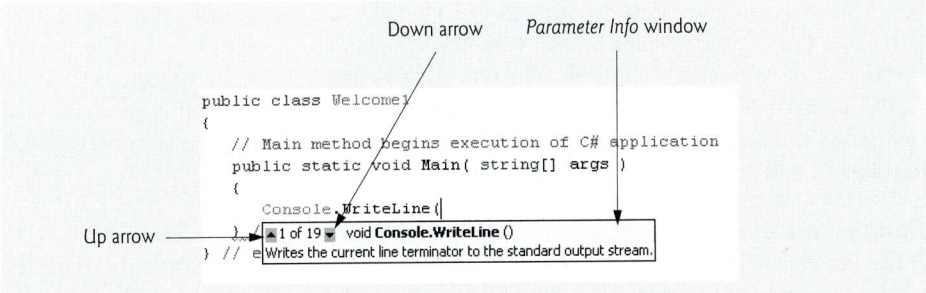

Fig. 3.8 | *Parameter Info* window.

similar tasks. The *Parameter Info* window indicates how many versions of the selected method are available and provides up and down arrows for scrolling through the different versions. For example, there are 19 versions of the WriteLine method—we use one of these 19 versions in our application. The *Parameter Info* window is one of the many features provided by the IDE to facilitate application development. In the next several chapters, you will learn more about the information displayed in these windows. The *Parameter Info* window is especially helpful when you want to see the different ways in which a method can be used. From the code in Fig. 3.1, we already know that we intend to display one string with WriteLine, so because you know exactly which version of WriteLine you want to use, you can simply close the *Parameter Info* window by pressing the *Esc* key.

Saving the Application

Select **File > Save All** to display the **Save Project** dialog (Fig. 3.9). In the **Location** text box, specify the directory where you want to save this project. We choose to save the project in the MyProjects directory on the C: drive. Select the **Create directory for solution** checkbox (to enable Visual Studio to create the directory if it does not already exist), and click **Save**.

Compiling and Running the Application

You are now ready to compile and execute your application. Depending on the type of application, the compiler may compile the code into files with a **.exe** (*executable*) *extension*, a **.dll** (*dynamic link library*) *extension* or one of several other extensions. Such files are called assemblies and are the packaging units for compiled C# code. These assemblies contain the Microsoft Intermediate Language (MSIL) code for the application.

To compile the application, select **Build > Build Solution**. If the application contains no syntax errors, your console application will compile into an executable file (named

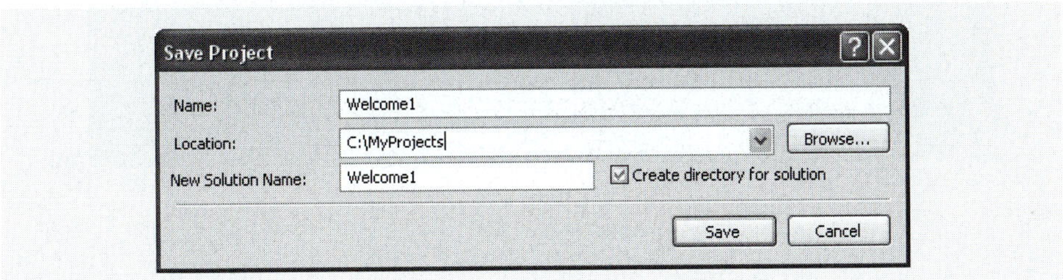

Fig. 3.9 | **Save Project** dialog.

Welcome1.exe, in the project's directory). To execute this console application (i.e., Welcome1.exe), select **Debug > Start Without Debugging** (or type *<Ctrl> F5*), which invokes the Main method (Fig. 3.1). The statement in line 10 of Main displays Welcome to C# Programming!. Figure 3.10 shows the results of executing this application. Note that the results are displayed in a console window. Leave the application open in Visual C# Express; we will go back to it later in this section.

Running the Application from the Command Prompt

As we mentioned at the beginning of the chapter, you can execute applications outside the IDE in a **Command Prompt**. This is useful when you simply want to run an application rather than open it for modification. To open the **Command Prompt**, select **Start > All Programs > Accessories > Command Prompt**. [*Note:* Windows 2000 users should replace **All Programs** with **Programs**.] The window (Fig. 3.11) displays copyright information, followed by a prompt that indicates the current directory. By default, the prompt specifies the current user's directory on the local machine (in our case, C:\Documents and Settings\deitel). On your machine, the folder name deitel will be replaced with your username. Enter the command cd (which stands for "change directory"), followed by the /d flag (to change drives if necessary), then the directory where the application's .exe file is located (i.e., the Release directory of your application). For example, the command cd /d C:\MyProjects\Welcome1\Welcome1\bin\Release (Fig. 3.12) changes the current directory, to the Welcome1 application's Release directory on the C: drive. The next prompt displays the new directory. After changing to the proper directory, you can run the compiled application by entering the name of the .exe file (i.e., Welcome1). The application will run to completion, then the prompt will display again, awaiting the next command. To close the **Command Prompt**, type exit (Fig. 3.12) and press *Enter*.

Note that Visual C# 2005 Express maintains a Debug and a Release directory in each project's bin directory. The Debug directory contains a version of the application that can be used with the debugger (see Appendix C, Using the Visual Studio 2005 Debugger). The Release directory contains an optimized version that you could provide to your clients. In the complete Visual Studio 2005, you can select the specific version you wish to build from the **Solution Configurations** drop-down list in the toolbars at the top of the IDE. The default is the Debug version.

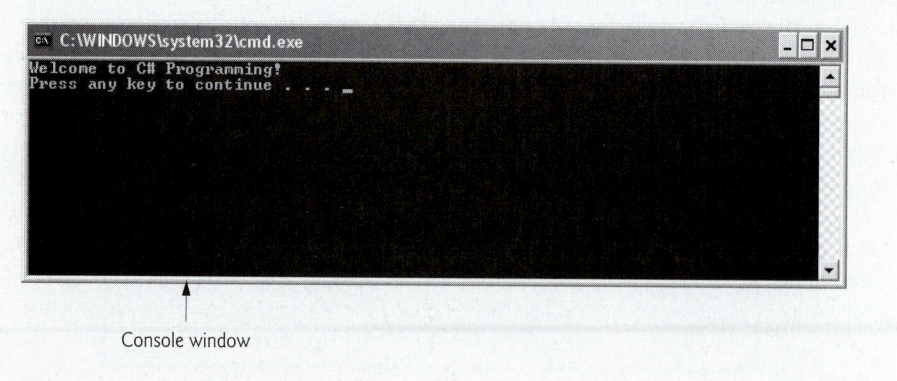

Console window

Fig. 3.10 | Executing the application shown in Fig. 3.1.

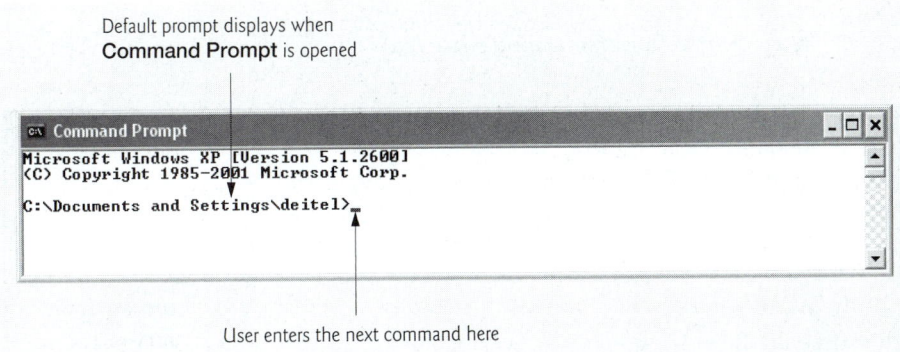

Fig. 3.11 | Executing the application shown in Fig. 3.1 from a **Command Prompt** window.

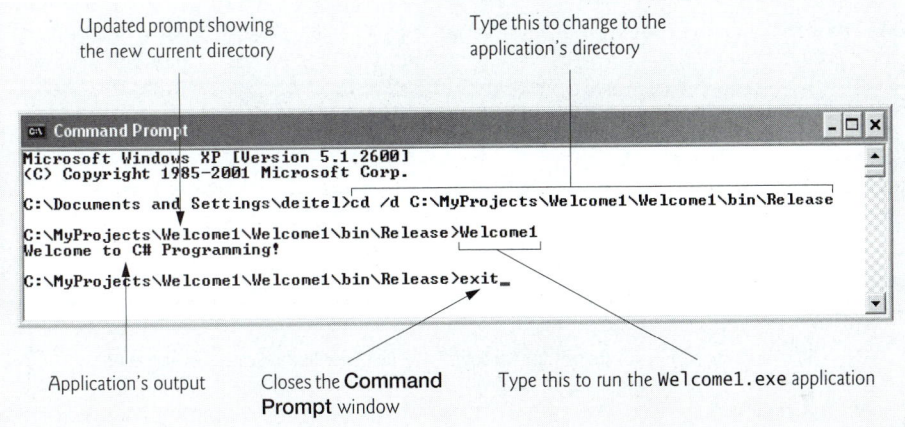

Fig. 3.12 | Executing the application shown in Fig. 3.1 from a **Command Prompt** window.

[*Note:* Many environments show **Command Prompt** windows with black backgrounds and white text. We adjusted these settings in our environment to make our screen captures more readable.]

Syntax Errors, Error Messages and the *Error List* *Window*
Go back to the application in Visual C# Express. When you type a line of code and press the *Enter* key, the IDE responds either by applying syntax-color highlighting or by generating a *syntax error*, which indicates a violation of Visual C#'s rules for creating correct applications (i.e., one or more statements are not written correctly). Syntax errors occur for various reasons, such as missing parentheses and misspelled keywords.

When a syntax error occurs, the IDE underlines the error in red and provides a description of the error in the *Error List window* (Fig. 3.13). If the **Error List** window is not visible in the IDE, select **View > Error List** to display it. In Figure 3.13, we intentionally omitted the first parenthesis in line 10. The first error contains the text "; expected" and specifies that the error is in column 25 of line 10. This error message appears when the compiler thinks that the line contains a complete statement, followed by a semicolon, and the beginning of another statement. The second error contains the same text, but specifies

Intentionally omitted parenthesis character (syntax error)

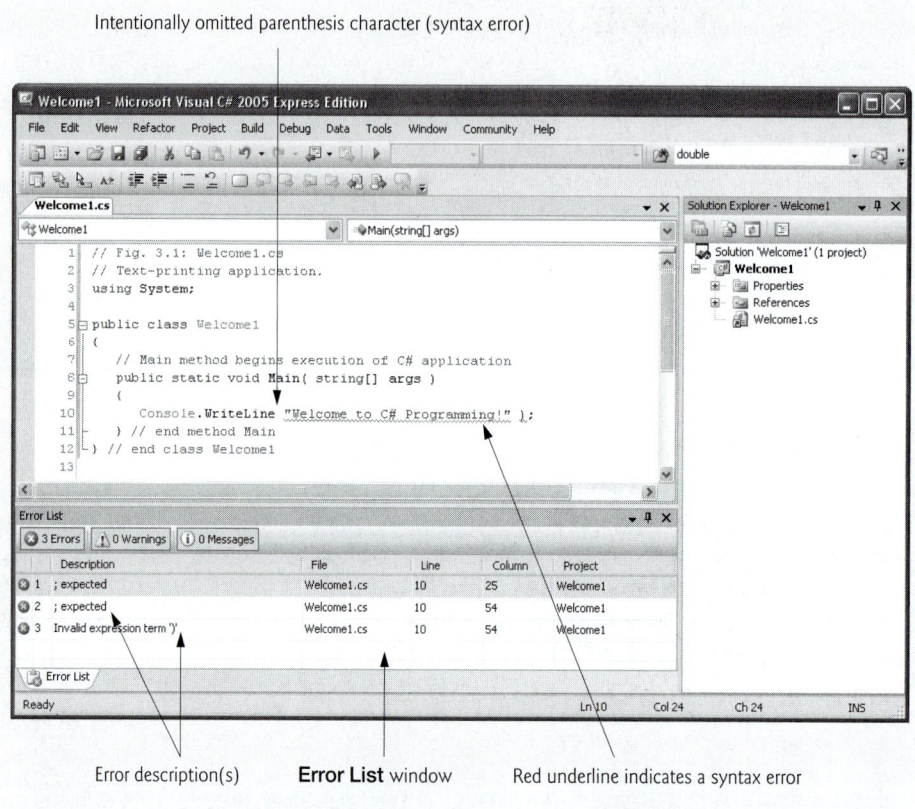

Error description(s)   **Error List** window   Red underline indicates a syntax error

Fig. 3.13 | Syntax errors indicated by the IDE.

that this error is in column 54 of line 10 because the compiler thinks that this is the end of the second statement. The third error has the text **"Invalid expression term ')'"** because the compiler is confused by the unmatched right parenthesis. Although we are attempting to include only one statement in line 10, the missing left parenthesis causes the compiler to incorrectly assume that there is more than one statement on that line, to misinterpret the right parenthesis and to generate *three* error messages.

Error-Prevention Tip 3.5

*One syntax error can lead to multiple entries in the **Error List** window. Each error that you address could eliminate several subsequent error messages when you recompile your application. So when you see an error you know how to fix, correct it and recompile—this may make several other errors disappear.*

3.4 Modifying Your Simple C# Application

This section continues our introduction to C# programming with two examples that modify the example of Fig. 3.1 to print text on one line by using several statements and to print text on several lines by using only one statement.

Displaying a Single Line of Text with Multiple Statements

"Welcome to C# Programming!" can be displayed several ways. Class Welcome2, shown in Fig. 3.14, uses two statements to produce the same output as that shown in Fig. 3.1. From this point forward, we highlight the new and key features in each code listing, as shown in lines 10–11 of Fig. 3.14.

The application is almost identical to Fig. 3.1. We discuss only the changes here. Line 2

```
// Printing one line of text with multiple statements.
```

is a comment stating the purpose of this application. Line 5 begins the Welcome2 class declaration.

Lines 10–11 of method Main

```
Console.Write( "Welcome to " );
Console.WriteLine( "C# Programming!" );
```

display one line of text in the console window. The first statement uses Console's method *Write* to display a string. Unlike WriteLine, after displaying its argument, Write does not position the screen cursor at the beginning of the next line in the console window—the next character the application displays will appear immediately after the last character that Write displays. Thus, line 11 positions the first character in its argument (the letter "C") immediately after the last character that line 10 displays (the space character before the string's closing double-quote character). Each Write statement resumes displaying characters from where the last Write statement displayed its last character.

Displaying Multiple Lines of Text with a Single Statement

A single statement can display multiple lines by using newline characters, which indicate to Console methods Write and WriteLine when they should position the screen cursor to the beginning of the next line in the console window. Like space characters and tab characters, newline characters are whitespace characters. The application of Fig. 3.15 outputs four lines of text, using newline characters to indicate when to begin each new line.

```
 1   // Fig. 3.14: Welcome2.cs
 2   // Printing one line of text with multiple statements.
 3   using System;
 4
 5   public class Welcome2
 6   {
 7      // Main method begins execution of C# application
 8      public static void Main( string[] args )
 9      {
10         Console.Write( "Welcome to " );
11         Console.WriteLine( "C# Programming!" );
12      } // end method Main
13   } // end class Welcome2
```

```
Welcome to C# Programming!
```

Fig. 3.14 | Printing one line of text with multiple statements.

```
 1    // Fig. 3.15: Welcome3.cs
 2    // Printing multiple lines with a single statement.
 3    using System;
 4
 5    public class Welcome3
 6    {
 7       // Main method begins execution of C# application
 8       public static void Main( string[] args )
 9       {
10          Console.WriteLine( "Welcome\nto\nC#\nProgramming!" );
11       } // end method Main
12    } // end class Welcome3
```

```
Welcome
to
C#
Programming!
```

Fig. 3.15 | Printing multiple lines with a single statement.

Most of the application is identical to the applications of Fig. 3.1 and Fig. 3.14, so we discuss only the changes here. Line 2

```
// Printing multiple lines with a single statement.
```

is a comment stating the purpose of this application. Line 5 begins the Welcome3 class declaration.

Line 10

```
Console.WriteLine( "Welcome\nto\nC#\nProgramming!" );
```

displays four separate lines of text in the console window. Normally, the characters in a string are displayed exactly as they appear in the double quotes. Note, however, that the two characters \ and n (repeated three times in the statement) do not appear on the screen. The *backslash* (\) is called an *escape character*. It indicates to C# that a "special character" is in the string. When a backslash appears in a string of characters, C# combines the next character with the backslash to form an *escape sequence.* The escape sequence \n represents the *newline character*. When a newline character appears in a string being output with Console methods, the newline character causes the screen cursor to move to the beginning of the next line in the console window. Figure 3.16 lists several common escape sequences and describes how they affect the display of characters in the console window.

Escape sequence	Description
\n	Newline. Positions the screen cursor at the beginning of the next line.
\t	Horizontal tab. Moves the screen cursor to the next tab stop.

Fig. 3.16 | Some common escape sequences. (Part 1 of 2.)

Escape sequence	Description
\r	Carriage return. Positions the screen cursor at the beginning of the current line—does not advance the cursor to the next line. Any characters output after the carriage return overwrite the characters previously output on that line.
\\	Backslash. Used to place a backslash character in a string.
\"	Double quote. Used to place a double-quote character (") in a string. For example, `Console.Write( "\"in quotes\"" );` displays `"in quotes"`

Fig. 3.16 | Some common escape sequences. (Part 2 of 2.)

3.5 Formatting Text with Console.Write and Console.WriteLine

Console methods Write and WriteLine also have the capability to display formatted data. Figure 3.17 outputs the strings "Welcome to" and "C# Programming!" with WriteLine. Line 10

```
Console.WriteLine( "{0}\n{1}", "Welcome to", "C# Programming!" );
```

calls method Console.WriteLine to display the application's output. The method call specifies three arguments. When a method requires multiple arguments, the arguments are separated with *commas* (,)—this is known as a *comma-separated list*.

 Good Programming Practice 3.7

Place a space after each comma (,) in an argument list to make applications more readable.

```
1   // Fig. 3.17: Welcome4.cs
2   // Printing multiple lines of text with string formatting.
3   using System;
4
5   public class Welcome4
6   {
7      // Main method begins execution of C# application
8      public static void Main( string[] args )
9      {
10         Console.WriteLine( "{0}\n{1}", "Welcome to", "C# Programming!" );
11      } // end method Main
12   } // end class Welcome4
```

```
Welcome to
C# Programming!
```

Fig. 3.17 | Printing multiple lines of text with string formatting.

Remember that all statements end with a semicolon (;). Therefore, line 10 represents only one statement. Large statements can be split over many lines, but there are some restrictions.

Common Programming Error 3.6

Splitting a statement in the middle of an identifier or a string is a syntax error.

Method WriteLine's first argument is a *format string* that may consist of *fixed text* and *format items*. Fixed text is output by WriteLine as we demonstrated in Fig. 3.1. Each format item is a placeholder for a value. Format items also may include optional formatting information.

Format items are enclosed in curly braces and contain a sequence of characters that tell the method which argument to use and how to format it. For example, the format item {0} is a placeholder for the first additional argument (because C# starts counting from 0), {1} is a placeholder for the second, etc. The format string in line 10 specifies that Write-Line should output two arguments and that the first one should be followed by a newline character. So this example substitutes "Welcome to" for the {0} and "C# Programming!" for the {1}. The output shows that two lines of text are displayed. Note that because braces in a formatted string normally indicate a placeholder for text substitution, you must type two left braces ({{) or two right braces (}}) to insert a single left or right brace into a formatted string, respectively. We introduce additional formatting features as they are needed in our examples.

3.6 Another C# Application: Adding Integers

Our next application reads (or inputs) two *integers* (whole numbers, like –22, 7, 0 and 1024) typed by a user at the keyboard, computes the sum of the values and displays the result. This application must keep track of the numbers supplied by the user for the calculation later in the application. Applications remember numbers and other data in the computer's memory and access that data through application elements called *variables*. The application of Fig. 3.18 demonstrates these concepts. In the sample output, we highlight data the user enters at the keyboard in bold.

Lines 1–2

```
// Fig. 3.18: Addition.cs
// Displaying the sum of two numbers input from the keyboard.
```

state the figure number, file name and purpose of the application.

Line 5

```
public class Addition
```

begins the declaration of class Addition. Remember that the body of each class declaration starts with an opening left brace (line 6), and ends with a closing right brace (line 26).

The application begins execution with method Main (lines 8–25). The left brace (line 9) marks the beginning of Main's body, and the corresponding right brace (line 25) marks the end of Main's body. Note that method Main is indented one level within the body of class Addition and that the code in the body of Main is indented another level for readability.

```
 1   // Fig. 3.18: Addition.cs
 2   // Displaying the sum of two numbers input from the keyboard.
 3   using System;
 4
 5   public class Addition
 6   {
 7      // Main method begins execution of C# application
 8      public static void Main( string[] args )
 9      {
10         int number1; // declare first number to add
11         int number2; // declare second number to add
12         int sum; // declare sum of number1 and number2
13
14         Console.Write( "Enter first integer: " ); // prompt user
15         // read first number from user
16         number1 = Convert.ToInt32( Console.ReadLine() );
17
18         Console.Write( "Enter second integer: " ); // prompt user
19         // read second number from user
20         number2 = Convert.ToInt32( Console.ReadLine() );
21
22         sum = number1 + number2; // add numbers
23
24         Console.WriteLine( "Sum is {0}", sum ); // display sum
25      } // end method Main
26   } // end class Addition
```

```
Enter first integer: 45
Enter second integer: 72
Sum is 117
```

Fig. 3.18 | Displaying the sum of two numbers input from the keyboard.

Line 10

```
int number1; // declare first number to add
```

is a *variable declaration statement* (also called a *declaration*) that specifies the name and type of a variable (number1) that is used in this application. A *variable* is a location in the computer's memory where a value can be stored for use later in an application. All variables must be declared with a *name* and a *type* before they can be used. A variable's name enables the application to access the value of the variable in memory—the name can be any valid identifier. (See Section 3.2 for identifier naming requirements.) A variable's type specifies what kind of information is stored at that location in memory. Like other statements, declaration statements end with a semicolon (;).

The declaration in line 10 specifies that the variable named number1 is of type *int*— it will hold *integer* values (whole numbers such as 7, –11, 0 and 31914). The range of values for an int is –2,147,483,648 (int.MinValue) to +2,147,483,647 (int.MaxValue). We will soon discuss types *float*, *double* and *decimal*, for specifying real numbers, and type *char*, for specifying characters. Real numbers contain decimal points, as in 3.4, 0.0 and –11.19. Variables of type float and double store approximations of real numbers in memory. Variables of type decimal store real numbers precisely (to 28–29 significant digits), so decimal variables are often used with monetary calculations. Variables of type char represent individual characters, such as an uppercase letter (e.g., A), a digit (e.g., 7), a special character (e.g., * or %) or an escape sequence (e.g., the newline character, \n). Types such as int, float, double, decimal and char are often called *simple types*. Simple-type names are keywords and must appear in all lowercase letters. Appendix L summarizes the characteristics of the thirteen simple types (bool, byte, sbyte, char, short, ushort, int, uint, long, ulong, float, double and decimal).

The variable declaration statements at lines 11–12

```
int number2; // declare second number to add
int sum; // declare sum of number1 and number2
```

similarly declare variables number2 and sum to be of type int.

Variable declaration statements can be split over several lines, with the variable names separated by commas (i.e., a comma-separated list of variable names). Several variables of the same type may be declared in one declaration or in multiple declarations. For example, lines 10–12 can also be written as follows:

```
int number1, // declare first number to add
    number2, // declare second number to add
    sum; // declare sum of number1 and number2
```

Good Programming Practice 3.8

Declare each variable on a separate line. This format allows a comment to be easily inserted next to each declaration.

Good Programming Practice 3.9

*Choosing meaningful variable names helps code to be **self-documenting** (i.e., one can understand the code simply by reading it rather than by reading documentation manuals or viewing an excessive number of comments).*

Good Programming Practice 3.10

*By convention, variable-name identifiers begin with a lowercase letter, and every word in the name after the first word begins with a capital letter. This naming convention is known as **camel casing**.*

Line 14

```
Console.Write( "Enter first integer: " ); // prompt user
```

uses Console.Write to display the message "Enter first integer: ". This message is called a *prompt* because it directs the user to take a specific action.

Line 16

```
number1 = Convert.ToInt32( Console.ReadLine() );
```

works in two steps. First, it calls the Console's **ReadLine** method. This method waits for the user to type a string of characters at the keyboard and press the *Enter* key to submit the string to the application. Then, the string is used as an argument to the **Convert** class's **ToInt32** method, which converts this sequence of characters into data of an type int. As we mentioned earlier in this chapter, some methods perform a task then return the result of that task. In this case, method ToInt32 returns the int representation of the user's input.

Technically, the user can type anything as the input value. ReadLine will accept it and pass it off to the ToInt32 method. This method assumes that the string contains a valid integer value. In this application, if the user types a noninteger value, a runtime logic error will occur and the application will terminate. Chapter 12, Exception Handling, discusses how to make your applications more robust by enabling them to handle such errors and continue executing. This is also known as making your application *fault tolerant*.

In line 16, the result of the call to method ToInt32 (an int value) is placed in variable number1 by using the *assignment operator*, =. The statement is read as "number1 gets the value returned by Convert.ToInt32." Operator = is called a *binary operator* because it has two *operands*—number1 and the result of the method call Convert.ToInt32. This statement is called an *assignment statement* because it assigns a value to a variable. Everything to the right of the assignment operator, =, is always evaluated before the assignment is performed.

Good Programming Practice 3.11

Place spaces on either side of a binary operator to make it stand out and make the code more readable.

Line 18

```
Console.Write( "Enter second integer: " ); // prompt user
```

prompts the user to enter the second integer. Line 20

```
number2 = Convert.ToInt32( Console.ReadLine() );
```

reads a second integer and assigns it to the variable number2.

Line 22

```
sum = number1 + number2; // add numbers
```

is an assignment statement that calculates the sum of the variables number1 and number2 and assigns the result to variable sum by using the assignment operator, =. The statement is read as "sum gets the value of number1 + number2." Most calculations are performed in assignment statements. When the application encounters the addition operator, it uses the values stored in the variables number1 and number2 to perform the calculation. In the preceding statement, the addition operator is a binary operator—its two *operands* are number1 and number2. Portions of statements that contain calculations are called *expressions*. In fact, an expression is any portion of a statement that has a value associated with it. For example, the value of the expression number1 + number2 is the sum of the numbers. Similarly, the value of the expression Console.ReadLine() is the string of characters typed by the user.

After the calculation has been performed, line 24

```
Console.WriteLine( "Sum is {0}", sum ); // display sum
```

uses method Console.WriteLine to display the sum. The format item {0} is a placeholder for the first argument after the format string. Other than the {0} format item, the remaining characters in the format string are all fixed text. So method WriteLine displays "Sum is ", followed by the value of sum (in the position of the {0} format item) and a newline.

Calculations can also be performed inside output statements. We could have combined the statements in lines 22 and 24 into the statement

```
Console.WriteLine( "Sum is {0}", ( number1 + number2 ) );
```

The parentheses around the expression number1 + number2 are not required—they are included to emphasize that the value of the expression number1 + number2 is output in the position of the {0} format item.

3.7 Memory Concepts

Variable names such as number1, number2 and sum actually correspond to *locations* in the computer's memory. Every variable has a *name*, a *type*, a *size* and a *value*.

In the addition application of Fig. 3.18, when the statement (line 16)

```
number1 = Convert.ToInt32( Console.ReadLine() );
```

executes, the number typed by the user is placed into a *memory location* to which the name number1 has been assigned by the compiler. Suppose that the user enters 45. The computer places that integer value into location number1, as shown in Fig. 3.19. Whenever a value is placed in a memory location, the value replaces the previous value in that location and the previous value is lost.

When the statement (line 20)

```
number2 = Convert.ToInt32( Console.ReadLine() );
```

executes, suppose that the user enters 72. The computer places that integer value into location number2. The memory now appears as shown in Fig. 3.20.

After the application of Fig. 3.18 obtains values for number1 and number2, it adds the values and places the sum into variable sum. The statement (line 22)

```
sum = number1 + number2; // add numbers
```

performs the addition, then replaces sum's previous value. After sum has been calculated, memory appears as shown in Fig. 3.21. Note that the values of number1 and number2 appear exactly as they did before they were used in the calculation of sum. These values were used, but not destroyed, as the computer performed the calculation—when a value is read from a memory location, the process is nondestructive.

| number1 | 45 |

Fig. 3.19 | Memory location showing the name and value of variable number1.

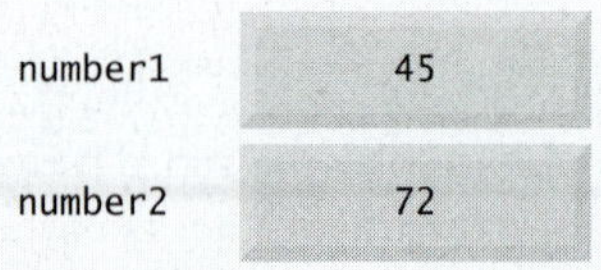

| number1 | 45 |
| number2 | 72 |

Fig. 3.20 | Memory locations after storing values for number1 and number2.

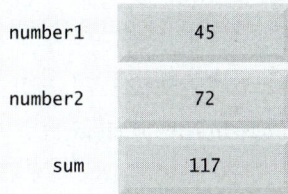

Fig. 3.21 | Memory locations after calculating and storing the sum of `number1` and `number2`.

3.8 Arithmetic

Most applications perform arithmetic calculations. The *arithmetic operators* are summarized in Fig. 3.22. Note the use of various special symbols not used in algebra. The *asterisk* (*) indicates multiplication, and the *percent sign* (%) is the *remainder operator* (called modulus in some languages), which we will discuss shortly. The arithmetic operators in Fig. 3.22 are binary operators—for example, the expression f + 7 contains the binary operator + and the two operands f and 7.

Integer division yields an integer quotient—for example, the expression 7 / 4 evaluates to 1, and the expression 17 / 5 evaluates to 3. Any fractional part in integer division is simply discarded (i.e., truncated)—no rounding occurs. C# provides the remainder operator, %, which yields the remainder after division. The expression x % y yields the remainder after x is divided by y. Thus, 7 % 4 yields 3, and 17 % 5 yields 2. This operator is most commonly used with integer operands, but can also be used with `floats`, `doubles`, and `decimals`. In the chapter's exercises and in later chapters, we consider several interesting applications of the remainder operator, such as determining whether one number is a multiple of another.

Arithmetic expressions must be written in *straight-line form* to facilitate entering applications into the computer. Thus, expressions such as "a divided by b" must be written as a / b, so that all constants, variables and operators appear in a straight line. The following algebraic notation is generally not acceptable to compilers:

$$\frac{a}{b}$$

C# operation	Arithmetic operator	Algebraic expression	C# expression
Addition	+	$f + 7$	f + 7
Subtraction	–	$p - c$	p – c
Multiplication	*	$b \cdot m$	b * m
Division	/	x / y or $\dfrac{x}{y}$ or $x \div y$	x / y
Remainder	%	$r \bmod s$	r % s

Fig. 3.22 | Arithmetic operators.

Parentheses are used to group terms in C# expressions in the same manner as in algebraic expressions. For example, to multiply a times the quantity b + c, we write

    a * (b + c)

If an expression contains *nested parentheses*, such as

    ((a + b) * c)

the expression in the innermost set of parentheses (a + b in this case) is evaluated first.

C# applies the operators in arithmetic expressions in a precise sequence determined by the following *rules of operator precedence*, which are generally the same as those followed in algebra (Fig. 3.23):

1. Multiplication, division and remainder operations are applied first. If an expression contains several such operations, the operators are applied from left to right. Multiplication, division and remainder operators have the same level of precedence.

2. Addition and subtraction operations are applied next. If an expression contains several such operations, the operators are applied from left to right. Addition and subtraction operators have the same level of precedence.

These rules enable C# to apply operators in the correct order. When we say that operators are applied from left to right, we are referring to their *associativity*. You will see that some operators associate from right to left. Figure 3.23 summarizes these rules of operator precedence. The table will be expanded as additional operators are introduced. A complete precedence chart is included in Appendix A.

Now let us consider several expressions in light of the rules of operator precedence. Each example lists an algebraic expression and its C# equivalent. The following is an example of an arithmetic mean (average) of five terms:

Algebra: $m = \dfrac{a + b + c + d + e}{5}$

C#:   m = (a + b + c + d + e) / 5;

Operator(s)	Operation(s)	Order of evaluation (associativity)
Evaluated first		
*	Multiplication	If there are several operators of this
/	Division	type, they are evaluated from left to
%	Remainder	right.
Evaluated next		
+	Addition	If there are several operators of this
–	Subtraction	type, they are evaluated from left to right.

Fig. 3.23 | Precedence of arithmetic operators.

The parentheses are required because division has higher precedence than addition. The entire quantity (a + b + c + d + e) is to be divided by 5. If the parentheses are erroneously omitted, we obtain a + b + c + d + e / 5, which evaluates as

$$a + b + c + d + \frac{e}{5}$$

The following is an example of the equation of a straight line:

Algebra: $y = mx + b$

C#:   y = m * x + b;

No parentheses are required. The multiplication operator is applied first because multiplication has a higher precedence than addition. The assignment occurs last because it has a lower precedence than multiplication or addition.

The following example contains remainder (%), multiplication, division, addition and subtraction operations:

Algebra: $z = pr\%q + w/x - y$

C#:   z = p * r % q + w / x - y;

              6   1   2   4   3   5

The circled numbers under the statement indicate the order in which C# applies the operators. The multiplication, remainder and division operations are evaluated first in left-to-right order (i.e., they associate from left to right), because they have higher precedence than addition and subtraction. The addition and subtraction operations are evaluated next. These operations are also applied from left to right.

To develop a better understanding of the rules of operator precedence, consider the evaluation of a second-degree polynomial ($y = ax^2 + bx + c$):

        y = a * x * x + b * x + c;

              6   1   2   4   3   5

The circled numbers indicate the order in which C# applies the operators. The multiplication operations are evaluated first in left-to-right order (i.e., they associate from left to right), because they have higher precedence than addition. The addition operations are evaluated next and are applied from left to right. There is no arithmetic operator for exponentiation in C#, so x^2 is represented as x * x. Section 6.4 shows an alternative for performing exponentiation in C#.

Suppose that a, b, c and x in the preceding second-degree polynomial are initialized (given values) as follows: a = 2, b = 3, c = 7 and x = 5. Figure 3.24 illustrates the order in which the operators are applied.

As in algebra, it is acceptable to place unnecessary parentheses in an expression to make the expression clearer. These are called *redundant parentheses*. For example, the preceding assignment statement might be parenthesized to highlight its terms as follows:

        y = (a * x * x) + (b * x) + c;

3.9 Decision Making: Equality and Relational Operators

A *condition* is an expression that can be either *true* or *false*. This section introduces a simple version of C#'s *if statement* that allows an application to make a *decision* based on the value of a condition. For example, the condition "grade is greater than or equal to 60" determines whether a student passed a test. If the condition in an if statement is true, the body of the if statement executes. If the condition is false, the body does not execute. We will see an example shortly.

Conditions in if statements can be formed by using the *equality operators* (==, and !=) and *relational operators* (>, <, >= and <=) summarized in Fig. 3.25. The two equality operators (== and !=) each have the same level of precedence, the relational operators (>, <, >= and <=) each have the same level of precedence, and the equality operators have lower precedence than the relational operators. They all associate from left to right.

The application of Fig. 3.26 uses six if statements to compare two integers entered by the user. If the condition in any of these if statements is true, the assignment statement associated with that if statement executes. The application uses the Console class to prompt for and read two lines of text from the user, extracts the integers from that text with the ToInt32 method of class Convert, and stores them in variables number1 and number2. Then the application compares the numbers and displays the results of the comparisons that are true.

The declaration of class Comparison begins at line 6

```
public class Comparison
```

The class's Main method (lines 9–39) begins the execution of the application.

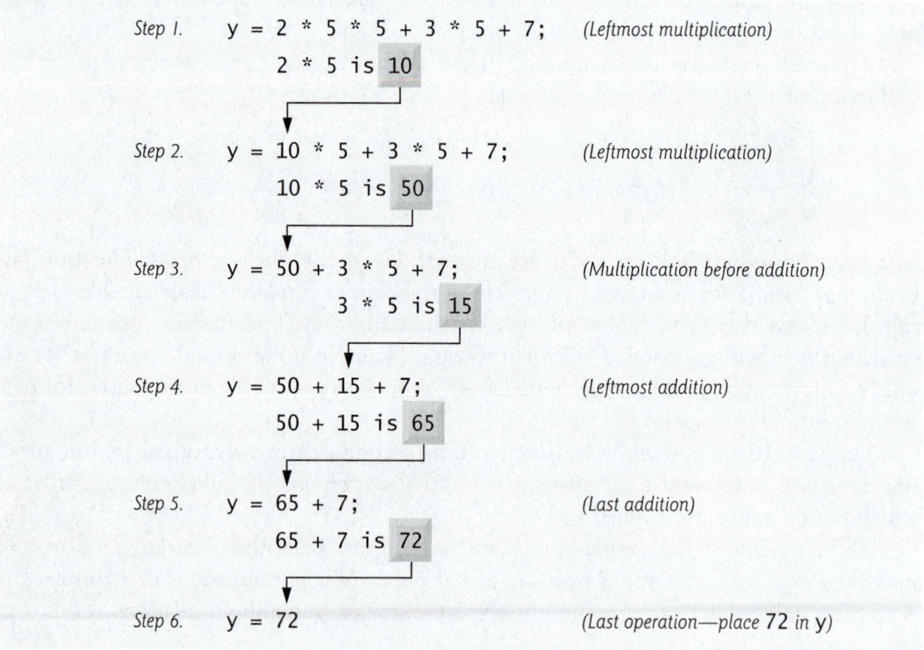

Step 1.	y = 2 * 5 * 5 + 3 * 5 + 7;	(Leftmost multiplication)
	2 * 5 is 10	
Step 2.	y = 10 * 5 + 3 * 5 + 7;	(Leftmost multiplication)
	10 * 5 is 50	
Step 3.	y = 50 + 3 * 5 + 7;	(Multiplication before addition)
	3 * 5 is 15	
Step 4.	y = 50 + 15 + 7;	(Leftmost addition)
	50 + 15 is 65	
Step 5.	y = 65 + 7;	(Last addition)
	65 + 7 is 72	
Step 6.	y = 72	(Last operation—place 72 in y)

Fig. 3.24 | Order in which a second-degree polynomial is evaluated.

Standard algebraic equality and relational operators	C# equality or relational operator	Sample C# condition	Meaning of C# condition
Equality operators			
=	==	x == y	x is equal to y
≠	!=	x != y	x is not equal to y
Relational operators			
>	>	x > y	x is greater than y
<	<	x < y	x is less than y
≥	>=	x >= y	x is greater than or equal to y
≤	<=	x <= y	x is less than or equal to y

Fig. 3.25 | Equality and relational operators.

```
1   // Fig. 3.26: Comparison.cs
2   // Comparing integers using if statements, equality operators,
3   // and relational operators.
4   using System;
5
6   public class Comparison
7   {
8      // Main method begins execution of C# application
9      public static void Main( string[] args )
10     {
11        int number1; // declare first number to compare
12        int number2; // declare second number to compare
13
14        //prompt user and read first number
15        Console.Write( "Enter first integer: " );
16        number1 = Convert.ToInt32( Console.ReadLine() );
17
18        //prompt user and read second number
19        Console.Write( "Enter second integer: " );
20        number2 = Convert.ToInt32( Console.ReadLine() );
21
22        if ( number1 == number2 )
23           Console.WriteLine( "{0} == {1}", number1, number2 );
24
25        if ( number1 != number2 )
26           Console.WriteLine( "{0} != {1}", number1, number2 );
27
28        if ( number1 < number2 )
29           Console.WriteLine( "{0} < {1}", number1, number2 );
```

Fig. 3.26 | Comparing integers using if statements, equality operators and relational operators. (Part 1 of 2.)

```
30
31          if ( number1 > number2 )
32             Console.WriteLine( "{0} > {1}", number1, number2 );
33
34          if ( number1 <= number2 )
35             Console.WriteLine( "{0} <= {1}", number1, number2 );
36
37          if ( number1 >= number2 )
38             Console.WriteLine( "{0} >= {1}", number1, number2 );
39       } // end method Main
40    } // end class Comparison
```

```
Enter first integer: 42
Enter second integer: 42
42 == 42
42 <= 42
42 >= 42
```

```
Enter first integer: 1000
Enter second integer: 2000
1000 != 2000
1000 < 2000
1000 <= 2000
```

```
Enter first integer: 2000
Enter second integer: 1000
2000 != 1000
2000 > 1000
2000 >= 1000
```

Fig. 3.26 | Comparing integers using if statements, equality operators and relational operators. (Part 2 of 2.)

Lines 11–12

```
int number1; // declare first number to compare
int number2; // declare second number to compare
```

declare the int variables used to store the values entered by the user.

Lines 14–16

```
// prompt user and read first number
Console.Write( "Enter first integer: " );
number1 = Convert.ToInt32( Console.ReadLine() );
```

prompt the user to enter the first integer and input the value. The input value is stored in variable number1.

Lines 18-20

```
// prompt user and read second number
Console.Write( "Enter second integer: " );
number2 = Convert.ToInt32( Console.ReadLine() );
```

perform the same task, except that the input value is stored in variable number2.

Lines 22–23

```
if ( number1 == number2 )
    Console.WriteLine( "{0} == {1}", number1, number2 );
```

compare the values of the variables `number1` and `number2` to determine whether they are equal. An `if` statement always begins with keyword `if`, followed by a condition in parentheses. An `if` statement expects one statement in its body. The indentation of the body statement shown here is not required, but it improves the code's readability by emphasizing that the statement in line 23 is part of the `if` statement that begins in line 22. Line 23 executes only if the numbers stored in variables `number1` and `number2` are equal (i.e., the condition is true). The `if` statements in lines 25–26, 28–29, 31–32, 34–35 and 37–38 compare `number1` and `number2` with the operators `!=`, `<`, `>`, `<=` and `>=`, respectively. If the condition in any of the `if` statements is true, the corresponding body statement executes.

Common Programming Error 3.7

Forgetting the left and/or right parentheses for the condition in an `if` statement is a syntax error—the parentheses are required.

Common Programming Error 3.8

Confusing the equality operator, `==`, with the assignment operator, `=`, can cause a logic error or a syntax error. The equality operator should be read as "is equal to," and the assignment operator should be read as "gets" or "gets the value of." To avoid confusion, some people read the equality operator as "double equals" or "equals equals."

Common Programming Error 3.9

It is a syntax error if the operators `==`, `!=`, `>=` and `<=` contain spaces between their symbols, as in `= =`, `! =`, `> =` and `< =`, respectively.

Common Programming Error 3.10

Reversing the operators `!=`, `>=` and `<=`, as in `=!`, `=>` and `=<`, is a syntax error.

Good Programming Practice 3.12

Indent an `if` statement's body to make it stand out and to enhance application readability.

Note that there is no semicolon (`;`) at the end of the first line of each `if` statement. Such a semicolon would result in a logic error at execution time. For example,

```
if ( number1 == number2 ); // logic error
    Console.WriteLine( "{0} == {1}", number1, number2 );
```

would actually be interpreted by C# as

```
if ( number1 == number2 )
    ; // empty statement

Console.WriteLine( "{0} == {1}", number1, number2 );
```

where the semicolon in the line by itself—called the ***empty statement***—is the statement to execute if the condition in the `if` statement is true. When the empty statement executes, no task is performed in the application. The application then continues with the output statement, which always executes, regardless of whether the condition is true or false, because the output statement is not part of the if statement.

Common Programming Error 3.11

Placing a semicolon immediately after the right parenthesis of the condition in an if statement is normally a logic error.

Note the use of whitespace in Fig. 3.26. Recall that whitespace characters, such as tabs, newlines and spaces, are normally ignored by the compiler. So statements may be split over several lines and may be spaced according to your preferences without affecting the meaning of an application. It is incorrect to split identifiers, strings, and multicharacter operators (like >=). Ideally, statements should be kept small, but this is not always possible.

Good Programming Practice 3.13

Place no more than one statement per line in an application. This format enhances readability.

Good Programming Practice 3.14

A lengthy statement can be spread over several lines. If a single statement must be split across lines, choose breaking points that make sense, such as after a comma in a comma-separated list, or after an operator in a lengthy expression. If a statement is split across two or more lines, indent all subsequent lines until the end of the statement.

Figure 3.27 shows the precedence of the operators introduced in this chapter. The operators are shown from top to bottom in decreasing order of precedence. All these operators, with the exception of the assignment operator, =, associate from left to right. Addition is left associative, so an expression like x + y + z is evaluated as if it had been written as (x + y) + z. The assignment operator, =, associates from right to left, so an expression like x = y = 0 is evaluated as if it had been written as x = (y = 0), which, as you will soon see, first assigns the value 0 to variable y and then assigns the result of that assignment, 0, to x.

Good Programming Practice 3.15

Refer to the operator precedence chart (the complete chart is in Appendix A) when writing expressions containing many operators. Confirm that the operations in the expression are performed in the order you expect. If you are uncertain about the order of evaluation in a complex expression, use parentheses to force the order, as you would do in algebraic expressions. Observe that some operators, such as assignment, =, associate from right to left rather than from left to right.

3.10 (Optional) Software Engineering Case Study: Examining the ATM Requirements Document

Now we begin our optional object-oriented design and implementation case study. The Software Engineering Case Study sections at the ends of this and the next several chapters will ease you into object orientation. We will develop software for a simple automated teller machine (ATM) system, providing you with a concise, carefully paced, complete design and implementation experience. In Chapters 4–9 and 11, we will perform the various steps of an object-oriented design (OOD) process using the UML, while relating these steps to the object-oriented concepts discussed in the chapters. Appendix J implements the ATM

Operators	Associativity	Type
* / %	left to right	multiplicative
+ –	left to right	additive
< <= > >=	left to right	relational
== !=	left to right	equality
=	right to left	assignment

Fig. 3.27 | Precedence and associativity of operations discussed.

using the techniques of object-oriented programming (OOP) in C# and presents the complete case study solution. This is not an exercise; rather, it is an end-to-end learning experience that concludes with a detailed walkthrough of the complete C# code that implements our design. It will begin to acquaint you with the kinds of substantial problems encountered in industry and their solutions.

We begin our design process by presenting a *requirements document* that specifies the overall purpose of the ATM system and *what* it must do. Throughout the case study, we refer to the requirements document to determine precisely what functionality the system must include.

Requirements Document

A small local bank intends to install a new automated teller machine (ATM) to allow users (i.e., bank customers) to perform basic financial transactions (Fig. 3.28). For simplicity, each user can have only one account at the bank. ATM users should be able to view their account balance, withdraw cash (i.e., take money out of an account) and deposit funds (i.e., place money into an account).

The user interface of the automated teller machine contains the following hardware components:

- a screen that displays messages to the user
- a keypad that receives numeric input from the user
- a cash dispenser that dispenses cash to the user
- a deposit slot that receives deposit envelopes from the user

The cash dispenser begins each day loaded with 500 $20 bills. [*Note:* Owing to the limited scope of this case study, certain elements of the ATM described here simplify various aspects of a real ATM. For example, a real ATM typically contains a device that reads a user's account number from an ATM card, whereas this ATM asks the user to type an account number on the keypad (which you will simulate with your personal computer's keypad). Also, a real ATM usually prints a paper receipt at the end of a session, but all output from this ATM appears on the screen.]

The bank wants you to develop software to perform the financial transactions initiated by bank customers through the ATM. The bank will integrate the software with the ATM's hardware at a later time. The software should simulate the functionality of the

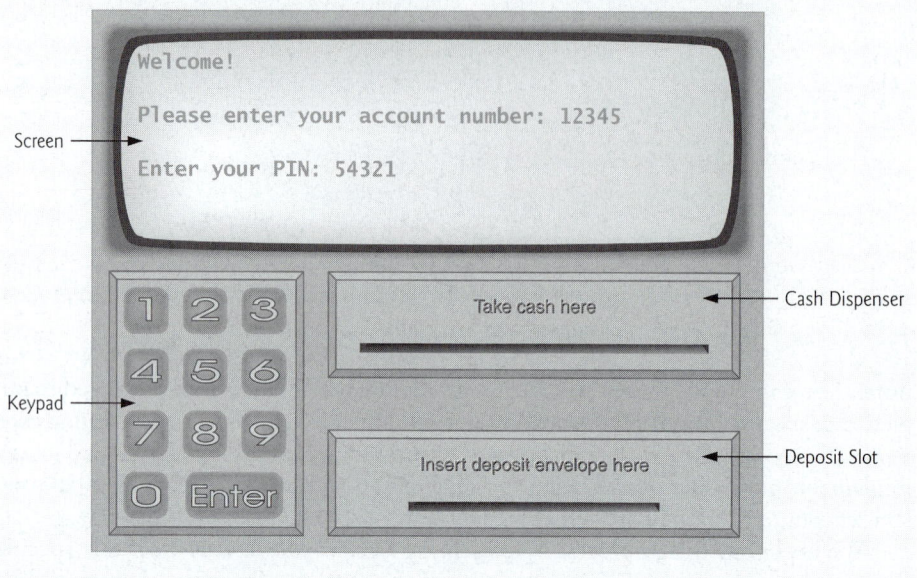

Fig. 3.28 | Automated teller machine user interface.

hardware devices (e.g., cash dispenser, deposit slot) in software components, but it need not concern itself with how these devices perform their duties. The ATM hardware has not been developed yet, so instead of writing your software to run on the ATM, you should develop a first version of the software to run on a personal computer. This version should use the computer's monitor to simulate the ATM's screen and the computer's keyboard to simulate the ATM's keypad.

An ATM session consists of authenticating a user (i.e., proving the user's identity) based on an account number and personal identification number (PIN), followed by creating and executing financial transactions. To authenticate a user and perform transactions, the ATM must interact with the bank's account information database. [*Note:* A database is an organized collection of data stored on a computer.] For each bank account, the database stores an account number, a PIN and a balance indicating the amount of money in the account. [*Note:* The bank plans to build only one ATM, so we do not need to worry about multiple ATMs accessing the database at the same time. Furthermore, we assume that the bank does not make any changes to the information in the database while a user is accessing the ATM. Also, any business system like an ATM faces reasonably complicated security issues that go well beyond the scope of a first- or second-semester programming course. We make the simplifying assumption, however, that the bank trusts the ATM to access and manipulate the information in the database without significant security measures.]

Upon approaching the ATM, the user should experience the following sequence of events (see Fig. 3.28):

1. The screen displays a welcome message and prompts the user to enter an account number.

2. The user enters a five-digit account number, using the keypad.

3. For authentication purposes, the screen prompts the user to enter the PIN (personal identification number) associated with the specified account number.

4. The user enters a five-digit PIN, using the keypad.

5. If the user enters a valid account number and the correct PIN for that account, the screen displays the main menu (Fig. 3.29). If the user enters an invalid account number or an incorrect PIN, the screen displays an appropriate message, then the ATM returns to *Step 1* to restart the authentication process.

After the ATM authenticates the user, the main menu (Fig. 3.29) displays a numbered option for each of the three types of transactions: balance inquiry (option 1), withdrawal (option 2) and deposit (option 3). The main menu also displays an option that allows the user to exit the system (option 4). The user then chooses either to perform a transaction (by entering 1, 2 or 3) or to exit the system (by entering 4). If the user enters an invalid option, the screen displays an error message, then redisplays the main menu.

If the user enters 1 to make a balance inquiry, the screen displays the user's account balance. To do so, the ATM must retrieve the balance from the bank's database.

The following actions occur when the user enters 2 to make a withdrawal:

1. The screen displays a menu (shown in Fig. 3.30) containing standard withdrawal amounts: $20 (option 1), $40 (option 2), $60 (option 3), $100 (option 4) and $200 (option 5). The menu also contains option 6 that allows the user to cancel the transaction.

2. The user enters a menu selection (1–6) using the keypad.

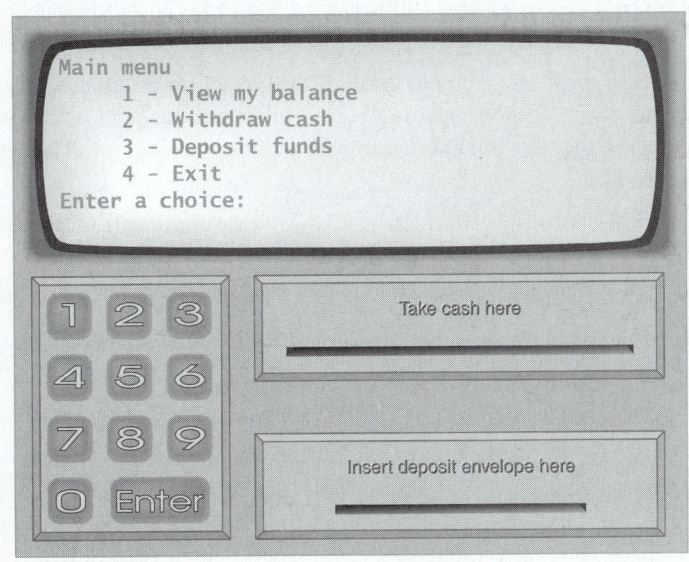

Fig. 3.29 | ATM main menu.

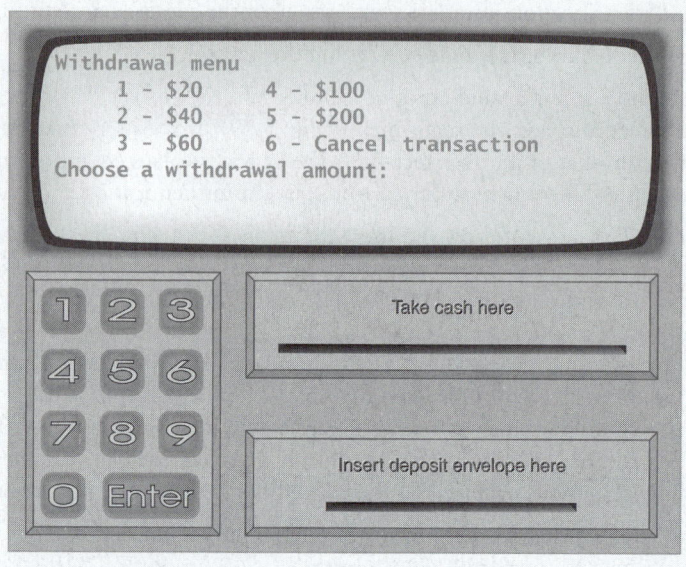

Fig. 3.30 | ATM withdrawal menu.

3. If the withdrawal amount chosen is greater than the user's account balance, the screen displays a message stating this and telling the user to choose a smaller amount. The ATM then returns to *Step 1*. If the withdrawal amount chosen is less than or equal to the user's account balance (i.e., an acceptable withdrawal amount), the ATM proceeds to *Step 4*. If the user chooses to cancel the transaction (option 6), the ATM displays the main menu (Fig. 3.29) and waits for user input.

4. If the cash dispenser contains enough cash to satisfy the request, the ATM proceeds to *Step 5*. Otherwise, the screen displays a message indicating the problem and telling the user to choose a smaller withdrawal amount. The ATM then returns to *Step 1*.

5. The ATM debits (i.e., subtracts) the withdrawal amount from the user's account balance in the bank's database.

6. The cash dispenser dispenses the desired amount of money to the user.

7. The screen displays a message reminding the user to take the money.

The following actions occur when the user enters 3 (from the main menu) to make a deposit:

1. The screen prompts the user to enter a deposit amount or to type 0 (zero) to cancel the transaction.

2. The user enters a deposit amount or 0, using the keypad. [*Note:* The keypad does not contain a decimal point or a dollar sign, so the user cannot type a real dollar amount (e.g., $147.25). Instead, the user must enter a deposit amount as a number of cents (e.g., 14725). The ATM then divides this number by 100 to obtain a number representing a dollar amount (e.g., $14725 \div 100 = 147.25$).]

3. If the user specifies a deposit amount, the ATM proceeds to *Step 4*. If the user chooses to cancel the transaction (by entering 0), the ATM displays the main menu (Fig. 3.29) and waits for user input.

4. The screen displays a message telling the user to insert a deposit envelope into the deposit slot.

5. If the deposit slot receives a deposit envelope within two minutes, the ATM credits (i.e., adds) the deposit amount to the user's account balance in the bank's database. [*Note:* This money is not immediately available for withdrawal. The bank first must verify the amount of cash in the deposit envelope, and any checks in the envelope must clear (i.e., money must be transferred from the check writer's account to the check recipient's account). When either of these events occurs, the bank appropriately updates the user's balance stored in its database. This occurs independently of the ATM system.] If the deposit slot does not receive a deposit envelope within two minutes, the screen displays a message that the system has canceled the transaction due to inactivity. The ATM then displays the main menu and waits for user input.

After the system successfully executes a transaction, the system should redisplay the main menu (Fig. 3.29) so that the user can perform additional transactions. If the user chooses to exit the system (by entering option 4), the screen should display a thank you message, then display the welcome message for the next user.

Analyzing the ATM System

The preceding statement presented a simplified requirements document. Typically, such a document is the result of a detailed process of *requirements gathering* that might include interviews with potential users of the system and specialists in fields related to the system. For example, a systems analyst who is hired to prepare a requirements document for banking software (e.g., the ATM system described here) might interview people who have used ATMs and financial experts to gain a better understanding of *what* the software must do. The analyst would use the information gained to compile a list of *system requirements* to guide systems designers.

The process of requirements gathering is a key task of the first stage of the software life cycle. The *software life cycle* specifies the stages through which software evolves from the time it is conceived to the time it is retired from use. These stages typically include analysis, design, implementation, testing and debugging, deployment, maintenance and retirement. Several software life cycle models exist, each with its own preferences and specifications for when and how often software engineers should perform the various stages. *Waterfall models* perform each stage once in succession, whereas *iterative models* may repeat one or more stages several times throughout a product's life cycle.

The analysis stage of the software life cycle focuses on precisely defining the problem to be solved. When designing any system, one must certainly *solve the problem right*, but of equal importance, one must *solve the right problem*. Systems analysts collect the requirements that indicate the specific problem to solve. Our requirements document describes our simple ATM system in sufficient detail that you do not need to go through an extensive analysis stage—it has been done for you.

To capture what a proposed system should do, developers often employ a technique known as *use case modeling*. This process identifies the *use cases* of the system, each of which represents a different capability that the system provides to its clients. For example, ATMs typically have several use cases, such as "View Account Balance," "Withdraw Cash," "Deposit Funds," "Transfer Funds Between Accounts" and "Buy Postage Stamps." The simplified ATM system we build in this case study requires only the first three use cases (Fig. 3.31).

Each use case describes a typical scenario in which the user uses the system. You have already read descriptions of the ATM system's use cases in the requirements document; the lists of steps required to perform each type of transaction (i.e., balance inquiry, withdrawal and deposit) actually described the three use cases of our ATM—"View Account Balance," "Withdraw Cash" and "Deposit Funds."

Use Case Diagrams

We now introduce the first of several UML diagrams in our ATM case study. We create a *use case diagram* to model the interactions between a system's clients (in this case study, bank customers) and the system. The goal is to show the kinds of interactions users have with a system without providing the details—these are shown in other UML diagrams (which we present throughout the case study). Use case diagrams are often accompanied by informal text that describes the use cases in more detail—like the text that appears in the requirements document. Use case diagrams are produced during the analysis stage of the software life cycle. In larger systems, use case diagrams are simple but indispensable tools that help system designers focus on satisfying the users' needs.

Figure 3.31 shows the use case diagram for our ATM system. The stick figure represents an *actor*, which defines the roles that an external entity—such as a person or another system—plays when interacting with the system. For our automated teller machine, the actor is a User who can view an account balance, withdraw cash and deposit funds using the ATM. The User is not an actual person, but instead comprises the roles that a real person—when playing the part of a User—can play while interacting with the ATM. Note that a use case diagram can include multiple actors. For example, the use case diagram for a real bank's ATM system might also include an actor named Administrator who refills the cash dispenser each day.

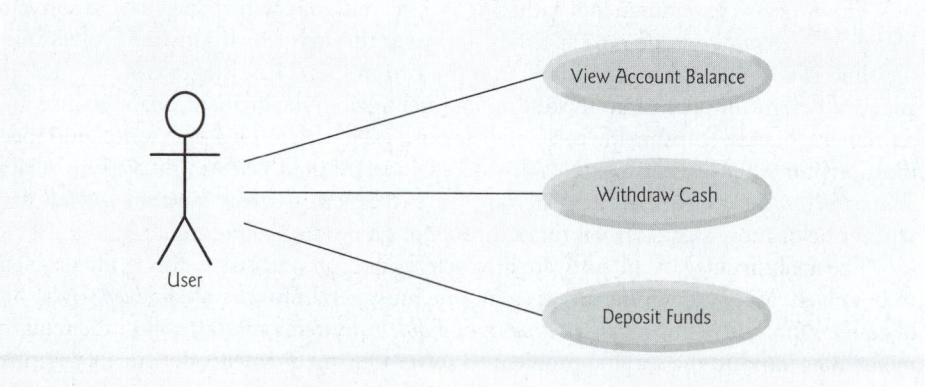

Fig. 3.31 | Use case diagram for the ATM system from the user's perspective.

We identify the actor in our system by examining the requirements document, which states, "ATM users should be able to view their account balance, withdraw cash and deposit funds." The actor in each of the three use cases is simply the User who interacts with the ATM. An external entity—a real person—plays the part of the User to perform financial transactions. Figure 3.31 shows one actor, whose name, User, appears below the actor in the diagram. The UML models each use case as an oval connected to an actor with a solid line.

Software engineers (more precisely, systems designers) must analyze the requirements document or a set of use cases, and design the system before programmers implement it in a particular programming language. During the analysis stage, systems designers focus on understanding the requirements document to produce a high-level specification that describes *what* the system is supposed to do. The output of the design stage—a *design specification*—should specify *how* the system should be constructed to satisfy these requirements. In the next several Software Engineering Case Study sections, we perform the steps of a simple OOD process on the ATM system to produce a design specification containing a collection of UML diagrams and supporting text. Recall that the UML is designed for use with any OOD process. Many such processes exist, the best known of which is the Rational Unified Process™ (RUP) developed by Rational Software Corporation (now a division of IBM). RUP is a rich process for designing "industrial strength" applications. For this case study, we present a simplified design process.

Designing the ATM System

We now begin the design stage of our ATM system. A *system* is a set of components that interact to solve a problem. For example, to perform the ATM system's designated tasks, our ATM system has a user interface (Fig. 3.28), contains software that executes financial transactions and interacts with a database of bank account information. *System structure* describes the system's objects and their interrelationships. *System behavior* describes how the system changes as its objects interact with one another. Every system has both structure and behavior—designers must specify both. There are several distinct types of system structures and behaviors. For example, the interactions among objects in the system differ from those between the user and the system, yet both constitute a portion of the system behavior.

The UML 2 specifies 13 diagram types for documenting system models. Each diagram type models a distinct characteristic of a system's structure or behavior—six diagram types relate to system structure; the remaining seven relate to system behavior. We list here only the six types of diagrams used in our case study—one of which (the class diagram) models system structure; the remaining five model system behavior. We overview the remaining seven UML diagram types in Appendix K, UML 2: Additional Diagram Types.

1. *Use case diagrams*, such as the one in Fig. 3.31, model the interactions between a system and its external entities (actors) in terms of use cases (system capabilities, such as "View Account Balance," "Withdraw Cash" and "Deposit Funds").

2. *Class diagrams*, which you will study in Section 4.11, model the classes, or "building blocks," used in a system. Each noun, or "thing," described in the requirements document is a candidate to be a class in the system (e.g., "account," "keypad"). Class diagrams help us specify the structural relationships between parts of the system. For example, the ATM system class diagram will, among other things, specify that the ATM is physically composed of a screen, a keypad, a cash dispenser and a deposit slot.

3. *State machine diagrams*, which you will study in Section 6.10, model the ways in which an object changes state. An object's *state* is indicated by the values of all the object's attributes at a given time. When an object changes state, it may subsequently behave differently in the system. For example, after validating a user's PIN, the ATM transitions from the "user not authenticated" state to the "user authenticated" state, at which point the ATM allows the user to perform financial transactions (e.g., view account balance, withdraw cash, deposit funds).

4. *Activity diagrams*, which you will also study in Section 6.10, model an object's *activity*—the object's workflow (sequence of events) during program execution. An activity diagram models the actions the object performs and specifies the order in which it performs these actions. For example, an activity diagram shows that the ATM must obtain the balance of the user's account (from the bank's account information database) before the screen can display the balance to the user.

5. *Communication diagrams* (called collaboration diagrams in earlier versions of the UML) model the interactions among objects in a system, with an emphasis on *what* interactions occur. You will learn in Section 8.14 that these diagrams show which objects must interact to perform an ATM transaction. For example, the ATM must communicate with the bank's account information database to retrieve an account balance.

6. *Sequence diagrams* also model the interactions among the objects in a system, but unlike communication diagrams, they emphasize *when* interactions occur. You will learn in Section 8.14 that these diagrams help show the order in which interactions occur in executing a financial transaction. For example, the screen prompts the user to enter a withdrawal amount before cash is dispensed.

In Section 4.11, we continue designing our ATM system by identifying the classes from the requirements document. We accomplish this by extracting key nouns and noun phrases from the requirements document. Using these classes, we develop our first draft of the class diagram that models the structure of our ATM system.

Internet and Web Resources

The following URLs provide information on object-oriented design with the UML.

www-306.ibm.com/software/rational/uml/

Lists frequently asked questions about the UML, provided by IBM Rational.

www.douglass.co.uk/documents/softdocwiz.com.UML.htm

Links to the Unified Modeling Language Dictionary, which defines all terms used in the UML.

www.agilemodeling.com/essays/umlDiagrams.htm

Provides in-depth descriptions and tutorials on each of the 13 UML 2 diagram types.

www-306.ibm.com/software/rational/offerings/design.html

IBM provides information about Rational software available for designing systems, and downloads of 30-day trial versions of several products, such as IBM Rational Rose® XDE (eXtended Development Environment) Developer.

www.embarcadero.com/products/describe/index.html

Provides a 15-day trial license for the Embarcadero Technologies® UML modeling tool Describe.™

`www.borland.com/together/index.html`

Provides a free 30-day license to download a trial version of Borland® Together® Control-Center™—a software development tool that supports the UML.

`www.ilogix.com/rhapsody/rhapsody.cfm`

Provides a free 30-day license to download a trial version of I-Logix Rhapsody®—a UML 2-based model-driven development environment.

`argouml.tigris.org`

Contains information and downloads for ArgoUML, a free open-source UML tool.

`www.objectsbydesign.com/books/booklist.html`

Lists books on the UML and object-oriented design.

`www.objectsbydesign.com/tools/umltools_byCompany.html`

Lists software tools that use the UML, such as IBM Rational Rose, Embarcadero Describe, Sparx Systems Enterprise Architect, I-Logix Rhapsody and Gentleware Poseidon for UML.

`www.ootips.org/ood-principles.html`

Provides answers to the question "What makes a good object-oriented design?"

`www.cetus-links.org/oo_uml.html`

Introduces the UML and provides links to numerous UML resources.

Recommended Readings

The following books provide information on object-oriented design with the UML.

Ambler, S. *The Elements of the UML 2.0 Style*. New York: Cambridge University Press, 2005.

Booch, G. *Object-Oriented Analysis and Design with Applications, Third Edition*. Boston: Addison-Wesley, 2004.

Eriksson, H., et al. *UML 2 Toolkit*. New York: John Wiley, 2003.

Kruchten, P. *The Rational Unified Process: An Introduction*. Boston: Addison-Wesley, 2004.

Larman, C. *Applying UML and Patterns: An Introduction to Object-Oriented Analysis and Design, Second Edition*. Upper Saddle River, NJ: Prentice Hall, 2002.

Roques, P. *UML in Practice: The Art of Modeling Software Systems Demonstrated Through Worked Examples and Solutions*. New York: John Wiley, 2004.

Rosenberg, D., and K. Scott. *Applying Use Case Driven Object Modeling with UML: An Annotated e-Commerce Example*. Reading, MA: Addison-Wesley, 2001.

Rumbaugh, J., I. Jacobson, and G. Booch. *The Complete UML Training Course*. Upper Saddle River, NJ: Prentice Hall, 2000.

Rumbaugh, J., I. Jacobson, and G. Booch. *The Unified Modeling Language Reference Manual*. Reading, MA: Addison-Wesley, 1999.

Rumbaugh, J., I. Jacobson, and G. Booch. *The Unified Software Development Process*. Reading, MA: Addison-Wesley, 1999.

Software Engineering Case Study Self-Review Exercises

3.1   Suppose we enabled a user of our ATM system to transfer money between two bank accounts. Modify the use case diagram of Fig. 3.31 to reflect this change.

3.2 _____ model the interactions among objects in a system with an emphasis on *when* these interactions occur.
  a) Class diagrams
  b) Sequence diagrams
  c) Communication diagrams
  d) Activity diagrams

3.3 Which of the following choices lists stages of a typical software life cycle in sequential order?
  a) design, analysis, implementation, testing
  b) design, analysis, testing, implementation
  c) analysis, design, testing, implementation
  d) analysis, design, implementation, testing

Answers to Software Engineering Case Study Self-Review Exercises

3.1 Figure 3.32 contains a use case diagram for a modified version of our ATM system that also allows users to transfer money between accounts.

3.2 b.

3.3 d.

3.11 Wrap-Up

You learned many important features of C# in this chapter, including displaying data on the screen in a command prompt, inputting data from the keyboard, performing calculations and making decisions. The applications presented here introduced you to basic programming concepts. As you will see in Chapter 4, C# applications typically contain just a few lines of code in method Main—these statements normally create the objects that perform the work of the application. In Chapter 4, you will learn how to implement your own classes and use objects of those classes in applications.

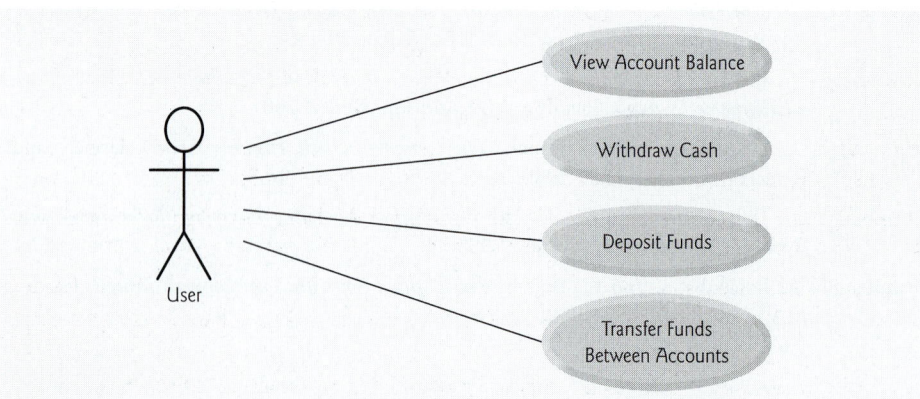

Fig. 3.32 | Use case diagram for a modified version of our ATM system that also allows users to transfer money between accounts.

Summary

Section 3.2 A Simple C# Application: Displaying a Line of Text

- Computer programmers create applications.

- Programmers insert comments to document applications and improve their readability. The C# compiler ignores comments.

- A comment that begins with // is called a single-line comment because the comment terminates at the end of the line on which it appears.

- Delimited comments can be spread over several lines and are delimited by /* and */. All text between the delimiters is ignored by the compiler.

- A programming language's syntax specifies the rules for creating a proper application in that language.

- A using directive helps the compiler locate a class that is used in an application.

- C# provides a rich set of predefined classes that you can reuse rather than "reinventing the wheel." These classes are grouped into namespaces—named collections of classes.

- Collectively, C#'s predefined namespaces are referred to as the .NET Framework Class Library.

- Programmers use blank lines and space characters to make applications easier to read. Together, blank lines, space characters and tab characters are known as whitespace. Space characters and tabs are known specifically as whitespace characters. Whitespace is ignored by the compiler.

- Every application in C# consists of at least one class declaration that is defined by the programmer (also known as a user-defined class).

- Keywords are reserved for use by C# and are always spelled with all lowercase letters.

- Keyword class introduces a class declaration and is immediately followed by the class name.

- By convention, all class names in C# begin with a capital letter and capitalize the first letter of each word they include (e.g., SampleClassName).

- A C# class name is an identifier—a series of characters consisting of letters, digits, and underscores (_) that does not begin with a digit and does not contain spaces.

- C# is case sensitive—that is, uppercase and lowercase letters are distinct.

- The body of every class declaration is delimited by braces, { and }.

- Method Main is the starting point of every C# application and is typically defined as:

  ```
  public static void Main( string[] args )
  ```

  otherwise, the compiler will not be able to create an executable application.

- Methods are able to perform tasks and return information when they complete their tasks. Keyword void indicates that a method will perform a task but will not return any information.

- Statements instruct the computer to perform actions.

- A sequence of characters in double quotation marks is called a string, a character string, a message or a string literal.

- The Console class allows C# applications to read and display characters in the console window.

- Method Console.WriteLine displays its argument in the console window, followed by a newline character to position the screen cursor to the beginning of the next line.

- Every statement ends with a semicolon.

Section 3.3 Creating Your Simple Application in Visual C# Express

- Visual C# Express provides many ways to personalize your coding experience. You can modify the editor settings to display line numbers or set code indentation.

- As you type characters, in some contexts Visual C# Express highlights the first member that matches all the characters typed, then displays a tool tip containing a description of that member. This IDE feature is called *IntelliSense*.

- To execute an application, select **Debug > Start Without Debugging**, which invokes the Main method.

- When you type a line of code and press the *Enter* key, the IDE responds either by applying syntax-color highlighting or by generating a syntax error, which indicates a violation of Visual C#'s rules for creating correct applications.

Section 3.4 Modifying Your Simple C# Application

- Console.Write displays its argument and positions the screen cursor immediately after the last character displayed.

- A backslash (\) in a string is an escape character. It indicates that a "special character" is to be displayed. C# combines the next character with the backslash to form an escape sequence. The escape sequence \n represents the newline character, which positions the cursor on the next line.

Section 3.5 Formatting Text with Console.Write and Console.WriteLine

- The Console.Write and Console.WriteLine methods can also display formatted data.

- When a method requires multiple arguments, the arguments are separated with commas (,)—this is known as a comma-separated list.

- Method Console.Write's first argument can be a format string that may consist of fixed text and format items. Fixed text is displayed normally. Each format item is a placeholder for a value.

- Format items are enclosed in curly braces and begin with a number that specifies an argument. The format item {0} is a placeholder for the first additional argument after the format string (because we start counting from 0), {1} is a placeholder for the second, etc.

Section 3.6 Another C# Application: Adding Integers

- Integers are whole numbers, like –22, 7, 0 and 1024.

- A variable declaration statement specifies the name and type of a variable.

- A variable is a location in the computer's memory where a value can be stored for use later in an application. All variables must be declared with a name and a type before they can be used.

- A variable's name enables the application to access the value of the variable in memory. A variable name can be any valid identifier.

- Like other statements, variable declaration statements end with a semicolon (;).

- Type int is used to declare variables that will hold integer values. The range of values for an int is –2,147,483,648 to +2,147,483,647.

- Types float, double, and decimal specify real numbers, and type char specifies character data. Real numbers are numbers that may contain decimal points, such as 3.4, 0.0 and –11.19. Variables of type char data represent individual characters, such as an uppercase letter (e.g., A), a digit (e.g., 7), a special character (e.g., * or %) or an escape sequence (e.g., the newline character, \n).

- Types such as int, float, double, decimal, and char are often called simple types. Simple-type names are keywords; thus, they must appear in all lowercase letters.

- A prompt directs the user to take a specific action.

- Console method ReadLine obtains a line of text for use in an application.

- Convert method `ToInt32` extracts an integer from a string of characters.
- The assignment operator, `=`, enables the application to give a value to a variable. Operator `=` is called a binary operator because it has two operands. An assignment statement uses an assignment operator to assign a value to a variable.
- Portions of statements that have values are called expressions.

Section 3.7 Memory Concepts
- Variable names correspond to locations in the computer's memory. Every variable has a name, a type, a size and a value.
- Whenever a value is placed in a memory location, the value replaces the previous value in that location. The previous value is lost.

Section 3.8 Arithmetic
- Most applications perform arithmetic calculations. The arithmetic operators are + (addition), - (subtraction, * (multiplication), / (division) and % (remainder).
- Integer division yields an integer quotient.
- The remainder operator, `%`, yields the remainder after division.
- Arithmetic expressions in C# must be written in straight-line form.
- If an expression contains nested parentheses, the innermost set of parentheses is evaluated first.
- C# applies the operators in arithmetic expressions in a precise sequence determined by the rules of operator precedence.
- When we say that operators are applied from left to right, we are referring to their associativity. Some operators associate from right to left.
- Redundant parentheses in an expression can make an expression clearer.

Section 3.9 Decision Making: Equality and Relational Operators
- A condition is an expression that can be either true or false. C#'s `if` statement allows an application to make a decision based on the value of a condition.
- Conditions in `if` statements can be formed by using the equality (`==` and `!=`) and relational (`>`, `<`, `>=` and `<=`) operators.
- An `if` statement always begins with keyword `if`, followed by a condition in parentheses, and expects one statement in its body.
- The empty statement is a statement that does not perform a task.

Terminology

addition operator (+)
application
argument
arithmetic operators (*, /, %, + and -)
assignment operator (=)
assignment statement
associativity of operators
backslash (\) escape character
binary operator
body of a class declaration
body of a method declaration
camel casing

case sensitive
char simple type
character string
class declaration
class keyword
class name
code walkthrough
comma (,)
comma-separated list
Command Prompt
comment
compilation error

Self-Review Exercises

3.1   Fill in the blanks in each of the following statements:
  a) A(n) _____ begins the body of every method, and a(n) _____ ends the body of every method.
  b) Every statement ends with a(n) _____.
  c) The _____ statement is used to make decisions.
  d) _____ begins a single-line comment.
  e) _____, _____ and _____ are called whitespace characters. Newline characters are also considered whitespace characters.
  f) _____ are reserved for use by C#.
  g) C# applications begin execution at method _____.
  h) Methods _____ and _____ display information in the console window.

3.2   State whether each of the following is *true* or *false*. If *false*, explain why.
  a) Comments cause the computer to print the text after the // on the screen when the application executes.
  b) All variables must be given a type when they are declared.
  c) C# considers the variables number and NuMbEr to be identical.
  d) The remainder operator (%) can be used only with integer operands.
  e) The arithmetic operators *, /, %, + and - all have the same level of precedence.

3.3   Write statements to accomplish each of the following tasks:
  a) Declare variables c, thisIsAVariable, q76354 and number to be of type int.
  b) Prompt the user to enter an integer.
  c) Input an integer and assign the result to int variable value.
  d) If the variable number is not equal to 7, display "The variable number is not equal to 7".
  e) Print "This is a C# application" on one line in the console window.
  f) Print "This is a C# application" on two lines in the console window. The first line should end with C#. Use method Console.WriteLine.
  g) Print "This is a C# application" on two lines in the console window. The first line should end with C#. Use method Console.WriteLine and two format items.

3.4   Identify and correct the errors in each of the following statements:
  a) if (c < 7);
          Console.WriteLine("c is less than 7");
  b) if (c => 7)
          Console.WriteLine("c is equal to or greater than 7");

3.5   Write declarations, statements or comments that accomplish each of the following tasks:
  a) State that an application will calculate the product of three integers.
  b) Declare the variables x, y, z and result to be of type int.
  c) Prompt the user to enter the first integer.
  d) Read the first integer from the user and store it in the variable x.
  e) Prompt the user to enter the second integer.
  f) Read the second integer from the user and store it in the variable y.
  g) Prompt the user to enter the third integer.
  h) Read the third integer from the user and store it in the variable z.
  i) Compute the product of the three integers contained in variables x, y and z, and assign the result to the variable result.
  j) Display the message "Product is", followed by the value of the variable result.

3.6   Using the statements you wrote in Exercise 3.5, write a complete application that calculates and prints the product of three integers.

Answers to Self-Review Exercises

3.1 a) left brace ({), right brace (}). b) semicolon (;). c) `if`. d) `//`. e) Blank lines, space characters, tab characters. f) Keywords. g) `Main`. h) `Console.WriteLine` and `Console.Write`.

3.2 a) False. Comments do not cause any action to be performed when the application executes. They are used to document applications and improve their readability.
  b) True.
  c) False. C# is case sensitive, so these variables are distinct.
  d) False. The remainder operator also can be used with noninteger operands in C#.
  e) False. The operators `*`, `/` and `%` are on the same level of precedence, and the operators `+` and `-` are on a lower level of precedence.

3.3 a) `int c, thisIsAVariable, q76354, number;`
  or
  `int c;`
  `int thisIsAVariable;`
  `int q76354;`
  `int number;`
  b) `Console.Write( "Enter an integer: " );`
  c) `value = Convert.ToInt32( Console.ReadLine() );`
  d) `if ( number != 7 )`
    `Console.WriteLine( "The variable number is not equal to 7" );`
  e) `Console.WriteLine( "This is a C# application" );`
  f) `Console.WriteLine( "This is a C#\napplication" );`
  g) `Console.WriteLine( "{0}\n{1}", "This is a C#", "application" );`

3.4 The solutions to Self-Review Exercise 3.4 are as follows:
  a) Error: Semicolon after the right parenthesis of the condition (`c < 7`) in the `if` statement.
    Correction: Remove the semicolon after the right parenthesis. [*Note*: As a result, the output statement will execute regardless of whether the condition in the `if` is true.]
  b) Error: The relational operator `=>` is incorrect. Correction: Change `=>` to `>=`.

3.5 a) `// Calculate the product of three integers`
  b) `int x, y, z, result;`
    or
    `int x;`
    `int y;`
    `int z;`
    `int result;`
  c) `Console.Write( "Enter first integer: " );`
  d) `x = Convert.ToInt32( Console.ReadLine() );`
  e) `Console.Write( "Enter second integer: " );`
  f) `y = Convert.ToInt32( Console.ReadLine() );`
  g) `Console.Write( "Enter third integer: ");`
  h) `z = Convert.ToInt32( Console.ReadLine() );`
  i) `result = x * y * z;`
  j) `Console.WriteLine( "Product is {0}", result );`

3.6 The solution to Exercise 3.6 is as follows:

```
1   // Exercise 3.6: Product.cs
2   // Calculating the product of three integers.
3   using System;
4
5   public class Product
6   {
7      public static void Main( string[] args )
8      {
9         int x; // declare first number to be entered by user
10        int y; // declare second number to be entered by user
11        int z; // declare third number to be entered by user
12        int result; // product of numbers
13
14        Console.Write( "Enter first integer: " ); // prompt for input
15        x = Convert.ToInt32( Console.ReadLine() ); // read first integer
16
17        Console.Write( "Enter second integer: " ); // prompt for input
18        y = Convert.ToInt32( Console.ReadLine() ); // read second integer
19
20        Console.Write( "Enter third integer: " ); // prompt for input
21        z = Convert.ToInt32( Console.ReadLine() ); // read third integer
22
23        result = x * y * z; // calculate the product of the numbers
24
25        Console.WriteLine( "Product is {0}", result );
26     } // end method Main
27  } // end class Product
```

```
Enter first integer: 10
Enter second integer: 20
Enter third integer: 30
Product is 6000
```

Exercises

3.7 Fill in the blanks in each of the following statements:

a) _____ are used to document an application and improve its readability.

b) A decision can be made in a C# application with a(n) _____.

c) Calculations are normally performed by _____ statements.

d) The arithmetic operators with the same precedence as multiplication are _____ and _____.

e) When parentheses in an arithmetic expression are nested, the _____ set of parentheses is evaluated first.

f) A location in the computer's memory that may contain different values at various times throughout the execution of an application is called a(n) _____.

3.8 Write C# statements that accomplish each of the following tasks:

a) Display the message "Enter an integer: ", leaving the cursor on the same line.

b) Assign the product of variables b and c to variable a.

c) State that an application performs a sample payroll calculation (i.e., use text that helps to document an application).

3.9 State whether each of the following is *true* or *false*. If *false*, explain why.
  a) C# operators are evaluated from left to right.
  b) The following are all valid variable names: _under_bar_, m928134, t5, j7, her_sales, his_account_total, a, b, c, z and z2.
  c) A valid C# arithmetic expression with no parentheses is evaluated from left to right.
  d) The following are all invalid variable names: 3g, 87, 67h2, h22 and 2h.

3.10 Assuming that x = 2 and y = 3, what does each of the following statements display?
  a) `Console.WriteLine( "x = {0}", x );`
  b) `Console.WriteLine( "Value of {0} + {0} is {1}", x, ( x + x ) );`
  c) `Console.Write( "x =" );`
  d) `Console.WriteLine( "{0} = {1}", ( x + y ), ( y + x ) );`

3.11 Which of the following C# statements contain variables whose values are modified?
  a) `p = i + j + k + 7;`
  b) `Console.WriteLine( "variables whose values are modified" );`
  c) `Console.WriteLine( "a = 5" );`
  d) `value = Convert.ToInt32( Console.ReadLine() );`

3.12 Given that $y = ax^3 + 7$, which of the following are correct C# statements for this equation?
  a) `y = a * x * x * x + 7;`
  b) `y = a * x * x * ( x + 7 );`
  c) `y = ( a * x ) * x * ( x + 7 );`
  d) `y = ( a * x ) * x * x + 7;`
  e) `y = a * ( x * x * x ) + 7;`
  f) `y = a * x * ( x * x + 7 );`

3.13 State the order of evaluation of the operators in each of the following C# statements and show the value of x after each statement is performed:
  a) `x = 7 + 3 * 6 / 2 - 1;`
  b) `x = 2 % 2 + 2 * 2 - 2 / 2;`
  c) `x = ( 3 * 9 * ( 3 + ( 9 * 3 / ( 3 ) ) ) );`

3.14 Write an application that displays the numbers 1 to 4 on the same line, with each pair of adjacent numbers separated by one space. Write the application using the following techniques:
  a) Use one `Console.WriteLine` statement.
  b) Use four `Console.Write` statements.
  c) Use one `Console.WriteLine` statement with four format items.

3.15 Write an application that asks the user to enter two integers, obtains them from the user and prints their sum, product, difference and quotient (division). Use the techniques shown in Fig. 3.18.

3.16 Write an application that asks the user to enter two integers, obtains them from the user and displays the larger number followed by the words "is larger". If the numbers are equal, print the message "These numbers are equal." Use the techniques shown in Fig. 3.26.

3.17 Write an application that inputs three integers from the user and displays the sum, average, product, and smallest and largest of the numbers. Use the techniques shown in Fig. 3.26. [*Note*: The calculation of the average in this exercise should result in an integer representation of the average. So if the sum of the values is 7, the average should be 2, not 2.3333....]

3.18 Write an application that displays a box, an oval, an arrow and a diamond using asterisks (*), as follows:

```
********      ***        *           *
*       *     *    *     ***        *  *
*       *     *    *      *****      *    *
*       *     *    *      *    *     *      *
*       *     *    *      *    *     *        *
*       *     *    *      *    *     *      *
*       *     *    *      *    *      *    *
*       *     *    *      *    *       *  *
********      ***        *            *
```

3.19   What does the following code print?

```
Console.WriteLine( "*\n**\n***\n****\n*****" );
```

3.20   What does the following code print?

```
Console.WriteLine( "*" );
Console.WriteLine( "***" );
Console.WriteLine( "*****" );
Console.WriteLine( "****" );
Console.WriteLine( "**" );
```

3.21   What does the following code print?

```
Console.Write( "*" );
Console.Write( "***" );
Console.Write( "*****" );
Console.Write( "****" );
Console.WriteLine( "**" );
```

3.22   What does the following code print?

```
Console.Write( "*" );
Console.WriteLine( "***" );
Console.WriteLine( "*****" );
Console.Write( "****" );
Console.WriteLine( "**" );
```

3.23   What does the following code print?

```
Console.WriteLine( "{0}\n{1}\n{2}", "*", "***", "*****" );
```

3.24   Write an application that reads five integers, then determines and prints the largest and smallest integers in the group. Use only the programming techniques you learned in this chapter.

3.25   Write an application that reads an integer and determines and prints whether it is odd or even. [*Hint*: Use the remainder operator. An even number is a multiple of 2. Any multiple of 2 leaves a remainder of 0 when divided by 2.]

3.26   Write an application that reads two integers, determines whether the first is a multiple of the second and prints the result. [*Hint*: Use the remainder operator.]

3.27   Write an application that displays a checkerboard pattern, as follows:

```
*  *  *  *  *  *  *  *
 *  *  *  *  *  *  *  *
*  *  *  *  *  *  *  *
 *  *  *  *  *  *  *  *
*  *  *  *  *  *  *  *
 *  *  *  *  *  *  *  *
*  *  *  *  *  *  *  *
 *  *  *  *  *  *  *  *
```

3.28   Here's a peek ahead. In this chapter, you have learned about integers and the type int. C# can also represent floating-point numbers that contain decimal points, such as 3.14159. Write an application that inputs from the user the radius of a circle as an integer and prints the circle's diameter, circumference and area using the floating-point value 3.14159 for π. Use the techniques shown in Fig. 3.18. [*Note:* You may also use the predefined constant Math.PI for the value of π. This constant is more precise than the value 3.14159. Class Math is defined in namespace System. Use the following formulas (*r* is the radius):

$$diameter = 2r$$
$$circumference = 2\pi r$$
$$area = \pi r^2$$

Do not store the results of each calculation in a variable. Rather, specify each calculation as the value that will be output in a Console.WriteLine statement. Note that the values produced by the circumference and area calculations are floating-point numbers. You will learn more about floating-point numbers in Chapter 4.

3.29   Here's another peek ahead. In this chapter, you have learned about integers and the type int. C# can also represent uppercase letters, lowercase letters and a considerable variety of special symbols. Every character has a corresponding integer representation. The set of characters a computer uses and the corresponding integer representations for those characters is called that computer's character set. You can indicate a character value in an application simply by enclosing that character in single quotes, as in 'A'.

You can determine the integer equivalent of a character by preceding that character with (int), as in

   (*int*) 'A'

The keyword int in parentheses is known as a cast operator, and the entire expression is called a cast expression. (You will learn about cast operators in Chapter 5.) The following statement outputs a character and its integer equivalent:

```
Console.WriteLine( "The character {0} has the value {1}",
    'A', ( ( int ) 'A' ) );
```

When the preceding statement executes, it displays the character A and the value 65 (from the Unicode[®] character set) as part of the string.

Using statements similar to the one shown earlier in this exercise, write an application that displays the integer equivalents of some uppercase letters, lowercase letters, digits and special symbols. Display the integer equivalents of the following: A B C a b c 0 1 2 $ * + / and the blank character.

3.30   Write an application that inputs one number consisting of five digits from the user, separates the number into its individual digits and prints the digits separated from one another by three spaces each. For example, if the user types in the number 42339, the application should print

```
4   2   3   3   9
```

Assume that the user enters the correct number of digits. What happens when you execute the application and type a number with more than five digits? What happens when you execute the application and type a number with fewer than five digits? [*Hint:* It is possible to do this exercise with the techniques you learned in this chapter. You will need to use both division and remainder operations to "pick off" each digit.]

3.31   Using only the programming techniques you learned in this chapter, write an application that calculates the squares and cubes of the numbers from 0 to 10 and prints the resulting values in table format, as shown below. All calculations should be done in terms of a variable x. [*Note:* This application does not require any input from the user.]

```
number  square  cube
0       0       0
1       1       1
2       4       8
3       9       27
4       16      64
5       25      125
6       36      216
7       49      343
8       64      512
9       81      729
10      100     1000
```

3.32   Write an application that inputs five numbers and determines and prints the number of negative numbers input, the number of positive numbers input and the number of zeros input.

4

Introduction to Classes and Objects

OBJECTIVES

In this chapter you will learn:

- What classes, objects, methods and instance variables are.

- How to declare a class and use it to create an object.

- How to implement a class's behaviors as methods.

- How to implement a class's attributes as instance variables and properties.

- How to call an object's methods to make the methods perform their tasks.

- The differences between instance variables of a class and local variables of a method.

- How to use a constructor to ensure that an object's data is initialized when the object is created.

- The differences between value types and reference types.

4.1 Introduction

We introduced the basic terminology and concepts of object-oriented programming in Section 1.17. In Chapter 3, you began to use those concepts to create simple applications that displayed messages to the user, obtained information from the user, performed calculations and made decisions. One common feature of every application in Chapter 3 was that all the statements that performed tasks were located in method Main. Typically, the applications you develop in this book will consist of two or more classes, each containing one or more methods. If you become part of a development team in industry, you might work on applications that contain hundreds, or even thousands, of classes. In this chapter, we present a simple framework for organizing object-oriented applications in C#.

First, we explain the concept of classes using a real-world example. Then we present five complete working applications to demonstrate how to create and use your own classes. The first four of these examples begin our case study on developing a grade-book class that instructors can use to maintain student test scores. This case study is enhanced over the next several chapters, culminating with the version presented in Chapter 8, Arrays. The last example in the chapter introduces the type decimal and uses it to declare monetary amounts in the context of a bank account class that maintains a customer's balance.

4.2 Classes, Objects, Methods, Properties and Instance Variables

Let's begin with a simple analogy to help you understand classes and their contents. Suppose you want to drive a car and make it go faster by pressing down on its accelerator pedal. What must happen before you can do this? Well, before you can drive a car, someone has to design it. A car typically begins as engineering drawings, similar to the blueprints used to design a house. These engineering drawings include the design for an accelerator pedal to make the car go faster. The pedal "hides" the complex mechanisms that actually make the car go faster, just as the brake pedal "hides" the mechanisms that slow the car and the steering wheel "hides" the mechanisms that turn the car. This enables people with little or no knowledge of how engines work to drive a car easily.

Unfortunately, you cannot drive the engineering drawings of a car. Before you can drive a car, the car must be built from the engineering drawings that describe it. A completed car will have an actual accelerator pedal to make the car go faster, but even that's not enough—the car will not accelerate on its own, so the driver must press the accelerator pedal.

Now let's use our car example to introduce the key programming concepts of this section. Performing a task in an application requires a method. The *method* describes the mechanisms that actually perform its tasks. The method hides from its user the complex tasks that it performs, just as the accelerator pedal of a car hides from the driver the complex mechanisms of making the car go faster. In C#, we begin by creating an application unit called a *class* to house (among other things) a method, just as a car's engineering drawings house (among other things) the design of an accelerator pedal. In a class, you provide one or more methods that are designed to perform the class's tasks. For example, a class that represents a bank account might contain one method to deposit money in an account, another to withdraw money from an account and a third to inquire what the current account balance is.

Just as you cannot drive an engineering drawing of a car, you cannot "drive" a class. Just as someone has to build a car from its engineering drawings before you can actually drive a car, you must build an *object* of a class before you can get an application to perform the tasks the class describes. That is one reason C# is known as an object-oriented programming language.

When you drive a car, pressing its gas pedal sends a message to the car to perform a task—make the car go faster. Similarly, you send *messages* to an object—each message is known as a *method call* and tells a method of the object to perform its task.

Thus far, we have used the car analogy to introduce classes, objects and methods. In addition to the capabilities a car provides, it also has many *attributes*, such as its color, the number of doors, the amount of gas in its tank, its current speed and its total miles driven (i.e., its odometer reading). Like the car's capabilities, these attributes are represented as part of a car's design in its engineering diagrams. As you drive a car, these attributes are always associated with the car. Every car maintains its own attributes. For example, each car knows how much gas is in its own gas tank, but not how much is in the tanks of other cars. Similarly, an object has attributes that are carried with the object as it is used in an application. These attributes are specified as part of the object's class. For example, a bank account object has a balance attribute that represents the amount of money in the account. Each bank account object knows the balance in the account it represents, but not the balances of the other accounts in the bank. Attributes are specified by the class's *instance variables*.

Notice that these attributes are not necessarily accessible directly. The car manufacturer does not want drivers to take apart the car's engine to observe the amount of gas in its tank. Instead, the driver can check the meter on the dashboard. The bank does not want its customers to walk into the vault to count the amount of money in an account. Instead, the customers talk to a bank teller. Similarly, you do not need to have access to an object's instance variables in order to use them. You can use the *properties* of an object. Properties contain *get accessors* for reading the values of variables, and *set accessors* for storing values into them.

The remainder of this chapter presents examples that demonstrate the concepts we introduced here in the context of the car analogy. The first four examples, summarized below, incrementally build a GradeBook class:

1. The first example presents a GradeBook class with one method that simply displays a welcome message when it is called. We show how to *create an object* of that class and call the method so that it displays the welcome message.

2. The second example modifies the first by allowing the method to receive a course name as an "argument" and by displaying the name as part of the welcome message.

3. The third example shows how to store the course name in a GradeBook object. For this version of the class, we also show how to use properties to set the course name and obtain the course name.

4. The fourth example demonstrates how the data in a GradeBook object can be initialized when the object is created—the initialization is performed by the class's constructor.

The last example in the chapter presents an Account class that reinforces the concepts presented in the first four examples and introduces the decimal type—a decimal number can contain a decimal point, as in 0.0345, –7.23 and 100.7, and is used for precise calculations, especially those involving monetary values. For this purpose, we present an Account class that represents a bank account and maintains its decimal balance. The class contains a method to credit a deposit to the account, thus increasing the balance, and a property to retrieve the balance and ensure that all values assigned to the balance are non-negative. The class's constructor initializes the balance of each Account object as the object is created. We create two Account objects and make deposits into each to show that each object maintains its own balance. The example also demonstrates how to input and display decimal numbers.

4.3 Declaring a Class with a Method and Instantiating an Object of a Class

We begin with an example that consists of classes GradeBook (Fig. 4.1) and GradeBook-Test (Fig. 4.2). Class GradeBook (declared in file GradeBook.cs) will be used to display a message on the screen (Fig. 4.2) welcoming the instructor to the grade-book application. Class GradeBookTest (declared in the file GradeBookTest.cs) is a testing class in which the Main method will create and use an object of class GradeBook. By convention, we declare classes GradeBook and GradeBookTest in separate files, such that each file's name matches the name of the class it contains.

To start, select **File > New Project...** to open the **New Project** dialog, then create a GradeBook **Console Application**. Delete all the code provided automatically by the IDE and replace it with the code in Fig. 4.1.

Class *GradeBook*

The GradeBook *class declaration* (Fig. 4.1) contains a DisplayMessage method (lines 8–11) that displays a message on the screen. Line 10 of the class displays the message. Recall that a class is like a blueprint—we need to make an object of this class and call its method to get line 10 to execute and display its message. (We do this in Fig. 4.2.)

```
 1   // Fig. 4.1: GradeBook.cs
 2   // Class declaration with one method.
 3   using System;
 4
 5   public class GradeBook
 6   {
 7      // display a welcome message to the GradeBook user
 8      public void DisplayMessage()
 9      {
10         Console.WriteLine( "Welcome to the Grade Book!" );
11      } // end method DisplayMessage
12   } // end class GradeBook
```

Fig. 4.1 | Class declaration with one method.

The class declaration begins in line 5. The keyword public is an *access modifier*. For now, we simply declare every class public. Every class declaration contains keyword class followed by the class's name. Every class's body is enclosed in a pair of left and right braces ({ and }), as in lines 6 and 12 of class GradeBook.

In Chapter 3, each class we declared had one method named Main. Class GradeBook also has one method—DisplayMessage (lines 8–11). Recall that Main is a special method that is always called automatically when you execute an application. Most methods do not get called automatically. As you will soon see, you must call method DisplayMessage to tell it to perform its task.

The method declaration begins with keyword public to indicate that the method is "available to the public"—that is, it can be called from outside the class declaration's body by methods of other classes. Keyword void—known as the method's *return type*—indicates that this method will not return (i.e., give back) any information to its *calling method* when it completes its task. When a method that specifies a return type other than void is called and completes its task, the method returns a result to its calling method. For example, when you go to an automated teller machine (ATM) and request your account balance, you expect the ATM to give you back a value that represents your balance. If you have a method Square that returns the square of its argument, you would expect the statement

    int result = Square(2);

to return 4 from method Square and assign 4 to variable result. If you have a method Maximum that returns the largest of three integer arguments, you would expect the statement

    int biggest = Maximum(27, 114, 51);

to return the value 114 from method Maximum and assign the value to variable biggest. You have already used methods that return information—for example, in Chapter 3 you used Console method ReadLine to input a string typed by the user at the keyboard. When ReadLine inputs a value, it returns that value for use in the application.

The name of the method, DisplayMessage, follows the return type (line 8). By convention, method names begin with an uppercase first letter, and all subsequent words in the name begin with a capital letter. The parentheses after the method name indicate that this is a method. An empty set of parentheses, as shown in line 8, indicates that this method does not require additional information to perform its task. Line 8 is commonly referred to as the *method header*. Every method's body is delimited by left and right braces, as in lines 9 and 11.

The body of a method contains statement(s) that perform the method's task. In this case, the method contains one statement (line 10) that displays the message "Welcome to the Grade Book!", followed by a newline in the console window. After this statement executes, the method has completed its task.

Next, we'd like to use class GradeBook in an application. As you learned in Chapter 3, method Main begins the execution of every application. Class GradeBook cannot begin an application because it does not contain Main. This was not a problem in Chapter 3, because every class you declared had a Main method. To fix this problem for the Grade-Book, we must either declare a separate class that contains a Main method or place a Main method in class GradeBook. To help you prepare for the larger applications you will encounter later in this book and in industry, we use a separate class (GradeBookTest in this example) containing method Main to test each new class we create in this chapter.

Adding a Class to a Visual C# Project

For each example in this chapter, you will add a class to your console application. To do this, right click the project name in the **Solution Explorer** and select **Add > New Item...** from the pop-up menu. In the **Add New Item** dialog that appears, select **Code File** and enter the name of your new file—in this case, GradeBookTest.cs. A new, blank file will be added to your project. Add the code from Fig. 4.2 to this file.

Class GradeBookTest

The GradeBookTest class declaration (Fig. 4.2) contains the Main method that controls our application's execution. Any class that contains a Main method (as shown in line 7) can be used to execute an application. This class declaration begins in line 4 and ends in line 15. The class contains only a Main method, which is typical of many classes that simply begin an application's execution.

```
1   // Fig. 4.2: GradeBookTest.cs
2   // Create a GradeBook object and call its DisplayMessage method.
3
4   public class GradeBookTest
5   {
6      // Main method begins program execution
7      public static void Main( string[] args )
8      {
9         // create a GradeBook object and assign it to myGradeBook
10        GradeBook myGradeBook = new GradeBook();
11
12        // call myGradeBook's DisplayMessage method
13        myGradeBook.DisplayMessage();
14     } // end Main
15  } // end class GradeBookTest
```

```
Welcome to the Grade Book!
```

Fig. 4.2 | Create a GradeBook object and call its DisplayMessage method.

Lines 7–14 declare method Main. A key part of enabling the method Main to begin the application's execution is the static keyword (line 7), which indicates that Main is a static method. A static method is special because it can be called without first creating an object of the class (in this case, GradeBookTest) in which the method is declared. We explain static methods in Chapter 7, Methods: A Deeper Look.

In this application, we'd like to call class GradeBook's DisplayMessage method to display the welcome message in the console window. Typically, you cannot call a method that belongs to another class until you create an object of that class, as shown in line 10. We begin by declaring variable myGradeBook. Note that the variable's type is GradeBook—the class we declared in Fig. 4.1. Each new class you create becomes a new type in C# that can be used to declare variables and create objects. New class types will be accessible to all classes in the same project. You can declare new class types as needed; this is one reason why C# is known as an *extensible language*.

Variable myGradeBook (line 10) is initialized with the result of the *object creation expression* new GradeBook(). The new operator creates a new object of the class specified to the right of the keyword (i.e., GradeBook). The parentheses to the right of the Grade-Book are required. As you will learn in Section 4.9, those parentheses in combination with a class name represent a call to a constructor, which is similar to a method, but is used only at the time an object is created to initialize the object's data. In that section you will see that data can be placed in parentheses to specify initial values for the object's data. For now, we simply leave the parentheses empty.

We can now use myGradeBook to call its method DisplayMessage. Line 13 calls the method DisplayMessage (lines 8–11 of Fig. 4.1) using variable myGradeBook followed by a *dot operator* (.), the method name DisplayMessage and an empty set of parentheses. This call causes the DisplayMessage method to perform its task. This method call differs from the method calls in Chapter 3 that displayed information in a console window—each of those method calls provided arguments that specified the data to display. At the beginning of line 13, "myGradeBook." indicates that Main should use the GradeBook object that was created on line 10. The empty parentheses in line 8 of Fig. 4.1 indicate that method DisplayMessage does not require additional information to perform its task. For this reason, the method call (line 13 of Fig. 4.2) specifies an empty set of parentheses after the method name to indicate that no arguments are being passed to method DisplayMessage. When method DisplayMessage completes its task, method Main continues executing at line 14. This is the end of method Main, so the application terminates.

UML Class Diagram for Class GradeBook
Figure 4.3 presents a *UML class diagram* for class GradeBook of Fig. 4.1. Recall from Section 1.17 that the UML is a graphical language used by programmers to represent their

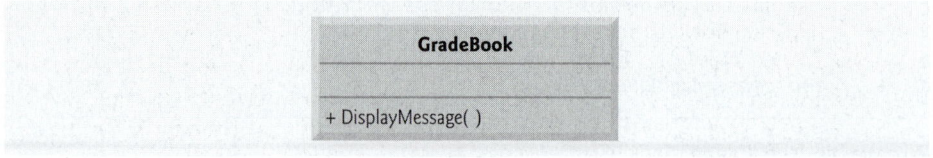

Fig. 4.3 | UML class diagram indicating that class GradeBook has a public DisplayMessage operation.

object-oriented systems in a standardized manner. In the UML, each class is modeled in a class diagram as a rectangle with three compartments. The top compartment contains the name of the class centered horizontally in boldface type. The middle compartment contains the class's attributes, which correspond to instance variables and properties in C#. In Fig. 4.3, the middle compartment is empty because the version of class GradeBook in Fig. 4.1 does not have any attributes. The bottom compartment contains the class's operations, which correspond to methods in C#. The UML models operations by listing the operation name followed by a set of parentheses. Class GradeBook has one method, DisplayMessage, so the bottom compartment of Fig. 4.3 lists one operation with this name. Method DisplayMessage does not require additional information to perform its tasks, so there are empty parentheses following DisplayMessage in the class diagram, just as they appeared in the method's declaration in line 8 of Fig. 4.1. The plus sign (+) in front of the operation name indicates that DisplayMessage is a public operation in the UML (i.e., a public method in C#). The plus sign is sometimes called the *public visibility symbol*. We will often use UML class diagrams to summarize a class's attributes and operations.

4.4 Declaring a Method with a Parameter

In our car analogy from Section 4.2, we discussed the fact that pressing a car's gas pedal sends a message to the car to perform a task—make the car go faster. But how fast should the car accelerate? As you know, the farther down you press the pedal, the faster the car accelerates. So the message to the car actually includes both the task to be performed and additional information that helps the car perform the task. This additional information is known as a *parameter*—the value of the parameter helps the car determine how fast to accelerate. Similarly, a method can require one or more parameters that represent additional information it needs to perform its task. A method call supplies values—called arguments—for each of the method's parameters. For example, the Console.WriteLine method requires an argument that specifies the data to be displayed in a console window. Similarly, to make a deposit into a bank account, a Deposit method specifies a parameter that represents the deposit amount. When the Deposit method is called, an argument value representing the deposit amount is assigned to the method's parameter. The method then makes a deposit of that amount, by increasing the account's balance.

Our next example declares class GradeBook (Fig. 4.4) with a DisplayMessage method that displays the course name as part of the welcome message. (See the sample execution in Fig. 4.5.) The new DisplayMessage method requires a parameter that represents the course name to output.

Before discussing the new features of class GradeBook, let's see how the new class is used from the Main method of class GradeBookTest (Fig. 4.5). Line 12 creates an object of class GradeBook and assigns it to variable myGradeBook. Line 15 prompts the user to enter a course name. Line 16 reads the name from the user and assigns it to the variable nameOfCourse, using Console method ReadLine to perform the input. The user types the course name and presses *Enter* to submit the course name to the application. Note that pressing *Enter* inserts a newline character at the end of the characters typed by the user. Method ReadLine reads characters typed by the user until the newline character is encountered, then returns a string containing the characters up to, but not including, the newline. The newline character is discarded.

```
 1   // Fig. 4.4: GradeBook.cs
 2   // Class declaration with a method that has a parameter.
 3   using System;
 4
 5   public class GradeBook
 6   {
 7      // display a welcome message to the GradeBook user
 8      public void DisplayMessage( string courseName )
 9      {
10         Console.WriteLine( "Welcome to the grade book for\n{0}!",
11            courseName );
12      } // end method DisplayMessage
13   } // end class GradeBook
```

Fig. 4.4 | Class declaration with a method that has a parameter.

```
 1   // Fig. 4.5: GradeBookTest.cs
 2   // Create GradeBook object and pass a string to
 3   // its DisplayMessage method.
 4   using System;
 5
 6   public class GradeBookTest
 7   {
 8      // Main method begins program execution
 9      public static void Main( string[] args )
10      {
11         // create a GradeBook object and assign it to myGradeBook
12         GradeBook myGradeBook = new GradeBook();
13
14         // prompt for and input course name
15         Console.WriteLine( "Please enter the course name:" );
16         string nameOfCourse = Console.ReadLine(); // read a line of text
17         Console.WriteLine(); // output a blank line
18
19         // call myGradeBook's DisplayMessage method
20         // and pass nameOfCourse as an argument
21         myGradeBook.DisplayMessage( nameOfCourse );
22      } // end Main
23   } // end class GradeBookTest
```

```
Please enter the course name:
CS101 Introduction to C# Programming

Welcome to the grade book for
CS101 Introduction to C# Programming!
```

Fig. 4.5 | Create GradeBook object and pass a string to its DisplayMessage method.

Line 21 calls myGradeBook's DisplayMessage method. The variable nameOfCourse in parentheses is the argument that is passed to method DisplayMessage so that the method can perform its task. Variable nameOfCourse's value in Main becomes the value of method DisplayMessage's parameter courseName in line 8 of Fig. 4.4. When you execute this application, notice that method DisplayMessage outputs the name you type as part of the welcome message (Fig. 4.5).

Software Engineering Observation 4.1

Normally, objects are created with new. One exception is a string literal that is contained in quotes, such as "hello". String literals are references to string objects that are implicitly created by C#.

More on Arguments and Parameters

When you declare a method, you must specify in the method's declaration whether the method requires data to perform its task. To do so, you place additional information in the method's *parameter list*, which is located in the parentheses that follow the method name. The parameter list may contain any number of parameters, including none at all. Empty parentheses following the method name (as in Fig. 4.1, line 8) indicate that a method does not require any parameters. In Fig. 4.4, DisplayMessage's parameter list (line 8) declares that the method requires one parameter. Each parameter must specify a type and an identifier. In this case, the type string and the identifier courseName indicate that method DisplayMessage requires a string to perform its task. At the time the method is called, the argument value in the call is assigned to the corresponding parameter (in this case, courseName) in the method header. Then, the method body uses the parameter courseName to access the value. Lines 10–11 of Fig. 4.4 display parameter courseName's value, using the {0} format item in WriteLine's first argument. Note that the parameter variable's name (Fig. 4.4, line 8) can be the same or different from the argument variable's name (Fig. 4.5, line 21).

A method can specify multiple parameters by separating each parameter from the next with a comma. The number of arguments in a method call must match the number of parameters in the parameter list of the called method's declaration. Also, the types of the arguments in the method call must be consistent with the types of the corresponding parameters in the method's declaration. (As you will learn in subsequent chapters, an argument's type and its corresponding parameter's type are not always required to be identical.) In our example, the method call passes one argument of type string (nameOfCourse is declared as a string in line 16 of Fig. 4.5), and the method declaration specifies one parameter of type string (line 8 in Fig. 4.4). So the type of the argument in the method call exactly matches the type of the parameter in the method header.

Common Programming Error 4.1

A compilation error occurs if the number of arguments in a method call does not match the number of parameters in the method declaration.

Common Programming Error 4.2

A compilation error occurs if the types of the arguments in a method call are not consistent with the types of the corresponding parameters in the method declaration.

Updated UML Class Diagram for Class GradeBook

The UML class diagram of Fig. 4.6 models class GradeBook of Fig. 4.4. Like Fig. 4.4, this GradeBook class contains public operation DisplayMessage. However, this version of DisplayMessage has a parameter. The UML models a parameter a bit differently from C#

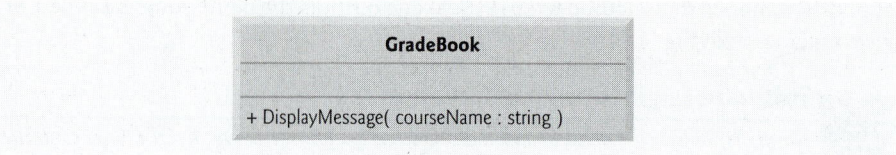

Fig. 4.6 | UML class diagram indicating that class GradeBook has a public DisplayMessage operation with a courseName parameter of type string.

by listing the parameter name, followed by a colon and the parameter type in the parentheses following the operation name. The UML has several data types that are similar to the C# types. For example, UML types String and Integer correspond to C# types string and int, respectively. Unfortunately, the UML does not provide types that correspond to every C# type. For this reason, and to avoid confusion between UML types and C# types, we use only C# types in our UML diagrams. Class Gradebook's method DisplayMessage (Fig. 4.4) has a string parameter named courseName, so Fig. 4.6 lists courseName : string between the parentheses following DisplayMessage.

Notes on using Directives
Notice the using directive in Fig. 4.5 (line 4). This indicates to the compiler that the application uses classes in the System namespace, like the Console class. Why do we need a using directive to use class Console, but not class GradeBook? There is a special relationship between classes that are compiled in the same project, like classes GradeBook and GradeBookTest. By default, such classes are considered to be in the same namespace. A using directive is not required when one class in a namespace uses another in the same namespace—such as when class GradeBookTest uses class GradeBook. You will see in Section 9.14 how to declare your own namespaces with the namespace keyword. For simplicity, our examples in this chapter do not declare a namespace. Any classes that are not explicitly placed in a namespace are implicitly placed in the so-called *global namespace*.

Actually, the using directive in line 4 is not required if we always refer to class Console as System.Console, which includes the full namespace and class name. This is known as the class's *fully qualified class name*. For example, line 15 could be written as

```
System.Console.WriteLine( "Please enter the course name:" );
```

Most C# programmers consider using fully qualified names to be cumbersome, and instead prefer to use using directives. The code generated by the Visual C# Form Designer uses fully qualified names.

4.5 Instance Variables and Properties
In Chapter 3, we declared all of an application's variables in the application's Main method. Variables declared in the body of a particular method are known as *local variables* and can be used only in that method. When a method terminates, the values of its local variables are lost. Recall from Section 4.2 that an object has attributes that are carried with the object as it is used in an application. Such attributes exist before a method is called on an object and after the method completes execution.

Attributes are represented as variables in a class declaration. Such variables are called *fields* and are declared inside a class declaration but outside the bodies of the class's method declarations. When each object of a class maintains its own copy of an attribute, the field that represents the attribute is also known as an instance variable—each object (instance) of the class has a separate instance of the variable in memory. [*Note:* In Chapter 9, Classes and Objects: A Deeper Look, we discuss another type of field called a static variable, where all objects of the same class share one copy of the variable.]

A class normally consists of one or more properties that manipulate the attributes that belong to a particular object of the class. The example in this section demonstrates a GradeBook class that contains a courseName instance variable to represent a particular GradeBook object's course name, and a CourseName property to manipulate courseName.

GradeBook *Class with an Instance Variable and a Property*

In our next application (Figs. 4.7–4.8), class GradeBook (Fig. 4.7) maintains the course name as an instance variable so that it can be used or modified at any time during an application's execution. The class also contains one method—DisplayMessage (lines 24–30)—and one property—CourseName (line 11–21). Recall from Chapter 2 that properties are used

```csharp
1   // Fig. 4.7: GradeBook.cs
2   // GradeBook class that contains a courseName instance variable,
3   // and a property to get and set its value.
4   using System;
5
6   public class GradeBook
7   {
8      private string courseName; // course name for this GradeBook
9
10     // property to get and set the course name
11     public string CourseName
12     {
13        get
14        {
15           return courseName;
16        } // end get
17        set
18        {
19           courseName = value;
20        } // end set
21     } // end property CourseName
22
23     // display a welcome message to the GradeBook user
24     public void DisplayMessage()
25     {
26        // use property CourseName to get the
27        // name of the course that this GradeBook represents
28        Console.WriteLine( "Welcome to the grade book for\n{0}!",
29           CourseName ); // display property CourseName
30     } // end method DisplayMessage
31  } // end class GradeBook
```

Fig. 4.7 | GradeBook class that contains a private instance variable, courseName and a public property to get and set its value.

to manipulate an object's attributes. For example, in that chapter, we used a Label's Text property to specify the text to display on the Label. In this example, we use a property in code rather than in the **Properties** window of the IDE. To do this, we first declare a property as a member of the GradeBook class. As you will soon see, the GradeBook's CourseName property can be used to store a course name in a GradeBook (in instance variable courseName) or retrieve the GradeBook's course name (from instance variable courseName). Method DisplayMessage—which now specifies no parameters—still displays a welcome message that includes the course name. However, the method now uses the CourseName property to obtain the course name from instance variable courseName.

A typical instructor teaches more than one course, each with its own course name. Line 8 declares courseName as a variable of type string. Line 8 is a declaration for an instance variable because the variable is declared in the body of the class (lines 7–31) but outside the bodies of the class's method (lines 24–30) and property (lines 11–21). Every instance (i.e., object) of class GradeBook contains one copy of each instance variable. For example, if there are two GradeBook objects, each object has its own copy of courseName (one per object). All the methods and properties of class GradeBook can directly manipulate its instance variable courseName, but it is considered good practice for methods of a class to use that class's properties to manipulate instance variables (as we do in line 29 of method DisplayMessage). The software engineering reasons for this will soon become clear.

Access Modifiers public and private

Most instance variable declarations are preceded with the keyword private (as in line 8). Like public, keyword private is an access modifier. Variables or methods declared with access modifier private are accessible only to methods of the class in which they are declared. Thus, variable courseName can be used only in property CourseName and method DisplayMessage of class GradeBook.

Software Engineering Observation 4.2

Precede every field and method declaration with an access modifier. As a rule of thumb, instance variables should be declared private and methods and properties should be declared public. If the access modifier is omitted before a member of a class, the member is implicitly declared private by default. (We will see that it is appropriate to declare certain methods private, if they will be accessed only by other methods of the class.)

Good Programming Practice 4.1

We prefer to list the fields of a class first, so that, as you read the code, you see the names and types of the variables before you see them used in the methods of the class. It is possible to list the class's fields anywhere in the class outside its method declarations, but scattering them can make code difficult to read.

Good Programming Practice 4.2

Placing a blank line between method and property declarations enhances application readability.

Declaring instance variables with access modifier private is known as *information hiding*. When an application creates (instantiates) an object of class GradeBook, variable courseName is encapsulated (hidden) in the object and can be accessed only by methods and properties of the object's class. In class GradeBook, the property CourseName manipulates the instance variable courseName.

Setting and Getting the Values of *private* Instance Variables

How can we allow a program to manipulate a class's private instance variables but ensure that they remain in a valid state? We need to provide controlled ways for programmers to "get" (i.e., retrieve) the value in an instance variable and "set" (i.e., modify) the value in an instance variable. For these purposes, programmers using languages other than C# normally use methods known as *get* and *set* methods. These methods typically are made public, and provide ways for the client to access or modify private data. Historically, these methods begin with the words "Get" and "Set"—in our class GradeBook, for example, if we were to use such methods they might be called GetCourseName and SetCourseName, respectively.

Although you can define methods like GetCourseName and SetCourseName, C# properties provide a more elegant solution. Next, we show how to declare and use properties.

GradeBook Class with a Property

The GradeBook class's CourseName *property declaration* is located in lines 11–21 of Fig. 4.7. The property begins in line 11 with an access modifier (in this case, public), followed by the type that the property represents (string) and the property's name (CourseName). Property names are normally capitalized.

Properties contain *accessors* that handle the details of returning and modifying data. A property declaration can contain a get accessor, a set accessor or both. The get accessor (lines 13–16) enables a client to read the value of private instance variable courseName; the set accessor (lines 17–20) enables a client to modify courseName.

After defining a property, you can use it like a variable in your code. For example, you can assign a value to a property using the = (assignment) operator. This executes the code in the property's set accessor to set the value of the corresponding instance variable. Similarly, referencing the property to use its value (for example, to display it on the screen) executes the code in the property's get accessor to obtain the corresponding instance variable's value. We show how to use properties shortly. By convention, we name each property with the capitalized name of the instance variable that it manipulates (e.g., CourseName is the property that represents instance variable courseName)—C# is case sensitive, so these are distinct identifiers.

get and set Accessors

Let us look more closely at property CourseName's get and set accessors (Fig. 4.7). The get accessor (lines 13–16) begins with the identifier ***get*** and is delimited by braces. The accessor's body contains a ***return statement***, which consists of the keyword ***return*** followed by an expression. The expression's value is returned to the client code that uses the property. In this example, the value of courseName is returned when the property CourseName is referenced. For example, the following statement

```
string theCourseName = gradeBook.CourseName;
```

where gradeBook is an object of class GradeBook, executes property CourseName's get accessor, which returns the value of instance variable courseName. That value is then stored in variable theCourseName. Note that property CourseName can be used as simply as if it were an instance variable. The property notation allows the client to think of the property as the underlying data. Again, the client cannot directly manipulate instance variable courseName because it is private.

The set accessor (lines 17–20) begins with the identifier *set* and is delimited by braces. When the property CourseName appears in an assignment statement, as in

```
gradeBook.CourseName = "CS100 Introduction to Computers";
```

the text "CS100 Introduction to Computers" is passed to an implicit parameter named value, and the set accessor executes. Notice that value is implicitly declared and initialized in the set accessor—it is a compilation error to declare a local variable value in this body. Line 19 stores this value in instance variable courseName. Note that set accessors do not return any data when they complete their tasks.

The statements inside the property in lines 15 and 19 (Fig. 4.7) each access course-Name even though it was declared outside the property. We can use instance variable courseName in the methods and properties of class GradeBook because courseName is an instance variable of the class. The order in which methods and properties are declared in a class does not determine when they are called at execution time, so you can declare method DisplayMessage (which uses property CourseName) before you declare property CourseName. Within the property itself, the get and set accessors can appear in any order, and either accessor can be omitted. In Chapter 9, we discuss how to omit either a set or get accessor to create so-called "read-only" and "write-only" properties, respectively.

Using Property CourseName in Method DisplayMessage

Method DisplayMessage (lines 24–30 of Fig. 4.7) does not receive any parameters. Lines 28–29 output a welcome message that includes the value of instance variable courseName. We do not reference courseName directly. Instead, we access property CourseName (line 29), which executes the property's get accessor, returning the value of courseName.

GradeBookTest Class That Demonstrates Class GradeBook

Class GradeBookTest (Fig. 4.8) creates a GradeBook object and demonstrates property CourseName. Line 11 creates a GradeBook object and assigns it to local variable myGrade-Book of type GradeBook. Lines 14–15 display the initial course name using the object's CourseName property—this executes the property's get accessor, which returns the value of courseName.

Note that the first line of the output shows an empty name (marked by ' '). Unlike local variables, which are not automatically initialized, every field has a *default initial value*—a value provided by C# when you do not specify the initial value. Thus, fields are not required to be explicitly initialized before they are used in an application—unless they must be initialized to values other than their default values. The default value for an instance variable of type string (like courseName) is null. When you display a string variable that contains the value null, no text is displayed on the screen. We will discuss the significance of null in Section 4.8.

Line 18 prompts the user to enter a course name. Local string variable theName (declared in line 19) is initialized with the course name entered by the user, which is returned by the call to ReadLine. Line 20 assigns theName to object myGradeBook's CourseName property. When a value is assigned to CourseName, the value specified (in this case, theName) is assigned to implicit parameter value of CourseName's set accessor (lines 17–20, Fig. 4.7). Then parameter value is assigned by the set accessor to instance variable courseName (line 19 of Fig. 4.7). Line 21 (Fig. 4.8) displays a blank line, then line 24 calls myGradeBook's DisplayMessage method to display the welcome message containing the course name.

```
 1   // Fig. 4.8: GradeBookTest.cs
 2   // Create and manipulate a GradeBook object.
 3   using System;
 4
 5   public class GradeBookTest
 6   {
 7      // Main method begins program execution
 8      public static void Main( string[] args )
 9      {
10         // create a GradeBook object and assign it to myGradeBook
11         GradeBook myGradeBook = new GradeBook();
12
13         // display initial value of CourseName
14         Console.WriteLine( "Initial course name is: '{0}'\n",
15            myGradeBook.CourseName );
16
17         // prompt for and read course name
18         Console.WriteLine( "Please enter the course name:" );
19         string theName = Console.ReadLine(); // read a line of text
20         myGradeBook.CourseName = theName; // set name using a property
21         Console.WriteLine(); // output a blank line
22
23         // display welcome message after specifying course name
24         myGradeBook.DisplayMessage();
25      } // end Main
26   } // end class GradeBookTest
```

```
Initial course name is: ''

Please enter the course name:
CS101 Introduction to C# Programming

Welcome to the grade book for
CS101 Introduction to C# Programming!
```

Fig. 4.8 | Create and manipulate a GradeBook object.

4.6 UML Class Diagram with a Property

Figure 4.9 contains an updated UML class diagram for the version of class GradeBook in Fig. 4.7. We model properties in the UML as attributes—the property (in this case, CourseName) is listed as a public attribute—as indicated by the plus (+) sign—preceded by the word "property" in *guillemets* (« and »). Using descriptive words in guillemets (called

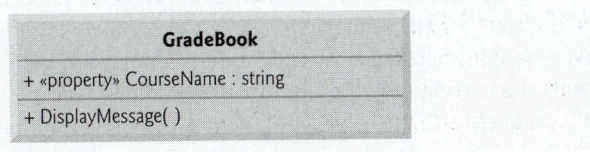

Fig. 4.9 | UML class diagram indicating that class GradeBook has a public CourseName property of type string and one public method.

stereotypes in the UML) helps distinguish properties from other attributes and operations. The UML indicates the type of the property by placing a colon and a type after the property name. The `get` and `set` accessors of the property are implied, so they are not listed in the UML diagram. Class `GradeBook` also contains one `public` method `DisplayMessage`, so the class diagram lists this operation in the third compartment. Recall that the plus (+) sign is the public visibility symbol.

In the preceding section, you learned how to declare a property in C# code. You saw that we typically name a property the same as the instance variable it manipulates, but with a capital first letter (e.g., property `CourseName` manipulates instance variable `courseName`). A class diagram helps you design a class, so it is not required to show every implementation detail of the class. Since, an instance variable that is manipulated by a property is really an implementation detail of that property, our class diagram does not show the `courseName` instance variable. A programmer implementing the `GradeBook` class based on this class diagram would create the instance variable `courseName` as part of the implementation process (as we did in Fig. 4.7).

In some cases, you may find it necessary to model the `private` instance variables of a class that are not properties. Like properties, instance variables are attributes of a class and are modeled in the middle compartment of a class diagram. The UML represents instance variables as attributes by listing the attribute name, followed by a colon and the attribute type. To indicate that an attribute is `private`, a class diagram would list the *private visibility symbol*—a minus sign (–)—before the attribute's name. For example, the instance variable `courseName` in Fig. 4.7 would be modeled as "- courseName : string" to indicate that it is a private attribute of type `string`.

4.7 Software Engineering with Properties and set and get Accessors

Using properties as described earlier in this chapter would seem to violate the notion of `private` data. Although providing a property with `get` and `set` accessors may appear to be the same as making its corresponding instance variable `public`, this is not the case. A `public` instance variable can be read or written by any property or method in the program. If an instance variable is `private`, the client code can access the instance variable only indirectly through the class's non-`private` properties or methods. This allows the class to control the manner in which the data is set or returned. For example, `get` and `set` accessors can translate between the format of the data used by the client and the format stored in the `private` instance variable.

Consider a `Clock` class that represents the time of day as a `private int` instance variable `time`, containing the number of seconds since midnight. Suppose the class provides a `Time` property of type `string` to manipulate this instance variable. Although `get` accessors typically return data exactly as it is stored in an object, they need not expose the data in this "raw" format. When a client refers to a `Clock` object's `Time` property, the property's `get` accessor could use instance variable `time` to determine the number of hours, minutes and seconds since midnight, then return the time as a `string` of the form `"HH:MM:SS"`. Similarly, suppose a `Clock` object's `Time` property is assigned a `string` of the form `"HH:MM:SS"`. Using the `string` capabilities presented in Chapter 16 and the method `Convert.ToInt32` presented in Section 3.6, the `Time` property's `set` accessor could convert this `string` to an `int` number of seconds since midnight and store the result in the `Clock` object's `private` instance variable `time`. The `Time` property's `set` accessor can also provide *data validation* capabilities that scrutinize attempts to modify the instance variable's value to ensure that the value it receives represents a valid time (e.g., `"12:30:45"` is valid but `"42:85:70"` is not). We demonstrate data validation in Section 4.10. So, although a property's accessors enable clients to manipulate `private` data, they carefully control those manipulations, and the object's `private` data remains safely encapsulated (i.e., hidden) in the object. This is not possible with `public` instance variables, which can easily be set by clients to invalid values.

Properties of a class should also be used by the class's own methods to manipulate the class's `private` instance variables, even though the methods can directly access the `private` instance variables. Accessing an instance variable via a property's accessors—as in the body of method `DisplayMessage` (Fig. 4.7, lines 28–29)—creates a more robust class that is easier to maintain and less likely to malfunction. If we decide to change the representation of instance variable `courseName` in some way, the declaration of method `DisplayMessage` does not require modification—only the bodies of property `CourseName`'s `get` and `set` accessors that directly manipulate the instance variable will need to change. For example, suppose we want to represent the course name as two separate instance variables—course-Number (e.g., `"CS101"`) and `courseTitle` (e.g., `"Introduction to C# Programming"`). The `DisplayMessage` method can still use property `CourseName`'s `get` accessor to obtain the full course name to display as part of the welcome message. In this case, the `get` accessor would need to build and return a `string` containing the `courseNumber`, followed by the course-`Title`. Method `DisplayMessage` would continue to display the complete course title "`CS101 Introduction to C# Programming`," because it is unaffected by the change to the class's instance variables.

Software Engineering Observation 4.3

Accessing `private` data through `set` and `get` accessors not only protects the instance variables from receiving invalid values, but also hides the internal representation of the instance variables from that class's clients. Thus, if representation of the data changes (often to reduce the amount of required storage or to improve performance), only the properties' implementations need to change—the clients' implementations need not change as long as the services provided by the properties are preserved.

4.8 Value Types vs. Reference Types

Types in C# are divided into two categories—*value types* and *reference types*. C#'s simple types are all value types. A variable of a value type (such as `int`) simply contains a value of that type. For example, Fig. 4.10 shows an `int` variable named `count` that contains the value 7.

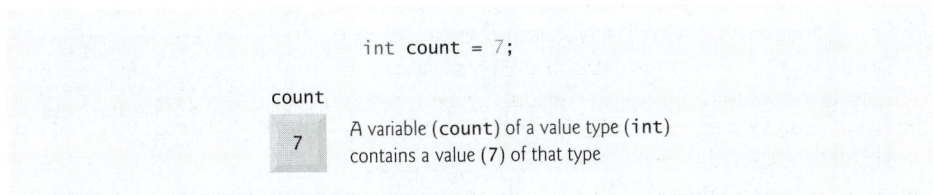

```
int count = 7;
```

count

| 7 |

A variable (`count`) of a value type (`int`) contains a value (7) of that type

Fig. 4.10 | Value type variable.

By contrast, a variable of a reference type (sometimes called a *reference*) contains the address of a location in memory where the data referred to by that variable is stored. Such a variable is said to *refer to an object* in the program. Line 11 of Fig. 4.8 creates a Grade-Book object, places it in memory and stores the object's memory address in reference variable myGradeBook of type GradeBook as shown in Fig. 4.11. Note that the GradeBook object is shown with its courseName instance variable.

Reference type instance variables (such as myGradeBook in Fig. 4.11) are initialized by default to the value *null*. string is a reference type. For this reason, string variable courseName is shown in Fig. 4.11 with an empty box representing the null-valued variable in memory.

A client of an object must use a reference to the object to *invoke* (i.e., call) the object's methods and access the object's properties. In Fig. 4.8, the statements in Main use variable myGradeBook, which contains the GradeBook object's reference, to send messages to the GradeBook object. These messages are calls to methods (like DisplayMessage) or references to properties (like CourseName) that enable the program to interact with GradeBook objects. For example, the statement (in line 20 of Fig. 4.8)

```
myGradeBook.CourseName = theName; // set name using a property
```

uses the reference myGradeBook to set the course name by assigning a value to property CourseName. This sends a message to the GradeBook object to invoke the CourseName property's set accessor. The message includes as an argument the value "CS101 Introduction to C# Programming" that CourseName's set accessor requires to perform its task. The set accessor uses this information to set the courseName instance variable. In Section 7.11, we discuss value types and reference types in detail.

Software Engineering Observation 4.4

A variable's declared type (e.g., int, double or GradeBook) indicates whether the variable is of a value or a reference type. If a variable's type is not one of the thirteen simple types, or an enum or a struct type (which we discuss in Section 7.10 and Chapter 16, respectively), then it is a reference type. For example, Account account1 indicates that account1 is a variable that can refer to an Account object.

4.9 Initializing Objects with Constructors

As mentioned in Section 4.5, when an object of class GradeBook (Fig. 4.7) is created, its instance variable courseName is initialized to null by default. What if you want to provide

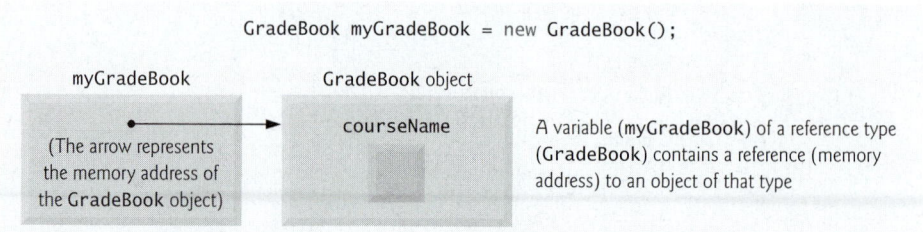

Fig. 4.11 | Reference type variable.

a course name when you create a GradeBook object? Each class you declare can provide a *constructor* that can be used to initialize an object of a class when the object is created. In fact, C# requires a constructor call for every object that is created. The new operator calls the class's constructor to perform the initialization. The constructor call is indicated by the class name, followed by parentheses. For example, line 11 of Fig. 4.8 first uses new to create a GradeBook object. The empty parentheses after "new GradeBook" indicate a call without arguments to the class's constructor. By default, the compiler provides a *default constructor* with no parameters in any class that does not explicitly include a constructor, so *every* class has a constructor.

When you declare a class, you can provide your own constructor to specify custom initialization for objects of your class. For example, you might want to specify a course name for a GradeBook object when the object is created, as in

```
GradeBook myGradeBook =
    new GradeBook( "CS101 Introduction to C# Programming" );
```

In this case, the argument "CS101 Introduction to C# Programming" is passed to the GradeBook object's constructor and used to initialize the courseName. Each time you create a different GradeBook object, you can provide a different course name. The preceding statement requires that the class provide a constructor with a string parameter. Figure 4.12 contains a modified GradeBook class with such a constructor.

```csharp
1   // Fig. 4.12: GradeBook.cs
2   // GradeBook class with a constructor to initialize the course name.
3   using System;
4
5   public class GradeBook
6   {
7      private string courseName; // course name for this GradeBook
8
9      // constructor initializes courseName with string supplied as argument
10     public GradeBook( string name )
11     {
12        CourseName = name; // initialize courseName using property
13     } // end constructor
14
15     // property to get and set the course name
16     public string CourseName
17     {
18        get
19        {
20           return courseName;
21        } // end get
22        set
23        {
24           courseName = value;
25        } // end set
26     } // end property CourseName
27
```

Fig. 4.12 | GradeBook class with a constructor to initialize the course name. (Part 1 of 2.)

```
28        // display a welcome message to the GradeBook user
29        public void DisplayMessage()
30        {
31           // use property CourseName to get the
32           // name of the course that this GradeBook represents
33           Console.WriteLine( "Welcome to the grade book for\n{0}!",
34              CourseName );
35        } // end method DisplayMessage
36     } // end class GradeBook
```

Fig. 4.12 | GradeBook class with a constructor to initialize the course name. (Part 2 of 2.)

Lines 10–13 declare the constructor for class GradeBook. A constructor must have the same name as its class. Like a method, a constructor specifies in its parameter list the data it requires to perform its task. Unlike a method, a constructor doesn't specify a return type. When you create a new object (with new), you place this data in the parentheses that follow the class name. Line 10 indicates that class GradeBook's constructor has a parameter called name of type string. In line 12, the name passed to the constructor is assigned to instance variable courseName via the CourseName property's set accessor.

Figure 4.13 demonstrates initializing GradeBook objects using this constructor. Lines 12–13 create and initialize a GradeBook object. The constructor of class GradeBook is called with the argument "CS101 Introduction to C# Programming" to initialize the course name. The object creation expression to the right of = in lines 12–13 returns a reference to the new object, which is assigned to variable gradeBook1. Lines 14–15 repeat this process for another GradeBook object, this time passing the argument "CS102 Data Structures in C#" to initialize the course name for gradeBook2. Lines 18–21 use each object's CourseName property to obtain the course names and show that they were indeed initialized when the objects were created. In the introduction to Section 4.5, you learned that each instance (i.e., object) of a class contains its own copy of the class's instance variables. The output confirms that each GradeBook maintains its own copy of instance variable courseName.

```
1     // Fig. 4.13: GradeBookTest.cs
2     // GradeBook constructor used to specify the course name at the
3     // time each GradeBook object is created.
4     using System;
5
6     public class GradeBookTest
7     {
8        // Main method begins program execution
9        public static void Main( string[] args )
10       {
11          // create GradeBook object
12          GradeBook gradeBook1 = new GradeBook( // invokes constructor
13             "CS101 Introduction to C# Programming" );
14          GradeBook gradeBook2 = new GradeBook( // invokes constructor
15             "CS102 Data Structures in C#" );
```

Fig. 4.13 | GradeBook constructor used to specify the course name at the time each GradeBook object is created. (Part 1 of 2.)

```
16
17          // display initial value of courseName for each GradeBook
18          Console.WriteLine( "gradeBook1 course name is: {0}",
19             gradeBook1.CourseName );
20          Console.WriteLine( "gradeBook2 course name is: {0}",
21             gradeBook2.CourseName );
22       } // end Main
23    } // end class GradeBookTest
```

```
gradeBook1 course name is: CS101 Introduction to C# Programming
gradeBook2 course name is: CS102 Data Structures in C#
```

Fig. 4.13 | GradeBook constructor used to specify the course name at the time each GradeBook object is created. (Part 2 of 2.)

Like methods, constructors also can take arguments. However, an important difference between constructors and methods is that constructors cannot return values—in fact, they cannot specify a return type (not even void). Normally, constructors are declared public. If a class does not include a constructor, the class's instance variables are initialized to their default values. If you declare any constructors for a class, C# will not create a default constructor for that class.

Error-Prevention Tip 4.1

Unless default initialization of your class's instance variables is acceptable, provide a constructor to ensure that your class's instance variables are properly initialized with meaningful values when each new object of your class is created.

Adding the Constructor to Class GradeBook's UML Class Diagram

The UML class diagram of Fig. 4.14 models class GradeBook of Fig. 4.12, which has a constructor that has a courseName parameter of type string. Like operations, the UML models constructors in the third compartment of a class in a class diagram. To distinguish a constructor from a class's operations, the UML places the word "constructor" between guillemets (« and ») before the constructor's name. It is customary to list constructors before other operations in the third compartment.

4.10 Floating-Point Numbers and Type `decimal`

In our next application, we depart temporarily from our GradeBook case study to declare a class called Account that maintains the balance of a bank account. Most account balances

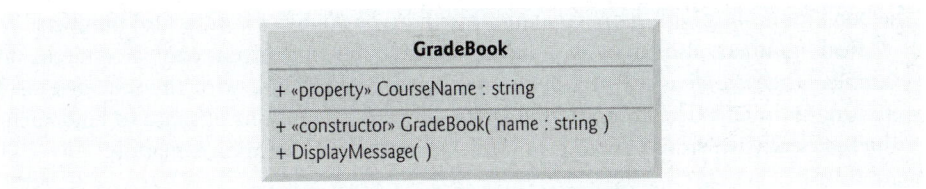

Fig. 4.14 | UML class diagram indicating that class GradeBook has a constructor with a name parameter of type string.

are not whole numbers (e.g., 0, –22 and 1024). For this reason, class `Account` represents the account balance as a real number (i.e., a number with a decimal point, such as 7.33, 0.0975 or 1000.12345). C# provides three simple types for storing real numbers in memory—`float`, *`double`*, and `decimal`. Types `float` and `double` are called *floating-point* types. The primary difference between them and `decimal` is that `decimal` variables store a limited range of real numbers precisely, whereas floating-point variables store only approximations of real numbers, but across a much greater range of values. Also, `double` variables can store numbers with larger magnitude and finer detail (i.e., more digits to the right of the decimal point—also known as the number's *precision*) than `float` variables. A key application of type `decimal` is representing monetary amounts.

Real Number Precision and Memory Requirements

Variables of type `float` represent *single-precision floating-point numbers* and have seven significant digits. Variables of type `double` represent *double-precision floating-point numbers*. These require twice as much memory as `float` variables and provide 15–16 significant digits—approximately double the precision of `float` variables. Furthermore, variables of type `decimal` require twice as much memory as `double` variables and provide 28–29 significant digits. For the range of values required by most applications, variables of type `float` should suffice for approximations, but you can use `double` or `decimal` to "play it safe." In some applications, even variables of type `double` and `decimal` will be inadequate—such applications are beyond the scope of this book.

Most programmers represent floating-point numbers with type `double`. In fact, C# treats all real numbers you type in an application's source code (such as 7.33 and 0.0975) as `double` values by default. Such values in the source code are known as *floating-point literals*. To type a *`decimal` literal*, you must type the letter "M" or "m" at the end of a real number (for example, 7.33M is a `decimal` literal rather than a `double`). Integer literals are implicitly converted into type `float`, `double` or `decimal` when they are assigned to a variable of one of these types. See Appendix L, Simple Types, for the ranges of values for `float`s, `double`s, `decimal`s and all the other simple types.

Although floating-point numbers are not always 100% precise, they have numerous applications. For example, when we speak of a "normal" body temperature of 98.6, we do not need to be precise to a large number of digits. When we read the temperature on a thermometer as 98.6, it may actually be 98.5999473210643. Calling this number simply 98.6 is fine for most applications involving body temperatures. Due to the imprecise nature of floating-point numbers, type `decimal` is preferred over the floating-point types whenever the calculations need to be exact, as with monetary calculations. In cases where approximation is enough, `double` is preferred over type `float` because `double` variables can represent floating-point numbers more accurately. For this reason, we use type `decimal` throughout the book for dealing with monetary amounts and type `double` for other real numbers.

Real numbers also arise as a result of division. In conventional arithmetic, for example, when we divide 10 by 3, the result is 3.3333333…, with the sequence of 3s repeating infinitely. The computer allocates only a fixed amount of space to hold such a value, so clearly the stored floating-point value can be only an approximation.

 Common Programming Error 4.3

Using floating-point numbers in a manner that assumes they are represented precisely can lead to logic errors.

Account Class with an Instance Variable of Type decimal

Our next application (Figs. 4.15–4.16) contains an oversimplified class named Account (Fig. 4.15) that maintains the balance of a bank account. A typical bank services many accounts, each with its own balance, so line 7 declares an instance variable named balance of type decimal. Variable balance is an instance variable because it is declared in the body of the class (lines 6–36) but outside the class's method and property declarations (lines 10–13, 16–19 and 22–35). Every instance (i.e., object) of class Account contains its own copy of balance.

Class Account contains a constructor, a method, and a property. Since it is common for someone opening an account to place money in the account immediately, the constructor (lines 10–13) receives a parameter initialBalance of type decimal that represents the account's starting balance. Line 12 assigns initialBalance to the property Balance, invoking Balance's set accessor to initialize the instance variable balance.

```csharp
1   // Fig. 4.15: Account.cs
2   // Account class with a constructor to
3   // initialize instance variable balance.
4
5   public class Account
6   {
7      private decimal balance; // instance variable that stores the balance
8
9      // constructor
10     public Account( decimal initialBalance )
11     {
12        Balance = initialBalance; // set balance using property
13     } // end Account constructor
14
15     // credit (add) an amount to the account
16     public void Credit( decimal amount )
17     {
18        Balance = Balance + amount; // add amount to balance
19     } // end method Credit
20
21     // a property to get and set the account balance
22     public decimal Balance
23     {
24        get
25        {
26           return balance;
27        } // end get
28        set
29        {
30           // validate that value is greater than or equal to 0;
31           // if it is not, balance is left unchanged
32           if ( value >= 0 )
33              balance = value;
34        } // end set
35     } // end property Balance
36  } // end class Account
```

Fig. 4.15 | Account class with a constructor to initialize instance variable balance.

Method Credit (lines 16–19) does not return any data when it completes its task, so its return type is void. The method receives one parameter named amount—a decimal value that is added to the property Balance. Line 18 uses both the get and set accessors of Balance. The expression Balance + amount invokes property Balance's get accessor to obtain the current value of instance variable balance, then adds amount to it. We then assign the result to instance variable balance by invoking the Balance property's set accessor (thus replacing the prior balance value).

Property Balance (lines 22–35) provides a get accessor, which allows clients of the class (i.e., other classes that use this class) to obtain the value of a particular Account object's balance. The property has type decimal (line 22). Balance also provides an enhanced set accessor.

In Section 4.5, we introduced properties whose set accessors allow clients of a class to modify the value of a private instance variable. In Fig. 4.7, class GradeBook defines property CourseName's set accessor to assign the value received in its parameter value to instance variable courseName (line 19). This CourseName property does not ensure that courseName contains only valid data.

The application of Figs. 4.15–4.16 enhances the set accessor of class Account's property Balance to perform this validation (also known as *validity checking*). Line 32 (Fig. 4.15) ensures that value is non-negative. If the value is greater than or equal to 0, the amount stored in value is assigned to instance variable balance in line 33. Otherwise, balance is left unchanged.

AccountTest Class to Use Class Account

Class AccountTest (Fig. 4.16) creates two Account objects (lines 10–11) and initializes them respectively with 50.00M and -7.53M (the decimal literals representing the real numbers 50.00 and -7.53). Note that the Account constructor (lines 10–13 of Fig. 4.15) references property Balance to initialize balance. In previous examples, the benefit of

```
 1   // Fig. 4.16: AccountTest.cs
 2   // Create and manipulate an Account object.
 3   using System;
 4
 5   public class AccountTest
 6   {
 7      // Main method begins execution of C# application
 8      public static void Main( string[] args )
 9      {
10         Account account1 = new Account( 50.00M ); // create Account object
11         Account account2 = new Account( -7.53M ); // create Account object
12
13         // display initial balance of each object using a property
14         Console.WriteLine( "account1 balance: {0:C}",
15            account1.Balance ); // display Balance property
16         Console.WriteLine( "account2 balance: {0:C}\n",
17            account2.Balance ); // display Balance property
18
```

Fig. 4.16 | Create and manipulate an Account object. (Part 1 of 2.)

```
19          decimal depositAmount; // deposit amount read from user
20
21          // prompt and obtain user input
22          Console.Write( "Enter deposit amount for account1: " );
23          depositAmount = Convert.ToDecimal( Console.ReadLine() );
24          Console.WriteLine( "adding {0:C} to account1 balance\n",
25             depositAmount );
26          account1.Credit( depositAmount ); // add to account1 balance
27
28          // display balances
29          Console.WriteLine( "account1 balance: {0:C}",
30             account1.Balance );
31          Console.WriteLine( "account2 balance: {0:C}\n",
32             account2.Balance );
33
34          // prompt and obtain user input
35          Console.Write( "Enter deposit amount for account2: " );
36          depositAmount = Convert.ToDecimal( Console.ReadLine() );
37          Console.WriteLine( "adding {0:C} to account2 balance\n",
38             depositAmount );
39          account2.Credit( depositAmount ); // add to account2 balance
40
41          // display balances
42          Console.WriteLine( "account1 balance: {0:C}", account1.Balance );
43          Console.WriteLine( "account2 balance: {0:C}", account2.Balance );
44       } // end Main
45    } // end class AccountTest
```

```
account1 balance: $50.00
account2 balance: $0.00

Enter deposit amount for account1: 49.99
adding $49.99 to account1 balance

account1 balance: $99.99
account2 balance: $0.00

Enter deposit amount for account2: 123.21
adding $123.21 to account2 balance

account1 balance: $99.99
account2 balance: $123.21
```

Fig. 4.16 | Create and manipulate an Account object. (Part 2 of 2.)

referencing the property in the constructor was not evident. Now, however, the constructor takes advantage of the validation provided by the set accessor of the Balance property. The constructor simply assigns a value to Balance rather than duplicating the set accessor's validation code. When line 11 of Fig. 4.16 passes an initial balance of -7.53 to the Account constructor, the constructor passes this value to the set accessor of property Balance, where the actual initialization occurs. This value is less than 0, so the set accessor does not modify balance, leaving this instance variable with its default value of 0.

Lines 14–17 in Fig. 4.16 output the balance in each `Account` by using the `Account`'s `Balance` property. When `Balance` is used for `account1` (line 15), the value of `account1`'s balance is returned by the `get` accessor in line 26 of Fig. 4.15 and displayed by the `Console.WriteLine` statement (Fig. 4.16, lines 14–15). Similarly, when property `Balance` is called for `account2` from line 17, the value of the `account2`'s balance is returned from line 26 of Fig. 4.15 and displayed by the `Console.WriteLine` statement (Fig. 4.16, lines 16–17). Note that the balance of `account2` is 0 because the constructor ensured that the account could not begin with a negative balance. The value is output by `WriteLine` with the format item `{0:C}`, which formats the account balance as a monetary amount. The : after the 0 indicates that the next character represents a *format specifier*, and the C format specifier after the : specifies a monetary amount (C is for currency). The cultural settings on the user's machine determine the format for displaying monetary amounts. For example, in the United States, 50 displays as $50.00. In Germany, 50 displays as 50,00€. Figure 4.17 lists a few other format specifiers in addition to C.

Line 19 declares local variable `depositAmount` to store each deposit amount entered by the user. Unlike the instance variable `balance` in class `Account`, the local variable `depositAmount` in `Main` is *not* initialized to 0 by default. However, this variable does not need to be initialized here because its value will be determined by the user's input.

Line 22 prompts the user to enter a deposit amount for `account1`. Line 23 obtains the input from the user by calling the `Console` class's `ReadLine` method, and then passing the `string` entered by the user to the `Convert` class's ***ToDecimal*** method, which returns the `decimal` value in this `string`. Lines 24–25 display the deposit amount. Line 26 calls object `account1`'s `Credit` method and supplies `depositAmount` as the method's argument. When the method is called, the argument's value is assigned to parameter `amount` of method

Format Specifier	Description
C or c	Formats the string as currency. Precedes the number with an appropriate currency symbol ($ in the US). Separates digits with an appropriate separator character (comma in the US) and sets the number of decimal places to two by default.
D or d	Formats the string as a decimal. Displays number as an integer.
N or n	Formats the string with commas and a default of two decimal places.
E or e	Formats the number using scientific notation with a default of six decimal places.
F or f	Formats the string with a fixed number of decimal places (two by default).
G or g	General. Formats the number normally with decimal places or using scientific notation, depending on context. If a format item does not contain a format specifier, format G is assumed implicitly.
X or x	Formats the string as hexadecimal.

Fig. 4.17 | `string` format specifiers.

Credit (lines 16–19 of Fig. 4.15), then method Credit adds that value to the balance (line 18 of Fig. 4.15). Lines 29–32 (Fig. 4.16) output the balances of both Accounts again to show that only account1's balance changed.

Line 35 prompts the user to enter a deposit amount for account2. Line 36 obtains the input from the user by calling Console class's ReadLine method, and passing the return value to the Convert class's ToDecimal method. Lines 37–38 display the deposit amount. Line 39 calls object account2's Credit method and supplies depositAmount as the method's argument, then method Credit adds that value to the balance. Finally, lines 42–43 output the balances of both Accounts again to show that only account2's balance changed.

set and get Accessors with Different Access Modifiers

By default, the get and set accessors of a property have the same access as the property—for example, for a public property, the accessors are public. It is possible to declare the get and set accessors with different access modifiers. In this case, one of the accessors must implicitly have the same access as the property and the other must be declared with a more restrictive access modifier than the property. For example, in a public property, the get accessor might be public and the set accessor might be private. We demonstrate this feature in Section 9.6.

Error-Prevention Tip 4.2

The benefits of data integrity are not automatic simply because instance variables are made private—you must provide appropriate validity checking and report the errors.

Error-Prevention Tip 4.3

set accessors that set the values of private data should verify that the intended new values are proper; if they are not, the set accessors should leave the instance variables unchanged and generate an error. We demonstrate how to gracefully generate errors in Chapter 12, Exception Handling.

UML Class Diagram for Class Account

The UML class diagram in Fig. 4.18 models class Account of Fig. 4.15. The diagram models the Balance property as a UML attribute of type decimal (because the corresponding C# property had type decimal). The diagram models class Account's constructor with a parameter initialBalance of type decimal in the third compartment of the class. The diagram models operation Credit in the third compartment with an amount parameter of type decimal (because the corresponding method has an amount parameter of C# type decimal).

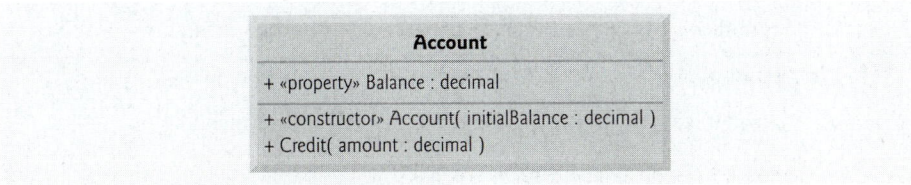

Fig. 4.18 | UML class diagram indicating that class Account has a public Balance property of type decimal, a constructor and a method.

4.11 (Optional) Software Engineering Case Study: Identifying the Classes in the ATM Requirements Document

Now we begin designing the ATM system that we introduced in Chapter 3. In this section, we identify the classes that are needed to build the ATM system by analyzing the nouns and noun phrases that appear in the requirements document. We introduce UML class diagrams to model the relationships between these classes. This is an important first step in defining the structure of our system.

Identifying the Classes in a System

We begin our object-oriented design (OOD) process by identifying the classes required to build the ATM system. We will eventually describe these classes using UML class diagrams and implement these classes in C#. First, we review the requirements document of Section 3.10 and find key nouns and noun phrases to help us identify classes that comprise the ATM system. We may decide that some of these nouns and noun phrases are attributes of other classes in the system. We may also conclude that some of the nouns and noun phrases do not correspond to parts of the system and thus should not be modeled at all. Additional classes may become apparent to us as we proceed through the design process. Figure 4.19 lists the nouns and noun phrases in the requirements document.

We create classes only for the nouns and noun phrases that have significance in the ATM system. We do not need to model "bank" as a class, because the bank is not a part of the ATM system—the bank simply wants us to build the ATM. "User" and "customer" also represent entities outside of the system—they are important because they interact with our ATM system, but we do not need to model them as classes in the ATM system. Recall that we modeled an ATM user (i.e., a bank customer) as the actor in the use case diagram of Fig. 3.31.

We do not model "$20 bill" or "deposit envelope" as classes. These are physical objects in the real world, but they are not part of what is being automated. We can adequately represent the presence of bills in the system using an attribute of the class that models the cash dispenser. (We assign attributes to classes in Section 5.14.) For example,

Nouns and noun phrases in the requirements document		
bank	money / funds	account number
ATM	screen	PIN
user	keypad	bank database
customer	cash dispenser	balance inquiry
transaction	$20 bill / cash	withdrawal
account	deposit slot	deposit
balance	deposit envelope	

Fig. 4.19 | Nouns and noun phrases in the requirements document.

the cash dispenser maintains a count of the number of bills it contains. The requirements document does not say anything about what the system should do with deposit envelopes after it receives them. We can assume that simply acknowledging the receipt of an envelope—an *operation* performed by the class that models the deposit slot—is sufficient to represent the presence of an envelope in the system. (We assign operations to classes in Section 7.15.)

In our simplified ATM system, representing various amounts of "money," including the "balance" of an account, as attributes of other classes seems most appropriate. Likewise, the nouns "account number" and "PIN" represent significant pieces of information in the ATM system. They are important attributes of a bank account. They do not, however, exhibit behaviors. Thus, we can most appropriately model them as attributes of an account class.

Though the requirements document frequently describes a "transaction" in a general sense, we do not model the broad notion of a financial transaction at this time. Instead, we model the three types of transactions (i.e., "balance inquiry," "withdrawal" and "deposit") as individual classes. These classes possess specific attributes needed to execute the transactions they represent. For example, a withdrawal needs to know the amount of money the user wants to withdraw. A balance inquiry, however, does not require any additional data. Furthermore, the three transaction classes exhibit unique behaviors. A withdrawal involves dispensing cash to the user, whereas a deposit involves receiving a deposit envelope from the user. [*Note:* In Section 11.9, we "factor out" common features of all transactions into a general "transaction" class using the object-oriented concepts of abstract classes and inheritance.]

We determine the classes for our system based on the remaining nouns and noun phrases from Fig. 4.19. Each of these refers to one or more of the following:

- ATM
- screen
- keypad
- cash dispenser
- deposit slot
- account
- bank database
- balance inquiry
- withdrawal
- deposit

The elements of this list are likely to be classes we will need to implement our system, although it's too early in our design process to claim that this list is complete.

We can now model the classes in our system based on the list we have created. We capitalize class names in the design process—a UML convention—as we will do when we write the actual C# code that implements our design. If the name of a class contains more than one word, we run the words together and capitalize each word (e.g., `MultipleWordName`). Using these conventions, we create classes `ATM`, `Screen`, `Keypad`, `CashDispenser`, `DepositSlot`,

Account, BankDatabase, BalanceInquiry, Withdrawal and Deposit. We construct our system using all of these classes as building blocks. Before we begin building the system, however, we must gain a better understanding of how the classes relate to one another.

Modeling Classes

The UML enables us to model, via *class diagrams*, the classes in the ATM system and their interrelationships. Figure 4.20 represents class ATM. In the UML, each class is modeled as a rectangle with three compartments. The top compartment contains the name of the class, centered horizontally and appearing in boldface. The middle compartment contains the class's attributes. (We discuss attributes in Section 5.14 and Section 6.10.) The bottom compartment contains the class's operations (discussed in Section 7.15). In Fig. 4.20, the middle and bottom compartments are empty, because we have not yet determined this class's attributes and operations.

Class diagrams also show the relationships between the classes of the system. Figure 4.21 shows how our classes ATM and Withdrawal relate to one another. For the moment, we choose to model only this subset of the ATM classes for simplicity. We present a more complete class diagram later in this section. Notice that the rectangles representing classes in this diagram are not subdivided into compartments. The UML allows the suppression of class attributes and operations in this manner, when appropriate, to create more readable diagrams. Such a diagram is said to be an *elided diagram*—one in which some information, such as the contents of the second and third compartments, is not modeled. We will place information in these compartments in Section 5.14 and Section 7.15.

In Fig. 4.21, the solid line that connects the two classes represents an *association*—a relationship between classes. The numbers near each end of the line are *multiplicity* values, which indicate how many objects of each class participate in the association. In this case, following the line from one end to the other reveals that, at any given moment, one ATM object participates in an association with either zero or one Withdrawal objects—zero if the current user is not performing a transaction or has requested a different type of transaction, and one if the user has requested a withdrawal. The UML can model many types of multiplicity. Figure 4.22 explains the multiplicity types.

An association can be named. For example, the word Executes above the line connecting classes ATM and Withdrawal in Fig. 4.21 indicates the name of that association.

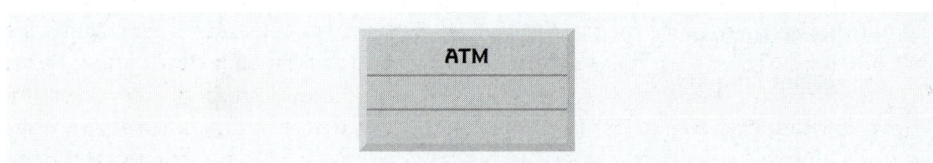

Fig. 4.20 | Representing a class in the UML using a class diagram.

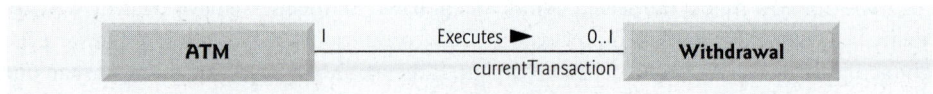

Fig. 4.21 | Class diagram showing an association among classes.

Symbol	Meaning
0	None
1	One
m	An integer value
0..1	Zero or one
m, n	m or n
$m..n$	At least m, but not more than n
*	Any nonnegative integer (zero or more)
0..*	Zero or more (identical to *)
1..*	One or more

Fig. 4.22 | Multiplicity types.

This part of the diagram reads "one object of class ATM executes zero or one objects of class Withdrawal." Note that association names are directional, as indicated by the filled arrowhead—so it would be improper, for example, to read the preceding association from right to left as "zero or one objects of class Withdrawal execute one object of class ATM."

The word currentTransaction at the Withdrawal end of the association line in Fig. 4.21 is a *role name*, which identifies the role the Withdrawal object plays in its relationship with the ATM. A role name adds meaning to an association between classes by identifying the role a class plays in the context of an association. A class can play several roles in the same system. For example, in a college personnel system, a person may play the role of "professor" when relating to students. The same person may take on the role of "colleague" when participating in a relationship with another professor, and "coach" when coaching student athletes. In Fig. 4.21, the role name currentTransaction indicates that the Withdrawal object participating in the Executes association with an object of class ATM represents the transaction currently being processed by the ATM. In other contexts, a Withdrawal object may take on other roles (e.g., the previous transaction). Notice that we do not specify a role name for the ATM end of the Executes association. Role names are often omitted in class diagrams when the meaning of an association is clear without them.

In addition to indicating simple relationships, associations can specify more complex relationships, such as objects of one class being composed of objects of other classes. Consider a real-world automated teller machine. What "pieces" does a manufacturer put together to build a working ATM? Our requirements document tells us that the ATM is composed of a screen, a keypad, a cash dispenser and a deposit slot.

In Fig. 4.23, the *solid diamonds* attached to the association lines of class ATM indicate that class ATM has a *composition* relationship with classes Screen, Keypad, CashDispenser and DepositSlot. Composition implies a whole/part relationship. The class that has the composition symbol (the solid diamond) on its end of the association line is the whole (in this case, ATM), and the classes on the other end of the association lines are the parts—in this case, classes Screen, Keypad, CashDispenser and DepositSlot. The compositions in

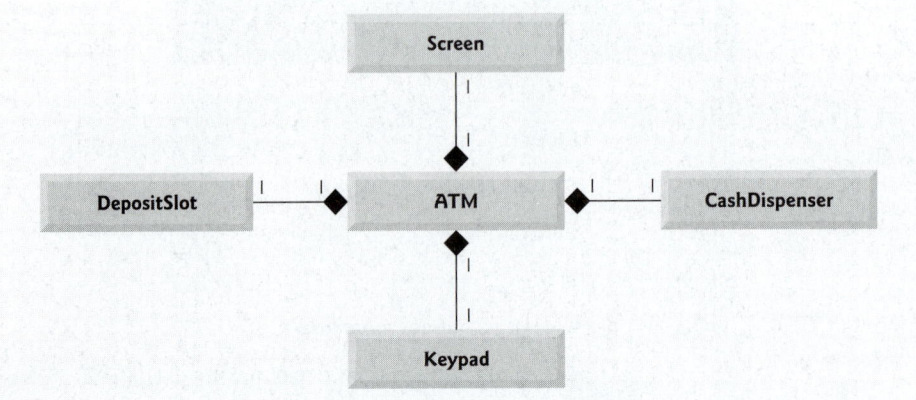

Fig. 4.23 | Class diagram showing composition relationships.

Fig. 4.23 indicate that an object of class ATM is formed from one object of class Screen, one object of class CashDispenser, one object of class Keypad and one object of class DepositSlot—the ATM "has a" screen, a keypad, a cash dispenser and a deposit slot. The *has-a relationship* defines composition. (We will see in the Software Engineering Case Study section in Chapter 11 that the *is-a* relationship defines inheritance.)

According to the UML specification, composition relationships have the following properties:

1. Only one class in the relationship can represent the whole (i.e., the diamond can be placed on only one end of the association line). For example, either the screen is part of the ATM or the ATM is part of the screen, but the screen and the ATM cannot both represent the whole in the relationship.

2. The parts in the composition relationship exist only as long as the whole, and the whole is responsible for the creation and destruction of its parts. For example, the act of constructing an ATM includes manufacturing its parts. Furthermore, if the ATM is destroyed, its screen, keypad, cash dispenser and deposit slot are also destroyed.

3. A part may belong to only one whole at a time, although the part may be removed and attached to another whole, which then assumes responsibility for the part.

The solid diamonds in our class diagrams indicate composition relationships that fulfill these three properties. If a "has-a" relationship does not satisfy one or more of these criteria, the UML specifies that hollow diamonds be attached to the ends of association lines to indicate *aggregation*—a weaker form of composition. For example, a personal computer and a computer monitor participate in an aggregation relationship—the computer "has a" monitor, but the two parts can exist independently, and the same monitor can be attached to multiple computers at once, thus violating the second and third properties of composition.

Figure 4.24 shows a class diagram for the ATM system. This diagram models most of the classes that we identified earlier in this section, as well as the associations between them that we can infer from the requirements document. [*Note:* Classes BalanceInquiry and Deposit participate in associations similar to those of class Withdrawal, so we have chosen

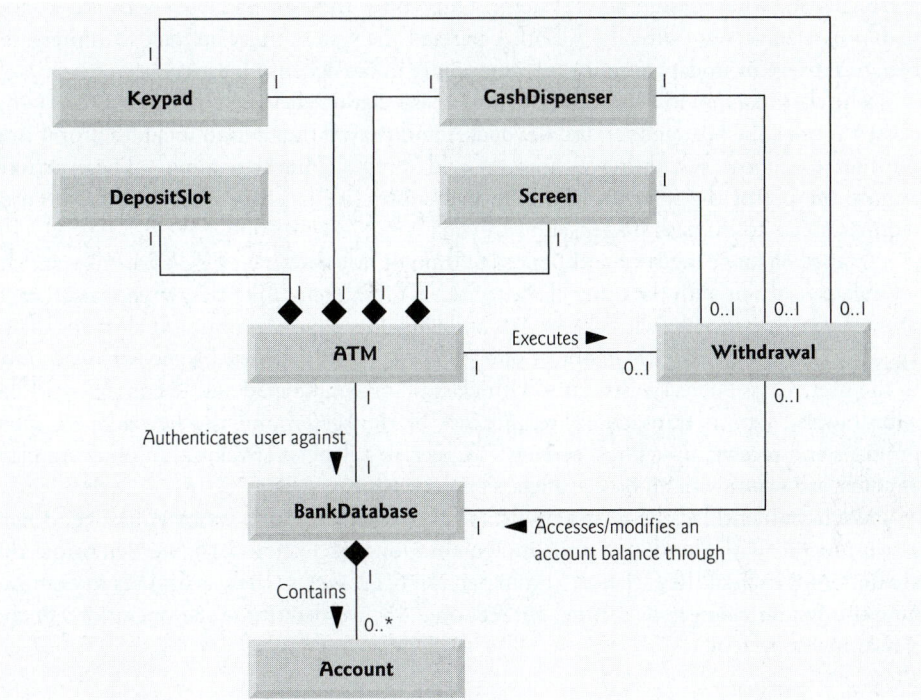

Fig. 4.24 | Class diagram for the ATM system model.

to omit them from this diagram for simplicity. In Chapter 11, we expand our class diagram to include all the classes in the ATM system.]

Figure 4.24 presents a graphical model of the structure of the ATM system. This class diagram includes classes BankDatabase and Account, and several associations that were not present in either Fig. 4.21 or Fig. 4.23. The class diagram shows that class ATM has a *one-to-one relationship* with class BankDatabase—one ATM object authenticates users against one BankDatabase object. In Fig. 4.24, we also model the fact that the bank's database contains information about many accounts—one object of class BankDatabase participates in a composition relationship with zero or more objects of class Account. Recall from Fig. 4.22 that the multiplicity value 0..* at the Account end of the association between class BankDatabase and class Account indicates that zero or more objects of class Account take part in the association. Class BankDatabase has a *one-to-many relationship* with class Account— the BankDatabase can contain many Accounts. Similarly, class Account has a *many-to-one relationship* with class BankDatabase—there can be many Accounts in the BankDatabase. Recall from Fig. 4.22 that the multiplicity value * is identical to 0..*.]

Figure 4.24 also indicates that if the user is performing a withdrawal, "one object of class Withdrawal accesses/modifies an account balance through one object of class BankDatabase." We could have created an association directly between class Withdrawal and class Account. The requirements document, however, states that the "ATM must interact with the bank's account information database" to perform transactions. A bank account contains sensitive information, and systems engineers must always consider the security of personal data when designing a system. Thus, only the `BankDatabase` can access and manipulate an account directly. All other parts of the system must interact with the database to retrieve or update account information (e.g., an account balance).

The class diagram in Fig. 4.24 also models associations between class `Withdrawal` and classes `Screen`, `CashDispenser` and `Keypad`. A withdrawal transaction includes prompting the user to choose a withdrawal amount and receiving numeric input. These actions require the use of the screen and the keypad, respectively. Dispensing cash to the user requires access to the cash dispenser.

Classes `BalanceInquiry` and `Deposit`, though not shown in Fig. 4.24, take part in several associations with the other classes of the ATM system. Like class `Withdrawal`, each of these classes associates with classes `ATM` and `BankDatabase`. An object of class `Balance-Inquiry` also associates with an object of class `Screen` to display the balance of an account to the user. Class `Deposit` associates with classes `Screen`, `Keypad` and `DepositSlot`. Like withdrawals, deposit transactions require use of the screen and the keypad to display prompts and receive inputs, respectively. To receive a deposit envelope, an object of class `Deposit` associates with an object of class `DepositSlot`.

We have identified the classes in our ATM system, although we may discover others as we proceed with the design and implementation. In Section 5.14, we determine the attributes for each of these classes, and in Section 6.10, we use these attributes to examine how the system changes over time. In Section 7.15, we determine the operations of the classes in our system.

Software Engineering Case Study Self-Review Exercises

4.1 Suppose we have a class `Car` that represents a car. Think of some of the different pieces that a manufacturer would put together to produce a whole car. Create a class diagram (similar to Fig. 4.23) that models some of the composition relationships of class `Car`.

4.2 Suppose we have a class `File` that represents an electronic document in a stand-alone, non-networked computer represented by class `Computer`. What sort of association exists between class `Computer` and class `File`?
  a) Class `Computer` has a one-to-one relationship with class `File`.
  b) Class `Computer` has a many-to-one relationship with class `File`.
  c) Class `Computer` has a one-to-many relationship with class `File`.
  d) Class `Computer` has a many-to-many relationship with class `File`.

4.3 State whether the following statement is *true* or *false*. If *false*, explain why: A UML class diagram in which a class's second and third compartments are not modeled is said to be an elided diagram.

4.4 Modify the class diagram of Fig. 4.24 to include class `Deposit` instead of class `Withdrawal`.

Answers to Software Engineering Case Study Self-Review Exercises

4.1 Figure 4.25 presents a class diagram that shows some of the composition relationships of a class `Car`.

4.2 c. In a computer network, this relationship could be many-to-many.

4.3 True.

4.4 Figure 4.26 presents a class diagram for the ATM including class `Deposit` instead of class `Withdrawal` (as in Fig. 4.24). Note that class `Deposit` does not associate with class `CashDispenser`, but does associate with class `DepositSlot`.

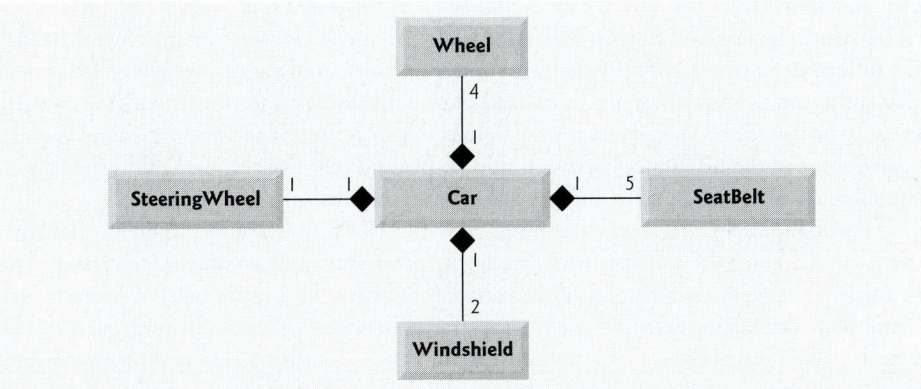

Fig. 4.25 | Class diagram showing some composition relationships of a class Car.

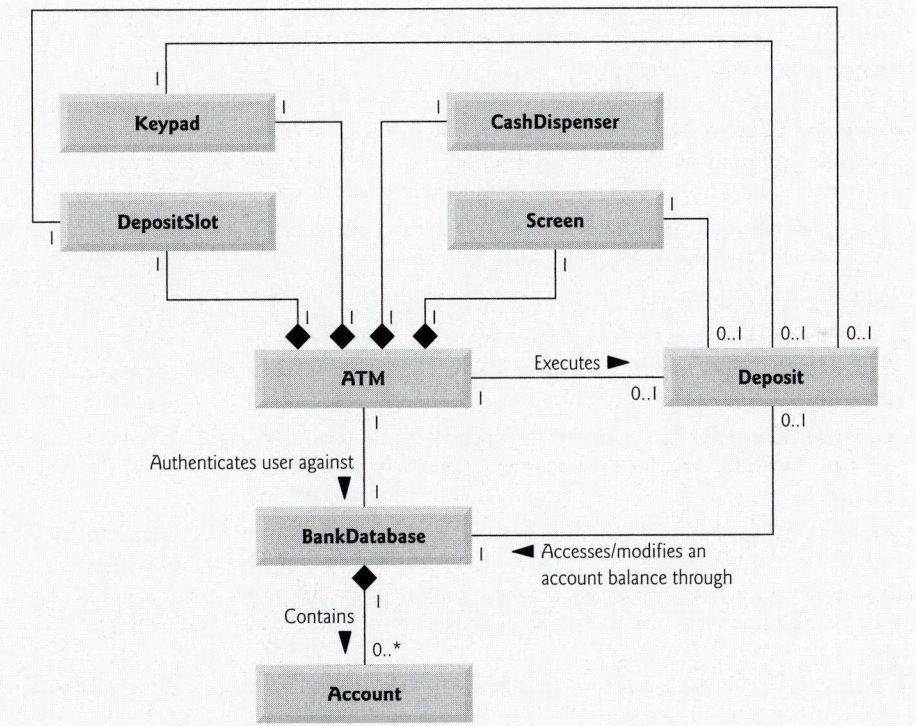

Fig. 4.26 | Class diagram for the ATM system model including class Deposit.

4.12 Wrap-Up

In this chapter, you learned the basic object-oriented concepts of classes, objects, methods, instance variables and properties—these will be used in most substantial C# applications you create. You learned how to declare instance variables of a class to maintain data for each object of the class, how to declare methods that operate on that data, and how to declare properties to obtain and set that data. We demonstrated how to call a method to tell it to perform its task and how to pass information to methods as arguments. We discussed the difference between a local variable of a method and an instance variable of a class and that only instance variables are initialized automatically. You also learned how to use a class's constructor to specify the initial values for an object's instance variables. We discussed some of the differences between value types and reference types. You learned about the value types `float`, `double` and `decimal` for storing real numbers.

Throughout the chapter, we showed how the UML can be used to create class diagrams that model the constructors, methods, properties and attributes of classes. You learned the value of declaring instance variables `private`, and using `public` properties to manipulate them. For example, we demonstrated how `set` accessors in properties can be used to validate an object's data and ensure that the object is maintained in a consistent state. In the next chapter we begin our introduction to control statements, which specify the order in which an application's actions are performed. You will use these in your methods to specify how they should perform their tasks.

Summary

Section 4.2 Classes, Objects, Methods, Properties and Instance Variables

- Methods perform tasks. Each method describes the mechanisms that actually perform its tasks. The method hides from its user the complex tasks that it performs.

- The application unit that houses a method is called a class. A class may contain one or more methods that are designed to perform the class's tasks.

- A method can perform a task and may return a result.

- An instance of a class is called an object.

- Each message sent to an object is known as a method call and tells a method of the object to perform its task.

- Each method can specify parameters that represent additional information the method requires to perform its task correctly. A method call supplies values—called arguments—for the method's parameters.

- An object has attributes that are carried with the object as it is used in an application. These attributes are specified as part of the object's class. Attributes are specified in classes by fields.

- An object has properties for accessing attributes. Properties contain `get` accessors for reading attributes, and `set` accessors for storing into them.

Section 4.3 Declaring a Class with a Method and Instantiating an Object of a Class

- Keyword `public` is an access modifier.

- Every class declaration contains keyword `class` followed immediately by the class's name.

- A method declaration that begins with keyword `public` indicates that the method is "available to the public"—that is, it can be called by other classes declared outside the class declaration.

- Keyword `void` indicates that a method will not return any information when it completes its task.

- By convention, method names begin with an uppercase first letter, and all subsequent words in the name begin with a capital first letter.

- Empty parentheses following a method name indicate that the method does not require any parameters to perform its task.
- Every method's body is delimited by left and right braces ({ and }).
- The body of a method contains statements that perform the method's task. After the statements execute, the method has completed its task.
- When you attempt to execute an application, C# looks for a Main method to begin execution.
- Typically, you cannot call a method that belongs to another class until you create an object of that class.
- Object creation expressions begin with the new operator and create new objects.
- To call a method of an object, follow the variable name with a dot operator (.), the method name and a set of parentheses containing the method's arguments.
- In the UML, each class is modeled in a class diagram as a rectangle with three compartments. The top compartment contains the name of the class, centered horizontally in boldface. The middle compartment contains the class's attributes, which correspond to fields in C#. The bottom compartment contains the class's operations, which correspond to methods and constructors in C#.
- The UML models operations by listing the operation name, followed by a set of parentheses. A plus sign (+) in front of the operation name indicates that the operation is a public operation in the UML (i.e., a public method in C#). The plus sign is called the public visibility symbol.

Section 4.4 Declaring a Method with a Parameter

- Methods often require additional information to perform their tasks. Such additional information is provided to methods via arguments in method calls.
- Console method ReadLine reads characters until a newline character is encountered, then returns the characters as a string.
- A method that requires data to perform its task must specify this in its declaration by placing additional information in the method's parameter list.
- Each parameter must specify both a type and an identifier.
- At the time a method is called, its arguments are assigned to its parameters. Then the method body uses the parameter variables to access the argument values.
- A method can specify multiple parameters by separating each parameter from the next with a comma.
- The number of arguments in the method call must match the number of parameters in the method declaration's parameter list. Also, the argument types in the method call must be consistent with the types of the corresponding parameters in the method's declaration.
- The UML models a parameter of an operation by listing the parameter name, followed by a colon and the parameter type between the parentheses following the operation name.
- Unfortunately, the UML does not provide types that correspond to every C# type. For this reason, and to avoid confusion between UML types and C# types, we use only C# types in our UML diagrams.
- There is a special relationship between classes that are compiled in the same project. By default, such classes are considered to be in the same namespace. A using directive is not required when one class in a namespace uses another in the same namespace.
- A using directive is not required if you always refer to a class with its fully qualified class name.

Section 4.5 Instance Variables and Properties

- Variables declared in the body of a particular method are known as local variables and can be used only in that method.

- A class normally consists of one or more methods that manipulate the attributes (data) that belong to a particular object of the class. Attributes are represented as instance variables in a class declaration. Such variables are declared inside a class declaration but outside the bodies of the class's method declarations.

- Each object (instance) of a class has a separate copy of each variable instance.

- Most instance variable declarations are preceded with the `private` access modifier. Variables or methods declared with access modifier `private` are accessible only to methods (and properties) of the class in which they are declared.

- Declaring instance variables with access modifier `private` is known as information hiding.

- Properties contain accessors that handle the details of modifying and returning data.

- Properties provide a controlled way for programmers to "get" (i.e., retrieve) the value in an instance variable and "set" (i.e., modify) the value in an instance variable.

- A property declaration can contain a `get` accessor, a `set` accessor or both. The `get` accessor typically enables a client to read the value of a `private` instance variable. The `set` accessor typically enables a client to modify that instance variable's value.

- After defining a property, you can use it the same way as you use a variable.

- Properties can scrutinize attempts to modify an instance variable's value (known as data validation), thus ensuring that the new value for that instance variable is valid.

- Using properties would seem to violate the notion of `private` data. However, a `set` accessor can provide data validation capabilities to ensure that the value is set properly; `get` and `set` accessors can translate between the format of the data used by the client and the format used in the `private` instance variable.

- A benefit of fields is that all the methods and properties of the class can use the fields. Another distinction between a field and a local variable is that a field has a default initial value provided by C# when you do not specify the field's initial value, but a local variable does not.

- The default value for a field of type `string` is `null`.

Section 4.6 UML Class Diagram with a Property

- We model properties in the UML as attributes, preceded by the word "property" in guillemets (« and »). Using descriptive words in guillemets (called stereotypes in the UML) helps distinguish properties from other attributes.

- A class diagram helps you design a class, so it is not required to show every implementation detail of the class. Since an instance variable that is manipulated by a property is really an implementation detail of that property, our class diagrams do not show instance variables.

- `private` class members are preceded by the minus (-) sign (the private visibility symbol) in the UML.

- The UML represents instance variables and properties as attributes by listing the attribute name, followed by a colon and the attribute type.

Section 4.8 Value Types vs. Reference Types

- Types are divided into two categories—value types and reference types.

- A variable of a value type contains data of that type.

- A variable of a reference type (sometimes called a reference) contains the address of a location in memory where an object is stored.

- Reference type instance variables are initialized by default to the value `null`.

Section 4.9 Initializing Objects with Constructors

- A constructor can be used to initialize an object of a class when the object is created.

- If no constructor is provided for a class, the compiler provides a default constructor with no parameters.

- Like operations, the UML models constructors in the third compartment of a class diagram. To distinguish a constructor from a class's operations, the UML places the word "constructor" between guillemets (« and ») before the constructor's name.

- Constructors can specify parameters but cannot specify return types.

Section 4.10 Floating-Point Numbers and Type `decimal`

- A real number is a number with a decimal point, such as 7.33, 0.0975 or 1000.12345. C# provides three simple types for storing real numbers in memory—`float`, `double`, and `decimal`.

- Types `float` and `double` are called floating-point types. The primary difference between them is that `decimal` variables store a limited range of real numbers precisely, but floating-point variables store approximations of real numbers across a much greater range.

- Variables of type `float` represent single-precision floating-point numbers and have seven significant digits. Variables of type `double` represent double-precision floating-point numbers. These require twice as much memory as `float` variables and provide 15–16 significant digits—approximately double the precision of `float` variables. Furthermore, variables of type `decimal` require twice as much memory as `double` variables and provide 28–29 significant digits.

- Real number values that appear in source code are known as floating-point literals and are type `double` by default.

- Convert method ToDecimal extracts a `decimal` value from a `string`.

- The : in a format item indicates that the next character represents a format specifier.

- The `C` format specifier specifies a monetary amount (`C` is for currency).

- Properties can be used to ensure that an object's instance variables contain valid data.

- It is possible to declare the `get` and `set` accessors of a property with different access modifiers. In this case, one of the accessors must implicitly have the same access as the property and the other must be declared with a more restrictive access modifier than the property; `private` is more restrictive than `public`.

Terminology

access modifier
attribute (UML)
`C` format specifier
calling method
class
class declaration
`class` keyword
client of an object or a class
compartment in a class diagram (UML)
constructor
create an object

`decimal` simple type
default constructor
default value
dot (.) operator
double-precision floating-point number
`double` simple type
field
`float` simple type
floating-point number
format specifier
get accessor

global namespace	precision of a floating-point value
guillemets, « and » (UML)	precision of a formatted floating-point number
information hiding	property
instance of a class (object)	`private` access modifier
instance variable	`public` access modifier
instantiate (or create) an object	`public` method
invoke a method	Read method of class `Console`
local variable	refer to an object
message	reference
method	reference type
method header	send a message
new operator	set accessor
`null` keyword	single-precision floating-point number
object (or instance)	`ToDecimal` method of class `Convert`
object creation expression	UML class diagram
operation (UML)	UML visibility symbol
parameter	`void` keyword
parameter list	

Self-Review Exercises

4.1 Fill in the blanks in each of the following:

a) A house is to a blueprint as a(n) _____ is to a class.

b) Every class declaration contains keyword _____ followed immediately by the class's name.

c) Operator _____ creates an object of the class specified to the right of the keyword.

d) Each parameter must specify both a(n) _____ and a(n) _____.

e) By default, classes that are not explicitly declared in a namespace are implicitly placed in the _____.

f) When each object of a class maintains its own copy of an attribute, the field that represents the attribute is also known as a(n) _____.

g) C# provides three simple types for storing real numbers—_____, _____ and _____.

h) Variables of type `double` represent _____ floating-point numbers.

i) `Convert` method _____ returns a `decimal` value.

j) Keyword `public` is a(n) _____.

k) Return type _____ indicates that a method will not return any information when it completes its task.

l) `Console` method _____ reads characters until a newline character is encountered, then returns those characters (not including the newline) as a `string`.

m) A(n) _____ is not required if you always refer to a class with its fully qualified class name.

n) Variables of type `float` represent _____ floating-point numbers.

o) The format specifier _____ is used to display values in a monetary format.

p) Types are either _____ types or _____ types.

4.2 State whether each of the following is *true* or *false*. If *false*, explain why.

a) By convention, method names begin with a lowercase first letter and all subsequent words in the name begin with a capital first letter.

b) A property's `get` accessor enables a client to modify the value of the instance variable associated with the property.

c) A using directive is not required when one class in a namespace uses another in the same namespace.

d) Empty parentheses following a method name in a method declaration indicate that the method does not require any parameters to perform its task.

e) After defining a property, you can use it the same way you use a method, but with empty parentheses because no arguments are passed to a property.

f) Variables or methods declared with access modifier `private` are accessible only to methods and properties of the class in which they are declared.

g) Variables declared in the body of a particular method are known as instance variables and can be used in all methods of the class.

h) A property declaration must contain both a `get` accessor and a `set` accessor.

i) The body of any method or property is delimited by left and right braces.

j) Local variables are initialized by default.

k) Reference-type instance variables are initialized by default to the value `null`.

l) Any class that contains `public static void Main( string[] args )` can be used to execute an application.

m) The number of arguments in the method call must match the number of parameters in the method declaration's parameter list.

n) Real number values that appear in source code are known as floating-point literals and are of type `float` by default.

4.3 What is the difference between a local variable and an instance variable?

4.4 Explain the purpose of a method parameter. What is the difference between a parameter and an argument?

Answers to Self-Review Exercises

4.1 a) object. b) `class`. c) `new`. d) type, name. e) global namespace. f) instance variable. g) `float`, `double`, `decimal`. h) double-precision. i) `ToDecimal`. j) access modifier. k) `void`. l) `ReadLine`. m) using directive. n) single-precision. o) `C`. p) value, reference.

4.2 a) False. By convention, method names begin with an uppercase first letter and all subsequent words in the name begin with a capital first letter. b) False. A property's `get` accessor enables a client to retrieve the value of the instance variable associated with the property. A property's `set` accessor enables a client to modify the value of the instance variable associated with the property. c) True. d) True. e) False. After defining a property, you can use it the same way you use a variable. f) True. g) False. Such variables are called local variables and can be used only in the method in which they are declared. h) False. A property declaration can contain a `get` accessor, a `set` accessor or both. i) True. j) False. Instance variables are initialized by default. k) True. l) True. m) True. n) False. Such literals are of type `double` by default.

4.3 A local variable is declared in the body of a method and can be used only from the point at which it is declared through the end of the method declaration. An instance variable is declared in a class, but not in the body of any of the class's methods. Every object (instance) of a class has a separate copy of the class's instance variables. Also, instance variables are accessible to all methods of the class. (We will see an exception to this in Chapter 9, Classes and Objects: A Deeper Look.)

4.4 A parameter represents additional information that a method requires to perform its task. Each parameter required by a method is specified in the method's declaration. An argument is the actual value that is passed to a method parameter when a method is called.

Exercises

4.5 What is the purpose of operator new? Explain what happens when this keyword is used in an application.

4.6 What is a default constructor? How are an object's instance variables initialized if a class has only a default constructor?

4.7 Explain the purpose of an instance variable.

4.8 Explain how an application could use class Console without using a using directive.

4.9 Explain why a class might provide a property for an instance variable.

4.10 Modify class GradeBook (Fig. 4.12) as follows:
   a) Include a second string instance variable that represents the name of the course's instructor.
   b) Provide a property with accessors to change the instructor's name and to retrieve it.
   c) Modify the constructor to specify two parameters—one for the course name and one for the instructor's name.
   d) Modify method DisplayMessage such that it first outputs the welcome message and course name, then outputs "This course is presented by: ", followed by the instructor's name.

Use your modified class in a test application that demonstrates the class's new capabilities.

4.11 Modify class Account (Fig. 4.15) to provide a method called Debit that withdraws money from an Account. Ensure that the debit amount does not exceed the Account's balance. If it does, the balance should be left unchanged and the method should print a message indicating "Debit amount exceeded account balance." Modify class AccountTest (Fig. 4.16) to test method Debit.

4.12 Create a class called Invoice that a hardware store might use to represent an invoice for an item sold at the store. An Invoice should include four pieces of information as instance variables—a part number (type string), a part description (type string), a quantity of the item being purchased (type int) and a price per item (decimal). Your class should have a constructor that initializes the four instance variables. Provide a property with a get and set accessor for each instance variable. In addition, provide a method named GetInvoiceAmount that calculates the invoice amount (i.e., multiplies the quantity by the price per item), then returns the amount as a decimal value. If the quantity is negative, it should be left unchanged. Similarly, if the price per item is negative, it should be left unchanged. Write a test application named InvoiceTest that demonstrates class Invoice's capabilities.

4.13 Create a class called Employee that includes three pieces of information as instance variables—a first name (type string), a last name (type string) and a monthly salary (decimal). Your class should have a constructor that initializes the three instance variables. Provide a property with a get and set accessor for each instance variable. If the monthly salary is negative, the set accessor should leave the instance variable unchanged. Write a test application named EmployeeTest that demonstrates class Employee's capabilities. Create two Employee objects and display each object's *yearly* salary. Then give each Employee a 10% raise and display each Employee's yearly salary again.

4.14 Create a class called Date that includes three pieces of information as instance variables—a month (type int), a day (type int) and a year (type int). Your class should have a constructor that initializes the three instance variables and assumes that the values provided are correct. Provide a property with a get and set accessor for each instance variable. Provide a method DisplayDate that displays the month, day and year separated by forward slashes (/). Write a test application named DateTest that demonstrates class Date's capabilities.

Let's all move one place on.
—Lewis Carroll

The wheel is come full circle.
—William Shakespeare

How many apples fell on Newton's head before he took the hint!
—Robert Frost

All the evolution we know of proceeds from the vague to the definite.
—Charles Sanders Peirce

Control Statements: Part 1

OBJECTIVES

In this chapter you will learn:

- To use basic problem-solving techniques.

- To develop algorithms through the process of top-down, stepwise refinement.

- To use the `if` and `if...else` selection statements to choose between alternative actions.

- To use the `while` repetition statement to execute statements in an application repeatedly.

- To use counter-controlled repetition and sentinel-controlled repetition.

- To use the increment, decrement and compound assignment operators.

5.1 Introduction

Before writing an application to solve a problem, it is essential to have a thorough understanding of the problem and a carefully planned approach to solving it. When writing an application, it is also essential to understand the types of building blocks that are available and to employ proven application-construction techniques. In this chapter and in Chapter 6, Control Statements: Part 2, we discuss these issues in our presentation of the theory and principles of structured programming. The concepts presented here are crucial to building classes and manipulating objects.

In this chapter, we introduce C#'s `if`, `if...else` and `while` control statements, three of the building blocks that allow you to specify the logic required for methods to perform their tasks. We devote a portion of the chapter (and Chapters 6 and 8) to further developing the `GradeBook` class introduced in Chapter 4. In particular, we add a method to the `GradeBook` class that uses control statements to calculate the average of a set of student grades. Another example demonstrates additional ways to combine control statements to solve a similar problem. We introduce C#'s compound assignment operators and explore its increment and decrement operators. These additional operators abbreviate and simplify many statements. Finally, we present an overview of C#'s simple types.

5.2 Algorithms

Any computing problem can be solved by executing a series of actions in a specific order. A *procedure* for solving a problem in terms of

1. the *actions* to execute and
2. the *order* in which these actions execute

is called an *algorithm*. The following example demonstrates that correctly specifying the order in which the actions execute is important.

Consider the "rise-and-shine algorithm" followed by one executive for getting out of bed and going to work: (1) Get out of bed; (2) take off pajamas; (3) take a shower; (4) get dressed; (5) eat breakfast; (6) carpool to work. This routine gets the executive to work well prepared to make critical decisions. Suppose that the same steps are performed in a slightly different order: (1) Get out of bed; (2) take off pajamas; (3) get dressed; (4) take a shower; (5) eat breakfast; (6) carpool to work. In this case, our executive shows up for work soaking wet.

Specifying the order in which statements (actions) execute in an application is called *program control*. This chapter investigates program control using C#'s *control statements*.

5.3 Pseudocode

Pseudocode is an informal language that helps programmers develop algorithms without having to worry about the strict details of C# language syntax. The pseudocode we present is particularly useful for developing algorithms that will be converted to structured portions of C# applications. Pseudocode is similar to everyday English—it is convenient and user friendly, but it is not an actual computer programming language.

Pseudocode does not execute on computers. Rather, it helps you "think out" an application before attempting to write it in a programming language, such as C#. This chapter provides several examples of how to use pseudocode to develop C# applications.

The style of pseudocode we present consists purely of characters, so you can create pseudocode using any text-editor application. A carefully prepared pseudocode application can easily be converted to a corresponding C# application. In many cases, this simply requires replacing pseudocode statements with C# equivalents.

Pseudocode normally describes only statements representing the actions that occur after you convert an application from pseudocode to C# and the application is run on a computer. Such actions might include input, output and calculations. We typically do not include variable declarations in our pseudocode, but some programmers do list variables and mention their purposes at the beginning of pseudocode programs.

5.4 Control Structures

Normally, statements in an application are executed one after the other in the order in which they are written. This process is called *sequential execution*. Various C# statements, which we will soon discuss, enable you to specify that the next statement to execute is not necessarily the next one in sequence. This is called *transfer of control*.

During the 1960s, it became clear that the indiscriminate use of transfers of control was the root of much difficulty experienced by software development groups. The blame was pointed at the *goto statement* (used in most programming languages of the time), which allows programmers to specify a transfer of control to one of a very wide range of possible destinations in an application (creating what is often called "spaghetti code"). The notion of so-called *structured programming* became almost synonymous with "goto elimination." We recommend that you avoid C#'s goto statement.

The research of Bohm and Jacopini[1] had demonstrated that applications could be written without goto statements. The challenge of the era for programmers was to shift their styles to "goto-less programming." Not until the 1970s did programmers start taking structured programming seriously. The results were impressive. Software development groups reported shorter development times, more frequent on-time delivery of systems and more frequent within-budget completion of software projects. The key to these successes was that structured applications were clearer, easier to debug and modify, and more likely to be bug free in the first place.

Bohm and Jacopini's work demonstrated that all applications could be written in terms of only three control structures—the *sequence structure*, the *selection structure* and the *repetition structure*. The term "control structures" comes from the field of computer science. When we introduce C#'s implementations of control structures, we will refer to them in the terminology of the *C# Language Specification* as "control statements."

Sequence Structure in C#

The sequence structure is built into C#. Unless directed otherwise, the computer executes C# statements one after the other in the order in which they are written—that is, in sequence. The UML *activity diagram* in Fig. 5.1 illustrates a typical sequence structure in which two calculations are performed in order. C# lets you have as many actions as you want in a sequence structure. As you will soon see, anywhere a single action may be placed, you may place several actions in sequence.

An activity diagram models the *workflow* (also called the *activity*) of a portion of a software system. Such workflows may include a portion of an algorithm, such as the sequence structure in Fig. 5.1. Activity diagrams are composed of special-purpose symbols, such as *action-state symbols* (rectangles with their left and right sides replaced with arcs curving outward), *diamonds* and *small circles*. These symbols are connected by *transition arrows*, which represent the flow of the activity—that is, the order in which the actions should occur.

Like pseudocode, activity diagrams help you develop and represent algorithms, although many programmers prefer pseudocode. Activity diagrams clearly show how control structures operate.

Consider the activity diagram for the sequence structure in Fig. 5.1. It contains two *action states* that represent actions to perform. Each action state contains an *action*

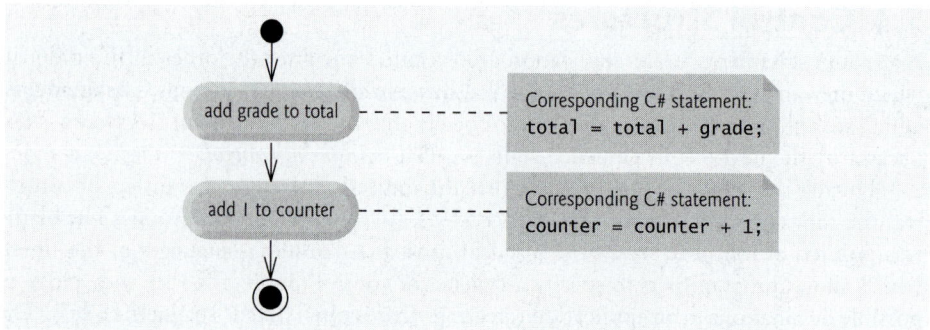

Fig. 5.1 | Sequence structure activity diagram.

---

1. Bohm, C., and G. Jacopini, "Flow Diagrams, Turing Machines, and Languages with Only Two Formation Rules," *Communications of the ACM*, Vol. 9, No. 5, May 1966, pp. 336–371.

expression—for example, "add grade to total" or "add 1 to counter"—that specifies a particular action to perform. Other actions might include calculations or input/output operations. The arrows in the activity diagram represent *transitions*, which indicate the order in which the actions represented by the action states occur. The portion of the application that implements the activities illustrated by the diagram in Fig. 5.1 first adds grade to total, then adds 1 to counter.

The *solid circle* located at the top of the activity diagram represents the activity's *initial state*—the beginning of the workflow before the application performs the modeled actions. The *solid circle surrounded by a hollow circle* that appears at the bottom of the diagram represents the *final state*—the end of the workflow after the application performs its actions.

Figure 5.1 also includes rectangles with the upper-right corners folded over. These are UML *notes* (like comments in C#)—explanatory remarks that describe the purpose of symbols in the diagram. Figure 5.1 uses UML notes to show the C# code associated with each action state in the activity diagram. A *dotted line* connects each note with the element that the note describes. Activity diagrams normally do not show the C# code that implements the activity. We use notes for this purpose here to illustrate how the diagram relates to C# code. For more information on the UML, see our optional case study, which appears in the Software Engineering Case Study sections at the ends of Chapters 1, 3–9 and 11, and visit www.uml.org.

Selection Structures in C#

C# has three types of selection structures, which from this point forward, we shall refer to as *selection statements*. These are discussed in this chapter and Chapter 6. The *if statement* either performs (selects) an action if a condition is true or skips the action if the condition is false. The *if...else* statement performs an action if a condition is true or performs a different action if the condition is false. The switch statement (Chapter 6) performs one of many different actions, depending on the value of an expression.

The if statement is called a *single-selection statement* because it selects or ignores a single action (or, as we will soon see, a single group of actions). The if...else statement is called a *double-selection statement* because it selects between two different actions (or groups of actions). The switch statement is called a *multiple-selection statement* because it selects among many different actions (or groups of actions).

Repetition Structures in C#

C# provides four repetition structures, which from this point forward, we shall refer to as *repetition statements* (also called *iteration statements* or *loops*). Repetition statements enable applications to perform statements repeatedly, depending on the value of a *loop-continuation condition*. The repetition statements are the while, do...while, for and foreach statements. (Chapter 6 presents the do...while and for statements. Chapter 8 discusses the foreach statement.) The while, for and foreach statements perform the action (or group of actions) in their bodies zero or more times—if the loop-continuation condition is initially false, the action (or group of actions) will not execute. The do...while statement performs the action (or group of actions) in its body one or more times.

The words if, else, switch, while, do, for and foreach are C# keywords. Recall that keywords are used to implement various C# features, such as control statements. Keywords cannot be used as identifiers, such as variable names. A complete list of C# keywords appears in Fig. 3.2.

Summary of Control Statements in C#

C# has only three kinds of structured control statements: the sequence statement, selection statement (three types) and repetition statement (four types). Every application is formed by combining as many sequence, selection and repetition statements as is appropriate for the algorithm the application implements. As with the sequence statement in Fig. 5.1, we can model each control statement as an activity diagram. Each diagram contains an initial state and a final state that represent a control statement's entry point and exit point, respectively. *Single-entry/single-exit control statements* make it easy to build applications—the control statements are "attached" to one another by connecting the exit point of one to the entry point of the next. This procedure is similar to the way in which a child stacks building blocks, so we call it *control-statement stacking*. You will learn that there is only one other way in which control statements may be connected: *control-statement nesting*, in which a control statement appears inside another control statement. Thus, algorithms in C# applications are constructed from only three kinds of structured control statements, combined in only two ways. This is the essence of simplicity.

5.5 if Single-Selection Statement

Applications use selection statements to choose among alternative courses of action. For example, suppose that the passing grade on an exam is 60. The pseudocode statement

> *if grade is greater than or equal to 60*
> *print "Passed"*

determines whether the condition "grade is greater than or equal to 60" is true or false. If the condition is true, "Passed" is printed, and the next pseudocode statement in order is "performed." (Remember that pseudocode is not a real programming language.) If the condition is false, the *Print* statement is ignored, and the next pseudocode statement in order is performed. The indentation of the second line of this selection statement is optional, but recommended, because it emphasizes the inherent structure of structured applications.

The preceding pseudocode *if* statement may be written in C# as

```
if ( grade >= 60 )
    Console.WriteLine( "Passed" );
```

Note that the C# code corresponds closely to the pseudocode. This is one of the properties of pseudocode that makes it such a useful application development tool.

Figure 5.2 illustrates the single-selection if statement. This activity diagram contains what is perhaps the most important symbol in an activity diagram—the diamond, or *decision symbol*, which indicates that a decision is to be made. The workflow will continue along a path determined by the symbol's associated *guard conditions*, which can be true or false. Each transition arrow emerging from a decision symbol has a guard condition (specified in square brackets next to the transition arrow). If a guard condition is true, the workflow enters the action state to which the transition arrow points. In Fig. 5.2, if the grade is greater than or equal to 60, the application prints "Passed" then transitions to the final state of this activity. If the grade is less than 60, the application immediately transitions to the final state without displaying a message.

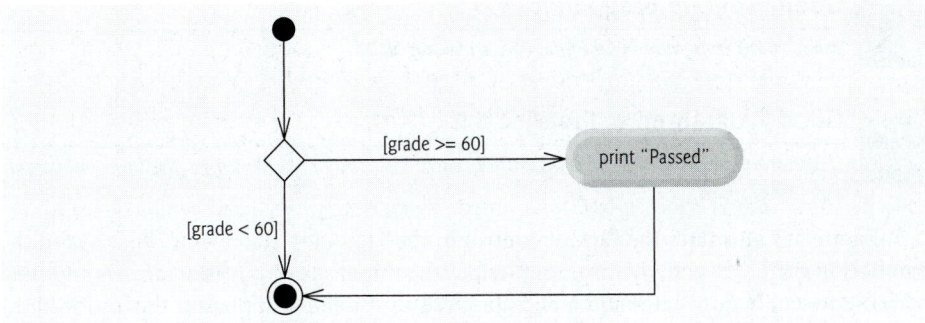

Fig. 5.2 | if single-selection statement UML activity diagram.

The if statement is a single-entry/single-exit control statement. You will see that the activity diagrams for the remaining control statements also contain initial states, transition arrows, action states that indicate actions to perform and decision symbols (with associated guard conditions) that indicate decisions to be made, and final states. This is consistent with the *action/decision model of programming* we have been emphasizing.

Envision seven bins, each containing only one type of C# control statement. The control statements are all empty. Your task is to assemble an application from as many of each type of control statement as the algorithm demands, combining the control statements in only two possible ways (stacking or nesting), then filling in the action states and decisions with action expressions and guard conditions appropriate for the algorithm. We will discuss in detail the variety of ways in which actions and decisions can be written.

5.6 if...else Double-Selection Statement

The if single-selection statement performs an indicated action only when the condition is true; otherwise, the action is skipped. The if...else double-selection statement allows you to specify an action to perform when the condition is true and a different action when the condition is false. For example, the pseudocode statement

> *if grade is greater than or equal to 60*
> > *print "Passed"*
> *else*
> > *print "Failed"*

prints "Passed" if the grade is greater than or equal to 60, but prints "Failed" if it is less than 60. In either case, after printing occurs, the next pseudocode statement in sequence is "performed."

The preceding *if...else* pseudocode statement can be written in C# as

```
if ( grade >= 60 )
   Console.WriteLine( "Passed" );
else
   Console.WriteLine( "Failed" );
```

Note that the body of the else part is also indented. Whatever indentation convention you choose should be applied consistently throughout your applications. It is difficult to read applications that do not obey uniform spacing conventions.

Good Programming Practice 5.1

Indent both body statements of an if...else statement.

Good Programming Practice 5.2

If there are several levels of indentation, each level should be indented the same additional amount of space.

Figure 5.3 illustrates the flow of control in the if...else statement. Once again, the symbols in the UML activity diagram (besides the initial state, transition arrows and final state) represent action states and a decision. We continue to emphasize this action/decision model of computing. Imagine again a deep bin containing as many empty if...else statements as might be needed to build any C# application. Your job is to assemble these if...else statements (by stacking and nesting) with any other control statements required by the algorithm. You fill in the action states and decision symbols with action expressions and guard conditions appropriate to the algorithm you are developing.

Conditional Operator (?:)

C# provides the *conditional operator* (?:), which can be used in place of an if...else statement. This is C#'s only *ternary operator*—this means that it takes three operands. Together, the operands and the ?: symbols form a *conditional expression.* The first operand (to the left of the ?) is a *boolean* expression (i.e., an expression that evaluates to a bool-type value—*true* or *false*), the second operand (between the ? and :) is the value of the conditional expression if the boolean expression is true and the third operand (to the right of the :) is the value of the conditional expression if the boolean expression is false. For example, the statement

```
Console.WriteLine( grade >= 60 ? "Passed" : "Failed" );
```

prints the value of WriteLine's conditional-expression argument. The conditional expression in this statement evaluates to the string "Passed" if the boolean expression grade >= 60 is true and evaluates to the string "Failed" if the boolean expression is false. Thus, this statement with the conditional operator performs essentially the same function as the if...else statement shown earlier in this section. You will see that conditional expressions can be used in some situations where if...else statements cannot.

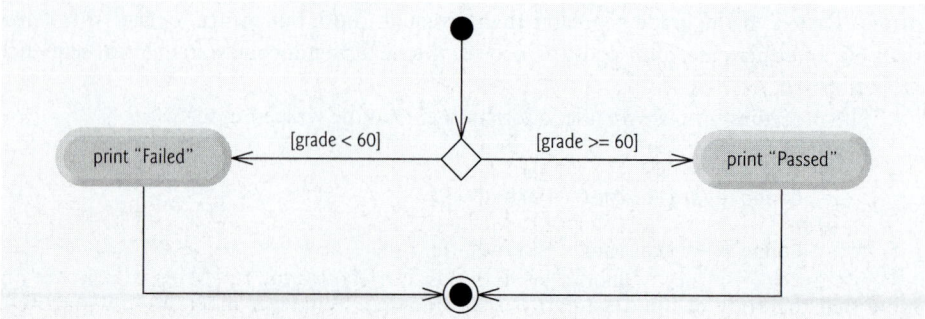

Fig. 5.3 | if...else double-selection statement UML activity diagram.

Good Programming Practice 5.3

Conditional expressions are more difficult to read than if...else statements and should be used to replace only simple if...else statements that choose between two values.

Good Programming Practice 5.4

When a conditional expression is inside a larger expression, it's good practice to parenthesize the conditional expression for clarity. Adding parentheses may also prevent operator precedence problems that could cause syntax errors.

Nested if...else Statements

An application can test multiple cases by placing if...else statements inside other if...else statements to create *nested if...else statements*. For example, the following pseudocode represents a nested if...else statement that prints A for exam grades greater than or equal to 90, B for grades in the range 80 to 89, C for grades in the range 70 to 79, D for grades in the range 60 to 69 and F for all other grades:

> *if grade is greater than or equal to 90*
> > *print "A"*
>
> *else*
> > *if grade is greater than or equal to 80*
> > > *print "B"*
> >
> > *else*
> > > *if grade is greater than or equal to 70*
> > > > *print "C"*
> > >
> > > *else*
> > > > *if grade is greater than or equal to 60*
> > > > > *print "D"*
> > > >
> > > > *else*
> > > > > *print "F"*

This pseudocode may be written in C# as

```
if ( grade >= 90 )
   Console.WriteLine( "A" );
else
   if ( grade >= 80 )
      Console.WriteLine( "B" );
   else
      if ( grade >= 70 )
         Console.WriteLine( "C" );
      else
         if ( grade >= 60 )
            Console.WriteLine( "D" );
         else
            Console.WriteLine( "F" );
```

If grade is greater than or equal to 90, the first four conditions will be true, but only the statement in the if-part of the first if...else statement will execute. After that statement executes, the else-part of the "outermost" if...else statement is skipped. Most C# programmers prefer to write the preceding if...else statement as

```
if ( grade >= 90 )
   Console.WriteLine( "A" );
else if ( grade >= 80 )
   Console.WriteLine( "B" );
else if ( grade >= 70 )
   Console.WriteLine( "C" );
else if ( grade >= 60 )
   Console.WriteLine( "D" );
else
   Console.WriteLine( "F" );
```

The two forms are identical except for the spacing and indentation, which the compiler ignores. The latter form is popular because it avoids deep indentation of the code to the right—such indentation often leaves little room on a line of code, forcing lines to be split and decreasing the readability of your code.

Dangling-else Problem

The C# compiler always associates an else with the immediately preceding if unless told to do otherwise by the placement of braces ({ and }). This behavior can lead to what is referred to as the *dangling-else problem*. For example,

```
if ( x > 5 )
   if ( y > 5 )
      Console.WriteLine( "x and y are > 5" );
else
   Console.WriteLine( "x is <= 5" );
```

appears to indicate that if x is greater than 5, the nested if statement determines whether y is also greater than 5. If so, the string "x and y are > 5" is output. Otherwise, it appears that if x is not greater than 5, the else part of the if...else outputs the string "x is <= 5".

Beware! This nested if...else statement does not execute as it appears. The compiler actually interprets the statement as

```
if ( x > 5 )
   if ( y > 5 )
      Console.WriteLine( "x and y are > 5" );
   else
      Console.WriteLine( "x is <= 5" );
```

in which the body of the first if is a nested if...else. The outer if statement tests whether x is greater than 5. If so, execution continues by testing whether y is also greater than 5. If the second condition is true, the proper string—"x and y are > 5"—is displayed. However, if the second condition is false, the string "x is <= 5" is displayed, even though we know that x is greater than 5.

To force the nested if...else statement to execute as it was originally intended, we must write it as follows:

```
if ( x > 5 )
{
   if ( y > 5 )
      Console.WriteLine( "x and y are > 5" );
}
else
   Console.WriteLine( "x is <= 5" );
```

The braces ({}) indicate to the compiler that the second `if` statement is in the body of the first `if` and that the `else` is associated with the *first* `if`. Exercises 5.27–5.28 investigate the dangling-`else` problem further.

Blocks

The `if` statement normally expects only one statement in its body. To include several statements in the body of an `if` (or the body of an `else` for an `if...else` statement), enclose the statements in braces ({ and }). A set of statements contained within a pair of braces is called a ***block***. A block can be placed anywhere in an application that a single statement can be placed.

The following example includes a block in the `else`-part of an `if...else` statement:

```
if ( grade >= 60 )
   Console.WriteLine( "Passed" );
else
{
   Console.WriteLine( "Failed" );
   Console.WriteLine( "You must take this course again." );
}
```

In this case, if `grade` is less than 60, the application executes both statements in the body of the `else` and prints

```
Failed.
You must take this course again.
```

Note the braces surrounding the two statements in the `else` clause. These braces are important. Without the braces, the statement

```
Console.WriteLine( "You must take this course again." );
```

would be outside the body of the `else`-part of the `if...else` statement and would execute regardless of whether the grade was less than 60.

Syntax errors (e.g., when one brace in a block is left out of the application) are caught by the compiler. A ***logic error*** (e.g., when both braces in a block are left out of the application) has its effect at execution time. A ***fatal logic error*** causes an application to fail and terminate prematurely. A ***nonfatal logic error*** allows an application to continue executing, but causes the application to produce incorrect results.

Common Programming Error 5.1

Forgetting one or both of the braces that delimit a block can lead to syntax errors or logic errors in an application.

Good Programming Practice 5.5

Always using braces in an `if...else` (or other) statement helps prevent their accidental omission, especially when adding statements to the `if`-part or the `else`-part at a later time. To avoid omitting one or both of the braces, some programmers type the beginning and ending braces of blocks before typing the individual statements within the braces.

Just as a block can be placed anywhere a single statement can be placed, it is also possible to have an empty statement. Recall from Section 3.9 that the empty statement is represented by placing a semicolon (;) where a statement would normally be.

Common Programming Error 5.2

Placing a semicolon after the condition in an if or if...else statement leads to a logic error in single-selection if statements and a syntax error in double-selection if...else statements (when the if-part contains an actual body statement).

5.7 `while` Repetition Statement

A *repetition statement* allows you to specify that an application should repeat an action while some condition remains true. The pseudocode statement

> *while there are more items on my shopping list*
> *purchase next item and cross it off my list*

describes the repetition that occurs during a shopping trip. The condition "there are more items on my shopping list" may be true or false. If it is true, then the action "Purchase next item and cross it off my list" is performed. This action will be performed repeatedly while the condition remains true. The statement(s) contained in the *while* repetition statement constitute the body of the *while* repetition statement, which may be a single statement or a block. Eventually, the condition will become false (when the last item on the shopping list has been purchased and crossed off the list). At this point, the repetition terminates, and the first statement after the repetition statement executes.

As an example of C#'s *while repetition statement*, consider a code segment designed to find the first power of 3 larger than 100. Suppose int variable product is initialized to 3. When the following while statement finishes executing, product contains the result:

```
int product = 3;

while ( product <= 100 )
   product = 3 * product;
```

When this while statement begins execution, the value of variable product is 3. Each repetition of the while statement multiplies product by 3, so product takes on the subsequent values 9, 27, 81 and 243 successively. When variable product becomes 243, the while statement condition—product <= 100—becomes false. This terminates the repetition, so the final value of product is 243. At this point, application execution continues with the next statement after the while statement.

Common Programming Error 5.3

*Not providing in the body of a while statement an action that eventually causes the condition in the while to become false normally results in a logic error called an **infinite loop**, in which the loop never terminates.*

The UML activity diagram in Fig. 5.4 illustrates the flow of control that corresponds to the preceding while statement. Once again, the symbols in the diagram (besides the initial state, transition arrows, the final state and three notes) represent an action state and a decision. This diagram also introduces the UML's *merge symbol*. The UML represents both the merge symbol and the decision symbol as diamonds. The merge symbol joins two flows of activity into one. In this diagram, the merge symbol joins the transitions from the initial state and the action state, so they both flow into the decision that determines whether the loop should begin (or continue) executing. The decision and merge symbols can be distinguished by the number of "incoming" and "outgoing" transition arrows. A decision symbol has one transition arrow pointing to the diamond and two or more transition arrows pointing out from the diamond to indicate possible transitions from that point. Each transition arrow pointing out of a decision symbol has a guard condition next to it. A merge symbol has two or more transition arrows pointing to the diamond and only one transition arrow pointing from the diamond, to indicate multiple activity flows merging to continue the activity. None of the transition arrows associated with a merge symbol have guard conditions.

Figure 5.4 clearly shows the repetition of the while statement discussed earlier in this section. The transition arrow emerging from the action state points back to the merge, from which program flow transitions back to the decision that is tested at the beginning of each repetition of the loop. The loop continues to execute until the guard condition product > 100 becomes true. Then the while statement exits (reaches its final state), and control passes to the next statement in sequence in the application.

5.8 Formulating Algorithms: Counter-Controlled Repetition

To illustrate how algorithms are developed, we modify the GradeBook class of Chapter 4 to solve two variations of a problem that averages student grades. Consider the following problem statement:

> *A class of 10 students took a quiz. The grades (integers in the range 0 to 100) for this quiz are available to you. Determine the class average on the quiz.*

The class average is equal to the sum of the grades divided by the number of students. The algorithm for solving this problem on a computer must input each grade, keep track of the total of all grades input, perform the averaging calculation and print the result.

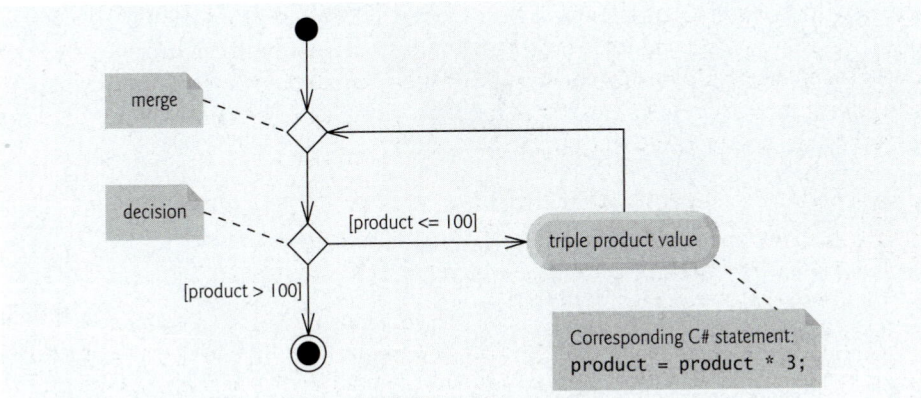

Fig. 5.4 | while repetition statement UML activity diagram.

Pseudocode Algorithm with Counter-Controlled Repetition

Let's use pseudocode to list the actions to execute and specify the order in which they should execute. We use *counter-controlled repetition* to input the grades one at a time. This technique uses a variable called a *counter* (or *control variable*) to control the number of times a set of statements will execute. Counter-controlled repetition is often called *definite repetition*, because the number of repetitions is known by the application before the loop begins executing. In this example, repetition terminates when the counter exceeds 10. This section presents a fully developed pseudocode algorithm (Fig. 5.5) and a version of class GradeBook (Fig. 5.6) that implements the algorithm in a C# method. The section then presents an application (Fig. 5.7) that demonstrates the algorithm in action. In Section 5.9, we demonstrate how to use pseudocode to develop such an algorithm from scratch.

Software Engineering Observation 5.1

Experience has shown that the most difficult part of solving a problem on a computer is developing the algorithm for the solution. Once a correct algorithm has been specified, the process of producing a working C# application from the algorithm is normally straightforward.

Note the references in the algorithm of Fig. 5.5 to a total and a counter. A *total* is a variable used to accumulate the sum of several values. A counter is a variable used to count—in this case, the grade counter indicates which of the 10 grades is about to be entered by the user. Variables used to store totals are normally initialized to zero before being used in an application.

Implementing Counter-Controlled Repetition in Class *GradeBook*

Class GradeBook (Fig. 5.6) contains a constructor (lines 11–14) that assigns a value to the class's instance variable courseName (declared in line 8) by using property CourseName. Lines 17–27 and 30–35 declare property CourseName and method DisplayMessage, respectively. Lines 38–64 declare method DetermineClassAverage, which implements the class-averaging algorithm described by the pseudocode in Fig. 5.5.

Lines 40–43 declare local variables total, gradeCounter, grade and average to be of type int. Variable grade stores the user input.

```
 1   set total to zero
 2   set grade counter to one
 3
 4   while grade counter is less than or equal to ten
 5       prompt the user to enter the next grade
 6       input the next grade
 7       add the grade into the total
 8       add one to the grade counter
 9
10   set the class average to the total divided by ten
11   print the class average
```

Fig. 5.5 | Pseudocode algorithm that uses counter-controlled repetition to solve the class-average problem.

Note that the declarations (in lines 40–43) appear in the body of method Determine-ClassAverage. Recall that variables declared in a method body are local variables and can be used only from the line of their declaration in the method to the closing right brace of the method declaration. A local variable's declaration must appear before the variable is used in that method. A local variable cannot be accessed outside the method in which it is declared.

```csharp
1    // Fig. 5.6: GradeBook.cs
2    // GradeBook class that solves class-average problem using
3    // counter-controlled repetition.
4    using System;
5
6    public class GradeBook
7    {
8       private string courseName; // name of course this GradeBook represents
9
10      // constructor initializes courseName
11      public GradeBook( string name )
12      {
13         CourseName = name; // initializes courseName by using property
14      } // end constructor
15
16      // property to get and set the course name
17      public string CourseName
18      {
19         get
20         {
21            return courseName;
22         } // end get
23         set
24         {
25            courseName = value; // set should validate
26         } // end set
27      } // end property CourseName
28
29      // display a welcome message to the GradeBook user
30      public void DisplayMessage()
31      {
32         // property CourseName gets the name of the course
33         Console.WriteLine( "Welcome to the grade book for\n{0}!\n",
34            CourseName );
35      } // end method DisplayMessage
36
37      // determine class average based on 10 grades entered by user
38      public void DetermineClassAverage()
39      {
40         int total; // sum of the grades entered by user
41         int gradeCounter; // number of the grade to be entered next
42         int grade; // grade value entered by the user
43         int average; // average of the grades
44
```

Fig. 5.6 | GradeBook class that solves the class-average problem using counter-controlled repetition. (Part 1 of 2.)

```
45        // initialization phase
46        total = 0; // initialize the total
47        gradeCounter = 1; // initialize the loop counter
48
49        // processing phase
50        while ( gradeCounter <= 10 ) // loop 10 times
51        {
52           Console.Write( "Enter grade: " ); // prompt the user
53           grade = Convert.ToInt32( Console.ReadLine() ); // read grade
54           total = total + grade; // add the grade to total
55           gradeCounter = gradeCounter + 1; // increment the counter by 1
56        } // end while
57
58        // termination phase
59        average = total / 10; // integer division yields integer result
60
61        // display total and average of grades
62        Console.WriteLine( "\nTotal of all 10 grades is {0}", total );
63        Console.WriteLine( "Class average is {0}", average );
64     } // end method DetermineClassAverage
65  } // end class GradeBook
```

Fig. 5.6 | GradeBook class that solves the class-average problem using counter-controlled repetition. (Part 2 of 2.)

In the versions of class GradeBook in this chapter, we simply read and process a set of grades. The averaging calculation is performed in method DetermineClassAverage using local variables—we do not preserve any information about student grades in instance variables of the class. In later versions of the class (in Chapter 8, Arrays), we maintain the grades in memory using an instance variable that refers to a data structure known as an array. This allows a GradeBook object to perform various calculations on the same set of grades without requiring the user to enter the grades multiple times.

Good Programming Practice 5.6

Separate declarations from other statements in methods with a blank line for readability.

We say that a variable is **definitely assigned** when the variable is assigned in every possible flow of control. Notice that each local variable declared in lines 40-43 is definitely assigned before it is used in calculations. The assignments (in lines 46–47) initialize total to 0 and gradeCounter to 1. Variables grade and average (for the user input and calculated average, respectively) need not be initialized here—their values are assigned as they are input or calculated later in the method.

Common Programming Error 5.4

Using the value of a local variable before it is definitely assigned results in a compilation error. All local variables must be definitely assigned before their values are used in expressions.

Error-Prevention Tip 5.1

Initialize each counter and total, either in its declaration or in an assignment statement. Totals are normally initialized to 0. Counters are normally initialized to 0 or 1, depending on how they are used (we will show examples of each).

Line 50 indicates that the `while` statement should continue looping (also called *iterating*) as long as the value of `gradeCounter` is less than or equal to 10. While this condition remains true, the `while` statement repeatedly executes the statements between the braces that delimit its body (lines 51–56).

Line 52 displays the prompt "`Enter grade: `" in the console window. Line 53 reads the grade entered by the user and assigns it to variable `grade`. Then line 54 adds the new grade entered by the user to the `total` and assigns the result to `total`, which replaces its previous value.

Line 55 adds 1 to `gradeCounter` to indicate that the application has processed a grade and is ready to input the next grade from the user. Incrementing `gradeCounter` eventually causes `gradeCounter` to exceed 10. At that point the `while` loop terminates because its condition (line 50) becomes false.

When the loop terminates, line 59 performs the averaging calculation and assigns its result to the variable `average`. Line 62 uses `Console`'s `WriteLine` method to display the text "`Total of all 10 grades is `" followed by variable `total`'s value. Line 63 then uses `WriteLine` to display the text "`Class average is `" followed by variable `average`'s value. Method `DetermineClassAverage` returns control to the calling method (i.e., `Main` in `GradeBookTest` of Fig. 5.7) after reaching line 64.

Class *GradeBookTest*
Class `GradeBookTest` (Fig. 5.7) creates an object of class `GradeBook` (Fig. 5.6) and demonstrates its capabilities. Lines 9–10 of Fig. 5.7 create a new `GradeBook` object and assign it to variable `myGradeBook`. The `string` in line 10 is passed to the `GradeBook` constructor (lines 11–14 of Fig. 5.6). Line 12 calls `myGradeBook`'s `DisplayMessage` method to display a welcome message to the user. Line 13 then calls `myGradeBook`'s `DetermineClassAverage` method to allow the user to enter 10 grades, for which the method then calculates and prints the average—the method performs the algorithm shown in Fig. 5.5.

```
 1   // Fig. 5.7: GradeBookTest.cs
 2   // Create GradeBook object and invoke its DetermineClassAverage method.
 3   public class GradeBookTest
 4   {
 5      public static void Main( string[] args )
 6      {
 7         // create GradeBook object myGradeBook and
 8         // pass course name to constructor
 9         GradeBook myGradeBook = new GradeBook(
10            "CS101 Introduction to C# Programming" );
11
12         myGradeBook.DisplayMessage(); // display welcome message
13         myGradeBook.DetermineClassAverage(); // find average of 10 grades
14      } // end Main
15   } // end class GradeBookTest
```

Fig. 5.7 | Create `GradeBook` object and invoke its `DetermineClassAverage` method. (Part 1 of 2.)

```
Welcome to the grade book for
CS101 Introduction to C# Programming!

Enter grade: 88
Enter grade: 79
Enter grade: 95
Enter grade: 100
Enter grade: 48
Enter grade: 88
Enter grade: 92
Enter grade: 83
Enter grade: 90
Enter grade: 85

Total of all 10 grades is 848
Class average is 84
```

Fig. 5.7 | Create `GradeBook` object and invoke its `DetermineClassAverage` method. (Part 2 of 2.)

Notes on Integer Division and Truncation

The averaging calculation performed by method `DetermineClassAverage` in response to the method call at line 13 in Fig. 5.7 produces an integer result. The application's output indicates that the sum of the grade values in the sample execution is 848, which when divided by 10, should yield the floating-point number 84.8. However, the result of the calculation `total / 10` (line 59 of Fig. 5.6) is the integer 84, because `total` and 10 are both integers. Dividing two integers results in *integer division*—any fractional part of the calculation is lost (i.e., *truncated*, not rounded). We will see how to obtain a floating-point result from the averaging calculation in the next section.

Common Programming Error 5.5

Assuming that integer division rounds (rather than truncates) can lead to incorrect results. For example, 7 ÷ 4, which yields 1.75 in conventional arithmetic, truncates to 1 in integer arithmetic, rather than rounding to 2.

5.9 Formulating Algorithms: Sentinel-Controlled Repetition

Let us generalize Section 5.8's class-average problem. Consider the following problem:

> *Develop a class-averaging application that processes grades for an arbitrary number of students each time it is run.*

In the previous class-average example, the problem statement specified the number of students, so the number of grades (10) was known in advance. In this example, no indication is given of how many grades the user will enter during the application's execution. The application must process an arbitrary number of grades. How can it determine when to stop the input of grades? How will it know when to calculate and print the class average?

One way to solve this problem is to use a special value called a *sentinel value* (also called a *signal value*, a *dummy value* or a *flag value*) to indicate "end of data entry." This is called *sentinel-controlled repetition.* The user enters grades until all legitimate grades have been entered. The user then types the sentinel value to indicate that no more grades will be entered. Sentinel-controlled repetition is often called *indefinite repetition* because the number of repetitions is not known by the application before the loop begins executing.

Clearly, a sentinel value must be chosen that cannot be confused with an acceptable input value. Grades on a quiz are nonnegative integers, so –1 is an acceptable sentinel value for this problem. Thus, a run of the class-average application might process a stream of inputs such as 95, 96, 75, 74, 89 and –1. The application would then compute and print the class average for the grades 95, 96, 75, 74 and 89. Since –1 is the sentinel value, it should not enter into the averaging calculation.

Common Programming Error 5.6

Choosing a sentinel value that is also a legitimate data value is a logic error.

Developing the Pseudocode Algorithm with Top-Down, Stepwise Refinement: The Top and First Refinement

We approach the class-average application with a technique called *top-down, stepwise refinement*, which is essential to the development of well-structured applications. We begin with a pseudocode representation of the *top*—a single statement that conveys the overall function of the application:

> *determine the class average for the quiz*

The top is, in effect, a *complete* representation of an application. Unfortunately, the top rarely conveys sufficient detail from which to write a C# application. So we now begin the refinement process. We divide the top into a series of smaller tasks and list these in the order in which they will be performed. This results in the following *first refinement*:

> *initialize variables*
> *input, sum and count the quiz grades*
> *calculate and print the class average*

This refinement uses only the sequence structure—the steps listed should execute in order, one after the other.

Software Engineering Observation 5.2

Each refinement, as well as the top itself, is a complete specification of the algorithm—only the level of detail varies.

Software Engineering Observation 5.3

Many applications can be divided logically into three phases: an initialization phase that initializes the variables; a processing phase that inputs data values and adjusts application variables (e.g., counters and totals) accordingly; and a termination phase that calculates and outputs the final results.

Proceeding to the Second Refinement

The preceding *Software Engineering Observation* is often all you need for the first refinement in the top-down process. To proceed to the next level of refinement, the *second re-*

finement, we specify individual variables. In this example, we need a running total of the numbers, a count of how many numbers have been processed, a variable to receive the value of each grade as it is input by the user and a variable to hold the calculated average. The pseudocode statement

> *initialize variables*

can be refined as follows:

> *initialize total to zero*
> *initialize counter to zero*

Only the variables *total* and *counter* need to be initialized before they are used. The variables *average* and *grade* (for the calculated average and the user input, respectively) need not be initialized, because their values will be replaced as they are calculated or input.

The pseudocode statement

> *input, sum and count the quiz grades*

requires a repetition structure (i.e., a loop) that successively inputs each grade. We do not know in advance how many grades are to be processed, so we will use sentinel-controlled repetition. The user enters grades one at a time. After entering the last grade, the user enters the sentinel value. The application tests for the sentinel value after each grade is input and terminates the loop when the user enters the sentinel value. The second refinement of the preceding pseudocode statement is then

> *prompt the user to enter the first grade*
> *input the first grade (possibly the sentinel)*
>
> *while the user has not yet entered the sentinel*
> > *add this grade into the running total*
> > *add one to the grade counter*
> > *prompt the user to enter the next grade*
> > *input the next grade (possibly the sentinel)*

In pseudocode, we do not use braces around the statements that form the body of the *while* structure. We simply indent the statements under the *while* to show that they belong to the *while*. Again, pseudocode is only an informal application-development aid.

The pseudocode statement

> *calculate and print the class average*

can be refined as follows:

> *if the counter is not equal to zero*
> > *set the average to the total divided by the counter*
> > *print the average*
> *else*
> > *print "No grades were entered"*

We are careful here to test for the possibility of division by zero—a logic error that, if undetected, would cause the application to fail or produce invalid output. The complete second refinement of the pseudocode for the class-average problem is shown in Fig. 5.8.

```
 1   initialize total to zero
 2   initialize counter to zero
 3
 4   prompt the user to enter the first grade
 5   input the first grade (possibly the sentinel)
 6
 7   while the user has not yet entered the sentinel
 8       add this grade into the running total
 9       add one to the grade counter
10       prompt the user to enter the next grade
11       input the next grade (possibly the sentinel)
12
13   if the counter is not equal to zero
14       set the average to the total divided by the counter
15       print the average
16   else
17       print "No grades were entered"
```

Fig. 5.8 | Class-average problem pseudocode algorithm with sentinel-controlled repetition.

Error-Prevention Tip 5.2

When performing division by an expression whose value could be zero, explicitly test for this possibility and handle it appropriately in your application (e.g., by printing an error message) rather than allowing the error to occur.

In Fig. 5.5 and Fig. 5.8, we included some completely blank lines and indentation in the pseudocode to make it more readable. The blank lines separate the pseudocode algorithms into their various phases and set off control statements, and the indentation emphasizes the bodies of the control statements.

The pseudocode algorithm in Fig. 5.8 solves the more general class-averaging problem. This algorithm was developed after only two refinements. Sometimes more refinements are necessary.

Software Engineering Observation 5.4

Terminate the top-down, stepwise refinement process when you have specified the pseudocode algorithm in sufficient detail for you to convert the pseudocode to C#. Normally, implementing the C# application is then straightforward.

Software Engineering Observation 5.5

Some experienced programmers write applications without ever using application-development tools like pseudocode. They feel that their ultimate goal is to solve the problem on a computer and that writing pseudocode merely delays the production of final outputs. Although this method may work for simple and familiar problems, it can lead to serious errors and delays in large, complex projects.

Implementing Sentinel-Controlled Repetition in Class GradeBook

Figure 5.9 shows the C# class GradeBook containing method DetermineClassAverage that implements the pseudocode algorithm of Fig. 5.8. Although each grade is an integer,

```
 1   // Fig. 5.9: GradeBook.cs
 2   // GradeBook class that solves class-average problem using
 3   // sentinel-controlled repetition.
 4   using System;
 5
 6   public class GradeBook
 7   {
 8      private string courseName; // name of course this GradeBook represents
 9
10      // constructor initializes courseName
11      public GradeBook( string name )
12      {
13         CourseName = name; // initialize courseName by using property
14      } // end constructor
15
16      // property to get and set the course name
17      public string CourseName
18      {
19        get
20        {
21           return courseName;
22        } // end get
23        set
24        {
25           courseName = value; // set should validate
26        } // end set
27      } // end property CourseName
28
29      // display a welcome message to the GradeBook user
30      public void DisplayMessage()
31      {
32         Console.WriteLine( "Welcome to the grade book for\n{0}!\n",
33            CourseName );
34      } // end method DisplayMessage
35
36      // determine the average of an arbitrary number of grades
37      public void DetermineClassAverage()
38      {
39         int total; // sum of grades
40         int gradeCounter; // number of grades entered
41         int grade; // grade value
42         double average; // number with decimal point for average
43
44         // initialization phase
45         total = 0; // initialize total
46         gradeCounter = 0; // initialize loop counter
47
48         // processing phase
49         // prompt for input and read grade from user
50         Console.Write( "Enter grade or -1 to quit: " );
51         grade = Convert.ToInt32( Console.ReadLine() );
```

Fig. 5.9 | GradeBook class that solves the class-average problem using sentinel-controlled repetition. (Part 1 of 2.)

```
52
53          // loop until sentinel value read from user
54          while ( grade != -1 )
55          {
56              total = total + grade; // add grade to total
57              gradeCounter = gradeCounter + 1; // increment counter
58
59              // prompt for input and read next grade from user
60              Console.Write( "Enter grade or -1 to quit: " );
61              grade = Convert.ToInt32( Console.ReadLine() );
62          } // end while
63
64          // termination phase
65          // if user entered at least one grade...
66          if ( gradeCounter != 0 )
67          {
68              // calculate average of all grades entered
69              average = ( double ) total / gradeCounter;
70
71              // display total and average (with two digits of precision)
72              Console.WriteLine( "\nTotal of the {0} grades entered is {1}",
73                  gradeCounter, total );
74              Console.WriteLine( "Class average is {0:F2}", average );
75          } // end if
76          else // no grades were entered, so output error message
77              Console.WriteLine( "No grades were entered" );
78      } // end method DetermineClassAverage
79   } // end class GradeBook
```

Fig. 5.9 | GradeBook class that solves the class-average problem using sentinel-controlled repetition. (Part 2 of 2.)

the averaging calculation is likely to produce a number with a decimal point—in other words, a real number or floating-point number. The type int cannot represent such a number, so this class uses type double to do so.

In this example, we see that control statements may be stacked on top of one another (in sequence) just as a child stacks building blocks. The while statement (lines 54–62) is followed in sequence by an if...else statement (lines 66–77). Much of the code in this application is identical to the code in Fig. 5.6, so we concentrate on the new features and issues.

Line 42 declares double variable average. This variable allows us to store the calculated class average as a floating-point number. Line 46 initializes gradeCounter to 0, because no grades have been entered yet. Remember that this application uses sentinel-controlled repetition to input the grades from the user. To keep an accurate record of the number of grades entered, the application increments gradeCounter only when the user inputs a valid grade value.

Program Logic for Sentinel-Controlled Repetition vs. Counter-Controlled Repetition
Compare the program logic for sentinel-controlled repetition in this application with that for counter-controlled repetition in Fig. 5.6. In counter-controlled repetition, each repetition of the while statement (e.g., lines 50–56 of Fig. 5.6) reads a value from the user, for

the specified number of repetitions. In sentinel-controlled repetition, the application reads the first value (lines 50–51 of Fig. 5.9) before reaching the while. This value determines whether the application's flow of control should enter the body of the while. If the condition of the while is false, the user entered the sentinel value, so the body of the while does not execute (because no grades were entered). If, on the other hand, the condition is true, the body begins execution, and the loop adds the grade value to the total (line 56) and adds 1 to gradeCounter (line 57). Then lines 60–61 in the loop's body input the next value from the user. Next, program control reaches the closing right brace of the body at line 62, so execution continues with the test of the while's condition (line 54). The condition uses the most recent grade input by the user to determine whether the loop's body should execute again. Note that the value of variable grade is always input from the user immediately before the application tests the while condition. This allows the application to determine whether the value just input is the sentinel value *before* the application processes that value (i.e., adds it to the total). If the sentinel value is input, the loop terminates; the application does *not* add –1 to the total.

Good Programming Practice 5.7

In a sentinel-controlled loop, the prompts requesting data entry should explicitly remind the user of the sentinel value.

After the loop terminates, the if...else statement at lines 66–77 executes. The condition at line 66 determines whether any grades were input. If none were input, the else part (lines 76–77) of the if...else statement executes and displays the message "No grades were entered", and the method returns control to the calling method.

Notice the while statement's block in Fig. 5.9 (lines 55–62). Without the braces, the loop would consider its body to be only the first statement, which adds the grade to the total. The last three statements in the block would fall outside the loop's body, causing the computer to interpret the code incorrectly as follows:

```
while ( grade != -1 )
   total = total + grade; // add grade to total
gradeCounter = gradeCounter + 1; // increment counter

// prompt for input and read next grade from user
Console.Write( "Enter grade or -1 to quit: " );
grade = Convert.ToInt32( Console.ReadLine() );
```

The preceding code would cause an infinite loop in the application if the user did not enter the sentinel -1 at line 51 (before the while statement).

Error-Prevention Tip 5.3

Omitting the braces that delimit a block can lead to logic errors, such as infinite loops. To prevent this problem, some programmers enclose the body of every control statement in braces even if the body contains only a single statement.

Explicitly and Implicitly Converting Between Simple Types
If at least one grade was entered, line 69 of Fig. 5.9 calculates the average of the grades. Recall from Fig. 5.6 that integer division yields an integer result. Even though variable average is declared as a double (line 42), the calculation

```
average = total / gradeCounter;
```

loses the fractional part of the quotient before the result of the division is assigned to average. This occurs because `total` and `gradeCounter` are both integers, and integer division yields an integer result. To perform a floating-point calculation with integer values,
we must temporarily treat these values as floating-point numbers for use in the calculation.
C# provides the ***unary cast operator*** to accomplish this task. Line 69 uses the **(double)**
cast operator—a unary operator—to create a *temporary* floating-point copy of its operand
`total` (which appears to the right of the operator). Using a cast operator in this manner is
called ***explicit conversion***. The value stored in `total` is still an integer.

The calculation now consists of a floating-point value (the temporary `double` version
of `total`) divided by the integer `gradeCounter`. C# knows how to evaluate only arithmetic
expressions in which the operands' types are identical. To ensure that the operands are of
the same type, C# performs an operation called ***promotion*** (or ***implicit conversion***) on
selected operands. For example, in an expression containing values of the types `int` and
`double`, the `int` values are promoted to `double` values for use in the expression. In this
example, the value of `gradeCounter` is promoted to type `double`, then floating-point division is performed and the result of the calculation is assigned to `average`. As long as the
`(double)` cast operator is applied to any variable in the calculation, the calculation will
yield a `double` result. Later in this chapter, we discuss all the simple types. You will learn
more about the promotion rules in Section 7.7.

Common Programming Error 5.7

*The cast operator can be used to convert between simple numeric types, such as `int` and `double`,
and between related reference types (as we discuss in Chapter 11, Polymorphism, Interfaces & Operator Overloading). Casting to the wrong type may cause compilation errors or runtime errors.*

Cast operators are available for all simple types. (We'll discuss cast operators for reference types in Chapter 11.) The cast operator is formed by placing parentheses around
the name of a type. This operator is a ***unary operator*** (i.e., an operator that takes only one
operand). In Chapter 3, we studied the binary arithmetic operators. C# also supports
unary versions of the plus (+) and minus (–) operators, so you can write expressions like
+5 or -7. Cast operators associate from right to left and have the same precedence as other
unary operators, such as unary + and unary -. This precedence is one level higher than that
of the ***multiplicative operators*** *, / and %. (See the operator precedence chart in
Appendix A.) We indicate the cast operator with the notation (*type*) in our precedence
charts, to indicate that any type name can be used to form a cast operator.

Line 74 outputs the class average using `Console`'s `WriteLine` method. In this example,
we decided that we'd like to display the class average rounded to the nearest hundredth
and output the average with exactly two digits to the right of the decimal point. The
format specifier F in `WriteLine`'s format item (line 74) indicates that variable `average`'s
value should be displayed as a real number. The number after the format specifier F represents the number of decimal places (in this case, 2) that should be output to the right of
the decimal point in the floating-point number—also known as the number's ***precision***.
Any floating point value output with F2 will be rounded to the hundredths position—for
example, 123.457 would be rounded to 123.46, and 27.333 would be rounded to 27.33.
In this application, the three grades entered during the sample execution of class `Grade-`
`BookTest` (Fig. 5.10) total 263, which yields the average 87.66666.... The format item
rounds the average to the hundredths position, and the average is displayed as `87.67`.

```
 1  // Fig. 5.10: GradeBookTest.cs
 2  // Create GradeBook object and invoke its DetermineClassAverage method.
 3  public class GradeBookTest
 4  {
 5     public static void Main( string[] args )
 6     {
 7        // create GradeBook object myGradeBook and
 8        // pass course name to constructor
 9        GradeBook myGradeBook = new GradeBook(
10           "CS101 Introduction to C# Programming" );
11
12        myGradeBook.DisplayMessage(); // display welcome message
13        myGradeBook.DetermineClassAverage(); // find average of grades
14     } // end Main
15  } // end class GradeBookTest
```

```
Welcome to the grade book for
CS101 Introduction to C# Programming!

Enter grade or -1 to quit: 96
Enter grade or -1 to quit: 88
Enter grade or -1 to quit: 79
Enter grade or -1 to quit: -1

Total of the 3 grades entered is 263
Class average is 87.67
```

Fig. 5.10 | Create GradeBook object and invoke its DetermineClassAverage method.

5.10 Formulating Algorithms: Nested Control Statements

For the next example, we once again formulate an algorithm by using pseudocode and top-down, stepwise refinement, and write a corresponding C# application. We have seen that control statements can be stacked on top of one another (in sequence). In this case study, we examine the only other structured way control statements can be connected, namely, by *nesting* one control statement within another.

Consider the following problem statement:

> *A college offers a course that prepares students for the state licensing exam for real estate brokers. Last year, 10 of the students who completed this course took the exam. The college wants to know how well its students did on the exam. You have been asked to write an application to summarize the results. You have been given a list of these 10 students. Next to each name is written a 1 if the student passed the exam or a 2 if the student failed.*

> *Your application should analyze the results of the exam as follows:*

> 1. *Input each test result (i.e., a 1 or 2). Display the message "Enter result" on the screen each time the application requests another test result.*

> 2. *Count the number of test results of each type.*

> 3. *Display a summary of the test results indicating the number of students who passed and the number who failed.*

> 4. *If more than eight students passed the exam, print the message "Raise tuition."*

After reading the problem statement, we make the following observations:

1. The application must process test results for 10 students. A counter-controlled loop can be used because the number of test results is known in advance.

2. Each test result has a numeric value—either a 1 or a 2. Each time the application reads a test result, the application must determine whether the number is a 1 or a 2. We test for a 1 in our algorithm. If the number is not a 1, we assume that it is a 2. (Exercise 5.24 considers the consequences of this assumption.)

3. Two counters are used to keep track of the exam results—one to count the number of students who passed the exam and one to count the number of students who failed the exam.

4. After the application has processed all the results, it must determine whether more than eight students passed the exam.

Let us proceed with top-down, stepwise refinement. We begin with a pseudocode representation of the top:

analyze exam results and decide whether tuition should be raised

Once again, the top is a *complete* representation of the application, but several refinements are likely to be needed before the pseudocode can evolve naturally into a C# application.

Our first refinement is

initialize variables
input the 10 exam results, and count passes and failures
print a summary of the exam results and decide whether tuition should be raised

Here too, even though we have a complete representation of the entire application, further refinement is necessary. We now specify individual variables. Counters are needed to record the passes and failures, a counter will be used to control the looping process and a variable is needed to store the user input. The variable in which the user input will be stored is not initialized at the start of the algorithm, because its value is read from the user during each repetition of the loop.

The pseudocode statement

initialize variables

can be refined as follows:

initialize passes to zero
initialize failures to zero
initialize student counter to one

Notice that only the counters are initialized at the start of the algorithm.

The pseudocode statement

input the 10 exam results, and count passes and failures

requires a loop that successively inputs the result of each exam. We know in advance that there are precisely 10 exam results, so counter-controlled looping is appropriate. Inside the loop (i.e., **nested** within the loop), a double-selection statement will determine whether each exam result is a pass or a failure and will increment the appropriate counter. The refinement of the preceding pseudocode statement is then

> *while student counter is less than or equal to 10*
>> *prompt the user to enter the next exam result*
>> *input the next exam result*
>>
>> *if the student passed*
>>> *add one to passes*
>> *else*
>>> *add one to failures*
>>
>> *add one to student counter*

We use blank lines to isolate the *if…else* control statement, which improves readability. The pseudocode statement

> *print a summary of the exam results and decide whether tuition should be raised*

can be refined as follows:

> *print the number of passes*
> *print the number of failures*
>
> *if more than eight students passed*
>> *print "Raise tuition"*

Complete Second Refinement of Pseudocode and Conversion to Class Analysis

The complete second refinement of the pseudocode appears in Fig. 5.11. Notice that blank lines are also used to set off the *while* statement for readability. This pseudocode is now sufficiently refined for conversion to C#. The C# class that implements the pseudocode algorithm is shown in Fig. 5.12, and two sample executions appear in Fig. 5.13.

```
 1    initialize passes to zero
 2    initialize failures to zero
 3    initialize student counter to one
 4
 5    while student counter is less than or equal to 10
 6        prompt the user to enter the next exam result
 7        input the next exam result
 8
 9        if the student passed
10            add one to passes
11        else
12            add one to failures
13
14        add one to student counter
15
16    print the number of passes
17    print the number of failures
18
19    if more than eight students passed
20        print "Raise tuition"
```

Fig. 5.11 | Pseudocode for the examination-results problem.

```
1    // Fig. 5.12: Analysis.cs
2    // Analysis of examination results, using nested control statements.
3    using System;
4
5    public class Analysis
6    {
7       public void ProcessExamResults()
8       {
9          // initializing variables in declarations
10         int passes = 0; // number of passes
11         int failures = 0; // number of failures
12         int studentCounter = 1; // student counter
13         int result; // one exam result from user
14
15         // process 10 students using counter-controlled repetition
16         while ( studentCounter <= 10 )
17         {
18            // prompt user for input and obtain value from user
19            Console.Write( "Enter result (1 = pass, 2 = fail): " );
20            result = Convert.ToInt32( Console.ReadLine() );
21
22            // if...else nested in while
23            if ( result == 1 ) // if result 1,
24               passes = passes + 1;
25            else // else result is not 1, so
26               failures = failures + 1; // increment failures
27
28            // increment studentCounter so loop eventually terminates
29            studentCounter = studentCounter + 1;
30         } // end while
31
32         // termination phase; prepare and display results
33         Console.WriteLine( "Passed: {0}\nFailed: {1}", passes, failures );
34
35         // determine whether more than 8 students passed
36         if ( passes > 8 )
37            Console.WriteLine( "Raise Tuition" );
38      } // end method ProcessExamResults
39   } // end class Analysis
```

Fig. 5.12 | Analysis of examination results, using nested control statements.

Lines 10–13 of Fig. 5.12 declare the variables that method ProcessExamResults of class Analysis uses to process the examination results. Several of these declarations use C#'s ability to incorporate variable initialization into declarations (passes is assigned 0, failures is assigned 0 and studentCounter is assigned 1). Looping applications may require initialization at the beginning of each repetition—such reinitialization would normally be performed by assignment statements rather than in declarations.

The while statement (lines 16–30) loops 10 times. During each repetition, the loop inputs and processes one exam result. Notice that the if...else statement (lines 23–26) for processing each result is nested in the while statement. If the result is 1, the if...else statement increments passes; otherwise, it assumes the result is 2 and increments failures. Line 29 increments studentCounter before the loop condition is tested again at line 16.

After 10 values have been input, the loop terminates and line 33 displays the number of passes and the number of failures. The if statement at lines 36–37 determines whether more than eight students passed the exam and, if so, outputs the message "Raise Tuition".

Error-Prevention Tip 5.4

Initializing local variables when they are declared helps you avoid compilation errors that might arise from attempts to use uninitialized data. While C# does not require that local variable initializations be incorporated into declarations, it does require that local variables be initialized before their values are used in an expression.

AnalysisTest *Class That Demonstrates Class* Analysis

Class AnalysisTest (Fig. 5.13) creates an Analysis object (line 7) and invokes the object's ProcessExamResults method (line 8) to process a set of exam results entered by the user. Figure 5.13 shows the input and output from two sample executions of the application. During the first sample execution, the condition at line 36 of method ProcessExamResults in Fig. 5.12 is true—more than eight students passed the exam, so the application outputs a message indicating that the tuition should be raised.

5.11 Compound Assignment Operators

C# provides several *compound assignment operators* for abbreviating assignment expressions. Any statement of the form

> *variable = variable operator expression*;

```
1   // Fig. 5.13: AnalysisTest.cs
2   // Test application for class Analysis.
3   public class AnalysisTest
4   {
5      public static void Main( string[] args )
6      {
7         Analysis application = new Analysis(); // create Analysis object
8         application.ProcessExamResults(); // call method to process results
9      } // end Main
10  } // end class AnalysisTest
```

```
Enter result (1 = pass, 2 = fail): 1
Enter result (1 = pass, 2 = fail): 2
Enter result (1 = pass, 2 = fail): 1
Enter result (1 = pass, 2 = fail): 1
Enter result (1 = pass, 2 = fail): 1
Enter result (1 = pass, 2 = fail): 1
Enter result (1 = pass, 2 = fail): 1
Enter result (1 = pass, 2 = fail): 1
Enter result (1 = pass, 2 = fail): 1
Enter result (1 = pass, 2 = fail): 1
Passed: 9
Failed: 1
Raise Tuition
```

Fig. 5.13 | Test application for class Analysis. (Part 1 of 2.)

```
Enter result (1 = pass, 2 = fail): 1
Enter result (1 = pass, 2 = fail): 2
Enter result (1 = pass, 2 = fail): 2
Enter result (1 = pass, 2 = fail): 2
Enter result (1 = pass, 2 = fail): 1
Enter result (1 = pass, 2 = fail): 1
Enter result (1 = pass, 2 = fail): 1
Enter result (1 = pass, 2 = fail): 1
Enter result (1 = pass, 2 = fail): 2
Enter result (1 = pass, 2 = fail): 2
Passed: 5
Failed: 5
```

Fig. 5.13 | Test application for class `Analysis`. (Part 2 of 2.)

where *operator* is one of the binary operators +, -, *, / or % (or others we discuss later in the text) can be written in the form

> *variable   operator=   expression*;

For example, you can abbreviate the statement

```
c = c + 3;
```

with the ***addition compound assignment operator***, ***+=***, as

```
c += 3;
```

The += operator adds the value of the expression on the right of the operator to the value of the variable on the left of the operator and stores the result in the variable on the left of the operator. Thus, the assignment expression c += 3 adds 3 to c. Figure 5.14 shows the arithmetic compound assignment operators, sample expressions using the operators and explanations of what the operators do.

Assignment operator	Sample expression	Explanation	Assigns
Assume: **int** c = 3, d = 5, e = 4, f = 6, g = 12;			
+=	c += 7	c = c + 7	10 to c
-=	d -= 4	d = d - 4	1 to d
*=	e *= 5	e = e * 5	20 to e
/=	f /= 3	f = f / 3	2 to f
%=	g %= 9	g = g % 9	3 to g

Fig. 5.14 | Arithmetic compound assignment operators.

5.12 Increment and Decrement Operators

C# provides two unary operators for adding 1 to or subtracting 1 from the value of a numeric variable. These are the unary *increment operator*, **++**, and the unary *decrement operator*, **--**, respectively, which are summarized in Fig. 5.15. An application can increment by 1 the value of a variable called c using the increment operator, ++, rather than the expression c = c + 1 or c += 1. An increment or decrement operator that is prefixed to (placed before) a variable is referred to as the *prefix increment operator* or *prefix decrement operator*, respectively. An increment or decrement operator that is postfixed to (placed after) a variable is referred to as the *postfix increment operator* or *postfix decrement operator*, respectively.

Incrementing (or decrementing) a variable with the prefix increment (or prefix decrement) operator causes it to be incremented (or decremented) by 1, and then the new value of the variable is used in the expression in which it appears. Incrementing (or decrementing) the variable with the postfix increment (or postfix decrement) operator causes the current value of the variable to be used in the expression in which it appears, and then the variable's value is incremented (or decremented) by 1.

Good Programming Practice 5.8

Unlike binary operators, the unary increment and decrement operators should (by convention) be placed next to their operands, with no intervening spaces.

Figure 5.16 demonstrates the difference between the prefix increment and postfix increment versions of the ++ increment operator. The decrement operator (--) works similarly. Note that this example contains only one class, with method Main performing all the class's work. In this chapter and in Chapter 4, you have seen examples consisting of two classes—one class containing methods that perform useful tasks and one containing method Main, which creates an object of the other class and calls its methods. In this example, we simply want to show the mechanics of the ++ operator, so we use only one class declaration containing method Main. Occasionally, when it makes no sense to try to create a reusable class to demonstrate a simple concept, we will use a mechanical example contained entirely within the Main method of a single class.

Operator	Called	Sample expression	Explanation
++	prefix increment	++a	Increment a by 1, then use the new value of a in the expression in which a resides.
++	postfix increment	a++	Use the current value of a in the expression in which a resides, then increment a by 1.
--	prefix decrement	--b	Decrement b by 1, then use the new value of b in the expression in which b resides.
--	postfix decrement	b--	Use the current value of b in the expression in which b resides, then decrement b by 1.

Fig. 5.15 | Increment and decrement operators.

```
1   // Fig. 5.16: Increment.cs
2   // Prefix increment and postfix increment operators.
3   using System;
4
5   public class Increment
6   {
7      public static void Main( string[] args )
8      {
9         int c;
10
11         // demonstrate postfix increment operator
12         c = 5; // assign 5 to c
13         Console.WriteLine( c ); // print 5
14         Console.WriteLine( c++ ); // print 5 again, then increment
15         Console.WriteLine( c ); // print 6
16
17         Console.WriteLine(); // skip a line
18
19         // demonstrate prefix increment operator
20         c = 5; // assign 5 to c
21         Console.WriteLine( c ); // print 5
22         Console.WriteLine( ++c ); // increment then print 6
23         Console.WriteLine( c ); // print 6 again
24      } // end Main
25   } // end class Increment
```

```
5
5
6

5
6
6
```

Fig. 5.16 | Prefix increment and postfix increment operators.

Line 12 initializes the variable c to 5, and line 13 outputs c's initial value. Line 14 outputs the value of the expression c++. This expression performs the postfix increment operation on the variable c, so c's original value (5) is output, then c's value is incremented. Thus, line 14 outputs c's initial value (5) again. Line 15 outputs c's new value (6) to prove that the variable's value was indeed incremented in line 14.

Line 20 resets c's value to 5, and line 21 outputs c's value. Line 22 outputs the value of the expression ++c. This expression performs the prefix increment operation on c, so its value is incremented, then the new value (6) is output. Line 23 outputs c's value again to show that the value of c is still 6 after line 22 executes.

The arithmetic compound assignment operators and the increment and decrement operators can be used to simplify statements. For example, the three assignment statements in Fig. 5.12 (lines 24, 26 and 29)

```
passes = passes + 1;
failures = failures + 1;
studentCounter = studentCounter + 1;
```

can be written more concisely with compound assignment operators as

```
passes += 1;
failures += 1;
studentCounter += 1;
```

and even more concisely with prefix increment operators as

```
++passes;
++failures;
++studentCounter;
```

or with postfix increment operators as

```
passes++;
failures++;
studentCounter++;
```

When incrementing or decrementing a variable in a statement by itself, the prefix increment and postfix increment forms have the same effect, and the prefix decrement and postfix decrement forms have the same effect. It is only when a variable appears in the context of a larger expression that the prefix increment and postfix increment have different effects (and similarly for the prefix decrement and postfix decrement).

Common Programming Error 5.8

Attempting to use the increment or decrement operator on an expression other than one to which a value can be assigned is a syntax error. For example, writing ++(x + 1) is a syntax error because (x + 1) is not a variable.

Figure 5.17 shows the precedence and associativity of the operators we have introduced to this point. The operators are shown from top to bottom in decreasing order of precedence. The second column describes the associativity of the operators at each level of precedence. The conditional operator (?:); the unary operators prefix increment (++), prefix decrement (--), plus (+) and minus (-); the cast operators; and the assignment operators =, +=, -=, *=, /= and %= associate from right to left. All the other operators in the operator precedence chart in Fig. 5.17 associate from left to right. The third column names the groups of operators.

5.13 Simple Types

The table in Appendix L, Simple Types, lists the thirteen *simple types* in C#. Like its predecessor languages C and C++, C# requires all variables to have a type. For this reason, C# is referred to as a *strongly typed language*.

In C and C++, programmers frequently have to write separate versions of applications to support different computer platforms, because the simple types are not guaranteed to be identical from computer to computer. For example, an int value on one machine might be represented by 16 bits (2 bytes) of memory, while an int value on another machine might be represented by 32 bits (4 bytes) of memory. In C#, int values are always 32 bits (4 bytes). In fact, *all* C# numeric types have fixed sizes, as is shown in Appendix L, Simple Types.

Operators						Associativity	Type
.	new	++*(postfix)*	--*(postfix)*			left to right	highest precedence
++	--	+	-	*(type)*		right to left	unary prefix
*	/	%				left to right	multiplicative
+	-					left to right	additive
<	<=	>	>=			left to right	relational
==	!=					left to right	equality
?:						right to left	conditional
=	+=	-=	*=	/=	%=	right to left	assignment

Fig. 5.17 | Precedence and associativity of the operators discussed so far.

Each type in Appendix L is listed with its size in bits (there are eight bits to a byte) and its range of values. Because the designers of C# want it to be maximally portable, they use internationally recognized standards for both character formats (Unicode; for more information, visit `www.unicode.org`) and floating-point numbers (IEEE 754; for more information, visit `grouper.ieee.org/groups/754/`).

Recall from Section 4.5 that variables of simple types declared outside of a method as fields of a class are automatically assigned default values unless explicitly initialized. Instance variables of types `char`, `byte`, `sbyte`, `short`, `ushort`, `int`, `uint`, `long`, `ulong`, `float`, `double`, and `decimal` are all given the value 0 by default. Instance variables of type `bool` are given the value `false` by default. Similarly, reference type instance variables are initialized by default to the value `null`.

5.14 (Optional) Software Engineering Case Study: Identifying Class Attributes in the ATM System

In Section 4.11, we began the first stage of an object-oriented design (OOD) for our ATM system—analyzing the requirements document and identifying the classes needed to implement the system. We listed the nouns and noun phrases in the requirements document and identified a separate class for each one that plays a significant role in the ATM system. We then modeled the classes and their relationships in a UML class diagram (Fig. 4.24). Classes have attributes (data) and operations (behaviors). Class attributes are implemented in C# programs as instance variables and properties, and class operations are implemented as methods and properties. In this section, we determine many of the attributes needed in the ATM system. In Section 6.10, we examine how these attributes represent an object's state. In Section 7.15, we determine the operations for our classes.

Identifying Attributes

Consider the attributes of some real-world objects: A person's attributes include height, weight and whether the person is left-handed, right-handed or ambidextrous. A radio's attributes include its station setting, its volume setting and its AM or FM setting. A car's attributes include its speedometer and odometer readings, the amount of gas in its tank and what gear it is in. A personal computer's attributes include its manufacturer (e.g., Dell, Gateway, Sun, Apple or IBM), type of screen (e.g., LCD or CRT), main memory size and hard disk size.

We can identify many attributes of the classes in our system by looking for descriptive words and phrases in the requirements document. For each one we find that plays a significant role in the ATM system, we create an attribute and assign it to one or more of the classes identified in Section 4.11. We also create attributes to represent any additional data that a class may need as such needs become clear throughout the design process.

Figure 5.18 lists the words or phrases from the requirements document that describe each class. For example, the requirements document describes the steps taken to obtain a "withdrawal amount," so we list "amount" next to class Withdrawal.

Figure 5.18 leads us to create one attribute of class ATM. Class ATM maintains information about the state of the ATM. The phrase "user is authenticated" describes a state of the ATM (we discuss states in detail in Section 6.10), so we include userAuthenticated as a bool *attribute* (i.e., an attribute that has a value of either true or false). This attribute indicates whether the ATM has successfully authenticated the current user—userAuthenticated must be true for the system to allow the user to perform transactions and access account information. This attribute helps ensure the security of the data in the system.

Class	Descriptive words and phrases
ATM	user is authenticated
BalanceInquiry	account number
Withdrawal	account number amount
Deposit	account number amount
BankDatabase	[no descriptive words or phrases]
Account	account number PIN balance
Screen	[no descriptive words or phrases]
Keypad	[no descriptive words or phrases]
CashDispenser	begins each day loaded with 500 $20 bills
DepositSlot	[no descriptive words or phrases]

Fig. 5.18 | Descriptive words and phrases from the ATM requirements document.

Classes `BalanceInquiry`, `Withdrawal` and `Deposit` share one attribute. Each transaction involves an "account number" that corresponds to the account of the user making the transaction. We assign integer attribute `accountNumber` to each transaction class to identify the account to which an object of the class applies.

Descriptive words and phrases in the requirements document also suggest some differences in the attributes required by each transaction class. The requirements document indicates that to withdraw cash or deposit funds, users must enter a specific "amount" of money to be withdrawn or deposited, respectively. Thus, we assign to classes `Withdrawal` and `Deposit` an attribute `amount` to store the value supplied by the user. The amounts of money related to a withdrawal and a deposit are defining characteristics of these transactions that the system requires for them to take place. Recall that C# represents monetary amounts with type `decimal`. Note that class `BalanceInquiry` does not need additional data to perform its task—it requires only an account number to indicate the account whose balance should be retrieved.

Class `Account` has several attributes. The requirements document states that each bank account has an "account number" and a "PIN," which the system uses for identifying accounts and authenticating users. We assign to class `Account` two integer attributes: `accountNumber` and `pin`. The requirements document also specifies that an account maintains a "balance" of the amount of money in the account, and that the money the user deposits does not become available for a withdrawal until the bank verifies the amount of cash in the deposit envelope and any checks in the envelope clear. An account must still record the amount of money that a user deposits, however. Therefore, we decide that an account should represent a balance using two `decimal` attributes—`availableBalance` and `totalBalance`. Attribute `availableBalance` tracks the amount of money that a user can withdraw from the account. Attribute `totalBalance` refers to the total amount of money that the user has "on deposit" (i.e., the amount of money available, plus the amount of cash deposits waiting to be verified or the amount of checks waiting to be cleared). For example, suppose an ATM user deposits $50.00 in cash into an empty account. The `totalBalance` attribute would increase to $50.00 to record the deposit, but the `availableBalance` would remain at $0 until a bank employee counts the amount of cash in the envelope and confirms the total. [*Note:* We assume that the bank updates the `availableBalance` attribute of an `Account` soon after the ATM transaction occurs, in response to confirming that $50 worth of cash was found in the deposit envelope. We assume that this update occurs through a transaction that a bank employee performs using a bank system other than the ATM. Thus, we do not discuss this transaction in our case study.]

Class `CashDispenser` has one attribute. The requirements document states that the cash dispenser "begins each day loaded with 500 $20 bills." The cash dispenser must keep track of the number of bills it contains to determine whether enough cash is on hand to satisfy withdrawal requests. We assign to class `CashDispenser` integer attribute `count`, which is initially set to 500.

For real problems in industry, there is no guarantee that requirements documents will be rich enough and precise enough for the object-oriented systems designer to determine all the attributes, or even all the classes. The need for additional classes, attributes and behaviors may become clear as the design process proceeds. As we progress through this case study, we too will continue to add, modify and delete information about the classes in our system.

Modeling Attributes

The class diagram in Fig. 5.19 lists some of the attributes for the classes in our system—the descriptive words and phrases in Fig. 5.18 helped us identify these attributes. For simplicity, Fig. 5.19 does not show the associations among classes—we showed these in Fig. 4.24. Systems designers commonly do this. Recall that in the UML, a class's attributes are placed in the middle compartment of the class's rectangle. We list each attribute's name and type separated by a colon (:), followed in some cases by an equal sign (=) and an initial value.

Consider the userAuthenticated attribute of class ATM:

```
userAuthenticated : bool = false
```

This attribute declaration contains three pieces of information about the attribute. The *attribute name* is userAuthenticated. The *attribute type* is bool. In C#, an attribute can be represented by a simple type, such as bool, int, double or decimal, or a class type—as discussed in Chapter 4. We have chosen to model only simple-type attributes in Fig. 5.19—we discuss the reasoning behind this decision shortly.

We can also indicate an initial value for an attribute. Attribute userAuthenticated in class ATM has an initial value of false. This indicates that the system initially does not consider the user to be authenticated. If an attribute has no initial value specified, only its

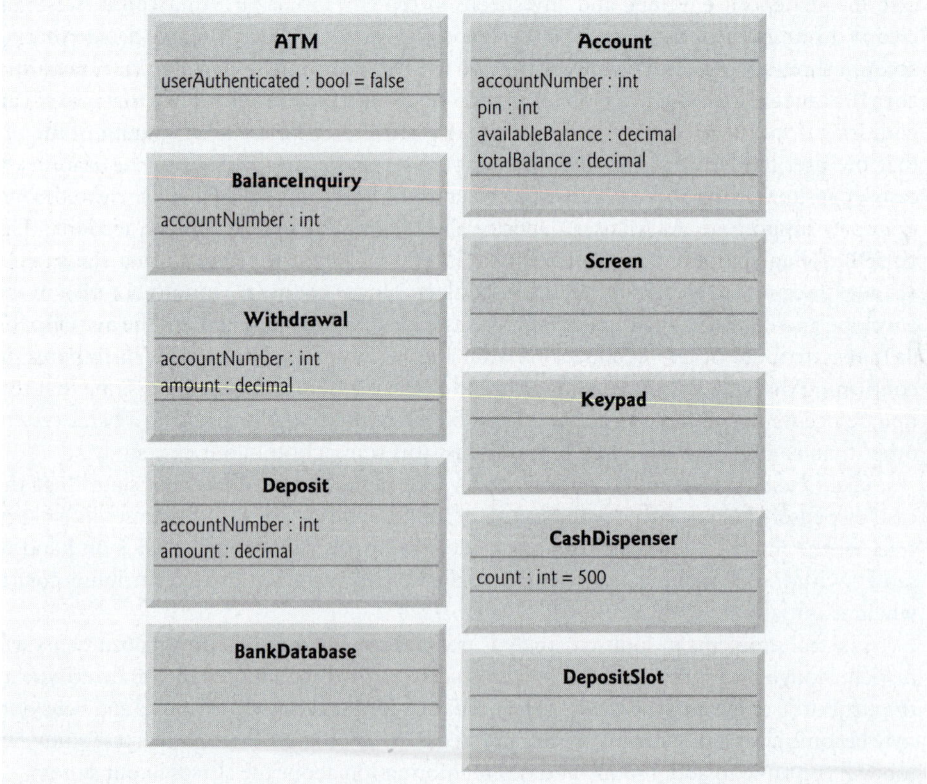

ATM	Account
userAuthenticated : bool = false	accountNumber : int pin : int availableBalance : decimal totalBalance : decimal

BalanceInquiry	Screen
accountNumber : int	

Withdrawal	Keypad
accountNumber : int amount : decimal	

Deposit	CashDispenser
accountNumber : int amount : decimal	count : int = 500

BankDatabase	DepositSlot

Fig. 5.19 | Classes with attributes.

name and type (separated by a colon) are shown. For example, the `accountNumber` attribute of class `BalanceInquiry` is an `int`. Here we show no initial value, because the value of this attribute is a number that we do not yet know. This number will be determined at execution time based on the account number entered by the current ATM user.

Figure 5.19 does not contain attributes for classes `Screen`, `Keypad` and `DepositSlot`. These are important components of our system for which our design process simply has not yet revealed any attributes. We may discover some, however, in the remaining phases of design or when we implement these classes in C#. This is perfectly normal.

Software Engineering Observation 5.6

Early in the design process, classes often lack attributes (and operations). Such classes should not be eliminated, however, because attributes (and operations) may become evident in the later phases of design and implementation.

Note that Fig. 5.19 also does not include attributes for class `BankDatabase`. We have chosen to include only simple-type attributes in Fig. 5.19 (and in similar class diagrams throughout the case study). A class-type attribute is modeled more clearly as an association (in particular, a composition) between the class with the attribute and the attribute's own class. For example, the class diagram in Fig. 4.24 indicates that class `BankDatabase` participates in a composition relationship with zero or more `Account` objects. From this composition, we can determine that when we implement the ATM system in C#, we will be required to create an attribute of class `BankDatabase` to hold zero or more `Account` objects. Similarly, we will assign attributes to class `ATM` that correspond to its composition relationships with classes `Screen`, `Keypad`, `CashDispenser` and `DepositSlot`. These composition-based attributes would be redundant if modeled in Fig. 5.19, because the compositions modeled in Fig. 4.24 already convey the fact that the database contains information about zero or more accounts and that an ATM is composed of a screen, keypad, cash dispenser and deposit slot. Software developers typically model these whole/part relationships as composition associations rather than as attributes required to implement the relationships.

The class diagram in Fig. 5.19 provides a solid basis for the structure of our model, but the diagram is not complete. In Section 6.10, we identify the states and activities of the objects in the model, and in Section 7.15 we identify the operations that the objects perform. As we present more of the UML and object-oriented design, we will continue to strengthen the structure of our model.

Software Engineering Case Study Self-Review Exercises

5.1 We typically identify the attributes of the classes in our system by analyzing the _____ in the requirements document.
  a) nouns and noun phrases
  b) descriptive words and phrases
  c) verbs and verb phrases
  d) All of the above.

5.2 Which of the following is not an attribute of an airplane?
  a) length
  b) wingspan
  c) fly
  d) number of seats

5.3 Describe the meaning of the following attribute declaration of class `CashDispenser` in the class diagram in Fig. 5.19:

```
count : int = 500
```

Answers to Software Engineering Case Study Self-Review Exercises

5.1 b.

5.2 c. Fly is an operation or behavior of an airplane, not an attribute.

5.3 This declaration indicates that attribute `count` is an `int` with an initial value of 500; `count` keeps track of the number of bills available in the `CashDispenser` at any given time.

5.15 Wrap-Up

This chapter presented basic problem-solving strategies that programmers use in building classes and developing methods for these classes. We demonstrated how to construct an algorithm (i.e., an approach to solving a problem), then how to refine the algorithm through several phases of pseudocode development, resulting in C# code that can be executed as part of a method. The chapter showed how to use top-down, stepwise refinement to plan out the specific actions that a method must perform and the order in which the method must perform these actions.

Only three types of control structures—sequence, selection and repetition—are needed to develop any problem-solving algorithm. Specifically, this chapter demonstrated the `if` single-selection statement, the `if...else` double-selection statement and the `while` repetition statement. These are some of the building blocks used to construct solutions to many problems. We used control-statement stacking to compute the total and the average of a set of student grades with counter- and sentinel-controlled repetition, and we used control-statement nesting to analyze and make decisions based on a set of exam results. We introduced C#'s compound assignment operators, as well as its increment and decrement operators. Finally, we discussed the simple types available to C# programmers. In Chapter 6, Control Statements: Part 2, we continue our discussion of control statements, introducing the `for`, `do...while` and `switch` statements.

Summary

Section 5.2 Algorithms
- An algorithm is a procedure for solving a problem in terms of the actions to execute and the order in which these actions execute.
- Specifying the order in which statements (actions) execute in an application is called program control.

Section 5.3 Pseudocode
- Pseudocode is an informal language that helps you develop algorithms without having to worry about the strict details of C# language syntax.
- A carefully prepared pseudocode application can easily be converted to a corresponding C# application.

Section 5.4 Control Structures

- There are three types of control structures—sequence, selection and repetition.
- The sequence structure is built into C#. Unless directed otherwise, the computer executes C# statements one after the other in the order in which they are written.
- Activity diagrams are part of the UML. An activity diagram models the workflow of a portion of a software system.
- Activity diagrams are composed of special-purpose symbols, such as action-state symbols, diamonds and small circles. These symbols are connected by transition arrows, which represent the flow of the activity.
- Like pseudocode, activity diagrams help you develop and represent algorithms. Activity diagrams clearly show how control structures operate.
- Action-state symbols (rectangles with their left and right sides replaced with arcs curving outward) represent actions to perform.
- The arrows in an activity diagram represent transitions, which indicate the order in which the actions represented by the action states occur.
- The solid circle located at the top of an activity diagram represents the activity's initial state. The solid circle surrounded by a hollow circle that appears at the bottom represents the final state.
- Rectangles with the upper-right corners folded over are UML notes (like comments in C#)—explanatory remarks that describe the purpose of symbols in the diagram.
- C# has three types of selection statements: the `if` statement, the `if...else` statement and the `switch` statement.
- The `if` statement is called a single-selection statement because it selects or ignores a single action.
- The `if...else` statement is called a double-selection statement because it selects between two different actions.
- The `switch` statement is called a multiple-selection statement because it selects among many different actions (or groups of actions).
- C# provides four repetition statements: the `while`, `do...while`, `for` and `foreach` statements.
- The `while`, `for` and `foreach` statements perform the actions in their bodies zero or more times.
- The `do...while` statement performs the actions in its body one or more times.
- Control statements may be connected in two ways: control-statement stacking and control-statement nesting.

Section 5.5 `if` Single-Selection Statement

- The `if` single-selection statement performs an indicated action only when the condition is true; otherwise, the action is skipped.
- In an activity diagram, the diamond, or decision symbol, indicates that a decision is to be made. The workflow will continue along a path determined by the symbol's associated guard conditions.
- When modelled by a UML activity diagram, all control statements contain initial states, transition arrows, action states and decision symbols.

Section 5.6 `if...else` Double-Selection Statement

- The `if...else` double-selection statement allows you to specify an action to perform when the condition is true and a different action when the condition is false.
- C# provides the conditional operator (`?:`), which can be used in place of an `if...else` statement. The conditional expression evaluates to the second operand if the first operand evaluates to `true`, and evaluates to the third operand if the first operand evaluates to `false`.

- To include several statements in the body of an `if` (or the body of an `else` for an `if...else` statement), enclose the statements in braces (`{` and `}`).

- A set of statements contained within a pair of braces is called a block. A block can be placed anywhere in an application that a single statement can be placed.

Section 5.7 `while` *Repetition Statement*

- A repetition statement allows you to specify that an application should repeat an action while some condition remains true.

- The format for the `while` repetition statement is

```
while ( condition )
    statement
```

Section 5.8 Formulating Algorithms: Counter-Controlled Repetition

- Counter-controlled repetition is a technique that uses a variable called a counter to control the number of times a set of statements will execute.

- We say that a variable is definitely assigned when the variable is assigned in every possible flow of control. Local variables must be definitely assigned before they are used in calculations.

- Dividing two integers results in integer division—any fractional part of the calculation is lost.

Section 5.9 Formulating Algorithms: Sentinel-Controlled Repetition

- Sentinel-controlled repetition is a technique that uses a special value called a sentinel value to indicate "end of data entry."

Section 5.10 Formulating Algorithms: Nested Control Statements

- The unary cast operator (`double`) creates a *temporary* floating-point copy of its operand. Using a cast operator in this manner is called explicit conversion.

- To ensure that both operands of a binary operator are of the same type, C# performs promotion on selected operands.

- The format specifier `F` indicates that a variable's value should be displayed as a real number. The number after the format specifier `F` represents the number's precision.

Section 5.11 Compound Assignment Operators

- C# provides several compound assignment operators for abbreviating assignment expressions, including `+=`, `-=`, `*=`, `/=` and `%=`.

Section 5.12 Increment and Decrement Operators

- C# provides the unary increment operator, `++`, and the unary decrement operator, `--`, for adding 1 to or subtracting 1 from the value of a numeric variable.

- Incrementing (or decrementing) a variable with the prefix increment (or prefix decrement) operator causes the variable to be incremented (decremented) by 1, and then the new value of the variable is used in the expression in which it appears. Incrementing (or decrementing) the variable with the postfix increment (or postfix decrement) operator causes the current value of the variable to be used in the expression in which it appears, and then the variable's value is incremented (decremented) by 1.

Section 5.13 Simple Types
- C# is a strongly typed language—that is, it requires all variables to have a type.

- Variables of simple types declared outside of a method as fields of a class are automatically assigned default values. Instance variables of types char, byte, sbyte, short, ushort, int, uint, long, ulong, float, double, and decimal are all given the value 0 by default. Instance variables of type bool are given the value false by default. Reference type instance variables are initialized by default to the value null.

Terminology

-- operator
?: operator
++ operator
action
action/decision model of programming
action expression (in the UML)
action state (in the UML)
action-state symbol (in the UML)
activity (in the UML)
activity diagram (in the UML)
addition compound assignment operator (+=)
algorithm
arithmetic compound assignment operators:
    +=, -=, *=, /= and %=
block
body of a loop
bool simple type
cast operator, (*type*)
compound assignment operator
conditional expression
conditional operator (?:)
control statement
control-statement nesting
control-statement stacking
control structure
control variable
counter
counter-controlled repetition
dangling-else problem
decision
decision symbol (in the UML)
decrement operator (--)
definite assignment
definite repetition
diamond (in the UML)
dotted line
double-selection statement
dummy value
explicit conversion
false
fatal logic error

final state (in the UML)
flag value
goto statement
guard condition (in the UML)
if statement
if...else statement
implicit conversion
increment operator (++)
indefinite repetition
infinite loop
initial state (in the UML)
initialization
integer division
instantiate an object
iterate
iteration statement
logic error
loop
loop-continuation condition
loop counter
merge symbol (in the UML)
multiple-selection statement
nested control statements
nested if...else statements
nonfatal logic error
note (in the UML)
order in which actions should execute
postfix decrement operator
postfix increment operator
prefix decrement operator
prefix increment operator
procedure
program control
promotion
pseudocode
refinement
repetition
repetition structure
selection structure
sentinel-controlled repetition
sentinel value

sequence structure
sequential execution
signal value
simple types
single-entry/single-exit control structures
single-selection statement
small circle (in the UML)
solid circle (in the UML)
solid circle surrounded by a hollow circle
(in the UML)
stacked control statements
strongly typed language
structured programming

syntax error
ternary operator
top-down stepwise refinement
total
transfer of control
transition (in the UML)
transition arrow (in the UML)
true
truncate
unary cast operator
unary operator
while statement
workflow

Self-Review Exercises

5.1 Fill in the blanks in each of the following statements:
   a) All applications can be written in terms of three types of control structures: _____, _____ and _____.
   b) The _____ statement is used to execute one action when a condition is true and another when that condition is false.
   c) Repeating a set of instructions a specific number of times is called _____ repetition.
   d) When it is not known in advance how many times a set of statements will be repeated, a(n) _____ value can be used to terminate the repetition.
   e) The _____ structure is built into C#—by default, statements execute in the order they appear.
   f) Instance variables of type int are given the value _____ by default.
   g) C# is a _____ language—it requires all variables to have a type.
   h) If the increment operator is _____ to a variable, the variable is incremented by 1 first, then its new value is used in the expression.

5.2 State whether each of the following is *true* or *false*. If *false*, explain why.
   a) An algorithm is a procedure for solving a problem in terms of the actions to execute and the order in which these actions execute.
   b) A set of statements contained within a pair of parentheses is called a block.
   c) A selection statement specifies that an action is to be repeated while some condition remains true.
   d) A nested control statement appears in the body of another control statement.
   e) C# provides the arithmetic compound assignment operators +=, -=, *=, /= and %= for abbreviating assignment expressions.
   f) Specifying the order in which statements (actions) execute in an application is called program control.
   g) The unary cast operator (double) creates a temporary integer copy of its operand.
   h) Instance variables of type bool are given the value true by default.
   i) Pseudocode helps you think out an application before attempting to write it in a programming language.

5.3 Write four different C# statements that each add 1 to int variable x.

5.4 Write C# statements to accomplish each of the following tasks:
   a) Assign the sum of x and y to z, and increment x by 1 after the calculation. Use only one statement.
   b) Test whether variable count is greater than 10. If it is, print "Count is greater than 10".

    c) Decrement the variable x by 1, then subtract it from the variable total. Use only one statement.

    d) Calculate the remainder after q is divided by divisor, and assign the result to q. Write this statement in two different ways.

5.5   Write a C# statement to accomplish each of the following tasks:

    a) Declare variables sum and x to be of type int.

    b) Assign 1 to variable x.

    c) Assign 0 to variable sum.

    d) Add variable x to variable sum, and assign the result to variable sum.

    e) Print "The sum is: ", followed by the value of variable sum.

5.6   Combine the statements that you wrote in Exercise 5.5 into a C# application that calculates and prints the sum of the integers from 1 to 10. Use a while statement to loop through the calculation and increment statements. The loop should terminate when the value of x becomes 11.

5.7   Determine the value of the variables in the following statement after the calculation is performed. Assume that when the statement begins executing, all variables are type int and have the value 5.

```
product *= x++;
```

5.8   Identify and correct the errors in each of the following sets of code:

    a)
```
while ( c <= 5 )
{
    product *= c;
    ++c;
```

    b)
```
if ( gender == 1 )
    Console.WriteLine( "Woman" );
else;
    Console.WriteLine( "Man" );
```

5.9   What is wrong with the following while statement?

```
while ( z >= 0 )
    sum += z;
```

Answers to Self-Review Exercises

5.1   a) sequence, selection, repetition. b) if...else. c) counter-controlled (or definite). d) sentinel, signal, flag or dummy. e) sequence. f) 0 (zero). g) strongly typed. h) prefixed.

5.2   a) True. b) False. A set of statements contained within a pair of braces ({ and }) is called a block. c) False. A repetition statement specifies that an action is to be repeated while some condition remains true. A selection statement determines whether an action is performed based on the truth or falsity of a condition. d) True. e) True. f) True. g) False. The unary cast operator (double) creates a temporary floating-point copy of its operand. h) False. Instance variables of type bool are given the value false by default. i) True.

5.3
```
x = x + 1;
x += 1;
++x;
x++;
```

5.4   a)
```
z = x++ + y;
```
    b)
```
if ( count > 10 )
    Console.WriteLine( "Count is greater than 10" );
```

c) total -= --x;
d) q %= divisor;
   q = q % divisor;

5.5   a) *int* sum, x;
       b) x = 1;
       c) sum = 0;
       d) sum += x; or sum = sum + x;
       e) Console.WriteLine("The sum is: {0}", sum);

5.6   The application is as follows:

```
1   // Ex. 5.6: Calculate.cs
2   // Calculate the sum of the integers from 1 to 10
3   using System;
4
5   public class Calculate
6   {
7      public static void Main( string[] args )
8      {
9         int sum;
10        int x;
11
12        x = 1; // initialize x to 1 for counting
13        sum = 0; // initialize sum to 0 for totaling
14
15        while ( x <= 10 ) // while x is less than or equal to 10
16        {
17           sum += x; // add x to sum
18           x++; // increment x
19        } // end while
20
21        Console.WriteLine( "The sum is: {0}", sum );
22     } // end Main
23  } // end class Calculate
```

```
The sum is: 55
```

5.7   product = 25, x = 6

5.8   a) Error: The closing right brace of the while statement's body is missing.
          Correction: Add a closing right brace after the statement ++c;.
       b) Error: The semicolon after else results in a logic error. The second output statement
          will always execute.
          Correction: Remove the semicolon after else.

5.9   The value of the variable z is never changed in the while statement. Therefore, an infinite
loop occurs if the loop-continuation condition (z >= 0) is initially true. To prevent an infinite loop,
z must be decremented so that it eventually becomes less than 0.

Exercises

5.10   Compare and contrast the if single-selection statement and the while repetition statement.
How are these two statements similar? How are they different?

5.11   Explain what happens when a C# application attempts to divide one integer by another. What happens to the fractional part of the calculation? How can you avoid that outcome?

5.12   Describe the two ways in which control statements can be combined.

5.13   What type of repetition would be appropriate for calculating the sum of the first 100 positive integers? What type of repetition would be appropriate for calculating the sum of an arbitrary number of positive integers? Briefly describe how each of these tasks could be performed.

5.14   What is the difference between the prefix increment operator and the postfix increment operator?

5.15   Identify and correct the errors in each of the following pieces of code. [*Note:* There may be more than one error in each piece of code.]

```
a) if ( age >= 65 );
       Console.WriteLine( "Age greater than or equal to 65" );
   else
       Console.WriteLine( "Age is less than 65 )";
b) int x = 1, total;
   while ( x <= 10 )
   {
       total += x;
       ++x;
   }
c) while ( x <= 100 )
       total += x;
       ++x;
d) while ( y > 0 )
   {
       Console.WriteLine( y );
       ++y;
```

5.16   What does the following application print?

```
1   // Ex. 5.16: Mystery.cs
2   using System;
3
4   public class Mystery
5   {
6      public static void Main( string[] args )
7      {
8         int y;
9         int x = 1;
10        int total = 0;
11
12        while ( x <= 10 )
13        {
14           y = x * x;
15           Console.WriteLine( y );
16           total += y;
17           x++;
18        } // end while
19
20        Console.WriteLine( "Total is {0}", total );
21     } // end Main
22  } // end class Mystery
```

For Exercise 5.17 through Exercise 5.20, perform each of the following steps:

 a) Read the problem statement.
 b) Formulate the algorithm using pseudocode and top-down, stepwise refinement.
 c) Write a C# application.
 d) Test, debug and execute the C# application.
 e) Process three complete sets of data.

5.17 Drivers are concerned with the mileage their automobiles get. One driver has kept track of several tankfuls of gasoline by recording the miles driven and gallons used for each tankful. Develop a C# application that will input the miles driven and gallons used (both as integers) for each tankful. The application should calculate and display the miles per gallon obtained for each tankful and print the combined miles per gallon obtained for all tankfuls up to this point. All averaging calculations should produce floating-point results. Display the results rounded to the nearest hundredth. Use the Console class's ReadLine method and sentinel-controlled repetition to obtain the data from the user.

5.18 Develop a C# application that will determine whether any of several department-store customers has exceeded the credit limit on a charge account. For each customer, the following facts are available:

 a) account number
 b) balance at the beginning of the month
 c) total of all items charged by the customer this month
 d) total of all credits applied to the customer's account this month
 e) allowed credit limit.

The application should input all these facts as integers, calculate the new balance (= *beginning balance + charges – credits*), display the new balance and determine whether the new balance exceeds the customer's credit limit. For those customers whose credit limit is exceeded, the application should display the message "Credit limit exceeded". Use sentinel-controlled repetition to obtain the data for each account.

5.19 A large company pays its salespeople on a commission basis. The salespeople receive $200 per week plus 9% of their gross sales for that week. For example, a salesperson who sells $5,000 worth of merchandise in a week receives $200 plus 9% of $5,000, or a total of $650. You have been supplied with a list of the items sold by each salesperson. The values of these items are as follows:

```
Item    Value
1       239.99
2       129.75
3        99.95
4       350.89
```

Develop a C# application that inputs one salesperson's items sold for the last week, then calculates and displays that salesperson's earnings. There is no limit to the number of items that can be sold by a salesperson.

5.20 Develop a C# application that will determine the gross pay for each of three employees. The company pays straight time for the first 40 hours worked by each employee and time-and-a-half for all hours worked in excess of 40 hours. You are given a list of the three employees of the company, the number of hours each employee worked last week and the hourly rate of each employee. Your application should input this information for each employee, then should determine and display the employee's gross pay. Use the Console class's ReadLine method to input the data.

5.21 The process of finding the maximum value (i.e., the largest of a group of values) is used frequently in computer applications. For example, an application that determines the winner of a sales contest would input the number of units sold by each salesperson. The salesperson who sells the most units wins the contest. Write a pseudocode application and then a C# application that inputs a series of 10 integers, then determines and prints the largest integer. Your application should use at least the following three variables:

a) `counter`: A counter to count to 10 (i.e., to keep track of how many numbers have been input and to determine when all 10 numbers have been processed).

b) `number`: The integer most recently input by the user.

c) `largest`: The largest number found so far.

5.22 Write a C# application that uses looping to print the following table of values:

```
N          10*N      100*N     1000*N

1          10        100       1000
2          20        200       2000
3          30        300       3000
4          40        400       4000
5          50        500       5000
```

5.23 Using an approach similar to that for Exercise 5.21, find the *two* largest values of the 10 values entered. [*Note:* You may input each number only once.]

5.24 Modify the application in Fig. 5.12 to validate its inputs. For any input, if the value entered is other than 1 or 2, keep looping until the user enters a correct value.

5.25 What does the following application print?

```csharp
1   // Ex. 5.25: Mystery2.cs
2   using System;
3
4   public class Mystery2
5   {
6      public static void Main( string[] args )
7      {
8         int count = 1;
9
10        while ( count <= 10 )
11        {
12           Console.WriteLine( count % 2 == 1 ? "****" : "++++++++" );
13           count++;
14        } // end while
15     } // end Main
16  } // end class Mystery2
```

5.26 What does the following application print?

```csharp
1   // Ex. 5.26: Mystery3.cs
2   using System;
3
4   public class Mystery3
5   {
6      public static void Main( string[] args )
7      {
8         int row = 10;
9         int column;
```

```
10
11          while ( row >= 1 )
12          {
13             column = 1;
14
15             while ( column <= 10 )
16             {
17                Console.Write( row % 2 == 1 ? "<" : ">" );
18                column++;
19             } // end while
20
21             row--;
22             Console.WriteLine();
23          } // end while
24       } // end Main
25    } // end class Mystery3
```

5.27   *(Dangling-else Problem)* Determine the output for each of the given sets of code when x is 9 and y, is 11 and when x is 11 and y is 9. Note that the compiler ignores the indentation in a C# application. Also, the C# compiler always associates an else with the immediately preceding if unless told to do otherwise by the placement of braces ({}). On first glance, you may not be sure which if an else matches—this situation is referred to as the "dangling-else problem." We have eliminated the indentation from the following code to make the problem more challenging. [*Hint:* Apply the indentation conventions you have learned.]

a)
```
if ( x < 10 )
if ( y > 10 )
Console.WriteLine( "*****" );
else
Console.WriteLine( "#####" );
Console.WriteLine( "$$$$$" );
```

b)
```
if ( x < 10 )
{
if ( y > 10 )
Console.WriteLine( "*****" );
}
else
{
Console.WriteLine( "#####" );
Console.WriteLine( "$$$$$" );
}
```

5.28   *(Another Dangling-else Problem)* Modify the given code to produce the output shown in each part of the problem. Use proper indentation techniques. Make no changes other than inserting braces and changing the indentation of the code. The compiler ignores indentation in a C# application. We have eliminated the indentation from the given code to make the problem more challenging. [*Note:* It is possible that no modification is necessary for some of the parts.]

```
if ( y == 8 )
if ( x == 5 )
Console.WriteLine( "@@@@@" );
else
Console.WriteLine( "#####" );
Console.WriteLine( "$$$$$" );
Console.WriteLine( "&&&&&" );
```

a) Assuming that x = 5 and y = 8, the following output is produced:

```
@@@@@
$$$$$
&&&&&
```

b) Assuming that x = 5 and y = 8, the following output is produced:

```
@@@@@
```

c) Assuming that x = 5 and y = 8, the following output is produced:

```
@@@@@
&&&&&
```

d) Assuming that x = 5 and y = 7, the following output is produced. [*Note:* The last three output statements after the else are all part of a block.]

```
#####
$$$$$
&&&&&
```

5.29   Write an application that prompts the user to enter the size of the side of a square, then displays a hollow square of that size made of asterisks. Your application should work for squares of all side lengths between 1 and 20. If the user enters a number less than 1 or greater than 20, your application should display a square of size 1 or 20, respectively.

5.30   *(Palindromes)* A palindrome is a sequence of characters that reads the same backward as forward. For example, each of the following five-digit integers is a palindrome: 12321, 55555, 45554 and 11611. Write an application that reads in a five-digit integer and determines whether it is a palindrome. If the number is not five digits long, display an error message and allow the user to enter a new value. [*Hint:* Use the remainder and division operators to pick off the number's digits one at a time, from right to left.]

5.31   Write an application that inputs an integer containing only 0s and 1s (i.e., a binary integer) and prints its decimal equivalent. [*Hint:* Picking the digits of a binary number is similar to picking the digits off a decimal number, which you did in Exercise 5.30. In the decimal number system, the rightmost digit has a positional value of 1 and the next digit to the left has a positional value of 10, then 100, then 1000 and so on. The decimal number 234 can be interpreted as 4 * 1 + 3 * 10 + 2 * 100. In the binary number system, the rightmost digit has a positional value of 1, the next digit to the left has a positional value of 2, then 4, then 8 and so on. The decimal equivalent of binary 1101 is 1 * 1 + 0 * 2 + 1 * 4 + 1 * 8, or 1 + 0 + 4 + 8, or 13.]

5.32   Write an application that uses only the output statements

```
Console.Write( "* " );
Console.Write( " " );
Console.WriteLine();
```

to display the checkerboard pattern that follows. Note that a `Console.WriteLine` method call with no arguments causes the application to output a single newline character. [*Hint:* Repetition statements are required.]

```
*  *  *  *  *  *  *
  *  *  *  *  *  *  *
*  *  *  *  *  *  *
  *  *  *  *  *  *  *
*  *  *  *  *  *  *
  *  *  *  *  *  *  *
*  *  *  *  *  *  *
  *  *  *  *  *  *  *
```

5.33 Write an application that keeps displaying in the console window the powers of the integer 2—namely, 2, 4, 8, 16, 32, 64 and so on. Loop 40 times. What happens when you run this application?

5.34 What is wrong with the following statement? Provide the correct statement to add one to the sum of x and y.

```
Console.WriteLine( ++(x + y) );
```

5.35 Write an application that reads three nonzero values entered by the user, then determines and prints whether they could represent the sides of a triangle.

5.36 Write an application that reads three nonzero integers, then determines and prints whether they could represent the sides of a right triangle.

5.37 A company wants to transmit data over the telephone, but is concerned that its phones may be tapped. It has asked you to write an application that will encrypt the data so that it may be transmitted more securely. All the data is transmitted as four-digit integers. Your application should read a four-digit integer entered by the user and encrypt it as follows: Replace each digit with the result of adding 7 to the digit and getting the remainder after dividing the new value by 10. Then swap the first digit with the third, and swap the second digit with the fourth. Then print the encrypted integer. Write a separate application that inputs an encrypted four-digit integer and decrypts it to form the original number.

5.38 The factorial of a non-negative integer n is written as $n!$ (pronounced "n factorial") and is defined as follows:

$$n! = n \cdot (n-1) \cdot (n-2) \cdot \ldots \cdot 1 \quad \text{(for values of } n \text{ greater than or equal to 1)}$$

and

$$n! = 1 \quad \text{(for } n = 0\text{)}$$

For example, $5! = 5 \cdot 4 \cdot 3 \cdot 2 \cdot 1$, which is 120.

a) Write an application that reads a non-negative integer and computes and prints its factorial.

b) Write an application that estimates the value of the mathematical constant e by using the formula

$$e = 1 + \frac{1}{1!} + \frac{1}{2!} + \frac{1}{3!} + \ldots$$

Note that the predefined constant Math.E (class Math is in the System namespace) provides a good approximation of e. Use the WriteLine method to output both your estimated value of e and Math.E for comparison.

c) Write an application that computes the value of e^x by using the formula

$$e^x = 1 + \frac{x}{1!} + \frac{x^2}{2!} + \frac{x^3}{3!} + \ldots$$

Compare the result of your calculation to the return value of the method call Math.Pow(Math.E, x). [*Note:* The predefined method Math.Pow takes two arguments, and raises the first argument to the power of the second. We discuss Math.Pow in Section 6.4.]

Control Statements: Part 2

Not everything that can be counted counts, and not every thing that counts can be counted.
—Albert Einstein

Who can control his fate?
—William Shakespeare

The used key is always bright.
—Benjamin Franklin

Intelligence ... is the faculty of making artificial objects, especially tools to make tools.
—Henri Bergson

Every advantage in the past is judged in the light of the final issue.
—Demosthenes

OBJECTIVES

In this chapter you will learn:

- The essentials of counter-controlled repetition.

- To use the `for` and `do...while` repetition statements to execute statements in an application repeatedly.

- To understand multiple selection using the `switch` selection statement.

- To use the `break` and `continue` program control statements to alter the flow of control.

- To use the logical operators to form complex conditional expressions in control statements.

6.1 Introduction

Chapter 5 began our introduction to the types of building blocks that are available for problem solving. We used those building blocks to employ proven application construction techniques. In this chapter, we continue our presentation of the theory and principles of structured programming by introducing all but one of C#'s remaining control statements. The control statements we study here and in Chapter 5 are helpful in building and manipulating objects.

In this chapter, we demonstrate C#'s for, do...while and switch statements. Through a series of short examples using while and for, we explore the essentials of counter-controlled repetition. We devote a portion of the chapter (and Chapter 8) to expanding the GradeBook class presented in Chapters 4 and 5. In particular, we create a version of class GradeBook that uses a switch statement to count the number of A, B, C, D and F grade equivalents in a set of numeric grades entered by the user. We introduce the break and continue program control statements. We discuss C#'s logical operators, which enable you to use more complex conditional expressions in control statements. Finally, we summarize C#'s control statements and the proven problem-solving techniques presented in this chapter and Chapter 5.

6.2 Essentials of Counter-Controlled Repetition

This section uses the while *repetition statement* introduced in Chapter 5 to formalize the elements required to perform counter-controlled repetition. Counter-controlled repetition requires

1. a *control variable* (or loop counter)

2. the *initial value* of the control variable

3. the *increment* (or *decrement*) by which the control variable is modified each time through the loop (also known as each *iteration of the loop*)

4. the *loop-continuation condition* that determines whether looping should continue.

To see these elements of counter-controlled repetition, consider the application of Fig. 6.1, which uses a loop to display the numbers from 1 through 10. Note that Fig. 6.1 contains only one method, Main, which does all of the class's work. For most applications in Chapters 4 and 5, we have encouraged the use of two separate files—one that declares a reusable class (e.g., Account) and one that instantiates one or more objects of that class (e.g., AccountTest) and demonstrates their functionality. Occasionally, however, it is more appropriate simply to create one class whose Main method concisely illustrates a basic concept. Throughout this chapter, we use several one-class examples like Fig. 6.1 to demonstrate the mechanics of various C# control statements.

In method Main of Fig. 6.1 (lines 7–18), the elements of counter-controlled repetition are defined in lines 9, 11 and 14. Line 9 declares the control variable (counter) as an int, reserves space for it in memory and sets its initial value to 1.

Line 13 in the while statement displays control variable counter's value during each iteration of the loop. Line 14 increments the control variable by 1 for each iteration of the loop. The loop-continuation condition in the while (line 11) tests whether the value of the control variable is less than or equal to 10 (the final value for which the condition is true). Note that the application performs the body of this while even when the control variable is 10. The loop terminates when the control variable exceeds 10 (i.e., counter becomes 11).

Common Programming Error 6.1

Because floating-point values may be approximate, controlling loops with floating-point variables may result in imprecise counter values and inaccurate termination tests.

Error-Prevention Tip 6.1

Control counting loops with integers.

```csharp
1  // Fig. 6.1: WhileCounter.cs
2  // Counter-controlled repetition with the while repetition statement.
3  using System;
4
5  public class WhileCounter
6  {
7     public static void Main( string[] args )
8     {
9        int counter = 1; // declare and initialize control variable
10
11       while ( counter <= 10 ) // loop-continuation condition
12       {
13          Console.Write( "{0}  ", counter );
14          counter++; // increment control variable
15       } // end while
16
17       Console.WriteLine(); // output a newline
18    } // end Main
19 } // end class WhileCounter
```

```
1 2 3 4 5 6 7 8 9 10
```

Fig. 6.1 | Counter-controlled repetition with the while repetition statement.

Good Programming Practice 6.1

Place blank lines above and below repetition and selection control statements, and indent the statement bodies to enhance readability.

The application in Fig. 6.1 can be made more concise by initializing counter to 0 in line 9 and incrementing counter in the while condition with the prefix increment operator as follows:

```
while ( ++counter <= 10 ) // loop-continuation condition
    Console.Write( "{0}  ", counter );
```

This code saves a statement (and eliminates the need for braces around the loop's body), because the while condition performs the increment before testing the condition. (Recall from Section 5.12 that the precedence of ++ is higher than that of <=.) Coding in such a condensed fashion might make code more difficult to read, debug, modify and maintain.

 Software Engineering Observation 6.1

"Keep it simple" is good advice for most of the code you will write.

6.3 for Repetition Statement

Section 6.2 presented the essentials of counter-controlled repetition. The while statement can be used to implement any counter-controlled loop. C# also provides the *for repetition statement*, which specifies the elements of counter-controlled-repetition in a single line of code. Figure 6.2 reimplements the application in Fig. 6.1 using the for statement.

The application's Main method operates as follows: when the for statement (lines 11–12) begins executing, control variable counter is declared and initialized to 1. (Recall from Section 6.2 that the first two elements of counter-controlled repetition are the control

```
 1   // Fig. 6.2: ForCounter.cs
 2   // Counter-controlled repetition with the for repetition statement.
 3   using System;
 4
 5   public class ForCounter
 6   {
 7      public static void Main( string[] args )
 8      {
 9         // for statement header includes initialization,
10         // loop-continuation condition and increment
11         for ( int counter = 1; counter <= 10; counter++ )
12            Console.Write( "{0}  ", counter );
13
14         Console.WriteLine(); // output a newline
15      } // end Main
16   } // end class ForCounter
```

```
1  2  3  4  5  6  7  8  9  10
```

Fig. 6.2 | Counter-controlled repetition with the for repetition statement.

variable and its initial value.) Next, the application checks the loop-continuation condition, counter <= 10, which is between the two required semicolons. Because the initial value of counter is 1, the condition initially is true. Therefore, the body statement (line 12) displays control variable counter's value, which is 1. After executing the loop's body, the application increments counter in the expression counter++, which appears to the right of the second semicolon. Then the loop-continuation test is performed again to determine whether the application should continue with the next iteration of the loop. At this point, the control variable value is 2, so the condition is still true (the final value is not exceeded)—and the application performs the body statement again (i.e., the next iteration of the loop). This process continues until the numbers 1 through 10 have been displayed and the counter's value becomes 11, causing the loop-continuation test to fail and repetition to terminate (after 10 repetitions of the loop body at line 12). Then the application performs the first statement after the for—in this case, line 14.

Note that Fig. 6.2 uses (in line 11) the loop-continuation condition counter <= 10. If you incorrectly specified counter < 10 as the condition, the loop would iterate only nine times—a common logic error called an ***off-by-one error***.

Common Programming Error 6.2

Using an incorrect relational operator or an incorrect final value of a loop counter in the loop-continuation condition of a repetition statement causes an off-by-one error.

Good Programming Practice 6.2

Using the final value in the condition of a while *or* for *statement with the* <= *relational operator helps avoid off-by-one errors. For a loop that prints the values 1 to 10, the loop-continuation condition should be* counter <= 10, *rather than* counter < 10 *(which causes an off-by-one error) or* counter < 11 *(which is correct). Many programmers prefer so-called zero-based counting, in which to count 10 times,* counter *would be initialized to zero and the loop-continuation test would be* counter < 10.

Figure 6.3 takes a closer look at the for statement in Fig. 6.2. The for's first line (including the keyword for and everything in parentheses after for)—line 11 in Fig. 6.2—is sometimes called the ***for statement header***, or simply the ***for header***. Note that the for header "does it all"—it specifies each of the items needed for counter-controlled repetition with a control variable. If there is more than one statement in the body of the for, braces are required to define the body of the loop.

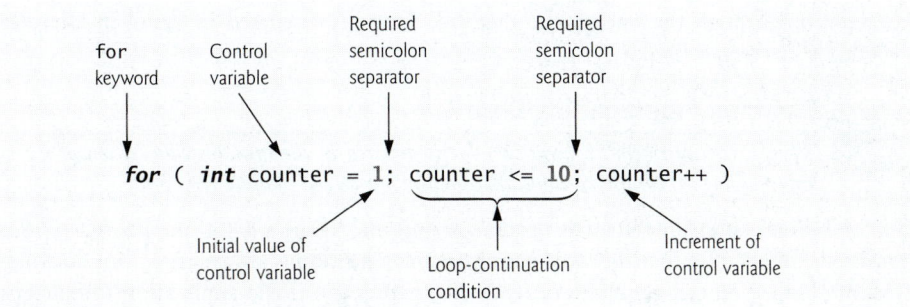

Fig. 6.3 | for statement header components.

The general format of the for statement is

> **for** (*initialization*; *loopContinuationCondition*; *increment*)
>   *statement*

where the *initialization* expression names the loop's control variable and provides its initial value, the *loopContinuationCondition* is the condition that determines whether looping should continue and the *increment* modifies the control variable's value (whether an increment or decrement), so that the loop-continuation condition eventually becomes false. The two semicolons in the for header are required. Note that we don't include a semicolon after *statement* because the semicolon is already assumed to be included in the notion of a *statement*.

Common Programming Error 6.3

Using commas instead of the two required semicolons in a for header is a syntax error.

In most cases, the for statement can be represented with an equivalent while statement as follows:

> *initialization*;
>
> **while** (*loopContinuationCondition*)
> {
>   *statement*
>   *increment*;
> }

In Section 6.7, we discuss a case in which a for statement cannot be represented with an equivalent while statement.

Typically, for statements are used for counter-controlled repetition, and while statements are used for sentinel-controlled repetition. However, while and for can each be used for either repetition type.

If the *initialization* expression in the for header declares the control variable (i.e., the control variable's type is specified before the variable name, as in Fig. 6.2), the control variable can be used only in that for statement—it will not exist outside the for statement. This restricted use of the name of the control variable is known as the variable's *scope*. The scope of a variable defines where it can be used in an application. For example, a local variable can be used only in the method that declares the variable and only from the point of declaration through the end of the method. Scope is discussed in detail in Chapter 7, Methods: A Deeper Look.

Common Programming Error 6.4

When a for statement's control variable is declared in the initialization section of the for's header, using the control variable after the for's body is a compilation error.

All three expressions in a for header are optional. If the *loopContinuationCondition* is omitted, C# assumes that the loop-continuation condition is always true, thus creating an infinite loop. You can omit the *initialization* expression if the application initializes the control variable before the loop—in this case, the scope of the control variable will not be limited to the loop. You can omit the *increment* expression if the application calculates the increment with statements in the loop's body or if no increment is needed. The increment expression in a for acts as if it were a stand-alone statement at the end of the for's body. Therefore, the expressions

```
counter = counter + 1
counter += 1
++counter
counter++
```

are equivalent increment expressions in a for statement. Many programmers prefer counter++ because it is concise and because a for loop evaluates its increment expression after its body executes—so the postfix increment form seems more natural. In this case, the variable being incremented does not appear in a larger expression, so the prefix and postfix increment operators have the same effect.

Performance Tip 6.1

There is a slight performance advantage to using the prefix increment operator, but if you choose the postfix increment operator because it seems more natural (as in a for header), optimizing compilers will generate MSIL code that uses the more efficient form anyway.

Good Programming Practice 6.3

In many cases, the prefix and postfix increment operators are both used to add 1 to a variable in a statement by itself. In these cases, the effect is exactly the same, except that the prefix increment operator has a slight performance advantage. Given that the compiler typically optimizes your code to help you get the best performance, use the idiom (prefix or postfix) with which you feel most comfortable in these situations.

Common Programming Error 6.5

Placing a semicolon immediately to the right of the right parenthesis of a for header makes that for's body an empty statement. This is normally a logic error.

Error-Prevention Tip 6.2

Infinite loops occur when the loop-continuation condition in a repetition statement never becomes false. To prevent this situation in a counter-controlled loop, ensure that the control variable is incremented (or decremented) during each iteration of the loop. In a sentinel-controlled loop, ensure that the sentinel value is eventually input.

The initialization, loop-continuation condition and increment portions of a for statement can contain arithmetic expressions. For example, assume that x = 2 and y = 10; if x and y are not modified in the body of the loop, then the statement

> *for* (*int* j = x; j <= 4 * x * y; j += y / x)

is equivalent to the statement

> *for* (*int* j = 2; j <= 80; j += 5)

The increment of a for statement may also be negative, in which case it is a decrement, and the loop counts downward.

If the loop-continuation condition is initially `false`, the application does not execute the `for` statement's body. Instead, execution proceeds with the statement following the `for`.

Applications frequently display the control variable value or use it in calculations in the loop body, but this use is not required. The control variable is commonly used to control repetition without being mentioned in the body of the `for`.

Error-Prevention Tip 6.3

Although the value of the control variable can be changed in the body of a for loop, avoid doing so, because this practice can lead to subtle errors.

The `for` statement's UML activity diagram is similar to that of the `while` statement (Fig. 5.4). Figure 6.4 shows the activity diagram of the `for` statement in Fig. 6.2. The diagram makes it clear that initialization occurs only once before the loop-continuation test is evaluated the first time, and that incrementing occurs each time through the loop after the body statement executes.

6.4 Examples Using the for Statement

The following examples show techniques for varying the control variable in a `for` statement. In each case, we write the appropriate `for` header. Note the change in the relational operator for loops that decrement the control variable.

a) Vary the control variable from 1 to 100 in increments of 1.

```
for ( int i = 1; i <= 100; i++ )
```

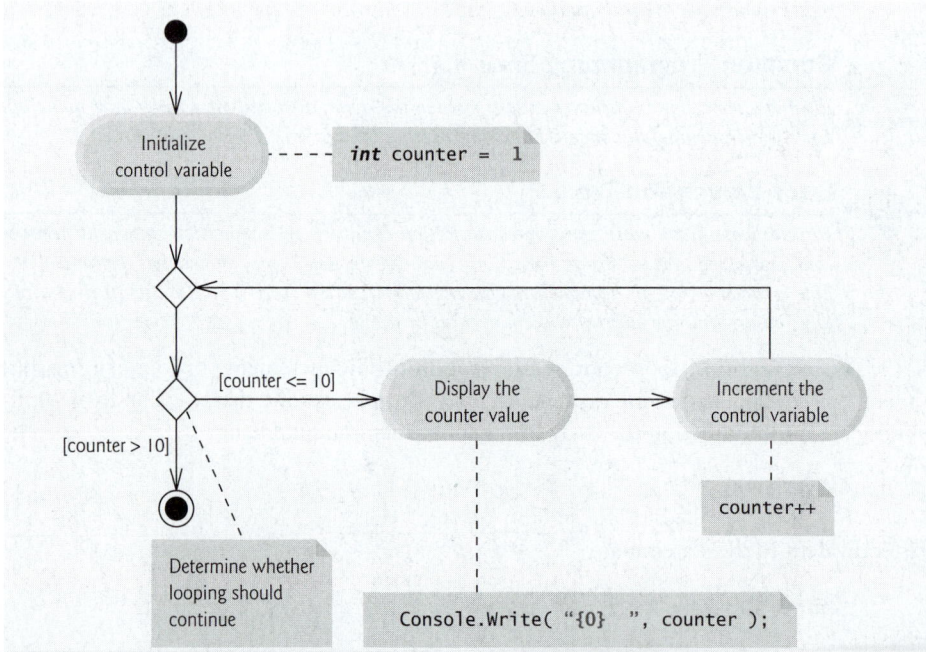

Fig. 6.4 | UML activity diagram for the `for` statement in Fig. 6.2.

b) Vary the control variable from 100 to 1 in decrements of 1.

```
for ( int i = 100; i >= 1; i-- )
```

c) Vary the control variable from 7 to 77 in increments of 7.

```
for ( int i = 7; i <= 77; i += 7 )
```

d) Vary the control variable from 20 to 2 in decrements of 2.

```
for ( int i = 20; i >= 2; i -= 2 )
```

e) Vary the control variable over the following sequence of values: 2, 5, 8, 11, 14, 17, 20.

```
for ( int i = 2; i <= 20; i += 3 )
```

f) Vary the control variable over the following sequence of values: 99, 88, 77, 66, 55, 44, 33, 22, 11, 0.

```
for ( int i = 99; i >= 0; i -= 11 )
```

Common Programming Error 6.6

Not using the proper relational operator in the loop-continuation condition of a loop that counts downward (e.g., using i <= 1 instead of i >= 1 in a loop counting down to 1) is a logic error.

Application: Summing the Even Integers from 2 to 20

We now consider two sample applications that demonstrate simple uses of for. The application in Fig. 6.5 uses a for statement to sum the even integers from 2 to 20 and store the result in an int variable called total.

```csharp
1   // Fig. 6.5: Sum.cs
2   // Summing integers with the for statement.
3   using System;
4
5   public class Sum
6   {
7      public static void Main( string[] args )
8      {
9         int total = 0; // initialize total
10
11         // total even integers from 2 through 20
12         for ( int number = 2; number <= 20; number += 2 )
13            total += number;
14
15         Console.WriteLine( "Sum is {0}", total ); // display results
16      } // end Main
17   } // end class Sum
```

```
Sum is 110
```

Fig. 6.5 | Summing integers with the for statement.

The *initialization* and *increment* expressions can be comma-separated lists of expressions that enable you to use multiple initialization expressions or multiple increment expressions. For example, the body of the for statement in lines 12–13 of Fig. 6.5 could be merged into the increment portion of the for header by using a comma as follows:

```
for ( int number = 2; number <= 20; total += number, number += 2 )
   ; // empty statement
```

Good Programming Practice 6.4

Limit the size of control statement headers to a single line if possible.

Good Programming Practice 6.5

Place only expressions involving the control variables in the initialization and increment sections of a for statement. Manipulations of other variables should appear either before the loop (if they execute only once, like initialization statements) or in the body of the loop (if they execute once per iteration of the loop, like increment or decrement statements).

Application: Compound Interest Calculations

The next application uses the for statement to compute compound interest. Consider the following problem:

A person invests $1,000 in a savings account yielding 5% interest, compounded yearly. Assuming that all the interest is left on deposit, calculate and print the amount of money in the account at the end of each year for 10 years. Use the following formula to determine the amounts:

$$a = p (1 + r)^n$$

where

p is the original amount invested (i.e., the principal)
r is the annual interest rate (e.g., use 0.05 for 5%)
n is the number of years
a is the amount on deposit at the end of the *n*th year.

This problem involves a loop that performs the indicated calculation for each of the 10 years the money remains on deposit. The solution is the application shown in Fig. 6.6. Lines 9–11 in method Main declare decimal variables amount and principal, and double variable rate. Lines 10–11 also initialize principal to 1000 (i.e., $1000.00) and rate to 0.05. C# treats real number constants like 0.05 as type double. Similarly, C# treats whole number constants like 7 and 1000 as type int. When principal is initialized to 1000, the value 1000 of type int is promoted to a decimal type implicitly—no cast is required.

Line 14 outputs the headers for the application's two columns of output. The first column displays the year, and the second column displays the amount on deposit at the end of that year. Note that we use the format item {1,20} to output the string "Amount on deposit". The integer 20 after the comma indicates that the value output should be displayed with a *field width* of 20—that is, WriteLine displays the value with at least 20 character positions. If the value to be output is less than 20 character positions wide (17 characters in this example), the value is *right justified* in the field by default (in this case the value is preceded by three blanks). If the year value to be output were more than four character positions wide, the field width would be extended to the right to accommodate

```
1   // Fig. 6.6: Interest.cs
2   // Compound-interest calculations with for.
3   using System;
4
5   public class Interest
6   {
7      public static void Main( string[] args )
8      {
9         decimal amount; // amount on deposit at end of each year
10        decimal principal = 1000; // initial amount before interest
11        double rate = 0.05; // interest rate
12
13        // display headers
14        Console.WriteLine( "{0}{1,20}", "Year", "Amount on deposit" );
15
16        // calculate amount on deposit for each of ten years
17        for ( int year = 1; year <= 10; year++ )
18        {
19           // calculate new amount for specified year
20           amount = principal *
21              ( ( decimal ) Math.Pow( 1.0 + rate, year ) );
22
23           // display the year and the amount
24           Console.WriteLine( "{0,4}{1,20:C}", year, amount );
25        } // end for
26     } // end Main
27  } // end class Interest
```

```
Year    Amount on deposit
   1           $1,050.00
   2           $1,102.50
   3           $1,157.63
   4           $1,215.51
   5           $1,276.28
   6           $1,340.10
   7           $1,407.10
   8           $1,477.46
   9           $1,551.33
  10           $1,628.89
```

Fig. 6.6 | Compound-interest calculations with for.

the entire value—this would push the amount field to the right, upsetting the neat columns of our tabular output. To indicate that output should be *left justified*, simply use a negative field width.

The for statement (lines 17–25) executes its body 10 times, varying control variable year from 1 to 10 in increments of 1. This loop terminates when control variable year becomes 11. (Note that year represents *n* in the problem statement.)

Classes provide methods that perform common tasks on objects. In fact, most methods must be called on a specific object. For example, to output a greeting in Fig. 4.2, we called method DisplayMessage on the myGradeBook object. Many classes also provide methods that perform common tasks and do not need to be called on objects. Such methods are called *static methods*. For example, C# does not include an exponentiation operator, so the designers of C#'s Math class defined `static` method Pow for raising a value to a power. You can call a `static` method by specifying the class name followed by the dot operator (`.`) and the method name, as in

    ClassName.*methodName*(*arguments*)

Note that `Console` methods `Write` and `WriteLine` are `static` methods. In Chapter 7, you will learn how to implement `static` methods in your own classes.

We use `static` method Pow of class Math to perform the compound interest calculation in Fig. 6.6. `Math.Pow(x, y)` calculates the value of x raised to the yth power. The method receives two `double` arguments and returns a `double` value. Lines 20–21 perform the calculation $a = p (1 + r)^n$, where a is the amount, p is the principal, r is the rate and n is the year. Notice that in this calculation, we need to multiply a `decimal` value (principal) by a `double` value (the return value of `Math.Pow`). C# will not implicitly convert `double` to a `decimal` type, or vice versa, because of the possible loss of information in either conversion, so line 21 contains a (`decimal`) cast operator that explicitly converts the `double` return value of `Math.Pow` to a `decimal`.

After each calculation, line 24 outputs the year and the amount on deposit at the end of that year. The year is output in a field width of four characters (as specified by {0,4}). The amount is output as a currency value with the format item {1,20:C}. The number 20 in the format item indicates that the value should be output right justified with a field width of 20 characters. The format specifier C specifies that the number should be formatted as currency.

Notice that we declared the variables `amount` and `principal` to be of type `decimal` rather than `double`. Recall that we introduced type `decimal` for monetary calculations in Section 4.10. We also use `decimal` in Fig. 6.6 for this purpose. You may be curious as to why we do this. We are dealing with fractional parts of dollars and thus need a type that allows decimal points in its values. Unfortunately, floating-point numbers of type `double` (or `float`) can cause trouble in monetary calculations. Two `double` dollar amounts stored in the machine could be 14.234 (which would normally be rounded to 14.23 for display purposes) and 18.673 (which would normally be rounded to 18.67 for display purposes). When these amounts are added, they produce the internal sum 32.907, which would normally be rounded to 32.91 for display purposes. Thus, your output could appear as

```
  14.23
+ 18.67
-------
  32.91
```

but a person adding the individual numbers as displayed would expect the sum to be 32.90. You have been warned! For people who work with programming languages that do not support a type for precise monetary calculations, Exercise 6.18 explores the use of integers to perform such calculations.

Good Programming Practice 6.6

Do not use variables of type `double` (or `float`) to perform precise monetary calculations; use type `decimal` instead. The imprecision of floating-point numbers can cause errors that will result in incorrect monetary values.

Note that the body of the `for` statement contains the calculation `1.0 + rate`, which appears as an argument to the `Math.Pow` method. In fact, this calculation produces the same result each time through the loop, so repeating the calculation in every iteration of the loop is wasteful.

Performance Tip 6.2

In loops, avoid calculations for which the result never changes—such calculations should typically be placed before the loop. [Note: Optimizing compilers will typically place such calculations outside loops in the compiled code.]

6.5 do...while Repetition Statement

The ***do...while repetition statement*** is similar to the `while` statement. In the `while`, the application tests the loop-continuation condition at the beginning of the loop, before executing the loop's body. If the condition is false, the body never executes. The `do...while` statement tests the loop-continuation condition *after* executing the loop's body; therefore, the body always executes at least once. When a `do...while` statement terminates, execution continues with the next statement in sequence. Figure 6.7 uses a `do...while` (lines 11–15) to output the numbers 1–10.

Line 9 declares and initializes control variable `counter`. Upon entering the `do...while` statement, line 13 outputs `counter`'s value, and line 14 increments `counter`. Then the application evaluates the loop-continuation test at the bottom of the loop (line 15). If the condition is true, the loop continues from the first body statement in the `do...while` (line 13). If the condition is false, the loop terminates, and the application continues with the next statement after the loop.

```
1   // Fig. 6.7: DoWhileTest.cs
2   // do...while repetition statement.
3   using System;
4
5   public class DoWhileTest
6   {
7      public static void Main( string[] args )
8      {
9         int counter = 1; // initialize counter
10
11         do
12         {
13            Console.Write( "{0}  ", counter );
14            counter++;
15         } while ( counter <= 10 ); // end do...while
16
17         Console.WriteLine(); // outputs a newline
18      } // end Main
19   } // end class DoWhileTest
```

```
1  2  3  4  5  6  7  8  9  10
```

Fig. 6.7 | do...while repetition statement.

Figure 6.8 contains the UML activity diagram for the do...while statement. This diagram makes it clear that the loop-continuation condition is not evaluated until after the loop performs the action state at least once. Compare this activity diagram with that of the while statement (Fig. 5.4). It is not necessary to use braces in the do...while repetition statement if there is only one statement in the body. However, most programmers include the braces, to avoid confusion between the while and do...while statements. For example,

> ***while*** (*condition*)

is normally the first line of a while statement. A do...while statement with no braces around a single-statement body appears as:

> ***do***
>   *statement*
> ***while*** (*condition*);

which can be confusing. A reader may misinterpret the last line—while(*condition*);— as a while statement containing an empty statement (the semicolon by itself). Thus, a do...while statement with one body statement is usually written as follows:

> ***do***
> {
>   *statement*
> } ***while*** (*condition*);

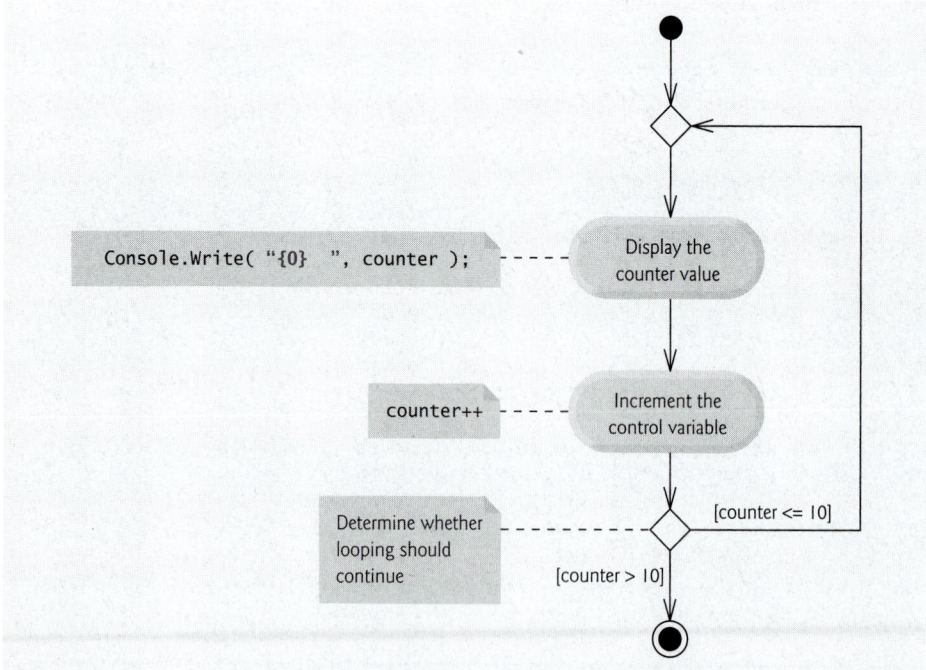

Fig. 6.8 | do...while repetition statement UML activity diagram.

![bug icon] **Error-Prevention Tip 6.4**

Always include braces in a do...while statement, even if they are not necessary. This helps eliminate ambiguity between while statements and do...while statements containing only one statement.

6.6 switch Multiple-Selection Statement

We discussed the if single-selection statement and the if...else double-selection statement in Chapter 5. C# provides the **switch multiple-selection** statement to perform different actions based on the possible values of an expression. Each action is associated with the value of a *constant integral expression* or a *constant string expression* that the variable or expression on which the switch is based may assume. A constant integral expression is any expression involving character and integer constants that evaluates to an integer value (i.e., values of type sbyte, byte, short, ushort, int, uint, long, ulong, and char). A constant string expression is any expression composed of string literals that always results in the same string.

GradeBook Class with switch Statement to Count A, B, C, D and F Grades.

Figure 6.9 contains an enhanced version of the GradeBook class introduced in Chapter 4 and further developed in Chapter 5. The version of the class we now present not only calculates the average of a set of numeric grades entered by the user, but uses a switch statement to determine whether each grade is the equivalent of an A, B, C, D or F and to increment the appropriate grade counter. The class also displays a summary of the number of students who received each grade. Figure 6.10 shows sample input and output of the GradeBookTest application that uses class GradeBook to process a set of grades.

```csharp
1   // Fig. 6.9: GradeBook.cs
2   // GradeBook class uses switch statement to count A, B, C, D and F grades.
3   using System;
4
5   public class GradeBook
6   {
7      private string courseName; // name of course this GradeBook represents
8      private int total; // sum of grades
9      private int gradeCounter; // number of grades entered
10     private int aCount; // count of A grades
11     private int bCount; // count of B grades
12     private int cCount; // count of C grades
13     private int dCount; // count of D grades
14     private int fCount; // count of F grades
15
16     // constructor initializes courseName;
17     // int instance variables are initialized to 0 by default
18     public GradeBook( string name )
19     {
20        CourseName = name; // initializes courseName
21     } // end constructor
```

Fig. 6.9 | GradeBook class that uses a switch statement to count A, B, C, D and F grades. (Part 1 of 3.)

```
22
23      // property that gets and sets the course name
24      public string CourseName
25      {
26        get
27        {
28          return courseName;
29        } // end get
30        set
31        {
32          courseName = value;
33        } // end set
34      } // end property CourseName
35
36      // display a welcome message to the GradeBook user
37      public void DisplayMessage()
38      {
39        // CourseName gets the name of the course
40        Console.WriteLine( "Welcome to the grade book for\n{0}!\n",
41          CourseName );
42      } // end method DisplayMessage
43
44      // input arbitrary number of grades from user
45      public void InputGrades()
46      {
47        int grade; // grade entered by user
48        string input; // text entered by the user
49
50        Console.WriteLine( "{0}\n{1}",
51          "Enter the integer grades in the range 0-100.",
52          "Type <Ctrl> z and press Enter to terminate input:" );
53
54        input = Console.ReadLine(); // read user input
55
56        // loop until user enters the end-of-file indicator (<Ctrl> z)
57        while ( input != null )
58        {
59          grade = Convert.ToInt32( input ); // read grade off user input
60          total += grade; // add grade to total
61          gradeCounter++; // increment number of grades
62
63          // call method to increment appropriate counter
64          IncrementLetterGradeCounter( grade );
65
66          input = Console.ReadLine(); // read user input
67        } // end while
68      } // end method InputGrades
69
70      // add 1 to appropriate counter for specified grade
71      private void IncrementLetterGradeCounter( int grade )
72      {
```

Fig. 6.9 | GradeBook class that uses a switch statement to count A, B, C, D and F grades. (Part 2 of 3.)

```
73        // determine which grade was entered
74        switch ( grade / 10 )
75        {
76           case 9: // grade was in the 90s
77           case 10: // grade was 100
78              aCount++; // increment aCount
79              break; // necessary to exit switch
80           case 8: // grade was between 80 and 89
81              bCount++; // increment bCount
82              break; // exit switch
83           case 7: // grade was between 70 and 79
84              cCount++; // increment cCount
85              break; // exit switch
86           case 6: // grade was between 60 and 69
87              dCount++; // increment dCount
88              break; // exit switch
89           default: // grade was less than 60
90              fCount++; // increment fCount
91              break; // exit switch
92        } // end switch
93     } // end method IncrementLetterGradeCounter
94
95     // display a report based on the grades entered by the user
96     public void DisplayGradeReport()
97     {
98        Console.WriteLine( "\nGrade Report:" );
99
100       // if user entered at least one grade...
101       if ( gradeCounter != 0 )
102       {
103          // calculate average of all grades entered
104          double average = ( double ) total / gradeCounter;
105
106          // output summary of results
107          Console.WriteLine( "Total of the {0} grades entered is {1}",
108             gradeCounter, total );
109          Console.WriteLine( "Class average is {0:F2}", average );
110          Console.WriteLine( "{0}A: {1}\nB: {2}\nC: {3}\nD: {4}\nF: {5}",
111             "Number of students who received each grade:\n",
112             aCount, // display number of A grades
113             bCount, // display number of B grades
114             cCount, // display number of C grades
115             dCount, // display number of D grades
116             fCount ); // display number of F grades
117       } // end if
118       else // no grades were entered, so output appropriate message
119          Console.WriteLine( "No grades were entered" );
120    } // end method DisplayGradeReport
121 } // end class GradeBook
```

Fig. 6.9 | GradeBook class that uses a switch statement to count A, B, C, D and F grades. (Part 3 of 3.)

Like earlier versions of the class, class GradeBook (Fig. 6.9) declares instance variable courseName (line 7), property CourseName (lines 24–34) to access courseName and method DisplayMessage (lines 37–42) to display a welcome message to the user. The class also contains a constructor (lines 18–21) that initializes the course name.

Class GradeBook also declares instance variables total (line 8) and gradeCounter (line 9), which keep track of the sum of the grades entered by the user and the number of grades entered, respectively. Lines 10–14 declare counter variables for each grade category. Class GradeBook maintains total, gradeCounter and the five letter-grade counters as instance variables so that these variables can be used or modified in any of the class's methods. Note that the class's constructor (lines 18–21) sets only the course name—the remaining seven instance variables are ints and are initialized to 0 by default.

Class GradeBook contains three additional methods—InputGrades, IncrementLetterGradeCounter and DisplayGradeReport. Method InputGrades (lines 45–68) reads an arbitrary number of integer grades from the user using sentinel-controlled repetition and updates instance variables total and gradeCounter. Method InputGrades calls method IncrementLetterGradeCounter (lines 71–93) to update the appropriate letter-grade counter for each grade entered. Class GradeBook also contains method DisplayGradeReport (lines 96–120), which outputs a report containing the total of all grades entered, the average of the grades and the number of students who received each letter grade. Let's examine these methods in more detail.

Lines 47–48 in method InputGrades declare variables grade and input, which will store the user's input first as a string (in the variable input) then convert it to an int to store in the variable grade. Lines 50–52 prompt the user to enter integer grades and to type *<Ctrl> z* then press *Enter* to terminate the input. The notation *<Ctrl> z* means to simultaneously press both the *Ctrl* key and the *z* key when typing in a Command Prompt. *<Ctrl> z* is the Windows key sequence for typing the ***end-of-file indicator***. This is one way to inform an application that there is no more data to input. (The end-of-file indicator is a system-dependent keystroke combination. On many non-Windows systems, end-of-file is entered by typing *<Ctrl> d*.) In Chapter 18, Files and Streams, we will see how the end-of-file indicator is used when an application reads its input from a file. [*Note:* Windows typically displays the characters ^Z in a Command Prompt when the end-of-file indicator is typed, as shown in the output of Fig. 6.10.]

Line 54 uses the ReadLine method to get the first line that the user entered and store it in variable input. The while statement (lines 57–67) processes this user input. The condition at line 57 checks if the value of input is a null reference. The Console class's ReadLine method will only return null if the user typed an end-of-file indicator. As long as the end-of-file indicator has not been typed, input will not contain a null reference, and the condition will pass.

Line 59 converts the string in input to an int type. Line 60 adds grade to total. Line 61 increments gradeCounter. The class's DisplayGradeReport method uses these variables to compute the average of the grades. Line 64 calls the class's IncrementLetterGradeCounter method (declared in lines 71–93) to increment the appropriate letter-grade counter, based on the numeric grade entered.

Method IncrementLetterGradeCounter contains a switch statement (lines 74–92) that determines which counter to increment. In this example, we assume that the user enters a valid grade in the range 0–100. A grade in the range 90–100 represents A, 80–89 represents B, 70–79 represents C, 60–69 represents D and 0–59 represents F. The switch statement consists of a block that contains a sequence of *case labels* and an optional *default label*. These are used in this example to determine which counter to increment based on the grade.

When the flow of control reaches the switch, the application evaluates the expression in the parentheses (grade / 10) following keyword switch. This is called the *switch expression*. The application compares the value of the switch expression with each case label. The switch expression in line 74 performs integer division, which truncates the fractional part of the result. Thus, when we divide any value in the range 0–100 by 10, the result is always a value from 0 to 10. We use several of these values in our case labels. For example, if the user enters the integer 85, the switch expression evaluates to int value 8. The switch compares 8 with each case. If a match occurs (case 8: at line 80), the application executes the statements for that case. For the integer 8, line 81 increments bCount, because a grade in the 80s is a B. The *break statement* (line 82) causes program control to proceed with the first statement after the switch—in this application, we reach the end of method IncrementLetterGradeCounter's body, so control returns to line 66 in method InputGrades (the first line after the call to IncrementLetterGradeCounter). This line uses the ReadLine method to read the next line entered by the user and assign it to the variable input. Line 67 marks the end of the body of the while loop that inputs grades (lines 57–67), so control flows to the while's condition (line 57) to determine whether the loop should continue executing based on the value just assigned to the variable input.

The cases in our switch explicitly test for the values 10, 9, 8, 7 and 6. Note the case labels at lines 76–77 that test for the values 9 and 10 (both of which represent the grade A). Listing case labels consecutively in this manner with no statements between them enables the cases to perform the same set of statements—when the switch expression evaluates to 9 or 10, the statements in lines 78–79 execute. The switch statement does not provide a mechanism for testing ranges of values, so every value to be tested must be listed in a separate case label. Note that each case can have multiple statements. The switch statement differs from other control statements in that it does not require braces around multiple statements in each case.

In C, C++, and many other programming languages that use the switch statement, the break statement is not required at the end of a case. Without break statements, each time a match occurs in the switch, the statements for that case and subsequent cases execute until a break statement or the end of the switch is encountered. This is often referred to as "falling through" to the statements in subsequent cases. This frequently leads to logic errors when you forget the break statement. For this reason, C# has a "no fall through" rule for cases in a switch—after the statements in a case execute, you are required to include a statement that terminates the case, such as a break, a return, or a throw. (We discuss the throw statement in Chapter 12.)

 Common Programming Error 6.7

Forgetting a break statement when one is needed in a switch is a syntax error.

If no match occurs between the switch expression's value and a case label, the statements after the default label (lines 90–91) execute. We use the default label in this example to process all switch-expression values that are less than 6—that is, all failing grades. If no match occurs and the switch does not contain a default label, program control simply continues with the first statement after the switch statement.

GradeBookTest Class That Demonstrates Class GradeBook

Class GradeBookTest (Fig. 6.10) creates a GradeBook object (lines 10–11). Line 13 invokes the object's DisplayMessage method to output a welcome message to the user. Line 14 invokes the object's InputGrades method to read a set of grades from the user and keep track of the sum of all the grades entered and the number of grades. Recall that method

```
 I   // Fig. 6.10: GradeBookTest.cs
 2   // Create GradeBook object, input grades and display grade report.
 3
 4   public class GradeBookTest
 5   {
 6      public static void Main( string[] args )
 7      {
 8         // create GradeBook object myGradeBook and
 9         // pass course name to constructor
10         GradeBook myGradeBook = new GradeBook(
11            "CS101 Introduction to C# Programming" );
12
13         myGradeBook.DisplayMessage(); // display welcome message
14         myGradeBook.InputGrades(); // read grades from user
15         myGradeBook.DisplayGradeReport(); // display report based on grades
16      } // end Main
17   } // end class GradeBookTest
```

```
Welcome to the grade book for
CS101 Introduction to C# Programming!

Enter the integer grades in the range 0-100.
Type <Ctrl> z and press Enter to terminate input:
99
92
45
100
57
63
76
14
92
^Z

Grade Report:
Total of the 9 grades entered is 638
Class average is 70.89
Number of students who received each grade:
A: 4
B: 0
C: 1
D: 1
F: 3
```

Fig. 6.10 | Create GradeBook object, input grades and display grade report.

InputGrades also calls method IncrementLetterGradeCounter to keep track of the number of students who received each letter grade. Line 15 invokes method DisplayGradeReport of class GradeBook, which outputs a report based on the grades entered. Line 101 of class GradeBook (Fig. 6.9) determines whether the user entered at least one grade—this avoids dividing by zero. If so, line 104 calculates the average of the grades. Lines 107–116 then output the total of all the grades, the class average and the number of students who received each letter grade. If no grades were entered, line 119 outputs an appropriate message. The output in Fig. 6.10 shows a sample grade report based on 9 grades.

Note that class GradeBookTest (Fig. 6.10) does not directly call GradeBook method IncrementLetterGradeCounter (lines 71–93 of Fig. 6.9). This method is used exclusively by method InputGrades of class GradeBook to update the appropriate letter-grade counter as each new grade is entered by the user. Method IncrementLetterGradeCounter exists solely to support the operations of class GradeBook's other methods and thus is declared private. Recall from Chapter 4 that methods declared with access modifier private can be called only by other methods of the class in which the private methods are declared. Such methods are commonly referred to as *utility methods* or *helper methods*, because they can be called only by other methods of that class and are used to support the operation of those methods.

switch *Statement UML Activity Diagram*

Figure 6.11 shows the UML activity diagram for the general switch statement. Every set of statements after a case label must end its execution in a break or return statement to terminate the switch statement after processing the case. Typically, you will use break statements. Figure 6.11 emphasizes this by including break statements in the activity diagram. The diagram makes it clear that the break statement at the end of a case causes control to exit the switch statement immediately.

Software Engineering Observation 6.2

Provide a default *label in switch statements. Cases not explicitly tested in a switch that lacks a* default *label are ignored. Including a* default *label focuses you on the need to process exceptional conditions.*

Good Programming Practice 6.7

Although each case *and the* default *label in a switch can occur in any order, place the* default *label last for clarity.*

When using the switch statement, remember that the expression after each case can be only a constant integral expression or a constant string expression—that is, any combination of constants that evaluates to a constant value of an integral or string type. An integer constant is simply an integer value (e.g., –7, 0 or 221). In addition, you can use *character constants*—specific characters in single quotes, such as 'A', '7' or '$'—which represent the integer values of characters. (Appendix D, ASCII Character Set, shows the integer values of the characters in the ASCII character set, which is a subset of the Unicode character set used by C#.) A string constant is a sequence of characters in double quotes, such as "Welcome to C# Programming!".

The expression in each case also can be a *constant*—a variable that contains a value which does not change for the entire application. Such a variable is declared with the keyword

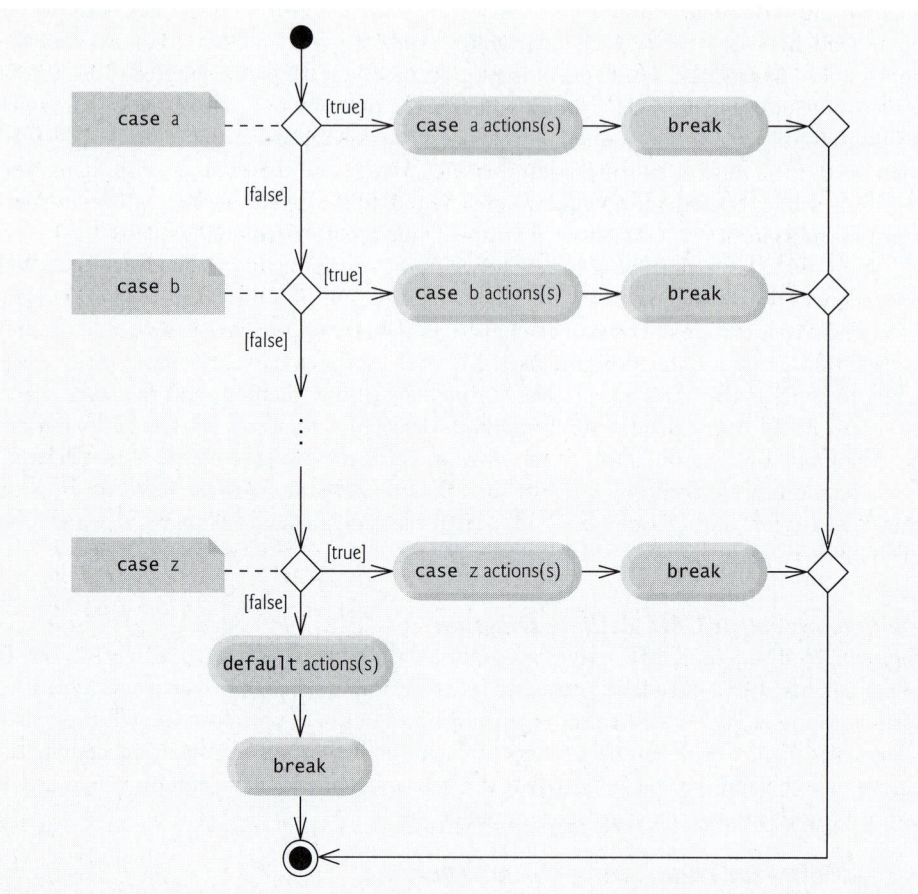

Fig. 6.11 | switch multiple-selection statement UML activity diagram with break statements.

const (discussed in Chapter 7, Methods: A Deeper Look). C# also has a feature called enumerations, which we also present in Chapter 7. Enumeration constants can also be used in case labels. In Chapter 11, Polymorphism, Interfaces & Operator Overloading, we present a more elegant way to implement switch logic—we use a technique called polymorphism to create applications that are often clearer, easier to maintain and easier to extend than applications using switch logic.

6.7 break and continue Statements

In addition to selection and repetition statements, C# provides statements break and continue to alter the flow of control. The preceding section showed how break can be used to terminate a switch statement's execution. This section discusses how to use break to terminate any repetition statement.

break Statement

The break statement, when executed in a while, for, do...while, switch, or foreach, causes immediate exit from that statement. Execution continues with the first statement after the control statement. Common uses of the break statement are to escape early from a repetition statement or to skip the remainder of a switch (as in Fig. 6.9). Figure 6.12 demonstrates a break statement exiting a for.

When the if nested at line 13 in the for statement (lines 11–17) determines that count is 5, the break statement at line 14 executes. This terminates the for statement, and the application proceeds to line 19 (immediately after the for statement), which displays a message indicating the value of the control variable when the loop terminated. The loop fully executes its body only four times instead of 10 because of the break.

continue Statement

The *continue statement*, when executed in a while, for, do...while, or foreach, skips the remaining statements in the loop body and proceeds with the next iteration of the loop. In while and do...while statements, the application evaluates the loop-continuation test immediately after the continue statement executes. In a for statement, the increment expression executes, then the application evaluates the loop-continuation test.

Figure 6.13 uses the continue statement in a for to skip the statement at line 14 when the nested if (line 11) determines that the value of count is 5. When the continue statement executes, program control continues with the increment of the control variable in the for statement (line 9).

```csharp
1   // Fig. 6.12: BreakTest.cs
2   // break statement exiting a for statement.
3   using System;
4
5   public class BreakTest
6   {
7      public static void Main( string[] args )
8      {
9         int count; // control variable also used after loop terminates
10
11        for ( count = 1; count <= 10; count++ ) // loop 10 times
12        {
13           if ( count == 5 ) // if count is 5,
14              break; // terminate loop
15
16           Console.Write( "{0} ", count );
17        } // end for
18
19        Console.WriteLine( "\nBroke out of loop at count = {0}", count );
20     } // end Main
21  } // end class BreakTest
```

```
1 2 3 4
Broke out of loop at count = 5
```

Fig. 6.12 | break statement exiting a for statement.

```
1   // Fig. 6.13: ContinueTest.cs
2   // continue statement terminating an iteration of a for statement.
3   using System;
4
5   public class ContinueTest
6   {
7      public static void Main( string[] args )
8      {
9         for ( int count = 1; count <= 10; count++ ) // loop 10 times
10        {
11           if ( count == 5 ) // if count is 5,
12              continue; // skip remaining code in loop
13
14           Console.Write( "{0} ", count );
15        } // end for
16
17        Console.WriteLine( "\nUsed continue to skip printing 5" );
18     } // end Main
19  } // end class ContinueTest
```

```
1 2 3 4 6 7 8 9 10
Used continue to skip printing 5
```

Fig. 6.13 | continue statement terminating an iteration of a for statement.

In Section 6.3, we stated that the while statement can be used in most cases in place of for. The one exception occurs when the increment expression in the while follows a continue statement. In this case, the increment does not execute before the application evaluates the repetition-continuation condition, so the while does not execute in the same manner as the for.

Software Engineering Observation 6.3

Some programmers feel that break and continue statements violate structured programming. Since the same effects are achievable with structured programming techniques, these programmers prefer not to use break or continue statements.

Software Engineering Observation 6.4

There is a tension between achieving quality software engineering and achieving the best-performing software. Often, one of these goals is achieved at the expense of the other. For all but the most performance-intensive situations, apply the following rule of thumb: First, make your code simple and correct; then make it fast and small, but only if necessary.

6.8 Logical Operators

The if, if...else, while, do...while and for statements each require a condition to determine how to continue an application's flow of control. So far, we have studied only *simple conditions*, such as count <= 10, number != sentinelValue and total > 1000. Simple conditions are expressed in terms of the relational operators >, <, >= and <=, and the equality operators == and !=. Each expression tests only one condition. To test multiple conditions in the process of making a decision, we performed these tests in separate statements or in nested if or if...else statements. Sometimes, control statements require more complex conditions to determine an application's flow of control.

C# provides *logical operators* to enable you to form more complex conditions by combining simple conditions. The logical operators are **&&** (conditional AND), **||** (conditional OR), **&** (boolean logical AND), **|** (boolean logical inclusive OR), **∧** (boolean logical exclusive OR) and **!** (logical negation).

Conditional AND (&&) Operator

Suppose that we wish to ensure at some point in an application that two conditions are *both* true before we choose a certain path of execution. In this case, we can use the **&&** (*conditional AND*) operator, as follows:

```
if ( gender == FEMALE && age >= 65 )
    seniorFemales++;
```

This if statement contains two simple conditions. The condition gender == FEMALE compares variable gender to constant FEMALE. This might be evaluated, for example, to determine whether a person is female. The condition age >= 65 might be evaluated to determine whether a person is a senior citizen. The if statement considers the combined condition

```
gender == FEMALE && age >= 65
```

which is true if and only if *both* simple conditions are true. If the combined condition is true, the if statement's body increments seniorFemales by 1. If either or both of the simple conditions are false, the application skips the increment. Some programmers find that the preceding combined condition is more readable when redundant parentheses are added, as in:

```
( gender == FEMALE ) && ( age >= 65 )
```

The table in Fig. 6.14 summarizes the && operator. The table shows all four possible combinations of false and true values for *expression1* and *expression2*. Such tables are called *truth tables*. C# evaluates all expressions that include relational operators, equality operators or logical operators to bool values—which are either true or false.

expression1	expression2	expression1 && expression2
false	false	false
false	true	false
true	false	false
true	true	true

Fig. 6.14 | && (conditional AND) operator truth table.

Conditional OR (||) Operator

Now suppose that we wish to ensure that *either or both* of two conditions are true before we choose a certain path of execution. In this case, we use the **||** (*conditional OR*) operator, as in the following application segment:

```
if ( ( semesterAverage >= 90 ) || ( finalExam >= 90 ) )
    Console.WriteLine ( "Student grade is A" );
```

This statement also contains two simple conditions. The condition semesterAverage >= 90 is evaluated to determine whether the student deserves an A in the course because of a solid performance throughout the semester. The condition finalExam >= 90 is evaluated to determine whether the student deserves an A in the course because of an outstanding performance on the final exam. The if statement then considers the combined condition

```
( semesterAverage >= 90 ) || ( finalExam >= 90 )
```

and awards the student an A if either or both of the simple conditions are true. The only time the message "Student grade is A" is *not* printed is when both of the simple conditions are false. Figure 6.15 is a truth table for operator conditional OR (||). Operator && has a higher precedence than operator ||. Both operators associate from left to right.

Short-Circuit Evaluation of Complex Conditions

The parts of an expression containing && or || operators are evaluated only until it is known whether the condition is true or false. Thus, evaluation of the expression

```
( gender == FEMALE ) && ( age >= 65 )
```

stops immediately if gender is not equal to FEMALE (i.e., at that point, it is certain that the entire expression is false) and continues if gender *is* equal to FEMALE (i.e., the entire expression could still be true if the condition age >= 65 is true). This feature of conditional AND and conditional OR expressions is called *short-circuit evaluation*.

Common Programming Error 6.8

In expressions using operator &&, a condition—which we refer to as the dependent condition—may require another condition to be true for the evaluation of the dependent condition to be meaningful. In this case, the dependent condition should be placed after the other condition, or an error might occur. For example, in the expression (i != 0) && (10 / i == 2), the second condition must appear after the first condition, or a divide-by-zero error might occur.

expression1	expression2	expression1 || expression2
false	false	false
false	true	true
true	false	true
true	true	true

Fig. 6.15 | || (conditional OR) operator truth table.

Boolean Logical AND (&) and Boolean Logical OR (|) Operators

The *boolean logical AND* (&) and *boolean logical inclusive OR* (|) operators work identically to the && (conditional AND) and || (conditional OR) operators, with one exception—the boolean logical operators always evaluate both of their operands (i.e., they do not perform short-circuit evaluation). Therefore, the expression

```
( gender == 1 ) & ( age >= 65 )
```

evaluates age >= 65 regardless of whether gender is equal to 1. This is useful if the right operand of the boolean logical AND or boolean logical inclusive OR operator has a required *side effect*—a modification of a variable's value. For example, the expression

```
( birthday == true ) | ( ++age >= 65 )
```

guarantees that the condition ++age >= 65 will be evaluated. Thus, the variable age is incremented in the preceding expression, regardless of whether the overall expression is true or false.

Error-Prevention Tip 6.5

For clarity, avoid expressions with side effects in conditions. The side effects may look clever, but they can make it harder to understand code and can lead to subtle logic errors.

Boolean Logical Exclusive OR (^)

A complex condition containing the *boolean logical exclusive OR* (^) operator (also called the *logical XOR operator*) is true *if and only if one of its operands is* true *and the other is* false. If both operands are true or both are false, the entire condition is false. Figure 6.16 is a truth table for the boolean logical exclusive OR operator (^). This operator is also guaranteed to evaluate both of its operands.

Logical Negation (!) Operator

The *!* (*logical negation*) operator enables you to "reverse" the meaning of a condition. Unlike the logical operators &&, ||, &, | and ^, which are binary operators that combine two conditions, the logical negation operator is a unary operator that has only a single condition as an operand. The logical negation operator is placed before a condition to choose a path of execution if the original condition (without the logical negation operator) is false, as in the code segment

```
if ( ! ( grade == sentinelValue ) )
   Console.WriteLine( "The next grade is {0}", grade );
```

expression1	expression2	expression1 ^ expression2
false	false	false
false	true	true
true	false	true
true	true	false

Fig. 6.16 | ^ (boolean logical exclusive OR) operator truth table.

which executes the `WriteLine` call only if `grade` is not equal to `sentinelValue`. The parentheses around the condition `grade == sentinelValue` are needed because the logical negation operator has a higher precedence than the equality operator.

In most cases, you can avoid using logical negation by expressing the condition differently with an appropriate relational or equality operator. For example, the previous statement may also be written as follows:

```
if ( grade != sentinelValue )
    Console.WriteLine( "The next grade is {0}", grade );
```

This flexibility can help you express a condition in a more convenient manner. Figure 6.17 is a truth table for the logical negation operator.

Logical Operators Example

Figure 6.18 demonstrates the logical operators and boolean logical operators by producing their truth tables. The output shows the expression that was evaluated and the `bool` result of that expression. Lines 10–14 produce the truth table for `&&` (conditional AND). Lines 17–21 produce the truth table for `||` (conditional OR). Lines 24–28 produce the truth table for `&` (boolean logical AND). Lines 31–36 produce the truth table for `|` (boolean logical inclusive OR). Lines 39–44 produce the truth table for `∧` (boolean logical exclusive OR). Lines 47–49 produce the truth table for `!` (logical negation).

Figure 6.19 shows the precedence and associativity of the C# operators introduced so far. The operators are shown from top to bottom in decreasing order of precedence.

6.9 Structured Programming Summary

Just as architects design buildings by employing the collective wisdom of their profession, so should programmers design applications. Our field is younger than architecture, and our collective wisdom is considerably sparser. We have learned that structured programming produces applications that are easier than unstructured applications to understand, test, debug, modify and even prove correct in a mathematical sense.

Figure 6.20 uses UML activity diagrams to summarize C#'s control statements. The initial and final states indicate the single entry point and the single exit point of each control statement. Arbitrarily connecting individual symbols in an activity diagram can lead to unstructured applications. Therefore, the programming profession has chosen a limited set of control statements that can be combined in only two simple ways to build structured applications.

expression	!expression
false	true
true	false

Fig. 6.17 | ! (logical negation) operator truth table.

```
 1   // Fig. 6.18: LogicalOperators.cs
 2   // Logical operators.
 3   using System;
 4
 5   public class LogicalOperators
 6   {
 7      public static void Main( string[] args )
 8      {
 9         // create truth table for && (conditional AND) operator
10         Console.WriteLine( "{0}\n{1}: {2}\n{3}: {4}\n{5}: {6}\n{7}: {8}\n",
11            "Conditional AND (&&)", "false && false", ( false && false ),
12            "false && true", ( false && true ),
13            "true && false", ( true && false ),
14            "true && true", ( true && true ) );
15
16         // create truth table for || (conditional OR) operator
17         Console.WriteLine( "{0}\n{1}: {2}\n{3}: {4}\n{5}: {6}\n{7}: {8}\n",
18            "Conditional OR (||)", "false || false", ( false || false ),
19            "false || true", ( false || true ),
20            "true || false", ( true || false ),
21            "true || true", ( true || true ) );
22
23         // create truth table for & (boolean logical AND) operator
24         Console.WriteLine( "{0}\n{1}: {2}\n{3}: {4}\n{5}: {6}\n{7}: {8}\n",
25            "Boolean logical AND (&)", "false & false", ( false & false ),
26            "false & true", ( false & true ),
27            "true & false", ( true & false ),
28            "true & true", ( true & true ) );
29
30         // create truth table for | (boolean logical inclusive OR) operator
31         Console.WriteLine( "{0}\n{1}: {2}\n{3}: {4}\n{5}: {6}\n{7}: {8}\n",
32            "Boolean logical inclusive OR (|)",
33            "false | false", ( false | false ),
34            "false | true", ( false | true ),
35            "true | false", ( true | false ),
36            "true | true", ( true | true ) );
37
38         // create truth table for ^ (boolean logical exclusive OR) operator
39         Console.WriteLine( "{0}\n{1}: {2}\n{3}: {4}\n{5}: {6}\n{7}: {8}\n",
40            "Boolean logical exclusive OR (^)",
41            "false ^ false", ( false ^ false ),
42            "false ^ true", ( false ^ true ),
43            "true ^ false", ( true ^ false ),
44            "true ^ true", ( true ^ true ) );
45
46         // create truth table for ! (logical negation) operator
47         Console.WriteLine( "{0}\n{1}: {2}\n{3}: {4}",
48            "Logical negation (!)", "!false", ( !false ),
49            "!true", ( !true ) );
50      } // end Main
51   } // end class LogicalOperators
```

Fig. 6.18 | Logical operators. (Part 1 of 2.)

```
Conditional AND (&&)
false && false: False
false && true: False
true && false: False
true && true: True

Conditional OR (||)
false || false: False
false || true: True
true || false: True
true || true: True

Boolean logical AND (&)
false & false: False
false & true: False
true & false: False
true & true: True

Boolean logical inclusive OR (|)
false | false: False
false | true: True
true | false: True
true | true: True

Boolean logical exclusive OR (^)
false ^ false: False
false ^ true: True
true ^ false: True
true ^ true: False

Logical negation (!)
!false: True
!true: False
```

Fig. 6.18 | Logical operators. (Part 2 of 2.)

Operators						Associativity	Type
.	new	++*(postfix)*	--*(postfix)*			left to right	highest precedence
++	--	+	-	!	*(type)*	right to left	unary prefix
*	/	%				left to right	multiplicative
+	-					left to right	additive
<	<=	>	>=			left to right	relational
==	!=					left to right	equality
&						left to right	boolean logical AND
^						left to right	boolean logical exclusive OR

Fig. 6.19 | Precedence/associativity of the operators discussed so far. (Part 1 of 2.)

Operators	Associativity	Type
|	left to right	boolean logical inclusive OR
&&	left to right	conditional AND
||	left to right	conditional OR
?:	right to left	conditional
= += -= *= /= %=	right to left	assignment

Fig. 6.19 | Precedence/associativity of the operators discussed so far. (Part 2 of 2.)

For simplicity, only *single-entry/single-exit control statements* are used—there is only one way to enter and only one way to exit each control statement. Connecting control statements in sequence to form structured applications is simple. The final state of one control statement is connected to the initial state of the next—that is, the control statements are placed one after another in an application in sequence. We call this "control-statement stacking." The rules for forming structured applications also allow for control statements to be nested.

Figure 6.21 shows the rules for forming structured applications. The rules assume that action states may be used to indicate any action. The rules also assume that we begin with the simplest activity diagram (Fig. 6.22) consisting of only an initial state, an action state, a final state and transition arrows.

Applying the rules in Fig. 6.21 always results in a properly structured activity diagram with a neat, building-block appearance. For example, repeatedly applying rule 2 to the simplest activity diagram results in an activity diagram containing many action states in sequence (Fig. 6.23). Rule 2 generates a stack of control statements, so let us call rule 2 the *stacking rule*. [*Note:* The vertical dashed lines in Fig. 6.23 are not part of the UML—we use them to separate the four activity diagrams that demonstrate the application of rule 2 of Fig. 6.21.]

Rule 3 is called the *nesting rule*. Repeatedly applying rule 3 to the simplest activity diagram results in an activity diagram with neatly *nested control statements*. For example, in Fig. 6.24, the action state in the simplest activity diagram is replaced with a double-selection (if...else) statement. Then rule 3 is applied again to the action states in the double-selection statement, replacing each of these action states with a double-selection statement. The dashed action-state symbols around each of the double-selection statements represent the action state that was replaced. [*Note:* The dashed arrows and dashed action state symbols shown in Fig. 6.24 are not part of the UML. They are used here to illustrate that any action state can be replaced with any control statement.]

Rule 4 generates larger, more involved and more deeply nested statements. The diagrams that emerge from applying the rules in Fig. 6.21 constitute the set of all possible structured activity diagrams and hence the set of all possible structured applications. The beauty of the structured approach is that we use only eight simple single-entry/single-exit control statements (counting the foreach statement, which we introduce in Section 8.6) and assemble them in only two simple ways.

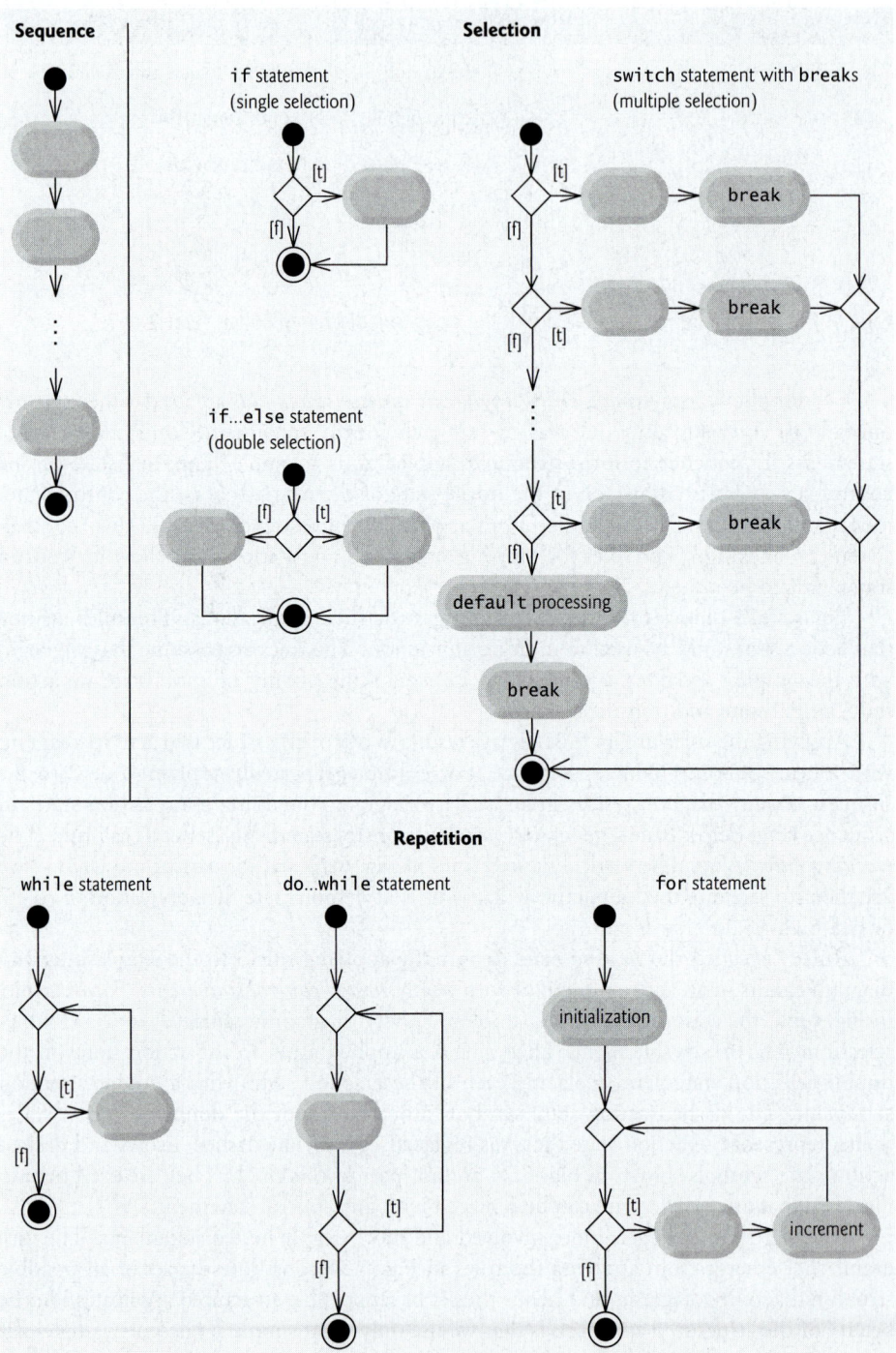

Fig. 6.20 | C#'s single-entry/single-exit sequence, selection and repetition statements.

Rules for Forming Structured Applications
1   Begin with the simplest activity diagram (Fig. 6.22).
2   Any action state can be replaced by two action states in sequence.
3   Any action state can be replaced by any control statement (sequence of action states, if, if…else, switch, while, do…while, for or foreach, which we will see in Chapter 8).
4   Rules 2 and 3 can be applied as often as necessary in any order.

Fig. 6.21 | Rules for forming structured applications.

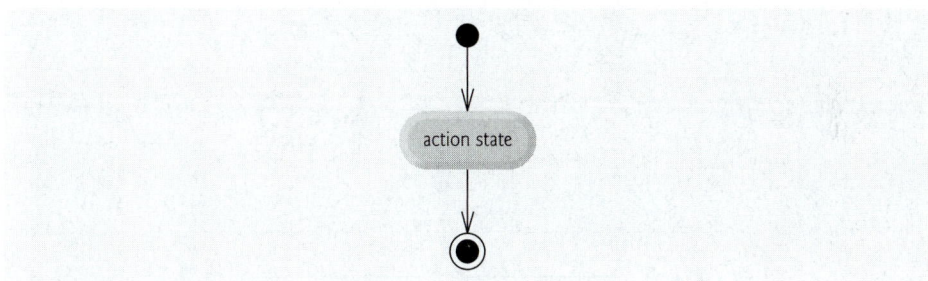

Fig. 6.22 | Simplest activity diagram.

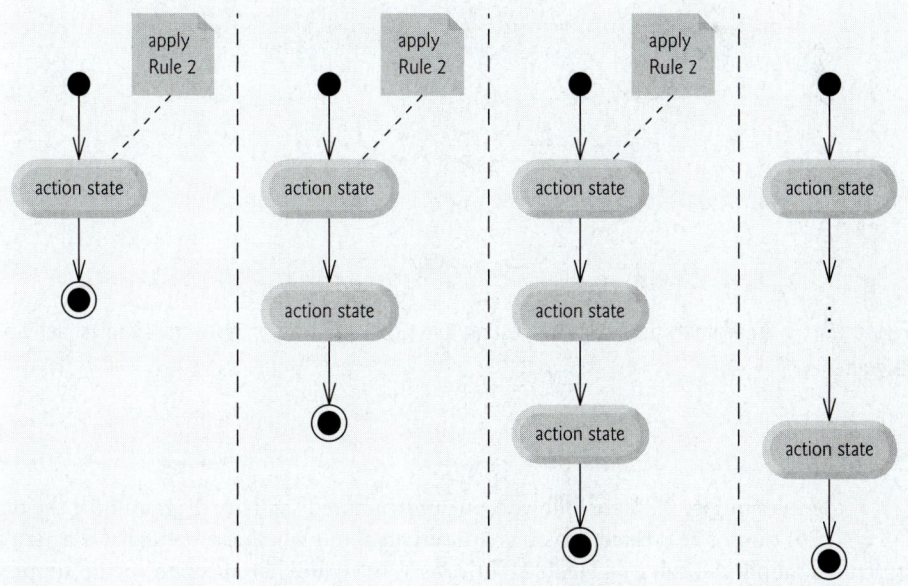

Fig. 6.23 | Repeatedly applying the stacking rule (Rule 2) of Fig. 6.21 to the simplest activity diagram.

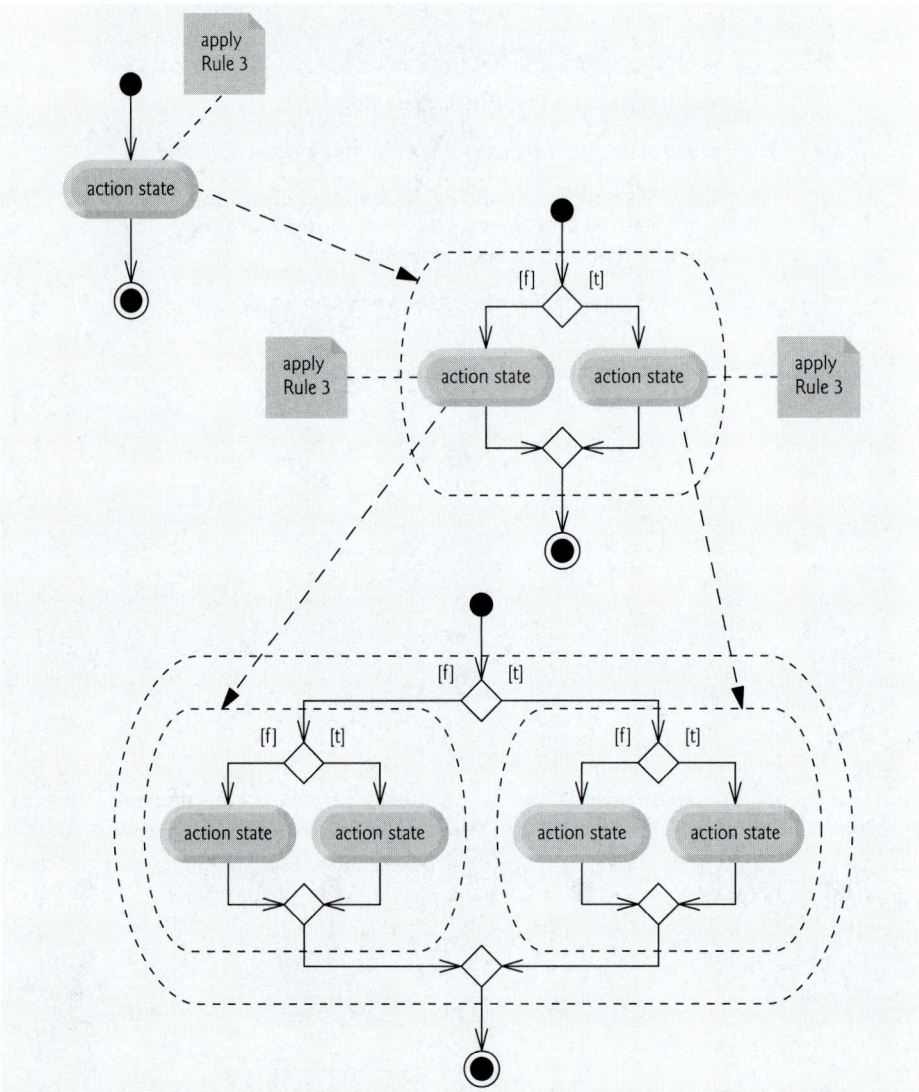

Fig. 6.24 | Repeatedly applying the nesting rule (Rule 3) of Fig. 6.21 to the simplest activity diagram.

If the rules in Fig. 6.21 are followed, an "unstructured" activity diagram (like the one in Fig. 6.25) cannot be created. If you are uncertain about whether a particular diagram is structured, apply the rules of Fig. 6.21 in reverse to reduce the diagram to the simplest activity diagram. If you can reduce it, the original diagram is structured; otherwise, it is not.

Structured programming promotes simplicity. Bohm and Jacopini have shown that only three forms of control are needed to implement any algorithm:

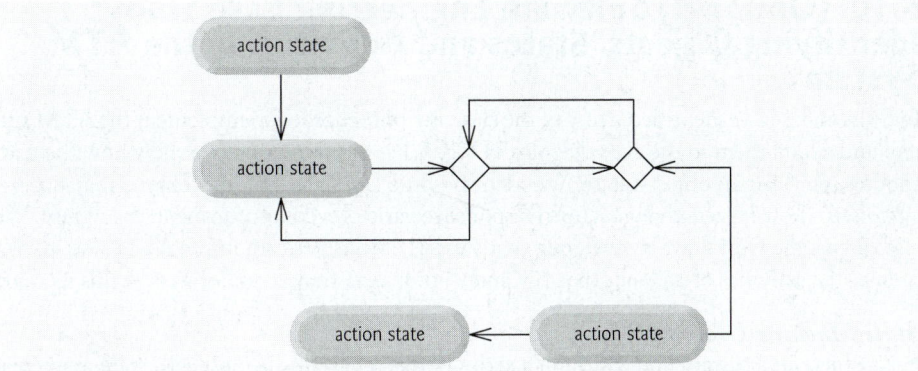

Fig. 6.25 | "Unstructured" activity diagram.

- sequence
- selection
- repetition

Sequence is trivial. Simply list the statements of the sequence in the order in which they should execute. Selection is implemented in one of three ways:

- `if` statement (single selection)
- `if...else` statement (double selection)
- `switch` statement (multiple selection)

In fact, it is straightforward to prove that the simple `if` statement is sufficient to provide any form of selection—everything that can be done with the `if...else` statement and the `switch` statement can be done by combining `if` statements (although perhaps not as clearly and efficiently).

Repetition is implemented in one of four ways:

- `while` statement
- `do...while` statement
- `for` statement
- `foreach` statement

It is straightforward to prove that the `while` statement is sufficient to provide any form of repetition. Everything that can be done with the `do...while`, `for` and `foreach` statements can be done with the `while` statement (although perhaps not as conveniently).

Combining these results illustrates that any form of control ever needed in a C# application can be expressed in terms of

- sequence structure
- `if` statement (selection)
- `while` statement (repetition)

and that these can be combined in only two ways—stacking and nesting. Indeed, structured programming is the essence of simplicity.

6.10 (Optional) Software Engineering Case Study: Identifying Objects' States and Activities in the ATM System

In Section 5.14, we identified many of the class attributes needed to implement the ATM system and added them to the class diagram in Fig. 5.19. In this section, we show how these attributes represent an object's state. We identify some key states that our objects may occupy and discuss how objects change state in response to various events occurring in the system. We also discuss the workflow, or *activities*, that various objects perform in the ATM system. We present the activities of BalanceInquiry and Withdrawal transaction objects in this section.

State Machine Diagrams

Each object in a system goes through a series of discrete states. An object's state at a given point in time is indicated by the values of the object's attributes at that time. *State machine diagrams* model key states of an object and show under what circumstances the object changes state. Unlike the class diagrams presented in earlier case study sections, which focused primarily on the *structure* of the system, state machine diagrams model some of the *behavior* of the system.

Figure 6.26 is a simple state machine diagram that models two of the states of an object of class ATM. The UML represents each state in a state machine diagram as a *rounded rectangle* with the name of the state placed inside it. A *solid circle* with an attached stick arrowhead designates the *initial state*. Recall that we modeled this state information as the bool attribute userAuthenticated in the class diagram of Fig. 5.19. This attribute is initialized to false, or the "User not authenticated" state, according to the state machine diagram.

The arrows with stick arrowheads indicate *transitions* between states. An object can transition from one state to another in response to various events that occur in the system. The name or description of the event that causes a transition is written near the line that corresponds to the transition. For example, the ATM object changes from the "User not authenticated" state to the "User authenticated" state after the bank database authenticates the user. Recall from the requirements document that the database authenticates a user by comparing the account number and PIN entered by the user with those of the corresponding account in the database. If the database indicates that the user has entered a valid account number and the correct PIN, the ATM object transitions to the "User authenticated" state and changes its userAuthenticated attribute to the value true. When the user exits the system by choosing the "exit" option from the main menu, the ATM object returns to the "User not authenticated" state in preparation for the next ATM user.

Software Engineering Observation 6.5

Software designers do not generally create state machine diagrams showing every possible state and state transition for all attributes—there are simply too many of them. State machine diagrams typically show only the most important or complex states and state transitions.

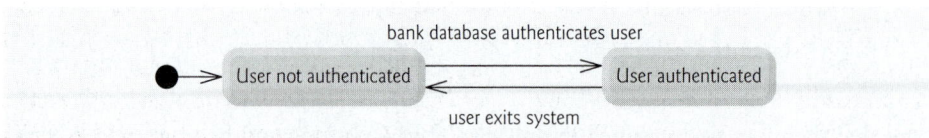

Fig. 6.26 | State machine diagram for some of the states of the ATM object.

Activity Diagrams

Like a state machine diagram, an activity diagram models aspects of system behavior. Unlike a state machine diagram, an activity diagram models an object's workflow (sequence of events) during application execution. An activity diagram models the actions to perform and in what order the object will perform them. Recall that we used UML activity diagrams to illustrate the flow of control for the control statements presented in Chapter 5 and Chapter 6.

The activity diagram in Fig. 6.27 models the actions involved in executing a Balance-Inquiry transaction. We assume that a BalanceInquiry object has already been initialized and assigned a valid account number (that of the current user), so the object knows which balance to retrieve. The diagram includes the actions that occur after the user selects a balance inquiry from the main menu and before the ATM returns the user to the main menu—a BalanceInquiry object does not perform or initiate these actions, so we do not model them here. The diagram begins with the retrieval of the available balance of the user's account from the database. Next, the BalanceInquiry retrieves the total balance of the account. Finally, the transaction displays the balances on the screen.

The UML represents an action in an activity diagram as an action state, which is modeled by a rectangle with its left and right sides replaced by arcs curving outward. Each action state contains an action expression—for example, "get available balance of user's account from database"—that specifies an action to perform. An arrow with a stick arrowhead connects two action states, indicating the order in which the actions represented by the action states occur. The solid circle (at the top of Fig. 6.27) represents the activity's initial state—the beginning of the workflow before the object performs the modeled actions. In this case, the transaction first executes the "get available balance of user's account from database" action expression. Second, the transaction retrieves the total balance. Finally, the transaction displays both balances on the screen. The solid circle enclosed in an open circle (at the bottom of Fig. 6.27) represents the final state—the end of the workflow after the object performs the modeled actions.

Figure 6.28 shows an activity diagram for a Withdrawal transaction. We assume that a Withdrawal object has been assigned a valid account number. We do not model the user selecting a withdrawal from the main menu or the ATM returning the user to the main menu, because these are not actions performed by a Withdrawal object. The transaction first displays a menu of standard withdrawal amounts (Fig. 3.30) and an option to cancel the transaction. The transaction then inputs a menu selection from the user. The activity flow now arrives at a decision symbol. This point determines the next action based on the associated guard conditions. If the user cancels the transaction, the system displays an appropriate message. Next, the cancellation flow reaches a merge symbol, where this activity flow joins the transaction's other possible activity flows (which we discuss shortly). Note that a merge can have any number of incoming transition arrows, but only one outgoing transition arrow. The decision at the bottom of the diagram determines whether the transaction should repeat from the beginning. When the user has canceled the transaction, the guard condition "cash dispensed or user canceled transaction" is true, so control transitions to the activity's final state.

If the user selects a withdrawal amount from the menu, amount (an attribute of class Withdrawal originally modeled in Fig. 5.19) is set to the value chosen by the user. The transaction next gets the available balance of the user's account (i.e., the availableBalance attribute of the user's Account object) from the database. The activity flow then arrives at another decision. If the requested withdrawal amount exceeds the user's available balance, the system displays an appropriate error message informing the user of the

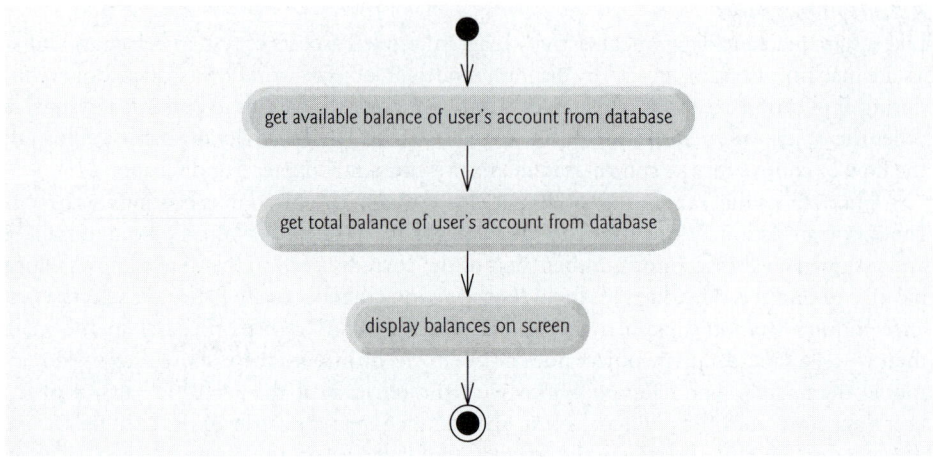

Fig. 6.27 | Activity diagram for a `BalanceInquiry` transaction.

problem. Control then merges with the other activity flows before reaching the decision at the bottom of the diagram. The guard condition "cash not dispensed and user did not cancel" is true, so the activity flow returns to the top of the diagram, and the transaction prompts the user to input a new amount.

If the requested withdrawal amount is less than or equal to the user's available balance, the transaction tests whether the cash dispenser has enough cash to satisfy the withdrawal request. If it does not, the transaction displays an appropriate error message and passes through the merge before reaching the final decision. Cash was not dispensed, so the activity flow returns to the beginning of the activity diagram, and the transaction prompts the user to choose a new amount. If sufficient cash is available, the transaction interacts with the database to debit the withdrawal amount from the user's account (i.e., subtract the amount from *both* the `availableBalance` and `totalBalance` attributes of the user's `Account` object). The transaction then dispenses the desired amount of cash and instructs the user to take the cash.

The main flow of activity next merges with the two error flows and the cancellation flow. In this case, cash was dispensed, so the activity flow reaches the final state.

We have taken the first steps in modeling the behavior of the ATM system and have shown how an object's attributes affect the object's activities. In Section 7.15, we investigate the operations of our classes to create a more complete model of the system's behavior.

Software Engineering Case Study Self-Review Exercises

6.1   State whether the following statement is *true* or *false*, and if *false*, explain why: State machine diagrams model structural aspects of a system.

6.2   An activity diagram models the _____ that an object performs and the order in which it performs them.
  a) actions
  b) attributes
  c) states
  d) state transitions

6.3   Based on the requirements document, create an activity diagram for a deposit transaction.

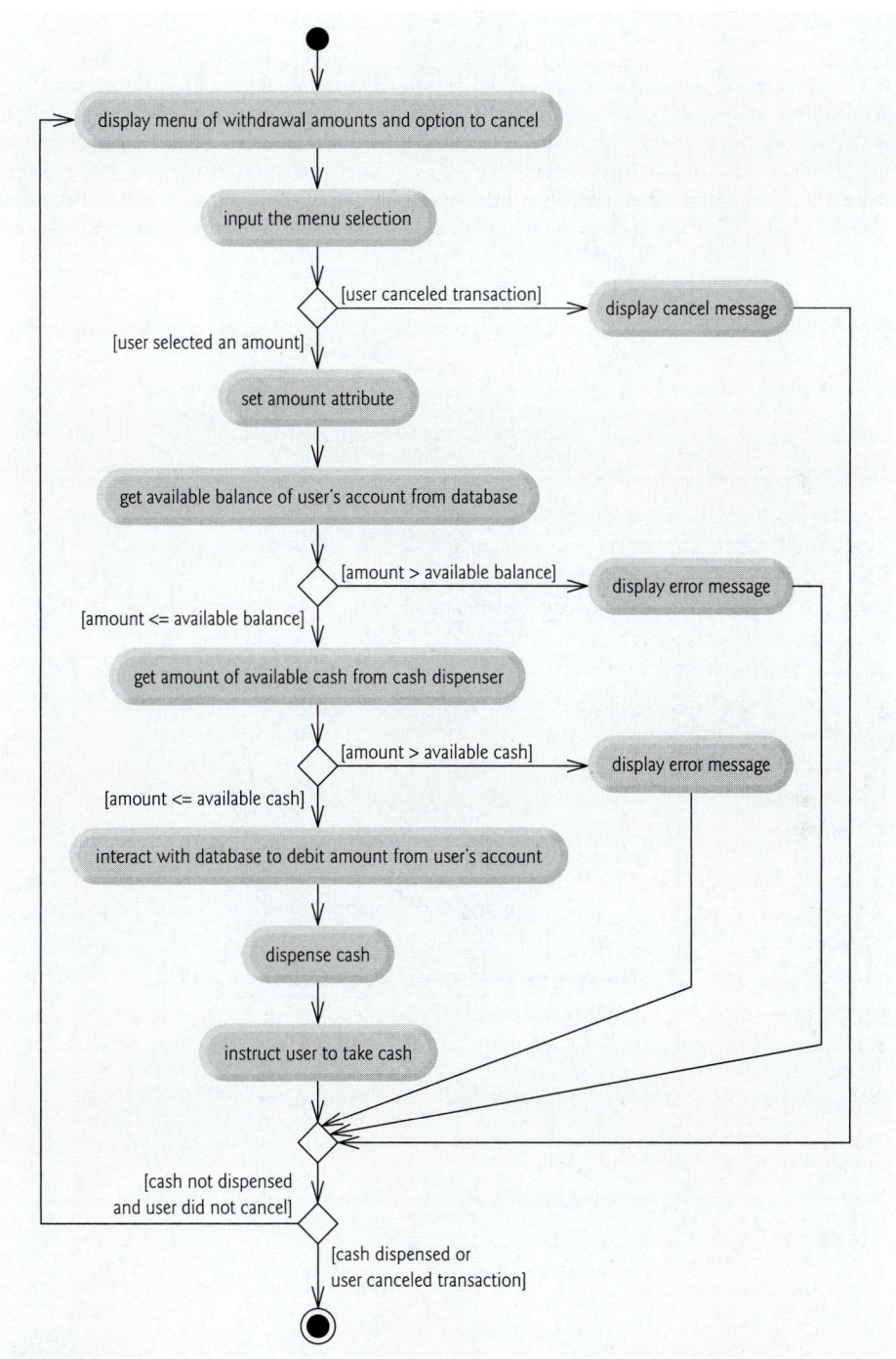

Fig. 6.28 | Activity diagram for a `Withdrawal` transaction.

Answers to Software Engineering Case Study Self-Review Exercises

6.1 False. State machine diagrams model some of the behaviors of a system.

6.2 a.

6.3 Figure 6.29 presents an activity diagram for a deposit transaction. The diagram models the actions that occur after the user chooses the deposit option from the main menu and before the ATM returns the user to the main menu. Recall that part of receiving a deposit amount from the user involves converting an integer number of cents to a dollar amount. Also recall that crediting a deposit amount to an account involves increasing only the `totalBalance` attribute of the user's `Account` object. The bank updates the `availableBalance` attribute of the user's `Account` object only

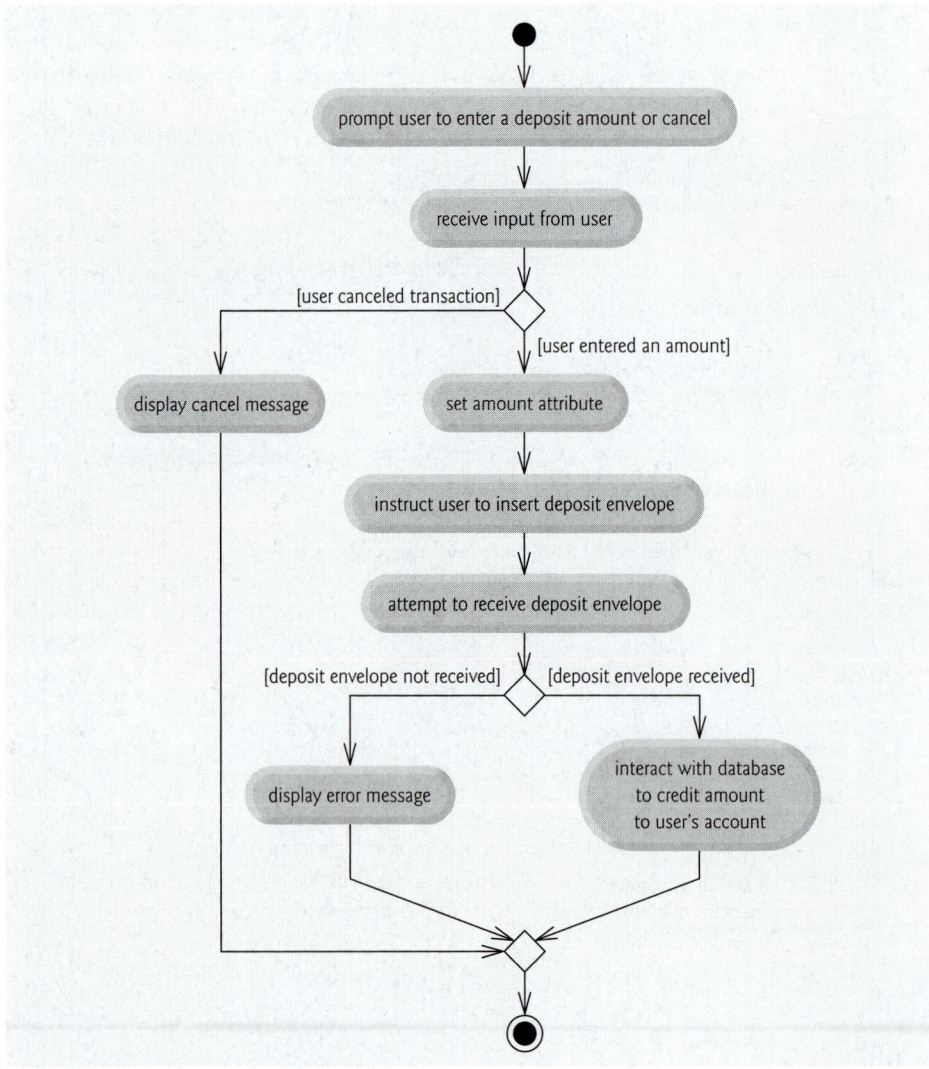

Fig. 6.29 | Activity diagram for a `Deposit` transaction.

after confirming the amount of cash in the deposit envelope and after the enclosed checks clear—this occurs independently of the ATM system.

6.11 Wrap-Up

Chapter 5 discussed the `if`, `if...else` and `while` control statements. In this chapter, we discussed the `for`, `do...while` and `switch` control statements. (We will discuss the `foreach` statement in Chapter 8). You learned that any algorithm can be developed using combinations of sequence (i.e., statements listed in the order in which they should execute), the three selection statements—`if`, `if...else` and `switch`—and the four repetition statements—`while`, `do...while`, `for` and `foreach`. You saw that the `for` and `do...while` statements are simply more convenient ways to express certain types of repetition. Similarly, we showed that the `switch` statement is a convenient notation for multiple selection, rather than using nested `if...else` statements. We discussed how you can combine various control statements by stacking and nesting them. We showed how to use the `break` and `continue` statements to alter the flow of control in repetition statements. You also learned about the logical operators, which enable you to use more complex conditional expressions in control statements.

In Chapter 4, we introduced the basic concepts of objects, classes and methods. Chapters 5 and 6 provided a thorough introduction to the control statements that you use to specify application logic in methods. In Chapter 7, we examine methods in greater depth.

Summary

Section 6.2 Essentials of Counter-Controlled Repetition

- Counter-controlled repetition requires a control variable, the initial value of the control variable, the increment (or decrement) by which the control variable is modified each time through the loop and the loop-continuation condition that determines whether looping should continue.

Section 6.3 for Repetition Statement

- The `for` header "does it all"—it specifies each of the items needed for counter-controlled repetition with a control variable. The general format of the `for` statement is

```
for ( initialization; loopContinuationCondition; increment )
    statement
```

where the *initialization* expression names the loop's control variable and provides its initial value, the *loopContinuationCondition* is the condition that determines whether looping should continue and the *increment* modifies the control variable's value so that the loop-continuation condition eventually becomes `false`.

- Typically, `for` statements are used for counter-controlled repetition, and `while` statements are used for sentinel-controlled repetition.

- The scope of a variable defines where it can be used in an application. For example, a local variable can be used only in the method that declares the variable and only from the point of declaration through the end of the method.

- The increment of a for statement may also be negative, in which case it is a decrement, and the loop counts downward.
- If the loop-continuation condition is initially false, the application does not execute the for statement's body.

Section 6.4 Examples Using the for Statement

- When a variable of type decimal is initialized to an int literal, the value of type int is promoted to a decimal type implicitly—no cast is required.
- In a format item, an integer *n* after a comma indicates that the value output should be displayed with a field width of *n*—that is, Write (or WriteLine) displays the value with at least *n* character positions.
- Values are right justified in a field by default. To indicate that values should be output left justified, simply use a negative field width.
- Methods that perform common tasks and do not need to be called on objects are called static methods.
- C# does not include an exponentiation operator. Instead, Math.Pow(x, y) calculates the value of *x* raised to the *y*th power. The method receives two double arguments and returns a double value.
- C# will not implicitly convert a double to a decimal type, or vice versa, because of the possible loss of information in either conversion. To perform this conversion, a cast operator is required.
- Floating-point numbers of type double (or float) can cause trouble in monetary calculations; use type decimal instead.

Section 6.5 do...while Repetition Statement

- The do...while statement tests the loop-continuation condition *after* executing the loop's body; therefore, the body always executes at least once.
- The do...while statement has the form:

```
do
{
    statement
} while ( condition );
```

Section 6.6 switch Multiple-Selection Statement

- The switch multiple-selection statement performs different actions based on the possible values of an expression.
- On Windows systems, *<Ctrl> z* is the key sequence for typing the end-of-file indicator, a system-dependent keystroke combination that the user enters to indicate that there is no more data to input.
- The switch statement consists of a block that contains a sequence of case labels and an optional default label.
- The expression in parentheses following keyword switch is the switch expression. The application compares the value of the switch expression (which must be a constant integral or string expression) with each case label. If a match occurs, the application executes the statements for that case.
- The switch statement does not provide a mechanism for testing ranges of values, so every value to be tested must be listed in a separate case label.

- After the statements in a case execute, you are required to include a statement that terminates the case, such as a break or a return.
- If no match occurs between the switch expression's value and a case label, the statements after the default label execute. If no match occurs and the switch does not contain a default label, program control simply continues with the first statement after the switch statement.

Section 6.7 break *and* continue *Statements*
- The break statement, when executed in a while, for, do...while, switch or foreach, causes immediate exit from that statement. Execution continues with the first statement after the control statement.
- The continue statement, when executed in a while, for, do...while or foreach, skips the remaining statements in the loop body and proceeds with the next iteration of the loop.

Section 6.8 *Logical Operators*
- Logical operators enable you to form more complex conditions by combining simple conditions. The logical operators are && (conditional AND), || (conditional OR), & (boolean logical AND), | (boolean logical inclusive OR), ∧ (boolean logical exclusive OR) and ! (logical negation).
- The && (conditional AND) operator ensures that two conditions are *both* true before we choose a certain path of execution.
- The || (conditional OR) operator ensures that *either or both* of two conditions are true before we choose a certain path of execution.
- The parts of an expression containing && or || operators are evaluated only until it is known whether the condition is true or false. This feature of conditional AND and conditional OR expressions is called short-circuit evaluation.
- The boolean logical AND (&) and boolean logical inclusive OR (|) operators work identically to the && (conditional AND) and || (conditional OR) operators, with one exception—the boolean logical operators always evaluate both of their operands (i.e., they do not perform short-circuit evaluation).
- A complex condition containing the boolean logical exclusive OR (∧) operator is true if and only if one of its operands is true and the other is false. If both operands are true or both are false, the entire condition is false.
- The ! (logical negation) operator enables you to "reverse" the meaning of a condition. The logical negation operator is placed before a condition to choose a path of execution if the original condition is false. In most cases, you can avoid using logical negation by expressing the condition differently with an appropriate relational or equality operator.

Section 6.9 *Structured Programming Summary*
- Any form of control ever needed in a C# application can be expressed in terms of sequence, the if statement (selection) and the while statement (repetition). These can be combined in only two ways—stacking and nesting.

Terminology

!, logical negation operator
&, boolean logical AND operator
&&, conditional AND operator
|, boolean logical OR operator
||, conditional OR operator
∧, boolean logical exclusive OR operator

boolean logical AND (&)
boolean logical exclusive OR (∧)
boolean logical inclusive OR (|)
break statement
case label in switch
character constant

conditional AND (&&)	logical operators
conditional OR (||)	logical XOR operator (^)
const keyword	loop-continuation condition
constant	multiple selection statement
constant integral expression	nested control statements
constant string expression	nesting rule
continue statement	off-by-one error
control variable	repetition statement
decrement a control variable	right justified
default label in switch	scope of a variable
do...while repetition statement	short-circuit evaluation
end-of-file indicator	side effect
field width	simple condition
for header	single-entry/single-exit control statements
for repetition statement	state machine diagram
for statement header	stacked control statements
foreach statement	stacking rule
helper method	static method
increment a control variable	switch expression
initial value of a control variable	switch selection statement
iteration of a loop	truth table
logical negation (!)	utility method

Self-Review Exercises

6.1 Fill in the blanks in each of the following statements:
 a) Typically, _____ statements are used for counter-controlled repetition and _____ statements are used for sentinel-controlled repetition.
 b) The do...while statement tests the loop-continuation condition _____ executing the loop's body; therefore, the body always executes at least once.
 c) The _____ statement selects among multiple actions based on the possible values of an integer variable or expression.
 d) The _____ statement, when executed in a repetition statement, skips the remaining statements in the loop body and proceeds with the next iteration of the loop.
 e) The _____ operator can be used to ensure that two conditions are *both* true before choosing a certain path of execution.
 f) If the loop-continuation condition in a for header is initially _____, the for statement's body does not execute.
 g) Methods that perform common tasks and do not need to be called on objects are called _____ methods.

6.2 State whether each of the following is *true* or *false*. If *false*, explain why.
 a) The default label is required in the switch selection statement.
 b) The break statement is required in every case of a switch statement.
 c) The expression ((x > y) && (a < b)) is true if either (x > y) is true or (a < b) is true.
 d) An expression containing the || operator is true if either or both of its operands are true.
 e) The integer after the comma (,) in a format item (e.g., {0,4}) indicates the field width of the displayed string.
 f) To test for a range of values in a switch statement, use a hyphen (–) between the start and end values of the range in a case label.
 g) Listing cases consecutively with no statements between them enables the cases to perform the same set of statements.

6.3   Write a C# statement or a set of C# statements to accomplish each of the following tasks:

a)   Sum the odd integers between 1 and 99, using a for statement. Assume that the integer variables sum and count have been declared.

b)   Calculate the value of 2.5 raised to the power of 3, using the Pow method.

c)   Print the integers from 1 to 20 using a while loop and the counter variable i. Assume that the variable i has been declared, but not initialized. Print only five integers per line. [*Hint:* Use the calculation i % 5. When the value of this expression is 0, print a newline character; otherwise, print a tab character. Assume that this code is an application. Use the Console.WriteLine() method to output the newline character, and use the Console.Write('\t') method to output the tab character.]

d)   Repeat part (c), using a for statement.

6.4   Find the error in each of the following code segments and explain how to correct it:

a)   i = 1;

```
while ( i <= 10 );
    i++;
}
```

b)
```
for ( k = 0.1; k != 1.0; k += 0.1 )
    Console.WriteLine( k );
```

c)
```
switch ( n )
{
    case 1:
        Console.WriteLine( "The number is 1" );
    case 2:
        Console.WriteLine( "The number is 2" );
        break;
    default:
        Console.WriteLine( "The number is not 1 or 2" );
        break;
}
```

d)   The following code should print the values 1 to 10:

```
n = 1;

while ( n < 10 )
    Console.WriteLine( n++ );
```

Answers to Self-Review Exercises

6.1   a) for, while. b) after. c) switch. d) continue. e) && (conditional AND) or & (boolean logical AND). f) false. g) static.

6.2   a) False. The default label is optional. If no default action is needed, then there is no need for a default label. b) False. You could terminate the case with other statements, such as a return. c) False. Both of the relational expressions must be true for this entire expression to be true when using the && operator. d) True. e) True. f) False. The switch statement does not provide a mechanism for testing ranges of values, so you must list every value to test in a separate case label. g) True.

6.3   a)
```
sum = 0;
for ( count = 1; count <= 99; count += 2 )
    sum += count;
```
b)   double result = Math.Pow(2.5, 3);

c) i = 1;

```
while ( i <= 20 )
{
    Console.Write( i );

    if ( i % 5 == 0 )
        Console.WriteLine();
    else
        Console.Write( '\t' );

    i++;
}
```

d)
```
for ( i = 1; i <= 20; i++ )
{
    Console.Write( i );

    if ( i % 5 == 0 )
        Console.WriteLine();
    else
        Console.Write( '\t' );
}
```

6.4   a) Error: The semicolon after the while header causes an infinite loop, and there is a missing left brace for the body of the while statement.
Correction: Remove the semicolon and add a { before the loop's body.

b) Error: Using a floating-point number to control a for statement may not work, because floating-point numbers are represented only approximately by most computers.
Correction: Use an integer, and perform the proper calculation in order to get the values you desire:

```
for ( k = 1; k < 10; k++ )
    Console.WriteLine( ( double ) k / 10 );
```

c) Error: case 1 cannot fall through into case 2.
Correction: Terminate the case in some way, such as adding a break statement at the end of the statements for the first case.

d) Error: An improper relational operator is used in the while repetition-continuation condition.
Correction: Use <= rather than <, or change 10 to 11.

Exercises

6.5   Describe the four basic elements of counter-controlled repetition.

6.6   Compare and contrast the while and for repetition statements.

6.7   Discuss a situation in which it would be more appropriate to use a do...while statement than a while statement. Explain why.

6.8   Compare and contrast the break and continue statements.

6.9   Find and correct the error(s) in each of the following segments of code:
a)
```
For ( i = 100, i >= 1, i++ )
    Console.WriteLine( i );
```
b) The following code should print whether integer value is odd or even:

```
switch ( value % 2 )
{
    case 0:
        Console.WriteLine( "Even integer" );
    case 1:
        Console.WriteLine( "Odd integer" );
}
```

c) The following code should output the odd integers from 19 to 1:

```
for ( int i = 19; i >= 1; i += 2 )
    Console.WriteLine( i );
```

d) The following code should output the even integers from 2 to 100:

```
counter = 2;

do
{
    Console.WriteLine( counter );
    counter += 2;
} while ( counter < 100 );
```

6.10   What does the following application do?

```
1   // Exercise 6.10 Solution: Printing.cs
2   using System;
3
4   public class Printing
5   {
6       public static void Main( string[] args )
7       {
8           for ( int i = 1; i <= 10; i++ )
9           {
10              for ( int j = 1; j <= 5; j++ )
11                  Console.Write( '@' );
12
13              Console.WriteLine();
14          } // end outer for
15      } // end Main
16  } // end class Printing
```

6.11   Write an application that finds the smallest of several integers. Assume that the first value read specifies the number of values to input from the user.

6.12   Write an application that calculates the product of the odd integers from 1 to 7.

6.13   *Factorials* are used frequently in probability problems. The factorial of a positive integer n (written $n!$ and pronounced "n factorial") is equal to the product of the positive integers from 1 to n. Write an application that evaluates the factorials of the integers from 1 to 5. Display the results in tabular format. What difficulty might prevent you from calculating the factorial of 20?

6.14   Modify the compound-interest application of Fig. 6.6 to repeat its steps for interest rates of 5, 6, 7, 8, 9 and 10%. Use a for loop to vary the interest rate.

6.15   Write an application that displays the following patterns separately, one below the other. Use for loops to generate the patterns. All asterisks (*) should be printed by a single statement of the form Console.Write('*'); which causes the asterisks to print side by side. A statement of the form `Console.WriteLine();` can be used to move to the next line. A statement of the form `Console.Write(' ');` can be used to display a space for the last two patterns. There should be no other output statements in the application. [*Hint:* The last two patterns require that each line begin with an appropriate number of blank spaces.]

```
(a)                    (b)                    (c)                    (d)

*                      **********             **********                      *
**                     *********              *********                      **
***                    ********               ********                      ***
****                   *******                *******                      ****
*****                  ******                 ******                      *****
******                 *****                  *****                      ******
*******                ****                   ****                      *******
********               ***                    ***                      ********
*********              **                     **                      *********
**********             *                      *                      **********
```

6.16   One interesting application of computers is to display graphs and bar charts. Write an application that reads three numbers between 1 and 30. For each number that is read, your application should display the same number of adjacent asterisks. For example, if your application reads the number 7, it should display *******.

6.17   A Web site sells three products whose retail prices are as follows: product 1, $2.98; product 2, $4.50; and product 3, $9.98. Write an application that reads a series of pairs of numbers as follows:

   a) product number
   b) quantity sold

Your application should use a `switch` statement to determine the retail price for each product. It should calculate and display the total retail value of all products sold. Use a sentinel-controlled loop to determine when the application should stop looping and display the final results.

6.18   In the future, you may work with other programming languages that do not have a type like `decimal` which supports precise monetary calculations. In those languages, you should perform such calculations using integers. Modify the application in Fig. 6.6 to use only integers to calculate the compound interest. Treat all monetary amounts as integral numbers of pennies. Then break the result into its dollars and cents portions by using the division and remainder operations, respectively. Insert a period between the dollars and the cents portions when you display the results.

6.19   Assume that i = 1, j = 2, k = 3 and m = 2. What does each of the following statements print?
   a) `Console.WriteLine( i == 1 );`
   b) `Console.WriteLine( j == 3 );`
   c) `Console.WriteLine( ( i >= 1 ) && ( j < 4 ) );`
   d) `Console.WriteLine( ( m <= 99 ) & ( k < m ) );`
   e) `Console.WriteLine( ( j >= i ) || ( k == m ) );`
   f) `Console.WriteLine( ( k + m < j ) | ( 3 - j >= k ) );`
   g) `Console.WriteLine( !( k > m ) );`

6.20   Calculate the value of π from the infinite series

$$\pi = 4 - \frac{4}{3} + \frac{4}{5} - \frac{4}{7} + \frac{4}{9} - \frac{4}{11} + \cdots$$

Print a table that shows the value of π approximated by computing one term of this series, by two terms, by three terms, and so on. How many terms of this series do you have to use before you first get 3.14? 3.141? 3.1415? 3.14159?

6.21 (*Pythagorean Triples*) A right triangle can have sides whose lengths are all integers. The set of three integer values for the lengths of the sides of a right triangle is called a Pythagorean triple. The lengths of the three sides must satisfy the relationship that the sum of the squares of two of the sides is equal to the square of the hypotenuse. Write an application to find all Pythagorean triples for side1, side2 and the hypotenuse, all no larger than 500. Use a triple-nested for loop that tries all possibilities. This method is an example of "brute-force" computing. You will learn in more advanced computer science courses that there are large numbers of interesting problems for which there is no known algorithmic approach other than using sheer brute force.

6.22 Modify Exercise 6.15 to combine your code from the four separate triangles of asterisks such that all four patterns print side by side. Make clever use of nested for loops.

6.23 Write an application that prints the following diamond shape. You may use output statements that print a single asterisk (*), a single space or a single newline character. Maximize your use of repetition (with nested for statements) and minimize the number of output statements.

```
    *
   ***
  *****
 *******
*********
 *******
  *****
   ***
    *
```

6.24 Modify the application you wrote in Exercise 6.23 to read an odd number in the range 1 to 19 to specify the number of rows in the diamond. Your application should then display a diamond of the appropriate size.

6.25 A criticism of the break statement and the continue statement is that each is unstructured. Actually, break statements and continue statements can always be replaced by structured statements, although doing so can be awkward. Describe in general how you would remove any break statement from a loop in an application and replace that statement with some structured equivalent. [*Hint:* The break statement exits a loop from the body of the loop. The other way to exit is by failing the loop-continuation test. Consider using in the loop-continuation test a second test that indicates "early exit because of a 'break' condition."] Use the technique you develop here to remove the break statement from the application in Fig. 6.12.

6.26 What does the following code segment do?

```
for ( int i = 1; i <= 5; i++ )
{
   for ( int j = 1; j <= 3; j++ )
   {
      for ( int k = 1; k <= 4; k++ )
         Console.Write( '*' );

      Console.WriteLine();
   } // end inner for

   Console.WriteLine();
} // end outer for
```

6.27 Describe in general how you would remove any continue statement from a loop in an application and replace it with some structured equivalent. Use the technique you develop here to remove the continue statement from the application in Fig. 6.13.

7

Methods:
A Deeper Look

Form ever follows function.
—Louis Henri Sullivan

E pluribus unum.
(One composed of many.)
—Virgil

O! call back yesterday, bid
time return.
—William Shakespeare

Call me Ishmael.
—Herman Melville

When you call me that,
smile!
—Owen Wister

Answer me in one word.
—William Shakespeare

There is a point at which
methods devour themselves.
—Frantz Fanon

Life can only be understood
backwards; but it must be
lived forwards.
—Soren Kierkegaard

OBJECTIVES

In this chapter you will learn:

- How **static** methods and variables are associated with an entire class rather than specific instances of the class.

- How the method call/return mechanism is supported by the method call stack and activation records.

- How to use random-number generation to implement game-playing applications.

- To understand how the visibility of declarations is limited to specific regions of applications.

- What method overloading is and how to create overloaded methods.

- What recursive methods are.

- The differences between passing method arguments by value and by reference.

7.1 Introduction

Most computer applications that solve real-world problems are much larger than the applications presented in the first few chapters of this book. Experience has shown that the best way to develop and maintain a large application is to construct it from small, simple pieces. This technique is called *divide and conquer.* We introduced methods in Chapter 4. In this chapter, we study methods in more depth. We emphasize how to declare and use methods to facilitate the design, implementation, operation and maintenance of large applications.

You will see that it is possible for certain methods, called `static` methods, to be called without the need for an object of the class to exist. You will learn how to declare a method with more than one parameter. You will also learn how C# is able to keep track of which method is currently executing, how value-type and reference-type arguments are passed to methods, how local variables of methods are maintained in memory and how a method knows where to return after it completes execution.

We discuss *simulation* techniques with random-number generation and develop a version of the casino dice game called craps that uses most of the programming techniques you have learned to this point in the book. In addition, you will learn to declare values that cannot change (i.e., constants). You will also learn to write methods that call themselves—this is called *recursion.*

Many of the classes you will use or create while developing applications will have more than one method of the same name. This technique, called *method overloading*, is used to implement methods that perform similar tasks but with different types or different numbers of arguments.

7.2 Packaging Code in C#

Three common ways of packaging code are methods, classes and namespaces. C# applications are written by combining new methods and classes that you write with predefined methods and classes available in the *.NET Framework Class Library* (also referred to as the *FCL*) and in various other class libraries. Related classes are often grouped into namespaces and compiled into class libraries so that they can be reused in other applications. You will learn how to create your own namespaces and class libraries in Chapter 9. The FCL provides many predefined classes that contain methods for performing common mathematical calculations, string manipulations, character manipulations, input/output operations, database operations, networking operations, file processing, error checking and many other useful operations.

Good Programming Practice 7.1

Familiarize yourself with the classes and methods provided by the FCL (msdn2.microsoft.com/ en-us/library/ms229335). In Section 7.8, we present an overview of several common namespaces.

Software Engineering Observation 7.1

Don't try to "reinvent the wheel." When possible, reuse FCL classes and methods. This reduces application development time and avoids introducing programming errors.

Methods (called *functions* or *procedures* in other programming languages) allow you to modularize an application by separating its tasks into self-contained units. You have declared methods in every application you have written. These methods are sometimes referred to as *user-defined methods*. The actual statements in the method bodies are written only once, can be reused from several locations in an application and are hidden from other methods.

There are several motivations for modularizing an application by means of methods. One is the "divide-and-conquer" approach, which makes application development more manageable by constructing applications from small, simple pieces. Another is *software reusability*—existing methods can be used as building blocks to create new applications. Often, you can create applications mostly by reusing existing methods rather than by building customized code. For example, in earlier applications, we did not have to define how to read data values from the keyboard—the FCL provides these capabilities in class Console. A third motivation is to avoid repeating code. Dividing an application into meaningful methods makes the application easier to debug and maintain.

Software Engineering Observation 7.2

To promote software reusability, every method should be limited to performing a single, well-defined task, and the name of the method should express that task effectively. Such methods make applications easier to write, debug, maintain and modify.

Error-Prevention Tip 7.1

A small method that performs one task is easier to test and debug than a larger method that performs many tasks.

Software Engineering Observation 7.3

If you cannot choose a concise name that expresses a method's task, your method might be attempting to perform too many diverse tasks. It is usually best to break such a method into several smaller methods.

As you know, a method is invoked by a method call, and when the called method completes its task, it either returns a result or simply control to the caller. An analogy to this application structure is the hierarchical form of management (Figure 7.1). A boss (the caller) asks a worker (the called method) to perform a task and report back (i.e., return) the results after completing the task. The boss method does not know how the worker method performs its designated tasks. The worker may also call other worker methods, unbeknownst to the boss. This "hiding" of implementation details promotes good software engineering. Figure 7.1 shows the boss method communicating with several worker methods in a hierarchical manner. The boss method divides the responsibilities among the various worker methods. Note that worker1 acts as a "boss method" to worker4 and worker5.

7.3 static Methods, static Variables and Class Math

Although most methods execute on specific objects in response to method calls, this is not always the case. Sometimes a method performs a task that does not depend on the contents of any object. Such a method applies to the class in which it is declared as a whole and is known as a static method. It is not uncommon for a class to contain a group of static methods to perform common tasks. For example, recall that we used static method Pow of class Math to raise a value to a power in Fig. 6.6. To declare a method as static, place the keyword static before the return type in the method's declaration. You call any static method by specifying the name of the class in which the method is declared, followed by the dot (.) operator and the method name, as in

ClassName.*methodName*(*arguments*)

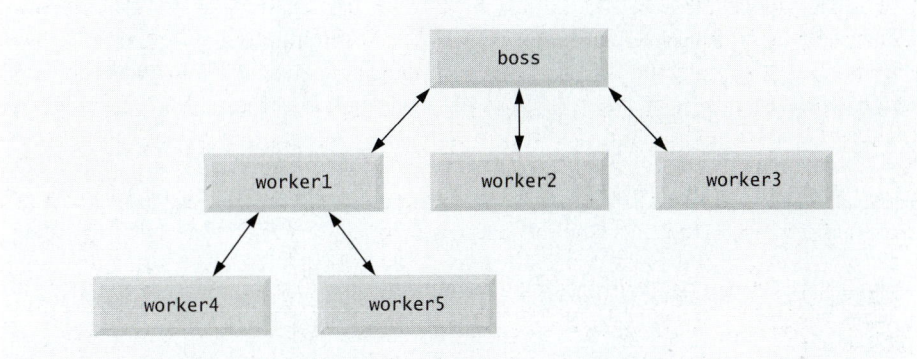

Fig. 7.1 | Hierarchical boss-method/worker-method relationship.

We use various methods of the Math class here to present the concept of static methods. Class Math (from the System namespace) provides a collection of methods that enable you to perform common mathematical calculations. For example, you can calculate the square root of 900.0 with the static method call

```
Math.Sqrt( 900.0 )
```

The preceding expression evaluates to 30.0. Method Sqrt takes an argument of type double and returns a result of type double. To output the value of the preceding method call in the console window, you might write the statement

```
Console.WriteLine( Math.Sqrt( 900.0 ) );
```

In this statement, the value that Sqrt returns becomes the argument to method Write-Line. Note that we did not create a Math object before calling method Sqrt. Also note that *all* of Math's methods are static—therefore, each is called by preceding the name of the method with the class name Math and the dot (.) operator. Similarly, Console method WriteLine is a static method of class Console, so we invoke the method by preceding its name with the class name Console and the dot (.) operator.

Method arguments may be constants, variables or expressions. If c = 13.0, d = 3.0 and f = 4.0, then the statement

```
Console.WriteLine( Math.Sqrt( c + d * f ) );
```

calculates and prints the square root of 13.0 + 3.0 * 4.0 = 25.0—namely, 5.0. Figure 7.2 summarizes several Math class methods. In the figure, x and y are of type double.

Method	Description	Example
Abs(x)	absolute value of x	Abs(23.7) is 23.7 Abs(0.0) is 0.0 Abs(-23.7) is 23.7
Ceiling(x)	rounds x to the smallest integer not less than x	Ceiling(9.2) is 10.0 Ceiling(-9.8) is -9.0
Cos(x)	trigonometric cosine of x (x in radians)	Cos(0.0) is 1.0
Exp(x)	exponential method e^x	Exp(1.0) is 2.71828 Exp(2.0) is 7.38906
Floor(x)	rounds x to the largest integer not greater than x	Floor(9.2) is 9.0 Floor(-9.8) is -10.0
Log(x)	natural logarithm of x (base e)	Log(Math.E) is 1.0 Log(Math.E * Math.E) is 2.0
Max(x, y)	larger value of x and y	Max(2.3, 12.7) is 12.7 Max(-2.3, -12.7) is -2.3

Fig. 7.2 | Math class methods. (Part 1 of 2.)

Method	Description	Example
Min(*x*, *y*)	smaller value of *x* and *y*	Min(2.3, 12.7) is 2.3 Min(-2.3, -12.7) is -12.7
Pow(*x*, *y*)	*x* raised to the power *y* (i.e., x^y)	Pow(2.0, 7.0) is 128.0 Pow(9.0, 0.5) is 3.0
Sin(*x*)	trigonometric sine of *x* (*x* in radians)	Sin(0.0) is 0.0
Sqrt(*x*)	square root of *x*	Sqrt(900.0) is 30.0
Tan(*x*)	trigonometric tangent of *x* (*x* in radians)	Tan(0.0) is 0.0

Fig. 7.2 | Math class methods. (Part 2 of 2.)

Math Class Constants PI and E

Class Math also declares two static variables that represent commonly used mathematical constants: ***Math.PI*** and ***Math.E***. The constant Math.PI (3.14159265358979323846) is the ratio of a circle's circumference to its diameter. The constant Math.E (2.7182818284590452354) is the base value for natural logarithms (calculated with static Math method Log). These variables are declared in class Math with the modifiers public and const. Making them public allows other programmers to use these variables in their own classes. Any variable declared with keyword ***const*** is a constant—its value cannot be changed after the constant is declared. Both PI and E are declared const because their values never change. Also, any constant is implicitly static (so it is a syntax error to declare a constant with keyword static explicitly). Making these constants static allows them to be accessed via the class name Math and the dot (.) operator, just like class Math's methods. Recall from Section 4.5 that when each object of a class maintains its own copy of an attribute, the variable that represents the attribute is also known as an instance variable—each object (instance) of the class has a separate instance of the variable in memory. There are variables for which each object of a class does *not* have a separate instance of the variable. That is the case with static variables. When objects of a class containing static variables are created, all the objects of that class share one copy of the class's static variables. Together the static variables and instance variables represent the *fields* of a class. You will learn more about static variables in Section 9.10.

Why Is Method Main Declared static?

Why must Main be declared static? During application startup when no objects of the class have been created, the Main method must be called to begin program execution. The Main method is sometimes called the application's *entry point*. Declaring Main as static allows the execution environment to invoke Main without creating an instance of the class. Method Main is often declared with the header:

> **public static void** Main(**string** args[])

When you execute your application from the command line, you type the application name, as in

> *ApplicationName argument1 argument2 ...*

In the preceding command, *argument1* and *argument2* are the ***command-line arguments*** to the application that specify a list of `strings` (separated by spaces) the execution environment will pass to the `Main` method of your application. Such arguments might be used to specify options (e.g., a file name) to run the application. As you will learn in Chapter 8, Arrays, your application can access those command-line arguments and use them to customize the application.

Additional Comments about Method `Main`
The header of a `Main` method does not need to appear exactly as we've shown. Applications that do not take command-line arguments may omit the `string[] args` parameter. The `public` keyword may also be omitted. In addition, you can declare `Main` with return type `int` (instead of `void`) to enable `Main` to return an error code with the `return` statement. A `Main` method declared with any one of these headers can be used as the application's entry point—but you can declare only one such `Main` method in each class.

In earlier chapters, most applications had one class that contained only `Main` and some examples had a second class that was used by `Main` to create and manipulate objects. Actually, any class can contain a `Main` method. In fact, each of our two-class examples could have been implemented as one class. For example, in the application in Fig. 6.9 and Fig. 6.10, method `Main` (lines 6–16 of Fig. 6.10) could have been taken as is and placed in class `GradeBook` (Fig. 6.9). The application results would be identical to those of the two-class version. You can place a `Main` method in every class you declare. Some programmers take advantage of this to build a small test application into each class they declare. However, if you declare more than one `Main` method among the classes of your project, you will need to indicate to the IDE which one you would like to be the application's entry point. You can do this by clicking the menu **Project > [ProjectName] Properties...** (where **[Project-Name]** is the name of your project) and selecting the class containing the `Main` method that should be the entry point from the **Startup object** list box.

7.4 Declaring Methods with Multiple Parameters

Chapters 4–6 presented classes containing simple methods that had at most one parameter. Methods often require more than one piece of information to perform their tasks. We now consider how to write your own methods with multiple parameters.

The application in Fig. 7.3 and Fig. 7.4 uses a user-defined method called `Maximum` to determine and return the largest of three `double` values that are input by the user. When the application begins execution, class `MaximumFinderTest`'s `Main` method (lines 6–10 of Fig. 7.4) creates an object of class `MaximumFinder` (line 8) and calls the object's `DetermineMaximum` method (line 9) to produce the application's output. In class `Maximum-Finder` (Fig. 7.3), lines 11–15 of method `DetermineMaximum` prompt the user to enter three `double` values and read them from the user. Line 18 calls method `Maximum` (declared in lines 25–38) to determine the largest of the three `double` values passed as arguments to the method. When method `Maximum` returns the result to line 18, the application assigns `Maximum`'s return value to local variable `result`. Then line 21 outputs the maximum value. At the end of this section, we'll discuss the use of operator + in line 21.

Consider the declaration of method `Maximum` (lines 25–38). Line 25 indicates that the method returns a `double` value, that the method's name is `Maximum` and that the method requires three `double` parameters (x, y and z) to accomplish its task. When a method has

```
1   // Fig. 7.3: MaximumFinder.cs
2   // User-defined method Maximum.
3   using System;
4
5   public class MaximumFinder
6   {
7      // obtain three floating-point values and determine maximum value
8      public void DetermineMaximum()
9      {
10        // prompt for and input three floating-point values
11        Console.WriteLine( "Enter three floating-point values,\n"
12           + " pressing 'Enter' after each one: " );
13        double number1 = Convert.ToDouble( Console.ReadLine() );
14        double number2 = Convert.ToDouble( Console.ReadLine() );
15        double number3 = Convert.ToDouble( Console.ReadLine() );
16
17        // determine the maximum value
18        double result = Maximum( number1, number2, number3 );
19
20        // display maximum value
21        Console.WriteLine( "Maximum is: " + result );
22     } // end method DetermineMaximum
23
24     // returns the maximum of its three double parameters
25     public double Maximum( double x, double y, double z )
26     {
27        double maximumValue = x; // assume x is the largest to start
28
29        // determine whether y is greater than maximumValue
30        if ( y > maximumValue )
31           maximumValue = y;
32
33        // determine whether z is greater than maximumValue
34        if ( z > maximumValue )
35           maximumValue = z;
36
37        return maximumValue;
38     } // end method Maximum
39  } // end class MaximumFinder
```

Fig. 7.3 | User-defined method `Maximum`.

more than one parameter, the parameters are specified as a comma-separated list. When `Maximum` is called in line 18 of Fig. 7.3, the parameter x is initialized with the value of the argument number1, the parameter y is initialized with the value of the argument number2 and the parameter z is initialized with the value of the argument number3. There must be one argument in the method call for each parameter (sometimes called a *formal parameter*) in the method declaration. Also, each argument must be consistent with the type of the corresponding parameter. For example, a parameter of type `double` can receive values like 7.35 (a `double`), 22 (an `int`) or –0.03456 (a `double`), but not `strings` like "hello". Section 7.7 discusses the argument types that can be provided in a method call for each parameter of a simple type.

```
 1   // Fig. 7.4: MaximumFinderTest.cs
 2   // Application to test class MaximumFinder.
 3   public class MaximumFinderTest
 4   {
 5      // application starting point
 6      public static void Main( string[] args )
 7      {
 8         MaximumFinder maximumFinder = new MaximumFinder();
 9         maximumFinder.DetermineMaximum();
10      } // end Main
11   } // end class MaximumFinderTest
```

```
Enter three floating-point values,
  pressing 'Enter' after each one:
3.33
2.22
1.11
Maximum is: 3.33
```

```
Enter three floating-point values,
  pressing 'Enter' after each one:
2.22
3.33
1.11
Maximum is: 3.33
```

```
Enter three floating-point values,
  pressing 'Enter' after each one:
1.11
2.22
867.5309
Maximum is: 867.5309
```

Fig. 7.4 | Application to test class `MaximumFinder`.

To determine the maximum value, we begin with the assumption that parameter x contains the largest value, so line 27 (Fig. 7.3) declares local variable maximumValue and initializes it with the value of parameter x. Of course, it is possible that parameter y or z contains the largest value, so we must compare each of these values with maximumValue. The if statement at lines 30–31 determines whether y is greater than maximumValue. If so, line 31 assigns y to maximumValue. The if statement at lines 34–35 determines whether z is greater than maximumValue. If so, line 35 assigns z to maximumValue. At this point, the largest of the three values resides in maximumValue, so line 37 returns that value to line 18. When program control returns to the point in the application where Maximum was called, Maximum's parameters x, y and z are no longer accessible in memory. Note that methods can return at most one value; the returned value can be a reference to an object that contains many values.

Note that result is a local variable in method DetermineMaximum because it is declared in the block that represents the method's body. Variables should be declared as fields of a class (i.e., as either instance variables or static variables of the class) only if they are required for use in more than one method of the class or if the application should save their values between calls to the class's methods.

Common Programming Error 7.1

Declaring method parameters of the same type as float x, y *instead of* float x, float y *is a syntax error—a type is required for each parameter in the parameter list.*

Software Engineering Observation 7.4

A method that has many parameters may be performing too many tasks. Consider dividing the method into smaller methods that perform the separate tasks. As a guideline, try to fit the method header on one line if possible.

Implementing Method Maximum *by Reusing Method* Math.Max

Recall from Fig. 7.2 that class Math has a Max method that can determine the larger of two values. The entire body of our maximum method could also be implemented with nested calls to Math.Max, as follows:

```
return Math.Max( x, Math.Max( y, z ) );
```

The leftmost call to Math.Max specifies arguments x and Math.Max(y, z). Before any method can be called, all its arguments must be evaluated to determine their values. If an argument is a method call, the method call must be performed to determine its return value. So, in the preceding statement, Math.Max(y, z) is evaluated first to determine the maximum of y and z. Then the result is passed as the second argument to the other call to Math.Max, which returns the larger of its two arguments. Using Math.Max in this manner is a good example of software reuse—we find the largest of three values by reusing Math.Max, which finds the larger of two values. Note how concise this code is compared to lines 27–37 of Fig. 7.3.

Assembling Strings with String Concatenation

C# allows string objects to be created by assembling smaller strings into larger strings using operator + (or the compound assignment operator +=). This is known as ***string concatenation***. When both operands of operator + are string objects, operator + creates a new string object in which a copy of the characters of the right operand are placed at the end of a copy of the characters in the left operand. For example, the expression "hello " + "there" creates the string "hello there" without disturbing the original strings.

In line 21 of Fig. 7.3, the expression "Maximum is: " + result uses operator + with operands of types string and double. Every value of a simple type in C# has a string representation. When one of the + operator's operands is a string, the other is implicitly converted to a string, then the two are concatenated. In line 21, the double value is implicitly converted to its string representation and placed at the end of the string "Maximum is: ". If there are any trailing zeros in a double value, these will be discarded when the number is converted to a string. Thus, the number 9.3500 would be represented as 9.35 in the resulting string.

For values of simple types used in string concatenation, the values are converted to strings. If a boolean is concatenated with a string, the bool is converted to the string "True" or "False" (note that each is capitalized). All objects have a ToString method that returns a `string` representation of the object. When an object is concatenated with a `string`, the object's `ToString` method is implicitly called to obtain the `string` representation of the object.

Line 21 of Fig. 7.3 could also be written using `string` formatting as

```
Console.WriteLine( "Maximum is: {0}", result );
```

As with `string` concatenation, using a format item to substitute an object into a `string` implicitly calls the object's `ToString` method to obtain the object's `string` representation. You will learn more about method `ToString` in Chapter 8, Arrays.

When a large `string` literal is typed into an application's source code, you can break that `string` into several smaller `strings` and place them on multiple lines for readability. The `strings` can be reassembled using either string concatenation or string formatting. We discuss the details of `strings` in Chapter 16, Strings, Characters and Regular Expressions.

 Common Programming Error 7.2

It is a syntax error to break a `string` literal across multiple lines in an application. If a `string` does not fit on one line, split the `string` into several smaller `strings` and use concatenation to form the desired `string`.

 Common Programming Error 7.3

Confusing the + operator used for string concatenation with the + operator used for addition can lead to strange results. The + operator is left-associative. For example, if integer variable y has the value 5, the expression "y + 2 = " + y + 2 results in the string "y + 2 = 52", not "y + 2 = 7", because first the value of y (5) is concatenated with the string "y + 2 = ", then the value 2 is concatenated with the new larger string "y + 2 = 5". The expression "y + 2 = " + (y + 2) produces the desired result "y + 2 = 7".

7.5 Notes on Declaring and Using Methods

You have seen three ways to call a method:

1. Using a method name by itself to call a method of the same class—such as `Maximum( number1, number2, number3 )` in line 18 of Fig. 7.3.

2. Using a variable that contains a reference to an object, followed by the dot (.) operator and the method name to call a non-`static` method of the referenced object—such as the method call in line 9 of Fig. 7.4, `maximumFinder.DetermineMaximum()`, which calls a method of class `MaximumFinder` from the `Main` method of `MaximumFinderTest`.

3. Using the class name and the dot (.) operator to call a `static` method of a class—such as `Math.Sqrt( 900.0 )` in Section 7.3.

Note that a `static` method can call only other `static` methods of the same class directly (i.e., using the method name by itself) and can manipulate only `static` variables in the same class directly. To access the class's non-`static` members, a `static` method must use a reference to an object of the class. Recall that `static` methods relate to a class as a whole, whereas non-`static` methods are associated with a specific instance (object) of the class and may manipulate the instance variables of that object. Many objects of a class, each with its own copies of the instance variables, may exist at the same time. Suppose a static method were to invoke a non-static method directly. How would the method know which object's instance variables to manipulate? What would happen if no objects of the class existed at the time the non-static method was invoked? Thus, C# does not allow a static method to access non-static members of the same class directly.

There are three ways to return control to the statement that calls a method. If the method does not return a result, control returns when the program flow reaches the method-ending right brace or when the statement

    return;

is executed. If the method returns a result, the statement

    return *expression*;

evaluates the *expression*, then returns the result (and control) to the caller.

Common Programming Error 7.4

Declaring a method outside the body of a class declaration or inside the body of another method is a syntax error.

Common Programming Error 7.5

Omitting the return type *in a method declaration is a syntax error.*

Common Programming Error 7.6

Placing a semicolon after the right parenthesis enclosing the parameter list of a method declaration is a syntax error.

Common Programming Error 7.7

Redeclaring a method parameter as a local variable in the method's body is a compilation error.

Common Programming Error 7.8

Forgetting to return a value from a method that should return a value is a compilation error. If a return type other than void *is specified, the method must contain a* return *statement that returns a value consistent with the method's* return type. *Returning a value from a method whose return type has been declared* void *is a compilation error.*

7.6 Method Call Stack and Activation Records

To understand how C# performs method calls, we first need to consider a data structure (i.e., collection of related data items) known as a *stack*. You can think of a stack as analogous to a pile of dishes. When a dish is placed on the pile, it is normally placed at the top (referred to as *pushing* the dish onto the stack). Similarly, when a dish is removed from the pile, it is always removed from the top (referred to as *popping* the dish off the stack). Stacks are known as *last-in-first-out (LIFO) data structures*—the last item pushed (inserted) on the stack is the first item popped off (removed from) the stack.

When an application calls a method, the called method must know how to return to its caller, so the return address of the calling method is pushed onto the ***program execution*** *stack* (sometimes referred to as the *method call stack*). If a series of method calls occurs, the successive return addresses are pushed onto the stack in last-in-first-out order so that each method can return to its caller.

The program execution stack also contains the memory for the local variables used in each invocation of a method during an application's execution. This data, stored as a portion of the program execution stack, is known as the *activation record* or *stack frame* of the method call. When a method call is made, the activation record for that method call is pushed onto the program execution stack. When the method returns to its caller, the activation record for this method call is popped off the stack, and those local variables are no longer known to the application. If a local variable holding a reference to an object is the only variable in the application with a reference to that object, when the activation record containing that local variable is popped off the stack, the object can no longer be accessed by the application and will eventually be deleted from memory during "garbage collection." We'll discuss garbage collection in Section 9.9.

Of course, the amount of memory in a computer is finite, so only a certain amount of memory can be used to store activation records on the program execution stack. If more method calls occur than can have their activation records stored on the program execution stack, an error known as a *stack overflow* occurs.

7.7 Argument Promotion and Casting

Another important feature of method calls is *argument promotion*—implicitly converting an argument's value to the type that the method expects to receive in its corresponding parameter. For example, an application can call Math method Sqrt with an integer argument even though the method expects to receive a double argument (but, as we will soon see, not vice versa). The statement

```
Console.WriteLine( Math.Sqrt( 4 ) );
```

correctly evaluates Math.Sqrt(4) and prints the value 2.0. The method declaration's parameter list causes C# to convert the int value 4 to the double value 4.0 before passing the value to Sqrt. Attempting these conversions may lead to compilation errors if C#'s *promotion rules* are not satisfied. The promotion rules specify which conversions are allowed—that is, which conversions can be performed without losing data. In the Sqrt example above, an int is converted to a double without changing its value. However, converting a double to an int truncates the fractional part of the double value—thus, part of the value is lost. Also, double variables can hold values much larger (and much smaller) than int variables, so assigning a double to an int can cause a loss of information when the double value doesn't fit in the int. Converting large integer types to small integer types (e.g., long to int) can also result in changed values.

The promotion rules apply to expressions containing values of two or more simple types and to simple-type values passed as arguments to methods. Each value is promoted to the appropriate type in the expression. (Actually, the expression uses a temporary copy of each value—the types of the original values remain unchanged.) Figure 7.5 lists the simple types alphabetically and the types to which each can be promoted. Note that values of all simple types can also be implicitly converted to type object. We demonstrate such implicit conversions in Chapter 25, Data Structures.

Type	Conversion types
bool	no possible implicit conversions to other simple types
byte	*ushort, short, uint, int, ulong, long, decimal, float* or *double*
char	*ushort, int, uint, long, ulong, decimal, float* or *double*
decimal	no possible implicit conversions to other simple types
double	no possible implicit conversions to other simple types
float	*double*
int	*long, decimal, float* or *double*
long	*decimal, float* or *double*
sbyte	*short, int, long, decimal, float* or *double*
short	*int, long, decimal, float* or *double*
uint	*ulong, long, decimal, float* or *double*
ulong	*decimal, float* or *double*
ushort	*uint, int, ulong, long, decimal, float* or *double*

Fig. 7.5 | Implicit conversions between simple types.

By default, C# does not allow you to implicitly convert values between simple types if the target type cannot represent the value of the original type (e.g., the int value 2000000 cannot be represented as a short, and any floating-point number with digits after its decimal point cannot be represented in an integer type such as long, int or short). Therefore, to prevent a compilation error in cases where information may be lost due to an implicit conversion between simple types, the compiler requires you to use a cast operator (introduced in Section 5.9) to explicitly force the conversion. This enables you to "take control" from the compiler. You essentially say, "I know this conversion might cause loss of information, but for my purposes here, that's fine." Suppose you create a method Square that calculates the square of an integer and thus requires an int argument. To call Square with a double argument named doubleValue, you would write the method call as Square((int) doubleValue). This method call explicitly casts (converts) the value of doubleValue to an integer for use in method Square. Thus, if doubleValue's value is 4.5, the method receives the value 4 and returns 16, not 20.25 (which does, unfortunately, result in the loss of information).

Common Programming Error 7.9

Converting a simple-type value to a value of another simple type may change the value if the promotion is not allowed. For example, converting a floating-point value to an integral value may introduce truncation errors (loss of the fractional part) in the result.

7.8 The Framework Class Library

Many predefined classes are grouped into categories of related classes called namespaces. Together, these namespaces are referred to as the .NET Framework Class Library, or the FCL.

Throughout the text, using directives allow us to use library classes from the FCL without specifying their fully-qualified names. For example, an application includes the declaration

> ***using*** System;

to allow an application to use the class names from the System namespace without fully qualifying their names. This allows you to use the **unqualified class name** Console, rather than the fully qualified class name System.Console, in your code. A great strength of C# is the large number of classes in the namespaces of the FCL. Some key FCL namespaces are described in Fig. 7.6, which represents only a small portion of the reusable classes in the FCL. When learning C#, spend a portion of your time browsing the namespaces and classes in the .NET documentation (msdn2.microsoft.com/en-us/library/ms229335).

Namespace	Description
System.Windows.Forms	Contains the classes required to create and manipulate GUIs. (Various classes in this namespace are discussed in Chapter 13, Graphical User Interface Concepts: Part 1, and Chapter 14, Graphical User Interface Concepts: Part 2.)
System.IO	Contains classes that enable programs to input and output data. (You will learn more about this namespace in Chapter 18, Files and Streams.)
System.Data	Contains classes that enable programs to access and manipulate databases (i.e., organized collections of data). (You will learn more about this namespace in Chapter 20, Database, SQL and ADO.NET.)
System.Web	Contains classes used for creating and maintaining Web applications, which are accessible over the Internet. (You will learn more about this namespace in Chapter 21, ASP.NET 2.0, Web Forms and Web Controls.)
System.Xml	Contains classes for creating and manipulating XML data. Data can be read from or written to XML files. (You will learn more about this namespace in Chapter 19, Extensible Markup Language (XML).)
System.Collections System.Collections.Generic	Contains classes that define data structures for maintaining collections of data. (You will learn more about this namespace in Chapter 27, Collections.)

Fig. 7.6 | FCL namespaces (a subset). (Part 1 of 2.)

Namespace	Description
System.Net	Contains classes that enable programs to communicate via computer networks like the Internet. (You will learn more about this namespace in Chapter 23, Networking: Streams-Based Sockets and Datagrams.)
System.Text	Contains classes and interfaces that enable programs to manipulate characters and strings. (You will learn more about this namespace in Chapter 16, Strings, Characters and Regular Expressions.)
System.Threading	Contains classes that enable programs to perform several tasks at the same time. (You will learn more about this namespace in Chapter 15, Multithreading.)
System.Drawing	Contains classes that enable programs to perform basic graphics processing, such as displaying shapes and arcs. (You will learn more about this namespace in Chapter 17, Graphics and Multimedia.)

Fig. 7.6 | FCL namespaces (a subset). (Part 2 of 2.)

The set of namespaces available in the FCL is quite large. In addition to the namespaces summarized in Fig. 7.6, the FCL contains namespaces for complex graphics, advanced graphical user interfaces, printing, advanced networking, security, database processing, multimedia, accessibility (for people with disabilities) and many other capabilities. The preceding URL for the .NET documentation provides an overview of the Framework Class Library's namespaces.

You can locate additional information about a predefined C# class's methods in the Framework Class Library Reference. When you visit this site, you will see an alphabetical listing of all the namespaces in the FCL. Locate the namespace and click its link to see an alphabetical listing of all its classes, with a brief description of each. Click a class's link to see a more complete description of the class. Click the **Methods** link in the left-hand column to see a listing of the class's methods.

Good Programming Practice 7.2

The online .NET Framework documentation is easy to search and provides many details about each class. As you learn each class in this book, you should review the class in the online documentation for additional information.

7.9 Case Study: Random-Number Generation

In this and the next section, we develop a nicely structured game-playing application with multiple methods. The application uses most of the control statements presented thus far in the book and introduces several new programming concepts.

There is something in the air of a casino that invigorates people—from the high rollers at the plush mahogany-and-felt craps tables to the quarter poppers at the one-armed bandits. It is the *element of chance*, the possibility that luck will convert a pocketful of money into a mountain of wealth. The element of chance can be introduced in an application via an object of class Random (of namespace System). Objects of class *Random* can produce random byte, int and double values. In the next several examples, we use objects of class Random to produce random numbers.

A new random-number generator object can be created as follows:

```
Random randomNumbers = new Random();
```

The random-number generator object can then be used to generate random byte, int and double values—we discuss only random int values here. For more information on the Random class, see msdn2.microsoft.com/en-us/library/ts6se2ek.

Consider the following statement:

```
int randomValue = randomNumbers.Next();
```

Method Next of class Random generates a random int value in the range 0 to +2,147,483,646, inclusive. If the Next method truly produces values at random, then every value in that range should have an equal chance (or probability) of being chosen each time method Next is called. The values returned by Next are actually *pseudorandom numbers*—a sequence of values produced by a complex mathematical calculation. The calculation uses the current time of day (which, of course, changes constantly) to *seed* the random-number generator such that each execution of an application yields a different sequence of random values.

The range of values produced directly by method Next often differs from the range of values required in a particular C# application. For example, an application that simulates coin tossing might require only 0 for "heads" and 1 for "tails." An application that simulates the rolling of a six-sided die might require random integers in the range 1–6. A video game that randomly predicts the next type of spaceship (out of four possibilities) that will fly across the horizon might require random integers in the range 1–4. For cases like these, class Random provides other versions of method Next. One receives an int argument and returns a value from 0 up to, but not including, the argument's value. For example, you might use the statement

```
int randomValue = randomNumbers.Next( 6 );
```

which returns 0, 1, 2, 3, 4 or 5. The argument 6—called the *scaling factor*—represents the number of unique values that Next should produce (in this case, six—0, 1, 2, 3, 4 and 5). This manipulation is called *scaling* the range of values produced by Random method Next.

Suppose we wanted to simulate a six-sided die that has the numbers 1–6 on its faces, not 0–5. Scaling the range of values alone is not enough. So we *shift* the range of numbers produced. We could do this by adding a *shifting value*—in this case 1—to the result of method Next, as in

```
face = 1 + randomNumbers.Next( 6 );
```

The shifting value (1) specifies the first value in the desired set of random integers. The preceding statement assigns to face a random integer in the range 1–6.

The third alternative of method Next provides a more intuitive way to express both shifting and scaling. This method receives two int arguments and returns a value from the first argument's value up to, but not including, the second argument's value. We could use this method to write a statement equivalent to our previous statement, as in

```
face = randomNumbers.Next( 1, 7 );
```

Rolling a Six-Sided Die

To demonstrate random numbers, let's develop an application that simulates 20 rolls of a six-sided die and displays each roll's value. Figure 7.7 shows two sample outputs, which confirm that the results of the preceding calculation are integers in the range 1–6 and that each run of the application can produce a different sequence of random numbers. The using directive in line 3 enables us to use class Random without fully qualifying its name. Line 9 creates the Random object randomNumbers to produce random values. Line 16 executes 20 times in a loop to roll the die. The if statement (lines 21–22) in the loop starts a new line of output after every five numbers, so the results can be presented on multiple lines.

```csharp
1    // Fig. 7.7: RandomIntegers.cs
2    // Shifted and scaled random integers.
3    using System;
4
5    public class RandomIntegers
6    {
7       public static void Main( string[] args )
8       {
9          Random randomNumbers = new Random(); // random number generator
10         int face; // stores each random integer generated
11
12         // loop 20 times
13         for ( int counter = 1; counter <= 20; counter++ )
14         {
15            // pick random integer from 1 to 6
16            face = randomNumbers.Next( 1, 7 );
17
18            Console.Write( "{0}  ", face ); // display generated value
19
20            // if counter is divisible by 5, start a new line of output
21            if ( counter % 5 == 0 )
22               Console.WriteLine();
23         } // end for
24      } // end Main
25   } // end class RandomIntegers
```

```
3  3  3  1  1
2  1  2  4  2
2  3  6  2  5
3  4  6  6  1
```

Fig. 7.7 | Shifted and scaled random integers. (Part 1 of 2.)

```
6   2   5   1   3
5   2   1   6   5
4   1   6   1   3
3   1   4   3   4
```

Fig. 7.7 | Shifted and scaled random integers. (Part 2 of 2.)

Rolling a Six-Sided Die 6000 Times

To show that the numbers produced by Next occur with approximately equal likelihood, let us simulate 6000 rolls of a die (Fig. 7.8). Each integer from 1 to 6 should appear approximately 1000 times.

As the two sample outputs show, the values produced by method Next enable the application to realistically simulate rolling a six-sided die. The application uses nested control statements (the switch is nested inside the for) to determine the number of times each side of the die occurred. The for statement (lines 21–47) iterates 6000 times. During each iteration, line 23 produces a random value from 1 to 6. This face value is then used as the switch expression (line 26) in the switch statement (lines 26–46). Based on the face value, the switch statement increments one of the six counter variables during each iteration of the loop. (In Chapter 8, Arrays, we show an elegant way to replace the entire switch statement in this application with a single statement.) Note that the switch statement has no default label because we have a case label for every possible die value that the expression in line 23 can produce. Run the application several times and observe the results. You'll see that every time you execute this application, it produces different results.

```csharp
1   // Fig. 7.8: RollDie.cs
2   // Roll a six-sided die 6000 times.
3   using System;
4
5   public class RollDie
6   {
7      public static void Main( string[] args )
8      {
9         Random randomNumbers = new Random(); // random number generator
10
11         int frequency1 = 0; // count of 1s rolled
12         int frequency2 = 0; // count of 2s rolled
13         int frequency3 = 0; // count of 3s rolled
14         int frequency4 = 0; // count of 4s rolled
15         int frequency5 = 0; // count of 5s rolled
16         int frequency6 = 0; // count of 6s rolled
17
18         int face; // stores most recently rolled value
19
20         // summarize results of 6000 rolls of a die
21         for ( int roll = 1; roll <= 6000; roll++ )
22         {
23            face = randomNumbers.Next( 1, 7 ); // number from 1 to 6
24
```

Fig. 7.8 | Roll a six-sided die 6000 times. (Part 1 of 2.)

```
25            // determine roll value 1-6 and increment appropriate counter
26            switch ( face )
27            {
28               case 1:
29                  frequency1++; // increment the 1s counter
30                  break;
31               case 2:
32                  frequency2++; // increment the 2s counter
33                  break;
34               case 3:
35                  frequency3++; // increment the 3s counter
36                  break;
37               case 4:
38                  frequency4++; // increment the 4s counter
39                  break;
40               case 5:
41                  frequency5++; // increment the 5s counter
42                  break;
43               case 6:
44                  frequency6++; // increment the 6s counter
45                  break;
46            } // end switch
47         } // end for
48
49         Console.WriteLine( "Face\tFrequency" ); // output headers
50         Console.WriteLine( "1\t{0}\n2\t{1}\n3\t{2}\n4\t{3}\n5\t{4}\n6\t{5}",
51            frequency1, frequency2, frequency3, frequency4,
52            frequency5, frequency6 );
53      } // end Main
54  } // end class RollDie
```

Face	Frequency
1	1039
2	994
3	991
4	970
5	978
6	1028

Face	Frequency
1	985
2	985
3	1001
4	1017
5	1002
6	1010

Fig. 7.8 | Roll a six-sided die 6000 times. (Part 2 of 2.)

7.9.1 Scaling and Shifting Random Numbers

Previously, we demonstrated the statement

```
face = randomNumbers.Next( 1, 7 );
```

which simulates the rolling of a six-sided die. This statement always assigns to variable face an integer in the range $1 \leq$ face < 7. The width of this range (i.e., the number of consecutive integers in the range) is 6, and the starting number in the range is 1. Referring to the preceding statement, we see that the width of the range is determined by the difference between the two integers passed to Random method Next, and the starting number of the range is the value of the first argument. We can generalize this result as

```
number = randomNumbers.Next( shiftingValue, shiftingValue + scalingFactor );
```

where *shiftingValue* specifies the first number in the desired range of consecutive integers and *scalingFactor* specifies how many numbers are in the range.

It is also possible to choose integers at random from sets of values other than ranges of consecutive integers. For this purpose, it is simpler to use the version of the Next method that takes only one argument. For example, to obtain a random value from the sequence 2, 5, 8, 11 and 14, you could use the statement

```
number = 2 + 3 * randomNumbers.Next( 5 );
```

In this case, randomNumberGenerator.Next(5) produces values in the range 0–4. Each value produced is multiplied by 3 to produce a number in the sequence 0, 3, 6, 9 and 12. We then add 2 to that value to shift the range of values and obtain a value from the sequence 2, 5, 8, 11 and 14. We can generalize this result as

```
number = shiftingValue +
        differenceBetweenValues * randomNumbers.Next( scalingFactor );
```

where *shiftingValue* specifies the first number in the desired range of values, *differenceBetweenValues* represents the difference between consecutive numbers in the sequence and *scalingFactor* specifies how many numbers are in the range.

7.9.2 Random-Number Repeatability for Testing and Debugging

As we mentioned earlier in Section 7.9, the methods of class Random actually generate pseudorandom numbers based on complex mathematical calculations. Repeatedly calling any of Random's methods produces a sequence of numbers that appears to be random. The calculation that produces the pseudorandom numbers uses the time of day as a *seed value* to change the sequence's starting point. Each new Random object seeds itself with a value based on the computer system's clock at the time the object is created, enabling each execution of an application to produce a different sequence of random numbers.

When debugging an application, it is sometimes useful to repeat the exact same sequence of pseudorandom numbers during each execution of the application. This repeatability enables you to prove that your application is working for a specific sequence of random numbers before you test the application with different sequences of random numbers. When repeatability is important, you can create a Random object as follows:

```
Random randomNumbers = new Random( seedValue );
```

The seedValue argument (type int) seeds the random-number calculation. If the same seedValue is used every time, the Random object produces the same sequence of random numbers.

Error-Prevention Tip 7.2

While an application is under development, create the Random *object with a specific seed value to produce a repeatable sequence of random numbers each time the application executes. If a logic error occurs, fix the error and test the application again with the same seed value—this allows you to reconstruct the same sequence of random numbers that caused the error. Once the logic errors have been removed, create the* Random *object without using a seed value, causing the* Random *object to generate a new sequence of random numbers each time the application executes.*

7.10 Case Study: A Game of Chance (Introducing Enumerations)

One popular game of chance is the dice game known as "craps," which is played in casinos and back alleys throughout the world. The rules of the game are straightforward:

> *You roll two dice. Each die has six faces, which contain one, two, three, four, five and six spots, respectively. After the dice have come to rest, the sum of the spots on the two upward faces is calculated. If the sum is 7 or 11 on the first throw, you win. If the sum is 2, 3 or 12 on the first throw (called "craps"), you lose (i.e., "the house" wins). If the sum is 4, 5, 6, 8, 9 or 10 on the first throw, that sum becomes your "point." To win, you must continue rolling the dice until you "make your point" (i.e., roll that same point value). You lose by rolling a 7 before making your point.*

The application in Fig. 7.9 and Fig. 7.10 simulates the game of craps, using methods to define the logic of the game. In the Main method of class CrapsTest (Fig. 7.10), line 7 creates an object of class Craps (Fig. 7.9), and line 8 calls its Play method to start the game. The Play method (Fig. 7.9, lines 24–70) calls the RollDice method (Fig. 7.9, lines 73–85) as needed to roll the two dice and compute their sum. The four sample outputs in Fig. 7.10 show winning on the first roll, losing on the first roll, winning on a subsequent roll and losing on a subsequent roll, respectively.

Let's discuss the declaration of class Craps in Fig. 7.9. In the rules of the game, the player must roll two dice on the first roll, and must do the same on all subsequent rolls. We declare method RollDice (lines 73–85) to roll the dice and compute and print their sum. Method RollDice is declared once, but it is called from two places (lines 30 and 54) in method Play, which contains the logic for one complete game of craps. Method Roll-Dice takes no arguments, so it has an empty parameter list. Each time it is called, RollDice returns the sum of the dice, so the return type int is indicated in the method header (line

```
 I   // Fig. 7.9: Craps.cs
 2   // Craps class simulates the dice game craps.
 3   using System;
 4
 5   public class Craps
 6   {
 7      // create random number generator for use in method RollDice
 8      private Random randomNumbers = new Random();
 9
10      // enumeration with constants that represent the game status
11      private enum Status { CONTINUE, WON, LOST }
```

Fig. 7.9 | Craps class simulates the dice game craps. (Part 1 of 3.)

```
12
13     // enumeration with constants that represent common rolls of the dice
14     private enum DiceNames
15     {
16        SNAKE_EYES = 2,
17        TREY = 3,
18        SEVEN = 7,
19        YO_LEVEN = 11,
20        BOX_CARS = 12
21     }
22
23     // plays one game of craps
24     public void Play()
25     {
26        // gameStatus can contain CONTINUE, WON or LOST
27        Status gameStatus = Status.CONTINUE;
28        int myPoint = 0; // point if no win or loss on first roll
29
30        int sumOfDice = RollDice(); // first roll of the dice
31
32        // determine game status and point based on first roll
33        switch ( ( DiceNames ) sumOfDice )
34        {
35           case DiceNames.SEVEN: // win with 7 on first roll
36           case DiceNames.YO_LEVEN: // win with 11 on first roll
37              gameStatus = Status.WON;
38              break;
39           case DiceNames.SNAKE_EYES: // lose with 2 on first roll
40           case DiceNames.TREY: // lose with 3 on first roll
41           case DiceNames.BOX_CARS: // lose with 12 on first roll
42              gameStatus = Status.LOST;
43              break;
44           default: // did not win or lose, so remember point
45              gameStatus = Status.CONTINUE; // game is not over
46              myPoint = sumOfDice; // remember the point
47              Console.WriteLine( "Point is {0}", myPoint );
48              break;
49        } // end switch
50
51        // while game is not complete
52        while ( gameStatus == Status.CONTINUE ) // game not WON or LOST
53        {
54           sumOfDice = RollDice(); // roll dice again
55
56           // determine game status
57           if ( sumOfDice == myPoint ) // win by making point
58              gameStatus = Status.WON;
59           else
60              // lose by rolling 7 before point
61              if ( sumOfDice == ( int ) DiceNames.SEVEN )
62                 gameStatus = Status.LOST;
63        } // end while
```

Fig. 7.9 | Craps class simulates the dice game craps. (Part 2 of 3.)

```
64
65        // display won or lost message
66        if ( gameStatus == Status.WON )
67           Console.WriteLine( "Player wins" );
68        else
69           Console.WriteLine( "Player loses" );
70     } // end method Play
71
72     // roll dice, calculate sum and display results
73     public int RollDice()
74     {
75        // pick random die values
76        int die1 = randomNumbers.Next( 1, 7 ); // first die roll
77        int die2 = randomNumbers.Next( 1, 7 ); // second die roll
78
79        int sum = die1 + die2; // sum of die values
80
81        // display results of this roll
82        Console.WriteLine( "Player rolled {0} + {1} = {2}",
83           die1, die2, sum );
84        return sum; // return sum of dice
85     } // end method RollDice
86  } // end class Craps
```

Fig. 7.9 | Craps class simulates the dice game craps. (Part 3 of 3.)

73). Although lines 76 and 77 look the same (except for the die names), they do not necessarily produce the same result. Each of these statements produces a random value in the range 1–6. Note that randomNumbers (used in lines 76 and 77) is not declared in the method. Rather it is declared as a private instance variable of the class and initialized in line 8. This enables us to create one Random object that is reused in each call to RollDice.

The game is reasonably involved. The player may win or lose on the first roll, or may win or lose on any subsequent roll. Method Play (lines 24–70) uses local variable gameStatus (line 27) to keep track of the overall game status, local variable myPoint (line 28) to store the "point" if the player does not win or lose on the first roll and local variable

```
 1   // Fig. 7.10: CrapsTest.cs
 2   // Application to test class Craps.
 3   public class CrapsTest
 4   {
 5      public static void Main( string[] args )
 6      {
 7         Craps game = new Craps();
 8         game.Play(); // play one game of craps
 9      } // end Main
10   } // end class CrapsTest
```

```
Player rolled 2 + 5 = 7
Player wins
```

Fig. 7.10 | Application to test class Craps. (Part 1 of 2.)

```
Player rolled 2 + 1 = 3
Player loses
```

```
Player rolled 4 + 6 = 10
Point is 10
Player rolled 1 + 3 = 4
Player rolled 1 + 3 = 4
Player rolled 2 + 3 = 5
Player rolled 4 + 4 = 8
Player rolled 6 + 6 = 12
Player rolled 4 + 4 = 8
Player rolled 4 + 5 = 9
Player rolled 2 + 6 = 8
Player rolled 6 + 6 = 12
Player rolled 6 + 4 = 10
Player wins
```

```
Player rolled 2 + 4 = 6
Point is 6
Player rolled 3 + 1 = 4
Player rolled 5 + 5 = 10
Player rolled 6 + 1 = 7
Player loses
```

Fig. 7.10 | Application to test class Craps. (Part 2 of 2.)

sumOfDice (line 30) to maintain the sum of the dice for the most recent roll. Note that myPoint is initialized to 0 to ensure that the application will compile. If you do not initialize myPoint, the compiler issues an error, because myPoint is not assigned a value in every branch of the switch statement—thus, the application could try to use myPoint before it is definitely assigned a value. By contrast, gameStatus does not require initialization because it *is* assigned a value in every branch of the switch statement—thus, it is guaranteed to be initialized before it is used. However, as good programming practice, we initialize it anyway.

Note that local variable gameStatus is declared to be of a new type called Status, which we declared in line 11. Type Status is declared as a private member of class Craps, because Status will be used only in that class. Status is a user-defined type called an *enumeration*, which declares a set of constants represented by identifiers. An enumeration is introduced by the keyword **enum** and a type name (in this case, Status). As with a class, braces ({ and }) delimit the body of an enum declaration. Inside the braces is a comma-separated list of *enumeration constants*. The enum constant names must be unique, but their underlying values need not be.

 Good Programming Practice 7.3

Use only uppercase letters in the names of constants. This makes the constants stand out in an application and reminds you that enumeration constants are not variables.

Variables of type Status should be assigned only one of the three constants declared in the enumeration. When the game is won, the application sets local variable gameStatus to Status.WON (lines 37 and 58). When the game is lost, the application sets local variable gameStatus to Status.LOST (lines 42 and 62). Otherwise, the application sets local variable gameStatus to Status.CONTINUE (line 45) to indicate that the dice must be rolled again.

Good Programming Practice 7.4

Using enumeration constants (like Status.WON, Status.LOST and Status.CONTINUE) rather than literal integer values (such as 0, 1 and 2) can make code easier to read and maintain.

Line 30 in method Play calls RollDice, which picks two random values from 1 to 6, displays the value of the first die, the value of the second die and the sum of the dice, and returns the sum of the dice. Method Play next enters the switch statement at lines 33–49, which uses the sumOfDice value from line 30 to determine whether the game has been won or lost, or whether it should continue with another roll.

The sums of the dice that would result in a win or loss on the first roll are declared in the DiceNames enumeration in lines 14–21. These are used in the cases of the switch statement. The identifier names use casino parlance for these sums. Notice that in the Dice-Names enumeration, a value is explicitly assigned to each identifier name. When the enum is declared, each constant in the enum declaration contains an underlying constant value of type int. If you do not assign a value to an identifier in the enum declaration, the compiler will do so. If the first enum constant is unassigned, the compiler gives it the value 0. If any other enum constant is unassigned, the compiler gives it a value equal to one more than the value of the preceding enum constant. For example, in the Status enumeration, the compiler implicitly assigns 0 to Status.WON, 1 to Status.CONTINUE and 2 to Status.LOST.

You could also declare an enum's underlying type to be byte, sbyte, short, ushort, int, uint, long or ulong by writing

> ***private enum*** MyEnum : *typeName* { *CONSTANT1*, *CONSTANT2*, ... }

where *typeName* represents one of the integral simple types.

If you need to compare a simple-type value to the underlying value of an enumeration constant, you must use a cast operator to make the two types match. In the switch statement at lines 33–49, we use the cast operator to convert the int value in sumOfDice to type DiceNames and compare it to each of the constants in DiceNames. Lines 35–36 determine whether the player won on the first roll with SEVEN (7) or YO_LEVEN (11). Lines 39–41 determine whether the player lost on the first roll with SNAKE_EYES (2), TREY (3) or BOX_CARS (12). After the first roll, if the game is not over, the default case (lines 44–48) saves sumOfDice in myPoint (line 46) and displays the point (line 47).

If we are still trying to "make our point" (i.e., the game is continuing from a prior roll), the loop in lines 52–63 executes. Line 54 rolls the dice again. If sumOfDice matches myPoint in line 57, line 58 sets gameStatus to Status.WON, and the loop terminates because the game is complete. In line 61, we use the cast operator (int) to obtain the underlying value of DiceNames.SEVEN so that we can compare it to sumOfDice. If sumOfDice is equal to SEVEN (7), line 62 sets gameStatus to Status.LOST, and the loop terminates because the game is over. When the game completes, lines 66–69 display a message indicating whether the player won or lost and the application terminates.

Note the use of the various program-control mechanisms we have discussed. The Craps class uses two methods—Play (called from CrapsTest.Main) and RollDice (called twice from Play)—and the switch, while, if...else and nested if control statements. Note also the use of multiple case labels in the switch statement to execute the same statements for sums of SEVEN and YO_LEVEN (lines 35–36) and for sums of SNAKE_EYES, TREY and BOX_CARS (lines 39–41).

7.11 Scope of Declarations

You have seen declarations of various C# entities, such as classes, methods, properties, variables and parameters. Declarations introduce names that can be used to refer to such C# entities. The *scope* of a declaration is the portion of the application that can refer to the declared entity by its unqualified name. Such an entity is said to be "in scope" for that portion of the application. This section introduces several important scope issues. For more scope information, see *Section 3.7, Scopes,* of the *C# Language Specification.*

The basic scope rules are as follows:

1. The scope of a parameter declaration is the body of the method in which the declaration appears.

2. The scope of a local-variable declaration is from the point at which the declaration appears to the end of the block containing the declaration.

3. The scope of a local-variable declaration that appears in the initialization section of a for statement's header is the body of the for statement and the other expressions in the header.

4. The scope of a method, property or field of a class is the entire body of the class. This enables non-static methods and properties of a class to use any of the class's fields, methods and properties, regardless of the order in which they are declared. Similarly, static methods and properties can use any of the static members of the class.

Any block may contain variable declarations. If a local variable or parameter in a method has the same name as a field, the field is hidden until the block terminates execution. In Chapter 9, we discuss how to access hidden fields.

Error-Prevention Tip 7.3

Use different names for fields and local variables to help prevent subtle logic errors that occur when a method is called and a local variable of the method hides a field of the same name in the class.

The application in Fig. 7.11 and Fig. 7.12 demonstrates scoping issues with fields and local variables. When the application begins execution, class ScopeTest's Main method (Fig. 7.12, lines 6–10) creates an object of class Scope (line 8) and calls the object's Begin method (line 9) to produce the application's output (shown in Fig. 7.12).

In class Scope (Fig. 7.11), line 8 declares and initializes the instance variable x to 1. This instance variable is hidden in any block (or method) that declares local variable named x. Method Begin (lines 12–31) declares local variable x (line 14) and initializes it to 5. This local variable's value is output to show that instance variable x (whose value is 1) is hidden in method Begin. The application declares two other methods—UseLocalVariable (lines 34–43) and UseInstanceVariable (lines 46–53)—that each take no arguments and do not return results. Method Begin calls each method twice (lines 19–28). Method UseLocalVariable declares local variable x (line 36). When UseLocalVariable is first called (line 19), it creates local variable x and initializes it to 25 (line 36), outputs the value of x (lines 38–39), increments x (line 40) and outputs the value of x again (lines 41–42). When UseLocalVariable is called a second time (line 25), it re-creates local variable x and re-initializes it to 25, so the output of each UseLocalVariable call is identical.

```csharp
1   // Fig. 7.11: Scope.cs
2   // Scope class demonstrates instance and local variable scopes.
3   using System;
4
5   public class Scope
6   {
7      // instance variable that is accessible to all methods of this class
8      private int x = 1;
9
10     // method Begin creates and initializes local variable x
11     // and calls methods UseLocalVariable and UseInstanceVariable
12     public void Begin()
13     {
14        int x = 5; // method's local variable x hides instance variable x
15
16        Console.WriteLine( "local x in method Begin is {0}", x );
17
18        // UseLocalVariable has its own local x
19        UseLocalVariable();
20
21        // UseInstanceVariable uses class Scope's instance variable x
22        UseInstanceVariable();
23
24        // UseLocalVariable reinitializes its own local x
25        UseLocalVariable();
26
27        // class Scope's instance variable x retains its value
28        UseInstanceVariable();
29
30        Console.WriteLine( "\nlocal x in method Begin is {0}", x );
31     } // end method Begin
32
33     // create and initialize local variable x during each call
34     public void UseLocalVariable()
35     {
36        int x = 25; // initialized each time UseLocalVariable is called
37
38        Console.WriteLine(
39           "\nlocal x on entering method UseLocalVariable is {0}", x );
40        x++; // modifies this method's local variable x
41        Console.WriteLine(
42           "local x before exiting method UseLocalVariable is {0}", x );
43     } // end method UseLocalVariable
44
```

Fig. 7.11 | Scope class demonstrates instance and local variable scopes. (Part 1 of 2.)

```
45      // modify class Scope's instance variable x during each call
46      public void UseInstanceVariable()
47      {
48         Console.WriteLine( "\ninstance variable x on entering {0} is {1}",
49            "method UseInstanceVariable", x );
50         x *= 10; // modifies class Scope's instance variable x
51         Console.WriteLine( "instance variable x before exiting {0} is {1}",
52            "method UseInstanceVariable", x );
53      } // end method UseInstanceVariable
54   } // end class Scope
```

Fig. 7.11 | Scope class demonstrates instance and local variable scopes. (Part 2 of 2.)

```
1    // Fig. 7.12: ScopeTest.cs
2    // Application to test class Scope.
3    public class ScopeTest
4    {
5       // application starting point
6       public static void Main( string[] args )
7       {
8          Scope testScope = new Scope();
9          testScope.Begin();
10      } // end Main
11   } // end class ScopeTest
```

```
local x in method Begin is 5

local x on entering method UseLocalVariable is 25
local x before exiting method UseLocalVariable is 26

instance variable x on entering method UseInstanceVariable is 1
instance variable x before exiting method UseInstanceVariable is 10

local x on entering method UseLocalVariable is 25
local x before exiting method UseLocalVariable is 26

instance variable x on entering method UseInstanceVariable is 10
instance variable x before exiting method UseInstanceVariable is 100

local x in method Begin is 5
```

Fig. 7.12 | Application to test class Scope.

Method UseInstanceVariable does not declare any local variables. Therefore, when
it refers to x, instance variable x (line 8) of the class is used. When method UseInstance-
Variable is first called (line 22), it outputs the value (1) of instance variable x (lines 48–
49), multiplies the instance variable x by 10 (line 50) and outputs the value (10) of instance
variable x again (lines 51–52) before returning. The next time method UseInstanceVariable is called (line 28), the instance variable has its modified value, 10, so the method outputs 10, then 100. Finally, in method Begin, the application outputs the value of local
variable x again (line 30) to show that none of the method calls modified Begin's local variable x, because the methods all referred to variables named x in other scopes.

7.12 Method Overloading

Methods of the same name can be declared in the same class, as long as they have different sets of parameters (determined by the number, types and order of the parameters). This is called *method overloading*. When an *overloaded method* is called, the C# compiler selects the appropriate method by examining the number, types and order of the arguments in the call. Method overloading is commonly used to create several methods with the same name that perform the same or similar tasks, but on different types or different numbers of arguments. For example, Math methods Min and Max (summarized in Section 7.3) are overloaded with 11 versions. These find the minimum and maximum, respectively, of two values of each of the 11 numeric simple types. Our next example demonstrates declaring and invoking overloaded methods. You will see examples of overloaded constructors in Chapter 9.

Declaring Overloaded Methods

In class MethodOverload (Fig. 7.13), we include two overloaded versions of a method called Square—one that calculates the square of an int (and returns an int) and one that calculates the square of a double (and returns a double). Although these methods have the same name and similar parameter lists and bodies, you can think of them simply as *different* methods. It may help to think of the method names as "Square of int" and "Square of double," respectively. When the application begins execution, class MethodOverloadTest's Main method (Fig. 7.14, lines 5–9) creates an object of class MethodOverload (line 7) and calls the object's TestOverloadedMethods method (line 8) to produce the application's output (Fig. 7.14).

In Fig. 7.13, line 10 invokes method Square with the argument 7. Literal integer values are treated as type int, so the method call in line 10 invokes the version of Square at lines 15–20 that specifies an int parameter. Similarly, line 11 invokes method Square with the argument 7.5. Literal real number values are treated as type double, so the method call in line 11 invokes the version of Square at lines 23–28 that specifies a double parameter. Each method first outputs a line of text to prove that the proper method was called in each case.

Notice that the overloaded methods in Fig. 7.13 perform the same calculation, but with two different types. C#'s new generics feature provides a mechanism for writing a single "generic method" that can perform the same tasks as an entire set of overloaded methods. We discuss generic methods in Chapter 26.

```
1   // Fig. 7.13: MethodOverload.cs
2   // Overloaded method declarations.
3   using System;
4
5   public class MethodOverload
6   {
7      // test overloaded square methods
8      public void TestOverloadedMethods()
9      {
10        Console.WriteLine( "Square of integer 7 is {0}", Square( 7 ) );
11        Console.WriteLine( "Square of double 7.5 is {0}", Square( 7.5 ) );
12     } // end method TestOverloadedMethods
```

Fig. 7.13 | Overloaded method declarations. (Part 1 of 2.)

```
13
14      // square method with int argument
15      public int Square( int intValue )
16      {
17         Console.WriteLine( "Called square with int argument: {0}",
18            intValue );
19         return intValue * intValue;
20      } // end method Square with int argument
21
22      // square method with double argument
23      public double Square( double doubleValue )
24      {
25         Console.WriteLine( "Called square with double argument: {0}",
26            doubleValue );
27         return doubleValue * doubleValue;
28      } // end method Square with double argument
29   } // end class MethodOverload
```

Fig. 7.13 | Overloaded method declarations. (Part 2 of 2.)

```
1    // Fig. 7.14: MethodOverloadTest.cs
2    // Application to test class MethodOverload.
3    public class MethodOverloadTest
4    {
5       public static void Main( string[] args )
6       {
7          MethodOverload methodOverload = new MethodOverload();
8          methodOverload.TestOverloadedMethods();
9       } // end Main
10   } // end class MethodOverloadTest
```

```
Called square with int argument: 7
Square of integer 7 is 49
Called square with double argument: 7.5
Square of double 7.5 is 56.25
```

Fig. 7.14 | Application to test class `MethodOverload`.

Distinguishing Between Overloaded Methods

The compiler distinguishes overloaded methods by their *signature*—a combination of the method's name, and the number, types and order of its parameters. The signature also includes the way those parameters are passed, which can be modified by the ref and out keywords that we discuss in Section 7.14. If the compiler looked only at method names during compilation, the code in Fig. 7.13 would be ambiguous—the compiler would not know how to distinguish between the two Square methods (lines 15–20 and 23–28). Internally, the compiler uses signatures to determine whether the methods in a class are unique in that class.

For example, in Fig. 7.13, the compiler will use the method signatures to distinguish between the "Square of int" method (the Square method that specifies an int parameter) and the "Square of double" method (the Square method that specifies a double parameter). If Method1's declaration begins as

$$void \; \texttt{Method1(} int \; \texttt{a, } float \; \texttt{b)}$$

then that method will have a different signature than the method declared beginning with

$$void \; \texttt{Method1(} float \; \texttt{a, } int \; \texttt{b)}$$

The order of the parameter types is important—the compiler considers the preceding two `Method1` headers to be distinct.

Return Types of Overloaded Methods

In discussing the logical names of methods used by the compiler, we did not mention the return types of the methods. This is because method *calls* cannot be distinguished by return type. The application in Fig. 7.15 illustrates the compiler errors generated when two methods have the same signature, but different return types. Overloaded methods can have the same or different return types if the methods have different parameter lists. Also, overloaded methods need not have the same number of parameters.

```
1   // Fig. 7.15: MethodOverload.cs
2   // Overloaded methods with identical signatures
3   // cause compilation errors, even if return types are different.
4   public class MethodOverloadError
5   {
6      // declaration of method Square with int argument
7      public int Square( int x )
8      {
9         return x * x;
10     }
11
12     // second declaration of method Square with int argument
13     // causes compilation error even though return types are different
14     public double Square( int y )
15     {
16        return y * y;
17     }
18  } // end class MethodOverloadError
```

	Description	File	Line	Column	Project
⊗ 1	Type 'MethodOverloadError' already defines a member called 'Square' with the same parameter types	MethodOverloadError	14	18	MethodOverloadError

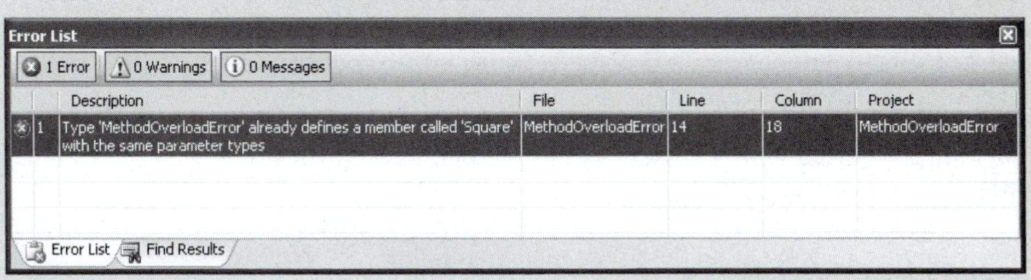

Fig. 7.15 | Overloaded methods with identical signatures cause compilation errors, even if return types are different.

Common Programming Error 7.10

Declaring overloaded methods with identical parameter lists is a compilation error regardless of whether the return types are different.

7.13 Recursion

The applications we have discussed thus far are generally structured as methods that call one another in a disciplined, hierarchical manner. For some problems, however, it is useful to have a method call itself. A ***recursive method*** is a method that calls itself, either directly or indirectly through another method.

We consider recursion conceptually first. Then we examine an application containing a recursive method. Recursive problem-solving approaches have a number of elements in common. When a recursive method is called to solve a problem, the method actually is capable of solving only the simplest case(s), or ***base case(s)***. If the method is called with a base case, the method returns a result. If the method is called with a more complex problem, the method divides the problem into two conceptual pieces: a piece that the method knows how to do and a piece that the method does not know how to do. To make recursion feasible, the latter piece must resemble the original problem, but be a slightly simpler or slightly smaller version of it. Because this new problem looks like the original problem, the method calls a fresh copy of itself to work on the smaller problem; this is referred to as a ***recursive call*** and is also called the ***recursion step***. The recursion step normally includes a `return` statement, because its result will be combined with the portion of the problem the method knew how to solve to form a result that will be passed back to the original caller.

The recursion step executes while the original call to the method is still active (i.e., while it has not finished executing). The recursion step can result in many more recursive calls, as the method divides each new subproblem into two conceptual pieces. For the recursion to terminate eventually, each time the method calls itself with a slightly simpler version of the original problem, the sequence of smaller and smaller problems must converge on the base case. At that point, the method recognizes the base case and returns a result to the previous copy of the method. A sequence of returns ensues until the original method call returns the result to the caller. This process sounds complex compared with the conventional problem solving we have performed to this point.

Recursive Factorial Calculations

As an example of recursion concepts at work, let us write a recursive application to perform a popular mathematical calculation. Consider the factorial of a nonnegative integer n, written $n!$ (and pronounced "n factorial"), which is the product

$$n \cdot (n-1) \cdot (n-2) \cdot \ldots \cdot 1$$

$1!$ is equal to 1 and $0!$ is defined to be 1. For example, $5!$ is the product $5 \cdot 4 \cdot 3 \cdot 2 \cdot 1$, which is equal to 120.

The factorial of an integer, `number`, greater than or equal to 0 can be calculated iteratively (nonrecursively) using the `for` statement as follows:

```
factorial = 1;

for ( int counter = number; counter >= 1; counter-- )
   factorial *= counter;
```

A recursive declaration of the factorial method is arrived at by observing the following relationship:

$$n! = n \cdot (n - 1)!$$

For example, 5! is clearly equal to 5 · 4!, as is shown by the following equations:

$$5! = 5 \cdot 4 \cdot 3 \cdot 2 \cdot 1$$
$$5! = 5 \cdot (4 \cdot 3 \cdot 2 \cdot 1)$$
$$5! = 5 \cdot (4!)$$

The evaluation of 5! would proceed as shown in Fig. 7.16. Figure 7.16(a) shows how the succession of recursive calls proceeds until 1! is evaluated to be 1, which terminates the recursion. Figure 7.16(b) shows the values returned from each recursive call to its caller until the value is calculated and returned.

Figure 7.17 uses recursion to calculate and print the factorials of the integers from 0 to 10. The recursive method Factorial (lines 16–24) first tests to determine whether a terminating condition (line 19) is true. If number is less than or equal to 1 (the base case), Factorial returns 1, no further recursion is necessary and the method returns. If number is greater than 1, line 23 expresses the problem as the product of number and a recursive call to Factorial evaluating the factorial of number - 1, which is a slightly simpler problem than the original calculation, Factorial(number).

Method Factorial (lines 16–24) receives a parameter of type long and returns a result of type long. As can be seen in Fig. 7.17, factorial values become large quickly. We chose type long (which can represent relatively large integers) so that the application could calculate factorials greater than 20!. Unfortunately, the Factorial method produces large values so quickly that factorial values soon exceed even the maximum value that can be

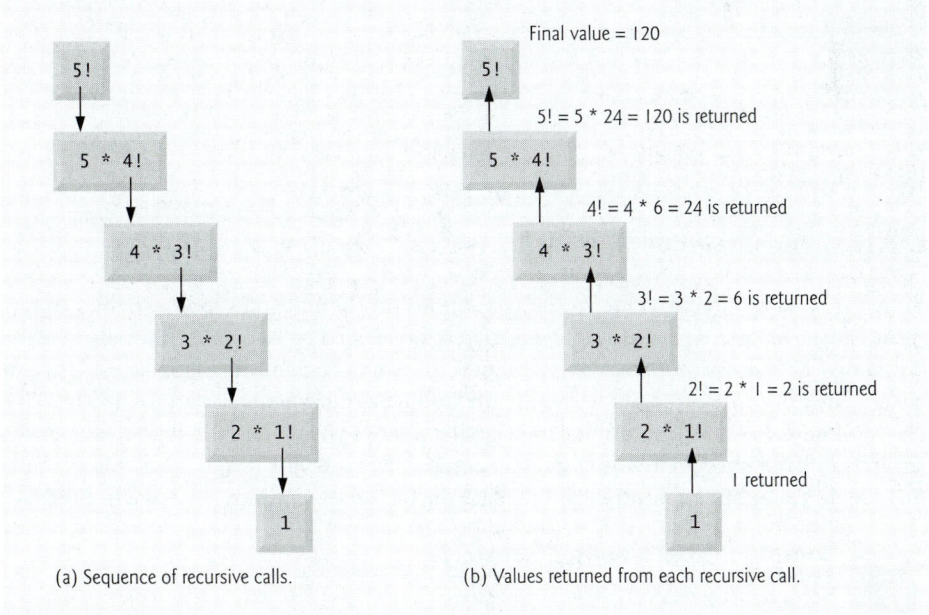

(a) Sequence of recursive calls.

(b) Values returned from each recursive call.

Fig. 7.16 | Recursive evaluation of 5!.

```
1   // Fig. 7.17: FactorialTest.cs
2   // Recursive Factorial method.
3   using System;
4
5   public class FactorialTest
6   {
7      public static void Main( string[] args )
8      {
9         // calculate the factorials of 0 through 10
10        for ( long counter = 0; counter <= 10; counter++ )
11           Console.WriteLine( "{0}! = {1}",
12              counter, Factorial( counter ) );
13     } // end method Main
14
15     // recursive declaration of method Factorial
16     public static long Factorial( long number )
17     {
18        // base case
19        if ( number <= 1 )
20           return 1;
21        // recursion step
22        else
23           return number * Factorial( number - 1 );
24     } // end method Factorial
25  } // end class FactorialTest
```

```
0! = 1
1! = 1
2! = 2
3! = 6
4! = 24
5! = 120
6! = 720
7! = 5040
8! = 40320
9! = 362880
10! = 3628800
```

Fig. 7.17 | Recursive `Factorial` method.

stored in a `long` variable. Due to the restrictions on the integral types, variables of type `float`, `double`, and `decimal` might ultimately be needed to calculate factorials of larger numbers. This situation points to a weakness in many programming languages—the languages are not easily extended to handle the unique requirements of various applications. As you know, C# is an extensible language that allows you to create a type that supports arbitrarily large integers if you wish. You could create a `HugeInteger` class, for example, that could enable an application to calculate the factorials of arbitrarily large numbers.

Common Programming Error 7.11

Either omitting the base case or writing the recursion step incorrectly so that it does not converge on the base case will cause infinite recursion, eventually exhausting memory. This error is analogous to the problem of an infinite loop in an iterative (nonrecursive) solution.

7.14 Passing Arguments: Pass-by-Value vs. Pass-by-Reference

Two ways to pass arguments to functions in many programming languages are *pass-by-value* and *pass-by-reference*. When an argument is passed by value (the default in C#), a *copy* of the argument's value is made and passed to the called function. Changes to the copy do not affect the original variable's value in the caller. This prevents the accidental side effects that so greatly hinder the development of correct and reliable software systems. Each argument that has been passed in the programs in this chapter so far has been passed by value. When an argument is passed by reference, the caller gives the method the ability to access and modify the caller's original variable.

Performance Tip 7.1

Pass-by-reference is good for performance reasons, because it can eliminate the pass-by-value overhead of copying large amounts of data.

Software Engineering Observation 7.5

Pass-by-reference can weaken security, because the called function can corrupt the caller's data.

To pass an object by reference into a method, simply provide as an argument in the method call the variable that refers to the object. Then, in the method body, reference the object using the parameter name. The parameter refers to the original object in memory, so the called method can access the original object directly.

Previously, we discussed the difference between value types and reference types. One of the major differences between them is that value-type variables store values, so specifying a value-type variable in a method call passes a copy of that variable's value to the method. Reference-type variables store references to objects, so specifying a reference-type variable as an argument passes the method a copy of the actual reference that refers to the object. Even though the reference itself is passed by value, the method can still use the reference it receives to modify the original object in memory. Similarly, when returning information from a method via a `return` statement, the method returns a copy of the value stored in a value-type variable or a copy of the reference stored in a reference-type variable. When a reference is returned, the calling method can use that reference to interact with the referenced object. So, in effect, objects are always passed by reference.

What if you would like to pass a variable by reference so the called method can modify the variable's value? To do this, C# provides keywords *ref* and *out*. Applying the `ref` keyword to a parameter declaration allows you to pass a variable to a method by reference— the called method will be able to modify the original variable in the caller. The `ref` keyword is used for variables that already have been initialized in the calling method. Normally, when a method call contains an uninitialized variable as an argument, the compiler generates an error. Preceding a parameter with keyword `out` creates an *output parameter*. This indicates to the compiler that the argument will be passed into the called method by reference and that the called method will assign a value to the original variable in the caller. If the method does not assign a value to the output parameter in every possible path of execution, the compiler generates an error. This also prevents the compiler from generating an error message for an uninitialized variable that is passed as an argument to a method. A method can return only one value to its caller via a return statement, but can return many values by specifying multiple output parameters.

You can also pass a reference-type variable by reference, which allows you to modify the passed reference-type variable so that it references a new object. Passing a reference by reference is a tricky but powerful technique that we discuss in Section 8.8.

The application in Figs. 7.18 and 7.19 uses the ref and out keywords to manipulate integer values. Class ReferenceAndOutputParameters (Fig. 7.18) contains three methods that calculate the square of an integer. Method SquareRef (lines 37–40) multiplies its parameter x by itself and assigns the new value to x. SquareRef's parameter x is declared as ref int, which indicates that the argument passed to this method must be an integer that is passed by reference. Because the argument is passed by reference, the assignment at line 39 modifies the original argument's value in the caller.

```csharp
1   // Fig. 7.18: ReferenceAndOutputParameters.cs
2   // Reference, output and value parameters.
3   using System;
4
5   class ReferenceAndOutputParameters
6   {
7      // call methods with reference, output and value parameters
8      public void DemonstrateReferenceAndOutputParameters()
9      {
10        int y = 5; // initialize y to 5
11        int z; // declares z, but does not initialize it
12
13        // display original values of y and z
14        Console.WriteLine( "Original value of y: {0}", y );
15        Console.WriteLine( "Original value of z: uninitialized\n" );
16
17        // pass y and z by reference
18        SquareRef( ref y ); // must use keyword ref
19        SquareOut( out z ); // must use keyword out
20
21        // display values of y and z after they are modified by
22        // methods SquareRef and SquareOut, respectively
23        Console.WriteLine( "Value of y after SquareRef: {0}", y );
24        Console.WriteLine( "Value of z after SquareOut: {0}\n", z );
25
26        // pass y and z by value
27        Square( y );
28        Square( z );
29
30        // display values of y and z after they are passed to method Square
31        // to demonstrate arguments passed by value are not modified
32        Console.WriteLine( "Value of y after Square: {0}", y );
33        Console.WriteLine( "Value of z after Square: {0}", z );
34     } // end method DemonstrateReferenceAndOutputParameters
35
36     // uses reference parameter x to modify caller's variable
37     void SquareRef( ref int x )
38     {
```

Fig. 7.18 | Reference, output and value parameters. (Part 1 of 2.)

```
39            x = x * x; // squares value of caller's variable
40        } // end method SquareRef
41
42        // uses output parameter x to assign a value
43        // to an uninitialized variable
44        void SquareOut( out int x )
45        {
46            x = 6; // assigns a value to caller's variable
47            x = x * x; // squares value of caller's variable
48        } // end method SquareOut
49
50        // parameter x receives a copy of the value passed as an argument,
51        // so this method cannot modify the caller's variable
52        void Square( int x )
53        {
54            x = x * x;
55        } // end method Square
56    } // end class ReferenceAndOutputParameters
```

Fig. 7.18 | Reference, output and value parameters. (Part 2 of 2.)

```
 1    // Fig. 7.19: ReferenceAndOutputParamtersTest.cs
 2    // Application to test class ReferenceAndOutputParameters.
 3    class ReferenceAndOutputParamtersTest
 4    {
 5        static void Main( string[] args )
 6        {
 7            ReferenceAndOutputParameters test =
 8                new ReferenceAndOutputParameters();
 9            test.DemonstrateReferenceAndOutputParameters();
10        } // end Main
11    } // end class ReferenceAndOutputParamtersTest
```

```
Original value of y: 5
Original value of z: uninitialized

Value of y after SquareRef: 25
Value of z after SquareOut: 36

Value of y after Square: 25
Value of z after Square: 36
```

Fig. 7.19 | Application to test class `ReferenceAndOutputParameters`.

Method `SquareOut` (lines 44–48) assigns its parameter the value 6 (line 46), then squares that value. `SquareOut`'s parameter is declared as `out int`, which indicates that the argument passed to this method must be an integer that is passed by reference and that the argument does not need to be initialized in advance.

Method `Square` (lines 52–55) multiplies its parameter x by itself and assigns the new value to x. When this method is called, a copy of the argument is passed to the parameter x. Thus, even though parameter x is modified in the method, the original value in the caller is not modified.

Method `DemonstrateReferenceAndOutputParameters` (lines 8–34) invokes methods `SquareRef`, `SquareOut` and `Square`. This method begins by initializing variable y to 5 and declaring, but not initializing, variable z. Lines 18–19 call methods `SquareRef` and `SquareOut`. Notice that when you pass a variable to a method with a reference parameter, you must precede the argument with the same keyword (`ref` or `out`) that was used to declare the reference parameter. Lines 23–24 display the values of y and z after the calls to `SquareRef` and `SquareOut`. Notice that y has been changed to 25 and z has been set to 36.

Lines 27–28 call method `Square` with y and z as arguments. In this case, both variables are passed by value—only copies of their values are passed to `Square`. As a result, the values of y and z remain 25 and 36, respectively. Lines 32–33 output the values of y and z to show that they were not modified.

Common Programming Error 7.12

The `ref` and `out` arguments in a method call must match the parameters specified in the method declaration; otherwise, a compilation error occurs.

Software Engineering Observation 7.6

By default, C# does not allow you to choose whether to pass each argument by value or by reference. Value-types are passed by value. Objects are not passed to methods; rather, references to objects are passed to methods. The references themselves are passed by value. When a method receives a reference to an object, the method can manipulate the object directly, but the reference value cannot be changed to refer to a new object. In Section 8.8, you'll see that references also can be passed by reference.

7.15 (Optional) Software Engineering Case Study: Identifying Class Operations in the ATM System

In the "Software Engineering Case Study" sections at the ends of Chapters 4–6, we performed the first few steps in the object-oriented design of our ATM system. In Chapter 4, we identified the classes that we will likely need to implement, and we created our first class diagram. In Chapter 5, we described some attributes of our classes. In Chapter 6, we examined our objects' states and modeled their state transitions and activities. In this section, we determine some of the class operations (or behaviors) needed to implement the ATM system.

Identifying Operations

An operation is a service that objects of a class provide to clients of the class. Consider the operations of some real-world objects. A radio's operations include setting its station and volume (typically invoked by a person adjusting the radio's controls). A car's operations include accelerating (invoked by the driver pressing the accelerator pedal), decelerating (invoked by the driver pressing the brake pedal or releasing the gas pedal), turning, and shifting gears. Software objects can offer operations as well—for example, a software graphics object might offer operations for drawing a circle, drawing a line and drawing a square. A spreadsheet software object might offer operations like printing the spreadsheet, totaling the elements in a row or column and graphing information in the spreadsheet as a bar chart or pie chart.

We can derive many of the operations of the classes in our ATM system by examining the verbs and verb phrases in the requirements document. We then relate each of these to particular classes in our system (Fig. 7.20). The verb phrases in Fig. 7.20 help us determine the operations of our classes.

Modeling Operations

To identify operations, we examine the verb phrases listed for each class in Fig. 7.20. The "executes financial transactions" phrase associated with class ATM implies that class ATM instructs transactions to execute. Therefore, classes BalanceInquiry, Withdrawal and Deposit each need an operation to provide this service to the ATM. We place this operation (which we have named Execute) in the third compartment of the three transaction classes in the updated class diagram of Fig. 7.21. During an ATM session, the ATM object will invoke the Execute operation of each transaction object to tell it to execute.

The UML represents operations (which are implemented as methods in C#) by listing the operation name, followed by a comma-separated list of parameters in parentheses, a colon and the return type:

$$operationName(\ parameter1, \ parameter2, \ \dots, \ parameterN \ ) \ : \ returnType$$

Each parameter in the comma-separated parameter list consists of a parameter name, followed by a colon and the parameter type:

$$parameterName \ : \ parameterType$$

For the moment, we do not list the parameters of our operations—we will identify and model the parameters of some of the operations shortly. For some of the operations,

Class	Verbs and verb phrases
ATM	executes financial transactions
BalanceInquiry	[none in the requirements document]
Withdrawal	[none in the requirements document]
Deposit	[none in the requirements document]
BankDatabase	authenticates a user, retrieves an account balance, credits an account, debits an account
Account	retrieves an account balance, credits a deposit amount to an account, debits a withdrawal amount to an account
Screen	displays a message to the user
Keypad	receives numeric input from the user
CashDispenser	dispenses cash, indicates whether it contains enough cash to satisfy a withdrawal request
DepositSlot	receives a deposit envelope

Fig. 7.20 | Verbs and verb phrases for each class in the ATM system.

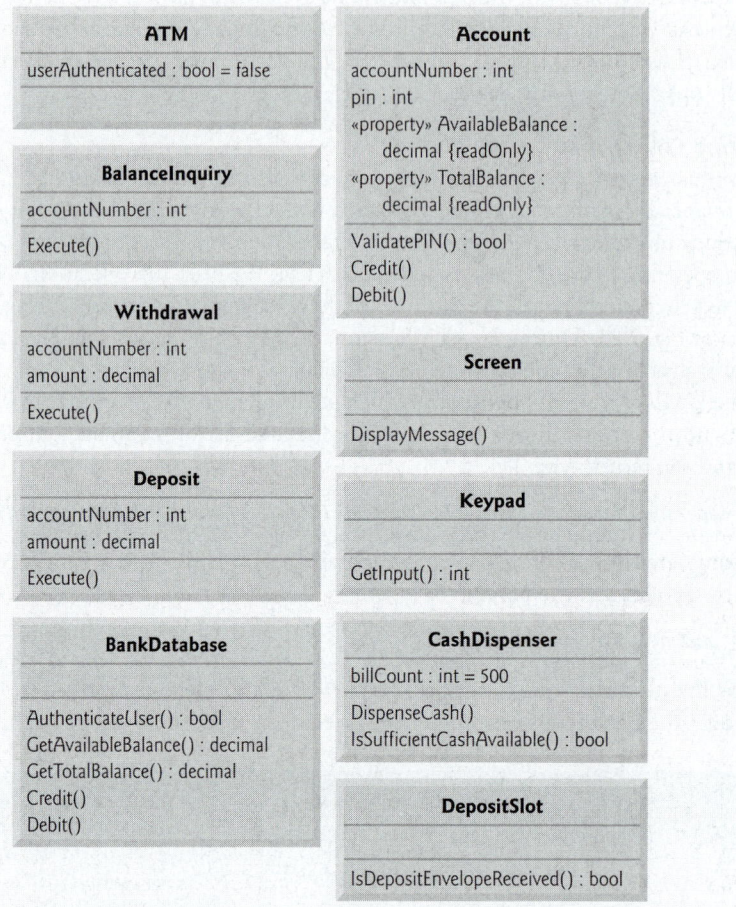

Fig. 7.21 | Classes in the ATM system with attributes and operations.

we do not yet know the return types, so we also omit them from the diagram. These omissions are perfectly normal at this point. As our design and implementation proceed, we will add the remaining return types.

Operations of Class *BankDatabase* and Class *Account*

Figure 7.20 lists the phrase "authenticates a user" next to class BankDatabase—the database is the object that contains the account information necessary to determine whether the account number and PIN entered by a user match those of an account at the bank. Therefore, class BankDatabase needs an operation that provides an authentication service to the ATM. We place the operation AuthenticateUser in the third compartment of class BankDatabase (Fig. 7.21). However, an object of class Account, not class BankDatabase, stores the account number and PIN that must be accessed to authenticate a user, so class Account must provide a service to validate a PIN obtained through user input against a PIN stored in an Account object. Therefore, we add a ValidatePIN operation to class Account. Note that we specify a return type of bool for the AuthenticateUser and ValidatePIN operations. Each operation returns a value indicating either that the operation was successful in performing its task (i.e., a return value of true) or that it was not successful (i.e., a return value of false).

Figure 7.20 lists several additional verb phrases for class BankDatabase: "retrieves an account balance," "credits an account" and "debits an account." Like "authenticates a user," these remaining phrases refer to services that the database must provide to the ATM, because the database holds all the account data used to authenticate a user and perform ATM transactions. However, objects of class Account actually perform the operations to which these phrases refer. Thus, class BankDatabase and class Account both need operations that correspond to each of these phrases. Recall from Section 4.11 that, because a bank account contains sensitive information, we do not allow the ATM to access accounts directly. The database acts as an intermediary between the ATM and the account data, preventing unauthorized access. As we will see in Section 8.14, class ATM invokes the operations of class BankDatabase, each of which in turn invokes corresponding operations (which are get accessors of read-only properties) in class Account.

The phrase "retrieves an account balance" suggests that classes BankDatabase and Account each need an operation that gets the balance. However, recall that Fig. 5.19 specified two attributes in class Account to represent a balance—availableBalance and totalBalance. A balance inquiry requires access to both balance attributes so that it can display them to the user, but a withdrawal needs to check only the value of availableBalance. To allow objects in the system to obtain these balance attributes individually from a specific Account object in the BankDatabase, we add operations GetAvailableBalance and GetTotalBalance to the third compartment of class BankDatabase (Fig. 7.21). We specify a return type of decimal for each of these operations, because the balances that they retrieve are of type decimal.

Once the BankDatabase knows which Account to access, the BankDatabase must be able to obtain each balance attribute individually from that Account. For this purpose, we could add operations GetAvailableBalance and GetTotalBalance to the third compartment of class Account (Fig. 7.21). However, in C#, simple operations such as getting the value of an attribute are typically performed by a property's get accessor (at least when that particular class "owns" the underlying attribute). This design is for a C# application, so rather than modeling operations GetAvailableBalance and GetTotalBalance, we model decimal properties AvailableBalance and TotalBalance in class Account. Properties are placed in the second compartment of a class diagram. These properties replace the availableBalance and totalBalance attributes that we modeled for class Account in Fig. 5.19. Recall from Chapter 4 that a property's accessors are implied—thus, they are not modeled in a class diagram. Figure 7.20 does not mention the need to set the balances, so Fig. 7.21 shows properties AvailableBalance and TotalBalance as read-only properties (i.e., they have only get accessors). To indicate a read-only property in the UML, we follow the property's type with "{readOnly}."

You may be wondering why we modeled AvailableBalance and TotalBalance *properties* in class Account, but modeled GetAvailableBalance and GetTotalBalance *operations* in class BankDatabase. Since there can be many Account objects in the BankDatabase, the ATM must specify which Account to access when invoking BankDatabase operations GetAvailableBalance and GetTotalBalance. The ATM does this by passing an account number argument to each BankDatabase operation. The get accessors of the properties you have seen in C# code cannot receive arguments. Thus, we modeled GetAvailableBalance and GetTotalBalance as operations in class BankDatabase so that we could specify parameters to which the ATM can pass arguments. Also, the underlying balance attributes are not owned by the BankDatabase, so get accessors are not appropriate here. We discuss the parameters for the BankDatabase operations shortly.

The phrases "credits an account" and "debits from an account" indicate that classes BankDatabase and Account must perform operations to update an account during deposits and withdrawals, respectively. We therefore assign Credit and Debit operations to classes BankDatabase and Account. You may recall that crediting an account (as in a deposit) adds an amount only to the Account's total balance. Debiting an account (as in a withdrawal), on the other hand, subtracts the amount from both the total and available balances. We hide these implementation details inside class Account. This is a good example of encapsulation and information hiding.

If this were a real ATM system, classes BankDatabase and Account would also provide a set of operations to allow another banking system to update a user's account balance after either confirming or rejecting all or part of a deposit. Operation ConfirmDepositAmount, for example, would add an amount to the Account's available balance, thus making deposited funds available for withdrawal. Operation RejectDepositAmount would subtract an amount from the Account's total balance to indicate that a specified amount, which had recently been deposited through the ATM and added to the Account's total balance, was invalidated (or checks may have "bounced"). The bank would invoke operation Reject-DepositAmout after determining either that the user failed to include the correct amount of cash or that any checks did not clear (i.e., they "bounced"). While adding these operations would make our system more complete, we do not include them in our class diagrams or implementation because they are beyond the scope of the case study.

Operations of Class Screen

Class Screen "displays a message to the user" at various times in an ATM session. All visual output occurs through the screen of the ATM. The requirements document describes many types of messages (e.g., a welcome message, an error message, a thank-you message) that the screen displays to the user. The requirements document also indicates that the screen displays prompts and menus to the user. However, a prompt is really just a message describing what the user should input next, and a menu is essentially a type of prompt consisting of a series of messages (i.e., menu options) displayed consecutively. Therefore, rather than provide class Screen with an individual operation to display each type of message, prompt and menu, we simply create one operation that can display any message specified by a parameter. We place this operation (DisplayMessage) in the third compartment of class Screen in our class diagram (Fig. 7.21). Note that we do not worry about the parameter of this operation at this time—we model the parameter momentarily.

Operations of Class Keypad

From the phrase "receives numeric input from the user" listed by class Keypad in Fig. 7.20, we conclude that class Keypad should perform a GetInput operation. Because the ATM's keypad, unlike a computer keyboard, contains only the numbers 0–9, we specify that this operation returns an integer value. Recall from the requirements document that in different situations, the user may be required to enter a different type of number (e.g., an account number, a PIN, the number of a menu option, a deposit amount as a number of cents). Class Keypad simply obtains a numeric value for a client of the class—it does not determine whether the value meets any specific criteria. Any class that uses this operation must verify that the user entered appropriate numbers and, if not, display error messages via class Screen). [*Note:* When we implement the system, we simulate the ATM's keypad with a computer keyboard, and for simplicity, we assume that the user does not enter non-numeric input using keys on the computer keyboard that do not appear on the ATM's keypad. In Chapter 16, Strings, Characters and Regular Expressions, you'll see how to examine inputs to determine if they are of particular types.]

Operations of Class CashDispenser and Class DepositSlot
Figure 7.20 lists "dispenses cash" for class CashDispenser. Therefore, we create operation DispenseCash and list it under class CashDispenser in Fig. 7.21. Class CashDispenser also "indicates whether it contains enough cash to satisfy a withdrawal request." Thus, we include IsSufficientCashAvailable, an operation that returns a value of type bool, in class CashDispenser. Figure 7.20 also lists "receives a deposit envelope" for class Deposit-Slot. The deposit slot must indicate whether it received an envelope, so we place the operation IsEnvelopeReceived, which returns a bool value, in the third compartment of class DepositSlot. [*Note:* A real hardware deposit slot would most likely send the ATM a signal to indicate that an envelope was received. We simulate this behavior, however, with an operation in class DepositSlot that class ATM can invoke to find out whether the deposit slot received an envelope.]

Operations of Class ATM
We do not list any operations for class ATM at this time. We are not yet aware of any services that class ATM provides to other classes in the system. When we implement the system in C# (Appendix J, ATM Case Study Code), however, operations of this class, and additional operations of the other classes in the system, may become apparent.

Identifying and Modeling Operation Parameters
So far, we have not been concerned with the parameters of our operations—we have attempted to gain only a basic understanding of the operations of each class. Let's now take a closer look at some operation parameters. We identify an operation's parameters by examining what data the operation requires to perform its assigned task.

Consider the AuthenticateUser operation of class BankDatabase. To authenticate a user, this operation must know the account number and PIN supplied by the user. Thus we specify that operation AuthenticateUser takes int parameters userAccountNumber and userPIN, which the operation must compare to the account number and PIN of an Account object in the database. We prefix these parameter names with user to avoid confusion between the operation's parameter names and the attribute names that belong to class Account. We list these parameters in the class diagram in Fig. 7.22, which models only class BankDatabase. [*Note:* It is perfectly normal to model only one class in a class diagram. In this case, we are most concerned with examining the parameters of this particular class, so we omit the other classes. In class diagrams later in the case study, parameters are no longer the focus of our attention, so we omit the parameters to save space. Remember, however, that the operations listed in these diagrams still have parameters.]

Recall that the UML models each parameter in an operation's comma-separated parameter list by listing the parameter name, followed by a colon and the parameter type. Figure 7.22 thus specifies, for example, that operation AuthenticateUser takes two parameters—userAccountNumber and userPIN, both of type int.

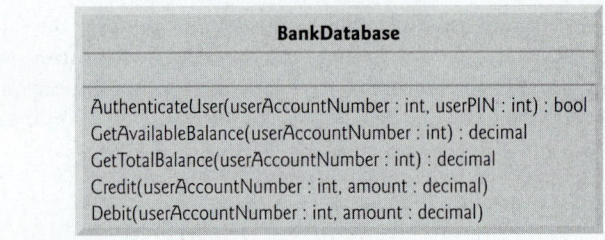

Fig. 7.22 | Class `BankDatabase` with operation parameters.

Class `BankDatabase` operations `GetAvailableBalance`, `GetTotalBalance`, `Credit` and `Debit` also each require a `userAccountNumber` parameter to identify the account to which the database must apply the operations, so we include these parameters in the class diagram. In addition, operations `Credit` and `Debit` each require a `decimal` parameter `amount` to specify the amount of money to be credited or debited, respectively.

The class diagram in Fig. 7.23 models the parameters of class `Account`'s operations. Operation `ValidatePIN` requires only a `userPIN` parameter, which contains the user-specified PIN to be compared with the PIN associated with the account. Like their counterparts in class `BankDatabase`, operations `Credit` and `Debit` in class `Account` each require a `decimal` parameter `amount` that indicates the amount of money involved in the operation. Note that class `Account`'s operations do not require an account number parameter—each of these operations can be invoked only on the `Account` object in which they are executing, so including a parameter to specify an `Account` is unnecessary.

Figure 7.24 models class `Screen` with a parameter specified for operation `DisplayMessage`. This operation requires only `string` parameter `message`, which indicates the text to be displayed.

The class diagram in Fig. 7.25 specifies that operation `DispenseCash` of class `CashDispenser` takes `decimal` parameter `amount` to indicate the amount of cash (in dollars) to be dispensed. Operation `IsSufficientCashAvailable` also takes `decimal` parameter `amount` to indicate the amount of cash in question.

Note that we do not discuss parameters for operation `Execute` of classes `BalanceInquiry`, `Withdrawal` and `Deposit`, operation `GetInput` of class `Keypad` and operation `IsEnvelopeReceived` of class `DepositSlot`. At this point in our design process, we cannot

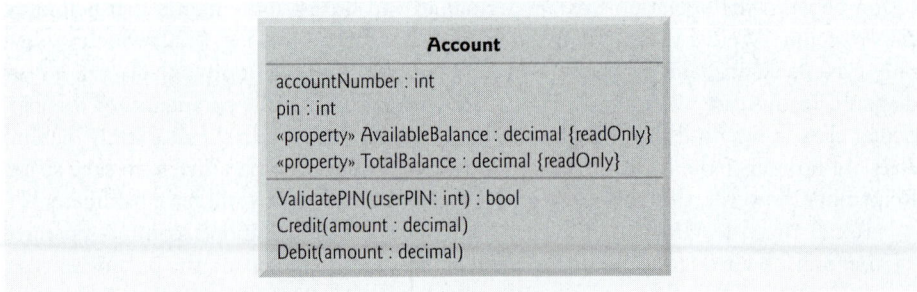

Fig. 7.23 | Class `Account` with operation parameters.

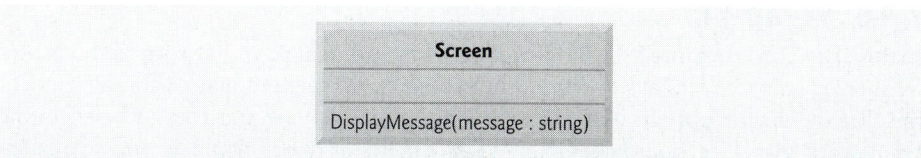

Fig. 7.24 | Class `Screen` with an operation parameter.

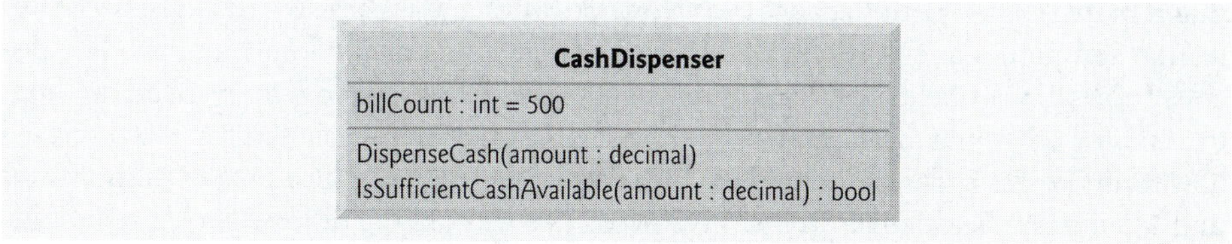

Fig. 7.25 | Class `CashDispenser` with operation parameters.

determine whether these operations require additional data to perform their tasks, so we leave their parameter lists empty. As we progress through the case study, we may decide to add parameters to these operations.

In this section, we have determined many of the operations performed by the classes in the ATM system. We have identified the parameters and return types of some of the operations. As we continue our design process, the number of operations belonging to each class may vary—we might find that new operations are needed or that some current operations are unnecessary—and we might determine that some of our class operations need additional parameters and different return types. Again, all of this is perfectly normal.

Software Engineering Case Study Self-Review Exercises

7.1   Which of the following is not a behavior?
 a) reading data from a file
 b) printing output
 c) text output
 d) obtaining input from the user

7.2   If you were to add to the ATM system an operation that returns the amount attribute of class `Withdrawal`, how and where would you specify this operation in the class diagram of Fig. 7.21?

7.3   Describe the meaning of the following operation listing that might appear in a class diagram for an object-oriented design of a calculator:

```
Add( x : int, y : int ) : int
```

Answers to Software Engineering Case Study Self-Review Exercises

7.1   c.

7.2   An operation that retrieves the amount attribute of class `Withdrawal` would typically be implemented as a get accessor of a property of class `Withdrawal`. The following would replace attribute amount in the attribute (i.e., second) compartment of class `Withdrawal`:

```
«property» Amount : decimal
```

7.3   This is an operation named `Add` that takes `int` parameters x and y and returns an `int` value. This operation would most likely sum its parameters x and y and return the result.

7.16 Wrap-Up

In this chapter, we discussed the difference between non-static and static methods, and we showed how to call static methods by preceding the method name with the name of the class in which it appears and the dot (.) operator. You saw that the Math class in the Framework Class Library provides many static methods to perform mathematical calculations. We presented several commonly used FCL namespaces. You learned how to use operator + to perform string concatenations. You also learned how to declare constant values in two ways—with the const keyword and with enum types. We demonstrated simulation techniques and used class Random to generate sets of random numbers. We discussed the scope of fields and local variables in a class. You saw how to overload methods in a class by providing methods with the same name but different signatures. We discussed how recursive methods call themselves, breaking larger problems into smaller subproblems until eventually the original problem is solved. You learned the differences between value types and reference types with respect to how they are passed to methods, and how to use the ref and out keywords to pass arguments by reference.

In Chapter 8, you will learn how to maintain lists and tables of data in arrays. You will see a more elegant implementation of the application that rolls a die 6000 times and two enhanced versions of our GradeBook case study. You will also learn how to access an application's command-line arguments that are passed to method Main when a console application begins execution.

Summary

Section 7.1 Introduction
- Experience has shown that the best way to develop and maintain a large application is to construct it from small, simple pieces. This technique is called divide and conquer.

Section 7.2 Packaging Code in C#
- Three common ways of packaging code are methods, classes and namespaces.
- Methods allow you to modularize an application by separating its tasks into self-contained units. The actual statements in the method bodies are written only once, can be reused from several locations in an application and are hidden from other methods.
- Dividing an application into meaningful methods makes the application easier to debug and maintain.

Section 7.3 static Methods, static Variables and Class Math
- You can call any static method by specifying the name of the class in which the method is declared, followed by the dot (.) operator and the method name, as in

    ClassName.*methodName*(*arguments*)

- Method arguments may be constants, variables or expressions.
- Any variable declared with keyword const is a constant—its value cannot be changed after the constant is declared.
- Class Math declares two constants that represent commonly used mathematical constants: Math.PI and Math.E. The constant Math.PI (3.14159265358979323846) is the ratio of a circle's circumference to its diameter. The constant Math.E (2.7182818284590452354) is the base value for natural logarithms.

- When each object of a class maintains its own copy of an attribute, each object (instance) of the class has a separate instance of the variable in memory. When objects of a class containing static variables are created, all objects of that class share one copy of the class's static variables.

- Together the static variables and instance variables represent the fields of a class.

- When you execute your application, you can specify a list of strings (separated by spaces) as command-line arguments. The execution environment will pass these arguments to the Main method of your application.

- If you declare more than one Main method among all the classes of your project, you will need to indicate which one you would like to be the application's entry point. You can do this by clicking the menu **Project > [ProjectName] Properties...** and selecting the class containing the Main method that should be the entry point from the **Startup object** list box.

Section 7.4 Declaring Methods with Multiple Parameters

- When a method has more than one parameter, the parameters are specified as a comma-separated list.

- When a method is called, each parameter is initialized with the value of the corresponding argument. There must be one argument in the method call for each parameter in the method declaration. Also, each argument must be consistent with the type of the corresponding parameter.

- When program control returns to the point in the application where a method was called, the method's parameters are no longer accessible in memory.

- Methods can return at most one value; the returned value can be a reference to an object that contains many values.

- C# allows string objects to be created by assembling smaller strings into larger strings using operator +. This is known as string concatenation.

- Every value of a simple type in C# has a string representation. When one of the + operator's operands is a string, the other is implicitly converted to a string, then the two are concatenated.

- All objects have a ToString method that returns a string representation of the object. When an object is concatenated with a string, the object's ToString method is implicitly called to obtain the string representation of the object.

Section 7.5 Notes on Declaring and Using Methods

- You have seen three ways to call a method—using a method name by itself to call another method of the same class; using a variable that contains a reference to an object, followed by the dot (.) operator and the method name to call a non-static method of the referenced object; and using the class name and the dot (.) operator to call a static method of a class.

- A static method can call only other static methods of the same class directly and can manipulate only static variables in the same class directly.

- There are three ways to return control to the statement that calls a method. If the method does not return a result, control returns when the program flow reaches the method-ending right brace or when the statement

    return;

is executed. If the method returns a result, the statement

    return *expression*;

evaluates the *expression*, then returns the result to the caller.

Section 7.6 Method Call Stack and Activation Records

- Stacks are known as last-in, first-out (LIFO) data structures—the last item pushed (inserted) on the stack is the first item popped off (removed from) the stack.

- When an application calls a method, the called method must know how to return to its caller, so the return address of the calling method is pushed onto the program execution stack. If a series of method calls occurs, the successive return addresses are pushed onto the stack in last-in-first-out order so that each method can return to its caller.

- The program execution stack also contains the memory for the local variables used in each invocation of a method during an application's execution. This data, stored as a portion of the program execution stack, is known as the activation record or stack frame of the method call.

- If a local variable holding a reference to an object is the only variable in the application with a reference to that object, when the activation record containing that local variable is popped off the stack, the object will eventually be deleted from memory during "garbage collection."

- The amount of memory in a computer is finite. If more method calls occur than can have their activation records stored on the program execution stack, stack overflow occurs.

Section 7.7 Argument Promotion and Casting

- Another important feature of method calls is argument promotion—implicitly converting an argument's value to the type that the method expects to receive in its corresponding parameter.

- The argument promotion rules apply to expressions containing values of two or more simple types and to simple-type values passed as arguments to methods.

- In cases where information may be lost due to conversion between simple types, the compiler requires you to use a cast operator to explicitly force the conversion.

Section 7.8 The Framework Class Library

- Many predefined classes are grouped into categories of related classes called namespaces. Together, these namespaces are referred to as the .NET Framework Class Library, or the FCL.

Section 7.9 Case Study: Random-Number Generation

- Method Next of class Random generates a random int value in the range 0 to +2,147,483,646, inclusive.

- Class Random provides other versions of method Next. One receives an int argument and returns a value from 0 up to, but not including, the argument's value. The other receives two int arguments and returns a value from the first argument's value up to, but not including, the second argument's value.

- The methods of class Random actually generate pseudorandom numbers based on complex mathematical calculations. The calculation that produces the pseudorandom numbers uses the time of day as a seed value to change the sequence's starting point.

- If the same seed value is used every time, the Random object produces the same sequence of random numbers.

Section 7.10 Case Study: A Game of Chance (Introducing Enumerations)

- An enumeration is introduced by the keyword enum and a type name. Braces delimit the body of an enum declaration. Inside the braces is a comma-separated list of enumeration constants. The enum constant names must be unique, but their underlying values need not be.

- Variables of an enum type should be assigned only constants of that enum type.

- By default, when an enum is declared, each constant in the enum declaration contains an underlying constant value of type int. If you do not assign a value to an identifier in the enum declaration, the compiler will do so. If the first enum constant is unassigned, the compiler gives it the value 0. If any other enum constant is unassigned, the compiler gives it a value equal to one more than the value of the preceding enum constant.

- If you need to compare a simple-type value to the underlying value of an enumeration constant, you must use a cast operator to make the two types match.

Section 7.11 Scope of Declarations

- The scope of a declaration is the portion of the application that can refer to the declared entity by its unqualified name.

- The scope of a parameter declaration is the body of the method in which the declaration appears.

- The scope of a local-variable declaration is from the point at which the declaration appears to the end of that block.

- The scope of a local-variable declaration that appears in the initialization section of a for statement's header is the body of the for statement and the other expressions in the header.

- The scope of a method, property or field of a class is the entire body of the class.

- Any block may contain variable declarations. If a local variable or parameter in a method has the same name as a field, the field is hidden until the block terminates execution.

Section 7.12 Method Overloading

- Methods of the same name can be declared in the same class, as long as they have different sets of parameters. This is called method overloading. When an overloaded method is called, the C# compiler selects the appropriate method by examining the number, types and order of the arguments in the call.

- The compiler distinguishes overloaded methods by their signature—a combination of the method's name and the number, types and order of its parameters. The signature also includes the way those parameters are passed, which can be modified by the ref and out keywords.

- The compiler will generate an error when two methods have the same signature but different return types. Overloaded methods can have the same or different return types if the methods have different parameter lists.

Section 7.13 Recursion

- A recursive method is a method that calls itself, either directly or indirectly through another method.

- When a recursive method is called to solve a problem, the method actually is capable of solving only the simplest case(s), or base case(s). If the method is called with a base case, the method returns a result.

- If the method is called with a more complex problem, the method divides the problem into two conceptual pieces: a piece that the method knows how to do and a piece that the method does not know how to do. Because this new problem looks like the original problem, the method calls a fresh copy of itself to work on the smaller problem; this procedure is referred to as a recursive call and is also called the recursion step.

- A recursive declaration of the factorial method is arrived at by observing the following relationship:

$$n! = n \cdot (n-1)!$$

Section 7.14 Passing Arguments: Pass-by-Value vs. Pass-by-Reference

- Two ways to pass arguments to functions in many programming languages are pass-by-value and pass-by-reference.

- When an argument is passed by value (the default in C#), a *copy* of the argument's value is passed to the called function. Changes to the copy do not affect the original variable's value in the caller.

- When an argument is passed by reference, the caller gives the method the ability to access and modify the caller's original data directly.

- Value-type variables store values, so specifying a value-type variable in a method call passes a copy of that variable's value to the method. Reference-type variables store references to objects, so specifying a reference-type variable as an argument passes the method a copy of the actual reference that refers to the object.

- When returning information from a method via a return statement, the method returns a copy of the value stored in a value-type variable or a copy of the reference stored in a reference-type variable.

- C# provides the keywords ref and out to pass variables by reference.

- A ref parameter indicates that a argument will be passed to the method by reference—the called method will be able to modify the original variable in the caller.

- An out parameter indicates that a possibly uninitialized variable will be passed into the method by reference and that the called method will assign a value to the original variable in the caller.

- A method can return only one value to its caller via a return statement, but can return many values by specifying multiple output (ref and/or out) parameters.

- When a variable is passed to a method with a reference parameter, you must precede the variable with the same keyword (ref or out) that was used to declare the reference parameter.

Terminology

.NET documentation
.NET Framework Class Library (FCL)
activation record
argument promotion
base case in recursion
block
comma-separated list of parameters
command-line argument
const keyword
constant
divide-and-conquer approach
element of chance
entry point of an application
enum keyword
enumeration
enumeration constant
field of a class
formal parameter
function

"hidden" fields
hide implementation details
hierarchical boss-method/worker-method
    relationship
implicit conversion
invoke a method
last-in, first-out (LIFO) data structure
local variable
Math.PI constant
Math.E constant
method call
method call stack
method declaration
method overloading
modularizing an application with methods
namespace
Next method of class Random
out keyword
output parameter

overloaded method
parameter
parameter list
pass by reference
pass by value
pop data from a stack
procedure
program execution stack
promotion rules
push data onto a stack
pseudorandom number
Random class
random numbers
ref keyword
recursion
recursion step
recursive call
recursive method

return keyword
reusable software components
scaling factor (with random numbers)
scope of a declaration
seed value (with random numbers)
shift a range (with random numbers)
shifting value (with random numbers)
signature of a method
simulation
simple type promotions
software reuse
stack
stack frame
stack overflow
string concatenation
unqualified name
user-defined method

Self-Review Exercises

7.1   Fill in the blanks in each of the following statements:

a) A method is invoked with a(n) _____.

b) A variable known only within the method in which it is declared is called a(n) _____.

c) The _____ statement in a called method can be used to pass the value of an expression back to the calling method.

d) The keyword _____ indicates that a method does not return a value.

e) Data can be added or removed only from the _____ of a stack.

f) Stacks are known as _____ data structures—the last item pushed (inserted) on the stack is the first item popped off (removed form) the stack.

g) The three ways to return control from a called method to a caller are _____, _____ and _____.

h) An object of class _____ produces random numbers.

i) The program execution stack contains the memory for local variables on each invocation of a method during an application's execution. This data, stored as a portion of the program execution stack, is known as the _____ or _____ of the method call.

j) If there are more method calls than can be stored on the program execution stack, an error known as a(n) _____ occurs.

k) The _____ of a declaration is the portion of an application that can refer to the entity in the declaration by its unqualified name.

l) It is possible to have several methods with the same name that each operate on different types or numbers of arguments. This feature is called method _____.

m) The program execution stack is also referred to as the _____ stack.

n) A method that calls itself either directly or indirectly is a(n) _____ method.

o) A recursive method typically has two components: one that provides a means for the recursion to terminate by testing for a(n) _____ case and one that expresses the problem as a recursive call for a slightly simpler problem than does the original call.

7.2 For the class Craps in Fig. 7.9, state the scope of each of the following entities:
  a) the variable randomNumbers.
  b) the variable die1.
  c) the method RollDice.
  d) the method Play.
  e) the variable sumOfDice.

7.3 Write an application that tests whether the examples of the Math class method calls shown in Fig. 7.2 actually produce the indicated results.

7.4 Give the method header for each of the following methods:
  a) Method Hypotenuse, which takes two double-precision, floating-point arguments side1 and side2 and returns a double-precision, floating-point result.
  b) Method Smallest, which takes three integers x, y and z and returns an integer.
  c) Method Instructions, which does not take any arguments and does not return a value. [*Note:* Such methods are commonly used to display instructions to a user.]
  d) Method IntToDouble, which takes integer argument number and returns a double value.

7.5 Find the error in each of the following code segments. Explain how to correct the error.
  a) ```
void G()
{
   Console.WriteLine("Inside method G");

   void H()
   {
      Console.WriteLine("Inside method H");
   }
}
```
  b) ```
int Sum( int x, int y )
{
   int result;
   result = x + y;
}
```
  c) ```
void F(float a);
{
   float a;
   Console.WriteLine(a);
}
```
  d) ```
void Product()
{
   int a = 6, b = 5, c = 4, result;
   result = a * b * c;
   Console.WriteLine( "Result is " + result );
   return result;
}
```

7.6 Write a complete C# application to prompt the user for the double radius of a sphere, and call method sphereVolume to calculate and display the volume of the sphere. Use the following statement to calculate the volume:

```
double volume = ( 4.0 / 3.0 ) * Math.PI * Math.Pow( radius, 3 )
```

Answers to Self-Review Exercises

7.1   a) method call. b) local variable. c) return. d) void. e) top. f) last-in-first-out (LIFO).
g) return; or return *expression*; or encountering the closing right brace of a method. h) Random.
i) activation record, stack frame. j) stack overflow. k) scope. l) overloading. m) method call. n)
recursive. o) base.

7.2   a) class body. b) block that defines method RollDice's body. c) class body. d) class body.
e) block that defines method Play's body.

7.3   The following solution demonstrates the Math class methods in Fig. 7.2:

```
1   // Exercise 7.3: MathTest.cs
2   // Testing the Math class methods.
3   using System;
4
5   public class MathTest
6   {
7      public static void Main( string[] args )
8      {
9         Console.WriteLine( "Math.Abs( 23.7 ) = {0}", Math.Abs( 23.7 ) );
10        Console.WriteLine( "Math.Abs( 0.0 ) = {0}", Math.Abs( 0.0 ) );
11        Console.WriteLine( "Math.Abs( -23.7 ) = {0}", Math.Abs( -23.7 ) );
12        Console.WriteLine( "Math.Ceiling( 9.2 ) = {0}",
13           Math.Ceiling( 9.2 ) );
14        Console.WriteLine( "Math.Ceiling( -9.8 ) = {0}",
15           Math.Ceiling( -9.8 ) );
16        Console.WriteLine( "Math.Cos( 0.0 ) = {0}", Math.Cos( 0.0 ) );
17        Console.WriteLine( "Math.Exp( 1.0 ) = {0}", Math.Exp( 1.0 ) );
18        Console.WriteLine( "Math.Exp( 2.0 ) = {0}", Math.Exp( 2.0 ) );
19        Console.WriteLine( "Math.Floor( 9.2 ) = {0}", Math.Floor( 9.2 ) );
20        Console.WriteLine( "Math.Floor( -9.8 ) = {0}",
21           Math.Floor( -9.8 ) );
22        Console.WriteLine( "Math.Log( Math.E ) = {0}",
23           Math.Log( Math.E ) );
24        Console.WriteLine( "Math.Log( Math.E * Math.E ) = {0}",
25           Math.Log( Math.E * Math.E ) );
26        Console.WriteLine( "Math.Max( 2.3, 12.7 ) = {0}",
27           Math.Max( 2.3, 12.7 ) );
28        Console.WriteLine( "Math.Max( -2.3, -12.7 ) = {0}",
29           Math.Max( -2.3, -12.7 ) );
30        Console.WriteLine( "Math.Min( 2.3, 12.7 ) = {0}",
31           Math.Min( 2.3, 12.7 ) );
32        Console.WriteLine( "Math.Min( -2.3, -12.7 ) = {0}",
33           Math.Min( -2.3, -12.7 ) );
34        Console.WriteLine( "Math.Pow( 2.0, 7.0 ) = {0}",
35           Math.Pow( 2.0, 7.0 ) );
36        Console.WriteLine( "Math.Pow( 9.0, 0.5 ) = {0}",
37           Math.Pow( 9.0, 0.5 ) );
38        Console.WriteLine( "Math.Sin( 0.0 ) = {0}", Math.Sin( 0.0 ) );
39        Console.WriteLine( "Math.Sqrt( 900.0 ) = {0}",
40           Math.Sqrt( 900.0 ) );
41        Console.WriteLine( "Math.Sqrt( 9.0 ) = {0}", Math.Sqrt( 9.0 ) );
42        Console.WriteLine( "Math.Tan( 0.0 ) = {0}", Math.Tan( 0.0 ) );
43      } // end Main
44   } // end class MathTest
```

```
Math.Abs( 23.7 ) = 23.7
Math.Abs( 0.0 ) = 0
Math.Abs( -23.7 ) = 23.7
Math.Ceiling( 9.2 ) = 10
Math.Ceiling( -9.8 ) = -9
Math.Cos( 0.0 ) = 1
Math.Exp( 1.0 ) = 2.71828182845905
Math.Exp( 2.0 ) = 7.38905609893065
Math.Floor( 9.2 ) = 9
Math.Floor( -9.8 ) = -10
Math.Log( Math.E ) = 1
Math.Log( Math.E * Math.E ) = 2
Math.Max( 2.3, 12.7 ) = 12.7
Math.Max( -2.3, -12.7 ) = -2.3
Math.Min( 2.3, 12.7 ) = 2.3
Math.Min( -2.3, -12.7 ) = -12.7
Math.Pow( 2.0, 7.0 ) = 128
Math.Pow( 9.0, 0.5 ) = 3
Math.Sin( 0.0 ) = 0
Math.Sqrt( 900.0 ) = 30
Math.Sqrt( 9.0 ) = 3
Math.Tan( 0.0 ) = 0
```

7.4 a) *double* Hypotenuse(*double* side1, *double* side2)
      b) *int* Smallest(*int* x, *int* y, *int* z)
      c) *void* Instructions()
      d) *double* IntToDouble(*int* number)

7.5 a) Error: Method H is declared within method G.
      Correction: Move the declaration of H outside the declaration of G.
      b) Error: The method is supposed to return an integer, but does not.
      Correction: Delete variable result and place the statement
         return x + y;
      in the method, or add the following statement at the end of the method body:
         return result;
      c) Error: The semicolon after the right parenthesis of the parameter list is incorrect, and
      the parameter a should not be redeclared in the method.
      Correction: Delete the semicolon after the right parenthesis of the parameter list, and
      delete the declaration float a;.
      d) Error: The method returns a value when it is not supposed to.
      Correction: Change the return type from void to int.

7.6 The following solution calculates the volume of a sphere, using the radius entered by the user:

```
 1    // Exercise 7.6: Sphere.cs
 2    // Calculate the volume of a sphere.
 3    using System;
 4
 5    public class Sphere
 6    {
 7       // obtain radius from user and display volume of sphere
 8       public void DetermineSphereVolume()
 9       {
```

```
10          Console.Write( "Enter radius of sphere: " );
11          double radius = Convert.ToDouble( Console.ReadLine() );
12
13          Console.WriteLine( "Volume is {0:F3}", SphereVolume( radius ) );
14       } // end method DetermineSphereVolume
15
16       // calculate and return sphere volume
17       public double SphereVolume( double radius )
18       {
19          double volume = ( 4.0 / 3.0 ) * Math.PI * Math.Pow( radius, 3 );
20          return volume;
21       } // end method SphereVolume
22    } // end class Sphere
```

```
1    // Exercise 7.6: SphereTest.cs
2    // Calculate the volume of a sphere.
3    public class SphereTest
4    {
5       // application starting point
6       public static void Main( string[] args )
7       {
8          Sphere mySphere = new Sphere();
9          mySphere.DetermineSphereVolume();
10      } // end Main
11   } // end class SphereTest
```

```
Enter radius of sphere: 4
Volume is 268.083
```

Exercises

7.7   What is the value of x after each of the following statements is executed?
   a) x = Math.Abs(7.5);
   b) x = Math.Floor(7.5);
   c) x = Math.Abs(0.0);
   d) x = Math.Ceiling(0.0);
   e) x = Math.Abs(-6.4);
   f) x = Math.Ceiling(-6.4);
   g) x = Math.Ceiling(-Math.Abs(-8 + Math.Floor(-5.5)));

7.8   A parking garage charges a $2.00 minimum fee to park for up to three hours. The garage charges an additional $0.50 per hour for each hour *or part thereof* in excess of three hours. The maximum charge for any given 24-hour period is $10.00. Assume that no car parks for longer than 24 hours at a time. Write an application that calculates and displays the parking charges for each customer who parked in the garage yesterday. You should enter the hours parked for each customer. The application should display the charge for the current customer and should calculate and display the running total of yesterday's receipts. The application should use method CalculateCharges to determine the charge for each customer.

7.9   An application of method Math.Floor is rounding a value to the nearest integer. The statement

```
y = Math.Floor( x + 0.5 );
```

will round the number x to the nearest integer and assign the result to y. Write an application that reads `double` values and uses the preceding statement to round each of the numbers to the nearest integer. For each number processed, display both the original number and the rounded number.

7.10   `Math.Floor` may be used to round a number to a specific decimal place. The statement

```
y = Math.Floor( x * 10 + 0.5 ) / 10;
```

rounds x to the tenths position (i.e., the first position to the right of the decimal point). The statement

```
y = Math.Floor( x * 100 + 0.5 ) / 100;
```

rounds x to the hundredths position (i.e., the second position to the right of the decimal point). Write an application that defines four methods for rounding a number x in various ways:

    a) `RoundToInteger( number )`
    b) `RoundToTenths( number )`
    c) `RoundToHundredths( number )`
    d) `RoundToThousandths( number )`

For each value read, your application should display the original value, the number rounded to the nearest integer, the number rounded to the nearest tenth, the number rounded to the nearest hundredth and the number rounded to the nearest thousandth.

7.11   Answer each of the following questions:

    a) What does it mean to choose numbers "at random?"
    b) Why is the `Random` class useful for simulating games of chance?
    c) Why is it often necessary to scale or shift the values produced by a `Random` object?
    d) Why is computerized simulation of real-world situations a useful technique?

7.12   Write statements that assign random integers to the variable n in the following ranges. Assume `Random randomNumbers = new Random()` has been defined and use the two-parameter version of the method `Random.Next`.

    a) $1 \le n \le 2$
    b) $1 \le n \le 100$
    c) $0 \le n \le 9$
    d) $1000 \le n \le 1112$
    e) $-1 \le n \le 1$
    f) $-3 \le n \le 11$

7.13   For each of the following sets of integers, write a single statement that will display a number at random from the set. Assume `Random randomNumbers = new Random()` has been defined and use the one-parameter version of method `Random.Next`.

    a) 2, 4, 6, 8, 10.
    b) 3, 5, 7, 9, 11.
    c) 6, 10, 14, 18, 22.

7.14   Write a method `IntegerPower( base, exponent )` that returns the value of

$$base^{\,exponent}$$

For example, `IntegerPower( 3, 4 )` calculates 3^4 (or 3 * 3 * 3 * 3). Assume that `exponent` is a positive, nonzero integer and that `base` is an integer. Method `IntegerPower` should use a `for` or `while` loop to control the calculation. Do not use any `Math`-library methods. Incorporate this method into an application that reads integer values for `base` and `exponent` and performs the calculation with the `IntegerPower` method.

7.15   Write method `Hypotenuse` that calculates the length of the hypotenuse of a right triangle when the lengths of the other two sides are given. (Use the sample data in Fig. 7.26.) The method should take two arguments of type `double` and return the hypotenuse as a `double`. Incorporate this method into an application that reads values for `side1` and `side2` and performs the calculation with the `Hypotenuse` method. Determine the length of the hypotenuse for each of the triangles in Fig. 7.26.

7.16   Write method `Multiple` that determines, for a pair of integers, whether the second integer is a multiple of the first. The method should take two integer arguments and return `true` if the second is a multiple of the first and `false` otherwise. Incorporate this method into an application that inputs a series of pairs of integers (one pair at a time) and determines whether the second value in each pair is a multiple of the first.

7.17   Write method `IsEven` that uses the remainder operator (%) to determine whether an integer is even. The method should take an integer argument, and return `true` if the integer is even and `false` otherwise. Incorporate this method into an application that inputs a sequence of integers (one at a time) and determines whether each is even or odd.

7.18   Write method `SquareOfAsterisks` that displays a solid square (the same number of rows and columns) of asterisks whose side length is specified in integer parameter `side`. For example, if `side` is 4, the method should display

```
****
****
****
****
```

Incorporate this method into an application that reads an integer value for `side` from the user and outputs the asterisks with the `SquareOfAsterisks` method.

7.19   Modify the method created in Exercise 7.18 to form the square out of whatever character is contained in character parameter `FillCharacter`. Thus, if `side` is 5 and `FillCharacter` is "#," the method should display

```
#####
#####
#####
#####
#####
```

[*Hint:* Use the expression `Convert.ToChar( Console.Read() )` to read a character from the user.]

7.20   Write an application that prompts the user for the radius of a circle and uses method `CircleArea` to calculate the area of the circle.

Triangle	Side 1	Side 2
1	3.0	4.0
2	5.0	12.0
3	8.0	15.0

Fig. 7.26 | Values for the sides of triangles in Exercise 7.15.

7.21 Write code segments that accomplish each of the following tasks:
  a) Calculate the integer part of the quotient when integer a is divided by integer b.
  b) Calculate the integer remainder when integer a is divided by integer b.
  c) Use the application pieces developed in parts (a) and (b) to write a method `DisplayDigits` that receives an integer between 1 and 99999 and displays it as a sequence of digits, separating each pair of digits by two spaces. For example, the integer 4562 should appear as

```
4  5  6  2
```

  d) Incorporate the method developed in part (c) into an application that inputs an integer and calls `DisplayDigits` by passing the method the integer entered. Display the results.

7.22 Implement the following integer methods:
  a) Method `Celsius` returns the Celsius equivalent of a Fahrenheit temperature, using the calculation

```
c = 5.0 / 9.0 * ( f - 32 );
```

  b) Method `Fahrenheit` returns the Fahrenheit equivalent of a Celsius temperature, using the calculation

```
f = 9.0 / 5.0 * c + 32;
```

  c) Use the methods from parts (a) and (b) to write an application that enables the user either to enter a Fahrenheit temperature and display the Celsius equivalent or to enter a Celsius temperature and display the Fahrenheit equivalent.

7.23 Write a method `Minimum3` that returns the smallest of three floating-point numbers. Use the `Math.Min` method to implement `Minimum3`. Incorporate the method into an application that reads three values from the user, determines the smallest value and displays the result.

7.24 An integer number is said to be a *perfect number* if its factors, including 1 (but not the number itself), sum to the number. For example, 6 is a perfect number, because 6 = 1 + 2 + 3. Write method `Perfect` that determines whether parameter `number` is a perfect number. Use this method in an application that determines and displays all the perfect numbers between 2 and 1000. Display the factors of each perfect number to confirm that the number is indeed perfect.

7.25 An integer is said to be *prime* if it is greater than 1 and divisible by only 1 and itself. For example, 2, 3, 5 and 7 are prime, but 4, 6, 8 and 9 are not.
  a) Write a method that determines whether a number is prime.
  b) Use this method in an application that determines and displays all the prime numbers less than 10,000.
  c) Initially, you might think that $n/2$ is the upper limit for which you must test to see whether a number is prime, but you need only go as high as the square root of n. Rewrite the application, and run it both ways.

7.26 Write a method that takes an integer value and returns the number with its digits reversed. For example, given the number 7631, the method should return 1367. Incorporate the method into an application that reads a value from the user and displays the result.

7.27 The *greatest common divisor* (*GCD*) of two integers is the largest integer that evenly divides each of the two numbers. Write method `Gcd` that returns the greatest common divisor of two integers. Incorporate the method into an application that reads two values from the user and displays the result.

7.28 Write method `QualityPoints` that inputs a student's average and returns 4 if the student's average is 90–100, 3 if the average is 80–89, 2 if the average is 70–79, 1 if the average is 60–69 and 0 if the average is lower than 60. Incorporate the method into an application that reads a value from the user and displays the result.

7.29 Write an application that simulates coin tossing. Let the application toss a coin each time the user chooses the "Toss Coin" menu option. Count the number of times each side of the coin appears. Display the results. The application should call a separate method `Flip` that takes no arguments and returns `false` for tails and `true` for heads. [*Note:* If the application realistically simulates coin tossing, each side of the coin should appear approximately half the time.]

7.30 Computers are playing an increasing role in education. Write an application that will help an elementary school student learn multiplication. Use a `Random` object to produce two positive one-digit integers. The application should then prompt the user with a question, such as

```
How much is 6 times 7?
```

The student then inputs the answer. Next, the application checks the student's answer. If it is correct, display the message `"Very good!"` and ask another multiplication question. If the answer is wrong, display the message `"No. Please try again."` and let the student try the same question repeatedly until the student finally gets it right. A separate method should be used to generate each new question. This method should be called once when the application begins execution and each time the user answers the question correctly.

7.31 The use of computers in education is referred to as computer-assisted instruction (CAI). One problem that develops in CAI environments is student fatigue. This problem can be eliminated by varying the computer's responses to hold the student's attention. Modify the application of Exercise 7.30 so that various comments are displayed for each correct answer and each incorrect answer as follows:

Responses to a correct answer:

```
Very good!
Excellent!
Nice work!
Keep up the good work!
```

Responses to an incorrect answer:

```
No. Please try again.
Wrong. Try once more.
Don't give up!
No. Keep trying.
```

Use random-number generation to choose a number from 1 to 4 that will be used to select an appropriate response to each answer. Use a `switch` statement to issue the responses.

7.32 More sophisticated computer-assisted instruction systems monitor the student's performance over a period of time. The decision to begin a new topic is often based on the student's success with previous topics. Modify the application of Exercise 7.31 to count the number of correct and incorrect responses typed by the student. After the student types 10 answers, your application should calculate the percentage of correct responses. If the percentage is lower than 75%, display `Please ask your instructor for extra help` and reset the application so another student can try it.

7.33 Write an application that plays "guess the number" as follows: Your application chooses the number to be guessed by selecting a random integer in the range 1 to 1000. The application displays the prompt `Guess a number between 1 and 1000`. The player inputs a first guess. If the player's guess is incorrect, your application should display Too high. Try again. or Too low. Try again. to help the player "zero in" on the correct answer. The application should prompt the user for the next guess. When the user enters the correct answer, display Congratulations. You guessed the number! and allow the user to choose whether to play again. [*Note:* The guessing technique employed in this problem is similar to a binary search, which is discussed in Chapter 24.]

7.34 Modify the application of Exercise 7.33 to count the number of guesses the player makes. If the number is 10 or fewer, display Either you know the secret or you got lucky! If the player guesses the number in 10 tries, display Aha! You know the secret! If the player makes more than 10 guesses, display You should be able to do better! Why should it take no more than 10 guesses? Well, with each "good guess," the player should be able to eliminate half of the numbers. Now show why any number from 1 to 1000 can be guessed in 10 or fewer tries.

7.35 Exercises 7.30—7.32 developed a computer-assisted instruction application to teach an elementary school student multiplication. Perform the following enhancements:
  a) Modify the application to allow the user to choose a "school grade-level" of 1 or 2. Grade level 1 means that the application should use only single-digit numbers in the problems. Grade level 2 means that the application should use numbers as large as two digits.
  b) Modify the application to allow the user to pick the type of arithmetic problems he or she wishes to study. An option of 1 means addition problems only, 2 means subtraction problems only, 3 means multiplication problems only, 4 means division problems only and 5 means a random mixture of problems of all these types.

7.36 Write method Distance to calculate the distance between two points *(x1, y1)* and *(x2, y2)*. All numbers and return values should be of type double. Incorporate this method into an application that enables the user to enter the coordinates of the points.

7.37 Modify the craps application of Fig. 7.9 to allow wagering. Initialize variable balance to 1000 dollars. Prompt the player to enter a wager. Check that wager is less than or equal to balance, and if it is not, have the user re-enter wager until a valid wager is entered. After a correct wager is entered, run one game of craps. If the player wins, increase balance by wager and display the new balance. If the player loses, decrease balance by wager, display the new balance, check whether balance has become zero and, if so, display the message "Sorry. You busted!"

7.38 Write an application that displays a table of the binary, octal, and hexadecimal equivalents of the decimal numbers in the range 1–256. If you are not familiar with these number systems, read Appendix B, Number Systems first.

7.39 Write recursive method Power(base, exponent) that, when called, returns

$base^{\,exponent}$

For example, Power(3, 4) = 3 * 3 * 3 * 3. Assume that exponent is an integer greater than or equal to 1. [*Hint:* The recursion step should use the relationship

$$base^{\,exponent} = base \cdot base^{\,exponent - 1}$$

and the terminating condition occurs when exponent is equal to 1, because

$base^1 = base$]

Incorporate this method into an application that enables the user to enter the base and exponent.

7.40 *(Towers of Hanoi)* Every budding computer scientist must grapple with certain classic problems, and the *Towers of Hanoi* (see Fig. 7.27) is one of the most famous. Legend has it that in a temple in the Far East, priests are attempting to move a stack of disks from one peg to another. The initial stack has 64 disks threaded onto one peg and arranged from bottom to top by decreasing size. The priests are attempting to move the stack from this peg to a second peg under the constraints

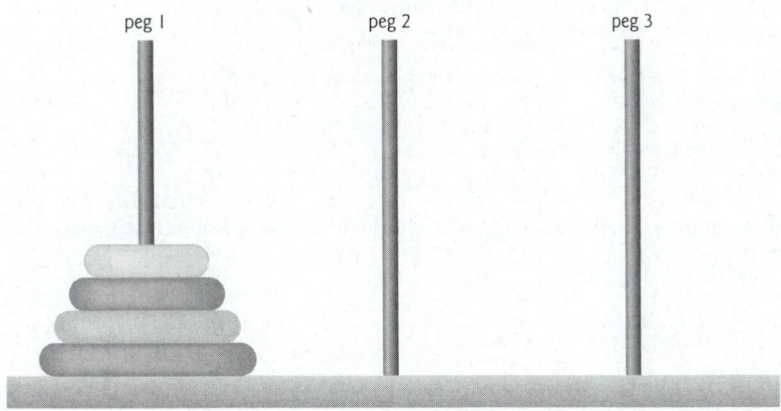

Fig. 7.27 | The Towers of Hanoi for the case with four disks.

that exactly one disk is moved at a time and at no time may a larger disk be placed above a smaller disk. A third peg is available for temporarily holding disks. Supposedly, the world will end when the priests complete their task, so there is little incentive for us to facilitate their efforts.

Let us assume that the priests are attempting to move the disks from peg 1 to peg 3. We wish to develop an algorithm that will print the precise sequence of peg-to-peg disk transfers.

If we were to approach this problem with conventional methods, we would rapidly find ourselves hopelessly knotted up in managing the disks. Instead, if we attack the problem with recursion in mind, it immediately becomes tractable. Moving n disks can be viewed in terms of moving only $n-1$ disks (hence the recursion) as follows:

a) Move $n-1$ disks from peg 1 to peg 2, using peg 3 as a temporary holding area.
b) Move the last disk (the largest) from peg 1 to peg 3.
c) Move the $n-1$ disks from peg 2 to peg 3, using peg 1 as a temporary holding area.

The process ends when the last task involves moving $n = 1$ disk (i.e., the base case). This task is accomplished by simply moving the disk, without the need for a temporary holding area.

Write an application to solve the Towers of Hanoi problem. Allow the user to enter the number of disks. Use a recursive Tower method with four parameters:

a) the number of disks to be moved,
b) the peg on which these disks are initially threaded,
c) the peg to which this stack of disks is to be moved, and
d) the peg to be used as a temporary holding area.

Your application should display the precise instructions it will take to move the disks from the starting peg to the destination peg. For example, to move a stack of three disks from peg 1 to peg 3, your application should print the following series of moves:

```
1 --> 3 (This notation means "Move one disk from peg 1 to peg 3.")
1 --> 2
3 --> 2
1 --> 3
2 --> 1
2 --> 3
1 --> 3
```

7.41   What does the following method do?

```
// Parameter b must be a positive
// integer to prevent infinite recursion
public int Mystery( int a, int b )
{
   if ( b == 1 )
      return a;
   else
      return a + Mystery( a, b - 1 );
}
```

7.42   Find the error in the following recursive method, and explain how to correct it:

```
public int Sum( int n )
{
   if ( n == 0 )
      return 0;
   else
      return n + Sum( n );
}
```

Arrays

*Now go, write it
before them in a table,
and note it in a book.*
—Isaiah 30:8

*To go beyond is as
wrong as to fall short.*
—Confucius

*Begin at the beginning, …
and go on till you come to
the end: then stop.*
—Lewis Carroll

OBJECTIVES

In this chapter you will learn:

■ What arrays are.

■ To use arrays to store data in and retrieve data from lists and tables of values.

■ To declare arrays, initialize arrays and refer to individual elements of arrays.

■ To use the **foreach** statement to iterate through arrays.

■ To pass arrays to methods.

■ To declare and manipulate multidimensional arrays.

■ To write methods that use variable-length argument lists.

■ To read command-line arguments into an application.

8.1 Introduction

This chapter introduces the important topic of *data structures*—collections of related data items. *Arrays* are data structures consisting of related data items of the same type. Arrays are fixed-length entities—they remain the same length once they are created, although an array variable may be reassigned such that it refers to a new array of a different length.

After discussing how arrays are declared, created and initialized, we present a series of examples that demonstrate several common array manipulations. We also present a case study that uses arrays to simulate shuffling and dealing playing cards for use in card game applications. The chapter demonstrates C#'s last structured control statement—the `foreach` repetition statement—which provides a concise notation for accessing the data in arrays (and other data structures as you will see in Chapter 27, Collections). Two sections of the chapter enhance the `GradeBook` case study from Chapters 4–6. In particular, we use arrays to enable the class to maintain a set of grades in memory and analyze student grades from multiple exams. These and other examples demonstrate the ways in which arrays allow you to organize and manipulate data.

8.2 Arrays

An array is a group of variables (called *elements*) containing values that all have the same type. Recall that types are divided into two categories—value types and reference types. Arrays are reference types. As you will see, what we typically think of as an array is actually a reference to an array instance in memory. The elements of an array can be either value types or reference types (including other arrays, as we will see in Section 8.10). To refer to a particular element in an array, we specify the name of the reference to the array and the position number of the element in the array. The position number of the element is called the element's *index*.

Figure 8.1 shows a logical representation of an integer array called c. This array contains 12 elements. An application refers to any one of these elements with an *array-access expression* that includes the name of the array, followed by the index of the particular element in *square brackets* ([]). The first element in every array has *index zero* and is sometimes called the *zeroth element*. Thus, the elements of array c are c[0], c[1], c[2] and so on. The highest index in array c is 11, which is one less than the number of elements in the array, because indices begin at 0. Array names follow the same conventions as other variable names.

An index must be a nonnegative integer and can be an expression. For example, if we assume that variable a is 5 and variable b is 6, then the statement

```
c[ a + b ] += 2;
```

adds 2 to array element c[11]. Note that an indexed array name is an array-access expression. Such expressions can be used on the left side of an assignment to place a new value into an array element. The array index must be a value of type int, uint, long or ulong, or a value of a type that can be implicitly promoted to one of these types.

Let's examine array c in Fig. 8.1 more closely. The *name* of the array is c. Every array instance knows its own length and provides access to this information with the Length property. For example, the expression c.Length uses array c's Length property to determine the length of the array. Note that the Length property of an array cannot be changed, because it does not provide a set accessor. The array's 12 elements are referred to as c[0], c[1], c[2], ..., c[11]. It is an error to refer to elements outside of this range, such as c[-1] or c[12]. The value of c[0] is -45, the value of c[1] is 6, the value of c[2] is 0, the value of c[7] is 62 and the value of c[11] is 78. To calculate the sum of the values

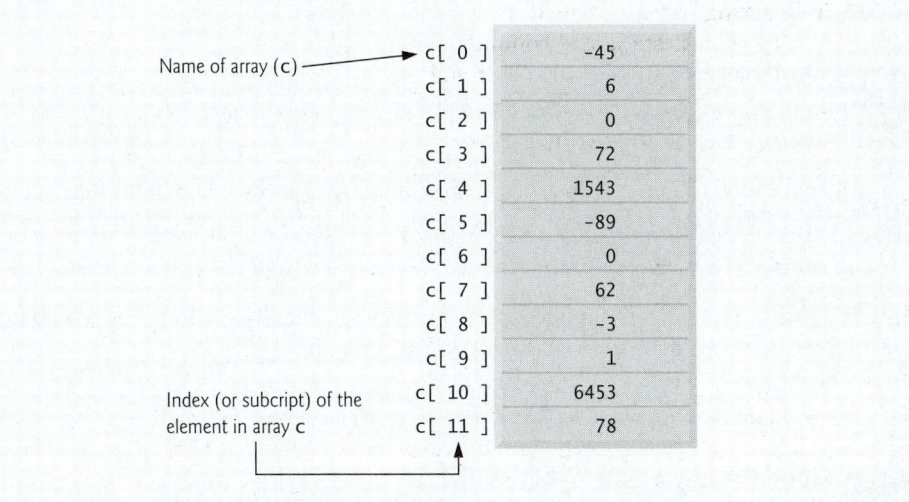

Fig. 8.1 | A 12-element array.

contained in the first three elements of array c and store the result in variable sum, we would write

```
sum = c[ 0 ] + c[ 1 ] + c[ 2 ];
```

To divide the value of c[6] by 2 and assign the result to the variable x, we would write

```
x = c[ 6 ] / 2;
```

8.3 Declaring and Creating Arrays

Array instances occupy space in memory. Like objects, arrays are created with keyword new. To create an array instance, you specify the type and the number of array elements and the number of elements as part of an *array-creation expression* that uses keyword new. Such an expression returns a reference that can be stored in an array variable. The following declaration and array-creation expression create an array object containing 12 int elements and store the array's reference in variable c:

```
int[] c = new int[ 12 ];
```

This expression can be used to create the array shown in Fig. 8.1 (but not the initial values in the array—we'll show how to initialize the elements of an array momentarily). This task also can be performed in two steps as follows:

```
int[] c; // declare the array variable
c = new int[ 12 ]; // create the array; assign to array variable
```

In the declaration, the square brackets following the variable type int indicate that c is a variable that will refer to an array of ints (i.e., c will store a reference to an array object). In the assignment statement, the array variable c receives the reference to a new array object of 12 int elements. When an array is created, each element of the array receives a default value—0 for the numeric simple-type elements, false for bool elements and null for references. As we will soon see, we can provide specific, nondefault initial element values when we create an array.

Common Programming Error 8.1

In an array declaration, specifying the number of elements in the square brackets of the declaration (e.g., int[12] c;) is a syntax error.

An application can create several arrays in a single declaration. The following declaration reserves 100 elements for string array b and 27 elements for string array x:

```
string[] b = new string[ 100 ], x = new string[ 27 ];
```

In this declaration, string[] applies to each variable in the declaration. For readability, we prefer to declare only one variable per declaration, as in:

```
string[] b = new string[ 100 ]; // create string array b
string[] x = new string[ 27 ]; // create string array x
```

Good Programming Practice 8.1

For readability, declare only one variable per declaration. Keep each declaration on a separate line and include a comment describing the variable being declared.

An application can declare arrays of value-type elements or reference-type elements. For example, every element of an int array is an int value, and every element of a string array is a reference to a string object.

8.4 Examples Using Arrays

This section presents several examples that demonstrate declaring arrays, creating arrays, initializing arrays and manipulating array elements.

Creating and Initializing an Array

The application of Fig. 8.2 uses keyword new to create an array of 10 int elements that are initially 0 (the default for int variables).

Line 9 declares array—a reference capable of referring to an array of int elements. Line 12 creates the 10-element array object and assigns its reference to variable array. Line 14 outputs the column headings. The first column contains the index (0–9) of each array element, and the second column contains the default value (0) of each array element and has a field width of 8.

```
1   // Fig. 8.2: InitArray.cs
2   // Creating an array.
3   using System;
4
5   public class InitArray
6   {
7      public static void Main( string[] args )
8      {
9         int[] array; // declare array named array
10
11        // create the space for array and initialize to default zeros
12        array = new int[ 10 ]; // 10 int elements
13
14        Console.WriteLine( "{0}{1,8}", "Index", "Value" ); // headings
15
16        // output each array element's value
17        for ( int counter = 0; counter < array.Length; counter++ )
18           Console.WriteLine( "{0,5}{1,8}", counter, array[ counter ] );
19     } // end Main
20  } // end class InitArray
```

```
Index    Value
    0        0
    1        0
    2        0
    3        0
    4        0
    5        0
    6        0
    7        0
    8        0
    9        0
```

Fig. 8.2 | Creating an array.

The for statement in lines 17–18 outputs the index number (represented by counter) and the value (represented by array[counter]) of each array element. Note that the loop control variable counter is initially 0—index values start at 0, so using zero-based counting allows the loop to access every element of the array. The for statement's loop-continuation condition uses the property array.Length (line 17) to obtain the length of the array. In this example, the length of the array is 10, so the loop continues executing as long as the value of control variable counter is less than 10. The highest index value of a 10-element array is 9, so using the less-than operator in the loop-continuation condition guarantees that the loop does not attempt to access an element beyond the end of the array (i.e., during the final iteration of the loop, counter is 9). We will soon see what happens when such an out-of-range index is encountered at execution time.

Using an Array Initializer

An application can create an array and initialize its elements with an *array initializer*, which is a comma-separated list of expressions (called an *initializer list*) enclosed in braces. In this case, the array length is determined by the number of elements in the initializer list. For example, the declaration

```
int[] n = { 10, 20, 30, 40, 50 };
```

creates a five-element array with index values 0, 1, 2, 3 and 4. Element n[0] is initialized to 10, n[1] is initialized to 20 and so on. This declaration does not require new to create the array object. When the compiler encounters an array declaration that includes an initializer list, the compiler counts the number of initializers in the list to determine the size of the array, then sets up the appropriate new operation "behind the scenes."

The application in Fig. 8.3 initializes an integer array with 10 values (line 10) and displays the array in tabular format. The code for displaying the array elements (lines 15–16) is identical to that in Fig. 8.2 (lines 17–18).

```
1   // Fig. 8.3: InitArray.cs
2   // Initializing the elements of an array with an array initializer.
3   using System;
4
5   public class InitArray
6   {
7      public static void Main( string[] args )
8      {
9         // initializer list specifies the value for each element
10        int[] array = { 32, 27, 64, 18, 95, 14, 90, 70, 60, 37 };
11
12        Console.WriteLine( "{0}{1,8}", "Index", "Value" ); // headings
13
14        // output each array element's value
15        for ( int counter = 0; counter < array.Length; counter++ )
16           Console.WriteLine( "{0,5}{1,8}", counter, array[ counter ] );
17      } // end Main
18   } // end class InitArray
```

Fig. 8.3 | Initializing the elements of an array with an array initializer. (Part 1 of 2.)

Index	Value
0	32
1	27
2	64
3	18
4	95
5	14
6	90
7	70
8	60
9	37

Fig. 8.3 | Initializing the elements of an array with an array initializer. (Part 2 of 2.)

Calculating a Value to Store in Each Array Element

Some applications calculate the value to be stored in each array element. The application in Fig. 8.4 creates a 10-element array and assigns to each element one of the even integers from 2 to 20 (2, 4, 6, ..., 20). Then the application displays the array in tabular format. The for statement at lines 13–14 calculates an array element's value by multiplying the current value of the for loop's control variable counter by 2, then adding 2.

Line 9 uses the modifier const to declare the constant ARRAY_LENGTH, whose value is 10. Constants must be initialized when they are declared and cannot be modified thereafter. Note that constants, like the enum constants introduced in Section 7.10, are declared with all capital letters by convention, to make them stand out in the code.

 Good Programming Practice 8.2

*Constants also are called **named constants**. Such variables often make applications more readable than applications that use literal values (e.g., 10)—a named constant such as ARRAY_LENGTH clearly indicates its purpose, whereas a literal value could have different meanings based on the context in which it is used. Another advantage to using named constants is that if the value of the constant must be changed, it is necessary to change it only in the declaration, thus reducing the cost of maintaining the code.*

```
 1  // Fig. 8.4: InitArray.cs
 2  // Calculating values to be placed into the elements of an array.
 3  using System;
 4
 5  public class InitArray
 6  {
 7     public static void Main( string[] args )
 8     {
 9        const int ARRAY_LENGTH = 10; // create a named constant
10        int[] array = new int[ ARRAY_LENGTH ]; // create array
11
12        // calculate value for each array element
13        for ( int counter = 0; counter < array.Length; counter++ )
14           array[ counter ] = 2 + 2 * counter;
15
```

Fig. 8.4 | Calculating values to be placed into the elements of an array. (Part 1 of 2.)

```
16            Console.WriteLine( "{0}{1,8}", "Index", "Value" ); // headings
17
18            // output each array element's value
19            for ( int counter = 0; counter < array.Length; counter++ )
20                Console.WriteLine( "{0,5}{1,8}", counter, array[ counter ] );
21        } // end Main
22  } // end class InitArray
```

```
Index    Value
    0        2
    1        4
    2        6
    3        8
    4       10
    5       12
    6       14
    7       16
    8       18
    9       20
```

Fig. 8.4 | Calculating values to be placed into the elements of an array. (Part 2 of 2.)

Common Programming Error 8.2

Assigning a value to a named constant after it has been initialized is a compilation error.

Common Programming Error 8.3

Attempting to declare a named constant without initializing it is a compilation error.

Summing the Elements of an Array

Often, the elements of an array represent a series of values to be used in a calculation. For example, if the elements of an array represent exam grades, an instructor may wish to total the elements of the array and use that total to calculate the class average for the exam. The GradeBook examples later in the chapter (Fig. 8.15 and Fig. 8.20) use this technique.

The application in Fig. 8.5 sums the values contained in a 10-element integer array. The application declares, creates and initializes the array at line 9. The for statement performs the calculations. [*Note:* The values supplied as array initializers are often read into an application, rather than specified in an initializer list. For example, an application could input the values from a user or from a file on disk (as discussed in Chapter 18, Files and Streams). Reading the data into an application makes the application more reusable, because it can be used with different sets of data.]

Using Bar Charts to Display Array Data Graphically

Many applications present data to users in a graphical manner. For example, numeric values are often displayed as bars in a bar chart. In such a chart, longer bars represent proportionally larger numeric values. One simple way to display numeric data graphically is with a bar chart that shows each numeric value as a bar of asterisks (*).

```
1   // Fig. 8.5: SumArray.cs
2   // Computing the sum of the elements of an array.
3   using System;
4
5   public class SumArray
6   {
7      public static void Main( string[] args )
8      {
9         int[] array = { 87, 68, 94, 100, 83, 78, 85, 91, 76, 87 };
10        int total = 0;
11
12        // add each element's value to total
13        for ( int counter = 0; counter < array.Length; counter++ )
14           total += array[ counter ];
15
16        Console.WriteLine( "Total of array elements: {0}", total );
17     } // end Main
18  } // end class SumArray
```

```
Total of array elements: 849
```

Fig. 8.5 | Computing the sum of the elements of an array.

Instructors often like to examine the distribution of grades on an exam. An instructor might graph the number of grades in each of several categories to visualize the grade distribution for the exam. Suppose the grades on an exam were 87, 68, 94, 100, 83, 78, 85, 91, 76 and 87. Note that there was one grade of 100, two grades in the 90s, four grades in the 80s, two grades in the 70s, one grade in the 60s and no grades below 60. Our next application (Fig. 8.6) stores this grade distribution data in an array of 11 elements, each corresponding to a category of grades. For example, array[0] indicates the number of grades in the range 0–9, array[7] indicates the number of grades in the range 70–79 and array[10] indicates the number of 100 grades. The two versions of class GradeBook later in the chapter (Fig. 8.15 and Fig. 8.20) contain code that calculates these grade frequencies based on a set of grades. For now, we manually create array by examining the set of grades and initializing the elements of array to the number of values in each range (line 9).

The application reads the numbers from the array and graphs the information as a bar chart. Each grade range is followed by a bar of asterisks indicating the number of grades in that range. To label each bar, lines 17–21 output a grade range (e.g., "70-79: ") based on the current value of counter. When counter is 10, line 18 outputs "   100:   " to align the colon with the other bar labels. When counter is not 10, line 20 uses the format items {0:D2} and {1:D2} to output the label of the grade range. The format specifier D indicates that the value should be formatted as an integer, and the number after the D indicates how many digits this formatted integer must contain. The 2 indicates that values with fewer than two digits should begin with a leading 0.

The nested for statement (lines 24–25) outputs the bars. Note the loop-continuation condition at line 24 (stars < array[counter]). Each time the application reaches the inner for, the loop counts from 0 up to one less than array[counter], thus using a value in array to determine the number of asterisks to display. In this example,

```csharp
1    // Fig. 8.6: BarChart.cs
2    // Bar chart printing application.
3    using System;
4
5    public class BarChart
6    {
7       public static void Main( string[] args )
8       {
9          int[] array = { 0, 0, 0, 0, 0, 0, 1, 2, 4, 2, 1 };
10
11         Console.WriteLine( "Grade distribution:" );
12
13         // for each array element, output a bar of the chart
14         for ( int counter = 0; counter < array.Length; counter++ )
15         {
16            // output bar labels ( "00-09: ", ..., "90-99: ", "100: " )
17            if ( counter == 10 )
18               Console.Write( "  100: " );
19            else
20               Console.Write( "{0:D2}-{1:D2}: ",
21                  counter * 10, counter * 10 + 9 );
22
23            // print bar of asterisks
24            for ( int stars = 0; stars < array[ counter ]; stars++ )
25               Console.Write( "*" );
26
27            Console.WriteLine(); // start a new line of output
28         } // end outer for
29      } // end Main
30   } // end class BarChart
```

```
Grade distribution:
00-09:
10-19:
20-29:
30-39:
40-49:
50-59:
60-69: *
70-79: **
80-89: ****
90-99: **
  100: *
```

Fig. 8.6 | Bar chart printing application.

array[0]–array[5] contain 0s because no students received a grade below 60. Thus, the application displays no asterisks next to the first six grade ranges.

Using the Elements of an Array as Counters

Sometimes, applications use counter variables to summarize data, such as the results of a survey. In Fig. 7.8, we used separate counters in our die-rolling application to track the number of times each face of a six-sided die appeared as the application rolled the die 6000 times. An array version of the application in Fig. 7.8 is shown in Fig. 8.7.

```
1   // Fig. 8.7: RollDie.cs
2   // Roll a six-sided die 6000 times.
3   using System;
4
5   public class RollDie
6   {
7      public static void Main( string[] args )
8      {
9         Random randomNumbers = new Random(); // random number generator
10        int[] frequency = new int[ 7 ]; // array of frequency counters
11
12        // roll die 6000 times; use die value as frequency index
13        for ( int roll = 1; roll <= 6000; roll++ )
14           ++frequency[ randomNumbers.Next( 1, 7 ) ];
15
16        Console.WriteLine( "{0}{1,10}", "Face", "Frequency" );
17
18        // output each array element's value
19        for ( int face = 1; face < frequency.Length; face++ )
20           Console.WriteLine( "{0,4}{1,10}", face, frequency[ face ] );
21     } // end Main
22  } // end class RollDie
```

```
Face Frequency
   1       956
   2       981
   3      1001
   4      1030
   5      1035
   6       997
```

Fig. 8.7 | Roll a six-sided die 6000 times.

Fig. 8.7 uses array frequency (line 10) to count the occurrences of each side of the die. *The single statement in line 14 of this application replaces lines 23–46 of Fig. 7.8.* Line 14 uses the random value to determine which frequency element to increment during each iteration of the loop. The calculation in line 14 produces random numbers from 1 to 6, so array frequency must be large enough to store six counters. We use a seven-element array in which we ignore frequency[0]—it is more logical to have the face value 1 increment frequency[1] than frequency[0]. Thus, each face value is used as an index for array frequency. We also replaced lines 50–52 of Fig. 7.8 by looping through array frequency to output the results (Fig. 8.7, lines 19–20).

Using Arrays to Analyze Survey Results

Our next example uses arrays to summarize the results of data collected in a survey:

> *Forty students were asked to rate the quality of the food in the student cafeteria on a scale of 1 to 10 (where 1 means awful and 10 means excellent). Place the 40 responses in an integer array and summarize the results of the poll.*

This is a typical array-processing application (see Fig. 8.8). We wish to summarize the number of responses of each type (i.e., 1 through 10). The array responses (lines 10–12) is a 40-element int array of the students' responses to the survey. We use 11-element array

```
1   // Fig. 8.8: StudentPoll.cs
2   // Poll analysis application.
3   using System;
4
5   public class StudentPoll
6   {
7      public static void Main( string[] args )
8      {
9         // array of survey responses
10        int[] responses = { 1, 2, 6, 4, 8, 5, 9, 7, 8, 10, 1, 6, 3, 8, 6,
11           10, 3, 8, 2, 7, 6, 5, 7, 6, 8, 6, 7, 5, 6, 6, 5, 6, 7, 5, 6,
12           4, 8, 6, 8, 10 };
13        int[] frequency = new int[ 11 ]; // array of frequency counters
14
15        // for each answer, select responses element and use that value
16        // as frequency index to determine element to increment
17        for ( int answer = 0; answer < responses.Length; answer++ )
18           ++frequency[ responses[ answer ] ];
19
20        Console.WriteLine( "{0}{1,10}", "Rating", "Frequency" );
21
22        // output each array element's value
23        for ( int rating = 1; rating < frequency.Length; rating++ )
24           Console.WriteLine( "{0,6}{1,10}", rating, frequency[ rating ] );
25     } // end Main
26  } // end class StudentPoll
```

```
Rating Frequency
    1         2
    2         2
    3         2
    4         2
    5         5
    6        11
    7         5
    8         7
    9         1
   10         3
```

Fig. 8.8 | Poll analysis application.

frequency (line 13) to count the number of occurrences of each response. Each element of the array is used as a counter for one of the survey responses and is initialized to 0 by default. As in Fig. 8.7, we ignore frequency[0].

The for loop at lines 17–18 takes the responses one at a time from array responses and increments one of the 10 counters in the frequency array (frequency[1] to frequency[10]). The key statement in the loop is line 18, which increments the appropriate frequency counter, depending on the value of responses[answer].

Let's consider several iterations of the for loop. When control variable answer is 0, the value of responses[answer] is the value of responses[0] (i.e., 1 in line 10), so the application interprets ++frequency[responses[answer]] as

    ++frequency[1]

which increments the value in frequency array element 1. To evaluate the expression, start with the value in the innermost set of square brackets, answer. Once you know answer's value (which is the value of the loop control variable in line 17), plug it into the expression and evaluate the next outer set of square brackets—i.e., responses[answer], which is a value selected from the responses array in lines 10–12. Then use the resulting value as the index for the frequency array to specify which counter to increment (line 18).

When answer is 1, responses[answer] is the value of responses[1], which is 2, so the application interprets ++frequency[responses[answer]] as

```
++frequency[ 2 ]
```

which increments the frequency array element 2.

When answer is 2, responses[answer] is the value of responses[2], which is 6, so the application interprets ++frequency[responses[answer]] as

```
++frequency[ 6 ]
```

which increments frequency array element 6, and so on. Regardless of the number of responses processed in the survey, the application requires only an 11-element array (in which we ignore element 0) to summarize the results, because all the response values are between 1 and 10, inclusive, and the index values for an 11-element array are 0 through 10.

If the data in the responses array had contained invalid values, such as 13, the application would have attempted to add 1 to frequency[13], which is outside the bounds of the array. In many programming languages, like C and C++, writing outside the bounds of an array is actually allowed and would overwrite arbitrary information in memory, often causing disastrous results. C# does not allow this—accessing any array element forces a check on the array index to ensure that it is valid (i.e., it must be greater than or equal to 0 and less than the length of the array). This is called ***bounds checking***. If an application uses an invalid index, the Common Language Runtime generates an exception (specifically, an ***IndexOutOfRangeException***) to indicate that an error occurred in the application at execution time. The condition in a control statement could determine whether an index is valid before allowing it to be used in an *array-access expression*, thus avoiding the exception.

Error-Prevention Tip 8.1

An exception indicates that an error has occurred in an application. You often can write code to recover from an exception and continue application execution, rather than abnormally terminating the application. Exception handling is discussed in Chapter 12.

Error-Prevention Tip 8.2

When writing code to loop through an array, ensure that the array index remains greater than or equal to 0 and less than the length of the array. The loop-continuation condition should prevent the accessing of elements outside this range.

8.5 Case Study: Card Shuffling and Dealing Simulation

The examples in the chapter thus far have used arrays containing value-type elements. This section uses random-number generation and an array of reference-type elements—namely, objects representing playing cards—to develop a class that simulates card shuffling and dealing. This class can then be used to implement applications that play card games. The exercises at the end of the chapter use the techniques developed here to build a poker application.

We first develop class Card (Fig. 8.9), which represents a playing card that has a face (e.g., "Ace", "Deuce", "Three", ..., "Jack", "Queen", "King") and a suit (e.g., "Hearts", "Diamonds", "Clubs", "Spades"). Next, we develop the DeckOfCards class (Fig. 8.10), which creates a deck of 52 playing cards in which each element is a Card object. Then we build a test application (Fig. 8.11) that demonstrates class DeckOfCards's card shuffling and dealing capabilities.

Class Card

Class Card (Fig. 8.9) contains two string instance variables—face and suit—that are used to store references to the face value and suit name for a specific Card. The constructor for the class (lines 9–13) receives two strings that it uses to initialize face and suit. Method ToString (lines 16–19) creates a string consisting of the face of the card, the string " of " and the suit of the card. Recall from Chapter 7 that the + operator can be used to concatenate (i.e., combine) several strings to form one larger string. Card's ToString method can be invoked explicitly to obtain a string representation of a Card object (e.g., "Ace of Spades"). The ToString method of an object is called implicitly in many cases when the object is used where a string is expected (e.g., when WriteLine outputs the object with a format item or when the object is concatenated to a string using the + operator). For this behavior to occur, ToString must be declared with the header exactly as shown in line 16 of Fig. 8.9. We will explain the purpose of the override keyword in more detail when we discuss inheritance in Chapter 10.

Class DeckOfCards

Class DeckOfCards (Fig. 8.10) declares an instance-variable array named deck that contains Card objects (line 7). Like simple-type array declarations, the declaration of an array of objects includes the type of the elements in the array, followed by square brackets and the name

```
1    // Fig. 8.9: Card.cs
2    // Card class represents a playing card.
3    public class Card
4    {
5       private string face; // face of card ("Ace", "Deuce", ...)
6       private string suit; // suit of card ("Hearts", "Diamonds", ...)
7
8       // two-parameter constructor initializes card's face and suit
9       public Card( string cardFace, string cardSuit )
10      {
11         face = cardFace; // initialize face of card
12         suit = cardSuit; // initialize suit of card
13      } // end two-parameter Card constructor
14
15      // return string representation of Card
16      public override string ToString()
17      {
18         return face + " of " + suit;
19      } // end method ToString
20   } // end class Card
```

Fig. 8.9 | Card class represents a playing card.

of the array variable (e.g., Card[] deck). Class DeckOfCards also declares int instance variable currentCard (line 8), representing the next Card to be dealt from the deck array, and named constant NUMBER_OF_CARDS (line 9), indicating the number of Cards in the deck (52).

The class's constructor instantiates the deck array (line 19) to be of size NUMBER_OF_CARDS. When first created, the elements of the deck array are null by default, so the constructor uses a for statement (lines 24–26) to fill the deck array with Cards. The for statement initializes control variable count to 0 and loops while count is less than deck.Length, causing count to take on each integer value from 0 to 51 (the indices of the deck array). Each Card is instantiated and initialized with two strings—one from the faces array (which contains the strings "Ace" through "King") and one from the suits array (which contains the strings "Hearts", "Diamonds", "Clubs" and "Spades"). The calculation count % 13 always results in a value from 0 to 12 (the 13 indices of the faces array in lines 15–16), and the calculation count / 13 always results in a value from 0 to 3 (the four indices of the suits array in line 17). When the deck array is initialized, it contains the Cards with faces "Ace" through "King" in order for each suit.

```
1    // Fig. 8.10: DeckOfCards.cs
2    // DeckOfCards class represents a deck of playing cards.
3    using System;
4
5    public class DeckOfCards
6    {
7       private Card[] deck; // array of Card objects
8       private int currentCard; // index of next Card to be dealt
9       private const int NUMBER_OF_CARDS = 52; // constant number of Cards
10      private Random randomNumbers; // random number generator
11
12      // constructor fills deck of Cards
13      public DeckOfCards()
14      {
15         string[] faces = { "Ace", "Deuce", "Three", "Four", "Five", "Six",
16            "Seven", "Eight", "Nine", "Ten", "Jack", "Queen", "King" };
17         string[] suits = { "Hearts", "Diamonds", "Clubs", "Spades" };
18
19         deck = new Card[ NUMBER_OF_CARDS ]; // create array of Card objects
20         currentCard = 0; // set currentCard so first Card dealt is deck[ 0 ]
21         randomNumbers = new Random(); // create random number generator
22
23         // populate deck with Card objects
24         for ( int count = 0; count < deck.Length; count++ )
25            deck[ count ] =
26               new Card( faces[ count % 13 ], suits[ count / 13 ] );
27      } // end DeckOfCards constructor
28
29      // shuffle deck of Cards with one-pass algorithm
30      public void Shuffle()
31      {
32         // after shuffling, dealing should start at deck[ 0 ] again
33         currentCard = 0; // reinitialize currentCard
34
```

Fig. 8.10 | DeckOfCards class represents a deck of playing cards. (Part 1 of 2.)

```
35          // for each Card, pick another random Card and swap them
36          for ( int first = 0; first < deck.Length; first++ )
37          {
38              // select a random number between 0 and 51
39              int second = randomNumbers.Next( NUMBER_OF_CARDS );
40
41              // swap current Card with randomly selected Card
42              Card temp = deck[ first ];
43              deck[ first ] = deck[ second ];
44              deck[ second ] = temp;
45          } // end for
46      } // end method Shuffle
47
48      // deal one Card
49      public Card DealCard()
50      {
51          // determine whether Cards remain to be dealt
52          if ( currentCard < deck.Length )
53              return deck[ currentCard++ ]; // return current Card in array
54          else
55              return null; // return null to indicate that all Cards were dealt
56      } // end method DealCard
57  } // end class DeckOfCards
```

Fig. 8.10 | DeckOfCards class represents a deck of playing cards. (Part 2 of 2.)

Method Shuffle (lines 30–46) shuffles the Cards in the deck. The method loops through all 52 Cards (array indices 0 to 51). For each Card, a number between 0 and 51 is picked randomly to select another Card. Next, the current Card object and the randomly selected Card object are swapped in the array. This exchange is performed by the three assignments in lines 42–44. The extra variable temp temporarily stores one of the two Card objects being swapped. The swap cannot be performed with only the two statements

```
deck[ first ] = deck[ second ];
deck[ second ] = deck[ first ];
```

If deck[first] is the "Ace" of "Spades" and deck[second] is the "Queen" of "Hearts", then after the first assignment, both array elements contain the "Queen" of "Hearts" and the "Ace" of "Spades" is lost—hence, the extra variable temp is needed. After the for loop terminates, the Card objects are randomly ordered. Only 52 swaps are made in a single pass of the entire array, and the array of Card objects is shuffled.

Method DealCard (lines 49–56) deals one Card in the array. Recall that currentCard indicates the index of the next Card to be dealt (i.e., the Card at the top of the deck). Thus, line 52 compares currentCard to the length of the deck array. If the deck is not empty (i.e., currentCard is less than 52), line 53 returns the top Card and increments current-Card to prepare for the next call to DealCard—otherwise, null is returned.

Shuffling and Dealing Cards

The application of Fig. 8.11 demonstrates the card dealing and shuffling capabilities of class DeckOfCards (Fig. 8.10). Line 10 creates a DeckOfCards object named myDeckOf-Cards. Recall that the DeckOfCards constructor creates the deck with the 52 Card objects

```
1   // Fig. 8.11: DeckOfCardsTest.cs
2   // Card shuffling and dealing application.
3   using System;
4
5   public class DeckOfCardsTest
6   {
7      // execute application
8      public static void Main( string[] args )
9      {
10        DeckOfCards myDeckOfCards = new DeckOfCards();
11        myDeckOfCards.Shuffle(); // place Cards in random order
12
13        // print all 52 Cards in the order in which they are dealt
14        for ( int i = 0; i < 13; i++ )
15        {
16           // deal and print 4 Cards
17           Console.WriteLine( "{0,-20}{1,-20}{2,-20}{3,-20}",
18              myDeckOfCards.DealCard(), myDeckOfCards.DealCard(),
19              myDeckOfCards.DealCard(), myDeckOfCards.DealCard() );
20        } // end for
21     } // end Main
22  } // end class DeckOfCardsTest
```

Ten of Hearts	Ace of Diamonds	Jack of Spades	Queen of Diamonds
Six of Clubs	Seven of Hearts	Deuce of Spades	Seven of Diamonds
Queen of Spades	King of Hearts	Nine of Hearts	Deuce of Clubs
Eight of Clubs	Five of Diamonds	Three of Hearts	Five of Hearts
Three of Spades	Four of Diamonds	Six of Hearts	Nine of Diamonds
Queen of Clubs	Deuce of Diamonds	Queen of Hearts	Four of Clubs
Seven of Spades	Four of Hearts	Three of Diamonds	Seven of Clubs
Ten of Clubs	Ten of Spades	Jack of Diamonds	Jack of Clubs
Nine of Clubs	Six of Diamonds	Eight of Hearts	Eight of Spades
King of Spades	Three of Clubs	King of Diamonds	Six of Spades
Jack of Hearts	Ace of Clubs	Five of Spades	Nine of Spades
Deuce of Hearts	Five of Clubs	Ten of Diamonds	Ace of Hearts
Ace of Spades	Four of Spades	Eight of Diamonds	King of Clubs

Fig. 8.11 | Card shuffling and dealing application.

in order by suit and face. Line 11 invokes myDeckOfCards's Shuffle method to rearrange the Card objects. The for statement in lines 14–20 deals all 52 Cards in the deck and prints them in four columns of 13 Cards each. Lines 17–19 deal and print four Card objects, each obtained by invoking myDeckOfCards's DealCard method. When WriteLine outputs a Card with string formatting, the Card's ToString method (declared in lines 16–19 of Fig. 8.9) is invoked implicitly. Because the field width is negative, the result is output *left* justified in a field of width 20.

8.6 foreach Statement

In previous examples, we demonstrated how to use counter-controlled for statements to iterate through the elements in an array. In this section, we introduce the ***foreach statement***, which iterates through the elements of an entire array or collection. This section discusses how to use the foreach statement to loop through an array. We show how to use the foreach statement with collections in Chapter 27, Collections. The syntax of a foreach statement is:

> **foreach** (*type identifier* **in** *arrayName*)
>   *statement*

where *type* and *identifier* are the type and name (e.g., int number) of the *iteration variable*, and *arrayName* is the array through which to iterate. The type of the iteration variable must match the type of the elements in the array. As the next example illustrates, the iteration variable represents successive values in the array on successive iterations of the foreach statement.

Figure 8.12 uses the foreach statement (lines 13–14) to calculate the sum of the integers in an array of student grades. The type specified is int, because array contains int values—therefore, the loop will select one int value from the array during each iteration. The foreach statement iterates through successive values in the array one-by-one. The foreach header can be read concisely as "for each iteration, assign the next element of array to int variable number, then execute the following statement." Thus, for each iteration, identifier number represents the next int value in the array. Lines 13–14 are equivalent to the following counter-controlled repetition used in lines 13–14 of Fig. 8.5 to total the integers in array:

> **for** (**int** counter = 0; counter < array.Length; counter++)
>   total += array[counter];

The foreach statement simplifies the code for iterating through an array. Note, however, that the foreach statement can be used only to access array elements—it cannot be used to modify elements. Any attempt to change the value of the iteration variable in the body of a foreach statement will cause a compilation error. If your application needs to modify elements, use the for statement.

```csharp
1   // Fig. 8.12: ForEachTest.cs
2   // Using foreach statement to total integers in an array.
3   using System;
4
5   public class ForEachTest
6   {
7      public static void Main( string[] args )
8      {
9         int[] array = { 87, 68, 94, 100, 83, 78, 85, 91, 76, 87 };
10        int total = 0;
11
12        // add each element's value to total
13        foreach ( int number in array )
14           total += number;
15
16        Console.WriteLine( "Total of array elements: {0}", total );
17     } // end Main
18  } // end class ForEachTest
```

```
Total of array elements: 849
```

Fig. 8.12 | Using the foreach statement to total integers in an array.

The foreach statement can be used in place of the for statement whenever code looping through an array does not require access to the counter indicating the index of the current array element. For example, totaling the integers in an array requires access only to the element values—the index of each element is irrelevant. However, if an application must use a counter for some reason other than simply to loop through an array (e.g., to print an index number next to each array element value, as in the examples earlier in this chapter), use the for statement.

8.7 Passing Arrays and Array Elements to Methods

To pass an array argument to a method, specify the name of the array without any brackets. For example, if array hourlyTemperatures is declared as

```
double[] hourlyTemperatures = new double[ 24 ];
```

then the method call

```
ModifyArray( hourlyTemperatures );
```

passes the reference of array hourlyTemperatures to method ModifyArray. Every array object "knows" its own length (and makes it available via its Length property). Thus, when we pass an array object's reference to a method, we need not pass the array length as an additional argument.

For a method to receive an array reference through a method call, the method's parameter list must specify an array parameter. For example, the method header for method ModifyArray might be written as

```
void ModifyArray( double[] b )
```

indicating that ModifyArray receives the reference of an array of doubles in parameter b. The method call passes array hourlyTemperature's reference, so when the called method uses the array variable b, it refers to the same array object as hourlyTemperatures in the calling method.

When an argument to a method is an entire array or an individual array element of a reference type, the called method receives a copy of the reference. However, when an argument to a method is an individual array element of a value type, the called method receives a copy of the element's value. To pass an individual array element to a method, use the indexed name of the array as an argument in the method call. If you want to pass a value-type array element to a method by reference, you must use the ref keyword as shown in Section 7.14, Passing Arguments: Pass-by-Value vs. Pass-by-Reference.

Figure 8.13 demonstrates the difference between passing an entire array and passing a value-type array element to a method. The foreach statement at lines 17–18 outputs the five elements of array (an array of int values). Line 20 invokes method ModifyArray, passing array as an argument. Method ModifyArray (lines 37–41) receives a copy of array's reference and uses the reference to multiply each of array's elements by 2. To prove that array's elements (in Main) were modified, the foreach statement at lines 24–25 outputs the five elements of array again. As the output shows, method ModifyArray doubled the value of each element.

Figure 8.13 next demonstrates that when a copy of an individual value-type array element is passed to a method, modifying the copy in the called method does not affect the

```csharp
1   // Fig. 8.13: PassArray.cs
2   // Passing arrays and individual array elements to methods.
3   using System;
4
5   public class PassArray
6   {
7      // Main creates array and calls ModifyArray and ModifyElement
8      public static void Main( string[] args )
9      {
10         int[] array = { 1, 2, 3, 4, 5 };
11
12         Console.WriteLine(
13            "Effects of passing reference to entire array:\n" +
14            "The values of the original array are:" );
15
16         // output original array elements
17         foreach ( int value in array )
18            Console.Write( "   {0}", value );
19
20         ModifyArray( array ); // pass array reference
21         Console.WriteLine( "\n\nThe values of the modified array are:" );
22
23         // output modified array elements
24         foreach ( int value in array )
25            Console.Write( "   {0}", value );
26
27         Console.WriteLine(
28            "\n\nEffects of passing array element value:\n" +
29            "array[3] before ModifyElement: {0}", array[ 3 ] );
30
31         ModifyElement( array[ 3 ] ); // attempt to modify array[ 3 ]
32         Console.WriteLine(
33            "array[3] after ModifyElement: {0}", array[ 3 ] );
34      } // end Main
35
36      // multiply each element of an array by 2
37      public static void ModifyArray( int[] array2 )
38      {
39         for ( int counter = 0; counter < array2.Length; counter++ )
40            array2[ counter ] *= 2;
41      } // end method ModifyArray
42
43      // multiply argument by 2
44      public static void ModifyElement( int element )
45      {
46         element *= 2;
47         Console.WriteLine(
48            "Value of element in ModifyElement: {0}", element );
49      } // end method ModifyElement
50   } // end class PassArray
```

Fig. 8.13 | Passing arrays and individual array elements to methods. (Part 1 of 2.)

```
Effects of passing reference to entire array:
The values of the original array are:
   1   2   3   4   5

The values of the modified array are:
   2   4   6   8   10

Effects of passing array element value:
array[3] before ModifyElement: 8
Value of element in ModifyElement: 16
array[3] after ModifyElement: 8
```

Fig. 8.13 | Passing arrays and individual array elements to methods. (Part 2 of 2.)

original value of that element in the calling method's array. To show the value of array[3] before invoking method ModifyElement, lines 27–29 output the value of array[3] which is 8. Line 31 calls method ModifyElement and passes array[3] as an argument. Remember that array[3] is actually one int value (8) in array. Therefore, the application passes a copy of the value of array[3]. Method ModifyElement (lines 44–49) multiplies the value received as an argument by 2, stores the result in its parameter element, then outputs the value of element (16). Since method parameters, like local variables, cease to exist when the method in which they are declared completes execution, the method parameter element is destroyed when method ModifyElement terminates. Thus, when the application returns control to Main, lines 32–33 output the unmodified value of array[3] (i.e., 8).

8.8 Passing Arrays by Value and by Reference

In C#, a variable that "stores" an object, such as an array, does not actually store the object itself. Instead, such a variable stores a reference to the object (i.e., the location in the computer's memory where the object itself is stored). The distinction between reference-type variables and value-type variables raises some subtle issues that you must understand to create secure, stable programs.

As you know, when an application passes an argument to a method, the called method receives a copy of that argument's value. Changes to the local copy in the called method do not affect the original variable in the caller. If the argument is of a reference type, the method makes a copy of the reference, not a copy of the actual object that is referenced. The local copy of the reference also refers to the original object in memory, which means that changes to the object in the called method affect the original object in memory.

Performance Tip 8.1

Passing arrays and other objects by reference makes sense for performance reasons. If arrays were passed by value, a copy of each element would be passed. For large, frequently passed arrays, this would waste time and would consume considerable storage for the copies of the arrays—both of these problems cause poor performance.

In Section 7.14, you learned that C# allows variables to be passed by reference with keyword ref. You can also use keyword ref to pass a reference-type variable by reference, which allows the called method to modify the original variable in the caller and make that variable refer to a different object in memory. This is a subtle capability, which if misused, can lead to problems. For instance, when a reference-type object like an array is passed with `ref`, the called method actually gains control over the reference itself, allowing the called method to replace the original reference in the caller with a different object, or even with `null`. Such behavior can lead to unpredictable effects, which can be disastrous in mission-critical applications. The application in Fig. 8.14 demonstrates the subtle difference between passing a reference by value and passing a reference by reference with keyword `ref`.

```csharp
1   // Fig. 8.14: ArrayReferenceTest.cs
2   // Testing the effects of passing array references
3   // by value and by reference.
4   using System;
5
6   public class ArrayReferenceTest
7   {
8      public static void Main( string[] args )
9      {
10        // create and initialize firstArray
11        int[] firstArray = { 1, 2, 3 };
12
13        // copy the reference in variable firstArray
14        int[] firstArrayCopy = firstArray;
15
16        Console.WriteLine(
17           "Test passing firstArray reference by value" );
18
19        Console.Write( "\nContents of firstArray " +
20           "before calling FirstDouble:\n\t" );
21
22        // print contents of firstArray
23        for ( int i = 0; i < firstArray.Length; i++ )
24           Console.Write( "{0} ", firstArray[ i ] );
25
26        // pass variable firstArray by value to FirstDouble
27        FirstDouble( firstArray );
28
29        Console.Write( "\n\nContents of firstArray after " +
30           "calling FirstDouble\n\t" );
31
32        // print contents of firstArray
33        for ( int i = 0; i < firstArray.Length; i++ )
34           Console.Write( "{0} ", firstArray[ i ] );
35
36        // test whether reference was changed by FirstDouble
37        if ( firstArray == firstArrayCopy )
38           Console.WriteLine(
39              "\n\nThe references refer to the same array" );
40        else
41           Console.WriteLine(
42              "\n\nThe references refer to different arrays" );
43
```

Fig. 8.14 | Passing an array reference by value and by reference. (Part 1 of 3.)

```
44          // create and initialize secondArray
45          int[] secondArray = { 1, 2, 3 };
46
47          // copy the reference in variable secondArray
48          int[] secondArrayCopy = secondArray;
49
50          Console.WriteLine( "\nTest passing secondArray " +
51             "reference by reference" );
52
53          Console.Write( "\nContents of secondArray " +
54             "before calling SecondDouble:\n\t" );
55
56          // print contents of secondArray before method call
57          for ( int i = 0; i < secondArray.Length; i++ )
58             Console.Write( "{0} ", secondArray[ i ] );
59
60          // pass variable secondArray by reference to SecondDouble
61          SecondDouble( ref secondArray );
62
63          Console.Write( "\n\nContents of secondArray " +
64             "after calling SecondDouble:\n\t" );
65
66          // print contents of secondArray after method call
67          for ( int i = 0; i < secondArray.Length; i++ )
68             Console.Write( "{0} ", secondArray[ i ] );
69
70          // test whether reference was changed by SecondDouble
71          if ( secondArray == secondArrayCopy )
72             Console.WriteLine(
73                "\n\nThe references refer to the same array" );
74          else
75             Console.WriteLine(
76                "\n\nThe references refer to different arrays" );
77       } // end method Main
78
79       // modify elements of array and attempt to modify reference
80       public static void FirstDouble( int[] array )
81       {
82          // double each element's value
83          for ( int i = 0; i < array.Length; i++ )
84             array[ i ] *= 2;
85
86          // create new object and assign its reference to array
87          array = new int[] { 11, 12, 13 };
88       } // end method FirstDouble
89
90       // modify elements of array and change reference array
91       // to refer to a new array
92       public static void SecondDouble( ref int[] array )
93       {
94          // double each element's value
95          for ( int i = 0; i < array.Length; i++ )
96             array[ i ] *= 2;
```

Fig. 8.14 | Passing an array reference by value and by reference. (Part 2 of 3.)

```
97
98          // create new object and assign its reference to array
99          array = new int[] { 11, 12, 13 };
100    } // end method SecondDouble
101  } // end class ArrayReferenceTest
```

```
Test passing firstArray reference by value

Contents of firstArray before calling FirstDouble:
        1 2 3

Contents of firstArray after calling FirstDouble
        2 4 6

The references refer to the same array

Test passing secondArray reference by reference

Contents of secondArray before calling SecondDouble:
        1 2 3

Contents of secondArray after calling SecondDouble:
        11 12 13

The references refer to different arrays
```

Fig. 8.14 | Passing an array reference by value and by reference. (Part 3 of 3.)

Lines 11 and 14 declare two integer array variables, firstArray and firstArrayCopy. Line 11 initializes firstArray with the values 1, 2 and 3. The assignment statement on line 14 copies the reference stored in firstArray to variable firstArrayCopy, causing these variables to reference the same array object in memory. We make the copy of the reference so that we can determine later whether reference firstArray gets overwritten. The for statement at lines 23–24 prints the contents of firstArray before it is passed to method FirstDouble (line 27) so that we can verify that the array is passed by reference (i.e., the called method indeed changes the array's contents).

The for statement in method FirstDouble (lines 83–84) multiplies the values of all the elements in the array by 2. Line 87 creates a new array containing the values 11, 12 and 13, and assigns the array's reference to parameter array in an attempt to overwrite reference firstArray in the caller—this, of course, does not happen, because the reference was passed by value. After method FirstDouble executes, the for statement at lines 33–34 prints the contents of firstArray, demonstrating that the values of the elements have been changed by the method (and confirming that in C# arrays are always passed by reference). The if...else statement at lines 37–42 uses the == operator to compare references firstArray (which we just attempted to overwrite) and firstArrayCopy. The expression in line 37 evaluates to true if the operands of operator == reference the same object. In this case, the object represented by firstArray is the array created in line 11—not the array created in method FirstDouble (line 87)—so the original reference stored in first-Array was not modified.

Lines 45–76 perform similar tests, using array variables secondArray and second-ArrayCopy, and method SecondDouble (lines 92–100). Method SecondDouble performs the same operations as FirstDouble, but receives its array argument using keyword ref. In this case, the reference stored in secondArray after the method call is a reference to the array created in line 99 of SecondDouble, demonstrating that a variable passed with keyword ref can be modified by the called method so that the variable in the caller actually points to a different object—in this case, an array created in SecondDouble. The if...else statement in lines 71–76 confirms that secondArray and secondArrayCopy no longer refer to the same array.

Software Engineering Observation 8.1

When a method receives a reference-type parameter by value, a copy of the object's reference is passed. This prevents a method from overwriting references passed to that method. In the vast majority of cases, protecting the caller's reference from modification is the desired behavior. If you encounter a situation where you truly want the called procedure to modify the caller's reference, pass the reference-type parameter using keyword ref—but, again, such situations are rare.

Software Engineering Observation 8.2

In C#, objects (including arrays) are passed by reference by default. So, a called method receiving a reference to an object in a caller can change the caller's object.

8.9 Case Study: Class GradeBook Using an Array to Store Grades

This section further evolves class GradeBook, introduced in Chapter 4 and expanded in Chapters 5–6. Recall that this class represents a grade book used by an instructor to store and analyze a set of student grades. Previous versions of the class process a set of grades entered by the user, but do not maintain the individual grade values in instance variables of the class. Thus, repeat calculations require the user to re-enter the same grades. One way to solve this problem would be to store each grade entered in an individual instance of the class. For example, we could create instance variables grade1, grade2, ..., grade10 in class GradeBook to store 10 student grades. However, the code to total the grades and determine the class average would be cumbersome, and the class would not be able to process any more than 10 grades at a time. In this section, we solve this problem by storing grades in an array.

Storing Student Grades in an Array in Class GradeBook

The version of class GradeBook (Fig. 8.15) presented here uses an array of integers to store the grades of several students on a single exam. This eliminates the need to repeatedly input the same set of grades. Array grades is declared as an instance variable in line 8—therefore, each GradeBook object maintains its own set of grades. The class's constructor (lines 11–15) has two parameters—the name of the course and an array of grades. When an application (e.g., class GradeBookTest in Fig. 8.16) creates a GradeBook object, the application passes an existing int array to the constructor, which assigns the array's reference to instance variable grades (line 14). The size of array grades is determined by the class that passes the array to the constructor. Thus, a GradeBook object can process a variable number of grades—as many as are in the array in the caller. The grade values in the passed array could have been input from a user at the keyboard or read from a file on disk (as discussed in Chapter 18). In our test application, we simply initialize an array with a set of grade values (Fig. 8.16, line 9). Once the grades are stored in instance variable grades of class GradeBook, all the class's methods can access the elements of grades as needed to perform various calculations.

```csharp
1   // Fig. 8.15: GradeBook.cs
2   // Grade book using an array to store test grades.
3   using System;
4
5   public class GradeBook
6   {
7      private string courseName; // name of course this GradeBook represents
8      private int[] grades; // array of student grades
9
10     // two-parameter constructor initializes courseName and grades array
11     public GradeBook( string name, int[] gradesArray )
12     {
13        CourseName = name; // initialize courseName
14        grades = gradesArray; // initialize grades array
15     } // end two-parameter GradeBook constructor
16
17     // property that gets and sets the course name
18     public string CourseName
19     {
20        get
21        {
22           return courseName;
23        } // end get
24        set
25        {
26           courseName = value;
27        } // end set
28     } // end property CourseName
29
30     // display a welcome message to the GradeBook user
31     public void DisplayMessage()
32     {
33        // CourseName property gets the name of the course
34        Console.WriteLine( "Welcome to the grade book for\n{0}!\n",
35           CourseName );
36     } // end method DisplayMessage
37
38     // perform various operations on the data
39     public void ProcessGrades()
40     {
41        // output grades array
42        OutputGrades();
43
44        // call method GetAverage to calculate the average grade
45        Console.WriteLine( "\nClass average is {0:F2}", GetAverage() );
46
```

Fig. 8.15 | Grade book using an array to store test grades. (Part 1 of 3.)

```
47          // call methods GetMinimum and GetMaximum
48          Console.WriteLine( "Lowest grade is {0}\nHighest grade is {1}\n",
49             GetMinimum(), GetMaximum() );
50
51          // call OutputBarChart to print grade distribution chart
52          OutputBarChart();
53       } // end method ProcessGrades
54
55       // find minimum grade
56       public int GetMinimum()
57       {
58          int lowGrade = grades[ 0 ]; // assume grades[ 0 ] is smallest
59
60          // loop through grades array
61          foreach ( int grade in grades )
62          {
63             // if grade lower than lowGrade, assign it to lowGrade
64             if ( grade < lowGrade )
65                lowGrade = grade; // new lowest grade
66          } // end for
67
68          return lowGrade; // return lowest grade
69       } // end method GetMinimum
70
71       // find maximum grade
72       public int GetMaximum()
73       {
74          int highGrade = grades[ 0 ]; // assume grades[ 0 ] is largest
75
76          // loop through grades array
77          foreach ( int grade in grades )
78          {
79             // if grade greater than highGrade, assign it to highGrade
80             if ( grade > highGrade )
81                highGrade = grade; // new highest grade
82          } // end for
83
84          return highGrade; // return highest grade
85       } // end method GetMaximum
86
87       // determine average grade for test
88       public double GetAverage()
89       {
90          int total = 0; // initialize total
91
92          // sum grades for one student
93          foreach ( int grade in grades )
94             total += grade;
95
96          // return average of grades
97          return ( double ) total / grades.Length;
98       } // end method GetAverage
99
```

Fig. 8.15 | Grade book using an array to store test grades. (Part 2 of 3.)

```
100    // output bar chart displaying grade distribution
101    public void OutputBarChart()
102    {
103       Console.WriteLine( "Grade distribution:" );
104
105       // stores frequency of grades in each range of 10 grades
106       int[] frequency = new int[ 11 ];
107
108       // for each grade, increment the appropriate frequency
109       foreach ( int grade in grades )
110          ++frequency[ grade / 10 ];
111
112       // for each grade frequency, print bar in chart
113       for ( int count = 0; count < frequency.Length; count++ )
114       {
115          // output bar label ( "00-09: ", ..., "90-99: ", "100: " )
116          if ( count == 10 )
117             Console.Write( "  100: " );
118          else
119             Console.Write( "{0:D2}-{1:D2}: ",
120                count * 10, count * 10 + 9 );
121
122          // print bar of asterisks
123          for ( int stars = 0; stars < frequency[ count ]; stars++ )
124             Console.Write( "*" );
125
126          Console.WriteLine(); // start a new line of output
127       } // end outer for
128    } // end method OutputBarChart
129
130    // output the contents of the grades array
131    public void OutputGrades()
132    {
133       Console.WriteLine( "The grades are:\n" );
134
135       // output each student's grade
136       for ( int student = 0; student < grades.Length; student++ )
137          Console.WriteLine( "Student {0,2}: {1,3}",
138             student + 1, grades[ student ] );
139    } // end method OutputGrades
140 } // end class GradeBook
```

Fig. 8.15 | Grade book using an array to store test grades. (Part 3 of 3.)

Method ProcessGrades (lines 39–53) contains a series of method calls that result in the output of a report summarizing the grades. Line 42 calls method OutputGrades to print the contents of array grades. Lines 136–138 in method OutputGrades use a for statement to output the student grades. A for statement, rather than a foreach, must be used in this case, because lines 137–138 use counter variable student's value to output each grade next to a particular student number (see Fig. 8.16). Although array indices start at 0, an instructor would typically number students starting at 1. Thus, lines 137–138 output student + 1 as the student number to produce grade labels "Student 1: ", "Student 2: " and so on.

Method ProcessGrades next calls method GetAverage (line 45) to obtain the average of the grades in the array. Method GetAverage (lines 88–98) uses a foreach statement to total the values in array grades before calculating the average. The iteration variable in the foreach's header (e.g., int grade) indicates that for each iteration, int variable grade takes on a value in array grades. Note that the averaging calculation in line 97 uses grades.Length to determine the number of grades being averaged.

Lines 48–49 in method ProcessGrades call methods GetMinimum and GetMaximum to determine the lowest and highest grades of any student on the exam, respectively. Each of these methods uses a foreach statement to loop through array grades. Lines 61–66 in method GetMinimum loop through the array, and lines 64–65 compare each grade to low-Grade. If a grade is less than lowGrade, lowGrade is set to that grade. When line 68 executes, lowGrade contains the lowest grade in the array. Method GetMaximum (lines 72–85) works the same way as method GetMinimum.

Finally, line 52 in method ProcessGrades calls method OutputBarChart to print a distribution chart of the grade data using a technique similar to that in Fig. 8.6. In that example, we manually calculated the number of grades in each category (i.e., 0–9, 10–19, ..., 90–99 and 100) by simply looking at a set of grades. In this example, lines 109–110 use a technique similar to that in Fig. 8.7 and Fig. 8.8 to calculate the frequency of grades in each category. Line 106 declares and creates array frequency of 11 ints to store the frequency of grades in each grade category. For each grade in array grades, lines 109–110 increment the appropriate element of the frequency array. To determine which element to increment, line 110 divides the current grade by 10 using integer division. For example, if grade is 85, line 110 increments frequency[8] to update the count of grades in the range 80–89. Lines 113–127 next print the bar chart (see Fig. 8.6) based on the values in array frequency. Like lines 24–25 of Fig. 8.6, lines 123–124 of Fig. 8.15 use a value in array frequency to determine the number of asterisks to display in each bar.

Class GradeBookTest That Demonstrates Class GradeBook

The application of Fig. 8.16 creates an object of class GradeBook (Fig. 8.15) using int array gradesArray (declared and initialized in line 9). Lines 11–12 pass a course name and gradesArray to the GradeBook constructor. Line 13 displays a welcome message, and line 14 invokes the GradeBook object's ProcessGrades method. The output reveals the summary of the 10 grades in myGradeBook.

Software Engineering Observation 8.3

*A **test harness** (or test application) is responsible for creating an object of the class being tested and providing it with data. This data could come from any of several sources. Test data can be placed directly into an array with an array initializer, it can come from the user at the keyboard, it can come from a file (as you will see in Chapter 18) or it can come from a network (as you will see in Chapter 23). After passing this data to the class's constructor to instantiate the object, the test harness should call the object to test its methods and manipulate its data. Gathering data in the test harness like this allows the class to manipulate data from several sources.*

8.10 Multidimensional Arrays

Multidimensional arrays with two dimensions are often used to represent *tables of values* consisting of information arranged in *rows* and *columns*. To identify a particular table element, we must specify two indices. By convention, the first identifies the element's row

```
 1    // Fig. 8.16: GradeBookTest.cs
 2    // Create GradeBook object using an array of grades.
 3    public class GradeBookTest
 4    {
 5       // Main method begins application execution
 6       public static void Main( string[] args )
 7       {
 8          // one-dimensional array of student grades
 9          int[] gradesArray = { 87, 68, 94, 100, 83, 78, 85, 91, 76, 87 };
10
11          GradeBook myGradeBook = new GradeBook(
12             "CS101 Introduction to C# Programming", gradesArray );
13          myGradeBook.DisplayMessage();
14          myGradeBook.ProcessGrades();
15       } // end Main
16    } // end class GradeBookTest
```

```
Welcome to the grade book for
CS101 Introduction to C# Programming!

The grades are:

Student  1:   87
Student  2:   68
Student  3:   94
Student  4:  100
Student  5:   83
Student  6:   78
Student  7:   85
Student  8:   91
Student  9:   76
Student 10:   87

Class average is 84.90
Lowest grade is 68
Highest grade is 100

Grade distribution:
00-09:
10-19:
20-29:
30-39:
40-49:
50-59:
60-69: *
70-79: **
80-89: ****
90-99: **
  100: *
```

Fig. 8.16 | Create a GradeBook object using an array of grades.

and the second its column. Arrays that require two indices to identify a particular element are called *two-dimensional arrays*. (Multidimensional arrays can have more than two dimensions, but arrays with more than two dimensions are beyond the scope of this book.) C# supports two types of two-dimensional arrays—*rectangular arrays* and *jagged arrays*.

Rectangular Arrays

Rectangular arrays are used to represent tables of information in the form of rows and columns, where each row has the same number of columns. Figure 8.17 illustrates a rectangular array named a containing three rows and four column—a three-by-four array. In general, an array with *m* rows and *n* columns is called an ***m-by-n array***.

Every element in array a is identified in Fig. 8.17 by an array-access expression of the form a[*row*, *column*]; a is the name of the array, and *row* and *column* are the indices that uniquely identify each element in array a by row and column number. Note that the names of the elements in row 0 all have a first index of 0, and the names of the elements in column 3 all have a second index of 3.

Like one-dimensional arrays, multidimensional arrays can be initialized with array initializers in declarations. A rectangular array b with two rows and two columns could be declared and initialized with ***nested array initializers*** as follows:

```
int[ , ] b = { { 1, 2 }, { 3, 4 } };
```

The initializer values are grouped by row in braces. So 1 and 2 initialize b[0, 0] and b[0, 1], respectively, and 3 and 4 initialize b[1, 0] and b[1, 1], respectively. The compiler counts the number of nested array initializers (represented by sets of two inner braces within the outer braces) in the array declaration to determine the number of rows in array b. The compiler counts the initializer values in the nested array initializer for a row to determine the number of columns (two) in that row. The compiler will generate an error if the number of initializers in each row is not the same, because every row of a rectangular array must have the same length.

Jagged Arrays

A *jagged array* is maintained as a one-dimensional array in which each element refers to a one-dimensional array. The manner in which jagged arrays are represented makes them quite flexible, because the lengths of the rows in the array need not be the same. For example, jagged arrays could be used to store a single student's exam grades across multiple classes, where the number of exams may vary from class to class.

We can access the elements in a jagged array by an array-access expression of the form *arrayName*[*row*][*column*]—similar to the array-access expression for rectangular

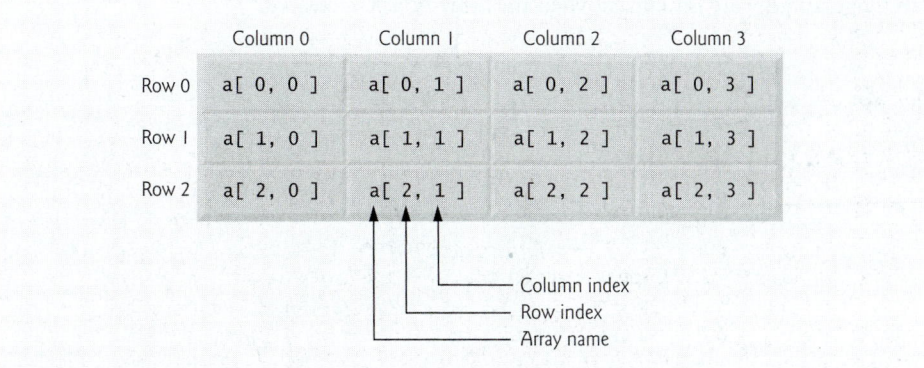

Fig. 8.17 | Rectangular array with three rows and four columns.

arrays, but with a separate set of square brackets for each dimension. A jagged array with three rows of different lengths could be declared and initialized as follows:

```
int[][] jagged = { new int[] { 1, 2 },
                   new int[] { 3 },
                   new int[] { 4, 5, 6 } };
```

In this statement, 1 and 2 initialize jagged[0][0] and jagged[0][1], respectively; 3 initializes jagged[1][0]; and 4, 5 and 6 initialize jagged[2][0], jagged[2][1] and jagged[2][2], respectively. Therefore, array jagged in the preceding declaration is actually composed of four separate one-dimensional arrays—one that represents the rows, one containing the values in the first row ({ 1, 2 }), one containing the value in the second row ({ 3 }) and one containing the values in the third row ({ 4, 5, 6 }). Thus, array jagged itself is an array of three elements, each reference to a one-dimensional array of int values.

Observe the differences between the array-creation expressions for rectangular arrays and jagged arrays. Two sets of square brackets follow the type of jagged, indicating that this is an array of int arrays. Furthermore, in the array initializer, C# requires the keyword new to create an array object for each row. Figure 8.18 illustrates the array reference jagged after it has been declared and initialized.

Creating Two-Dimensional Arrays with Array-Creation Expressions

A rectangular array can be created with an array-creation expression. For example, the following lines declare array b and assign it a reference to a three-by-four rectangular array:

```
int[ , ] b;
b = new int[ 3, 4 ];
```

In this case, we use the literal values 3 and 4 to specify the number of rows and number of columns, respectively, but this is not required—applications can also use variables and expressions to specify array dimensions. As with one-dimensional arrays, the elements of a rectangular array are initialized when the array object is created.

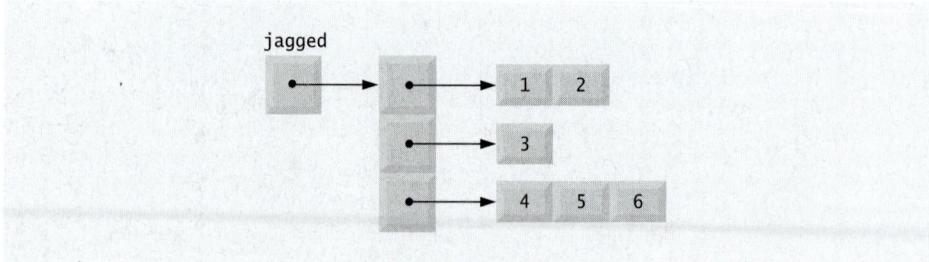

Fig. 8.18 | Jagged array with three rows of different lengths.

A jagged array cannot be completely created with a single array creation expression. The following statement is a syntax error:

```
int[][] c = new int[ 2 ][ 5 ]; // error
```

Instead, each one-dimensional array in the jagged array must be initialized separately. A jagged array can be created as follows:

```
int[][] c;
c = new int[ 2 ][ ]; // create 2 rows
c[ 0 ] = new int[ 5 ]; // create 5 columns for row 0
c[ 1 ] = new int[ 3 ]; // create 3 columns for row 1
```

The preceding statements create a jagged array with two rows. Row 0 has five columns, and row 1 has three columns.

Two-Dimensional Array Example: Displaying Element Values

Figure 8.19 demonstrates initializing rectangular and jagged arrays with array initializers and using nested for loops to *traverse* the arrays (i.e., visit every element of each array).

Class InitArray's Main method declares two arrays. The declaration of rectangular (line 12) uses nested array initializers to initialize row 0 of the array to the values 1, 2 and 3, and the row 1 to the values 4, 5 and 6. The declaration of jagged (lines 17–19) uses nested initializers of different lengths. In this case, the initializer uses the keyword new to create a one-dimensional array for each row. Row 0 is initialized to have two elements with

```
 1   // Fig. 8.19: InitArray.cs
 2   // Initializing rectangular and jagged arrays.
 3   using System;
 4
 5   public class InitArray
 6   {
 7      // create and output rectangular and jagged arrays
 8      public static void Main( string[] args )
 9      {
10         // with rectangular arrays,
11         // every column must be the same length.
12         int[ , ] rectangular = { { 1, 2, 3 }, { 4, 5, 6 } };
13
14         // with jagged arrays,
15         // we need to use "new int[]" for every row,
16         // but every column does not need to be the same length.
17         int[][] jagged = { new int[] { 1, 2 },
18                            new int[] { 3 },
19                            new int[] { 4, 5, 6 } };
20
21         OutputArray( rectangular ); // displays array rectangular by row
22         Console.WriteLine(); // output a blank line
23         OutputArray( jagged ); // displays array jagged by row
24      } // end Main
25
```

Fig. 8.19 | Initializing jagged and rectangular arrays. (Part 1 of 2.)

```
26      // output rows and columns of a rectangular array
27      public static void OutputArray( int[ , ] array )
28      {
29         Console.WriteLine( "Values in the rectangular array by row are" );
30
31         // loop through array's rows
32         for ( int row = 0; row < array.GetLength( 0 ); row++ )
33         {
34            // loop through columns of current row
35            for ( int column = 0; column < array.GetLength( 1 ); column++ )
36               Console.Write( "{0}  ", array[ row, column ] );
37
38            Console.WriteLine(); // start new line of output
39         } // end outer for
40      } // end method OutputArray
41
42      // output rows and columns of a jagged array
43      public static void OutputArray( int[][] array )
44      {
45         Console.WriteLine( "Values in the jagged array by row are" );
46
47         // loop through array's rows
48         for ( int row = 0; row < array.Length; row++ )
49         {
50            // loop through columns of current row
51            for ( int column = 0; column < array[ row ].Length; column++ )
52               Console.Write( "{0}  ", array[ row ][ column ] );
53
54            Console.WriteLine(); // start new line of output
55         } // end outer for
56      } // end method OutputArray
57   } // end class InitArray
```

```
Values in the rectangular array by row are
1  2  3
4  5  6

Values in the jagged array by row are
1  2
3
4  5  6
```

Fig. 8.19 | Initializing jagged and rectangular arrays. (Part 2 of 2.)

values 1 and 2, respectively. Row 1 is initialized to have one element with value 3. Row 2 is initialized to have three elements with the values 4, 5 and 6, respectively.

Method OutputArray has been overloaded with two versions. The first version (lines 27–40) specifies the array parameter as int[,] array to indicate that it takes a rectangular array. The second version (lines 43–56) takes a jagged array, because its array parameter is listed as int[][] array.

Line 21 invokes method OutputArray with argument rectangular, so the version of OutputArray at lines 27–40 is called. The for statement (lines 32–39) outputs the rows of a rectangular array. The loop-continuation condition of each for statement (lines 32 and 35) uses the rectangular array's GetLength method to obtain the length of each dimension. The dimensions are numbered starting from 0. So the method call GetLength(0) on array returns the size of the first dimension of the array (the number of rows), and the call GetLength(1) returns the size of the second dimension (the number of columns).

Line 23 invokes method OutputArray with argument jagged, so the version of OutputArray at lines 43–56 is called. The for statement (lines 48–55) outputs the rows of a jagged array. In the loop-continuation condition of the outer for statement (line 48), we use the property array.Length to determine the number of rows in the array. In the inner for statement (line 51), we use the property array[row].Length to determine the number of columns in the current row of the array. This condition enables the loop to determine the exact number of columns in each row.

Common Multidimensional-Array Manipulations Performed with for *Statements*

Many common array manipulations use for statements. As an example, the following for statement sets all the elements in row 2 of rectangular array a in Fig. 8.17 to 0:

```
for ( int column = 0; column < a.GetLength( 1 ); column++)
    a[ 2, column ] = 0;
```

We specified row 2; therefore, we know that the first index is always 2 (0 is the first row, and 1 is the second row). This for loop varies only the second index (i.e., the column index). The preceding for statement is equivalent to the assignment statements

```
a[ 2, 0 ] = 0;
a[ 2, 1 ] = 0;
a[ 2, 2 ] = 0;
a[ 2, 3 ] = 0;
```

The following nested for statement totals the values of all the elements in array a:

```
int total = 0;

for ( int row = 0; row < a.GetLength( 0 ); row++ )
{
    for ( int column = 0; column < a.GetLength( 1 ); column++ )
        total += a[ row, column ];
} // end outer for
```

These nested for statements total the array elements one row at a time. The outer for statement begins by setting the row index to 0 so that row 0's elements can be totaled by the inner for statement. The outer for then increments row to 1 so that row 1's elements can be totaled. Then the outer for increments row to 2 so that row 2's elements can be totaled. The variable total can be displayed when the outer for statement terminates. In the next example, we show how to process a rectangular array in a more concise manner using foreach statements.

8.11 Case Study: Class GradeBook Using a Rectangular Array

In Section 8.9, we presented class GradeBook (Fig. 8.15), which used a one-dimensional array to store student grades on a single exam. In most courses, students take several exams. Instructors are likely to want to analyze grades across the entire course, both for a single student and for the class as a whole.

Storing Student Grades in a Rectangular Array in Class GradeBook

Figure 8.20 contains a version of class GradeBook that uses a rectangular array grades to store the grades of a number of students on multiple exams. Each row of the array represents a single student's grades for the entire course, and each column represents the grades for the whole class on one of the exams the students took during the course. An application such as GradeBookTest (Fig. 8.21) passes the array as an argument to the GradeBook constructor. In this example, we use a 10-by-3 array containing 10 students' grades on three exams. Five methods perform array manipulations to process the grades. Each method is similar to its counterpart in the earlier one-dimensional array version of class GradeBook (Fig. 8.15). Method GetMinimum (lines 54–68) determines the lowest grade of any student for the semester. Method GetMaximum (lines 71–85) determines the highest grade of any student for the semester. Method GetAverage (lines 88–100) determines a particular student's semester average. Method OutputBarChart (lines 103–132) outputs a bar chart of the distribution of all student grades for the semester. Method OutputGrades (lines 135–159) outputs the two-dimensional array in tabular format, along with each student's semester average.

```
1   // Fig. 8.20: GradeBook.cs
2   // Grade book using rectangular array to store grades.
3   using System;
4
5   public class GradeBook
6   {
7      private string courseName; // name of course this grade book represents
8      private int[ , ] grades; // rectangular array of student grades
9
10     // two-parameter constructor initializes courseName and grades array
11     public GradeBook( string name, int[ , ] gradesArray )
12     {
13        CourseName = name; // initialize courseName
14        grades = gradesArray; // initialize grades array
15     } // end two-parameter GradeBook constructor
16
17     // property that gets and sets the course name
18     public string CourseName
19     {
20        get
21        {
22           return courseName;
23        } // end get
24        set
25        {
26           courseName = value;
27        } // end set
28     } // end property CourseName
29
30     // display a welcome message to the GradeBook user
31     public void DisplayMessage()
32     {
```

Fig. 8.20 | Grade book using rectangular array to store grades. (Part 1 of 4.)

```
33          // CourseName property gets the name of the course
34          Console.WriteLine( "Welcome to the grade book for\n{0}!\n",
35             CourseName );
36       } // end method DisplayMessage
37
38       // perform various operations on the data
39       public void ProcessGrades()
40       {
41          // output grades array
42          OutputGrades();
43
44          // call methods GetMinimum and GetMaximum
45          Console.WriteLine( "\n{0} {1}\n{2} {3}\n",
46             "Lowest grade in the grade book is", GetMinimum(),
47             "Highest grade in the grade book is", GetMaximum() );
48
49          // output grade distribution chart of all grades on all tests
50          OutputBarChart();
51       } // end method ProcessGrades
52
53       // find minimum grade
54       public int GetMinimum()
55       {
56          // assume first element of grades array is smallest
57          int lowGrade = grades[ 0, 0 ];
58
59          // loop through elements of rectangular grades array
60          foreach ( int grade in grades )
61          {
62             // if grade less than lowGrade, assign it to lowGrade
63             if ( grade < lowGrade )
64                lowGrade = grade;
65          } // end foreach
66
67          return lowGrade; // return lowest grade
68       } // end method GetMinimum
69
70       // find maximum grade
71       public int GetMaximum()
72       {
73          // assume first element of grades array is largest
74          int highGrade = grades[ 0, 0 ];
75
76          // loop through elements of rectangular grades array
77          foreach ( int grade in grades )
78          {
79             // if grade greater than highGrade, assign it to highGrade
80             if ( grade > highGrade )
81                highGrade = grade;
82          } // end foreach
83
```

Fig. 8.20 | Grade book using rectangular array to store grades. (Part 2 of 4.)

```
84          return highGrade; // return highest grade
85      } // end method GetMaximum
86
87      // determine average grade for particular student
88      public double GetAverage( int student )
89      {
90          // get the number of grades per student
91          int amount = grades.GetLength( 1 );
92          int total = 0; // initialize total
93
94          // sum grades for one student
95          for ( int exam = 0; exam < amount; exam++ )
96              total += grades[ student, exam ];
97
98          // return average of grades
99          return ( double ) total / amount;
100     } // end method GetAverage
101
102     // output bar chart displaying overall grade distribution
103     public void OutputBarChart()
104     {
105         Console.WriteLine( "Overall grade distribution:" );
106
107         // stores frequency of grades in each range of 10 grades
108         int[] frequency = new int[ 11 ];
109
110         // for each grade in GradeBook, increment the appropriate frequency
111         foreach ( int grade in grades )
112         {
113             ++frequency[ grade / 10 ];
114         } // end foreach
115
116         // for each grade frequency, print bar in chart
117         for ( int count = 0; count < frequency.Length; count++ )
118         {
119             // output bar label ( "00-09: ", ..., "90-99: ", "100: " )
120             if ( count == 10 )
121                 Console.Write( "  100: " );
122             else
123                 Console.Write( "{0:D2}-{1:D2}: ",
124                     count * 10, count * 10 + 9 );
125
126             // print bar of asterisks
127             for ( int stars = 0; stars < frequency[ count ]; stars++ )
128                 Console.Write( "*" );
129
130             Console.WriteLine(); // start a new line of output
131         } // end outer for
132     } // end method OutputBarChart
133
134     // output the contents of the grades array
135     public void OutputGrades()
136     {
```

Fig. 8.20 | Grade book using rectangular array to store grades. (Part 3 of 4.)

```
137        Console.WriteLine( "The grades are:\n" );
138        Console.Write( "                " ); // align column heads
139
140        // create a column heading for each of the tests
141        for ( int test = 0; test < grades.GetLength( 1 ); test++ )
142           Console.Write( "Test {0}  ", test + 1 );
143
144        Console.WriteLine( "Average" ); // student average column heading
145
146        // create rows/columns of text representing array grades
147        for ( int student = 0; student < grades.GetLength( 0 ); student++ )
148        {
149           Console.Write( "Student {0,2}", student + 1 );
150
151           // output student's grades
152           for ( int grade = 0; grade < grades.GetLength( 1 ); grade++ )
153              Console.Write( "{0,8}", grades[ student, grade ] );
154
155           // call method GetAverage to calculate student's average grade;
156           // pass row number as the argument to GetAverage
157           Console.WriteLine( "{0,9:F2}", GetAverage( student ) );
158        } // end outer for
159     } // end method OutputGrades
160  } // end class GradeBook
```

Fig. 8.20 | Grade book using rectangular array to store grades. (Part 4 of 4.)

Methods GetMinimum, GetMaximum and OutputBarChart each loop through array grades using the foreach statement—for example, the foreach statement from method GetMinimum (lines 60–65). To find the lowest overall grade, this foreach statement iterates through rectangular array grades and compares each element to variable lowGrade. If a grade is less than lowGrade, lowGrade is set to that grade.

When the foreach statement traverses the elements of the grades array, it looks at each element of the first row in order by index, then each element of the second row in order by index and so on. The foreach statement in lines 60–65 traverses the elements of grade in the same order as the following equivalent code, expressed with nested for statements:

```
for ( int row = 0; row < grades.GetLength( 0 ); row++ )
   for ( int column = 0; column < grades.GetLength( 1 ); column++ )
   {
      if ( grades[ row, column ] < lowGrade )
         lowGrade = grades[ row, column ];
   }
```

When the foreach statement completes, lowGrade contains the lowest grade in the rectangular array. Method GetMaximum works similarly to method GetMinimum.

Method OutputBarChart in Fig. 8.20 displays the grade distribution as a bar chart. Note that the syntax of the foreach statement (lines 111–114) is identical for one-dimensional and two-dimensional arrays.

Method OutputGrades (lines 135–159) uses nested for statements to output values of the array grades, in addition to each student's semester average. The output in Fig. 8.21 shows the result, which resembles the tabular format of an instructor's physical grade book.

Lines 141–142 print the column headings for each test. We use the for statement rather than the foreach statement here so that we can identify each test with a number. Similarly, the for statement in lines 147–158 first outputs a row label using a counter variable to identify each student (line 149). Although array indices start at 0, note that lines 142 and 149 output test + 1 and student + 1, respectively, to produce test and student numbers starting at 1 (see Fig. 8.21). The inner for statement in lines 152–153 uses the outer for statement's counter variable student to loop through a specific row of array grades and output each student's test grade. Finally, line 157 obtains each student's semester average by passing the row index of grades (i.e., student) to method GetAverage.

Method GetAverage (lines 88–100) takes one argument—the row index for a particular student. When line 157 calls GetAverage, the argument is int value student, which specifies the particular row of rectangular array grades. Method GetAverage calculates the sum of the array elements on this row, divides the total by the number of test results and returns the floating-point result as a double value (line 99).

Class GradeBookTest That Demonstrates Class GradeBook

The application in Fig. 8.21 creates an object of class GradeBook (Fig. 8.20) using the two-dimensional array of ints named gradesArray (declared and initialized in lines 9–18). Lines 20–21 pass a course name and gradesArray to the GradeBook constructor. Lines 22–23 then invoke myGradeBook's DisplayMessage and ProcessGrades methods to display a welcome message and obtain a report summarizing the students' grades for the semester, respectively.

```
1   // Fig. 8.21: GradeBookTest.cs
2   // Create GradeBook object using a rectangular array of grades.
3   public class GradeBookTest
4   {
5      // Main method begins application execution
6      public static void Main( string[] args )
7      {
8         // rectangular array of student grades
9         int[ , ] gradesArray = { { 87, 96, 70 },
10                                 { 68, 87, 90 },
11                                 { 94, 100, 90 },
12                                 { 100, 81, 82 },
13                                 { 83, 65, 85 },
14                                 { 78, 87, 65 },
15                                 { 85, 75, 83 },
16                                 { 91, 94, 100 },
17                                 { 76, 72, 84 },
18                                 { 87, 93, 73 } };
19
20         GradeBook myGradeBook = new GradeBook(
21            "CS101 Introduction to C# Programming", gradesArray );
22         myGradeBook.DisplayMessage();
23         myGradeBook.ProcessGrades();
24      } // end Main
25   } // end class GradeBookTest
```

Fig. 8.21 | Create GradeBook object using a rectangular array of grades. (Part 1 of 2.)

```
Welcome to the grade book for
CS101 Introduction to C# Programming!

The grades are:

            Test 1  Test 2  Test 3  Average
Student  1    87      96      70     84.33
Student  2    68      87      90     81.67
Student  3    94     100      90     94.67
Student  4   100      81      82     87.67
Student  5    83      65      85     77.67
Student  6    78      87      65     76.67
Student  7    85      75      83     81.00
Student  8    91      94     100     95.00
Student  9    76      72      84     77.33
Student 10    87      93      73     84.33

Lowest grade in the grade book is 65
Highest grade in the grade book is 100

Overall grade distribution:
00-09:
10-19:
20-29:
30-39:
40-49:
50-59:
60-69: ***
70-79: ******
80-89: ***********
90-99: *******
  100: ***
```

Fig. 8.21 | Create GradeBook object using a rectangular array of grades. (Part 2 of 2.)

8.12 Variable-Length Argument Lists

Variable-length argument lists allow you to create methods that receive an arbitrary number of arguments. A one-dimensional array-type argument preceded by the keyword **params** in a method's parameter list indicates that the method receives a variable number of arguments with the type of the array's elements. This use of a params modifier can occur only in the last entry of the parameter list. While you can use method overloading and array passing to accomplish much of what is accomplished with "varargs"—another name for variable-length argument lists—using the params modifier is more concise.

Figure 8.22 demonstrates method Average (lines 8–17), which receives a variable-length sequence of doubles (line 8). C# treats the variable-length argument list as a one-dimensional array whose elements are all of the same type. Hence, the method body can manipulate the parameter numbers as an array of doubles. Lines 13–14 use the foreach loop to walk through the array and calculate the total of the doubles in the array. Line 16 accesses numbers.Length to obtain the size of the numbers array for use in the averaging calculation. Lines 31, 33 and 35 in Main call method Average with two, three and four arguments, respectively. Method Average has a variable-length argument list, so it can average as many double arguments as the caller passes. The output reveals that each call to method Average returns the correct value.

```
1   // Fig. 8.22: VarargsTest.cs
2   // Using variable-length argument lists.
3   using System;
4
5   public class VarargsTest
6   {
7      // calculate average
8      public static double Average( params double[] numbers )
9      {
10        double total = 0.0; // initialize total
11
12        // calculate total using the foreach statement
13        foreach ( double d in numbers )
14           total += d;
15
16        return total / numbers.Length;
17     } // end method Average
18
19     public static void Main( string[] args )
20     {
21        double d1 = 10.0;
22        double d2 = 20.0;
23        double d3 = 30.0;
24        double d4 = 40.0;
25
26        Console.WriteLine(
27           "d1 = {0:F1}\nd2 = {1:F1}\nd3 = {2:F1}\nd4 = {3:F1}\n",
28           d1, d2, d3, d4 );
29
30        Console.WriteLine( "Average of d1 and d2 is {0:F1}",
31           Average( d1, d2 ) );
32        Console.WriteLine( "Average of d1, d2 and d3 is {0:F1}",
33           Average( d1, d2, d3 ) );
34        Console.WriteLine( "Average of d1, d2, d3 and d4 is {0:F1}",
35           Average( d1, d2, d3, d4 ) );
36     } // end Main
37  } // end class VarargsTest
```

```
d1 = 10.0
d2 = 20.0
d3 = 30.0
d4 = 40.0

Average of d1 and d2 is 15.0
Average of d1, d2 and d3 is 20.0
Average of d1, d2, d3 and d4 is 25.0
```

Fig. 8.22 | Using variable-length argument lists.

Common Programming Error 8.4

Using the params modifier with a parameter in the middle of a method parameter list is a syntax error. The params modifier may be used only with the last parameter of the parameter list.

8.13 Using Command-Line Arguments

On many systems, it is possible to pass arguments from the command line (these are known as *command-line arguments*) to an application by including a parameter of type string[] (i.e., an array of strings) in the parameter list of Main, exactly as we have done in every application in the book. By convention, this parameter is named args (Fig. 8.23, line 7). When an application is executed from the Command Prompt, the execution environment passes the command-line arguments that appear after the application name to the application's Main method as strings in the one-dimensional array args. The number of arguments passed from the command line is obtained by accessing the array's Length property. For example, the command "MyApplication a b" passes two command-line arguments to application MyApplication. Note that command-line arguments are separated by white space, not commas. When the preceding command executes, the Main method entry point receives the two-element array args (i.e., args.Length is 2) in which args[0] contains the string "a" and args[1] contains the string "b". Common uses of command-line arguments include passing options and file names to applications.

Figure 8.23 uses three command-line arguments to initialize an array. When the application executes, if args.Length is not 3, the application prints an error message and terminates (lines 10–13). Otherwise, lines 16–32 initialize and display the array based on the values of the command-line arguments.

```
1   // Fig. 8.23: InitArray.cs
2   // Using command-line arguments to initialize an array.
3   using System;
4
5   public class InitArray
6   {
7      public static void Main( string[] args )
8      {
9         // check number of command-line arguments
10        if ( args.Length != 3 )
11           Console.WriteLine(
12              "Error: Please re-enter the entire command, including\n" +
13              "an array size, initial value and increment." );
14        else
15        {
16           // get array size from first command-line argument
17           int arrayLength = Convert.ToInt32( args[ 0 ] );
18           int[] array = new int[ arrayLength ]; // create array
19
20           // get initial value and increment from command-line argument
21           int initialValue = Convert.ToInt32( args[ 1 ] );
22           int increment = Convert.ToInt32( args[ 2 ] );
23
24           // calculate value for each array element
25           for ( int counter = 0; counter < array.Length; counter++ )
26              array[ counter ] = initialValue + increment * counter;
27
28           Console.WriteLine( "{0}{1,8}", "Index", "Value" );
29
```

Fig. 8.23 | Using command-line arguments to initialize an array. (Part 1 of 2.)

```
30              // display array index and value
31              for ( int counter = 0; counter < array.Length; counter++ )
32                  Console.WriteLine( "{0,5}{1,8}", counter, array[ counter ] );
33          } // end else
34      } // end Main
35  } // end class InitArray
```

```
C:\Examples\ch08\fig08_21>InitArray.exe
Error: Please re-enter the entire command, including
an array size, initial value and increment.
```

```
C:\Examples\ch08\fig08_21>InitArray.exe 5 0 4
Index    Value
    0        0
    1        4
    2        8
    3       12
    4       16
```

```
C:\Examples\ch08\fig08_21>InitArray.exe 10 1 2
Index    Value
    0        1
    1        3
    2        5
    3        7
    4        9
    5       11
    6       13
    7       15
    8       17
    9       19
```

Fig. 8.23 | Using command-line arguments to initialize an array. (Part 2 of 2.)

The command-line arguments become available to Main as strings in args. Line 17 gets args[0]—a string that specifies the array size—and converts it to an int value, which the application uses to create the array in line 18. The static method ToInt32 of class Convert converts its string argument to an int.

Lines 21–22 convert the args[1] and args[2] command-line arguments to int values and store them in initialValue and increment, respectively. Lines 25–26 calculate the value for each array element.

The output of the first sample execution indicates that the application received an insufficient number of command-line arguments. The second sample execution uses command-line arguments 5, 0 and 4 to specify the size of the array (5), the value of the first element (0) and the increment of each value in the array (4), respectively. The corresponding output indicates that these values create an array containing the integers 0, 4, 8, 12 and 16. The output from the third sample execution illustrates that the command-line arguments 10, 1 and 2 produce an array whose 10 elements are the nonnegative odd integers from 1 to 19.

8.14 (Optional) Software Engineering Case Study: Collaboration Among Objects in the ATM System

When two objects communicate with each other to accomplish a task, they are said to *collaborate*. A *collaboration* consists of an object of one class sending a *message* to an object of another class. Messages are sent in C# via method calls. In this section, we concentrate on the collaborations (interactions) among the objects in our ATM system.

In Section 7.15, we determined many of the operations of the classes in our system. In this section, we concentrate on the messages that invoke these operations. To identify the collaborations in the system, we return to the requirements document of Section 3.10. Recall that this document specifies the activities that occur during an ATM session (e.g., authenticating a user, performing transactions). The steps used to describe how the system must perform each of these tasks are our first indication of the collaborations in our system. As we proceed through this and the remaining Software Engineering Case Study sections, we may discover additional collaborations.

Identifying the Collaborations in a System

We begin to identify the collaborations in the system by carefully reading the sections of the requirements document that specify what the ATM should do to authenticate a user and to perform each transaction type. For each action or step described in the requirements document, we decide which objects in our system must interact to achieve the desired result. We identify one object as the sending object (i.e., the object that sends the message) and another as the receiving object (i.e., the object that offers that operation to clients of the class). We then select one of the receiving object's operations (identified in Section 7.15) that must be invoked by the sending object to produce the proper behavior. For example, the ATM displays a welcome message when idle. We know that an object of class Screen displays a message to the user via its DisplayMessage operation. Thus, we decide that the system can display a welcome message by employing a collaboration between the ATM and the Screen in which the ATM sends a DisplayMessage message to the Screen by invoking the DisplayMessage operation of class Screen. [*Note:* To avoid repeating the phrase "an object of class…," we refer to each object simply by using its class name preceded by an article (e.g., "a," "an" or "the")—for example, "the ATM" refers to an object of class ATM.]

Figure 8.24 lists the collaborations that can be derived from the requirements document. For each sending object, we list the collaborations in the order in which they are discussed in the requirements document. We list each collaboration involving a unique sender, message and recipient only once, even though the collaboration may occur several times during an ATM session. For example, the first row in Fig. 8.24 indicates that the ATM collaborates with the Screen whenever the ATM needs to display a message to the user.

Let's consider the collaborations in Fig. 8.24. Before allowing a user to perform any transactions, the ATM must prompt the user to enter an account number, then to enter a PIN. It accomplishes each of these tasks by sending a DisplayMessage message to the Screen. Both of these actions refer to the same collaboration between the ATM and the Screen, which is already listed in Fig. 8.24. The ATM obtains input in response to a prompt by sending a GetInput message to the Keypad. Next the ATM must determine whether the user-specified account number and PIN match those of an account in the database. It does so by sending an AuthenticateUser message to the BankDatabase. Recall that the Bank-Database cannot authenticate a user directly—only the user's Account (i.e., the Account

An object of class...	sends the message...	to an object of class...
ATM	DisplayMessage	Screen
	GetInput	Keypad
	AuthenticateUser	BankDatabase
	Execute	BalanceInquiry
	Execute	Withdrawal
	Execute	Deposit
BalanceInquiry	GetAvailableBalance	BankDatabase
	GetTotalBalance	BankDatabase
	DisplayMessage	Screen
Withdrawal	DisplayMessage	Screen
	GetInput	Keypad
	GetAvailableBalance	BankDatabase
	IsSufficientCashAvailable	CashDispenser
	Debit	BankDatabase
	DispenseCash	CashDispenser
Deposit	DisplayMessage	Screen
	GetInput	Keypad
	IsDepositEnvelopeReceived	DepositSlot
	Credit	BankDatabase
BankDatabase	ValidatePIN	Account
	AvailableBalance (get)	Account
	TotalBalance (get)	Account
	Debit	Account
	Credit	Account

Fig. 8.24 | Collaborations in the ATM system.

that contains the account number specified by the user) can access the user's PIN to authenticate the user. Figure 8.24 therefore lists a collaboration in which the Bank-Database sends a ValidatePIN message to an Account.

After the user is authenticated, the ATM displays the main menu by sending a series of DisplayMessage messages to the Screen and obtains input containing a menu selection by sending a GetInput message to the Keypad. We have already accounted for these collaborations. After the user chooses a type of transaction to perform, the ATM executes the transaction by sending an Execute message to an object of the appropriate transaction class (i.e., a BalanceInquiry, a Withdrawal or a Deposit). For example, if the user chooses to perform a balance inquiry, the ATM sends an Execute message to a BalanceInquiry.

Further examination of the requirements document reveals the collaborations involved in executing each transaction type. A BalanceInquiry retrieves the amount of money available in the user's account by sending a GetAvailableBalance message to the BankDatabase, which sends a get message to an Account's AvailableBalance property to access the available balance. Similarly, the BalanceInquiry retrieves the amount of money on deposit by sending a `GetTotalBalance` message to the `BankDatabase`, which sends a get message to an `Account`'s `TotalBalance` property to access the total balance on deposit. To display both measures of the user's balance at the same time, the `BalanceInquiry` sends `DisplayMessage` messages to the `Screen`.

A `Withdrawal` sends `DisplayMessage` messages to the `Screen` to display a menu of standard withdrawal amounts (i.e., $20, $40, $60, $100, $200). The `Withdrawal` sends a `GetInput` message to the `Keypad` to obtain the user's menu selection. Next, the `Withdrawal` determines whether the requested withdrawal amount is less than or equal to the user's account balance. The `Withdrawal` obtains the amount of money available in the user's account by sending a `GetAvailableBalance` message to the `BankDatabase`. The `Withdrawal` then tests whether the cash dispenser contains enough cash by sending an `IsSufficientCashAvailable` message to the `CashDispenser`. A `Withdrawal` sends a `Debit` message to the `BankDatabase` to decrease the user's account balance. The `Bank-Database` in turn sends the same message to the appropriate `Account`. Recall that debiting an `Account` decreases both the total balance and the available balance. To dispense the requested amount of cash, the `Withdrawal` sends a `DispenseCash` message to the `CashDispenser`. Finally, the `Withdrawal` sends a `DisplayMessage` message to the `Screen`, instructing the user to take the cash.

A `Deposit` responds to an `Execute` message first by sending a `DisplayMessage` message to the `Screen` to prompt the user for a deposit amount. The `Deposit` sends a `GetInput` message to the `Keypad` to obtain the user's input. The `Deposit` then sends a `DisplayMessage` message to the `Screen` to tell the user to insert a deposit envelope. To determine whether the deposit slot received an incoming deposit envelope, the `Deposit` sends an `IsDepositEnvelopeReceived` message to the `DepositSlot`. The `Deposit` updates the user's account by sending a `Credit` message to the `BankDatabase`, which subsequently sends a `Credit` message to the user's `Account`. Recall that crediting an `Account` increases the total balance but not the available balance.

Interaction Diagrams
Now that we have identified a set of possible collaborations between the objects in our ATM system, let us graphically model these interactions. The UML provides several types of *interaction diagrams* that model the behavior of a system by modeling how objects interact with one another. The *communication diagram* emphasizes *which objects* participate in collaborations. [*Note:* Communication diagrams were called *collaboration diagrams* in earlier versions of the UML.] Like the communication diagram, the *sequence diagram* shows collaborations among objects, but it emphasizes *when* messages are sent between objects.

Communication Diagrams
Figure 8.25 shows a communication diagram that models the ATM executing a `Balance-Inquiry`. Objects are modeled in the UML as rectangles containing names in the form

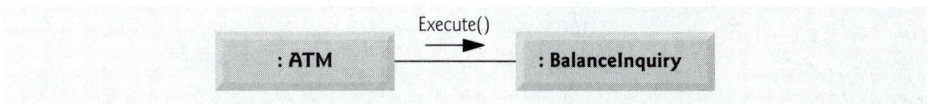

Fig. 8.25 | Communication diagram of the ATM executing a balance inquiry.

objectName : ClassName. In this example, which involves only one object of each type, we disregard the object name and list only a colon followed by the class name. Specifying the name of each object in a communication diagram is recommended when modeling multiple objects of the same type. Communicating objects are connected with solid lines, and messages are passed between objects along these lines in the direction shown by arrows with filled arrowheads. The name of the message, which appears next to the arrow, is the name of an operation (i.e., a method) belonging to the receiving object—think of the name as a service that the receiving object provides to sending objects (its "clients").

The filled arrow in Fig. 8.25 represents a message—or *synchronous call*—in the UML and a method call in C#. This arrow indicates that the flow of control is from the sending object (the ATM) to the receiving object (a BalanceInquiry). Since this is a synchronous call, the sending object cannot send another message, or do anything at all, until the receiving object processes the message and returns control (and possibly a return value) to the sending object. The sender just waits. For example, in Fig. 8.25, the ATM calls method Execute of a BalanceInquiry and cannot send another message until Execute finishes and returns control to the ATM. [*Note:* If this were an *asynchronous call*, represented by a stick arrowhead, the sending object would not have to wait for the receiving object to return control—it would continue sending additional messages immediately following the asynchronous call. Such calls are beyond the scope of this book.]

Sequence of Messages in a Communication Diagram

Figure 8.26 shows a communication diagram that models the interactions among objects in the system when an object of class BalanceInquiry executes. We assume that the object's accountNumber attribute contains the account number of the current user. The collaborations

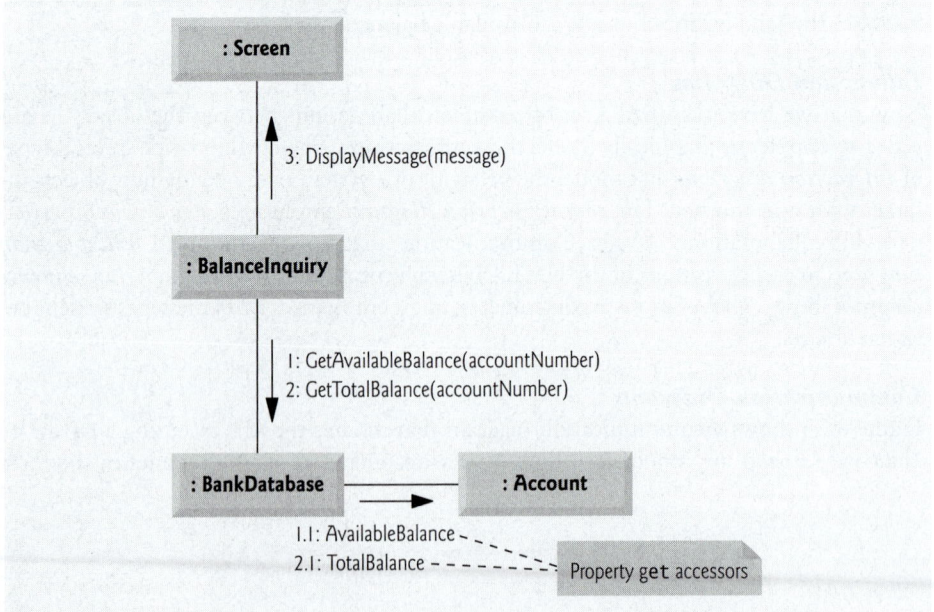

Fig. 8.26 | Communication diagram for executing a BalanceInquiry.

in Fig. 8.26 begin after the ATM sends an Execute message to a BalanceInquiry (i.e., the interaction modeled in Fig. 8.25). The number to the left of a message name indicates the order in which the message is passed. The *sequence of messages* in a communication diagram progresses in numerical order from least to greatest. In this diagram, the numbering starts with message 1 and ends with message 3. The BalanceInquiry first sends a GetAvailableBalance message to the BankDatabase (message 1), then sends a GetTotalBalance message to the BankDatabase (message 2). Within the parentheses following a message name, we can specify a comma-separated list of the names of the arguments sent with the message (i.e., arguments in a C# method call)—the BalanceInquiry passes attribute accountNumber with its messages to the BankDatabase to indicate which Account's balance information to retrieve. Recall from Fig. 7.22 that operations GetAvailableBalance and GetTotalBalance of class BankDatabase each require a parameter to identify an account. The BalanceInquiry next displays the available balance and the total balance to the user by passing a DisplayMessage message to the Screen (message 3) that includes a parameter indicating the message to be displayed.

Note that Fig. 8.26 models two additional messages passing from the BankDatabase to an Account (message 1.1 and message 2.1). To provide the ATM with the two balances of the user's Account (as requested by messages 1 and 2), the BankDatabase must send get messages to the Account's AvailableBalance and TotalBalance properties. A message passed within the handling of another message is called a *nested message*. The UML recommends using a decimal numbering scheme to indicate nested messages. For example, message 1.1 is the first message nested in message 1—the BankDatabase sends the get message to the Account's AvailableBalance property during BankDatabase's processing of a GetAvailableBalance message. [*Note:* If the BankDatabase needed to pass a second nested message while processing message 1, the second message would be numbered 1.2.] A message may be passed only when all the nested messages from the previous message have been passed. For example, the BalanceInquiry passes message 3 to the Screen only after messages 2 and 2.1 have been passed, in that order.

The nested numbering scheme used in communication diagrams helps clarify precisely when and in what context each message is passed. For example, if we numbered the five messages in Fig. 8.26 using a flat numbering scheme (i.e., 1, 2, 3, 4, 5), someone looking at the diagram might not be able to determine that BankDatabase passes the get message to an Account's AvailableBalance property (message 1.1) *during* the BankDatabase's processing of message 1, as opposed to *after* completing the processing of message 1. The nested decimal numbers make it clear that the get message (message 1.1) is passed to an Account's AvailableBalance property within the handling of the GetAvailableBalance message (message 1) by the BankDatabase.

Sequence Diagrams

Communication diagrams emphasize the participants in collaborations but model their timing a bit awkwardly. A sequence diagram helps model the timing of collaborations more clearly. Figure 8.27 shows a sequence diagram modeling the sequence of interactions that occur when a Withdrawal executes. The dotted line extending down from an object's rectangle is that object's *lifeline*, which represents the progression of time. Actions typically occur along an object's lifeline in chronological order from top to bottom—an action near the top happens before one near the bottom.

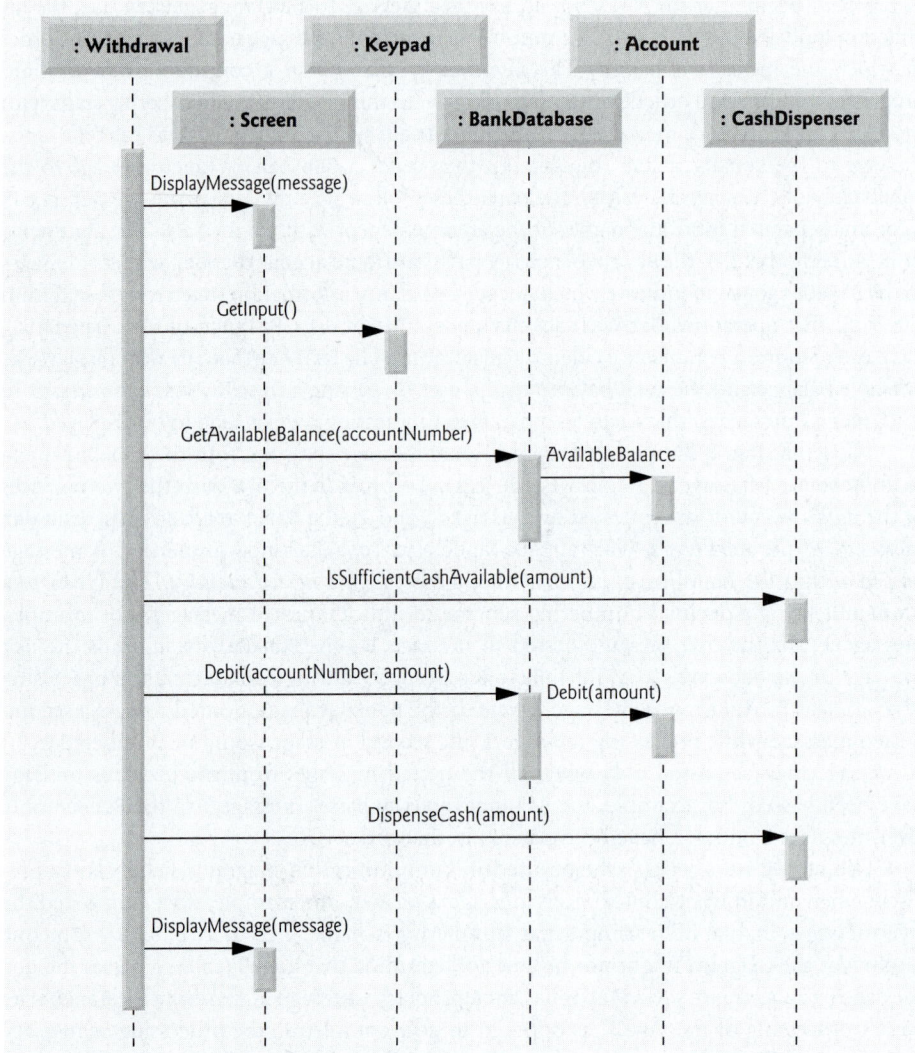

Fig. 8.27 | Sequence diagram that models a `Withdrawal` executing.

Message passing in sequence diagrams is similar to message passing in communication diagrams. An arrow with a filled arrowhead extending from the sending object to the receiving object represents a message between two objects. The arrowhead points to an activation on the receiving object's lifeline. An **activation**, shown as a thin vertical rectangle, indicates that an object is executing. When an object returns control, a return message, represented as a dashed line with a stick arrowhead, extends from the activation of the object returning control to the activation of the object that initially sent the message. To eliminate clutter, we omit the return-message arrows—the UML allows this practice to make diagrams more readable. Like communication diagrams, sequence diagrams can indicate message parameters between the parentheses following a message name.

The sequence of messages in Fig. 8.27 begins when a `Withdrawal` prompts the user to choose a withdrawal amount by sending a `DisplayMessage` message to the `Screen`. The `Withdrawal` then sends a `GetInput` message to the `Keypad`, which obtains input from the user. We have already modeled the control logic involved in a `Withdrawal` in the activity diagram of Fig. 6.28, so we do not show this logic in the sequence diagram of Fig. 8.27. Instead, we model the best-case scenario, in which the balance of the user's account is greater than or equal to the chosen withdrawal amount, and the cash dispenser contains a sufficient amount of cash to satisfy the request. For information on how to model control logic in a sequence diagram, please refer to the Web resources and recommended readings listed at the end of Section 3.10.

After obtaining a withdrawal amount, the `Withdrawal` sends a `GetAvailableBalance` message to the `BankDatabase`, which in turn sends a `get` message to the `Account`'s `AvailableBalance` property. Assuming that the user's account has enough money available to permit the transaction, the `Withdrawal` next sends an `IsSufficientCashAvailable` message to the `CashDispenser`. Assuming that there is enough cash available, the `Withdrawal` decreases the balance of the user's account (both the total balance and the available balance) by sending a `Debit` message to the `BankDatabase`. The `BankDatabase` responds by sending a `Debit` message to the user's `Account`. Finally, the `Withdrawal` sends a `DispenseCash` message to the `CashDispenser` and a `DisplayMessage` message to the `Screen`, telling the user to remove the cash from the machine.

We have identified collaborations among objects in the ATM system and modeled some of these collaborations using UML interaction diagrams—communication diagrams and sequence diagrams. In the next Software Engineering Case Study section (Section 9.17), we enhance the structure of our model to complete a preliminary object-oriented design, then we begin implementing the ATM system in C#.

Software Engineering Case Study Self-Review Exercises

8.1   A(n) _____ consists of an object of one class sending a message to an object of another class.
- a) association
- b) aggregation
- c) collaboration
- d) composition

8.2   Which form of interaction diagram emphasizes *what* collaborations occur? Which form emphasizes *when* collaborations occur?

8.3   Create a sequence diagram that models the interactions among objects in the ATM system that occur when a `Deposit` executes successfully. Explain the sequence of messages modeled by the diagram.

Answers to Software Engineering Case Study Self-Review Exercises

8.1   c.

8.2   Communication diagrams emphasize *what* collaborations occur. Sequence diagrams emphasize *when* collaborations occur.

8.3   Figure 8.28 presents a sequence diagram that models the interactions between objects in the ATM system that occur when a `Deposit` executes successfully. Figure 8.28 indicates that a `Deposit` first sends a `DisplayMessage` message to the `Screen` (to ask the user to enter a deposit amount).

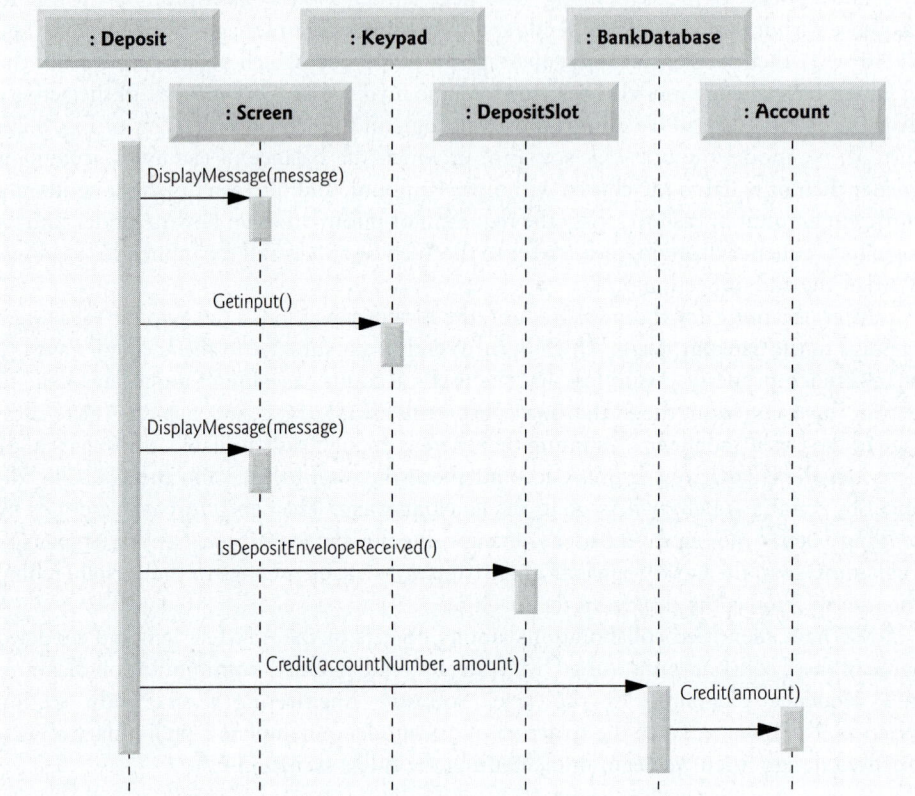

Fig. 8.28 | Sequence diagram that models a Deposit executing.

Next, the Deposit sends a GetInput message to the Keypad to receive the amount the user will be depositing. The Deposit then prompts the user (to insert a deposit envelope) by sending a Display-Message message to the Screen. The Deposit next sends an IsDepositEnvelopeReceived message to the DepositSlot to confirm that the deposit envelope has been received by the ATM. Finally, the Deposit increases the total balance (but not the available balance) of the user's Account by sending a Credit message to the BankDatabase. The BankDatabase responds by sending the same message to the user's Account.

8.15 Wrap-Up

This chapter began our introduction to data structures, exploring the use of arrays to store data in and retrieve data from lists and tables of values. The chapter examples demonstrated how to declare arrays, initialize arrays and refer to individual elements of arrays. The chapter introduced the foreach statement as an additional means (besides the for statement) for iterating through arrays. We showed how to pass arrays to methods and how to declare and manipulate multidimensional arrays. Finally, the chapter showed how to write methods that use variable-length argument lists and how to read arguments passed to an application from the command line.

We continue our coverage of data structures in Chapter 25, Data Structures, which introduces dynamic data structures, such as lists, queues, stacks and trees, that can grow and shrink as applications execute. Chapter 26, Generics, presents one of C#'s new features—generics—which provides the means to create general models of methods and classes that can be declared once, but used with many different data types. Chapter 27, Collections, introduces the data structure classes provided by the .NET Framework, some of which use generics to allow you to specify the exact types of objects that a particular data structure will store. You can use these predefined data structures instead of building your own. Chapter 27 discusses many data structure classes, including `Hashtable` and `ArrayList`, which are array-like data structures that can grow and shrink in response to an application's changing storage requirements. The .NET Framework also provides class `Array`, which contains utility methods for array manipulation. Chapter 27 uses several `static` methods of class `Array` to perform such manipulations as sorting and searching the data in an array.

We have now introduced the basic concepts of classes, objects, control statements, methods and arrays. In Chapter 9, we take a deeper look at classes and objects.

Summary

Section 8.1 Introduction
- Arrays are data structures consisting of related data items of the same type. Arrays are fixed-length entities—they remain the same length once they are created.

Section 8.2 Arrays
- Arrays are reference types. What we typically think of as an array is actually a reference to an array instance in memory. The elements of an array can be either value types or reference types (including other arrays).

- To refer to a particular element in an array, we specify the name of the reference to the array and the index (i.e., the position number) of the element in the array.

- An application refers to an array element with an *array-access expression* that includes the name of the array, followed by the index of the particular element in square brackets (`[]`).

- The first element in every array has index zero and is sometimes called the zeroth element.

- Every array instance knows its own length and provides access to this information with the `Length` property.

Section 8.3 Declaring and Creating Arrays
- To create an array instance, you specify the type and the number of array elements as part of an *array-creation expression* that uses keyword `new`. The following declaration and *array-creation expression* create an array object containing 12 `int` elements:

    ```
    int[] a = new int[ 12 ];
    ```

- When an array is created, each element of the array receives a default value—0 for the numeric simple-type elements, `false` for `bool` elements and `null` for references.

- An application can declare arrays of any type. Every element of a value-type array contains a value of the array's declared type. In an array of a reference type, every element is a reference to an object of the array's declared type.

Section 8.4 Examples Using Arrays

- An application can create an array and initialize its elements with an array initializer, which is a comma-separated list of expressions (called an initializer list) enclosed in braces.

- Constants must be initialized when they are declared and cannot be modified thereafter.

- In a format item, a D format specifier indicates that the value should be formatted as an integer, and the number after the D indicates how many digits this formatted integer must contain.

- When a C# application executes, accessing any array element forces a check on the array index to ensure that it is valid (i.e., it must be greater than or equal to 0 and less than the length of the array). This is called bounds checking. If an application uses an invalid index, the Common Language Runtime generates an exception (specifically, an IndexOutOfRangeException) to indicate that an error occurred in the application at execution time.

Section 8.5 Case Study: Card Shuffling and Dealing Simulation

- The ToString method of an object is called implicitly in many cases when the object is used where a string is expected.

Section 8.6 foreach Statement

- The foreach statement iterates through the elements of an entire array or collection. The syntax of a foreach statement is:

    foreach (*type identifier* **in** *arrayName*)
        statement

  where *type* and *identifier* are the type and name of the iteration variable, and *arrayName* is the array through which to iterate.

- The foreach header can be read concisely as "for each iteration, assign the next element of the array to the iteration variable, then execute the following statement."

- The foreach statement can be used only to access array elements, but it cannot be used to modify elements. Any attempt to change the value of the iteration variable in the body of a foreach statement will cause a compilation error.

Section 8.7 Passing Arrays and Array Elements to Methods

- When an argument to a method is an entire array or an individual array element of a reference type, the called method receives a copy of the reference. However, when an argument to a method is an individual array element of a value type, the called method receives a copy of the element's value.

Section 8.8 Passing Arrays by Value and by Reference

- Passing arrays and other objects by reference makes sense for performance reasons. If arrays were passed by value, a copy of each element would be passed. For large, frequently passed arrays, this would waste time and would consume considerable storage.

- When a reference-type object is passed with ref, the called method actually gains control over the reference itself, allowing the called method to replace the original reference in the caller with a different object or even with null.

- If you encounter a situation where you truly want the called procedure to modify the caller's reference, pass the reference-type parameter using keyword ref—but such situations are rare.

Section 8.10 Multidimensional Arrays

- Two-dimensional arrays are often used to represent tables of values consisting of information arranged in rows and columns. To identify a particular table element, we must specify two indices.

- C# supports two types of two-dimensional arrays—rectangular arrays and jagged arrays.

- Rectangular arrays are used to represent tables of information in the form of rows and columns, where each row has the same number of columns.

- Elements in rectangular array a are identified by an array-access expression of the form a[row, column].

- A rectangular array could be declared and initialized with array initializers of the form:

  arrayType[,] *arrayName* = { {*row0 initializer*}, {*row1 initializer*}, ... };

  provided that each row of the rectangular array must have the same length.

- A jagged array is maintained as a one-dimensional array in which each element refers to a one-dimensional array.

- The lengths of the rows in a jagged array need not be the same.

- We can access the elements in a jagged array *arrayName* by an array-access expression of the form *arrayName*[*row*][*column*].

- A jagged array can be declared and initialized in the form:

  arrayType[][] *arrayName* = { **new** *arrayType*[] {*row0 initializer*},
  new *arrayType*[] {*row1 initializer*},
  ... };

- A rectangular array can be created with an array-creation expression of the form

  arrayType[,] *arrayName* = **new** *arrayType*[*numRows*, *numColumns*];

Section 8.11 Case Study: Class GradeBook Using a Rectangular Array

- When the foreach statement traverses the elements of a rectangular array, it looks at each element of the first row in order by index, then each element of the second row in order by index and so on.

Section 8.12 Variable-Length Argument Lists

- A one-dimensional array-type argument preceded by the keyword params in a method's parameter list indicates that the method receives a variable number of arguments with the type of the array's elements.

- The params modifier can appear only in the last entry of the parameter list.

- C# treats the variable-length argument list as a one-dimensional array whose elements are all of the same type.

Section 8.13 Using Command-Line Arguments

- When an application is executed from the Command Prompt, the execution environment passes the command-line arguments that appear after the application name to the application's Main method as strings in a one-dimensional array.

Terminology

a[i]
a[i,j]
a[i][j]

array
array-access expression
array-creation expression

array initializer

bounds checking

column index

column of an array

command-line arguments

const keyword

constant

data structure

declare a constant

declare an array

element of an array

foreach statement

index

index zero

IndexOutOfRangeException

initialize an array

initializer list

iteration variable

jagged array

Length property of an array

m-by-*n* array

multidimensional array

name of an array

named constant

nested array initializers

off-by-one error

one-dimensional array

out-of-bounds array index

override keyword

params modifier

pass-by-reference

pass-by-value

passing an array to a method

rectangular array

row index

row of an array

square brackets, []

table of values

tabular format

test harness

traverse an array

two-dimensional array

value of an element

variable-length argument list

zeroth element

Self-Review Exercises

8.1 Fill in the blank(s) in each of the following statements:

a) Lists and tables of values can be stored in _____.

b) An array is a group of _____ (called elements) containing values that all have the same _____.

c) The _____ statement allows you to iterate through the elements in an array without using a counter.

d) The number used to refer to a particular element of an array is called the element's _____.

e) An array that uses two indices is referred to as a(n) _____ array.

f) Use the foreach statement _____ to walk through double array numbers.

g) Command-line arguments are stored in _____.

h) Use the expression _____ to receive the total number of arguments in a command line. Assume that command-line arguments are stored in string[] args.

i) Given the command MyApplication test, the first command-line argument is _____.

j) A(n) _____ in the parameter list of a method indicates that the method can receive a variable number of arguments.

8.2 Determine whether each of the following is *true* or *false*. If *false*, explain why.

a) A single array can store values of many different types.

b) An array index should normally be of type float.

c) An individual array element that is passed to a method and modified in that method will contain the modified value when the called method completes execution.

d) Command-line arguments are separated by commas.

8.3   Perform the following tasks for an array called `fractions`:
   a)   Declare constant `ARRAY_SIZE` initialized to 10.
   b)   Declare array `fractions` with `ARRAY_SIZE` elements of type `double`, and initialize the elements to 0.
   c)   Name the element of the array with index 3.
   d)   Assign the value `1.667` to the array element with index 9.
   e)   Assign the value `3.333` to the array element with index 6.
   f)   Sum all the elements of the array, using a `for` statement. Declare integer variable x as a control variable for the loop.

8.4   Perform the following tasks for an array called `table`:
   a)   Declare and create the array as a rectangular integer array that has three rows and three columns. Assume that constant `ARRAY_SIZE` has been declared to be 3.
   b)   How many elements does the array contain?
   c)   Use a `for` statement to initialize each element of the array to the sum of its indices. Assume that integer variables x and y are declared as control variables.

8.5   Find and correct the error in each of the following code segments:
   a)   ```
        const int ARRAY_SIZE = 5;
        ARRAY_SIZE = 10;
        ```
   b)   ```
        Assume int[] b = new int[ 10 ];
        for ( int i = 0; i <= b.Length; i++ )
           b[ i ] = 1;
        ```
   c)   ```
        Assume int[,] a = { { 1, 2 }, { 3, 4 } };
           a[1][1] = 5;
        ```

# Answers to Self-Review Exercises

**8.1**    a) arrays. b) variables, type. c) `foreach`. d) index (or position number). e) two-dimensional. f) `foreach ( double d in numbers )`. g) an array of `string`s, usually called `args`. h) `args.Length`. i) test. j) `params` modifier.

**8.2**    a)   False. An array can store only values of the same type.
   b)   False. An array index must be an integer or an integer expression.
   c)   For individual value-type elements of an array: False. A called method receives and manipulates a copy of the value of such an element, so modifications do not affect the original value. If the reference of an array is passed to a method, however, modifications to the array elements made in the called method are indeed reflected in the original. For individual elements of a reference type: True. A called method receives a copy of the reference of such an element, and changes to the referenced object will be reflected in the original array element.
   d)   False. Command-line arguments are separated by white space.

**8.3**    a)   `const int ARRAY_SIZE = 10;`
   b)   `double[] fractions = new double[ ARRAY_SIZE ];`
   c)   `fractions[ 3 ]`
   d)   `fractions[ 9 ] = 1.667;`
   e)   `fractions[ 6 ] = 3.333;`
   f)   ```
        double total = 0.0;
        for ( int x = 0; x < fractions.Length; x++ )
           total += fractions[ x ];
        ```

8.4   a)   `int[ , ] table = new int[ ARRAY_SIZE, ARRAY_SIZE ];`
   b)   Nine.

c) ```
for (int x = 0; x < table.GetLength(0); x++)
    for (int y = 0; y < table.GetLength(1); y++)
        table[x, y] = x + y;
```

8.5  a) Error: Assigning a value to a constant after it has been initialized.
     Correction: Assign the correct value to the constant in a const int ARRAY_SIZE declaration or declare another variable.
  b) Error: Referencing an array element outside the bounds of the array (b[10]).
     Correction: Change the <= operator to <.
  c) Error: Array indexing is performed incorrectly.
     Correction: Change the statement to a[ 1, 1 ] = 5;.

## Exercises

8.6  Fill in the blanks in each of the following statements:
  a) One-dimensional array p contains four elements. The names of those elements are _____, _____, _____ and _____.
  b) Naming an array, stating its type and specifying the number of dimensions in the array is called _____ the array.
  c) In a two-dimensional array, the first index identifies the _____ of an element and the second index identifies the _____ of an element.
  d) An *m*-by-*n* array contains _____ rows, _____ columns and _____ elements.
  e) The name of the element in row 3 and column 5 of jagged array d is _____.

8.7  Determine whether each of the following is *true* or *false*. If *false*, explain why.
  a) To refer to a particular location or element within an array, we specify the name of the array and the value of the particular element.
  b) An array declaration reserves memory for the array.
  c) To indicate that 100 locations should be reserved for integer array p, the programmer writes the declaration
     p[ 100 ];
  d) An application that initializes the elements of a 15-element array to 0 must contain at least one for statement.
  e) An application that totals the elements of a two-dimensional array must contain nested for statements.

8.8  Write C# statements to accomplish each of the following tasks:
  a) Display the value of the element of character array f with index 6.
  b) Initialize each of the five elements of one-dimensional integer array g to 8.
  c) Total the 100 elements of floating-point array c.
  d) Copy 11-element array a into the first portion of array b, which contains 34 elements.
  e) Determine and display the smallest and largest values contained in 99-element floating-point array w.

8.9  Consider the two-by-three rectangular integer array t.
  a) Write a statement that declares and creates t.
  b) How many rows does t have?
  c) How many columns does t have?
  d) How many elements does t have?
  e) Write the names of all the elements in row 1 of t.
  f) Write the names of all the elements in column 2 of t.
  g) Write a single statement that sets the element of t in row 0 and column 1 to zero.
```

h) Write a sequence of statements that initializes each element of t to 1. Do not use a repetition statement.

i) Write a nested for statement that initializes each element of t to 3.

j) Write a nested for statement that inputs values for the elements of t from the user.

k) Write a sequence of statements that determines and displays the smallest value in t.

l) Write a statement that displays the elements of row 0 of t.

m) Write a statement that totals the elements of column 2 of t.

n) Write a sequence of statements that displays the contents of t in tabular format. List the column indices as headings across the top, and list the row indices at the left of each row.

8.10 *(Sales Commissions)* Use a one-dimensional array to solve the following problem: A company pays its salespeople on a commission basis. The salespeople receive $200 per week plus 9% of their gross sales for that week. For example, a salesperson who grosses $5000 in sales in a week receives $200 plus 9% of $5000, or a total of $650. Write an application (using an array of counters) that determines how many of the salespeople earned salaries in each of the following ranges (assume that each salesperson's salary is truncated to an integer amount):

a) $200–299

b) $300–399

c) $400–499

d) $500–599

e) $600–699

f) $700–799

g) $800–899

h) $900–999

i) $1000 and over

Summarize the results in tabular format.

8.11 Write statements that perform the following one-dimensional-array operations:

a) Set the three elements of integer array counts to 0.

b) Add 1 to each of the four elements of integer array bonus.

c) Display the five values of integer array bestScores in column format.

8.12 *(Duplicate Elimination)* Use a one-dimensional array to solve the following problem: Write an application that inputs five numbers, each of which is between 10 and 100, inclusive. As each number is read, display it only if it is not a duplicate of a number already read. Provide for the "worst case," in which all five numbers are different. Use the smallest possible array to solve this problem. Display the complete set of unique values input after the user inputs each new value.

8.13 List the elements of three-by-five jagged array sales in the order in which they are set to 0 by the following code segment:

```
for ( int row = 0; row < sales.Length; row++ )
{
   for ( int col = 0; col < sales[row].Length; col++ )
   {
      sales[ row ][ col ] = 0;
   }
}
```

8.14 Write an application that calculates the product of a series of integers that are passed to method product using a variable-length argument list. Test your method with several calls, each with a different number of arguments.

8.15 Rewrite Fig. 8.2 so that the size of the array is specified by the first command-line argument. If no command-line argument is supplied, use 10 as the default size of the array.

8.16 Write an application that uses a foreach statement to sum the double values passed by the command-line arguments. [*Hint:* Use static method ToDouble of class Convert to convert a string to a double value.]

8.17 *(Dice Rolling)* Write an application to simulate the rolling of two dice. The application should use an object of class Random once to roll the first die and again to roll the second die. The sum of the two values should then be calculated. Each die can show an integer value from 1 to 6, so the sum of the values will vary from 2 to 12, with 7 being the most frequent sum and 2 and 12 being the least frequent sums. Figure 8.29 shows the 36 possible combinations of the two dice. Your application should roll the dice 36,000 times. Use a one-dimensional array to tally the number of times each possible sum appears. Display the results in tabular format. Determine whether the totals are reasonable (e.g., there are six ways to roll a 7, so approximately one-sixth of the rolls should be 7).

8.18 *(Game of Craps)* Write an application that runs 1000 games of craps (Fig. 7.9) and answers the following questions:
   a) How many games are won on the first roll, second roll, …, twentieth roll and after the twentieth roll?
   b) How many games are lost on the first roll, second roll, …, twentieth roll and after the twentieth roll?
   c) What are the chances of winning at craps? [*Note:* You should discover that craps is one of the fairest casino games.]
   d) What is the average length of a game of craps?

8.19 *(Airline Reservations System)* A small airline has just purchased a computer for its new automated reservations system. You have been asked to develop the new system. You are to write an application to assign seats on each flight of the airline's only plane (capacity: 10 seats).

Your application should display the following alternatives: Please type 1 for First Class and Please type 2 for Economy. If the user types 1, your application should assign a seat in the first-class section (seats 1–5). If the user types 2, your application should assign a seat in the economy section (seats 6–10).

Use a one-dimensional array of simple type bool to represent the seating chart of the plane. Initialize all the elements of the array to false to indicate that all the seats are empty. As each seat is assigned, set the corresponding element of the array to true to indicate that the seat is no longer available.

Your application should never assign a seat that has already been assigned. When the economy section is full, your application should ask the person if it is acceptable to be placed in the first-class section (and vice versa). If yes, make the appropriate seat assignment. If no, display the message "Next flight leaves in 3 hours."

	1	2	3	4	5	6
1	2	3	4	5	6	7
2	3	4	5	6	7	8
3	4	5	6	7	8	9
4	5	6	7	8	9	10
5	6	7	8	9	10	11
6	7	8	9	10	11	12

Fig. 8.29 | The 36 possible sums of two dice.

8.20 *(Total Sales)* Use a rectangular array to solve the following problem: A company has three salespeople (1 to 3) who sell five different products (1 to 5). Once a day, each salesperson passes in a slip for each type of product sold. Each slip contains the following:

a) The salesperson number
b) The product number
c) The total dollar value of that product sold that day

Thus, each salesperson passes in between 0 and 5 sales slips per day. Assume that the information from all of the slips for last month is available. Write an application that will read all the information for last month's sales and summarize the total sales by salesperson and by product. All totals should be stored in rectangular array `sales`. After processing all the information for last month, display the results in tabular format, with each column representing a particular salesperson and each row representing a particular product. Cross-total each row to get the total sales of each product for last month. Cross-total each column to get the total sales by salesperson for last month. Your tabular output should include these cross-totals to the right of the totaled rows and below the totaled columns.

8.21 *(Turtle Graphics)* The Logo language made the concept of *turtle graphics* famous. Imagine a mechanical turtle that walks around the room under the control of a C# application. The turtle holds a pen in one of two positions—up or down. While the pen is down, the turtle traces out shapes as it moves, and while the pen is up, the turtle moves about freely without writing anything. In this problem, you will simulate the operation of the turtle and create a computerized sketchpad.

Use 20-by-20 rectangular array `floor` that is initialized to 0. Read commands from an array that contains them. Keep track at all times of the current position of the turtle and whether the pen is currently up or down. Assume that the turtle always starts at position (0, 0) of the floor with its pen up. The set of turtle commands your application must process are shown in Fig. 8.30.

Suppose that the turtle is somewhere near the center of the floor. The following "application" would draw and display a 12-by-12 square, leaving the pen in the up position:

```
2
5,12
3
5,12
3
5,12
3
5,12
1
6
9
```

Command	Meaning
1	Pen up
2	Pen down
3	Turn right
4	Turn left
5,10	Move forward 10 spaces (replace 10 for a different number of spaces)

Fig. 8.30 | Turtle graphics commands. (Part 1 of 2.)

Command	Meaning
6	Display the 20-by-20 array
9	End of data (sentinel)

Fig. 8.30 | Turtle graphics commands. (Part 2 of 2.)

As the turtle moves with the pen down, set the appropriate elements of array floor to 1s. When the 6 command (display the array) is given, wherever there is a 1 in the array, display an asterisk or any character you choose. Wherever there is a 0, display a blank.

Write an application to implement the turtle graphics capabilities discussed here. Write several turtle graphics applications to draw interesting shapes. Add other commands to increase the power of your turtle graphics language.

8.22 (*Knight's Tour*) One of the more interesting puzzlers for chess buffs is the Knight's Tour problem, originally proposed by the mathematician Euler. Can the chess piece called the knight move around an empty chessboard and touch each of the 64 squares once and only once? We study this intriguing problem in depth here.

The knight makes only L-shaped moves (two spaces in one direction and one space in a perpendicular direction). Thus, as shown in Fig. 8.31, from a square near the middle of an empty chessboard, the knight (labeled K) can make eight different moves (numbered 0 through 7).

a) Draw an eight-by-eight chessboard on a sheet of paper, and attempt a Knight's Tour by hand. Put a 1 in the starting square, a 2 in the second square, a 3 in the third and so on. Before starting the tour, estimate how far you think you will get, remembering that a full tour consists of 64 moves. How far did you get? Was this close to your estimate?

b) Now let us develop an application that will move the knight around a chessboard. The board is represented by eight-by-eight rectangular array board. Each square is initialized to zero. We describe each of the eight possible moves in terms of their horizontal and vertical components. For example, a move of type 0, as shown in Fig. 8.31, consists of moving two squares horizontally to the right and one square vertically upward. A move of type 2 consists of moving one square horizontally to the left and two squares vertically

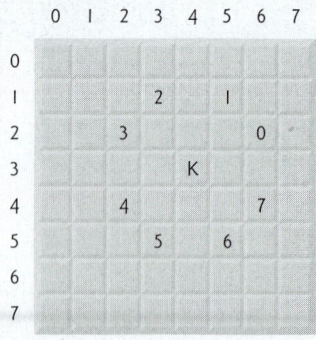

Fig. 8.31 | The eight possible moves of the knight.

upward. Horizontal moves to the left and vertical moves upward are indicated with negative numbers. The eight moves may be described by two one-dimensional arrays, horizontal and vertical, as follows:

```
horizontal[ 0 ] = 2        vertical[ 0 ] = -1
horizontal[ 1 ] = 1        vertical[ 1 ] = -2
horizontal[ 2 ] = -1       vertical[ 2 ] = -2
horizontal[ 3 ] = -2       vertical[ 3 ] = -1
horizontal[ 4 ] = -2       vertical[ 4 ] = 1
horizontal[ 5 ] = -1       vertical[ 5 ] = 2
horizontal[ 6 ] = 1        vertical[ 6 ] = 2
horizontal[ 7 ] = 2        vertical[ 7 ] = 1
```

Let variables currentRow and currentColumn indicate the row and column, respectively, of the knight's current position. To make a move of type moveNumber, where moveNumber is between 0 and 7, your application should use the statements

```
currentRow += vertical[ moveNumber ];
currentColumn += horizontal[ moveNumber ];
```

Write an application to move the knight around the chessboard. Keep a counter that varies from 1 to 64. Record the latest count in each square the knight moves to. Test each potential move to see if the knight has already visited that square. Test every potential move to ensure that the knight does not land off the chessboard. Run the application. How many moves did the knight make?

c) After attempting to write and run a Knight's Tour application, you have probably developed some valuable insights. We will use these insights to develop a *heuristic* (or "rule of thumb") for moving the knight. Heuristics do not guarantee success, but a carefully developed heuristic greatly improves the chance of success. You may have observed that the outer squares are more troublesome than the squares nearer the center of the board. In fact, the most troublesome and inaccessible squares are the four corners.

Intuition may suggest that you should attempt to move the knight to the most troublesome squares first and leave open those that are easiest to get to, so that when the board gets congested near the end of the tour, there will be a greater chance of success.

We could develop an "accessibility heuristic" by classifying each of the squares according to how accessible it is and always moving the knight (using the knight's L-shaped moves) to the most inaccessible square. We label two-dimensional array accessibility with numbers indicating from how many squares each particular square is accessible. On a blank chessboard, each of the 16 squares nearest the center is rated as 8, each corner square is rated as 2, and the other squares have accessibility numbers of 3, 4 or 6 as follows:

```
2  3  4  4  4  4  3  2
3  4  6  6  6  6  4  3
4  6  8  8  8  8  6  4
4  6  8  8  8  8  6  4
4  6  8  8  8  8  6  4
4  6  8  8  8  8  6  4
3  4  6  6  6  6  4  3
2  3  4  4  4  4  3  2
```

Write a new version of the Knight's Tour, using the accessibility heuristic. The knight should always move to the square with the lowest accessibility number. In case of a tie, the knight may move to any of the tied squares. Therefore, the tour may begin in any of the four corners. [*Note:* As the knight moves around the chessboard as more squares become occupied, your application should reduce the accessibility numbers. In this way, at any given time during the tour, each available square's accessibility number will remain equal to precisely the number of squares from which that square may be reached.] Run this version of your application. Did you get a full tour? Modify the application to run 64 tours, one starting from each square of the chessboard. How many full tours did you get?

d) Write a version of the Knight's Tour application that, when encountering a tie between two or more squares, decides what square to choose by looking ahead to those squares reachable from the "tied" squares. Your application should move to the tied square for which the next move would arrive at the square with the lowest accessibility number.

8.23 (*Knight's Tour: Brute-Force Approaches*) In part (c) of Exercise 8.22, we developed a solution to the Knight's Tour problem. The approach used, called the "accessibility heuristic," generates many solutions and executes efficiently.

As computers continue to increase in power, we will be able to solve more problems with sheer computer power and relatively unsophisticated algorithms. Let us call this approach "brute-force" problem solving.

a) Use random-number generation to enable the knight to walk around the chessboard (in its legitimate L-shaped moves) at random. Your application should run one tour and display the final chessboard. How far did the knight get?

b) Most likely, the application in part (a) produced a relatively short tour. Now modify your application to attempt 1000 tours. Use a one-dimensional array to keep track of the number of tours of each length. When your application finishes attempting the 1000 tours, it should display this information in neat tabular format. What was the best result?

c) Most likely, the application in part (b) gave you some "respectable" tours, but no full tours. Now let your application run until it produces a full tour. Once again, keep a table of the number of tours of each length, and display this table when the first full tour is found. How many tours did your application attempt before producing a full tour? How much time did it take?

d) Compare the brute-force version of the Knight's Tour with the accessibility-heuristic version. Which required a more careful study of the problem? Which algorithm was more difficult to develop? Which required more computer power? Could we be certain (in advance) of obtaining a full tour with the accessibility-heuristic approach? Could we be certain (in advance) of obtaining a full tour with the brute-force approach? Argue the pros and cons of brute-force problem solving in general.

8.24 (*Eight Queens*) Another puzzler for chess buffs is the Eight Queens problem, which asks the following: Is it possible to place eight queens on an empty chessboard so that no queen is "attacking" any other (i.e., no two queens are in the same row, in the same column or along the same diagonal)? Use the thinking developed in Exercise 8.22 to formulate a heuristic for solving the Eight Queens problem. Run your application. [*Hint:* It is possible to assign a value to each square of the chessboard to indicate how many squares of an empty chessboard are "eliminated" if a queen is placed in that square. Each of the corners would be assigned the value 22, as demonstrated by Fig. 8.32. Once these "elimination numbers" are placed in all 64 squares, an appropriate heuristic might be as follows: Place the next queen in the square with the smallest elimination number. Why is this strategy intuitively appealing?]

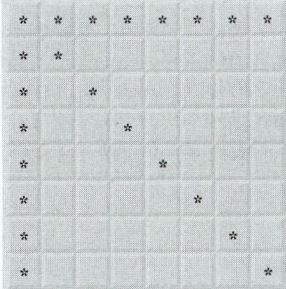

Fig. 8.32 | The 22 squares eliminated by placing a queen in the upper left corner.

8.25 (*Eight Queens: Brute-Force Approaches*) In this exercise, you will develop several brute-force approaches to solving the Eight Queens problem introduced in Exercise 8.24.

  a) Use the random brute-force technique developed in Exercise 8.23 to solve the Eight Queens problem.

  b) Use an exhaustive technique (i.e., try all possible combinations of eight queens on the chessboard) to solve the Eight Queens problem.

8.26 (*Knight's Tour: Closed-Tour Test*) In the Knight's Tour (Exercise 8.22), a full tour occurs when the knight makes 64 moves, touching each square of the chessboard once and only once. A closed tour occurs when the 64th move is one move away from the square in which the knight started the tour. Modify the application you wrote in Exercise 8.22 to test for a closed tour if a full tour has occurred.

8.27 (*Sieve of Eratosthenes*) A prime number is any integer greater than 1 that is evenly divisible only by itself and 1. The Sieve of Eratosthenes is a method of finding prime numbers. It operates as follows:

  a) Create a simple type `bool` array with all elements initialized to `true`. Array elements with prime indices will remain `true`. All other array elements will eventually be set to `false`.

  b) Starting with array index 2, determine whether a given element is `true`. If so, loop through the remainder of the array and set to `false` every element whose index is a multiple of the index for the element with value `true`. Then continue the process with the next element with value `true`. For array index 2, all elements beyond element 2 in the array with indices that are multiples of 2 (indices 4, 6, 8, 10, etc.) will be set to `false`; for array index 3, all elements beyond element 3 in the array with indices that are multiples of 3 (indices 6, 9, 12, 15, etc.) will be set to `false`; and so on.

When this process completes, the array elements that are still `true` indicate that the index is a prime number. These indices can be displayed. Write an application that uses an array of 1000 elements to determine and display the prime numbers between 2 and 999. Ignore array elements 0 and 1.

8.28 (*Simulation: The Tortoise and the Hare*) In this problem, you will re-create the classic race of the tortoise and the hare. You will use random-number generation to develop a simulation of this memorable event.

  Our contenders begin the race at square 1 of 70 squares. Each square represents a possible position along the race course. The finish line is at square 70. The first contender to reach or pass square 70 is rewarded with a pail of fresh carrots and lettuce. The course weaves its way up the side of a slippery mountain, so occasionally the contenders lose ground.

A clock ticks once per second. With each tick of the clock, your application should adjust the position of the animals according to the rules in Fig. 8.33. Use variables to keep track of the positions of the animals (i.e., position numbers are 1–70). Start each animal at position 1 (the "starting gate"). If an animal slips left before square 1, move it back to square 1.

Generate the percentages in Fig. 8.33 by producing a random integer i in the range $1 \leq i \leq 10$. For the tortoise, perform a "fast plod" when $1 \leq i \leq 5$, a "slip" when $6 \leq i \leq 7$ or a "slow plod" when $8 \leq i \leq 10$. Use a similar technique to move the hare.

Begin the race by displaying

```
ON YOUR MARK, GET SET
BANG !!!!!
AND THEY'RE OFF !!!!!
```

Then, for each tick of the clock (i.e., each repetition of a loop), display a 70-position line showing the letter T in the position of the tortoise and the letter H in the position of the hare. Occasionally, the contenders will land on the same square. In this case, the tortoise bites the hare, and your application should display OUCH!!! beginning at that position. All output positions other than the T, the H or the OUCH!!! (in case of a tie) should be blank.

After each line is displayed, test for whether either animal has reached or passed square 70. If so, display the winner and terminate the simulation. If the tortoise wins, display TORTOISE WINS!!! YAY!!! If the hare wins, display Hare wins. Yuch. If both animals win on the same tick of the clock, you may want to favor the tortoise (the "underdog"), or you may want to display It's a tie. If neither animal wins, perform the loop again to simulate the next tick of the clock. When you are ready to run your application, assemble a group of fans to watch the race. You'll be amazed at how involved your audience gets!

Later in the book, we introduce a number of C# capabilities, such as graphics, images, animation, sound and multithreading. As you study those features, you might enjoy enhancing your tortoise-and-hare contest simulation.

8.29 *(Card Shuffling and Dealing)* Modify the application of Fig. 8.11 to deal a five-card poker hand. Then modify class DeckOfCards of Fig. 8.10 to include methods that determine whether a hand contains

    a) a pair

    b) two pairs

Animal	Move type	Percentage of the time	Actual move
Tortoise	Fast plod	50%	3 squares to the right
	Slip	20%	6 squares to the left
	Slow plod	30%	1 square to the right
Hare	Sleep	20%	No move at all
	Big hop	20%	9 squares to the right
	Big slip	10%	12 squares to the left
	Small hop	30%	1 square to the right
	Small slip	20%	2 squares to the left

Fig. 8.33 | Rules for adjusting the positions of the tortoise and the hare.

    c) three of a kind (e.g., three jacks)

    d) four of a kind (e.g., four aces)

    e) a flush (i.e., all five cards of the same suit)

    f) a straight (i.e., five cards of consecutive face values)

    g) a full house (i.e., two cards of one face value and three cards of another face value)

[*Hint:* Add methods `GetFace` and `GetSuit` to class `Card` of Fig. 8.9.]

8.30 *(Card Shuffling and Dealing)* Use the methods developed in Exercise 8.29 to write an application that deals two five-card poker hands, evaluates each hand and determines which is the better hand.

Special Section: Building Your Own Computer

In the next several problems, we take a temporary diversion from the world of high-level language programming to "peel open" a computer and look at its internal structure. We introduce machine-language programming and write several machine-language programs. To make this an especially valuable experience, we then build a computer (through the technique of software-based simulation) on which you can execute your machine-language programs.

8.31 *(Machine-Language Programming)* Let us create a computer called the Simpletron. As its name implies, it is a simple, but powerful, machine. The Simpletron runs programs written in the only language it directly understands: Simpletron Machine Language, or SML for short.

    The Simpletron contains an *accumulator*—a special register in which information is put before the Simpletron uses that information in calculations or examines it in various ways. All the information in the Simpletron is handled in terms of *words*. A word is a signed four-digit decimal number, such as +3364, -1293, +0007 and -0001. The Simpletron is equipped with a 100-word memory, and these words are referenced by their location numbers 00, 01, ..., 99.

    Before running an SML program, we must *load*, or place, the code into memory. The first instruction (or statement) of every SML program is always placed in location 00. The simulator will start executing at this location.

    Each instruction written in SML occupies one word of the Simpletron's memory (hence, instructions are signed four-digit decimal numbers). We shall assume that the sign of an SML instruction is always plus, but the sign of a data word may be either plus or minus. Each location in the Simpletron's memory may contain an instruction, a data value used by a program or an unused (and hence undefined) area of memory. The first two digits of each SML instruction are the *operation code* specifying the operation to be performed. SML operation codes are summarized in Fig. 8.34.

Operation code	Meaning
Input/output operations:	
`const int READ = 10;`	Read a word from the keyboard into a specific location in memory.
`const int WRITE = 11;`	Write a word from a specific location in memory to the screen.
Load/store operations:	
`const int LOAD = 20;`	Load a word from a specific location in memory into the accumulator.

Fig. 8.34 | Simpletron Machine Language (SML) operation codes. (Part 1 of 2.)

Operation code	Meaning
const int STORE = 21;	Store a word from the accumulator into a specific location in memory.
Arithmetic operations:	
const int ADD = 30;	Add a word from a specific location in memory to the word in the accumulator (leave the result in the accumulator).
const int SUBTRACT = 31;	Subtract a word from a specific location in memory from the word in the accumulator (leave the result in the accumulator).
const int DIVIDE = 32;	Divide a word from a specific location in memory into the word in the accumulator (leave result in the accumulator).
const int MULTIPLY = 33;	Multiply a word from a specific location in memory by the word in the accumulator (leave the result in the accumulator).
Transfer of control operations:	
const int BRANCH = 40;	Branch to a specific location in memory.
const int BRANCHNEG = 41;	Branch to a specific location in memory if the accumulator is negative.
const int BRANCHZERO = 42;	Branch to a specific location in memory if the accumulator is zero.
const int HALT = 43;	Halt. The program has completed its task.

Fig. 8.34 | Simpletron Machine Language (SML) operation codes. (Part 2 of 2.)

The last two digits of an SML instruction are the *operand*—the address of the memory location containing the word to which the operation applies. Let's consider several simple SML programs.

The first SML program (Fig. 8.35) reads two numbers from the keyboard, then computes and displays their sum. The instruction +1007 reads the first number from the keyboard and places it

Location	Number	Instruction
00	+1007	(Read A)
01	+1008	(Read B)
02	+2007	(Load A)

Fig. 8.35 | SML program that reads two integers and computes their sum. (Part 1 of 2.)

Location	Number	Instruction
03	+3008	(Add B)
04	+2109	(Store C)
05	+1109	(Write C)
06	+4300	(Halt)
07	+0000	(Variable A)
08	+0000	(Variable B)
09	+0000	(Result C)

Fig. 8.35 | SML program that reads two integers and computes their sum. (Part 2 of 2.)

into location 07 (which has been initialized to 0). Then instruction +1008 reads the next number into location 08. The *load* instruction, +2007, puts the first number into the accumulator, and the *add* instruction, +3008, adds the second number to the number in the accumulator. *All SML arithmetic instructions leave their results in the accumulator.* The *store* instruction, +2109, places the result in memory location 09, from which the *write* instruction, +1109, takes the number and displays it (as a signed four-digit decimal number). The *halt* instruction, +4300, terminates execution.

The second SML program (Fig. 8.36) reads two numbers from the keyboard and determines and displays the larger value. Note the use of the instruction +4107 as a conditional transfer of control, much the same as C#'s if statement.

Location	Number	Instruction
00	+1009	(Read A)
01	+1010	(Read B)
02	+2009	(Load A)
03	+3110	(Subtract B)
04	+4107	(Branch negative to 07)
05	+1109	(Write A)
06	+4300	(Halt)
07	+1110	(Write B)
08	+4300	(Halt)
09	+0000	(Variable A)
10	+0000	(Variable B)

Fig. 8.36 | SML program that reads two integers and determines the larger.

Now write SML programs to accomplish each of the following tasks:

a) Use a sentinel-controlled loop to read positive numbers and compute and print their sum. Terminate input when a negative number is entered.

b) Use a counter-controlled loop to read seven numbers, some positive and some negative, then compute and display their average.

c) Read a series of numbers, then determine and display the largest number. The first number read indicates how many numbers should be processed.

8.32 (*Computer Simulator*) In this problem, you are going to build your own computer. No, you will not be soldering components together. Rather, you will use the powerful technique of *software-based simulation* to create an object-oriented *software model* of the Simpletron of Exercise 8.31. Your Simpletron simulator will turn the computer you are using into a Simpletron, and you will actually be able to run, test and debug the SML programs you wrote in Exercise 8.31.

When you run your Simpletron simulator, it should begin by displaying:

```
*** Welcome to Simpletron! ***
*** Please enter your program one instruction ***
*** ( or data word ) at a time into the input ***
*** text field. I will display the location   ***
*** number and a question mark (?). You then   ***
*** type the word for that location. Enter     ***
*** -99999 to stop entering your program.      ***
```

Your application should simulate the memory of the Simpletron with one-dimensional array memory of 100 elements. Now assume that the simulator is running, and let us examine the dialog as we enter the program of Fig. 8.36 (Exercise 8.31):

```
00 ? +1009
01 ? +1010
02 ? +2009
03 ? +3110
04 ? +4107
05 ? +1109
06 ? +4300
07 ? +1110
08 ? +4300
09 ? +0000
10 ? +0000
11 ? -99999
```

Your program should display the memory location followed by a question mark. Each of the values to the right of a question mark is input by the user. When the sentinel value -99999 is input, the program should display the following:

```
*** Program loading completed ***
*** Program execution begins   ***
```

The SML program has now been placed (or loaded) in array memory. Now the Simpletron executes the SML program. Execution begins with the instruction in location 00 and, as in C#, continues sequentially, unless directed to some other part of the program by a transfer of control.

Use variable accumulator to represent the accumulator register. Use variable instructionCounter to keep track of the location in memory that contains the instruction being performed. Use variable operationCode to indicate the operation currently being performed (i.e., the left two digits of the instruction word). Use variable operand to indicate the memory location on which the current instruction operates. Thus, operand is the rightmost two digits of the instruction currently being performed. Do not execute instructions directly from memory. Rather, transfer the next instruction to be performed from memory to a variable called `instructionRegister`. Then "pick off" the left two digits and place them in `operationCode`, and "pick off" the right two digits and place them in `operand`. When the Simpletron begins execution, the special registers are all initialized to zero.

Now, let us "walk through" execution of the first SML instruction, +1009 in memory location 00. This procedure is called an *instruction execution cycle*.

The `instructionCounter` tells us the location of the next instruction to be performed. We *fetch* the contents of that location from `memory` by using the C# statement

```
instructionRegister = memory[ instructionCounter ];
```

The operation code and the operand are extracted from the instruction register by the statements

```
operationCode = instructionRegister / 100;
operand = instructionRegister % 100;
```

Now the Simpletron must determine that the operation code is actually a *read* (versus a *write*, a *load*, etc.). A `switch` differentiates among the 12 operations of SML. In the `switch` statement, the behavior of various SML instructions is simulated as shown in Fig. 8.37. We discuss branch instructions shortly and leave the others to you.

When the SML program completes execution, the name and contents of each register, as well as the complete contents of memory, should be displayed. Such a printout is often called a memory dump. To help you program your dump method, a sample dump format is shown in Fig. 8.38. Note that a dump after executing a Simpletron program would show the actual values of instructions and data values at the moment execution terminated.

Let us proceed with the execution of our program's first instruction—namely, the +1009 in location 00. As we have indicated, the `switch` statement simulates this task by prompting the user to enter a value, reading the value and storing it in memory location `memory[ operand ]`. The value is then read into location 09.

At this point, simulation of the first instruction is completed. All that remains is to prepare the Simpletron to execute the next instruction. Since the instruction just performed was not a transfer of control, we need merely increment the instruction-counter register as follows:

```
instructionCounter++;
```

This action completes the simulated execution of the first instruction. The entire process (i.e., the instruction execution cycle) begins anew with the fetch of the next instruction to execute.

Instruction	Description
read:	Display the prompt `"Enter an integer"`, then input the integer and store it in location `memory[ operand ]`.
load:	`accumulator = memory[ operand ];`
add:	`accumulator += memory[ operand ];`
halt:	This instruction displays the message `*** Simpletron execution terminated ***`

Fig. 8.37 | Behavior of several SML instructions in the Simpletron.

```
REGISTERS:
accumulator            +0000
instructionCounter        00
instructionRegister    +0000
operationCode             00
operand                   00

MEMORY:
        0     1     2     3     4     5     6     7     8     9
 0  +0000 +0000 +0000 +0000 +0000 +0000 +0000 +0000 +0000 +0000
10  +0000 +0000 +0000 +0000 +0000 +0000 +0000 +0000 +0000 +0000
20  +0000 +0000 +0000 +0000 +0000 +0000 +0000 +0000 +0000 +0000
30  +0000 +0000 +0000 +0000 +0000 +0000 +0000 +0000 +0000 +0000
40  +0000 +0000 +0000 +0000 +0000 +0000 +0000 +0000 +0000 +0000
50  +0000 +0000 +0000 +0000 +0000 +0000 +0000 +0000 +0000 +0000
60  +0000 +0000 +0000 +0000 +0000 +0000 +0000 +0000 +0000 +0000
70  +0000 +0000 +0000 +0000 +0000 +0000 +0000 +0000 +0000 +0000
80  +0000 +0000 +0000 +0000 +0000 +0000 +0000 +0000 +0000 +0000
90  +0000 +0000 +0000 +0000 +0000 +0000 +0000 +0000 +0000 +0000
```

Fig. 8.38 | A sample memory dump.

Now let us consider how the branching instructions—the transfers of control—are simulated. All we need to do is adjust the value in the instruction counter appropriately. Therefore, the unconditional branch instruction (40) is simulated within the `switch` as

```
instructionCounter = operand;
```

The conditional "branch if accumulator is zero" instruction is simulated as

```
if ( accumulator == 0 )
    instructionCounter = operand;
```

At this point, you should implement your Simpletron simulator and run each of the SML programs you wrote in Exercise 8.31. If you desire, you may embellish SML with additional features and provide for these features in your simulator.

Your simulator should check for various types of errors. During the program-loading phase, for example, each number the user types into the Simpletron's memory must be in the range -9999 to +9999. Your simulator should test that each number entered is in this range and, if not, keep prompting the user to re-enter the number until the user enters a correct number.

During the execution phase, your simulator should check for various serious errors, such as attempts to divide by zero, attempts to execute invalid operation codes and accumulator overflows (i.e., arithmetic operations resulting in values larger than +9999 or smaller than -9999). Such serious errors are called *fatal errors*. When a fatal error is detected, your simulator should display an error message, such as

```
*** Attempt to divide by zero ***
*** Simpletron execution abnormally terminated ***
```

and should display a full computer dump in the format we discussed previously. This treatment will help the user locate the error in the program.

8.33   (*Simpletron Simulator Modifications*) In Exercise 8.32, you wrote a software simulation of a computer that executes programs written in Simpletron Machine Language (SML). In this exercise, we propose several modifications and enhancements to the Simpletron Simulator. In Exercise 25.10 and Exercise 25.11, we propose building a compiler that converts programs written in a high-level programming language (a variation of Basic) to Simpletron Machine Language. Some of the following modifications and enhancements may be required to execute the programs produced by the compiler:

a) Extend the Simpletron Simulator's memory to contain 1000 memory locations to enable the Simpletron to handle larger programs.

b) Allow the simulator to perform remainder calculations. This modification requires an additional SML instruction.

c) Allow the simulator to perform exponentiation calculations. This modification requires an additional SML instruction.

d) Modify the simulator to use hexadecimal values rather than integer values to represent SML instructions.

e) Modify the simulator to allow output of a newline. This modification requires an additional SML instruction.

f) Modify the simulator to process floating-point values in addition to integer values.

g) Modify the simulator to handle string input. [*Hint:* Each Simpletron word can be divided into two groups, each holding a two-digit integer. Each two-digit integer represents the ASCII (see Appendix D) decimal equivalent of a character. Add a machine-language instruction that will input a string and store the string beginning at a specific Simpletron memory location. The first half of the word at that location will be a count of the number of characters in the string (i.e., the length of the string). Each succeeding half-word contains one ASCII character expressed as two decimal digits. The machine-language instruction converts each character into its ASCII equivalent and assigns it to a half-word.]

h) Modify the simulator to handle output of strings stored in the format of *Part g*. [*Hint:* Add a machine-language instruction that will display a string beginning at a certain Simpletron memory location. The first half of the word at that location is a count of the number of characters in the string (i.e., the length of the string). Each succeeding half-word contains one ASCII character expressed as two decimal digits. The machine-language instruction checks the length and displays the string by translating each two-digit number into its equivalent character.]

9

Classes and Objects: A Deeper Look

OBJECTIVES

In this chapter you will learn:

- Encapsulation and data hiding.
- The concepts of data abstraction and abstract data types (ADTs).
- To use keyword `this`.
- To use indexers to access members of a class.
- To use `static` variables and methods.
- To use `readonly` fields.
- To take advantage of C#'s memory management features.
- How to create a class library.
- When to use the `internal` access modifier.

9.1 Introduction

In our discussions of object-oriented applications in the preceding chapters, we introduced many basic concepts and terminology that relate to C# object-oriented programming (OOP). We also discussed our application development methodology: We selected appropriate variables and methods for each application and specified the manner in which an object of our class collaborated with objects of classes in the .NET Framework Class Library to accomplish the application's overall goals.

In this chapter, we take a deeper look at building classes, controlling access to members of a class and creating constructors. We discuss composition—a capability that allows a class to have references to objects of other classes as members. We reexamine the use of properties and explore indexers as an alternative notation for accessing the members of a class. The chapter also discusses static class members and readonly instance variables in detail. We investigate issues such as software reusability, data abstraction and encapsulation. Finally, we explain how to organize classes in assemblies to help manage large applications and promote reuse, then show a special relationship between classes in the same assembly.

Chapter 10, Object-Oriented Programming: Inheritance, and Chapter 11, Polymorphism, Interfaces & Operator Overloading, introduce two additional key object-oriented programming technologies.

9.2 Time Class Case Study

Time1 Class Declaration

Our first example consists of two classes—Time1 (Fig. 9.1) and Time1Test (Fig. 9.2). Class Time1 represents the time of day. Class Time1Test is a testing class in which the Main method creates an object of class Time1 and invokes its methods. The output of this application appears in Fig. 9.2.

Class Time1 contains three private instance variables of type int (Fig. 9.1, lines 5–7)—hour, minute and second—that represent the time in universal-time format (24-hour clock format, in which hours are in the range 0–23). Class Time1 contains public methods SetTime (lines 11–16), ToUniversalString (lines 19–23) and ToString (lines 26–31). These methods are the public *services* or the public *interface* that the class provides to its clients.

In this example, class Time1 does not declare a constructor, so the class has a default constructor that is supplied by the compiler. Each instance variable implicitly receives the default value 0 for an int. Note that when instance variables are declared in the class body they can be initialized using the same initialization syntax as a local variable.

```
 1   // Fig. 9.1: Time1.cs
 2   // Time1 class declaration maintains the time in 24-hour format.
 3   public class Time1
 4   {
 5      private int hour; // 0 - 23
 6      private int minute; // 0 - 59
 7      private int second; // 0 - 59
 8
 9      // set a new time value using universal time; ensure that
10      // the data remains consistent by setting invalid values to zero
11      public void SetTime( int h, int m, int s )
12      {
13         hour = ( ( h >= 0 && h < 24 ) ? h : 0 ); // validate hour
14         minute = ( ( m >= 0 && m < 60 ) ? m : 0 ); // validate minute
15         second = ( ( s >= 0 && s < 60 ) ? s : 0 ); // validate second
16      } // end method SetTime
17
18      // convert to string in universal-time format (HH:MM:SS)
19      public string ToUniversalString()
20      {
21         return string.Format( "{0:D2}:{1:D2}:{2:D2}",
22            hour, minute, second );
23      } // end method ToUniversalString
24
25      // convert to string in standard-time format (H:MM:SS AM or PM)
26      public override string ToString()
27      {
28         return string.Format( "{0}:{1:D2}:{2:D2} {3}",
29            ( ( hour == 0 || hour == 12 ) ? 12 : hour % 12 ),
30            minute, second, ( hour < 12 ? "AM" : "PM" ) );
31      } // end method ToString
32   } // end class Time1
```

Fig. 9.1 | Time1 class declaration maintains the time in 24-hour format.

Method SetTime (lines 11–16) is a public method that declares three int parameters and uses them to set the time. A conditional expression tests each argument to determine whether the value is in a specified range. For example, the hour value (line 13) must be greater than or equal to 0 and less than 24, because universal-time format represents hours as integers from 0 to 23 (e.g., 1 PM is hour 13 and 11 PM is hour 23; midnight is hour 0 and noon is hour 12). Similarly, both minute and second values (lines 14 and 15) must be greater than or equal to 0 and less than 60. Any out-of-range values are set to 0 to ensure that a Time1 object always contains consistent data—that is, the object's data values are always kept in range, even if the values provided as arguments to method SetTime are incorrect. In this example, 0 is a consistent value for hour, minute and second.

A value passed to SetTime is a correct value if that value is in the allowed range for the member it is initializing. So, any number in the range 0–23 would be a correct value for the hour. A correct value is always a consistent value. However, a consistent value is not necessarily a correct value. If SetTime sets hour to 0 because the argument received was out of range, then SetTime is taking an incorrect value and making it consistent, so the object remains in a consistent state at all times. In this case, the application might want to indicate that the object is incorrect. In Chapter 12, Exception Handling, you will learn techniques that enable your classes to indicate when incorrect values are received.

Software Engineering Observation 9.1

Methods and properties that modify the values of private variables should verify that the intended new values are proper. If they are not, they should place the private variables in an appropriate consistent state.

Method ToUniversalString (lines 19–23) takes no arguments and returns a string in universal-time format, consisting of six digits—two for the hour, two for the minute and two for the second. For example, if the time were 1:30:07 PM, method ToUniversalString would return 13:30:07. The return statement (lines 21–22) uses static method *Format* of class string to return a string containing the formatted hour, minute and second values, each with two digits and, where needed, a leading 0 (specified with the D2 format specifier—which pads the integer with 0s if it has less than two digits). Method Format is similar to the string formatting in method Console.Write, except that Format returns a formatted string rather than displaying it in a console window. The formatted string is returned by method ToUniversalString.

Method ToString (lines 26–31) takes no arguments and returns a string in standard-time format, consisting of the hour, minute and second values separated by colons and followed by an AM or PM indicator (e.g., 1:27:06 PM). Like method ToUniversalString, method ToString uses static string method Format to format the minute and second as two-digit values with leading 0s, if necessary. Line 29 uses a conditional operator (?:) to determine the value for hour in the string—if the hour is 0 or 12 (AM or PM), it appears as 12—otherwise, the hour appears as a value from 1 to 11. The conditional operator in line 30 determines whether AM or PM will be returned as part of the string.

Recall from Section 7.4 that all objects in C# have a ToString method that returns a string representation of the object. We chose to return a string containing the time in standard-time format. Method ToString is called implicitly when an object's value is output with a format item in a call to Console.Write. Remember that to enable objects to be converted to their string representations, we need to declare method ToString with keyword override—the reason for this will become clear when we discuss inheritance in Chapter 10.

Using Class Time1

As you learned in Chapter 4, each class you declare represents a new type in C#. Therefore, after declaring class Time1, we can use it as a type in declarations such as

```
Time1 sunset; // sunset can hold a reference to a Time1 object
```

The Time1Test application class (Fig. 9.2) uses class Time1. Line 10 creates a Time1 object and assigns it to local variable time. Note that new invokes class Time1's default constructor, since Time1 does not declare any constructors. Lines 13–17 output the time, first in universal-time format (by invoking time's ToUniversalString method in line 14), then in standard-time format (by explicitly invoking time's ToString method in line 16) to confirm that the Time1 object was initialized properly.

```
 1   // Fig. 9.2: Time1Test.cs
 2   // Time1 object used in an application.
 3   using System;
 4
 5   public class Time1Test
 6   {
 7      public static void Main( string[] args )
 8      {
 9         // create and initialize a Time1 object
10         Time1 time = new Time1(); // invokes Time1 constructor
11
12         // output string representations of the time
13         Console.Write( "The initial universal time is: " );
14         Console.WriteLine( time.ToUniversalString() );
15         Console.Write( "The initial standard time is: " );
16         Console.WriteLine( time.ToString() );
17         Console.WriteLine(); // output a blank line
18
19         // change time and output updated time
20         time.SetTime( 13, 27, 6 );
21         Console.Write( "Universal time after SetTime is: " );
22         Console.WriteLine( time.ToUniversalString() );
23         Console.Write( "Standard time after SetTime is: " );
24         Console.WriteLine( time.ToString() );
25         Console.WriteLine(); // output a blank line
26
27         // set time with invalid values; output updated time
28         time.SetTime( 99, 99, 99 );
29         Console.WriteLine( "After attempting invalid settings:" );
30         Console.Write( "Universal time: " );
31         Console.WriteLine( time.ToUniversalString() );
32         Console.Write( "Standard time: " );
33         Console.WriteLine( time.ToString() );
34      } // end Main
35   } // end class Time1Test
```

Fig. 9.2 | Time1 object used in an application. (Part 1 of 2.)

```
The initial universal time is: 00:00:00
The initial standard time is: 12:00:00 AM

Universal time after SetTime is: 13:27:06
Standard time after SetTime is: 1:27:06 PM

After attempting invalid settings:
Universal time: 00:00:00
Standard time: 12:00:00 AM
```

Fig. 9.2 | `Time1` object used in an application. (Part 2 of 2.)

Line 20 invokes method `SetTime` of the `time` object to change the time. Then lines 21–25 output the time again in both formats to confirm that the time was set correctly.

To illustrate that method `SetTime` maintains the object in a consistent state, line 28 calls method `SetTime` with invalid arguments of 99 for the `hour`, `minute` and `second`. Lines 29–33 output the time again in both formats to confirm that `SetTime` maintains the object's consistent state, then the application terminates. The last two lines of the application's output show that the time is reset to midnight—the initial value of a `Time1` object—after an attempt to set the time with three out-of-range values.

Notes on the `Time1` Class Declaration
Consider several issues of class design with respect to class `Time1`. The instance variables `hour`, `minute` and `second` are each declared `private`. The actual data representation used within the class is of no concern to the class's clients. For example, it would be perfectly reasonable for `Time1` to represent the time internally as the number of seconds since midnight or the number of minutes and seconds since midnight. Clients could use the same `public` methods and properties to get the same results without being aware of this. (Exercise 9.5 asks you to represent the time as the number of seconds since midnight and show that there is indeed no change visible to the clients of the class.)

Software Engineering Observation 9.2

Classes simplify programming because the client can use only the `public` members exposed by the class. Such members are usually client oriented rather than implementation oriented. Clients are neither aware of, nor involved in, a class's implementation. Clients generally care about what the class does but not how the class does it. (Clients do, of course, care that the class operates correctly and efficiently.)

Software Engineering Observation 9.3

Interfaces change less frequently than implementations. When an implementation changes, implementation-dependent code must change accordingly. Hiding the implementation reduces the possibility that other application parts will become dependent on class-implementation details.

9.3 Controlling Access to Members
The access modifiers `public` and `private` control access to a class's variables and methods. (In Section 9.15 and Chapter 10, we will introduce the additional access modifiers `inter-`

nal and protected, respectively.) As we stated in Section 9.2, the primary purpose of public methods is to present to the class's clients a view of the services the class provides (the class's public interface). Clients of the class need not be concerned with how the class accomplishes its tasks. For this reason, a class's private variables and methods (i.e., the class's implementation details) are not directly accessible to the class's clients.

Figure 9.3 demonstrates that private class members are not directly accessible outside the class. Lines 9–11 attempt to access directly private instance variables hour, minute and second of Time1 object time. When this application is compiled, the compiler generates error messages stating that these private members are not accessible. [*Note:* This application assumes that the Time1 class from Fig. 9.1 is used.]

> ### Common Programming Error 9.1
>
> *An attempt by a method that is not a member of a class to access a private member of that class is a compilation error.*

Notice that members of a class—for instance, methods and instance variables—do not need to be explicitly declared private. If a class member is not declared with an access modifier, it has private access by default. We always explicitly declare private members.

9.4 Referring to the Current Object's Members with the this Reference

Every object can access a reference to itself with keyword this (also called the this *reference*). When a non-static method is called for a particular object, the method's body implicitly uses keyword this to refer to the object's instance variables and other methods. As

```
1   // Fig. 9.3: MemberAccessTest.cs
2   // Private members of class Time1 are not accessible.
3   public class MemberAccessTest
4   {
5      public static void Main( string[] args )
6      {
7         Time1 time = new Time1(); // create and initialize Time1 object
8
9         time.hour = 7; // error: hour has private access in Time1
10        time.minute = 15; // error: minute has private access in Time1
11        time.second = 30; // error: second has private access in Time1
12     } // end Main
13   } // end class MemberAccessTest
```

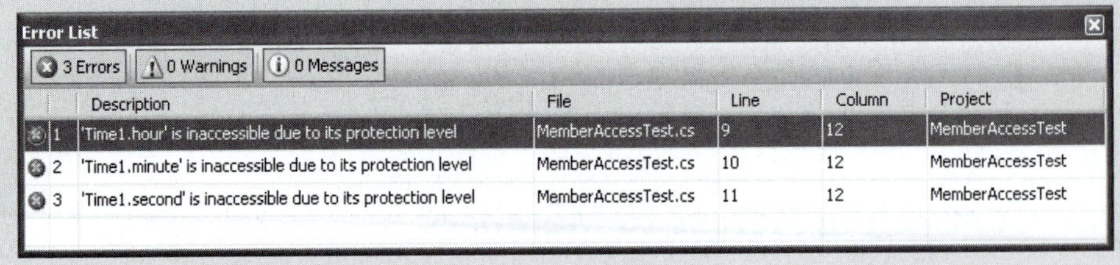

	Description	File	Line	Column	Project
1	'Time1.hour' is inaccessible due to its protection level	MemberAccessTest.cs	9	12	MemberAccessTest
2	'Time1.minute' is inaccessible due to its protection level	MemberAccessTest.cs	10	12	MemberAccessTest
3	'Time1.second' is inaccessible due to its protection level	MemberAccessTest.cs	11	12	MemberAccessTest

Error List — 3 Errors — 0 Warnings — 0 Messages

Fig. 9.3 | Private members of class Time1 are not accessible.

you will see in Fig. 9.4, you can also use keyword this *explicitly* in a non-static method's body. Section 9.5 and Section 9.6 show two more interesting uses of keyword this. Section 9.10 explains why keyword this cannot be used in a static method.

We now demonstrate implicit and explicit use of the this reference to enable class ThisTest's Main method to display the private data of a class SimpleTime object (Fig. 9.4). For the sake of brevity, we declare two classes in one file—class ThisTest is declared in lines 5–12, and class SimpleTime is declared in lines 15–48.

Class SimpleTime (lines 15–48) declares three private instance variables—hour, minute and second (lines 17–19). The constructor (lines 24–29) receives three int arguments to initialize a SimpleTime object. Note that for the constructor we used parameter names that are identical to the class's instance variable names (lines 17–19). We don't recommend this practice, but we did it here to hide the corresponding instance variables so that we could illustrate explicit use of the this reference. Recall from Section 7.11 that if a method contains a local variable with the same name as a field, that method will refer to the local variable rather than the field. In this case, the local variable hides the field in the method's scope. However, the method can use the this reference to refer to the hidden instance variable explicitly, as shown in lines 26–28 for SimpleTime's hidden instance variables.

Method BuildString (lines 32–37) returns a string created by a statement that uses the this reference explicitly and implicitly. Line 35 uses the this reference explicitly to

```
 1    // Fig. 9.4: ThisTest.cs
 2    // this used implicitly and explicitly to refer to members of an object.
 3    using System;
 4
 5    public class ThisTest
 6    {
 7       public static void Main( string[] args )
 8       {
 9          SimpleTime time = new SimpleTime( 15, 30, 19 );
10          Console.WriteLine( time.BuildString() );
11       } // end Main
12    } // end class ThisTest
13
14    // class SimpleTime demonstrates the "this" reference
15    public class SimpleTime
16    {
17       private int hour; // 0-23
18       private int minute; // 0-59
19       private int second; // 0-59
20
21       // if the constructor uses parameter names identical to
22       // instance variable names the "this" reference is
23       // required to distinguish between names
24       public SimpleTime( int hour, int minute, int second )
25       {
26          this.hour = hour; // set "this" object's hour instance variable
27          this.minute = minute; // set "this" object's minute
28          this.second = second; // set "this" object's second
29       } // end SimpleTime constructor
```

Fig. 9.4 | this used implicitly and explicitly to refer to members of an object. (Part I of 2.)

```
30
31      // use explicit and implicit "this" to call ToUniversalString
32      public string BuildString()
33      {
34          return string.Format( "{0,24}: {1}\n{2,24}: {3}",
35              "this.ToUniversalString()", this.ToUniversalString(),
36              "ToUniversalString()", ToUniversalString() );
37      } // end method BuildString
38
39      // convert to string in universal-time format (HH:MM:SS)
40      public string ToUniversalString()
41      {
42          // "this" is not required here to access instance variables,
43          // because method does not have local variables with same
44          // names as instance variables
45          return string.Format( "{0:D2}:{1:D2}:{2:D2}",
46              this.hour, this.minute, this.second );
47      } // end method ToUniversalString
48  } // end class SimpleTime
```

```
this.ToUniversalString(): 15:30:19
    ToUniversalString(): 15:30:19
```

Fig. 9.4 | this used implicitly and explicitly to refer to members of an object. (Part 2 of 2.)

call method ToUniversalString. Line 36 uses the this reference implicitly to call the same method. Note that both lines perform the same task. Programmers typically do not use the this reference explicitly to reference other methods in the current object. Also, note that line 46 in method ToUniversalString explicitly uses the this reference to access each instance variable. This is not necessary here, because the method does not have any local variables that hide the instance variables of the class.

Common Programming Error 9.2

It is often a logic error when a method contains a parameter or local variable that has the same name as an instance variable of the class. In such a case, use reference this if you wish to access the instance variable of the class—otherwise, the method parameter or local variable will be referenced.

Error-Prevention Tip 9.1

Avoid method parameter names or local variable names that conflict with field names. This helps prevent subtle, hard-to-locate bugs.

Class ThisTest (Fig. 9.4, lines 5–12) demonstrates class SimpleTime. Line 9 creates an instance of class SimpleTime and invokes its constructor. Line 10 invokes the object's BuildString method, then displays the results.

Performance Tip 9.1

C# conserves memory by maintaining only one copy of each method per class—this method is invoked by every object of the class. Each object, on the other hand, has its own copy of the class's instance variables (i.e., non-static variables). Each method of the class implicitly uses the this reference to determine the specific object of the class to manipulate.

9.5 Indexers

Chapter 4 introduced properties as a way to access a class's private data in a controlled manner via the properties' get and set accessors. Sometimes a class encapsulates lists of data such as arrays. Such a class can use keyword this to define property-like class members called *indexers* that allow array-style indexed access to lists of elements. With "conventional" C# arrays, the index must be an integer value. A benefit of indexers is that you can define both integer indices and non-integer indices. For example, you could allow client code to manipulate data using strings as indices that represent the data items' names or descriptions. When manipulating "conventional" C# array elements, the array element access operator always returns a value of the same type—i.e., the type of the array. Indexers are more flexible— they can return any type, even one that is different from the type of the underlying data.

Although an indexer's element access operator is used like an array element access operator, indexers are defined like properties in a class. Unlike properties, for which you can choose an appropriate property name, indexers must be defined with keyword this. Indexers have the general form:

```
accessModifier returnType this[ IndexType1 name1 , IndexType2 name2 , ... ]
{
    get
    {
        // use name1, name2, ... here to get data
    }
    set
    {
        // use name1, name2, ... here to set data
    }
}
```

The *IndexType* parameters specified in the brackets ([]) are accessible to the get and set accessors. These accessors define how to use the index (or indices) to retrieve or modify the appropriate data member. As with properties, the indexer's get accessor must return a value of type *returnType* and the set accessor can use the implicit parameter value to reference the value that should be assigned to the element.

Common Programming Error 9.3

Declaring indexers as static is a syntax error.

The application of Figs. 9.5 and 9.6 contains two classes—class Box represents a box with a length, a width and a height, and class BoxTest demonstrates class Box's indexers.

The private data members of class Box are string array names (line 6), which contains the names (i.e., "length", "width" and "height") for the dimensions of a Box, and double array dimensions (line 7), which contains the size of each dimension. Each element in array names corresponds to an element in array dimensions (e.g., dimensions[2] contains the height of the Box).

Box defines two indexers (lines 18–33 and lines 36–59) that each return a double value representing the size of the dimension specified by the indexer's parameter. Indexers can be overloaded like methods. The first indexer uses an int index to manipulate an element in the dimensions array. The second indexer uses a string index representing the name of the dimension to manipulate an element in the `dimensions` array. Each indexer returns -1 if its get accessor encounters an invalid subscript. Each indexer's set accessor assigns `value` to the appropriate element of `dimensions` only if the index is valid. Normally, you would have an indexer throw an exception if it receives an invalid index. We discuss how to throw exceptions in Chapter 12, Exception Handling.

Notice that the `string` indexer uses a `while` structure to search for a matching `string` in the `names` array (lines 42–44 and lines 52–54). If a match is found, the indexer manipulates the corresponding element in array `dimensions` (lines 46 and 57).

Class `BoxTest` (Fig. 9.6) manipulates the `private` data members of class `Box` through `Box`'s indexers. Local variable `box` is declared at line 10, and initialized to a new instance of class `Box`. We use the `Box` constructor to initialize `box` with dimensions of 30, 30, and 30. Lines 14–16 use the indexer declared with parameter `int` to obtain the three dimensions of `box`, and display them with `WriteLine`. The expression `box[0]` (line 14) implicitly calls the `get` accessor of the indexer to obtain the value of `box`'s `private` instance variable `dimensions[0]`. Similarly, the assignment to `box[0]` in line 20 implicitly calls the `set` accessor in lines 28–32 of Fig. 9.5. The `set` accessor implicitly sets its `value` parameter to 10, then sets `dimensions[0]` to `value` (10). Lines 24 and 28–30 in Fig. 9.6 take similar actions, using the overloaded indexer with a `string` parameter to manipulate the same data.

```csharp
 1   // Fig. 9.5: Box.cs
 2   // Box class definition represents a box with length,
 3   // width and height dimensions with indexers.
 4   public class Box
 5   {
 6      private string[] names = { "length", "width", "height" };
 7      private double[] dimensions = new double[ 3 ];
 8
 9      // constructor
10      public Box( double length, double width, double height )
11      {
12         dimensions[ 0 ] = length;
13         dimensions[ 1 ] = width;
14         dimensions[ 2 ] = height;
15      }
16
17      // indexer to access dimensions by integer index number
18      public double this[ int index ]
19      {
20         get
21         {
22            // validate index to get
23            if ( ( index < 0 ) || ( index >= dimensions.Length ) )
24               return -1;
25            else
26               return dimensions[ index ];
27         } // end get
28         set
29         {
```

Fig. 9.5 | Box class definition represents a box with length, width and height dimensions with indexers. (Part 1 of 2.)

```
30              if ( index >= 0 && index < dimensions.Length )
31                 dimensions[ index ] = value;
32           } // end set
33        } // end numeric indexer
34
35        // indexer to access dimensions by their string names
36        public double this[ string name ]
37        {
38           get
39           {
40              // locate element to get
41              int i = 0;
42              while ( ( i < names.Length ) &&
43                 ( name.ToLower() != names[ i ] ) )
44                 i++;
45
46              return ( i == names.Length ) ? -1 : dimensions[ i ];
47           } // end get
48           set
49           {
50              // locate element to set
51              int i = 0;
52              while ( ( i < names.Length ) &&
53                 ( name.ToLower() != names[ i ] ) )
54                 i++;
55
56              if ( i != names.Length )
57                 dimensions[ i ] = value;
58           } // end set
59        } // end string indexer
60     } // end class Box
```

Fig. 9.5 | Box class definition represents a box with length, width and height dimensions with indexers. (Part 2 of 2.)

```
1   // Fig. 9.6: BoxTest.cs
2   // Indexers provide access to a Box object's members.
3   using System;
4
5   public class BoxTest
6   {
7      public static void Main( string[] args )
8      {
9         // create a box
10        Box box = new Box( 30, 30, 30 );
11
12        // show dimensions with numeric indexers
13        Console.WriteLine( "Created a box with the dimensions:" );
14        Console.WriteLine( "box[ 0 ] = {0}", box[ 0 ] );
15        Console.WriteLine( "box[ 1 ] = {0}", box[ 1 ] );
16        Console.WriteLine( "box[ 2 ] = {0}", box[ 2 ] );
17
```

Fig. 9.6 | Indexers provide access to an object's members. (Part 1 of 2.)

```
18        // set a dimension with the numeric indexer
19        Console.WriteLine( "\nSetting box[ 0 ] to 10...\n" );
20        box[ 0 ] = 10;
21
22        // set a dimension with the string indexer
23        Console.WriteLine( "Setting box[ \"width\" ] to 20...\n" );
24        box[ "width" ] = 20;
25
26        // show dimensions with string indexers
27        Console.WriteLine( "Now the box has the dimensions:" );
28        Console.WriteLine( "box[ \"length\" ] = {0}", box[ "length" ] );
29        Console.WriteLine( "box[ \"width\" ] = {0}", box[ "width" ] );
30        Console.WriteLine( "box[ \"height\" ] = {0}", box[ "height" ] );
31     } // end method Main
32  } // end class BoxTest
```

```
Created a box with the dimensions:
box[ 0 ] = 30
box[ 1 ] = 30
box[ 2 ] = 30

Setting box[ 0 ] to 10...

Setting box[ "width" ] to 20...

Now the box has the dimensions:
box[ "length" ] = 10
box[ "width" ] = 20
box[ "height" ] = 30
```

Fig. 9.6 | Indexers provide access to an object's members. (Part 2 of 2.)

9.6 Time Class Case Study: Overloaded Constructors

As you know, you can declare your own constructor to specify how objects of a class should be initialized. Next, we demonstrate a class with several *overloaded constructors* that enable objects of that class to be initialized in different ways. To overload constructors, simply provide multiple constructor declarations with different signatures. Recall from Section 7.12 that the compiler differentiates signatures by the number, types and order of the parameters in each signature.

Class Time2 with Overloaded Constructors

By default, instance variables hour, minute and second of class Time1 (Fig. 9.1) are initialized to their default values of 0 (which is midnight in universal time). Class Time1 does not enable the class's clients to initialize the time with specific non-zero values. Class Time2 (Fig. 9.7) contains five overloaded constructors for conveniently initializing its objects in a variety of ways. The constructors ensure that each Time2 object begins in a consistent state. In this application, four of the constructors invoke a fifth constructor, which in turn calls method SetTime. Method SetTime invokes the set accessors of properties Hour, Minute and Second, which ensure that the value supplied for hour is in the range 0 to 23 and that the values for minute and second are each in the range 0 to 59. If a value is out

```
 1   // Fig. 9.7: Time2.cs
 2   // Time2 class declaration with overloaded constructors.
 3   public class Time2
 4   {
 5      private int hour; // 0 - 23
 6      private int minute; // 0 - 59
 7      private int second; // 0 - 59
 8
 9      // Time2 parameterless constructor: initializes each instance variable
10      // to zero; ensures that Time2 objects start in a consistent state
11      public Time2() : this( 0, 0, 0 ) { }
12
13      // Time2 constructor: hour supplied, minute and second defaulted to 0
14      public Time2( int h ) : this( h, 0, 0 ) { }
15
16      // Time2 constructor: hour and minute supplied, second defaulted to 0
17      public Time2( int h, int m ) : this( h, m, 0 ) { }
18
19      // Time2 constructor: hour, minute and second supplied
20      public Time2( int h, int m, int s )
21      {
22         SetTime( h, m, s ); // invoke SetTime to validate time
23      } // end Time2 three-parameter constructor
24
25      // Time2 constructor: another Time2 object supplied
26      public Time2( Time2 time )
27         : this( time.Hour, time.Minute, time.Second ) { }
28
29      // set a new time value using universal time; ensure that
30      // the data remains consistent by setting invalid values to zero
31      public void SetTime( int h, int m, int s )
32      {
33         Hour = h; // set the Hour property
34         Minute = m; // set the Minute property
35         Second = s; // set the Second property
36      } // end method SetTime
37
38      // Properties for getting and setting
39      // property that gets and sets the hour
40      public int Hour
41      {
42         get
43         {
44            return hour;
45         } // end get
46         // make writing inaccessible outside the class
47         private set
48         {
49            hour = ( ( value >= 0 && value < 24 ) ? value : 0 );
50         } // end set
51      } // end property Hour
```

Fig. 9.7 | Time2 class declaration with overloaded constructors. (Part I of 2.)

```
52
53      // property that gets and sets the minute
54      public int Minute
55      {
56         get
57         {
58            return minute;
59         } // end get
60         // make writing inaccessible outside the class
61         private set
62         {
63            minute = ( ( value >= 0 && value < 60 ) ? value : 0 );
64         } // end set
65      } // end property Minute
66
67      // property that gets and sets the second
68      public int Second
69      {
70         get
71         {
72            return second;
73         } // end get
74         // make writing inaccessible outside the class
75         private set
76         {
77            second = ( ( value >= 0 && value < 60 ) ? value : 0 );
78         } // end set
79      } // end property Second
80
81      // convert to string in universal-time format (HH:MM:SS)
82      public string ToUniversalString()
83      {
84         return string.Format(
85            "{0:D2}:{1:D2}:{2:D2}", Hour, Minute, Second );
86      } // end method ToUniversalString
87
88      // convert to string in standard-time format (H:MM:SS AM or PM)
89      public override string ToString()
90      {
91         return string.Format( "{0}:{1:D2}:{2:D2} {3}",
92            ( ( Hour == 0 || Hour == 12 ) ? 12 : Hour % 12 ),
93            Minute, Second, ( Hour < 12 ? "AM" : "PM" ) );
94      } // end method ToString
95   } // end class Time2
```

Fig. 9.7 | Time2 class declaration with overloaded constructors. (Part 2 of 2.)

of range, it is set to 0 by the corresponding property (once again ensuring that each instance variable remains in a consistent state). The compiler invokes the appropriate constructor by matching the number and types of the arguments specified in the constructor call with the number and types of the parameters specified in each constructor declaration. Note that class Time2 also provides properties for each instance variable.

Class Time2's Constructors

Line 11 declares a *parameterless constructor*—a constructor invoked without arguments. Note that this constructor has an empty body, as indicated by the empty set of curly braces after the constructor header. Instead, we introduce a use of the `this` reference that is allowed only in the constructor's header. In line 11, the usual constructor header is followed by a colon (`:`), then the keyword `this`. The `this` reference is used in method-call syntax (along with the three `int` arguments) to invoke the `Time2` constructor that takes three `int` arguments (lines 20–23). The parameterless constructor passes values of 0 for the `hour`, `minute` and `second` to the constructor with three `int` parameters. The use of the `this` reference as shown here is called a *constructor initializer*. Constructor initializers are a popular way to reuse initialization code provided by one of the class's constructors rather than defining similar code in another constructor's body. We use this syntax in four of the five `Time2` constructors to make the class easier to maintain. If we needed to change how objects of class `Time2` are initialized, only the constructor that the class's other constructors call would need to be modified. Even that constructor might not need modification—it simply calls the `SetTime` method to perform the actual initialization, so it is possible that the changes the class might require would be localized to this method.

Line 14 declares a `Time2` constructor with a single `int` parameter representing the hour, which is passed with 0 for the `minute` and `second` to the constructor at lines 20–23. Line 17 declares a `Time2` constructor that receives two `int` parameters representing the hour and `minute`, which are passed with 0 for the `second` to the constructor at lines 20–23. Like the parameterless constructor, each of these constructors invokes the constructor at lines 20–23 to minimize code duplication. Lines 20–23 declare the `Time2` constructor that receives three `int` parameters representing the hour, `minute` and `second`. This constructor calls `SetTime` to initialize the instance variables to consistent values. `SetTime`, in turn, invokes the set accessors of properties `Hour`, `Minute` and `Second`.

Common Programming Error 9.4

A constructor can call methods of the class. Be aware that the instance variables might not yet be in a consistent state, because the constructor is in the process of initializing the object. Using instance variables before they have been initialized properly is a logic error.

Lines 26–27 declare a `Time2` constructor that receives a `Time2` reference to another `Time2` object. In this case, the values from the `Time2` argument are passed to the three-parameter constructor at lines 20–23 to initialize the `hour`, `minute` and `second`. Note that line 27 could have directly accessed the `hour`, `minute` and `second` instance variables of the constructor's `time` argument with the expressions `time.hour`, `time.minute` and `time.second`—even though `hour`, `minute` and `second` are declared as `private` variables of class `Time2`.

Software Engineering Observation 9.4

When one object of a class has a reference to another object of the same class, the first object can access all the second object's data and methods (including those that are `private`).

Notes Regarding Class Time2's Methods, Properties and Constructors

Note that `Time2`'s properties are accessed throughout the body of the class. In particular, method `SetTime` assigns values to properties `Hour`, `Minute` and `Second` in lines 33–35, and methods `ToUniversalString` and `ToString` use properties `Hour`, `Minute` and `Second` in line 85 and lines 92–93, respectively. In each case, these methods could have accessed the class's `private` data directly without using the properties. However, consider changing the representation of the time from three `int` values (requiring 12 bytes of memory) to a single `int` value representing the total number of seconds that have elapsed since midnight (requiring only 4 bytes of memory). If we make such a change, only the bodies of the methods that access the `private` data directly would need to change—in particular, the individual properties `Hour`, `Minute` and `Second`. There would be no need to modify the bodies of methods `SetTime`, `ToUniversalString` or `ToString`, because they do not access the `private` data directly. Designing the class in this manner reduces the likelihood of programming errors when altering the class's implementation.

Similarly, each `Time2` constructor could be written to include a copy of the appropriate statements from method `SetTime`. Doing so may be slightly more efficient, because the extra constructor call and the call to `SetTime` are eliminated. However, duplicating statements in multiple methods or constructors makes changing the class's internal data representation more difficult and error-prone. Having the `Time2` constructors call the three-parameter constructor (or even call `SetTime` directly) requires any changes to the implementation of `SetTime` to be made only once.

Software Engineering Observation 9.5

When implementing a method of a class, use the class's properties to access the class's `private` data. This simplifies code maintenance and reduces the likelihood of errors.

Also notice that class `Time2` takes advantage of access modifiers to ensure that clients of the class must use the appropriate methods and properties to access `private` data. In particular, the properties `Hour`, `Minute` and `Second` declare `private` `set` accessors (lines 47, 61 and 75, respectively) to restrict the use of the `set` accessors to members of the class. We declare these `private` for the same reasons that we declare the instance variables `private`— to simplify code maintenance and ensure that the data remains in a consistent state. Although the methods in class `Time2` still have all the advantages of using the `set` accessors to perform validation, clients of the class must use the `SetTime` method to modify this data. The `get` accessors of properties `Hour`, `Minute` and `Second` are implicitly declared `public` because their properties are declared `public`—when there is no access modifier before a `get` or `set` accessor, the accessor inherits the access modifier preceding the property name.

Using Class Time2's Overloaded Constructors

Class `Time2Test` (Fig. 9.8) creates six `Time2` objects (lines 9–14) to invoke the overloaded `Time2` constructors. Line 9 shows that the parameterless constructor (line 11 of Fig. 9.7) is invoked by placing an empty set of parentheses after the class name when allocating a `Time2` object with `new`. Lines 10–14 of the application demonstrate passing arguments to the other `Time2` constructors. C# invokes the appropriate overloaded constructor by matching the number and types of the arguments specified in the constructor call with the number and types of the parameters specified in each constructor declaration. Line 10 invokes the constructor at line 14 of Fig. 9.7. Line 11 invokes the constructor at line 17 of Fig. 9.7. Lines 12–13 invoke the constructor at lines 20–23 of Fig. 9.7. Line 14 invokes the constructor at lines 26–27 of Fig. 9.7. The application displays the `string` representation of each initialized `Time2` object to confirm that each was initialized properly.

9.7 Default and Parameterless Constructors

Every class must have at least one constructor. Recall from Section 4.9 that if you do not provide any constructors in a class's declaration, the compiler creates a default constructor that takes no arguments when it is invoked. In Section 10.4.1, you will learn that the default constructor implicitly performs a special task.

The compiler will not create a default constructor for a class that explicitly declares at least one constructor. In this case, if you want to be able to invoke the constructor with no

```csharp
1   // Fig. 9.8: Time2Test.cs
2   // Overloaded constructors used to initialize Time2 objects.
3   using System;
4
5   public class Time2Test
6   {
7      public static void Main( string[] args )
8      {
9         Time2 t1 = new Time2(); // 00:00:00
10        Time2 t2 = new Time2( 2 ); // 02:00:00
11        Time2 t3 = new Time2( 21, 34 ); // 21:34:00
12        Time2 t4 = new Time2( 12, 25, 42 ); // 12:25:42
13        Time2 t5 = new Time2( 27, 74, 99 ); // 00:00:00
14        Time2 t6 = new Time2( t4 ); // 12:25:42
15
16        Console.WriteLine( "Constructed with:\n" );
17        Console.WriteLine( "t1: all arguments defaulted" );
18        Console.WriteLine( "   {0}", t1.ToUniversalString() ); // 00:00:00
19        Console.WriteLine( "   {0}\n", t1.ToString() ); // 12:00:00 AM
20
21        Console.WriteLine(
22           "t2: hour specified; minute and second defaulted" );
23        Console.WriteLine( "   {0}", t2.ToUniversalString() ); // 02:00:00
24        Console.WriteLine( "   {0}\n", t2.ToString() ); // 2:00:00 AM
25
26        Console.WriteLine(
27           "t3: hour and minute specified; second defaulted" );
28        Console.WriteLine( "   {0}", t3.ToUniversalString() ); // 21:34:00
29        Console.WriteLine( "   {0}\n", t3.ToString() ); // 9:34:00 PM
30
31        Console.WriteLine( "t4: hour, minute and second specified" );
32        Console.WriteLine( "   {0}", t4.ToUniversalString() ); // 12:25:42
33        Console.WriteLine( "   {0}\n", t4.ToString() ); // 12:25:42 PM
34
35        Console.WriteLine( "t5: all invalid values specified" );
36        Console.WriteLine( "   {0}", t5.ToUniversalString() ); // 00:00:00
37        Console.WriteLine( "   {0}\n", t5.ToString() ); // 12:00:00 AM
38
39        Console.WriteLine( "t6: Time2 object t4 specified" );
40        Console.WriteLine( "   {0}", t6.ToUniversalString() ); // 12:25:42
41        Console.WriteLine( "   {0}", t6.ToString() ); // 12:25:42 PM
42     } // end Main
43  } // end class Time2Test
```

Fig. 9.8 | Overloaded constructors used to initialize Time2 objects. (Part 1 of 2.)

```
Constructed with:

t1: all arguments defaulted
    00:00:00
    12:00:00 AM

t2: hour specified; minute and second defaulted
    02:00:00
    2:00:00 AM

t3: hour and minute specified; second defaulted
    21:34:00
    9:34:00 PM

t4: hour, minute and second specified
    12:25:42
    12:25:42 PM

t5: all invalid values specified
    00:00:00
    12:00:00 AM

t6: Time2 object t4 specified
    12:25:42
    12:25:42 PM
```

Fig. 9.8 | Overloaded constructors used to initialize Time2 objects. (Part 2 of 2.)

arguments, you must declare a parameterless constructor—as in line 11 of Fig. 9.7. Like a default constructor, a parameterless constructor is invoked with empty parentheses. Note that the Time2 parameterless constructor explicitly initializes a Time2 object by passing to the three-parameter constructor 0 for each parameter. Since 0 is the default value for int instance variables, the parameterless constructor in this example could actually omit the constructor initializer. In this case, each instance variable would receive its default value when the object is created. If we omit the parameterless constructor, clients of this class would not be able to create a Time2 object with the expression new Time2().

Common Programming Error 9.5

If a class has constructors, but none of the public constructors are parameterless constructors, and an application attempts to call a parameterless constructor to initialize an object of the class, a compilation error occurs. A constructor can be called with no arguments only if the class does not have any constructors (in which case the default constructor is called) or if the class has a public parameterless constructor.

Common Programming Error 9.6

Only constructors can have the same name as the class. Declaring a method, property or field with the same name as the class is a compilation error.

9.8 Composition

A class can have references to objects of other classes as members. Such a capability is called *composition* and is sometimes referred to as a ***has-a relationship***. For example, an object of class AlarmClock needs to know the current time and the time when it is supposed to sound its alarm, so it is reasonable to include two references to Time objects as members of the AlarmClock object.

Software Engineering Observation 9.6

One form of software reuse is composition, in which a class has as members references to objects of other classes.

Our example of composition contains three classes—Date (Fig. 9.9), Employee (Fig. 9.10) and EmployeeTest (Fig. 9.11). Class Date (Fig. 9.9) declares instance variables month, day and year (lines 7–9) to represent a date. The constructor receives three int parameters. Line 15 implicitly invokes the set accessor of property Month (lines 41–50) to validate the month—an out-of-range value is set to 1 to maintain a consistent state. Line 16 similarly uses property Year to set the year—but notice that the set accessor of Year (lines 28–31) assumes that the value for year is correct and does not validate it. Line 17 uses property Day (lines 54–78), which validates and assigns the value for day based on the current month and year (by using properties Month and Year in turn to obtain the values of month and year). Note that the order of initialization is important because the set accessor of property Day validates the value for day based on the assumption that month and year are correct. Line 66 determines whether the day is correct based on the number of days in the particular Month. If the day is not correct, lines 69–70 determine whether the Month is February, the day is 29 and the Year is a leap year. Otherwise, if the parameter value does not contain a correct value for day, line 75 sets day to 1 to maintain the Date in a consistent state. Note that line 18 in the constructor outputs the this reference as a string. Since this is a reference to the current Date object, the object's ToString method (lines 81–84) is called implicitly to obtain the object's string representation.

Class Employee (Fig. 9.10) has instance variables firstName, lastName, birthDate and hireDate. Members birthDate and hireDate (lines 7–8) are references to Date objects, demonstrating that a class can have as instance variables references to objects of other classes. The Employee constructor (lines 11–18) takes four parameters—first, last, dateOfBirth and dateOfHire. The objects referenced by parameters dateOfBirth and dateOfHire are assigned to the Employee object's birthDate and hireDate instance variables, respectively. Note that when class Employee's ToString method is called, it returns a string containing the string representations of the two Date objects. Each of these strings is obtained with an implicit call to the Date class's ToString method.

```csharp
1   // Fig. 9.9: Date.cs
2   // Date class declaration.
3   using System;
4
5   public class Date
6   {
7      private int month; // 1-12
8      private int day; // 1-31 based on month
9      private int year; // any year (could validate)
10
```

Fig. 9.9 | Date class declaration. (Part 1 of 3.)

```
11      // constructor: use property Month to confirm proper value for month;
12      // use property Day to confirm proper value for day
13      public Date( int theMonth, int theDay, int theYear )
14      {
15         Month = theMonth; // validate month
16         Year = theYear; // could validate year
17         Day = theDay; // validate day
18         Console.WriteLine( "Date object constructor for date {0}", this );
19      } // end Date constructor
20
21      // property that gets and sets the year
22      public int Year
23      {
24         get
25         {
26            return year;
27         } // end get
28         private set // make writing inaccessible outside the class
29         {
30            year = value; // could validate
31         } // end set
32      } // end property Year
33
34      // property that gets and sets the month
35      public int Month
36      {
37         get
38         {
39            return month;
40         } // end get
41         private set // make writing inaccessible outside the class
42         {
43            if ( value > 0 && value <= 12 ) // validate month
44               month = value;
45            else // month is invalid
46            {
47               Console.WriteLine( "Invalid month ({0}) set to 1.", value );
48               month = 1; // maintain object in consistent state
49            } // end else
50         } // end set
51      } // end property Month
52
53      // property that gets and sets the day
54      public int Day
55      {
56         get
57         {
58            return day;
59         } // end get
60         private set // make writing inaccessible outside the class
61         {
62            int[] daysPerMonth =
63               { 0, 31, 28, 31, 30, 31, 30, 31, 31, 30, 31, 30, 31 };
```

Fig. 9.9 | Date class declaration. (Part 2 of 3.)

```
64
65          // check if day in range for month
66          if ( value > 0 && value <= daysPerMonth[ Month ] )
67             day = value;
68          // check for leap year
69          else if ( Month == 2 && value == 29 &&
70             ( Year % 400 == 0 || ( Year % 4 == 0 && Year % 100 != 0 ) ) )
71             day = value;
72          else
73          {
74             Console.WriteLine( "Invalid day ({0}) set to 1.", value );
75             day = 1; // maintain object in consistent state
76          } // end else
77       } // end set
78    } // end property Day
79
80    // return a string of the form month/day/year
81    public override string ToString()
82    {
83       return string.Format( "{0}/{1}/{2}", Month, Day, Year );
84    } // end method ToString
85 } // end class Date
```

Fig. 9.9 | Date class declaration. (Part 3 of 3.)

```
1  // Fig. 9.10: Employee.cs
2  // Employee class with references to other objects.
3  public class Employee
4  {
5     private string firstName;
6     private string lastName;
7     private Date birthDate;
8     private Date hireDate;
9
10    // constructor to initialize name, birth date and hire date
11    public Employee( string first, string last,
12       Date dateOfBirth, Date dateOfHire )
13    {
14       firstName = first;
15       lastName = last;
16       birthDate = dateOfBirth;
17       hireDate = dateOfHire;
18    } // end Employee constructor
19
20    // convert Employee to string format
21    public override string ToString()
22    {
23       return string.Format( "{0}, {1}  Hired: {2}  Birthday: {3}",
24          lastName, firstName, hireDate, birthDate );
25    } // end method ToString
26 } // end class Employee
```

Fig. 9.10 | Employee class with references to other objects.

Class `EmployeeTest` (Fig. 9.11) creates two `Date` objects (lines 9–10) to represent an `Employee`'s birthday and hire date, respectively. Line 11 creates an `Employee` and initializes its instance variables by passing to the constructor two `string`s (representing the `Employee`'s first and last names) and two `Date` objects (representing the birthday and hire date). Line 13 implicitly invokes the `Employee`'s `ToString` method to display the values of its instance variables and demonstrate that the object was initialized properly.

9.9 Garbage Collection and Destructors

Every object you create uses various system resources, such as memory. In many programming languages, these system resources are reserved for the object's use until they are explicitly released. If all the references to the object that manages the resource are lost before the resource is explicitly released, the application can no longer access the resource to release it. This is known as a *resource leak*.

We need a disciplined way to give resources back to the system when they are no longer needed, thus avoiding resource leaks. The Common Language Runtime (CLR) performs automatic memory management by using a *garbage collector* to reclaim the memory occupied by objects that are no longer in use, so the memory can be used for other objects. When there are no more references to an object, the object becomes *eligible for destruction*. Every object has a special member, called a *destructor*, that is invoked by the garbage collector to perform *termination housekeeping* on an object just before the garbage collector reclaims the object's memory. A destructor is declared like a parameterless constructor, except that its name is the class name, preceded by a tilde (~), and it has no access modifier in its header. After the garbage collector calls the object's destructor, the object becomes *eligible for garbage collection*. The memory for such an object can be reclaimed by the garbage collector. *Memory leaks*, which are common in other languages like C and C++ (because memory is not automatically reclaimed in those languages), are

```
1   // Fig. 9.11: EmployeeTest.cs
2   // Composition demonstration.
3   using System;
4
5   public class EmployeeTest
6   {
7      public static void Main( string[] args )
8      {
9         Date birth = new Date( 7, 24, 1949 );
10        Date hire = new Date( 3, 12, 1988 );
11        Employee employee = new Employee( "Bob", "Blue", birth, hire );
12
13        Console.WriteLine( employee );
14     } // end Main
15  } // end class EmployeeTest
```

```
Date object constructor for date 7/24/1949
Date object constructor for date 3/12/1988
Blue, Bob  Hired: 3/12/1988  Birthday: 7/24/1949
```

Fig. 9.11 | Composition demonstration.

less likely in C# (but some can still happen in subtle ways). Other types of resource leaks can occur. For example, an application could open a file on disk to modify the file's contents. If the application does not close the file, no other application can modify (or possibly even use) the file until the application that opened the file completes.

A problem with the garbage collector is that it is not guaranteed to perform its tasks at a specified time. Therefore, the garbage collector may call the destructor any time after the object becomes eligible for destruction, and may reclaim the memory any time after the destructor executes. In fact, neither may happen before an application terminates. Thus, it is unclear if, or when, the destructor will be called. For this reason, most programmers should avoid using destructors. In Section 9.10, we demonstrate a situation in which we use a destructor. We will also demonstrate some of the static methods of class *GC* (in namespace System), which allow us to exert some control over the garbage collector and when destructors are called.

> ### Software Engineering Observation 9.7
> *A class that uses system resources, such as files on disk, should provide a method to eventually release the resources. Many FCL classes provide Close or Dispose methods for this purpose.*

9.10 static Class Members

Every object has its own copy of all the instance variables of the class. In certain cases, only one copy of a particular variable should be shared by all objects of a class. A static *variable* is used in such cases. A static variable represents *classwide information*—all objects of the class share the same piece of data. The declaration of a static variable begins with the keyword static.

Let's motivate static data with an example. Suppose that we have a video game with Martians and other space creatures. Each Martian tends to be brave and willing to attack other space creatures when it is aware that there are at least four other Martians present. If fewer than five Martians are present, each Martian becomes cowardly. Thus each Martian needs to know the martianCount. We could endow class Martian with martianCount as an instance variable. If we do this, every Martian will have a separate copy of the instance variable, and every time we create a new Martian, we will have to update the instance variable martianCount in every Martian. This wastes space on redundant copies, wastes time updating the separate copies and is error prone. Instead, we declare martianCount to be static, making martianCount classwide data. Every Martian can access the martianCount as if it were an instance variable of class Martian, but only one copy of the static martianCount is maintained. This saves space. We save time by having the Martian constructor increment the static martianCount—there is only one copy, so we do not have to increment separate copies of martianCount for each Martian object.

> ### Software Engineering Observation 9.8
> *Use a static variable when all objects of a class must use the same copy of the variable.*

The scope of a static variable is the body of its class. A class's public static members can be accessed by qualifying the member name with the class name and the dot (.) operator, as in Math.PI. A class's private static class members can be accessed only through the methods and properties of the class. Actually, static class members exist even when no objects of the class exist—they are available as soon as the class is loaded into memory at execution time. To access a private static member from outside its class, a public static method or property can be provided.

Common Programming Error 9.7

It is a compilation error to access or invoke a static member by referencing it through an instance of the class, like a non-static member.

Software Engineering Observation 9.9

Static variables and methods exist, and can be used, even if no objects of that class have been instantiated.

Our next application declares two classes—Employee (Fig. 9.12) and EmployeeTest (Fig. 9.13). Class Employee declares private static variable count (Fig. 9.12, line 10), and public static property Count (lines 52–58). We omit the set accessor of property Count to make the property read-only—we do not want clients of the class to be able to

```
1   // Fig. 9.12: Employee.cs
2   // Static variable used to maintain a count of the number of
3   // Employee objects in memory.
4   using System;
5
6   public class Employee
7   {
8      private string firstName;
9      private string lastName;
10     private static int count = 0; // number of objects in memory
11
12     // initialize employee, add 1 to static count and
13     // output string indicating that constructor was called
14     public Employee( string first, string last )
15     {
16        firstName = first;
17        lastName = last;
18        count++; // increment static count of employees
19        Console.WriteLine( "Employee constructor: {0} {1}; count = {2}",
20           FirstName, LastName, Count );
21     } // end Employee constructor
22
23     // subtract 1 from static count when the garbage collector
24     // calls destructor to clean up object;
25     // confirm that destructor was called
26     ~Employee()
27     {
28        count--; // decrement static count of employees
29        Console.WriteLine( "Employee destructor: {0} {1}; count = {2}",
30           FirstName, LastName, Count );
31     } // end destructor
32
```

Fig. 9.12 | static variable used to maintain a count of the number of Employee objects in memory. (Part 1 of 2.)

```
33        // read-only property that gets the first name
34        public string FirstName
35        {
36           get
37           {
38              return firstName;
39           } // end get
40        } // end property FirstName
41
42        // read-only property that gets the last name
43        public string LastName
44        {
45           get
46           {
47              return lastName;
48           } // end get
49        } // end property LastName
50
51        // read-only property that gets the employee count
52        public static int Count
53        {
54           get
55           {
56              return count;
57           } // end get
58        } // end property Count
59     } // end class Employee
```

Fig. 9.12 | static variable used to maintain a count of the number of Employee objects in memory. (Part 2 of 2.)

modify count. The static variable count is initialized to 0 in line 10. If a static variable is not initialized, the compiler assigns a default value to the variable—in this case 0, the default value for type int. Variable count maintains a count of the number of objects of class Employee currently in memory. This includes objects that are already inaccessible from the application, but have not yet had their destructors invoked by the garbage collector.

When Employee objects exist, member count can be used in any method of an Employee object—this example increments count in the constructor (line 18) and decrements it in the destructor (line 28). When no objects of class Employee exist, member count can still be referenced, but only through a call to public static property Count (lines 52–58), as in Employee.Count, which evaluates to the number of Employee objects currently in memory.

Note that the Employee class has a destructor (lines 26–31). This destructor is included to decrement static variable count, then show when the garbage collector executes in this application. Unlike constructors and methods, the destructor cannot be invoked explicitly by any programmer-written code. It can only be invoked by the garbage collector, so it does not need an access modifier—in fact, it is a syntax error to include one.

EmployeeTest method Main (Fig. 9.13) instantiates two Employee objects (lines 14–15). When each Employee object's constructor is invoked, lines 16–17 of Fig. 9.12 assign the Employee's first name and last name to instance variables firstName and lastName.

Note that these two statements do not make copies of the original string arguments. Actually, string objects in C# are immutable—they cannot be modified after they are created. Therefore, it is safe to have many references to one string object. This is not normally the case for objects of most other classes in C#. If string objects are immutable, you might wonder why we are able to use operators + and += to concatenate string objects. String concatenation operations actually result in a new string object containing the concatenated values. The original string objects are not modified.

```csharp
1   // Fig. 9.13: EmployeeTest.cs
2   // Static member demonstration.
3   using System;
4
5   public class EmployeeTest
6   {
7      public static void Main( string[] args )
8      {
9         // show that count is 0 before creating Employees
10        Console.WriteLine( "Employees before instantiation: {0}",
11           Employee.Count );
12
13        // create two Employees; count should become 2
14        Employee e1 = new Employee( "Susan", "Baker" );
15        Employee e2 = new Employee( "Bob", "Blue" );
16
17        // show that count is 2 after creating two Employees
18        Console.WriteLine( "\nEmployees after instantiation: {0}",
19           Employee.Count );
20
21        // get names of Employees
22        Console.WriteLine( "\nEmployee 1: {0} {1}\nEmployee 2: {2} {3}\n",
23           e1.FirstName, e1.LastName,
24           e2.FirstName, e2.LastName );
25
26        // in this example, there is only one reference to each Employee,
27        // so the following statements cause the CLR to mark each
28        // Employee object as being eligible for destruction
29        e1 = null; // object e1 no longer needed
30        e2 = null; // object e2 no longer needed
31
32        GC.Collect(); // ask for garbage collection to occur now
33        // wait until the destructors
34        // finish writing to the console
35        GC.WaitForPendingFinalizers();
36
37        // show Employee count after calling garbage collector and
38        // waiting for all destructors to finish
39        Console.WriteLine( "\nEmployees after destruction: {0}",
40           Employee.Count );
41     } // end Main
42  } // end class EmployeeTest
```

Fig. 9.13 | static member demonstration. (Part 1 of 2.)

```
Employees before instantiation: 0
Employee constructor: Susan Baker; count = 1
Employee constructor: Bob Blue; count = 2

Employees after instantiation: 2

Employee 1: Susan Baker
Employee 2: Bob Blue

Employee destructor: Bob Blue; count = 1
Employee destructor: Susan Baker; count = 0

Employees after destruction: 0
```

Fig. 9.13 | static member demonstration. (Part 2 of 2.)

When Main has finished using the two Employee objects, references e1 and e2 are set to null at lines 29–30, so they no longer refer to the objects that were instantiated on lines 14–15. The objects become "eligible for garbage collection" because there are no more references to them in the application.

Eventually, the garbage collector might reclaim the memory for these objects (or the operating system will reclaim the memory when the application terminates). C# does not guarantee when, or even whether, the garbage collector will execute, so in line 32, this application explicitly calls the garbage collector using static method Collect of class GC to indicate that the garbage collector should make a "best-effort" attempt to reclaim objects that are inaccessible. This is just a best effort—it is possible that no objects or only a subset of the eligible objects will be collected. When method Collect returns, this does *not* indicate that the garbage collector has finished searching for memory to reclaim. The garbage collector may still, in fact, be executing. For this reason, we call static method ***WaitForPendingFinalizers*** of class GC. If the garbage collector has marked any objects eligible for destruction, invoking WaitforPendingFinalizers in line 35 stops the execution of the Main method until the destructors of these objects have been completely executed.

In Fig. 9.13's sample output, the garbage collector did reclaim the objects formerly referenced by e1 and e2 before lines 39–40 displayed the current Employee count. The last output line indicates that the number of Employee objects in memory is 0 after the call to GC.Collect(). The third- and second-to-last lines of the output show that the Employee object for Bob Blue was destructed before the Employee object for Susan Baker. The output on your system may differ, because the garbage collector is not guaranteed to execute when GC.Collect() is called, nor is it guaranteed to collect objects in a specific order. In fact, if you omit the call to WaitForPendingFinalizers, it is likely that lines 39–40 will execute before the garbage collector has a chance to call the destructors.

[*Note:* A method declared static cannot access non-static class members directly, because a static method can be called even when no objects of the class exist. For the same reason, the this reference cannot be used in a static method—the this reference must refer to a specific object of the class, and when a static method is called, there might not be any objects of its class in memory. The this reference is required to allow a method of a class to access non-static members of the same class.]

Common Programming Error 9.8

A compilation error occurs if a static method calls an instance (non-static) method in the same class by using only the method name. Similarly, a compilation error occurs if a static method attempts to access an instance variable in the same class by using only the variable name.

Common Programming Error 9.9

Referring to the this reference in a static method is a syntax error.

9.11 readonly Instance Variables

The **principle of least privilege** is fundamental to good software engineering. In the context of an application, the principle states that code should be granted only the amount of privilege and access needed to accomplish its designated task, but no more. Let us see how this principle applies to instance variables.

Some instance variables need to be modifiable, and some do not. In Section 8.4, we introduced keyword const for declaring constants. These constants must be initialized to a constant value when they are declared. Suppose, however, we want to initialize a constant belonging to an object in the object's constructor. C# provides keyword **readonly** to specify that an instance variable of an object is not modifiable and that any attempt to modify it after the object is constructed is an error. For example,

```
private readonly int INCREMENT;
```

declares readonly instance variable INCREMENT of type int. Like constants, readonly variables are declared with all capital letters by convention. Although readonly instance variables can be initialized when they are declared, this is not required. Readonly variables can be initialized by each of the class's constructors. The constructor can assign values to a readonly instance variable multiple times—the variable doesn't become unmodifiable until after the constructor completes execution.

Software Engineering Observation 9.10

Declaring an instance variable as readonly helps enforce the principle of least privilege. If an instance variable should not be modified after the object is constructed, declare it to be readonly to prevent modification.

Members that are declared as const must be assigned values at compile time. Therefore, const members can be initialized only with other constant values, such as integers, string literals, characters and other const members. Constant members with values that cannot be determined at compile time must be declared with keyword readonly, so they can be initialized at execution time. Variables that are readonly can be initialized with more complex expressions, such as an array initializer or a method call that returns a value or a reference to an object.

Our next example contains two classes—class Increment (Fig. 9.14) and class IncrementTest (Fig. 9.15). Class Increment contains a readonly instance variable of type int named INCREMENT (Fig. 9.14, line 6). Note that the readonly variable is not initialized in its declaration, so it should be initialized by the class's constructor (lines 10–13). If the class provides multiple constructors, every constructor should initialize the readonly variable. If a constructor does not initialize the readonly variable, the variable receives the same default value as any other instance variable (0 for numeric simple types, false for bool types and null for reference types), and the compiler generates a warning. In Fig. 9.14, the constructor receives int parameter incrementValue and assigns its value to INCREMENT (line 12). If class Increment's constructor does not initialize INCREMENT (if line 12 were omitted), the compiler would give the warning:

```
Field 'Increment.INCREMENT' is never assigned to, and will always
have its default value 0
```

Application class IncrementTest creates an object of class Increment (Fig. 9.15, line 9) and provides as the argument to the constructor the value 5, which is assigned to the readonly variable INCREMENT. Lines 11 and 16 implicitly invoke class Increment's ToString method, which returns a formatted string describing the value of private instance variable total.

Common Programming Error 9.10

Attempting to modify a readonly instance variable anywhere but its declaration or the object's constructors is a compilation error.

Error-Prevention Tip 9.2

Attempts to modify a readonly instance variable are caught at compilation time rather than causing execution-time errors. It is always preferable to get bugs out at compile time, if possible, rather than allowing them to slip through to execution time (where studies have found that repairing is often many times more costly).

```csharp
1   // Fig. 9.14: Increment.cs
2   // readonly instance variable in a class.
3   public class Increment
4   {
5      // readonly instance variable (uninitialized)
6      private readonly int INCREMENT;
7      private int total = 0; // total of all increments
8
9      // constructor initializes readonly instance variable INCREMENT
10     public Increment( int incrementValue )
11     {
12        INCREMENT = incrementValue; // initialize readonly variable (once)
13     } // end Increment constructor
14
15     // add INCREMENT to total
16     public void AddIncrementToTotal()
17     {
18        total += INCREMENT;
19     } // end method AddIncrementToTotal
20
21     // return string representation of an Increment object's data
22     public override string ToString()
23     {
24        return string.Format( "total = {0}", total );
25     } // end method ToString
26  } // end class Increment
```

Fig. 9.14 | readonly instance variable in a class.

```
 1    // Fig. 9.15: IncrementTest.cs
 2    // readonly instance variable initialized with a constructor argument.
 3    using System;
 4
 5    public class IncrementTest
 6    {
 7       public static void Main( string[] args )
 8       {
 9          Increment incrementer = new Increment( 5 );
10
11          Console.WriteLine( "Before incrementing: {0}\n", incrementer );
12
13          for ( int i = 1; i <= 3; i++ )
14          {
15             incrementer.AddIncrementToTotal();
16             Console.WriteLine( "After increment {0}: {1}", i, incrementer );
17          } // end for
18       } // end Main
19    } // end class IncrementTest
```

```
Before incrementing: total = 0

After increment 1: total = 5
After increment 2: total = 10
After increment 3: total = 15
```

Fig. 9.15 | `readonly` instance variable initialized with a constructor argument.

Software Engineering Observation 9.11

If a `readonly` instance variable is initialized to a constant only in its declaration, it is not necessary to have a separate copy of the instance variable for every object of the class. The variable should be declared `const` instead. Constants declared with `const` are implicitly `static`, so there will only be one copy for the entire class.

9.12 Software Reusability

Programmers concentrate on crafting new classes and reusing existing classes. Many class libraries exist, and others are being developed worldwide. Software is then constructed from existing, well-defined, carefully tested, well-documented, portable, performance-tuned, widely available components. This kind of software reusability speeds the development of powerful, high-quality software. *Rapid application development (RAD)* is of great interest today.

Microsoft provides C# programmers with thousands of classes in the .NET Framework Class Library to help them implement C# applications. The .NET Framework enables C# developers to work to achieve true reusability and rapid application development. C# programmers can focus on the task at hand when developing their applications and leave the lower-level details to the classes of the FCL. For example, to write an application that draws graphics, an FCL programmer does not require knowledge of graphics on every computer platform where the application will execute. Instead, the programmer can concentrate on learning .NET's graphics capabilities (which are quite substantial and growing) and write a C# application that draws the graphics, using FCL classes such as those in the `System.Drawing` namespace. When the application executes on a given computer, it is the job of the CLR to translate the MSIL commands compiled from the C# code into commands that the local computer can understand.

The FCL classes enable C# programmers to bring new applications to market faster by using preexisting, tested components. Not only does this reduce development time, it also improves the programmer's ability to debug and maintain applications. To take advantage of C#'s many capabilities, it is essential that programmers familiarize themselves with the variety of classes in the .NET Framework. There are many Web-based resources at `msdn2.microsoft.com` to help you with this task. The primary resource for learning about the FCL is the .NET Framework Reference in the MSDN library, which can be found at

> `msdn2.microsoft.com/en-us/library/ms229335`

In addition, `msdn2.microsoft.com` provides many other resources, including tutorials, articles and sites specific to individual C# topics.

Good Programming Practice 9.1

Avoid reinventing the wheel. Study the capabilities of the FCL. If the FCL contains a class that meets your application's requirements, use that class rather than create your own.

To realize the full potential of software reusability, we need to improve cataloging schemes, licensing schemes, protection mechanisms that prevent master copies of classes from being corrupted, description schemes that system designers use to determine whether existing classes meet their needs, browsing mechanisms that determine what classes are available and how closely they meet software developer requirements, and the like. Many interesting research and development problems have been solved and many more need to be solved. These problems will likely be solved because the potential value of increased software reuse is enormous.

9.13 Data Abstraction and Encapsulation

Classes normally hide the details of their implementation from their clients. This is called *information hiding*. As an example, let us consider the stack data structure introduced in Section 7.6. Recall that a stack is a last-in, first-out (LIFO) data structure—the last item pushed (inserted) on the stack is the first item popped (removed) off the stack.

Stacks can be implemented with arrays and with other data structures, such as linked lists. (We discuss stacks and linked lists in Chapter 25, Data Structures, and Chapter 27, Collections.) A client of a stack class need not be concerned with the stack's implementation. The client knows only that when data items are placed in the stack, they will be recalled in last-in, first-out order. The client cares about what functionality a stack offers, not about how that functionality is implemented. This concept is referred to as *data abstraction*. Although programmers might know the details of a class's implementation, they should not write code that depends on these details. This enables a particular class (such as one that implements a stack and its *push* and *pop* operations) to be replaced with another version without affecting the rest of the system. As long as the `public` services of the class do not change (i.e., every original method still has the same name, return type and parameter list in the new class declaration), the rest of the system is not affected.

Most programming languages emphasize actions. In these languages, data exists to support the actions that applications must take. Data is "less interesting" than actions. Data is "crude." Only a few simple types exist, and it is difficult for programmers to create their own types. C# and the object-oriented style of programming elevate the importance of data. The primary activities of object-oriented programming in C# are the creation of types (e.g., classes) and the expression of the interactions among objects of those types. To create languages that emphasize data, the programming-languages community needed to formalize some notions about data. The formalization we consider here is the notion of *abstract data types (ADTs)*, which improve the application-development process.

Consider simple type `int`, which most people would associate with an integer in mathematics. Actually, an `int` is an abstract representation of an integer. Unlike mathematical integers, computer `int`s are fixed in size. For example, simple type `int` in C# is limited to the range −2,147,483,648 to +2,147,483,647. If the result of a calculation falls outside this range, an error occurs, and the computer responds in some manner. It might, for example, "quietly" produce an incorrect result, such as a value too large to fit in an `int` variable—commonly called *arithmetic overflow*. It also might throw an exception, called an `OverflowException`. (We discuss the two ways of dealing with arithmetic overflow in Section 12.8.) Mathematical integers do not have this problem. Therefore, the computer `int` is only an approximation of the real-world integer. The same is true of `double` and other simple types.

We have taken the notion of `int` for granted until this point, but we now consider it from a new perspective. Types like `int`, `double`, and `char` are all examples of abstract data types. They are representations of real-world concepts to some satisfactory level of precision within a computer system.

An ADT actually captures two notions: a *data representation* and the *operations* that can be performed on that data. For example, in C#, an `int` contains an integer value (data) and provides addition, subtraction, multiplication, division and remainder operations— division by zero is undefined. C# programmers use classes to implement abstract data types.

Software Engineering Observation 9.12

Programmers create types through the class mechanism. New types can be designed to be as convenient to use as the simple types. This marks C# as an extensible language. Although the language is easy to extend via new types, the programmer cannot alter the base language itself.

Another abstract data type we discuss is a *queue*, which is similar to a "waiting line." Computer systems use many queues internally. A queue offers well-understood behavior to its clients: Clients place items in a queue one at a time via an *enqueue* operation, then get them back one at a time via a *dequeue* operation. A queue returns items in *first-in, first-out (FIFO)* order, which means that the first item inserted in a queue is the first item removed from the queue. Conceptually, a queue can become infinitely long, but real queues are finite.

The queue hides an internal data representation that keeps track of the items currently waiting in line, and it offers operations to its clients (*enqueue* and *dequeue*). The clients are not concerned about the implementation of the queue—they simply depend on the queue to operate "as advertised." When a client enqueues an item, the queue should accept that item and place it in some kind of internal FIFO data structure. Similarly, when the client wants the next item from the front of the queue, the queue should remove the item from its internal representation and deliver it in FIFO order (i.e., the item that has been in the queue the longest should be returned by the next dequeue operation).

The queue ADT guarantees the integrity of its internal data structure. Clients cannot manipulate this data structure directly—only the queue ADT has access to its internal data. Clients are able to perform only allowable operations on the data representation— the ADT rejects operations that its public interface does not provide. We will discuss stacks and queues in greater depth in Chapter 25, Data Structures.

9.14 Time Class Case Study: Creating Class Libraries

In almost every example in the text, we have seen that classes from preexisting libraries, such as the .NET Framework Class Library, can be imported into a C# application. Each class in the FCL belongs to a namespace that contains a group of related classes. As applications become more complex, namespaces help you manage the complexity of application components. Class libraries and namespaces also facilitate software reuse by enabling applications to add classes from other namespaces (as we have done in most examples). This section introduces how to create your own class libraries.

Steps for Declaring and Using a Reusable Class

Before a class can be used in multiple applications, it must be placed in a class library to make it reusable. Figure 9.16 shows how to specify the namespace in which a class should be placed in the library. Figure 9.19 shows how to use our class library in an application. The steps for creating a reusable class are:

1. Declare a public class. If the class is not public, it can be used only by other classes in the same assembly.

2. Choose a namespace name and add a ***namespace*** *declaration* to the source-code file for the reusable class declaration.

3. Compile the class into a class library.

4. Add a reference to the class library in an application.

5. Specify a using directive for the namespace of the reusable class and use the class.

Step 1: Creating a public Class

For *Step 1* in this discussion, we use the public class Time1 declared in Fig. 9.1. No modifications have been made to the implementation of the class, so we will not discuss its implementation details again here.

Step 2: Adding the namespace Declaration

For *Step 2*, we add a namespace declaration to Fig. 9.1. The new version is shown in Fig. 9.16. Line 3 declares a namespace named Chapter09. Placing the Time1 class inside the namespace declaration indicates that the class is part of the specified namespace. The namespace name is part of the fully qualified class name, so the name of class Time1 is actually Chapter09.Time1. You can use this fully qualified name in your applications, or you can write a using directive (as we will see shortly) and use its ***simple name*** (the unqualified

```
1   // Fig. 9.16: Time1.cs
2   // Time1 class declaration in a namespace.
3   namespace Chapter09
4   {
5      public class Time1
6      {
7         private int hour;   // 0 - 23
8         private int minute; // 0 - 59
9         private int second; // 0 - 59
10
11        // set a new time value using universal time; ensure that
12        // the data remains consistent by setting invalid values to zero
13        public void SetTime( int h, int m, int s )
14        {
15           hour = ( ( h >= 0 && h < 24 ) ? h : 0 ); // validate hour
16           minute = ( ( m >= 0 && m < 60 ) ? m : 0 ); // validate minute
17           second = ( ( s >= 0 && s < 60 ) ? s : 0 ); // validate second
18        } // end method SetTime
19
20        // convert to string in universal-time format (HH:MM:SS)
21        public string ToUniversalString()
22        {
23           return string.Format( "{0:D2}:{1:D2}:{2:D2}",
24              hour, minute, second );
25        } // end method ToUniversalString
26
27        // convert to string in standard-time format (H:MM:SS AM or PM)
28        public override string ToString()
29        {
30           return string.Format( "{0}:{1:D2}:{2:D2} {3}",
31              ( ( hour == 0 || hour == 12 ) ? 12 : hour % 12 ),
32              minute, second, ( hour < 12 ? "AM" : "PM" ) );
33        } // end method ToString
34     } // end class Time1
35  } // end namespace Chapter09
```

Fig. 9.16 | Time1 class declaration in a namespace.

class name—Time1) in the application. If another namespace also contains a Time1 class, the fully qualified class names can be used to distinguish between the classes in the application and prevent a *name conflict* (also called a *name collision*).

Only namespace declarations, using directives, comments and C# attributes (first used in Chapter 18) can appear outside the braces of a type declaration (e.g., classes and enumerations). Only class declarations declared public will be reusable by clients of the class library. Non-public classes are typically placed in a library to support the public reusable classes in that library.

Step 3: Compiling the Class Library

Step 3 is to compile the class into a class library. To create a class library in Visual C# Express, we must create a new project by clicking the **File** menu, selecting **New Project...** and choosing **Class Library** from the list of templates, as shown in Fig. 9.17. Then add the code from Fig. 9.16 into the new project (either by copying our code from the book's examples

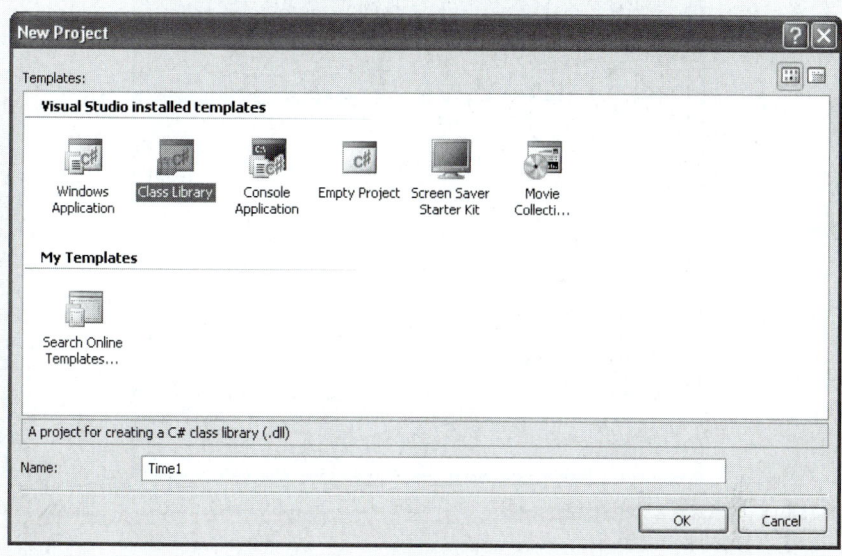

Fig. 9.17 | Creating a **Class Library** Project.

or by typing the code yourself). In the projects you've created so far, the C# compiler created an executable .exe containing the application. When you compile a **Class Library** project, the compiler creates a *.dll file*, known as a *dynamic link library*—a type of assembly that you can reference from other applications.

Step 4: Adding a Reference to the Class Library

Once the class is compiled and stored in the class library file, the library can be referenced from any application by indicating to the Visual C# Express IDE where to find the class library file (*Step 4*). Create a new (empty) project and right-click the project name in the **Solution Explorer** window. Select **Add Reference...** from the pop-up menu that appears. The dialog box that appears will contain a list of class libraries from the .NET Framework. Some class libraries, like the one containing the System namespace, are so common that they are added to your application implicitly. The ones in this list are not.

In the **Add Reference...** dialog box, click the **Browse** tab. Recall from Section 3.3 that when you build an application, Visual C# 2005 places the .exe file in the bin\Release folder in the directory of your application. When you build a class library, Visual C# places the .dll file in the same place. In the **Browse** tab, you can navigate to the directory containing the class library file you created in *Step 3*, as shown in Fig. 9.18. Select the .dll file and click **OK**.

Step 5: Using the Class from an Application

Add a new code file to your application and enter the code for class Time1NamespaceTest (Fig. 9.19). Now that you've added a reference to your class library in this application, your Time1 class can be used by Time1NamespaceTest (*Step 5*) without adding the Time1.cs source code file to the project.

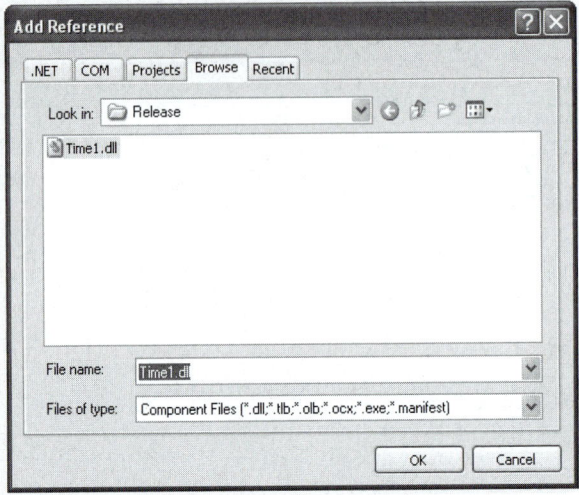

Fig. 9.18 | Adding a Reference.

In Fig. 9.19, the using directive in line 3 specifies that we'd like to use the class(es) of namespace Chapter09 in this file. Class Time1NamespaceTest is in the global namespace of this application because the class's file does not contain a namespace declaration. Since the two classes are in different namespaces, the using directive at line 3 allows class Time1NamespaceTest to use class Time1 as if it was in the same namespace.

Recall from Section 4.4 that we could omit the using directive in line 4 if we always referred to class Console by its fully qualified class name, System.Console. Similarly, we could omit the using directive in line 3 for namespace Chapter09 if we changed the Time1 declaration in line 11 of Fig. 9.19 to use class Time1's fully qualified name, as in:

```
Chapter09.Time1 time = new Chapter09.Time1();
```

```
 1   // Fig. 9.19: Time1NamespaceTest.cs
 2   // Time1 object used in an application.
 3   using Chapter09;
 4   using System;
 5
 6   public class Time1NamespaceTest
 7   {
 8      public static void Main( string[] args )
 9      {
10         // create and initialize a Time1 object
11         Time1 time = new Time1(); // calls Time1 constructor
12
13         // output string representations of the time
14         Console.Write( "The initial universal time is: " );
15         Console.WriteLine( time.ToUniversalString() );
16         Console.Write( "The initial standard time is: " );
17         Console.WriteLine( time.ToString() );
18         Console.WriteLine(); // output a blank line
```

Fig. 9.19 | Time1 object used in an application. (Part 1 of 2.)

```
19
20          // change time and output updated time
21          time.SetTime( 13, 27, 6 );
22          Console.Write( "Universal time after SetTime is: " );
23          Console.WriteLine( time.ToUniversalString() );
24          Console.Write( "Standard time after SetTime is: " );
25          Console.WriteLine( time.ToString() );
26          Console.WriteLine(); // output a blank line
27
28          // set time with invalid values; output updated time
29          time.SetTime( 99, 99, 99 );
30          Console.WriteLine( "After attempting invalid settings:" );
31          Console.Write( "Universal time: " );
32          Console.WriteLine( time.ToUniversalString() );
33          Console.Write( "Standard time: " );
34          Console.WriteLine( time.ToString() );
35       } // end Main
36    } // end class Time1NamespaceTest
```

```
The initial universal time is: 00:00:00
The initial standard time is: 12:00:00 AM

Universal time after SetTime is: 13:27:06
Standard time after SetTime is: 1:27:06 PM

After attempting invalid settings:
Universal time: 00:00:00
Standard time: 12:00:00 AM
```

Fig. 9.19 | Time1 object used in an application. (Part 2 of 2.)

9.15 internal Access

Classes can be declared with only two access modifiers—public and internal. If there is no access modifier in the class declaration, the class defaults to *internal access*. This allows the class to be used by all code in the same assembly as the class, but not by code in other assemblies. Within the same assembly as the class, this is equivalent to public access. However, if a class library is referenced from an application, the library's internal classes will be inaccessible from the code of the application. Similarly, methods, instance variables and other members of a class declared internal are accessible to all code compiled in the same assembly, but not to code in other assemblies.

The application in Fig. 9.20 demonstrates internal access. The application contains two classes in one source-code file—the InternalAccessTest application class (lines 6–22) and the InternalData class (lines 25–43).

In the InternalData class declaration, lines 27–28 declare the instance variables number and message with the internal access modifier—class InternalData has access internal by default, so there is no need for an access modifier. The InternalAccessTest's static Main method creates an instance of the InternalData class (line 10) to demonstrate modifying the InternalData instance variables directly (as shown in lines 16–17). Within the same assembly, internal access is equivalent to public access. The

```
1   // Fig. 9.20: InternalAccessTest.cs
2   // Members declared internal in a class are accessible by other classes
3   // in the same assembly.
4   using System;
5
6   public class InternalAccessTest
7   {
8      public static void Main( string[] args )
9      {
10        InternalData internalData = new InternalData();
11
12        // output string representation of internalData
13        Console.WriteLine( "After instantiation:\n{0}", internalData );
14
15        // change internal access data in internalData
16        internalData.number = 77;
17        internalData.message = "Goodbye";
18
19        // output string representation of internalData
20        Console.WriteLine( "\nAfter changing values:\n{0}", internalData );
21     } // end Main
22  } // end class InternalAccessTest
23
24  // class with internal access instance variables
25  class InternalData
26  {
27     internal int number; // internal-access instance variable
28     internal string message; // internal-access instance variable
29
30     // constructor
31     public InternalData()
32     {
33        number = 0;
34        message = "Hello";
35     } // end InternalData constructor
36
37     // return InternalData object string representation
38     public override string ToString()
39     {
40        return string.Format(
41           "number: {0}; message: {1}", number, message );
42     } // end method ToString
43  } // end class InternalData
```

```
After instantiation:
number: 0; message: Hello

After changing values:
number: 77; message: Goodbye
```

Fig. 9.20 | Members declared `internal` in a class are accessible by other classes in the same assembly.

results can be seen in the output window. If we compile this class into a `.dll` class library file and reference it from a new application, that application will have access to `public` class `InternalAccessTest`, but not to `internal` class `InternalData`, or its `internal` members.

9.16 Class View and Object Browser

Now that we have introduced key concepts of object-oriented programming, we present two features that Visual Studio provides to facilitate the design of object-oriented applications—*Class View* and *Object Browser*.

Using the Class View Window

The **Class View** displays the fields and methods for all classes in a project. To access this feature, select **Class View** from the **View** menu. Figure 9.21 shows the **Class View** for the Time1 project of Fig. 9.1 (class Time1) and Fig. 9.2 (class TimeTest1). The view follows a hierarchical structure, positioning the project name (Time1) as the root and including a series of nodes that represent the classes, variables and methods in the project. If a plus sign (+) appears to the left of a node, that node can be expanded to show other nodes. If a minus sign (–) appears to the left of a node, that node can be collapsed. According to the **Class View**, project Time1 contains class Time1 and class TimeTest1 as children. When class Time1 is selected, the class's members appear in the lower half of the window. Class Time1 contains methods SetTime, ToString and ToUniversalString (indicated by purple boxes) and instance variables hour, minute and second (indicated by blue boxes). The lock icons, placed to the left of the blue box icons for the instance variables, specify that the variables are private. Class TimeTest1 contains method Main. Note that both class Time1 and class TimeTest1 contain the **Base Types** node. If you expand this node, you will see class object in each case, because each class inherits from class `System.Object` (discussed in Chapter 10).

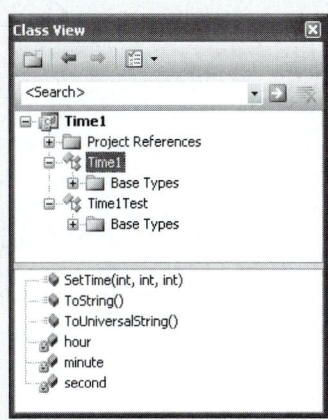

Fig. 9.21 | **Class View** of class Time1 (Fig. 9.1) and class TimeTest (Fig. 9.2).

Using the Object Browser

Visual C# Express's **Object Browser** lists all classes in the C# library. You can use the **Object Browser** to learn about the functionality provided by a specific class. To open the **Object Browser**, select **Other Windows** from the **View** menu and click **Object Browser**. Figure 9.22 depicts the **Object Browser** when the user navigates to the Math class in namespace System in the assembly mscorlib (Microsoft Core Library). [*Note:* Be careful not to confuse the System namespace with the assembly named System. The System assembly describes other members of the System namespace, but class System.Math is in mscorlib.] The **Object Browser** lists all methods provided by class Math in the upper-right frame—this offers you "instant access" to information regarding the functionality of various objects. If you click the name of a member in the upper-right frame, a description of that member appears in the lower-right frame. Note also that the **Object Browser** lists in the left frame all classes of the FCL. The **Object Browser** can be a quick mechanism to learn about a class or a method of a class. Remember that you can also view the complete description of a class or a method in the online documentation available through the **Help** menu in Visual C# Express.

9.17 (Optional) Software Engineering Case Study: Starting to Program the Classes of the ATM System

In the Software Engineering Case Study sections in Chapters 1 and 3–8, we introduced the fundamentals of object orientation and developed an object-oriented design for our ATM system. In Chapters 4–7, we introduced object-oriented programming in C#. In Chapter 8, we took a deeper look at the details of programming with classes. We now begin implementing our object-oriented design by converting class diagrams to C# code. In the final Software Engineering Case Study section (Section 11.9), we modify the code to incorporate the object-oriented concepts of inheritance and polymorphism. We present the full C# code implementation in Appendix J.

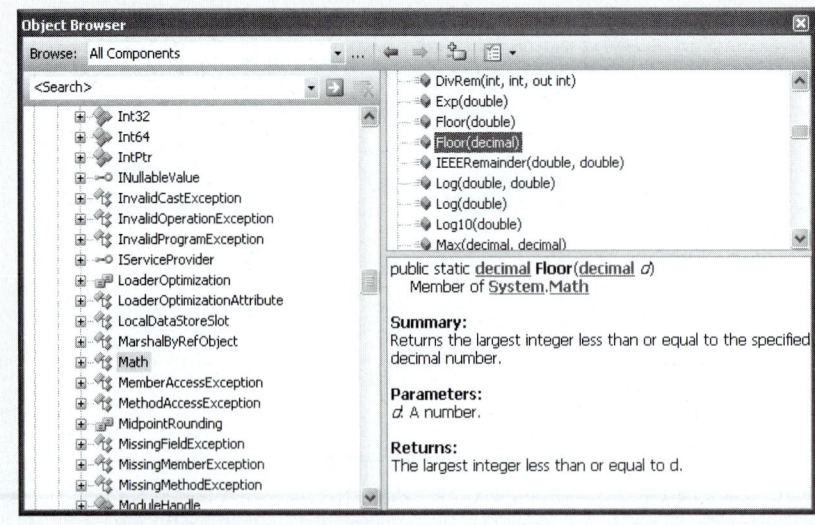

Fig. 9.22 | **Object Browser** for class Math.

Visibility

We now apply access modifiers to the members of our classes. In Chapter 4, we introduced access modifiers `public` and `private`. Access modifiers determine the *visibility*, or accessibility, of an object's attributes and operations to other objects. Before we can begin implementing our design, we must consider which attributes and methods of our classes should be `public` and which should be `private`.

In Chapter 4, we observed that attributes normally should be `private` and that methods invoked by clients of a class should be `public`. Methods that are called only by other methods of the class as "utility functions," however, should be `private`. The UML employs *visibility markers* for modeling the visibility of attributes and operations. Public visibility is indicated by placing a plus sign (+) before an operation or an attribute; a minus sign (–) indicates private visibility. Figure 9.23 shows our updated class diagram with visibility markers included. [*Note:* We do not include any operation parameters in Fig. 9.23. This is perfectly normal. Adding visibility markers does not affect the parameters already modeled in the class diagrams of Figs. 7.21–7.25.]

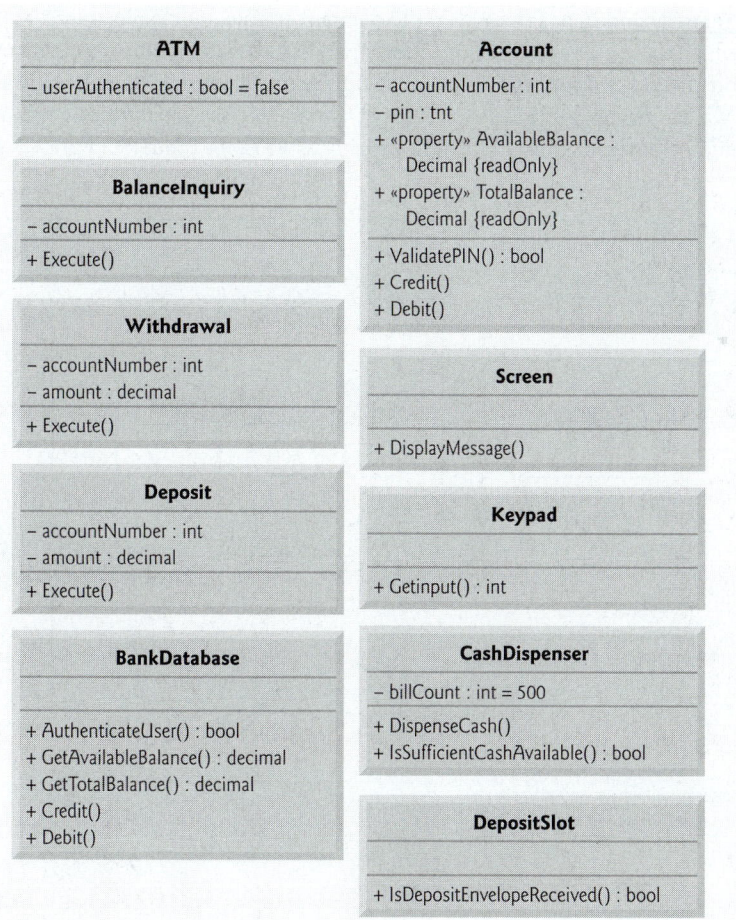

Fig. 9.23 | Class diagram with visibility markers.

Navigability

Before we begin implementing our design in C#, we introduce an additional UML notation. The class diagram in Fig. 9.24 further refines the relationships among classes in the ATM system by adding navigability arrows to the association lines. *Navigability arrows* (represented as arrows with stick arrowheads in the class diagram) indicate in which direction an association can be traversed and are based on the collaborations modeled in communication and sequence diagrams (see Section 8.14). When implementing a system designed using the UML, programmers use navigability arrows to help determine which objects need references to other objects. For example, the navigability arrow pointing from class ATM to class Bank-Database indicates that we can navigate from the former to the latter, thereby enabling the ATM to invoke the BankDatabase's operations. However, since Fig. 9.24 does not contain a navigability arrow pointing from class BankDatabase to class ATM, the BankDatabase cannot access the ATM's operations. Note that associations in a class diagram that have navigability arrows at both ends or do not have navigability arrows at all indicate *bidirectional navigability*—navigation can proceed in either direction across the association.

Like the class diagram of Fig. 4.24, the class diagram of Fig. 9.24 omits classes BalanceInquiry and Deposit to keep the diagram simple. The navigability of the associations in which these classes participate closely parallels the navigability of class Withdrawal's associations. Recall from Section 4.11 that BalanceInquiry has an association with class Screen. We can navigate from class BalanceInquiry to class Screen along this association, but we cannot navigate from class Screen to class BalanceInquiry. Thus, if we were to

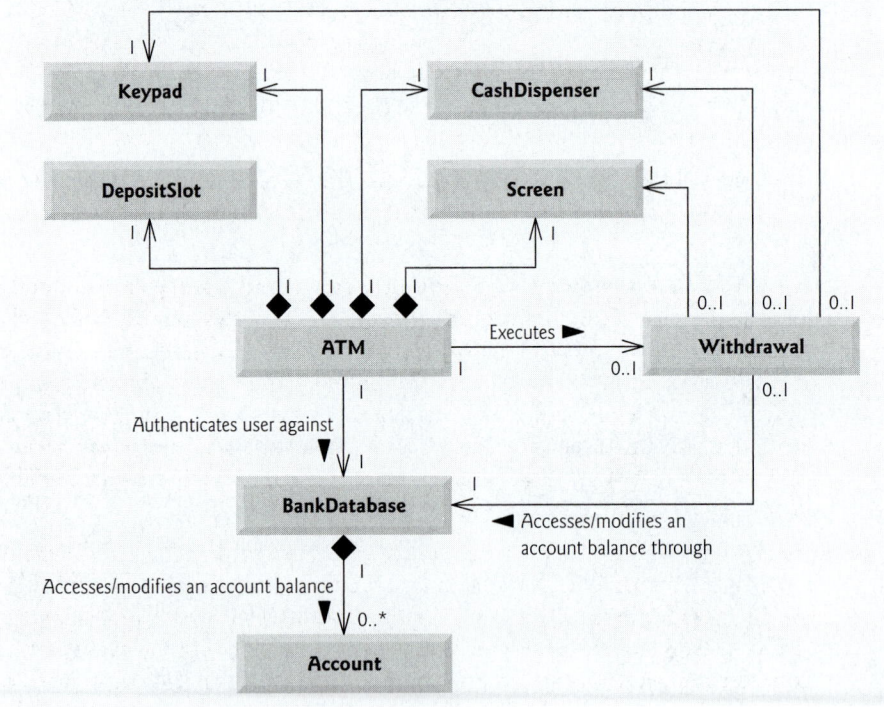

Fig. 9.24 | Class diagram with navigability arrows.

model class `BalanceInquiry` in Fig. 9.24, we would place a navigability arrow at class `Screen`'s end of this association. Also recall that class `Deposit` associates with classes `Screen`, `Keypad` and `DepositSlot`. We can navigate from class `Deposit` to each of these classes, but not vice versa. We therefore would place navigability arrows at the `Screen`, `Keypad` and `DepositSlot` ends of these associations. [*Note:* We model these additional classes and associations in our final class diagram in Section 11.9, after we have simplified the structure of our system by incorporating the object-oriented concept of inheritance.]

Implementing the ATM System from Its UML Design

We are now ready to begin implementing the ATM system. We first convert the classes in the diagrams of Fig. 9.23 and Fig. 9.24 into C# code. This code will represent the "skeleton" of the system. In Chapter 11, we modify the code to incorporate the object-oriented concept of inheritance. In Appendix J, ATM Case Study Code, we present the complete working C# code that implements our object-oriented design.

As an example, we begin to develop the code for class `Withdrawal` from our design of class `Withdrawal` in Fig. 9.23. We use this figure to determine the attributes and operations of the class. We use the UML model in Fig. 9.24 to determine the associations among classes. We follow these four guidelines for each class:

1. Use the name located in the first compartment of a class in a class diagram to declare the class as a `public` class with an empty parameterless constructor—we include this constructor simply as a placeholder to remind us that most classes will need one or more constructors. In Appendix J, when we complete a working version of this class, we add any necessary arguments and code to the body of the constructor. Class `Withdrawal` initially yields the code in Fig. 9.25. [*Note:* If we find that the class's instance variables require only default initialization, we will remove the empty parameterless constructor because it is unnecessary.]

2. Use the attributes located in the class's second compartment to declare the instance variables. The `private` attributes `accountNumber` and `amount` of class `Withdrawal` yield the code in Fig. 9.26.

3. Use the associations described in the class diagram to declare references to other objects. According to Fig. 9.24, `Withdrawal` can access one object of class `Screen`, one object of class `Keypad`, one object of class `CashDispenser` and one object of class `BankDatabase`. Class `Withdrawal` must maintain references to these objects to send messages to them, so lines 10–13 of Fig. 9.27 declare the appropriate references as `private` instance variables. In the implementation of class `Withdrawal` in Appendix J, a constructor initializes these instance variables with references to the actual objects.

4. Use the operations located in the third compartment of Fig. 9.23 to declare the shells of the methods. If we have not yet specified a return type for an operation, we declare the method with return type `void`. Refer to the class diagrams of Figs. 7.21–7.25 to declare any necessary parameters. Adding the `public` operation `Execute` (which has an empty parameter list) in class `Withdrawal` yields the code in lines 23–26 of Fig. 9.28. [*Note:* We code the bodies of the methods when we implement the complete ATM system in Appendix J.]

```
 1   // Fig. 9.25: Withdrawal.cs
 2   // Class Withdrawal represents an ATM withdrawal transaction
 3   public class Withdrawal
 4   {
 5      // parameterless constructor
 6      public Withdrawal()
 7      {
 8         // constructor body code
 9      } // end constructor
10   } // end class Withdrawal
```

Fig. 9.25 | Initial C# code for class `Withdrawal` based on Figs. 9.23 and 9.24.

```
 1   // Fig. 9.26: Withdrawal.cs
 2   // Class Withdrawal represents an ATM withdrawal transaction
 3   public class Withdrawal
 4   {
 5      // attributes
 6      private int accountNumber; // account to withdraw funds from
 7      private decimal amount; // amount to withdraw from account
 8
 9      // parameterless constructor
10      public Withdrawal()
11      {
12         // constructor body code
13      } // end constructor
14   } // end class Withdrawal
```

Fig. 9.26 | C# incorporating `private` variables for class `Withdrawal` based on Figs. 9.23 and 9.24.

```
 1   // Fig. 9.27: Withdrawal.cs
 2   // Class Withdrawal represents an ATM withdrawal transaction
 3   public class Withdrawal
 4   {
 5      // attributes
 6      private int accountNumber; // account to withdraw funds from
 7      private decimal amount; // amount to withdraw
 8
 9      // references to associated objects
10      private Screen screen; // ATM's screen
11      private Keypad keypad; // ATM's keypad
12      private CashDispenser cashDispenser; // ATM's cash dispenser
13      private BankDatabase bankDatabase; // account information database
14
15      // parameterless constructor
16      public Withdrawal()
17      {
18         // constructor body code
19      } // end constructor
20   } // end class Withdrawal
```

Fig. 9.27 | C# code incorporating `private` reference handles for the associations of class `Withdrawal` based on Figs. 9.23 and 9.24.

```
 1    // Fig. 9.28: Withdrawal.cs
 2    // Class Withdrawal represents an ATM withdrawal transaction
 3    public class Withdrawal
 4    {
 5       // attributes
 6       private int accountNumber; // account to withdraw funds from
 7       private decimal amount; // amount to withdraw
 8
 9       // references to associated objects
10       private Screen screen; // ATM's screen
11       private Keypad keypad; // ATM's keypad
12       private CashDispenser cashDispenser; // ATM's cash dispenser
13       private BankDatabase bankDatabase; // account information database
14
15       // parameterless constructor
16       public Withdrawal()
17       {
18          // constructor body code
19       } // end constructor
20
21       // operations
22       // perform transaction
23       public void Execute()
24       {
25          // Execute method body code
26       } // end method Execute
27    } // end class Withdrawal
```

Fig. 9.28 | C# code incorporating method `Execute` in class `Withdrawal` based on Figs. 9.23 and 9.24.

Software Engineering Observation 9.13

Many UML modeling tools can convert UML-based designs into C# code, considerably speeding up the implementation process. For more information on these "automatic" code generators, refer to the Web resources listed at the end of Section 3.10.

This concludes our discussion of the basics of generating class files from UML diagrams. In the final Software Engineering Case Study section (Section 11.9), we demonstrate how to modify the code in Fig. 9.28 to incorporate the object-oriented concepts of inheritance and polymorphism, which we present in Chapters 10 and 11, respectively.

Software Engineering Case Study Self-Review Exercises

9.1   State whether the following statement is *true* or *false*, and if *false*, explain why: If an attribute of a class is marked with a minus sign (-) in a class diagram, the attribute is not directly accessible outside of the class.

9.2   In Fig. 9.24, the association between the `ATM` and the `Screen` indicates:
    a)   that we can navigate from the `Screen` to the `ATM`.
    b)   that we can navigate from the `ATM` to the `Screen`.
    c)   Both a and b; the association is bidirectional.
    d)   None of the above.

9.3   Write C# code to begin implementing the design for class `Account`.

Answers to Software Engineering Case Study Self-Review Exercises

9.1 True. The minus sign (–) indicates private visibility.

9.2 b.

9.3 The design for class Account yields the code in Fig. 9.29. Note that we include private instance variables availableBalance and totalBalance to store the data that properties AvailableBalance and TotalBalance, and methods Credit and Debit, will manipulate.

```csharp
1  // Fig. 9.29: Account.cs
2  // Class Account represents a bank account.
3  public class Account
4  {
5     private int accountNumber; // account number
6     private int pin; // PIN for authentication
7     private decimal availableBalance; // available withdrawal amount
8     private decimal totalBalance; // funds available + pending deposit
9
10    // parameterless constructor
11    public Account()
12    {
13       // constructor body code
14    } // end constructor
15
16    // validates user PIN
17    public bool ValidatePIN()
18    {
19       // ValidatePIN method body code
20    } // end method ValidatePIN
21
22    // read-only property that gets the available balance
23    public decimal AvailableBalance
24    {
25       get
26       {
27          // AvailableBalance get accessor body code
28       } // end get
29    } // end property AvailableBalance
30
31    // read-only property that gets the total balance
32    public decimal TotalBalance
33    {
34       get
35       {
36          // TotalBalance get accessor body code
37       } // end get
38    } // end property TotalBalance
39
40    // credits the account
41    public void Credit()
42    {
43       // Credit method body code
44    } // end method Credit
```

Fig. 9.29 | C# code for class Account based on Figs. 9.23 and 9.24. (Part 1 of 2.)

```
45
46      // debits the account
47      public void Debit()
48      {
49          // Debit method body code
50      } // end method Debit
51  } // end class Account
```

Fig. 9.29 | C# code for class `Account` based on Figs. 9.23 and 9.24. (Part 2 of 2.)

9.18 Wrap-Up

In this chapter, we discussed additional class concepts. The `Time` class case study presented a complete class declaration consisting of `private` data, overloaded `public` constructors for initialization flexibility, properties for manipulating the class's data and methods that returned `string` representations of a `Time` object in two different formats. You learned that every class can declare a `ToString` method that returns a `string` representation of an object of the class and that this method is invoked implicitly when an object of a class is output as a `string`.

You learned that the `this` reference is used implicitly in a class's non-`static` methods to access the class's instance variables and other non-`static` methods. You saw explicit uses of the `this` reference to access the class's members (including hidden fields) and learned how to use keyword `this` in a constructor to call another constructor of the class. You also learned how to declare indexers with the `this` keyword, allowing you to access the data of an object in much the same manner as you access the elements of an array.

You saw that a class can have references to objects of other classes as members—a concept known as composition. You learned about C#'s garbage collection capability and how it reclaims the memory of objects that are no longer used. We explained the motivation for `static` variables in a class, and demonstrated how to declare and use `static` variables and methods in your own classes. You also learned how to declare and initialize `readonly` variables.

We showed how to create a class library for reuse and how to use the classes of the library in an application. You learned that classes declared without an access modifier are given `internal` access by default. You saw that classes in an assembly can access the `internal`-access members of the other classes in the same assembly. We also showed how to use Visual Studio's **Class Library** and **Object Browser** windows to navigate the classes of the FCL and your own applications to discover information about those classes.

In the next chapter, you will learn another key object-oriented programming technology—inheritance. You will see that all classes in C# are related directly or indirectly to the `object` class. You will also begin to understand how inheritance enables you to build more powerful applications faster.

Summary

Section 9.2 Time Class Case Study

- The `public` methods of a class are the `public` services or the `public` interface that the class provides to its clients.
- Objects should always contain consistent data—that is, the object's data values should always be kept in range, even if the values provided as arguments to methods are incorrect.

- Methods and properties that modify the values of private variables should verify that the intended new values are proper. If they are not, they should place the private variables in an appropriate consistent state.

- The actual data representation used within the class is of no concern to the class's clients. This allows you to change the implementation of the class. Clients could use the same public methods and properties to get the same results without being aware of this change.

- Clients are neither aware of, nor involved in, a class's implementation. Clients generally care about *what* the class does but not *how* the class does it.

Section 9.3 Controlling Access to Members

- Access modifiers public and private control access to a class's variables and methods. A class's private variables and methods are not directly accessible to the class's clients.

- If a client attempts to use the private members of another class, the compiler generates error messages stating that these private members are not accessible.

- If a class member is not declared with an access modifier, it has private access by default.

Section 9.4 Referring to the Current Object's Members with the this Reference

- Every object can access a reference to itself with keyword this. When a non-static method is called for a particular object, the method's body implicitly uses keyword this to refer to the object's instance variables and other methods.

- If a method contains a local variable with the same name as a field, that method will refer to the local variable rather than the field. However, a non-static method can use the this reference to refer to a hidden instance variable explicitly.

- Avoid method parameter names or local variable names that conflict with field names. This helps prevent subtle, hard-to-locate bugs.

Section 9.5 Indexers

- A class can use keyword this to define indexers that allow array-style indexed access to lists of elements in a class.

- A benefit of indexers is that you can define both integer indices and non-integer indices. For example, you could allow client code to manipulate data using strings as indices that represent the data items' names or descriptions.

- Indexers have the general form:

```
accessModifier returnType this[ IndexType1 name1, IndexType2 name2, … ]
{
   get
   {
      // use name1, name2, ... here to get data
   }
   set
   {
      // use name1, name2, ... here to set data
   }
}
```

As with properties, an indexer's get accessor must return a value of type *returnType*, and the set accessor can use the implicit parameter value to reference the value that should be assigned to the element.

Section 9.6 Time Class Case Study: Overloaded Constructors

- To overload constructors, provide multiple constructor declarations with different signatures.
- Following the constructor header with the constructor initializer : this (*args*) invokes the matching overloaded constructor in the same class.
- Constructor initializers are a popular way to reuse initialization code provided by one of the class's constructors rather than defining similar code in another constructor's body.
- When one object of a class has a reference to another object of the same class, the first object can access all the second object's data and methods (including those that are private).
- When implementing a method of a class, use the class's properties to access the class's private data. This simplifies code maintenance and reduces the likelihood of errors.

Section 9.7 Default and Parameterless Constructors

- Every class must have at least one constructor. If there are no constructors in a class's declaration, the compiler creates a default constructor for the class.
- The compiler will not create a default constructor for a class that explicitly declares at least one constructor. In this case, if you want to be able to invoke the constructor with no arguments, you must declare a parameterless constructor.

Section 9.8 Composition

- A class can have references to objects of other classes as members. Such a capability is called composition and is sometimes referred to as a *has-a* relationship.

Section 9.9 Garbage Collection and Destructors

- Every object you create uses various system resources, such as memory. The CLR performs automatic memory management by using a garbage collector to reclaim the memory occupied by objects that are no longer in use.
- The destructor is invoked by the garbage collector to perform termination housekeeping on an object just before the garbage collector reclaims the object's memory.
- Memory leaks are common in other languages like C and C++ (because memory is not automatically reclaimed in those languages), which are less likely in C#.
- A problem with the garbage collector is that it is not guaranteed to perform its tasks at a specified time. Therefore, the garbage collector may call the destructor any time after the object becomes eligible for destruction, making it unclear when, or if, the destructor will be called.

Section 9.10 static Class Members

- A static variable represents classwide information—all objects of the class share the same piece of data.
- The scope of a static variable is the body of its class. A class's public static members can be accessed by qualifying the member name with the class name and the dot (.) operator, as in Math.PI.
- Static class members exist even when no objects of the class exist—they are available as soon as the class is loaded into memory at execution time.
- Unlike constructors and methods, the destructor cannot be invoked explicitly by any programmer-written code. It can only be invoked by the garbage collector.
- String objects in C# are immutable—they cannot be modified after they are created. Therefore, it is safe to have many references to one string object.

- If the garbage collector has marked any objects eligible for destruction, invoking `WaitforPending-Finalizers` stops execution until the destructors of these objects have been completely executed.

- Static method `Collect` of class `GC` (in namespace `System`) indicates that the garbage collector should make a "best-effort" attempt to reclaim objects that are inaccessible. This is just a best effort—it is possible that no objects or only a subset of the eligible objects will be collected.

- A method declared `static` cannot access non-`static` class members directly, because a `static` method can be called even when no objects of the class exist. For the same reason, the `this` reference cannot be used in a `static` method.

Section 9.11 readonly *Instance Variables*
- The principle of least privilege is fundamental to good software engineering. In the context of an application, the principle states that code should be granted only the amount of privilege and access needed to accomplish its designated task, but no more.

- Any attempt to modify a `readonly` instance variable after its object is constructed is an error.

- Although `readonly` instance variables can be initialized when they are declared, this is not required. Readonly variables can be initialized by each of the class's constructors.

- Members that are declared as `const` must be assigned values at compile time. Constant members with values that cannot be determined at compile time must be declared with keyword `readonly`, so they can be initialized at execution time.

Section 9.12 *Software Reusability*
- The FCL classes enable C# programmers to bring new applications to market faster by using pre-existing, tested components. Not only does this reduce development time, it also improves the programmer's ability to debug and maintain applications.

- Avoid reinventing the wheel. Study the capabilities of the FCL. If the FCL contains a class that meets your application's requirements, use that class rather than create your own.

Section 9.13 *Data Abstraction and Encapsulation*
- Classes normally hide the details of their implementation from their clients. This is called information hiding.

- The client cares about what functionality a class offers, not about how that functionality is implemented. This concept is referred to as data abstraction. Although programmers might know the details of a class's implementation, they should not write code that depends on these details.

- C# and the object-oriented style of programming elevate the importance of data. The primary activities of object-oriented programming in C# are the creation of types (e.g., classes) and the expression of the interactions among objects of those types.

- Types like `int`, `double`, and `char` are all examples of abstract data types. They are representations of real-world notions to some satisfactory level of precision within a computer system.

- An ADT actually captures two notions: A data representation and the operations that can be performed on that data.

Section 9.14 *Time Class Case Study: Creating Class Libraries*
- Class libraries and namespaces facilitate software reuse by enabling applications to add classes from other namespaces.

- Before a class can be used in multiple applications, it must be placed in a class library to make it reusable.

- When you compile a class library, the compiler will create a `.dll` file, known as a dynamic link library—a type of assembly that you can reference from other applications.

Section 9.15 *internal Access*
- The `internal` access modifier gives access to all code in the same assembly as the declaration. If a class library is referenced from an application, the library's `internal` classes and members will be inaccessible from the code of the application.

Section 9.16 *Class View and Object Browser*
- The **Class View** displays the variables and methods for all classes in a project. The view follows a hierarchical structure, positioning the project name as the root and including a series of nodes that represent the classes, variables and methods in the project.

- The **Object Browser** lists in the left window all classes of the FCL. The **Object Browser** can be a quick mechanism to learn about a class or method of a class.

Terminology

abstract data type (ADT)	`internal` access modifier
access modifier	indexer
accessor	last-in, first-out (LIFO) data structure
arithmetic overflow	memory leak
attribute (in the UML)	name collision
behavior	name conflict
class library	namespace declaration
Class View	**Object Browser**
classwide information	overloaded constructors
`Collect` method of class `GC`	parameterless constructor
composition	pop
constructor initializer	principle of least privilege
data abstraction	`private` access modifier
data representation	`public` access modifier
dequeue	`public` interface
destructor	`public` service
`.dll` file	push
dynamic link library	queue data structure
eligible for destruction	rapid application development (RAD)
eligible for garbage collection	`readonly` instance variable
enqueue	resource leak
extensible language	service of a class
first-in, first-out (FIFO) data structure	simple name of a class, field or method
`Format` method of class `string`	`static` variable
fully qualified class name	stack data structure
garbage collector	termination housekeeping
`GC` class of namespace `System`	`this` keyword
has-a relationship	unmodifiable variable
information hiding	`WaitForPendingFinalizers` method of class `GC`

Self-Review Exercises

9.1   Fill in the blanks in each of the following statements:

      a) `string` class `static` method _____ is similar to method `Console.Write`, but returns a formatted `string` rather than displaying a `string` in a console window.

      b) If a method contains a local variable with the same name as one of its class's fields, the local variable _____ the field in that method's scope.

c) The _____ is called by the garbage collector just before it reclaims an object's memory.

d) If a class declares constructors, the compiler will not create a(n) _____.

e) An object's _____ method can be called implicitly when an object appears in code where a string is needed.

f) Composition is sometimes referred to as a(n) _____ relationship.

g) A(n) _____ variable represents classwide information that is shared by all the objects of the class.

h) The _____ states that code should be granted only the amount of access needed to accomplish its designated task.

i) Declaring an instance variable with keywords _____ or _____ specifies that the variable is not modifiable.

j) A(n) _____ consists of a data representation and the operations that can be performed on the data.

k) Adding a(n) _____ to a class library allows the application to use the classes from that class library.

l) The compiler builds a class library project into a type of assembly called a(n) _____.

m) The public methods of a class are also known as the class's _____ or _____.

n) System.GC class static method _____ indicates that the garbage collector should make a best-effort attempt to reclaim objects that are eligible for garbage collection.

o) An object that contains _____ has data values that are always kept in range.

Answers to Self-Review Exercises

9.1 a) Format. b) hides. c) destructor. d) default constructor. e) ToString. f) *has-a*. g) static. h) principle of least privilege. i) const, readonly. j) abstract data type (ADT). k) reference. l) dynamic link library. m) public services, public interface. n) Collect. o) consistent data.

Exercises

9.2 Explain the notion of internal access in C#.

9.3 What happens when a return type, even void, is specified for a constructor?

9.4 *(Rectangle Class)* Create class Rectangle. The class has attributes length and width, each of which defaults to 1. It has read-only properties that calculate the Perimeter and the Area of the rectangle. It has properties for both length and width. The set accessors should verify that length and width are each floating-point numbers greater than 0.0 and less than 20.0. Write an application to test class Rectangle.

9.5 *(Modifying the Internal Data Representation of a Class)* It would be perfectly reasonable for the Time2 class of Fig. 9.7 to represent the time internally as the number of seconds since midnight rather than the three integer values hour, minute and second. Clients could use the same public methods and properties to get the same results. Modify the Time2 class of Fig. 9.7 to implement the Time2 as the number of seconds since midnight and show that no change is visible to the clients of the class by using the same test application from Fig. 9.8.

9.6 *(Savings Account Class)* Create class SavingsAccount. Use static variable annualInterestRate to store the annual interest rate for all account holders. Each object of the class contains a private instance variable savingsBalance, indicating the amount the saver currently has on deposit. Provide method CalculateMonthlyInterest to calculate the monthly interest by multiplying the savingsBalance by annualInterestRate divided by 12—this interest should be added to savingsBalance. Provide static method ModifyInterestRate to set the annualInterestRate to a new value. Write an application to test class SavingsAccount. Create two savingsAccount objects, saver1 and saver2, with balances of $2000.00 and $3000.00, respectively. Set annualInterestRate to 4%, then calculate the monthly interest and print the new balances for both savers. Then set the annualInterestRate to 5%, calculate the next month's interest and print the new balances for both savers.

9.7 *(Enhancing Class Time2)* Modify class Time2 of Fig. 9.7 to include a Tick method that increments the time stored in a Time2 object by one second. Provide method IncrementMinute to increment the minute and method IncrementHour to increment the hour. The Time2 object should always remain in a consistent state. Write an application that tests the Tick method, the Increment-Minute method and the IncrementHour method to ensure that they work correctly. Be sure to test the following cases:

    a) incrementing to the next minute,
    b) incrementing to the next hour and
    c) incrementing to the next day (i.e., 11:59:59 PM to 12:00:00 AM).

9.8 *(Enhancing Class Date)* Modify class Date of Fig. 9.9 to perform error checking on the initializer values for instance variables month, day and year (class Date currently validates only the month and day). Provide method NextDay to increment the day by 1. The Date object should always remain in a consistent state. Write an application that tests the NextDay method in a loop that prints the date during each iteration of the loop to illustrate that the NextDay method works correctly. Test the following cases:

    a) incrementing to the next month and
    b) incrementing to the next year.

9.9 *(Complex Numbers)* Create a class called Complex for performing arithmetic with complex numbers. Complex numbers have the form

    realPart + imaginaryPart * i

where *i* is

$$\sqrt{-1}$$

Write an application to test your class. Use floating-point variables to represent the private data of the class. Provide a constructor that enables an object of this class to be initialized when it is declared. Provide a parameterless constructor with default values in case no initializers are provided. Provide public methods that perform the following operations:

    a) Add two Complex numbers: The real parts are added together and the imaginary parts are added together.
    b) Subtract two Complex numbers: The real part of the right operand is subtracted from the real part of the left operand, and the imaginary part of the right operand is subtracted from the imaginary part of the left operand.
    c) Return a string representation of a Complex number in the form (a, b), where a is the real part and b is the imaginary part.

9.10 *(Date and Time Class)* Create class DateAndTime that combines the modified Time2 class of Exercise 9.7 and the modified Date class of Exercise 9.8. Modify method IncrementHour to call method NextDay if the time is incremented to the next day. Modify methods ToString and ToUniversalString to output the date and time. Write an application to test the new class DateAndTime. Specifically, test incrementing the time to the next day.

9.11 *(Enhanced Rectangle Class)* Create a more sophisticated Rectangle class than the one you created in Exercise 9.4. This class stores only the Cartesian coordinates of the four corners of the rectangle. The constructor calls a SetCoordinates method that accepts four sets of coordinates and verifies that each of these is in the first quadrant with no single *x*- or *y*-coordinate larger than 20.0.

The method also verifies that the supplied coordinates specify a rectangle. Provide read-only properties that get the Length, Width, Perimeter and Area—but do not store these values in instance variables. Write get accessors that calculate and return these values. The length is the larger of the two dimensions. Include methods IsRectangle and IsSquare that determine whether this is a rectangle and square, respectively. Write an application to test class Rectangle.

9.12   *(Set of Integers)* Create class IntegerSet. Each IntegerSet object can hold integers in the range 0–100. The set is represented by an array of bools. Array element a[i] is true if integer *i* is in the set. Array element a[j] is false if integer *j* is not in the set. The parameterless constructor initializes the array to the "empty set" (i.e., a set whose array representation contains all false values).

Provide the following methods:

a)   Method Union creates a third set that is the set-theoretic union of two existing sets (i.e., an element of the third set's array is set to true if that element is true in either or both of the existing sets—otherwise, the element of the third set is set to false).

b)   Method Intersection creates a third set which is the set-theoretic intersection of two existing sets (i.e., an element of the third set's array is set to false if that element is false in either or both of the existing sets—otherwise, the element of the third set is set to true).

c)   Method InsertElement inserts a new integer *k* into a set (by setting a[k] to true).

d)   Method DeleteElement deletes integer *m* (by setting a[m] to false).

e)   Method ToString returns a string containing a set as a list of numbers separated by spaces. Include only those elements that are present in the set. Use --- to represent an empty set.

f)   Method IsEqualTo determines whether two sets are equal.

Write an application to test class IntegerSet. Instantiate several IntegerSet objects. Test that all your methods work properly.

9.13   *(Date Class)* Create class Date with the following capabilities:

a)   Output the date in multiple formats, such as

```
MM/DD/YYYY
June 14, 1992
DDD YYYY
```

b)   Use overloaded constructors to create Date objects initialized with dates of the formats in part (a). In the first case, the constructor should receive three integer values. In the second case, it should receive a string and two integer values. In the third case it should receive two integer values, the first of which represents the day number in the year. [*Hint:* To convert the string representation of the month to a numeric value, declare a string array of month names in order and iterate through the array, comparing the string to each element. Use the index of the matching month name to calculate the month's numeric value.]

9.14   *(Rational Numbers)* Create a class called Rational for performing arithmetic with fractions. Write an application to test your class. Use integer variables to represent the private instance variables of the class—the numerator and the denominator. Provide a constructor that enables an object of this class to be initialized when it is declared. The constructor should store the fraction in reduced form. The fraction

2/4

is equivalent to 1/2 and would be stored in the object as 1 in the numerator and 2 in the denominator. Provide a parameterless constructor with default values in case no initializers are provided.

Provide `public` methods that perform each of the following operations (all calculation results should be stored in a reduced form):

a) Add two `Rational` numbers.

b) Subtract two `Rational` numbers.

c) Multiply two `Rational` numbers.

d) Divide two `Rational` numbers.

e) Print `Rational` numbers in the form a/b, where a is the numerator and b is the denominator.

f) Print `Rational` numbers in floating-point format. (Consider providing formatting capabilities that enable the user of the class to specify the number of digits of precision to the right of the decimal point.)

9.15 *(Huge Integer Class)* Create a class `HugeInteger` which uses a 40-element array of digits to store integers as large as 40 digits each. Provide methods `Input`, `ToString`, `Add` and `Subtract`. For comparing `HugeInteger` objects, provide the following methods: `IsEqualTo`, `IsNotEqualTo`, `IsGreaterThan`, `IsLessThan`, `IsGreaterThanOrEqualTo` and `IsLessThanOrEqualTo`. Each of these is a method that returns `true` if the relationship holds between the two `HugeInteger` objects and returns `false` if the relationship does not hold. Provide method `IsZero`. If you feel ambitious, also provide methods `Multiply`, `Divide` and `Remainder`.

9.16 *(Tic-Tac-Toe)* Create class `TicTacToe` that will enable you to write a complete application to play the game of Tic-Tac-Toe. The class contains a `private` 3-by-3 rectangular array of integers. The constructor should initialize the empty board to all 0s. Allow two human players. Wherever the first player moves, place a 1 in the specified square, and place a 2 wherever the second player moves. Each move must be to an empty square. After each move, determine whether the game has been won and whether it is a draw. If you feel ambitious, modify your application so that the computer makes the moves for one of the players. Also, allow the player to specify whether he or she wants to go first or second. If you feel exceptionally ambitious, develop an application that will play three-dimensional Tic-Tac-Toe on a 4-by-4-by-4 board.

10

Object-Oriented Programming: Inheritance

OBJECTIVES

In this chapter you will learn:

- How inheritance promotes software reusability.

- The concepts of base classes and derived classes.

- To create a derived class that inherits attributes and behaviors from a base class.

- To use access modifier **protected** to give derived class methods access to base class members.

- To access base class members with **base**.

- How constructors are used in inheritance hierarchies.

- The methods of class **object**, the direct or indirect base class of all classes.

10.1 Introduction

This chapter continues our discussion of object-oriented programming (OOP) by introducing one of its primary features—*inheritance*, which is a form of software reuse in which a new class is created by absorbing an existing class's members and enhancing them with new or modified capabilities. With inheritance, programmers save time during application development by reusing proven and debugged high-quality software. This also increases the likelihood that a system will be implemented effectively.

When creating a class, rather than declaring completely new members, you can designate that the new class should inherit the members of an existing class. The existing class is called the *base class*, and the new class is the *derived class.* Each derived class can become the base class for future derived classes.

A derived class normally adds its own fields and methods. Therefore, a derived class is more specific than its base class and represents a more specialized group of objects. Typically, the derived class exhibits the behaviors of its base class and additional behaviors that are specific to the derived class.

The *direct base class* is the base class from which the derived class explicitly inherits. An *indirect base class* is any class above the direct base class in the *class hierarchy*, which defines the inheritance relationships among classes. The class hierarchy begins with class object (which is the C# alias for System.Object in the Framework Class Library), which *every* class directly or indirectly *extends* (or "inherits from"). Section 10.7 lists the methods of class object, which every other class inherits. In the case of *single inheritance,* a class is derived from one direct base class. C#, unlike C++, does not support multiple inheritance (which occurs when a class is derived from more than one direct base class). In Chapter 11, Polymorphism, Interfaces & Operator Overloading, we explain how you can use interfaces to realize many of the benefits of multiple inheritance while avoiding the associated problems.

Experience in building software systems indicates that significant amounts of code deal with closely related special cases. When programmers are preoccupied with special cases, the details can obscure the big picture. With object-oriented programming, programmers can, when appropriate, focus on the commonalities among objects in the system rather than the special cases.

We distinguish between the **is-a relationship** and the **has-a relationship**. *Is-a* represents inheritance. In an *is-a* relationship, an object of a derived class can also be treated as an object of its base class. For example, a car *is a* vehicle, and a truck *is a* vehicle. By contrast, *has-a* represents composition (see Chapter 9). In a *has-a* relationship, an object contains as members references to other objects. For example, a car *has a* steering wheel, and a car object *has a* reference to a steering wheel object.

New classes can inherit from classes in **class libraries**. Organizations develop their own class libraries and can take advantage of others available worldwide. Some day, most new software likely will be constructed from **standardized reusable components**, just as automobiles and most computer hardware are constructed today. This will facilitate the development of more powerful, abundant and economical software.

10.2 Base Classes and Derived Classes

Often, an object of one class *is an* object of another class as well. For example, in geometry, a rectangle *is a* quadrilateral (as are squares, parallelograms and trapezoids). Thus, class `Rectangle` can be said to inherit from class `Quadrilateral`. In this context, class `Quadrilateral` is a base class and class `Rectangle` is a derived class. A rectangle *is a* specific type of quadrilateral, but it is incorrect to claim that every quadrilateral *is a* rectangle—the quadrilateral could be a parallelogram or some other shape. Figure 10.1 lists several simple examples of base classes and derived classes—note that base classes tend to be "more general," and derived classes tend to be "more specific."

Because every derived class object *is an* object of its base class, and one base class can have many derived classes, the set of objects represented by a base class is typically larger than the set of objects represented by any of its derived classes. For example, the base class `Vehicle` represents all vehicles—cars, trucks, boats, bicycles and so on. By contrast, derived class `Car` represents a smaller, more specific subset of vehicles.

Base class	Derived classes
Student	GraduateStudent, UndergraduateStudent
Shape	Circle, Triangle, Rectangle
Loan	CarLoan, HomeImprovementLoan, MortgageLoan
Employee	Faculty, Staff, HourlyWorker, CommissionWorker
BankAccount	CheckingAccount, SavingsAccount

Fig. 10.1 | Inheritance examples.

Inheritance relationships form tree-like hierarchical structures (Figs. 10.2 and 10.3). A base class exists in a hierarchical relationship with its derived classes. When classes participate in inheritance relationships, they become "affiliated" with other classes. A class becomes either a base class, supplying members to other classes, or a derived class, inheriting its members from another class. In some cases, a class is both a base class and a derived class.

Let us develop a sample class hierarchy, also called an *inheritance hierarchy* (Fig. 10.2). The UML class diagram of Fig. 10.2 shows a university community that has many types of members, including employees, students and alumni. Employees are either faculty members or staff members. Faculty members are either administrators (such as deans and department chairpersons) or teachers. Note that the hierarchy could contain many other classes. For example, students can be graduate or undergraduate students. Undergraduate students can be freshmen, sophomores, juniors or seniors.

Each arrow with a hollow triangular arrowhead in the hierarchy diagram represents an *is-a* relationship. As we follow the arrows in this class hierarchy, we can state, for instance, that "an Employee *is a* CommunityMember" and "a Teacher *is a* Faculty member." CommunityMember is the direct base class of Employee, Student and Alumnus, and is an indirect base class of all the other classes in the diagram. Starting from the bottom of the diagram, the reader can follow the arrows and apply the *is-a* relationship up to the topmost base class. For example, an Administrator *is a* Faculty member, *is an* Employee and *is a* CommunityMember.

Now consider the Shape inheritance hierarchy in Fig. 10.3. This hierarchy begins with base class Shape, which is extended by derived classes TwoDimensionalShape and Three-DimensionalShape—Shapes are either TwoDimensionalShapes or ThreeDimensional-Shapes. The third level of this hierarchy contains some specific TwoDimensionalShapes and ThreeDimensionalShapes. As in Fig. 10.2, we can follow the arrows from the bottom of the class diagram to the topmost base class in this class hierarchy to identify several *is-a* relationships. For instance, a Triangle *is a* TwoDimensionalShape and *is a* Shape, while a Sphere *is a* ThreeDimensionalShape and *is a* Shape. Note that this hierarchy could contain many other classes. For example, ellipses and trapezoids are TwoDimensionalShapes.

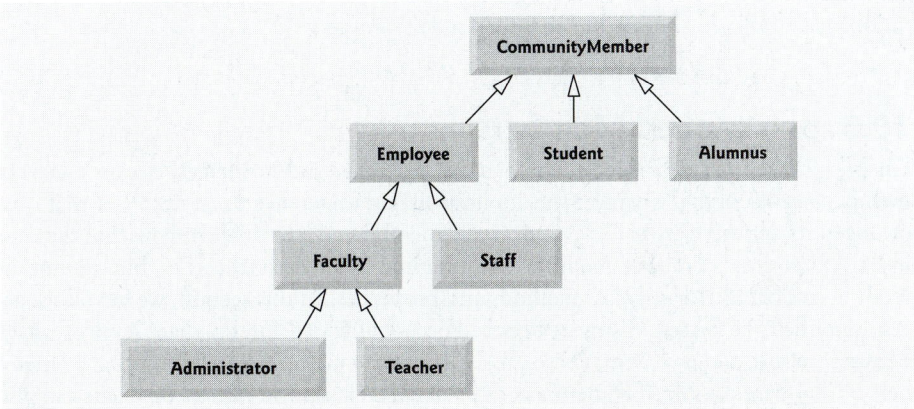

Fig. 10.2 | UML class diagram showing an inheritance hierarchy for university CommunityMembers.

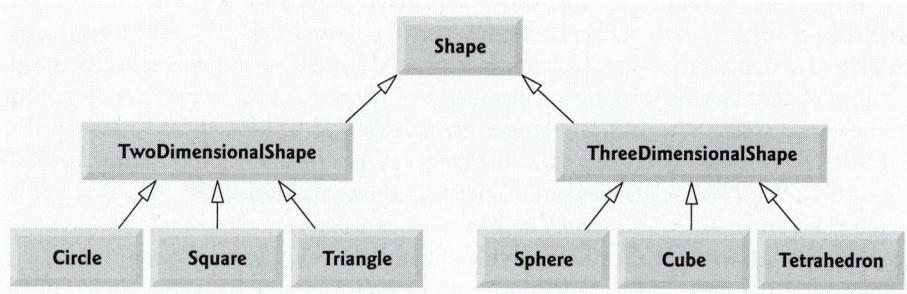

Fig. 10.3 | UML class diagram showing an inheritance hierarchy for Shapes.

Not every class relationship is an inheritance relationship. In Chapter 9, we discussed the *has-a* relationship, in which classes have members that are references to objects of other classes. Such relationships create classes by composition of existing classes. For example, given the classes Employee, BirthDate and TelephoneNumber, it is improper to say that an Employee *is a* BirthDate or that an Employee *is a* TelephoneNumber. However, an Employee *has a* BirthDate, and an Employee *has a* TelephoneNumber.

It is possible to treat base class objects and derived class objects similarly—their commonalities are expressed in the members of the base class. Objects of all classes that extend a common base class can be treated as objects of that base class (i.e., such objects have an *is-a* relationship with the base class). However, base class objects cannot be treated as objects of their derived classes. For example, all cars are vehicles, but not all vehicles are cars (the other vehicles could be trucks, planes or bicycles, for example). In this chapter and in Chapter 11, Polymorphism, Interfaces & Operator Overloading, we consider many examples of *is-a* relationships.

One problem with inheritance is that a derived class can inherit methods that it does not need or should not have. Even when a base class method is appropriate for a derived class, that derived class often needs a customized version of the method. In such cases, the derived class can **override** (redefine) the base class method with an appropriate implementation, as we will see often in the chapter's code examples.

10.3 protected Members

Chapter 9 discussed access modifiers public, private, and internal. A class's public members are accessible wherever the application has a reference to an object of that class or one of its derived classes. A class's private members are accessible only within the class itself. A base class's private members are inherited by its derived classes, but are not directly accessible by derived class methods and properties. In this section, we introduce access modifier protected. Using protected access offers an intermediate level of access between public and private. A base class's protected members can be accessed by members of that base class *and* by members of its derived classes. (Members of a class can also be declared **protected internal**. A base class's protected internal members can be accessed by members of that base class, by members of its derived classes *and* by any class in the same assembly.)

All non-`private` base class members retain their original access modifier when they become members of the derived class (i.e., `public` members of the base class become `public` members of the derived class, and `protected` members of the base class become `protected` members of the derived class).

Derived class methods can refer to `public` and `protected` members inherited from the base class simply by using the member names. When a derived class method overrides a base class method, the base class version of the method can be accessed from the derived class by preceding the base class method name with the keyword `base` and the dot (`.`) operator. We discuss accessing overridden members of the base class in Section 10.4.

Software Engineering Observation 10.1

Methods of a derived class cannot directly access `private` members of the base class. A derived class can change the state of `private` base class fields only through non-private methods and properties provided in the base class.

Software Engineering Observation 10.2

Declaring `private` fields in a base class helps you test, debug and correctly modify systems. If a derived class could access its base class's `private` fields, classes that inherit from that base class could access the fields as well. This would propagate access to what should be `private` fields, and the benefits of information hiding would be lost.

10.4 Relationship between Base Classes and Derived Classes

In this section, we use an inheritance hierarchy containing types of employees in a company's payroll application to discuss the relationship between a base class and its derived classes. In this company, commission employees (who will be represented as objects of a base class) are paid a percentage of their sales, while base-salaried commission employees (who will be represented as objects of a derived class) receive a base salary plus a percentage of their sales.

We divide our discussion of the relationship between commission employees and base-salaried commission employees into five examples. The first declares class `CommissionEmployee`, which directly inherits from class `object` and declares as `private` instance variables a first name, last name, social security number, commission rate and gross (i.e., total) sales amount.

The second example declares class `BasePlusCommissionEmployee`, which also directly inherits from class `object` and declares as `private` instance variables a first name, last name, social security number, commission rate, gross sales amount and base salary. We create the latter class by writing every line of code the class requires—we will soon see that it is much more efficient to create this class by inheriting from class `CommissionEmployee`.

The third example declares a separate `BasePlusCommissionEmployee2` class that extends class `CommissionEmployee` (i.e., a `BasePlusCommissionEmployee2` *is a* `CommissionEmployee` who also has a base salary). We show that base class methods must be explicitly declared `virtual` if they are to be overridden by methods in derived classes. `BasePlusCommissionEmployee2` attempts to access class `CommissionEmployee`'s `private` members—this results in compilation errors, because a derived class cannot access its base class's `private` instance variables.

The fourth example shows that if base class CommissionEmployee's instance variables are declared as protected, a BasePlusCommissionEmployee3 class that extends class CommissionEmployee2 can access that data directly. For this purpose, we declare class CommissionEmployee2 with protected instance variables. All of the BasePlus-CommissionEmployee classes contain identical functionality, but we show how the class BasePlusCommissionEmployee3 is easier to create and manage.

After we discuss the convenience of using protected instance variables, we create the fifth example, which sets the CommissionEmployee instance variables back to private in class CommissionEmployee3 to enforce good software engineering. Then we show how a separate BasePlusCommissionEmployee4 class, which extends class Commission-Employee3, can use CommissionEmployee3's public methods to manipulate Commission-Employee3's private instance variables.

10.4.1 Creating and Using a CommissionEmployee Class

We begin by declaring class CommissionEmployee (Fig. 10.4). Line 3 begins the class declaration. The colon (:) followed by class name object at the end of the declaration header indicates that class CommissionEmployee extends class object (System.Object in the FCL). C# programmers use inheritance to create classes from existing classes. In fact, every class in C# (except object) extends an existing class. Because class CommissionEmployee extends class object, class CommissionEmployee inherits the methods of class object—class object does not have any fields. Every C# class directly or indirectly inherits object's methods. If a class does not specify that it inherits from another class, the new class implicitly inherits from object. For this reason, programmers typically do not include ": object" in their code—we do so in this example for demonstration purposes.

```
1   // Fig. 10.4: CommissionEmployee.cs
2   // CommissionEmployee class represents a commission employee.
3   public class CommissionEmployee : object
4   {
5      private string firstName;
6      private string lastName;
7      private string socialSecurityNumber;
8      private decimal grossSales; // gross weekly sales
9      private decimal commissionRate; // commission percentage
10
11     // five-parameter constructor
12     public CommissionEmployee( string first, string last, string ssn,
13        decimal sales, decimal rate )
14     {
15        // implicit call to object constructor occurs here
16        firstName = first;
17        lastName = last;
18        socialSecurityNumber = ssn;
19        GrossSales = sales; // validate gross sales via property
20        CommissionRate = rate; // validate commission rate via property
21     } // end five-parameter CommissionEmployee constructor
22
```

Fig. 10.4 │ CommissionEmployee class represents a commission employee. (Part 1 of 3.)

```
23        // read-only property that gets commission employee's first name
24        public string FirstName
25        {
26           get
27           {
28              return firstName;
29           } // end get
30        } // end property FirstName
31
32        // read-only property that gets commission employee's last name
33        public string LastName
34        {
35           get
36           {
37              return lastName;
38           } // end get
39        } // end property LastName
40
41        // read-only property that gets
42        // commission employee's social security number
43        public string SocialSecurityNumber
44        {
45           get
46           {
47              return socialSecurityNumber;
48           } // end get
49        } // end property SocialSecurityNumber
50
51        // property that gets and sets commission employee's gross sales
52        public decimal GrossSales
53        {
54           get
55           {
56              return grossSales;
57           } // end get
58           set
59           {
60              grossSales = ( value < 0 ) ? 0 : value;
61           } // end set
62        } // end property GrossSales
63
64        // property that gets and sets commission employee's commission rate
65        public decimal CommissionRate
66        {
67           get
68           {
69              return commissionRate;
70           } // end get
71           set
72           {
73              commissionRate = ( value > 0 && value < 1 ) ? value : 0;
74           } // end set
75        } // end property CommissionRate
```

Fig. 10.4 | CommissionEmployee class represents a commission employee. (Part 2 of 3.)

```
76
77      // calculate commission employee's pay
78      public decimal Earnings()
79      {
80         return commissionRate * grossSales;
81      } // end method Earnings
82
83      // return string representation of CommissionEmployee object
84      public override string ToString()
85      {
86         return string.Format(
87            "{0}: {1} {2}\n{3}: {4}\n{5}: {6:C}\n{7}: {8:F2}",
88            "commission employee", FirstName, LastName,
89            "social security number", SocialSecurityNumber,
90            "gross sales", GrossSales, "commission rate", CommissionRate );
91      } // end method ToString
92   } // end class CommissionEmployee
```

Fig. 10.4 | CommissionEmployee class represents a commission employee. (Part 3 of 3.)

Software Engineering Observation 10.3

The compiler sets the base class of a class to object when the class declaration does not explicitly extend a base class.

The public services of class CommissionEmployee include a constructor (lines 12–21) and methods Earnings (lines 78–81) and ToString (lines 84–91). Lines 24–75 declare public properties for manipulating the class's instance variables firstName, lastName, socialSecurityNumber, grossSales and commissionRate (declared in lines 5–9). Class CommissionEmployee declares each of its instance variables as private, so objects of other classes cannot directly access these variables. Declaring instance variables as private and providing public properties to manipulate and validate them helps enforce good software engineering. The set accessors of properties GrossSales and CommissionRate, for example, validate their arguments before assigning the values to instance variables gross-Sales and commissionRate, respectively.

Constructors are not inherited, so class CommissionEmployee does not inherit class object's constructor. However, class CommissionEmployee's constructor calls class object's constructor implicitly. In fact, the first task of any derived class's constructor is to call its direct base class's constructor, either explicitly or implicitly (if no constructor call is specified), to ensure that the instance variables inherited from the base class are initialized properly. The syntax for calling a base class constructor explicitly is discussed in Section 10.4.3. If the code does not include an explicit call to the base class constructor, The compiler generates an implicit call to the base class's default or parameterless constructor. The comment in line 15 of Fig. 10.4 indicates where the implicit call to the base class object's default constructor is made (you do not write the code for this call). Class object's default (empty) constructor does nothing. Note that even if a class does not have constructors, the default constructor that the compiler implicitly declares for the class will call the base class's default or parameterless constructor. Class object is the only class that does not have a base class.

After the implicit call to object's constructor occurs, lines 16–20 of CommissionEmployee's constructor assign values to the class's instance variables. Note that we do not validate the values of arguments first, last and ssn before assigning them to the corresponding instance variables. We certainly could validate the first and last names—perhaps by ensuring that they are of a reasonable length. Similarly, a social security number could be validated to ensure that it contains nine digits, with or without dashes (e.g., 123-45-6789 or 123456789).

Method Earnings (lines 78–81) calculates a CommissionEmployee's earnings. Line 80 multiplies the commissionRate by the grossSales and returns the result.

Method ToString (lines 84–91) is special—it is one of the methods that every class inherits directly or indirectly from class object, which is the root of the C# class hierarchy. Section 10.7 summarizes class object's methods. Method ToString returns a string representing an object. This method is called implicitly by an application whenever an object must be converted to a string representation, such as in Console's Write method or string method Format using a format item. Class object's ToString method returns a string that includes the name of the object's class. It is primarily a placeholder that can be (and typically is) overridden by a derived class to specify an appropriate string representation of the data in a derived class object. Method ToString of class CommissionEmployee overrides (redefines) class object's ToString method. When invoked, CommissionEmployee's ToString method uses string method Format to return a string containing information about the CommissionEmployee. We use format specifier C to format grossSales as currency and the format specifier F2 to format the commissionRate with two digits of precision to the right of the decimal point. To override a base class method, a derived class must declare a method with keyword **override** and with the same signature (method name, number of parameters and parameter types) and return type as the base class method—object's ToString method takes no parameters and returns type string, so CommissionEmployee declares ToString with no parameters and return type string.

Common Programming Error 10.1

It is a compilation error to override a method with a different access modifier. Notice that overriding a method with a more restrictive access modifier would break the is-a relationship. If a public method could be overridden as a protected or private method, the derived class objects would not be able to respond to the same method calls as base class objects. Once a method is declared in a base class, the method must have the same access modifier for all that class's direct and indirect derived classes.

Figure 10.5 tests class CommissionEmployee. Lines 10–11 instantiate a CommissionEmployee object and invoke CommissionEmployee's constructor (lines 12–21 of Fig. 10.4)

```
1   // Fig. 10.5: CommissionEmployeeTest.cs
2   // Testing class CommissionEmployee.
3   using System;
4
5   public class CommissionEmployeeTest
6   {
7      public static void Main( string[] args )
8      {
9         // instantiate CommissionEmployee object
10        CommissionEmployee employee = new CommissionEmployee( "Sue",
11           "Jones", "222-22-2222", 10000.00M, .06M );
```

Fig. 10.5 | Testing class CommissionEmployee. (Part 1 of 2.)

```
12
13          // display commission employee data
14          Console.WriteLine(
15             "Employee information obtained by properties and methods: \n" );
16          Console.WriteLine( "{0} {1}", "First name is",
17             employee.FirstName );
18          Console.WriteLine( "{0} {1}", "Last name is",
19             employee.LastName );
20          Console.WriteLine( "{0} {1}", "Social security number is",
21             employee.SocialSecurityNumber );
22          Console.WriteLine( "{0} {1:C}", "Gross sales are",
23             employee.GrossSales );
24          Console.WriteLine( "{0} {1:F2}", "Commission rate is",
25             employee.CommissionRate );
26          Console.WriteLine( "{0} {1:C}", "Earnings are",
27             employee.Earnings() );
28
29          employee.GrossSales = 5000.00M; // set gross sales
30          employee.CommissionRate = .1M; // set commission rate
31
32          Console.WriteLine( "\n{0}:\n\n{1}",
33             "Updated employee information obtained by ToString", employee );
34          Console.WriteLine( "earnings: {0:C}", employee.Earnings() );
35       } // end Main
36    } // end class CommissionEmployeeTest
```

```
Employee information obtained by properties and methods:

First name is Sue
Last name is Jones
Social security number is 222-22-2222
Gross sales are $10,000.00
Commission rate is 0.06
Earnings are $600.00

Updated employee information obtained by ToString:

commission employee: Sue Jones
social security number: 222-22-2222
gross sales: $5,000.00
commission rate: 0.10
earnings: $500.00
```

Fig. 10.5 | Testing class `CommissionEmployee`. (Part 2 of 2.)

to initialize it with "Sue" as the first name, "Jones" as the last name, "222-22-2222" as the social security number, 10000.00M as the gross sales amount and .06M as the commission rate. We append the M suffix to the gross sales amount and the commission rate to indicate that these should be interpreted as decimal literals, rather than doubles. Lines 16–25 use CommissionEmployee's properties to retrieve the object's instance variable values for output. Lines 26–27 output the amount calculated by the Earnings method. Lines 29–30 invoke the set accessors of the object's GrossSales and CommissionRate properties to change the values of instance variables grossSales and commissionRate. Lines 32–33 output the string representation of the updated CommissionEmployee. Note that when an object is output using a format item, the object's ToString method is invoked implicitly to obtain the object's string representation. Line 34 outputs the earnings again.

10.4.2 Creating a BasePlusCommissionEmployee Class without Using Inheritance

We now discuss the second part of our introduction to inheritance by declaring and testing (completely new and independent) class BasePlusCommissionEmployee (Fig. 10.6), which contains a first name, last name, social security number, gross sales amount, commission rate and base salary. Class BasePlusCommissionEmployee's public services include a BasePlusCommissionEmployee constructor (lines 14–24) and methods Earnings (lines 99–102) and ToString (lines 105–113). Lines 28–96 declare public properties for the class's private instance variables firstName, lastName, socialSecurityNumber, grossSales, commissionRate and baseSalary (declared in lines 6–11). These variables, properties and methods encapsulate all the necessary features of a base-salaried commission employee. Note the similarity between this class and class CommissionEmployee (Fig. 10.4)—in this example, we do not yet exploit that similarity.

Note that class BasePlusCommissionEmployee does not specify that it extends object with the syntax ": object" in line 4, so the class implicitly extends object. Also note that, like class CommissionEmployee's constructor (lines 12–21 of Fig. 10.4), class BasePlusCommissionEmployee's constructor invokes class object's default constructor implicitly, as noted in the comment in line 17 of Fig. 10.6.

```
 1    // Fig. 10.6: BasePlusCommissionEmployee.cs
 2    // BasePlusCommissionEmployee class represents an employee that receives
 3    // a base salary in addition to a commission.
 4    public class BasePlusCommissionEmployee
 5    {
 6       private string firstName;
 7       private string lastName;
 8       private string socialSecurityNumber;
 9       private decimal grossSales; // gross weekly sales
10       private decimal commissionRate; // commission percentage
11       private decimal baseSalary; // base salary per week
12
13       // six-parameter constructor
14       public BasePlusCommissionEmployee( string first, string last,
15          string ssn, decimal sales, decimal rate, decimal salary )
16       {
17          // implicit call to object constructor occurs here
18          firstName = first;
19          lastName = last;
20          socialSecurityNumber = ssn;
21          GrossSales = sales; // validate gross sales via property
22          CommissionRate = rate; // validate commission rate via property
23          BaseSalary = salary; // validate base salary via property
24       } // end six-parameter BasePlusCommissionEmployee constructor
```

Fig. 10.6 | BasePlusCommissionEmployee class represents an employee that receives a base salary in addition to a commission. (Part 1 of 3.)

```
25
26      // read-only property that gets
27      // base-salaried commission employee's first name
28      public string FirstName
29      {
30         get
31         {
32            return firstName;
33         } // end get
34      } // end property FirstName
35
36      // read-only property that gets
37      // base-salaried commission employee's last name
38      public string LastName
39      {
40         get
41         {
42            return lastName;
43         } // end get
44      } // end property LastName
45
46      // read-only property that gets
47      // base-salaried commission employee's social security number
48      public string SocialSecurityNumber
49      {
50         get
51         {
52            return socialSecurityNumber;
53         } // end get
54      } // end property SocialSecurityNumber
55
56      // property that gets and sets
57      // base-salaried commission employee's gross sales
58      public decimal GrossSales
59      {
60         get
61         {
62            return grossSales;
63         } // end get
64         set
65         {
66            grossSales = ( value < 0 ) ? 0 : value;
67         } // end set
68      } // end property GrossSales
69
70      // property that gets and sets
71      // base-salaried commission employee's commission rate
72      public decimal CommissionRate
73      {
74         get
75         {
```

Fig. 10.6 | BasePlusCommissionEmployee class represents an employee that receives a base salary in addition to a commission. (Part 2 of 3.)

```
76              return commissionRate;
77          } // end get
78          set
79          {
80              commissionRate = ( value > 0 && value < 1 ) ? value : 0;
81          } // end set
82      } // end property CommissionRate
83
84      // property that gets and sets
85      // base-salaried commission employee's base salary
86      public decimal BaseSalary
87      {
88          get
89          {
90              return baseSalary;
91          } // end get
92          set
93          {
94              baseSalary = ( value < 0 ) ? 0 : value;
95          } // end set
96      } // end property BaseSalary
97
98      // calculate earnings
99      public decimal Earnings()
100     {
101         return BaseSalary + ( CommissionRate * GrossSales );
102     } // end method earnings
103
104     // return string representation of BasePlusCommissionEmployee
105     public override string ToString()
106     {
107         return string.Format(
108             "{0}: {1} {2}\n{3}: {4}\n{5}: {6:C}\n{7}: {8:F2}\n{9}: {10:C}",
109             "base-salaried commission employee", FirstName, LastName,
110             "social security number", SocialSecurityNumber,
111             "gross sales", GrossSales, "commission rate", CommissionRate,
112             "base salary", BaseSalary );
113     } // end method ToString
114 } // end class BasePlusCommissionEmployee
```

Fig. 10.6 | BasePlusCommissionEmployee class represents an employee that receives a base salary in addition to a commission. (Part 3 of 3.)

Class BasePlusCommissionEmployee's Earnings method (lines 99–102) computes the earnings of a base-salaried commission employee. Line 101 returns the result of adding the employee's base salary to the product of the commission rate and the employee's gross sales.

Class BasePlusCommissionEmployee overrides object method ToString to return a string containing the BasePlusCommissionEmployee's information (lines 105–113). Once again, we use format specifier C to format the gross sales and base salary as currency and format specifier F2 to format the commission rate with two digits of precision to the right of the decimal point (line 108).

Figure 10.7 tests class BasePlusCommissionEmployee. Lines 10–12 instantiate a Base-PlusCommissionEmployee object and pass "Bob", "Lewis", "333-33-3333", 5000.00M, .04M and 300.00M to the constructor as the first name, last name, social security number, gross sales, commission rate and base salary, respectively. Lines 17–30 use BasePlus-CommissionEmployee's properties and methods to retrieve the values of the object's instance variables and calculate the earnings for output. Line 32 invokes the object's BaseSalary property to change the base salary. Property BaseSalary's set accessor (Fig. 10.6, lines 92–95) ensures that instance variable baseSalary is not assigned a negative value, because an employee's base salary cannot be negative. Lines 34–35 of Fig. 10.7 invoke the object's ToString method implicitly to get the object's string representation.

```
1   // Fig. 10.7: BasePlusCommissionEmployeeTest.cs
2   // Testing class BasePlusCommissionEmployee.
3   using System;
4
5   public class BasePlusCommissionEmployeeTest
6   {
7      public static void Main( string[] args )
8      {
9         // instantiate BasePlusCommissionEmployee object
10        BasePlusCommissionEmployee employee =
11           new BasePlusCommissionEmployee( "Bob", "Lewis",
12           "333-33-3333", 5000.00M, .04M, 300.00M );
13
14        // display base-salaried commission employee data
15        Console.WriteLine(
16           "Employee information obtained by properties and methods: \n" );
17        Console.WriteLine( "{0} {1}", "First name is",
18           employee.FirstName );
19        Console.WriteLine( "{0} {1}", "Last name is",
20           employee.LastName );
21        Console.WriteLine( "{0} {1}", "Social security number is",
22           employee.SocialSecurityNumber );
23        Console.WriteLine( "{0} {1:C}", "Gross sales are",
24           employee.GrossSales );
25        Console.WriteLine( "{0} {1:F2}", "Commission rate is",
26           employee.CommissionRate );
27        Console.WriteLine( "{0} {1:C}", "Earnings are",
28           employee.Earnings() );
29        Console.WriteLine( "{0} {1:C}", "Base salary is",
30           employee.BaseSalary );
31
32        employee.BaseSalary = 1000.00M; // set base salary
33
34        Console.WriteLine( "\n{0}:\n\n{1}",
35           "Updated employee information obtained by ToString", employee );
36        Console.WriteLine( "earnings: {0:C}", employee.Earnings() );
37     } // end Main
38  } // end class BasePlusCommissionEmployeeTest
```

Fig. 10.7 | Testing class BasePlusCommissionEmployee. (Part 1 of 2.)

```
Employee information obtained by properties and methods:

First name is Bob
Last name is Lewis
Social security number is 333-33-3333
Gross sales are $5,000.00
Commission rate is 0.04
Earnings are $500.00
Base salary is $300.00

Updated employee information obtained by ToString:

base-salaried commission employee: Bob Lewis
social security number: 333-33-3333
gross sales: $5,000.00
commission rate: 0.04
base salary: $1,000.00
earnings: $1,200.00
```

Fig. 10.7 | Testing class `BasePlusCommissionEmployee`. (Part 2 of 2.)

Note that much of the code for class `BasePlusCommissionEmployee` (Fig. 10.6) is similar, if not identical, to the code for class `CommissionEmployee` (Fig. 10.4). For example, in class `BasePlusCommissionEmployee`, private instance variables `firstName` and `lastName` and properties `FirstName` and `LastName` are identical to those of class `CommissionEmployee`. Classes `CommissionEmployee` and `BasePlusCommissionEmployee` also both contain private instance variables `socialSecurityNumber`, `commissionRate` and `grossSales`, as well as properties to manipulate these variables. In addition, the `BasePlusCommission-Employee` constructor is almost identical to that of class `CommissionEmployee`, except that `BasePlusCommissionEmployee`'s constructor also sets the `baseSalary`. The other additions to class `BasePlusCommissionEmployee` are private instance variable `baseSalary` and property `BaseSalary`. Class `BasePlusCommissionEmployee`'s `ToString` method is nearly identical to that of class `CommissionEmployee`, except that `BasePlusCommissionEmployee`'s `ToString` also formats the value of instance variable `baseSalary` as currency.

We literally copied the code from class `CommissionEmployee` and pasted it into class `BasePlusCommissionEmployee`, then modified class `BasePlusCommissionEmployee` to include a base salary, and methods and properties that manipulate the base salary. This "copy-and-paste" approach is often error prone and time consuming. Worse yet, it can spread many physical copies of the same code throughout a system, creating a code-maintenance nightmare. Is there a way to "absorb" the members of one class in a way that makes them part of other classes without copying code? In the next several examples, we answer this question, using a more elegant approach to building classes, namely inheritance.

 Error-Prevention Tip 10.1

Copying and pasting code from one class to another can spread errors across multiple source code files. To avoid duplicating code (and possibly errors) in situations where you want one class to "absorb" the members of another class, use inheritance rather than the "copy-and-paste" approach.

Software Engineering Observation 10.4

With inheritance, the common members of all the classes in the hierarchy are declared in a base class. When changes are required for these common features, you need only to make the changes in the base class—derived classes then inherit the changes. Without inheritance, changes would need to be made to all the source code files that contain a copy of the code in question.

10.4.3 Creating a CommissionEmployee–BasePlusCommissionEmployee Inheritance Hierarchy

Now we declare class BasePlusCommissionEmployee2 (Fig. 10.8), which extends class CommissionEmployee (Fig. 10.4). A BasePlusCommissionEmployee2 object *is a* CommissionEmployee (because inheritance passes on the capabilities of class CommissionEmployee), but class BasePlusCommissionEmployee2 also has instance variable baseSalary (Fig. 10.8, line 5). The colon (:) in line 3 of the class declaration indicates inheritance. As a derived class, BasePlusCommissionEmployee2 inherits the members of class CommissionEmployee and can access those members that are non-private. The constructor of class CommissionEmployee is not inherited. Thus, the public services of BasePlusCommissionEmployee2 include its constructor (lines 9–14), public methods and properties inherited from class CommissionEmployee, property BaseSalary (lines 18–28), method Earnings (lines 31–35) and method ToString (lines 38–47).

```
 1    // Fig. 10.8: BasePlusCommissionEmployee2.cs
 2    // BasePlusCommissionEmployee2 inherits from class CommissionEmployee.
 3    public class BasePlusCommissionEmployee2 : CommissionEmployee
 4    {
 5       private decimal baseSalary; // base salary per week
 6
 7       // six-parameter derived class constructor
 8       // with call to base class CommissionEmployee constructor
 9       public BasePlusCommissionEmployee2( string first, string last,
10          string ssn, decimal sales, decimal rate, decimal salary )
11          : base( first, last, ssn, sales, rate )
12       {
13          BaseSalary = salary; // validate base salary via property
14       } // end six-parameter BasePlusCommissionEmployee2 constructor
15
16       // property that gets and sets
17       // base-salaried commission employee's base salary
18       public decimal BaseSalary
19       {
20          get
21          {
22             return baseSalary;
23          } // end get
24          set
25          {
26             baseSalary = ( value < 0 ) ? 0 : value;
27          } // end set
28       } // end property BaseSalary
```

Fig. 10.8 | BasePlusCommissionEmployee2 inherits from class CommissionEmployee. (Part 1 of 2.)

```
29
30      // calculate earnings
31      public override decimal Earnings()
32      {
33          // not allowed: commissionRate and grossSales private in base class
34          return baseSalary + ( commissionRate * grossSales );
35      } // end method Earnings
36
37      // return string representation of BasePlusCommissionEmployee2
38      public override string ToString()
39      {
40          // not allowed: attempts to access private base class members
41          return string.Format(
42              "{0}: {1} {2}\n{3}: {4}\n{5}: {6:C}\n{7}: {8:F2}\n{9}: {10:C}",
43              "base-salaried commission employee", firstName, lastName,
44              "social security number", socialSecurityNumber,
45              "gross sales", grossSales, "commission rate", commissionRate,
46              "base salary", baseSalary );
47      } // end method ToString
48  } // end class BasePlusCommissionEmployee2
```

				Error List					⊠
🔴 1 Error	⚠ 0 Warnings	ⓘ 0 Messages							
	Description				File	Line	Column	Project	
⊗ 1	'BasePlusCommissionEmployee2.Earnings()': cannot override inherited member 'CommissionEmployee.Earnings()' because it is not marked virtual, abstract, or override				BasePlusComn	31	28	BasePlusCommissionEmployee2	

Fig. 10.8 | BasePlusCommissionEmployee2 inherits from class CommissionEmployee. (Part 2 of 2.)

Each derived class constructor must implicitly or explicitly call its base class constructor to ensure that the instance variables inherited from the base class are initialized properly. BasePlusCommissionEmployee2's six-parameter constructor explicitly calls class CommissionEmployee's five-parameter constructor to initialize the base class portion of a BasePlusCommissionEmployee2 object (i.e., variables firstName, lastName, social-SecurityNumber, grossSales and commissionRate). Line 11 in the header of BasePlusCommissionEmployee2's six-parameter constructor invokes the CommissionEmployee's five-parameter constructor (declared at lines 12–21 of Fig. 10.4) by using a constructor initializer. In Section 9.6, we used constructor initializers with keyword this to call overloaded constructors in the same class. In line 11 of Fig. 10.8, we use a constructor initializer with keyword base to invoke the base class constructor. The arguments first, last, ssn, sales and rate are used to initialize base class members firstName, lastName, socialSecurityNumber, grossSales and commissionRate, respectively. If BasePlus-CommissionEmployee2's constructor did not invoke CommissionEmployee's constructor explicitly, C# would attempt to invoke class CommissionEmployee's parameterless or default constructor—but the class does not have such a constructor, so the compiler would issue an error. When a base class contains a parameterless constructor, you can use base() in the constructor initializer to call that constructor explicitly, but this is rarely done.

Common Programming Error 10.2

A compilation error occurs if a derived class constructor calls one of its base class constructors with arguments that do not match the number and types of parameters specified in one of the base class constructor declarations.

Lines 31–35 of Fig. 10.8 declare method Earnings using keyword override to override the CommissionEmployee's Earnings method, as we did with method ToString in previous examples. Line 31 causes a compilation error indicating that we cannot override the base class's Earnings method because it was not explicitly "marked virtual, abstract, or override." The *virtual* and abstract keywords indicate that a base class method can be overridden in derived classes. (As you will learn in Section 11.4, abstract methods are implicitly virtual.) The override modifier declares that a derived class method overrides a virtual or abstract base class method. This modifier also implicitly declares the derived class method virtual and allows it to be overridden in derived classes further down the inheritance hierarchy.

If we add the keyword virtual to the declaration of method Earnings in Fig. 10.4 and recompile, other compilation errors appear. As shown in Fig. 10.9, the compiler generates additional errors for line 34 of Fig. 10.8 because base class CommissionEmployee's instance variables commissionRate and grossSales are private—derived class BasePlusCommissionEmployee2's methods are not allowed to access base class CommissionEmployee's private instance variables. Note that we used red text in Fig. 10.8 to indicate erroneous code. The compiler issues additional errors at lines 43–45 of BasePlusCommissionEmployee2's ToString method for the same reason. The errors in BasePlusCommissionEmployee2 could have been prevented by using the public properties inherited from class CommissionEmployee. For example, line 34 could have invoked the get accessors of properties CommissionRate and GrossSales to access CommissionEmployee's private instance variables commissionRate and grossSales, respectively. Lines 43–45 also could have used appropriate properties to retrieve the values of the base class's instance variables.

Error List					⊠
⊗ 7 Errors	⚠ 0 Warnings	ⓘ 0 Messages			
	Description	File	Line	Column	Project
⊗ 1	'CommissionEmployee.commissionRate' is inaccessible due to its protection level	BasePlusCc	34	29	BasePlusCommission Employee2
⊗ 2	'CommissionEmployee.grossSales' is inaccessible due to its protection level	BasePlusCc	34	46	BasePlusCommission Employee2
⊗ 3	'CommissionEmployee.firstName' is inaccessible due to its protection level	BasePlusCc	43	47	BasePlusCommission Employee2
⊗ 4	'CommissionEmployee.lastName' is inaccessible due to its protection level	BasePlusCc	43	58	BasePlusCommission Employee2
⊗ 5	'CommissionEmployee.socialSecurityNumber' is inaccessible due to its protection level	BasePlusCc	44	36	BasePlusCommission Employee2
⊗ 6	'CommissionEmployee.grossSales' is inaccessible due to its protection level	BasePlusCc	45	25	BasePlusCommission Employee2
⊗ 7	'CommissionEmployee.commissionRate' is inaccessible due to its protection level	BasePlusCc	45	56	BasePlusCommission Employee2

Fig. 10.9 | Compilation errors generated by BasePlusCommissionEmployee2 (Fig. 10.8) after declaring the Earnings method in Fig. 10.4 with keyword virtual.

10.4.4 CommissionEmployee–BasePlusCommissionEmployee Inheritance Hierarchy Using protected Instance Variables

To enable class BasePlusCommissionEmployee to directly access base class instance variables firstName, lastName, socialSecurityNumber, grossSales and commissionRate, we can declare those members as protected in the base class. As we discussed in Section 10.3, a base class's protected members *are* inherited by all derived classes of that base class. Class CommissionEmployee2 (Fig. 10.10) is a modification of class CommissionEmployee (Fig. 10.4) that declares instance variables firstName, lastName, socialSecurityNumber, grossSales and commissionRate as protected rather than private (Fig. 10.10, lines 5–9). As discussed in Section 10.4.3, we also declare the Earnings method virtual in line 78 so

```
1   // Fig. 10.10: CommissionEmployee2.cs
2   // CommissionEmployee2 with protected instance variables.
3   public class CommissionEmployee2
4   {
5      protected string firstName;
6      protected string lastName;
7      protected string socialSecurityNumber;
8      protected decimal grossSales; // gross weekly sales
9      protected decimal commissionRate; // commission percentage
10
11     // five-parameter constructor
12     public CommissionEmployee2( string first, string last, string ssn,
13        decimal sales, decimal rate )
14     {
15        // implicit call to object constructor occurs here
16        firstName = first;
17        lastName = last;
18        socialSecurityNumber = ssn;
19        GrossSales = sales; // validate gross sales via property
20        CommissionRate = rate; // validate commission rate via property
21     } // end five-parameter CommissionEmployee2 constructor
22
23     // read-only property that gets commission employee's first name
24     public string FirstName
25     {
26        get
27        {
28           return firstName;
29        } // end get
30     } // end property FirstName
31
32     // read-only property that gets commission employee's last name
33     public string LastName
34     {
35        get
36        {
37           return lastName;
38        } // end get
39     } // end property LastName
40
```

Fig. 10.10 | CommissionEmployee2 with protected instance variables. (Part 1 of 2.)

```csharp
41      // read-only property that gets
42      // commission employee's social security number
43      public string SocialSecurityNumber
44      {
45         get
46         {
47            return socialSecurityNumber;
48         } // end get
49      } // end property SocialSecurityNumber
50
51      // property that gets and sets commission employee's gross sales
52      public decimal GrossSales
53      {
54         get
55         {
56            return grossSales;
57         } // end get
58         set
59         {
60            grossSales = ( value < 0 ) ? 0 : value;
61         } // end set
62      } // end property GrossSales
63
64      // property that gets and sets commission employee's commission rate
65      public decimal CommissionRate
66      {
67         get
68         {
69            return commissionRate;
70         } // end get
71         set
72         {
73            commissionRate = ( value > 0 && value < 1 ) ? value : 0;
74         } // end set
75      } // end property CommissionRate
76
77      // calculate commission employee's pay
78      public virtual decimal Earnings()
79      {
80         return commissionRate * grossSales;
81      } // end method Earnings
82
83      // return string representation of CommissionEmployee object
84      public override string ToString()
85      {
86         return string.Format(
87            "{0}: {1} {2}\n{3}: {4}\n{5}: {6:C}\n{7}: {8:F2}",
88            "commission employee", firstName, lastName,
89            "social security number", socialSecurityNumber,
90            "gross sales", grossSales, "commission rate", commissionRate );
91      } // end method ToString
92   } // end class CommissionEmployee2
```

Fig. 10.10 | CommissionEmployee2 with protected instance variables. (Part 2 of 2.)

that BasePlusCommissionEmployee can override the method. Other than the change in the class name (and thus the change in the constructor name) to CommissionEmployee2, the rest of the class declaration in Fig. 10.10 is identical to that of Fig. 10.4.

We could have declared the base class CommissionEmployee2's instance variables firstName, lastName, socialSecurityNumber, grossSales and commissionRate as public to enable derived class BasePlusCommissionEmployee2 to access the base class instance variables. However, declaring public instance variables is poor software engineering, because it allows unrestricted access to the instance variables, greatly increasing the chance of errors. With protected instance variables, the derived class gets access to the instance variables, but classes that are not derived from the base class cannot access its variables directly.

Class BasePlusCommissionEmployee3 (Fig. 10.11) is a modification of class BasePlusCommissionEmployee2 (Fig. 10.8) that extends CommissionEmployee2 (line 4) rather than class CommissionEmployee. Objects of class BasePlusCommissionEmployee3 inherit CommissionEmployee2's protected instance variables firstName, lastName, socialSecurityNumber, grossSales and commissionRate—all these variables are now protected members of BasePlusCommissionEmployee3. As a result, the compiler does not generate errors when compiling line 34 of method Earnings and lines 42–44 of method ToString. If another class extends BasePlusCommissionEmployee3, the new derived class also inherits the protected members.

Class BasePlusCommissionEmployee3 does not inherit class CommissionEmployee2's constructor. However, class BasePlusCommissionEmployee3's six-parameter constructor (lines 10–15) calls class CommissionEmployee2's five-parameter constructor with a constructor initializer. BasePlusCommissionEmployee3's six-parameter constructor must explicitly call the five-parameter constructor of class CommissionEmployee2, because CommissionEmployee2 does not provide a parameterless constructor that could be invoked implicitly.

```
1   // Fig. 10.11: BasePlusCommissionEmployee3.cs
2   // BasePlusCommissionEmployee3 inherits from CommissionEmployee2 and has
3   // access to CommissionEmployee2's protected members.
4   public class BasePlusCommissionEmployee3 : CommissionEmployee2
5   {
6      private decimal baseSalary; // base salary per week
7
8      // six-parameter derived class constructor
9      // with call to base class CommissionEmployee constructor
10     public BasePlusCommissionEmployee3( string first, string last,
11        string ssn, decimal sales, decimal rate, decimal salary )
12        : base( first, last, ssn, sales, rate )
13     {
14        BaseSalary = salary; // validate base salary via property
15     } // end six-parameter BasePlusCommissionEmployee3 constructor
16
```

Fig. 10.11 | BasePlusCommissionEmployee3 inherits from CommissionEmployee2 and has access to CommissionEmployee2's protected members. (Part 1 of 2.)

```
17      // property that gets and sets
18      // base-salaried commission employee's base salary
19      public decimal BaseSalary
20      {
21         get
22         {
23            return baseSalary;
24         } // end get
25         set
26         {
27            baseSalary = ( value < 0 ) ? 0 : value;
28         } // end set
29      } // end property BaseSalary
30
31      // calculate earnings
32      public override decimal Earnings()
33      {
34         return baseSalary + ( commissionRate * grossSales );
35      } // end method Earnings
36
37      // return string representation of BasePlusCommissionEmployee3
38      public override string ToString()
39      {
40         return string.Format(
41            "{0}: {1} {2}\n{3}: {4}\n{5}: {6:C}\n{7}: {8:F2}\n{9}: {10:C}",
42            "base-salaried commission employee", firstName, lastName,
43            "social security number", socialSecurityNumber,
44            "gross sales", grossSales, "commission rate", commissionRate,
45            "base salary", baseSalary );
46      } // end method ToString
47   } // end class BasePlusCommissionEmployee3
```

Fig. 10.11 | BasePlusCommissionEmployee3 inherits from CommissionEmployee2 and has access to CommissionEmployee2's protected members. (Part 2 of 2.)

Figure 10.12 uses a BasePlusCommissionEmployee3 object to perform the same tasks that Fig. 10.7 performed on a BasePlusCommissionEmployee object (Fig. 10.6). Note that the outputs of the two applications are identical. Although we declared class BasePlusCommissionEmployee without using inheritance and declared class BasePlusCommissionEmployee3 using inheritance, both classes provide the same functionality. The source code for class BasePlusCommissionEmployee3, which is 47 lines, is considerably shorter than that for class BasePlusCommissionEmployee, which is 114 lines, because class BasePlusCommissionEmployee3 inherits most of its functionality from CommissionEmployee2, whereas class BasePlusCommissionEmployee inherits only class object's functionality. Also, there is now only one copy of the commission employee functionality declared in class CommissionEmployee2. This makes the code easier to maintain, modify and debug, because the code related to a commission employee exists only in class CommissionEmployee2.

In this example, we declared base class instance variables as protected so that derived classes could inherit them. Inheriting protected instance variables slightly increases performance, because we can directly access the variables in the derived class without incurring the overhead of invoking the `set` or `get` accessors of the corresponding property. In most cases, however, it is better to use `private` instance variables to encourage proper software engineering, and leave code optimization issues to the compiler. Your code will be easier to maintain, modify and debug.

Using `protected` instance variables creates several potential problems. First, the derived class object can set an inherited variable's value directly without using the property's set accessor. Therefore, a derived class object can assign an invalid value to the variable, thus leaving the object in an inconsistent state. For example, if we were to declare `CommissionEmployee3`'s instance variable `grossSales` as `protected`, a derived class object (e.g., `BasePlusCommissionEmployee`) could then assign a negative value to `grossSales`.

```
1   // Fig. 10.12: BasePlusCommissionEmployeeTest3.cs
2   // Testing class BasePlusCommissionEmployee3.
3   using System;
4
5   public class BasePlusCommissionEmployeeTest3
6   {
7      public static void Main( string[] args )
8      {
9         // instantiate BasePlusCommissionEmployee3 object
10        BasePlusCommissionEmployee3 basePlusCommissionEmployee =
11           new BasePlusCommissionEmployee3( "Bob", "Lewis",
12           "333-33-3333", 5000.00M, .04M, 300.00M );
13
14        // display base-salaried commission employee data
15        Console.WriteLine(
16           "Employee information obtained by properties and methods: \n" );
17        Console.WriteLine( "{0} {1}", "First name is",
18           basePlusCommissionEmployee.FirstName );
19        Console.WriteLine( "{0} {1}", "Last name is",
20           basePlusCommissionEmployee.LastName );
21        Console.WriteLine( "{0} {1}", "Social security number is",
22           basePlusCommissionEmployee.SocialSecurityNumber );
23        Console.WriteLine( "{0} {1:C}", "Gross sales are",
24           basePlusCommissionEmployee.GrossSales );
25        Console.WriteLine( "{0} {1:F2}", "Commission rate is",
26           basePlusCommissionEmployee.CommissionRate );
27        Console.WriteLine( "{0} {1:C}", "Earnings are",
28           basePlusCommissionEmployee.Earnings() );
29        Console.WriteLine( "{0} {1:C}", "Base salary is",
30           basePlusCommissionEmployee.BaseSalary );
31
32        basePlusCommissionEmployee.BaseSalary = 1000.00M; // set base salary
33
34        Console.WriteLine( "\n{0}:\n\n{1}",
35           "Updated employee information obtained by ToString",
36           basePlusCommissionEmployee );
37        Console.WriteLine( "earnings: {0:C}",
38           basePlusCommissionEmployee.Earnings() );
39     } // end Main
40  } // end class BasePlusCommissionEmployeeTest3
```

Fig. 10.12 | Testing class `BasePlusCommissionEmployee3`. (Part 1 of 2.)

```
Employee information obtained by properties and methods:

First name is Bob
Last name is Lewis
Social security number is 333-33-3333
Gross sales are $5,000.00
Commission rate is 0.04
Earnings are $500.00
Base salary is $300.00

Updated employee information obtained by ToString:

base-salaried commission employee: Bob Lewis
social security number: 333-33-3333
gross sales: $5,000.00
commission rate: 0.04
base salary: $1,000.00
earnings: $1,200.00
```

Fig. 10.12 | Testing class `BasePlusCommissionEmployee3`. (Part 2 of 2.)

The second problem with using `protected` instance variables is that derived class methods are more likely to be written to depend on the base class's data implementation. In practice, derived classes should depend only on the base class services (i.e., non-private methods and properties) and not on the base class data implementation. With `protected` instance variables in the base class, we may need to modify all the derived classes of the base class if the base class implementation changes. For example, if for some reason we were to change the names of instance variables `firstName` and `lastName` to `first` and `last`, then we would have to do so for all occurrences in which a derived class directly references base class instance variables `firstName` and `lastName`. In such a case, the software is said to be *fragile* or *brittle*, because a small change in the base class can "break" derived class implementation. You should be able to change the base class implementation while still providing the same services to the derived classes. Of course, if the base class services change, we must reimplement our derived classes.

> ### Software Engineering Observation 10.5
>
> *Declaring base class instance variables `private` (as opposed to protected) enables the base class implementation of these instance variables to change without affecting derived class implementations.*

10.4.5 CommissionEmployee–BasePlusCommissionEmployee Inheritance Hierarchy Using private Instance Variables

We now reexamine our hierarchy once more, this time using the best software engineering practices. Class `CommissionEmployee3` (Fig. 10.13) declares instance variables `firstName`, `lastName`, `socialSecurityNumber`, `grossSales` and `commissionRate` as `private` (lines 5–9) and provides public properties `FirstName`, `LastName`, `SocialSecurityNumber`, `GrossSales` and `GrossSales` for manipulating these values. Note that methods `Earnings` (lines 78–81) and `ToString` (lines 84–91) use the class's properties to obtain the values of its instance variables. If we decide to change the instance variable names, the `Earnings` and

```
 1   // Fig. 10.13: CommissionEmployee3.cs
 2   // CommissionEmployee3 class represents a commission employee.
 3   public class CommissionEmployee3
 4   {
 5      private string firstName;
 6      private string lastName;
 7      private string socialSecurityNumber;
 8      private decimal grossSales; // gross weekly sales
 9      private decimal commissionRate; // commission percentage
10
11      // five-parameter constructor
12      public CommissionEmployee3( string first, string last, string ssn,
13         decimal sales, decimal rate )
14      {
15         // implicit call to object constructor occurs here
16         firstName = first;
17         lastName = last;
18         socialSecurityNumber = ssn;
19         GrossSales = sales; // validate gross sales via property
20         CommissionRate = rate; // validate commission rate via property
21      } // end five-parameter CommissionEmployee3 constructor
22
23      // read-only property that gets commission employee's first name
24      public string FirstName
25      {
26         get
27         {
28            return firstName;
29         } // end get
30      } // end property FirstName
31
32      // read-only property that gets commission employee's last name
33      public string LastName
34      {
35         get
36         {
37            return lastName;
38         } // end get
39      } // end property LastName
40
41      // read-only property that gets
42      // commission employee's social security number
43      public string SocialSecurityNumber
44      {
45         get
46         {
47            return socialSecurityNumber;
48         } // end get
49      } // end property SocialSecurityNumber
50
51      // property that gets and sets commission employee's gross sales
52      public decimal GrossSales
53      {
```

Fig. 10.13 | CommissionEmployee3 class represents a commission employee. (Part 1 of 2.)

```
54          get
55          {
56             return grossSales;
57          } // end get
58          set
59          {
60             grossSales = ( value < 0 ) ? 0 : value;
61          } // end set
62       } // end property GrossSales
63
64       // property that gets and sets commission employee's commission rate
65       public decimal CommissionRate
66       {
67          get
68          {
69             return commissionRate;
70          } // end get
71          set
72          {
73             commissionRate = ( value > 0 && value < 1 ) ? value : 0;
74          } // end set
75       } // end property CommissionRate
76
77       // calculate commission employee's pay
78       public virtual decimal Earnings()
79       {
80          return CommissionRate * GrossSales;
81       } // end method Earnings
82
83       // return string representation of CommissionEmployee object
84       public override string ToString()
85       {
86          return string.Format(
87             "{0}: {1} {2}\n{3}: {4}\n{5}: {6:C}\n{7}: {8:F2}",
88             "commission employee", FirstName, LastName,
89             "social security number", SocialSecurityNumber,
90             "gross sales", GrossSales, "commission rate", CommissionRate );
91       } // end method ToString
92    } // end class CommissionEmployee3
```

Fig. 10.13 | CommissionEmployee3 class represents a commission employee. (Part 2 of 2.)

ToString declarations will not require modification—only the bodies of the properties that directly manipulate the instance variables will need to change. Note that these changes occur solely within the base class—no changes to the derived class are needed. Localizing the effects of changes like this is a good software engineering practice. Derived class BasePlusCommissionEmployee4 (Fig. 10.14) inherits CommissionEmployee3's non-private members and can access the private base class members via its public properties.

Class BasePlusCommissionEmployee4 (Fig. 10.14) has several changes to its method implementations that distinguish it from class BasePlusCommissionEmployee3 (Fig. 10.11). Methods Earnings (Fig. 10.14, lines 33–36) and ToString (lines 39–43) each invoke property BaseSalary's get accessor to obtain the base salary value, rather than

```
1    // Fig. 10.14: BasePlusCommissionEmployee4.cs
2    // BasePlusCommissionEmployee4 inherits from CommissionEmployee3 and has
3    // access to CommissionEmployee3's private data via
4    // its public properties.
5    public class BasePlusCommissionEmployee4 : CommissionEmployee3
6    {
7       private decimal baseSalary; // base salary per week
8
9       // six-parameter derived class constructor
10      // with call to base class CommissionEmployee3 constructor
11      public BasePlusCommissionEmployee4( string first, string last,
12         string ssn, decimal sales, decimal rate, decimal salary )
13         : base( first, last, ssn, sales, rate )
14      {
15         BaseSalary = salary; // validate base salary via property
16      } // end six-parameter BasePlusCommissionEmployee4 constructor
17
18      // property that gets and sets
19      // base-salaried commission employee's base salary
20      public decimal BaseSalary
21      {
22         get
23         {
24            return baseSalary;
25         } // end get
26         set
27         {
28            baseSalary = ( value < 0 ) ? 0 : value;
29         } // end set
30      } // end property BaseSalary
31
32      // calculate earnings
33      public override decimal Earnings()
34      {
35         return BaseSalary + base.Earnings();
36      } // end method Earnings
37
38      // return string representation of BasePlusCommissionEmployee4
39      public override string ToString()
40      {
41         return string.Format( "{0} {1}\n{2}: {3:C}",
42            "base-salaried", base.ToString(), "base salary", BaseSalary );
43      } // end method ToString
44   } // end class BasePlusCommissionEmployee4
```

Fig. 10.14 | BasePlusCommissionEmployee4 inherits from CommissionEmployee3 and has access to CommissionEmployee3's private data via its public properties.

accessing baseSalary directly. If we decide to rename instance variable baseSalary, only the body of property BaseSalary will need to change.

Class BasePlusCommissionEmployee4's Earnings method (Fig. 10.14, lines 33–36) overrides class CommissionEmployee3's Earnings method (Fig. 10.13, lines 78–81) to calculate the earnings of a base-salaried commission employee. The new version obtains the portion of the employee's earnings based on commission alone by calling CommissionEmployee3's Earnings method with the expression base.Earnings() (Fig. 10.14, line 35). BasePlusCommissionEmployee4's Earnings method then adds the base salary to this value to calculate the total earnings of the employee. Note the syntax used to invoke an overridden base class method from a derived class—place the keyword base and the dot (.) operator before the base class method name. This method invocation is a good software engineering practice—by having BasePlusCommissionEmployee4's Earnings method invoke CommissionEmployee3's Earnings method to calculate part of a BasePlusCommissionEmployee4 object's earnings, we avoid duplicating the code and reduce code-maintenance problems.

Common Programming Error 10.3

When a base class method is overridden in a derived class, the derived class version often calls the base class version to do a portion of the work. Failure to prefix the base class method name with the keyword base and the dot (.) operator when referencing the base class's method causes the derived class method to call itself, creating an error called infinite recursion. Recursion, used correctly, is a powerful capability, as you learned in Section 7.13, Recursion.

Common Programming Error 10.4

The use of "chained" base references to refer to a member (a method, property or variable) several levels up the hierarchy—as in base.base.Earnings()—is a compilation error.

Similarly, BasePlusCommissionEmployee4's ToString method (Fig. 10.14, lines 39–43) overrides class CommissionEmployee3's ToString method (Fig. 10.13, lines 84–91) to return a string representation that is appropriate for a base-salaried commission employee. The new version creates part of a BasePlusCommissionEmployee4 object's string representation (i.e., the string "commission employee" and the values of class CommissionEmployee3's private instance variables) by calling CommissionEmployee3's ToString method with the expression base.ToString() (Fig. 10.14, line 42). BasePlusCommissionEmployee4's ToString method then outputs the remainder of a BasePlusCommissionEmployee4 object's string representation (i.e., the value of class BasePlusCommissionEmployee4's base salary).

Figure 10.15 performs the same manipulations on a BasePlusCommissionEmployee4 object as did Fig. 10.7 and Fig. 10.12 on objects of classes BasePlusCommissionEmployee

```csharp
1   // Fig. 10.15: BasePlusCommissionEmployeeTest4.cs
2   // Testing class BasePlusCommissionEmployee4.
3   using System;
4
5   public class BasePlusCommissionEmployeeTest4
6   {
7      public static void Main( string[] args )
8      {
9         // instantiate BasePlusCommissionEmployee3 object
10        BasePlusCommissionEmployee4 employee =
11           new BasePlusCommissionEmployee4( "Bob", "Lewis",
12           "333-33-3333", 5000.00M, .04M, 300.00M );
```

Fig. 10.15 | Testing class BasePlusCommissionEmployee4. (Part 1 of 2.)

```
13
14          // display base-salaried commission employee data
15          Console.WriteLine(
16             "Employee information obtained by properties and methods: \n" );
17          Console.WriteLine( "{0} {1}", "First name is",
18             employee.FirstName );
19          Console.WriteLine( "{0} {1}", "Last name is",
20             employee.LastName );
21          Console.WriteLine( "{0} {1}", "Social security number is",
22             employee.SocialSecurityNumber );
23          Console.WriteLine( "{0} {1:C}", "Gross sales are",
24             employee.GrossSales );
25          Console.WriteLine( "{0} {1:F2}", "Commission rate is",
26             employee.CommissionRate );
27          Console.WriteLine( "{0} {1:C}", "Earnings are",
28             employee.Earnings() );
29          Console.WriteLine( "{0} {1:C}", "Base salary is",
30             employee.BaseSalary );
31
32          employee.BaseSalary = 1000.00M; // set base salary
33
34          Console.WriteLine( "\n{0}:\n\n{1}",
35             "Updated employee information obtained by ToString", employee );
36          Console.WriteLine( "earnings: {0:C}", employee.Earnings() );
37       } // end Main
38    } // end class BasePlusCommissionEmployeeTest4
```

```
Employee information obtained by properties and methods:

First name is Bob
Last name is Lewis
Social security number is 333-33-3333
Gross sales are $5,000.00
Commission rate is 0.04
Earnings are $500.00
Base salary is $300.00

Updated employee information obtained by ToString:

base-salaried commission employee: Bob Lewis
social security number: 333-33-3333
gross sales: $5,000.00
commission rate: 0.04
base salary: $1,000.00
earnings: $1,200.00
```

Fig. 10.15 | Testing class `BasePlusCommissionEmployee4`. (Part 2 of 2.)

and `BasePlusCommissionEmployee3`, respectively. Although each "base-salaried commission employee" class behaves identically, class `BasePlusCommissionEmployee4` is the best engineered. By using inheritance and by using properties that hide the data and ensure consistency, we have efficiently and effectively constructed a well-engineered class.

In this section, you saw an evolutionary set of examples that was carefully designed to teach key capabilities for good software engineering with inheritance. You learned how to create a derived class using inheritance, how to use `protected` base class members to enable a derived class to access inherited base class instance variables and how to override base class methods to provide versions that are more appropriate for derived class objects. In addition, you applied software-engineering techniques from Chapter 4, Chapter 9 and this chapter to create classes that are easy to maintain, modify and debug.

10.5 Constructors in Derived Classes

As we explained in the preceding section, instantiating a derived class object begins a chain of constructor calls in which the derived class constructor, before performing its own tasks, invokes its direct base class's constructor either explicitly (via a constructor initializer with the `base` reference) or implicitly (calling the base class's default constructor or parameterless constructor). Similarly, if the base class is derived from another class (as every class except `object` is), the base class constructor invokes the constructor of the next class up in the hierarchy, and so on. The last constructor called in the chain is always the constructor for class `object`. The original derived class constructor's body finishes executing last. Each base class's constructor manipulates the base class instance variables that the derived class object inherits. For example, consider again the `CommissionEmployee3`–`BasePlusCommissionEmployee4` hierarchy from Fig. 10.13 and Fig. 10.14. When an application creates a `BasePlusCommissionEmployee4` object, the `BasePlusCommissionEmployee4` constructor is called. That constructor calls `CommissionEmployee3`'s constructor, which in turn implicitly calls `object`'s constructor. Class `object`'s constructor has an empty body, so it immediately returns control to `CommissionEmployee3`'s constructor, which then initializes the `private` instance variables of `CommissionEmployee3` that are part of the `BasePlusCommissionEmployee4` object. When `CommissionEmployee3`'s constructor completes execution, it returns control to `BasePlus-CommissionEmployee4`'s constructor, which initializes the `BasePlusCommissionEmployee4` object's `baseSalary`.

Software Engineering Observation 10.6

When an application creates a derived class object, the derived class constructor immediately calls the base class constructor (explicitly, via `base`, or implicitly). The base class constructor's body executes to initialize the base class's instance variables that are part of the derived class object, then the derived class constructor's body executes to initialize the derived class-only instance variables. Even if a constructor does not assign a value to an instance variable, the variable is still initialized to its default value (i.e., 0 for simple numeric types, `false` for `bools` and `null` for references).

Our next example revisits the commission employee hierarchy by declaring a `CommissionEmployee4` class (Fig. 10.16) and a `BasePlusCommissionEmployee5` class (Fig. 10.17). Each class's constructor prints a message when invoked, enabling us to observe the order in which the constructors in the hierarchy execute.

Class `CommissionEmployee4` (Fig. 10.16) contains the same features as the version of the class shown in Fig. 10.13. We modified the constructor (lines 14–25) to output text when it is invoked. Note that concatenating `this` with a `string` literal (line 24) implicitly invokes the `ToString` method of the object being constructed to obtain the object's `string` representation.

```csharp
1   // Fig. 10.16: CommissionEmployee4.cs
2   // CommissionEmployee4 class represents a commission employee.
3   using System;
4
5   public class CommissionEmployee4
6   {
7      private string firstName;
8      private string lastName;
9      private string socialSecurityNumber;
10     private decimal grossSales; // gross weekly sales
11     private decimal commissionRate; // commission percentage
12
13     // five-parameter constructor
14     public CommissionEmployee4( string first, string last, string ssn,
15        decimal sales, decimal rate )
16     {
17        // implicit call to object constructor occurs here
18        firstName = first;
19        lastName = last;
20        socialSecurityNumber = ssn;
21        GrossSales = sales; // validate gross sales via property
22        CommissionRate = rate; // validate commission rate via property
23
24        Console.WriteLine( "\nCommissionEmployee4 constructor:\n" + this );
25     } // end five-parameter CommissionEmployee4 constructor
26
27     // read-only property that gets commission employee's first name
28     public string FirstName
29     {
30        get
31        {
32           return firstName;
33        } // end get
34     } // end property FirstName
35
36     // read-only property that gets commission employee's last name
37     public string LastName
38     {
39        get
40        {
41           return lastName;
42        } // end get
43     } // end property LastName
44
45     // read-only property that gets
46     // commission employee's social security number
47     public string SocialSecurityNumber
48     {
49        get
50        {
51           return socialSecurityNumber;
52        } // end get
53     } // end property SocialSecurityNumber
```

Fig. 10.16 | CommissionEmployee4 class represents a commission employee. (Part 1 of 2.)

```
54
55      // property that gets and sets commission employee's gross sales
56      public decimal GrossSales
57      {
58         get
59         {
60            return grossSales;
61         } // end get
62         set
63         {
64            grossSales = ( value < 0 ) ? 0 : value;
65         } // end set
66      } // end property GrossSales
67
68      // property that gets and sets commission employee's commission rate
69      public decimal CommissionRate
70      {
71         get
72         {
73            return commissionRate;
74         } // end get
75         set
76         {
77            commissionRate = ( value > 0 && value < 1 ) ? value : 0;
78         } // end set
79      } // end property CommissionRate
80
81      // calculate commission employee's pay
82      public virtual decimal Earnings()
83      {
84         return CommissionRate * GrossSales;
85      } // end method Earnings
86
87      // return string representation of CommissionEmployee object
88      public override string ToString()
89      {
90         return string.Format(
91            "{0}: {1} {2}\n{3}: {4}\n{5}: {6:C}\n{7}: {8:F2}",
92            "commission employee", FirstName, LastName,
93            "social security number", SocialSecurityNumber,
94            "gross sales", GrossSales, "commission rate", CommissionRate );
95      } // end method ToString
96   } // end class CommissionEmployee4
```

Fig. 10.16 | CommissionEmployee4 class represents a commission employee. (Part 2 of 2.)

Class BasePlusCommissionEmployee5 (Fig. 10.17) is almost identical to BasePlus-CommissionEmployee4 (Fig. 10.14), except that BasePlusCommissionEmployee5's constructor outputs text when invoked. As in CommissionEmployee4 (Fig. 10.16), we concatenate this with a string literal to implicitly obtain the object's string representation.

Figure 10.18 demonstrates the order in which constructors are called for objects of classes that are part of an inheritance hierarchy. Method Main begins by instantiating CommissionEmployee4 object employee1 (lines 10–11). Next, lines 14–16 instantiate

BasePlusCommissionEmployee5 object employee2. This invokes the CommissionEmployee4 constructor, which prints output with the values passed from the BasePlusCommissionEmployee5 constructor, then performs the output specified in the BasePlusCommissionEmployee5 constructor. Lines 19–21 then instantiate BasePlusCommissionEmployee5 object employee3. Again, the CommissionEmployee4 and BasePlusCommissionEmployee5 constructors are both called. In each case, the body of the CommissionEmployee4 constructor executes before the body of the BasePlusCommissionEmployee5 constructor. Note that employee2 is constructed completely before construction of employee3 begins.

```csharp
1   // Fig. 10.17: BasePlusCommissionEmployee5.cs
2   // BasePlusCommissionEmployee5 class declaration.
3   using System;
4
5   public class BasePlusCommissionEmployee5 : CommissionEmployee4
6   {
7      private decimal baseSalary; // base salary per week
8
9      // six-parameter derived class constructor
10     // with call to base class CommissionEmployee4 constructor
11     public BasePlusCommissionEmployee5( string first, string last,
12        string ssn, decimal sales, decimal rate, decimal salary )
13        : base( first, last, ssn, sales, rate )
14     {
15        BaseSalary = salary; // validate base salary via property
16
17        Console.WriteLine(
18           "\nBasePlusCommissionEmployee5 constructor:\n" + this );
19     } // end six-parameter BasePlusCommissionEmployee5 constructor
20
21     // property that gets and sets
22     // base-salaried commission employee's base salary
23     public decimal BaseSalary
24     {
25        get
26        {
27           return baseSalary;
28        } // end get
29        set
30        {
31           baseSalary = ( value < 0 ) ? 0 : value;
32        } // end set
33     } // end property BaseSalary
34
35     // calculate earnings
36     public override decimal Earnings()
37     {
38        return BaseSalary + base.Earnings();
39     } // end method Earnings
40
```

Fig. 10.17 | BasePlusCommissionEmployee5 class declaration. (Part 1 of 2.)

```
41      // return string representation of BasePlusCommissionEmployee5
42      public override string ToString()
43      {
44          return string.Format( "{0} {1}\n{2}: {3:C}",
45              "base-salaried", base.ToString(), "base salary", BaseSalary );
46      } // end method ToString
47  } // end class BasePlusCommissionEmployee5
```

Fig. 10.17 | BasePlusCommissionEmployee5 class declaration. (Part 2 of 2.)

10.6 Software Engineering with Inheritance

This section discusses customizing existing software with inheritance. When a new class extends an existing class, the new class inherits the members of the existing class. We can customize the new class to meet our needs by including additional members and by overriding base class members. Doing this does not require the derived class programmer to change the base class's source code. C# simply requires access to the compiled base class code, so it can compile and execute any application that uses or extends the base class. This powerful capability is attractive to independent software vendors (ISVs), who can develop proprietary classes for sale or license and make them available to users in class libraries. Users then can derive new classes from these library classes rapidly, without accessing the ISVs' proprietary source code.

```
1   // Fig. 10.18: ConstructorTest.cs
2   // Display order in which base class and derived class constructors
3   // are called.
4   using System;
5
6   public class ConstructorTest
7   {
8       public static void Main( string[] args )
9       {
10          CommissionEmployee4 employee1 = new CommissionEmployee4( "Bob",
11              "Lewis", "333-33-3333", 5000.00M, .04M );
12
13          Console.WriteLine();
14          BasePlusCommissionEmployee5 employee2 =
15              new BasePlusCommissionEmployee5( "Lisa", "Jones",
16              "555-55-5555", 2000.00M, .06M, 800.00M );
17
18          Console.WriteLine();
19          BasePlusCommissionEmployee5 employee3 =
20              new BasePlusCommissionEmployee5( "Mark", "Sands",
21              "888-88-8888", 8000.00M, .15M, 2000.00M );
22      } // end Main
23  } // end class ConstructorTest
```

Fig. 10.18 | Display order in which base class and derived class constructors are called. (Part 1 of 2.)

```
CommissionEmployee4 constructor:
commission employee: Bob Lewis
social security number: 333-33-3333
gross sales: $5,000.00
commission rate: 0.04


CommissionEmployee4 constructor:
base-salaried commission employee: Lisa Jones
social security number: 555-55-5555
gross sales: $2,000.00
commission rate: 0.06
base salary: $0.00

BasePlusCommissionEmployee5 constructor:
base-salaried commission employee: Lisa Jones
social security number: 555-55-5555
gross sales: $2,000.00
commission rate: 0.06
base salary: $800.00


CommissionEmployee4 constructor:
base-salaried commission employee: Mark Sands
social security number: 888-88-8888
gross sales: $8,000.00
commission rate: 0.15
base salary: $0.00

BasePlusCommissionEmployee5 constructor:
base-salaried commission employee: Mark Sands
social security number: 888-88-8888
gross sales: $8,000.00
commission rate: 0.15
base salary: $2,000.00
```

Fig. 10.18 | Display order in which base class and derived class constructors are called. (Part 2 of 2.)

Software Engineering Observation 10.7

Despite the fact that inheriting from a class does not require access to the class's source code, developers often insist on seeing the source code to understand how the class is implemented. They may, for example, want to ensure that they are extending a class that performs well and is implemented securely.

Sometimes, students have difficulty appreciating the scope of the problems faced by designers who work on large-scale software projects in industry. People experienced with such projects say that effective software reuse improves the software development process. Object-oriented programming facilitates software reuse, potentially shortening development time. The availability of substantial and useful class libraries delivers the maximum benefits of software reuse through inheritance. The FCL class libraries that are used by C#

tend to be rather general purpose. Many special-purpose class libraries exist and more are being created.

Software Engineering Observation 10.8

At the design stage in an object-oriented system, the designer often finds that certain classes are closely related. The designer should "factor out" common members and place them in a base class. Then the designer should use inheritance to develop derived classes, specializing them with capabilities beyond those inherited from the base class.

Software Engineering Observation 10.9

Declaring a derived class does not affect its base class's source code. Inheritance preserves the integrity of the base class.

Software Engineering Observation 10.10

Just as designers of non-object-oriented systems should avoid method proliferation, designers of object-oriented systems should avoid class proliferation. Such proliferation creates management problems and can hinder software reusability, because in a huge class library it becomes difficult for a client to locate the most appropriate classes. The alternative is to create fewer classes that provide more substantial functionality, but such classes might prove cumbersome.

Performance Tip 10.1

If derived classes are larger than they need to be (i.e., contain too much functionality), memory and processing resources might be wasted. Extend the base class that contains the functionality that is closest to what is needed.

Reading derived class declarations can be confusing, because inherited members are not declared explicitly in the derived classes, but are nevertheless present in them. A similar problem exists in documenting derived class members.

10.7 Class object

As we discussed earlier in this chapter, all classes inherit directly or indirectly from the object class (System.Object in the FCL), so its seven methods are inherited by all other classes. Figure 10.19 summarizes object's methods.

We discuss several of object's methods throughout this book (as indicated in the table). You can learn more about object's methods in object's online documentation in the Framework Class Library Reference at:

msdn2.microsoft.com/en-us/library/system.object_members

All array types implicitly inherit from class Array in the System namespace, which in turn extends class object. As a result, like all other objects, an array inherits the members of class object. For more information about the class Array, please see Array's documentation in the FCL Reference, at:

msdn2.microsoft.com/en-us/library/system.array_members

Method	Description
Equals	This method compares two objects for equality and returns true if they are equal and false otherwise. The method takes any object as an argument. When objects of a particular class must be compared for equality, the class should override method Equals to compare the contents of the two objects. The method's implementation should meet the following requirements: • It should return false if the argument is null. • It should return true if an object is compared to itself, as in object1.Equals(object1). • It should return true only if both object1.Equals(object2) and object2.Equals(object1) would return true. • For three objects, if object1.Equals(object2) returns true and object2.Equals(object3) returns true, then object1.Equals(object3) should also return true. • A class that overrides the method Equals should also override the method GetHashCode to ensure that equal objects have identical hashcodes. The default Equals implementation determines only whether two references *refer to the same object* in memory.
Finalize	This method cannot be explicitly declared or called. When a class contains a destructor, the compiler implicitly renames it to override the protected method Finalize, which is called only by the garbage collector before it reclaims an object's memory. The garbage collector is not guaranteed to reclaim an object, thus it is not guaranteed that an object's Finalize method will execute. When a derived class's Finalize method executes, it performs its task, then invokes the base class's Finalize method. Finalize's default implementation is a placeholder that simply invokes the base class's Finalize method.
GetHashCode	A hashtable is a data structure that relates one object, called the key, to another object, called the value. We discuss Hashtable in Chapter 27, Collections. When initially inserting a value into a hashtable, the key's GetHashCode method is called. The hashcode value returned is used by the hashtable to determine the location at which to insert the corresponding value. The key's hashcode is also used by the hashtable to locate the key's corresponding value.
GetType	Every object knows its own type at execution time. Method GetType (used in Section 11.5) returns an object of class Type (namespace System) that contains information about the object's type, such as its class name (obtained from Type property FullName).
Memberwise-Clone	This protected method, which takes no arguments and returns an object reference, makes a copy of the object on which it is called. The implementation of this method performs a *shallow copy*—instance variable values in one object are copied into another object of the same type. For reference types, only the references are copied.

Fig. 10.19 | object methods that are inherited directly or indirectly by all classes. (Part 1 of 2.)

Method	Description
Reference-Equals	This static method takes two object arguments and returns true if two objects are the same instance or if they are null references. Otherwise, it returns false.
ToString	This method (introduced in Section 7.4) returns a string representation of an object. The default implementation of this method returns the namespace followed by a dot and the class name of the object's class.

Fig. 10.19 | object methods that are inherited directly or indirectly by all classes. (Part 2 of 2.)

10.8 Wrap-Up

This chapter introduced inheritance—the ability to create classes by absorbing an existing class's members and enhancing them with new capabilities. You learned the notions of base classes and derived classes and created a derived class that inherits members from a base class. The chapter introduced access modifier protected; derived class methods can access protected base class members. You learned how to access base class members with base. You also saw how constructors are used in inheritance hierarchies. Finally, you learned about the methods of class object, the direct or indirect base class of all classes.

In Chapter 11, Polymorphism, Interfaces & Operator Overloading, we build on our discussion of inheritance by introducing polymorphism—an object-oriented concept that enables us to write applications that handle, in a more general manner, objects of a wide variety of classes related by inheritance. After studying Chapter 11, you will be familiar with classes, objects, encapsulation, inheritance and polymorphism—the most essential aspects of object-oriented programming.

Summary

Section 10.1 Introduction

- Inheritance is a form of software reuse in which a new class is created by absorbing an existing class's members and enhancing them with new or modified capabilities. With inheritance, programmers save time during application development by reusing proven and debugged high-quality software.
- A derived class is more specific than its base class and represents a more specialized group of objects.
- The *is-a* relationship represents inheritance. In an *is-a* relationship, an object of a derived class can also be treated as an object of its base class.

Section 10.2 Base Classes and Derived Classes

- Inheritance relationships form tree-like hierarchical structures. A base class exists in a hierarchical relationship with its derived classes.
- Objects of all classes that extend a common base class can be treated as objects of that base class. However, base class objects cannot be treated as objects of their derived classes.

- When a base class method is inherited by a derived class, that derived class often needs a customized version of the method. In such cases, the derived class can override the base class method with an appropriate implementation.

Section 10.3 protected Members

- Using protected access offers an intermediate level of access between public and private. A base class's protected members can be accessed by members of that base class *and* by members of its derived classes.

- All non-private base class members retain their original access modifier when they become members of the derived class.

- Methods of a derived class cannot directly access private members of the base class.

Section 10.4.1 Creating and Using a CommissionEmployee Class

- A colon (:) followed by a base class name at the end of a class declaration header indicates that the declared class extends the base class.

- If a class does not specify that it inherits from another class, the new class implicitly inherits from object.

- The first task of any derived class's constructor is to call its direct base class's constructor, either explicitly or implicitly (if no constructor call is specified).

- Constructors are not inherited. Note that even if a class does not have constructors, the default constructor that the compiler implicitly declares for the class will call the base class's default or parameterless constructor.

- Method ToString is one of the methods that every class inherits directly or indirectly from class object, which is the root of the C# class hierarchy.

- To override a base class method, a derived class must declare a method with keyword override and with the same signature (method name, number of parameters and parameter types) and return type as the base class method.

- It is a compilation error to override a method with a different access modifier.

Section 10.4.2 Creating a BasePlusCommissionEmployee Class without Using Inheritance

- Copying and pasting code from one class to another can spread errors across multiple source code files. To avoid duplicating code (and possibly errors) in situations where you want one class to "absorb" the members of another class, use inheritance.

Section 10.4.3 Creating a CommissionEmployee–BasePlusCommissionEmployee Inheritance Hierarchy

- The virtual and abstract keywords indicate that a base class method can be overridden in derived classes.

- The override modifier declares that a derived class method overrides a virtual or abstract base class method. This modifier also implicitly declares the derived class method virtual.

- When a base class's instance variables are private, a derived class's methods are not allowed to access them.

Section 10.4.4 CommissionEmployee–BasePlusCommissionEmployee Inheritance Hierarchy Using protected Instance Variables

- Inheriting protected instance variables slightly increases performance, because we can directly access the variables in the derived class without incurring the overhead of invoking the set or get accessors of the corresponding property.

- Software is said to be fragile or brittle when a small change in the base class can "break" derived class implementation. You should be able to change the base class implementation while still providing the same services to the derived classes.

- Declaring base class instance variables private enables the base class implementation of these instance variables to change without affecting derived class implementations.

Section 10.4.5 CommissionEmployee–BasePlusCommissionEmployee Inheritance Hierarchy Using private Instance Variables

- Place the keyword base and the dot (.) operator before the base class method name to invoke an overridden base class method from a derived class.

- Failure to prefix the base class method name with the keyword base and the dot (.) operator when referencing the base class's method causes the derived class method to call itself, creating an error called infinite recursion.

Section 10.5 Constructors in Derived Classes

- Instantiating a derived class object begins a chain of constructor calls. The last constructor called in the chain is always the constructor for class object. The original derived class constructor's body finishes executing last.

Section 10.6 Software Engineering with Inheritance

- We can customize new classes to meet our needs by including additional members and by overriding base class members. This powerful capability is attractive to independent software vendors (ISVs), who can develop proprietary classes for sale or license and make them available to users in class libraries.

Section 10.7 Class object

- All classes in C# inherit directly or indirectly from the object class, so its seven methods are inherited by all other classes. These methods are Equals, Finalize, GetHashCode, GetType, MemberwiseClone, ReferenceEquals and ToString.

- All array types implicitly inherit from class Array in the System namespace, which in turn extends class object. As a result, like all other objects, an array inherits the members of class object.

Terminology

base class
base class constructor
base class constructor call syntax
base class parameterless constructor
base keyword
brittle software
class hierarchy
class library
composition
deep copy

derived class
derived class constructor
direct base class
Equals method of class object
extend a base class
Finalize method of class object
fragile software
GetHashCode method of class object
GetType method of class object
has-a relationship

hierarchical relationship	override keyword
hierarchy diagram	override (redefine) a base class method
indirect base class	private base class member
inheritance	protected base class member
inheritance hierarchy	protected internal access modifier
inherited member	protected access modifier
inherited method	public base class member
invoke a base class constructor	ReferenceEquals method of class object
invoke a base class method	single inheritance
is-a relationship	shallow copy
MemberwiseClone method of class object	software reuse
object class	standardized reusable components
object of a derived class	ToString method of class object
object of a base class	virtual keyword

Self-Review Exercises

10.1 Fill in the blanks in each of the following statements:
a) _____ is a form of software reusability in which new classes acquire the members of existing classes and enhance those classes with new capabilities.
b) A base class's _____ members can be accessed only in the base class declaration and in derived class declarations.
c) In a(n) _____ relationship, an object of a derived class can also be treated as an object of its base class.
d) In a(n) _____ relationship, a class object has references to objects of other classes as members.
e) In single inheritance, a base class exists in a(n) _____ relationship with its derived classes.
f) A base class's _____ members are accessible anywhere that the application has a reference to an object of that base class or to an object of any of its derived classes.
g) When an object of a derived class is instantiated, a base class _____ is called implicitly or explicitly.
h) Derived class constructors can call base class constructors via the _____ keyword.

10.2 State whether each of the following is *true* or *false*. If a statement is *false*, explain why.
a) Base class constructors are not inherited by derived classes.
b) A *has-a* relationship is implemented via inheritance.
c) A Car class has *is-a* relationships with the SteeringWheel and Brakes classes.
d) Inheritance encourages the reuse of proven high-quality software.
e) When a derived class redefines a base class method by using the same signature and return type, the derived class is said to overload that base class method.

Answers to Self-Review Exercises

10.1 a) Inheritance. b) protected. c) *is-a* or inheritance. d) *has-a* or composition. e) hierarchical. f) public. g) constructor. h) base.

10.2 a) True. b) False. A *has-a* relationship is implemented via composition. An *is-a* relationship is implemented via inheritance. c) False. These are examples of *has-a* relationships. Class Car has an *is-a* relationship with class Vehicle. d) True. e) False. This is known as overriding, not overloading.

Exercises

10.3 Many applications written with inheritance could be written with composition instead, and vice versa. Rewrite class BasePlusCommissionEmployee4 (Fig. 10.14) of the CommissionEmployee3–BasePlusCommissionEmployee4 hierarchy to use composition rather than inheritance.

10.4 Discuss the ways in which inheritance promotes software reuse, saves time during application development and helps prevent errors.

10.5 Draw a UML class diagram for an inheritance hierarchy for students at a university similar to the hierarchy shown in Fig. 10.2. Use Student as the base class of the hierarchy, then extend Student with classes UndergraduateStudent and GraduateStudent. Continue to extend the hierarchy as deeply (i.e., as many levels) as possible. For example, Freshman, Sophomore, Junior and Senior might extend UndergraduateStudent, and DoctoralStudent and MastersStudent might be derived classes of GraduateStudent. After drawing the hierarchy, discuss the relationships that exist between the classes. [*Note:* You do not need to write any code for this exercise.]

10.6 The world of shapes is much richer than the shapes included in the inheritance hierarchy of Fig. 10.3. Write down all the shapes you can think of—both two-dimensional and three-dimensional—and form them into a more complete Shape hierarchy with as many levels as possible. Your hierarchy should have class Shape at the top. Class TwoDimensionalShape and class ThreeDimensionalShape should extend Shape. Add additional derived classes, such as Quadrilateral and Sphere, at their correct locations in the hierarchy as necessary.

10.7 Some programmers prefer not to use protected access, because they believe it breaks the encapsulation of the base class. Discuss the relative merits of using protected access vs. using private access in base classes.

10.8 Write an inheritance hierarchy for classes Quadrilateral, Trapezoid, Parallelogram, Rectangle and Square. Use Quadrilateral as the base class of the hierarchy. Make the hierarchy as deep (i.e., as many levels) as possible. Specify the instance variables, properties and methods for each class. The private instance variables of Quadrilateral should be the *x-y* coordinate pairs for the four endpoints of the Quadrilateral. Write an application that instantiates objects of your classes and outputs each object's area (except Quadrilateral).

10.9 (*Package Inheritance Hierarchy*) Package-delivery services, such as FedEx®, DHL® and UPS®, offer a number of different shipping options, each with specific costs associated. Create an inheritance hierarchy to represent various types of packages. Use Package as the base class of the hierarchy, then include classes TwoDayPackage and OvernightPackage that derive from Package. Base class Package should include private instance variables representing the name, address, city, state and ZIP code for the package's sender and recipient, and instance variables that store the weight (in ounces) and cost per ounce to ship the package. Package's constructor should initialize these private instance variables with public properties. Ensure that the weight and cost per ounce contain positive values. Package should provide a public method CalculateCost that returns a decimal indicating the cost associated with shipping the package. Package's CalculateCost method should determine the cost by multiplying the weight by the cost per ounce. Derived class TwoDayPackage should inherit the functionality of base class Package, but also include an instance variable that represents a flat fee that the shipping company charges for two-day delivery service. TwoDayPackage's constructor should receive a value to initialize this instance variable. TwoDayPackage should redefine method CalculateCost so that it computes the shipping cost by adding the flat fee to the weight-based cost calculated by base class Package's CalculateCost method. Class OvernightPackage should inherit directly from class Package and contain an instance variable representing an additional fee per ounce charged for overnight-delivery service. OvernightPackage should redefine method CalculateCost so that it adds the additional fee per ounce to the standard cost per ounce before calculating the shipping cost. Write a test application that creates objects of each type of Package and tests method CalculateCost.

10.10 *(Account Inheritance Hierarchy)* Create an inheritance hierarchy that a bank might use to represent customers' bank accounts. All customers at this bank can deposit (i.e., credit) money into their accounts and withdraw (i.e., debit) money from their accounts. More specific types of accounts also exist. Savings accounts, for instance, earn interest on the money they hold. Checking accounts, on the other hand, charge a fee per transaction.

Create base class Account and derived classes SavingsAccount and CheckingAccount that inherit from class Account. Base class Account should include one private instance variable of type decimal to represent the account balance. The class should provide a constructor that receives an initial balance and uses it to initialize the instance variable with a public property. The property should validate the initial balance to ensure that it is greater than or equal to 0.0. If not, the balance should be set to 0.0, and the set accessor should display an error message, indicating that the initial balance was invalid. The class should provide two public methods. Method Credit should add an amount to the current balance. Method Debit should withdraw money from the Account and ensure that the debit amount does not exceed the Account's balance. If it does, the balance should be left unchanged, and the method should print the message "Debit amount exceeded account balance." The class should also provide a get accessor in property Balance that returns the current balance.

Derived class SavingsAccount should inherit the functionality of an Account, but also include a decimal instance variable indicating the interest rate (percentage) assigned to the Account. SavingsAccount's constructor should receive the initial balance, as well as an initial value for the interest rate. SavingsAccount should provide public method CalculateInterest that returns a decimal indicating the amount of interest earned by an account. Method CalculateInterest should determine this amount by multiplying the interest rate by the account balance. [*Note:* SavingsAccount should inherit methods Credit and Debit without redefining them.]

Derived class CheckingAccount should inherit from base class Account and include a decimal instance variable that represents the fee charged per transaction. CheckingAccount's constructor should receive the initial balance, as well as a parameter indicating a fee amount. Class CheckingAccount should redefine methods Credit and Debit so that they subtract the fee from the account balance whenever either transaction is performed successfully. CheckingAccount's versions of these methods should invoke the base-class Account version to perform the updates to an account balance. CheckingAccount's Debit method should charge a fee only if money is actually withdrawn (i.e., the debit amount does not exceed the account balance). [*Hint:* Define Account's Debit method so that it returns a bool indicating whether money was withdrawn. Then use the return value to determine whether a fee should be charged.]

After defining the classes in this hierarchy, write an application that creates objects of each class and tests their methods. Add interest to the SavingsAccount object by first invoking its CalculateInterest method, then passing the returned interest amount to the object's Credit method.

11

Polymorphism, Interfaces & Operator Overloading

One Ring to rule them all,
One Ring to find them,
One Ring to bring them all
and in the darkness bind
them.

—John Ronald Reuel Tolkien

General propositions do not
decide concrete cases.

—Oliver Wendell Holmes

A philosopher of imposing
stature doesn't think in a
vacuum. Even his most
abstract ideas are, to some
extent, conditioned by
what is or is not known
in the time when he lives.

—Alfred North Whitehead

Why art thou cast down,
O my soul?

—Psalms 42:5

OBJECTIVES

In this chapter you will learn:

- The concept of polymorphism and how it enables you to "program in the general."

- To use overridden methods to effect polymorphism.

- To distinguish between abstract and concrete classes.

- To declare abstract methods to create abstract classes.

- How polymorphism makes systems extensible and maintainable.

- To determine an object's type at execution time.

- To create `sealed` methods and classes.

- To declare and implement interfaces.

- To overload operators to enable them to manipulate objects.

Outline

11.1 Introduction

We now continue our study of object-oriented programming by explaining and demonstrating *polymorphism* with inheritance hierarchies. Polymorphism enables us to "program in the general" rather than "program in the specific." In particular, polymorphism enables us to write applications that process objects that share the same base class in a class hierarchy as if they are all objects of the base class.

Consider the following example of polymorphism. Suppose we create an application that simulates the movement of several types of animals for a biological study. Classes Fish, Frog and Bird represent the three types of animals under investigation. Imagine that each of these classes extends base class Animal, which contains a method Move and maintains an animal's current location as *x-y* coordinates. Each derived class implements method Move.

Our application maintains an array of references to objects of the various `Animal` derived classes. To simulate the animals' movements, the application sends each object the same message once per second—namely, `Move`. However, each specific type of `Animal` responds to a `Move` message in a unique way—a `Fish` might swim three feet, a `Frog` might jump five feet and a `Bird` might fly 10 feet. The application issues the same message (i.e., `Move`) to each animal object generically, but each object knows how to modify its *x-y* coordinates appropriately for its specific type of movement. Relying on each object to know how to "do the right thing" (i.e., do what is appropriate for that type of object) in response to the same method call is the key concept of polymorphism. The same message (in this case, `Move`) sent to a variety of objects has "many forms" of results—hence the term polymorphism.

With polymorphism, we can design and implement systems that are easily extensible— new classes can be added with little or no modification to the general portions of the application, as long as the new classes are part of the inheritance hierarchy that the application processes generically. The only parts of an application that must be altered to accommodate new classes are those that require direct knowledge of the new classes that the programmer adds to the hierarchy. For example, if we extend class `Animal` to create class `Tortoise` (which might respond to a `Move` message by crawling one inch), we need to write only the `Tortoise` class and the part of the simulation that instantiates a `Tortoise` object. The portions of the simulation that process each `Animal` generically can remain the same.

This chapter has several parts. First, we discuss common examples of polymorphism. We then provide a live-code example demonstrating polymorphic behavior. As you will soon see, you will use base class references to manipulate both base class objects and derived class objects polymorphically.

We then present a case study that revisits the employee hierarchy of Section 10.4.5. We develop a simple payroll application that polymorphically calculates the weekly pay of several different types of employees using each employee's `Earnings` method. Though the earnings of each type of employee are calculated in a specific way, polymorphism allows us to process the employees "in the general." In the case study, we enlarge the hierarchy to include two new classes—`SalariedEmployee` (for people paid a fixed weekly salary) and `HourlyEmployee` (for people paid an hourly salary and "time-and-a-half" for overtime). We declare a common set of functionality for all the classes in the updated hierarchy in an "abstract" class, `Employee`, from which classes `SalariedEmployee`, `HourlyEmployee` and `CommissionEmployee` inherit directly and class `BasePlusCommissionEmployee4` inherits indirectly. As you will soon see, when we invoke each employee's `Earnings` method off a base class `Employee` reference, the correct earnings calculation is performed due to C#'s polymorphic capabilities.

Occasionally, when performing polymorphic processing, we need to program "in the specific." Our `Employee` case study demonstrates that an application can determine the type of an object at execution time and act on that object accordingly. In the case study, we use these capabilities to determine whether a particular employee object *is a* `BasePlus-CommissionEmployee`. If so, we increase that employee's base salary by 10%.

The chapter continues with an introduction to C# interfaces. An interface describes a set of methods and properties that can be called on an object, but does not provide concrete implementations for them. Programmers can declare classes that *implement* (i.e., provide concrete implementations for the methods and properties of) one or more interfaces. Each interface member must be declared in all the classes that implement the interface. Once a class implements an interface, all objects of that class have an *is-a* relationship with the interface type, and all objects of the class are guaranteed to provide the functionality described by the interface. This is true of all derived classes of that class as well.

Interfaces are particularly useful for assigning common functionality to possibly unrelated classes. This allows objects of unrelated classes to be processed polymorphically—objects of classes that implement the same interface can respond to the same method calls. To demonstrate creating and using interfaces, we modify our payroll application to create a general accounts-payable application that can calculate payments due for the earnings of company employees and for invoice amounts to be billed for purchased goods. As you will see, interfaces enable polymorphic capabilities similar to those enabled by inheritance.

This chapter ends with an introduction to operator overloading. In previous chapters, we declared our own classes and used methods to perform tasks on objects of those classes. Operator overloading allows us to define the behavior of the built-in operators, such as +, - and <, when used on objects of our own classes. This provides a much more convenient notation than calling methods for performing tasks on objects.

11.2 Polymorphism Examples

We now consider several additional examples of polymorphism. If class Rectangle is derived from class Quadrilateral (a four-sided shape), then a Rectangle is a more specific version of a Quadrilateral. Any operation (e.g., calculating the perimeter or the area) that can be performed on a Quadrilateral object can also be performed on a Rectangle object. These operations also can be performed on other Quadrilaterals, such as Squares, Parallelograms and Trapezoids. The polymorphism occurs when an application invokes a method through a base class variable—at execution time, the correct derived class version of the method is called, based on the type of the referenced object. You will see a simple code example that illustrates this process in Section 11.3.

As another example, suppose we design a video game that manipulates objects of many different types, including objects of classes Martian, Venusian, Plutonian, SpaceShip and LaserBeam. Imagine that each class inherits from the common base class SpaceObject, which contains method Draw. Each derived class implements this method. A screen-manager application maintains a collection (e.g., a SpaceObject array) of references to objects of the various classes. To refresh the screen, the screen manager periodically sends each object the same message—namely, Draw. However, each object responds in a unique way. For example, a Martian object might draw itself in red with the appropriate number of antennae. A SpaceShip object might draw itself as a bright silver flying saucer. A LaserBeam object might draw itself as a bright red beam across the screen. Again, the same message (in this case, Draw) sent to a variety of objects has "many forms" of results.

A polymorphic screen manager might use polymorphism to facilitate adding new classes to a system with minimal modifications to the system's code. Suppose we want to add Mercurian objects to our video game. To do so, we must build a Mercurian class that extends SpaceObject and provides its own Draw method implementation. When objects of class Mercurian appear in the SpaceObject collection, the screen manager code invokes method Draw, exactly as it does for every other object in the collection, regardless of its type. So the new Mercurian objects simply "plug right in" without any modification of the screen manager code by the programmer. Thus, without modifying the system (other than to build new classes and modify the code that creates new objects), programmers can use polymorphism to include additional types that might not have been envisioned when the system was created.

Software Engineering Observation 11.1

Polymorphism promotes extensibility: Software that invokes polymorphic behavior is independent of the object types to which messages are sent. New object types that can respond to existing method calls can be incorporated into a system without requiring modification of the base system. Only client code that instantiates new objects must be modified to accommodate new types.

11.3 Demonstrating Polymorphic Behavior

Section 10.4 created a commission employee class hierarchy, in which class BasePlusCommissionEmployee inherited from class CommissionEmployee. The examples in that section manipulated CommissionEmployee and BasePlusCommissionEmployee objects by using references to them to invoke their methods. We aimed base class references at base class objects and derived class references at derived class objects. These assignments are natural and straightforward—base class references are intended to refer to base class objects, and derived class references are intended to refer to derived class objects. However, other assignments are possible.

In the next example, we aim a base class reference at a derived class object. We then show how invoking a method on a derived class object via a base class reference invokes the derived class functionality—the type of the *actual referenced object*, not the type of the *reference*, determines which method is called. This example demonstrates the key concept that an object of a derived class can be treated as an object of its base class. This enables various interesting manipulations. An application can create an array of base class references that refer to objects of many derived class types. This is allowed because each derived class object *is an* object of its base class. For instance, we can assign the reference of a BasePlusCommissionEmployee object to a base class CommissionEmployee variable because a BasePlusCommissionEmployee *is a* CommissionEmployee—so we can treat a BasePlusCommissionEmployee as a CommissionEmployee.

A base class object is not an object of any of its derived classes. For example, we cannot assign the reference of a CommissionEmployee object to a derived class BasePlusCommissionEmployee variable because a CommissionEmployee is not a BasePlusCommissionEmployee—a CommissionEmployee does not, for example, have a baseSalary instance variable and does not have a BaseSalary property. The *is-a* relationship applies from a derived class to its direct and indirect base classes, but not vice versa.

It turns out that the compiler does allow the assignment of a base class reference to a derived class variable if we explicitly cast the base class reference to the derived class type—a technique we discuss in greater detail in Section 11.5.6. Why would we ever want to perform such an assignment? A base class reference can be used to invoke only the methods declared in the base class—attempting to invoke derived-class-only methods through a base class reference results in compilation errors. If an application needs to perform a derived-class-specific operation on a derived class object referenced by a base class variable, the application must first cast the base class reference to a derived class reference through a technique known as *downcasting*. This enables the application to invoke derived class methods that are not in the base class. We present a concrete example of downcasting in Section 11.5.6.

The example in Fig. 11.1 demonstrates three ways to use base class and derived class variables to store references to base class and derived class objects. The first two are straightforward—as in Section 10.4, we assign a base class reference to a base class variable, and we assign a derived class reference to a derived class variable. Then we demonstrate the relationship between derived classes and base classes (i.e., the *is-a* relationship) by assigning

```csharp
 1   // Fig. 11.1: PolymorphismTest.cs
 2   // Assigning base class and derived class references to base class and
 3   // derived class variables.
 4   using System;
 5
 6   public class PolymorphismTest
 7   {
 8      public static void Main( string[] args )
 9      {
10         // assign base class reference to base class variable
11         CommissionEmployee3 commissionEmployee = new CommissionEmployee3(
12            "Sue", "Jones", "222-22-2222", 10000.00M, .06M );
13
14         // assign derived class reference to derived class variable
15         BasePlusCommissionEmployee4 basePlusCommissionEmployee =
16            new BasePlusCommissionEmployee4( "Bob", "Lewis",
17            "333-33-3333", 5000.00M, .04M, 300.00M );
18
19         // invoke ToString and Earnings on base class object
20         // using base class variable
21         Console.WriteLine( "{0} {1}:\n\n{2}\n{3}: {4:C}\n",
22            "Call CommissionEmployee3's ToString with base class reference",
23            "to base class object", commissionEmployee.ToString(),
24            "earnings", commissionEmployee.Earnings() );
25
26         // invoke ToString and Earnings on derived class object
27         // using derived class variable
28         Console.WriteLine( "{0} {1}:\n\n{2}\n{3}: {4:C}\n",
29            "Call BasePlusCommissionEmployee4's ToString with derived class",
30            "reference to derived class object",
31            basePlusCommissionEmployee.ToString(),
32            "earnings", basePlusCommissionEmployee.Earnings() );
33
34         // invoke ToString and Earnings on derived class object
35         // using base class variable
36         CommissionEmployee3 commissionEmployee2 =
37            basePlusCommissionEmployee;
38         Console.WriteLine( "{0} {1}:\n\n{2}\n{3}: {4:C}",
39            "Call BasePlusCommissionEmployee4's ToString with base class",
40            "reference to derived class object",
41            commissionEmployee2.ToString(), "earnings",
42            commissionEmployee2.Earnings() );
43      } // end Main
44   } // end class PolymorphismTest
```

Fig. 11.1 | Assigning base class and derived class references to base class and derived class variables. (Part 1 of 2.)

```
Call CommissionEmployee3's ToString with base class reference to base class
object:

commission employee: Sue Jones
social security number: 222-22-2222
gross sales: $10,000.00
commission rate: 0.06
earnings: $600.00

Call BasePlusCommissionEmployee4's ToString with derived class reference to
derived class object:

base-salaried commission employee: Bob Lewis
social security number: 333-33-3333
gross sales: $5,000.00
commission rate: 0.04
base salary: $300.00
earnings: $500.00

Call BasePlusCommissionEmployee4's ToString with base class reference to de-
rived class object:

base-salaried commission employee: Bob Lewis
social security number: 333-33-3333
gross sales: $5,000.00
commission rate: 0.04
base salary: $300.00
earnings: $500.00
```

Fig. 11.1 | Assigning base class and derived class references to base class and derived class variables. (Part 2 of 2.)

a derived class reference to a base class variable. [*Note:* This application uses classes CommissionEmployee3 and BasePlusCommissionEmployee4 from Fig. 10.13 and Fig. 10.14, respectively.]

In Fig. 11.1, lines 11–12 create a new CommissionEmployee3 object and assign its reference to a CommissionEmployee3 variable. Lines 15–17 create a new BasePlusCommissionEmployee4 object and assign its reference to a BasePlusCommissionEmployee4 variable. These assignments are natural—for example, a CommissionEmployee3 variable's primary purpose is to hold a reference to a CommissionEmployee3 object. Lines 21–24 use the reference commissionEmployee to invoke methods ToString and Earnings. Because commissionEmployee refers to a CommissionEmployee3 object, base class CommissionEmployee3's version of the methods are called. Similarly, lines 28–32 use basePlusCommissionEmployee to invoke the methods ToString and Earnings on the BasePlusCommissionEmployee4 object. This invokes derived class BasePlusCommissionEmployee4's version of the methods.

Lines 36–37 then assign the reference to derived class object basePlusCommissionEmployee to a base class CommissionEmployee3 variable, which lines 38–42 use to invoke methods ToString and Earnings. A base class variable that contains a reference to a derived class object and is used to call a virtual method actually calls the overriding derived class version of the method. Hence, commissionEmployee2.ToString() in line 41 actually calls class `BasePlusCommissionEmployee4`'s `ToString` method. The compiler allows this "crossover" because an object of a derived class *is an* object of its base class (but not vice versa). When the compiler encounters a method call made through a variable, the compiler determines if the method can be called by checking the *variable's* class type. If that class contains the proper method declaration (or inherits one), the compiler allows the call to be compiled. At execution time, *the type of the object to which the variable refers* determines the actual method to use.

11.4 Abstract Classes and Methods

When we think of a class type, we assume that applications will create objects of that type. In some cases, however, it is useful to declare classes for which the programmer never intends to instantiate objects. Such classes are called *abstract classes*. Because they are used only as base classes in inheritance hierarchies, we refer to them as *abstract base classes*. These classes cannot be used to instantiate objects, because as you will soon see, abstract classes are incomplete—derived classes must declare the "missing pieces." We demonstrate abstract classes in Section 11.5.1.

The purpose of an abstract class is primarily to provide an appropriate base class from which other classes can inherit, and thus share a common design. In the `Shape` hierarchy of Fig. 10.3, for example, derived classes inherit the notion of what it means to be a `Shape`—common attributes such as `location`, `color` and `borderThickness`, and behaviors such as `Draw`, `Move`, `Resize` and `ChangeColor`. Classes that can be used to instantiate objects are called *concrete classes*. Such classes provide implementations of *every* method they declare (some of the implementations can be inherited). For example, we could derive concrete classes `Circle`, `Square` and `Triangle` from abstract base class `TwoDimensionalShape`. Similarly, we could derive concrete classes `Sphere`, `Cube` and `Tetrahedron` from abstract base class `ThreeDimensionalShape`. Abstract base classes are too general to create real objects—they specify only what is common among derived classes. We need to be more specific before we can create objects. For example, if you send the `Draw` message to abstract class `TwoDimensionalShape`, the class knows that two-dimensional shapes should be drawable, but it does not know what specific shape to draw, so it cannot implement a real `Draw` method. Concrete classes provide the specifics that make it reasonable to instantiate objects.

Not all inheritance hierarchies contain abstract classes. However, programmers often write client code that uses only abstract base class types to reduce client code's dependencies on a range of specific derived class types. For example, a programmer can write a method with a parameter of an abstract base class type. When called, such a method can be passed an object of any concrete class that directly or indirectly extends the base class specified as the parameter's type.

Abstract classes sometimes constitute several levels of the hierarchy. For example, the Shape hierarchy of Fig. 10.3 begins with abstract class `Shape`. On the next level of the hierarchy are two more abstract classes, `TwoDimensionalShape` and `ThreeDimensionalShape`. The next level of the hierarchy declares concrete classes for `TwoDimensionalShape`s (`Circle`, `Square` and `Triangle`) and for `ThreeDimensionalShape`s (`Sphere`, `Cube` and `Tetrahedron`).

You make a class abstract by declaring it with keyword `abstract`. An abstract class normally contains one or more *abstract methods*. An abstract method is one with keyword `abstract` in its declaration, as in

```
public abstract void Draw(); // abstract method
```

Abstract methods do not provide implementations. A class that contains abstract methods must be declared as an abstract class even if that class contains concrete (non-abstract) methods. Each concrete derived class of an abstract base class also must provide concrete implementations of the base class's abstract methods. We show an example of an abstract class with an abstract method in Fig. 11.4.

Properties can also be declared abstract, then overridden in derived classes with the override keyword, just like methods. This allows an abstract base class to specify common properties of its derived classes. Abstract property declarations have the form:

```
public abstract PropertyType MyProperty
{
    get;
    set;
} // end abstract property
```

The semicolons after the get and set keywords indicate that we provide no implementation for these accessors. An abstract property may omit implementations for the get accessor, the set accessor or both. Concrete derived classes must provide implementations for *every* accessor declared in the abstract property. When both get and set accessors are specified (as above), every concrete derived class must implement both. If one accessor is omitted, the derived class is not allowed to implement that accessor. Doing so causes a compilation error.

Constructors and static methods cannot be declared abstract. Constructors are not inherited, so an abstract constructor could never be implemented. Similarly, derived classes cannot override static methods, so an abstract static method could never be implemented.

Software Engineering Observation 11.2

An abstract class declares common attributes and behaviors of the various classes that inherit from it, either directly or indirectly, in a class hierarchy. An abstract class typically contains one or more abstract methods or properties that concrete derived classes must override. The instance variables, concrete methods and concrete properties of an abstract class are subject to the normal rules of inheritance.

Common Programming Error 11.1

Attempting to instantiate an object of an abstract class is a compilation error.

Common Programming Error 11.2

Failure to implement a base class's abstract methods and properties in a derived class is a compilation error unless the derived class is also declared abstract.

Although we cannot instantiate objects of abstract base classes, you will soon see that we *can* use abstract base classes to declare variables that can hold references to objects of any concrete classes derived from those abstract classes. Applications typically use such variables to manipulate derived class objects polymorphically. Also, you can use abstract base class names to invoke static methods declared in those abstract base classes.

Polymorphism is particularly effective for implementing so-called layered software systems. In operating systems, for example, each type of physical device could operate quite differently from the others. Even so, common commands can read or write data from and to the devices. For each device, the operating system uses a piece of software called a device driver to control all communication between the system and the device. The write message sent to a device driver object needs to be interpreted specifically in the context of that driver and how it manipulates a specific device. However, the write call itself really is no different from the write to any other device in the system: Place some number of bytes from memory onto that device. An object-oriented operating system might use an abstract base class to provide an "interface" appropriate for all device drivers. Then, through inheritance from that abstract base class, derived classes are formed that all behave similarly. The device driver methods are declared as abstract methods in the abstract base class. The implementations of these abstract methods are provided in the derived classes that correspond to the specific types of device drivers. New devices are always being developed, often long after the operating system has been released. When you buy a new device, it comes with a device driver provided by the device vendor. The device is immediately operational after you connect it to your computer and install the device driver. This is another elegant example of how polymorphism makes systems extensible.

It is common in object-oriented programming to declare an *iterator class* that can traverse all the objects in a collection, such as an array (Chapter 8) or an ArrayList (Chapter 27, Collections). For example, an application can print an ArrayList of objects by creating an iterator object and using it to obtain the next list element each time the iterator is called. Iterators often are used in polymorphic programming to traverse a collection that contains references to objects of various classes in an inheritance hierarchy. (Chapters 26–27 present a thorough treatment of C#'s new "generics" capabilities, ArrayList and iterators.) An ArrayList of references to objects of class TwoDimensionalShape, for example, could contain references to objects from derived classes Square, Circle, Triangle and so on. Calling method Draw for each TwoDimensionalShape object off a TwoDimensionalShape variable would polymorphically draw each object correctly on the screen.

11.5 Case Study: Payroll System Using Polymorphism

This section reexamines the CommissionEmployee-BasePlusCommissionEmployee hierarchy that we explored throughout Section 10.4. Now we use an abstract method and polymorphism to perform payroll calculations based on the type of employee. We create an enhanced employee hierarchy to solve the following problem:

> *A company pays its employees on a weekly basis. The employees are of four types: Salaried employees are paid a fixed weekly salary regardless of the number of hours worked, hourly employees are paid by the hour and receive overtime pay for all hours worked in excess of 40 hours, commission employees are paid a percentage of their sales, and salaried-commission employees receive a base salary plus a percentage of their sales. For the current pay period, the company has decided to reward salaried-commission employees by adding 10% to their base salaries. The company wants to implement a C# application that performs its payroll calculations polymorphically.*

We use abstract class Employee to represent the general concept of an employee. The classes that extend Employee are SalariedEmployee, CommissionEmployee and HourlyEmployee. Class BasePlusCommissionEmployee—which extends CommissionEmployee—

represents the last employee type. The UML class diagram in Fig. 11.2 shows the inheritance hierarchy for our polymorphic employee payroll application. Note that abstract class `Employee` is italicized, as per the convention of the UML.

Abstract base class `Employee` declares the "interface" to the hierarchy—that is, the set of methods that an application can invoke on all `Employee` objects. We use the term "interface" here in a general sense to refer to the various ways applications can communicate with objects of any `Employee` derived class. Be careful not to confuse the general notion of an "interface" with the formal notion of a C# interface, the subject of Section 11.7. Each employee, regardless of the way his or her earnings are calculated, has a first name, a last name and a social security number, so `private` instance variables `firstName`, `lastName` and `socialSecurityNumber` appear in abstract base class `Employee`.

> **Software Engineering Observation 11.3**
>
> *A derived class can inherit "interface" or "implementation" from a base class. Hierarchies designed for **implementation inheritance** tend to have their functionality high in the hierarchy—each new derived class inherits one or more methods that were implemented in a base class, and the derived class uses the base class implementations. Hierarchies designed for **interface inheritance** tend to have their functionality lower in the hierarchy—a base class specifies one or more abstract methods that must be declared for each concrete class in the hierarchy, and the individual derived classes override these methods to provide derived-class-specific implementations.*

The following sections implement the `Employee` class hierarchy. The first section implements `abstract` base class `Employee`. The next four sections each implement one of the concrete classes. The sixth section implements a test application that builds objects of all these classes and processes those objects polymorphically.

11.5.1 Creating Abstract Base Class Employee

Class `Employee` (Fig. 11.4) provides methods `Earnings` and `ToString`, in addition to the properties that manipulate `Employee`'s instance variables. An `Earnings` method certainly applies generically to all employees. But each earnings calculation depends on the employee's class. So we declare `Earnings` as `abstract` in base class `Employee`, because a default implementation does not make sense for that method—there is not enough information to determine what amount `Earnings` should return. Each derived class overrides `Earnings` with an appropriate implementation. To calculate an employee's earnings, the application

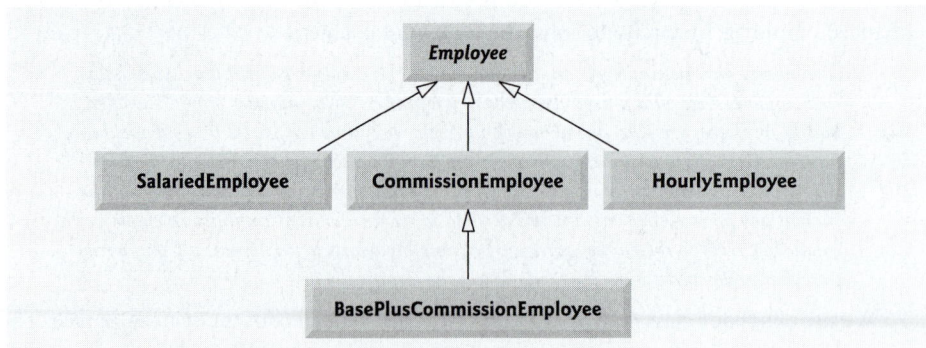

Fig. 11.2 | `Employee` hierarchy UML class diagram.

assigns a reference to the employee's object to a base class `Employee` variable, then invokes the `Earnings` method on that variable. We maintain an array of `Employee` variables, each of which holds a reference to an `Employee` object (of course, there cannot be `Employee` objects because `Employee` is an abstract class—because of inheritance, however, all objects of all derived classes of `Employee` may nevertheless be thought of as `Employee` objects). The application iterates through the array and calls method `Earnings` for each `Employee` object. C# processes these method calls polymorphically. Including `Earnings` as an abstract method in `Employee` forces every directly derived concrete class of `Employee` to override `Earnings` with a method that performs an appropriate pay calculation.

Method `ToString` in class `Employee` returns a `string` containing the first name, last name and social security number of the employee. Each derived class of `Employee` overrides method `ToString` to create a string representation of an object of that class containing the employee's type (e.g., `"salaried employee:"`), followed by the rest of the employee's information.

The diagram in Fig. 11.3 shows each of the five classes in the hierarchy down the left side and methods `Earnings` and `ToString` across the top. For each class, the diagram shows the desired results of each method. [*Note:* We do not list base class `Employee`'s properties because they are not overridden in any of the derived classes—each of these properties is inherited and used "as is" by each of the derived classes.]

	Earnings	ToString
Employee	abstract	*firstName lastName* social security number: *SSN*
Salaried- Employee	weeklySalary	salaried employee: *firstName lastName* social security number: *SSN* weekly salary: *weeklysalary*

Hourly-
Employee
	If hours <= 40
	    wage * hours
	If hours > 40
	    40 * wage +
	    (hours - 40) *
	    wage * 1.5
		hourly employee: *firstName lastName*
		social security number: *SSN*
		hourly wage: *wage*
		hours worked: *hours*

Commission- Employee	commissionRate * grossSales	commission employee: *firstName lastName* social security number: *SSN* gross sales: *grossSales* commission rate: *commissionRate*
BasePlus- Commission- Employee	(commissionRate * grossSales) + baseSalary	base salaried commission employee: *firstName lastName* social security number: *SSN* gross sales: *grossSales* commission rate: *commissionRate* base salary: *baseSalary*

Fig. 11.3 | Polymorphic interface for the `Employee` hierarchy classes.

Let us consider class Employee's declaration (Fig. 11.4). The class includes a constructor that takes the first name, last name and social security number as arguments (lines 10–15); read-only properties for obtaining the first name, last name and social security number (lines 18–24, 27–33 and 36–42, respectively); method ToString (lines 45–49), which uses properties to return the string representation of Employee; and abstract method Earnings (line 52), which must be implemented by concrete derived classes. Note that the Employee constructor does not validate the social security number in this example. Normally, such validation should be provided.

```csharp
1   // Fig. 11.4: Employee.cs
2   // Employee abstract base class.
3   public abstract class Employee
4   {
5      private string firstName;
6      private string lastName;
7      private string socialSecurityNumber;
8
9      // three-parameter constructor
10     public Employee( string first, string last, string ssn )
11     {
12        firstName = first;
13        lastName = last;
14        socialSecurityNumber = ssn;
15     } // end three-parameter Employee constructor
16
17     // read-only property that gets employee's first name
18     public string FirstName
19     {
20        get
21        {
22           return firstName;
23        } // end get
24     } // end property FirstName
25
26     // read-only property that gets employee's last name
27     public string LastName
28     {
29        get
30        {
31           return lastName;
32        } // end get
33     } // end property LastName
34
35     // read-only property that gets employee's social security number
36     public string SocialSecurityNumber
37     {
38        get
39        {
40           return socialSecurityNumber;
41        } // end get
42     } // end property SocialSecurityNumber
```

Fig. 11.4 | Employee abstract base class. (Part 1 of 2.)

```
43
44      // return string representation of Employee object, using properties
45      public override string ToString()
46      {
47         return string.Format( "{0} {1}\nsocial security number: {2}",
48            FirstName, LastName, SocialSecurityNumber );
49      } // end method ToString
50
51      // abstract method overridden by derived classes
52      public abstract decimal Earnings(); // no implementation here
53   } // end abstract class Employee
```

Fig. 11.4 | Employee abstract base class. (Part 2 of 2.)

Why did we declare Earnings as an abstract method? It simply does not make sense to provide an implementation of this method in class Employee. We cannot calculate the earnings for a general Employee—we first must know the specific Employee type to determine the appropriate earnings calculation. By declaring this method abstract, we indicate that each concrete derived class *must* provide an appropriate Earnings implementation and that an application will be able to use base class Employee variables to invoke method Earnings polymorphically for any type of Employee.

11.5.2 Creating Concrete Derived Class SalariedEmployee

Class SalariedEmployee (Fig. 11.5) extends class Employee (line 3) and overrides Earnings (lines 28–31), which makes SalariedEmployee a concrete class. The class includes a constructor (lines 8–12) that takes a first name, a last name, a social security number and a weekly salary as arguments; property WeeklySalary to manipulate instance variable weeklySalary, including a set accessor that ensures we assign only non-negative values to weeklySalary (lines 15–25); method Earnings (lines 28–31) to calculate a SalariedEmployee's earnings; and method ToString (lines 34–38), which returns a string including the employee's type, namely, "salaried employee: ", followed by employee-specific information produced by base class Employee's ToString method and SalariedEmployee's WeeklySalary property. Class SalariedEmployee's constructor passes the first name, last name and social security number to the Employee constructor (line 9) via a constructor initializer to initialize the private instance variables not inherited from the base class. Method Earnings overrides Employee's abstract method Earnings to provide a concrete implementation that returns the SalariedEmployee's weekly salary. If we do not implement Earnings, class SalariedEmployee must be declared abstract—otherwise, a compilation error occurs (and, of course, we want SalariedEmployee to be a concrete class).

Method ToString (lines 34–38) of class SalariedEmployee overrides Employee method ToString. If class SalariedEmployee did not override ToString, SalariedEmployee would have inherited the Employee version of ToString. In that case, SalariedEmployee's ToString method would simply return the employee's full name and social security number, which does not adequately represent a SalariedEmployee. To produce a complete string representation of a SalariedEmployee, the derived class's ToString method returns "salaried employee: ", followed by the base class Employee-specific information (i.e., first name, last name and social security number) obtained by invoking

```
1   // Fig. 11.5: SalariedEmployee.cs
2   // SalariedEmployee class that extends Employee.
3   public class SalariedEmployee : Employee
4   {
5      private decimal weeklySalary;
6
7      // four-parameter constructor
8      public SalariedEmployee( string first, string last, string ssn,
9         decimal salary ) : base( first, last, ssn )
10     {
11        WeeklySalary = salary; // validate salary via property
12     } // end four-parameter SalariedEmployee constructor
13
14     // property that gets and sets salaried employee's salary
15     public decimal WeeklySalary
16     {
17        get
18        {
19           return weeklySalary;
20        } // end get
21        set
22        {
23           weeklySalary = ( ( value >= 0 ) ? value : 0 ); // validation
24        } // end set
25     } // end property WeeklySalary
26
27     // calculate earnings; override abstract method Earnings in Employee
28     public override decimal Earnings()
29     {
30        return WeeklySalary;
31     } // end method Earnings
32
33     // return string representation of SalariedEmployee object
34     public override string ToString()
35     {
36        return string.Format( "salaried employee: {0}\n{1}: {2:C}",
37           base.ToString(), "weekly salary", WeeklySalary );
38     } // end method ToString
39  } // end class SalariedEmployee
```

Fig. 11.5 | SalariedEmployee class that extends Employee.

the base class's ToString (line 37)—this is a nice example of code reuse. The string representation of a SalariedEmployee also contains the employee's weekly salary, obtained by using the class's WeeklySalary property.

11.5.3 Creating Concrete Derived Class HourlyEmployee

Class HourlyEmployee (Fig. 11.6) also extends class Employee (line 3). The class includes a constructor (lines 9–15) that takes as arguments a first name, a last name, a social security number, an hourly wage and the number of hours worked. Lines 18–28 and 31–42 declare properties Wage and Hours for instance variables wage and hours, respectively. The set accessor in property Wage (lines 24–27) ensures that wage is non-negative, and the set accessor

```
 1    // Fig. 11.6: HourlyEmployee.cs
 2    // HourlyEmployee class that extends Employee.
 3    public class HourlyEmployee : Employee
 4    {
 5       private decimal wage; // wage per hour
 6       private decimal hours; // hours worked for the week
 7
 8       // five-parameter constructor
 9       public HourlyEmployee( string first, string last, string ssn,
10          decimal hourlyWage, decimal hoursWorked )
11          : base( first, last, ssn )
12       {
13          Wage = hourlyWage; // validate hourly wage via property
14          Hours = hoursWorked; // validate hours worked via property
15       } // end five-parameter HourlyEmployee constructor
16
17       // property that gets and sets hourly employee's wage
18       public decimal Wage
19       {
20          get
21          {
22             return wage;
23          } // end get
24          set
25          {
26             wage = ( value >= 0 ) ? value : 0; // validation
27          } // end set
28       } // end property Wage
29
30       // property that gets and sets hourly employee's hours
31       public decimal Hours
32       {
33          get
34          {
35             return hours;
36          } // end get
37          set
38          {
39             hours = ( ( value >= 0 ) && ( value <= 168 ) ) ?
40                   value : 0; // validation
41          } // end set
42       } // end property Hours
43
44       // calculate earnings; override Employee's abstract method Earnings
45       public override decimal Earnings()
46       {
47          if ( Hours <= 40 ) // no overtime
48             return Wage * Hours;
49          else
50             return ( 40 * Wage ) + ( ( Hours - 40 ) * Wage * 1.5M );
51       } // end method Earnings
52
```

Fig. 11.6 | HourlyEmployee class that extends Employee. (Part 1 of 2.)

```
53        // return string representation of HourlyEmployee object
54        public override string ToString()
55        {
56            return string.Format(
57                "hourly employee: {0}\n{1}: {2:C}; {3}: {4:F2}",
58                base.ToString(), "hourly wage", Wage, "hours worked", Hours );
59        } // end method ToString
60    } // end class HourlyEmployee
```

Fig. 11.6 | HourlyEmployee class that extends Employee. (Part 2 of 2.)

in property Hours (lines 37–41) ensures that hours is in the range 0–168 (the total number of hours in a week) inclusive. Class HourlyEmployee also includes method Earnings (lines 45–51) to calculate an HourlyEmployee's earnings; and method ToString (lines 54–59), which returns the employee's type, namely, "hourly employee: ", and employee-specific information. Note that the HourlyEmployee constructor, like the SalariedEmployee constructor, passes the first name, last name and social security number to the base class Employee constructor (line 11) to initialize the base class's private instance variables. Also, method ToString calls base class method ToString (line 58) to obtain the Employee-specific information (i.e., first name, last name and social security number)—this is another nice example of code reuse.

11.5.4 Creating Concrete Derived Class CommissionEmployee

Class CommissionEmployee (Fig. 11.7) extends class Employee (line 3). The class includes a constructor (lines 9–14) that takes a first name, a last name, a social security number, a sales amount and a commission rate; properties (lines 17–28 and 31–41) for instance variables commissionRate and grossSales, respectively; method Earnings (lines 44–47) to calculate a CommissionEmployee's earnings; and method ToString (lines 50–55), which returns the employee's type, namely, "commission employee: ", and employee-specific information.

```
1     // Fig. 11.7: CommissionEmployee.cs
2     // CommissionEmployee class that extends Employee.
3     public class CommissionEmployee : Employee
4     {
5         private decimal grossSales; // gross weekly sales
6         private decimal commissionRate; // commission percentage
7
8         // five-parameter constructor
9         public CommissionEmployee( string first, string last, string ssn,
10            decimal sales, decimal rate ) : base( first, last, ssn )
11        {
12            GrossSales = sales; // validate gross sales via property
13            CommissionRate = rate; // validate commission rate via property
14        } // end five-parameter CommissionEmployee constructor
15
16        // property that gets and sets commission employee's commission rate
17        public decimal CommissionRate
18        {
```

Fig. 11.7 | CommissionEmployee class that extends Employee. (Part 1 of 2.)

```
19              get
20              {
21                  return commissionRate;
22              } // end get
23              set
24              {
25                  commissionRate = ( value > 0 && value < 1 ) ?
26                              value : 0; // validation
27              } // end set
28          } // end property CommissionRate
29
30          // property that gets and sets commission employee's gross sales
31          public decimal GrossSales
32          {
33              get
34              {
35                  return grossSales;
36              } // end get
37              set
38              {
39                  grossSales = ( value >= 0 ) ? value : 0; // validation
40              } // end set
41          } // end property GrossSales
42
43          // calculate earnings; override abstract method Earnings in Employee
44          public override decimal Earnings()
45          {
46              return CommissionRate * GrossSales;
47          } // end method Earnings
48
49          // return string representation of CommissionEmployee object
50          public override string ToString()
51          {
52              return string.Format( "{0}: {1}\n{2}: {3:C}\n{4}: {5:F2}",
53                  "commission employee", base.ToString(),
54                  "gross sales", GrossSales, "commission rate", CommissionRate );
55          } // end method ToString
56      } // end class CommissionEmployee
```

Fig. 11.7 | CommissionEmployee class that extends Employee. (Part 2 of 2.)

The CommissionEmployee's constructor also passes the first name, last name and social security number to the Employee constructor (line 10) to initialize Employee's private instance variables. Method ToString calls base class method ToString (line 53) to obtain the Employee-specific information (i.e., first name, last name and social security number).

11.5.5 Creating Indirect Concrete Derived Class BasePlusCommissionEmployee

Class BasePlusCommissionEmployee (Fig. 11.8) extends class CommissionEmployee (line 3) and therefore is an indirect derived class of class Employee. Class BasePlusCommissionEmployee has a constructor (lines 8–13) that takes as arguments a first name, a last name, a social security number, a sales amount, a commission rate and a base salary. It then passes the first name, last name, social security number, sales amount and commission rate to the CommissionEmployee constructor (line 10) to initialize the base class's private data members. BasePlusCommissionEmployee also contains property BaseSalary (lines 17–27) to manipulate instance variable baseSalary. Method Earnings (lines 30–33) calculates a BasePlusCommissionEmployee's earnings. Note that line 32 in method Earnings calls base class CommissionEmployee's Earnings method to calculate the commission-based portion of the employee's earnings. This is another nice example of code reuse. BasePlusCommissionEmployee's ToString method (lines 36–40) creates a string representation of a BasePlusCommissionEmployee that contains "base-salaried", followed by the string obtained by invoking base class CommissionEmployee's ToString method (another example of code reuse), then the base salary. The result is a string beginning with "base-salaried commission employee", followed by the rest of the BasePlusCommissionEmployee's information. Recall that CommissionEmployee's ToString method obtains the employee's first name, last name and social security number by invoking the ToString method of its base class (i.e., Employee)—yet another example of code reuse. Note that BasePlusCommissionEmployee's ToString initiates a chain of method calls that span all three levels of the Employee hierarchy.

```csharp
1   // Fig. 11.8: BasePlusCommissionEmployee.cs
2   // BasePlusCommissionEmployee class that extends CommissionEmployee.
3   public class BasePlusCommissionEmployee : CommissionEmployee
4   {
5      private decimal baseSalary; // base salary per week
6
7      // six-parameter constructor
8      public BasePlusCommissionEmployee( string first, string last,
9         string ssn, decimal sales, decimal rate, decimal salary )
10        : base( first, last, ssn, sales, rate )
11     {
12        BaseSalary = salary; // validate base salary via property
13     } // end six-parameter BasePlusCommissionEmployee constructor
14
15     // property that gets and sets
16     // base-salaried commission employee's base salary
17     public decimal BaseSalary
18     {
19        get
20        {
21           return baseSalary;
22        } // end get
23        set
24        {
25           baseSalary = ( value >= 0 ) ? value : 0; // validation
26        } // end set
27     } // end property BaseSalary
28
```

Fig. 11.8 | BasePlusCommissionEmployee class that extends CommissionEmployee. (Part 1 of 2.)

```
29        // calculate earnings; override method Earnings in CommissionEmployee
30        public override decimal Earnings()
31        {
32           return BaseSalary + base.Earnings();
33        } // end method Earnings
34
35        // return string representation of BasePlusCommissionEmployee object
36        public override string ToString()
37        {
38           return string.Format( "{0} {1}; {2}: {3:C}",
39              "base-salaried", base.ToString(), "base salary", BaseSalary );
40        } // end method ToString
41     } // end class BasePlusCommissionEmployee
```

Fig. 11.8 | BasePlusCommissionEmployee class that extends CommissionEmployee. (Part 2 of 2.)

11.5.6 Polymorphic Processing, Operator is and Downcasting

To test our Employee hierarchy, the application in Fig. 11.9 creates an object of each of the four concrete classes SalariedEmployee, HourlyEmployee, CommissionEmployee and BasePlusCommissionEmployee. The application manipulates these objects, first via variables of each object's own type, then polymorphically, using an array of Employee variables. While processing the objects polymorphically, the application increases the base salary of each BasePlusCommissionEmployee by 10% (this, of course, requires determining the object's type at execution time). Finally, the application polymorphically determines and outputs the type of each object in the Employee array. Lines 10–20 create objects of each of the

```
1     // Fig. 11.9: PayrollSystemTest.cs
2     // Employee hierarchy test application.
3     using System;
4
5     public class PayrollSystemTest
6     {
7        public static void Main( string[] args )
8        {
9           // create derived class objects
10          SalariedEmployee salariedEmployee =
11             new SalariedEmployee( "John", "Smith", "111-11-1111", 800.00M );
12          HourlyEmployee hourlyEmployee =
13             new HourlyEmployee( "Karen", "Price",
14             "222-22-2222", 16.75M, 40.0M );
15          CommissionEmployee commissionEmployee =
16             new CommissionEmployee( "Sue", "Jones",
17             "333-33-3333", 10000.00M, .06M );
18          BasePlusCommissionEmployee basePlusCommissionEmployee =
19             new BasePlusCommissionEmployee( "Bob", "Lewis",
20             "444-44-4444", 5000.00M, .04M, 300.00M );
21
22          Console.WriteLine( "Employees processed individually:\n" );
```

Fig. 11.9 | Employee hierarchy test application. (Part 1 of 3.)

```
23
24          Console.WriteLine( "{0}\n{1}: {2:C}\n",
25             salariedEmployee, "earned", salariedEmployee.Earnings() );
26          Console.WriteLine( "{0}\n{1}: {2:C}\n",
27             hourlyEmployee, "earned", hourlyEmployee.Earnings() );
28          Console.WriteLine( "{0}\n{1}: {2:C}\n",
29             commissionEmployee, "earned", commissionEmployee.Earnings() );
30          Console.WriteLine( "{0}\n{1}: {2:C}\n",
31             basePlusCommissionEmployee,
32             "earned", basePlusCommissionEmployee.Earnings() );
33
34          // create four-element Employee array
35          Employee[] employees = new Employee[ 4 ];
36
37          // initialize array with Employees of derived types
38          employees[ 0 ] = salariedEmployee;
39          employees[ 1 ] = hourlyEmployee;
40          employees[ 2 ] = commissionEmployee;
41          employees[ 3 ] = basePlusCommissionEmployee;
42
43          Console.WriteLine( "Employees processed polymorphically:\n" );
44
45          // generically process each element in array employees
46          foreach ( Employee currentEmployee in employees )
47          {
48             Console.WriteLine( currentEmployee ); // invokes ToString
49
50             // determine whether element is a BasePlusCommissionEmployee
51             if ( currentEmployee is BasePlusCommissionEmployee )
52             {
53                // downcast Employee reference to
54                // BasePlusCommissionEmployee reference
55                BasePlusCommissionEmployee employee =
56                   ( BasePlusCommissionEmployee ) currentEmployee;
57
58                employee.BaseSalary *= 1.10M;
59                Console.WriteLine(
60                   "new base salary with 10% increase is: {0:C}",
61                   employee.BaseSalary );
62             } // end if
63
64             Console.WriteLine(
65                "earned {0:C}\n", currentEmployee.Earnings() );
66          } // end foreach
67
68          // get type name of each object in employees array
69          for ( int j = 0; j < employees.Length; j++ )
70             Console.WriteLine( "Employee {0} is a {1}", j,
71                employees[ j ].GetType() );
72       } // end Main
73    } // end class PayrollSystemTest
```

Fig. 11.9 | Employee hierarchy test application. (Part 2 of 3.)

```
Employees processed individually:

salaried employee: John Smith
social security number: 111-11-1111
weekly salary: $800.00
earned: $800.00

hourly employee: Karen Price
social security number: 222-22-2222
hourly wage: $16.75; hours worked: 40.00
earned: $670.00

commission employee: Sue Jones
social security number: 333-33-3333
gross sales: $10,000.00
commission rate: 0.06
earned: $600.00

base-salaried commission employee: Bob Lewis
social security number: 444-44-4444
gross sales: $5,000.00
commission rate: 0.04; base salary: $300.00
earned: $500.00

Employees processed polymorphically:

salaried employee: John Smith
social security number: 111-11-1111
weekly salary: $800.00
earned $800.00

hourly employee: Karen Price
social security number: 222-22-2222
hourly wage: $16.75; hours worked: 40.00
earned $670.00

commission employee: Sue Jones
social security number: 333-33-3333
gross sales: $10,000.00
commission rate: 0.06
earned $600.00

base-salaried commission employee: Bob Lewis
social security number: 444-44-4444
gross sales: $5,000.00
commission rate: 0.04; base salary: $300.00
new base salary with 10% increase is: $330.00
earned $530.00

Employee 0 is a SalariedEmployee
Employee 1 is a HourlyEmployee
Employee 2 is a CommissionEmployee
Employee 3 is a BasePlusCommissionEmployee
```

Fig. 11.9 | Employee hierarchy test application. (Part 3 of 3.)

four concrete `Employee` derived classes. Lines 24–32 output the string representation and earnings of each of these objects. Note that each object's `ToString` method is called implicitly by `Write` when the object is output as a `string` with format items.

Line 35 declares `employees` and assigns it an array of four `Employee` variables. Lines 38–41 assign a `SalariedEmployee` object, an `HourlyEmployee` object, a `Commission-Employee` object and a `BasePlusCommissionEmployee` object to `employees[ 0 ]`, `employees[ 1 ]`, `employees[ 2 ]` and `employees[ 3 ]`, respectively. Each assignment is allowed, because a `SalariedEmployee` *is an* `Employee`, an `HourlyEmployee` *is an* `Employee`, a `CommissionEmployee` *is an* `Employee` and a `BasePlusCommissionEmployee` *is an* `Employee`. Therefore, we can assign the references of `SalariedEmployee`, `HourlyEmployee`, `CommissionEmployee` and `BasePlusCommissionEmployee` objects to base class `Employee` variables, even though `Employee` is an abstract class.

Lines 46–66 iterate through array `employees` and invoke methods `ToString` and `Earnings` with `Employee` variable `currentEmployee`, which is assigned the reference to a different `Employee` in the array during each iteration. The output illustrates that the appropriate methods for each class are indeed invoked. All calls to method's `ToString` and `Earnings` are resolved at execution time, based on the type of the object to which `currentEmployee` refers. This process is known as ***dynamic binding*** or ***late binding***. For example, line 48 implicitly invokes method `ToString` of the object to which `currentEmployee` refers. As a result of dynamic binding, the CLR decides which class's `ToString` method to call at execution time rather than at compile time. Note that only the methods of class `Employee` can be called via an `Employee` variable—and `Employee`, of course, includes the methods of class `object`, such as `ToString`. (Section 10.7 discussed the set of methods that all classes inherit from class `object`.) A base class reference can be used to invoke only methods of the base class.

We perform special processing on `BasePlusCommissionEmployee` objects—as we encounter them, we increase their base salary by 10%. When processing objects polymorphically, we typically do not need to worry about the "specifics," but to adjust the base salary, we do have to determine the specific type of each `Employee` object at execution time. Line 51 uses the `is` operator to determine whether a particular `Employee` object's type is `BasePlusCommissionEmployee`. The condition in line 51 is true if the object referenced by `currentEmployee` *is a* `BasePlusCommissionEmployee`. This would also be true for any object of a `BasePlusCommissionEmployee` derived class (if there were any) because of the *is-a* relationship a derived class has with its base class. Lines 55–56 downcast `currentEmployee` from type `Employee` to type `BasePlusCommissionEmployee`—this cast is allowed only if the object has an *is-a* relationship with `BasePlusCommissionEmployee`. The condition at line 51 ensures that this is the case. This cast is required if we are to use derived class `BasePlusCommissionEmployee`'s `BaseSalary` property on the current `Employee` object—attempting to invoke a derived-class-only method directly on a base class reference is a compilation error.

Common Programming Error 11.3

Assigning a base class variable to a derived class variable (without an explicit downcast) is a compilation error.

Software Engineering Observation 11.4

If at execution time the reference to a derived class object has been assigned to a variable of one of its direct or indirect base classes, it is acceptable to cast the reference stored in that base class variable back to a reference of the derived class type. Before performing such a cast, use the is operator to ensure that the object is indeed an object of an appropriate derived class type.

Common Programming Error 11.4

When downcasting an object, an InvalidCastException (of namespace System) occurs if at execution time the object does not have an is-a relationship with the type specified in the cast operator. An object can be cast only to its own type or to the type of one of its base classes.

If the is expression in line 51 is true, the if statement (lines 51–62) performs the special processing required for the BasePlusCommissionEmployee object. Using Base-PlusCommissionEmployee variable employee, line 58 uses the derived-class-only property BaseSalary to retrieve and update the employee's base salary with the 10% raise.

Lines 64–65 invoke method Earnings on currentEmployee, which calls the appropriate derived class object's Earnings method polymorphically. Note that obtaining the earnings of the SalariedEmployee, HourlyEmployee and CommissionEmployee polymorphically in lines 64–65 produces the same result as obtaining these employees' earnings individually in lines 24–32. However, the earnings amount obtained for the BasePlus-CommissionEmployee in lines 64–65 is higher than that obtained in lines 30–32, due to the 10% increase in its base salary.

Lines 69–71 display each employee's type as a string. Every object in C# knows its own class and can access this information through method **GetType**, which all classes inherit from class object. Method GetType returns an object of class Type (of namespace System), which contains information about the object's type, including its class name, the names of its public methods, and the name of its base class. Line 71 invokes method Get-Type on the object to get its runtime class (i.e., a Type object that represents the object's type). Then method ToString is implicitly invoked on the object returned by GetType. The Type class's ToString method returns the class name.

In the previous example, we avoid several compilation errors by downcasting an Employee variable to a BasePlusCommissionEmployee variable in lines 55–56. If we remove the cast operator (BasePlusCommissionEmployee) from line 56 and attempt to assign Employee variable currentEmployee directly to BasePlusCommissionEmployee variable employee, we receive a "Cannot implicitly convert type" compilation error. This error indicates that the attempt to assign the reference of base class object commissionEmployee to derived class variable basePlusCommissionEmployee is not allowed without an appropriate cast operator. The compiler prevents this assignment because a CommissionEmployee is not a BasePlusCommissionEmployee—again, the *is-a* relationship applies only between the derived class and its base classes, not vice versa.

Similarly, if lines 58 and 61 use base class variable currentEmployee, rather than derived class variable employee, to use derived-class-only property BaseSalary, we receive an "'Employee' does not contain a definition for 'BaseSalary'" compilation error on each of these lines. Attempting to invoke derived-class-only methods on a base class reference is not allowed. While lines 58 and 61 execute only if is in line 51 returns true to indicate that currentEmployee has been assigned a reference to a BasePlusCommission-Employee object, we cannot attempt to use derived class BasePlusCommissionEmployee property `BaseSalary` with base class `Employee` reference `currentEmployee`. The compiler would generate errors in lines 58 and 61, because `BaseSalary` is not a base class member and cannot be used with a base class variable. Although the actual method that is called depends on the object's type at execution time, a variable can be used to invoke only those methods that are members of that variable's type, which the compiler verifies. Using a base class `Employee` variable, we can invoke only methods and properties found in class `Employee`—methods `Earnings` and `ToString`, and properties `FirstName`, `LastName` and `SocialSecurityNumber`.

11.5.7 Summary of the Allowed Assignments Between Base Class and Derived Class Variables

Now that you have seen a complete application that processes diverse derived class objects polymorphically, we summarize what you can and cannot do with base class and derived class objects and variables. Although a derived class object also *is a* base class object, the two objects are nevertheless different. As discussed previously, derived class objects can be treated as if they are base class objects. However, the derived class can have additional derived-class-only members. For this reason, assigning a base class reference to a derived class variable is not allowed without an explicit cast—such an assignment would leave the derived class members undefined for a base class object.

We have discussed four ways to assign base class and derived class references to variables of base class and derived class types:

1. Assigning a base class reference to a base class variable is straightforward.

2. Assigning a derived class reference to a derived class variable is straightforward.

3. Assigning a derived class reference to a base class variable is safe, because the derived class object *is an* object of its base class. However, this reference can be used to refer only to base class members. If this code refers to derived-class-only members through the base class variable, the compiler reports errors.

4. Attempting to assign a base class reference to a derived class variable is a compilation error. To avoid this error, the base class reference must be cast to a derived class type explicitly. At execution time, if the object to which the reference refers is not a derived class object, an exception will occur. (For more on exception handling, see Chapter 12, Exception Handling.) The `is` operator can be used to ensure that such a cast is performed only if the object is a derived class object.

11.6 `sealed` Methods and Classes

We saw in Section 10.4 that only methods declared `virtual`, `override` or `abstract` can be overridden in derived classes. A method declared *sealed* in a base class cannot be overridden in a derived class. Methods that are declared `private` are implicitly `sealed`, because it is impossible to override them in a derived class (though the derived class can declare a new method with the same signature as the `private` method in the base class). Methods that are declared `static` also are implicitly `sealed`, because `static` methods cannot be overridden either. A derived class method declared both `override` and `sealed` can override a base class method, but cannot be overridden in derived classes further down the inheritance hierarchy.

A `sealed` method's declaration can never change, so all derived classes use the same method implementation, and calls to `sealed` methods are resolved at compile time—this is known as *static binding*. Since the compiler knows that `sealed` methods cannot be overridden, it can often optimize code by removing calls to `sealed` methods and replacing them with the expanded code of their declarations at each method-call location—a technique known as *inlining the code*.

Performance Tip 11.1

The compiler can decide to inline a `sealed` method call and will do so for small, simple `sealed` methods. Inlining does not violate encapsulation or information hiding, but does improve performance because it eliminates the overhead of making a method call.

A class that is declared `sealed` cannot be a base class (i.e., a class cannot extend a `sealed` class). All methods in a `sealed` class are implicitly `sealed`. Class `string` is a `sealed` class. This class cannot be extended, so applications that use `strings` can rely on the functionality of `string` objects as specified in the FCL.

Common Programming Error 11.5

Attempting to declare a derived class of a `sealed` class is a compilation error.

Software Engineering Observation 11.5

In the FCL, the vast majority of classes are not declared `sealed`. This enables inheritance and polymorphism—the fundamental capabilities of object-oriented programming.

11.7 Case Study: Creating and Using Interfaces

Our next example (Figs. 11.11–11.15) reexamines the payroll system of Section 11.5. Suppose that the company involved wishes to perform several accounting operations in a single accounts-payable application—in addition to calculating the payroll earnings that must be paid to each employee, the company must also calculate the payment due on each of several invoices (i.e., bills for goods purchased). Though applied to unrelated things (i.e., employees and invoices), both operations have to do with calculating some kind of payment amount. For an employee, the payment refers to the employee's earnings. For an invoice, the payment refers to the total cost of the goods listed on the invoice. Can we calculate such different things as the payments due for employees and invoices polymorphically in a single application? Does C# offer a capability that requires that unrelated classes implement a set of common methods (e.g., a method that calculates a payment amount)? C# interfaces offer exactly this capability.

Interfaces define and standardize the ways in which people and systems can interact with one another. For example, the controls on a radio serve as an interface between a radio's users and its internal components. The controls allow users to perform a limited set of operations (e.g., changing the station, adjusting the volume, choosing between AM and FM), and different radios may implement the controls in different ways (e.g., using push buttons, dials, voice commands). The interface specifies *what* operations a radio must permit users to perform but does not specify *how* the operations are performed. Similarly, the interface between a driver and a car with a manual transmission includes the steering wheel, the gear shift, the clutch pedal, the gas pedal and the brake pedal. This same interface is found in nearly all manual-transmission cars, enabling someone who knows how to drive one particular manual-transmission car to drive just about any manual transmission car. The components of each individual car may look a bit different, but the general purpose is the same—to allow people to drive the car.

Software objects also communicate via interfaces. A C# interface describes a set of methods that can be called on an object, to tell the object to perform some task or return some piece of information, for example. The next example introduces an interface named `IPayable` that describes the functionality of any object that must be capable of being paid and thus must offer a method to determine the proper payment amount due. An *interface declaration* begins with the keyword `interface` and can contain only abstract methods, properties, indexers and events (events are discussed in Chapter 13, Graphical User Interface Concepts: Part 1.) All interface members are implicitly declared both `public` and `abstract`. In addition, each interface can extend one or more other interfaces to create a more elaborate interface that other classes can implement.

Common Programming Error 11.6

It is a compilation error to declare an interface member `public` or `abstract` explicitly, because they are redundant in interface member declarations. It is also a compilation error to specify any implementation details, such as concrete method declarations, in an interface.

To use an interface, a class must specify that it *implements* the interface by listing the interface after the colon (:) in the class declaration. Note that this is the same syntax used to indicate inheritance from a base class. A concrete class implementing the interface must declare each member of the interface with the signature specified in the interface declaration. A class that implements an interface but does not implement all the interface's members is an abstract class—it must be declared `abstract` and must contain an `abstract` declaration for each unimplemented member of the interface. Implementing an interface is like signing a contract with the compiler that states, "I will provide an implementation for all the members specified by the interface, or I will declare them `abstract`."

Common Programming Error 11.7

Failing to declare any member of an interface in a class that implements the interface results in a compilation error.

An interface is typically used when disparate (i.e., unrelated) classes need to share common methods. This allows objects of unrelated classes to be processed polymorphically—objects of classes that implement the same interface can respond to the same method calls. Programmers can create an interface that describes the desired functionality, then implement this interface in any classes requiring that functionality. For example, in the accounts-payable application developed in this section, we implement interface `IPayable` in any class that must be able to calculate a payment amount (e.g., `Employee`, `Invoice`).

An interface often is used in place of an `abstract` class when there is no default implementation to inherit—that is, no fields and no default method implementations. Like `public abstract` classes, interfaces are typically `public` types, so they are normally declared in files by themselves with the same name as the interface and the `.cs` filename extension.

11.7.1 Developing an IPayable Hierarchy

To build an application that can determine payments for employees and invoices alike, we first create an interface named IPayable. Interface IPayable contains method GetPaymentAmount that returns a decimal amount that must be paid for an object of any class that implements the interface. Method GetPaymentAmount is a general purpose version of method Earnings of the Employee hierarchy—method Earnings calculates a payment amount specifically for an Employee, while GetPaymentAmount can be applied to a broad range of unrelated objects. After declaring interface IPayable, we introduce class Invoice, which implements interface IPayable. We then modify class Employee such that it also implements interface IPayable. Finally, we update Employee derived class SalariedEmployee to "fit" into the IPayable hierarchy (i.e., rename SalariedEmployee method Earnings as GetPaymentAmount).

Good Programming Practice 11.1

By convention, the name of an interface begins with "I". This helps distinguish interfaces from classes, improving code readability.

Good Programming Practice 11.2

When declaring a method in an interface, choose a method name that describes the method's purpose in a general manner, because the method may be implemented by a broad range of unrelated classes.

Classes Invoice and Employee both represent things for which the company must be able to calculate a payment amount. Both classes implement IPayable, so an application can invoke method GetPaymentAmount on Invoice objects and Employee objects alike. This enables the polymorphic processing of Invoices and Employees required for our company's accounts-payable application.

The UML class diagram in Fig. 11.10 shows the interface and class hierarchy used in our accounts-payable application. The hierarchy begins with interface IPayable. The UML distinguishes an interface from a class by placing the word "interface" in guillemets (« and ») above the interface name. The UML expresses the relationship between a class and an interface through a *realization*. A class is said to "realize," or implement, an interface. A class diagram models a realization as a dashed arrow with a hollow arrowhead pointing from the implementing class to the interface. The diagram in Fig. 11.10 indicates that classes Invoice and Employee each realize (i.e., implement) interface IPayable. Note that as in the class diagram of Fig. 11.2, class Employee appears in italics, indicating that it is an abstract class. Concrete class SalariedEmployee extends Employee and inherits its base class's realization relationship with interface IPayable.

11.7.2 Declaring Interface IPayable

The declaration of interface IPayable begins in Fig. 11.11 at line 3. Interface IPayable contains public abstract method GetPaymentAmount (line 5). Note that the method cannot be explicitly declared public or abstract. Interface IPayable has only one method, but interfaces can have any number of members. In addition, method GetPaymentAmount has no parameters, but interface methods can have parameters.

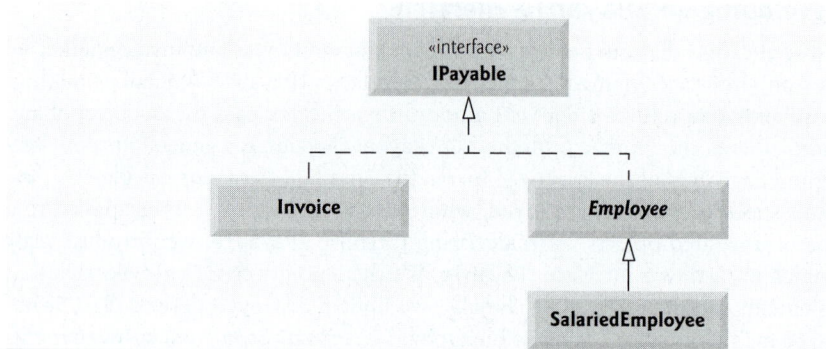

Fig. 11.10 | IPayable interface and class hierarchy UML class diagram.

```
1    // Fig. 11.11: IPayable.cs
2    // IPayable interface declaration.
3    public interface IPayable
4    {
5        decimal GetPaymentAmount(); // calculate payment; no implementation
6    } // end interface IPayable
```

Fig. 11.11 | IPayable interface declaration.

11.7.3 Creating Class Invoice

We now create class Invoice (Fig. 11.12) to represent a simple invoice that contains billing information for one kind of part. The class declares private instance variables partNumber, partDescription, quantity and pricePerItem (lines 5–8) that indicate the part number, the description of the part, the quantity of the part ordered and the price per item. Class Invoice also contains a constructor (lines 11–18), properties (lines 21–70) that manipulate the class's instance variables and a ToString method (lines 73–79) that returns a string representation of an Invoice object. Note that the set accessors of properties Quantity (lines 53–56) and PricePerItem (lines 66–69) ensure that quantity and pricePerItem are assigned only non-negative values.

Line 3 of Fig. 11.12 indicates that class Invoice implements interface IPayable. Like all classes, class Invoice also implicitly extends object. C# does not allow derived classes to inherit from more than one base class, but it does allow a class to inherit from a base class and implement any number of interfaces. All objects of a class that implement multiple interfaces have the *is-a* relationship with each implemented interface type. To implement more than one interface, use a comma-separated list of interface names after the colon (:) in the class declaration, as in:

> **public class** *ClassName* : *BaseClassName*, *FirstInterface*, *SecondInterface*, ...

When a class inherits from a base class and implements one or more interfaces, the class declaration must list the base class name before any interface names.

Class Invoice implements the one method in interface IPayable—method GetPaymentAmount is declared in lines 82–85. The method calculates the amount required to pay the invoice. The method multiplies the values of quantity and pricePerItem (obtained through the appropriate properties) and returns the result (line 84). This method satisfies the implementation requirement for the method in interface IPayable— we have fulfilled the interface contract with the compiler.

```csharp
1   // Fig. 11.12: Invoice.cs
2   // Invoice class implements IPayable.
3   public class Invoice : IPayable
4   {
5       private string partNumber;
6       private string partDescription;
7       private int quantity;
8       private decimal pricePerItem;
9
10      // four-parameter constructor
11      public Invoice( string part, string description, int count,
12          decimal price )
13      {
14          PartNumber = part;
15          PartDescription = description;
16          Quantity = count; // validate quantity via property
17          PricePerItem = price; // validate price per item via property
18      } // end four-parameter Invoice constructor
19
20      // property that gets and sets the part number on the invoice
21      public string PartNumber
22      {
23          get
24          {
25              return partNumber;
26          } // end get
27          set
28          {
29              partNumber = value; // should validate
30          } // end set
31      } // end property PartNumber
32
33      // property that gets and sets the part description on the invoice
34      public string PartDescription
35      {
36          get
37          {
38              return partDescription;
39          } // end get
40          set
41          {
42              partDescription = value; // should validate
43          } // end set
44      } // end property PartDescription
45
```

Fig. 11.12 | Invoice class implements IPayable. (Part 1 of 2.)

```
46      // property that gets and sets the quantity on the invoice
47      public int Quantity
48      {
49         get
50         {
51            return quantity;
52         } // end get
53         set
54         {
55            quantity = ( value < 0 ) ? 0 : value; // validate quantity
56         } // end set
57      } // end property Quantity
58
59      // property that gets and sets the price per item
60      public decimal PricePerItem
61      {
62         get
63         {
64            return pricePerItem;
65         } // end get
66         set
67         {
68            pricePerItem = ( value < 0 ) ? 0 : value; // validate price
69         } // end set
70      } // end property PricePerItem
71
72      // return string representation of Invoice object
73      public override string ToString()
74      {
75         return string.Format(
76            "{0}: \n{1}: {2} ({3}) \n{4}: {5} \n{6}: {7:C}",
77            "invoice", "part number", PartNumber, PartDescription,
78            "quantity", Quantity, "price per item", PricePerItem );
79      } // end method ToString
80
81      // method required to carry out contract with interface IPayable
82      public decimal GetPaymentAmount()
83      {
84         return Quantity * PricePerItem; // calculate total cost
85      } // end method GetPaymentAmount
86   } // end class Invoice
```

Fig. 11.12 | Invoice class implements IPayable. (Part 2 of 2.)

11.7.4 Modifying Class Employee to Implement Interface IPayable

We now modify class Employee to implement interface IPayable. Figure 11.13 contains the modified Employee class. This class declaration is identical to that of Fig. 11.4 with two exceptions. First, line 3 of Fig. 11.13 indicates that class Employee now implements interface IPayable. Second, since Employee now implements interface IPayable, we must rename Earnings to GetPaymentAmount throughout the Employee hierarchy. As with method Earnings in the version of class Employee in Fig. 11.4, however, it does not make sense to implement method GetPaymentAmount in class Employee, because we cannot calculate the earnings payment owed to a general Employee—first, we must know the specific type of Employee. In Fig. 11.4, we declared method Earnings as abstract for this reason, and as a result, class Employee had to be declared abstract. This forced each Employee derived class to override Earnings with a concrete implementation.

In Fig. 11.13, we handle this situation the same way. Recall that when a class implements an interface, the class makes a contract with the compiler stating that the class either will implement each of the methods in the interface or will declare them abstract. If the latter option is chosen, we must also declare the class abstract. As we discussed in

```
1   // Fig. 11.13: Employee.cs
2   // Employee abstract base class.
3   public abstract class Employee : IPayable
4   {
5      private string firstName;
6      private string lastName;
7      private string socialSecurityNumber;
8
9      // three-parameter constructor
10     public Employee( string first, string last, string ssn )
11     {
12        firstName = first;
13        lastName = last;
14        socialSecurityNumber = ssn;
15     } // end three-parameter Employee constructor
16
17     // read-only property that gets employee's first name
18     public string FirstName
19     {
20        get
21        {
22           return firstName;
23        } // end get
24     } // end property FirstName
25
26     // read-only property that gets employee's last name
27     public string LastName
28     {
29        get
30        {
31           return lastName;
32        } // end get
33     } // end property LastName
34
35     // read-only property that gets employee's social security number
36     public string SocialSecurityNumber
37     {
38        get
39        {
40           return socialSecurityNumber;
41        } // end get
42     } // end property SocialSecurityNumber
```

Fig. 11.13 | Employee abstract base class. (Part 1 of 2.)

```
43
44      // return string representation of Employee object
45      public override string ToString()
46      {
47         return string.Format( "{0} {1}\nsocial security number: {2}",
48            FirstName, LastName, SocialSecurityNumber );
49      } // end method ToString
50
51      // Note: We do not implement IPayable method GetPaymentAmount here so
52      // this class must be declared abstract to avoid a compilation error.
53      public abstract decimal GetPaymentAmount();
54   } // end abstract class Employee
```

Fig. 11.13 | Employee abstract base class. (Part 2 of 2.)

Section 11.4, any concrete derived class of the abstract class must implement the abstract methods of the base class. If the derived class does not do so, it too must be declared abstract. As indicated by the comments in lines 51–52, class Employee of Fig. 11.13 does not implement method GetPaymentAmount, so the class is declared abstract.

11.7.5 Modifying Class SalariedEmployee for Use in the IPayable Hierarchy

Figure 11.14 contains a modified version of class SalariedEmployee that extends Employee and implements method GetPaymentAmount. This version of SalariedEmployee is identical

```
 1   // Fig. 11.14: SalariedEmployee.cs
 2   // SalariedEmployee class that extends Employee.
 3   public class SalariedEmployee : Employee
 4   {
 5      private decimal weeklySalary;
 6
 7      // four-parameter constructor
 8      public SalariedEmployee( string first, string last, string ssn,
 9         decimal salary ) : base( first, last, ssn )
10      {
11         WeeklySalary = salary; // validate salary via property
12      } // end four-parameter SalariedEmployee constructor
13
14      // property that gets and sets salaried employee's salary
15      public decimal WeeklySalary
16      {
17         get
18         {
19            return weeklySalary;
20         } // end get
21         set
22         {
23            weeklySalary = value < 0 ? 0 : value; // validation
24         } // end set
25      } // end property WeeklySalary
```

Fig. 11.14 | SalariedEmployee class that extends Employee. (Part 1 of 2.)

```
26
27      // calculate earnings; implement interface IPayable method
28      // that was abstract in base class Employee
29      public override decimal GetPaymentAmount()
30      {
31         return WeeklySalary;
32      } // end method GetPaymentAmount
33
34      // return string representation of SalariedEmployee object
35      public override string ToString()
36      {
37         return string.Format( "salaried employee: {0}\n{1}: {2:C}",
38            base.ToString(), "weekly salary", WeeklySalary );
39      } // end method ToString
40   } // end class SalariedEmployee
```

Fig. 11.14 | SalariedEmployee class that extends Employee. (Part 2 of 2.)

to that of Fig. 11.5 with the exception that the version here implements method GetPaymentAmount (lines 29–32) instead of method Earnings. The two methods contain the same functionality but have different names. Recall that the IPayable version of the method has a more general name to be applicable to possibly disparate classes. The remaining Employee derived classes (e.g., HourlyEmployee, CommissionEmployee and BasePlusCommissionEmployee) also must be modified to contain method GetPaymentAmount in place of Earnings to reflect the fact that Employee now implements IPayable. We leave these modifications as an exercise and use only SalariedEmployee in our test application in this section.

When a class implements an interface, the same *is-a* relationship provided by inheritance applies. For example, class Employee implements IPayable, so we can say that an Employee *is an* IPayable, as are any classes that extend Employee. SalariedEmployee objects, for instance, are IPayable objects. As with inheritance relationships, an object of a class that implements an interface may be thought of as an object of the interface type. Objects of any classes derived from the class that implements the interface can also be thought of as objects of the interface type. Thus, just as we can assign the reference of a SalariedEmployee object to a base class Employee variable, we can assign the reference of a SalariedEmployee object to an interface IPayable variable. Invoice implements IPayable, so an Invoice object also *is an* IPayable object, and we can assign the reference of an Invoice object to an IPayable variable.

Software Engineering Observation 11.6

Inheritance and interfaces are similar in their implementation of the is-a *relationship. An object of a class that implements an interface may be thought of as an object of that interface type. An object of any derived classes of a class that implements an interface also can be thought of as an object of the interface type.*

Software Engineering Observation 11.7

The is-a *relationship that exists between base classes and derived classes, and between interfaces and the classes that implement them, holds when passing an object to a method. When a method parameter receives a variable of a base class or interface type, the method polymorphically processes the object received as an argument.*

11.7.6 Using Interface IPayable to Process Invoices and Employees Polymorphically

PayableInterfaceTest (Fig. 11.15) illustrates that interface IPayable can be used to process a set of Invoices and Employees polymorphically in a single application. Line 10 declares payableObjects and assigns it an array of four IPayable variables. Lines 13–14 assign the references of Invoice objects to the first two elements of payableObjects. Lines 15–18 assign the references of SalariedEmployee objects to the remaining two elements of payableObjects. These assignments are allowed because an Invoice *is an* IPayable, a SalariedEmployee *is an* Employee and an Employee *is an* IPayable. Lines 24–29 use a foreach statement to process each IPayable object in payableObjects polymorphically, printing the object as a string, along with the payment due. Note that line 27 implicitly invokes method ToString off an IPayable interface reference, even though ToString is not declared in interface IPayable—all references (including those of interface types) refer to objects that extend object and therefore have a ToString method. Line 28 invokes IPayable method GetPaymentAmount to obtain the payment amount for each object in payableObjects, regardless of the actual type of the object. The output reveals that the method calls in lines 27–28 invoke the appropriate class's implementation of methods ToString and GetPaymentAmount. For instance, when currentEmployee refers to an Invoice during the first iteration of the foreach loop, class Invoice's ToString and GetPaymentAmount methods execute.

> **Software Engineering Observation 11.8**
>
> *All methods of class object can be called by using a reference of an interface type—the reference refers to an object, and all objects inherit the methods of class object.*

```
1   // Fig. 11.15: PayableInterfaceTest.cs
2   // Tests interface IPayable with disparate classes.
3   using System;
4
5   public class PayableInterfaceTest
6   {
7      public static void Main( string[] args )
8      {
9         // create four-element IPayable array
10        IPayable[] payableObjects = new IPayable[ 4 ];
11
12        // populate array with objects that implement IPayable
13        payableObjects[ 0 ] = new Invoice( "01234", "seat", 2, 375.00M );
14        payableObjects[ 1 ] = new Invoice( "56789", "tire", 4, 79.95M );
15        payableObjects[ 2 ] = new SalariedEmployee( "John", "Smith",
16           "111-11-1111", 800.00M );
17        payableObjects[ 3 ] = new SalariedEmployee( "Lisa", "Barnes",
18           "888-88-8888", 1200.00M );
19
20        Console.WriteLine(
21           "Invoices and Employees processed polymorphically:\n" );
22
```

Fig. 11.15 | Tests interface IPayable with disparate classes. (Part 1 of 2.)

```
23          // generically process each element in array payableObjects
24          foreach ( IPayable currentPayable in payableObjects )
25          {
26             // output currentPayable and its appropriate payment amount
27             Console.WriteLine( "{0} \n{1}: {2:C}\n", currentPayable,
28                "payment due", currentPayable.GetPaymentAmount() );
29          } // end foreach
30      } // end Main
31  } // end class PayableInterfaceTest
```

```
Invoices and Employees processed polymorphically:

invoice:
part number: 01234 (seat)
quantity: 2
price per item: $375.00
payment due: $750.00

invoice:
part number: 56789 (tire)
quantity: 4
price per item: $79.95
payment due: $319.80

salaried employee: John Smith
social security number: 111-11-1111
weekly salary: $800.00
payment due: $800.00

salaried employee: Lisa Barnes
social security number: 888-88-8888
weekly salary: $1,200.00
payment due: $1,200.00
```

Fig. 11.15 | Tests interface IPayable with disparate classes. (Part 2 of 2.)

11.7.7 Common Interfaces of the .NET Framework Class Library

In this section, we overview several common interfaces in the .NET Framework Class Library. These interfaces are implemented and used in the same manner as those you create (e.g., interface IPayable in Section 11.7.2). The FCL's interfaces enable you to extend many important aspects of C# with your own classes. Figure 11.16 overviews several commonly used FCL interfaces.

11.8 Operator Overloading

Manipulations of class objects are accomplished by sending messages (in the form of method calls) to the objects. This method-call notation is cumbersome for certain kinds of classes, especially mathematical classes. For these classes, it would be convenient to use C#'s rich set of built-in operators to specify object manipulations. In this section, we show how to enable these operators to work with class objects—via a process called *operator overloading*.

Interface	Description
IComparable	As you learned in Chapter 3, C# contains several comparison operators (e.g., <, <=, >, >=, ==, !=) that allow you to compare simple-type values. In Section 11.8 you will see that these operators can be defined to compare two objects. Interface IComparable can also be used to allow objects of a class that implements the interface to be compared to one another. The interface contains one method, CompareTo, that compares the object that calls the method to the object passed as an argument to the method. Classes must implement CompareTo to return a value indicating whether the object on which it is invoked is less than (negative integer return value), equal to (0 return value) or greater than (positive integer return value) the object passed as an argument, using any criteria specified by the programmer. For example, if class Employee implements IComparable, its CompareTo method could compare Employee objects by their earnings amounts. Interface IComparable is commonly used for ordering objects in a collection such as an array. We use IComparable in Chapter 26, Generics, and Chapter 27, Collections.
IComponent	Implemented by any class that represents a component, including Graphical User Interface (GUI) controls (such as buttons or labels). Interface IComponent defines the behaviors that components must implement. We discuss IComponent and many GUI controls that implement this interface in Chapter 13, Graphical User Interface Concepts: Part 1, and Chapter 14, Graphical User Interface Concepts: Part 2.
IDisposable	Implemented by classes that must provide an explicit mechanism for releasing resources. Some resources can be used by only one program at a time. In addition, some resources, such as files on disk, are unmanaged resources that, unlike memory, cannot be released by the garbage collector. Classes that implement interface IDisposable provide a Dispose method that can be called to explicitly release resources. We discuss IDisposable briefly in Chapter 12, Exception Handling. You can learn more about this interface at msdn2.microsoft.com/en-us/library/aax125c9. The MSDN article *Implementing a Dispose Method* at msdn2.microsoft.com/en-us/library/fs2xkftw discusses the proper implementation of this interface in your classes.
IEnumerator	Used for iterating through the elements of a collection (such as an array) one element at a time. Interface IEnumerator contains method MoveNext to move to the next element in a collection, method Reset to move to the position before the first element and property Current to return the object at the current location. We use IEnumerator in Chapter 27, Collections.

Fig. 11.16 | Common interfaces of the .NET Framework Class Library.

Software Engineering Observation 11.9

Use operator overloading when it makes an application clearer than accomplishing the same operations with explicit method calls.

C# enables you to overload most operators to make them sensitive to the context in which they are used. Some operators are overloaded frequently, especially the various arithmetic operators, such as + and -. The job performed by overloaded operators also can be performed by explicit method calls, but operator notation often is more natural. Figures 11.17 and 11.18 provide an example of using operator overloading with a ComplexNumber class.

Class ComplexNumber (Fig. 11.17) overloads the plus (+), minus (-) and multiplication (*) operators to enable programs to add, subtract and multiply instances of class ComplexNumber using common mathematical notation. Lines 8–9 declare instance variables for the real and imaginary parts of the complex number.

```csharp
1   // Fig. 11.17: ComplexNumber.cs
2   // Class that overloads operators for adding, subtracting
3   // and multiplying complex numbers.
4   using System;
5
6   public class ComplexNumber
7   {
8      private double real; // real component of the complex number
9      private double imaginary; // imaginary component of the complex number
10
11     // constructor
12     public ComplexNumber( double a, double b )
13     {
14        real = a;
15        imaginary = b;
16     } // end constructor
17
18     // return string representation of ComplexNumber
19     public override string ToString()
20     {
21        return string.Format( "({0} {1} {2}i)",
22           Real, ( Imaginary < 0 ? "-" : "+" ), Math.Abs( Imaginary ) );
23     } // end method ToString
24
25     // read-only property that gets the real component
26     public double Real
27     {
28        get
29        {
30           return real;
31        } // end get
32     } // end property Real
33
```

Fig. 11.17 | Class that overloads operators for adding, subtracting and multiplying complex numbers. (Part 1 of 2.)

```
34      // read-only property that gets the imaginary component
35      public double Imaginary
36      {
37         get
38         {
39            return imaginary;
40         } // end get
41      } // end property Imaginary
42
43      // overload the addition operator
44      public static ComplexNumber operator+(
45         ComplexNumber x, ComplexNumber y )
46      {
47         return new ComplexNumber( x.Real + y.Real,
48            x.Imaginary + y.Imaginary );
49      } // end operator +
50
51      // overload the subtraction operator
52      public static ComplexNumber operator-(
53         ComplexNumber x, ComplexNumber y )
54      {
55         return new ComplexNumber( x.Real - y.Real,
56            x.Imaginary - y.Imaginary );
57      } // end operator -
58
59      // overload the multiplication operator
60      public static ComplexNumber operator*(
61         ComplexNumber x, ComplexNumber y )
62      {
63         return new ComplexNumber(
64            x.Real * y.Real - x.Imaginary * y.Imaginary,
65            x.Real * y.Imaginary + y.Real * x.Imaginary );
66      } // end operator *
67   } // end class ComplexNumber
```

Fig. 11.17 | Class that overloads operators for adding, subtracting and multiplying complex numbers. (Part 2 of 2.)

Lines 44–49 overload the plus operator (+) to perform addition of ComplexNumbers. Keyword *operator*, followed by an operator symbol, indicates that a method overloads the specified operator. Methods that overload binary operators must take two arguments. The first argument is the left operand, and the second argument is the right operand. Class ComplexNumber's overloaded plus operator takes two ComplexNumber references as arguments and returns a ComplexNumber that represents the sum of the arguments. Note that this method is marked public and static, which is required for overloaded operators. The body of the method (lines 47–48) performs the addition and returns the result as a new Complex-Number. Notice that we do not modify the contents of either of the original operands passed as arguments x and y. This matches our intuitive sense of how this operator should behave—adding two numbers does not modify either of the original numbers. Lines 52–66 provide similar overloaded operators for subtracting and multiplying ComplexNumbers.

Software Engineering Observation 11.10

Overload operators to perform the same function or similar functions on class objects as the operators perform on objects of simple types. Avoid non-intuitive use of operators.

Software Engineering Observation 11.11

At least one argument of an overloaded operator method must be a reference to an object of the class in which the operator is overloaded. This prevents programmers from changing how operators work on simple types.

Class `ComplexTest` (Fig. 11.18) demonstrates the overloaded operators for adding, subtracting and multiplying `ComplexNumbers`. Lines 14–27 prompt the user to enter two complex numbers, then use this input to create two `ComplexNumbers` and assign them to variables x and y.

```csharp
1   // Fig 11.18: OperatorOverloading.cs
2   // Overloading operators for complex numbers.
3   using System;
4
5   public class ComplexTest
6   {
7      public static void Main( string[] args )
8      {
9         // declare two variables to store complex numbers
10        // to be entered by user
11        ComplexNumber x, y;
12
13        // prompt the user to enter the first complex number
14        Console.Write( "Enter the real part of complex number x: " );
15        double realPart = Convert.ToDouble( Console.ReadLine() );
16        Console.Write(
17           "Enter the imaginary part of complex number x: " );
18        double imaginaryPart = Convert.ToDouble( Console.ReadLine() );
19        x = new ComplexNumber( realPart, imaginaryPart );
20
21        // prompt the user to enter the second complex number
22        Console.Write( "\nEnter the real part of complex number y: " );
23        realPart = Convert.ToDouble( Console.ReadLine() );
24        Console.Write(
25           "Enter the imaginary part of complex number y: " );
26        imaginaryPart = Convert.ToDouble( Console.ReadLine() );
27        y = new ComplexNumber( realPart, imaginaryPart );
28
29        // display the results of calculations with x and y
30        Console.WriteLine();
31        Console.WriteLine( "{0} + {1} = {2}", x, y, x + y );
32        Console.WriteLine( "{0} - {1} = {2}", x, y, x - y );
33        Console.WriteLine( "{0} * {1} = {2}", x, y, x * y );
34     } // end method Main
35  } // end class ComplexTest
```

Fig. 11.18 | Overloading operators for complex numbers. (Part 1 of 2.)

```
Enter the real part of complex number x: 2
Enter the imaginary part of complex number x: 4

Enter the real part of complex number y: 4
Enter the imaginary part of complex number y: -2

(2 + 4i) + (4 - 2i) = (6 + 2i)
(2 + 4i) - (4 - 2i) = (-2 + 6i)
(2 + 4i) * (4 - 2i) = (16 + 12i)
```

Fig. 11.18 | Overloading operators for complex numbers. (Part 2 of 2.)

Lines 31–33 add, subtract and multiply x and y with the overloaded operators, then output the results. In line 31, we perform the addition by using the plus operator with ComplexNumber operands x and y. Without operator overloading, the expression x + y would not make sense—the compiler would not know how two objects should be added. This expression makes sense here because we've defined the plus operator for two ComplexNumbers in lines 44–49 of Fig. 11.17. When the two ComplexNumbers are "added" in line 31 of Fig. 11.18, this invokes the operator+ declaration, passing the left operand as the first argument and the right operand as the second argument. When we use the subtraction and multiplication operators in lines 32–33, their respective overloaded operator declarations are invoked similarly.

Notice that the result of each calculation is a reference to a new ComplexNumber object. When this new object is passed to the Console class's WriteLine method, its ToString method (lines 19–23 of Fig. 11.17) is implicitly invoked. We do not need to assign an object to a reference-type variable to invoke its ToString method. Line 31 of Fig. 11.18 could be rewritten to explicitly invoke the ToString method of the object created by the overloaded plus operator, as in:

```
Console.WriteLine( "{0} + {1} = {2}", x, y, ( x + y ).ToString() );
```

11.9 (Optional) Software Engineering Case Study: Incorporating Inheritance and Polymorphism into the ATM System

We now revisit our ATM system design to see how it might benefit from inheritance and polymorphism. To apply inheritance, we first look for commonality among classes in the system. We create an inheritance hierarchy to model similar classes in an elegant and efficient manner that enables us to process objects of these classes polymorphically. We then modify our class diagram to incorporate the new inheritance relationships. Finally, we demonstrate how the inheritance aspects of our updated design are translated into C# code.

In Section 4.11, we encountered the problem of representing a financial transaction in the system. Rather than create one class to represent all transaction types, we created three distinct transaction classes—BalanceInquiry, Withdrawal and Deposit—to represent the transactions that the ATM system can perform. The class diagram of Fig. 11.19 shows the attributes and operations of these classes. Note that they have one private attribute (accountNumber) and one public operation (Execute) in common. Each class requires attribute accountNumber to specify the account to which the transaction applies.

one object of each of the four `Employee` derived classes. If the object currently being processed is a `BasePlusCommissionEmployee`, the application should increase the `BasePlusCommissionEmployee`'s base salary by 10%. Finally, the application should output the payment amount for each object. Complete the following steps to create the new application:

a) Modify classes `HourlyEmployee` (Fig. 11.6) and `CommissionEmployee` (Fig. 11.7) to place them in the `IPayable` hierarchy as derived classes of the version of `Employee` (Fig. 11.13) that implements `IPayable`. [*Hint:* Change the name of method `Earnings` to `GetPaymentAmount` in each derived class.]

b) Modify class `BasePlusCommissionEmployee` (Fig. 11.8) such that it extends the version of class `CommissionEmployee` created in *Part a*.

c) Modify `PayableInterfaceTest` (Fig. 11.15) to polymorphically process two `Invoices`, one `SalariedEmployee`, one `HourlyEmployee`, one `CommissionEmployee` and one `BasePlusCommissionEmployee`. First, output a string representation of each `IPayable` object. Next, if an object is a `BasePlusCommissionEmployee`, increase its base salary by 10%. Finally, output the payment amount for each `IPayable` object.

11.13 (*Package Inheritance Hierarchy*) Use the `Package` inheritance hierarchy created in Exercise 10.9 to create an application that displays the address information and calculates the shipping costs for several `Packages`. The application should contain an array of `Package` objects of classes `TwoDayPackage` and `OvernightPackage`. Loop through the array to process the `Packages` polymorphically. For each `Package`, use properties to obtain the address information of the sender and the recipient, then print the two addresses as they would appear on mailing labels. Also, call each `Package`'s `CalculateCost` method and print the result. Keep track of the total shipping cost for all `Packages` in the array, and display this total when the loop terminates.

11.14 (*Polymorphic Banking Program Using `Account` Hierarchy*) Develop a polymorphic banking application using the `Account` hierarchy created in Exercise 10.10. Create an array of `Account` references to `SavingsAccount` and `CheckingAccount` objects. For each `Account` in the array, allow the user to specify an amount of money to withdraw from the `Account` using method `Debit` and an amount of money to deposit into the `Account` using method `Credit`. As you process each `Account`, determine its type. If an `Account` is a `SavingsAccount`, calculate the amount of interest owed to the `Account` using method `CalculateInterest`, then add the interest to the account balance using method `Credit`. After processing an `Account`, print the updated account balance obtained by using base class property `Balance`.

12

Exception Handling

> *It is common sense to take a method and try it. If it fails, admit it frankly and try another. But above all, try something.*
> —Franklin Delano Roosevelt

> *O! throw away the worser part of it, And live the purer with the other half.*
> —William Shakespeare

> *If they're running and they don't look where they're going I have to come out from somewhere and catch them.*
> —J. D. Salinger

> *And oftentimes excusing of a fault Doth make the fault the worse by the excuse.*
> —William Shakespeare

> *O infinite virtue! com'st thou smiling from the world's great snare uncaught?*
> —William Shakespeare

OBJECTIVES

In this chapter you will learn:

- What exceptions are and how they are handled.
- When to use exception handling.
- To use `try` blocks to delimit code in which exceptions might occur.
- To `throw` exceptions to indicate a problem.
- To use `catch` blocks to specify exception handlers.
- To use the `finally` block to release resources.
- The .NET exception class hierarchy.
- `Exception` properties.
- To create user-defined exceptions.

12.1 Introduction

In this chapter, we introduce *exception handling*. An *exception* is an indication of a problem that occurs during a program's execution. The name "exception" comes from the fact that, although the problem can occur, it occurs infrequently. If the "rule" is that a statement normally executes correctly, then the occurrence of a problem represents the "exception to the rule." Exception handling enables programmers to create applications that can resolve (or handle) exceptions. In many cases, handling an exception allows a program to continue executing as if no problems were encountered. However, more severe problems may prevent a program from continuing normal execution, instead requiring the program to notify the user of the problem, then terminate in a controlled manner. The features presented in this chapter enable programmers to write clear, ***robust*** and more ***fault-tolerant programs*** (i.e., programs that are able to deal with problems that may arise and continue executing). The style and details of C# exception handling are based in part on the work of Andrew Koenig and Bjarne Stroustrup. "Best practices" for exception handling in Visual C# 2005 are specified in the Visual Studio documentation.[1]

 Error-Prevention Tip 12.1

Exception handling helps improve a program's fault tolerance.

This chapter begins with an overview of exception-handling concepts and demonstrations of basic exception-handling techniques. The chapter also overviews .NET's excep-

---

1. "Best Practices for Handling Exceptions [C#]," *.NET Framework Developer's Guide*, Visual Studio .NET Online Help. Available at `msdn2.microsoft.com/library/seyhszts(en-us,vs.80).aspx`.

tion-handling class hierarchy. Programs typically request and release resources (such as files on disk) during program execution. Often, the supply of these resources is limited, or the resources can be used by only one program at a time. We demonstrate a part of the exception-handling mechanism that enables a program to use a resource, then guarantee that the resource will be released for use by other programs, even if an exception occurs. The chapter demonstrates several properties of class System.Exception (the base class of all exception classes) and discusses how you can create and use your own exception classes.

12.2 Exception Handling Overview

Programs frequently test conditions to determine how program execution should proceed. Consider the following pseudocode:

> *Perform a task*
>
> *If the preceding task did not execute correctly*
> *Perform error processing*
>
> *Perform next task*
>
> *If the preceding task did not execute correctly*
> *Perform error processing*
>
> …

In this pseudocode, we begin by performing a task; then we test whether that task executed correctly. If not, we perform error processing. Otherwise, we continue with the next task. Although this form of error handling works, intermixing program logic with error-handling logic can make programs difficult to read, modify, maintain and debug—especially in large applications.

Exception handling enables programmers to remove error-handling code from the "main line" of the program's execution, improving program clarity and enhancing modifiability. Programmers can decide to handle any exceptions they choose—all exceptions, all exceptions of a certain type or all exceptions of a group of related types (i.e., exception types that are related through an inheritance hierarchy). Such flexibility reduces the likelihood that errors will be overlooked, thus making programs more robust.

With programming languages that do not support exception handling, programmers often delay writing *error-processing code* and sometimes forget to include it. This results in less robust software products. C# enables programmers to deal with exception handling easily from the beginning of a project.

12.3 Example: Divide by Zero Without Exception Handling

First we demonstrate what happens when errors arise in a console application that does not use exception handling. Figure 12.1 inputs two integers from the user, then divides the first integer by the second using integer division to obtain an int result. In this example, we will see that an exception is *thrown* (i.e., an exception occurs) when a method detects a problem and is unable to handle it.

```
 1    // Fig. 12.1: DivideByZeroNoExceptionHandling.cs
 2    // An application that attempts to divide by zero.
 3    using System;
 4
 5    class DivideByZeroNoExceptionHandling
 6    {
 7       static void Main()
 8       {
 9          // get numerator and denominator
10          Console.Write( "Please enter an integer numerator: " );
11          int numerator = Convert.ToInt32( Console.ReadLine() );
12          Console.Write( "Please enter an integer denominator: " );
13          int denominator = Convert.ToInt32( Console.ReadLine() );
14
15          // divide the two integers, then display the result
16          int result = numerator / denominator;
17          Console.WriteLine( "\nResult: {0:D} / {1:D} = {2:D}",
18             numerator, denominator, result );
19       } // end Main
20    } // end class DivideByZeroNoExceptionHandling
```

```
Please enter an integer numerator: 100
Please enter an integer denominator: 7

Result: 100 / 7 = 14
```

```
Please enter an integer numerator: 100
Please enter an integer denominator: 0

Unhandled Exception: System.DivideByZeroException:
   Attempted to divide by zero.
   at DivideByZeroNoExceptionHandling.Main()
      in C:\examples\ch12\Fig12_01\DivideByZeroNoExceptionHandling\
      DivideByZeroNoExceptionHandling.cs:line 16
```

```
Please enter an integer numerator: 100
Please enter an integer denominator: hello

Unhandled Exception: System.FormatException:
   Input string was not in a correct format.
   at System.Number.StringToNumber(String str, NumberStyles options,
      NumberBuffer& number, NumberFormatInfo info, Boolean parseDecimal)
   at System.Number.ParseInt32(String s, NumberStyles style,
      NumberFormatInfo info)
   at System.Convert.ToInt32(String value)
   at DivideByZeroNoExceptionHandling.Main()
      in C:\examples\ch12\Fig12_01\DivideByZeroNoExceptionHandling\
      DivideByZeroNoExceptionHandling.cs:line 13
```

Fig. 12.1 | Integer division without exception handling.

Running the Application

In most of the examples we have created so far, the application appears to run the same with or without debugging. As we discuss shortly, the example in Fig. 12.1 might cause errors, depending on the user's input. If you run this application using the **Debug > Start Debugging** menu option, the program pauses at the line where an exception occurs and displays the Exception Assistant, allowing you to analyze the current state of the program and debug it. We discuss the Exception Assistant in Section 12.4.3. We discuss debugging in detail in Appendix C.

In this example, we do not wish to debug the application; we simply want to see what happens when errors arise. For this reason, we execute this application from a Command Prompt window. Select **Start > All Programs > Accessories > Command Prompt** to open a Command Prompt window, then use the `cd` command to change to the application's `Debug` directory. For example, if this application resides in the directory `C:\examples\ch12\Fig12_01\DivideByZeroNoExceptionHandling` on your system, you would type

```
cd /d C:\examples\ch12\Fig12_01\DivideByZeroNoExceptionHandling
\bin\Debug
```

in the Command Prompt, then press *Enter* to change to the application's `Debug` directory. To execute the application, type

```
DivideByZeroNoExceptionHandling.exe
```

in the Command Prompt, then press *Enter*. If an error arises during execution, a dialog is displayed indicating that the application has encountered a problem and needs to close. The dialog also asks whether you'd like to send information about this error to Microsoft. Since we are creating this error for demonstration purposes, you should click **Don't Send**. [*Note:* On some systems a **Just-In-Time Debugging** dialog is displayed instead. If this occurs, simply click the **No** button to dismiss the dialog.] At this point, an error message describing the problem is displayed in the Command Prompt. We formatted the error messages in Fig. 12.1 for readability. [*Note:* Selecting **Debug > Start Without Debugging** (or *<Ctrl> F5*) to run the application from Visual Studio executes the application's so-called release version. The error messages produced by this version of the application may differ from those shown in Fig. 12.1 due to optimizations that the compiler performs to create an application's release version.]

Analyzing the Results

The first sample execution in Fig. 12.1 shows a successful division. In the second sample execution, the user enters 0 as the denominator. Note that several lines of information are displayed in response to the invalid input. This information—known as a *stack trace*—includes the exception name (`System.DivideByZeroException`) in a descriptive message indicating the problem that occurred and the path of execution that led to the exception, method by method. This information helps you debug a program. The first line of the error message specifies that a `DivideByZeroException` has occurred. When *division by zero* in integer arithmetic occurs, the CLR throws a ***DivideByZeroException*** (namespace System). The text after the name of the exception, "`Attempted to divide by zero,`" indicates that this exception occurred as a result of an attempt to divide by zero. Division by zero is not allowed in integer arithmetic. [*Note:* Division by zero with floating-point values is allowed. Such a calculation results in the value infinity, which is represented by either constant *Double.PositiveInfinity* or constant *Double.NegativeInfinity*, depending on whether the numerator is positive or negative. These values are displayed as `Infinity` or `-Infinity`. If both the numerator and denominator are zero, the result of the calculation is the constant *Double.NaN* ("not a number"), which is returned when a calculation's result is undefined.]

Each "at" line in the stack trace indicates a line of code in the particular method that was executing when the exception occurred. The "at" line contains the namespace, class name and method name in which the exception occurred (`DivideByZeroNoException-Handling.Main`), the location and name of the file in which the code resides (`C:\examples\ch12\Fig12_01\DivideByZeroNoExceptionHandling\DivideByZeroNoException Handling.cs:line 16`) and the line of code where the exception occurred. In this case, the stack trace indicates that the `DivideByZeroException` occurred when the program was executing line 16 of method `Main`. The first "at" line in the stack trace indicates the exception's ***throw point***—the initial point at which the exception occurred (i.e., line 16 in `Main`). This information makes it easy for the programmer to see where the exception originated, and what method calls were made to get to that point in the program.

Now, let's look at a more detailed stack trace. In the third sample execution, the user enters the string `"hello"` as the denominator. This causes a `FormatException`, and another stack trace is displayed. Our earlier examples that read numeric values from the user assumed that the user would input an integer value. However, a user could erroneously input a noninteger value. A *FormatException* (namespace `System`) occurs, for example, when `Convert` method `ToInt32` receives a string that does not represent a valid integer. Starting from the last "at" line in the stack trace, we see that the exception was detected in line 13 of method `Main`. The stack trace also shows the other methods that led to the exception being thrown—`Convert.ToInt32`, `Number.ParseInt32` and `Number.StringToNumber`. To perform its task, `Convert.ToInt32` calls method `Number.ParseInt32`, which in turn calls `Number.StringToNumber`. The throw point occurs in `Number.StringToNumber`, as indicated by the first "at" line in the stack trace.

Note that in the sample executions in Fig. 12.1, the program also terminates when exceptions occur and stack traces are displayed. This does not always happen—sometimes a program may continue executing even though an exception has occurred and a stack trace has been printed. In such cases, the application may produce incorrect results. The next section demonstrates how to handle exceptions to enable the program to run to normal completion.

12.4 Example: Handling `DivideByZeroExceptions` and `FormatExceptions`

Let us consider a simple example of exception handling. The application in Fig. 12.2 uses exception handling to process any `DivideByZeroExceptions` and `FormatExceptions` that might arise. The application displays two `TextBoxes` in which the user can type integers. When the user presses **Click To Divide**, the program invokes event handler `DivideButton_Click` (lines 17–48), which obtains the user's input, converts the input values to type `int` and divides the first number (`numerator`) by the second number (`denominator`). Assuming that the user provides integers as input and does not specify 0 as the

```
1    // Fig. 12.2: DivideByZeroTest.cs
2    // Exception handlers for FormatException and DivideByZeroException.
3    using System;
4    using System.Windows.Forms;
5
6    namespace DivideByZeroTest
7    {
8       public partial class DivideByZeroTestForm : Form
9       {
10          public DivideByZeroTestForm()
11          {
12             InitializeComponent();
13          } // end constructor
14
15          // obtain 2 integers from the user
16          // and divide numerator by denominator
17          private void DivideButton_Click( object sender, EventArgs e )
18          {
19             OutputLabel.Text = ""; // clear Label OutputLabel
20
21             // retrieve user input and calculate quotient
22             try
23             {
24                // Convert.ToInt32 generates FormatException
25                // if argument is not an integer
26                int numerator = Convert.ToInt32( NumeratorTextBox.Text );
27                int denominator = Convert.ToInt32( DenominatorTextBox.Text );
28
29                // division generates DivideByZeroException
30                // if denominator is 0
31                int result = numerator / denominator;
32
33                // display result in OutputLabel
34                OutputLabel.Text = result.ToString();
35             } // end try
36             catch ( FormatException )
37             {
38                MessageBox.Show( "You must enter two integers.",
39                   "Invalid Number Format", MessageBoxButtons.OK,
40                   MessageBoxIcon.Error );
41             } // end catch
42             catch ( DivideByZeroException divideByZeroExceptionParameter )
43             {
44                MessageBox.Show( divideByZeroExceptionParameter.Message,
45                   "Attempted to Divide by Zero", MessageBoxButtons.OK,
46                   MessageBoxIcon.Error );
47             } // end catch
48          } // end method DivideButton_Click
49       } // end class DivideByZeroTestForm
50    } // end namespace DivideByZeroTest
```

Fig. 12.2 | Exception handlers for FormatException and DivideByZeroException. (Part 1 of 2.)

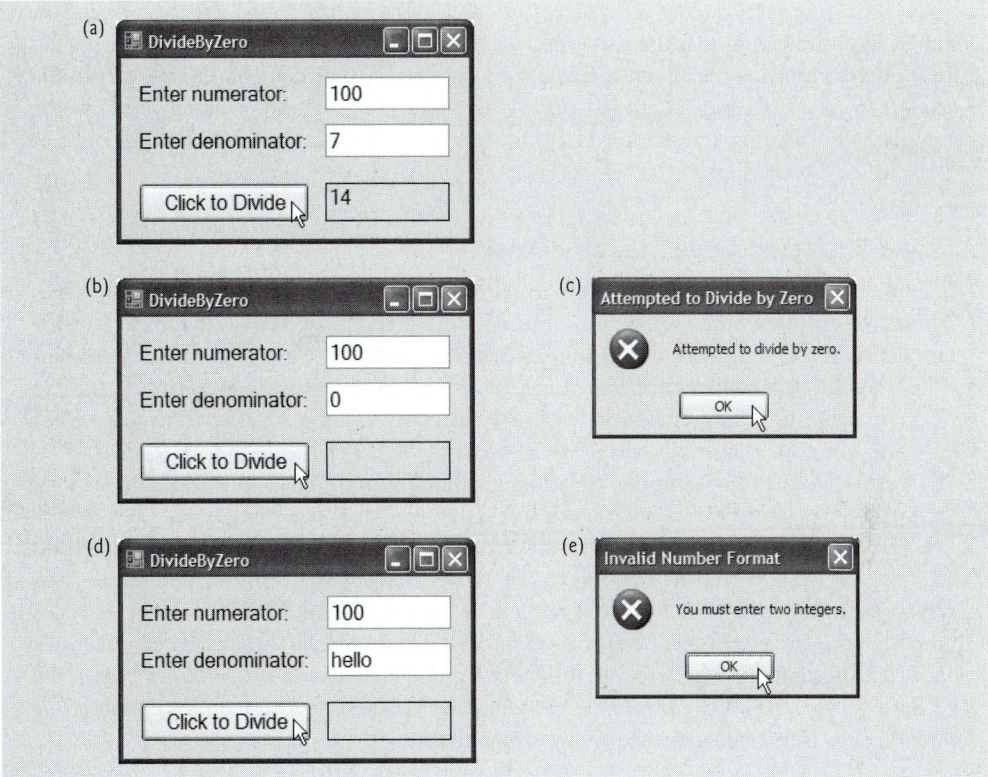

Fig. 12.2 | Exception handlers for `FormatException` and `DivideByZeroException`. (Part 2 of 2.)

denominator for the division, `DivideButton_Click` displays the division result in `Output-Label`. However, if the user inputs a noninteger value or supplies 0 as the denominator, an exception occurs. This program demonstrates how to *catch* and *handle* (i.e., deal with) such exceptions—in this case, displaying an error message and allowing the user to enter another set of values.

Before we discuss the details of the program, let's consider the sample output windows in Fig. 12.2. The window in Fig. 12.2(a) shows a successful calculation, in which the user enters the numerator 100 and the denominator 7. Note that the result (14) is an int, because integer division always yields an int result. The next two windows, Fig. 12.2(b) and Fig. 12.2(c), demonstrate the result of an attempt to divide by zero. In integer arithmetic, the CLR tests for division by zero and generates a `DivideByZeroException` if the denominator is zero. The program detects the exception and displays the error message dialog in Fig. 12.2(c) indicating the attempt to divide by zero. The last two output windows, Fig. 12.2(d) and Fig. 12.2(e), depict the result of inputting a non-int value—in this case, the user enters `"hello"` in the second `TextBox`, as shown in Fig. 12.2(d). When the user clicks **Click To Divide**, the program attempts to convert the input `strings` into int values using method `Convert.ToInt32` (lines 26–27). If an argument passed to `Convert.ToInt32` cannot be converted to an int value, the method throws a `FormatExcep-`

tion. The program catches the exception and displays the error message dialog in Fig. 12.2(e) indicating that the user must enter two ints. Notice that we did not include a parameter name for the catch at line 36. In the catch's block, we do not use any information from the FormatException object. Omitting the parameter name prevents the compiler from issuing a warning which indicates that we declared a variable, but did not use it in the catch block.

12.4.1 Enclosing Code in a try Block

Now we consider the user interactions and flow of control that yield the results shown in the sample output windows. The user inputs values into the TextBoxes that represent the numerator and denominator, then presses **Click To Divide**. At this point, the program invokes method DivideButton_Click. Line 19 assigns the empty string to OutputLabel to clear any prior result in preparation for a new calculation. Lines 22–35 define a *try block* enclosing the code that might throw exceptions, as well as the code that is skipped when an exception occurs. For example, the program should not display a new result in Output-Label (line 34) unless the calculation in line 31 completes successfully.

The two statements that read the ints from the TextBoxes (lines 26–27) call method Convert.ToInt32 to convert strings to int values. This method throws a FormatException if it cannot convert its string argument to an int. If lines 26–27 convert the values properly (i.e., no exceptions occur), then line 31 divides the numerator by the denominator and assigns the result to variable result. If denominator is 0, line 31 causes the CLR to throw a DivideByZeroException. If line 31 does not cause an exception to be thrown, then line 34 displays the result of the division.

12.4.2 Catching Exceptions

Exception-handling code appears in a *catch block*. In general, when an exception occurs in a try block, a corresponding catch block catches the exception and handles it. The try block in this example is followed by two catch blocks—one that handles a Format-Exception (lines 36–41) and one that handles a DivideByZeroException (lines 42–47). A catch block specifies an exception parameter representing the exception that the catch block can handle. The catch block can use the parameter's identifier (which is chosen by the programmer) to interact with a caught exception object. If there is no need to use the exception object in the catch block, the exception parameter's identifier can be omitted. The type of the catch's parameter is the type of the exception that the catch block handles. Optionally, programmers can include a catch block that does not specify an exception type or an identifier—such a catch block (known as a *general catch clause*) catches all exception types. At least one catch block and/or a *finally block* (discussed in Section 12.6) must immediately follow a try block.

In Fig. 12.2, the first catch block catches FormatExceptions (thrown by method Convert.ToInt32), and the second catch block catches DivideByZeroExceptions (thrown by the CLR). If an exception occurs, the program executes only the first matching catch block. Both exception handlers in this example display an error message dialog. After either catch block terminates, program control continues with the first statement after the last catch block (the end of the method, in this example). We will soon take a deeper look at how this flow of control works in exception handling.

12.4.3 Uncaught Exceptions

An *uncaught exception* is an exception for which there is no matching catch block. You saw the results of uncaught exceptions in the second and third outputs of Fig. 12.1. Recall that when exceptions occur in that example, the application terminates early (after displaying the exception's stack trace). The result of an uncaught exception depends on how you execute the program—Fig. 12.1 demonstrated the results of an uncaught exception when an application is executed in a Command Prompt. If you run the application from Visual Studio with debugging and the runtime environment detects an uncaught exception, the application pauses, and a window called the ***Exception Assistant*** appears indicating where the exception occurred, the type of the exception and links to helpful information on handling the exception. Figure 12.3 shows the Exception Assistant that is displayed if the user attempts to divide by zero in the application of Fig. 12.1.

12.4.4 Termination Model of Exception Handling

When a method called in a program or the CLR detects a problem, the method or the CLR throws an exception. Recall that the point in the program at which an exception occurs is called the throw point—this is an important location for debugging purposes (as we demonstrate in Section 12.7). If an exception occurs in a try block (such as a FormatException being thrown as a result of the code in line 27 in Fig. 12.2), the try block terminates immediately, and program control transfers to the first of the following catch blocks in which the exception parameter's type matches the type of the thrown exception. In Fig. 12.2, the first catch block catches FormatExceptions (which occur if input of an invalid type is entered); the second catch block catches DivideByZeroExceptions (which occur if an attempt is made to divide by zero). After the exception is handled, program control does not return to the throw point because the try block has expired (which also causes any of its local variables to go out of scope). Rather, control resumes after the last catch block. This is known as the ***termination model of exception handling***. [*Note:* Some languages use the ***resumption model of exception handling***, in which after an exception is handled, control resumes just after the throw point.]

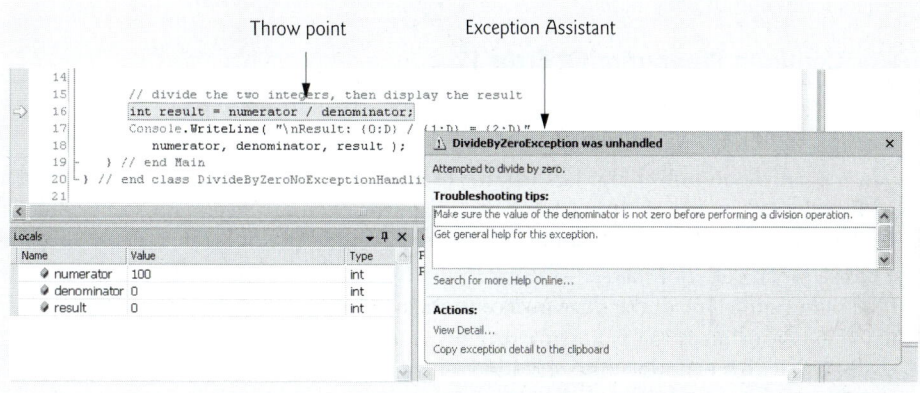

Fig. 12.3 | Exception Assistant.

Common Programming Error 12.1

Logic errors can occur if you assume that after an exception is handled, control will return to the first statement after the throw point.

If no exceptions occur in the try block, the program of Fig. 12.2 successfully completes the try block by ignoring the catch blocks in lines 36–41 and 42–47, and passing line 47. Then the program executes the first statement following the try and catch blocks. In this example, the program reaches the end of event handler DivideButton_Click (line 48), so the method terminates, and the program awaits the next user interaction.

The try block and its corresponding catch and finally blocks together form a ***try statement***. It is important not to confuse the terms "try block" and "try statement"—the term "try block" refers to the block of code following the keyword try (but before any catch or finally blocks), while the term "try statement" includes all the code from the opening try keyword to the end of the last catch or finally block. This includes the try block, as well as any associated catch blocks and finally block.

As with any other block of code, when a try block terminates, local variables defined in the block go out of scope. If a try block terminates due to an exception, the CLR searches for the first catch block that can process the type of exception that occurred. The CLR locates the matching catch by comparing the type of the thrown exception to each catch's parameter type. A match occurs if the types are identical or if the thrown exception's type is a derived class of the catch's parameter type. Once an exception is matched to a catch block, the code in that block executes and the other catch blocks in the try statement are ignored.

12.4.5 Flow of Control When Exceptions Occur

In the sample output of Fig. 12.2(b), the user inputs hello as the denominator. When line 27 executes, Convert.ToInt32 cannot convert this string to an int, so Convert.ToInt32 throws a FormatException object to indicate that the method was unable to convert the string to an int. When the exception occurs, the try block expires (terminates). Next, the CLR attempts to locate a matching catch block. A match occurs with the catch block in line 36, so the exception handler executes and the program ignores all other exception handlers following the try block.

Common Programming Error 12.2

Specifying a comma-separated list of parameters in a catch block is a syntax error. A catch block can have at most one parameter.

In the sample output of Fig. 12.2(d), the user inputs 0 as the denominator. When the division in line 31 executes, a DivideByZeroException occurs. Once again, the try block terminates, and the program attempts to locate a matching catch block. In this case, the first catch block does not match—the exception type in the catch-handler declaration is not the same as the type of the thrown exception, and FormatException is not a base class of DivideByZeroException. Therefore the program continues to search for a matching catch block, which it finds in line 42. Line 44 displays the value of property ***Message*** of class Exception, which contains the error message. Note that our program never "sets" this error message attribute. This is done by the CLR when it creates the exception object.

12.5 .NET Exception Hierarchy

In C#, the exception-handling mechanism allows only objects of class *Exception* (namespace System) and its derived classes to be thrown and caught. Note, however, that C# programs may interact with software components written in other .NET languages (such as C++) that do not restrict exception types. The general catch clause can be used to catch such exceptions.

This section overviews several of the .NET Framework's exception classes and focuses exclusively on exceptions that derived from class Exception. In addition, we discuss how to determine whether a particular method throws exceptions.

12.5.1 Classes ApplicationException and SystemException

Class *Exception* of namespace System is the base class of the .NET Framework exception class hierarchy. Two of the most important classes derived from Exception are *ApplicationException* and *SystemException*. ApplicationException is a base class that programmers can extend to create exception classes that are specific to their applications. We show how to create user-defined exception classes in Section 12.8. Programs can recover from most ApplicationExceptions and continue execution.

The CLR generates SystemExceptions, which can occur at any point during program execution. Many of these exceptions can be avoided if applications are coded properly. For example, if a program attempts to access an *out-of-range array index*, the CLR throws an exception of type *IndexOutOfRangeException* (a derived class of SystemException). Similarly, an exception occurs when a program uses an object reference to manipulate an object that does not yet exist (i.e., the reference has a value of null). Attempting to use a null reference causes a *NullReferenceException* (another derived class of SystemException). You saw earlier in this chapter that a DivideByZeroException occurs in integer division when a program attempts to divide by zero.

Other SystemException types thrown by the CLR include *OutOfMemoryException*, *StackOverflowException* and *ExecutionEngineException*. These are thrown when the something goes wrong that causes the CLR to become unstable. In some cases, such exceptions cannot even be caught. In general, it is best to simply log such exceptions then terminate your application.

A benefit of the exception class hierarchy is that a catch block can catch exceptions of a particular type or—because of the *is-a* relationship of inheritance—can use a base-class type to catch exceptions in a hierarchy of related exception types. For example, Section 12.4.2 discussed the catch block with no parameter, which catches exceptions of all types (including those that are not derived from Exception). A catch block that specifies a parameter of type Exception can catch all exceptions that derive from Exception, because Exception is the base class of all exception classes. The advantage of this approach is that the exception handler can access the caught exception's information via the parameter in the catch. We demonstrated accessing the information in an exception in line 44 of Fig. 12.2. We'll say more about accessing exception information in Section 12.7.

Using inheritance with exceptions enables an catch block to catch related exceptions using a concise notation. A set of exception handlers could catch each derived-class exception type individually, but catching the base-class exception type is more concise. However, this technique makes sense only if the handling behavior is the same for a base class and all derived classes. Otherwise, catch each derived-class exception individually.

Common Programming Error 12.3

It is a compilation error if a catch block that catches a base-class exception is placed before a catch block for any of that class's derived-class types. If this were allowed, the base-class catch block would catch all base-class and derived-class exceptions, so the derived-class exception handler would never execute.

12.5.2 Determining Which Exceptions a Method Throws

How do we determine that an exception might occur in a program? For methods contained in the .NET Framework classes, read the detailed descriptions of the methods in the online documentation. If a method throws an exception its description contains a section called **Exceptions** that specifies the types of exceptions the method throws and briefly describes possible causes for the exceptions. For example, search for "Convert.ToInt32 method" in the **Index** of the Visual Studio online documentation (use the **.NET Framework** filter). Select the document entitled **Convert.ToInt32 Method (System)**. In the document that describes the method, click the link **Convert.ToInt32(String)**. In the document that appears, the **Exceptions** section (near the bottom of the document) indicates that method Convert.ToInt32 throws two exception types—FormatException and OverflowException—and describes the reason why each might occur.

Software Engineering Observation 12.1

If a method throws exceptions, statements that invoke the method directly or indirectly should be placed in try blocks, and those exceptions should be caught and handled.

It is more difficult to determine when the CLR throws exceptions. Such information appears in the *C# Language Specification*. This document defines C#'s syntax and specifies cases in which exceptions are thrown. Figure 12.2 demonstrated that the CLR throws a DivideByZeroException in integer arithmetic when a program attempts to divide by zero. Section 7.7.2 of the language specification (14.7.2 in the ECMA version) discusses the division operator and when DivideByZeroExceptions occur.

12.6 finally Block

Programs frequently request and release resources dynamically (i.e., at execution time). For example, a program that reads a file from disk first makes a file-open request (as we'll see in Chapter 18, Files and Streams). If that request succeeds, the program reads the contents of the file. Operating systems typically prevent more than one program from manipulating a file at once. Therefore, when a program finishes processing a file, the program should close the file (i.e., release the resource) so other programs can use it. If the file is not closed, a *resource leak* occurs. In such a case, the file resource is not available to other programs, possibly because a program using the file has not closed it.

In programming languages such as C and C++, in which the programmer (not the language) is responsible for dynamic memory management, the most common type of resource leak is a *memory leak*. A memory leak occurs when a program allocates memory (as C# programmers do via keyword new), but does not deallocate the memory when it is no longer needed. Normally, this is not an issue in C#, because the CLR performs garbage collection of memory that is no longer needed by an executing program (Section 9.10). However, other kinds of resource leaks (such as unclosed files) can occur.

Error-Prevention Tip 12.2

The CLR does not completely eliminate memory leaks. The CLR will not garbage collect an object until the program contains no more references to that object. Thus, memory leaks can occur if programmers inadvertently keep references to unwanted objects.

Moving Resource Release Code to a finally Block

Typically, exceptions occur when processing resources that require explicit release. For example, a program that processes a file might receive IOExceptions during the processing. For this reason, file processing code normally appears in a try block. Regardless of whether a program experiences exceptions while processing a file, the program should close the file when it is no longer needed. Suppose a program places all resource request and resource release code in a try block. If no exceptions occur, the try block executes normally and releases the resources after using them. However, if an exception occurs, the try block may expire before the resource-release code can execute. We could duplicate all the resource release code in each of the catch blocks, but this would make the code more difficult to modify and maintain. We could also place the resource release code after the try statement; however, if the try block terminates due to a return statement, code following the try statement would never execute.

To address these problems, C#'s exception handling mechanism provides the finally block, which is guaranteed to execute regardless of whether the try block executes successfully or an exception occurs. This makes the finally block an ideal location in which to place resource-release code for resources that are acquired and manipulated in the corresponding try block. If the try block executes successfully, the finally block executes immediately after the try block terminates. If an exception occurs in the try block, the finally block executes immediately after a catch block completes. If the exception is not caught by a catch block associated with the try block, or if a catch block associated with the try block throws an exception itself, the finally block executes before the exception is processed by the next enclosing try block (if there is one). By placing the resource release code in a finally block, we ensure that even if the program terminates due to an uncaught exception, the resource will be deallocated. Note that local variables in a try block cannot be accessed in the corresponding finally block. For this reason, variables that must be accessed in both a try block and its corresponding finally block should be declared before the try block.

Error-Prevention Tip 12.3

A finally block typically contains code to release resources acquired in the corresponding try block, which makes the finally block an effective mechanism for eliminating resource leaks.

Performance Tip 12.1

As a rule, resources should be released as soon as they are no longer needed in a program. This makes them available for reuse promptly.

If one or more catch blocks follow a try block, the finally block is optional. However, if no catch blocks follow a try block, a finally block must appear immediately after the try block. If any catch blocks follow a try block, the finally block (if there is one) appears after the last catch block. Only whitespace and comments can separate the blocks in a try statement.

Common Programming Error 12.4

Placing the `finally` *block before a* `catch` *block is a syntax error.*

Demonstrating the `finally` Block

The application in Fig. 12.4 demonstrates that the `finally` block always executes, regardless of whether an exception occurs in the corresponding `try` block. The program consists of method `Main` (lines 8–47) and four other methods that `Main` invokes to demonstrate `finally`. These methods are `DoesNotThrowException` (lines 50–67), `ThrowException-WithCatch` (lines 70–89), `ThrowExceptionWithoutCatch` (lines 92–108) and `ThrowExceptionCatchRethrow` (lines 111–136).

```
1   // Fig. 12.4: UsingExceptions.cs
2   // Using finally blocks.
3   // Demonstrate that finally always executes.
4   using System;
5
6   class UsingExceptions
7   {
8      static void Main()
9      {
10        // Case 1: No exceptions occur in called method
11        Console.WriteLine( "Calling DoesNotThrowException" );
12        DoesNotThrowException();
13
14        // Case 2: Exception occurs and is caught in called method
15        Console.WriteLine( "\nCalling ThrowExceptionWithCatch" );
16        ThrowExceptionWithCatch();
17
18        // Case 3: Exception occurs, but is not caught in called method
19        // because there is no catch block.
20        Console.WriteLine( "\nCalling ThrowExceptionWithoutCatch" );
21
22        // call ThrowExceptionWithoutCatch
23        try
24        {
25           ThrowExceptionWithoutCatch();
26        } // end try
27        catch
28        {
29           Console.WriteLine( "Caught exception from " +
30              "ThrowExceptionWithoutCatch in Main" );
31        } // end catch
32
33        // Case 4: Exception occurs and is caught in called method,
34        // then rethrown to caller.
35        Console.WriteLine( "\nCalling ThrowExceptionCatchRethrow" );
```

Fig. 12.4 | `finally` blocks always execute, regardless of whether an exception occurs. (Part 1 of 4.)

```
36
37         // call ThrowExceptionCatchRethrow
38         try
39         {
40            ThrowExceptionCatchRethrow();
41         } // end try
42         catch
43         {
44            Console.WriteLine( "Caught exception from " +
45               "ThrowExceptionCatchRethrow in Main" );
46         } // end catch
47      } // end method Main
48
49      // no exceptions thrown
50      static void DoesNotThrowException()
51      {
52         // try block does not throw any exceptions
53         try
54         {
55            Console.WriteLine( "In DoesNotThrowException" );
56         } // end try
57         catch
58         {
59            Console.WriteLine( "This catch never executes" );
60         } // end catch
61         finally
62         {
63            Console.WriteLine( "finally executed in DoesNotThrowException" );
64         } // end finally
65
66         Console.WriteLine( "End of DoesNotThrowException" );
67      } // end method DoesNotThrowException
68
69      // throws exception and catches it locally
70      static void ThrowExceptionWithCatch()
71      {
72         // try block throws exception
73         try
74         {
75            Console.WriteLine( "In ThrowExceptionWithCatch" );
76            throw new Exception( "Exception in ThrowExceptionWithCatch" );
77         } // end try
78         catch ( Exception exceptionParameter )
79         {
80            Console.WriteLine( "Message: " + exceptionParameter.Message );
81         } // end catch
82         finally
83         {
84            Console.WriteLine(
85               "finally executed in ThrowExceptionWithCatch" );
86         } // end finally
```

Fig. 12.4 | finally blocks always execute, regardless of whether an exception occurs. (Part 2 of 4.)

```
87
88          Console.WriteLine( "End of ThrowExceptionWithCatch" );
89    } // end method ThrowExceptionWithCatch
90
91    // throws exception and does not catch it locally
92    static void ThrowExceptionWithoutCatch()
93    {
94       // throw exception, but do not catch it
95       try
96       {
97          Console.WriteLine( "In ThrowExceptionWithoutCatch" );
98          throw new Exception( "Exception in ThrowExceptionWithoutCatch" );
99       } // end try
100      finally
101      {
102         Console.WriteLine( "finally executed in " +
103            "ThrowExceptionWithoutCatch" );
104      } // end finally
105
106      // unreachable code; logic error
107      Console.WriteLine( "End of ThrowExceptionWithoutCatch" );
108   } // end method ThrowExceptionWithoutCatch
109
110   // throws exception, catches it and rethrows it
111   static void ThrowExceptionCatchRethrow()
112   {
113      // try block throws exception
114      try
115      {
116         Console.WriteLine( "In ThrowExceptionCatchRethrow" );
117         throw new Exception( "Exception in ThrowExceptionCatchRethrow" );
118      } // end try
119      catch ( Exception exceptionParameter )
120      {
121         Console.WriteLine( "Message: " + exceptionParameter.Message );
122
123         // rethrow exception for further processing
124         throw;
125
126         // unreachable code; logic error
127      } // end catch
128      finally
129      {
130         Console.WriteLine( "finally executed in " +
131            "ThrowExceptionCatchRethrow" );
132      } // end finally
133
134      // any code placed here is never reached
135      Console.WriteLine( "End of ThrowExceptionCatchRethrow" );
136   } // end method ThrowExceptionCatchRethrow
137 } // end class UsingExceptions
```

Fig. 12.4 | `finally` blocks always execute, regardless of whether an exception occurs. (Part 3 of 4.)

```
Calling DoesNotThrowException
In DoesNotThrowException
finally executed in DoesNotThrowException
End of DoesNotThrowException

Calling ThrowExceptionWithCatch
In ThrowExceptionWithCatch
Message: Exception in ThrowExceptionWithCatch
finally executed in ThrowExceptionWithCatch
End of ThrowExceptionWithCatch

Calling ThrowExceptionWithoutCatch
In ThrowExceptionWithoutCatch
finally executed in ThrowExceptionWithoutCatch
Caught exception from ThrowExceptionWithoutCatch in Main

Calling ThrowExceptionCatchRethrow
In ThrowExceptionCatchRethrow
Message: Exception in ThrowExceptionCatchRethrow
finally executed in ThrowExceptionCatchRethrow
Caught exception from ThrowExceptionCatchRethrow in Main
```

Fig. 12.4 | finally blocks always execute, regardless of whether an exception occurs. (Part 4 of 4.)

Line 12 of Main invokes method DoesNotThrowException. The try block for this method outputs a message (line 55). Because the try block does not throw any exceptions, program control ignores the catch block (lines 57–60) and executes the finally block (lines 61–64), which outputs a message. At this point, program control continues with the first statement after the close of the finally block (line 66) which outputs a message indicating that the end of the method has been reached. Then, program control returns to Main.

Throwing Exceptions Using the *throw* Statement

Line 16 of Main invokes method ThrowExceptionWithCatch (lines 70–89), which begins in its try block (lines 73–77) by outputting a message. Next, the try block creates an Exception object and uses a ***throw statement*** to throw the exception object (line 76). Executing the throw statement indicates that an exception has occurred. So far you have only caught exceptions thrown by called methods. You can throw exceptions by using the throw statement. Just as with exceptions thrown by the FCL's methods and the CLR, this indicates to client applications that an error has occurred. A throw statement specifies an object to be thrown. The operand of a throw statement can be of type Exception or of any type derived from class Exception.

Common Programming Error 12.5

It is a compilation error if the argument of a throw—an exception object—is not of class Exception or one of its derived classes.

The string passed to the constructor becomes the exception object's error message. When a throw statement in a try block executes, the try block expires immediately, and program control continues with the first matching catch block (lines 78–81) following the try block. In this example, the type thrown (Exception) matches the type specified in the catch, so line 80 outputs a message indicating the exception that occurred. Then, the finally block (lines 82–86) executes and outputs a message. At this point, program control continues with the first statement after the close of the finally block (line 88), which outputs a message indicating that the end of the method has been reached. Program control then returns to Main. In line 80, note that we use the exception object's Message property to retrieve the error message associated with the exception (i.e., the message passed to the Exception constructor). Section 12.7 discusses several properties of class Exception.

Lines 23–31 of Main define a try statement in which Main invokes method ThrowExceptionWithoutCatch (lines 92–108). The try block enables Main to catch any exceptions thrown by ThrowExceptionWithoutCatch. The try block in lines 95–99 of ThrowExceptionWithoutCatch begins by outputting a message. Next, the try block throws an Exception (line 98) and expires immediately.

Normally, program control would continue at the first catch following this try block. However, this try block does not have any catch blocks. Therefore, the exception is not caught in method ThrowExceptionWithoutCatch. Program control proceeds to the finally block (lines 100–104), which outputs a message. At this point, program control returns to Main—any statements appearing after the finally block (e.g., line 107) do not execute. In this example, such statements could cause logic errors, because the exception thrown in line 98 is not caught. In Main, the catch block in lines 27–31 catches the exception and displays a message indicating that the exception was caught in Main.

Rethrowing Exceptions

Lines 38–46 of Main define a try statement in which Main invokes method ThrowExceptionCatchRethrow (lines 111–136). The try statement enables Main to catch any exceptions thrown by ThrowExceptionCatchRethrow. The try statement in lines 114–132 of ThrowExceptionCatchRethrow begins by outputting a message. Next, the try block throws an Exception (line 117). The try block expires immediately, and program control continues at the first catch (lines 119–127) following the try block. In this example, the type thrown (Exception) matches the type specified in the catch, so line 121 outputs a message indicating where the exception occurred. Line 124 uses the throw statement to *rethrow* the exception. This indicates that the catch block performed partial processing of the exception and now is passing the exception back to the calling method (in this case, Main) for further processing.

You can also rethrow an exception with a version of the throw statement which takes an operand that is the reference to the exception that was caught. It is important to note, however, that this form of throw statement resets the throw point, so the original throw point's stack trace information is lost. Section 12.7 demonstrates using a throw statement with an operand from a catch block. In that section, you will see that after an exception is caught, you can create and throw a different type of exception object from the catch block and you can include the original exception as part of the new exception object. Class library designers often do this to customize the exception types thrown from methods in their class libraries or to provide additional debugging information.

The exception handling in method ThrowExceptionCatchRethrow does not complete, because the program cannot run code in the catch block placed after the invocation of the throw statement in line 124. Therefore, method ThrowExceptionCatchRethrow terminates and returns control to Main. Once again, the finally block (lines 128–132) executes and outputs a message before control returns to Main. When control returns to Main, the catch block in lines 42–46 catches the exception and displays a message indicating that the exception was caught. Then the program terminates.

Returning After a finally Block

Note that the next statement to execute after a finally block terminates depends on the exception-handling state. If the try block successfully completes, or if a catch block catches and handles an exception, the program continues its execution with the next statement after the finally block. However, if an exception is not caught, or if a catch block rethrows an exception, program control continues in the next enclosing try block. The enclosing try could be in the calling method or in one of its callers. It also is possible to nest a try statement in a try block; in such a case, the outer try statement's catch blocks would process any exceptions that were not caught in the inner try statement. If a try block executes and has a corresponding finally block, the finally block executes even if the try block terminates due to a return statement. The return occurs after the execution of the finally block.

Common Programming Error 12.6

Throwing an exception from a finally block can be dangerous. If an uncaught exception is awaiting processing when the finally block executes, and the finally block throws a new exception that is not caught in the finally block, the first exception is lost, and the new exception is passed to the next enclosing try block.

Error-Prevention Tip 12.4

When placing code that can throw an exception in a finally block, always enclose the code in a try statement that catches the appropriate exception types. This prevents the loss of any uncaught and rethrown exceptions that occur before the finally block executes.

Software Engineering Observation 12.2

Do not place try blocks around every statement that might throw an exception, because this can make programs difficult to read. It is better to place one try block around a significant portion of code, and follow this try block with catch blocks that handle each of the possible exceptions. Then follow the catch blocks with a single finally block. Separate try blocks should be used when it is important to distinguish between multiple statements that can throw the same exception type.

The using Statement

Recall from earlier in this section that resource-release code should be placed in a finally block to ensure that a resource is released, regardless of whether there were exceptions when the resource was used in the corresponding try block. An alternative notation—the *using* statement (not to be confused with the using directive for using namespaces)—simplifies writing code in which you obtain a resource, use the resource in a try block and release the resource in a corresponding finally block. For example, a file processing application (Chapter 18) could process a file with a using statement to ensure that the file is closed properly when it is no longer needed. The resource must be an object that implements the `IDisposable` interface and therefore has a `Dispose` method. The general form of a `using` statement would be

```
using ( ExampleObject exampleObject = new ExampleObject() )
{
    exampleObject.SomeMethod();
}
```

where `ExampleObject` is a class that implements the `IDisposable` interface. This code creates an object of type `ExampleObject` and uses it in a statement, then calls its `Dispose` method to release any resources used by the object. The `using` statement implicitly places the code in its body in a `try` block with a corresponding `finally` block that calls the object's `Dispose` method. For instance, the preceding code is equivalent to

```
{
    ExampleObject exampleObject = new ExampleObject();

    try
    {
        exampleObject.SomeMethod();
    }
    finally
    {
        if ( exampleObject != null )
            ( ( IDisposable ) exampleObject ).Dispose();
    }
}
```

Note that the `if` statement ensures that `exampleObject` still references an object; otherwise, a `NullReferenceException` might occur. You can read more about the `using` statement in the *C# Language Specification* Section 8.13 (Section 15.13 in the ECMA version).

12.7 Exception Properties

As we discussed in Section 12.5, exception types derive from class `Exception`, which has several properties. These frequently are used to formulate error messages indicating a caught exception. Two important properties are `Message` and ***StackTrace***. Property `Message` stores the error message associated with an `Exception` object. This message can be a default message associated with the exception type or a customized message passed to an `Exception` object's constructor when the `Exception` object is thrown. Property `StackTrace` contains a `string` that represents the ***method-call stack***. Recall that the runtime environment at all times keeps a list of open method calls that have been made but have not yet returned. The `StackTrace` represents the series of methods that have not finished processing at the time the exception occurs.

Error-Prevention Tip 12.5

A stack trace shows the complete method-call stack at the time an exception occurred. This enables the programmer to view the series of method calls that led to the exception. Information in the stack trace includes the names of the methods on the call stack at the time of the exception, the names of the classes in which the methods are defined and the names of the namespaces in which the classes are defined. If the program database (PDB) file that contains the debugging information for the method is available, the stack trace also includes line numbers; the first line number indicates the throw point, and subsequent line numbers indicate the locations from which the methods in the stack trace were called. PDB files are created by the IDE to maintain the debugging information for your projects.

Property InnerException

Another property used frequently by class-library programmers is ***InnerException***. Typically, class library programmers "wrap" exception objects caught in their code so that they then can throw new exception types that are specific to their libraries. For example, a programmer implementing an accounting system might have some account-number processing code in which account numbers are input as strings but represented as ints in the code. Recall that a program can convert strings to int values with Convert.ToInt32, which throws a FormatException when it encounters an invalid number format. When an invalid account number format occurs, the accounting system programmer might wish to employ a different error message than the default message supplied by FormatException or might wish to indicate a new exception type, such as InvalidAccountNumberFormatException. In such cases, the programmer would provide code to catch the FormatException, then create an appropriate type of Exception object in the catch block and pass the original exception as one of the constructor arguments. The original exception object becomes the InnerException of the new exception object. When an InvalidAccountNumberFormatException occurs in code that uses the accounting system library, the catch block that catches the exception can obtain a reference to the original exception via property InnerException. Thus the exception indicates both that the user specified an invalid account number and that the problem was an invalid number format. If the InnerException property is null, this indicates that the exception was not caused by another exception.

Other Exception Properties

Class Exception provides other properties, including ***HelpLink***, ***Source*** and ***TargetSite***. Property HelpLink specifies the location of the help file that describes the problem that occurred. This property is null if no such file exists. Property Source specifies the name of the application where the exception occurred. Property TargetSite specifies the method where the exception originated.

Demonstrating Exception Properties and Stack Unwinding

Our next example (Fig. 12.5) demonstrates properties Message, StackTrace and InnerException, and method ToString, of class Exception. In addition, the example introduces *stack unwinding*—when an exception is thrown but not caught in a particular scope, the method-call stack is "unwound," and an attempt is made to catch the exception in the

```
1   // Fig. 12.5: Properties.cs
2   // Stack unwinding and Exception class properties.
3   // Demonstrates using properties Message, StackTrace and InnerException.
4   using System;
5
```

Fig. 12.5 | Exception properties and stack unwinding. (Part 1 of 3.)

```
 6   class Properties
 7   {
 8      static void Main()
 9      {
10         // call Method1; any Exception generated is caught
11         // in the catch block that follows
12         try
13         {
14            Method1();
15         } // end try
16         catch ( Exception exceptionParameter )
17         {
18            // output the string representation of the Exception, then output
19            // properties InnerException, Message and StackTrace
20            Console.WriteLine( "exceptionParameter.ToString: \n{0}\n",
21               exceptionParameter.ToString() );
22            Console.WriteLine( "exceptionParameter.Message: \n{0}\n",
23               exceptionParameter.Message );
24            Console.WriteLine( "exceptionParameter.StackTrace: \n{0}\n",
25               exceptionParameter.StackTrace );
26            Console.WriteLine( "exceptionParameter.InnerException: \n{0}\n",
27               exceptionParameter.InnerException.ToString() );
28         } // end catch
29      } // end method Main
30
31      // calls Method2
32      static void Method1()
33      {
34         Method2();
35      } // end method Method1
36
37      // calls Method3
38      static void Method2()
39      {
40         Method3();
41      } // end method Method2
42
43      // throws an Exception containing an InnerException
44      static void Method3()
45      {
46         // attempt to convert string to int
47         try
48         {
49            Convert.ToInt32( "Not an integer" );
50         } // end try
51         catch ( FormatException formatExceptionParameter )
52         {
53            // wrap FormatException in new Exception
54            throw new Exception( "Exception occurred in Method3",
55               formatExceptionParameter );
56         } // end catch
57      } // end method Method3
58   } // end class Properties
```

Fig. 12.5 | Exception properties and stack unwinding. (Part 2 of 3.)

```
exceptionParameter.ToString:
System.Exception: Exception occurred in Method3 --->
   System.FormatException: Input string was not in a correct format.
   at System.Number.StringToNumber(String str, NumberStyles options,
      NumberBuffer& number, NumberFormatInfo info, Boolean parseDecimal)
   at System.Number.ParseInt32(String s, NumberStyles style,
      NumberFormatInfo info)
   at System.Convert.ToInt32(String value)
   at Properties.Method3() in C:\examples\ch12\Fig12_04\Properties\
      Properties.cs:line 49
   --- End of inner exception stack trace ---
   at Properties.Method3() in C:\examples\ch12\Fig12_04\Properties\
      Properties.cs:line 54
   at Properties.Method2() in C:\examples\ch12\Fig12_04\Properties\
      Properties.cs:line 40
   at Properties.Method1() in C:\examples\ch12\Fig12_04\Properties\
      Properties.cs:line 34
   at Properties.Main() in C:\examples\ch12\Fig12_04\Properties\
      Properties.cs:line 14

exceptionParameter.Message:
Exception occurred in Method3

exceptionParameter.StackTrace:
   at Properties.Method3() in C:\examples\ch12\Fig12_04\Properties\
      Properties.cs:line 54
   at Properties.Method2() in C:\examples\ch12\Fig12_04\Properties\
      Properties.cs:line 40
   at Properties.Method1() in C:\examples\ch12\Fig12_04\Properties\
      Properties.cs:line 34
   at Properties.Main() in C:\examples\ch12\Fig12_04\Properties\
      Properties.cs:line 14

exceptionParameter.InnerException:
System.FormatException: Input string was not in a correct format.
   at System.Number.StringToNumber(String str, NumberStyles options,
      NumberBuffer& number, NumberFormatInfo info, Boolean parseDecimal)
   at System.Number.ParseInt32(String s, NumberStyles style,
      NumberFormatInfo info)
   at System.Convert.ToInt32(String value)
   at Properties.Method3() in C:\examples\ch12\Fig12_04\Properties\
      Properties.cs:line 49
```

Fig. 12.5 | Exception properties and stack unwinding. (Part 3 of 3.)

next outer try block. We keep track of the methods on the call stack as we discuss property StackTrace and the stack-unwinding mechanism. To see the proper stack trace, you should execute this program using steps similar to those presented in Section 12.3.

Program execution begins with Main, which becomes the first method on the method call stack. Line 14 of the try block in Main invokes Method1 (declared in lines 32–35), which becomes the second method on the stack. If Method1 throws an exception, the catch block in lines 16–28 handles the exception and outputs information about the exception that occurred. Line 34 of Method1 invokes Method2 (lines 38–41), which becomes the third method on the stack. Then line 40 of Method2 invokes Method3 (lines 44–57), which becomes the fourth method on the stack.

At this point, the method-call stack (from top to bottom) for the program is:

```
Method3
Method2
Method1
Main
```

The method called most recently (`Method3`) appears at the top of the stack; the first method called (`Main`) appears at the bottom. The `try` statement (lines 47–56) in `Method3` invokes method `Convert.ToInt32` (line 49), which attempts to convert a `string` to an `int`. At this point, `Convert.ToInt32` becomes the fifth and final method on the call stack.

Throwing an `Exception` *with an* `InnerException`

Because the argument to `Convert.ToInt32` is not in `int` format, line 49 throws a `FormatException` that is caught in line 51 of `Method3`. The exception terminates the call to `Convert.ToInt32`, so the method is removed (or unwound) from the method-call stack. The `catch` block in `Method3` then creates and throws an `Exception` object. The first argument to the `Exception` constructor is the custom error message for our example, "Exception occurred in Method3." The second argument is the `InnerException`—the `FormatException` that was caught. The `StackTrace` for this new exception object reflects the point at which the exception was thrown (lines 54–55). Now `Method3` terminates, because the exception thrown in the `catch` block is not caught in the method body. Thus, control returns to the statement that invoked `Method3` in the prior method in the call stack (`Method2`). This removes, or *unwinds,* `Method3` from the method-call stack.

When control returns to line 40 in `Method2`, the CLR determines that line 40 is not in a `try` block. Therefore the exception cannot be caught in `Method2`, and `Method2` terminates. This unwinds `Method2` from the call stack and returns control to line 28 in `Method1`.

Here again, line 34 is not in a `try` block, so `Method1` cannot catch the exception. The method terminates and is unwound from the call stack, returning control to line 14 in `Main`, which *is* located in a `try` block. The `try` block in `Main` expires and the `catch` block (lines 16–28) catches the exception. The `catch` block uses method `ToString` and properties `Message`, `StackTrace` and `InnerException` to create the output. Note that stack unwinding continues until a `catch` block catches the exception or the program terminates.

Displaying Information About the `Exception`

The first block of output (which we reformatted for readability) in Fig. 12.5 contains the exception's `string` representation, which is returned from method `ToString`. The `string` begins with the name of the exception class followed by the `Message` property value. The next four items present the stack trace of the `InnerException` object. The remainder of the block of output shows the `StackTrace` for the exception thrown in `Method3`. Note that the `StackTrace` represents the state of the method-call stack at the throw point of the exception, rather than at the point where the exception eventually is caught. Each `StackTrace` line that begins with "at" represents a method on the call stack. These lines indicate the method in which the exception occurred, the file in which the method resides and the line number of the throw point in the file. Note that the inner-exception information includes the inner exception stack trace.

Error-Prevention Tip 12.6

When catching and rethrowing an exception, provide additional debugging information in the rethrown exception. To do so, create an `Exception` object containing more specific debugging information, then pass the original caught exception to the new exception object's constructor to initialize the `InnerException` property.

The next block of output (two lines) simply displays the `Message` property's value (`Exception occurred in Method3`) of the exception thrown in `Method3`.

The third block of output displays the `StackTrace` property of the exception thrown in `Method3`. Note that this `StackTrace` property contains the stack trace starting from line 54 in `Method3`, because that is the point at which the `Exception` object was created and thrown. The stack trace always begins from the exception's throw point.

Finally, the last block of output displays the `string` representation of the `InnerException` property, which includes the namespace and class name of the exception object, as well as its `Message` and `StackTrace` properties.

12.8 User-Defined Exception Classes

In many cases, you can use existing exception classes from the .NET Framework Class Library to indicate exceptions that occur in your programs. However, in some cases, you might wish to create new exception classes specific to the problems that occur in your programs. *User-defined exception classes* should derive directly or indirectly from class `ApplicationException` of namespace `System`.

Good Programming Practice 12.1

Associating each type of malfunction with an appropriately named exception class improves program clarity.

Software Engineering Observation 12.3

Before creating a user-defined exception class, investigate the existing exceptions in the .NET Framework Class Library to determine whether an appropriate exception type already exists.

Figures 12.6 and 12.7 demonstrate a user-defined exception class. Class `Negative-NumberException` (Fig. 12.6) is a user-defined exception class representing exceptions that occur when a program performs an illegal operation on a negative number, such as attempting to calculate its square root.

According to "Best Practices for Handling Exceptions [C#]," user-defined exceptions should extend class `ApplicationException`, have a class name that ends with "Exception" and define three constructors: a parameterless constructor; a constructor that receives a `string` argument (the error message); and a constructor that receives a `string` argument and an `Exception` argument (the error message and the inner exception object). Defining these three constructors makes your exception class more flexible, allowing other programmers to easily use and extend it.

`NegativeNumberExceptions` most frequently occur during arithmetic operations, so it seems logical to derive class `NegativeNumberException` from class `Arithmetic-Exception`. However, class `ArithmeticException` derives from class `SystemException`—the category of exceptions thrown by the CLR. Recall that user-defined exception classes should inherit from `ApplicationException` rather than `SystemException`.

```
 1    // Fig. 12.6: NegativeNumberException.cs
 2    // NegativeNumberException represents exceptions caused by
 3    // illegal operations performed on negative numbers.
 4    using System;
 5
 6    namespace SquareRootTest
 7    {
 8       class NegativeNumberException : ApplicationException
 9       {
10          // default constructor
11          public NegativeNumberException()
12             : base( "Illegal operation for a negative number" )
13          {
14             // empty body
15          } // end default constructor
16
17          // constructor for customizing error message
18          public NegativeNumberException( string messageValue )
19             : base( messageValue )
20          {
21             // empty body
22          } // end one-argument constructor
23
24          // constructor for customizing the exception's error
25          // message and specifying the InnerException object
26          public NegativeNumberException( string messageValue,
27             Exception inner )
28             : base( messageValue, inner )
29          {
30             // empty body
31          } // end two-argument constructor
32       } // end class NegativeNumberException
33    } // end namespace SquareRootTest
```

Fig. 12.6 | ApplicationException derived class thrown when a program performs an illegal operation on a negative number.

Class SquareRootForm (Fig. 12.7) demonstrates our user-defined exception class. The application enables the user to input a numeric value, then invokes method SquareRoot (lines 17–25) to calculate the square root of that value. To perform this calculation, SquareRoot invokes class Math's Sqrt method, which receives a double value as its argument. Normally, if the argument is negative, method Sqrt returns NaN. In this program, we would like to prevent the user from calculating the square root of a negative number. If the numeric value that the user enters is negative, method SquareRoot throws a NegativeNumberException (lines 21–22). Otherwise, SquareRoot invokes class Math's method Sqrt to compute the square root (line 24).

When the user inputs a value and clicks the **Square Root** button, the program invokes event handler SquareRootButton_Click (lines 28–53). The try statement (lines 33–52) attempts to invoke SquareRoot using the value input by the user. If the user input is not a valid number, a FormatException occurs, and the catch block in lines 40–45 processes the exception. If the user inputs a negative number, method SquareRoot throws a NegativeNumberException (lines 21–22); the catch block in lines 46–52 catches and handles this type of exception.

```
1    // Fig. 12.7: SquareRootTest.cs
2    // Demonstrating a user-defined exception class.
3    using System;
4    using System.Windows.Forms;
5
6    namespace SquareRootTest
7    {
8       public partial class SquareRootForm : Form
9       {
10          public SquareRootForm()
11          {
12             InitializeComponent();
13          } // end constructor
14
15          // computes square root of parameter; throws
16          // NegativeNumberException if parameter is negative
17          public double SquareRoot( double value )
18          {
19             // if negative operand, throw NegativeNumberException
20             if ( value < 0 )
21                throw new NegativeNumberException(
22                   "Square root of negative number not permitted" );
23             else
24                return Math.Sqrt( value ); // compute square root
25          } // end method SquareRoot
26
27          // obtain user input, convert to double, calculate square root
28          private void SquareRootButton_Click( object sender, EventArgs e )
29          {
30             OutputLabel.Text = ""; // clear OutputLabel
31
32             // catch any NegativeNumberException thrown
33             try
34             {
35                double result =
36                   SquareRoot( Convert.ToDouble( InputTextBox.Text ) );
37
38                OutputLabel.Text = result.ToString();
39             } // end try
40             catch ( FormatException formatExceptionParameter )
41             {
42                MessageBox.Show( formatExceptionParameter.Message,
43                   "Invalid Number Format", MessageBoxButtons.OK,
44                   MessageBoxIcon.Error );
45             } // end catch
46             catch ( NegativeNumberException
47                negativeNumberExceptionParameter )
48             {
```

Fig. 12.7 | SquareRootForm class throws an exception if an error occurs when calculating the square root. (Part 1 of 2.)

```
49              MessageBox.Show( negativeNumberExceptionParameter.Message,
50                 "Invalid Operation", MessageBoxButtons.OK,
51                 MessageBoxIcon.Error );
52          } // end catch
53      } // end method SquareRootButton_Click
54    } // end class SquareRootForm
55  } // end namespace SquareRootTest
```

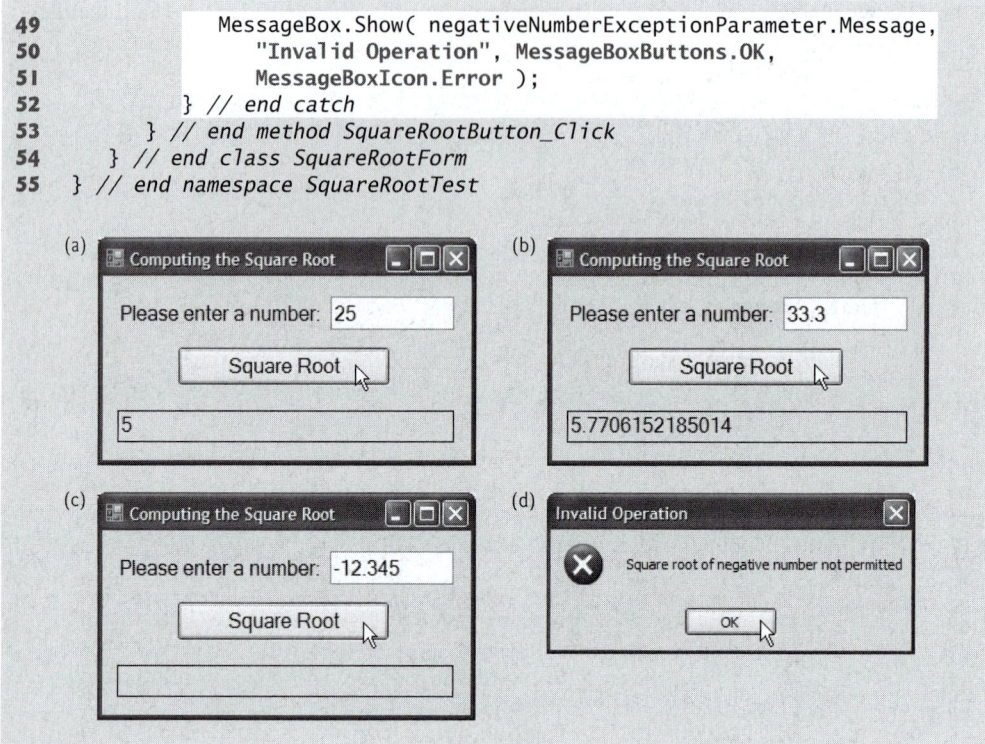

Fig. 12.7 | SquareRootForm class throws an exception if an error occurs when calculating the square root. (Part 2 of 2.)

12.9 Wrap-Up

In this chapter, you learned how to use exception handling to deal with errors in an application. We demonstrated that exception handling enables you to remove error-handling code from the "main line" of the program's execution. You saw exception handling in the context of a divide-by-zero example. You learned how to use try blocks to enclose code that may throw an exception, and how to use catch blocks to deal with exceptions that may arise. We discussed the termination model of exception handling, in which after an exception is handled, program control does not return to the throw point. We also discussed several important classes of the .NET Exception hierarchy, including ApplicationException (from which user-defined exception classes are derived) and SystemException. Next you learned how to use the finally block to release resources whether or not an exception occurs, and how to throw and rethrow exceptions with the throw statement. We also discussed how the using statement can be used to automate the process of releasing a resource. You then learned how to obtain information about an exception using Exception properties Message, StackTrace and InnerException, and method ToString. You learned how to create your own exception classes. In the next two chapters, we present an in-depth treatment of graphical user interfaces. In these chapters and throughout the rest of the book, we use exception handling to make our examples more robust, while still demonstrating new features of the language.

Summary

Section 12.1 Introduction

- An exception is an indication of a problem that occurs during a program's execution.
- Exception handling enables programmers to create applications that can resolve (or handle) exceptions.

Section 12.2 Exception Handling Overview

- Intermixing program logic with error-handling logic can make programs difficult to read, modify, maintain and debug—especially in large applications.
- Exception handling enables programmers to remove error-handling code from the "main line" of the program's execution, improving program clarity and enhancing modifiability.
- C# enables programmers to deal with exception handling easily from the beginning of a project.

Section 12.3 Example: Divide by Zero Without Exception Handling

- An exception is thrown when a method or the CLR detects a problem and is unable to handle it.
- A stack trace includes the name of the exception in a descriptive message that indicates the problem that occurred and the complete method-call stack at the time the exception occurred.
- Division by zero is not allowed in integer arithmetic.
- Division by zero is allowed with floating-point values. Such a calculation results in the value infinity, which is represented by either constant `Double.PositiveInfinity` or constant `Double.NegativeInfinity`, depending on whether the numerator is positive or negative. If both the numerator and denominator are zero, the result of the calculation is the constant `Double.NaN`.
- When division by zero occurs in integer arithmetic, a `DivideByZeroException` is thrown.
- A `FormatException` occurs when `Convert` method `ToInt32` receives a string that does not represent a valid integer.

Section 12.4 Example: Handling `DivideByZeroException`s and `FormatException`s

- A `try` block encloses the code that might throw exceptions, as well as the code that should not execute if an exception occurs.
- A `catch` block can specify an identifier representing the exception that the `catch` block can handle. A general `catch` clause (i.e., `catch()`) catches all exception types, but cannot access exception information.
- At least one `catch` block and/or a `finally` block must immediately follow the `try` block.
- An uncaught exception is an exception that occurs for which there is no matching `catch` block.
- When a method called in a program detects an exception, or when the CLR detects a problem, the method or the CLR throws an exception.
- The point in the program at which an exception occurs is called the throw point.
- If an exception occurs in a `try` block, the `try` block terminates immediately, and program control transfers to the first of the following `catch` blocks in which the exception parameter's type matches the type of the thrown exception.
- After the exception is handled, program control does not return to the throw point because the `try` block has expired (which also causes any of its local variables to be lost). Instead control resumes after the last `catch` block. This is known as the termination model of exception handling.
- The `try` block and its corresponding `catch` and `finally` blocks together form a `try` statement.

- The CLR locates the matching catch by comparing the thrown exception's type to each catch's exception-parameter type. A match occurs if the types are identical or if the thrown exception's type is a derived class of the exception-parameter type.
- Once an exception is matched to a catch block, the other catch blocks are ignored.

Section 12.5 .NET Exception Hierarchy

- The C# exception-handling mechanism allows objects only of class Exception and its derived classes to be thrown and caught.
- Class Exception of namespace System is the base class of the .NET Framework Class Library exception class hierarchy.
- Two of the most important classes derived from Exception are ApplicationException and SystemException.
- ApplicationException is the base class that you should extend to create exception classes that are specific to your applications.
- The CLR generates SystemExceptions, which can occur at any point during the execution of the program. Many of these exceptions can be avoided if applications are coded properly.
- A benefit of using the exception class hierarchy is that a catch block can catch exceptions of a particular type or—because of the *is-a* relationship of inheritance—can use a base-class type to catch exceptions in a hierarchy of related exception types.
- A catch block that specifies an exception parameter of type Exception can catch all exceptions that derive from Exception, because Exception is the base class of all exception classes.
- Using inheritance with exceptions enables an exception handler to catch related exceptions using a concise notation.

Section 12.6 finally Block

- The most common type of resource leak is a memory leak.
- A memory leak occurs when a program allocates memory but does not deallocate the memory when it is no longer needed. Normally, this is not an issue in C#, because the CLR performs garbage collection of memory that is no longer needed by an executing program.
- C#'s exception handling mechanism provides the finally block, which is guaranteed to execute if program control enters the corresponding try block.
- The finally block executes regardless of whether the corresponding try block executes successfully or an exception occurs. This makes the finally block an ideal location in which to place resource-release code for resources acquired and manipulated in the corresponding try block.
- If the try block executes successfully, the finally block executes immediately after the try block terminates. If an exception occurs in the try block, the finally block executes immediately after a catch block completes.
- If the exception is not caught by a catch block associated with the try block, or if a catch block associated with the try block throws an exception, the finally block executes before the exception is processed by the next enclosing try block (if there is one).
- The throw statement can be used to rethrow an exception, indicating that a catch block performed partial processing of the exception and now is passing the exception back to the calling method for further processing.
- If a try block executes and has a corresponding finally block, the finally block always executes—even if the try block terminates due to a return statement. The return occurs after the execution of the finally block.

- The using statement simplifies writing code in which you obtain a resource, use the resource in a try block and release the resource in a corresponding finally block.

Section 12.7 Exception Properties
- Property Message of class Exception stores the error message associated with an Exception object.
- Property StackTrace of class Exception contains a string that represents the method-call stack.
- Another Exception property used frequently by class library programmers is InnerException. Typically, you use this property to "wrap" exception objects caught in your code so that you then can throw new exception types specific to your libraries.
- When an exception is thrown but not caught in a particular scope, the method-call stack is "unwound," and an attempt is made to catch the exception in the next outer try block—this is known as stack unwinding.

Section 12.8 User-Defined Exception Classes
- User-defined exception classes should derive directly or indirectly from class ApplicationException of namespace System.
- User-defined exceptions should extend ApplicationException, have a class name that ends with "Exception" and define a parameterless constructor, a constructor that receives a string argument (the error message), and a constructor that receives a string argument and an Exception argument (the error message and the inner exception object).

Terminology

ApplicationException class
catch an exception
catch block
divide by zero
DivideByZeroException class
error-processing code
exception
Exception Assistant
Exception class
exception handling
fault-tolerant program
finally block
FormatException class
general catch clause
handle an exception
HelpLink property of class Exception
IndexOutOfRangeException class
InnerException property of class Exception
memory leak
Message property of class Exception
method call stack
NullReferenceException class

out-of-range array index
resource leak
resumption model of exception handling
rethrow an exception
robust program
Source property of class Exception
stack trace
stack unwinding
StackTrace property of class Exception
SystemException class
TargetSite property of class Exception
termination model of exception handling
throw an exception
throw point
throw statement
try block
try statement
uncaught exception
unwind a method from call stack
user-defined exception class
using statement

Self-Review Exercises

12.1   Fill in the blanks in each of the following statements:

    a) A method is said to _____ an exception when that method detects that a problem has occurred.

b) When present, the _____ block associated with a try block always executes.

c) Exception classes are derived from class _____ .

d) The statement that throws an exception is called the _____ of the exception.

e) C# uses the _____ model of exception handling as opposed to the _____ model of exception handling.

f) An uncaught exception in a method causes the method to _____ from the method-call stack.

g) Method Convert.ToInt32 can throw a(n) _____ exception if its argument is not a valid integer value.

12.2   State whether each of the following is *true* or *false*. If *false*, explain why.

a) Exceptions always are handled in the method that initially detects the exception.

b) User-defined exception classes should extend class SystemException.

c) Accessing an out-of-bounds array index causes the CLR to throw an exception.

d) A finally block is optional after a try block that does not have any corresponding catch blocks.

e) A finally block that appears in a method is guaranteed to execute.

f) It is possible to return to the throw point of an exception using keyword return.

g) Exceptions can be rethrown.

h) Property Message of class Exception returns a string indicating the method from which the exception was thrown.

Answers to Self-Review Exercises

12.1   a) throw. b) finally. c) Exception. d) throw point. e) termination, resumption. f) unwind. g) FormatException.

12.2   a) False. Exceptions can be handled by other methods on the method-call stack. b) False. User-defined exception classes should extend class ApplicationException. c) True. d) False. A try block that does not have any catch blocks requires a finally block. e) False. The finally block executes only if program control enters the corresponding try block. f) False. return causes control to return to the caller. g) True. h) False. Property Message of class Exception returns a string representing the error message.

Exercises

12.3   Use inheritance to create an exception base class and various exception-derived classes. Write a program to demonstrate that the catch specifying the base class catches derived-class exceptions.

12.4   Write a program that demonstrates how various exceptions are caught with

```
catch ( Exception exceptionParameter )
```

12.5   To demonstrate the importance of the order of exception handlers, write two programs, one with correct ordering of catch blocks (i.e., place the base-class exception handler after all derived-class exception handlers) and another with improper ordering (i.e., place the base-class exception handler before the derived-class exception handlers). What happens when you attempt to compile the second program.

12.6   Exceptions can be used to indicate problems that occur when an object is being constructed. Write a program that shows a constructor passing information about constructor failure to an exception handler. The exception thrown also should contain the arguments sent to the constructor.

12.7   Write a program that demonstrates rethrowing an exception.

12.8   Write a program demonstrating that a method with its own try block does not have to catch every possible exception that occurs within the try block—some exceptions can slip through to, and be handled in, other scopes.

12.9   Write a program that throws an exception from a deeply nested method. The catch block should follow the try block that encloses the call chain. The exception caught should be one you defined yourself. In catching the exception, display the exception's message and stack trace.

12.10   Create a GUI application that displays images in a PictureBox. Allow the user to enter the path of the image in a TextBox and click a Button to display the image. If the user enters an invalid file path, a FileNotFoundException will occur. Use exception handling so that a default image will be displayed if an invalid path is entered. Whether a valid path is entered or not, clear the TextBox where the user enters input. Three images have been provided in the examples folder for this chapter in the Ex12_10 directory. Use the image named image0.bmp as the default image. You can use the other two images to test entering a valid path. [*Note:* You will need to specify that you are using the System.IO namespace for this exercise.]

12.11   Create a GUI application that inputs miles driven and gallons used, and calculates miles per gallon. The example should use exception handling to process the FormatExceptions that occur when converting the strings in the TextBoxes to doubles. If invalid data is entered, a MessageBox should be displayed informing the user.

12.12   Create a **Vending Machine** application (Fig. 12.8) that displays images for four snacks and corresponding Labels that indicate numbers for each snack (the snacks should be numbered 0–3). Use a string array that contains the names of each snack. The GUI should contain a TextBox in which the user specifies the number of the desired snack. When the **Dispense Snack** Button is clicked, the name of the selected snack (retrieved from the array) should be displayed. If the user enters a snack value not in the range 0–3, an IndexOutOfRangeException will occur. Use exception handling so that whenever an IndexOutOfRangeException occurs, a MessageBox is displayed indicating the proper range of values. Also handle any possible FormatExceptions that may occur. The images used in this application can be found in the examples folder for this chapter, in the Ex12_12 directory.

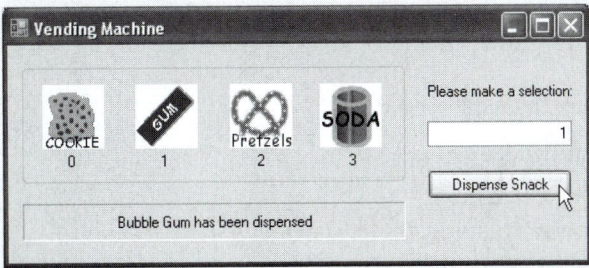

Fig. 12.8 | **Vending Machine** application.

13

Graphical User Interface Concepts: Part 1

… the wisest prophets make sure of the event first.
—Horace Walpole

…The user should feel in control of the computer; not the other way around. This is achieved in applications that embody three qualities: responsiveness, permissiveness, and consistency.
—Inside Macintosh, Volume 1
Apple Computer, Inc. 1985

All the better to see you with my dear.
—The Big Bad Wolf to Little Red Riding Hood

OBJECTIVES

In this chapter you will learn:

- Design principles of graphical user interfaces (GUIs).

- How to create graphical user interfaces.

- How to process events that are generated by user interactions with GUI controls.

- The namespaces that contain the classes for graphical user interface controls and event handling.

- How to create and manipulate `Button`, `Label`, `RadioButton`, `CheckBox`, `TextBox`, `Panel` and `NumericUpDown` controls.

- How to add descriptive `ToolTips` to GUI controls.

- How to process mouse and keyboard events.

13.1 Introduction

A graphical user interface (GUI) allows a user to interact visually with a program. A GUI (pronounced "GOO-ee") gives a program a distinctive "look" and "feel." Providing different applications with a consistent set of intuitive user-interface components enables users to become productive with each application faster.

Look-and-Feel Observation 13.1

Consistent user interfaces enable a user to learn new applications more quickly because the applications have the same "look" and "feel."

As an example of a GUI, consider Fig. 13.1, which shows an Internet Explorer Web browser window containing various GUI controls. Near the top of the window, there is a menu bar containing the menus **File**, **Edit**, **View**, **Favorites**, **Tools** and **Help**. Below the menu bar is a set of buttons, each of which has a defined task in Internet Explorer, such as going back to the previously viewed Web page, printing the current page or refreshing the page. Below these buttons lies a combobox, in which users can type the locations of Web sites that they wish to visit. To the left of the combobox is a label (**Address**) that indicates the combobox's purpose (in this case, entering the location of a Web site). Scrollbars are located at the right side and bottom of the window. Usually, scrollbars appear when a window contains more information than can be displayed in the window's viewable area. Scrollbars enable a user to view different portions of the window's contents. These controls form a user-friendly interface through which the user interacts with the Internet Explorer Web browser.

Label   Button   Menu   Title bar   Menu bar   Combobox   Scrollbars

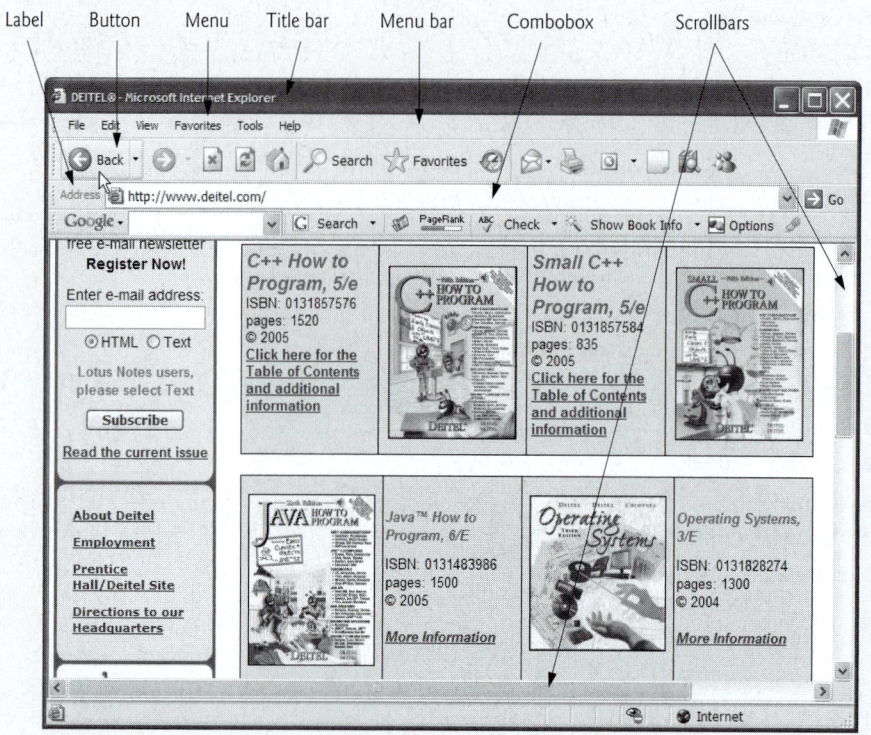

Fig. 13.1 | GUI controls in an Internet Explorer window.

GUIs are built from GUI controls (which are sometimes called *components* or *widgets*—short for *window gadgets*). GUI controls are objects that can display information on the screen or enable users to interact with an application via the mouse, keyboard or some other form of input (such as voice commands). Several common GUI controls are listed in Fig. 13.2—in the sections that follow and in Chapter 14, we discuss each of these in detail. Chapter 14 also explores the features and properties of additional GUI controls.

Control	Description
Label	Displays images or uneditable text.
TextBox	Enables the user to enter data via the keyboard. It can also be used to display editable or uneditable text.
Button	Triggers an event when clicked with the mouse.
CheckBox	Specifies an option that can be selected (checked) or unselected (not checked).
ComboBox	Provides a drop-down list of items from which the user can make a selection either by clicking an item in the list or by typing in a box.

Fig. 13.2 | Some basic GUI controls. (Part 1 of 2.)

Control	Description
ListBox	Provides a list of items from which the user can make a selection by clicking an item in the list. Multiple elements can be selected.
Panel	A container in which controls can be placed and organized.
NumericUpDown	Enables the user to select from a range of input values.

Fig. 13.2 | Some basic GUI controls. (Part 2 of 2.)

13.2 Windows Forms

Windows Forms are used to create the GUIs for programs. A Form is a graphical element that appears on your computer's desktop; it can be a dialog, a window or an *MDI window* (*multiple document interface window*)—discussed in Chapter 14, Graphical User Interface Concepts: Part 2. A *component* is an instance of a class that implements the *IComponent interface*, which defines the behaviors that components must implement, such as how the component is loaded. A control, such as a Button or Label, has a graphical representation at runtime. Some components lack graphical representations (e.g., class Timer of namespace System.Windows.Forms—see Chapter 14). Such, components are not visible at run time.

Figure 13.3 displays the Windows Forms controls and components from the C# **Toolbox**. The controls and components are organized into categories by functionality. Selecting the category **All Windows Forms** at the top of the **Toolbox** allows you to view all the controls and components from the other tabs in one list (as shown in Fig. 13.3). In this chapter and the next, we discuss many of these controls and components. To add a control or component to a Form, select that control component or from the **Toolbox** and drag it on the Form. To deselect a control or component, select the **Pointer** item in the **Toolbox** (the icon at the top of the list). When the **Pointer** item is selected, you cannot accidentally add a new control to the Form.

When there are several windows on the screen, the *active window* is the frontmost and has a highlighted title bar—typically darker blue than the other windows on the screen. A window becomes the active window when the user clicks somewhere inside it. The active window is said to "have the *focus*." For example, in Visual Studio the active window is the **Toolbox** when you are selecting an item from it, or the **Properties** window when you are editing a control's properties.

A Form is a *container* for controls and components. When you drag a control or component from the **Toolbox** on the Form, Visual Studio generates code that instantiates the object and sets its basic properties. This code is updated when the control or component's properties are modified in the IDE. If a control or component is removed from the Form, the generated code for that control is deleted. The generated code is placed by the IDE in a separate file using partial classes. Although we could write this code ourselves, it is much easier to create and modify controls and components using the **Toolbox** and **Properties** windows and allow Visual Studio to handle the details. We introduced visual programming concepts in Chapter 2. In this chapter and the next, we use visual programming to build more substantial GUIs.

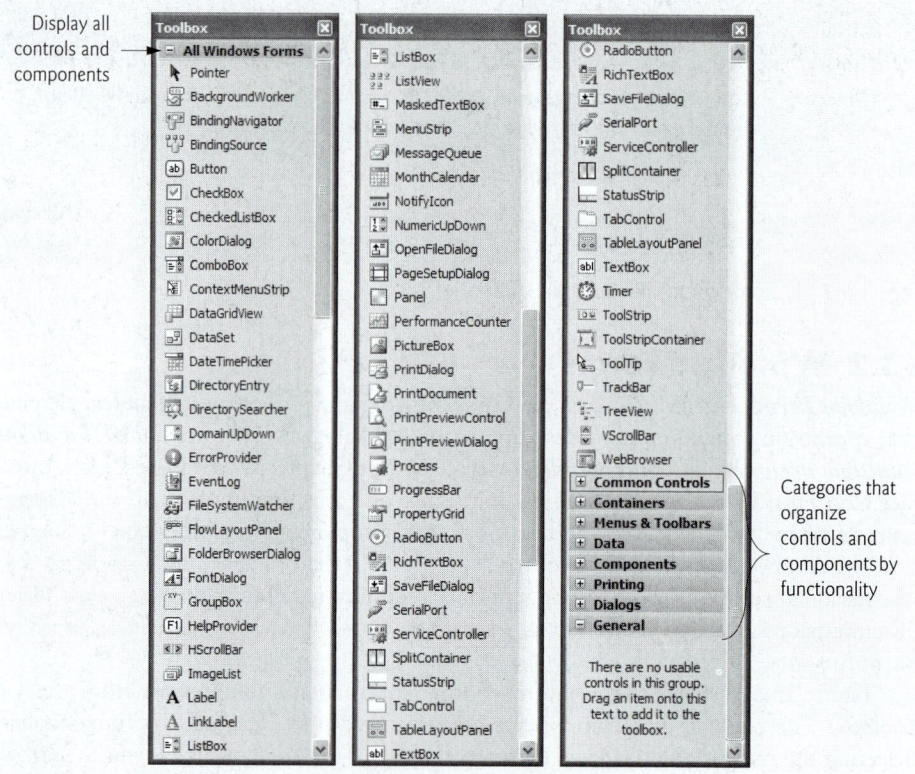

Fig. 13.3 | Components and controls for Windows Forms.

Each control or component we present in this chapter is located in namespace `System.Windows.Forms`. To create a Windows application, you generally create a Windows `Form`, set its properties, add controls to the `Form`, set their properties and implement event handlers (methods) that respond to events generated by the controls. Figure 13.4 lists common `Form` properties, methods and events.

Form properties, methods and events	Description
Common Properties	
`AcceptButton`	`Button` that is clicked when *Enter* is pressed.
`AutoScroll`	`Boolean` value that allows or disallows scrollbars when needed.
`CancelButton`	`Button` that is clicked when the *Escape* key is pressed.
`FormBorderStyle`	Border style for the `Form` (e.g., none, single, three-dimensional).

Fig. 13.4 | Common `Form` properties, methods and events. (Part 1 of 2.)

Form properties, methods and events	Description
Font	Font of text displayed on the Form, and the default font for controls added to the Form.
Text	Text in the Form's title bar.
Common Methods	
Close	Closes a Form and releases all resources, such as the memory used for the Form's controls and components. A closed Form cannot be reopened.
Hide	Hides a Form, but does not destroy the Form or release its resources.
Show	Displays a hidden Form.
Common Event	
Load	Occurs before a Form is displayed to the user. The handler for this event is displayed in the Visual Studio editor when you double click the Form in the Visual Studio designer.

Fig. 13.4 | Common Form properties, methods and events. (Part 2 of 2.)

When we create controls and event handlers, Visual Studio generates much of the GUI-related code. In visual programming, the IDE maintains GUI-related code and you write the bodies of the event handlers to indicate what actions the program should take when particular events occur.

13.3 Event Handling

Normally, a user interacts with an application's GUI to indicate the tasks that the application should perform. For example, when you write an e-mail in an e-mail application, clicking the **Send** button tells the application to send the e-mail to the specified e-mail addresses. GUIs are *event driven*. When the user interacts with a GUI component, the interaction—known as an *event*—drives the program to perform a task. Common events (user interactions) that might cause an application to perform a task include clicking a Button, typing in a TextBox, selecting an item from a menu, closing a window and moving the mouse. A method that performs a task in response to an event is called an *event handler*, and the overall process of responding to events is known as *event handling*.

13.3.1 A Simple Event-Driven GUI

The Form in the application of Fig. 13.5 contains a Button that a user can click to display a MessageBox. You have already created several GUI examples that execute an event handler in response to clicking a Button. In this example, we discuss Visual Studio's auto-generated code in more depth.

Using the techniques presented earlier in the book, create a Form containing a Button. First, create a new Windows application and add a Button to the Form. In the **Properties**

```
 1   // Fig. 13.5: SimpleEventExampleForm.cs
 2   // Using Visual Studio to create event handlers.
 3   using System;
 4   using System.Windows.Forms;
 5
 6   // Form that shows a simple event handler
 7   public partial class SimpleEventExampleForm : Form
 8   {
 9      // default constructor
10      public SimpleEventExampleForm()
11      {
12         InitializeComponent();
13      } // end constructor
14
15      // handles click event of Button clickButton
16      private void clickButton_Click( object sender, EventArgs e )
17      {
18         MessageBox.Show( "Button was clicked." );
19      } // end method clickButton_Click
20   } // end class SimpleEventExampleForm
```

Fig. 13.5 | Simple event-handling example using visual programming.

window for the Button, set the (Name) property to clickButton and the Text property to Click Me. You'll notice that we use a convention in which each variable name we create for a control ends with the control's type. For example, in the variable name clickButton, "Button" is the control's type.

When the user clicks the Button in this example, we want the application to respond by displaying a MessageBox. To do this, you must create an event handler for the Button's Click event. You can create this event handler by double clicking the Button on the Form, which declares the following empty event handler in the program code:

```
private void clickButton_Click( object sender, EventArgs e )
{

} // end method clickButton_Click
```

By convention, C# names the event-handler method as *controlName_eventName* (e.g., clickButton_Click). The clickButton_Click event handler executes when the user clicks the clickButton control.

Each event handler receives two parameters when it is called. The first—an object reference named sender—is a reference to the object that generated the event. The second is a reference to an event arguments object of type EventArgs (or one of its derived classes), which is typically named e. This object contains additional information about the event that occurred. EventArgs is the base class of all classes that represent event information.

Software Engineering Observation 13.1

You should not expect return values from event handlers—event handlers are designed to execute code based on an action and return control to the main program.

Good Programming Practice 13.1

Use the event-handler naming convention controlName_eventName, *so method names are meaningful. Such names tell users what event a method handles for what control. This convention is not required, but it makes your code easier to read, understand, modify and maintain.*

To display a MessageBox in response to the event, insert the statement

```
MessageBox.Show( "Button was clicked." );
```

in the event handler's body. The resulting event handler appears in lines 16–19 of Fig. 13.5. When you execute the application and click the Button, a MessageBox appears displaying the text "Button was clicked".

13.3.2 Another Look at the Visual Studio Generated Code

Visual Studio generates the code that creates and initializes the GUI that you build in the GUI design window. This auto-generated code is placed in the Designer.cs file of the Form (SimpleEventExampleForm.Designer.cs in this example). You can open this file by expanding the node for the file you are currently working in (SimpleEventExampleForm.cs) and double clicking the file name that ends with Designer.cs. Figs. 13.6 and 13.7 show this file's contents. The IDE collapses the code in lines 21–53 of Fig. 13.7 by default.

Now that you have studied classes and objects in detail, this code will be easier to understand. Since this code is created and maintained by Visual Studio, you generally don't need to look at it. In fact, you do not need to understand most of the code shown here to build GUI applications. However, we now take a closer look to help you understand how GUI applications work.

```
SimpleEventExampleForm.Designer.cs

SimpleEventExampleForm                          components

 1   partial class SimpleEventExampleForm
 2   {
 3       /// <summary>
 4       /// Required designer variable.
 5       /// </summary>
 6       private System.ComponentModel.IContainer components = null;
 7
 8       /// <summary>
 9       /// Clean up any resources being used.
10       /// </summary>
11       /// <param name="disposing">true if managed resources should be disposed; otherwise,
12       protected override void Dispose(bool disposing)
13       {
14           if (disposing && (components != null))
15           {
16               components.Dispose();
17           }
18           base.Dispose(disposing);
19       }
20
```

Fig. 13.6 | First half of the Visual Studio generated code file.

```
SimpleEventExampleForm.Designer.cs                                        ▾ ✕

SimpleEventExampleForm                         ▾  🔧 components                ▾

21   #region Windows Form Designer generated code
22
23   /// <summary>
24   /// Required method for Designer support - do not modify
25   /// the contents of this method with the code editor.
26   /// </summary>
27   private void InitializeComponent()
28   {
29       this.clickButton = new System.Windows.Forms.Button();
30       this.SuspendLayout();
31       //
32       // clickButton
33       //
34       this.clickButton.Location = new System.Drawing.Point(84, 28);
35       this.clickButton.Name = "clickButton";
36       this.clickButton.Size = new System.Drawing.Size(75, 29);
37       this.clickButton.TabIndex = 0;
38       this.clickButton.Text = "Click Me";
39       this.clickButton.Click += new System.EventHandler(this.clickButton_Click);
40       //
41       // SimpleEventExample
42       //
43       this.AutoScaleDimensions = new System.Drawing.SizeF(6F, 13F);
44       this.AutoScaleMode = System.Windows.Forms.AutoScaleMode.Font;
45       this.ClientSize = new System.Drawing.Size(242, 84);
46       this.Controls.Add(this.clickButton);
47       this.Name = "SimpleEventExample";
48       this.Text = "Simple Event Example";
49       this.ResumeLayout(false);
50
51   }
52
53   #endregion
54
55   private System.Windows.Forms.Button clickButton;
56   }
```

Fig. 13.7 | Second half of the Visual Studio generated code file.

The auto-generated code that defines the GUI is actually part of the Form's class—in this case, SimpleEventExampleForm. Line 1 of Fig. 13.6 uses the partial modifier, which allows this class to be split among multiple files. Line 55 contains the declaration of the Button control clickButton that we created in **Design** mode. Note that the control is declared as an instance variable of class SimpleEventExampleForm. By default, all variable declarations for controls created through C#'s design window have a private access modifier. The code also includes the Dispose method for releasing resources (lines 12–19) and method InitializeComponent (lines 27–51), which contains the code that creates the Button, then sets some of the Button's and the Form's properties. The property values correspond to the values set in the **Properties** window for each control. Note that Visual Studio adds comments to the code that it generates, as in lines 31–33. Line 39 was generated when we created the event handler for the Button's Click event.

Method InitializeComponent is called when the Form is created, and establishes such properties as the Form title, the Form size, control sizes and text. Visual Studio also uses the code in this method to create the GUI you see in design view. Changing the code in InitializeComponent may prevent Visual Studio from displaying the GUI properly.

Error-Prevention Tip 13.1

The code generated by building a GUI in **Design** *mode is not meant to be modified directly, and doing so can result in an application that functions incorrectly. You should modify control properties through the* **Properties** *window.*

13.3.3 Delegates and the Event-Handling Mechanism

The control that generates an event is known as the *event sender*. An event-handling method—known as the *event receiver*—responds to a particular event that a control generates. When the event occurs, the event sender calls its event receiver to perform a task (i.e., to "handle the event").

The .NET event-handling mechanism allows you to choose your own names for event-handling methods. However, each event-handling method must declare the proper parameters to receive information about the event that it handles. Since you can choose your own method names, an event sender such as a Button cannot know in advance which method will respond to its events. So, we need a mechanism to indicate which method is the event receiver for an event.

Delegates

Event handlers are connected to a control's events via special objects called ***delegates***. A delegate object holds a reference to a method with a signature that is specified by the delegate type's declaration. GUI controls have predefined delegates that correspond to every event they can generate. For example, the delegate for a Button's Click event is of type EventHandler (namespace System). If you look at this type in the online help documentation, you will see that it is declared as follows:

```
public delegate void EventHandler( object sender, EventArgs e );
```

This uses the ***delegate*** keyword to declare a delegate type named EventHandler, which can hold references to methods that return void and receive two parameters—one of type object (the event sender) and one of type EventArgs. If you compare the delegate declaration with clickButton_Click's header (Fig. 13.5, line 16), you will see that this event handler indeed meets the requirements of the EventHandler delegate. Note that the preceding declaration actually creates an entire class for you. The details of this special class's declaration are handled by the compiler.

Indicating the Method that a Delegate Should Call

An event sender calls a delegate object like a method. Since each event handler is declared as a delegate, the event sender can simply call the appropriate delegate when an event occurs—a Button calls its EventHandler delegate in response to a click. The delegate's job is to invoke the appropriate method. To enable the clickButton_Click method to be called, Visual Studio assigns clickButton_Click to the delegate, as shown in line 39 of Fig. 13.7. This code is added by Visual Studio when you double click the Button control in **Design** mode. The expression

```
new System.EventHandler(this.clickButton_Click);
```

creates an EventHandler delegate object and initializes it with the clickButton_Click method. Line 39 uses the += operator to add the delegate to the Button's Click event. This indicates that clickButton_Click will respond when a user clicks the Button. Note that the += operator is overloaded by the delegate class that is created by the compiler.

You can actually specify that several different methods should be invoked in response to an event by adding other delegates to the Button's Click event with statements similar to line 39 of Fig. 13.7. Event delegates are *multicast*—they represent a set of delegate objects that all have the same signature. Multicast delegates enable several methods to be called in response to a single event. When an event occurs, the event sender calls every method referenced by the multicast delegate. This is known as *event multicasting*. Event delegates derive from class ***MulticastDelegate***, which derives from class ***Delegate*** (both from namespace System).

13.3.4 Other Ways to Create Event Handlers

In all the GUI applications you have created so far, you double clicked a control on the Form to create an event handler for that control. This technique creates an event handler for a control's *default event*—the event that is most frequently used with that control. Typically, controls can generate many different types of events, and each type can have its own event handler. For instance, you already created Click event handlers for Buttons by double clicking a Button in design view (Click is the default event for a Button). However your application can also provide an event handler for a Button's MouseHover event, which occurs when the mouse pointer remains positioned over the Button. We now discuss how to create an event handler for an event that is not a control's default event.

Using the Properties Window to Create Event Handlers

You can create additional event handlers through the **Properties** window. If you select a control on the Form, then click the **Events** icon (the lightning bolt icon in Fig. 13.8) in the **Properties** window, all the events for that control are listed in the window. You can double click an event's name to display the event handler in the editor, if the event handler already exists, or to create the event handler. You can also select an event, then use the drop-down list to its right to choose an existing method that should be used as the event handler for that event. The methods that appear in this drop-down list are the class's methods that have the proper signature to be an event handler for the selected event. You can return to viewing the properties of a control by selecting the **Properties** icon (Fig. 13.8).

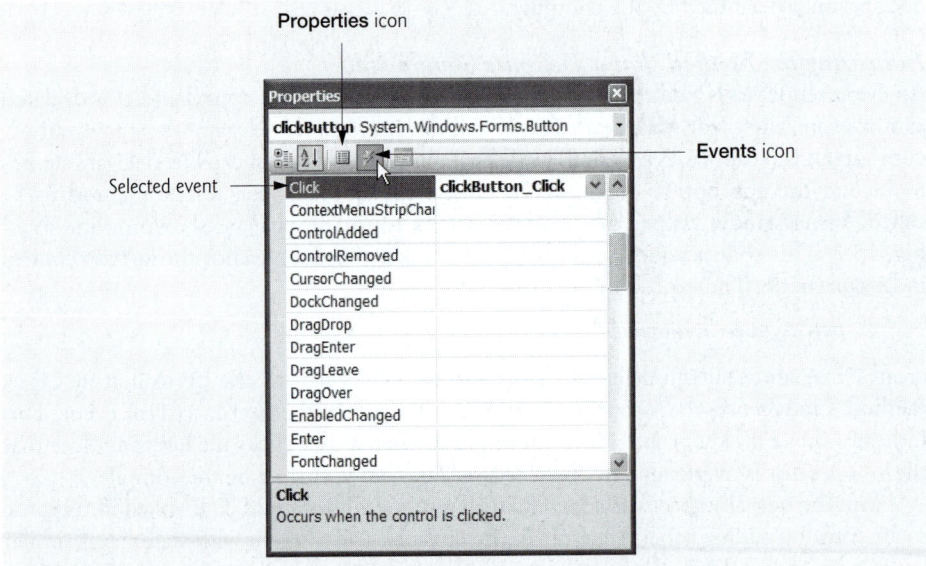

Fig. 13.8 | Viewing events for a Button control in the **Properties** window.

13.3.5 Locating Event Information

Read the Visual Studio documentation to learn about the different events raised by a control. To do this, select **Help > Index**. In the window that appears, select **.NET Framework** in the **Filtered by** drop-down list and enter the name of the control's class in the **Index** window. To ensure that you are selecting the proper class, enter the fully qualified class name as shown in Fig. 13.9 for class `System.Windows.Forms.Button`. Once you select a control's class in the documentation, a list of all the class's members is displayed. This list includes the events that the class can generate. In Fig. 13.9, we scrolled to class `Button`'s events. Click the name of an event to view its description and examples of its use (Fig. 13.10). Notice that the `Click` event is listed as a member of class `Control`, because class `Button`'s `Click` event is inherited from class `Control`.

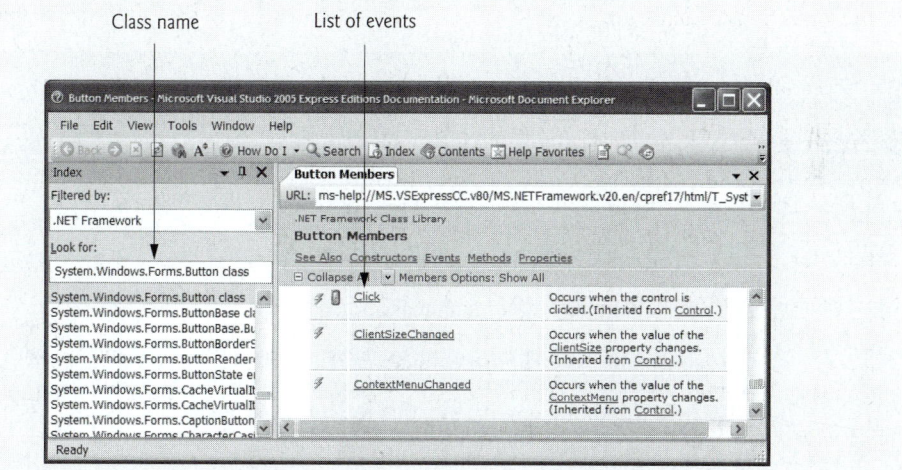

Fig. 13.9 | List of `Button` events.

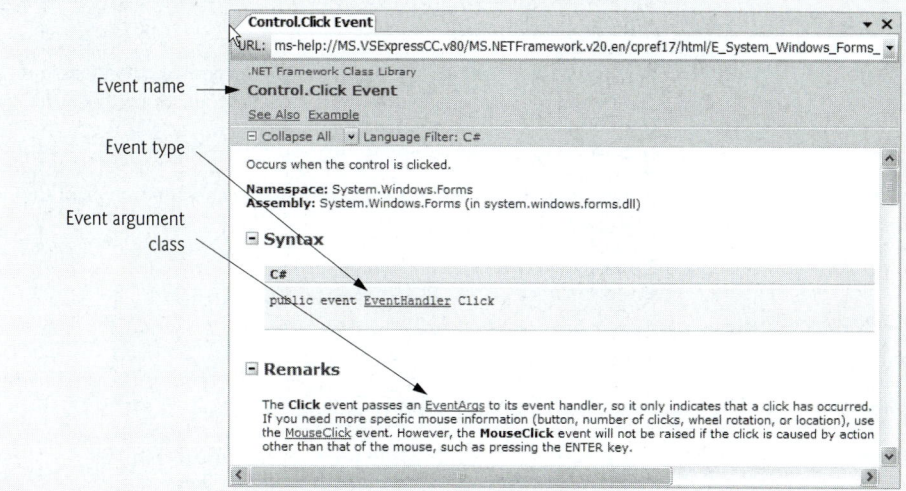

Fig. 13.10 | `Click` event details.

13.4 Control Properties and Layout

This section overviews properties that are common to many controls. Controls derive from class **Control** (namespace System.Windows.Forms). Figure 13.11 lists some of class Control's properties and methods. The properties shown here can be set for many controls. For example, the Text property specifies the text that appears on a control. The location of this text varies depending on the control. In a Windows Form, the text appears in the title bar, but the text of a Button appears on its face.

The **Focus** method transfers the focus to a control and makes it the *active control*. When you press the *Tab* key in an executing Windows application, controls receive the focus in the order specified by their **TabIndex** property. This property is set by Visual Studio based on the order in which controls are added to a Form, but you can change the tabbing order. TabIndex is helpful for users who enter information in many controls, such

Class Control properties and methods	Description
Common Properties	
BackColor	The control's background color.
BackgroundImage	The control's background image.
Enabled	Specifies whether the control is enabled (i.e., if the user can interact with it). Typically, portions of a disabled control appear "grayed out" as a visual indication to the user that the control is disabled.
Focused	Indicates whether the control has the focus.
Font	The Font used to display the control's text.
ForeColor	The control's foreground color. This usually determines the color of the text in the Text property.
TabIndex	The tab order of the control. When the *Tab* key is pressed, the focus transfers between controls based on the tab order. You can set this order.
TabStop	If true, then a user can give focus to this control via the *Tab* key.
Text	The text associated with the control. The location and appearance of the text vary depending on the type of control.
Visible	Indicates whether the control is visible.
Common Methods	
Focus	Acquires the focus.
Hide	Hides the control (sets the Visible property to false).
Show	Shows the control (sets the Visible property to true).

Fig. 13.11 | Class Control properties and methods.

as a set of TextBoxes that represent a user's name, address and telephone number. The user can enter information, then quickly select the next control by pressing the *Tab* key.

The **Enabled** property indicates whether the user can interact with a control to generate an event. Often, if a control is disabled, it is because an option is unavailable to the user at that time. For example, text editor applications often disable the "paste" command until the user copies some text. In most cases, a disabled control's text appears in gray (rather than in black). You can also hide a control from the user without disabling the control by setting the Visible property to false or by calling method Hide. In each case, the control still exists but is not visible on the Form.

You can use anchoring and docking to specify the layout of controls inside a container (such as a Form). *Anchoring* causes controls to remain at a fixed distance from the sides of the container even when the container is resized. Anchoring enhances the user experience. For example, if the user expects a control to appear in a particular corner of the application, anchoring ensures that the control will always be in that corner—even if the user resizes the Form. *Docking* attaches a control to a container such that the control stretches across an entire side. For example, a button docked to the top of a container stretches across the entire top of that container, regardless of the width of the container.

When parent containers are resized, anchored controls are moved (and possibly resized) so that the distance from the sides to which they are anchored does not vary. By default, most controls are anchored to the top-left corner of the Form. To see the effects of anchoring a control, create a simple Windows application that contains two Buttons. Anchor one control to the right and bottom sides by setting the **Anchor** property as shown in Fig. 13.12. Leave the other control unanchored. Execute the application and enlarge the Form. Notice that the Button anchored to the bottom-right corner is always the same distance from the Form's bottom-right corner (Fig. 13.13), but that the other control stays its original distance from the top-left corner of the Form.

Sometimes, it is desirable for a control to span an entire side of the Form, even when the Form is resized. For example, a control such as a status bar typically should remain at the bottom of the Form. Docking allows a control to span an entire side (left, right, top or bottom) of its parent container or to fill the entire container. When the parent control is resized, the docked control resizes as well. In Fig. 13.14, a Button is docked at the top of the Form (spanning the top portion). When the Form is resized, the Button is resized to the

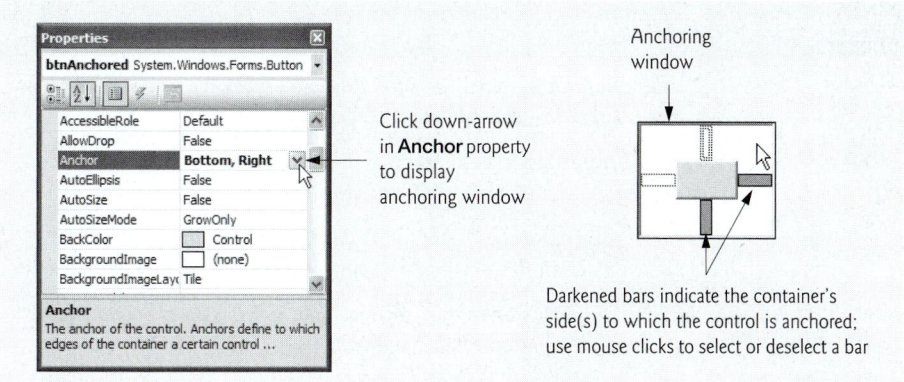

Fig. 13.12 | Manipulating the **Anchor** property of a control.

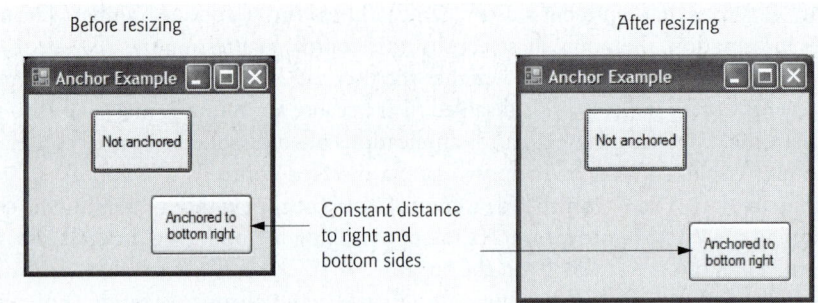

Fig. 13.13 | Anchoring demonstration.

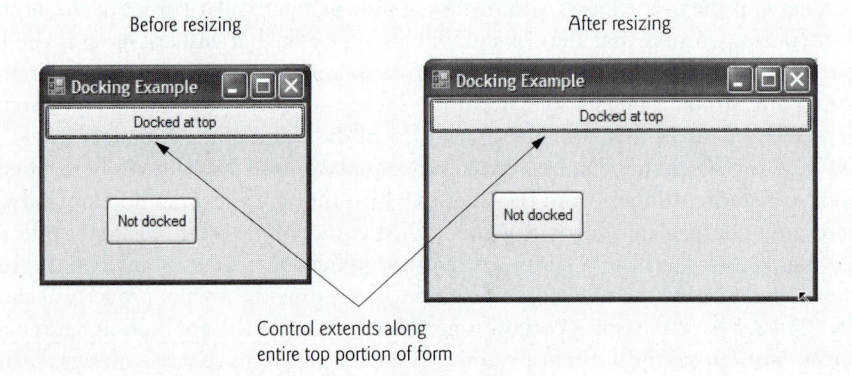

Fig. 13.14 | Docking a `Button` to the top of a `Form`.

Form's new width. Forms have a ***Padding*** property that specifies the distance between the docked controls and the Form edges. This property specifies four values (one for each side), and each value is set to 0 by default. Some common control layout properties are summarized in Fig. 13.15.

Control layout properties	Description
Anchor	Causes a control to remain at a fixed distance from the side(s) of the container even when the container is resized.
Dock	Allows a control to span one side of its container or to fill the entire container.
Padding	Sets the space between a container's edges and docked controls. The default is 0, causing the control to appear flush with the containe's sides.
Location	Specifies the location (as a set of coordinates) of the upper-left corner of the control, in relation to its container.

Fig. 13.15 | `Control` layout properties. (Part 1 of 2.)

Control layout properties	Description
Size	Specifies the size of the control in pixels as a Size object, which has properties Width and Height.
MinimumSize, MaximumSize	Indicates the minimum and maximum size of a Control, respectively.

Fig. 13.15 | Control layout properties. (Part 2 of 2.)

The Anchor and Dock properties of a Control are set with respect to the Control's parent container, which could be a Form or another parent container (such as a Panel; discussed in Section 13.6). The minimum and maximum Form (or other Control) sizes can be set via properties *MinimumSize* and *MaximumSize*, respectively. Both are of type *Size*, which has properties *Width* and *Height* to specify the size of the Form. Properties MinimumSize and MaximumSize allow you to design the GUI layout for a given size range. The user cannot make a Form smaller than the size specified by property MinimumSize and cannot make a Form larger than the size specified by property MaximumSize. To set a Form to a fixed size (where the Form cannot be resized by the user), set its minimum and maximum size to the same value or set its FormBorderStyle property to FixedSingle.

Look-and-Feel Observation 13.2

For resizable Forms, ensure that the GUI layout appears consistent across various Form sizes.

Using Visual Studio To Edit a GUI's Layout

Visual Studio provides tools that help you with GUI layout. You may have noticed when dragging a control across a Form, that blue lines (known as *snap lines*) appear to help you position the control with respect to other controls (Fig. 13.16) and the Form's edges. This new feature of Visual Studio 2005 makes the control you are dragging appear to "snap into

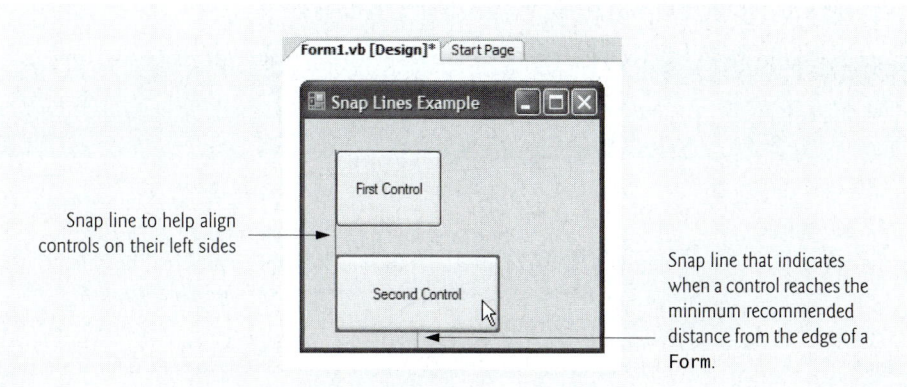

Fig. 13.16 | Snap lines in Visual Studio 2005.

place" alongside other controls. Visual Studio also provides the **Format** menu, which contains several options for modifying your GUI's layout. The **Format** menu does not appear in the IDE unless you select a control (or set of controls) in design view. When you select multiple controls, you can use the **Format** menu's **Align** submenu to align the controls. The **Format** menu also enables you to modify the amount of space between controls or to center a control on the Form.

13.5 Labels, TextBoxes and Buttons

Labels provide text information (as well as optional images) and are defined with class Label (a derived class of Control). A Label displays text that the user cannot directly modify. A Label's text can be changed programmatically by modifying the Label's Text property. Figure 13.17 lists common Label properties.

A textbox (class TextBox) is an area in which either text can be displayed by a program or the user can type text via the keyboard. A *password TextBox* is a TextBox that hides the information entered by the user. As the user types characters, the password TextBox masks the user input by displaying a character you specify (usually *). If you set the **Password-Char** property, the TextBox becomes a password TextBox. Users often encounter both types of TextBoxes, when logging into a computer or Web site—the username TextBox allows users to input their usernames; the password TextBox allows users to enter their passwords. Figure 13.18 lists the common properties and a common event of TextBoxes.

Common Label properties	Description
Font	The font of the text on the Label.
Text	The text on the Label.
TextAlign	The alignment of the Label's text on the control—horizontally (left, center or right) and vertically (top, middle or bottom).

Fig. 13.17 | Common Label properties.

TextBox properties and events	Description
Common Properties	
AcceptsReturn	If true in a multiline TextBox, pressing *Enter* in the TextBox creates a new line. If false, pressing *Enter* is the same as pressing the default Button on the Form. The default Button is the one assigned to a Form's AcceptButton property.
Multiline	If true, the TextBox can span multiple lines. The default value is false.

Fig. 13.18 | TextBox properties and events. (Part 1 of 2.)

TextBox properties and events	Description
PasswordChar	When this property is set to a character, the TextBox becomes a password box, and the specified character masks each character the user type. If no character is specified, the TextBox displays the typed text.
ReadOnly	If true, the TextBox has a gray background, and its text cannot be edited. The default value is false.
ScrollBars	For multiline textboxes, this property indicates which scrollbars appear (None, Horizontal, Vertical or Both).
Text	The TextBox's text content.
Common Event	
TextChanged	Generated when the text changes in a TextBox (i.e., when the user adds or deletes characters). When you double click the TextBox control in **Design** mode, an empty event handler for this event is generated.

Fig. 13.18 | TextBox properties and events. (Part 2 of 2.)

A button is a control that the user clicks to trigger a specific action or to select an option in a program. As you will see, a program can use several types of buttons, such as *checkboxes* and *radio buttons*. All the button classes derive from class **ButtonBase** (namespace System.Windows.Forms), which defines common button features. In this section, we discuss class Button, which typically enables a user to issue a command to an application. Figure 13.19 lists common properties and a common event of class Button.

Button properties and events	Description
Common Properties	
Text	Specifies the text displayed on the Button face.
FlatStyle	Modifies a Button's appearance—attribute Flat (for the Button to display without a three-dimensional appearance), Popup (for the Button to appear flat until the user moves the mouse pointer over the Button), Standard (three-dimensional) and System, where the Button's appearance is controlled by the operating system. The default value is Standard.
Common Event	
Click	Generated when the user clicks the Button. When you double click a Button in design view, an empty event handler for this event is created.

Fig. 13.19 | Button properties and event.

Look-and-Feel Observation 13.3

Although Labels, TextBoxes *and other controls can respond to mouse clicks,* Buttons *are more natural for this purpose.*

Figure 13.20 uses a TextBox, a Button and a Label. The user enters text into a password box and clicks the Button, causing the text input to be displayed in the Label. Normally, we would not display this text—the purpose of password TextBoxes is to hide the text being entered by the user. When the user clicks the **Show Me** Button, this application retrieves the text that the user typed in the password TextBox and displays it in another TextBox.

First, create the GUI by dragging the controls (a TextBox, a Button and a Label) on the Form. Once the controls are positioned, change their names in the **Properties** window from the default values—textBox1, button1 and label1—to the more descriptive displayPasswordLabel, displayPasswordButton and inputPasswordTextBox. The (Name) property in the **Properties** window enables us to change the variable name for a control. Visual Studio creates the necessary code and places it in method InitializeComponent of the partial class in the file LabelTextBoxButtonTestForm.Designer.cs.

```csharp
 1   // Fig. 13.20: LabelTextBoxButtonTestForm.cs
 2   // Using a TextBox, Label and Button to display
 3   // the hidden text in a password TextBox.
 4   using System;
 5   using System.Windows.Forms;
 6
 7   // Form that creates a password TextBox and
 8   // a Label to display TextBox contents
 9   public partial class LabelTextBoxButtonTestForm : Form
10   {
11      // default constructor
12      public LabelTextBoxButtonTestForm()
13      {
14         InitializeComponent();
15      } // end constructor
16
17      // display user input in Label
18      private void displayPasswordButton_Click(
19         object sender, EventArgs e )
20      {
21         // display the text that the user typed
22         displayPasswordLabel.Text = inputPasswordTextBox.Text;
23      } // end method displayPasswordButton_Click
24   } // end class LabelTextBoxButtonTestForm
```

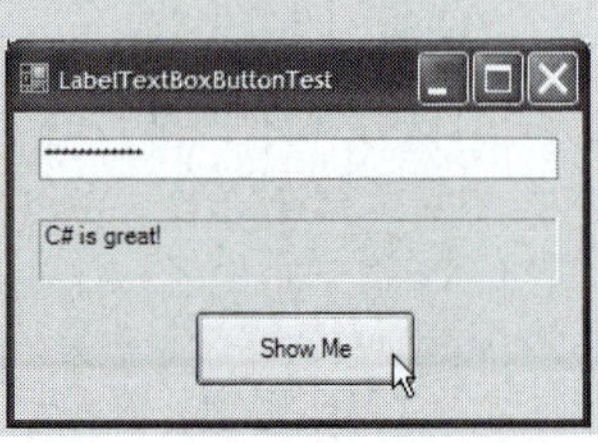

Fig. 13.20 | Program to display hidden text in a password box.

We then set displayPasswordButton's Text property to "Show Me" and clear the Text of displayPasswordLabel and inputPasswordTextBox so that they are blank when the program begins executing. The BorderStyle property of displayPasswordLabel is set to Fixed3D, giving our Label a three-dimensional appearance. The BorderStyle property of all TextBoxes is set to Fixed3D by default. The password character for inputPassword-TextBox is set by assigning the asterisk character (*) to the PasswordChar property. This property accepts only one character.

We create an event handler for displayPasswordButton by double clicking this control in **Design** mode. We add line 22 to the event handler's body. When the user clicks the **Show Me** Button in the executing application, line 22 obtains the text entered by the user in inputPasswordTextBox and displays the text in displayPasswordLabel.

13.6 GroupBoxes and Panels

GroupBoxes and *Panels* arrange controls on a GUI. GroupBoxes and Panels are typically used to group several controls of similar functionality or several controls that are related in a GUI. All of the controls in a GroupBox or Panel move together when the GroupBox or Panel is moved.

The primary difference between these two controls is that GroupBoxes can display a caption (i.e., text) and do not include scrollbars, whereas Panels can include scrollbars and do not include a caption. GroupBoxes have thin borders by default; Panels can be set so that they also have borders by changing their BorderStyle property. Figures 13.21–13.22 list the common properties of GroupBoxes and Panels, respectively.

Look-and-Feel Observation 13.4

Panels and GroupBoxes can contain other Panels and GroupBoxes for more complex layouts.

GroupBox properties	Description
Controls	The set of controls that the GroupBox contains.
Text	Specifies the caption text displayed at the top of the GroupBox.

Fig. 13.21 | GroupBox properties.

Panel properties	Description
AutoScroll	Indicates whether scrollbars appear when the Panel is too small to display all of its controls. The default value is false.
BorderStyle	Sets the border of the Panel. The default value is None; other options are Fixed3D and FixedSingle.
Controls	The set of controls that the Panel contains.

Fig. 13.22 | Panel properties.

Look-and-Feel Observation 13.5

You can organize a GUI by anchoring and docking controls inside a GroupBox or Panel. The GroupBox or Panel then can be anchored or docked inside a Form. This divides controls into functional "groups" that can be arranged easily.

To create a GroupBox, drag its icon from the **Toolbox** onto a Form. Then, drag new controls from the **Toolbox** into the GroupBox. These controls are added to the GroupBox's **Controls** property and become part of the GroupBox. The GroupBox's Text property specifies the caption.

To create a Panel, drag its icon from the **Toolbox** onto the Form. You can then add controls directly to the Panel by dragging them from the **Toolbox** onto the Panel. To enable the scrollbars, set the Panel's AutoScroll property to true. If the Panel is resized and cannot display all of its controls, scrollbars appear (Fig. 13.23). The scrollbars can be used to view all the controls in the Panel—both at design time and at execution time. In Fig. 13.23, we set the Panel's BorderStyle property to FixedSingle so that you can see the Panel in the Form.

Look-and-Feel Observation 13.6

Use Panels with scrollbars to avoid cluttering a GUI and to reduce the GUI's size.

The program in Fig. 13.24 uses a GroupBox and a Panel to arrange Buttons. When these Buttons are clicked, their event handlers change the text on a Label.

The GroupBox (named mainGroupBox) has two Buttons—hiButton (which displays the text **Hi**) and byeButton (which displays the text **Bye**). The Panel (named mainPanel) also has two Buttons, leftButton (which displays the text **Far Left**) and rightButton (which displays the text **Far Right**). The mainPanel has its AutoScroll property set to true, allowing scrollbars to appear when the contents of the Panel require more space

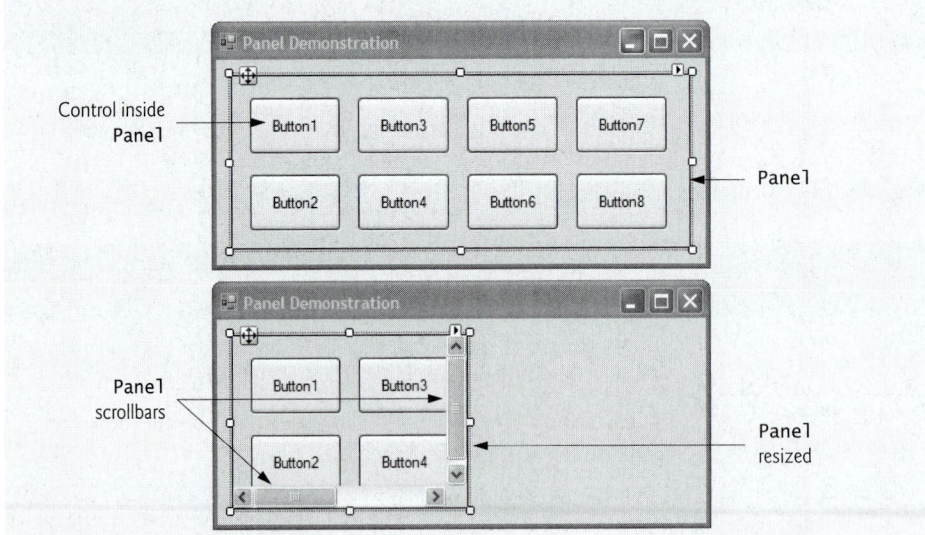

Fig. 13.23 | Creating a Panel with scrollbars.

```
 1   // Fig. 13.24: GroupboxPanelExampleForm.cs
 2   // Using GroupBoxes and Panels to hold Buttons.
 3   using System;
 4   using System.Windows.Forms;
 5
 6   // Form that displays a GroupBox and a Panel
 7   public partial class GroupBoxPanelExampleForm : Form
 8   {
 9      // default constructor
10      public GroupBoxPanelExampleForm()
11      {
12         InitializeComponent();
13      } // end constructor
14
15      // event handler for Hi Button
16      private void hiButton_Click( object sender, EventArgs e )
17      {
18         messageLabel.Text = "Hi pressed"; // change text in Label
19      } // end method hiButton_Click
20
21      // event handler for Bye Button
22      private void byeButton_Click( object sender, EventArgs e )
23      {
24         messageLabel.Text = "Bye pressed"; // change text in Label
25      } // end method byeButton_Click
26
27      // event handler for Far Left Button
28      private void leftButton_Click( object sender, EventArgs e )
29      {
30         messageLabel.Text = "Far left pressed"; // change text in Label
31      } // end method leftButton_Click
32
33      // event handler for Far Right Button
34      private void rightButton_Click( object sender, EventArgs e )
35      {
36         messageLabel.Text = "Far right pressed"; // change text in Label
37      } // end method rightButton_Click
38   } // end class GroupBoxPanelExampleForm
```

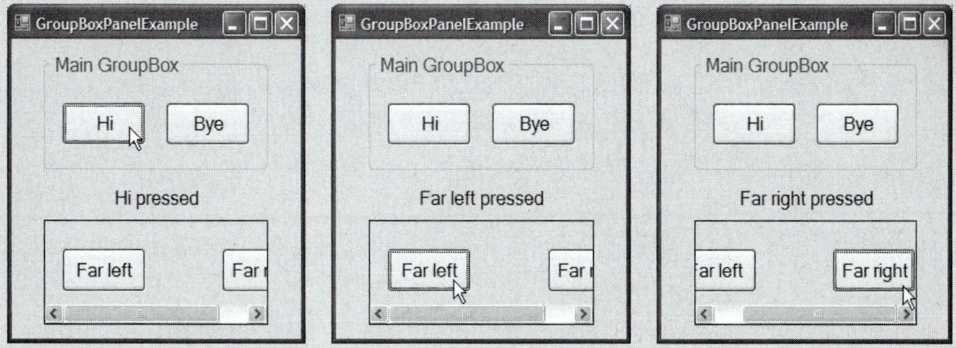

Fig. 13.24 | Using GroupBoxes and Panels to arrange Buttons.

than the Panel's visible area. The Label (named messageLabel) is initially blank. To add controls to mainGroupBox or mainPanel, Visual Studio calls method Add of each container's Controls property. This code is placed in the partial class located in the file Group-BoxPanelExampleForm.Designer.cs.

The event handlers for the four Buttons are located in lines 16–37. We added a line in each event handler (lines 18, 24, 30 and 36) to change the text of messageLabel to indicate which Button the user pressed.

13.7 CheckBoxes and RadioButtons

C# has two types of *state buttons* that can be in the on/off or true/false states—*CheckBoxes* and *RadioButtons*. Like class Button, classes CheckBox and RadioButton are derived from class ButtonBase.

CheckBoxes

A CheckBox is a small square that either is blank or contains a check mark. When the user clicks a CheckBox to select it, a check mark appears in the box. If the user clicks CheckBox again to deselect it, the check mark is removed. Any number of CheckBoxes can be selected at a time. A list of common CheckBox properties and events appears in Fig. 13.25.

CheckBox properties and events	Description
Common Properties	
Checked	Indicates whether the CheckBox is checked (contains a check mark) or unchecked (blank). This property returns a Boolean value.
CheckState	Indicates whether the CheckBox is checked or unchecked with a value from the CheckState enumeration (Checked, Unchecked or Indeterminate). Indeterminate is used when it is unclear whether the state should be Checked or Unchecked. For example, in Microsoft Word, when you select a paragraph that contains several character formats, then go to **Format > Font**, some of the CheckBoxes appear in the Indeterminate state. When CheckState is set to Indeterminate, the CheckBox is usually shaded.
Text	Specifies the text displayed to the right of the CheckBox.
Common Events	
CheckedChanged	Generated when the Checked property changes. This is a CheckBox's default event. When a user double clicks the CheckBox control in design view, an empty event handler for this event is generated.
CheckStateChanged	Generated when the CheckState property changes.

Fig. 13.25 | CheckBox properties and events.

The program in Fig. 13.26 allows the user to select CheckBoxes to change a Label's font style. The event handler for one CheckBox applies bold and the event handler for the other applies italic. If both CheckBoxes are selected, the font style is set to bold and italic. Initially, neither CheckBox is checked.

The boldCheckBox has its Text property set to Bold. The italicCheckBox has its Text property set to Italic. The Text property of outputLabel is set to Watch the font style change. After creating the controls, we define their event handlers. Double clicking the CheckBoxes at design time creates empty CheckedChanged event handlers.

To change the font style on a Label, you must set its Font property to a new **_Font object_** (lines 21–23 and 31–33). The Font constructor that we use here takes the font name, size and style as arguments. The first two arguments—outputLabel.Font.Name and outputLabel.Font.Size—use outputLabel's original font name and size. The style is specified with a member of the **_FontStyle enumeration_**, which contains Regular, Bold, Italic, Strikeout and Underline. (The Strikeout style displays text with a line through

```
 1   // Fig. 13.26: CheckBoxTestForm.cs
 2   // Using CheckBoxes to toggle italic and bold styles.
 3   using System;
 4   using System.Drawing;
 5   using System.Windows.Forms;
 6
 7   // Form contains CheckBoxes to allow the user to modify sample text
 8   public partial class CheckBoxTestForm : Form
 9   {
10      // default constructor
11      public CheckBoxTestForm()
12      {
13         InitializeComponent();
14      } // end constructor
15
16      // toggle the font style between bold and
17      // not bold based on the  current setting
18      private void boldCheckBox_CheckedChanged(
19         object sender, EventArgs e )
20      {
21         outputLabel.Font =
22            new Font( outputLabel.Font.Name, outputLabel.Font.Size,
23            outputLabel.Font.Style ^ FontStyle.Bold );
24      } // end metod boldCheckBox_CheckedChanged
25
26      // toggle the font style between italic and
27      // not italic based on the current setting
28      private void italicCheckBox_CheckedChanged(
29         object sender, EventArgs e )
30      {
31         outputLabel.Font =
32            new Font( outputLabel.Font.Name, outputLabel.Font.Size,
33            outputLabel.Font.Style ^ FontStyle.Italic );
34      } // end method italicCheckBox_CheckedChanged
35   } // end class CheckBoxTestForm
```

Fig. 13.26 | Using CheckBoxes to change font styles. (Part 1 of 2.)

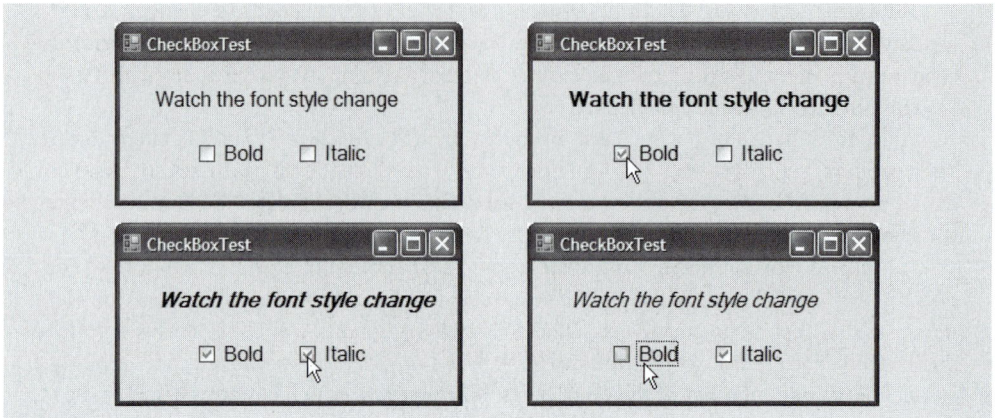

Fig. 13.26 | Using CheckBoxes to change font styles. (Part 2 of 2.)

it.) A Font object's **Style** property is read-only, so it can be set only when the Font object is created.

Styles can be combined via ***bitwise operators***—operators that perform manipulation on bits of information. Recall from Chapter 1 that all data is represented in the computer as combinations of 0s and 1s. Each 0 or 1 represents a bit. FontStyle has a System.FlagAttribute, meaning that the FontStyle bit values are selected in a way that allows us to combine different FontStyle elements to create compound styles, using bitwise operators. These styles are not mutually exclusive, so we can combine different styles and remove them without affecting the combination of previous FontStyle elements. We can combine these various font styles, using either the logical OR (|) operator or the logical exclusive OR (∧) operator. When the logical OR operator is applied to two bits, if at least one bit of the two has the value 1, then the result is 1. Combining styles using the conditional OR operator works as follows. Assume that FontStyle.Bold is represented by bits 01 and that FontStyle.Italic is represented by bits 10. When we use the conditional OR (||) to combine the styles, we obtain the bits 11.

```
01  =  Bold
10  =  Italic
--
11  =  Bold and Italic
```

The conditional OR operator helps create style combinations. However, what happens if we want to undo a style combination, as we did in Fig. 13.26?

The logical exclusive OR operator enables us to combine styles and to undo existing style settings. When logical exclusive OR is applied to two bits, if both bits have the same value, then the result is 0. If both bits are different, then the result is 1.

Combining styles using logical exclusive OR works as follows. Assume, again, that FontStyle.Bold is represented by bits 01 and that FontStyle.Italic is represented by bits 10. When we use logical exclusive OR (∧) on both styles, we obtain the bits 11.

```
01  =  Bold
10  =  Italic
--
11  =  Bold and Italic
```

Now, suppose that we would like to remove the FontStyle.Bold style from the previous combination of FontStyle.Bold and FontStyle.Italic. The easiest way to do so is to reapply the logical exclusive OR (^) operator to the compound style and FontStyle.Bold.

```
11   =   Bold and Italic
01   =   Bold
--
10   =   Italic
```

This is a simple example. The advantages of using bitwise operators to combine FontStyle values become more evident when we consider that there are five different FontStyle values (Bold, Italic, Regular, Strikeout and Underline), resulting in 16 different FontStyle combinations. Using bitwise operators to combine font styles greatly reduces the amount of code required to check all possible font combinations.

In Fig. 13.26, we need to set the FontStyle so that the text appears in bold if it was not bold originally, and vice versa. Notice that line 23 uses the bitwise logical exclusive OR operator to do this. If outputLabel.Font.Style is bold, then the resulting style is not bold. If the text is originally italic, the resulting style is bold and italic, rather than just bold. The same applies for FontStyle.Italic in line 33.

If we did not use bitwise operators to compound FontStyle elements, we would have to test for the current style and change it accordingly. For example, in event handler boldCheckBox_CheckChanged, we could test for the regular style and make it bold; test for the bold style and make it regular; test for the italic style and make it bold italic; and test for the italic bold style and make it italic. This is cumbersome because, for every new style we add, we double the number of combinations. Adding a CheckBox for underline would require testing eight additional styles. Adding a CheckBox for strikeout would require testing 16 additional styles.

RadioButtons

Radio buttons (defined with class RadioButton) are similar to CheckBoxes in that they also have two states—*selected* and *not selected* (also called *deselected*). However, RadioButtons normally appear as a *group*, in which only one RadioButton can be selected at a time. Selecting one RadioButton in the group forces all the others to be deselected. Therefore, RadioButtons are used to represent a set of *mutually exclusive* options (i.e., a set in which multiple options cannot be selected at the same time).

Look-and-Feel Observation 13.7

Use RadioButtons when the user should choose only one option in a group.

Look-and-Feel Observation 13.8

Use CheckBoxes when the user should be able to choose multiple options in a group.

All RadioButtons added to a container become part of the same group. To separate RadioButtons into several groups, the RadioButtons must be added to GroupBoxes or Panels. The common properties and a common event of class RadioButton are listed in Fig. 13.27.

RadioButton properties and events	Description
Common Properties	
Checked	Indicates whether the RadioButton is checked.
Text	Specifies the RadioButton's text.
Common Event	
CheckedChanged	Generated every time the RadioButton is checked or unchecked. When you double click a RadioButton control in design view, an empty event handler for this event is generated.

Fig. 13.27 | RadioButton properties and events.

Software Engineering Observation 13.2

Forms, GroupBoxes, and Panels can act as logical groups for RadioButtons. The RadioButtons within each group are mutually exclusive to each other, but not to RadioButtons in different logical groups.

The program in Fig. 13.28 uses RadioButtons to enable users to select options for a MessageBox. After selecting the desired attributes, the user presses the **Display** Button to display the MessageBox. A Label in the lower-left corner shows the result of the MessageBox (i.e., which Button the user clicked—**Yes**, **No**, **Cancel**, etc.).

To store the user's choices, we create and initialize the iconType and buttonType objects (lines 11–12). Object iconType is of type MessageBoxIcon, and can have values Asterisk, Error, Exclamation, Hand, Information, None, Question, Stop and Warning. The sample output shows only Error, Exclamation, Information and Question icons.

Object buttonType is of type MessageBoxButtons, and can have values AbortRetryIgnore, OK, OKCancel, RetryCancel, YesNo and YesNoCancel. The name indicates the options that are presented to the user in the MessageBox. The sample output windows show MessageBoxes for all of the MessageBoxButtons enumeration values.

We created two GroupBoxes, one for each set of enumeration values. The GroupBox captions are **Button Type** and **Icon**. The GroupBoxes contain RadioButtons for the corresponding enumeration options, and the RadioButtons' Text properties are set appropriately. Because the RadioButtons are grouped, only one RadioButton can be selected from each GroupBox. There is also a Button (displayButton) labeled **Display**. When a user clicks this Button, a customized MessageBox is displayed. A Label (displayLabel) displays which Button the user pressed within the MessageBox.

The event handler for the RadioButtons handles the CheckedChanged event of each RadioButton. When a RadioButton contained in the **Button Type** GroupBox is checked, the checked RadioButton's corresponding event handler sets buttonType to the appropriate value. Lines 21–45 contain the event handling for these RadioButtons. Similarly, when the user checks the RadioButtons belonging to the **Icon** GroupBox, the event handlers associated with these events (lines 48–80) set iconType to its corresponding value.

```
 1   // Fig. 13.28: RadioButtonsTestForm.cs
 2   // Using RadioButtons to set message window options.
 3   using System;
 4   using System.Windows.Forms;
 5
 6   // Form contains several RadioButtons--user chooses one
 7   // from each group to create a custom MessageBox
 8   public partial class RadioButtonsTestForm : Form
 9   {
10      // create variables that store the user's choice of options
11      private MessageBoxIcon iconType;
12      private MessageBoxButtons buttonType;
13
14      // default constructor
15      public RadioButtonsTestForm()
16      {
17         InitializeComponent();
18      } // end constructor
19
20      // change Buttons based on option chosen by sender
21      private void buttonType_CheckedChanged( object sender, EventArgs e )
22      {
23         if ( sender == okButton ) // display OK Button
24            buttonType = MessageBoxButtons.OK;
25
26         // display OK and Cancel Buttons
27         else if ( sender == okCancelButton )
28            buttonType = MessageBoxButtons.OKCancel;
29
30         // display Abort, Retry and Ignore Buttons
31         else if ( sender == abortRetryIgnoreButton )
32            buttonType = MessageBoxButtons.AbortRetryIgnore;
33
34         // display Yes, No and Cancel Buttons
35         else if ( sender == yesNoCancelButton )
36            buttonType = MessageBoxButtons.YesNoCancel;
37
38         // display Yes and No Buttons
39         else if ( sender == yesNoButton )
40            buttonType = MessageBoxButtons.YesNo;
41
42         // only on option left--display Retry and Cancel Buttons
43         else
44            buttonType = MessageBoxButtons.RetryCancel;
45      } // end method buttonType_Changed
46
47      // change Icon based on option chosen by sender
48      private void iconType_CheckedChanged( object sender, EventArgs e )
49      {
50         if ( sender == asteriskButton ) // display asterisk Icon
51            iconType = MessageBoxIcon.Asterisk;
52
```

Fig. 13.28 | Using RadioButtons to set message-window options. (Part 1 of 4.)

```
53        // display error Icon
54        else if ( sender == errorButton )
55           iconType = MessageBoxIcon.Error;
56
57        // display exclamation point Icon
58        else if ( sender == exclamationButton )
59           iconType = MessageBoxIcon.Exclamation;
60
61        // display hand Icon
62        else if ( sender == handButton )
63           iconType = MessageBoxIcon.Hand;
64
65        // display information Icon
66        else if ( sender == informationButton )
67           iconType = MessageBoxIcon.Information;
68
69        // display question mark Icon
70        else if ( sender == questionButton )
71           iconType = MessageBoxIcon.Question;
72
73        // display stop Icon
74        else if ( sender == stopButton )
75           iconType = MessageBoxIcon.Stop;
76
77        // only one option left--display warning Icon
78        else
79           iconType = MessageBoxIcon.Warning;
80     } // end method iconType_CheckChanged
81
82     // display MessageBox and Button user pressed
83     private void displayButton_Click( object sender, EventArgs e )
84     {
85        // display MessageBox and store
86        // the value of the Button that was pressed
87        DialogResult result = MessageBox.Show(
88           "This is your Custom MessageBox.", "Custom MessageBox",
89           buttonType, iconType, 0, 0 );
90
91        // check to see which Button was pressed in the MessageBox
92        // change text displayed accordingly
93        switch (result)
94        {
95           case DialogResult.OK:
96              displayLabel.Text = "OK was pressed.";
97              break;
98           case DialogResult.Cancel:
99              displayLabel.Text = "Cancel was pressed.";
100             break;
101          case DialogResult.Abort:
102             displayLabel.Text = "Abort was pressed.";
103             break;
```

Fig. 13.28 | Using RadioButtons to set message-window options. (Part 2 of 4.)

```
104           case DialogResult.Retry:
105               displayLabel.Text = "Retry was pressed.";
106               break;
107           case DialogResult.Ignore:
108               displayLabel.Text = "Ignore was pressed.";
109               break;
110           case DialogResult.Yes:
111               displayLabel.Text = "Yes was pressed.";
112               break;
113           case DialogResult.No:
114               displayLabel.Text = "No was pressed.";
115               break;
116       } // end switch
117     } // end method displayButton_Click
118 } // end class RadioButtonsTestForm
```

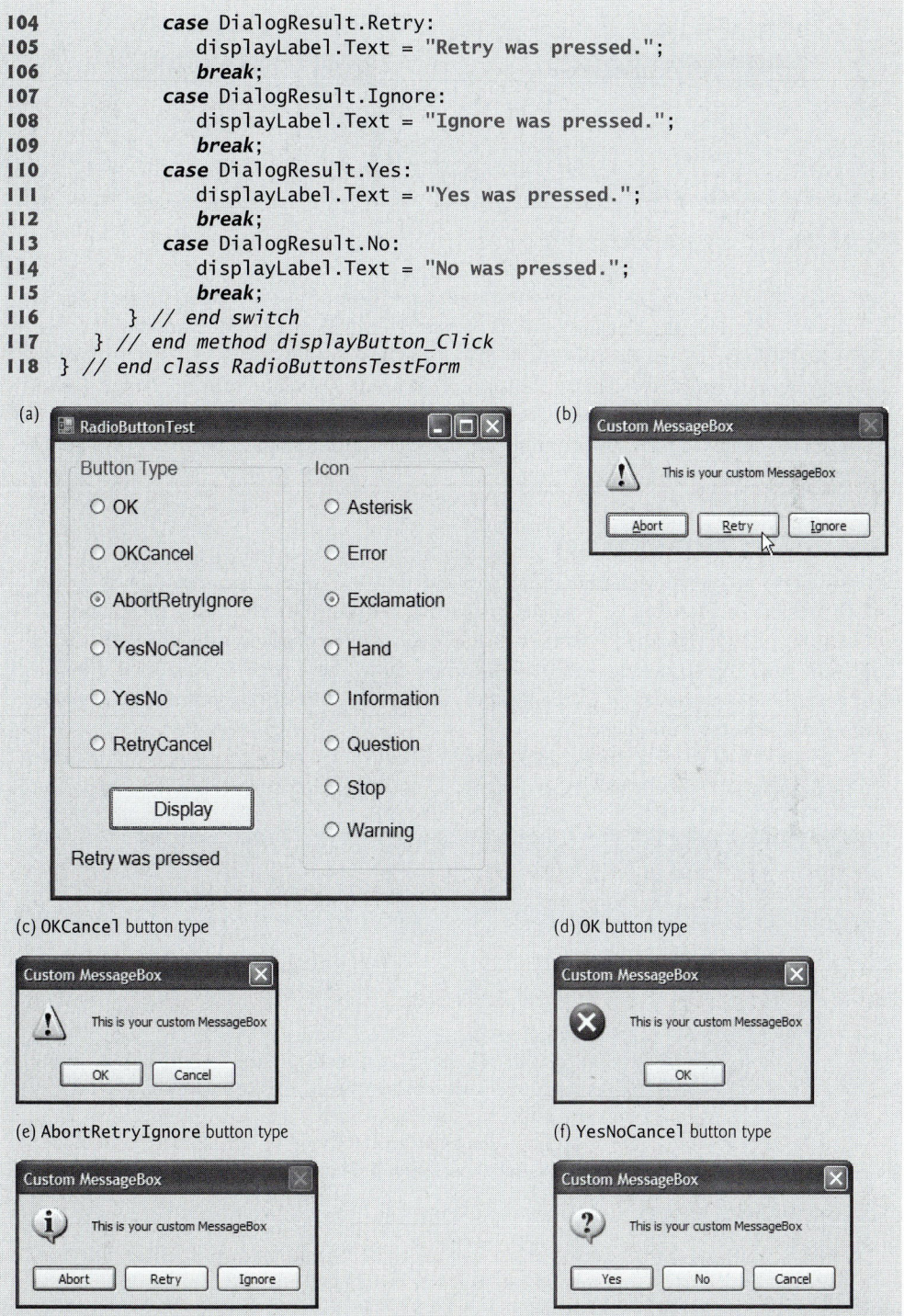

Fig. 13.28 | Using RadioButtons to set message-window options. (Part 3 of 4.)

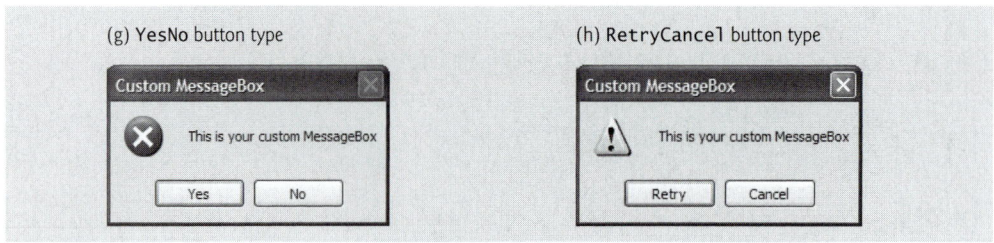

Fig. 13.28 | Using RadioButtons to set message-window options. (Part 4 of 4.)

The Click event handler for displayButton (lines 83–117) creates a MessageBox (lines 87–89). The MessageBox options are specified with the values stored in iconType and buttonType. When the user clicks one of the MessageBox's buttons, the result of the message box is returned to the application. This result is a value from the *DialogResult enumeration* that contains Abort, Cancel, Ignore, No, None, OK, Retry or Yes. The switch statement in lines 93–116 tests for the result and sets displayLabel.Text appropriately.

13.8 PictureBoxes

A PictureBox displays an image. The image can be one of several formats, such as bitmap, GIF (Graphics Interchange Format) and JPEG. (Images are discussed in Chapter 17, Graphics and Multimedia.) A PictureBox's Image property specifies the image that is displayed, and the SizeMode property indicates how the image is displayed (Normal, StretchImage, Autosize or CenterImage). Figure 13.29 describes common PictureBox properties and a common event.

Figure 13.30 uses a PictureBox named imagePictureBox to display one of three bitmap images—image0, image1 or image2. These images are located in the images direc-

PictureBox properties and event	Description
Common Properties	
Image	Sets the image to display in the PictureBox.
SizeMode	Enumeration that controls image sizing and positioning. Values are Normal (default), StretchImage, AutoSize and CenterImage. Normal places the image in the top-left corner of the PictureBox, and CenterImage puts the image in the middle. These two options truncate the image if it is too large. StretchImage resizes the image to fit in the PictureBox. AutoSize resizes the PictureBox to hold the image.
Common Event	
Click	Occurs when the user clicks the control. When you double click this control in the designer, an event handler is generated for this event.

Fig. 13.29 | PictureBox properties and event.

```
 1   // Fig. 13.30: PictureBoxTestForm.cs
 2   // Using a PictureBox to display images.
 3   using System;
 4   using System.Drawing;
 5   using System.Windows.Forms;
 6   using System.IO;
 7
 8   // Form to display different images when PictureBox is clicked
 9   public partial class PictureBoxTestForm : Form
10   {
11      private int imageNum = -1; // determines which image is displayed
12
13      // default constructor
14      public PictureBoxTestForm()
15      {
16         InitializeComponent();
17      } // end constructor
18
19      // change image whenever Next Button is clicked
20      private void nextButton_Click( object sender, EventArgs e )
21      {
22         imageNum = ( imageNum + 1 ) % 3; // imageNum cycles from 0 to 2
23
24         // create Image object from file, display in PicutreBox
25         imagePictureBox.Image = Image.FromFile(
26            Directory.GetCurrentDirectory() + @"\images\image" +
27            imageNum + ".bmp" );
28      } // end method nextButton_Click
29   } // end class PictureBoxTestForm
```

Fig. 13.30 | Using a PictureBox to display images. (Part 1 of 2.)

Fig. 13.30 │ Using a `PictureBox` to display images. (Part 2 of 2.)

tory in the project's `bin/Debug` and `bin/Release` directories. Whenever a user clicks the **Next Image** `Button`, the image changes to the next image in sequence. When the last image is displayed and the user clicks the **Next Image** `Button`, the first image is displayed again. Inside event handler `nextButton_Click` (lines 20–28), we use an `int` (`imageNum`) to store the number of the image we want to display. We then set the `Image` property of `imagePic-tureBox` to an `Image` (lines 25–27).

13.9 ToolTips

In Chapter 2, we demonstrated tool tips—the helpful text that appears when the mouse hovers over an item in a GUI. Recall that the tool tips displayed in Visual Studio help you become familiar with the IDE's features and serve as useful reminders for each toolbar icon's functionality. Many programs use tool tips to remind users of each control's purpose. For example, Microsoft Word has tool tips that help users determine the purpose of the application's icons. This section demonstrates how use the ***ToolTip component*** to add tool tips to your applications. Figure 13.31 describes common properties and a common event of class `ToolTip`.

ToolTip properties and events	Description
Common Properties	
`AutoPopDelay`	The amount of time (in milliseconds) that the tool tip appears while the mouse is over a control.
`InitialDelay`	The amount of time (in milliseconds) that a mouse must hover over a control before a tool tip appears.

Fig. 13.31 │ `ToolTip` properties and events. (Part 1 of 2.)

ToolTip properties and events	Description
ReshowDelay	The amount of time (in milliseconds) between which two different tool tips appear (when the mouse is moved from one control to another).
Common Event	
Draw	Raised when the tool tip is displayed. This event allows programmers to modify the appearance of the tool tip.

Fig. 13.31 | ToolTip properties and events. (Part 2 of 2.)

When you add a ToolTip component from the **Toolbox**, it appears in the ***component tray***—the gray region below the Form in **Design** mode. Once a ToolTip is added to a Form, a new property appears in the **Properties** window for the Form's other controls. This property appears in the **Properties** window as **ToolTip on**, followed by the name of the ToolTip component. For instance, if our Form's ToolTip were named helpfulToolTip, you would set a control's **ToolTip on helpfulToolTip** property value to specify the control's tool tip text. Figure 13.32 demonstrates the ToolTip component. For this example, we create a GUI containing two Labels, so we can demonstrate different tool tip text for each Label. To make the sample outputs clearer, we set the BorderStyle property of each Label to FixedSingle, which displays a solid border. Since there is no event-handling code in this example, the class in Fig. 13.32 contains only a constructor.

In this example, we named the ToolTip component labelsToolTip. Figure 13.33 shows the ToolTip in the component tray. We set the tool tip text for the first Label to "First Label" and the tool tip text for the second Label to "Second Label". Figure 13.34 demonstrates setting the tool tip text for the first Label.

```
 1   // Fig. 13.32: ToolTipExampleForm.cs
 2   // Demonstrating the ToolTip component.
 3   using System;
 4   using System.Windows.Forms;
 5
 6   public partial class ToolTipExampleForm : Form
 7   {
 8      // default constructor
 9      public ToolTipExampleForm()
10      {
11         InitializeComponent();
12      } // end constructor
13
14      // no event handlers needed for this example
15
16   } // end class ToolTipExampleForm
```

Fig. 13.32 | Demonstrating the ToolTip component. (Part 1 of 2.)

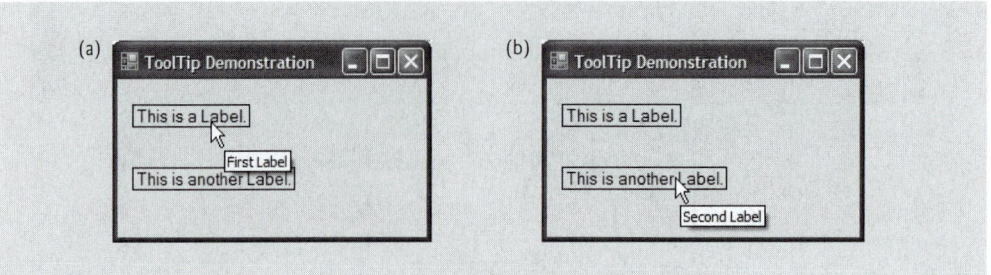

Fig. 13.32 | Demonstrating the ToolTip component. (Part 2 of 2.)

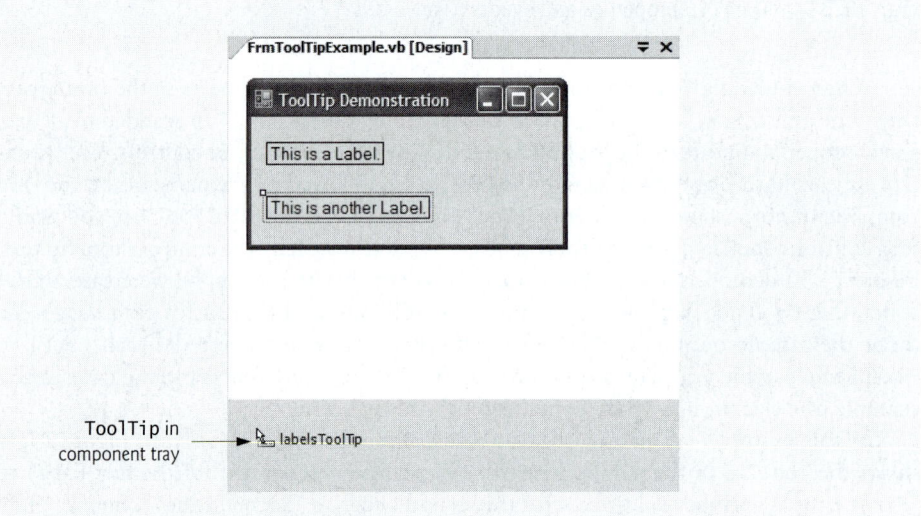

Fig. 13.33 | Demonstrating the component tray.

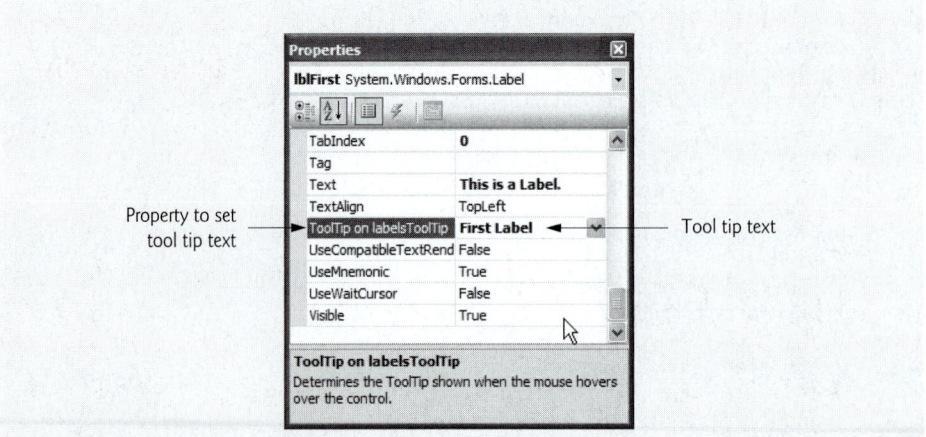

Fig. 13.34 | Setting a control's tool tip text.

13.10 NumericUpDown Control

At times, we will want to restrict a user's input choices to a specific range of numeric values. This is the purpose of the **NumericUpDown control**. This control appears as a TextBox, with two small Buttons on the right side—one with an up arrow and one with a down arrow. By default, a user can type numeric values into this control as if it were a TextBox or click the up and down arrows to increase or decrease the value in the control, respectively. The largest and smallest values in the range are specified with the **Maximum** and **Minimum** properties, respectively (both of type decimal). The **Increment** property (also of type decimal) specifies by how much the current number in the control changes when the user clicks the control's up and down arrows. Figure 13.35 describes common properties and a common event of class NumericUpDown.

Figure 13.36 demonstrates using a NumericUpDown control for a GUI that calculates interest rate. The calculations performed in this application are similar to those performed in Fig. 6.6. TextBoxes are used to input the principal and interest rate amounts, and a

NumericUpDown properties and event	Description
Common Properties	
Increment	Specifies by how much the current number in the control changes when the user clicks the control's up and down arrows.
Maximum	Largest value in the control's range.
Minimum	Smallest value in the control's range.
UpDownAlign	Modifies the alignment of the up and down Buttons on the NumericUpDown control. This property can be used to display these Buttons either to the left or to the right of the control.
Value	The numeric value currently displayed in the control.
Common Event	
ValueChanged	This event is raised when the value in the control is changed. This is the default event for the NumericUpDown control.

Fig. 13.35 | NumericUpDown properties and event.

```
1   // Fig. 13.36: interestCalculatorForm.cs
2   // Demonstrating the NumericUpDown control.
3   using System;
4   using System.Windows.Forms;
5
6   public partial class interestCalculatorForm : Form
7   {
```

Fig. 13.36 | Demonstrating the NumericUpDown control. (Part 1 of 2.)

```
 8      // default constructor
 9      public interestCalculatorForm()
10      {
11         InitializeComponent();
12      } // end constructor
13
14      private void calculateButton_Click(
15         object sender, EventArgs e )
16      {
17         // declare variables to store user input
18         decimal principal; // store principal
19         double rate; // store interest rate
20         int year; // store number of years
21         decimal amount; // store amount
22         string output; // store output
23
24         // retrieve user input
25         principal = Convert.ToDecimal( principalTextBox.Text );
26         rate = Convert.ToDouble( interestTextBox.Text );
27         year = Convert.ToInt32( yearUpDown.Value );
28
29         // set output header
30         output = "Year\tAmount on Deposit\r\n";
31
32         // calculate amount after each year and append to output
33         for ( int yearCounter = 1; yearCounter <= year;  yearCounter++ )
34         {
35            amount =  principal *
36               ( ( decimal ) Math.Pow( ( 1 + rate / 100 ), yearCounter ) );
37            output += ( yearCounter + "\t" +
38               string.Format( "{0:C}", amount ) + "\r\n" );
39         } // end for
40
41         displayTextBox.Text = output; // display result
42      } // end method calculateButton_Click
43   } // end class interestCalculatorForm
```

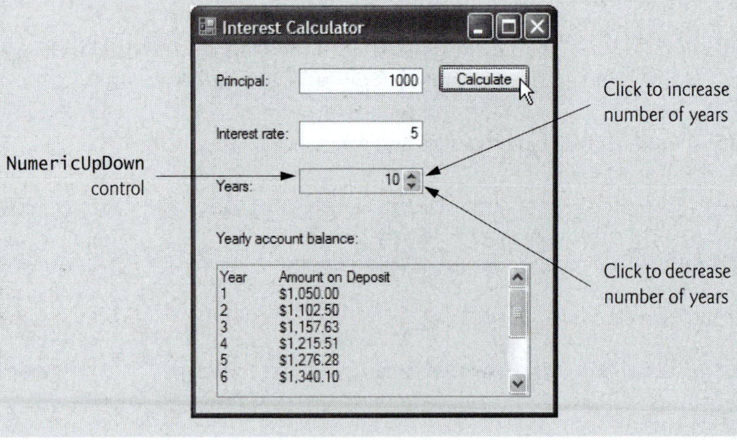

Fig. 13.36 | Demonstrating the NumericUpDown control. (Part 2 of 2.)

NumericUpDown control is used to input the number of years for which we want to calculate interest.

For the NumericUpDown control named yearUpDown, we set the Minimum property to 1 and the Maximum property to 10. We left the Increment property set to 1, its default value. These settings specify that users can enter a number of years in the range 1 to 10 in increments of 1. If we had set the Increment to 0.5, we could also input values such as 1.5 or 2.5. We set the NumericUpDown's *ReadOnly property* to true to indicate that the user can cannot type a number into the control to make a selection. Thus, the user must click the up and down arrows to modify the value in the control. By default, the ReadOnly property is set to false. The output for this application is displayed in a multiline read-only TextBox with a vertical scrollbar, so the user can scroll through the entire output.

13.11 Mouse-Event Handling

This section explains how to handle *mouse events*, such as *clicks*, *presses* and *moves*, which are generated when the user interacts with a control via the mouse. Mouse events can be handled for any control that derives from class System.Windows.Forms.Control. For most mouse events, information about the event is passed to the event-handling method through an object of class *MouseEventArgs*, and the delegate used to create the mouse-event handlers is *MouseEventHandler*. Each mouse-event-handling method for these events requires an object and a MouseEventArgs object as arguments.

Class MouseEventArgs contains information related to the mouse event, such as the mouse pointer's *x*- and *y*-coordinates, the mouse button pressed (Right, Left or Middle) and the number of times the mouse was clicked. Note that the *x*- and *y*-coordinates of the MouseEventArgs object are relative to the control that generated the event—i.e., point *(0,0)* represents the upper-left corner of the control where the mouse event occurred. Several common mouse events are described in Fig. 13.37.

Mouse events and event arguments
Mouse Events with Event Argument of Type EventArgs
MouseEnter   Occurs when the mouse cursor enters the control's boundaries.
MouseLeave   Occurs when the mouse cursor leaves the control's boundaries.
Mouse Events with Event Argument of Type MouseEventArgs
MouseDown   Occurs when a mouse button is pressed while the mouse cursor is within a control's boundaries.
MouseHover   Occurs when the mouse cursor hovers within the control's boundaries.
MouseMove   Occurs when the mouse cursor is moved while in the control's boundaries.
MouseUp   Occurs when a mouse button is released when the cursor is over the control's boundaries.

Fig. 13.37 | Mouse events and event arguments. (Part 1 of 2.)

Mouse events and event arguments	
Class MouseEventArgs Properties	
Button	Specifies which mouse button was pressed (Left, Right, Middle or none).
Clicks	The number of times that the mouse button was clicked.
X	The *x*-coordinate within the control where the event occurred.
Y	The *y*-coordinate within the control where the event occurred.

Fig. 13.37 | Mouse events and event arguments. (Part 2 of 2.)

Figure 13.38 uses mouse events to draw on a Form. Whenever the user drags the mouse (i.e., moves the mouse while a mouse button is pressed), small circles appear on the Form at the position where each mouse event occurs during the drag operation.

In line 10, the program declares variable shouldPaint, which determines whether to draw on the Form. We want the program to draw only while the mouse button is pressed

```
1   // Fig 13.38: PainterForm.cs
2   // Using the mouse to draw on a Form.
3   using System;
4   using System.Drawing;
5   using System.Windows.Forms;
6
7   // creates a Form that is a drawing surface
8   public partial class PainterForm : Form
9   {
10     bool shouldPaint = false; // determines whether to paint
11
12     // default constructor
13     public PainterForm()
14     {
15        InitializeComponent();
16     } // end constructor
17
18     // should paint when mouse button is pressed down
19     private void PainterForm_MouseDown( object sender, MouseEventArgs e )
20     {
21        // indicate that user is dragging the mouse
22        shouldPaint = true;
23     } // end method PainterForm_MouseDown
24
25     // stop painting when mouse button is released
26     private void PainterForm_MouseUp( object sender, MouseEventArgs e )
27     {
28        // indicate that user released the mouse button
29        shouldPaint = false;
30     } // end method PainterForm_MouseUp
```

Fig. 13.38 | Using the mouse to draw on a Form. (Part 1 of 2.)

```
31
32       // draw circle whenever mouse moves with its button held down
33       private void PainterForm_MouseMove( object sender, MouseEventArgs e )
34       {
35          if ( shouldPaint ) // check if mouse button is being pressed
36          {
37             // draw a circle where the mouse pointer is present
38             Graphics graphics = CreateGraphics();
39             graphics.FillEllipse(
40                new SolidBrush( Color.BlueViolet ), e.X, e.Y, 4, 4 );
41             graphics.Dispose();
42          } // end if
43       } // end method PainterForm_MouseMove
44    } // end class PainterForm
```

Fig. 13.38 | Using the mouse to draw on a Form. (Part 2 of 2.)

(i.e., held down). Thus, when the user clicks or holds down a mouse button, the system generates a MouseDown event, and the event handler (lines 19–23) sets shouldPaint to true. When the user releases the mouse button, the system generates a MouseUp event, shouldPaint is set to false in the PainterForm_MouseUp event handler (lines 26–30) and the program stops drawing. Unlike MouseMove events, which occur continuously as the user moves the mouse, the system generates a MouseDown event only when a mouse button is first pressed and generates a MouseUp event only when a mouse button is released.

Whenever the mouse moves over a control, the MouseMove event for that control occurs. Inside the PainterForm_MouseMove event handler (lines 33–43), the program draws only if shouldPaint is true (i.e., a mouse button is pressed). Line 38 calls inherited Form method CreateGraphics to create a *Graphics* object that allows the program to draw on the Form. Class Graphics provides methods that draw various shapes. For example, lines 39–40 use method *FillEllipse* to draw a circle. The first parameter to method FillEllipse in this case is an object of class *SolidBrush*, which specifies the solid color that will fill the shape. The color is provided as an argument to class SolidBrush's constructor. Type *Color* contains numerous predefined color constants—we selected Color.BlueViolet. FillEllipse draws an oval in a bounding rectangle that is specified by the x- and y-coordinates of its upper-left corner, its width and its height—the final four arguments to the method. The x- and y-coordinates represent the location of the mouse event and can be taken from the mouse-event arguments (e.X and e.Y). To draw a circle, we set the width and height of the bounding rectangle so that they are equal—in this example, both are 4 pixels. `Graphics`, `SolidBrush` and `Color` are all part of the namespace `System.Drawing`. We discuss class `Graphics` and its methods in depth in Chapter 17.

13.12 Keyboard-Event Handling

Key events occur when keyboard keys are pressed and released. Such events can be handled for any control that inherits from `System.Windows.Forms.Control`. There are three key events—KeyPress, KeyUp and KeyDown. The **KeyPress** event occurs when the user presses a key that represents an ASCII character. The specific key can be determined with property **KeyChar** of the event handler's **KeyPressEventArgs** argument. ASCII is a 128-character set of alphanumeric symbols, a full listing of which can be found in Appendix D.

The KeyPress event does not indicate whether *modifier keys* (e.g., *Shift*, *Alt* and *Ctrl*) were pressed when a key event occurred. If this information is important, the **KeyUp** or **Key-Down** events can be used. The **KeyEventArgs** argument for each of these events contains information about modifier keys. Often, modifier keys are used in conjunction with the mouse to select or highlight information. Figure 13.39 lists important key event information. Several properties return values from the **Keys enumeration**, which provides constants that specify the various keys on a keyboard. Like the `FontStyle` enumeration (Section 13.7), the Keys enumeration is a `System.FlagAttribute`, so the enumeration's constants can be combined to indicate multiple keys pressed at the same time.

Keyboard events and event arguments	
Key Events with Event Arguments of Type `KeyEventArgs`	
`KeyDown`	Generated when a key is initially pressed.
`KeyUp`	Generated when a key is released.
Key Event with Event Argument of Type `KeyPressEventArgs`	
`KeyPress`	Generated when a key is pressed.
Class `KeyPressEventArgs` *Properties*	
`KeyChar`	Returns the ASCII character for the key pressed.
`Handled`	Indicates whether the `KeyPress` event was handled.
Class `KeyEventArgs` *Properties*	
`Alt`	Indicates whether the *Alt* key was pressed.
`Control`	Indicates whether the *Ctrl* key was pressed.
`Shift`	Indicates whether the *Shift* key was pressed.
`Handled`	Indicates whether the event was handled.
`KeyCode`	Returns the key code for the key as a value from the Keys enumeration. This does not include modifier-key information. It is used to test for a specific key.

Fig. 13.39 | Keyboard events and event arguments. (Part 1 of 2.)

Keyboard events and event arguments	
KeyData	Returns the key code for a key combined with modifier information as a Keys value. This property contains all information about the pressed key.
KeyValue	Returns the key code as an int, rather than as a value from the Keys enumeration. This property is used to obtain a numeric representation of the pressed key. The int value is known as a Windows virtual key code.
Modifiers	Returns a Keys value indicating any pressed modifier keys (*Alt*, *Ctrl* and *Shift*). This property is used to determine modifier-key information only.

Fig. 13.39 | Keyboard events and event arguments. (Part 2 of 2.)

Figure 13.40 demonstrates the use of the key-event handlers to display a key pressed by a user. The program is a Form with two Labels that displays the pressed key on one Label and modifier key information on the other.

```
1   // Fig. 13.40: KeyDemoForm.cs
2   // Displaying information about the key the user pressed.
3       System;
4       System.Windows.Forms;
5
6   // Form to display key information when key is pressed
7                   KeyDemoForm : Form
8   {
9      // default constructor
10         KeyDemoForm()
11     {
12        InitializeComponent();
13     } // end constructor
14
15     // display the character pressed using KeyChar
16             KeyDemoForm_KeyPress(           sender, KeyPressEventArgs e )
17     {
18        charLabel.Text = "Key pressed: " + e.KeyChar;
19     } // end method KeyDemoForm_KeyPress
20
21     // display modifier keys, key code, key data and key value
22             KeyDemoForm_KeyDown(           sender, KeyEventArgs e )
23     {
24        keyInfoLabel.Text =
25          "Alt: " + ( e.Alt ? "Yes" : "No" ) + '\n' +
26          "Shift: " + ( e.Shift ? "Yes" : "No" ) + '\n' +
27          "Ctrl: " + ( e.Control ? "Yes" : "No" ) + '\n' +
28          "KeyCode: " + e.KeyCode + '\n' +
29          "KeyData: " + e.KeyData + '\n' +
30          "KeyValue: " + e.KeyValue;
31     } // end method KeyDemoForm_KeyDown
32
```

Fig. 13.40 | Demonstrating keyboard events. (Part 1 of 2.)

```
33        // clear Labels when key released
34                 KeyDemoForm_KeyUp(          sender, KeyEventArgs e )
35        {
36           charLabel.Text = "";
37           keyInfoLabel.Text = "";
38        } // end method KeyDemoForm_KeyUp
39     } // end class KeyDemoForm
```

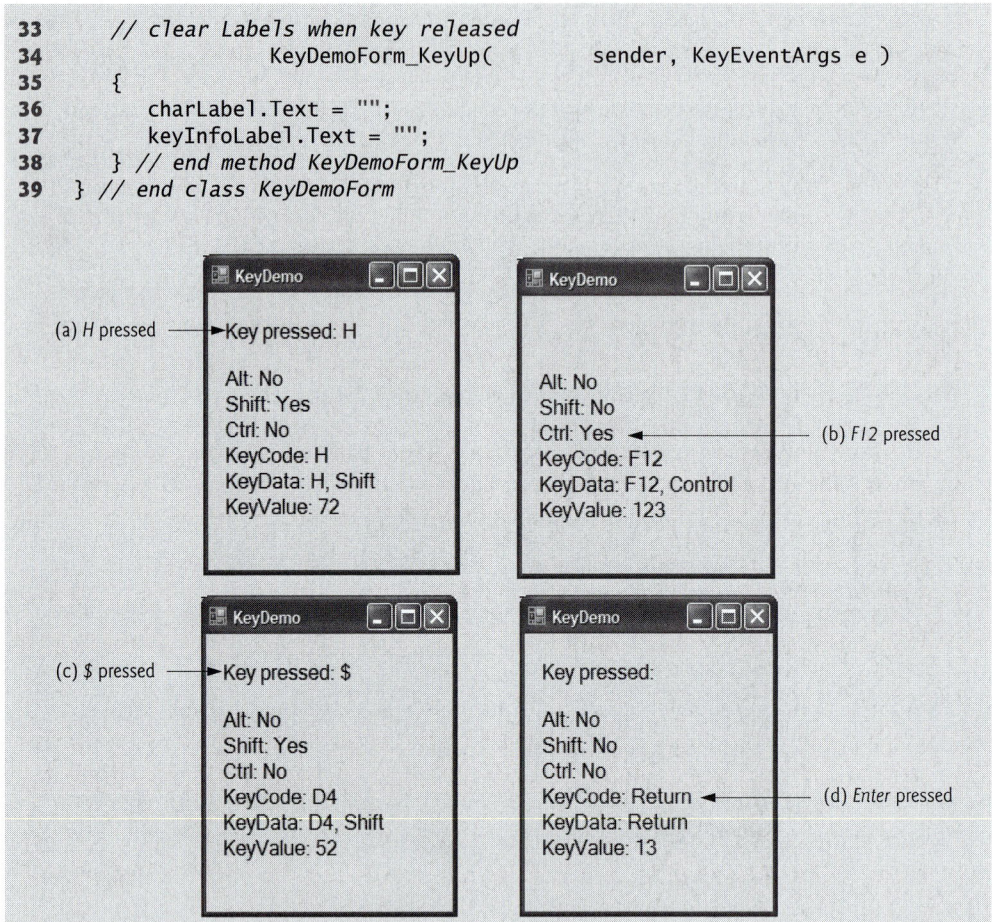

Fig. 13.40 | Demonstrating keyboard events. (Part 2 of 2.)

Initially, the two Labels (charLabel and keyInfoLabel) are empty. Control char-Label displays the character value of the key pressed, whereas keyInfoLabel displays information relating to the pressed key. Because the KeyDown and KeyPress events convey different information, the Form (KeyDemoForm) handles both.

The KeyPress event handler (lines 16–19) accesses the KeyChar property of the Key-PressEventArgs object. This returns the pressed key as a char and which we then display in charLabel (line 18). If the pressed key is not an ASCII character, then the KeyPress event will not occur, and charLabel will not display any text. ASCII is a common encoding format for letters, numbers, punctuation marks and other characters. It does not support keys such as the *function keys* (like *F1*) or the modifier keys (*Alt*, *Ctrl* and *Shift*).

The KeyDown event handler (lines 22–31) displays information from its KeyEventArgs object. The event handler tests for the *Alt*, *Shift* and *Ctrl* keys by using the Alt, Shift and Control properties, each of which returns a bool value—true if the corresponding key is pressed and false otherwise. The event handler then displays the KeyCode, KeyData and KeyValue properties.

The KeyCode property returns a Keys enumeration value (line 28). The KeyCode property returns the pressed key, but does not provide any information about modifier keys. Thus, both a capital and a lowercase "a" are represented as the *A* key.

The KeyData property (line 29) also returns a Keys enumeration value, but this property includes data about modifier keys. Thus, if "A" is input, the KeyData shows that both the *A* key and the *Shift* key were pressed. Lastly, KeyValue (line 30) returns the key code of the pressed key as an int. This int is the **key code**, which provides an int value for a wide range of keys and for mouse buttons. The Windows virtual key code is useful when one is testing for non-ASCII keys (such as *F12*).

The KeyUp event handler (lines 34–38) clears both Labels when the key is released. As we can see from the output, non-ASCII keys are not displayed in charLabel, because the KeyPress event is not generated. However, the KeyDown event still is generated, and keyInfoLabel displays information about the key that is pressed. The Keys enumeration can be used to test for specific keys by comparing the key pressed to a specific KeyCode.

Software Engineering Observation 13.3

To cause a control to react when a particular key is pressed (such as Enter*), handle a key event and test for the pressed key. To cause a* Button *to be clicked when the* Enter *key is pressed on a Form, set the Form's AcceptButton property.*

13.13 Wrap-Up

This chapter introduced several common GUI controls. We discussed event handling in detail, and showed how to create event handlers. We also discussed how delegates are used to connect event handlers to the events of specific controls. You learned how to use a control's properties and Visual Studio to specify the layout of your GUI. We then demostrated several controls, beginning with Labels, Buttons and TextBoxes. You learned how to use GroupBoxes and Panels to organize other controls. We then demonstrated CheckBoxes and RadioButtons, which are state buttons that allow users to select among several options. We displayed images in PictureBox controls, displayed helpful text on a GUI with ToolTip components and specified a range of input values for users with a NumericUpDown control. We then demonstrated how to handle mouse and keyboard events. The next chapter introduces additional GUI controls. You will learn how to add menus to your GUIs and create Windows applications that display multiple Forms.

Summary

Section 13.1 Introduction

- A graphical user interface (GUI) allows a user to interact visually with a program.
- By providing different applications with a consistent set of intuitive user-interface components, GUIs enable users to become productive with each application faster.
- GUIs are built from GUI controls.
- GUI controls are objects that can display information on the screen or enable users to interact with an application via the mouse, keyboard or some other form of input.

Section 13.2 Windows Forms

- Windows Forms are used to create the GUIs for programs.

- A Form is a graphical element that appears on the desktop; it can be a dialog, a window or an MDI (multiple document interface) window.

- A component is an instance of a class that implements the IComponent interface, which defines the behaviors that components must implement, such as how the component is loaded.

- A control has a graphical representation at runtime.

- Some components lack graphical representations (e.g., class Timer of namespace System.Windows.Forms). Such, components are not visible at runtime.

- When there are several windows on the screen, the active window is the frontmost and has a highlighted title bar—typically darker blue than the other windows on the screen. A window becomes the active window when the user clicks somewhere inside it.

- The active window is said to "have the focus."

- A Form is a container for controls and components.

Section 13.3 Event Handling

- Normally, a user interacts with an application's GUI to indicate the tasks that the application should perform.

- GUIs are event driven.

- When the user interacts with a GUI component, the interaction—known as an event—drives the program to perform a task. Common events include clicking a Button, typing in a TextBox, selecting an item from a menu, closing a window and moving the mouse.

- A method that performs a task in response to an event is called an event handler, and the overall process of responding to events is known as event handling.

Section 13.3.1 A Simple Event-Driven GUI

- By convention, event-handler methods are named as *controlName_eventName*.

- An event handler executes only when the user performs the specific event.

- Each event handler receives two parameters when it is called. The first—an object reference named sender—is a reference to the object that generated the event. The second is a reference to an event arguments object of type EventArgs (or one of its derived classes), which is typically named e. This object contains additional information about the event that occurred.

- EventArgs is the base class of all classes that represent event information.

Section 13.3.2 Another Look at the Visual Studio Generated Code

- Visual Studio generates the code that creates and initializes the GUI that you build in the GUI design window. This auto-generated code is placed in the Designer.cs file of the Form.

- The auto-generated code that defines the GUI is part of the Form's class. The use of the partial modifier in the class declaration allows the class to be split among multiple files.

- The Designer.cs file contains the declarations of the controls you create in **Design** mode. By default, all variable declarations for controls created through C#'s design window have a private access modifier.

- The Designer.cs file includes the Dispose method for releasing resources and method InitializeComponent, which sets the properties of the Form and its controls.

- Visual Studio uses the code in InitializeComponent to create the GUI you see in design view. Changing the code in this method may prevent Visual Studio from displaying the GUI properly.

Section 13.3.3 Delegates and the Event-Handling Mechanism

- The control that generates an event is known as the event sender.
- An event-handling method—known as the event receiver—responds to a particular event that a control generates.
- When an event occurs, the event sender calls its event receiver to perform a task.
- The .NET event-handling mechanism allows you to choose your own names for event-handling methods. However, each event-handling method must declare the proper parameters to receive information about the event that it handles.
- Event handlers are connected to a control's events via special objects called delegates.
- A delegate object holds a reference to a method with a signature specified by the delegate type's declaration.
- GUI controls have predefined delegates that correspond to every event they can generate.
- An event sender calls a delegate object like a method.
- Since each event handler is declared as a delegate, the event sender can simply call the appropriate delegate when an event occurs. The delegate's job is to invoke the appropriate method.
- Event delegates represent a set of delegate objects that all have the same signature.
- When an event occurs, the event sender calls every method referenced by a multicast delegate. This is known as event multicasting. Multicast delegates enable several methods to be called in response to a single event.
- Event delegates derive from class `MulticastDelegate`, which derives from class `Delegate` (both from namespace `System`).

Section 13.3.4 Other Ways to Create Event Handlers

- Double-clicking a control on the `Form` creates an event handler for a control's default event.
- Typically, controls can generate many different events, and each can have its own event handler.
- You can create additional event handlers through the **Properties** window.
- If you select a control on the `Form`, then click the **Events** icon (the lightning bolt icon) in the **Properties** window, all the events for that control are listed in the window. You can double click an event's name to display the event handler in the editor, if the event handler already exists, or to create the corresponding event handler.
- You can select an event, then use the drop-down list to its right to choose an existing method that should be used as the event handler for that event. The methods that appear in this drop-down list are the class's methods that have the proper signature to be an event handler for the selected event.

Section 13.3.5 Locating Event Information

- Read the Visual Studio documentation to learn about the different events raised by a control.
- To do this, select **Help > Index**. In the window that appears, select **.NET Framework** in the **Filtered by::** drop-down list and enter the name of the control's class in the **Index** window. To ensure that you are selecting the proper class, enter the fully qualified class name.
- Once you select a control's class in the documentation, a list of all the class's members are displayed. This list includes the events that the class can generate.
- Click the name of an event to view its description and examples of its use.

Section 13.4 Control Properties and Layout

- Controls derive from class Control (of namespace System.Windows.Forms).

- The Focus method transfers the focus to a control and makes it the active control.

- The Enabled property indicates whether the user can interact with a control to generate an event.

- A programmer can hide a control from the user without disabling the control by setting the Visible property to false or by calling method Hide.

- Anchoring causes controls to remain at a fixed distance from the sides of the container even when the control is resized.

- Docking attaches a control to a container such that the control stretches across an entire side.

- Forms have a Padding property that specifies the distance between the docked controls and the Form edges.

- The Anchor and Dock properties of a Control are set with respect to the Control's parent container, which could be a Form or other parent container (such as a Panel).

- The minimum and maximum Form (or other Control) sizes can be set via properties MinimumSize and MaximumSize, respectively.

- When dragging a control across a Form, blue lines (known as snap lines) appear to help you position the control with respect to other controls and the Form's edges.

- Visual Studio also provides the **Format** menu, which contains several options for modifying your GUI's layout.

Section 13.5 Labels, TextBoxes and Buttons

- Labels provide text information (as well as optional images) that the user cannot directly modify.

- A textbox (class TextBox) is an area in which text either can be displayed by a program or in which the user can type text via the keyboard.

- A password TextBox is a TextBox that hides the information entered by the user. As the user types characters, the password TextBox masks the user input by displaying a character you specify (usually *). If you set the PasswordChar property, the TextBox becomes a password TextBox.

- A button is a control that the user clicks to trigger a specific action in a program or to select an option.

- All the button classes derive from class ButtonBase (namespace System.Windows.Forms), which defines common button features.

Section 13.6 GroupBoxes and Panels

- GroupBoxes and Panels arrange controls on a GUI.

- GroupBoxes and Panels are typically used to group several controls of similar functionality or several controls that are related in a GUI.

- GroupBoxes can display a caption (i.e., text) and do not include scrollbars, whereas Panels can include scrollbars and do not include a caption.

- GroupBoxes have thin borders by default; Panels can be set so that they also have borders, by changing their BorderStyle property.

- The controls of a GroupBox or Panel are added to the container's Controls property.

- To enable a Panel's scrollbars, set the Panel's AutoScroll property to true. If the Panel is resized and cannot display all of its controls, scrollbars appear.

Section 13.7 CheckBoxes and RadioButtons

- CheckBoxes and RadioButtons can be in the on/off or true/false states.

- Classes CheckBox and RadioButton are derived from class ButtonBase.

- A CheckBox is a small square that either is blank or contains a check mark. When a CheckBox is selected, a check mark appears in the box. Any number of CheckBoxes can be selected at a time.

- Styles can be combined via bitwise operators, such as the conditional OR (||) operator or the logical exclusive OR (∧) operator.

- RadioButtons (defined with class RadioButton) are similar to CheckBoxes in that they also have two states: selected and not selected (also called deselected).

- RadioButtons normally appear as a group, in which only one RadioButton can be selected at a time. The selection of one RadioButton in the group forces all the others to be deselected. Therefore, RadioButtons are used to represent a set of mutually exclusive options.

- All RadioButtons added to a container become part of the same group.

Section 13.8 PictureBoxes

- A PictureBox displays an image.

- The Image property specifies the image that is displayed

- The SizeMode property indicates how the image is displayed (Normal, StretchImage, Autosize or CenterImage).

Section 13.9 ToolTips

- Tool tips help you become familiar with the IDE's features and serve as useful reminders for each toolbar icon's functionality. This property appears in the **Properties** window as **ToolTip on** followed by the name of the ToolTip component.

- Once a ToolTip is added to a Form, a new property appears in the **Properties** window for the other controls on the Form.

- The ToolTip component can be used to add tool tips to your application.

- The component tray is the gray region below the Form in **Design** mode.

Section 13.10 NumericUpDown Control

- At times you will want to restrict a user's input choices to a specific range of numeric values. This is the purpose of the NumericUpDown control.

- The NumericUpDown control appears as a TextBox, with two small Buttons on the right side, one with an up arrow and one with a down arrow. By default, a user can type numeric values into this control as if it were a TextBox or click the up and down arrows to increase or decrease the value in the control, respectively.

- The largest and smallest values in the range are specified with the Maximum and Minimum properties, respectively (both are of type decimal).

- The Increment property of type decimal) specifies by how much the current number in the control changes when the user clicks the control's up and down arrows.

- Setting a NumericUpDown control's ReadOnly property to true specifies that the user can only use the up and down arrows to modify the value in the NumericUpDown control.

Section 13.11 Mouse-Event Handling

- This section explains how to handle mouse events, such as clicks, presses and moves, which are generated when the mouse interacts with a control.

- Mouse events can be handled for any control that derives from class System.Windows.Forms.Control.
- Class MouseEventArgs contains information related to the mouse event, such as the *x*- and *y*-coordinates of the mouse pointer, the mouse button pressed (Right, Left or Middle) and the number of times the mouse was clicked.
- Whenever the user clicks or holds down a mouse button, the system generates a MouseDown event.
- When the user releases the mouse button (to complete a "click" operation), the system generates a single MouseUp event.
- Whenever the mouse moves over a control, the MouseMove event for that control is raised.

Section 13.12 Keyboard-Event Handling
- Key events occur when keys on the keyboard are pressed and released.
- There are three key events—KeyPress, KeyUp and KeyDown.
- The KeyPress event occurs when the user presses a key that represents an ASCII character. The specific key can be determined with property KeyChar of the event handler's KeyPressEventArgs argument.
- The KeyPress event does not indicate whether modifier keys (e.g., *Shift*, *Alt* and *Ctrl*) were pressed when a key event occurred. If this information is important, the KeyUp or KeyDown events can be used.
- The KeyEventArgs argument for each Key event contains information about modifier keys. Several properties returns values from the Keys enumeration, which provides constants that specify the various keys on a keyboard.
- The KeyCode property returns the pressed key, but does not provide any information about modifier keys.
- The KeyData property returns a Keys enumeration value, including data about modifier keys.

Terminology

active control
active window
anchor a control
bitwise operator
Button properties and events
Button property of class MouseEventArgs
ButtonBase class
checkbox
CheckBox class
Checked property of class CheckBox
Checked property of class RadioButton
CheckedChanged event of class CheckBox
CheckedChanged event of class RadioButton
CheckState property of class CheckBox
CheckStateChanged event of class CheckBox
Color structure
component
component tray
container
Control class

Controls property of a container
default event
delegate
delegate class
delegate keyword
deselected state
DialogResult enumeration
dock a control
Dock property of class Control
Enabled property of class Control
event
event-driven programming
event handler
event handling
event multicasting
event receiver
event sender
FillEllipse method of class Graphics
FlatStyle property of class Button
focus

Focus method of class Control
Font class
FontStyle enumeration
Graphics class
Height property of structure Size
IComponent interface
Increment property of class NumericUpDown
key code
key event
KeyChar property of class KeyPressEventArgs
KeyCode property of class KeyEventArgs
KeyData property of class KeyEventArgs
KeyDown event of class Control
KeyEventArgs class
KeyPress event of class Control
KeyPressEventArgs class
Keys enumeration
KeyUp event of class Control
KeyValue property of class KeyEventArgs
Maximum property of class NumericUpDown
MaximumSize property of class Control
Minimum property of class NumericUpDown
MinimumSize property of class Control
modifier key
mouse click
mouse event
mouse move
mouse press
MouseDown event of class Control
MouseEventArgs class
MouseEventHandler delegate
MouseMove event of class Control

MouseUp event of class Control
multicast delegate
MulticastDelegate class
multiple document interface (MDI) window
mutual exclusion
"not-selected" state
NumericUpDown class
Padding property of class Control
Panel class
password TextBox
PasswordChar property of class TextBox
radio button
radio button group
RadioButton class
ReadOnly property of class NumericUpDown
selected state
Size property of class Control
Size structure
snap line
SolidBrush class
state button
Style property of class Font
TabIndex property of class Control
TabStop property of class Control
ToolTip class
UpDownAlign property of class NumericUpDown
Value property of class NumericUpDown
Visible property of class Control
widget
Width property of structure Size
window gadget
Windows Form

Self-Review Exercises

13.1 State whether each of the following is *true* or *false*. If *false*, explain why.
   a) The KeyData property includes data about modifier keys.
   b) Windows Forms commonly are used to create GUIs.
   c) A Form is a container.
   d) All Forms, components and controls are classes.
   e) CheckBoxes are used to represent a set of mutually exclusive options.
   f) A Label displays text that a user running an application can edit.
   g) Button presses generate events.
   h) All mouse events use the same event arguments class.
   i) Visual Studio can register an event and create an empty event handler.
   j) The NumericUpDown control is used to specify a range of input values.
   k) A control's tool tip text is set with the ToolTip property of class Control.

13.2 Fill in the blanks in each of the following statements:
   a) The active control is said to have the _____.
   b) The Form acts as a(n) _____ for the controls that are added.

    c) GUIs are _____ driven.

    d) Every method that handles the same event must have the same _____.

    e) A(n) _____ TextBox masks user input with a character used repeatedly.

    f) Class _____ and class _____ help arrange controls on a GUI and provide logical groups for radio buttons.

    g) Typical mouse events include _____, _____ and _____.

    h) _____ events are generated when a key on the keyboard is pressed or released.

    i) The modifier keys are _____, _____ and _____.

    j) A(n) _____ event or delegate can call multiple methods.

Answers To Self-Review Exercises

13.1 a) True. b) True. c) True. d) True. e) False. RadioButtons are used to represent a set of mutually exclusive options. f) False. A Label's text cannot be edited by the user. g) True. h) False. Some mouse events use EventArgs, others use MouseEventArgs. i) True. j) True. k) False. A control's tool tip text is set using a ToolTip component that must be added to the application.

13.2 a) focus. b) container. c) event. d) signature. e) password. f) GroupBox, Panel. g) mouse clicks, mouse presses, mouse moves. h) Key. i) *Shift, Ctrl, Alt.* j) multicast.

Exercises

13.3 Extend the program in Fig. 13.26 to include a CheckBox for every font-style option. [*Hint:* Use logical exclusive OR (∧) rather than testing for every bit explicitly.]

13.4 Create the GUI in Fig. 13.41 (you do not have to provide functionality).

13.5 Create the GUI in Fig. 13.42 (you do not have to provide functionality).

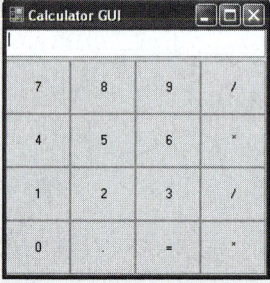

Fig. 13.41 | Calculator GUI.

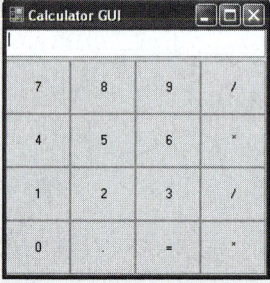

Fig. 13.42 | Printer GUI.

13.6   Write a temperature conversion program that converts from Fahrenheit to Celsius. The Fahrenheit temperature should be entered from the keyboard (via a TextBox). A Label should be used to display the converted temperature. Use the following formula for the conversion:

Celsius = (5 / 9) x (Fahrenheit – 32)

13.7   Extend the program of Fig. 13.38 to include options for changing the size and color of the lines drawn. Create a GUI similar to Fig. 13.43. The user should be able to draw on the application's Panel. To retrieve a Graphics object for drawing, call method *panelName*.CreateGraphics(), substituting in the name of your Panel.

13.8   Write a program that plays "guess the number" as follows: Your program chooses the number to be guessed by selecting an int at random in the range 1–1000. The program then displays the following text in a label:

```
I have a number between 1 and 1000--can you guess my number?
Please enter your first guess.
```

A TextBox should be used to input the guess. As each guess is input, the background color should change to red or blue. Red indicates that the user is getting "warmer," blue that the user is getting "colder." A Label should display either "Too High" or "Too Low," to help the user zero in on the correct answer. When the user guesses the correct answer, display "Correct!" in a message box, change the Form's background color to green and disable the TextBox. Recall that a TextBox (like other controls) can be disabled by setting the control's Enabled property to false. Provide a Button that allows the user to play the game again. When the Button is clicked, generate a new random number, change the background to the default color and enable the TextBox.

13.9   Write an application that allows users to process orders for fuzzy dice. The application should calculate the total price of the order, including tax and shipping. TextBoxes for inputting the order number, the customer name and the shipping address are provided. Initially, these fields contain text that describes their purpose. Provide CheckBoxes for selecting the fuzzy-dice color and TextBoxes for inputting the quantities of fuzzy dice to order. The application should update the total cost, tax and shipping when the user changes any one of the three **Quantity** fields' values. The application should also contain a Button that when clicked, returns all fields to their original values. Use 5% for the tax rate. Shipping charges are $1.50 for up to 20 pairs of dice. If more than 20 pairs of dice are ordered, shipping is free. All fields must be filled out at the top, and an item must be checked for the user to enter a quantity for that item.

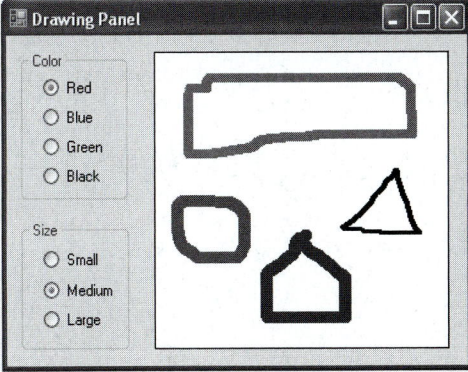

Fig. 13.43 | Drawing Panel GUI.

14

Graphical User Interface Concepts: Part 2

> *I claim not to have controlled events, but confess plainly that events have controlled me.*
> —Abraham Lincoln

> *Capture its reality in paint!*
> —Paul Cézanne

> *An actor entering through the door, you've got nothing. But if he enters through the window, you've got a situation.*
> —Billy Wilder

> *But, soft! what light through yonder window breaks? It is the east, and Juliet is the sun!*
> —William Shakespeare

OBJECTIVES

In this chapter you will learn:

- To create menus, tabbed windows and multiple document interface (MDI) programs.
- To use the `ListView` and `TreeView` controls for displaying information.
- To create hyperlinks using the `LinkLabel` control.
- To display lists of information in `ListBox` and `ComboBox` controls.
- To input date and time data with the `DateTimePicker`.
- To create custom controls.

14.1 Introduction

This chapter continues our study of GUIs. We begin our discussion with menus, which present users with logically organized commands (or options). Next, we discuss how to input and display dates and times using the `MonthCalendar` and `DateTimePicker` controls. We show how to develop menus with the tools provided by Visual Studio. We also introduce `LinkLabel`s—powerful GUI components that enable the user to visit one of several destinations, such as a file on the current machine or a Web page, by simply clicking the mouse.

We demonstrate how to manipulate a list of values via a `ListBox` and how to combine several checkboxes in a `CheckedListBox`. We also create drop-down lists using `ComboBox`es and display data hierarchically with a `TreeView` control. You will learn two other important GUI components—tab controls and multiple document interface (MDI) windows. These components enable you to create real-world programs with sophisticated GUIs.

Visual Studio provides a large set of GUI components, several of which are discussed in this (and the previous) chapter. Visual Studio also enables you to design custom controls and add those controls to the **ToolBox**, as we demonstrate in the last example of this chapter. The techniques presented in this chapter form the groundwork for creating more substantial GUIs and custom controls.

14.2 Menus

Menus provide groups of related commands for Windows applications. Although these commands depend on the program, some—such as **Open** and **Save**—are common to many applications. Menus are an integral part of GUIs, because they organize commands without "cluttering" the GUI.

In Fig. 14.1, an expanded menu from Visual Studio lists various commands (called *menu items*), plus *submenus* (menus within a menu). Notice that the top-level menus appear in the left portion of the figure, whereas any submenus or menu items are displayed to the right. The menu that contains a menu item is called that menu item's *parent menu*. A menu item that contains a submenu is considered to be the parent of that submenu.

All menu items can have *Alt* key shortcuts (also called *access shortcuts* or *hotkeys*), which are accessed by pressing *Alt* and the underlined letter (for example, *Alt F* typically expands the **File** menu). Menus that are not top-level menus can have shortcut keys as well (combinations of *Ctrl*, *Shift*, *Alt*, *F1*, *F2*, letter keys, etc.). Some menu items display check marks, usually indicating that multiple options on the menu can be selected at once.

To create a menu, open the **Toolbox** and drag a *MenuStrip* control onto the Form. This creates a menu bar across the top of the Form (below the title bar) and places a MenuStrip icon in the component tray. To select the MenuStrip, click this icon. You can now use **Design** mode to create and edit menus for your application. Menus, like other controls, have properties and events, which can be accessed through the **Properties** window.

To add menu items to the menu, click the **Type Here** TextBox (Fig. 14.2) and type the menu item's name. This action adds an entry to the menu of type *ToolStripMenuItem*. After you press the *Enter* key, the menu item name is added to the menu. Then more **Type Here** TextBoxes appear, allowing you to add items underneath or to the side of the original menu item (Fig. 14.3).

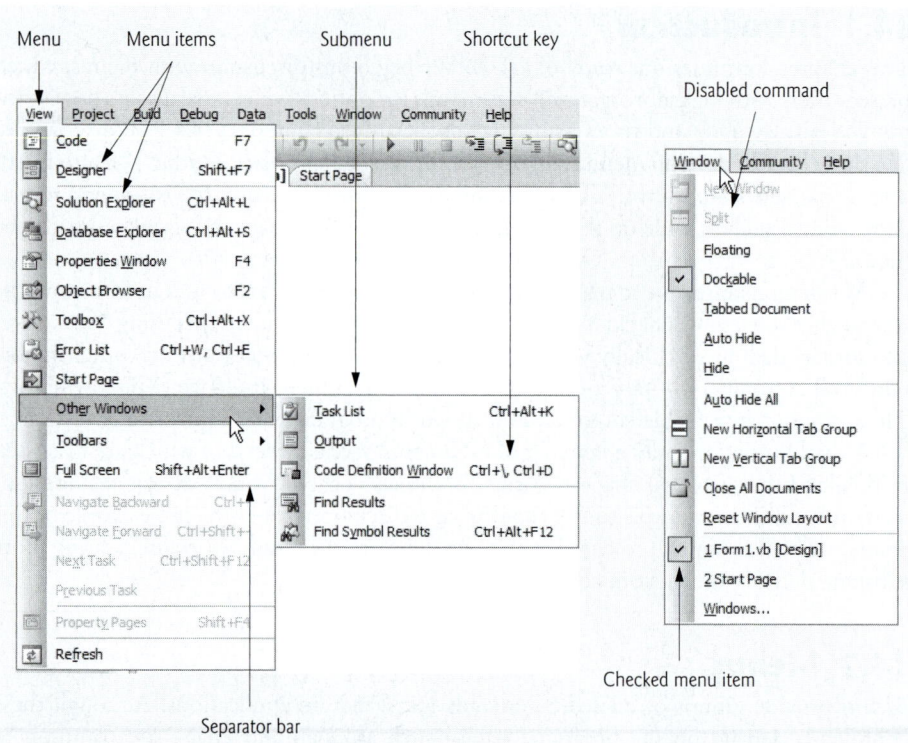

Fig. 14.1 | Menus, submenus and menu items.

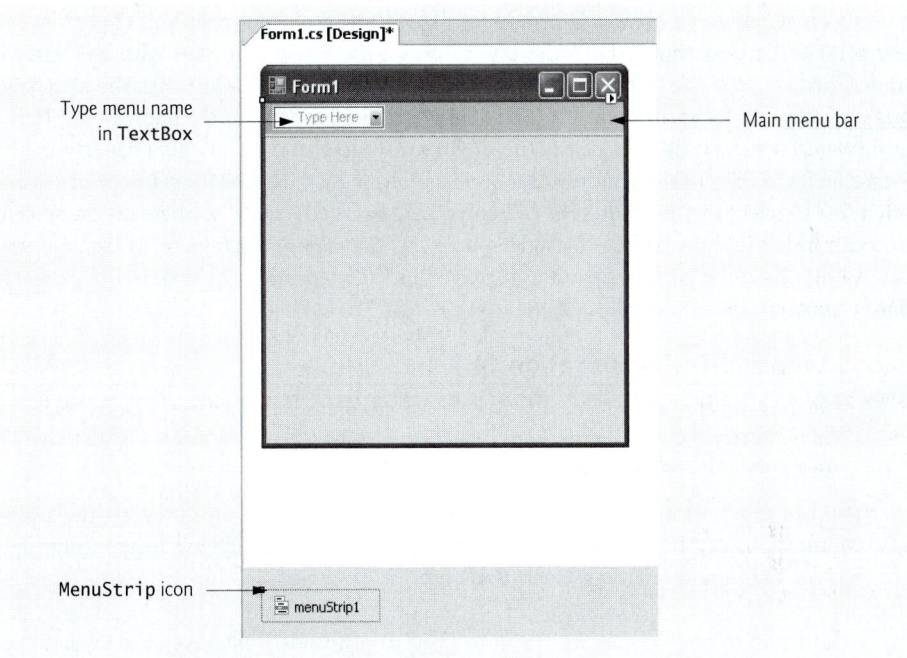

Fig. 14.2 | Editing menus in Visual Studio.

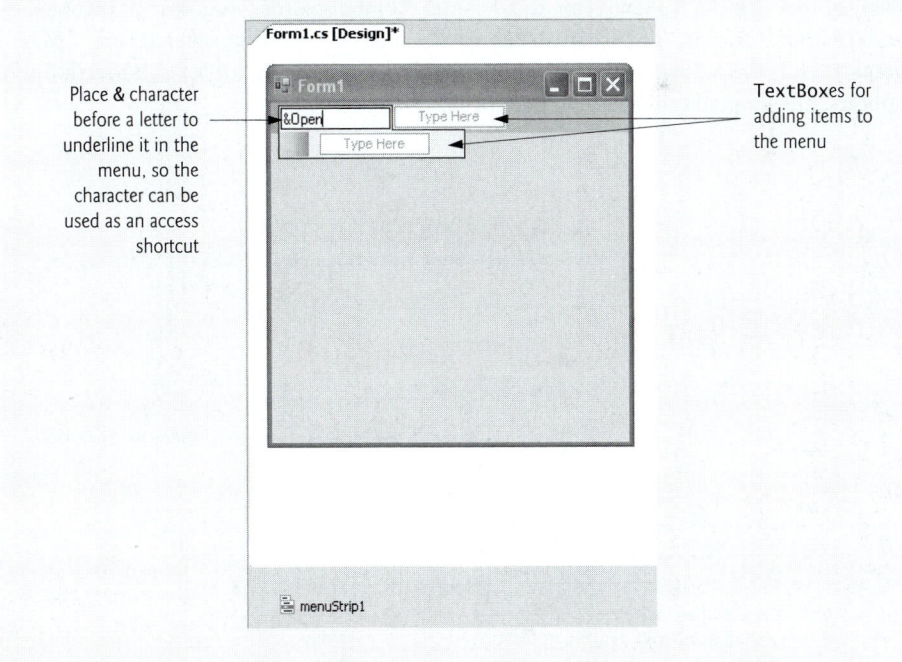

Fig. 14.3 | Adding ToolStripMenuItems to a MenuStrip.

To create an *access shortcut* (or *keyboard shortcut*), type an ampersand (&) before the character to be underlined. For example, to create the **File** menu item with the letter **F** underlined, type &File. To display an ampersand, type &&. To add other shortcut keys (e.g., *<Ctrl>-F9*) for menu items, set the ***ShortcutKeys*** property of the appropriate Tool-StripMenuItems. To do this, select the down arrow to the right of this property in the **Properties** window. In the window that appears (Fig. 14.4), use the CheckBoxes and drop-down list to select the shortcut keys. When you are finished, click elsewhere on the screen. You can hide the shortcut keys by setting property ***ShowShortcutKeys*** to false, and you can modify how the control keys are displayed in the menu item by modifying property ***ShortcutKeyDisplayString***.

Look-and-Feel Observation 14.1

Buttons can have access shortcuts. Place the & symbol immediately before the desired character in the Button's label. To press the button by using its access key in the running application, the user presses Alt and the underlined character.

You can remove a menu item by selecting it with the mouse and pressing the *Delete* key. Menu items can be grouped logically by *separator bars*, which are inserted by right clicking the menu and selecting **Insert Separator** or by typing "-" for the text of a menu item.

In addition to text, Visual Studio allows you to easily add TextBoxes and ComboBoxes (drop-down lists) as menu items. When adding an item in **Design** mode, you may have noticed that before you enter text for a new item, you are provided with a drop-down list. Clicking the down arrow (Fig. 14.5) allows you to select the type of item to add—**Menu-Item** (of type ToolStripMenuItem, the default), **ComboBox** (of type ToolStripComboBox) and **TextBox** (of type ToolStripTextBox). We focus on ToolStripMenuItems. [*Note:* If you view this drop-down list for menu items that are not on the top level, a fourth option appears, allowing you to insert a separator bar.]

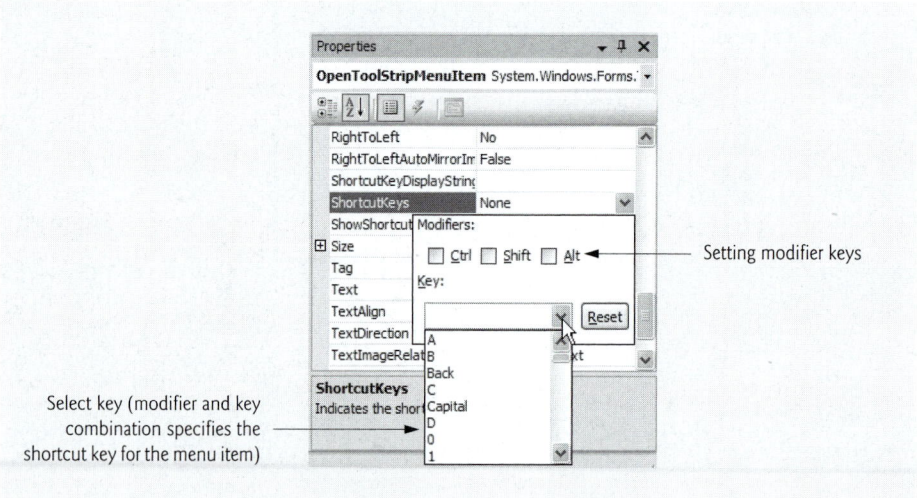

Fig. 14.4 | Setting a menu item's shortcut keys.

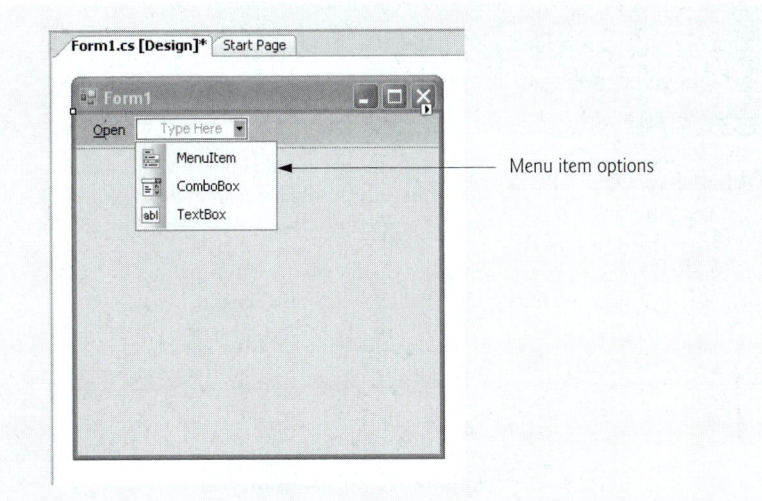

Fig. 14.5 | Menu item options.

ToolStripMenuItems generate a *Click* event when selected. To create an empty Click event handler, double click the menu item in **Design** mode. Common actions in response to these events include displaying dialogs and setting properties. Common menu properties and a common event are summarized in Fig. 14.6.

MenuStrip and ToolStripMenuItem properties and an event	Description
MenuStrip Properties	
MenuItems	Contains the top-level menu items for this MenuStrip.
HasChildren	Indicates whether MenuStrip has any child controls (menu items).
RightToLeft	Causes text to display from right to left. This is useful for languages that are read from right to left.
ToolStripMenuItem Properties	
Checked	Indicates whether a menu item is checked. The default value is false, meaning that the menu item is unchecked.
CheckOnClick	Indicates that a menu item should appear checked or unchecked as the item is clicked.
Index	Specifies an item's position in its parent menu. A value of 0 places the MenuItem at the beginning of the menu.
MenuItems	Lists the submenu items for a particular menu item.

Fig. 14.6 | MenuStrip and ToolStripMenuItem properties and an event. (Part 1 of 2.)

MenuStrip and ToolStripMenuItem properties and an event	Description
ShortcutKey-DisplayString	Specifies text that should appear beside a menu item for a shortcut key. If left blank, the key names are displayed. Otherwise, the text in this property is displayed for the shortcut key.
ShortcutKeys	Specifies the shortcut key for the menu item (e.g., *<Ctrl>-F9* is equivalent to clicking a specific item).
ShowShortcutKeys	Indicates whether a shortcut key is shown beside menu item text. The default is true, which displays the shortcut key.
Text	Specifies the menu item's text. To create an *Alt* access shortcut, precede a character with & (e.g., &File to specify a menu named **File** with the letter **F** underlined).
Common ToolStripMenuItem Event	
Click	Generated when an item is clicked or a shortcut key is used. This is the default event when the menu is double clicked in the designer.

Fig. 14.6 | MenuStrip and ToolStripMenuItem properties and an event. (Part 2 of 2.)

Look-and-Feel Observation 14.2

*It is a convention to place an ellipsis (...) after the name of a menu item that when selected, displays a dialog (e.g. **Save As...**). Menu items that produce an immediate action without prompting the user for more information (e.g. **Save**) should not have an ellipsis following their name.*

Class MenuTestForm (Fig. 14.7) creates a simple menu on a Form. The Form has a top-level **File** menu with menu items **About** (which displays a MessageBox) and **Exit** (which terminates the program). The program also includes a **Format** menu, which contains menu items that change the format of the text on a Label. The **Format** menu has submenus **Color** and **Font**, which change the color and font of the text on a Label.

```
1   // Fig. 14.7: MenuTestForm.cs
2   // Using Menus to change font colors and styles.
3   using System;
4   using System.Drawing;
5   using System.Windows.Forms;
6
7   // our Form contains a Menu that changes the font color
8   // and style of the text displayed in Label
9   public partial class MenuTestForm : Form
10  {
11     // default constructor
12     public MenuTestForm()
13     {
```

Fig. 14.7 | Menus for changing text font and color. (Part 1 of 5.)

```
14          InitializeComponent();
15       } // end constructor
16
17       // display MessageBox when About ToolStripMenuItem is selected
18       private void aboutToolStripMenuItem_Click( object sender, EventArgs e )
19       {
20          MessageBox.Show(
21             "This is an example\nof using menus.",
22             "About", MessageBoxButtons.OK, MessageBoxIcon.Information );
23       } // end method aboutToolStripMenuItem_Click
24
25       // exit program when Exit ToolStripMenuItem is selected
26       private void exitToolStripMenuItem_Click( object sender, EventArgs e )
27       {
28          Application.Exit();
29       } // end method exitToolStripMenuItem_Click
30
31       // reset checkmarks for Color ToolStripMenuItems
32       private void ClearColor()
33       {
34          // clear all checkmarks
35          blackToolStripMenuItem.Checked = false;
36          blueToolStripMenuItem.Checked = false;
37          redToolStripMenuItem.Checked = false;
38          greenToolStripMenuItem.Checked = false;
39       } // end method ClearColor
40
41       // update Menu state and color display black
42       private void blackToolStripMenuItem_Click( object sender, EventArgs e )
43       {
44          // reset checkmarks for Color ToolStripMenuItems
45          ClearColor();
46
47          // set Color to Black
48          displayLabel.ForeColor = Color.Black;
49          blackToolStripMenuItem.Checked = true;
50       } // end method blackToolStripMenuItem_Click
51
52       // update Menu state and color display blue
53       private void blueToolStripMenuItem_Click( object sender, EventArgs e )
54       {
55          // reset checkmarks for Color ToolStripMenuItems
56          ClearColor();
57
58          // set Color to Blue
59          displayLabel.ForeColor = Color.Blue;
60          blueToolStripMenuItem.Checked = true;
61       } // end method blueToolStripMenuItem_Click
62
63       // update Menu state and color display red
64       private void redToolStripMenuItem_Click( object sender, EventArgs e )
65       {
```

Fig. 14.7 | Menus for changing text font and color. (Part 2 of 5.)

```
66          // reset checkmarks for Color ToolStripMenuItems
67          ClearColor();
68
69          // set Color to Red
70          displayLabel.ForeColor = Color.Red;
71          redToolStripMenuItem.Checked = true;
72       } // end method redToolStripMenuItem_Click
73
74       // update Menu state and color display green
75       private void greenToolStripMenuItem_Click( object sender, EventArgs e )
76       {
77          // reset checkmarks for Color ToolStripMenuItems
78          ClearColor();
79
80          // set Color to Green
81          displayLabel.ForeColor = Color.Green;
82          greenToolStripMenuItem.Checked = true;
83       } // end method greenToolStripMenuItem_Click
84
85       // reset checkmarks for Font ToolStripMenuItems
86       private void ClearFont()
87       {
88          // clear all checkmarks
89          timesToolStripMenuItem.Checked = false;
90          courierToolStripMenuItem.Checked = false;
91          comicToolStripMenuItem.Checked = false;
92       } // end method ClearFont
93
94       // update Menu state and set Font to Times New Roman
95       private void timesToolStripMenuItem_Click( object sender, EventArgs e )
96       {
97          // reset checkmarks for Font ToolStripMenuItems
98          ClearFont();
99
100         // set Times New Roman font
101         timesToolStripMenuItem.Checked = true;
102         displayLabel.Font = new Font(
103            "Times New Roman", 14, displayLabel.Font.Style );
104      } // end method timesToolStripMenuItem_Click
105
106      // update Menu state and set Font to Courier
107      private void courierToolStripMenuItem_Click(
108         object sender, EventArgs e )
109      {
110         // reset checkmarks for Font ToolStripMenuItems
111         ClearFont();
112
113         // set Courier font
114         courierToolStripMenuItem.Checked = true;
115         displayLabel.Font = new Font(
116            "Courier", 14, displayLabel.Font.Style );
117      } // end method courierToolStripMenuItem_Click
```

Fig. 14.7 | Menus for changing text font and color. (Part 3 of 5.)

```
118
119      // update Menu state and set Font to Comic Sans MS
120      private void comicToolStripMenuItem_Click( object sender, EventArgs e )
121      {
122         // reset checkmarks for Font ToolStripMenuItems
123         ClearFont();
124
125         // set Comic Sans font
126         comicToolStripMenuItem.Checked = true;
127         displayLabel.Font = new Font(
128            "Comic Sans MS", 14, displayLabel.Font.Style );
129      } // end method comicToolStripMenuItem_Click
130
131      // toggle checkmark and toggle bold style
132      private void boldToolStripMenuItem_Click( object sender, EventArgs e )
133      {
134         // toggle checkmark
135         boldToolStripMenuItem.Checked = !boldToolStripMenuItem.Checked;
136
137         // use logical exlusive OR to toggle bold, keep all other styles
138         displayLabel.Font = new Font(
139            displayLabel.Font.FontFamily, 14,
140            displayLabel.Font.Style ^ FontStyle.Bold );
141      } // end method boldToolStripMenuItem_Click
142
143      // toggle checkmark and toggle italic style
144      private void italicToolStripMenuItem_Click(
145         object sender, EventArgs e )
146      {
147         // toggle checkmark
148         italicToolStripMenuItem.Checked = !italicToolStripMenuItem.Checked;
149
150         // use logical exclusive OR to toggle italic, keep all other styles
151         displayLabel.Font = new Font(
152            displayLabel.Font.FontFamily, 14,
153            displayLabel.Font.Style ^ FontStyle.Italic );
154      } // end method italicToolStripMenuItem_Click
155   } // end class MenuTestForm
```

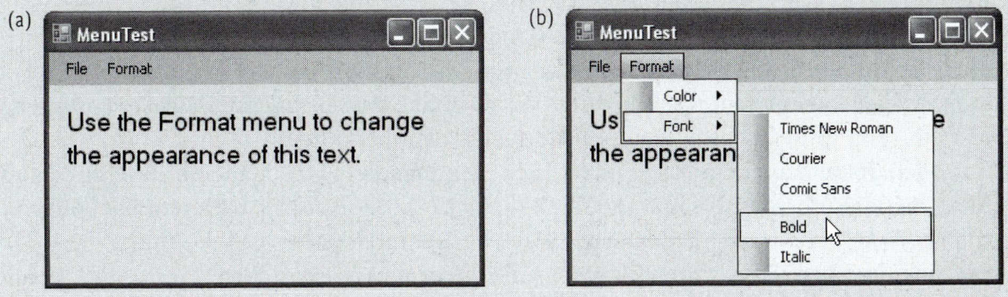

Fig. 14.7 | Menus for changing text font and color. (Part 4 of 5.)

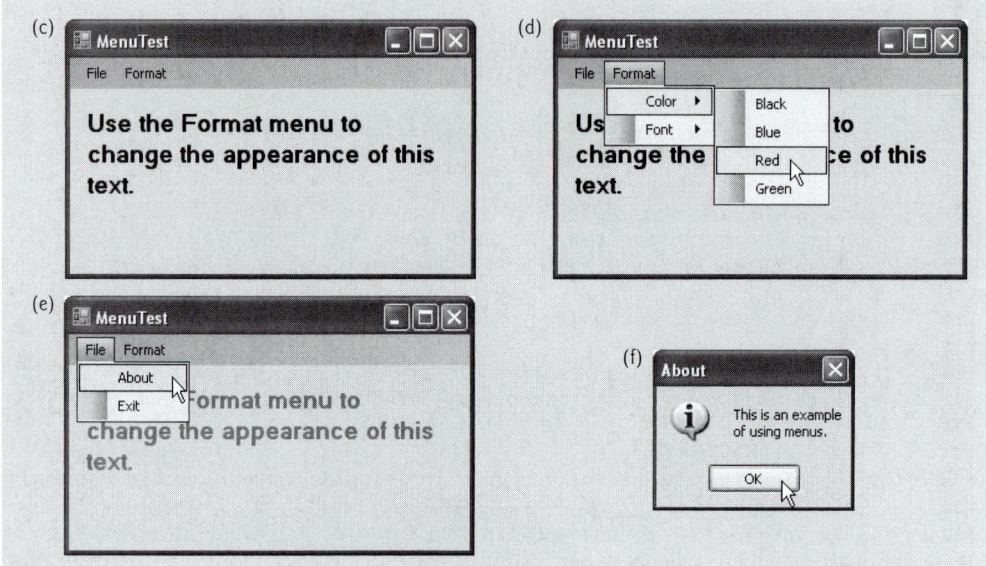

Fig. 14.7 | Menus for changing text font and color. (Part 5 of 5.)

To create this GUI, begin by dragging the MenuStrip from the **ToolBox** onto the Form. Then use **Design** mode to create the menu structure shown in the sample outputs. The **File** menu (fileToolStripMenuItem) has menu items **About** (aboutToolStripMenu-Item) and **Exit** (exitToolStripMenuItem); the **Format** menu (formatToolStripMenuItem) has two submenus. The first submenu, **Color** (colorToolStripMenuItem), contains menu items **Black** (blackToolStripMenuItem), **Blue** (blueToolStripMenuItem), **Red** (redTool-StripMenuItem) and **Green** (greenToolStripMenuItem). The second submenu, **Font** (fontToolStripMenuItem), contains menu items **Times New Roman** (timesToolStrip-MenuItem), **Courier** (courierToolStripMenuItem), **Comic Sans** (comicToolStripMenu-Item), a separator bar (dashToolStripMenuItem), **Bold** (boldToolStripMenuItem) and Italic (italicToolStripMenuItem).

The **About** menu item in the **File** menu displays a MessageBox when clicked (lines 18–23). The **Exit** menu item closes the application through static method *Exit* of class *Application* (line 28). Class Application's static methods control program execution. Method Exit causes our application to terminate.

We made the items in the **Color** submenu (**Black**, **Blue**, **Red** and **Green**) mutually exclusive—the user can select only one at a time (we explain how we did this shortly). To indicate that a menu item is selected, we will set each **Color** menu item's *Checked* property to true. This causes a check to appear to the left of a menu item.

Each **Color** menu item has its own Click event handler. The method handler for color **Black** is blackToolStripMenuItem_Click (lines 42–50). Similarly, the event handlers for colors **Blue**, **Red** and **Green** are blueToolStripMenuItem_Click (lines 53–61), redToolStripMenuItem_Click (lines 64–72) and greenToolStripMenuItem_Click (lines 75–83), respectively. Each **Color** menu item must be mutually exclusive, so each event handler calls method ClearColor (lines 32–39) before setting its corresponding Checked property to true. Method ClearColor sets the Checked property of each color MenuItem to false, effectively preventing more than one menu item from being selected at a time. In the designer, we initially set the **Black** menu item's Checked property to true, because at the start of the program, the text on the Form is black.

> **Software Engineering Observation 14.1**
>
> *The mutual exclusion of menu items is not enforced by the MenuStrip, even when the Checked property is true. You must program this behavior.*

The **Font** menu contains three menu items for fonts (**Courier**, **Times New Roman** and **Comic Sans**) and two menu items for font styles (**Bold** and **Italic**). We added a separator bar between the font and font-style menu items to indicate that these are separate options. A Font object can specify only one font at a time but can set multiple styles at once (e.g., a font can be both bold and italic). We set the font menu items to display checks. As with the **Color** menu, we must enforce mutual exclusion of these items in our event handlers.

Event handlers for font menu items **TimesRoman**, **Courier** and **ComicSans** are timesToolStripMenuItem_Click (lines 95–104), courierToolStripMenuItem_Click (lines 107–117) and comicToolStripMenuItem_Click (lines 120–129), respectively. These event handlers behave in a manner similar to that of the event handlers for the **Color** menu items. Each event handler clears the Checked properties for all font menu items by calling method ClearFont (lines 86–92), then sets the Checked property of the menu item that raised the event to true. This enforces the mutual exclusion of the font menu items. In the designer, we initially set the **Times New Roman** menu item's Checked property to true, because this is the original font for the text on the Form. The event handlers for the **Bold** and **Italic** menu items (lines 132–154) use the bitwise logical exclusive OR (^) operator to combine font styles, as we discussed in Chapter 13.

14.3 MonthCalendar Control

Many applications must perform date and time calculations. The .NET Framework provides two controls that allow an application to retrieve date and time information—the MonthCalendar and DateTimePicker (Section 14.4) controls.

The *MonthCalendar* (Fig. 14.8) control displays a monthly calendar on the Form. The user can select a date from the currently displayed month, or can use the provided links to navigate to another month. When a date is selected, it is highlighted. Multiple dates can be selected by clicking dates on the calendar while holding down the *Shift* key. The default event for this control is *DateChanged*, which is generated when a new date is selected. Properties are provided that allow you to modify the appearance of the calendar, how many dates can be selected at once, and the minimum and maximum dates that may be selected. MonthCalendar properties and a common event are summarized in Fig. 14.9.

14.4 DateTimePicker Control

The *DateTimePicker* control (see output of Fig. 14.11) is similar to the MonthCalendar control, but displays the calendar when a down arrow is selected. The DateTimePicker can be used to retrieve date and time information from the user. The DateTimePicker is also more customizable than a MonthCalendar control—more properties are provided to edit the look and feel of the drop-down calendar. Property *Format* specifies the user's selection options using the *DateTimePickerFormat* enumeration. The values in this enumeration

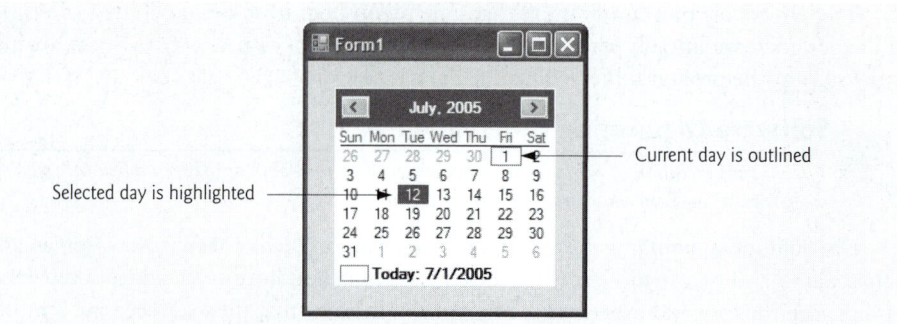

Current day is outlined

Selected day is highlighted

Fig. 14.8 | `MonthCalendar` control.

MonthCalendar properties and an event	Description
MonthCalendar Properties	
`FirstDayOfWeek`	Sets which day of the week is the first displayed for each week in the calendar.
`MaxDate`	The last date that can be selected.
`MaxSelectionCount`	The maximum number of dates that can be selected at once.
`MinDate`	The first date that can be selected.
`MonthlyBoldedDates`	An array of dates that will displayed in bold in the calendar.
`SelectionEnd`	The last of the dates selected by the user.
`SelectionRange`	The dates selected by the user.
`SelectionStart`	The first of the dates selected by the user.
Common MonthCalendar Event	
`DateChanged`	Generated when a date is selected in the calendar.

Fig. 14.9 | `MonthCalendar` properties and an event.

are **Long** (displays the date in long format, as in **Friday, July 1, 2005**), **Short** (displays the date in short format, as in **7/1/2005**), **Time** (displays a time value, as in **11:48:02 PM**) and **Custom** (indicates that a custom format will be used). If value `Custom` is used, the display in the `DateTimePicker` is specified using property **CustomFormat**. The default event for this control is **ValueChanged**, which occurs when the selected value (whether a date or a time) is changed. `DateTimePicker` properties and a common event are summarized in Fig. 14.10.

Figure 14.11 demonstrates using the `DateTimePicker` control to select an item's drop-off time. Many companies use such functionality. For instance, several online DVD rental companies specify the day a movie is sent out, and the estimated time that the movie

DateTimePicker properties and an event	Description
DateTimePicker Properties	
CalendarForeColor	Sets the text color for the calendar.
CalendarMonth-Background	Sets the calendar's background color.
CustomFormat	Sets the custom format string for the user's options.
Format	Sets the format of the date and/or time used for the user's options.
MaxDate	The maximum date and time that can be selected.
MinDate	The minimum date and time that can be selected.
ShowCheckBox	Indicates if a CheckBox should be displayed to the left of the selected date and time.
ShowUpDown	Used to indicate that the control should have up and down Buttons. This is helpful for instances when the DateTimePicker is used to select a time—the Buttons can be used to increase or decrease hour, minute and second values.
Value	The data selected by the user.
Common DateTimePicker Event	
ValueChanged	Generated when the Value property changes, including when the user selects a new date or time.

Fig. 14.10 | DateTimePicker properties and an event.

will arrive at your home. In this application, the user selects a drop-off day, and then an estimated arrival date is displayed. The date is always two days after drop off, three days if a Sunday is reached (mail is not delivered on Sunday).

```csharp
1   // Fig. 14.11: DateTimePickerForm.cs
2   // Using a DateTimePicker to select a drop off time.
3   using System;
4   using System.Windows.Forms;
5
6   public partial class DateTimePickerForm : Form
7   {
8      // default constructor
9      public DateTimePickerForm()
10     {
11        InitializeComponent();
12     } // end constructor
13
```

Fig. 14.11 | Demonstrating DateTimePicker. (Part 1 of 2.)

```
14      private void dateTimePickerDropOff_ValueChanged(
15         object sender, EventArgs e )
16      {
17         DateTime dropOffDate = dateTimePickerDropOff.Value;
18
19         // add extra time when items are dropped off around Sunday
20         if ( dropOffDate.DayOfWeek == DayOfWeek.Friday ||
21            dropOffDate.DayOfWeek == DayOfWeek.Saturday ||
22            dropOffDate.DayOfWeek == DayOfWeek.Sunday )
23
24            //estimate three days for delivery
25            outputLabel.Text = dropOffDate.AddDays( 3 ).ToLongDateString();
26         else
27            // otherwise estimate only two days for delivery
28            outputLabel.Text = dropOffDate.AddDays( 2 ).ToLongDateString();
29      } // end method dateTimePickerDropOff_ValueChanged
30
31      private void DateTimePickerForm_Load( object sender, EventArgs e )
32      {
33         // user cannot select days before today
34         dateTimePickerDropOff.MinDate = DateTime.Today;
35
36         // user can only select days of this year
37         dateTimePickerDropOff.MaxDate = DateTime.Today.AddYears( 1 );
38      } // end method DateTimePickerForm_Load
39   } // end class DateTimePickerForm
```

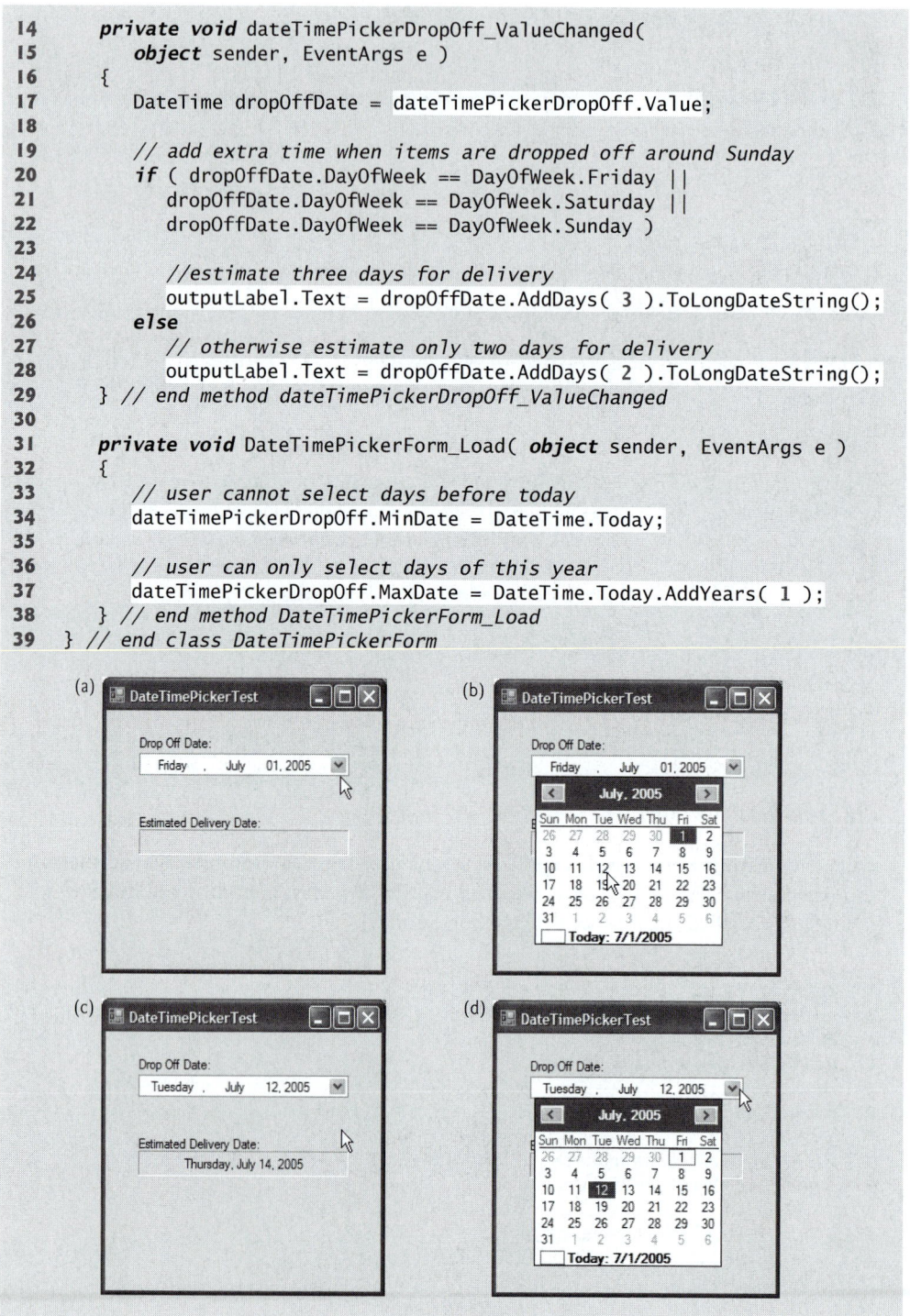

Fig. 14.11 | Demonstrating `DateTimePicker`. (Part 2 of 2.)

The DateTimePicker (dateTimePickerDropOff) has its Format property set to Long, so the user can select a date and not a time in this application. When the user selects a date, the ValueChanged event occurs. The event handler for this event (lines 14–29) first retrieves the selected date from the DateTimePicker's *Value* property (line 17). Lines 20–22 use the DateTime structure's *DayOfWeek* property to determine the day of the week on which the selected date falls. The day values are represented using the *DayOfWeek* enumeration. Lines 25 and 28 use DateTime's *AddDays* method to increase the date by two days or three days, respectively. The resulting date is then displayed in Long format using method *ToLongDateString*.

In this application, we do not want the user to be able to select a drop-off day before the current day, or one that is more than a year into the future. To enforce this, we set the DateTimePicker's *MinDate* and *MaxDate* properties when the Form is loaded (lines 34 and 37). Property Today returns the current day, and method *AddYears* (with an argument of 1) is used to specify a date one year in the future.

Let's take a closer look at the output. This application begins by displaying the current date (Fig. 14.11(a)). In Fig. 14.11(b), we selected the 12th of July. In Fig. 14.11(c), the estimated arrival date is displayed as the 14th. Figure 14.11(d) shows that the 12th, after it is selected, is highlighted in the calendar.

14.5 LinkLabel Control

The *LinkLabel* control displays links to other resources, such as files or Web pages (Fig. 14.12). A LinkLabel appears as underlined text (colored blue by default). When the mouse moves over the link, the pointer changes to a hand; this is similar to the behavior of a hyperlink in a Web page. The link can change color to indicate whether the link is new, previously visited or active. When clicked, the LinkLabel generates a *LinkClicked* event (see Fig. 14.13). Class LinkLabel is derived from class Label and therefore inherits all of class Label's functionality.

> **Look-and-Feel Observation 14.3**
>
> *A LinkLabel is the preferred control for indicating that the user can click a link to jump to a resource such as a Web page, though other controls can perform similar tasks.*

Class LinkLabelTestForm (Fig. 14.14) uses three LinkLabels to link to the C: drive, the Deitel Web site (www.deitel.com) and the Notepad application, respectively. The Text properties of the LinkLabel's driveLinkLabel, deitelLinkLabel and notepadLinkLabel describe each link's purpose.

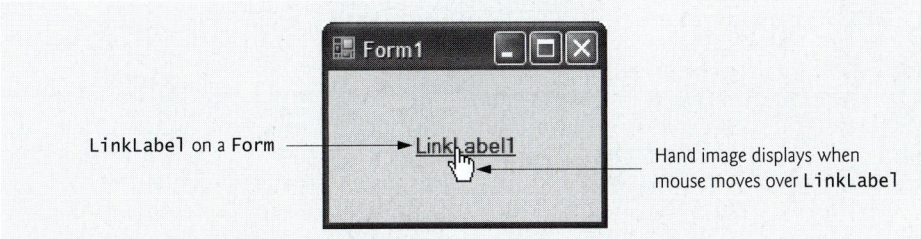

Fig. 14.12 | LinkLabel control in running program.

LinkLabel properties and event	Description
Common Properties	
ActiveLinkColor	Specifies the color of the active link when clicked.
LinkArea	Specifies which portion of text in the LinkLabel is part of the link.
LinkBehavior	Specifies the link's behavior, such as how the link appears when the mouse is placed over it.
LinkColor	Specifies the original color of all links before they have been visited. The default color is set by the system, but is usually blue.
LinkVisited	If true, the link appears as though it has been visited (its color is changed to that specified by property VisitedLinkColor). The default value is false.
Text	Specifies the control's text.
UseMnemonic	If true, the & character in the Text property acts as a shortcut (similar to the *Alt* shortcut in menus).
VisitedLinkColor	Specifies the color of visited links. The default color is set by the system, but is usually purple.
Common Event	*(Event arguments LinkLabelLinkClickedEventArgs)*
LinkClicked	Generated when the link is clicked. This is the default event when the control is double clicked in **Design** mode.

Fig. 14.13 | LinkLabel properties and an event.

```
 1    // Fig. 14.14: LinkLabelTestForm.cs
 2    // Using LinkLabels to create hyperlinks.
 3    using System;
 4    using System.Windows.Forms;
 5
 6    // Form using LinkLabels to browse the C:\ drive,
 7    // load a webpage and run Notepad
 8    public partial class LinkLabelTestForm : Form
 9    {
10       // default constructor
11       public LinkLabelTestForm()
12       {
13          InitializeComponent();
14       } // end constructor
15
```

Fig. 14.14 | LinkLabels used to link to a drive, a Web page and an application. (Part 1 of 3.)

```
16       // browse C:\ drive
17       private void driveLinkLabel_LinkClicked( object sender,
18          LinkLabelLinkClickedEventArgs e )
19       {
20          // change LinkColor after it has been clicked
21          driveLinkLabel.LinkVisited = true;
22
23          System.Diagnostics.Process.Start( @"C:\" );
24       } // end method driveLinkLabel_LinkClicked
25
26       // load www.deitel.com in web browser
27       private void deitelLinkLabel_LinkClicked( object sender,
28          LinkLabelLinkClickedEventArgs e )
29       {
30          // change LinkColor after it has been clicked
31          deitelLinkLabel.LinkVisited = true;
32
33          System.Diagnostics.Process.Start(
34             "IExplore", "http://www.deitel.com" );
35       } // end method deitelLinkLabel_LinkClicked
36
37       // run application Notepad
38       private void notepadLinkLabel_LinkClicked( object sender,
39          LinkLabelLinkClickedEventArgs e )
40       {
41          // change LinkColor after it has been clicked
42          notepadLinkLabel.LinkVisited = true;
43
44          // program called as if in run
45          // menu and full path not needed
46          System.Diagnostics.Process.Start( "notepad" );
47       } // end method driveLinkLabel_LinkClicked
48    } // end class LinkLabelTestForm
```

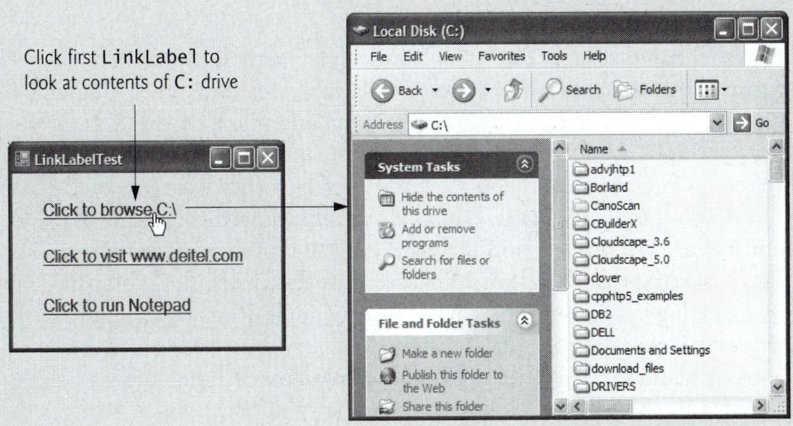

Fig. 14.14 | LinkLabels used to link to a drive, a Web page and an application. (Part 2 of 3.)

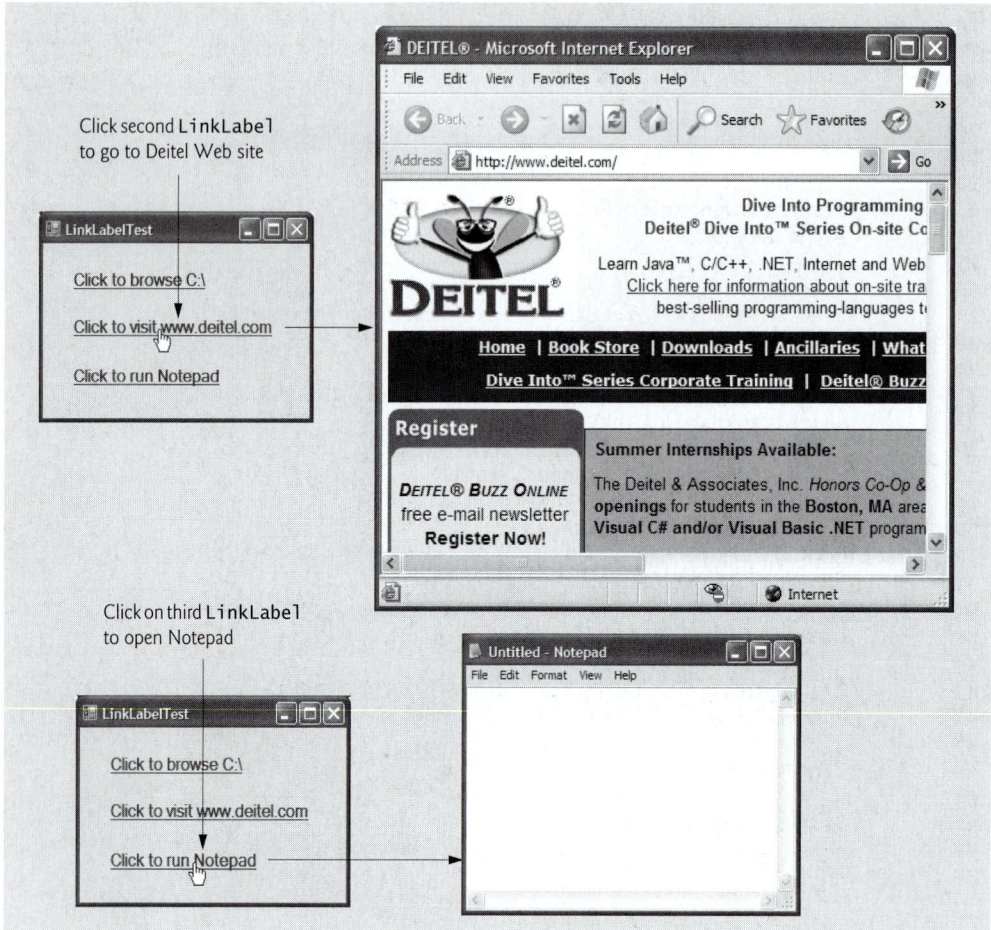

Fig. 14.14 | LinkLabels used to link to a drive, a Web page and an application. (Part 3 of 3.)

The event handlers for the LinkLabels call method ***Start*** of class ***Process*** (namespace ***System.Diagnostics***), which allows you to execute other programs from an application. Method Start can take one argument, the file to open (a string), or two arguments, the application to run and its command-line arguments (two strings). Method Start's arguments can be in the same form as if they were provided for input to the Windows **Run** command (**Start > Run...**). For applications that are known to Windows, full path names are not needed, and the .exe extension often can be omitted. To open a file that has a file type that Windows recognizes, simply use the file's full path name. The Windows operating system must be able to use the application associated with the given file's extension to open the file.

The event handler for driveLinkLabel's LinkClicked event browses the C: drive (lines 17–24). Line 21 sets the LinkVisited property to true, which changes the link's color from blue to purple (the LinkVisited colors can be configured through the **Proper- ties** window in Visual Studio). The event handler then passes @"C:\" to method Start (line 23), which opens a **Windows Explorer** window. The @ symbol that we placed before

"C:\" indicates that all characters in the string should be interpreted literally. Thus, the backslash within the string is not considered to be the first character of an escape sequence. This simplifies strings that represent directory paths, since you do not need to use \\ for each \ character in the path.

The event handler for deitelLinkLabel's LinkClicked event (lines 27–35) opens the Web page www.deitel.com in Internet Explorer. We achieve this by passing the Web page address as a string (lines 33–34), which opens Internet Explorer. Line 31 sets the LinkVisited property to true.

The event handler for notepadLinkLabel's LinkClicked event (lines 38–47) opens the Notepad application. Line 42 sets the LinkVisited property to true so the link appears as a visited link. Line 46 passes the argument "notepad" to method Start, which runs notepad.exe. Note that in line 46, the .exe extension is not required—Windows can determine whether it recognizes the argument given to method Start as an executable file.

14.6 ListBox Control

The *ListBox* control allows the user to view and select from multiple items in a list. List-Boxes are static GUI entities, which means that items must be added to the list programmatically. The user can be provided with TextBoxes and Buttons with which to specify items to be added to the list, but the actual additions must be performed in code. The *CheckedListBox* control (Section 14.7) extends a ListBox by including CheckBoxes next to each item in the list. This allows users to place checks on multiple items at once, as is possible with CheckBox controls. (Users also can select multiple items from a ListBox by setting the ListBox's *SelectionMode* property, which is discussed shortly.) Figure 14.15 displays a ListBox and a CheckedListBox. In both controls, scrollbars appear if the number of items exceeds the ListBox's viewable area.

Figure 14.16 lists common ListBox properties and methods, and a common event. The SelectionMode property determines the number of items that can be selected. This property has the possible values *None*, *One*, *MultiSimple* and *MultiExtended* (from the

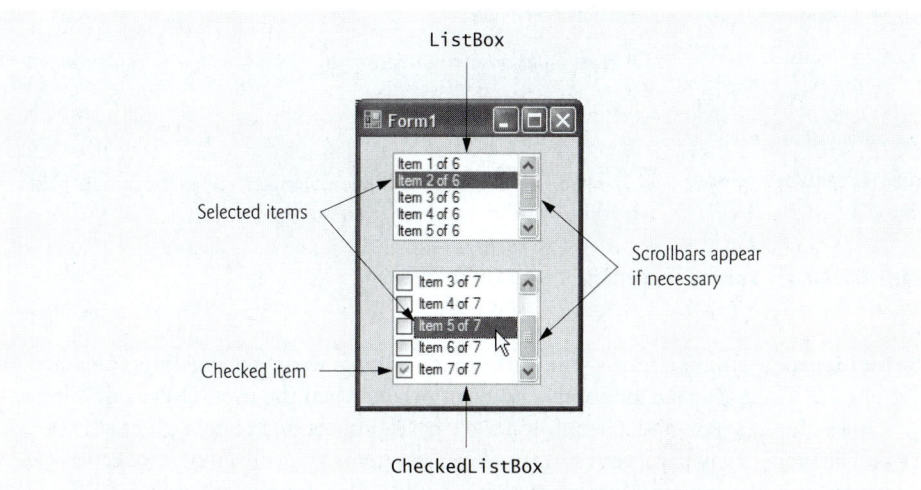

Fig. 14.15 | ListBox and CheckedListBox on a Form.

ListBox properties, methods and an event	Description
Common Properties	
Items	The collection of items in the ListBox.
MultiColumn	Indicates whether the ListBox can break a list into multiple columns. Multiple columns eliminate vertical scrollbars from the display.
SelectedIndex	Returns the index of the selected item. If no items have been selected, the property returns -1. If the user selects multiple items, this property returns only one of the selected indices. For this reason, if multiple items are selected, you should use property SelectedIndices.
SelectedIndices	Returns a collection containing the indices for all selected items.
SelectedItem	Returns a reference to the selected item. If multiple items are selected, it returns the item with the lowest index number.
SelectedItems	Returns a collection of the selected item(s).
SelectionMode	Determines the number of items that can be selected, and the means through which multiple items can be selected. Values None, One, MultiSimple (multiple selection allowed) or MultiExtended (multiple selection allowed using a combination of arrow keys or mouse clicks and *Shift* and *Ctrl* keys).
Sorted	Indicates whether items are sorted alphabetically. Setting this property's value to true sorts the items. The default value is false.
Common Methods	
ClearSelected	Deselects every item.
GetSelected	Takes an index as an argument, and returns true if the corresponding item is selected.
Common Event	
SelectedIndexChanged	Generated when the selected index changes. This is the default event when the control is double clicked in the designer.

Fig. 14.16 | ListBox properties, methods and an event.

SelectionMode enumeration)—the differences among these settings are explained in Fig. 14.16. The *SelectedIndexChanged* event occurs when the user selects a new item.

Both the ListBox and CheckedListBox have properties Items, SelectedItem and SelectedIndex. Property *Items* returns all the list items as a collection. Collections are a common way of managing lists of objects in the .NET framework. Many .NET GUI components (e.g., ListBoxes) use collections to expose lists of internal objects (e.g., items contained within a ListBox). We discuss collections further in Chapter 27. The collection returned by property Items is represented as an object of type ***ObjectCollection***. Property ***SelectedItem*** returns the ListBox's currently selected item. If the user can select multiple items, use collection ***SelectedItems*** to return all the selected items as a collection. Property ***SelectedIndex*** returns the index of the selected item—if there could be more than one, use property ***SelectedIndices***. If no items are selected, property Selected-Index returns -1. Method ***GetSelected*** takes an index and returns true if the corresponding item is selected.

To add items to a ListBox or to a CheckedListBox, we must add objects to its Items collection. This can be accomplished by calling method Add to add a string to the ListBox's or CheckedListBox's Items collection. For example, we could write

> *myListBox*.Items.Add(*myListItem*)

to add string *myListItem* to ListBox *myListBox*. To add multiple objects, you can either call method Add multiple times or call method AddRange to add an array of objects. Classes ListBox and CheckedListBox each call the submitted object's ToString method to determine the Label for the corresponding object's entry in the list. This allows you to add different objects to a ListBox or a CheckedListBox that later can be returned through properties SelectedItem and SelectedItems.

Alternatively, you can add items to ListBoxes and CheckedListBoxes visually by examining the Items property in the **Properties** window. Clicking the ellipsis button opens the **String Collection Editor**, which contains a text area for adding items; each item appears on a separate line (Fig. 14.17). Visual Studio then writes code to add these strings to the Items collection inside method InitializeComponent.

Figure 14.18 uses class ListBoxTestForm to add, remove and clear items from ListBox displayListBox. Class ListBoxTestForm uses TextBox inputTextBox to allow the user to type in a new item. When the user clicks the **Add** Button, the new item appears in displayListBox. Similarly, if the user selects an item and clicks **Remove**, the item is deleted. When clicked, **Clear** deletes all entries in displayListBox. The user terminates the application by clicking **Exit**.

The addButton_Click event handler (lines 18–22) calls method ***Add*** of the Items collection in the ListBox. This method takes a string as the item to add to displayListBox.

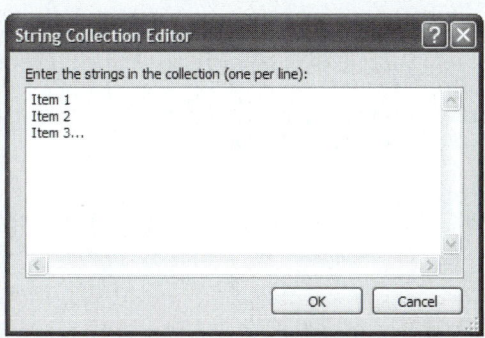

Fig. 14.17 | String Collection Editor.

In this case, the `string` used is the user-input text, or `inputTextBox.Text` (line 20). After the item is added, `inputTextBox.Text` is cleared (line 21).

The `removeButton_Click` event handler (lines 25–30) uses method **RemoveAt** to remove an item from the `ListBox`. Event handler `removeButton_Click` first uses property `SelectedIndex` to determine which index is selected. If `SelectedIndex` is not –1 (i.e., an item is selected) line 29 removes the item that corresponds to the selected index.

```
1   // Fig. 14.18: ListBoxTestForm.cs
2   // Program to add, remove and clear ListBox items
3   using System;
4   using System.Windows.Forms;
5
6   // Form uses a TextBox and Buttons to add,
7   // remove, and clear ListBox items
8   public partial class ListBoxTestForm : Form
9   {
10      // default constructor
11      public ListBoxTestForm()
12      {
13         InitializeComponent();
14      } // end constructor
15
16      // add new item to ListBox (text from input TextBox)
17      // and clear input TextBox
18      private void addButton_Click( object sender, EventArgs e )
19      {
20         displayListBox.Items.Add( inputTextBox.Text );
21         inputTextBox.Clear();
22      } // end method addButton_Click
23
24      // remove item if one is selected
25      private void removeButton_Click( object sender, EventArgs e )
26      {
27         // check if item is selected, remove if selected
28         if ( displayListBox.SelectedIndex != -1 )
29            displayListBox.Items.RemoveAt( displayListBox.SelectedIndex );
30      } // end method removeButton_Click
31
32      // clear all items in ListBox
33      private void clearButton_Click( object sender, EventArgs e )
34      {
35         displayListBox.Items.Clear();
36      } // end method clearButton_Click
37
38      // exit application
39      private void exitButton_Click( object sender, EventArgs e )
40      {
41         Application.Exit();
42      } // end method exitButton_Click
43   } // end class ListBoxTestForm
```

Fig. 14.18 | Program that adds, removes and clears `ListBox` items. (Part 1 of 2.)

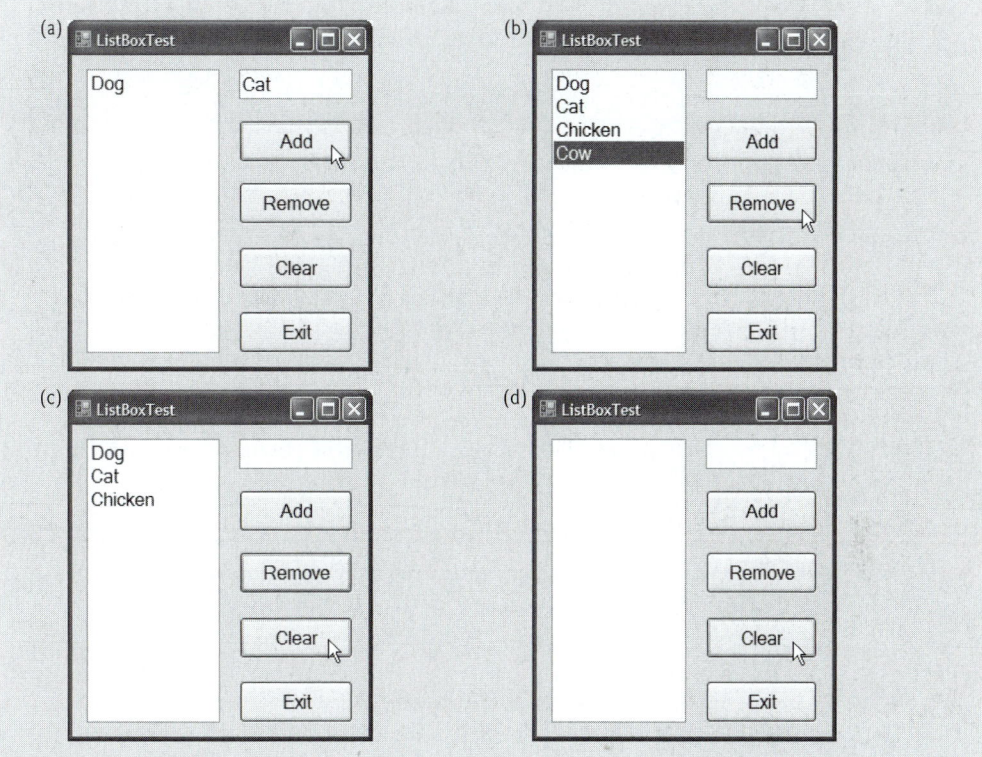

Fig. 14.18 | Program that adds, removes and clears ListBox items. (Part 2 of 2.)

The clearButton_Click event handler (lines 33–36) calls method *Clear* of the Items collection (line 35). This removes all the entries in displayListBox. Finally, event handler exitButton_Click (lines 39–42) terminates the application by calling method Application.Exit (line 41).

14.7 CheckedListBox Control

The CheckedListBox control derives from class ListBox and includes a CheckBox next to each item. As in ListBoxes, items can be added via methods Add and AddRange or through the **String Collection Editor**. CheckedListBoxes imply that multiple items can be selected, and the only possible values for the SelectionMode property are None and One. One allows multiple selection, because CheckBoxes imply that there are no logical restrictions on the items—the user can select as many items as required. Thus, the only choice is whether to give the user multiple selection or no selection at all. This keeps the CheckedListBox's behavior consistent with that of CheckBoxes. Common properties, events and methods of CheckedListBoxes appear in Fig. 14.19.

Common Programming Error 14.1

*The IDE displays an error message if you attempt to set the SelectionMode property to Multi-Simple or MultiExtended in the **Properties** window of a CheckedListBox. If this value is set programmatically, a runtime error occurs.*

CheckedListBox properties, methods and events	Description
Common Properties	*(All the ListBox properties, methods and events are inherited by CheckedListBox.)*
CheckedItems	Contains the collection of items that are checked. This is distinct from the selected item, which is highlighted (but not necessarily checked). [*Note:* There can be at most one selected item at any given time.]
CheckedIndices	Returns indices for all checked items.
SelectionMode	Determines how many items can be checked. The only possible values are One (allows multiple checks to be placed) or None (does not allow any checks to be placed).
Common Method	
GetItemChecked	Takes an index and returns true if the corresponding item is checked.
Common Event (Event arguments ItemCheckEventArgs)	
ItemCheck	Generated when an item is checked or unchecked.
ItemCheckEventArgs Properties	
CurrentValue	Indicates whether the current item is checked or unchecked. Possible values are Checked, Unchecked and Indeterminate.
Index	Returns the zero-based index of the item that changed.
NewValue	Specifies the new state of the item.

Fig. 14.19 | CheckedListBox properties, methods and events.

Event ***ItemCheck*** occurs whenever a user checks or unchecks a CheckedListBox item. Event argument properties CurrentValue and NewValue return CheckState values for the current and new state of the item, respectively. A comparison of these values allows you to determine whether the CheckedListBox item was checked or unchecked. The CheckedListBox control retains the SelectedItems and SelectedIndices properties (it inherits them from class ListBox). However, it also includes properties CheckedItems and CheckedIndices, which return information about the checked items and indices.

In Fig. 14.20, class CheckedListBoxTestForm uses a CheckedListBox and a ListBox to display a user's selection of books. The CheckedListBox allows the user to select multiple titles. In the **String Collection Editor**, items were added for some Deitel books: C++, Java™, Visual Basic, Internet & WWW, Perl, Python, Wireless Internet and Advanced Java (the acronym HTP stands for "How to Program"). The ListBox (named display-ListBox) displays the user's selection. In the screenshots accompanying this example, the CheckedListBox appears to the left, the ListBox on the right.

```
 1   // Fig. 14.20: CheckedListBoxTestForm.cs
 2   // Using the checked ListBox to add items to a display ListBox
 3   using System;
 4   using System.Windows.Forms;
 5
 6   // Form uses a checked ListBox to add items to a display ListBox
 7   public partial class CheckedListBoxTestForm : Form
 8   {
 9      // default constructor
10      public CheckedListBoxTestForm()
11      {
12         InitializeComponent();
13      } // end constructor
14
15      // item about to change
16      // add or remove from display ListBox
17      private void inputCheckedListBox_ItemCheck(
18         object sender, ItemCheckEventArgs e )
19      {
20         // obtain reference of selected item
21         string item = inputCheckedListBox.SelectedItem.ToString();
22
23         // if item checked add to ListBox
24         // otherwise remove from ListBox
25         if ( e.NewValue == CheckState.Checked )
26            displayListBox.Items.Add( item );
27         else
28            displayListBox.Items.Remove( item );
29      } // end method inputCheckedListBox_ItemCheck
30   } // end class CheckedListBoxTestForm
```

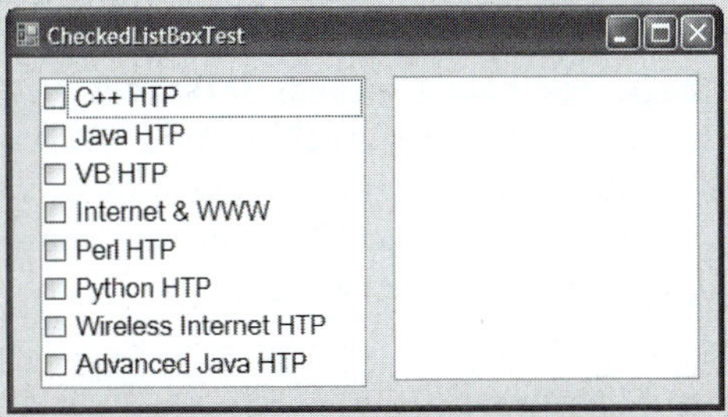

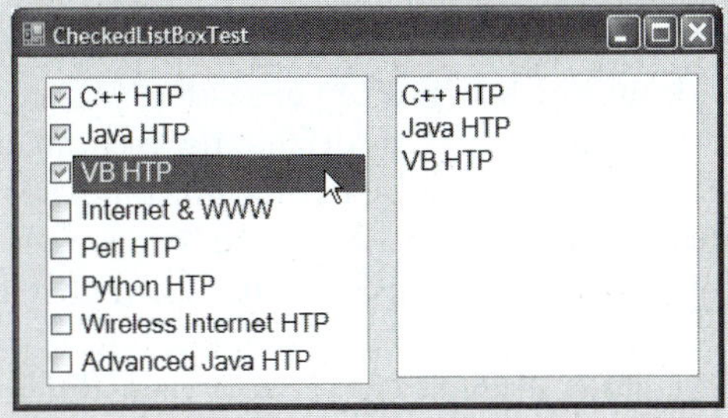

Fig. 14.20 | CheckedListBox and ListBox used in a program to display a user selection. (Part I of 2.)

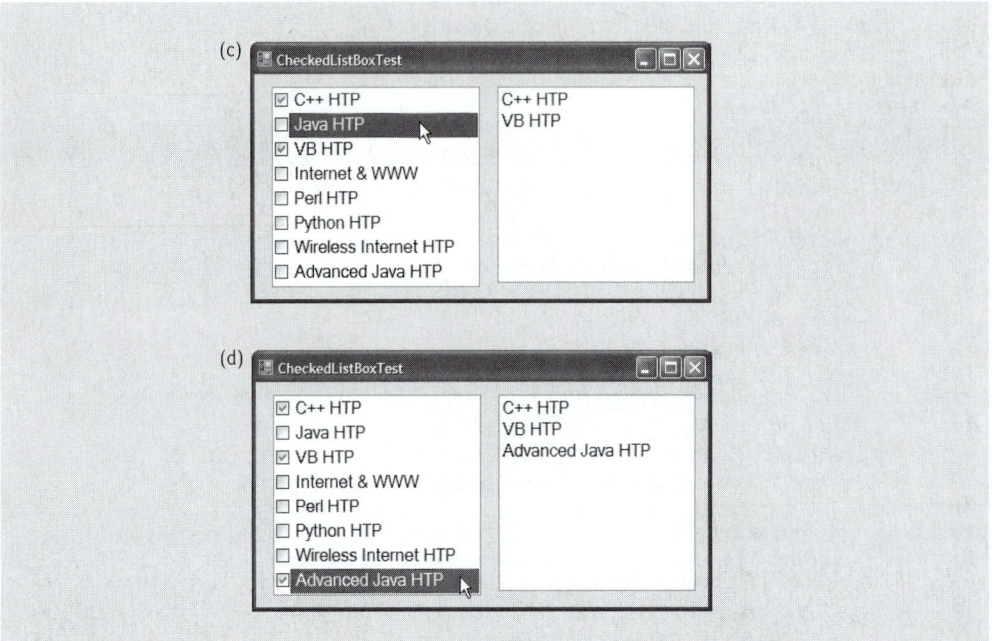

Fig. 14.20 | CheckedListBox and ListBox used in a program to display a user selection. (Part 2 of 2.)

When the user checks or unchecks an item in inputCheckedListBox, an ItemCheck event occurs and event handler inputCheckedListBox_ItemCheck (lines 17–29) executes. An if...else statement (lines 25–28) determines whether the user checked or unchecked an item in the CheckedListBox. Line 25 uses the NewValue property to determine whether the item is being checked (CheckState.Checked). If the user checks an item, line 26 adds the checked entry to the ListBox displayListBox. If the user unchecks an item, line 28 removes the corresponding item from displayListBox. This event handler was created by selecting the CheckedListBox in **Design** mode, viewing the control's events in the **Properties** window and double clicking the ItemCheck event.

14.8 ComboBox Control

The *ComboBox* control combines TextBox features with a *drop-down list*—a GUI component that contains a list from which a value can be selected. A ComboBox usually appears as a TextBox with a down arrow to its right. By default, the user can enter text into the Text-Box or click the down arrow to display a list of predefined items. If a user chooses an element from this list, that element is displayed in the TextBox. If the list contains more elements than can be displayed in the drop-down list, a scrollbar appears. The maximum number of items that a drop-down list can display at one time is set by property *MaxDrop-DownItems*. Figure 14.21 shows a sample ComboBox in three different states.

As with the ListBox control, you can add objects to collection Items programmatically, using methods Add and AddRange, or visually, with the **String Collection Editor**. Figure 14.22 lists common properties and a common event of class ComboBox.

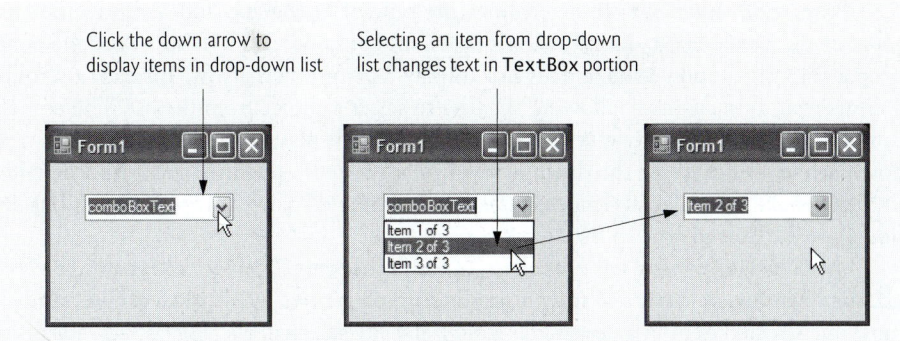

Fig. 14.21 | ComboBox demonstration.

Look-and-Feel Observation 14.4

Use a ComboBox to save space on a GUI. A disadvantage is that, unlike with a ListBox, the user cannot see available items without expanding the drop-down list.

ComboBox properties and an event	Description
Common Properties	
DropDownStyle	Determines the type of ComboBox. Value Simple means that the text portion is editable, and the list portion is always visible. Value Drop-Down (the default) means that the text portion is editable, but the user must click an arrow button to see the list portion. Value Drop-DownList means that the text portion is not editable, and the user must click the arrow button to see the list portion.
Items	The collection of items in the ComboBox control.
MaxDropDownItems	Specifies the maximum number of items (between 1 and 100) that the drop-down list can display. If the number of items exceeds the maximum number of items to display, a scrollbar appears.
SelectedIndex	Returns the index of the selected item. If there is no selected item, -1 is returned.
SelectedItem	Returns a reference to the selected item.
Sorted	Indicates whether items are sorted alphabetically. Setting this property's value to true sorts the items. The default is false.
Common Event	
SelectedIndexChanged	Generated when the selected index changes (such as when a different item is selected). This is the default event when control is double clicked in the designer.

Fig. 14.22 | ComboBox properties and an event.

Property ***DropDownStyle*** determines the type of ComboBox, and is represented as a value of the ***ComboBoxStyle*** enumeration, which contains values Simple, DropDown and DropDownList. Option ***Simple*** does not display a drop-down arrow. Instead, a scrollbar appears next to the control, allowing the user to select a choice from the list. The user also can type in a selection. Style ***DropDown*** (the default) displays a drop-down list when the down arrow is clicked (or the down-arrow key is pressed). The user can type a new item in the ComboBox. The last style is ***DropDownList***, which displays a drop-down list but does not allow the user to type in the TextBox.

The ComboBox control has properties ***Items*** (a collection), ***SelectedItem*** and ***SelectedIndex***, which are similar to the corresponding properties in ListBox. There can be at most one selected item in a ComboBox. If no items are selected, then SelectedIndex is -1. When the selected item changes, a ***SelectedIndexChanged*** event occurs.

Class ComboBoxTestForm (Fig. 14.23) allows users to select a shape to draw—circle, ellipse, square or pie (in both filled and unfilled versions)—by using a ComboBox. The ComboBox in this example is uneditable, so the user cannot type in the TextBox.

```
1   // Fig. 14.23: ComboBoxTestForm.cs
2   // Using ComboBox to select a shape to draw.
3   using System;
4   using System.Drawing;
5   using System.Windows.Forms;
6
7   // Form uses a ComboBox to select different shapes to draw
8   public partial class ComboBoxTestForm : Form
9   {
10      // default constructor
11      public ComboBoxTestForm()
12      {
13         InitializeComponent();
14      } // end constructor
15
16      // get index of selected shape, draw shape
17      private void imageComboBox_SelectedIndexChanged(
18         object sender, EventArgs e )
19      {
20         // create graphics object, Pen and SolidBrush
21         Graphics myGraphics = base.CreateGraphics();
22
23         // create Pen using color DarkRed
24         Pen myPen = new Pen( Color.DarkRed );
25
26         // create SolidBrush using color DarkRed
27         SolidBrush mySolidBrush = new SolidBrush( Color.DarkRed );
28
29         // clear drawing area setting it to color white
30         myGraphics.Clear( Color.White );
31
32         // find index, draw proper shape
33         switch ( imageComboBox.SelectedIndex )
34         {
```

Fig. 14.23 | ComboBox used to draw a selected shape. (Part 1 of 2.)

```
35            case 0: // case Circle is selected
36               myGraphics.DrawEllipse( myPen, 50, 50, 150, 150 );
37               break;
38            case 1: // case Rectangle is selected
39               myGraphics.DrawRectangle( myPen, 50, 50, 150, 150 );
40               break;
41            case 2: // case Ellipse is selected
42               myGraphics.DrawEllipse( myPen, 50, 85, 150, 115 );
43               break;
44            case 3: // case Pie is selected
45               myGraphics.DrawPie( myPen, 50, 50, 150, 150, 0, 45 );
46               break;
47            case 4: // case Filled Circle is selected
48               myGraphics.FillEllipse( mySolidBrush, 50, 50, 150, 150 );
49               break;
50            case 5: // case Filled Rectangle is selected
51               myGraphics.FillRectangle( mySolidBrush, 50, 50, 150, 150 );
52               break;
53            case 6: // case Filled Ellipse is selected
54               myGraphics.FillEllipse( mySolidBrush, 50, 85, 150, 115 );
55               break;
56            case 7: // case Filled Pie is selected
57               myGraphics.FillPie( mySolidBrush, 50, 50, 150, 150, 0, 45 );
58               break;
59         } // end switch
60
61         myGraphics.Dispose(); // release the Graphics object
62      } // end method imageComboBox_SelectedIndexChanged
63   } // end class ComboBoxTestForm
```

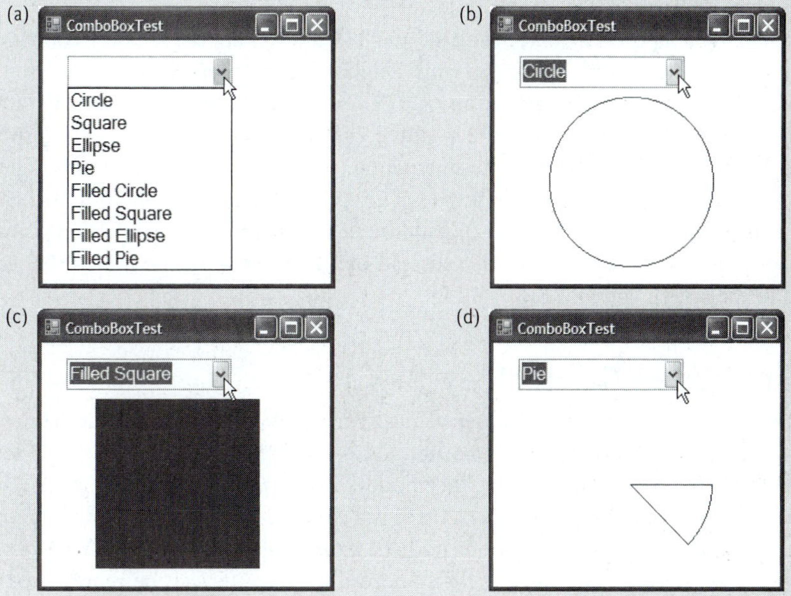

Fig. 14.23 | ComboBox used to draw a selected shape. (Part 2 of 2.)

Look-and-Feel Observation 14.5

Make lists (such as ComboBoxes) editable only if the program is designed to accept user-submitted elements. Otherwise, the user might try to enter a custom item that is improper for the purposes of your application.

After creating ComboBox imageComboBox, make it uneditable by setting its DropDown-Style to DropDownList in the **Properties** window. Next, add items Circle, Square, Ellipse, Pie, Filled Circle, Filled Square, Filled Ellipse and Filled Pie to the Items collection using the **String Collection Editor**. Whenever the user selects an item from imageComboBox, a SelectedIndexChanged event occurs and event handler imageComboBox_SelectedIndexChanged (lines 17–60) executes. Lines 21–27 create a Graphics object, a Pen and a SolidBrush, which are used to draw on the Form. The Graphics object (line 21) allows a pen or brush to draw on a component using one of several Graphics methods. The Pen object (line 24) is used by methods DrawEllipse, DrawRectangle and DrawPie (lines 36, 39, 42 and 45) to draw the outlines of their corresponding shapes. The SolidBrush object (line 27) is used by methods FillEllipse, FillRectangle and FillPie (lines 48, 51, 54 and 57) to fill their corresponding solid shapes. Line 30 colors the entire Form White, using Graphics method *Clear*. These methods are discussed in greater detail in Chapter 17, .

The application draws a shape based on the selected item's index. The switch statement (lines 33–59) uses imageComboBox.SelectedIndex to determine which item the user selected. Graphics method *DrawEllipse* (line 36) takes a Pen, the *x*- and *y*-coordinates of the center and the width and height of the ellipse to draw. The origin of the coordinate system is in the upper-left corner of the Form; the *x*-coordinate increases to the right, and the *y*-coordinate increases downward. A circle is a special case of an ellipse (with the width and height equal). Line 36 draws a circle. Line 42 draws an ellipse that has different values for width and height.

Class Graphics method *DrawRectangle* (line 39) takes a Pen, the *x*- and *y*-coordinates of the upper-left corner and the width and height of the rectangle to draw. Method *DrawPie* (line 45) draws a pie as a portion of an ellipse. The ellipse is bounded by a rectangle. Method DrawPie takes a Pen, the *x*- and *y*-coordinates of the upper-left corner of the rectangle, its width and height, the start angle (in degrees) and the sweep angle (in degrees) of the pie. Angles increase clockwise. The *FillEllipse* (lines 48 and 54), *FillRectangle* (line 51) and *FillPie* (line 57) methods are similar to their unfilled counterparts, except that they take a SolidBrush instead of a Pen. Some of the drawn shapes are illustrated in the screen shots of Fig. 14.23.

14.9 TreeView Control

The *TreeView* control displays *nodes* hierarchically in a *tree*. Traditionally, nodes are objects that contain values and can refer to other nodes. A *parent node* contains *child nodes*, and the child nodes can be parents to other nodes. Two child nodes that have the same parent node are considered *sibling nodes*. A tree is a collection of nodes, usually organized in a hierarchical manner. The first parent node of a tree is the *root* node (a TreeView can have multiple roots). For example, the file system of a computer can be represented as a tree. The top-level directory (perhaps C:) would be the root, each subfolder of C: would be a child node and each child folder could have its own children. TreeView controls are useful for displaying hierarchal information, such as the file structure that we just mentioned. We cover nodes and trees in greater detail in Chapter 25, Data Structures. Figure 14.24 displays a sample TreeView control on a Form.

A parent node can be expanded or collapsed by clicking the plus box or minus box to its left. Nodes without children do not have these boxes.

The nodes in a TreeView are instances of class **TreeNode**. Each TreeNode has a **Nodes collection** (type **TreeNodeCollection**), which contains a list of other TreeNodes—known as its children. The Parent property returns a reference to the parent node (or null if the node is a root node). Figure 14.25 and Fig. 14.26 list the common properties of TreeViews and TreeNodes, common TreeNode methods and a common TreeView event.

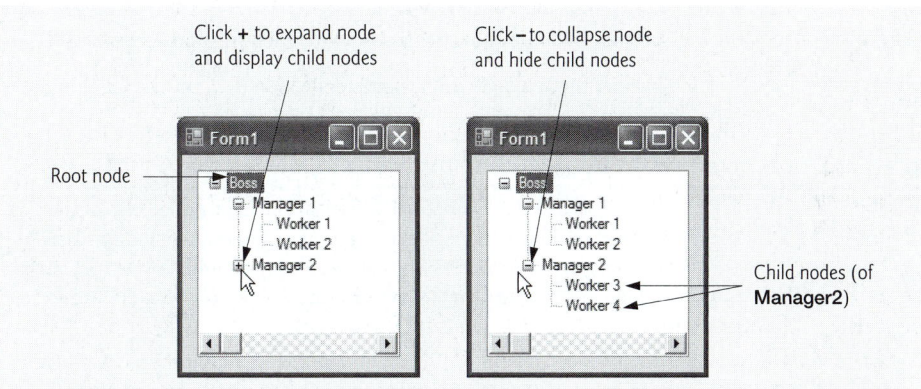

Fig. 14.24 | TreeView displaying a sample tree.

TreeView properties and an event	Description
Common Properties	
CheckBoxes	Indicates whether CheckBoxes appear next to nodes. A value of true displays CheckBoxes. The default value is false.
ImageList	Specifies an ImageList object containing the node icons. An *ImageList* object is a collection that contains Image objects.
Nodes	Lists the collection of TreeNodes in the control. It contains methods Add (adds a TreeNode object), Clear (deletes the entire collection) and Remove (deletes a specific node). Removing a parent node deletes all of its children.
SelectedNode	The selected node.
*Common Event (Event arguments **TreeViewEventArgs**)*	
AfterSelect	Generated after selected node changes. This is the default event when the control is double clicked in the designer.

Fig. 14.25 | TreeView properties and an event.

TreeNode properties and methods	Description
Common Properties	
Checked	Indicates whether the TreeNode is checked (CheckBoxes property must be set to true in the parent TreeView).
FirstNode	Specifies the first node in the Nodes collection (i.e., the first child in the tree).
FullPath	Indicates the path of the node, starting at the root of the tree.
ImageIndex	Specifies the index of the image shown when the node is deselected.
LastNode	Specifies the last node in the Nodes collection (i.e., the last child in the tree).
NextNode	Next sibling node.
Nodes	Collection of TreeNodes contained in the current node (i.e., all the children of the current node). It contains methods Add (adds a TreeNode object), Clear (deletes the entire collection) and Remove (deletes a specific node). Removing a parent node deletes all of its children.
PrevNode	Previous sibling node.
SelectedImageIndex	Specifies the index of the image to use when the node is selected.
Text	Specifies the TreeNode's text.
Common Methods	
Collapse	Collapses a node.
Expand	Expands a node.
ExpandAll	Expands all the children of a node.
GetNodeCount	Returns the number of child nodes.

Fig. 14.26 | TreeNode properties and methods.

To add nodes to the TreeView visually, click the ellipsis next to the Nodes property in the **Properties** window. This opens the **TreeNode Editor** (Fig. 14.27), which displays an empty tree representing the TreeView. There are Buttons to create a root, and to add or delete a node. To the right are the properties of current node. Here you can rename the node.

To add nodes programmatically, first create a root node. Create a new TreeNode object and pass it a string to display. Then call method Add to add this new TreeNode to the TreeView's Nodes collection. Thus, to add a root node to TreeView *myTreeView*, write

```
myTreeView.Nodes.Add( new TreeNode( rootLabel ) );
```

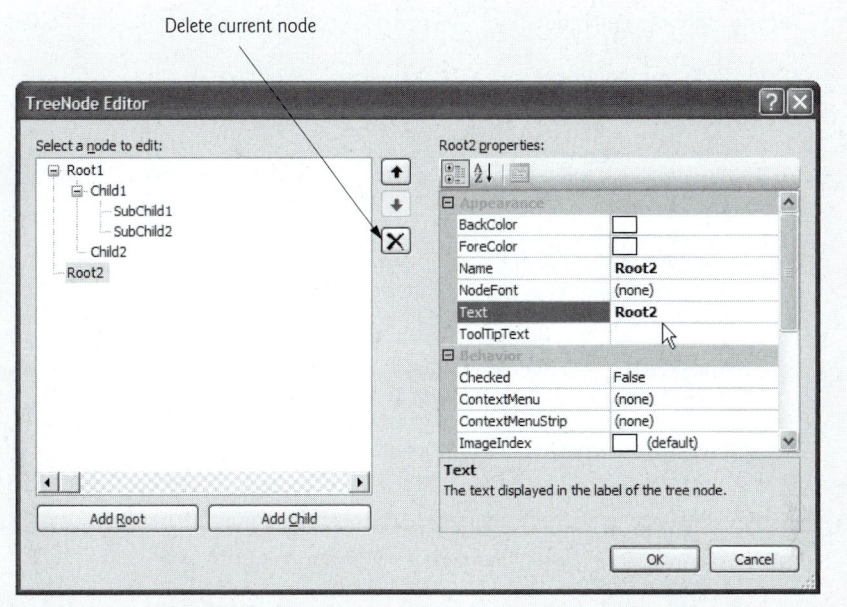

Fig. 14.27 | TreeNode Editor.

where *myTreeView* is the TreeView to which we are adding nodes, and *rootLabel* is the text to display in *myTreeView*. To add children to a root node, add new TreeNodes to its Nodes collection. We select the appropriate root node from the TreeView by writing

    myTreeView.Nodes[*myIndex*]

where *myIndex* is the root node's index in *myTreeView*'s Nodes collection. We add nodes to child nodes through the same process by which we added root nodes to *myTreeView*. To add a child to the root node at index *myIndex*, write

    myTreeView.Nodes[*myIndex*].Nodes.Add(**new** TreeNode(*ChildLabel*));

Class TreeViewDirectoryStructureForm (Fig. 14.28) uses a TreeView to display the contents of a directory chosen by the user. A TextBox and a Button are used to specify the directory. First, enter the full path of the directory you want to display. Then click the

```
1   // Fig. 14.28: TreeViewDirectoryStructureForm.cs
2   // Using TreeView to display directory structure.
3   using System;
4   using System.Windows.Forms;
5   using System.IO;
6
7   // Form uses TreeView to display directory structure
8   public partial class TreeViewDirectoryStructureForm : Form
9   {
```

Fig. 14.28 | TreeView used to display directories. (Part 1 of 3.)

```
10      string substringDirectory; // store last part of full path name
11
12      // default constructor
13      public TreeViewDirectoryStructureForm()
14      {
15         InitializeComponent();
16      } // end constructor
17
18      // populate current node with subdirectories
19      public void PopulateTreeView(
20         string directoryValue, TreeNode parentNode )
21      {
22         // array stores all subdirectories in the directory
23         string[] directoryArray =
24            Directory.GetDirectories( directoryValue );
25
26         // populate current node with subdirectories
27         try
28         {
29            // check to see if any subdirectories are present
30            if ( directoryArray.Length != 0 )
31            {
32               // for every subdirectory, create new TreeNode,
33               // add as a child of current node and recursively
34               // populate child nodes with subdirectories
35               foreach ( string directory in directoryArray )
36               {
37                  // obtain last part of path name from the full path name
38                  // by finding the last occurence of "\" and returning the
39                  // part of the path name that comes after this occurence
40                  substringDirectory = directory.Substring(
41                     directory.LastIndexOf( '\\' ) + 1,
42                     directory.Length - directory.LastIndexOf( '\\' ) - 1 );
43
44                  // create TreeNode for current directory
45                  TreeNode myNode = new TreeNode( substringDirectory );
46
47                  // add current directory node to parent node
48                  parentNode.Nodes.Add( myNode );
49
50                  // recursively populate every subdirectory
51                  PopulateTreeView( directory, myNode );
52               } // end foreach
53            } // end if
54         } //end try
55
56         // catch exception
57         catch ( UnauthorizedAccessException )
58         {
59            parentNode.Nodes.Add( "Access denied" );
60         } // end catch
61      } // end method PopulateTreeView
```

Fig. 14.28 | TreeView used to display directories. (Part 2 of 3.)

```
62
63      // handles enterButton click event
64      private void enterButton_Click( object sender, EventArgs e )
65      {
66         // clear all nodes
67         directoryTreeView.Nodes.Clear();
68
69         // check if the directory entered by user exists
70         // if it does then fill in the TreeView,
71         // if not display error MessageBox
72         if ( Directory.Exists( inputTextBox.Text ) )
73         {
74            // add full path name to directoryTreeView
75            directoryTreeView.Nodes.Add( inputTextBox.Text );
76
77            // insert subfolders
78            PopulateTreeView(
79               inputTextBox.Text, directoryTreeView.Nodes[ 0 ] );
80         }
81         // display error MessageBox if directory not found
82         else
83            MessageBox.Show( inputTextBox.Text + " could not be found.",
84               "Directory Not Found", MessageBoxButtons.OK,
85               MessageBoxIcon.Error );
86      } // end method enterButton_Click
87   } // end class TreeViewDirectoryStructureForm
```

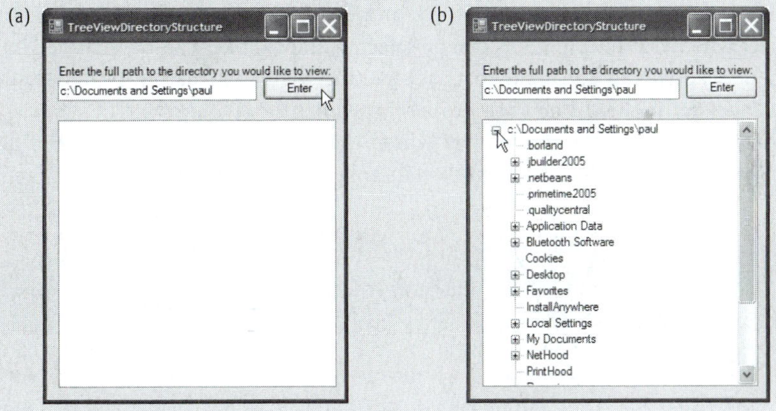

Fig. 14.28 | TreeView used to display directories. (Part 3 of 3.)

Button to set the specified directory as the root node in the TreeView. Each subdirectory of this directory becomes a child node. This layout is similar to that used in **Windows Explorer**. Folders can be expanded or collapsed by clicking the plus or minus boxes that appear to their left.

When the user clicks the enterButton, all the nodes in directoryTreeView are cleared (line 67). Then the path entered in inputTextBox is used to create the root node. Line 75 adds the directory to directoryTreeView as the root node, and lines 78–79 call method PopulateTreeView (lines 19–61), which takes a directory (a string) and a parent node. Method `PopulateTreeView` then creates child nodes corresponding to the subdirectories of the directory it receives as an argument.

Method `PopulateTreeView` (lines 19–61) obtains a list of subdirectories, using method **`GetDirectories`** of class `Directory` (namespace `System.IO`) in lines 23–24. Method `GetDirectories` takes a `string` (the current directory) and returns an array of `strings` (the subdirectories). If a directory is not accessible for security reasons, an `UnauthorizedAccessException` is thrown. Lines 57–60 catch this exception and add a node containing "`Access Denied`" instead of displaying the subdirectories.

If there are accessible subdirectories, lines 40–42 use the `Substring` method to increase readability by shortening the full path name to just the directory name. Next, each `string` in the `directoryArray` is used to create a new child node (line 45). We use method `Add` (line 48) to add each child node to the parent. Then method `PopulateTreeView` is called recursively on every subdirectory (line 51), which eventually populates the `TreeView` with the entire directory structure. Note that our recursive algorithm may cause a delay when the program loads large directories. However, once the folder names are added to the appropriate `Nodes` collection, they can be expanded and collapsed without delay. In the next section, we present an alternate algorithm to solve this problem.

14.10 `ListView` Control

The **`ListView`** control is similar to a `ListBox` in that both display lists from which the user can select one or more items (an example of a `ListView` can be found in Fig. 14.31). The important difference between the two classes is that a `ListView` can display icons next to the list items (controlled by its `ImageList` property). Property **`MultiSelect`** (a `Boolean`) determines whether multiple items can be selected. CheckBoxes can be included by setting property **`CheckBoxes`** (a `Boolean`) to `true`, making the `ListView`'s appearance similar to that of a `CheckedListBox`. The **`View`** property specifies the layout of the `ListBox`. Property **`Activation`** determines the method by which the user selects a list item. The details of these properties and the `ItemActivate` event are explained in Fig. 14.29.

ListView properties and an event	Description
Common Properties	
Activation	Determines how the user activates an item. This property takes a value in the `ItemActivation` enumeration. Possible values are `OneClick` (single-click activation), `TwoClick` (double-click activation, item changes color when selected) and `Standard` (double-click activation, item does not change color).
CheckBoxes	Indicates whether items appear with CheckBoxes. `true` displays CheckBoxes. The default is `false`.
LargeImageList	Specifies the `ImageList` containing large icons for display.

Fig. 14.29 | `ListView` properties and an event. (Part 1 of 2.)

ListView properties and an event	Description
Items	Returns the collection of ListViewItems in the control.
MultiSelect	Determines whether multiple selection is allowed. The default is true, which enables multiple selection.
SelectedItems	Gets the collection of selected items.
SmallImageList	Specifies the ImageList containing small icons for display.
View	Determines appearance of ListViewItems. Possible values are LargeIcon (large icon displayed, items can be in multiple columns), SmallIcon (small icon displayed, items can be in multiple columns), List (small icons displayed, items appear in a single column), Details (like List, but multiple columns of information can be displayed per item) and Tile (large icons displayed, information provided to right of icon, valid only in Windows XP or later).
Common Event	
ItemActivate	Generated when an item in the ListView is activated. Does not contain the specifics of which item is activated.

Fig. 14.29 | ListView properties and an event. (Part 2 of 2.)

ListView allows you to define the images used as icons for ListView items. To display images, an ImageList component is required. Create one by dragging it to a Form from the **ToolBox**. Then, select the ***Images*** property in the **Properties** window to display the **Image Collection Editor** (Fig. 14.30). Here you can browse for images that you wish to add to the ImageList, which contains an array of Images. Once the images have been defined, set property SmallImageList of the ListView to the new ImageList object. Property ***SmallImageList*** specifies the image list for the small icons. Property ***LargeImageList*** sets the ImageList for large icons. The items in a ListView are each of type ***ListViewItem***.

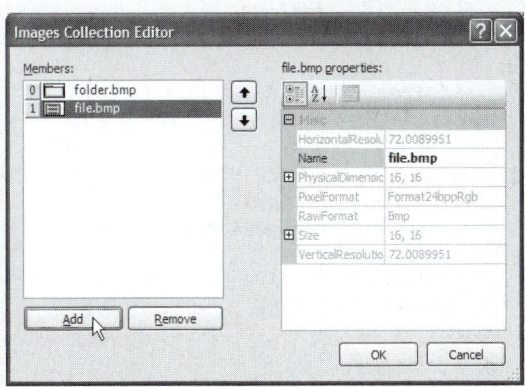

Fig. 14.30 | **Image Collection Editor** window for an ImageList component.

Icons for the ListView items are selected by setting the item's ***ImageIndex*** property to the appropriate index.

Class ListViewTestForm (Fig. 14.31) displays files and folders in a ListView, along with small icons representing each file or folder. If a file or folder is inaccessible because of permission settings, a MessageBox appears. The program scans the contents of the directory as it browses, rather than indexing the entire drive at once.

To display icons beside list items, create an ImageList for the ListView browser-ListView. First, drag and drop an ImageList on the Form and open the **Image Collection Editor**. Select our two simple bitmap images, provided in the bin\Release folder of this example—one for a folder (array index 0) and the other for a file (array index 1). Then set the object browserListView property SmallImageList to the new ImageList in the **Properties** window.

```
 1   // Fig. 14.31: ListViewTestForm.cs
 2   // Displaying directories and their contents in ListView.
 3   using System;
 4   using System.Drawing;
 5   using System.Windows.Forms;
 6   using System.IO;
 7
 8   // Form contains a ListView which displays
 9   // folders and files in a directory
10   public partial class ListViewTestForm : Form
11   {
12      // store current directory
13      string currentDirectory = Directory.GetCurrentDirectory();
14
15      // default constructor
16      public ListViewTestForm()
17      {
18         InitializeComponent();
19      } // end constructor
20
21      // browse directory user clicked or go up one level
22      private void browserListView_Click( object sender, EventArgs e )
23      {
24         // ensure an item is selected
25         if ( browserListView.SelectedItems.Count != 0 )
26         {
27            // if first item selected, go up one level
28            if ( browserListView.Items[ 0 ].Selected )
29            {
30               // create DirectoryInfo object for directory
31               DirectoryInfo directoryObject =
32                  new DirectoryInfo( currentDirectory );
33
34               // if directory has parent, load it
35               if ( directoryObject.Parent != null )
36                  LoadFilesInDirectory( directoryObject.Parent.FullName );
37            } // end if
```

Fig. 14.31 | ListView displaying files and folders. (Part 1 of 4.)

```
38
39              // selected directory or file
40              else
41              {
42                  // directory or file chosen
43                  string chosen = browserListView.SelectedItems[ 0 ].Text;
44
45                  // if item selected is directory, load selected directory
46                  if ( Directory.Exists( currentDirectory + @"\" + chosen ) )
47                  {
48                      // if currently in C:\, do not need '\'; otherwise we do
49                      if ( currentDirectory == @"C:\" )
50                          LoadFilesInDirectory( currentDirectory + chosen );
51                      else
52                          LoadFilesInDirectory(
53                              currentDirectory + @"\" + chosen );
54                  } // end if
55              } // end else
56
57          // update displayLabel
58          displayLabel.Text = currentDirectory;
59      } // end if
60  } // end method browserListView_Click
61
62  // display files/subdirectories of current directory
63  public void LoadFilesInDirectory( string currentDirectoryValue )
64  {
65      // load directory information and display
66      try
67      {
68          // clear ListView and set first item
69          browserListView.Items.Clear();
70          browserListView.Items.Add( "Go Up One Level" );
71
72          // update current directory
73          currentDirectory = currentDirectoryValue;
74          DirectoryInfo newCurrentDirectory =
75              new DirectoryInfo( currentDirectory );
76
77          // put files and directories into arrays
78          DirectoryInfo[] directoryArray =
79              newCurrentDirectory.GetDirectories();
80          FileInfo[] fileArray = newCurrentDirectory.GetFiles();
81
82          // add directory names to ListView
83          foreach ( DirectoryInfo dir in directoryArray )
84          {
85              // add directory to ListView
86              ListViewItem newDirectoryItem =
87                  browserListView.Items.Add( dir.Name );
88
89              newDirectoryItem.ImageIndex = 0;   // set directory image
90          } // end foreach
```

Fig. 14.31 | ListView displaying files and folders. (Part 2 of 4.)

```
 91
 92            // add file names to ListView
 93            foreach ( FileInfo file in fileArray )
 94            {
 95               // add file to ListView
 96               ListViewItem newFileItem =
 97                  browserListView.Items.Add( file.Name );
 98
 99               newFileItem.ImageIndex = 1;  // set file image
100            } // end foreach
101         } // end try
102
103         // access denied
104         catch ( UnauthorizedAccessException )
105         {
106            MessageBox.Show( "Warning: Some fields may not be " +
107               "visible due to permission settings",
108               "Attention", 0, MessageBoxIcon.Warning );
109         } // end catch
110      } // end method LoadFilesInDirectory
111
112      // handle load event when Form displayed for first time
113      private void ListViewTestForm_Load( object sender, EventArgs e )
114      {
115         // set Image list
116         Image folderImage = Image.FromFile(
117            currentDirectory + @"\images\folder.bmp" );
118
119         Image fileImage = Image.FromFile(
120            currentDirectory + @"\images\file.bmp" );
121
122         fileFolder.Images.Add( folderImage );
123         fileFolder.Images.Add( fileImage );
124
125         // load current directory into browserListView
126         LoadFilesInDirectory( currentDirectory );
127         displayLabel.Text = currentDirectory;
128      } // end method ListViewTestForm_Load
129   } // end class ListViewTestForm
```

(a)

ListViewTest

Now in Directory: C:\Documents and Settings

```
   Go Up One Level
🗀 Administrator
🗀 All Users
🗀 Default User
🗀 LocalService
🗀 NetworkService
🗀 test
```

Fig. 14.31 | ListView displaying files and folders. (Part 3 of 4.)

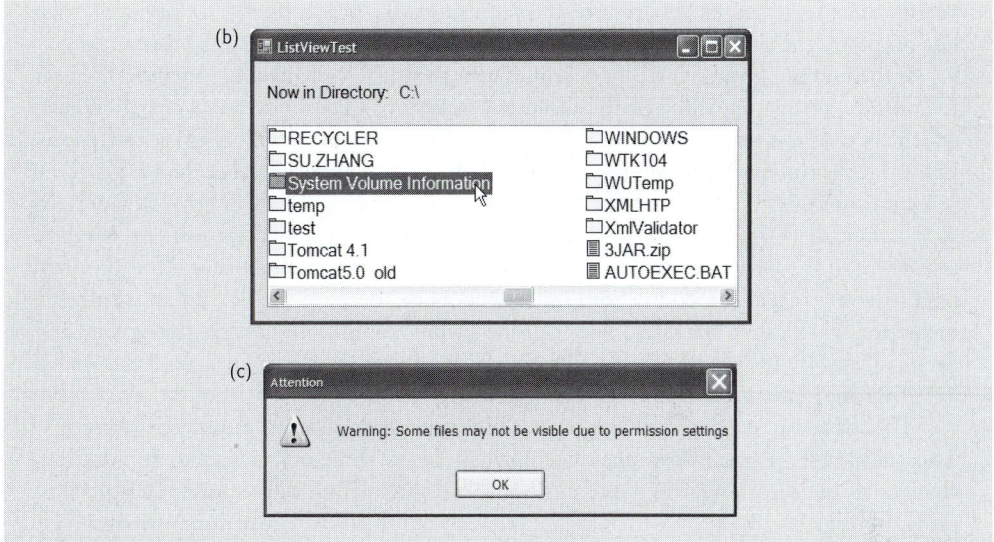

Fig. 14.31 | ListView displaying files and folders. (Part 4 of 4.)

Method LoadFilesInDirectory (lines 63–110) populates browserListView with the directory passed to it (currentDirectoryValue). It clears browserListView and adds the element "Go Up One Level". When the user clicks this element, the program attempts to move up one level (we see how shortly). The method then creates a DirectoryInfo object initialized with the string currentDirectory (lines 74–75). If permission is not given to browse the directory, an exception is thrown (and caught in line 104). Method Load-FilesInDirectory works differently from method PopulateTreeView in the previous program (Fig. 14.28). Instead of loading all the folders on the hard drive, method Load-FilesInDirectory loads only the folders in the current directory.

Class *DirectoryInfo* (namespace System.IO) enables us to browse or manipulate the directory structure easily. Method *GetDirectories* (line 79) returns an array of DirectoryInfo objects containing the subdirectories of the current directory. Similarly, method *GetFiles* (line 80) returns an array of class *FileInfo* objects containing the files in the current directory. Property *Name* (of both class DirectoryInfo and class FileInfo) contains only the directory or file name, such as temp instead of C:\myfolder\temp. To access the full name, use property *FullName*.

Lines 83–90 and lines 93–100 iterate through the subdirectories and files of the current directory and add them to browserListView. Lines 89 and 99 set the ImageIndex properties of the newly created items. If an item is a directory, we set its icon to a directory icon (index 0); if an item is a file, we set its icon to a file icon (index 1).

Method browserListView_Click (lines 22–60) responds when the user clicks control browserListView. Line 25 checks whether anything is selected. If a selection has been made, line 28 determines whether the user chose the first item in browserListView. The first item in browserListView is always **Go up one level**; if it is selected, the program attempts to go up a level. Lines 31–32 create a DirectoryInfo object for the current directory. Line 35 tests property Parent to ensure that the user is not at the root of the directory tree. Property *Parent* indicates the parent directory as a DirectoryInfo object; if no parent directory exists, `Parent` returns the value `null`. If a parent does directory exist, then line 36 passes the full name of the parent directory to method `LoadFilesInDirectory`.

If the user did not select the first item in `browserListView`, lines 40–55 allow the user to continue navigating through the directory structure. Line 43 creates `string chosen`, which receives the text of the selected item (the first item in collection `SelectedItems`). Line 46 determines whether the user has selected a valid directory (rather than a file). The program combines variables `currentDirectory` and `chosen` (the new directory), separated by a backslash (\), and passes this value to class `Directory`'s method ***Exists***. Method `Exists` returns `true` if its `string` parameter is a directory. If this occurs, the program passes the `string` to method `LoadFilesInDirectory`. Because the `C:\` directory already includes a backslash, a backslash is not needed when combining `currentDirectory` and `chosen` (line 50). However, other directories must include the slash (lines 52–53). Finally, `displayLabel` is updated with the new directory (line 58).

This program loads quickly, because it indexes only the files in the current directory. This means that a small delay may occur when a new directory is loaded. In addition, changes in the directory structure can be shown by reloading a directory. The previous program (Fig. 14.28) may have a large initial delay as it loads an entire directory structure. This type of trade-off is typical in the software world.

Software Engineering Observation 14.2

When designing applications that run for long periods of time, you might choose a large initial delay to improve performance throughout the rest of the program. However, in applications that run for only short periods of time, developers often prefer fast initial loading times and small delays after each action.

14.11 TabControl Control

The ***TabControl*** control creates tabbed windows, such as the ones we have seen in Visual Studio (Fig. 14.32). This allows you to specify more information in the same space on a `Form`.

`TabControl`s contain ***TabPage*** objects, which are similar to `Panel`s and `GroupBox`es in that `TabPage`s also can contain controls. You first add controls to the `TabPage` objects, then add the `TabPage`s to the `TabControl`. Only one `TabPage` is displayed at a time. To add objects to the `TabPage` and the `TabControl`, write

> *myTabPage*.`Controls.Add(`*myControl*`)`
> *myTabControl*.`Controls.Add(`*myTabPage*`)`

These statements call method `Add` of the `Controls` collection. The example adds `TabControl` *myControl* to `TabPage` *myTabPage*, then adds *myTabPage* to *myTabControl*. Alternatively, we can use method `AddRange` to add an array of `TabPage`s or controls to a `TabControl` or `TabPage`, respectively. Figure 14.33 depicts a sample `TabControl`.

You can add `TabControl`s visually by dragging and dropping them onto a `Form` in **Design** mode. To add `TabPage`s in **Design** mode, right click the `TabControl` and select **Add Tab** (Fig. 14.34). Alternatively, click the ***TabPages*** property in the **Properties** window, and add tabs in the dialog that appears. To change a tab label, set the ***Text*** property of the `TabPage`. Note that clicking the tabs selects the `TabControl`—to select the `TabPage`, click the control area underneath the tabs. You can add controls to the `TabPage` by dragging and dropping

Tab windows

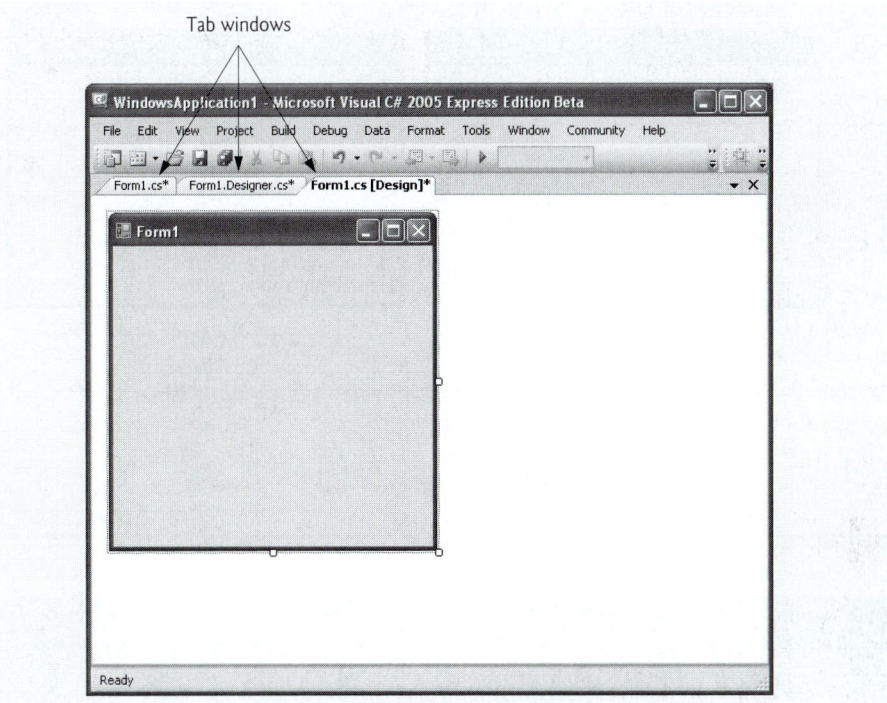

Fig. 14.32 | Tabbed windows in Visual Studio.

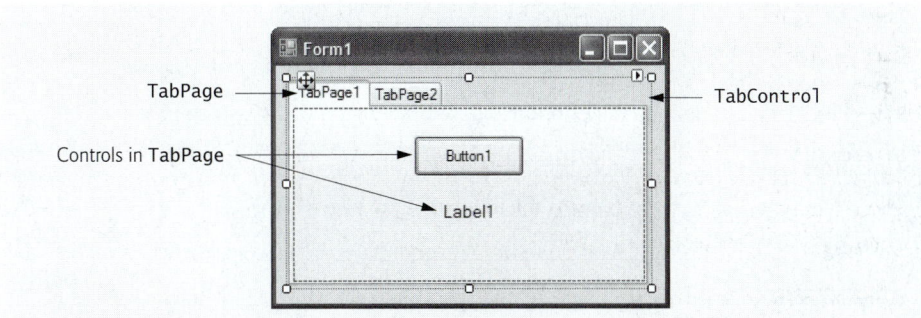

Fig. 14.33 | TabControl with TabPages example.

items from the **ToolBox**. To view different TabPages, click the appropriate tab (in either design or run mode). Common properties and a common event of TabControls are described in Fig. 14.35.

Each TabPage generates a Click event when its tab is clicked. Event handlers for this event can be created by double clicking the body of the TabPage.

Class UsingTabsForm (Fig. 14.36) uses a TabControl to display various options relating to the text on a label (**Color**, **Size** and **Message**). The last TabPage displays an **About** message, which describes the use of TabControls.

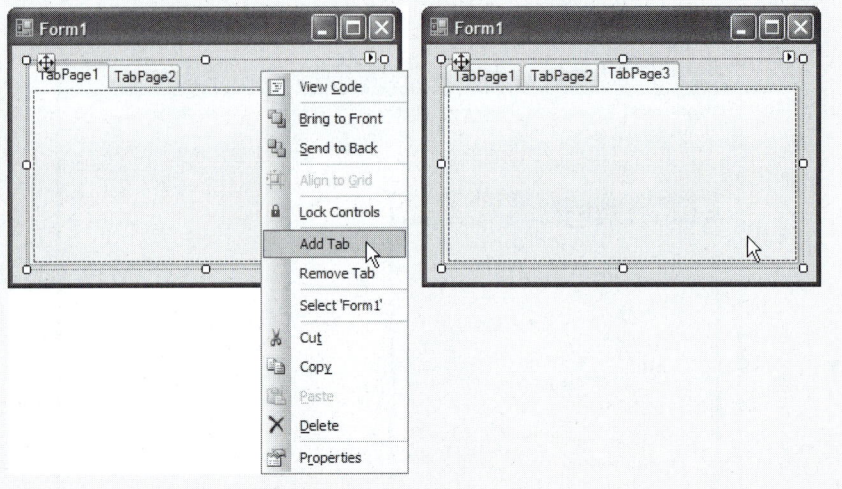

Fig. 14.34 | TabPages added to a `TabControl`.

TabControl properties and an event	Description
Common Properties	
ImageList	Specifies images to be displayed on tabs.
ItemSize	Specifies the tab size.
Multiline	Indicates whether multiple rows of tabs can be displayed.
SelectedIndex	Index of the selected `TabPage`.
SelectedTab	The selected `TabPage`.
TabCount	Returns the number of tab pages.
TabPages	Collection of `TabPages` within the `TabControl`.
Common Event	
SelectedIndexChanged	Generated when `SelectedIndex` changes (i.e., another `TabPage` is selected).

Fig. 14.35 | `TabControl` properties and an event.

```
1   // Fig. 14.36: UsingTabsForm.cs
2   // Using TabControl to display various font settings.
3   using System;
4   using System.Drawing;
```

Fig. 14.36 | `TabControl` used to display various font settings. (Part 1 of 3.)

```
5    using System.Windows.Forms;
6
7    // Form uses Tabs and RadioButtons to display various font settings
8    public partial class UsingTabsForm : Form
9    {
10      // default constructor
11      public UsingTabsForm()
12      {
13         InitializeComponent();
14      } // end constructor
15
16      // event handler for Black RadioButton
17      private void blackRadioButton_CheckedChanged(
18         object sender, EventArgs e )
19      {
20         displayLabel.ForeColor = Color.Black; // change font color to black
21      } // end method blackRadioButton_CheckedChanged
22
23      // event handler for Red RadioButton
24      private void redRadioButton_CheckedChanged(
25         object sender, EventArgs e )
26      {
27         displayLabel.ForeColor = Color.Red; // change font color to red
28      } // end method redRadioButton_CheckedChanged
29
30      // event handler for Green RadioButton
31      private void greenRadioButton_CheckedChanged(
32         object sender, EventArgs e )
33      {
34         displayLabel.ForeColor = Color.Green; // change font color to green
35      } // end method greenRadioButton_CheckedChanged
36
37      // event handler for 12 point RadioButton
38      private void size12RadioButton_CheckedChanged(
39         object sender, EventArgs e )
40      {
41         // change font size to 12
42         displayLabel.Font = new Font( displayLabel.Font.Name, 12 );
43      } // end method size12RadioButton_CheckedChanged
44
45      // event handler for 16 point RadioButton
46      private void size16RadioButton_CheckedChanged(
47         object sender, EventArgs e )
48      {
49         // change font size to 16
50         displayLabel.Font = new Font( displayLabel.Font.Name, 16 );
51      } // end method size16RadioButton_CheckedChanged
52
53      // event handler for 20 point RadioButton
54      private void size20RadioButton_CheckedChanged(
55         object sender, EventArgs e )
56      {
```

Fig. 14.36 | TabControl used to display various font settings. (Part 2 of 3.)

```
57        // change font size to 20
58        displayLabel.Font = new Font( displayLabel.Font.Name, 20 );
59     } // end method size20RadioButton_CheckedChanged
60
61     // event handler for  Hello! RadioButton
62     private void helloRadioButton_CheckedChanged(
63        object sender, EventArgs e )
64     {
65        displayLabel.Text = "Hello!"; // change text to Hello!
66     } // end method helloRadioButton_CheckedChanged
67
68     // event handler for Goodbye! RadioButton
69     private void goodbyeRadioButton_CheckedChanged(
70        object sender, EventArgs e )
71     {
72        displayLabel.Text = "Goodbye!"; // change text to Goodbye!
73     } // end method goodbyeRadioButton_CheckedChanged
74  } // end class UsingTabsForm
```

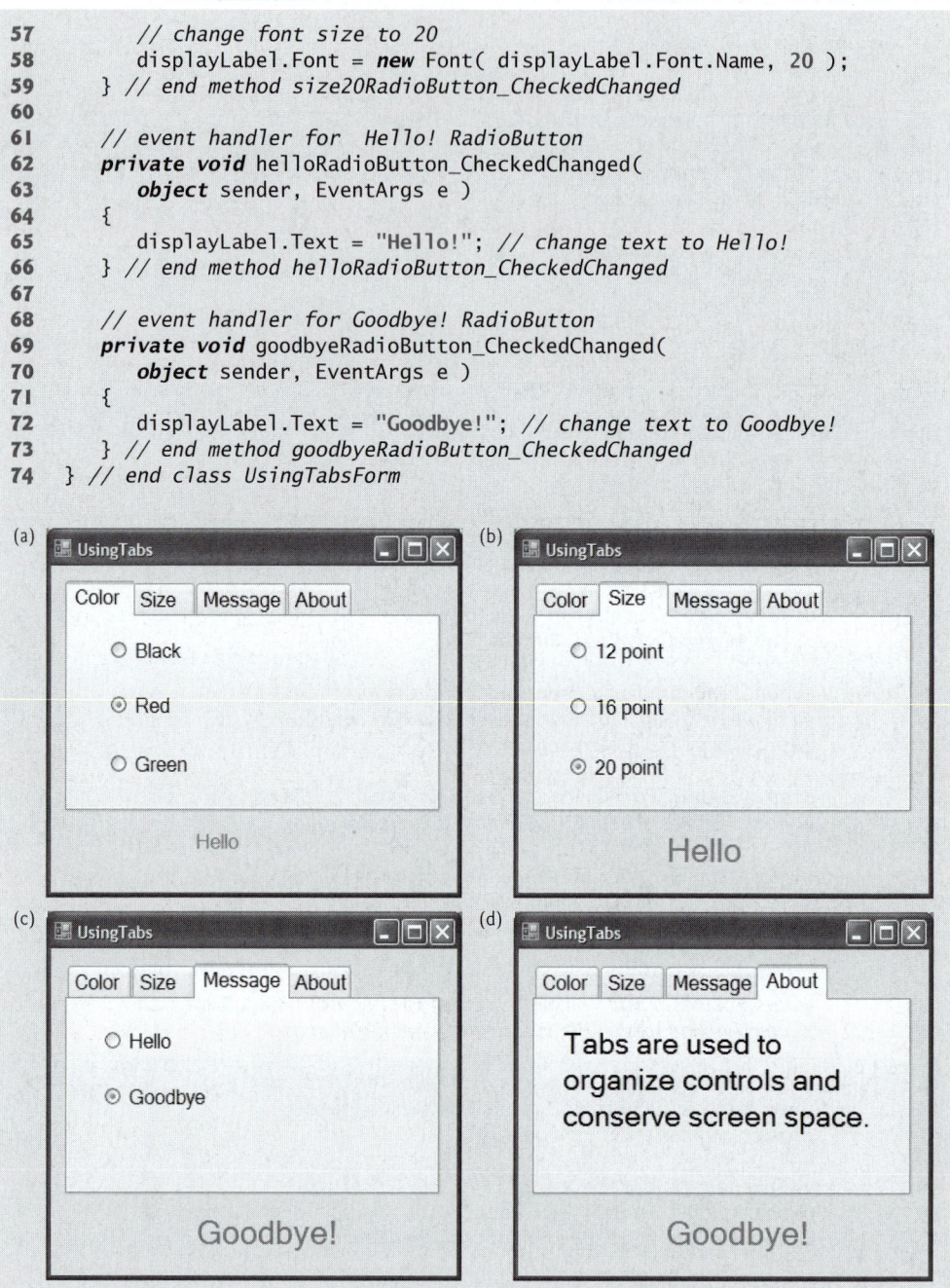

Fig. 14.36 | TabControl used to display various font settings. (Part 3 of 3.)

The textOptionsTabControl and the colorTabPage, sizeTabPage, messageTabPage and aboutTabPage are created in the designer (as described previously). The colorTabPage contains three RadioButtons for the colors black (blackRadioButton), red (redRadioButton) and green (greenRadioButton). This TabPage is displayed in Fig. 14.36(a). The Check-Changed event handler for each RadioButton updates the color of the text in displayLabel (lines 20, 27 and 34). The sizeTabPage (Fig. 14.36(b)) has three RadioButtons, corresponding to font sizes 12 (size12RadioButton), 16 (size16RadioButton) and 20 (size20RadioButton), which change the font size of displayLabel—lines 42, 50 and 58, respectively. The messageTabPage (Fig. 14.36(c)) contains two RadioButtons for the messages **Hello!** (helloRadioButton) and **Goodbye!** (goodbyeRadioButton). The two RadioButtons determine the text on displayLabel (lines 65 and 72, respectively). The aboutTabPage (Fig. 14.36(d)) contains a Label (messageLabel) describing the purpose of TabControls.

Software Engineering Observation 14.3

A TabPage *can act as a container for a single logical group of* RadioButtons, *enforcing their mutual exclusivity. To place multiple* RadioButton *groups inside a single* TabPage, *you should group* RadioButtons *within* Panels *or* GroupBoxes *contained within the* TabPage.

14.12 Multiple Document Interface (MDI) Windows

In previous chapters, we have built only *single document interface (SDI)* applications. Such programs (including Microsoft's Notepad and Paint) can support only one open window or document at a time. SDI applications usually have limited abilities—Paint and Notepad, for example, have limited image- and text-editing features. To edit multiple documents, the user must execute another instance of the SDI application.

Most recent applications are *multiple document interface (MDI)* programs, which allow users to edit multiple documents at once (e.g. Microsoft Office products). MDI programs also tend to be more complex—PaintShop Pro and Photoshop have a greater number of image-editing features than does Paint.

The main application window of an MDI program is called the *parent window*, and each window inside the application is referred to as a *child window*. Although an MDI application can have many child windows, each has only one parent window. Furthermore, a maximum of one child window can be active at once. Child windows cannot be parents themselves and cannot be moved outside their parent. Otherwise, a child window behaves like any other window (with regard to closing, minimizing, resizing, etc.). A child window's functionality can be different from the functionality of other child windows of the parent. For example, one child window might allow the user to edit images, another might allow the user to edit text and a third might display network traffic graphically, but all could belong to the same MDI parent. Figure 14.37 depicts a sample MDI application.

To create an MDI Form, create a new Form and set its ***IsMdiContainer*** property to true. The Form changes appearance, as in Fig. 14.38.

Next, create a child Form class to be added to the Form. To do this, right click the project in the **Solution Explorer**, select **Project > Add Windows Form...** and name the file. Edit the Form as you like. To add the child Form to the parent, we must create a new child Form object, set its ***MdiParent*** property to the parent Form and call the child Form's Show method. In general, to add a child Form to a parent, write

```
ChildFormClass childForm = New ChildFormClass();
childForm.MdiParent = parentForm;
childForm.Show();
```

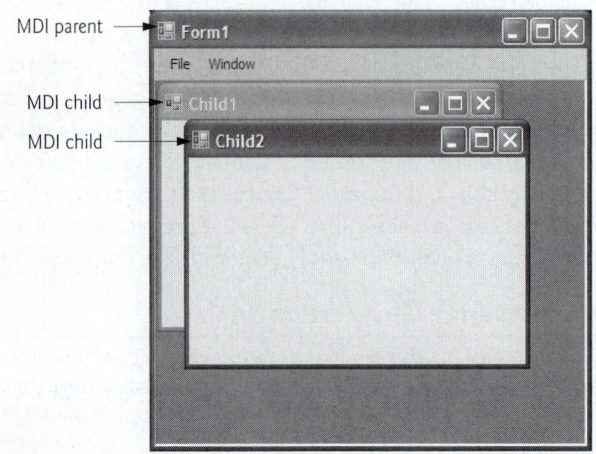

Fig. 14.37 | MDI parent window and MDI child windows.

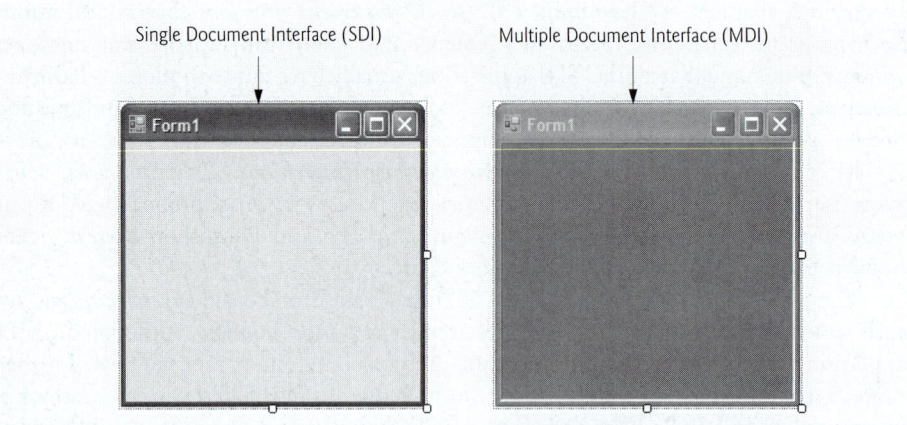

Fig. 14.38 | SDI and MDI forms.

In most cases, the parent Form creates the child, so the *parentForm* reference is this. The code to create a child usually lies inside an event handler, which creates a new window in response to a user action. Menu selections (such as **File**, followed by a submenu option of **New**, followed by a submenu option of **Window**) are common techniques for creating new child windows.

Class Form property **MdiChildren** returns an array of child Form references. This is useful if the parent window wants to check the status of all its children (for example, ensuring that all are saved before the parent closes). Property **ActiveMdiChild** returns a reference to the active child window; it returns Nothing if there are no active child windows. Other features of MDI windows are described in Fig. 14.39.

Child windows can be minimized, maximized and closed independently of each other and the parent window. Figure 14.40 shows two images: one containing two minimized child windows and a second containing a maximized child window. When the parent is

MDI Form properties, a method and an event	Description
Common MDI Child Properties	
IsMdiChild	Indicates whether the Form is an MDI child. If true, Form is an MDI child (read-only property).
MdiParent	Specifies the MDI parent Form of the child.
Common MDI Parent Properties	
ActiveMdiChild	Returns the Form that is the currently active MDI child (returns null if no children are active).
IsMdiContainer	Indicates whether a Form can be an MDI parent. If true, the Form can be an MDI parent. The default value is false.
MdiChildren	Returns the MDI children as an array of Forms.
Common Method	
LayoutMdi	Determines the display of child forms on an MDI parent. The method takes as a parameter an MdiLayout enumeration with possible values ArrangeIcons, Cascade, TileHorizontal and TileVertical. Figure 14.42 depicts the effects of these values.
Common Event	
MdiChildActivate	Generated when an MDI child is closed or activated.

Fig. 14.39 | MDI parent and MDI child properties, method and event.

minimized or closed, the child windows are minimized or closed as well. Notice that the title bar in Fig. 14.40(b) is **Form1 - [Child2]**. When a child window is maximized, its title bar text is inserted into the parent window's title bar. When a child window is minimized or maximized, its title bar displays a restore icon, which can be used to return the child window to its previous size (its size before it was minimized or maximized).

C# provides a property that helps track which child windows are open in an MDI container. Property *MdiWindowListItem* of class MenuStrip specifies which menu, if any, displays a list of open child windows. When a new child window is opened, an entry is added to the list (as in the first screen of Figure 14.41). If nine or more child windows are open, the list includes the option **More Windows...**, which allows the user to select a window from a list in a dialog.

 Good Programming Practice 14.1

When creating MDI applications, include a menu that displays a list of the open child windows. This helps the user select a child window quickly, rather than having to search for it in the parent window.

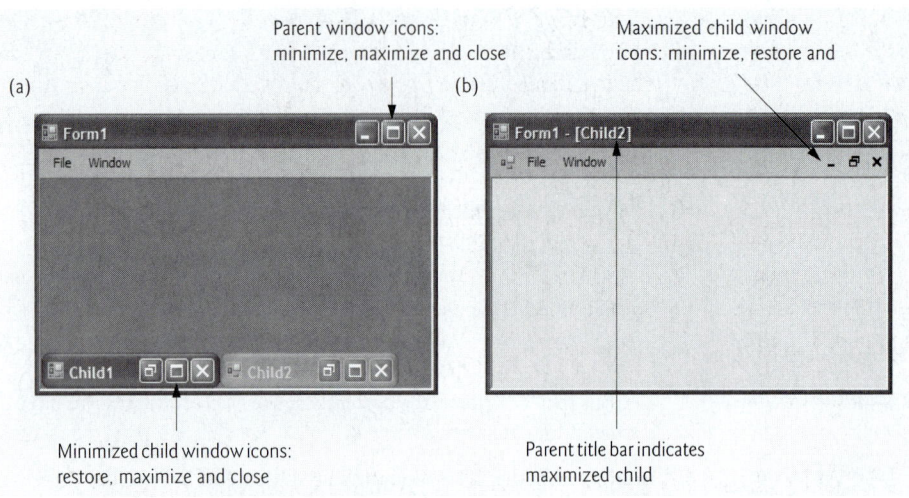

Fig. 14.40 | Minimized and maximized child windows.

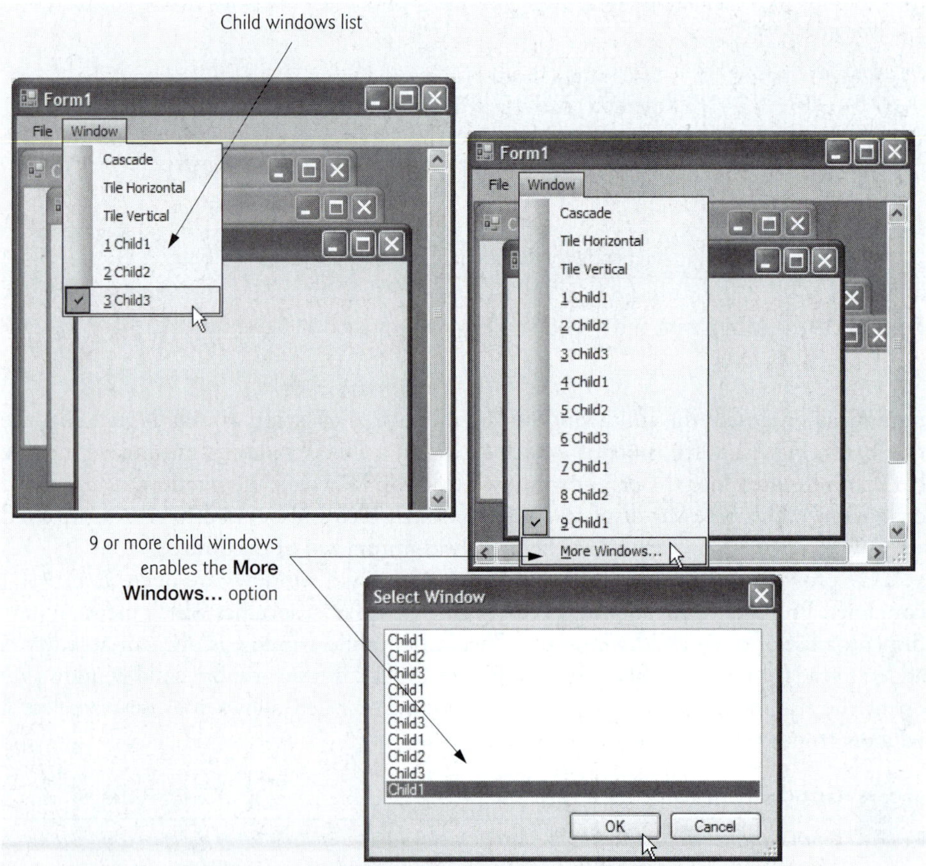

Fig. 14.41 | `MenuItem` property `MdiList` example.

MDI containers allow you to organize the placement ofs child windows. The child windows in an MDI application can be arranged by calling method **LayoutMdi** of the parent Form. Method LayoutMdi takes a **MdiLayout** enumeration, which can have values **ArrangeIcons**, **Cascade**, **TileHorizontal** and **TileVertical**. *Tiled windows* completely fill the parent and do not overlap; such windows can be arranged horizontally (value Tile-Horizontal) or vertically (value TileVertical). *Cascaded windows* (value Cascade) overlap—each is the same size and displays a visible title bar, if possible. Value Arrange-Icons arranges the icons for any minimized child windows. If minimized windows are scattered around the parent window, value ArrangeIcons orders them neatly at the bottom-left corner of the parent window. Figure 14.42 illustrates the values of the Mdi-Layout enumeration.

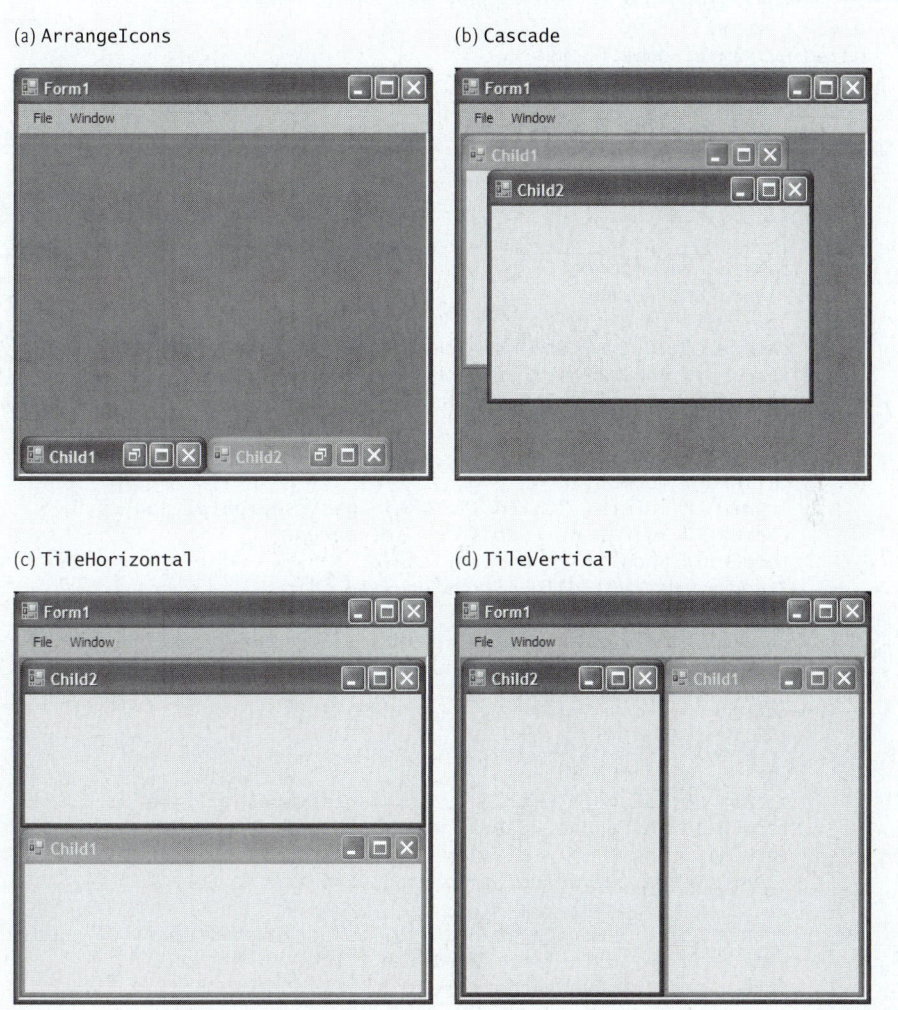

(a) ArrangeIcons

(b) Cascade

(c) TileHorizontal

(d) TileVertical

Fig. 14.42 | MdiLayout enumeration values.

Class `UsingMDIForm` (Fig. 14.43) demonstrates MDI windows. Class `UsingMDIForm` uses three instances of child Form `ChildForm` (Fig. 14.44), each containing a `PictureBox` that displays an image. The parent MDI Form contains a menu enabling users to create and arrange child Forms.

The program in Fig. 14.43 is the application. The MDI parent Form, which is created first, contains two top-level menus. The first of these menus, **File** (`fileToolStripMenu-Item`), contains both an **Exit** item (`exitToolStripMenuItem`) and a **New** submenu (`new-ToolStripMenuItem`) consisting of items for each child window. The second menu, **Window** (`windowToolStripMenuItem`), provides options for laying out the MDI children, plus a list of the active MDI children.

```csharp
1   // Fig. 14.43: UsingMDIForm.cs
2   // Demonstrating use of MDI parent and child windows.
3   using System;
4   using System.Windows.Forms;
5
6   // Form demonstrates the use of MDI parent and child windows
7   public partial class UsingMDIForm : Form
8   {
9      // default constructor
10     public UsingMDIForm()
11     {
12        InitializeComponent();
13     } // end constructor
14
15     // create Child 1 window when child1ToolStrip MenuItem is clicked
16     private void child1ToolStripMenuItem_Click(
17        object sender, EventArgs e )
18     {
19        // create new child
20        ChildForm formChild =
21           new ChildForm( "Child 1", @"\images\csharphtp1.jpg" );
22        formChild.MdiParent = this; // set parent
23        formChild.Show(); // display child
24     } // end method child1ToolStripMenuItem_Click
25
26     // create Child 2 window when child2ToolStripMenuItem is clicked
27     private void child2ToolStripMenuItem_Click(
28        object sender, EventArgs e )
29     {
30        // create new child
31        ChildForm formChild =
32           new ChildForm( "Child 2", @"\images\vbnethtp2.jpg" );
33        formChild.MdiParent = this; // set parent
34        formChild.Show(); // display child
35     } // end method child2ToolStripMenuItem_Click
36
37     // create Child 3 window when child3ToolStripMenuItem is clicked
38     private void child3ToolStripMenuItem_Click(
39        object sender, EventArgs e )
40     {
```

Fig. 14.43 | MDI parent-window class. (Part 1 of 3.)

```
41        // create new child
42        Child formChild =
43           new Child( "Child 3", @"\images\pythonhtp1.jpg" );
44        formChild.MdiParent = this; // set parent
45        formChild.Show(); // display child
46     } // end method child3ToolStripMenuItem_Click
47
48     // exit application
49     private void exitToolStripMenuItem_Click( object sender, EventArgs e )
50     {
51        Application.Exit();
52     } // end method exitToolStripMenuItem_Click
53
54     // set Cascade layout
55     private void cascadeToolStripMenuItem_Click(
56        object sender, EventArgs e )
57     {
58        this.LayoutMdi( MdiLayout.Cascade );
59     } // end method cascadeToolStripMenuItem_Click
60
61     // set TileHorizontal layout
62     private void tileHorizontalToolStripMenuItem_Click(
63        object sender, EventArgs e )
64     {
65        this.LayoutMdi( MdiLayout.TileHorizontal );
66     } // end method tileHorizontalToolStripMenuItem
67
68     // set TileVertical layout
69     private void tileVerticalToolStripMenuItem_Click(
70        object sender, EventArgs e )
71     {
72        this.LayoutMdi( MdiLayout.TileVertical );
73     } // end method tileVerticalToolStripMenuItem_Click
74  } // end class UsingMDIForm
```

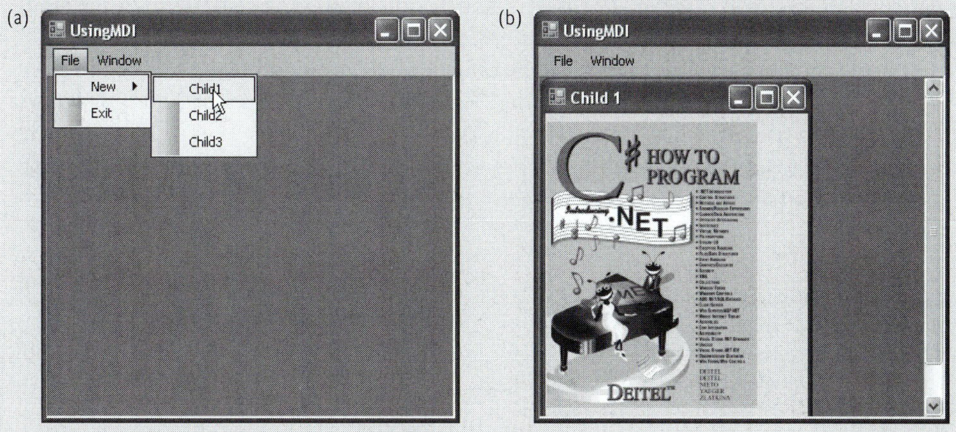

Fig. 14.43 | MDI parent-window class. (Part 2 of 3.)

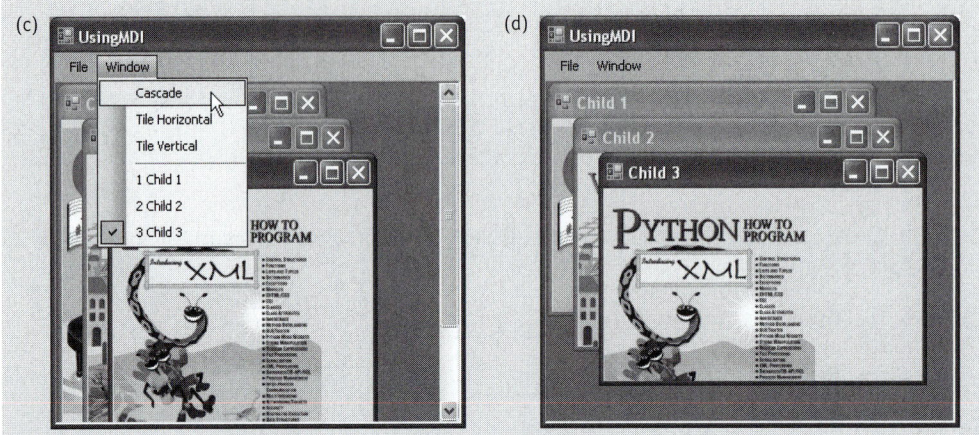

Fig. 14.43 | MDI parent-window class. (Part 3 of 3.)

In the **Properties** window, we set the Form's IsMdiContainer property to true, making the Form an MDI parent. In addition, we set the MenuStrip's MdiWindowListItem property to windowToolStripMenuItem. This enables the **Window** menu to contain the list of child MDI windows.

The **Cascade** menu item (cascadeToolStripMenuItem) has an event handler (cascadeToolStripMenuItem_Click, lines 55–59) that arranges the child windows in a cascading manner. The event handler calls method LayoutMdi with the argument Cascade from the MdiLayout enumeration (line 58).

The **Tile Horizontal** menu item (tileHorizontalToolStripMenuItem) has an event handler (tileHorizontalToolStripMenuItem_Click, lines 62–66) that arranges the child windows in a horizontal manner. The event handler calls method LayoutMdi with the argument TileHorizontal from the MdiLayout enumeration (line 65).

Finally, the **Tile Vertical** menu item (tileVerticalToolStripMenuItem) has an event handler (tileVerticalToolStripMenuItem_Click, lines 69–73) that arranges the child windows in a vertical manner. The event handler calls method LayoutMdi with the argument TileVertical from the MdiLayout enumeration (line 72).

At this point, the application is still incomplete—we must define the MDI child class. To do this, right click the project in the **Solution Explorer** and select **Add > Windows Form…**. Then name the new class in the dialog as ChildForm (Fig. 14.44). Next, we add a PictureBox (picDisplay) to ChildForm. In the constructor, line 15 sets the title bar text. Lines 18–19 set ChildForm's Image property to an Image, using method FromFile.

```
1   // Fig. 14.44: ChildForm.cs
2   // Child window of MDI parent.
3   using System;
4   using System.Drawing;
5   using System.Windows.Forms;
6   using System.IO;
7
```

Fig. 14.44 | MDI child ChildForm. (Part 1 of 2.)

```
 8   public partial class ChildForm : Form
 9   {
10      public ChildForm( string title, string fileName )
11      {
12         // Required for Windows Form Designer support
13         InitializeComponent();
14
15         Text = title; // set title text
16
17         // set image to display in pictureBox
18         picDisplay.Image = Image.FromFile(
19            Directory.GetCurrentDirectory() + fileName );
20      } // end constructor
21   } // end class ChildForm
```

Fig. 14.44 | MDI child `ChildForm`. (Part 2 of 2.)

After the MDI child class is defined, the parent MDI Form (Fig. 14.43) can create new child windows. The event handlers in lines 16–46 create a new child Form corresponding to the menu item clicked. Lines 20–21, 31–32 and 42–43 create new instances of Child-Form. Lines 22, 33 and 44 set each Child's MdiParent property to the parent Form. Lines 23, 34 and 45 call method Show to display each child Form.

14.13 Visual Inheritance

Chapter 10 discussed how to create classes by inheriting from other classes. We have also used inheritance to create Forms that display a GUI, by deriving our new Form classes from class System.Windows.Forms.Form. This is an example of *visual inheritance*. The derived Form class contains the functionality of its Form base class, including any base-class properties, methods, variables and controls. The derived class also inherits all visual aspects—such as sizing, component layout, spacing between GUI components, colors and fonts—from its base class.

Visual inheritance enables you to achieve visual consistency across applications. For example, you could define a base Form that contains a product's logo, a specific background color, a predefined menu bar and other elements. You then could use the base Form throughout an application for uniformity and branding.

Class VisualInheritanceForm (Fig. 14.45) derives from Form. The output depicts the workings of the program. The GUI contains two Labels with text **Bugs, Bugs, Bugs** and **Copyright 2006, by deitel.com.**, as well as one Button displaying the text **Learn More**. When a user presses the **Learn More** Button, method learnMoreButton_Click (lines 16–22) is invoked. This method displays a MessageBox that provides some informative text.

```
1   // Fig. 14.45: VisualInheritanceForm.cs
2   // Base Form for use with visual inheritance.
3   using System;
4   using System.Windows.Forms;
```

Fig. 14.45 | Class VisualInheritanceForm, which inherits from class Form, contains a Button (**Learn More**). (Part 1 of 2.)

```
5
6    // base Form used to demonstrate visual inheritance
7    public partial class VisualInheritanceForm : Form
8    {
9        // default constructor
10       public VisualInheritanceForm()
11       {
12           InitializeComponent();
13       } // end constructor
14
15       // display MessageBox when Button is clicked
16       private void learnMoreButton_Click( object sender, EventArgs e )
17       {
18           MessageBox.Show(
19               "Bugs, Bugs, Bugs is a product of deitel.com",
20               "Learn More", MessageBoxButtons.OK,
21               MessageBoxIcon.Information );
22       } // end method learnMoreButton_Click
23   } // end class VisualInheritanceForm
```

Fig. 14.45 | Class `VisualInheritanceForm`, which inherits from class `Form`, contains a Button (**Learn More**). (Part 2 of 2.)

To allow other `Form`s to inherit from `VisualInheritanceForm`, we must package `VisualInheritanceForm` as a `.dll` (class library). Right click the project name in the **Solution Explorer** and select **Properties**, then choose the **Application** tab. In the **Output type** drop-down list, change **Windows Application** to **Class Library**. Building the project produces the `.dll`.

To visually inherit from `VisualInheritanceForm`, first create a new Windows application. In this application, add a reference to the `.dll` you just created (located in the previous application's `bin/Release` folder). Then open the file that defines the new application's GUI and modify the first line of the class so that it inherits from class `VisualInheritanceForm`. Note that you will only need to specify the class name. In **design** view, the new application's `Form` should now display the controls of the base `Form` (Fig. 14.46). We can still add more components to the `Form`.

Class `VisualInheritanceTestForm` (Fig. 14.47) is a derived class of `VisualInheritanceForm`. The output illustrates the functionality of the program. The GUI contains those components derived from class `VisualInheritanceForm`, as well as an additional Button with text **Learn The Program**. When a user presses this Button, method

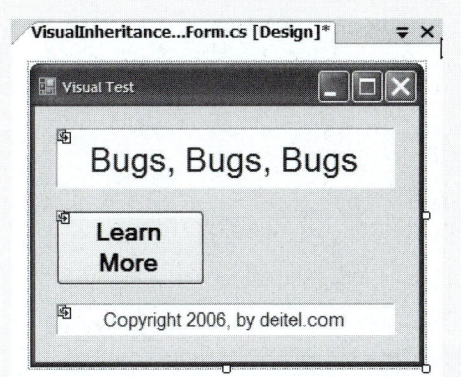

Fig. 14.46 | Form demonstrating visual inheritance.

learnProgramButton_Click (lines 17–22) is invoked. This method displays another MessageBox providing different informative text.

Figure 14.47 demonstrates that the components, their layouts and the functionality of base-class VisualInheritanceForm (Fig. 14.45) are inherited by VisualInheritanceTestForm. If a user clicks the button **Learn More**, the base class event handler learnMoreButton_Click displays a MessageBox. VisualInheritanceForm uses a private access modifier to declare its controls, so class VisualInheritanceTestForm cannot modify the controls inherited from class VisualInheritanceForm.

```
 1   // Fig. 14.47: VisualInheritanceTestForm.cs
 2   // Derived Form using visual inheritance.
 3   using System;
 4   using System.Windows.Forms;
 5
 6   // derived form using visual inheritance
 7   public partial class VisualInheritanceTestForm :
 8      VisualInheritanceForm   // code for inheritance
 9   {
10      // default constructor
11      public VisualInheritanceTestForm()
12      {
13         InitializeComponent();
14      } // end constructor
15
16      // display MessageBox when Button is clicked
17      private void learnProgramButton_Click(object sender, EventArgs e)
18      {
19         MessageBox.Show( "This program was created by Deitel & Associates",
20            "Learn the Program", MessageBoxButtons.OK,
21            MessageBoxIcon.Information );
22      } // end method learnProgramButton_Click
23   } // end class VisualInheritanceTestForm
```

Fig. 14.47 | Class VisualInheritanceTestForm, which inherits from class VisualInheritanceForm, contains an additional Button. (Part 1 of 2.)

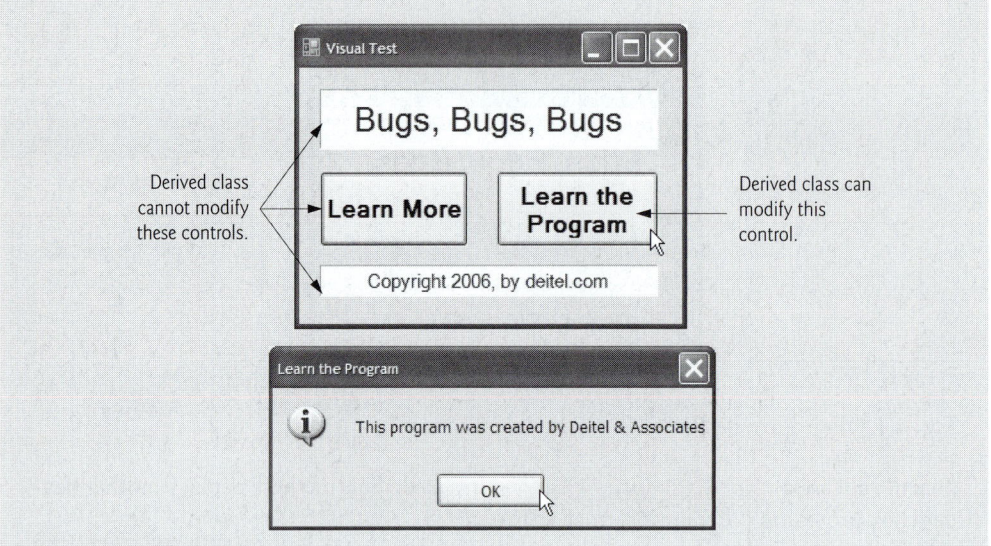

Fig. 14.47 | Class `VisualInheritanceTestForm`, which inherits from class `VisualInheritanceForm`, contains an additional `Button`. (Part 2 of 2.)

14.14 User-Defined Controls

The .NET Framework allows you to create *custom controls*. These custom controls appear in the user's **Toolbox** and can be added to `Forms`, `Panels` or `GroupBoxes` in the same way that we add `Buttons`, `Labels` and other predefined controls. The simplest way to create a custom control is to derive a class from an existing control, such as a `Label`. This is useful if you want to add functionality to an existing control, rather than having to reimplement the existing control to include the desired functionality. For example, you can create a new type of `Label` that behaves like a normal `Label` but has a different appearance. You accomplish this by inheriting from class `Label` and overriding method `OnPaint`.

All controls contain method **`OnPaint`**, which the system calls when a component must be redrawn (such as when the component is resized). Method `OnPaint` is passed a **`PaintEventArgs`** object, which contains graphics information—property **`Graphics`** is the graphics object used to draw, and property **`ClipRectangle`** defines the rectangular boundary of the control. Whenever the system raises the `Paint` event, our control's base class catches the event. Through polymorphism, our control's `OnPaint` method is called. Our base class's `OnPaint` implementation is not called, so we must call it explicitly from our `OnPaint` implementation before we execute our custom-paint code. In most cases, you want to do this to ensure that the original painting code executes in addition to the code you define in the custom control's class. Alternately, if we do not wish to let the base class `OnPaint` method execute, we do not call it.

To create a new control composed of existing controls, use class **`UserControl`**. Controls added to a custom control are called *constituent controls*. For example, a programmer could create a `UserControl` composed of a `Button`, a `Label` and a `TextBox`, each associated with some functionality (for example, the `Button` setting the `Label`'s text to that contained in the `TextBox`). The `UserControl` acts as a container for the controls added to it. The `UserControl` contains constituent controls, so it does not determine how these constituent controls are displayed. Method `OnPaint` of the `UserControl` cannot be overridden. To control the appearance of each constituent control, you must handle each control's `Paint` event. The `Paint` event handler is passed a `PaintEventArgs` object, which can be used to draw graphics (lines, rectangles, etc.) on the constituent controls.

Using another technique, a programmer can create a brand new control by inheriting from class `Control`. This class does not define any specific behavior; that task is left to you. Instead, class `Control` handles the items associated with all controls, such as events and sizing handles. Method `OnPaint` should contain a call to the base class's `OnPaint` method, which calls the `Paint` event handlers. You must then add code that draws custom graphics inside the overridden `OnPaint` method when drawing the control. This technique allows for the greatest flexibility, but also requires the most planning. All three approaches are summarized in Fig. 14.48.

We create a "clock" control in Fig. 14.49. This is a `UserControl` composed of a `Label` and a `Timer`—whenever the `Timer` raises an event, the `Label` is updated to reflect the current time.

Timers (`System.Windows.Forms` namespace) are invisible components that reside on a Form, generating *Tick* events at a set interval. This interval is set by the `Timer`'s *Interval*

Custom control techniques and PaintEventArgs properties	Description
Custom Control Techniques	
Inherit from Windows Forms control	You can do this to add functionality to a pre-existing control. If you override method `OnPaint`, call the base class's `OnPaint` method. Note that you only can add to the original control's appearance, not redesign it.
Create a `UserControl`	You can create a `UserControl` composed of multiple pre-existing controls (e.g., to combine their functionality). Note that you cannot override the `OnPaint` methods of custom controls. Instead, you must place drawing code in a `Paint` event handler. Again, note that you only can add to the original control's appearance, not redesign it
Inherit from class `Control`	Define a brand new control. Override method `OnPaint`, then call base class method `OnPaint` and include methods to draw the control. With this method you can customize control appearance and functionality.
PaintEventArgs Properties	
`Graphics`	The graphics object of the control. It is used to draw on the control.
`ClipRectangle`	Specifies the rectangle indicating the boundary of the control.

Fig. 14.48 | Custom control creation.

```
1    // Fig. 14.49: ClockUserControl.cs
2    // User-defined control with a timer and a Label.
3    using System;
4    using System.Windows.Forms;
5
6    // UserControl that displays the time on a Label
7    public partial class ClockUserControl : UserControl
8    {
9       // default constructor
10      public ClockUserControl()
11      {
12         InitializeComponent();
13      } // end constructor
14
15      // update Label at every tick
16      private void clockTimer_Tick(object sender, EventArgs e)
17      {
18         // get current time (Now), convert to string
19         displayLabel.Text = DateTime.Now.ToLongTimeString();
20      } // end method clockTimer_Tick
21   } // end class ClockUserControl
```

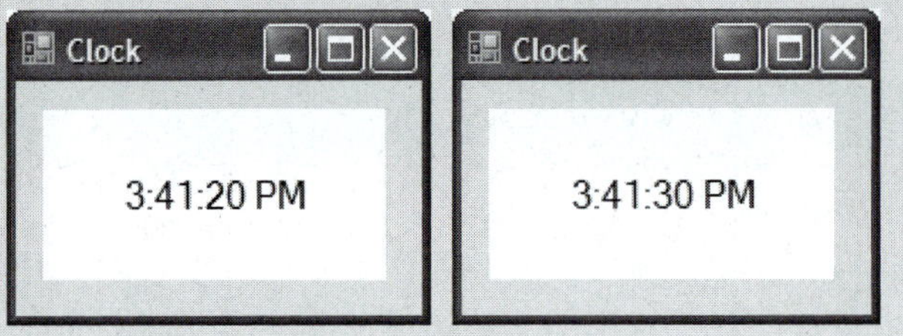

Fig. 14.49 | UserControl-defined clock.

property, which defines the number of milliseconds (thousandths of a second) between events. By default, timers are disabled and do not generate events.

This application contains a user control (ClockUserControl) and a Form that displays the user control. We begin by creating a Windows application. Next, we create a User-Control class for the project by selecting **Project > Add User Control....** This displays a dialog from which we can select the type of control to add—user controls are already selected. We then name the file (and the class) ClockUserControl. Our empty Clock-UserControl is displayed as a grey rectangle.

You can treat this control like a Windows Form, meaning that you can add controls using the **ToolBox** and set properties using the **Properties** window. However, instead of creating an application, you are simply creating a new control composed of other controls. Add a Label (displayLabel) and a Timer (clockTimer) to the UserControl. Set the Timer interval to 1000 milliseconds and set displayLabel's text with each event (lines 16–20). To generate events, clockTimer must be enabled by setting property Enabled to true in the **Properties** window.

Structure *DateTime* (namespace System) contains property *Now*, which is the current time. Method *ToLongTimeString* converts Now to a string containing the current hour, minute and second (along with AM or PM). We use this to set the time in `displayLabel` in line 19.

Once created, our clock control appears as an item on the **ToolBox**. You may need to switch to the application's `Form` before the item appears in the **ToolBox**. To use the control, simply drag it to the `Form` and run the Windows application. We gave the `ClockUserControl` object a white background to make it stand out in the `Form`. Figure 14.49 shows the output of `ClockForm`, which contains our `ClockUserControl`. There are no event handlers in `ClockForm`, so we show only the code for `ClockUserControl`.

Visual Studio allows you to share custom controls with other developers. To create a `UserControl` that can be exported to other solutions, do the following:

1. Create a new **Class Library** project.

2. Delete `Class1.cs`, initially provided with the application.

3. Right click the project in the **Solution Explorer** and select **Add > User Control....** In the dialog that appears, name the user control file and click **Add**.

4. Inside the project, add controls and functionality to the `UserControl` (Fig. 14.50).

5. Build the project. Visual Studio creates a `.dll` file for the `UserControl` in the output directory (`bin/Release`). The file is not executable; class libraries are used to define classes that are reused in other executable applications.

6. Create a new Windows application.

7. In the new Windows application, right click the **ToolBox** and select **Choose Items....** In the **Choose Toolbox Items** dialog that appears, click **Browse....** Browse for the `.dll` file from the class library created in *Steps 1–5*. The item will then appear in the **Choose Toolbox Items** dialog (Fig. 14.51). If it is not already checked, check this item. Click **OK** to add the item to the **Toolbox**. This control can now be added to the `Form` as if it were any other control (Fig. 14.52).

14.15 Wrap-Up

Many of today's commercial applications provide GUIs that are easy to use and manipulate. Because of this demand for user-friendly GUIs, the ability to design sophisticated GUIs is an essential programming skill. Visual Studio's IDE makes GUI development quick and easy. In Chapters 13 and 14, we presented basic GUI development techniques. In Chapter 14, we demonstrated how to create menus, which provide users easy access to

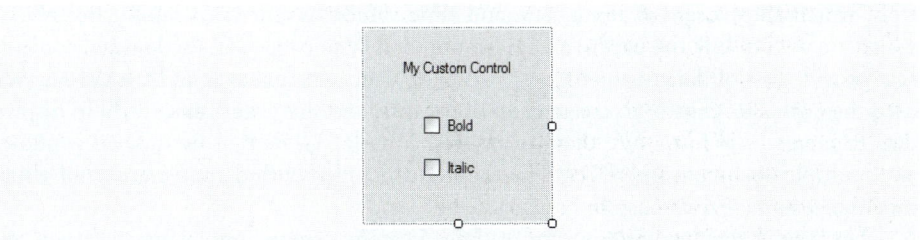

Fig. 14.50 | Custom-control creation.

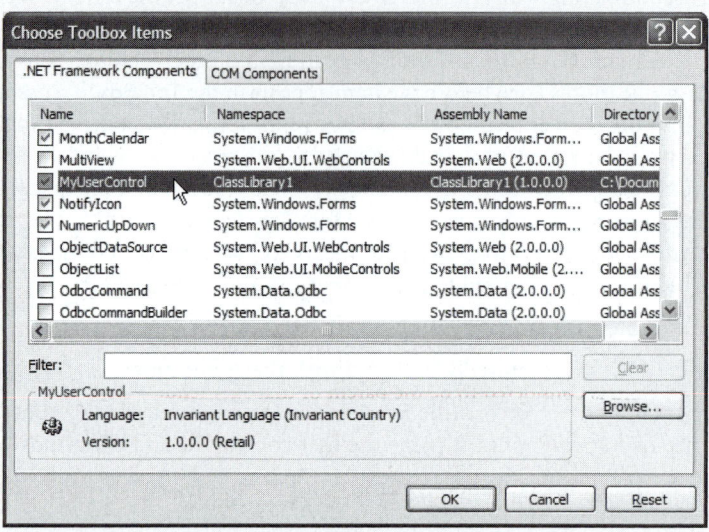

Fig. 14.51 | Custom control added to the **ToolBox**.

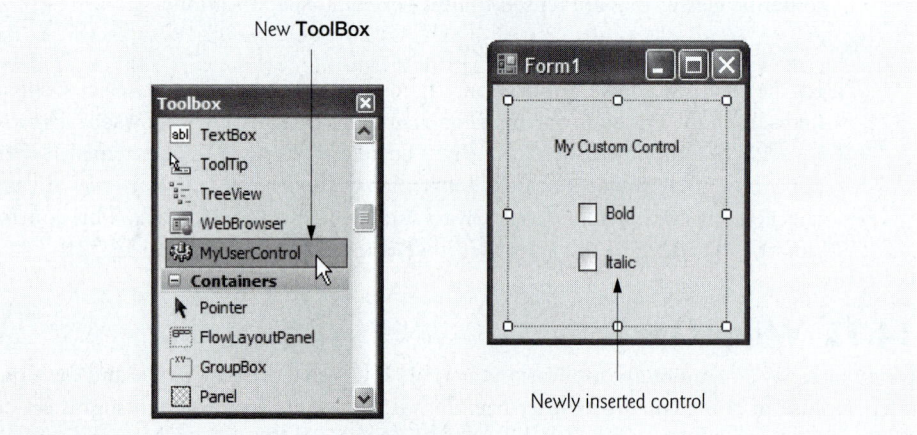

Fig. 14.52 | Custom control added to a Form.

an application's functionality. You learned the DateTimePicker and MonthCalendar controls, which allow users to input date and time values. We demonstrated LinkLabels, which are used to link the user to an application or a Web page. You used several controls that provide lists of data to the user—ListBoxes, CheckedListBoxes and ListViews. We used the ComboBox control to create drop-down lists, and the TreeView control to display data in hierarchical form. We then introduced complex GUIs that use tabbed windows and multiple document interfaces. The chapter concluded with demonstrations of visual inheritance and creating custom controls.

The next chapter explores multithreading. In many programming languages, you can create multiple threads, enabling several activities to proceed in parallel.

Summary

Section 14.1 Introduction
- Menus present users with several logically organized commands (or options).
- Visual Studio enables you to design custom controls and add those controls to the **ToolBox**.

Section 14.2 Menus
- Menus provide groups of related commands for Windows applications.
- Menus organize commands without "cluttering" the GUI.
- An expanded menu lists various commands (called menu items), plus submenus (menus within a menu).
- A menu that contains a menu item is called that menu item's parent menu. A menu item that contains a submenu is considered to be the parent of that submenu.
- All menu items can have *Alt* key shortcuts (also called access shortcuts or hotkeys), which are accessed by pressing *Alt* and the underlined letter.
- Menus that are not top-level menus can have shortcut keys as well (combinations of *Ctrl*, *Shift*, *Alt*, *F1*, *F2*, letter keys, etc.).
- Some menu items display check marks, indicating that multiple options on the menu can be selected at once.
- The `MenuStrip` control is used to create menus in a GUI.
- Top-level menus and their menu items are represented using type `ToolStripMenuItem`.
- To create an access shortcut, type an ampersand (&) before the character to be underlined.
- To add other shortcut keys, set the `ShortcutKeys` property of the `ToolStripMenuItem`.
- You can hide the shortcut keys by setting property `ShowShortcutKeys` to `false`, and you can modify how the control keys are displayed in the menu item by modifying property `ShortcutKeyDisplayString`.
- A menu item's `Checked` property is used to display a check to the left of the menu item.

Section 14.3 `MonthCalendar` Control
- The `MonthCalendar` control displays a monthly calendar.
- The user can select a date from the currently displayed month or use the links to navigate to another month.
- A `MonthCalendar`'s `DateChanged` event occurs when a new date is selected.

Section 14.4 `DateTimePicker` Control
- The `DateTimePicker` control can be used to retrieve date and/or time information from the user.
- Property `Format` of class `DateTimePicker` specifies the user's selection options using the `DateTimePickerFormat` enumeration.
- The `DateTimePicker`'s `ValueChanged` event is raised when the selected value (whether a date or a time) is changed.

Section 14.5 `LinkLabel` Control
- The `LinkLabel` control displays links to other resources, such as files or Web pages.
- A `LinkLabel` appears as underlined text (colored blue by default). When the mouse moves over the link, the pointer changes to a hand; this is similar to a hyperlink in a Web page.

- The link can change color to indicate whether the link is new, previously visited or active.
- When clicked, the LinkLabel generates a LinkClicked event.

Section 14.6 ListBox Control
- The ListBox control allows the user to view and select items in a list.
- ListBox property SelectionMode determines the number of items that can be selected. This property has the possible values None, One, MultiSimple and MultiExtended (from the SelectionMode enumeration).
- The SelectedIndexChanged event of class ListBox occurs when the user selects a new item.
- Property Items returns all the list items as a collection.
- Property SelectedItem returns the currently selected item.
- To add items to a ListBox, add objects to its Items collection. Call method Add to add a string to the ListBox's Items collection.
- You can add items to ListBoxes and CheckedListBoxes visually by examining the Items property in the **Properties** window.

Section 14.7 CheckedListBox Control
- The CheckedListBox control extends a ListBox by including CheckBoxes next to each item.
- As in ListBoxes, items can be added via methods Add and AddRange or through the **String Collection Editor**.
- CheckedListBoxes imply that multiple items can be selected.
- Event ItemCheck of class CheckedListBox occurs whenever a user checks or unchecks a CheckedListBox item.

Section 14.8 ComboBox Control
- The ComboBox control combines TextBox features with a drop-down list.
- The maximum number of items that a drop-down list can display at one time is set by property MaxDropDownItems.
- As with the ListBox control, you can add objects to collection Items programmatically, using methods Add and AddRange, or visually, with the **String Collection Editor**.
- Property DropDownStyle determines the type of ComboBox, and is represented as a value of the ComboBoxStyle enumeration, which contains values Simple, DropDown and DropDownList.
- There can be at most one selected item in a ComboBox (if none, then SelectedIndex is -1).
- When the selected item changes in a ComboBox, a SelectedIndexChanged event occurs.

Section 14.9 TreeView Control
- The TreeView control displays nodes hierarchically in a tree.
- Traditionally, nodes are objects that contain values and can refer to other nodes.
- A parent node contains child nodes, and the child nodes can be parents to other nodes.
- Two child nodes that have the same parent node are considered sibling nodes.
- A tree is a collection of nodes, usually organized in a hierarchical manner. The first parent node of a tree is the root node.
- TreeView controls are useful for displaying hierarchical information.
- In a TreeView, a parent node can be expanded or collapsed by clicking the plus box or minus box to its left. Nodes without children do not have these boxes.

- The nodes displayed in a TreeView are instances of class TreeNode.
- Each TreeNode has a Nodes collection (type TreeNodeCollection), which contains a list of other TreeNodes—its children.
- To add nodes to the TreeView visually, click the ellipsis next to the Nodes property in the **Properties** window. This opens the **TreeNode Editor**, which displays an empty tree representing the TreeView.
- To add nodes programmatically, must create a root TreeNode object and pass it a string to display. Then call method Add to add this new TreeNode to the TreeView's Nodes collection.

Section 14.10 *ListView Control*
- The ListView control is similar to a ListBox in that both display lists from which the user can select one or more items. The important difference between the two classes is that a ListView can display icons alongside the list items.
- Property MultiSelect (a bool) determines whether multiple items can be selected.
- To display images, an ImageList component is required.
- Property SmallImageList of class ListView sets the ImageList for the small icons.
- Property LargeImageList of class ListView sets the ImageList for large icons.
- The items in a ListView are each of type ListViewItem.

Section 14.11 *TabControl Control*
- The TabControl control creates tabbed windows, such as the ones we have seen in Visual Studio. This allows you to specify more information in the same space on a Form.
- TabControls contain TabPage objects, which are similar to Panels and GroupBoxes in that TabPages also can contain controls.
- Only one TabPage is displayed at a time.
- You can add TabControls visually by dragging and dropping them on a Form in **Design** mode.
- To add TabPages in **Design** mode, right click the TabControl and select **Add Tab**, or click the TabPages property in the **Properties** window, and add tabs in the dialog that appears.
- Each TabPage raises a Click event when its tab is clicked.

Section 14.12 *Multiple Document Interface (MDI) Windows*
- Multiple document interface (MDI) programs enable users to edit multiple documents at once.
- The application window of an MDI program is called the parent window, and each window inside the application is referred to as a child window.
- Child windows cannot be parents themselves and cannot be moved outside their parent.
- To create an MDI Form, create a new Form and set its IsMdiContainer property to true.
- To add a child Form to the parent, create a new child Form object, set its MdiParent property to the parent Form and call the child Form's Show method.
- Child windows can be minimized, maximized and closed independently of each other and of the parent window.
- Property MdiWindowListItem of class MenuStrip specifies which menu, if any, displays a list of open child windows.
- MDI containers allow you to organize the placement of child windows. The child windows in an MDI application can be arranged by calling method LayoutMdi of the parent Form.

Section 14.13 Visual Inheritance

- Visual inheritance allows you to create a new Form by inheriting from an existing Form. The derived Form class contains the functionality of its base class.

- Visual inheritance enables you to achieve visual consistency across applications by reusing code.

- A Form can inherit from another Form as long as that Form (or its compiled .d11) is included in the project.

Section 14.14 User-Defined Controls

- The .NET Framework allows you to create custom controls.

- Custom controls appear in the user's **Toolbox** and can be added to Forms, Panels or GroupBoxes in the same way that Buttons, Labels and other predefined controls are added.

- The simplest way to create a custom control is to derive a class from an existing control, such as a Label. This is useful if you want to add functionality to an existing control, rather than having to reimplement the existing control to include the desired functionality.

- To create a new control composed of existing controls, use class UserControl.

- Controls added to a custom control are called constituent controls.

- A programmer can create a brand new control by inheriting from class Control. This class does not define any specific behavior; that task is left to you.

- Timers are invisible components that reside on a Form, generating Tick events at a set interval. This interval is set by the Timer's Interval property, which defines the number of milliseconds (thousandths of a second) between events.

Terminology

Activation property of class ListView
ActiveMdiChild property of class Form
Add method of class ObjectCollection
AddDays method of struct DateTime
AddYears method of struct DateTime
ArrangeIcons value of enumeration MdiLayout
Cascade value of enumeration MdiLayout
cascaded window
CheckBoxes property of class ListView
Checked property of class ToolStripMenuItem
CheckedListBox class
child node
child window
Clear method of class Graphics
Clear method of class ObjectCollection
Click event of class ToolStripMenuItem
ClipRectangle property of class
    PaintEventArgs
ComboBox class
ComboBoxStyle enumeration
constituent controls
custom controls
Custom value of enumeration
    DateTimePickerFormat
CustomFormat property of class DateTimePicker

DateChanged event of class MonthCalendar
DateTime struct
DateTimePicker class
DateTimePickerFormat enumeration
DayOfWeek enumeration
DayOfWeek property of class DateTime
DirectoryInfo class
DrawEllipse method of class Graphics
DrawPie method of class Graphics
DrawRectangle method of class Graphics
drop-down list
DropDown value of enumeration ComboBoxStyle
DropDownList value of enumeration
    ComboBoxStyle
DropDownStyle property of class ComboBox
Exit method of class Application
FileInfo class
FillEllipse method of class Graphics
FillPie method of class Graphics
FillRectangle method of class Graphics
Format property of class DateTimePicker
FullName property of class DirectoryInfo
FullName property of class FileInfo
GetDirectories method of class DirectoryInfo
GetFiles method of class DirectoryInfo

ToolStripMenuItem class
tree
TreeNode class
TreeNodeCollection type
TreeView class
TreeViewEventArgs class

UserControl class
Value property of class DateTimePicker
ValueChanged event of class DateTimePicker
View property of class ListView
visual inheritance

Self-Review Exercises

14.1 State whether each of the following is *true* or *false*. If *false*, explain why.
   a) Menus provide groups of related classes.
   b) Menu items can display ComboBoxes, checkmarks and access shortcuts.
   c) The ListBox control allows only single selection (like a RadioButton).
   d) A ComboBox control typically has a drop-down list.
   e) Deleting a parent node in a TreeView control deletes its child nodes.
   f) The user can select only one item in a ListView control.
   g) A TabPage can act as a container for RadioButtons.
   h) An MDI child window can have MDI children.
   i) MDI child windows can be moved outside the boundaries of their parent window.
   j) There are two basic ways to create a customized control.

14.2 Fill in the blanks in each of the following statements:
   a) Method _____ of class Process can open files and Web pages, similar to the **Run...** command in Windows.
   b) If more elements appear in a ComboBox than can fit, a(n) _____ appears.
   c) The top-level node in a TreeView is the _____ node.
   d) A(n) _____ and a(n) _____ can display icons contained in an ImageList control.
   e) The _____ property allows a menu to display a list of active child windows.
   f) Class _____ allows you to combine several controls into a single, custom control.
   g) The _____ saves space by layering TabPages on top of each other.
   h) The _____ window layout option makes all MDI windows the same size and layers them so every title bar is visible (if possible).
   i) _____ are typically used to display hyperlinks to other resources, files or Web pages.

Answers to Self-Review Exercises

14.1 a) False. Menus provide groups of related commands. b) True. c) False. Both controls can have single or multiple selection. d) True. e) True. f) False. The user can select one or more items. g) True. h) False. Only an MDI parent window can have MDI children. An MDI parent window cannot be an MDI child. i) False. MDI child windows cannot be moved outside their parent window. j) False. There are three ways: 1) Derive from an existing control, 2) use a UserControl or 3) derive from Control and create a control from scratch.

14.2 a) Start. b) scrollbar. c) root. d) ListView, TreeView. e) MdiList. f) UserControl. g) TabControl. h) Cascade. i) LinkLabels.

Exercises

14.3 Write a program that displays the names of 15 states in a ComboBox. When an item is selected from the ComboBox, remove it.

14.4   Modify your solution to the previous exercise to add a ListBox. When the user selects an item from the ComboBox, remove the item from the ComboBox and add it to the ListBox. Your program should check to ensure that the ComboBox contains at least one item. If it does not, print a message, using a message box, then terminate program execution when the user dismisses the message box.

14.5   Write a program that allows the user to enter strings in a TextBox. Each string input is added to a ListBox. As each string is added to the ListBox, ensure that the strings are in sorted order. [*Note:* Use property Sorted.]

14.6   Create a file browser (similar to Windows Explorer) based on the programs in Fig. 14.14, Fig. 14.28 and Fig. 14.31. The file browser should have a TreeView, which allows the user to browse directories. There should also be a ListView, which displays the contents (all subdirectories and files) of the directory being browsed. Double clicking a file in the ListView should open it, and double clicking a directory in either the ListView or the TreeView should browse it. If a file or directory cannot be accessed because of its permission settings, notify the user.

14.7   Create an MDI text editor. Each child window should contain a multiline RichTextBox. The MDI parent should have a **Format** menu, with submenus to control the size, font and color of the text in the active child window. Each submenu should have at least three options. In addition, the parent should have a **File** menu, with menu items **New** (create a new child), **Close** (close the active child) and **Exit** (exit the application). The parent should have a **Window** menu to display a list of the open child windows and their layout options.

14.8   Create a UserControl called LoginPasswordUserControl. The LoginPasswordUserControl contains a Label (loginLabel) that displays string "Login:", a TextBox (loginTextBox) where the user inputs a login name, a Label (passwordLabel) that displays the string "Password:" and finally, a TextBox (passwordTextBox) where a user inputs a password (do not forget to set property PasswordChar to "*" in the TextBox's **Properties** window). LoginPasswordUserControl must provide Public read-only properties Login and Password that allow an application to retrieve the user input from loginTextBox and passwordTextBox. The UserControl must be exported to an application that displays the values input by the user in LoginPasswordUserControl.

14.9   A restaurant wants an application that calculates a table's bill. The application should display all the menu items from Fig. 14.53 in four ComboBoxes. Each ComboBox should contain a category of food offered by the restaurant (Beverage, Appetizer, Main Course and Dessert). The user can choose from one of these ComboBoxes to add an item to a table's bill. As each item is selected in the ComboBoxes, add the price of that item to the bill. The user can click the Clear Button to restore the Subtotal:, Tax: and Total: fields to $0.00.

Name	Category	Price
Soda	Beverage	$1.95
Tea	Beverage	$1.50
Coffee	Beverage	$1.25
Mineral Water	Beverage	$2.95
Juice	Beverage	$2.50
Milk	Beverage	$1.50

Fig. 14.53 | Food items and prices. (Part 1 of 2.)

Name	Category	Price
Buffalo Wings	Appetizer	$5.95
Buffalo Fingers	Appetizer	$6.95
Potato Skins	Appetizer	$8.95
Nachos	Appetizer	$8.95
Mushroom Caps	Appetizer	$10.95
Shrimp Cocktail	Appetizer	$12.95
Chips and Salsa	Appetizer	$6.95
Seafood Alfredo	Main Course	$15.95
Chicken Alfredo	Main Course	$13.95
Chicken Picatta	Main Course	$13.95
Turkey Club	Main Course	$11.95
Lobster Pie	Main Course	$19.95
Prime Rib	Main Course	$20.95
Shrimp Scampi	Main Course	$18.95
Turkey Dinner	Main Course	$13.95
Stuffed Chicken	Main Course	$14.95
Apple Pie	Dessert	$5.95
Sundae	Dessert	$3.95
Carrot Cake	Dessert	$5.95
Mud Pie	Dessert	$4.95
Apple Crisp	Dessert	$5.95

Fig. 14.53 | Food items and prices. (Part 2 of 2.)

14.10 Create an application that contains three TabPages. On the first TabPage, place a CheckedList-Box with six items. On the second TabPage, place six TextBoxes. On the last TabPage, place six LinkLabels. The user's selections on the first TabPage should specify which of the six LinkLabels will be displayed. To hide or display a LinkLabel's value, use its Visible property. Use the second TabPage to modify the Web page that is opened by the LinkLabels. [*Note:* To change the LinkLabels' Visible properties, you will need to change the currently displayed TabPage to the last one. To do this, use the TabPage's SelectedTab property.]

14.11 Create an MDI application with child windows that each have a Panel for drawing. Add menus to the MDI application that allow the user to modify the size and color of the paint brush. When running this application, be aware that if one of the windows overlaps another, the Panel will be cleared.

15

Multithreading

OBJECTIVES

In this chapter you will learn:

- What threads are and why they are useful.
- How threads enable you to manage concurrent activities.
- The life cycle of a thread.
- Thread priorities and scheduling.
- To create and execute `Thread`s.
- Thread synchronization.
- What producer/consumer relationships are and how they are implemented with multithreading.
- To display output from multiple threads in a GUI.

15.1 Introduction

It would be nice if we could perform one action at a time and perform it well, but that is usually difficult to do. The human body performs a great variety of operations *in parallel*—or, as we will say throughout this chapter, *concurrently*. Respiration, blood circulation and digestion, for example, can occur concurrently. All the senses—sight, touch, smell, taste and hearing—can be employed at once. Computers, too, perform operations concurrently. It is common for your computer to be compiling a program, sending a file to a printer and receiving electronic mail messages over a network concurrently.

Ironically, most programming languages do not enable programmers to specify concurrent activities. Rather, programming languages generally provide only a simple set of control statements that enable programmers to perform one action at a time, proceeding to the next action after the previous one has finished. Historically, the type of concurrency that computers perform today generally has been implemented as operating system "primitives" available only to highly experienced "systems programmers."

The Ada programming language, developed by the United States Department of Defense, made concurrency primitives widely available to defense contractors building military command-and-control systems. However, Ada has not been widely used in academia and commercial industry.

The .NET Framework Class Library provides concurrency primitives. You specify that applications contain "*threads of execution*," each of which designates a portion of a program that may execute concurrently with other threads—this capability is called multithreading. Multithreading is available to all .NET programming languages, including C#, Visual Basic and Visual C++. The .NET Framework Class Library includes multithreading capabilities in namespace *System.Threading*.

Performance Tip 15.1

A problem with single-threaded applications is that lengthy activities must complete before other activities can begin. In a multithreaded application, threads can be distributed across multiple processors (if they are available) so that multiple tasks are performed concurrently, allowing the application to operate more efficiently. Multithreading can also increase performance on single-processor systems that simulate concurrency—when one thread cannot proceed, another can use the processor.

We discuss many applications of *concurrent programming*. When programs download large files, such as audio clips or video clips over the Internet, users do not want to wait until an entire clip downloads before starting the playback. To solve this problem, we can put multiple threads to work—one thread downloads a clip, while another plays the clip. These activities proceed concurrently. To avoid choppy playback, we *synchronize* the threads so that the player thread does not begin until there is a sufficient amount of the clip in memory to keep the player thread busy.

Another example of multithreading is the CLR's automatic garbage collection. C and C++ require programmers to reclaim dynamically allocated memory explicitly. The CLR provides a garbage-collector thread, which reclaims dynamically allocated memory that is no longer needed.

Good Programming Practice 15.1

Set an object reference to null *when the program no longer needs that object. This enables the garbage collector to determine at the earliest possible moment that the object can be garbage collected. If such an object has other references to it, that object cannot be collected.*

Writing multithreaded programs can be tricky. Although the human mind can perform functions concurrently, people find it difficult to jump between parallel "trains of thought." To see why multithreading can be difficult to program and understand, try the following experiment: Open three books to page 1 and try reading the books concurrently. Read a few words from the first book, then read a few words from the second book, then read a few words from the third book, then loop back and read the next few words from the first book, etc. After this experiment, you will appreciate the challenges of multithreading—switching between books, reading briefly, remembering your place in each book, moving the book you are reading closer so you can see it, pushing books you are not reading aside and, amid all this chaos, trying to comprehend the content of the books!

15.2 Thread States: Life Cycle of a Thread

At any time, a thread is said to be in one of several thread states that are illustrated in the UML state diagram of Fig. 15.1. This section discusses these states and the transitions between states. Two classes critical for multithreaded applications are *Thread* and *Monitor* (System.Threading namespace). This section also discusses several methods of classes Thread and Monitor that cause state transitions. A few of the terms in the diagram are discussed in later sections.

A Thread object begins its life cycle in the *Unstarted* state when the program creates the object and passes a *ThreadStart* delegate to the object's constructor. The ThreadStart delegate, which specifies the actions the thread will perform during its life cycle, must be initialized with a method that returns void and takes no arguments. [*Note:* .NET 2.0 also includes a ParameterizedThreadStart delegate to which you can pass a method that takes arguments. For more information, visit the site msdn2.microsoft.com/en-us/library/xzehzsds.] The thread remains in the *Unstarted* state until the program calls the Thread's *Start* method, which places the thread in the *Running* state and immediately returns control to the part of the program that called Start. Then the newly *Running* thread and any other threads in the program can execute concurrently on a multiprocessor system or share the processor on a system with a single processor.

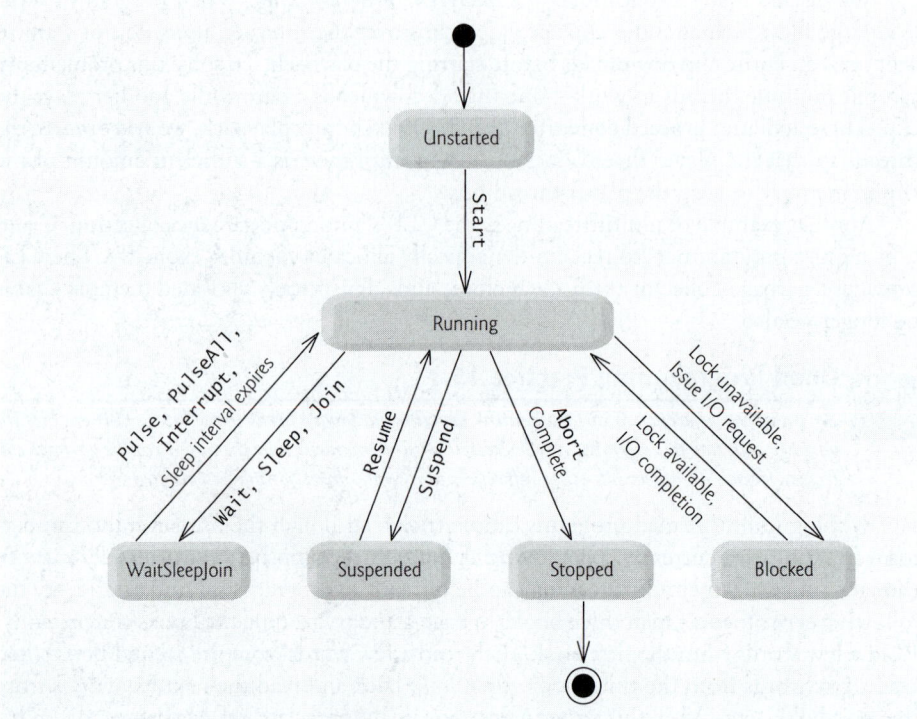

Fig. 15.1 | Thread life cycle.

While in the *Running* state, the thread may not actually be executing all the time. The thread executes in the *Running* state only when the operating system assigns a processor to the thread. When a *Running* thread receives a processor for the first time, the thread begins executing the method specified by its ThreadStart delegate.

A *Running* thread enters the **Stopped** (or **Aborted**) state when its ThreadStart delegate terminates, which normally indicates that the thread has completed its task. Note that a program can force a thread into the *Stopped* state by calling Thread method **Abort** on the appropriate Thread object. Method Abort throws a **ThreadAbortException** in the thread, normally causing the thread to terminate. When a thread is in the *Stopped* state and there are no references to the thread object, the garbage collector can remove the thread object from memory. [*Note:* Internally, when a thread's Abort method is called, the thread actually enters the **AbortRequested** state before entering the *Stopped* state. The thread remains in the *AbortRequested* state while waiting to receive the pending ThreadAbortException. When Abort is called, if the thread is in the *WaitSleepJoin*, *Suspended* or *Blocked* state, the thread resides in its current state and the *AbortRequested* state, and cannot receive the ThreadAbortException until it leaves its current state.]

A thread is considered **Blocked** if it is unable to use a processor even if one is available. For example, a thread becomes blocked when it issues an input/output (I/O) request. The operating system blocks the thread from executing until the operating system can complete the I/O request for which the thread is waiting. At that point, the thread returns to the *Running* state, so it can resume execution. Another case in which a thread becomes blocked is in thread synchronization (Section 15.5). A thread being synchronized must acquire a lock on an object by calling Monitor method **Enter**. If a lock is not available, the thread is blocked until the desired lock becomes available. [*Note:* The *Blocked* state is not an actual state in .NET. It is a conceptual state that describes a thread that is not *Running.*]

There are three ways in which a *Running* thread enters the **WaitSleepJoin** state. If a thread encounters code that it cannot execute yet (normally because a condition is not satisfied), the thread can call Monitor method **Wait** to enter the *WaitSleepJoin* state. Once in this state, a thread returns to the *Running* state when another thread invokes Monitor method **Pulse** or **PulseAll**. Method Pulse moves the next waiting thread back to the *Running* state. Method PulseAll moves all waiting threads back to the *Running* state.

A *Running* thread can call Thread method **Sleep** to enter the *WaitSleepJoin* state for a period of milliseconds specified as the argument to Sleep. A sleeping thread returns to the *Running* state when its designated sleep time expires. Sleeping threads cannot use a processor, even if one is available.

Any thread that enters the *WaitSleepJoin* state by calling Monitor method Wait or by calling Thread method Sleep also leaves the *WaitSleepJoin* state and returns to the *Running* state if the sleeping or waiting Thread's **Interrupt** method is called by another thread in the program. The Interrupt method causes a ThreadInterruptionException to be thrown in the interrupted thread.

If a thread cannot continue executing (we will call this the dependent thread) unless another thread terminates, the dependent thread calls the other thread's **Join** method to "join" the two threads. When two threads are "joined," the dependent thread leaves the *WaitSleepJoin* state and re-enters the *Running* state when the other thread finishes execution (enters the **Stopped** state).

If a *Running* Thread's **Suspend** method is called, the *Running* thread enters the **Suspended** state. A *Suspended* thread returns to the *Running* state when another thread in the program invokes the *Suspended* thread's **Resume** method. [*Note:* Internally, when a thread's Suspend method is called, the thread actually enters the **SuspendRequested** state before entering the *Suspended* state. The thread remains in the *SuspendRequested* state while waiting to respond to the Suspend request. If the thread is in the *WaitSleepJoin* state or is blocked when its Suspend method is called, the thread resides in its current state and the *SuspendRequested* state, and cannot respond to the Suspend request until it leaves its current state.] Methods Suspend and Resume are now deprecated and should not be used. In Section 15.9, we show how to emulate these methods using thread synchronization.

If a thread's **IsBackground** property is set to true, the thread resides in the **Background** state (not shown in Fig. 15.1). A thread can reside in the *Background* state and any other state simultaneously. A process must wait for all **foreground threads** (threads not in the *Background* state) to finish executing and enter the *Stopped* state before the process can terminate. However, if the only threads remaining in a process are *Background threads*, the CLR terminates each thread by invoking its Abort method, and the process terminates.

15.3 Thread Priorities and Thread Scheduling

Every thread has a priority in the range between ThreadPriority.Lowest to ThreadPriority.Highest. These values come from the **ThreadPriority** enumeration (namespace System.Threading), which consists of the values **Lowest**, **BelowNormal**, **Normal**, **AboveNormal** and **Highest**. By default, each thread has priority Normal.

The Windows operating system supports a concept, called timeslicing, that enables threads of equal priority to share a processor. Without timeslicing, each thread in a set of equal-priority threads runs to completion (unless the thread leaves the *Running* state and enters the *WaitSleepJoin*, *Suspended* or *Blocked* state) before the thread's peers get a chance to execute. With timeslicing, each thread receives a brief burst of processor time, called a quantum, during which the thread can execute. At the completion of the quantum, even if the thread has not finished executing, the processor is taken away from that thread and given to the next thread of equal priority, if one is available.

The job of the ***thread scheduler*** is to keep the highest-priority thread running at all times and, if there is more than one highest-priority thread, to ensure that all such threads execute for a quantum in round-robin fashion. Figure 15.2 illustrates the ***multilevel priority queue*** for threads. In Fig. 15.2, assuming a single-processor computer, threads A and B each execute for a quantum in round-robin fashion until both threads complete execution. This means that A gets a quantum of time to run. Then B gets a quantum. Then A gets another quantum. Then B gets another quantum. This continues until one thread completes. The processor then devotes all its power to the thread that remains (unless another thread of that priority is started). Next, thread C runs to completion. Threads D, E and F each execute for a quantum in round-robin fashion until they all complete execution. This process continues until all threads run to completion. Note that, depending on the operating system, new higher-priority threads could postpone—possibly indefinitely—the execution of lower-priority threads. Such indefinite postponement often is referred to more colorfully as starvation.

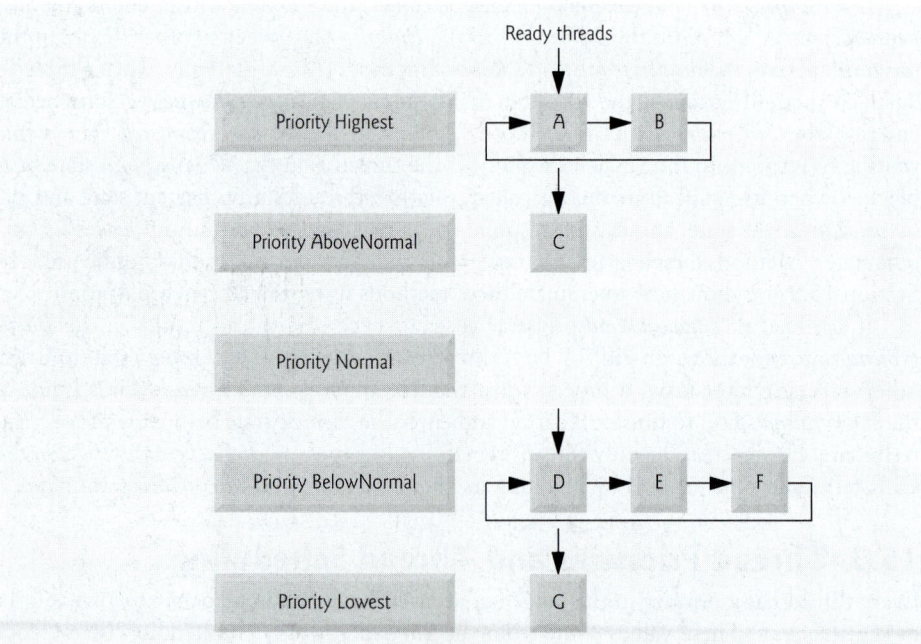

Fig. 15.2 | Thread-priority scheduling.

A thread's priority can be adjusted with the ***Priority*** property, which accepts values from the ThreadPriority enumeration. If the value specified is not one of the valid thread-priority constants, an ArgumentException occurs.

A thread executes until it dies, becomes *Blocked* for I/O (or some other reason), calls Sleep, calls Monitor method Wait or Join, is pre-empted by a thread of higher priority or has its ***quantum expire***. A thread with a higher priority than the *Running* thread can become *Running* (and hence pre-empt the first *Running* thread) if a sleeping thread wakes up, if I/O completes for a thread that *Blocked* for that I/O, if either Pulse or PulseAll is called on an object on which Wait was called, if a thread is Resumed from the *Suspended* state or if a thread to which the high-priority thread was joined completes.

15.4 Creating and Executing Threads

Figure 15.3 demonstrates basic threading techniques, including constructing Thread objects and the use of the Thread class's static method ***Sleep***. The program creates three threads of execution, each with the default priority Normal. Each thread displays a message indicating that it is going to sleep for a random interval of from 0 to 5000 milliseconds, then goes to sleep. When each thread awakens, the thread displays its name, indicates that it is done sleeping, terminates and enters the *Stopped* state. You will see that method Main (i.e., the Main *thread of execution*) terminates before the application terminates. The program consists of two classes—ThreadTester (lines 7–35), which creates the three threads, and MessagePrinter (lines 38–64), which defines a Print method containing the actions each thread will perform.

Objects of class MessagePrinter (lines 38–64) control the life cycle of each of the three threads created in class ThreadTester's Main method. Class MessagePrinter con-

```
1   // Fig. 15.3: ThreadTester.cs
2   // Multiple threads printing at different intervals.
3   using System;
4   using System.Threading;
5
6   // class ThreadTester demonstrates basic threading concepts
7   class ThreadTester
8   {
9      static void Main( string[] args )
10     {
11        // Create and name each thread. Use MessagePrinter's
12        // Print method as argument to ThreadStart delegate.
13        MessagePrinter printer1 = new MessagePrinter();
14        Thread thread1 = new Thread ( new ThreadStart( printer1.Print ) );
15        thread1.Name = "thread1";
16
17        MessagePrinter printer2 = new MessagePrinter();
18        Thread thread2 = new Thread ( new ThreadStart( printer2.Print ) );
19        thread2.Name = "thread2";
20
21        MessagePrinter printer3 = new MessagePrinter();
22        Thread thread3 = new Thread ( new ThreadStart( printer3.Print ) );
```

Fig. 15.3 | Threads sleeping and printing. (Part 1 of 3.)

```
23          thread3.Name = "thread3";
24
25          Console.WriteLine( "Starting threads" );
26
27          // call each thread's Start method to place each
28          // thread in Running state
29          thread1.Start();
30          thread2.Start();
31          thread3.Start();
32
33          Console.WriteLine( "Threads started\n" );
34       } // end method Main
35    } // end class ThreadTester
36
37    // Print method of this class used to control threads
38    class MessagePrinter
39    {
40       private int sleepTime;
41       private static Random random = new Random();
42
43       // constructor to initialize a MessagePrinter object
44       public MessagePrinter()
45       {
46          // pick random sleep time between 0 and 5 seconds
47          sleepTime = random.Next( 5001 ); // 5001 milliseconds
48       } // end constructor
49
50       // method Print controls thread that prints messages
51       public void Print()
52       {
53          // obtain reference to currently executing thread
54          Thread current = Thread.CurrentThread;
55
56          // put thread to sleep for sleepTime amount of time
57          Console.WriteLine( "{0} going to sleep for {1} milliseconds",
58             current.Name, sleepTime );
59          Thread.Sleep( sleepTime ); // sleep for sleepTime milliseconds
60
61          // print thread name
62          Console.WriteLine( "{0} done sleeping", current.Name );
63       } // end method Print
64    } // end class MessagePrinter
```

```
Starting threads
thread1 going to sleep for 1603 milliseconds
thread2 going to sleep for 2355 milliseconds
thread3 going to sleep for 285 milliseconds
Threads started

thread3 done sleeping
thread1 done sleeping
thread2 done sleeping
```

Fig. 15.3 | Threads sleeping and printing. (Part 2 of 3.)

```
Starting threads
thread1 going to sleep for 4245 milliseconds
thread2 going to sleep for 1466 milliseconds
Threads started

thread3 going to sleep for 1929 milliseconds
thread2 done sleeping
thread3 done sleeping
thread1 done sleeping
```

Fig. 15.3 | Threads sleeping and printing. (Part 3 of 3.)

sists of instance variable `sleepTime` (line 40), `static` variable `random` (line 41), a constructor (lines 44–48) and a `Print` method (lines 51–63). Variable `sleepTime` stores a random integer value chosen when a new `MessagePrinter` object's constructor is called. Each thread controlled by a `MessagePrinter` object sleeps for the amount of time specified by the corresponding `MessagePrinter` object's `sleepTime`.

The `MessagePrinter` constructor (lines 44–48) initializes `sleepTime` to a random number of milliseconds from 0 up to, but not including, 5001 (i.e., from 0 to 5000).

Method `Print` begins by obtaining a reference to the currently executing thread (line 54) via class `Thread`'s `static` property **CurrentThread**. The currently executing thread is the one that invokes method `Print`. Next, lines 57–58 display a message indicating the name of the currently executing thread and stating that the thread is going to sleep for a certain number of milliseconds. Note that line 58 uses the currently executing thread's **Name** property to obtain the thread's name (set in method `Main` when each thread is created). Line 59 invokes `static` `Thread` method `Sleep` to place the thread in the *WaitSleepJoin* state. At this point, the thread loses the processor, and the system allows another thread to execute if one is ready to run. When the thread awakens, it re-enters the *Running* state and waits to be assigned a processor by the thread scheduler. When the `Message-Printer` object enters the *Running* state again, line 62 outputs the thread's name in a message that indicates the thread is done sleeping, and method `Print` terminates.

Class `ThreadTester`'s `Main` method (lines 9–34) creates three objects of class `MessagePrinter`, at lines 13, 17 and 21, respectively. Lines 14, 18 and 22 create and initialize three `Thread` objects. Note that each `Thread`'s constructor receives a `ThreadStart` delegate as an argument. A `ThreadStart` delegate represents a method with no arguments and a `void` return type that specifies the actions a thread will perform. Line 14 initializes the `ThreadStart` delegate for `thread1` with `printer1`'s `Print` method. When `thread1` enters the *Running* state for the first time, `thread1` will invoke `printer1`'s `Print` method to perform the tasks specified in method `Print`'s body. Thus, `thread1` will print its name, display the amount of time for which it will go to sleep, sleep for that amount of time, wake up and display a message indicating that the thread is done sleeping. At that point, method `Print` will terminate. A thread completes its task when the method specified by its `ThreadStart` delegate terminates, at which point the thread enters the *Stopped* state. When `thread2` and `thread3` enter the *Running* state for the first time, they invoke the `Print` methods of `printer2` and `printer3`, respectively. `thread2` and `thread3` perform the same tasks as `thread1` by executing the `Print` methods of the objects to which `printer2` and `printer3` refer (each of which has its own randomly chosen sleep time). Lines 15, 19 and 23 set each `Thread`'s `Name` property, which we use for output purposes.

Lines 29–31 invoke each `Thread`'s `Start` method to place the threads in the *Running* state. Method `Start` returns immediately from each invocation, then line 33 outputs a message indicating that the threads were started, and the `Main` thread of execution terminates. The program itself does not terminate, however, because there are still non-background threads that are alive (i.e., the threads are *Running* and have not yet reached the *Stopped* state). The program will not terminate until its last non-background thread dies. When the system assigns a processor to a thread, the thread enters the *Running* state and calls the method specified by the thread's `ThreadStart` delegate. In this program, each thread invokes method `Print` of the appropriate `MessagePrinter` object to perform the tasks discussed previously.

Note that the sample outputs for this program show each thread and the thread's sleep time in milliseconds as the thread goes to sleep. The thread with the shortest sleep time normally awakens first, then indicates that it is done sleeping and terminates. In Section 15.8, we discuss multithreading issues that could prevent the thread with the shortest sleep time from awakening first (none of this is guaranteed). Notice in the second sample output that `thread1` and `thread2` were able to report their sleep times before `Main` could output its final message. This means that the main thread's quantum ended before it could finish executing `Main`, and `thread1` and `thread2` each got a chance to execute.

15.5 Thread Synchronization and Class `Monitor`

Often, multiple threads of execution manipulate shared data. If threads with access to shared data simply read that data, then any number of threads could access that data simultaneously and no problems would arise. However, when multiple threads share data and that data is modified by one or more of those threads, then indeterminate results may occur. If one thread is in the process of updating the data and another thread tries to update it too, the data will reflect only the later update. If the data is an array or other data structure in which the threads could update separate parts of the data concurrently, it is possible that part of the data will reflect the information from one thread while part of the data will reflect information from another thread. When this happens, the program has difficulty determining when the data has been updated properly.

The problem can be solved by giving one thread at a time exclusive access to code that manipulates the shared data. During that time, other threads wishing to manipulate the data should be kept waiting. When the thread with exclusive access to the data completes its data manipulations, one of the waiting threads should be allowed to proceed. In this fashion, each thread accessing the shared data excludes all other threads from doing so simultaneously. This is called *mutual exclusion* or thread synchronization.

C# uses the .NET Framework's monitors to perform synchronization. Class `Monitor` provides the methods for locking objects to implement synchronized access to shared data. Locking an object means that only one thread can access that object at a time. When a thread wishes to acquire exclusive control over an object, the thread invokes `Monitor` method `Enter` to *acquire the lock* on that data object. Each object has a SyncBlock that maintains the state of that object's lock. Methods of class Monitor use the data in an object's SyncBlock to determine the state of the lock for that object. After acquiring the lock for an object, a thread can manipulate that object's data. While the object is locked, all other threads attempting to acquire the lock on that object are blocked from acquiring the lock—such threads enter the *Blocked* state. When the thread that locked the shared object no longer requires the lock, that thread invokes Monitor method **Exit** to release the lock. This updates the SyncBlock of the shared object to indicate that the lock for the object is available again. At this point, if there is a thread that was previously blocked from acquiring the lock on the shared object, that thread acquires the lock to begin its processing of the object. If all threads with access to an object attempt to acquire the object's lock before manipulating the object, only one thread at a time will be allowed to manipulate the object. This helps ensure the integrity of the data.

Common Programming Error 15.1

Make sure that all code that updates a shared object locks the object before doing so. Otherwise, a thread calling a method that does not lock the object can make the object unstable even when another thread has acquired the lock for the object.

Common Programming Error 15.2

Deadlock occurs when a waiting thread (let us call this thread1) cannot proceed because it is waiting (either directly or indirectly) for another thread (let us call this thread2) to proceed, while simultaneously thread2 cannot proceed because it is waiting (either directly or indirectly) for thread1 to proceed. Two threads are waiting for each other, so the actions that would enable either thread to continue execution never occur.

C# provides another means of manipulating an object's lock—keyword **lock**. Placing lock before a block of code (designated with braces) as in

```
lock ( objectReference )
{
    // code that requires synchronization goes here
}
```

obtains the lock on the object to which the *objectReference* in parentheses refers. The *objectReference* is the same reference that normally would be passed to Monitor methods Enter, Exit, Pulse and PulseAll. When a lock block terminates for any reason, C# releases the lock on the object to which the *objectReference* refers. We explain lock further in Section 15.8.

If a thread that owns the lock on an object determines that it cannot continue with its task until some condition is satisfied, the thread should call Monitor method Wait and pass as an argument the object on which the thread will wait until the thread can perform its task. Calling method Monitor.Wait from a thread releases the lock the thread has on the object that Wait receives as an argument and places that thread in the *WaitSleepJoin* state for that object. A thread in the *WaitSleepJoin* state of a specific object leaves that state when a separate thread invokes Monitor method Pulse or PulseAll with that object as an argument. Method Pulse transitions the object's first waiting thread from the *WaitSleepJoin* state to the *Running* state. Method PulseAll transitions all threads in the object's *WaitSleepJoin* state to the *Running* state. The transition to the *Running* state enables the thread (or threads) to get ready to continue executing.

There is a difference between threads waiting to acquire an object's lock and threads waiting in an object's *WaitSleepJoin* state. Threads that call Monitor method Wait with an object as an argument are placed in that object's *WaitSleepJoin* state. Threads that are simply waiting to acquire the lock enter the conceptual *Blocked* state and wait until the object's lock becomes available. Then, a *Blocked* thread can acquire the object's lock.

Monitor methods Enter, Exit, Wait, Pulse and PulseAll all take a reference to an object—usually keyword this—as their argument.

Common Programming Error 15.3

A thread in the WaitSleepJoin *state cannot re-enter the* Running *state to continue execution until a separate thread invokes* Monitor *method* Pulse *or* PulseAll *with the appropriate object as an argument. If this does not occur, the waiting thread will wait forever—essentially the equivalent of deadlock.*

Error-Prevention Tip 15.2

When multiple threads manipulate a shared object using monitors, ensure that if one thread calls Monitor *method* Wait *to enter the* WaitSleepJoin *state for the shared object, a separate thread eventually will call* Monitor *method* Pulse *to transition the thread waiting on the shared object back to the* Running *state. If multiple threads may be waiting for the shared object, a separate thread can call* Monitor *method* PulseAll *as a safeguard to ensure that all waiting threads have another opportunity to perform their tasks. If this is not done, indefinite postponement or deadlock could occur.*

Performance Tip 15.2

Synchronization to achieve correctness in multithreaded programs can make programs run more slowly, as a result of monitor overhead and the frequent transitioning of threads between the WaitSleepJoin *and* Running *states. There is not much to say, however, for highly efficient, yet incorrect multithreaded programs!*

15.6 Producer/Consumer Relationship without Thread Synchronization

In a producer/consumer relationship, the *producer* portion of an application generates data and the *consumer* portion of an application uses that data. In a multithreaded producer/consumer relationship, a producer thread calls a produce method to generate data and place it in a shared region of memory, called a buffer. A consumer thread calls a consume method to read that data. If the producer wishes to put the next data in the buffer but determines that the consumer has not yet read the previous data from the buffer, the producer thread should call Wait. Otherwise, the consumer would never see the previous data, which would be lost to that application. When the consumer thread reads the data, it should call Pulse to allow a waiting producer to proceed, since there is now free space in the buffer. If a consumer thread finds the buffer empty or finds that the previous data has already been read, the consumer should call Wait. Otherwise, the consumer might read "garbage" from the buffer, or the consumer might process a previous data item more than once—each of these possibilities results in a logic error in the application. When the producer places the next data into the buffer, the producer should call Pulse to allow the consumer thread to proceed and read that data.

Let us consider how logic errors can arise if we do not synchronize access among multiple threads manipulating shared data. Consider a producer/consumer relationship in which a producer thread writes a sequence of numbers (we use 1–10) into a shared buffer—a memory location shared between multiple threads. The consumer thread reads this data from the shared buffer, then displays the data. We display in the program's output the values that the producer writes (produces) and that the consumer reads (consumes). Figures 15.4–15.8 demonstrate a producer thread and a consumer thread accessing a single shared int variable without any synchronization. The producer thread writes to the variable; the consumer thread reads from it. We would like each value the producer thread writes to the shared variable to be consumed exactly once by the consumer thread. However, the threads in this example are not synchronized. Therefore, data can be lost if the producer places new data in the variable before the consumer consumes the previous data. Also, data can be incorrectly repeated if the consumer consumes data again before the producer produces the next value. If the consumer attempts to read before the producer produces the first value, the consumer reads garbage. To show these possibilities, the consumer thread in the example keeps a total of all the values it reads. The producer thread produces values from 1 to 10. If the consumer reads each value produced once and only once, the total would be 55. However, when you execute this program several times, you will see that the total is rarely, if ever, 55. Also, to emphasize our point, the producer and consumer threads in the example each sleep for random intervals of up to three seconds between performing their tasks. Thus, we do not know exactly when the producer thread will attempt to write a new value, nor do we know when the consumer thread will attempt to read a value.

The program consists of interface Buffer (Fig. 15.4) and classes Producer (Fig. 15.5), Consumer (Fig. 15.6), UnsynchronizedBuffer (Fig. 15.7) and UnsynchronizedBuffer-Test (Fig. 15.8). Interface Buffer declares an int property called Buffer. Any implementation of Buffer must provide a get accessor and a set accessor for this property to allow the producer and consumer to access the shared data.

Class Producer (Figure 15.5) consists of instance variable sharedLocation (line 10) of type Buffer, instance variable randomSleepTime (line 11) of type Random, a constructor (lines 14–18) to initialize the instance variables and a Produce method (lines 21–33). The

```
 1   // Fig. 15.4: Buffer.cs
 2   // Interface for a shared buffer of int.
 3   using System;
 4
 5   // this interface represents a shared buffer
 6   public interface Buffer
 7   {
 8      // property Buffer
 9      int Buffer
10      {
11         get;
12         set;
13      } // end property Buffer
14   } // end interface Buffer
```

Fig. 15.4 | Buffer interface used in producer/consumer examples.

constructor initializes instance variable sharedLocation to refer to the Buffer object received from method Main as the parameter shared. The producer thread in this program executes the tasks specified in method Produce of class Producer. The for statement in method Produce (lines 25–29) loops 10 times. Each iteration of the loop first invokes Thread method Sleep to place the producer thread in the *WaitSleepJoin* state for a random time interval between 0 and 3 seconds. When the thread awakens, line 28 assigns the value of control variable count to sharedLocation's Buffer property. When the loop completes, lines 31–32 display a line of text in the console window indicating that the thread finished producing data and that the thread is terminating. The Produce method then terminates, and the producer thread enters the *Stopped* state.

Class Consumer (Figure 15.6) consists of instance variable sharedLocation (line 10) of type Buffer, instance variable randomSleepTime (line 11) of type Random, a constructor (lines 14–18) to initialize the instance variables and a Consume method (lines 21–36). The constructor initializes sharedLocation to refer to the Buffer object received from Main as

```
1   // Fig. 15.5: Producer.cs
2   // Producer produces 10 integer values in the shared buffer.
3   using System;
4   using System.Threading;
5
6   // class Producer's Produce method controls a thread that
7   // stores values from 1 to 10 in sharedLocation
8   public class Producer
9   {
10      private Buffer sharedLocation;
11      private Random randomSleepTime;
12
13      // constructor
14      public Producer( Buffer shared, Random random )
15      {
16         sharedLocation = shared;
17         randomSleepTime = random;
18      } // end constructor
19
20      // store values 1-10 in object sharedLocation
21      public void Produce()
22      {
23         // sleep for random interval up to 3000 milliseconds
24         // then set sharedLocation's Buffer property
25         for ( int count = 1; count <= 10; count++ )
26         {
27            Thread.Sleep( randomSleepTime.Next( 1, 3001 ) );
28            sharedLocation.Buffer = count;
29         } // end for
30
31         Console.WriteLine( "{0} done producing.\nTerminating {0}.",
32            Thread.CurrentThread.Name );
33      } // end method Produce
34   } // end class Producer
```

Fig. 15.5 | Producer represents the producer thread in a producer/consumer relationship.

the parameter shared. The consumer thread in this program performs the tasks specified in class Consumer's Consume method. The method contains a for statement (lines 27–31) that loops ten times. Each iteration of the loop invokes Thread method Sleep to put the consumer thread into the *WaitSleepJoin* state for a random time interval between 0 and 3 seconds. Next, line 30 gets the value of sharedLocation's Buffer property and adds the value to variable sum. When the loop completes, lines 33–35 display a line in the console window indicating the sum of all values read. Again, ideally the total should be 55, but because access to the shared data is not synchronized, this sum will almost never appear. The Consume method then terminates, and the consumer thread enters the *Stopped* state.

We use method Sleep in this example's threads to emphasize the fact that in multi-threaded applications, it is unclear when each thread will perform its task and for how long it will perform that task when it has the processor. Normally, these thread-scheduling

```
1   // Fig. 15.6: Consumer.cs
2   // Consumer consumes 10 integer values from the shared buffer.
3   using System;
4   using System.Threading;
5
6   // class Consumer's Consume method controls a thread that
7   // loops 10 times and reads a value from sharedLocation
8   public class Consumer
9   {
10      private Buffer sharedLocation;
11      private Random randomSleepTime;
12
13      // constructor
14      public Consumer( Buffer shared, Random random )
15      {
16          sharedLocation = shared;
17          randomSleepTime = random;
18      } // end constructor
19
20      // read sharedLocation's value ten times
21      public void Consume()
22      {
23          int sum = 0;
24
25          // sleep for random interval up to 3000 milliseconds then
26          // add sharedLocation's Buffer property value to sum
27          for ( int count = 1; count <= 10; count++ )
28          {
29              Thread.Sleep( randomSleepTime.Next( 1, 3001 ) );
30              sum += sharedLocation.Buffer;
31          } // end for
32
33          Console.WriteLine(
34              "{0} read values totaling: {1}.\nTerminating {0}.",
35              Thread.CurrentThread.Name, sum );
36      } // end method Consume
37   } // end class Consumer
```

Fig. 15.6 | Consumer represents the consumer thread in a producer/consumer relationship.

issues are the job of the computer's operating system. In this program, our thread's tasks are quite simple—for the producer, loop 10 times and perform an assignment statement; for the consumer, loop 10 times and add a value to variable sum. Without the Sleep method call, and if the producer executes first, the producer would most likely complete its task before the consumer ever gets a chance to execute. If the consumer executes first, it would consume -1 ten times, then terminate before the producer could produce the first real value.

Class UnsynchronizedBuffer (Figure 15.7) implements interface Buffer (line 7) and consists of instance variable buffer (line 10) and property Buffer (lines 13–27), which provides get and set accessors. Property Buffer's accessors do not synchronize access to instance variable buffer. Note that each accessor uses class Thread's static property CurrentThread to obtain a reference to the currently executing thread, then uses that thread's Name property to obtain the thread's name for output purposes.

Class UnsynchronizedBufferTest (Figure 15.8) defines a Main method (lines 11–36) that instantiates a shared UnsynchronizedBuffer object (line 14) and a Random object (line 17) for generating random sleep times. These are used as arguments to the constructors for the objects of classes Producer (line 20) and Consumer (line 21). The Unsynchronized-Buffer object contains the data that will be shared between the producer and consumer

```
1   // Fig. 15.7: UnsynchronizedBuffer.cs
2   // An unsynchronized shared buffer implementation.
3   using System;
4   using System.Threading;
5
6   // this class represents a single shared int
7   public class UnsynchronizedBuffer : Buffer
8   {
9      // buffer shared by producer and consumer threads
10     private int buffer = -1;
11
12     // property Buffer
13     public int Buffer
14     {
15        get
16        {
17           Console.WriteLine( "{0} reads {1}",
18              Thread.CurrentThread.Name, buffer );
19           return buffer;
20        } // end get
21        set
22        {
23           Console.WriteLine( "{0} writes {1}",
24              Thread.CurrentThread.Name, value );
25           buffer = value;
26        } // end set
27     } // end property Buffer
28  } // end class UnsynchronizedBuffer
```

Fig. 15.7 | UnsynchronizedBuffer maintains the shared integer variable that is accessed by a producer thread and a consumer thread via property Buffer.

threads. Because UnsynchronizedBuffer implements the Buffer interface, the Producer and Consumer constructors can each take an UnsynchronizedBuffer object and assign it to their respective Buffer variables named sharedLocation. Lines 25–27 create and name producerThread. The ThreadStart delegate for producerThread specifies that the thread will execute method Produce of object producer. Lines 29–31 create and name the consumerThread. The ThreadStart delegate for the consumerThread specifies that the thread will execute method Consume of object consumer. Finally, lines 34–35 place the two threads in the *Running* state by invoking each thread's Start method, then the thread executing Main terminates.

Ideally, we would like every value produced by the Producer object to be consumed exactly once by the Consumer object. However, when we study the first output of

```
1   // Fig. 15.8: UnsynchronizedBufferTest.cs
2   // Showing multiple threads modifying a shared object without
3   // synchronization.
4   using System;
5   using System.Threading;
6
7   // this class creates producer and consumer threads
8   class UnsynchronizedBufferTest
9   {
10     // create producer and consumer threads and start them
11     static void Main( string[] args )
12     {
13       // create shared object used by threads
14       UnsynchronizedBuffer shared = new UnsynchronizedBuffer();
15
16       // Random object used by each thread
17       Random random = new Random();
18
19       // create Producer and Consumer objects
20       Producer producer = new Producer( shared, random );
21       Consumer consumer = new Consumer( shared, random );
22
23       // create threads for producer and consumer and set
24       // delegates for each thread
25       Thread producerThread =
26          new Thread( new ThreadStart( producer.Produce ) );
27       producerThread.Name = "Producer";
28
29       Thread consumerThread =
30          new Thread( new ThreadStart( consumer.Consume ) );
31       consumerThread.Name = "Consumer";
32
33       // start each thread
34       producerThread.Start();
35       consumerThread.Start();
36     } // end Main
37   } // end class UnsynchronizedBufferTest
```

Fig. 15.8 | Producer and consumer threads accessing a shared object without synchronization. (Part I of 2.)

```
Consumer reads -1
Producer writes 1
Consumer reads 1
Producer writes 2
Consumer reads 2
Consumer reads 2
Producer writes 3
Consumer reads 3
Consumer reads 3
Producer writes 4
Consumer reads 4
Producer writes 5
Consumer reads 5
Consumer reads 5
Producer writes 6
Consumer reads 6
Consumer read values totaling: 30.
Terminating Consumer.
Producer writes 7
Producer writes 8
Producer writes 9
Producer writes 10
Producer done producing.
Terminating Producer.
```

```
Producer writes 1
Producer writes 2
Consumer reads 2
Consumer reads 2
Producer writes 3
Producer writes 4
Consumer reads 4
Consumer reads 4
Producer writes 5
Consumer reads 5
Producer writes 6
Consumer reads 6
Producer writes 7
Consumer reads 7
Producer writes 8
Consumer reads 8
Producer writes 9
Producer writes 10
Producer done producing.
Terminating Producer.
Consumer reads 10
Consumer reads 10
Consumer read values totaling: 58.
Terminating Consumer.
```

Fig. 15.8 | Producer and consumer threads accessing a shared object without synchronization. (Part 2 of 2.)

Fig. 15.8, we see that the consumer retrieved a value (–1) before the producer ever placed a value in the shared buffer and that the values 2, 3 and 5 were consumed twice each. The consumer finished executing before the producer had an opportunity to produce the values 7, 8, 9 and 10. Therefore, those four values were lost, and an incorrect sum resulted. In the second output, we see that the value 1 was lost, because the values 1 and 2 were produced before the consumer thread could read the value 1. The values 3 and 9 were also lost and the values 4 and 10 were consumed twice each, also resulting in an incorrect sum. This example clearly demonstrates that access to shared data by concurrent threads must be controlled carefully; otherwise, a program may produce incorrect results.

To solve the problems of lost data and data consumed more than once in the previous example, we will (in Figs. 15.9 and 15.10) synchronize the access of the concurrent producer and consumer threads to the code that manipulates the shared data by using Monitor class methods Enter, Wait, Pulse and Exit. When a thread uses synchronization to access a shared object, the object is *locked*, so no other thread can acquire the lock for that shared object at the same time.

15.7 Producer/Consumer Relationship with Thread Synchronization

Figures 15.9 and 15.10 demonstrate a producer and a consumer accessing a shared cell of memory with synchronization, so that the consumer consumes only after the producer produces a value and the producer produces a new value only after the consumer consumes the previous value produced. This examples reuses interface Buffer (Fig. 15.4) and classes Producer (Fig. 15.5) and Consumer (Fig. 15.6) from the previous example. [*Note:* In this example, we demonstrate synchronization with class Monitor's Enter and Exit methods. In the next example, we demonstrate the same concepts via a lock block.]

Class SynchronizedBuffer (Figure 15.9) implements interface Buffer and contains two instance variables—buffer (line 10) and occupiedBufferCount (line 13). Also, property Buffer's get (lines 18–61) and set (lines 62–93) accessors now use methods of class Monitor to synchronize access to instance variable buffer. Thus, each object of class SynchronizedBuffer has a SyncBlock to maintain synchronization. Instance variable occupiedBufferCount is known as a condition variable—property Buffer's accessors use this int in conditions to determine whether it is the producer's or the consumer's turn to perform a task. If occupiedBufferCount is 0, property Buffer's set accessor can place a value into variable buffer, because the variable currently does not contain information—but this means that property Buffer's get accessor cannot read the value of buffer. If occupiedBufferCount is 1, the Buffer property's get accessor can read a value from variable buffer, because the variable does contain information, but property Buffer's set accessor cannot place a value into buffer.

```
1  // Fig. 15.9: SynchronizedBuffer.cs
2  // A synchronized shared buffer implementation.
3  using System;
4  using System.Threading;
5
```

Fig. 15.9 | SynchronizedBuffer synchronizes access to a shared integer. (Part 1 of 3.)

```
 6     // this class represents a single shared int
 7     public class SynchronizedBuffer : Buffer
 8     {
 9         // buffer shared by producer and consumer threads
10         private int buffer = -1;
11
12         // occupiedBufferCount maintains count of occupied buffers
13         private int occupiedBufferCount = 0;
14
15         // property Buffer
16         public int Buffer
17         {
18             get
19             {
20                 // obtain lock on this object
21                 Monitor.Enter( this );
22
23                 // if there is no data to read, place invoking
24                 // thread in WaitSleepJoin state
25                 if ( occupiedBufferCount == 0 )
26                 {
27                     Console.WriteLine(
28                         Thread.CurrentThread.Name + " tries to read." );
29                     DisplayState( "Buffer empty. " +
30                         Thread.CurrentThread.Name + " waits." );
31                     Monitor.Wait( this ); // enter WaitSleepJoin state
32                 } // end if
33
34                 // indicate that producer can store another value
35                 // because consumer is about to retrieve a buffer value
36                 --occupiedBufferCount;
37
38                 DisplayState( Thread.CurrentThread.Name + " reads " + buffer );
39
40                 // tell waiting thread (if there is one) to
41                 // become ready to execute (Running state)
42                 Monitor.Pulse( this );
43
44                 // Get copy of buffer before releasing lock.
45                 // It is possible that the producer could be
46                 // assigned the processor immediately after the
47                 // monitor is released and before the return
48                 // statement executes. In this case, the producer
49                 // would assign a new value to buffer before the
50                 // return statement returns the value to the
51                 // consumer. Thus, the consumer would receive the
52                 // new value. Making a copy of buffer and
53                 // returning the copy ensures that the
54                 // consumer receives the proper value.
55                 int bufferCopy = buffer;
56
57                 // release lock on this object
58                 Monitor.Exit( this );
```

Fig. 15.9 | SynchronizedBuffer synchronizes access to a shared integer. (Part 2 of 3.)

```
59
60              return bufferCopy;
61          } // end get
62      set
63      {
64          // acquire lock for this object
65          Monitor.Enter( this );
66
67          // if there are no empty locations, place invoking
68          // thread in WaitSleepJoin state
69          if ( occupiedBufferCount == 1 )
70          {
71              Console.WriteLine(
72                  Thread.CurrentThread.Name + " tries to write." );
73              DisplayState( "Buffer full. " +
74                  Thread.CurrentThread.Name + " waits." );
75              Monitor.Wait( this ); // enter WaitSleepJoin state
76          } // end if
77
78          // set new buffer value
79          buffer = value;
80
81          // indicate consumer can retrieve another value
82          // because producer has just stored a buffer value
83          ++occupiedBufferCount;
84
85          DisplayState( Thread.CurrentThread.Name + " writes " + buffer );
86
87          // tell waiting thread (if there is one) to
88          // become ready to execute (Running state)
89          Monitor.Pulse( this );
90
91          // release lock on this object
92          Monitor.Exit( this );
93      } // end set
94  } // end property Buffer
95
96  // display current operation and buffer state
97  public void DisplayState( string operation )
98  {
99      Console.WriteLine( "{0,-35}{1,-9}{2}\n",
100         operation, buffer, occupiedBufferCount );
101 } // end method DisplayState
102 } // end class SynchronizedBuffer
```

Fig. 15.9 | SynchronizedBuffer synchronizes access to a shared integer. (Part 3 of 3.)

As in the previous example, the producer thread performs the tasks specified in the producer object's Produce method. When line 28 of Fig. 15.5 sets the value of shared-Location's property Buffer, the producer thread invokes the set accessor at lines 62–93 of Fig. 15.9. Line 65 invokes Monitor method Enter with the argument this to acquire the lock on the SynchronizedBuffer object. The if statement (lines 69–76) determines whether occupiedBufferCount is 1. If this condition is true, lines 71–72 output a message indicating that the producer thread is trying to write a value, and lines 73–74 invoke method DisplayState (lines 97–101) to output another message indicating that the buffer is full and that the producer thread waits. Line 75 invokes Monitor method Wait with the argument this to place the calling thread (i.e., the producer) in the *WaitSleepJoin* state for the SynchronizedBuffer object. This also *releases the lock* on the Synchro-nizedBuffer object. The *WaitSleepJoin* state for an object is maintained by that object's SyncBlock. Now another thread can invoke an accessor method of the Synchronized-Buffer object's Buffer property.

The producer thread remains in the *WaitSleepJoin* state until the thread is notified by the consumer's call to Monitor method Pulse that it may proceed—at which point the thread returns to the *Running* state and waits for the system to assign a processor to the thread. When the thread returns to the *Running* state, the thread implicitly reacquires the lock on the SynchronizedBuffer object, and the set accessor continues executing with the next statement after Wait. Line 79 assigns value to buffer. Line 83 increments the occupiedBufferCount to indicate that the shared buffer now contains a value (i.e., a con-sumer can read the value, and a producer cannot yet put another value there). Line 85 invokes method DisplayState to output a line to the console window indicating that the producer is writing a new value into the buffer. Line 89 invokes Monitor method Pulse with the SynchronizedBuffer object (this) as an argument. If there are any waiting threads in that object's SyncBlock, the first waiting thread enters the *Running* state, indi-cating that the thread can now attempt its task again (as soon as the thread is assigned a processor). The Pulse method returns immediately. Line 92 invokes Monitor method Exit to release the lock on the SynchronizedBuffer object, and the set accessor returns to its caller (i.e., the Produce method of the Producer).

Common Programming Error 15.4

Forgetting to release the lock on an object when that lock is no longer needed is a logic error. This will prevent the threads in your program from acquiring the lock to proceed with their tasks. These threads will be forced to wait (unnecessarily, because the lock is no longer needed). Such waiting can lead to deadlock and indefinite postponement.

The get and set accessors are implemented similarly. As in the previous example, the consumer thread performs the tasks specified in the consumer object's Consume method. The consumer thread gets the value of the SynchronizedBuffer object's Buffer property (line 30 of Fig. 15.6) by invoking the get accessor at lines 18–61 of Fig. 15.9. Line 21 invokes Monitor method Enter to acquire the lock on the SynchronizedBuffer object.

The if statement at lines 25–32 determines whether occupiedBufferCount is 0. If this condition is true, lines 27–28 output a message indicating that the consumer thread is trying to read a value, and lines 29–30 invoke method DisplayState to output another message indicating that the buffer is empty and that the consumer thread waits. Line 31 invokes Monitor method Wait with the argument this to place the calling thread (i.e., the consumer) in the *WaitSleepJoin* state for the SynchronizedBuffer object and releases the lock on the object. Now another thread can invoke an accessor method of the Synchro-nizedBuffer object's Buffer property.

The consumer thread object remains in the *WaitSleepJoin* state until the thread is noti-fied by the producer's call to Monitor method Pulse that it may proceed—at which point the thread returns to the *Running* state and waits for the system to assign a processor to the thread. When the thread re-enters the *Running* state, the thread implicitly reacquires the lock on the SynchronizedBuffer object, and the get accessor continues executing with the next statement after Wait. Line 36 decrements occupiedBufferCount to indicate that the shared buffer is now empty (i.e., a consumer cannot read the value, but a producer can place another value in the shared buffer), line 38 outputs a line to the console window indicating the value the consumer is reading and line 42 invokes Monitor method Pulse with the SynchronizedBuffer object as an argument. If there are any waiting threads in that object's SyncBlock, the first waiting thread enters the *Running* state, indicating that the thread can now attempt its task again (as soon as the thread is assigned a processor). The Pulse method returns immediately. Line 55 gets a copy of buffer before releasing the lock. This is necessary because it is possible that the producer could be assigned the processor immediately after the lock is released (line 58) and before the return statement executes (line 60). In this case, the producer would assign a new value to buffer before the return statement returns the value to the consumer and the consumer receives the new value. Making a copy of buffer and returning the copy ensures that the consumer receives the proper value. Line 58 invokes Monitor method Exit to release the lock on the SynchronizedBuffer object, and the get accessor returns bufferCopy to its caller.

Class SynchronizedBufferTest (Fig. 15.10) is nearly identical to class UnsynchronizedBufferTest (Fig. 15.8). SynchronizedBufferTest's Main method declares shared as an object of class SynchronizedBuffer (line 14) and also displays header information for the output (lines 20–22).

```
1   // Fig. 15.10: SynchronizedBufferTest.cs
2   // Showing multiple threads modifying a shared object with
3   // synchronization.
4   using System;
5   using System.Threading;
6
7   // this class creates producer and consumer threads
8   class SynchronizedBufferTest
9   {
10      // create producer and consumer threads and start them
11      static void Main( string[] args )
12      {
13         // create shared object used by threads
14         SynchronizedBuffer shared = new SynchronizedBuffer();
15
16         // Random object used by each thread
17         Random random = new Random();
18
19         // output column heads and initial buffer state
20         Console.WriteLine( "{0,-35}{1,-9}{2}\n",
21            "Operation", "Buffer", "Occupied Count" );
22         shared.DisplayState( "Initial state" );
23
24         // create Producer and Consumer objects
25         Producer producer = new Producer( shared, random );
```

Fig. 15.10 | Producer and consumer threads accessing a shared object with synchronization. (Part 1 of 4.)

```
26          Consumer consumer = new Consumer( shared, random );
27
28          // create threads for producer and consumer and set
29          // delegates for each thread
30          Thread producerThread =
31              new Thread( new ThreadStart( producer.Produce ) );
32          producerThread.Name = "Producer";
33
34          Thread consumerThread =
35              new Thread( new ThreadStart( consumer.Consume ) );
36          consumerThread.Name = "Consumer";
37
38          // start each thread
39          producerThread.Start();
40          consumerThread.Start();
41      } // end Main
42  } // end class SynchronizedBufferTest
```

Operation	Buffer	Occupied Count
Initial state	-1	0
Producer writes 1	1	1
Consumer reads 1	1	0
Consumer tries to read. Buffer empty. Consumer waits.	1	0
Producer writes 2	2	1
Consumer reads 2	2	0
Producer writes 3	3	1
Producer tries to write. Buffer full. Producer waits.	3	1
Consumer reads 3	3	0
Producer writes 4	4	1
Consumer reads 4	4	0
Consumer tries to read. Buffer empty. Consumer waits.	4	0
Producer writes 5	5	1
Consumer reads 5	5	0
Producer writes 6	6	1

(continued...)

Fig. 15.10 | Producer and consumer threads accessing a shared object with synchronization. (Part 2 of 4.)

Consumer reads 6	6	0
Producer writes 7	7	1
Consumer reads 7	7	0
Producer writes 8	8	1
Producer tries to write. Buffer full. Producer waits.	8	1
Consumer reads 8	8	0
Producer writes 9	9	1
Consumer reads 9	9	0
Consumer tries to read. Buffer empty. Consumer waits.	9	0
Producer writes 10	10	1
Producer done producing. Terminating Producer. Consumer reads 10	10	0
Consumer read values totaling: 55. Terminating Consumer.		

Operation	Buffer	Occupied Count
Initial state	-1	0
Consumer tries to read. Buffer empty. Consumer waits.	-1	0
Producer writes 1	1	1
Consumer reads 1	1	0
Consumer tries to read. Buffer empty. Consumer waits.	1	0
Producer writes 2	2	1
Consumer reads 2	2	0
Producer writes 3	3	1
Consumer reads 3	3	0

(continued...)

Fig. 15.10 | Producer and consumer threads accessing a shared object with synchronization. (Part 3 of 4.)

Producer writes 4	4	1
Producer tries to write. Buffer full. Producer waits.	4	1
Consumer reads 4	4	0
Producer writes 5	5	1
Producer tries to write. Buffer full. Producer waits.	5	1
Consumer reads 5	5	0
Producer writes 6	6	1
Consumer reads 6	6	0
Producer writes 7	7	1
Consumer reads 7	7	0
Producer writes 8	8	1
Consumer reads 8	8	0
Consumer tries to read. Buffer empty. Consumer waits.	8	0
Producer writes 9	9	1
Consumer reads 9	9	0
Consumer tries to read. Buffer empty. Consumer waits.	9	0
Producer writes 10	10	1
Consumer reads 10	10	0
Producer done producing. Terminating Producer. Consumer read values totaling: 55. Terminating Consumer.		

Fig. 15.10 | Producer and consumer threads accessing a shared object with synchronization. (Part 4 of 4.)

Study the two sample outputs in Fig. 15.10. Observe that every integer produced is consumed exactly once—no values are lost and no values are consumed more than once. This occurs because the producer and consumer cannot perform tasks unless it is "their turn." The producer must go first; the consumer must wait if the producer has not produced since the consumer last consumed; and the producer must wait if the consumer has not yet consumed the value the producer most recently produced. Execute this program

```
Producer writes 10 (buffers occupied: 2)
buffers:   10    8    9
         ---- ---- ----
               W    R
Producer done producing.
Terminating Producer.

Consumer reads 9 (buffers occupied: 1)
buffers:   10    8    9
         ---- ---- ----
           R    W
Consumer reads 10 (buffers occupied: 0)
buffers:   10    8    9
         ---- ---- ----
              WR
Consumer read values totaling: 55.
Terminating Consumer.
```

Fig. 15.12 | Producer and consumer threads accessing a circular buffer. (Part 4 of 4.)

15.9 Multithreading with GUIs

The nature of multithreaded programming prevents you from knowing exactly when a thread will execute. Windows form components are not *thread safe*—if multiple threads manipulate a Windows GUI component, the results may not be correct. To ensure that threads manipulate GUI components in a thread-safe manner, all interactions with GUI components should be performed by the *User Interface thread* (also known as the *UI thread*)—the thread that creates and maintains the GUI. Class Control provides method *Invoke* to help with this process. Method Invoke specifies GUI processing statements that the UI thread should execute. The method receives as its arguments a delegate representing a method that will modify the GUI and an optional array of objects representing the parameters to the method. At some point after Invoke is called, the UI thread will execute the method represented by the delegate, passing the contents of the object array as the method's arguments.

Our next example (Figs. 15.13 and 15.14) uses separate threads to modify the content displayed in a Windows GUI. This example also demonstrates how to use thread synchronization to *suspend* a thread (i.e., temporarily prevent it from executing) and to *resume* a suspended thread. The GUI for the application contains three Labels and three Check-Boxes. Each thread in the program displays random characters in a particular Label. The user can temporarily suspend a thread by clicking the appropriate CheckBox and can resume the thread's execution by clicking the same CheckBox again.

Class RandomLetters (Fig. 15.13) contains method GenerateRandomCharacters (lines 33–58), which takes no arguments and returns void. Line 36 uses static Thread property currentThread to determine the currently executing thread, then uses the thread's Name property to get the thread's name. Each executing thread is assigned a name that includes the number of the thread in the Main method (see the output of Fig. 15.14). Lines 38–57 are an infinite loop. [*Note:* In earlier chapters, we have said that infinite loops are bad programming because the application will not terminate. In this case, the infinite loop is in a separate thread from the main thread. When the application window is closed in this example, all the threads created by the main thread are closed as well, including threads (such as this one) that are executing infinite loops.] In each iteration of the loop, the thread sleeps for a random interval from 0 to 1 second (line 41).

When the thread awakens, line 43 locks this RandomLetters object, so we can determine whether the thread has been suspended (i.e., the user clicked the corresponding CheckBox). Lines 45–48 loop while the bool variable suspended remains true. Line 47 calls Monitor method Wait on this RandomLetters object to temporarily release the lock and place this thread into the *WaitSleepJoin* state. When this thread is Pulsed (i.e., the user clicks the corresponding CheckBox again), it moves back to the *Running* state. If suspended is false, the thread resumes execution. If suspended is still true, the loop executes again and the thread re-enters the *WaitSleepJoin* state.

```csharp
1   // Fig. 15.13: RandomLetters.cs
2   // Writes a random letter to a label
3   using System;
4   using System.Windows.Forms;
5   using System.Drawing;
6   using System.Threading;
7
8   public class RandomLetters
9   {
10      private static Random generator = new Random(); // for random letters
11      private bool suspended = false; // true if thread is suspended
12      private Label output; // Label to display  output
13      private string threadName; // name of the current thread
14
15      // RandomLetters constructor
16      public RandomLetters( Label label )
17      {
18         output = label;
19      } // end RandomLetters constructor
20
21      // delegate that allows method DisplayCharacter to be called
22      // in the thread that creates and maintains the GUI
23      private delegate void DisplayDelegate( char displayChar );
24
25      // method DisplayCharacter sets the Label's Text property
26      private void DisplayCharacter( char displayChar )
27      {
28         // output character in Label
29         output.Text = threadName + ": " + displayChar;
30      } // end method DisplayCharacter
31
32      // place random characters in GUI
33      public void GenerateRandomCharacters()
34      {
35         // get name of executing thread
36         threadName = Thread.CurrentThread.Name;
37
```

Fig. 15.13 | Class RandomLetters outputs random letters and can be suspended. (Part 1 of 2.)

```
38            while ( true ) // infinite loop; will be terminated from outside
39            {
40               // sleep for up to 1 second
41               Thread.Sleep( generator.Next( 1001 ) );
42
43               lock ( this ) // obtain lock
44               {
45                  while ( suspended ) // loop until not suspended
46                  {
47                     Monitor.Wait( this ); // suspend thread execution
48                  } // end while
49               } // end lock
50
51               // select random uppercase letter
52               char displayChar = ( char ) ( generator.Next( 26 ) + 65 );
53
54               // display character on corresponding Label
55               output.Invoke( new DisplayDelegate( DisplayCharacter ),
56                  new object[] { displayChar } );
57            } // end while
58         } // end method GenerateRandomCharacters
59
60         // change the suspended/running state
61         public void Toggle()
62         {
63            suspended = !suspended; // toggle bool controlling state
64
65            // change label color on suspend/resume
66            output.BackColor = suspended ? Color.Red : Color.LightGreen;
67
68            lock ( this ) // obtain lock
69            {
70               if ( !suspended ) // if thread resumed
71                  Monitor.Pulse( this );
72            } // end lock
73         } // end method Toggle
74      } // end class RandomLetters
```

Fig. 15.13 | Class `RandomLetters` outputs random letters and can be suspended. (Part 2 of 2.)

Line 52 generates a random uppercase character. Lines 55–56 call method `Invoke`, passing to it a new `DisplayDelegate` containing method `DisplayCharacter` and a new array of `object`s that contains the randomly generated letter. Line 23 declares a delegate type named `DisplayDelegate`, which represents methods that take a char argument and do not return a value. Method `DisplayCharacter` (lines 26–30) meets those requirements—it receives a char parameter named `displayChar` and does not return a value. The call to `Invoke` in lines 55–56 will cause the UI thread to call `DisplayCharacter` with the randomly generated letter as the argument. At that time, line 29 will replace the text in the Label associated with this `RandomLetters` object with the name of the `Thread` executing this `RandomLetters` object's `GenerateRandomCharacters` method and the randomly generated letter.

When the user clicks the CheckBox to the right of a particular Label, the corresponding thread should be suspended (temporarily prevented from executing) or resumed (allowed to continue executing). Suspending and resuming a thread can be implemented by using thread synchronization and Monitor methods Wait and Pulse. Lines 61–73 declare method Toggle, which will change the suspended/resumed state of the current thread. Line 63 reverses the value of bool variable suspended. Line 66 changes the background color of the Label by assigning a color to Label property BackColor. If the thread is suspended, the background color will be Color.Red. If the thread is running, the background color will be Color.LightGreen. Method Toggle is called from the event handler in Fig. 15.14, so its tasks will be performed in the UI thread—thus, there is no need to use Invoke for line 66. Line 68 locks this RandomLetters object, so we can determine whether the thread should resume execution. If so, line 71 calls method Pulse on this RandomLetters object to alert the thread that was placed in the *WaitSleepJoin* state by the Wait method call in line 47.

Note that the if statement in line 70 does not have an associated else. If this condition fails, it means that the thread has just been suspended. When this happens, a thread executing at line 45 will enter the while loop, and line 47 will suspend the thread with a call to method Wait.

Class GUIThreads (Fig. 15.14) displays three Labels and three CheckBoxes. A separate thread of execution is associated with each Label and CheckBox pair. Each thread randomly displays letters from the alphabet in its corresponding Label object. Lines 21, 28 and 35 create three new RandomLetters objects. Lines 22–23, 29–30 and 36–37 create three new Threads that will execute the RandomLetters objects' GenerateRandomCharacters methods. Lines 24, 31 and 38 assign each Thread a name, and lines 25, 32 and 39 Start the Threads.

```
1   // Fig. 15.14: GUIThreads.cs
2   // Demonstrates using threads in a GUI
3   using System;
4   using System.Windows.Forms;
5   using System.Threading;
6
7   public partial class GUIThreadsForm : Form
8   {
9      public GUIThreadsForm()
10     {
11        InitializeComponent();
12     } // end constructor
13
14     private RandomLetters letter1; // first RandomLetters object
15     private RandomLetters letter2; // second RandomLetters object
16     private RandomLetters letter3; // third RandomLetters object
17
18     private void GUIThreadsForm_Load( object sender, EventArgs e )
19     {
20        // create first thread
21        letter1 = new RandomLetters( thread1Label );
```

Fig. 15.14 | GUIThreads demonstrates multithreading in a GUI application. (Part 1 of 2.)

```
22          Thread firstThread = new Thread(
23             new ThreadStart( letter1.GenerateRandomCharacters ) );
24          firstThread.Name = "Thread 1";
25          firstThread.Start();
26
27          // create second thread
28          letter2 = new RandomLetters( thread2Label );
29          Thread secondThread = new Thread(
30             new ThreadStart( letter2.GenerateRandomCharacters ) );
31          secondThread.Name = "Thread 2";
32          secondThread.Start();
33
34          // create third thread
35          letter3 = new RandomLetters( thread3Label );
36          Thread thirdThread = new Thread(
37             new ThreadStart( letter3.GenerateRandomCharacters ) );
38          thirdThread.Name = "Thread 3";
39          thirdThread.Start();
40       } // end method GUIThreadsForm_Load
41
42       // close all threads associated with this application
43       private void GUIThreadsForm_FormClosing( object sender,
44          FormClosingEventArgs e )
45       {
46          System.Environment.Exit( System.Environment.ExitCode );
47       } // end method GUIThreadsForm_FormClosing
48
49       // suspend or resume the corresponding thread
50       private void threadCheckBox_CheckedChanged( object sender,
51          EventArgs e )
52       {
53          if ( sender == thread1CheckBox )
54             letter1.Toggle();
55          else if ( sender == thread2CheckBox )
56             letter2.Toggle();
57          else if ( sender == thread3CheckBox )
58             letter3.Toggle();
59       } // end method threadCheckBox_CheckedChanged
60    } // end class GUIThreadsForm
```

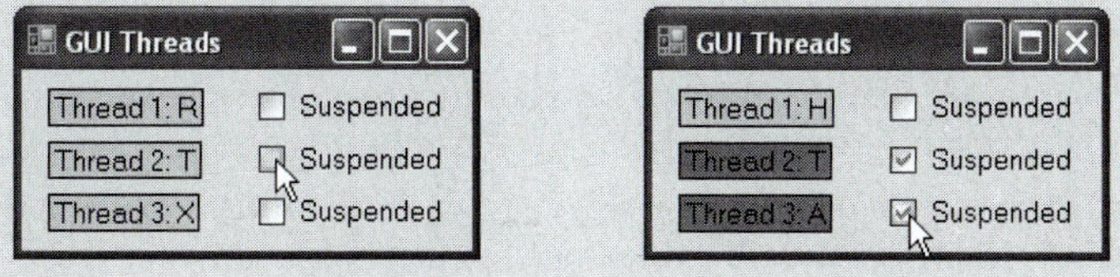

Fig. 15.14 | GUIThreads demonstrates multithreading in a GUI application. (Part 2 of 2.)

If the user clicks the **Suspended** CheckBox next to a particular Label, event handler threadCheckBox_CheckedChanged (lines 50–59) determines which CheckBox generated the event and calls its associated RandomLetters object's Toggle method to suspend or resume the thread.

Lines 43–47 define the GUIThreadsForm_FormClosing event handler, which calls method Exit of class System.Environment with the ExitCode property as as argument. This causes all other threads in this application to terminate. Otherwise, only the UI thread would be terminated when the user closes this application; Thread1, Thread2 and Thread3 would continue executing forever.

15.10 Wrap-Up

In this chapter, you learned basic capabilities of the .NET framework that enable you to specify concurrent tasks in your programs. We discussed how to create threads of execution using class Thread and ThreadStart delegates—both from the System.Threading namespace.

We discussed several applications of concurrent programming. In particular, you learned about problems that may occur when multiple threads share the same data. We demonstrated how to synchronize threads using the capabilities of class Monitor to ensure that data is accessed an manipulated properly by multiple threads. We also showed how to implement shared data as a circular buffer to enable threads to operate more efficiently.

Next, you learned that GUI components are not thread safe, so all changes to GUI components should be performed in the user interface thread that creates and maintains the GUI. We showed how to use Control method Invoke and a delegate to allow a thread to specify tasks that the user interface thread should perform on GUI components. This enabled multiple threads to modify GUI components in a thread-safe manner. In the next chapter, you will learn about the .NET framework's string, character and regular expression processing capabilities.

Summary

Section 15.1 Introduction

- Computers perform operations concurrently. It is common for your computer to compile a program, send a file to a printer and receive electronic mail messages over a network concurrently.
- Historically, the type of concurrency that computers perform today generally has been implemented as operating system "primitives" available only to experienced "systems programmers."
- The Ada programming language, developed by the United States Department of Defense, made concurrency primitives widely available.
- The .NET Framework Class Library provides concurrency primitives in the System.Threading namespace.
- Each thread designates a portion of a program that may execute concurrently with other threads—this capability is called multithreading.
- An example of multithreading is the CLR's a garbage-collector thread which reclaims dynamically allocated memory that is no longer needed.

Section 15.2 Thread States: Life Cycle of a Thread

- At any time, a thread is said to be in one of several thread states.
- A Thread object begins its life cycle in the *Unstarted* state when the program creates the object and passes a ThreadStart delegate to the object's constructor.

- A `ThreadStart` delegate, which specifies the actions the thread will perform during its life cycle, must be initialized with a method that returns `void` and takes no arguments.

- A thread remains in the *Unstarted* state until the program calls the `Thread`'s `Start` method, which places the thread in the *Running* state and immediately returns control to the part of the program that called `Start`.

- While in the *Running* state, a thread may not actually be executing all the time. The thread executes in the *Running* state only when the operating system assigns a processor to the thread.

- When a *Running* thread receives a processor for the first time, the thread begins executing the method specified by its `ThreadStart` delegate.

- A *Running* thread enters the *Stopped* (or *Aborted*) state when its `ThreadStart` delegate terminates, which normally indicates that the thread has completed its task.

- A program can force a thread into the *Stopped* state by calling `Thread` method `Abort` on the appropriate `Thread` object. Method `Abort` throws a `ThreadAbortException` in the thread, normally causing the thread to terminate.

- When a thread is in the *Stopped* state and there are no references to the thread object, the garbage collector can remove the thread object from memory.

- A thread is considered to be *Blocked* if it is unable to use a processor even if one is available.

- If a thread encounters code that it cannot execute yet, the thread can call `Monitor` method `Wait` to enter the *WaitSleepJoin* state. Once in this state, a thread returns to the *Running* state when another thread invokes `Monitor` method `Pulse` or `PulseAll`. Method `Pulse` moves the next waiting thread back to the *Running* state; `PulseAll` moves all waiting threads back.

- A *Running* thread can call `Thread` method `Sleep` to enter the *WaitSleepJoin* state for a specified period of milliseconds. The thread returns to the *Running* state when its sleep time expires.

- Any thread that enters the *WaitSleepJoin* state also returns to the *Running* state if the `Thread`'s `Interrupt` method is called by another thread in the program. This causes a `ThreadInterruption-Exception` to be thrown in the interrupted thread.

- If a thread cannot continue executing (we will call this the dependent thread) unless another thread terminates, the dependent thread calls the other thread's `Join` method to "join" the two threads. The dependent thread leaves the *WaitSleepJoin* state and re-enters the *Running* state when the other thread finishes execution (enters the *Stopped* state).

- If a *Running* `Thread`'s `Suspend` method is called, the *Running* thread enters the *Suspended* state. A *Suspended* thread returns to the *Running* state when another thread in the program invokes the *Suspended* thread's `Resume` method. Methods `Suspend` and `Resume` are now deprecated.

- If a thread's `IsBackground` property is set to `true`, the thread resides in the *Background* state. A thread can reside in the *Background* state and any other state simultaneously.

- A process must wait for all foreground threads to enter the *Stopped* state before the process can terminate. If the only threads remaining in a process are *Background threads*, the CLR terminates those threads by invoking their `Abort` methods, and the process terminates.

Section 15.3 Thread Priorities and Thread Scheduling

- Every thread has a priority in the range between `ThreadPriority.Lowest` to `ThreadPriority.Highest`. These values come from the `ThreadPriority` enumeration (namespace `System.Threading`), which consists of the values `Lowest`, `BelowNormal`, `Normal`, `AboveNormal` and `Highest`. By default, each thread has priority `Normal`.

- The Windows operating system supports a concept, called timeslicing, that enables threads of equal priority to share a processor.

- Without timeslicing, each thread in a set of equal-priority threads runs to completion (unless the thread leaves the *Running* state and enters the *WaitSleepJoin*, *Suspended* or *Blocked* state) before the thread's peers get a chance to execute.

- With timeslicing, each thread receives a brief burst of processor time, called a quantum, during which the thread can execute. At the completion of the quantum, the processor is taken away from that thread and given to the next thread of equal priority, if one is available.

- The job of the thread scheduler is to keep the highest-priority thread running at all times and, if there is more than one highest-priority thread, to ensure that all such threads execute for a quantum in round-robin fashion.

- A thread's priority can be adjusted with the `Priority` property, which accepts values from the `ThreadPriority` enumeration. If the value specified is not one of the valid thread-priority constants, an `ArgumentException` occurs.

- A thread executes until it dies, becomes *Blocked*, calls `Sleep`, calls `Monitor` method `Wait` or `Join`, is preempted by a thread of higher priority or has its quantum expire.

- A thread with a higher priority than the *Running* thread can preempt the *Running* thread.

Section 15.4 Creating and Executing Threads

- Class `Thread`'s `static` property `CurrentThread` returns the currently executing thread.

- `Thread` property `Name` specifies the name of the thread.

- `Thread`'s `static` method `Sleep` places a thread into the *WaitSleepJoin* state for a specified number of milliseconds. At this point, the thread loses the processor, and the system allows another thread to execute if one is ready to run. When the thread awakens, it re-enters the *Running* state and waits for the thread scheduler to assign a processor to the thread.

- A `Thread` constructor receives as an argument a `ThreadStart` delegate that represents a method with no arguments and a `void` return type, and specifies the actions the thread will perform.

- `Thread` method `Start` places a thread in the *Running* state. Method `Start` returns immediately.

- When the system assigns a processor to a thread for the first time, the thread calls the method specified by the thread's `ThreadStart` delegate.

Section 15.5 Thread Synchronization and Class `Monitor`

- When multiple threads share data and that data is modified by one or more of those threads, then indeterminate results may occur. The problem can be solved by giving one thread at a time exclusive access to code that manipulates the shared data. During that time, other threads wishing to manipulate the data should be kept waiting. When the thread with exclusive access to the data completes its data manipulations, one of the waiting threads should be allowed to proceed. In this fashion, each thread accessing the shared data excludes all other threads from doing so simultaneously. This is called mutual exclusion or thread synchronization.

- Class `Monitor` provides the methods for locking objects to implement synchronized access to shared data. Locking an object means that only one thread can access that object at a time.

- When a thread wishes to acquire exclusive control over an object, the thread invokes `Monitor` method `Enter` to acquire the lock on that data object.

- Each object has a SyncBlock that maintains the state of that object's lock. Methods of class `Monitor` use the data in an object's SyncBlock to determine the state of the lock for that object.

- While an object is locked, all other threads attempting to acquire the lock on that object are blocked from acquiring the lock—such threads enter the *Blocked* state.

- When the thread that locked a shared object no longer requires the lock, that thread invokes `Monitor` method `Exit` to release the lock. This updates the SyncBlock of the shared object to indicate that the lock for the object is available again. If a thread was previously blocked from acquiring the lock on the shared object, that thread acquires the lock to begin its processing of the object.

• C# provides another means of manipulating an object's lock—keyword `lock`. Placing `lock` before a block of code obtains the lock on the object specified in parentheses after keyword `lock`. This is the same object that normally would be passed to class `Monitor`'s methods. When a `lock` block terminates for any reason, C# releases the lock on the object.

• If a thread that owns the lock on an object determines that it cannot continue with its task until some condition is satisfied, the thread should call `Monitor` method `Wait` and pass as an argument the object on which the thread will wait. This releases the lock the thread has on that object and places that thread into the *WaitSleepJoin* state for that object.

• A thread in the *WaitSleepJoin* state leaves that state when a separate thread invokes `Monitor` method `Pulse` or `PulseAll` with the object on which the thread is waiting as an argument. Method `Pulse` transitions the object's first waiting thread to the *Running* state; `PulseAll` transitions all the object's waiting threads to the *Running* state.

• There is a difference between threads waiting to acquire an object's lock and threads waiting in the *WaitSleepJoin* state. Threads that call `Monitor` method `Wait` with an object as an argument are placed in the *WaitSleepJoin* state. Threads that are simply waiting to acquire the object's lock enter the conceptual *Blocked* state and wait until that lock becomes available.

Section 15.6 Producer/Consumer Relationship without Thread Synchronization

• In a producer/consumer relationship, the producer portion of an application generates data, and the consumer portion of an application uses that data.

• In a multithreaded producer/consumer relationship, a producer thread calls a produce method to generate data and place it in a shared region of memory, called a buffer. A consumer thread calls a consume method to read that data. If the producer wishes to put the next data in the buffer but determines that the consumer has not yet read the previous data from the buffer, the producer thread should call `Wait`. Otherwise, the consumer would never see the previous data, which would be lost to that application. When the consumer thread reads the data, it should call `Pulse` to allow a waiting producer to proceed since there is now free space in the buffer. If a consumer thread finds the buffer empty or finds that the previous data has already been read, the consumer should call `Wait`. Otherwise, the consumer might read "garbage" from the buffer, or the consumer might process a previous data item more than once—each of these possibilities results in a logic error in the application. When the producer places the next data into the buffer, the producer should call `Pulse` to allow the consumer thread to proceed and read that data.

Section 15.8 Producer/Consumer Relationship: Circular Buffer

• If producer and consumer threads operate at different speeds, one will spend more (or most) of its time waiting. If the producer thread produces values faster than the consumer can consume those values, then the producer thread waits for the consumer, because there are no other locations in memory to place the next value. Similarly, if the consumer consumes faster than the producer can produce values, the consumer waits until the producer places the next value into the shared location in memory.

• Even when we have threads that operate at the same relative speeds, those threads over a period of time may become "out of sync," causing one of the threads to wait for the other. When threads wait, programs become less productive, user-interactive programs become less responsive and network applications suffer longer delays because the processor is not used efficiently.

• To minimize the waiting for threads that share resources and operate at the same relative speeds, we can implement a circular buffer that provides extra locations in which the producer can place values (if it "gets ahead" of the consumer) and from which the consumer can retrieve those values (if it "catches up" to the producer).

- A circular buffer would be inappropriate if the producer and consumer operate at different speeds. If the consumer always executes faster than the producer, then a buffer with one location is enough. Additional locations would waste memory. If the producer always executes faster, a buffer with an infinite number of locations would be required to absorb the extra production.

- The key to using a circular buffer is to define it with enough extra cells to handle the anticipated "extra" production.

Section 15.9 Multithreading with GUIs

- To ensure that threads manipulate GUI components in a thread-safe manner, all interactions with GUI components should be performed by the User Interface thread. Class `Control` provides method `Invoke` to help with this process. Method `Invoke` specifies GUI processing statements that the UI thread should execute. The method receives as its arguments a `delegate` representing a method that will modify the GUI and an optional array of `object`s representing the parameters to the method. At some point after `Invoke` is called, the UI thread will execute the method represented by the `delegate`, passing to the contents of the `object` array as the method's arguments.

- Suspending and resuming a thread can be implemented by using thread synchronization and `Monitor` methods `Wait` and `Pulse`.

Terminology

Abort method of class Thread
Aborted state
Abort Requested state
AboveNormal constant of the ThreadPriority
    enumeration
accessing shared data with synchronization
acquire the lock for an object
Background state
BelowNormal constant of the ThreadPriority
    enumeration
Blocked state
Blocked thread
buffer
circular buffer
concurrency
concurrent producer and consumer threads
concurrent programming
condition variable
consumer thread
CurrentThread property of class Thread
deadlock
Enter method of class Monitor
Exit method of class Monitor
foreground thread
garbage collection
garbage-collector thread
Highest constant of the ThreadPriority enu-
    meration

indefinite postponement
I/O completion
I/O request
I/O blocking
Interrupt method of class Thread
Invoke method of class Control
IsBackground method of class Thread
Join method of class Thread
life cycle of a thread
lock keyword
locking objects
Lowest constant of the ThreadPriority enu-
    meration
Monitor class
multilevel priority queue
multithreading
mutual exclusion
Name property of class Thread
Normal constant of the ThreadPriority enu-
    meration
Priority property of class Thread
priority scheduling
producer thread
producer/consumer relationship
Pulse method of class Monitor
PulseAll method of class Monitor
quantum
quantum expiration

release a lock	SyncBlock
resume a suspended thread	synchronized block of code
Resume method of class Thread	System.Threading namespace
Running state	Thread class
scheduling	thread of execution
shared buffer	thread safe
sleep interval expires	thread scheduler
Sleep method of class Thread	thread state
sleeping thread	ThreadAbortException
Start method of class Thread	ThreadPriority enumeration
starvation	ThreadStart delegate
Stopped state	timeslicing
suspend a thread	*Unstarted* state
Suspend method of class Thread	User Interface (UI) thread
Suspended state	Wait method of class Monitor
Suspended Requested state	*WaitSleepJoin* state

Self-Review Exercises

15.1 Fill in the blanks in each of the following statements:
a) Monitor methods _____ and _____ acquire and release the lock on an object.
b) Among a group of equal-priority threads, each thread receives a brief burst of time called a(n) _____, during which the thread has the processor and can perform its tasks.
c) C# provides a _____ thread that reclaims dynamically allocated memory.
d) Four reasons a thread that is alive is not in the *Running* state are _____, _____, _____ and _____.
e) A thread enters the _____ state when the method that controls the thread's life cycle terminates.
f) A thread's priority must be one of the ThreadPriority constants _____, _____, _____, _____ and _____.
g) To wait for a designated number of milliseconds then resume execution, a thread should call the _____ method of class Thread.
h) Method _____ of class Monitor transitions a thread from the *WaitSleepJoin* state to the *Running* state.
i) A(n) _____ block automatically acquires the lock on an object as the program control enters the block and releases the lock on that object when the block terminates.
j) Class Monitor provides methods that _____ access to shared data.

15.2 State whether each of the following is *true* or *false*. If *false*, explain why.
a) A thread cannot execute if it is in the *Stopped* state.
b) In C#, a higher-priority thread entering (or re-entering) the *Running* state will preempt threads of lower priority.
c) The code that a thread executes is defined in its Main method.
d) A thread in the *WaitSleepJoin* state always returns to the *Running* state when Monitor method Pulse is called.
e) Method Sleep of class Thread does not consume processor time while a thread sleeps.
f) A blocked thread can be placed in the *Running* state by Monitor method Pulse.
g) Class Monitor's Wait, Pulse and PulseAll methods can be used in any block of code.
h) The programmer must place a call to Monitor method Exit in a lock block to relinquish the lock.
i) When Monitor class method Wait is called within a locked block, the lock for that block is released and the thread that called Wait is placed in the *WaitSleepJoin* state.

Answers to Self-Review Exercises

15.1 a) Enter, Exit. b) timeslice or quantum. c) garbage collector. d) waiting, sleeping, suspended, blocked for input/output. e) *Stopped*. f) Lowest, BelowNormal, Normal, AboveNormal, Highest. g) Sleep. h) Pulse. i) lock. j) synchronize.

15.2 a) True. b) True. c) False. The code that a thread executes is defined in the method specified by the thread's ThreadStart delegate. d) False. A thread may be in the *WaitSleepJoin* state for several reasons. Calling Pulse moves a thread from the *WaitSleepJoin* state to the *Running* state only if the thread entered the *WaitSleepJoin* state as the result of a call to Monitor method Wait. e) True. f) False. A thread is blocked by the operating system and returns to the *Running* state when the operating system determines that the thread can continue executing (e.g., when an I/O request completes or when a lock the thread attempted to acquire becomes available). g) False. Class Monitor methods can be called only if the thread performing the call currently owns the lock on the object each method receives as an argument. h) False. A lock block implicitly relinquishes the lock when the thread completes execution of the lock block. i) True.

Exercises

15.3 *(Bouncing Ball)* Write a program that bounces a blue ball inside a Panel. The ball should begin moving with a MouseClick event. When the ball hits the edge of the Panel, it should bounce off the edge and continue in the opposite direction. The ball's position should be updated using a Thread and redrawn periodically using another Thread. Use float variables to maintain the ball's position, radius and velocity. Draw the ball using the FillEllipse method of class Graphics (see Fig. 13.38). Remember to terminate all Threads when the user closes the application.

15.4 *(Enhanced Bouncing Ball)* Modify the program in Exercise 15.3 to add a new ball each time the user clicks the mouse. Provide for a maximum of 10 balls. Use a separate Thread to control the movements of each ball, plus an additional Thread to periodically redraw all of the balls. Randomly choose the color and size for each new ball.

15.5 *(Bouncing Balls with Shadows)* Modify the program in Exercise 15.4 to add shadows. As a ball moves, draw a solid black oval at the bottom of the Panel. You may consider adding a 3-D effect by increasing or decreasing the size of the shadow depending upon the vertical position of the ball.

15.6 *(Bouncing Balls with Collision Detection)* Modify the program in Exercise 15.4 or Exercise 15.5 to bounce the balls off each other when they collide. A collision should occur between two balls when the distance between the centers of those two balls is less than the sum of the two balls' radii. When a collision between two balls occurs, use the following equations to modify each ball's velocity:

$$distance = \sqrt{(x1 - x2)^2 + (y1 - y2)^2}$$

$$overlap = (\,radius1 + radius2\,) - distance$$

$$xVelocity1 = xVelocity1 + (\,x1 - x2\,) * (\,overlap\,/\,distance\,) * 0.5$$

$$yVelocity1 = yVelocity1 + (\,y1 - y2\,) * (\,overlap\,/\,distance\,) * 0.5$$

$$xVelocity2 = xVelocity2 + (\,x2 - x1\,) * (\,overlap\,/\,distance\,) * 0.5$$

$$yVelocity2 = yVelocity2 + (\,y2 - y1\,) * (\,overlap\,/\,distance\,) * 0.5$$

[*Note:* Ensure that *distance* does not equal zero.]

Strings, Characters and Regular Expressions

The chief defect of Henry King
Was chewing little bits of string.
—Hilaire Belloc

Vigorous writing is concise. A sentence should contain no unnecessary words, a paragraph no unnecessary sentences.
—William Strunk, Jr.

I have made this letter longer than usual, because I lack the time to make it short.
—Blaise Pascal

The difference between the almost-right word & the right word is really a large matter—it's the difference between the lightning bug and the lightning.
—Mark Twain

Mum's the word.
—Miguel de Cervantes, *Don Quixote de la Mancha*

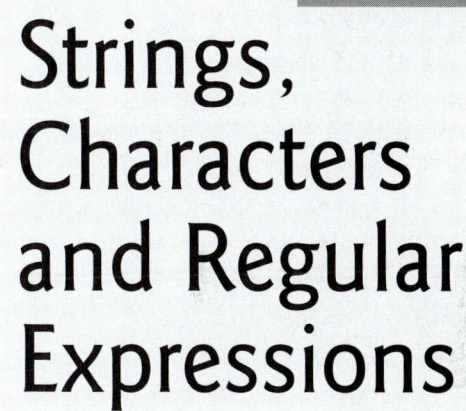

OBJECTIVES

In this chapter you will learn:

- To create and manipulate immutable character string objects of class **string**.

- To create and manipulate mutable character string objects of class **StringBuilder**.

- To manipulate character objects of struct **Char**.

- To use regular expressions in conjunction with classes **Regex** and **Match**.

16.1 Introduction

This chapter introduces the FCL's string- and character-processing capabilities, and demonstrates how to use regular expressions to search for patterns in text. The techniques presented in this chapter can be employed in text editors, word processors, page-layout software, computerized typesetting systems and other kinds of text-processing software. Previous chapters presented some basic string-processing capabilities. In this chapter, we discuss in detail the text-processing capabilities of class `string` and type `Char` from the `System` namespace and class `StringBuilder` from the `System.Text` namespace.

We begin with an overview of the fundamentals of characters and strings in which we discuss character constants and string literals. We then provide examples of class `string`'s many constructors and methods. The examples demonstrate how to determine the length of strings, copy strings, access individual characters in strings, search strings, obtain substrings from larger strings, compare strings, concatenate strings, replace characters in strings and convert strings to uppercase or lowercase letters.

Next, we introduce class `StringBuilder`, which is used to build strings dynamically. We demonstrate `StringBuilder` capabilities for determining and specifying the size of a `StringBuilder`, as well as appending, inserting, removing and replacing characters in a `StringBuilder` object. We then introduce the character-testing methods of struct `Char` that enable a program to determine whether a character is a digit, a letter, a lowercase letter, an uppercase letter, a punctuation mark or a symbol other than a punctuation mark. Such methods are useful for validating individual characters in user input. In addition, type Char provides methods for converting a character to uppercase or lowercase.

The chapter concludes with a discussion of regular expressions. We discuss classes Regex and Match from the System.Text.RegularExpressions namespace as well as the symbols that are used to form regular expressions. We then demonstrate how to find patterns in a string, match entire strings to patterns, replace characters in a string that match a pattern and split strings at delimiters specified as a pattern in a regular expression.

16.2 Fundamentals of Characters and Strings

Characters are the fundamental building blocks of C# source code. Every program is composed of characters that, when grouped together meaningfully, create a sequence that the compiler interprets as instructions describing how to accomplish a task. In addition to normal characters, a program also can contain *character constants*. A character constant is a character that is represented as an integer value, called a *character code*. For example, the integer value 122 corresponds to the character constant 'z'. The integer value 10 corresponds to the newline character '\n'. Character constants are established according to the *Unicode character set*, an international character set that contains many more symbols and letters than does the ASCII character set (listed in Appendix F). To learn more about Unicode, see Appendix E.

A string is a series of characters treated as a unit. These characters can be uppercase letters, lowercase letters, digits and various *special characters:* +, -, *, /, $ and others. A string is an object of class string in the System namespace.[1] We write *string literals*, also called *string constants*, as sequences of characters in double quotation marks, as follows:

```
"John Q. Doe"
"9999 Main Street"
"Waltham, Massachusetts"
"(201) 555-1212"
```

A declaration can assign a string literal to a string reference. The declaration

```
string color = "blue";
```

initializes string reference color to refer to the string literal object "blue".

Performance Tip 16.1

If there are multiple occurrences of the same string literal object in an application, a single copy of the string literal object will be referenced from each location in the program that uses that string literal. It is possible to share the object in this manner, because string literal objects are implicitly constant. Such sharing conserves memory.

On occasion, a string will contain multiple backslash characters (this often occurs in the name of a file). To avoid excessive backslash characters, it is possible to exclude escape sequences and interpret all the characters in a string literally, using the @ character. Back-

---

1. C# provides the string keyword as an alias for class String. In this book, we use the term string.

slashes within the double quotation marks following the @ character are not considered escape sequences, but rather regular backslash characters. Often this simplifies programming and makes the code easier to read. For example, consider the string "C:\MyFolder\MySubFolder\MyFile.txt" with the following assignment:

> *string* file = "C:\\MyFolder\\MySubFolder\\MyFile.txt";

Using the verbatim string syntax, the assignment can be altered to

> *string* file = @"C:\MyFolder\MySubFolder\MyFile.txt";

This approach also has the advantage of allowing strings to span multiple lines by preserving all newlines, spaces and tabs.

16.3 string Constructors

Class string provides eight constructors for initializing strings in various ways. Figure 16.1 demonstrates the use of three of the constructors.

```
1   // Fig. 16.1: StringConstructor.cs
2   // Demonstrating string class constructors.
3   using System;
4
5   class StringConstructor
6   {
7      public static void Main()
8      {
9         string originalString, string1, string2,
10           string3, string4;
11        char[] characterArray =
12           { 'b', 'i', 'r', 't', 'h', ' ', 'd', 'a', 'y' };
13
14        // string initialization
15        originalString = "Welcome to C# programming!";
16        string1 = originalString;
17        string2 = new string( characterArray );
18        string3 = new string( characterArray, 6, 3 );
19        string4 = new string( 'C', 5 );
20
21        Console.WriteLine( "string1 = " + "\"" + string1 + "\"\n" +
22           "string2 = " + "\"" + string2 + "\"\n" +
23           "string3 = " + "\"" + string3 + "\"\n" +
24           "string4 = " + "\"" + string4 + "\"\n" );
25     } // end method Main
26  } // end class StringConstructor
```

```
string1 = "Welcome to C# programming!"
string2 = "birth day"
string3 = "day"
string4 = "CCCCC"
```

Fig. 16.1 | string constructors.

Lines 9–10 declare the strings originalString, string1, string2, string3 and string4. Lines 11–12 allocate the char array characterArray, which contains nine characters. Line 15 assigns string literal "Welcome to C# programming!" to string reference originalString. Line 16 sets string1 to reference the same string literal.

Line 17 assigns to string2 a new string, using the string constructor that takes a character array as an argument. The new string contains a copy of the characters in array characterArray.

Software Engineering Observation 16.1

In most cases, it is not necessary to make a copy of an existing string. All strings are immutable—their character contents cannot be changed after they are created. Also, if there are one or more references to a string (or any object for that matter), the object cannot be reclaimed by the garbage collector.

Line 18 assigns to string3 a new string, using the string constructor that takes a char array and two int arguments. The second argument specifies the starting index position (the *offset*) from which characters in the array are to be copied. The third argument specifies the number of characters (the *count*) to be copied from the specified starting position in the array. The new string contains a copy of the specified characters in the array. If the specified offset or count indicates that the program should access an element outside the bounds of the character array, an ArgumentOutOfRangeException is thrown.

Line 19 assigns to string4 a new string, using the string constructor that takes as arguments a character and an int specifying the number of times to repeat that character in the string.

16.4 string Indexer, Length Property and CopyTo Method

The application in Fig. 16.2 presents the string indexer, which facilitates the retrieval of any character in the string, and the string property Length, which returns the length of the string. The string method CopyTo copies a specified number of characters from a string into a char array.

```csharp
// Fig. 16.2: StringMethods.cs
// Using the indexer, property Length and method CopyTo
// of class string.
using System;

class StringMethods
{
    public static void Main()
    {
        string string1;
        char[] characterArray;

        string1 = "hello there";
        characterArray = new char[ 5 ];

```

Fig. 16.2 | string indexer, Length property and CopyTo method. (Part 1 of 2.)

```
16        // output string1
17        Console.WriteLine( "string1: \"" + string1 + "\"" );
18
19        // test Length property
20        Console.WriteLine( "Length of string1: " + string1.Length );
21
22        // loop through characters in string1 and display reversed
23        Console.Write( "The string reversed is: " );
24
25        for ( int i = string1.Length - 1; i >= 0; i-- )
26           Console.Write( string1[ i ] );
27
28        // copy characters from string1 into characterArray
29        string1.CopyTo( 0, characterArray, 0, characterArray.Length );
30        Console.Write( "\nThe character array is: " );
31
32        for ( int i = 0; i < characterArray.Length; i++ )
33           Console.Write( characterArray[ i ] );
34
35        Console.WriteLine( "\n" );
36     } // end method Main
37  } // end class StringMethods
```

```
string1: "hello there"
Length of string1: 11
The string reversed is: ereht olleh
The character array is: hello
```

Fig. 16.2 | string indexer, Length property and CopyTo method. (Part 2 of 2.)

This application determines the length of a string, displays its characters in reverse order and copies a series of characters from the string to a character array.

Line 20 uses string property Length to determine the number of characters in string1. Like arrays, strings always know their own size.

Lines 25–26 write the characters of string1 in reverse order using the string indexer. The string indexer treats a string as an array of chars and returns the character at a specific position in the string. The indexer receives an integer argument as the *position number* and returns the character at that position. As with arrays, the first element of a string is considered to be at position 0.

Common Programming Error 16.1

Attempting to access a character that is outside a string's bounds (i.e., an index less than 0 or an index greater than or equal to the string's length) results in an IndexOutOfRangeException.

Line 29 uses string method CopyTo to copy the characters of string1 into a character array (characterArray). The first argument given to method CopyTo is the index from which the method begins copying characters in the string. The second argument is the character array into which the characters are copied. The third argument is the index specifying the starting location at which the method begins placing the copied characters into the character array. The last argument is the number of characters that the method will copy from the string. Lines 32–33 output the char array contents one character at a time.

16.5 Comparing strings

The next two examples demonstrate various methods for comparing strings. To understand how one string can be "greater than" or "less than" another string, consider the process of alphabetizing a series of last names. The reader would, no doubt, place "Jones" before "Smith", because the first letter of "Jones" comes before the first letter of "Smith" in the alphabet. The alphabet is more than just a set of 26 letters—it is an ordered list of characters in which each letter occurs in a specific position. For example, Z is more than just a letter of the alphabet; Z is specifically the twenty-sixth letter of the alphabet.

Computers can order characters alphabetically because the characters are represented internally as Unicode numeric codes. When comparing two strings, C# simply compares the numeric codes of the characters in the strings.

Class string provides several ways to compare strings. The application in Fig. 16.3 demonstrates the use of method Equals, method CompareTo and the equality operator (==).

```csharp
 1   // Fig. 16.3: StringCompare.cs
 2   // Comparing strings
 3   using System;
 4
 5   class StringCompare
 6   {
 7      public static void Main()
 8      {
 9         string string1 = "hello";
10         string string2 = "good bye";
11         string string3 = "Happy Birthday";
12         string string4 = "happy birthday";
13
14         // output values of four strings
15         Console.WriteLine( "string1 = \"" + string1 + "\"" +
16            "\nstring2 = \"" + string2 + "\"" +
17            "\nstring3 = \"" + string3 + "\"" +
18            "\nstring4 = \"" + string4 + "\"\n" );
19
20         // test for equality using Equals method
21         if ( string1.Equals( "hello" ) )
22            Console.WriteLine( "string1 equals \"hello\"" );
23         else
24            Console.WriteLine( "string1 does not equal \"hello\"" );
25
26         // test for equality with ==
27         if ( string1 == "hello" )
28            Console.WriteLine( "string1 equals \"hello\"" );
29         else
30            Console.WriteLine( "string1 does not equal \"hello\"" );
31
32         // test for equality comparing case
33         if ( string.Equals( string3, string4 ) ) // static method
34            Console.WriteLine( "string3 equals string4" );
35         else
36            Console.WriteLine( "string3 does not equal string4" );
```

Fig. 16.3 | string test to determine equality. (Part 1 of 2.)

```
37
38              // test CompareTo
39              Console.WriteLine ( "\nstring1.CompareTo( string2 ) is " +
40                  string1.CompareTo( string2 ) + "\n" +
41                  "string2.CompareTo( string1 ) is " +
42                  string2.CompareTo( string1 ) + "\n" +
43                  "string1.CompareTo( string1 ) is " +
44                  string1.CompareTo( string1 ) + "\n" +
45                  "string3.CompareTo( string4 ) is " +
46                  string3.CompareTo( string4 ) + "\n" +
47                  "string4.CompareTo( string3 ) is " +
48                  string4.CompareTo( string3 ) + "\n\n" );
49      } // end method Main
50  } // end class StringCompare
```

```
string1 = "hello"
string2 = "good bye"
string3 = "Happy Birthday"
string4 = "happy birthday"

string1 equals "hello"
string1 equals "hello"
string3 does not equal string4

string1.CompareTo( string2 ) is 1
string2.CompareTo( string1 ) is -1
string1.CompareTo( string1 ) is 0
string3.CompareTo( string4 ) is 1
string4.CompareTo( string3 ) is -1
```

Fig. 16.3 | string test to determine equality. (Part 2 of 2.)

The condition in the if statement (line 21) uses string method Equals to compare string1 and literal string "hello" to determine whether they are equal. Method Equals (inherited from object and overridden in string) tests any two objects for equality (i.e., checks whether the objects contain identical contents). The method returns true if the objects are equal and false otherwise. In this instance, the preceding condition returns true, because string1 references string literal object "hello". Method Equals uses a *lexicographical comparison*—the integer Unicode values that represent each character in each string are compared. A comparison of the string "hello" with the string "HELLO" would return false, because the numeric representations of lowercase letters are different from the numeric representations of corresponding uppercase letters.

The condition in line 27 uses the equality operator (==) to compare string string1 with the literal string "hello" for equality. In C#, the equality operator also uses a lexicographical comparison to compare two strings. Thus, the condition in the if statement evaluates to true, because the values of string1 and "hello" are equal.

We present the test for string equality between string3 and string4 (line 33) to illustrate that comparisons are indeed case sensitive. Here, static method Equals is used to compare the values of two strings. "Happy Birthday" does not equal "happy birthday", so the condition of the if statement fails, and the message "string3 does not equal string4" is output (line 36).

Lines 40–48 use `string` method `CompareTo` to compare `strings`. Method `CompareTo` returns 0 if the `strings` are equal, a negative value if the `string` that invokes `CompareTo` is less than the `string` that is passed as an argument and a positive value if the `string` that invokes `CompareTo` is greater than the `string` that is passed as an argument. Method `CompareTo` uses a lexicographical comparison.

Notice that `CompareTo` considers `string3` to be larger than `string4`. The only difference between these two `strings` is that `string3` contains two uppercase letters in positions where `string4` contains lowercase letters.

The application in Fig. 16.4 shows how to test whether a `string` instance begins or ends with a given `string`. Method `StartsWith` determines whether a `string` instance starts with the `string` text passed to it as an argument. Method `EndsWith` determines whether a `string` instance ends with the `string` text passed to it as an argument. Class `stringStartEnd`'s `Main` method defines an array of `strings` (called `strings`), which contains `"started"`, `"starting"`, `"ended"` and `"ending"`. The remainder of method `Main` tests the elements of the array to determine whether they start or end with a particular set of characters.

Line 14 uses method `StartsWith`, which takes a `string` argument. The condition in the `if` statement determines whether the `string` at index `i` of the array starts with the characters `"st"`. If so, the method returns `true`, and `strings[ i ]` is output along with a message.

```csharp
1   // Fig. 16.4: StringStartEnd.cs
2   // Demonstrating StartsWith and EndsWith methods.
3   using System;
4
5   class StringStartEnd
6   {
7      public static void Main()
8      {
9         string[] strings =
10           { "started", "starting", "ended", "ending" };
11
12        // test every string to see if it starts with "st"
13        for ( int i = 0; i < strings.Length; i++ )
14           if ( strings[ i ].StartsWith( "st" ) )
15              Console.WriteLine( "\"" + strings[ i ] + "\"" +
16                 " starts with \"st\"" );
17
18        Console.WriteLine( "" );
19
20        // test every string to see if it ends with "ed"
21        for ( int i = 0; i < strings.Length; i++ )
22           if ( strings[ i ].EndsWith( "ed" ) )
23              Console.WriteLine( "\"" + strings[ i ] + "\"" +
24                 " ends with \"ed\"" );
25
26        Console.WriteLine( "" );
27     } // end method Main
28  } // end class StringStartEnd
```

Fig. 16.4 | StartsWith and EndsWith methods. (Part 1 of 2.)

```
"started" starts with "st"
"starting" starts with "st"

"started" ends with "ed"
"ended" ends with "ed"
```

Fig. 16.4 | StartsWith and EndsWith methods. (Part 2 of 2.)

Line 22 uses method EndsWith, which also takes a string argument. The condition in the if statement determines whether the string at index i of the array ends with the characters "ed". If so, the method returns true, and strings[i] is displayed along with a message.

16.6 Locating Characters and Substrings in strings

In many applications, it is necessary to search for a character or set of characters in a string. For example, a programmer creating a word processor would want to provide capabilities for searching through documents. The application in Fig. 16.5 demonstrates some of the many versions of string methods IndexOf, IndexOfAny, LastIndexOf and LastIndexOfAny, which search for a specified character or substring in a string. We perform all searches in this example on the string letters (initialized with "abcdefghijkl-mabcdefghijklm") located in method Main of class StringIndexMethods.

Lines 14, 16 and 18 use method IndexOf to locate the first occurrence of a character or substring in a string. If it finds a character, IndexOf returns the index of the specified character in the string; otherwise, IndexOf returns -1. The expression in line 16 uses a version of method IndexOf that takes two arguments—the character to search for and the starting index at which the search of the string should begin. The method does not examine any characters that occur prior to the starting index (in this case, 1). The expression in line 18 uses another version of method IndexOf that takes three arguments—the character to search for, the index at which to start searching and the number of characters to search.

Lines 22, 24 and 26 use method LastIndexOf to locate the last occurrence of a character in a string. Method LastIndexOf performs the search from the end of the string to the beginning of the string. If it finds the character, LastIndexOf returns the index of the specified character in the string; otherwise, LastIndexOf returns -1. There are three versions of LastIndexOf. The expression in line 22 uses the version of method LastIndexOf that takes as an argument the character for which to search. The expression in line 24 uses the version of method LastIndexOf that takes two arguments—the character for which to search and the highest index from which to begin searching backward for the character. The expression in line 26 uses a third version of method LastIndexOf that takes three arguments—the character for which to search, the starting index from which to start searching backward and the number of characters (the portion of the string) to search.

Lines 29–44 use versions of IndexOf and LastIndexOf that take a string instead of a character as the first argument. These versions of the methods perform identically to those described above except that they search for sequences of characters (or substrings) that are specified by their string arguments.

```
 1   // Fig. 16.5: StringIndexMethods.cs
 2   // Using string searching methods.
 3   using System;
 4
 5   class StringIndexMethods
 6   {
 7      public static void Main()
 8      {
 9         string letters = "abcdefghijklmabcdefghijklm";
10         char[] searchLetters = { 'c', 'a', '$' };
11
12         // test IndexOf to locate a character in a string
13         Console.WriteLine( "First 'c' is located at index " +
14            letters.IndexOf( 'c' ) );
15         Console.WriteLine( "First 'a' starting at 1 is located at index " +
16            letters.IndexOf( 'a', 1 ) );
17         Console.WriteLine( "First '$' in the 5 positions starting at 3 " +
18            "is located at index " + letters.IndexOf( '$', 3, 5 ) );
19
20         // test LastIndexOf to find a character in a string
21         Console.WriteLine( "\nLast 'c' is located at index " +
22            letters.LastIndexOf( 'c' ) );
23         Console.WriteLine( "Last 'a' up to position 25 is located at " +
24            "index " + letters.LastIndexOf( 'a', 25 ) );
25         Console.WriteLine( "Last '$' in the 5 positions starting at 15 " +
26            "is located at index " + letters.LastIndexOf( '$', 15, 5 ) );
27
28         // test IndexOf to locate a substring in a string
29         Console.WriteLine( "\nFirst \"def\" is located at index " +
30            letters.IndexOf( "def" ) );
31         Console.WriteLine( "First \"def\" starting at 7 is located at " +
32            "index " + letters.IndexOf( "def", 7 ) );
33         Console.WriteLine( "First \"hello\" in the 15 positions " +
34            "starting at 5 is located at index " +
35            letters.IndexOf( "hello", 5, 15 ) );
36
37         // test LastIndexOf to find a substring in a string
38         Console.WriteLine( "\nLast \"def\" is located at index " +
39            letters.LastIndexOf( "def" ) );
40         Console.WriteLine( "Last \"def\" up to position 25 is located " +
41            "at index " + letters.LastIndexOf( "def", 25 ) );
42         Console.WriteLine( "Last \"hello\" in the 15 positions " +
43            "ending at 20 is located at index " +
44            letters.LastIndexOf( "hello", 20, 15 ) );
45
46         // test IndexOfAny to find first occurrence of character in array
47         Console.WriteLine( "\nFirst 'c', 'a' or '$' is " +
48            "located at index " + letters.IndexOfAny( searchLetters ) );
49         Console.WriteLine( "First 'c', 'a' or '$' starting at 7 is " +
50            "located at index " + letters.IndexOfAny( searchLetters, 7 ) );
51         Console.WriteLine( "First 'c', 'a' or '$' in the 5 positions " +
52            "starting at 7 is located at index " +
53            letters.IndexOfAny( searchLetters, 7, 5 ) );
```

Fig. 16.5 | Searching for characters and substrings in `strings`. (Part 1 of 2.)

```
54
55          // test LastIndexOfAny to find last occurrence of character
56          // in array
57          Console.WriteLine( "\nLast 'c', 'a' or '$' is " +
58             "located at index " + letters.LastIndexOfAny( searchLetters ) );
59          Console.WriteLine( "Last 'c', 'a' or '$' up to position 1 is " +
60             "located at index " +
61             letters.LastIndexOfAny( searchLetters, 1 ) );
62          Console.WriteLine( "Last 'c', 'a' or '$' in the 5 positions " +
63             "ending at 25 is located at index " +
64             letters.LastIndexOfAny( searchLetters, 25, 5 ) );
65       } // end method Main
66    } // end class StringIndexMethods
```

```
First 'c' is located at index 2
First 'a' starting at 1 is located at index 13
First '$' in the 5 positions starting at 3 is located at index -1

Last 'c' is located at index 15
Last 'a' up to position 25 is located at index 13
Last '$' in the 5 positions starting at 15 is located at index -1

First "def" is located at index 3
First "def" starting at 7 is located at index 16
First "hello" in the 15 positions starting at 5 is located at index -1

Last "def" is located at index 16
Last "def" up to position 25 is located at index 16
Last "hello" in the 15 positions ending at 20 is located at index -1

First 'c', 'a' or '$' is located at index 0
First 'c', 'a' or '$' starting at 7 is located at index 13
First 'c', 'a' or '$' in the 5 positions starting at 7 is located at index -1

Last 'c', 'a' or '$' is located at index 15
Last 'c', 'a' or '$' up to position 1 is located at index 0
Last 'c', 'a' or '$' in the 5 positions ending at 25 is located at index -1
```

Fig. 16.5 | Searching for characters and substrings in `string`s. (Part 2 of 2.)

Lines 47–64 use methods `IndexOfAny` and `LastIndexOfAny`, which take an array of characters as the first argument. These versions of the methods also perform identically to those described above except that they return the index of the first occurrence of any of the characters in the character array argument.

Common Programming Error 16.2

In the overloaded methods `LastIndexOf` and `LastIndexOfAny` that take three parameters, the second argument must be greater than or equal to the third. This might seem counterintuitive, but remember that the search moves from the end of the string toward the start of the string.

16.7 Extracting Substrings from `string`s

Class `string` provides two `Substring` methods, which are used to create a new `string` by copying part of an existing `string`. Each method returns a new `string`. The application in Fig. 16.6 demonstrates the use of both methods.

```
 1   // Fig. 16.6: SubString.cs
 2   // Demonstrating the string Substring method.
 3   using System;
 4
 5   class SubString
 6   {
 7      public static void Main()
 8      {
 9         string letters = "abcdefghijklmabcdefghijklm";
10
11         // invoke Substring method and pass it one parameter
12         Console.WriteLine( "Substring from index 20 to end is \"" +
13            letters.Substring( 20 ) + "\"" );
14
15         // invoke Substring method and pass it two parameters
16         Console.WriteLine( "Substring from index 0 of length 6 is \"" +
17            letters.Substring( 0, 6 ) + "\"" );
18      } // end method Main
19   } // end class SubString
```

```
Substring from index 20 to end is "hijklm"
Substring from index 0 of length 6 is "abcdef"
```

Fig. 16.6 | Substrings generated from strings.

The statement in line 13 uses the Substring method that takes one int argument. The argument specifies the starting index from which the method copies characters in the original string. The substring returned contains a copy of the characters from the starting index to the end of the string. If the index specified in the argument is outside the bounds of the string, the program throws an ArgumentOutOfRangeException.

The second version of method Substring (line 17) takes two int arguments. The first argument specifies the starting index from which the method copies characters from the original string. The second argument specifies the length of the substring to be copied. The substring returned contains a copy of the specified characters from the original string.

16.8 Concatenating strings

The + operator (discussed in Chapter 3, Introduction to C# Programming) is not the only way to perform string concatenation. The static method Concat of class string (Fig. 16.7) concatenates two strings and returns a new string containing the combined characters from both original strings. Line 16 appends the characters from string2 to the end of a copy of string1, using method Concat. The statement in line 16 does not modify the original strings.

16.9 Miscellaneous string Methods

Class string provides several methods that return modified copies of strings. The application in Fig. 16.8 demonstrates the use of these methods, which include string methods Replace, ToLower, ToUpper and Trim.

```
1    // Fig. 16.7: SubConcatenation.cs
2    // Demonstrating string class Concat method.
3    using System;
4
5    class StringConcatenation
6    {
7       public static void Main()
8       {
9          string string1 = "Happy ";
10         string string2 = "Birthday";
11
12         Console.WriteLine( "string1 = \"" + string1 + "\"\n" +
13            "string2 = \"" + string2 + "\"" );
14         Console.WriteLine(
15            "\nResult of string.Concat( string1, string2 ) = " +
16            string.Concat( string1, string2 ) );
17         Console.WriteLine( "string1 after concatenation = " + string1 );
18      } // end method Main
19   } // end class StringConcatenation
```

```
string1 = "Happy "
string2 = "Birthday"

Result of string.Concat( string1, string2 ) = Happy Birthday
string1 after concatenation = Happy
```

Fig. 16.7 | Concat static method.

```
1    // Fig. 16.8: StringMethods2.cs
2    // Demonstrating string methods Replace, ToLower, ToUpper, Trim,
3    // and ToString.
4    using System;
5
6    class StringMethods2
7    {
8       public static void Main()
9       {
10         string string1 = "cheers!";
11         string string2 = "GOOD BYE ";
12         string string3 = "   spaces   ";
13
14         Console.WriteLine( "string1 = \"" + string1 + "\"\n" +
15            "string2 = \"" + string2 + "\"\n" +
16            "string3 = \"" + string3 + "\"" );
17
18         // call method Replace
19         Console.WriteLine(
20            "\nReplacing \"e\" with \"E\" in string1: \"" +
21            string1.Replace( 'e', 'E' ) + "\"" );
22
```

Fig. 16.8 | string methods Replace, ToLower, ToUpper and Trim. (Part 1 of 2.)

```
23          // call ToLower and ToUpper
24          Console.WriteLine( "\nstring1.ToUpper() = \"" +
25             string1.ToUpper() + "\"\nstring2.ToLower() = \"" +
26             string2.ToLower() + "\"" );
27
28          // call Trim method
29          Console.WriteLine( "\nstring3 after trim = \"" +
30             string3.Trim() + "\"" );
31
32          Console.WriteLine( "\nstring1 = \"" + string1 + "\"" );
33       } // end method Main
34    } // end class StringMethods2
```

```
string1 = "cheers!"
string2 = "GOOD BYE "
string3 = "    spaces    "

Replacing "e" with "E" in string1: "chEErs!"

string1.ToUpper() = "CHEERS!"
string2.ToLower() = "good bye "

string3 after trim = "spaces"

string1 = "cheers!"
```

Fig. 16.8 | string methods Replace, ToLower, ToUpper and Trim. (Part 2 of 2.)

Line 21 uses string method Replace to return a new string, replacing every occurrence in string1 of character 'e' with 'E'. Method Replace takes two arguments—a string for which to search and another string with which to replace all matching occurrences of the first argument. The original string remains unchanged. If there are no occurrences of the first argument in the string, the method returns the original string.

string method ToUpper generates a new string (line 25) that replaces any lowercase letters in string1 with their uppercase equivalents. The method returns a new string containing the converted string; the original string remains unchanged. If there are no characters to convert, the original string is returned. Line 26 uses string method ToLower to return a new string in which any uppercase letters in string2 are replaced by their lowercase equivalents. The original string is unchanged. As with ToUpper, if there are no characters to convert to lowercase, method ToLower returns the original string.

Line 30 uses string method Trim to remove all whitespace characters that appear at the beginning and end of a string. Without otherwise altering the original string, the method returns a new string that contains the string, but omits leading or trailing whitespace characters. Another version of method Trim takes a character array and returns a string that does not contain the characters in the array argument.

16.10 Class StringBuilder

The string class provides many capabilities for processing strings. However a string's contents can never change. Operations that seem to concatenate strings are in fact assigning string references to newly created strings (e.g., the += operator creates a new string and assigns the initial string reference to the newly created string).

The next several sections discuss the features of class StringBuilder (namespace System.Text), used to create and manipulate dynamic string information—i.e., mutable strings. Every StringBuilder can store a certain number of characters that is specified by its capacity. Exceeding the capacity of a StringBuilder causes the capacity to expand to accommodate the additional characters. As we will see, members of class StringBuilder, such as methods Append and AppendFormat, can be used for concatenation like the operators + and += for class string.

Performance Tip 16.2

Objects of class string are immutable (i.e., constant strings), whereas object of class String-Builder are mutable. C# can perform certain optimizations involving strings (such as the sharing of one string among multiple references), because it knows these objects will not change.

Class StringBuilder provides six overloaded constructors. Class StringBuilderConstructor (Fig. 16.9) demonstrates three of these overloaded constructors.

Line 12 employs the no-parameter StringBuilder constructor to create a StringBuilder that contains no characters and has a default initial capacity of 16 characters. Line 13 uses the StringBuilder constructor that takes an int argument to create a StringBuilder that contains no characters and has the initial capacity specified in the int argument (i.e., 10). Line 14 uses the StringBuilder constructor that takes a string argument to create a StringBuilder containing the characters of the string argument. The initial capacity is the smallest power of two greater than or equal to the number of characters in the argument string, with a minimum of 16. Lines 16–18 implicitly use StringBuilder method ToString to obtain string representations of the StringBuilders' contents.

```
1   // Fig. 16.9: StringBuilderConstructor.cs
2   // Demonstrating StringBuilder class constructors.
3   using System;
4   using System.Text;
5
6   class StringBuilderConstructor
7
8      public static void Main()
9      {
10        StringBuilder buffer1, buffer2, buffer3;
11
12        buffer1 = new StringBuilder();
13        buffer2 = new StringBuilder( 10 );
14        buffer3 = new StringBuilder( "hello" );
15
16        Console.WriteLine( "buffer1 = \"" + buffer1 + "\"" );
17        Console.WriteLine( "buffer2 = \"" + buffer2 + "\"" );
18        Console.WriteLine( "buffer3 = \"" + buffer3 + "\"" );
19     } // end method Main
20  } // end class StringBuilderConstructor
```

Fig. 16.9 | StringBuilder class constructors. (Part 1 of 2.)

```
buffer1 = ""
buffer2 = ""
buffer3 = "hello"
```

Fig. 16.9 | StringBuilder class constructors. (Part 2 of 2.)

16.11 Length and Capacity Properties, EnsureCapacity Method and Indexer of Class StringBuilder

Class StringBuilder provides the Length and Capacity properties to return the number of characters currently in a StringBuilder and the number of characters that a StringBuilder can store without allocating more memory, respectively. These properties also can increase or decrease the length or the capacity of the StringBuilder.

Method EnsureCapacity allows you to reduce the number of times that a StringBuilder's capacity must be increased. The method doubles the StringBuilder instance's current capacity. If this doubled value is greater than the value that the programmer wishes to ensure, that value becomes the new capacity. Otherwise, EnsureCapacity alters the capacity to make it equal to the requested number. For example, if the current capacity is 17 and we wish to make it 40, 17 multiplied by 2 is not greater than 40, so the call will result in a new capacity of 40. If the current capacity is 23 and we wish to make it 40, 23 will be multiplied by 2 to result in a new capacity of 46. Both 40 and 46 are greater than or equal to 40, so a capacity of 40 is indeed ensured by method EnsureCapacity. The program in Fig. 16.10 demonstrates the use of these methods and properties.

```
1   // Fig. 16.10: StringBuilderFeatures.cs
2   // Demonstrating some features of class StringBuilder.
3   using System;
4   using System.Text;
5
6   class StringBuilderFeatures
7   {
8      public static void Main()
9      {
10         StringBuilder buffer =
11            new StringBuilder( "Hello, how are you?" );
12
13         // use Length and Capacity properties
14         Console.WriteLine( "buffer = " + buffer +
15            "\nLength = " + buffer.Length +
16            "\nCapacity = " + buffer.Capacity );
17
18         buffer.EnsureCapacity( 75 ); // ensure a capacity of at least 75
19         Console.WriteLine( "\nNew capacity = " +
20            buffer.Capacity );
21
```

Fig. 16.10 | StringBuilder size manipulation. (Part 1 of 2.)

```
22          // truncate StringBuilder by setting Length property
23          buffer.Length = 10;
24          Console.Write( "\nNew length = " +
25             buffer.Length + "\nbuffer = " );
26
27          // use StringBuilder indexer
28          for ( int i = 0; i < buffer.Length; i++ )
29             Console.Write( buffer[ i ] );
30
31          Console.WriteLine( "\n" );
32      } // end method Main
33   } // end class StringBuilderFeatures
```

```
buffer = Hello, how are you?
Length = 19
Capacity = 32

New capacity = 75

New length = 10
buffer = Hello, how
```

Fig. 16.10 | StringBuilder size manipulation. (Part 2 of 2.)

The program contains one StringBuilder, called buffer. Lines 10–11 of the program use the StringBuilder constructor that takes a string argument to instantiate the StringBuilder and initialize its value to "Hello, how are you?". Lines 13–16 output the content, length and capacity of the StringBuilder. In the output window, notice that the capacity of the StringBuilder is initially 32. Remember, the StringBuilder constructor that takes a string argument creates a StringBuilder object with an initial capacity that is the smallest power of two greater than or equal to the number of characters in the string passed as an argument.

Line 18 expands the capacity of the StringBuilder to a minimum of 75 characters. The current capacity (32) multiplied by two is less than 75, so method EnsureCapacity increases the capacity to 75. If new characters are added to a StringBuilder so that its length exceeds its capacity, the capacity grows to accommodate the additional characters in the same manner as if method EnsureCapacity had been called.

Line 23 uses property Length to set the length of the StringBuilder to 10. If the specified length is less than the current number of characters in the StringBuilder, the contents of the StringBuilder are truncated to the specified length. If the specified length is greater than the number of characters currently in the StringBuilder, space characters are appended to the StringBuilder until the total number of characters in the StringBuilder is equal to the specified length.

Common Programming Error 16.3

Assigning null *to a* string *reference can lead to logic errors if you attempt to compare* null *to an empty* string*. The keyword* null *is a value that represents a null reference (i.e., a reference that does not refer to an object), not an empty* string *(which is a* string *object that is of length 0 and contains no characters).*

16.12 Append and AppendFormat Methods of Class StringBuilder

Class `StringBuilder` provides 19 overloaded `Append` methods that allow various types of values to be added to the end of a `StringBuilder`. The FCL provides versions for each of the simple types and for character arrays, `string`s and `object`s. (Remember that method `ToString` produces a `string` representation of any `object`.) Each of the methods takes an argument, converts it to a `string` and appends it to the `StringBuilder`. Figure 16.11 demonstrates the use of several `Append` methods.

Lines 22–40 use 10 different overloaded `Append` methods to attach the string representations of objects created in lines 10–18 to the end of the `StringBuilder`. `Append` behaves similarly to the + operator, which is used to concatenate `string`s.

Class `StringBuilder` also provides method `AppendFormat`, which converts a `string` to a specified format, then appends it to the `StringBuilder`. The example in Fig. 16.12 demonstrates the use of this method.

Line 14 creates a `string` that contains formatting information. The information enclosed in braces specifies how to format a specific piece of data. Formats have the form {X[,Y][:FormatString]}, where X is the number of the argument to be formatted, counting from zero. Y is an optional argument, which can be positive or negative, indicating how many characters should be in the result. If the resulting `string` is less than the number Y, the `string` will be padded with spaces to make up for the difference. A positive integer aligns the `string` to the right; a negative integer aligns it to the left. The optional `FormatString` applies a particular format to the argument—currency, decimal or scientific, among others. In this case, "{0}" means the first argument will be printed out. "{1:C}" specifies that the second argument will be formatted as a currency value.

Line 23 shows a version of `AppendFormat` that takes two parameters—a `string` specifying the format and an array of objects to serve as the arguments to the format `string`. The argument referred to by "{0}" is in the object array at index 0.

```
 1    // Fig. 16.11: StringBuilderAppend.cs
 2    // Demonstrating StringBuilder Append methods.
 3    using System;
 4    using System.Text;
 5
 6    class StringBuilderAppend
 7    {
 8       public static void Main( string[] args )
 9       {
10          object objectValue = "hello";
11          string stringValue = "good bye";
12          char[] characterArray = { 'a', 'b', 'c', 'd', 'e', 'f' };
13          bool booleanValue = true;
14          char characterValue = 'Z';
15          int integerValue = 7;
16          long longValue = 1000000;
17          float floatValue = 2.5F; // F suffix indicates that 2.5 is a float
18          double doubleValue = 33.333;
19          StringBuilder buffer = new StringBuilder();
```

Fig. 16.11 | Append methods of `StringBuilder`. (Part 1 of 2.)

```
20
21          // use method Append to append values to buffer
22          buffer.Append( objectValue );
23          buffer.Append( " " );
24          buffer.Append( stringValue );
25          buffer.Append( " " );
26          buffer.Append( characterArray );
27          buffer.Append( " " );
28          buffer.Append( characterArray, 0, 3 );
29          buffer.Append( " " );
30          buffer.Append( booleanValue );
31          buffer.Append( " " );
32          buffer.Append( characterValue );
33          buffer.Append( " " );
34          buffer.Append( integerValue );
35          buffer.Append( " " );
36          buffer.Append( longValue );
37          buffer.Append( " " );
38          buffer.Append( floatValue );
39          buffer.Append( " " );
40          buffer.Append( doubleValue );
41
42          Console.WriteLine( "buffer = " + buffer.ToString() + "\n" );
43       } // end method Main
44    } // end class StringBuilderAppend
```

```
buffer = hello  good bye  abcdef  abc  True  Z  7  1000000  2.5  33.333
```

Fig. 16.11 | Append methods of `StringBuilder`. (Part 2 of 2.)

```
1    // Fig. 16.12: StringBuilderAppendFormat.cs
2    // Demonstrating method AppendFormat.
3    using System;
4    using System.Text;
5
6    class StringBuilderAppendFormat
7    {
8       public static void Main( string[] args )
9       {
10          StringBuilder buffer = new StringBuilder();
11          string string1, string2;
12
13          // formatted string
14          string1 = "This {0} costs: {1:C}.\n";
15
16          // string1 argument array
17          object[] objectArray = new object[ 2 ];
18
19          objectArray[ 0 ] = "car";
20          objectArray[ 1 ] = 1234.56;
21
```

Fig. 16.12 | StringBuilder's AppendFormat method. (Part 1 of 2.)

```
22          // append to buffer formatted string with argument
23          buffer.AppendFormat( string1, objectArray );
24
25          // formatted string
26          string2 = "Number:{0:d3}.\n" +
27             "Number right aligned with spaces:{0, 4}.\n" +
28             "Number left aligned with spaces:{0, -4}.";
29
30          // append to buffer formatted string with argument
31          buffer.AppendFormat( string2, 5 );
32
33          // display formatted strings
34          Console.WriteLine( buffer.ToString() );
35       } // end method Main
36    } // end class StringBuilderAppendFormat
```

```
This car costs: $1,234.56.
Number:005.
Number right aligned with spaces:    5.
Number left aligned with spaces:5   .
```

Fig. 16.12 | StringBuilder's AppendFormat method. (Part 2 of 2.)

Lines 26–28 define another string used for formatting. The first format "{0:d3}", specifies that the first argument will be formatted as a three-digit decimal, meaning any number that has fewer than three digits will have leading zeros placed in front to make up the difference. The next format, "{0, 4}", specifies that the formatted string should have four characters and should be right aligned. The third format, "{0, -4}", specifies that the strings should be aligned to the left. For more formatting options, please refer to the online help documentation.

Line 31 uses a version of AppendFormat that takes two parameters—a string containing a format and an object to which the format is applied. In this case, the object is the number 5. The output of Fig. 16.12 displays the result of applying these two versions of AppendFormat with their respective arguments.

16.13 Insert, Remove and Replace Methods of Class StringBuilder

Class StringBuilder provides 18 overloaded Insert methods to allow various types of data to be inserted at any position in a StringBuilder. The class provides versions for each of the simple types and for character arrays, strings and objects. Each method takes its second argument, converts it to a string and inserts the string into the StringBuilder in front of the character in the position specified by the first argument. The index specified by the first argument must be greater than or equal to 0 and less than the length of the StringBuilder; otherwise, the program throws an ArgumentOutOfRangeException.

Class StringBuilder also provides method Remove for deleting any portion of a StringBuilder. Method Remove takes two arguments—the index at which to begin deletion and the number of characters to delete. The sum of the starting index and the number of characters to be deleted must always be less than the length of the StringBuilder; otherwise, the program throws an ArgumentOutOfRangeException. The Insert and Remove methods are demonstrated in Fig. 16.13.

```cs
1   // Fig. 16.13: StringBuilderInsertRemove.cs
2   // Demonstrating methods Insert and Remove of the
3   // StringBuilder class.
4   using System;
5   using System.Text;
6
7   class StringBuilderInsertRemove
8   {
9      public static void Main()
10     {
11        object objectValue = "hello";
12        string stringValue = "good bye";
13        char[] characterArray = { 'a', 'b', 'c', 'd', 'e', 'f' };
14        bool booleanValue = true;
15        char characterValue = 'K';
16        int integerValue = 7;
17        long longValue = 10000000;
18        float floatValue = 2.5F; // F suffix indicates that 2.5 is a float
19        double doubleValue = 33.333;
20        StringBuilder buffer = new StringBuilder();
21
22        // insert values into buffer
23        buffer.Insert( 0, objectValue );
24        buffer.Insert( 0, "   " );
25        buffer.Insert( 0, stringValue );
26        buffer.Insert( 0, "   " );
27        buffer.Insert( 0, characterArray );
28        buffer.Insert( 0, "   " );
29        buffer.Insert( 0, booleanValue );
30        buffer.Insert( 0, "   " );
31        buffer.Insert( 0, characterValue );
32        buffer.Insert( 0, "   " );
33        buffer.Insert( 0, integerValue );
34        buffer.Insert( 0, "   " );
35        buffer.Insert( 0, longValue );
36        buffer.Insert( 0, "   " );
37        buffer.Insert( 0, floatValue );
38        buffer.Insert( 0, "   " );
39        buffer.Insert( 0, doubleValue );
40        buffer.Insert( 0, "   " );
41
42        Console.WriteLine( "buffer after Inserts: \n" + buffer + "\n" );
43
44        buffer.Remove( 10, 1 ); // delete 2 in 2.5
45        buffer.Remove( 4, 4 );  // delete .333 in 33.333
46
47        Console.WriteLine( "buffer after Removes:\n" + buffer.ToString() );
48     } // end method Main
49  } // end class StringBuilderInsertRemove
```

Fig. 16.13 | StringBuilder text insertion and removal. (Part 1 of 2.)

```
buffer after Inserts:
  33.333  2.5  10000000  7  K  True  abcdef  good bye  hello

buffer after Removes:
  33  .5  10000000  7  K  True  abcdef  good bye  hello
```

Fig. 16.13 | StringBuilder text insertion and removal. (Part 2 of 2.)

Another useful method included with StringBuilder is Replace. Replace searches for a specified string or character and substitutes another string or character in its place. Figure 16.14 demonstrates this method.

Line 18 uses method Replace to replace all instances of the string "Jane" with the string "Greg" in builder1. Another overload of this method takes two characters as parameters and replaces each occurrence of the first character with the second character. Line 19 uses an overload of Replace that takes four parameters, the first two of which are characters and the second two of which are ints. The method replaces all instances of the first character with the second character, beginning at the index specified by the first int and continuing for a count specified by the second int. Thus, in this case, Replace looks

```
 1   // Fig. 16.14: StringBuilderReplace.cs
 2   // Demonstrating method Replace.
 3   using System;
 4   using System.Text;
 5
 6   class StringBuilderReplace
 7   {
 8      public static void Main()
 9      {
10         StringBuilder builder1 =
11            new StringBuilder( "Happy Birthday Jane" );
12         StringBuilder builder2 =
13            new StringBuilder( "good bye greg" );
14
15         Console.WriteLine( "Before replacements:\n" +
16            builder1.ToString() + "\n" + builder2.ToString() );
17
18         builder1.Replace( "Jane", "Greg" );
19         builder2.Replace( 'g', 'G', 0, 5 );
20
21         Console.WriteLine( "\nAfter replacements:\n" +
22            builder1.ToString() + "\n" + builder2.ToString() );
23      } // end method Main
24   } // end class StringBuilderReplace
```

```
Before Replacements:
Happy Birthday Jane
good bye greg

After replacements:
Happy Birthday Greg
Good bye greg
```

Fig. 16.14 | StringBuilder text replacement.

through only five characters, starting with the character at index 0. As the output illustrates, this version of Replace replaces g with G in the word "good", but not in "greg". This is because the gs in "greg" are not in the range indicated by the int arguments (i.e., between indexes 0 and 4).

16.14 Char Methods

C# provides a type called a *struct* (short for structure) that is similar to a class. Although structs and classes are comparable in many ways, structs represent value types. Like classes, structs can have methods and properties, and can use the access modifiers public and private. Also, struct members are accessed via the member access operator (.).

The simple types are actually aliases for struct types. For instance, an int is defined by struct System.Int32, a long by System.Int64 and so on. All struct types derive from class *ValueType*, which in turn derives from object. Also, all struct types are implicitly sealed, so they do not support virtual or abstract methods, and their members cannot be declared protected or protected internal.

In this section, we present struct *Char*,[2] which is the struct for characters. Most Char methods are static, take at least one character argument and perform either a test or a manipulation on the character. We present several of these methods in the next example. Figure 16.15 demonstrates static methods that test characters to determine whether they are of a specific character type and static methods that perform case conversions on characters.

```
1   // Fig. 16.15: StaticCharMethods.cs
2   // Demonstrates static character testing methods
3   // from Char struct
4   using System;
5   using System.Windows.Forms;
6
7   public partial class StaticCharMethodsForm : Form
8   {
9      // default constructor
10     public StaticCharMethodsForm()
11     {
12        InitializeComponent();
13     } // end constructor
14
15     // handle analyzeButton_Click
16     private void analyzeButton_Click( object sender, EventArgs e )
17     {
18        // convert string entered to type char
19        char character = Convert.ToChar( inputTextBox.Text );
20        string output;
21
```

Fig. 16.15 | Char's static character-testing and case-conversion methods. (Part 1 of 2.)

---

2. Just as keyword string is an alias for class String, keyword char is an alias for struct Char. In this text, we use the term Char when calling a static method of struct Char and the term char elsewhere.

```
22        output = "is digit: " +
23           Char.IsDigit( character ) + "\r\n";
24        output += "is letter: " +
25           Char.IsLetter( character ) + "\r\n";
26        output += "is letter or digit: " +
27           Char.IsLetterOrDigit( character ) + "\r\n";
28        output += "is lower case: " +
29           Char.IsLower( character ) + "\r\n";
30        output += "is upper case: " +
31           Char.IsUpper( character ) + "\r\n";
32        output += "to upper case: " +
33           Char.ToUpper( character ) + "\r\n";
34        output += "to lower case: " +
35           Char.ToLower( character ) + "\r\n";
36        output += "is punctuation: " +
37           Char.IsPunctuation( character ) + "\r\n";
38        output += "is symbol: " + Char.IsSymbol( character );
39        outputTextBox.Text = output;
40     } // end method analyzeButton_Click
41  } // end class StaticCharMethodsForm
```

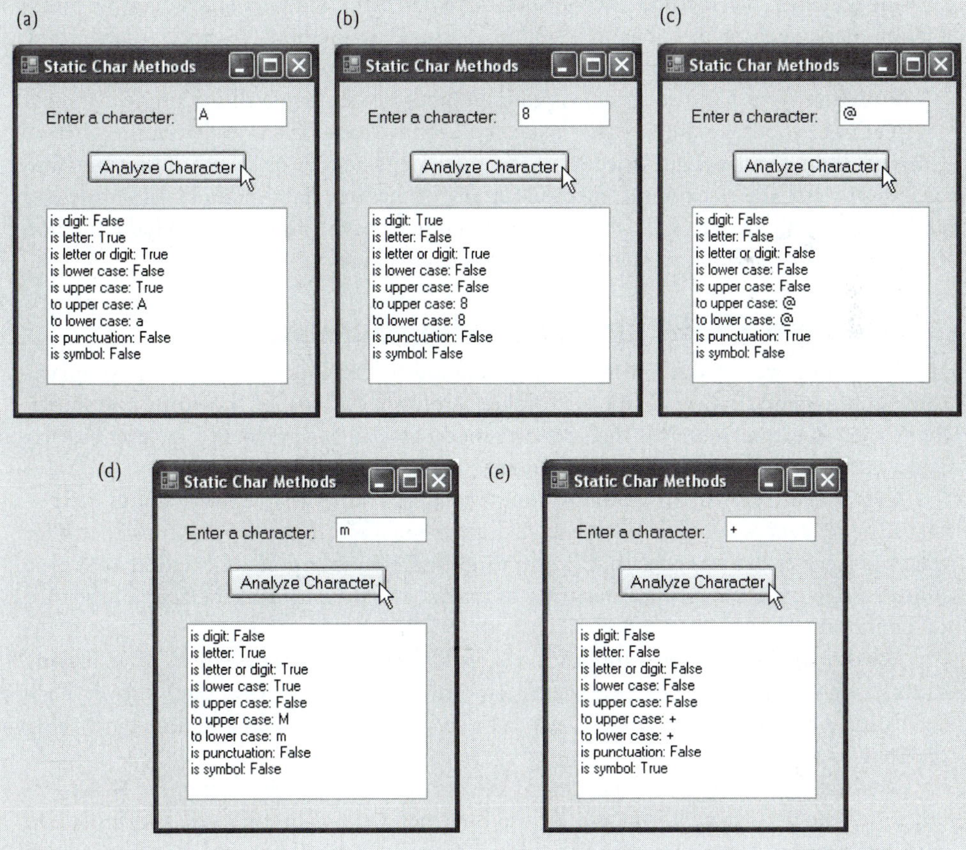

(a)

Static Char Methods

Enter a character: A

   Analyze Character

is digit: False
is letter: True
is letter or digit: True
is lower case: False
is upper case: True
to upper case: A
to lower case: a
is punctuation: False
is symbol: False

(b)

Static Char Methods

Enter a character: 8

   Analyze Character

is digit: True
is letter: False
is letter or digit: True
is lower case: False
is upper case: False
to upper case: 8
to lower case: 8
is punctuation: False
is symbol: False

(c)

Static Char Methods

Enter a character: @

   Analyze Character

is digit: False
is letter: False
is letter or digit: False
is lower case: False
is upper case: False
to upper case: @
to lower case: @
is punctuation: True
is symbol: False

(d)

Static Char Methods

Enter a character: m

   Analyze Character

is digit: False
is letter: True
is letter or digit: True
is lower case: True
is upper case: False
to upper case: M
to lower case: m
is punctuation: False
is symbol: False

(e)

Static Char Methods

Enter a character: +

   Analyze Character

is digit: False
is letter: False
is letter or digit: False
is lower case: False
is upper case: False
to upper case: +
to lower case: +
is punctuation: False
is symbol: True

Fig. 16.15 | Char's static character-testing and case-conversion methods. (Part 2 of 2.)

This Windows application contains a prompt, a TextBox in which the user can input a character, a button that the user can press after entering a character and a second TextBox that displays the output of our analysis. When the user clicks the **Analyze Character** button, event handler analyzeButton_Click (lines 16–40) is invoked. This event handler converts the input from a string to a char, using method Convert.ToChar (line 19).

Line 23 uses Char method IsDigit to determine whether character is defined as a digit. If so, the method returns true; otherwise, it returns false (note again that bool values are output capitalized). Line 25 uses Char method IsLetter to determine whether character character is a letter. Line 27 uses Char method IsLetterOrDigit to determine whether character character is a letter or a digit.

Line 29 uses Char method IsLower to determine whether character character is a lowercase letter. Line 31 uses Char method IsUpper to determine whether character character is an uppercase letter. Line 33 uses Char method ToUpper to convert character character to its uppercase equivalent. The method returns the converted character if the character has an uppercase equivalent; otherwise, the method returns its original argument. Line 35 uses Char method ToLower to convert character character to its lowercase equivalent. The method returns the converted character if the character has a lowercase equivalent; otherwise, the method returns its original argument.

Line 37 uses Char method IsPunctuation to determine whether character is a punctuation mark, such as "!", ":" or ")". Line 38 uses Char method IsSymbol to determine whether character character is a symbol, such as "+", "=" or "^".

Structure type Char also contains other methods not shown in this example. Many of the static methods are similar—for instance, IsWhiteSpace is used to determine whether a certain character is a whitespace character (e.g., newline, tab or space). The struct also contains several public instance methods; many of these, such as methods ToString and Equals, are methods that we have seen before in other classes. This group includes method CompareTo, which is used to compare two character values with one another.

16.15 Card Shuffling and Dealing Simulation

In this section, we use random-number generation to develop a program that simulates card shuffling and dealing. These techniques can form the basis of programs that implement specific card games. We include several exercises at the end of this chapter that require card shuffling and dealing capabilities.

Class Card (Fig. 16.16) contains two string instance variables—face and suit—that store references to the face value and suit name of a specific card. The constructor for the class receives two strings that it uses to initialize face and suit. Method ToString (lines 16–19) creates a string consisting of the face of the card and the suit of the card to identify the card when it is dealt.

We develop the DeckForm application (Fig. 16.17), which creates a deck of 52 playing cards, using Card objects. Users can deal each card by clicking the **Deal Card** button. Each dealt card is displayed in a Label. Users can also shuffle the deck at any time by clicking the **Shuffle Cards** button.

Method DeckForm_Load (lines 19–31 of Fig. 16.17) uses a for statement (lines 29–30) to fill the deck array with Cards. Note that each Card is instantiated and initialized with two strings—one from the faces array (strings "Ace" through "King") and one from the suits array ("Hearts", "Diamonds", "Clubs" or "Spades"). The calculation i %

```
 1   // Fig. 16.16: Card.cs
 2   // Stores suit and face information on each card.
 3   using System;
 4
 5   public class Card
 6   {
 7      private string face;
 8      private string suit;
 9
10      public Card( string faceValue, string suitValue )
11      {
12         face = faceValue;
13         suit = suitValue;
14      } // end constructor
15
16      public override string ToString()
17      {
18         return face + " of " + suit;
19      } // end method ToString
20   } // end class Card
```

Fig. 16.16 | Card class.

13 always results in a value from 0 to 12 (the thirteen subscripts of the faces array), and the calculation i / 13 always results in a value from 0 to 3 (the four subscripts in the suits array). The initialized deck array contains the cards with faces Ace through King for each suit.

When the user clicks the **Deal Card** button, event handler dealButton_Click (lines 34–50) invokes method DealCard (defined in lines 75–90) to get the next card in the deck array. If the deck is not empty, the method returns a Card object reference; otherwise, it returns null. If the reference is not null, lines 42–43 display the Card in displayLabel and display the card number in statusLabel.

```
 1   // Fig. 16.17: DeckForm.cs
 2   // Simulating card shuffling and dealing.
 3   using System;
 4   using System.Windows.Forms;
 5
 6   public partial class DeckForm : Form
 7   {
 8      private Card[] deck = new Card[ 52 ]; // deak of 52 cards
 9      private int currentCard; // count which card was just dealt
10
11      // default constructor
12      public DeckForm()
13      {
14         // Required for Windows Form Designer support
15         InitializeComponent();
16      } // end constructor
17
```

Fig. 16.17 | Card shuffling and dealing simulation. (Part 1 of 4.)

```
18      // handles form at load time
19      private void DeckForm_Load( object sender, EventArgs e )
20      {
21          string[] faces = { "Ace", "Deuce", "Three", "Four", "Five",
22                              "Six", "Seven", "Eight", "Nine", "Ten",
23                              "Jack", "Queen", "King" };
24          string[] suits = { "Hearts", "Diamonds", "Clubs", "Spades" };
25
26          currentCard = -1; // no cards have been dealt
27
28          // initialize deck
29          for ( int i = 0; i < deck.Length; i++ )
30              deck[ i ] = new Card( faces[ i % 13 ], suits[ i / 13 ] );
31      } // end method DeckForm_Load
32
33      // handles dealButton Click
34      private void dealButton_Click( object sender, EventArgs e )
35      {
36          Card dealt = DealCard();
37
38          // if dealt card is null, then no cards left
39          // player must shuffle cards
40          if ( dealt != null )
41          {
42              displayLabel.Text = dealt.ToString();
43              statusLabel.Text = "Card #: " + currentCard;
44          } // end if
45          else
46          {
47              displayLabel.Text = "NO MORE CARDS TO DEAL";
48              statusLabel.Text = "Shuffle cards to continue";
49          } // end else
50      } // end method dealButton_Click
51
52      // shuffle cards
53      private void Shuffle()
54      {
55          Random randomNumber = new Random();
56          Card temporaryValue;
57
58          currentCard = -1;
59
60          // swap each card with randomly selected card (0-51)
61          for ( int i = 0; i < deck.Length; i++ )
62          {
63              int j = randomNumber.Next( 52 );
64
65              // swap cards
66              temporaryValue = deck[ i ];
67              deck[ i ] = deck[ j ];
68              deck[ j ] = temporaryValue;
69          } // end for
```

Fig. 16.17 | Card shuffling and dealing simulation. (Part 2 of 4.)

```
70
71          dealButton.Enabled = true; // shuffled deck can now deal cards
72      } // end method Shuffle
73
74      // deal a card if the deck is not empty
75      private Card DealCard()
76      {
77          // if there is a card to deal then deal it
78          // otherwise signal that cards need to be shuffled by
79          // disabling dealButton and returning null
80          if ( currentCard + 1 < deck.Length )
81          {
82              currentCard++; // increment count
83              return deck[ currentCard ]; // return new card
84          } // end if
85          else
86          {
87              dealButton.Enabled = false; // empty deck cannot deal cards
88              return null; // do not return a card
89          } // end else
90      } // end method DealCard
91
92      // handles shuffleButton Click
93      private void shuffleButton_Click( object sender, EventArgs e )
94      {
95          displayLabel.Text = "SHUFFLING...";
96          Shuffle();
97          displayLabel.Text = "DECK IS SHUFFLED";
98      } // end method shuffleButton_Click
99  } // end class DeckForm
```

(a)

Card Dealing Program

Deal Card   Shuffle Cards

King of Spades

Card #: 51

(b)

Card Dealing Program

Deal Card   Shuffle Cards

NO MORE CARDS TO DEAL

Shuffle cards to continue

Fig. 16.17 | Card shuffling and dealing simulation. (Part 3 of 4.)

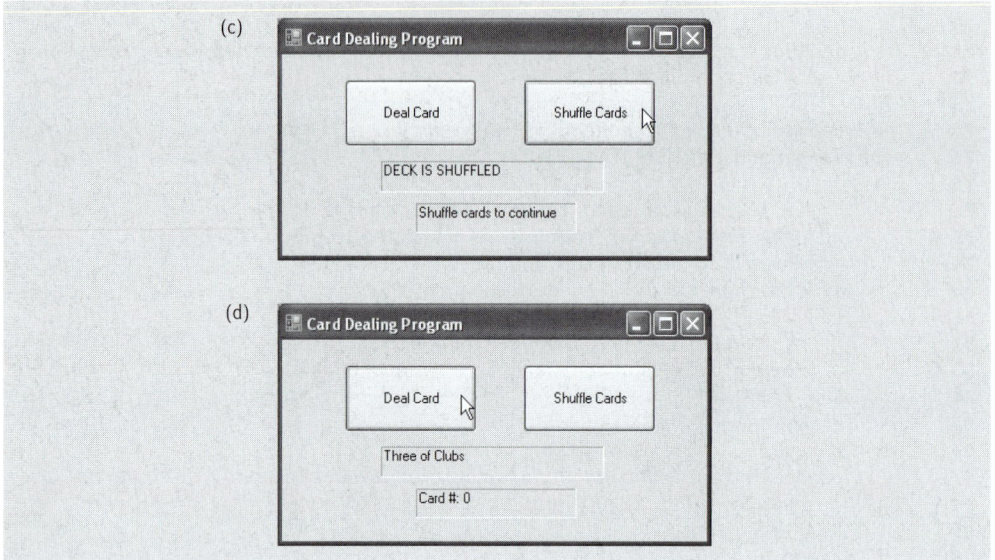

Fig. 16.17 | Card shuffling and dealing simulation. (Part 4 of 4.)

If DealCard returns null, the string "NO MORE CARDS TO DEAL" is displayed in dis-playLabel, and the string "Shuffle cards to continue" is displayed in statusLabel.

When the user clicks the **Shuffle Cards** button, event handler shuffleButton_Click (lines 93–98) invokes method Shuffle (defined on lines 53–72) to shuffle the cards. The method loops through all 52 cards (array subscripts 0–51). For each card, the method randomly picks a number in the range 0–51. Then the current Card object and the randomly selected Card object are swapped in the array. To shuffle the cards, method Shuffle makes a total of only 52 swaps during a single pass of the entire array. When the shuffling is complete, displayLabel displays the string "DECK IS SHUFFLED".

16.16 Regular Expressions and Class Regex

Regular expressions are specially formatted strings used to find patterns in text. They can be useful during information validation, to ensure that data is in a particular format. For example, a ZIP code must consist of five digits, and a last name must start with a capital letter. Compilers use regular expressions to validate the syntax of programs. If the program code does not match the regular expression, the compiler indicates that there is a syntax error.

The .NET Framework provides several classes to help developers recognize and manipulate regular expressions. Class Regex (of the System.Text.RegularExpressions namespace) represents an immutable regular expression. Regex *method* Match returns an object of *class* Match that represents a single regular expression match. Regex also provides method Matches, which finds all matches of a regular expression in an arbitrary string and returns an object of the class MatchCollection object containing all the Matches. A collection is a data structure, similar to an array and can be used with a foreach statement to iterate through the collection's elements. We discuss collections in more detail in

Chapter 27, Collections. To use class Regex, you should add a using directive for the namespace System.Text.RegularExpressions.

Regular Expression Character Classes

The table in Fig. 16.18 specifies some *character classes* that can be used with regular expressions. Please do not confuse a character class with a C# class declaration. A character class is simply an escape sequence that represents a group of characters that might appear in a string.

A *word character* is any alphanumeric character or underscore. A whitespace character is a space, a tab, a carriage return, a newline or a form feed. A digit is any numeric character. Regular expressions are not limited to the character classes in Fig. 16.18. As you will see in our first example, regular expressions can use other notations to search for complex patterns in strings.

16.16.1 Regular Expression Example

The program of Fig. 16.19 tries to match birthdays to a regular expression. For demonstration purposes, the expression matches only birthdays that do not occur in April and that belong to people whose names begin with "J".

Character class	Matches	Character class	Matches
\d	any digit	\D	any non-digit
\w	any word character	\W	any non-word character
\s	any whitespace	\S	any non-whitespace

Fig. 16.18 | Character classes.

```
1   // Fig. 16.19: RegexMatches.cs
2   // Demonstrating Class Regex.
3   using System;
4   using System.Text.RegularExpressions;
5
6   class RegexMatches
7   {
8      public static void Main()
9      {
10        // create regular expression
11        Regex expression =
12           new Regex( @"J.*\d[0-35-9]-\d\d-\d\d" );
13
14        string string1 = "Jane's Birthday is 05-12-75\n" +
15           "Dave's Birthday is 11-04-68\n" +
16           "John's Birthday is 04-28-73\n" +
17           "Joe's Birthday is 12-17-77";
```

Fig. 16.19 | Regular expressions checking birthdays. (Part 1 of 2.)

```
18
19          // match regular expression to string and
20          // print out all matches
21          foreach ( Match myMatch in expression.Matches( string1 ) )
22             Console.WriteLine( myMatch );
23       } // end method Main
24    } // end class RegexMatches
```

```
Jane's Birthday is 05-12-75
Joe's Birthday is 12-17-77
```

Fig. 16.19 | Regular expressions checking birthdays. (Part 2 of 2.)

Lines 11–12 create a `Regex` object and pass a regular expression pattern string to the `Regex` constructor. Note that we precede the string with `@`. Recall that backslashes within the double quotation marks following the `@` character are regular backslash characters, not the beginning of escape sequences. To define the regular expression without prefixing `@` to the string, you would need to escape every backslash character, as in

"J.*\\d[0-35-9]-\\d\\d-\\d\\d"

which makes the regular expression more difficult to read.

The first character in the regular expression, `"J"`, is a literal character. Any `string` matching this regular expression is required to start with `"J"`. In a regular expression, the dot character `"."` matches any single character except a newline character. When the dot character is followed by an asterisk, as in `".*"`, the regular expression matches any number of unspecified characters except newlines. In general, when the operator `"*"` is applied to a pattern, the pattern will match zero or more occurrences. By contrast, applying the operator `"+"` to a pattern causes the pattern to match one or more occurrences. For example, both `"A*"` and `"A+"` will match `"A"`, but only `"A*"` will match an empty `string`.

As indicated in Fig. 16.18, `"\d"` matches any numeric digit. To specify sets of characters other than those that belong to a predefined character class, characters can be listed in square brackets, `[]`. For example, the pattern `"[aeiou]"` matches any vowel. Ranges of characters are represented by placing a dash (-) between two characters. In the example, `"[0-35-9]"` matches only digits in the ranges specified by the pattern—i.e., any digit between 0 and 3 or between 5 and 9; therefore, it matches any digit except 4. You can also specify that a pattern should match anything other than the characters in the brackets. To do so, place ^ as the first character in the brackets. It is important to note that `"[^4]"` is not the same as `"[0-35-9]"`; `"[^4]"` matches any non-digit and digits other than 4.

Although the `"-"` character indicates a range when it is enclosed in square brackets, instances of the `"-"` character outside grouping expressions are treated as literal characters. Thus, the regular expression in line 12 searches for a `string` that starts with the letter `"J"`, followed by any number of characters, followed by a two-digit number (of which the second digit cannot be 4), followed by a dash, another two-digit number, a dash and another two-digit number.

Lines 21–22 use a `foreach` statement to iterate through the `MatchCollection` returned by the `expression` object's `Matches` method, which received `string1` as an argument. The elements in the `MatchCollection` are `Match` objects, so the `foreach` statement declares variable myMatch to be of type Match. For each Match, line 22 outputs the text that matched the regular expression. The output in Fig. 16.19 indicates the two matches that were found in string1. Notice that both matches conform to the pattern specified by the regular expression.

Quantifiers

The asterisk (*) in line 12 of Fig. 16.19 is more formally called a *quantifier*. Figure 16.20 lists various quantifiers that you can place after a pattern in a regular expression and the purpose of each quantifier.

We have already discussed how the asterisk (*) and plus (+) quantifiers work. The question mark (?) quantifier matches zero or one occurrences of the pattern that it quantifies. A set of braces containing one number ({n}) matches exactly n occurrences of the pattern it quantifies. We demonstrate this quantifier in the next example. Including a comma after the number enclosed in braces matches at least n occurrences of the quantified pattern. The set of braces containing two numbers ({n,m}), matches between n and m occurrences (inclusively) of the pattern that it qualifies. All of the quantifiers are *greedy*— they will match as many occurrences of the pattern as possible until the pattern fails to make a match. If a quantifier is followed by a question mark (?), the quantifier becomes *lazy* and will match as few occurrences as possible as long as there is a successful match.

16.16.2 Validating User Input with Regular Expressions

The Windows application in Fig. 16.21 presents a more involved example that uses regular expressions to validate name, address and telephone number information input by a user.

When a user clicks the **OK** button, the program checks to make sure that none of the fields is empty (lines 19–22). If one or more fields are empty, the program displays a message to the user (lines 25–26) that all fields must be filled in before the program can validate the input information. Line 27 calls lastNameTextBox's Focus method to place the cursor in the lastNameTextBox. The program then exits the event handler (line 28). If there are no empty fields, lines 32–105 validate the user input. Lines 32–40 validate the last name by calling static method Match of class Regex, passing both the string to validate and the regular expression as arguments. Method Match returns a Match object. This

Quantifier	Matches
*	Matches zero or more occurrences of the preceding pattern.
+	Matches one or more occurrences of the preceding pattern.
?	Matches zero or one occurrences of the preceding pattern.
{n}	Matches exactly n occurrences of the preceding pattern.
{n,}	Matches at least n occurrences of the preceding pattern.
{n,m}	Matches between n and m (inclusive) occurrences of the preceding pattern.

Fig. 16.20 | Quantifiers used in regular expressions.

object contains a Success property that indicates whether method Match's first argument matched the pattern specified by the regular expression in the second argument. If the value of Success is false (i.e., there was no match), lines 36–37 display an error message, line 38 sets the focus back to the lastNameTextBox so that the user can retype the input and line 39 terminates the event handler. If there is a match, the event handler proceeds to validate the first name. This process continues until the event handler validates the user input in all the TextBoxes or until a validation fails. If all of the fields contain valid information, the program displays a message dialog stating this, and the program exits when the user dismisses the dialog.

```
1   // Fig. 16.21: Validate.cs
2   // Validate user information using regular expressions.
3   using System;
4   using System.Text.RegularExpressions;
5   using System.Windows.Forms;
6
7   public partial class ValidateForm : Form
8   {
9      // default constructor
10     public ValidateForm()
11     {
12        InitializeComponent();
13     } // end constructor
14
15     // handles OkButton Click event
16     private void okButton_Click( object sender, EventArgs e )
17     {
18        // ensures no TextBoxes are empty
19        if ( lastNameTextBox.Text == "" || firstNameTextBox.Text == "" ||
20           addressTextBox.Text == "" || cityTextBox.Text == "" ||
21           stateTextBox.Text == "" || zipCodeTextBox.Text == "" ||
22           phoneTextBox.Text == "" )
23        {
24           // display popup box
25           MessageBox.Show( "Please fill in all fields", "Error",
26              MessageBoxButtons.OK, MessageBoxIcon.Error );
27           lastNameTextBox.Focus(); // set focus to lastNameTextBox
28           return;
29        } // end if
30
31        // if last name format invalid show message
32        if ( !Regex.Match( lastNameTextBox.Text,
33           "^[A-Z][a-zA-Z]*$" ).Success )
34        {
35           // last name was incorrect
36           MessageBox.Show( "Invalid last name", "Message",
37              MessageBoxButtons.OK, MessageBoxIcon.Error );
38           lastNameTextBox.Focus();
39           return;
40        } // end if
41
```

Fig. 16.21 | Validating user information using regular expressions. (Part 1 of 4.)

```
42        // if first name format invalid show message
43        if ( !Regex.Match( firstNameTextBox.Text,
44           "^[A-Z][a-zA-Z]*$" ).Success )
45        {
46           // first name was incorrect
47           MessageBox.Show( "Invalid first name", "Message",
48              MessageBoxButtons.OK, MessageBoxIcon.Error );
49           firstNameTextBox.Focus();
50           return;
51        } // end if
52
53        // if address format invalid show message
54        if ( !Regex.Match( addressTextBox.Text,
55           @"^[0-9]+\s+([a-zA-Z]+|[a-zA-Z]+\s[a-zA-Z]+)$" ).Success )
56        {
57           // address was incorrect
58           MessageBox.Show( "Invalid address", "Message",
59              MessageBoxButtons.OK, MessageBoxIcon.Error );
60           addressTextBox.Focus();
61           return;
62        } // end if
63
64        // if city format invalid show message
65        if ( !Regex.Match( cityTextBox.Text,
66           @"^([a-zA-Z]+|[a-zA-Z]+\s[a-zA-Z]+)$" ).Success )
67        {
68           // city was incorrect
69           MessageBox.Show( "Invalid city", "Message",
70              MessageBoxButtons.OK, MessageBoxIcon.Error );
71           cityTextBox.Focus();
72           return;
73        } // end if
74
75        // if state format invalid show message
76        if ( !Regex.Match( stateTextBox.Text,
77           @"^([a-zA-Z]+|[a-zA-Z]+\s[a-zA-Z]+)$" ).Success )
78        {
79           // state was incorrect
80           MessageBox.Show( "Invalid state", "Message",
81              MessageBoxButtons.OK, MessageBoxIcon.Error );
82           stateTextBox.Focus();
83           return;
84        } // end if
85
86        // if zip code format invalid show message
87        if ( !Regex.Match( zipCodeTextBox.Text, @"^\d{5}$" ).Success )
88        {
89           // zip was incorrect
90           MessageBox.Show( "Invalid zip code", "Message",
91              MessageBoxButtons.OK, MessageBoxIcon.Error );
92           zipCodeTextBox.Focus();
93           return;
94        } // end if
```

Fig. 16.21 | Validating user information using regular expressions. (Part 2 of 4.)

```
95
96          // if phone number format invalid show message
97          if ( !Regex.Match( phoneTextBox.Text,
98             @"^[1-9]\d{2}-[1-9]\d{2}-\d{4}$" ).Success )
99          {
100             // phone number was incorrect
101             MessageBox.Show( "Invalid phone number", "Message",
102                MessageBoxButtons.OK, MessageBoxIcon.Error );
103             phoneTextBox.Focus();
104             return;
105          } // end if
106
107          // information is valid, signal user and exit application
108          this.Hide(); // hide main window while MessageBox displays
109          MessageBox.Show( "Thank You!", "Information Correct",
110             MessageBoxButtons.OK, MessageBoxIcon.Information );
111          Application.Exit();
112       } // end method okButton_Click
113    } // end class ValidateForm
```

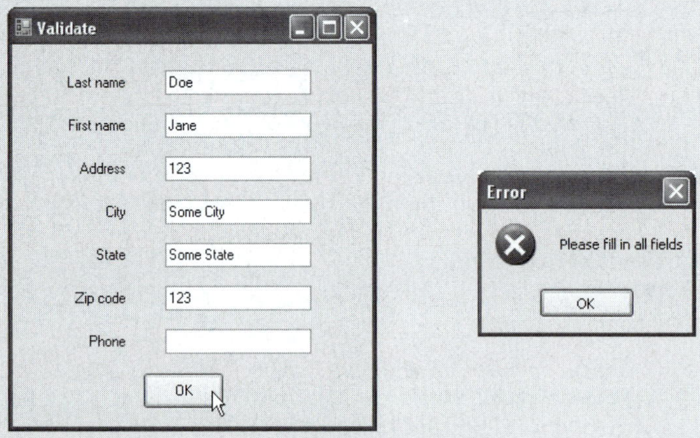

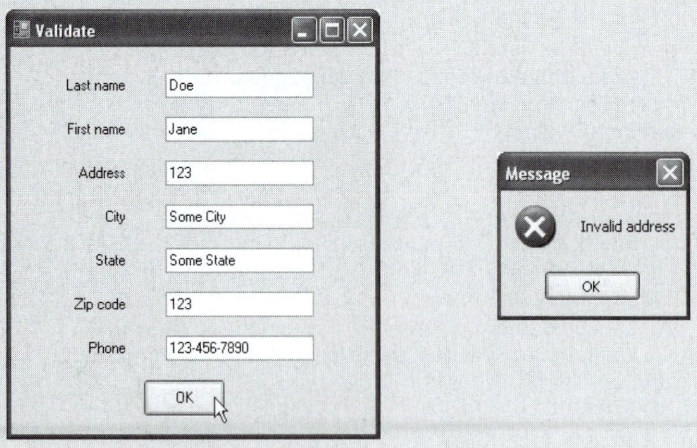

Fig. 16.21 | Validating user information using regular expressions. (Part 3 of 4.)

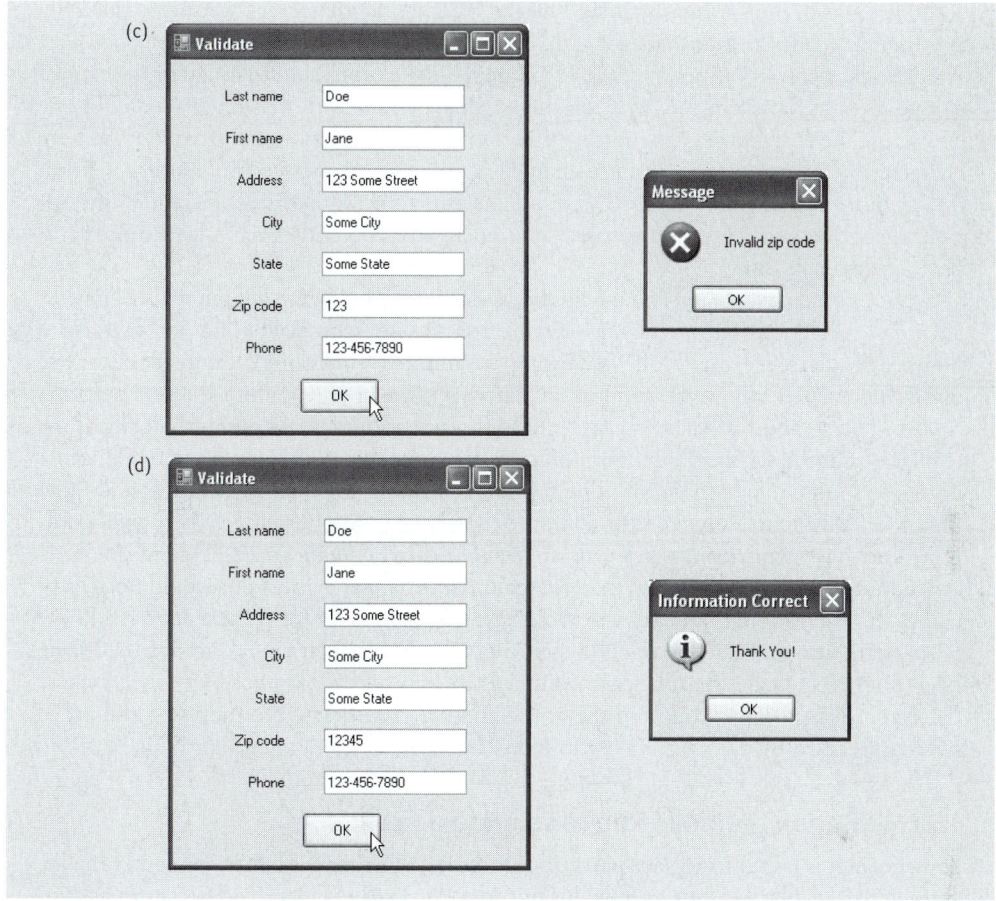

Fig. 16.21 | Validating user information using regular expressions. (Part 4 of 4.)

In the previous example, we searched a string for substrings that matched a regular expression. In this example, we want to ensure that the entire string in each TextBox conforms to a particular regular expression. For example, we want to accept "Smith" as a last name, but not "9@Smith#". In a regular expression that begins with a "^" character and ends with a "$" character, the characters "^" and "$" represent the beginning and end of a string, respectively. These characters force a regular expression to return a match only if the entire string being processed matches the regular expression.

The regular expression in line 33 uses the square bracket and range notation to match an uppercase first letter, followed by letters of any case—a-z matches any lowercase letter, and A-Z matches any uppercase letter. The * quantifier signifies that the second range of characters may occur zero or more times in the string. Thus, this expression matches any string consisting of one uppercase letter, followed by zero or more additional letters.

The notation \s matches a single whitespace character (lines 55, 66 and 77). The expression \d{5}, used in the **Zip** (zip code) field, matches any five digits (line 87). Note that without the "^" and "$" characters, the regular expression would match any five consecutive digits in the string. By including the "^" and "$" characters, we ensure that only five-digit zip codes are allowed.

The character "|" (lines 55, 66 and 77) matches the expression to its left or the expression to its right. For example, Hi (John|Jane) matches both Hi John and Hi Jane. In line 55, we use the character "|" to indicate that the address can contain a word of one or more characters *or* a word of one or more characters followed by a space and another word of one or more characters. Note the use of parentheses to group parts of the regular expression. Quantifiers may be applied to patterns enclosed in parentheses to create more complex regular expressions.

The **Last name** and **First name** fields both accept strings of any length that begin with an uppercase letter. The regular expression for the **Address** field (line 55) matches a number of at least one digit, followed by a space and then either one or more letters or else one or more letters followed by a space and another series of one or more letters. Therefore, "10 Broadway" and "10 Main Street" are both valid addresses. As currently formed, the regular expression in line 55 does not match an address that does not start with a number or that has more than two words. The regular expressions for the **City** (line 66) and **State** (line 77) fields match any word of at least one character or, alternatively, any two words of at least one character if the words are separated by a single space. This means both Waltham and West Newton would match. Again, these regular expressions would not accept names that have more than two words. The regular expression for the **Zip code** field (line 87) ensures that the zip code is a five-digit number. The regular expression for the **Phone** field (line 98) indicates that the phone number must be of the form xxx-yyy-yyyy, where the xs represent the area code and the ys the number. The first x and the first y cannot be zero, as specified by the range [1-9] in each case.

16.16.3 Regex methods `Replace` and `Split`

Sometimes it is useful to replace parts of one string with another or to split a string according to a regular expression. For this purpose, the Regex class provides static and instance versions of methods Replace and Split, which are demonstrated in Fig. 16.22.

```csharp
1   // Fig. 16.22: RegexSubstitution.cs
2   // Using Regex method Replace.
3   using System;
4   using System.Text.RegularExpressions;
5
6   class RegexSubstitution
7   {
8      public static void Main()
9      {
10         string testString1 =
11            "This sentence ends in 5 stars *****";
12         string output = "";
13         string testString2 = "1, 2, 3, 4, 5, 6, 7, 8";
14         Regex testRegex1 = new Regex( @"\d" );
15         string[] result;
16
```

Fig. 16.22 | Regex methods `Replace` and `Split`. (Part 1 of 2.)

```
17          Console.WriteLine( "Original string: " +
18             testString1 );
19          testString1 = Regex.Replace( testString1, @"\*", "^" );
20          Console.WriteLine( "^ substituted for *: " + testString1 );
21          testString1 = Regex.Replace( testString1, "stars",
22             "carets" );
23          Console.WriteLine( "\"carets\" substituted for \"stars\": " +
24             testString1 );
25          Console.WriteLine( "Every word replaced by \"word\": " +
26             Regex.Replace( testString1, @"\w+", "word" ) );
27          Console.WriteLine( "\nOriginal string: " + testString2 );
28          Console.WriteLine( "Replace first 3 digits by \"digit\": " +
29             testRegex1.Replace( testString2, "digit", 3 ) );
30          Console.Write( "string split at commas [" );
31
32          result = Regex.Split( testString2, @",\s" );
33
34          foreach ( string resultString in result )
35             output += "\"" + resultString + "\", ";
36
37          // Delete ", " at the end of output string
38          Console.WriteLine( output.Substring( 0, output.Length - 2 ) + "]" );
39       } // end method Main
40    } // end class RegexSubstitution
```

```
Original string: This sentence ends in 5 stars *****
^ substituted for *: This sentence ends in 5 stars ^^^^^
"carets" substituted for "stars": This sentence ends in 5 carets ^^^^^
Every word replaced by "word": word word word word word word ^^^^^

Original string: 1, 2, 3, 4, 5, 6, 7, 8
Replace first 3 digits by "digit": digit, digit, digit, 4, 5, 6, 7, 8
string split at commas ["1", "2", "3", "4", "5", "6", "7", "8"]
```

Fig. 16.22 | Regex methods `Replace` and `Split`. (Part 2 of 2.)

Method `Replace` replaces text in a `string` with new text wherever the original `string` matches a regular expression. We use two versions of this method in Fig. 16.22. The first version (line 19) is `static` and takes three parameters—the `string` to modify, the `string` containing the regular expression to match and the replacement `string`. Here, `Replace` replaces every instance of "*" in `testString1` with "^". Notice that the regular expression (@"*") precedes character * with a backslash, \. Normally, * is a quantifier indicating that a regular expression should match any number of occurrences of a preceding pattern. However, in line 19, we want to find all occurrences of the literal character *; to do this, we must escape character * with character \. By escaping a special regular expression character with a \, we tell the regular-expression matching engine to find the actual character * rather than use it as a quantifier.

The second version of method `Replace` (line 29) is an instance method that uses the regular expression passed to the constructor for `testRegex1` (line 14) to perform the replacement operation. Line 14 instantiates `testRegex1` with argument @"\d". The call to instance method `Replace` in line 29 takes three arguments—a `string` to modify, a `string` containing the replacement text and an `int` specifying the number of replacements to make. In this case, line 29 replaces the first three instances of a digit (`"\d"`) in `testString2` with the text `"digit"`.

Method `Split` divides a `string` into several substrings. The original `string` is broken at delimiters that match a specified regular expression. Method `Split` returns an array containing the substrings. In line 32, we use the `static` version of method `Split` to separate a `string` of comma-separated integers. The first argument is the `string` to split; the second argument is the regular expression that represents the delimiter. The regular expression `@",\s"` separates the substrings at each comma. By matching any whitespace characters (`\s*` in the regular expression), we eliminate extra spaces from the resulting substrings.

16.17 Wrap-Up

In this chapter, you learned about the FCL's string and character processing capabilities. We overviewed the fundamentals of characters and strings. You saw how to determine the length of strings, copy strings, access the individual characters in strings, search strings, obtain substrings from larger strings, compare strings, concatenate strings, replace characters in strings and convert strings to uppercase or lowercase letters.

We showed how to use class `StringBuilder` to build strings dynamically. You learned how to determine and specify the size of a `StringBuilder` object, and how to append, insert, remove and replace characters in a `StringBuilder` object. We then introduced the character testing methods of type `Char` that enable a program to determine whether a character is a digit, a letter, a lowercase letter, an uppercase letter, a punctuation mark or a symbol other than a punctuation mark, and the methods for converting a character to uppercase or lowercase.

Finally, we discussed classes `Regex` and `Match` from the `System.Text.Regular-Expressions` namespace and the symbols that are used to form regular expressions. You learned how to find patterns in a string and match entire strings to patterns with `Regex` methods `Match` and `Matches`, how to replace characters in a string with `Regex` method `Replace` and how to split strings at delimiters with `Regex` method `Split`. In the next chapter, you will learn how to add graphics and other multimedia capabilities to your Windows applications.

Summary

Section 16.2 Fundamentals of Characters and Strings
- Characters are the fundamental building blocks of C# program code. Every program is composed of a sequence of characters that is interpreted by the compiler as a series of instructions used to accomplish a task.
- A `string` is a series of characters treated as a single unit. A `string` may include letters, digits and the various special characters: +, -, *, /, $ and others.

Section 16.5 Comparing `strings`
- All characters correspond to numeric codes. When the computer compares two `strings`, it actually compares the Unicode values of the characters in the `strings`.

- Method `Equals` uses a lexicographical comparison—if a certain `string` has a higher value than another `string`, it would be found later in a dictionary.

- Method `CompareTo` returns 0 if the strings are equal, a negative number if the `string` that invokes `CompareTo` is less than the `string` passed as an argument and a positive number if the `string` that invokes `CompareTo` is greater than the `string` passed as an argument. Method `CompareTo` uses a lexicographical comparison.

- `string` method `StartsWith` determines whether a `string` starts with the characters specified as an argument. `string` method `EndsWith` determines whether a `string` ends with the characters specified as an argument.

Section 16.6 Locating Characters and Substrings in `strings`

- `string` method `IndexOf` locates the first occurrence of a character or a substring in a `string`. Method `LastIndexOf` locates the last occurrence of a character or a substring in a `string`.

Section 16.7 Extracting Substrings from `strings`

- Class `string` provides two `Substring` methods to enable a new `string` to be created by copying part of an existing `string`.

Section 16.8 Concatenating `strings`

- The static method `Concat` of class `string` concatenates two `strings` and returns a new `string` containing the characters from both original `strings`.

Section 16.9 Miscellaneous `string` Methods

- Methods `Replace`, `ToUpper`, `ToLower`, `Trim` and `Remove` are provided for more advanced string manipulation.

Section 16.10 Class `StringBuilder`

- The `string` class provides many capabilities for processing strings. Once a `string` is created, its contents can never change. Class `StringBuilder` is available for creating and manipulating strings that can change.

Section 16.11 Length and Capacity Properties, EnsureCapacity Method and Indexer of Class `StringBuilder`

- Class `StringBuilder` provides `Length` and `Capacity` properties to return the number of characters currently in a `StringBuilder` and the number of characters that can be stored in a `StringBuilder` without allocating more memory, respectively. These properties also can be used to increase or decrease the length or the capacity of the `StringBuilder`.

- Method `EnsureCapacity` allows you to guarantee that a `StringBuilder` has a minimum capacity. Method `EnsureCapacity` attempts to double the capacity. If this value is greater than the value that you wish to ensure, this will be the new capacity. Otherwise, `EnsureCapacity` alters the capacity to make it equal to the requested number.

Section 16.12 Append and AppendFormat Methods of Class `StringBuilder`

- Class `StringBuilder` provides 19 overloaded `Append` methods to allow various types of values to be added to the end of a `StringBuilder`. Versions are provided for each of the simple types and for character arrays, `strings` and `Objects`.

- The braces in a format string specify how to format a specific piece of information. Formats have the form {X[,Y][:FormatString]}, where X is the number of the argument to be formatted, counting from zero. Y is an optional argument, which can be positive or negative. Y indicates how many characters should be in the result of formatting. If the resulting string has fewer characters than this number, it will be padded with spaces to make up for the difference. A positive integer means the string will be right aligned; a negative one means the string will be left aligned. The optional FormatString indicates what kind of formatting should be applied to the argument—currency, decimal, or scientific, among others.

Section 16.13 Insert, Remove *and* Replace *Methods of Class* StringBuilder

- Class StringBuilder provides 18 overloaded Insert methods to allow various types of values to be inserted at any position in a StringBuilder. Versions are provided for each of the simple types and for character arrays, strings and Objects.
- Class StringBuilder also provides method Remove for deleting any portion of a StringBuilder.
- StringBuilder method Replace searches for a specified string or character and substitutes another in its place.

Section 16.14 Char *Methods*

- C# provides a type called a struct (short for structure) that is similar to a class.
- structs represent value types.
- Like classes, structs can have methods and properties, and can use the access modifiers public and private.
- struct members are accessed via the member access operator (.).
- The simple types are actually aliases for struct types.
- All struct types derive from class ValueType, which in turn derives from object.
- All struct types are implicitly sealed, so they do not support virtual or abstract methods, and their members cannot be declared protected or protected internal.
- Char is a struct that represents characters.
- Method Char.Parse converts string data into a character.
- Method Char.IsDigit determines whether a character is a defined Unicode digit.
- Method Char.IsLetter determines whether a character is a letter.
- Method Char.IsLetterOrDigit determines whether a character is a letter or a digit.
- Method Char.IsLower determines whether a character is a lowercase letter, if appropriate.
- Method Char.IsUpper determines whether a character is an uppercase letter, if appropriate.
- Method Char.ToUpper converts a lowercase character to its uppercase equivalent.
- Method Char.ToLower converts an uppercase character to its lowercase equivalent.
- Method Char.IsPunctuation determines whether a character is a punctuation mark.
- Method Char.IsSymbol determines whether a character is a symbol.
- Method Char.IsWhiteSpace determines whether a character is a whitespace character.
- Method Char.CompareTo compares two character values.

Section 16.16 Regular Expressions and Class Regex

- Regular expressions find patterns in text.
- The .NET Framework provides class Regex to aid developers in recognizing and manipulating regular expressions. Regex provides method Match, which returns an object of class Match. This object represents a single match in a regular expression. Regex also provides the method Matches, which finds all matches of a regular expression in an arbitrary string and returns a MatchCollection—a set of Matches.

- Classes `Regex` and `Match` are in namespace `System.Text.RegularExpressions`.
- In general, applying the quantifier `*` to any expression will match zero or more occurrences of that expression, and applying the quantifier `+` will match one or more occurrences of that expression.
- A character class is an escape sequence that matches one in a specific group of characters.
- The pattern `"[0-35-9]"` is a regular expression that matches any digit 0-3 and 5-9, i.e. any digit except 4.
- The character `"."` matches any character other than a newline.
- The characters `"^"` and `"$"` match the positions at the beginning and end of a string, respectively.
- The character `"|"` matches the expression to its left *or* to its right. For example, `"Hi (John|Jane)"` matches both `"Hi John"` and `"Hi Jane"`.
- Method `Replace` replaces with a specified `string` those substrings in a `string` that match a certain regular expression.

Terminology

\d
\w
\s
\D
\W
\S
$
^@ verbatim string character
+ operator
+= concatenation operator
== equality operator
alphabetizing
Append method of class `StringBuilder`
AppendFormat method of class `StringBuilder`
ArgumentOutOfRangeException
Capacity property of `StringBuilder`
char array
Char struct
Chars property of class `string`
character
character class, in regular expressions
character constant
CompareTo method of class `string`
CompareTo method of struct `Char`
Concat method of class `string`
CopyTo method of class `string`
Enabled property of class `Control`
EndsWith method of class `string`
EnsureCapacity method of class `StringBuilder`
Equals method of class `string`
Equals method of struct `Char`
format string
greedy quantifier

immutable string
IndexOf method of class `string`
IndexOfAny method of class `string`
Insert method of class `StringBuilder`
IsDigit method of struct `Char`
IsLetter method of struct `Char`
IsLetterOrDigit method of struct `Char`
IsLower method of struct `Char`
IsPunctuation method of struct `Char`
IsSymbol method of struct `Char`
IsUpper method of struct `Char`
IsWhiteSpace method of struct `Char`
LastIndexOf method of class `string`
LastIndexOfAny method of class `string`
lazy quantifier
Length property of class `string`
Length property of class `StringBuilder`
lexicographical comparison
Match class
MatchCollection class
page-layout software
quantifier, in regular expressions
random-number generation
Regex class for regular expressions
regular expression
Remove method of class `StringBuilder`
Replace method of class `Regex`
Replace method of class `string`
Replace method of class `StringBuilder`
special characters
Split method of class `Regex`
StartsWith method of class `string`
string class
string literal

string reference	ToString method of class string
StringBuilder class	ToString method of StringBuilder
struct keyword	ToUpper method of class string
Substring method of class string	ToUpper method of struct Char
Success property of class Match	trailing whitespace characters
System namespace	Trim method of class string
System.Text namespace	Unicode character set
System.Text.RegularExpressions namespace	ValueType class
text editor	verbatim string syntax
ToLower method of class string	whitespace character
ToLower method of struct Char	word character

Self-Review Exercises

16.1 State whether each of the following is *true* or *false*. If *false*, explain why.

a) When strings are compared with ==, the result is true if the strings contain the same values.

b) A string can be modified after it is created.

c) StringBuilder method EnsureCapacity sets the StringBuilder instance's length to the argument's value.

d) Method Equals and the equality operator work the same for strings.

e) Method Trim removes all whitespace at the beginning and the end of a string.

f) A regular expression matches a string to a pattern.

g) It is always better to use strings, rather than StringBuilders, because strings containing the same value will reference the same object in memory.

h) string method ToUpper creates a new string with the first letter capitalized.

i) The expression \d in a regular expression denotes all letters.

16.2 Fill in the blanks in each of the following statements:

a) To concatenate strings, use the _____ operator, StringBuilder method _____ or String method _____.

b) Method Compare of class string uses a(n) _____ comparison of strings.

c) Class Regex is located in namespace _____.

d) StringBuilder method _____ first formats the specified string, then concatenates it to the end of the StringBuilder.

e) If the arguments to a Substring method call are out of range, a(n) _____ exception is thrown.

f) Regex method _____ changes all occurrences of a pattern in a string to a specified string.

g) A C in a format string means to output the number as _____.

h) Regular expression quantifier _____ matches zero or more occurrences of an expression.

i) Regular expression operator _____ inside square brackets will not match any of the characters in that set of brackets.

Answers to Self-Review Exercises

16.1 a) True. b) False. strings are immutable; they cannot be modified after they are created. StringBuilder objects can be modified after they are created. c) False. EnsureCapacity sets the instance's capacity to either double the current capacity or the value of its argument, whichever is larg-

To begin drawing in C#, we first must understand GDI+'s *coordinate system* (Fig. 17.2), a scheme for identifying every point on the screen. By default, the upper-left corner of a GUI component (such as a `Panel` or a `Form`) has the coordinates (0, 0). A coordinate pair has both an *x-coordinate* (the *horizontal coordinate*) and a *y-coordinate* (the *vertical coordinate*). The *x*-coordinate is the horizontal distance (to the right) from the upper-left corner. The *y*-coordinate is the vertical distance (downward) from the upper-left corner. The *x-axis* defines every horizontal coordinate, and the *y-axis* defines every vertical coordinate. Programmers position text and shapes on the screen by specifying their (*x*, *y*) coordinates. Coordinate units are measured in pixels ("picture elements"), which are the smallest units of *resolution* on a display monitor.

Portability Tip 17.1

Different display monitors have different resolutions, so the density of pixels on such monitors will vary. This might cause the sizes of graphics to appear different on different monitors.

The `System.Drawing` namespace provides several structures that represent sizes and locations in the coordinate system. The *Point* structure represents the *x-y* coordinates of a point on a two-dimensional plane. The *Rectangle* structure defines the loading width and height of a rectangular shape. The `Size` structure represents the width and height of a shape.

17.3 Graphics Contexts and Graphics Objects

A C# *graphics context* represents a drawing surface that enables drawing on the screen. A `Graphics` object manages a graphics context by controlling how information is drawn. `Graphics` objects contain methods for drawing, font manipulation, color manipulation and other graphics-related actions. Every derived class of `System.Windows.Forms.Form` inherits a `virtual` *OnPaint* method in which most graphics operations are performed. The arguments to the `OnPaint` method include a *PaintEventArgs* object from which we can obtain a `Graphics` object for the `Form`. We must obtain the `Graphics` object on each call to the method, because the properties of the graphics context that the graphics object represents could change. Method `OnPaint` triggers the `Control`'s *Paint* event.

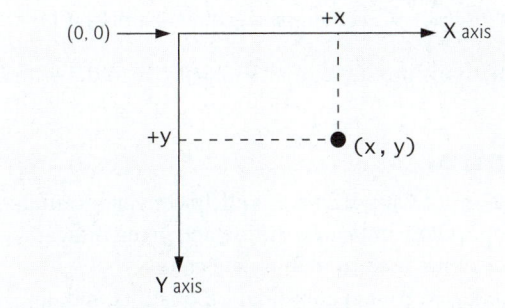

Fig. 17.2 | GDI+ coordinate system. Units are measured in pixels.

When drawing on a Form, you can override method OnPaint to retrieve a Graphics object from argument PaintEventArgs or to create a new Graphics object associated with the appropriate surface. We demonstrate these drawing techniques in C# later in the chapter.

To override the inherited OnPaint method, use the following method header:

protected override void OnPaint(PaintEventArgs e)

Next, extract the incoming Graphics object from argument PaintEventArg, as in:

Graphics graphicsObject = e.Graphics;

Variable graphicsObject can now be used to draw shapes and strings on the form.

Calling the OnPaint method raises the Paint event. Instead of overriding the OnPaint method, programmers can add an event handler for the Paint event. Visual Studio .NET generates the Paint event handler in this form:

protected void MyEventHandler_Paint(
  object sender, PaintEventArgs e)

Programmers seldom call the OnPaint method directly, because drawing graphics is an *event-driven process*. An event—such as covering, uncovering or resizing a window—calls the OnPaint method of that Form. Similarly, when any control (such as a TextBox or Label) is displayed, that control's OnPaint method is called.

You can force a call to OnPaint by calling a Control's **Invalidate** method. This method refreshes a control and implicitly repaints all its graphical components. Class Control has several overloaded Invalidate methods that allow programmers to update portions of a control.

Performance Tip 17.1

Calling the Invalidate method to refresh the Control can be inefficient if only a small portion of a Control needs refreshing. Calling Invalidate with a Rectangle parameter refreshes only the area designated by the rectangle. This improves program performance.

Controls, such as Labels and Buttons, do not have their own graphics contexts, but you can create them. To draw on a control, first create a graphics object by invoking the control's CreateGraphics method, as in:

Graphics *graphicsObject* = *controlName*.CreateGraphics();

Now you can use the methods provided in class Graphics to draw on the control.

17.4 Color Control

Colors can enhance a program's appearance and help convey meaning. For example, a red traffic light indicates stop, yellow indicates caution and green indicates go. Structure Color defines methods and constants used to manipulate colors.

Every color can be created from a combination of alpha, red, green and blue components (called *ARGB values*). All four ARGB components are bytes that represent integer values in the range 0 to 255. The alpha value determines the opacity of the color. For example, the alpha value 0 represents a transparent color, and the value 255 represents an opaque color. Alpha values between 0 and 255 result in a weighted blending effect of the color's *RGB value* with that of any background color, causing a semitransparent effect. The first number in the RGB value defines the amount of red in the color, the second defines the amount of green and the third defines the amount of blue. The larger the value, the greater the amount of that particular color. C# enables programmers to choose from almost 17 million colors. If a particular computer cannot display all these colors, it will display the color closest to the one specified. Figure 17.3 summarizes some predefined Color constants (all are public and static), and Fig. 17.4 describes several Color methods and properties. For a complete list of predefined Color constants, methods and properties, see the online documentation for the Color structure (msdn2.microsoft.com/en-us/library/system.drawing.color).

Constants in structure Color	RGB value	Constants in structure Color	RGB value
Orange	255, 200, 0	White	255, 255, 255
Pink	255, 175, 175	Gray	128, 128, 128
Cyan	0, 255, 255	DarkGray	64, 64, 64
Magenta	255, 0, 255	Red	255, 0, 0
Yellow	255, 255, 0	Green	0, 255, 0
Black	0, 0, 0	Blue	0, 0, 255

Fig. 17.3 | Color structure static constants and their RGB values.

Structure Color methods and properties	Description
Common Methods	
FromArgb	A static method that creates a color based on red, green and blue values expressed as ints from 0 to 255. The overloaded version allows specification of alpha, red, green and blue values.
FromName	A static method that creates a color from a name, passed as a string.
Common Properties	
A	A byte between 0 and 255, representing the alpha component.
R	A byte between 0 and 255, representing the red component.
G	A byte between 0 and 255, representing the green component.
B	A byte between 0 and 255, representing the blue component.

Fig. 17.4 | Color structure members.

The table in Fig. 17.4 describes two *FromArgb* method calls. One takes three int arguments, and one takes four int arguments (all argument values must be between 0 and 255, inclusive). Both take int arguments specifying the amount of red, green and blue. The overloaded version also allows the user to specify the alpha component; the three-argument version defaults the alpha to 255 (opaque). Both methods return a Color object. Color properties *A*, *R*, *G* and *B* return bytes that represent int values from 0 to 255, corresponding to the amounts of alpha, red, green and blue, respectively.

Programmers draw shapes and strings with Brushes and Pens. A Pen, which functions similarly to an ordinary pen, is used to draw lines. Most drawing methods require a Pen object. The overloaded Pen constructors allow programmers to specify the colors and widths of the lines that they wish to draw. The System.Drawing namespace also provides a Pens class containing predefined Pens.

All classes derived from abstract class Brush define objects that color the interiors of graphical shapes. For example, the SolidBrush constructor takes a Color object—the color to draw. In most Fill methods, Brushes fill a space with a color, pattern or image. Figure 17.5 summarizes various Brushes and their functions.

Manipulating Colors

Figure 17.6 demonstrates several of the methods and properties described in Fig. 17.4. It displays two overlapping rectangles, allowing you to experiment with color values, color names and alpha values (for transparency).

Class	Description
HatchBrush	Fills a region with a pattern. The pattern is defined by a member of the *HatchStyle enumeration*, a foreground color (with which the pattern is drawn) and a background color.
LinearGradientBrush	Fills a region with a gradual blend of one color to another. Linear gradients are defined along a line. They can be specified by the two colors, the angle of the gradient and either the width of a rectangle or two points.
SolidBrush	Fills a region with one color that is specified by a Color object.
TextureBrush	Fills a region by repeating a specified Image across the surface.

Fig. 17.5 | Classes that derive from class Brush.

```
1   // Fig 17.6: ShowColors.cs
2   // Color value and alpha demonstration.
3   using System;
4   using System.Drawing;
5   using System.Windows.Forms;
6
7   public partial class ShowColors : Form
8   {
```

Fig. 17.6 | Color value and alpha demonstration. (Part 1 of 3.)

```
 9        // color for back rectangle
10        private Color backColor = Color.Wheat;
11
12        // color for front rectangle
13        private Color frontColor = Color.FromArgb( 100, 0, 0, 255 );
14
15        // default constructor
16        public ShowColors()
17        {
18           InitializeComponent();
19        } // end constructor
20
21        // override Form OnPaint method
22        protected override void OnPaint( PaintEventArgs e )
23        {
24           Graphics graphicsObject = e.Graphics; // get graphics
25
26           // create text brush
27           SolidBrush textBrush = new SolidBrush( Color.Black );
28
29           // create solid brush
30           SolidBrush brush = new SolidBrush( Color.White );
31
32           // draw white background
33           graphicsObject.FillRectangle( brush, 4, 4, 275, 180 );
34
35           // display name of backColor
36           graphicsObject.DrawString( backColor.Name, this.Font,
37              textBrush, 40, 5 );
38
39           // set brush color and display back rectangle
40           brush.Color = backColor;
41           graphicsObject.FillRectangle( brush, 45, 20, 150, 120 );
42
43           // display Argb values of front color
44           graphicsObject.DrawString( "Alpha: " + frontColor.A +
45              " Red: " + frontColor.R + " Green: " + frontColor.G +
46              " Blue: " + frontColor.B, this.Font, textBrush, 55, 165 );
47
48           // set brush color and display front rectangle
49           brush.Color = frontColor;
50           graphicsObject.FillRectangle( brush, 65, 35, 170, 130 );
51        } // end method OnPaint
52
53        // handle colorNameButton click event
54        private void colorNameButton_Click( object sender, EventArgs e )
55        {
56           // set backColor to color specified in text box
57           backColor = Color.FromName( colorNameTextBox.Text );
58
59           Invalidate(); // refresh Form
60        } // end method colorNameButton_Click
61
```

Fig. 17.6 | Color value and alpha demonstration. (Part 2 of 3.)

```
62        // handle colorValueButton click event
63        private void colorValueButton_Click( object sender, EventArgs e )
64        {
65           // obtain new front color from text boxes
66           frontColor = Color.FromArgb(
67              Convert.ToInt32( alphaTextBox.Text ),
68              Convert.ToInt32( redTextBox.Text ),
69              Convert.ToInt32( greenTextBox.Text ),
70              Convert.ToInt32( blueTextBox.Text ) );
71
72           Invalidate(); // refresh Form
73        } // end method colorValueButton_Click
74     } // end class ShowColors
```

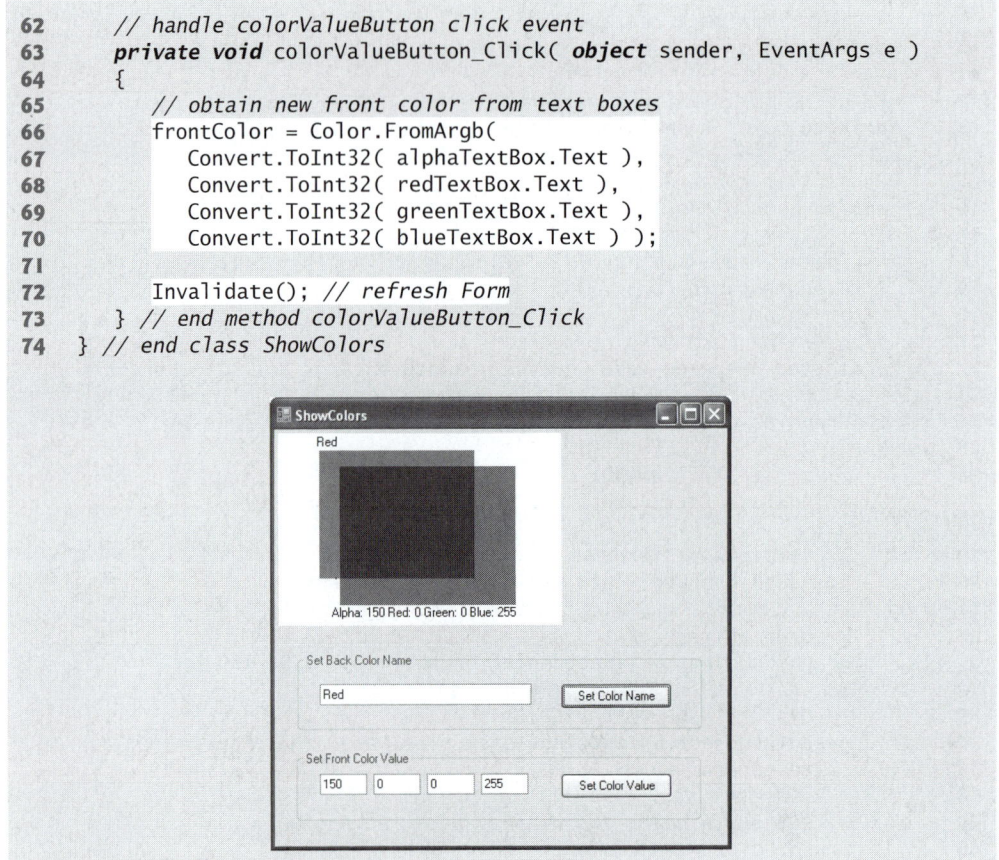

Fig. 17.6 | Color value and alpha demonstration. (Part 3 of 3.)

When the application begins executing, its Form is displayed. This results in a call to ShowColors's OnPaint method to paint the Form's contents. Line 24 gets a reference to PaintEventArgs e's Graphics object and assigns it to graphicsObject. Lines 27 and 30 create a black and a white SolidBrush for drawing solid shapes on the Form. Class *Solid-Brush* derives from abstract base class Brush, so a SolidBrush can be passed to any method that expects a Brush parameter.

Line 33 uses Graphics method FillRectangle to draw a solid white rectangle using the SolidBrush created in line 30. FillRectangle takes as parameters a Brush, the *x*- and *y*-coordinates of the rectangle's upper-left corner, and the width and height of the rectangle. Lines 36–37 display the Name property of backColor with Graphics method *Draw-String*. There are several overloaded DrawString methods; the version demonstrated in lines 36–37 takes as arguments the string to display, the display Font, the Brush to use for drawing and the *x*- and *y*-coordinates of the location for the string's first character.

Lines 40–41 assign the backColor value to brush's Color property and display a rectangle. Lines 44–46 extract and display frontColor's ARGB values and draw a string containing those values. Lines 49–50 assign the frontColor value to brush's Color property, then draw a filled rectangle in the frontColor that overlaps the rectangle drawn at line 41.

Button event handler colorNameButton_Click (lines 54–60) uses class Color's static method *FromName* to create a new Color object from the colorName that a user enters in a TextBox. This Color is assigned to backColor (line 57). Then line 59 invokes the Form's Invalidate method to indicate that the Form should be repainted, which results in a call to OnPaint to update the Form on the screen.

Button event handler colorValueButton_Click (lines 63–73) uses Color method FromArgb to construct a new Color object from the ARGB values that a user specifies via TextBoxes, then assigns the newly created Color to frontColor. Line 72 invokes the Form's Invalidate method to indicate that the Form should be repainted, which results in a call to OnPaint to update the Form on the screen.

If the user assigns an alpha value between 0 and 255 for the frontColor, the effects of alpha blending are apparent. In the sample output, the red back rectangle blends with the blue front rectangle to create purple where the two overlap. Note that you cannot change the characteristics of an existing Color object. To use a different color, create a new Color object.

Using the ColorDialog to Select Colors from a Color Palette

The predefined GUI component *ColorDialog* is a dialog box that allows users to select from a palette of available colors or to create custom colors. Figure 17.7 demonstrates the ColorDialog. When a user selects a color and presses **OK**, the application retrieves the user's selection via the ColorDialog's *Color* property.

```
1   // Fig. 17.7: ShowColorsComplex.cs
2   // ColorDialog used to change background and text color.
3   using System;
4   using System.Drawing;
5   using System.Windows.Forms;
6
7   // allows users to change colors using a ColorDialog
8   public partial class ShowColorsComplex : Form
9   {
10      // create ColorDialog object
11      private static ColorDialog colorChooser = new ColorDialog();
12
13      // default constructor
14      public ShowColorsComplex()
15      {
16         InitializeComponent();
17      } // end constructor
18
19      // change text color
20      private void textColorButton_Click( object sender, EventArgs e )
21      {
22         // get chosen color
23         DialogResult result = colorChooser.ShowDialog();
24
25         if ( result == DialogResult.Cancel )
26            return;
27
```

Fig. 17.7 | ColorDialog used to change background and text color. (Part 1 of 2.)

```
28          // assign forecolor to result of dialog
29          backgroundColorButton.ForeColor = colorChooser.Color;
30          textColorButton.ForeColor = colorChooser.Color;
31      } // end method textColorButton_Click
32
33      // change background color
34      private void backgroundColorButton_Click( object sender, EventArgs e )
35      {
36          // show ColorDialog and get result
37          colorChooser.FullOpen = true;
38          DialogResult result = colorChooser.ShowDialog();
39
40          if ( result == DialogResult.Cancel )
41              return;
42
43          // set background color
44          this.BackColor = colorChooser.Color;
45      } // end method backgroundColorButton_Click
46  } // end class ShowColorsComplex
```

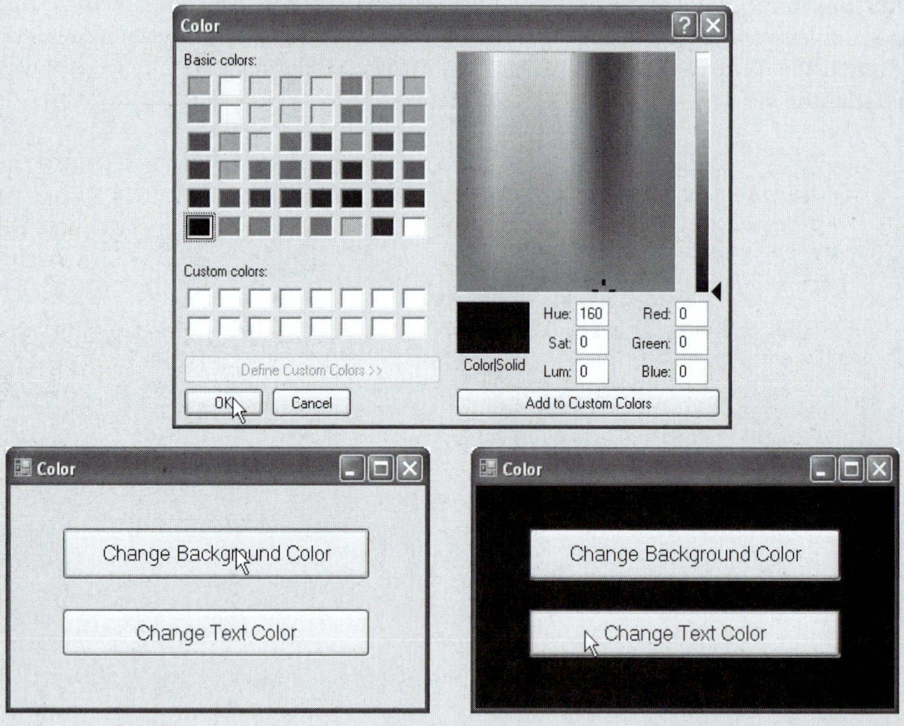

Fig. 17.7 | ColorDialog used to change background and text color. (Part 2 of 2.)

The GUI for this application contains two Buttons. The backgroundColorButton allows the user to change the form background color. The textColorButton allows the user to change the button text colors. Line 11 creates a private static ColorDialog named colorChooser, which is used in the event handlers for both Buttons.

Lines 20–31 define the `textColorButtonClick` event handler, which invokes `color-Chooser`'s `ShowDialog` method (line 23) to display the dialog. The dialog's `Color` property stores the user's selection. Lines 29–30 set the text color of both buttons to the selected color.

Lines 34–45 define the `backgroundColorButtonClick` event handler, which modifies the background color of the form by setting its `BackColor` property to the dialog's `Color` property (line 44). The method sets the `ColorDialog`'s ***FullOpen*** property to `true` (line 37), so the dialog displays all available colors, as shown in the screen capture in Fig. 17.7. When `FullOpen` is `false`, the dialog shows only the color swatches.

Users are not restricted to the `ColorDialog`'s 48 color swatches. To create a custom color, users can click anywhere in the `ColorDialog`'s large rectangle, which displays various color shades. Adjust the slider, hue and other features to refine the color. When finished, click the **Add to Custom Colors** button, which adds the custom color to a square in the **Custom Colors** section of the dialog. Clicking **OK** sets the `Color` property of the `ColorDialog` to that color.

17.5 Font Control

This section introduces methods and constants that are related to font control. The properties of Font objects cannot be modified. If you need a different Font, you must create a new Font object. There are many overloaded versions of the Font constructor for initializing Font objects. Some properties of class Font are summarized in Fig. 17.8.

Note that the ***Size*** property returns the font size as measured in design units, whereas ***SizeInPoints*** returns the font size as measured in points (the more common measurement). ***Design units*** allow the font size to be specified in one of several units of measurement, such as inches or millimeters. Some versions of the Font constructor accept a

Property	Description
Bold	Returns `true` if the font is bold.
FontFamily	Returns the Font's FontFamily—a grouping structure to organize fonts and define their similar properties.
Height	Returns the height of the font.
Italic	Returns `true` if the font is italic.
Name	Returns the font's name as a `string`.
Size	Returns a `float` value indicating the current font size measured in design units (design units are any specified unit of measurement for the font).
SizeInPoints	Returns a `float` value indicating the current font size measured in points.
Strikeout	Returns `true` if the font is in strikeout format.
Underline	Returns `true` if the font is underlined.

Fig. 17.8 | Font class read-only properties.

GraphicsUnit argument. GraphicsUnit is an enumeration that allows you to specify the unit of measurement that describes the font size. Members of the GraphicsUnit enumeration include *Point* (1/72 inch), *Display* (1/75 inch), *Document* (1/300 inch), *Millimeter*, *Inch* and *Pixel*. If this argument is provided, the Size property contains the size of the font as measured in the specified design unit, and the SizeInPoints property contains the corresponding size of the font in points. For example, if we create a Font having size 1 and specify the unit of measurement as GraphicsUnit.Inch, the Size property will be 1 and the SizeInPoints property will be 72, because there are 72 points in an inch. The default measurement for the font size is GraphicsUnit.Point (thus, the Size and SizeInPoints properties will be equal).

Class Font has several constructors. Most require a font name, which is a string representing a font currently supported by the system. Common fonts include *Microsoft SansSerif* and *Serif*. Most Font constructors also require as arguments the *font size* and *font style*. The font style is specified with a constant from the *FontStyle* enumeration (*Bold*, *Italic*, *Regular*, *Strikeout* and *Underline*, or a combination of these). You can combine font styles with the | operator, as in FontStyle.Italic | FontStyle.Bold, which makes a font both italic and bold. Graphics method *DrawString* sets the current drawing font—the font in which the text displays—to its Font argument.

Common Programming Error 17.1

Specifying a font that is not available on a system is a logic error. If this occurs, C# will substitute that system's default font.

Drawing Strings in Different Fonts

The program in Fig. 17.9 displays text in different fonts and sizes. The program uses the Font constructor to initialize the Font objects (lines 24, 28, 32 and 36). Each call to the Font constructor passes a font name (e.g., Arial, Times New Roman, Courier New or Tahoma) as a string, a font size (a float) and a FontStyle object (style). Graphics method DrawString sets the font and draws the text at the specified location. Note that line 20 creates a DarkBlue SolidBrush object (brush). All strings drawn with that brush appear in DarkBlue.

```
I    // Fig. 17.9 UsingFonts.cs
2    // Fonts and FontStyles.
3    using System;
4    using System.Drawing;
5    using System.Windows.Forms;
6
7    // demonstrate font constructors and properties
8    public partial class UsingFonts : Form
9    {
10      // default constructor
11      public UsingFonts()
12      {
13         InitializeComponent();
14      } // end constructor
15
```

Fig. 17.9 | Fonts and FontStyles. (Part 1 of 2.)

```
16      // demonstrate various font and style settings
17      protected override void OnPaint( PaintEventArgs paintEvent )
18      {
19         Graphics graphicsObject = paintEvent.Graphics;
20         SolidBrush brush = new SolidBrush( Color.DarkBlue );
21
22         // arial, 12 pt bold
23         FontStyle style = FontStyle.Bold;
24         Font arial = new Font( "Arial" , 12, style );
25
26         // times new roman, 12 pt regular
27         style = FontStyle.Regular;
28         Font timesNewRoman = new Font( "Times New Roman", 12, style );
29
30         // courier new, 16 pt bold and italic
31         style = FontStyle.Bold | FontStyle.Italic;
32         Font courierNew = new Font( "Courier New", 16, style );
33
34         // tahoma, 18 pt strikeout
35         style = FontStyle.Strikeout;
36         Font tahoma = new Font( "Tahoma", 18, style );
37
38         graphicsObject.DrawString( arial.Name +
39            " 12 point bold.", arial, brush, 10, 10 );
40
41         graphicsObject.DrawString( timesNewRoman.Name +
42            " 12 point plain.", timesNewRoman, brush, 10, 30 );
43
44         graphicsObject.DrawString( courierNew.Name +
45            " 16 point bold and italic.", courierNew,
46            brush, 10, 54 );
47
48         graphicsObject.DrawString( tahoma.Name +
49            " 18 point strikeout.", tahoma, brush, 10, 75 );
50      } // end method OnPaint
51   } // end class UsingFonts
```

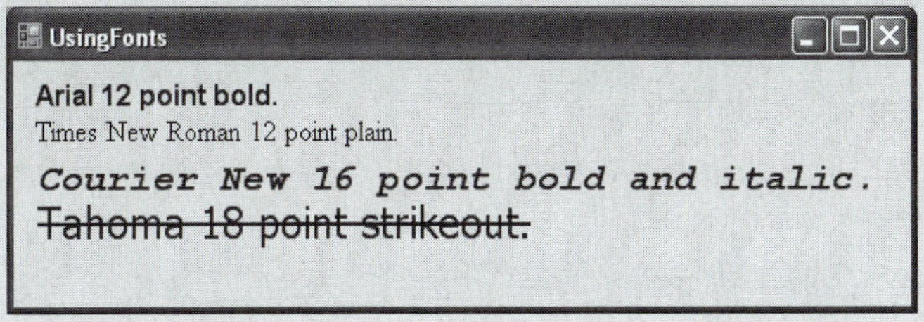

Fig. 17.9 | Fonts and FontStyles. (Part 2 of 2.)

Font Metrics

You can determine precise information about a font's *metrics* (or properties), such as *height*, *descent* (the amount that characters dip below the baseline), *ascent* (the amount that characters rise above the baseline) and *leading* (the difference between the ascent of one line and the decent of the previous line). Figure 17.10 illustrates these font metrics.

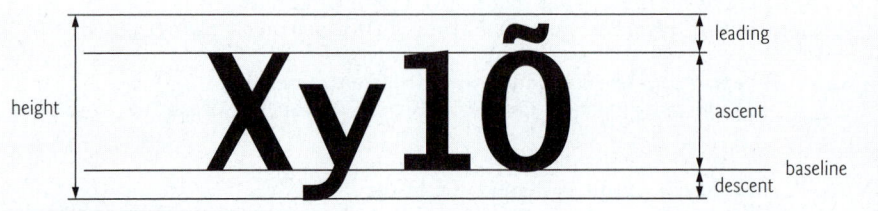

Fig. 17.10 | Font metrics illustration.

Class `FontFamily` defines characteristics common to a group of related fonts. Class `FontFamily` provides several methods used to determine the font metrics that are shared by members of a particular family. These methods are summarized in Fig. 17.11.

The program in Fig. 17.12 displays the metrics of two fonts. Line 23 creates `Font` object `arial` and sets it to 12-point Arial font. Line 24 uses `Font` property `FontFamily` to obtain object `arial`'s `FontFamily` object. Lines 27–28 output the `string` representation of the font. Lines 30–44 then use methods of class `FontFamily` to obtain the ascent, descent, height and leading of the font and draw strings containing that information. Lines 47–68 repeat this process for font `sansSerif`, a `Font` object derived from the MS Sans Serif `FontFamily`.

Method	Description
GetCellAscent	Returns an int representing the ascent of a font as measured in design units.
GetCellDescent	Returns an int representing the descent of a font as measured in design units.
GetEmHeight	Returns an int representing the height of a font as measured in design units.
GetLineSpacing	Returns an int representing the distance between two consecutive lines of text as measured in design units.

Fig. 17.11 | `FontFamily` methods that return font-metric information.

```
1   // Fig 17.12: UsingFontMetrics.cs
2   // Displaying font metric information
3   using System;
4   using System.Drawing;
5   using System.Windows.Forms;
6
7   // display font information
8   public partial class UsingFontMetrics : Form
9   {
```

Fig. 17.12 | FontFamily class used to obtain font-metric information. (Part 1 of 3.)

```
10      // default constructor
11      public UsingFontMetrics()
12      {
13         InitializeComponent();
14      } // end constructor
15
16      // displays font information
17      protected override void OnPaint( PaintEventArgs paintEvent )
18      {
19         Graphics graphicsObject = paintEvent.Graphics;
20         SolidBrush brush = new SolidBrush( Color.DarkBlue );
21
22         // Arial font metrics
23         Font arial = new Font( "Arial", 12 );
24         FontFamily family = arial.FontFamily;
25
26         // display Arial font metrics
27         graphicsObject.DrawString( "Current Font: " +
28            arial, arial, brush, 10, 10 );
29
30         graphicsObject.DrawString( "Ascent: " +
31            family.GetCellAscent( FontStyle.Regular ), arial,
32            brush, 10, 30 );
33
34         graphicsObject.DrawString( "Descent: " +
35            family.GetCellDescent( FontStyle.Regular ), arial,
36            brush, 10, 50 );
37
38         graphicsObject.DrawString( "Height: " +
39            family.GetEmHeight( FontStyle.Regular ), arial,
40            brush, 10, 70 );
41
42         graphicsObject.DrawString( "Leading: " +
43            family.GetLineSpacing( FontStyle.Regular ), arial,
44            brush, 10, 90 );
45
46         // display Sans Serif font metrics
47         Font sanSerif = new Font( "Microsoft Sans Serif",
48            14, FontStyle.Italic );
49         family = sanSerif.FontFamily;
50
51         graphicsObject.DrawString( "Current Font: " +
52            sanSerif, sanSerif, brush, 10, 130 );
53
54         graphicsObject.DrawString( "Ascent: " +
55            family.GetCellAscent( FontStyle.Regular ), sanSerif,
56            brush, 10, 150 );
57
58         graphicsObject.DrawString( "Descent: " +
59            family.GetCellDescent( FontStyle.Regular ), sanSerif,
60            brush, 10, 170 );
61
```

Fig. 17.12 | FontFamily class used to obtain font-metric information. (Part 2 of 3.)

```
62          graphicsObject.DrawString( "Height: " +
63              family.GetEmHeight( FontStyle.Regular ), sanSerif,
64              brush, 10, 190 );
65
66          graphicsObject.DrawString( "Leading: " +
67              family.GetLineSpacing( FontStyle.Regular ), sanSerif,
68              brush, 10, 210 );
69      } // end method OnPaint
70  } // end class UsingFontMetrics
```

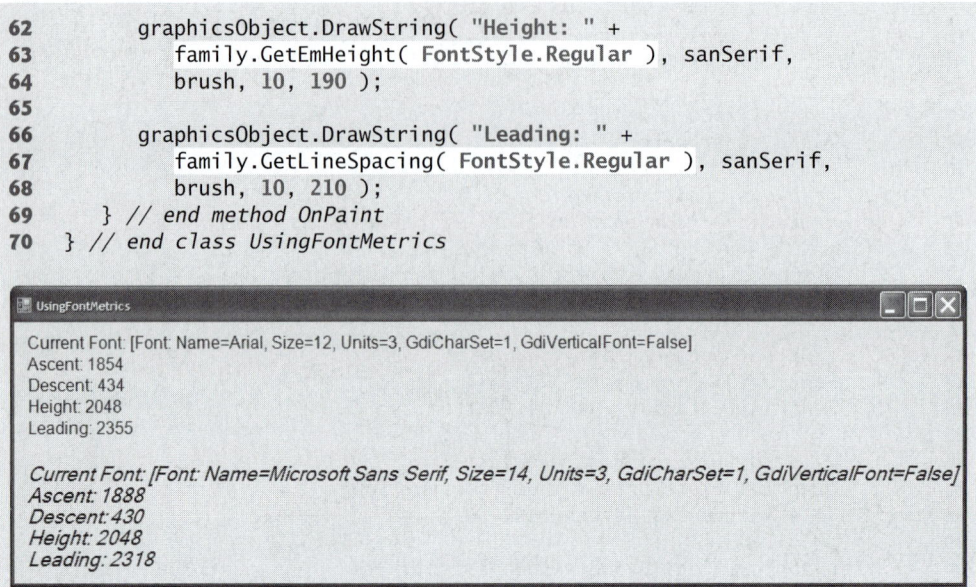

Fig. 17.12 | FontFamily class used to obtain font-metric information. (Part 3 of 3.)

17.6 Drawing Lines, Rectangles and Ovals

This section presents Graphics methods for drawing lines, rectangles and ovals. Each of the drawing methods has several overloaded versions. Methods that draw hollow shapes typically require as arguments a Pen and four ints. Methods that draw solid shapes typically require as arguments a Brush and four ints. The first two int arguments represent the coordinates of the upper-left corner of the shape (or its enclosing area), and the last two ints indicate the shape's (or enclosing area's) width and height. Figure 17.13 summarizes several Graphics methods and their parameters. [*Note:* Many of these methods are overloaded—consult the documentation for a complete listing (msdn2.microsoft.com/en-us/library/system.drawing.graphics).]

Graphics Drawing Methods and Descriptions
DrawLine(Pen p, *int* x1, *int* y1, *int* x2, *int* y2) Draws a line from (x1, y1) to (x2, y2). The Pen determines the line's color, style and width.
DrawRectangle(Pen p, *int* x, *int* y, *int* width, *int* height) Draws a rectangle of the specified width and height. The top-left corner of the rectangle is at point (x, y). The Pen determines the rectangle's color, style and border width.
FillRectangle(Brush b, *int* x, *int* y, *int* width, *int* height) Draws a solid rectangle of the specified width and height. The top-left corner of the rectangle is at point (x, y). The Brush determines the fill pattern inside the rectangle.

Fig. 17.13 | Graphics methods that draw lines, rectangles and ovals. (Part 1 of 2.)

Graphics Drawing Methods and Descriptions

DrawEllipse(Pen p, *int* x, *int* y, *int* width, *int* height)
Draws an ellipse inside a bounding rectangle of the specified width and height. The top-left corner of the bounding rectangle is located at (x, y). The Pen determines the color, style and border width of the ellipse.

FillEllipse(Brush b, *int* x, *int* y, *int* width, *int* height)
Draws a filled ellipse inside a bounding rectangle of the specified width and height. The top-left corner of the bounding rectangle is located at (x, y). The Brush determines the pattern inside the ellipse.

Fig. 17.13 | Graphics methods that draw lines, rectangles and ovals. (Part 2 of 2.)

The application in Fig. 17.14 draws lines, rectangles and ellipses. In this application, we also demonstrate methods that draw filled and unfilled shapes.

```csharp
1   // Fig. 17.14: LinesRectanglesOvals.cs
2   // Demonstrating lines, rectangles and ovals.
3   using System;
4   using System.Drawing;
5   using System.Windows.Forms;
6
7   // draw shapes on Form
8   public partial class LinesRectanglesOvals : Form
9   {
10      // default constructor
11      public LinesRectanglesOvals()
12      {
13         InitializeComponent();
14      } // end constructor
15
16      // override Form OnPaint method
17      protected override void OnPaint( PaintEventArgs paintEvent )
18      {
19         // get graphics object
20         Graphics g = paintEvent.Graphics;
21         SolidBrush brush = new SolidBrush( Color.Blue );
22         Pen pen = new Pen( Color.AliceBlue );
23
24         // create filled rectangle
25         g.FillRectangle( brush, 90, 30, 150, 90 );
26
27         // draw lines to connect rectangles
28         g.DrawLine( pen, 90, 30, 110, 40 );
29         g.DrawLine( pen, 90, 120, 110, 130 );
30         g.DrawLine( pen, 240, 30, 260, 40 );
31         g.DrawLine( pen, 240, 120, 260, 130 );
```

Fig. 17.14 | Demonstration of methods that draw lines, rectangles and ellipses. (Part 1 of 2.)

```
32
33          // draw top rectangle
34          g.DrawRectangle( pen, 110, 40, 150, 90 );
35
36          // set brush to red
37          brush.Color = Color.Red;
38
39          // draw base Ellipse
40          g.FillEllipse( brush, 280, 75, 100, 50 );
41
42          // draw connecting lines
43          g.DrawLine( pen, 380, 55, 380, 100 );
44          g.DrawLine( pen, 280, 55, 280, 100 );
45
46          // draw Ellipse outline
47          g.DrawEllipse( pen, 280, 30, 100, 50 );
48       } // end method OnPaint
49    } // end class LinesRectanglesOvals
```

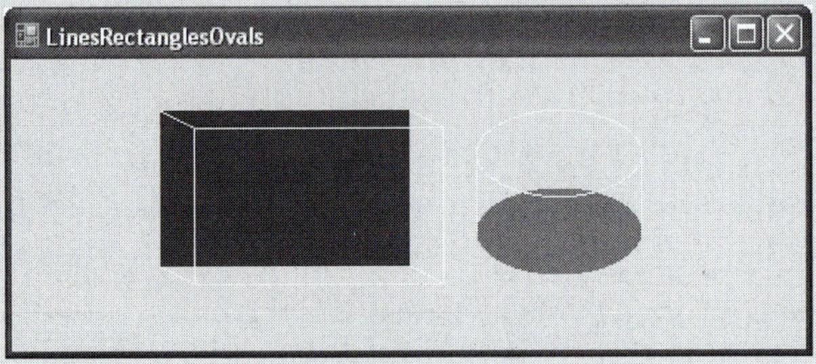

Fig. 17.14 | Demonstration of methods that draw lines, rectangles and ellipses. (Part 2 of 2.)

Methods *FillRectangle* and *DrawRectangle* (lines 25 and 34) draw rectangles on the screen. For each method, the first argument specifies the drawing object to use. The FillRectangle method uses a Brush object (in this case, an instance of SolidBrush—a class that derives from Brush), whereas the DrawRectangle method uses a Pen object. The next two arguments specify the coordinates of the upper-left corner of the *bounding rectangle*, which represents the area in which the rectangle will be drawn. The fourth and fifth arguments specify the rectangle's width and height. Method DrawLine (lines 28–31) takes a Pen and two pairs of ints, specifying the start and end of a line. The method then draws a line, using the Pen object.

Methods *FillEllipse* and *DrawEllipse* (lines 40 and 47) each provide overloaded versions that take five arguments. In both methods, the first argument specifies the drawing object to use. The next two arguments specify the upper-left coordinates of the bounding rectangle representing the area in which the ellipse will be drawn. The last two arguments specify the bounding rectangle's width and height, respectively. Figure 17.15 depicts an ellipse bounded by a rectangle. The ellipse touches the midpoint of each of the four sides of the bounding rectangle. The bounding rectangle is not displayed on the screen.

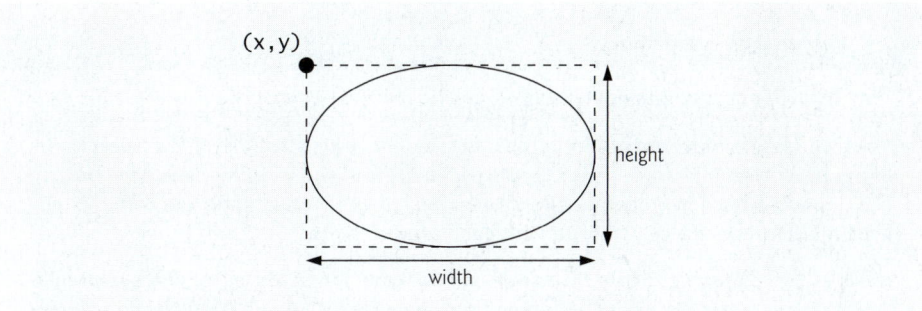

Fig. 17.15 | Ellipse bounded by a rectangle.

17.7 Drawing Arcs

Arcs are portions of ellipses and are measured in degrees, beginning at a *starting angle* and continuing for a specified number of degrees called the *arc angle*. An arc is said to *sweep* (traverse) its arc angle, beginning from its starting angle. Arcs that sweep in a clockwise direction are measured in positive degrees, whereas arcs that sweep in a counterclockwise direction are measured in negative degrees. Figure 17.16 depicts two arcs. Note that the arc at the left of the figure sweeps upward from zero degrees to approximately –110 degrees. Similarly, the arc at the right of the figure sweeps downward from zero degrees to approximately 110 degrees.

Notice the dashed boxes around the arcs in Fig. 17.16. Each arc is drawn as part of an oval (the rest of which is not visible). When drawing an oval, we specify the oval's dimensions in the form of a bounding rectangle that encloses the oval. The boxes in Fig. 17.16 correspond to these bounding rectangles. The Graphics methods used to draw arcs— *DrawArc*, *DrawPie* and *FillPie*—are summarized in Fig. 17.17.

The program in Fig. 17.18 draws six images (three arcs and three filled pie slices) to demonstrate the arc methods listed in Fig. 17.17. To illustrate the bounding rectangles that determine the sizes and locations of the arcs, the arcs are displayed inside red rectangles that have the same *x-y* coordinates, width and height arguments as those that define the bounding rectangles for the arcs.

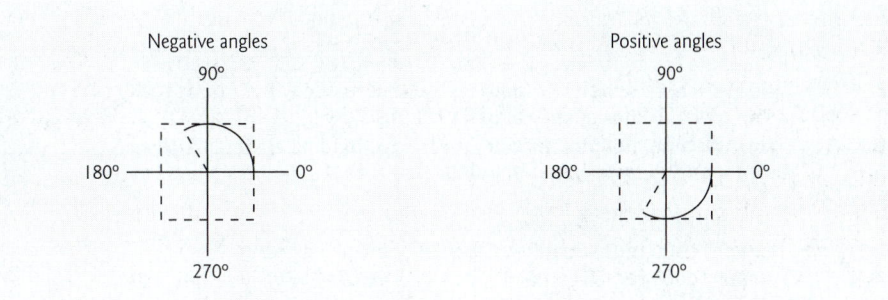

Fig. 17.16 | Positive and negative arc angles.

Graphics Methods And Descriptions

Note: Many of these methods are overloaded—consult the documentation for a complete listing.

DrawArc(Pen p, *int* x, *int* y, *int* width, *int* height, *int* startAngle, *int* sweepAngle)
Draws an arc beginning from angle startAngle (in degrees) and sweeping sweepAngle degrees.
The ellipse is defined by a bounding rectangle of width, height and upper-left corner (x,y).
The Pen determines the color, border width and style of the arc.

DrawPie(Pen p, *int* x, *int* y, *int* width, *int* height, *int* startAngle, *int* sweepAngle)
Draws a pie section of an ellipse beginning from angle startAngle (in degrees) and sweeping
sweepAngle degrees. The ellipse is defined by a bounding rectangle of width, height and
upper-left corner (x,y). The Pen determines the color, border width and style of the arc.

FillPie(Brush b, *int* x, *int* y, *int* width, *int* height, *int* startAngle,
    int sweepAngle)
Functions similarly to DrawPie, except draws a solid arc (i.e., a sector). The Brush determines
the fill pattern for the solid arc.

Fig. 17.17 | Graphics methods for drawing arcs.

```
 1   // Fig. 17.18: DrawingArcs.cs
 2   // Drawing various arcs on a Form.
 3   using System;
 4   using System.Drawing;
 5   using System.Windows.Forms;
 6
 7   // draws various arcs
 8   public partial class DrawArcs : Form
 9   {
10      // default constructor
11      public DrawArcs()
12      {
13         InitializeComponent();
14      } // end constructor
15
16      // draw arcs
17      private void DrawArcs_Paint( object sender, PaintEventArgs e )
18      {
19         // get graphics object
20         Graphics graphicsObject = e.Graphics;
21         Rectangle rectangle1 = new Rectangle( 15, 35, 80, 80 );
22         SolidBrush brush1 = new SolidBrush( Color.Firebrick );
23         Pen pen1 = new Pen( brush1, 1 );
24         SolidBrush brush2 = new SolidBrush( Color.DarkBlue );
25         Pen pen2 = new Pen( brush2, 1 );
26
27         // start at 0 and sweep 360 degrees
28         graphicsObject.DrawRectangle( pen1, rectangle1 );
29         graphicsObject.DrawArc( pen2, rectangle1, 0, 360 );
```

Fig. 17.18 | Drawing various arcs on a Form. (Part 1 of 2.)

```
30
31        // start at 0 and sweep 110 degrees
32        rectangle1.Location = new Point( 100, 35 );
33        graphicsObject.DrawRectangle( pen1, rectangle1 );
34        graphicsObject.DrawArc( pen2, rectangle1, 0, 110 );
35
36        // start at 0 and sweep -270 degrees
37        rectangle1.Location = new Point( 185, 35 );
38        graphicsObject.DrawRectangle( pen1, rectangle1 );
39        graphicsObject.DrawArc( pen2, rectangle1, 0, -270 );
40
41        // start at 0 and sweep 360 degrees
42        rectangle1.Location = new Point( 15, 120 );
43        rectangle1.Size = new Size( 80, 40 );
44        graphicsObject.DrawRectangle( pen1, rectangle1 );
45        graphicsObject.FillPie( brush2, rectangle1, 0, 360 );
46
47        // start at 270 and sweep -90 degrees
48        rectangle1.Location = new Point( 100, 120 );
49        graphicsObject.DrawRectangle( pen1, rectangle1 );
50        graphicsObject.FillPie( brush2, rectangle1, 270, -90 );
51
52        // start at 0 and sweep -270 degrees
53        rectangle1.Location = new Point( 185, 120 );
54        graphicsObject.DrawRectangle( pen1, rectangle1 );
55        graphicsObject.FillPie( brush2, rectangle1, 0, -270 );
56    } // end method DrawArcs_Paint
57 } // end class DrawArcs
```

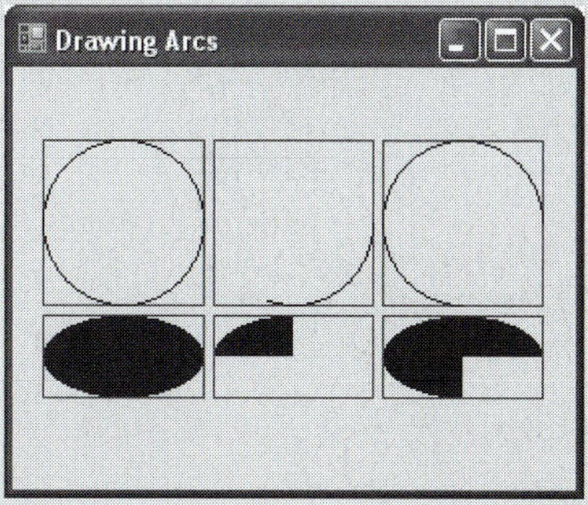

Fig. 17.18 | Drawing various arcs on a Form. (Part 2 of 2.)

Lines 20–25 create the objects that we need to draw various arcs—a Graphics object, a Rectangle, SolidBrushes and Pens. Lines 28–29 then draw a rectangle and an arc inside the rectangle. The arc sweeps 360 degrees, forming a circle. Line 32 changes the location of the Rectangle by setting its Location property to a new Point. The Point constructor takes as arguments the *x*- and *y*-coordinates of the new point. The Location property determines the upper-left corner of the Rectangle. After drawing the rectangle, the program draws an arc that starts at 0 degrees and sweeps 110 degrees. Because the angles increase in a clockwise direction, the arc sweeps downward.

Lines 37–39 perform similar functions, except that the specified arc sweeps –270 degrees. The Size property of a Rectangle determines the arc's height and width. Line 43 sets the Size property to a new Size object, which changes the size of the rectangle.

The remainder of the program is similar to the portions described above, except that a SolidBrush is used with method FillPie. The resulting arcs, which are filled, can be seen in the bottom half of the sample output (Fig. 17.18).

17.8 Drawing Polygons and Polylines

Polygons are multisided shapes. There are several Graphics methods used to draw polygons—*DrawLines* draws a series of connected lines, *DrawPolygon* draws a closed polygon and *FillPolygon* draws a solid polygon. These methods are described in Fig. 17.19. The program in Fig. 17.20 allows users to draw polygons and connected lines via the methods listed in Fig. 17.19.

Method	Description
DrawLines	Draws a series of connected lines. The coordinates of each point are specified in an array of Point objects. If the last point is different from the first point, the figure is not closed.
DrawPolygon	Draws a polygon. The coordinates of each point are specified in an array of Point objects. If the last point is different from the first point, those two points are connected to close the polygon.
FillPolygon	Draws a solid polygon. The coordinates of each point are specified in an array of Point objects. If the last point is different from the first point, those two points are connected to close the polygon.

Fig. 17.19 | Graphics methods for drawing polygons.

```
1   // Fig. 17.20: DrawPolygons.cs
2   // Demonstrating polygons.
3   using System;
4   using System.Collections;
5   using System.Drawing;
6   using System.Windows.Forms;
7
8   // demonstrating polygons
9   public partial class PolygonForm : Form
10  {
11     // default constructor
12     public PolygonForm()
13     {
14        InitializeComponent();
15     } // end constructor
16
```

Fig. 17.20 | Polygon-drawing demonstration. (Part 1 of 4.)

```
17      // contains list of polygon vertices
18      private ArrayList points = new ArrayList();
19
20      // initialize default pen and brush
21      Pen pen = new Pen( Color.DarkBlue );
22      SolidBrush brush = new SolidBrush( Color.DarkBlue );
23
24      // draw panel mouse down event handler
25      private void drawPanel_MouseDown( object sender, MouseEventArgs e )
26      {
27         // add mouse position to vertex list
28         points.Add( new Point( e.X, e.Y ) );
29         drawPanel.Invalidate(); // refresh panel
30      } // end method drawPanel_MouseDown
31
32      // draw panel Paint event handler
33      private void drawPanel_Paint( object sender, PaintEventArgs e )
34      {
35         // get graphics object for panel
36         Graphics graphicsObject = e.Graphics;
37
38         // if arraylist has 2 or more points, display shape
39         if ( points.Count > 1 )
40         {
41            // get array for use in drawing functions
42            Point[] pointArray =
43               ( Point[] ) points.ToArray( points[ 0 ].GetType() );
44
45            if ( lineOption.Checked )
46               graphicsObject.DrawLines( pen, pointArray );
47            else if ( polygonOption.Checked )
48               graphicsObject.DrawPolygon( pen, pointArray );
49            else if ( filledPolygonOption.Checked )
50               graphicsObject.FillPolygon( brush, pointArray );
51         } // end if
52      } // end method drawPanel_Paint
53
54      // handle clearButton click event
55      private void clearButton_Click( object sender, EventArgs e )
56      {
57         points.Clear(); // remove points
58         drawPanel.Invalidate(); // refresh panel
59      } // end method clearButton_Click
60
61      // handle polygon RadioButton CheckedChanged event
62      private void polygonOption_CheckedChanged(
63         object sender, System.EventArgs e )
64      {
65         drawPanel.Invalidate(); // refresh panel
66      } // end method polygonOption_CheckedChanged
67
```

Fig. 17.20 | Polygon-drawing demonstration. (Part 2 of 4.)

```
68      // handle line ReadioButton CheckedChanged event
69      private void lineOption_CheckedChanged(
70         object sender, System.EventArgs e )
71      {
72         drawPanel.Invalidate(); // refresh panel
73      } // end method lineOption_CheckedChanged
74
75      // handle filled polygon RadioButton CheckedChanged event
76      private void filledPolygonOption_CheckedChanged(
77         object sender, System.EventArgs e )
78      {
79         drawPanel.Invalidate(); // refresh panel
80      } // end method filledPolygonOption_CheckedChanged
81
82      // handle colorButton Click event
83      private void colorButton_Click( object sender, EventArgs e )
84      {
85         // create new color dialog
86         ColorDialog dialogColor = new ColorDialog();
87
88         // show dialog and obtain result
89         DialogResult result = dialogColor.ShowDialog();
90
91         // return if user cancels
92         if ( result == DialogResult.Cancel )
93            return;
94
95         pen.Color = dialogColor.Color;   // set pen to color
96         brush.Color = dialogColor.Color; // set brush
97         drawPanel.Invalidate(); // refresh panel;
98      } // end method colorButton_Click
99   } // end class PolygonForm
```

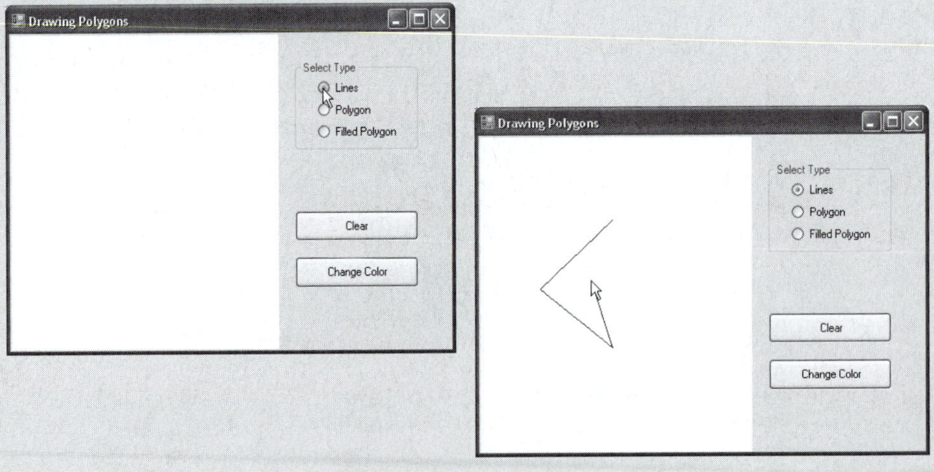

Fig. 17.20 | Polygon-drawing demonstration. (Part 3 of 4.)

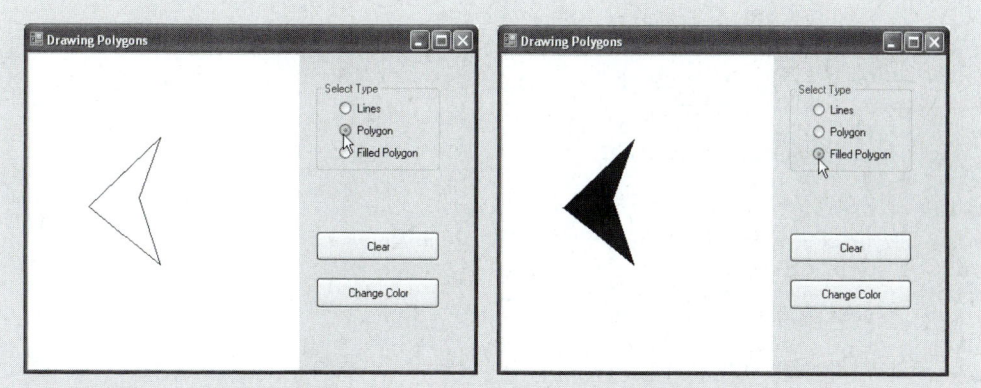

Fig. 17.20 | Polygon-drawing demonstration. (Part 4 of 4.)

To allow the user to specify a variable number of points, line 18 declares **ArrayList** points as a container for our Point objects. An ArrayList is similar to an array, but an ArrayList can grow dynamically to accommodate more elements. Lines 21–22 declare the Pen and Brush used to color our shapes. The MouseDown event handler (lines 25–30) for drawPanel stores mouse-click locations in points with ArrayList method **Add** (line 28). The event handler then calls method Invalidate of drawPanel (line 29) to ensure that the panel refreshes to accommodate the new point. Method drawPanel_Paint (lines 33–52) handles the Panel's Paint event. It obtains the Panel's Graphics object (line 36) and, if the ArrayList points contains two or more Points (line 39), displays the polygon with the method that the user selected via the GUI radio buttons (lines 45–50). In lines 42–43, we extract an array from the ArrayList via method **ToArray**. Method ToArray can take a single argument to determine the type of the returned array; we obtain the type from the first element in the ArrayList by calling the element's GetType method.

Method clearButton_Click (lines 55–59) handles the **Clear** button's Click event by calling ArrayList method **Clear** (causing the old list to be erased) and refreshing the display. Lines 62–80 define the event handlers for each radio button's CheckedChanged event. Each method invalidates drawPanel to ensure that the panel is repainted to reflect the selected shape type. Event handler colorButton_Click (83–98) allows the user to select a new drawing color with a ColorDialog, using the techniques demonstrated in Fig. 17.7.

17.9 Advanced Graphics Capabilities

C# offers many additional graphics capabilities. The Brush hierarchy, for example, also includes **HatchBrush**, **LinearGradientBrush**, **PathGradientBrush** and **TextureBrush**.

Gradients, Line Styles and Fill Patterns

The program in Fig. 17.21 demonstrates several graphics features, such as dashed lines, thick lines and the ability to fill shapes with various patterns. These represent just a few of the additional capabilities of the System.Drawing namespace.

Lines 18–88 define the DrawShapesForm Paint event handler. Lines 25–27 create an object of class LinearGradientBrush named linearBrush. A LinearGradientBrush (namespace System.Drawing.Drawing2D) enables users to draw with a color gradient. The

```
 1   // Fig. 17.21: DrawShapes.cs
 2   // Drawing various shapes on a Form.
 3   using System;
 4   using System.Drawing;
 5   using System.Drawing.Drawing2D;
 6   using System.Windows.Forms;
 7
 8   // draws shapes with different brushes
 9   public partial class DrawShapesForm : Form
10   {
11      // default constructor
12      public DrawShapesForm()
13      {
14         InitializeComponent();
15      } // end constructor
16
17      // draw various shapes on Form
18      private void DrawShapesForm_Paint( object sender, PaintEventArgs e )
19      {
20         // references to object we will use
21         Graphics graphicsObject = e.Graphics;
22
23         // ellipse rectangle and gradient brush
24         Rectangle drawArea1 = new Rectangle( 5, 35, 30, 100 );
25         LinearGradientBrush linearBrush =
26            new LinearGradientBrush( drawArea1, Color.Blue,
27               Color.Yellow, LinearGradientMode.ForwardDiagonal );
28
29         // draw ellipse filled with a blue-yellow gradient
30         graphicsObject.FillEllipse( linearBrush, 5, 30, 65, 100 );
31
32         // pen and location for red outline rectangle
33         Pen thickRedPen = new Pen( Color.Red, 10 );
34         Rectangle drawArea2 = new Rectangle( 80, 30, 65, 100 );
35
36         // draw thick rectangle outline in red
37         graphicsObject.DrawRectangle( thickRedPen, drawArea2 );
38
39         // bitmap texture
40         Bitmap textureBitmap = new Bitmap( 10, 10 );
41
42         // get bitmap graphics
43         Graphics graphicsObject2 =
44            Graphics.FromImage( textureBitmap );
45
46         // brush and pen used throughout program
47         SolidBrush solidColorBrush =
48            new SolidBrush( Color.Red );
49         Pen coloredPen = new Pen( solidColorBrush );
50
51         // fill textureBitmap with yellow
52         solidColorBrush.Color = Color.Yellow;
53         graphicsObject2.FillRectangle( solidColorBrush, 0, 0, 10, 10 );
```

Fig. 17.21 | Shapes drawn on a form. (Part 1 of 2.)

```
54
55          // draw small black rectangle in textureBitmap
56          coloredPen.Color = Color.Black;
57          graphicsObject2.DrawRectangle( coloredPen, 1, 1, 6, 6 );
58
59          // draw small blue rectangle in textureBitmap
60          solidColorBrush.Color = Color.Blue;
61          graphicsObject2.FillRectangle( solidColorBrush, 1, 1, 3, 3 );
62
63          // draw small red square in textureBitmap
64          solidColorBrush.Color = Color.Red;
65          graphicsObject2.FillRectangle( solidColorBrush, 4, 4, 3, 3 );
66
67          // create textured brush and
68          // display textured rectangle
69          TextureBrush texturedBrush =
70             new TextureBrush( textureBitmap );
71          graphicsObject.FillRectangle( texturedBrush, 155, 30, 75, 100 );
72
73          // draw pie-shaped arc in white
74          coloredPen.Color = Color.White;
75          coloredPen.Width = 6;
76          graphicsObject.DrawPie( coloredPen, 240, 30, 75, 100, 0, 270 );
77
78          // draw lines in green and yellow
79          coloredPen.Color = Color.Green;
80          coloredPen.Width = 5;
81          graphicsObject.DrawLine( coloredPen, 395, 30, 320, 150 );
82
83          // draw a rounded, dashed yellow line
84          coloredPen.Color = Color.Yellow;
85          coloredPen.DashCap = DashCap.Round;
86          coloredPen.DashStyle = DashStyle.Dash;
87          graphicsObject.DrawLine( coloredPen, 320, 30, 395, 150 );
88       } // end method DrawShapesForm_Paint
89    } // end class DrawShapesForm
```

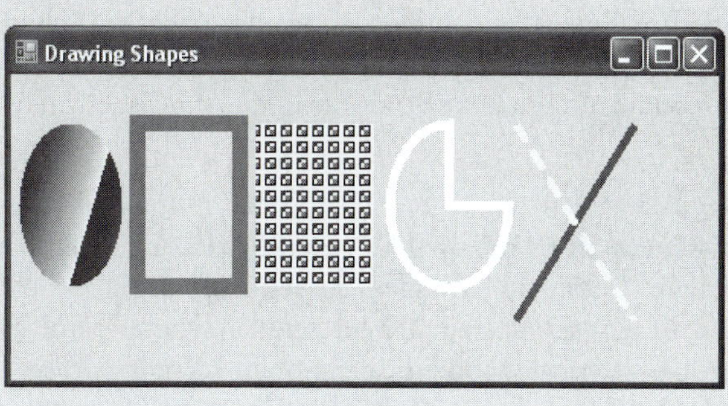

Fig. 17.21 | Shapes drawn on a form. (Part 2 of 2.)

LinearGradientBrush used in this example takes four arguments—a Rectangle, two Colors and a member of enumeration LinearGradientMode. In C#, all linear gradients are defined along a line that determines the gradient endpoints. This line can be specified either by the starting and ending points or by the diagonal of a rectangle. The first argument, Rectangle drawArea1, represents the endpoints of the linear gradient—the upper-left corner is the starting point and the bottom-right corner is the ending point. The second and third arguments specify the colors that the gradient will use. In this case, the color of the ellipse will gradually change from Color.Blue to Color.Yellow. The last argument, a type from the enumeration **LinearGradientMode**, specifies the linear gradient's direction. In our case, we use **LinearGradientMode.ForwardDiagonal**, which creates a gradient from the upper-left to the lower-right corner. We then use Graphics method FillEllipse in line 30 to draw an ellipse with linearBrush; the color gradually changes from blue to yellow, as described above.

In line 33, we create Pen object thickRedPen. We pass to thickRedPen's constructor Color.Red and int argument 10, indicating that we want thickRedPen to draw red lines that are 10 pixels wide.

Line 40 creates a new **Bitmap** image, which initially is empty. Class Bitmap can produce images in color and gray scale; this particular Bitmap is 10 pixels wide and 10 pixels tall. Method **FromImage** (line 43–44) is a static member of class Graphics and retrieves the Graphics object associated with an Image, which may be used to draw on an image. Lines 52–65 draw on the Bitmap a pattern consisting of black, blue, red and yellow rectangles and lines. A TextureBrush is a brush that fills the interior of a shape with an image, rather than a solid color. In line 71, TextureBrush object textureBrush fills a rectangle with our Bitmap. The TextureBrush constructor used in lines 69–70 takes as an argument an image that defines its texture.

Next, we draw a pie-shaped arc with a thick white line. Lines 74–75 set coloredPen's color to White and modify its width to be six pixels. We then draw the pie on the form by specifying the Pen, the x-coordinate, y-coordinate, width and height of the bounding rectangle and the start and sweep angles.

Lines 79–81 draw a five-pixel-wide green line. Finally, lines 85–86 use enumerations **DashCap** and **DashStyle** (namespace System.Drawing.Drawing2D) to specify settings for a dashed line. Line 85 sets the **DashCap** property of coloredPen (not to be confused with the DashCap enumeration) to a member of the DashCap enumeration. The DashCap enumeration specifies the styles for the start and end of a dashed line. In this case, we want both ends of the dashed line to be rounded, so we use **DashCap.Round**. Line 86 sets the **DashStyle** property of coloredPen (not to be confused with the DashStyle enumeration) to **DashStyle.Dash**, indicating that we want our line to consist entirely of dashes.

General Paths

Our next example demonstrates the use of a *general path*. A general path is a shape constructed from straight lines and complex curves. An object of class **GraphicsPath** (namespace System.Drawing.Drawing2D) represents a general path. The GraphicsPath class provides functionality that enables the creation of complex shapes from vector-based primitive graphics objects. A GraphicsPath object consists of figures defined by simple shapes. The start point of each vector-graphics object (such as a line or arc) that is added to the path is connected by a straight line to the end point of the previous object. When called, the **CloseFigure** method attaches the final vector-graphic object end point to the initial starting point for the current figure by a straight line, then starts a new figure. Method StartFigure begins a new figure within the path without closing the previous figure.

The program of Fig. 17.22 draws general paths in the shape of five-pointed stars. Lines 26–29 define two int arrays, representing the *x*- and *y*-coordinates of the points in the star, and line 32 defines GraphicsPath object star. A loop (lines 35–37) then creates lines to connect the points of the star and adds these lines to star. We use GraphicsPath method **AddLine** to append a line to the shape. The arguments of AddLine specify the coordinates for the line's endpoints; each new call to AddLine adds a line from the previous point to the current point. Line 40 uses GraphicsPath method CloseFigure to complete the shape.

```csharp
1   // Fig. 17.22: DrawStarsForm.cs
2   // Using paths to draw stars on the form.
3   using System;
4   using System.Drawing;
5   using System.Drawing.Drawing2D;
6   using System.Windows.Forms;
7
8   // draws randomly colored stars
9   public partial class DrawStarsForm : Form
10  {
11     // default constructor
12     public DrawStarsForm()
13     {
14        InitializeComponent();
15     } // end constructor
16
17     // create path and draw stars along it
18     private void DrawStarsForm_Paint(object sender, PaintEventArgs e)
19     {
20        Graphics graphicsObject = e.Graphics;
21        Random random = new Random();
22        SolidBrush brush =
23           new SolidBrush( Color.DarkMagenta );
24
25        // x and y points of the path
26        int[] xPoints =
27           { 55, 67, 109, 73, 83, 55, 27, 37, 1, 43 };
28        int[] yPoints =
29           { 0, 36, 36, 54, 96, 72, 96, 54, 36, 36 };
30
31        // create graphics path for star;
32        GraphicsPath star = new GraphicsPath();
33
34        // create star from series of points
35        for ( int i = 0; i <= 8; i += 2 )
36           star.AddLine( xPoints[ i ], yPoints[ i ],
37              xPoints[ i + 1 ], yPoints[ i + 1 ] );
38
39        // close the shape
40        star.CloseFigure();
41
```

Fig. 17.22 | Paths used to draw stars on a form. (Part 1 of 2.)

```
42          // translate the origin to (150, 150)
43          graphicsObject.TranslateTransform( 150, 150 );
44
45          // rotate the origin and draw stars in random colors
46          for ( int i = 1; i <= 18; i++ )
47          {
48              graphicsObject.RotateTransform( 20 );
49
50              brush.Color = Color.FromArgb(
51                  random.Next( 200, 255 ), random.Next( 255 ),
52                  random.Next( 255 ), random.Next( 255 ) );
53
54              graphicsObject.FillPath( brush, star );
55          } // end for
56      } // end method DrawStarsForm_Paint
57  } // end class DrawStarsForm
```

Fig. 17.22 | Paths used to draw stars on a form. (Part 2 of 2.)

Line 43 sets the origin of the Graphics object. The arguments to method TranslateTransform indicate that the origin should be translated to the coordinates (150, 150). The loop in lines 46–55 draws the star 18 times, rotating it around the origin. Line 48 uses Graphics method *RotateTransform* to move to the next position on the form; the argument specifies the rotation angle in degrees. Graphics method FillPath (line 54) then draws a filled version of the star with the Brush created in lines 50–52. The application determines the SolidBrush's color randomly, using Random method Next.

17.10 Introduction to Multimedia

C# offers many convenient ways to include images and animations in programs. People who entered the computing field decades ago used computers primarily to perform arithmetic calculations. As the discipline evolves, we are realizing the importance of computers' data-manipulation capabilities. We are seeing many exciting new three-dimensional applications. Multimedia programming is an entertaining and innovative field, but one that presents many challenges

Multimedia applications demand extraordinary computing power. Today's ultrafast processors make multimedia-based applications commonplace. As the market for multimedia explodes, users are purchasing the faster processors, larger memories and wider communications bandwidths needed to support multimedia applications. This benefits the computer and communications industries, which provide the hardware, software and services fueling the multimedia revolution.

In the remaining sections of this chapter, we introduce basic image processing and other multimedia features and capabilities. Section 17.11 discusses how to load, display and scale images; Section 17.12 demonstrates image animation; Section 17.13 presents the video capabilities of the Windows Media Player control; and Section 17.14 explores Microsoft Agent technology.

17.11 Loading, Displaying and Scaling Images

C#'s multimedia capabilities include graphics, images, animations and video. Previous sections demonstrated C#'s vector-graphics capabilities; this section presents image manipulation. The application in Fig. 17.23 loads an Image (System.Drawing namespace), then allows the user to scale the Image to a specified width and height.

```csharp
 1   // Fig. 17.23: DisplayLogoForm.cs
 2   // Displaying and resizing an image
 3   using System;
 4   using System.Drawing;
 5   using System.Windows.Forms;
 6
 7   // displays an image and allows the user to resize it
 8   public partial class DisplayLogoForm : Form
 9   {
10      private Image image = Image.FromFile( @"images\Logo.gif" );
11      private Graphics graphicsObject;
12
13      public DisplayLogoForm()
14      {
15         InitializeComponent();
16         graphicsObject = this.CreateGraphics();
17      }
18
19      // handle setButton Click event
20      private void setButton_Click( object sender, EventArgs e )
21      {
22         // get user input
23         int width = Convert.ToInt32( widthTextBox.Text );
24         int height = Convert.ToInt32( heightTextBox.Text );
25
```

Fig. 17.23 | Image resizing. (Part 1 of 2.)

```
26          // if dimensions specified are too large
27          // display problem
28          if ( width > 375 || height > 225 )
29          {
30             MessageBox.Show( " Height or Width too large" );
31             return;
32          } // end if
33
34          // clear the Form then draw the image
35          graphicsObject.Clear( this.BackColor );
36          graphicsObject.DrawImage( image, 5, 5, width, height );
37       } // end method setButton_Click
38    } // end class DisplayLogoForm
```

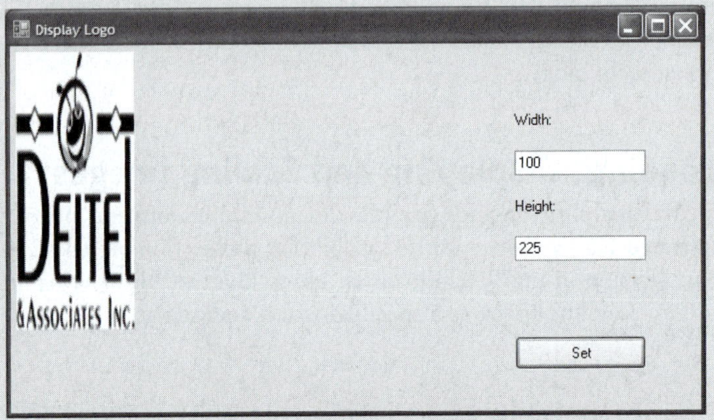

Fig. 17.23 | Image resizing. (Part 2 of 2.)

Line 10 declares Image variable image and uses static Image method *FromFile* to load an image from a file on disk. Line 16 uses the Form's *CreateGraphics* method to create a Graphics object for drawing on the Form. Method CreateGraphics is inherited from class Control. When you click the **Set** Button, lines 28–32 validate the width and height to ensure that they are not too large. If the parameters are valid, line 35 calls

Graphics method *Clear* to paint the entire Form in the current background color. Line 36 calls Graphics method *DrawImage*, passing as arguments the image to draw, the *x*-coordinate of the image's upper-left corner, the *y*-coordinate of the image's upper-left corner, the width of the image and the height of the image. If the width and height do not correspond to the image's original dimensions, the image is scaled to fit the new width and height.

17.12 Animating a Series of Images

The next example animates a series of images stored in an array. The application uses the same technique to load and display Images as shown in Fig. 17.23.

The animation in Fig. 17.24 uses a PictureBox, which contains the images that we animate. We use a Timer to cycle through the images and display a new image every 50 milliseconds. Variable count keeps track of the current image number and increases by one every time we display a new image. The array includes 30 images (numbered 0–29); when the application reaches image 29, it returns to image 0. The 30 images are located in the images folder inside the project's bin/Debug and bin/Release directories.

```
1   // Fig. 17.24: LogoAnimator.cs
2   // Program that animates a series of images.
3   using System;
4   using System.Drawing;
5   using System.Windows.Forms;
6
7   // animates a series of 30 images
8   public partial class LogoAnimator : Form
9   {
10     private Image[] images = new Image[ 30 ];
11     private int count = -1;
12
13     // LogoAnimator constructor
14     public LogoAnimator()
15     {
16        InitializeComponent();
17
18        for ( int i = 0; i < 30; i++ )
19           images[ i ] = Image.FromFile( @"images\deitel" + i + ".gif" );
20
21        logoPictureBox.Image = images[ 0 ]; // display first image
22
23        // set PictureBox to be the same size as Image
24        logoPictureBox.Size = logoPictureBox.Image.Size;
25     } // end LogoAnimator constructor
26
27     // event handler for timer's Tick event
28     private void timer_Tick( object sender, EventArgs e )
29     {
30        count = ( count + 1 ) % 30; // increment counter
31        logoPictureBox.Image = images[ count ]; // display next image
32     } // end method timer_Tick
33   } // end class LogoAnimator
```

Fig. 17.24 | Animation of a series of images. (Part 1 of 2.)

Fig. 17.24 │ Animation of a series of images. (Part 2 of 2.)

Lines 18–19 load each of 30 images and place them in an array of Images. Line 21 places the first image in the PictureBox. Line 24 modifies the size of the PictureBox so that it is equal to the size of the Image it is displaying. The event handler for timer's Tick event (line 28–32) responds to each event by displaying the next image from the array.

> ### Performance Tip 17.2
>
> *It is more efficient to load an animation's frames as one image than to load each image separately. (A painting program, such as Adobe Photoshop®, or Jasc® Paint Shop Pro™, can be used to combine the animation's frames into one image.) If the images are being loaded separately from the Web, each loaded image requires a separate connection to the site on which the images are stored; this process can result in poor performance.*

Chess Example

The following chess example demonstrates techniques for two-dimensional **collision detection**, selecting single frames from a multiframe image, and **regional invalidation**, refreshing only the parts of the screen that have changed, to increase performance. Two-dimensional collision detection enables a program to detect whether two shapes overlap or whether a point is contained within a shape. In the next example, we demonstrate the simplest form of collision detection, which determines whether a point (the mouse-click location) is contained within a rectangle (a chess-piece image).

Class ChessPiece (Fig. 17.25) represents the individual chess pieces. Lines 10–18 define a public enumeration of constants that identify each chess-piece type. The constants also serve to identify the location of each piece in the chess-piece image file. Rectangle object targetRectangle (lines 24–25) identifies the image location on the chessboard. The x and y properties of the rectangle are assigned in the ChessPiece constructor, and all chess-piece images have a width and height of 75 pixels.

The ChessPiece constructor (lines 28–39) receives the chess-piece type, its x and y location and the Bitmap containing all chess-piece images. Rather than loading the chess-piece image within the class, we allow the calling class to pass the image. This increases the flexibility of the class by allowing the user to change images. Lines 36–38 extract a sub-image that contains only the current piece's bitmap data. Our chess-piece images are defined in a specific manner: One image contains six chess-piece images, each defined within a 75-pixel block, resulting in a total image size of 450-by-75. We obtain a single

```
 1    // Fig. 17.25 : ChessPiece.cs
 2    // Class that represents chess piece attributes.
 3    using System;
 4    using System.Drawing;
 5
 6    // represents a chess piece
 7    class ChessPiece
 8    {
 9       // define chess-piece type constants
10       public enum Types
11       {
12          KING,
13          QUEEN,
14          BISHOP,
15          KNIGHT,
16          ROOK,
17          PAWN
18       } // end enum Types
19
20       private int currentType; // this object's type
21       private Bitmap pieceImage; // this object's image
22
23       // default display location
24       private Rectangle targetRectangle =
25          new Rectangle( 0, 0, 75, 75 );
26
27       // construct piece
28       public ChessPiece( int type, int xLocation,
29          int yLocation, Bitmap sourceImage )
30       {
31          currentType = type; // set current type
32          targetRectangle.X = xLocation; // set current x location
33          targetRectangle.Y = yLocation; // set current y location
34
35          // obtain pieceImage from section of sourceImage
36          pieceImage = sourceImage.Clone(
37             new Rectangle( type * 75, 0, 75, 75 ),
38             System.Drawing.Imaging.PixelFormat.DontCare );
39       } // end method ChessPiece
40
41       // draw chess piece
42       public void Draw( Graphics graphicsObject )
43       {
44          graphicsObject.DrawImage( pieceImage, targetRectangle );
45       } // end method Draw
46
47       // obtain this piece's location rectangle
48       public Rectangle GetBounds()
49       {
50          return targetRectangle;
51       } // end method GetBounds
52
```

Fig. 17.25 │ Class that represents chess piece attributes. (Part 1 of 2.)

```
53        // set this piece's location
54        public void SetLocation( int xLocation, int yLocation )
55        {
56            targetRectangle.X = xLocation;
57            targetRectangle.Y = yLocation;
58        } // end method SetLocation
59    } // end class ChessPiece
```

Fig. 17.25 | Class that represents chess piece attributes. (Part 2 of 2.)

image via Bitmap's Clone method, which allows us to specify a rectangle image location and the desired pixel format. The location is a 75-by-75 pixel block with its upper-left corner x equal to 75 * type and the corresponding y equal to 0. For the pixel format, we specify constant DontCare, causing the format to remain unchanged.

Method Draw (lines 42–45) causes the ChessPiece to draw pieceImage in the targetRectangle using the Graphics object passed as Draw's argument. Method GetBounds (lines 48–51) returns the targetRectangle object for use in collision detection, and method SetLocation (lines 54–58) allows the calling class to specify a new piece location.

Class ChessGame (Fig. 17.26) defines the game and graphics code for our chess game. Lines 11–15 define instance variables the program requires. ArrayList chessTile (line 11) stores the board tile images. ArrayList chessPieces (line 12) stores all active ChessPiece objects, and int selectedIndex (line 13) identifies the index in chessPieces of the currently selected piece. The board (line 14) is an 8-by-8, two-dimensional int array corresponding to the squares of a chess board. Each board element is an integer from 0 to 3 that corresponds to an index in chessTile and is used to specify the chessboard-square image. const TILESIZE (line 15) defines the size of each tile in pixels.

```
1    // Fig. 17.26: ChessGame.cs
2    // Chess Game graphics code.
3    using System;
4    using System.Collections;
5    using System.Drawing;
6    using System.Windows.Forms;
7
8    // allows 2 players to play chess
9    public partial class ChessGame : Form
10   {
11       private ArrayList chessTile = new ArrayList(); // for tile images
12       private ArrayList chessPieces = new ArrayList(); // for chess pieces
13       private int selectedIndex = -1; // index for selected piece
14       private int[ , ] board = new int[ 8, 8 ]; // board array
15       private const int TILESIZE = 75; // chess tile size in pixels
16
17       // default constructor
18       public ChessGame()
19       {
20           // Required for Windows Form Designer support
21           InitializeComponent();
22       } // end constructor
```

Fig. 17.26 | Chess-game code. (Part 1 of 7.)

```
23
24       // load tile bitmaps and reset game
25       private void ChessGame_Load( object sender, EventArgs e )
26       {
27          // load chess board tiles
28          chessTile.Add( Bitmap.FromFile( @"images\lightTile1.png" ) );
29          chessTile.Add( Bitmap.FromFile( @"images\lightTile2.png" ) );
30          chessTile.Add( Bitmap.FromFile( @"images\darkTile1.png" ) );
31          chessTile.Add( Bitmap.FromFile( @"images\darkTile2.png" ) );
32
33          ResetBoard(); // initialize board
34          Invalidate(); // refresh form
35       } // end method ChessGame_Load
36
37       // initialize pieces to start and rebuild board
38       private void ResetBoard()
39       {
40          int current = -1;
41          ChessPiece piece;
42          Random random = new Random();
43          bool light = false;
44          int type;
45
46          chessPieces.Clear(); // ensure empty arraylist
47
48          // load whitepieces image
49          Bitmap whitePieces =
50             ( Bitmap ) Image.FromFile( @"images\whitePieces.png" );
51
52          // load blackpieces image
53          Bitmap blackPieces =
54             ( Bitmap ) Image.FromFile( @"images\blackPieces.png" );
55
56          // set whitepieces to be drawn first
57          Bitmap selected = whitePieces;
58
59          // traverse board rows in outer loop
60          for ( int row = 0; row <= board.GetUpperBound( 0 ); row++ )
61          {
62             // if at bottom rows, set to black pieces images
63             if ( row > 5 )
64                selected = blackPieces;
65
66             // traverse board columns in inner loop
67             for ( int column = 0;
68                column <= board.GetUpperBound( 1 ); column++ )
69             {
70                // if first or last row, organize pieces
71                if ( row == 0 || row == 7 )
72                {
73                   switch ( column )
74                   {
```

Fig. 17.26 | Chess-game code. (Part 2 of 7.)

```
75                        case 0:
76                        case 7: // set current piece to rook
77                            current = ( int ) ChessPiece.Types.ROOK;
78                            break;
79                        case 1:
80                        case 6: // set current piece to knight
81                            current = ( int ) ChessPiece.Types.KNIGHT;
82                            break;
83                        case 2:
84                        case 5: // set current piece to bishop
85                            current = ( int ) ChessPiece.Types.BISHOP;
86                            break;
87                        case 3: // set current piece to king
88                            current = ( int ) ChessPiece.Types.KING;
89                            break;
90                        case 4: // set current piece to queen
91                            current = ( int ) ChessPiece.Types.QUEEN;
92                            break;
93                    } // end switch
94
95                    // create current piece at start position
96                    piece = new ChessPiece( current,
97                        column * TILESIZE, row * TILESIZE, selected );
98
99                    chessPieces.Add( piece ); // add piece to arraylist
100                } // end if
101
102                // if second or seventh row, organize pawns
103                if ( row == 1 || row == 6 )
104                {
105                    piece = new ChessPiece(
106                        ( int ) ChessPiece.Types.PAWN,
107                        column * TILESIZE, row * TILESIZE, selected );
108                    chessPieces.Add( piece ); // add piece to arraylist
109                } // end if
110
111                type = random.Next( 0, 2 ); // determine board piece type
112
113                if ( light ) // set light tile
114                {
115                    board[ row, column ] = type;
116                    light = false;
117                }
118                else // set dark tile
119                {
120                    board[ row, column ] = type + 2;
121                    light = true;
122                }
123            } // end for loop for columns
124
125            light = !light; // account for new row tile color switch
126        } // end for loop for rows
127    } // end method ResetBoard
```

Fig. 17.26 | Chess-game code. (Part 3 of 7.)

```
128
129      // display board in form OnPaint event
130      private void ChessGame_Paint( object sender, PaintEventArgs e )
131      {
132         Graphics graphicsObject = e.Graphics; // obtain graphics object
133         graphicsObject.TranslateTransform( 0, 24 ); // adjust origin
134
135         for ( int row = 0; row <= board.GetUpperBound( 0 ); row++ )
136         {
137            for ( int column = 0;
138               column <= board.GetUpperBound( 1 ); column++)
139            {
140               // draw image specified in board array
141               graphicsObject.DrawImage(
142                  ( Image ) chessTile[ board[ row, column ] ],
143                  new Point( TILESIZE * column, ( TILESIZE * row ) ) );
144            } // end for loop for columns
145         } // end for loop for rows
146      } // end method ChessGame_Paint
147
148      // return index of piece that intersects point
149      // optionally exclude a value
150      private int CheckBounds( Point point, int exclude )
151      {
152         Rectangle rectangle; // current bounding rectangle
153
154         for ( int i = 0; i < chessPieces.Count; i++ )
155         {
156            // get piece rectangle
157            rectangle = GetPiece( i ).GetBounds();
158
159            // check if rectangle contains point
160            if ( rectangle.Contains( point ) && i != exclude )
161               return i;
162         } // end for
163
164         return -1;
165      } // end method CheckBounds
166
167      // handle pieceBox paint event
168      private void pieceBox_Paint(
169         object sender, System.Windows.Forms.PaintEventArgs e )
170      {
171         // draw all pieces
172         for ( int i = 0; i < chessPieces.Count; i++ )
173            GetPiece( i ).Draw( e.Graphics );
174      } // end method pieceBox_Paint
175
176      // handle pieceBox MouseDown event
177      private void pieceBox_MouseDown(
178         object sender, System.Windows.Forms.MouseEventArgs e )
179      {
```

Fig. 17.26 | Chess-game code. (Part 4 of 7.)

```
180            // determine selected piece
181            selectedIndex = CheckBounds( new Point( e.X, e.Y ), -1 );
182         } // end method pieceBox_MouseDown
183
184         // if piece is selected, move it
185         private void pieceBox_MouseMove(
186            object sender, System.Windows.Forms.MouseEventArgs e )
187         {
188            if ( selectedIndex > -1 )
189            {
190               Rectangle region = new Rectangle(
191                  e.X - TILESIZE * 2, e.Y - TILESIZE * 2,
192                  TILESIZE * 4, TILESIZE * 4 );
193
194               // set piece center to mouse
195               GetPiece( selectedIndex ).SetLocation(
196                  e.X - TILESIZE / 2, e.Y - TILESIZE / 2 );
197
198               pieceBox.Invalidate( region ); // refresh region
199            } // end if
200         } // end method pieceBox_MouseMove
201
202         // on mouse up deselect piece and remove taken piece
203         private void pieceBox_MouseUp( object sender, MouseEventArgs e )
204         {
205            int remove = -1;
206
207            // if chess piece was selected
208            if ( selectedIndex > -1 )
209            {
210               Point current = new Point( e.X, e.Y );
211               Point newPoint = new Point(
212                  current.X - ( current.X % TILESIZE ),
213                  current.Y - ( current.Y % TILESIZE ) );
214
215               // check bounds with point, exclude selected piece
216               remove = CheckBounds( current, selectedIndex );
217
218               // snap piece into center of closest square
219               GetPiece( selectedIndex ).SetLocation( newPoint.X, newPoint.Y );
220               selectedIndex = -1; // deselect piece
221
222               // remove taken piece
223               if ( remove > -1 )
224                  chessPieces.RemoveAt( remove );
225            } // end if
226
227            pieceBox.Invalidate(); // ensure artifact removal
228         } // end method pieceBox_MouseUp
229
```

Fig. 17.26 | Chess-game code. (Part 5 of 7.)

```
230     // helper function to convert
231     // ArrayList object to ChessPiece
232     private ChessPiece GetPiece( int i )
233     {
234        return ( ChessPiece ) chessPieces[ i ];
235     } // end method GetPiece
236
237     // handle NewGame menu option click
238     private void newGameItem_Click(
239        object sender, System.EventArgs e )
240     {
241        ResetBoard(); // reinitialize board
242        Invalidate(); // refresh form
243     } // end method newGameItem_Click
244  } // end class ChessGame
```

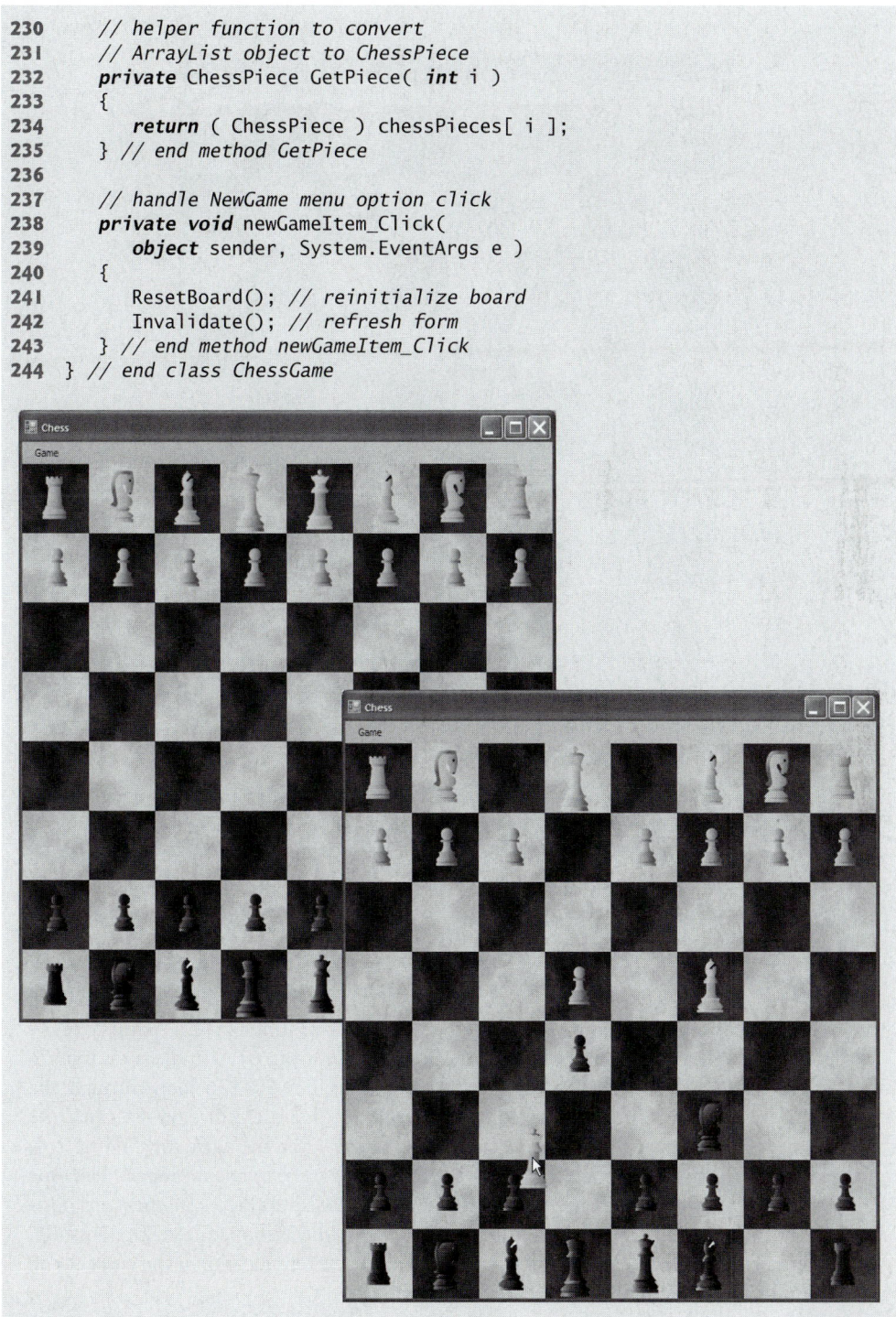

Fig. 17.26 | Chess-game code. (Part 6 of 7.)

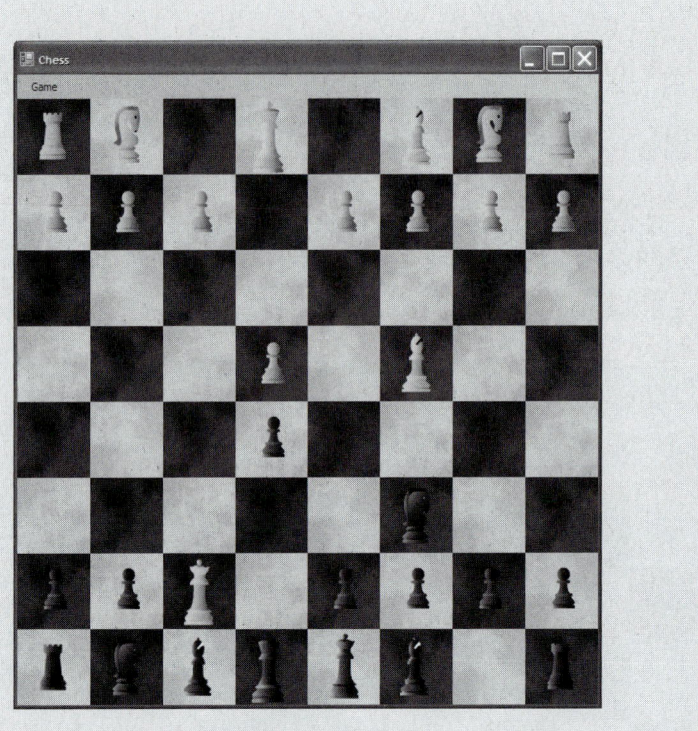

Fig. 17.26 | Chess-game code. (Part 7 of 7.)

The chess game GUI consists of Form ChessGame, the area in which we draw the tiles; Panel pieceBox, the area in which we draw the pieces (note that pieceBox's background color is set to "transparent"); and a Menu that allows the user to begin a new game. Although the pieces and tiles could have been drawn on the same form, doing so would decrease performance. We would be forced to refresh the board and all the pieces every time we refreshed the control.

The ChessGame_Load event handler (lines 25–35) loads four tile images into chessTile—two light tiles and two dark tiles for variety. It then calls method ResetBoard to refresh the Form and begin the game. Method ResetBoard (lines 38–127) clears chess-Pieces, loads images for both the black and the white chess-piece sets and creates Bitmap selected to define the currently selected Bitmap set. Lines 60–126 loop through the board's 64 positions, setting the tile color and piece for each tile. Lines 63–64 cause the currently selected image to switch to the blackPieces after the fifth row. If the row counter is on the first or last row, lines 71–100 add a new piece to chessPieces. The type of the piece is based on the current column we are initializing. Pieces in chess are positioned in the following order, from left to right: rook, knight, bishop, queen, king, bishop, knight and rook. Lines 103–109 add a new pawn at the current location if the current row is second or seventh.

A chessboard is defined by alternating light and dark tiles across a row in a pattern where the color that starts each row is equal to the color of the last tile of the previous row.

Lines 113–122 assign the current board-tile color to an element in the board array. Based on the alternating value of bool variable light and the results of the random operation on line 111, we assign an int to the board to determine the color of that tile—0 and 1 represent light tiles; 2 and 3 represent dark tiles. Line 125 inverts the value of light at the end of each row to maintain the staggered effect of a chessboard.

Method ChessGame_Paint (lines 130–146) handles the Form's Paint event and draws the tiles according to their values in the board array. Since the default height of a Menu-Strip is 24 pixels, we use the *TranslateTransform* method of class Graphics to shift the origin of the Form down 24 pixels (line 133). This shift prevents the top row of tiles from being hidden behind the MenuStrip. Method pieceBox_Paint (lines 168–174), which handles the Paint event for the pieceBox Panel, iterates through each element of the chessPiece ArrayList and calls its Draw method.

The pieceBox MouseDown event handler (lines 177–182) calls CheckBounds (lines 150–165) with the location of the mouse to determine whether the user selected a piece.

The pieceBox MouseMove event handler (lines 185–200) moves the selected piece with the mouse. Lines 190–192 define a region of the Panel that spans two tiles in every direction from the pointer. As mentioned previously, Invalidate is slow. This means that the pieceBox MouseMove event handler might be called several times before the Invalidate method completes. If a user working on a slow computer moves the mouse quickly, the application could leave behind *artifacts*. An artifact is any unintended visual abnormality in a graphical program. By causing the program to refresh a two-square rectangle, which should suffice in most cases, we achieve a significant performance enhancement over an entire component refresh during each MouseMove event. Lines 195–196 set the selected piece location to the mouse-cursor position, adjusting the location to center the image on the mouse. Line 198 invalidates the region defined in lines 190–192 so that it will be refreshed.

Lines 203–228 define the pieceBox MouseUp event handler. If a piece has been selected, lines 208–225 determine the index in chessPieces of any piece collision, remove the collided piece, snap (align) the current piece to a valid location and deselect the piece. We check for piece collisions to allow the chess piece to "take" other chess pieces. Line 216 checks whether any piece (excluding the currently selected piece) is beneath the current mouse location. If a collision is detected, the returned piece index is assigned to remove. Lines 211–213 determine the closest valid chess tile and "snaps" the selected piece to that location. If remove contains a positive value, line 224 removes the object at that index from the chessPieces ArrayList. Finally, the entire Panel is invalidated in line 227 to display the new piece location and remove any artifacts created during the move.

Method CheckBounds (lines 150–165) is a collision-detection helper method; it iterates through ArrayList chessPieces and returns the index of any piece's rectangle that contains the point passed to the method (the mouse location, in this example). Check-Bounds uses Rectangle method Contains to determine whether a point is in the Rectangle. Method CheckBounds optionally can exclude a single piece index (to ignore the selected index in the pieceBox MouseUp event handler, in this example).

Lines 232–235 define helper function GetPiece, which simplifies the conversion from objects in ArrayList chessPieces to ChessPiece types. Method newGameItem_Click (lines 238–243) handles the NewGame menu item click event, calls RefreshBoard to reset the game and invalidates the entire form.

17.13 Windows Media Player

The *Windows Media Player control* enables an application to play video and sound in many *multimedia formats*. These include *MPEG* (*Motion Pictures Experts Group*) audio and video, *AVI* (*audio-video interleave*) video, *WAV* (*Windows wave-file format*) audio and *MIDI* (*Musical Instrument Digital Interface*) audio. Users can find pre-existing audio and video on the Internet, or they can create their own files, using available sound and graphics packages.

The application in Fig. 17.27 demonstrates the Windows Media Player control. To use this control, you must add the control to the **Toolbox**. First select **Tools > Choose Toolbox Items...** to display the **Choose Toolbox Items** dialog. Click the **COM components** tab, then scroll down and select the option **Windows Media Player**. Click the **OK** button to dismiss the dialog. The Windows Media Player control now appears at the bottom of the **Toolbox**.

The Windows Media Player control provides several buttons that allow the user to play the current file, pause, stop, play the previous file, rewind, forward and play the next file. The control also includes a volume control and trackbars to select a specific position in the media file.

Our application provides a **File** menu containing the **Open** and **Exit** menu items. When a user chooses **Open** from the **File** menu, event handler openItem_Click (lines 15–

```
1   // Fig. 17.27: MediaPlayerTest.cs
2   // Windows Media Player control used to play media files.
3   using System;
4   using System.Windows.Forms;
5
6   public partial class MediaPlayer : Form
7   {
8      // default constructor
9      public MediaPlayer()
10     {
11        InitializeComponent();
12     } // end constructor
13
14     // open new media file in Windows Media Player
15     private void openItem_Click( object sender, EventArgs e )
16     {
17        openMediaFileDialog.ShowDialog();
18
19        // load and play the media clip
20        player.URL = openMediaFileDialog.FileName;
21     } // end method openItem_Click
22
23     // exit program when exit menu item is clicked
24     private void exitItem_Click( object sender, EventArgs e )
25     {
26        Application.Exit();
27     } // end method exitItem_Click
28  } // end class MediaPlayer
```

Fig. 17.27 | Windows Media Player demonstration. (Part 1 of 2.)

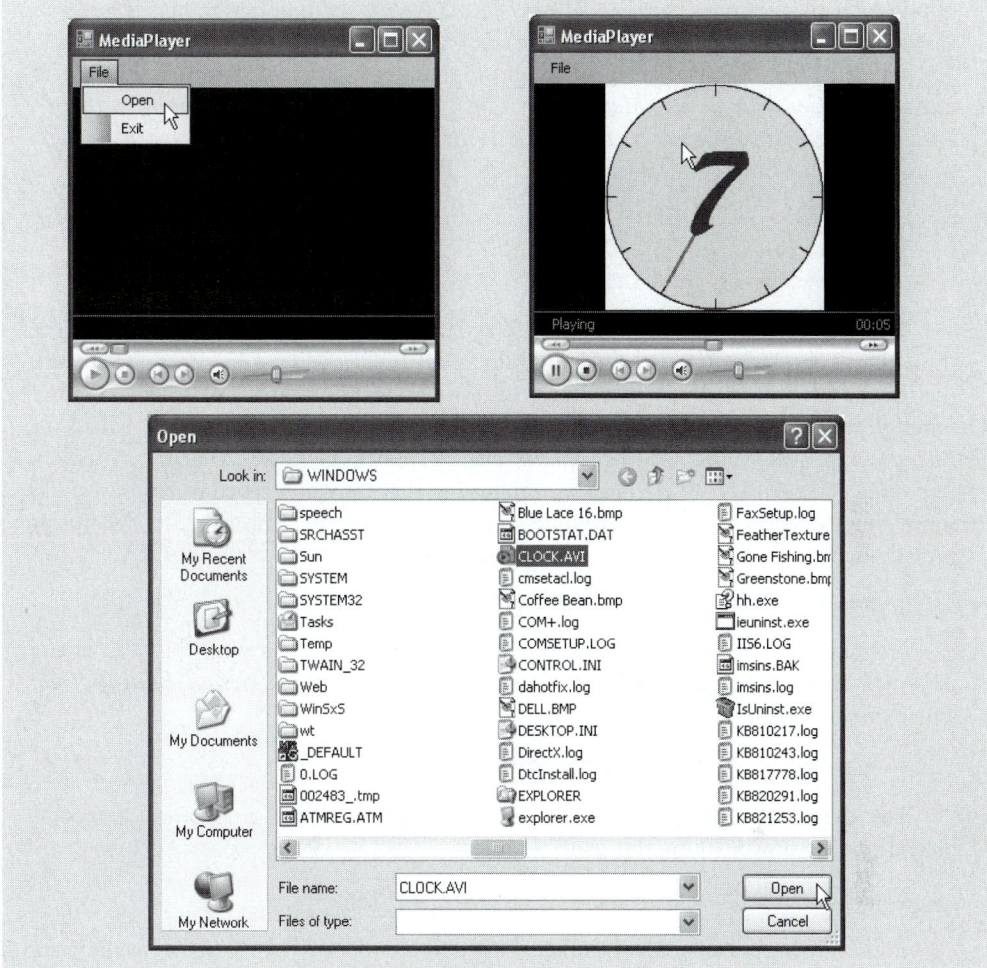

Fig. 17.27 | Windows Media Player demonstration. (Part 2 of 2.)

21) executes. An OpenFileDialog box displays (line 17) to allow the user to select a file. The program then sets the URL property of the player (the Windows Media Player control object of type *AxMediaPlayer*) to the name of the file chosen by the user. The URL property specifies the file that Windows Media Player is currently using.

The exitItem_Click event handler (lines 24–27) executes when the user selects **Exit** from the **File** menu. This event handler simply calls Application.Exit to terminate the application. We provide sample audio and video files in the directory that contains this example.

17.14 Microsoft Agent

Microsoft Agent is a technology used to add *interactive animated characters* to Windows applications or Web pages. Microsoft Agent characters can speak and respond to user input via speech recognition and synthesis. Microsoft employs its Agent technology in applications such as Word, Excel and PowerPoint. Agents in these programs aid users in finding answers to questions and in understanding how the applications function.

The Microsoft Agent control provides programmers with access to four predefined characters—*Genie* (a genie), *Merlin* (a wizard), *Peedy* (a parrot) and *Robby* (a robot). Each character has a unique set of animations that programmers can use in their applications to illustrate different points and functions. For instance, the Peedy character-animation set includes different flying animations, which the programmer might use to move Peedy on the screen. Microsoft provides basic information on Agent technology at

    www.microsoft.com/msagent

Microsoft Agent technology enables users to interact with applications and Web pages through speech, the most natural form of human communication. To understand speech, the control uses a *speech recognition engine*—an application that translates vocal sound input from a microphone to language that the computer understands. The Microsoft Agent control also uses a *text-to-speech engine*, which generates characters' spoken responses. A text-to-speech engine is an application that translates typed words into audio sound that users hear through headphones or speakers connected to a computer. Microsoft provides speech recognition and text-to-speech engines for several languages at

    www.microsoft.com/msagent/downloads/user.asp

Programmers can even create their own animated characters with the help of the *Microsoft Agent Character Editor* and the *Microsoft Linguistic Sound Editing Tool*. These products are available free for download from

    www.microsoft.com/msagent/downloads/developer.asp

This section introduces the basic capabilities of the Microsoft Agent control. For complete details on downloading this control, visit

    www.microsoft.com/msagent/downloads/user.asp

The following example, Peedy's Pizza Palace, was developed by Microsoft to illustrate the capabilities of the Microsoft Agent control. Peedy's Pizza Palace is an online pizza shop where users can place their orders via voice input. The Peedy character interacts with users by helping them choose toppings and calculating the totals for their orders. You can view this example at

    agent.microsoft.com/agent2/sdk/samples/html/peedypza.htm

To run the example, you must go to www.microsoft.com/msagent/downloads/user.asp and download and install the Peedy character file, a text-to-speech engine and a speech-recognition engine.

When the window opens, Peedy introduces himself (Fig. 17.28), and the words he speaks appear in a cartoon bubble above his head. Notice that Peedy's animations correspond to the words he speaks.

Programmers can synchronize character animations with speech output to illustrate a point or to convey a character's mood. For instance, Fig. 17.29 depicts Peedy's *Pleased* animation. The Peedy character-animation set includes eighty-five different animations, each of which is unique to the Peedy character.

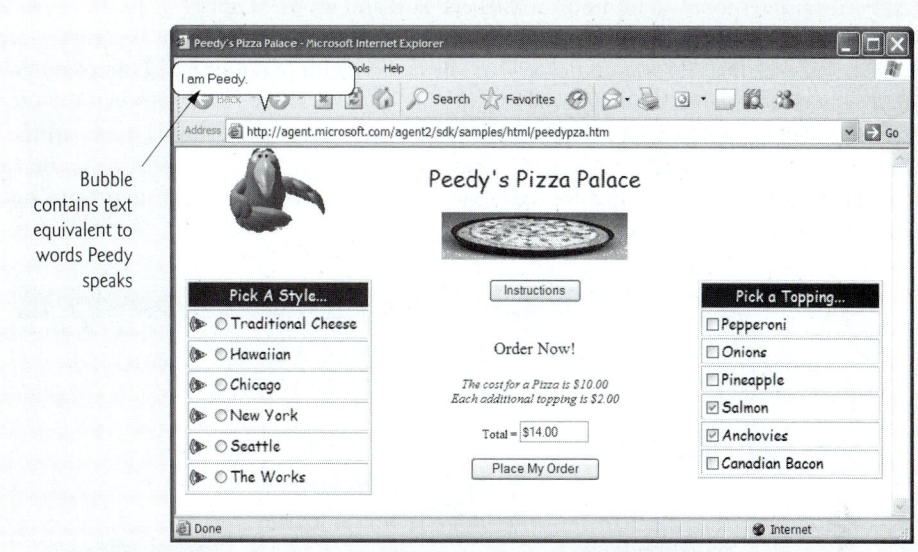

Fig. 17.28 | Peedy introducing himself when the window opens.

Look-and-Feel Observation 17.1

Agent characters remain on top of all active windows while a Microsoft Agent application is running. Their motions are not limited by the boundaries of the browser or application window.

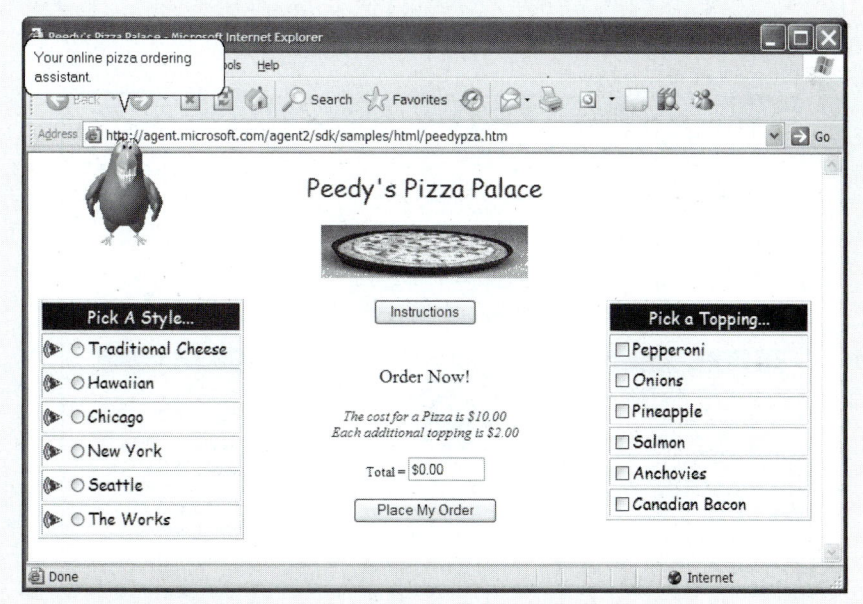

Fig. 17.29 | Peedy's *Pleased* animation.

Peedy also responds to input from the keyboard and mouse. Figure 17.30 shows what happens when a user clicks Peedy with the mouse pointer. Peedy jumps up, ruffles his feathers and exclaims, "Hey, that tickles!" or "Be careful with that pointer!" Users can relocate Peedy on the screen by dragging him with the mouse. However, even when the user moves Peedy to a different part of the screen, he continues to perform his preset animations and location changes.

Many location changes involve animations. For instance, Peedy can hop from one screen location to another, or he can fly (Fig. 17.31).

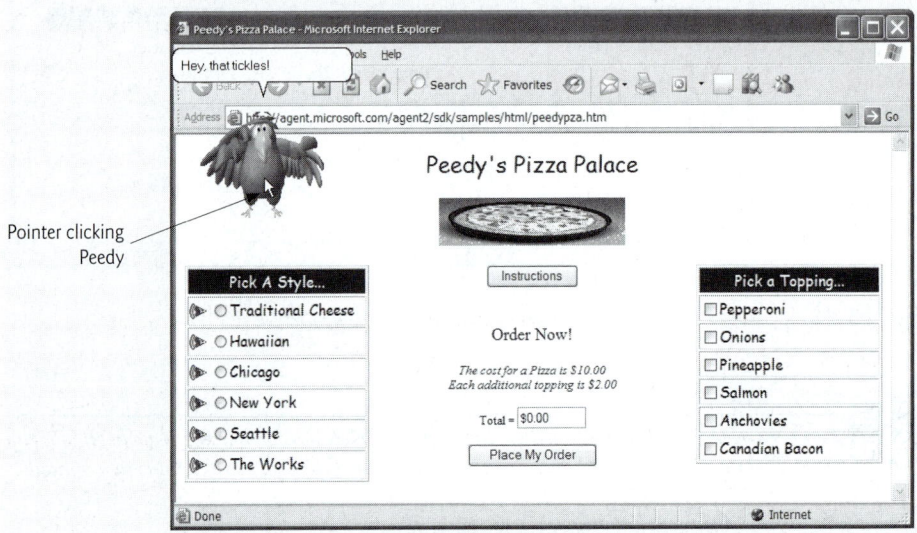

Fig. 17.30 | Peedy's reaction when he is clicked.

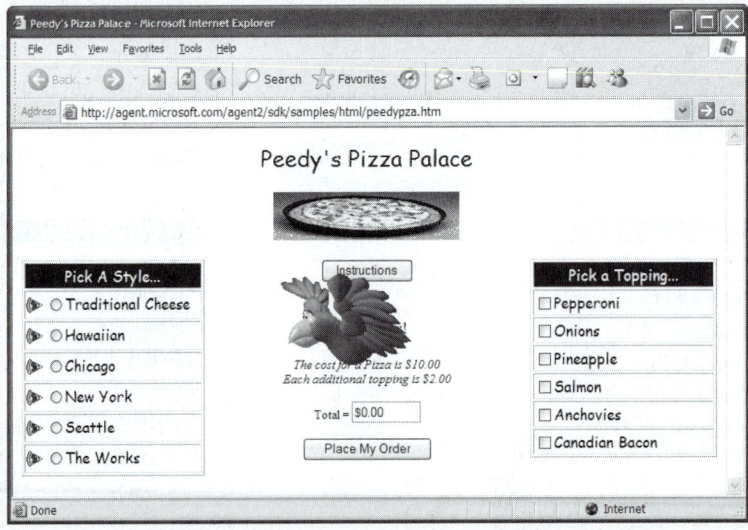

Fig. 17.31 | Peedy flying animation.

Once Peedy completes the ordering instructions, a tool tip appears beneath him indicating that he is listening for a voice command (Fig. 17.32). You can enter the type of pizza to order either by speaking the style name into a microphone or by clicking the radio button corresponding to your choice.

If you choose speech input, a box appears below Peedy displaying the words that Peedy "heard" (i.e., the words translated to the program by the speech-recognition engine). Once he recognizes your input, Peedy gives you a description of the selected pizza. Figure 17.33 shows what happens when you choose **Seattle** as the pizza style.

Peedy then asks you to choose additional toppings. Again, you can either speak or use the mouse to make a selection. Checkboxes corresponding to toppings that come with the selected pizza style are checked for you. Figure 17.34 shows what happens when you choose anchovies as an additional topping. Peedy makes a wisecrack about your choice.

You can submit the order either by pressing the **Place My Order** button or by speaking "Place order" into the microphone. Peedy recounts the order while writing down the order items on his notepad (Fig. 17.35). He then calculates the figures on his calculator and reports the total price (Fig. 17.36).

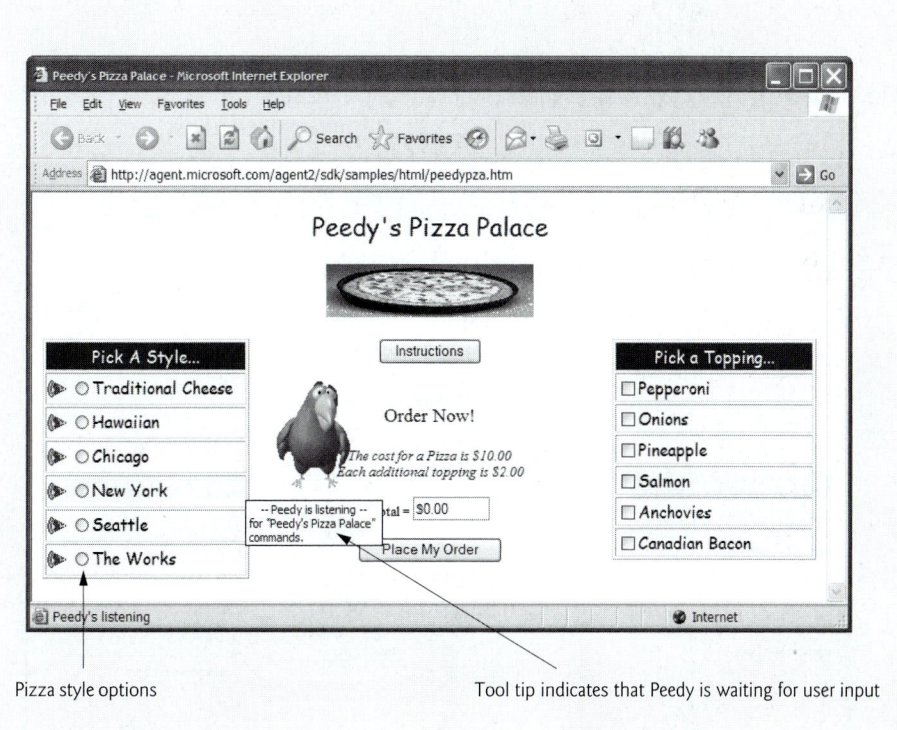

Pizza style options   Tool tip indicates that Peedy is waiting for user input

Fig. 17.32 | Peedy waiting for speech input.

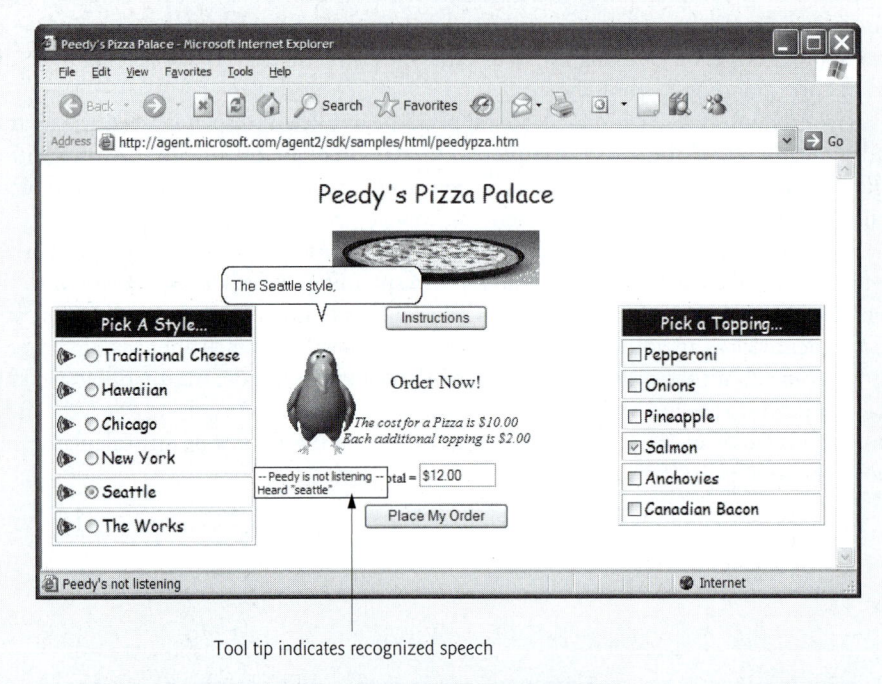

Tool tip indicates recognized speech

Fig. 17.33 | Peedy repeating a request for Seattle-style pizza.

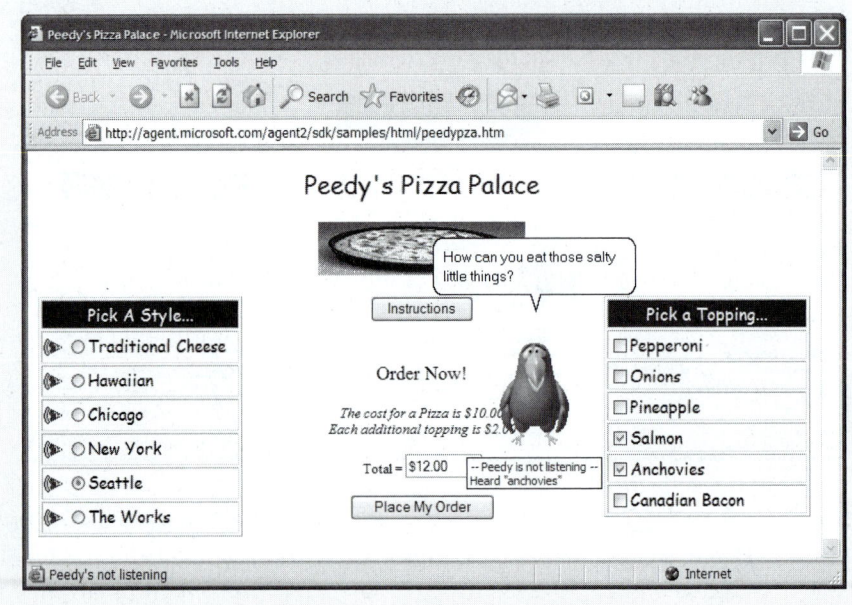

Fig. 17.34 | Peedy repeating a request for anchovies as an additional topping.

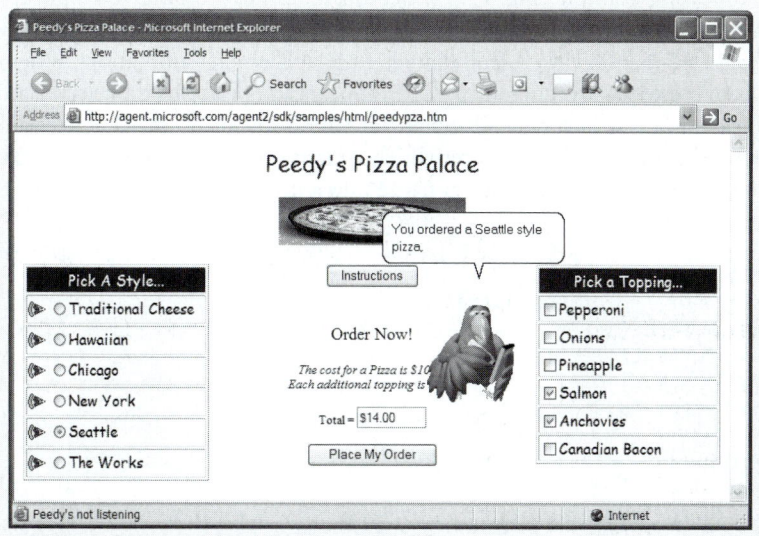

Fig. 17.35 | Peedy recounting the order.

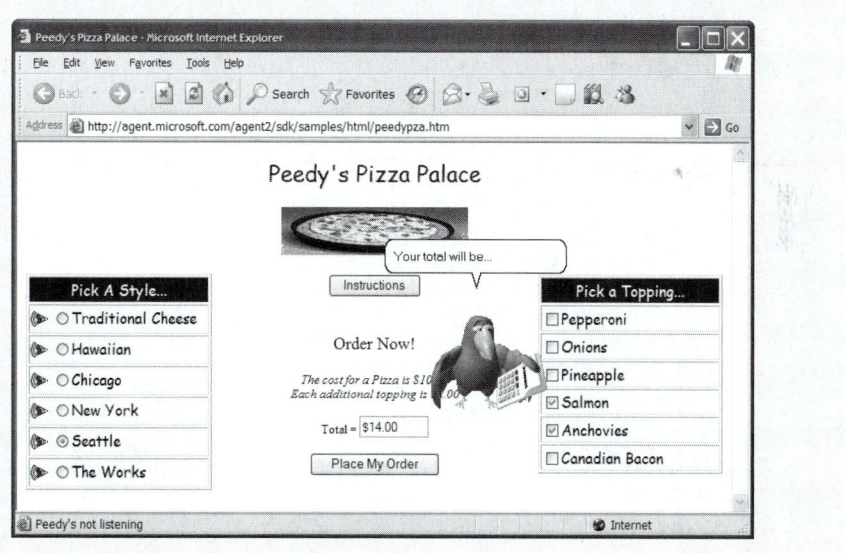

Fig. 17.36 | Peedy calculating the total.

Creating an Application That Uses Microsoft Agent

[*Note:* Before running this example, you must first download and install the Microsoft Agent control, a speech-recognition engine, a text-to-speech engine and the four character definitions from the Microsoft Agent Web site, as we discussed at the beginning of this section.]

The following example (Fig. 17.37) demonstrates how to build a simple application with the Microsoft Agent control. This application contains two drop-down lists from which the user can choose an Agent character and a character animation. When the user chooses from these lists, the chosen character appears and performs the selected animation. The application uses speech recognition and synthesis to control the character animations and speech—you can tell the character which animation to perform by pressing the *Scroll Lock* key, then speaking the animation name into a microphone.

```csharp
1   // Fig. 17.28: Agent.cs
2   // Microsoft Agent demonstration.
3   using System;
4   using System.Collections;
5   using System.Windows.Forms;
6   using System.IO;
7
8   public partial class Agent : Form
9   {
10      // current agent object
11      private AgentObjects.IAgentCtlCharacter speaker;
12
13      // default constructor
14      public Agent()
15      {
16         InitializeComponent();
17
18         // initialize the characters
19         try
20         {
21            // load characters into agent object
22            mainAgent.Characters.Load( "Genie",
23               @"C:\windows\msagent\chars\Genie.acs" );
24            mainAgent.Characters.Load( "Merlin",
25               @"C:\windows\msagent\chars\Merlin.acs" );
26            mainAgent.Characters.Load( "Peedy",
27               @"C:\windows\msagent\chars\Peedy.acs" );
28            mainAgent.Characters.Load( "Robby",
29               @"C:\windows\msagent\chars\Robby.acs" );
30
31            // set current character to Genie and show him
32            speaker = mainAgent.Characters[ "Genie" ];
33            GetAnimationNames(); // obtain an animation name list
34            speaker.Show( 0 ); // display Genie
35            characterCombo.SelectedText = "Genie";
36         } // end try
37         catch ( FileNotFoundException )
38         {
39            MessageBox.Show( "Invalid character location",
40               "Error", MessageBoxButtons.OK, MessageBoxIcon.Error );
41         } // end catch
42      } // end constructor
43
```

Fig. 17.37 | Microsoft Agent demonstration. (Part 1 of 5.)

```
44      // event handler for Speak Button
45      private void speakButton_Click( object sender, EventArgs e )
46      {
47         // if textbox is empty, have the character ask
48         // user to type the words into the TextBox; otherwise,
49         // have the character say the words in the TextBox
50         if ( speechTextBox.Text == "" )
51            speaker.Speak(
52               "Please, type the words you want me to speak", "" );
53         else
54            speaker.Speak( speechTextBox.Text, "" );
55      } // end method speakButton_Click
56
57      // event handler for Agent control's ClickEvent
58      private void mainAgent_ClickEvent(
59         object sender, AxAgentObjects._AgentEvents_ClickEvent e )
60      {
61         speaker.Play( "Confused" );
62         speaker.Speak( "Why are you poking me?", "" );
63         speaker.Play( "RestPose" );
64      } // end method mainAgent_ClickEvent
65
66      // ComboBox changed event, switch active agent character
67      private void characterCombo_SelectedIndexChanged(
68         object sender, EventArgs e )
69      {
70         ChangeCharacter( characterCombo.Text );
71      } // end method characterCombo_SelectedIndexChanged
72
73      // utility method to change characters
74      private void ChangeCharacter( string name )
75      {
76         speaker.StopAll( "Play" );
77         speaker.Hide( 0 );
78         speaker = mainAgent.Characters[ name ];
79
80         // regenerate animation name list
81         GetAnimationNames();
82         speaker.Show( 0 );
83      } // end method ChangeCharacter
84
85      // get animation names and store in ArrayList
86      private void GetAnimationNames()
87      {
88         // ensure thread safety
89         lock ( this )
90         {
91            // get animation names
92            IEnumerator enumerator = mainAgent.Characters[
93               speaker.Name ].AnimationNames.GetEnumerator();
94
95            string voiceString;
```

Fig. 17.37 | Microsoft Agent demonstration. (Part 2 of 5.)

```
96
97          // clear actionsCombo
98          actionsCombo.Items.Clear();
99          speaker.Commands.RemoveAll();
100
101         // copy enumeration to ArrayList
102         while ( enumerator.MoveNext() )
103         {
104             // remove underscores in speech string
105             voiceString = ( string ) enumerator.Current;
106             voiceString = voiceString.Replace( "_", "underscore" );
107
108             actionsCombo.Items.Add( enumerator.Current );
109
110             // add all animations as voice enabled commands
111             speaker.Commands.Add( ( string ) enumerator.Current,
112                 enumerator.Current, voiceString, true, false );
113         } // end while
114
115         // add custom command
116         speaker.Commands.Add( "MoveToMouse", "MoveToMouse",
117             "MoveToMouse", true, true );
118     } // end lock
119 } // end method GetAnimationNames
120
121 // user selects new action
122 private void actionsCombo_SelectedIndexChanged(
123     object sender, EventArgs e )
124 {
125     speaker.StopAll( "Play" );
126     speaker.Play( actionsCombo.Text );
127     speaker.Play( "RestPose" );
128 } // end method actionsCombo_SelectedIndexChanged
129
130 // event handler for Agent commands
131 private void mainAgent_Command(
132     object sender, AxAgentObjects._AgentEvents_CommandEvent e )
133 {
134     // get UserInput object
135     AgentObjects.IAgentCtlUserInput command =
136         ( AgentObjects.IAgentCtlUserInput ) e.userInput;
137
138     // change character if user speaks character name
139     if ( command.Voice == "Peedy" || command.Voice == "Robby" ||
140         command.Voice == "Merlin" || command.Voice == "Genie" )
141     {
142         ChangeCharacter( command.Voice );
143         return;
144     } // end if
145
146     // send agent to mouse
147     if ( command.Voice == "MoveToMouse" )
148     {
```

Fig. 17.37 | Microsoft Agent demonstration. (Part 3 of 5.)

```
149            speaker.MoveTo( Convert.ToInt16( Cursor.Position.X - 60 ),
150               Convert.ToInt16( Cursor.Position.Y - 60 ), 5 );
151            return;
152         } // end if
153
154         // play new animation
155         speaker.StopAll( "Play" );
156         speaker.Play( command.Name );
157      }
158 } // end class Agent
```

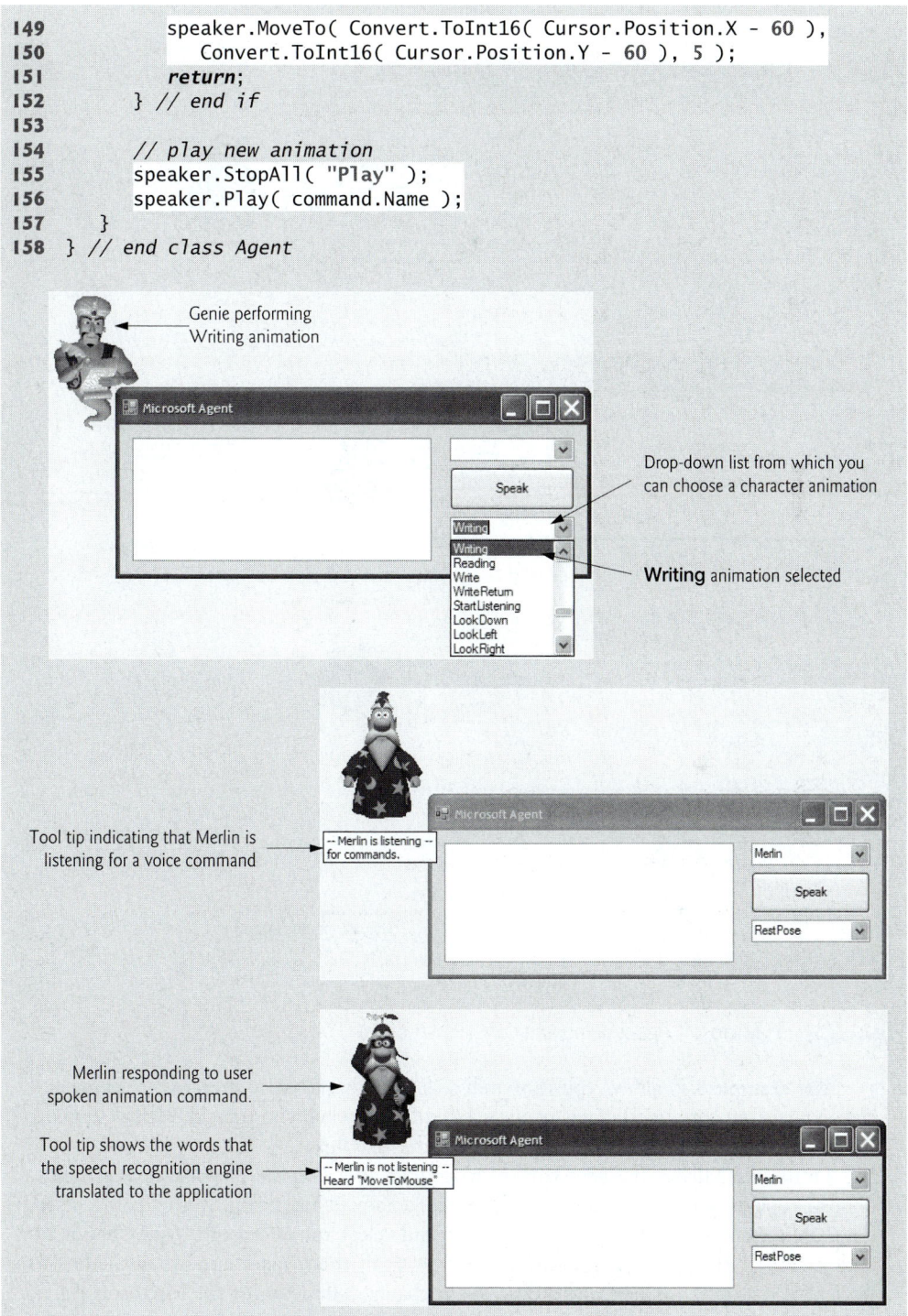

Fig. 17.37 | Microsoft Agent demonstration. (Part 4 of 5.)

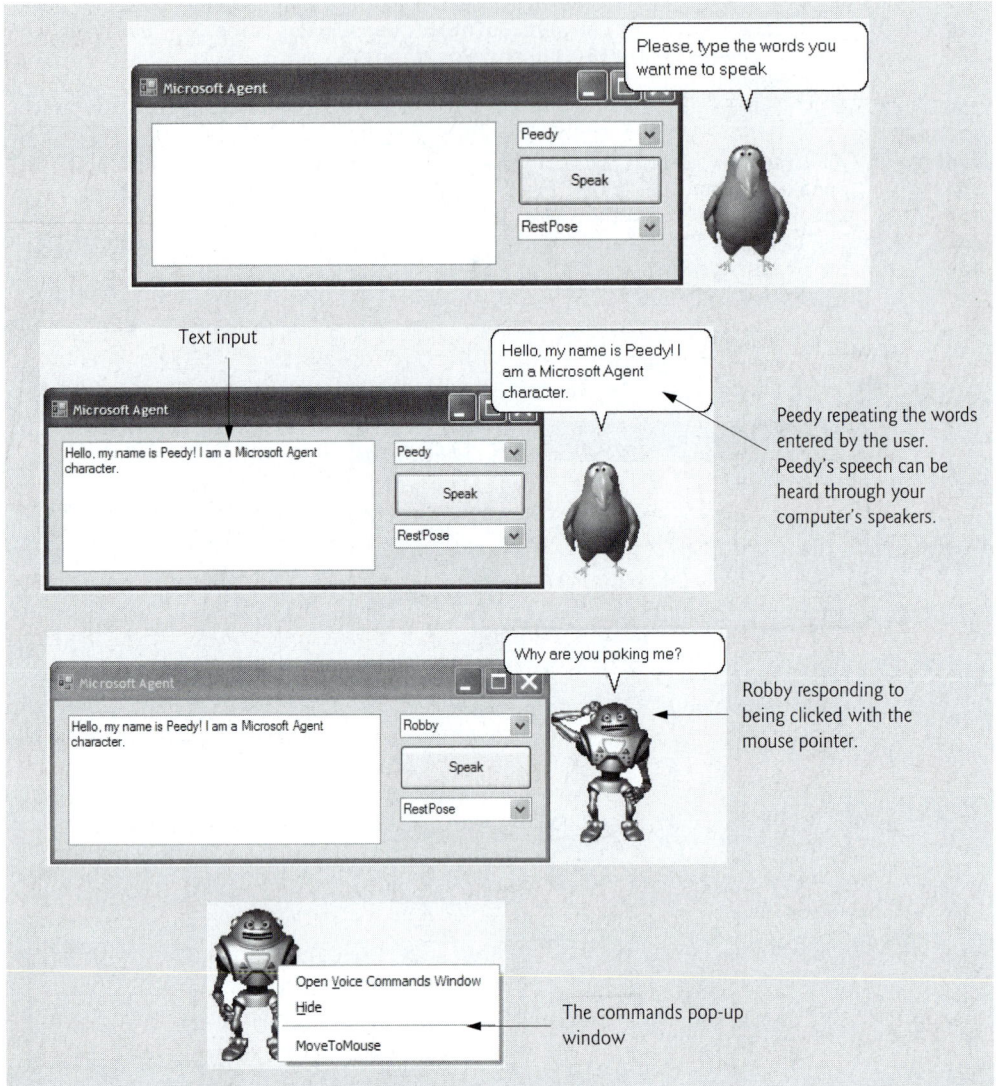

Fig. 17.37 | Microsoft Agent demonstration. (Part 5 of 5.)

The example also allows you to switch to a new character by speaking its name and creates a custom command, `MoveToMouse`. In addition, when you press the **Speak** `Button`, the characters speak any text that you typed in the `TextBox`.

To use the Microsoft Agent control, you must add it to the **Toolbox**. Select **Tools > Choose Toolbox Items...** to display the **Choose Toolbox Items** dialog. In the dialog, select the **COM Components** tab, then scroll down and select the **Microsoft Agent Control 2.0** option. When this option is selected properly, a small check mark appears in the box to the left of the option. Click **OK** to dismiss the dialog. The icon for the Microsoft Agent control now appears at the bottom of the **Toolbox**. Drag the **Microsoft Agent Control 2.0** control onto your `Form` and name the object `mainAgent`.

In addition to the Microsoft Agent object `mainAgent` (of type *AxAgent*) that manages the characters, you also need a variable of type *IAgentCtlCharacter* to represent the current character. We create this variable, named `speaker`, in line 11.

When you execute this program, class `Agent`'s constructor (lines 14–42) loads the character descriptions for the predefined animated characters (lines 22–29). If the specified location of the characters is incorrect, or if any character is missing, a `FileNotFoundException` is thrown. By default, the character descriptions are stored in `C:\Windows\msagent\chars`. If your system uses another name for the `Windows` directory, you'll need to modify the paths in lines 22–29.

Lines 32–34 set Genie as the default character, obtain all animation names via our utility method `GetAnimationNames` and call `IAgentCtlCharacter` method *Show* to display the character. We access characters through property *Characters* of `mainAgent`, which contains all characters that have been loaded. We use the indexer of the `Characters` property to specify the name of the character that we wish to load (Genie).

Responding to the Agent Control's `ClickEvent`
When a user clicks the character (i.e., pokes it with the mouse), event handler `mainAgent_ClickEvent` (lines 58–64) executes. First, `speaker` method *Play* plays an animation. This method accepts as an argument a `string` representing one of the predefined animations for the character (a list of animations for each character is available at the Microsoft Agent Web site; each character provides over 70 animations). In our example, the argument to `Play` is `"Confused"`—this animation is defined for all four characters, each of which expresses this emotion in a unique way. The character then speaks, `"Why are you poking me?"` via a call to method `Speak`. Finally, we play the `RestPose` animation, which returns the character to its neutral, resting pose.

Obtaining a Character's List of Animations and Defining Its Commands
The list of valid commands for a character is contained in property `Commands` of the `IAgentCtlCharacter` object (`speaker`, in this example). The commands for an Agent character can be viewed in the **Commands** pop-up window, which displays when the user right-clicks an Agent character (the last screenshot in Fig. 17.37). Method `Add` of property `Commands` adds a new command to the command list. Method `Add` takes three `string` arguments and two `bool` arguments. The first `string` argument identifies the name of the command, which we use to identify the command programmatically. The second `string` defines the command name as it appears in the **Commands** pop-up window. The third `string` defines the voice input that triggers the command. The first `bool` specifies whether the command is active, and the second `bool` indicates whether the command is visible in the **Commands** pop-up window. A command is triggered when the user selects the command from the **Commands** pop-up window or speaks the voice input into a microphone. Command logic is handled in the `Command` event handler of the `AxAgent` control (`mainAgent`, in this example). In addition, Agent defines several global commands that have predefined functions (for example, speaking a character name causes that character to appear).

Method `GetAnimationNames` (lines 86–119) fills the `actionsCombo` ComboBox with the current character's animation listing and defines the valid commands that can be used with the character. The method contains a `lock` block to prevent errors resulting from rapid character changes. The method uses an `IEnumerator` (lines 92–93) to obtain the current character's animations. Lines 98–99 clear the existing items in the ComboBox and the character's Commands property. Lines 102–113 iterate through all items in the animation-name enumerator. For each animation, line 105 assigns the animation name to string voiceString. Line 106 removes any underscore characters (_) and replaces them with the string "underscore"; this changes the string so that a user can pronounce and employ it as a command activator. Line 108 adds the animation's name to the actionsCombo ComboBox. The Add method of the Commands property (lines 111–112) adds a new command to the current character. In this example, we add every animation name as a command. Each call to Add receives the animation name as both the name of the command and the string that appears in the **Commands** pop-up window. The third argument is the voice command, and the last two arguments enable the command but indicate that it is not available via the **Commands** pop-up window. Thus, the command can be activated only by voice input. Lines 116–117 create a new command, named MoveToMouse, which is visible in the **Commands** pop-up window.

Responding to Selections from the actionsCombo ComboBox
After the GetAnimationNames method has been called, the user can select a value from the actionsCombo ComboBox. Event handler actionsCombo_SelectedIndexChanged (lines 122–128) stops any current animation, then plays the animation that the user selected from the ComboBox, followed by the RestPose animation.

Speaking the Text Typed by the User
You can also type text in the TextBox and click **Speak**. This causes event handler speakButton_Click (line 45–55) to call speaker method Speak, supplying as an argument the text in speechTextBox. If the user clicks **Speak** without providing text, the character speaks, "Please, type the words you want me to speak".

Changing Characters
At any point in the program, the user can choose a different character from the charactersCombo ComboBox. When this happens, the SelectedIndexChanged event handler for characterCombo (lines 67–71) executes. The event handler calls method Change-Character (lines 74–83) with the text in the characterCombo as an argument. Method ChangeCharacter stops any current animation, then calls the Hide method of speaker (line 77) to remove the current character from view. Line 78 assigns the newly selected character to speaker, line 81 generates the character's animation names and commands, and line 82 displays the character via a call to method Show.

Responding to Commands
Each time a user presses the *Scroll Lock* key and speaks into a microphone or selects a command from the **Commands** pop-up window, event handler mainAgent_Command (lines 131–157) is called. This method is passed an argument of type AxAgentObjects._AgentEvents_CommandEvent, which contains a single property, userInput. The userInput property returns an Object that can be converted to type AgentObjects.IAgentCtlUserInput. Lines 135–136 assign the userInput object to an IAgentCtlUserInput object named command, which is used to identify the command, so the program can respond appropriately. Lines 139–144 use method ChangeCharacter to change the current Agent character if the user speaks a character name. Microsoft Agent always will show a character when a user speaks its name; however, by controlling the char-

acter change, we can ensure that only one Agent character is displayed at a time. Lines 147–152 move the character to the current mouse location if the user invokes the Move-ToMouse command. Agent method **MoveTo** takes *x*- and *y*-coordinate arguments and moves the character to the specified screen position, applying appropriate movement animations. For all other commands, we Play the command name as an animation in line 156.

17.15 Wrap-Up

This chapter began with an introduction to the .NET framework's drawing capabilities. We then presented more powerful drawing capabilities, such as changing the styles of lines used to draw shapes and controlling the colors and patterns of filled shapes.

Next, you learned techniques for manipulating images and creating smooth animations. We discussed class Image, which can store and manipulate images of various formats. We explained how to combine the graphical rendering capabilities covered in the early sections of the chapter with those for image manipulation.

You also learned how to incorporate the Windows Media Player control in an application to play audio or video. Finally, we demonstrated Microsoft Agent—a technology for adding interactive animated characters to applications or Web pages—then showed how to incorporate Microsoft Agent in an application to add speech synthesis and recognition capabilities. In the next chapter, we discuss file processing techniques than enable programs to store and retrieve data from persistent storage, such as your computer's hard disk. We also explore several types of streams included in Visual Studio .NET.

Summary

Section 17.1 Introduction

- The FCL contains many sophisticated drawing capabilities as part of namespace System.Drawing and the other namespaces that make up the .NET resource GDI+.
- GDI+ is an API that provides classes for creating two-dimensional vector graphics, manipulating fonts and inserting images.

Section 17.2 Drawing Classes and the Coordinate System

- Namespaces System.Drawing and System.Drawing.Drawing2D contain the most commonly used GDI+ components.
- Class Graphics contains methods used for drawing strings, lines, rectangles and other shapes on a Control. These methods usually require a Pen or Brush object to render a shape. A Pen draws shape outlines; a Brush draws solid objects.
- The Color structure contains numerous static properties, which set the colors of various graphical components, plus methods that allow users to create new colors.
- Class Font contains properties that define unique fonts.
- Class FontFamily contains methods for obtaining font information.
- GDI+'s coordinate system identifies points on the screen. The upper-left corner of a control has the coordinates (0, 0). The *x*-coordinate is the horizontal distance to the right from the upper-left corner. The *y*-coordinate is the vertical distance downward from the upper-left corner. The *x*-axis defines every horizontal coordinate, and the *y*-axis defines every vertical coordinate.
- Programmers position text and shapes on the screen by specifying their coordinates, which are measured in pixels—the smallest units of resolution on a display monitor.

- The Point structure represents the *x-y* coordinates of a point on a two-dimensional plane.
- The Rectangle structure defines the location, width and height of a rectangular shape.
- The Size structure represents the width and height of a shape.

Section 17.3 Graphics Contexts and Graphics Objects

- A graphics context represents a drawing surface that enables drawing on the screen. A Graphics object manages a graphics context by controlling how information is drawn.
- Every derived class of Form inherits a virtual OnPaint method in which most graphics operations are performed. The OnPaint method triggers the Control's Paint event. Instead of overriding the OnPaint method, you can add an event handler for the Paint event.
- You can force a call to OnPaint by calling a Control's Invalidate method to indicate that the control should be refreshed.
- To draw on a control, first create a graphics object by invoking the control's CreateGraphics method, then use the Graphics object's methods to draw on the control.

Section 17.4 Color Control

- Structure Color defines methods and constants used to manipulate colors.
- Every color can be created from a combination of alpha, red, green and blue components (called ARGB values). All four ARGB values are integer values in the range 0–255.
- The alpha value determines the opacity of the color. The alpha value 0 represents a transparent color, and the value 255 represents an opaque color. Alpha values between 0 and 255 result in a weighted blending effect of the color's RGB value with that of any background color, causing a semitransparent effect.
- The first number in the RGB value defines the amount of red in the color, the second defines the amount of green and the third defines the amount of blue. The larger the value, the greater the amount of that particular color.
- Method FromArgb has three- and four-parameter versions (all argument values must be int between 0 and 255, inclusive). Both take int arguments specifying the amount of red, green and blue. The four-argument version also allows the user to specify the alpha component; the three-argument version defaults the alpha to 255 (opaque). Both methods return a Color object.
- A Pen is used to draw lines. Most drawing methods require a Pen object. The overloaded Pen constructors allow programmers to specify the colors and widths of the lines that they wish to draw.
- The System.Drawing namespace provides a Pens class containing predefined Pens.
- Derived classes of Brush define objects that color the interiors of graphical shapes.
- The SolidBrush constructor takes a Color object representing the color to draw.
- Fill methods use Brushes to fill a space with a color, pattern or image.
- Graphics method FillRectangle draws a filled-in rectangle. FillRectangle takes as parameters a Brush, the *x*- and *y*-coordinates of the rectangle's upper-left corner and its width and height.
- There are several overloaded DrawString methods; one takes as arguments the string to display, the display Font, the Brush to use for drawing and the coordinates of the string's first character.
- Class Color's static method FromName creates a new Color object from a string.
- ColorDialog is a dialog box that allows users to select from a palette of available colors or to create custom colors. An application retrieves the user's selection via the ColorDialog's Color property.
- Setting ColorDialog's FullOpen property to true indicates that the dialog should display all available colors. When FullOpen is false, the dialog shows only color swatches.

Section 17.5 Font Control

- A Font's Size property returns the font size as measured in design units, whereas property SizeInPoints returns the font size as measured in points. Design units allow the font size to be specified in one of several units of measurement, such as inches or millimeters.

- Some Font constructors accept a GraphicsUnit enumeration argument that allows you to specify the unit of measurement for the font size. Members of the GraphicsUnit enumeration include Point (1/72 inch), Display (1/75 inch), Document (1/300 inch), Millimeter, Inch and Pixel.

- Most Font constructors require a font name, the font size and the font style. The font style is specified with a constant from the FontStyle enumeration (Bold, Italic, Regular, Strikeout and Underline, or a combination of these). You can combine font styles with the | operator.

- You can determine a font's metrics, such as height, descent, ascent and leading.

- Class FontFamily defines characteristics common to a group of related fonts. Class FontFamily provides methods to determine the font metrics shared by members of a particular family.

Section 17.6 Drawing Lines, Rectangles and Ovals

- Methods that draw hollow shapes typically require as arguments a Pen and four ints. Methods that draw solid shapes typically require as arguments a Brush and four ints. the ints represent the bounding box of the shape.

- Methods FillRectangle and DrawRectangle draw rectangles. For each method, the first argument specifies the drawing object to use—for FillRectangle a Brush object and for DrawRectangle method a Pen object. The last four arguments represent the rectangle's bounding box.

- Method DrawLine takes a Pen and two pairs of ints that specify the start and end of a line. The method then draws a line, using the Pen object.

- Methods FillEllipse and DrawEllipse draw ellipse. For each method, the first argument specifies the drawing object to use. The last four arguments represent the ellipse's bounding box. The ellipse touches the midpoint of each of the four sides of the bounding rectangle.

Section 17.7 Drawing Arcs

- Arcs are portions of ellipses and are measured in degrees, beginning at a starting angle and continuing for a specified number of degrees called the arc angle. Arcs that sweep in a clockwise direction are measured in positive degrees. Arcs that sweep in a counterclockwise direction are measured in negative degrees.

- The Point constructor takes as arguments the *x*- and *y*-coordinates of the new point.

- The Location property determines the upper-left corner of the Rectangle.

- The Size property of a Rectangle determines the arc's height and width.

Section 17.8 Drawing Polygons and Polylines

- Polygons are multisided shapes. There are several Graphics methods used to draw polygons— DrawLines draws a series of connected points, DrawPolygon draws a closed polygon and FillPolygon draws a solid polygon.

- An ArrayList is similar to an array, but an ArrayList can grow dynamically to accommodate more elements.

- ArrayList method ToArray returns an array representing an ArrayList's contents. The method takes a single argument that determine the type of the returned array.

- ArrayList method Clear erases the contents of an ArrayList.

Section 17.9 Advanced Graphics Capabilities

- The Brush hierarchy includes HatchBrush, LinearGradientBrush, PathGradientBrush and TextureBrush.
- Graphics features such as dashed lines, thick lines and the ability to fill shapes with various patterns represent just a few of the capabilities of the System.Drawing namespace.
- Class LinearGradientBrush (System.Drawing.Drawing2D) enables drawing with a color gradient. One of its constructors takes four arguments—a Rectangle, two Colors and a member of enumeration LinearGradientMode. All linear gradients are defined along a line that determines the gradient endpoints. This line can be specified either by the starting and ending points or by the diagonal of a rectangle. The Rectangle argument represents the endpoints of the linear gradient—the upper-left corner is the starting point and the bottom-right corner is the ending point. The second and third arguments specify the colors that the gradient will use. The last argument, a type from the enumeration LinearGradientMode, specifies the gradient's direction. LinearGradientMode.ForwardDiagonal creates a gradient from the upper-left to the lower-right corner.
- Class Bitmap can produce images in color and gray scale. Graphics method FromImage retrieves the Graphics object associated with an Image, which may be used to draw on the image.
- A TextureBrush is a brush that fills the interior of a shape with an image, rather than a solid color. The TextureBrush constructor takes as an argument an image that defines its texture.
- Enumerations DashCap and DashStyle (System.Drawing.Drawing2D namespace) specify settings for a dashed line.
- The DashCap enumeration specifies the styles for the start and end of a dashed line.
- The DashStyle enumeration specifies the dash styles for a line.
- A GraphicsPath (System.Drawing.Drawing2D namespace) represents a general path. The class provides functionality for creating complex shapes from vector-based primitive graphics objects.
- GraphicsPath method CloseFigure attaches the final vector-graphic object end point to the initial starting point for the current figure by a straight line, then starts a new figure. Method StartFigure begins a new figure within the path without closing the previous figure.
- GraphicsPath method AddLine appends a line to the shape.
- Method TranslateTransform sets the origin of a Graphics object.
- Graphics method RotateTransform enables you to rotate drawing positions around the origin.
- Graphics method FillPath draws a filled version of a GraphicsPath.

Section 17.10 Introduction to Multimedia

- Multimedia applications demand extraordinary computing power. Today's ultrafast processors make multimedia-based applications commonplace.

Section 17.11 Loading, Displaying and Scaling Images

- Image method FromFile loads an image from a file on disk.
- Graphics method Clear paints the entire Form in the current background color.
- Graphics method DrawImage receives as arguments the image to draw, the *x*- and *y*-coordinates of the image's upper-left corner, the width of the image and the height of the image. The image is scaled to fit the specified width and height.

Section 17.12 Animating a Series of Images

- Two-dimensional collision detection enables a program to detect whether two shapes overlap or whether a point is contained within a shape. Rectangle method Contains is useful for determining whether a point is inside a rectangular area.

- If a user working with graphics on a slow computer moves the mouse quickly, the application could leave behind artifacts (unintended visual abnormalities).

Section 17.13 Windows Media Player
- The Windows Media Player control enables an application to play video and sound in many multimedia formats, including MPEG, AVI, WAV and MIDI.
- To use the Windows Media Player control, you must add the control to the **Toolbox**. Select **Tools > Choose Toolbox Items...** to display the **Choose Toolbox Items** dialog. Click the **COM components** tab then select the option **Windows Media Player**. Click the **OK** button to dismiss the dialog. The **Windows Media Player** control now appears at the bottom of the **Toolbox**.
- The Windows Media Player control provides several buttons that allow the user to play the current file, pause, stop, play the previous file, rewind, forward and play the next file. The control also includes a volume control and trackbars to select a specific position in the media file.
- The URL property of a Windows Media Player control object (type AxMediaPlayer) specifies the file that Windows Media Player is currently using.

Section 17.14 Microsoft Agent
- Microsoft Agent is a technology used to add interactive animated characters to Windows applications or Web pages. Microsoft Agent characters can speak and respond to user input via speech recognition and synthesis.
- There are four predefined characters—Genie (a genie), Merlin (a wizard), Peedy (a parrot) and Robby (a robot). Each has a unique set of animations.
- The control uses a speech recognition engine to translate vocal sound input from a microphone to language that the computer understands. The Microsoft Agent control also uses a text-to-speech engine, which generates characters' spoken responses.
- Programmers can synchronize character animations with speech output to illustrate a point or to convey a character's mood.
- Agent characters also respond to input from the keyboard and mouse.
- You can issue spoken commands to an Agent character by pressing the *Scroll Lock* key, then speaking into a microphone.
- To use the Microsoft Agent control, you must add it to the **Toolbox**. Select **Tools > Choose Toolbox Items...** to display the **Choose Toolbox Items** dialog. In the dialog, select the **COM Components** tab, then select the **Microsoft Agent Control 2.0** option. Click **OK** to dismiss the dialog. The icon for the Microsoft Agent control now appears at the bottom of the **Toolbox**.
- A variable of type IAgentCtlCharacter represents the current Agent character in a program.
- By default, the character descriptions are stored in C:\Windows\msagent\chars.
- IAgentCtlCharacter method Show displays a character.
- AxAgent control property Characters contains all characters that have been loaded. Use the indexer of the Characters property to specify the name of the character you want to access.
- When a user clicks a character, the AxAgent control's ClickEvent event handler executes.
- IAgentCtlCharacter method Play plays an animation. This method accepts as an argument a string representing one of the predefined animations for the character.
- The list of valid commands for a character is contained in property **Commands** of the IAgentCtlCharacter object. The commands for an Agent character can be viewed in the Commands pop-up window, which displays when the user right-clicks an Agent character.

- Method `Add` of property `Commands` adds a new command to the command list. Method `Add` takes three `string` arguments and two `bool` arguments. The first `string` identifies the name of the command, which we use to identify the command programmatically. The second `string` defines the command name as it appears in the **Commands** pop-up window. The third `string` defines the voice input that triggers the command. The first `bool` specifies whether the command is active, and the second `bool` indicates whether the command is visible in the **Commands** pop-up window.

- A command is triggered when the user selects the command from the **Commands** pop-up window or speaks the voice input into a microphone. Command logic is handled in the `Command` event handler of the `AxAgent` control.

- `IAgentCtlCharacter` method `Speak` receives a `string` that the character should speak.

- `IAgentCtlCharacter` method `MoveTo` moves the character to the specified position on the screen.

Terminology

A property of structure `Color`
`AboutBox` method of `AxMediaPlayer`
`Add` method of class `ArrayList`
`AddLine` method of class `GraphicsPath`
animation
arc angle
artifact
ARGB values
`ArrayList` class
audio-video interleave (AVI)
`AxAgent` class
`AxMediaPlayer` class
`B` property of structure `Color`
bandwidth
`Bitmap` class
`Black` static property of structure `Color`
`Blue` static property of structure `Color`
`Bold` member of enumeration `FontStyle`
`Bold` property of class `Font`
bounding rectangle for an oval
`Brush` class
`Characters` property of class `AxAgent`
`Clear` method of class `ArrayList`
closed polygon
`CloseFigure` method of class `GraphicsPath`
collision detection
color constants
color manipulation
`Color` methods and properties
`Color` property of class `ColorDialog`
`Color` structure
`ColorDialog` class
complex curve
connected lines
coordinate system

coordinates (0, 0)
`CreateGraphics` method of class `Graphics`
customizing the **Toolbox**
`Cyan` static property of structure `Color`
`DarkBlue` static property of structure `Color`
`DarkGray` static property of structure `Color`
`Dash` member of enumeration `DashStyle`
`DashCap` enumeration
`DashCap` property of class `Pen`
dashed lines
`DashStyle` enumeration
`DashStyle` property of class `Pen`
default font
degree
design units
`GetCellDescent` method of class `FontFamily`
`GetEmHeight` method of `FontFamily`
`GetLineSpacing` method of class `FontFamily`
`Display` member of enumeration `GraphicsUnit`
display monitor
`Document` member of enumeration
     `GraphicsUnit`
`DrawArc` method of class `Graphics`
`DrawEllipse` method of class `Graphics`
`DrawLine` method of class `Graphics`
`DrawLines` method of class `Graphics`
`DrawPie` method of class `Graphics`
`DrawPolygon` method of class `Graphics`
`DrawRectangle` method of class `Graphics`
`DrawString` method of class `Graphics`
event-driven process
fill a shape with color
`FillEllipse` method of class `Graphics`
fill shape
`FillPath` method of class `Graphics`

SizeInPoints property of class Font
solid arc
solid polygon
solid rectangle
SolidBrush class
speech-recognition engine
starting angle
straight line
Strikeout member of enumeration FontStyle
Strikeout property of class Font
sweep
System.Drawing namespace
System.Drawing.Drawing2D namespace
text-to-speech engine
TextureBrush class
three-dimensional application
Tick event of class Timer

Timer class
ToArray method of class Arraylist
TranslateTransform method of class Graphics
two-dimensional shape
Underline member of enumeration FontStyle
Underline property of class Font
upper-left corner of a GUI component
URL property of class AxMediaPlayer
vertical coordinate
White static property of structure Color
Windows Media Player
Windows wave file format (WAV)
x-axis
x-coordinate
y-axis
y-coordinate
Yellow static property of structure Color

Self-Review Exercises

17.1 State whether each of the following is *true* or *false*. If *false*, explain why.
  a) A Font object's size can be changed by setting its Size property.
  b) In the C# coordinate system, *x*-values increase from left to right.
  c) Method FillPolygon draws a solid polygon with a specified Brush.
  d) Method DrawArc allows negative angles.
  e) Font property Size returns the size of the current font in centimeters.
  f) Pixel coordinate (0, 0) is located at the exact center of the monitor.
  g) A HatchBrush is used to draw lines.
  h) A Color is defined by its alpha, red, green and violet content.
  i) Every Control has an associated Graphics object.
  j) Method OnPaint is inherited by every Form.

17.2 Fill in the blanks in each of the following statements:
  a) Class _____ is used to draw lines of various colors and thicknesses.
  b) Classes _____ and _____ define the fill for a shape in such a way that the fill gradually changes from one color to another.
  c) Method _____ of class Graphics draws a line between two points.
  d) ARGB is short for _____, _____, _____ and _____.
  e) Font sizes usually are measured in units called _____.
  f) Class _____ fills a shape using a pattern drawn in a Bitmap.
  g) _____ _____ _____ allows an application to play multimedia files.
  h) Class _____ defines a path consisting of lines and curves.
  i) C#'s drawing capabilities are part of the namespaces _____ and _____.
  j) Method _____ loads an image from a disk into an Image object.

Answers to Self-Review Exercises

17.1 a) False. Size is a read-only property. b) True. c) True. d) True. e) False. It returns the size of the current Font in design units. f) False. The coordinate (0,0) corresponds to the upper-left corner of a GUI component on which drawing occurs. g) False. A Pen is used to draw lines, a Hatch-Brush fills a shape with a hatch pattern. h) False. A color is defined by its alpha, red, green and blue content. i) True. j) True.

4. Hourly pay rate

5. Number of exemptions claimed

6. Year-to-date earnings

7. Amount of taxes withheld

In the preceding example, each field is associated with the same employee. A file is a group of related records.[1] A company's payroll file normally contains one record for each employee. A payroll file for a small company might contain only 22 records, whereas one for a large company might contain 100,000 records. It is not unusual for a company to have many files, some containing millions, billions or even trillions of characters of information.

To facilitate the retrieval of specific records from a file, at least one field in each record is chosen as a *record key*, which identifies a record as belonging to a particular person or entity and distinguishes that record from all others. For example, in a payroll record, the employee identification number normally would be the record key.

There are many ways to organize records in a file. A common organization is called a *sequential file,* in which records typically are stored in order by a record-key field. In a payroll file, records usually are placed in order by employee identification number. The first employee record in the file contains the lowest employee identification number, and subsequent records contain increasingly higher ones.

Most businesses use many different files to store data. For example, a company might have payroll files, accounts-receivable files (listing money due from clients), accounts-payable files (listing money due to suppliers), inventory files (listing facts about all the items handled by the business) and many other files. A group of related files often are stored in a *database*. A collection of programs designed to create and manage databases is called a *database management system (DBMS)*. We discuss databases in Chapter 20.

18.3 Files and Streams

C# views each file as a sequential *stream* of bytes (Fig. 18.2). Each file ends either with an *end-of-file marker* or at a specific byte number that is recorded in a system-maintained administrative data structure. When a file is opened, an object is created and a stream is associated with the object. When a program executes, the runtime environment creates three stream objects that are accessible via properties **Console.Out**, **Console.In** and **Console.Error**, respectively. These objects facilitate communication between a program and a particular file or device. Console.In refers to the *standard input stream object*, which

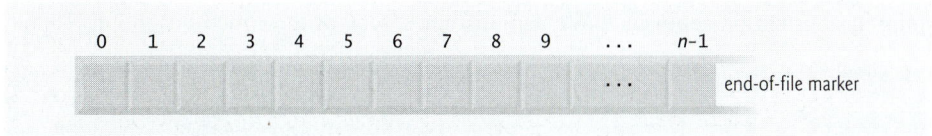

Fig. 18.2 | C#'s view of an *n*-byte file.

---

1. Generally, a file can contain arbitrary data in arbitrary formats. In some operating systems, a file is viewed as nothing more than a collection of bytes, and any organization of the bytes in a file (such as organizing the data into records) is a view created by the application programmer.

enables a program to input data from the keyboard. `Console.Out` refers to the *standard output stream object*, which enables a program to output data to the screen. `Console.Error` refers to the *standard error stream object*, which enables a program to output error messages to the screen. We have been using `Console.Out` and `Console.In` in our console applications—`Console` methods `Write` and `WriteLine` use `Console.Out` to perform output, and `Console` methods `Read` and `ReadLine` use `Console.In` to perform input.

There are many file-processing classes in the FCL. The `System.IO` namespace includes stream classes such as *StreamReader* (for text input from a file), *StreamWriter* (for text output to a file) and *FileStream* (for both input from and output to a file). These stream classes inherit from abstract classes *TextReader*, *TextWriter* and `Stream`, respectively. Actually, properties `Console.In` and `Console.Out` are of type `TextReader` and `TextWriter`, respectively. The system creates objects of `TextReader` and `TextWriter` derived classes to initialize `Console` properties `Console.In` and `Console.Out`.

Abstract class *Stream* provides functionality for representing streams as bytes. Classes `FileStream`, *MemoryStream* and *BufferedStream* (all from namespace `System.IO`) inherit from class `Stream`. Class `FileStream` can be used to write data to and read data from files. Class `MemoryStream` enables the transfer of data directly to and from memory—this is much faster than reading from and writing to external devices. Class `BufferedStream` uses *buffering* to transfer data to or from a stream. Buffering is an I/O performance enhancement technique, in which each output operation is directed to a region in memory, called a *buffer*, that is large enough to hold the data from many output operations. Then actual transfer to the output device is performed in one large *physical output operation* each time the buffer fills. The output operations directed to the output buffer in memory often are called *logical output operations*. Buffering can also be used to speed input operations by initially reading more data than is required into a buffer, so subsequent reads get data from memory rather than an external device.

In this chapter, we use key stream classes to implement file processing programs that create and manipulate sequential-access files. In Chapter 23, Networking: Streams-Based Sockets and Datagrams, we use stream classes to implement networking applications.

18.4 Classes `File` and `Directory`

Information is stored in files, which are organized in directories. Classes `File` and `Directory` enable programs to manipulate files and directories on disk. Class *File* can determine information about files and can be used to open files for reading or writing. We discuss techniques for writing to and reading from files in subsequent sections.

Figure 18.3 lists several of class `File`'s `static` methods for manipulating and determining information about files. We demonstrate several of these methods in Fig. 18.5.

static Method	Description
AppendText	Returns a `StreamWriter` that appends text to an existing file or creates a file if one does not exist.
Copy	Copies a file to a new file.

Fig. 18.3 | `File` class `static` methods (partial list). (Part 1 of 2.)

static Method	Description
Create	Creates a file and returns its associated FileStream.
CreateText	Creates a text file and returns its associated StreamWriter.
Delete	Deletes the specified file.
Exists	Returns true if the specified file exists and false otherwise.
GetCreationTime	Returns a DateTime object representing when the file was created.
GetLastAccessTime	Returns a DateTime object representing when the file was last accessed.
GetLastWriteTime	Returns a DateTime object representing when the file was last modified.
Move	Moves the specified file to a specified location.
Open	Returns a FileStream associated with the specified file and equipped with the specified read/write permissions.
OpenRead	Returns a read-only FileStream associated with the specified file.
OpenText	Returns a StreamReader associated with the specified file.
OpenWrite	Returns a read/write FileStream associated with the specified file.

Fig. 18.3 | File class static methods (partial list). (Part 2 of 2.)

Class ***Directory*** provides capabilities for manipulating directories. Figure 18.4 lists some of class Directory's static methods for directory manipulation. Figure 18.5 demonstrates several of these methods, as well. The ***DirectoryInfo*** object returned by method ***CreateDirectory*** contains information about a directory. Much of the information contained in class DirectoryInfo also can be accessed via the methods of class Directory.

static Method	Description
CreateDirectory	Creates a directory and returns its associated DirectoryInfo object.
Delete	Deletes the specified directory.
Exists	Returns true if the specified directory exists and false otherwise.
GetDirectories	Returns a string array containing the names of the subdirectories in the specified directory.
GetFiles	Returns a string array containing the names of the files in the specified directory.
GetCreationTime	Returns a DateTime object representing when the directory was created.
GetLastAccessTime	Returns a DateTime object representing when the directory was last accessed.

Fig. 18.4 | Directory class static methods. (Part 1 of 2.)

static Method	Description
GetLastWriteTime	Returns a DateTime object representing when items were last written to the directory.
Move	Moves the specified directory to a specified location.

Fig. 18.4 | Directory class static methods. (Part 2 of 2.)

Demonstrating Classes File and Directory

Class FileTestForm (Fig. 18.5) uses File and Directory methods to access file and directory information. This Form contains the control inputTextBox, in which the user enters a file or directory name. For each key that the user presses while typing in the TextBox, the program calls event handler inputTextBox_KeyDown (lines 17–74). If the user presses the *Enter* key (line 20), this method displays either the file's or directory's contents, depending on the text the user input. (If the user does not press the *Enter* key, this method returns without displaying any content.) Line 28 uses File method Exists to determine whether the user-specified text is the name of an existing file. If so, line 32 invokes private method GetInformation (lines 77–97), which calls File methods GetCreationTime (line 86), GetLastWriteTime (line 90) and GetLastAccessTime (line 94) to access file information. When method GetInformation returns, line 38 instantiates a StreamReader for reading text from the file. The StreamReader constructor takes as an argument a string containing the name of the file to open. Line 39 calls StreamReader method ReadToEnd to read the entire contents of the file as a string, then appends the string to outputTextBox.

```
1    // Fig 18.5: FileTestForm.cs
2    // Using classes File and Directory.
3    using System;
4    using System.Windows.Forms;
5    using System.IO;
6
7    // displays contents of files and directories
8    public partial class FileTestForm : Form
9    {
10       // parameterless constructor
11       public FileTestForm()
12       {
13          InitializeComponent();
14       } // end constructor
15
16       // invoked when user presses key
17       private void inputTextBox_KeyDown( object sender, KeyEventArgs e )
18       {
19          // determine whether user pressed Enter key
20          if ( e.KeyCode == Keys.Enter )
21          {
22             string fileName; // name of file or directory
23
```

Fig. 18.5 | Testing classes File and Directory. (Part 1 of 3.)

```
24              // get user-specified file or directory
25              fileName = inputTextBox.Text;
26
27              // determine whether fileName is a file
28              if ( File.Exists( fileName ) )
29              {
30                 // get file's creation date,
31                 // modification date, etc.
32                 outputTextBox.Text = GetInformation( fileName );
33
34                 // display file contents through StreamReader
35                 try
36                 {
37                    // obtain reader and file contents
38                    StreamReader stream = new StreamReader( fileName );
39                    outputTextBox.Text += stream.ReadToEnd();
40                 } // end try
41                 // handle exception if StreamReader is unavailable
42                 catch ( IOException )
43                 {
44                    MessageBox.Show( "Error reading from file", "File Error",
45                       MessageBoxButtons.OK, MessageBoxIcon.Error );
46                 } // end catch
47              } // end if
48              // determine whether fileName is a directory
49              else if ( Directory.Exists( fileName ) )
50              {
51                 string[] directoryList;  // array for directories
52
53                 // get directory's creation date,
54                 // modification date, etc.
55                 outputTextBox.Text = GetInformation( fileName );
56
57                 // obtain file/directory list of specified directory
58                 directoryList = Directory.GetDirectories( fileName );
59
60                 outputTextBox.Text += "\r\n\r\nDirectory contents:\r\n";
61
62                 // output directoryList contents
63                 for ( int i = 0; i < directoryList.Length; i++ )
64                    outputTextBox.Text += directoryList[ i ] + "\r\n";
65              } // end else if
66              else
67              {
68                 // notify user that neither file nor directory exists
69                 MessageBox.Show( inputTextBox.Text +
70                    " does not exist", "File Error",
71                    MessageBoxButtons.OK, MessageBoxIcon.Error );
72              } // end else
73           } // end if
74        } // end method inputTextBox_KeyDown
75
```

Fig. 18.5 | Testing classes File and Directory. (Part 2 of 3.)

```
76      // get information on file or directory
77      private string GetInformation( string fileName )
78      {
79         string information;
80
81         // output that file or directory exists
82         information = fileName + " exists\r\n\r\n";
83
84         // output when file or directory was created
85         information += "Created: " +
86            File.GetCreationTime( fileName ) + "\r\n";
87
88         // output when file or directory was last modified
89         information += "Last modified: " +
90            File.GetLastWriteTime( fileName ) + "\r\n";
91
92         // output when file or directory was last accessed
93         information += "Last accessed: " +
94            File.GetLastAccessTime( fileName ) + "\r\n" + "\r\n";
95
96         return information;
97      } // end method GetInformation
98   } // end class FileTestForm
```

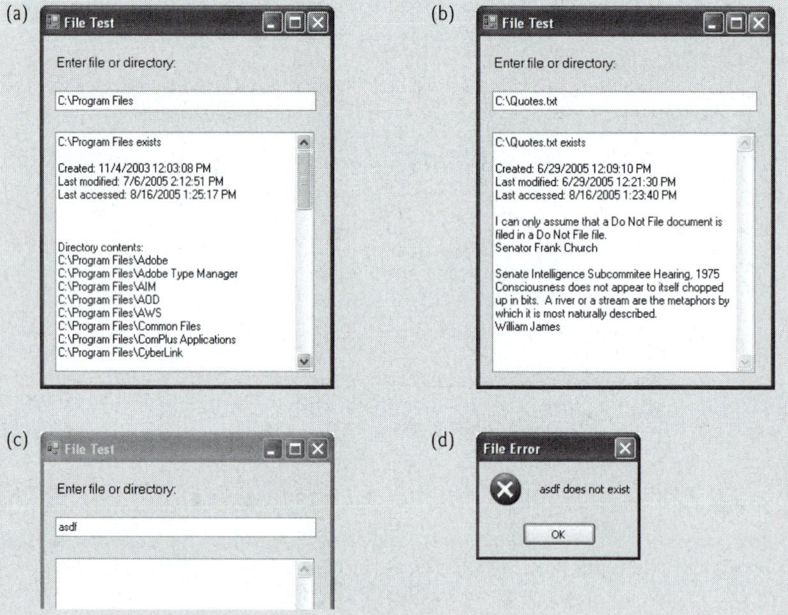

(a)

(b)

(c)

(d)

Fig. 18.5 | Testing classes File and Directory. (Part 3 of 3.)

If line 28 determines that the user-specified text is not a file, line 49 determines whether it is a directory using Directory method *Exists*. If the user specified an existing directory, line 55 invokes method GetInformation to access the directory information.

Line 58 calls Directory method ***GetDirectories*** to obtain a string array containing the names of subdirectories in the specified directory. Lines 63–64 display each element in the string array. Note that, if line 49 determines that the user-specified text is not a directory name, lines 69–71 notify the user (via a MessageBox) that the name the user entered does not exist as a file or directory.

Finding Directories with Regular Expressions

We now consider another example that uses C#'s file- and directory-manipulation capabilities. Class FileSearchForm (Fig. 18.6) uses classes File and Directory, and regular expression capabilities, to report the number of files of each file type that exist in the specified directory path. The program also serves as a "clean-up" utility—when the program encounters a file that has the .bak filename extension (i.e., a backup file), the program displays a MessageBox asking the user whether that file should be removed, then responds appropriately to the user's input.

```
1   // Fig 18.6: FileSearchForm.cs
2   // Using regular expressions to determine file types.
3   using System;
4   using System.Windows.Forms;
5   using System.IO;
6   using System.Text.RegularExpressions;
7   using System.Collections.Specialized;
8
9   // uses regular expressions to determine file types
10  public partial class FileSearchForm : Form
11  {
12     string currentDirectory = Directory.GetCurrentDirectory();
13     string[] directoryList; // subdirectories
14     string[] fileArray;
15
16     // store extensions found and number found
17     NameValueCollection found = new NameValueCollection();
18
19     // parameterless constructor
20     public FileSearchForm()
21     {
22        InitializeComponent();
23     } // end constructor
24
25     // invoked when user types in text box
26     private void inputTextBox_KeyDown( object sender, KeyEventArgs e )
27     {
28        // determine whether user pressed Enter
29        if ( e.KeyCode == Keys.Enter )
30           searchButton_Click( sender, e );
31     } // end method inputTextBox_KeyDown
32
33     // invoked when user clicks "Search Directory" button
34     private void searchButton_Click( object sender, EventArgs e )
35     {
```

Fig. 18.6 | Regular expression used to determine file types. (Part 1 of 4.)

```
36          // check for user input; default is current directory
37          if ( inputTextBox.Text != "" )
38          {
39             // verify that user input is valid directory name
40             if ( Directory.Exists( inputTextBox.Text ) )
41             {
42                currentDirectory = inputTextBox.Text;
43
44                // reset input text box and update display
45                directoryLabel.Text = "Current Directory:" +
46                   "\r\n" + currentDirectory;
47             } // end if
48             else
49             {
50                // show error if user does not specify valid directory
51                MessageBox.Show( "Invalid Directory", "Error",
52                   MessageBoxButtons.OK, MessageBoxIcon.Error );
53             } // end else
54          } // end if
55
56          // clear text boxes
57          inputTextBox.Text = "";
58          outputTextBox.Text = "";
59
60          SearchDirectory( currentDirectory );   // search directory
61
62          // summarize and print results
63          foreach ( string current in found )
64          {
65             outputTextBox.Text += "* Found " +
66                found[ current ] + " " + current + " files.\r\n";
67          } // end foreach
68
69          // clear output for new search
70          found.Clear();
71       } // end method searchButton_Click
72
73       // search directory using regular expression
74       private void SearchDirectory( string currentDirectory )
75       {
76          // for file name without directory path
77          try
78          {
79             string fileName = "";
80
81             // regular expression for extensions matching pattern
82             Regex regularExpression = new Regex(
83                @"[a-zA-Z0-9]+\.(?<extension>\w+)" );
84
85             // stores regular-expression match result
86             Match matchResult;
87
88             string fileExtension; // holds file extensions
```

Fig. 18.6 | Regular expression used to determine file types. (Part 2 of 4.)

```
 89
 90            // number of files with given extension in directory
 91            int extensionCount;
 92
 93            // get directories
 94            directoryList = Directory.GetDirectories( currentDirectory );
 95
 96            // get list of files in current directory
 97            fileArray = Directory.GetFiles( currentDirectory );
 98
 99            // iterate through list of files
100            foreach ( string myFile in fileArray )
101            {
102               // remove directory path from file name
103               fileName = myFile.Substring( myFile.LastIndexOf( @"\" ) + 1 );
104
105               // obtain result for regular-expression search
106               matchResult = regularExpression.Match( fileName );
107
108               // check for match
109               if ( matchResult.Success )
110                  fileExtension = matchResult.Result( "${extension}" );
111               else
112                  fileExtension = "[no extension]";
113
114               // store value from container
115               if ( found[ fileExtension ] == null )
116                  found.Add( fileExtension, "1" );
117               else
118               {
119                  extensionCount = Int32.Parse( found[ fileExtension ] ) + 1;
120                  found[ fileExtension ] = extensionCount.ToString();
121               } // end else
122
123               // search for backup( .bak ) files
124               if ( fileExtension == "bak" )
125               {
126                  // prompt user to delete ( .bak ) file
127                  DialogResult result =
128                     MessageBox.Show( "Found backup file " +
129                     fileName + ". Delete?", "Delete Backup",
130                     MessageBoxButtons.YesNo, MessageBoxIcon.Question );
131
132                  // delete file if user clicked 'yes'
133                  if ( result == DialogResult.Yes )
134                  {
135                     File.Delete( myFile );
136                     extensionCount = Int32.Parse( found[ "bak" ] ) - 1;
137                     found[ "bak" ] = extensionCount.ToString();
138                  } // end if
139               } // end if
140            } // end foreach
141
```

Fig. 18.6 | Regular expression used to determine file types. (Part 3 of 4.)

```
142              // recursive call to search files in subdirectory
143              foreach ( string myDirectory in directoryList )
144                  SearchDirectory( myDirectory );
145          } // end try
146          // handle exception if files have unauthorized access
147          catch ( UnauthorizedAccessException )
148          {
149              MessageBox.Show( "Some files may not be visible" +
150                  " due to permission settings", "Warning",
151                  MessageBoxButtons.OK, MessageBoxIcon.Information );
152          } // end catch
153      } // end method SearchDirectory
154  } // end class FileSearchForm
```

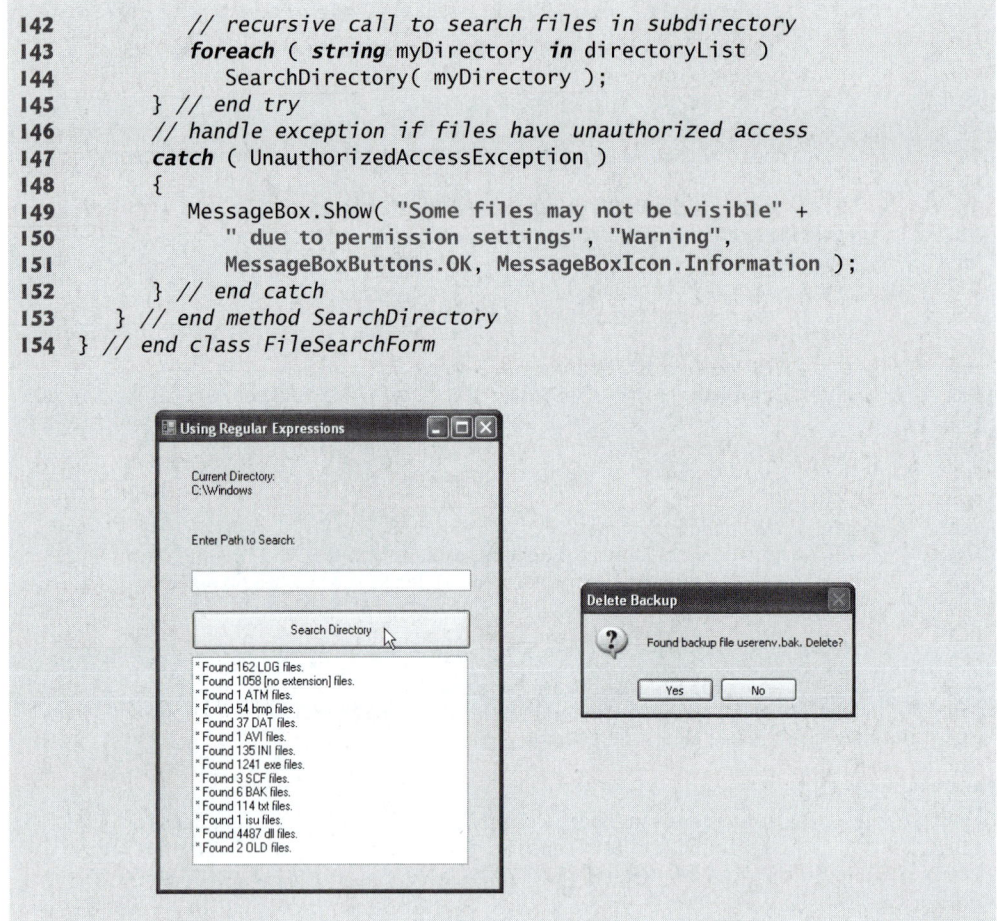

Fig. 18.6 | Regular expression used to determine file types. (Part 4 of 4.)

When the user presses the *Enter* key or clicks the **Search Directory** button, the program invokes method searchButton_Click (lines 34–71), which searches recursively through the directory path that the user provides. If the user inputs text in the TextBox, line 40 calls Directory method Exists to determine whether that text is a valid directory path and name. If not, lines 51–52 notify the user of the error.

If the user specifies a valid directory, line 60 passes the directory name as an argument to private method SearchDirectory (lines 74–153). This method locates files that match the regular expression defined in lines 82–83. This regular expression matches any sequence of numbers or letters followed by a period and one or more letters. Notice the substring of format (?<extension>\w+) in the argument to the Regex constructor (line 83). This indicates that the part of the string that matches \w+ (i.e., the filename extension that appears after a period in the file name) should be placed in the regular expression variable named extension. This variable's value is retrieved later from Match object matchResult to obtain the filename extension so we can summarize the types of files in the directory.

Line 94 calls `Directory` method `GetDirectories` to retrieve the names of all subdirectories that belong to the current directory. Line 97 calls `Directory` method **GetFiles** to store in `string` array `fileArray` the names of files in the current directory. The `foreach` loop in lines 100–140 searches for all files with extension .bak. The loop at lines 143–144 then calls `SearchDirectory` recursively (line 144) for each subdirectory in the current directory. Line 103 eliminates the directory path, so the program can test only the file name when using the regular expression. Line 106 uses `Regex` method `Match` to match the regular expression with the file name, then assigns the result to `Match` object `matchResult`. If the match is successful, line 110 uses `Match` method `Result` to assign to `fileExtension` the value of the regular expression variable `extension` from object `matchResult`. If the match is unsuccessful, line 112 sets `fileExtension` to `"[no extension]"`.

Class `FileSearchForm` uses an instance of class `NameValueCollection` (declared in line 17) to store each filename-extension type and the number of files for each type. A **NameValueCollection** (namespace `System.Collections.Specialized`) contains a collection of key-value pairs of `string`s, and provides method `Add` to add a key-value pair to the collection. The indexer for this class can index according to the order that the items were added or according to the keys. Line 115 uses `NameValueCollection` `found` to determine whether this is the first occurrence of the filename extension (the expression returns `null` if the collection does not contain a key-value pair for the specified `fileExtension`). If this is the first occurrence, line 116 adds that extension to `found` as a key with the value 1. Otherwise, line 119 increments the value associated with the extension in `found` to indicate another occurrence of that file extension, and line 120 assigns the new value to the key-value pair.

Line 124 determines whether `fileExtension` equals "bak"—i.e., whether the file is a backup file. If so, lines 127–130 prompt the user to indicate whether the file should be removed; if the user clicks **Yes** (line 133), lines 135–137 delete the file and decrement the value for the "bak" file type in `found`.

Lines 143–144 call method `SearchDirectory` for each subdirectory. Using recursion, we ensure that the program performs the same logic for finding .bak files in each subdirectory. After each subdirectory has been checked for .bak files, method `SearchDirectory` completes, and lines 63–67 display the results.

18.5 Creating a Sequential-Access Text File

C# imposes no structure on files. Thus, the concept of a "record" does not exist in C# files. This means that you must structure files to meet the requirements of your applications. In the next few examples, we use text and special characters to organize our own concept of a "record."

Class *BankUIForm*

The following examples demonstrate file processing in a bank-account maintenance application. These programs have similar user interfaces, so we created reusable class `BankUIForm` (Fig. 18.7 from the Visual Studio Form designer) to encapsulate a base-class GUI (see the screen capture in Fig. 18.7). Class `BankUIForm` contains four `Label`s and four `TextBox`es. Methods `ClearTextBoxes` (lines 26–40), `SetTextBoxValues` (lines 43–61) and `GetTextBoxValues` (lines 64–75) clear, set the values of and get the values of the text in the `TextBox`es, respectively.

```
1   // Fig. 18.7: BankUIForm.cs
2   // A reusable Windows Form for the examples in this chapter.
3   using System;
4   using System.Windows.Forms;
5
6   public partial class BankUIForm : Form
7   {
8      protected int TextBoxCount = 4; // number of TextBoxes on Form
9
10     // enumeration constants specify TextBox indices
11     public enum TextBoxIndices
12     {
13        ACCOUNT,
14        FIRST,
15        LAST,
16        BALANCE
17     } // end enum
18
19     // parameterless constructor
20     public BankUIForm()
21     {
22        InitializeComponent();
23     } // end constructor
24
25     // clear all TextBoxes
26     public void ClearTextBoxes()
27     {
28        // iterate through every Control on form
29        for ( int i = 0; i < Controls.Count; i++ )
30        {
31           Control myControl = Controls[ i ]; // get control
32
33           // determine whether Control is TextBox
34           if ( myControl is TextBox )
35           {
36              // clear Text property ( set to empty string )
37              myControl.Text = "";
38           } // end if
39        } // end for
40     } // end method ClearTextBoxes
41
42     // set text box values to string array values
43     public void SetTextBoxValues( string[] values )
44     {
45        // determine whether string array has correct length
46        if ( values.Length != TextBoxCount )
47        {
48           // throw exception if not correct length
49           throw( new ArgumentException( "There must be " +
50              ( TextBoxCount + 1 ) + " strings in the array" ) );
51        } // end if
```

Fig. 18.7 | Base class for GUIs in our file-processing applications. (Part 1 of 2.)

```
52          // set array values if array has correct length
53          else
54          {
55              // set array values to text box values
56              accountTextBox.Text = values[ ( int ) TextBoxIndices.ACCOUNT ];
57              firstNameTextBox.Text = values[ ( int ) TextBoxIndices.FIRST ];
58              lastNameTextBox.Text = values[ ( int ) TextBoxIndices.LAST ];
59              balanceTextBox.Text = values[ ( int ) TextBoxIndices.BALANCE ];
60          } // end else
61      } // end method SetTextBoxValues
62
63      // return text box values as string array
64      public string[] GetTextBoxValues()
65      {
66          string[] values = new string[ TextBoxCount ];
67
68          // copy text box fields to string array
69          values[ ( int ) TextBoxIndices.ACCOUNT ] = accountTextBox.Text;
70          values[ ( int ) TextBoxIndices.FIRST ] = firstNameTextBox.Text;
71          values[ ( int ) TextBoxIndices.LAST ] = lastNameTextBox.Text;
72          values[ ( int ) TextBoxIndices.BALANCE ] = balanceTextBox.Text;
73
74          return values;
75      } // end method GetTextBoxValues
76  } // end class BankUIForm
```

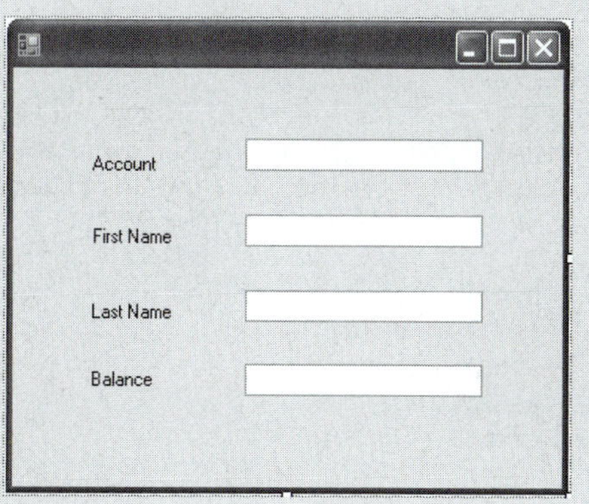

Fig. 18.7 | Base class for GUIs in our file-processing applications. (Part 2 of 2.)

To reuse class BankUIForm, you must compile the GUI into a DLL by creating a project of type **Windows Control Library** (we named it BankLibrary). This library is provided with the code for this chapter. You might need to change references to this library in our examples when you copy them to your system, since the library most likely will reside in a different location on your system.

Class Record
Figure 18.8 contains class Record that Fig. 18.9, Fig. 18.11 and Fig. 18.12 use for maintaining the information in each record that is written to or read from a file. This class also belongs to the BankLibrary DLL, so it is located in the same project as class BankUIForm.

Class Record contains private instance variables account, firstName, lastName and balance (lines 9–12), which collectively represent all the information for a record. The parameterless constructor (lines 15–17) sets these members by calling the four-argument constructor with 0 for the account number, empty strings ("") for the first and last name and 0.0M for the balance. The four-argument constructor (lines 20–27) sets these members to the specified parameter values. Class Record also provides properties Account (lines 30–40), FirstName (lines 43–53), LastName (lines 56–66) and Balance (lines 69–79) for accessing each record's account number, first name, last name and balance, respectively.

```
1   // Fig. 18.8: Record.cs
2   // Serializable class that represents a data record.
3   using System;
4   using System.Collections.Generic;
5   using System.Text;
6
7   public class Record
8   {
9      private int account;
10     private string firstName;
11     private string lastName;
12     private decimal balance;
13
14     // parameterless constructor sets members to default values
15     public Record() : this( 0, "", "", 0.0M )
16     {
17     } // end constructor
18
19     // overloaded constructor sets members to parameter values
20     public Record( int accountValue, string firstNameValue,
21        string lastNameValue, decimal balanceValue )
22     {
23        Account = accountValue;
24        FirstName = firstNameValue;
25        LastName = lastNameValue;
26        Balance = balanceValue;
27     } // end constructor
28
29     // property that gets and sets Account
30     public int Account
31     {
32        get
33        {
34           return account;
35        } // end get
36        set
37        {
38           account = value;
39        } // end set
40     } // end property Account
41
```

Fig. 18.8 | Record for sequential-access file-processing applications. (Part 1 of 2.)

```
42        // property that gets and sets FirstName
43        public string FirstName
44        {
45           get
46           {
47              return firstName;
48           } // end get
49           set
50           {
51              firstName = value;
52           } // end set
53        } // end property FirstName
54
55        // property that gets and sets LastName
56        public string LastName
57        {
58           get
59           {
60              return lastName;
61           } // end get
62           set
63           {
64              lastName = value;
65           } // end set
66        } // end property LastName
67
68        // property that gets and sets Balance
69        public decimal Balance
70        {
71           get
72           {
73              return balance;
74           } // end get
75           set
76           {
77              balance = value;
78           } // end set
79        } // end property Balance
80     } // end class Record
```

Fig. 18.8 | Record for sequential-access file-processing applications. (Part 2 of 2.)

Using a Character Stream to Create an Output File

Class `CreateFileForm` (Fig. 18.9) uses instances of class `Record` to create a sequential-access file that might be used in an accounts receivable system—i.e., a program that organizes data regarding money owed by a company's credit clients. For each client, the program obtains an account number and the client's first name, last name and balance (i.e., the amount of money that the client owes to the company for previously received goods and services). The data obtained for each client constitutes a record for that client. In this application, the account number is used as the record key—files are created and maintained in account-number order. This program assumes that the user enters records in accountnumber order. However, a comprehensive accounts receivable system would provide a sorting capability, so the user could enter the records in any order.

Class CreateFileForm either creates or opens a file (depending on whether one exists), then allows the user to write records to that file. The using directive in line 6 enables us to use the classes of the BankLibrary namespace; this namespace contains class BankUIForm, from which class CreateFileForm inherits (line 8). Class CreateFileForm's GUI enhances that of class BankUIForm with buttons **Save As**, **Enter** and **Exit**.

When the user clicks the **Save As** button, the program invokes the event handler saveButton_Click (lines 20–63). Line 23 instantiates an object of class *SaveFileDialog* (namespace System.Windows.Forms). Objects of this class are used for selecting files (see the second screen in Fig. 18.9). Line 24 calls SaveFileDialog method ShowDialog to display the dialog. When displayed, a SaveFileDialog prevents the user from interacting with any other window in the program until the user closes the SaveFileDialog by clicking either **Save** or **Cancel**. Dialogs that behave in this manner are called *modal dialogs*. The user selects the appropriate drive, directory and file name, then clicks **Save**. Method *ShowDialog* returns a DialogResult specifying which button (**Save** or **Cancel**) the user clicked to close the dialog. This is assigned to DialogResult variable result (line 24). Line 30 tests whether the user clicked **Cancel** by comparing this value to DialogResult.Cancel. If the values are equal, method saveButton_Click returns (line 31). Otherwise, line 33 uses SaveFileDialog property FileName to obtain the user-selected file.

```
1   // Fig. 18.9: CreateFileForm.cs
2   // Creating a sequential-access file.
3   using System;
4   using System.Windows.Forms;
5   using System.IO;
6   using BankLibrary;
7
8   public partial class CreateFileForm : BankUIForm
9   {
10     private StreamWriter fileWriter; // writes data to text file
11     private FileStream output; // maintains connection to file
12
13     // parameterless constructor
14     public CreateFileForm()
15     {
16        InitializeComponent();
17     } // end constructor
18
19     // event handler for Save Button
20     private void saveButton_Click( object sender, EventArgs e )
21     {
22        // create dialog box enabling user to save file
23        SaveFileDialog fileChooser = new SaveFileDialog();
24        DialogResult result = fileChooser.ShowDialog();
25        string fileName; // name of file to save data
26
27        fileChooser.CheckFileExists = false; // allow user to create file
```

Fig. 18.9 | Creating and writing to a sequential-access file. (Part 1 of 5.)

```
28
29          // exit event handler if user clicked "Cancel"
30          if ( result == DialogResult.Cancel )
31            return;
32
33          fileName = fileChooser.FileName; // get specified file name
34
35          // show error if user specified invalid file
36          if ( fileName == "" || fileName == null )
37            MessageBox.Show( "Invalid File Name", "Error",
38              MessageBoxButtons.OK, MessageBoxIcon.Error );
39          else
40          {
41            // save file via FileStream if user specified valid file
42            try
43            {
44              // open file with write access
45              output = new FileStream( fileName,
46                FileMode.OpenOrCreate, FileAccess.Write );
47
48              // sets file to where data is written
49              fileWriter = new StreamWriter( output );
50
51              // disable Save button and enable Enter button
52              saveButton.Enabled = false;
53              enterButton.Enabled = true;
54            } // end try
55            // handle exception if there is a problem opening the file
56            catch ( IOException )
57            {
58              // notify user if file does not exist
59              MessageBox.Show( "Error opening file", "Error",
60                MessageBoxButtons.OK, MessageBoxIcon.Error );
61            } // end catch
62          } // end else
63        } // end method saveButton_Click
64
65        // handler for enterButton Click
66        private void enterButton_Click( object sender, EventArgs e )
67        {
68          // store TextBox values string array
69          string[] values = GetTextBoxValues();
70
71          // Record containing TextBox values to serialize
72          Record record = new Record();
73
74          // determine whether TextBox account field is empty
75          if ( values[ ( int ) TextBoxIndices.ACCOUNT ] != "" )
76          {
77            // store TextBox values in Record and serialize Record
78            try
79            {
```

Fig. 18.9 | Creating and writing to a sequential-access file. (Part 2 of 5.)

```
80                  // get account number value from TextBox
81                  int accountNumber = Int32.Parse(
82                     values[ ( int ) TextBoxIndices.ACCOUNT ] );
83
84                  // determine whether accountNumber is valid
85                  if ( accountNumber > 0 )
86                  {
87                     // store TextBox fields in Record
88                     record.Account = accountNumber;
89                     record.FirstName = values[ ( int ) TextBoxIndices.FIRST ];
90                     record.LastName =  values[ ( int ) TextBoxIndices.LAST ];
91                     record.Balance = Decimal.Parse(
92                        values[ ( int ) TextBoxIndices.BALANCE ] );
93
94                     // write Record to file, fields separated by commas
95                     fileWriter.WriteLine(
96                        record.Account + "," + record.FirstName + "," +
97                        record.LastName + "," + record.Balance );
98                  } // end if
99                  else
100                 {
101                    // notify user if invalid account number
102                    MessageBox.Show( "Invalid Account Number", "Error",
103                       MessageBoxButtons.OK, MessageBoxIcon.Error );
104                 } // end else
105              } // end try
106              // notify user if error occurs in serialization
107              catch ( IOException )
108              {
109                 MessageBox.Show( "Error Writing to File", "Error",
110                    MessageBoxButtons.OK, MessageBoxIcon.Error );
111              } // end catch
112              // notify user if error occurs regarding parameter format
113              catch ( FormatException )
114              {
115                 MessageBox.Show( "Invalid Format", "Error",
116                    MessageBoxButtons.OK, MessageBoxIcon.Error );
117              } // end catch
118           } // end if
119
120        ClearTextBoxes(); // clear TextBox values
121     } // end method enterButton_Click
122
123     // handler for exitButton Click
124     private void exitButton_Click( object sender, EventArgs e )
125     {
126        // determine whether file exists
127        if ( output != null )
128        {
129           try
130           {
131              fileWriter.Close(); // close StreamWriter
```

Fig. 18.9 | Creating and writing to a sequential-access file. (Part 3 of 5.)

```
132          output.Close(); // close file
133       } // end try
134       // notify user of error closing file
135       catch ( IOException )
136       {
137          MessageBox.Show( "Cannot close file", "Error",
138             MessageBoxButtons.OK, MessageBoxIcon.Error );
139       } // end catch
140    } // end if
141
142    Application.Exit();
143    } // end method exitButton_Click
144 } // end class CreateFileForm
```

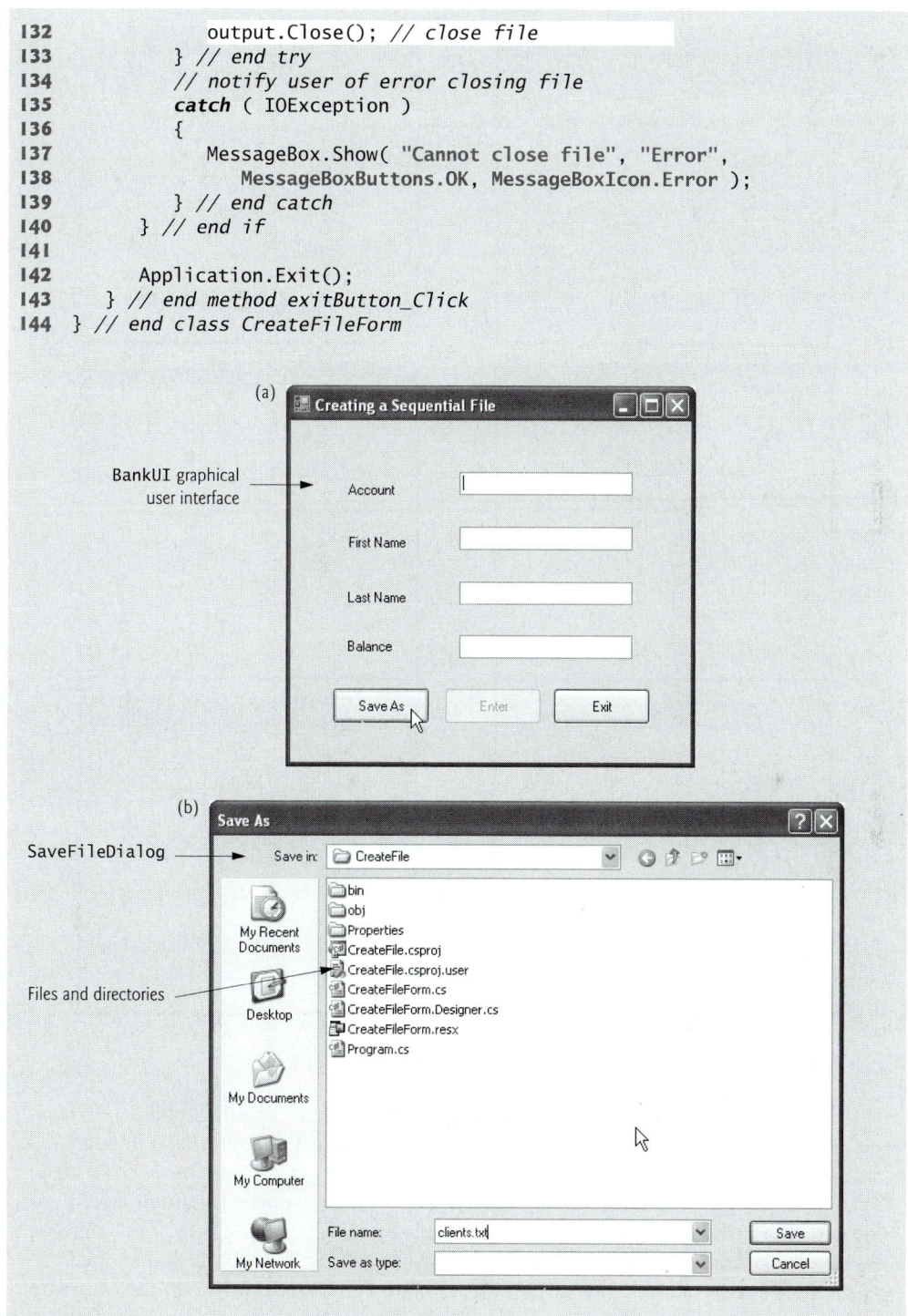

Fig. 18.9 | Creating and writing to a sequential-access file. (Part 4 of 5.)

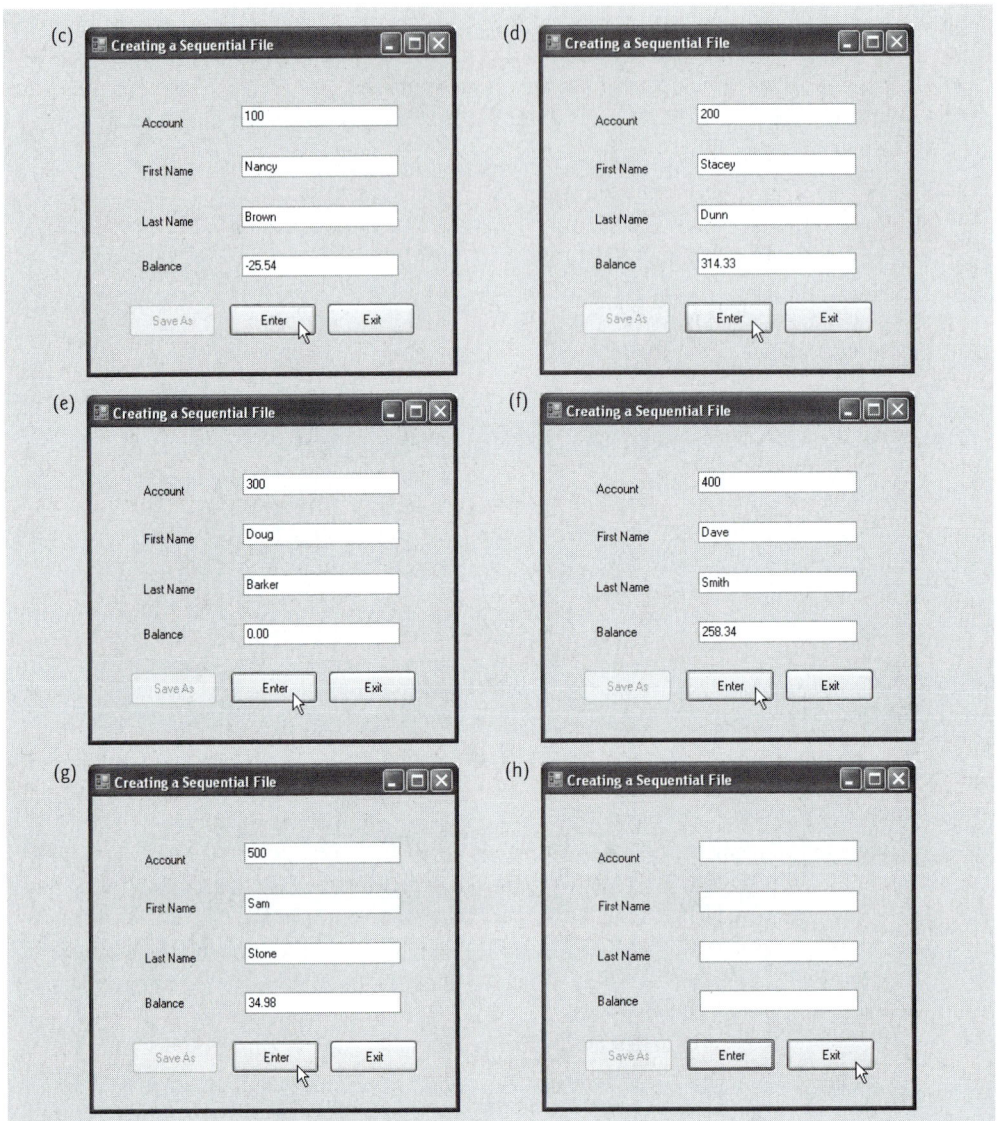

Fig. 18.9 | Creating and writing to a sequential-access file. (Part 5 of 5.)

You can open files to perform text manipulation by creating objects of class FileStream. In this example, we want the file to be opened for output, so lines 45–46 create a FileStream object. The FileStream constructor that we use receives three arguments—a string containing the path and name of the file to open, a constant describing how to open the file and a constant describing the file permissions. The constant FileMode.OpenOrCreate (line 46) indicates that the FileStream object should open the file if the file exists or create the file if it does not exist. There are other FileMode constants describing how to open files; we introduce these constants as we use them in examples. The constant FileAccess.Write indicates that the program can perform only write operations with the FileStream object. There are two other constants for the third constructor parameter—FileAccess.Read for read-only access and FileAccess.ReadWrite for both read and write access. Line 56 catches an ***IOException*** if there is a problem opening the file or creating the StreamWriter. If so, the program displays an error message (lines 59–60). If no exception occurs, the file is open for writing.

Good Programming Practice 18.1

*When opening files, use the **FileAccess enumeration** to control user access to these files.*

Common Programming Error 18.1

Failure to open a file before attempting to reference it in a program is a logic error.

After the user types information in each TextBox, the user clicks the **Enter** button, which calls event handler enterButton_Click (lines 66–121) to save the data from the TextBoxes into the user-specified file. If the user entered a valid account number (i.e., an integer greater than zero), lines 88–92 store the TextBox values in an object of type Record (created at line 72). If the user entered invalid data in one of the TextBoxes (such as non-numeric characters in the **Balance** field), the program throws a FormatException. The catch block in lines 113–117 handles such exceptions by notifying the user (via a MessageBox) of the improper format.

If the user entered valid data, lines 95–97 write the record to the file by invoking method WriteLine of the StreamWriter object that was created at line 49. Method WriteLine writes a sequence of characters to a file. The StreamWriter object is constructed with a FileStream argument that specifies the file to which the StreamWriter will output text. Class StreamWriter belongs to the System.IO namespace.

When the user clicks the **Exit** button, event handler exitButton_Click (lines 124–143) exits the application. Line 131 closes the StreamWriter, and line 132 closes the FileStream, then line 142 terminates the program. Note that the call to method Close is located in a try block. Method ***Close*** throws an IOException if the file or stream cannot be closed properly. In this case, it is important to notify the user that the information in the file or stream might be corrupted.

Performance Tip 18.1

Close each file explicitly when the program no longer needs to reference the file. This can reduce resource usage in programs that continue executing long after they finish using a specific file. The practice of explicitly closing files also improves program clarity.

Performance Tip 18.2

Releasing resources explicitly when they are no longer needed makes them immediately available for reuse by other programs, thus improving resource utilization.

In the sample execution for the program in Fig. 18.9, we entered information for the five accounts shown in Fig. 18.10. The program does not depict how the data records are rendered in the file. To verify that the file has been created successfully, we create a program in the next section to read and display the file. Since this is a text file, you can actually open the file in any text editor to see its contents.

Account Number	First Name	Last Name	Balance
100	Nancy	Brown	−25.54
200	Stacey	Dunn	314.33
300	Doug	Barker	0.00
400	Dave	Smith	258.34
500	Sam	Stone	34.98

Fig. 18.10 | Sample data for the program of Fig. 18.9.

18.6 Reading Data from a Sequential-Access Text File

The previous section demonstrated how to create a file for use in sequential-access applications. In this section, we discuss how to read (or retrieve) data sequentially from a file.

Class ReadSequentialAccessFileForm (Fig. 18.11) reads records from the file created by the program in Fig. 18.9, then displays the contents of each record. Much of the code in this example is similar to that of Fig. 18.9, so we discuss only the unique aspects of the application.

```
1   // Fig. 18.11: ReadSequentialAccessFileForm.cs
2   // Reading a sequential-access file.
3   using System;
4   using System.Windows.Forms;
5   using System.IO;
6   using BankLibrary;
7
8   public partial class ReadSequentialAccessFileForm : BankUIForm
9   {
10      private FileStream input; // maintains connection to a file
11      private StreamReader fileReader; // reads data from a text file
12
13      // paramterless constructor
14      public ReadSequentialAccessFileForm()
15      {
16         InitializeComponent();
17      } // end constructor
18
19      // invoked when user clicks the Open button
20      private void openButton_Click( object sender, EventArgs e )
21      {
22         // create dialog box enabling user to open file
23         OpenFileDialog fileChooser = new OpenFileDialog();
24         DialogResult result = fileChooser.ShowDialog();
25         string fileName; // name of file containing data
26
```

Fig. 18.11 | Reading sequential-access files. (Part 1 of 4.)

```
27          // exit event handler if user clicked Cancel
28          if ( result == DialogResult.Cancel )
29             return;
30
31          fileName = fileChooser.FileName; // get specified file name
32          ClearTextBoxes();
33
34          // show error if user specified invalid file
35          if ( fileName == "" || fileName == null )
36             MessageBox.Show( "Invalid File Name", "Error",
37                MessageBoxButtons.OK, MessageBoxIcon.Error );
38          else
39          {
40             // create FileStream to obtain read access to file
41             input = new FileStream( fileName, FileMode.Open,
42                FileAccess.Read );
43
44             // set file from where data is read
45             fileReader = new StreamReader( input );
46
47             openButton.Enabled = false; // disable Open File button
48             nextButton.Enabled = true; // enable next record button
49          } // end else
50       } // end method openButton_Click
51
52       // invoked when user clicks Next button
53       private void nextButton_Click( object sender, EventArgs e )
54       {
55          try
56          {
57             // get next record available in file
58             string inputRecord = fileReader.ReadLine();
59             string[] inputFields; // will store individual pieces of data
60
61             if ( inputRecord != null )
62             {
63                inputFields = inputRecord.Split( ',' );
64
65                Record record = new Record(
66                   Convert.ToInt32( inputFields[ 0 ] ), inputFields[ 1 ],
67                   inputFields[ 2 ], Convert.ToDecimal( inputFields[ 3 ] ) );
68
69                // copy string array values to TextBox values
70                SetTextBoxValues( inputFields );
71             } // end if
72             else
73             {
74                fileReader.Close(); // close StreamReader
75                input.Close(); // close FileStream if no Records in file
76                openButton.Enabled = true; // enable Open File button
77                nextButton.Enabled = false; // disable Next Record button
78                ClearTextBoxes();
79
```

Fig. 18.11 | Reading sequential-access files. (Part 2 of 4.)

```
80              // notify user if no Records in file
81              MessageBox.Show( "No more records in file", "",
82                 MessageBoxButtons.OK, MessageBoxIcon.Information );
83           } // end else
84        } // end try
85        catch ( IOException )
86        {
87           MessageBox.Show( "Error Reading from File", "Error",
88              MessageBoxButtons.OK, MessageBoxIcon.Error );
89        } // end catch
90     } // end method nextButton_Click
91  } // end class readSequentialAccessFileForm
```

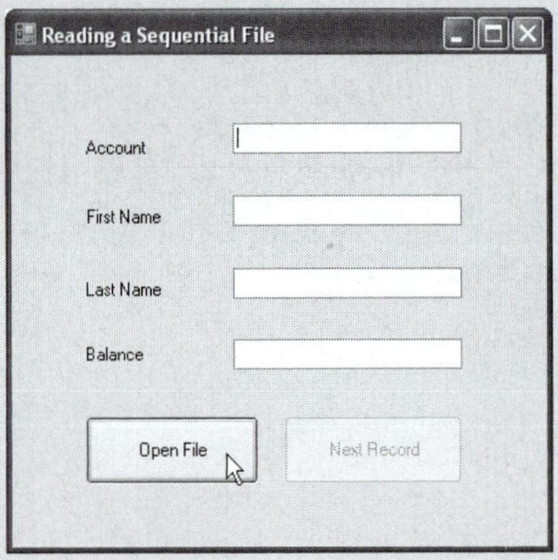

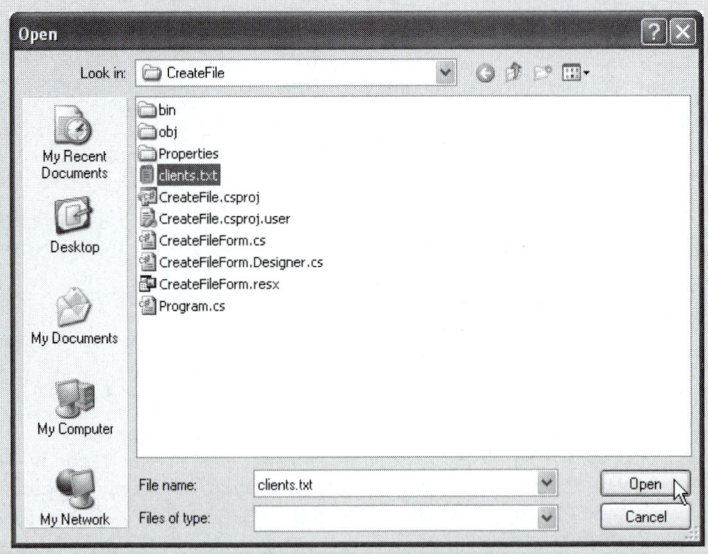

Fig. 18.11 | Reading sequential-access files. (Part 3 of 4.)

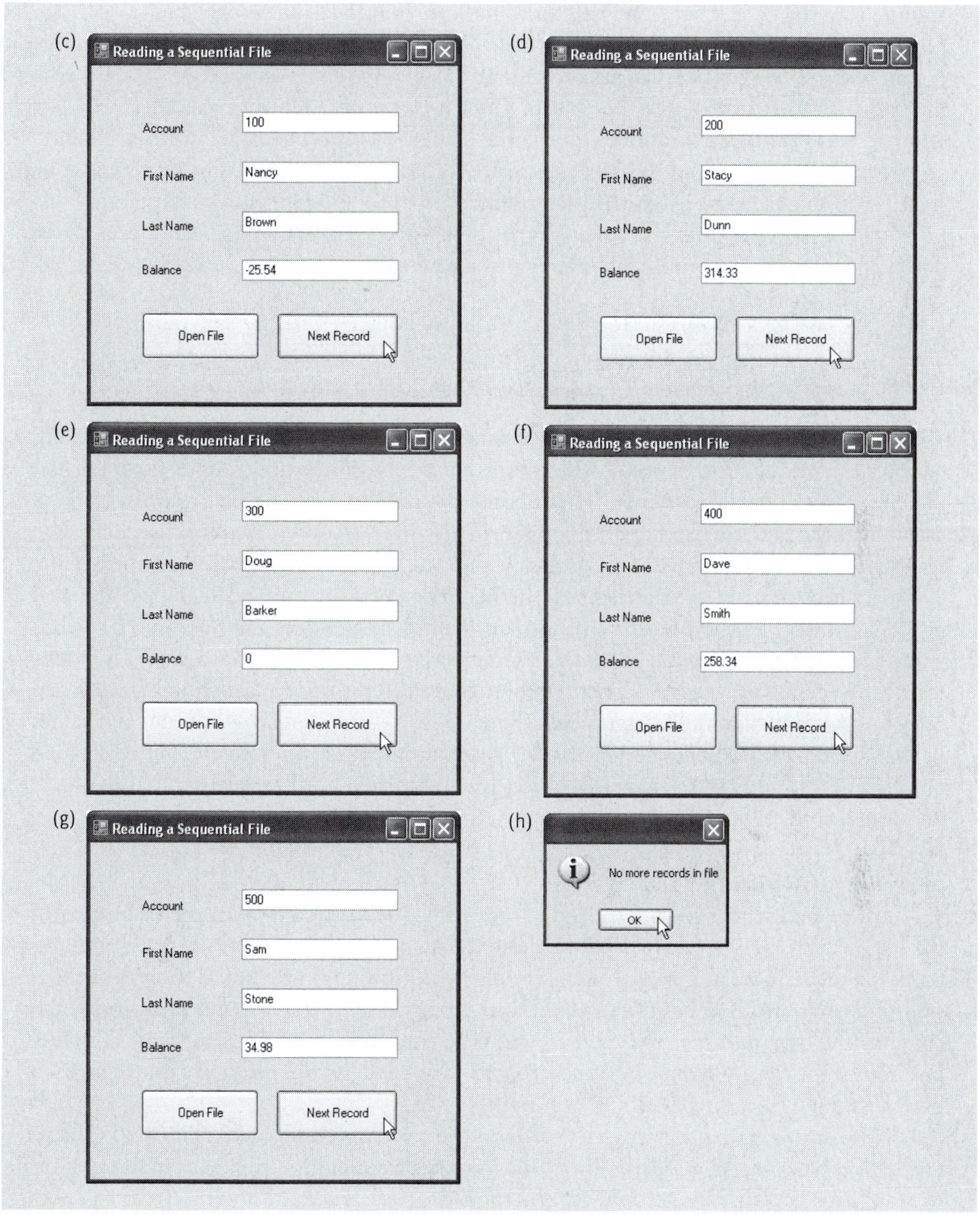

Fig. 18.11 | Reading sequential-access files. (Part 4 of 4.)

When the user clicks the **Open File** button, the program calls event handler open-Button_Click (lines 20–50). Line 23 creates an *OpenFileDialog*, and line 24 calls its *ShowDialog* method to display the **Open** dialog (see the second screenshot in Fig. 18.11). The behavior and GUI for the **Save** and **Open** dialog types are identical, except that **Save** is replaced by **Open**. If the user inputs a valid file name, lines 41–42 create a FileStream object and assign it to reference input. We pass constant FileMode.Open as the second argument to the FileStream constructor to indicate that the FileStream should open the file if it exists or should throw a FileNotFoundException if the file does not exist. (In this example, the FileStream constructor will not throw a FileNotFoundException, because the OpenFileDialog requires the user to enter a name of a file that exists.) In the last example (Fig. 18.9), we wrote text to the file using a FileStream object with write-only access. In this example (Fig. 18.11), we specify read-only access to the file by passing constant FileAccess.Read as the third argument to the FileStream constructor. This FileStream object is used to create a StreamReader object in line 45. The FileStream object specifies the file from which the StreamReader object will read text.

Error-Prevention Tip 18.1

Open a file with the FileAccess.Read file-open mode if the contents of the file should not be modified. This prevents unintentional modification of the contents.

When the user clicks the **Next Record** button, the program calls event handler nextButton_Click (lines 53–90), which reads the next record from the user-specified file. (The user must click **Next Record** after opening the file to view the first record.) Line 58 calls StreamReader method ReadLine to read the next record. If an error occurs while reading the file, an IOException is thrown (caught at line 85), and the user is notified (line 87–88). Otherwise, line 61 determines whether StreamReader method ReadLine returned null (i.e., there is no more text in the file). If not, line 63 uses method Split of class string to separate the stream of characters that was read from the file into strings that represent the Record's properties. These properties are then stored by constructing a Record object using the properties as arguments (lines 65–67). Line 70 displays the Record values in the TextBoxes. If ReadLine returns null, the program closes both the StreamReader object (line 74) and the FileStream object (line 75), then notifies the user that there are no more records (lines 81–82).

Searching a Sequential-Access File

To retrieve data sequentially from a file, programs normally start from the beginning of the file, reading consecutively until the desired data is found. It sometimes is necessary to process a file sequentially several times (from the beginning of the file) during the execution of a program. A FileStream object can reposition its ***file-position pointer*** (which contains the byte number of the next byte to be read from or written to the file) to any position in the file. When a FileStream object is opened, its file-position pointer is set to byte position 0 (i.e., the beginning of the file)

We now present a program that builds on the concepts employed in Fig. 18.11. Class CreditInquiryForm (Fig. 18.12) is a credit-inquiry program that enables a credit manager to search for and display account information for those customers with credit balances (i.e., customers to whom the company owes money), zero balances (i.e., customers who do not owe the company money) and debit balances (i.e., customers who owe the company money for previously received goods and services). We use a RichTextBox in the program to display the account information. RichTextBoxes provide more functionality than regular TextBoxes—for example, RichTextBoxes offer method Find for searching individual strings and method LoadFile for displaying file contents. Classes RichTextBox and TextBox both inherit from abstract class System.Windows.Forms.TextBoxBase. We chose a RichTextBox in this example, because it displays multiple lines of text by default, whereas a regular TextBox displays only one. Alternatively, we could have specified that a TextBox object display multiple lines of text by setting its Multiline property to true.

```
1   // Fig. 18.12: CreditInquiryForm.cs
2   // Read a file sequentially and display contents based on
3   // account type specified by user ( credit, debit or zero balances ).
4   using System;
5   using System.Windows.Forms;
6   using System.IO;
7   using BankLibrary;
8
9   public partial class CreditInquiryForm : Form
10  {
11     private FileStream input; // maintains the connection to the file
12     private StreamReader fileReader; // reads data from text file
13
14     // name of file that stores credit, debit and zero balances
15     private string fileName;
16
17     // parameterless constructor
18     public CreditInquiryForm()
19     {
20        InitializeComponent();
21     } // end constructor
22
23     // invoked when user clicks Open File button
24     private void openButton_Click( object sender, EventArgs e )
25     {
26        // create dialog box enabling user to open file
27        OpenFileDialog fileChooser = new OpenFileDialog();
28        DialogResult result = fileChooser.ShowDialog();
29
30        // exit event handler if user clicked Cancel
31        if ( result == DialogResult.Cancel )
32           return;
33
34        fileName = fileChooser.FileName; // get name from user
35
36        // show error if user specified invalid file
37        if ( fileName == "" || fileName == null )
38           MessageBox.Show( "Invalid File Name", "Error",
39              MessageBoxButtons.OK, MessageBoxIcon.Error );
40        else
41        {
42           // create FileStream to obtain read access to file
43           input = new FileStream( fileName,
44              FileMode.Open, FileAccess.Read );
45
46           // set file from where data is read
47           fileReader = new StreamReader( input );
48
```

Fig. 18.12 | Credit-inquiry program. (Part 1 of 5.)

```
49          // enable all GUI buttons, except for Open File button
50          openButton.Enabled = false;
51          creditButton.Enabled = true;
52          debitButton.Enabled = true;
53          zeroButton.Enabled = true;
54       } // end else
55    } // end method openButton_Click
56
57    // invoked when user clicks credit balances,
58    // debit balances or zero balances button
59    private void getBalances_Click( object sender, System.EventArgs e )
60    {
61       // convert sender explicitly to object of type button
62       Button senderButton = ( Button )sender;
63
64       // get text from clicked Button, which stores account type
65       string accountType = senderButton.Text;
66
67       // read and display file information
68       try
69       {
70          // go back to the beginning of the file
71          input.Seek( 0, SeekOrigin.Begin );
72
73          displayTextBox.Text = "The accounts are:\r\n";
74
75          // traverse file until end of file
76          while ( true )
77          {
78             string[] inputFields; // will store individual pieces of data
79             Record record; // store each Record as file is read
80             decimal balance; // store each Record's balance
81
82             // get next Record available in file
83             string inputRecord = fileReader.ReadLine();
84
85             // when at the end of file, exit method
86             if ( inputRecord == null )
87                return;
88
89             inputFields = inputRecord.Split( ',' ); // parse input
90
91             // create Record from input
92             record = new Record(
93                Convert.ToInt32( inputFields[ 0 ] ), inputFields[ 1 ],
94                inputFields[ 2 ], Convert.ToDecimal( inputFields[ 3 ] ) );
95
96             // store record's last field in balance
97             balance = record.Balance;
98
99             // determine whether to display balance
100            if ( ShouldDisplay( balance, accountType ) )
101            {
```

Fig. 18.12 | Credit-inquiry program. (Part 2 of 5.)

```
102                    // display record
103                    string output = record.Account + "\t" +
104                        record.FirstName + "\t" + record.LastName + "\t";
105
106                    // display balance with correct monetary format
107                    output += string.Format( "{0:F}", balance ) + "\r\n";
108
109                    displayTextBox.Text += output; // copy output to screen
110                } // end if
111            } // end while
112        } // end try
113        // handle exception when file cannot be read
114        catch ( IOException )
115        {
116            MessageBox.Show( "Cannot Read File", "Error",
117                MessageBoxButtons.OK, MessageBoxIcon.Error );
118        } // end catch
119    } // end method getBalances_Click
120
121    // determine whether to display given record
122    private bool ShouldDisplay( decimal balance, string accountType )
123    {
124        if ( balance > 0 )
125        {
126            // display credit balances
127            if ( accountType == "Credit Balances" )
128                return true;
129        } // end if
130        else if ( balance < 0 )
131        {
132            // display debit balances
133            if ( accountType == "Debit Balances" )
134                return true;
135        } // end else if
136        else // balance == 0
137        {
138            // display zero balances
139            if ( accountType == "Zero Balances" )
140                return true;
141        } // end else
142
143        return false;
144    } // end method ShouldDisplay
145
146    // invoked when user clicks Done button
147    private void doneButton_Click( object sender, EventArgs e )
148    {
149        // determine whether file exists
150        if ( input != null )
151        {
152            // close file and StreamReader
153            try
154            {
```

Fig. 18.12 | Credit-inquiry program. (Part 3 of 5.)

```
155                input.Close();
156                fileReader.Close();
157            } // end try
158            // handle exception if FileStream does not exist
159            catch( IOException )
160            {
161                // notify user of error closing file
162                MessageBox.Show( "Cannot close file", "Error",
163                    MessageBoxButtons.OK, MessageBoxIcon.Error );
164            } // end catch
165        } // end if
166
167        Application.Exit();
168    } // end method doneButton_Click
169 } // end class CreditInquiryForm
```

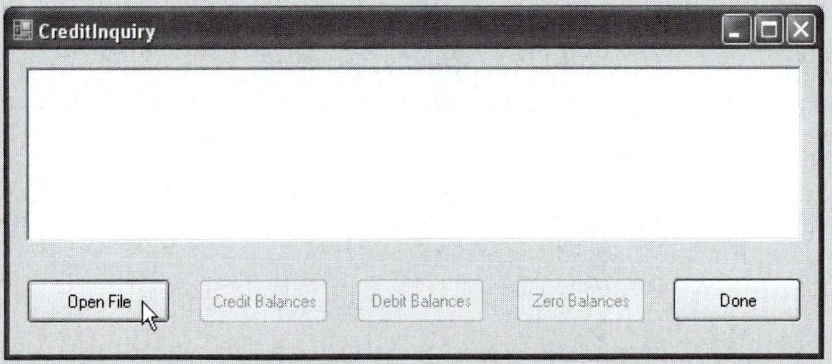

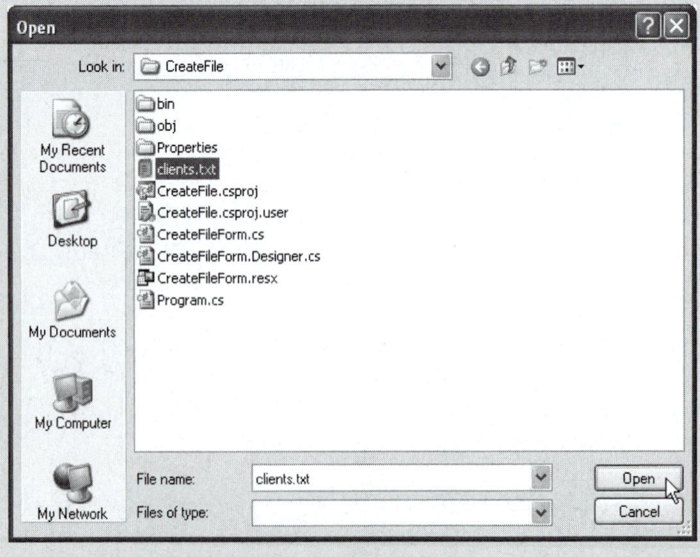

Fig. 18.12 | Credit-inquiry program. (Part 4 of 5.)

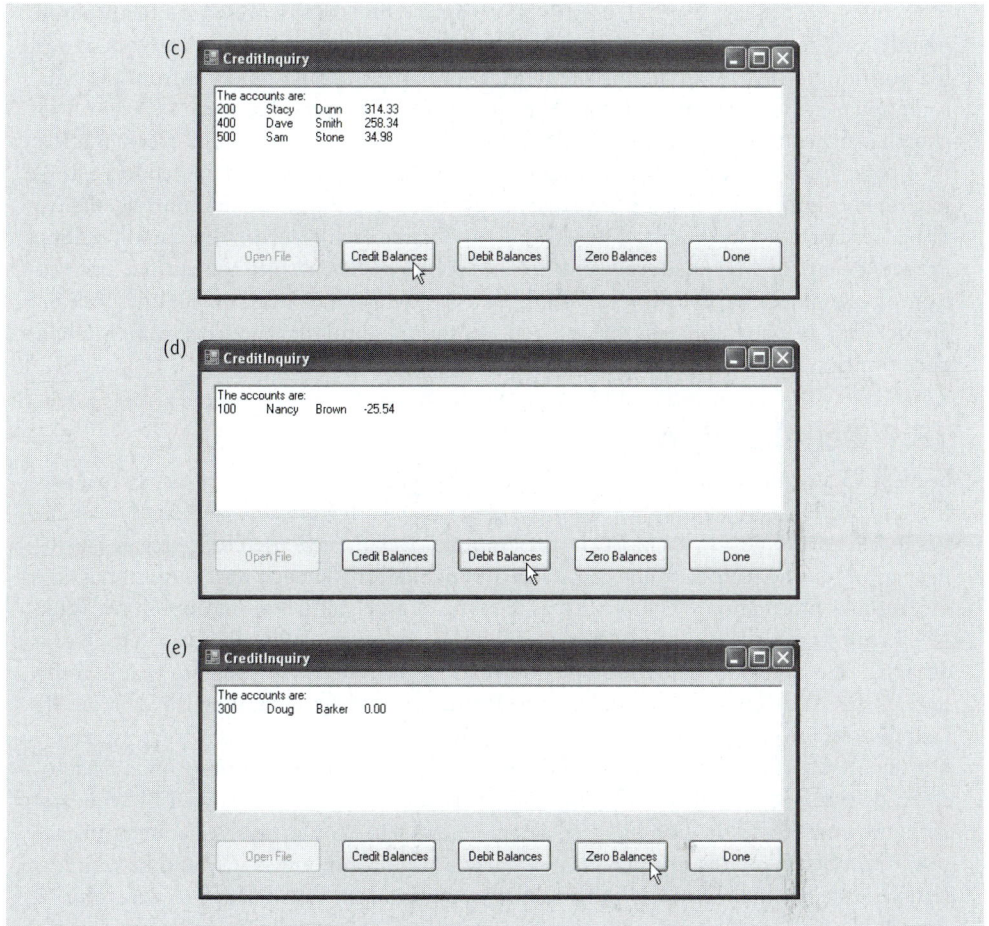

Fig. 18.12 | Credit-inquiry program. (Part 5 of 5.)

The program displays buttons that enable a credit manager to obtain credit information. The **Open File** button opens a file for gathering data. The **Credit Balances** button displays a list of accounts that have credit balances, the **Debit Balances** button displays a list of accounts that have debit balances and the **Zero Balances** button displays a list of accounts that have zero balances. The **Done** button exits the application.

When the user clicks the **Open File** button, the program calls the event handler openButton_Click (lines 24–55). Line 27 creates an OpenFileDialog, and line 28 calls its ShowDialog method to display the **Open** dialog, in which the user selects the file to open. Lines 43–44 create a FileStream object with read-only file access and assign it to reference input. Line 47 creates a StreamReader object that we use to read text from the FileStream.

When the user clicks **Credit Balances**, **Debit Balances** or **Zero Balances**, the program invokes method getBalances_Click (lines 59–119). Line 62 casts the sender parameter, which is an object reference to the control that generated the event, to a Button object. Line 65 extracts the Button object's text, which the program uses to determine which type of accounts to display. Line 71 uses FileStream method **Seek** to reset the file-position pointer back to the beginning of the file. FileStream method Seek allows you to reset the file-position pointer by specifying the number of bytes it should be offset from the file's beginning, end or current position. The part of the file you want to be offset from is chosen using constants from the **SeekOrigin** enumeration. In this case, our stream is offset by 0 bytes from the file's beginning (SeekOrigin.Begin). Lines 76–111 define a while loop that uses private method ShouldDisplay (lines 122–144) to determine whether to display each record in the file. The while loop obtains each record by repeatedly calling StreamReader method ReadLine (line 83) and splitting the text into tokens that are used to initialize object record (lines 89–94). Line 86 determines whether the file-position pointer has reached the end of the file. If so, the program returns from method getBalances_Click (line 87).

18.7 Serialization

Section 18.5 demonstrated how to write the individual fields of a Record object to a text file, and Section 18.6 demonstrated how to read those fields from a file and place their values in a Record object in memory. In the examples, Record was used to aggregate the information for one record. When the instance variables for a Record were output to a disk file, certain information was lost, such as the type of each value. For instance, if the value "3" is read from a file, there is no way to tell if the value came from an int, a string or a decimal. We have only data, not type information, on disk. If the program that is going to read this data "knows" what object type the data corresponds to, then the data can be read directly into objects of that type. For example, in Fig. 18.9, we know that we are inputting an int (the account number), followed by two strings (the first and last name) and a decimal (the balance). We also know that these values are separated by commas, with only one record on each line. So, we are able to parse the strings and convert the account number to an int and the balance to a decimal. Sometimes it would be easier to read or write entire objects. C# provides such a mechanism, called *object serialization*. A *serialized object* is an object represented as a sequence of bytes that includes the object's data, as well as information about the object's type and the types of data stored in the object. After a serialized object has been written to a file, it can be read from the file and *deserialized*—that is, the type information and bytes that represent the object and its data can be used to recreate the object in memory.

Class **BinaryFormatter** (namespace **System.Runtime.Serialization.Formatters. Binary**) enables entire objects to be written to or read from a stream. BinaryFormatter method **Serialize** writes an object's representation to a file. BinaryFormatter method **Deserialize** reads this representation from a file and reconstructs the original object. Both methods throw a **SerializationException** if an error occurs during serialization or deserialization. Both methods require a Stream object (e.g., the FileStream) as a parameter so that the BinaryFormatter can access the correct stream. As you will see in Chapter 23, Networking: Streams-Based Sockets and Datagrams, serialization can be used to transmit objects between applications over a network.

In Sections 18.8 and 18.9, we create and manipulate sequential-access files using object serialization. Object serialization is performed with byte-based streams, so the sequential files created and manipulated will be binary files. Binary files are not human readable. For this reason, we write a separate application that reads and displays serialized objects.

18.8 Creating a Sequential-Access File Using Object Serialization

We begin by creating and writing serialized objects to a sequential-access file. In this section, we reuse much of the code from Section 18.5, so we focus only on the new features.

Defining the RecordSerializable Class

Let us begin by modifying our Record class (Fig. 18.8) so that objects of this class can be serialized. Class RecordSerializable (Fig. 18.13) is marked with the *[Serializable]* attribute (line 5), which indicates to the CLR that objects of class Record can be serialized. The classes for objects that we wish to write to or read from a stream must include this attribute in their declarations or must implement interface *ISerializable*. Class RecordSerializable contains private data members account, firstName, lastName and balance. This class also provides public properties for accessing the private fields.

In a class that is marked with the [Serializable] attribute or that implements interface ISerializable, you must ensure that every instance variable of the class is also serializable. All simple-type variables and strings are serializable. For variables of reference types, you must check the class declaration (and possibly its base classes) to ensure that the type is serializable. By default, array objects are serializable. However, if the array contains references to other objects, those objects may or may not be serializable.

```
1    // Fig. 18.13: RecordSerializable.cs
2    // Serializable class that represents a data record.
3    using System;
4
5    [ Serializable ]
6    public class RecordSerializable
7    {
8       private int account;
9       private string firstName;
10      private string lastName;
11      private decimal balance;
12
13      // parameterless constructor sets members to default values
14      public RecordSerializable()
15         : this( 0, "", "", 0.0M )
16      {
17      } // end constructor
18
19      // overloaded constructor sets members to parameter values
20      public RecordSerializable( int accountValue, string firstNameValue,
21         string lastNameValue, decimal balanceValue )
22      {
23         Account = accountValue;
24         FirstName = firstNameValue;
25         LastName = lastNameValue;
26         Balance = balanceValue;
27      } // end constructor
28
```

Fig. 18.13 | RecordSerializable class for serializable objects. (Part 1 of 2.)

```
29          // property that gets and sets Account
30          public int Account
31          {
32             get
33             {
34                return account;
35             } // end get
36             set
37             {
38                account = value;
39             } // end set
40          } // end property Account
41
42          // property that gets and sets FirstName
43          public string FirstName
44          {
45             get
46             {
47                return firstName;
48             } // end get
49             set
50             {
51                firstName = value;
52             } // end set
53          } // end property FirstName
54
55          // property that gets and sets LastName
56          public string LastName
57          {
58             get
59             {
60                return lastName;
61             } // end get
62             set
63             {
64                lastName = value;
65             } // end set
66          } // end property LastName
67
68          // property that gets and sets Balance
69          public decimal Balance
70          {
71             get
72             {
73                return balance;
74             } // end get
75             set
76             {
77                balance = value;
78             } // end set
79          } // end property Balance
80    } // end class RecordSerializable
```

Fig. 18.13 | RecordSerializable class for serializable objects. (Part 2 of 2.)

Using a Serialization Stream to Create an Output File

Now let's create a sequential-access file with serialization (Fig. 18.14). Line 13 creates a BinaryFormatter for writing serialized objects. Lines 48–49 open the FileStream to which this program writes the serialized objects. The string argument that is passed to the FileStream's constructor represents the name and path of the file to be opened. This specifies the file to which the serialized objects will be written.

Common Programming Error 18.2

It is a logic error to open an existing file for output when the user wishes to preserve the file. The original file's contents will be lost.

This program assumes that data is input correctly and in the proper record-number order. Event handler enterButton_Click (lines 66–119) performs the write operation. Line 72 creates a RecordSerializable object, which is assigned values in lines 88–92. Line 95 calls method Serialize to write the RecordSerializable object to the output file. Method Serialize takes the FileStream object as the first argument so that the BinaryFormatter can write its second argument to the correct file. Note that only one statement is required to write the entire object.

In the sample execution for the program in Fig. 18.14, we entered information for five accounts—the same information shown in Fig. 18.10. The program does not show how the data records actually appear in the file. Remember that we are now using binary files, which are not human readable. To verify that the file was created successfully, the next section presents a program to read the file's contents.

```csharp
 1   // Fig 18.14: CreateFileForm.cs
 2   // Creating a sequential-access file using serialization.
 3   using System;
 4   using System.Windows.Forms;
 5   using System.IO;
 6   using System.Runtime.Serialization.Formatters.Binary;
 7   using System.Runtime.Serialization;
 8   using BankLibrary;
 9
10   public partial class CreateFileForm : BankUIForm
11   {
12      // object for serializing Records in binary format
13      private BinaryFormatter formatter = new BinaryFormatter();
14      private FileStream output; // stream for writing to a file
15
16      // parameterless constructor
17      public CreateFileForm()
18      {
19         InitializeComponent();
20      } // end constructor
21
22      // handler for saveButton_Click
23      private void saveButton_Click( object sender, EventArgs e )
24      {
```

Fig. 18.14 | Sequential file created using serialization. (Part 1 of 5.)

```
25        // create dialog box enabling user to save file
26        SaveFileDialog fileChooser = new SaveFileDialog();
27        DialogResult result = fileChooser.ShowDialog();
28        string fileName; // name of file to save data
29
30        fileChooser.CheckFileExists = false; // allow user to create file
31
32        // exit event handler if user clicked "Cancel"
33        if ( result == DialogResult.Cancel )
34           return;
35
36        fileName = fileChooser.FileName; // get specified file name
37
38        // show error if user specified invalid file
39        if ( fileName == "" || fileName == null )
40           MessageBox.Show( "Invlaid File Name", "Error",
41              MessageBoxButtons.OK, MessageBoxIcon.Error );
42        else
43        {
44           // save file via FileStream if user specified valid file
45           try
46           {
47              // open file with write access
48              output = new FileStream( fileName,
49                 FileMode.OpenOrCreate, FileAccess.Write );
50
51              // disable Save button and enable Enter button
52              saveButton.Enabled = false;
53              enterButton.Enabled = true;
54           } // end try
55           // handle exception if there is a problem opening the file
56           catch ( IOException )
57           {
58              // notify user if file does not exist
59              MessageBox.Show( "Error opening file", "Error",
60                 MessageBoxButtons.OK, MessageBoxIcon.Error );
61           } // end catch
62        } // end else
63     } // end method saveButton_Click
64
65     // handler for enterButton Click
66     private void enterButton_Click( object sender, EventArgs e )
67     {
68        // store TextBox values string array
69        string[] values = GetTextBoxValues();
70
71        // Record containing TextBox values to serialize
72        RecordSerializable record = new RecordSerializable();
73
74        // determine whether TextBox account field is empty
75        if ( values[ ( int ) TextBoxIndices.ACCOUNT ] != "" )
76        {
```

Fig. 18.14 | Sequential file created using serialization. (Part 2 of 5.)

```
77                  // store TextBox values in Record and serialize Record
78              try
79              {
80                  // get account number value from TextBox
81                  int accountNumber = Int32.Parse(
82                      values[ ( int ) TextBoxIndices.ACCOUNT ] );
83
84                  // determine whether accountNumber is valid
85                  if ( accountNumber > 0 )
86                  {
87                      // store TextBox fields in Record
88                      record.Account = accountNumber;
89                      record.FirstName = values[ ( int ) TextBoxIndices.FIRST ];
90                      record.LastName = values[ ( int ) TextBoxIndices.LAST ];
91                      record.Balance = Decimal.Parse( values[
92                          ( int ) TextBoxIndices.BALANCE ] );
93
94                      // write Record to FileStream ( serialize object )
95                      formatter.Serialize( output, record );
96                  } // end if
97                  else
98                  {
99                      // notify user if invalid account number
100                     MessageBox.Show( "Invalid Account Number", "Error",
101                         MessageBoxButtons.OK, MessageBoxIcon.Error );
102                 } // end else
103             } // end try
104             // notify user if error occurs in serialization
105             catch ( SerializationException )
106             {
107                 MessageBox.Show( "Error Writing to File", "Error",
108                     MessageBoxButtons.OK, MessageBoxIcon.Error );
109             } // end catch
110             // notify user if error occurs regarding parameter format
111             catch ( FormatException )
112             {
113                 MessageBox.Show( "Invalid Format", "Error",
114                     MessageBoxButtons.OK, MessageBoxIcon.Error );
115             } // end catch
116         } // end if
117
118         ClearTextBoxes(); // clear TextBox values
119     } // end method enterButton_Click
120
121     // handler for exitButton Click
122     private void exitButton_Click( object sender, EventArgs e )
123     {
124         // determine whether file exists
125         if ( output != null )
126         {
127             // close file
128             try
129             {
```

Fig. 18.14 | Sequential file created using serialization. (Part 3 of 5.)

```
130              output.Close();
131          } // end try
132          // notify user of error closing file
133          catch ( IOException )
134          {
135              MessageBox.Show( "Cannot close file", "Error",
136                  MessageBoxButtons.OK, MessageBoxIcon.Error );
137          } // end catch
138      } // end if
139
140      Application.Exit();
141   } // end method exitButton_Click
142 } // end class CreateFileForm
```

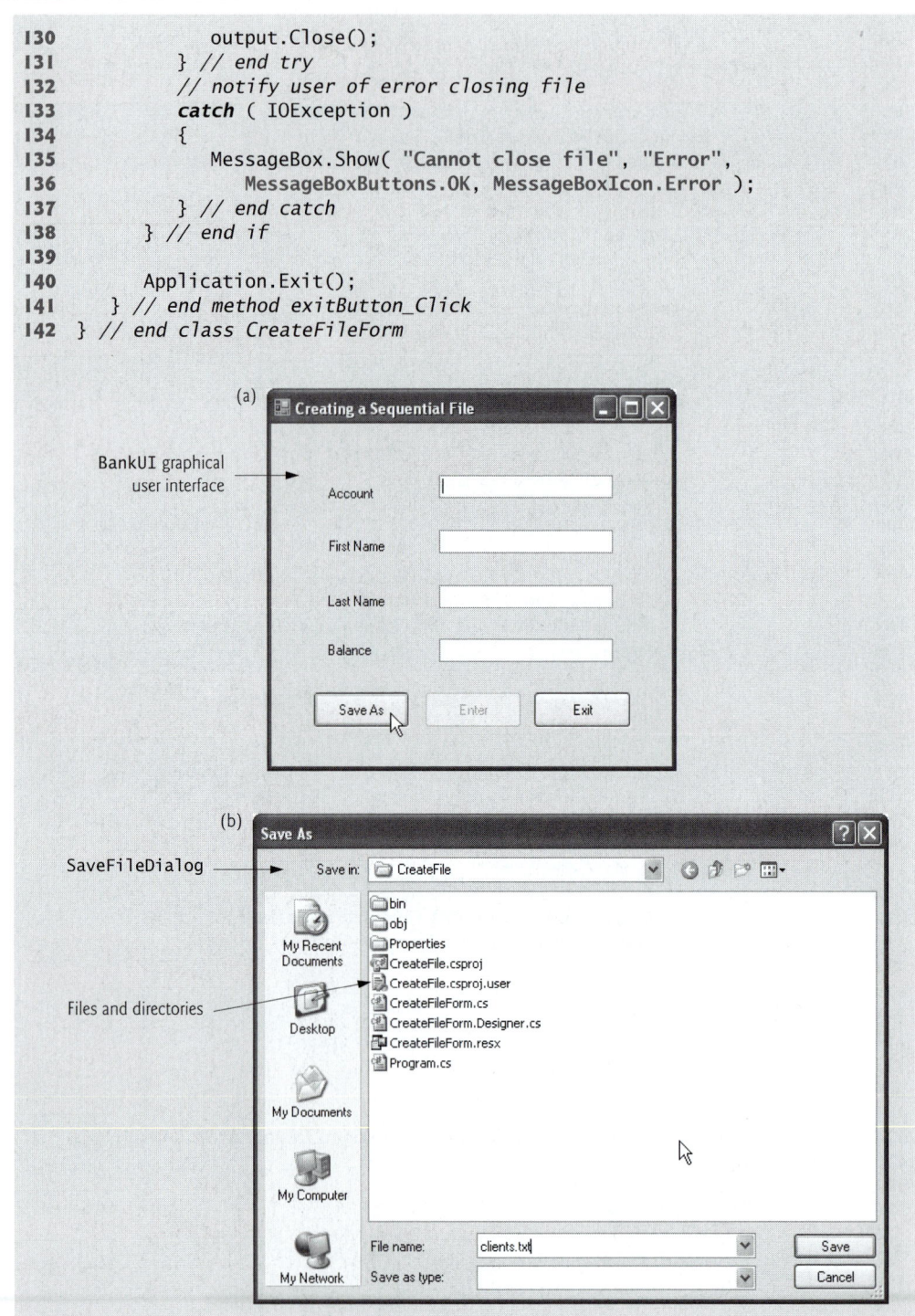

Fig. 18.14 | Sequential file created using serialization. (Part 4 of 5.)

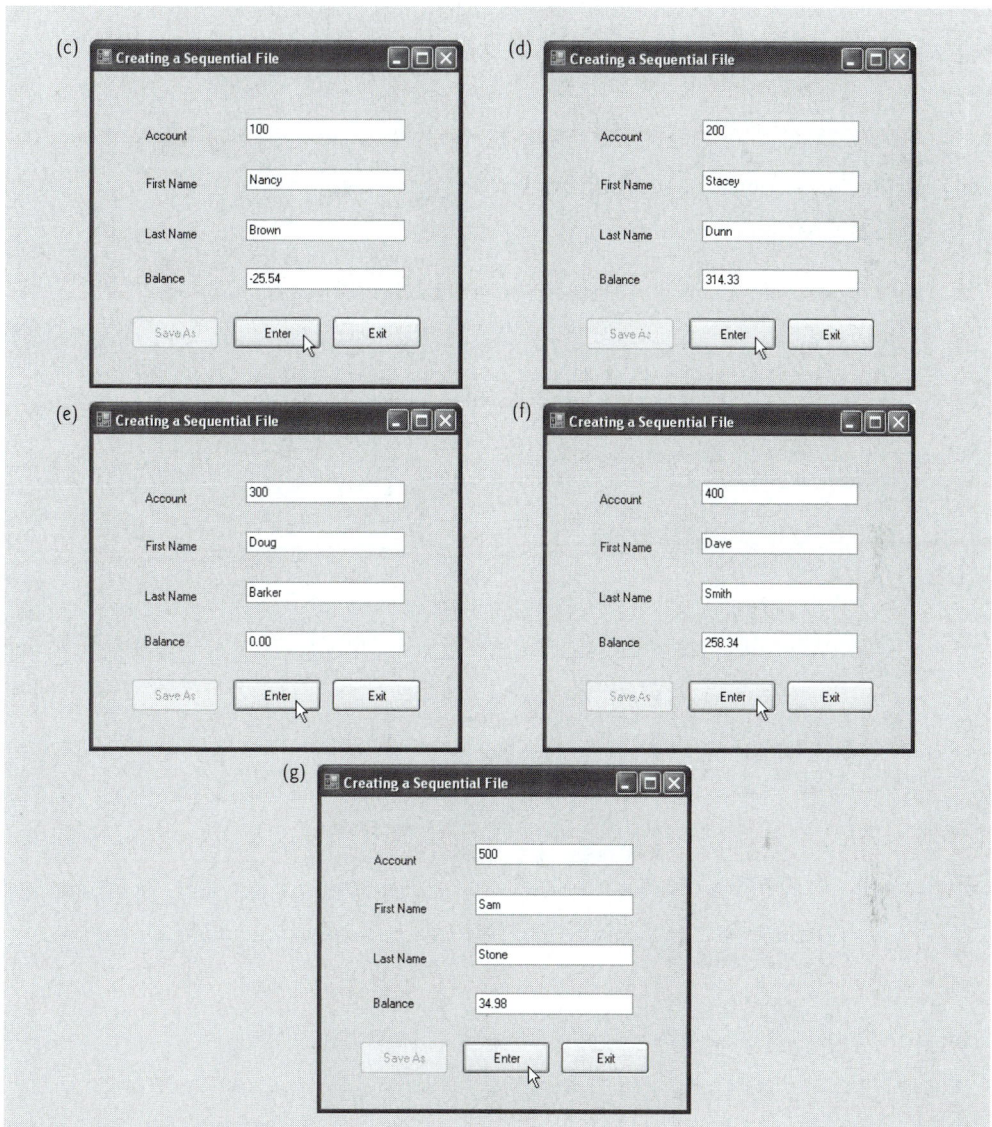

Fig. 18.14 | Sequential file created using serialization. (Part 5 of 5.)

18.9 Reading and Deserializing Data from a Sequential-Access Text File

The preceding section showed how to create a sequential-access file using object serialization. In this section, we discuss how to read serialized objects sequentially from a file.

Figure 18.15 reads and displays the contents of the file created by the program in Fig. 18.14. Line 13 creates the BinaryFormatter that will be used to read objects. The program opens the file for input by creating a FileStream object (lines 44–45). The name of the file to open is specified as the first argument to the FileStream constructor.

```
1   // Fig. 18.15: ReadSequentialAccessFileForm.cs
2   // Reading a sequential-access file using deserialization.
3   using System;
4   using System.Windows.Forms;
5   using System.IO;
6   using System.Runtime.Serialization.Formatters.Binary;
7   using System.Runtime.Serialization;
8   using BankLibrary;
9
10  public partial class ReadSequentialAccessFileForm : BankUIForm
11  {
12     // object for deserializing Record in binary format
13     private BinaryFormatter reader = new BinaryFormatter();
14     private FileStream input; // stream for reading from a file
15
16     // parameterless constructor
17     public ReadSequentialAccessFileForm()
18     {
19        InitializeComponent();
20     } // end constructor
21
22     // invoked when user clicks Open button
23     private void openButton_Click( object sender, EventArgs e )
24     {
25        // create dialog box enabling user to open file
26        OpenFileDialog fileChooser = new OpenFileDialog();
27        DialogResult result = fileChooser.ShowDialog();
28        string fileName; // name of file containing data
29
30        // exit event handler if user clicked Cancel
31        if ( result == DialogResult.Cancel )
32           return;
33
34        fileName = fileChooser.FileName; // get specified file name
35        ClearTextBoxes();
36
37        // show error if user specified invalid file
38        if ( fileName == "" || fileName == null )
39           MessageBox.Show( "Invalid File Name", "Error",
40              MessageBoxButtons.OK, MessageBoxIcon.Error );
41        else
42        {
43           // create FileStream to obtain read access to file
44           input = new FileStream(
45              fileName, FileMode.Open, FileAccess.Read );
46
47           openButton.Enabled = false; // disable Open File button
48           nextButton.Enabled = true;  // enable Next Record button
49        } // end else
50     } // end method openButton_Click
51
```

Fig. 18.15 | Sequential file read using deserialzation. (Part 1 of 4.)

```
52      // invoked when user clicks Next button
53      private void nextButton_Click( object sender, EventArgs e )
54      {
55         // deserialize Record and store data in TextBoxes
56         try
57         {
58            // get next RecordSerializable available in file
59            RecordSerializable record =
60               ( RecordSerializable ) reader.Deserialize( input );
61
62            // store Record values in temporary string array
63            string[] values = new string[] {
64               record.Account.ToString(),
65               record.FirstName.ToString(),
66               record.LastName.ToString(),
67               record.Balance.ToString()
68            };
69            // copy string array values to TextBox values
70            SetTextBoxValues( values );
71         } // end try
72         // handle exception when there are no Records in file
73         catch( SerializationException )
74         {
75            input.Close(); // close FileStream if no Records in file
76            openButton.Enabled = true; // enable Open File button
77            nextButton.Enabled = false; // disable Next Record button
78
79            ClearTextBoxes();
80
81            // notify user if no Records in file
82            MessageBox.Show( "No more records in file", "",
83               MessageBoxButtons.OK, MessageBoxIcon.Information );
84         } // end catch
85      } // end method nextButton_Click
86   } // end class readSequentialAccessFileForm
```

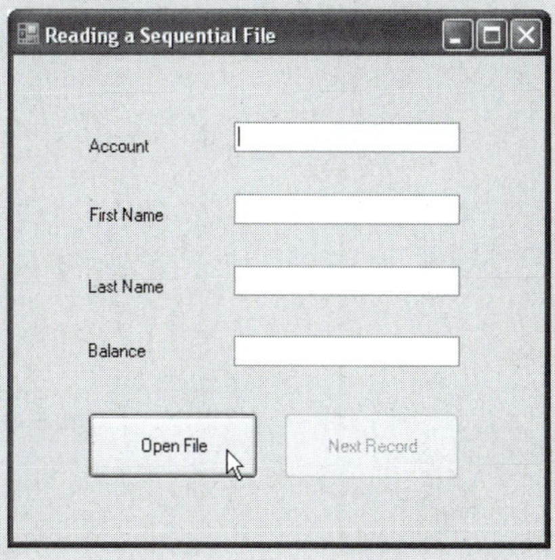

Fig. 18.15 | Sequential file read using deserialzation. (Part 2 of 4.)

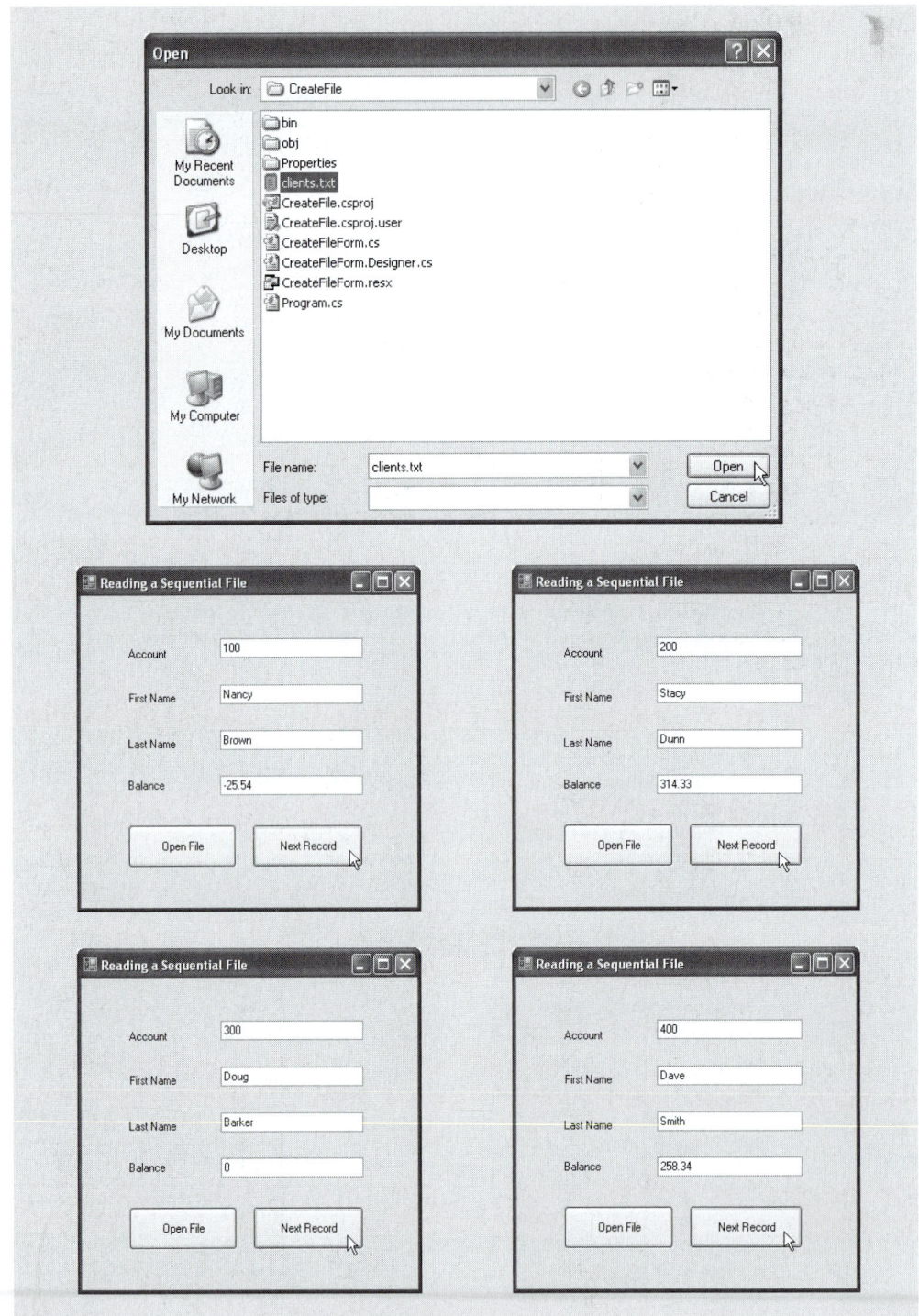

Fig. 18.15 | Sequential file read using deserialzation. (Part 3 of 4.)

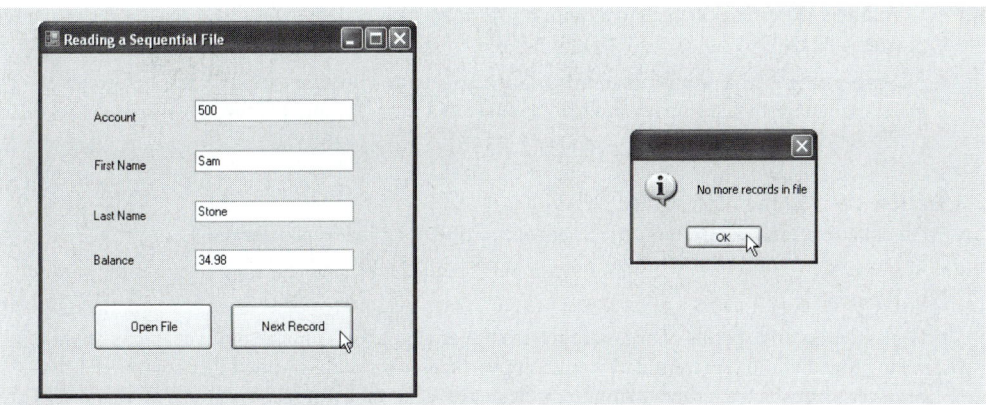

Fig. 18.15 | Sequential file read using deserialzation. (Part 4 of 4.)

The program reads objects from a file in event handler `nextButton_Click` (lines 53–85). We use method `Deserialize` (of the `BinaryFormatter` created in line 13) to read the data (lines 59–60). Note that we cast the result of `Deserialize` to type `RecordSerializable` (line 60)—this cast is necessary, because `Deserialize` returns a reference of type `object` and we need to access properties that belong to class `RecordSerializable`. If an error occurs during deserialization, a `SerializationException` is thrown, and the `FileStream` object is closed (line 75).

18.10 Wrap-Up

In this chapter, you learned how to use file processing to manipulate persistent data. You learned that data is stored in computers as 0s and 1s, and that combinations of these values are used to form bytes, fields, records and eventually files. We overviewed the differences between character-based and byte-based streams, as well as several file-processing classes from the `System.IO` namespace. You used class `File` to manipulate files and class `Directory` to manipulate directories. Next, you learned how to use sequential-access file processing to manipulate records in text files. We then discussed the differences between text-file processing and object serialization, and used serialization to store entire objects in and retrieve entire objects from files.

In the next chapter, we present Extensible Markup Language (XML)—a widely supported technology for describing data. Using XML, we can describe any type of data, such as mathematical formulas, music and financial reports. We'll demonstrate how to describe data with XML and how to write program that can process XML encoded data.

Summary

Section 18.1 Introduction

- Files are used for long-term retention of large amounts of data, even after the program that created the data terminates.

- Data maintained in files often is called persistent data.

- Computers store files on secondary storage devices, such as magnetic disks, optical disks and magnetic tapes.
- File processing is one of a programming language's most important capabilities, because it enables a language to support commercial applications that typically process massive amounts of persistent data.

Section 18.2 Data Hierarchy
- All data items that computers process are reduced to combinations of 0s and 1s.
- The smallest data item that computers support is called a bit and can assume either the value 0 or the value 1.
- Digits, letters and special symbols are referred to as characters. The set of all characters used to write programs and represent data items on a particular computer is called that computer's character set. Every character in a computer's character set is represented as a pattern of 0s and 1s.
- Bytes are composed of eight bits
- Characters in C# are Unicode characters, which are composed of 2 bytes.
- Just as characters are composed of bits, fields are composed of characters. A field is a group of characters that conveys meaning.
- Typically, a record is composed of several related fields.
- A file is a group of related records.
- At least one field in each record is chosen as a record key, which identifies a record as belonging to a particular person or entity and distinguishes that record from all others.
- The most common type of file organization is a sequential file, in which records typically are stored in order by record-key field.
- A group of related files is called a database. A collection of programs designed to create and manage databases is called a database management system (DBMS).

Section 18.3 Files and Streams
- C# views each file as a sequential stream of bytes.
- Each file ends either with an end-of-file marker or at a specific byte number that is recorded in a system-maintained administrative data structure.
- Files are opened by creating an object that has a stream associated with it.
- Streams provide communication channels between files and programs.
- To perform file processing in C#, the System.IO namespace must be referenced. This namespace includes definitions for stream classes such as StreamReader (for text input from a file), StreamWriter (for text output to a file) and FileStream (for both input from and output to a file).
- Class Stream provides functionality for representing streams as bytes. This class is abstract, so objects of this class cannot be instantiated.
- Classes FileStream, MemoryStream and BufferedStream (all from namespace System.IO) inherit from class Stream.
- Class FileStream can be used to read data to and write data from sequential-access files.
- Class MemoryStream enables the transfer of data directly to and from memory—this is much faster than other types of data transfer (e.g., to and from disk).
- Class BufferedStream uses buffering to transfer data to or from a stream. Buffering is an I/O performance enhancement technique, in which each output operation is directed to a region in memory, called a buffer, that is large enough to hold the data from many output operations.

Then actual transfer to the output device is performed in one large physical output operation each time the buffer fills. The output operations directed to the output buffer in memory often are called logical output operations. Buffering can also be used to speed input operations.

Section 18.4 Classes `File` and `Directory`

- Information on computers is stored in files, which are organized in directories. Classes `File` and `Directory` enable programs to manipulate files and directories on disk.

- Class `File` provides `static` methods determining information about files and can be used to open files for reading or writing.

- Class `Directory` provides `static` methods for manipulating directories.

- The `DirectoryInfo` object returned by `Directory` method `CreateDirectory` contains information about a directory. Much of the information contained in class `DirectoryInfo` also can be accessed via the methods of class `Directory`.

- `File` method `Exists` determines whether a `string` is the name of an existing file.

- A `StreamReader` can be used to read text from a file. The `StreamReader` constructor takes as an argument a `string` containing the name of the file to open. `StreamReader` method `ReadToEnd` reads the entire contents of a file.

- `Directory` method `Exists` determines whether a `string` is the name of an existing directory.

- `Directory` method `GetDirectories` obtains a `string` array containing the names of subdirectories in the specified directory.

- A `NameValueCollection` (namespace `System.Collections.Specialized`) contains a collection of key-value pairs of `string`s, and provides method `Add` to add a key-value pair to the collection. The indexer for this class can index according to the order that the items were added or according to the keys.

Section 18.5 Creating a Sequential-Access Text File

- C# imposes no structure on files. Thus, concepts like that of a "record" do not exist in C# files. This means that you must structure files to meet the requirements of your applications.

- When displayed, a `SaveFileDialog` prevents the user from interacting with any other window in the program until the user closes the `SaveFileDialog` by clicking either **Save** or **Cancel**. Dialogs that behave in this manner are called modal dialogs.

- There is a `FileStream` constructor that receives three arguments—a `string` containing the name of the file to be opened, a constant describing how to open the file and a constant describing the file permissions.

- The `StreamWriter` object is constructed with a `FileStream` argument that specifies the file to which `StreamWriter` outputs text.

- Class `StreamWriter` belongs to the `System.IO` namespace.

Section 18.6 Reading Data from a Sequential-Access Text File

- Data are stored in files so that they can be retrieved for processing when they are needed.

- To retrieve data sequentially from a file, programs normally start from the beginning of the file, reading data consecutively until the desired data is found. It sometimes is necessary to process a file sequentially several times during the execution of a program.

- An `OpenFileDialog` allows a user to select files to open. Method `ShowDialog` displays the dialog.

- `FileStream` method `Seek` allows you to reset the file-position pointer by specifying the number of bytes it should be offset from the file's beginning, end or current position. The part of the file you want to be offset from is chosen using constants from the `SeekOrigin` enumeration.

Section 18.7 Serialization

- A serialized object is represented as a sequence of bytes that includes the object's data, as well as information about the object's type and the types of data stored in the object.

- After a serialized object has been written to a file, it can be read from the file and deserialized (recreated in memory).

- Class `BinaryFormatter` (namespace `System.Runtime.Serialization.Formatters.Binary`), which supports the `ISerializable` interface, enables entire objects to be read from or written to a stream.

- `BinaryFormatter` methods `Serialize` and `Deserialize` write objects to and read objects from streams, respectively.

- Both method `Serialize` and method `Deserialize` require a `Stream` object (e.g., the `FileStream`) as a parameter so that the `BinaryFormatter` can access the correct file.

Section 18.8 Creating a Sequential-Access File Using Object Serialization

- Classes that are marked with the `Serializable` attribute indicate to the CLR that objects of the class can be serialized. Objects that we wish to write to or read from a stream must include this attribute in their class definitions.

- In a serializable class, you must ensure that every instance variable of the class is also serializable. By default, all simple-type variables are serializable. For reference-type variables, you must check the declaration of the class (and possibly its superclasses) to ensure that the type is serializable.

Section 18.9 Reading and Deserializing Data from a Sequential-Access Text File

- Method `Deserialize` (of class `BinaryFormatter`) reads a serialized object from a stream and reforms the object in memory.

- Method `Deserialize` returns a reference of type `object` which must be cast to the appropriate type to manipulate the object.

- If an error occurs during deserialization, a `SerializationException` is thrown.

Terminology

binary digit (bit)
`BinaryFormatter` class
`BinaryReader` class
`BinaryWriter` class
bit manipulation
buffer
`BufferedStream` class
buffering
character
character set
`Close` method of class `StreamWriter`
closing a file
`Console` class
`Copy` method of class `File`
`Create` method of class `File`
`CreateDirectory` method of class `Directory`
`CreateText` method of class `File`
data hierarchy
database

database management system (DBMS)
`Delete` method of class `Directory`
`Delete` method of class `File`
`Deserialize` method of class `BinaryFormatter`
`Directory` class
`DirectoryInfo` class
end-of-file marker
`Error` property of class `Console`
`Exists` method of class `Directory`
field
file
`File` class
file-processing programs
`FileAccess` enumeration
file-position pointer
`FileStream` class
fixed-length records
`GetCreationTime` method of class `Directory`
`GetCreationTime` method of class `File`

GetDirectories method of class `Directory`
GetFiles method of class `Directory`
GetLastAccessTime method of class `Directory`
GetLastAccessTime method of class `File`
GetLastWriteTime method of class `Directory`
GetLastWriteTime method of class `File`
In property of class `Console`
IOException
ISerializable interface
logical output operator
MemoryStream class
modal dialog
Move method of class `Directory`
Move method of class `File`
NameValueCollection class
object serialization
Open method of class `File`
OpenFileDialog class
OpenRead method of class `File`
OpenText method of class `File`
OpenWrite method of class `File`
Out property of class `Console`
pattern of 0s and 1s
persistent data
physical output operation
Read method of class `Console`
ReadLine method of class `Console`
ReadLine method of class `StreamReader`
record
record key

regular expression
SaveFileDialog class
secondary storage devices
Seek method of class `FileStream`
SeekOrigin enumeration
sequential-access file
Serializable attribute
SerializationException
Serialize method of class `BinaryFormatter`
OpenFileDialog
ShowDialog method of class `SaveFileDialog`
standard error stream object
standard input stream object
standard output stream object
Stream class
stream of bytes
StreamReader class
StreamWriter class
System.IO namespace
System.Runtime.Serialization.Formatters.Binary namespace
TextReader class
TextWriter class
transaction-processing system
Windows Control Library project
Write method of class `BinaryWriter`
Write method of class `Console`
Write method of class `StreamWriter`
WriteLine method of class `Console`
WriteLine method of class `StreamWriter`

Self-Review Exercises

18.1   State whether each of the following is *true* or *false*. If *false*, explain why.
    a) Creating instances of classes `File` and `Directory` is impossible.
    b) Typically, a sequential file stores records in order by the record-key field.
    c) Class `StreamReader` inherits from class `Stream`.
    d) Any class can be serialized to a file.
    e) Method `Seek` of class `FileStream` always seeks relative to the beginning of a file.
    f) Classes `StreamReader` and `StreamWriter` are used with sequential-access files.
    g) You cannot instantiate objects of type `Stream`.

18.2   Fill in the blanks in each of the following statements:
    a) Ultimately, all data items processed by a computer are reduced to combinations of _____ and _____.
    b) The smallest data item a computer can process is called a(n) _____.
    c) A(n) _____ is a group of related records.
    d) Digits, letters and special symbols are collectively referred to as _____.
    e) A group of related files is called a(n) _____.
    f) `StreamReader` method _____ reads a line of text from a file.
    g) `StreamWriter` method _____ writes a line of text to a file.

h) Method `Serialize` of class `BinaryFormatter` takes a(n) _____ and a(n) _____ as arguments.

i) The _____ namespace contains most of C#'s file-processing classes.

j) The _____ namespace contains the `BinaryFormatter` class.

Answers to Self-Review Exercises

18.1 a) True. b) True. c) False. Class `StreamReader` inherits from class `TextReader`. d) False. Only classes with the `Serializable` attribute can be serialized. e) False. It seeks relative to the `Seek-Origin` enumeration member that is passed as one of the arguments. f.) True. g) True.

18.2 a) 0s, 1s. b) bit. c) file. d) characters. e) database. f) `ReadLine`. g) `WriteLine`. h) `Stream`, object. i) `System.IO`. j) `System.Runtime.Serialization.Formatters.Binary`.

Exercises

18.3 Create a program that stores student grades in a text file. The file should contain the name, ID number, class taken and grade of every student. Allow the user to load a grade file and display its contents in a read-only `TextBox`. The entries should be displayed in the following format:

```
LastName, FirstName:  ID#  Class  Grade
```

We list some sample data below:

```
Jones, Bob: 1 "Introduction to Computer Science" "A-"
Johnson, Sarah: 2 "Data Structures" "B+"
Smith, Sam: 3 "Data Structures" "C"
```

18.4 Modify the previous program to use objects of a class that can be serialized to and deserialized from a file.

18.5 Extend classes `StreamReader` and `StreamWriter`. Make the class that derives from `StreamReader` have methods `ReadInteger`, `ReadBoolean` and `ReadString`. Make the class that derives from `StreamWriter` have methods `WriteInteger`, `WriteBoolean` and `WriteString`. Think about how to design the writing methods so that the reading methods will be able to read what was written. Design `WriteInteger` and `WriteBoolean` to write `strings` of uniform size so that `ReadInteger` and `ReadBoolean` can read those values accurately. Make sure `ReadString` and `WriteString` use the same character(s) to separate `strings`.

18.6 Create a program that combines the ideas of Fig. 18.9 and Fig. 18.11 to allow a user to write records to and read records from a file. Add an extra field of type `bool` to the record to indicate whether the account has overdraft protection.

18.7 *(Telephone-Number Word Generator)* Standard telephone keypads contain the digits zero through nine. The numbers two through nine each have three letters associated with them (Fig. 18.16). Many people find it difficult to memorize phone numbers, so they use the correspondence between digits and letters to develop seven-letter words that correspond to their phone numbers. For example, a person whose telephone number is 686-2377 might use the correspondence indicated in Fig. 18.16 to develop the seven-letter word "NUMBERS." Every seven-letter word corresponds to exactly one seven-digit telephone number. A restaurant wishing to increase its takeout business could surely do so with the number 825-3688 (i.e., "TAKEOUT").

Every seven-letter phone number corresponds to many different seven-letter words. Unfortunately, most of these words represent unrecognizable juxtapositions of letters. It is possible, however, that the owner of a barbershop would be pleased to know that the shop's telephone number, 424-7288, corresponds to "HAIRCUT." The owner of a liquor store would no doubt be delighted

Digit	Letter
2	A B C
3	D E F
4	G H I
5	J K L
6	M N O
7	P R S
8	T U V
9	W X Y

Fig. 18.16 | Letters that correspond to the numbers on a telephone keypad .

to find that the store's number, 233-7226, corresponds to "BEERCAN." A veterinarian with the phone number 738-2273 would be pleased to know that the number corresponds to the letters "PETCARE." An automotive dealership would be pleased to know that its phone number, 639-2277, corresponds to "NEWCARS."

Write a GUI program that, given a seven-digit number, uses a StreamWriter object to write to a file every possible seven-letter word combination corresponding to that number. There are 2,187 (3^7) such combinations. Avoid phone numbers with the digits 0 and 1.

18.8 *(Student Poll)* Figure 8.8 contains an array of survey responses that is hard-coded into the program. Suppose we wish to process survey results that are stored in a file. First, create a Windows Form that prompts the user for survey responses and outputs each response to a file. Use Stream-Writer to create a file called numbers.txt. Each integer should be written using method Write. Then add a TextBox that will output the frequency of survey responses. You should modify the code in Fig. 8.8 to read the survey responses from numbers.txt. The responses should be read from the file by using a StreamReader. Class string's split method should be used to split the input string into separate responses, then each response should be converted to an integer. The program should continue to read responses until it reaches the end of file. The results should be output to the TextBox.

19

Extensible Markup Language (XML)

*Knowing trees, I understand
the meaning of patience.
Knowing grass, I can
appreciate persistence.*
—Hal Borland

*Like everything
metaphysical, the harmony
between thought and reality
is to be found in the
grammar of the language.*
—Ludwig Wittgenstein

*I played with an idea, and
grew willful; tossed it into
the air; transformed it; let it
escape and recaptured it;
made it iridescent with
fancy, and winged it with
paradox.*
—Oscar Wilde

OBJECTIVES

In this chapter you will learn:

- To mark up data using XML.

- How XML namespaces help provide unique XML element and attribute names.

- To create DTDs and schemas for specifying and validating the structure of an XML document.

- To create and use simple XSL style sheets to render XML document data.

- To retrieve and modify XML data programmatically using .NET Framework classes.

- To validate XML documents against schemas using class `XmlReader`.

- To transform XML documents into XHTML using class `XslCompiledTransform`.

19.1 Introduction

The *Extensible Markup Language* (*XML*) was developed in 1996 by the *World Wide Web Consortium's* (*W3C's*) XML Working Group. XML is a widely supported *open technology* (i.e., nonproprietary technology) for describing data that has become the standard format for data exchanged between applications over the Internet.

The .NET Framework uses XML extensively. The Framework Class Library provides an extensive set of XML-related classes, and much of Visual Studio's internal implementation also employs XML. Sections 19.2–19.6 introduce XML and XML-related technologies—XML namespaces for providing unique XML element and attribute names, and Document Type Definitions (DTDs) and XML Schemas for validating XML documents. These sections are required to support the use of XML in Chapters 20–22. Sections 19.7–19.10 present additional XML technologies and key .NET Framework classes for creating and manipulating XML documents programmatically—this material is optional but recommended for readers who plan to employ XML in their own C# applications.

19.2 XML Basics

XML permits document authors to create *markup* (i.e., a text-based notation for describing data) for virtually any type of information. This enables document authors to create entirely new markup languages for describing any type of data, such as mathematical formulas, software-configuration instructions, chemical molecular structures, music, news, recipes and financial reports. XML describes data in a way that both human beings and computers can understand.

Figure 19.1 is a simple XML document that describes information for a baseball player. We focus on lines 5–11 to introduce basic XML syntax. You will learn about the other elements of this document in Section 19.3.

XML documents contain text that represents content (i.e., data), such as John (line 6 of Fig. 19.1), and *elements* that specify the document's structure, such as firstName (line 6 of Fig. 19.1). XML documents delimit elements with *start tags* and *end tags*. A start tag

```
1   <?xml version = "1.0"?>
2   <!-- Fig. 19.1: player.xml -->
3   <!-- Baseball player structured with XML -->
4
5   <player>
6      <firstName>John</firstName>
7
8      <lastName>Doe</lastName>
9
10     <battingAverage>0.375</battingAverage>
11  </player>
```

Fig. 19.1 | XML that describes a baseball player's information.

consists of the element name in *angle brackets* (e.g., <player> and <firstName> in lines 5 and 6, respectively). An end tag consists of the element name preceded by a *forward slash* (/) in angle brackets (e.g., </firstName> and </player> in lines 6 and 11, respectively). An element's start and end tags enclose text that represents a piece of data (e.g., the firstName of the player—John—in line 6, which is enclosed by the <firstName> start tag and </firstName> end tag). Every XML document must have exactly one *root element* that contains all the other elements. In Fig. 19.1, player (lines 5–11) is the root element.

Some XML-based markup languages include XHTML (Extensible HyperText Markup Language—HTML's replacement for marking up Web content), MathML (for mathematics), VoiceXML™ (for speech), CML (Chemical Markup Language—for chemistry) and XBRL (Extensible Business Reporting Language—for financial data exchange). These markup languages are called XML *vocabularies* and provide a means for describing particular types of data in standardized, structured ways.

Massive amounts of data are currently stored on the Internet in a variety of formats (e.g., databases, Web pages, text files). Based on current trends, it is likely that much of this data, especially that which is passed between systems, will soon take the form of XML. Organizations see XML as the future of data encoding. Information technology groups are planning ways to integrate XML into their systems. Industry groups are developing custom XML vocabularies for most major industries that will allow computer-based business applications to communicate in common languages. For example, Web services, which we discuss in Chapter 22, allow Web-based applications to exchange data seamlessly through standard protocols based on XML.

The next generation of the Internet and World Wide Web will almost certainly be built on a foundation of XML, which will permit the development of more sophisticated Web-based applications. As is discussed in this chapter, XML allows you to assign meaning to what would otherwise be random pieces of data. As a result, programs can "understand" the data they manipulate. For example, a Web browser might view a street address listed on a simple HTML Web page as a string of characters without any real meaning. In an XML document, however, this data can be clearly identified (i.e., marked up) as an address. A program that uses the document can recognize this data as an address and provide links to a map of that location, driving directions from that location or other location-specific information. Likewise, an application can recognize names of people, dates, ISBN numbers and any other type of XML-encoded data. Based on this data, the application can present users with other related information, providing a richer, more meaningful user experience.

Viewing and Modifying XML Documents

XML documents are highly portable. Viewing or modifying an XML document—which is a text file that ends with the **.xml** filename extension—does not require special software, although many software tools exist, and new ones are frequently released that make it more convenient to develop XML-based applications. Any text editor that supports ASCII/Unicode characters can open XML documents for viewing and editing. Also, most Web browsers can display XML documents in a formatted manner that makes it easier to see the XML's structure. We demonstrate this using Internet Explorer in Section 19.3. One important characteristic of XML is that it is both human readable and machine readable.

Processing XML Documents

Processing an XML document requires software called an **XML parser** (or **XML processor**). A parser makes the document's data available to applications. While reading the contents of an XML document, a parser checks that the document follows the syntax rules specified by the W3C's XML Recommendation (www.w3.org/XML). XML syntax requires a single root element, a start tag and end tag for each element, and properly nested tags (i.e., the end tag for a nested element must appear before the end tag of the enclosing element). Furthermore, XML is case sensitive, so the proper capitalization must be used in elements. A document that conforms to this syntax is a **well-formed XML document**, and is syntactically correct. We present fundamental XML syntax in Section 19.3. If an XML parser can process an XML document successfully, that XML document is well formed. Parsers can provide access to XML-encoded data in well-formed documents only.

Often, XML parsers are built into software such as Visual Studio or available for download over the Internet. Popular parsers include **Microsoft XML Core Services** (**MSXML**), the Apache Software Foundation's **Xerces** (xml.apache.org) and the opensource **Expat XML Parser** (expat.sourceforge.net). In this chapter, we use MSXML.

Validating XML Documents

An XML document can optionally reference a **Document Type Definition** (**DTD**) or a **schema** that defines the proper structure of the XML document. When an XML document references a DTD or a schema, some parsers (called **validating parsers**) can read the DTD/schema and check that the XML document follows the structure defined by the DTD/schema. If the XML document conforms to the DTD/schema (i.e., the document has the appropriate structure), the XML document is **valid**. For example, if in Fig. 19.1 we were referencing a DTD that specifies that a player element must have firstName, lastName and battingAverage elements, then omitting the lastName element (line 8 in Fig. 19.1) would cause the XML document player.xml to be invalid. However, the XML document would still be well formed, because it follows proper XML syntax (i.e., it has one root element, and each element has a start tag and an end tag). By definition, a valid XML document is well formed. Parsers that cannot check for document conformity against DTDs/schemas are **nonvalidating parsers**—they determine only whether an XML document is well formed, not whether it is valid.

We discuss validation, DTDs and schemas, as well as the key differences between these two types of structural specifications, in Sections 19.5 and 19.6. For now, note that schemas are XML documents themselves, whereas DTDs are not. As you will learn in Section 19.6, this difference presents several advantages in using schemas over DTDs.

Software Engineering Observation 19.1

DTDs and schemas are essential for business-to-business (B2B) transactions and mission-critical systems. Validating XML documents ensures that disparate systems can manipulate data structured in standardized ways and prevents errors caused by missing or malformed data.

Formatting and Manipulating XML Documents

XML documents contain only data, not formatting instructions, so applications that process XML documents must decide how to manipulate or display each document's data. For example, a PDA (personal digital assistant) may render an XML document differently than a wireless phone or a desktop computer. You can use *Extensible Stylesheet Language* (*XSL*) to specify rendering instructions for different platforms. We discuss XSL in Section 19.7.

XML-processing programs can also search, sort and manipulate XML data using technologies such as XSL. Some other XML-related technologies are XPath (XML Path Language—a language for accessing parts of an XML document), XSL-FO (XSL Formatting Objects—an XML vocabulary used to describe document formatting) and XSLT (XSL Transformations—a language for transforming XML documents into other documents). We present XSLT in Section 19.7. We also introduce XPath in Section 19.7, then discuss it in greater detail in Section 19.8.

19.3 Structuring Data

In this section and throughout this chapter, we create our own XML markup. XML allows you to describe data precisely in a well-structured format.

XML Markup for an Article

In Fig. 19.2, we present an XML document that marks up a simple article using XML. The line numbers shown are for reference only and are not part of the XML document.

```
1   <?xml version = "1.0"?>
2   <!-- Fig. 19.2: article.xml -->
3   <!-- Article structured with XML -->
4
5   <article>
6      <title>Simple XML</title>
7
8      <date>May 5, 2005</date>
9
10     <author>
11        <firstName>John</firstName>
12        <lastName>Doe</lastName>
13     </author>
14
15     <summary>XML is pretty easy.</summary>
16
```

Fig. 19.2 | XML used to mark up an article. (Part 1 of 2.)

```
17        <content>
18            In this chapter, we present a wide variety of examples that use XML.
19        </content>
20    </article>
```

Fig. 19.2 | XML used to mark up an article. (Part 2 of 2.)

This document begins with an ***XML declaration*** (line 1), which identifies the document as an XML document. The ***version attribute*** specifies the XML version to which the document conforms. The current XML standard is version 1.0. Though the W3C released a version 1.1 specification in February 2004, this newer version is not yet widely supported. The W3C may continue to release new versions as XML evolves to meet the requirements of different fields.

Portability Tip 19.1

Documents should include the XML declaration to identify the version of XML used. A document that lacks an XML declaration might be assumed to conform to the latest version of XML—when it does not, errors could result.

Common Programming Error 19.1

Placing whitespace characters before the XML declaration is an error.

XML comments (lines 2–3), which begin with `<!--` and end with `-->`, can be placed almost anywhere in an XML document. XML comments can span to multiple lines—an end marker on each line is not needed; the end marker can appear on a subsequent line as long as there is exactly one end marker (`-->`) for each begin marker (`<!--`). As in a C# program, comments are used in XML for documentation purposes. Line 4 is a blank line. As in a C# program, blank lines, whitespaces and indentation are used in XML to improve readability. Later you will see that the blank lines are normally ignored by XML parsers.

Common Programming Error 19.2

In an XML document, each start tag must have a matching end tag; omitting either tag is an error. Soon, you will learn how such errors are detected.

Common Programming Error 19.3

XML is case sensitive. Using different cases for the start tag and end tag names for the same element is a syntax error.

In Fig. 19.2, `article` (lines 5–20) is the root element. The lines that precede the root element (lines 1–4) are the XML ***prolog***. In an XML prolog, the XML declaration must appear before the comments and any other markup.

The elements we used in the example do not come from any specific markup language. Instead, we chose the element names and markup structure that best describe our particular data. You can invent elements to mark up your data. For example, element `title` (line 6) contains text that describes the article's title (e.g., `Simple XML`). Similarly, `date` (line 8), `author` (lines 10–13), `firstName` (line 11), `lastName` (line 12), `summary` (line 15) and `content` (lines 17–19) contain text that describes the date, author, the author's first name, the author's last name, a summary and the content of the document, respectively. XML element names can be of any length and may contain letters, digits, underscores, hyphens and periods. However, they must begin with either a letter or an underscore, and they should not begin with "xml" in any combination of uppercase and lowercase letters (e.g., XML, Xml, xMl) as this is reserved for use in the XML standards.

Common Programming Error 19.4

Using a whitespace character in an XML element name is an error.

Good Programming Practice 19.1

XML element names should be meaningful to humans and should not use abbreviations.

XML elements are *nested* to form hierarchies—with the root element at the top of the hierarchy. This allows document authors to create parent/child relationships between data. For example, elements title, date, author, summary and content are nested within article. Elements firstName and lastName are nested within author. Figure 19.21 shows the hierarchy of Fig. 19.2.

Common Programming Error 19.5

Nesting XML tags improperly is a syntax error. For example, <x><y>hello</x></y> is an error, because the </y> tag must precede the </x> tag.

Any element that contains other elements (e.g., article or author) is a *container element*. Container elements also are called *parent elements*. Elements nested inside a container element are *child elements* (or children) of that container element.

Viewing an XML Document in Internet Explorer

The XML document in Fig. 19.2 is simply a text file named article.xml. This document does not contain formatting information for the article. This is because XML is a technology for describing the structure of data. Formatting and displaying data from an XML document are application-specific issues. For example, when the user loads article.xml in Internet Explorer (IE), MSXML (Microsoft XML Core Services) parses and displays the document's data. Internet Explorer uses a built-in *style sheet* to format the data. Note that the resulting format of the data (Fig. 19.3) is similar to the format of the listing in Fig. 19.2. In Section 19.7, we show how to create style sheets to transform your XML data into various formats suitable for display.

Note the minus sign (–) and plus sign (+) in the screen shots of Fig. 19.3. Although these symbols are not part of the XML document, Internet Explorer places them next to every container element. A minus sign indicates that Internet Explorer is displaying the container element's child elements. Clicking the minus sign next to an element collapses that element (i.e., causes Internet Explorer to hide the container element's children and replace the minus sign with a plus sign). Conversely, clicking the plus sign next to an element expands that element (i.e., causes Internet Explorer to display the container element's children and replace the plus sign with a minus sign). This behavior is similar to viewing the directory structure using Windows Explorer. In fact, a directory structure often is modeled as a series of tree structures, in which the *root* of a tree represents a drive letter (e.g., C:), and *nodes* in the tree represent directories. Parsers often store XML data as tree structures to facilitate efficient manipulation, as discussed in Section 19.8.

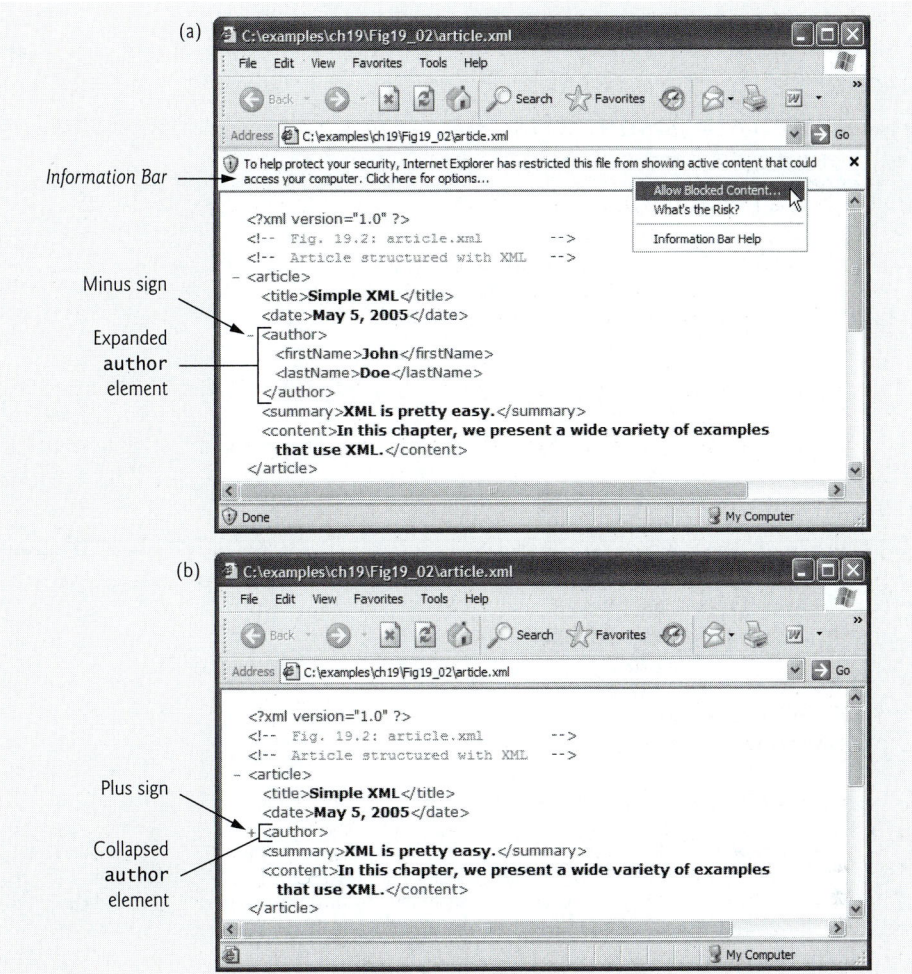

Information Bar

Minus sign

Expanded
author
element

Plus sign

Collapsed
author
element

Fig. 19.3 | `article.xml` displayed by Internet Explorer.

[*Note:* In Windows XP Service Pack 2, by default Internet Explorer displays all the XML elements in expanded view, and clicking the minus sign (Fig. 19.3(a) does not do anything. So by default, Windows will not be able to collapse the element. To enable this functionality, right click the *Information Bar* just below the **Address** field and select **Allow Blocked Content...**. Then click **Yes** in the popup window that appears.]

XML Markup for a Business Letter

Now that we have seen a simple XML document, let's examine a more complex XML document that marks up a business letter (Fig. 19.4). Again, we begin the document with the XML declaration (line 1) that states the XML version to which the document conforms.

Line 5 specifies that this XML document references a DTD. Recall from Section 19.2 that DTDs define the structure of the data for an XML document. For example, a DTD specifies the elements and parent-child relationships between elements permitted in an XML document.

```
 1   <?xml version = "1.0"?>
 2   <!-- Fig. 19.4: letter.xml -->
 3   <!-- Business letter marked up as XML -->
 4
 5   <!DOCTYPE letter SYSTEM "letter.dtd">
 6
 7   <letter>
 8      <contact type = "sender">
 9         <name>Jane Doe</name>
10         <address1>Box 12345</address1>
11         <address2>15 Any Ave.</address2>
12         <city>Othertown</city>
13         <state>Otherstate</state>
14         <zip>67890</zip>
15         <phone>555-4321</phone>
16         <flag gender = "F" />
17      </contact>
18
19      <contact type = "receiver">
20         <name>John Doe</name>
21         <address1>123 Main St.</address1>
22         <address2></address2>
23         <city>Anytown</city>
24         <state>Anystate</state>
25         <zip>12345</zip>
26         <phone>555-1234</phone>
27         <flag gender = "M" />
28      </contact>
29
30      <salutation>Dear Sir:</salutation>
31
32      <paragraph>It is our privilege to inform you about our new database
33         managed with XML. This new system allows you to reduce the
34         load on your inventory list server by having the client machine
35         perform the work of sorting and filtering the data.
36      </paragraph>
37
38      <paragraph>Please visit our Web site for availability
39         and pricing.
40      </paragraph>
41
42      <closing>Sincerely,</closing>
43      <signature>Ms. Jane Doe</signature>
44   </letter>
```

Fig. 19.4 | Business letter marked up as XML.

Error-Prevention Tip 19.1

An XML document is not required to reference a DTD, but validating XML parsers can use a DTD to ensure that the document has the proper structure.

Portability Tip 19.2

Validating an XML document helps guarantee that independent developers will exchange data in a standardized form that conforms to the DTD.

The DTD reference (line 5) contains three items, the name of the root element that the DTD specifies (`letter`); the keyword *SYSTEM* (which denotes an *external DTD*—a DTD declared in a separate file, as opposed to a DTD declared locally in the same file); and the DTD's name and location (i.e., `letter.dtd` in the current directory). DTD document filenames typically end with the *.dtd* extension. We discuss DTDs and `letter.dtd` in detail in Section 19.5.

Several tools (many of which are free) validate documents against DTDs and schemas (discussed in Section 19.5 and Section 19.6, respectively). Microsoft's *XML Validator* is available free of charge from the **Download Sample** link at

```
msdn.microsoft.com/archive/en-us/samples/internet/
xml/xml_validator/default.asp
```

This validator can validate XML documents against both DTDs and Schemas. To install it, run the downloaded executable file `xml_validator.exe` and follow the steps to complete the installation. Once the installation is successful, open the `validate_js.htm` file located in your XML Validator installation directory in IE to validate your XML documents. We installed the XML Validator at `C:\XMLValidator` (Fig. 19.5). The output (Fig. 19.6) shows the results of validating the document using Microsoft's XML Validator. Visit `www.w3.org/XML/Schema` for a list of additional validation tools.

Root element `letter` (lines 7–44 of Fig. 19.4) contains the child elements `contact`, `contact`, `salutation`, `paragraph`, `paragraph`, `closing` and `signature`. In addition to being placed between tags, data also can be placed in *attributes*—name-value pairs that appear within the angle brackets of start tags. Elements can have any number of attributes (separated by spaces) in their start tags. The first `contact` element (lines 8–17) has an attribute named `type` with *attribute value* `"sender"`, which indicates that this `contact` element identifies the letter's sender. The second `contact` element (lines 19–28) has attribute `type` with value `"receiver"`, which indicates that this `contact` element identifies

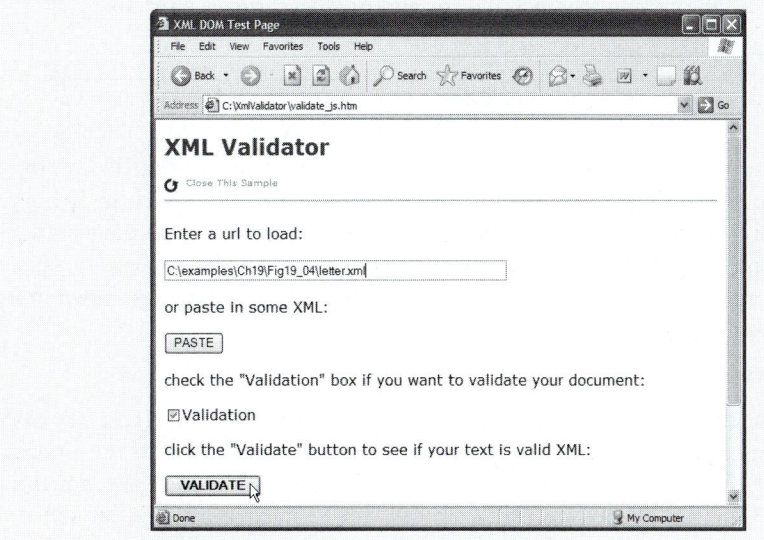

Fig. 19.5 | Validating an XML document with Microsoft's XML Validator.

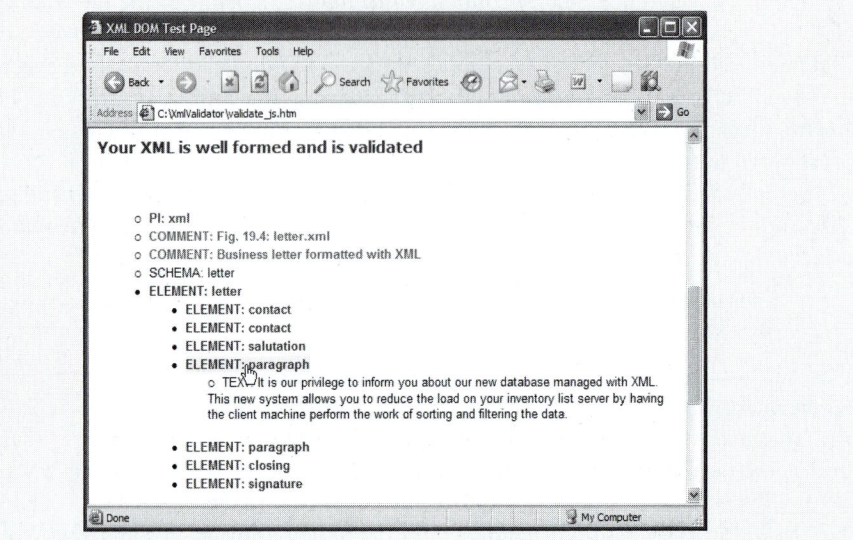

Fig. 19.6 | Validation result using Microsoft's XML Validator.

the letter's recipient. Like element names, attribute names are case sensitive, can be any length, may contain letters, digits, underscores, hyphens and periods, and must begin with either a letter or an underscore character. A `contact` element stores various items of information about a contact, such as the contact's name (represented by element `name`), address (represented by elements `address1`, `address2`, `city`, `state` and `zip`), phone number (represented by element `phone`) and gender (represented by attribute `gender` of element `flag`). Element `salutation` (line 30) marks up the letter's salutation. Lines 32–40 mark up the letter's body using two `paragraph` elements. Elements `closing` (line 42) and `signature` (line 43) mark up the closing sentence and the author's "signature," respectively.

Common Programming Error 19.6

Failure to enclose attribute values in double ("") or single (' ') quotes is a syntax error.

Line 16 introduces the *empty element* `flag`. An empty element is one that does not contain any content. Instead, an empty element sometimes contains data in attributes. Empty element `flag` contains an attribute that indicates the gender of the contact (represented by the parent `contact` element). Document authors can close an empty element either by placing a slash immediately preceding the right angle bracket, as shown in line 16, or by explicitly writing an end tag, as in line 22

```
<address2></address2>
```

Note that the `address2` element in line 22 is empty because there is no second part to this contact's address. However, we must include this element to conform to the structural rules specified in the XML document's DTD—`letter.dtd` (which we present in Section 19.5). This DTD specifies that each `contact` element must have an `address2` child element (even if it is empty). In Section 19.5, you will learn how DTDs indicate that certain elements are required while others are optional.

19.4 XML Namespaces

XML allows document authors to create custom elements. This extensibility can result in *naming collisions* among elements in an XML document that each have the same name. For example, we may use the element book to mark up data about a Deitel publication. A stamp collector may use the element book to mark up data about a book of stamps. Using both of these elements in the same document could create a naming collision, making it difficult to determine which kind of data each element contains.

An XML *namespace* is a collection of element and attribute names. Like C# namespaces, XML namespaces provide a means for document authors to unambiguously refer to elements with the same name (i.e., prevent collisions). For example,

> **<*subject*>**Math**</*subject*>**

and

> **<*subject*>**Cardiology**</*subject*>**

use element subject to mark up data. In the first case, the subject is something one studies in school, whereas in the second case, the subject is a field of medicine. Namespaces can differentiate these two subject elements. For example

> **<*school:subject*>**Math**</*school:subject*>**

and

> **<*medical:subject*>**Cardiology**</*medical:subject*>**

Both school and medical are *namespace prefixes*. A document author places a namespace prefix and colon (:) before an element name to specify the namespace to which that element belongs. Document authors can create their own namespace prefixes using virtually any name except the reserved namespace prefix xml. In the next subsections, we demonstrate how document authors ensure that namespaces are unique.

Common Programming Error 19.7

Attempting to create a namespace prefix named xml in any mixture of uppercase and lowercase letters is a syntax error—the xml namespace prefix is reserved for internal use by XML itself.

Differentiating Elements with Namespaces

Figure 19.7 demonstrates namespaces. In this document, namespaces differentiate two distinct elements—the file element related to a text file and the file document related to an image file.

Lines 6–7 use the XML-namespace reserved attribute *xmlns* to create two namespace prefixes—text and image. Each namespace prefix is bound to a series of characters called a *Uniform Resource Identifier* (*URI*) that uniquely identifies the namespace. Document authors create their own namespace prefixes and URIs. A URI is a way to identifying a resource, typically on the Internet. Two popular types of URI are *Uniform Resource Name* (*URN*) and *Uniform Resource Locator* (*URL*).

To ensure that namespaces are unique, document authors must provide unique URIs. In this example, we use the text urn:deitel:textInfo and urn:deitel:imageInfo as

```
 1   <?xml version = "1.0"?>
 2   <!-- Fig. 19.7: namespace.xml -->
 3   <!-- Demonstrating namespaces -->
 4
 5   <text:directory
 6      xmlns:text = "urn:deitel:textInfo"
 7      xmlns:image = "urn:deitel:imageInfo">
 8
 9      <text:file filename = "book.xml">
10         <text:description>A book list</text:description>
11      </text:file>
12
13      <image:file filename = "funny.jpg">
14         <image:description>A funny picture</image:description>
15         <image:size width = "200" height = "100" />
16      </image:file>
17   </text:directory>
```

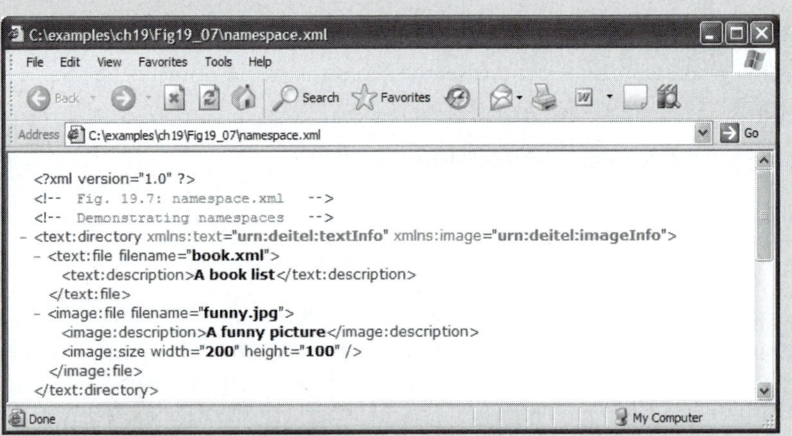

Fig. 19.7 | XML namespaces demonstration.

URIs. These URIs employ the URN scheme frequently used to identify namespaces. Under this naming scheme, a URI begins with "urn:", followed by a unique series of additional names separated by colons.

Another common practice is to use URLs, which specify the location of a file or a resource on the Internet. For example, www.deitel.com is the URL that identifies the home page of the Deitel & Associates Web site. Using URLs guarantees that the namespaces are unique because the domain names (e.g., www.deitel.com) are guaranteed to be unique. For example, lines 5–7 could be rewritten as

```
<text:directory
   xmlns:text = "http://www.deitel.com/xmlns-text"
   xmlns:image = "http://www.deitel.com/xmlns-image">
```

where URLs related to the Deitel & Associates, Inc. domain name serve as URIs to identify the text and image namespaces. The parser does not visit these URLs, nor do these URLs need to refer to actual Web pages. They each simply represent a unique series of characters used to differentiate URI names. In fact, any string can represent a namespace. For example, our `image` namespace URI could be `hgjfkdlsa4556`, in which case our prefix assignment would be

```
xmlns:image = "hgjfkdlsa4556"
```

Lines 9–11 use the `text` namespace prefix for elements `file` and `description`. Note that the end tags must also specify the namespace prefix `text`. Lines 13–16 apply namespace prefix `image` to the elements `file`, `description` and `size`. Note that attributes do not require namespace prefixes (although they can have them), because each attribute is already part of an element that specifies the namespace prefix. For example, attribute `filename` (line 9) is implicitly part of namespace `text` because its element (i.e., `file`) specifies the `text` namespace prefix.

Specifying a Default Namespace

To eliminate the need to place namespace prefixes in each element, document authors may specify a *default namespace* for an element and its children. Figure 19.8 demonstrates using a default namespace (`urn:deitel:textInfo`) for element `directory`.

```xml
 1  <?xml version = "1.0"?>
 2  <!-- Fig. 19.8: defaultnamespace.xml -->
 3  <!-- Using default namespaces -->
 4
 5  <directory xmlns = "urn:deitel:textInfo"
 6      xmlns:image = "urn:deitel:imageInfo">
 7
 8      <file filename = "book.xml">
 9          <description>A book list</description>
10      </file>
11
12      <image:file filename = "funny.jpg">
13          <image:description>A funny picture</image:description>
14          <image:size width = "200" height = "100" />
15      </image:file>
16  </directory>
```

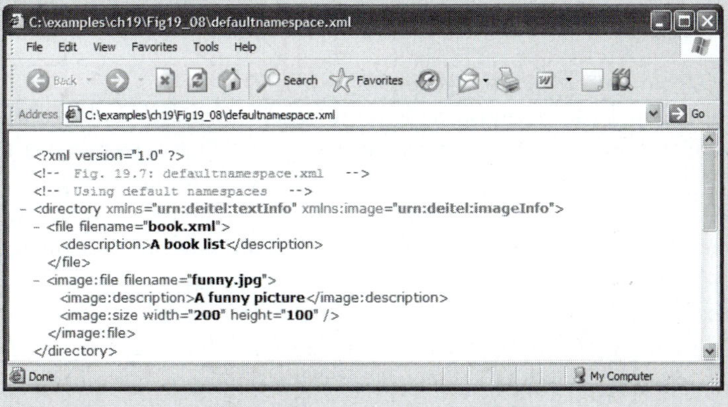

Fig. 19.8 | Default namespace demonstration.

Line 5 defines a default namespace using attribute `xmlns` with a URI as its value. Once we define this default namespace, child elements belonging to the namespace need not be qualified by a namespace prefix. Thus, element `file` (lines 8–10) is in the default namespace `urn:deitel:textInfo`. Compare this to lines 8–10 of Fig. 19.7, where we had to prefix the `file` and `description` element names with the namespace prefix `text`.

The default namespace applies to the `directory` element and all elements that are not qualified with a namespace prefix. However, we can use a namespace prefix to specify a different namespace for particular elements. For example, the `file` element in lines 12–15 includes the `image` namespace prefix, indicating that this element is in the `urn:deitel:imageInfo` namespace, not the default namespace.

Namespaces in XML Vocabularies

XML-based languages, such as XML Schema (Section 19.6), Extensible Stylesheet Language (XSL) (Section 19.7) and BizTalk (`www.microsoft.com/biztalk`), often use namespaces to identify their elements. Each of these vocabularies defines special-purpose elements that are grouped in namespaces. These namespaces help prevent naming collisions between predefined elements and user-defined elements.

19.5 Document Type Definitions (DTDs)

Document Type Definitions (DTDs) are one of two main types of documents you can use to specify XML document structure. Section 19.6 presents W3C XML Schema documents, which provide an improved method of specifying XML document structure.

 Software Engineering Observation 19.2

XML documents can have many different structures, and for this reason an application cannot be certain whether a particular document it receives is complete, ordered properly, and not missing data. DTDs and schemas (Section 19.6) solve this problem by providing an extensible way to describe XML document structure. Applications should use DTDs or schemas to confirm whether XML documents are valid.

 Software Engineering Observation 19.3

*Many organizations and individuals are creating DTDs and schemas for a broad range of applications. These collections—called **repositories**—are available free for download from the Web (e.g., `www.xml.org`, `www.oasis-open.org`).*

Creating a Document Type Definition

Figure 19.4 presented a simple business letter marked up with XML. Recall that line 5 of `letter.xml` references a DTD—`letter.dtd` (Fig. 19.9). This DTS specifies the business letter's element types and attributes, and their relationships to one another.

A DTD describes the structure of an XML document and enables an XML parser to verify whether an XML document is valid (i.e., whether its elements contain the proper attributes and appear in the proper sequence). DTDs allow users to check document structure and to exchange data in a standardized format. A DTD expresses the set of rules for document structure using an EBNF (Extended Backus-Naur Form) grammar. [*Note:* EBNF grammars are commonly used to define programming languages. For more information on EBNF grammars, please see `en.wikipedia.org/wiki/EBNF` or `www.garshol.priv.no/download/text/bnf.html`.]

has a corresponding end tag, the document contains only one root element, etc.), and a valid document contains the proper elements with the proper attributes in the proper sequence. An XML document cannot be valid unless it is well formed.

When a document fails to conform to a DTD or a schema, the Microsoft XML Validator displays an error message. For example, the DTD in Fig. 19.9 indicates that a contact element must contain the child element name. A document that omits this child element is still well formed, but is not valid. In such a scenario, Microsoft XML Validator displays the error message shown in Fig. 19.10.

19.6 W3C XML Schema Documents

In this section, we introduce schemas for specifying XML document structure and validating XML documents. Many developers in the XML community believe that DTDs are not flexible enough to meet today's programming needs. For example, DTDs lack a way of indicating what specific type of data (e.g., numeric, text) an element can contain and DTDs are not themselves XML documents. These and other limitations have led to the development of schemas.

Unlike DTDs, schemas do not use EBNF grammar. Instead, schemas use XML syntax and are actually XML documents that programs can manipulate. Like DTDs, schemas are used by validating parsers to validate documents.

In this section, we focus on the W3C's *XML Schema* vocabulary (note the capital "S" in "Schema"). We use the term XML Schema in the rest of the chapter whenever we refer to W3C's XML Schema vocabulary. For the latest information on XML Schema, visit www.w3.org/XML/Schema. For tutorials on XML Schema concepts beyond what we present here, visit www.w3schools.com/schema/default.asp.

A DTD describes an XML document's structure, not the content of its elements. For example,

> *<quantity>*5*</quantity>*

contains character data. If the document that contains element quantity references a DTD, an XML parser can validate the document to confirm that this element indeed does contain PCDATA content. However, the parser cannot validate that the content is numeric; DTDs do not provide this capability. So, unfortunately, the parser also considers

> *<quantity>*hello*</quantity>*

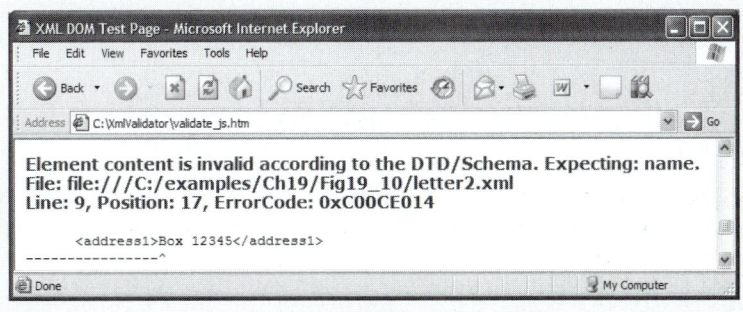

Fig. 19.10 | XML Validator displaying an error message.

to be valid. An application that uses the XML document containing this markup should test that the data in element `quantity` is numeric and take appropriate action if it is not.

XML Schema enables schema authors to specify that element `quantity`'s data must be numeric or, even more specifically, an integer. A parser validating the XML document against this schema can determine that 5 conforms and `hello` does not. An XML document that conforms to a schema document is *schema valid*, and one that does not conform is *schema invalid*. Schemas are XML documents and therefore must themselves be valid.

Validating Against an XML Schema Document

Figure 19.11 shows a schema-valid XML document named `book.xml`, and Fig. 19.12 shows the pertinent XML Schema document (`book.xsd`) that defines the structure for `book.xml`. By convention, schemas use the *.xsd* extension. We used an online XSD schema validator provided by Microsoft at

> apps.gotdotnet.com/xmltools/xsdvalidator

to ensure that the XML document in Fig. 19.11 conforms to the schema in Fig. 19.12. To validate the schema document itself (i.e., `book.xsd`) and produce the output shown in Fig. 19.12, we used an online XSV (XML Schema Validator) provided by the W3C at

> www.w3.org/2001/03/webdata/xsv

These tools are free and enforce the W3C's specifications regarding XML Schemas and schema validation. Section 19.12 lists several online XML Schema validators.

```
 1   <?xml version = "1.0"?>
 2   <!-- Fig. 19.11: book.xml -->
 3   <!-- Book list marked up as XML -->
 4
 5   <deitel:books xmlns:deitel = "http://www.deitel.com/booklist">
 6      <book>
 7         <title>Visual Basic 2005 How to Program, 3/e</title>
 8      </book>
 9
10      <book>
11         <title>Visual C# 2005 How to Program</title>
12      </book>
13
14      <book>
15         <title>Java How to Program, 6/e</title>
16      </book>
17
18      <book>
19         <title>C++ How to Program, 5/e</title>
20      </book>
21
22      <book>
23         <title>Internet and World Wide Web How to Program, 3/e</title>
24      </book>
25   </deitel:books>
```

Fig. 19.11 | Schema-valid XML document describing a list of books.

```
 1   <?xml version = "1.0"?>
 2   <!-- Fig. 19.12: book.xsd          -->
 3   <!-- Simple W3C XML Schema document -->
 4
 5   <schema xmlns = "http://www.w3.org/2001/XMLSchema"
 6      xmlns:deitel = "http://www.deitel.com/booklist"
 7      targetNamespace = "http://www.deitel.com/booklist">
 8
 9      <element name = "books" type = "deitel:BooksType"/>
10
11      <complexType name = "BooksType">
12         <sequence>
13            <element name = "book" type = "deitel:SingleBookType"
14               minOccurs = "1" maxOccurs = "unbounded"/>
15         </sequence>
16      </complexType>
17
18      <complexType name = "SingleBookType">
19         <sequence>
20            <element name = "title" type = "string"/>
21         </sequence>
22      </complexType>
23   </schema>
```

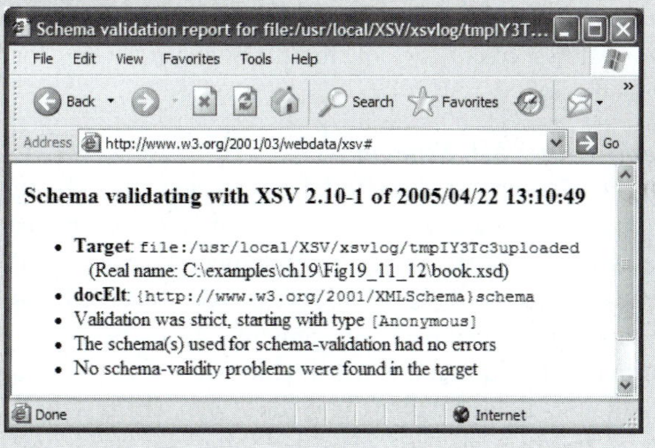

Fig. 19.12 | XML Schema document for `book.xml`.

Figure 19.11 contains markup describing several Deitel books. The `books` element (line 5) has the namespace prefix `deitel`, indicating that the `books` element is a part of the `http://www.deitel.com/booklist` namespace. Note that we declare the namespace prefix `deitel` in line 5.

Creating an XML Schema Document

Figure 19.12 presents the XML Schema document that specifies the structure of `book.xml` (Fig. 19.11). This document defines an XML-based language (i.e., a vocabulary) for writing XML documents about collections of books. The schema defines the elements, attributes and parent-child relationships that such a document can (or must) include. The schema also specifies the type of data that these elements and attributes may contain.

Root element *schema* (Fig. 19.12, lines 5–23) contains elements that define the structure of an XML document such as book.xml. Line 5 specifies as the default namespace the standard W3C XML Schema namespace URI—*http://www.w3.org/2001/XMLSchema*. This namespace contains predefined elements (e.g., root element schema) that comprise the XML Schema vocabulary—the language used to write an XML Schema document.

Portability Tip 19.3

W3C XML Schema authors specify URI http://www.w3.org/2001/XMLSchema when referring to the XML Schema namespace. This namespace contains predefined elements that comprise the XML Schema vocabulary. Specifying this URI ensures that validation tools correctly identify XML Schema elements and do not confuse them with those defined by document authors.

Line 6 binds the URI http://www.deitel.com/booklist to namespace prefix deitel. As we discuss momentarily, the schema uses this namespace to differentiate names created by us from names that are part of the XML Schema namespace. Line 7 also specifies http://www.deitel.com/booklist as the *targetNamespace* of the schema. This attribute identifies the namespace of the XML vocabulary that this schema defines. Note that the targetNamespace of book.xsd is the same as the namespace referenced in line 5 of book.xml (Fig. 19.11). This is what "connects" the XML document with the schema that defines its structure. When an XML schema validator examines book.xml and book.xsd, it will recognize that book.xml uses elements and attributes from the http://www.deitel.com/booklist namespace. The validator also will recognize that this namespace is the namespace defined in book.xsd (i.e., the schema's targetNamespace). Thus the validator knows where to look for the structural rules for the elements and attributes used in book.xml.

Defining an Element in XML Schema

In XML Schema, the *element* tag (line 9) defines an element to be included in an XML document that conforms to the schema. In other words, element specifies the actual *elements* that can be used to mark up data. Line 9 defines the books element, which we use as the root element in book.xml (Fig. 19.11). Attributes *name* and *type* specify the element's name and data type, respectively. An element's data type indicates the data that the element may contain. Possible data types include XML Schema–defined types (e.g., string, double) and user-defined types (e.g., BooksType, which is defined in lines 11–16). Figure 19.13 lists several of XML Schema's many built-in types. For a complete list of built-in types, see Section 3 of the specification found at www.w3.org/TR/xmlschema-2.

In this example, books is defined as an element of data type deitel:BooksType (line 9). BooksType is a user-defined type (lines 11–16) in the http://www.deitel.com/booklist namespace and therefore must have the namespace prefix deitel. It is not an existing XML Schema data type.

Two categories of data type exist in XML Schema—*simple types* and *complex types*. Simple and complex types differ only in that simple types cannot contain attributes or child elements and complex types can.

A user-defined type that contains attributes or child elements must be defined as a complex type. Lines 11–16 use element *complexType* to define BooksType as a complex type that has a child element named book. The sequence element (lines 12–15) allows you to specify the sequential order in which child elements must appear. The element (lines 13–14) nested within the complexType element indicates that a BooksType element (e.g.,

XML Schema Data Type(s)	Description	Ranges or Structures	Examples
string	A character string.		"hello"
boolean	True or false.	true, false	true
decimal	A decimal numeral.	$i * (10^n)$, where i is an integer and n is an integer that is less than or equal to zero.	5, -12, -45.78
float	A floating-point number.	$m * (2^e)$, where m is an integer whose absolute value is less than 2^{24} and e is an integer in the range -149 to 104. Plus three additional numbers: positive infinity, negative infinity and not-a-number (NaN).	0, 12, -109.375, NaN
double	A floating-point number.	$m * (2^e)$, where m is an integer whose absolute value is less than 2^{53} and e is an integer in the range -1075 to 970. Plus three additional numbers: positive infinity, negative infinity and not-a-number (NaN).	0, 12, -109.375, NaN
long	A whole number.	-9223372036854775808 to 9223372036854775807, inclusive	1234567890, -1234567890
int	A whole number.	-2147483648 to 2147483647, inclusive	1234567890, -1234567890
short	A whole number.	-32768 to 32767, inclusive	12, -345
date	A date consisting of a year, month and day.	yyyy-mm with an optional dd and an optional time zone, where yyyy is four digits long and mm and dd are two digits long.	2005-05-10
time	A time consisting of hours, minutes and seconds.	hh:mm:ss with an optional time zone, where hh, mm and ss are two digits long.	16:30:25-05:00

Fig. 19.13 | Some XML Schema data types.

books) can contain child elements named book of type deitel:SingleBookType (defined in lines 18–22). Attribute *minOccurs* (line 14), with value 1, specifies that elements of type

BooksType must contain a minimum of one book element. Attribute *maxOccurs* (line 14), with value *unbounded*, specifies that elements of type BooksType may have any number of book child elements.

Lines 18–22 define the complex type SingleBookType. An element of this type contains a child element named title. Line 20 defines element title to be of simple type string. Recall that elements of a simple type cannot contain attributes or child elements. The schema end tag (</schema>, line 23) declares the end of the XML Schema document.

A Closer Look at Types in XML Schema

Every element in XML Schema has a type. Types include the built-in types provided by XML Schema (Fig. 19.13) or user-defined types (e.g., SingleBookType in Fig. 19.12).

Every simple type defines a *restriction* on an XML Schema-defined type or a restriction on a user-defined type. Restrictions limit the possible values that an element can hold.

Complex types are divided into two groups—those with *simple content* and those with *complex content*. Both can contain attributes, but only complex content can contain child elements. Complex types with simple content must extend or restrict some other existing type. Complex types with complex content do not have this limitation. We demonstrate complex types with each kind of content in the next example.

The schema document in Fig. 19.14 creates both simple types and complex types. The XML document in Fig. 19.15 (laptop.xml) follows the structure defined in Fig. 19.14 to describe parts of a laptop computer. A document such as laptop.xml that conforms to a schema is known as an *XML instance document*—the document is an instance (i.e., example) of the schema.

Line 5 declares the default namespace to be the standard XML Schema namespace—any elements without a prefix are assumed to be in the XML Schema namespace. Line 6

```
 1   <?xml version = "1.0"?>
 2   <!-- Fig. 19.14: computer.xsd -->
 3   <!-- W3C XML Schema document   -->
 4
 5   <schema xmlns = "http://www.w3.org/2001/XMLSchema"
 6      xmlns:computer = "http://www.deitel.com/computer"
 7      targetNamespace = "http://www.deitel.com/computer">
 8
 9      <simpleType name = "gigahertz">
10         <restriction base = "decimal">
11            <minInclusive value = "2.1"/>
12         </restriction>
13      </simpleType>
14
15      <complexType name = "CPU">
16         <simpleContent>
17            <extension base = "string">
18               <attribute name = "model" type = "string"/>
19            </extension>
20         </simpleContent>
21      </complexType>
22
```

Fig. 19.14 | XML Schema document defining simple and complex types. (Part 1 of 2.)

```
23        <complexType name = "portable">
24          <all>
25            <element name = "processor" type = "computer:CPU"/>
26            <element name = "monitor" type = "int"/>
27            <element name = "CPUSpeed" type = "computer:gigahertz"/>
28            <element name = "RAM" type = "int"/>
29          </all>
30          <attribute name = "manufacturer" type = "string"/>
31        </complexType>
32
33        <element name = "laptop" type = "computer:portable"/>
34      </schema>
```

Fig. 19.14 | XML Schema document defining simple and complex types. (Part 2 of 2.)

```
1   <?xml version = "1.0"?>
2   <!-- Fig. 19.15: laptop.xml            -->
3   <!-- Laptop components marked up as XML -->
4
5   <computer:laptop xmlns:computer = "http://www.deitel.com/computer"
6      manufacturer = "IBM">
7
8      <processor model = "Centrino">Intel</processor>
9      <monitor>17</monitor>
10     <CPUSpeed>2.4</CPUSpeed>
11     <RAM>256</RAM>
12  </computer:laptop>
```

Fig. 19.15 | XML document using the laptop element defined in computer.xsd.

binds the namespace prefix computer to the namespace http://www.deitel.com/computer. Line 7 identifies this namespace as the targetNamespace—the namespace being defined by the current XML Schema document.

To design the XML elements for describing laptop computers, we first create a simple type in lines 9–13 using the ***simpleType*** element. We name this simpleType gigahertz because it will be used to describe the clock speed of the processor in gigahertz. Simple types are restrictions of a type typically called a ***base type***. For this simpleType, line 10 declares the base type as decimal, and we restrict the value to be at least 2.1 by using the ***minInclusive*** element in line 11.

Next, we declare a complexType named CPU that has ***simpleContent*** (lines 16–20). Remember that a complex type with simple content can have attributes but not child elements. Also recall that complex types with simple content must extend or restrict some XML Schema type or user-defined type. The ***extension*** element with attribute ***base*** (line 17) sets the base type to string. In this complexType, we extend the base type string with an attribute. The ***attribute*** element (line 18) gives the complexType an attribute of type string named model. Thus an element of type CPU must contain string text (because the base type is string) and may contain a model attribute that is also of type string.

Lastly we define type portable, which is a complexType with complex content (lines 23–31). Such types are allowed to have child elements and attributes. The element ***all*** (lines 24–29) encloses elements that must each be included once in the corresponding XML instance document. These elements can be included in any order. This complex type holds four elements—processor, monitor, CPUSpeed and RAM. They are given types CPU, int, gigahertz and int, respectively. When using types CPU and gigahertz, we must include the namespace prefix computer, because these user-defined types are part of the computer namespace (http://www.deitel.com/computer)—the namespace defined in the current document (line 7). Also, portable contains an attribute defined in line 30. The attribute element indicates that elements of type portable contain an attribute of type string named manufacturer.

Line 33 declares the actual element that uses the three types defined in the schema. The element is called laptop and is of type portable. We must use the namespace prefix computer in front of portable.

We have now created an element named laptop that contains child elements processor, monitor, CPUSpeed and RAM, and an attribute manufacturer. Figure 19.15 uses the laptop element defined in the computer.xsd schema. Once again, we used an online XSD schema validator (apps.gotdotnet.com/xmltools/xsdvalidator) to ensure that this XML instance document adheres to the schema's structural rules.

Line 5 declares namespace prefix computer. The laptop element requires this prefix because it is part of the http://www.deitel.com/computer namespace. Line 6 sets the laptop's manufacturer attribute, and lines 8–11 use the elements defined in the schema to describe the laptop's characteristics.

In this section, we introduced W3C XML Schema documents for defining the structure of XML documents, and we validated XML instance documents against schemas using an online XSD schema validator. Section 19.9 demonstrates programmatically validating XML documents against schemas using .NET Framework classes. This allows you to ensure that a C# program manipulates only valid documents—manipulating an invalid document that is missing required pieces of data could cause errors in the program.

19.7 (Optional) Extensible Stylesheet Language and XSL Transformations

Extensible Stylesheet Language (*XSL*) documents specify how programs are to render XML document data. XSL is a group of three technologies—*XSL-FO* (*XSL Formatting Objects*), *XPath* (*XML Path Language*) and *XSLT* (*XSL Transformations*). XSL-FO is a vocabulary for specifying formatting, and XPath is a string-based language of expressions used by XML and many of its related technologies for effectively and efficiently locating structures and data (such as specific elements and attributes) in XML documents.

The third portion of XSL—XSL Transformations (XSLT)—is a technology for transforming XML documents into other documents—i.e., transforming the structure of the XML document data to another structure. XSLT provides elements that define rules for transforming one XML document to produce a different XML document. This is useful when you want to use data in multiple applications or on multiple platforms, each of which may be designed to work with documents written in a particular vocabulary. For example, XSLT allows you to convert a simple XML document to an *XHTML* (*Extensible HyperText Markup Language*) document that presents the XML document's data (or a subset of the data) formatted for display in a Web browser. (See Fig. 19.16 for a sample "before" and "after" view of such a transformation.) XHTML is the W3C technical recommendation that replaces HTML for marking up Web content. For more information on XHTML, see Appendix F, Introduction to XHTML: Part 1, and Appendix G, Introduction to XHTML: Part 2, and visit www.w3.org.

Transforming an XML document using XSLT involves two tree structures—the *source tree* (i.e., the XML document to be transformed) and the *result tree* (i.e., the XML document to be created). XPath is used to locate parts of the source tree document that match *templates* defined in an *XSL style sheet*. When a match occurs (i.e., a node matches a template), the matching template executes and adds its result to the result tree. When there are no more matches, XSLT has transformed the source tree into the result tree. The XSLT does not analyze every node of the source tree; it selectively navigates the source tree using XPath's `select` and `match` attributes. For XSLT to function, the source tree must be properly structured. Schemas, DTDs and validating parsers can validate document structure before using XPath and XSLTs.

A Simple XSL Example

Figure 19.16 lists an XML document that describes various sports. The output shows the result of the transformation (specified in the XSLT template of Fig. 19.17) rendered by Internet Explorer 6.

```
 1  <?xml version = "1.0"?>
 2  <?xml:stylesheet type = "text/xsl" href = "sports.xsl"?>
 3
 4  <!-- Fig. 19.16: sports.xml -->
 5  <!-- Sports Database -->
 6
 7  <sports>
 8     <game id = "783">
 9        <name>Cricket</name>
10
11        <paragraph>
12           More popular among commonwealth nations.
13        </paragraph>
14     </game>
15
16     <game id = "239">
17        <name>Baseball</name>
18
19        <paragraph>
20           More popular in America.
21        </paragraph>
22     </game>
23
24     <game id = "418">
25        <name>Soccer (Futbol)</name>
26
27        <paragraph>
28           Most popular sport in the world.
29        </paragraph>
30     </game>
31  </sports>
```

Fig. 19.16 | XML document that describes various sports. (Part 1 of 2.)

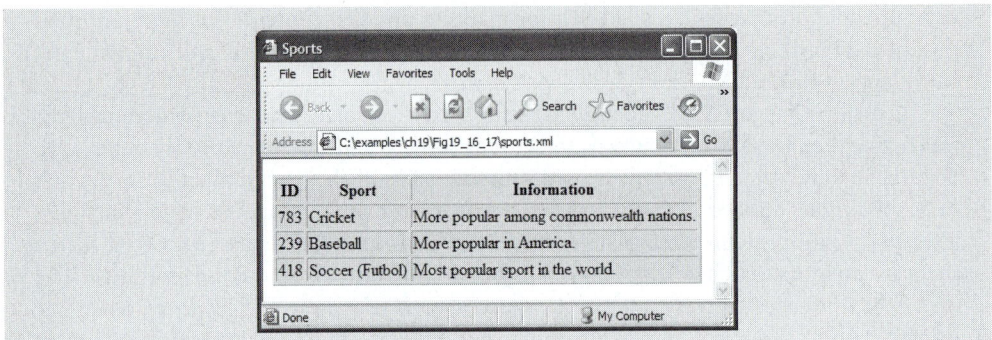

Fig. 19.16 | XML document that describes various sports. (Part 2 of 2.)

To perform transformations, an XSLT processor is required. Popular XSLT processors include Microsoft's MSXML and the Apache Software Foundation's *Xalan 2* (xml.apache.org). The XML document shown in Fig. 19.16 is transformed into an XHTML document by MSXML when the document is loaded in Internet Explorer. MSXML is both an XML parser and an XSLT processor.

Line 2 (Fig. 19.16) is a *processing instruction* (*PI*) that references the XSL style sheet sports.xsl (Fig. 19.17). A processing instruction is embedded in an XML document and provides application-specific information to whichever XML processor the application uses. In this particular case, the processing instruction specifies the location of an XSLT document with which to transform the XML document. The characters *<?* and *?>* (line 2, Fig. 19.16) delimit a processing instruction, which consists of a *PI target* (e.g., xml:stylesheet) and a *PI value* (e.g., type = "text/xsl" href = "sports.xsl"). The PI value's type attribute specifies that sports.xsl is a text/xsl file (i.e., a text file containing XSL content). The href attribute specifies the name and location of the style sheet to apply—in this case, sports.xsl in the current directory.

Software Engineering Observation 19.5

XSL enables document authors to separate data presentation (specified in XSL documents) from data description (specified in XML documents).

Figure 19.17 shows the XSL document for transforming the structured data of the XML document of Fig. 19.16 into an XHTML document for presentation. By convention, XSL documents have the filename extension *.xsl*.

Lines 6–7 begin the XSL style sheet with the *stylesheet* start tag. Attribute *version* specifies the XSLT version to which this document conforms. Line 7 binds namespace prefix *xsl* to the W3C's XSLT URI (i.e., http://www.w3.org/1999/XSL/Transform).

Lines 9–12 use element *xsl:output* to write an XHTML document type declaration (DOCTYPE) to the result tree (i.e., the XML document to be created). The DOCTYPE identifies XHTML as the type of the resulting document. Attribute method is assigned "xml", which indicates that XML is being output to the result tree. (Recall that XHTML is a type of XML.) Attribute *omit-xml-declaration* specifies whether the transformation should write the XML declaration to the result tree. In this case, we do not want to omit the XML declaration, so we assign to this attribute the value "no". Attributes doctype-system and doctype-public write the DOCTYPE DTD information to the result tree.

```
 1    <?xml version = "1.0"?>
 2    <!-- Fig. 19.17: sports.xsl -->
 3    <!-- A simple XSLT transformation -->
 4
 5    <!-- reference XSL style sheet URI -->
 6    <xsl:stylesheet version = "1.0"
 7       xmlns:xsl = "http://www.w3.org/1999/XSL/Transform">
 8
 9       <xsl:output method = "xml" omit-xml-declaration = "no"
10          doctype-system =
11             "http://www.w3c.org/TR/xhtml1/DTD/xhtml1-strict.dtd"
12          doctype-public = "-//W3C//DTD XHTML 1.0 Strict//EN"/>
13
14       <xsl:template match = "/"> <!-- match root element -->
15
16       <html xmlns = "http://www.w3.org/1999/xhtml">
17          <head>
18             <title>Sports</title>
19          </head>
20
21          <body>
22             <table border = "1" bgcolor = "wheat">
23                <thead>
24                   <tr>
25                      <th>ID</th>
26                      <th>Sport</th>
27                      <th>Information</th>
28                   </tr>
29                </thead>
30
31                <!-- insert each name and paragraph element value -->
32                <!-- into a table row. -->
33                <xsl:for-each select = "/sports/game">
34                   <tr>
35                      <td><xsl:value-of select = "@id"/></td>
36                      <td><xsl:value-of select = "name"/></td>
37                      <td><xsl:value-of select = "paragraph"/></td>
38                   </tr>
39                </xsl:for-each>
40             </table>
41          </body>
42       </html>
43
44       </xsl:template>
45    </xsl:stylesheet>
```

Fig. 19.17 | XSLT that creates elements and attributes in an XHTML document.

XSLT uses *templates* (i.e., *xsl:template* elements) to describe how to transform particular nodes from the source tree to the result tree. A template is applied to nodes that are specified in the required match attribute. Line 14 uses the *match* attribute to select the *document root* (i.e., the conceptual part of the document that contains the root element and everything below it) of the XML source document (i.e., sports.xml). The XPath character **/** (a forward slash) always selects the document root. Recall that XPath is a string-based language used to locate parts of an XML document easily. In XPath, a leading forward slash specifies that we are using *absolute addressing* (i.e., we are starting from the root and defining paths down the source tree). In the XML document of Fig. 19.16, the child nodes of the document root are the two processing instruction nodes (lines 1–2), the two comment nodes (lines 4–5) and the sports element node (lines 7–31). The template in Fig. 19.17, line 14, matches a node (i.e., the root node), so the contents of the template are now added to the result tree.

The MSXML processor writes the XHTML in lines 16–29 (Fig. 19.17) to the result tree exactly as it appears in the XSL document. Now the result tree consists of the DOCTYPE definition and the XHTML code from lines 16–29. Lines 33–39 use element ***xsl:for-each*** to iterate through the source XML document, searching for game elements. The xsl:for-each element is similar to C#'s foreach statement. Attribute ***select*** is an XPath expression that specifies the nodes (called the *node set*) on which the xsl:for-each operates. Again, the first forward slash means that we are using absolute addressing. The forward slash between sports and game indicates that game is a child node of sports. Thus, the xsl:for-each finds game nodes that are children of the sports node. The XML document sports.xml contains only one sports node, which is also the document root node. After finding the elements that match the selection criteria, the xsl:for-each processes each element with the code in lines 34–38 (these lines produce one row in a table each time they execute) and places the result of lines 34–38 in the result tree.

Line 35 uses element ***value-of*** to retrieve attribute id's value and place it in a td element in the result tree. The XPath symbol **@** specifies that id is an attribute node of the context node game. Lines 36–37 place the name and paragraph element values in td elements and insert them in the result tree. When an XPath expression has no beginning forward slash, the expression uses *relative addressing*. Omitting the beginning forward slash tells the ***xsl:value-of select*** statements to search for name and paragraph elements that are children of the context node, not the root node. Due to the last XPath expression selection, the current context node is game, which indeed has an id attribute, a name child element and a paragraph child element.

Using XSLT to Sort and Format Data

Figure 19.18 presents an XML document (sorting.xml) that marks up information about a book. Note that several elements of the markup describing the book appear out of order (e.g., the element describing Chapter 3 appears before the element describing Chapter 2). We arranged them this way purposely to demonstrate that the XSL style sheet referenced in line 5 (sorting.xsl) can sort the XML file's data for presentation purposes.

```
1   <?xml version = "1.0"?>
2   <!-- Fig. 19.18: sorting.xml -->
3   <!-- XML document containing book information -->
4
5   <?xml:stylesheet type = "text/xsl" href = "sorting.xsl"?>
6
7   <book isbn = "999-99999-9-X">
8      <title>Deitel&apos;s XML Primer</title>
```

Fig. 19.18 | XML document containing book information. (Part 1 of 2.)

```
 9
10     <author>
11        <firstName>Jane</firstName>
12        <lastName>Blue</lastName>
13     </author>
14
15     <chapters>
16        <frontMatter>
17           <preface pages = "2" />
18           <contents pages = "5" />
19           <illustrations pages = "4" />
20        </frontMatter>
21
22        <chapter number = "3" pages = "44">Advanced XML</chapter>
23        <chapter number = "2" pages = "35">Intermediate XML</chapter>
24        <appendix number = "B" pages = "26">Parsers and Tools</appendix>
25        <appendix number = "A" pages = "7">Entities</appendix>
26        <chapter number = "1" pages = "28">XML Fundamentals</chapter>
27     </chapters>
28
29     <media type = "CD" />
30  </book>
```

Fig. 19.18 | XML document containing book information. (Part 2 of 2.)

Figure 19.19 presents an XSL document (`sorting.xsl`) for transforming `sorting.xml` (Fig. 19.18) to XHTML. Recall that an XSL document navigates a source tree and builds a result tree. In this example, the source tree is XML, and the output tree is XHTML. Line 14 of Fig. 19.19 matches the root element of the document in Fig. 19.18. Line 15 outputs an `html` start tag to the result tree. The `<xsl:apply-templates/>` element (line 16) specifies that the XSLT processor is to apply the `xsl:templates` defined in this XSL document to the current node's (i.e., the document root's) children. The content from the applied templates is output in the `html` element that ends at line 17. Lines 21–84 specify a template that matches element `book`. The template indicates how to format the information contained in `book` elements of `sorting.xml` (Fig. 19.18) as XHTML.

```
 1   <?xml version = "1.0"?>
 2   <!-- Fig. 19.19: sorting.xsl -->
 3   <!-- Transformation of book information into XHTML -->
 4
 5   <xsl:stylesheet version = "1.0"
 6      xmlns:xsl = "http://www.w3.org/1999/XSL/Transform">
 7
 8      <!-- write XML declaration and DOCTYPE DTD information -->
 9      <xsl:output method = "xml" omit-xml-declaration = "no"
10         doctype-system = "http://www.w3.org/TR/xhtml11/DTD/xhtml11.dtd"
11         doctype-public = "-//W3C//DTD XHTML 1.1//EN"/>
12
```

Fig. 19.19 | XSL document that transforms `sorting.xml` into XHTML. (Part 1 of 3.)

```
13       <!-- match document root -->
14       <xsl:template match = "/">
15          <html xmlns = "http://www.w3.org/1999/xhtml">
16             <xsl:apply-templates/>
17          </html>
18       </xsl:template>
19
20       <!-- match book -->
21       <xsl:template match = "book">
22          <head>
23             <title>ISBN <xsl:value-of select = "@isbn"/> -
24                <xsl:value-of select = "title"/></title>
25          </head>
26
27          <body>
28             <h1 style = "color: blue"><xsl:value-of select = "title"/></h1>
29             <h2 style = "color: blue">by
30                <xsl:value-of select = "author/lastName"/>,
31                <xsl:value-of select = "author/firstName"/></h2>
32
33             <table style = "border-style: groove; background-color: wheat">
34
35                <xsl:for-each select = "chapters/frontMatter/*">
36                   <tr>
37                      <td style = "text-align: right">
38                         <xsl:value-of select = "name()"/>
39                      </td>
40
41                      <td>
42                         ( <xsl:value-of select = "@pages"/> pages )
43                      </td>
44                   </tr>
45                </xsl:for-each>
46
47                <xsl:for-each select = "chapters/chapter">
48                   <xsl:sort select = "@number" data-type = "number"
49                      order = "ascending"/>
50                   <tr>
51                      <td style = "text-align: right">
52                         Chapter <xsl:value-of select = "@number"/>
53                      </td>
54
55                      <td>
56                         <xsl:value-of select = "text()"/>
57                         ( <xsl:value-of select = "@pages"/> pages )
58                      </td>
59                   </tr>
60                </xsl:for-each>
61
62                <xsl:for-each select = "chapters/appendix">
63                   <xsl:sort select = "@number" data-type = "text"
64                      order = "ascending"/>
```

Fig. 19.19 | XSL document that transforms sorting.xml into XHTML. (Part 2 of 3.)

```
65                    <tr>
66                        <td style = "text-align: right">
67                            Appendix <xsl:value-of select = "@number"/>
68                        </td>
69
70                        <td>
71                            <xsl:value-of select = "text()"/>
72                            ( <xsl:value-of select = "@pages"/> pages )
73                        </td>
74                    </tr>
75                </xsl:for-each>
76            </table>
77
78            <br /><p style = "color: blue">Pages:
79            <xsl:variable name = "pagecount"
80                select = "sum(chapters//*/@pages)"/>
81            <xsl:value-of select = "$pagecount"/>
82            <br />Media Type: <xsl:value-of select = "media/@type"/></p>
83        </body>
84    </xsl:template>
85 </xsl:stylesheet>
```

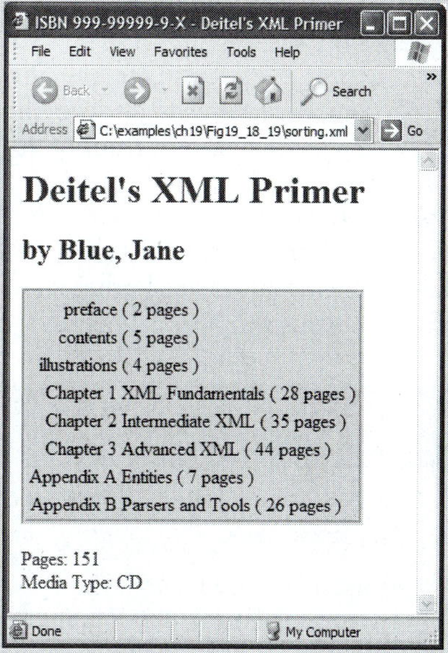

Fig. 19.19 | XSL document that transforms `sorting.xml` into XHTML. (Part 3 of 3.)

Lines 23–24 create the title for the XHTML document. We use the book's ISBN (from attribute `isbn`) and the contents of element `title` to create the string that appears in the browser window's title bar (**ISBN 999-99999-9-X - Deitel's XML Primer**).

Line 28 creates a header element that contains the book's title. Lines 29–31 create a header element that contains the book's author. Because the context node (i.e., the current node being processed) is book, the XPath expression `author/lastName` selects the author's last name, and the expression `author/firstName` selects the author's first name.

Line 35 selects each element (indicated by an asterisk) that is a child of element frontMatter. Line 38 calls *node-set function **name*** to retrieve the current node's element name (e.g., preface). The current node is the context node specified in the xsl:for-each (line 35). Line 42 retrieves the value of the pages attribute of the current node.

Line 47 selects each chapter element. Lines 48–49 use element ***xsl:sort*** to sort chapters by number in ascending order. Attribute ***select*** selects the value of attribute number in context node chapter. Attribute ***data-type***, with value "number", specifies a numeric sort, and attribute ***order***, with value "ascending", specifies ascending order. Attribute data-type also accepts the value "text" (line 63), and attribute order also accepts the value "descending". Line 56 uses *node-set function **text*** to obtain the text between the chapter start and end tags (i.e., the name of the chapter). Line 57 retrieves the value of the pages attribute of the current node. Lines 62–75 perform similar tasks for each appendix.

Lines 79–80 use an *XSL variable* to store the value of the book's total page count and output the page count to the result tree. Attribute ***name*** specifies the variable's name (i.e., pagecount), and attribute select assigns a value to the variable. Function ***sum*** (line 80) totals the values for all page attribute values. The two slashes between chapters and * indicate a *recursive descent*—the MSXML processor will search for elements that contain an attribute named pages in all descendant nodes of chapters. The XPath expression

```
//*
```

selects all the nodes in an XML document. Line 81 retrieves the value of the newly created XSL variable pagecount by placing a dollar sign in front of its name.

Summary of XSL Style Sheet Elements

This section's examples used several predefined XSL elements to perform various operations. Figure 19.20 lists these elements and several other commonly used XSL elements. For more information on these elements and XSL in general, see www.w3.org/Style/XSL.

Element	Description
`<xsl:apply-templates>`	Applies the templates of the XSL document to the children of the current node.
`<xsl:apply-templates match = "expression">`	Applies the templates of the XSL document to the children of *expression*. The value of the attribute match (i.e., *expression*) must be an XPath expression that specifies elements.
`<xsl:template>`	Contains rules to apply when a specified node is matched.
`<xsl:value-of select = "expression">`	Selects the value of an XML element and adds it to the output tree of the transformation. The required select attribute contains an XPath expression.
`<xsl:for-each select = "expression">`	Applies a template to every node selected by the XPath specified by the select attribute.

Fig. 19.20 | XSL style sheet elements. (Part 1 of 2.)

Element	Description
`<xsl:sort select = "`*expression*`">`	Used as a child element of an `<xsl:apply-templates>` or `<xsl:for-each>` element. Sorts the nodes selected by the `<xsl:apply-template>` or `<xsl:for-each>` element so that the nodes are processed in sorted order.
`<xsl:output>`	Has various attributes to define the format (e.g., XML, XHTML), version (e.g., 1.0, 2.0), document type and media type of the output document. This tag is a top-level element—it can be used only as a child element of an `xml:stylesheet`.
`<xsl:copy>`	Adds the current node to the output tree.

Fig. 19.20 | XSL style sheet elements. (Part 2 of 2.)

This section introduced Extensible Stylesheet Language (XSL) and showed how to create XSL transformations to convert XML documents from one format to another. We showed how to transform XML documents to XHTML documents for display in a Web browser. Recall that these transformations are performed by MSXML, Internet Explorer's built-in XML parser and XSLT processor. In most business applications, XML documents are transferred between business partners and are transformed to other XML vocabularies programmatically. In Section 19.10, we demonstrate how to perform XSL transformations using the `XslCompiledTransform` class provided by the .NET Framework.

19.8 (Optional) Document Object Model (DOM)

Although an XML document is a text file, retrieving data from the document using traditional sequential file processing techniques is neither practical nor efficient, especially for adding and removing elements dynamically.

Upon successfully parsing a document, some XML parsers store document data as tree structures in memory. Figure 19.21 illustrates the tree structure for the root element of the document `article.xml` discussed in Fig. 19.2. This hierarchical tree structure is called a *Document Object Model* (*DOM*) *tree*, and an XML parser that creates this type of structure is known as a *DOM parser*. Each element name (e.g., `article`, `date`, `firstName`) is represented by a node. A node that contains other nodes (called *child nodes* or children) is called a *parent node* (e.g., `author`). A parent node can have many children, but a child node can have only one parent node. Nodes that are peers (e.g., `firstName` and `lastName`) are called *sibling nodes*. A node's *descendant nodes* include its children, its children's children and so on. A node's *ancestor nodes* include its parent, its parent's parent and so on.

The DOM tree has a single *root node*, which contains all the other nodes in the document. For example, the root node of the DOM tree that represents `article.xml` (Fig. 19.2) contains a node for the XML declaration (line 1), two nodes for the comments (lines 2–3) and a node for the XML document's root element `article` (line 5).

Classes for creating, reading and manipulating XML documents are located in the C# namespace *System.Xml*. This namespace also contains additional namespaces that provide other XML-related operations.

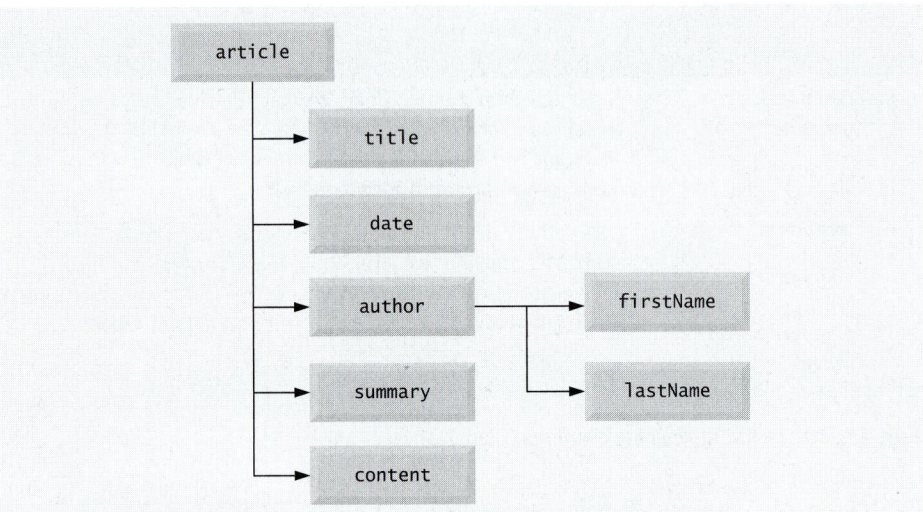

Fig. 19.21 | Tree structure for the document `article.xml` of Fig. 19.2.

Reading an XML Document with an *XmlReader*

In this section, we present several examples that use DOM trees. Our first example, the program in Fig. 19.22, loads the XML document presented in Fig. 19.2 and displays its data in a text box. This example uses class *XmlReader* to iterate through each node in the XML document.

Line 5 is a using declaration for the System.Xml namespace, which contains the XML classes used in this example. Class XmlReader is an abstract class that defines the interface for reading XML documents. We cannot create an XmlReader object directly. Instead, we must invoke XmlReader's static method *Create* to obtain an XmlReader reference (line 21). Before doing so, however, we must prepare an XmlReaderSettings object that specifies how we would like the XmlReader to behave (line 20). In this example, we use the default settings of the properties of an XmlReaderSettings object. Later, you will learn how to set certain properties of the XmlReaderSettings class to instruct the XmlReader to perform validation, which it does not do by default. The static method Create receives as arguments the name of the XML document to read and an XmlReaderSettings object. In this example the XML document article.xml (Fig. 19.2) is opened when method

```
1    // Fig. 19.22: XmlReaderTest.cs
2    // Reading an XML document.
3    using System;
4    using System.Windows.Forms;
5    using System.Xml;
6
7    namespace XmlReaderTest
8    {
9       public partial class XmlReaderTestForm : Form
10      {
```

Fig. 19.22 | XmlReader iterating through an XML document. (Part 1 of 3.)

```
11          public XmlReaderTestForm()
12          {
13             InitializeComponent();
14          } // end constructor
15
16          // read XML document and display its content
17          private void XmlReaderTestForm_Load( object sender, EventArgs e )
18          {
19             // create the XmlReader object
20             XmlReaderSettings settings = new XmlReaderSettings();
21             XmlReader reader = XmlReader.Create( "article.xml", settings );
22
23             int depth = -1; // tree depth is -1, no indentation
24
25             while ( reader.Read() ) // display each node's content
26             {
27                switch ( reader.NodeType )
28                {
29                   case XmlNodeType.Element: // XML Element, display its name
30                      depth++; // increase tab depth
31                      TabOutput( depth ); // insert tabs
32                      OutputTextBox.Text += "<" + reader.Name + ">\r\n";
33
34                      // if empty element, decrease depth
35                      if ( reader.IsEmptyElement )
36                         depth--;
37                      break;
38                   case XmlNodeType.Comment: // XML Comment, display it
39                      TabOutput( depth ); // insert tabs
40                      OutputTextBox.Text += "<!--" + reader.Value + "-->\r\n";
41                      break;
42                   case XmlNodeType.Text: // XML Text, display it
43                      TabOutput( depth ); // insert tabs
44                      OutputTextBox.Text += "\t" + reader.Value + "\r\n";
45                      break;
46
47                   // XML XMLDeclaration, display it
48                   case XmlNodeType.XmlDeclaration:
49                      TabOutput( depth ); // insert tabs
50                      OutputTextBox.Text += "<?" + reader.Name + " " +
51                         reader.Value + "?>\n";
52                      break;
53                   case XmlNodeType.EndElement: // XML EndElement, display it
54                      TabOutput( depth ); // insert tabs
55                      OutputTextBox.Text += "</" + reader.Name + ">\r\n";
56                      depth--; // decrement depth
57                      break;
58                } // end switch
59             } // end while
60          } // end method XmlReaderTextForm_Load
61
```

Fig. 19.22 | XmlReader iterating through an XML document. (Part 2 of 3.)

```
62          // insert tabs
63          private void TabOutput( int number )
64          {
65             for ( int i = 0; i < number; i++ )
66                OutputTextBox.Text += "\t";
67          } // end method TabOutput
68       } // end class XmlReaderTestForm
69    } // end namespace XmlReaderTest
```

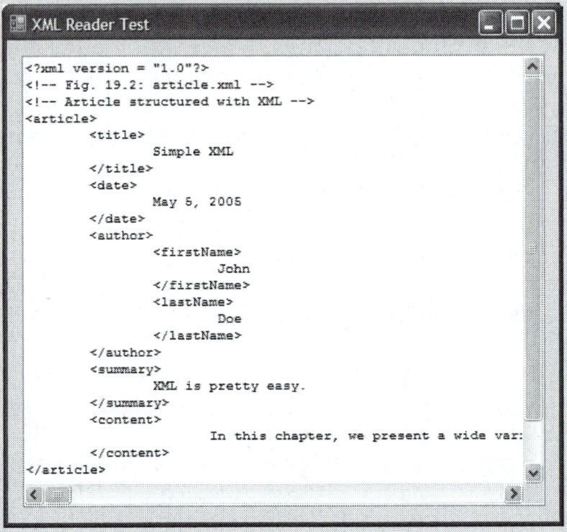

Fig. 19.22 | XmlReader iterating through an XML document. (Part 3 of 3.)

Create is invoked in line 21. Once the XmlReader is created, the XML document's contents can be read programmatically.

Method **Read** of XmlReader reads one node from the DOM tree. By calling this method in the while loop condition (line 27), reader Reads all the document nodes. The switch statement (lines 27–58) processes each node. Either the Name property (lines 32, 50 and 55), which contains the node's name, or the Value property (lines 40 and 44), which contains the node's data, is formatted and concatenated to the string assigned to the TextBox's Text property. The XmlReader's NodeType property specifies whether the node is an element, comment, text, XML declaration or end element. Note that each case specifies a node type using **XmlNodeType** enumeration constants. For example, XmlNode-Type.Element (line 31) indicates the start tag of an element.

The displayed output emphasizes the structure of the XML document. Variable depth (line 23) maintains the number of tab characters to indent each element. The depth is incremented each time the program encounters an Element and is decremented each time the program encounters an EndElement or empty element. We use a similar technique in the next example to emphasize the tree structure of the XML document being displayed.

Displaying a DOM Tree Graphically in a *TreeView* Control

XmlReaders do not provide features for displaying their content graphically. In this example, we display an XML document's contents using a **TreeView** control. We use class **TreeNode** to represent each node in the tree. Class TreeView and class TreeNode are part of the `System.Windows.Forms` namespace. `TreeNodes` are added to the `TreeView` to emphasize the structure of the XML document.

The C# program in Fig. 19.23 demonstrates how to manipulate a DOM tree programmatically to display it graphically in a `TreeView` control. The GUI for this application contains a `TreeView` control named `xmlTreeView` (declared in `XmlDom.Designer.cs`). The application loads `letter.xml` (Fig. 19.24) into `XmlReader` (line 27), then displays the document's tree structure in the `TreeView` control. [*Note:* The version of `letter.xml` in Fig. 19.24 is nearly identical to the one in Fig. 19.4, except that Fig. 19.24 does not reference a DTD as line 5 of Fig. 19.4 does.]

In `XmlDomForm`'s Load event handler (lines 19–34), lines 23–24 create an `XmlReaderSettings` object and set its *IgnoreWhitespace* property to `true` so that the insignificant

```
I    // Fig. 19.23: XmlDom.cs
2    // Demonstrates DOM tree manipulation.
3    using System;
4    using System.Windows.Forms;
5    using System.Xml;
6
7    namespace XmlDom
8    {
9       public partial class XmlDomForm : Form
10      {
11         public XmlDomForm()
12         {
13            InitializeComponent();
14         } // end constructor
15
16         private TreeNode tree; // TreeNode reference
17
18         // initialize instance variables
19         private void XmlDomForm_Load( object sender, EventArgs e )
20         {
21            // create Xml ReaderSettings and
22            // set the IgnoreWhitespace property
23            XmlReaderSettings settings = new XmlReaderSettings();
24            settings.IgnoreWhitespace = true;
25
26            // create XmlReader object
27            XmlReader reader = XmlReader.Create( "letter.xml", settings );
28
29            tree = new TreeNode(); // instantiate TreeNode
30
31            tree.Text = "letter.xml"; // assign name to TreeNode
32            xmlTreeView.Nodes.Add( tree ); // add TreeNode to TreeView
33            BuildTree( reader, tree ); // build node and tree hierarchy
34         } // end method XmlDomForm_Load
35
36         // construct TreeView based on DOM tree
37         private void BuildTree( XmlReader reader, TreeNode treeNode )
38         {
```

Fig. 19.23 | DOM structure of an XML document displayed in a `TreeView`. (Part 1 of 3.)

```
39              // treeNode to add to existing tree
40              TreeNode newNode = new TreeNode();
41
42              while ( reader.Read() )
43              {
44                  // build tree based on node type
45                  switch ( reader.NodeType )
46                  {
47                      // if Text node, add its value to tree
48                      case XmlNodeType.Text:
49                          newNode.Text = reader.Value;
50                          treeNode.Nodes.Add( newNode );
51                          break;
52                      case XmlNodeType.EndElement: // if EndElement, move up tree
53                          treeNode = treeNode.Parent;
54                          break;
55
56                      // if new element, add name and traverse tree
57                      case XmlNodeType.Element:
58
59                          // determine if element contains content
60                          if ( !reader.IsEmptyElement )
61                          {
62                              // assign node text, add newNode as child
63                              newNode.Text = reader.Name;
64                              treeNode.Nodes.Add( newNode );
65
66                              // set treeNode to last child
67                              treeNode = newNode;
68                          } // end if
69                          else // do not traverse empty elements
70                          {
71                              // assign NodeType string to newNode
72                              // and add it to tree
73                              newNode.Text = reader.NodeType.ToString();
74                              treeNode.Nodes.Add( newNode );
75                          } // end else
76                          break;
77                      default: // all other types, display node type
78                          newNode.Text = reader.NodeType.ToString();
79                          treeNode.Nodes.Add( newNode );
80                          break;
81                  } // end switch
82
83                  newNode = new TreeNode();
84              } // end while
85
86              // update TreeView control
87              xmlTreeView.ExpandAll(); // expand tree nodes in TreeView
88              xmlTreeView.Refresh(); // force TreeView to update
89          } // end method BuildTree
90      } // end class XmlDomForm
91  } // end namespace XmlDom
```

Fig. 19.23 | DOM structure of an XML document displayed in a `TreeView`. (Part 2 of 3.)

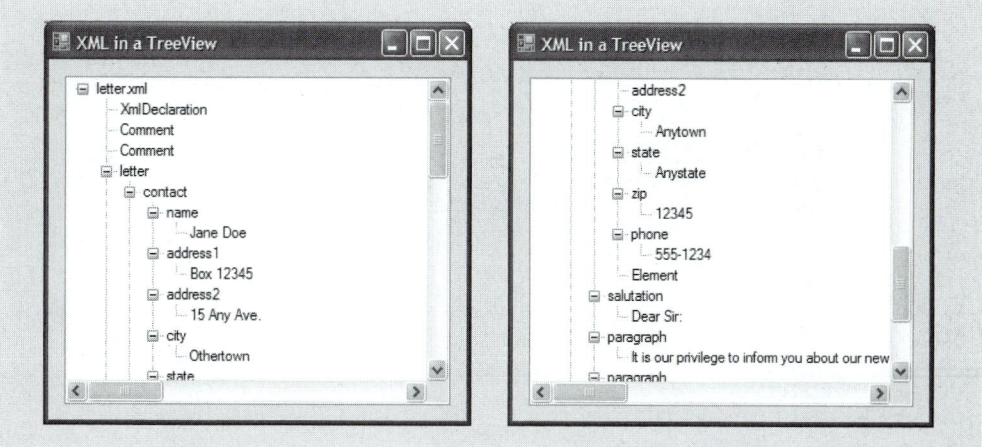

Fig. 19.23 | DOM structure of an XML document displayed in a `TreeView`. (Part 3 of 3.)

whitespaces in the XML document are ignored. Line 27 then invokes static `XmlReader` method `Create` to parse and load `letter.xml`.

Line 29 creates the `TreeNode tree` (declared in line 16). This `TreeNode` is used as a graphical representation of a DOM tree node in the `TreeView` control. Line 31 assigns the XML document's name (i.e., `letter.xml`) to tree's `Text` property. Line 32 calls method `Add` to add the new `TreeNode` to the `TreeView`'s `Nodes` collection. Line 33 calls method `BuildTree` to update the `TreeView` so that it displays source's complete DOM tree.

Method `BuildTree` (lines 37–89) receives an `XmlReader` for reading the XML document and a `TreeNode` referencing the current location in the tree (i.e., the `TreeNode` most recently added to the `TreeView` control). Line 40 declares `TreeNode` reference `newNode`, which will be used for adding new nodes to the `TreeView`. Lines 42–84 iterate through each node in the XML document's DOM tree.

The `switch` statement in lines 45–81 adds a node to the `TreeView`, based on the `Xml-Reader`'s current node. When a text node is encountered, the `Text` property of the new `TreeNode`—`newNode`—is assigned the current node's value (line 49). Line 50 adds this `TreeNode` to `treeNode`'s node list (i.e., adds the node to the `TreeView` control).

Line 52 matches an `EndElement` node type. This `case` moves up the tree to the current node's parent because the end of an element has been encountered. Line 53 accesses `treeNode`'s **Parent** property to retrieve the node's current parent.

Line 57 matches `Element` node types. Each non-empty `Element` `NodeType` (line 60) increases the depth of the tree; thus, we assign the current `reader` `Name` to the `newNode`'s `Text` property and add the `newNode` to `treeNode`'s node list (lines 63–64). Line 67 assigns the `newNode`'s reference to `treeNode` to ensure that `treeNode` refers to the last child `TreeNode` in the node list. If the current `Element` node is an empty element (line 69), we assign to the `newNode`'s `Text` property the string representation of the `NodeType` (line 73). Next, the `newNode` is added to the `treeNode` node list (line 74). The default `case` (lines 77–80) assigns the string representation of the node type to the `newNode` `Text` property, then adds the `newNode` to the `TreeNode` node list.

After the entire DOM tree is processed, the `TreeNode` node list is displayed in the `TreeView` control (lines 87–88). `TreeView` method **ExpandAll** causes all the nodes of the

```
 1    <?xml version = "1.0"?>
 2    <!-- Fig. 19.24: letter.xml -->
 3    <!-- Business letter formatted with XML -->
 4
 5    <letter>
 6       <contact type = "sender">
 7          <name>Jane Doe</name>
 8          <address1>Box 12345</address1>
 9          <address2>15 Any Ave.</address2>
10          <city>Othertown</city>
11          <state>Otherstate</state>
12          <zip>67890</zip>
13          <phone>555-4321</phone>
14          <flag gender = "F" />
15       </contact>
16
17       <contact type = "receiver">
18          <name>John Doe</name>
19          <address1>123 Main St.</address1>
20          <address2></address2>
21          <city>Anytown</city>
22          <state>Anystate</state>
23          <zip>12345</zip>
24          <phone>555-1234</phone>
25          <flag gender = "M" />
26       </contact>
27
28       <salutation>Dear Sir:</salutation>
29
30       <paragraph>It is our privilege to inform you about our new database
31          managed with XML. This new system allows you to reduce the
32          load on your inventory list server by having the client machine
33          perform the work of sorting and filtering the data.
34       </paragraph>
35
36       <paragraph>Please visit our Web site for availability
37          and pricing.
38       </paragraph>
39
40       <closing>Sincerely,</closing>
41       <signature>Ms. Doe</signature>
42    </letter>
```

Fig. 19.24 | Business letter marked up as XML.

tree to be displayed. TreeView method **Refresh** updates the display to show the newly added TreeNodes. Note that while the application is running, clicking nodes (i.e., the **+** or **–** boxes) in the TreeView either expands or collapses them.

Locating Data in XML Documents with XPath

Although XmlReader includes methods for reading and modifying node values, it is not the most efficient means of locating data in a DOM tree. The Framework Class Library provides class **XPathNavigator** in the **System.Xml.XPath** namespace for iterating through node lists that match search criteria, which are written as XPath expressions. Recall that

XPath (XML Path Language) provides a syntax for locating specific nodes in XML documents effectively and efficiently. XPath is a string-based language of expressions used by XML and many of its related technologies (such as XSLT, discussed in Section 19.7).

Figure 19.25 uses an XPathNavigator to navigate an XML document and uses a TreeView control and TreeNode objects to display the XML document's structure. In this example, the TreeNode node list is updated each time the XPathNavigator is positioned to a new node, rather than displaying the entire DOM tree at once. Nodes are added to and deleted from the TreeView to reflect the XPathNavigator's location in the DOM tree. Figure 19.26 shows the XML document sports.xml that we use in this example. [*Note:* The versions of sports.xml presented in Fig. 19.26 and Fig. 19.16 are nearly identical. In the current example, we do not want to apply an XSLT, so we omit the processing instruction found in line 2 of Fig. 19.16.]

```
1   // Fig. 19.25: PathNavigator.cs
2   // Demonstrates class XPathNavigator.
3   using System;
4   using System.Windows.Forms;
5   using System.Xml.XPath; // contains XPathNavigator
6
7   namespace PathNavigator
8   {
9      public partial class PathNavigatorForm : Form
10     {
11        public PathNavigatorForm()
12        {
13           InitializeComponent();
14        } // end constructor
15
16        private XPathNavigator xPath; // navigator to traverse document
17
18        // references document for use by XPathNavigator
19        private XPathDocument document;
20
21        // references TreeNode list used by TreeView control
22        private TreeNode tree;
23
24        // initialize variables and TreeView control
25        private void PathNavigatorForm_Load( object sender, EventArgs e )
26        {
27           // load XML document
28           document = new XPathDocument( "sports.xml" );
29           xPath = document.CreateNavigator(); // create navigator
30           tree = new TreeNode(); // create root node for TreeNodes
31
32           tree.Text = xPath.NodeType.ToString(); // #root
33           pathTreeView.Nodes.Add( tree ); // add tree
34
35           // update TreeView control
36           pathTreeView.ExpandAll(); // expand tree node in TreeView
37           pathTreeView.Refresh(); // force TreeView update
```

Fig. 19.25 | XPathNavigator navigating selected nodes. (Part 1 of 5.)

```
38              pathTreeView.SelectedNode = tree; // highlight root
39          } // end method PathNavigatorForm_Load
40
41          // process selectButton_Click event
42          private void selectButton_Click( object sender, EventArgs e )
43          {
44              XPathNodeIterator iterator; // enables node iteration
45
46              try // get specified node from ComboBox
47              {
48                  // select specified node
49                  iterator = xPath.Select( selectComboBox.Text );
50                  DisplayIterator( iterator ); // print selection
51              } // end try
52              // catch invalid expressions
53              catch ( System.Xml.XPath.XPathException argumentException )
54              {
55                  MessageBox.Show( argumentException.Message, "Error",
56                      MessageBoxButtons.OK, MessageBoxIcon.Error );
57              } // end catch
58          } // end method selectButton_Click
59
60          // traverse to first child on firstChildButton_Click event
61          private void firstChildButton_Click( object sender, EventArgs e )
62          {
63              TreeNode newTreeNode;
64
65              // move to first child
66              if ( xPath.MoveToFirstChild() )
67              {
68                  newTreeNode = new TreeNode(); // create new node
69
70                  // set node's Text property to
71                  // either navigator's name or value
72                  DetermineType( newTreeNode, xPath );
73
74                  // add nodes to TreeNode node list
75                  tree.Nodes.Add( newTreeNode );
76                  tree = newTreeNode; // assign tree newTreeNode
77
78                  // update TreeView control
79                  pathTreeView.ExpandAll(); // expand node in TreeView
80                  pathTreeView.Refresh(); // force TreeView to update
81                  pathTreeView.SelectedNode = tree; // highlight root
82              } // end if
83              else // node has no children
84                  MessageBox.Show( "Current Node has no children.",
85                      "", MessageBoxButtons.OK, MessageBoxIcon.Information );
86          } // end method firstChildButton_Click
87
88          // traverse to node's parent on parentButton_Click event
89          private void parentButton_Click( object sender, EventArgs e )
90          {
```

Fig. 19.25 | XPathNavigator navigating selected nodes. (Part 2 of 5.)

```
 91                    // move to parent
 92                    if ( xPath.MoveToParent() )
 93                    {
 94                       tree = tree.Parent;
 95
 96                       // get number of child nodes, not including sub trees
 97                       int count = tree.GetNodeCount( false );
 98
 99                       // remove all children
100                       for ( int i = 0; i < count; i++ )
101                          tree.Nodes.Remove( tree.FirstNode ); // remove child node
102
103                       // update TreeView control
104                       pathTreeView.ExpandAll(); // expand node in TreeView
105                       pathTreeView.Refresh(); // force TreeView to update
106                       pathTreeView.SelectedNode = tree; // highlight root
107                    } // end if
108                    else // if node has no parent (root node)
109                       MessageBox.Show( "Current node has no parent.", "",
110                          MessageBoxButtons.OK, MessageBoxIcon.Information );
111                 } // end method parentButton_Click
112
113                 // find next sibling on nextButton_Click event
114                 private void nextButton_Click( object sender, EventArgs e )
115                 {
116                    // declare and initialize two TreeNodes
117                    TreeNode newTreeNode = null;
118                    TreeNode newNode = null;
119
120                    // move to next sibling
121                    if ( xPath.MoveToNext() )
122                    {
123                       newTreeNode = tree.Parent; // get parent node
124
125                       newNode = new TreeNode(); // create new node
126
127                       // decide whether to display current node
128                       DetermineType( newNode, xPath );
129                       newTreeNode.Nodes.Add( newNode ); // add to parent node
130
131                       tree = newNode; // set current position for display
132
133                       // update TreeView control
134                       pathTreeView.ExpandAll(); // expand node in Tree''''View
135                       pathTreeView.Refresh(); // force TreeView to update
136                       pathTreeView.SelectedNode = tree; // highlight root
137                    } // end if
138                    else // node has no additional siblings
139                       MessageBox.Show( "Current node is last sibling.", "",
140                          MessageBoxButtons.OK, MessageBoxIcon.Information );
141                 } // end method nextButton_Click
```

Fig. 19.25 | XPathNavigator navigating selected nodes. (Part 3 of 5.)

```
142
143        // get previous sibling on previousButton_Click
144        private void previousButton_Click( object sender, EventArgs e )
145        {
146            TreeNode parentTreeNode = null;
147
148            // move to previous sibling
149            if ( xPath.MoveToPrevious() )
150            {
151                parentTreeNode = tree.Parent; // get parent node
152                parentTreeNode.Nodes.Remove( tree ); // delete current node
153                tree = parentTreeNode.LastNode; // move to previous node
154
155                // update TreeView control
156                pathTreeView.ExpandAll(); // expand tree node in TreeView
157                pathTreeView.Refresh(); // force TreeView to update
158                pathTreeView.SelectedNode = tree; // highlight root
159            } // end if
160            else // if current node has no previous siblings
161                MessageBox.Show( "Current node is first sibling.", "",
162                    MessageBoxButtons.OK, MessageBoxIcon.Information );
163        } // end method previousButton_Click
164
165        // print values for XPathNodeIterator
166        private void DisplayIterator( XPathNodeIterator iterator )
167        {
168            selectTextBox.Clear();
169
170            // prints selected node's values
171            while ( iterator.MoveNext() )
172                selectTextBox.Text += iterator.Current.Value.Trim() + "\r\n";
173        } // end method DisplayIterator
174
175        // determine if TreeNode should display current node name or value
176        private void DetermineType( TreeNode node, XPathNavigator xPath )
177        {
178            switch ( xPath.NodeType ) // determine NodeType
179            {
180                case XPathNodeType.Element: // if Element, get its name
181                    // get current node name, and remove whitespaces
182                    node.Text = xPath.Name.Trim();
183                    break;
184                default: // obtain node values
185                    // get current node value and remove whitespaces
186                    node.Text = xPath.Value.Trim();
187                    break;
188            } // end switch
189        } // end method DetermineType
190    } // end class PathNavigatorForm
191 } // end namespace PathNavigator
```

Fig. 19.25 | XPathNavigator navigating selected nodes. (Part 4 of 5.)

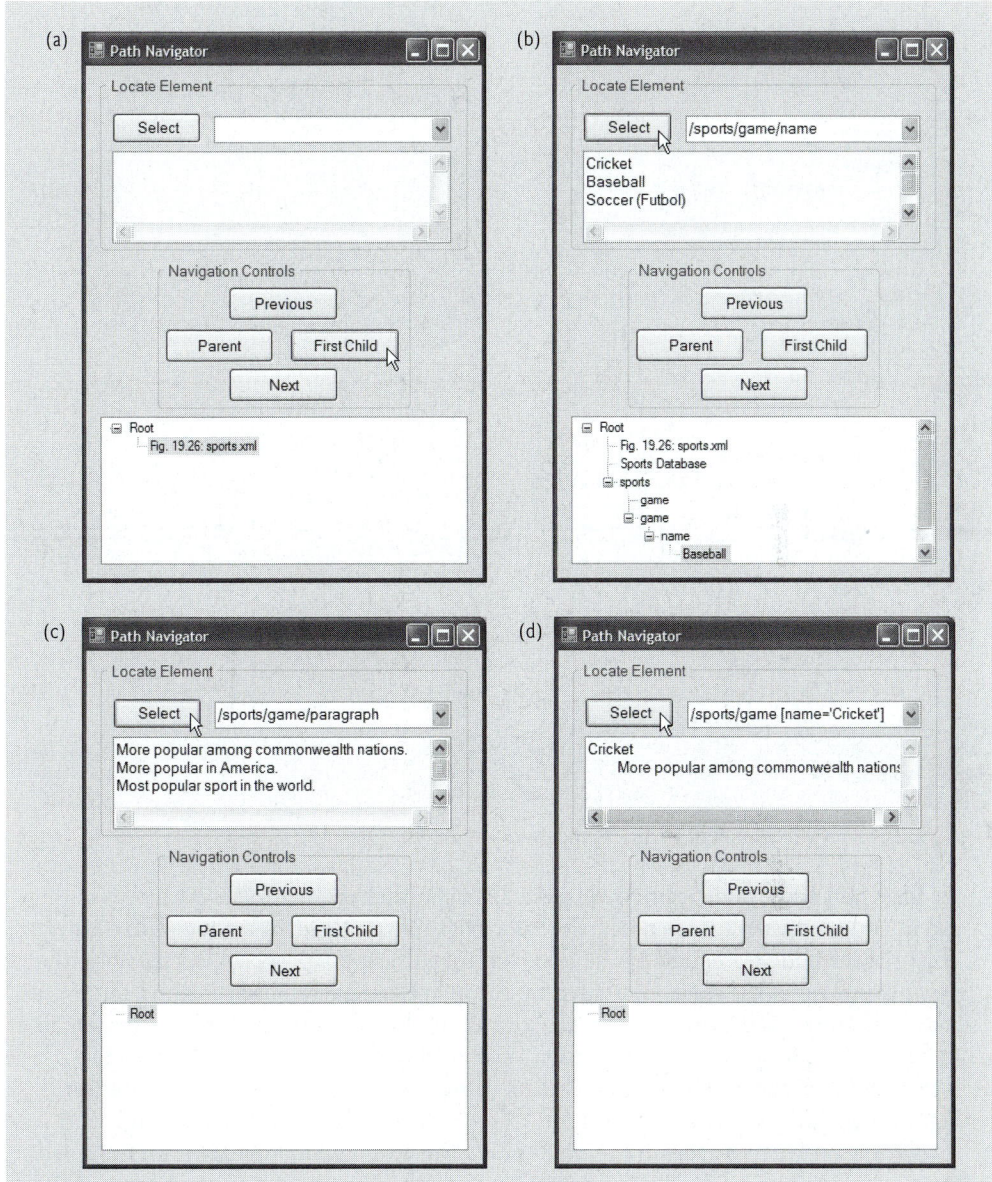

Fig. 19.25 | XPathNavigator navigating selected nodes. (Part 5 of 5.)

The program of Fig. 19.25 loads XML document sports.xml (Fig. 19.26) into an **XPathDocument** object by passing the document's file name to the XPathDocument constructor (line 28). Method **CreateNavigator** (line 29) creates and returns an XPathNavigator reference to the XPathDocument's tree structure.

The navigation methods of XPathNavigator are **MoveToFirstChild** (line 66), **MoveToParent** (line 92), **MoveToNext** (line 121) and **MoveToPrevious** (line 149). Each method performs the action that its name implies. Method MoveToFirstChild moves to

```
 1   <?xml version = "1.0"?>
 2   <!-- Fig. 19.26: sports.xml -->
 3   <!-- Sports Database        -->
 4
 5   <sports>
 6      <game id = "783">
 7         <name>Cricket</name>
 8
 9         <paragraph>
10            More popular among commonwealth nations.
11         </paragraph>
12      </game>
13
14      <game id = "239">
15         <name>Baseball</name>
16
17         <paragraph>
18            More popular in America.
19         </paragraph>
20      </game>
21
22      <game id = "418">
23         <name>Soccer (Futbol)</name>
24
25         <paragraph>
26            Most popular sport in the world.
27         </paragraph>
28      </game>
29   </sports>
```

Fig. 19.26 | XML document that describes various sports.

the first child of the node referenced by the XPathNavigator, MoveToParent moves to the parent node of the node referenced by the XPathNavigator, MoveToNext moves to the next sibling of the node referenced by the XPathNavigator and MoveToPrevious moves to the previous sibling of the node referenced by the XPathNavigator. Each method returns a bool indicating whether the move was successful. In this example, we display a warning in a MessageBox whenever a move operation fails. Furthermore, each method is called in the event handler of the button that matches its name (e.g., clicking the **First Child** button in Fig. 19.25(a) triggers firstChildButton_Click, which calls MoveToFirstChild).

Whenever we move forward using XPathNavigator, as with MoveToFirstChild and MoveToNext, nodes are added to the TreeNode node list. The private method Determine-Type (lines 176–189) determines whether to assign the Node's *Name* property or *Value* property to the TreeNode (lines 182 and 186). Whenever MoveToParent is called, all the children of the parent node are removed from the display. Similarly, a call to MoveToPrevious removes the current sibling node. Note that the nodes are removed only from the TreeView, not from the tree representation of the document.

The selectButton_Click event handler (lines 42–58) corresponds to the **Select** button. XPathNavigator method Select (line 49) takes search criteria in the form of either an *XPathExpression* or a string that represents an XPath expression, and returns as an XPathNodeIterator object any node that matches the search criteria. Figure 19.27

XSLT processor included in Internet Explorer (i.e., MSXML) performed the transformations.

Performing an XSL Transformation in C# Using the .NET Framework

Figure 19.30 applies the style sheet sports.xsl (Fig. 19.17) to sports.xml (Fig. 19.26) programmatically. The result of the transformation is written to an XHTML file on disk and displayed in a text box. Figure 19.30(c) shows the resulting XHTML document (sports.html) when it is viewed in Internet Explorer.

Line 5 is a using declaration for the **System.Xml.Xsl** namespace, which contains class **XslCompiledTransform** for applying XSLT style sheets to XML documents. Line 17 declares XslCompiledTransform reference transformer. An object of this type serves as an

```
 1   // Fig. 19.30: TransformTest.cs
 2   // Applying an XSLT style sheet to an XML document.
 3   using System;
 4   using System.Windows.Forms;
 5   using System.Xml.Xsl; // contains class XslCompiledTransform
 6
 7   namespace TransformTest
 8   {
 9      public partial class TransformTestForm : Form
10      {
11         public TransformTestForm()
12         {
13            InitializeComponent();
14         } // end constructor
15
16         // applies the transformation
17         private XslCompiledTransform transformer;
18
19         // initialize variables
20         private void TransformTestForm_Load( object sender, EventArgs e )
21         {
22            transformer = new XslCompiledTransform(); // create transformer
23
24            // load and compile the style sheet
25            transformer.Load( "sports.xsl" );
26         } // end method TransformTestForm_Load
27
28         // transform XML data on transformButton_Click event
29         private void transformButton_Click( object sender, EventArgs e )
30         {
31            // perform the transformation and store the result in new file
32            transformer.Transform( "sports.xml", "sports.html" );
33
34            // read and display the XHTML document's text in a Textbox
35            consoleTextBox.Text =
36               System.IO.File.ReadAllText( "sports.html" );
37         } // end method transformButton_Click
38      } // end class TransformTestForm
39   } // end namespace TransformTest
```

Fig. 19.30 | XSLT style sheet applied to an XML document. (Part 1 of 2.)

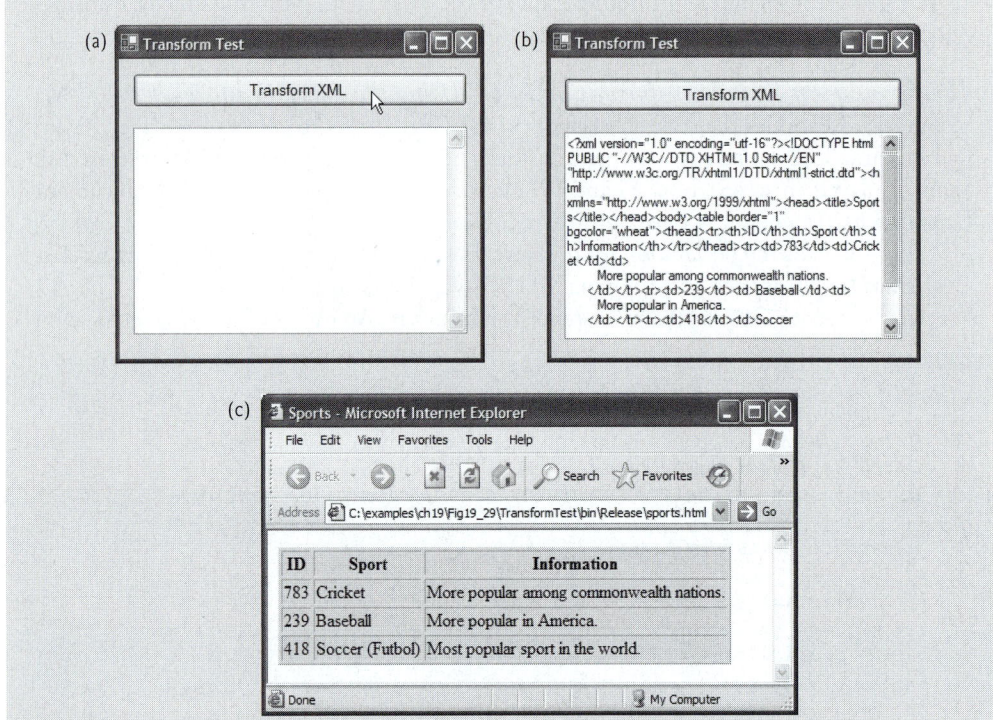

Fig. 19.30 | XSLT style sheet applied to an XML document. (Part 2 of 2.)

XSLT processor (like MSXML in earlier examples) to transform XML data from one format to another.

In event handler `TransformTestForm_Load` (lines 20–26), line 22 creates a new `XslCompiledTransform` object. Then line 25 calls the `XslCompiledTransform` object's ***Load*** method, which parses and loads the style sheet that this application uses. This method takes an argument specifying the name and location of the style sheet—`sports.xsl` (Fig. 19.17) located in the current directory.

Event handler `transformButton_Click` (lines 29–37) calls method ***Transform*** of class `XslCompiledTransform` to apply the style sheet (`sports.xsl`) to `sports.xml` (line 32). This method takes two `string` arguments—the first specifies the XML file to which the style sheet should be applied, and the second specifies the file in which the result of the transformation should be stored on disk. Thus the `Transform` method call in line 32 transforms `sports.xml` to XHTML and writes the result to disk as the file `sports.html`. Figure 19.30(c) shows the new XHTML document rendered in Internet Explorer. Note that the output is identical to that of Fig. 19.16—in the current example, though, the XHTML is stored on disk rather than generated dynamically by MSXML.

After applying the transformation, the program displays the content of the newly created `sports.html` file in the `txtConsole` TextBox, as shown in Fig. 19.30(b). Lines 35–36 obtain the text of the file by passing its name to method `ReadAllText` of the `System.IO.File` class provided by the FCL to simplify file-processing tasks on the local system.

19.11 Wrap-Up

In this chapter, we studied Extensible Markup Language and several of its related technologies. We began by discussing some basic XML terminology, introducing the concepts of markup, XML vocabularies and XML parsers (validating and nonvalidating). We then demonstrated how to describe and structure data in XML, illustrating these points with examples marking up an article and a business letter.

The chapter discussed the concept of an XML namespace. You learned that each namespace has a unique name that provides a means for document authors to unambiguously refer to elements with the same name (i.e., prevent naming collisions). We presented examples of defining two namespaces in the same document, as well as setting the default namespace for a document.

We also discussed how to create DTDs and schemas for specifying and validating the structure of an XML document. We showed how to use various tools to confirm whether XML documents are valid (i.e., conform to a DTD or schema).

The chapter also demonstrated how to create and use XSL documents to specify rules for converting XML documents between formats. Specifically, you learned how to format and sort XML data as XHTML for display in a Web browser.

The final sections of the chapter presented more advanced uses of XML in C# applications. We demonstrated how to retrieve and display data from an XML document using various classes of the .NET Framework. We illustrated how a Document Object Model (DOM) tree represents each element of an XML document as a node in the tree. The chapter also demonstrated reading data from an XML document using the XmlReader class, displaying DOM trees graphically and locating data in XML documents with XPath. Finally, we showed how to use .NET Framework classes XmlReader and XslCompiledTransform to perform schema validation and XSL transformations, respectively.

In Chapter 20, we begin our discussion of databases, which organize data in such a way that the data can be selected and updated quickly. We introduce Structured Query Language (SQL) for writing simple database queries (i.e., searches) and ADO.NET for manipulating information in a database through C#. You will learn how to create XML documents based on data in a database.

19.12 Web Resources

www.w3.org/XML
The W3C (World Wide Web Consortium) facilitates the development of common protocols to ensure interoperability on the Web. Its XML page includes information about upcoming events, publications, software, discussion groups and the latest developments in XML.

www.xml.org
xml.org is a reference for XML, DTDs, schemas and namespaces.

www.w3.org/Style/XSL
This W3C site provides information on XSL, including such topics as XSL development, learning XSL, XSL-enabled tools, the XSL specification, FAQs and XSL history.

www.w3.org/TR
This is the W3C technical reports and publications site. It contains links to working drafts, proposed recommendations and other resources.

www.xmlbooks.com
This site provides a list of XML books recommended by Charles Goldfarb, one of the original designers of GML (General Markup Language), from which SGML, HTML and XML were derived.

`www.xml-zone.com`

The DevX XML Zone is a complete resource for XML information. This site includes FAQs, news, articles and links to other XML sites and newsgroups.

`wdvl.internet.com/Authoring/Languages/XML`

The Web Developer's Virtual Library XML site includes tutorials, FAQs, the latest news and extensive links to XML sites and software downloads.

`www.xml.com`

This site provides the latest news and information about XML, conference listings, links to XML Web resources organized by topic, tools and other resources.

`msdn.microsoft.com/xml/default.aspx`

The MSDN XML Development Center features articles on XML, Ask-the-Experts chat sessions, samples, demos, newsgroups and other helpful information.

`www.oasis-open.org/cover/xml.html`

This site includes links to several FAQs, online resources, industry initiatives, demos, conferences and tutorials.

`www-106.ibm.com/developerworks/xml`

The IBM developerWorks XML site is a great resource for developers that provides news, tools, a library, case studies and information about XML-related events and standards.

`www.devx.com/projectcool/door/7051`

The Project Cool DevX site includes several tutorials covering introductory through advanced XML topics.

`www.ucc.ie/xml`

This site provides a detailed XML FAQ. Developers can read responses to some popular questions or submit their own questions through the site.

`www.w3.org/XML/Schema`

This W3C site provides information on XML Schema, including links, tools, resources and the XML Schema specification.

`tools.decisionsoft.com/schemaValidate.html`

DecisionSoft provides a free online XML Schema validator from DecisionSoft.

`www.sun.com/software/xml/developers/multischema/`

The Web page for downloading the Sun Multi-Schema XML Validator (MSV), which validates XML documents against several kinds of schemas.

`en.wikipedia.org/wiki/EBNF`

This site provides detailed information about Extended Backus-Naur Form (EBNF).

`www.garshol.priv.no/download/text/bnf.html`

This site introduces Backus-Naur Form (BNF) and EBNF, and discusses the differences between these notations.

`www.w3schools.com/schema/default.asp`

This site provides an XML Schema tutorial.

`www.w3.org/2001/03/webdata/xsv`

This is an online tool for validating XML Schema documents.

`apps.gotdotnet.com/xmltools/xsdvalidator`

This is an online tool for validating XML documents against an XML Schema.

`www.w3.org/TR/xmlschema-2`

This is part 2 of the W3C XML Schema specification, which defines the data types allowed in an XML Schema.

Summary

Section 19.1 Introduction
- XML is a portable, widely supported, open (i.e., nonproprietary) technology for data storage and exchange.
- The Framework Class Library provides an extensive set of XML-related classes. Much of Visual Studio's internal implementation also employs XML.

Section 19.2 XML Basics
- XML documents are readable by both humans and machines.
- XML permits document authors to create custom markup for any type of information. This enables document authors to create entirely new markup languages that describe specific types of data, including mathematical formulas, chemical molecular structures, music and recipes.
- An XML parser is responsible for identifying components of XML documents (typically files with the .xml extension) and then storing those components in a data structure for manipulation.
- An XML document can optionally reference a Document Type Definition (DTD) or schema that defines the XML document's structure.
- An XML document that conforms to a DTD/schema (i.e., has the appropriate structure) is valid.
- If an XML parser (validating or nonvalidating) can process an XML document successfully, that XML document is well formed.

Section 19.3 Structuring Data
- An XML document begins with an optional XML declaration, which identifies the document as an XML document. The version attribute specifies the version of XML syntax used in the document.
- XML comments begin with <!-- and end with -->.
- An XML document contains text that represents its content (i.e., data) and elements that specify its structure. XML documents delimit an element with start and end tags.
- The root element of an XML document encompasses all its other elements.
- XML element names can be of any length and can contain letters, digits, underscores, hyphens and periods. However, they must begin with either a letter or an underscore, and they should not begin with "xml" in any combination of uppercase and lowercase letters as this is reserved for use in the XML standards.
- When a user loads an XML document in Internet Explorer, MSXML parses the document, and Internet Explorer uses a style sheet to format the data for display.
- Internet Explorer displays minus (–) or plus (+) signs next to all container elements. A minus sign indicates that all child elements are being displayed. When clicked, a minus sign becomes a plus sign (which collapses the container element and hides all the children), and vice versa.
- Data can be placed between tags or in attributes (name-value pairs that appear within the angle brackets of start tags). Elements can have any number of attributes.

Section 19.4 XML Namespaces
- XML allows document authors to create their own markup, and as a result, naming collisions (i.e., two different elements that have the same name) can occur. XML namespaces provide a means for document authors to prevent collisions.
- Each namespace prefix is bound to a uniform resource identifier (URI) that uniquely identifies the namespace. A URI is a series of characters that differentiate names. Document authors create

their own namespace prefixes. Any name can be used as a namespace prefix but the namespace prefix `xml` is reserved for use in XML standards.

- To eliminate the need to place a namespace prefix in each element, authors can specify a default namespace for an element and its children. We declare a default namespace using keyword `xmlns` with a URI (Uniform Resource Identifier) as its value.

- Document authors commonly use URLs (Uniform Resource Locators) for URIs, because domain names (e.g., `deitel.com`) in URLs must be unique.

Section 19.5 Document Type Definitions (DTDs)

- DTDs and schemas specify documents' element types and attributes, and their relationships to one another.

- DTDs and schemas enable an XML parser to verify whether an XML document is valid (i.e., its elements contain the proper attributes and appear in the proper sequence).

- A DTD expresses the set of rules for document structure using an EBNF (Extended Backus-Naur Form) grammar.

- In a DTD, an `ELEMENT` element type declaration defines the rules for an element. An `ATTLIST` attribute-list declaration defines attributes for a particular element.

Section 19.6 W3C XML Schema Documents

- Unlike DTDs, schemas do not use EBNF grammar. Instead, they use XML syntax and are themselves XML documents that programs can manipulate.

- Unlike DTDs, XML Schema documents can specify what type of data (e.g., numeric, text) an element can contain.

- An XML document that conforms to a schema document is schema valid.

- Two categories of data types exist in XML Schema: simple types and complex types. Simple types cannot contain attributes or child elements; complex types can.

- Every simple type defines a restriction on an XML Schema–defined schema data type or on a user-defined type.

- Complex types can have either simple content or complex content. Both simple content and complex content can contain attributes, but only complex content can contain child elements.

- Whereas complex types with simple content must extend or restrict some other existing type, complex types with complex content do not have this limitation.

Section 19.7 (Optional) Extensible Stylesheet Language and XSL Transformations

- XSL can convert XML into any text-based document. XSL documents have the extension `.xsl`.

- XPath is a string-based language of expressions used by XML and many of its related technologies for effectively and efficiently locating structures and data (such as specific elements and attributes) in XML documents.

- XPath is used to locate parts of the source tree document that match templates defined in an XSL style sheet. When a match occurs (i.e., a node matches a template), the matching template executes and adds its result to the result tree. When there are no more matches, XSLT has transformed the source tree into the result tree.

- The XSLT does not analyze every node of the source tree; it selectively navigates the source tree using XPath's `select` and `match` attributes.

- For XSLT to function, the source tree must be properly structured. Schemas, DTDs and validating parsers can validate document structure before using XPath and XSLTs.

- XSL style sheets can be connected directly to an XML document by adding an xml:stylesheet processing instruction to the XML document.

- Two tree structures are involved in transforming an XML document using XSLT—the source tree (the XML document being transformed) and the result tree (the result of the transformation).

- The XPath character / (a forward slash) always selects the document root. In XPath, a leading forward slash specifies that we are using absolute addressing.

- When an XPath expression has no beginning forward slash, the expression uses relative addressing.

- XSL element value-of retrieves an attribute's value. The @ symbol specifies an attribute node.

- XSL node-set function name retrieves the current node's element name.

- XSL node-set function text retrieves the text between an element's start and end tags.

- The XPath expression //* selects all the nodes in an XML document.

Section 19.8 (Optional) Document Object Model (DOM)

- Upon successfully parsing a document, some XML parsers store document data as tree structures in memory. This hierarchical tree structure is called a Document Object Model (DOM) tree, and an XML parser that creates this type of structure is known as a DOM parser.

- In the DOM, each element name represents a node. A node that contains children is called a parent node. A parent node can have many children, but a child node can have only one parent node. Nodes that are peers are called sibling nodes.

- A node's descendant nodes include its children, its children's children and so on. A node's ancestor nodes include its parent, its parent's parent and so on.

- The DOM tree has a single root node that contains all the other nodes in the document.

- Namespace System.Xml contains classes for creating, reading and manipulating XML documents.

- Class XmlReader is an abstract class that defines the interface for reading XML documents.

- XmlReader's static method Create obtains a new XmlReader object.

- An XmlReaderSettings object specifies how we would like the XmlReader to behave.

- By default, an XmlReader does not perform validation.

- Method Create receives as arguments the name of the XML document to read and an XmlReaderSettings object.

- An XML document is opened when method Create is invoked to create an XmlReader object. The document can then be read programmatically.

- Method Read of XmlReader reads one node from the DOM tree.

- The Name property contains the node's name, the Value property contains the node's data and the NodeType property contains the node's type (i.e., element, comment, text).

- A TreeView control can be used to display an XML document's contents graphically. Objects of class TreeNode represent each node in the tree.

- Class XPathNavigator in the System.Xml.XPath namespace can iterate through node lists that match search criteria written as XPath expressions.

- XPath provides a syntax for locating specific nodes in XML documents. XPath is a string-based language of expressions used by XML and many of its related technologies.

- XPathNavigator method MoveToFirstChild moves to the first child of the node referenced by the XPathNavigator, MoveToParent moves to the parent node of the node referenced by the XPath-Navigator, MoveToNext moves to the next sibling of the node referenced by the XPathNavigator and MoveToPrevious moves to the previous sibling of the node referenced by the XPathNavigator.

Section 19.9 (Optional) Schema Validation with Class XmlReader

- Class XmlReader can validate an XML document as it reads and parses the document.
- Class XmlSchemaSet stores a collection of schemas against which an XmlReader can validate.
- XmlReader static method Create returns a reference to an XmlReader object created based on an XmlReaderSettings object that specifies how the XmlReader is to behave.
- Setting XmlReaderSettings's ValidationType property to ValidationType.Schema indicates that the XmlReader is to perform validation against an XML Schema as it reads an XML document.
- The Schemas property of an XmlReaderSettings object sets the schema(s) used to validate the document read by the XmlReader.
- If created with XmlReaderSettings property ValidationType set to ValidationType.Schema, an XmlReader validates each node in an XML document with each call to the object's Read method.
- When an XmlReader encounters an invalid node, the method registered with its XmlReaderSettings object's ValidationEventHandler is called.

Section 19.10 (Optional) XSLT with Class XslCompiledTransform

- The System.Xml.Xsl namespace contains class XslCompiledTransform for applying XSLT style sheets to XML documents.
- XslCompiledTransform method Load loads and compiles a style sheet.
- XslCompiledTransform method Transform applies the compiled style sheet to a specified XML document. This method takes two string arguments: the name of the XML file to which the style sheet should be applied and the name of the file to store the transformation result.

Terminology

Sections 19.1–19.6

/ forward slash (end tag of XML element)
<!-- and --> XML comment delimiters
all element
angle brackets (<>)
asterisk (*) occurrence indicator
ATTLIST attribute-list declaration
attribute of XML element
attribute value
base attribute of element restriction
base attribute of element extension
base type
CDATA keyword
character data
character entity reference
child element
complex content in XML Schema
complex type

complexType element
container element
default namespace
Document Type Definition (DTD)
.dtd filename extension
element element (XML Schema)
ELEMENT element type declaration
empty element
EMPTY keyword
end tag
Export XML parser
Extensible HyperText Markup Language (XHTML)
Extensible Markup Language (XML)
Extensible Stylesheet Language (XSL)
extension element
external DTD

#FIXED keyword
forward slash character (/)
#IMPLIED keyword
markup
maxOccurs attribute of element element
Microsoft XML Core Services (MSXML)
minInclusive element
minOccurs attribute of element element
name attribute of element element
namespace prefix
naming collision
nested element
node
nonvalidating XML parser
occurrence indicator
open technology
parent element
parsed character data
parser
#PCDATA keyword
plus sign (+) occurrence indicator
prolog of an XML document
question mark (?) occurrence indicator
#REQUIRED keyword
restriction on built-in schema data type
root
root element (XML)
schema
schema element
schema repository
schema-valid XML document
schema-invalid XML document

simple content in XML Schema
simple type
simpleContent XML Schema element
simpleType XML Schema element
start tag
style sheet
SYSTEM keyword in XML
targetNamespace attribute of schema element
type attribute of element element
unbounded value of attribute maxOccurs
Uniform Resource Identifier (URI)
Uniform Resource Locator (URL)
Uniform Resource Name (URN)
valid XML document
validating XML parser
version attribute in an XML declaration
well-formed XML document
World Wide Web Consortium (W3C)
Xerces
XML comment
XML declaration
XML element
.xml filename extension
XML instance document
XML namespace
XML parser
XML processor
XML Schema
XML Validator
XML vocabulary
xmlns attribute in an XML document
.xsd filename extension

Sections 19.7–19.10

/ forward slash character (XPath)
@ XPath attribute symbol
<? and ?> XML delimiters
absolute addressing
Add method of XML Schema set class
ancestor node
child node
context node
Create method of XmlReader class
CreateNavigator method of class
    XPathDocument
Current property of class XPathnodeIterator
data-type attribute of xsl:sort element
descendant node
Document Object Model (DOM)
document root

DOM parser
ExpandAll method of TreeView class
Extensible Hyper Text Markup Language
    (XHTML)
IgnoreWhitespace property of class
    XmlReaderSettings
Load method of XslCompiledTransform class
match attribute of xsl:template element
MoveNext method of class XPathNodeIterator
MoveToFirstChild method of class
    XPathNavigator
MoveToNext method of class XPathNavigator
MoveToParent method of class XPathNavigator
MoveToPrevious method of class
    XPathNavigator
name node-set function

node-set function
node set of an `xsl:for-each` element
order attribute of `xsl:sort` element
parent node
Parent property of `TreeNode` class
PI target
PI value
processing instruction (PI)
Read method of `XmlReader` class
recursive descent
Refresh method `TreeView` class
relative addressing
result tree (XSLT)
root node
Schemas property of `XmlReaderSettings` class
select attribute of `xsl:for-each` element
sibling node
source tree (XSLT)
stylesheet start tag
sum function (XSL)
`System.Xml` namespace
`System.Xml.XPath` namespace
`System.Xml.Xsl` namespace
text node-set function
`TreeNode` class
`TreeView` control
Transform method of class
    `XslCompiledTransform`

type attribute in a processing instruction
`ValidationEventHandler` of `settings` object
`ValidationType` property of class
    `XmlReaderSettings`
`ValidationType.Schema`
version attribute of `xsl:stylesheet` element
Xalan 2
`XmlNodeType` enumeration
XML Path Language (XPath)
`XmlReader` class
`XmlReaderSettings` class
`XmlSchemaSet` class
`XPathDocument` class
`XPathExpression` class
`XPathNavigator` class
`XslCompiledTransform` class
`.xsl` filename extension
XSL Formatting Objects (XSL-FO)
XSL style sheet
XSL template
XSL Transformations (XSLT)
XSL variable
`xsl:for-each` element
`xsl:output` element
`xsl:sort` element
`xsl:stylesheet` element
`xsl:template` element
`xsl:value-of` element

Self-Review Exercises

Sections 19.1–19.6

19.1   Which of the following are valid XML element names? (Select all that apply.)
    a) `yearBorn`
    b) `year.Born`
    c) `year Born`
    d) `year-Born1`
    e) `2_year_born`
    f) `_year_born_`

19.2   State which of the following statements are *true* and which are *false*. If *false*, explain why.
    a) XML is a technology for creating markup languages.
    b) XML markup is delimited by forward and backward slashes (/ and \).
    c) All XML start tags must have corresponding end tags.
    d) Parsers check an XML document's syntax.
    e) XML does not support namespaces.
    f) When creating XML elements, document authors must use the set of XML tags provided by the W3C.
    g) The pound character (#), dollar sign ($), ampersand (&) and angle brackets (< and >) are examples of XML reserved characters.

19.3 Fill in the blanks for each of the following:
    a) _____ help prevent naming collisions.
    b) _____ embed application-specific information into an XML document.
    c) _____ is Microsoft's XML parser.
    d) XSL element _____ writes a DOCTYPE to the result tree.
    e) XML Schema documents have root element _____.
    f) XSL element _____ is the root element in an XSL document.
    g) XSL element _____ selects specific XML elements using repetition.

19.4 State which of the following statements are *true* and which are *false*. If *false*, explain why.
    a) XML is not case sensitive.
    b) Xml Schemas are better than DTDs, because DTDs lack a way of indicating what specific type of data (e.g., numeric, text) an element can contain and DTDs are not themselves XML documents.
    c) DTDs are written using an XML vocabulary.
    d) Schema is a technology for locating information in an XML document.

19.5 In Fig. 19.2, we subdivided the author element into more detailed pieces. How might you subdivide the date element? Use the date May 5, 2005, as an example.

Sections 19.7–19.10

19.6 Write a processing instruction that includes style sheet wap.xsl for use in Internet Explorer.

19.7 Fill in the blanks for each of the following:
    a) Nodes that contain other nodes are called _____ nodes.
    b) Nodes that are peers are called _____ nodes.
    c) Class XmlReader is a(n) _____ class that defines the interface for reading XML documents.

19.8 Write an XPath expression that locates contact nodes in letter.xml (Fig. 19.4).

19.9 Describe method Select of class XPathNavigator.

Answers to Self-Review Exercises

Sections 19.1–19.6

19.1 a, b, d, f. [Choice c is incorrect because it contains a space. Choice e is incorrect because the first character is a number.]

19.2 a) True. b) False. In an XML document, markup text is delimited by tags enclosed in angle brackets (< and >) with a forward slash just after the < in the end tag. c) True. d) True. e) False. XML does support namespaces. f) False. When creating tags, document authors can use any valid name but should avoid ones that begin with the reserved word xml (also XML, Xml, etc.). g) False. XML reserved characters include the ampersand (&), the left-angle bracket (<) and the right-angle bracket (>), but not # and $.

19.3 a) Namespaces. b) Processing instructions. c) MSXML. d) xsl:output. e) schema. f) xsl:stylesheet. g) xsl:for-each.

19.4 a) False. XML is case sensitive. b) True. c) False. DTDs use EBNF grammar, which is not XML syntax. d) False. XPath is a technology for locating information in an XML document. XML Schema provides a means for type checking XML documents and verifying their validity.

19.5   *<date>*
       *<month>*May*</month>*
       *<day>*5*</day>*
       *<year>*2005*</year>*
    </date>.

Sections 19.7–19.10

19.6   *<?xsl:stylesheet type* = "text/xsl" *href* = "wap.xsl"*?>*

19.7   a) parent. b) sibling. c) abstract.

19.8   /letter/contact.

19.9   Method `Select` receives as an argument either an `XPathExpression` or a `string` containing an `XPathExpression`, to select nodes referenced by the navigator.

Exercises

Sections 19.1–19.6

19.10   *(Nutrition Information XML Document)* Create an XML document that marks up the nutrition facts for a package of Grandma White's cookies. A package of cookies has a serving size of 1 package and the following nutritional value per serving: 260 calories, 100 fat calories, 11 grams of fat, 2 grams of saturated fat, 5 milligrams of cholesterol, 210 milligrams of sodium, 36 grams of total carbohydrates, 2 grams of fiber, 15 grams of sugars and 5 grams of protein. Name this document `nutrition.xml`. Load the XML document into Internet Explorer. [*Hint:* Your markup should contain elements describing the product name, serving size/amount, calories, sodium, cholesterol, proteins, etc. Mark up each nutrition fact/ingredient listed above.]

19.11   *(Nutrition Information XML Schema)* Write an XML Schema document (`nutrition.xsd`) specifying the structure of the XML document created in Exercise 19.10.

Sections 19.7–19.10

19.12   *(Nutrition Information XSL Style Sheet)* Write an XSL style sheet for your solution to Exercise 19.10 that displays the nutritional facts in an XHTML table. Modify Fig. 19.30 (`TransformTest.cs`) to output an XHTML file, `nutrition.html`. Render `nutrition.html` in a Web browser.

19.13   *(Validation Against Multiple Schemas)* Alter Fig. 19.28 (`ValidationTest.cs`) to validate a selected XML file against multiple schemas—`book.xsd` and `nutrition.xsd` (Exercise 19.11). Allow the user to select either `book.xml`, `fail.xml` or `nutrition.xml` (Exercise 19.10). [*Hint:* You can add multiple schema documents to an `XmlSchemaSet`.]

19.14   *(XmlReaderTest Modification)* Modify `XmlReaderTest` (Fig. 19.22) to display `article.xml` (Fig. 19.2) in a `TreeView` instead of in a `TextBox`.

19.15   *(Sorting XSLT Modification)* Modify Fig. 19.19 (`sorting.xsl`) to sort by the number of pages rather than by chapter number. Save the modified document as `sorting_byPage.xsl`.

19.16   *(TransformTest Modification)* Modify `TransformTest` (Fig. 19.30) to use `sorting.xml` (Fig. 19.18), `sorting.xsl` (Fig. 19.19) and `sorting_byPage.xsl` (from Exercise 19.15). Display the result of transforming `sorting.xml` into two XHTML files, `sorting_byChapter.html` and `sorting_byPage.html`. [*Hint:* Remove the `xml:stylesheet` processing instruction from line 5 of `sorting.xml` before attempting to transform the file programmatically.]

20

Database, SQL and ADO.NET

OBJECTIVES

In this chapter you will learn:

- The relational database model.
- To write basic database queries in SQL.
- To add data sources to projects.
- To use the IDE's drag-and-drop capabilities to display database tables in applications.
- To use the classes of namespaces **System.Data** and **System.Data.SqlClient** to manipulate databases.
- To use ADO.NET's disconnected object model to store data from a database in local memory.
- To create XML documents from data sources.

20.1 Introduction

A *database* is an organized collection of data. Many strategies exist for organizing data to facilitate easy access and manipulation. A *database management system* (*DBMS*) provides mechanisms for storing, organizing, retrieving and modifying data for many users. Database management systems allow access to and storage of data independently of the internal representation of the data.

Today's most popular database systems are *relational databases*. A language called *SQL*—pronounced "sequel," or as its individual letters—is the international standard language used almost universally with relational databases to perform *queries* (i.e., to request information that satisfies given criteria) and to manipulate data. In this book, we pronounce SQL as "sequel."

Some popular *relational database management systems* (*RDBMS*) are Microsoft SQL Server, Oracle, Sybase, IBM DB2 and PostgreSQL. We provide URLs for these systems in Section 20.11, Web Resources. MySQL (www.mysql.com) is an increasingly popular open-source RDBMS that can be downloaded and used freely by non-commercial users. You may also be familiar with Microsoft Access—a relational database system that is part of Microsoft Office. In this chapter, we use *Microsoft SQL Server 2005 Express*—a free version of SQL Server 2005 that is installed when you install Visual C# 2005. We will refer to SQL Server 2005 Express simply as SQL Server from this point forward.

A programming language connects to and interacts with a relational database via a *database interface*—software that facilitates communication between a database management system and a program. C# programs communicate with databases and manipulate their data through *ADO.NET*. The current version of ADO.NET is 2.0. Section 20.5 presents an overview of ADO.NET's object model and the relevant namespaces and classes that allow you to work with databases in C#. However, as you will learn in subsequent sections, most of the work required to communicate with a database using ADO.NET 2.0 is performed by the IDE itself. You will work primarily with the IDE's visual programming tools and wizards, which simplify the process of connecting to and manipulating a database. Throughout this chapter, we refer to ADO.NET 2.0 simply as ADO.NET.

This chapter introduces general concepts of relational databases and SQL, then explores ADO.NET and the IDE's tools for accessing data sources. The examples in Sections 20.6–20.9 demonstrate how to build applications that use databases to store information. In the next two chapters, you will see other practical database applications. Chapter 21, ASP.NET 2.0, Web Forms and Web Controls, presents a Web-based bookstore case study that retrieves user and book information from a database. Chapter 22, Web Services, uses a database to store airline reservation data for a Web service (i.e., a software component that can be accessed remotely over a network).

20.2 Relational Databases

A *relational database* is a logical representation of data that allows the data to be accessed independently of its physical structure. A relational database organizes data in *tables*. Figure 20.1 illustrates a sample Employees table that might be used in a personnel system. The table stores the attributes of employees. Tables are composed of *rows* and *columns* in which values are stored. This table consists of six rows and five columns. The Number column of each row in this table is the table's *primary key*—a column (or group of columns) in a table that requires a unique value that cannot be duplicated in other rows. This guarantees that a primary key value can be used to uniquely identify a row. A primary key that is composed of two or more columns is known as a *composite key*. Good examples of primary key columns in other applications are an employee ID number in a payroll system and a part number in an inventory system—values in each of these columns are guaranteed to be unique. The rows in Fig. 20.1 are displayed in order by primary key. In this case, the rows are listed in increasing (ascending) order, but they could also be listed in decreasing (descending) order or in no particular order at all. As we will demonstrate in an upcoming example, programs can specify ordering criteria when requesting data from a database.

Each column represents a different data attribute. Rows are normally unique (by primary key) within a table, but some column values may be duplicated between rows. For example, three different rows in the Employees table's Department column contain the number 413, indicating that these employees work in the same department.

Different database users are often interested in different data and different relationships among the data. Most users require only subsets of the rows and columns. To obtain these subsets, programs use SQL to define queries that select subsets of the data from a table. For example, a program might select data from the Employees table to create a query result that shows where each department is located, in increasing order by Department number (Fig. 20.2). SQL queries are discussed in Section 20.4. In Section 20.7, you will learn how to use the IDE's **Query Builder** to create SQL queries.

Table Employees

	Number	Name	Department	Salary	Location
	23603	Jones	413	1100	New Jersey
	24568	Kerwin	413	2000	New Jersey
Row	34589	Larson	642	1800	Los Angeles
	35761	Myers	611	1400	Orlando
	47132	Neumann	413	9000	New Jersey
	78321	Stephens	611	8500	Orlando

Primary key   Column

Fig. 20.1 | Employees table sample data.

Department	Location
413	New Jersey
611	Orlando
642	Los Angeles

Fig. 20.2 | Result of selecting distinct Department and Location data from the Employees table.

20.3 Relational Database Overview: Books Database

We now overview relational databases in the context of a simple Books database. The database stores information about some recent Deitel publications. First, we overview the tables of the Books database. Then we introduce database concepts, such as how to use SQL to retrieve information from the Books database and to manipulate the data. We provide the database file—Books.mdf—with the examples for this chapter (downloadable from www.deitel.com/books/csharphtp2/). SQL Server database files typically end with the .mdf ("master data file") filename extension. Section 20.6 explains how to use this file in an application.

Authors Table of the Books Database
The database consists of three tables: Authors, AuthorISBN and Titles. The Authors table (described in Fig. 20.3) consists of three columns that maintain each author's unique ID number, first name and last name, respectively. Figure 20.4 contains the data from the Authors table. We list the rows in order by the table's primary key—AuthorID. You will learn how to sort data by other criteria (e.g., in alphabetical order by last name) using SQL's ORDER BY clause in Section 20.4.3.

Titles Table of the Books Database
The Titles table (described in Fig. 20.5) consists of four columns that maintain information about each book in the database, including the ISBN, title, edition number and copyright year. Figure 20.6 contains the data from the Titles table.

Column	Description
AuthorID	Author's ID number in the database. In the Books database, this integer column is defined as an *identity* column, also known as an ***autoincremented*** column—for each row inserted in the table, the AuthorID value is increased by 1 automatically to ensure that each row has a unique AuthorID. This is the primary key.
FirstName	Author's first name (a string).
LastName	Author's last name (a string).

Fig. 20.3 | Authors table of the Books database.

AuthorID	FirstName	LastName
1	Harvey	Deitel
2	Paul	Deitel
3	Andrew	Goldberg
4	David	Choffnes

Fig. 20.4 | Data from the Authors table of the Books database.

Column	Description
ISBN	ISBN of the book (a string). The table's primary key. ISBN is an abbreviation for "International Standard Book Number"—a numbering scheme that publishers worldwide use to give every book a unique identification number.
Title	Title of the book (a string).
EditionNumber	Edition number of the book (an integer).
Copyright	Copyright year of the book (a string).

Fig. 20.5 | Titles table of the Books database.

ISBN	Title	Edition-Number	Copy-right
0131426443	C How to Program	4	2004
0131450913	Internet & World Wide Web How to Program	3	2004

Fig. 20.6 | Data from the Titles table of the Books database. (Part I of 2.)

ISBN	Title	Edition-Number	Copy-right
0131483986	Java How to Program	6	2005
0131525239	Visual C# 2005 How to Program	2	2006
0131828274	Operating Systems	3	2004
0131857576	C++ How to Program	5	2005
0131869000	Visual Basic 2005 How to Program	3	2006

Fig. 20.6 | Data from the Titles table of the Books database. (Part 2 of 2.)

AuthorISBN *Table of the Books Database*

The AuthorISBN table (described in Fig. 20.7) consists of two columns that maintain IS-BNs for each book and their corresponding authors' ID numbers. This table associates authors with their books. The AuthorID column is a *foreign key*—a column in this table that matches the primary key column in another table (i.e., AuthorID in the Authors table). The ISBN column is also a foreign key—it matches the primary key column (i.e., ISBN) in the Titles table. Together the AuthorID and ISBN columns in this table form a composite primary key. Every row in this table uniquely matches one author to one book's ISBN. Figure 20.8 contains the data from the AuthorISBN table of the Books database.

Column	Description
AuthorID	The author's ID number, a foreign key to the Authors table.
ISBN	The ISBN for a book, a foreign key to the Titles table.

Fig. 20.7 | AuthorISBN table of the Books database.

AuthorID	ISBN	AuthorID	ISBN
1	0131869000	2	0131450913
1	0131525239	2	0131426443
1	0131483986	2	0131857576
1	0131857576	2	0131483986
1	0131426443	2	0131525239
1	0131450913	2	0131869000
1	0131828274	3	0131450913
2	0131828274	4	0131828274

Fig. 20.8 | Data from the AuthorISBN table of Books.

Foreign Keys

Foreign keys can be specified when creating a table. A foreign key helps maintain the ***Rule of Referential Integrity***—every foreign key value must appear as another table's primary key value. This enables the DBMS to determine whether the AuthorID value for a particular row of the AuthorISBN table is valid. Foreign keys also allow related data in multiple tables to be selected from those tables—this is known as *joining* the data. (You will learn how to join data using SQL's INNER JOIN operator in Section 20.4.4.) There is a ***one-to-many relationship*** between a primary key and a corresponding foreign key (e.g., one author can write many books). This means that a foreign key can appear many times in its own table, but can appear only once (as the primary key) in another table. For example, the ISBN 0131450913 can appear in several rows of AuthorISBN (because this book has several authors), but can appear only once in Titles, where ISBN is the primary key.

Entity-Relationship Diagram for the **Books** *Database*

Figure 20.9 is an *entity-relationship* (*ER*) *diagram* for the Books database. This diagram shows the tables in the database and the relationships among them. The first compartment in each box contains the table's name. The names in italic font are primary keys (e.g., *AuthorID* in the Authors table). A table's primary key uniquely identifies each row in the table. Every row must have a value in the primary key column, and the value of the key must be unique in the table. This is known as the ***Rule of Entity Integrity***. Note that the names AuthorID and ISBN in the AuthorISBN table are both italic—together these form a composite primary key for the AuthorISBN table.

 Common Programming Error 20.1

Not providing a value for every column in a primary key breaks the Rule of Entity Integrity and causes the DBMS to report an error.

 Common Programming Error 20.2

Providing the same value for the primary key in multiple rows breaks the Rule of Entity Integrity and causes the DBMS to report an error.

The lines connecting the tables in Fig. 20.9 represent the relationships among the tables. Consider the line between the Authors and AuthorISBN tables. On the Authors end of the line, there is a 1, and on the AuthorISBN end, there is an infinity symbol (∞). This indicates a one-to-many relationship—for each author in the Authors table, there can be an arbitrary number of ISBNs for books written by that author in the AuthorISBN table

Fig. 20.9 | Entity-relationship diagram for the Books database.

(i.e., an author can write any number of books). Note that the relationship line links the AuthorID column in the Authors table (where AuthorID is the primary key) to the AuthorID column in the AuthorISBN table (where AuthorID is a foreign key)—the line between the tables links the primary key to the matching foreign key.

Common Programming Error 20.3

Providing a foreign-key value that does not appear as a primary-key value in another table breaks the Rule of Referential Integrity and causes the DBMS to report an error.

The line between the Titles and AuthorISBN tables illustrates a one-to-many relationship—a book can be written by many authors. Note that the line between the tables links the primary key ISBN in table Titles to the corresponding foreign key in table AuthorISBN. The relationships in Fig. 20.9 illustrate that the sole purpose of the AuthorISBN table is to provide a many-to-many relationship between the Authors and Titles tables—an author can write many books, and a book can have many authors.

20.4 SQL

We now overview SQL in the context of the Books database. Later in the chapter, you will build C# applications that execute SQL queries and access their results using ADO.NET technology. Though the Visual C# IDE provides visual tools that hide some of the SQL used to manipulate databases, it is nevertheless important to understand SQL basics. Knowing the types of operations you can perform will help you develop more advanced database-intensive applications.

Figure 20.10 lists some common *SQL keywords* used to form complete *SQL statements*—we discuss these keywords in the next several subsections. Other SQL keywords exist, but they are beyond the scope of this text. For additional information on SQL, please refer to the URLs listed in Section 20.11, Web Resources.

SQL keyword	Description
SELECT	Retrieves data from one or more tables.
FROM	Specifies the tables involved in a query. Required in every query.
WHERE	Specifies optional criteria for selection that determine the rows to be retrieved, deleted or updated.
ORDER BY	Specifies optional criteria for ordering rows (e.g., ascending, descending).
INNER JOIN	Specifies optional operator for merging rows from multiple tables.
INSERT	Inserts rows in a specified table.
UPDATE	Updates rows in a specified table.
DELETE	Deletes rows from a specified table.

Fig. 20.10 | Common SQL keywords.

20.4.1 Basic SELECT Query

Let us consider several SQL queries that retrieve information from database Books. A SQL *query* "selects" rows and columns from one or more tables in a database. Such selections are performed by queries with the **SELECT** keyword. The basic form of a **SELECT** *query* is

> **SELECT** * **FROM** *tableName*

in which the asterisk (*) indicates that all the columns from the *tableName* table should be retrieved. For example, to retrieve all the data in the Authors table, use

> **SELECT** * **FROM** Authors

Note that the rows of the Authors table are not guaranteed to be returned in any particular order. You will learn how to specify criteria for sorting rows in Section 20.4.3.

Most programs do not require all the data in a table. To retrieve only specific columns from a table, replace the asterisk (*) with a comma-separated list of the column names. For example, to retrieve only the columns AuthorID and LastName for all the rows in the Authors table, use the query

> **SELECT** AuthorID, LastName **FROM** Authors

This query returns only the data listed in Fig. 20.11.

20.4.2 WHERE Clause

When users search a database for rows that satisfy certain *selection criteria* (formally called *predicates*), only rows that satisfy the selection criteria are selected. SQL uses the optional **WHERE** *clause* in a query to specify the selection criteria for the query. The basic form of a query with selection criteria is

> **SELECT** *columnName1*, *columnName2*, ... **FROM** *tableName* **WHERE** *criteria*

For example, to select the Title, EditionNumber and Copyright columns from table Titles for which the Copyright date is more recent than 2004, use the query

> **SELECT** Title, EditionNumber, Copyright
> **FROM** Titles
> **WHERE** Copyright > '2004'

Figure 20.12 shows the result of the preceding query.

AuthorID	LastName
1	Deitel
2	Deitel
3	Goldberg
4	Choffnes

Fig. 20.11 | AuthorID and LastName data from the Authors table.

Title	EditionNumber	Copyright
Java How to Program	6	2005
Visual C# 2005 How to Program	2	2006
C++ How to Program	5	2005
Visual Basic 2005 How to Program	3	2006

Fig. 20.12 | Titles with copyright dates after 2004 from table `Titles`.

The WHERE clause criteria can contain the relational operators <, >, <=, >=, = (equality), <> (inequality) and LIKE, as well as the logical operators AND, OR and NOT (discussed in Section 20.4.6). Operator **LIKE** is used for *pattern matching* with wildcard characters *percent* (**%**) and *underscore* (_). Pattern matching allows SQL to search for strings that match a given pattern.

A pattern that contains a percent character (%) searches for strings that have zero or more characters at the percent character's position in the pattern. For example, the following query locates the rows of all the authors whose last names start with the letter D:

```
SELECT AuthorID, FirstName, LastName
FROM Authors
WHERE LastName LIKE 'D%'
```

The preceding query selects the two rows shown in Fig. 20.13, because two of the four authors in our database have a last name starting with the letter D (followed by zero or more characters). The % in the WHERE clause's LIKE pattern indicates that any number of characters can appear after the letter D in the LastName column. Note that the pattern string is surrounded by single-quote characters.

An underscore (_) in the pattern string indicates a single wildcard character at that position in the pattern. For example, the following query locates the rows of all the authors whose last names start with any character (specified by _), followed by the letter h, followed by any number of additional characters (specified by %):

```
SELECT AuthorID, FirstName, LastName
FROM Authors
WHERE LastName LIKE '_h%'
```

The preceding query produces the row shown in Fig. 20.14, because only one author in our database has a last name that contains the letter h as its second letter.

AuthorID	FirstName	LastName
1	Harvey	Deitel
2	Paul	Deitel

Fig. 20.13 | Authors from the `Authors` table whose last names start with D.

AuthorID	FirstName	LastName
4	David	Choffnes

Fig. 20.14 | The only author from the Authors table whose last name contains **h** as the second letter.

20.4.3 ORDER BY Clause

The rows in the result of a query can be sorted into ascending or descending order by using the optional **ORDER BY** *clause*. The basic form of a query with an ORDER BY clause is

> **SELECT** *columnName1*, *columnName2*, ... **FROM** *tableName* **ORDER BY** *column* **ASC**
> **SELECT** *columnName1*, *columnName2*, ... **FROM** *tableName* **ORDER BY** *column* **DESC**

where **ASC** specifies ascending order (lowest to highest), **DESC** specifies descending order (highest to lowest) and *column* specifies the column on which the sort is based. For example, to obtain the list of authors in ascending order by last name (Fig. 20.15), use the query

> **SELECT** AuthorID, FirstName, LastName
> **FROM** Authors
> **ORDER BY** LastName **ASC**

The default sorting order is ascending, so ASC is optional in the preceding query.

To obtain the same list of authors in descending order by last name (Fig. 20.16), use the query

> **SELECT** AuthorID, FirstName, LastName
> **FROM** Authors
> **ORDER BY** LastName **DESC**

Multiple columns can be used for sorting with an ORDER BY clause of the form

> **ORDER BY** *column1 sortingOrder*, *column2 sortingOrder*, ...

where *sortingOrder* is either ASC or DESC. Note that the *sortingOrder* does not have to be identical for each column. For example, the query

> **SELECT** Title, EditionNumber, Copyright
> **FROM** Titles
> **ORDER BY** Copyright **DESC**, Title **ASC**

AuthorID	FirstName	LastName
4	David	Choffnes
1	Harvey	Deitel
2	Paul	Deitel
3	Andrew	Goldberg

Fig. 20.15 | Authors from table Authors in ascending order by LastName.

AuthorID	FirstName	LastName
3	Andrew	Goldberg
1	Harvey	Deitel
2	Paul	Deitel
4	David	Choffnes

Fig. 20.16 | Authors from table `Authors` in descending order by `LastName`.

returns the rows of the `Titles` table sorted first in descending order by copyright date, then in ascending order by title (Fig. 20.17). This means that rows with higher `Copyright` values are returned before rows with lower `Copyright` values, and any rows that have the same `Copyright` values are sorted in ascending order by title.

The `WHERE` and `ORDER BY` clauses can be combined in one query. For example, the query

```
SELECT ISBN, Title, EditionNumber, Copyright
FROM Titles
WHERE Title LIKE '%How to Program'
ORDER BY Title ASC
```

returns the ISBN, `Title`, `EditionNumber` and `Copyright` of each book in the `Titles` table that has a `Title` ending with "How to Program" and sorts them in ascending order by `Title`. The query results are shown in Fig. 20.18.

20.4.4 Merging Data from Multiple Tables: INNER JOIN

Database designers typically *normalize* databases—i.e., split related data into separate tables to ensure that a database does not store redundant data. For example, the `Books` database has tables `Authors` and `Titles`. We use an `AuthorISBN` table to store "links"

Title	EditionNumber	Copyright
Visual Basic 2005 How to Program	3	2006
Visual C# 2005 How to Program	2	2006
C++ How to Program	5	2005
Java How to Program	6	2005
C How to Program	4	2004
Internet & World Wide Web How to Program	3	2004
Operating Systems	3	2004

Fig. 20.17 | Data from `Titles` in descending order by `Copyright` and ascending order by `Title`.

ISBN	Title	EditionNumber	Copyright
0131426443	C How to Program	4	2004
0131857576	C++ How to Program	5	2005
0131450913	Internet & World Wide Web How to Program	3	2004
0131483986	Java How to Program	6	2005
0131869000	Visual Basic 2005 How to Program	3	2006
0131525239	Visual C# 2005 How to Program	2	2006

Fig. 20.18 | Books from table `Titles` whose titles end with `How to Program` in ascending order by `Title`.

between authors and titles. If we did not separate this information into individual tables, we would need to include author information with each entry in the `Titles` table. This would result in the database storing duplicate author information for authors who wrote more than one book.

Often, it is desirable to merge data from multiple tables into a single result. This is referred to as joining the tables, and is specified by an ***INNER JOIN** operator* in the query. An `INNER JOIN` merges rows from two tables by testing for matching values in a column that is common to the tables. The basic form of an `INNER JOIN` is:

> ***SELECT*** *columnName1, columnName2, ...*
> ***FROM*** *table1* ***INNER JOIN*** *table2*
>   ***ON*** *table1.columnName = table2.columnName*

The ***ON** clause* of the `INNER JOIN` specifies the columns from each table that are compared to determine which rows are merged. For example, the following query produces a list of authors accompanied by the ISBNs for books written by each author:

> ***SELECT*** FirstName, LastName, ISBN
> ***FROM*** Authors ***INNER JOIN*** AuthorISBN
>   ***ON*** Authors.AuthorID = AuthorISBN.AuthorID
> ***ORDER BY*** LastName, FirstName

The query combines the `FirstName` and `LastName` columns from table `Authors` and the `ISBN` column from table `AuthorISBN`, sorting the results in ascending order by `LastName` and `FirstName`. Note the use of the syntax *tableName.columnName* in the `ON` clause. This syntax (called a *qualified name*) specifies the columns from each table that should be compared to join the tables. The "*tableName.*" syntax is required if the columns have the same name in both tables. The same syntax can be used in any query to distinguish columns that have the same name in different tables.

Common Programming Error 20.4

In a SQL query, failure to qualify names for columns that have the same name in two or more tables is an error.

As always, the query can contain an ORDER BY clause. Figure 20.19 depicts the results of the preceding query, ordered by LastName and FirstName.

20.4.5 INSERT Statement

The **INSERT** *statement* inserts a row into a table. The basic form of this statement is

```
INSERT INTO tableName ( columnName1, columnName2, ..., columnNameN )
VALUES ( value1, value2, ..., valueN )
```

where *tableName* is the table in which to insert the row. The *tableName* is followed by a comma-separated list of column names in parentheses (this list is not required if the IN-SERT operation specifies a value for every column of the table in the correct order). The list of column names is followed by the SQL keyword **VALUES** and a comma-separated list of values in parentheses. The values specified here must match up with the columns specified after the table name in both order and type (e.g., if *columnName1* is supposed to be the FirstName column, then *value1* should be a string in single quotes representing the first name). Always explicitly list the columns when inserting rows—if the order of the columns in the table changes, using only VALUES may cause an error. The INSERT statement

```
INSERT INTO Authors ( FirstName, LastName )
VALUES ( 'Sue', 'Smith' )
```

FirstName	LastName	ISBN
David	Choffnes	0131828274
Harvey	Deitel	0131869000
Harvey	Deitel	0131525239
Harvey	Deitel	0131483986
Harvey	Deitel	0131857576
Harvey	Deitel	0131426443
Harvey	Deitel	0131450913
Harvey	Deitel	0131828274
Paul	Deitel	0131869000
Paul	Deitel	0131525239
Paul	Deitel	0131483986
Paul	Deitel	0131857576
Paul	Deitel	0131426443
Paul	Deitel	0131450913
Paul	Deitel	0131828274
Andrew	Goldberg	0131450913

Fig. 20.19 | Authors and ISBNs for their books in ascending order by LastName and FirstName.

inserts a row into the Authors table. The statement indicates that the values 'Sue' and 'Smith' are provided for the FirstName and LastName columns, respectively.

We do not specify an AuthorID in this example because AuthorID is an identity column in the Authors table (see Fig. 20.3). For every row added to this table, SQL Server assigns a unique AuthorID value that is the next value in an autoincremented sequence (i.e., 1, 2, 3 and so on). In this case, Sue Smith would be assigned AuthorID number 5. Figure 20.20 shows the Authors table after the INSERT operation. Not every DBMS supports identity or autoincremented columns.

Common Programming Error 20.5

It is an error to specify a value for an identity column.

Common Programming Error 20.6

SQL uses the single-quote (') character to delimit strings. To specify a string containing a single quote (e.g., O'Malley) in a SQL statement, there must be two single quotes in the position where the single-quote character appears in the string (e.g., 'O''Malley'). The first of the two single-quote characters acts as an escape character for the second. Not escaping single-quote characters in a string that is part of a SQL statement is a syntax error.

20.4.6 UPDATE Statement

An **UPDATE statement** modifies data in a table. The basic form of the UPDATE statement is

```
UPDATE tableName
SET columnName1 = value1, columnName2 = value2, ..., columnNameN = valueN
WHERE criteria
```

where *tableName* is the table to update. The *tableName* is followed by keyword **SET** and a comma-separated list of column name-value pairs in the format *columnName = value*. The optional WHERE clause provides criteria that determine which rows to update. Though not required, the WHERE clause is typically used, unless a change is to be made to every row. The UPDATE statement

```
UPDATE Authors
SET LastName = 'Jones'
WHERE LastName = 'Smith' AND FirstName = 'Sue'
```

AuthorID	FirstName	LastName
1	Harvey	Deitel
2	Paul	Deitel
3	Andrew	Goldberg
4	David	Choffnes
5	Sue	Smith

Fig. 20.20 | Table Authors after an INSERT operation.

updates a row in the Authors table. Keyword *AND* is a logical operator that, like the C# &&
operator, returns true *if and only if* both of its operands are true. Thus, the preceding statement assigns to LastName the value Jones for the row in which LastName is equal to Smith
and FirstName is equal to Sue. [*Note:* If there are multiple rows with the first name "Sue"
and the last name "Smith," this statement modifies all such rows to have the last name
"Jones."] Figure 20.21 shows the Authors table after the UPDATE operation has taken place.
SQL also provides other logical operators, such as *OR* and *NOT*, which behave like their C#
counterparts.

20.4.7 DELETE Statement

A *DELETE statement* removes rows from a table. The basic form of a DELETE statement is

> *DELETE FROM* tableName *WHERE* criteria

where *tableName* is the table from which to delete. The optional WHERE clause specifies the
criteria used to determine which rows to delete. The DELETE statement

```
DELETE FROM Authors
WHERE LastName = 'Jones' AND FirstName = 'Sue'
```

deletes the row for Sue Jones in the Authors table. DELETE statements can delete multiple
rows if the rows all meet the criteria in the WHERE clause. Figure 20.22 shows the Authors
table after the DELETE operation has taken place.

AuthorID	FirstName	LastName
1	Harvey	Deitel
2	Paul	Deitel
3	Andrew	Goldberg
4	David	Choffnes
5	Sue	Jones

Fig. 20.21 | Table Authors after an UPDATE operation.

AuthorID	FirstName	LastName
1	Harvey	Deitel
2	Paul	Deitel
3	Andrew	Goldberg
4	David	Choffnes

Fig. 20.22 | Table Authors after a DELETE operation.

SQL Wrap-Up

This concludes our SQL introduction. We demonstrated several commonly used SQL keywords, formed SQL queries that retrieved data from databases and formed other SQL statements that manipulated data in a database. Next, we introduce the ADO.NET object model, which allows C# applications to interact with databases. As you will see, ADO.NET objects manipulate databases using SQL statements like those presented here.

20.5 ADO.NET Object Model

The *ADO.NET object model* provides an API for accessing database systems programmatically. ADO.NET was created for the .NET framework to replace Microsoft's ActiveX Data Objects™ (ADO) technology. As will be discussed in the next section, the IDE features visual programming tools that simplify the process of using a database in your projects. While you may not need to work directly with many ADO.NET objects to develop simple applications, basic knowledge of how the ADO.NET object model works is important for understanding data access in C#.

Namespaces `System.Data`, `System.Data.OleDb` *and* `System.Data.SqlClient`

Namespace **`System.Data`** is the root namespace for the ADO.NET API. The other important ADO.NET namespaces, **`System.Data.OleDb`** and **`System.Data.SqlClient`**, contain classes that enable programs to connect with and manipulate *data sources*—locations that contain data, such as a database or an XML file. Namespace `System.Data.OleDb` contains classes that are designed to work with any data source, whereas `System.Data.SqlClient` contains classes that are optimized to work with Microsoft SQL Server databases. The chapter examples manipulate SQL Server 2005 Express databases, so we use the classes of namespace `System.Data.SqlClient`. SQL Server Express 2005 is provided with Visual C# 2005 Express. It can also be downloaded from `msdn.microsoft.com/vstudio/express/sql/default.aspx`.

An object of class **`SqlConnection`** (namespace `System.Data.SqlClient`) represents a connection to a data source—specifically a SQL Server database. A `SqlConnection` object keeps track of the location of the data source and any settings that specify how the data source is to be accessed. A connection is either *active* (i.e., open and permitting data to be sent to and retrieved from the data source) or *closed*.

An object of class **`SqlCommand`** (namespace `System.Data.SqlClient`) represents a SQL command that a DBMS can execute on a database. A program can use `SqlCommand` objects to manipulate a data source through a `SqlConnection`. The program must open the connection to the data source before executing one or more `SqlCommands` and close the connection once no further access to the data source is required. A connection that remains active for some length of time to permit multiple data operations is known as a *persistent connection*.

Class **`DataTable`** (namespace `System.Data`) represents a table of data. A `DataTable` contains a collection of **`DataRows`** that represent the table's data. A `DataTable` also has a collection of **`DataColumns`** that describe the columns in a table. DataRow and DataColumn are both located in namespace `System.Data`. An object of class **`System.Data.DataSet`**, which consists of a set of `DataTables` and the relationships among them, represents a *cache* of data—data that a program stores temporarily in local memory. The structure of a `DataSet` mimics the structure of a relational database.

ADO.NET's Disconnected Model

An advantage of using class `DataSet` is that it is *disconnected*—the program does not need a persistent connection to the data source to work with data in a `DataSet`. Instead, the program connects to the data source to *populate the `DataSet`* (i.e., fill the `DataSet`'s Data-Tables with data), but disconnects from the data source immediately after retrieving the desired data. The program then accesses and potentially manipulates the data stored in the `DataSet`. The program operates on this local cache of data, rather than the original data in the data source. If the program makes changes to the data in the `DataSet` that need to be permanently saved in the data source, the program reconnects to the data source to perform an update then disconnects promptly. Thus the program does not require any active, persistent connection to the data source.

An object of class ***SqlDataAdapter*** (namespace `System.Data.SqlClient`) connects to a SQL Server data source and executes SQL statements to both populate a `DataSet` and update the data source based on the current contents of a `DataSet`. A `SqlDataAdapter` maintains a `SqlConnection` object that it opens and closes as needed to perform these operations using `SqlCommands`. We demonstrate populating `DataSets` and updating data sources later in this chapter.

20.6 Programming with ADO.NET: Extracting Information from a Database

In this section, we demonstrate how to connect to a database, query the database and display the result of the query. You will notice that there is little code in this section. The IDE provides visual programming tools and wizards that simplify accessing data in your projects. These tools establish database connections and create the ADO.NET objects necessary to view and manipulate the data through GUI controls. The example in this section connects to the SQL Server `Books` database that we have discussed throughout this chapter. The `Books.mdf` file that contains the database can be found with the chapter's examples (www.deitel.com/books/csharpforprogrammers2).

20.6.1 Displaying a Database Table in a `DataGridView`

This example performs a simple query on the `Books` database that retrieves the entire Authors table and displays the data in a ***DataGridView*** (a control from namespace `System.Windows.Forms` that can display a data source in a GUI—see the output in Fig. 20.32 later in this section). First, we demonstrate how to connect to the `Books` database and include it as a data source in your project. Once the `Books` database is established as a data source, you can display the data from the `Authors` table in a `DataGridView` simply by dragging and dropping items in the project's **Design** view.

Step 1: Creating the Project
Create a new Windows Application named `DisplayTable`. Change the `Form` name to `DisplayTableForm` and change the source file name to `DisplayTable.cs`. Then set the `Form`'s **Text** property to `Display Table`.

Step 2: Adding a Data Source to the Project
To interact with a data source (e.g., a database), you must add it to the project using the **Data Sources** *window*, which lists the data that your project can access. Open the **Data**

Sources window (Fig. 20.23) by selecting **Data > Show Data Sources** or by clicking the tab to the right of the tab for the **Solution Explorer**. In the **Data Sources** window, click **Add New Data Source...** to open the ***Data Source Configuration Wizard*** (Fig. 20.24). This wizard guides you through connecting to a database and choosing the parts of the database you will want to access in your project.

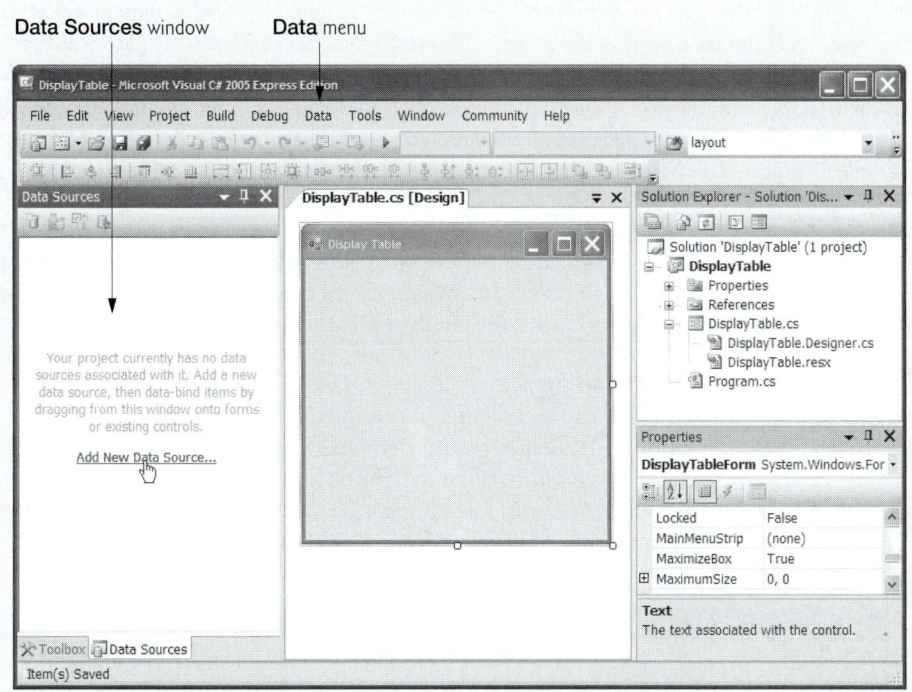

Fig. 20.23 | Adding a data source to a project.

Fig. 20.24 | Choosing the data source type in the **Data Source Configuration Wizard**.

Step 3: Choosing the Data Source Type to Add to the Project

The first screen of the **Data Source Configuration Wizard** (Fig. 20.24) asks you to choose the data source type you wish to include in the project. Select **Database** and click **Next >**.

Step 4: Adding a New Database Connection

You must next choose the connection that will be used to connect to the database (i.e., the actual *source* of the data). Click **New Connection...** to open the **Add Connection** dialog (Fig. 20.25). If the **Data Source** is not set to **Microsoft SQL Server Database File (SqlClient)**, click **Change...**, select **Microsoft SQL Server Database File** and click **OK**. In the **Add Connection** dialog, click **Browse...**, locate the Books.mdf database file on your computer, select it and click **Open**. You can click **Test Connection** to verify that the IDE can connect to the database through SQL Server. Click **OK** to create the connection.

Step 5: Choosing the Books.mdf Data Connection

Now that you have created a connection to the Books.mdf database, you can select and use this connection to access the database. Click **Next >** to set the connection, then click **Yes** when asked whether you want to move the database file to your project (Fig. 20.26).

Step 6: Saving the Connection String

The next screen (Fig. 20.27) asks you whether you want to save the connection string to the application configuration file. A *connection string* specifies the path to a database file on disk, as well as some additional settings that determine how to access the database. Saving the connection string in a configuration file makes it easy to change the connection settings at a later time. Leave the default selections and click **Next >** to proceed.

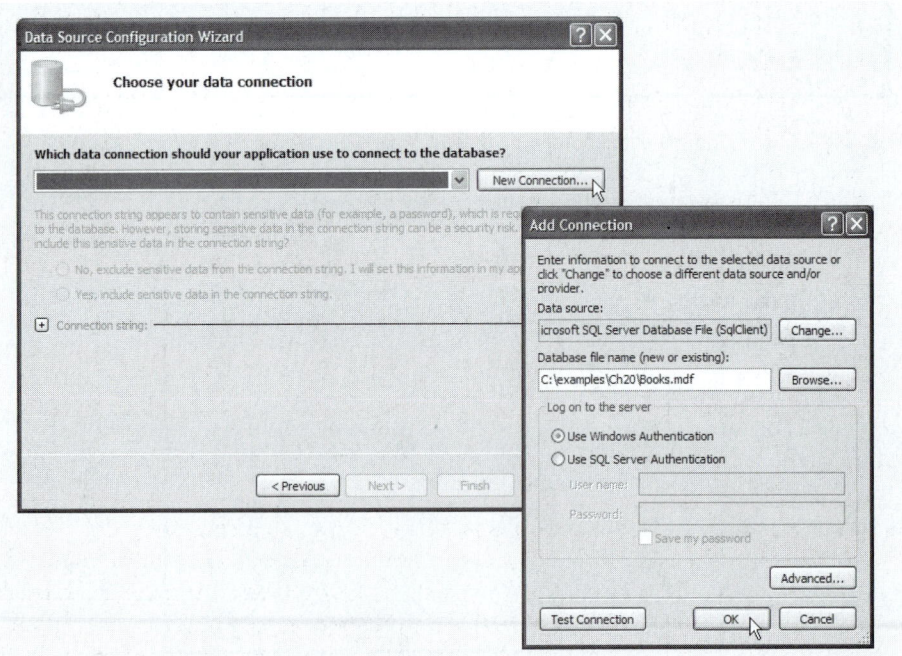

Fig. 20.25 | Adding a new data connection.

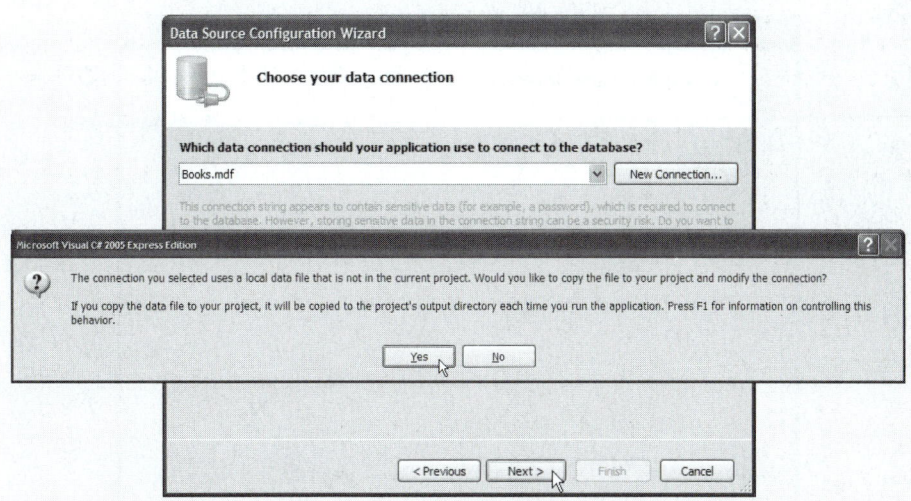

Fig. 20.26 | Choosing the `Books.mdf` data connection.

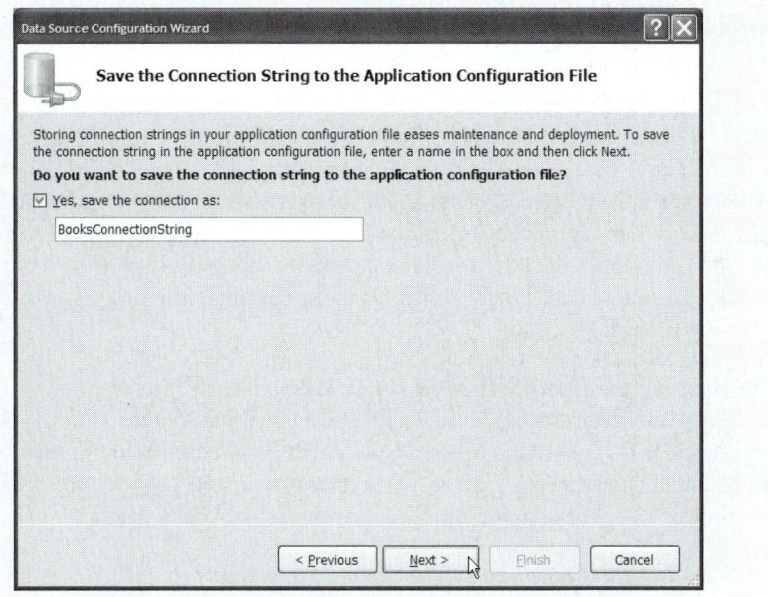

Fig. 20.27 | Saving the connection string to the application configuration file.

Step 7: Selecting the Database Objects to Include in Your DataSet

The IDE retrieves information about the database you selected and prompts you to select the database objects (i.e., the parts of the database) that you want your project to be able to access (Fig. 20.28). Recall that programs typically access a database's contents through a cache of the data, which is stored in a DataSet. In response to your selections in this screen, the IDE will generate a class derived from System.Data.DataSet that is designed

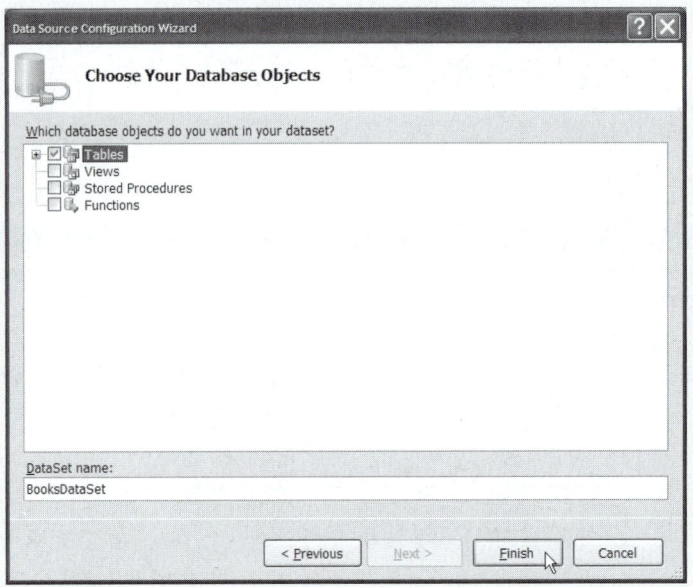

Fig. 20.28 | Choosing the database objects to include in the DataSet.

specifically to store data from the Books database. Click the checkbox to the left of **Tables** to indicate that the custom DataSet should cache (i.e., locally store) the data from all the tables in the Books database—Authors, AuthorISBN and Titles. [*Note:* You can also expand the **Tables** node to select specific tables. The other database objects listed do not contain any data in our sample Books database and are beyond the scope of the book.] By default, the IDE names the DataSet BooksDataSet, though it is possible to specify a different name in this screen. Finally, click **Finish** to complete the process of adding a data source to the project.

Step 8: Viewing the Data Source in the Data Sources *Window*
Notice that a **BooksDataSet** node now appears in the **Data Sources** window (Fig. 20.29) with child nodes for each table in the Books database—these nodes represent the DataTables of the BooksDataSet. Expand the **Authors** node and you will see the table's columns—the DataSet's structure mimics that of the actual Books database.

Step 9: Viewing the Database in the Solution Explorer
Books.mdf is now listed as a node in the **Solution Explorer** (Fig. 20.30), indicating that the database is now part of this project. In addition, the **Solution Explorer** now lists a new node named BooksDataSet.xsd. You learned in Chapter 19 that a file with the .xsd extension is an XML Schema document, which specifies the structure of a set of XML documents. The IDE uses an XML Schema document to represent a DataSet's structure, including the tables that comprise the DataSet and the relationships among them. When you added the Books database as a data source, the IDE created the BooksDataSet.xsd file based on the structure of the Books database. The IDE then generated class BooksDataSet from the schema (i.e., structure) described by the .xsd file.

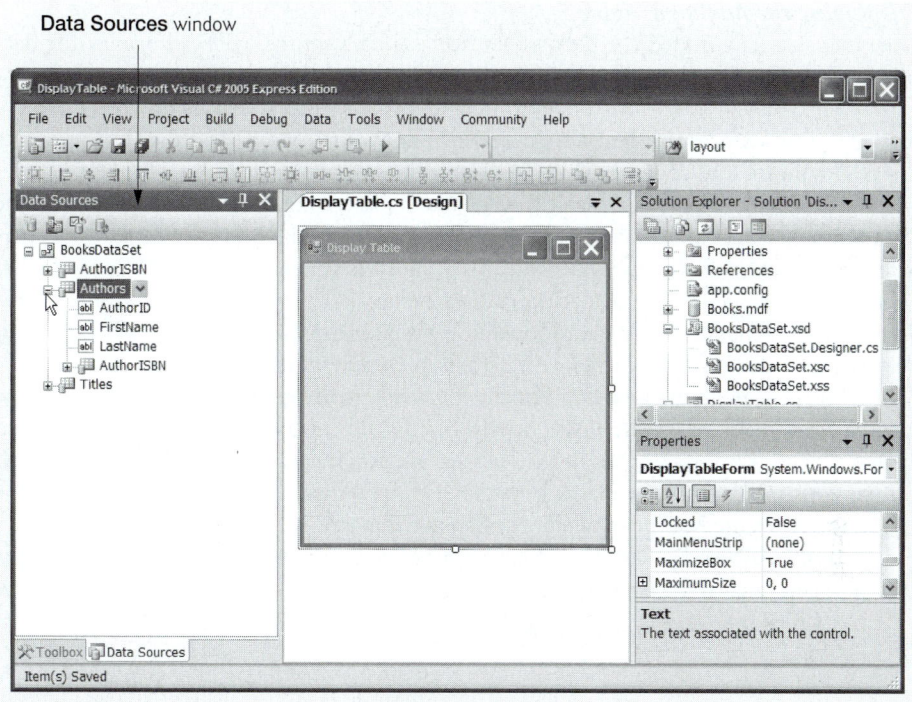

Fig. 20.29 | Viewing a data source listed in the **Data Sources** window.

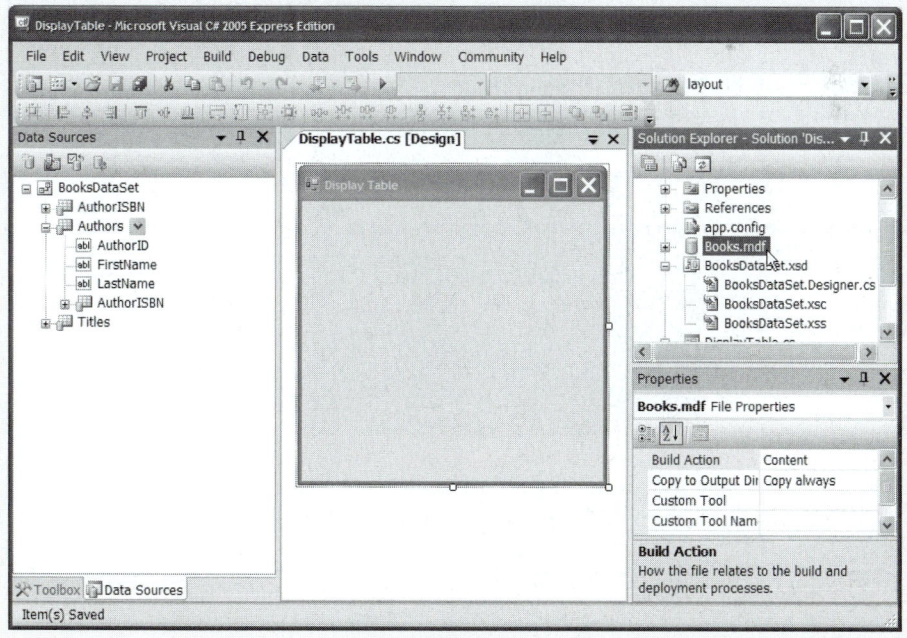

Fig. 20.30 | Viewing a database listed in the **Solution Explorer**.

Displaying the Authors Table

Now that you have added the Books database as a data source, you can display the data from the database's Authors table in your program. The IDE provides design tools that allow you to display data from a data source on a Form without writing any code. Simply drag and drop items from the **Data Sources** window onto a Form, and the IDE generates the GUI controls and code necessary to display the selected data source's content.

To display the Authors table of the Books database, drag the Authors node from the **Data Sources** window to the Form. Figure 20.31 presents the **Design** view after we performed this action and resized the controls. The IDE generates two GUI controls that appear on DisplayTableForm—authorsBindingNavigator and authorsDataGridView. The IDE also generates several additional non-visual components that appear in the *component tray*—the gray region below the Form in **Design** view. We use the IDE's default names for these autogenerated components (and others throughout the chapter) to show exactly what the IDE creates. We briefly discuss the authorsBindingNavigator and authorsDataGridView controls here. The next section discusses all of the autogenerated components in detail and explains how the IDE uses these components to connect the GUI controls to the Authors table of the Books database.

A *DataGridView* displays data organized in rows and columns that correspond to the rows and columns of the underlying data source. In this case, the DataGridView displays

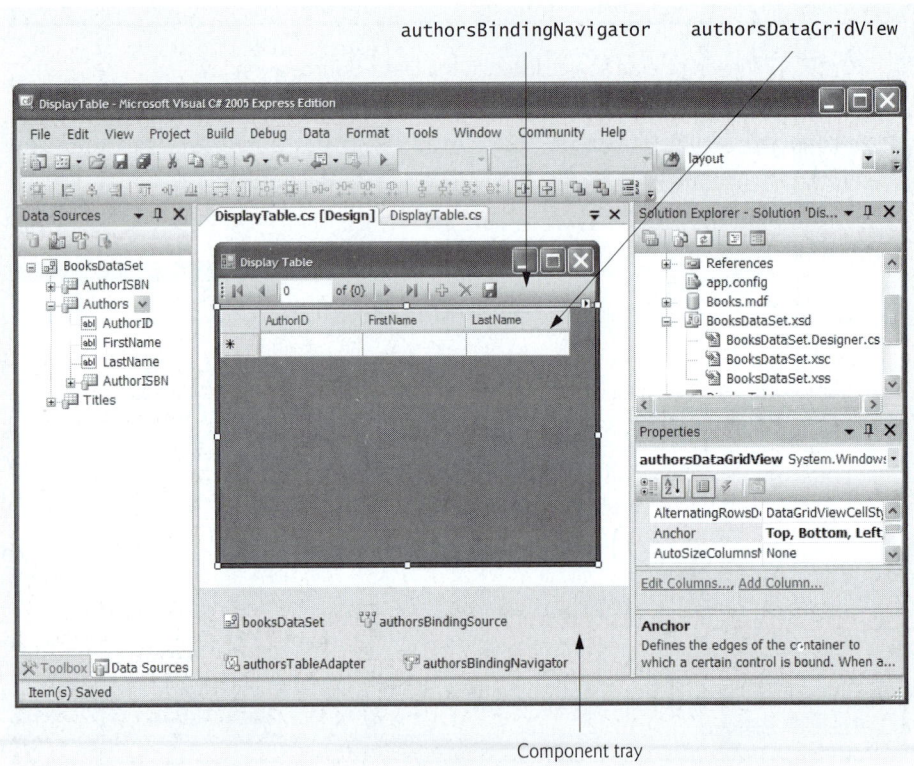

Fig. 20.31 | **Design** view after dragging the Authors data source node to the Form.

the data of the Authors table, so the control has columns named AuthorID, FirstName and LastName. In **Design** view, the control does not display any rows of actual data below the column headers. The data is retrieved from the database and displayed in the DataGrid-View only at runtime. Execute the program. When the Form loads, the DataGridView contains four rows of data—one for each row of the Authors table (Fig. 20.32).

The strip of buttons below the title bar of the window is a ***BindingNavigator***, which enables users to browse and manipulate data displayed by another GUI control (in this case, a DataGridView) on the Form. A BindingNavigator's buttons resemble the controls on a CD or DVD player and allow you to move to the first row of data, the preceding row, the next row and the last row. The control also displays the currently selected row number in a text box. You can use this text box to enter the number of a row that you want to select. The authorsBindingNavigator in this example allows you to "navigate" the Authors table displayed in the authorsDataGridView. Clicking the buttons or entering a value in the text box causes the DataGridView to select the appropriate row. An arrow in the Data-GridView's leftmost column indicates the currently selected row.

A BindingNavigator also has buttons that allow you to add a new row, delete a row and save changes back to the underlying data source (in this case, the Authors table of the Books database). Clicking the button with the yellow plus icon ( ) adds a new row to the DataGridView. However, simply typing values in the FirstName and LastName columns does not insert a new row in the Authors table. To add the new row to the database on disk, click the **Save** button (the button with the disk icon,). Clicking the button with the red **X** ( ) deletes the currently selected row from the DataGridView. Again, you must click the **Save** button to make the change in the database. Test these buttons. Execute the program and add a new row, then save the changes and close the program. When you restart the program, you should see that the new row was saved to the database and appears in the DataGridView. Now delete the new row and click the **Save** button. Close and restart the program to see that the new row no longer exists in the database.

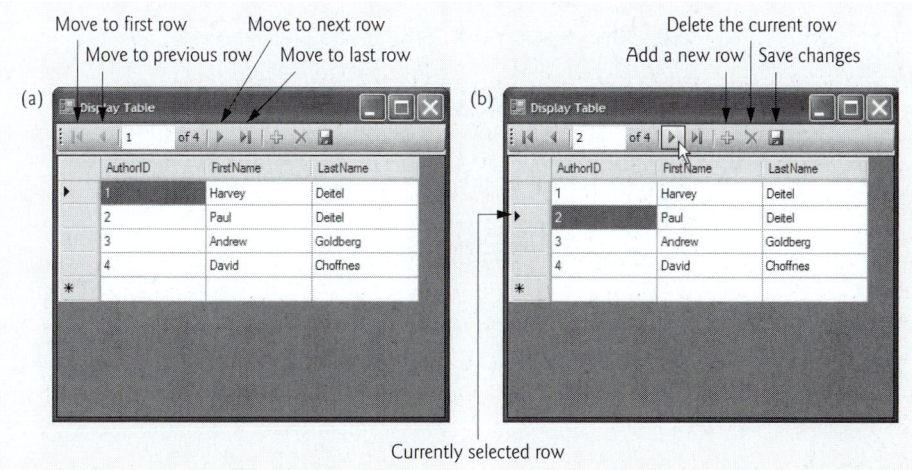

Fig. 20.32 | Displaying the Authors table in a DataGridView.

20.6.2 How Data Binding Works

The technique through which GUI controls are connected to data sources is known as *data binding*. The IDE allows controls, such as a DataGridView, to be bound to a data source, such as a DataSet that represents a table in a database. Any changes you make through the application to the underlying data source will automatically be reflected in the way the data is presented in the data-bound control (e.g., the DataGridView). Likewise, modifying the data in the data-bound control and saving the changes updates the underlying data source. In the current example, the DataGridView is bound to the DataTable of the BooksDataSet that represents the Authors table in the database. Dragging the Authors node from the **Data Sources** window to the Form caused the IDE to create this data binding for you, using several autogenerated components (i.e., objects) in the component tray. Figure 20.33 models these objects and their associations, which the following sections examine in detail to explain how data binding works.

BooksDataSet

As discussed in Section 20.6.1, adding the Books database to the project enabled the IDE to generate the BooksDataSet. Recall that a DataSet represents a cache of data that mimics the structure of a relational database. You can explore the structure of the BooksDataSet

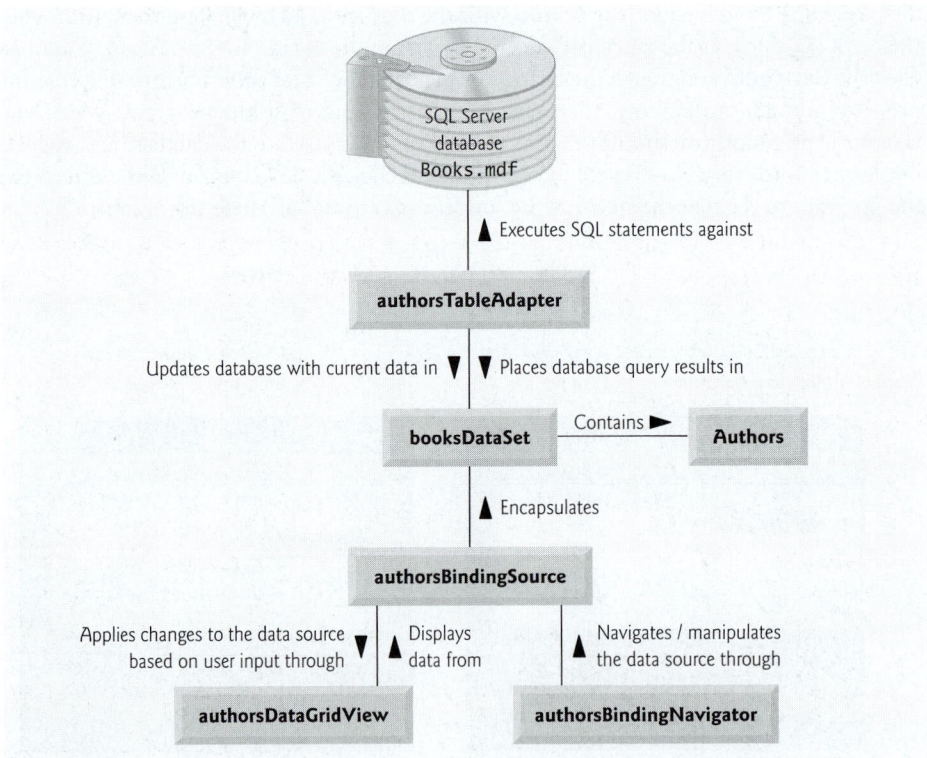

Fig. 20.33 | Data binding architecture used to display the Authors table of the Books database in a GUI.

in the **Data Sources** window. A DataSet's structure can be determined at execution time or at design time. An *untyped DataSet*'s structure (i.e., the tables that comprise it and the relationships among them) is determined at execution time based on the result of a specific query. Tables and column values are accessed using indices into collections of DataTables and DataRows, respectively. The type of each piece of data in an untyped DataSet is unknown at design time. BooksDataSet, however, is created by the IDE at design time as a *strongly typed DataSet*. BooksDataSet (a derived class of DataSet) contains objects of classes derived from DataTable that represent the tables in the Books database. BooksDataSet provides properties corresponding to the objects whose names match those of the underlying tables. For example, booksDataSet.Authors represents a cache of the data in the Authors table. Each DataTable contains a collection of DataRows. Each DataRow contains members whose names and types correspond to those of the columns of the underlying database table. Thus, booksDataSet.Authors[0].AuthorID refers to the AuthorID of the first row of the Authors table in the Books database. Note that zero-based indices are used to access DataRows in a DataTable.

The booksDataSet object in the component tray is an object of the BooksDataSet class. When you indicate that you want to display the contents of the Authors table on the Form, the IDE generates a BooksDataSet object to store the data that Form will display. This is the data to which the DataGridView will be bound. The DataGridView does not display data from the database directly. Instead, it displays the contents of a BooksDataSet object. As we discuss shortly, the AuthorsTableAdapter fills the BooksDataSet object with data retrieved from the database by executing a SQL query.

AuthorsTableAdapter

The AuthorsTableAdapter is the component that interacts with the Books database on disk (i.e., the Books.mdf file). When other components need to retrieve data from the database or write data to the database, they invoke the methods of the AuthorsTableAdapter. Class AuthorsTableAdapter is generated by the IDE when you drag a table from the Books database onto the Form. The authorsTableAdapter object in the component tray is an object of this class. The AuthorsTableAdapter is responsible for filling the BooksDataSet with the Authors data from the database—this stores a copy of the Authors table in local memory. As you will soon see, this cached copy can be modified during program execution. Thus, the AuthorsTableAdapter is also responsible for updating the database when the data in the BooksDataSet changes.

Class AuthorsTableAdapter encapsulates a SqlDataAdapter object, which contains SqlCommand objects that specify how the SqlDataAdapter selects, inserts, updates and deletes data in the database. Recall from Section 20.5 that a SqlCommand object must have a SqlConnection object through which the SqlCommand can communicate with a database. In this example, the AuthorsTableAdapter sets the Connection property of each of the SqlDataAdapter's SqlCommand objects, based on the connection string that refers to the Books database.

To interact with the database, the AuthorsTableAdapter invokes the methods of its SqlDataAdapter, each of which executes the appropriate SqlCommand object. For example, to fill the BooksDataSet's Authors table, the AuthorsTableAdapter's Fill method invokes its SqlDataAdapter's Fill method, which executes a SqlCommand object representing the SELECT query

> *SELECT* AuthorID, FirstName, LastName *FROM* Authors

This query selects all the rows and columns of the Authors table and places them in books-DataSet.Authors. You will see an example of authorsTableAdapter's Fill method being invoked shortly.

authorsBindingSource *and* authorsDataGridView

The authorsBindingSource object (an object of class *BindingSource*) identifies a data source that a program can bind to a control and serves as an intermediary between a data-bound GUI control and its data source. In this example, the IDE uses a BindingSource object to connect the authorsDataGridView to booksDataSet.Authors. To achieve this data binding, the IDE first sets authorsBindingSource's *DataSource* property to Books-DataSet. This property specifies the DataSet that contains the data to be bound. The IDE then sets the *DataMember* property to Authors. This property identifies a specific table within the DataSource. After configuring the authorsBindingSource object, the IDE assigns this object to authorsDataGridView's *DataSource* property to indicate what the Da-taGridView will display.

A BindingSource object also manages the interaction between a data-bound GUI control and its underlying data source. If you edit the data displayed in a DataGridView and want to save changes to the data source, your code must invoke the *EndEdit* method of the BindingSource object. This method applies the changes made to the data through the GUI control (i.e., the pending changes) to the data source bound to that control. Note that this updates only the DataSet—an additional step is required to permanently update the database itself. You will see an example of this shortly, when we present the code generated by the IDE in the DisplayTable.cs file.

authorsBindingNavigator

Recall that a BindingNavigator allows you to move through (i.e., navigate) and manipulate (i.e., add or delete rows) data bound to a control on a Form. A BindingNavigator communicates with a BindingSource (specified in the BindingNavigator's *BindingSource* property) to carry out these actions in the underlying data source (i.e., the DataSet). The BindingNavigator does not interact with the data-bound control. Instead, it invokes BindingSource methods that cause the data-bound control to update its presentation of the data. For example, when you click the BindingNavigator's button to add a new row, the BindingNavigator invokes a method of the BindingSource. The BindingSource then adds a new row to its associated DataSet. Once this DataSet is modified, the DataGrid-View displays the new row, because the DataGridView and the BindingNavigator are bound to the same BindingSource object (and thus the same DataSet).

Examining the Autogenerated Code for DisplayTableForm

Figure 20.34 presents the code for DisplayTableForm. Note that you do not need to write any of this code—the IDE generates it when you drag and drop the Authors table from the **Data Sources** window onto the Form. We modified the autogenerated code to add comments, split long lines for display purposes and remove unnecessary using declarations. The IDE also generates a considerable amount of additional code, such as the code that defines classes BooksDataSet and AuthorsTableAdapter, as well as the designer code that declares the autogenerated objects in the component tray. The additional IDE-gen-

```csharp
 1    // Fig. 20.34: DisplayTable.cs
 2    // Displays data from a database table in a DataGridView.
 3    using System;
 4    using System.Windows.Forms;
 5
 6    namespace DisplayTable
 7    {
 8       public partial class DisplayTableForm : Form
 9       {
10          public DisplayTableForm()
11          {
12             InitializeComponent();
13          } // end constructor
14
15          // Click event handler for the Save Button in the
16          // BindingNavigator saves the changes made to the data
17          private void authorsBindingNavigatorSaveItem_Click(
18             object sender, EventArgs e )
19          {
20             this.Validate();
21             this.authorsBindingSource.EndEdit();
22             this.authorsTableAdapter.Update( this.booksDataSet.Authors );
23          } // end method authorsBindingNavigatorSaveItem_Click
24
25          // loads data into the booksDataSet.Authors table,
26          // which is then displayed in the DataGridView
27          private void DisplayTableForm_Load( object sender, EventArgs e )
28          {
29             // TODO: This line of code loads data into the
30             // 'booksDataSet.Authors' table. You can move, or remove it,
31             // as needed.
32             this.authorsTableAdapter.Fill( this.booksDataSet.Authors );
33          } // end method DisplayTableForm_Load
34       } // end class DisplayTableForm
35    } // end namespace DisplayTable
```

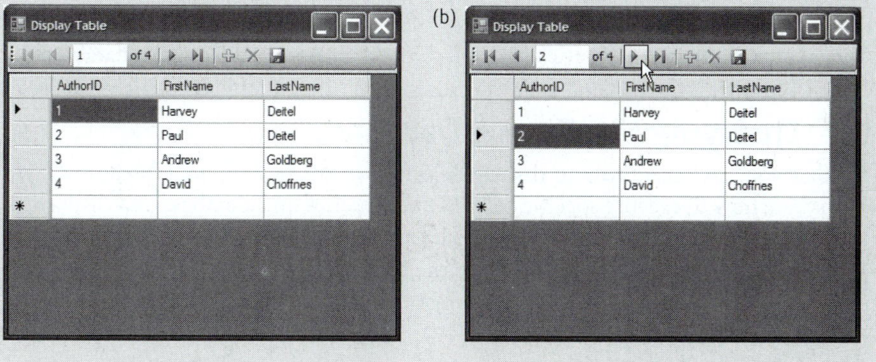

Fig. 20.34 | Auto-generated code for displaying data from a database table in a `DataGridView` control.

erated code resides in files visible in the **Solution Explorer** when you select **Show All Files**. We present only the code in `DisplayTable.cs`, because it is the only file you'll need to modify.

Lines 17–23 contain the `Click` event handler for the **Save** button in the Authors-BindingNavigator. Recall that you click this button to save changes made to the data in the `DataGridView` in the underlying data source (i.e., the `Authors` table of the `Books` database). Saving the changes is a two-step process:

1. The `DataSet` associated with the `DataGridView` (indicated by its `BindingSource`) must be updated to include any changes made by the user.

2. The database on disk must be updated to match the new contents of the `DataSet`.

Before the event handler saves any changes, line 21 invokes `this.Validate()` to validate the controls on the `Form`. If you implement `Validating` or `Validated` events for any of `Form`'s controls, these events enable you to validate user input and potentially indicate errors for invalid data. Line 21 invokes `authorsBindingSource`'s ***EndEdit*** method to ensure that the object's associated data source (`booksDataSet.Authors`) is updated with any changes made by the user to the currently selected row in the `DataGridView` (e.g., adding a row, changing a column value). Any changes to other rows were applied to the `DataSet` when you selected another row. Line 22 invokes `authorsTableAdapter`'s ***Update*** method to write the modified version of the `Authors` table (in memory) to the SQL Server database on disk. The `Update` method executes the SQL statements (encapsulated in `Sql-Command` objects) necessary to make the database's `Authors` table match books-DataSet.Authors.

The `Load` event handler for `DisplayTableForm` (lines 27–33) executes when the program loads. This event handler fills the in-memory `DataSet` with data from the SQL Server database on disk. Once the `DataSet` is filled, the GUI control bound to it can display its data. Line 32 calls `authorsTableAdapter`'s ***Fill*** method to retrieve information from the database, placing this information in the `DataSet` member provided as an argument. Recall that `authorsTableAdapter` was generated by the IDE to execute `SqlCom-mands` over the connection we created within the **Data Source Configuration Wizard**. Thus, the `Fill` method here executes a `SELECT` statement to retrieve all the rows of the `Authors` table of the `Books` database, then places the result of this query in `booksDataSet.Authors`. Recall that `authorsDataGridView`'s `DataSource` property is set to `authorsBindingSource` (which references `booksDataSet.Authors`). Thus, after this data source is loaded, the `authorsDataGridView` automatically displays the data retrieved from the database.

20.7 Querying the Books Database

Now that you have seen how to display an entire database table in a `DataGridView`, we demonstrate how to execute specific SQL `SELECT` queries on a database and display the results. Although this example only queries the data, the application could be modified easily to execute other SQL statements. Perform the following steps to build the example application, which executes custom queries against the `Titles` table of the `Books` database.

Step 1: Creating the Project
Create a new Windows Application named `DisplayQueryResult`. Rename the `Form` `DisplayQueryResultForm` and name its source file `DisplayQueryResult.cs`, then set the `Form`'s **Text** property to `Display Query Result`.

Step 2: Adding a Data Source to the Project
Perform the steps in Section 20.6.1 to include the Books database as a data source in the project.

Step 3: Creating a `DataGridView` ***to Display the*** `Titles` ***Table***
Drag the `Titles` node from the **Data Sources** window onto the Form to create a DataGrid-View that will display the entire contents of the `Titles` table.

Step 4: Adding Custom Queries to the `TitlesTableAdapter`
Recall that invoking a `TableAdapter`'s `Fill` method populates the `DataSet` passed as an argument with the entire contents of the database table that corresponds to that Table-Adapter. To populate a `DataSet` member (i.e., a `DataTable`) with only a portion of a table (e.g., books with copyright dates of 2006), you must add a method to the `TableAdapter` that fills the specified `DataTable` with the results of a custom query. The IDE provides the ***TableAdapter Query Configuration Wizard*** to perform this task. To open this wizard, first right click the `BooksDataSet.xsd` node in the **Solution Explorer** and choose **View Designer**. You can also click the **Edit DataSet with Designer** icon (🔛). Either of these actions opens the ***Dataset Designer*** (Fig. 20.35), which displays a visual representation of the `BooksDataSet` (i.e., the tables `AuthorISBN`, `Authors` and `Titles` and the relationships among them). The **Dataset Designer** lists each table's columns and the autogenerated `TableAdapter` that accesses the table. Select the `TitlesTableAdapter` by clicking its name, then right click the name and select **Add Query...** to begin the **TableAdapter Query Configuration Wizard** (Fig. 20.36).

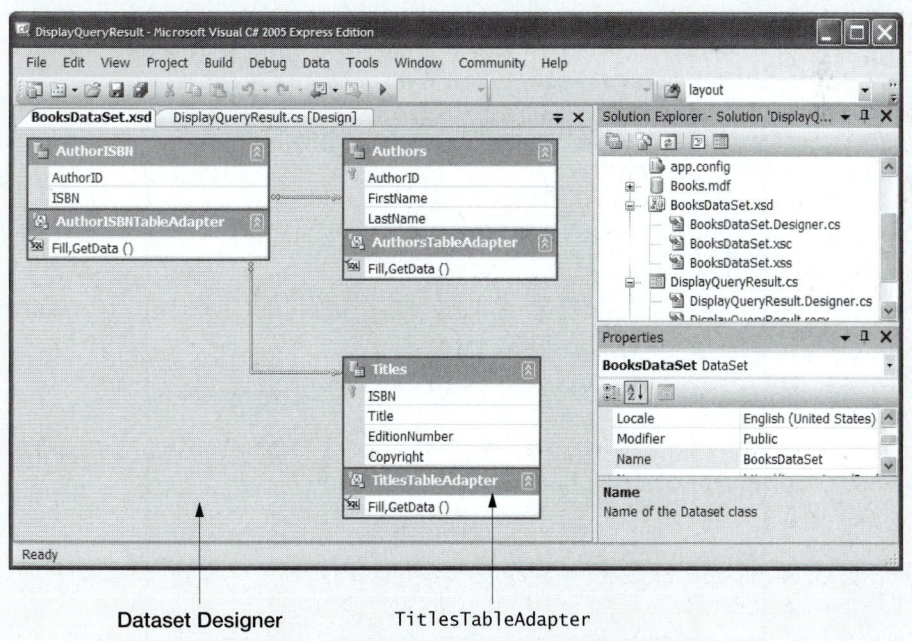

Fig. 20.35 | Viewing the BooksDataSet in the **Dataset Designer**.

Step 5: Choosing How the TableAdapter Should Access the Database

On the first screen of the wizard (Fig. 20.36), keep the default option **Use SQL Statements** and click **Next**.

Step 6: Choosing a Query Type

On the next screen of the wizard (Fig. 20.37), keep the default option **SELECT which re-turns rows** and click **Next**.

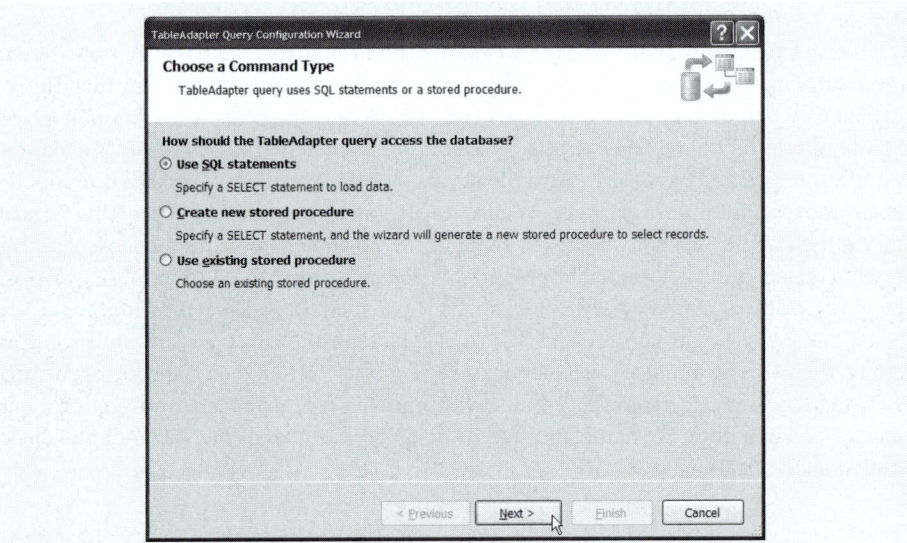

Fig. 20.36 │ **TableAdapter Query Configuration Wizard** to add a query to a `TableAdapter`.

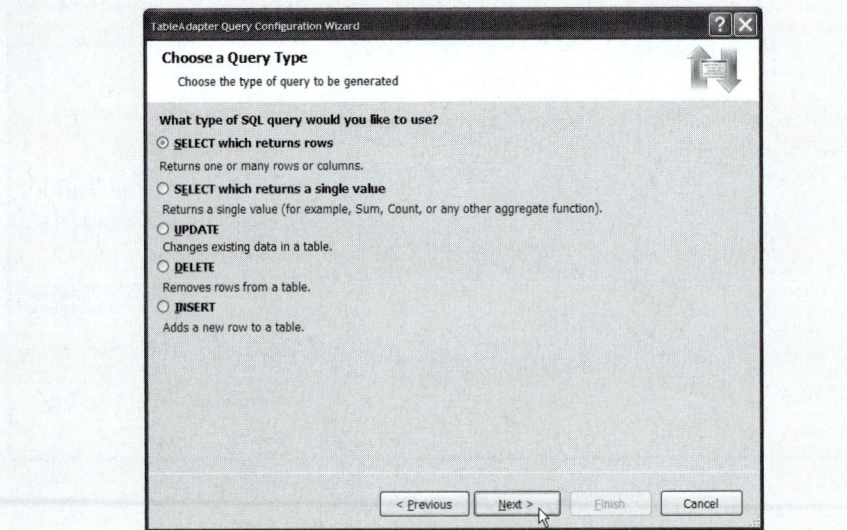

Fig. 20.37 │ Choosing the type of query to be generated for the `TableAdapter`.

Step 7: Specifying a SELECT Statement for the Query

The next screen (Fig. 20.38) asks you to enter a query that will be used to retrieve data from the Books database. Note that the default SELECT prefixes Titles with "dbo.". This prefix stands for "database owner" and indicates that the table Titles belongs to the database owner (i.e., you). In cases where you need to reference a table owned by another user of the system, this prefix would be replaced by the owner's username. You can modify the SQL statement in the text box here (using the SQL syntax discussed in Section 20.4), or you can click **Query Builder...** to design and test the query using a visual tool.

Step 8: Building a Query with Query Builder

Click the **Query Builder...** button to open the ***Query Builder*** (Fig. 20.39). The top portion of the **Query Builder** window contains a box listing the columns of the Titles table. By default, each column is checked (Fig. 20.39(a)), indicating that each column should be returned by the query. The middle portion of the window contains a table in which each row corresponds to a column in the Titles table. To the right of the column names are columns in which you can enter values or make selections to modify the query. For example, to create a query that selects only books that are copyright 2006, enter the value 2006 in the **Filter** column of the Copyright row. Note that the **Query Builder** modifies your input to be "= '2006'" and adds an appropriate WHERE clause to the SELECT statement displayed in the middle of Fig. 20.39(b). Click the **Execute Query** button to test the query and display the results in the bottom portion of the **Query Builder** window. For more **Query Builder** information, see msdn2.microsoft.com/library/ms172013.aspx.

Step 9: Closing the Query Builder

Click **OK** to close the **Query Builder** and return to the **TableAdapter Query Configuration Wizard** (Fig. 20.40), which now displays the SQL query created in the preceding step. Click **Next** to continue.

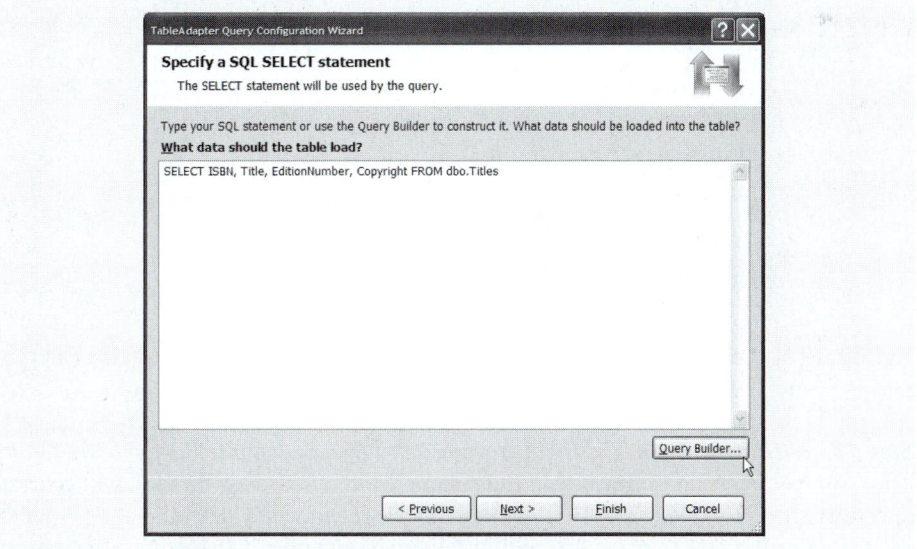

Fig. 20.38 | Specifying a SELECT statement for the query.

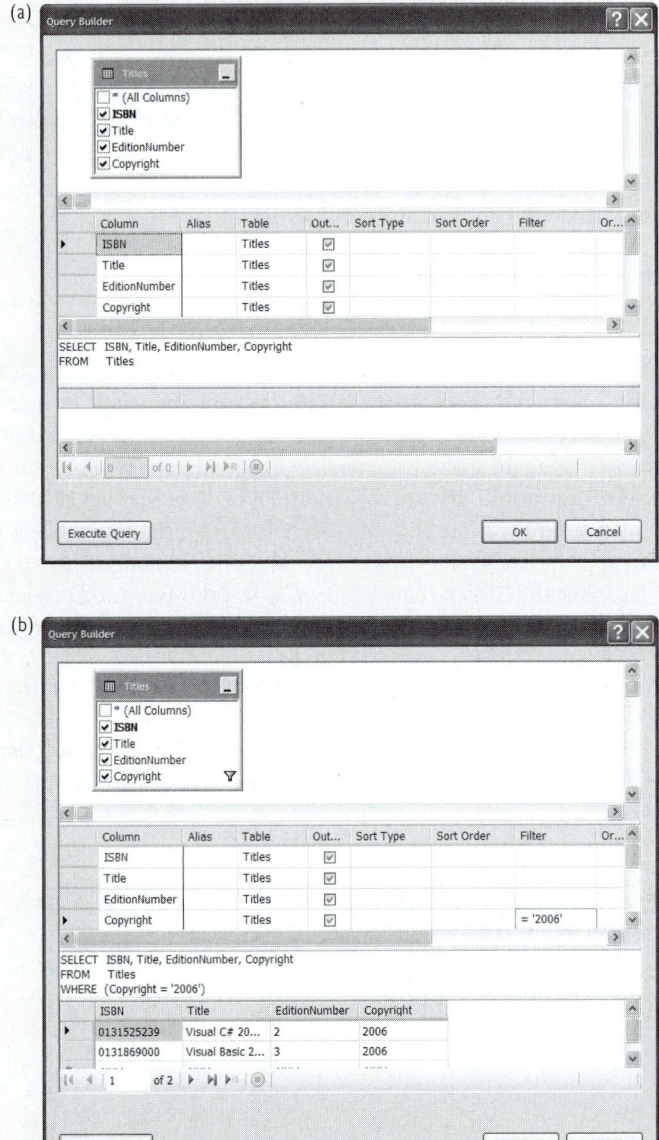

Fig. 20.39 | **Query Builder** after adding a WHERE clause by entering a value in the **Filter** column.

Step 10: Setting the Names of the Autogenerated Methods That Perform the Query

After you specify the SQL query, you must name the methods that the IDE will generate to perform the query (Fig. 20.41). Two methods are generated by default—a "Fill method" that fills a DataTable parameter with the query result and a "Get method" that returns a new DataTable filled with the query result. The text boxes to enter names for these meth-

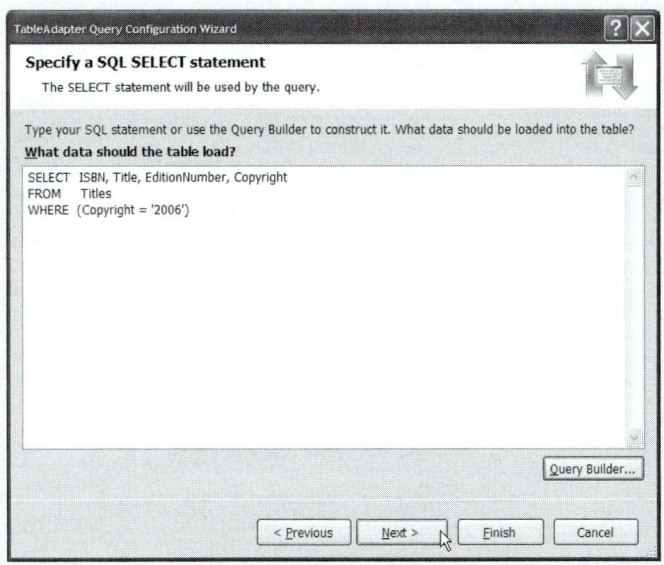

Fig. 20.40 | The SELECT statement created by the **Query Builder**.

ods are prepopulated with FillBy and GetDataBy, respectively. Modify these names to FillWithCopyright2006 and GetDataWithCopyright2006, as shown in Fig. 20.41. Finally, click **Finish** to complete the wizard and return to the **Dataset Designer** (Fig. 20.42). Note that these methods are now listed in the TitlesTableAdapter section of the box representing the Titles table.

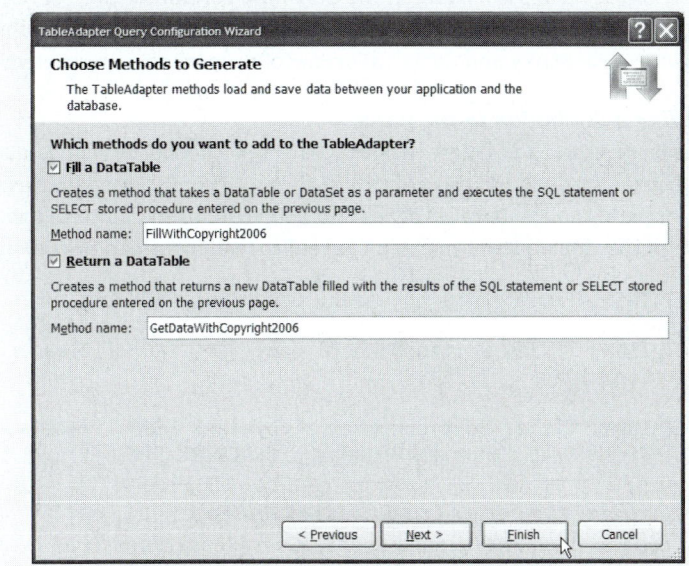

Fig. 20.41 | Specifying names for the methods to be added to the TitlesTableAdapter.

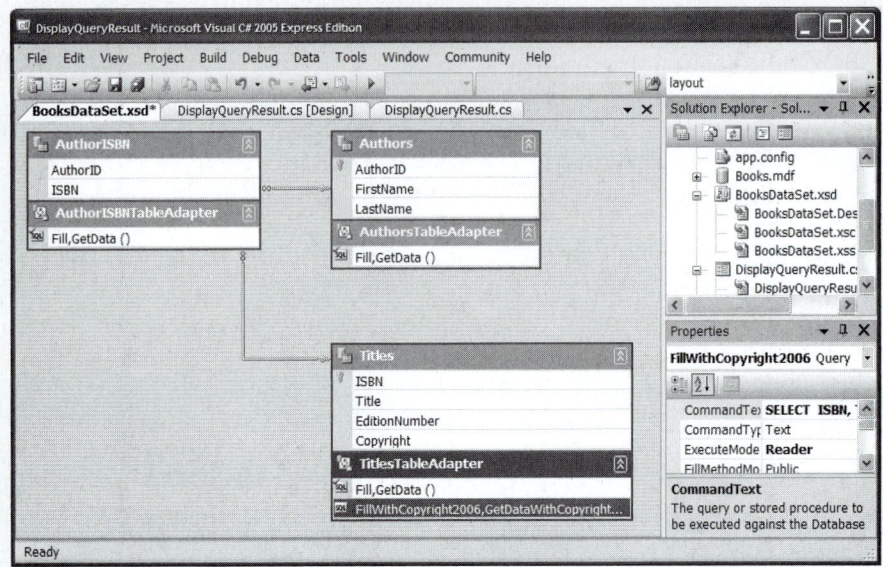

Fig. 20.42 | **Dataset Designer** after adding Fill and Get methods to the TitlesTableAdapter.

Step 11: Adding an Additional Query

Repeat *Steps 4–10* to add another query that selects all books whose titles end with the text "How to Program" and sorts the results by title in ascending order (see Section 20.4.3). In the **Query Builder**, enter LIKE '%How to Program' in the Title row's **Filter** column. To specify the sort order, select **Ascending** in the **Sort Type** column of the Title row. In the final step of the **TableAdapter Query Configuration Wizard**, name the Fill and Get methods FillWithHowToProgramBooks and GetDataForHowToProgramBooks, respectively.

Step 12: Adding a ComboBox to the Form

Return to **Design** view and add below the DataGridView a ComboBox named queriesComboBox to the Form. Users will use this control to choose a SELECT query to execute, whose result will be displayed in the DataGridView. Add three items to queriesComboBox—one to match each of the three queries that the TitlesTableAdapter can now perform:

```
SELECT ISBN, Title, EditionNumber, Copyright FROM Titles

SELECT ISBN, Title, EditionNumber, Copyright FROM Titles
WHERE (Copyright = '2006')

SELECT ISBN, Title, EditionNumber, Copyright FROM Titles
WHERE (Title LIKE '%How to Program') ORDER BY Title
```

Step 13: Customizing the Form's Load Event Handler

Add a line of code to the autogenerated DisplayQueryResultForm_Load event handler, which sets the initial SelectedIndex of the queriesComboBox to 0. Recall that the Load event handler calls the Fill method by default, which executes the first query (the item in index 0). Thus, setting the SelectedIndex causes the ComboBox to display the query that is initially performed when DisplayQueryResultForm first loads.

Step 14: Programming an Event Handler for the ComboBox

Next you must write code that will execute the appropriate query each time the user chooses a different item from queriesComboBox. Double click queriesComboBox in **Design** view to generate a queriesComboBox_SelectedIndexChanged event handler (lines 42–61) in the DisplayQueryResult.cs file (Fig. 20.43). Then to the event handler add a switch statement that invokes the method of titlesTableAdapter that executes the query associated with the ComboBox's current selection (lines 47–60). Recall that method Fill (line 50) executes a SELECT query that selects all rows, method FillWithCopyright2006 (lines 53–54) executes a SELECT query that selects all rows in which the copyright year is 2006 and method FillWithHowToProgramBooks (lines 57–58) executes a query that selects all rows that have "How to Program" at the end of their titles and sorts them in ascending order by title. Each method fills BooksDataSet.Titles with only those rows returned by the corresponding query. Thanks to the data binding relationships created by the IDE, refilling booksDataSet.Titles causes the TitlesDataGridView to display the selected query's result with no additional code.

```
 1   // Fig. 20.43: DisplayQueryResult.cs
 2   // Displays the result of a user-selected query in a DataGridView.
 3   using System;
 4   using System.Windows.Forms;
 5
 6   namespace DisplayQueryResult
 7   {
 8      public partial class DisplayQueryResultForm : Form
 9      {
10         public DisplayQueryResultForm()
11         {
12            InitializeComponent();
13         } // end DisplayQueryResultForm constructor
14
15         // Click event handler for the Save Button in the
16         // BindingNavigator saves the changes made to the data
17         private void titlesBindingNavigatorSaveItem_Click(
18            object sender, EventArgs e )
19         {
20            this.Validate();
21            this.titlesBindingSource.EndEdit();
22            this.titlesTableAdapter.Update( this.booksDataSet.Titles );
23         } // end method titlesBindingNavigatorSaveItem_Click
24
25         // loads data into the booksDataSet.Titles table,
26         // which is then displayed in the DataGridView
27         private void DisplayQueryResultForm_Load(
28            object sender, EventArgs e )
29         {
```

Fig. 20.43 | Displaying the result of a user-selected query in a DataGridView. (Part 1 of 3.)

```
30              // TODO: This line of code loads data into the
31              // 'booksDataSet.Titles' table. You can move, or remove it,
32              // as needed.
33              this.titlesTableAdapter.Fill( this.booksDataSet.Titles );
34
35              // set the ComboBox to show the default query that
36              // selects all books from the Titles table
37              queriesComboBox.SelectedIndex = 0;
38          } // end method DisplayQueryResultForm_Load
39
40          // loads data into the booksDataSet.Titles table based on
41          // user-selected query
42          private void queriesComboBox_SelectedIndexChanged(
43              object sender, EventArgs e )
44          {
45              // fill the Titles DataTable with
46              // the result of the selected query
47              switch ( queriesComboBox.SelectedIndex )
48              {
49                  case 0: // all books
50                      titlesTableAdapter.Fill( booksDataSet.Titles );
51                      break;
52                  case 1: // books with copyright year 2006
53                      titlesTableAdapter.FillWithCopyright2006(
54                          booksDataSet.Titles );
55                      break;
56                  case 2: // How to Program books, sorted by Title
57                      titlesTableAdapter.FillWithHowToProgramBooks(
58                          booksDataSet.Titles );
59                      break;
60              } // end switch
61          } // end method queriesComboBox_SelectedIndexChanged
62      } // end class DisplayQueryResultForm
63  } // end namespace DisplayQueryResult
```

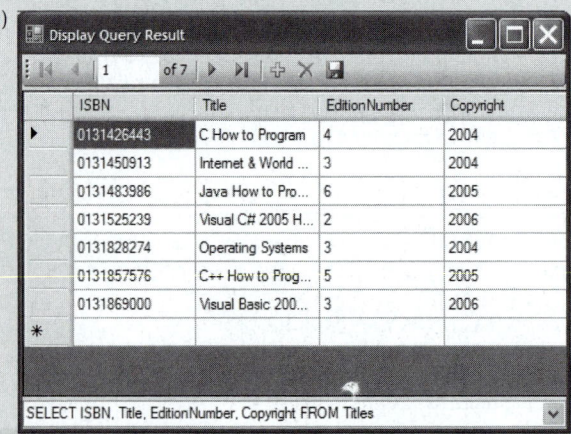

(a)

Fig. 20.43 | Displaying the result of a user-selected query in a DataGridView. (Part 2 of 3.)

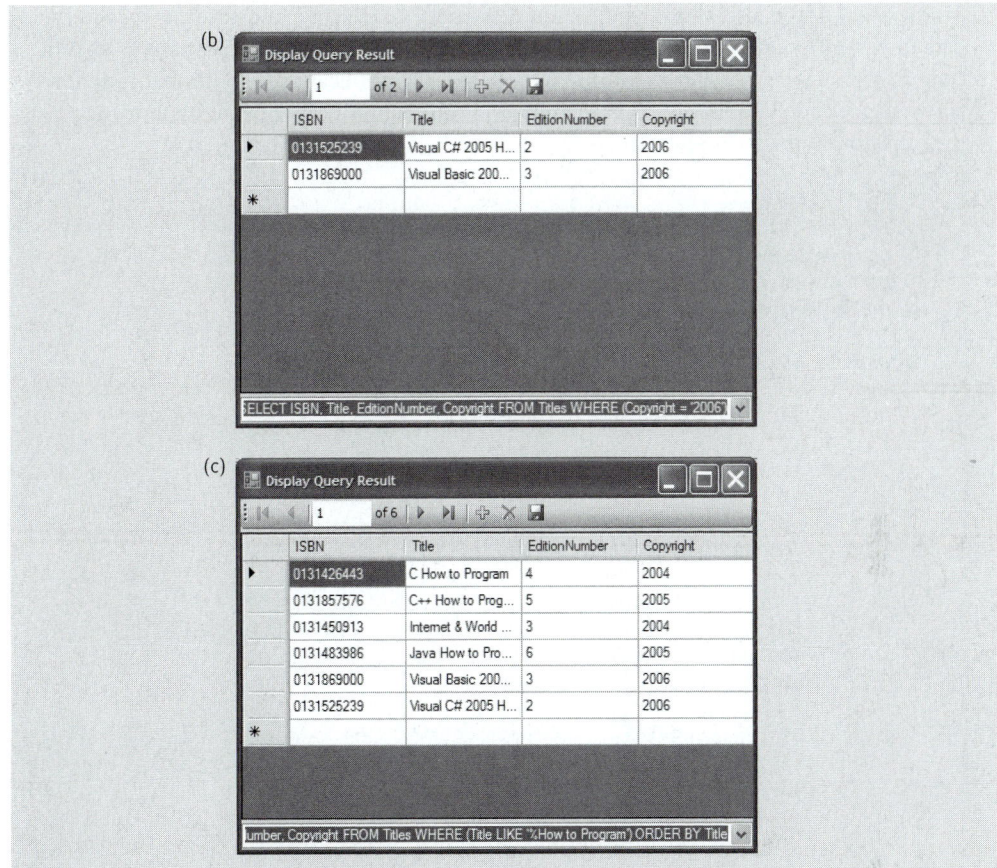

Fig. 20.43 | Displaying the result of a user-selected query in a `DataGridView`. (Part 3 of 3.)

Figure 20.43 also displays the output for `DisplayQueryResultForm`. Figure 20.43(a) depicts the result of retrieving all rows from the `Titles` table. Figure 20.43(b) demonstrates the second query, which retrieves only rows for books with a 2006 copyright. Finally, Fig. 20.43(c) demonstrates the third query, which selects rows for How to Program books and sorts them in ascending order by title.

20.8 Programming with ADO.NET: Address Book Case Study

Our next example implements a simple address book application that enables users to insert rows into, locate rows from and update the SQL Server database `AddressBook.mdf` (located in the chapter's examples directory on the CD that accompanies the book).

The `AddressBook` application (Fig. 20.44) provides a GUI through which users can execute SQL statements on the database. However, instead of displaying a database table in a `DataGridView`, this example presents data from a table one row at a time, using a set of `TextBox`es that display the values of each of the row's columns. A `BindingNavigator` allows you to control which row of the table is currently in view at any given time. The

BindingNavigator also allows you to add new rows, delete row, and save changes to the data in view. Note that lines 17–34 in Fig. 20.44 are similar to the corresponding lines of code in the chapter's earlier examples. We discuss the application's additional functionality and the code in lines 38–53 that supports it momentarily. We begin by showing you the steps to create this application.

```
1   // Fig. 20.44: AddressBook.cs
2   // Allows users to manipulate an address book.
3   using System;
4   using System.Windows.Forms;
5
6   namespace AddressBook
7   {
8      public partial class AddressBookForm : Form
9      {
10        public AddressBookForm()
11        {
12           InitializeComponent();
13        } // end AddressBookForm constructor
14
15        // Click event handler for the Save Button in the
16        // BindingNavigator saves the changes made to the data
17        private void addressesBindingNavigatorSaveItem_Click(
18           object sender, EventArgs e )
19        {
20           this.Validate();
21           this.addressesBindingSource.EndEdit();
22           this.addressesTableAdapter.Update(
23              this.addressBookDataSet.Addresses );
24        } // end method bindingNavigatorSaveItem_Click
25
26        // loads data into the addressBookDataSet.Addresses table
27        private void AddressBookForm_Load( object sender, EventArgs e )
28        {
29           // TODO: This line of code loads data into the
30           // 'addressBookDataSet.Addresses' table. You can move,
31           // or remove it, as needed.
32           this.addressesTableAdapter.Fill(
33              this.addressBookDataSet.Addresses );
34        } // end method AddressBookForm_Load
35
36        // loads data for the rows with the specified last name
37        // into the addressBookDataSet.Addresses table
38        private void findButton_Click( object sender, EventArgs e )
39        {
40           // fill the DataSet's DataTable with only rows
41           // containing the user-specified last name
42           addressesTableAdapter.FillByLastName(
43              addressBookDataSet.Addresses, findTextBox.Text );
44        } // end method findButton_Click
```

Fig. 20.44 | AddressBook application that allows you to manipulate entries in an address book database. (Part 1 of 2.)

```
45
46          // reloads addressBookDataSet.Addresses with all rows
47          private void browseAllButton_Click( object sender, EventArgs e )
48          {
49              // fill the DataSet's DataTable with all rows in the database
50              addressesTableAdapter.Fill( addressBookDataSet.Addresses );
51
52              findTextBox.Text = ""; // clear Find TextBox
53          } // end method browseAllButton_Click
54      } // end class AddressBookForm
55 } // end namespace AddressBook
```

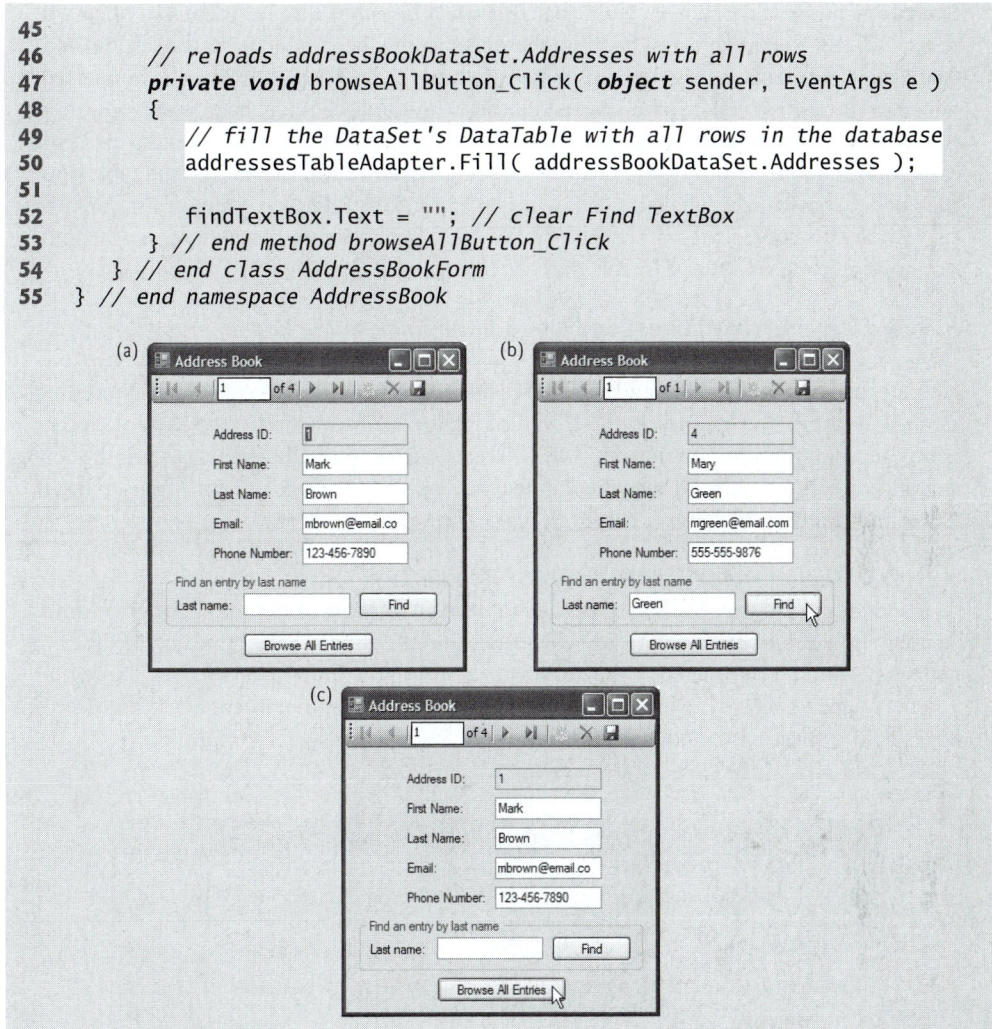

Fig. 20.44 | AddressBook application that allows you to manipulate entries in an address book database. (Part 2 of 2.)

Step 1: Adding the Database to the Project

As in the preceding examples, you must begin by adding the database to the project. After adding the AddressBook.mdf as a data source, the **Data Sources** window will list Address-BookDataSet, which contains a table named Addresses.

Step 2: Indicating that the IDE Should Create a Set of Labels and TextBoxes to Display Each Row of Data

In the earlier sections, you dragged a node from the **Data Sources** window to the Form to create a DataGridView bound to the data source member represented by that node. The IDE allows you to specify the type of control(s) that it creates when you drag and drop a data source member onto a Form. In **Design** view, click the Addresses node in the **Data**

Sources window (Fig. 20.45). Note that this node becomes a drop-down list when you select it. Click the down arrow to view the items in the list. The icon to the left of **Data-GridView** will initially be highlighted in blue, because the default control to be bound to a table is a DataGridView (as you saw in the earlier examples). Select the **Details** option in the drop-down list to indicate that the IDE should create a set of Label–TextBox pairs for each column name–column value pair when you drag and drop the Addresses table onto the Form. (You will see what this looks like in Fig. 20.46.) The drop-down list contains suggestions for controls to display the table's data, but you can also choose the **Customize...** option to select other controls that are capable of being bound to a table's data.

Step 3: Dragging the *Addresses* Data Source Node to the *Form*
Drag the Addresses node from the **Data Sources** window to the Form (Fig. 20.46). The IDE creates a series of Labels and TextBoxes because you selected **Details** in the preceding step. As in the earlier examples, the IDE also creates a BindingNavigator and the other components in the component tray. The IDE sets the text of each Label based on the corresponding column name in the table in the database, and uses regular expressions to insert spaces into multiword column names to make the Labels more readable.

Step 4: Making the *AddressID TextBox* *ReadOnly*
The AddressID column of the Addresses table is an auto-incremented identity column, so users should not be allowed to edit the values in this column. Select the TextBox for the AddressID and set its ReadOnly property to true using the **Properties** window. Note that you may need to click in an empty part of the Form to deselect the other Labels and Text-Boxes before selecting the AddressID TextBox.

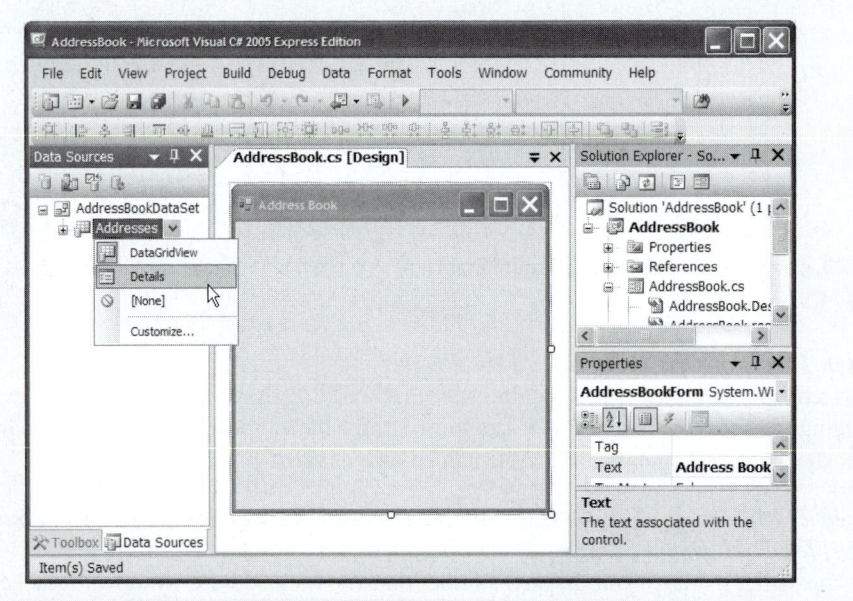

Fig. 20.45 | Selecting the control(s) to be created when dragging and dropping a data source member onto the Form.

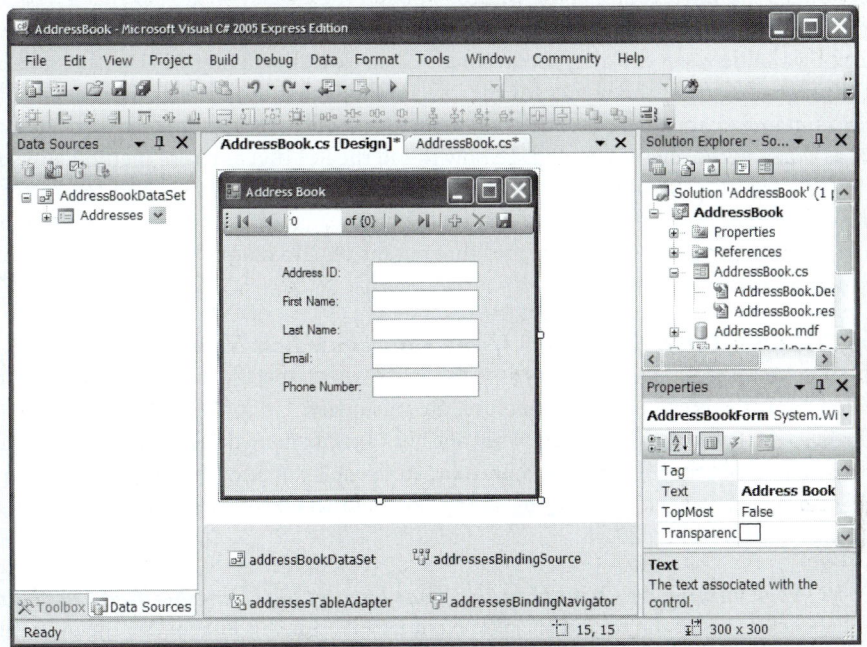

Fig. 20.46 | Displaying a table on a Form using a series of Labels and TextBoxes.

Step 5: Running the Application

Run the application and experiment with the controls in the BindingNavigator at the top of the window. Like the previous examples, this example fills a DataSet object (specifically an AddressBookDataSet object) with all the rows of a database table (i.e., Addresses). However, only a single row of the DataSet appears at any given time. The CD- or DVD-like buttons of the BindingNavigator allow you to change the currently displayed row (i.e., change the values in each of the TextBoxes). The buttons to add a row, delete a row and save changes also perform their designated tasks. Adding a row clears the TextBoxes and makes a new auto-incremented ID (i.e., 5) appear in the TextBox to the right of **Address ID**. After entering some data, click the **Save** button to record the new row in the database. After closing and restarting the application, there should still be five rows. Delete the new row by clicking the appropriate button, then save the changes.

Step 6: Adding a Query to the AddressesTableAdapter

While the BindingNavigator allows you to browse the address book, it would be more convenient to be able to find a specific entry by last name. To add this functionality to the application, you must add a new query to the AddressesTableAdapter using the **Table-Adapter Query Configuration Wizard**. Click the **Edit DataSet with Designer** icon (⌨) in the **Data Sources** window. Select the box representing the AddressesTableAdapter. Right click the TableAdapter's name and select **Add Query....** In the **TableAdapter Query Config-uration Wizard**, keep the default option **Use SQL Statements** and click **Next**. On the next screen, keep the default option **SELECT which returns rows** and click **Next**. Rather than use the **Query Builder** to form your query (as we did in the preceding example), modify the query directly in the text box in the wizard. Append the clause "WHERE LastName = @last-Name" to the end of the default query. Note that @lastName is a parameter that will be replaced by a value when the query is executed. Click **Next**, then enter FillByLastName and GetDataByLastName as the names for the two methods that the wizard will generate. The query contains a parameter, so each of these methods will take a parameter to set the value of @lastName in the query. You will see how to call the FillByLastName method and specify a value for @lastName shortly. Click **Finish** to complete the wizard and return to the **Dataset Designer** (Fig. 20.47). Note that the newly created Fill and Get methods appear under the AddressesTableAdapter and that parameter @lastName is listed to the right of the method names.

Step 7: Adding Controls to Allow Users to Specify a Last Name to Locate
Now that you have created a query to locate rows with a specific last name, add controls to allow users to enter a last name and execute this query. Go to **Design** view (Fig. 20.48) and add to the Form a Label named findLabel, a TextBox named findTextBox and a Button named findButton. Place these controls in a GroupBox named findGroupBox, then set its Text property to Find an entry by last name. Set the Text properties of the Label and Button as shown in Fig. 20.48.

Step 8: Programming an Event Handler That Locates the User-Specified Last Name
Double click findButton to add a Click event handler for this Button. In the event handler, write the following lines of code (lines 42–43 of Fig. 20.44):

```
addressesTableAdapter.FillByLastName(
    addressBookDataSet.Addresses, findTextBox.Text );
```

The FillByLastName method replaces the current data in addressBookDataSet.Addresses with data for only those rows with the last name entered in findTextBox. Note that when invoking FillByLastName, you must pass the DataTable to be filled, as well as an argument specifying the last name to find. This argument becomes the value of the

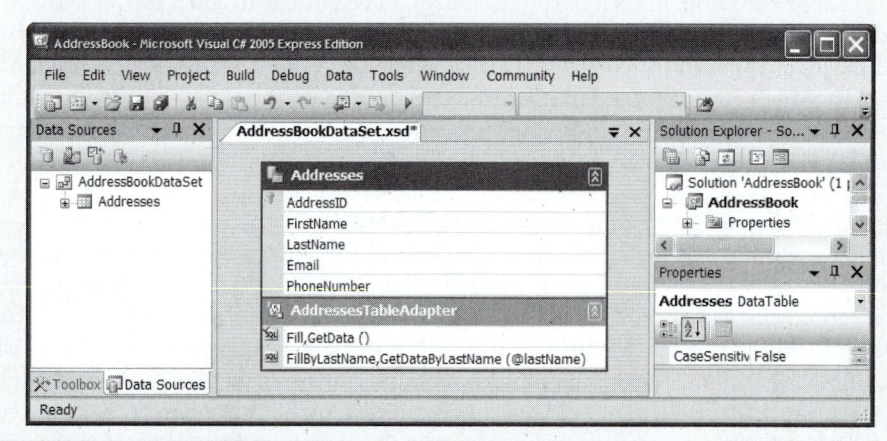

Fig. 20.47 | **Dataset Designer** for the AddressBookDataSet after adding a query to AddressesTableAdapter.

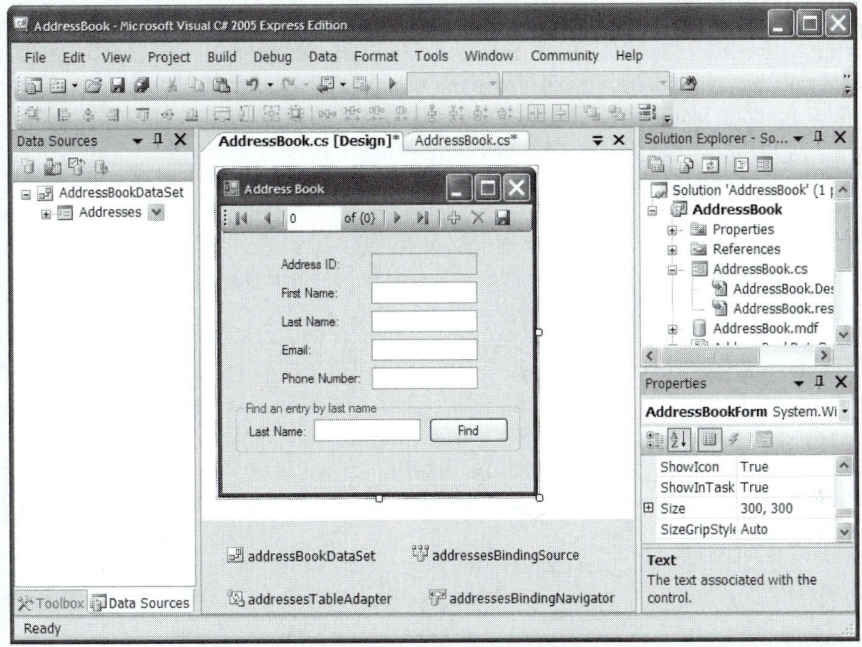

Fig. 20.48 | **Design** view after adding controls to locate a last name in the address book.

@lastName parameter in the SELECT statement created in *Step 6*. Start the application to test the new functionality. Note that when you search for a specific entry (i.e., enter a last name and click **Find**), the BindingNavigator allows the user to browse only the rows containing the specified last name. This is because the data source bound to the Form's controls (i.e., addressBookDataSet.Addresses) has changed and now contains only a limited number of rows.

Step 9: Allowing the User to Return to Browsing All Rows in the Database
To allow users to return to browsing all the rows after searching for specific rows, add a Button named browseAllButton below the findGroupBox. Double click browseAllButton to add a Click event handler to the code. Set the Text property of browseAllButton to **Browse All Entries** in the **Properties** window. Add a line of code that calls addressesTableAdapter.Fill(addressBookDataSet.Addresses) to refill the Addresses DataTable with all the rows from the table in the database (line 50 of Fig. 20.44). Also, add a line of code that clears the Text property of findTextBox (line 52). Start the application. Find a specific last name as in the previous step, then click the browseAllButton button to test the new functionality.

Data Binding in the AddressBook Application
Dragging and dropping the Addresses node from the **Data Sources** window onto AddressBookForm in this example caused the IDE to generate several components in the component tray. These serve the same purposes as those generated for the earlier examples that use the Books database. In this case, addressBookDataSet is an object of a strongly

typed DataSet, AddressBookDataSet, whose structure mimics that of the AddressBook database. addressesBindingSource is a BindingSource object that refers to the Addresses table of the AddressBookDataSet. addressesTableAdapter encapsulates a SqlDataAdapter object configured with SqlCommand objects that execute SQL statements against the AddressBook database. Finally, addressesBindingNavigator is bound to the addressesBindingSource object, thus allowing you to indirectly manipulate the Addresses table of the AddressBookDataSet.

In each of the earlier examples using a DataGridView to display all the rows of a database table, the DataGridView's BindingSource property was set to the corresponding BindingSource object. In this example, you selected **Details** from the drop-down list for the Addresses table in the **Data Sources** window, so the values from a single row of the table appear on the Form in a set of TextBoxes. The IDE sets up the data binding in this example by binding each TextBox to a specific column of the Addresses DataTable in the AddressBookDataSet. To do this, the IDE sets the TextBox's *DataBindings.Text* property. You can view this property by clicking the plus sign next to **(DataBindings)** in the **Properties** window (Fig. 20.49). Clicking the drop-down list for this property allows you to choose a BindingSource object and a property (i.e., column) within the associated data source to bind to the TextBox.

Consider the TextBox that displays the FirstName value—named firstNameTextBox by the IDE. This control's DataBindings.Text property is set to the FirstName property

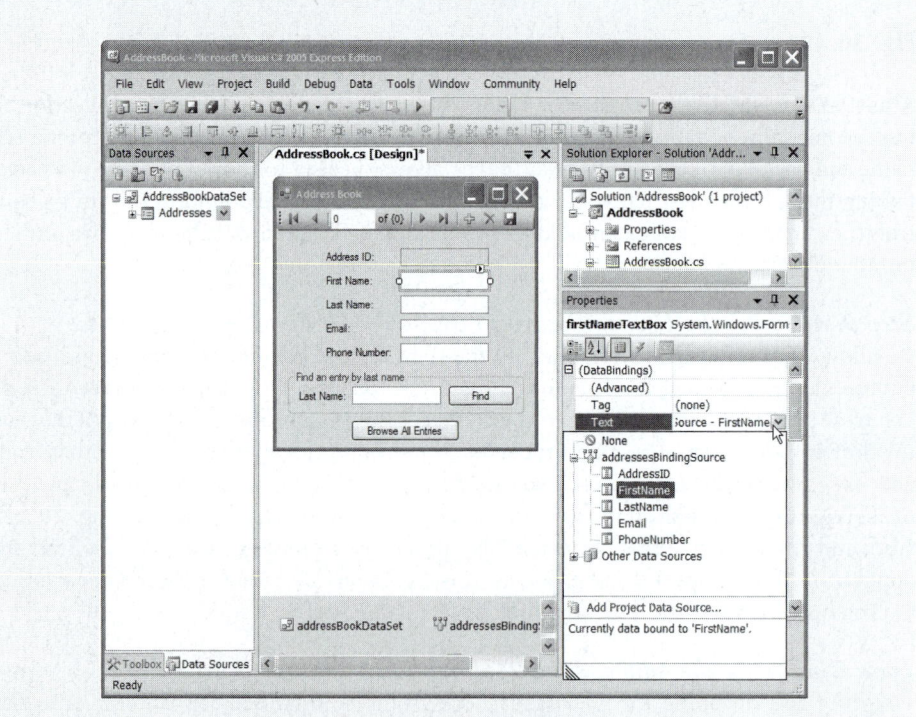

Fig. 20.49 | Viewing the DataBindings.Text property of a TextBox in the **Properties** window.

of the AddressesBindingSource (which refers to AddressBookDataSet.Addresses). Thus, firstNameTextBox always displays the value of the FirstName column in the currently selected row of addressBookDataSet.Addresses. Each IDE-created TextBox on the Form is configured in a similar manner. Browsing the address book with the AddressesBindingNavigator changes the current position in addressBookDataSet.Addresses and thus changes the values displayed in each TextBox. Regardless of changes to the contents of addressBookDataSet.Addresses, the TextBoxes remain bound to the same properties of the DataTable and always display the appropriate data. Note that the TextBoxes do not display any values if the cached version of Addresses is empty (i.e., if there are no rows in the DataTable because the query that filled the DataTable returned no rows).

20.9 Using a DataSet to Read and Write XML

A powerful feature of ADO.NET is its ability to convert data stored in a data source to XML for exchanging data between applications in a portable format. Class DataSet of namespace System.Data provides methods *WriteXml*, *ReadXml* and *GetXml*, which enable developers to create XML documents from data sources and to convert data from XML into data sources.

Writing Data from a Data Source to an XML Document
The application of Fig. 20.50 populates a DataSet with statistics about baseball players, then writes the data to an XML document. The application also displays the XML in a TextBox.

```
 1   // Fig. 20.50: XMLWriter.cs
 2   // Demonstrates generating XML from an ADO.NET DataSet.
 3   using System;
 4   using System.Windows.Forms;
 5
 6   namespace XMLWriter
 7   {
 8      public partial class XMLWriterForm : Form
 9      {
10         public XMLWriterForm()
11         {
12            InitializeComponent();
13         } // end XMLWriterForm constructor
14
15         // Click event handler for the Save Button in the
16         // BindingNavigator saves the changes made to the data
17         private void playersBindingNavigatorSaveItem_Click(
18            object sender, EventArgs e )
19         {
20            this.Validate();
21            this.playersBindingSource.EndEdit();
22            this.playersTableAdapter.Update( this.baseballDataSet.Players );
23         } // end method bindingNavigatorSaveItem_Click
24
```

Fig. 20.50 | Writing the XML representation of a DataSet to a file. (Part 1 of 2.)

```
25      // loads data into the baseballDataSet.Players table
26      private void XMLWriterForm_Load( object sender, EventArgs e )
27      {
28         // TODO: This line of code loads data into the
29         // 'baseballDataSet.Players' table. You can move,
30         // or remove it, as needed.
31         this.playersTableAdapter.Fill( this.baseballDataSet.Players );
32      }
33
34      // write XML representation of DataSet when Button clicked
35      private void writeButton_Click( object sender, EventArgs e )
36      {
37         // set the namespace for this DataSet
38         // and the resulting XML document
39         baseballDataSet.Namespace = "http://www.deitel.com/baseball";
40
41         // write XML representation of DataSet to a file
42         baseballDataSet.WriteXml( "Players.xml" );
43
44         // display XML representation in TextBox
45         outputTextBox.Text += "Writing the following XML:\r\n" +
46            baseballDataSet.GetXml() + "\r\n";
47      } // end method writeButton_Click
48   } // end class XMLWriterForm
49 } // end namespace XMLWriter
```

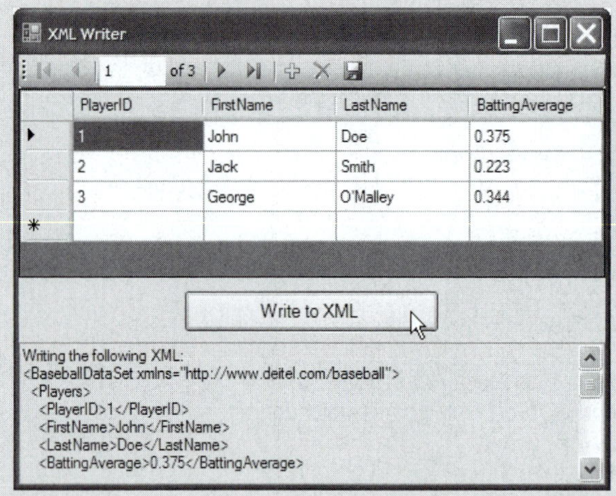

Fig. 20.50 | Writing the XML representation of a **DataSet** to a file. (Part 2 of 2.)

We created this GUI by first adding the **Baseball.mdf** database (located in the chapter's examples directory) to the project, then dragging the **Players** node from the **Data Sources** window to the **Form**. This action created the **BindingNavigator** and **Data-GridView** seen in the output of Fig. 20.50. We then added the **Button** **writeButton** and the **TextBox** **outputTextBox**. The XML representation of the **Players** table should not be edited and will span more lines than the **TextBox** can display at once, so we set output-

TextBox's ReadOnly and MultiLine properties to true and its ScrollBars property to Vertical. Create the event handler for writeButton by double clicking it in **Design** view.

The autogenerated XMLWriterForm_Load event handler (lines 26–32) calls method Fill of class PlayersTableAdapter to populate baseballDataSet with data from the Players table in the Baseball database. Note that the IDE binds the DataGridView to baseballDataSet.Players (through the PlayersBindingSource) to display the information to the user.

Lines 35–47 define the event handler for the **Write to XML** button. When the user clicks this button, line 39 sets baseballDataSet's *Namespace* property to specify a namespace for the DataSet and any XML documents based on the DataSet (see Section 19.4 to learn about XML namespaces). Line 42 invokes DataSet method WriteXml, which generates an XML representation of the data contained in the DataSet, then writes the XML to the specified file. This file is created in the project's bin/Debug or bin/Release directory, depending on how you executed the program. Lines 45–46 then display this XML representation, obtained by invoking DataSet method *GetXml*, which returns a string containing the XML.

Examining an XML Document Generated By DataSet Method WriteXml
Figure 20.51 presents the Players.xml document generated by DataSet method WriteXml in Fig. 20.50. Note that the BaseballDataSet root element (line 2) declares the document's default namespace to be the namespace specified in line 39 of Fig. 20.50. Each Players element represents a record in the Players table. The PlayerID, FirstName, LastName and BattingAverage elements correspond to the columns with these names in the Players database table.

```xml
1    <?xml version="1.0" standalone="yes"?>
2    <BaseballDataSet xmlns="http://www.deitel.com/baseball">
3       <Players>
4          <PlayerID>1</PlayerID>
5          <FirstName>John</FirstName>
6          <LastName>Doe</LastName>
7          <BattingAverage>0.375</BattingAverage>
8       </Players>
9       <Players>
10         <PlayerID>2</PlayerID>
11         <FirstName>Jack</FirstName>
12         <LastName>Smith</LastName>
13         <BattingAverage>0.223</BattingAverage>
14      </Players>
15      <Players>
16         <PlayerID>3</PlayerID>
17         <FirstName>George</FirstName>
18         <LastName>O'Malley</LastName>
19         <BattingAverage>0.344</BattingAverage>
20      </Players>
21   </BaseballDataSet>
```

Fig. 20.51 | XML document generated from BaseballDataSet in XMLWriter.

20.10 Wrap-Up

This chapter introduced relational databases, SQL, ADO.NET and the IDE's visual programming tools for working with databases. You examined the contents of a simple `Books` database and learned about the relationships among the tables in the database. You then learned basic SQL to retrieve data from, add new data to, and update data in a database.

You learned about the classes of namespaces `System.Data` and `System.Data.Sql-Client` that allow programs to connect to a database, then access and manipulate its data. The chapter also explained ADO.NET's disconnected model, which enables a program to store data from a database temporarily in local memory as a `DataSet`.

The second part of the chapter focused on using the IDE's tools and wizards to access and manipulate data sources like a database in C# GUI applications. You learned how to add data sources to projects and how to use the IDE's drag-and-drop capabilities to display database tables in applications. We showed how the IDE hides from you the SQL used to interact with the database. We also demonstrated adding custom queries to GUI applications so that you can display only those rows of data that meet specific criteria. Finally, you learned how to write data from a data source to an XML file.

In the next chapter, we demonstrate how to build Web applications using Microsoft's ASP.NET technology. We also introduce the concept of a three-tier application, in which an application is divided into three pieces that can reside on the same computer or can be distributed among separate computers across a network such as the Internet. As will be discussed, one of these tiers—the information tier—typically stores data in an RDBMS like SQL Server.

20.11 Web Resources

`msdn.microsoft.com/sql/`
The SQL Server Developer Center provides up-to-date product information, downloads, articles and community forums.

`msdn.microsoft.com/vstudio/express/sql/default.aspx`
The home page for SQL Server 2005 Express provides how-to articles, blogs, newsgroups and other valuable resources.

`msdn2.microsoft.com/library/system.data.aspx`
Microsoft's documentation for the `System.Data` namespace.

`msdn.microsoft.com/SQL/sqlreldata/TSQL/default.aspx`
Microsoft's SQL language reference guide.

`msdn2.microsoft.com/library/ms172013.aspx`
Microsoft's documentation for the **Query Builder** and other visual database tools.

`www.w3schools.com/sql/default.asp`
The W3C's SQL tutorial presents basic and advanced SQL features with examples.

`www.sql.org`
This SQL portal provides links to many resources, including SQL syntax, tips, tutorials, books, magazines, discussion groups, companies with SQL services, SQL consultants and free software.

`www.oracle.com/database/index.html`
The home page for Oracle's database management systems.

`www.sybase.com`
The home page for the Sybase database management system.

www-306.ibm.com/software/data/db2/
The home page for IBM's DB2 database management system.

www.postgresql.org
The home page for the PostgreSQL database management system.

www.mysql.com
The home page for the MySQL database server.

Summary

Section 20.1 Introduction
- A database is an organized collection of data. A database management system (DBMS) provides mechanisms for storing, organizing, retrieving and modifying data for many users.
- Today's most popular database management systems are relational database management systems (RDBMS).
- SQL is the international standard language used almost universally with relational database systems to perform queries and manipulate data.
- Programs connect to, and interact with, relational databases via an interface—software that facilitates communications between a database management system and a program.
- C# programs communicate with databases and manipulate their data through ADO.NET.

Section 20.2 Relational Databases
- A relational database stores data in tables. Tables are composed of rows and columns in which values are stored.
- A primary key provides a unique value that cannot be duplicated in other rows of the same table. The primary key uniquely identifies each row.
- Each row of a table represents a record.
- Each column of a table represents a different attribute.
- The primary key can be composed of more than one column.

Section 20.3 Relational Database Overview: Books Database
- A foreign key is a column (or columns) in a table that matches the primary key column in another table.
- The foreign key helps maintain the Rule of Referential Integrity: Every foreign key value must appear as another table's primary key value. Foreign keys enable information from multiple tables to be joined together. There is a one-to-many relationship between a primary key and its corresponding foreign key.
- Every column in a primary key must have a value, and the value of the primary key must be unique. This is known as the Rule of Entity Integrity.
- A one-to-many relationship between tables indicates that a row in one table can have many related rows in a separate table.

Section 20.4 SQL
- SQL provides a rich set of language constructs that enable programmers to define complex queries to retrieve data from a database.

Section 20.4.1 Basic SELECT Query

- The basic form of a SELECT query is

      SELECT * FROM *tableName*

  where the asterisk (*) indicates that all columns from *tableName* should be selected and *tableName* specifies the table in the database from which rows will be retrieved.

- To retrieve specific columns from a table, replace the asterisk (*) with a comma-separated list of column names. Specifying columns explicitly guarantees that they are always returned in the specified order, even if the actual order in the table(s) is different.

Section 20.4.2 WHERE Clause

- The optional WHERE clause in a query specifies the selection criteria for the query. The basic form of a query with selection criteria is

      SELECT *columnName1*, *columnName2*, … FROM *tableName* WHERE *criteria*

- The WHERE clause can contain operators <, >, <=, >=, =, <> and LIKE. Operator LIKE is used for string pattern matching with wildcard characters percent (%) and underscore (_).

- A percent character (%) in a pattern indicates that a string matching the pattern can have zero or more characters at the percent character's location in the pattern.

- An underscore (_) in the pattern string indicates a single character at that position in the pattern.

Section 20.4.3 ORDER BY Clause

- The result of a query can be sorted in ascending or descending order using the optional ORDER BY clause. The simplest form of an ORDER BY clause is

      SELECT *columnName1*, *columnName2*, … FROM *tableName* ORDER BY *column* ASC
      SELECT *columnName1*, *columnName2*, … FROM *tableName* ORDER BY *column* DESC

  where ASC specifies ascending order, DESC specifies descending order and *column* specifies the column on which the sort is based. The default sorting order is ascending, so ASC is optional.

- Multiple columns can be used for ordering purposes with an ORDER BY clause of the form

      ORDER BY *column1 sortingOrder*, *column2 sortingOrder*, …

- The WHERE and ORDER BY clauses can be combined in one query. If used, ORDER BY must be the last clause in the query.

Section 20.4.4 Merging Data from Multiple Tables: INNER JOIN

- An INNER JOIN merges rows from two tables by testing for matching values in a column that is common to the tables. The basic form for the INNER JOIN operator is:

      SELECT *columnName1, columnName2, …*
      FROM *table1* INNER JOIN *table2*
          ON *table1.columnName* = *table2.columnName*

  The ON clause specifies the columns from each table that are compared to determine which rows are joined.

- If a SQL statement uses columns with the same name from multiple tables, the column names must be fully qualified by prefixing them with their table names and a dot (.).

Section 20.4.5 INSERT Statement

- An INSERT statement inserts a new row into a table. The basic form of this statement is

      INSERT INTO *tableName* (*columnName1*, *columnName2*, …, *columnNameN*)
      VALUES (*value1*, *value2*, …, *valueN*)

where *tableName* is the table in which to insert the row. The *tableName* is followed by a comma-separated list of column names in parentheses. The list of column names is followed by the SQL keyword VALUES and a comma-separated list of values in parentheses.

- SQL uses single quotes (') as the delimiter for strings. To specify a string containing a single quote in SQL, the single quote must be escaped with another single quote.

Section 20.4.6 UPDATE Statement
- An UPDATE statement modifies data in a table. The basic form of an UPDATE statement is

    UPDATE *tableName*
    SET *columnName1* = *value1*, *columnName2* = *value2*, ..., *columnNameN* = *valueN*
    WHERE *criteria*

  where *tableName* is the table in which to update data. The *tableName* is followed by keyword SET and a comma-separated list of column name/value pairs in the format *columnName = value*. The optional WHERE clause *criteria* determines which rows to update. If the WHERE clause is omitted, the UPDATE applies to all rows of the table.

Section 20.4.7 DELETE Statement
- A DELETE statement removes rows from a table. The simplest form for a DELETE statement is

    DELETE FROM *tableName* **WHERE** *criteria*

  where *tableName* is the table from which to delete a row (or rows). The optional WHERE *criteria* determines which rows to delete. If the WHERE clause is omitted, the DELETE applies to all rows of the table.

Section 20.5 ADO.NET Object Model
- The ADO.NET object model provides an API for accessing database systems programmatically.
- Namespace System.Data is the root namespace for the ADO.NET API.
- The other important namespaces for ADO.NET, System.Data.OleDb and System.Data.SqlClient, contain classes that enable programs to connect with and modify data sources (i.e., locations that contain data, such as a database or an XML file).
- An object of class SqlConnection of namespace System.Data.SqlClient represents a connection to a data source—specifically a SQL Server database.
- An object of class SqlCommand of namespace System.Data.SqlClient represents an arbitrary SQL command to be executed against a data source.
- Class DataTable of namespace System.Data represents a table of data.
- A DataTable contains a collection of DataRows that represent the table's data.
- A DataTable has a collection of DataColumns that describe the columns in a table.
- DataRow and DataColumn are both located in namespace System.Data.
- An object of class System.Data.DataSet, which consists of a set of DataTables and the relationships among them, represents a cache of data—data that a program stores temporarily in local memory. The structure of a DataSet mimics the structure of a relational database.
- A program does not need a persistent connection to a data source to work with data in a DataSet—it is disconnected from the database.
- An object of class SqlDataAdapter (of namespace System.Data.SqlClient) connects to a data source and executes SQL statements to both populate a DataSet and update the data source based on the current contents of a DataSet.

Section 20.6 Programming with ADO.NET: Extracting Information from a Database

- The IDE provides several visual programming tools and wizards that make accessing data in your projects easy. These tools establish database connections and create the ADO.NET objects necessary to view and manipulate the data through GUI controls.

Section 20.6.1 Displaying a Database Table in a `DataGridView`

- A `DataGridView` is a control from namespace `System.Windows.Forms` that can display a data source in a GUI. A `DataGridView` displays data organized in rows and columns that correspond to the rows and columns of the underlying data source.
- To interact with a data source (e.g., a database), you must add it to the project using the Data Sources window.
- The **Data Source Configuration Wizard** guides you through connecting to a database and choosing the parts of the database you will want to access in your project.
- A connection string specifies the path to a database file on disk, as well as additional settings that determine how the database is accessed.
- Adding a data source causes the IDE to generate a class derived from `System.Data.DataSet` that is designed specifically to store data from that data source.
- The component tray is the gray region below a `Form` in **Design** view that lists the nonvisual components used by a GUI application.
- A `BindingNavigator` provides several ways for users to browse and manipulate data displayed by another GUI control (e.g, a `DataGridView`) on a `Form`.

Section 20.6.2 How Data Binding Works

- The technique through which GUI controls are tied to data sources is known as data binding.
- The structure of an untyped `DataSet` (i.e., the tables that comprise it and the relationships among them) is determined at runtime based on the results of a specific query. The structure of a strongly typed `DataSet` is known at compile time, because it is created specifically to store data from a particular data source.
- A `TableAdapter` is a component responsible for interacting with a database on disk. When other components need to retrieve data from the database or write data to the database, they invoke the methods of the `TableAdapter`.
- A `TableAdapter` encapsulates a `SqlDataAdapter` object, which contains `SqlCommand` objects that specify how the `SqlDataAdapter` selects, inserts, updates and deletes data in the database.
- A `BindingSource` identifies a data source that a program can bind to a control, and serves as an intermediary between the data source and the corresponding data-bound GUI control.
- The `EndEdit` method of a `BindingSource` object applies the changes made to data through a GUI control (i.e., the pending changes) to the data source bound to that control.
- A `TableAdapter`'s `Fill` method retrieves information from the database and places this information in the `DataSet` member provided as an argument.

Section 20.7 Querying the Books Database

- The **TableAdapter Query Configuration Wizard** adds methods to a `TableAdapter` that fill the specified `DataTable` with the results of a custom query.
- The **Dataset Designer** displays a visual representation of a `DataSet` (i.e., the tables it contains and the relationships among them).
- The **Query Builder** allows you to design and test a SQL query for use by a `TableAdapter`.

Section 20.8 Programming with ADO.NET: Address Book Case Study

- Selecting the **Details** option in the drop-down list next to a node in the **Data Sources** window indicates that the IDE should create a set of Label–TextBox pairs for each column name–column value pair when that node is dragged and dropped onto the Form.

- An @ symbol in a query created in the **TableAdapter Query Configuration Wizard** is used to indicate a parameter that will be replaced by a value when the query is executed.

Section 20.9 Using a DataSet to Read and Write XML

- A powerful feature of ADO.NET is its ability to readily convert data stored in a data source to XML and vice versa.

- Method WriteXml of class DataSet writes the XML representation of the DataSet instance to the file specified by the string argument passed to the method.

- Method ReadXml of class DataSet reads the XML representation of the file specified by the string argument passed to it into its own DataSet.

- Method GetXml of class DataSet returns a string containing the XML representation of a DataSet.

Terminology

% SQL wildcard character
_ SQL wildcard character
active database connection
ADO.NET
ADO.NET object model
AND SQL operator
ASC (ascending order)
auto-incremented database column
BindingNavigator class
BindingSource class
BindingSource property of class
    BindingNavigator
cache of data in local memory
closed database connection
column in a relational database
component tray
composite key
connection string
data binding
data source
Data Source Configuration Wizard
Data Sources window
database
database interface
database management system (DBMS)
DataBindings.Text property of class TextBox
DataGridView class
DataMember property of class BindingSource
DataSet class
Dataset Designer
DataSource property of class BindingSource

DataSource property of class DataGridView
DataTable class
DELETE SQL statement
DESC (descending order)
disconnected model
EndEdit method of class BindingSource
entity-relationship (ER) diagram
Fill method of a TableAdapter
foreign key in a database table
GetXml method of class DataSet
identity column in a database table
INNER JOIN SQL operator
INSERT SQL statement
joining database tables
LIKE SQL clause
Microsoft SQL Server 2005 Express
Namespace property of class DataSet
normalizing a database
NOT SQL operator
ON SQL clause in an INNER JOIN SQL operation
one-to-many relationship
open database connection
OR SQL operator
ORDER BY SQL clause
pattern matching
persistent database connection
populating a DataSet
predicate in a SQL WHERE clause
primary key in a database table
qualified name of a database table
query of a database

Query Builder

ReadXml method of class DataSet

relational database

relational database management system
    (RDBMS)

row in a relational database

Rule of Entity Integrity

Rule of Referential Integrity

SELECT SQL query

selection criteria in a WHERE SQL clause

SET SQL clause

SQL

SQL keyword

SQL statement

SqlCommand class

SqlConnection class

SqlDataAdapter class

strongly typed DataSet

System.Data namespace

System.Data.OleDb namespace

System.Data.SqlClient namespace

table in a relational database

TableAdapter

TableAdapter Query Configuration Wizard

untyped DataSet

Update method of a TableAdapter

UPDATE SQL statement

VALUES SQL clause

WHERE SQL clause

WriteXml method of class DataSet

Self-Review Exercises

20.1 Fill in the blanks in each of the following statements:
  a) The international standard database query language is _____.
  b) A table in a relational database consists of _____ and _____ in which values are stored.
  c) The _____ uniquely identifies each row in a relational database table.
  d) A relational database can be manipulated in C# as a(n) _____ object, which stores a cache of the database's data.
  e) A(n) _____ control displays data in rows and columns that correspond to the rows and columns of the underlying data source.
  f) The optional _____ clause in a SQL SELECT query specifies selection criteria for the query.
  g) The optional _____ clause in a SQL SELECT query specifies the order in which rows are sorted in a query.
  h) Merging data from multiple relational database tables is called _____ the data.
  i) A(n) _____ is a column (or group of columns) in a relational database table that matches the primary key column in another table.
  j) Namespace _____ contains classes that are optimized to work with Microsoft SQL Server databases.
  k) Namespace _____ is the root namespace for the ADO.NET API.
  l) An object of class _____ in the System.Data.SqlClient namespace represents a SQL statement that can be executed against a data source.
  m) A(n) _____ object serves as an intermediary between a data source and its corresponding data-bound GUI control.

20.2 State whether each of the following is *true* or *false*. If *false*, explain why.
  a) Only the SQL UPDATE statement can change the data in a database.
  b) Providing the same value for a foreign key in multiple rows breaks the Rule of Entity Integrity.
  c) Providing a foreign-key value that does not appear as a primary-key value in another table breaks the Rule of Referential Integrity.
  d) The result of a query can be sorted in ascending or descending order.
  e) SQL SELECT queries can merge data from multiple relational database tables.
  f) A SQL DELETE statement deletes only one row in a relational database table.

g) A BindingNavigator object can Fill a DataSet.

h) Class DataSet of namespace System.Data provides methods that enable developers to create XML documents from DataSets.

Answers to Self-Review Exercises

20.1 a) SQL. b) rows, columns. c) primary key. d) DataSet. e) DataGridView. f) WHERE. g) ORDER BY. h) joining. i) foreign key. j) System.Data.SqlClient. k) System.Data. l) SqlCommand. m) BindingSource.

20.2 a) False. INSERT and DELETE statements also change the database. Do not confuse the SQL UPDATE statement with the Update method of a TableAdapter. b) False. Multiple rows can have the same value for a foreign key. Providing the same value for the primary key in multiple rows breaks the Rule of Entity Integrity—doing so prevents each row from being identified uniquely. c) True. d) True. e) True. f) False. A DELETE statement deletes all rows satisfying the selection criteria in its WHERE clause. g) False. A BindingNavigator allows users to browse and manipulate data displayed by another GUI control. A TableAdapter can Fill a DataSet. h) True.

Exercises

20.3 (*DisplayTable Application Modification*) Modify the **DisplayTable** application in Section 20.6 to contain a TextBox and a Button that allow the user to search for specific authors by last name. Include a Label to identify the TextBox. Using the techniques presented in Section 20.8, add a query to the AuthorsTableAdapter that takes a parameter specifying the last name of the author to locate. When the user clicks the Button, the application should execute this query by passing the value entered in the TextBox to the appropriate Fill method of the AuthorsTableAdapter.

20.4 (*DisplayQueryResult Application Modification*) Modify the **DisplayQueryResult** application in Section 20.7 to contain a TextBox and a Button that allow the user to perform a search of the book titles in the Titles table of the Books database. Use a Label to identify the TextBox. When the user clicks the Button, the application should execute and display the result of a query that selects all the rows in which the search term entered by the user in the TextBox appears anywhere in the Title column. For example, if the user enters the search term "Visual," the DataGridView should display the rows for *Visual Basic 2005 How to Program* and *Visual C# 2005 How to Program*. If the user enters "Systems," the DataGridView should display only the row for *Operating Systems*. [*Hint:* Build a query that uses pattern matching with the % wildcard character. SQL supports string concatenation with the + operator, so you can combine '%' with a parameter by placing a + between them.]

20.5 (*Baseball Database Application*) Build an application that executes a query against the Players table of the Baseball database from Section 20.9. Display the table in a DataGridView, and add a TextBox and Button to allow the user to search for a specific player by last name. Use a Label to identify the TextBox. Clicking the Button should execute the appropriate query.

20.6 (*Baseball Database Application Modification*) Modify Exercise 20.5 to allow the user to locate players with batting averages in a specific range. Add a TextBox txtMinimum for the minimum batting average (0.000 by default) and a TextBox txtMaximum for the maximum batting average (1.000 by default). Use a Label to identify the TextBox. Add a Button for executing a query that selects rows from the Players table in which the BattingAverage column is greater than or equal to the specified minimum value and less than or equal to the specified maximum value. [*Hint:* Use method Decimal.Parse to convert the values of txtMinimum and txtMaximum to Decimal values before passing them to the appropriate Fill method of the PlayersTableAdapter.]

21

ASP.NET 2.0, Web Forms and Web Controls

If any man will draw up his case, and put his name at the foot of the first page, I will give him an immediate reply. Where he compels me to turn over the sheet, he must wait my leisure.
—Lord Sandwich

Rule One: Our client is always right
Rule Two: If you think our client is wrong, see Rule One.
—Anonymous

A fair question should be followed by a deed in silence.
—Dante Alighieri

You will come here and get books that will open your eyes, and your ears, and your curiosity, and turn you inside out or outside in.
—Ralph Waldo Emerson

OBJECTIVES

In this chapter you will learn:

- Web application development using ASP.NET.

- To create Web Forms.

- To create ASP.NET applications consisting of multiple Web Forms.

- To maintain state information about a user with session tracking and cookies.

- To use the **Web Site Administration Tool** to modify Web application configuration settings.

- To control user access to Web applications using forms authentication and ASP.NET login controls.

- To use databases in ASP.NET applications.

- To design a master page and content pages to create a uniform look-and-feel for a Web site.

21.1 Introduction

In previous chapters, we used Windows Forms and Windows controls to develop Windows applications. In this chapter, we introduce **_Web application development_** with Microsoft's **_ASP.NET 2.0_** technology. Web-based applications create Web content for Web browser clients. This Web content includes Extensible HyperText Markup Language (XHTML), client-side scripting, images and binary data. Readers not familiar with XHTML should first read Appendix F, Introduction to XHTML: Part 1, and Appendix G, Introduction to XHTML: Part 2, before studying this chapter.

We present several examples that demonstrate Web application development using **_Web Forms_**, **_Web controls_** (also called **_ASP.NET server controls_**) and C# programming. Web Form files have the filename extension **_.aspx_** and contain the Web page's GUI. You customize Web Forms by adding Web controls including labels, text boxes, images, buttons and other GUI components. The Web Form file represents the Web page that is sent to the client browser. From this point onward, we refer to Web Form files as **_ASPX files_**.

Every ASPX file created in Visual Studio has a corresponding class written in a .NET language, such as C#. This class contains event handlers, initialization code, utility methods and other supporting code. The file that contains this class is called the *code-behind file* and provides the ASPX file's programmatic implementation.

To develop the code and GUIs in this chapter, we used Microsoft Visual Web Developer 2005 Express—an IDE designed for developing ASP.NET Web applications. Visual Web Developer and Visual C# 2005 Express share many common features and visual programming tools that simplify building complex applications, such as those that access a database (presented in Sections 21.7 and 21.8). The full version of Visual Studio 2005 includes the functionality of Visual Web Developer, so the instructions we present for Visual Web Developer also apply to Visual Studio 2005. Note that you must install either Visual Web Developer 2005 Express (available from msdn.microsoft.com/vstudio/express/vwd/default.aspx) or a complete version of Visual Studio 2005 to implement the programs in this chapter and Chapter 22, Web Services. The site www.deitel.com/books/csharphtp2/ provides instructions for running the ASP.NET 2.0 examples presented in this chapter if you do not wish to recreate them.

21.2 Simple HTTP Transactions

Web application development requires a basic understanding of networking and the World Wide Web. In this section, we discuss the *Hypertext Transfer Protocol* (*HTTP*) and what occurs behind the scenes when a browser displays a Web page. HTTP specifies a set of *methods* and *headers* that allow clients and servers to interact and exchange information in a uniform and predictable manner.

In its simplest form, a Web page is nothing more than an XHTML document—a plain text file containing *markup* (i.e., *tags*) that describe to a Web browser how to display and format the document's information. For example, the XHTML markup

```
<title>My Web Page</title>
```

indicates that the browser should display the text between the **<title>** *start tag* and the **</title>** *end tag* in the browser's title bar. XHTML documents also can contain *hypertext* data (usually called *hyperlinks*), which links to different pages or to other parts of the same page. When the user activates a hyperlink (usually by clicking it with the mouse), the requested Web page loads into the user's browser window.

Any XHTML document available for viewing over the Web has a corresponding Uniform Resource Locator (URL). A URL is an address indicating the location of an Internet resource, such as an XHTML document. The URL contains information that directs a browser to the resource that the user wishes to access. Computers that run *Web server* software make such resources available. When requesting ASP.NET Web applications, the Web server is usually Microsoft *Internet Information Services* (*IIS*). As we discuss shortly, it is also possible to test ASP.NET applications using the ASP.NET Development Server built into Visual Web Developer.

Let us examine the components of the URL

```
http://www.deitel.com/books/downloads.html
```

The http:// indicates that the resource is to be obtained using the HTTP protocol. The middle portion, www.deitel.com, is the server's fully qualified *hostname*—the name of the computer on which the resource resides. This computer usually is referred to as the *host*, because it houses and maintains resources. The hostname www.deitel.com is translated into an *IP address* (68.236.123.125), which identifies the server in a manner similar to how a telephone number uniquely defines a particular phone line. The hostname is translated into an IP address by a *domain name system* (*DNS*) *server*—a computer that maintains a database of hostnames and their corresponding IP addresses. This translation operation is called a *DNS lookup*.

The remainder of the URL (i.e., /books/downloads.html) specifies both the name of the requested resource (the XHTML document downloads.html) and its path, or location (/books), on the Web server. The path could specify the location of an actual directory on the Web server's file system. However, for security reasons, the path often specifies the location of a *virtual directory*. In such systems, the server translates the virtual directory into a real location on the server (or on another computer on the server's network), thus hiding the true location of the resource. Some resources are created dynamically and do not reside anywhere on the server computer. The hostname in the URL for such a resource specifies the correct server, and the path and resource information identify the location of the resource with which to respond to the client's request.

When given a URL, a Web browser performs a simple HTTP transaction to retrieve and display the Web page found at that address. Figure 21.1 illustrates the transaction in detail. This transaction consists of interaction between the Web browser (the client side) and the Web server application (the server side).

In Fig. 21.1, the Web browser sends an HTTP request to the server. The request (in its simplest form) is

```
GET /books/downloads.html HTTP/1.1
```

The word *GET* is an HTTP method indicating that the client wishes to obtain a resource from the server. The remainder of the request provides the path name of the resource (an XHTML document) and the protocol's name and version number (HTTP/1.1).

Any server that understands HTTP (version 1.1) can translate this request and respond appropriately. Figure 21.2 depicts the results of a successful request. The server first responds by sending a line of text that indicates the HTTP version, followed by a numeric code and a phrase describing the status of the transaction. For example,

```
HTTP/1.1 200 OK
```

indicates success, whereas

```
HTTP/1.1 404 Not found
```

informs the client that the Web server could not locate the requested resource.

The server then sends one or more *HTTP headers,* which provide additional information about the data that will be sent. In this case, the server is sending an XHTML text document, so the HTTP header for this example reads:

```
Content-type: text/html
```

The information provided in this header specifies the *Multipurpose Internet Mail Extensions* (*MIME*) type of the content that the server is transmitting to the browser. MIME is an Internet standard that specifies data formats so that programs can interpret data correctly. For example, the MIME type text/plain indicates that the sent information is text

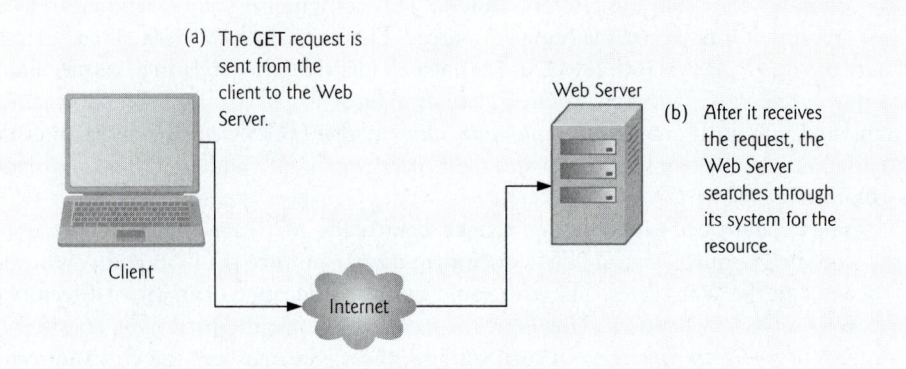

Fig. 21.1 | Client interacting with Web server. *Step 1:* The GET request.

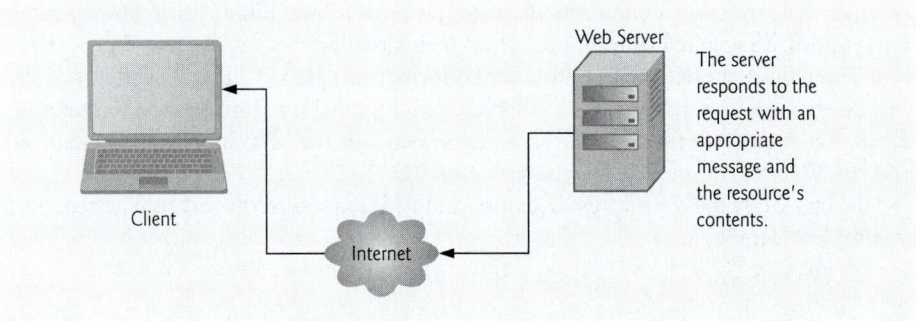

Fig. 21.2 | Client interacting with Web server. *Step 2:* The HTTP response.

that can be displayed directly, without any interpretation of the content as XHTML markup. Similarly, the MIME type image/jpeg indicates that the content is a JPEG image. When the browser receives this MIME type, it attempts to display the image.

The header or set of headers is followed by a blank line, which indicates to the client that the server is finished sending HTTP headers. The server then sends the contents of the requested XHTML document (downloads.html). The server terminates the connection when the resource transfer is complete. At this point, the client-side browser parses the XHTML markup it has received and *renders* (or displays) the results.

21.3 Multitier Application Architecture

Web-based applications are *multitier applications* (sometimes referred to as *n-tier applications*). Multitier applications divide functionality into separate *tiers* (i.e., logical groupings of functionality). Although tiers can be located on the same computer, the tiers of Web-based applications typically reside on separate computers. Figure 21.3 presents the basic structure of a three-tier Web-based application.

The *information tier* (also called the *data tier* or the *bottom tier*) maintains data pertaining to the application. This tier typically stores data in a relational database management system (RDBMS). We discussed RDBMSs in Chapter 20. For example, a retail store

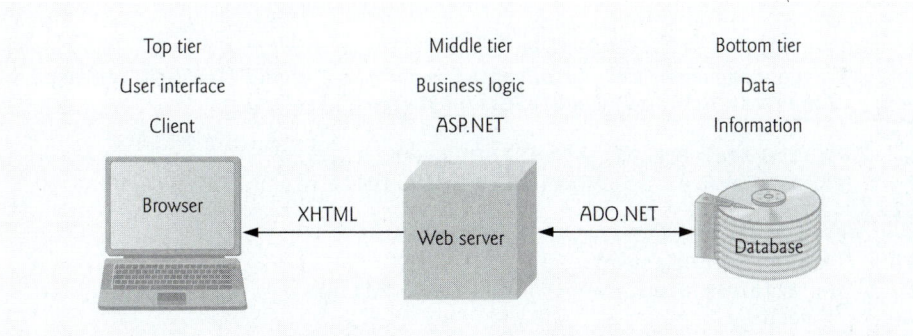

Fig. 21.3 | Three-tier architecture.

might have a database for storing product information, such as descriptions, prices and quantities in stock. The same database also might contain customer information, such as user names, billing addresses and credit card numbers. This tier can contain multiple databases, which together comprise the data needed for our application.

The *middle tier* implements *business logic*, *controller logic* and *presentation logic* to control interactions between the application's clients and the application's data. The middle tier acts as an intermediary between data in the information tier and the application's clients. The middle-tier controller logic processes client requests (such as requests to view a product catalog) and retrieves data from the database. The middle-tier presentation logic then processes data from the information tier and presents the content to the client. Web applications typically present data to clients as XHTML documents.

Business logic in the middle tier enforces *business rules* and ensures that data is reliable before the server application updates the database or presents the data to users. Business rules dictate how clients can and cannot access application data, and how applications process data. For example, a business rule in the middle tier of a retail store's Web-based application might ensure that all product quantities remain positive. A client request to set a negative quantity in the bottom tier's product information database would be rejected by the middle tier's business logic.

The *client tier*, or *top tier*, is the application's user interface, which gathers input and displays output. Users interact directly with the application through the user interface, which is typically a Web browser, keyboard and mouse. In response to user actions (e.g., clicking a hyperlink), the client tier interacts with the middle tier to make requests and to retrieve data from the information tier. The client tier then displays the data retrieved from the middle tier to the user. The client tier never directly interacts with the information tier.

21.4 Creating and Running a Simple Web-Form Example

Our first example displays the Web server's time of day in a browser window. When run, this program displays the text A Simple Web Form Example, followed by the Web server's time. As mentioned previously, the program consists of two related files—an ASPX file (Fig. 21.4) and a C# code-behind file (Fig. 21.5). We first display the markup, code and output, then we carefully guide you through the step-by-step process of creating this program. [*Note*: The markup in Fig. 21.4 and other ASPX file listings in this chapter is the

```
 I    <%-- Fig. 21.4: WebTime.aspx --%>
 2    <%-- A page that displays the current time in a Label. --%>
 3    <%@ Page Language="C#" AutoEventWireup="true" CodeFile="WebTime.aspx.cs"
 4       Inherits="WebTime" EnableSessionState="False" %>
 5
 6    <!DOCTYPE html PUBLIC "-//W3C//DTD XHTML 1.1//EN"
 7       "http://www.w3.org/TR/xhtml11/DTD/xhtml11.dtd">
 8
 9    <html xmlns="http://www.w3.org/1999/xhtml">
10       <head runat="server">
11          <title>A Simple Web Form Example</title>
12       </head>
13       <body>
14          <form id="form1" runat="server">
15             <div>
16                <h2>Current time on the Web server:</h2>
17                <p>
18                   <asp:Label ID="timeLabel" runat="server" BackColor="Black"
19                      Font-Size="XX-Large" ForeColor="Yellow"
20                      EnableViewState="False"></asp:Label>
21                </p>
22             </div>
23          </form>
24       </body>
25    </html>
```

Fig. 21.4 | ASPX file that displays the Web server's time.

same as the markup that appears in Visual Web Developer, but we have reformatted the markup for presentation purposes to make the code more readable.]

Visual Web Developer generates all the markup shown in Fig. 21.4 when you set the Web page's title, type text in the Web Form, drag a Label onto the Web Form and set the properties of the page's text and the Label. We show these steps shortly.

21.4.1 Examining an ASPX File

The ASPX file contains other information in addition to XHTML. Lines 1–2 are *ASP.NET comments* that indicate the figure number, the file name and the purpose of the file. ASP.NET comments begin with **<%--** and terminate with **--%>**. We added these comments to the file. Lines 3–4 use a *Page* directive (in an ASPX file a *directive* is delimited by **<%@** and **%>**) to specify information needed by ASP.NET to process this file. The *Language* attribute of the Page directive specifies the language of the code-behind file as C#; the code-behind file (i.e., the *CodeFile*) is WebTime.aspx.cs. Note that a code-behind file name usually consists of the full ASPX file name (e.g., WebTime.aspx) followed by the .cs extension.

The *AutoEventWireup* attribute (line 3) determines how Web Form events are handled. When AutoEventWireup is set to true, ASP.NET determines which methods in the class are called in response to an event generated by the Page. For example, ASP.NET will call methods Page_Load and Page_Init in the code-behind file to handle the Page's Load and Init events respectivel. (We discuss these events later in the chapter.)

The ***Inherits*** attribute (line 4) specifies the class in the code-behind file from which this ASP.NET class inherits—in this case, `WebTime`. We say more about `Inherits` momentarily. [*Note:* We explicitly set the ***EnableSessionState*** attribute (line 4) to `False`. We explain the significance of this attribute later in the chapter. The IDE sometimes generates attribute values (e.g., `True` and `False`) and control names (as you will see later in the chapter) that do not adhere to our standard code capitalization conventions (i.e., `true` and `false`). However, unlike C# code, ASP.NET markup is not case-sensitive, so using a different case is not problematic. To remain consistent with the code generated by the IDE, we do not modify these values in our code listings or in our accompanying discussions.]

For this first ASPX file, we provide a brief discussion of the XHTML markup. We do not discuss the majority of the XHTML contained in subsequent ASPX files. Lines 6–7 contain the document type declaration, which specifies the document element name (`HTML`) and the `PUBLIC` Uniform Resource Identifier (URI) for the DTD that defines the XHTML vocabulary.

Lines 9–10 contain the `<html>` and `<head>` start tags, respectively. XHTML documents have the root element `html` and mark up information about the document in the `head` element. Also note that the `html` element specifies the XML namespace of the document using the `xmlns` attribute (see Section 19.4).

Line 11 sets the title of this Web page. We demonstrate how to set the title through a property in the IDE shortly. Notice the ***runat*** attribute in line 10, which is set to ***"server"***. This attribute indicates that when a client requests this ASPX file, ASP.NET processes the `head` element and its nested elements on the server and generates the corresponding XHTML, which is then sent to the client. In this case, the XHTML sent to the client will be identical to the markup in the ASPX file. However, as you will see, ASP.NET can generate complex XHTML markup from simple elements in an ASPX file.

Line 13 contains the `<body>` start tag, which begins the body of the XHTML document; the body contains the main content that the browser displays. The `form` that contains our XHTML text and controls is defined in lines 14–23. Again, the `runat` attribute in the `form` element indicates that this element executes on the server, which generates equivalent XHTML and sends it to the client. Lines 15–22 contain a `div` element that groups the elements of the form in a block of markup.

Line 16 is an `h2` heading element that contains text indicating the purpose of the Web page. As we demonstrate shortly, the IDE generates this element in response to typing text directly in the Web Form and selecting the text as a second-level heading.

Lines 17–21 contain a `p` element to mark up content to be displayed as a paragraph in the browser. Lines 18–20 mark up a label Web control. The properties that we set in the **Properties** window, such as `Font-Size` and `BackColor` (i.e., background color), are attributes here. The ***ID*** attribute (line 18) assigns a name to the control so that it can be manipulated programmatically in the code-behind file. We set the control's ***EnableView-State*** attribute (line 20) to `False`. We explain the significance of this attribute later in the chapter.

The ***asp: tag prefix*** in the declaration of the ***Label*** tag (line 18) indicates that the label is an ASP.NET Web control, not an XHTML element. Each Web control maps to a corresponding XHTML element (or group of elements)—when processing a Web control on the server, ASP.NET generates XHTML markup that will be sent to the client to represent that control in a Web browser.

Portability Tip 21.1

The same Web control can map to different XHTML elements, depending on the client browser and the Web control's property settings.

In this example, the asp:Label control maps to the XHTML **span** element (i.e., ASP.NET creates a span element to represent this control in the client's Web browser). A span element contains text that is displayed in a Web page. This particular element is used because span elements allow formatting styles to be applied to text. Several of the property values that were applied to our label are represented as part of the style attribute of the span element. You will soon see what the generated span element's markup looks like.

The Web control in this example contains the runat="server" attribute–value pair (line 18), because this control must be processed on the server so that the server can translate the control into XHTML that can be rendered in the client browser. If this attribute pair is not present, the asp:Label element is written as text to the client (i.e., the control is not converted into a span element and does not render properly).

21.4.2 Examining a Code-Behind File

Figure 21.5 presents the code-behind file. Recall that the ASPX file in Fig. 21.4 references this file in line 3.

Line 13 begins the declaration of class WebTime. Recall from Chapter 9 that a class declaration can span multiple source-code files and that the separate portions of the class declaration in each file are known as partial classes. The partial modifier in line 13 of Fig. 21.5 indicates that the code-behind file actually is a partial class. We discuss the remaining portion of this class shortly.

```
 1   // Fig. 21.5: WebTime.aspx.cs
 2   // Code-behind file for a page that displays the current time.
 3   using System;
 4   using System.Data;
 5   using System.Configuration;
 6   using System.Web;
 7   using System.Web.Security;
 8   using System.Web.UI;
 9   using System.Web.UI.WebControls;
10   using System.Web.UI.WebControls.WebParts;
11   using System.Web.UI.HtmlControls;
12
13   public partial class WebTime : System.Web.UI.Page
14   {
15      // initializes the contents of the page
16      protected void Page_Init( object sender, EventArgs e )
17      {
18         // display the server's current time in timeLabel
19         timeLabel.Text = string.Format( "{0:D2}:{1:D2}:{2:D2}",
20            DateTime.Now.Hour, DateTime.Now.Minute, DateTime.Now.Second );
21      } // end method Page_Init
22   } // end class WebTime
```

Fig. 21.5 | Code-behind file for a page that displays the Web server's time. (Part 1 of 2.)

Fig. 21.5 | Code-behind file for a page that displays the Web server's time. (Part 2 of 2.)

Line 13 indicates that WebTime inherits from class *Page* in namespace *System.Web.UI*. This namespace contains classes and controls that assist in building Web-based applications. Class Page provides event handlers and objects necessary for creating Web-based applications. In addition to class Page (from which all Web applications directly or indirectly inherit), System.Web.UI also includes class *Control*—the base class that provides common functionality for all Web controls.

Lines 16–21 define method *Page_Init*, which handles the page's *Init* event. This event—the first event raised after a page is requested—indicates that the page is ready to be initialized. The only initialization required for this page is setting timeLabel's Text property to the time on the server (i.e., the computer on which this code executes). The statement in lines 19–20 retrieves the current time and formats it as *HH:MM:SS*. For example, 9 AM is formatted as 09:00:00, and 2:30 PM is formatted as 14:30:00. Notice that the code-behind file can access timeLabel (the ID of the Label in the ASPX file) programmatically, even though the file does not contain a declaration for a variable named timeLabel. You will learn why momentarily.

21.4.3 Relationship Between an ASPX File and a Code-Behind File

How are the ASPX and code-behind files used to create the Web page that is sent to the client? First, recall that class WebTime is the base class specified in line 3 of the ASPX file (Fig. 21.4). This class (partially declared in the code-behind file) inherits from Page, which defines the general functionality of a Web page. Partial class WebTime inherits this functionality and defines some of its own (i.e., displaying the current time). The code-behind file contains the code to display the time, whereas the ASPX file contains the code to define the GUI.

When a client requests an ASPX file, ASP.NET creates two classes behind the scenes. Recall that the code-behind file contains a partial class named WebTime. The first file ASP.NET generates is another partial class containing the remainder of class WebTime, based on the markup in the ASPX file. For example, WebTime.aspx contains a Label Web control with ID timeLabel, so the generated partial class would contain a declaration for a Label variable named timeLabel. This partial class might look like

```
public partial class WebTime
{
    protected System.Web.UI.WebControls.Label timeLabel;
}
```

Note that a `Label` is a Web control defined in namespace *`System.Web.UI.WebControls`*, which contains Web controls for designing a page's user interface. Web controls in this namespace derive from class *`WebControl`*. When compiled, the preceding partial class declaration containing Web control declarations combines with the code-behind file's partial class declaration to form the complete `WebTime` class. This explains why line 19 in method `Page_Init` of `WebTime.aspx.cs` (Fig. 21.5) can access `timeLabel`, which is created in lines 18–20 of `WebTime.aspx` (Fig. 21.4)—method `Page_Init` and control `timeLabel` are actually members of the same class, but defined in separate partial classes.

The second class generated by ASP.NET is based on the ASPX file that defines the page's visual representation. This new class inherits from class `WebTime`, which defines the page's logic. The first time the Web page is requested, this class is compiled, and an instance is created. This instance represents our page—it creates the XHTML that is sent to the client. The assembly created from our compiled classes is placed within a subdirectory of

```
C:\WINDOWS\Microsoft.NET\Framework\VersionNumber\
    Temporary ASP.NET Files\WebTime
```

where *VersionNumber* is the version number of the .NET Framework (e.g., `v2.0.50215`) installed on your computer.

Performance Tip 21.1

Once an instance of the Web page has been created, multiple clients can use it to access the page—no recompilation is necessary. The project will be recompiled only when you modify the application; changes are detected by the runtime environment, and the project is recompiled to reflect the altered content.

21.4.4 How the Code in an ASP.NET Web Page Executes

Let's look briefly at how the code for our Web page executes. When an instance of the page is created, the `Init` event occurs first, invoking method `Page_Init`. Method `Page_Init` can contain code needed to initialize objects and other aspects of the page. After `Page_Init` executes, the *Load* event occurs, and the *`Page_Load`* event handler executes. Although not present in this example, this event is inherited from class `Page`. You will see examples of the `Page_Load` event handler later in the chapter. After this event handler finishes executing, the page processes events that are generated by the page's controls, such as user interactions with the GUI. When the Web Form object is ready for garbage collection, an *Unload* event occurs, which calls the *`Page_Unload`* event handler. This event, too, is inherited from class `Page`. `Page_Unload` typically contains code that releases resources used by the page.

21.4.5 Examining the XHTML Generated by an ASP.NET Application

Figure 21.6 shows the XHTML generated by ASP.NET when `WebTime.aspx` (Fig. 21.4) is requested by a client Web browser. To view this XHTML, select **View > Source** in Internet Explorer. [*Note:* We added the XHTML comments in lines 1–2 and reformatted the XHTML to conform to our coding conventions.]

The contents of this page are similar to those of the ASPX file. Lines 7–9 define a document header comparable to that in Fig. 21.4. Lines 10–28 define the body of the docu-

```
 1    <!-- Fig. 21.6: WebTime.html -->
 2    <!-- The XHTML generated when WebTime.aspx is loaded. -->
 3    <!DOCTYPE html PUBLIC "-//W3C//DTD XHTML 1.1//EN"
 4       "http://www.w3.org/TR/xhtml11/DTD/xhtml11.dtd">
 5
 6    <html xmlns="http://www.w3.org/1999/xhtml">
 7       <head>
 8          <title>A Simple Web Form Example</title>
 9       </head>
10       <body>
11          <form method="post" action="WebTime.aspx" id="form1">
12             <div>
13                <input type="hidden" name="__VIEWSTATE"
14                   id="__VIEWSTATE" value=
15                   "/wEPDwUJODExMDE5NzY5ZGQ4n4mht8D7Eqxn73tM5LDnstPlCg==" />
16             </div>
17
18             <div>
19                <h2>Current time on the Web server:</h2>
20                <p>
21                   <span id="timeLabel" style="color:Yellow;
22                      background-color:Black;font-size:XX-Large;">
23                      17:13:52
24                   </span>
25                </p>
26             </div>
27          </form>
28       </body>
29    </html>
```

Fig. 21.6 | XHTML response when the browser requests `WebTime.aspx`.

ment. Line 11 begins the form, a mechanism for collecting user information and sending it to the Web server. In this particular program, the user does not submit data to the Web server for processing; however, processing user data is a crucial part of many applications that is facilitated by the form. We demonstrate how to submit data to the server in later examples.

XHTML forms can contain visual and nonvisual components. Visual components include clickable buttons and other GUI components with which users interact. Nonvisual components, called *hidden inputs*, store data, such as e-mail addresses, that the document author specifies. One of these hidden inputs is defined in lines 13–15. We discuss the precise meaning of this hidden input later in the chapter. Attribute *method* of the form element (line 11) specifies the method by which the Web browser submits the form to the server. The *action* attribute identifies the name and location of the resource that will be requested when this form is submitted—in this case, `WebTime.aspx`. Recall that the ASPX file's form element contained the runat="server" attribute–value pair (line 14 of Fig. 21.4). When the form is processed on the server, the runat attribute is removed. The method and action attributes are added, and the resulting XHTML form is sent to the client browser.

In the ASPX file, the form's Label (i.e., timeLabel) is a Web control. Here, we are viewing the XHTML created by our application, so the form contains a span element (lines 21–24 of Fig. 21.6) to represent the text in the label. In this particular case, ASP.NET maps the *Label* Web control to an XHTML span element. The formatting options that were specified as properties of timeLabel, such as the font size and color of the text in the *Label*, are now specified in the style attribute of the span element.

Notice that only those elements in the ASPX file marked with the runat="server" attribute–value pair or specified as Web controls are modified or replaced when the file is processed by the server. The pure XHTML elements, such as the h2 in line 19, are sent to the browser exactly as they appear in the ASPX file.

21.4.6 Building an ASP.NET Web Application

Now that we have presented the ASPX file, the code-behind file and the resulting Web page sent to the Web browser, we outline the process by which we created this application. To build the WebTime application, perform the following steps in Visual Web Developer:

Step 1: Creating the Web Application Project
Select **File > New Web Site...** to display the **New Web Site** dialog (Fig. 21.7). In this dialog, select **ASP.NET Web Site** in the **Templates** pane. Below this pane, the **New Web Site** dialog contains two fields with which you can specify the type and location of the Web application you are creating. If it is not already selected, select **HTTP** from the drop-down list closest to **Location**. This indicates that the Web application should be configured to run as an IIS application using HTTP (either on your computer or on a remote computer). We want our project to be located in http://localhost, which is the URL for IIS's root directory (this URL corresponds to the C:\InetPub\wwwroot directory on your machine). The name *localhost* indicates that the client and server reside on the same machine. If the Web server were located on a different machine, localhost would be replaced with the appropriate IP address or hostname. By default, Visual Web Developer sets the location where the Web site will be created to http://localhost/WebSite, which we change to http://localhost/WebTime.

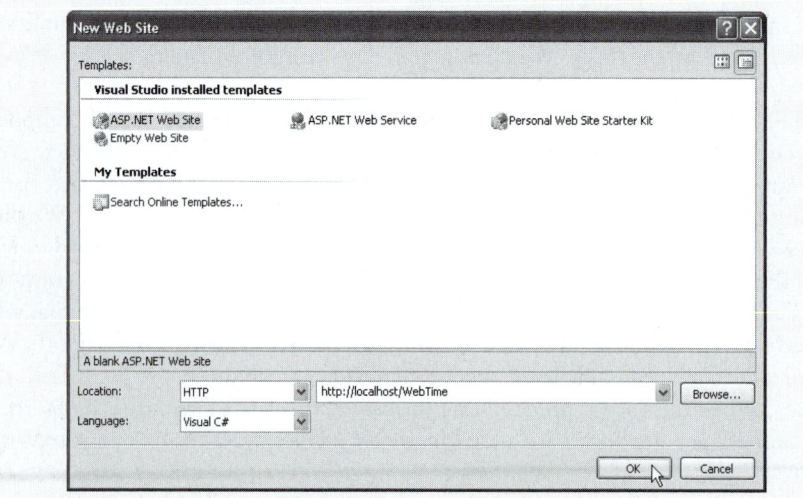

Fig. 21.7 | Creating an **ASP.NET Web Site** in Visual Web Developer.

If you do not have access to IIS, you can select **File System** from the drop-down list next to **Location** to create the Web application in a folder on your computer. You will be able to test the application using Visual Web Developer's internal ASP.NET Development Server, but you will not be able to access the application remotely over the Internet.

The **Language** drop-down list in the **New Web Site** dialog allows you to specify the language (i.e., Visual Basic, Visual C# or Visual J#) in which you will write the code-behind file(s) for the Web application. Change the setting to Visual C#. Click **OK** to create the Web application project. This action creates the directory C:\Inetpub\wwwroot\ WebTime and makes it accessible through the URL http://localhost/WebTime. This action also creates a WebTime directory in the Visual Studio 2005/Projects directory of your Windows user's My Documents directory to store the project's solution files (e.g., WebTime.sln).

Step 2: *Examining the* Solution Explorer *of the Newly Created Project*
The next several figures describe the new project's content, begining with the **Solution Explorer** shown in Fig. 21.8. Like Visual C# 2005 Express, Visual Web Developer creates several files when a new project is created. An ASPX file (i.e., Web Form) named Default.aspx is created for each new **ASP.NET Web Site** project. This file is open by default in the Web Forms Designer in **Source** mode when the project first loads (we discuss this momentarily). As mentioned previously, a code-behind file is included as part of the project. Visual Web Developer creates a code-behind file named Default.aspx.cs. To open the ASPX file's code-behind file, right click the ASPX file and select **View Code** or click the **View Code** button at the top of the **Solution Explorer**. Alternatively, you can expand the node for the ASPX file to reveal the node for the code-behind file (see Fig. 21.8). You can also choose to list all the files in the project individually (instead of nested) by clicking the **Nest Related Files** button—this option is turned on by default, so clicking the button toggles the option off.

The **Properties** and **Refresh** buttons in Visual Web Developer's **Solution Explorer** behave like those in Visual C# 2005 Express. Visual Web Developer's **Solution Explorer** also contains three additional buttons—**View Designer**, **Copy Web Site** and **ASP.NET Configuration**. The **View Designer** button allows you to open the Web Form in **Design** mode, which we discuss shortly. The **Copy Web Site** button opens a dialog that allows you to move the files in this project to another location, such as a remote Web server. This is useful if you are developing the application on your local computer, but want to make it available to the public from a different location. Finally, the **ASP.NET Configuration** button takes you to a Web page called the **Web Site Administration Tool**, where you can manipulate various settings and security options for your application. We discuss this tool in greater detail in Section 21.8.

Step 3: *Examining the* Toolbox *in Visual Web Developer*
Figure 21.9 shows the **Toolbox** displayed in the IDE when the project loads. Figure 21.9(a) displays the beginning of the **Standard** list of Web controls, and Fig. 21.9(b) displays the remaining Web controls, as well as the list of **Data** controls used in ASP.NET. We discuss specific controls in Fig. 21.9 as they are used throughout the chapter. Notice that some controls in the **Toolbox** are similar to the Windows controls presented earlier in the book.

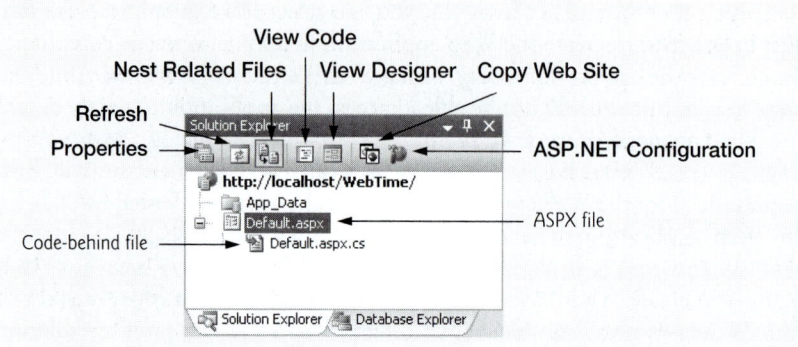

Fig. 21.8 | **Solution Explorer** window for project `WebTime`.

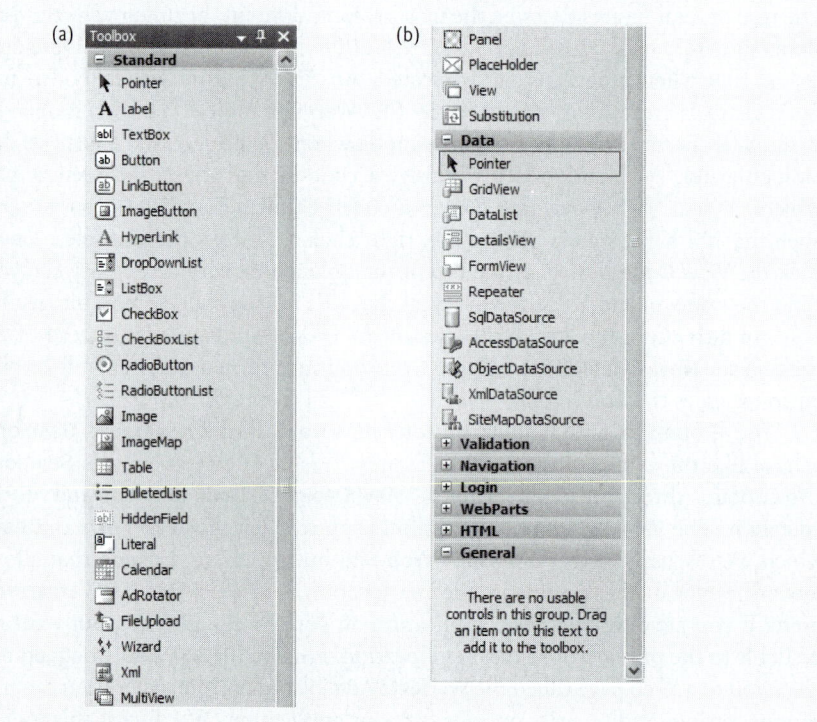

Fig. 21.9 | **Toolbox** in Visual Web Developer.

Step 4: Examining the Web Forms Designer

Figure 21.10 shows the Web Forms Designer in **Source** mode, which appears in the center of the IDE. When the project loads for the first time, the Web Forms Designer displays the auto-generated ASPX file (i.e., `Default.aspx`) in **Source** mode, which allows you to view and edit the markup that comprises the Web page. The markup listed in Fig. 21.10 was created by the IDE and serves as a template that we will modify shortly. Clicking the **Design** button in the lower-left corner of the Web Forms Designer switches to **Design** mode (Fig. 21.11), which allows you to drag and drop controls from the **Toolbox** on the Web Form. You can also type at the current cursor location to add text to the Web page. We demonstrate this shortly. In response to such actions, the IDE generates the appropriate markup in the ASPX file. Notice that **Design** mode indicates the XHTML element where the cursor is currently located. Clicking the **Source** button returns the Web Forms Designer to **Source** mode, where you can see the generated markup.

Step 5: Examining the Code-Behind File in the IDE

The next figure (Fig. 21.12) displays Default.aspx.cs—the code-behind file generated by Visual Web Developer for Default.aspx. Right click the ASPX file in the **Solution Explorer** and select **View Code** to open the code-behind file. When it is first created, this file contains nothing more than a partial class declaration with an empty Page_Load event handler. We will add the Page_Init event handler to this code momentarily.

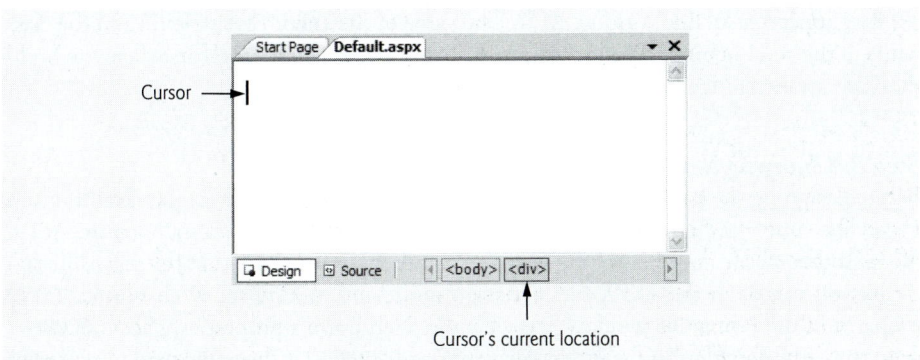

```
Start Page   Default.aspx                                            ▼ ✕

Client Objects & Events          ▼    (No Events)                       ▼

 1    <%@ Page Language="C#" AutoEventWireup="true"
 2        CodeFile="Default.aspx.cs" Inherits="_Default" %>
 3
 4    <!DOCTYPE html PUBLIC "-//W3C//DTD XHTML 1.1//EN"
 5        "http://www.w3.org/TR/xhtml11/DTD/xhtml11.dtd">
 6
 7    <html xmlns="http://www.w3.org/1999/xhtml" >
 8    <head runat="server">
 9        <title>Untitled Page</title>
10    </head>
11    <body>
12        <form id="form1" runat="server">
13        <div>
14
15        </div>
16        </form>
17    </body>
18    </html>
19
```

Source mode button

Design mode button → 🖵 Design   ⊞ Source

Fig. 21.10 | **Source** mode of the Web Forms Designer.

```
Start Page   Default.aspx                          ▼ ✕

Cursor → |




🖵 Design   ⊞ Source    ◀ <body> <div>          ▶
```

Cursor's current location

Fig. 21.11 | **Design** mode of the Web Forms Designer.

```
Default.aspx.cs   Start Page   Default.aspx                          ▾ ✕
_Default                          ▾  Page_Load(object sender, EventArgs e)  ▾
  1  using System;
  2  using System.Data;
  3  using System.Configuration;
  4  using System.Web;
  5  using System.Web.Security;
  6  using System.Web.UI;
  7  using System.Web.UI.WebControls;
  8  using System.Web.UI.WebControls.WebParts;
  9  using System.Web.UI.HtmlControls;
 10
 11  public partial class _Default : System.Web.UI.Page
 12  {
 13      protected void Page_Load( object sender, EventArgs e )
 14      {
 15
 16      }
 17  }
```

Fig. 21.12 | Code-behind file for `Default.aspx` generated by Visual Web Developer.

Step 6: Renaming the ASPX File

We have displayed the contents of the default ASPX and code-behind files. We now rename these files. Right click the ASPX file in the **Solution Explorer** and select **Rename**. Enter the new file name `WebTime.aspx` and press *Enter*. This updates the name of both the ASPX file and the code-behind file. Note that the `CodeFile` attribute of `WebTime.aspx`'s `Page` directive is also updated by the IDE.

Step 7: Renaming the Class in the Code-Behind File and Updating the ASPX File

Although renaming the ASPX file causes the name of the code-behind file to change, this action does not affect the name of the partial class declared in the code-behind file. Open the code-behind file and change the class name from `_Default` (line 11 in Fig. 21.12) to `WebTime`, so the partial class declaration appears as in line 13 of Fig. 21.5. Recall that this class is also referenced by the `Page` directive of the ASPX file. Using the Web Forms Designer's **Source** mode, modify the `Inherits` attribute of the `Page` directive in `WebTime.aspx`, so it appears as in line 4 of Fig. 21.4. The value of the `Inherits` attribute and the class name in the code-behind file must be identical; otherwise, you'll get errors when you build the Web application.

Step 8: Changing the Title of the Page

Before designing the content of the Web Form, we change its title from the default `Untitled Page` (line 9 of Fig. 21.10) to `A Simple Web Form Example`. To do so, open the ASPX file in **Source** mode and modify the text between the start and end `<title>` tags. Alternatively, you can open the ASPX file in **Design** mode and modify the Web Form's *Title* property in the **Properties** window. To view the Web Form's properties, select DOCUMENT from the drop-down list in the **Properties** window; *DOCUMENT* is the name used to represent the Web Form in the **Properties** window.

Step 9: Designing the Page

Designing a Web Form is as simple as designing a Windows Form. To add controls to the page, you can drag-and-drop them from the **Toolbox** onto the Web Form in **Design** mode. Like the Web Form itself, each control is an object that has properties, methods and events. You can set these properties and events visually using the **Properties** window or programmatically in the code-behind file. However, unlike working with a Windows Form, you can type text directly on a Web Form at the cursor location or insert XHTML elements using menu commands.

Controls and other elements are placed sequentially on a Web Form, much like how text and images are placed in a document using word processing software like Microsoft Word. Controls are placed one after another in the order in which you drag-and-drop them onto the Web Form. The cursor indicates the point at which text and XHTML elements will be inserted. If you want to position a control between existing text or controls, you can drop the control at a specific position within the existing elements. You can also rearrange existing controls using drag-and-drop actions. The positions of controls and other elements are relative to the Web Form's upper-left corner. This type of layout is known as *relative positioning*.

An alternate type of layout is known as *absolute positioning*, in which controls are located exactly where they are dropped on the Web Form. You can enable absolute positioning in **Design** mode by selecting **Layout > Position > Auto-position Options....**, then clicking the first checkbox in the **Positioning options** pane of the **Options** dialog that appears.

Portability Tip 21.2

Absolute positioning is discouraged, because pages designed in this manner may not render correctly on computers with different screen resolutions and font sizes. This could cause absolutely positioned elements to overlap each other or display off-screen, requiring the client to scroll to see the full page content.

In this example, we use one piece of text and one Label. To add the text to the Web Form, click the blank Web Form in **Design** mode and type Current time on the Web server:. Visual Web Developer is a *WYSIWYG* (*What You See Is What You Get*) editor—whenever you make a change to a Web Form in **Design** mode, the IDE creates the markup (visible in **Source** mode) necessary to achieve the desired visual effects seen in **Design** mode. After adding the text to the Web Form, switch to **Source** mode. You should see that the IDE added this text to the div element that appears in the ASPX file by default. Back in **Design** mode, highlight the text you added. From the **Block Format** drop-down list (see Fig. 21.13), choose **Heading 2** to format this text as a heading that will appear bold in a font slightly larger than the default. This action causes the IDE to enclose the newly added text in an h2 element. Finally, click to the right of the text and press the *Enter* key to move the cursor to a new paragraph. This action generates an empty p element in the ASPX file's markup. The IDE should now look like Fig. 21.13.

You can place a Label on a Web Form either by draging-and-dropping or by double clicking the **Toolbox**'s **Label** control. Be sure the cursor is in the newly created paragraph, then add a Label that will be used to display the time. Using the **Properties** window, set the (ID) property of the Label to timeLabel. We delete timeLabel's text, because this text is set programmatically in the code-behind file. When a Label does not contain text, the

Block Format drop-down list

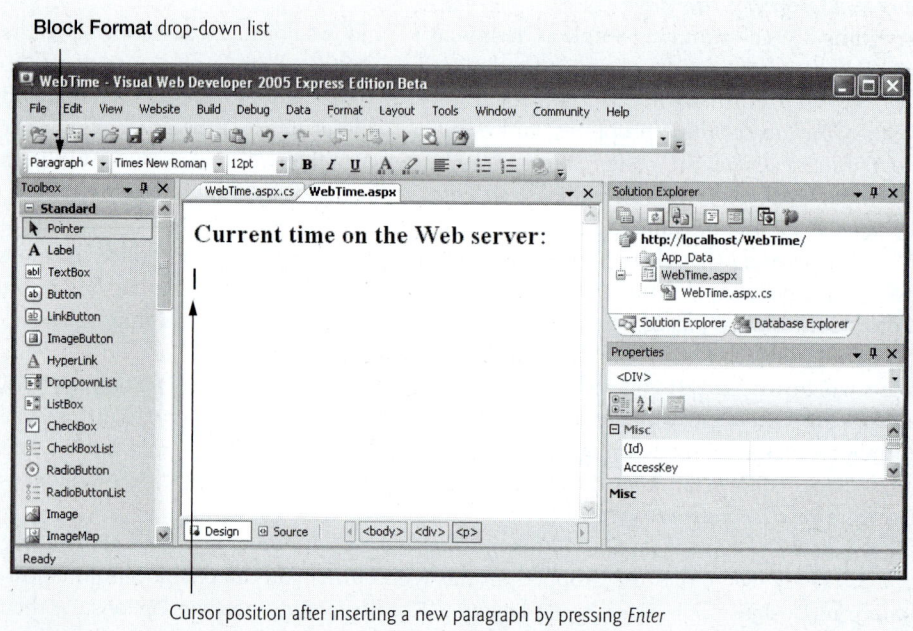

Cursor position after inserting a new paragraph by pressing *Enter*

Fig. 21.13 | `WebTime.aspx` after inserting text and a new paragraph.

name is displayed in square brackets in the Web Forms Designer (Fig. 21.14), but is not displayed at execution time. The label name is a placeholder for design and layout purposes. We set `timeLabel`'s `BackColor`, `ForeColor` and `Font-Size` properties to `Black`, `Yellow` and `XX-Large`, respectively. To change font properties, expand the `Font` node in the **Properties** window, then change each relevant property individually. Once the `Label`'s properties are set in the **Properties** window, Visual Web Developer updates the ASPX file's contents. Figure 21.14 shows the IDE after these properties are set.

Next, set the `Label`'s `EnableViewState` property to `False`. Finally, select `DOCUMENT` from the drop-down list in the **Properties** window and set the Web Form's `EnableSessionState` property to `False`. We discuss both of these properties later in the chapter.

Step 10: Adding Page Logic

Once the user interface has been designed, C# code must be added to the code-behind file. Open `WebTime.aspx.cs` by double clicking its node in the **Solution Explorer**. In this example, we add a `Page_Init` event handler (lines 16–21 of Fig. 21.5) to the code-behind file. Recall that `Page_Init` handles the `Init` event and contains code to initialize the page. The statement in lines 19–20 of Fig. 21.5 programmatically sets the text of `timeLabel` to the current time on the server.

Step 11: Running the Program

After the Web Form is created, you can view it several ways. First, you can select **Debug > Start Without Debugging**, which runs the application by opening a browser window. If you created the application on your local IIS server (as we did in this example), the URL shown in the browser will be `http://localhost/WebTime/WebTime.aspx` (Fig. 21.5), indicating

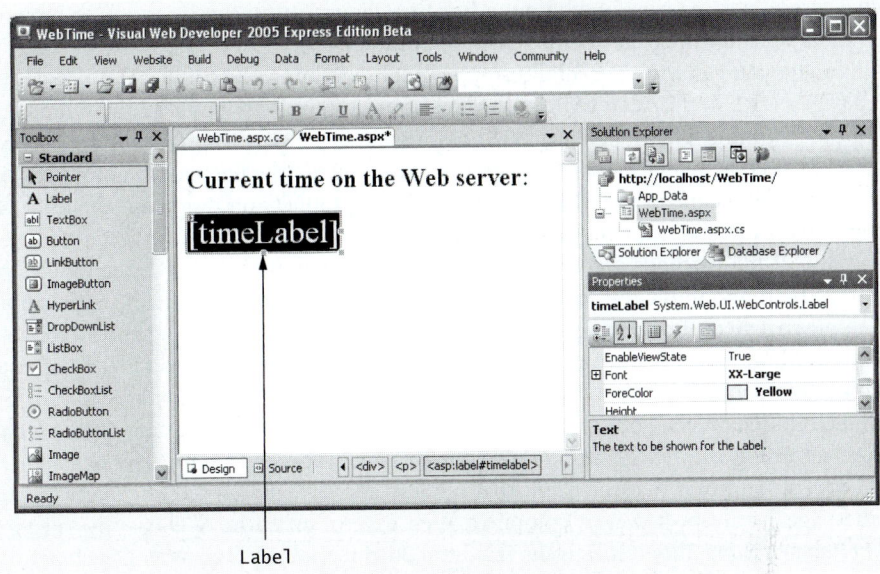

Label

Fig. 21.14 | WebTime.aspx after adding a Label and setting its properties.

that the Web page (the ASPX file) is located within the virtual directory WebTime on the local IIS Web server. IIS must be running to test the Web site in a browser. IIS can be started by executing inetmgr.exe from **Start > Run...**, right clicking **Default Web Site** and selecting **Start**. [*Note:* You might need to expand the node representing your computer to display the **Default Web Site**.]

Note that if you created the ASP.NET application on the local file system, the URL shown in the browser will be http://localhost:*PortNumber*/WebTime/WebTime.aspx, where *PortNumber* is the number of the randomly assigned port on which Visual Web Developer's built-in test server runs. The IDE assigns the port number on a per solution basis. This URL indicates that the WebTime project folder is being accessed through the root directory of the test server running at localhost:*PortNumber*. When you select **Debug > Start Without Debugging**, a tray icon appears near the bottom-right of your screen next to the computer's date and time to show that the **ASP.NET Development Server** is running. The server stops when you exit Visual Web Developer.

You also can select **Debug > Start Debugging** to view the Web page in a Web browser with debugging enabled. Note that you cannot debug a Web site unless debugging is explicitly enabled by the *Web.config* file—a file that stores configuration settings for an ASP.NET Web application. You will rarely need to manually create or modify Web.config. The first time you select **Debug > Start Debugging** in a project, a dialog appears and asks whether you want the IDE to generate the necessary Web.config file and add it to the project, then the IDE enters **Running** mode. You can exit **Running** mode by selecting **Debug > Stop Debugging** in Visual Web Developer or by closing the browser window that is displaying the Web site.

You also can right click either the Web Forms Designer or the ASPX file name (in the **Solution Explorer**) and select *View In Browser* to open a browser window and load the Web page. Right clicking the ASPX file in the **Solution Explorer** and selecting **Browse**

With... also opens the page in a browser, but first allows you to specify the Web browser that should display the page and its screen resolution.

Finally, you can run your application by opening a browser window and typing the Web page's URL in the **Address** field. When testing an ASP.NET application on the same computer running IIS, type `http://localhost/`*ProjectFolder*`/`*PageName*`.aspx`, where *ProjectFolder* is the folder in which the page resides (usually the name of the project), and *PageName* is the name of the ASP.NET page. If your application resides on the local file system, you must first start the **ASP.NET Development Server** by running the application using one of the methods described above. Then you can type the URL (including the *PortNumber* found in the test server's tray icon) in the browser to execute the application.

Note that all of these methods of running the application compile the project for you. In fact, ASP.NET compiles your Web page whenever it changes between HTTP requests. For example, suppose you browse the page, then modify the ASPX file or add code to the code-behind file. When you reload the page, ASP.NET recompiles the page on the server before returning the HTTP response to the browser. This important new behavior of ASP.NET 2.0 ensures that the client that requests the page always sees the latest version of the page. You can, however, compile a Web page or an entire Web site by selecting **Build Page** or **Build Site**, respectively, from the **Build** menu in Visual Web Developer.

If you would like to test your Web application over a network, you may need to change your Windows Firewall settings. For security reasons, Windows Firewall does not allow remote access to a Web server on your local computer by default. To change this, open the Windows Firewall utility in the Windows Control Panel. Click the **Advanced** tab and select your network connection from the **Network Connection Settings** list, then click **Settings....** On the **Services** tab of the **Advanced Settings** dialog, ensure that **Web Server (HTTP)** is checked.

21.5 Web Controls

This section introduces some of the Web controls located in the **Standard** section of the **Toolbox** (Fig. 21.9). Figure 21.15 summarizes some of the Web controls used in the chapter examples.

Web Control	Description
Label	Displays text that the user cannot edit.
TextBox	Gathers user input and displays text.
Button	Triggers an event when clicked.
HyperLink	Displays a hyperlink.
DropDownList	Displays a drop-down list of choices from which a user can select an item.
RadioButtonList	Groups radio buttons.
Image	Displays images (e.g., GIF and JPG).

Fig. 21.15 | Commonly used Web controls .

21.5.1 Text and Graphics Controls

Figure 21.16 depicts a simple form for gathering user input. This example uses all the controls listed in Fig. 21.15, except Label, which you used in Section 21.4. Note that all the code in Fig. 21.16 was generated by Visual Web Developer in response to actions performed in **Design** mode. [*Note:* This example does not contain any functionality—i.e., no action occurs when the user clicks **Register**. We ask the reader to provide the functionality as an exercise. In successive examples, we demonstrate how to add functionality to many of these Web controls.]

```
 1   <%-- Fig. 21.16: WebControls.aspx --%>
 2   <%-- Registration form that demonstrates Web controls. --%>
 3   <%@ Page Language="C#" AutoEventWireup="true"
 4      CodeFile="WebControls.aspx.cs" Inherits="WebControls"
 5      EnableSessionState="False" %>
 6
 7   <!DOCTYPE html PUBLIC "-//W3C//DTD XHTML 1.1//EN"
 8      "http://www.w3.org/TR/xhtml11/DTD/xhtml11.dtd">
 9
10   <html xmlns="http://www.w3.org/1999/xhtml">
11      <head runat="server">
12         <title>Web Controls Demonstration</title>
13      </head>
14      <body>
15         <form id="form1" runat="server">
16            <div>
17               <h3>This is a sample registration form.</h3>
18               <p><em>Please fill in all fields and click Register.</em></p>
19               <p>
20                  <asp:Image ID="UserInformationImage" runat="server"
21                     ImageUrl="~/Images/user.png" EnableViewState="False" />
22                
23                  <span style="color: teal">
24                     Please fill out the fields below.</span>
25               </p>
26               <table>
27                  <tr>
28                     <td style="width: 230px; height: 21px" valign="top">
29                        <asp:Image ID="FirstNameImage" runat="server"
30                           ImageUrl="~/Images/fname.png"
31                           EnableViewState="False" />
32                        <asp:TextBox ID="FirstNameTextBox" runat="server"
33                           EnableViewState="False"></asp:TextBox>
34                     </td>
35                     <td style="width: 231px; height: 21px" valign="top">
36                        <asp:Image ID="LastNameImage" runat="server"
37                           ImageUrl="~/Images/lname.png"
38                           EnableViewState="False" />
39                        <asp:TextBox ID="LastNameTextBox" runat="server"
40                           EnableViewState="False"></asp:TextBox>
41                     </td>
42                  </tr>
```

Fig. 21.16 | Web Form that demonstrates Web controls. (Part 1 of 3.)

```
43                      <tr>
44                          <td style="width: 230px" valign="top">
45                              <asp:Image ID="EmailImage" runat="server"
46                                  ImageUrl="~/Images/email.png"
47                                  EnableViewState="False" />
48                              <asp:TextBox ID="EmailTextBox" runat="server"
49                                  EnableViewState="False"></asp:TextBox>
50                          </td>
51                          <td style="width: 231px" valign="top">
52                              <asp:Image ID="PhoneImage" runat="server"
53                                  ImageUrl="~/Images/phone.png"
54                                  EnableViewState="False" />
55                              <asp:TextBox ID="PhoneTextBox" runat="server"
56                                  EnableViewState="False"></asp:TextBox><br />
57                              Must be in the form (555) 555-5555.
58                          </td>
59                      </tr>
60                  </table>
61                  <p>
62                      <asp:Image ID="PublicationsImage" runat="server"
63                          ImageUrl="~/Images/publications.png"
64                          EnableViewState="False" />
65                       
66                      <span style="color: teal">
67                          Which book would you like information about?</span>
68                  </p>
69                  <p>
70                      <asp:DropDownList ID="BooksDropDownList" runat="server"
71                          EnableViewState="False">
72                          <asp:ListItem>Visual Basic 2005 How to Program 3e
73                              </asp:ListItem>
74                          <asp:ListItem>Visual C# 2005 How to Program 2e
75                              </asp:ListItem>
76                          <asp:ListItem>Java How to Program 6e</asp:ListItem>
77                          <asp:ListItem>C++ How to Program 5e</asp:ListItem>
78                          <asp:ListItem>XML How to Program 1e</asp:ListItem>
79                      </asp:DropDownList>
80                  </p>
81                  <p>
82                      <asp:HyperLink ID="BooksHyperLink" runat="server"
83                          NavigateUrl="http://www.deitel.com" Target="_blank"
84                          EnableViewState="False">
85                          Click here to view more information about our books
86                      </asp:HyperLink>
87                  </p>
88                  <p>
89                      <asp:Image ID="OSImage" runat="server"
90                          ImageUrl="~/Images/os.png" EnableViewState="False" />
91                       
92                      <span style="color: teal">
93                          Which operating system are you using?</span>
94                  </p>
```

Fig. 21.16 | Web Form that demonstrates Web controls. (Part 2 of 3.)

```
95                    <p>
96                        <asp:RadioButtonList ID="OperatingSystemRadioButtonList"
97                            runat="server" EnableViewState="False">
98                            <asp:ListItem>Windows XP</asp:ListItem>
99                            <asp:ListItem>Windows 2000</asp:ListItem>
100                           <asp:ListItem>Windows NT</asp:ListItem>
101                           <asp:ListItem>Linux</asp:ListItem>
102                           <asp:ListItem>Other</asp:ListItem>
103                       </asp:RadioButtonList>
104                   </p>
105                   <p>
106                       <asp:Button ID="RegisterButton" runat="server"
107                           Text="Register" EnableViewState="False" />
108                   </p>
109               </div>
110           </form>
111       </body>
112   </html>
```

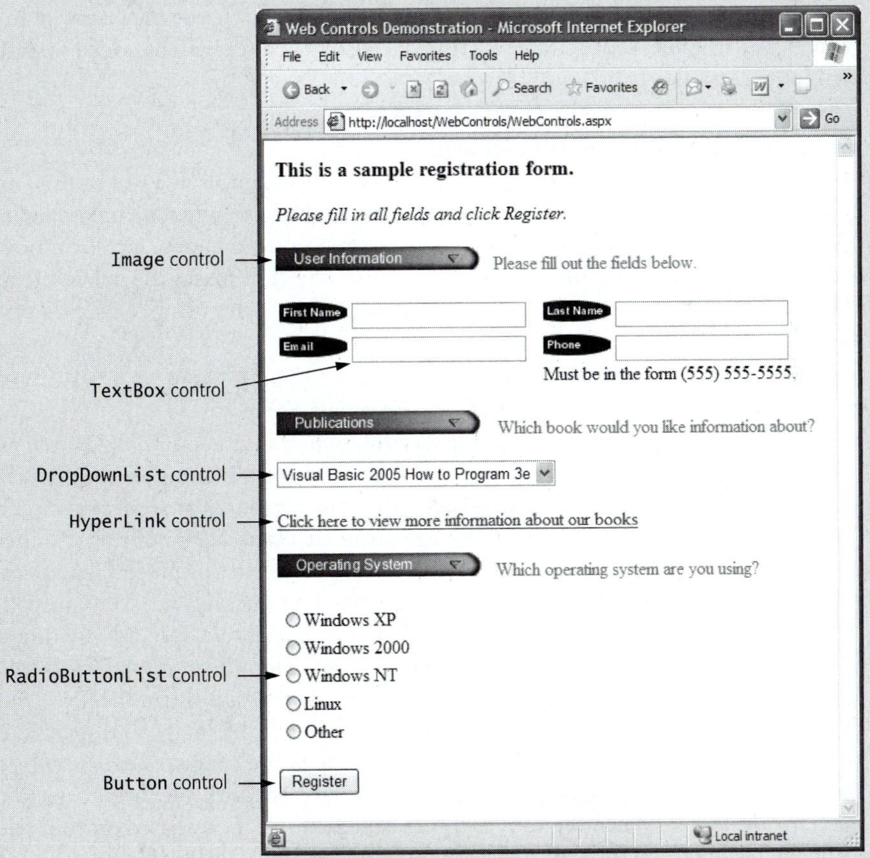

Fig. 21.16 | Web Form that demonstrates Web controls. (Part 3 of 3.)

Before discussing the Web controls used in this ASPX file, we explain the XHTML that creates the layout seen in Fig. 21.16. The page contains an h3 heading element (line 17), followed by a series of additional XHTML blocks. We place most of the Web controls inside p elements (i.e., paragraphs), but we use an XHTML table element (lines 26–60) to organize the Image and TextBox controls in the user information section of the page. In the preceding section, we described how to add heading elements and paragraphs visually without manipulating any XHTML in the ASPX file directly. Visual Web Developer allows you to add a table in a similar manner.

Adding an XHTML Table to a Web Form

To create a table with two rows and two columns in **Design** mode, select the **Insert Table** command from the **Layout** menu. In the **Insert Table** dialog that appears, make sure the **Custom** radio button is selected. In the **Layout** group box, change the values of the **Rows** and **Columns** combo boxes to 2. By default, the contents of a table cell are aligned vertically in the middle of the cell. We changed the vertical alignment of all cells in the table by clicking the **Cell Properties...** button, then selecting **top** from the **Vertical align** combo box in the resulting dialog. This causes the content of each table cell to align with the top of the cell. Click **OK** to close the **Cell Properties** dialog, then click **OK** to close the **Insert Table** dialog and create the table. Once a table is created, controls and text can be added to particular cells to create a neatly organized layout.

Setting the Color of Text on a Web Form

Notice that some of the instructions to the user on the form appear in a teal color. To set the color of a specific piece of text, highlight the text and select **Format > Foreground color...**. In the **Color Picker** dialog, click the **Named Colors** tab and choose a color from the palette shown. Click **OK** to apply the color. Note that the IDE places the colored text in an XHTML span element (e.g., lines 23–24) and applies the color using the span's style attribute.

Examining Web Controls on a Sample Registration Form

Lines 20–21 of Fig. 21.16 define an *Image* control, which inserts an image into a Web page. The images used in this example are located in the chapter's examples directory. You can download the examples from www.deitel.com/books/csharpforprogrammers2. Before an image can be displayed on a Web page using an Image Web control, the image must first be added to the project. We added an Images folder to this project (and to each example project in the chapter that uses images) by right clicking the location of the project in the **Solution Explorer**, selecting **Add Folder > Regular Folder** and entering the folder name Images. We then added each of the images used in the example to this folder by right clicking the folder, selecting **Add Existing Item...** and browsing for the files to add.

The *ImageUrl* property (line 21) specifies the location of the image to display in the Image control. To select an image, click the ellipsis next to the ImageUrl property in the **Properties** window and use the **Select Image** dialog to browse for the desired image in the project's Images folder. When the IDE fills in the ImageUrl property based on your selection, it includes a tilde and forward slash (~/) at the beginning of the ImageUrl—this indicates that the Images folder is in the root directory of the project (i.e., http://localhost/WebControls, whose physical path is C:\Inetpub\wwwroot\WebControls).

Lines 26–60 contain the table element created by the steps discussed previously. Each td element contains an Image control and a **TextBox** control, which allows you to obtain text from the user and display text to the user. For example, lines 32–33 define a TextBox control used to collect the user's first name.

Lines 70–79 define a **DropDownList**. This control is similar to the ComboBox Windows control. When a user clicks the drop-down list, it expands and displays a list from which the user can make a selection. Each item in the drop-down list is defined by a **ListItem** element (lines 72–78). After dragging a DropDownList control onto a Web Form, you can add items to it using the **ListItem Collection Editor**. This process is similar to customizing a ListBox in a Windows application. In Visual Web Developer, you can access the **ListItem Collection Editor** by clicking the ellipsis next to the Items property of the DropDownList. It can also be accessed using the **DropDownList Tasks** menu, which is opened by clicking the small arrowhead that appears in the upper-right corner of the control in **Design** mode (Fig. 21.17). This menu is called a *smart tag menu*. Visual Web Developer displays smart tag menus for many ASP.NET controls to facilitate performing common tasks. Clicking **Edit Items...** in the **DropDownList Tasks** menu opens the **ListItem Collection Editor**, which allows you to add ListItem elements to the DropDownList.

The **HyperLink** control (lines 82–86 of Fig. 21.16) adds a hyperlink to a Web page. The **NavigateUrl** property (line 83) of this control specifies the resource (i.e., http://www.deitel.com) that is requested when a user clicks the hyperlink. Setting the **Target** property to _blank specifies that the requested Web page should open in a new browser window. By default, HyperLink controls cause pages to open in the same browser window.

Lines 96–103 define a **RadioButtonList** control, which provides a series of radio buttons from which the user can select only one. Like options in a DropDownList, individual radio buttons are defined by ListItem elements. Note that, like the **DropDownList Tasks** smart tag menu, the **RadioButtonList Tasks** smart tag menu also provides an **Edit Items...** link to open the **ListItem Collection Editor**.

The final Web control in Fig. 21.16 is a **Button** (lines 106–107). Like a Button Windows control, a Button Web control represents a button that triggers an action when clicked. A Button Web control typically maps to an input XHTML element with attribute type set to "button". As stated earlier, clicking the **Register** button in this example does not do anything.

21.5.2 AdRotator Control

Web pages often contain product or service advertisements, which usually consist of images. Although Web site authors want to include as many sponsors as possible, Web pages can display only a limited number of advertisements. To address this problem, ASP.NET provides the **AdRotator** Web control for displaying advertisements. Using advertisement data located in an XML file, the AdRotator control randomly selects an image to display

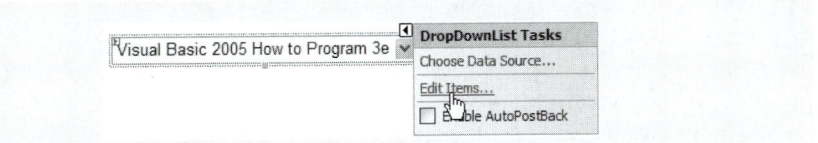

Fig. 21.17 | **DropDownList Tasks** smart tag menu.

and generates a hyperlink to the Web page associated with that image. Browsers that do not support images display alternate text that is specified in the XML document. If a user clicks the image or substituted text, the browser loads the Web page associated with that image.

Demonstrating the AdRotator Web Control

Figure 21.18 demonstrates the AdRotator Web control. In this example, the "advertisements" that we rotate are the flags of 10 countries. When a user clicks the displayed flag image, the browser is redirected to a Web page containing information about the country that the flag represents. If a user refreshes the browser or requests the page again, one of the eleven flags is again chosen at random and displayed.

The ASPX file in Fig. 21.18 is similar to that in Fig. 21.4. However, instead of XHTML text and a Label, this page contains XHTML text (i.e., the h3 element in line 17) and one AdRotator control named countryRotator (lines 19–21). This page also contains an XmlDataSource control (lines 22–24), which supplies the data to the AdRotator control. The background attribute of the page's body element (line 14) is set to display the image background.png, located in the project's Images folder. To specify this file, click the ellipsis provided next to the Background property of DOCUMENT in the **Properties** window and use the resulting dialog to browse for background.png.

```
1   <%-- Fig. 21.18: FlagRotator.aspx --%>
2   <%-- A Web Form that displays flags using an AdRotator control. --%>
3   <%@ Page Language="C#" AutoEventWireup="true"
4      CodeFile="FlagRotator.aspx.cs" Inherits="FlagRotator"
5      EnableSessionState="False" %>
6
7   <!DOCTYPE html PUBLIC "-//W3C//DTD XHTML 1.1//EN"
8      "http://www.w3.org/TR/xhtml11/DTD/xhtml11.dtd">
9
10  <html xmlns="http://www.w3.org/1999/xhtml" >
11     <head runat="server">
12        <title>Flag Rotator</title>
13     </head>
14     <body background="Images/background.png">
15        <form id="form1" runat="server">
16           <div>
17              <h3>AdRotator Example</h3>
18              <p>
19                 <asp:AdRotator ID="countryRotator" runat="server"
20                    DataSourceID="adXmlDataSource"
21                    EnableViewState="False" />
22                 <asp:XmlDataSource ID="adXmlDataSource" runat="server"
23                    DataFile="~/App_Data/AdRotatorInformation.xml">
24                 </asp:XmlDataSource>
25              </p>
26           </div>
27        </form>
28     </body>
29  </html>
```

Fig. 21.18 | Web Form that demonstrates the AdRotator Web control. (Part 1 of 2.)

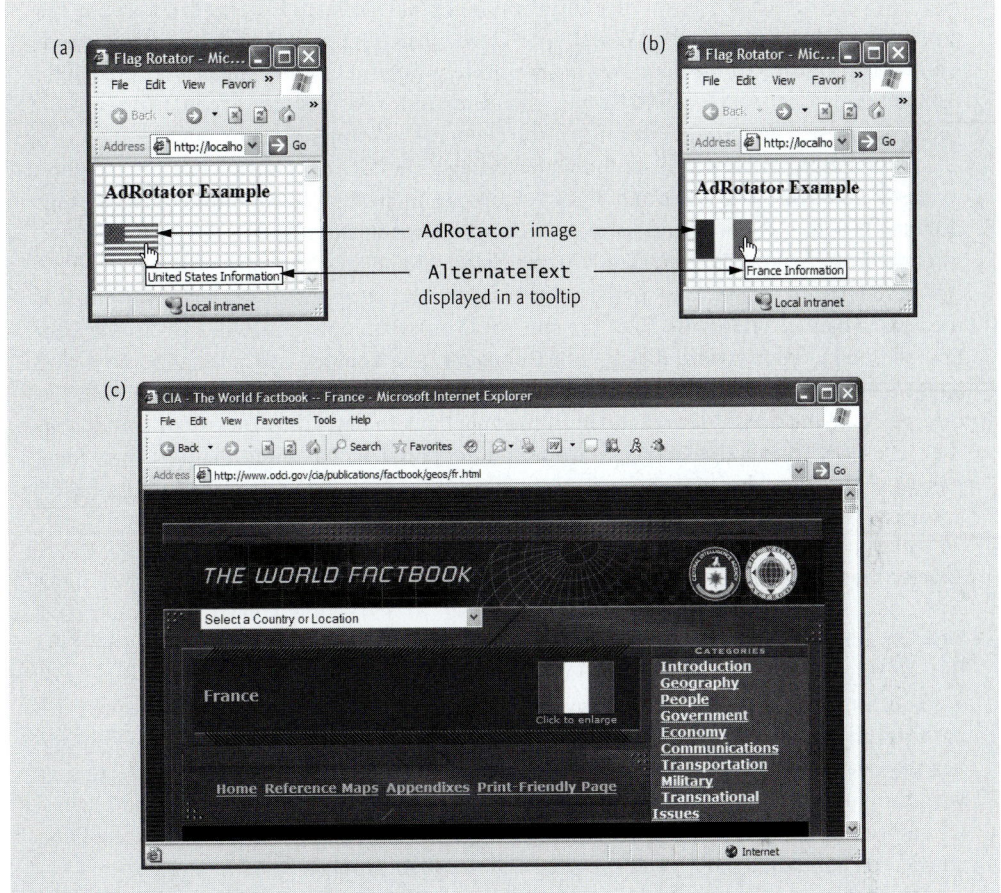

Fig. 21.18 | Web Form that demonstrates the AdRotator Web control. (Part 2 of 2.)

You do not need to add any code to the code-behind file, because the AdRotator control does "all the work." The output depicts two different requests. Figure 21.18(a) shows the first time the page is requested, when the American flag is shown. In the second request, as shown in Fig. 21.18(b), the French flag is displayed. Figure 21.18(c) depicts the Web page that loads when the French flag is clicked.

Connecting Data to an AdRotator Control

An AdRotator control accesses an XML file (presented shortly) to determine what advertisement (i.e., flag) image, hyperlink URL and alternate text to display and include in the page. To connect the AdRotator control to the XML file, we create an *XmlDataSource* control—one of several ASP.NET data controls (found in the **Data** section of the **Toolbox**) that encapsulate data sources and make such data available for Web controls. An XmlDataSource references an XML file containing data that will be used in an ASP.NET application. Later in the chapter, you will learn more about data-bound Web controls, as well as the SqlDataSource control, which retrieves data from a SQL Server database, and the ObjectDataSource control, which encapsulates an object that makes data available.

To build this example, we first add the XML file `AdRotatorInformation.xml` to the project. Each project created in Visual Web Developer contains an `App_Data` folder, which is intended to store all the data used by the project. Right click this folder in the **Solution Explorer** and select **Add Existing Item...**, then browse for `AdRotatorInformation.xml` on your computer. (We provide this file in the chapter's examples directory.)

After adding the XML file to the project, drag an `AdRotator` control from the **Toolbox** to the Web Form. The **AdRotator Tasks** smart tag menu will open automatically. From this menu, select **<New Data Source...>** from the **Choose Data Source** drop-down list to start the **Data Source Configuration Wizard**. Select **XML File** as the data-source type. This causes the wizard to create an `XmlDataSource` with the `ID` specified in the bottom half of the wizard dialog. We set the `ID` of the control to `adXmlDataSource`. Click **OK** in the **Data Source Configuration Wizard** dialog. The **Configure Data Source - adXmlDataSource** dialog appears next. In this dialog's **Data File** section, click **Browse...** and, in the **Select XML File** dialog, locate the XML file you added to the `App_Data` folder. Click **OK** to exit this dialog, then click **OK** to exit the **Configure Data Source - adXmlDataSource** dialog. After completing these steps, the `AdRotator` is configured to use the XML file to determine which advertisements to display.

Examining an XML File Containing Advertisement Information

XML document `AdRotatorInformation.xml` (Fig. 21.19)—or any XML document used with an `AdRotator` control—must contain one *Advertisements* root element (lines 4–94). Within that element can be several *Ad* elements (e.g., lines 5–12), each of which provides information about a different advertisement. Element *ImageUrl* (line 6) specifies the path (location) of the advertisement's image, and element *NavigateUrl* (lines 7–9) specifies the URL for the Web page that loads when a user clicks the advertisement. Note that we reformatted this file for presentation purposes. The actual XML file cannot contain any whitespace before or after the URL in the `NavigateUrl` element, or the whitespace will be considered part of the URL, and the page will not load properly.

```
 1    <?xml version="1.0" encoding="utf-8"?>
 2    <!-- Fig. 21.19: AdRotatorInformation.xml -->
 3    <!-- XML file containing advertisement information. -->
 4    <Advertisements>
 5       <Ad>
 6          <ImageUrl>Images/france.png</ImageUrl>
 7          <NavigateUrl>
 8             http://www.odci.gov/cia/publications/factbook/geos/fr.html
 9          </NavigateUrl>
10          <AlternateText>France Information</AlternateText>
11          <Impressions>1</Impressions>
12       </Ad>
13
14       <Ad>
15          <ImageUrl>Images/germany.png</ImageUrl>
16          <NavigateUrl>
17             http://www.odci.gov/cia/publications/factbook/geos/gm.html
18          </NavigateUrl>
```

Fig. 21.19 | File containing advertisement information used in `AdRotator` example. (Part 1 of 3.)

```
19          <AlternateText>Germany Information</AlternateText>
20          <Impressions>1</Impressions>
21      </Ad>
22
23      <Ad>
24          <ImageUrl>Images/italy.png</ImageUrl>
25          <NavigateUrl>
26              http://www.odci.gov/cia/publications/factbook/geos/it.html
27          </NavigateUrl>
28          <AlternateText>Italy Information</AlternateText>
29          <Impressions>1</Impressions>
30      </Ad>
31
32      <Ad>
33          <ImageUrl>Images/spain.png</ImageUrl>
34          <NavigateUrl>
35              http://www.odci.gov/cia/publications/factbook/geos/sp.html
36          </NavigateUrl>
37          <AlternateText>Spain Information</AlternateText>
38          <Impressions>1</Impressions>
39      </Ad>
40
41      <Ad>
42          <ImageUrl>Images/latvia.png</ImageUrl>
43          <NavigateUrl>
44              http://www.odci.gov/cia/publications/factbook/geos/lg.html
45          </NavigateUrl>
46          <AlternateText>Latvia Information</AlternateText>
47          <Impressions>1</Impressions>
48      </Ad>
49
50      <Ad>
51          <ImageUrl>Images/peru.png</ImageUrl>
52          <NavigateUrl>
53              http://www.odci.gov/cia/publications/factbook/geos/pe.html
54          </NavigateUrl>
55          <AlternateText>Peru Information</AlternateText>
56          <Impressions>1</Impressions>
57      </Ad>
58
59      <Ad>
60          <ImageUrl>Images/senegal.png</ImageUrl>
61          <NavigateUrl>
62              http://www.odci.gov/cia/publications/factbook/geos/sg.html
63          </NavigateUrl>
64          <AlternateText>Senegal Information</AlternateText>
65          <Impressions>1</Impressions>
66      </Ad>
67
68      <Ad>
69          <ImageUrl>Images/sweden.png</ImageUrl>
```

Fig. 21.19 | File containing advertisement information used in AdRotator example. (Part 2 of 3.)

```
70          <NavigateUrl>
71              http://www.odci.gov/cia/publications/factbook/geos/sw.html
72          </NavigateUrl>
73          <AlternateText>Sweden Information</AlternateText>
74          <Impressions>1</Impressions>
75      </Ad>
76
77      <Ad>
78          <ImageUrl>Images/thailand.png</ImageUrl>
79          <NavigateUrl>
80              http://www.odci.gov/cia/publications/factbook/geos/th.html
81          </NavigateUrl>
82          <AlternateText>Thailand Information</AlternateText>
83          <Impressions>1</Impressions>
84      </Ad>
85
86      <Ad>
87          <ImageUrl>Images/unitedstates.png</ImageUrl>
88          <NavigateUrl>
89              http://www.odci.gov/cia/publications/factbook/geos/us.html
90          </NavigateUrl>
91          <AlternateText>United States Information</AlternateText>
92          <Impressions>1</Impressions>
93      </Ad>
94  </Advertisements>
```

Fig. 21.19 | File containing advertisement information used in `AdRotator` example. (Part 3 of 3.)

The *AlternateText* element (line 10) nested in each Ad element contains text that displays in place of the image when the browser cannot locate or render the image for some reason (i.e., the file is missing, or the browser is not capable of displaying it). The AlternatenateText element's text is also a tooltip that Internet Explorer displays when a user places the mouse pointer over the image (Fig. 21.18). The *Impressions* element (line 56) specifies how often a particular image appears, relative to the other images. An advertisement that has a higher Impressions value displays more frequently than an advertisement with a lower value. In our example, the advertisements display with equal probability, because the value of each Impressions element is set to 1.

21.5.3 Validation Controls

This section introduces a different type of Web control, called a *validation control* (or *validator)*, which determines whether the data in another Web control is in the proper format. For example, validators could determine whether a user has provided information in a required field or whether a ZIP-code field contains exactly five digits. Validators provide a mechanism for validating user input on the client. When the XHTML for our page is created, the validator is converted into *ECMAScript*[1] that performs the validation. ECMAScript is a scripting language that enhances the functionality and appearance of Web pages. ECMAScript is typically executed on the client. Some clients do not support scripting or disable scripting. However, for security reasons, validation is always performed on the server—whether or not the script executes on the client.

Validating Input in a Web Form

The example in this section prompts the user to enter a name, e-mail address and phone number. A Web site could use a form like this to collect contact information from site visitors. After the user enters any data, but before the data is sent to the Web server, validators ensure that the user entered a value in each field and that the e-mail address and phone number values are in an acceptable format. In this example, (555) 123-4567, 555-123-4567 and 123-4567 are all considered valid phone numbers. Once the data is submitted, the Web server responds by displaying an appropriate message and an XHTML table repeating the submitted information. Note that a real business application would typically store the submitted data in a database or a in file on the server. We simply send the data back to the form to demonstrate that the server received the data.

Figure 21.20 presents the ASPX file. Like the Web Form in Fig. 21.16, this Web Form uses a `table` to organize the page's contents. Lines 24–25, 36–37 and 56–57 define `TextBox`es for retrieving the user's name, e-mail address and phone number, respectively, and line 75 defines a **Submit** button. Lines 77–79 create a `Label` named `outputLabel` that displays the response from the server when the user successfully submits the form. Notice that `outputLabel`'s *Visible* property is initially set to `False`, so the `Label` does not appear in the client's browser when the page loads for the first time.

```
 1   <%-- Fig. 21.20: Validation.aspx --%>
 2   <%-- Form that demonstrates using validators to validate user input. --%>
 3   <%@ Page Language="C#" AutoEventWireup="true"
 4      CodeFile="Validation.aspx.cs" Inherits="Validation" %>
 5
 6   <!DOCTYPE html PUBLIC "-//W3C//DTD XHTML 1.1//EN"
 7      "http://www.w3.org/TR/xhtml11/DTD/xhtml11.dtd">
 8
 9   <html xmlns="http://www.w3.org/1999/xhtml" >
10      <head runat="server">
11         <title>Demonstrating Validation Controls</title>
12      </head>
13      <body>
14         <form id="form1" runat="server">
15            <div>
16               Please fill out the following form.<br />
17               <em>All fields are required and must
18                  contain valid information.</em><br />
19               <br />
20               <table>
21                  <tr>
22                     <td style="width: 100px" valign="top">Name:</td>
```

Fig. 21.20 | Validators used in a Web Form that retrieves user's contact information. (Part 1 of 4.)

---

1. ECMAScript (commonly known as JavaScript) is a scripting standard developed by ECMA International. Both Netscape's JavaScript and Microsoft's JScript implement the ECMAScript standard, but each provides additional features beyond the specification. For information on the current ECMAScript standard, visit www.ecma-international.org/publications/standards/Ecma-262.htm. See www.mozilla.org/js for information on JavaScript and msdn.microsoft.com/library/en-us/script56/html/js56jsoriJScript.asp for information on JScript.

```
23                        <td style="width: 450px" valign="top">
24                           <asp:TextBox ID="nameTextBox" runat="server">
25                           </asp:TextBox><br />
26                           <asp:RequiredFieldValidator ID="nameInputValidator"
27                              runat="server" ControlToValidate="nameTextBox"
28                              ErrorMessage="Please enter your name."
29                              Display="Dynamic"></asp:RequiredFieldValidator>
30                        </td>
31                     </tr>
32                     <tr>
33                        <td style="width: 100px" valign="top">
34                           E-mail address:</td>
35                        <td style="width: 450px" valign="top">
36                           <asp:TextBox ID="emailTextBox" runat="server">
37                           </asp:TextBox>
38                            e.g., user@domain.com<br />
39                           <asp:RequiredFieldValidator ID="emailInputValidator"
40                              runat="server" ControlToValidate="emailTextBox"
41                              ErrorMessage="Please enter your e-mail address."
42                              Display="Dynamic"></asp:RequiredFieldValidator>
43                           <asp:RegularExpressionValidator
44                              ID="emailFormatValidator" runat="server"
45                              ControlToValidate="emailTextBox"
46                              ErrorMessage="Please enter an e-mail address in a
47                              valid format." Display="Dynamic"
48                              ValidationExpression=
49                              "\w+([-+.']\w+)*@\w+([-.]\w+)*\.\w+([-.]\w+)*">
50                           </asp:RegularExpressionValidator>
51                        </td>
52                     </tr>
53                     <tr>
54                        <td style="width: 100px" valign="top">Phone number:</td>
55                        <td style="width: 450px" valign="top">
56                           <asp:TextBox ID="phoneTextBox" runat="server">
57                           </asp:TextBox>
58                            e.g., (555) 555-1234<br />
59                           <asp:RequiredFieldValidator ID="phoneInputValidator"
60                              runat="server" ControlToValidate="phoneTextBox"
61                              ErrorMessage="Please enter your phone number."
62                              Display="Dynamic"></asp:RequiredFieldValidator>
63                           <asp:RegularExpressionValidator
64                              ID="phoneFormatValidator" runat="server"
65                              ControlToValidate="phoneTextBox"
66                              ErrorMessage="Please enter a phone number in a
67                              valid format." Display="Dynamic"
68                              ValidationExpression=
69                              "((\(\d{3}\) ?)|(\d{3}-))?\d{3}-\d{4}">
70                           </asp:RegularExpressionValidator>
71                        </td>
72                     </tr>
73                  </table>
74                  <br />
```

Fig. 21.20 | Validators used in a Web Form that retrieves user's contact information. (Part 2 of 4.)

```
75                <asp:Button ID="submitButton" runat="server" Text="Submit" />
76                <br /><br />
77                <asp:Label ID="outputLabel" runat="server"
78                    Text="Thank you for your submission."
79                    Visible="False"></asp:Label>
80            </div>
81        </form>
82    </body>
83 </html>
```

(a)

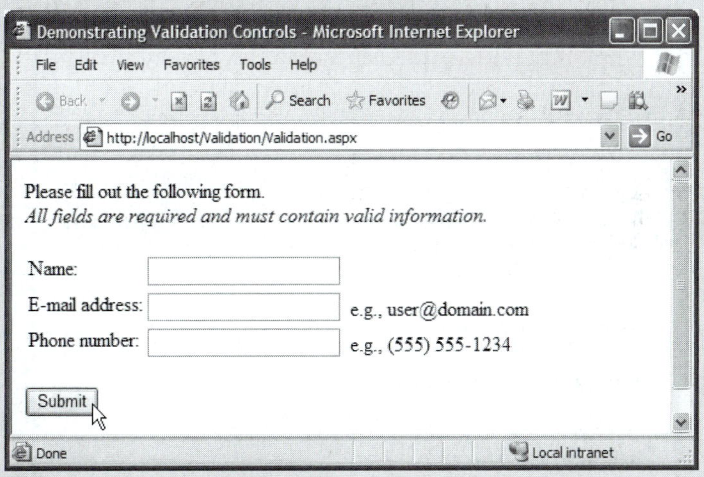

(b)

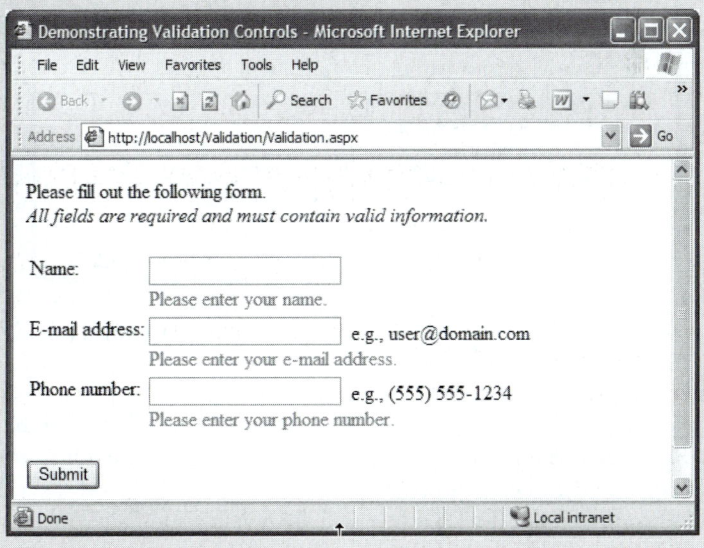

Fig. 21.20 | Validators used in a Web Form that retrieves user's contact information. (Part 3 of 4.)

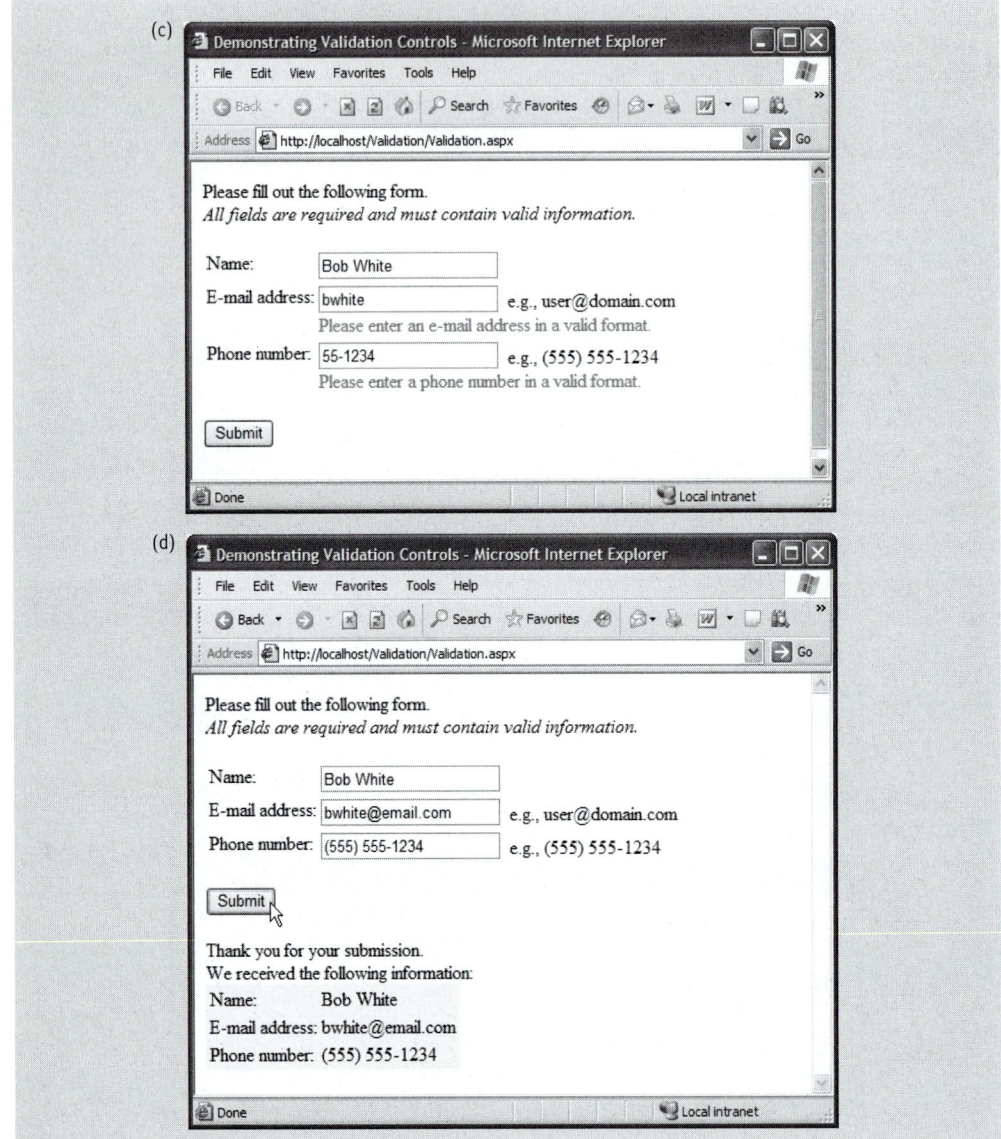

Fig. 21.20 | Validators used in a Web Form that retrieves user's contact information. (Part 4 of 4.)

Using RequiredFieldValidator Controls

In this example, we use three **RequiredFieldValidator** controls (found in the **Validation** section of the **Toolbox**) to ensure that the name, e-mail address and phone number Text-Boxes are not empty when the form is submitted. A RequiredFieldValidator makes an input control a required field. If such a field is empty, validation fails. For example, lines 26–29 define RequiredFieldValidator nameInputValidator, which confirms that nameTextBox is not empty. Line 27 associates nameTextBox with nameInputValidator by setting the validator's **ControlToValidate** property to nameTextBox. This indicates that nameInputValidator verifies the nameTextBox's contents. Property ***ErrorMessage***'s text (line 28) is displayed on the Web Form if the validation fails. If the user does not input any data in nameTextBox and attempts to submit the form, the ErrorMessage text is displayed in red. Because we set the control's ***Display*** property to Dynamic (line 29), the validator takes up space on the Web Form only when validation fails—space is allocated dynamically when validation fails, causing the controls below the validator to shift downward to accommodate the ErrorMessage, as seen in Fig. 21.20(a)–(c).

Using RegularExpressionValidator Controls

This example also uses ***RegularExpressionValidator*** controls to match the e-mail address and phone number entered by the user against regular expressions. (Regular expressions are introduced in Chapter 16.) These controls determine whether the e-mail address and phone number were each entered in a valid format. For example, lines 43–50 create a RegularExpressionValidator named emailFormatValidator. Line 45 sets property ControlToValidate to emailTextBox to indicate that emailFormatValidator verifies the emailTextBox's contents.

A RegularExpressionValidator's ***ValidationExpression*** property specifies the regular expression that validates the ControlToValidate's contents. Clicking the ellipsis next to property ValidationExpression in the **Properties** window displays the **Regular Expression Editor** dialog, which contains a list of **Standard expressions** for phone numbers, ZIP codes and other formatted information. You can also write your own custom expression. For the emailFormatValidator, we selected the standard expression **Internet e-mail address**, which uses the validation expression

$$\w+([-+.']\w+)*@\w+([-.]\w+)*\.\w+([-.]\w+)*$$

This regular expression indicates that an e-mail address is valid if the part of the address before the @ symbol contains one or more word characters (i.e., alphanumeric characters or underscores), followed by zero or more strings comprised of a hyphen, plus sign, period or apostrophe and additional word characters. After the @ symbol, a valid e-mail address must contain one or more groups of word characters potentially separated by hyphens or periods, followed by a required period and another group of one or more word characters potentially separated by hyphens or periods. For example, bob.white@email.com, bob-white@my-email.com and bob's-personal.email@white.email.com are all valid e-mail addresses. If the user enters text in the emailTextBox that does not have the correct format and either clicks in a different text box or attempts to submit the form, the ErrorMessage text is displayed in red.

We also use RegularExpressionValidator phoneFormatValidator (lines 63–70) to ensure that the phoneTextBox contains a valid phone number before the form is submitted. In the **Regular Expression Editor** dialog, we select **U.S. phone number**, which assigns

$$((\(\d{3}\) ?)|(\d{3}-))?\d{3}-\d{4}$$

to the ValidationExpression property. This expression indicates that a phone number can contain a three-digit area code either in parentheses and followed by an optional space or without parentheses and followed by required hyphen. After an optional area code, a phone number must contain three digits, a hyphen and another four digits. For example, (555) 123-4567, 555-123-4567 and 123-4567 are all valid phone numbers.

If all five validators are successful (i.e., each TextBox is filled in, and the e-mail address and phone number provided are valid), clicking the **Submit** button sends the form's data to the server. As shown in Fig. 21.20(d), the server then responds by displaying the submitted data in the outputLabel (lines 77–79).

Examining the Code-Behind File for a Web Form That Receives User Input
Figure 21.21 depicts the code-behind file for the ASPX file in Fig. 21.20. Notice that this code-behind file does not contain any implementation related to the validators. We say more about this soon.

```
1   // Fig. 21.21: Validation.aspx.cs
2   // Code-behind file for the form demonstrating validation controls.
3   using System;
4   using System.Data;
5   using System.Configuration;
6   using System.Web;
7   using System.Web.Security;
8   using System.Web.UI;
9   using System.Web.UI.WebControls;
10  using System.Web.UI.WebControls.WebParts;
11  using System.Web.UI.HtmlControls;
12
13  public partial class Validation : System.Web.UI.Page
14  {
15     // Page_Load event handler executes when the page is loaded
16     protected void Page_Load( object sender, EventArgs e )
17     {
18        // if this is not the first time the page is loading
19        // (i.e., the user has already submitted form data)
20        if ( IsPostBack )
21        {
22           // retrieve the values submitted by the user
23           string name = Request.Form[ "nameTextBox" ];
24           string email = Request.Form[ "emailTextBox" ];
25           string phone = Request.Form[ "phoneTextBox" ];
26
27           // create a table indicating the submitted values
28           outputLabel.Text +=
29              "<br />We received the following information:" +
30              "<table style=\"background-color: yellow\">" +
31              "<tr><td>Name: </td><td>" + name + "</td></tr>" +
32              "<tr><td>E-mail address: </td><td>" + email + "</td></tr>" +
33              "<tr><td>Phone number: </td><td>" + phone + "</td></tr>" +
34              "<table>";
35
36           outputLabel.Visible = true; // display the output message
37        } // end if
38     } // end method Page_Load
39  } // end class Validation
```

Fig. 21.21 | Code-behind file for a Web Form that obtains a user's contact information.

Web programmers using ASP.NET often design their Web pages so that the current page reloads when the user submits the form; this enables the program to receive input, process it as necessary and display the results in the same page when it is loaded the second time. These pages usually contain a form that when submitted, sends the values of all the controls to the server and causes the current page to be requested again. This event is known as a *postback*. Line 20 uses the ***IsPostBack*** property of class Page to determine whether the page is being loaded due to a postback. The first time that the Web page is requested, IsPostBack is false, and the page displays only the form for user input. When the postback occurs (from the user clicking **Submit**), IsPostBack is true.

Lines 23–25 use the ***Request*** object to retrieve the values of nameTextBox, email-TextBox and phoneTextBox from the NameValueCollection ***Form***. When data is posted to the Web server, the XHTML form's data is accessible to the Web application through the Request object's Form array. Lines 28–34 append to outputLabel's Text a line break, an additional message and an XHTML table containing the submitted data so the user knows that the server received the data correctly. In a real business application, the data would be stored in a database or file at this point in the application. Line 36 sets the outputLabel's Visible property to true, so the user can see the thank you message and submitted data.

Examining the Client-Side XHTML for a Web Form with Validation

Figure 21.22 shows the XHTML and ECMAScript sent to the client browser when Validation.aspx loads after the postback. To view this code, select **View > Source** in Internet Explorer. Lines 25–36, lines 100–171 and lines 180–218 contain the ECMAScript that provides the implementation for the validation controls and for performing the postback. ASP.NET generates this ECMAScript. You do not need to be able to create or even understand ECMAScript—the functionality defined for the controls in our application is converted to working ECMAScript for us.

In earlier ASPX files, we explicitly set the EnableViewState attribute of each Web control to False. This attribute determines whether a Web control's value persists (i.e., is retained) when a postback occurs. By default, this attribute is True, which indicates that the control's value persists. In Fig. 21.20(d), notice that the values entered by the user still appear in the text boxes after the postback occurs. A hidden input in the XHTML document (lines 14–22 of Fig. 21.22) contains the data of the controls on this page. This element is always named __*VIEWSTATE* and stores the controls' data as an encoded string.

> **Performance Tip 21.2**
>
> *Setting EnableViewState to False reduces the amount of data passed to the Web server with each request.*

```
1   <!-- Fig. 21.22: Validation.html -->
2   <!-- The XHTML and ECMAScript generated for Validation.aspx -->
3   <!DOCTYPE html PUBLIC "-//W3C//DTD XHTML 1.1//EN"
4      "http://www.w3.org/TR/xhtml11/DTD/xhtml11.dtd">
5
6   <html xmlns="http://www.w3.org/1999/xhtml" >
```

Fig. 21.22 | XHTML and ECMAScript generated by ASP.NET and sent to the browser when Validation.aspx is requested. (Part 1 of 6.)

```
7    <head>
8       <title>Demonstrating Validation Controls</title>
9    </head>
10   <body>
11      <form method="post" action="Validation.aspx"
12         onsubmit="javascript:return WebForm_OnSubmit();" id="form1">
13         <div>
14            <input type="hidden" name="__VIEWSTATE" id="__VIEWSTATE"
15               value="/wEPDwUJODc5MTExMzA4D2QWAgIDD2QWAgITDw8WBB4EVGV4dAWQ
16               AlRoYW5rIHlvdSBmb3IgeW91ciBzdWJtaXNzaW9uLjxiciAvPldlIHJlY2V
17               pdmVkIHRoZSBmb2xsb3dpbmcgaW5mb3JtYXRpb246PHRhYmxlIHN0eWxlPS
18               JiYWNrZ3JvdW5kLWNvbG9yOiB5ZWxsb3ciPjx0cj48dGQ+TmFtZTogPC90Z
19               D48dGQ+Qm9iPC90ZD48L3RyPjx0cj48dGQ+RS1tYWlsIGFkZHJlc3M6IDwv
20               dGQ+PHRkPmJ3J3aGl0ZUBlbWFpbC5jb208L3RkPjwvdHI+PHRyPjx0ZD5QaG9
21               uZSBudW1iZXI6IDwvdGQ+PHRkPig1NTUpIDU1NS0xMjM0PC90ZD48L3RyPj
22               wvdGFibGU+HgdWaXNpYmxlZ2RkZHiyTaX3DhELahxLUxCHnaZuvuMd" />
23         </div>
24
25         <script src="/Validation/WebResource.axd?d=kpdxzzpROgHb8glw78d_
26            hfkpmflQLBVBMoL34vcFGS41&amp;t=632494248729409088"
27            type="text/javascript"></script>
28
29         <script type="text/javascript">
30         <!--
31            function WebForm_OnSubmit() {
32               if (ValidatorOnSubmit() == false) return false;
33                  return true;
34            }
35         // -->
36         </script>
37
38         <div>
39            Please fill out the following form.<br />
40            <em>All fields are required and must
41               contain valid information.</em><br />
42            <br />
43            <table>
44               <tr>
45                  <td style="width: 100px" valign="top">Name:</td>
46                  <td style="width: 450px" valign="top">
47                     <input name="nameTextBox" type="text"
48                        id="nameTextBox" /><br />
49                     <span id="nameInputValidator" style="color:Red;
50                        display:none;">Please enter your name.</span>
51                  </td>
52               </tr>
53               <tr>
54                  <td style="width: 100px" valign="top">
55                     E-mail address:</td>
56                  <td style="width: 450px" valign="top">
```

Fig. 21.22 | XHTML and ECMAScript generated by ASP.NET and sent to the browser when Validation.aspx is requested. (Part 2 of 6.)

```
57              <input name="emailTextBox" type="text"
58                  id="emailTextBox" />
59               e.g., user@domain.com<br />
60              <span id="emailInputValidator" style="color:Red;
61                  display:none;">Please enter your e-mail address.
62              </span>
63              <span id="emailFormatValidator" style="color:Red;
64                  display:none;">Please enter an e-mail address in a
65                  valid format.</span>
66          </td>
67        </tr>
68        <tr>
69          <td style="width: 100px" valign="top">Phone number:</td>
70          <td style="width: 450px" valign="top">
71              <input name="phoneTextBox" type="text"
72                  id="phoneTextBox" />
73               e.g., (555) 555-1234<br />
74              <span id="phoneInputValidator" style="color:Red;
75                  display:none;">Please enter your phone number.
76              </span>
77              <span id="phoneFormatValidator" style="color:Red;
78                  display:none;">Please enter a phone number in a
79                  valid format.</span>
80          </td>
81        </tr>
82      </table>
83      <br />
84      <input type="submit" name="submitButton" value="Submit"
85          onclick="javascript:WebForm_DoPostBackWithOptions(
86          new WebForm_PostBackOptions(&quot;submitButton&quot;,
87          &quot;&quot;, true, &quot;&quot;, &quot;&quot;,
88          false, false))" id="submitButton" />
89      <br /><br />
90      <span id="outputLabel">Thank you for your submission.<br />
91          We received the following information:
92          <table style="background-color: yellow">
93          <tr><td>Name: </td><td>Bob</td></tr>
94          <tr><td>E-mail address: </td><td>bwhite@email.com</td></tr>
95          <tr><td>Phone number: </td><td>(555) 555-1234</td></tr>
96          </table>
97      </span>
98    </div>
99
100   <script type="text/javascript">
101   <!--
102       var Page_Validators = new Array(
103           document.getElementById("nameInputValidator"),
104           document.getElementById("emailInputValidator"),
105           document.getElementById("emailFormatValidator"),
106           document.getElementById("phoneInputValidator"),
107           document.getElementById("phoneFormatValidator"));
```

Fig. 21.22 | XHTML and ECMAScript generated by ASP.NET and sent to the browser when `Validation.aspx` is requested. (Part 3 of 6.)

```
108          // -->
109          </script>
110
111          <script type="text/javascript">
112          <!--
113              var nameInputValidator =
114                  document.all ? document.all["nameInputValidator"] :
115                  document.getElementById("nameInputValidator");
116              nameInputValidator.controltovalidate = "nameTextBox";
117              nameInputValidator.errormessage = "Please enter your name.";
118              nameInputValidator.display = "Dynamic";
119              nameInputValidator.evaluationfunction =
120                  "RequiredFieldValidatorEvaluateIsValid";
121              nameInputValidator.initialvalue = "";
122
123              var emailInputValidator =
124                  document.all ? document.all["emailInputValidator"] :
125                  document.getElementById("emailInputValidator");
126              emailInputValidator.controltovalidate = "emailTextBox";
127              emailInputValidator.errormessage =
128                  "Please enter your e-mail address.";
129              emailInputValidator.display = "Dynamic";
130              emailInputValidator.evaluationfunction =
131                  "RequiredFieldValidatorEvaluateIsValid";
132              emailInputValidator.initialvalue = "";
133
134              var emailFormatValidator =
135                  document.all ? document.all["emailFormatValidator"] :
136                  document.getElementById("emailFormatValidator");
137              emailFormatValidator.controltovalidate = "emailTextBox";
138              emailFormatValidator.errormessage =
139                  "Please enter an e-mail address in a \r\n          " +
140                  "          valid format.";
141              emailFormatValidator.display = "Dynamic";
142              emailFormatValidator.evaluationfunction =
143                  "RegularExpressionValidatorEvaluateIsValid";
144              emailFormatValidator.validationexpression =
145                  "\\w+([-+.\']\\w+)*@\\w+([-.]\\w+)*\\.\\w+([-.]\\w+)*";
146
147              var phoneInputValidator =
148                  document.all ? document.all["phoneInputValidator"] :
149                  document.getElementById("phoneInputValidator");
150              phoneInputValidator.controltovalidate = "phoneTextBox";
151              phoneInputValidator.errormessage =
152                  "Please enter your phone number.";
153              phoneInputValidator.display = "Dynamic";
154              phoneInputValidator.evaluationfunction =
155                  "RequiredFieldValidatorEvaluateIsValid";
156              phoneInputValidator.initialvalue = "";
157
```

Fig. 21.22 | XHTML and ECMAScript generated by ASP.NET and sent to the browser when
`Validation.aspx` is requested. (Part 4 of 6.)

```
158            var phoneFormatValidator =
159                document.all ? document.all["phoneFormatValidator"] :
160                document.getElementById("phoneFormatValidator");
161            phoneFormatValidator.controltovalidate = "phoneTextBox";
162            phoneFormatValidator.errormessage =
163                "Please enter a phone number in a \r\n            " +
164                "        valid format.";
165            phoneFormatValidator.display = "Dynamic";
166            phoneFormatValidator.evaluationfunction =
167                "RegularExpressionValidatorEvaluateIsValid";
168            phoneFormatValidator.validationexpression =
169                "((\\(\\(\\d{3}\\) ?)|(\\d{3}-))?\\d{3}-\\d{4}";
170        // -->
171        </script>
172
173        <div>
174            <input type="hidden" name="__EVENTTARGET"
175                id="__EVENTTARGET" value="" />
176            <input type="hidden" name="__EVENTARGUMENT"
177                id="__EVENTARGUMENT" value="" />
178        </div>
179
180        <script type="text/javascript">
181        <!--
182            var theForm = document.forms['form1'];
183
184            if (!theForm) {
185                theForm = document.form1;
186            }
187
188            function __doPostBack(eventTarget, eventArgument) {
189                if (!theForm.onsubmit || (theForm.onsubmit() != false)) {
190                    theForm.__EVENTTARGET.value = eventTarget;
191                    theForm.__EVENTARGUMENT.value = eventArgument;
192                    theForm.submit();
193                }
194            }
195        // -->
196        </script>
197
198        <script src="/Validation/WebResource.axd?d=2vO6TLcUQjFB3X5GN16w
199            bg2&amp;t=632494248729409088" type="text/javascript"></script>
200
201        <script type="text/javascript">
202        <!--
203            var Page_ValidationActive = false;
204
205            if (typeof(ValidatorOnLoad) == "function") {
206                ValidatorOnLoad();
207            }
208
```

Fig. 21.22 | XHTML and ECMAScript generated by ASP.NET and sent to the browser when Validation.aspx is requested. (Part 5 of 6.)

```
209                    function ValidatorOnSubmit() {
210                        if (Page_ValidationActive) {
211                            return ValidatorCommonOnSubmit();
212                        }
213                        else {
214                            return true;
215                        }
216                    }
217                // -->
218                </script>
219            </form>
220        </body>
221    </html>
```

Fig. 21.22 | XHTML and ECMAScript generated by ASP.NET and sent to the browser when `Validation.aspx` is requested. (Part 6 of 6.)

21.6 Session Tracking

Originally, critics accused the Internet and e-business of failing to provide the kind of customized service typically experienced in "brick-and-mortar" stores. To address this problem, e-businesses began to establish mechanisms by which they could personalize users' browsing experiences, tailoring content to individual users while enabling them to bypass irrelevant information. Businesses achieve this level of service by tracking each customer's movement through the Internet and combining the collected data with information provided by the consumer, including billing information, personal preferences, interests and hobbies.

Personalization

Personalization makes it possible for e-businesses to communicate effectively with their customers and also improves users' ability to locate desired products and services. Companies that provide content of particular interest to users can establish relationships with customers and build on those relationships over time. Furthermore, by targeting consumers with personal offers, recommendations, advertisements, promotions and services, e-businesses create customer loyalty. Web sites can use sophisticated technology to allow visitors to customize home pages to suit their individual needs and preferences. Similarly, online shopping sites often store personal information for customers, tailoring notifications and special offers to their interests. Such services encourage customers to visit sites more frequently and make purchases more regularly.

Privacy

A trade-off exists, however, between personalized e-business service and protection of privacy. Some consumers embrace the idea of tailored content, but others fear the possible adverse consequences if the info they provide to e-businesses is released or collected by tracking technologies. Consumers and privacy advocates ask: What if the e-business to which we give personal data sells or gives that information to another organization without our knowledge? What if we do not want our actions on the Internet—a supposedly anonymous medium—to be tracked and recorded by unknown parties? What if unauthorized parties gain access to sensitive private data, such as credit-card numbers or medical history?

All of these are questions that must be debated and addressed by programmers, consumers, e-businesses and lawmakers alike.

Recognizing Clients

To provide personalized services to consumers, e-businesses must be able to recognize clients when they request information from a site. As we have discussed, the request/response system on which the Web operates is facilitated by HTTP. Unfortunately, HTTP is a stateless protocol—it does not support persistent connections that would enable Web servers to maintain state information regarding particular clients. This means that Web servers cannot determine whether a request comes from a particular client or whether the same or different clients generate a series of requests. To circumvent this problem, sites can provide mechanisms by which they identify individual clients. A session represents a unique client on a Web site. If the client leaves a site and then returns later, the client will still be recognized as the same user. To help the server distinguish among clients, each client must identify itself to the server. Tracking individual clients, known as ***session tracking***, can be achieved in a number of ways. One popular technique uses cookies (Section 21.6.1); another uses ASP.NET's `HttpSessionState` object (Section 21.6.2). Additional session-tracking techniques include the use of `input form` elements of type `"hidden"` and URL rewriting. Using `"hidden"` form elements, a Web Form can write session-tracking data into a `form` in the Web page that it returns to the client in response to a prior request. When the user submits the form in the new Web page, all the form data, including the `"hidden"` fields, is sent to the form handler on the Web server. When a Web site performs URL rewriting, the Web Form embeds session-tracking information directly in the URLs of hyperlinks that the user clicks to send subsequent requests to the Web server.

Note that our previous examples set the Web Form's `EnableSessionState` property to `False`. However, because we wish to use session tracking in the following examples, we keep this property's default setting—`True`.

21.6.1 Cookies

Cookies provide Web developers with a tool for personalizing Web pages. A cookie is a piece of data stored in a small text file on the user's computer. A cookie maintains information about the client during and between browser sessions. The first time a user visits the Web site, the user's computer might receive a cookie; this cookie is then reactivated each time the user revisits that site. The collected information is intended to be an anonymous record containing data that is used to personalize the user's future visits to the site. For example, cookies in a shopping application might store unique identifiers for users. When a user adds items to an online shopping cart or performs another task resulting in a request to the Web server, the server receives a cookie containing the user's unique identifier. The server then uses the unique identifier to locate the shopping cart and perform any necessary processing.

In addition to identifying users, cookies also can indicate clients' shopping preferences. When a Web Form receives a request from a client, the Web Form can examine the cookie(s) it sent to the client during previous communications, identify the client's preferences and immediately display products of interest to the client.

Every HTTP-based interaction between a client and a server includes a header containing information either about the request (when the communication is from the client to the server) or about the response (when the communication is from the server to the client). When a Web Form receives a request, the header includes information such as the request type (e.g., `Get`) and any cookies that have been sent previously from the server to be stored on the client machine. When the server formulates its response, the header information contains any cookies the server wants to store on the client computer and other information, such as the MIME type of the response.

The *expiration date* of a cookie determines how long the cookie remains on the client's computer. If you do not set an expiration date for a cookie, the Web browser maintains the cookie for the duration of the browsing session. Otherwise, the Web browser maintains the cookie until the expiration date occurs. When the browser requests a resource from a Web server, cookies previously sent to the client by that Web server are returned to the Web server as part of the request formulated by the browser. Cookies are deleted when they *expire*.

Portability Tip 21.3

Clients may disable cookies in their Web browsers to ensure that their privacy is protected. Such clients will experience difficulty using Web applications that depend on cookies to maintain state information.

Using Cookies to Provide Book Recommendations

The next Web application demonstrates the use of cookies. The example contains two pages. In the first page (Figs. 21.23–21.24), users select a favorite programming language from a group of radio buttons and submit the XHTML form to the Web server for processing. The Web server responds by creating a cookie that stores a record of the chosen language, as well as the ISBN number for a book on that topic. The server then returns an XHTML document to the browser, allowing the user either to select another favorite programming language or to view the second page in our application (Figs. 21.25 and 21.26), which lists recommended books pertaining to the programming language that the user selected previously. When the user clicks the hyperlink, the cookies previously stored on the client are read and used to form the list of book recommendations.

The ASPX file in Fig. 21.23 contains five radio buttons (lines 21–27) with the values **Visual Basic 2005**, **Visual C# 2005**, **C**, **C++**, and **Java**. Recall that you can set the values of radio buttons via the **ListItem Collection Editor**, which is opened either by clicking the

```
 1   <%-- Fig. 21.23: Options.aspx --%>
 2   <%-- Allows client to select programming languages and access --%>
 3   <%-- book recommendations. --%>
 4   <%@ Page Language="C#" AutoEventWireup="true"
 5      CodeFile="Options.aspx.cs" Inherits="Options" %>
 6
 7   <!DOCTYPE html PUBLIC "-//W3C//DTD XHTML 1.1//EN"
 8      "http://www.w3.org/TR/xhtml11/DTD/xhtml11.dtd">
 9
10   <html xmlns="http://www.w3.org/1999/xhtml" >
11      <head runat="server">
12         <title>Cookies</title>
13      </head>
```

Fig. 21.23 | ASPX file that presents a list of programming languages. (Part 1 of 3.)

```
14      <body>
15        <form id="form1" runat="server">
16          <div>
17            <asp:Label ID="promptLabel" runat="server" Font-Bold="True"
18              Font-Size="Large" Text="Select a programming language:">
19            </asp:Label>
20
21            <asp:RadioButtonList ID="languageList" runat="server">
22              <asp:ListItem>Visual Basic 2005</asp:ListItem>
23              <asp:ListItem>Visual C# 2005</asp:ListItem>
24              <asp:ListItem>C</asp:ListItem>
25              <asp:ListItem>C++</asp:ListItem>
26              <asp:ListItem>Java</asp:ListItem>
27            </asp:RadioButtonList>
28
29            <asp:Button ID="submitButton" runat="server" Text="Submit" />
30
31            <asp:Label ID="responseLabel" runat="server" Font-Bold="True"
32              Font-Size="Large" Text="Welcome to cookies!"
33              Visible="False"></asp:Label>
34            <br /><br />
35
36            <asp:HyperLink ID="languageLink" runat="server"
37              Visible="False" NavigateUrl="~/Options.aspx">
38              Click here to choose another language</asp:HyperLink>
39            <br /><br />
40
41            <asp:HyperLink ID="recommendationsLink" runat="server"
42              Visible="False" NavigateUrl="~/Recommendations.aspx">
43              Click here to get book recommendations</asp:HyperLink>
44          </div>
45        </form>
46      </body>
47    </html>
```

(a)

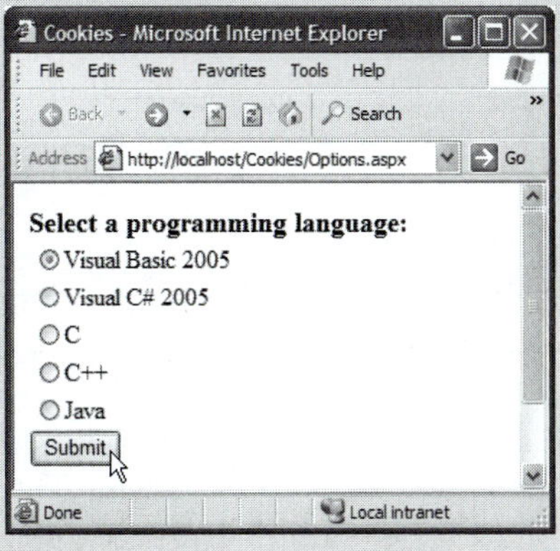

Fig. 21.23 | ASPX file that presents a list of programming languages. (Part 2 of 3.)

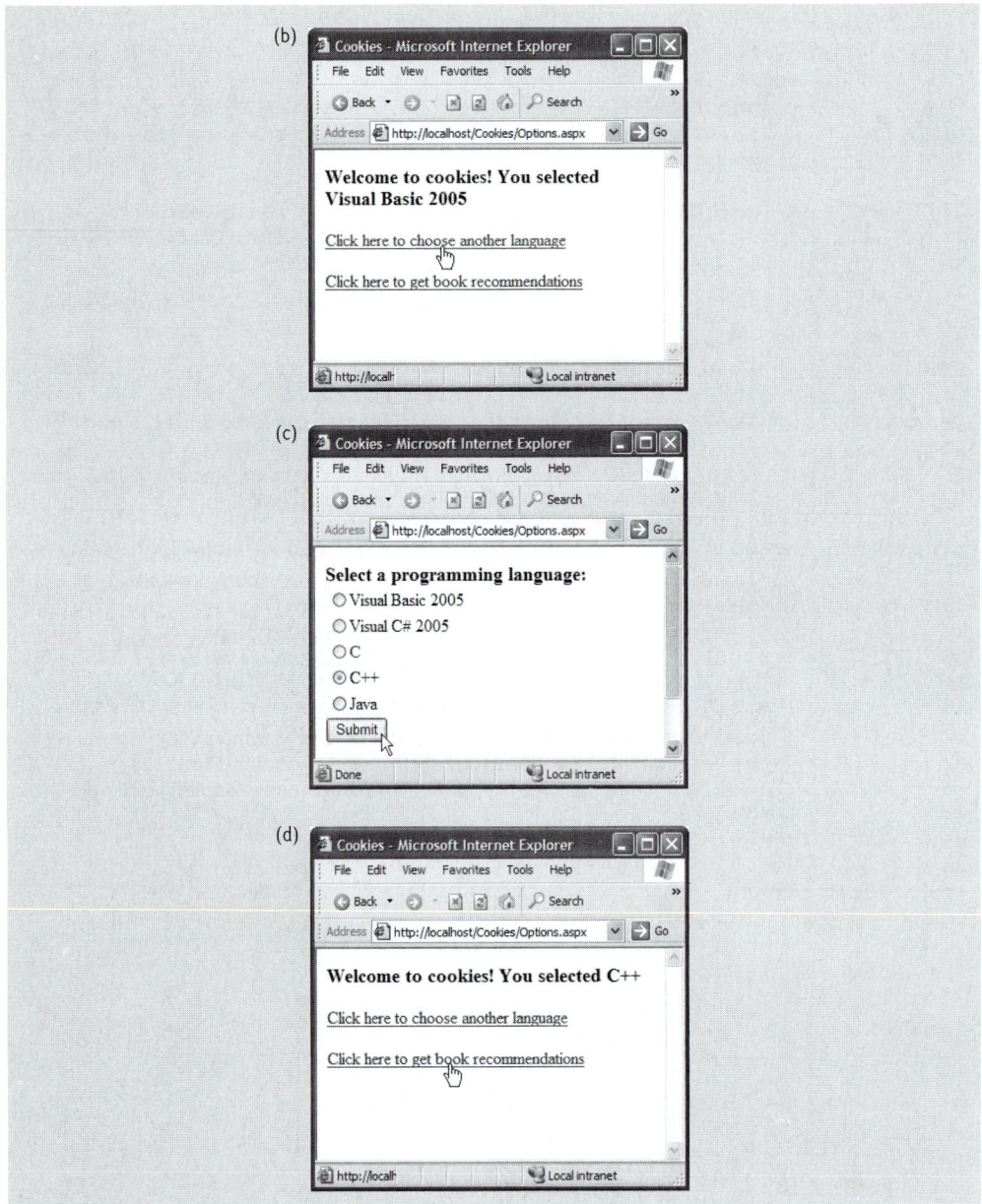

Fig. 21.23 | ASPX file that presents a list of programming languages. (Part 3 of 3.)

RadioButtonList's Items property in the **Properties** window or by clicking the **Edit Items...** link in the **RadioButtonList Tasks** smart tag menu. The user selects a programming language by clicking one of the radio buttons. The page contains a **Submit** button, which when clicked, creates a cookie containing a record of the selected language. Once created, this cookie is added to the HTTP response header, and a postback occurs. Each time the user chooses a language and clicks **Submit**, a cookie is written to the client.

When the postback occurs, certain controls are hidden and others are displayed. The Label, RadioButtonList and Button used to select a language are hidden. Toward the bottom of the page, a Label and two HyperLinks are displayed. One link requests this page (lines 36–38), and the other requests Recommendations.aspx (lines 41–43). Notice that clicking the first hyperlink (the one that requests the current page) does not cause a postback to occur. The file Options.aspx is specified in the NavigateUrl property of the hyperlink. When the hyperlink is clicked, this page is requested as a completely new request. Recall that earlier in the chapter, we set NavigateUrl to a remote Web site (http://www.deitel.com). To set this property to a page within the same ASP.NET application, click the ellipsis button next to the NavigateUrl property in the **Properties** window to open the **Select URL** dialog. Use this dialog to select a page within your project as the destination for the HyperLink.

Adding and Linking to a New Web Form

Setting the NavigateUrl property to a page in the current application requires that the destination page exist already. Thus, to set the NavigateUrl property of the second link (the one that requests the page with book recommendations) to Recommendations.aspx, you must first create this file by right clicking the project location in the **Solution Explorer** and selecting **Add New Item...** from the menu that appears. In the **Add New Item** dialog, select **Web Form** from the **Templates** pane and change the name of the file to Recommendations.aspx. Finally, check the box labeled **Place code in separate file** to indicate that the IDE should create a code-behind file for this ASPX file. Click **Add** to create the file. (We discuss the contents of this ASPX file and code-behind file shortly.) Once the Recommendations.aspx file exists, you can select it as the NavigateUrl value for a HyperLink in the **Select URL** dialog.

Writing Cookies in a Code-Behind File

Figure 21.24 presents the code-behind file for Options.aspx (Fig. 21.23). This file contains the code that writes a cookie to the client machine when the user selects a programming language. The code-behind file also modifies the appearance of the page in response to a postback.

```
1   // Fig. 21.24: Options.aspx.cs
2   // Processes user's selection of a programming language
3   // by displaying links and writing a cookie to the user's machine.
4   using System;
5   using System.Data;
6   using System.Configuration;
7   using System.Web;
8   using System.Web.Security;
9   using System.Web.UI;
10  using System.Web.UI.WebControls;
11  using System.Web.UI.WebControls.WebParts;
12  using System.Web.UI.HtmlControls;
13  public partial class Options : System.Web.UI.Page
14  {
```

Fig. 21.24 | Code-behind file that writes a cookie to the client. (Part 1 of 3.)

```
15    // stores values to represent books as cookies
16    private System.Collections.Hashtable books =
17       new System.Collections.Hashtable();
18
19    // initializes the Hashtable of values to be stored as cookies
20    protected void Page_Init( object sender, EventArgs e )
21    {
22       books.Add( "Visual Basic 2005", "0-13-186900-0" );
23       books.Add( "Visual C# 2005", "0-13-152523-9" );
24       books.Add( "C", "0-13-142644-3" );
25       books.Add( "C++", "0-13-185757-6" );
26       books.Add( "Java", "0-13-148398-6" );
27    } // end method Page_Init
28
29    // if postback, hide form and display links to make additional
30    // selections or view recommendations
31    protected void Page_Load( object sender, EventArgs e )
32    {
33       if ( IsPostBack )
34       {
35          // user has submitted information, so display message
36          // and appropriate hyperlinks
37          responseLabel.Visible = true;
38          languageLink.Visible = true;
39          recommendationsLink.Visible = true;
40
41          // hide other controls used to make language selection
42          promptLabel.Visible = false;
43          languageList.Visible = false;
44          submitButton.Visible = false;
45
46          // if the user made a selection, display it in responseLabel
47          if ( languageList.SelectedItem != null )
48             responseLabel.Text += " You selected " +
49                languageList.SelectedItem.Text.ToString();
50          else
51             responseLabel.Text += " You did not select a language.";
52       } // end if
53    } // end method Page_Load
54
55    // write a cookie to record the user's selection
56    protected void submitButton_Click( object sender, EventArgs e )
57    {
58       // if the user made a selection
59       if ( languageList.SelectedItem != null )
60       {
61          string language = languageList.SelectedItem.ToString();
62
63          // get ISBN number of book for the given language
64          string ISBN = books[ language ].ToString();
65
66          // create cookie using language-ISBN name-value pair
67          HttpCookie cookie = new HttpCookie( language, ISBN );
```

Fig. 21.24 | Code-behind file that writes a cookie to the client. (Part 2 of 3.)

```
68
69              // add cookie to response to place it on the user's machine
70              Response.Cookies.Add( cookie );
71         } // end if
72     } // end method submitButton_Click
73 } // end class Options
```

Fig. 21.24 | Code-behind file that writes a cookie to the client. (Part 3 of 3.)

Lines 16–17 create books as a Hashtable (namespace System.Collections)—a data structure that stores *key–value pairs*. A program uses the key to store and retrieve the associated value in the Hashtable. In this example, the keys are strings containing the programming languages' names, and the values are strings containing the ISBN numbers for the recommended books. Class Hashtable provides method **Add**, which takes as arguments a key and a value. A value that is added via method Add is placed in the Hashtable at a location determined by the key. The value for a specific Hashtable entry can be determined by indexing the Hashtable with that value's key. The expression

> *HashtableName*[*keyName*]

returns the value in the key–value pair in which *keyName* is the key. For example, the expression books[language] in line 64 returns the value that corresponds to the key contained in language. Class Hashtable is discussed in detail in Chapter 25, Data Structures.

Clicking the **Submit** button creates a cookie if a language is selected and causes a postback to occur. In the submitButton_Click event handler (lines 56–72), a new cookie object (of type **HttpCookie**) is created to store the language and its corresponding ISBN number (line 67). This cookie is then Added to the **Cookies** collection sent as part of the HTTP response header (line 70). The postback causes the condition in the if statement of Page_Load (line 33) to evaluate to true, and lines 37–51 execute. Lines 37–39 reveal the initially hidden controls responseLabel, languageLink and recommendationsLink. Lines 42–44 hide the controls used to obtain the user's language selection. Line 47 determines whether the user selected a language. If so, that language is displayed in responseLabel (lines 48–49). Otherwise, text indicating that a language was not selected is displayed in responseLabel (line 51).

Displaying Book Recommendations Based on Cookie Values

After the postback of Options.aspx, the user may request a book recommendation. The book recommendation hyperlink forwards the user to Recommendations.aspx (Fig. 21.25) to display the recommendations based on the user's language selections.

```
1  <%-- Fig. 21.25: Recommendations.aspx --%>
2  <%-- Displays book recommendations using cookies. --%>
3  <%@ Page Language="C#" AutoEventWireup="true"
4     CodeFile="Recommendations.aspx.cs" Inherits="Recommendations" %>
5
6  <!DOCTYPE html PUBLIC "-//W3C//DTD XHTML 1.1//EN"
7     "http://www.w3.org/TR/xhtml11/DTD/xhtml11.dtd">
```

Fig. 21.25 | ASPX file that displays book recommendations based on cookies. (Part 1 of 2.)

```
 8
 9    <html xmlns="http://www.w3.org/1999/xhtml" >
10       <head runat="server">
11          <title>Book Recommendations</title>
12       </head>
13       <body>
14          <form id="form1" runat="server">
15             <div>
16                <asp:Label ID="recommendationsLabel"
17                   runat="server" Text="Recommendations"
18                   Font-Bold="True" Font-Size="X-Large">
19                </asp:Label><br /><br />
20
21                <asp:ListBox ID="booksListBox" runat="server" Height="125px"
22                   Width="450px"></asp:ListBox><br /><br />
23
24                <asp:HyperLink ID="languageLink" runat="server"
25                   NavigateUrl="~/Options.aspx">
26                   Click here to choose another language
27                </asp:HyperLink>
28             </div>
29          </form>
30       </body>
31    </html>
```

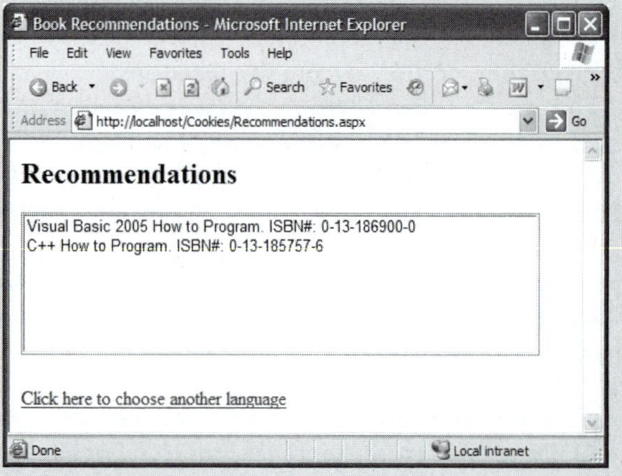

Fig. 21.25 | ASPX file that displays book recommendations based on cookies. (Part 2 of 2.)

Recommendations.aspx contains a Label (lines 16–19), a ListBox (lines 21–22) and a HyperLink (lines 24–27). The Label displays the text **Recommendations** if the user has selected one or more languages; otherwise, it displays **No Recommendations**. The ListBox displays the recommendations created by the code-behind file, which is shown in Fig. 21.26. The HyperLink allows the user to return to Options.aspx to select additional languages.

Code-Behind File That Creates Book Recommendations From Cookies

In the code-behind file Recommendations.aspx.cs (Fig. 21.26), method Page_Init (lines 17–40) retrieves the cookies from the client, using the Request object's **Cookies** property

```
 1    // Fig. 21.26: Recommendations.aspx.cs
 2    // Creates book recommendations based on cookies.
 3    using System;
 4    using System.Data;
 5    using System.Configuration;
 6    using System.Collections;
 7    using System.Web;
 8    using System.Web.Security;
 9    using System.Web.UI;
10    using System.Web.UI.WebControls;
11    using System.Web.UI.WebControls.WebParts;
12    using System.Web.UI.HtmlControls;
13
14    public partial class Recommendations : System.Web.UI.Page
15    {
16       // read cookies and populate ListBox with any book recommendations
17       protected void Page_Init( object sender, EventArgs e )
18       {
19          // retrieve client's cookies
20          HttpCookieCollection cookies = Request.Cookies;
21
22          // if there are cookies, list the appropriate books and ISBN numbers
23          if ( cookies.Count != 0 )
24          {
25             for ( int i = 0; i < cookies.Count; i++ )
26                booksListBox.Items.Add( cookies[ i ].Name +
27                   " How to Program. ISBN#: " + cookies[ i ].Value );
28          } // end if
29          else
30          {
31             // if there are no cookies, then no language was chosen, so
32             // display appropriate message and clear and hide booksListBox
33             recommendationsLabel.Text = "No Recommendations";
34             booksListBox.Items.Clear();
35             booksListBox.Visible = false;
36
37             // modify languageLink because no language was selected
38             languageLink.Text = "Click here to choose a language";
39          } // end else
40       } // end method Page_Init
41    } // end class Recommendations
```

Fig. 21.26 | Reading cookies from a client to determine book recommendations.

(line 20). This returns a collection of type **HttpCookieCollection**, containing cookies that have previously been written to the client. Cookies can be read by an application only if they were created in the domain in which the application is running—a Web server can never access cookies created outside the domain associated with that server. For example, a cookie created by a Web server in the deitel.com domain cannot be read by a Web server in any other domain.

Line 23 determines whether at least one cookie exists. Lines 25–27 add the information in the cookie(s) to the booksListBox. The for statement retrieves the name and value of each cookie using i, the statement's control variable, to determine the current value in the cookie collection. The *Name* and *Value* properties of class HttpCookie, which contain the language and corresponding ISBN, respectively, are concatenated with " How to Program. ISBN# " and added to the ListBox. Lines 33–38 execute if no language was selected. We summarize some commonly used HttpCookie properties in Fig. 21.27.

21.6.2 Session Tracking with HttpSessionState

C# provides session-tracking capabilities in the Framework Class Library's *HttpSessionState* class. To demonstrate basic session-tracking techniques, we modified Fig. 21.26 so that it uses HttpSessionState objects. Figure 21.28 presents the ASPX file, and Fig. 21.29 presents the code-behind file. The ASPX file is similar to that presented in Fig. 21.23, except Fig. 21.28 contains two additional Labels (lines 35–36 and lines 38–39), which we discuss shortly.

Every Web Form includes an HttpSessionState object, which is accessible through property *Session* of class Page. Throughout this section, we use property Session to manipulate our page's HttpSessionState object. When the Web page is requested, an HttpSessionState object is created and assigned to the Page's Session property. As a result, we often refer to property Session as the Session object.

Properties	Description
Domain	Returns a string containing the cookie's domain (i.e., the domain of the Web server running the application that wrote the cookie). This determines which Web servers can receive the cookie. By default, cookies are sent to the Web server that originally sent the cookie to the client. Changing the Domain property causes the cookie to be returned to a Web server other than the one that originally wrote it.
Expires	Returns a DateTime object indicating when the browser can delete the cookie.
Name	Returns a string containing the cookie's name.
Path	Returns a string containing the path to a directory on the server (i.e., the Domain) to which the cookie applies. Cookies can be "targeted" to specific directories on the Web server. By default, a cookie is returned only to applications operating in the same directory as the application that sent the cookie or a subdirectory of that directory. Changing the Path property causes the cookie to be returned to a directory other than the one from which it was originally written.
Secure	Returns a bool value indicating whether the cookie should be transmitted through a secure protocol. The value true causes a secure protocol to be used.
Value	Returns a string containing the cookie's value.

Fig. 21.27 | HttpCookie properties.

```
 1    <%-- Fig. 21.28: Options.aspx --%>
 2    <%-- Allows client to select programming languages and access --%>
 3    <%-- book recommendations. --%>
 4    <%@ Page Language="C#" AutoEventWireup="true"
 5       CodeFile="Options.aspx.cs" Inherits="Options" %>
 6
 7    <!DOCTYPE html PUBLIC "-//W3C//DTD XHTML 1.1//EN"
 8       "http://www.w3.org/TR/xhtml11/DTD/xhtml11.dtd">
 9
10    <html xmlns="http://www.w3.org/1999/xhtml" >
11       <head runat="server">
12          <title>Sessions</title>
13       </head>
14       <body>
15          <form id="form1" runat="server">
16             <div>
17                <asp:Label ID="promptLabel" runat="server" Font-Bold="True"
18                   Font-Size="Large" Text="Select a programming language:">
19                </asp:Label>
20
21                <asp:RadioButtonList ID="languageList" runat="server">
22                   <asp:ListItem>Visual Basic 2005</asp:ListItem>
23                   <asp:ListItem>Visual C# 2005</asp:ListItem>
24                   <asp:ListItem>C</asp:ListItem>
25                   <asp:ListItem>C++</asp:ListItem>
26                   <asp:ListItem>Java</asp:ListItem>
27                </asp:RadioButtonList>
28
29                <asp:Button ID="submitButton" runat="server" Text="Submit" />
30
31                <asp:Label ID="responseLabel" runat="server" Font-Bold="True"
32                   Font-Size="Large" Text="Welcome to sessions!"
33                   Visible="False"></asp:Label><br /><br />
34
35                <asp:Label ID="idLabel" runat="server" Visible="False">
36                </asp:Label><br /><br />
37
38                <asp:Label ID="timeoutLabel" runat="server" Visible="False">
39                </asp:Label><br /><br />
40
41                <asp:HyperLink ID="languageLink" runat="server"
42                   Visible="False" NavigateUrl="~/Options.aspx">
43                   Click here to choose another language
44                </asp:HyperLink><br /><br />
45
46                <asp:HyperLink ID="recommendationsLink" runat="server"
47                   Visible="False" NavigateUrl="~/Recommendations.aspx">
48                   Click here to get book recommendations</asp:HyperLink>
49             </div>
50          </form>
51       </body>
52    </html>
```

Fig. 21.28 | ASPX file that presents a list of programming languages. (Part 1 of 3.)

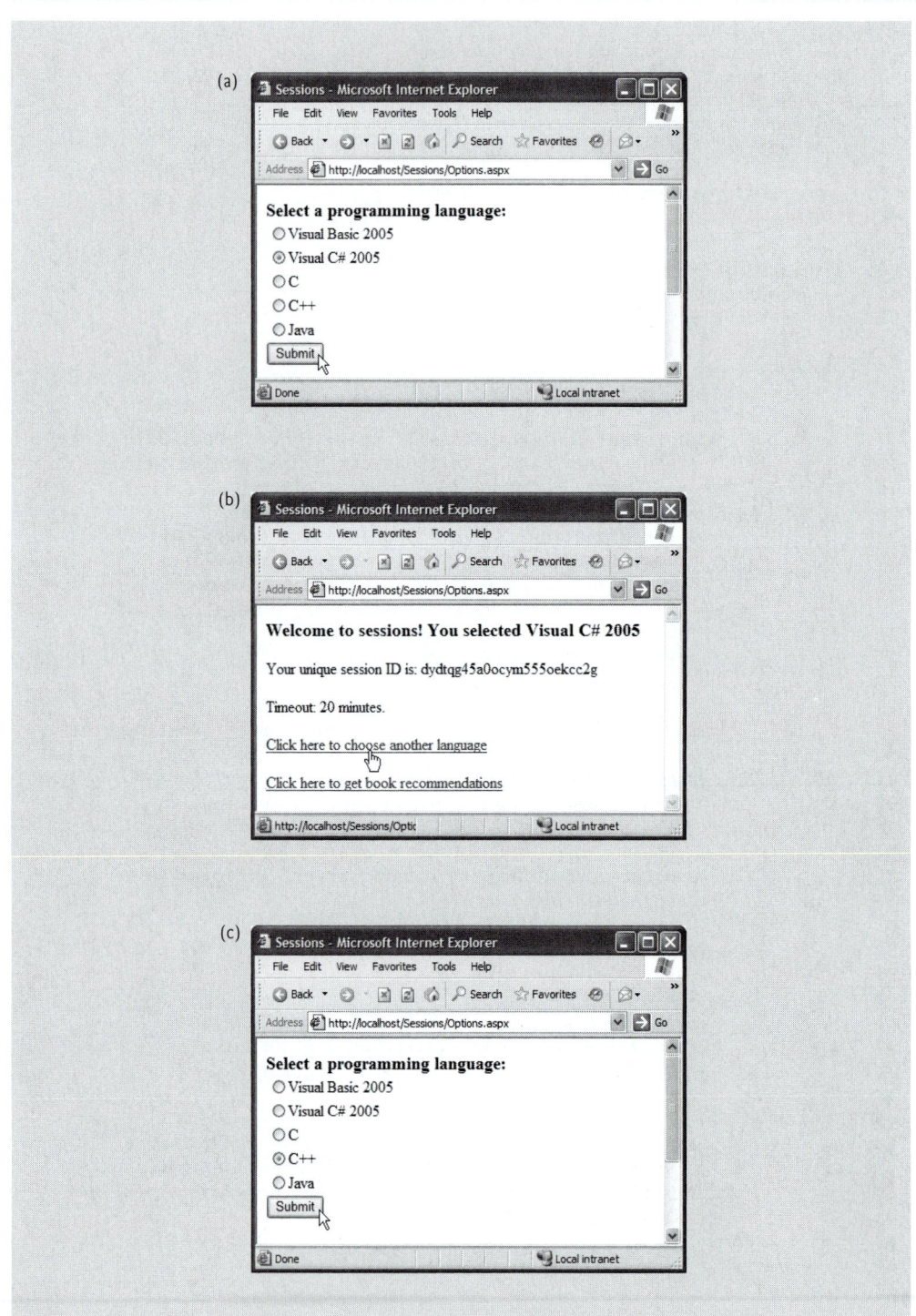

Fig. 21.28 | ASPX file that presents a list of programming languages. (Part 2 of 3.)

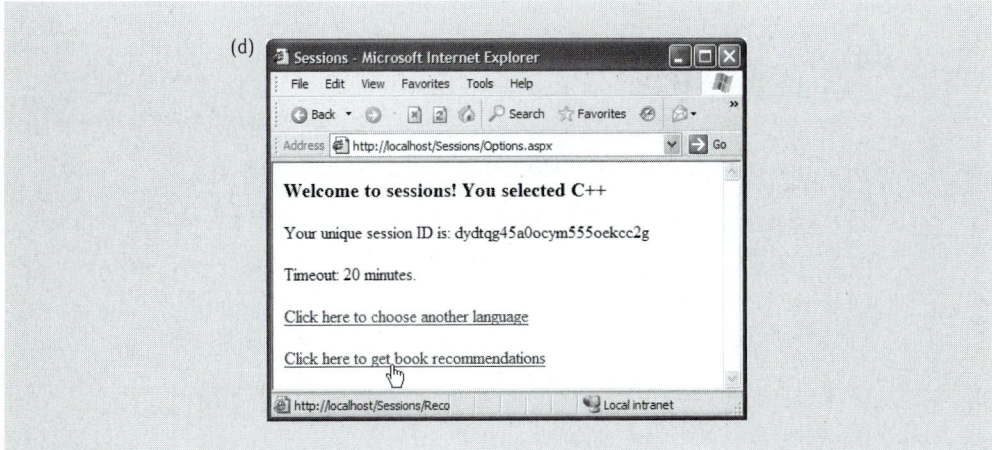

Fig. 21.28 | ASPX file that presents a list of programming languages. (Part 3 of 3.)

Adding Session Items

When the user presses **Submit** on the Web Form, submitButton_Click is invoked in the code-behind file (Fig. 21.29). Method submitButton_Click responds by adding a key–value pair to our Session object, specifying the language chosen and the ISBN number for a book on that language. These key–value pairs are often referred to as *session items*. Next, a postback occurs. Each time the user clicks **Submit**, submitButton_Click adds a new session item to the HttpSessionState object. Because much of this example is identical to the last example, we concentrate on the new features.

Software Engineering Observation 21.1

A Web Form should not use instance variables to maintain client state information, because each new request or postback, is handled by a new instance of the page. Web Forms should maintain client state information in HttpSessionState objects, because such objects are specific to each client.

```
1   // Fig. 21.29: Options.aspx.cs
2   // Processes user's selection of a programming language
3   // by displaying links and writing a cookie to the user's machine.
4   using System;
5   using System.Data;
6   using System.Configuration;
7   using System.Web;
8   using System.Web.Security;
9   using System.Web.UI;
10  using System.Web.UI.WebControls;
11  using System.Web.UI.WebControls.WebParts;
12  using System.Web.UI.HtmlControls;
13  public partial class Options : System.Web.UI.Page
14  {
```

Fig. 21.29 | Creates a session item for each programming language selected by the user on the ASPX page. (Part 1 of 3.)

```
15        // stores values to represent books as cookies
16        private System.Collections.Hashtable books =
17           new System.Collections.Hashtable();
18
19        //initializes the Hashtable of values to be stored as cookies
20        protected void Page_Init( object sender, EventArgs e )
21        {
22           books.Add( "Visual Basic 2005", "0-13-186900-0" );
23           books.Add( "Visual C# 2005", "0-13-152523-9" );
24           books.Add( "C", "0-13-142644-3" );
25           books.Add( "C++", "0-13-185757-6" );
26           books.Add( "Java", "0-13-148398-6" );
27        } // end method Page_Init
28
29        // if postback, hide form and display links to make additional
30        // selections or view recommendations
31        protected void Page_Load( object sender, EventArgs e )
32        {
33           if ( IsPostBack )
34           {
35              // user has submitted information, so display appropriate labels
36              // and hyperlinks
37              responseLabel.Visible = true;
38              idLabel.Visible = true;
39              timeoutLabel.Visible = true;
40              languageLink.Visible = true;
41              recommendationsLink.Visible = true;
42
43              // hide other controls used to make language selection
44              promptLabel.Visible = false;
45              languageList.Visible = false;
46              submitButton.Visible = false;
47
48              // if the user made a selection, display it in responseLabel
49              if ( languageList.SelectedItem != null )
50                 responseLabel.Text += " You selected " +
51                    languageList.SelectedItem.Text.ToString();
52              else
53                 responseLabel.Text += " You did not select a language.";
54
55              // display session ID
56              idLabel.Text = "Your unique session ID is: " + Session.SessionID;
57
58              // display the timeout
59              timeoutLabel.Text = "Timeout: " + Session.Timeout + " minutes.";
60           } // end if
61        } // end method Page_Load
62
63        // write a cookie to record the user's selection
64        protected void submitButton_Click( object sender, EventArgs e )
65        {
```

Fig. 21.29 | Creates a session item for each programming language selected by the user on the ASPX page. (Part 2 of 3.)

```
66            // if the user made a selection
67            if ( languageList.SelectedItem != null )
68            {
69                string language = languageList.SelectedItem.ToString();
70
71                // get ISBN number of book for the given language
72                string ISBN = books[ language ].ToString();
73
74                Session.Add( language, ISBN ); // add name/value pair to Session
75            } // end if
76        } // end method submitButton_Click
77    } // end class Options
```

Fig. 21.29 | Creates a session item for each programming language selected by the user on the ASPX page. (Part 3 of 3.)

Like a cookie, an HttpSessionState object can store name–value pairs. These session items are placed in an HttpSessionState object by calling method **Add**. Line 74 calls Add to place the language and its corresponding recommended book's ISBN number in the HttpSessionState object. If the application calls method Add to add an attribute that has the same name as an attribute previously stored in a session, the object associated with that attribute is replaced.

Software Engineering Observation 21.2

One of the primary benefits of using HttpSessionState objects (rather than cookies) is that HttpSessionState objects can store any type of object (not just Strings) as attribute values. This provides you with increased flexibility in determining the type of state information to maintain for clients.

The application handles the postback event (lines 33–60) in method Page_Load. Here, we retrieve information about the current client's session from the Session object's properties and display this information in the Web page. The ASP.NET application contains information about the HttpSessionState object for the current client. Property **SessionID** (line 56) contains the *unique session ID*—a sequence of random letters and numbers. The first time a client connects to the Web server, a unique session ID is created for that client. When the client makes additional requests, the client's session ID is compared with the session IDs stored in the Web server's memory to retrieve the HttpSessionState object for that client. Property **Timeout** (line 59) specifies the maximum amount of time that an HttpSessionState object can be inactive before it is discarded. Figure 21.30 lists some common HttpSessionState properties.

Properties	Description
Count	Specifies the number of key–value pairs in the Session object.
IsNewSession	Indicates whether this is a new session (i.e., whether the session was created during loading of this page).

Fig. 21.30 | HttpSessionState properties. (Part 1 of 2.)

Properties	Description
IsReadOnly	Indicates whether the Session object is read-only.
Keys	Returns a collection containing the Session object's keys.
SessionID	Returns the session's unique ID.
Timeout	Specifies the maximum number of minutes during which a session can be inactive (i.e., no requests are made) before the session expires. By default, this property is set to 20 minutes.

Fig. 21.30 | HttpSessionState properties. (Part 1 of 2.)

Displaying Recommendations Based on Session Values

As in the cookies example, this application provides a link to Recommendations.aspx (Fig. 21.31), which displays a list of book recommendations based on the user's language selections. Lines 21–22 define a ListBox Web control that is used to present the recommendations to the user.

```
1   <%-- Fig. 21.31: Recommendations.aspx --%>
2   <%-- Displays book recommendations using sessions. --%>
3   <%@ Page Language="C#" AutoEventWireup="true"
4      CodeFile="Recommendations.aspx.cs" Inherits="Recommendations" %>
5
6   <!DOCTYPE html PUBLIC "-//W3C//DTD XHTML 1.1//EN"
7      "http://www.w3.org/TR/xhtml11/DTD/xhtml11.dtd">
8
9   <html xmlns="http://www.w3.org/1999/xhtml" >
10     <head runat="server">
11        <title>Book Recommendations</title>
12     </head>
13     <body>
14        <form id="form1" runat="server">
15           <div>
16              <asp:Label ID="recommendationsLabel"
17                 runat="server" Text="Recommendations"
18                 Font-Bold="True" Font-Size="X-Large">
19              </asp:Label><br /><br />
20
21              <asp:ListBox ID="booksListBox" runat="server" Height="125px"
22                 Width="450px"></asp:ListBox><br /><br />
23
24              <asp:HyperLink ID="languageLink" runat="server"
25                 NavigateUrl="~/Options.aspx">
26                 Click here to choose another language
27              </asp:HyperLink>
28           </div>
29        </form>
30     </body>
31   </html>
```

Fig. 21.31 | Session-based book recommendations displayed in a ListBox. (Part 1 of 2.)

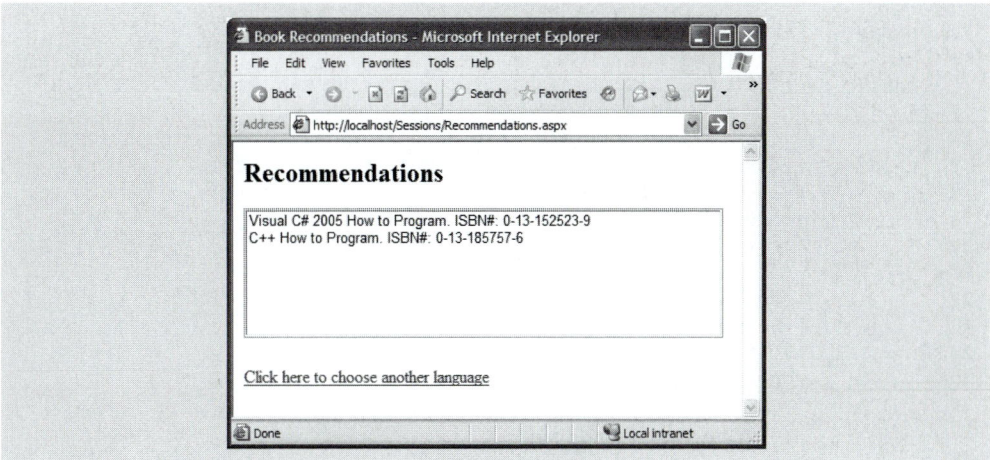

Fig. 21.31 | Session-based book recommendations displayed in a ListBox. (Part 2 of 2.)

Code-Behind File That Creates Book Recommendations from a Session

Figure 21.32 presents the code-behind file for Recommendations.aspx. Event handler Page_Init (lines 17–47) retrieves the session information. If a user has not selected a language on Options.aspx, our Session object's **Count** property will be 0. This property provides the number of session items contained in a Session object. If Session object's Count property is 0 (i.e., no language was selected), then we display the text **No Recommendations** and update the Text of the HyperLink back to Options.aspx.

If the user has chosen a language, the for statement (lines 25–34) iterates through our Session object's session items, temporarily storing each key name (line 27). The value in a key–value pair is retrieved from the Session object by indexing the Session object with the key name, using the same process by which we retrieved a value from our Hashtable in the preceding section.

Line 27 accesses the **Keys** property of class HttpSessionState, which returns a collection containing all the keys in the session. Line 27 indexes this collection to retrieve the current key. Lines 31–33 concatenate keyName's value to the string " How to Program. ISBN#: " and the value from the Session object for which keyName is the key. This string is the recommendation that appears in the ListBox.

```
1    // Fig. 21.32: Recommendations.aspx.cs
2    // Creates book recommendations based on a session object.
3    using System;
4    using System.Data;
5    using System.Configuration;
6    using System.Collections;
7    using System.Web;
8    using System.Web.Security;
9    using System.Web.UI;
10   using System.Web.UI.WebControls;
11   using System.Web.UI.WebControls.WebParts;
```

Fig. 21.32 | Session data used to provide book recommendations to the user. (Part 1 of 2.)

```
12    using System.Web.UI.HtmlControls;
13
14    public partial class Recommendations : System.Web.UI.Page
15    {
16       // read cookies and populate ListBox with any book recommendations
17       protected void Page_Init( object sender, EventArgs e )
18       {
19          // stores a key name found in the Session object
20          string keyName;
21
22          // determine whether Session contains any information
23          if ( Session.Count != 0 )
24          {
25             for ( int i = 0; i < Session.Count; i++ )
26             {
27                keyName = Session.Keys[ i ]; // store current key name
28
29                // use current key to display one
30                // of session's name-value pairs
31                booksListBox.Items.Add( keyName +
32                   " How to Program. ISBN#: " +
33                   Session[ keyName ].ToString() );
34             } // end for
35          } // end if
36          else
37          {
38             // if there are no session items, no language was chosen, so
39             // display appropriate message and clear and hide booksListBox
40             recommendationsLabel.Text = "No Recommendations";
41             booksListBox.Items.Clear();
42             booksListBox.Visible = false;
43
44             // modify languageLink because no language was selected
45             languageLink.Text = "Click here to choose a language";
46          } // end else
47       } // end method Page_Init
48    } // end class Recommendations
```

Fig. 21.32 | Session data used to provide book recommendations to the user. (Part 2 of 2.)

21.7 Case Study: Connecting to a Database in ASP.NET

Many Web sites allow users to provide feedback about the Web site in a *guestbook*. Typically, users click a link on the Web site's home page to request the guestbook page. This page usually consists of an XHTML form that contains fields for the user's name, e-mail address, message/feedback and so on. Data submitted on the guestbook form is then stored in a database located on the Web server's machine.

In this section, we create a guestbook Web Form application. This example's GUI is slightly more complex than that of earlier examples. It contains a *GridView* ASP.NET data control, as shown in Fig. 21.33, which displays all the entries in the guestbook in tabular format. We explain how to create and configure this data control shortly. Note that the GridView displays **abc** in **Design** mode to indicate string data that will be retrieved from a data source at runtime.

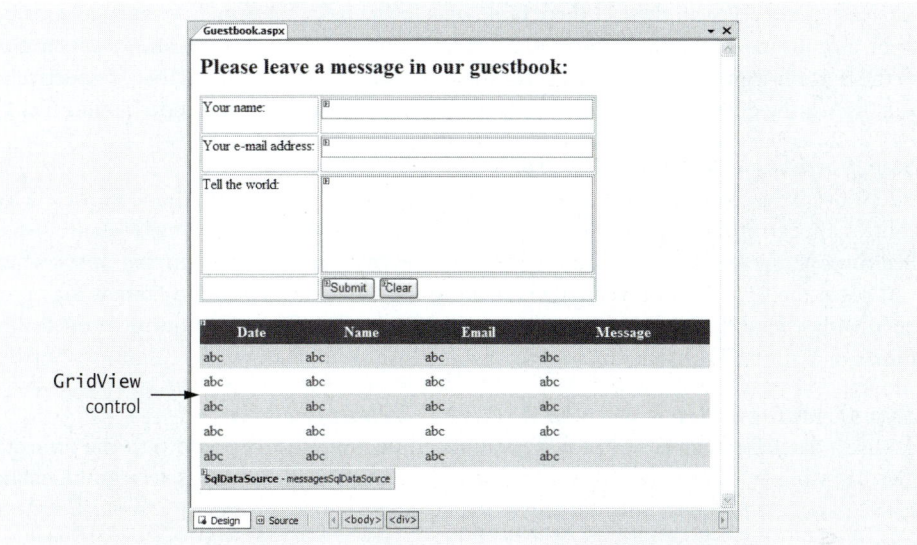

Fig. 21.33 | Guestbook application GUI in **Design** mode.

The XHTML form presented to the user consists of a name field, an e-mail address field and a message field. The form also contains a **Submit** button to send the data to the server and a **Clear** button to reset each of the fields on the form. The application stores the guestbook information in a SQL Server database called Guestbook.mdf located on the Web server. (We provide this database in the examples directory for this chapter. You can download the examples from www.deitel.com/books/csharpforprogrammers2.) Below the XHTML form, the GridView displays the data (i.e., guestbook entries) in the database's Messages table.

21.7.1 Building a Web Form That Displays Data from a Database

We now explain how to build this GUI and set up the data binding between the GridView control and the database. Many of these steps are similar to those performed in Chapter 20 to access and interact with a database in a Windows application. We present the ASPX file generated from the GUI later in the section, and we discuss the related code-behind file in the next section. To build the guestbook application, perform the following steps:

Step 1: Creating the Project
Create an **ASP.NET Web Site** named Guestbook and rename the ASPX file Guestbook.aspx. Rename the class in the code-behind file Guestbook, and update the Page directive in the ASPX file accordingly.

Step 2: Creating the Form for User Input
In **Design** mode for the ASPX file, add the text Please leave a message in our guestbook: formatted as a navy blue h2 header. As discussed in Section 21.5.1, insert an XHTML table with two columns and four rows, configured so that the text in each cell aligns with the top of the cell. Place the appropriate text (see Fig. 21.33) in the top three cells in the table's left column. Then place TextBoxes named nameTextBox, emailTextBox

and messageTextBox in the top three table cells in the right column. Set messageTextBox to be a multiline TextBox. Finally, add Buttons named submitButton and clearButton to the bottom-right table cell. Set the buttons' captions to Submit and Clear, respectively. We discuss the event handlers for these buttons when we present the code-behind file.

Step 3: Adding a GridView Control to the Web Form

Add a GridView named messagesGridView that will display the guestbook entries. This control appears in the **Data** section of the **Toolbox**. The colors for the GridView are specified through the **Auto Format...** link in the **GridView Tasks** smart tag menu that opens when you place the GridView on the page. Clicking this link causes an **Auto Format** dialog to open with several choices. In this example, we chose **Simple**. We show how to set the GridView's data source (i.e., where it gets the data to display in its rows and columns) shortly.

Step 4: Adding a Database to an ASP.NET Web Application

To use a database in an ASP.NET Web application, you must first add it to the project's App_Data folder. Right click this folder in the **Solution Explorer** and select **Add Existing Item....** Locate the Guestbook.mdf file in the chapter's examples directory, then click **Add**.

Step 5: Binding the GridView to the Messages Table of the Guestbook Database

Now that the database is part of the project, we can configure the GridView to display its data. Open the **GridView Tasks** smart tag menu, then select **<New data source...>** from the **Choose Data Source** drop-down list. In the **Data Source Configuration Wizard** that appears, select **Database**. In this example, we use a *SqlDataSource* control that allows the application to interact with the Guestbook database. Set the ID of the data source to messagesSql-DataSource and click **OK** to begin the **Configure Data Source** wizard. In the **Choose Your Data Connection** screen, select Guestbook.mdf from the drop-down list (Fig. 21.34), then click **Next >** twice to continue to the **Configure the Select Statement** screen.

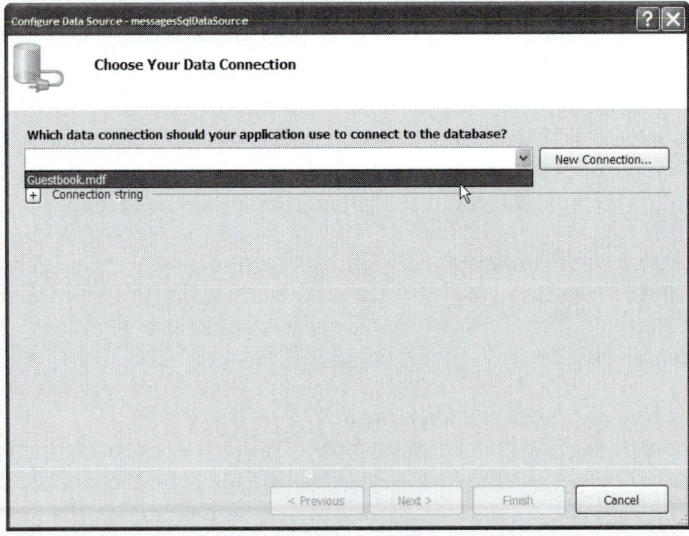

Fig. 21.34 | **Change Data Source** dialog in Visual Web Developer.

The **Configure the Select Statement** screen (Fig. 21.35) allows you to specify which data the `SqlDataSource` should retrieve from the database. Your choices on this page design a SELECT statement, shown in the bottom pane of the dialog. The **Name** drop-down list identifies a table in the database. The `Guestbook` database contains only one table named `Messages`, which is selected by default. In the **Columns** pane, click the checkbox marked with an asterisk (*) to indicate that you want to retrieve the data from all the columns in the **Message** table. Click the **Advanced** button, then check the box next to **Generate UPDATE, INSERT and DELETE statements**. This configures the `SqlDataSource` control to allow us to insert new data into the database. We discuss inserting new guestbook entries based on users' form submissions shortly. Click **OK**, then click **Next >** to continue the **Configure Data Source** wizard.

The next screen of the wizard allows you to test the query that you just designed. Click **Test Query** to preview the data that will be retrieved by the `SqlDataSource` (shown in Fig. 21.36).

Finally, click **Finish** to complete the wizard. Notice that a control named `messagesSqlDataSource` now appears on the Web Form directly below the `GridView` (Fig. 21.37). This control is represented in **Design** mode as a gray box containing its type and name. This control will *not* appear on the Web page—the gray box simply provides a way to manipulate the control visually through **Design** mode. Also notice that the `GridView` now has column headers that correspond to the columns in the `Messages` table and that the rows each contain either a number (which signifies an autoincremented column) or **abc** (which indicates string data). The actual data from the `Guestbook` database file will appear in these rows when the ASPX file is executed and viewed in a Web browser.

Step 6: Modifying the Columns of the Data Source Displayed in the `GridView`

It is not necessary for site visitors to see the `MessageID` column when viewing past guestbook entries—this column is merely a unique primary key required by the `Messages` table within the database. Thus, we modify the `GridView` so that this column does not display

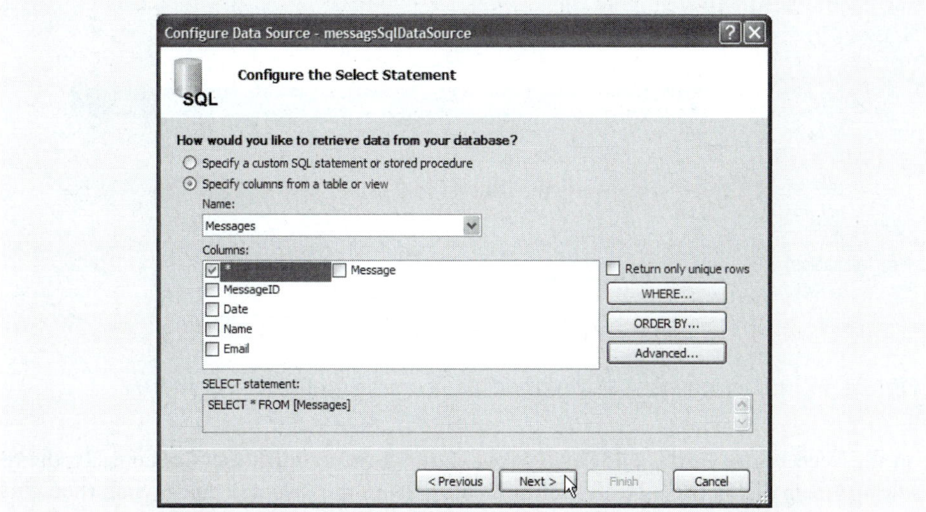

Fig. 21.35 | Configuring the SELECT statement used by the `SqlDataSource` to retrieve data.

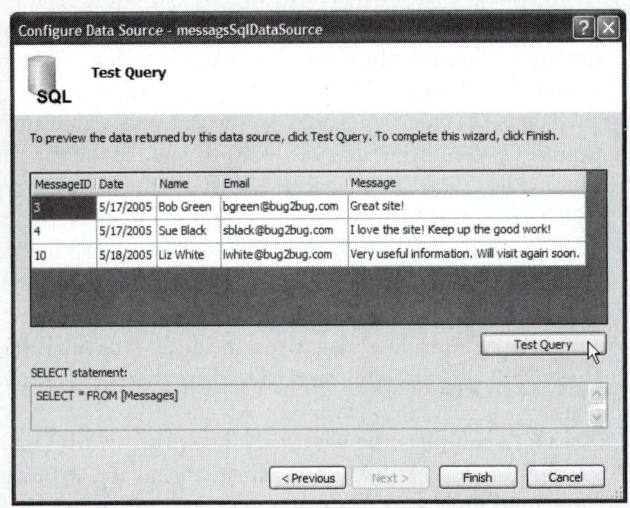

Fig. 21.36 | Previewing the data retrieved by the `SqlDataSource`.

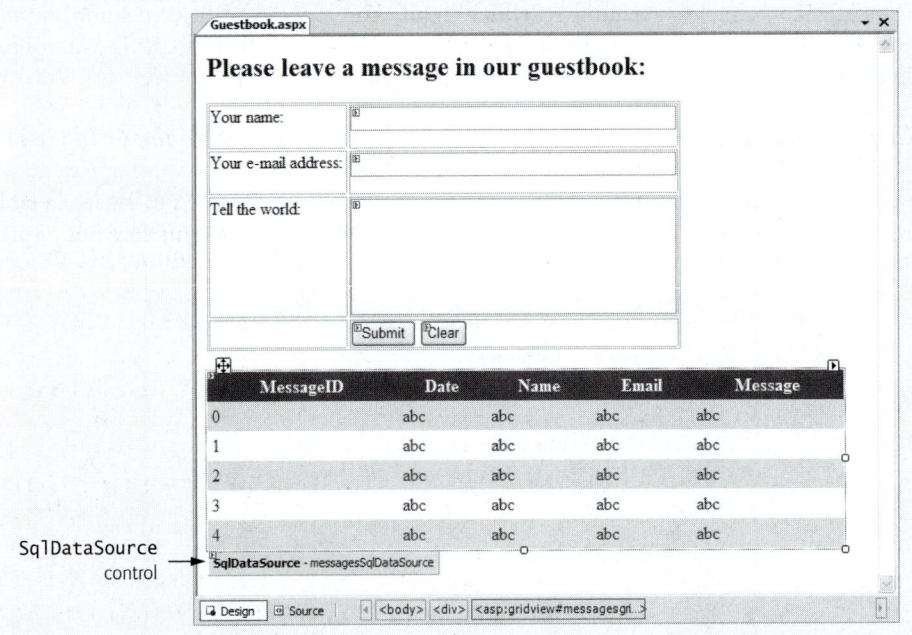

Fig. 21.37 | **Design** mode displaying `SqlDataSource` control for a `GridView`.

on the Web Form. In the **GridView Tasks** smart tag menu, click **Edit Columns.** In the resulting **Fields** dialog (Fig. 21.38), select **MessageID** in the **Selected fields** pane, then click the **X**. This removes the `MessageID` column from the `GridView`. Click **OK** to return to the main IDE window. The `GridView` should now appear as in Fig. 21.33.

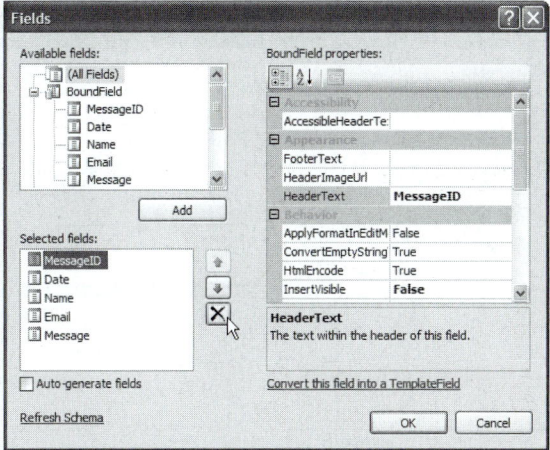

Fig. 21.38 | Removing the `MessageID` column from the `GridView`.

Step 7: Modifying the Way the *SqlDataSource* Control Inserts Data

When you create a `SqlDataSource` in the manner described here, it is configured to permit INSERT SQL operations against the database table from which it gathers data. You must specify the values to insert either programmatically or through other controls on the Web Form. In this example, we wish to insert the data entered by the user in the `nameTextBox`, `emailTextBox` and `messageTextBox` controls. We also want to insert the current date—we will specify the date to insert programmatically in the code-behind file, which we present shortly.

To configure the `SqlDataSource` to allow such an insertion, click the ellipsis button next to the ***InsertQuery*** property of the `messagesSqlDataSource` control in the **Properties** window. The **Command and Parameter Editor** (Fig. 21.39) that appears displays the INSERT command used by the `SqlDataSource` control. This command contains parameters `@Date`, `@Name`, `@Email` and `@Message`. You must provide values for these parameters before they are inserted into the database. Each parameter is listed in the **Parameters** section of the **Command and Parameter Editor**. Because we will set the **Date** parameter programmatically, we do not modify it here. For each of the remaining three parameters, select the parameter, then select **Control** from the **Parameter source** drop-down list. This indicates that the value of the parameter should be taken from a control. The **ControlID** drop-down list contains all the controls on the Web Form. Select the appropriate control for each parameter, then click **OK**. Now the `SqlDataSource` is configured to insert the user's name, e-mail address and message in the `Messages` table of the `Guestbook` database. We show how to set the date parameter and initiate the insert operation when the user clicks **Submit** shortly.

ASPX File for a Web Form That Interacts with a Database

The ASPX file generated by the guestbook GUI (and `messagesSqlDataSource` control) is shown in Fig. 21.40. This file contains a large amount of generated markup. We discuss only those parts that are new or noteworthy for the current example. Lines 20–58 contain the XHTML and ASP.NET elements that comprise the form that gathers user input. The

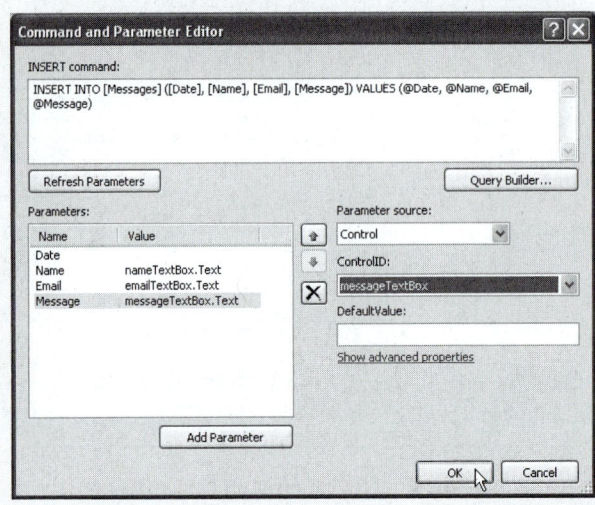

Fig. 21.39 | Setting up INSERT parameters based on control values.

GridView control appears in lines 61–87. The `<asp:GridView>` start tag (lines 61–65) contains properties that set various aspects of the GridView's appearance and behavior, such as whether grid lines should be displayed between rows and columns. The **DataSourceID** property identifies the data source that is used to fill the GridView with data at runtime. Lines 66–76 contain nested elements that define the styles used to format the GridView's rows. The IDE configured these styles based on your selection of the **Simple** style in the **Auto Format** dialog for the GridView.

```
 1   <%-- Fig. 21.40: Guestbook.aspx --%>
 2   <%-- Guestbook Web application with a form for users to submit --%>
 3   <%-- guestbook entries and a GridView to view existing entries. --%>
 4   <%@ Page Language="C#" AutoEventWireup="true"
 5      CodeFile="Guestbook.aspx.cs" Inherits="Guestbook" %>
 6
 7   <!DOCTYPE html PUBLIC "-//W3C//DTD XHTML 1.1//EN"
 8      "http://www.w3.org/TR/xhtml11/DTD/xhtml11.dtd">
 9
10   <html xmlns="http://www.w3.org/1999/xhtml" >
11      <head runat="server">
12         <title>Guestbook</title>
13      </head>
14      <body>
15         <form id="form1" runat="server">
16            <div>
17               <h2><span style="color: navy">
18                  Please leave a message in our guestbook:</span></h2>
19
```

Fig. 21.40 | ASPX file for the guestbook application. (Part 1 of 4.)

```
20              <table>
21                <tr>
22                  <td style="width: 130px; height: 21px" valign="top">
23                    Your name: <br />
24                  </td>
25                  <td style="width: 300px; height: 21px" valign="top">
26                    <asp:TextBox ID="nameTextBox" runat="server"
27                      Width="300px"></asp:TextBox>
28                  </td>
29                </tr>
30                <tr>
31                  <td style="width: 130px" valign="top">
32                    Your e-mail address: <br />
33                  </td>
34                  <td style="width: 300px" valign="top">
35                    <asp:TextBox ID="emailTextBox" runat="server"
36                      Width="300px"></asp:TextBox></td>
37                </tr>
38                <tr>
39                  <td style="width: 130px" valign="top">
40                    Tell the world: <br />
41                  </td>
42                  <td style="width: 300px" valign="top">
43                    <asp:TextBox ID="messageTextBox" runat="server"
44                      Height="100px" Rows="8" Width="300px">
45                    </asp:TextBox>
46                  </td>
47                </tr>
48                <tr>
49                  <td style="width: 130px" valign="top">
50                  </td>
51                  <td style="width: 300px" valign="top">
52                    <asp:Button ID="submitButton" runat="server"
53                      Text="Submit" />
54                    <asp:Button ID="clearButton" runat="server"
55                      Text="Clear" />
56                  </td>
57                </tr>
58              </table>
59              <br />
60
61              <asp:GridView ID="messagesGridView" runat="server"
62                AutoGenerateColumns="False" CellPadding="4"
63                ForeColor="#333333" GridLines="None"
64                DataSourceID="messagesSqlDataSource" Width="600px"
65                DataKeyNames="MessageID">
66                <FooterStyle BackColor="#1C5E55" Font-Bold="True"
67                  ForeColor="White" />
68                <RowStyle BackColor="#E3EAEB" />
69                <PagerStyle BackColor="#666666" ForeColor="White"
70                  HorizontalAlign="Center" />
71                <SelectedRowStyle BackColor="#C5BBAF" Font-Bold="True"
72                  ForeColor="#333333" />
```

Fig. 21.40 | ASPX file for the guestbook application. (Part 2 of 4.)

```
73              <HeaderStyle BackColor="#1C5E55" Font-Bold="True"
74                  ForeColor="White" />
75              <EditRowStyle BackColor="#7C6F57" />
76              <AlternatingRowStyle BackColor="White" />
77              <Columns>
78                  <asp:BoundField DataField="Date" HeaderText="Date"
79                      SortExpression="Date" />
80                  <asp:BoundField DataField="Name" HeaderText="Name"
81                      SortExpression="Name" />
82                  <asp:BoundField DataField="Email" HeaderText="Email"
83                      SortExpression="Email" />
84                  <asp:BoundField DataField="Message" HeaderText="Message"
85                      SortExpression="Message" />
86              </Columns>
87          </asp:GridView>
88
89          <asp:SqlDataSource ID="messagesSqlDataSource" runat="server"
90              ConnectionString=
91                  "<%$ ConnectionStrings:GuestbookConnectionString %>"
92              SelectCommand="SELECT * FROM [Messages]"
93              DeleteCommand="DELETE FROM [Messages] WHERE
94                  [MessageID] = @original_MessageID"
95              InsertCommand="INSERT INTO [Messages]
96                  ([Date], [Name], [Email], [Message]) VALUES
97                  (@Date, @Name, @Email, @Message)"
98              UpdateCommand="UPDATE [Messages] SET [Date] = @Date,
99                  [Name] = @Name, [Email] = @Email, [Message] = @Message
100                 WHERE [MessageID] = @original_MessageID">
101             <DeleteParameters>
102                 <asp:Parameter Name="original_MessageID" Type="Int32" />
103             </DeleteParameters>
104             <UpdateParameters>
105                 <asp:Parameter Name="Date" Type="String" />
106                 <asp:Parameter Name="Name" Type="String" />
107                 <asp:Parameter Name="Email" Type="String" />
108                 <asp:Parameter Name="Message" Type="String" />
109                 <asp:Parameter Name="original_MessageID" Type="Int32" />
110             </UpdateParameters>
111             <InsertParameters>
112                 <asp:Parameter Name="Date" Type="String" />
113                 <asp:ControlParameter ControlID="nameTextBox"
114                     Name="Name" PropertyName="Text" Type="String" />
115                 <asp:ControlParameter ControlID="emailTextBox"
116                     Name="Email" PropertyName="Text" Type="String" />
117                 <asp:ControlParameter ControlID="messageTextBox"
118                     Name="Message" PropertyName="Text" Type="String" />
119             </InsertParameters>
120         </asp:SqlDataSource>
121     </div>
122     </form>
123     </body>
124 </html>
```

Fig. 21.40 | ASPX file for the guestbook application. (Part 3 of 4.)

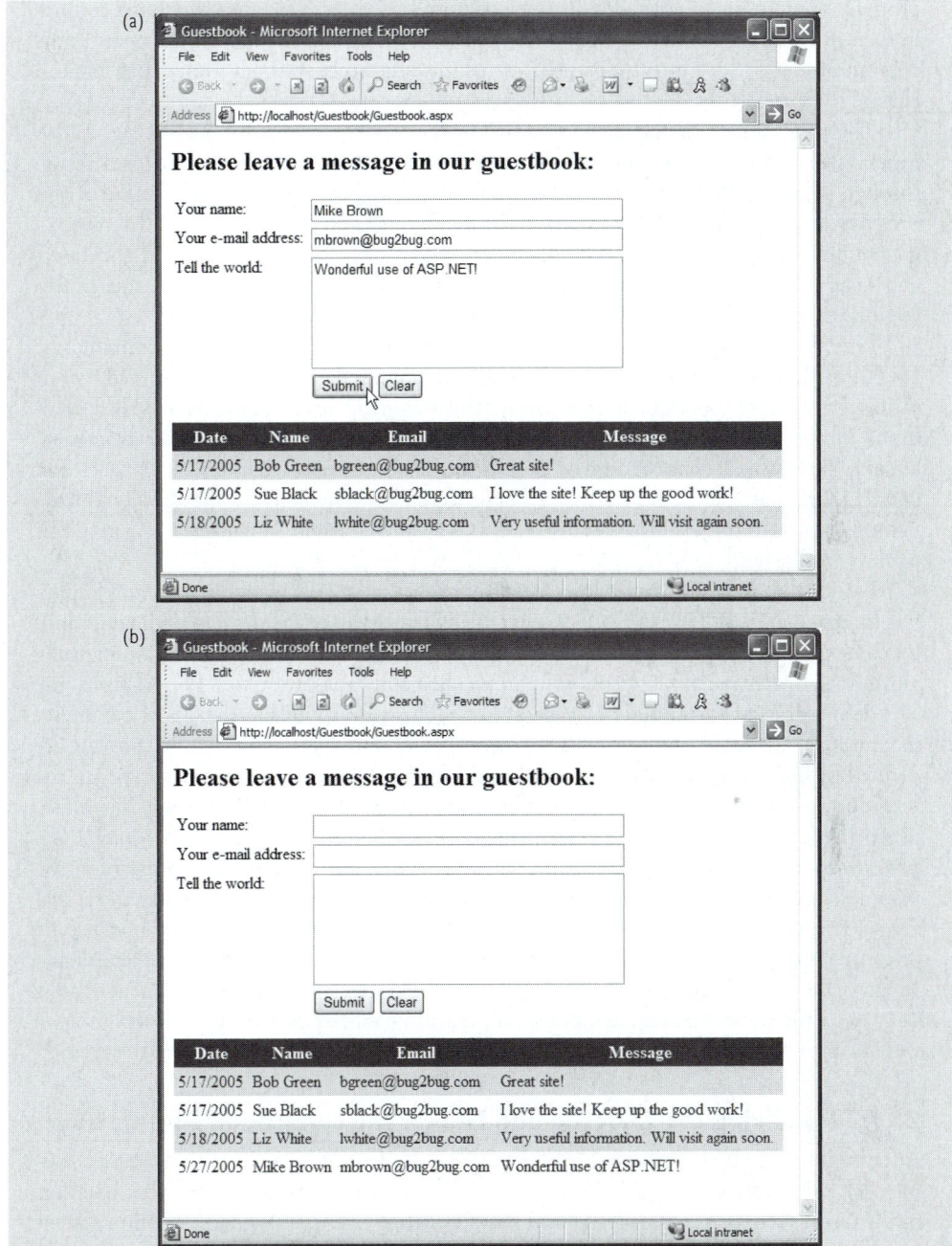

Fig. 21.40 | ASPX file for the guestbook application. (Part 4 of 4.)

Lines 77–86 define the Columns that appear in the GridView. Each column is represented as a ***BoundField***, because the values in the columns are bound to values retrieved from the data source (i.e., the Messages table of the Guestbook database). The DataField property of each BoundField identifies the column in the data source to which the column in the GridView is bound. The HeaderText property indicates the text that appears as the column header. By default, this is the name of the column in the data source, but you can change this property as desired.

The messagesSqlDataSource is defined by the markup in lines 89–120 in Fig. 21.40. Lines 90–91 contain a *ConnectionString* property, which indicates the connection through which the SqlDataSource control interacts with the database. The value of this property uses an *ASP.NET expression*, delimited by *<%$* and *%>*, to access the Guestbook-ConnectionString stored in the ConnectionStrings section of the application's Web.config configuration file. Recall that we created this connection string earlier in this section using the **Configure Data Source** wizard.

Line 92 defines the SqlDataSource's *SelectCommand* property, which contains the SELECT SQL statement used to retrieve the data from the database. As determined by our actions in the **Configure Data Source** wizard, this statement retrieves the data in all the columns in all the rows of the Messages table. Lines 93–100 define the *DeleteCommand*, *InsertCommand* and *UpdateCommand* properties, which contain the DELETE, INSERT and UPDATE SQL statements, respectively. These were also generated by the **Configure Data Source** wizard. In this example, we use only the InsertCommand. We discuss invoking this command shortly.

Notice that the SQL commands used by the SqlDataSource contain several parameters (prefixed with @). Lines 101–119 contain elements that define the name, the type and, for some parameters, the source of the parameter. Parameters that are set programmatically are defined by *Parameter* elements containing Name and Type properties. For example, line 112 defines the Date parameter of Type String. This corresponds to the @Date parameter in the InsertCommand (line 97). Parameters that obtain their values from controls are defined by *ControlParameter* elements. Lines 113–118 contain markup that sets up the relationships between the INSERT parameters and the Web Form's TextBoxes. We established these relationships in the **Command and Parameter Editor** (Fig. 21.39). Each ControlParameter contains a ControlID property indicating the control from which the parameter gets its value. The PropertyName specifies the property that contains the actual value to be used as the parameter value. The IDE sets the PropertyName based on the type of control specified by the ControlID (indirectly via the **Command and Parameter Editor**). In this case, we use only TextBoxes, so the PropertyName of each ControlParameter is Text (e.g., the value of parameter @Name comes from nameTextBox.Text). However, if we were using a DropDownList, for example, the PropertyName would be SelectedValue.

21.7.2 Modifying the Code-Behind File for the Guestbook Application

After building the Web Form and configuring the data controls used in this example, double click the **Submit** and **Clear** buttons to create their corresponding Click event handlers in the Guestbook.aspx.cs code-behind file (Fig. 21.41). The IDE generates empty event handlers, so we must add the appropriate code to make these buttons work properly. The event handler for clearButton (lines 43–48) clears each TextBox by setting its Text property to an empty string. This resets the form for a new guestbook submission.

Lines 17–40 contain the event-handling code for submitButton, which adds the user's information to the Messages table of the Guestbook database. Recall that we configured messagtesSqlDataSource's INSERT command to use the values of the TextBoxes on the Web Form as the parameter values inserted into the database. We have not yet specified the date value to be inserted, though. Lines 20–22 assign a `string` representation of

```csharp
 1  // Fig. 21.41: Guestbook.aspx.cs
 2  // Code-behind file that defines event handlers for the guestbook.
 3  using System;
 4  using System.Data;
 5  using System.Configuration;
 6  using System.Web;
 7  using System.Web.Security;
 8  using System.Web.UI;
 9  using System.Web.UI.WebControls;
10  using System.Web.UI.WebControls.WebParts;
11  using System.Web.UI.HtmlControls;
12
13  public partial class Guestbook : System.Web.UI.Page
14  {
15     // Submit Button adds a new guestbook entry to the database,
16     // clears the form and displays the updated list of guestbook entries
17     protected void submitButton_Click( object sender, EventArgs e )
18     {
19        // create a date parameter to store the current date
20        System.Web.UI.WebControls.Parameter date =
21           new System.Web.UI.WebControls.Parameter(
22           "Date", TypeCode.String, DateTime.Now.ToShortDateString() );
23
24        // set the @Date parameter to the date parameter
25        messagesSqlDataSource.InsertParameters.RemoveAt( 0 );
26        messagesSqlDataSource.InsertParameters.Add( date );
27
28        // execute an INSERT SQL statement to add a new row to the
29        // Messages table in the Guestbook database that contains the
30        // current date and the user's name, e-mail address and message
31        messagesSqlDataSource.Insert();
32
33        // clear the TextBoxes
34        nameTextBox.Text = "";
35        emailTextBox.Text = "";
36        messageTextBox.Text = "";
37
38        // update the GridView with the new database table contents
39        messagesGridView.DataBind();
40     } // end method submitButton_Click
41
42     // Clear Button clears the Web Form's TextBoxes
43     protected void clearButton_Click( object sender, EventArgs e )
44     {
45        nameTextBox.Text = "";
46        emailTextBox.Text = "";
47        messageTextBox.Text = "";
48     } // end method clearButton_Click
49  } // end class Guestbook
```

Fig. 21.41 | Code-behind file for the guestbook application.

the current date (e.g., "5/27/05") to a new object of type `Parameter`. This `Parameter` object is identified as "Date" and is given the current date as a default value. The `SqlData-Source`'s `InsertParameters` collection contains an item named `Date`, which we `Remove` in line 25 and replace in line 26 by `Add`ing our `date` parameter. Invoking `SqlDataSource` method `Insert` in line 31 executes the `INSERT` command against the database, thus adding a row to the `Messages` table. After the data is inserted into the database, lines 34–36 clear the `TextBox`es, and line 39 invokes `messagesGridView`'s `DataBind` method to refresh the data that the `GridView` displays. This causes `messagesSqlDataSource` (the data source of the `GridView`) to execute its `SELECT` command to obtain the `Messages` table's newly updated data.

21.8 Case Study: Secure Books Database Application

This case study presents a Web application in which a user logs into a secure Web site to view a list of publications by an author of the user's choosing. The application consists of several ASPX files. Section 21.8.1 presents the working application and explains the purpose of each of its Web pages. Section 21.8.2 provides step-by-step instructions to guide you through building the application and presents the markup in the ASPX files as they are created.

21.8.1 Examining the Completed Secure Books Database Application

This example uses a technique known as *forms authentication* to protect a page so that only users known to the Web site can access it. Such users are known as the site's members. Authentication is a crucial tool for sites that allow only members to enter the site or a portion of the site. In this application, Web site visitors must log in before they are allowed to view the publications in the `Books` database. The first page that a user would typically request is `Login.aspx` (Fig. 21.42). You will soon learn to create this page using a `Login` control, one of several *ASP.NET login controls* that help create secure applications using authentication. These controls are found in the **Login** section of the **Toolbox**.

Fig. 21.42 | `Login.aspx` page of the secure books database application.

The Login.aspx page allows a site visitor to enter an existing user name and password to log into the Web site. A first-time visitor must click the link below the **Log In** button to create a new user before attempting to log in. Doing so redirects the visitor to CreateNewUser.aspx (Fig. 21.43), which contains a CreateUserWizard control that presents the visitor with a user registration form. We discuss the CreateUserWizard control in detail in Section 21.8.2. In Fig. 21.43, we use the password pa$$word for testing purposes—as you will learn, the CreateUserWizard requires that the password contain special characters for security purposes. Clicking **Create User** establishes a new user account. Once the new user account is created, the user is automatically logged in and shown a success message (Fig. 21.44).

Fig. 21.43 | CreateNewUser.aspx page of the secure book database application.

Fig. 21.44 | Message displayed to indicate that a user account was created successfully.

Clicking the **Continue** button on the confirmation page sends the user to Books.aspx (Fig. 21.45), which provides a drop-down list of authors and a table containing the ISBNs, titles, edition numbers and copyright years of books in the database. By default, all the books by Harvey Deitel are displayed. Links appear at the bottom of the table that allow you to access additional pages of data. When the user chooses an author, a postback occurs, and the page is updated to display information about books written by the selected author (Fig. 21.46).

Note that once the user creates an account and is logged in, Books.aspx displays a welcome message customized for the particular logged-in user. As you will soon see, a LoginName control provides this functionality. After you add this control to the page, ASP.NET handles the details of determining the user name.

Clicking the **Click here to log out** link logs the user out, then sends the user back to Login.aspx (Fig. 21.47). As you will learn, this link is created by a LoginStatus control, which handles the details of logging the user out of the page. To view the book listing again, the user must log in through Login.aspx. The Login control on this page receives the user name and password entered by a visitor. ASP.NET then compares these values with user names and passwords stored in a database on the server. If there is a match, the visitor is *authenticated* (i.e., the user's identity is confirmed). We explain the authentication process in detail in Section 21.8.2. When an existing user is successfully authenticated, Login.aspx redirects the user to Books.aspx (Fig. 21.45). If the user's login attempt fails, an appropriate error message is displayed (Fig. 21.48).

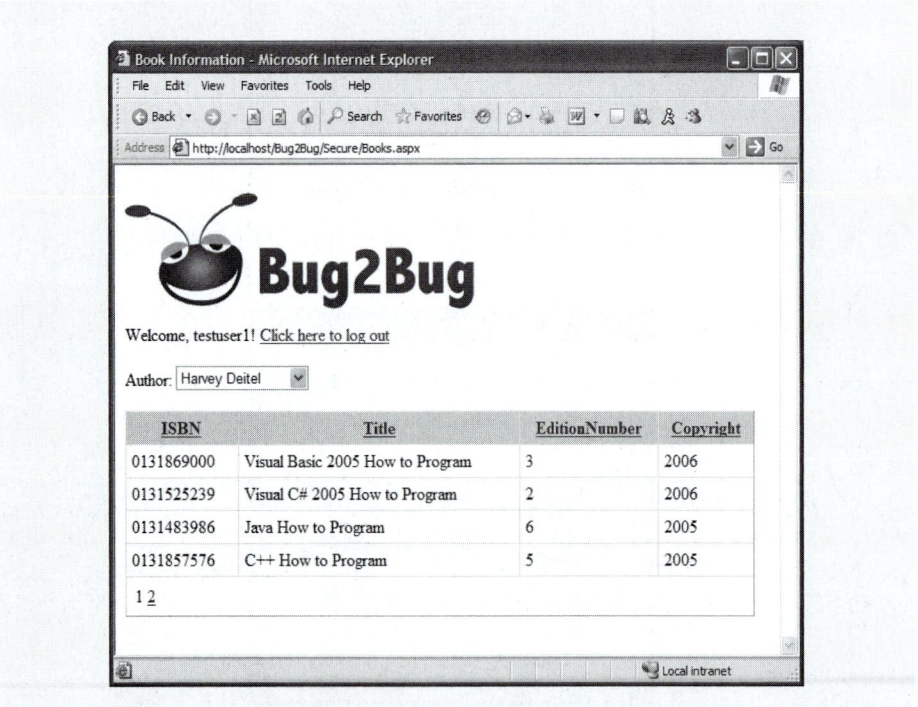

Fig. 21.45 | Books.aspx displaying books by Harvey Deitel (by default).

Fig. 21.46 | `Books.aspx` displaying books by Andrew Goldberg.

Fig. 21.47 | Logging in using the `Login` control.

Notice that `Login.aspx`, `CreateNewUser.aspx` and `Books.aspx` share the same page header containing the Bug2Bug logo image. Instead of placing this image at the top of each page, we use a *master page* to achieve this. As we demonstrate shortly, a master page defines common GUI elements that are inherited by each page in a set of *content pages*. Just as C# classes can inherit instance variables and methods from existing classes, content pages inherit elements from master pages—this is known as *visual inheritance*.

21.8.2 Creating the Secure Books Database Application

Now that you are familiar with how this application behaves, we demonstrate how to create it from scratch. Thanks to the rich set of login and data controls provided by

Fig. 21.48 | Error message displayed for an unsuccessful login attempt using the Login control.

ASP.NET, you will not have to write *any* code to create this application. In fact, the application does not contain any code-behind files. All of the functionality is specified through properties of controls, many of which are set through wizards and other visual programming tools. ASP.NET hides the details of authenticating users against a database of user names and passwords, displaying appropriate success or error messages and redirecting the user to the correct page based on the authentication results. We now discuss the steps you must perform to create the secure books database application.

Step 1: Creating the Web Site

Create a new **ASP.NET Web Site** at http://localhost/Bug2Bug as described previously. We will explicitly create each of the ASPX files that we need in this application, so delete the IDE-generated Default.aspx file (and its corresponding code-behind file) by selecting Default.aspx in the **Solution Explorer** and pressing the *Delete* key. Click **OK** in the confirmation dialog to delete these files.

Step 2: Setting Up the Web Site's Folders

Before building any of the pages in the Web site, we create folders to organize its contents. First, create an Images folder and add the bug2bug.png file to it. This image can be found in the examples directory for this chapter. Next, add the Books.mdf database file (which can also be found in the examples directory) to the project's App_Data folder. We show how to retrieve data from this database later in the section.

Step 3: Configuring the Application's Security Settings

In this application, we want to ensure that only authenticated users are allowed to access Books.aspx (created in *Step 9* and *Step 10*) to view the information in the database. Previously, we created all of our ASPX pages in the Web application's root directory (e.g., http://localhost/*ProjectName*). By default, any Web site visitor (regardless of whether the visitor is authenticated) can view pages in the root directory. ASP.NET allows you to restrict access to particular folders of a Web site. We do not want to restrict access to the root of the Web site, however, because all users must be able to view `Login.aspx` and `CreateNewUser.aspx` to log in and create user accounts, respectively. Thus, if we want to restrict access to `Books.aspx`, it must reside in a directory other than the root directory. Create a folder named `Secure`. Later in the section, we will create `Books.aspx` in this folder. First, let's enable forms authentication in our application and configure the `Secure` folder to restrict access to authenticated users only.

Select **Website > ASP.NET Configuration** to open the ***Web Site Administration Tool*** in a Web browser (Fig. 21.49). This tool allows you to configure various options that determine how your application behaves. Click either the **Security** link or the **Security** tab to open a Web page in which you can set security options (Fig. 21.50), such as the type of authentication the application should use. In the **Users** column, click **Select authentication type**. On the resulting page (Fig. 21.51), select the radio button next to **From the internet** to indicate that users will log in via a form on the Web site in which the user can enter a username and password (i.e., the application will use forms authentication). The default setting—**From a local network**—relies on users' Windows user names and passwords for authentication purposes. Click the **Done** button to save this change.

Now that forms authentication is enabled, the **Users** column on the main page of the **Web Site Administration Tool** (Fig. 21.52) provides links to create and manage users. As you saw in Section 21.8.1, our application provides the `CreateNewUser.aspx` page in which users can create their own accounts. Thus, while it is possible to create users through the **Web Site Administration Tool**, we do not do so here.

Even though no users exist at the moment, we configure the `Secure` folder to grant access only to authenticated users (i.e., deny access to all unauthenticated users). Click the **Create access rules** link in the **Access Rules** column of the **Web Site Administration Tool**

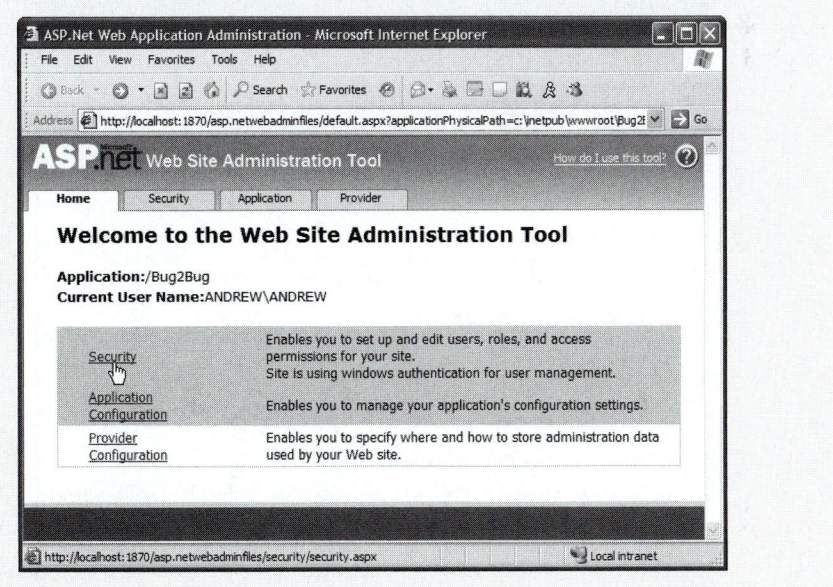

Fig. 21.49 | **Web Site Administration Tool** for configuring a Web application.

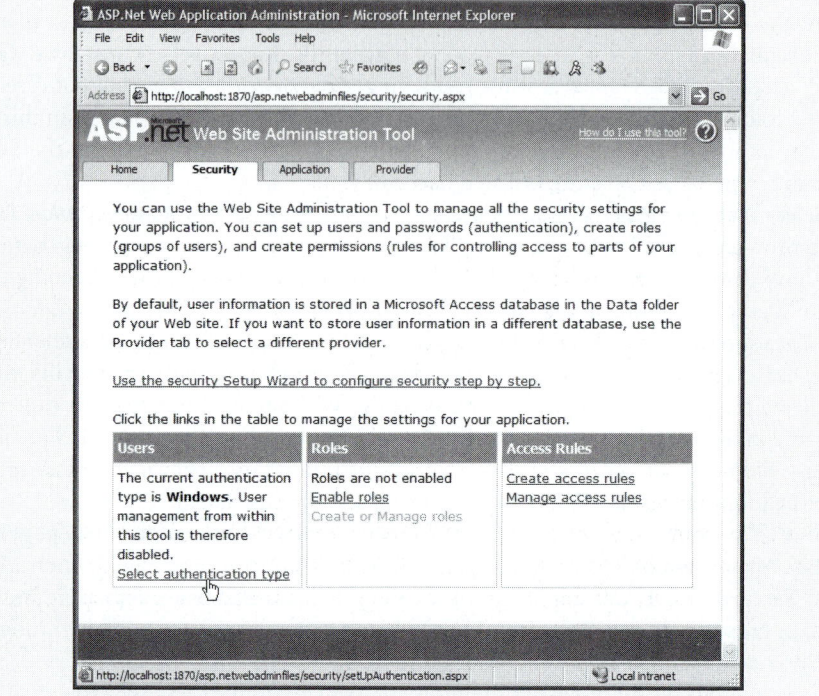

Fig. 21.50 │ Security page of the **Web Site Administration Tool**.

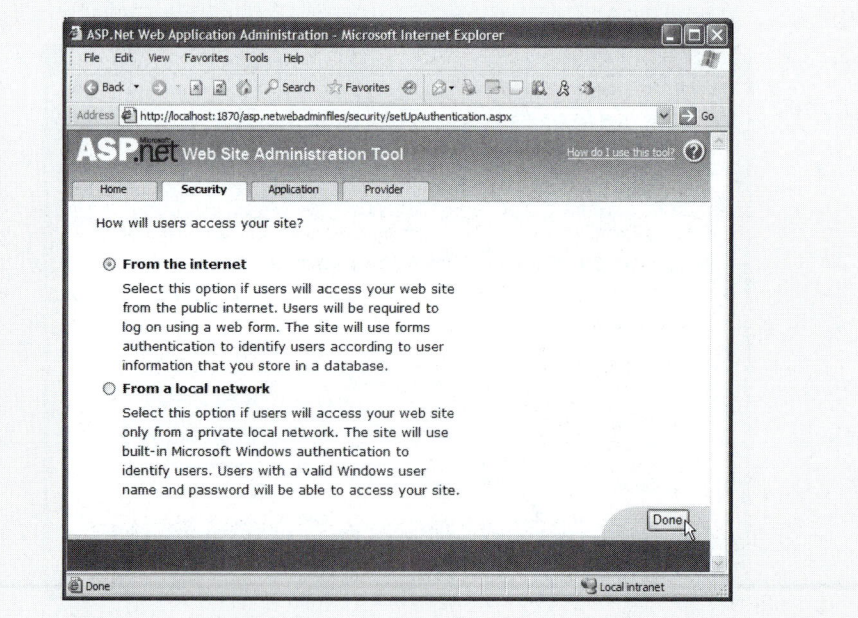

Fig. 21.51 │ Choosing the type of authentication used by an ASP.NET Web application.

(Fig. 21.52) to view the **Add New Access Rule** page (Fig. 21.53). This page is used to create an *access rule*—a rule that grants or denies access to a particular Web application directory for a specific user or group of users. Click the Secure directory in the left column of the page to identify the directory to which our access rule applies. In the middle column, select the radio button marked **Anonymous users** to specify that the rule applies to users who have not been authenticated. Finally, select **Deny** in the right column, labeled **Permission**, then click **OK**. This rule indicates that *anonymous users* (i.e., users who have not identified themselves by logging in) should be denied access to any pages in the Secure directory (e.g., Books.aspx). By default, anonymous users who attempt to load a page in the Secure directory are redirected to the Login.aspx page so that they can identify themselves. Note that because we did not set up any access rules for the Bug2Bug root directory, anonymous users may still access pages there (e.g., Login.aspx, CreateNewUser.aspx). We create these pages momentarily.

Step 4: Examining the Auto-Generated Web.config Files
We have now configured the application to use forms authentication and created an access rule to ensure that only authenticated users can access the Secure folder. Before creating the Web site's content, we examine how the changes made through the **Web Site Administration Tool** appear in the IDE. Recall that Web.config is an XML file used for application configuration, such as enabling debugging or storing database connection strings. Visual Web Developer generates two Web.config files in response to our actions using the

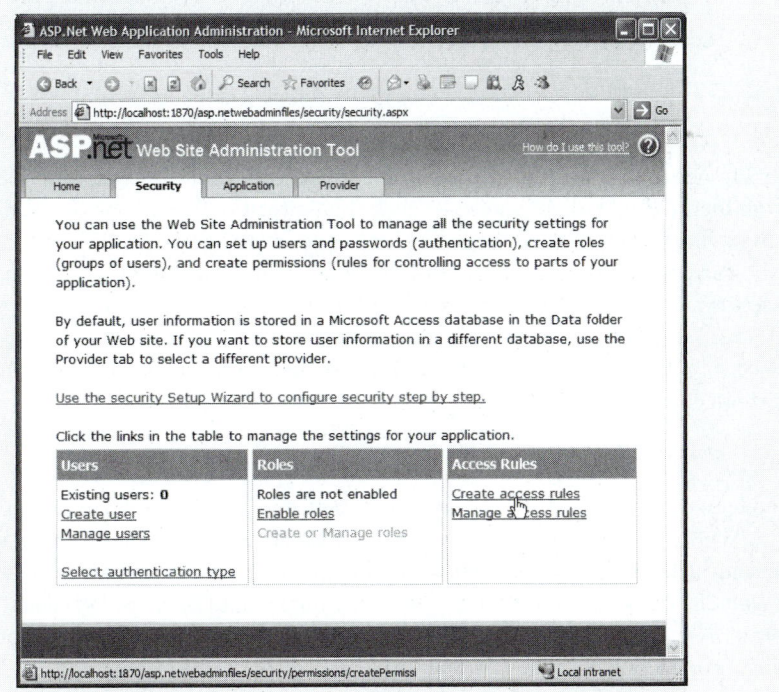

Fig. 21.52 | Main page of the **Web Site Administration Tool** after enabling forms authentication.

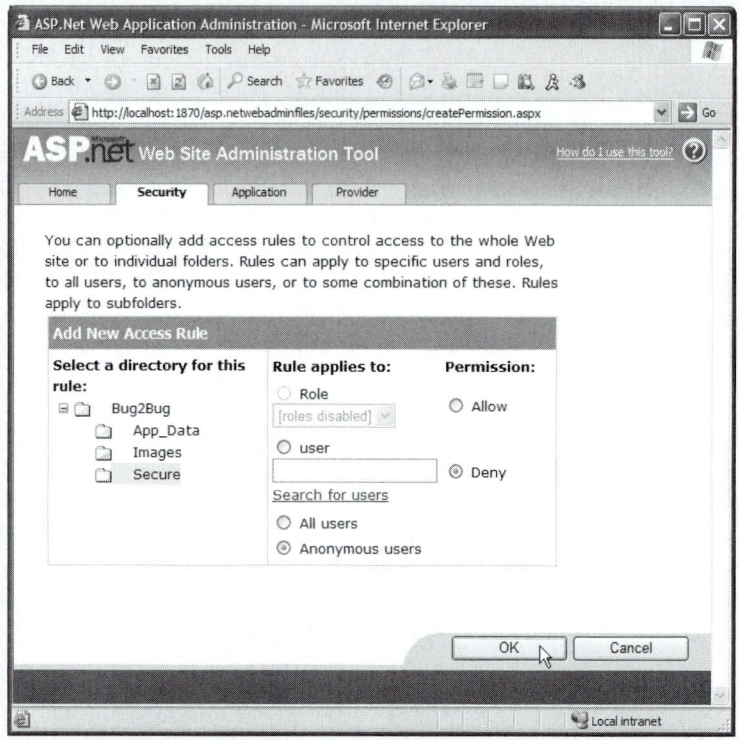

Fig. 21.53 | **Add New Access Rule** page used to configure directory access.

Web Site Administration Tool—one in the application's root directory and one in the Secure folder. [*Note:* You may need to click the **Refresh** button in the **Solution Explorer** to see these files.] In an ASP.NET application, a page's configuration settings are determined by the current directory's Web.config file. The settings in this file take precedence over the settings in the root directory's Web.config file.

After setting the authentication type for the Web application, the IDE generates a Web.config file at http://localhost/Bug2Bug/Web.config, which contains an ***authentication*** element

```
<authentication mode="Forms" />
```

This element appears in the root directory's Web.config file, so the setting applies to the entire Web site. The value "Forms" of the ***mode*** attribute specifies that we want to use forms authentication. Had we left the authentication type set to **From a local network** in the **Web Site Administration Tool**, the mode attribute would be set to "Windows". Note that "Forms" is the default mode in a Web.config file generated for another purpose, such as saving a connection string.

After creating the access rule for the Secure folder, the IDE generates a second Web.config file in that folder. This file contains an ***authorization*** element that indicates who is; and who is not, authorized to access this folder over the Web. In this application, we want to allow only authenticated users to access the contents of the Secure folder, so the authorization element appears as

```
<authorization>
    <deny users="?" />
</authorization>
```

Rather than grant permission to each individual authenticated user, we deny access to those who are not authenticated (i.e., those who have not logged in). The **deny** element inside the authorization element specifies the users to whom we wish to deny access. When the users attribute's value is set to "?", all anonymous (i.e., unauthenticated) users are denied access to the folder. Thus, an unauthenticated user will not be able to load http://localhost/ Bug2Bug/Secure/Books.aspx. Instead, such a user will be redirected to the Login.aspx page—when a user is denied access to a part of a site, ASP.NET by default sends the user to a page named Login.aspx in the application's root directory.

Step 5: Creating a Master Page

Now that you have established the application's security settings, you can create the application's Web pages. We begin with the master page, which defines the elements we want to appear on each page. A master page is like a base class in a visual inheritance hierarchy, and content pages are like derived classes. The master page contains placeholders for custom content created in each content page. The content pages visually inherit the master page's content, then add content in place of the master page's placeholders.

For example, you might want to include a *navigation bar* (i.e., a series of buttons for navigating a Web site) on every page of a site. If the site encompasses a large number of pages, adding markup to create the navigation bar for each page can be time consuming. Moreover, if you subsequently modify the navigation bar, every page on the site that uses it must be updated. By creating a master page, you can specify the navigation bar markup in one file and have it appear on all the content pages, with only a few lines of markup. If the navigation bar changes, only the master page changes—any content pages that use it are updated the next time the page is requested.

In this example, we want the Bug2Bug logo to appear as a header at the top of every page, so we will place an Image control in the master page. Each subsequent page we create will be a content page based on this master page and thus will include the header. To create a master page, right click the location of the Web site in the **Solution Explorer** and select **Add New Item....** In the **Add New Item** dialog, select **Master Page** from the template list and specify Bug2Bug.master as the filename. Master pages have the filename extension **.master** and, like Web Forms, can optionally use a code-behind file to define additional functionality. In this example, we do not need to specify any code for the master page, so leave the box labeled **Place code in a separate file** unchecked. Click **Add** to create the page.

The IDE opens the master page in **Source** mode (Fig. 21.54) when the file is first created. [*Note:* We added a line break in the DOCTYPE element for presentation purposes.] The markup for a master page is almost identical to that of a Web Form. One difference is that a master page contains a *Master* directive (line 1 in Fig. 21.54), which specifies that this file defines a master page using the indicated Language for any code. Because we chose not to use a code-behind file, the master page also contains a *script* element (lines 6–8). Code that would usually be placed in a code-behind file can be placed in a script element.

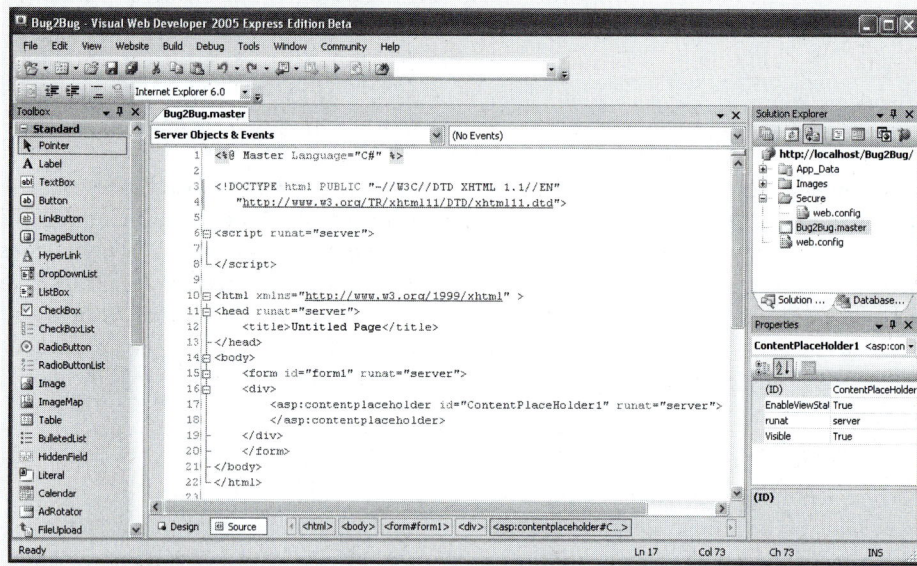

Fig. 21.54 | Master page in **Source** mode.

However, we remove the script element from this page, because we do not need to write any additional code. After deleting this block of markup, set the title of the page to Bug2Bug. Finally, notice that the master page contains a ***ContentPlaceHolder*** control in lines 17–18. This control serves as a placeholder for content that will be defined by a content page. You will see how to define content to replace the ContentPlaceHolder shortly.

At this point, you can edit the master page in **Design** mode (Fig. 21.55) as if it were an ASPX file. Notice that the ContentPlaceHolder control appears as a large rectangle with a gray bar indicating the control's type and ID. Using the **Properties** window, change the ID of this control to bodyContent.

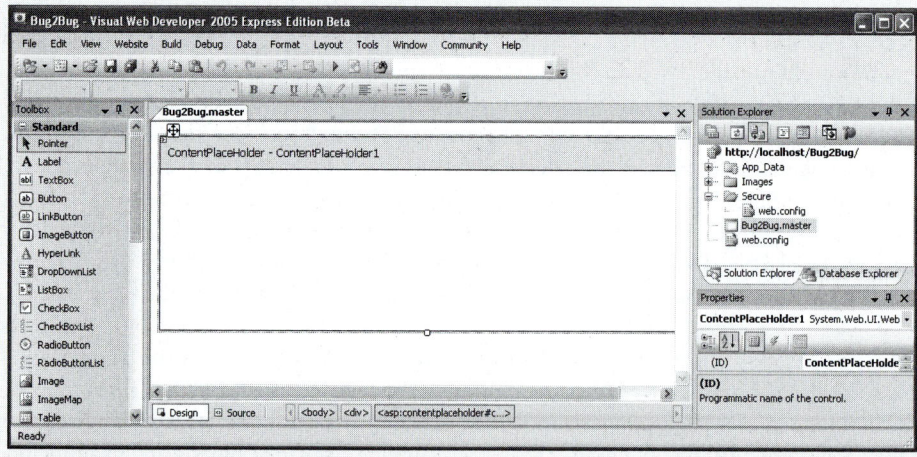

Fig. 21.55 | Master page in **Design** mode.

To create a header in the master page that will appear at the top of each content page, we insert a table into the master page. Place the cursor to the left of the ContentPlace-Holder and select **Layout > Insert Table**. In the **Insert Table** dialog, click the **Template** radio button, then select **Header** from the drop-down list of available table templates. Click **OK** to create a table that fills the page and contains two rows. Drag and drop the Content-PlaceHolder into the bottom table cell. Change the valign property of this cell to top, so the ContentPlaceHolder vertically aligns with the top of the cell. Next, set the Height of the top table cell to 130. Add to this cell an Image control named headerImage with its ImageUrl property set to the bug2bug.png file in the project's Images folder. (You can also simply drag the image from the **Solution Explorer** into the top cell.) Figure 21.56 shows the markup and **Design** view of the completed master page. As you will see in *Step 6*, a content page based on this master page displays the logo image defined here, as well as the content designed for that specific page (in place of the ContentPlaceHolder).

```
1   <%-- Fig. 21.56: Bug2Bug.master --%>
2   <%-- Master page that defines common features of all pages in the --%>
3   <%-- secure book database application. --%>
4   <%@ Master Language="C#" %>
5
6   <!DOCTYPE html PUBLIC "-//W3C//DTD XHTML 1.1//EN"
7       "http://www.w3.org/TR/xhtml11/DTD/xhtml11.dtd">
8
9   <html xmlns="http://www.w3.org/1999/xhtml" >
10      <head runat="server">
11          <title>Bug2Bug</title>
12      </head>
13      <body>
14          <form id="form1" runat="server">
15              <div>
16                  <table border="0" cellpadding="0" cellspacing="0"
17                      style="width: 100%; height: 100%">
18                      <tr>
19                          <td height="130">
20                              <asp:Image ID="headerImage" runat="server"
21                                  ImageUrl="~/Images/bug2bug.png" />
22                          </td>
23                      </tr>
24                      <tr>
25                          <td valign="top">
26                              <asp:contentplaceholder id="bodyContent"
27                                  runat="server">
28                              </asp:contentplaceholder>
29                          </td>
30                      </tr>
31                  </table>
32              </div>
33          </form>
34      </body>
35  </html>
```

Fig. 21.56 | Bug2Bug.master page that defines a logo image header for all pages in the secure book database application. (Part 1 of 2.)

Fig. 21.56 | Bug2Bug.master page that defines a logo image header for all pages in the secure book database application. (Part 2 of 2.)

Step 6: Creating a Content Page

We now create a content page based on Bug2Bug.master. We begin by building Create-NewUser.aspx. To create this file, right click the master page in the **Solution Explorer** and select **Add Content Page**. This action causes a Default.aspx file, configured to use the master page, to be added to the project. Rename this file CreateNewUser.aspx, then open it in **Source** mode (Fig. 21.57). Note that this file contains a Page directive with a Language property, a MasterPageFile property and a Title property. The Page directive indicates the *MasterPageFile* on which the content page builds. In this case, the MasterPageFile property is set to "~/Bug2Bug.master" to indicate that the current file builds on the master page we just created. The *Title* property specifies the title that will be displayed in the Web browser's title bar when the content page is loaded. This value, which we set to Create a New User, replaces the value (i.e., Bug2Bug) set in the title element of the master page.

Because CreateNewUser.aspx's Page directive specifies Bug2Bug.master as the page's MasterPageFile, the content page implicitly contains the contents of the master page,

```
CreateNewUser.aspx   Bug2Bug.master
Server Objects & Events                    (No Events)
  1  <%@ Page Language="C#" MasterPageFile="~/Bug2Bug.master"
  2      Title="Create a New User" %>
  3
  4  <asp:Content ID="Content1" ContentPlaceHolderID="bodyContent"
  5      Runat="Server">
  6  </asp:Content>
  7
 Design    Source      <Page>
```

Fig. 21.57 | Content page CreateNewUser.aspx in **Source** mode.

such as the DOCTYPE, html and body elements. The content page file does not duplicate the XHTML elements found in the master page. Instead, the content page contains a *Content* control (lines 4–6 in Fig. 21.57), in which we will place page-specific content that will replace the master page's ContentPlaceHolder when the content page is requested. The ContentPlaceHolderID property of the Content control identifies the ContentPlace-Holder in the master page that the control should replace—in this case, bodyContent.

The relationship between a content page and its master page is more evident in **Design** mode (Fig. 21.58). The shaded region contains the contents of the master page Bug2Bug.master as they will appear in CreateNewUser.aspx when rendered in a Web browser. The only editable part of this page is the Content control, which appears in place of the master page's ContentPlaceHolder.

Step 7: Adding a CreateUserWizard Control to a Content Page

Recall from Section 21.8.1 that CreateNewUser.aspx is the page in our Web site that allows first-time visitors to create user accounts. To provide this functionality, we use a *CreateUserWizard* control. Place the cursor inside the Content control in **Design** mode and double click CreateUserWizard in the **Login** section of the **Toolbox** to add it to the page at the current cursor position. You can also drag-and-drop the control onto the page. To change the CreateUserWizard's appearance, open the **CreateUserWizard Tasks** smart tag menu, and click **Auto Format**. Select the **Professional** color scheme.

As discussed previously, a CreateUserWizard provides a registration form that site visitors can use to create a user account. ASP.NET handles the details of creating a SQL Server database (named ASPNETDB.MDF and located in the App_Data folder) to store the user names, passwords and other account information of the application's users. ASP.NET also enforces a default set of requirements for filling out the form. Each field on the form is required, the password must contain at least seven characters, including at least one non-alphanumeric character, and the two passwords entered must match. The form also asks for a security question and answer that can be used to identify a user in case the account's password needs to be reset or recovered.

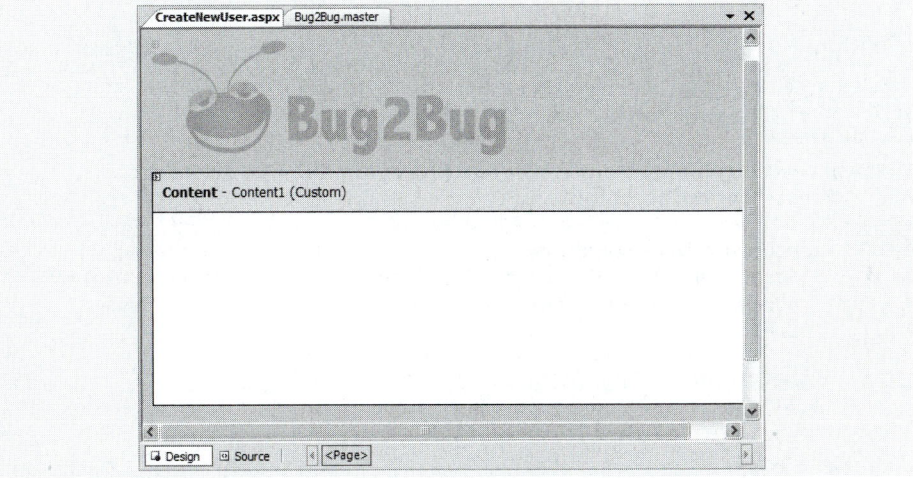

Fig. 21.58 | Content page CreateNewUser.aspx in **Design** mode.

After the user fills in the form's fields and clicks the **Create User** button to submit the account information, ASP.NET verifies that all the form's requirements were fulfilled and attempts to create the user account. If an error occurs (e.g., the user name already exists), the CreateUserWizard displays a message below the form. If the account is created successfully, the form is replaced by a confirmation message and a button that allows the user to continue. You can view this confirmation message in **Design** mode by selecting **Complete** from the **Step** drop-down list in the **CreateUserWizard Tasks** smart tag menu.

When a user account is created, ASP.NET automatically logs the user into the site (we say more about the login process shortly). At this point, the user is authenticated and allowed to access the Secure folder. After we create Books.aspx later in this section, we set the CreateUserWizard's ContinueDestinationPageUrl property to ~/Secure/Books.aspx to indicate that the user should be redirected to Books.aspx after clicking the **Continue** button on the confirmation page.

Figure 21.59 presents the completed CreateNewUser.aspx file (reformatted for readability). Inside the Content control, the CreateUserWizard control is defined by the markup in lines 9–40. The start tag (lines 9–12) contains several properties that specify formatting styles for the control, as well as the ContinueDestinationPageUrl property, which you will set later in the chapter. Lines 14–32 contain elements that define additional styles used to format specific parts of the control. Finally, lines 34–39 specify the wizard's two steps—CreateUserWizardStep and CompleteWizardStep—in a WizardSteps element. CreateUserWizardStep and CompleteWizardStep are classes that encapsulate the details of creating a user and issuing a confirmation message.

The sample outputs in Fig. 21.59(a) and Fig. 21.59(b) demonstrate successfully creating a user account with CreateNewUser.aspx. We use the password pa$$word for testing purposes. This password satisfies the minimum length and special character requirement imposed by ASP.NET, but in a real application, you should use a password that is more difficult for someone to guess. Figure 21.59(c) illustrates the error message that appears when you attempt to create a second user account with the same user name—ASP.NET requires that each user name be unique.

```
 1    <%-- Fig. 21.59: CreateNewUser.aspx --%>
 2    <%-- Content page using a CreateUserWizard control to register users. --%>
 3    <%@ Page Language="C#" MasterPageFile="~/Bug2Bug.master"
 4       Title="Create a New User" %>
 5
 6    <asp:Content ID="Content1" ContentPlaceHolderID="bodyContent"
 7       Runat="Server">
 8
 9       <asp:CreateUserWizard ID="CreateUserWizard1" runat="server"
10          BackColor="#F7F6F3" BorderColor="#E6E2D8" BorderStyle="Solid"
11          BorderWidth="1px" Font-Names="Verdana" Font-Size="0.8em"
12          ContinueDestinationPageUrl="~/Secure/Books.aspx">
13
14          <SideBarStyle BackColor="#5D7B9D" BorderWidth="0px"
15             Font-Size="0.9em" VerticalAlign="Top" />
```

Fig. 21.59 | CreateNewUser.aspx content page that provides a user registration form. (Part 1 of 3.)

```
16        <SideBarButtonStyle BorderWidth="0px" Font-Names="Verdana"
17           ForeColor="White" />
18        <NavigationButtonStyle BackColor="#FFFBFF" BorderColor="#CCCCCC"
19           BorderStyle="Solid" BorderWidth="1px" Font-Names="Verdana"
20           ForeColor="#284775" />
21        <HeaderStyle BackColor="#5D7B9D" BorderStyle="Solid"
22           Font-Bold="True" Font-Size="0.9em"
23           ForeColor="White" HorizontalAlign="Left" />
24        <CreateUserButtonStyle BackColor="#FFFBFF" BorderColor="#CCCCCC"
25           BorderStyle="Solid" BorderWidth="1px" Font-Names="Verdana"
26           ForeColor="#284775" />
27        <ContinueButtonStyle BackColor="#FFFBFF" BorderColor="#CCCCCC"
28           BorderStyle="Solid" BorderWidth="1px" Font-Names="Verdana"
29           ForeColor="#284775" />
30        <StepStyle BorderWidth="0px" />
31        <TitleTextStyle BackColor="#5D7B9D" Font-Bold="True"
32           ForeColor="White" />
33
34        <WizardSteps>
35           <asp:CreateUserWizardStep runat="server">
36           </asp:CreateUserWizardStep>
37           <asp:CompleteWizardStep runat="server">
38           </asp:CompleteWizardStep>
39        </WizardSteps>
40     </asp:CreateUserWizard>
41  </asp:Content>
```

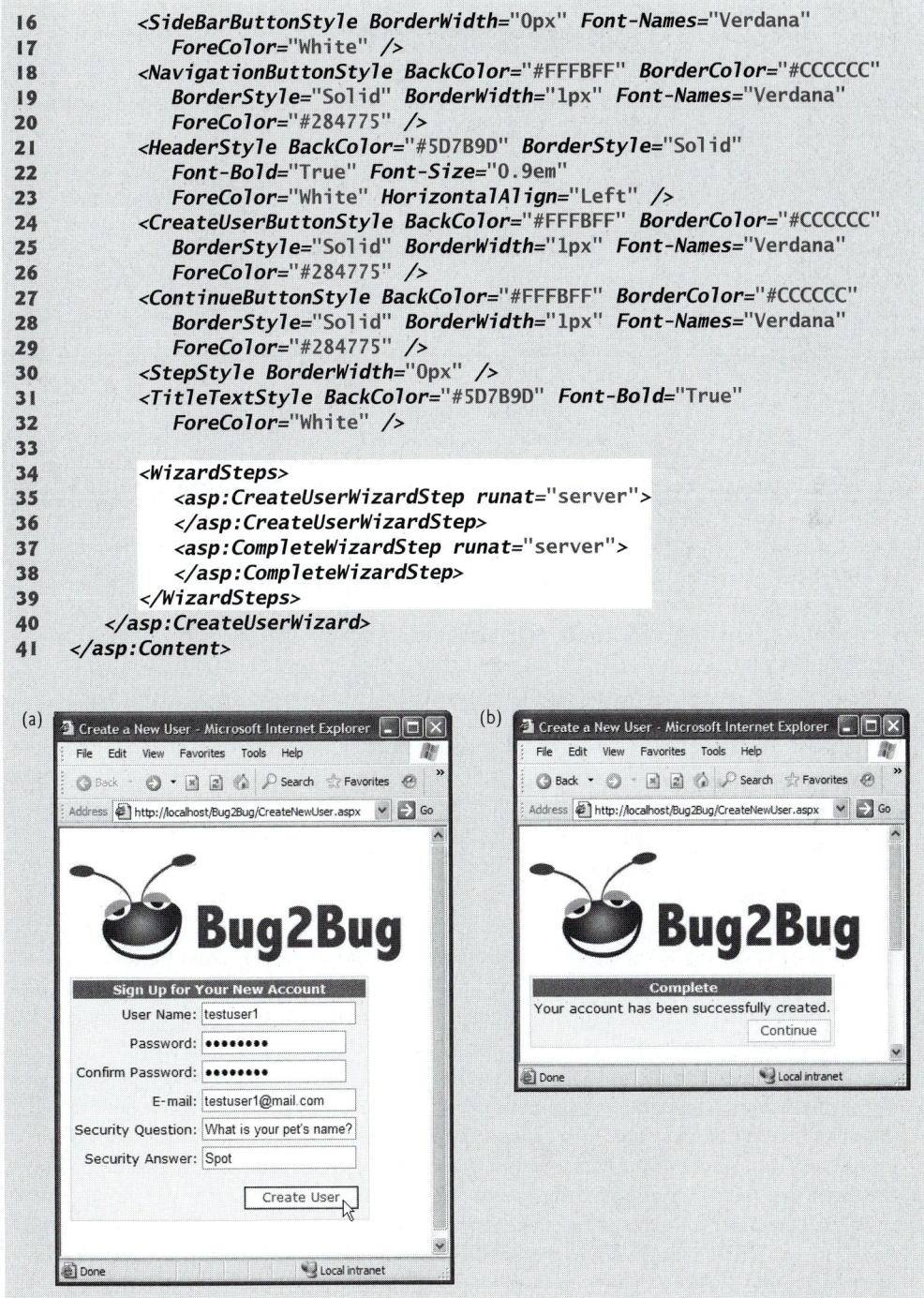

Fig. 21.59 | CreateNewUser.aspx content page that provides a user registration form. (Part 2 of 3.)

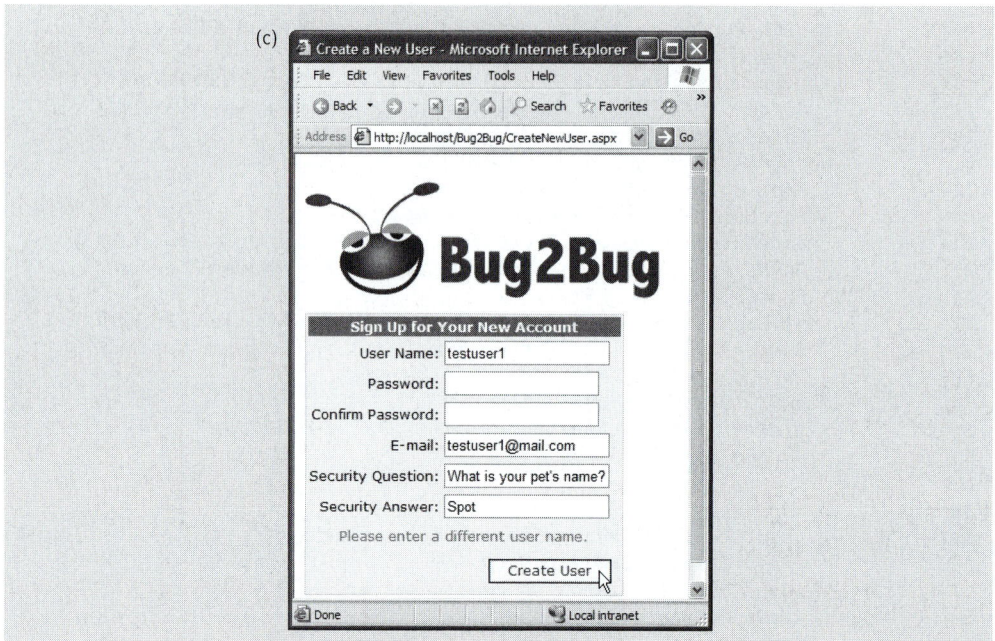

Fig. 21.59 | CreateNewUser.aspx content page that provides a user registration form. (Part 3 of 3.)

Step 8: Creating a Login Page

Recall from Section 21.8.1 that Login.aspx is the page in our Web site that allows returning visitors to log into their user accounts. To create this functionality, add another content page named Login.aspx and set its title to Login. In **Design** mode, drag a *Login* control (located in the **Login** section of the **Toolbox**) to the page's Content control. Open the **Auto Format** dialog from the **Login Tasks** smart tag menu and set the control's color scheme to **Professional**.

Next, configure the Login control to display a link to the page for creating new users. Set the Login control's CreateUserUrl property to CreateNewUser.aspx by clicking the ellipsis button to the right of this property and selecting the CreateNewUser.aspx file in the resulting dialog. Then set the CreateUserText property to Click here to create a new user. These property values cause a link to appear in the Login control.

Finally, we change the value of the Login control's DisplayRememberMe property to False. By default, the control displays a checkbox and the text Remember me next time. This can be used to allow a user to remain authenticated beyond a single browser session on the user's current computer. However, we want to require that users log in each time they visit the site, so we disable this option.

The Login control encapsulates the details of logging a user into a Web application (i.e., authenticating a user). When a user enters a user name and password, then clicks the **Log In** button, ASP.NET determines whether the information provided match those of an account in the membership database (i.e., ASPNETDB.MDF created by ASP.NET). If they match, the user is authenticated (i.e., the user's identity is confirmed), and the browser is redirected to the page specified by the Login control's DestinationPageUrl property. We set this property to the Books.aspx page after creating it in the next section. If the user's identity cannot be confirmed (i.e., the user is not authenticated), the Login control displays an error message (see Fig. 21.60), and the user can attempt to log in again.

Figure 21.60 presents the completed Login.aspx file. Note that, as in CreateNew-User.aspx, the Page directive indicates that this content page inherits content from Bug2Bug.master. In the Content control that replaces the master page's ContentPlace-Holder with ID bodyContent, lines 8–22 create a Login control. Note the CreateUser-

```
1   <%-- Fig. 21.60: Login.aspx --%>
2   <%-- Content page using a Login control that authenticates users. --%>
3   <%@ Page Language="C#" MasterPageFile="~/Bug2Bug.master" Title="Login" %>
4
5   <asp:Content ID="Content1" ContentPlaceHolderID="bodyContent"
6      Runat="Server">
7
8      <asp:Login ID="Login1" runat="server" BackColor="#F7F6F3"
9         BorderColor="#E6E2D8" BorderPadding="4" BorderStyle="Solid"
10        BorderWidth="1px" CreateUserText="Click here to create a new user"
11        CreateUserUrl="~/CreateNewUser.aspx"
12        DestinationPageUrl="~/Secure/Books.aspx" DisplayRememberMe="False"
13        Font-Names="Verdana" Font-Size="0.8em" ForeColor="#333333">
14
15        <LoginButtonStyle BackColor="#FFFBFF" BorderColor="#CCCCCC"
16           BorderStyle="Solid" BorderWidth="1px" Font-Names="Verdana"
17           Font-Size="0.8em" ForeColor="#284775" />
18        <TextBoxStyle Font-Size="0.8em" />
19        <TitleTextStyle BackColor="#5D7B9D" Font-Bold="True"
20           Font-Size="0.9em" ForeColor="White" />
21        <InstructionTextStyle Font-Italic="True" ForeColor="Black" />
22     </asp:Login>
23  </asp:Content>
```

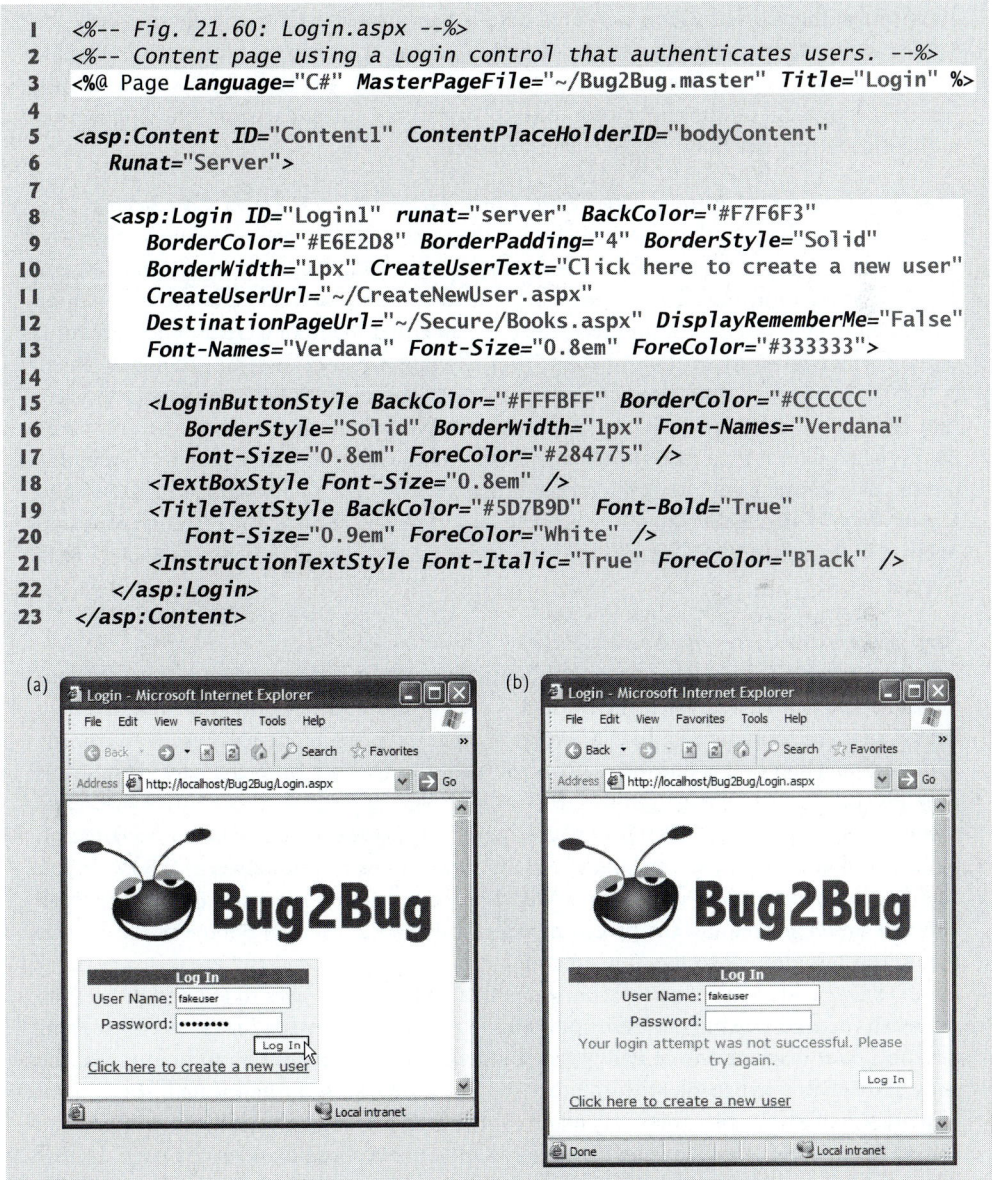

Fig. 21.60 | Login.aspx content page using a Login control.

Text and CreateUserUrl properties (lines 10–11) that we set using the **Properties** window. Line 12 in the start tag for the Login control contains the DestinationPageUrl (you will set this property in the next step) and the DisplayRememberMe property, which we set to False. The elements in lines 15–21 define various formatting styles applied to parts of the control. Note that all of the functionality related to actually logging the user in or displaying error messages is completely hidden from you.

When a user enters the user name and password of an existing user account, ASP.NET authenticates the user and writes to the client an *encrypted* cookie containing information about the authenticated user. Encrypted data is data translated into a code that only the sender and receiver can understand—thereby keeping it private. The encrypted cookie contains a string user name and a bool value that specifies whether this cookie should persist (i.e., remain on the client's computer) beyond the current session. Our application authenticates the user only for the current session.

Step 9: Creating a Content Page That Only Authenticated Users Can Access
A user who has been authenticated will be redirected to Books.aspx. We now create the Books.aspx file in the Secure folder—the folder for which we set an access rule denying access to anonymous users. If an unauthenticated user requests this file, the user will be redirected to Login.aspx. From there, the user can either log in or a create a new account, both of which will authenticate the user, thus allowing the user to return to Books.aspx.

To create Books.aspx, right click the Secure folder in the **Solution Explorer** and select **Add New Item....** In the resulting dialog, select **Web Form** and specify the file name Books.aspx. Check the box **Select Master Page** to indicate that this Web Form should be created as a content page that references a master page, then click **Add**. In the **Select a Master Page** dialog, select Bug2Bug.master and click **OK**. The IDE creates the file and opens it in **Source** mode. Change the Title property of the Page directive to Book Information.

Step 10: Customizing the Secure Page
To customize the Books.aspx page for a particular user, we add a welcome message containing a *LoginName* control, which displays the current authenticated user name. Open Books.aspx in **Design** mode. In the Content control, type Welcome followed by a comma and a space. Then drag a LoginName control from the **Toolbox** onto the page. When this page executes on the server, the text [UserName] that appears in this control in **Design** mode will be replaced by the current user name. In **Source** mode, type an exclamation point (!) directly after the LoginName control (with no spaces in between). [*Note:* If you add the exclamation point in **Design** mode, the IDE may insert extra spaces or a line break between this character and the preceding control. Entering the ! in **Source** mode ensures that it appears adjacent to the user's name.]

Next, we add a LoginStatus control, which will allow the user to log out of the Web site when finished viewing the listing of books in the database. A *LoginStatus* control renders on a Web page in one of two ways—by default, if the user is not authenticated, the control displays a hyperlink with the text Login; if the user is authenticated, the control displays a hyperlink with the text Logout. Each link performs the stated action. Add a LoginStatus control to the page by dragging it from the **Toolbox** onto the page. In this example, any user who reaches this page must already be authenticated, so the control will always render as a Logout link. The **LoginStatus Tasks** smart tag menu allows you switch between the control's **Views**. Select the **Logged In** view to see the Logout link. To change the actual text of this link, modify the control's LogoutText property to Click here to log out. Next, set the LogoutAction property to RedirectToLoginPage.

Step 11: Connecting the CreateUserWizard and Login Controls to the Secure Page

Now that we have created Books.aspx, we can specify that this is the page to which the CreateUserWizard and Login controls redirect users after they are authenticated. Open CreateNewUser.aspx in **Design** mode and set the CreateUserWizard control's Continue-DestinationPageUrl property to Books.aspx. Next, open Login.aspx and select Books.aspx as the DestinationPageUrl of the Login control.

At this point, you can run the Web application by selecting **Debug > Start Without Debugging**. First, create a user account on CreateNewUser.aspx, then notice how the LoginName and LoginStatus controls appear on Books.aspx. Next, log out of the site and log back in using Login.aspx.

Step 12: Generating a DataSet Based on the Books.mdf Database

We now begin to add the content (i.e., book information) to the secure page Books.aspx. This page will provide a DropDownList containing authors' names and a GridView displaying information about books written by the author selected in the DropDownList. A user will select an author from the DropDownList to cause the GridView to display information about only the books written by the selected author. As you will see, we create this functionality entirely in **Design** mode without writing any code.

To work with the Books database, we use an approach slightly different than in the preceding case study in which we accessed the Guestbook database using a SqlDataSource control. Here we use an *ObjectDataSource* control, which encapsulates an object that provides access to a data source. Recall that in Chapter 20, we accessed the Books database in a Windows application using TableAdapters configured to communicate with the database file. These TableAdapters placed a cached copy of the database's data in a DataSet, which the application then accessed. We use a similar approach in this example. An ObjectDataSource can encapsulate a TableAdapter and use its methods to access the data in the database. This helps separate the data-access logic from the presentation logic. As you will see shortly, the SQL statements used to retrieve data do not appear in the ASPX page when using an ObjectDataSource.

The first step in accessing data using an ObjectDataSource is to create a DataSet that contains the data from the Books database required by the application. In Visual C# 2005 Express, this occurs automatically when you add a data source to a project. In Visual Web Developer, however, you must explicitly generate the DataSet. Right click the project's location in the **Solution Explorer** and select **Add New Item...** In the resulting dialog, select **DataSet** and specify BooksDataSet.xsd as the file name, then click **Add**. A dialog will appear that asks you whether the DataSet should be placed in an App_Code folder—a folder whose contents are compiled and made available to all parts of the project. Click **Yes** for the IDE to create this folder to store BooksDataSet.xsd.

Step 13: Creating and Configuring an AuthorsTableAdapter

Once the DataSet is added, the **Dataset Designer** will appear, and the **TableAdapter Configuration Wizard** will open. Recall from Chapter 20 that this wizard allows you to configure a TableAdapter for filling a DataTable in a DataSet with data from a database. The

Books.aspx page requires two sets of data—a list of authors that will be displayed in the page's DropDownList (created shortly) and a list of books written by a specific author. We focus on the first set of data here—the authors. Thus, we use the **TableAdapter Configuration Wizard** first to configure an AuthorsTableAdapter. In the next step, we will configure a TitlesTableAdapter.

In the **TableAdapter Configuration Wizard**, select Books.mdf from the drop-down list. Then click **Next >** twice to save the connection string in the application's Web.config file and move to the **Choose a Command Type** screen.

In the wizard's **Choose a Command Type** screen, select **Use SQL statements** and click **Next >**. The next screen allows you to enter a SELECT statement for retrieving data from the database, which will then be placed in an Authors DataTable within the Books-DataSet. Enter the SQL statement

> **SELECT** AuthorID, FirstName + ' ' + LastName **AS** Name **FROM** Authors

in the text box on the **Enter a SQL Statement** screen. This query selects the AuthorID of each row. This query's result will also contain a column named Name that is created by concatenating each row's FirstName and LastName, separated by a space. The **AS** SQL keyword allows you to generate a column in a query result—called an *alias*—that contains the result of a SQL expression (e.g., FirstName + ' ' + LastName). You will soon see how we use the result of this query to populate the DropDownList with items containing the authors' full names.

After entering the SQL statement, click the **Advanced Options...** button and uncheck **Generate Insert, Update and Delete statements**, since this application does not need to modify the database's contents. Click **OK** to close the **Advanced Options** dialog. Click **Next >** to advance to the **Choose Methods to Generate** screen. Leave the default names and click **Finish**. Notice that the **DataSet Designer** (Fig. 21.61) now displays a DataTable named Authors with AuthorID and Name members, and Fill and GetData methods.

Step 14: Creating and Configuring a TitlesTableAdapter

Books.aspx needs to access a list of books by a specific author and a list of authors. Thus we must create a TitlesTableAdapter that will retrieve the desired information from the database's Titles table. Right click the **Dataset Designer** and from the menu that appears, select **Add > TableAdapter...** to launch the **TableAdapter Configuration Wizard**. Make sure the BooksConnectionString is selected as the connection in the wizard's first screen, then click **Next >**. Choose **Use SQL statements** and click **Next >**.

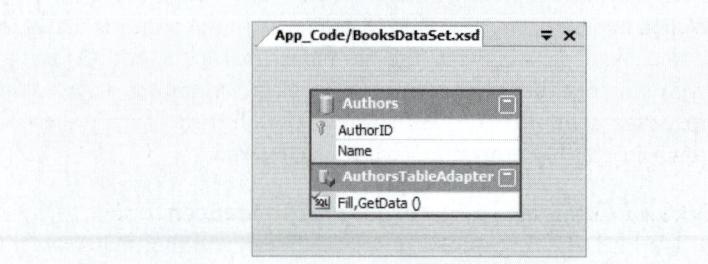

Fig. 21.61 | Authors DataTable in the **Dataset Designer**.

In the **Enter a SQL Statement** screen, open the **Advanced Options** dialog and uncheck **Generate Insert, Update and Delete statements**, then click **OK**. Our application allows users to filter the books displayed by the author's name, so we need to build a query that takes an `AuthorID` as a parameter and returns the rows in the `Titles` table for books written by that author. To build this complex query, click the **Query Builder...** button.

In the **Add Table** dialog that appears, select **AuthorISBN** and click **Add**. Then **Add** the **Titles** table, too. Our query will require access to data in both of these tables. Click **Close** to exit the **Add Table** dialog. In the top pane of the **Query Builder** window (Fig. 21.62), check the box marked *** (All Columns)** in the **Titles** table. Next, in the middle pane, add a row with **Column** set to `AuthorISBN.AuthorID`. Uncheck the **Output** box, because we do not want the **AuthorID** to appear in our query result. Add an `@authorID` parameter in the **Filter** column of the newly added row. The SQL statement generated by these actions retrieves information about all books written by the author specified by parameter `@authorID`. The statement first merges the data from the `AuthorISBN` and `Titles` tables. The `INNER JOIN` clause specifies that the `ISBN` columns of each table are compared to determine which rows are merged. The `INNER JOIN` results in a temporary table containing the columns of both tables. The outer portion of the SQL statement selects the book information from this temporary table for a specific author (i.e., all rows in which the `AuthorID` column is equal to `@authorID`).

Click **OK** to exit the **Query Builder**, then in the **TableAdapter Configuration Wizard**, click **Next >**. On the **Choose Methods to Generate** screen, enter `FillByAuthorID` and `Get-DataByAuthorID` as the names of the two methods to be generated for the `TitlesTable-Adapter`. Click **Finish** to exit the wizard. You should now see a `Titles` DataTable in the **Dataset Designer** (Fig. 21.63).

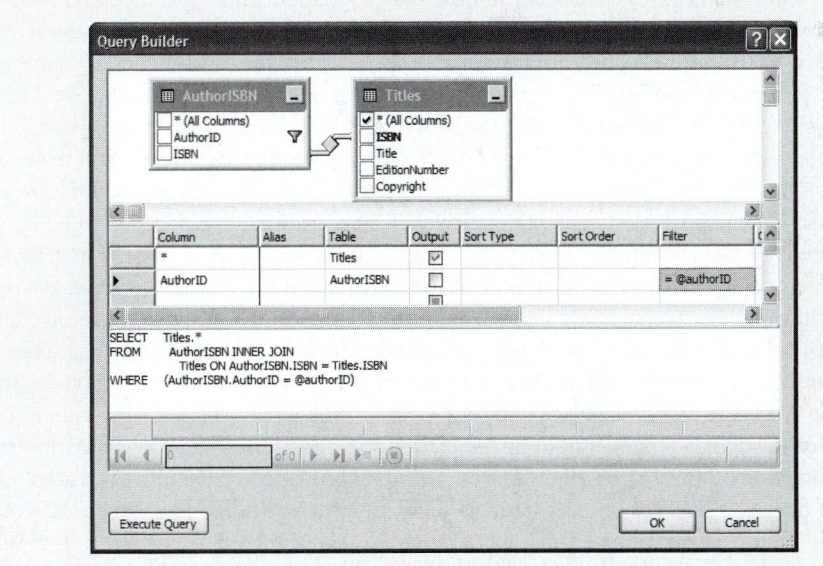

Fig. 21.62 | **Query Builder** for designing a query that selects books written by a particular author.

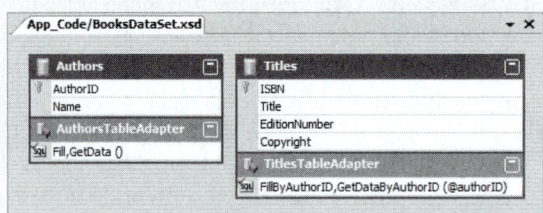

Fig. 21.63 | Dataset Designer after adding the `TitlesTableAdapter`.

Step 15: Adding a DropDownList Containing Authors' First and Last Names

Now that we have created a `BooksDataSet` and configured the necessary `TableAdapters`, we add controls to `Books.aspx` that will display the data on the Web page. We first add the `DropDownList` from which users can select an author. Open `Books.aspx` in **Design** mode, then add the text `Author:` and a `DropDownList` control named `authorsDropDownList` in the page's `Content` control, below the existing content. The `DropDownList` initially displays the text `[Unbound]`. We now bind the list to a data source, so the list displays the author information placed in the `BooksDataSet` by the `AuthorsTableAdapter`. In the **DropDownList Tasks** smart tag menu, click **Choose Data Source...** to start the **Data Source Configuration Wizard**. Select **<New data source...>** from the **Select a data source** drop-down list in the first screen of the wizard. Doing so opens the **Choose a Data Source Type** screen. Select **Object** and set the ID to `authorsObjectDataSource`, then click **OK**.

An `ObjectDataSource` accesses data through another object, often called a ***business object***. Recall from Section 21.3 that the middle tier of a three-tier application contains business logic that controls the way an application's top tier user interface (in this case, `Books.aspx`) accesses the bottom tier's data (in this case, the `Books.mdf` database file). Thus, a business object represents the middle tier of an application and mediates interactions between the other two tiers. In an ASP.NET Web application, a `TableAdapter` typically serves as the business object that retrieves the data from the bottom-tier database and makes it available to the top-tier user interface through a `DataSet`. In the **Choose a Business Object** screen of the **Configure Data Source** wizard (Fig. 21.64), select `BooksDataSet-TableAdapters.AuthorsTableAdapter`. [*Note:* You may need to save the project to see the `AuthorsTableAdapter`.] `BooksDataSetTableAdapters` is a namespace declared by the IDE when you create `BooksDataSet`. Click **Next >** to continue.

The **Define Data Methods** screen (Fig. 21.65) allows you to specify which method of the business object (in this case, `AuthorsTableAdapter`) should be used to obtain the data accessed through the `ObjectDataSource`. You can choose only methods that return data, so the only choice provided is the `GetData` method, which returns an `AuthorsDataTable`. Click **Finish** to close the **Configure Data Source** wizard and return to the **Data Source Configuration Wizard** for the `DropDownList` (Fig. 21.66). The newly created data source (i.e., `authorsObjectDataSource`) should be selected in the top drop-down list. The other two drop-down lists on this screen allow you to configure how the `DropDownList` control uses the data from the data source. Set `Name` as the data field to display and `AuthorID` as the data field to use as the value. Thus, when `authorsDropDownList` is rendered in a Web browser, the list items will display the names of the authors, but the underlying values associated with each item will be the `AuthorID`s of the authors. Finally, click **OK** to bind the `DropDownList` to the specified data.

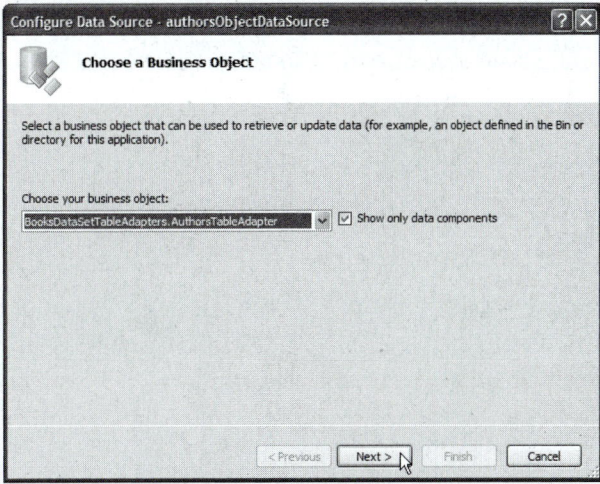

Fig. 21.64 | Choosing a business object for an `ObjectDataSource`.

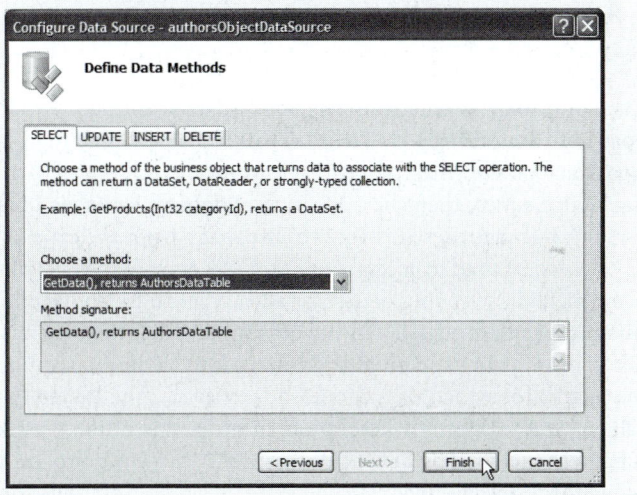

Fig. 21.65 | Choosing a data method of a business object for use with an `ObjectDataSource`.

The last step in configuring the `DropDownList` on `Books.aspx` is to set the control's **_AutoPostBack_** property to `True`. This property indicates that a postback occurs each time the user selects an item in the `DropDownList`. As you will see shortly, this causes the page's `GridView` (created in the next step) to display new data.

Step 16: Creating a `GridView` to Display the Selected Author's Books
We now add a `GridView` to `Books.aspx` for displaying the book information by the author selected in the `authorsDropDownList`. Add a `GridView` named `titlesGridView` below the other controls in the page's `Content` control.

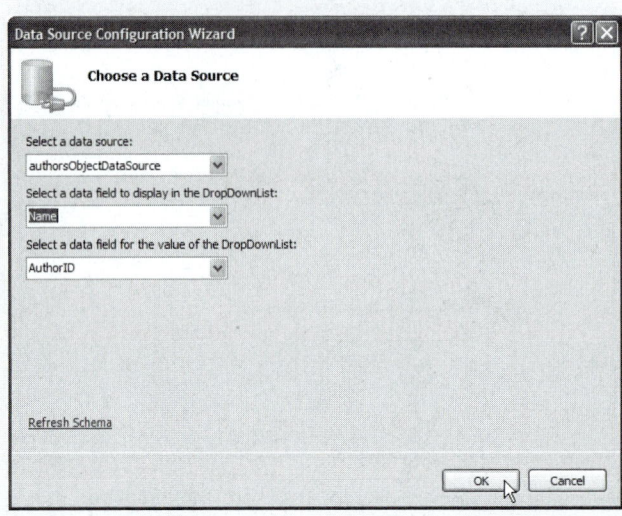

Fig. 21.66 | Choosing a data source for a `DropDownList`.

To bind the `GridView` to data from the `Books` database, select **<New data source...>** from the **Choose Data Source** drop-down list in the **GridView Tasks** smart tag menu. When the **Data Source Configuration Wizard** opens, select **Object** and set the ID of the data source to `titlesObjectDataSource`, then click **OK**. In the **Choose a Business Object** screen, select the `BooksDataSetTableAdapters.TitlesTableAdapter` from the drop-down list to indicate the object that will be used to access the data. Click **Next >**. In the **Define Data Methods** screen, leave the default selection of `GetDataByAuthorID` as the method that will be invoked to obtain the data for display in the `GridView`. Click **Next >**.

Recall that `TitlesTableAdapter` method `GetDataByAuthorID` requires a parameter to indicate the `AuthorID` for which data should be retrieved. The **Define Parameters** screen (Fig. 21.67) allows you to specify where to obtain the value of the `@authorID` parameter in the SQL statement executed by `GetDataByAuthorID`. Select **Control** from the **Parameter source** drop-down list. Select `authorsDropDownList` as the **ControlID** (i.e., the ID of the parameter source control). Next, enter 1 as the **DefaultValue**, so books by Harvey Deitel (who has `AuthorID 1` in the database) display when the page first loads (i.e., before the user has made any selections using the `authorsDropDownList`). Finally, click **Finish** to exit the wizard. The `GridView` is now configured to display the data retrieved by `TitlesTableAdapter.GetDataByAuthorID`, using the value of the current selection in `authorsDropDownList` as the parameter. Thus, when the user selects a new author and a postback occurs, the `GridView` displays a new set of data.

Now that the `GridView` is tied to a data source, we modify several of the control's properties to adjust its appearance and behavior. Set the `GridView`'s `CellPadding` property to 5, set the `BackColor` of the `AlternatingRowStyle` to `LightYellow`, and set the `BackColor` of the `HeaderStyle` to `LightGreen`. Change the `Width` of the control to 600px to accommodate long data values.

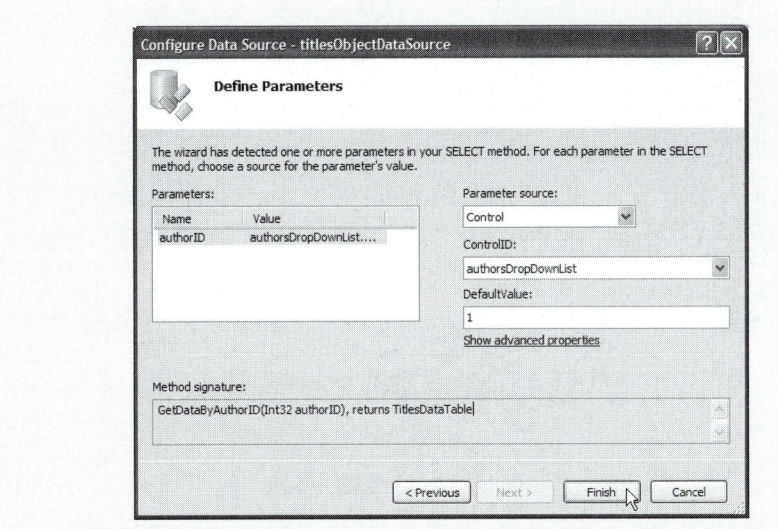

Fig. 21.67 | Choosing the data source for a parameter in a business object's data method.

Next, in the **GridView Tasks** smart tag menu, check **Enable Sorting**. This causes the column headings in the GridView to turn into hyperlinks that allow users to sort the data in the GridView. For example, clicking the Titles heading in the Web browser will cause the displayed data to appear sorted in alphabetical order. Clicking this heading a second time will cause the data to be sorted in reverse alphabetical order. ASP.NET hides from you the details required to achieve this functionality.

Finally, in the **GridView Tasks** smart tag menu, check **Enable Paging**. This causes the GridView to split across multiple pages. The user can click the numbered links at the bottom of the GridView control to display a different page of data. GridView's **PageSize** property determines the number of entries per page. Set the PageSize property to 4 using the **Properties** window so that the GridView displays only four books per page. This technique for displaying data makes the site more readable and enables pages to load more quickly (because less data is displayed at one time). Note that, as with sorting data in a GridView, you do not need to add any code to achieve paging functionality. Fig. 21.68 displays the completed Books.aspx file in **Design** mode.

Step 17: Examining the Markup in Books.aspx

Figure 21.69 presents the markup in Books.aspx (reformatted for readability). Aside from the exclamation point in line 9, which we added manually in **Source** mode, all the remaining markup was generated by the IDE in response to the actions we performed in **Design** mode. The Content control (lines 6–55) defines page-specific content that will replace the ContentPlaceHolder named bodyContent. Recall that this control is located in the master page specified in line 3. Line 9 creates the LoginName control, which displays the authenticated user's name when the page is requested and viewed in a browser. Lines 10–12 create the LoginStatus control. Recall that this control is configured to redirect the user to the login page after logging out (i.e., clicking the hyperlink with the LogoutText).

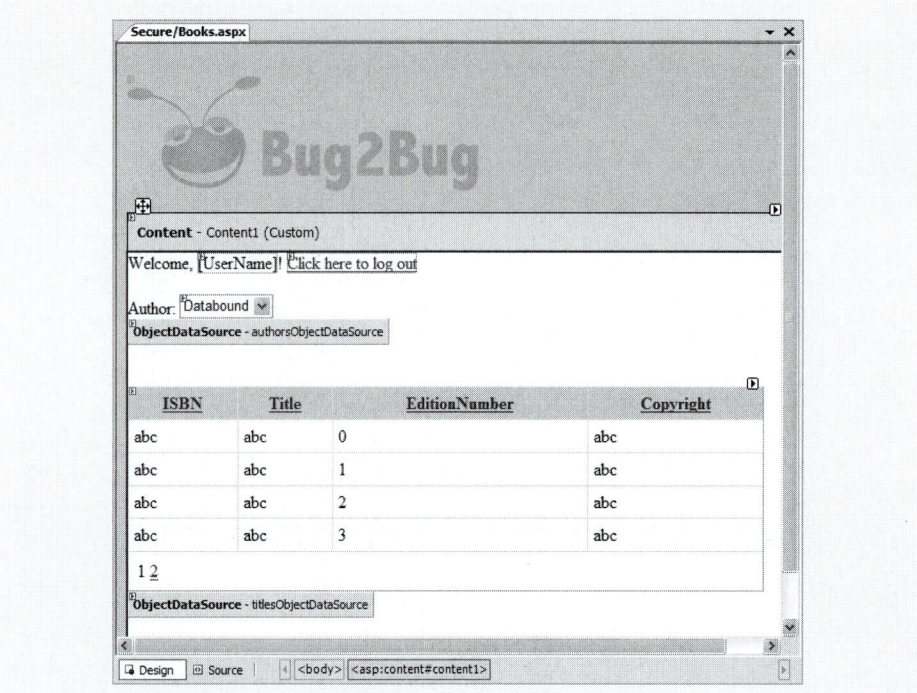

Fig. 21.68 | Completed `Books.aspx` in **Design** mode.

Lines 15–18 define the `DropDownList` that displays the names of the authors in the Books database. Line 16 contains the control's `AutoPostBack` property, which indicates that changing the selected item in the list causes a postback to occur. The `DataSourceID` property in line 16 specifies that the `DropDownList`'s items are created based on the data obtained through the `authorsObjectDataSource` (defined in lines 20–23). Line 21 specifies that this `ObjectDataSource` accesses the Books database by calling method `GetData` of the `BooksDataSet`'s `AuthorsTableAdapter` (line 22).

Lines 25–43 create the `GridView` that displays information about the books written by the selected author. The start tag (lines 25–28) indicates that paging (with a page size of 4) and sorting are enabled in the `GridView`. The `AutoGenerateColumns` property indicates whether the columns in the `GridView` are generated at runtime based on the fields in the data source. This property is set to `False`, because the IDE-generated `Columns` element (lines 30–39) already specifies the columns for the `GridView` using `BoundFields`. Lines 45–54 define the `ObjectDataSource` used to fill the `GridView` with data. Recall that we configured `titlesObjectDataSource` to use method `GetDataByAuthorID` of the `BooksDataSet`'s `TitlesTableAdapter` for this purpose. The `ControlParameter` in lines 50–52 specifies that the value of method `GetDataByAuthorID`'s parameter comes from the `SelectedValue` property of the `authorsDropDownList`.

Figure 21.69(a) depicts the default appearance of `Books.aspx` in a Web browser. Because the `DefaultValue` property (line 51) of the `ControlParameter` for the `titlesObjectDataSource` is set to 1, books by the author with `AuthorID 1` (i.e., Harvey Deitel) are displayed when the page first loads. Note that the `GridView` displays paging links below

```
 1   <%-- Fig. 21.69: Books.aspx --%>
 2   <%-- Displays information from the Books database. --%>
 3   <%@ Page Language="C#" MasterPageFile="~/Bug2Bug.master"
 4      Title="Book Information" %>
 5
 6   <asp:Content ID="Content1" ContentPlaceHolderID="bodyContent"
 7      Runat="Server">
 8
 9      Welcome, <asp:LoginName ID="LoginName1" runat="server" />!
10      <asp:LoginStatus ID="LoginStatus1" runat="server"
11         LogoutAction="RedirectToLoginPage"
12         LogoutText="Click here to log out" /><br /><br />
13
14      Author:
15      <asp:DropDownList ID="authorsDropDownList" runat="server"
16         AutoPostBack="True" DataSourceID="authorsObjectDataSource"
17         DataTextField="Name" DataValueField="AuthorID">
18      </asp:DropDownList>
19
20      <asp:ObjectDataSource ID="authorsObjectDataSource"
21         runat="server" SelectMethod="GetData"
22         TypeName="BooksDataSetTableAdapters.AuthorsTableAdapter">
23      </asp:ObjectDataSource><br /><br />
24
25      <asp:GridView ID="titlesGridView" runat="server" AllowPaging="True"
26         AllowSorting="True" AutoGenerateColumns="False" CellPadding="5"
27         DataKeyNames="ISBN" DataSourceID="titlesObjectDataSource"
28         PageSize="4" Width="600px">
29
30         <Columns>
31            <asp:BoundField DataField="ISBN"
32               HeaderText="ISBN" ReadOnly="True" SortExpression="ISBN" />
33            <asp:BoundField DataField="Title"
34               HeaderText="Title" SortExpression="Title" />
35            <asp:BoundField DataField="EditionNumber"
36               HeaderText="EditionNumber" SortExpression="EditionNumber" />
37            <asp:BoundField DataField="Copyright"
38               HeaderText="Copyright" SortExpression="Copyright" />
39         </Columns>
40
41         <HeaderStyle BackColor="LightGreen" />
42         <AlternatingRowStyle BackColor="LightYellow" />
43      </asp:GridView>
44
45      <asp:ObjectDataSource ID="titlesObjectDataSource" runat="server"
46         SelectMethod="GetDataByAuthorID"
47         TypeName="BooksDataSetTableAdapters.TitlesTableAdapter">
48
49         <SelectParameters>
50            <asp:ControlParameter ControlID="authorsDropDownList"
51               DefaultValue="1" Name="authorID"
52               PropertyName="SelectedValue" Type="Int32" />
```

Fig. 21.69 | Markup for the completed Books.aspx file. (Part 1 of 3.)

```
53              </SelectParameters>
54          </asp:ObjectDataSource>
55      </asp:Content>
```

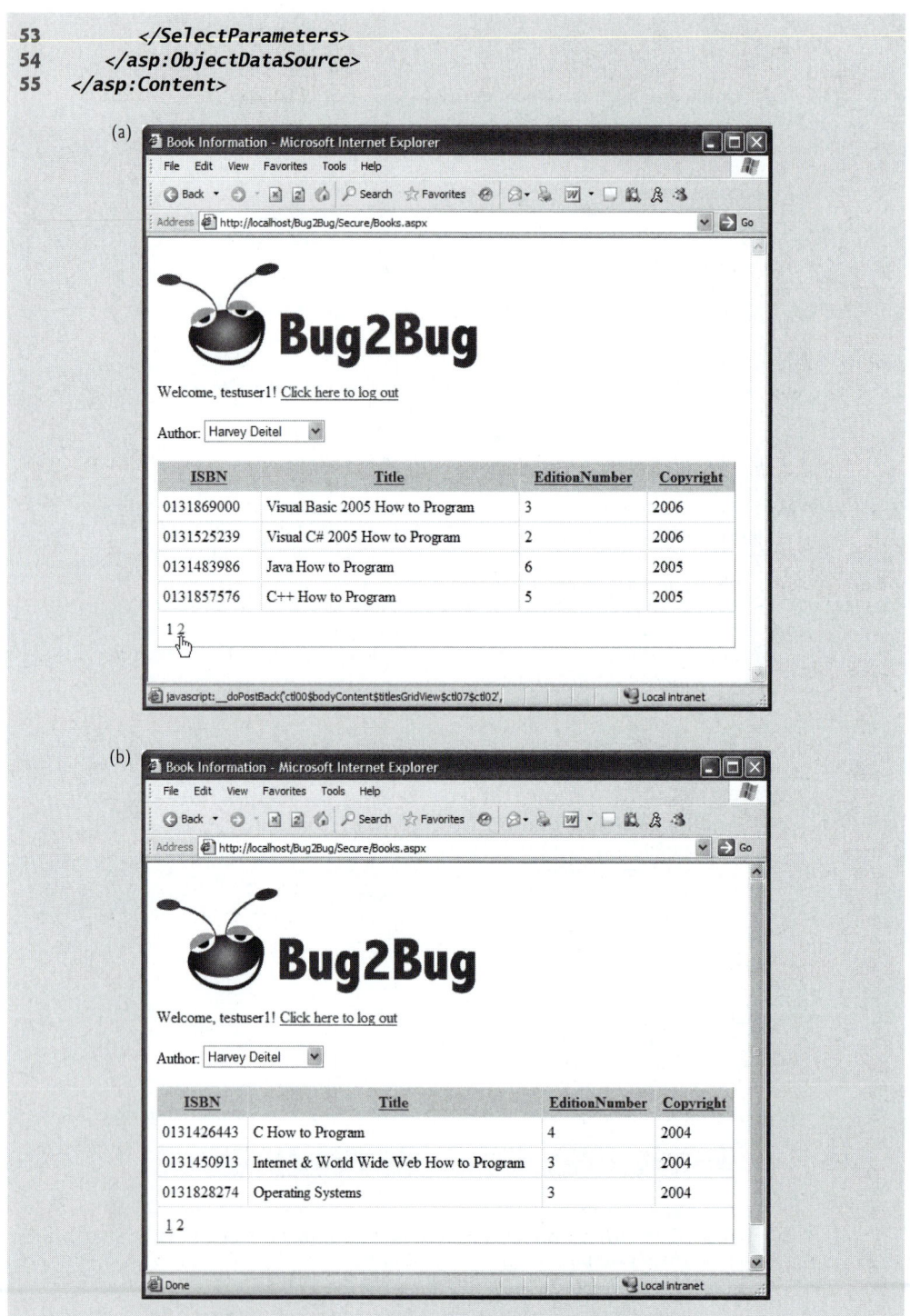

Fig. 21.69 | Markup for the completed `Books.aspx` file. (Part 2 of 3.)

Fig. 21.69 | Markup for the completed `Books.aspx` file. (Part 3 of 3.)

the data, because the number of rows of data returned by `GetDataByAuthorID` is greater than the page size. Figure 21.69(b) shows the `GridView` after clicking the 2 link to view the second page of data. Figure 21.69(c) presents `Books.aspx` after the user selects a different author from the `authorsDropDownList`. The data fits on one page, so the `GridView` does not display paging links.

21.9 Wrap-Up

In this chapter, we introduced Web application development using ASP.NET and Visual Web Developer 2005 Express. We began by discussing the simple HTTP transactions that take place when you request and receive a Web page through a Web browser. You then learned about the three tiers (i.e., the client or top tier, the business logic or middle tier and the information or bottom tier) that comprise most Web applications.

We then explained the role of ASPX files (i.e., Web Form files) and code-behind files, and the relationship between them. We discussed how ASP.NET compiles and executes Web applications so that they can be displayed as XHTML in a Web browser. You also learned how to build an ASP.NET Web application using the Visual Web Developer IDE.

The chapter demonstrated several common ASP.NET Web controls used for displaying text and images on a Web Form. You learned how to use an `AdRotator` control to display randomly selected images. We also discussed validation controls, which allow you to ensure that user input on a Web page satisfies certain requirements.

We discussed the benefits of maintaining state information about a user across multiple pages of a Web site. We then demonstrated how you can include such functionality in a Web application using either cookies or session tracking with `HttpSessionState` objects.

Finally, the chapter presented two case studies on building ASP.NET applications that interact with databases. First, we showed how to build a guestbook application that allows users to submit comments about a Web site. You learned how to save the user input in a SQL Server database and how to display past submissions on the Web page.

The second case study demonstrated how to build an application that requires users to log in before accessing information from the Books database discussed in Chapter 20. You used the **Web Site Administration Tool** to configure the application to use forms authentication and prevent anonymous users from accessing the book information. This case study explained how to use the Login, CreateUserWizard, LoginName and Login-Status controls to simplify user authentication. You also learned to create a uniform look-and-feel for a Web site using one master page and several content pages.

In the next chapter, we continue our coverage of ASP.NET technology with an introduction to Web services, which allow methods on one machine to call methods on other machines via common data formats and protocols, such as XML and HTTP. You will learn how Web services promote software reusability and interoperability across multiple computers on a network such as the Internet.

21.10 Web Resources

`beta.asp.net`
This official Microsoft site overviews ASP.NET and provides a link for downloading Visual Web Developer. This site includes ASP.NET articles, links to useful ASP.NET resources and lists of books on Web development with ASP.NET.

`beta.asp.net/QuickStartv20/aspnet/`
The ASP.NET QuickStart Tutorial from Microsoft provides code samples and discussion of fundamental ASP.NET topics.

`beta.asp.net/guidedtour2/`
This guided tour of Visual Web Developer 2005 Express introduces key features in the IDE used to develop ASP.NET Web applications.

`www.15seconds.com`
This site offers ASP.NET news, articles, code samples, FAQs and links to valuable community resources, such as an ASP.NET message board and a mailing list.

`aspalliance.com`
This community site contains ASP.NET articles, tutorials and examples.

`aspadvice.com`
This site provides access to many e-mail lists where anyone can ask and respond to questions about ASP.NET and related technologies.

`www.asp101.com/aspdotnet/`
This site overviews ASP.NET and includes articles, code examples, a discussion board and links to ASP.NET resources. The code samples build on many of the techniques presented in the chapter, such as session tracking and connecting to a database.

`www.411asp.net`
This resource site provides programmers with ASP.NET tutorials and code samples. The community pages allow programmers to ask questions, answer questions and post messages.

`www.123aspx.com`
This site offers a directory of links to ASP.NET resources. The site also includes daily and weekly newsletters.

Summary

Section 21.1 Introduction

- Microsoft's ASP.NET technology is used for Web application development.
- Web-based applications create Web content for Web browser clients. This Web content includes XHTML, client-side scripting, images and binary data.
- A Web Form file represents a Web page that is sent to the client browser. Web Form files have the filename extension .aspx and contain a Web page's GUI. You customize Web Forms by adding Web controls.
- Every ASPX file created in Visual Studio has a corresponding class written in a .NET language. The file that contains this class is called the code-behind file and provides the ASPX file's programmatic implementation.

Section 21.2 Simple HTTP Transactions

- HTTP specifies a set of methods and headers that allow clients and servers to interact and exchange information in a uniform and predictable way.
- In its simplest form, a Web page is nothing more than an XHTML document. This document is a plain text file containing markup that describes to a Web browser how to display and format the document's information.
- Any XHTML document available for viewing over the Web has a corresponding URL.
- Computers that run Web server software make Internet resources such as Web pages available.
- The hostname is the name of the computer on which the resource resides. This computer usually is referred to as the host, because it houses and maintains resources.
- An IP address identifies a server in a manner similar to how a telephone number uniquely defines a particular phone line.
- MIME is an Internet standard that specifies the way in which certain types of data must be formatted so that programs can interpret the data correctly. Popular MIME types include text/plain and image/jpeg.

Section 21.3 Multitier Application Architecture

- Web applications are multitier applications (sometimes referred to as *n*-tier applications). Multitier applications divide functionality into separate tiers (i.e., logical groupings of functionality).
- The information tier, or bottom tier, maintains data pertaining to the application.
- The middle tier implements business logic, controller logic and presentation logic to control interactions between the application's clients and the application's data.
- The client tier, or top tier, is the application's user interface, which is typically a Web browser.

Section 21.4 Creating and Running a Simple Web-Form Example

- An ASP.NET Web Form consists of an ASPX file and a C# code-behind file.
- Visual Web Developer generates markup when you change a Web Form's properties and when you add text or controls to a Web Form.

Section 21.4.1 Examining an ASPX File

- ASP.NET comments begin with <%-- and terminate with --%>.
- A Page directive (delimited by <%@ and %>) specifies information needed by ASP.NET to process an ASPX file. The CodeFile attribute of the Page directive indicates the name of the corresponding code-behind file. The Language attribute specifies the .NET language used in this file.

- When a control's runat attribute is set to "server", the control is processed by ASP.NET on the server, generating an XHTML equivalent.
- The asp: tag prefix in a control declaration indicates that a control is an ASP.NET Web control.
- Each Web control maps to a corresponding XHTML element (or group of elements)—when processing a Web control on the server, ASP.NET generates XHTML markup that will be sent to the client to represent that control in a Web browser.

Section 21.4.2 Examining a Code-Behind File
- The code-behind file is a partial class.
- Namespace System.Web.UI contains classes for the creation of Web applications and controls.
- Class Page defines a standard Web page, providing event handlers and objects necessary for creating Web-based applications. All Web applications directly or indirectly inherit from class Page.
- Class Control is the base class that provides common functionality for all Web controls.
- Method Page_Init handles the Init event, which indicates that a page is ready to be initialized.

Section 21.4.3 Relationship Between an ASPX File and a Code-Behind File
- When a client requests an ASPX file, ASP.NET creates two classes behind the scenes.
- The first file ASP.NET generates is another partial class, based on the markup in the ASPX file, containing the remaining portion of the class partially defined by the code-behind file.
- The second class generated by ASP.NET is based on the ASPX file that is used to create the visual aspect of the page. This new class inherits from the class defined by the ASPX file and the code-behind file, which defines the logic of the page. The first time the Web page is requested, this class is compiled, and an instance is created. This instance represents our page—it creates the XHTML that is sent to the client.
- Namespace System.Web.UI.WebControls contains Web controls (derived from class WebControl) for designing a page's user interface.

Section 21.4.4 How the Code in an ASP.NET Web Page Executes
- When an instance of a page is created, the Init event occurs first, invoking method Page_Init. After Page_Init executes, the Load event occurs and the Page_Load event handler executes. This event handler is inherited from class Page and is typically overridden to perform any processing that is necessary to restore data from previous requests.
- After Page_Load finishes executing, the page processes any events raised by the page's controls.
- When a Web Form object is ready for garbage collection, an Unload event occurs. Event handler Page_Unload is inherited from class Page and contains any code that releases resources.

Section 21.4.5 Examining the XHTML Generated by an ASP.NET Application
- A form is a mechanism for collecting user information and sending it to the Web server.
- XHTML forms can contain visual and nonvisual components.
- Nonvisual components in an XHTML form, called hidden inputs, store any data that the document author specifies.

Section 21.4.6 Building an ASP.NET Web Application
- The name localhost indicates that the client and server reside on the same machine. If the Web server were located on a different machine, localhost would be replaced with the appropriate IP address or hostname.
- DOCUMENT is the name used to represent a Web Form in the **Properties** window.

- The Web Forms Designer's **Source** mode allows you to view the markup that represents the user interface of a page. The **Design** mode allows you to view the page as it will look and modify it by dragging and dropping controls from the **Toolbox** onto the Web Form.

- Controls and other elements are placed sequentially on a Web Form, much like how text and images are placed in a document using word processing software like Microsoft Word. The positions of controls and other elements are relative to the Web Form's upper-left corner, so this type of layout is known as relative positioning.

- An alternate type of layout is known as absolute positioning, in which controls are located exactly where they are dropped on the Web Form.

- Visual Web Developer is a WYSIWYG (What You See Is What You Get) editor—whenever you make a change to a Web Form in **Design** mode, the IDE creates the markup (visible in **Source** mode) necessary to achieve the desired visual effects seen in **Design** mode.

- Web.config is a file that stores configuration settings for an ASP.NET Web application.

Section 21.5 Web Controls
- The **Standard** section of the **Toolbox** in Visual Web Developer contains several Web controls.

Section 21.5.1 Text and Graphics Controls
- The **Insert Table** command from the **Layout** menu in **Design** mode allows you to add an XHTML table to a Web Form.

- An Image control inserts an image into a Web page. The ImageUrl property specifies the file location of the image to display.

- A TextBox control allows the you to obtain text from the user and display text to the user.

- A DropDownList control provides a list of options to the user. Each item in the drop-down list is defined by a ListItem element.

- Visual Web Developer displays smart tag menus for many ASP.NET controls to facilitate performing common tasks. A smart tag menu is opened by clicking the small arrowhead that appears in the upper-right corner of the control in **Design** mode.

- A HyperLink control adds a hyperlink to a Web page. The NavigateUrl property of this control specifies the resource that is requested when a user clicks the hyperlink.

- A RadioButtonList control provides a series of radio buttons for the user.

Section 21.5.2 AdRotator Control
- ASP.NET provides the AdRotator Web control for displaying advertisements (or any other images). Using data from an XML file, the AdRotator control randomly selects an image to display and generates a hyperlink to the Web page associated with that image.

- An XmlDataSource references an XML file containing data that will be used in an ASP.NET application. The **AdRotator Tasks** smart tag menu allows you to create a new XmlDataSource that retrieves advertisement data from an XML file.

- The advertisement file used for an AdRotator control contains Ad elements, each of which provides information about a different advertisement.

- Element ImageUrl in an advertisement file specifies the path (location) of the advertisement's image, and element NavigateUrl specifies the URL that loads when a user clicks the advertisement.

- The AlternateText element contains text that displays in place of the image when the browser cannot locate or render the image for some reason.

- Element Impressions specifies how often an image appears, relative to the other images.

Section 21.5.3 Validation Controls

- A validation control (or validator) determines whether the data in another Web control is in the proper format. Validators provide a mechanism for validating user input on the client.

- When the XHTML for a page is created, a validator is converted into ECMAScript. ECMAScript is a scripting language that enhances the functionality and appearance of Web pages.

- The Visible property of a control indicates whether the control appears in the client's browser.

- A RequiredFieldValidator ensures that a control receives user input before a form is submitted.

- A validator's ControlToValidate property indicates which control will be validated.

- A validator's ErrorMessage property contains text to be displayed if the validation fails.

- A RegularExpressionValidator matches a Web control's content against a regular expression. The regular expression that validates the input is assigned to property ValidationExpression.

- Web programmers using ASP.NET often design their Web pages so that the current page reloads when the user submits the form. This event is known as a postback.

- A Page's IsPostBack property determines whether the page is being loaded due to a postback.

- When data is posted to the Web server, the XHTML form's data is accessible to the Web application through the Request object's Form array.

- The EnableViewState attribute determines whether a Web control's state persists (i.e., is retained) when a postback occurs.

Section 21.6 Session Tracking

- Personalization makes it possible for e-businesses to communicate effectively with their customers and also improves users' ability to locate desired products and services.

- To provide personalized services to consumers, e-businesses must be able to recognize clients when they request information from a site.

- The request/response system on which the Web operates is facilitated by HTTP. Unfortunately, HTTP is a stateless protocol—it does not support persistent connections that would enable Web servers to maintain state information regarding particular clients.

- A session represents a unique client on a Web site. If the client leaves a site and then returns later, the client will still be recognized as the same user. To help the server distinguish among clients, each client must identify itself to the server.

- Tracking individual clients is known as session tracking.

Section 21.6.1 Cookies

- A cookie is a piece of data stored in a small text file on the user's computer. A cookie maintains information about the client during and between browser sessions.

- A cookie object is of type HttpCookie. Properties Name and Value of class HttpCookie can be used to retrieve the key and value in a key–value pair (both strings) in a cookie.

- Cookies are sent and received as a collection of type HttpCookieCollection. An application on a server can write cookies to a client using the Response object's Cookies property. Cookies can be accessed programmatically using the Request object's Cookies property. Cookies can be read by an application only if they were created in the domain in which the application is running.

- When a Web Form receives a request, the header includes information such as the request type and any cookies that have been sent previously from the server to be stored on the client machine.

- When the server formulates its response, the header information includes any cookies the server wants to store on the client computer.

- The expiration date of a cookie determines how long the cookie remains on the client's computer. If you do not set an expiration date for a cookie, the Web browser maintains the cookie for the duration of the browsing session.

- Clients can disable cookies in their browsers. If they do this, they may not be able to use certain Web applications.

Section 21.6.2 Session Tracking with HttpSessionState

- C# provides session-tracking capabilities in class HttpSessionState. Every Web Form includes an HttpSessionState object, which is accessible through property Session of class Page.

- When the Web page is requested, an HttpSessionState object is created and assigned to the Page's Session property. Thus, Page property Session is often known as the Session object.

- The Session object's key–value pairs are often referred to as session items.

- Session items are placed into an HttpSessionState object by calling method Add.

- HttpSessionState objects can store any type of object (not just strings) as attribute values. This provides increased flexibility in maintaining client state information.

- Property SessionID contains the unique session ID. The first time a client connects to the Web server, a unique session ID is created for that client. When the client makes additional requests, the client's session ID is compared with the session IDs stored in the Web server's memory to retrieve the HttpSessionState object for that client.

- Property Timeout specifies the maximum amount of time that an HttpSessionState object can be inactive before it is discarded.

- Property Count provides the number of session items contained in a Session object.

- Indexing the Session object with a key name retrieves the corresponding value.

- Property Keys of class HttpSessionState returns a collection containing all the session's keys.

Section 21.7 Case Study: Connecting to a Database in ASP.NET

- A GridView ASP.NET data control displays data on a Web Form in a tabular format.

Section 21.7.1 Building a Web Form That Displays Data from a Database

- A GridView's colors can be set using the **Auto Format…** link in the **GridView Tasks** smart tag menu.

- A database used by an ASP.NET Web site should be located in the project's App_Data folder.

- A SqlDataSource control allows a Web application to interact with a database.

- When a SqlDataSource is configured to perform INSERT SQL operations against the database table from which it gathers data, you must specify the values to insert either programmatically or through other controls on the Web Form.

- The **Command and Parameter Editor**, accessed by clicking the ellipsis next to a SqlDataSource's InsertQuery property, allows you to specify that parameter values come from controls.

- Each column in a GridView is represented as a BoundField.

- SqlDataSource property ConnectionString indicates the connection through which the SqlDataSource control interacts with the database.

- An ASP.NET expression, delimited by <%$ and %>, can be used to access a connection string stored in an application's Web.config configuration file.

Section 21.7.2 Modifying the Code-Behind File for the Guestbook Application

- A `SqlDataSource`'s `InsertParameters` collection contains an item corresponding to each parameter in the `SqlDataSource`'s `INSERT` command. Setting the `DefaultValue` of this `Item` allows you to set the value to be inserted.

- `SqlDataSource` method `Insert` executes the control's `INSERT` command against the database.

- `GridView` method `DataBind` refreshes the information displayed in the `GridView`.

Section 21.8.1 Examining the Completed Secure Books Database Application

- Forms authentication is a technique that protects a page so that only users known to the Web site can access it. Such users are known as the site's members.

- ASP.NET login controls help create secure applications using authentication. These controls are found in the **Login** section of the **Toolbox**.

- When a user's identity is confirmed, the user is said to have been authenticated.

- A master page defines common GUI elements that are inherited by each page in a set of content pages. Just as C# classes can inherit instance variables and methods from existing classes, content pages inherit elements from master pages—this is known as visual inheritance.

Section 21.8.2 Creating the Secure Books Database Application

- ASP.NET hides the details of authenticating users, displaying appropriate success or error messages and redirecting the user to the correct page based on the authentication results.

- The **Web Site Administration Tool** allows you to configure an application's security settings, add site users and create access rules that determine who is allowed to access the site.

- By default, anonymous users who attempt to load a page in a directory to which they are denied access are redirected to a page named `Login.aspx` so that they can identify themselves.

- In an ASP.NET application, a page's configuration settings are determined by the current directory's `Web.config` file. The settings in this file take precedence over the settings in the root directory's `Web.config` file.

- A master page contains placeholders for custom content created in a content page, which visually inherits the master page's content, then adds content in place of the placeholders.

- Master pages have the filename extension `.master` and, like Web Forms, can optionally use a code-behind file to define additional functionality.

- A `Master` directive in an ASPX file specifies that the file defines a master page.

- A `ContentPlaceHolder` control serves as a placeholder for page-specific content defined by a content page using a `Content` control. The `Content` control will appear in place of the master page's `ContentPlaceHolder` when the content page is requested.

- A `CreateUserWizard` control provides a registration form that site visitors can use to create a user account. ASP.NET handles the details of creating a SQL Server database to store the user names, passwords and other account information of the application's users.

- A `Login` control encapsulates the details of logging a user into a Web application (i.e., authenticating a user by comparing the provided user name and password with those of an account in the ASP.NET-created membership database). If the user is authenticated, the browser is redirected to the page specified by the `Login` control's `DestinationPageUrl` property. If the user is not authenticated, the `Login` control displays an error message.

- ASP.NET writes to the client an encrypted cookie containing data about an authenticated user.

- Encrypted data is data translated into a code that only the sender and receiver can understand.

- A `LoginName` control displays the current authenticated user name on a Web Form.

- A `LoginStatus` control renders on a Web page in one of two ways—by default, if the user is not authenticated (the **Logged Out** view), the control displays a hyperlink with the text `Login`; if the user is authenticated (the **Logged In** view), the control displays a hyperlink with the text `Logout`. The `LogoutText` determines the text of the link in the **Logged In** view.

- An `ObjectDataSource` control encapsulates a business object that provides access to a data source. A business object (e.g., a `TableAdapter`) represents the middle tier of an application and mediates interactions between the bottom tier and the top tier.

- The `AS` SQL keyword allows you to generate a column in a query result—called an alias—that contains the result of a SQL expression.

- A `DropDownList`'s `AutoPostBack` property indicates whether a postback occurs each time the user selects an item.

- When you **Enable Sorting** for a `GridView`, the column headings in the `GridView` turn into hyperlinks that allow users to sort the data it displays.

- When you **Enable Paging** for a `GridView`, the `GridView` divides its data among multiple pages. The user can click the numbered links at the bottom of the `GridView` control to display a different page of data. `GridView`'s `PageSize` property determines the number of entries per page.

Terminology

<%-- --%> ASP.NET delimiters
<%$ %> ASP.NET expression delimiters
<%@ %> ASP.NET directive delimiters
absolute positioning
access rule in ASP.NET
action attribute of XHTML element `form`
Ad XML element in an `AdRotator` advertisement
    file
Add method of class `Hashtable`
Add method of class `HttpSessionState`
`AdRotator` ASP.NET Web control
`Advertisements` XML element in an `AdRotator`
    advertisement file
alias in SQL
`AlternateText` element in an `AdRotator`
    advertisement file
anonymous user
AS SQL keyword
asp: tag prefix
ASP.NET 20
ASP.NET comment
ASP.NET expression
ASP.NET login control
ASP.NET server control
ASP.NET Web Site in Visual Web Developer
ASPX file
.aspx filename extension
authenticating a user
`authentication` element in `Web.config`
`authorization` element in `Web.config`
`AutoEventWireup` attribute of ASP.NET page

`AutoPostBack` property of a `DropDownList`
bottom tier
`BoundField` ASP.NET element
Build Page command in Visual Web Developer
Build Site command in Visual Web Developer
business logic
business object
business rule
`Button` ASP.NET Web control
client tier
code-behind file
`CodeFile` attribute in a `Page` directive
`ConnectionString` property of a `SqlDataSource`
`Content` ASP.NET control
content page in ASP.NET
`ContentPlaceHolder` ASP.NET control
`Control` class
controller logic
`ControlParameter` ASP.NET element
`ControlToValidate` property of a validation
    control
cookie
`Cookies` collection of the `Response` object
`Cookies` property of class `Request`
`Count` property of class `HttpSessionState`
`CreateUserWizard` ASP.NET login control
data tier
`DataSourceID` property of a `GridView`
`DeleteCommand` property of a `SqlDataSource`
`deny` element in `Web.config`
Design mode in Visual Web Developer

22

Web Services

OBJECTIVES

In this chapter you will learn:

- What a Web service is.
- How to create Web services.
- The important part that XML and the XML-based Simple Object Access Protocol play in enabling Web services.
- The elements that comprise Web services, such as service descriptions and discovery files.
- How to create a client that uses a Web service.
- How to use Web services with Windows applications and Web applications.
- How to use session tracking in Web services to maintain state information for the client.
- How to pass user-defined types to a Web service.

22.1 Introduction

This chapter introduces Web services, which promote software reusability in distributed systems where applications execute across multiple computers on a network. A *Web service* is a class that allows its methods to be called by methods on other machines via common data formats and protocols, such as XML (see Chapter 19) and HTTP. In .NET, the over-the-network method calls are commonly implemented through the *Simple Object Access Protocol (SOAP)*, an XML-based protocol describing how to mark up requests and responses so that they can be transferred via protocols such as HTTP. Using SOAP, applications represent and transmit data in a standardized XML-based format.

Microsoft is encouraging software vendors and e-businesses to deploy Web services. As increasing numbers of organizations worldwide have connected to the Internet, the concept of applications that call methods across a network has become more practical. Web services represent the next step in object-oriented programming—rather than developing software from a small number of class libraries provided at one location, programmers can access Web service class libraries distributed worldwide.

Performance Tip 22.1

Web services are not the best solution for certain performance-intensive applications, because applications that invoke Web services experience network delays. Also, data transfers are typically larger because data is transmitted in text-based XML formats.

Web services facilitate collaboration and allow businesses to grow. By purchasing Web services and using extensive free Web services that are relevant to their businesses, companies can spend less time developing new applications. E-businesses can use Web services to provide their customers with enhanced shopping experiences. Consider an online music store. The store's Web site provides links to information about various CDs, enabling users to purchase the CDs or to learn about the artists. Another company that sells concert tickets provides a Web service that displays upcoming concert dates for various artists, then allows users to buy tickets. By consuming the concert-ticket Web service on its site, the online music store can provide an additional service to its customers and increase its site traffic. The company that sells concert tickets also benefits from the business relationship by selling more tickets and possibly by receiving revenue from the online music store for the use of its Web service. Many Web services are provided at no charge. For example, Amazon and Google offer free Web services that you can use in your own applications to access the information they provide.

Visual Web Developer and the .NET Framework provide a simple, user-friendly way to create Web services. In this chapter, we show how to use these tools to create, deploy and use Web services. For each example, we provide the code for the Web service, then present an application that uses the Web service. Our first examples analyze Web services and how they work in Visual Web Developer. Then we demonstrate Web services that use more sophisticated features, such as session tracking (discussed in Chapter 21) and manipulating objects of user-defined types.

As in Chapter 21, we distinguish between Visual C# 2005 Express and Visual Web Developer 2005 Express in this chapter. We create Web services in Visual Web Developer, and we create client applications that use these Web services using both Visual C# 2005 and Visual Web Developer 2005. The full version of Visual Studio 2005 includes the functionality of both Express editions.

22.2 .NET Web Services Basics

A Web service is a software component stored on one machine that can be accessed by an application (or other software component) on another machine over a network. The machine on which the Web service resides is referred to as a *remote machine*. The application (i.e., the client) that accesses the Web service sends a method call over a network to the remote machine, which processes the call and returns a response over the network to the application. This kind of distributed computing benefits various systems. For example, an application without direct access to certain data on another system might be able to retrieve this data via a Web service. Similarly, an application lacking the processing power necessary to perform specific computations could use a Web service to take advantage of another system's superior resources.

A Web service is typically implemented as a class. In previous chapters, we included a class in a project either by defining the class in the project or by adding a reference to a compiled DLL. All the pieces of an application resided on one machine. When a client uses a Web service, the class (and its compiled DLL) is stored on a remote machine—a compiled version of the Web service class is not placed in the current application's directory. We discuss what happens shortly.

Requests to and responses from Web services created with Visual Web Developer are typically transmitted via SOAP. So any client capable of generating and processing SOAP messages can interact with a Web service, regardless of the language in which the Web service is written. We say more about SOAP in Section 22.3.

It is possible for Web services to limit access to authorized clients. See the Web Resources at the end of the chapter for links to information on standard mechanisms and protocols addressing Web service security concerns.

Web services have important implications for *business-to-business* (*B2B*) *transactions*. They enable businesses to conduct transactions via standardized, widely available Web services rather than relying on proprietary applications. Web services and SOAP are platform and language independent, so companies can collaborate via Web services without worrying about the compatibility of their hardware, software and communications technologies. Companies such as Amazon, Google, eBay and many others are using Web services to their advantage. To read case studies of Web services used in business, visit `msdn.microsoft.com/webservices/understanding/casestudies/default.aspx`.

22.2.1 Creating a Web Service in Visual Web Developer

To create a Web service in Visual Web Developer, you first create a project of type **ASP.NET Web Service**. Visual Web Developer then generates the following:

- files to contain the Web service code (which implements the Web service)
- an *ASMX file* (which provides access to the Web service)
- a *DISCO file* (which potential clients use to discover the Web service)

Figure 22.1 displays the files that comprise a Web service. When you create an **ASP.NET Web Service** application in Visual Web Developer, the IDE typically generates several additional files. We show only those files that are specific to Web services applications. We discuss these files in Section 22.2.2.

Visual Web Developer generates code files for the Web service class and any other code that is part of the Web service implementation. In the Web service class, you define the methods that your Web service makes available to client applications. Like ASP.NET Web applications, ASP.NET Web services can be tested using Visual Web Developer's built-in test server. However, to make an ASP.NET Web service publicly accessible to clients outside Visual Web Developer, you must deploy the Web service to a Web server such as an Internet Information Services (IIS) Web server.

Methods in a Web service are invoked through a *Remote Procedure Call* (*RPC*). These methods, which are marked with the **WebMethod** attribute, are often referred to as *Web service methods* or simply *Web methods*—we refer to them as Web methods from this point forward. Declaring a method with attribute WebMethod makes the method accessible to other classes through RPCs and is known as *exposing* a Web method. We discuss the details of exposing Web methods in Section 22.4.

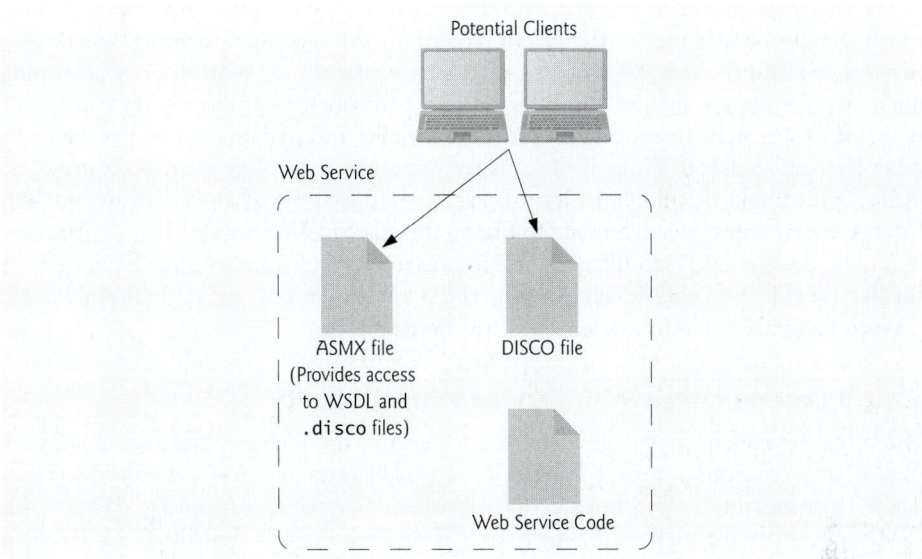

Fig. 22.1 | Web service components.

22.2.2 Discovering Web Services

Once you implement a Web service, compile it and deploy it on a Web server (discussed in Section 22.4), a client application can *consume* (i.e., use) the Web service. However, clients must be able to find the Web service and learn about its capabilities. *Discovery of Web services* (*DISCO*) is a Microsoft-specific technology used to locate Web services on a server. Four types of DISCO files facilitate the discovery process: .disco files, .vsdisco files, .discomap files and .map files.

DISCO files consist of XML markup that describes for clients the location of Web services. A .disco file is accessed via a Web service's ASMX page and contains markup specifying references to the documents that define various Web services. The resulting data that is returned from accessing a .disco file is placed in the .discomap file.

A .vsdisco file is placed in a Web service's application directory and behaves in a slightly different manner. When a potential client requests a .vsdisco file, XML markup describing the locations of Web services is generated dynamically, then returned to the client. First, the .NET Framework searches for Web services in the directory in which the .vsdisco file is located, as well as that directory's subdirectories. The .NET Framework then generates XML (using the same syntax as that of a .disco file) that contains references to all the Web services found in this search.

Note that a .vsdisco file does not store the markup generated in response to a request. Instead, the .vsdisco file on disk contains configuration settings that specify the .vsdisco file's behavior. For example, developers can specify in the .vsdisco file certain directories that should *not* be searched when a client requests a .vsdisco file. Although a developer can open a .vsdisco file in a text editor and examine its contents, this is rarely necessary—a .vsdisco file is intended to be requested (i.e., viewed in a browser) by clients over the Web. Every time this occurs, new markup is generated and displayed.

Using .vsdisco files benefits developers in several ways. These files contain only a small amount of data and provide up-to-date information about a server's available Web services. However, .vsdisco files generate more overhead (i.e., require more processing) than .disco files do, because a search must be performed every time a .vsdisco file is accessed. Thus, some developers find it more beneficial to update .disco files manually. Many systems use both types of files. As we discuss shortly, Web services created using ASP.NET contain the functionality to generate a .disco file when it is requested. This .disco file contains references only to files in the current Web service. Thus, a developer typically places a .vsdisco file at the root of a server; when accessed, this file locates the .disco files for Web services anywhere on the system and uses the markup found in these .disco files to return information about the entire system.

22.2.3 Determining a Web Service's Functionality

After locating a Web service, the client must determine the Web service's functionality and how to use it. For this purpose, Web services normally contain a *service description*. This is an XML document that conforms to the *Web Service Description Language* (*WSDL*)—an XML vocabulary that defines the methods a Web service makes available and how clients interact with them. The WSDL document also specifies lower-level information that clients might need, such as the required formats for requests and responses.

WSDL documents are not meant to be read by developers; rather, WSDL documents are meant to be read by applications, so they know how to interact with the Web services described in the documents. Visual Web Developer generates an ASMX file when a Web service is constructed. Files with the *.asmx* filename extension are ASP.NET Web service files and are executed by ASP.NET on a Web server (e.g., IIS). When viewed in a Web browser, an ASMX file presents Web method descriptions and links to test pages that allow users to execute sample calls to these methods. We explain these test pages in greater detail later in this section. The ASMX file also specifies the Web service's implementation class, and optionally the code-behind file in which the Web service is defined and the assemlies referenced by the Web service. When the Web server receives a request for the Web service, it accesses the ASMX file, which, in turn, invokes the Web service implementation. To view more technical information about the Web service, developers can access the WSDL file (which is generated by ASP.NET). We show how to do this shortly.

The ASMX page in Fig. 22.2 displays information about the HugeInteger Web service that we create in Section 22.4. This Web service is designed to perform calculations with integers that contain a maximum of 100 digits. Most programming languages cannot easily perform calculations using integers this large. The Web service provides client applications with methods that take two "huge integers" and determine their sum, their difference, which one is larger or smaller and whether the two numbers are equal. Note that the top of the page provides a link to the Web service's **Service Description**. ASP.NET generates the WSDL service description from the code you write to define the Web service. Client programs use a Web service's service description to validate Web method calls when the client programs are compiled.

ASP.NET generates WSDL information dynamically rather than creating an actual WSDL file. If a client requests the Web service's WSDL description (either by appending *?WSDL* to the ASMX file's URL or by clicking the **Service Description** link), ASP.NET generates the WSDL description, then returns it to the client for display in the Web browser.

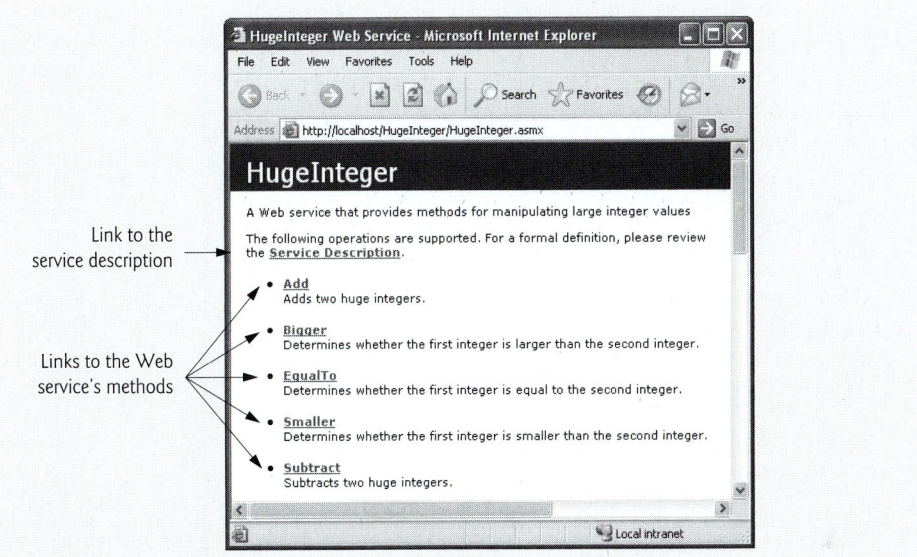

Link to the
service description

Links to the Web
service's methods

Fig. 22.2 | ASMX file rendered in a Web browser.

Generating the WSDL description dynamically ensures that clients receive the most current information about the Web service. It is common for an XML document (such as a WSDL description) to be created dynamically and not saved to disk.

When a user clicks the **Service Description** link at the top of the ASMX page in Fig. 22.2, the browser displays the generated WSDL document containing the service description for our `HugeInteger` Web service (Fig. 22.3).

22.2.4 Testing a Web Service's Methods

Below the **Service Description** link, the ASMX page shown in Fig. 22.2 lists the methods that the Web service offers. Clicking any method name requests a test page that describes the method (Fig. 22.4). The test page allows users to test the method by entering parameter values and clicking the **Invoke** button. (We discuss the process of testing a Web method shortly.) Below the **Invoke** button, the page displays sample request-and-response messages using SOAP and HTTP POST. These protocols are two options for sending and receiving messages in Web services. The protocol that transmits request-and-response messages is also known as the Web service's *wire format* or *wire protocol*, because it defines how information is sent "along the wire." SOAP is the more commonly used wire format, because SOAP messages can be sent using several transport protocols, whereas HTTP POST must use HTTP. When you test a Web service via an ASMX page (as in Fig. 22.4), the ASMX page uses HTTP POST to test the Web service methods. Later in this chapter, when we use Web services in our C# programs, we employ SOAP—the default protocol for .NET Web services.

Figure 22.4 depicts the test page for the `HugeInteger` Web method `Bigger`. From this page, users can test the method by entering values in the **first:** and **second:** fields, then clicking **Invoke**. The method executes, and a new Web browser window opens, displaying an XML document that contains the result (Fig. 22.5).

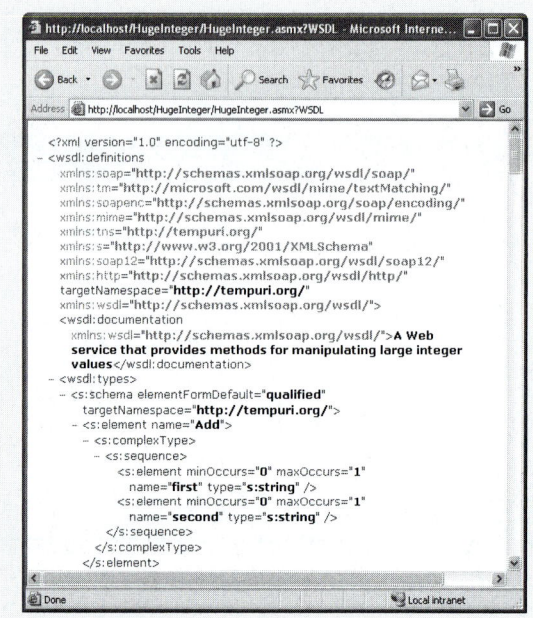

Fig. 22.3 | Service description for our HugeInteger Web service.

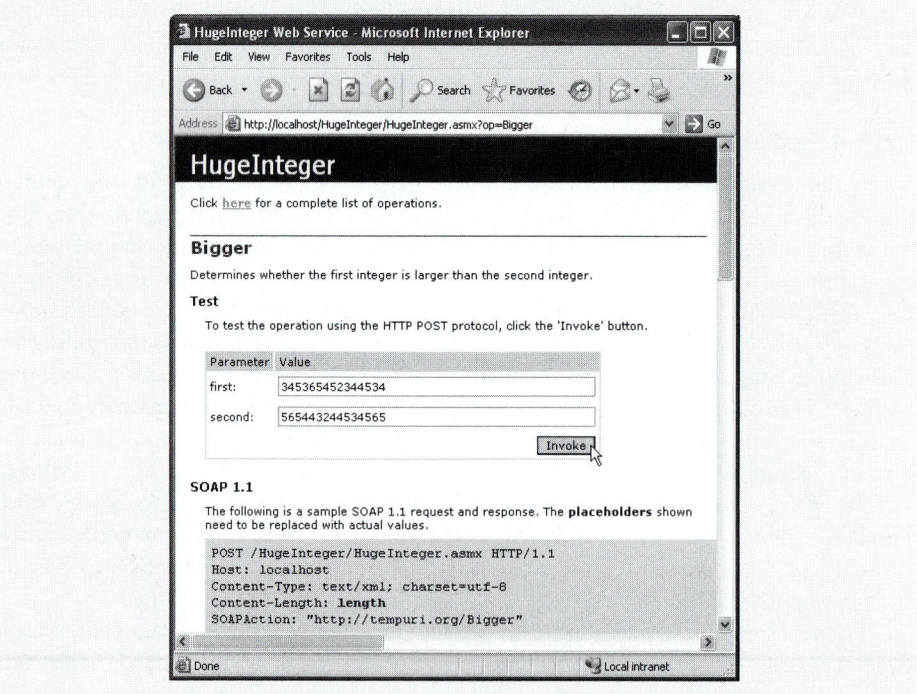

Fig. 22.4 | Invoking a Web method from a Web browser.

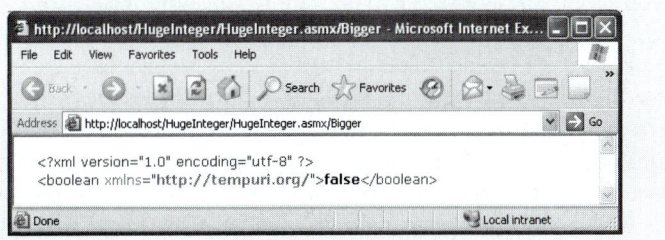

Fig. 22.5 | Results of invoking a Web method from a Web browser.

 Error-Prevention Tip 22.1

Using the ASMX page of a Web service to test and debug methods can help you make the Web service more reliable and robust.

22.2.5 Building a Client to Use a Web Service

Now that we have discussed the different files that comprise a .NET Web service, let's examine the parts of a .NET Web service client (Fig. 22.6). A .NET client can be any type of .NET application, such as a Windows application, a console application or a Web application. You can enable a client application to consume a Web service by *adding a Web reference* to the client. This process adds files to the client application that allow the client to access the Web service. This section discusses Visual C# 2005, but the discussion also applies to Visual Web Developer.

To add a Web reference in Visual C# 2005, right click the project name in the **Solution Explorer** and select **Add Web Reference…**. In the resulting dialog, specify the Web service to consume. Visual C# 2005 then adds an appropriate Web reference to the client application. We demonstrate adding Web references in more detail in Section 22.4.

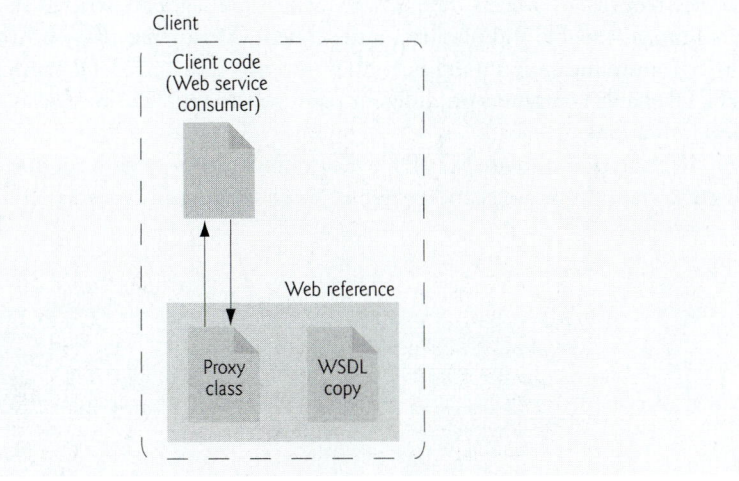

Fig. 22.6 | .NET Web service client after a Web reference has been added.

When you specify the Web service you want to consume, Visual C# 2005 accesses the Web service's WSDL information and copies it into a WSDL file that is stored in the client project's Web References folder. This file is visible when you instruct Visual C# 2005 to **Show All Files**. [*Note:* A copy of the WSDL file provides the client application with local access to the Web service's description. To ensure that the WSDL file is up-to-date, Visual C# 2005 provides an **Update Web Reference** option (available by right clicking the Web reference in the **Solution Explorer**), which updates the files in the Web References folder.] The WSDL information is used to create a *proxy class*, which handles all the "plumbing" required for Web method calls (i.e., the networking details and the formation of SOAP messages). Whenever the client application calls a Web method, the application actually calls a corresponding method in the proxy class. This method has the same name and parameters as the Web method that is being called, but formats the call to be sent as a request in a SOAP message. The Web service receives this request as a SOAP message, executes the method call and sends back the result as another SOAP message. When the client application receives the SOAP message containing the response, the proxy class deserializes it and returns the results as the return value of the Web method that was called. Figure 22.7 depicts the interactions among the client code, proxy class and Web service.

The .NET environment hides most of these details from you. Many aspects of Web service creation and consumption—such as generating WSDL files, proxy classes and DISCO files—are handled by Visual Web Developer, Visual C# 2005 and ASP.NET. Although developers are relieved of the tedious process of creating these files, they can still modify the files if necessary. This is required only when developing advanced Web services—none of our examples require modifications to these files.

22.3 Simple Object Access Protocol (SOAP)

The Simple Object Access Protocol (SOAP) is a platform-independent protocol that uses XML to make remote procedure calls, typically over HTTP. Each request and response is packaged in a *SOAP message*—an XML message containing the information that a Web service requires to process the message. SOAP messages are written in XML so that they are human readable and platform independent. Most *firewalls*—security barriers that restrict communication among networks—do not restrict HTTP traffic. Thus, XML and HTTP enable computers on different platforms to send and receive SOAP messages with few limitations.

Web services also use SOAP for the extensive set of types it supports. The wire format used to transmit requests and responses must support all types passed between the appli-

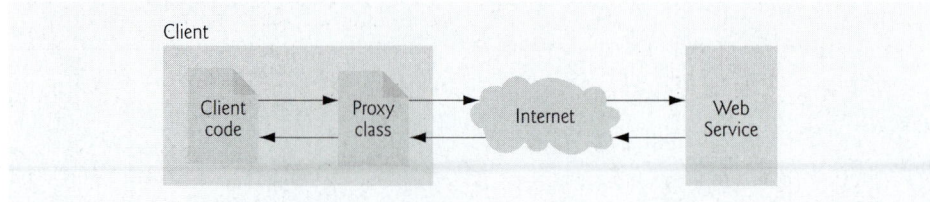

Fig. 22.7 | Interaction between a Web service client and a Web service.

cations. SOAP types include the primitive types (e.g., Integer), as well as DateTime, Xml-Node and others. SOAP can also transmit arrays of all these types. In addition, DataSets can be serialized into SOAP. In Section 22.7, you will see that you can transmit user-defined types in SOAP messages.

When a program invokes a Web method, the request and all relevant information are packaged in a SOAP message and sent to the server on which the Web service resides. When the Web service receives this SOAP message, it begins to process the contents (contained in a *SOAP envelope*), which specify the method that the client wishes to execute and any arguments the client is passing to that method. This process of interpreting a SOAP message's contents is known as *parsing a SOAP message*. After the Web service receives and parses a request, the proper method is called with the specified arguments (if there are any), and the response is sent back to the client in another SOAP message. The client parses the response to retrieve the result of the method call.

The SOAP request in Fig. 22.8 was taken from the test page for the HugeInteger Web service's Bigger method (Fig. 22.4). Visual C# 2005 creates such a message when a client wishes to execute the HugeInteger Web service's Bigger method. If the client is a Web application, Visual Web Developer creates the SOAP message. The message in Fig. 22.8 contains placeholders (length in line 4 and string in lines 16–17) representing values specific to a particular call to Bigger. If this were a real SOAP request, elements first and second (lines 16–17) would each contain an actual value passed from the client to the Web service, rather than the placeholder string. For example, if this envelope were transmitting the request from Fig. 22.4, element first and element second would contain the numbers displayed in the figure, and placeholder length (line 4) would contain the length of the SOAP message. Most programmers do not manipulate SOAP messages directly, but instead allow the .NET framework to handle the transmission details.

```
 1   POST /HugeInteger/HugeInteger.asmx HTTP/1.1
 2   Host: localhost
 3   Content-Type: text/xml; charset=utf-8
 4   Content-Length: length
 5   SOAPAction: "http://www.deitel.com/Bigger"
 6
 7   <?xml version="1.0" encoding="utf-8"?>
 8
 9   <soap:Envelope
10      xmlns:xsi="http://www.w3.org/2001/XMLSchema-instance"
11      xmlns:xsd="http://www.w3.org/2001/XMLSchema"
12      xmlns:soap="http://schemas.xmlsoap.org/soap/envelope/">
13
14     <soap:Body>
15        <Bigger xmlns="http://www.deitel.com">
16           <first>string</first>
17           <second>string</second>
18        </Bigger>
19     </soap:Body>
20   </soap:Envelope>
```

Fig. 22.8 | SOAP request message for the HugeInteger Web service.

22.4 Publishing and Consuming Web Services

This section presents several examples of creating (also known as *publishing*) and using (also known as *consuming*) Web services. Recall that an application that consumes a Web service actually consists of two parts—a proxy class representing the Web service and a client application that accesses the Web service via an instance of the proxy class. The instance of the proxy class passes a Web method's arguments from the client application to the Web service. When the Web method completes its task, the instance of the proxy class receives the result and parses it for the client application. Visual C# 2005 and Visual Web Developer create these proxy classes for you. We demonstrate this momentarily.

22.4.1 Defining the HugeInteger Web Service

Figure 22.9 presents the code-behind file for the HugeInteger Web service that you will build in Section 22.4.2. When creating Web services in Visual Web Developer, you work almost exclusively in the code-behind file. As we mentioned earlier, this Web service is designed to perform calculations with integers that have a maximum of 100 digits. long variables cannot handle integers of this size (i.e., an overflow occurs). The Web service provides methods that take two "huge integers" (represented as strings) and determine their sum, their difference, which one is larger or smaller and whether the two numbers are equal. You can think of these methods as *services* available to programmers of other applications via the *Web* (hence the term Web services). Any programmer can access this Web service, use the methods and thus avoid writing 172 lines of code.

```
1   // Fig. 22.9: HugeInteger.cs
2   // HugeInteger Web service performs operations on large integers.
3   using System;
4   using System.Web;
5   using System.Web.Services;
6   using System.Web.Services.Protocols;
7
8   [ WebService( Namespace = "http://www.deitel.com/",
9      Description = "A Web service that provides methods for" +
10     " manipulating large integer values" ) ]
11  [ WebServiceBinding( ConformsTo = WsiProfiles.BasicProfile1_1 ) ]
12  public class HugeInteger : System.Web.Services.WebService
13  {
14     private const int MAXIMUM = 100; // maximum number of digits
15     public int[] number; // array representing the huge integer
16
17     // default constructor
18     public HugeInteger()
19     {
20        number = new int[ MAXIMUM ];
21     } // end default constructor
22
23     // indexer that accepts an integer parameter
24     public int this[ int index ]
25     {
```

Fig. 22.9 | HugeInteger Web service. (Part 1 of 4.)

```
26        get
27        {
28           return number[ index ];
29        } // end get
30
31        set
32        {
33           number[ index ] = value;
34        } // end set
35     } // end indexer
36
37     // returns string representation of HugeInteger
38     public override string ToString()
39     {
40        string returnString = "";
41
42        foreach ( int i in number )
43           returnString = i + returnString;
44
45        return returnString;
46     } // end method ToString
47
48     // creates HugeInteger based on argument
49     public static HugeInteger FromString( string value )
50     {
51        // create temporary HugeInteger to be returned by the method
52        HugeInteger parsedInteger = new HugeInteger();
53
54        for ( int i = 0 ; i < value.Length; i++ )
55           parsedInteger[ i ] = Int32.Parse(
56              value[ value.Length - i - 1 ].ToString() );
57
58        return parsedInteger;
59     } // end method FromString
60
61     // WebMethod that adds integers represented by the string arguments
62     [ WebMethod( Description = "Adds two huge integers." ) ]
63     public string Add( string first, string second )
64     {
65        int carry = 0;
66        HugeInteger operand1 = HugeInteger.FromString( first );
67        HugeInteger operand2 = HugeInteger.FromString( second );
68        HugeInteger result = new HugeInteger(); // stores result of addition
69
70        // perform addition algorithm for each digit
71        for ( int i = 0; i < MAXIMUM; i++ )
72        {
73           // add two digits in same column,
74           // result is their sum plus carry from
75           // previous operation modulo 10
76           result[ i ] =
77              ( operand1[ i ] + operand2[ i ] + carry ) % 10;
78
```

Fig. 22.9 | HugeInteger Web service. (Part 2 of 4.)

```
79         // set carry to remainder of dividing sums of two digits by 10
80         carry = ( operand1[ i ] + operand2[ i ] + carry ) / 10;
81      } // end for
82
83      return result.ToString();
84   } // end method Add
85
86   // WebMethod that subtracts integers
87   // represented by the string arguments
88   [ WebMethod( Description = "Subtracts two huge integers." ) ]
89   public string Subtract( string first, string second )
90   {
91      HugeInteger operand1 = HugeInteger.FromString( first );
92      HugeInteger operand2 = HugeInteger.FromString( second );
93      HugeInteger result = new HugeInteger();
94
95      // subtract bottom digit from top digit
96      for ( int i = 0; i < MAXIMUM; i++ )
97      {
98         // if top digit is smaller than bottom digit we need to borrow
99         if ( operand1[ i ] < operand2[ i ] )
100            Borrow( operand1, i );
101
102         // subtract bottom from top
103         result[ i ] = operand1[ i ] - operand2[ i ];
104      } // end for
105
106      return result.ToString();
107   } // end method Subtract
108
109   // borrow 1 from next digit
110   private void Borrow( HugeInteger hugeInteger, int place )
111   {
112      // if no place to borrow from, signal problem
113      if ( place >= MAXIMUM - 1 )
114         throw new ArgumentException();
115
116      // otherwise if next digit is zero, borrow from column to left
117      else if ( hugeInteger[ place + 1 ] == 0 )
118         Borrow( hugeInteger, place + 1 );
119
120      // add ten to current place because we borrowed and subtract
121      // one from previous digit--this is the digit we borrowed from
122      hugeInteger[ place ] += 10;
123      hugeInteger[ place + 1 ]--;
124   } // end method Borrow
125
126   // WebMethod that returns true if first integer is bigger than second
127   [ WebMethod( Description = "Determines whether the first integer is " +
128      "larger than the second integer." ) ]
129   public bool Bigger( string first, string second )
130   {
131      char[] zeros = { '0' };
```

Fig. 22.9 | HugeInteger Web service. (Part 3 of 4.)

```
132
133        try
134        {
135            // if elimination of all zeros from result
136            // of subtraction is an empty string,
137            // numbers are equal, so return false, otherwise return true
138            if ( Subtract( first, second ).Trim( zeros ) == "" )
139                return false;
140            else
141                return true;
142        } // end try
143        // if ArgumentException occurs,
144        // first number was smaller, so return false
145        catch ( ArgumentException exception )
146        {
147            return false;
148        } // end catch
149    } // end method Bigger
150
151    // WebMethod returns true if first integer is smaller than second
152    [ WebMethod( Description = "Determines whether the first integer " +
153        "is smaller than the second integer." ) ]
154    public bool Smaller( string first, string second )
155    {
156        // if second is bigger than first, then first is smaller than second
157        return Bigger( second, first );
158    } // end method Smaller
159
160    // WebMethod that returns true if two integers are equal
161    [ WebMethod( Description = "Determines whether the first integer " +
162        "is equal to the second integer." ) ]
163    public bool EqualTo( string first, string second )
164    {
165        // if either first is bigger than second,
166        // or first is smaller than second, they are not equal
167        if ( Bigger( first, second ) || Smaller( first, second ) )
168            return false;
169        else
170            return true;
171    } // end method EqualTo
172 } // end class HugeInteger
```

Fig. 22.9 | HugeInteger Web service. (Part 4 of 4.)

Lines 8–10 contain a *WebService* attribute. Attaching this attribute to a Web service class declaration allows you to specify the Web service's namespace and description. Like an XML namespace (see Section 19.4), a Web service's namespace is used by client applications to differentiate that Web service from others available on the Web. Line 8 assigns http://www.deitel.com as the Web service's namespace using the WebService attribute's *Namespace* property. Lines 9–10 use the WebService attribute's *Description* property to describe the Web service's purpose—this appears in the ASMX page (Fig. 22.2).

Visual Web Developer places line 11 in all newly created Web services. This line indicates that the Web service conforms to the *Basic Profile 1.1* (*BP 1.1*) developed by the *Web*

Services Interoperability Organization (*WS-I*), a group dedicated to promoting interoperability among Web services developed on different platforms with different programming languages. BP 1.1 is a document that defines best practices for various aspects of Web service creation and consumption (www.WS-I.org). As we discussed in Section 22.2, the .NET environment hides many of these details from you. Setting the *WebServiceBinding* attribute's *ConformsTo* property to *WsiProfiles.BasicProfile1_1* instructs Visual Web Developer to perform its "behind-the-scenes" work, such as generating WSDL and ASMX files, in conformance with the guidelines laid out in BP 1.1. For more information on Web services interoperabilty and the Basic Profile 1.1, visit the WS-I Web site at www.ws-i.org.

By default, each new Web service class created in Visual Web Developer inherits from class `System.Web.Services.WebService` (line 12). Although a Web service need not derive from class `WebService`, this class provides members that are useful in determining information about the client and the Web service itself. Several methods in class `Huge-Integer` are tagged with the `WebMethod` attribute (lines 62, 88, 127, 152 and 161), which exposes a method so that it can be called remotely. When this attribute is absent, the method is not accessible to clients that consume the Web service. Note that this attribute, like the `WebService` attribute, contains a `Description` property that allows the ASMX page to display information about the method (see these descriptions shown in Fig. 22.2).

Common Programming Error 22.1

Failing to expose a method as a Web method by declaring it with the `WebMethod` attribute prevents clients of the Web service from accessing the method.

Portability Tip 22.1

Specify a namespace for each Web service so that it can be uniquely identified by clients. In general, you should use your company's domain name as the Web service's namespace, since company domain names are guaranteed to be unique.

Portability Tip 22.2

Specify descriptions for a Web service and its Web methods so that the Web service's clients can view information about the service in the service's ASMX page.

Common Programming Error 22.2

No method with the `WebMethod` attribute can be declared `static`—for a client to access a Web method, an instance of that Web service must exist.

Lines 24–35 define an indexer, which enables us to access any digit in a `HugeInteger`. Lines 62–84 and 88–107 define Web methods `Add` and `Subtract`, which perform addition and subtraction, respectively. Method `Borrow` (lines 110–124) handles the case in which the digit that we are currently examining in the left operand is smaller than the corresponding digit in the right operand. For instance, when we subtract 19 from 32, we usually examine the numbers in the operands digit-by-digit, starting from the right. The number 2 is smaller than 9, so we add 10 to 2 (resulting in 12). After borrowing, we can subtract 9 from 12, resulting in 3 for the rightmost digit in the solution. We then subtract 1 from the 3 in 32—the next digit to the left (i.e., the digit we borrowed from). This leaves a 2 in the tens place. The corresponding digit in the other operand is now the 1 in 19. Subtracting 1 from 2 yields 1, making the corresponding digit in the result 1. The final result, when the digits are put together, is 13. Method `Borrow` is the method that adds 10 to the appropriate digits and subtracts 1 from the digits to the left. This is a utility method that is not intended to be called remotely, so it is not qualified with attribute `WebMethod`.

Recall that Fig. 22.2 presented a screen capture of the ASMX page `HugeInteger.asmx` for which the code-behind file `HugeInteger.cs` (Fig. 22.9) defines Web methods. A client application can invoke only the five methods listed in the screen capture in Fig. 22.2 (i.e., the methods qualified with the `WebMethod` attribute in Fig. 22.9).

22.4.2 Building a Web Service in Visual Web Developer

We now show you how to create the `HugeInteger` Web service. In the following steps, you will create an **ASP.NET Web Service** project that executes on your computer's local IIS Web server. To create the `HugeInteger` Web service in Visual Web Developer, perform the following steps:

Step 1: Creating the Project
To begin, we must create a project of type **ASP.NET Web Service**. Select **File > New Web Site...** to display the **New Web Site** dialog (Fig. 22.10). Select **ASP.NET Web Service** in the **Templates** pane. Select **HTTP** from the **Location** drop-down list to indicate that the files should be placed on a Web server. By default, Visual Web Developer indicates that it will place the files on the local machine's IIS Web server in a virtual directory named `WebSite` (`http://localhost/WebSite`). Replace the name `WebSite` with `HugeInteger` for this example. Next, select **Visual C#** from the **Language** drop-down list to indicate that you will use Visual C# to build this Web service. Visual Web Developer places the Web service project's solution file (`.sln`) in the `Projects` subfolder within the current Windows user's `My Documents\Visual Studio 2005` folder. If you do not have access to an IIS Web server to build and test the examples in this chapter, you can select **File System** from the **Location** drop-down list. In this case, Visual Web Developer will place your Web service's files on your local hard disk. You will then be able to test the Web service using Visual Web Developer's built-in Web server.

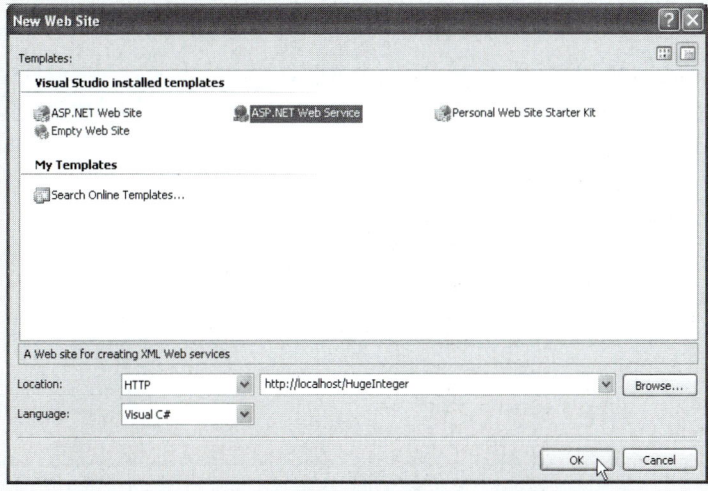

Fig. 22.10 | Creating an **ASP.NET Web Service** in Visual Web Developer.

Step 2: Examining the Newly Created Project

When the project is created, the code-behind file Service.cs, which contains code for a simple Web service (Fig. 22.11) is displayed by default. If the code-behind file is not open, it can be opened by double clicking the file in the **App_Code** directory listed in the **Solution Explorer**. Visual Web Developer includes four using declarations that are helpful for developing Web services (lines 1–4). By default, a new code-behind file defines a class named Service that is marked with the WebService and WebServiceBinding attributes (lines 6–7). The class contains a sample Web method named HelloWorld (lines 14–17). This method is a placeholder that you will replace with your own method(s).

Step 3: Modifying and Renaming the Code-Behind File

To create the HugeInteger Web service developed in this section, modify Service.cs by replacing all of the sample code provided by Visual Web Developer with all of the code from the HugeInteger code-behind file (Fig. 22.9). Then rename the file HugeInteger.cs (by right clicking the file in the **Solution Explorer** and choosing **Rename**).

Step 4: Examining the ASMX File

The **Solution Explorer** lists one file—Service.asmx—in addition to the code-behind file. Recall from Fig. 22.2 that a Web service's ASMX page, when accessed through a Web browser, displays information about the Web service's methods and provides access to the Web service's WSDL information. However, if you open the ASMX file on disk, you will see that it actually contains only

```
<%@ WebService Language="C#" CodeBehind="~/App_Code/Service.cs"
    Class="Service" %>
```

to indicate the programming language in which the Web service's code-behind file is written, the code-behind file's location and the class that defines the Web service. When you

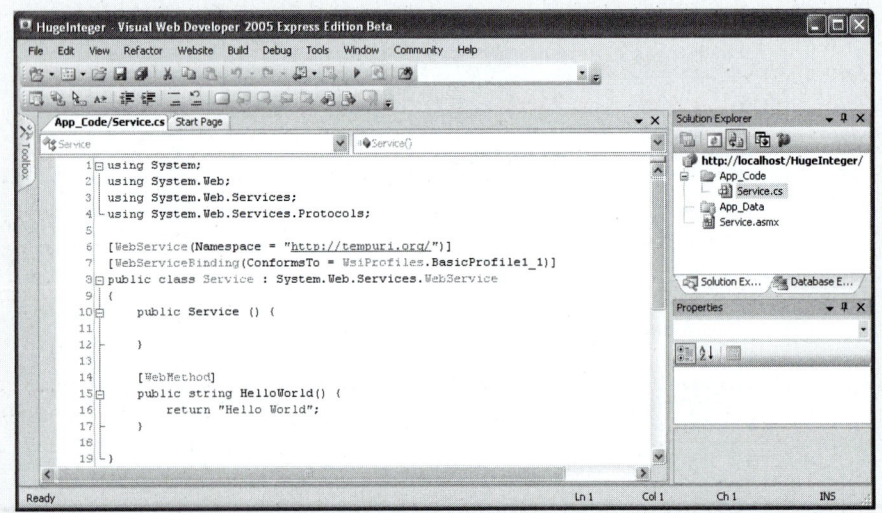

Fig. 22.11 | Code view of a Web service.

request the ASMX page through IIS, ASP.NET uses this information to generate the content displayed in the Web browser (i.e., the list of Web methods and their descriptions).

Step 5: Modifying the ASMX File
Whenever you change the name of the code-behind file or the name of the class that defines the Web service, you must modify the ASMX file accordingly. Thus, after defining class `HugeInteger` in the code-behind file `HugeInteger.cs`, modify the ASMX file to contain the lines

```
<%@ WebService Language="C#" CodeBehind="~/App_Code/HugeInteger.cs"
    Class="HugeInteger" %>
```

 Error-Prevention Tip 22.2

Update the Web service's ASMX file appropriately whenever the name of a Web service's code-behind file or the class name changes. Visual Web Developer creates the ASMX file, but does not automatically update it when you make changes to other files in the project.

Step 6: Renaming the ASMX File
The final step in creating the `HugeInteger` Web service is to rename the ASMX file `HugeInteger.asmx`.

22.4.3 Deploying the HugeInteger Web Service
The Web service is already deployed because we created the `HugeInteger` Web service directly on our computer's local IIS server. You can choose **Build Web Site** from the **Build** menu to ensure that the Web service compiles without errors. You can also test the Web service directly from Visual Web Developer by selecting **Start Without Debugging** from the **Debug** menu. This opens a browser window that contains the ASMX page shown in Fig. 22.2. Clicking the link for a particular `HugeInteger` Web service method displays a Web page like the one in Fig. 22.4 that allows you to test the method. Note that you can also access the Web service's ASMX page from your computer by typing the following URL in a Web browser

```
http://localhost/HugeInteger/HugeInteger.asmx
```

Accessing the HugeInteger Web Service's ASMX Page from Another Computer
Eventually, you will want other clients to be able to access and use your Web service. If you deploy the Web service on an IIS Web server, a client can connect to that server to access the Web service with a URL of the form

```
http://host/HugeInteger/HugeInteger.asmx
```

where *host* is the hostname or IP address of the Web server. To access the Web service from another computer in your company's or school's local area network, you can replace *host* with the actual name of the computer on which IIS is running.

If you have the Windows XP Service Pack 2 operating system on the computer running IIS, that computer may not allow requests from other computers by default. If you wish to allow other computers to connect to your computer's Web server, perform the following steps:

1. Select **Start > Control Panel** to open your system's **Control Panel** window, then double click **Windows Firewall** to view the **Windows Firewall** settings dialog.

2. In the **Windows Firewall** settings dialog, click the **Advanced** tab, select **Local Area Connection** (or your network connection's name, if it is different) in the **Network Connection Settings** list box and click the **Settings...** button to display the **Advanced Settings** dialog.

3. In the **Advanced Settings** dialog, ensure that the checkbox for **Web Server (HTTP)** is checked to allow clients on other computers to submit requests to your computer's Web server.

4. Click **OK** in the **Advanced Settings** dialog, then click **OK** in the **Windows Firewall** settings dialog.

Accessing the HugeInteger Web Service's ASMX Page When the Web Service Executes in Visual Web Developer's Built-in Web Server

Recall from *Step 1* of Section 22.4.2 that if you do not have access to an IIS server to deploy and test your Web service, you can create the Web service on your computer's hard disk and use Visual Web Developer's built-in Web server to test the Web service. In this case, when you select **Start Without Debugging** from the **Debug** menu, Visual Web Developer executes its built-in Web server, then opens a Web browser containing the Web service's ASMX page so that you can test the Web service.

Web servers typically receive requests on port 80. To ensure that Visual Web Developer's built-in Web server does not conflict with another Web server running on your local computer, Visual Web Developer's Web server receives requests on a randomly selected port number. When a Web server receives requests on a port number other than port 80, the port number must be specified as part of the request. In this case, the URL to access the HugeInteger Web service's ASMX page would be of the form

```
http://host:portNumber/HugeInteger/HugeInteger.asmx
```

where *host* is the hostname or IP address of the computer on which Visual Web Developer's built-in Web server is running and *portNumber* is the specific port on which the Web server receives requests. You can see this port number in your Web browser's **Address** field when you test the Web service from Visual Web Developer. Unfortunately, Web services executed using Visual Web Developer's built-in server cannot be accessed over a network.

22.4.4 Creating a Client to Consume the HugeInteger Web Service

Now that we have defined and deployed our Web service, we demonstrate how to consume it from a client application. In this section, you will create a Windows application as the client using Visual C# 2005. After creating the client application, you will add a proxy class to the project that allows the client to access the Web service. Recall that the proxy class (or proxy) is generated from the Web service's WSDL file and enables the client to call Web methods over the Internet. The proxy class handles all the details of communicating with the Web service. The proxy class is hidden from you by default—you can view it in the **Solution Explorer** by clicking the **Show All Files** button. The proxy class's purpose is to make clients think that they are calling the Web methods directly.

This example demonstrates how to create a Web service client and generate a proxy class that allows the client to access the `HugeInteger` Web service. You will begin by creating a project and adding a Web reference to it. When you add the Web reference, Visual C# 2005 will generate the appropriate proxy class. You will then create an instance of the proxy class and use it to call the Web service's methods. First, create a Windows application in Visual C# 2005, then perform the following steps:

Step 1: Opening the Add Web Reference *Dialog*
Right click the project name in the **Solution Explorer** and select **Add Web Reference...** (Fig. 22.12).

Step 2: Locating *Web Services on Your Computer*
In the **Add Web Reference** dialog that appears (Fig. 22.13), click **Web services on the local machine** to locate Web references stored on the IIS Web server on your local computer (`http://localhost`). This server's files are located at `C:\Inetpub\wwwroot` by default. Note that the **Add Web Reference** dialog allows you to search for Web services in several different locations. Many companies that provide Web services simply distribute the exact URLs at which their Web services can be accessed. For this reason, the **Add Web Reference** dialog also allows you to enter the specific URL of a Web service in the **URL** field.

Step 3: Choosing the *Web Service to Reference*
Select the `HugeInteger` Web service from the list of available Web services (Fig. 22.14).

Step 4: Adding the *Web Reference*
Add the Web reference by clicking the **Add Reference** button (Fig. 22.15).

Step 5: Viewing the Web Reference in the *Solution Explorer*
The **Solution Explorer** (Fig. 22.16) should now contain a **Web References** folder with a node named after the domain name where the Web service is located. In this case, the

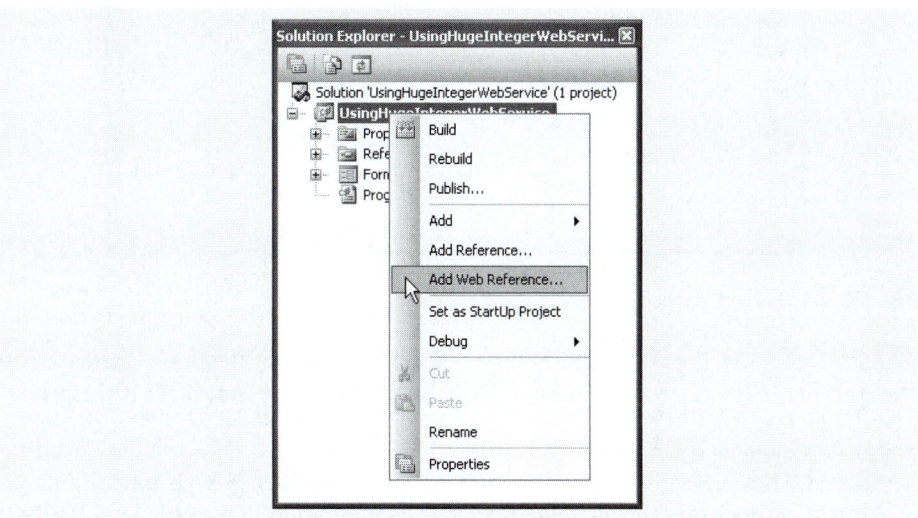

Fig. 22.12 | Adding a Web service reference to a project.

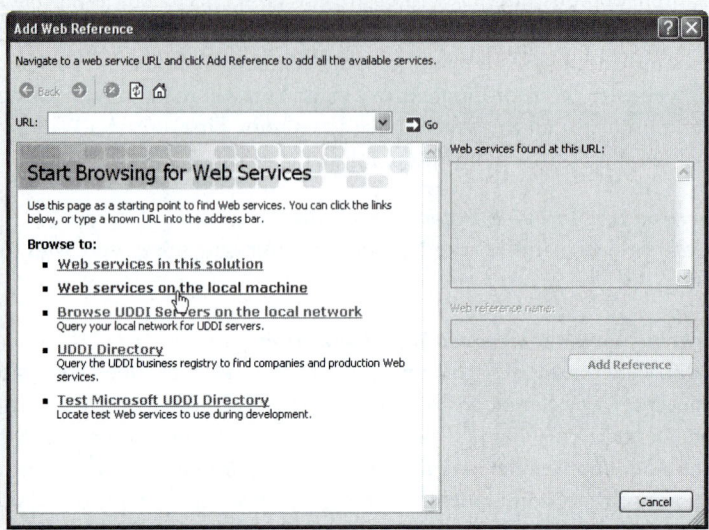

Fig. 22.13 | **Add Web Reference** dialog.

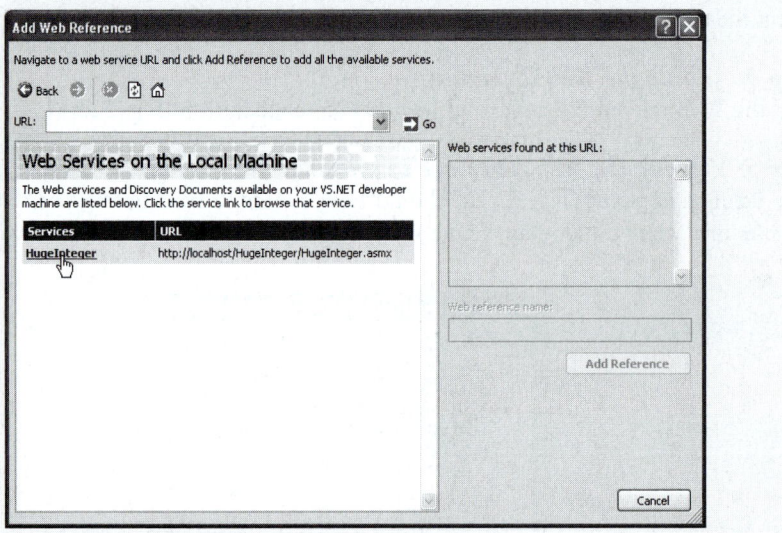

Fig. 22.14 | Web services located on `localhost`.

name is `localhost` because we are using the local Web server. When we reference class `HugeInteger` in the client application, we will do so through the `localhost` namespace.

Notes on Creating a Client to Consume a Web Service
The steps we just presented also apply to adding Web references to Web applications created in Visual Web Developer. We present a Web application that consumes a Web service in Section 22.6.

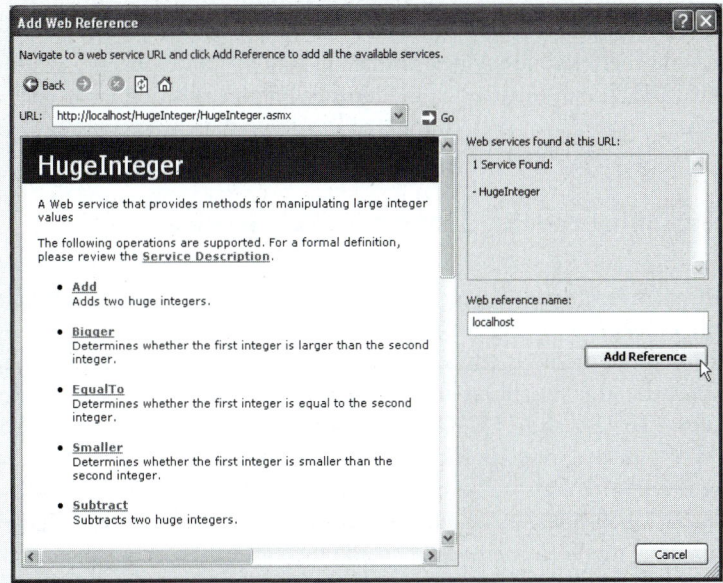

Fig. 22.15 | Web reference selection and description.

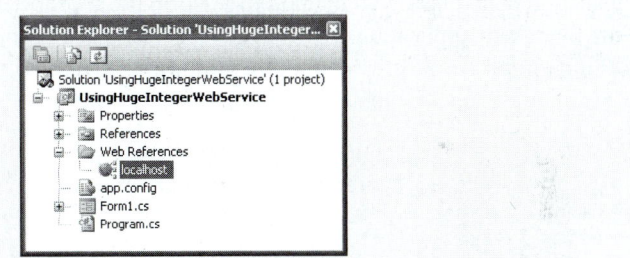

Fig. 22.16 | **Solution Explorer** after adding a Web reference to a project.

When creating a client to consume a Web service, add the Web reference first so that Visual C# 2005 (or Visual Web Developer) can recognize an object of the Web service proxy class. Once you add the Web reference to the client, it can access the Web service through an object of the proxy class. The proxy class (named `HugeInteger`) is located in namespace `localhost`, so you must use `localhost.HugeInteger` to reference this class. Although you must create an object of the proxy class to access the Web service, you do not need access to the proxy class's code. As we show in Section 22.4.5, you can invoke the proxy object's methods as if it were an object of the Web service class.

The steps that we described in this section work well if you know the appropriate Web service reference. However, what if you are trying to locate a new Web service? Two common technologies facilitate this process—*Universal Description, Discovery and Integration* (*UDDI*) and Discovery of Web services (DISCO). We discussed DISCO in Section 22.2. UDDI is an ongoing project for developing a set of specifications that define how Web services should be published so that programmers searching for Web services can find them. Microsoft and its partners are working on this project to help programmers locate Web services that conform to certain specifications, allowing developers to find Web services through search engines similar to Yahoo!® and Google™. You can learn more about UDDI and view a demonstration by visiting www.uddi.org and uddi.microsoft.com. These sites contain search tools that make finding Web services convenient.

22.4.5 Consuming the HugeInteger Web Service

The Windows Form in Fig. 22.17 uses the HugeInteger Web service to perform computations with positive integers up to 100 digits long. Line 22 declares variable remoteInteger of type localhost.HugeInteger. This variable is used in each of the application's event handlers to call methods of the HugeInteger Web service. The proxy object is created and assigned to this variable at line 31 in the Form's Load event handler. Lines 52–53, 66–67, 95–96, 116–117 and 135–136 in the various button event handlers invoke methods of the Web service. Note that each call is made on the local proxy object, which then communicates with the Web service on the client's behalf. If you downloaded the example from www.deitel.com/books/csharpforprogrammers2, you might need to regenerate the proxy by removing the Web reference, then adding it again. To do so, right click **localhost** in the **Web References** folder in the **Solution Explorer** and select option **Delete**. Then follow the instructions in the preceding section to add the Web reference to the project.

The user inputs two integers, each up to 100 digits long. Clicking a button causes the application to invoke a Web method to perform the appropriate task and return the result. Note that client application UsingHugeIntegerService cannot perform operations using 100-digit numbers directly. Instead the application creates string representations of these

```
1   // Fig. 22.17: UsingHugeIntegerService.cs
2   // Using the HugeInteger Web Service.
3   using System;
4   using System.Collections.Generic;
5   using System.ComponentModel;
6   using System.Data;
7   using System.Drawing;
8   using System.Text;
9   using System.Windows.Forms;
10  using System.Web.Services.Protocols;
11
12  namespace UsingHugeIntegerWebService
13  {
14     public partial class UsingHugeIntegerServiceForm : Form
15     {
16        public UsingHugeIntegerServiceForm()
17        {
18           InitializeComponent();
19        } // end constructor
20
21        // declare a reference to Web service
22        private localhost.HugeInteger remoteInteger;
```

Fig. 22.17 | Using the HugeInteger Web service. (Part 1 of 5.)

```
23
24        private char[] zeros = { '0' }; // character to trim from strings
25
26        // instantiates object to interact with Web service
27        private void UsingHugeIntegerServiceForm_Load( object sender,
28           EventArgs e )
29        {
30           // instantiate remoteInteger
31           remoteInteger = new localhost.HugeInteger();
32        } // end method UsingHugeIntegerServiceForm_Load
33
34        // adds two numbers input by user
35        private void addButton_Click( object sender, EventArgs e )
36        {
37           // make sure numbers do not exceed 100 digits and that both
38           // are not 100 digits long, which would result in overflow
39           if ( firstTextBox.Text.Length > 100 ||
40              secondTextBox.Text.Length > 100 ||
41              ( firstTextBox.Text.Length == 100 &&
42              secondTextBox.Text.Length == 100) )
43           {
44              MessageBox.Show( "HugeIntegers must not be more " +
45                 "than 100 digits\r\nBoth integers cannot be " +
46                 "of length 100: this causes an overflow", "Error",
47                 MessageBoxButtons.OK, MessageBoxIcon.Information );
48              return;
49           } // end if
50
51           // perform addition
52           resultLabel.Text = remoteInteger.Add(
53              firstTextBox.Text, secondTextBox.Text ).TrimStart( zeros );
54        } // end method addButton_Click
55
56        // subtracts two numbers input by user
57        private void subtractButton_Click( object sender, EventArgs e )
58        {
59           // make sure HugeIntegers do not exceed 100 digits
60           if ( SizeCheck( firstTextBox, secondTextBox ) )
61              return;
62
63           // perform subtraction
64           try
65           {
66              string result = remoteInteger.Subtract(
67                 firstTextBox.Text, secondTextBox.Text ).TrimStart( zeros );
68
69              if ( result == "" )
70                 resultLabel.Text = "0";
71              else
72                 resultLabel.Text = result;
73
74           } // end try
75
```

Fig. 22.17 | Using the `HugeInteger` Web service. (Part 2 of 5.)

```
76          // if WebMethod throws an exception,
77          // then first argument was smaller than second
78          catch ( SoapException exception )
79          {
80             MessageBox.Show(
81                "First argument was smaller than the second" );
82          } // end catch
83       } // end method subtractButton_Click
84
85       // determines whether first number
86       // input by user is larger than second
87       private void largerButton_Click( object sender, EventArgs e )
88       {
89          // make sure HugeIntegers do not exceed 100 digits
90          if ( SizeCheck( firstTextBox, secondTextBox ) )
91             return;
92
93          // call Web-service method to determine if
94          // first integer is larger than the second
95          if ( remoteInteger.Bigger( firstTextBox.Text,
96             secondTextBox.Text ) )
97             resultLabel.Text = firstTextBox.Text.TrimStart( zeros ) +
98                " is larger than " +
99                secondTextBox.Text.TrimStart( zeros );
100         else
101            resultLabel.Text = firstTextBox.Text.TrimStart( zeros ) +
102               " is not larger than " +
103               secondTextBox.Text.TrimStart( zeros );
104      } // end method largerButton_Click
105
106      // determines whether first number
107      // input by user is smaller than second
108      private void smallerButton_Click( object sender, EventArgs e )
109      {
110         // make sure HugeIntegers do not exceed 100 digits
111         if ( SizeCheck( firstTextBox, secondTextBox ) )
112            return;
113
114         // call Web-service method to determine if
115         // first integer is smaller than second
116         if ( remoteInteger.Smaller( firstTextBox.Text,
117            secondTextBox.Text ) )
118            resultLabel.Text = firstTextBox.Text.TrimStart( zeros ) +
119               " is smaller than " +
120               secondTextBox.Text.TrimStart( zeros );
121         else
122            resultLabel.Text = firstTextBox.Text.TrimStart( zeros ) +
123               " is not smaller than " +
124               secondTextBox.Text.TrimStart( zeros );
125      } // end method smallerButton_Click
126
127      // determines whether two numbers input by user are equal
128      private void equalButton_Click( object sender, EventArgs e )
```

Fig. 22.17 | Using the HugeInteger Web service. (Part 3 of 5.)

```
129         {
130            // make sure HugeIntegers do not exceed 100 digits
131            if ( SizeCheck( firstTextBox, secondTextBox ) )
132               return;
133
134            // call Web-service method to determine if integers are equal
135            if ( remoteInteger.EqualTo( firstTextBox.Text,
136               secondTextBox.Text ) )
137               resultLabel.Text = firstTextBox.Text.TrimStart( zeros ) +
138                  " is equal to " + secondTextBox.Text.TrimStart( zeros );
139            else
140               resultLabel.Text = firstTextBox.Text.TrimStart( zeros ) +
141                  " is not equal to " +
142                  secondTextBox.Text.TrimStart( zeros );
143         } // end method equalButton_Click
144
145         // determines whether numbers input by user are too big
146         private bool SizeCheck( TextBox first, TextBox second )
147         {
148            // display an error message if either number has too many digits
149            if ( ( first.Text.Length > 100 ) ||
150               ( second.Text.Length > 100 ) )
151            {
152               MessageBox.Show( "HugeIntegers must be less than 100 digits" ,
153                  "Error", MessageBoxButtons.OK, MessageBoxIcon.Information);
154               return true;
155            } // end if
156
157            return false;
158         } // end method SizeCheck
159      } // end class UsingHugeIntegerServiceForm
160   } // end namespace UsingHugeIntegerWebService
```

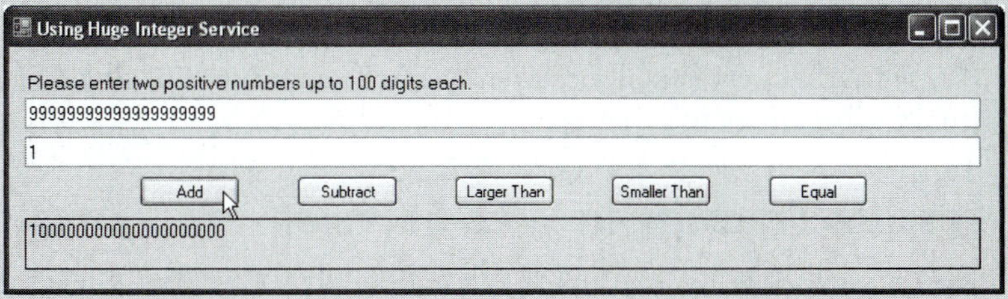

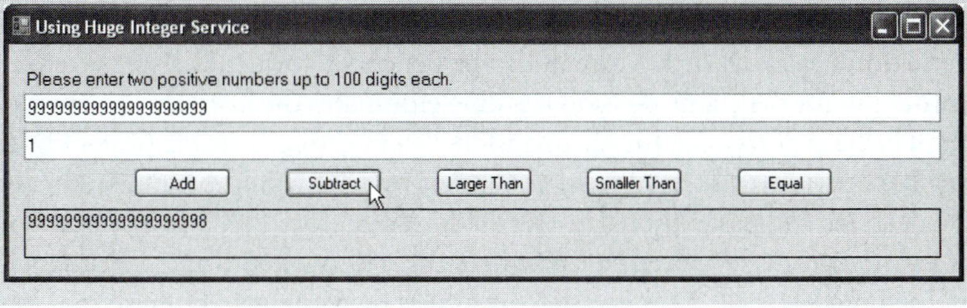

Fig. 22.17 | Using the `HugeInteger` Web service. (Part 4 of 5.)

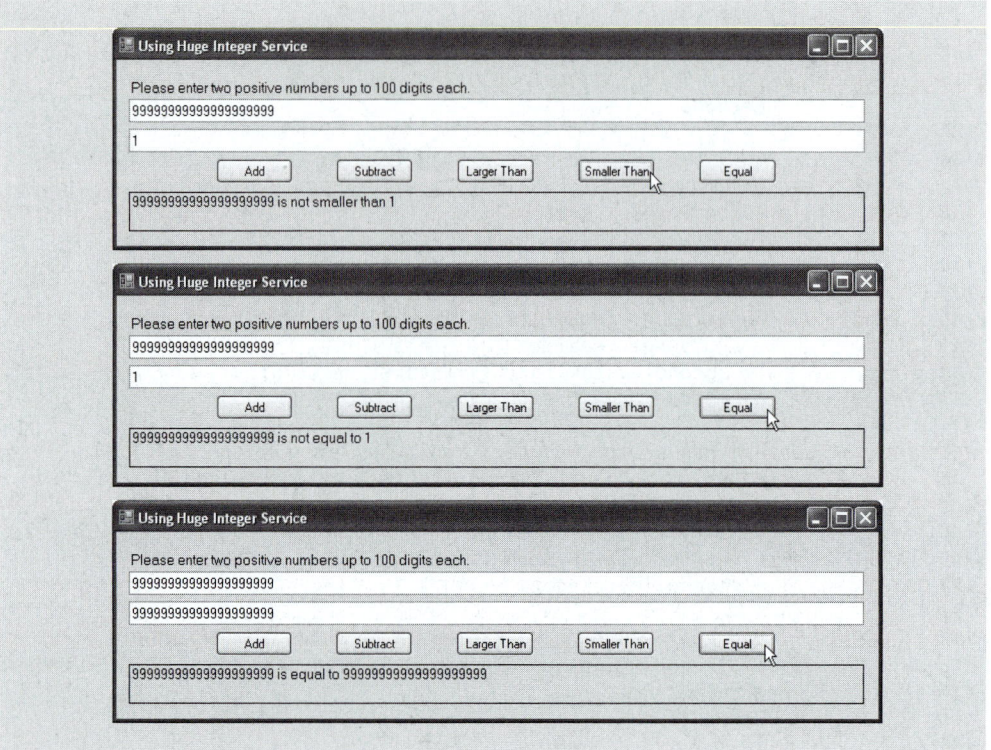

Fig. 22.17 | Using the `HugeInteger` Web service. (Part 5 of 5.)

numbers and passes them as arguments to Web methods that handle such tasks for the client. It then uses the return value of each operation to display an appropriate message.

Note that the application eliminates leading zeros in the numbers before displaying them by calling `string` method `TrimStart`. Like `string` method `Trim` (discussed in Chapter 16), `TrimStart` removes all occurrences of characters specified by a `char` array (line 24) from the beginning of a `string`.

22.5 Session Tracking in Web Services

In Chapter 21, we described the advantages of maintaining information about users to personalize their experiences. In particular, we discussed session tracking using cookies and `HttpSessionState` objects. We will now incorporate session tracking into a Web service. Suppose a client application needs to call several methods from the same Web service, possibly several times each. In such a case, it can be beneficial for the Web service to maintain state information for the client. Session tracking eliminates the need for information about the client to be passed between the client and the Web service multiple times. For example, a Web service providing access to local restaurant reviews would benefit from storing the client user's street address. Once the user's address is stored in a session variable, Web methods can return personalized, localized results without requiring that the address be passed in each method call. This not only improves performance, but also requires less effort on the part of the programmer—less information is passed in each method call.

22.5.1 Creating a Blackjack Web Service

Storing session information can provide client programmers with a more intuitive Web service. Our next example is a Web service that assists programmers in developing a blackjack card game (Fig. 22.18). The Web service provides Web methods to deal a card and to evaluate a hand of cards. After presenting the Web service, we use it to serve as the dealer for a game of blackjack (Fig. 22.19). The blackjack Web service uses a session variable to maintain a unique deck of cards for each client application. Several clients can use the service at the same time, but Web method calls made by a specific client use only the deck stored in that client's session. Our example uses a simple subset of casino blackjack rules:

Two cards each are dealt to the dealer and the player. The player's cards are dealt face up. Only the first of the dealer's cards is dealt face up. Each card has a value. A card numbered 2 through 10 is worth its face value. Jacks, queens and kings each count as 10. Aces can count as 1 or 11—whichever value is more beneficial to the player (as we will soon see). If the sum of the player's two initial cards is 21 (i.e., the player was dealt a card valued at 10 and an ace, which counts as 11 in this situation), the player has "blackjack" and immediately wins the game. Otherwise, the player can begin taking additional cards one at a time. These cards are dealt face up, and the player decides when to stop taking cards. If the player "busts" (i.e., the sum of the player's cards exceeds 21), the game is over, and the player loses. When the player is satisfied with the current set of cards, the player "stays" (i.e., stops taking cards), and the dealer's hidden card is revealed. If the dealer's total is 16 or less, the dealer must take another card; otherwise, the dealer must stay. The dealer must continue to take cards until the sum of the dealer's cards is greater than or equal to 17. If the dealer exceeds 21, the player wins. Otherwise, the hand with the higher point total wins. If the dealer and the player have the same point total, the game is a "push" (i.e., a tie), and no one wins.

The Web service (Fig. 22.18) provides methods to deal a card and to determine the point value of a hand. We represent each card as a `string` consisting of a digit (e.g., 1–13) representing the card's face (e.g., ace through king), followed by a space and a digit (e.g., 0–3) representing the card's suit (e.g., clubs, diamonds, hearts or spades). For example, the jack of hearts is represented as `"11 2"`, and the two of clubs is represented as `"2 0"`. After deploying the Web service, we create a Windows application that uses the `BlackjackService`'s Web methods to implement a game of blackjack. To create and deploy this Web service follow the steps presented in Sections 22.4.2–22.4.3 for the `HugeInteger` service.

```
1   // Fig. 22.18: BlackjackService.cs
2   // Blackjack Web Service deals and counts cards.
3   using System;
4   using System.Web;
5   using System.Web.Services;
6   using System.Web.Services.Protocols;
7   using System.Collections;
8
9   [ WebService( Namespace = "http://www.deitel.com/", Description =
10     "A Web service that deals and counts cards for the game Blackjack" ) ]
11  [ WebServiceBinding( ConformsTo = WsiProfiles.BasicProfile1_1 ) ]
```

Fig. 22.18 | Blackjack Web service. (Part 1 of 3.)

```
12   public class BlackjackService : System.Web.Services.WebService
13   {
14      // deals card that has not yet been dealt
15      [ WebMethod( EnableSession = true,
16         Description="Deal a new card from the deck." ) ]
17      public string DealCard()
18      {
19         string card = "2 2";
20
21         // get client's deck
22         ArrayList deck = ( ArrayList )( Session[ "deck" ] );
23         card = Convert.ToString( deck[ 0 ] );
24         deck.RemoveAt( 0 );
25         return card;
26      } // end method DealCard
27
28      // creates and shuffles a deck of cards
29      [ WebMethod( EnableSession = true,
30         Description="Create and shuffle a deck of cards." ) ]
31      public void Shuffle()
32      {
33         object temporary; // holds card temporarily during swapping
34         Random randomObject = new Random(); // generates random numbers
35         int newIndex; // index of randomly selected card
36         ArrayList deck = new ArrayList(); // stores deck of cards (strings)
37
38         // generate all possible cards
39         for ( int i = 1; i <= 13; i++ ) // loop through face values
40            for ( int j = 0; j <= 3; j++ ) // loop through suits
41               deck.Add( i + " " + j ); // add card (string) to deck
42
43         // shuffles deck by swapping each card with another card randomly
44         for ( int i = 0; i < deck.Count; i++ )
45         {
46            // get random index
47            newIndex = randomObject.Next( deck.Count - 1 );
48            temporary = deck[ i ]; // save current card in temporary variable
49            deck[ i ] = deck[ newIndex ]; // copy randomly selected card
50            deck[ newIndex ] = temporary; // copy current card back into deck
51         } // end for
52
53         // add this deck to user's session state
54         Session.Add( "deck", deck );
55      } // end method Shuffle
56
57      // computes value of hand
58      [ WebMethod( Description =
59         "Compute a numerical value for the current hand." ) ]
60      public int GetHandValue( string dealt )
61      {
62         // split string containing all cards
63         char[] tab = { '\t' };
```

Fig. 22.18 | Blackjack Web service. (Part 2 of 3.)

```
64        string[] cards = dealt.Split( tab ); // get array of cards
65        int total = 0; // total value of cards in hand
66        int face; // face of the current card
67        int aceCount = 0; // number of aces in hand
68
69        // loop through the cards in the hand
70        foreach ( string drawn in cards )
71        {
72           // get face of card
73           face = Int32.Parse( drawn.Substring( 0, drawn.IndexOf( " " ) ) );
74
75           switch ( face )
76           {
77              case 1: // if ace, increment aceCount
78                 aceCount++;
79                 break;
80              case 11: // if jack add 10
81              case 12: // if queen add 10
82              case 13: // if king add 10
83                 total += 10;
84                 break;
85              default: // otherwise, add value of face
86                 total += face;
87                 break;
88           } // end switch
89        } // end foreach
90
91        // if there are any aces, calculate optimum total
92        if ( aceCount > 0 )
93        {
94           // if it is possible to count one ace as 11, and the rest
95           // as 1 each, do so; otherwise, count all aces as 1 each
96           if ( total + 11 + aceCount - 1 <= 21 )
97              total += 11 + aceCount - 1;
98           else
99              total += aceCount;
100       } // end if
101
102       return total;
103    } // end method GetHandValue
104 } // end class BlackjackService
```

Fig. 22.18 | `Blackjack` Web service. (Part 3 of 3.)

Lines 15–16 define method `DealCard` as a Web method. Setting property **_EnableSession_** to `True` indicates that session information should be maintained and should be accessible to this method. This is required only for methods that must access the session information. Doing so allows the Web service to use an `HttpSessionState` object (named `Session` by ASP.NET) to maintain the deck of cards for each client application that uses this Web service (line 22). We can use `Session` to store objects for a specific client between method calls. We discussed session state in detail in Chapter 21.

Method DealCard removes a card from the deck and sends it to the client. Without using a session variable, the deck of cards would need to be passed back and forth with each method call. Using session state make the method easy to call (it requires no arguments), and avoids the overhead of sending the deck over the network multiple times.

At this point, our Web service contains methods that use session variables. However, the Web service still cannot determine which session variables belong to which user. If two clients successfully call the DealCard method, the same deck would be manipulated. To avoid this problem, the Web service automatically creates a cookie to uniquely identify each client. A Web browser client that has cookie handling enabled stores cookies automatically. A non-browser client application that consumes this Web service must create a **CookieContainer** object to store cookies sent from the server. We discuss this in more detail in Section 22.5.2, when we examine the blackjack Web service's client.

Web method DealCard (lines 15–26) selects a card from the deck and sends it to the client. The method first obtains the current user's deck as an ArrayList from the Web service's Session object (line 22). After obtaining the user's deck, DealCard removes the top card from the deck (line 24) and returns the card's value as a string (line 25).

Method Shuffle (lines 29–55) generates an ArrayList representing a deck of cards, shuffles it and stores the shuffled cards in the client's Session object. Lines 39–41 use nested for statements to generate strings in the form "*face suit*" to represent each possible card in a deck. Lines 44–51 shuffle the deck by swapping each card with another card selected at random. Line 54 adds the ArrayList to the Session object to maintain the deck between method calls from a particular client.

Method GetHandValue (lines 58–103) determines the total value of the cards in a hand by trying to attain the highest score possible without going over 21. Recall that an ace can be counted as either 1 or 11, and all face cards count as 10.

As you will see in Fig. 22.19, the client application maintains a hand of cards as a string in which each card is separated by a tab character. Line 64 tokenizes the hand of cards (represented by dealt) into individual cards by calling string method Split and passing to it an array that contains the delimiter characters (in this case, just a tab). Split uses the delimiter characters to separate tokens in the string. Lines 70–89 count the value of each card. Line 73 retrieves the first integer—the face—and uses that value in the switch statement (lines 75–88). If the card is an ace, the method increments variable ace-Count. We discuss how this variable is used shortly. If the card is an 11, 12 or 13 (jack, queen or king), the method adds 10 to the total value of the hand (line 83). If the card is anything else, the method increases the total by that value (line 86).

Because an ace can have either of two values, additional logic is required to process aces. Lines 92–100 of method GetHandValue process the aces after all the other cards. If a hand contains several aces, only one ace can be counted as 11 (if two aces each are counted as 11, the hand would have a losing value of 22). The condition in line 96 determines whether counting one ace as 11 and the rest as 1 will result in a total that does not exceed 21. If this is possible, line 97 adjusts the total accordingly. Otherwise, line 99 adjusts the total, counting each ace as 1.

Method GetHandValue maximizes the value of the current cards without exceeding 21. Imagine, for example, that the dealer has a 7 and receives an ace. The new total could be either 8 or 18. However, GetHandValue always maximizes the value of the cards without going over 21, so the new total is 18.

22.5.2 Consuming the Blackjack Web Service

Now we use the blackjack Web service in a Windows application (Fig. 22.19). This application uses an instance of `BlackjackService` (declared in line 18 and created in line 47) to

```
1   // Fig. 22.19: Blackjack.cs
2   // Blackjack game that uses the Blackjack Web service.
3   using System;
4   using System.Collections.Generic;
5   using System.ComponentModel;
6   using System.Data;
7   using System.Drawing;
8   using System.Text;
9   using System.Windows.Forms;
10  using System.Net;
11  using System.Collections;
12
13  namespace Blackjack
14  {
15     public partial class BlackjackForm : Form
16     {
17        // reference to Web service
18        private localhost.BlackjackService dealer;
19
20        // string representing the dealer's cards
21        private string dealersCards;
22
23        // string representing the player's cards
24        private string playersCards;
25        private ArrayList cardBoxes; // list of PictureBoxes for card images
26        private int currentPlayerCard; // player's current card number
27        private int currentDealerCard; // dealer's current card number
28
29        // enum representing the possible game outcomes
30        public enum GameStatus
31        {
32           PUSH, // game ends in a tie
33           LOSE, // player loses
34           WIN, // player wins
35           BLACKJACK // player has blackjack
36        } // end enum GameStatus
37
38        public BlackjackForm()
39        {
40           InitializeComponent();
41        } // end constructor
42
43        // sets up the game
44        private void BlackjackForm_Load( object sender, EventArgs e )
45        {
46           // instantiate object allowing communication with Web service
47           dealer = new localhost.BlackjackService();
48
```

Fig. 22.19 | Blackjack game that uses the `Blackjack` Web service. (Part 1 of 8.)

```
49              // allow session state
50              dealer.CookieContainer = new CookieContainer();
51              cardBoxes = new ArrayList();
52
53              // put PictureBoxes into cardBoxes
54              cardBoxes.Add( pictureBox1 );
55              cardBoxes.Add( pictureBox2 );
56              cardBoxes.Add( pictureBox3 );
57              cardBoxes.Add( pictureBox4 );
58              cardBoxes.Add( pictureBox5 );
59              cardBoxes.Add( pictureBox6 );
60              cardBoxes.Add( pictureBox7 );
61              cardBoxes.Add( pictureBox8 );
62              cardBoxes.Add( pictureBox9 );
63              cardBoxes.Add( pictureBox10 );
64              cardBoxes.Add( pictureBox11 );
65              cardBoxes.Add( pictureBox12 );
66              cardBoxes.Add( pictureBox13 );
67              cardBoxes.Add( pictureBox14 );
68              cardBoxes.Add( pictureBox15 );
69              cardBoxes.Add( pictureBox16 );
70              cardBoxes.Add( pictureBox17 );
71              cardBoxes.Add( pictureBox18 );
72              cardBoxes.Add( pictureBox19 );
73              cardBoxes.Add( pictureBox20 );
74              cardBoxes.Add( pictureBox21 );
75              cardBoxes.Add( pictureBox22 );
76          } // end method BlackjackForm_Load
77
78          // deals cards to dealer while dealer's total is less than 17,
79          // then computes value of each hand and determines winner
80          private void DealerPlay()
81          {
82              // while value of dealer's hand is below 17,
83              // dealer must take cards
84              while ( dealer.GetHandValue( dealersCards ) < 17 )
85              {
86                  dealersCards += '\t' + dealer.DealCard(); // deal new card
87
88                  // update GUI to show new card
89                  DisplayCard( currentDealerCard, "" );
90                  currentDealerCard++;
91                  MessageBox.Show( "Dealer takes a card" );
92              } // end while
93
94              int dealersTotal = dealer.GetHandValue( dealersCards );
95              int playersTotal = dealer.GetHandValue( playersCards );
96
97              // if dealer busted, player wins
98              if ( dealersTotal > 21 )
99              {
100                 GameOver( GameStatus.WIN );
```

Fig. 22.19 | Blackjack game that uses the Blackjack Web service. (Part 2 of 8.)

```
101              return;
102          } // end if
103
104          // if dealer and player have not exceeded 21,
105          // higher score wins; equal scores is a push.
106          if ( dealersTotal > playersTotal )
107              GameOver( GameStatus.LOSE );
108          else if ( playersTotal > dealersTotal )
109              GameOver( GameStatus.WIN );
110          else
111              GameOver( GameStatus.PUSH );
112      } // end method DealerPlay
113
114      // displays card represented by cardValue in specified PictureBox
115      public void DisplayCard( int card, string cardValue )
116      {
117          // retrieve appropriate PictureBox from ArrayList
118          PictureBox displayBox = ( PictureBox )( cardBoxes[ card ] );
119
120          // if string representing card is empty,
121          // set displayBox to display back of card
122          if ( cardValue == "" )
123          {
124              displayBox.Image =
125                  Image.FromFile( "blackjack_images/cardback.png" );
126              return;
127          } // end if
128
129          // retrieve face value of card from cardValue
130          string face = cardValue.Substring( 0, cardValue.IndexOf( " " ) );
131
132          // retrieve the suit of the card from cardValue
133          string suit =
134              cardValue.Substring( cardValue.IndexOf( " " ) + 1 );
135
136          char suitLetter; // suit letter used to form image file name
137
138          // determine the suit letter of the card
139          switch ( Convert.ToInt32( suit ) )
140          {
141              case 0: // clubs
142                  suitLetter = 'c';
143                  break;
144              case 1: // diamonds
145                  suitLetter = 'd';
146                  break;
147              case 2: // hearts
148                  suitLetter = 'h';
149                  break;
150              default: // spades
151                  suitLetter = 's';
152                  break;
153          } // end switch
```

Fig. 22.19 | Blackjack game that uses the Blackjack Web service. (Part 3 of 8.)

```
154
155          // set displayBox to display appropriate image
156          displayBox.Image = Image.FromFile(
157             "blackjack_images/" + face + suitLetter + ".png" );
158      } // end method DisplayCard
159
160      // displays all player cards and shows
161      // appropriate game status message
162      public void GameOver( GameStatus winner )
163      {
164         char[] tab = { '\t' };
165         string[] cards = dealersCards.Split( tab );
166
167         // display all the dealer's cards
168         for ( int i = 0; i < cards.Length; i++ )
169            DisplayCard( i, cards[ i ] );
170
171         // display appropriate status image
172         if ( winner == GameStatus.PUSH ) // push
173            statusPictureBox.Image =
174               Image.FromFile( "blackjack_images/tie.png" );
175         else if ( winner == GameStatus.LOSE ) // player loses
176            statusPictureBox.Image =
177               Image.FromFile( "blackjack_images/lose.png" );
178         else if ( winner == GameStatus.BLACKJACK )
179            // player has blackjack
180            statusPictureBox.Image =
181               Image.FromFile( "blackjack_images/blackjack.png" );
182         else // player wins
183            statusPictureBox.Image =
184               Image.FromFile( "blackjack_images/win.png" );
185
186         // display final totals for dealer and player
187         dealerTotalLabel.Text =
188            "Dealer: " + dealer.GetHandValue( dealersCards );
189         playerTotalLabel.Text =
190            "Player: " + dealer.GetHandValue( playersCards );
191
192         // reset controls for new game
193         stayButton.Enabled = false;
194         hitButton.Enabled = false;
195         dealButton.Enabled = true;
196      } // end method GameOver
197
198      // deal two cards each to dealer and player
199      private void dealButton_Click( object sender, EventArgs e )
200      {
201         string card; // stores a card temporarily until added to a hand
202
203         // clear card images
204         foreach ( PictureBox cardImage in cardBoxes )
205            cardImage.Image = null;
206
```

Fig. 22.19 | Blackjack game that uses the Blackjack Web service. (Part 4 of 8.)

```
207          statusPictureBox.Image = null; // clear status image
208          dealerTotalLabel.Text = ""; // clear final total for dealer
209          playerTotalLabel.Text = ""; // clear final total for player
210
211          // create a new, shuffled deck on the remote machine
212          dealer.Shuffle();
213
214          // deal two cards to player
215          playersCards = dealer.DealCard(); // deal a card to player's hand
216
217          // update GUI to display new card
218          DisplayCard( 11, playersCards );
219          card = dealer.DealCard(); // deal a second card
220          DisplayCard( 12, card ); // update GUI to display new card
221          playersCards += '\t' + card; // add second card to player's hand
222
223          // deal two cards to dealer, only display face of first card
224          dealersCards = dealer.DealCard(); // deal a card to dealer's hand
225          DisplayCard( 0, dealersCards ); // update GUI to display new card
226          card = dealer.DealCard(); // deal a second card
227          DisplayCard( 1, "" ); // update GUI to show face-down card
228          dealersCards += '\t' + card; // add second card to dealer's hand
229
230          stayButton.Enabled = true; // allow player to stay
231          hitButton.Enabled = true; // allow player to hit
232          dealButton.Enabled = false; // disable Deal Button
233
234          // determine the value of the two hands
235          int dealersTotal = dealer.GetHandValue( dealersCards );
236          int playersTotal = dealer.GetHandValue( playersCards );
237
238          // if hands equal 21, it is a push
239          if ( dealersTotal == playersTotal && dealersTotal == 21 )
240             GameOver( GameStatus.PUSH );
241          else if ( dealersTotal == 21 ) // if dealer has 21, dealer wins
242             GameOver( GameStatus.LOSE );
243          else if ( playersTotal == 21 ) // player has blackjack
244             GameOver( GameStatus.BLACKJACK );
245
246          // next dealer card has index 2 in cardBoxes
247          currentDealerCard = 2;
248
249          // next player card has index 13 in cardBoxes
250          currentPlayerCard = 13;
251       } // end method dealButton_Click
252
253       // deal another card to player
254       private void hitButton_Click( object sender, EventArgs e )
255       {
256          // get player another card
257          string card = dealer.DealCard(); // deal new card
258          playersCards += '\t' + card; // add new card to player's hand
259
```

Fig. 22.19 | Blackjack game that uses the Blackjack Web service. (Part 5 of 8.)

```
260              // update GUI to show new card
261              DisplayCard( currentPlayerCard, card );
262              currentPlayerCard++;
263
264              // determine the value of the player's hand
265              int total = dealer.GetHandValue( playersCards );
266
267              // if player exceeds 21, house wins
268              if ( total > 21 )
269                 GameOver( GameStatus.LOSE );
270
271              // if player has 21,
272              // they cannot take more cards, and dealer plays
273              if ( total == 21 )
274              {
275                 hitButton.Enabled = false;
276                 DealerPlay();
277              } // end if
278           } // end method hitButton_Click
279
280           // play the dealer's hand after the play chooses to stay
281           private void stayButton_Click( object sender, EventArgs e )
282           {
283              stayButton.Enabled = false; // disable Stay Button
284              hitButton.Enabled = false; // display Hit Button
285              dealButton.Enabled = true; // re-enable Deal Button
286              DealerPlay(); // player chose to stay, so play the dealer's hand
287           } // end method stayButton_Click
288        } // end class BlackjackForm
289     } // end namespace Blackjack
```

a) Initial cards dealt to the player and the dealer when the user pressed the **Deal** button.

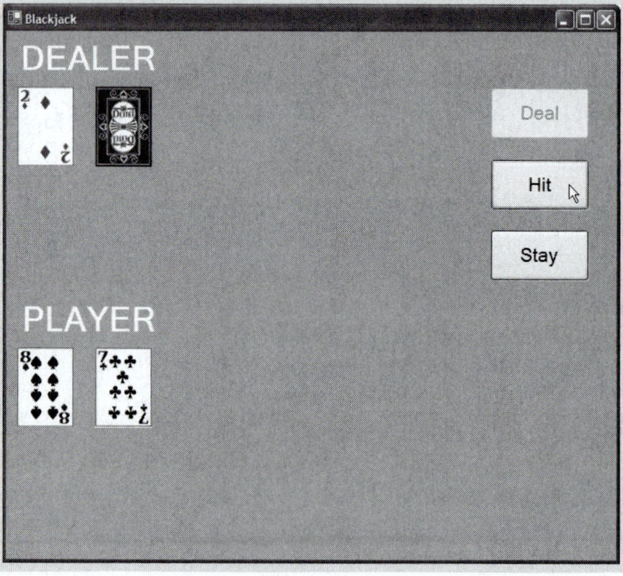

Fig. 22.19 | Blackjack game that uses the Blackjack Web service. (Part 6 of 8.)

b) Cards after the player pressed the **Hit** button twice, then the **Stay** button. In this case, the player won the game with a higher total than the dealer.

c) Cards after the player pressed the **Hit** button once, then the **Stay** button. In this case, the player busted (exceeded 21) and the dealer won the game.

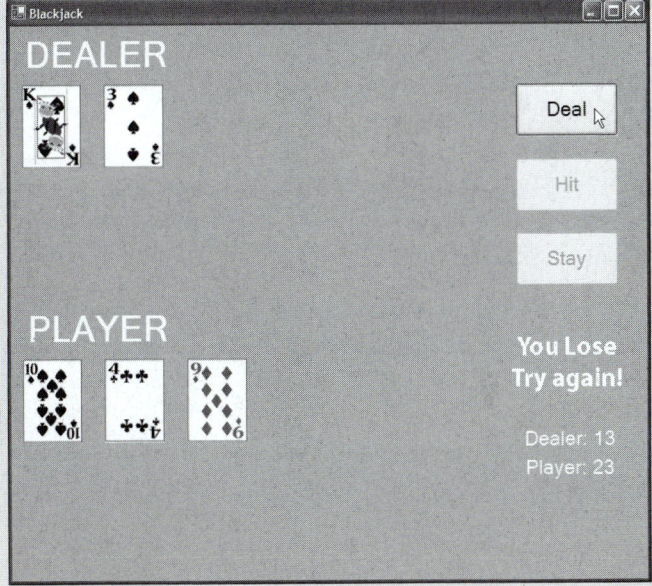

Fig. 22.19 | Blackjack game that uses the `Blackjack` Web service. (Part 7 of 8.)

d) Cards after the player pressed the **Deal** button. In this case, the player won with Blackjack because the first two cards were an ace and a card with a value of 10 (a jack in this case).

e) Cards after the player pressed the **Stay** button. In this case, the player and dealer push—they have the same card total.

Fig. 22.19 | Blackjack game that uses the `Blackjack` Web service. (Part 8 of 8.)

represent the dealer. The Web service keeps track of the player's and the dealer's cards (i.e., all the cards that have been dealt).

Each player has 11 PictureBoxes—the maximum number of cards that can be dealt without automatically exceeding 21 (i.e., four aces, four twos and three threes). These PictureBoxes are placed in an ArrayList (lines 54–75), so we can index the ArrayList during the game to determine the PictureBox that will display a particular card image.

In Section 22.5.1, we mentioned that the client must provide a way to accept cookies created by the Web service to uniquely identify users. Line 50 in BlackjackForm's Load event handler creates a new CookieContainer object for the dealer's CookieContainer property. A CookieContainer (namespace System.Net) stores the information from a cookie (created by the Web service) in a Cookie object in the CookieContainer. The Cookie contains a unique identifier that the Web service can use to recognize the client when the client makes future requests. As part of each request, the cookie is automatically sent back to the server. If the client did not create a CookieContainer object, the Web service would create a new Session object for each request, and the user's state information would not persist across requests.

Method GameOver (lines 162–196) displays all the dealer's cards, shows the appropriate message in the status PictureBox and displays the final point totals of both the dealer and the player. Method GameOver receives as an argument a member of the GameStatus enumeration (defined in lines 30–36). The enumeration represents whether the player tied, lost or won the game; its four members are PUSH, LOSE, WIN and BLACKJACK.

When the player clicks the **Deal** button (whose event handler appears in lines 199–251), all of the PictureBoxes and the Labels displaying the final point totals are cleared. Next, the deck is shuffled, and the player and dealer receive two cards each. If the player and the dealer both obtain scores of 21, the program calls method GameOver, passing GameStatus.PUSH. If only the player has 21 after the first two cards are dealt, the program passes GameStatus.BLACKJACK to method GameOver. If only the dealer has 21, the program passes GameStatus.LOSE to method GameOver.

If dealButton_Click does not call GameOver, the player can take more cards by clicking the **Hit** button. The event handler for this button is in lines 254–278. Each time a player clicks **Hit**, the program deals the player one more card and displays it in the GUI. If the player exceeds 21, the game is over, and the player loses. If the player has exactly 21, the player is not allowed to take any more cards, and method DealerPlay (lines 80–112) is called, causing the dealer to keep taking cards until the dealer's hand has a value of 17 or more (lines 84–92). If the dealer exceeds 21, the player wins (line 100); otherwise, the values of the hands are compared, and GameOver is called with the appropriate argument (lines 106–111).

Clicking the **Stay** button indicates that a player does not want to be dealt another card. The event handler for this button (lines 281–287) disables the **Hit** and **Stay** buttons, then calls method DealerPlay.

Method DisplayCard (lines 115–158) updates the GUI to display a newly dealt card. The method takes as arguments an integer representing the index of the PictureBox in the ArrayList that must have its image set, and a string representing the card. An empty string indicates that we wish to display the card face down. If method DisplayCard receives a string that's not empty, the program extracts the face and suit from the string and uses this information to find the correct image. The switch statement (lines 139–153) converts the number representing the suit to an integer and assigns the appropriate character to suitLetter (c for clubs, d for diamonds, h for hearts and s for spades). The character in suitLetter is used to complete the image's file name (lines 156–157).

22.6 Using Web Forms and Web Services

Our prior examples accessed Web services from Visual C# 2005 Windows applications. However, we can just as easily use them in Web applications created with Visual Web Developer. In fact, because Web-based businesses are becoming increasingly prevalent, it is common for Web applications to consume Web services. Figure 22.20 presents an airline reservation Web service that receives information regarding the type of seat a customer wishes to reserve and makes a reservation if such a seat is available. Later in this section, we present a Web application that allows a customer to specify a reservation request, then uses the airline reservation Web service to attempt to execute the request.

The airline reservation Web service has a single Web method—Reserve (lines 24–42)—which searches its seat database (Tickets.mdf) to locate a seat matching a user's request. If it finds an appropriate seat, Reserve updates the database, makes the reservation and returns true; otherwise, no reservation is made, and the method returns false. Note that the statements at lines 28–29 and line 37, which query and update the database, use objects of classes TicketsDataSet and TicketsDataSetTableAdapters.SeatsTableAdapter. Recall from Chapter 20 that DataSet and TableAdapter classes are created for you when you use the **DataSet Designer** to add a DataSet to a project. We discuss the steps for adding the TicketsDataSet in Section 22.6.1.

Reserve takes two arguments—a string representing the desired seat type (i.e., Window, Middle or Aisle) and a string representing the desired class type (i.e., Economy

```
1   // Fig. 22.20: ReservationService.cs
2   // Airline reservation Web Service.
3   using System;
4   using System.Web;
5   using System.Web.Services;
6   using System.Web.Services.Protocols;
7
8   [ WebService( Namespace = "http://www.deitel.com/", Description =
9      "Service that enables a user to reserve a seat on a plane." ) ]
10  [ WebServiceBinding( ConformsTo = WsiProfiles.BasicProfile1_1 ) ]
11  public class ReservationService : System.Web.Services.WebService
12  {
13     // create TicketsDataSet object for
14     // caching data from the Tickets database
15     private TicketsDataSet ticketsDataSet = new TicketsDataSet();
16
17     // create SeatsTableAdapter for interacting with the database
18     private TicketsDataSetTableAdapters.SeatsTableAdapter
19        SeatsTableAdapter =
20        new TicketsDataSetTableAdapters.SeatsTableAdapter();
21
```

Fig. 22.20 | Airline reservation Web service. (Part I of 2.)

```
22        // checks database to determine whether matching seat is available
23        [ WebMethod( Description = "Method to reserve a seat." ) ]
24        public bool Reserve( string seatType, string classType )
25        {
26            // fill TicketsDataSet.Seats with rows that represent untaken
27            // seats that match the specified seatType and classType
28            SeatsTableAdapter.FillByTypeAndClass(
29                ticketsDataSet.Seats, seatType, classType );
30
31            // if the number of seats returned is nonzero,
32            // obtain the first matching seat number and mark it as taken
33            if ( ticketsDataSet.Seats.Count != 0 )
34            {
35                string seatNumber = ticketsDataSet.Seats[ 0 ].Number;
36
37                SeatsTableAdapter.UpdateSeatAsTaken( seatNumber );
38                return true; // seat was reserved
39            } // end if
40
41            return false; // no seat was reserved
42        } // end method Reserve
43    } // end class ReservationService
```

Fig. 22.20 | Airline reservation Web service. (Part 2 of 2.)

or First). Our database contains four columns—the seat number (i.e., 1–10), the seat type (i.e., Window, Middle or Aisle), the class type (i.e., Economy or First) and a column containing either 1 (true) or 0 (false) to indicate whether the seat is taken. Lines 28–29 retrieve the seat numbers of any available seats matching the requested seat and class type. This statement fills the Seats table in ticketsDataSet with the results of the query

```
SELECT Number
FROM Seats
WHERE (Taken = 0) AND (Type = @type) AND (Class = @class)
```

The parameters @type and @class in the query are replaced with values of the seatType and classType arguments to SeatsTableAdapter method FillByTypeAndClass. In line 33, if the number of rows in the Seats table (ticketsDataSet.Seats.Count) is not zero, there was at least one seat that matched the user's request. In this case, the Web service reserves the first matching seat number. We obtain the seat number in line 35 by accessing the Seats table's first element (i.e., Seats[0]—the first row in the table), then obtaining the value of that row's Number column. Line 37 invokes the SeatsTableAdapter method UpdateSeatAsTaken and passes to it seatNumber—the seat to reserve. Method Update-SeatAsTaken uses the UPDATE statement

```
UPDATE Seats
SET Taken = 1
WHERE (Number = @number)
```

to mark the seat as taken in the database by replacing parameter @number with the value of seatNumber. Method Reserve returns true (line 38) to indicate that the reservation was successful. If there are no matching seats (line 33), Reserve returns false (line 41) to indicate that no seats matched the user's request.

22.6.1 Adding Data Components to a Web Service

We now use Visual Web Developer's tools to configure a DataSet that allows our Web service to interact with the Tickets.mdf SQL Server database file that is provided in the example folder for Fig. 22.20. We will add a new DataSet to the project, then configure the DataSet's TableAdapter using the **TableAdapter Configuration Wizard**. We will use the wizard to select the data source (Tickets.mdf) and to create the SQL statements necessary to support the database operations discussed in Fig. 22.20's description. The following steps for configuring the DataSet and its corresponding TableAdapter are similar to those you saw in Chapters 20–21.

Step 1: Create ReservationService and Add a DataSet to the Project
Begin by creating an ASP.NET Web Service project named ReservationService. Rename the file Service.cs as ReservationService.cs and replace its code with the code in Fig. 22.20. Next, add a DataSet named TicketsDataSet to the project. Right click the **App_Code** folder in the **Solution Explorer** and select **Add New Item...** from the pop-up menu. In the **Add New Item** dialog, select **DataSet**, specify TicketsDataSet.xsd in the **Name** field and click **Add**. This displays the TicketsDataSet in design view and opens the **TableAdapter Configuration Wizard**. When you add a DataSet to a project, the IDE creates appropriate TableAdapter classes for interacting with the database tables.

Step 2: Select the Data Source and Create a Connection
We use the **TableAdapter Configuration Wizard** in the next several steps to configure a TableAdapter for manipulating the Seats table in the Tickets.mdf database. Now, we select the database. In the **TableAdapter Configuration Wizard**, click the **New Connection...** button to display the **Add Connection** dialog. In this dialog, specify **Microsoft SQL Server Database File** as the **Data source**, then click the **Browse...** button to display the **Select SQL Server Database File** dialog. Locate Tickets.mdf on your computer, select it and click the **Open** button to return to the **Add Connection** dialog. Click the **Test Connection** button to test the database connection, then click **OK** to return to the **TableAdapter Configuration Wizard**. Click the **Next >** button, then click **Yes** when you are asked whether you would like to add the file to your project and modify the connection. Click **Next >** to save the connection string in the application configuration file.

Step 3: Open the Query Builder and Add the Seats Table from Tickets.mdf
Now we must specify how the TableAdapter will access the database. In this example, we will use SQL statements, so choose **Use SQL Statements**, then click **Next >**. Click **Query Builder...** to display the **Query Builder** and **Add Table** dialogs. Before building a SQL query, we must specify the table(s) to use in the query. The Tickets.mdf database contains only one table, named Seats. Select this table from the **Tables** tab and click **Add**. Click **Close** to close the **Add Table** dialog.

Step 4: Configure a SELECT Query to Obtain Available Seats
Now let's create a query which selects seats that are not already reserved and that match a particular type and class. Begin by selecting **Number** from the **Seats** table at the top of the **Query Builder** dialog. Next, we must specify the criteria for selecting seats. In the middle of the **Query Builder** dialog, click the cell below **Number** in the **Column** column and select **Taken**. In the **Filter** column of this row, type 0 (i.e., false) to indicate that we should select

only seat numbers that are not taken. In the next row, select **Type** in the **Column** column and specify @type as the **Filter** to indicate that the filter value will be specified as an argument to the method that implements this query. In the next row, select **Class** in the **Column** column and specify @class as the **Filter** to indicate that this filter value also will be specified as a method argument. Uncheck the checkboxes in the **Output** column for the **Taken, Type** and **Class** rows. The **Query Builder** dialog should now appear as shown in Fig. 22.21. Click **OK** to close the **Query Builder** dialog. Click the **Next >** button to choose the methods to generate. For the method name under **Fill a DataTable**, type FillByType-AndClass. For the method name under **Return a DataTable**, type GetDataByTypeAnd-Class. Click the **Finish** button to generate these methods.

Step 5: Add Another Query to the SeatsTableAdapter for the TicketsDataSet

The last two steps we need to perform create an UPDATE query that reserves a seat. In the design area for the TicketsDataSet, click **SeatsTableAdapter** to select it, then right click it and select **Add Query...** to display the **TableAdapter Query Configuration Wizard**. Select **Use SQL Statements** and click the **Next >** button. Select **Update** as the query type and click the **Next >** button. Delete the existing UPDATE query. Click **Query Builder...** to display the **Query Builder** and **Add Table** dialogs. Then add the Seats table as we did in *Step 3* and click **Close** to return to the **Query Builder** dialog.

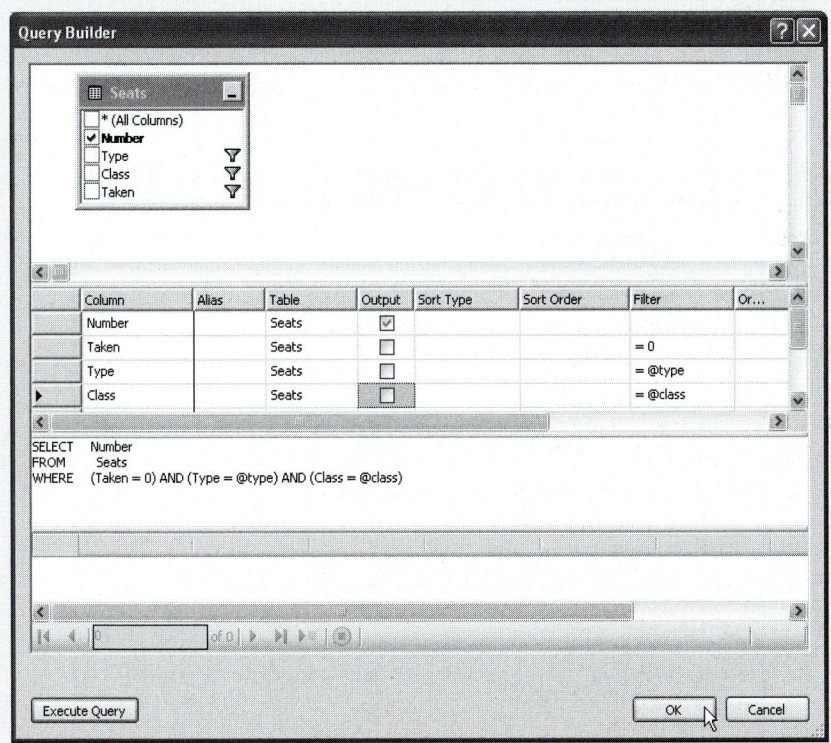

Fig. 22.21 | **QueryBuilder** dialog specifying a SELECT query that selects seats that are not already reserved and that match a particular type and class.

Step 6: Configure an UPDATE Statement to Reserve a Seat
In the **Query Builder** dialog, select the **Taken** column from the **Seats** table at the top of the dialog. In the middle of the dialog, place the value 1 (i.e., true) in the **New Value** column for the **Taken** row. In the row below **Taken**, select **Number**, uncheck the checkbox in the **Set** column and specify @number as the **Filter** value to indicate that the seat number will be specified as an argument to the method that implements this query. The **Query Builder** dialog should now appear as shown in Fig. 22.22. Click **OK** in the **Query Builder** dialog to return to the **TableAdapter Query Configuration Wizard**. Then click the **Next >** button to choose the name of the method that will perform the UPDATE query. Name the method UpdateSeatAsTaken, then click **Finish** to close the **TableAdapter Query Configuration Wizard**. At this point, you can use the ReservationService.asmx page to test the Web service's Reserve method. To do so, select **Start Without Debugging** from the **Debug** menu. In Section 22.6.2, we build a Web form to consume this Web service.

22.6.2 Creating a Web Form to Interact with the Airline Reservation Web Service

Figure 22.23 presents the ASPX listing for a Web Form through which users can select seat types. This page allows users to reserve a seat on the basis of its class (Economy or First) and location (Aisle, Middle or Window) in a row of seats. The page then uses the airline reservation Web service to carry out users' requests. If the database request is not successful, the user is instructed to modify the request and try again.

This page defines two DropDownList objects and a Button. One DropDownList (lines 22–27) displays all the seat types from which users can select. The second (lines 29–32)

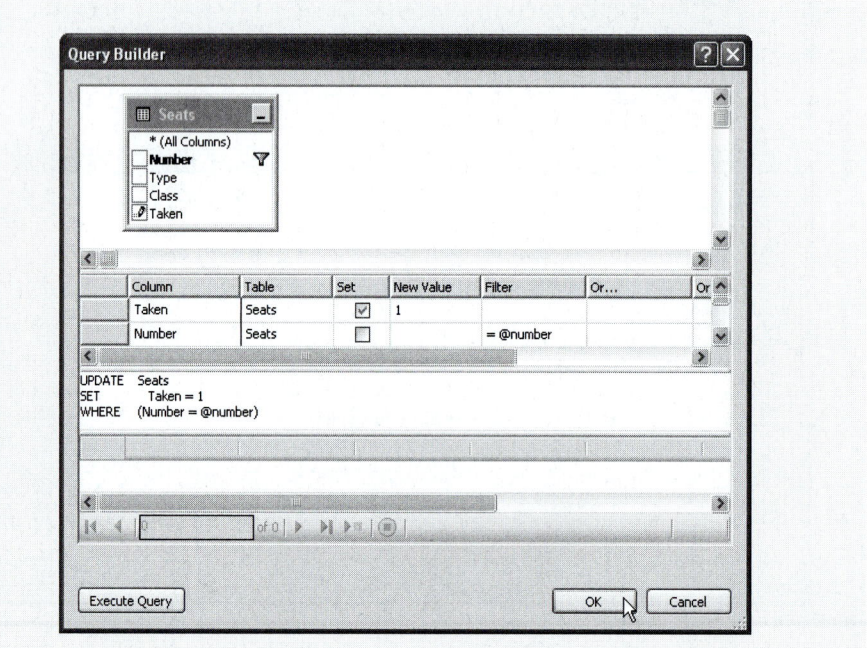

Fig. 22.22 | QueryBuilder dialog specifying an UPDATE statement that reserves a seat.

```
 1    <%-- Fig. 22.23: ReservationClient.aspx              --%>
 2    <%-- Web Form that allows users to reserve seats on a plane. --%>
 3    <%@ Page Language="C#" AutoEventWireup="true"
 4       CodeFile="ReservationClient.aspx.cs"
 5       Inherits="ReservationClient" %>
 6
 7    <!DOCTYPE html PUBLIC "-//W3C//DTD XHTML 1.1//EN"
 8       "http://www.w3.org/TR/xhtml11/DTD/xhtml11.dtd">
 9
10    <html xmlns="http://www.w3.org/1999/xhtml" >
11       <head runat="server">
12          <title>Ticket Reservation</title>
13       </head>
14
15       <body>
16          <form id="form1" runat="server">
17             <div>
18                <asp:Label ID="instructionsLabel" runat="server"
19                   Text="Please select the seat type and class to reserve:">
20                </asp:Label><br /><br />
21
22                <asp:DropDownList ID="seatList" runat="server"
23                   Height="22px" Width="100px">
24                   <asp:ListItem>Aisle</asp:ListItem>
25                   <asp:ListItem>Middle</asp:ListItem>
26                   <asp:ListItem>Window</asp:ListItem>
27                </asp:DropDownList>     
28
29                <asp:DropDownList ID="classList" runat="server" Width="100px">
30                   <asp:ListItem>Economy</asp:ListItem>
31                   <asp:ListItem>First</asp:ListItem>
32                </asp:DropDownList>     
33
34                <asp:Button ID="reserveButton" runat="server" Height="24px"
35                   OnClick="reserveButton_Click"
36                   Text="Reserve" Width="102px" /><br /><br />
37
38                <asp:Label ID="errorLabel" runat="server" ForeColor="#C00000"
39                   Height="19px" Width="343px"></asp:Label>
40             </div>
41          </form>
42       </body>
43    </html>
```

Fig. 22.23 | ASPX file that takes reservation information.

provides choices for the class type. Users click the Button named reserveButton (lines 34–36) to submit requests after making selections from the DropDownLists. The page also defines an initially blank Label named errorLabel (lines 38–39), which displays an appropriate message if no seat matching the user's selection is available. The code-behind file (Fig. 22.24) attaches an event handler to reserveButton.

Lines 16–17 of Fig. 22.24 create a ReservationService object. (Recall that you must add a Web reference to this Web service.) When the user clicks **Reserve** (Fig. 22.25), the reserveButton_Click event handler (lines 20–42 of Fig. 22.24) executes, and the page reloads. The event handler calls the Web service's Reserve method and passes to it the selected seat and class type as arguments (lines 23–24). If Reserve returns true, the application displays a message thanking the user for making a reservation (line 34); otherwise, errorLabel notifies the user that the type of seat requested is not available and instructs the user to try again (lines 39–40). Use the techniques presented in Chapter 21 to build this ASP.NET Web Form.

```
 1   // Fig. 22.24: ReservationClient.aspx.cs
 2   // ReservationClient code behind file.
 3   using System;
 4   using System.Data;
 5   using System.Configuration;
 6   using System.Web;
 7   using System.Web.Security;
 8   using System.Web.UI;
 9   using System.Web.UI.WebControls;
10   using System.Web.UI.WebControls.WebParts;
11   using System.Web.UI.HtmlControls;
12
13   public partial class ReservationClient : System.Web.UI.Page
14   {
15      // object of proxy type used to connect to Reservation Web service
16      private localhost.ReservationService ticketAgent =
17         new localhost.ReservationService();
18
19      // attempt to reserve the selected type of seat
20      protected void reserveButton_Click( object sender, EventArgs e )
21      {
22         // if WebMethod returned true, signal success
23         if ( ticketAgent.Reserve( seatList.SelectedItem.Text,
24            classList.SelectedItem.Text ) )
25         {
26            // hide other controls
27            instructionsLabel.Visible = false;
28            seatList.Visible = false;
29            classList.Visible = false;
30            reserveButton.Visible = false;
31            errorLabel.Visible = false;
32
33            // display message indicating success
34            Response.Write( "Your reservation has been made. Thank you." );
35         } // end if
36         else // WebMethod returned false, so signal failure
37         {
38            // display message in the initially blank errorLabel
39            errorLabel.Text = "This type of seat is not available. " +
40               "Please modify your request and try again.";
41         } // end else
42      } // end method reserveButton_Click
43   } // end class ReservationClient
```

Fig. 22.24 | Code-behind file for the reservation page.

a) Selecting a seat.

b) Seat reserved successfully.

c) Attempting to reserve another seat.

d) No seats match the requested type and class.

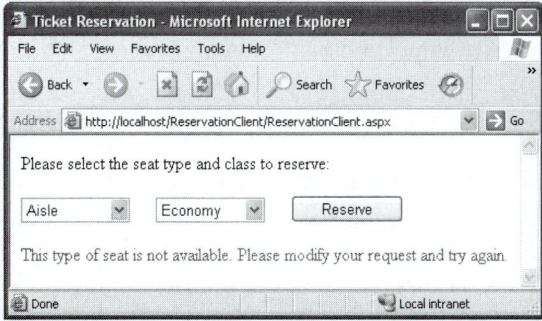

Fig. 22.25 | Ticket reservation Web Form sample execution.

22.7 User-Defined Types in Web Services

The Web methods we have demonstrated so far all received and returned simple type values. It is also possible to process user-defined types—known as *custom types*—in a Web service. These types can be passed to or returned from Web methods. Web service clients also can use these user-defined types, because the proxy class created for the client contains the type definitions.

This section presents an `EquationGenerator` Web service that generates random arithmetic equations of type `Equation`. The client is a math-tutoring application that inputs information about the mathematical question that the user wishes to attempt (addition, subtraction or multiplication) and the skill level of the user (1 specifies equations using one-digit numbers, 2 specifies equations involving two-digit numbers and 3 specifies equations containing three-digit numbers). The Web service then generates an equation consisting of random numbers with the proper number of digits. The client application receives the `Equation` and displays the sample question to the user in a Windows Form.

Serialization of User-Defined Types

We mentioned earlier that all types passed to and from Web services must be supported by SOAP. How, then, can SOAP support a type that is not even created yet? Custom types that are sent to or from a Web service are serialized, enabling them to be passed in XML format. This process is referred to as *XML serialization*.

Requirements for User-Defined Types Used with Web Methods

Classes that are used to specify return types and parameter types for Web methods must meet several requirements:

1. They must provide a `public` default or parameterless constructor. When a Web service or Web service consumer receives an XML serialized object, the .NET Framework must be able to call this constructor as part of the process of deserializing the object (i.e., converting it back to a C# object).

2. Properties and instance variables that should be serialized in XML format must be declared `public`. (Note that the `public` properties can be used to provide access to `private` instance variables.)

3. Properties that should be serialized must provide both `get` and `set` accessors (even if they have empty bodies). Read-only properties are not serialized.

Any data that is not serialized simply receives its default value (or the value provided by the default or parameterless constructor) when an object of the class is deserialized.

Common Programming Error 22.3

Failure to define a default or parameterless `public` constructor for a type being passed to or returned from a Web method is a runtime error.

Common Programming Error 22.4

Defining only the `get` or `set` accessor of a property for a user-defined type being passed to or returned from a Web method results in a property that is inaccessible to the client.

Software Engineering Observation 22.1

Clients of a Web service can access only the service's public members. The programmer can provide public properties to allow access to private data.

Defining Class Equation

We define class `Equation` in Fig. 22.26. Lines 28–46 define a constructor that takes three arguments—two `int`s representing the left and right operands and a `string` that represents the arithmetic operation to perform. The constructor sets the `leftOperand`, `rightOperand` and `operationType` instance variables, then calculates the appropriate result. The parameterless constructor (lines 21–25) calls the three-argument constructor (lines 28–46) and passes some default values. We do not use the parameterless constructor explicitly, but the XML serialization mechanism uses it when objects of this class are deserialized. Because we provide a constructor with parameters, we must explicitly define the parameterless constructor in this class so that objects of the class can be passed to or returned from Web methods.

```
 1   // Fig. 22.26: Equation.cs
 2   // Class Equation that contains information about an equation.
 3   using System;
 4   using System.Data;
 5   using System.Configuration;
 6   using System.Web;
 7   using System.Web.Security;
 8   using System.Web.UI;
 9   using System.Web.UI.WebControls;
10   using System.Web.UI.WebControls.WebParts;
11   using System.Web.UI.HtmlControls;
12
13   public class Equation
14   {
15      private int leftOperand; // number to the left of the operator
16      private int rightOperand; // number to the right of the operator
17      private int resultValue; // result of the operation
18      private string operationType; // type of the operation
19
20      // required default constructor
21      public Equation()
22         : this( 0, 0, "+" )
23      {
24         // empty body
25      } // end default constructor
26
27      // three-argument constructor for class Equation
28      public Equation( int leftValue, int rightValue, string type )
29      {
30         leftOperand = leftValue;
31         rightOperand = rightValue;
32         operationType = type;
33
34         switch ( operationType ) // perform appropriate operation
35         {
```

Fig. 22.26 | Class that stores equation information. (Part 1 of 3.)

```
36             case "+": // addition
37                 resultValue = leftOperand + rightOperand;
38                 break;
39             case "-": // subtraction
40                 resultValue = leftOperand - rightOperand;
41                 break;
42             case "*": // multiplication
43                 resultValue = leftOperand * rightOperand;
44                 break;
45         } // end switch
46     } // end three-argument constructor
47
48     // return string representation of the Equation object
49     public override string ToString()
50     {
51         return leftOperand.ToString() + " " + operationType + " " +
52             rightOperand.ToString() + " = " + resultValue.ToString();
53     } // end method ToString
54
55     // property that returns a string representing left-hand side
56     public string LeftHandSide
57     {
58         get
59         {
60             return leftOperand.ToString() + " " + operationType + " " +
61                 rightOperand.ToString();
62         } // end get
63
64         set // required set accessor
65         {
66             // empty body
67         } // end set
68     } // end property LeftHandSide
69
70     // property that returns a string representing right-hand side
71     public string RightHandSide
72     {
73         get
74         {
75             return resultValue.ToString();
76         } // end get
77
78         set // required set accessor
79         {
80             // empty body
81         } // end set
82     } // end property RightHandSide
83
84     // property to access the left operand
85     public int Left
86     {
87         get
88         {
```

Fig. 22.26 | Class that stores equation information. (Part 2 of 3.)

```
89          return leftOperand;
90        } // end get
91
92        set
93        {
94           leftOperand = value;
95        } // end set
96     } // end property Left
97
98     // property to access the right operand
99     public int Right
100    {
101       get
102       {
103          return rightOperand;
104       } // end get
105
106       set
107       {
108          rightOperand = value;
109       } // end set
110    } // end property Right
111
112    // property to access the result of applying
113    // an operation to the left and right operands
114    public int Result
115    {
116       get
117       {
118          return resultValue;
119       } // end get
120
121       set
122       {
123          resultValue = value;
124       } // end set
125    } // end property Result
126
127    // property to access the operation
128    public string Operation
129    {
130       get
131       {
132          return operationType;
133       } // end get
134
135       set
136       {
137          operationType = value;
138       } // end set
139    } // end property Operation
140 } // end class Equation
```

Fig. 22.26 | Class that stores equation information. (Part 3 of 3.)

Class Equation defines properties LeftHandSide (lines 56–68), RightHandSide (lines 71–82), Left (lines 85–96), Right (lines 99–110), Result (lines 114–125) and Operation (lines 128–139). The client of the Web service does not need to modify the values of properties LeftHandSide and RightHandSide. However, recall that a property can be serialized only if it has both a get and a set accessor—this is true even if the set accessor has an empty body. LeftHandSide (lines 56–68) returns a string representing everything to the left of the equals (=) sign in the equation, and RightHandSide (lines 71–82) returns a string representing everything to the right of the equals (=) sign. Left (lines 85–96) returns the int to the left of the operator (known as the left operand), and Right (lines 99–110) returns the int to the right of the operator (known as the right operand). Result (lines 114–125) returns the solution to the equation, and Operation (lines 128–139) returns the operator in the equation. The client in this case study does not use the RightHandSide property, but we included it in case future clients choose to use it.

Creating the EquationGenerator Web Service

Figure 22.27 presents the EquationGenerator Web service, which creates random, customized Equations. This Web service contains only method GenerateEquation (lines 16–32), which takes two parameters—a string representing the mathematical operation (addition, subtraction or multiplication) and an int representing the difficulty level.

```
1   // Fig. 22.27: Generator.cs
2   // Web Service to generate random equations based on a specified
3   // operation and difficulty level.
4   using System;
5   using System.Web;
6   using System.Web.Services;
7   using System.Web.Services.Protocols;
8
9   [ WebService( Namespace = "http://www.deitel.com/", Description =
10      "Web service that generates a math equation." ) ]
11  [ WebServiceBinding( ConformsTo = WsiProfiles.BasicProfile1_1 ) ]
12  public class Generator : System.Web.Services.WebService
13  {
14      // Method to generate a math equation
15      [ WebMethod( Description = "Method to generate a math equation." ) ]
16      public Equation GenerateEquation( string operation, int level )
17      {
18          // find maximum and minimum number to be used
19          int maximum = Convert.ToInt32( Math.Pow( 10, level ) );
20          int minimum = Convert.ToInt32( Math.Pow( 10, level - 1 ) );
21
22          // object to generate random numbers
23          Random randomObject = new Random();
24
25          // create equation consisting of two random
26          // numbers between minimum and maximum parameters
27          Equation equation = new Equation(
28              randomObject.Next( minimum, maximum ),
29              randomObject.Next( minimum, maximum ), operation );
```

Fig. 22.27 | Web service that generates random equations. (Part 1 of 2.)

```
30
31          return equation;
32        } // end method GenerateEquation
33      } // end class Generator
```

Fig. 22.27 | Web service that generates random equations. (Part 2 of 2.)

Testing the EquationGenerator Web Service

Figure 22.28 shows the result of testing the EquationGenerator Web service. Note that the return value from our Web method is XML-encoded. However, this example differs from previous ones in that the XML specifies the values for all public properties and data of the object that is being returned. The return object has been serialized in XML. Our proxy class takes this return value and deserializes it into an object of class Equation, then passes it to the client.

Note that an Equation object is *not* being passed between the Web service and the client. Rather, the information in the object is being sent as XML-encoded data. Clients

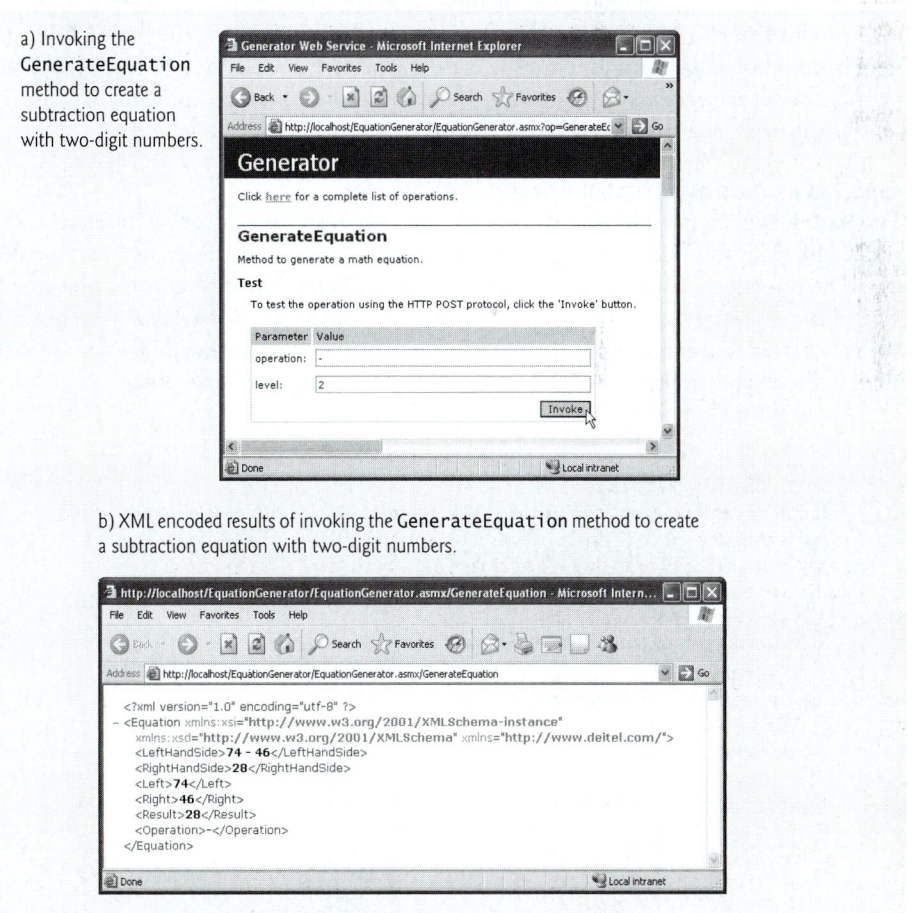

a) Invoking the GenerateEquation method to create a subtraction equation with two-digit numbers.

b) XML encoded results of invoking the GenerateEquation method to create a subtraction equation with two-digit numbers.

Fig. 22.28 | Returning an XML serialized object from a Web method.

created using .NET will take the information and create a new Equation object. Clients created on other platforms, however, may use the information differently. Readers creating clients on other platforms should check the Web services documentation for the specific platform they are using, to see how their clients may process custom types.

Let's examine Web method GenerateEquation more closely. Lines 19–20 of Fig. 22.27 define the upper and lower bounds for the random numbers that the method uses to generate an Equation. To set these limits, the program first calls static method Pow of class Math—this method raises its first argument to the power of its second argument. To calculate the value of maximum (the upper bound for any randomly generated numbers used to form an Equation), the program raises 10 to the power of the specified level argument (line 19). If level is 1, maximum is 10; if level is 2, maximum is 100; and if level is 3, maximum is 1000. Variable minimum's value is determined by raising 10 to a power one less than level (line 20). This calculates the smallest number with level digits. If level is 1, minimum is 1; if level is 2, minimum is 10; and if level is 3, minimum is 100.

Lines 27–29 create a new Equation object. The program calls Random method Next, which returns an int that is greater than or equal to the specified lower bound, but less than the specified upper bound. This method generates a left operand value that is greater than or equal to minimum but less than maximum (i.e., a number with level digits). The right operand is another random number with the same characteristics. Line 29 passes the string operation received by GenerateEquation to the Equation constructor. Line 31 returns the new Equation object to the client.

Consuming the *EquationGenerator* Web Service

The MathTutor application (Fig. 22.29) uses the EquationGenerator Web service. The application calls the Web service's GenerateEquation method to create an Equation object. The tutor then displays the left-hand side of the Equation and waits for user input. This example accesses classes Generator and Equation from the localhost namespace—both are placed in this namespace by default when the proxy is generated. We declare variables of these types at lines 22–23. Line 23 also creates the Generator proxy.

```
1   // Fig. 22.29: MathTutor.cs
2   // Math tutoring program using Web service to generate random equations.
3   using System;
4   using System.Collections.Generic;
5   using System.ComponentModel;
6   using System.Data;
7   using System.Drawing;
8   using System.Text;
9   using System.Windows.Forms;
10
11  namespace MathTutor
12  {
13      public partial class MathTutorForm : Form
14      {
15          public MathTutorForm()
16          {
```

Fig. 22.29 | Math-tutoring application. (Part 1 of 4.)

```
17          InitializeComponent();
18      } // end constructor
19
20      private string operation = "+";
21      private int level = 1;
22      private localhost.Equation equation;
23      private localhost.Generator generator = new localhost.Generator();
24
25      // generates new equation when user clicks button
26      private void generateButton_Click( object sender, EventArgs e )
27      {
28          // generate equation using current operation and level
29          equation = generator.GenerateEquation( operation, level );
30
31          // display left-hand side of equation
32          questionLabel.Text = equation.LeftHandSide;
33
34          okButton.Enabled = true;
35          answerTextBox.Enabled = true;
36      } // end method generateButton_Click
37
38      // check user's answer
39      private void okButton_Click( object sender, EventArgs e )
40      {
41          // determine correct result from Equation object
42          int answer = equation.Result;
43
44          if ( answerTextBox.Text == "" )
45              return;
46
47          // get user's answer
48          int userAnswer = Int32.Parse( answerTextBox.Text );
49
50          // determine whether user's answer is correct
51          if ( answer == userAnswer )
52          {
53              questionLabel.Text = ""; // clear question
54              answerTextBox.Text = ""; // clear answer
55              okButton.Enabled = false; // disable OK button
56              MessageBox.Show( "Correct! Good job!" );
57          } // end if
58          else
59              MessageBox.Show( "Incorrect. Try again." );
60      } // end method okButton_Click
61
62      // set difficulty level to 1
63      private void levelOneRadioButton_CheckedChanged( object sender,
64          EventArgs e )
65      {
66          level = 1;
67      } // end method levelOneRadioButton_CheckedChanged
68
```

Fig. 22.29 | Math-tutoring application. (Part 2 of 4.)

```
69         // set difficulty level to 2
70         private void levelTwoRadioButton_CheckedChanged( object sender,
71            EventArgs e )
72         {
73            level = 2;
74         } // end method levelTwoRadioButton_CheckedChanged
75
76         // set difficulty level to 3
77         private void levelThreeRadioButton_CheckedChanged( object sender,
78            EventArgs e )
79         {
80            level = 3;
81         } // end method levelThreeRadioButton_CheckedChanged
82
83         // set the operation to addition
84         private void additionRadioButton_CheckedChanged( object sender,
85            EventArgs e )
86         {
87            operation = "+";
88            generateButton.Text =
89               "Generate " + additionRadioButton.Text + " Example";
90         } // end method additionRadioButton_CheckedChanged
91
92         // set the operation to subtraction
93         private void subtractionRadioButton_CheckedChanged( object sender,
94            EventArgs e )
95         {
96            operation = "-";
97            generateButton.Text = "Generate " +
98               subtractionRadioButton.Text + " Example";
99         } // end method subtractionRadioButton_CheckedChanged
100
101        // set the operation to multiplication
102        private void multiplicationRadioButton_CheckedChanged(
103           object sender, EventArgs e )
104        {
105           operation = "*";
106           generateButton.Text = "Generate " +
107              multiplicationRadioButton.Text + " Example";
108        } // end method multiplicationRadioButton_CheckedChanged
109     } // end class MathTutorForm
110  } // end namespace MathTutor
```

a) Generating a level 1 addition equation.

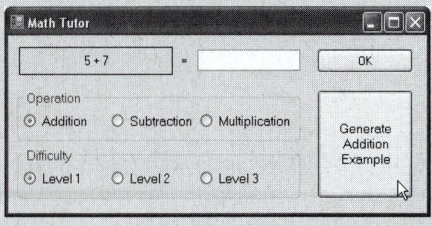

Fig. 22.29 | Math-tutoring application. (Part 3 of 4.)

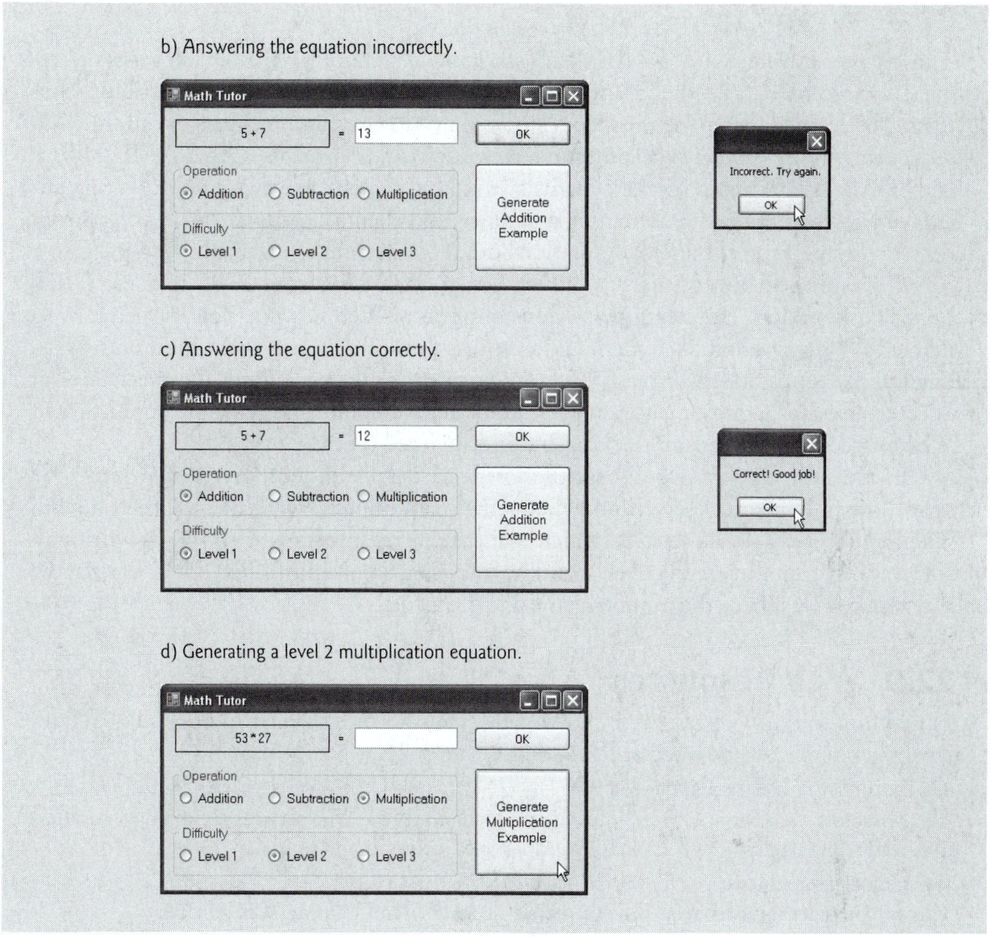

b) Answering the equation incorrectly.

c) Answering the equation correctly.

d) Generating a level 2 multiplication equation.

Fig. 22.29 | Math-tutoring application. (Part 4 of 4.)

The math-tutoring application displays an equation and waits for the user to enter an answer. The default setting for the difficulty level is **1**, but the user can change this by choosing a level from the RadioButtons in the GroupBox labeled **Difficulty**. Clicking any of the levels invokes the corresponding RadioButton's CheckedChanged event handler (lines 63–81), which sets integer level to the level selected by the user. Although the default setting for the question type is **Addition**, the user also can change this by selecting one of the RadioButtons in the GroupBox labeled **Operation**. Doing so invokes the corresponding operation's event handlers in lines 84–108, which assigns to string operation the symbol corresponding to the user's selection. Each event handler also updates the Text property of the **Generate** button to match the newly selected operation.

Event handler generateButton_Click (lines 26–36) invokes EquationGenerator method GenerateEquation (line 29). After receiving an Equation object from the Web service, the handler displays the left-hand side of the equation in questionLabel (line 32) and enables OkButton so that the user can enter an answer. When the user clicks **OK**, OkButton_Click (lines 39–60) checks whether the user provided the correct answer.

22.8 Wrap-Up

This chapter introduced ASP.NET Web services—a technology that enables users to request and receive data via the Internet and promotes software reusability in distributed systems. You learned that a Web service is a class that allows client machines to call the Web service's methods remotely via common data formats and protocols, such as XML, HTTP and SOAP. We discussed several benefits of this kind of distributed computing—e.g., clients can access certain data on remote machines, and clients lacking the processing power necessary to perform specific computations can leverage remote machines' resources.

We explained how Visual C# 2005, Visual Web Developer 2005 and the .NET Framework facilitate the creation and consumption of Web services. You learned how to define Web services and Web methods, as well as how to consume them from both Windows applications and ASP.NET Web applications. After explaining the mechanics of Web services through our HugeInteger example, we demonstrated more sophisticated Web services that use session tracking and user-defined types.

In the next chapter, we discuss the low-level details of computer networking. We show how to implement servers and clients that communicate with one another, how to send and receive data via sockets (which make such transmissions as simple as writing to and reading from files, respectively), and how to create a multithreaded server for playing a networked version of the popular game Tic-Tac-Toe.

22.9 Web Resources

In addition to the Web resources shown here, you should also refer to the ASP.NET-related Web resources provided at the end of Chapter 21.

msdn.microsoft.com/webservices
The Microsoft Web Services Developer Center includes .NET Web services technology specifications and white papers as well as XML/SOAP articles, columns and links.

www.webservices.org
This site provides industry-related news, articles, resources and links on Web services.

www-130.ibm.com/developerworks/webservices
IBM's site for service-oriented architecture (SOA) and Web services includes articles, downloads, demos and discussion forums regarding Web services technology.

www.w3.org/TR/wsdl
This site provides extensive documentation on WSDL, including a thorough discussion of Web services–related technologies such as XML, SOAP, HTTP and MIME types in the context of WSDL.

www.w3.org/TR/soap
This site provides extensive documentation on SOAP messages, using SOAP with HTTP and SOAP security issues.

www.uddi.com
The Universal Description, Discovery and Integration site provides discussions, specifications, white papers and general information on UDDI.

www.ws-i.org
The Web Services Interoperability Organization's Web site provides detailed information regarding efforts to build Web services based on standards that promote interoperability and true platform independence.

webservices.xml.com/security
This site contains articles about Web services security issues and standard security protocols.

Summary

Section 22.1 Introduction

- Web services promote software reusability in distributed systems where applications execute across multiple computers on a network.

- Simple Object Access Protocol (SOAP) is an XML-based protocol that describes how to mark up requests and responses so that they can be transferred via protocols such as HTTP.

- Web services represent the next step in object-oriented programming. Programmers can develop applications using Web service class libraries distributed worldwide.

Section 22.2 .NET Web Services Basics

- A Web service is a software component stored on one machine that can be accessed by an application (or other software component) on another machine over a network using standard Internet protocols.

- The machine on which a Web service resides is referred to as a remote machine.

- A client that accesses a Web service sends a method call over a network to the remote machine, which processes the call and returns a response over the network to the client.

- Requests to and responses from Web services created with Visual Web Developer are typically transmitted via SOAP. Any client capable of generating and processing SOAP messages can interact with a Web service, regardless of the language in which the Web service is written.

- Web services and SOAP are platform and language independent, so companies can collaborate via Web services without worrying about the compatibility of their hardware, software and communications technologies.

Section 22.2.1 Creating a Web Service in Visual Web Developer

- To create a Web service in Visual Web Developer, you first create a project of type **ASP.NET Web Service**. Visual Web Developer then generates files to contain the Web service code and an ASMX file (which provides access to the Web service).

- A Web service class defines the methods that the Web service makes available to clients.

- ASP.NET Web services can be tested using Visual Web Developer's built-in test server. However, to make an ASP.NET Web service publicly accessible to clients on other computers, you must deploy the Web service to a Web server such as Internet Information Services (IIS).

- Methods marked with the `WebMethod` attribute are invoked through Remote Procedure Calls (RPCs). These methods are often referred to as Web service methods or simply Web methods.

Section 22.2.2 Discovering Web Services

- A client application can consume (i.e., use) a published Web service.

- Clients must be able to find a Web service and learn about its capabilities before consuming it. DISCO is a Microsoft-specific technology used to locate Web services on a server.

- DISCO files consist of XML markup that describes for clients the location of Web services.

- A `.disco` file is accessed via a Web service's ASMX page and contains markup specifying references to the documents that define various Web services.

- When a client requests a `.vsdisco` file, the .NET Framework searches for Web services in the directory containing the `.vsdisco` file (and its subdirectories), then generates XML (using the same syntax as that of a `.disco` file) that contains references to all the Web services found.

- A developer typically places a `.vsdisco` file at the root of a server; when accessed, this file locates the `.disco` files for Web services anywhere on the system and uses the markup found in these `.disco` files to return information about the entire system.

Section 22.2.3 Determining a Web Service's Functionality

- Web services normally contain a service description—an XML document that conforms to the Web Service Description Language (WSDL). WSDL is an XML vocabulary that defines the methods that a Web service makes available and how clients can interact with them.

- WSDL documents are meant to be read by applications, so they know how to interact with the Web services described in the documents.

- Visual Web Developer generates an ASMX file when a Web service is constructed, to offer a more human-understandable description of the Web service. Files with the .asmx filename extension are ASP.NET Web service files and are executed by ASP.NET on a Web server (e.g., IIS).

- When viewed in a Web browser, an ASMX file presents descriptions of Web methods and links to test pages that allow users to execute sample calls to these methods.

- If a client requests the Web service's WSDL description (either by appending ?WSDL to the ASMX file's URL or by clicking the **Service Description** link in an ASMX page), ASP.NET generates the WSDL description, then returns it to the client for display in the Web browser.

Section 22.2.4 Testing a Web Service's Methods

- The protocol that transmits request and response messages is known as the Web service's wire format or wire protocol because it defines how information is sent "along the wire."

- SOAP is a popular wire format, because SOAP messages can be sent using several wire protocols.

Section 22.2.5 Building a Client to Use a Web Service

- For a client application to consume a Web service, you must add to the client application a Web reference that refers to the Web service.

- To add a Web reference in Visual C# 2005, right click the project name in the **Solution Explorer** and select **Add Web Reference...**. In the resulting dialog, specify the Web service to consume.

- When you specify the Web service you want to consume, Visual C# 2005 accesses the Web service's WSDL information and copies it to a WSDL file that is stored in the client project's Web References folder. This file is visible when you instruct Visual C# 2005 to **Show All Files**.

- To ensure that the WSDL file is up-to-date, right click the Web reference in the **Solution Explorer** and select **Update Web Reference** to update the files in the **Web References** folder.

- The WSDL information is used to create a proxy class, which handles all the "plumbing" required for Web method calls (i.e., the networking details and the formation of SOAP messages).

- When a client calls a Web method, the client actually calls a corresponding method in the proxy class that has the same name and parameters as the Web method. The proxy formats the call to be sent as a request in a SOAP message. The Web service receives this request as a SOAP message, executes the method call and sends back the result as another SOAP message. When the client application receives the SOAP message containing the response, the proxy class decodes it and returns the results as the return value of the Web method that was called.

Section 22.3 Simple Object Access Protocol (SOAP)

- The Simple Object Access Protocol (SOAP) is a platform-independent protocol that uses XML to make remote procedure calls.

- Each request and response is packaged in a SOAP message containing the information that a Web service requires to process the message.

- SOAP supports an extensive set of types—the primitive types, DataSet, DateTime, XmlNode and others. SOAP can also transmit arrays of these types and objects of user-defined types.

- When a program invokes a Web method, the request and all relevant information are packaged in a SOAP message and sent to the server on which the Web service resides.

- A Web service receives a SOAP message and parses its contents (contained in a SOAP envelope) to determine the method that the client wishes to execute and the method's arguments.

- After a Web service parses a SOAP message, the proper method is called and the response is sent back to the client in another SOAP message. The client parses the response to retrieve the result.

Section 22.4 Publishing and Consuming Web Services

- Creating a Web service is also known as publishing the Web service.

- Using a Web service is also known as consuming the Web service.

- An application that consumes a Web service consists of a proxy class representing the Web service and a client application that accesses the Web service via an instance of the proxy class.

- The proxy passes a Web method's arguments from the client to the Web service. When the Web method completes its task, the proxy receives the result and parses it for the client application.

Section 22.4.1 Defining the HugeInteger Web Service

- The WebService attribute specifies a Web service class's namespace and description. Namespaces help clients differentiate between Web services. The WebService attribute's Namespace property specifies the namespace—usually a company's domain name, since all domain names are guaranteed to be unique. The Description property describes the Web service's purpose.

- By default, Visual Web Developer sets the WebServiceBinding attribute to indicate that the Web service conforms to the Basic Profile 1.1 (BP 1.1) developed by the Web Services Interoperability Organization (WS-I), a group dedicated to promoting interoperability among Web services developed on different platforms with different programming languages. BP 1.1 defines best practices for various aspects of creating and consuming Web services. Setting the WebServiceBinding attribute's ConformsTo property to WsiProfiles.BasicProfile1_1 instructs ASP.NET to generate WSDL and ASMX files, in conformance with BP 1.1 guidelines.

- Web service classes created in Visual Web Developer inherit from System.Web.Services.WebService, which provides members that are useful in determining information about the client and the Web service itself.

- The WebMethod attribute exposes a Web method so that it can be called remotely. When this attribute is absent, the method is not accessible to clients that consume the Web service.

- The WebMethod attribute's Description property allows the ASMX page to display information about the method.

Section 22.4.2 Building a Web Service in Visual Web Developer

- To create an **ASP.NET Web Service** project, first select **File > New Web Site...** to display the **New Web Site** dialog. In this dialog, select **ASP.NET Web Service** in the **Templates** pane. Select **HTTP** from the **Location** drop-down list to indicate that the files should be placed on a Web server. By default, Visual Web Developer places the files on the local machine's IIS Web server in a virtual directory named WebSite1 (http://localhost/WebSite1). Replace the name WebSite1 with your Web service's name. Next, select **Visual C#** from the **Language** drop-down list to build the Web service with C#. The Web service project's solution file (.sln) is placed in the Projects subfolder within the current Windows user's My Documents\Visual Studio 2005 folder.

- If you do not have access to an IIS Web server to build and test your Web services, you can select **File System** from the **Location** drop-down list to place your Web service's files on your local hard disk. You can test the Web service using Visual Web Developer's built-in Web server.

- When an **ASP.NET Web Service** project is created, the code-behind file `Service.cs` contains code for a simple Web service named `Service` that contains a sample Web method named `HelloWorld`. This method is a placeholder that you will replace with your own method(s).

- The ASMX file displayed in the **Solution Explorer** indicates the programming language in which the Web service's code-behind file is written, the location of the code-behind file and the class that defines the Web service. When you request the ASMX page through IIS, ASP.NET uses this information to generate the list of Web methods and their descriptions.

- If you change the name of the code-behind file or the name of the class that defines the Web service, you must modify the ASMX file accordingly.

Section 22.4.3 Deploying the HugeInteger Web Service

- When you create a Web service directly on your computer's local IIS server, the Web service is already deployed.

- Choose **Build Web Site** from the **Build** menu to ensure that a Web service compiles without errors.

- You can test the Web service directly from Visual Web Developer by selecting **Start Without Debugging** from the **Debug** menu. This opens a browser window that contains the Web service's ASMX page. Click the link for a particular Web service method to display a Web page that allows you to test the method.

- If you deploy a Web service on an IIS Web server, a client can connect to that server to access the Web service with a URL of the form

  `http://host/WebServiceName/WebServiceName.asmx`

  where *host* is the hostname or IP address of the Web server. To access the Web service from another computer in your company's or school's local area network, replace *host* with the actual name of the computer on which IIS is running.

- If you have the Windows XP Service Pack 2 operating system on the computer running IIS, that computer may not allow requests from other computers by default. To allow other computers to connect to your computer's Web server, select **Start > Control Panel** to open your system's **Control Panel** window, then double click **Windows Firewall** to view the **Windows Firewall** settings dialog. In the **Windows Firewall** settings dialog, click the **Advanced** tab, select **Local Area Connection** (or your network connection's name if it is different) in the **Network Connection Settings** list box and click the **Settings...** button to display the **Advanced Settings** dialog. In the **Advanced Settings** dialog, ensure that the checkbox for **Web Server (HTTP)** is checked to allow clients on other computers to submit requests to your computer's Web server. Click **OK** in the **Advanced Settings** dialog, then click **OK** in the **Windows Firewall** settings dialog.

- To access a Web service that is running in Visual Web Developer's built-in Web server, you must specify the randomly generated port number chosen by Visual Web Developer, as in

  `http://host:portNumber/WebServiceName/WebServiceName.asmx`

  where *host* is the hostname or IP address of the computer on which Visual Web Developer's built-in Web server is running and *portNumber* is the specific port on which the Web server receives requests. You can see this port number in your Web browser's **Address** field when you test the Web service from Visual Web Developer.

Section 22.4.4 Creating a Client to Consume the HugeInteger Web Service

- A client uses a proxy class to communicate with a Web service. The proxy class's purpose is to make clients think they are calling the Web methods directly.

- When you add a Web reference, Visual C# 2005 generates an appropriate proxy class. You create an instance of the proxy class and use it to call the Web service's methods.

- To add a Web reference, right click the project name in the **Solution Explorer** and select **Add Web Reference....** In the **Add Web Reference** dialog that appears, click **Web services on the local machine** to locate Web references stored on IIS Web server on your local computer (http://localhost). Select the Web service from the list of available Web services, then click the **Add Reference** button. The **Solution Explorer** should now contain a **Web References** folder with a node named after the domain name where the Web service is located (localhost when using the local Web server).

- When creating a client to consume a Web service, add the Web reference first so that Visual C# 2005 (or Visual Web Developer) can recognize an object of the Web service proxy class.

- Universal Description, Discovery and Integration (UDDI) is a technology for locating new Web services. UDDI is an ongoing project for developing a set of specifications that define how Web services should be published so that programmers searching for Web services can find them.

Section 22.5 Session Tracking in Web Services
- Using session tracking eliminates the need for information about the client to be passed between the client and the Web service multiple times.

Section 22.5.1 Creating a Blackjack Web Service
- Storing session information can provide client programmers with a more intuitive Web service.

- Setting a WebMethod attribute's EnableSession property to True indicates that session information should be maintained in an HttpSessionState object (named Session by ASP.NET).

- A Web service that uses session tracking creates cookies to identify each of its clients uniquely. A non-browser client application that wishes to use such a Web service must create a CookieContainer object to store cookies. A client Web browser with cookie handling enabled stores cookies automatically.

- An ArrayList is a dynamic array—its size can change at execution time. ArrayList method Add places an object in the ArrayList, and ArrayList method RemoveAt removes the element in the ArrayList at the index specified by its argument, thus reducing the size of the ArrayList by one.

Section 22.5.2 Consuming the Blackjack Web Service
- An object of class CookieContainer (namespace System.Net) stores the information from a cookie (created by a Web service that uses session tracking) in a Cookie object in the CookieContainer.

- A Cookie contains a unique identifier that a Web service can use to recognize the client when the client makes future requests. The cookie is sent back to the server with each request.

- If a client does not create a CookieContainer object when consuming a Web service that uses session tracking, the Web service creates a new Session object for each request, and the user's state information does not persist across requests.

Section 22.6 Using Web Forms and Web Services
- It is common for Web applications to consume Web services.

- You can use the **TableAdapter Configuration Wizard** to select a data source and to create the SQL statements necessary to support the database operations of your Web service.

- To add a DataSet to your Web service, right click the **App_Code** folder in the **Solution Explorer** and select **Add New Item...** from the pop-up menu. In the **Add New Item** dialog, select **DataSet**, specify the name of your DataSet in the **Name** field and click **Add**. This displays the DataSet in design view and opens the **TableAdapter Configuration Wizard**.

Section 22.7 User-Defined Types in Web Services

- It is possible to process user-defined types (also known as custom types) in a Web service. These types can be passed to or returned from Web methods. Web service clients also can use these user-defined types, because the proxy class created for the client contains these type definitions.

- Custom types that are sent to or from a Web service are serialized, enabling them to be passed in XML format. This process is referred to as XML serialization.

- Classes that are used to specify Web method return types and parameter types must provide a `public` default or parameterless constructor. Properties and instance variables that should be serialized in XML format must be declared `public`. Properties that should be serialized must provide both `get` and `set` accessors. Read-only properties are not serialized. Data that is not serialized simply receives its default value when an object of the class is deserialized.

Terminology

Add method of class `ArrayList`
Add Web Reference dialog
`ArrayList` class
`.asmx` filename extension
ASMX page
ASP.NET Web Service project
business-to-business (B2B) transactions
`ConformsTo` property of a `WebServiceBinding` attribute
consume a Web service
`CookieContainer` class
custom type
`Description` property of a `WebMethod` attribute
`Description` property of a `WebService` attribute
`.disco` file
`.discomap` file
Discovery of Web services (DISCO)
`EnableSession` property of a `WebMethod` attribute
expose a Web method
firewall
`.map` file
`Namespace` property of a `WebService` attribute
parse a SOAP message
proxy class for a Web service
publish a Web service
remote machine
Remote Procedure Call (RPC)
`RemoveAt` method of class `ArrayList`

request a Web service's WSDL description
service description for a Web service
session tracking in Web services
Simple Object Access Protocol (SOAP)
SOAP envelope
SOAP message
`System.Net` namespace
TableAdapter Configuration Wizard
Universal Description, Discovery and Integration (UDDI)
user-defined types in Web services
`.vsdisco` file
Web method
Web references
Web service
Web Service Description Language (WSDL)
Web service method
Web Services Interoperability Organization (WS-I)
`WebMethod` attribute
`WebService` attribute
`WebService` class
`WebServiceBinding` attribute
wire format
wire protocol
WS-I Basic Profile 1.1 (BP 1.1)
`WsiProfiles.BasicProfile1_1`
XML serialization

Self-Review Exercises

22.1 State whether each of the following is *true* or *false*. If *false*, explain why.
  a) The purpose of a Web service is to create objects of a class located on a remote machine. This class then can be instantiated and used on the local machine.
  b) You must explicitly create the proxy class after you add a Web reference to a client application.

c) A proxy class communicating with a Web service normally uses SOAP to send and receive messages.

d) A client application can invoke only those methods of a Web service that are tagged with the `WebMethod` attribute.

e) To enable session tracking in a Web method, no action is required other than setting the `EnableSession` property to `true` in the `WebMethod` attribute.

f) Web methods cannot be declared `static`.

g) A user-defined type used in a Web service must define both `get` and `set` accessors for any property that will be serialized.

22.2 Fill in the blanks for each of the following statements:

a) When messages are sent between an application and a Web service, each message is placed in a(n) _____.

b) A Web service can derive from class _____ to inherit members that determine information about the user, the application and other topics relevant to the Web service.

c) The class that defines a Web service is located in the _____ file for that Web service.

d) Web service requests are typically transported over the Internet via the _____ protocol.

e) To add a description for a Web method in an ASMX page, the _____ property of the `WebMethod` attribute is used.

f) _____ transforms an object into a format that can be sent between a Web service and a client.

g) By default, a proxy class is defined in a namespace whose name is that of the _____ in which the Web service is defined.

Answers to Self-Review Exercises

22.1 a) False. Web services are used to execute methods on remote machines. The Web service receives the arguments it needs to execute a particular method, executes the method and returns the result to the caller. b) False. The proxy is created by Visual C# or Visual Web Developer when you add the Web reference. The proxy class itself is hidden from you. c) True. d) True. e) False. A `CookieContainer` also must be created on the client side if the client is not a Web browser. f) True. g) True.

22.2 a) SOAP message or SOAP envelope. b) `System.Web.Services.WebService`. c) code-behind. d) HTTP. e) `Description`. f) XML serialization. g) domain.

Exercises

22.3 *(Phone Book Web Service)* Create a Web service that stores phone book entries in a database (`PhoneBook.mdf`, which is provided in the examples directory for this chapter) and a client application that consumes this service. Give the client user the capability to enter a new contact (Web method `AddEntry`) and to find contacts by last name (Web method `GetEntries`). Pass only simple types as arguments to the Web service. Add a `DataSet` to the Web service project to enable the Web service to interact with the database. The `GetEntries` Web method should return an array of `strings` that contains the matching phone book entries. Each `string` in the array should consist of the last name, first name and phone number for one phone book entry. When configuring the `PhoneBookDataSetTableAdapters.PhoneBookTableAdapter` that provides access to the `PhoneBook.mdf` database, first set up the SELECT query that will be used by the `GetEntries` Web method. Then, when you add the INSERT statement to the `TableAdapter`, the **TableAdapter Configuration Wizard** will preconfigure the INSERT statement for you. You will simply need to name the PhoneBook-

DataSetTableAdapters.PhoneBookTableAdapter method that will perform the INSERT operation. The SELECT query that will find a phone book entry by last name should be:

```
SELECT LastName, FirstName, PhoneNumber
FROM PhoneBook
WHERE (LastName = @lastName)
```

The INSERT statement that inserts a new entry into the PhoneBook.mdf database should be:

```
INSERT INTO [PhoneBook] ([LastName], [FirstName], [PhoneNumber])
VALUES (@LastName, @FirstName, @PhoneNumber)
```

[*Note:* The **TableAdapter Configuration Wizard** adds the square brackets around each table name and column name by default when it configures the INSERT statement.]

22.4 *(Phone Book Web Service Modification)* Modify Exercise 22.3 so that it uses a class named PhoneBookEntry to represent a row in the database. The client application should provide objects of type PhoneBookEntry to the Web service when adding contacts and should receive objects of type PhoneBookEntry when searching for contacts.

22.5 *(Blackjack Web Service Modification)* Modify the blackjack Web service example in Section 22.5 to include class Card. Change Web method DealCard so that it returns an object of type Card. Also modify the client application to keep track of what cards have been dealt by using Card objects. Your Card class should include properties to determine the face and suit of the card.

22.6 *(Airline Reservation Web Service Modification)* Modify the airline reservation Web service in Section 22.6 so that it contains two separate Web methods—one that allows users to view all available seats, and another that allows users to reserve a particular seat that is currently available. Use an object of type Ticket to pass information to and from the Web service. The Web service must be able to handle cases in which two users view available seats, one reserves a seat and the second user tries to reserve the same seat, not knowing that it is now taken. To obtain the list of available seats, configure the SeatsTableAdapter with the SELECT query:

```
SELECT  Number, Type, Class
FROM    Seats
WHERE   (Taken = 0)
```

The names of the methods that execute this query should be FillWithAvailableSeats and GetAvailableSeats. To determine whether a specific seat is available, add the following SELECT query to the SeatsTableAdapter:

```
SELECT  Number
FROM    Seats
WHERE   (Number = @number) AND (Taken = 0)
```

The names of the methods that execute this query should be FillWithSpecificSeat and GetSpecificSeat. Finally, to reserve a specific seat, add the following UPDATE to the SeatsTableAdapter:

```
UPDATE Seats
SET    Taken = 1
WHERE  (Number = @number) AND (Taken = 0)
```

The name of the method that executes this UPDATE should be UpdateSeatAsTaken.

23

Networking: Streams-Based Sockets and Datagrams

If the presence of electricity can be made visible in any part of a circuit, I see no reason why intelligence may not be transmitted instantaneously by electricity.
—Samuel F. B. Morse

Protocol is everything.
—Francois Giuliani

What networks of railroads, highways and canals were in another age, the networks of telecommunications, information and computerization ... are today.
—Bruno Kreisky

The port is near, the bells I hear, the people all exulting.
—Walt Whitman

OBJECTIVES

In this chapter you will learn:

- To implement networking applications that use sockets and datagrams.

- To implement clients and servers that communicate with one another.

- To implement network-based collaborative applications.

- To construct a multithreaded server.

- To use the **WebBrowser** control to add Web browsing capabilities to any application.

- To use .NET remoting to enable an application executing on one computer to invoke methods from an application executing on a different computer.

23.1 Introduction

There is much excitement about the Internet and the Web. The Internet ties the information world together. The Web makes the Internet easy to use and gives it the flair and sizzle of multimedia. Organizations see the Internet and the Web as crucial to their information-systems strategies. The .NET FCL provides a number of built-in networking capabilities that make it easy to develop Internet- and Web-based applications. Programs can search the world for information and collaborate with programs running on other computers internationally, nationally or just within an organization.

In Chapter 21, ASP.NET 2.0, Web Forms and Web Controls, and Chapter 22, Web Services, we began our presentation of C#'s networking and distributed-computing capabilities. We discussed ASP.NET, Web Forms and Web services—high-level networking technologies that enable programmers to develop distributed applications. In this chapter, we focus on the underlying networking technologies that support C#'s ASP.NET and Web services capabilities.

This chapter begins with an overview of the communication techniques and technologies used to transmit data over the Internet. Next, we present the basic concepts of establishing a connection between two applications using streams of data that are similar to File I/O. This connection-oriented approach enables programs to communicate with one another as easily as writing to and reading from files on disk. Then we present a simple chat application that uses these techniques to send messages between a client and a server. The chapter continues with a presentation and an example of connectionless techniques for transmitting data between applications that is less reliable than establishing a connection between applications, but much more efficient. Such techniques are typically used in applications such as streaming audio and video over the Internet. Next, we present an example of a client-server Tic-Tac-Toe game that demonstrates how to create a simple multithreaded server. Then this chapter demonstrates the new `WebBrowser` control for adding Web browsing capabilities to any application. The chapter completes with a brief introduction to .NET remoting which, like Web services (Chapter 22) enable distributed computing over networks.

23.2 Connection-Oriented vs. Connectionless Communication

There are two primary approaches to communicating between applications—*connection oriented* and *connectionless*. Connection-oriented communications are similar to the telephone system, in which a connection is established and held for the length of the session. Connectionless services are similar to the postal service, in which two letters mailed from the same place and to the same destination may actually take two dramatically different paths through the system and even arrive at different times, or not at all.

In a connection-oriented approach, computers send each other control information—through a technique called *handshaking*—to initiate an end-to-end connection. The Internet is an *unreliable network*, which means that data sent across the Internet may be damaged or lost. Data is sent in *packets*, which contain pieces of the data along with information that helps the Internet route the packets to the proper destination. The Internet does not guarantee anything about the packets sent; they could arrive corrupted or out of order, as duplicates or not at all. The Internet makes only a "best effort" to deliver packets. A connection-oriented approach ensures reliable communications on unreliable networks, guaranteeing that sent packets will arrive at the intended receiver undamaged and be reassembled in the correct sequence.

In a connectionless approach, the two computers do not handshake before transmission, and reliability is not guaranteed—data sent may never reach the intended recipient. A connectionless approach, however, avoids the overhead associated with handshaking and enforcing reliability—less information often needs to be passed between the hosts.

23.3 Protocols for Transporting Data

There are many protocols for communicating between applications. *Protocols* are sets of rules that govern how two entities should interact. In this chapter, we focus on Transmission Control Protocol (TCP) and User Datagram Protocol (UDP). .NET's TCP and UDP networking capabilities are defined in the **System.Net.Sockets** namespace.

Transmission Control Protocol (TCP) is a connection-oriented communication protocol which guarantees that sent packets will arrive at the intended receiver undamaged and in the correct sequence. TCP allows protocols like HTTP (Chapter 21) to send information across a network as simply and reliably as writing to a file on a local computer. If packets of information don't arrive at the recipient, TCP ensures that the packets are sent again. If the packets arrive out of order, TCP reassembles them in the correct order transparently to the receiving application. If duplicate packets arrive, TCP discards them.

Applications that do not require TCP's reliable end-to-end transmission guaranty typically use the connectionless *User Datagram Protocol (UDP)*. UDP incurs the minimum overhead necessary to communicate between applications. UDP makes no guarantees that packets, called *datagrams*, will reach their destination or arrive in their original order.

There are benefits to using UDP over TCP. UDP has little overhead because UDP datagrams do not need to carry the information that TCP packets carry to ensure reliability. UDP also reduces network traffic relative to TCP due to the absence of handshaking, retransmissions, etc.

Unreliable communication is acceptable in many situations. First, reliability is not necessary for some applications, so the overhead imposed by a protocol that guarantees reliability can be avoided. Second, some applications, such as streaming audio and video, can tolerate occasional datagram loss. This usually results in a small pause (or "hiccup") in the audio or video being played. If the same application were run over TCP, a lost segment could cause a significant pause, since the protocol would wait until the lost segment was retransmitted and delivered correctly before continuing. Finally, applications that need to implement their own reliability mechanisms different from those provided by TCP can build such mechanisms over UDP.

23.4 Establishing a Simple TCP Server (Using Stream Sockets)

Typically, with TCP, a server "waits" for a connection request from a client. Often, the server program contains a control statement or block of code that executes continuously until the server receives a request. On receiving a request, the server establishes a connection to the client. The server then uses this connection—managed by an object of class *Socket*—to handle future requests from that client and to send data to the client. Since programs that communicate via TCP process the data they send and receive as streams of bytes, programmers sometimes refer to Sockets as "stream Sockets."

Establishing a simple server with TCP and stream sockets requires five steps. First, create an object of class TcpListener of namespace System.Net.Sockets. This class represents a TCP stream socket through which a server can listen for requests. Creating a new TcpListener, as in

```
TcpListener server = new TcpListener( ipAddress, port );
```

binds (assigns) the server application to the specified *port number*. A port number is a numeric identifier that an application uses to identify itself at a given *network address*, also known as an *Internet Protocol Address* (*IP Address*). IP addresses identify computers on the Internet. In fact, Web-site names, such as www.deitel.com, are aliases for IP addresses. An IP address is represented by an object of class *IPAddress* of namespace *System.Net*. Any application that performs networking identifies itself via an *IP address/ port number pair*—no two applications can have the same port number at a given IP address. Explicitly binding a socket to a connection port (using method Bind of class Socket) is usually unnecessary, because class TcpListener and other classes discussed in this chapter do it automatically, along with other socket-initialization operations.

> ### Software Engineering Observation 23.1
> *Port numbers can have values between 0 and 65535. Many operating systems reserve port numbers below 1024 for system services (such as e-mail and Web servers). Applications must be granted special privileges to use these reserved port numbers.*

To receive requests, TcpListener first must listen for them. The second step in the connection process is to call TcpListener's Start method, which causes the TcpListener object to begin listening for connection requests. The server listens indefinitely for a request—i.e., the execution of the server-side application waits until some client attempts to connect with it. The server creates a connection to the client when it receives a connection request. An object of class Socket (namespace System.Net.Sockets) manages a con-

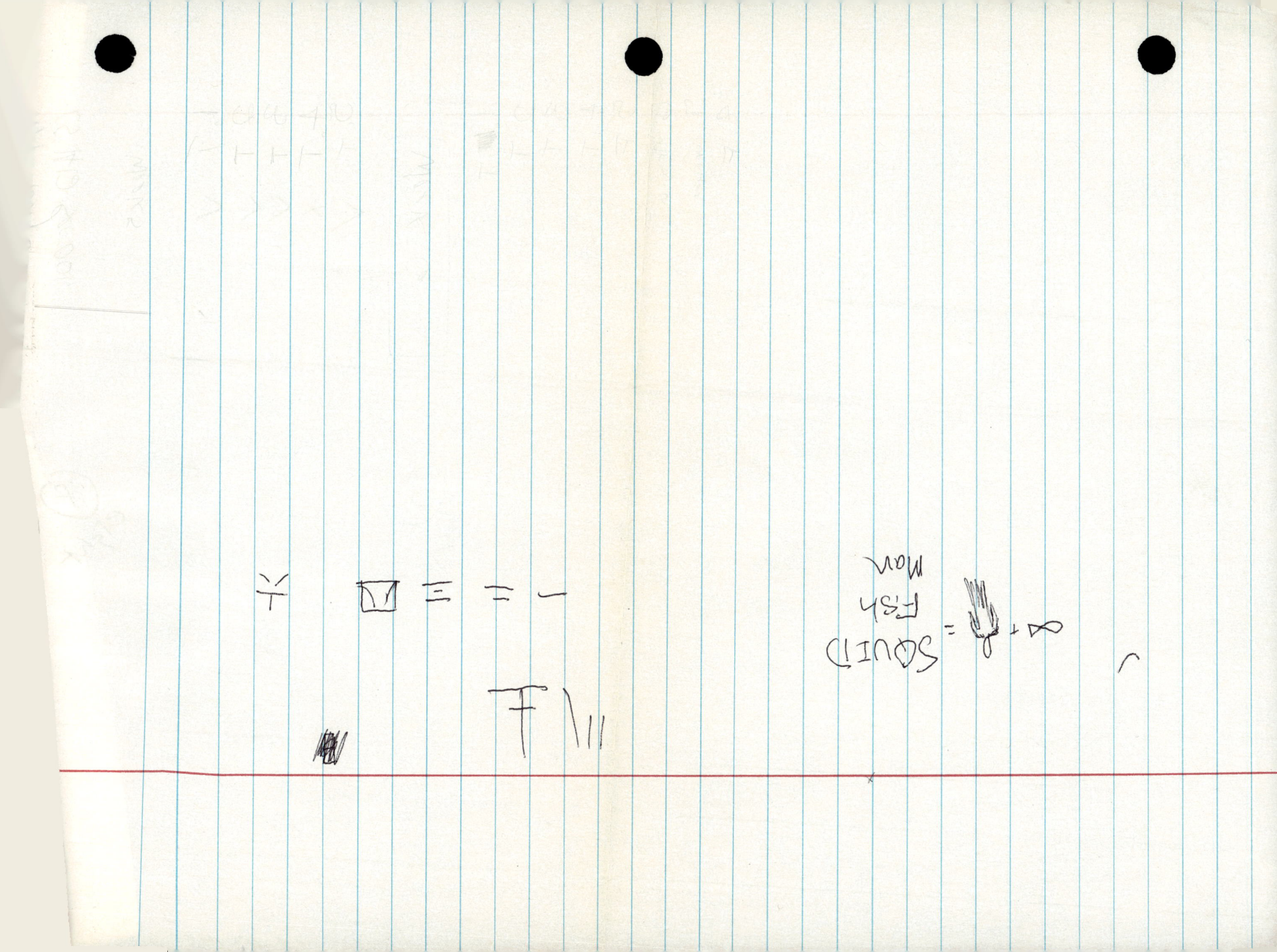

Week5

1. T ✓
2. T ✓
3. T ✓
4. T ✗
5. T ✓

Week 6

1. T ✓
2. T ✓
3. T ✓
4. T ✓
5. F ✓
6. has-a ✓
7. concrete ✓
8. F ✓

10
ten

nection to a client. Method `AcceptSocket` of class `TcpListener` accepts a connection request. This method returns a `Socket` object upon connection, as in the statement

```
Socket connection = server.AcceptSocket();
```

When the server receives a request, `AcceptSocket` calls method `Accept` of the `TcpListener`'s underlying `Socket` to make the connection. This is an example of how networking complexity is hidden from the programmer. You simply place the preceding statement in a server-side program—the classes of namespace `System.Net.Sockets` handle the details of accepting requests and establishing connections.

The third step establishes the streams used for communication with the client. In this step, we create a `NetworkStream` object that uses the `Socket` object representing the connection to perform the actual sending and receiving of data. In our forthcoming example, we use this `NetworkStream` object to create a `BinaryWriter` and a `BinaryReader` that will be used to send information to and receive information from the client, respectively.

Step four is the processing phase, in which the server and client communicate using the connection established in the third step. In this phase, the client uses `BinaryWriter` method `Write` and `BinaryReader` method `ReadString` to perform the appropriate communications.

The fifth step is the connection-termination phase. When the client and server have finished communicating, the server calls method `Close` of the `BinaryReader`, `BinaryWriter`, `NetworkStream` and `Socket` to terminate the connection. The server can then return to step two to wait for the next connection request. Note that the documentation for class `Socket` recommends that you call method `Shutdown` before method `Close` to ensure that all data is sent and received before the `Socket` closes.

One problem associated with the server scheme described in this section is that step four **blocks** other requests while processing the connected client's request, so no other client can connect with the server while the code that defines the processing phase is executing. The most common technique for addressing this problem is to use multithreaded servers, which place the processing-phase code in a separate thread. For each connection request the server receives, it creates a `Thread` to process the connection, leaving its `TcpListener` (or `Socket`) free to receive other connections. We demonstrate a multithreaded server in Section 23.8.

Software Engineering Observation 23.2

Multithreaded servers can efficiently manage simultaneous connections with multiple clients. This architecture is precisely what popular UNIX and Windows network servers use.

Software Engineering Observation 23.3

A multithreaded server can be implemented to create a thread that manages network I/O across a Socket object returned by method AcceptSocket. A multithreaded server also can be implemented to maintain a pool of threads that manage network I/O across newly created Sockets.

Performance Tip 23.1

In high-performance systems with abundant memory, a multithreaded server can be implemented to create a pool of threads. These threads can be assigned quickly to handle network I/O across multiple Sockets. Thus, when a connection is received, the server does not incur the overhead of thread creation.

23.5 Establishing a Simple TCP Client (Using Stream Sockets)

There are four steps to creating a simple TCP client. First, we create an object of class Tcp-Client (namespace System.Net.Sockets) to connect to the server. The connection is established by calling TcpClient method Connect. One overloaded version of this method takes two arguments—the server's IP address and its port number—as in:

```
TcpClient client = new TcpClient();
client.Connect( serverAddress, serverPort );
```

The *serverPort* is an int that represents the port number to which the server application is bound to listen for connection requests. The *serverAddress* can be either an IPAddress instance (that encapsulates the server's IP address) or a string that specifies the server's hostname or IP address. Method Connect also has an overloaded version to which you can pass an IPEndPoint object that represents an IP address/port number pair. TcpClient method Connect calls Socket method Connect to establish the connection. If the connection is successful, TcpClient method Connect returns a positive integer; otherwise, it returns 0.

In step two, the TcpClient uses its GetStream method to get a NetworkStream so that it can write to and read from the server. We then use the NetworkStream object to create a BinaryWriter and a BinaryReader that will be used to send information to and receive information from the server, respectively.

The third step is the processing phase, in which the client and the server communicate. In this phase of our example, the client uses BinaryWriter method Write and Binary-Reader method ReadString to perform the appropriate communications. Using a process similar to that used by servers, a client can employ threads to prevent blocking of communication with other servers while processing data from one connection.

After the transmission is complete, step four requires the client to close the connection by calling method Close on each of BinaryReader, BinaryWriter, NetworkStream and TcpClient. This closes each of the streams and the TcpClient's Socket to terminate the connection with the server. At this point, a new connection can be established through method Connect, as we have described.

23.6 Client/Server Interaction with Stream-Socket Connections

The applications in Fig. 23.1 and Fig. 23.2 use the classes and techniques discussed in the previous two sections to construct a simple *client/server chat application*. The server waits for a client's request to make a connection. When a client application connects to the server, the server application sends an array of bytes to the client, indicating that the connection was successful. The client then displays a message notifying the user that a connection has been established.

Both the client and the server applications contain TextBoxes that enable users to type messages and send them to the other application. When either the client or the server sends the message "TERMINATE," the connection between the client and the server terminates. The server then waits for another client to request a connection. Figure 23.1 and Fig. 23.2 provide the code for classes Server and Client, respectively. Figure 23.2 also contains screen captures displaying the execution between the client and the server.

ChatServerForm Class

We begin by discussing class ChatServerForm (Fig. 23.1). In the constructor, line 27 creates a Thread that will accept connections from clients. The ThreadStart delegate object that is passed as the constructor's argument specifies which method the Thread should execute. Line 28 starts the Thread, which uses the ThreadStart delegate to invoke method RunServer (lines 104–179). This method initializes the server to receive connection requests and process connections. Line 115 instantiates a TcpListener object to listen for a connection request from a client at port 50000 (Step 1). Line 118 then calls TcpListener method Start, which causes the TcpListener to begin waiting for requests (Step 2).

```csharp
1   // Fig. 23.1: ChatServer.cs
2   // Set up a server that will receive a connection from a client, send a
3   // string to the client, chat with the client and close the connection.
4   using System;
5   using System.Windows.Forms;
6   using System.Threading;
7   using System.Net;
8   using System.Net.Sockets;
9   using System.IO;
10
11  public partial class ChatServerForm : Form
12  {
13     public ChatServerForm()
14     {
15        InitializeComponent();
16     } // end constructor
17
18     private Socket connection; // Socket for accepting a connection
19     private Thread readThread; // Thread for processing incoming messages
20     private NetworkStream socketStream; // network data stream
21     private BinaryWriter writer; // facilitates writing to the stream
22     private BinaryReader reader; // facilitates reading from the stream
23
24     // initialize thread for reading
25     private void ChatServerForm_Load( object sender, EventArgs e )
26     {
27        readThread = new Thread( new ThreadStart( RunServer ) );
28        readThread.Start();
29     } // end method CharServerForm_Load
30
31     // close all threads associated with this application
32     private void ChatServerForm_FormClosing( object sender,
33        FormClosingEventArgs e )
34     {
35        System.Environment.Exit( System.Environment.ExitCode );
36     } // end method CharServerForm_FormClosing
37
38     // delegate that allows method DisplayMessage to be called
39     // in the thread that creates and maintains the GUI
40     private delegate void DisplayDelegate( string message );
41
```

Fig. 23.1 | Server portion of a client/server stream-socket connection. (Part 1 of 4.)

```
42    // method DisplayMessage sets displayTextBox's Text property
43    // in a thread-safe manner
44    private void DisplayMessage( string message )
45    {
46       // if modifying displayTextBox is not thread safe
47       if ( displayTextBox.InvokeRequired )
48       {
49          // use inherited method Invoke to execute DisplayMessage
50          // via a delegate
51          Invoke( new DisplayDelegate( DisplayMessage ),
52             new object[] { message } );
53       } // end if
54       else // OK to modify displayTextBox in current thread
55          displayTextBox.Text += message;
56    } // end method DisplayMessage
57
58    // delegate that allows method DisableInput to be called
59    // in the thread that creates and maintains the GUI
60    private delegate void DisableInputDelegate( bool value );
61
62    // method DisableInput sets inputTextBox's ReadOnly property
63    // in a thread-safe manner
64    private void DisableInput( bool value )
65    {
66       // if modifying inputTextBox is not thread safe
67       if ( inputTextBox.InvokeRequired )
68       {
69          // use inherited method Invoke to execute DisableInput
70          // via a delegate
71          Invoke( new DisableInputDelegate( DisableInput ),
72             new object[] { value } );
73       } // end if
74       else // OK to modify inputTextBox in current thread
75          inputTextBox.ReadOnly = value;
76    } // end method DisableInput
77
78    // send the text typed at the server to the client
79    private void inputTextBox_KeyDown( object sender, KeyEventArgs e )
80    {
81       // send the text to the client
82       try
83       {
84          if ( e.KeyCode == Keys.Enter && inputTextBox.ReadOnly == false )
85          {
86             writer.Write( "SERVER>>> " + inputTextBox.Text );
87             displayTextBox.Text += "\r\nSERVER>>> " + inputTextBox.Text;
88
89             // if the user at the server signaled termination
90             // sever the connection to the client
91             if ( inputTextBox.Text == "TERMINATE" )
92                connection.Close();
93
```

Fig. 23.1 | Server portion of a client/server stream-socket connection. (Part 2 of 4.)

```
94              inputTextBox.Clear(); // clear the user's input
95           } // end if
96        } // end try
97        catch ( SocketException )
98        {
99           displayTextBox.Text += "\nError writing object";
100        } // end catch
101     } // end method inputTextBox_KeyDown
102
103     // allows a client to connect; displays text the client sends
104     public void RunServer()
105     {
106        TcpListener listener;
107        int counter = 1;
108
109        // wait for a client connection and display the text
110        // that the client sends
111        try
112        {
113           // Step 1: create TcpListener
114           IPAddress local = IPAddress.Parse( "127.0.0.1" );
115           listener = new TcpListener( local, 50000 );
116
117           // Step 2: TcpListener waits for connection request
118           listener.Start();
119
120           // Step 3: establish connection upon client request
121           while ( true )
122           {
123              DisplayMessage( "Waiting for connection\r\n" );
124
125              // accept an incoming connection
126              connection = listener.AcceptSocket();
127
128              // create NetworkStream object associated with socket
129              socketStream = new NetworkStream( connection );
130
131              // create objects for transferring data across stream
132              writer = new BinaryWriter( socketStream );
133              reader = new BinaryReader( socketStream );
134
135              DisplayMessage( "Connection " + counter + " received.\r\n" );
136
137              // inform client that connection was successfull
138              writer.Write( "SERVER>>> Connection successful" );
139
140              DisableInput( false ); // enable inputTextBox
141
142              string theReply = "";
143
144              // Step 4: read string data sent from client
145              do
146              {
```

Fig. 23.1 | Server portion of a client/server stream-socket connection. (Part 3 of 4.)

```
147                    try
148                    {
149                        // read the string sent to the server
150                        theReply = reader.ReadString();
151
152                        // display the message
153                        DisplayMessage( "\r\n" + theReply );
154                    } // end try
155                    catch ( Exception )
156                    {
157                        // handle exception if error reading data
158                        break;
159                    } // end catch
160                } while ( theReply != "CLIENT>>> TERMINATE"  &&
161                    connection.Connected );
162
163                DisplayMessage( "\r\nUser terminated connection\r\n" );
164
165                // Step 5: close connection
166                writer.Close();
167                reader.Close();
168                socketStream.Close();
169                connection.Close();
170
171                DisableInput( true ); // disable InputTextBox
172                counter++;
173            } // end while
174        } // end try
175        catch ( Exception error )
176        {
177            MessageBox.Show( error.ToString() );
178        } // end catch
179    } // end method RunServer
180 } // end class ChatServerForm
```

Fig. 23.1 | Server portion of a client/server stream-socket connection. (Part 4 of 4.)

Accepting the Connection and Establishing the Streams

Lines 121–173 declare an infinite loop that begins by establishing the connection requested by the client (Step 3). Line 126 calls method AcceptSocket of the TcpListener object, which returns a Socket upon successful connection. The thread in which method Accept-Socket is called blocks (i.e., stops executing) until a connection is established. The returned Socket object manages the connection. Line 129 passes this Socket object as an argument to the constructor of a NetworkStream object, which provides access to streams across a network. In this example, the NetworkStream object uses the streams of the specified Socket. Lines 132–133 create instances of the BinaryWriter and BinaryReader classes for writing and reading data. We pass the NetworkStream object as an argument to each constructor—BinaryWriter can write bytes to the NetworkStream, and BinryReader can read bytes from NetworkStream. Line 135 calls DisplayMessage, indicating that a connection was received. Next, we send a message to the client indicating that the connection was received. BinaryWriter method Write has many overloaded versions that write data of various types to a stream. Line 138 uses method Write to send to the client a string notifying the user of a successful connection. This completes Step 3.

Receiving Messages from the Client

Next, we begin the processing phase (Step 4). Lines 145–161 declare a do...while statement that executes until the server receives a message indicating connection termination (i.e., CLIENT>>> TERMINATE). Line 150 uses BinaryReader method ReadString to read a string from the stream. Method ReadString blocks until a string is read. This is the reason that we execute method RunServer in a separate Thread (created at lines 27–28, when the Form loads). This Thread ensures that our Server application's user can continue to interact with the GUI to send messages to the client, even when this thread is blocked while awaiting a message from the client.

Modifying GUI Controls from Separate Threads

Windows Form controls are not thread safe—a control that is modified from multiple threads is not guaranteed to be modified correctly. The Visual Studio 2005 Documentation[1] recommends that only the thread which created the GUI should modify the controls. Class Control provides method ***Invoke*** to help ensure this. Invoke takes two arguments—a delegate representing a method that will modify the GUI and an array of objects representing the parameters of the method. At some point after Invoke is called, the thread that originally created the GUI will (when it's not executing any other code) execute the method represented by the delegate, passing the contents of the object array as the method's arguments.

Line 40 declares a delegate type named DisplayDelegate, which represents methods that take a string argument and do not return a value. Method DisplayMessage (lines 44–56) meets those requirements—it receives a string parameter named message and does not return a value. The if statement in line 47 tests displayTextBox's ***Invoke-Required*** property (inherited from class Control), which returns true if the current thread is not allowed to modify this control directly and returns false otherwise. If the current thread executing method DisplayMessage is not the thread that created the GUI, then the if condition evaluates to true and lines 51–52 call method Invoke, passing to it a new DisplayDelegate representing the method DisplayMessage *itself* and a new object array consisting of the string argument message. This causes the thread that created the GUI to call method DisplayMessage again at a later time with the same string argument as the original call. When that call occurs from the thread that created the GUI, the method *is* allowed to modify displayTextBox directly, so the else body (line 55) executes and appends message to displayTextBox's Text property.

Lines 60–76 provide a delegate definition, DisableInputDelegate, and a method, DisableInput, to allow any thread to modify the ReadOnly property of inputTextBox using the same techniques. A thread calls DisableInput with a bool argument (true to disable; false to enable). If DisableInput is not allowed to modify the control from the current thread, DisableInput calls method Invoke. This causes the thread that created the GUI to call DisableInput at a later time and set inputTextBox.ReadOnly to the value of the bool argument.

---

1. The MSDN article "How to: Make Cross-Thread Calls to Windows Forms Controls" can be found at msdn2.microsoft.com/library/ms171728(en-us,vs.80).aspx.

Terminating the Connection with the Client

When the chat is complete, lines 166–169 close the BinaryWriter, BinaryReader, NetworkStream and Socket (Step 5) by invoking their respective Close methods. The server then waits for another client connection request by returning to the beginning of the while loop (line 121).

Sending Messages to the Client

When the server application's user enters a string in the TextBox and presses the *Enter* key, event handler inputTextBox_KeyDown (lines 79–101) reads the string and sends it via method Write of class BinaryWriter. If a user terminates the server application, line 92 calls method Close of the Socket object to close the connection.

Terminating the Server Application

Lines 32–36 define event handler ChatServerForm_FormClosing for the FormClosing event. The event closes the application and calls method Exit of class Environment with parameter ExitCode to terminate all threads. Method Exit of class Environment closes all threads associated with the application.

ChatClientForm Class

Figure 23.2 lists the code for the ChatClientForm class. Like the ChatServerForm object, the ChatClientForm object creates a Thread (lines 26–27) in its constructor to handle all incoming messages. ChatClientForm method RunClient (lines 96–151) connects to the ChatServerForm, receives data from the ChatServerForm and sends data to the ChatServerForm. Lines 106–107 instantiate a TcpClient object, then call its Connect method to establish a connection (Step 1). The first argument to method Connect is the name of the server—in our case, the server's name is "localhost", meaning that the server is located on the same machine as the client. The localhost is also known as the *loopback IP address* and is equivalent to the IP address 127.0.0.1. This value sends the data transmission back to the sender's IP address. [*Note*: We chose to demonstrate the client/server relationship by connecting between programs that are executing on the same computer (localhost). Normally, this argument would contain the Internet address of another computer.] The second argument to method Connect is the server port number. This number must match the port number at which the server waits for connections.

```
1   // Fig. 23.2: ChatClient.cs
2   // Set up a client that will send information to and
3   // read information from a server.
4   using System;
5   using System.Windows.Forms;
6   using System.Threading;
7   using System.Net.Sockets;
8   using System.IO;
9
10  public partial class ChatClientForm : Form
11  {
```

Fig. 23.2 | Client portion of a client/server stream-socket connection. (Part 1 of 5.)

```
118
119          // loop until server signals termination
120          do
121          {
122             // Step 3: processing phase
123             try
124             {
125                // read message from server
126                message = reader.ReadString();
127                DisplayMessage( "\r\n" + message );
128             } // end try
129             catch ( Exception )
130             {
131                // handle exception if error in reading server data
132                System.Environment.Exit( System.Environment.ExitCode );
133             } // end catch
134          } while ( message != "SERVER>>> TERMINATE" );
135
136          // Step 4: close connection
137          writer.Close();
138          reader.Close();
139          output.Close();
140          client.Close();
141
142          Application.Exit();
143       } // end try
144       catch ( Exception error )
145       {
146          // handle exception if error in establishing connection
147          MessageBox.Show( error.ToString(), "Connection Error",
148             MessageBoxButtons.OK, MessageBoxIcon.Error );
149          System.Environment.Exit( System.Environment.ExitCode );
150       } // end catch
151    } // end method RunClient
152 } // end class ChatClientForm
```

(a)

Chat Server

Waiting for connection
Connection 1 received.

(b)

Chat Client

Hi to person at the server

Attempting connection

Got I/O streams

SERVER>>> Connection successful

Fig. 23.2 | Client portion of a client/server stream-socket connection. (Part 4 of 5.)

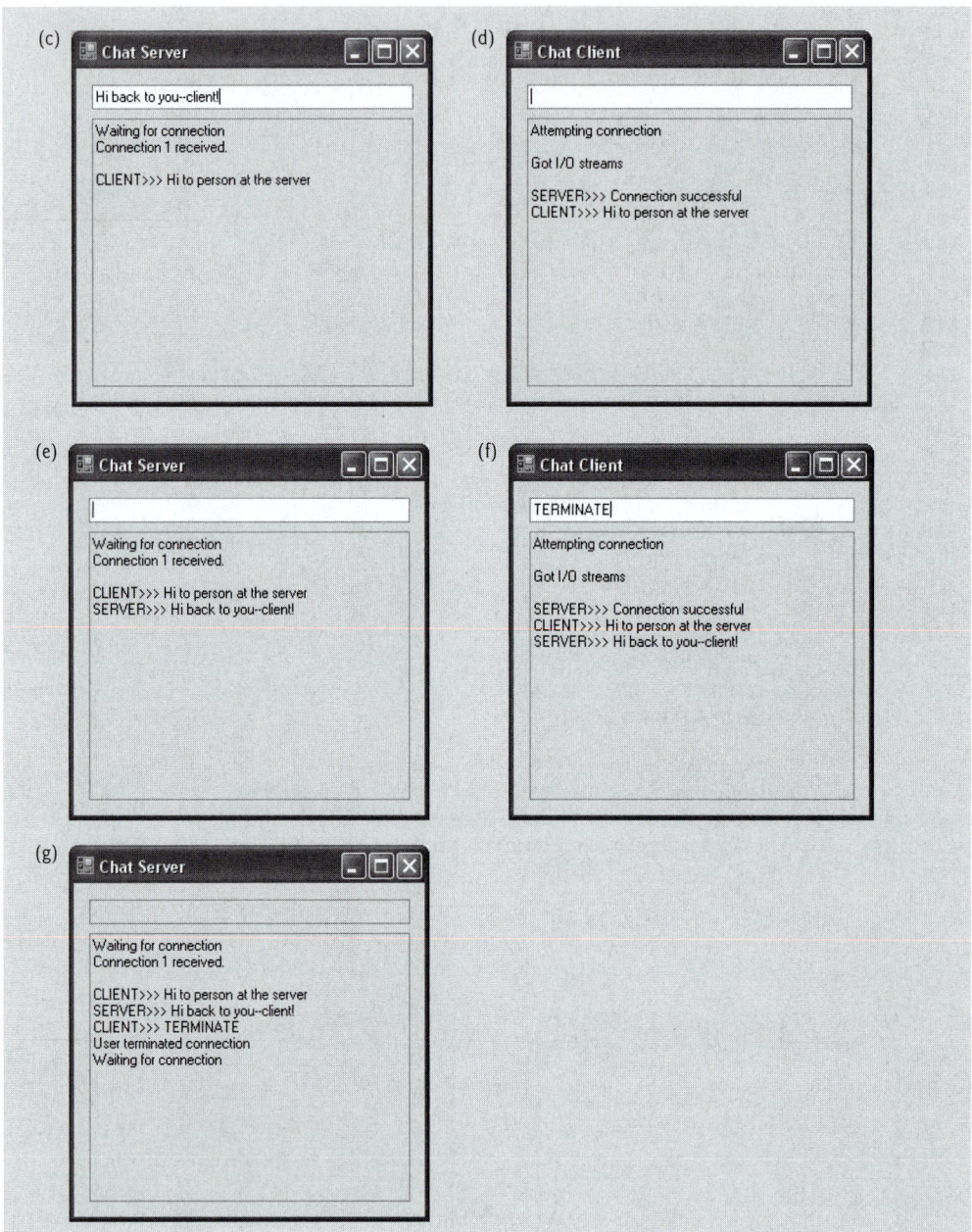

Fig. 23.2 | Client portion of a client/server stream-socket connection. (Part 5 of 5.)

The ChatClientForm uses a NetworkStream to send data to and receive data from the server. The client obtains the NetworkStream in line 110 through a call to TcpClient method GetStream (Step 2). The do...while statement in lines 120–134 loops until the client receives the connection-termination message (SERVER>>> TERMINATE). Line 126 uses BinaryReader method ReadString to obtain the next message from the server (Step 3).

Line 127 displays the message, and lines 137–140 close the BinaryWriter, BinaryReader, NetworkStream and TcpClient objects (Step 4).

Lines 39–75 declare DisplayDelegate, DisplayMessage, DisableInputDelegate and DisableInput just as in lines 40–76 of Fig. 23.1. These once again are used to ensure that the GUI is modified by only the thread that created the GUI controls.

When the user of the client application enters a string in the TextBox and presses the *Enter* key, event handler inputTextBox_KeyDown (lines 78–93) reads the string from the TextBox and sends it via BinaryWriter method Write. Notice here that the ChatServerForm receives a connection, processes it, closes it and waits for the next one. In a real-world application, a server would likely receive a connection, set up the connection to be processed as a separate thread of execution and wait for new connections. The separate threads that process existing connections could then continue to execute while the server concentrates on new connection requests.

23.7 Connectionless Client/Server Interaction with Datagrams

Up to this point, we have discussed connection-oriented, streams-based transmissions using the TCP protocol to ensure that the packets of data are transmitted reliably. Now, we consider connectionless transmission using datagrams and UDP.

Connectionless transmission via datagrams resembles the method by which the postal service carries and delivers mail. Connectionless transmission bundles and sends information in packets called datagrams, which can be thought of as similar to letters you send through the mail. If a large message will not fit in one envelope, that message is broken into separate message pieces and placed in separate, sequentially numbered envelopes. All the letters are mailed at once. The letters might arrive in order, out of order or not at all. The person at the receiving end reassembles the message pieces in sequential order before attempting to interpret the message. If the message is small enough to fit in one envelope, the sequencing problem is eliminated, but it is still possible that the message will never arrive. (Unlike with postal mail, duplicate of datagrams could reach receiving computers.) C# provides the UdpClient class for connectionless transmission. Like TcpListener and TcpClient, UdpClient uses methods from class Socket. The UdpClient methods Send and Receive transmit data with Socket's SendTo method and read data with Socket's ReceiveFrom method, respectively.

The programs in Fig. 23.3 and Fig. 23.4 use datagrams to send packets of information between client and server applications. In the PacketClient application, the user types a message into a TextBox and presses *Enter*. The client converts the message to a byte array and sends it to the server. The server receives the packet and displays the packet's information, then ***echoes***, or returns, the packet to the client. When the client receives the packet, the client displays the packet's information. In this example, the implementations of the PacketClientForm and PacketServerForm classes are similar.

PacketServerForm Class
The code in Fig. 23.3 defines the PacketServerForm for this application. Line 23 in the Load event handler for class PacketServerForm creates an instance of the UdpClient class that receives data at port 50000. This initializes the underlying Socket for communica-

tions. Line 24 creates an instance of class IPEndPoint to hold the IP address and port number of the client(s) that transmit to PacketServerForm. The first argument to the IPEndPoint constructor is an IPAddress object; the second argument is the port number of the endpoint. These values are both 0, because we need only instantiate an empty IPEndPoint object. The IP addresses and port numbers of clients are copied into the IPEndPoint when datagrams are received from clients.

```
1   // Fig. 23.3: PacketServer.cs
2   // Set up a server that will receive packets from a
3   // client and send the packets back to the client.
4   using System;
5   using System.Windows.Forms;
6   using System.Net;
7   using System.Net.Sockets;
8   using System.Threading;
9
10  public partial class PacketServerForm : Form
11  {
12     public PacketServerForm()
13     {
14        InitializeComponent();
15     } // end constructor
16
17     private UdpClient client;
18     private IPEndPoint receivePoint;
19
20     // initialize variables and thread for receiving packets
21     private void PacketServerForm_Load( object sender, EventArgs e )
22     {
23        client = new UdpClient( 50000 );
24        receivePoint = new IPEndPoint( new IPAddress( 0 ), 0 );
25        Thread readThread =
26           new Thread( new ThreadStart( WaitForPackets ) );
27        readThread.Start();
28     } // end method PacketServerForm_Load
29
30     // shut down the server
31     private void PacketServerForm_FormClosing( object sender,
32        FormClosingEventArgs e )
33     {
34        System.Environment.Exit( System.Environment.ExitCode );
35     } // end method PacketServerForm_FormClosing
36
37     // delegate that allows method DisplayMessage to be called
38     // in the thread that creates and maintains the GUI
39     private delegate void DisplayDelegate( string message );
40
41     // method DisplayMessage sets displayTextBox's Text property
42     // in a thread-safe manner
43     private void DisplayMessage( string message )
44     {
```

Fig. 23.3 | Server-side portion of connectionless client/server computing. (Part 1 of 2.)

```
45          // if modifying displayTextBox is not thread safe
46          if ( displayTextBox.InvokeRequired )
47          {
48             // use inherited method Invoke to execute DisplayMessage
49             // via a delegate
50             Invoke( new DisplayDelegate( DisplayMessage ),
51                new object[] { message } );
52          } // end if
53          else // OK to modify displayTextBox in current thread
54             displayTextBox.Text += message;
55       } // end method DisplayMessage
56
57       // wait for a packet to arrive
58       public void WaitForPackets()
59       {
60          while ( true )
61          {
62             // set up packet
63             byte[] data = client.Receive( ref receivePoint );
64             DisplayMessage( "\r\nPacket received:" +
65                "\r\nLength: " + data.Length +
66                "\r\nContaining: " +
67                System.Text.Encoding.ASCII.GetString( data ) );
68
69             // echo information from packet back to client
70             DisplayMessage( "\r\n\r\nEcho data back to client..." );
71             client.Send( data, data.Length, receivePoint );
72             DisplayMessage( "\r\nPacket sent\r\n" );
73          } // end while
74       } // end method WaitForPackets
75    } // end class PacketServerForm
```

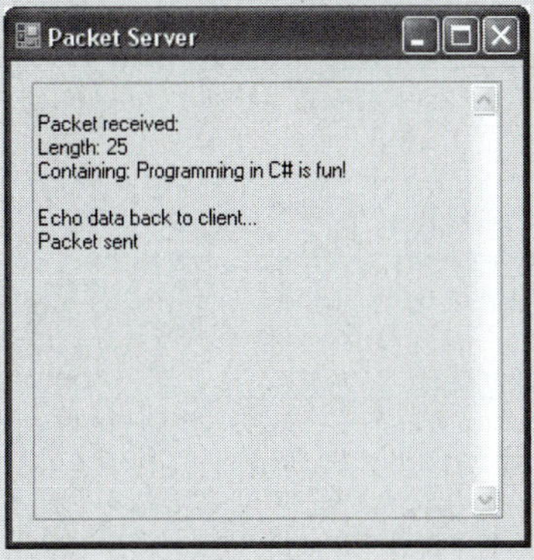

Fig. 23.3 | Server-side portion of connectionless client/server computing. (Part 2 of 2.)

Lines 39–55 define `DisplayDelegate` and `DisplayMessage`, allowing any thread to modify `displayTextBox`'s Text property.

`PacketServerForm` method `WaitForPackets` (lines 58–74) executes an infinite loop while waiting for data to arrive at the `PacketServerForm`. When information arrives, `Udp-Client` method `Receive` (line 63) receives a byte array from the client. We pass to

Receive the IPEndPoint object created in the constructor—this provides the method with an IPEndPoint to which the program copies the client's IP address and port number. This program will compile and run without an exception even if the reference to the IPEnd-Point object is null, because method Receive initializes the IPEndPoint if it is null.

Lines 64–67 update the PacketServerForm's display to include the packet's information and content. Line 71 echoes the data back to the client, using UdpClient method Send. This version of Send takes three arguments—the byte array to send, an int representing the array's length and the IPEndPoint to which to send the data. We use array data returned by method Receive as the data, the length of array data as the length and the IPEndPoint passed to method Receive as the data's destination. The IP address and port number of the client that sent the data are stored in receivePoint, so merely passing receivePoint to Send allows PacketServerForm to respond to the client.

PacketClientForm Class

Class PacketClientForm (Fig. 23.4) works similarly to class PacketServerForm, except that the Client object sends packets only when the user types a message in a TextBox and presses the *Enter* key. When this occurs, the program calls event handler inputTextBox_KeyDown (lines 58–75). Line 68 converts the string that the user entered in the TextBox to a byte array. Line 71 calls UdpClient method Send to send the byte array to the PacketServerForm that is located on localhost (i.e., the same machine). We specify the port as 50000, which we know to be PacketServerForm's port.

Lines 39–55 define DisplayDelegate and DisplayMessage, allowing any thread to modify displayTextBox's Text property.

Line 24 instantiates a UdpClient object to receive packets at port 50001—we choose port 50001 because the PacketServerForm already occupies port 50000. Method WaiFor-Packets of class PacketClientForm (lines 78–90) uses an infinite loop to wait for these packets. UdpClient method Receive blocks until a packet of data is received (line 83). The blocking performed by method Receive does not prevent class PacketClientForm from performing other services (e.g., handling user input), because a separate thread runs method WaitForPackets.

```
1   // Fig. 23.4: PacketClient.cs
2   // Set up a client that sends packets to a server and receives
3   // packets from a server.
4   using System;
5   using System.Windows.Forms;
6   using System.Net;
7   using System.Net.Sockets;
8   using System.Threading;
9
10  public partial class PacketClientForm : Form
11  {
12     public PacketClientForm()
13     {
14        InitializeComponent();
15     } // end constructor
16
```

Fig. 23.4 | Client portion of connectionless client/server computing. (Part 1 of 3.)

```
17      private UdpClient client;
18      private IPEndPoint receivePoint;
19
20      // initialize variables and thread for receiving packets
21      private void PacketClientForm_Load( object sender, EventArgs e )
22      {
23          receivePoint = new IPEndPoint( new IPAddress( 0 ), 0 );
24          client = new UdpClient( 50001 );
25          Thread thread =
26              new Thread( new ThreadStart( WaitForPackets ) );
27          thread.Start();
28      } // end method PacketClientForm_Load
29
30      // shut down the client
31      private void PacketClientForm_FormClosing( object sender,
32          FormClosingEventArgs e )
33      {
34          System.Environment.Exit( System.Environment.ExitCode );
35      } // end method PacketClientForm_FormClosing
36
37      // delegate that allows method DisplayMessage to be called
38      // in the thread that creates and maintains the GUI
39      private delegate void DisplayDelegate( string message );
40
41      // method DisplayMessage sets displayTextBox's Text property
42      // in a thread-safe manner
43      private void DisplayMessage( string message )
44      {
45          // if modifying displayTextBox is not thread safe
46          if ( displayTextBox.InvokeRequired )
47          {
48              // use inherited method Invoke to execute DisplayMessage
49              // via a delegate
50              Invoke( new DisplayDelegate( DisplayMessage ),
51                  new object[] { message } );
52          } // end if
53          else // OK to modify displayTextBox in current thread
54              displayTextBox.Text += message;
55      } // end method DisplayMessage
56
57      // send a packet
58      private void inputTextBox_KeyDown( object sender, KeyEventArgs e )
59      {
60          if ( e.KeyCode == Keys.Enter )
61          {
62              // create packet (datagram) as string
63              string packet = inputTextBox.Text;
64              displayTextBox.Text +=
65                  "\r\nSending packet containing: " + packet;
66
67              // convert packet to byte array
68              byte[] data = System.Text.Encoding.ASCII.GetBytes( packet );
69
```

Fig. 23.4 | Client portion of connectionless client/server computing. (Part 2 of 3.)

```
70          // send packet to server on port 50000
71          client.Send( data, data.Length, "127.0.0.1", 50000 );
72          displayTextBox.Text += "\r\nPacket sent\r\n";
73          inputTextBox.Clear();
74       } // end if
75    } // end method inputTextBox_KeyDown
76
77    // wait for packets to arrive
78    public void WaitForPackets()
79    {
80       while ( true )
81       {
82          // receive byte array from server
83          byte[] data = client.Receive( ref receivePoint );
84
85          // output packet data to TextBox
86          DisplayMessage( "\r\nPacket received:" +
87             "\r\nLength: " + data.Length + "\r\nContaining: " +
88             System.Text.Encoding.ASCII.GetString( data ) + "\r\n" );
89       } // end while
90    } // end method WaitForPackets
91 } // end class PacketClientForm
```

(a) Packet Client window before sending a packet to the server

(b) Packet Client window after sending a packet to the server and receiving it back

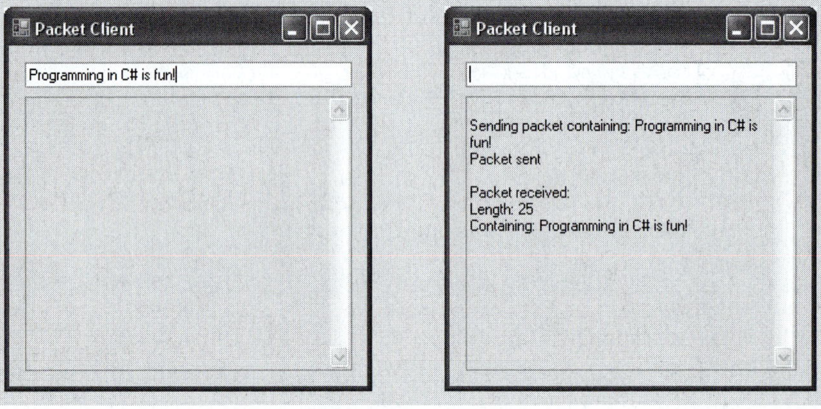

Fig. 23.4 | Client portion of connectionless client/server computing. (Part 3 of 3.)

When a packet arrives, lines 86–88 display its contents in the TextBox. The user can type information in the PacketClientForm window's TextBox and press the *Enter* key at any time, even while a packet is being received. The event handler for the TextBox processes the event and sends the data to the server.

23.8 Client/Server Tic-Tac-Toe Using a Multithreaded Server

In this section, we present a networked version of the popular game Tic-Tac-Toe, implemented with stream sockets and client/server techniques. The program consists of a Tic-

TacToeServer application (Fig. 23.5) and a TicTacToeClient application (Fig. 23.6). The TicTacToeServer allows two TicTacToeClient instances to connect to the server and play Tic-Tac-Toe against each other. We depict the output in Fig. 23.6. When the server receives a client connection, lines 78–87 of Fig. 23.5 create instances of class Player to process each client in a separate thread of execution. This enables the server to handle requests from both clients. The server assigns value "X" to the first client that connects (player X makes the first move), then assigns value "O" to the second client. Throughout the game, the server maintains information regarding the status of the board so that the server can validate players' requested moves. However, neither the server nor the client can establish whether a player has won the game—in this application, method GameOver (lines 139–143) always returns false. Each Client maintains its own GUI version of the Tic-Tac-Toe board to display the game. The clients can place marks only in empty squares on the board. Class Square (Fig. 23.7) is used to define squares on the Tic-Tac-Toe board.

TicTacToeServerForm Class

TicTacToeServerForm (Fig. 23.5) uses its Load event handler (lines 27–37) to create a byte array to store the moves the players have made (line 29). The program creates an array of two references to Player objects (line 30) and an array of two references to Thread objects (line 31). Each element in both arrays corresponds to a Tic-Tac-Toe player. Variable currentPlayer is set to 0 (line 32), which corresponds to player "X". In our program, player "X" makes the first move. Lines 35–36 create and start Thread getPlayers, which the TicTacToeServerForm uses to accept connections so that the current Thread does not block while awaiting players.

```
1    // Fig. 23.5: TicTacToeServer.cs
2    // This class maintains a game of Tic-Tac-Toe for two
3    // client applications.
4    using System;
5    using System.Windows.Forms;
6    using System.Net;
7    using System.Net.Sockets;
8    using System.Threading;
9    using System.IO;
10
11   public partial class TicTacToeServerForm : Form
12   {
13      public TicTacToeServerForm()
14      {
15         InitializeComponent();
16      } // end constructor
17
18      private byte[] board; // the local representation of the game board
19      private Player[] players; // two Player objects
20      private Thread[] playerThreads; // Threads for client interaction
21      private TcpListener listener; // listen for client connection
22      private int currentPlayer; // keep track of whose turn it is
```

Fig. 23.5 | Server side of client/server Tic-Tac-Toe program. (Part 1 of 6.)

```
23      private Thread getPlayers; // Thread for acquiring client connections
24      internal bool disconnected = false; // true if the server closes
25
26      // initialize variables and thread for receiving clients
27      private void TicTacToeServerForm_Load( object sender, EventArgs e )
28      {
29         board = new byte[ 9 ];
30         players = new Player[ 2 ];
31         playerThreads = new Thread[ 2 ];
32         currentPlayer = 0;
33
34         // accept connections on a different thread
35         getPlayers = new Thread( new ThreadStart( SetUp ) );
36         getPlayers.Start();
37      } // end method TicTacToeServerForm_Load
38
39      // notify Players to stop Running
40      private void TicTacToeServerForm_FormClosing( object sender,
41         FormClosingEventArgs e )
42      {
43         disconnected = true;
44         System.Environment.Exit( System.Environment.ExitCode );
45      } // end method TicTacToeServerForm_FormClosing
46
47      // delegate that allows method DisplayMessage to be called
48      // in the thread that creates and maintains the GUI
49      private delegate void DisplayDelegate( string message );
50
51      // method DisplayMessage sets displayTextBox's Text property
52      // in a thread-safe manner
53      internal void DisplayMessage( string message )
54      {
55         // if modifying displayTextBox is not thread safe
56         if ( displayTextBox.InvokeRequired )
57         {
58            // use inherited method Invoke to execute DisplayMessage
59            // via a delegate
60            Invoke( new DisplayDelegate( DisplayMessage ),
61               new object[] { message } );
62         } // end if
63         else // OK to modify displayTextBox in current thread
64            displayTextBox.Text += message;
65      } // end method DisplayMessage
66
67      // accepts connections from 2 players
68      public void SetUp()
69      {
70         DisplayMessage( "Waiting for players...\r\n" );
71
72         // set up Socket
73         listener =
74            new TcpListener( IPAddress.Parse( "127.0.0.1" ), 50000 );
75         listener.Start();
```

Fig. 23.5 | Server side of client/server Tic-Tac-Toe program. (Part 2 of 6.)

```
76
77        // accept first player and start a player thread
78        players[ 0 ] = new Player( listener.AcceptSocket(), this, 0 );
79        playerThreads[ 0 ] =
80           new Thread( new ThreadStart( players[ 0 ].Run ) );
81        playerThreads[ 0 ].Start();
82
83        // accept second player and start another player thread
84        players[ 1 ] = new Player( listener.AcceptSocket(), this, 1 );
85        playerThreads[ 1 ] =
86           new Thread( new ThreadStart( players[ 1 ].Run ) );
87        playerThreads[ 1 ].Start();
88
89        // let the first player know that the other player has connected
90        lock ( players[ 0 ] )
91        {
92           players[ 0 ].threadSuspended = false;
93           Monitor.Pulse( players[ 0 ] );
94        } // end lock
95     } // end method SetUp
96
97     // determine if a move is valid
98     public bool ValidMove( int location, int player )
99     {
100       // prevent another thread from making a move
101       lock ( this )
102       {
103          // while it is not the current player's turn, wait
104          while ( player != currentPlayer )
105             Monitor.Wait( this );
106
107          // if the desired square is not occupied
108          if ( !IsOccupied( location ) )
109          {
110             // set the board to contain the current player's mark
111             board[ location ] = ( byte ) ( currentPlayer == 0 ?
112                'X' : 'O' );
113
114             // set the currentPlayer to be the other player
115             currentPlayer = ( currentPlayer + 1 ) % 2;
116
117             // notify the other player of the move
118             players[ currentPlayer ].OtherPlayerMoved( location );
119
120             // alert the other player that it's time to move
121             Monitor.Pulse( this );
122             return true;
123          } // end if
124          else
125             return false;
126       } // end lock
127    } // end method ValidMove
128
```

Fig. 23.5 | Server side of client/server Tic-Tac-Toe program. (Part 3 of 6.)

```csharp
129     // determines whether the specified square is occupied
130     public bool IsOccupied( int location )
131     {
132         if ( board[ location ] == 'X' || board[ location ] == 'O' )
133             return true;
134         else
135             return false;
136     } // end method IsOccupied
137
138     // determines if the game is over
139     public bool GameOver()
140     {
141         // place code here to test for a winner of the game
142         return false;
143     } // end method GameOver
144 } // end class TicTacToeServerForm
145
146 // class Player represents a tic-tac-toe player
147 public class Player
148 {
149     internal Socket connection; // Socket for accepting a connection
150     private NetworkStream socketStream; // network data stream
151     private TicTacToeServerForm server; // reference to server
152     private BinaryWriter writer; // facilitates writing to the stream
153     private BinaryReader reader; // facilitates reading from the stream
154     private int number; // player number
155     private char mark; // player's mark on the board
156     internal bool threadSuspended = true; // if waiting for other player
157
158     // constructor requiring Socket, TicTacToeServerForm and int
159     // objects as arguments
160     public Player( Socket socket, TicTacToeServerForm serverValue,
161         int newNumber )
162     {
163         mark = (newNumber == 0 ? 'X' : 'O');
164         connection = socket;
165         server = serverValue;
166         number = newNumber;
167
168         // create NetworkStream object for Socket
169         socketStream = new NetworkStream( connection );
170
171         // create Streams for reading/writing bytes
172         writer = new BinaryWriter( socketStream );
173         reader = new BinaryReader( socketStream );
174     } // end constructor
175
176     // signal other player of move
177     public void OtherPlayerMoved( int location )
178     {
179         // signal that opponent moved
180         writer.Write( "Opponent moved." );
```

Fig. 23.5 | Server side of client/server Tic-Tac-Toe program. (Part 4 of 6.)

```
181            writer.Write( location ); // send location of move
182        } // end method OtherPlayerMoved
183
184        // allows the players to make moves and receive moves
185        // from the other player
186        public void Run()
187        {
188            bool done = false;
189
190            // display on the server that a connection was made
191            server.DisplayMessage( "Player " + ( number == 0 ? 'X' : 'O' )
192                + " connected\r\n" );
193
194            // send the current player's mark to the client
195            writer.Write( mark );
196
197            // if number equals 0 then this player is X,
198            // otherwise O must wait for X's first move
199            writer.Write( "Player " + ( number == 0 ?
200                "X connected.\r\n" : "O connected, please wait.\r\n" ) );
201
202            // X must wait for another player to arrive
203            if ( mark == 'X' )
204            {
205                writer.Write( "Waiting for another player." );
206
207                // wait for notification from server that another
208                // player has connected
209                lock ( this )
210                {
211                    while ( threadSuspended )
212                        Monitor.Wait( this );
213                } // end lock
214
215                writer.Write( "Other player connected. Your move." );
216            } // end if
217
218            // play game
219            while ( !done )
220            {
221                // wait for data to become available
222                while ( connection.Available == 0 )
223                {
224                    Thread.Sleep( 1000 );
225
226                    if ( server.disconnected )
227                        return;
228                } // end while
229
230                // receive data
231                int location = reader.ReadInt32();
232
```

Fig. 23.5 | Server side of client/server Tic-Tac-Toe program. (Part 5 of 6.)

```
233            // if the move is valid, display the move on the
234            // server and signal that the move is valid
235            if ( server.ValidMove( location, number ) )
236            {
237               server.DisplayMessage( "loc: " + location + "\r\n" );
238               writer.Write( "Valid move." );
239            } // end if
240            else // signal that the move is invalid
241               writer.Write( "Invalid move, try again." );
242
243            // if game is over, set done to true to exit while loop
244            if ( server.GameOver() )
245               done = true;
246         } // end while loop
247
248         // close the socket connection
249         writer.Close();
250         reader.Close();
251         socketStream.Close();
252         connection.Close();
253      } // end method Run
254   } // end class Player
```

Fig. 23.5 | Server side of client/server Tic-Tac-Toe program. (Part 6 of 6.)

Lines 49–65 define `DisplayDelegate` and `DisplayMessage`, allowing any thread to modify `displayTextBox`'s `Text` property. This time, the `DisplayMessage` method is declared as `internal`, so it can be called inside a method of class `Player` through a `TicTacToeServerForm` reference.

Thread `getPlayers` executes method `SetUp` (lines 68–95), which creates a `TcpListener` object to listen for requests on port 50000 (lines 73–75). This object then listens for connection requests from the first and second players. Lines 78 and 84 instantiate `Player` objects representing the players, and lines 79–81 and 85–87 create two `Threads` that execute the `Run` methods of each `Player` object.

The `Player` constructor (Fig. 23.5, lines 160–174) receives as arguments a reference to the `Socket` object (i.e., the connection to the client), a reference to the `TicTacToeServerForm` object and an `int` indicating the player number (from which the constructor infers the mark, "X" or "O" used by that player). In this case study, `TicTacToeServerForm` calls method `Run` (lines 186–253) after instantiating a `Player` object. Lines 191–200 notify the server of a successful connection and send to the client the `char` that the client will place on the board when making a move. If `Run` is executing for `Player` "X", lines 205–215 execute, causing `Player` "X" to wait for a second player to connect. Lines 211–212 define a `while` statement that suspends the `Player` "X" `Thread` until the server signals that `Player` "O" has connected. The server notifies the `Player` of the connection by setting the `Player`'s `threadSuspended` variable to `false` (line 92). When `threadSuspended` becomes `false`, `Player` exits the `while` statement at lines 211–212.

Method `Run` executes the `while` statement at lines 219–24), enabling the user to play the game. Each iteration of this statement waits for the client to send an `int` specifying where on the board to place the "X" or "O"—the `Player` then places the mark on the board, if the specified mark location is valid (e.g., that location does not already contain a mark). Note that the while statement continues execution only if bool variable done is false. This variable is set to true by event handler TicTacToeServerForm_FormClosing of class TicTacToeServerForm, which is invoked when the server closes the connection.

Line 222 of Fig. 23.5 begins a while statement that loops until Socket property Available indicates that there is information to receive from the Socket (or until the server disconnects from the client). If there is no information, the Thread goes to sleep for one second. On awakening, the Thread uses property Disconnected to check whether server variable disconnected is true (line 226). If the value is true, the Thread exits the method (thus terminating the Thread); otherwise, the Thread loops again. However, if property Available indicates that there is data to receive, the while statement of lines 222–228 terminates, enabling the information to be processed.

This information contains an int representing the location in which the client wants to place a mark. Line 231 calls method ReadInt32 of the BinaryReader object (which reads from the NetworkStream created with the Socket) to read this int. Line 235 then passes the int to TicTacToeServerForm method ValidMove. If this method validates the move, the Player places the mark in the desired location.

Method ValidMove (lines 98–127) sends to the client a message indicating whether the move was valid. Locations on the board correspond to numbers from 0–8 (0–2 for the top row, 3–5 for the middle and 6–8 for the bottom). All statements in method ValidMove are enclosed in a lock statement that allows only one move to be attempted at a time. This prevents two players from modifying the game's state information simultaneously. If the Player attempting to validate a move is not the current player (i.e., the one allowed to make a move), that Player is placed in a *Wait* state until it is that Player's turn to move. If the user attempts to place a mark on a location that already contains a mark, method ValidMove returns false. However, if the user has selected an unoccupied location (line 108), lines 111–112 place the mark on the local representation of the board. Line 118 notifies the other Player that a move has been made, and line 121 invokes the Pulse method so that the waiting Player can validate a move. The method then returns true to indicate that the move is valid.

When a TicTacToeClientForm application (Fig. 23.6) executes, it creates a TextBox to display messages from the server and the Tic-Tac-Toe board representation. The board is created out of nine Square objects (Fig. 23.7) that contain Panels on which the user can click, indicating the position on the board in which to place a mark. The TicTacToeClientForm's Load event handler (lines 30–58) opens a connection to the server (line 50) and obtains a reference to the connection's associated NetworkStream object from TcpClient (line 51). Lines 56–57 start a thread to read messages sent from the server to the client. The server passes messages (for example, whether each move is valid) to method ProcessMessage (lines 179–215). If the message indicates that a move is valid (line 184), the client sets its Mark to the current square (the square that the user clicked) and repaints the board. If the message indicates that a move is invalid (line 190), the client notifies the user to click a different square. If the message indicates that the opponent made a move (line 197), line 200 reads an int from the server specifying where on the board the client should place the opponent's Mark. TicTacToeClientForm includes a delegate/method pair for allowing threads to modify idLabel's Text property (lines 97–113), as well as DisplayDelegate and DisplayMesage for modifying displayTextBox's Text property (lines 77–93).

```csharp
 1   // Fig. 23.6: TicTacToeClient.cs
 2   // Client for the TicTacToe program.
 3   using System;
 4   using System.Drawing;
 5   using System.Windows.Forms;
 6   using System.Net.Sockets;
 7   using System.Threading;
 8   using System.IO;
 9
10   public partial class TicTacToeClientForm : Form
11   {
12      public TicTacToeClientForm()
13      {
14         InitializeComponent();
15      } // end constructor
16
17      private Square[ , ] board; // local representation of the game board
18      private Square currentSquare; // the Square that this player chose
19      private Thread outputThread; // Thread for receiving data from server
20      private TcpClient connection; // client to establish connection
21      private NetworkStream stream; // network data stream
22      private BinaryWriter writer; // facilitates writing to the stream
23      private BinaryReader reader; // facilitates reading from the stream
24      private char myMark; // player's mark on the board
25      private bool myTurn; // is it this player's turn?
26      private SolidBrush brush; // brush for drawing X's and O's
27      private bool done = false; // true when game is over
28
29      // initialize variables and thread for connecting to server
30      private void TicTacToeClientForm_Load( object sender, EventArgs e )
31      {
32         board = new Square[ 3, 3 ];
33
34         // create 9 Square objects and place them on the board
35         board[ 0, 0 ] = new Square( board0Panel, ' ', 0 );
36         board[ 0, 1 ] = new Square( board1Panel, ' ', 1 );
37         board[ 0, 2 ] = new Square( board2Panel, ' ', 2 );
38         board[ 1, 0 ] = new Square( board3Panel, ' ', 3 );
39         board[ 1, 1 ] = new Square( board4Panel, ' ', 4 );
40         board[ 1, 2 ] = new Square( board5Panel, ' ', 5 );
41         board[ 2, 0 ] = new Square( board6Panel, ' ', 6 );
42         board[ 2, 1 ] = new Square( board7Panel, ' ', 7 );
43         board[ 2, 2 ] = new Square( board8Panel, ' ', 8 );
44
45         // create a SolidBrush for writing on the Squares
46         brush = new SolidBrush( Color.Black );
47
48         // make connection to server and get the associated
49         // network stream
50         connection = new TcpClient( "127.0.0.1", 50000 );
51         stream = connection.GetStream();
52         writer = new BinaryWriter( stream );
53         reader = new BinaryReader( stream );
```

Fig. 23.6 | Client side of client/server Tic-Tac-Toe program. (Part 1 of 7.)

```
54
55         // start a new thread for sending and receiving messages
56         outputThread = new Thread( new ThreadStart( Run ) );
57         outputThread.Start();
58      } // end method TicTacToeClientForm_Load
59
60      // repaint the Squares
61      private void TicTacToeClientForm_Paint( object sender,
62         PaintEventArgs e )
63      {
64         PaintSquares();
65      } // end method TicTacToeClientForm_Load
66
67      // game is over
68      private void TicTacToeClientForm_FormClosing( object sender,
69         FormClosingEventArgs e )
70      {
71         done = true;
72         System.Environment.Exit( System.Environment.ExitCode );
73      } // end TicTacToeClientForm_FormClosing
74
75      // delegate that allows method DisplayMessage to be called
76      // in the thread that creates and maintains the GUI
77      private delegate void DisplayDelegate( string message );
78
79      // method DisplayMessage sets displayTextBox's Text property
80      // in a thread-safe manner
81      private void DisplayMessage( string message )
82      {
83         // if modifying displayTextBox is not thread safe
84         if ( displayTextBox.InvokeRequired )
85         {
86            // use inherited method Invoke to execute DisplayMessage
87            // via a delegate
88            Invoke( new DisplayDelegate( DisplayMessage ),
89               new object[] { message } );
90         } // end if
91         else // OK to modify displayTextBox in current thread
92            displayTextBox.Text += message;
93      } // end method DisplayMessage
94
95      // delegate that allows method ChangeIdLabel to be called
96      // in the thread that creates and maintains the GUI
97      private delegate void ChangeIdLabelDelegate( string message );
98
99      // method ChangeIdLabel sets displayTextBox's Text property
100     // in a thread-safe manner
101     private void ChangeIdLabel( string label )
102     {
103        // if modifying idLabel is not thread safe
104        if ( idLabel.InvokeRequired )
105        {
```

Fig. 23.6 | Client side of client/server Tic-Tac-Toe program. (Part 2 of 7.)

```
106            // use inherited method Invoke to execute ChangeIdLabel
107            // via a delegate
108            Invoke( new ChangeIdLabelDelegate( ChangeIdLabel ),
109               new object[] { label } );
110         } // end if
111         else // OK to modify idLabel in current thread
112            idLabel.Text = label;
113      } // end method ChangeIdLabel
114
115      // draws the mark of each square
116      public void PaintSquares()
117      {
118         Graphics g;
119
120         // draw the appropriate mark on each panel
121         for ( int row = 0; row < 3; row++ )
122         {
123            for ( int column = 0; column < 3; column++ )
124            {
125               // get the Graphics for each Panel
126               g = board[ row, column ].SquarePanel.CreateGraphics();
127
128               // draw the appropriate letter on the panel
129               g.DrawString( board[ row, column ].Mark.ToString(),
130                  board0Panel.Font, brush, 10, 8 );
131            } // end for
132         } // end for
133      } // end method PaintSquares
134
135      // send location of the clicked square to server
136      private void square_MouseUp( object sender,
137         System.Windows.Forms.MouseEventArgs e )
138      {
139         // for each square check if that square was clicked
140         for ( int row = 0; row < 3; row++ )
141         {
142            for ( int column = 0; column < 3; column++ )
143            {
144               if ( board[ row, column ].SquarePanel == sender )
145               {
146                  CurrentSquare = board[ row, column ];
147
148                  // send the move to the server
149                  SendClickedSquare( board[ row, column ].Location );
150               } // end if
151            } // end for
152         } // end for
153      } // end method square_MouseUp
154
155      // control thread that allows continuous update of the
156      // TextBox display
157      public void Run()
158      {
```

Fig. 23.6 | Client side of client/server Tic-Tac-Toe program. (Part 3 of 7.)

```
159         // first get players's mark (X or O)
160         myMark = reader.ReadChar();
161         ChangeIdLabel( "You are player \"" + myMark + "\"" );
162         myTurn = ( myMark == 'X' ? true : false );
163
164         // process incoming messages
165         try
166         {
167             // receive messages sent to client
168             while ( !done )
169                 ProcessMessage( reader.ReadString() );
170         } // end try
171         catch ( IOException )
172         {
173             MessageBox.Show( "Server is down, game over", "Error",
174                 MessageBoxButtons.OK, MessageBoxIcon.Error );
175         } // end catch
176     } // end method Run
177
178     // process messages sent to client
179     public void ProcessMessage( string message )
180     {
181         // if the move the player sent to the server is valid
182         // update the display, set that square's mark to be
183         // the mark of the current player and repaint the board
184         if ( message == "Valid move." )
185         {
186             DisplayMessage( "Valid move, please wait.\r\n" );
187             currentSquare.Mark = myMark;
188             PaintSquares();
189         } // end if
190         else if ( message == "Invalid move, try again." )
191         {
192             // if the move is invalid, display that and it is now
193             // this player's turn again
194             DisplayMessage( message + "\r\n" );
195             myTurn = true;
196         } // end else if
197         else if ( message == "Opponent moved." )
198         {
199             // if opponent moved, find location of their move
200             int location = reader.ReadInt32();
201
202             // set that square to have the opponents mark and
203             // repaint the board
204             board[ location / 3, location % 3 ].Mark =
205                 ( myMark == 'X' ? 'O' : 'X' );
206             PaintSquares();
207
208             DisplayMessage( "Opponent moved.  Your turn.\r\n" );
209
```

Fig. 23.6 | Client side of client/server Tic-Tac-Toe program. (Part 4 of 7.)

```
210              // it is now this player's turn
211              myTurn = true;
212          } // end else if
213          else
214              DisplayMessage( message + "\r\n" ); // display message
215      } // end method ProcessMessage
216
217      // sends the server the number of the clicked square
218      public void SendClickedSquare( int location )
219      {
220          // if it is the current player's move right now
221          if ( myTurn )
222          {
223              // send the location of the move to the server
224              writer.Write( location );
225
226              // it is now the other player's turn
227              myTurn = false;
228          } // end if
229      } // end method SendClickedSquare
230
231      // write-only property for the current square
232      public Square CurrentSquare
233      {
234          set
235          {
236              currentSquare = value;
237          } // end set
238      } // end property CurrentSquare
239  } // end class TicTacToeClientForm
```

At the start of the game.

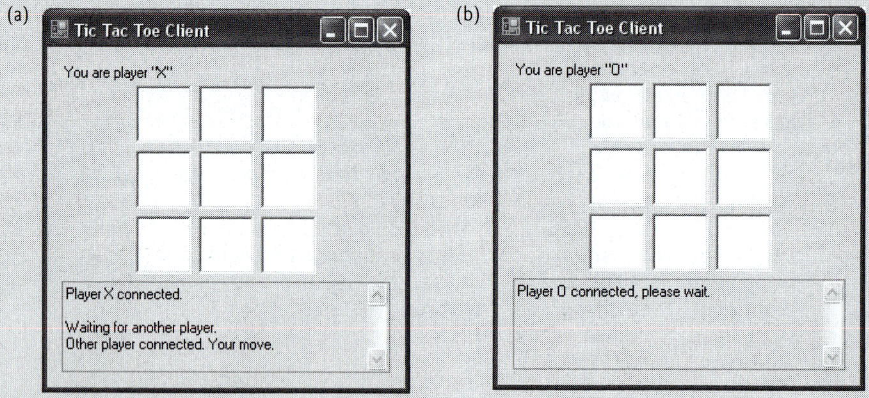

(a)

(b)

Fig. 23.6 | Client side of client/server Tic-Tac-Toe program. (Part 5 of 7.)

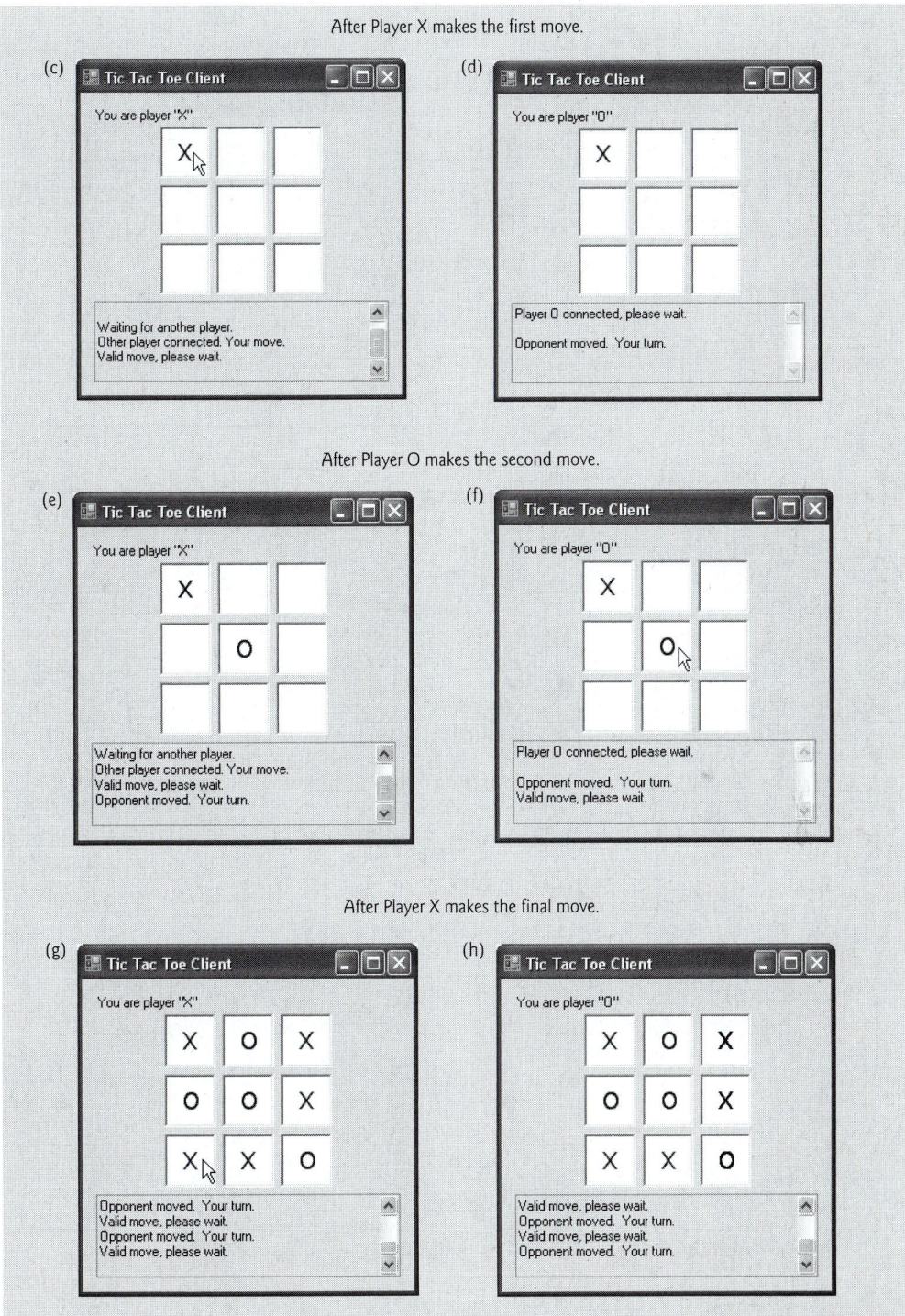

Fig. 23.6 | Client side of client/server Tic-Tac-Toe program. (Part 6 of 7.)

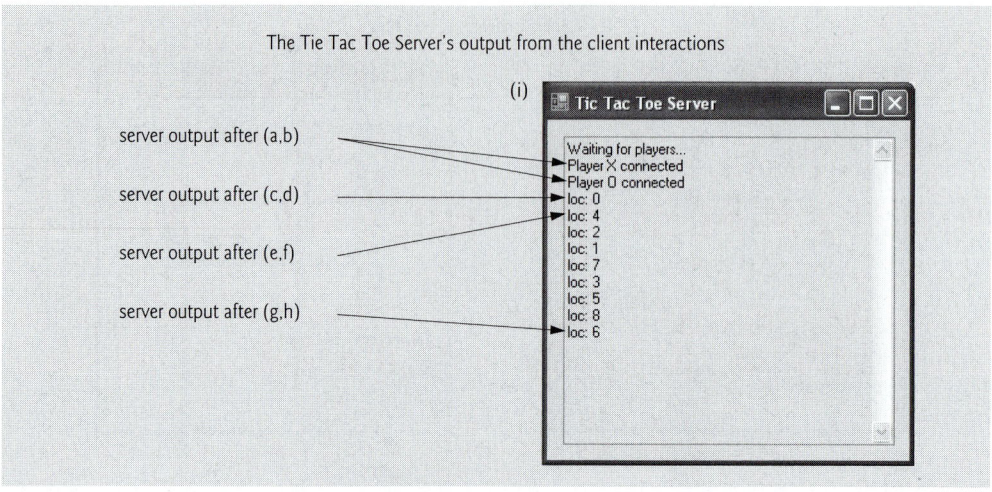

The Tie Tac Toe Server's output from the client interactions

server output after (a,b)

server output after (c,d)

server output after (e,f)

server output after (g,h)

(i)

Fig. 23.6 | Client side of client/server Tic-Tac-Toe program. (Part 7 of 7.)

```
 1   // Fig. 23.7: Square.cs
 2   // A Square on the TicTacToe board.
 3   using System.Windows.Forms;
 4
 5   // the representation of a square in a tic-tac-toe grid
 6   public class Square
 7   {
 8      private Panel panel; // GUI Panel that represents this Square
 9      private char mark; // player's mark on this Square (if any)
10      private int location; // location on the board of this Square
11
12      // constructor
13      public Square( Panel newPanel, char newMark, int newLocation )
14      {
15         panel = newPanel;
16         mark = newMark;
17         location = newLocation;
18      } // end constructor
19
20      // property SquarePanel; the panel which the square represents
21      public Panel SquarePanel
22      {
23         get
24         {
25            return panel;
26         } // end get
27      } // end property SquarePanel
28
29      // property Mark; the mark on the square
30      public char Mark
31      {
```

Fig. 23.7 | Class Square. (Part 1 of 2.)

```
32          get
33          {
34              return mark;
35          } // end get
36          set
37          {
38              mark = value;
39          } // end set
40      } // end property Mark
41
42      // property Location; the square's location on the board
43      public int Location
44      {
45          get
46          {
47              return location;
48          } // end get
49      } // end property Location
50  } // end class Square
```

Fig. 23.7 | Class Square. (Part 2 of 2.)

23.9 WebBrowser Control

With FCL 2.0, Microsoft introduced the WebBrowser control, which enables applications to incorporate Web browsing capabilities. The control provides methods for navigating Web pages and maintains its own history of Web sites visited. It also generates events as the user interacts with the content displayed in the control, so your application can respond to events such as the user clicking the links displayed in the content.

Figure 23.8 demonstrates the WebBrowser control's capabilities. Class BrowserForm provides the basic functionality of a Web browser, allowing the user to navigate to a URL, to move backward and forward through the history of visited sites and to reload the current Web page.

```
1   // Fig. 23.8: Browser.cs
2   // WebBrowser control example.
3   using System;
4   using System.Windows.Forms;
5
6   public partial class BrowserForm : Form
7   {
8       public BrowserForm()
9       {
10          InitializeComponent();
11      } // end constructor
12
13      // navigate back one page
14      private void backButton_Click( object sender, EventArgs e )
15      {
```

Fig. 23.8 | WebBrowser control example. (Part 1 of 3.)

```
16          webBrowser.GoBack();
17       } // end method backButton_Click
18
19       // navigate forward one page
20       private void forwardButton_Click( object sender, EventArgs e )
21       {
22          webBrowser.GoForward();
23       } // end method forwardButton_Click
24
25       // stop loading the current page
26       private void stopButton_Click( object sender, EventArgs e )
27       {
28          webBrowser.Stop();
29       } // end method stopButton_Click
30
31       // reload the current page
32       private void reloadButton_Click( object sender, EventArgs e )
33       {
34          webBrowser.Refresh();
35       } // end method reloadButton_Click
36
37       // navigate to the user's home page
38       private void homeButton_Click( object sender, EventArgs e )
39       {
40          webBrowser.GoHome();
41       } // end method homeButton_Click
42
43       // if the user pressed enter, navigate to the specified URL
44       private void navigationTextBox_KeyDown( object sender,
45          KeyEventArgs e )
46       {
47          if ( e.KeyCode == Keys.Enter )
48             webBrowser.Navigate( navigationTextBox.Text );
49       } // end method navigationTextBox_KeyDown
50
51       // enable stopButton while the current page is loading
52       private void webBrowser_Navigating( object sender,
53          WebBrowserNavigatingEventArgs e )
54       {
55          stopButton.Enabled = true;
56       } // end method webBrowser_Navigating
57
58       // update the status text
59       private void webBrowser_StatusTextChanged( object sender,
60          EventArgs e )
61       {
62          statusTextBox.Text = webBrowser.StatusText;
63       } // end method webBrowser_StatusTextChanged
64
65       // update the ProgressBar for how much of the page has been loaded
66       private void webBrowser_ProgressChanged( object sender,
67          WebBrowserProgressChangedEventArgs e )
68       {
```

Fig. 23.8 | WebBrowser control example. (Part 2 of 3.)

```
69        pageProgressBar.Value =
70           ( int ) ( ( 100 * e.CurrentProgress ) / e.MaximumProgress );
71     } // end method webBrowser_ProgressChanged
72
73     // update the web browser's controls appropriately
74     private void webBrowser_DocumentCompleted( object sender,
75        WebBrowserDocumentCompletedEventArgs e )
76     {
77        // set the text in navigationTextBox to the current page's URL
78        navigationTextBox.Text = webBrowser.Url.ToString();
79
80        // enable or disable backButton and forwardButton
81        backButton.Enabled = webBrowser.CanGoBack;
82        forwardButton.Enabled = webBrowser.CanGoForward;
83
84        // disable stopButton
85        stopButton.Enabled = false;
86
87        // clear the pageProgressBar
88        pageProgressBar.Value = 0;
89     } // end method webBrowser_DocumentCompleted
90
91     // update the title of the Browser
92     private void webBrowser_DocumentTitleChanged( object sender,
93        EventArgs e )
94     {
95        this.Text = webBrowser.DocumentTitle + " - Browser";
96     } // end method webBrowser_DocumentTitleChanged
97  } // end class BrowserForm
```

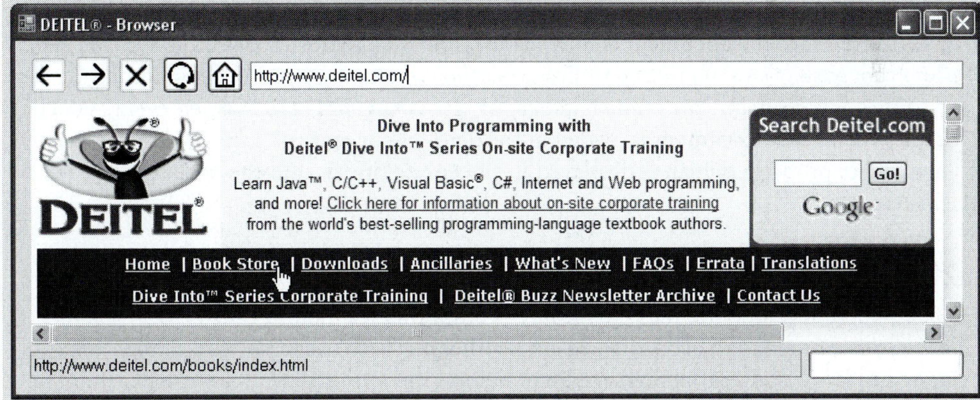

Fig. 23.8 | WebBrowser control example. (Part 3 of 3.)

Lines 14–41 define five Click event handlers, one for each of the five navigation Buttons that appear at the top of the Form. Each event handler calls a corresponding Web-Browser method. WebBrowser method **GoBack** (line 16) causes the control to navigate back to the previous page in the navigation history. Method **GoForward** (line 22) causes the control to navigate forward to the next page in the navigation history. Method **Stop** (line 28) causes the control to stop loading the current page. Method **Refresh** (line 34) causes the control to reload the current page. Method **GoHome** (line 40) causes the control to navigate to the user's home page, as defined under Internet Explorer's settings (under **Tools > Internet Options...** in the **Home page** section).

The TextBox to the right of the navigation buttons allows the user to enter the URL of a Web site to browse. When the user types each keystroke in the TextBox, the event handler at lines 44–49 executes. If the key pressed was *Enter*, line 48 calls WebBrowser method **Navigate** to retrieve the document at the specified URL.

The WebBrowser control generates a **Navigating** event when the WebBrowser starts loading a new page. When this occurs, the event handler at lines 52–56 executes, and line 55 enables stopButton so that the user can cancel the loading of the Web page.

Typically, a user can see the status of a loading Web page at the bottom of the browser window. For this reason, we include a TextBox control (named statusTextBox) and a ProgressBar control (named pageProgressBar) at the bottom of our Form. The Web-Browser control generates a **StatusTextChanged** event when the WebBrowser's **Status-Text** property changes. The event handler for this event (lines 59–63) assigns the new contents of the control's StatusText property to statusTextBox's Text property (line 62), so the user can monitor the WebBrowser's status messages. The control generates a **ProgressChanged** event when the WebBrowser control's page-loading progress is updated. The ProgressChanged event handler (lines 66–71) updates pageProgressBar's Value (lines 69–70) to reflect how much of the current document has been loaded.

When the WebBrowser finishes loading a document, the control generates a **DocumentCompleted** event. This executes the event handler at lines 74–89. Line 78 updates the contents of navigationTextBox so that it shows the URL of the currently loaded page (WebBrowser property Url). This is particularly important if the user browses to another Web page by clicking a link in the existing page. Lines 81–82 use properties **CanGoBack** and **CanGoForward** to determine whether the back and forward buttons should be enabled or disabled. Since the document is now loaded, line 85 disables stopButton. Line 88 sets pageProgressBar's Value to 0 to indicate that no content is currently being loaded.

Lines 92–96 define an event handler for the **DocumentTitleChanged** event, which occurs when a new document is loaded in the WebBrowser control. Line 95 sets Browser-Form's Text property (which is displayed in the Form's title bar) to the WebBrowser's current **DocumentTitle**.

23.10 .NET Remoting

The .NET framework provides a distributed computing technology called *.NET remoting* that allows a program to access objects on another machine over a network. .NET remoting is similar in concept to RMI (remote method invocation) in Java and RPC (remote procedure call) in procedural programming languages. .NET remoting is also similar to Web services (Chapter 22) with a few key differences. With Web services, a client application communicates with a Web service that is hosted by a Web server. The client and the Web service can be written in any language, as long as they can transmit messages in SOAP. With .NET remoting, a client application communicates with a server application, both of which must be written in .NET languages. Using .NET remoting, a client and a server can communicate via method calls and objects can be transmitted between applications—a process known as *marshaling* the objects.

Channels

The client and the server are able to communicate with one another through *channels*. Channels typically use either the HTTP protocol or the TCP protocol to transmit messages. The advantage of an *HTTP channel* is that firewalls usually permit HTTP connections by default, while they normally block unfamiliar TCP connections. The advantage of a *TCP channel* is better performance than an HTTP channel. In a .NET remoting application, the client and the server each create a channel, and both channels must use the same protocol to communicate with one another. In our example, we use HTTP channels.

Marshaling

There are two ways to marshal an object—by value and by reference. *Marshal by value* requires that the object be *serializable*—that is, capable of being represented as a formated message that can be sent between applications through a channel. The receiving end of the channel *deserializes* the object to obtain a copy of the original object. To enable an object to be serialized and deserialized, its class must either be declared with attribute [Serializable] or must implement interface ISerializable.

Marshal by reference requires that the object's class extend class **MarshalByRefObject** of namespace System. An object that is marshaled by reference is referred to as a *remote object*, and its class is referred to as a *remote class*. When an object is marshaled by reference, the object itself is not transmitted. Instead, two *proxy* objects are created—a *transparent proxy* and a *real proxy*. The transparent proxy provides all the public services of a remote object. Typically, a client calls the methods and properties of the transparent proxy as if it were the remote object. The transparent proxy then calls the Invoke method of the real proxy. This sends the appropriate message from the client channel to the server channel. The server receives this message and performs the specified method call or accesses the specified property on the actual object, which resides on the server. In our example, we marshal a remote object by reference.

Weather Information Application Using .NET Remoting

We now present a .NET remoting example that downloads the *Traveler's Forecast* weather information from the National Weather Service Web site:

```
http://iwin.nws.noaa.gov/iwin/us/traveler.html
```

[*Note:* As we developed this example, the National Weather Service indicated that the information provided on the *Traveler's Forecast* Web page would be provided by a Web service in the near future. The information we use in this example depends directly on the format of the *Traveler's Forecast* Web page. If you have trouble running this example, please refer to the FAQ page at www.deitel.com/faq.html. This potential problem demonstrates a benefit of using Web services or .NET remoting to implement distributed computing applications that may change in the future. Separating the server part of the application that depends on the format of an outside data source from the client part of the application allows the server implementation to be updated without requiring any changes to the client.]

Our .NET remoting application consists of five components:

1. Serializable class CityWeather, which represents the weather report for one city.

2. Interface `Report`, which declares a property `Reports` that the marshaled object provides to a client application to obtain a collection of `CityWeather` objects.

3. Remote class `ReportInfo`, which extends class `MarshalByRefObject`, implements interface `Report` and will be instantiated only on the server.

4. A `WeatherServer` application that sets up a server channel and makes the `ReportInfo` class available at a particular URI (uniform resource identifier).

5. A `WeatherClient` application that sets up a client channel and requests a `ReportInfo` object from the `WeatherServer` to retrieve the day's weather report.

Class CityWeather

Class `CityWeather` (Fig. 23.9) contains weather information for one city. Class `CityWeather` is declared in namespace `Weather` (line 5) for reusability and will be published in the `Weather.dll` class library file that both the server application and the client application must reference. For this reason, you should place this class (and interface `Report` from Fig. 23.10) in a class library project. Class `CityWeather` is declared with attribute `Serializable` (line 7), which indicates that an object of class `CityWeather` can be marshaled by value. This is necessary because `CityWeather` objects will be returned by the `ReportInfo` object's `Reports` property, and the return values of the methods and properties declared by a remote class must themselves be marshaled by value from the server to the client. (The argument values in method calls will also be marshaled by value from the client to the server.) So when the client calls a `get` accessor that returns `CityWeather` objects, the server channel will serialize the `CityWeather` objects in a message that the client channel can deserialize to create copies of the original `CityWeather` objects. Class `CityWeather` also implements interface `IComparable` (line 8) so that an `ArrayList` of `CityWeather` objects can be sorted alphabetically.

```csharp
1   // Fig. 23.9: CityWeather.cs
2   // Class representing the weather information for one city.
3   using System;
4
5   namespace Weather
6   {
7      [ Serializable ]
8      public class CityWeather : IComparable
9      {
10         private string cityName;
11         private string description;
12         private string temperature;
13
14         public CityWeather( string city, string information,
15            string degrees )
16         {
17            cityName = city;
18            description = information;
19            temperature = degrees;
20         } // end constructor
21
```

Fig. 23.9 | Class `CityWeather`. (Part 1 of 2.)

```
22              // read-only property that gets city's name
23              public string CityName
24              {
25                 get
26                 {
27                    return cityName;
28                 } // end get
29              } // end property CityName
30
31              // read-only property that gets city's weather description
32              public string Description
33              {
34                 get
35                 {
36                    return description;
37                 } // end get
38              } // end property Description
39
40              // read-only property that gets city's temperature
41              public string Temperature
42              {
43                 get
44                 {
45                    return temperature;
46                 } // end get
47              } // end property Temperature
48
49              // implementation of CompareTo method for alphabetizing
50              public int CompareTo( object other )
51              {
52                 return string.Compare(
53                    CityName, ( ( CityWeather ) other ).CityName );
54              } // end method Compare
55
56              // return string representation of this CityWeather object
57              // (used to display the weather report on the server console)
58              public override string ToString()
59              {
60                 return cityName + " | " + temperature + " | " + description;
61              } // end method ToString
62           } // end class CityWeather
63        } // end namespace Weather
```

Fig. 23.9 | Class CityWeather. (Part 2 of 2.)

CityWeather contains three instance variables (lines 10–12) for storing the city's name, high/low temperatures and weather condition description. The CityWeather constructor (lines 14–20) initializes the three instance variables. Lines 23–47 declare three read-only properties that allow the values of the three instance variables to be retrieved. CityWeather implements IComparable, so it must declare a method called CompareTo that takes an object reference and returns an int (lines 50–54). Also, we want to alphabetize CityWeather objects by their cityNames, so CompareTo calls string method Compare with the cityNames of the two CityWeather objects. Class CityWeather also overrides the

`ToString` method to display information for this city (lines 58–61). Method `ToString` is used by the server application to display the weather information retrieved from the *Traveler's Forecast* Web page in the console.

Interface Report

Figure 23.10 shows the code for interface `Report`. Interface `Report` is also declared in namespace `Weather` (line 7) and will be included with class `CityWeather` in the `Weather.dll` class library file, so it can be used in both the client and server applications. `Report` declares a read-only property (lines 11–14) with a `get` accessor that returns an `ArrayList` of `CityWeather` objects. The client application will use this property to retrieve the information in the weather report—each city's name, high/low temperature and weather condition.

Class ReportInfo

Remote class `ReportInfo` (Fig. 23.11) implements interface `Report` (line 10) of namespace `Weather` (specified by the `using` directive in line 8). `ReportInfo` also extends base class `MarshalByRefObject`. Class `ReportInfo` is part of the remote `WeatherServer` application and will not be directly available to the client application.

```
1   // Fig. 23.10: Report.cs
2   // Interface that defines a property for getting
3   // the information in a weather report.
4   using System;
5   using System.Collections;
6
7   namespace Weather
8   {
9      public interface Report
10     {
11        ArrayList Reports
12        {
13           get;
14        } // end property Reports
15     } // end interface Report
16  } // end namespace Weather
```

Fig. 23.10 | Interface `Report` in namespace `Weather`.

```
1   // Fig. 23.11: ReportInfo.cs
2   // Class that implements interface Report, retrieves
3   // and returns data on weather
4   using System;
5   using System.Collections;
6   using System.IO;
7   using System.Net;
8   using Weather;
9
```

Fig. 23.11 | Class `ReportInfo`, which implements interface `Report`, is marshaled by reference. (Part I of 3.)

```
10   public class ReportInfo : MarshalByRefObject, Report
11   {
12      private ArrayList cityList; // cities, temperatures, descriptions
13
14      public ReportInfo()
15      {
16         cityList = new ArrayList();
17
18         // create WebClient to get access to Web page
19         WebClient myClient = new WebClient();
20
21         // get StreamReader for response so we can read page
22         StreamReader input = new StreamReader( myClient.OpenRead(
23            "http://iwin.nws.noaa.gov/iwin/us/traveler.html" ) );
24
25         string separator1 = "TAV12"; // indicates first batch of cities
26         string separator2 = "TAV13"; // indicates second batch of cities
27
28         // locate separator1 in Web page
29         while ( !input.ReadLine().StartsWith( separator1 ) ); // do nothing
30         ReadCities( input ); // read the first batch of cities
31
32         // locate separator2 in Web page
33         while ( !input.ReadLine().StartsWith( separator2 ) ); // do nothing
34         ReadCities( input ); // read the second batch of cities
35
36         cityList.Sort(); // sort list of cities by alphabetical order
37         input.Close(); // close StreamReader to NWS server
38
39         // display the data on the server side
40         Console.WriteLine( "Data from NWS Web site:" );
41
42         foreach ( CityWeather city in cityList )
43         {
44            Console.WriteLine( city );
45         } // end foreach
46      } // end constructor
47
48      // utility method that reads a batch of cities
49      private void ReadCities( StreamReader input )
50      {
51         // day format and night format
52         string dayFormat =
53            "CITY            WEA     HI/LO    WEA      HI/LO";
54         string nightFormat =
55            "CITY            WEA     LO/HI    WEA      LO/HI";
56         string inputLine = "";
57
58         // locate header that begins weather information
59         do
60         {
```

Fig. 23.11 | Class ReportInfo, which implements interface Report, is marshaled by reference. (Part 2 of 3.)

```
61          inputLine = input.ReadLine();
62      } while ( !inputLine.Equals( dayFormat ) &&
63          !inputLine.Equals( nightFormat ) );
64
65      inputLine = input.ReadLine(); // get first city's data
66
67      // while there are more cities to read
68      while ( inputLine.Length > 28 )
69      {
70          // create CityWeather object for city
71          CityWeather weather = new CityWeather(
72              inputLine.Substring( 0, 16 ),
73              inputLine.Substring( 16, 7 ),
74              inputLine.Substring( 23, 7 ) );
75
76          cityList.Add( weather ); // add to ArrayList
77          inputLine = input.ReadLine(); // get next city's data
78      } // end while
79   } // end method ReadCities
80
81   // property for getting the cities' weather reports
82   public ArrayList Reports
83   {
84      get
85      {
86          return cityList;
87      } // end get
88   } // end property Reports
89 } // end class ReportInfo
```

Fig. 23.11 | Class `ReportInfo`, which implements interface `Report`, is marshaled by reference. (Part 3 of 3.)

Lines 14–46 declare the `ReportInfo` constructor. Line 19 creates a **`WebClient`** (namespace `System.Net`) object to interact with a data source that is specified by a URL—in this case, the URL for the NWS *Traveler's Forecast* page (`http://iwin.nws.noaa.gov/iwin/us/traveler.html`). Lines 22–23 call `WebClient` method `OpenRead`, which returns a `Stream` that the program can use to read data containing the weather information from the specified URL. This `Stream` is used to create a `StreamReader` object, so the program can read the Web page's HTML markup line-by-line.

The section of the Web page in which we are interested consists of two batches of cities—Albany through Reno, and Salt Lake City through Washington, D.C. The first batch occurs in a section that starts with the `string` "TAV12," while the second batch occurs in a section that starts with the `string` "TAV13." We declare variables `separator1` and `separator2` to store these strings. Line 29 reads the HTML markup one line at a time until "TAV12" is encountered. Once "TAV12" is reached, the program calls utility method `ReadCities` to read a batch of cities into `ArrayList` `cityList`. Next, line 33 reads the HTML markup one line at a time until "TAV13" is encountered, and line 34 makes another call to method `ReadCities` to read the second batch of cities. Line 36 calls method *Sort* of class `ArrayList` to sort the `CityWeather` objects in alphabetical order by city name. Line

37 closes the `StreamReader` connection to the Web site. Lines 42–45 output the weather information for each city to the server application's console display.

Lines 49–79 declare utility method `ReadCities`, which takes a `StreamReader` object and reads the information for each city, creates a `CityWeather` object for it and places the `CityWeather` object in `cityList`. The `do...while` statement (lines 59–63) continues to read the page one line at a time until it finds the header line that begins the weather forecast table. This line starts with either `dayFormat` (lines 52–53), indicating the header for the daytime information, or `nightFormat` (lines 54–55), indicating the header for the nighttime information. Because the line could be in either format based on the time of day, the loop-continuation condition checks for both. Line 65 reads the next line from the Web page, which is the first line containing temperature information.

The `while` statement (lines 68–78) creates a new `CityWeather` object to represent the current city. It parses the `string` containing the current weather data, separating the city name, the weather condition and the temperature. The `CityWeather` object is added to `cityList`. Then the next line from the page is read and stored in `inputLine` for the next iteration. This process continues while the length of the `string` read from the Web page is greater than 28 (the lines containing weather data are all longer than 28 characters). The first line shorter than this signals the end of that forecast section in the Web page.

Read-only property `Reports` (lines 82–88) implements the `Report` interface's `Reports` property to return `cityList`. The client application will remotely call this property to retrieve the day's weather report.

Class *WeatherServer*

Figure 23.12 contains the code for the server application. The `using` directives in lines 5–7 specify .NET remoting namespaces ***System.Runtime.Remoting***, ***System.Runtime.Remoting.Channels*** and ***System.Runtime.Remoting.Channels.Http***. The first two namespaces are required for .NET remoting, and the third is required for HTTP channels. Namespace `System.Runtime.Remoting.Channels.Http` requires the project to reference the `System.Runtime.Remoting` assembly, which can be found under the **.NET** tab in the **Add References** menu. The `using` directive at line 8 specifies namespace `Weather`, which contains interface `Report`. Remember to add a reference to `Weather.dll` in this project.

```
1   // Fig. 23.12: WeatherServer.cs
2   // Server application that uses .NET remoting to send
3   // weather report information to a client
4   using System;
5   using System.Runtime.Remoting;
6   using System.Runtime.Remoting.Channels;
7   using System.Runtime.Remoting.Channels.Http;
8   using Weather;
9
10  class WeatherServer
11  {
12     static void Main( string[] args )
13     {
14        // establish HTTP channel
15        HttpChannel channel = new HttpChannel( 50000 );
```

Fig. 23.12 | Class `WeatherServer` exposes remote class `ReportInfo`. (Part 1 of 2.)

```
16                ChannelServices.RegisterChannel( channel, false );
17
18                // register ReportInfo class
19                RemotingConfiguration.RegisterWellKnownServiceType(
20                   typeof( ReportInfo ), "Report",
21                   WellKnownObjectMode.Singleton );
22
23                Console.WriteLine( "Press Enter to terminate server." );
24                Console.ReadLine();
25          } // end Main
26       } // end class WeatherServer
```

Fig. 23.12 | Class `WeatherServer` exposes remote class `ReportInfo`. (Part 2 of 2.)

Lines 15–16 in `Main` register an HTTP channel on the current machine at port 50000. This is the port number that clients will use to connect to the `WeatherServer` remotely. The argument `false` at line 16 indicates that we do not wish to enable security, which is beyond the scope of this introduction. Lines 19–21 register the `ReportInfo` class type at the "Report" URI as a `Singleton` remote class. If a remote class is registered as *Singleton*, one remote object will be created when the first client requests that remote class, and that remote object will service all clients. The alternative mode is *SingleCall*, where one remote object is created for each individual remote method call to the remote class. [*Note:* A `Singleton` remote object does not have an infinite lifetime; it will be garbage collected after being idle for 5 minutes. A new `Singleton` remote object will be created if another client requests one later.] The `ReportInfo` remote class is now available to clients at the URI "`http://IPAddress:50000/Report`" where *IPAddress* is the IP address of the computer on which the server is running. The channel remains open as long as the server application continues running, so line 24 waits for the user running the server application to press **Enter** before terminating the application.

Class WeatherClientForm

`WeatherClientForm` (Fig. 23.13) is a Windows application that uses .NET remoting to retrieve weather information from `WeatherServer` and displays the information in a graphical, easy-to-read manner. The GUI contains 43 `Label`s—one for each city in the *Traveler's Forecast*. All the `Label`s are placed in a `Panel` with a vertical scrollbar. Each `Label` displays

```
 1   // Fig. 23.13: WeatherClient.cs
 2   // Client that uses .NET remoting to retrieve a weather report.
 3   using System;
 4   using System.Collections;
 5   using System.Drawing;
 6   using System.Windows.Forms;
 7   using System.Runtime.Remoting;
 8   using System.Runtime.Remoting.Channels;
 9   using System.Runtime.Remoting.Channels.Http;
10   using Weather;
```

Fig. 23.13 | The Weather Client accesses a `ReportInfo` object remotely and displays the weather report. (Part 1 of 3.)

```
11
12   public partial class WeatherClientForm : Form
13   {
14      public WeatherClientForm()
15      {
16         InitializeComponent();
17      } // end constructor
18
19      // retrieve weather data
20      private void WeatherClientForm_Load( object sender, EventArgs e )
21      {
22         // setup HTTP channel, does not need to provide a port number
23         HttpChannel channel = new HttpChannel();
24         ChannelServices.RegisterChannel( channel, false );
25
26         // obtain a proxy for an object that implements interface Report
27         Report info = ( Report ) RemotingServices.Connect(
28            typeof( Report ), "http://localhost:50000/Report" );
29
30         // retrieve an ArrayList of CityWeather objects
31         ArrayList cities = info.Reports;
32
33         // create array and populate it with every Label
34         Label[] cityLabels = new Label[ 43 ];
35         int labelCounter = 0;
36
37         foreach ( Control control in displayPanel.Controls )
38         {
39            if ( control is Label )
40            {
41               cityLabels[ labelCounter ] = ( Label ) control;
42               ++labelCounter; // increment Label counter
43            } // end if
44         } // end foreach
45
46         // create Hashtable and populate with all weather conditions
47         Hashtable weather = new Hashtable();
48         weather.Add( "SUNNY", "sunny" );
49         weather.Add( "PTCLDY", "pcloudy" );
50         weather.Add( "CLOUDY", "mcloudy" );
51         weather.Add( "MOCLDY", "mcloudy" );
52         weather.Add( "TSTRMS", "rain" );
53         weather.Add( "RAIN", "rain" );
54         weather.Add( "SNOW", "snow" );
55         weather.Add( "VRYHOT", "vryhot" );
56         weather.Add( "FAIR", "fair" );
57         weather.Add( "RNSNOW", "rnsnow" );
58         weather.Add( "SHWRS", "showers" );
59         weather.Add( "WINDY", "windy" );
60         weather.Add( "NOINFO", "noinfo" );
61         weather.Add( "MISG", "noinfo" );
```

Fig. 23.13 | The Weather Client accesses a `ReportInfo` object remotely and displays the weather report. (Part 2 of 3.)

```
62          weather.Add( "DRZL", "rain" );
63          weather.Add( "HAZE", "noinfo" );
64          weather.Add( "SMOKE", "mcloudy" );
65          weather.Add( "SNOWSHWRS", "snow" );
66          weather.Add( "FLRRYS", "snow" );
67          weather.Add( "FOG", "noinfo" );
68
69          // create the font for the text output
70          Font font = new Font( "Courier New", 8, FontStyle.Bold );
71
72          // for every city
73          for ( int i = 0; i < cities.Count; i++ )
74          {
75             // use array cityLabels to find the next Label
76             Label currentCity = cityLabels[ i ];
77
78             // use ArrayList cities to find the next CityWeather object
79             CityWeather city = ( CityWeather ) cities[ i ];
80
81             // set current Label's image to image
82             // corresponding to the city's weather condition -
83             // find correct image name in Hashtable weather
84             currentCity.Image = new Bitmap( @"images\" +
85                weather[ city.Description.Trim() ] + ".png" );
86             currentCity.Font = font; // set font of Label
87             currentCity.ForeColor = Color.White; // set text color of Label
88
89             // set Label's text to city name and temperature
90             currentCity.Text = "\r\n " + city.CityName + city.Temperature;
91          } // end for
92       } // end method WeatherClientForm_Load
93    } // end class WeatherClientForm
```

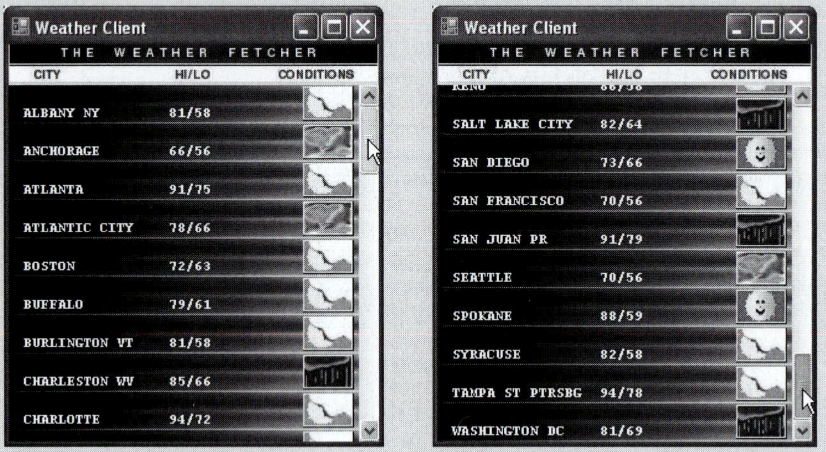

Fig. 23.13 | The Weather Client accesses a `ReportInfo` object remotely and displays the weather report. (Part 3 of 3.)

the weather information for one city. Lines 7–9 are using directives for the namespaces that are required to perform .NET remoting. For this project, you must add references to the System.Runtime.Remoting assembly and the Weather.dll file we created earlier.

Method WeatherClientForm_Load (lines 20–92) retrieves the weather information when this Windows application loads. Line 23 creates an HTTP channel without specifying a port number. This causes the HttpChannel constructor to choose any available port number on the client computer. A specific port number is not necessary because this application does not have its own clients that need to know the port number in advance. Line 24 registers the channel on the client computer. This will allow the server to send information back to the client. Lines 27–28 declare a Report variable and assign to it a proxy for a Report object instantiated by the server. This proxy allows the client to remotely call ReportInfo's properties by redirecting method calls to the server. *Remoting-Services* method *Connect* connects to the server and returns a reference to the proxy for the Report object. Note that we are executing the client and the server on the same computer, so we use localhost in the URL that represents the server application. To connect to a WeatherServer on a different computer, you must modify this URL accordingly. Line 31 retrieves the ArrayList of CityWeather objects generated by the ReportInfo constructor (lines 14–46 of Fig. 23.11). Variable cities now refers to an ArrayList of City-Weather objects that contains the information taken from the *Traveler's Forecast* Web page.

Because the application presents weather data for so many cities, we must establish a way to organize the information in the Labels and to ensure that each weather description is accompanied by an appropriate image. The program uses an array to store all the Labels, and a Hashtable (discussed further in Chapter 27, Collections) to store weather descriptions and the names of their corresponding images. A *Hashtable* stores key–value pairs, in which both the key and the value can be any type of object. Method *Add* adds key–value pairs to a Hashtable. The class also provides an indexer to return the value for a particular key in the Hashtable. Line 34 creates an array of Label references, and lines 35–44 place the Labels we created in the designer in the array so that they can be accessed programmatically to display weather information for individual cities. Line 47 creates Hashtable object weather to store pairs of weather conditions and the names for images associated with those conditions. Note that a given weather description name does not necessarily correspond to the name of the PNG file containing the correct image. For example, both "TSTRMS" and "RAIN" weather conditions use the rain.png image file.

Lines 73–91 set each Label so that it contains a city name, the current temperature in the city and an image corresponding to the weather conditions for that city. Line 76 retrieves the Label that will display the weather information for the next city. Line 79 uses ArrayList cities to retrieve the CityWeather object that contains the weather information for the city. Lines 84–85 set the Label's image to the PNG image that corresponds to the city's weather conditions. This is done by eliminating any spaces in the description string by calling string method Trim and retrieving the name of the PNG image from the weather Hashtable. Lines 86–87 set Label properties to achieve the visual effect seen in the sample output. Line 90 sets the Text property to display the city's name and high/low temperatures. [*Note:* To preserve the layout of the client application's window, we set the MaximumSize and MinimumSize properties of the Windows Form to the same value so that the user cannot resize the window.]

Web Resources for .NET Remoting

This section provided a basic introduction to .NET remoting. There is much more to this powerful .NET framework capability. The following Web sites provide additional information for readers who wish to investigate these capabilities further. In addition, searching for ".NET remoting" with most search engines yields many additional resources.

`msdn.microsoft.com/library/en-us/cpguide/html/cpconaccessingobjectsinotherap-plicationdomainsusingnetremoting.asp`

The *.NET Framework Developer's Guide* on the MSDN Web site provides detailed information on .NET remoting, including articles that include choosing between ASP.NET and .NET remoting, an overview of .NET remoting, advanced .NET remoting techniques and .NET remoting examples.

`msdn.microsoft.com/library/en-us/dndotnet/html/introremoting.asp`

This site offers a general overview of .NET remoting capabilties.

`search.microsoft.com/search/results.aspx?qu=.net+remoting`

This `microsoft.com` search provides links to many .NET remoting articles and resources.

23.11 Wrap-Up

In this chapter, we presented both connection-oriented and connectionless networking techniques. You learned that the Internet is an "unreliable" network that simply transmits packets of data. We discussed two protocols for transmitting packets over the Internet—Transmission Control Protocol (TCP) and User Datagram Protocol (UDP). You learned that TCP is a connection-oriented communication protocol that guarantees that sent packets will arrive at the intended receiver undamaged and in the correct sequence. You also learned that UDP is typically used in performance-oriented applications because it incurs minimum overhead for communicating between applications. We presented some of C#'s capabilities for implementing communications with TCP and UDP. We showed how to create a simple client/server chat application using stream sockets. We then showed how to send datagrams between a client and a server. You also saw a multithreaded Tic-Tac-Toe server that allowed two clients to connect simultaneously to the server and play Tic-Tac-Toe against one another. We presented the new `WebBrowser` control, which allows you to add Web browsing capabilities to your Windows applications. Finally, we demonstrated .NET remoting, a technology that allows a client application to remotely access the properties and methods of an object instantiated by a server application. In Chapter 24, Searching and Sorting, we discuss how to create methods that can order array elements in ascending or descending order, and that can search for values in arrays.

Summary

Section 23.1 Introduction

- The Internet ties the information world together.
- The Web makes the Internet easy to use and gives it the flair and sizzle of multimedia.

Section 23.2 Connection-Oriented vs. Connectionless Communication

- There are two primary approaches to communicating between applications—connection oriented and connectionless.

- Connection-oriented communications are similar to the telephone system, in which a connection is established and held for the length of the session.

- Connectionless services are similar to the postal service, in which two letters mailed from one place to the same destination may actually take two dramatically different paths through the system and even arrive at different times, or not at all.

- Data is sent by TCP in packets, which contain pieces of the data, along with information that helps the Internet route the packets to the proper destination.

- The Internet does not guarantee anything about the packets sent; they could arrive corrupted or out of order, as duplicates or not at all. The Internet makes only a "best effort" to deliver packets.

- A connection-oriented approach guarantees that sent packets will arrive at the intended receiver undamaged and be reassembled into the correct sequence.

- In a connectionless approach, data sent may never reach the intended recipient. A connectionless approach, however, avoids the overhead associated with handshaking and enforcing reliability— less information often needs to be passed between the hosts.

Section 23.3 Protocols for Transporting Data
- Protocols are sets of rules that govern how two entities should interact.

- C#'s Transmission Control Protocol (TCP) and User Datagram Protocol (UDP) networking capabilities are defined by classes of the System.Net.Sockets namespace.

- Transmission Control Protocol (TCP) is a connection-oriented communication protocol that guarantees that sent packets will arrive at the intended receiver undamaged and in the correct sequence.

- If packets of information don't arrive at the recipient, TCP ensures that the packets are sent again. If packets arrive out of order, TCP reassembles them into the correct order transparently to the application receiving the data. If duplicate packets arrive, TCP discards the duplicates.

- Applications that do not require reliable end-to-end transmission typically use the connectionless User Datagram Protocol (UDP).

- UDP makes no guarantees that packets, called datagrams, will reach their destination or arrive in their original order.

- UDP has little overhead because UDP datagrams do not need to carry the information that TCP packets carry to ensure reliability.

Section 23.4 Establishing a Simple TCP Server (Using Stream Sockets)
- Class IPAddress represents an Internet Protocol (IP) address.

- Establishing a simple server with TCP and stream sockets in C# requires several steps. Step 1 is to create a TcpListener object. This class represents a TCP stream socket that a server can use to receive connections. To receive connections, the TcpListener must be listening for them. For the TcpListener to listen for client connections, its Start method must be called (Step 2). TcpListener method AcceptSocket blocks indefinitely until a connection is established, at which point it returns a Socket (Step 3). Step 4 is the processing phase, in which the server and the client communicate via streams maintained by a NetworkStream object. When the client and server have finished communicating, the server closes the connection (Step 5). The server can then wait for another client's connection.

- A port number is a numeric ID number that an application uses to identify itself at a given network address.

- An individual application running on a computer is identified by an IP address/port number pair. Hence, no two processes can have the same port number at a given IP address.

Section 23.5 Establishing a Simple TCP Client (Using Stream Sockets)

- Class `IPEndPoint` represents an endpoint on a network.

- Establishing a simple client requires four steps. In Step 1, we create a `TcpClient` to connect to the server. This connection is established through a call to the `TcpClient` method `Connect` containing two arguments—the server's IP address and the port number. In Step 2, the `TcpClient` uses method `GetStream` to get a `NetworkStream` to write to and read from the server. Step 3 is the processing phase, in which the client and the server communicate. In Step 4, the client closes the connection.

Section 23.7 Connectionless Client/Server Interaction with Datagrams

- Class `UdpClient` is provided for connectionless transmission of data.

- Class `UdpClient` methods `Send` and `Receive` are used to transmit data.

Section 23.8 Client/Server Tic-Tac-Toe Using a Multithreaded Server

- Multithreaded servers can manage many simultaneous connections with multiple clients.

Section 23.9 `WebBrowser` Control

- The `WebBrowser` control provides Web browsing functionality and maintains its own navigation history.

- `WebBrowser` methods `GoBack`, `GoForward`, `GoHome` and `Navigate` are used for Web navigation. Method `Stop` cancels loading of the current page, and method `Refresh` reloads the current page.

- Many `WebBrowser` events, including `StatusTextChanged`, `ProgressChanged` and `DocumentTitleChanged`, indicate changes in `WebBrowser` properties. The `Navigating` event occurs when the `WebBrowser` starts loading a page and the `DocumentCompleted` event occurs when the page is finished loading.

Section 23.10 .NET Remoting

- .NET remoting is a distributed computing technology that allows a program to access objects on another machine over a network.

- .NET remoting is similar in concept to RMI (remote method invocation) in Java and RPC (remote procedure calls) in procedural programming languages.

- Marshal by value requires that the object be serializable, capable of being represented as a formatted message which the server can send through a channel to the client. To enable an object to be serialized and deserialized, its class must either be declared with the attribute [`Serializable`] or must implement interface `ISerializable`.

- Marshal by reference requires that the object's class extend class `MarshalByRefObject`. An object that is marshaled by reference is referred to as a remote object, and its class is referred to as a remote class.

- When an object is marshaled by reference, the client creates two proxy objects, a transparent proxy and a real proxy. The client application calls the methods and properties of the transparent proxy as if it were the remote object itself. The transparent proxy calls the real proxy to send a message to the server to perform the appropriate actions on the actual object.

- The parameters and return values of the methods and properties declared by a remote class will themselves be marshaled by value.

- Namespaces `System.Runtime.Remoting` and `System.Runtime.Remoting.Channels` are required for .NET remoting. Namespace `System.Runtime.Remoting.Channels.Http` is required for HTTP channels and is found in reference `System.Runtime.Remoting`.

- Class `HttpChannel` represents an HTTP channel. Its constructor takes an `int` port number. `static` method `RegisterChannel` of class `ChannelServices` takes an object of a class that implements interface `IChannel`, such as `HttpChannel`, and registers it on the local machine.

- `static` method `RegisterWellKnownServiceType` of class `RemotingConfiguration` takes a `Type`, a URI extension and a mode, `Singleton` or `SingleCall`, as arguments and makes the class type available to respond to clients that clients access the class at that URI.

- A `Singleton` remote class instantiates one remote object to service all clients. A `SingleCall` remote class instantiates one remote object for each individual method call.

- `static` method `Connect` of class `RemotingServices` takes a `Type` and a URI as arguments and returns a reference to the transparent proxy that enables method calls to the remote object.

- A `Hashtable` stores key–value pairs, in which both the key and the value can be any type of object. Method `Add` adds key–value pairs to a `Hashtable`. The indexer returns the value with which a particular key was placed in the `Hashtable`.

Terminology

Refresh method of WebBrowser

remote class

RemotingService class

Send method of class UdpClient

SendTo method of class Socket

Serializable attribute

serialize

server

SingleCall

Singleton

socket

Socket class

Sort method of class ArrayList

Start method of class TcpListener

StatusText property of WebBrowser

StatusTextChanged event of WebBrowser

Stop method of WebBrowser

stream socket

streams-based transmission

System.Net namespace

System.Net.Sockets namespace

SystemRuntime.Remoting namespace

SystemRuntime.Remoting.Channels

System.RuntimeRemoting.Channels HTTP
  namespace

TCP channel

TcpClient class

TcpListener class

Transmission Control Protocol (TCP)

transparent proxy

UdpClient class

unreliable network

Uniform Resource Identifier (URI)

User Datagram Protocol (UDP)

WebBrowser control

WebClient class

Write method of class BinaryWriter

Self-Review Exercises

23.1   State whether each of the following is *true* or *false*. If *false*, explain why.
   a) UDP is a connection-oriented protocol.
   b) Packet transmission over a network is reliable—packets are guaranteed to arrive in sequence.
   c) TCP is preferred over UDP when applications require reliable packet transmission.
   d) Each TcpListener can accept only one connection.
   e) A TcpListener can listen for connections at more than one port at a time.
   f) A UdpClient can send information only to one particular port.
   g) Clients must know the port number at which the server is waiting for connections in order to connect to the server.
   h) The WebBrowser control can be used in any Windows application.
   i) When an object is marshaled by reference, a copy of that object is created and sent to the client.
   j) A Singleton remote class instantiates one remote object for each client.

23.2   Fill in the blanks in each of the following statements:
   a) Many of C#'s networking classes are contained in namespaces _____ and _____.
   b) Class _____ is used for unreliable but fast datagram transmission.
   c) An object of class _____ represents an Internet Protocol (IP) address.
   d) The two socket types discussed in this chapter are _____ and _____ sockets.
   e) The acronym TCP stands for _____.
   f) Class _____ listens for connections from clients.
   g) Class _____ connects to servers.
   h) Class _____ provides access to stream data on a network.
   i) Method _____ causes a WebBrowser to go to a particular URL.
   j) A serializable class must either be declared with attribute _____ or extend class _____.
   k) The _____ provides all the public services of the remote object being marshaled by reference.

Answers to Self-Review Exercises

23.1   a) False. UDP is a connectionless protocol, and TCP is a connection-oriented protocol. b) False. Packets can be lost, arrive out of order or even be duplicated. c) True. d) False. `TcpListener`'s `AcceptSocket` method may be called as often as necessary—each call will accept a new connection. e) False. A `TcpListener` can listen for connections at only one port at a time. f) False. A `UdpClient` can send information to any port represented by an `IPEndPoint`. g) True. h) True. i) False. When an object is marshaled by reference, the client application accesses the original remote object on the server, not a local copy. j) False. A `Singleton` remote class instantiates one remote object to service all clients.

23.2   a) System.Net, System.Net.Sockets. b) UdpClient. c) IPAddress. d) stream, datagram. e) Transmission Control Protocol. f) TcpListener. g) TcpClient. h) NetworkStream. i) Navigate. j) Serializable, ISerializable. k) transparent proxy.

Exercises

23.3   Use a socket connection to allow a client to specify a text file's name and have the server send the contents of the file or indicate that the file does not exist.

23.4   Modify Exercise 23.3 to allow the client to modify the contents of the file and send the file back to the server for storage. The user can edit the file in a `TextBox`, then click an `Update file on server` button to send the file back to the server.

23.5   Multithreaded servers are quite popular today, especially because of the increasing use of multiprocessing servers. Modify the simple server application presented in Section 23.6 to be a multithreaded server. Then use several client applications and have each of them connect to the server simultaneously. Use a `HashTable` (namespace System.Collections) to store the client threads. `HashTable` provides several properties and methods of use in this exercise. Property `Keys` returns an `ICollection` of keys currently found in the `HashTable`. Each key can then be used in the `HashTable`'s indexer to retrieve the corresponding value. Method `Add` places its arguments—a key and a value— into the `HashTable`. Method `Remove` deletes its argument—the key—from the `HashTable`.

23.6   Create a client/server application for the game of Hangman, using socket connections. The server should randomly pick a word or phrase from a file. After connecting, the client should be allowed to begin guessing. If a client guesses incorrectly five times, the game is over. Display the original phrase or word on the server. Display dashes (for letters that have not been guessed yet) and the letters that have been guessed in the word or phrase on the client.

23.7   Modify the previous exercise to be a connectionless game using datagrams.

23.8   (*Checkers Game*) In the text, we presented a Tic-Tac-Toe program controlled by a multithreaded server. Develop a checkers program modeled after the Tic-Tac-Toe program. The two users should alternate making moves. Your program should mediate the players' moves, determining whose turn it is and allowing only valid moves. The players themselves will determine when the game is over.

23.9   (*Networked Morse Code*) Perhaps the most famous of all coding schemes is the Morse code, developed by Samuel Morse in the 1830s for use with the telegraph system. The Morse code assigns a series of dots and dashes to each letter of the alphabet, each digit and a few special characters (such as period, comma, colon and semicolon). In sound-oriented systems, the dot represents a short sound and the dash represents a long sound. Other representations of dots and dashes are used with light-oriented systems and signal-flag systems.

Separation between words is indicated by a space, or quite simply, the absence of a dot or dash. In a sound-oriented system, a space is indicated by a short period of time during which no sound is transmitted. The international version of the Morse code appears in Fig. 23.14.

Character	Code	Character	Code
A	.-	T	-
B	-...	U	..-
C	-.-.	V	...-
D	-..	W	.--
E	.	X	-..-
F	..-.	Y	-.--
G	--.	Z	--..
H	....		
I	..	Digits	
J	.---	1	.----
K	-.-	2	..---
L	.-..	3	...--
M	--	4	....-
N	-.	5	.....
O	---	6	-....
P	.--.	7	--...
Q	--.-	8	---..
R	.-.	9	----.
S	...	0	-----

Fig. 23.14 | English letters of the alphabet and decimal digits as expressed in international Morse code.

Write a client/server application in which two clients can send Morse code messages to each other through a multithreaded server application. The client application should allow the user to type English-language phrases in a TextBox. When the user sends the message, the client application encodes the text in Morse code and sends the coded message through the server to the other client. Use one blank between each Morse-coded letter and three blanks between each Morse-coded word. When messages are received, they should be decoded and displayed as normal characters and as Morse code. The client should have one TextBox for typing and one TextBox for displaying the other client's messages.

23.10 Write a bulletin board application that uses .NET remoting. Create a remote object that will allow the client application to list all available bulletins, retrieve the text of any bulletin and post a new bulletin. Each bulletin should be stored in a .txt file in the server's directory. Refer to Chapter 18, Files and Streams.

23.11 Write a quiz application that uses .NET remoting. Store one quiz question in a text file on the server machine. Allow the client to retrieve the question from the server and send an answer back to the server. You may wish to store records of who answered the quiz question correctly so the server operator can keep score.

Searching and Sorting

OBJECTIVES

In this chapter you will learn:

- To search for a given value in an array using the linear search and binary search algorithm.

- To sort arrays using the iterative selection and insertion sort algorithms.

- To sort arrays using the recursive merge sort algorithm.

- To determine the efficiency of searching and sorting algorithms.

24.1 Introduction

Searching data involves determining whether a value (referred to as the ***search key***) is present in the data and, if so, finding the value's location. Two popular search algorithms are the simple linear search and the faster, but more complex, binary search. *Sorting* places data in order, based on one or more ***sort keys***. A list of names could be sorted alphabetically, bank accounts could be sorted by account number, employee payroll records could be sorted by social security number and so on. This chapter introduces two simple sorting algorithms, the selection sort and the insertion sort, along with the more efficient, but more complex, merge sort. Figure 24.1 summarizes the searching and sorting algorithms discussed in this book.

Chapter	Algorithm	Location
Searching Algorithms:		
24	Linear Search	Section 24.2.1
	Binary Search	Section 24.2.2
	Recursive Linear Search	Exercise 24.8
	Recursive Binary Search	Exercise 24.9
27	BinarySearch method of class `Array`	Fig. 27.3
	Contains method of classes `ArrayList` and `Stack`	Fig. 27.4
	ContainsKey method of class `HashTable`	Fig. 27.7
Sorting Algorithms:		
24	Selection Sort	Section 24.3.1
	Insertion Sort	Section 24.3.2
	Recursive Merge Sort	Section 24.3.3

Fig. 24.1 | Searching and sorting capabilities in this text. (Part 1 of 2.)

Chapter	Algorithm	Location
	Bubble Sort	Exercises 24.5–24.6
	Bucket Sort	Exercise 24.7
	Recursive Quicksort	Exercise 24.10
24, 27	Sort method of classes Array and ArrayList	Fig. 24.4, Figs. 27.3–27.4

Fig. 24.1 | Searching and sorting capabilities in this text. (Part 2 of 2.)

24.2 Searching Algorithms

Looking up a phone number, accessing a Web site and checking the definition of a word in a dictionary all involve searching large amounts of data. The next two sections discuss two common search algorithms—one that is easy to program yet relatively inefficient and one that is relatively efficient but more complex to program.

24.2.1 Linear Search

The *linear search algorithm* searches each element in an array sequentially. If the search key does not match an element in the array, the algorithm tests each element and, when the end of the array is reached, informs the user that the search key is not present. If the search key is in the array, the algorithm tests each element until it finds one that matches the search key and returns the index of that element.

As an example, consider an array containing the following values

    34   56   2   10   77   51   93   30   5   52

and an application that is searching for 51. Using the linear search algorithm, the application first checks whether 34 matches the search key. It does not, so the algorithm checks whether 56 matches the search key. The application continues moving through the array sequentially, testing 2, then 10, then 77. When the application tests 51, which matches the search key, the application returns the index 5, which is the location of 51 in the array. If, after checking every array element, the application determines that the search key does not match any element in the array, the application returns a sentinel value (e.g. -1). If there are duplicate values in the array, linear search returns the index of the first element in the array that matches the search key.

Figure 24.2 declares class LinearArray. This class has two private instance variables—an array of ints named data, and a static Random object named generator to fill the array with randomly generated ints. When an object of class LinearArray is instantiated, the constructor (lines 12–19) creates and initializes the array data with random ints in the range 10–99.

Lines 22–30 perform the linear search. The search key is passed to parameter searchKey. Lines 25–27 loop through the elements in the array. Line 26 compares each element in the array with searchKey. If the values are equal, line 27 returns the index of the element. If the loop ends without finding the value, line 29 returns -1. Lines 33–43 declare method ToString, which returns a string representation of the array for printing.

```
1    // Fig 24.2: LinearArray.cs
2    // Class that contains an array of random integers and a method
3    // that will search that array sequentially.
4    using System;
5
6    public class LinearArray
7    {
8       private int[] data; // array of values
9       private static Random generator = new Random();
10
11      // create array of given size and fill with random integers
12      public LinearArray( int size )
13      {
14         data = new int[ size ]; // create space for array
15
16         // fill array with random ints in range 10-99
17         for ( int i = 0; i < size; i++ )
18            data[ i ] = generator.Next( 10, 100 );
19      } // end LinearArray constructor
20
21      // perform a linear search on the data
22      public int LinearSearch( int searchKey )
23      {
24         // loop through array sequentially
25         for ( int index = 0; index < data.Length; index++ )
26            if ( data[ index ] == searchKey )
27               return index; // return index of integer
28
29         return -1; // integer was not found
30      } // end method LinearSearch
31
32      // method to output values in array
33      public override string ToString()
34      {
35         string temporary = "";
36
37         // iterate through array
38         foreach ( int element in data )
39            temporary += element + " ";
40
41         temporary += "\n"; // add newline character
42         return temporary;
43      } // end method ToString
44   } // end class LinearArray
```

Fig. 24.2 | Class that contains an array of random integers and a method that searches that array sequentially.

Figure 24.3 creates LinearArray object searchArray containing an array of 10 ints (line 13) and allows the user to search the array for specific elements. Lines 17–18 prompt the user for the search key and store it in searchInt. Lines 21–37 then loop until the searchInt is equal to -1. The array holds ints from 10–99 (line 18 of Fig. 24.2). Line 24 calls method LinearSearch to determine whether searchInt is in the array. If searchInt

```
1   // Fig 24.3: LinearSearchTest.cs
2   // Sequentially search an array for an item.
3   using System;
4
5   public class LinearSearchTest
6   {
7      public static void Main( string[] args )
8      {
9         int searchInt; // search key
10        int position; // location of search key in array
11
12        // create array and output it
13        LinearArray searchArray = new LinearArray( 10 );
14        Console.WriteLine( searchArray ); // print array
15
16        // input first int from user
17        Console.Write( "Please enter an integer value (-1 to quit): " );
18        searchInt = Convert.ToInt32( Console.ReadLine() );
19
20        // repeatedly input an integer; -1 terminates the application
21        while ( searchInt != -1 )
22        {
23           // perform linear search
24           position = searchArray.LinearSearch( searchInt );
25
26           if ( position != -1 ) // integer was not found
27              Console.WriteLine(
28                 "The integer {0} was found in position {1}.\n",
29                 searchInt, position );
30           else // integer was found
31              Console.WriteLine( "The integer {0} was not found.\n",
32                 searchInt );
33
34           // input next int from user
35           Console.Write( "Please enter an integer value (-1 to quit): " );
36           searchInt = Convert.ToInt32( Console.ReadLine() );
37        } // end while
38     } // end Main
39  } // end class LinearSearchTest
```

```
64 90 84 62 28 68 55 27 78 73

Please enter an integer value (-1 to quit): 78
The integer 78 was found in position 8.

Please enter an integer value (-1 to quit): 64
The integer 64 was found in position 0.

Please enter an integer value (-1 to quit): 65
The integer 65 was not found.

Please enter an integer value (-1 to quit): -1
```

Fig. 24.3 | Sequentially searching an array for an item.

is found, LinearSearch returns the position of the element, which the application outputs in lines 27–29. If searchInt is not in the array, LinearSearch returns -1, and the application notifies the user (lines 31–32). Lines 35–36 retrieve the next integer from the user.

Efficiency of Linear Search

Searching algorithms all accomplish the same goal—finding an element that matches a given search key, if such an element, in fact, exists. There are, however, a number of things that differentiate search algorithms from another. The major difference is the amount of effort they require to complete the search. One way to describe this effort is with **Big O notation**, which is a measure of the worst-case run time for an algorithm—that is, how hard an algorithm may have to work to solve a problem. For searching and sorting algorithms, this is particularly dependent on how many data elements there are.

Suppose an algorithm is designed to test whether the first element of an array is equal to the second element of the array. If the array has 10 elements, this algorithm requires one comparison. If the array has 1,000 elements, the algorithm still requires one comparison. In fact, the algorithm is completely independent of the number of elements in the array. This algorithm is said to have a **constant run time**, which is represented in Big O notation as $O(1)$. An algorithm that is $O(1)$ does not necessarily require only one comparison. $O(1)$ just means that the number of comparisons is *constant*—it does not grow as the size of the array increases. An algorithm that tests whether the first element of an array is equal to any of the next three elements is still $O(1)$ even though it requires three comparisons.

An algorithm that tests whether the first element of an array is equal to *any* of the other elements of the array will require at most $n - 1$ comparisons, where n is the number of elements in the array. If the array has 10 elements, this algorithm requires up to nine comparisons. If the array has 1,000 elements, this algorithm requires up to 999 comparisons. As n grows larger, the n part of the expression "dominates" and subtracting one becomes inconsequential. Big O is designed to highlight these dominant terms and ignore terms that become unimportant as n grows. For this reason, an algorithm that requires a total of $n - 1$ comparisons (such as the one we described earlier) is said to be $O(n)$. An $O(n)$ algorithm is referred to as having a **linear run time**. $O(n)$ is often pronounced "on the order of n" or more simply "order n."

Now suppose you have an algorithm that tests whether *any* element of an array is duplicated elsewhere in the array. The first element must be compared with every other element in the array. The second element must be compared with every other element except the first (it already compared to the first). The third element must be compared with every other element except the first two. In the end, this algorithm will end up making $(n - 1) + (n - 2) + \ldots + 2 + 1$ or $n^2/2 - n/2$ comparisons. As n increases, the n^2 term dominates and the n term becomes inconsequential. Again, Big O notation highlights the n^2 term, leaving $n^2/2$. But as we will soon see, constant factors are omitted in Big O notation.

Big O is concerned with how an algorithm's run time grows in relation to the number of items processed. Suppose an algorithm requires n^2 comparisons. With four elements, the algorithm will require 16 comparisons; with eight elements, the algorithm will require 64 comparisons. With this algorithm, doubling the number of elements quadruples the number of comparisons. Consider a similar algorithm requiring $n^2/2$ comparisons. With four elements, the algorithm will require eight comparisons; with eight elements, the algorithm will require 32 comparisons. Again, doubling the number of elements quadruples the number of comparisons. Both of these algorithms grow as the square of n, so Big O ignores the constant, and both algorithms are considered to be $O(n^2)$, which is referred to as *quadratic run time* and pronounced "on the order of *n*-squared" or more simply "order *n*-squared."

When *n* is small, $O(n^2)$ algorithms (running on today's billion-operation-per-second personal computers) will not noticeably affect performance. But as *n* grows, you will start to notice the performance degradation. An $O(n^2)$ algorithm running on a million-element array would require a trillion "operations" (where each could actually require several machine instructions to execute). This could require a few hours to execute. A billion-element array would require a quintillion operations, a number so large that the algorithm could take decades! $O(n^2)$ algorithms are easy to write, as you will see in this chapter. You will also see algorithms with more favorable Big O measures. These efficient algorithms often take a bit more cleverness and effort to create, but their superior performance can be well worth the extra effort, especially as *n* gets large and algorithms are compounded into larger applications.

The linear search algorithm runs in $O(n)$ time. The worst case in this algorithm is that every element must be checked to determine whether the search item exists in the array. If the size of the array is doubled, the number of comparisons that the algorithm must perform is also doubled. Note that linear search can provide outstanding performance if the element matching the search key happens to be at or near the front of the array. But we seek algorithms that perform well, on average, across all searches, including those where the element matching the search key is near the end of the array.

Linear search is the easiest search algorithm to program, but it can be slow compared to other search algorithms. If an application needs to perform many searches on large arrays, it may be better to implement a different, more efficient algorithm, such as the binary search, which we present in the next section.

Performance Tip 24.1

Sometimes the simplest algorithms perform poorly. Their virtue is that they are easy to program, test and debug. Sometimes more complex algorithms are required to realize maximum performance.

24.2.2 Binary Search

The *binary search algorithm* is more efficient than the linear search algorithm, but it requires that the array be sorted. The first iteration of this algorithm tests the middle element in the array. If this matches the search key, the algorithm ends. Assuming the array is sorted in ascending order, if the search key is less than the middle element, the search key cannot match any element in the second half of the array and the algorithm continues with only the first half of the array (i.e., the first element up to, but not including, the middle element). If the search key is greater than the middle element, the search key cannot match any element in the first half of the array, and the algorithm continues with only the second half of the array (i.e., the element after the middle element through the last element). Each iteration tests the middle value of the remaining portion of the array, called a *subarray*. A subarray can have no elements, or it can encompass the entire array. If the search key does not match the element, the algorithm eliminates half of the remaining elements. The algorithm ends either by finding an element that matches the search key or reducing the subarray to zero size.

As an example, consider the sorted 15-element array

2   3   5   10   27   30   34   51   56   65   77   81   82   93   99

and a search key of 65. An application implementing the binary search algorithm would first check whether 51 is the search key (because 51 is the middle element of the array). The search key (65) is larger than 51, so 51 is "discarded" (i.e., eliminated from consideration) along with the first half of the array (all elements smaller than 51.) Next, the algorithm checks whether 81 (the middle element of the remainder of the array) matches the search key. The search key (65) is smaller than 81, so 81 is discarded along with the elements larger than 81. After just two tests, the algorithm has narrowed the number of values to check to three (56, 65 and 77). The algorithm then checks 65 (which indeed matches the search key), and returns the index of the array element containing 65. This algorithm required just three comparisons to determine whether the search key matched an element of the array. Using a linear search algorithm would have required 10 comparisons. [*Note:* In this example, we have chosen to use an array with 15 elements so that there will always be an obvious middle element in the array. With an even number of elements, the middle of the array lies between two elements. We implement the algorithm to chose the higher of the two elements.]

Figure 24.4 declares class `BinaryArray`. This class is similar to `LinearArray`—it has two `private` instance variables, a constructor, a search method (`BinarySearch`), a `RemainingElements` method (which creates a `string` containing the elements not yet searched) and a `ToString` method. Lines 12–21 declare the constructor. After initializing the array with random `int`s from 10–99 (lines 17–18), line 20 calls method `Array.Sort` on the array data. Method ***Sort*** is a `static` method of class `Array` that sorts the elements in an array in ascending order. Recall that the binary search algorithm works only on sorted arrays.

Lines 24–56 declare method `BinarySearch`. The search key is passed into parameter `searchElement` (line 24). Lines 26–28 calculate the `low` end index, `high` end index and `middle` index of the portion of the array that the application is currently searching. At the beginning of the method, the `low` end is 0, the `high` end is the length of the array minus 1 and the `middle` is the average of these two values. Line 29 initializes the `location` of the element to -1—the value that will be returned if the element is not found. Lines 31–53 loop until `low` is greater than `high` (this occurs when the element is not found) or `location` does not equal -1 (indicating that the search key was found). Line 43 tests whether the value in the `middle` element is equal to `searchElement`. If this is true, line 44 assigns `middle` to `location`. Then the loop terminates, and `location` is returned to the caller. Each iteration of the loop tests a single value (line 43) and eliminates half of the remaining values in the array (line 48 or 50).

```
1   // Fig 24.4: BinaryArray.cs
2   // Class that contains an array of random integers and a method
3   // that uses binary search to find an integer.
4   using System;
5
6   public class BinaryArray
7   {
8       private int[] data; // array of values
9       private static Random generator = new Random();
10
```

Fig. 24.4 | Class that contains an array of random integers and a method that uses binary search to find an integer. (Part 1 of 3.)

```
11      // create array of given size and fill with random integers
12      public BinaryArray( int size )
13      {
14         data = new int[ size ]; // create space for array
15
16         // fill array with random ints in range 10-99
17         for ( int i = 0; i < size; i++ )
18            data[ i ] = generator.Next( 10, 100 );
19
20         Array.Sort( data );
21      } // end BinaryArray constructor
22
23      // perform a binary search on the data
24      public int BinarySearch( int searchElement )
25      {
26         int low = 0; // low end of the search area
27         int high = data.Length - 1; // high end of the search area
28         int middle = ( low + high + 1 ) / 2; // middle element
29         int location = -1; // return value; -1 if not found
30
31         do // loop to search for element
32         {
33            // print remaining elements of array
34            Console.Write( RemainingElements( low, high ) );
35
36            // output spaces for alignment
37            for ( int i = 0; i < middle; i++ )
38               Console.Write( "   " );
39
40            Console.WriteLine( " * " ); // indicate current middle
41
42            // if the element is found at the middle
43            if ( searchElement == data[ middle ] )
44               location = middle; // location is the current middle
45
46            // middle element is too high
47            else if ( searchElement < data[ middle ] )
48               high = middle - 1; // eliminate the higher half
49            else // middle element is too low
50               low = middle + 1; // eliminate the lower half
51
52            middle = ( low + high + 1 ) / 2; // recalculate the middle
53         } while ( ( low <= high ) && ( location == -1 ) );
54
55         return location; // return location of search key
56      } // end method BinarySearch
57
58      // method to output certain values in array
59      public string RemainingElements( int low, int high )
60      {
61         string temporary = "";
```

Fig. 24.4 | Class that contains an array of random integers and a method that uses binary search to find an integer. (Part 2 of 3.)

```
62
63          // output spaces for alignment
64          for ( int i = 0; i < low; i++ )
65             temporary += "   ";
66
67          // output elements left in array
68          for ( int i = low; i <= high; i++ )
69             temporary += data[ i ] + " ";
70
71          temporary += "\n";
72          return temporary;
73       } // end method RemainingElements
74
75       // method to output values in array
76       public override string ToString()
77       {
78          return RemainingElements( 0, data.Length - 1 );
79       } // end method ToString
80    } // end class BinaryArray
```

Fig. 24.4 | Class that contains an array of random integers and a method that uses binary search to find an integer. (Part 3 of 3.)

Lines 22–40 of Fig. 24.5 loop until the user enters -1. For each other number the user enters, the application performs a binary search to determine whether the number matches an element in the array. The first line of output from this application is the array of ints, in increasing order. When the user instructs the application to search for 72, the application first tests the middle element (indicated by * in the sample output of Fig. 24.5), which is 52. The search key is greater than 52, so the application eliminates from consideration the first half of the array and tests the middle element from the second half of the array. The search key is smaller than 82, so the application eliminates from consideration the second half of the subarray, leaving only three elements. Finally, the application checks 72 (which matches the search key) and returns the index 9.

```
1    // Fig 24.5: BinarySearchTest.cs
2    // Use binary search to locate an item in an array.
3    using System;
4
5    public class BinarySearchTest
6    {
7       public static void Main( string[] args )
8       {
9          int searchInt; // search key
10         int position; // location of search key in array
11
12         // create array and output it
13         BinaryArray searchArray = new BinaryArray( 15 );
14         Console.WriteLine( searchArray );
15
```

Fig. 24.5 | Using binary search to locate an item in an array. (Part 1 of 2.)

```
16          // prompt and input first int from user
17          Console.Write( "Please enter an integer value (-1 to quit): " );
18          searchInt = Convert.ToInt32( Console.ReadLine() );
19          Console.WriteLine();
20
21          // repeatedly input an integer; -1 terminates the application
22          while ( searchInt != -1 )
23          {
24              // use binary search to try to find integer
25              position = searchArray.BinarySearch( searchInt );
26
27              // return value of -1 indicates integer was not found
28              if ( position == -1 )
29                  Console.WriteLine( "The integer {0} was not found.\n",
30                      searchInt );
31              else
32                  Console.WriteLine(
33                      "The integer {0} was found in position {1}.\n",
34                      searchInt, position);
35
36              // prompt and input next int from user
37              Console.Write( "Please enter an integer value (-1 to quit): " );
38              searchInt = Convert.ToInt32( Console.ReadLine() );
39              Console.WriteLine();
40          } // end while
41      } // end Main
42  } // end class BinarySearchTest
```

```
12 17 22 25 30 39 40 52 56 72 76 82 84 91 93

Please enter an integer value (-1 to quit): 72

12 17 22 25 30 39 40 52 56 72 76 82 84 91 93
                        *
                        56 72 76 82 84 91 93
                                 *
                        56 72 76
                           *
The integer 72 was found in position 9.

Please enter an integer value (-1 to quit): 13

12 17 22 25 30 39 40 52 56 72 76 82 84 91 93
                  *
12 17 22 25 30 39 40
         *
12 17 22
   *
12
*
The integer 13 was not found.

Please enter an integer value (-1 to quit): -1
```

Fig. 24.5 | Using binary search to locate an item in an array. (Part 2 of 2.)

Efficiency of Binary Search

In the worst-case scenario, searching a sorted array of 1,023 elements will take only 10 comparisons when using a binary search. Repeatedly dividing 1,023 by 2 (because after each comparison, we are able to eliminate half of the array) and rounding down (because we also remove the middle element) yields the values 511, 255, 127, 63, 31, 15, 7, 3, 1 and 0. The number 1023 ($2^{10} - 1$) is divided by 2 only 10 times to get the value 0, which indicates that there are no more elements to test. Dividing by 2 is equivalent to one comparison in the binary-search algorithm. Thus, an array of 1,048,575 ($2^{20} - 1$) elements takes a maximum of 20 comparisons to find the key, and an array of one billion elements (which is less than $2^{30} - 1$) takes a maximum of 30 comparisons to find the key. This is a tremendous improvement in performance over the linear search. For a one-billion-element array, this is a difference between an average of 500 million comparisons for the linear search and a maximum of only 30 comparisons for the binary search! The maximum number of comparisons needed for the binary search of any sorted array is the exponent of the first power of 2 greater than the number of elements in the array, which is represented as $\log_2 n$. All logarithms grow at roughly the same rate, so in Big O notation the base can be omitted. This results in a big O of *O(log n)* for a binary search, which is also known as *logarithmic run time*.

24.3 Sorting Algorithms

Sorting data (i.e., placing the data in some particular order, such as ascending or descending) is one of the most important computing applications. A bank sorts all checks by account number so that it can prepare individual bank statements at the end of each month. Telephone companies sort their lists of accounts by last name and, further, by first name to make it easy to find phone numbers. Virtually every organization must sort some data—often, massive amounts of it. Sorting data is an intriguing, compute-intensive problem that has attracted substantial research efforts.

An important item to understand about sorting is that the end result—the sorted array—will be the same no matter which (correct) algorithm you use to sort the array. The choice of algorithm affects only the run time and memory use of the application. The rest of the chapter introduces three common sorting algorithms. The first two—selection sort and insertion sort—are simple to program, but inefficient. The last algorithm—merge sort—is a much faster algorithm than selection sort and insertion sort, but is more difficult to program. We focus on sorting arrays of simple-type data, namely ints. It is possible to sort arrays of objects as well—we discuss this in Chapter 27, Collections.

24.3.1 Selection Sort

Selection sort is a simple, but inefficient, sorting algorithm. The first iteration of the algorithm selects the smallest element in the array and swaps it with the first element. The second iteration selects the second-smallest item (which is the smallest item of the remaining elements) and swaps it with the second element. The algorithm continues until the last iteration selects the second-largest element and swaps it with the second-to-last index, leaving the largest element in the last index. After the *i*th iteration, the smallest *i* items of the array will be sorted in increasing order in the first *i* elements of the array.

As an example, consider the array

    34   56   4   10   77   51   93   30   5   52

An application that implements selection sort first determines the smallest element (4) of this array which is contained in index 2. The application swaps 4 with 34, resulting in

> 4   56   34   10   77   51   93   30   5   52

The application then determines the smallest value of the remaining elements (all elements except 4), which is 5, contained in index 8. The application swaps 5 with 56, resulting in

> 4   5   34   10   77   51   93   30   56   52

On the third iteration, the application determines the next smallest value (10) and swaps it with 34.

> 4   5   10   34   77   51   93   30   56   52

The process continues until the array is fully sorted.

> 4   5   10   30   34   51   52   56   77   93

Note that after the first iteration, the smallest element is in the first position. After the second iteration, the two smallest elements are in order in the first two positions. After the third iteration, the three smallest elements are in order in the first three positions.

Figure 24.6 declares the SelectionSort class. This class has two private instance variables—an array of ints named data and a static Random object generator to generate random integers to fill the array. When an object of class SelectionSort is instantiated, the constructor (lines 12–19) creates and initializes array data with random ints in the range 10–99.

```
1   // Fig 24.6: SelectionSort.cs
2   // Class that creates an array filled with random integers.
3   // Provides a method to sort the array with selection sort.
4   using System;
5
6   public class SelectionSort
7   {
8      private int[] data; // array of values
9      private static Random generator = new Random();
10
11     // create array of given size and fill with random integers
12     public SelectionSort( int size )
13     {
14        data = new int[ size ]; // create space for array
15
16        // fill array with random ints in range 10-99
17        for ( int i = 0; i < size; i++ )
18           data[ i ] = generator.Next( 10, 100 );
19     } // end SelectionSort constructor
20
```

Fig. 24.6 | Class that creates an array filled with random integers and selection sorts the array. (Part 1 of 3.)

```
21    // sort array using selection sort
22    public void Sort()
23    {
24       int smallest; // index of smallest element
25
26       // loop over data.Length - 1 elements
27       for ( int i = 0; i < data.Length - 1; i++ )
28       {
29          smallest = i; // first index of remaining array
30
31          // loop to find index of smallest element
32          for ( int index = i + 1; index < data.Length; index++ )
33             if ( data[ index ] < data[ smallest ] )
34                smallest = index;
35
36          Swap( i, smallest ); // swap smallest element into position
37          PrintPass( i + 1, smallest ); // output pass of algorithm
38       } // end outer for
39    } // end method Sort
40
41    // helper method to swap values in two elements
42    public void Swap( int first, int second )
43    {
44       int temporary = data[ first ]; // store first in temporary
45       data[ first ] = data[ second ]; // replace first with second
46       data[ second ] = temporary; // put temporary in second
47    } // end method Swap
48
49    // print a pass of the algorithm
50    public void PrintPass( int pass, int index )
51    {
52       Console.Write( "after pass {0}: ", pass );
53
54       // output elements through the selected item
55       for ( int i = 0; i < index; i++ )
56          Console.Write( data[ i ] + "  " );
57
58       Console.Write( data[ index ] + "* " ); // indicate swap
59
60       // finish outputting array
61       for ( int i = index + 1; i < data.Length; i++ )
62          Console.Write( data[ i ] + "  " );
63
64       Console.Write( "\n                " ); // for alignment
65
66       // indicate amount of array that is sorted
67       for( int j = 0; j < pass; j++ )
68          Console.Write( "--  " );
69       Console.WriteLine( "\n" ); // skip a line in output
70    } // end method PrintPass
71
```

Fig. 24.6 | Class that creates an array filled with random integers and selection sorts the array. (Part 2 of 3.)

```
72        // method to output values in array
73        public override string ToString()
74        {
75            string temporary = "";
76
77            // iterate through array
78            foreach ( int element in data )
79                temporary += element + "   ";
80
81            temporary += "\n"; // add newline character
82            return temporary;
83        } // end method ToString
84    } // end class SelectionSort
```

Fig. 24.6 | Class that creates an array filled with random integers and selection sorts the array. (Part 3 of 3.)

Lines 22–39 declare the Sort method. Line 24 declares variable smallest, which will store the index of the smallest element in the remaining array. Lines 27–38 loop data.Length - 1 times. Line 29 initializes the index of the smallest element to the current item. Lines 32–34 loop over the remaining elements in the array. For each of these elements, line 33 compares its value to the value of the smallest element. If the current element is smaller than the smallest element, line 34 assigns the current element's index to smallest. When this loop finishes, smallest will contain the index of the smallest element in the remaining array. Line 36 calls method Swap (lines 42–47) to place the smallest remaining element in the next spot in the array.

Line 10 of Fig. 24.7 creates a SelectionSort object with 10 elements. Line 13 implicitly calls method ToString to output the unsorted object. Line 15 calls method Sort (lines 22–39 of Fig. 24.6), which sorts the elements using selection sort. Then lines 17–18 output the sorted object. The output uses dashes to indicate the portion of the array that is sorted after each pass. An asterisk is placed next to the position of the element that was swapped with the smallest element on that pass. On each pass, the element next to the asterisk and the element above the rightmost set of dashes were the two values that were swapped.

```
1    // Fig 24.7: SelectionSortTest.cs
2    // Test the selection sort class.
3    using System;
4
5    public class SelectionSortTest
6    {
7        public static void Main( string[] args )
8        {
9            // create object to perform selection sort
10           SelectionSort sortArray = new SelectionSort( 10 );
11
12           Console.WriteLine( "Unsorted array:" );
13           Console.WriteLine( sortArray ); // print unsorted array
```

Fig. 24.7 | Testing the selection sort class. (Part 1 of 2.)

```
14
15        sortArray.Sort(); // sort array
16
17        Console.WriteLine( "Sorted array:" );
18        Console.WriteLine( sortArray ); // print sorted array
19     } // end Main
20  } // end class SelectionSortTest
```

```
Unsorted array:
86  97  83  45  19  31  86  13  57  61

after pass 1: 13  97  83  45  19  31  86  86* 57  61
              --

after pass 2: 13  19  83  45  97* 31  86  86  57  61
              --  --

after pass 3: 13  19  31  45  97  83* 86  86  57  61
              --  --  --

after pass 4: 13  19  31  45* 97  83  86  86  57  61
              --  --  --  --

after pass 5: 13  19  31  45  57  83  86  86  97* 61
              --  --  --  --  --

after pass 6: 13  19  31  45  57  61  86  86  97  83*
              --  --  --  --  --  --

after pass 7: 13  19  31  45  57  61  83  86  97  86*
              --  --  --  --  --  --  --

after pass 8: 13  19  31  45  57  61  83  86* 97  86
              --  --  --  --  --  --  --  --

after pass 9: 13  19  31  45  57  61  83  86  86  97*
              --  --  --  --  --  --  --  --  --

Sorted array:
13  19  31  45  57  61  83  86  86  97
```

Fig. 24.7 | Testing the selection sort class. (Part 2 of 2.)

Efficiency of Selection Sort

The selection sort algorithm runs in $O(n^2)$ time. Method Sort in lines 22–39 of Fig. 24.6, which implements the selection sort algorithm, contains nested for loops. The outer for loop (lines 27–38) iterates over the first $n-1$ elements in the array, swapping the smallest remaining item to its sorted position. The inner for loop (lines 32–34) iterates over each item in the remaining array, searching for the smallest element. This loop executes $n-1$ times during the first iteration of the outer loop, $n-2$ times during the second iteration, then $n-3, ..., 3, 2, 1$. This inner loop will iterate a total of $n(n-1)/2$ or $(n^2-n)/2$. In Big O notation, smaller terms drop out and constants are ignored, leaving a final Big O of $O(n^2)$.

24.3.2 Insertion Sort

Insertion sort is another simple, but inefficient, sorting algorithm. The first iteration of this algorithm takes the second element in the array and, if it is less than the first element, swaps it with the first element. The second iteration looks at the third element and inserts it in the correct position with respect to the first two elements, so all three elements are in order. At the ith iteration of this algorithm, the first i elements in the original array will be sorted.

Consider as an example the following array, which is identical to the array used in the discussions of selection sort and merge sort.

34   56   4   10   77   51   93   30   5   52

An application that implements the insertion sort algorithm first looks at the first two elements of the array, 34 and 56. These two elements are already in order, so the application continues (if they were out of order, it would swap them).

In the next iteration, the application looks at the third value, 4. This value is less than 56, so the application stores 4 in a temporary variable and moves 56 one element to the right. The application then checks and determines that 4 is less than 34, so it moves 34 one element to the right. The application has now reached the beginning of the array, so it places 4 in the zeroth element. The array now is

4   34   56   10   77   51   93   30   5   52

In the next iteration, the application stores the value 10 in a temporary variable. Then the application compares 10 to 56 and moves 56 one element to the right because it is larger than 10. The application then compares 10 to 34, moving 34 one element to the right. When the application compares 10 to 4, it observes that 10 is larger than 4 and places 10 in element 1. The array now is

4   10   34   56   77   51   93   30   5   52

Using this algorithm, at the ith iteration, the first i elements of the original array are sorted. They may not be in their final locations, however, because smaller values may be located later in the array.

Figure 24.8 declares the `InsertionSort` class. Lines 22–46 declare the `Sort` method. Line 24 declares variable `insert`, which holds the element to be inserted while the other elements are moved. Lines 27–45 loop through `data.Length - 1` items in the array. In each iteration, line 30 stores in variable `insert` the value of the element that will be inserted in the sorted portion of the array. Line 33 declares and initializes variable `moveItem`, which keeps track of where to insert the element. Lines 36–41 loop to locate the correct position to insert the element. The loop will terminate either when the application reaches the front of the array or when it reaches an element that is less than the value to be inserted. Line 39 moves an element to the right, and line 40 decrements the position at which to insert the next element. After the loop ends, line 43 inserts the element in place. Figure 24.9 is the same as Fig. 24.7 except that it creates and uses an `InsertionSort` object. The output of this application uses dashes to indicate the portion of the array that is sorted after each pass. An asterisk is placed next to the element that was inserted in place on that pass.

```
1    // Fig 24.8: InsertionSort.cs
2    // Class that creates an array filled with random integers.
3    // Provides a method to sort the array with insertion sort.
4    using System;
5
6    public class InsertionSort
7    {
8       private int[] data; // array of values
9       private static Random generator = new Random();
10
11      // create array of given size and fill with random integers
12      public InsertionSort( int size )
13      {
14         data = new int[ size ]; // create space for array
15
16         // fill array with random ints in range 10-99
17         for ( int i = 0; i < size; i++ )
18            data[ i ] = generator.Next( 10, 100 );
19      } // end InsertionSort constructor
20
21      // sort array using insertion sort
22      public void Sort()
23      {
24         int insert; // temporary variable to hold element to insert
25
26         // loop over data.Length - 1 elements
27         for ( int next = 1; next < data.Length; next++ )
28         {
29            // store value in current element
30            insert = data[ next ];
31
32            // initialize location to place element
33            int moveItem = next;
34
35            // search for place to put current element
36            while ( moveItem > 0 && data[ moveItem - 1 ] > insert )
37            {
38               // shift element right one slot
39               data[ moveItem ] = data[ moveItem - 1 ];
40               moveItem--;
41            } // end while
42
43            data[ moveItem ] = insert; // place inserted element
44            PrintPass( next, moveItem ); // output pass of algorithm
45         } // end for
46      } // end method Sort
47
48      // print a pass of the algorithm
49      public void PrintPass( int pass, int index )
50      {
51         Console.Write( "after pass {0}: ", pass );
```

Fig. 24.8 | Class that creates an array filled with random integers and insertion sorts them. (Part 1 of 2.)

```
52
53          // output elements till swapped item
54          for ( int i = 0; i < index; i++ )
55             Console.Write( data[ i ] + "  " );
56
57          Console.Write( data[ index ] + "* " ); // indicate swap
58
59          // finish outputting array
60          for ( int i = index + 1; i < data.Length; i++ )
61             Console.Write( data[ i ] + "  " );
62
63          Console.Write( "\n                  " ); // for alignment
64
65          // indicate amount of array that is sorted
66          for( int i = 0; i <= pass; i++ )
67             Console.Write( "--  " );
68          Console.WriteLine( "\n" ); // skip a line in output
69       } // end method PrintPass
70
71       // method to output values in array
72       public override string ToString()
73       {
74          string temporary = "";
75
76          // iterate through array
77          foreach ( int element in data )
78             temporary += element + "  ";
79
80          temporary += "\n"; // add newline character
81          return temporary;
82       } // end method ToString
83    } // end class InsertionSort
```

Fig. 24.8 | Class that creates an array filled with random integers and insertion sorts them. (Part 2 of 2.)

```
1     // Fig 24.9: InsertionSortTest.cs
2     // Test the insertion sort class.
3     using System;
4
5     public class InsertionSortTest
6     {
7        public static void Main( string[] args )
8        {
9           // create object to perform insertion sort
10          InsertionSort sortArray = new InsertionSort( 10 );
11
12          Console.WriteLine( "Unsorted array:" );
13          Console.WriteLine( sortArray ); // print unsorted array
14
15          sortArray.Sort(); // sort array
```

Fig. 24.9 | Testing the insertion sort class. (Part 1 of 2.)

```
16
17              Console.WriteLine( "Sorted array:" );
18              Console.WriteLine( sortArray ); // print sorted array
19        } // end Main
20    } // end class InsertionSortTest
```

```
Unsorted array:
12   27   36   28   33   92   11   93   59   62

after pass 1: 12   27* 36   28   33   92   11   93   59   62
              --   --

after pass 2: 12   27   36* 28   33   92   11   93   59   62
              --   --   --

after pass 3: 12   27   28* 36   33   92   11   93   59   62
              --   --   --   --

after pass 4: 12   27   28   33* 36   92   11   93   59   62
              --   --   --   --   --

after pass 5: 12   27   28   33   36   92* 11   93   59   62
              --   --   --   --   --   --

after pass 6: 11* 12   27   28   33   36   92   93   59   62
              --   --   --   --   --   --   --

after pass 7: 11   12   27   28   33   36   92   93* 59   62
              --   --   --   --   --   --   --   --

after pass 8: 11   12   27   28   33   36   59* 92   93   62
              --   --   --   --   --   --   --   --   --

after pass 9: 11   12   27   28   33   36   59   62* 92   93
              --   --   --   --   --   --   --   --   --   --

Sorted array:
11   12   27   28   33   36   59   62   92   93
```

Fig. 24.9 | Testing the insertion sort class. (Part 2 of 2.)

Efficiency of Insertion Sort

The insertion sort algorithm also runs in $O(n^2)$ time. Like selection sort, the implementation of insertion sort (lines 22–46 of Fig. 24.8) contains nested loops. The for loop (lines 27–45) iterates data.Length - 1 times, inserting an element in the appropriate position in the elements sorted so far. For the purposes of this application, data.Length - 1 is equivalent to $n - 1$ (as data.Length is the size of the array). The while loop (lines 36–41) iterates over the preceding elements in the array. In the worst case, this while loop will require $n - 1$ comparisons. Each individual loop runs in $O(n)$ time. In Big O notation, nested loops mean that you must multiply the number of iterations of each loop. For each iteration of an outer loop, there will be a certain number of iterations of the inner loop. In this algorithm, for each $O(n)$ iterations of the outer loop, there will be $O(n)$ iterations of the inner loop. Multiplying these values results in a Big O of $O(n^2)$.

24.3.3 Merge Sort

Merge sort is an efficient sorting algorithm, but is conceptually more complex than selection sort and insertion sort. The merge sort algorithm sorts an array by splitting it into two equal-sized subarrays, sorting each subarray and merging them in one larger array. With an odd number of elements, the algorithm creates the two subarrays such that one has one more element than the other.

The implementation of merge sort in this example is recursive. The base case is an array with one element. A one-element array is, of course, sorted, so merge sort immediately returns when it is called with a one-element array. The recursion step splits an array in two approximately equal-length pieces, recursively sorts them and merges the two sorted arrays in one larger, sorted array.

Suppose the algorithm has already merged smaller arrays to create sorted arrays A:

4   10   34   56   77

and B:

5   30   51   52   93

Merge sort combines these two arrays in one larger, sorted array. The smallest element in A is 4 (located in the zeroth element of A). The smallest element in B is 5 (located in the zeroth element of B). In order to determine the smallest element in the larger array, the algorithm compares 4 and 5. The value from A is smaller, so 4 becomes the first element in the merged array. The algorithm continues by comparing 10 (the second element in A) to 5 (the first element in B). The value from B is smaller, so 5 becomes the second element in the larger array. The algorithm continues by comparing 10 to 30, with 10 becoming the third element in the array, and so on.

Lines 22–25 of Fig. 24.10 declare the Sort method. Line 24 calls method SortArray with 0 and data.Length - 1 as the arguments—these are the beginning and ending indices of the array to be sorted. These values tell method SortArray to operate on the entire array.

Method SortArray is declared in lines 28–49. Line 31 tests the base case. If the size of the array is 1, the array is already sorted, so the method simply returns immediately. If the size of the array is greater than 1, the method splits the array in two, recursively calls method SortArray to sort the two subarrays and merges them. Line 43 recursively calls method SortArray on the first half of the array, and line 44 recursively calls method Sort-Array on the second half of the array. When these two method calls return, each half of the array has been sorted. Line 47 calls method Merge (lines 52–91) on the two halves of the array to combine the two sorted arrays in one larger sorted array.

Lines 64–72 in method Merge loop until the application reaches the end of either subarray. Line 68 tests which element at the beginning of the arrays is smaller. If the element in the left array is smaller, line 69 places it in position in the combined array. If the element in the right array is smaller, line 71 places it in position in the combined array. When the while loop has completed (line 72), one entire subarray is placed in the combined array, but the other subarray still contains data. Line 75 tests whether the left array has reached the end. If so, lines 77–78 fill the combined array with the remaining elements of the right array. If the left array has not reached the end, then the right array has, and lines 81–82 fill the combined array with the remaining elements of the left array. Finally, lines 85–86 copy the combined array into the original array. Figure 24.11 creates and uses a MergeSort object. The output from this application displays the splits and merges performed by merge sort, showing the progress of the sort at each step of the algorithm.

```
1   // Figure 24.10: MergeSort.cs
2   // Class that creates an array filled with random integers.
3   // Provides a method to sort the array with merge sort.
4   using System;
5
6   public class MergeSort
7   {
8      private int[] data; // array of values
9      private static Random generator = new Random();
10
11     // create array of given size and fill with random integers
12     public MergeSort( int size )
13     {
14        data = new int[ size ]; // create space for array
15
16        // fill array with random ints in range 10-99
17        for ( int i = 0; i < size; i++ )
18           data[ i ] = generator.Next( 10, 100 );
19     } // end MergeSort constructor
20
21     // calls recursive SortArray method to begin merge sorting
22     public void Sort()
23     {
24        SortArray( 0, data.Length - 1 ); // sort entire array
25     } // end method Sort
26
27     // splits array, sorts subarrays and merges subarrays into sorted array
28     private void SortArray( int low, int high )
29     {
30        // test base case; size of array equals 1
31        if ( ( high - low ) >= 1 ) // if not base case
32        {
33           int middle1 = ( low + high ) / 2; // calculate middle of array
34           int middle2 = middle1 + 1; // calculate next element over
35
36           // output split step
37           Console.WriteLine( "split:   " + Subarray( low, high ) );
38           Console.WriteLine( "         " + Subarray( low, middle1 ) );
39           Console.WriteLine( "         " + Subarray( middle2, high ) );
40           Console.WriteLine();
41
42           // split array in half; sort each half (recursive calls)
43           SortArray( low, middle1 ); // first half of array
44           SortArray( middle2, high ); // second half of array
45
```

Fig. 24.10 | Class that creates an array filled with random integers and merge sorts the array. (Part 1 of 3.)

```
46          // merge two sorted arrays after split calls return
47          Merge( low, middle1, middle2, high );
48       } // end if
49    } // end method SortArray
50
51    // merge two sorted subarrays into one sorted subarray
52    private void Merge( int left, int middle1, int middle2, int right )
53    {
54       int leftIndex = left; // index into left subarray
55       int rightIndex = middle2; // index into right subarray
56       int combinedIndex = left; // index into temporary working array
57       int[] combined = new int[ data.Length ]; // working array
58
59       // output two subarrays before merging
60       Console.WriteLine( "merge:   " + Subarray( left, middle1 ) );
61       Console.WriteLine( "         " + Subarray( middle2, right ) );
62
63       // merge arrays until reaching end of either
64       while ( leftIndex <= middle1 && rightIndex <= right )
65       {
66          // place smaller of two current elements into result
67          // and move to next space in arrays
68          if ( data[ leftIndex ] <= data[ rightIndex ] )
69             combined[ combinedIndex++ ] = data[ leftIndex++ ];
70          else
71             combined[ combinedIndex++ ] = data[ rightIndex++ ];
72       } // end while
73
74       // if left array is empty
75       if ( leftIndex == middle2 )
76          // copy in rest of right array
77          while ( rightIndex <= right )
78             combined[ combinedIndex++ ] = data[ rightIndex++ ];
79       else // right array is empty
80          // copy in rest of left array
81          while ( leftIndex <= middle1 )
82             combined[ combinedIndex++ ] = data[ leftIndex++ ];
83
84       // copy values back into original array
85       for ( int i = left; i <= right; i++ )
86          data[ i ] = combined[ i ];
87
88       // output merged array
89       Console.WriteLine( "          " + Subarray( left, right ) );
90       Console.WriteLine();
91    } // end method Merge
92
93    // method to output certain values in array
94    public string Subarray( int low, int high )
95    {
96       string temporary = "";
```

Fig. 24.10 | Class that creates an array filled with random integers and merge sorts the array. (Part 2 of 3.)

```
 97
 98          // output spaces for alignment
 99          for ( int i = 0; i < low; i++ )
100             temporary += "   ";
101
102          // output elements left in array
103          for ( int i = low; i <= high; i++ )
104             temporary += " " + data[ i ];
105
106          return temporary;
107       } // end method Subarray
108
109       // method to output values in array
110       public override string ToString()
111       {
112          return Subarray( 0, data.Length - 1 );
113       } // end method ToString
114    } // end class MergeSort
```

Fig. 24.10 | Class that creates an array filled with random integers and merge sorts the array. (Part 3 of 3.)

Efficiency of Merge Sort

Merge sort is a far more efficient algorithm than either insertion sort or selection sort when sorting large sets of data. Consider the first (nonrecursive) call to method SortArray. This results in two recursive calls to method SortArray with subarrays each approximately half the size of the original array, and a single call to method Merge. This call to method Merge requires, at worst, $n - 1$ comparisons to fill the original array, which is $O(n)$. (Recall that

```
 1    // Figure 24.11: MergeSortTest.cs
 2    // Test the merge sort class.
 3    using System;
 4
 5    public class MergeSortTest
 6    {
 7       public static void Main( string[] args )
 8       {
 9          // create object to perform merge sort
10          MergeSort sortArray = new MergeSort( 10 );
11
12          // print unsorted array
13          Console.WriteLine( "Unsorted: {0}\n", sortArray );
14
15          sortArray.Sort(); // sort array
16
17          // print sorted array
18          Console.WriteLine( "Sorted: {0}", sortArray );
19       } // end Main
20    } // end class MergeSortTest
```

Fig. 24.11 | Testing the merge sort class. (Part 1 of 3.)

```
Unsorted:  36 38 81 93 85 72 31 11 33 74

split:     36 38 81 93 85 72 31 11 33 74
           36 38 81 93 85
                         72 31 11 33 74

split:     36 38 81 93 85
           36 38 81
                   93 85

split:     36 38 81
           36 38
                 81

split:     36 38
           36
              38

merge:     36
              38
           36 38

merge:     36 38
                 81
           36 38 81

split:           93 85
                 93
                    85

merge:           93
                    85
                 85 93

merge:     36 38 81
                    85 93
           36 38 81 85 93

split:                   72 31 11 33 74
                         72 31 11
                                  33 74

split:                   72 31 11
                         72 31
                               11

split:                   72 31
                         72
                            31

merge:                   72
                            31
                         31 72
```

(continued …)

Fig. 24.11 | Testing the merge sort class. (Part 2 of 3.)

```
merge:                      31 72
                                11
                            11 31 72

split:                            33 74
                                  33
                                       74

merge:                            33
                                       74
                                  33 74

merge:                   11 31 72
                                       33 74
                         11 31 33 72 74

merge:      36 38 81 85 93
                               11 31 33 72 74
              11 31 33 36 38 72 74 81 85 93

Sorted:    11 31 33 36 38 72 74 81 85 93
```

Fig. 24.11 | Testing the merge sort class. (Part 3 of 3.)

each element in the array can be chosen by comparing one element from each of the suar-rays.) The two calls to method SortArray result in four more recursive calls to SortArray, each with a subarray approximately a quarter the size of the original array, along with two calls to method Merge. These two calls to method Merge each require, at worst, $n/2 - 1$ comparisons for a total number of comparisons of $(n/2 - 1) + (n/2 - 1) = n - 2$, which is $O(n)$. This process continues, each call to SortArray generating two additional calls to method SortArray and a call to Merge, until the algorithm has split the array in one-element subarrays. At each level, $O(n)$ comparisons are required to merge the subarrays. Each level splits the size of the arrays in half, so doubling the size of the array requires only one more level. Quadrupling the size of the array requires only two more levels. This pattern is logarithmic and results in $\log_2 n$ levels. This results in a total efficiency of $O(n \log n)$. Figure 24.12 summarizes many of the searching and sorting algorithms covered in this book and lists the Big O of each. Figure 24.13 lists the Big O values we have covered in this chapter, along with a number of values for n to highlight the differences in the growth rates.

Algorithm	Location	Big O
Searching Algorithms:		
Linear Search	Section 24.2.1	$O(n)$
Binary Search	Section 24.2.2	$O(\log n)$
Recursive Linear Search	Exercise 24.8	$O(n)$

Fig. 24.12 | Searching and sorting algorithms with Big O values. (Part 1 of 2.)

Algorithm	Location	Big O
Recursive Binary Search	Exercise 24.9	$O(\log n)$
Sorting Algorithms:		
Selection Sort	Section 24.3.1	$O(n^2)$
Insertion Sort	Section 24.3.2	$O(n^2)$
Merge Sort	Section 24.3.3	$O(n \log n)$
Bubble Sort	Exercises 24.5–24.6	$O(n^2)$

Fig. 24.12 | Searching and sorting algorithms with Big O values. (Part 2 of 2.)

$n =$	$O(\log n)$	$O(n)$	$O(n \log n)$	$O(n^2)$
1	0	1	0	1
2	1	2	2	4
3	1	3	3	9
4	1	4	4	16
5	1	5	5	25
10	1	10	10	100
100	2	100	200	10000
1,000	3	1000	3000	10^6
1,000,000	6	1000000	6000000	10^{12}
1,000,000,000	9	1000000000	9000000000	10^{18}

Fig. 24.13 | Number of comparisons for common Big O notations.

24.4 Wrap-Up

In this chapter, you learned how to search for items in arrays and how to sort arrays so that their elements are arranged in order. We discussed two searching algorithms (linear search and binary search) and three sorting algorithms (selection sort, insertion sort and merge sort). You learned that linear search can operate on any set of data, but that binary search requires the data to be sorted first. You also learned that the simplest searching and sorting algorithms can exhibit poor performance. We introduced Big O notation—a measure of the efficiency of algorithms—and used it to compare the efficiency of the algorithms we discussed. In the next chapter, you will learn about dynamic data structures that can grow or shrink at execution time.

Summary

Section 24.1 Introduction
- Searching data involves determining whether a search key is present in the data and, if so, finding its location.
- Sorting involves arranging data in order.

Section 24.2.1 Linear Search
- The linear search algorithm searches each element in an array sequentially until it finds the element that matches the search key. If the search key is not in the array, the algorithm tests each element in the array, and when the end of the array is reached, informs the user that the search key is not present. If the search key is in the array, linear search tests each element sequentially until it finds the correct item.
- One way to describe the efficiency of an algorithm is with Big O notation (*O*), which indicates how hard an algorithm may have to work to solve a problem.
- For searching and sorting algorithms, Big O is often dependent on how many elements are in the data.
- An $O(n)$ algorithm is referred to as having a linear run time.
- Big O is designed to highlight dominant factors and ignore terms that become unimportant with high *n* values. Big O notation is concerned with the growth rate of algorithm run times, so constants are ignored.
- The linear search algorithm runs in $O(n)$ time.
- The worst case in linear search is that every element must be checked to determine whether the search item exists. This occurs if the search key is the last element in the array or is not present.

Section 24.2.2 Binary Search
- The binary search algorithm is more efficient than the linear search algorithm, but it requires that an array be sorted.
- The first iteration of binary search tests the middle element in the array. If this is the search key, the algorithm returns its location. If the search key is less than the middle element, binary search continues with the first half of the array. If the search key is greater than the middle element, binary search continues with the second half of the array. Each iteration of binary search tests the middle value of the remaining array and, if the element is not found, eliminates half of the remaining elements.
- Binary search is a more efficient searching algorithm than linear search because binary search with each comparison eliminates from consideration half of the elements in the array.
- Binary search runs in $O(\log n)$ time because each step removes half of the remaining elements.

Section 24.3.1 Selection Sort
- The selection sort is a simple, but inefficient, sorting algorithm.
- The first iteration of the selection sort selects the smallest element in the array and swaps it with the first element. The second iteration of selection sort selects the second-smallest item (which is the smallest remaining item) and swaps it with the second element. Selection sort continues until the largest element is in the last index. At the *i*th iteration of selection sort, the smallest *i* items of the whole array are sorted into the first *i* indices.
- The selection sort algorithm runs in $O(n^2)$ time.

Section 24.3.2 Insertion Sort

- The first iteration of insertion sort takes the second element in the array and, if it is less than the first element, swaps it with the first element. The second iteration of insertion sort looks at the third element and inserts it in the correct position with respect to the first two elements. After the ith iteration of insertion sort, the first i elements in the original array are sorted.

- The insertion sort algorithm runs in $O(n^2)$ time.

Section 24.3.3 Merge Sort

- Merge sort is a sorting algorithm that is faster, but more complex to implement, than selection sort and insertion sort.

- The merge sort algorithm sorts an array by splitting it into two equal-sized subarrays, sorting each subarray recursively and merging the subarrays into one larger array.

- Merge sort's base case is an array with one element. A one-element array is already sorted.

- Merge sort performs the merge by looking at the first element in each array, which is also the smallest element in the array. Merge sort takes the smallest of these and places it in the first element of the larger array. If there are still elements in the subarray, merge sort looks at the second element in that subarray (which is now the smallest element remaining) and compares it to the first element in the other subarray. Merge sort continues this process until the larger array is filled.

- In the worst case, the first call to merge sort has to make $O(n)$ comparisons to fill the n slots in the final array.

- The merging portion of the merge sort algorithm is performed on two subarrays, each of approximately size $n/2$. Creating each of these subarrays requires $n/2 - 1$ comparisons for each subarray, or $O(n)$ comparisons total. This pattern continues as each level works on twice as many arrays, but each is half the size of the previous array. Similar to binary search, this halving results in log n levels for a total efficiency of $O(n \log n)$.

Terminology

Big O notation	$O(n)$
binary search	$O(n^2)$
constant run time	search key
efficiency of algorithms	quadratic run time
insertion sort	search key
linear run time	searching
linear search	selection sort
logarithmic run time	sort key
merge sort	Sort method of class `Array`
$O(1)$	sorting
$O(\log n)$	subarray
$O(n \log n)$	swapping values

Self-Review Exercises

24.1   Fill in the blanks in each of the following statements:
   a) A selection sort application would take approximately _____ times as long to run on a 128-element array as on a 32-element array.
   b) The efficiency of merge sort is _____.

24.2   What key aspect of both the binary search and the merge sort accounts for the logarithmic portion of their respective Big Os?

24.3 In what sense is the insertion sort superior to the merge sort? In what sense is the merge sort superior to the insertion sort?

24.4 In the text, we say that after the merge sort splits the array into two subarrays, it then sorts these two subarrays and merges them. Why might someone be puzzled by our statement that "it then sorts these two subarrays"?

Answers to Self-Review Exercises

24.1 a) 16, because an $O(n^2)$ algorithm takes 16 times as long to sort four times as much information. b) $O(n \log n)$.

24.2 Both of these algorithms incorporate "halving"—somehow reducing something by half. The binary search eliminates from consideration one half of the array after each comparison. The merge sort splits the array in half each time it is called.

24.3 The insertion sort is easier to understand and to program than the merge sort. The merge sort is far more efficient ($O(n \log n)$) than the insertion sort ($O(n^2)$).

24.4 In a sense, it does not really sort these two subarrays. It simply keeps splitting the original array in half until it provides a one-element subarray, which is, of course, sorted. It then builds up the original two subarrays by merging these one-element arrays to form larger subarrays, which are then merged until the whole array has been sorted.

Exercises

24.5 *(Bubble Sort)* Implement the bubble sort—another simple, yet inefficient, sorting technique. It is called bubble sort or sinking sort because smaller values gradually "bubble" their way to the top of the array (i.e., toward the first element) like air bubbles rising in water, while the larger values sink to the bottom (end) of the array. The technique uses nested loops to make several passes through the array. Each pass compares successive pairs of elements. If a pair is in increasing order (or the values are equal), the bubble sort leaves the values as they are. If a pair is in decreasing order, the bubble sort swaps their values in the array.

The first pass compares the first two elements of the array and swaps them if necessary. It then compares the second and third elements in the array. The end of this pass compares the last two elements in the array and swaps them if necessary. After one pass, the largest element will be in the last index. After two passes, the largest two elements will be in the last two indices. Explain why bubble sort is an $O(n^2)$ algorithm.

24.6 *(Enhanced Bubble Sort)* Make the following simple modifications to improve the performance of the bubble sort you developed in Exercise 24.5:
   a) After the first pass, the largest number is guaranteed to be in the highest-numbered element of the array; after the second pass, the two highest numbers are "in place"; and so on. Instead of making nine comparisons on every pass, modify the bubble sort to make eight comparisons on the second pass, seven on the third pass and so on.
   b) The data in the array may already be in the proper order or near-proper order, so why make nine passes if fewer will suffice? Modify the sort to check at the end of each pass whether any swaps have been made. If none have been made, the data must already be in the proper order, so the application should terminate. If swaps have been made, at least one more pass is needed.

24.7 *(Bucket Sort)* A bucket sort begins with a one-dimensional array of positive integers to be sorted and a two-dimensional array of integers with rows indexed from 0 to 9 and columns indexed from 0 to $n - 1$, where n is the number of values to be sorted. Each row of the two-dimensional array is referred to as a *bucket*. Write a class named BucketSort containing a method called Sort that operates as follows:

a) Place each value of the one-dimensional array into a row of the bucket array, based on the value's "ones" (right-most) digit. For example, 97 is placed in row 7, 3 is placed in row 3 and 100 is placed in row 0. This procedure is called a *distribution pass*.

b) Loop through the bucket array row by row, and copy the values back to the original array. This procedure is called a *gathering pass*. The new order of the preceding values in the one-dimensional array is 100, 3 and 97.

c) Repeat this process for each subsequent digit position (tens, hundreds, thousands, etc.).

On the second (tens digit) pass, 100 is placed in row 0, 3 is placed in row 0 (because 3 has no tens digit) and 97 is placed in row 9. After the gathering pass, the order of the values in the one-dimensional array is 100, 3 and 97. On the third (hundreds digit) pass, 100 is placed in row 1, 3 is placed in row 0 and 97 is placed in row 0 (after the 3). After this last gathering pass, the original array is in sorted order.

Note that the two-dimensional array of buckets is 10 times the length of the integer array being sorted. This sorting technique provides better performance than a bubble sort, but requires much more memory—the bubble sort requires space for only one additional element of data. This comparison is an example of the space–time trade-off: The bucket sort uses more memory than the bubble sort, but performs better. This version of the bucket sort requires copying all the data back to the original array on each pass. Another possibility is to create a second two-dimensional bucket array and repeatedly swap the data between the two bucket arrays.

24.8 (*Recursive Linear Search*) Modify Fig. 24.2 to use recursive method `RecursiveLinearSearch` to perform a linear search of the array. The method should receive the search key and starting index as arguments. If the search key is found, return its index in the array; otherwise, return –1. Each call to the recursive method should check one index in the array.

24.9 (*Recursive Binary Search*) Modify Fig. 24.4 to use recursive method `RecursiveBinarySearch` to perform a binary search of the array. The method should receive the search key, starting index and ending index as arguments. If the search key is found, return its index in the array. If the search key is not found, return –1.

24.10 (*Quicksort*) The recursive sorting technique called quicksort uses the following basic algorithm for a one-dimensional array of values:

a) *Partitioning Step*: Take the first element of the unsorted array and determine its final location in the sorted array (i.e., all values to the left of the element in the array are less than the element, and all values to the right of the element in the array are greater than the element—we show how to do this below). We now have one element in its proper location and two unsorted subarrays.

b) *Recursive Step*: Perform *Step 1* on each unsorted subarray.

Each time *Step 1* is performed on a subarray, another element is placed in its final location in the sorted array, and two unsorted subarrays are created. When a subarray consists of one element, that element is in its final location (because a one-element array is already sorted).

The basic algorithm seems simple enough, but how do we determine the final position of the first element of each subarray? As an example, consider the following set of values (the element in bold is the partitioning element—it will be placed in its final location in the sorted array):

37 2 6 4 89 8 10 12 68 45

a) Starting from the right-most element of the array, compare each element with 37 until an element less than 37 is found, then swap 37 and that element. The first element less than 37 is 12, so 37 and 12 are swapped. The new array is

12 2 6 4 89 8 10 *37* 68 45

Element 12 is in italics to indicate that it was just swapped with 37.

b) Starting from the left of the array, but beginning with the element after 12, compare each element with 37 until an element greater than 37 is found—then swap 37 and that element. The first element greater than 37 is 89, so 37 and 89 are swapped. The new array is

>   12   2   6   4   *37*   8   10   *89*   68   45

c) Starting from the right, but beginning with the element before 89, compare each element with 37 until an element less than 37 is found—then swap 37 and that element. The first element less than 37 is 10, so 37 and 10 are swapped. The new array is

>   12   2   6   4   *10*   8   *37*   89   68   45

d) Starting from the left, but beginning with the element after 10, compare each element with 37 until an element greater than 37 is found—then swap 37 and that element. There are no more elements greater than 37, so when we compare 37 with itself, we know that 37 has been placed in its final location of the sorted array. Every value to the left of 37 is smaller than it, and every value to the right of 37 is larger than it.

Once the partition has been applied on the previous array, there are two unsorted subarrays. The subarray with values less than 37 contains 12, 2, 6, 4, 10 and 8. The subarray with values greater than 37 contains 89, 68 and 45. The sort continues recursively with both subarrays being partitioned in the same manner as the original array.

Based on the preceding discussion, write recursive method `QuickSortHelper` to sort a one-dimensional integer array. The method should receive as arguments a starting index and an ending index in the original array being sorted.

25

Data Structures

OBJECTIVES

In this chapter you will learn:

- To form linked data structures using references, self-referential classes and recursion.

- How boxing and unboxing enable simple-type values to be used where **object**s are expected in a program.

- To create and manipulate dynamic data structures, such as linked lists, queues, stacks and binary trees.

- Various important applications of linked data structures.

- To create reusable data structures with classes, inheritance and composition.

25.1 Introduction

This chapter begins our three-chapter treatment of data structures. The *data structures* that we have studied thus far have had fixed sizes, such as one- and two-dimensional arrays. This chapter introduces *dynamic data structures* that grow and shrink at execution time. Linked lists are collections of data items "lined up in a row"—users can make insertions and deletions anywhere in a linked list. Stacks are important in compilers and operating systems; insertions and deletions are made at only one end—its *top*. Queues represent waiting lines; insertions are made at the back (also referred to as the *tail*) of a queue, and deletions are made from the front (also referred to as the *head*) of a queue. *Binary trees* facilitate high-speed searching and sorting of data, efficient elimination of duplicate data items, representation of file system directories and compilation of expressions into machine language. These data structures have many other interesting applications as well.

We will discuss each of these major types of data structures and implement programs that create and manipulate them. We use classes, inheritance and composition to create and package these data structures for reusability and maintainability. In Chapter 26, we introduce generics, which allow you to declare data structures that can be automatically adapted to contain data of any type. In Chapter 27, Collections, we discuss C#'s predefined classes that implement various data structures.

The chapter examples are practical programs that will be useful in more advanced courses and in industrial applications. The programs focus on reference manipulation. The exercises offer a rich collection of useful applications.

25.2 Simple-Type `struct`s, Boxing and Unboxing

The data structures we discuss in this chapter store `object` references. However, as you will soon see, we are able to store both simple- and reference-type values in these data structures. This section discusses the mechanisms that enable simple-type values to be manipulated as objects.

Simple-Type `struct`s

Each simple type (Appendix L, Simple Types) has a corresponding **struct** in namespace `System` that declares the simple type. These structs are called `Boolean`, `Byte`, `SByte`, `Char`,

Decimal, Double, Single, Int32, UInt32, Int64, UInt64, Int16 and UInt16. Types declared with keyword struct are implicitly value types.

Simple types are actually aliases for their corresponding structs, so a variable of a simple type can be declared using either the keyword for that simple type or the struct name—e.g., int and Int32 are interchangeable. The methods related to a simple type are located in the corresponding struct (e.g., method Parse, which converts a string to an int value, is located in struct Int32). Refer to the documentation for the corresponding struct type to see the methods available for manipulating values of that type.

Boxing and Unboxing Conversions

All simple-type structs inherit from class *ValueType* in namespace System. Class Value-Type inherits from class object. Thus, any simple-type value can be assigned to an object variable; this is referred to as a *boxing conversion*. In a boxing conversion, the simple-type value is copied into an object so that the simple-type value can be manipulated as an object. Boxing conversions can be performed either explicitly or implicitly as shown in the following statements:

```
int i = 5; // create an int value
object object1 = ( object ) i; // explicitly box the int value
object object2 = i; // implicitly box the int value
```

After executing the preceding code, both object1 and object2 refer to two different objects that contain a copy of the integer value in int variable i.

An *unboxing conversion* can be used to explicitly convert an object reference to a simple value as shown in the following statement:

```
int int1 = ( int ) object1; // explicitly unbox the int value
```

Explicitly attempting to unbox an object reference that does not refer to the correct simple value type causes an *InvalidCastException.*

In Chapter 26, Generics, and Chapter 27, Collections, we discuss C#'s generics and generic collections. As you will see, generics eliminate the overhead of boxing and unboxing conversions by enabling us to create and use collections of specific value types.

25.3 Self-Referential Classes

A *self-referential class* contains a reference member that refers to an object of the same class type. For example, the class declaration in Fig. 25.1 defines the shell of a self-referential class named Node. This type has two private instance variables—integer data and Node reference next. Member next references an object of type Node, an object of the same type as the one being declared here—hence, the term "self-referential class." Member next is referred to as a *link* (i.e., next can be used to "tie" an object of type Node to another object of the same type). Class Node also has two properties—one for instance variable data (named Data) and another for instance variable next (named Next).

Self-referential objects can be linked together to form useful data structures, such as lists, queues, stacks and trees. Figure 25.2 illustrates two self-referential objects linked together to form a linked list. A backslash (representing a null reference) is placed in the

```
 I    // Fig. 25.1: Fig25_01.cs
 2    // A self-referential class.
 3    class Node
 4    {
 5       private int data; // store integer data
 6       private Node next; // store reference to next Node
 7
 8       public Node( int dataValue )
 9       {
10          // constructor body
11       } // end constructor
12
13       public int Data
14       {
15          get
16          {
17             // get body
18          } // end get
19          set
20          {
21             // set body
22          } // end set
23       } // end property Data
24
25       public Node Next
26       {
27          get
28          {
29             // get body
30          } // end get
31          set
32          {
33             // set body
34          } // end set
35       } // end property Next
36    } // end class Node
```

Fig. 25.1 | Self-referential Node class declaration.

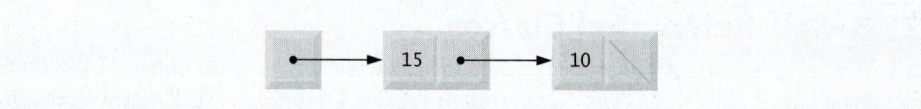

Fig. 25.2 | Self-referential class objects linked together.

link member of the second self-referential object to indicate that the link does not refer to another object. The backslash is for illustration purposes; it does not correspond to the backslash character in C#. A null reference normally indicates the end of a data structure.

 Common Programming Error 25.1

Not setting the link in the last node of a list to null is a logic error.

Creating and maintaining dynamic data structures requires *dynamic memory alloca-tion*—a program's ability to obtain more memory space at execution time to hold new nodes and to release space no longer needed. As you learned in Section 9.9, C# programs do not explicitly release dynamically allocated memory—rather, C# performs automatic garbage collection.

The new operator is essential to dynamic memory allocation. Operator new takes as an operand the type of the object being dynamically allocated and returns a reference to an object of that type. For example, the statement

```
Node nodeToAdd = new Node( 10 );
```

allocates the appropriate amount of memory to store a Node and stores a reference to this object in nodeToAdd. If no memory is available, new throws an OutOfMemoryException. The constructor argument 10 specifies the Node object's data.

The following sections discuss lists, stacks, queues and trees. These data structures are created and maintained with dynamic memory allocation and self-referential classes.

Good Programming Practice 25.1

When creating a large number of objects, test for an OutOfMemoryException. Perform appropriate error processing if the requested memory is not allocated.

25.4 Linked Lists

A *linked list* is a linear collection (i.e., a sequence) of self-referential class objects, called *nodes*, connected by reference links—hence, the term "linked" list. A program accesses a linked list via a reference to the first node of the list. Each subsequent node is accessed via the link-reference member stored in the previous node. By convention, the link reference in the last node of a list is set to null to mark the end of the list. Data is stored in a linked list dynamically—that is, each node is created as necessary. A node can contain data of any type, including references to objects of other classes. Stacks and queues are also linear data structures—in fact, they are constrained versions of linked lists. Trees are non-linear data structures.

Lists of data can be stored in arrays, but linked lists provide several advantages. A linked list is appropriate when the number of data elements to be represented in the data structure is unpredictable. Unlike a linked list, the size of a conventional C# array cannot be altered, because the array size is fixed at creation time. Conventional arrays can become full, but linked lists become full only when the system has insufficient memory to satisfy dynamic memory allocation requests.

Performance Tip 25.1

An array can be declared to contain more elements than the number of items expected, possibly wasting memory. Linked lists provide better memory utilization in these situations, because they can grow and shrink at execution time.

Performance Tip 25.2

After locating the insertion point for a new item in a sorted linked list, inserting an element in the list is fast—only two references have to be modified. All existing nodes remain at their current locations in memory.

Programmers can maintain linked lists in sorted order simply by inserting each new element at the proper point in the list (locating the proper insertion point does take time). They do not need to move existing list elements.

Performance Tip 25.3

The elements of an array are stored contiguously in memory to allow immediate access to any array element—the address of any element can be calculated directly from its index. Linked lists do not afford such immediate access to their elements—an element can be accessed only by traversing the list from the front.

Normally linked-list nodes are not stored contiguously in memory. Rather, the nodes are logically contiguous. Figure 25.3 illustrates a linked list with several nodes.

Performance Tip 25.4

Using linked data structures and dynamic memory allocation (instead of arrays) for data structures that grow and shrink at execution time can save memory. Keep in mind, however, that reference links occupy space, and dynamic memory allocation incurs the overhead of method calls.

Linked List Implementation

The program of Figs. 25.4 and 25.5 uses an object of class List to manipulate a list of miscellaneous object types. The Main method of class ListTest (Fig. 25.5) creates a list of objects, inserts objects at the beginning of the list using List method InsertAtFront, inserts objects at the end of the list using List method InsertAtBack, deletes objects from the front of the list using List method RemoveFromFront and deletes objects from the end of the list using List method RemoveFromBack. After each insertion and deletion operation, the program invokes List method Print to display the current list contents. If an attempt is made to remove an item from an empty list, an EmptyListException occurs. A detailed discussion of the program follows.

Performance Tip 25.5

Insertion and deletion in a sorted array can be time consuming—all the elements following the inserted or deleted element must be shifted appropriately.

The program consists of four classes—ListNode (Fig. 25.4, lines 8–49), List (lines 52–165), EmptyListException (lines 168–174) and ListTest (Fig. 25.5). The classes in Fig. 25.4 create a linked-list library (defined in namespace LinkedListLibrary) that can be reused throughout this chapter. You should place the code of Fig. 25.4 in its own class library project as we described in Section 9.14.

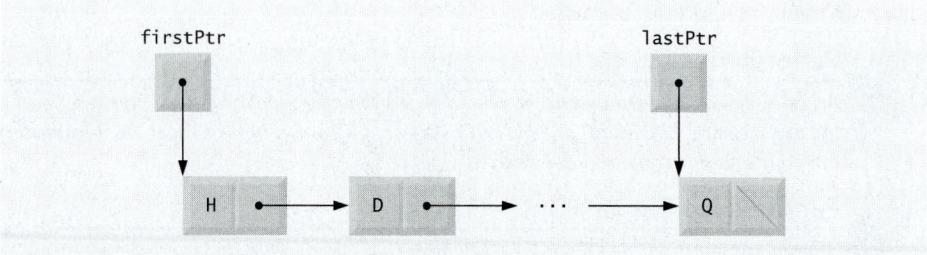

Fig. 25.3 | Linked list graphical representation.

Encapsulated in each List object is a linked list of ListNode objects. Class ListNode (Fig. 25.4, lines 8–49) contains two instance variables—data and next. Member data can refer to any object. [*Note:* Typically, a data structure will contain data of only one type, or data of any type derived from one base type.] In this example, we use data of various types derived from object to demonstrate that our List class can store data of any type. Member next stores a reference to the next ListNode object in the linked list. The List-Node constructors (lines 15–18 and 22–26) enable us to initialize a ListNode that will be placed at the end of a List or before a specific ListNode in a List, respectively. A List accesses the ListNode member variables via properties Next (lines 29–39) and Data (lines 42–48), respectively.

```csharp
1   // Fig. 25.4: LinkedListLibrary.cs
2   // Class ListNode and class List declarations.
3   using System;
4
5   namespace LinkedListLibrary
6   {
7      // class to represent one node in a list
8      class ListNode
9      {
10        private object data; // stores data for this node
11        private ListNode next; // stores a reference to the next node
12
13        // constructor to create ListNode that refers to dataValue
14        // and is last node in list
15        public ListNode( object dataValue )
16           : this( dataValue, null )
17        {
18        } // end default constructor
19
20        // constructor to create ListNode that refers to dataValue
21        // and refers to next ListNode in List
22        public ListNode( object dataValue, ListNode nextNode )
23        {
24           data = dataValue;
25           next = nextNode;
26        } // end constructor
27
28        // property Next
29        public ListNode Next
30        {
31           get
32           {
33              return next;
34           } // end get
35           set
36           {
37              next = value;
38           } // end set
39        } // end property Next
```

Fig. 25.4 | ListNode, List and EmptyListException classes. (Part 1 of 4.)

```
40
41        // property Data
42        public object Data
43        {
44           get
45           {
46              return data;
47           } // end get
48        } // end property Data
49     } // end class ListNode
50
51     // class List declaration
52     public class List
53     {
54        private ListNode firstNode;
55        private ListNode lastNode;
56        private string name; // string like "list" to display
57
58        // construct empty List with specified name
59        public List( string listName )
60        {
61           name = listName;
62           firstNode = lastNode = null;
63        } // end constructor
64
65        // construct empty List with "list" as its name
66        public List()
67           : this( "list" )
68        {
69        } // end constructor default
70
71        // Insert object at front of List. If List is empty,
72        // firstNode and lastNode will refer to same object.
73        // Otherwise, firstNode refers to new node.
74        public void InsertAtFront( object insertItem )
75        {
76           if ( IsEmpty() )
77              firstNode = lastNode = new ListNode( insertItem );
78           else
79              firstNode = new ListNode( insertItem, firstNode );
80        } // end method InsertAtFront
81
82        // Insert object at end of List. If List is empty,
83        // firstNode and lastNode will refer to same object.
84        // Otherwise, lastNode's Next property refers to new node.
85        public void InsertAtBack( object insertItem )
86        {
87           if ( IsEmpty() )
88              firstNode = lastNode = new ListNode( insertItem );
89           else
90              lastNode = lastNode.Next = new ListNode( insertItem );
91        } // end method InsertAtBack
```

Fig. 25.4 | ListNode, List and EmptyListException classes. (Part 2 of 4.)

```
 92
 93        // remove first node from List
 94        public object RemoveFromFront()
 95        {
 96           if ( IsEmpty() )
 97              throw new EmptyListException( name );
 98
 99           object removeItem = firstNode.Data; // retrieve data
100
101           // reset firstNode and lastNode references
102           if ( firstNode == lastNode )
103              firstNode = lastNode = null;
104           else
105              firstNode = firstNode.Next;
106
107           return removeItem; // return removed data
108        } // end method RemoveFromFront
109
110        // remove last node from List
111        public object RemoveFromBack()
112        {
113           if ( IsEmpty() )
114              throw new EmptyListException( name );
115
116           object removeItem = lastNode.Data; // retrieve data
117
118           // reset firstNode and lastNode references
119           if ( firstNode == lastNode )
120              firstNode = lastNode = null;
121           else
122           {
123              ListNode current = firstNode;
124
125              // loop while current node is not lastNode
126              while ( current.Next != lastNode )
127                 current = current.Next; // move to next node
128
129              // current is new lastNode
130              lastNode = current;
131              current.Next = null;
132           } // end else
133
134           return removeItem; // return removed data
135        } // end method RemoveFromBack
136
137        // return true if List is empty
138        public bool IsEmpty()
139        {
140           return firstNode == null;
141        } // end method IsEmpty
142
```

Fig. 25.4 | ListNode, List and EmptyListException classes. (Part 3 of 4.)

```
143         // output List contents
144         public void Print()
145         {
146            if ( IsEmpty() )
147            {
148               Console.WriteLine( "Empty " + name );
149               return;
150            } // end if
151
152            Console.Write( "The " + name + " is: " );
153
154            ListNode current = firstNode;
155
156            // output current node data while not at end of list
157            while ( current != null )
158            {
159               Console.Write( current.Data + " " );
160               current = current.Next;
161            } // end while
162
163            Console.WriteLine( "\n" );
164         } // end method Print
165      } // end class List
166
167      // class EmptyListException declaration
168      public class EmptyListException : ApplicationException
169      {
170         public EmptyListException( string name )
171            : base( "The " + name + " is empty" )
172         {
173         } // end constructor
174      } // end class EmptyListException
175   } // end namespace LinkedListLibrary
```

Fig. 25.4 | ListNode, List and EmptyListException classes. (Part 4 of 4.)

Class List (lines 52–165) contains private instance variables firstNode (a reference to the first ListNode in a List) and lastNode (a reference to the last ListNode in a List). The constructors (lines 59–63 and 66–69) initialize both references to null and enable us to specify the List's name for output purposes. InsertAtFront (lines 74–80), InsertAt-Back (lines 85–91), RemoveFromFront (lines 94–108) and RemoveFromBack (lines 111–135) are the primary methods of class List. Method IsEmpty (lines 138–141) is a *predicate method* that determines whether the list is empty (i.e., the reference to the first node of the list is null). Predicate methods typically test a condition and do not modify the object on which they are called. If the list is empty, method IsEmpty returns true; otherwise, it returns false. Method Print (lines 144–164) displays the list's contents. A detailed discussion of class List's methods follows Fig. 25.5.

Class EmptyListException (lines 168–174) defines an exception class that we use to indicate illegal operations on an empty List.

Class ListTest (Fig. 25.5) uses the linked-list library to create and manipulate a linked list. [*Note:* In the project containing Fig. 25.5, you must add a reference to the class library containing the classes in Fig. 25.4. If you use our existing example, you may need to update this reference.] Line 11 creates a new List object and assigns it to variable list. Lines 14–17 create data to add to the list. Lines 20–27 use List insertion methods to insert these values and use List method Print to output the contents of list after each insertion. Note that the values of the simple-type variables are implicitly boxed in lines 20, 22 and 24 where object references are expected. The code inside the try block (lines 33–50) removes objects via List deletion methods, outputs each removed object and outputs list after every deletion. If there is an attempt to remove an object from an empty list, the catch at lines 51–54 catches the EmptyListException and displays an error message.

```csharp
// Fig. 25.5: ListTest.cs
// Testing class List.
using System;
using LinkedListLibrary;

// class to test List class functionality
class ListTest
{
   static void Main( string[] args )
   {
      List list = new List(); // create List container

      // create data to store in List
      bool aBoolean = true;
      char aCharacter = '$';
      int anInteger = 34567;
      string aString = "hello";

      // use List insert methods
      list.InsertAtFront( aBoolean );
      list.Print();
      list.InsertAtFront( aCharacter );
      list.Print();
      list.InsertAtBack( anInteger );
      list.Print();
      list.InsertAtBack( aString );
      list.Print();

      // use List remove methods
      object removedObject;

      // remove data from list and print after each removal
      try
      {
         removedObject = list.RemoveFromFront();
         Console.WriteLine( removedObject + " removed" );
         list.Print();

         removedObject = list.RemoveFromFront();
         Console.WriteLine( removedObject + " removed" );
         list.Print();

```

Fig. 25.5 | Linked list demonstration. (Part 1 of 2.)

```
43              removedObject = list.RemoveFromBack();
44              Console.WriteLine( removedObject + " removed" );
45              list.Print();
46
47              removedObject = list.RemoveFromBack();
48              Console.WriteLine( removedObject + " removed" );
49              list.Print();
50          } // end try
51          catch ( EmptyListException emptyListException )
52          {
53              Console.Error.WriteLine( "\n" + emptyListException );
54          } // end catch
55      } // end method Main
56  } // end class ListTest
```

```
The list is: True

The list is: $ True

The list is: $ True 34567

The list is: $ True 34567 hello

$ removed
The list is: True 34567 hello

True removed
The list is: 34567 hello

hello removed
The list is: 34567

34567 removed
Empty list
```

Fig. 25.5 | Linked list demonstration. (Part 2 of 2.)

Method *InsertAtFront*

Over the next several pages, we discuss each of the methods of class List in detail. Method InsertAtFront (Fig. 25.4, lines 74–80) places a new node at the front of the list. The method consists of three steps:

1. Call IsEmpty to determine whether the list is empty (line 76).

2. If the list is empty, set both firstNode and lastNode to refer to a new ListNode initialized with insertItem (line 77). The ListNode constructor at lines 15–18 of Fig. 25.4 calls the ListNode constructor at lines 22–26, which sets instance variable data to refer to the object passed as the first argument and sets the next reference to null.

3. If the list is not empty, the new node is "linked" into the list by setting firstNode to refer to a new ListNode object initialized with insertItem and firstNode (line 79). When the ListNode constructor (lines 22–26) executes, it sets instance variable data to refer to the object passed as the first argument and performs the insertion by setting the next reference to the ListNode passed as the second argument.

In Fig. 25.6, part (a) shows a list and a new node during the InsertAtFront operation and before the new node is linked into the list. The dashed lines and arrows in part (b) illustrate *Step 3* of the InsertAtFront operation, which enables the node containing 12 to become the new list front.

Method *InsertAtBack*

Method InsertAtBack (Fig. 25.4, lines 85–91) places a new node at the back of the list. The method consists of three steps:

1. Call IsEmpty to determine whether the list is empty (line 87).

2. If the list is empty, set both firstNode and lastNode to refer to a new ListNode initialized with insertItem (line 88). The ListNode constructor at lines 15–18 calls the ListNode constructor at lines 22–26, which sets instance variable data to refer to the object passed as the first argument and sets the next reference to null.

3. If the list is not empty, link the new node into the list by setting lastNode and lastNode.next to refer to a new ListNode object initialized with insertItem (line 90). When the ListNode constructor (lines 15–18) executes, it calls the constructor at lines 22–26, which sets instance variable data to refer to the object passed as an argument and sets the next reference to null.

In Fig. 25.7, part (a) shows a list and a new node during the InsertAtBack operation; before the new node has been linked into the list. The dashed lines and arrows in part (b) illustrate *Step 3* of method InsertAtBack, which enables a new node to be added to the end of a list that is not empty.

Method *RemoveFromFront*

Method RemoveFromFront (Fig. 25.4, lines 94–108) removes the front node of the list and returns a reference to the removed data. The method throws an EmptyListException (line 97) if the programmer tries to remove a node from an empty list. Otherwise, the method

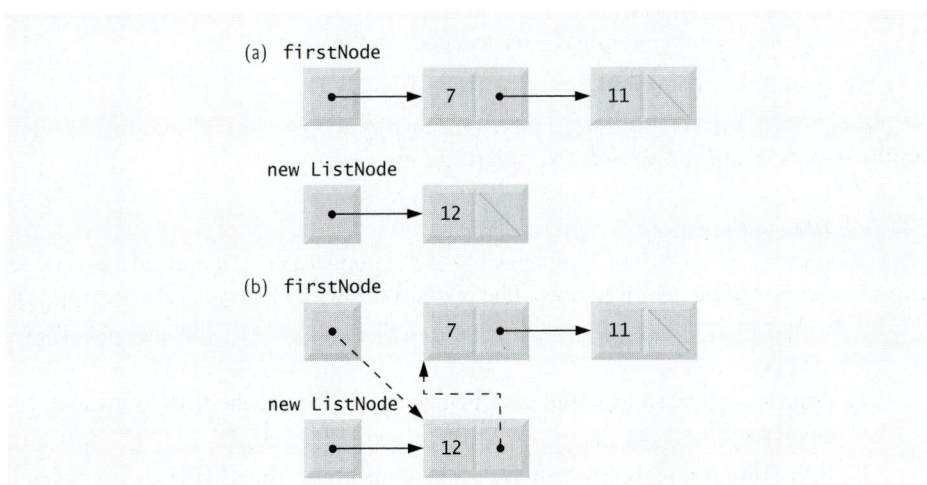

Fig. 25.6 | InsertAtFront operation.

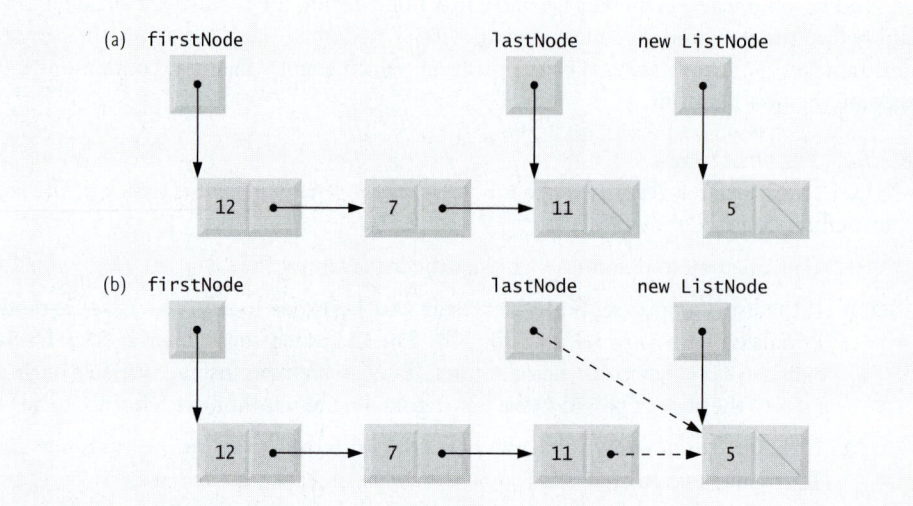

Fig. 25.7 | InsertAtBack operation.

returns a reference to the removed data. After determining that a List is not empty, the method consists of four steps to remove the first node:

1. Assign firstNode.Data (the data being removed from the list) to variable removeItem (line 99).

2. If the objects to which firstNode and lastNode refer are the same object, the list has only one element, so the method sets firstNode and lastNode to null (line 103) to remove the node from the list (leaving the list empty).

3. If the list has more than one node, the method leaves reference lastNode as is and assigns firstNode.Next to firstNode (line 105). Thus, firstNode references the node that was previously the second node in the List.

4. Return the removeItem reference (line 107).

In Fig. 25.8, part (a) illustrates a list before a removal operation. The dashed lines and arrows in part (b) show the reference manipulations.

Method RemoveFromBack
Method RemoveFromBack (Fig. 25.4, lines 111–135) removes the last node of a list and returns a reference to the removed data. The method throws an EmptyListException (line 114) if the program attempts to remove a node from an empty list. The method consists of several steps:

1. Assign lastNode.Data (the data being removed from the list) to variable removeItem (line 116).

2. If firstNode and lastNode refer to the same object (line 119), the list has only one element, so the method sets firstNode and lastNode to null (line 120) to remove that node from the list (leaving the list empty).

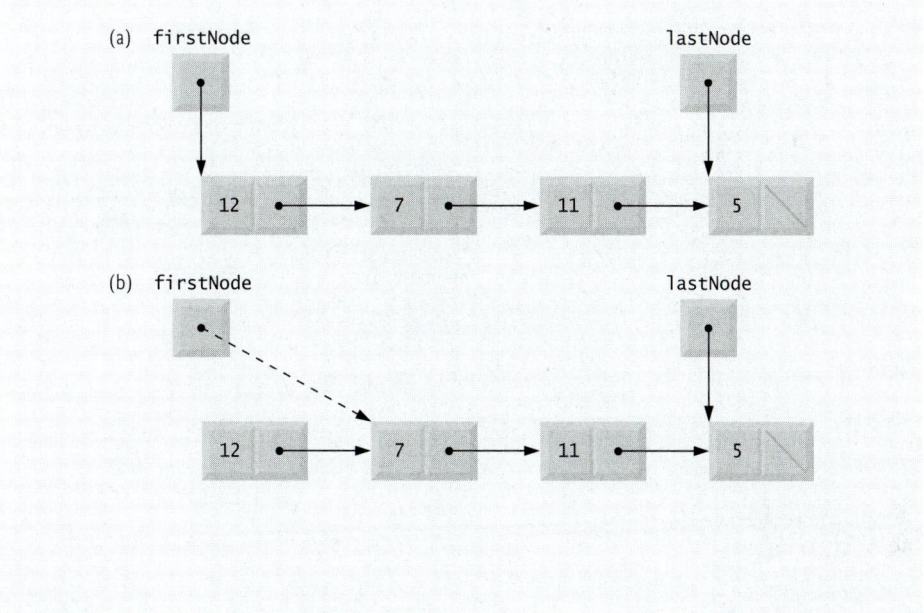

Fig. 25.8 | RemoveFromFront operation.

3. If the list has more than one node, create `ListNode` variable `current` and assign it `firstNode` (line 123).

4. Now "walk the list" with `current` until it references the node before the last node. The `while` loop (lines 126–127) assigns `current.Next` to `current` as long as `current.Next` is not equal to `lastNode`.

5. After locating the second-to-last node, assign `current` to `lastNode` (line 130) to update which node is last in the list.

6. Set `current.Next` to `null` (line 131) to remove the last node from the list and terminate the list at the current node.

7. Return the `removeItem` reference (line 134).

In Fig. 25.9, part (a) illustrates a list before a removal operation. The dashed lines and arrows in part (b) show the reference manipulations.

Method Print

Method `Print` (Fig. 25.4, lines 144–164) first determines whether the list is empty (line 146). If so, `Print` displays a `string` consisting of the string `"Empty "` and the list's name, then returns control to the calling method. Otherwise, `Print` outputs the data in the list. The method prints a `string` consisting of the string `"The "`, the list's name and the string `" is: "`. Then line 154 creates `ListNode` variable `current` and initializes it with `firstNode`. While `current` is not `null`, there are more items in the list. Therefore, the method displays `current.Data` (line 159), then assigns `current.Next` to `current` (line 160) to move to the next node in the list.

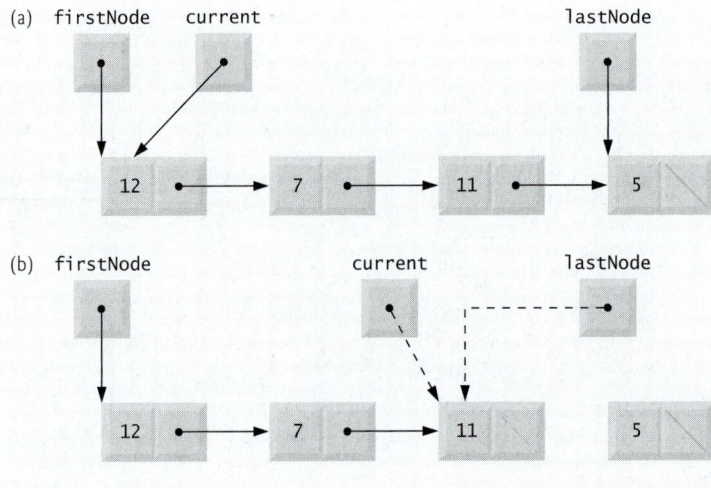

Fig. 25.9 | RemoveFromBack operation.

Linear and Circular Singly Linked and Doubly Linked Lists

The kind of linked list we have been discussing is a *singly linked list*—the list begins with a reference to the first node, and each node contains a reference to the next node "in sequence." This list terminates with a node whose reference member has the value null. A singly linked list may be traversed in only one direction.

A *circular, singly linked list* (Fig. 25.10) begins with a reference to the first node, and each node contains a reference to the next node. The "last node" does not contain a null reference; rather, the reference in the last node points back to the first node, thus closing the "circle."

A *doubly linked list* (Fig. 25.11) allows traversals both forward and backward. Such a list is often implemented with two "start references"—one that refers to the first element of the list to allow front-to-back traversal of the list and one that refers to the last element

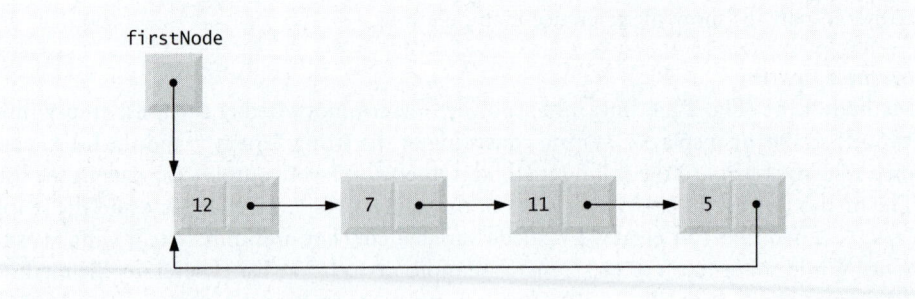

Fig. 25.10 | Circular, singly linked list.

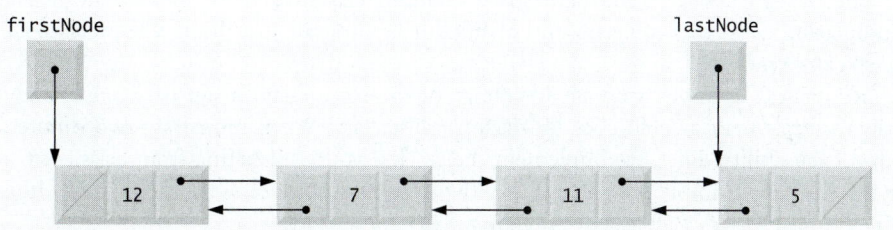

Fig. 25.11 | Doubly linked list.

to allow back-to-front traversal. Each node has both a forward reference to the next node in the list and a backward reference to the previous node in the list. If your list contains an alphabetized telephone directory, for example, a search for someone whose name begins with a letter near the front of the alphabet might begin from the front of the list. A search for someone whose name begins with a letter near the end of the alphabet might begin from the back of the list.

In a *circular, doubly linked list* (Fig. 25.12), the forward reference of the last node refers to the first node, and the backward reference of the first node refers to the last node, thus closing the "circle."

25.5 Stacks

A *stack* is a constrained version of a linked list—a stack receives new nodes and releases nodes only at the top. For this reason, a stack is referred to as a *last-in-first-out (LIFO)* data structure.

The primary operations to manipulate a stack are *push* and *pop*. Operation push adds a new node to the top of the stack. Operation pop removes a node from the top of the stack and returns the data item from the popped node.

Stacks have many interesting applications. For example, when a program calls a method, the called method must know how to return to its caller, so the return address is pushed onto the method call stack. If a series of method calls occurs, the successive return values are pushed onto the stack in last-in, first-out order so that each method can return to its caller. Stacks support recursive method calls in the same manner that they do conventional non-recursive method calls.

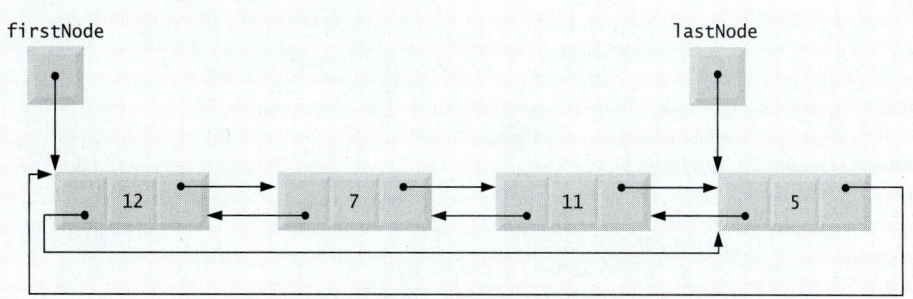

Fig. 25.12 | Circular, doubly linked list.

The `System.Collections` namespace contains class `Stack` for implementing and manipulating stacks that can grow and shrink during program execution. Chapters 26–27 discuss class `Stack`.

In our next example, we take advantage of the close relationship between lists and stacks to implement a stack class by reusing a list class. We demonstrate two different forms of reusability. First, we implement the stack class by inheriting from class `List` of Fig. 25.4. Then we implement an identically performing stack class through composition by including a `List` object as a `private` member of a stack class.

Stack Class That Inherits from `List`

The program of Figs. 25.13 and 25.14 creates a stack class by inheriting from class `List` of Fig. 25.4 (line 9). We want the stack to have methods `Push`, `Pop`, `IsEmpty` and `Print`. Essentially, these are the methods `InsertAtFront`, `RemoveFromFront`, `IsEmpty` and `Print` of class `List`. Of course, class `List` contains other methods (such as `InsertAtBack` and `RemoveFromBack`) that we would rather not make accessible through the `public` interface of the stack. It is important to remember that all methods in the `public` interface of class `List` are also `public` methods of the derived class `StackInheritance` (Fig. 25.13).

```
1   // Fig. 25.13: StackInheritanceLibrary.cs
2   // Implementing a stack by inheriting from class List.
3   using System;
4   using LinkedListLibrary;
5
6   namespace StackInheritanceLibrary
7   {
8      // class StackInheritance inherits class List's capabilities
9      public class StackInheritance : List
10     {
11        // pass name "stack" to List constructor
12        public StackInheritance()
13           : base( "stack" )
14        {
15        } // end constructor
16
17        // place dataValue at top of stack by inserting
18        // dataValue at front of linked list
19        public void Push( object dataValue )
20        {
21           InsertAtFront(dataValue);
22        } // end method Push
23
24        // remove item from top of stack by removing
25        // item at front of linked list
26        public object Pop()
27        {
28           return RemoveFromFront();
29        } // end method Pop
30     } // end class StackInheritance
31  } // end namespace StackInheritanceLibrary
```

Fig. 25.13 | StackInheritance extends class List.

The implementation of each StackInheritance method calls the appropriate List method—method Push calls InsertAtFront, method Pop calls RemoveFromFront. Class StackInheritance does not define methods IsEmpty and Print, because StackInheritance inherits these methods from class List into StackInheritance's public interface. Note that class StackInheritance uses namespace LinkedListLibrary (Fig. 25.4); thus, the class library that defines StackInheritance must have a reference to the LinkedListLibrary class library.

StackInheritanceTest's Main method (Fig. 25.14) uses class StackInheritance to create a stack of objects called stack (line 12). Lines 15–18 define four values that will be pushed onto the stack and popped off the stack. The program pushes onto the stack (lines 21, 23, 25 and 27) a bool containing true, a char containing '$', an int containing 34567 and a string containing "hello". An infinite while loop (lines 33–38) pops the elements from the stack. When the stack is empty, method Pop throws an EmptyListException, and the program displays the exception's stack trace, which shows the program-execution stack at the time the exception occurred. The program uses method Print (inherited by StackInheritance from class List) to output the contents of the stack after each operation. Note that class StackInheritanceTest uses namespace LinkedListLibrary (Fig. 25.4) and namespace StackInheritanceLibrary (Fig. 25.13); thus, the solution for class StackInheritanceTest must have references to both class libraries.

```csharp
1   // Fig. 25.14: StackInheritanceTest.cs
2   // Testing class StackInheritance.
3   using System;
4   using StackInheritanceLibrary;
5   using LinkedListLibrary;
6
7   // demonstrate functionality of class StackInheritance
8   class StackInheritanceTest
9   {
10     static void Main( string[] args )
11     {
12        StackInheritance stack = new StackInheritance();
13
14        // create objects to store in the stack
15        bool aBoolean = true;
16        char aCharacter = '$';
17        int anInteger = 34567;
18        string aString = "hello";
19
20        // use method Push to add items to stack
21        stack.Push( aBoolean );
22        stack.Print();
23        stack.Push( aCharacter );
24        stack.Print();
25        stack.Push( anInteger );
26        stack.Print();
27        stack.Push( aString );
28        stack.Print();
29
```

Fig. 25.14 | Using class StackInheritance. (Part 1 of 2.)

```
30          // remove items from stack
31          try
32          {
33             while ( true )
34             {
35                object removedObject = stack.Pop();
36                Console.WriteLine( removedObject + " popped" );
37                stack.Print();
38             } // end while
39          } // end try
40          catch ( EmptyListException emptyListException )
41          {
42             // if exception occurs, print stack trace
43             Console.Error.WriteLine( emptyListException.StackTrace );
44          } // end catch
45       } // end Main
46    } // end class StackInheritanceTest
```

```
The stack is: True

The stack is: $ True

The stack is: 34567 $ True

The stack is: hello 34567 $ True

hello popped
The stack is: 34567 $ True

34567 popped
The stack is: $ True

$ popped
The stack is: True

True popped
Empty stack
   at LinkedListLibrary.List.RemoveFromFront()
   at StackInheritanceLibrary.StackInheritance.Pop()
   at StackInheritanceTest.StackInheritanceTest.Main(String[] args)
      in C:\examples\ch25\Fig25_14\StackInheritanceTest\
      StackInheritanceTest.cs:line 35
```

Fig. 25.14 | Using class StackInheritance. (Part 2 of 2.)

Stack Class That Contains a Reference to a List

Another way to implement a stack class is by reusing a list class through composition. The class in Fig. 25.15 uses a private object of class List (line 11) in the declaration of class StackComposition. Composition enables us to hide the methods of class List that should not be in our stack's public interface by providing public interface methods only to the required List methods. This class implements each stack method by delegating its work to an appropriate List method. StackComposition's methods call List methods InsertAtFront, RemoveFromFront, IsEmpty and Print. In this example, we do not show class StackCompositionTest, because the only difference in this example is that we change the

```
1    // Fig. 25.15: StackCompositionLibrary.cs
2    // StackComposition declaration with composed List object.
3    using System;
4    using LinkedListLibrary;
5
6    namespace StackCompositionLibrary
7    {
8       // class StackComposition encapsulates List's capabilities
9       public class StackComposition
10      {
11         private List stack;
12
13         // construct empty stack
14         public StackComposition()
15         {
16            stack = new List( "stack" );
17         } // end constructor
18
19         // add object to stack
20         public void Push( object dataValue )
21         {
22            stack.InsertAtFront( dataValue );
23         } // end method Push
24
25         // remove object from stack
26         public object Pop()
27         {
28            return stack.RemoveFromFront();
29         } // end method Pop
30
31         // determine whether stack is empty
32         public bool IsEmpty()
33         {
34            return stack.IsEmpty();
35         } // end method IsEmpty
36
37         // output stack contents
38         public void Print()
39         {
40            stack.Print();
41         } // end method Print
42      } // end class StackComposition
43   } // end namespace StackCompositionLibrary
```

Fig. 25.15 | StackComposition class encapsulates functionality of class List.

name of the stack class from StackInheritance to StackComposition. If you execute the application from the code on the CD that accompanies this book, you will see that the output is identical.

25.6 Queues

Another commonly used data structure is the queue. A queue is similar to a checkout line in a supermarket—the cashier services the person at the beginning of the line first. Other customers enter the line only at the end and wait for service. Queue nodes are removed only from the head (or front) of the queue and are inserted only at the tail (or end). For this reason, a queue is a *first-in, first-out* (*FIFO*) data structure. The insert and remove operations are known as *enqueue* and *dequeue*.

Queues have many uses in computer systems. Most computers have only a single processor, so only one application at a time can be serviced. Each application requiring processor time is placed in a queue. The application at the front of the queue is the next to receive service. Each application gradually advances to the front as the applications before it receive service.

Queues are also used to support *print spooling*. For example, a single printer might be shared by all users of a network. Many users can send print jobs to the printer, even when the printer is already busy. These print jobs are placed in a queue until the printer becomes available. A program called a *spooler* manages the queue to ensure that as each print job completes, the next print job is sent to the printer.

Information packets also wait in queues in computer networks. Each time a packet arrives at a network node, it must be routed to the next node along the path to the packet's final destination. The routing node routes one packet at a time, so additional packets are enqueued until the router can route them.

A file server in a computer network handles file-access requests from many clients throughout the network. Servers have a limited capacity to service requests from clients. When that capacity is exceeded, client requests wait in queues.

Queue Class That Inherits from List

The program of Figs. 25.16 and 25.17 creates a queue class by inheriting from a list class. We want the QueueInheritance class (Fig. 25.16) to have methods Enqueue, Dequeue, IsEmpty and Print. Essentially, these are the methods InsertAtBack, RemoveFromFront, IsEmpty and Print of class List. Of course, the list class contains other methods (such as InsertAtFront and RemoveFromBack) that we would rather not make accessible through the public interface to the queue class. Remember that all methods in the public interface of the List class are also public methods of the derived class QueueInheritance.

```
1   // Fig. 25.16: QueueInheritanceLibrary.cs
2   // Implementing a queue by inheriting from class List.
3   using System;
4   using LinkedListLibrary;
5
6   namespace QueueInheritanceLibrary
7   {
8      // class QueueInheritance inherits List's capabilities
9      public class QueueInheritance : List
10     {
11        // pass name "queue" to List constructor
12        public QueueInheritance()
13           : base( "queue" )
14        {
15        } // end constructor
16
```

Fig. 25.16 | QueueInheritance extends class List. (Part 1 of 2.)

```
17          // place dataValue at end of queue by inserting
18          // dataValue at end of linked list
19          public void Enqueue( object dataValue )
20          {
21              InsertAtBack( dataValue );
22          } // end method Enqueue
23
24          // remove item from front of queue by removing
25          // item at front of linked list
26          public object Dequeue()
27          {
28              return RemoveFromFront();
29          } // end method Dequeue
30      } // end class QueueInheritance
31  } // end namespace QueueInheritanceLibrary
```

Fig. 25.16 | QueueInheritance extends class List. (Part 2 of 2.)

The implementation of each QueueInheritance method calls the appropriate List method—method Enqueue calls InsertAtBack and method Dequeue calls RemoveFrom-Front. Calls to IsEmpty and Print invoke the base-class versions that were inherited from class List into QueueInheritance's public interface. Note that class QueueInheritance uses namespace LinkedListLibrary (Fig. 25.4); thus, the class library for QueueInher-itance must have a reference to the LinkedListLibrary class library.

Class QueueInheritanceTest's Main method (Fig. 25.17) creates a QueueInher-itance object called queue. Lines 15–18 define four values that will be enqueued and dequeued. The program enqueues (lines 21, 23, 25 and 27) a bool containing true, a char containing '$', an int containing 34567 and a string containing "hello". Note that class QueueInheritanceTest uses namespace LinkedListLibrary and namespace QueueInheritanceLibrary; thus, the solution for class StackInheritanceTest must have references to both class libraries.

```
1   // Fig. 25.17: QueueTest.cs
2   // Testing class QueueInheritance.
3   using System;
4   using QueueInheritanceLibrary;
5   using LinkedListLibrary;
6
7   // demonstrate functionality of class QueueInheritance
8   class QueueTest
9   {
10      static void Main( string[] args )
11      {
12          QueueInheritance queue = new QueueInheritance();
13
14          // create objects to store in the stack
15          bool aBoolean = true;
16          char aCharacter = '$';
17          int anInteger = 34567;
```

Fig. 25.17 | Queue created by inheritance. (Part 1 of 2.)

```
18          string aString = "hello";
19
20          // use method Enqueue to add items to queue
21          queue.Enqueue( aBoolean );
22          queue.Print();
23          queue.Enqueue( aCharacter );
24          queue.Print();
25          queue.Enqueue( anInteger );
26          queue.Print();
27          queue.Enqueue( aString );
28          queue.Print();
29
30          // use method Dequeue to remove items from queue
31          object removedObject = null;
32
33          // remove items from queue
34          try
35          {
36             while ( true )
37             {
38                removedObject = queue.Dequeue();
39                Console.WriteLine( removedObject + " dequeued" );
40                queue.Print();
41             } // end while
42          } // end try
43          catch ( EmptyListException emptyListException )
44          {
45             // if exception occurs, print stack trace
46             Console.Error.WriteLine( emptyListException.StackTrace );
47          } // end catch
48       } // end method Main
49    } // end class QueueTest
```

```
The queue is: True

The queue is: True $

The queue is: True $ 34567

The queue is: True $ 34567 hello

True dequeued
The queue is: $ 34567 hello

$ dequeued
The queue is: 34567 hello

34567 dequeued
The queue is: hello

hello dequeued
Empty queue
   at LinkedListLibrary.List.RemoveFromFront()
   at QueueInheritanceLibrary.QueueInheritance.Dequeue()
   at QueueTest.QueueTest.Main(String[] args)
      in C:\examples\ch25\Fig25_17\QueueTest.cs:line 38
```

Fig. 25.17 | Queue created by inheritance. (Part 2 of 2.)

An infinite while loop (lines 36–41) dequeues the elements from the queue in FIFO order. When there are no objects left to dequeue, method Dequeue throws an Empty-ListException, and the program displays the exception's stack trace, which shows the program execution stack at the time the exception occurred. The program uses method Print (inherited from class List) to output the contents of the queue after each operation. Note that class QueueInheritanceTest uses namespace LinkedListLibrary (Fig. 25.4) and namespace QueueInheritanceLibrary (Fig. 25.16); thus, the solution for class QueueInheritanceTest must have references to both class libraries.

25.7 Trees

Linked lists, stacks and queues are *linear data structures* (i.e., *sequences*). A *tree* is a non-linear, two-dimensional data structure with special properties. Tree nodes contain two or more links.

Basic Terminology

This section discusses *binary trees* (Fig. 25.18)—trees whose nodes all contain two links (none, one or both of which may be null). The *root node* is the first node in a tree. Each link in the root node refers to a *child*. The *left child* is the first node in the *left subtree*, and the *right child* is the first node in the *right subtree*. The children of a specific node are called *siblings*. A node with no children is called a *leaf node*. Computer scientists normally draw trees from the root node down—exactly the opposite of the way most trees grow in nature.

 Common Programming Error 25.2

Not setting to null the links in leaf nodes of a tree is a common logic error.

Binary Search Trees

In our binary tree example, we create a special binary tree called a *binary search tree*. A binary search tree (with no duplicate node values) has the characteristic that the values in

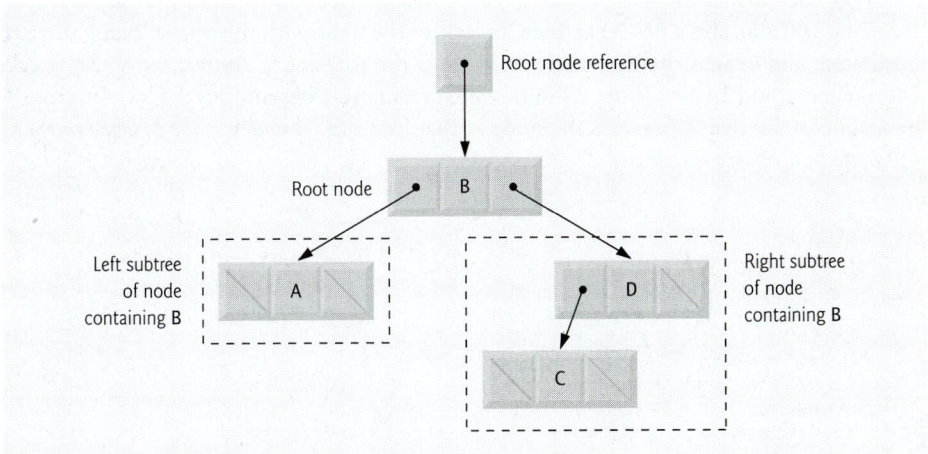

Fig. 25.18 | Binary tree graphical representation.

any left subtree are less than the value in the subtree's *parent node*, and the values in any right subtree are greater than the value in the subtree's parent node. Figure 25.19 illustrates a binary search tree with 9 integer values. Note that the shape of the binary search tree that corresponds to a set of data can depend on the order in which the values are inserted into the tree.

25.7.1 Binary Search Tree of Integer Values

The application of Figs. 25.20 and 25.21 creates a binary search tree of integers and traverses it (i.e., walks through all its nodes) in three ways—using recursive *inorder, preorder* and *postorder* traversals. The program generates 10 random numbers and inserts each into the tree. Figure 25.20 defines class Tree in namespace BinaryTreeLibrary for reuse purposes. Figure 25.21 defines class TreeTest to demonstrate class Tree's functionality. Method Main of class TreeTest instantiates an empty Tree object, then randomly generates 10 integers and inserts each value in the binary tree by calling Tree method InsertNode. The program then performs preorder, inorder and postorder traversals of the tree. We will discuss these traversals shortly.

Class TreeNode (lines 8–81 of Fig. 25.20) is a self-referential class containing three private data members—leftNode and rightNode of type TreeNode and data of type int. Initially, every TreeNode is a leaf node, so the constructor (lines 15–19) initializes references leftNode and rightNode to null. Properties LeftNode (lines 22–32), Data (lines 35–45) and RightNode (lines 48–58) provide access to a ListNode's private data members. We discuss TreeNode method Insert (lines 62–80) shortly.

Class Tree (lines 84–170 of Fig. 25.20) manipulates objects of class TreeNode. Class Tree has as private data root (line 86)—a reference to the root node of the tree. The class contains public method InsertNode (lines 97–103) to insert a new node in the tree and public methods PreorderTraversal (lines 106–109), InorderTraversal (lines 128–131) and PostorderTraversal (lines 150–153) to begin traversals of the tree. Each of these methods calls a separate recursive utility method to perform the traversal operations on the internal representation of the tree. The Tree constructor (lines 89–92) initializes root to null to indicate that the tree initially is empty.

Tree method InsertNode (lines 97–103) first determines whether the tree is empty. If so, line 100 allocates a new TreeNode, initializes the node with the integer being inserted in the tree and assigns the new node to root. If the tree is not empty, InsertNode calls TreeNode method Insert (lines 62–80), which recursively determines the location for the new node in the tree and inserts the node at that location. *A node can be inserted only as a leaf node in a binary search tree.*

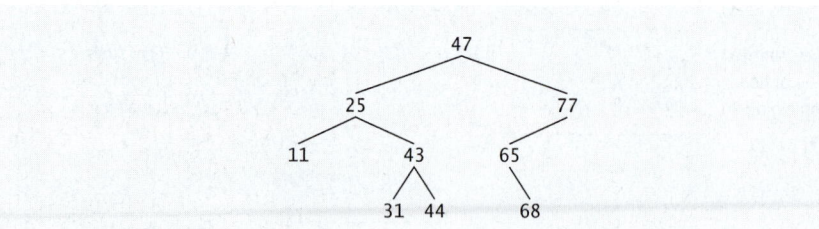

Fig. 25.19 | Binary search tree containing 9 values.

```
1    // Fig. 25.20: BinaryTreeLibrary.cs
2    // Declaration of class TreeNode and class Tree.
3    using System;
4
5    namespace BinaryTreeLibrary
6    {
7       // class TreeNode declaration
8       class TreeNode
9       {
10          private TreeNode leftNode; // link to left child
11          private int data; // data stored in node
12          private TreeNode rightNode; // link to right child
13
14          // initialize data and make this a leaf node
15          public TreeNode( int nodeData )
16          {
17             data = nodeData;
18             leftNode = rightNode = null; // node has no children
19          } // end constructor
20
21          // LeftNode property
22          public TreeNode LeftNode
23          {
24             get
25             {
26                return leftNode;
27             } // end get
28             set
29             {
30                leftNode = value;
31             } // end set
32          } // end property LeftNode
33
34          // Data property
35          public int Data
36          {
37             get
38             {
39                return data;
40             } // end get
41             set
42             {
43                data = value;
44             } // end set
45          } // end property Data
46
47          // RightNode property
48          public TreeNode RightNode
49          {
50             get
51             {
```

Fig. 25.20 | TreeNode and Tree classes for a binary search tree. (Part 1 of 4.)

```
52              return rightNode;
53          } // end get
54          set
55          {
56              rightNode = value;
57          } // end set
58      } // end property RightNode
59
60      // insert TreeNode into Tree that contains nodes;
61      // ignore duplicate values
62      public void Insert( int insertValue )
63      {
64          if ( insertValue < data ) // insert in left subtree
65          {
66              // insert new TreeNode
67              if ( leftNode == null )
68                  leftNode = new TreeNode( insertValue );
69              else // continue traversing left subtree
70                  leftNode.Insert( insertValue );
71          } // end if
72          else if ( insertValue > data ) // insert in right subtree
73          {
74              // insert new TreeNode
75              if ( rightNode == null )
76                  rightNode = new TreeNode( insertValue );
77              else // continue traversing right subtree
78                  rightNode.Insert( insertValue );
79          } // end else if
80      } // end method Insert
81  } // end class TreeNode
82
83  // class Tree declaration
84  public class Tree
85  {
86      private TreeNode root;
87
88      // construct an empty Tree of integers
89      public Tree()
90      {
91          root = null;
92      } // end constructor
93
94      // Insert a new node in the binary search tree.
95      // If the root node is null, create the root node here.
96      // Otherwise, call the insert method of class TreeNode.
97      public void InsertNode( int insertValue )
98      {
99          if ( root == null )
100             root = new TreeNode( insertValue );
101         else
102             root.Insert( insertValue );
103     } // end method InsertNode
```

Fig. 25.20 | TreeNode and Tree classes for a binary search tree. (Part 2 of 4.)

```
104
105        // begin preorder traversal
106        public void PreorderTraversal()
107        {
108            PreorderHelper( root );
109        } // end method PreorderTraversal
110
111        // recursive method to perform preorder traversal
112        private void PreorderHelper( TreeNode node )
113        {
114            if ( node == null )
115                return;
116
117            // output node data
118            Console.Write( node.Data + " " );
119
120            // traverse left subtree
121            PreorderHelper( node.LeftNode );
122
123            // traverse right subtree
124            PreorderHelper( node.RightNode );
125        } // end method PreorderHelper
126
127        // begin inorder traversal
128        public void InorderTraversal()
129        {
130            InorderHelper( root );
131        } // end method InorderTraversal
132
133        // recursive method to perform inorder traversal
134        private void InorderHelper( TreeNode node )
135        {
136            if ( node == null )
137                return;
138
139            // traverse left subtree
140            InorderHelper( node.LeftNode );
141
142            // output node data
143            Console.Write( node.Data + " " );
144
145            // traverse right subtree
146            InorderHelper( node.RightNode );
147        } // end method InorderHelper
148
149        // begin postorder traversal
150        public void PostorderTraversal()
151        {
152            PostorderHelper( root );
153        } // end method PostorderTraversal
154
```

Fig. 25.20 | TreeNode and Tree classes for a binary search tree. (Part 3 of 4.)

```
155         // recursive method to perform postorder traversal
156         private void PostorderHelper( TreeNode node )
157         {
158            if ( node == null )
159               return;
160
161            // traverse left subtree
162            PostorderHelper( node.LeftNode );
163
164            // traverse right subtree
165            PostorderHelper( node.RightNode );
166
167            // output node data
168            Console.Write( node.Data + " " );
169         } // end method PostorderHelper
170      } // end class Tree
171   } // end namespace BinaryTreeLibrary
```

Fig. 25.20 | TreeNode and Tree classes for a binary search tree. (Part 4 of 4.)

```
1    // Fig. 25.21: TreeTest.cs
2    // This program tests class Tree.
3    using System;
4    using BinaryTreeLibrary;
5
6    // class TreeTest declaration
7    public class TreeTest
8    {
9       // test class Tree
10      static void Main( string[] args )
11      {
12         Tree tree = new Tree();
13         int insertValue;
14
15         Console.WriteLine( "Inserting values: " );
16         Random random = new Random();
17
18         // insert 10 random integers from 0-99 in tree
19         for ( int i = 1; i <= 10; i++ )
20         {
21            insertValue = random.Next( 100 );
22            Console.Write( insertValue + " " );
23
24            tree.InsertNode( insertValue );
25         } // end for
26
27         // perform preorder traversal of tree
28         Console.WriteLine( "\n\nPreorder traversal" );
29         tree.PreorderTraversal();
30
```

Fig. 25.21 | Creating and traversing a binary tree. (Part 1 of 2.)

```
31        // perform inorder traversal of tree
32        Console.WriteLine( "\n\nInorder traversal" );
33        tree.InorderTraversal();
34
35        // perform postorder traversal of tree
36        Console.WriteLine( "\n\nPostorder traversal" );
37        tree.PostorderTraversal();
38     } // end method Main
39  } // end class TreeTest
```

```
Inserting values:
39 69 94 47 50 72 55 41 97 73

Preorder traversal
39 69 47 41 50 55 94 72 73 97

Inorder traversal
39 41 47 50 55 69 72 73 94 97

Postorder traversal
41 55 50 47 73 72 97 94 69 39
```

Fig. 25.21 | Creating and traversing a binary tree. (Part 2 of 2.)

TreeNode method Insert compares the value to insert with the data value in the root node. If the insert value is less than the root-node data, the program determines whether the left subtree is empty (line 67). If so, line 68 allocates a new TreeNode, initializes it with the integer being inserted and assigns the new node to reference leftNode. Otherwise, line 70 recursively calls Insert for the left subtree to insert the value into the left subtree. If the insert value is greater than the root-node data, the program determines whether the right subtree is empty (line 75). If so, line 76 allocates a new TreeNode, initializes it with the integer being inserted and assigns the new node to reference rightNode. Otherwise, line 78 recursively calls Insert for the right subtree to insert the value in the right subtree.

Methods InorderTraversal, PreorderTraversal and PostorderTraversal call helper methods InorderHelper (lines 134–147), PreorderHelper (lines 112–125) and PostorderHelper (lines 156–169), respectively, to traverse the tree and print the node values. The purpose of the helper methods in class Tree is to allow the programmer to start a traversal without needing to obtain a reference to the root node first, then call the recursive method with that reference. Methods InorderTraversal, PreorderTraversal and PostorderTraversal simply take private variable root and pass it to the appropriate helper method to initiate a traversal of the tree. For the following discussion, we use the binary search tree shown in Fig. 25.22.

Inorder Traversal Algorithm
Method InorderHelper (lines 134–147) defines the steps for an inorder traversal. Those steps are as follows:

1. If the argument is null, return immediately.

2. Traverse the left subtree with a call to InorderHelper (line 140).

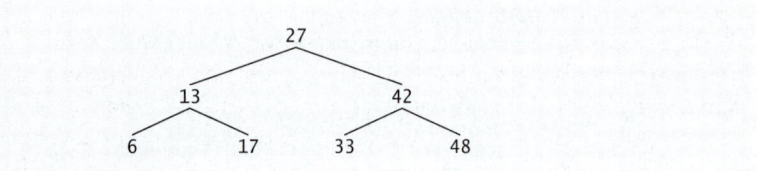

Fig. 25.22 | Binary search tree.

3. Process the value in the node (line 143).

4. Traverse the right subtree with a call to `InorderHelper` (line 146).

The inorder traversal does not process the value in a node until the values in that node's left subtree are processed. The inorder traversal of the tree in Fig. 25.22 is

        6 13 17 27 33 42 48

Note that the inorder traversal of a binary search tree prints the node values in ascending order. The process of creating a binary search tree actually sorts the data (when coupled with an inorder traversal)—thus, this process is called the *binary tree sort*.

Preorder Traversal Algorithm

Method `PreorderHelper` (lines 112–125) defines the steps for a preorder traversal. Those steps are as follows:

1. If the argument is `null`, return immediately.

2. Process the value in the node (line 118).

3. Traverse the left subtree with a call to `PreorderHelper` (line 121).

4. Traverse the right subtree with a call to `PreorderHelper` (line 124).

The preorder traversal processes the value in each node as the node is visited. After processing the value in a given node, the preorder traversal processes the values in the left subtree, then the values in the right subtree. The preorder traversal of the tree in Fig. 25.22 is

        27 13 6 17 42 33 48

Postorder Traversal Algorithm

Method `PostorderHelper` (lines 156–169) defines the steps for a postorder traversal. Those steps are as follows:

1. If the argument is `null`, return immediately.

2. Traverse the left subtree with a call to `PostorderHelper` (line 162).

3. Traverse the right subtree with a call to `PostorderHelper` (line 165).

4. Process the value in the node (line 168).

The postorder traversal processes the value in each node after the values of all that node's children are processed. The postorder traversal of the tree in Fig. 25.22 is

        6 17 13 33 48 42 27

Duplicate Elimination

The binary search tree facilitates *duplicate elimination.* While building a tree, the insertion operation recognizes attempts to insert a duplicate value, because a duplicate follows the same "go left" or "go right" decisions on each comparison as the original value did. Thus, the insertion operation eventually compares the duplicate with a node containing the same value. At this point, the insertion operation might simply discard the duplicate value.

Searching a binary tree for a value that matches a key value is fast, especially for *tightly packed* binary trees. In a tightly packed binary tree, each level contains about twice as many elements as the previous level. Figure 25.22 is a tightly packed binary tree. A binary search tree with n elements has a minimum of $\log_2 n$ levels. Thus, at most $\log_2 n$ comparisons are required either to find a match or to determine that no match exists. Searching a (tightly packed) 1000-element binary search tree requires at most 10 comparisons, because $2^{10} > 1000$. Searching a (tightly packed) 1,000,000-element binary search tree requires at most 20 comparisons, because $2^{20} > 1,000,000$.

Overview of the Binary Tree Exercises

The chapter exercises present algorithms for other binary tree operations, such as deleting an item from a binary tree and performing a *level-order traversal of a binary tree.* The level-order traversal of a binary tree visits the nodes of the tree row by row, starting at the root-node level. On each level of the tree, a level-order traversal visits the nodes from left to right.

25.7.2 Binary Search Tree of `IComparable` Objects

The binary tree example in Section 25.7.1 works nicely when all the data is of type `int`. Suppose that you want to manipulate a binary tree of double values. You could rewrite the `TreeNode` and `Tree` classes with different names and customize the classes to manipulate `double` values. Similarly, for each data type you could create customized versions of classes `TreeNode` and `Tree`. This results in a proliferation of code, which can become difficult to manage and maintain.

Ideally, we would like to define the functionality of a binary tree once and reuse that functionality for many data types. Languages like Java™ and C# provide polymorphic capabilities that enable all objects to be manipulated in a uniform manner. Using such capabilities enables us to design a more flexible data structure. The new version of C#, C# 2.0, provides these capabilities with generics (Chapter 26).

In our next example, we take advantage of C#'s polymorphic capabilities by implementing `TreeNode` and `Tree` classes that manipulate objects of any type that implements interface **`IComparable`** (namespace `System`). It is imperative that we be able to compare objects stored in a binary search, so we can determine the path to the insertion point of a new node. Classes that implement `IComparable` define method **`CompareTo`**, which compares the object that invokes the method with the object that the method receives as an argument. The method returns an `int` value less than zero if the calling object is less than the argument object, zero if the objects are equal and a positive value if the calling object is greater than the argument object. Also, both the calling and argument objects must be of the same data type; otherwise, the method throws an `ArgumentException`.

The program of Figs. 25.23 and 25.24 enhances the program from Section 25.7.1 to manipulate IComparable objects. One restriction on the new versions of classes TreeNode and Tree in Fig. 25.23 is that each Tree object can contain objects of only one data type (e.g., all strings or all doubles). If a program attempts to insert multiple data types in the same Tree object, ArgumentExceptions will occur. We modified only six lines of code in class TreeNode (lines 12, 16, 36, 63, 65 and 73) and one line of code in class Tree (line 98) to enable processing of IComparable objects. With the exception of lines 65 and 73, all other changes simply replaced the type int with the type IComparable. Lines 65 and 73 previously used the < and > operators to compare the value being inserted with the value in a given node. These lines now compare IComparable objects via the interface's CompareTo method, then test the method's return value to determine whether it is less than zero (the calling object is less than the argument object) or greater than zero (the calling object is greater than the argument object), respectively. [*Note:* If this class were written using generics, the type of data, int or IComparable, could be replaced at compile time by any other type that implements the necessary operators and methods.]

```csharp
1   // Fig. 25.23: BinaryTreeLibrary2.cs
2   // Declaration of class TreeNode and class Tree for IComparable
3   // objects.
4   using System;
5
6   namespace BinaryTreeLibrary2
7   {
8      // class TreeNode declaration
9      class TreeNode
10     {
11        private TreeNode leftNode; // link to left child
12        private IComparable data; // data stored in node
13        private TreeNode rightNode; // link to right subtree
14
15        // initialize data and make this a leaf node
16        public TreeNode( IComparable nodeData )
17        {
18           data = nodeData;
19           leftNode = rightNode = null;   // node has no children
20        } // end constructor
21
22        // LeftNode property
23        public TreeNode LeftNode
24        {
25           get
26           {
27              return leftNode;
28           } // end get
29           set
30           {
31              leftNode = value;
32           } // end set
33        } // end property LeftNode
34
```

Fig. 25.23 | TreeNode and Tree classes for manipulating IComparable objects. (Part 1 of 4.)

```
35        // Data property
36        public IComparable Data
37        {
38           get
39           {
40              return data;
41           } // end get
42           set
43           {
44              data = value;
45           } // end set
46        } // end property Data
47
48        // RightNode property
49        public TreeNode RightNode
50        {
51           get
52           {
53              return rightNode;
54           } // end get
55           set
56           {
57              rightNode = value;
58           } // end set
59        } // end property Right Node
60
61        // insert TreeNode into Tree that contains nodes;
62        // ignore duplicate values
63        public void Insert( IComparable insertValue )
64        {
65           if ( insertValue.CompareTo( data ) < 0 )
66           {
67              // insert in left subtree
68              if ( leftNode == null )
69                 leftNode = new TreeNode( insertValue );
70              else // continue traversing left subtree
71                 leftNode.Insert( insertValue );
72           } // end if
73           else if ( insertValue.CompareTo( data ) > 0 )
74           {
75              // insert in right subtree
76              if ( rightNode == null )
77                 rightNode = new TreeNode( insertValue );
78              else // continue traversing right subtree
79                 rightNode.Insert( insertValue );
80           } // end else if
81        } // end method Insert
82     } // end class TreeNode
83
84     // class Tree declaration
85     public class Tree
86     {
87        private TreeNode root;
```

Fig. 25.23 | TreeNode and Tree classes for manipulating IComparable objects. (Part 2 of 4.)

```
88
89          // construct an empty Tree of integers
90          public Tree()
91          {
92             root = null;
93          } // end constructor
94
95          // Insert a new node in the binary search tree.
96          // If the root node is null, create the root node here.
97          // Otherwise, call the insert method of class TreeNode.
98          public void InsertNode( IComparable insertValue )
99          {
100            if ( root == null )
101               root = new TreeNode( insertValue );
102            else
103               root.Insert( insertValue );
104         } // end method InsertNode
105
106         // begin preorder traversal
107         public void PreorderTraversal()
108         {
109            PreorderHelper( root );
110         } // end method PreorderTraversal
111
112         // recursive method to perform preorder traversal
113         private void PreorderHelper( TreeNode node )
114         {
115            if ( node == null )
116               return;
117
118            // output node data
119            Console.Write( node.Data + " " );
120
121            // traverse left subtree
122            PreorderHelper( node.LeftNode );
123
124            // traverse right subtree
125            PreorderHelper( node.RightNode );
126         } // end method PreorderHelper
127
128         // begin inorder traversal
129         public void InorderTraversal()
130         {
131            InorderHelper( root );
132         } // end method InorderTraversal
133
134         // recursive method to perform inorder traversal
135         private void InorderHelper( TreeNode node )
136         {
137            if ( node == null )
138               return;
139
```

Fig. 25.23 | TreeNode and Tree classes for manipulating IComparable objects. (Part 3 of 4.)

```
140         // traverse left subtree
141         InorderHelper( node.LeftNode );
142
143         // output node data
144         Console.Write( node.Data + " " );
145
146         // traverse right subtree
147         InorderHelper( node.RightNode );
148      } // end method InorderHelper
149
150      // begin postorder traversal
151      public void PostorderTraversal()
152      {
153         PostorderHelper( root );
154      } // end method PostorderTraversal
155
156      // recursive method to perform postorder traversal
157      private void PostorderHelper( TreeNode node )
158      {
159         if ( node == null )
160            return;
161
162         // traverse left subtree
163         PostorderHelper( node.LeftNode );
164
165         // traverse right subtree
166         PostorderHelper( node.RightNode );
167
168         // output node data
169         Console.Write( node.Data + " " );
170      } // end method PostorderHelper
171
172   } // end class Tree
173 } // end namespace BinaryTreeLibrary2
```

Fig. 25.23 | TreeNode and Tree classes for manipulating IComparable objects. (Part 4 of 4.)

Class TreeTest (Fig. 25.24) creates three Tree objects to store int, double and string values, all of which the .NET Framework defines as IComparable types. The program populates the trees with the values in arrays intArray (line 12), doubleArray (lines 13–14) and stringArray (lines 15–16), respectively.

```
1  // Fig. 25.24: TreeTest.cs
2  // This program tests class Tree.
3  using System;
4  using BinaryTreeLibrary2;
5
6  // class TreeTest declaration
7  public class TreeTest
8  {
```

Fig. 25.24 | Demonstrating class Tree with IComparable objects. (Part 1 of 3.)

```
 9      // test class Tree
10      static void Main( string[] args )
11      {
12         int[] intArray = { 8, 2, 4, 3, 1, 7, 5, 6 };
13         double[] doubleArray =
14            { 8.8, 2.2, 4.4, 3.3, 1.1, 7.7, 5.5, 6.6 };
15         string[] stringArray = { "eight", "two", "four",
16            "three", "one", "seven", "five", "six" };
17
18         // create int Tree
19         Tree intTree = new Tree();
20         populateTree( intArray, intTree, "intTree" );
21         traverseTree( intTree, "intTree" );
22
23         // create double Tree
24         Tree doubleTree = new Tree();
25         populateTree( doubleArray, doubleTree, "doubleTree" );
26         traverseTree( doubleTree, "doubleTree" );
27
28         // create string Tree
29         Tree stringTree = new Tree();
30         populateTree( stringArray, stringTree, "stringTree" );
31         traverseTree( stringTree, "stringTree" );
32      } // end Main
33
34      // populate Tree with array elements
35      static void populateTree( Array array, Tree tree, string name )
36      {
37         Console.WriteLine( "\nInserting into " + name + ":" );
38
39         foreach ( IComparable data in array )
40         {
41            Console.Write( data + " " );
42            tree.InsertNode( data );
43         } // end foreach
44      } // end method populateTree
45
46      // insert perform traversals
47      static void traverseTree( Tree tree, string treeType )
48      {
49         // perform preorder traveral of tree
50         Console.WriteLine( "\n\nPreorder traversal of " + treeType );
51         tree.PreorderTraversal();
52
53         // perform inorder traveral of tree
54         Console.WriteLine( "\n\nInorder traversal of " + treeType );
55         tree.InorderTraversal();
56
57         // perform postorder traveral of tree
58         Console.WriteLine( "\n\nPostorder traversal of " + treeType );
59         tree.PostorderTraversal();
60      } // end method traverseTree
61   } // end class TreeTest
```

Fig. 25.24 | Demonstrating class **Tree** with IComparable objects. (Part 2 of 3.)

```
Inserting into intTree:
8 2 4 3 1 7 5 6

Preorder traversal of intTree
8 2 1 4 3 7 5 6

Inorder traversal of intTree
1 2 3 4 5 6 7 8

Postorder traversal of intTree
1 3 6 5 7 4 2 8

Inserting into doubleTree:
8.8 2.2 4.4 3.3 1.1 7.7 5.5 6.6

Preorder traversal of doubleTree
8.8 2.2 1.1 4.4 3.3 7.7 5.5 6.6

Inorder traversal of doubleTree
1.1 2.2 3.3 4.4 5.5 6.6 7.7 8.8

Postorder traversal of doubleTree
1.1 3.3 6.6 5.5 7.7 4.4 2.2 8.8

Inserting into stringTree:
eight two four three one seven five six

Preorder traversal of stringTree
eight two four five three one seven six

Inorder traversal of stringTree
eight five four one seven six three two

Postorder traversal of stringTree
five six seven one three four two eight
```

Fig. 25.24 | Demonstrating class `Tree` with IComparable objects. (Part 3 of 3.)

Method `PopulateTree` (lines 35–44) receives as arguments an `Array` containing the initializer values for the `Tree`, a `Tree` in which the array elements will be placed and a `string` representing the `Tree` name, then inserts each `Array` element into the `Tree`. Method `TraverseTree` (lines 47–60) receives as arguments a `Tree` and a `string` representing the `Tree` name, then outputs the preorder, inorder and postorder traversals of the `Tree`. Note that the inorder traversal of each `Tree` outputs the data in sorted order regardless of the data type stored in the `Tree`. Our polymorphic implementation of class Tree invokes the appropriate data type's `CompareTo` method to determine the path to each value's insertion point by using the standard binary search tree insertion rules. Also, notice that the `Tree` of `string`s appears in alphabetical order.

25.8 Wrap-Up

In this chapter, you learned that simple types are value-type `struct`s, but can still be used anywhere `object`s are expected in a program due to boxing and unboxing conversions.

You learned that linked lists are collections of data items that are "linked together in a chain." You also learned that a program can perform insertions and deletions anywhere in a linked list (though our implementation only performed insertions and deletions at the ends of the list). We demonstrated that the stack and queue data structures are constrained versions of lists. For stacks, you saw that insertions and deletions are made only at the top—so stacks are known as last-in-first out (LIFO) data structures. For queues, which represent waiting lines, you saw that insertions are made at the tail and deletions are made from the head—so queues are known as first-in-first out (FIFO) data structures. We also presented the binary tree data structure. You saw a binary search tree that facilitated high-speed searching and sorting of data and efficient duplicate elimination. In the next chapter, we introduce generics, which allow you to declare a family of classes and methods that implement the same functionality on any type.

Summary

Section 25.1 Introduction
• Dynamic data structures can grow and shrink at execution time.

Section 25.2 Simple-Type `structs`, Boxing and Unboxing
• All simple-type names are aliases for corresponding `structs` in namespace `System`.
• Each simple type `struct` declares methods for manipulating the corresponding simple-type values.
• Each struct that represents a simple type inherits from class `ValueType` in namespace `System`.
• A boxing conversion creates an object that contains a copy of a simple-type value.
• An unboxing conversion retrieves a simple-type value from an object.

Section 25.3 Self-Referential Classes
• A self-referential class contains a data member that refers to an object of the same class type. Self-referential objects can be linked to form data structures, such as lists, queues, stacks and trees.
• Creating and maintaining dynamic data structures requires dynamic memory allocation—a program's ability to obtain more memory at execution time (to hold new nodes) and to release memory no longer needed.
• Operator new takes as an operand the type of the object being dynamically allocated, calls the appropriate constructor to initialize the object and returns a reference to the new object. If no memory is available, new throws an `OutOfMemoryException`.

Section 25.4 Linked Lists
• A linked list is a linear collection (i.e., a sequence) of self-referential class objects called nodes, connected by reference links.
• A node can contain instance variables of any type, including references to objects of other classes.
• A linked list is accessed via a reference to the first node of the list. Each subsequent node is accessed via the link-reference member stored in the previous node.
• By convention, the link reference in the last node of a list is set to `null` to mark the end of the list.

Section 25.5 Stacks
• Stacks are important in compilers and operating systems.

- A stack is a constrained version of a linked list—new nodes can be added to and removed from a stack only at the top. A stack is referred to as a last-in, first-out (LIFO) data structure.
- The primary stack operations are push and pop. Operation push adds a new node to the top of the stack. Operation pop removes a node from the top of the stack and returns the data object from the popped node.

Section 25.6 Queues
- Queues represent waiting lines. Insertions occur at the back (also referred to as the tail) of a queue, and deletions occur from the front (also referred to as the head) of a queue.
- A queue is similar to a checkout line in a supermarket: The first person in line is served first; other customers enter the line at the end and wait to be served.
- Queue nodes are removed only from the head of the queue and are inserted only at the tail of the queue. For this reason, a queue is referred to as a first-in, first-out (FIFO) data structure.
- The insert and remove operations for a queue are known as enqueue and dequeue.

Section 25.7 Trees
- Binary trees facilitate high-speed searching and sorting of data.
- Tree nodes contain two or more links.
- A binary tree is a tree whose nodes all contain two links. The root node is the first node in a tree.
- Each link in the root node refers to a child. The left child is the root node of the left subtree, and the right child is the root node of the right subtree.
- The children of a node are called siblings. A node with no children is called a leaf node.
- A binary search tree (with no duplicate node values) has the characteristic that the values in any left subtree are less than the value in that subtree's parent node, and the values in any right subtree are greater than the value in that subtree's parent node.
- A node can be inserted only as a leaf node in a binary search tree.
- An inorder traversal of a binary search tree processes the node values in ascending order.
- The process of creating a binary search tree actually sorts the data (when coupled with an inorder traversal)—hence, the term "binary tree sort."
- In a preorder traversal, the value in each node is processed as the node is visited. After the value in a given node is processed, the values in the left subtree are processed, then the values in the right subtree are processed.
- In a postorder traversal, the value in each node is processed after the node's left and right subtrees are processed.
- The binary search tree facilitates duplicate elimination. As the tree is created, attempts to insert a duplicate value are recognized because a duplicate follows the same "go left" or "go right" decisions on each comparison as the original value did. Thus, the duplicate eventually is compared with a node containing the same value. The duplicate value may simply be discarded at this point.

Terminology

ArgumentException	circular, doubly linked list
binary search tree	circular, singly linked list
binary tree	collection
binary tree sort	CompareTo method of interface IComparable
boxing conversion	data structures
child node	dequeue

doubly linked list
duplicate elimination
dynamic data structures
enqueue
first-in-first-out (FIFO) data structure
head of a queue
IComparable interface
inorder traversal
InvalidCastException
last-in-last-out (LIFO) data structure
leaf mode
left child mode
left subtree
level-order traversal of a binary tree
linear data structure
link
linked list
node
OutOfMemoryException
parent node
pop on a stack
postorder traversal

predicate method
preordered traversal
print spooling
push on a stack
queue
right child node
right subtree
root node
searching
self-referential class
sibling node
simple type
singly linked list
sorting
spooler
stack
struct
tail of a queue
top of a stack
tightly packed binary tree
unboxing conversion
ValueType class

Self-Review Exercises

25.1   State whether each of the following is *true* or *false*. If *false*, explain why.

a) In a queue, the first item to be added is the last item to be removed.

b) Trees can have no more than two child nodes per node.

c) A tree node with no children is called a leaf node.

d) Linked-list nodes are stored contiguously in memory.

e) The primary operations of the stack data structure are enqueue and dequeue.

f) Lists, stacks and queues are linear data structures.

25.2   Fill in the blanks in each of the following statements:

a) A(n) _____ class is used to define nodes that form dynamic data structures, which can grow and shrink at execution time.

b) Operator _____ allocates memory dynamically; this operator returns a reference to the allocated memory.

c) A(n) _____ is a constrained version of a linked list in which nodes can be inserted and deleted only from the start of the list; this data structure returns node values in last-in, first-out order.

d) A queue is a(n) _____ data structure, because the first nodes inserted are the first nodes removed.

e) A(n) _____ is a constrained version of a linked list in which nodes can be inserted only at the end of the list and deleted only from the start of the list.

f) A(n) _____ is a nonlinear, two-dimensional data structure that contains nodes with two or more links.

g) The nodes of a(n) _____ tree contain two link members.

h) The tree-traversal algorithm that processes the node and then processes all the nodes to its left followed by all the nodes to its right is called _____.

Answers to Self-Review Exercises

25.1   a) False. A queue is a first-in, first-out data structure—the first item added is the first item removed. b) False. In general, trees may have as many child nodes per node as is necessary. Only binary trees are restricted to no more than two child nodes per node. c) True. d) False. Linked-list nodes are logically contiguous, but they need not be stored in a physically contiguous memory space. e) False. Those are the primary operations of a queue. The primary operations of a stack are push and pop. f) True.

25.2   a) self-referential. b) new. c) stack. d) first-in, first-out (FIFO). e) queue. f) tree. g) binary. h) preorder.

Exercises

25.3   Write a program that merges two ordered list objects of integers into a single ordered list object of integers. Method Merge of class ListMerge should receive references to each of the list objects to be merged and should return a reference to the merged list object.

25.4   Write a program that inputs a line of text and uses a stack object to print the line reversed.

25.5   Write a program that uses a stack to determine whether a string is a palindrome (i.e., the string is spelled identically backward and forward). The program should ignore capitalization, spaces and punctuation.

25.6   Stacks are used by compilers in the process of evaluating expressions and in generating machine language code. In this and the next exercise, we investigate how compilers evaluate arithmetic expressions consisting only of constants, operators and parentheses.

Humans generally write expressions like 3 + 4 and 7 / 9, in which the operator (+ or / here) is written between its operands—this is called *infix notation*. Computers "prefer" *postfix notation*, in which the operator is written to the right of its two operands. The preceding infix expressions would appear in postfix notation as 3 4 + and 7 9 /, respectively.

To evaluate a complex infix expression, a compiler would first convert the expression to postfix notation, then evaluate the postfix version of the expression. Each of these algorithms requires only a single left-to-right pass of the expression. Each algorithm uses a stack object in support of its operation, and in each algorithm the stack is used for a different purpose.

In this exercise, you will write a C# version of the infix-to-postfix conversion algorithm. In the next exercise, you will write a C# version of the postfix expression evaluation algorithm. In a later exercise, you will discover that code you write in this exercise can help you implement a complete working compiler.

Write class InfixToPostfixConverter to convert an ordinary infix arithmetic expression (assume a valid expression is entered), with single-digit integers, such as

    (6 + 2) * 5 - 8 / 4

to a postfix expression. The postfix version of the preceding infix expression (note that no parentheses are needed) is

    6 2 + 5 * 8 4 / -

The program should read the expression into StringBuilder infix, then use class StackInheritance (implemented in Fig. 25.13) to help create the postfix expression in StringBuilder postfix. The algorithm for creating a postfix expression is as follows:
   a) Push a left parenthesis '(' on the stack.
   b) Append a right parenthesis ')' to the end of infix.

c) While the stack is not empty, read `infix` from left to right and do the following:

If the current character in `infix` is a digit, append it to `postfix`.

If the current character in `infix` is a left parenthesis, push it onto the stack.

If the current character in `infix` is an operator:

Pop operators (if there are any) at the top of the stack while they have equal or higher precedence than the current operator, and append the popped operators to `postfix`.

Push the current character in `infix` onto the stack.

If the current character in `infix` is a right parenthesis:

Pop operators from the top of the stack and append them to `postfix` until a left parenthesis is at the top of the stack.

Pop (and discard) the left parenthesis from the stack.

The following arithmetic operations are allowed in an expression:

+   addition
-    subtraction
*   multiplication
/   division
^   exponentiation
%   modulus

Some of the methods you may want to provide in your program follow:

a) Method `ConvertToPostfix`, which converts the infix expression to postfix notation.

b) Method `IsOperator`, which determines whether c is an operator.

c) Method `Precedence`, which determines whether the precedence of `operator1` (from the infix expression) is less than, equal to or greater than the precedence of `operator2` (from the stack). The method returns `true` if `operator1` has lower precedence than or equal precedence to `operator2`. Otherwise, `false` is returned.

25.7   Write class `PostfixEvaluator`, which evaluates a postfix expression (assume it is valid) such as

        6 2 + 5 * 8 4 / -

The program should read a postfix expression consisting of digits and operators into a `String-Builder`. Using the stack class from Exercise 25.6, the program should scan the expression and evaluate it. The algorithm (for single-digit numbers) is as follows:

a) Append a right parenthesis (`')'`) to the end of the postfix expression. When the right-parenthesis character is encountered, no further processing is necessary.

b) When the right-parenthesis character has not been encountered, read the expression from left to right.

If the current character is a digit, do the following:

Push its integer value on the stack (the integer value of a digit character is its value in the computer's character set minus the value of `'0'` in Unicode).

Otherwise, if the current character is an *operator*:

Pop the two top elements of the stack into variables x and y.

Calculate y *operator* x.

Push the result of the calculation onto the stack.

c) When the right parenthesis is encountered in the expression, pop the top value of the stack. This is the result of the postfix expression.

[*Note:* In part (b) above (based on the sample expression at the beginning of this exercises), if the operator is `'/'`, the top of the stack is 4 and the next element in the stack is 8, then pop 4 into x, pop 8 into y, evaluate 8 / 4 and push the result, 2, back on the stack. This note also applies to operator `'-'`.] The arithmetic operations allowed in an expression are:

+   addition
-   subtraction
*   multiplication
/   division
^   exponentiation
%   modulus

You may want to provide the following methods:

    a) Method `EvaluatePostfixExpression`, which evaluates the postfix expression.
    b) Method `Calculate`, which evaluates the expression op1 *operator* op2.

25.8 (*Binary Tree Delete*) In this exercise, we discuss deleting items from binary search trees. The deletion algorithm is not as straightforward as the insertion algorithm. There are three cases that are encountered when deleting an item—the item is contained in a leaf node (i.e., it has no children), the item is contained in a node that has one child or the item is contained in a node that has two children.

If the item to be deleted is contained in a leaf node, the node is deleted and the reference in the parent node is set to `null`.

If the item to be deleted is contained in a node with one child, the reference in the parent node is set to reference the child node and the node containing the data item is deleted. This causes the child node to take the place of the deleted node in the tree.

The last case is the most difficult. When a node with two children is deleted, another node in the tree must take its place. However, the reference in the parent node cannot be assigned to reference one of the children of the node to be deleted. In most cases, the resulting binary search tree would not adhere to the following characteristic of binary search trees (with no duplicate values): *The values in any left subtree are less than the value in the parent node, and the values in any right subtree are greater than the value in the parent node.*

Which node is used as a *replacement node* to maintain this characteristic—the node containing the largest value in the tree less than the value in the node being deleted or the node containing the smallest value in the tree greater than the value in the node being deleted? Let us consider the node with the smaller value. In a binary search tree, the largest value less than a parent's value is located in the left subtree of the parent node and is guaranteed to be contained in the rightmost node of the subtree. This node is located by walking down the left subtree to the right until the reference to the right child of the current node is null. We are now referencing the replacement node, which is either a leaf node or a node with one child to its left. If the replacement node is a leaf node, the steps to perform the deletion are as follows:

    a) Store the reference to the node to be deleted in a temporary reference variable.
    b) Set the reference in the parent of the node being deleted to reference the replacement node.
    c) Set the reference in the parent of the replacement node to `null`.
    d) Set the reference to the right subtree in the replacement node to reference the right subtree of the node to be deleted.
    e) Set the reference to the left subtree in the replacement node to reference the left subtree of the node to be deleted.

The deletion steps for a replacement node with a left child are similar to those for a replacement node with no children, but the algorithm also must move the child into the replacement node's position in the tree. If the replacement node is a node with a left child, the steps to perform the deletion are as follows:

    a) Store the reference to the node to be deleted in a temporary reference variable.
    b) Set the reference in the parent of the node being deleted to reference the replacement node.
    c) Set the reference in the parent of the replacement node reference to the left child of the replacement node.

d) Set the reference to the right subtree in the replacement node reference to the right subtree of the node to be deleted.

e) Set the reference to the left subtree in the replacement node to reference the left subtree of the node to be deleted.

Write method DeleteNode, which takes as its argument the value of the node to be deleted. Method DeleteNode should locate in the tree the node containing the value to be deleted and use the algorithms discussed here to delete the node. If the value is not found in the tree, the method should print a message that indicates whether the value is deleted. Modify the program of Fig. 25.21 to use this method. After deleting an item, call methods InorderTraversal, PreorderTraversal and PostorderTraversal to confirm that the delete operation was performed correctly.

25.9 (*Level-Order Binary Tree Traversal*) The program of Fig. 25.21 illustrated three recursive methods of traversing a binary tree—inorder, preorder, and postorder traversals. This exercise presents the *level-order traversal* of a binary tree, in which the node values are printed level-by-level, starting at the root-node level. The nodes on each level are printed from left to right. The level-order traversal is not a recursive algorithm. It uses a queue object to control the output of the nodes. The algorithm is as follows:

a) Insert the root node in the queue.

b) While there are nodes left in the queue, do the following:

Get the next node in the queue.

Print the node's value.

If the reference to the left child of the node is not null:

Insert the left child node in the queue.

If the reference to the right child of the node is not null:

Insert the right child node in the queue.

Write method LevelOrderTraversal to perform a level-order traversal of a binary tree object. Modify the program of Fig. 25.21 to use this method. [*Note:* You also will need to use the queue-processing methods of Fig. 25.16 in this program.]

Generics

OBJECTIVES

In this chapter you will learn:

- To create generic methods that perform identical tasks on arguments of different types.
- To create a generic **Stack** class that can be used to store objects of any class or interface type.
- To understand how to overload generic methods with non-generic methods or with other generic methods.
- To understand the **new()** constraint of a type parameter.
- To apply multiple constraints to a type parameter.
- The relationship between generics and inheritance.

26.1 Introduction

In Chapter 25, we presented data structures that stored and manipulated `object` references. You could store any `object` in our data structures. One inconvenient aspect of storing `object` references occurs when retrieving them from a collection. An application normally needs to process specific types of objects. As a result, the `object` references obtained from a collection typically need to be downcast to an appropriate type to allow the application to process the objects correctly. In addition, data of value types (e.g., `int` and `double`) must be boxed to be manipulated with `object` references, which increases the overhead of processing such data. Also, processing all data as type `object` limits the C# compiler's ability to perform type checking.

Though we can easily create data structures that manipulate any type of data as `objects` (as we did in Chapter 25), it would be nice if we could detect type mismatches at compile time—this is known as *compile-time type safety*. For example, if a `Stack` should store only `int` values, attempting to push a `string` onto that `Stack` should cause a compile-time error. Similarly, a `Sort` method should be able to compare elements that are all guaranteed to have the same type. If we create type-specific versions of class `Stack` class and method `Sort`, the C# compiler would certainly be able to ensure compile-time type safety. However, this would require that we create many copies of the same basic code.

This chapter discusses one of C#'s newest features—*generics*—which provides the means to create the general models mentioned above. *Generic methods* enable you to specify, with a single method declaration, a set of related methods. *Generic classes* enable you to specify, with a single class declaration, a set of related classes. Similarly, *generic interfaces* enable you to specify, with a single interface declaration, a set of related interfaces. Generics provide compile-time type safety. [*Note:* You can also implement generic `structs` and `delegates`. For more information, see the C# language specification.]

We can write a generic method for sorting an array of objects, then invoke the generic method separately with an `int` array, a `double` array, a `string` array and so on, to sort each different type of array. The compiler performs *type checking* to ensure that the array passed to the sorting method contains only elements of the same type. We can write a single generic `Stack` class that manipulates a stack of objects, then instantiate `Stack` objects for a stack of `int`s, a stack of `double`s, a stack of `string`s and so on. The compiler performs type checking to ensure that the `Stack` stores only elements of the same type.

This chapter presents examples of generic methods and generic classes. It also considers the relationships between generics and other C# features, such as overloading and inheritance. Chapter 27, Collections, discusses the .NET Framework's generic and non-generic collections classes. A collection is a data structure that maintains a group of related objects or values. The .NET Framework collection classes use generics to allow you to specify the exact types of object that a particular collection will store.

26.2 Motivation for Generic Methods

Overloaded methods are often used to perform similar operations on different types of data. To motivate generic methods, let's begin with an example (Fig. 26.1) that contains three overloaded PrintArray methods (lines 23–29, lines 32–38 and lines 41–47). These methods display the elements of an int array, a double array and a char array, respectively. Soon, we will reimplement this program more concisely and elegantly using a single generic method.

```csharp
 1   // Fig. 26.1: OverloadedMethods.cs
 2   // Using overloaded methods to print arrays of different types.
 3   using System;
 4
 5   class OverloadedMethods
 6   {
 7      static void Main( string[] args )
 8      {
 9         // create arrays of int, double and char
10         int[] intArray = { 1, 2, 3, 4, 5, 6 };
11         double[] doubleArray = { 1.1, 2.2, 3.3, 4.4, 5.5, 6.6, 7.7 };
12         char[] charArray = { 'H', 'E', 'L', 'L', 'O' };
13
14         Console.WriteLine( "Array intArray contains:" );
15         PrintArray( intArray ); // pass an int array argument
16         Console.WriteLine( "Array doubleArray contains:" );
17         PrintArray( doubleArray ); // pass a double array argument
18         Console.WriteLine( "Array charArray contains:" );
19         PrintArray( charArray ); // pass a char array argument
20      } // end Main
21
22      // output int array
23      static void PrintArray( int[] inputArray )
24      {
25         foreach ( int element in inputArray )
26            Console.Write( element + " " );
27
28         Console.WriteLine( "\n" );
29      } // end method PrintArray
30
31      // output double array
32      static void PrintArray( double[] inputArray )
33      {
34         foreach ( double element in inputArray )
35            Console.Write( element + " " );
36
```

Fig. 26.1 | Displaying arrays of different types using overloaded methods. (Part 1 of 2.)

```
37          Console.WriteLine( "\n" );
38      } // end method PrintArray
39
40      // output char array
41      static void PrintArray( char[] inputArray )
42      {
43          foreach ( char element in inputArray )
44              Console.Write( element + " " );
45
46          Console.WriteLine( "\n" );
47      } // end method PrintArray
48  } // end class OverloadedMethods
```

```
Array intArray contains:
1 2 3 4 5 6

Array doubleArray contains:
1.1 2.2 3.3 4.4 5.5 6.6 7.7

Array charArray contains:
H E L L O
```

Fig. 26.1 | Displaying arrays of different types using overloaded methods. (Part 2 of 2.)

The program begins by declaring and initializing three arrays—six-element int array intArray (line 10), seven-element double array doubleArray (line 11) and five-element char array charArray (line 12). Then, lines 14–19 output the arrays.

When the compiler encounters a method call, it attempts to locate a method declaration that has the same method name and parameters that match the argument types in the method call. In this example, each PrintArray call exactly matches one of the PrintArray method declarations. For example, line 15 calls PrintArray with intArray as its argument. At compile time, the compiler determines argument intArray's type (i.e., int[]), attempts to locate a method named PrintArray that specifies a single int[] parameter (which it finds at lines 23–29) and sets up a call to that method. Similarly, when the compiler encounters the PrintArray call at line 17, it determines argument doubleArray's type (i.e., double[]), then attempts to locate a method named PrintArray that specifies a single double[] parameter (which it finds at lines 32–38) and sets up a call to that method. Finally, when the compiler encounters the PrintArray call at line 19, it determines argument charArray's type (i.e., char[]), then attempts to locate a method named PrintArray that specifies a single char[] parameter (which it finds at lines 41–47) and sets up a call to that method.

Study each PrintArray method. Note that the array element type (int, double or char) appears in two locations in each method—the method header (lines 23, 32 and 41) and the foreach statement header (lines 25, 34 and 43). If we replace the element types in each method with a generic name—we chose E to represent the "element" type—then all three methods would look like the one in Fig. 26.2. It appears that if we can replace the array element type in each of the three methods with a single "generic type parameter," then we should be able to declare one PrintArray method that can display the elements of *any* array. The method in Fig. 26.2 will not compile, because its syntax is not correct. We declare a generic PrintArray method with the proper syntax in Fig. 26.3.

```
1   static void PrintArray( E[] inputArray )
2   {
3       foreach ( E element in inputArray )
4           Console.Write( element + " " );
5
6       Console.WriteLine( "\n" );
7   } // end method PrintArray
```

Fig. 26.2 | PrintArray method in which actual type names are replaced by convention with the generic name E.

26.3 Generic Method Implementation

If the operations performed by several overloaded methods are identical for each argument type, the overloaded methods can be more compactly and conveniently coded using a generic method. You can write a single generic method declaration that can be called at different times with arguments of different types. Based on the types of the arguments passed to the generic method, the compiler handles each method call appropriately.

Figure 26.3 reimplements the application of Fig. 26.1 using a generic PrintArray method (lines 24–30). Note that the PrintArray method calls in lines 16, 18 and 20 are identical to those of Fig. 26.1, the outputs of the two applications are identical and the code in Fig. 26.3 is 17 lines shorter than the code in Fig. 26.1. As illustrated in Fig. 26.3, generics enable us to create and test our code once, then reuse that code for many different types of data. This demonstrates the expressive power of generics.

Line 24 begins method PrintArray's declaration. All generic method declarations have a *type parameter list* delimited by angle brackets *(< E > in this example)* that follows

```
1    // Fig. 26.3: GenericMethod.cs
2    // Using overloaded methods to print arrays of different types.
3    using System;
4    using System.Collections.Generic;
5
6    class GenericMethod
7    {
8        static void Main( string[] args )
9        {
10           // create arrays of int, double and char
11           int[] intArray = { 1, 2, 3, 4, 5, 6 };
12           double[] doubleArray = { 1.1, 2.2, 3.3, 4.4, 5.5, 6.6, 7.7 };
13           char[] charArray = { 'H', 'E', 'L', 'L', 'O' };
14
15           Console.WriteLine( "Array intArray contains:" );
16           PrintArray( intArray ); // pass an int array argument
17           Console.WriteLine( "Array doubleArray contains:" );
18           PrintArray( doubleArray ); // pass a double array argument
19           Console.WriteLine( "Array charArray contains:" );
20           PrintArray( charArray ); // pass a char array argument
21       } // end Main
22
```

Fig. 26.3 | Printing array elements using generic method PrintArray. (Part 1 of 2.)

```
23      // output array of all types
24      static void PrintArray< E >( E[] inputArray )
25      {
26          foreach ( E element in inputArray )
27              Console.Write( element + " " );
28
29          Console.WriteLine( "\n" );
30      } // end method PrintArray
31  } // end class GenericMethod
```

```
Array intArray contains:
1 2 3 4 5 6

Array doubleArray contains:
1.1 2.2 3.3 4.4 5.5 6.6 7.7

Array charArray contains:
H E L L O
```

Fig. 26.3 | Printing array elements using generic method `PrintArray`. (Part 2 of 2.)

the method's name. Each type parameter list contains one or more *type parameters,* separated by commas. A type parameter is an identifier that is used in place of actual type names. The type parameters can be used to declare the return type, the parameter types and the local variable types in a generic method declaration; the type parameters act as placeholders for the types of the arguments passed to the generic method. A generic method's body is declared like that of any other method. Note that the type parameter names throughout the method declaration must match those declared in the type parameter list. For example, line 26 declares `element` in the `foreach` statement as type E, which matches the type parameter (E) declared in line 24. Also, a type parameter can be declared only once in the type parameter list but can appear more than once in the method's parameter list. Type parameter names need not be unique among different generic methods.

Common Programming Error 26.1

If you forget to include the type parameter list when declaring a generic method, the compiler will not recognize the type parameter names when they are encountered in the method. This results in compilation errors.

Method `PrintArray`'s type parameter list (line 24) declares type parameter E as the placeholder for the array element type that `PrintArray` will output. Note that E appears in the parameter list as the array element type (line 24). The `foreach` statement header (line 26) also uses E as the `element` type. These are the same two locations where the overloaded `PrintArray` methods of Fig. 26.1 specified `int`, `double` or `char` as the array element type. The remainder of `PrintArray` is identical to the version presented in Fig. 26.1.

Good Programming Practice 26.1

It is recommended that type parameters be specified as individual capital letters. Typically, a type parameter that represents the type of an element in an array (or other collection) is named E for "element" or T for "type."

As in Fig. 26.1, the program of Fig. 26.3 begins by declaring and initializing six-element `int` array `intArray` (line 11), seven-element `double` array `doubleArray` (line 12) and five-element char array charArray (line 13). Then each array is output by calling Print-Array (lines 16, 18 and 20)—once with argument intArray, once with argument doubleArray and once with argument charArray.

When the compiler encounters a method call such as line 16, it analyzes the set of methods (both non-generic and generic) that might match the method call looking for a method that matches the call exactly. If there are no exact matches, the compiler picks the best match. If there are no matching methods, or if there is more than one best match, the compiler generates an error. The complete details of method call resolution can be found in Section 14.5.5.1 of the Ecma C# Language Specification

```
www.ecma-international.org/publications/files/ECMA-ST/Ecma-334.pdf
```

or Section 20.9.7 of the Microsoft C# Language Specification 2.0

```
msdn.microsoft.com/vcsharp/programming/language/
```

In the case of line 16, the compiler determines that an exact match occurs if the type parameter E in lines 24 and 26 of method PrintArray's declaration is replaced with the type of the elements in the method call's argument intArray (i.e., int). Then, the compiler sets up a call to PrintArray with the int as the *type argument* for the type parameter E. This is known as the *type inferencing* process. The same process is repeated for the calls to method PrintArray in lines 18 and 20.

Common Programming Error 26.2

If the compiler cannot find a single non-generic or generic method declaration that is a best match for a method call, or if there are multiple best matches, a compilation error occurs.

You can also use *explicit type arguments* to indicate the exact type that should be used to call a generic function. For example, line 16 could be written as

```
PrintArray< int >( intArray ); // pass an int array argument
```

The preceding method call explicitly provides the type argument (int) that should be used to replace type parameter E in lines 24 and 26 of the PrintArray method's declaration.

The compiler also determines whether the operations performed on the method's type parameters can be applied to elements of the type stored in the array argument. The only operation performed on the array elements in this example is to output the string representation of the elements. Line 27 performs an implicit conversion for every value type array element and an implicit ToString call on every reference type array element. Since all objects have a ToString method, the compiler is satisfied that line 27 performs a valid operation for any array element.

By declaring PrintArray as a generic method in Fig. 26.3, we eliminated the need for the overloaded methods of Fig. 26.1, saving 17 lines of code and creating a reusable method that can output the string representations of the elements in *any* array, not just arrays of int, double or char elements.

26.4 Type Constraints

In this section, we present a generic Maximum method that determines and returns the largest of its three arguments (all of the same type). The generic method in this example uses the type parameter to declare both the method's return type and its parameters. Normally, when comparing values to determine which one is greater, you would use the > operator. However, this operator is not overloaded for use with every type that is built into the FCL or that might be defined by extending those types. Generic code is restricted to performing operations that are guaranteed to work for every possible type. Thus, an expression like variable1 < variable2 is not allowed unless the compiler can ensure that the operator < is provided for every type that will ever be used in the generic code. Similarly, you cannot call a method on a generic-type variable unless the compiler can ensure that all types that will ever be used in the generic code support that method.

IComparable< E > Interface

It is possible to compare two objects of the same type if that type implements the generic interface IComparable< T > (of namespace System). A benefit of implementing interface IComparable< T > is that IComparable< T > objects can be used with the sorting and searching methods of classes in the System.Collections.Generic namespace—we discuss those methods in Chapter 27, Collections. The structures in the FCL that correspond to the simple types all implement this interface. For example, the structure for simple type double is Double and the structure for simple type int is Int32—both Double and Int32 implement the IComparable interface. Types that implement IComparable< T > must declare a CompareTo method for comparing objects. For example, if we have two ints, int1 and int2, they can be compared with the expression:

```
int1.CompareTo( int2 )
```

Method CompareTo must return 0 if the objects are equal, a negative integer if int1 is less than int2 or a positive integer if int1 is greater than int2. It is the responsibility of the programmer who declares a type that implements IComparable< T > to declare method CompareTo such that it compares the contents of two objects of that type and returns the appropriate result.

Specifying Type Constraints

Even though IComparable objects can be compared, they cannot be used with generic code by default, because not all types implement interface IComparable< T >. However, we can restrict the types that can be used with a generic method or class to ensure that they meet certain requirements. This feature—known as a ***type constraint***—restricts the type of the argument supplied to a particular type parameter. Figure 26.4 declares method Maximum (lines 20–33) with a type constraint that requires each of the method's arguments to be of type IComparable< T >. This restriction is important because not all objects can be compared. However, all IComparable< T > objects are guaranteed to have a CompareTo method that can be used in method Maximum to determine the largest of its three arguments.

Generic method Maximum uses type parameter T as the return type of the method (line 20), as the type of method parameters x, y and z (line 20), and as the type of local variable max (line 22). Generic method Maximum's ***where*** clause (after the parameter list in line 20) specifies the type constraint for type parameter T. In this case, the clause where T : IComparable< T > indicates that this method requires the type arguments to implement interface IComparable< T >. If no type constraint is specified, the default type constraint is object.

```
 1    // Fig 26.4: MaximumTest.cs
 2    // Generic method maximum returns the largest of three objects.
 3    using System;
 4
 5    class MaximumTest
 6    {
 7       static void Main( string[] args )
 8       {
 9          Console.WriteLine( "Maximum of {0}, {1} and {2} is {3}\n",
10             3, 4, 5, Maximum( 3, 4, 5 ) );
11          Console.WriteLine( "Maximum of {0}, {1} and {2} is {3}\n",
12             6.6, 8.8, 7.7, Maximum( 6.6, 8.8, 7.7 ) );
13          Console.WriteLine( "Maximum of {0}, {1} and {2} is {3}\n",
14             "pear", "apple", "orange",
15             Maximum( "pear", "apple", "orange" ) );
16       } // end Main
17
18       // generic function determines the
19       // largest of the IComparable objects
20       static T Maximum< T >( T x, T y, T z ) where T : IComparable < T >
21       {
22          T max = x; // assume x is initially the largest
23
24          // compare y with max
25          if ( y.CompareTo( max ) > 0 )
26             max = y; // y is the largest so far
27
28          // compare z with max
29          if ( z.CompareTo( max ) > 0 )
30             max = z; // z is the largest
31
32          return max; // return largest object
33       } // end method Maximum
34    } // end class MaximumTest
```

```
Maximum of 3, 4 and 5 is 5

Maximum of 6.6, 8.8 and 7.7 is 8.8

Maximum of pear, apple and orange is pear
```

Fig. 26.4 | Generic method Maximum with a type constraint on its type parameter.

C# provides several kinds of type constraints. A *class constraint* indicates that the type argument must be an object of a specific base class or one of its subclasses. An *interface constraint* indicates that the type argument's class must implement a specific interface. The type constraint in line 20 is an interface constraint, because IComparable< T > is an interface. You can specify that the type argument must be a reference type or a value type by using the *reference type constraint* (**class**) or the *value type constraint* (**struct**), respectively. Finally, you can specify a *constructor constraint*—**new()**—to indicate that the generic code can use operator new to create new objects of the type represented by the type parameter. If a type parameter is specified with a constructor constraint, the type argument's class must provide `public` a parameterless or default constructor to ensure that objects of the class can be created without passing constructor arguments; otherwise, a compilation error occurs.

It is possible to apply *multiple constraints* to a type parameter. To do so, simply provide a comma-separated list of constraints in the `where` clause. If you have a class constraint, reference type constraint or value type constraint, it must be listed first—only one of these types of constraints can be used for each type parameter. Interface constraints (if any) are listed next. The constructor constraint is listed last (if there is one).

Analyzing the Code

Method `Maximum` assumes that its first argument (x) is the largest and assigns it to local variable max (line 22). Next, the `if` statement at lines 25–26 determines whether y is greater than max. The condition invokes y's `CompareTo` method with the expression y.`CompareTo( max )`. If y is greater than max, then y is assigned to variable max (line 26). Similarly, the statement at lines 29–30 determines whether z is greater than max. If so, line 30 assigns z to max. Then, line 32 returns max to the caller.

In `Main` (lines 7–16), line 10 calls `Maximum` with the integers 3, 4 and 5. Generic method `Maximum` is a match for this call, but its arguments must implement interface `IComparable< T >` to ensure that they can be compared. Type `int` is a synonym for `struct` `Int32`, which implements interface `IComparable< int >`. Thus, `int`s (and other simple types) are valid arguments to method `Maximum`.

Line 12 passes three `double` arguments to `Maximum`. Again, this is allowed because `double` is a synonym for the `Double` `struct`, which implements `IComparable< double >`. Line 15 passes `Maximum` three `string`s, which are also `IComparable< string >` objects. Note that we intentionally placed the largest value in a different position in each method call (lines 10, 12 and 15) to show that the generic method always finds the maximum value, regardless of its position in the argument list and regardless of the inferred type argument.

26.5 Overloading Generic Methods

A generic method may be *overloaded*. A class can provide two or more generic methods with the same name but different method parameters. For example, we could provide a second version of generic method `PrintArray` (Fig. 26.3) with the additional parameters `lowIndex` and `highIndex` that specify the portion of the array to output (see Exercise 26.8). A generic method can also be overloaded by another generic method with the same method name and a different number of type parameters, or by a generic method with different numbers of type parameters and method parameters.

A generic method can be overloaded by non-generic methods that have the same method name and number of parameters. When the compiler encounters a method call, it searches for the method declaration that most precisely matches the method name and the argument types specified in the call. For example, generic method `PrintArray` of Fig. 26.3 could be overloaded with a version specific to `string`s that outputs the `string`s in neat, tabular format (see Exercise 26.9). If the compiler cannot match a method call to either a non-generic method or a generic method, or if there is ambiguity due to multiple possible matches, the compiler generates an error. Generic methods can also be overloaded by non-generic methods that have the same method name but a different number of method parameters.

26.6 Generic Classes

The concept of a data structure (e.g., a stack), that contains data elements can be understood independently of the element type it manipulates. A generic class provides a means for describing a class in a type-independent manner. We can then instantiate type-specific objects of the generic class. This capability is an opportunity for software reusability.

Once you have a generic class, you can use a simple, concise notation to indicate the actual type(s) that should be used in place of the class's type parameter(s). At compilation time, the compiler ensures the type safety of your code, and the runtime system replaces type parameters with actual arguments to enable your client code to interact with the generic class.

One generic Stack class, for example, could be the basis for creating many Stack classes (e.g., "Stack of double," "Stack of int," "Stack of char," "Stack of Employee"). Figure 26.5 presents a generic Stack class declaration. A generic class declaration is similar to a non-generic class declaration, except that the class name is followed by a type parameter list (line 5) and, in this case, a constraint on its type parameter (which we will discuss shortly). Type parameter E represents the element type the Stack will manipulate. As with generic methods, the type parameter list of a generic class can have one or more type parameters separated by commas. (You will create a generic class with two type parameters in Exercise 26.11.) Type parameter E is used throughout the Stack class declaration (Fig. 26.5) to represent the element type. Class Stack declares variable elements as an array of type E (line 8). This array (created at line 20 or 22) will store the Stack's elements. [*Note:* This example implements a Stack as an array. As you have seen in Chapter 25, Data Structures, Stacks also are commonly implemented as linked lists.]

```
1   // Fig. 26.5: Stack.cs
2   // Generic class Stack
3   using System;
4
5   class Stack< E >
6   {
7      private int top; // location of the top element
8      private E[] elements; // array that stores Stack elements
9
10     // parameterless constructor creates a Stack of the default size
11     public Stack() : this( 10 ) // default stack size
12     {
13        // empty constructor; calls constructor at line 17 to perform init
14     } // end Stack constructor
15
16     // constructor creates a Stack of the specified number of elements
17     public Stack( int stackSize )
18     {
19        if ( stackSize > 0 ) // validate stackSize
20           elements = new E[ stackSize ]; // create stackSize elements
21        else
22           elements = new E[ 10 ]; // create 10 elements
23
```

Fig. 26.5 | Generic class Stack declaration. (Part 1 of 2.)

```
24          top = -1; // Stack initially empty
25      } // end Stack constructor
26
27      // push element onto the Stack; if successful, return true
28      // otherwise, throw FullStackException
29      public void Push( E pushValue )
30      {
31          if ( top == elements.Length - 1 ) // Stack is full
32              throw new FullStackException( String.Format(
33                  "Stack is full, cannot push {0}", pushValue ) );
34
35          top++; // increment top
36          elements[ top ] = pushValue; // place pushValue on Stack
37      } // end method Push
38
39      // return the top element if not empty
40      // else throw EmptyStackException
41      public E Pop()
42      {
43          if ( top == -1 ) // Stack is empty
44              throw new EmptyStackException( "Stack is empty, cannot pop" );
45
46          top--; // decrement top
47          return elements[ top + 1 ]; // return top value
48      } // end method Pop
49  } // end class Stack
```

Fig. 26.5 | Generic class `Stack` declaration. (Part 2 of 2.)

Class `Stack` has two constructors. The parameterless constructor (lines 11–14) passes the default stack size (10) to the one-argument constructor, using the syntax `this` (line 11) to invoke another constructor in the same class. The one-argument constructor (lines 17–25) validates the `stackSize` argument and creates an array of the specified `stackSize` (if it is greater than 0) or an array of 10 elements, otherwise.

Method `Push` (lines 29–37) first determines whether an attempt is being made to push an element onto a full `Stack`. If so, lines 32–33 throw a `FullStackException` (declared in Fig. 26.6). If the `Stack` is not full, line 35 increments the `top` counter to indicate the new top position, and line 36 places the argument in that location of array `elements`.

Method `Pop` (lines 41–48) first determines whether an attempt is being made to pop an element from an empty `Stack`. If so, line 44 throws an `EmptyStackException` (declared in Fig. 26.7). Otherwise, line 46 decrements the `top` counter to indicate the new top position, and line 47 returns the original top element of the `Stack`.

Classes `FullStackException` (Fig. 26.6) and `EmptyStackException` (Fig. 26.7) each provide a parameterless constructor and a one-argument constructor of exception classes (as discussed in Section 12.8). The parameterless constructor sets the default error message, and the one-argument constructor sets a custom error message.

As with generic methods, when a generic class is compiled, the compiler performs type checking on the class's type parameters to ensure that they can be used with the code in the generic class. The constraints determine the operations that can be performed on the type parameters. The runtime system replaces the type parameters with the actual types at

```
1    // Fig. 26.6: FullStackException.cs
2    // Indicates a stack is full.
3    using System;
4
5    class FullStackException : ApplicationException
6    {
7       // parameterless constructor
8       public FullStackException() : base( "Stack is full" )
9       {
10         // empty constructor
11      } // end FullStackException constructor
12
13      // one-parameter constructor
14      public FullStackException( string exception ) : base( exception )
15      {
16         // empty constructor
17      } // end FullStackException constructor
18   } // end class FullStackException
```

Fig. 26.6 | FullStackException class declaration.

```
1    // Fig. 26.7: EmptyStackException.cs
2    // Indicates a stack is empty
3    using System;
4
5    class EmptyStackException : ApplicationException
6    {
7       // parameterless constructor
8       public EmptyStackException() : base( "Stack is empty" )
9       {
10         // empty constructor
11      } // end EmptyStackException constructor
12
13      // one-parameter constructor
14      public EmptyStackException( string exception ) : base( exception )
15      {
16         // empty constructor
17      } // end EmptyStackException constructor
18   } // end class EmptyStackException
```

Fig. 26.7 | EmptyStackException class declaration.

runtime. For class Stack (Fig. 26.5), no type constraint is specified, so the default type constraint, object, is used. The scope of a generic class's type parameter is the entire class.

Now, let's consider an application (Fig. 26.8) that uses the Stack generic class. Lines 13–14 declare variables of type Stack< double > (pronounced "Stack of double") and Stack< int > (pronounced "Stack of int"). The types double and int are the Stack's type arguments. The compiler replaces the type parameters in the generic class so that the compiler can perform type checking. Method Main instantiates objects doubleStack of size 5 (line 18) and intStack of size 10 (line 19), then calls methods TestPushDouble (lines 28–48), TestPopDouble (lines 51–73), TestPushInt (lines 76–96) and TestPopInt (lines 99–121) to manipulate the two Stacks in this example.

```
 1    // Fig. 26.8: StackTest.cs
 2    // Stack generic class test program.
 3    using System;
 4
 5    class StackTest
 6    {
 7       // create arrays of doubles and ints
 8       static double[] doubleElements =
 9          new double[]{ 1.1, 2.2, 3.3, 4.4, 5.5, 6.6 };
10       static int[] intElements =
11          new int[]{ 1, 2, 3, 4, 5, 6, 7, 8, 9, 10, 11 };
12
13       static Stack< double > doubleStack; // stack stores double objects
14       static Stack< int > intStack; // stack stores int objects
15
16       static void Main( string[] args )
17       {
18          doubleStack = new Stack< double >( 5 ); // Stack of doubles
19          intStack = new Stack< int >( 10 ); // Stack of ints
20
21          TestPushDouble(); // push doubles onto doubleStack
22          TestPopDouble(); // pop doubles from doubleStack
23          TestPushInt(); // push ints onto intStack
24          TestPopInt(); // pop ints from intStack
25       } // end Main
26
27       // test Push method with doubleStack
28       static void TestPushDouble()
29       {
30          // push elements onto stack
31          try
32          {
33             Console.WriteLine( "\nPushing elements onto doubleStack" );
34
35             // push elements onto stack
36             foreach ( double element in doubleElements )
37             {
38                Console.Write( "{0:F1} ", element );
39                doubleStack.Push( element ); // push onto doubleStack
40             } // end foreach
41          } // end try
42          catch ( FullStackException exception )
43          {
44             Console.Error.WriteLine();
45             Console.Error.WriteLine( "Message: " + exception.Message );
46             Console.Error.WriteLine( exception.StackTrace );
47          } // end catch
48       } // end method TestPushDouble
49
50       // test Pop method with doubleStack
51       static void TestPopDouble()
52       {
```

Fig. 26.8 | Generic class Stack test program. (Part 1 of 3.)

```
53          // pop elements from stack
54          try
55          {
56             Console.WriteLine( "\nPopping elements from doubleStack" );
57
58             double popValue; // store element removed from stack
59
60             // remove all elements from Stack
61             while ( true )
62             {
63                popValue = doubleStack.Pop(); // pop from doubleStack
64                Console.Write( "{0:F1} ", popValue );
65             } // end while
66          } // end try
67          catch ( EmptyStackException exception )
68          {
69             Console.Error.WriteLine();
70             Console.Error.WriteLine( "Message: " + exception.Message );
71             Console.Error.WriteLine( exception.StackTrace );
72          } // end catch
73       } // end method TestPopDouble
74
75       // test Push method with intStack
76       static void TestPushInt()
77       {
78          // push elements onto stack
79          try
80          {
81             Console.WriteLine( "\nPushing elements onto intStack" );
82
83             // push elements onto stack
84             foreach ( int element in intElements )
85             {
86                Console.Write( "{0} ", element );
87                intStack.Push( element ); // push onto intStack
88             } // end foreach
89          } // end try
90          catch ( FullStackException exception )
91          {
92             Console.Error.WriteLine();
93             Console.Error.WriteLine( "Message: " + exception.Message );
94             Console.Error.WriteLine( exception.StackTrace );
95          } // end catch
96       } // end method TestPushInt
97
98       // test Pop method with intStack
99       static void TestPopInt()
100      {
101         // pop elements from stack
102         try
103         {
104            Console.WriteLine( "\nPopping elements from intStack" );
```

Fig. 26.8 | Generic class Stack test program. (Part 2 of 3.)

```
105
106            int popValue; // store element removed from stack
107
108            // remove all elements from Stack
109            while ( true )
110            {
111               popValue = intStack.Pop(); // pop from intStack
112               Console.Write( "{0} ", popValue );
113            } // end while
114         } // end try
115         catch ( EmptyStackException exception )
116         {
117            Console.Error.WriteLine();
118            Console.Error.WriteLine( "Message: " + exception.Message );
119            Console.Error.WriteLine( exception.StackTrace );
120         } // end catch
121      } // end method TestPopInt
122   } // end class StackTest
```

```
Pushing elements onto doubleStack
1.1 2.2 3.3 4.4 5.5 6.6
Message: Stack is full, cannot push 6.6
   at Stack`1.Push(E pushValue) in
      C:\Examples\ch25\Fig25_05\Stack\Stack.cs:line 32
   at StackTest.TestPushDouble() in
      C:\Examples\ch25\Fig25_05\Stack\StackTest.cs:line 39

Popping elements from doubleStack
5.5 4.4 3.3 2.2 1.1
Message: Stack is empty, cannot pop
   at Stack`1.Pop() in C:\Examples\ch25\Fig25_05\Stack\Stack.cs:line 44
   at StackTest.TestPopDouble() in
      C:\Examples\ch25\Fig25_05\Stack\StackTest.cs:line 63

Pushing elements onto intStack
1 2 3 4 5 6 7 8 9 10 11
Message: Stack is full, cannot push 11
   at Stack`1.Push(E pushValue) in
      C:\Examples\ch25\Fig25_05\Stack\Stack.cs:line 32
   at StackTest.TestPushInt() in
      C:\Examples\ch25\Fig25_05\Stack\StackTest.cs:line 87

Popping elements from intStack
10 9 8 7 6 5 4 3 2 1
Message: Stack is empty, cannot pop
   at Stack`1.Pop() in C:\Examples\ch25\Fig25_05\Stack\Stack.cs:line 44
   at StackTest.TestPopInt() in
      C:\Examples\ch25\Fig25_05\Stack\StackTest.cs:line 111
```

Fig. 26.8 | Generic class Stack test program. (Part 3 of 3.)

Method TestPushDouble (lines 28–48) invokes method Push to place the double values 1.1, 2.2, 3.3, 4.4 and 5.5 stored in array doubleElements onto doubleStack. The for statement terminates when the test program attempts to Push a sixth value onto doubleStack (which is full, because doubleStack can store only five elements). In this case, the method throws a FullStackException (Fig. 26.6) to indicate that the Stack is full. Lines 42–47 catch this exception, and print the message and stack trace information. The stack trace indicates the exception that occurred and shows that Stack method Push generated the exception at lines 34–35 of the file Stack.cs (Fig. 26.5). The trace also shows that method Push was called by StackTest method TestPushDouble at line 39 of Stack-Test.cs. This information enables you to determine the methods that were on the method call stack at the time that the exception occurred. Because the program catches the exception, the C# runtime environment considers the exception to have been handled, and the program can continue executing.

Method TestPopDouble (lines 51–73) invokes Stack method Pop in an infinite while loop to remove all the values from the stack. Note in the output that the values are popped off in last-in-first-out order—this, of course, is the defining characteristic of stacks. The while loop (lines 61–65) continues until the stack is empty. An EmptyStackException occurs when an attempt is made to pop from the empty stack. This causes the program to proceed to the catch block (lines 67–72) and handle the exception, so the program can continue executing. When the test program attempts to Pop a sixth value, the doubleStack is empty, so method Pop throws an EmptyStackException.

Method TestPushInt (lines 76–96) invokes Stack method Push to place values onto intStack until it is full. Method TestPopInt (lines 99–121) invokes Stack method Pop to remove values from intStack until it is empty. Once again, note that the values pop off in last-in-first-out order.

Creating Generic Methods to Test Class Stack< E >

Note that the code in methods TestPushDouble and TestPushInt is almost identical for pushing values onto a Stack< double > or a Stack< int >, respectively. Similarly the code in methods TestPopDouble and TestPopInt is almost identical for popping values from a Stack< double > or a Stack< int >, respectively. This presents another opportunity to use generic methods. Figure 26.9 declares generic method TestPush (lines 32–53) to perform the same tasks as TestPushDouble and TestPushInt in Fig. 26.8—that is, Push values onto a Stack< E > . Similarly, generic method TestPop (lines 55–77) performs the same tasks as TestPopDouble and TestPopInt in Fig. 26.8—that is, Pop values off a Stack< E >. Note that the output of Fig. 26.9 precisely matches the output of Fig. 26.8.

```
1    // Fig 26.9: StackTest.cs
2    // Stack generic class test program.
3    using System;
4    using System.Collections.Generic;
5
6    class StackTest
7    {
8       // create arrays of doubles and ints
9       static double[] doubleElements =
10          new double[]{ 1.1, 2.2, 3.3, 4.4, 5.5, 6.6 };
11      static int[] intElements =
12          new int[]{ 1, 2, 3, 4, 5, 6, 7, 8, 9, 10, 11 };
```

Fig. 26.9 | Passing a generic type Stack to a generic method. (Part 1 of 3.)

```
13
14     static Stack< double >doubleStack; // stack stores double objects
15     static Stack< int >intStack; // stack stores int objects
16
17     static void Main( string[] args )
18     {
19        doubleStack = new Stack< double >( 5 ); // Stack of doubles
20        intStack = new Stack< int >( 10 ); // Stack of ints
21
22        // push doubles onto doubleStack
23        TestPush( "doubleStack", doubleStack, doubleElements );
24        // pop doubles from doubleStack
25        TestPop( "doubleStack", doubleStack );
26        // push ints onto intStack
27        TestPush( "intStack", intStack, intElements );
28        // pop ints from intStack
29        TestPop( "intStack", intStack );
30     } // end Main
31
32     static void TestPush< E >( string name, Stack< E > stack,
33        IEnumerable< E > elements )
34     {
35        // push elements onto stack
36        try
37        {
38           Console.WriteLine( "\nPushing elements onto " + name );
39
40           // push elements onto stack
41           foreach ( E element in elements )
42           {
43              Console.Write( "{0} ", element );
44              stack.Push( element ); // push onto stack
45           } // end foreach
46        } // end try
47        catch ( FullStackException exception )
48        {
49           Console.Error.WriteLine();
50           Console.Error.WriteLine( "Message: " + exception.Message );
51           Console.Error.WriteLine( exception.StackTrace );
52        } // end catch
53     } // end method TestPush
54
55     static void TestPop< E >( string name, Stack< E > stack )
56     {
57        // push elements onto stack
58        try
59        {
60           Console.WriteLine( "\nPopping elements from " + name );
61
62           E popValue; // store element removed from stack
63
```

Fig. 26.9 | Passing a generic type Stack to a generic method. (Part 2 of 3.)

```
64              // remove all elements from Stack
65              while ( true )
66              {
67                  popValue = stack.Pop(); // pop from stack
68                  Console.Write( "{0} ", popValue );
69              } // end while
70          } // end try
71          catch ( EmptyStackException exception )
72          {
73              Console.Error.WriteLine();
74              Console.Error.WriteLine( "Message: " + exception.Message );
75              Console.Error.WriteLine( exception.StackTrace );
76          } // end catch
77      } // end TestPop
78  } // end class StackTest
```

```
Pushing elements onto doubleStack
1.1 2.2 3.3 4.4 5.5 6.6
Message: Stack is full, cannot push 6.6
    at Stack`1.Push(E pushValue) in
        C:\Examples\ch25\Fig25_05\Stack\Stack.cs:line 35
    at StackTest.TestPush[E](String name, Stack`1 stack, IEnumerable`1
        elements) in C:\Examples\ch25\Fig25_05\Stack\StackTest.cs:line 44

Popping elements from doubleStack
5.5 4.4 3.3 2.2 1.1
Message: Stack is empty, cannot pop
    at Stack`1.Pop() in C:\Examples\ch25\Fig25_05\Stack\Stack.cs:line 49
    at StackTest.TestPop[E](String name, Stack`1 stack) in
        C:\Examples\ch25\Fig25_05\Stack\StackTest.cs:line 67

Pushing elements onto intStack
1 2 3 4 5 6 7 8 9 10 11
Message: Stack is full, cannot push 11
    at Stack`1.Push(E pushValue) in
        C:\Examples\ch25\Fig25_05\Stack\Stack.cs:line 35
    at StackTest.TestPush[E](String name, Stack`1 stack, IEnumerable`1
        elements) in C:\Examples\ch25\Fig25_05\Stack\StackTest.cs:line 44

Popping elements from intStack
10 9 8 7 6 5 4 3 2 1
Message: Stack is empty, cannot pop
    at Stack`1.Pop() in C:\Examples\ch25\Fig25_05\Stack\Stack.cs:line 49
    at StackTest.TestPop[E](String name, Stack`1 stack) in
        C:\Examples\ch25\Fig25_05\Stack\StackTest.cs:line 67
```

Fig. 26.9 | Passing a generic type Stack to a generic method. (Part 3 of 3.)

Method Main (lines 17–30) creates the Stack< double > (line 19) and Stack< int > (line 20) objects. Lines 23–29 invoke generic methods TestPush and TestPop to test the Stack objects.

Generic method TestPush (lines 32–53) uses type parameter E (specified at line 32) to represent the data type stored in the Stack. The generic method takes three arguments—a string that represents the name of the Stack object for output purposes, an object of type Stack< E > and an IEnumerable< E >—the type of elements that will be Pushed onto Stack< E >. Note that the compiler enforces consistency between the type of the Stack and the elements that will be pushed onto the Stack when Push is invoked, which is the type argument of the generic method call. Generic method TestPop (lines 55–77) takes two arguments—a string that represents the name of the Stack object for output purposes and an object of type Stack< E >. Notice that the type parameter E used in both TestPush and TestPop methods has a new constraint, because both methods take an object of type Stack< E > and the type parameter in the Stack generic class declaration has a new constraint (line 5 in Fig. 26.5). This ensures that the objects that TestPush and TestPop manipulate can be used with generic Stack class, which requires objects stored in the Stack to have a default or parameterless public constructor.

26.7 Notes on Generics and Inheritance

Generics can be used with inheritance in several ways:

- A generic class can be derived from a non-generic class. For example, class object (which is not a generic class) is a direct or indirect base class of every generic class.

- A generic class can be derived from another generic class. Recall that in Chapter 25, the non-generic Stack class (Fig. 25.12) inherits from the non-generic List class (Fig. 25.5). You could also create a generic Stack class by inheriting from a generic List class.

- A non-generic class can be derived from a generic class. For example, you can implement a non-generic AddressList class that inherits from a generic List class and stores only Address objects.

26.8 Wrap-Up

This chapter introduced generics—one of C#'s newest capabilities. We discussed how generics ensure compile-time type safety by checking for type mismatches at compile time. You learned that the compiler will allow generic code to compile only if all operations performed on the type parameters in the generic code are supported for all types that could be used with the generic code. You also learned how to declare generic methods and classes using type parameters. We demonstrated how to use a type constraint to specify the requirements for a type parameter—a key component of compile-time type safety. We discussed several kinds of type constraints, including reference type constraints, value type constraints, class constraints, interface constraints and constructor constraints. You learned that a constructor constraint indicates that the type argument must provide a public parameterless or default constructor so that objects of that type can be created with new. We also discussed how to implement multiple type constraints for a type parameter. We showed how generics improve code reuse. Finally, we mentioned several ways to use generics in inheritance. In the next chapter, we demonstrate the .NET FCL's collection classes, interfaces and algorithms. Collection classes are pre-built data structures that you can reuse in your applications, saving you time. We present both generic collections and the older, non-generic collections.

Summary

Section 26.1 Introduction
- Generic methods enable you to specify, with a single method declaration, a set of related methods.
- Generic classes enable you to specify, with a single class declaration, a set of related classes.
- Generic interfaces enable you to specify, with a single interface declaration, a set of related interfaces.
- Generics provide compile-time type safety.

Section 26.2 Motivation for Generic Methods
- Overloaded methods are often used to perform similar operations on different types of data.
- When the compiler encounters a method call, it attempts to locate a method declaration that has the same method name and parameters that match the argument types in the method call.

Section 26.3 Generic Method Implementation
- If the operations performed by several overloaded methods are identical for each argument type, the overloaded methods can be more compactly and conveniently coded using a generic method.
- You can write a single generic method declaration that can be called at different times with arguments of different types. Based on the types of the arguments passed to the generic method, the compiler handles each method call appropriately.
- All generic method declarations have a type parameter list delimited by angle brackets that follows the method's name. Each type parameter list contains one or more type parameters, separated by commas.
- A type parameter is used in place of actual type names. The type parameters can be used to declare the return type, parameter types and local variable types in a generic method declaration; the type parameters act as placeholders for the types of the arguments passed to the method.
- A generic method's body is declared like that of any other method. The type parameter names throughout the method declaration must match those declared in the type parameter list.
- A type parameter can be declared only once in the type parameter list but can appear more than once in the method's parameter list. Type parameter names need not be unique among different generic methods.
- When the compiler encounters a method call, it analyzes the set of methods (both non-generic and generic) that might match the method call looking for a method that matches the call exactly. If there are no exact matches, the compiler picks the best match. If there are no matching methods, or if there is more than one best match, the compiler generates an error.
- The complete details of method call resolution can be found in Section 14.5.5.1 of the Ecma C# Language Specification

    www.ecma-international.org/publications/files/ECMA-ST/Ecma-334.pdf

  or Section 20.9.7 of the Microsoft C# Language Specification 2.0

    msdn.microsoft.com/vcsharp/programming/language/

- You can use explicit type arguments to indicate the exact type that should be used to call a generic function. For example, the method call `PrintArray< int >( intArray );` explicitly provides the type argument (`int`) that should be used to replace type parameter `E` in lines 24 and 26 of the `PrintArray` method's declaration.

Section 26.4 Type Constraints

- Generic code is restricted to performing operations that are guaranteed to work for every possible type. Thus, an expression like `variable1 < variable2` is not allowed unless the compiler can ensure that the operator `<` is provided for every type that will ever be used in the generic code. Similarly, you cannot call a method on a generic-type variable unless the compiler can ensure that all types that will ever be used in the generic code support that method.

- It is possible to compare two objects of the same type if that type implements the generic interface `IComparable< T >` (of namespace `System`), which declares method `CompareTo`.

- `IComparable< T >` objects can be used with the sorting and searching methods of classes in the `System.Collections.Generic` namespace.

- The structures in the FCL that correspond to the simple types all implement interface `IComparable< T >`.

- It is the responsibility of the programmer who declares a type that implements `IComparable< T >` to declare method `CompareTo` such that it compares the contents of two objects of that type and returns the appropriate result.

- You can restrict the types that can be used with a generic method or class to ensure that they meet certain requirements. This feature—known as a type constraint—restricts the type of the argument supplied to a particular type parameter. For example, the clause `where T : IComparable< T >` indicates that the type arguments must implement interface `IComparable< T >`. If no type constraint is specified, the default type constraint is `object`.

- A class constraint indicates that the type argument must be an object of a specific base class or one of its subclasses.

- An interface constraint indicates that the type argument's class must implement a specific interface.

- You can specify that the type argument must be a reference type or a value type by using the reference type constraint (`class`) or the value type constraint (`struct`), respectively.

- You can specify a constructor constraint—`new()`—to indicate that the generic code can use operator `new` to create new objects of the type represented by the type parameter. If a type parameter is specified with a constructor constraint, the type argument's class must provide `public` a parameterless or default constructor to ensure that objects of the class can be created without passing constructor arguments; otherwise, a compilation error occurs.

- It is possible to apply multiple constraints to a type parameter by providing a comma-separated list of constraints in the `where` clause.

- If you have a class constraint, reference type constraint or value type constraint, it must be listed first—only one of these types of constraints can be used for each type parameter. Interface constraints (if any) are listed next. The constructor constraint is listed last (if there is one).

Section 26.5 Overloading Generic Methods

- A generic method may be overloaded. A class can provide two or more generic methods with the same name but different method parameters.

- A generic method can also be overloaded by another generic method with the same method name and a different number of type parameters, or by a generic method with different numbers of type parameters and method parameters.

- A generic method can be overloaded by non-generic methods that have the same method name and number of parameters. When the compiler encounters a method call, it searches for the method declaration that most precisely matches the method name and the argument types specified in the call.

- Generic methods can also be overloaded by non-generic methods that have the same method name but a different number of method parameters.

Section 26.6 Generic Classes
- A generic class provides a means for describing a class in a type-independent manner.
- Once you have a generic class, you can use a simple, concise notation to indicate the actual type(s) that should be used in place of the class's type parameter(s). At compilation time, the compiler ensures the type safety of your code, and the runtime system replaces type parameters with actual arguments to enable your client code to interact with the generic class.
- A generic class declaration is similar to a non-generic class declaration, except that the class name is followed by a type parameter list and possibly constraints on its type parameter.
- As with generic methods, the type parameter list of a generic class can have one or more type parameters separated by commas.
- When a generic class is compiled, the compiler performs type checking on the class's type parameters to ensure that they can be used with the code in the generic class. The constraints determine the operations that can be performed on the type parameters.

Section 26.7 Notes on Generics and Inheritance
- A generic class can be derived from a non-generic class.
- A generic class can be derived from another generic class.
- A non-generic class can be derived from a generic class.

Terminology

class constraint	multiple constraints
CompareTo method of interface IComparable	new() (constructor) constraint
compile-time type safety	overloading generic methods
constructor constraint (new())	reference type constraint (class)
default type constraint (object) of a type parameter	scope of a type parameter
explicit type argument	type argument
generic class	type checking
generic interface	type constraint
generic method	type inference
generics	type parameter
IComparable< T > interface	type parameter list
interface constraint	value type constraint (struct)
	where clause

Self-Review Exercises

26.1 State whether each of the following is *true* or *false*. If *false*, explain why.
a) A generic method cannot have the same method name as a non-generic method.
b) All generic method declarations have a type parameter list that immediately precedes the method name.
c) A generic method can be overloaded by another generic method with the same method name but a different number of type parameters.
d) A type parameter can be declared only once in the type parameter list but can appear more than once in the method's parameter list.
e) Type parameter names among different generic methods must be unique.

    f)   The scope of a generic class's type parameter is the entire class.

    g)   A type parameter can have at most one interface constraint, but multiple class constraints.

26.2   Fill in the blanks in each of the following:

    a)   _____ enable you to specify, with a single method declaration, a set of related methods; _____ enable you to specify, with a single class declaration, a set of related classes.

    b)   A type parameter list is delimited by _____.

    c)   The _____ of a generic method can be used to specify the types of the arguments to the method, to specify the return type of the method and to declare variables within the method.

    d)   The statement "`Stack< int > objectStack = new Stack< int >();`" indicates that objectStack stores _____.

    e)   In a generic class declaration, the class name is followed by a(n) _____.

    f)   The _____ constraint requires that the type argument must have a `public` parameterless constructor.

Answers to Self-Review Exercises

26.1   a) False. A generic method can be overloaded by non-generic methods with the same or a different number of arguments. b) False. All generic method declarations have a type parameter list that immediately follows the method's name. c) True. d) True. e) False. Type parameter names among different generic methods need not be unique. f) True. g) False. A type parameter can have at most one class constraint, but multiple interface constraints.

26.2   a)   Generic methods, Generic classes. b) angle brackets. c) type parameters. d) `int`s. e) type parameter list. f) `new`.

Exercises

26.3   Explain the use of the following notation in a C# program:

```
public class Array< E >
```

26.4   How can generic methods be overloaded?

26.5   The compiler performs a matching process to determine which method to call when a method is invoked. Under what circumstances does an attempt to make a match result in a compile-time error?

26.6   Explain why a C# program might use the statement

```
Array< Employee > workerList = new Array< Employee >();
```

26.7   Write a generic method, `Search`, that implements the linear search algorithm. Method `Search` should compare the search key with each element in the array until the search key is found or until the end of the array is reached. If the search key is found, return its location in the array; otherwise, return -1. Write a test application that inputs and searches an `int` array and a `double` array. Provide buttons that the user can click to randomly generate `int` and `double` values. Display the generated values in a `TextBox`, so the user knows what values they can search for [*Hint:* Use (`E : IComparable< E >`) in the `where` clause for method `Search` so that you can use method `CompareTo` to compare the search key to the elements in the array.]

26.8   Overload generic method `PrintArray` of Fig. 26.3 so that it takes two additional `int` arguments: `lowIndex` and `highIndex`. A call to this method prints only the designated portion of the array. Validate `lowIndex` and `highIndex`. If either is out-of-range, or if `highIndex` is less than or equal to `lowIndex`, the overloaded `PrintArray` method should throw an `InvalidIndexException`; otherwise, `PrintArray` should return the number of elements printed. Then modify `Main` to exercise both versions of `PrintArray` on arrays `intArray`, `doubleArray` and `charArray`. Test all capabilities of both versions of `PrintArray`.

26.9 Overload generic method `PrintArray` of Fig. 26.3 with a non-generic version that prints an array of strings in neat, tabular format, as shown in the sample output that follows:

```
Array stringArray contains:
one      two      three    four
five     six      seven    eight
```

26.10 Write a simple generic version of method `IsEqualTo` that compares its two arguments with the `Equals` method, and returns `true` if they are equal and `false` otherwise. Use this generic method in a program that calls `IsEqualTo` with a variety of simple types, such as `object` or `int`. What result do you get when you attempt to run this program?

26.11 Write a generic class `Pair` which has two type parameters, `F` and `S`, representing the type of the first and second element of the pair, respectively. Add properties (with `Get` and `Set` accessors) for the first and second elements of the pair. [*Hint:* The class header should be `public class Pair< F, S >`.]

26.12 Convert classes `TreeNode` and `Tree` from Figs. 25.19 and 25.20 into generic classes. To insert an object in a `Tree`, the object must be compared to the objects in existing `TreeNode`s. For this reason, classes `TreeNode` and `Tree` should specify `IComparable< E >` as the interface constraint of each class's type parameter. After modifying classes `TreeNode` and `Tree`, write a test application that creates three `Tree` objects—one that stores `int`s, one that stores `double`s and one that stores `string`s. Insert 10 values into each tree. Then output the preorder, inorder and postorder traversals for each `Tree`.

26.13 Modify your test program from Exercise 26.12 to use generic method `TestTree` to test the three `Tree` objects. The method should be called three times—once for each `Tree` object.

27

Collections

> *The shapes a bright container can contain!*
> —Theodore Roethke

> *Not by age but by capacity is wisdom acquired.*
> —Titus Maccius Plautus

> *It is a riddle wrapped in a mystery inside an enigma.*
> —Winston Churchill

> *I think this is the most extraordinary collection of talent, of human knowledge, that has ever been gathered together at the White House—with the possible exception of when Thomas Jefferson dined alone.*
> —John F. Kennedy

OBJECTIVES

In this chapter you will learn:

- The non-generic and generic collections that are provided by the .NET Framework.

- To use class **Array**'s **static** methods to manipulate arrays.

- To use enumerators to "walk through" a collection.

- To use the **foreach** statement with the .NET collections.

- To use non-generic collection classes **ArrayList**, **Stack**, and **Hashtable**.

- To use generic collection classes **SortedDictionary** and **LinkedList**.

- To use synchronization wrappers to make collections safe in multithreaded applications.

27.1 Introduction

In Chapter 25, we discussed how to create and manipulate data structures. The discussion was "low level," in the sense that we painstakingly created each element of each data structure dynamically with new and modified the data structures by directly manipulating their elements and references to their elements. In this chapter, we consider the prepackaged data-structure classes provided by the .NET Framework. These classes are known as *collection classes*—they store collections of data. Each instance of one of these classes is a *collection* of items. Some examples of collections are the cards you hold in a card game, the songs stored in your computer, the real-estate records in your local registry of deeds (which map book numbers and page numbers to property owners), and the players on your favorite sports team.

Collection classes enable programmers to store sets of items by using existing data structures, without concern for how they are implemented. This is a nice example of code reuse. Programmers can code faster and expect excellent performance, maximizing execution speed and minimizing memory consumption. In this chapter, we discuss the collection interfaces that list the capabilities of each collection type, the implementation classes and the *enumerators* that "walk through" collections.

The .NET Framework provides three namespaces dedicated to collections. The `System.Collections` namespace contains collections that store references to objects. The newer ***System.Collections.Generic*** namespace contains generic classes to store collections of specified types. The newer ***System.Collections.Specialized*** namespace contains several collections that support specific types, such as strings and bits. You can learn more about this namespace at msdn2.microsoft.com/en-us/library/system.collections.specialized.aspx. The collections in these namespaces provide standardized, reusable components; you do not need to write your own collection classes. These collections are written for broad reuse. They are tuned for rapid execution and for efficient use of memory. As new data structures and algorithms are developed that fit this framework, a large base of programmers already will be familiar with the interfaces and algorithms implemented by those data structures.

27.2 Collections Overview

All collection classes in the .NET Framework implement some combination of the collection interfaces. These interfaces declare the operations to be performed generically on various types of collections. Figure 27.1 lists some of the interfaces of the .NET Framework collections. All the interfaces in Fig. 27.1 are declared in namespace System.Collections and have generic analogues in namespace System.Collections.Generic. Implementations of these interfaces are provided within the framework. Programmers may also provide implementations specific to their own requirements.

In earlier versions of C#, the .NET Framework primarily provided the collection classes in the System.Collections and System.Collections.Specialized namespaces. These classes stored and manipulated object references. You could store any object in a collection. One inconvenient aspect of storing object references occurs when retrieving them from a collection. An application normally needs to process specific types of objects. As a result, the object references obtained from a collection typically need to be downcast to an appropriate type to allow the application to process the objects correctly.

The .NET Framework 2.0 now also includes the System.Collections.Generic namespace, which uses the generics capabilities we introduced in Chapter 26. Many of these new classes are simply generic counterparts of the classes in namespace System.Collections. This means that you can specify the exact type that will be stored in a collection. You also receive the benefits of compile-time type checking—the compiler ensures that you are using appropriate types with your collection and, if not, issues compile-time error messages. Also, once you specify the type stored in a collection, any item you retrieve from the collection will have the correct type. This eliminates the need for explicit type casts that can throw InvalidCastExceptions at execution time if the referenced object is not of the appropriate type. This also eliminates the overhead of explicit casting, improving efficiency.

Interface	Description
ICollection	The root interface in the collections hierarchy from which interfaces IList and IDictionary inherit. Contains a Count property to determine the size of a collection and a CopyTo method for copying a collection's contents into a traditional array.
IList	An ordered collection that can be manipulated like an array. Provides an indexer for accessing elements with an int index. Also has methods for searching and modifying a collection, including Add, Remove, Contains and IndexOf.
IDictionary	A collection of values, indexed by an arbitrary "key" object. Provides an indexer for accessing elements with an object index and methods for modifying the collection (e.g. Add, Remove). IDictionary property Keys contains the objects used as indices, and property Values contains all the stored objects.
IEnumerable	An object that can be enumerated. This interface contains exactly one method, GetEnumerator, which returns an IEnumerator object (discussed in Section 27.3). ICollection implements IEnumerable, so all collection classes implement IEnumerable directly or indirectly.

Fig. 27.1 | Some common collection interfaces.

In this chapter, we demonstrate six collection classes—*Array*, *ArrayList*, *Stack*, *Hashtable*, generic *SortedDictionary*, and generic *LinkedList*—plus built-in array capabilities. Namespace System.Collections provides several other data structures, including *BitArray* (a collection of true/false values), *Queue* and *SortedList* (a collection of key/value pairs that are sorted by key and can be accessed either by key or by index). Figure 27.2 summarizes many of the collection classes. We also discuss the IEnumerator interface. Collection classes can create enumerators that allow programmers to walk through the collections. Although these enumerators have different implementations, they all implement the IEnumerator interface so that they can be processed polymorphically. As we will soon see, the foreach statement is simply a convenient notation for using an enumerator. In the next section, we begin our discussion by examining enumerators and the collections capabilities for array manipulation.

Class	Implements	Description
System namespace:		
Array	IList	The base class of all conventional arrays. See Section 27.3.
System.Collections namespace:		
ArrayList	IList	Mimics conventional arrays, but will grow or shrink as needed to accommodate the number of elements. See Section 27.4.1.
BitArray	ICollection	A memory-efficient array of bools.
Hashtable	IDictionary	An unordered collection of key–value pairs that can be accessed by key. See Section 27.4.3.
Queue	ICollection	A first-in first-out collection. See Section 25.6.
SortedList	IDictionary	A generic Hashtable that sorts data by keys and can be accessed either by key or by index.
Stack	ICollection	A last-in, first-out collection. See Section 27.4.2.
System.Collections.Generic namespace:		
Dictionary< K, E >	IDictionary< K, E >	A generic, unordered collection of key–value pairs that can be accessed by key.
LinkedList< E >	ICollection< E >	A doubly linked list. See Section 27.5.2.
List< E >	IList< E >	A generic ArrayList.

Fig. 27.2 | Some collection classes of the .NET Framework. (Part 1 of 2.)

Class	Implements	Description
Queue< E >	ICollection< E >	A generic Queue.
SortedDictionary< K, E >	IDictionary< K, E >	A Dictionary that sorts the data by the keys in a binary tree. See Section 27.5.1.
SortedList< K, E >	IDictionary< K, E >	A generic SortedList.
Stack< E >	ICollection< E >	A generic Stack.

[Note: *All collection classes directly or indirectly implement* ICollection *and* IEnumerable *(or the equivalent generic interfaces* ICollection< E > *and* IEnumerable< E > *for generic collections).*]

Fig. 27.2 | Some collection classes of the .NET Framework. (Part 2 of 2.)

27.3 Class Array and Enumerators

Chapter 8 presented basic array-processing capabilities. All arrays implicitly inherit from abstract base class Array (namespace System), which defines property Length, which specifies the number of elements in the array. In addition, class Array provides static methods that provide algorithms for processing arrays. Typically, class Array overloads these methods—for example, Array method Reverse can reverse the order of the elements in an entire array or can reverse the elements in a specified range of elements in an array. For a complete list of class Array's static methods visit:

msdn2.microsoft.com/en-us/library/system.array.aspx

Figure 27.3 demonstrates several static methods of class Array.

```
1   // Fig. 27.3: UsingArray.cs
2   // Array class static methods for common array manipulations.
3   using System;
4   using System.Collections;
5
6   // demonstrate algorithms of class Array
7   public class UsingArray
8   {
9      private static int[] intValues = { 1, 2, 3, 4, 5, 6 };
10     private static double[] doubleValues = { 8.4, 9.3, 0.2, 7.9, 3.4 };
11     private static int[] intValuesCopy;
12
13     // method Main demonstrates class Array's methods
14     public static void Main( string[] args )
15     {
16        intValuesCopy = new int[ intValues.Length ]; // defaults to zeroes
17
18        Console.WriteLine( "Initial array values:\n" );
19        PrintArrays(); // output initial array contents
```

Fig. 27.3 | Array class used to perform common array manipulations. (Part 1 of 3.)

```
20
21        // sort doubleValues
22        Array.Sort( doubleValues );
23
24        // copy intValues into intValuesCopy
25        Array.Copy( intValues, intValuesCopy, intValues.Length );
26
27        Console.WriteLine( "\nArray values after Sort and Copy:\n" );
28        PrintArrays(); // output array contents
29        Console.WriteLine();
30
31        // search for 5 in intValues
32        int result = Array.BinarySearch( intValues, 5 );
33        if ( result >= 0 )
34           Console.WriteLine( "5 found at element {0} in intValues",
35              result );
36        else
37           Console.WriteLine( "5 not found in intValues" );
38
39        // search for 8763 in intValues
40        result = Array.BinarySearch( intValues, 8763 );
41        if ( result >= 0 )
42           Console.WriteLine( "8763 found at element {0} in intValues",
43              result );
44        else
45           Console.WriteLine( "8763 not found in intValues" );
46     } // end method Main
47
48     // output array content with enumerators
49     private static void PrintArrays()
50     {
51        Console.Write( "doubleValues: " );
52
53        // iterate through the double array with an enumerator
54        IEnumerator enumerator = doubleValues.GetEnumerator();
55
56        while ( enumerator.MoveNext() )
57           Console.Write( enumerator.Current + " " );
58
59        Console.Write( "\nintValues: " );
60
61        // iterate through the int array with an enumerator
62        enumerator = intValues.GetEnumerator();
63
64        while ( enumerator.MoveNext() )
65           Console.Write( enumerator.Current + " " );
66
67        Console.Write( "\nintValuesCopy: " );
68
69        // iterate through the second int array with a foreach statement
70        foreach ( int element in intValuesCopy )
71           Console.Write( element + " " );
72
```

Fig. 27.3 | Array class used to perform common array manipulations. (Part 2 of 3.)

```
73            Console.WriteLine();
74        } // end method PrintArrays
75    } // end class UsingArray
```

```
Initial array values:

doubleValues: 8.4 9.3 0.2 7.9 3.4
intValues: 1 2 3 4 5 6
intValuesCopy: 0 0 0 0 0 0

Array values after Sort and Copy:

doubleValues: 0.2 3.4 7.9 8.4 9.3
intValues: 1 2 3 4 5 6
intValuesCopy: 1 2 3 4 5 6

5 found at element 4 in intValues
8763 not found in intValues
```

Fig. 27.3 | Array class used to perform common array manipulations. (Part 3 of 3.)

The using directives in lines 3–4 include the namespaces System (for classes Array and Console) and System.Collections (for interface IEnumerator, which we discuss shortly). References to the assemblies for these namespaces are implicitly included in every application, so we do not need to add any new references to the project file.

Our test class declares three static array variables (lines 9–11). The first two lines initialize intValues and doubleValues to an int and double array, respectively. Static variable intValuesCopy is intended to demonstrate the Array's Copy method, so it is left with the default value null—it does not yet refer to an array.

Line 16 initializes intValuesCopy to an int array with the same length as array intValues. Line 19 calls the PrintArrays method (lines 49–74) to output the initial contents of all three arrays. We discuss the PrintArrays method shortly. We can see from the output of Fig. 27.3 that each element of array intValuesCopy is initialized to the default value 0.

Line 22 uses static Array method *Sort* to sort array doubleValues. When this method returns, the array contains its original elements sorted in ascending order.

Line 25 uses static Array method *Copy* to copy elements from array intValues to array intValuesCopy. The first argument is the array to copy (intValues), the second argument is the destination array (intValuesCopy) and the third argument is an int representing the number of elements to copy (in this case, intValues.Length specifies all elements).

Lines 32 and 40 invoke static Array method *BinarySearch* to perform binary searches on array intValues. Method BinarySearch receives the *sorted* array in which to search and the key for which to search. The method returns the index in the array at which it finds the key (or a negative number if the key was not found). Notice that BinarySearch assumes that it receives a sorted array. Its behavior on an unsorted array is unpredictable. Chapter 24, Searching and Sorting, discusses binary searching in detail.

Common Programming Error 27.1

Passing an unsorted array to BinarySearch is a logic error—the value returned is undefined.

The PrintArrays method (lines 49–74) uses class Array's methods to loop though each array. In line 54, the GetEnumerator method obtains an enumerator for array intValues. Recall that Array implements the **IEnumerable** interface. All arrays inherit implicitly from Array, so both the int[] and double[] array types implement IEnumerable interface method **GetEnumerator**, which returns an enumerator that can iterate over the collection. Interface **IEnumerator** (which all enumerators implement) defines methods **MoveNext** and **Reset** and property **Current**. MoveNext moves the enumerator to the next element in the collection. The first call to MoveNext positions the enumerator at the first element of the collection. MoveNext returns true if there is at least one more element in the collection; otherwise, the method returns false. Method Reset positions the enumerator before the first element of the collection. Methods MoveNext and Reset throw an **InvalidOperationException** if the contents of the collection are modified in any way after the enumerator is created. Property Current returns the object at the current location in the collection.

Common Programming Error 27.2

If a collection is modified after an enumerator is created for that collection, the enumerator immediately becomes invalid—any methods called with the enumerator after this point throw InvalidOperationExceptions. For this reason, enumerators are said to be "fail fast."

When an enumerator is returned by the GetEnumerator method in line 54, it is initially positioned *before* the first element in Array doubleValues. Then when line 56 calls MoveNext in the first iteration of the while loop, the enumerator advances to the first element in doubleValues. The while statement in lines 56–57 loops over each element until the enumerator passes the end of doubleValues and MoveNext returns false. In each iteration, we use the enumerator's Current property to obtain and output the current array element. Lines 62–65 iterate over array intValues.

Notice that PrintArrays is called twice (lines 19 and 28), so GetEnumerator is called twice on doubleValues. The GetEnumerator method (lines 54 and 62) always returns an enumerator positioned before the first element. Also notice that the IEnumerator property Current is read-only. Enumerators cannot be used to modify the contents of collections, only to obtain the contents.

Lines 70–71 use a foreach statement to iterate over the collection elements like an enumerator. In fact, the foreach statement behaves exactly like an enumerator. Both loop over the elements of an array one-by-one in a well-defined order. Neither allows you to modify the elements during the iteration. This is not a coincidence. The foreach statement implicitly obtains an enumerator via the GetEnumerator method and uses the enumerator's MoveNext method and Current property to traverse the collection, just as we did explicitly in lines 54–57. For this reason, we can use the foreach statement to iterate over *any* collection that implements the IEnumerable interface—not just arrays. We demonstrate this functionality in the next section when we discuss class ArrayList.

Other static Array methods include **Clear** (to set a range of elements to 0 or null), **CreateInstance** (to create a new array of a specified type), **IndexOf** (to locate the first occurrence of an object in an array or portion of an array), **LastIndexOf** (to locate the last occurrence of an object in an array or portion of an array) and **Reverse** (to reverse the contents of an array or portion of an array).

27.4 Non-Generic Collections

The System.Collections namespace in the .NET Framework Class Library is the primary source for non-generic collections. These classes provide standard implementations of many of the data structures discussed in Chapter 25 with collections that store references of type object. In this section, we demonstrate classes ArrayList, Stack and Hashtable.

27.4.1 Class ArrayList

In most programming languages, conventional arrays have a fixed size—they cannot be changed dynamically to conform to an application's execution-time memory requirements. In some applications, this fixed-size limitation presents a problem for programmers. They must choose between using fixed-size arrays that are large enough to store the maximum number of elements the application may require and using dynamic data structures that can grow and shrink the amount of memory required to store data in response to the changing requirements of an application at execution time.

The .NET Framework's *ArrayList* collection class mimics the functionality of conventional arrays and provides dynamic resizing of the collection through the class's methods. At any time, an ArrayList contains a certain number of elements less than or equal to its *capacity*—the number of elements currently reserved for the ArrayList. An application can manipulate the capacity with ArrayList property Capacity. If an ArrayList needs to grow, it by default doubles its Capacity.

Performance Tip 27.1

As with linked lists, inserting additional elements into an ArrayList whose current size is less than its capacity is a fast operation.

Performance Tip 27.2

It is a slow operation to insert an element into an ArrayList that needs to grow larger to accommodate a new element. An ArrayList that is at its capacity must have its memory reallocated and the existing values copied into it.

Performance Tip 27.3

If storage is at a premium, use method TrimToSize of class ArrayList to trim an ArrayList to its exact size. This will optimize an ArrayList's memory use. Be careful—if the application needs to insert additional elements, the process will be slower because the ArrayList must grow dynamically (trimming leaves no room for growth).

Performance Tip 27.4

The default capacity increment, doubling the size of the ArrayList, may seem to waste storage, but doubling is an efficient way for an ArrayList to grow quickly to "about the right size." This is a much more efficient use of time than growing the ArrayList by one element at a time in response to insert operations.

ArrayLists store references to objects. All classes derive from class object, so an ArrayList can contain objects of any type. Figure 27.4 lists some useful methods and properties of class ArrayList.

Method or Property	Description
Add	Adds an object to the ArrayList and returns an int specifying the index at which the object was added.
Capacity	Property that gets and sets the number of elements for which space is currently reserved in the ArrayList.
Clear	Removes all the elements from the ArrayList.
Contains	Returns true if the specified object is in the ArrayList; otherwise, returns false.
Count	Read-only property that gets the number of elements stored in the ArrayList.
IndexOf	Returns the index of the first occurrence of the specified object in the ArrayList.
Insert	Inserts an object at the specified index.
Remove	Removes the first occurrence of the specified object.
RemoveAt	Removes an object at the specified index.
RemoveRange	Removes a specified number of elements starting at a specified index in the ArrayList.
Sort	Sorts the ArrayList.
TrimToSize	Sets the Capacity of the ArrayList to the number of elements the ArrayList currently contains (Count).

Fig. 27.4 | Some methods and properties of class ArrayList.

Figure 27.5 demonstrates class ArrayList and several of its methods. Class Array-List belongs to the System.Collections namespace (line 4). Lines 8–11 declare two arrays of strings (colors and removeColors) that we will use to fill two ArrayList objects. Recall from Section 9.11 that constants must be initialized at compile-time, but readonly variables can be initialized at execution time. Arrays are objects created at execution time, so we declare colors and removeColors with readonly—not const—to make them unmodifiable. When the application begins execution, we create an ArrayList with an initial capacity of one element and store it in variable list (line 16). The foreach statement in lines 20–21 adds the five elements of array colors to list via ArrayList's **Add** method, so list grows to accommodate these new elements. Line 25 uses ArrayList's overloaded constructor to create a new ArrayList initialized with the contents of array removeColors, then assigns it to variable removeList. This constructor can initialize the contents of an ArrayList with the elements of any ICollection passed to it. Many of the collection classes have such a constructor. Notice that the constructor call in line 25 performs the task of lines 20–21.

Line 28 calls method DisplayInformation (lines 38–55) to output the contents of the list. This method uses a foreach statement to traverse the elements of an ArrayList. As we discussed in Section 27.3, the foreach statement is a convenient shorthand for calling ArrayList's GetEnumerator method and using an enumerator to traverse the elements of the collection. Also, we must use an iteration variable of type object because class ArrayList is non-generic and stores references to objects.

```csharp
1   // Fig. 27.5: ArrayListTest.cs
2   // Using class ArrayList.
3   using System;
4   using System.Collections;
5
6   public class ArrayListTest
7   {
8      private static readonly string[] colors =
9         { "MAGENTA", "RED", "WHITE", "BLUE", "CYAN" };
10     private static readonly string[] removeColors =
11        { "RED", "WHITE", "BLUE" };
12
13     // create ArrayList, add colors to it and manipulate it
14     public static void Main( string[] args )
15     {
16        ArrayList list = new ArrayList( 1 ); // initial capacity of 1
17
18        // add the elements of the colors array
19        // to the ArrayList list
20        foreach ( string color in colors )
21           list.Add( color ); // add color to the ArrayList list
22
23        // add elements in the removeColors array to
24        // the ArrayList removeList with the ArrayList constructor
25        ArrayList removeList = new ArrayList( removeColors );
26
27        Console.WriteLine( "ArrayList: " );
28        DisplayInformation( list ); // output the list
29
30        // remove from ArrayList list the colors in removeList
31        RemoveColors( list, removeList );
32
33        Console.WriteLine( "\nArrayList after calling RemoveColors: " );
34        DisplayInformation( list ); // output list contents
35     } // end method Main
36
37     // displays information on the contents of an array list
38     private static void DisplayInformation( ArrayList arrayList )
39     {
40        // iterate through array list with a foreach statement
41        foreach ( object element in arrayList )
42           Console.Write( "{0} ", element ); // invokes ToString
43
```

Fig. 27.5 | Using class ArrayList. (Part 1 of 2.)

```
44          // display the size and capacity
45          Console.WriteLine( "\nSize = {0}; Capacity = {1}",
46             arrayList.Count, arrayList.Capacity );
47
48          int index = arrayList.IndexOf( "BLUE" );
49
50          if ( index != -1 )
51             Console.WriteLine( "The array list contains BLUE at index {0}.",
52                index );
53          else
54             Console.WriteLine( "The array list does not contain BLUE." );
55       } // end method DisplayInformation
56
57       // remove colors specified in secondList from firstList
58       private static void RemoveColors( ArrayList firstList,
59          ArrayList secondList )
60       {
61          // iterate through second ArrayList like an array
62          for ( int count = 0; count < secondList.Count; count++ )
63             firstList.Remove( secondList[ count ] );
64       } // end method RemoveColors
65    } // end class ArrayListTest
```

```
ArrayList:
MAGENTA RED WHITE BLUE CYAN
Size = 5; Capacity = 8
The array list contains BLUE at index 3.

ArrayList after calling RemoveColors:
MAGENTA CYAN
Size = 2; Capacity = 8
The array list does not contain BLUE.
```

Fig. 27.5 | Using class `ArrayList`. (Part 2 of 2.)

We use the **Count** and **Capacity** properties in line 46 to display the current number of elements and the maximum number of elements that can be stored without allocating more memory to the `ArrayList`. The output of Fig. 27.5 indicates that the `ArrayList` has capacity 8—recall that an `ArrayList` doubles its capacity whenever it needs more space.

In line 48, we invoke method **IndexOf** to determine the position of the `string` "BLUE" in `arrayList` and store the result in local variable `index`. `IndexOf` returns -1 if the element is not found. The `if` statement in lines 50–54 checks if `index` is -1 to determine whether `arrayList` contains "BLUE". If it does, we output its index. `ArrayList` also provides method **Contains**, which simply returns `true` if an object is in the `ArrayList`, and `false` otherwise. Method `Contains` is preferred if we do not need the index of the element.

Performance Tip 27.5

`ArrayList` methods `IndexOf` and `Contains` each perform a linear search, which is a costly operation for large `ArrayLists`. If the `ArrayList` is sorted, use `ArrayList` method `BinarySearch` to perform a more efficient search. Method `BinarySearch` returns the index of the element, or a negative number if the element is not found.

After method DisplayInformation returns, we call method RemoveColors (lines 58–64) with the two ArrayLists. The for statement in lines 62–63 iterates over ArrayList secondList. Line 63 uses an indexer to access an ArrayList element—by following the ArrayList reference name with square brackets ([]) containing the desired index of the element. An ArgumentOutOfRangeException occurs if the specified index is not both greater than 0 and less than the number of elements currently stored in the ArrayList (specified by the ArrayList's Count property).

We use the indexer to obtain each of secondList's elements, then remove each one from firstList with the *Remove* method. This method deletes a specified item from an ArrayList by performing a linear search and removing (only) the first occurrence of the specified object. All subsequent elements shift toward the beginning of the ArrayList to fill the emptied position.

After the call to RemoveColors, line 34 again outputs the contents of list, confirming that the elements of removeList were, indeed, removed.

27.4.2 Class Stack

The Stack class implements a stack data structure and provides much of the functionality that we defined in our own implementation in Section 25.3. Refer to that section for a discussion of stack data structure concepts. We created a test application in Fig. 25.11 to demonstrate the StackInheritance data structure that we developed. We adapt Fig. 25.14 in Fig. 27.6 to demonstrate the .NET Framework collection class Stack.

The using directive in line 4 allows us to use the Stack class with its unqualified name from the System.Collections namespace. Line 10 creates a Stack with the default initial capacity (10 elements). As one might expect, class Stack has methods Push and Pop to perform the basic stack operations.

Method Push takes an object as an argument and inserts it at the top of the Stack. If the number of items on the Stack (the Count property) is equal to the capacity at the time of the Push operation, the Stack grows to accommodate more objects. Lines 19–26 use method Push to add four elements (a bool, a char, an int and a string) to the stack and invoke method PrintStack (lines 50–64) after each Push to output the contents of the stack. Notice that this non-generic Stack class can store only references to objects, so each of the value-type items—the bool, the char and the int—are implicitly boxed before they are added to the Stack. (Namespace System.Collections.Generic provides a generic Stack class that has many of the same methods and properties used in Fig. 27.6.)

Method PrintStack (lines 50–64) uses Stack property Count (implemented to fulfill the contract of interface ICollection) to obtain the number of elements in stack. If the stack is not empty (i.e., Count is not equal to 0), we use a foreach statement to iterate over the stack and output its contents by implicitly invoking the ToString method of each element. The foreach statement implicitly invokes Stack's GetEnumerator method, which we could have called explicitly to traverse the stack via an enumerator.

Method *Peek* returns the value of the top stack element, but does not remove the element from the Stack. We use Peek at line 30 to obtain the top object of the Stack, then output that object, implicitly invoking the object's ToString method. An InvalidOperationException occurs if the Stack is empty when the application calls Peek. (We do not need an exception handling block because we know the stack is not empty here.)

```
1   // Fig. 27.6: StackTest.cs
2   // Demonstrating class Stack.
3   using System;
4   using System.Collections;
5
6   public class StackTest
7   {
8      public static void Main( string[] args )
9      {
10        Stack stack = new Stack(); // default Capacity of 10
11
12        // create objects to store in the stack
13        bool aBoolean = true;
14        char aCharacter = '$';
15        int anInteger = 34567;
16        string aString = "hello";
17
18        // use method Push to add items to (the top of) the stack
19        stack.Push( aBoolean );
20        PrintStack( stack );
21        stack.Push( aCharacter );
22        PrintStack( stack );
23        stack.Push( anInteger );
24        PrintStack( stack );
25        stack.Push( aString );
26        PrintStack( stack );
27
28        // check the top element of the stack
29        Console.WriteLine( "The top element of the stack is {0}\n",
30           stack.Peek() );
31
32        // remove items from stack
33        try
34        {
35           while ( true )
36           {
37              object removedObject = stack.Pop();
38              Console.WriteLine( removedObject + " popped" );
39              PrintStack( stack );
40           } // end while
41        } // end try
42        catch ( InvalidOperationException exception )
43        {
44           // if exception occurs, print stack trace
45           Console.Error.WriteLine( exception );
46        } // end catch
47     } // end Main
48
49     // print the contents of a stack
50     private static void PrintStack( Stack stack )
51     {
```

Fig. 27.6 | Demonstrating class Stack. (Part 1 of 2.)

```
52          if ( stack.Count == 0 )
53             Console.WriteLine( "stack is empty\n" ); // the stack is empty
54          else
55          {
56             Console.Write( "The stack is: " );
57
58             // iterate through the stack with a foreach statement
59             foreach ( object element in stack )
60                Console.Write( "{0} ", element ); // invokes ToString
61
62             Console.WriteLine( "\n" );
63          } // end else
64       } // end method PrintStack
65    } // end class StackTest
```

```
The stack is: True

The stack is: $ True

The stack is: 34567 $ True

The stack is: hello 34567 $ True

The top element of the stack is hello

hello popped
The stack is: 34567 $ True

34567 popped
The stack is: $ True

$ popped
The stack is: True

True popped
stack is empty

System.InvalidOperationException: Stack empty.
   at System.Collections.Stack.Pop()
   at StackTest.Main(String[] args) in C:\examples\ch27\
         fig27_06\StackTest\StackTest.cs:line 37
```

Fig. 27.6 | Demonstrating class Stack. (Part 2 of 2.)

Method Pop takes no arguments—it removes and returns the object currently on top of the Stack. An infinite loop (lines 35–40) pops objects off the stack and outputs them until the stack is empty. When the application calls Pop on the empty stack, an Invalid-OperationException is thrown. The catch block (lines 42–46) outputs the exception, implicitly invoking the InvalidOperationException's ToString method to obtain its error message and stack trace.

Common Programming Error 27.3

Attempting to Peek or Pop an empty Stack (a Stack whose Count property is 0) causes an In-validOperationException.

Although Fig. 27.6 does not demonstrate it, class `Stack` also has method `Contains`, which returns `true` if the `Stack` contains the specified object, and returns `false` otherwise.

27.4.3 Class `Hashtable`

When an application creates objects of new or existing types, it needs to manage those objects efficiently. This includes sorting and retrieving objects. Sorting and retrieving information with arrays is efficient if some aspect of your data directly matches the key value and if those keys are unique and tightly packed. If you have 100 employees with nine-digit Social Security numbers and you want to store and retrieve employee data by using the Social Security number as a key, it would nominally require an array with 999,999,999 elements, because there are 999,999,999 unique nine-digit numbers. If you have an array that large, you could get very high performance storing and retrieving employee records by simply using the Social Security number as the array index, but it would be a large waste of memory.

Many applications have this problem—either the keys are of the wrong type (i.e., not non-negative integers), or they are of the right type, but they are sparsely spread over a large range.

What is needed is a high-speed scheme for converting keys such as Social Security numbers and inventory part numbers to unique array indices. Then, when an application needs to store something, the scheme could convert the application key rapidly to an index and the record of information could be stored at that location in the array. Retrieval occurs the same way—once the application has a key for which it wants to retrieve the data record, the application simply applies the conversion to the key, which produces the array subscript where the data resides in the array and retrieves the data.

The scheme we describe here is the basis of a technique called *hashing*, in which we store data in a data structure called a *hash table*. Why the name? Because, when we convert a key into an array subscript, we literally scramble the bits, making a "hash" of the number. The number actually has no real significance beyond its usefulness in storing and retrieving this particular data record.

A glitch in the scheme occurs when *collisions* occur (i.e., two different keys "hash into" the same cell, or element, in the array). Since we cannot sort two different data records to the same space, we need to find an alternative home for all records beyond the first that hash to a particular array subscript. One scheme for doing this is to "hash again" (i.e., to reapply the hashing transformation to the key to provide a next candidate cell in the array). The hashing process is designed to be quite random, so the assumption is that with just a few hashes, an available cell will be found.

Another scheme uses one hash to locate the first candidate cell. If the cell is occupied, successive cells are searched linearly until an available cell is found. Retrieval works the same way—the key is hashed once, the resulting cell is checked to determine whether it contains the desired data. If it does, the search is complete. If it does not, successive cells are searched linearly until the desired data is found.

The most popular solution to hash-table collisions is to have each cell of the table be a hash "bucket"—typically, a linked list of all the key–value pairs that hash to that cell. This is the solution that the .NET Framework's *Hashtable* class implements.

The *load factor* affects the performance of hashing schemes. The load factor is the ratio of the number of objects stored in the hash table to the total number of cells of the hash table. As this ratio gets higher, the chance of collisions tends to increase.

Performance Tip 27.6

*The load factor in a hash table is a classic example of a **space/time trade-off**. By increasing the load factor, we get better memory utilization, but the application runs slower due to increased hashing collisions. By decreasing the load factor, we get better application speed because of reduced hashing collisions, but we get poorer memory utilization because a larger portion of the hash table remains empty.*

Computer science students study hashing schemes in courses called "Data Structures" and "Algorithms." Recognizing the value of hashing, the .NET Framework provides class Hashtable to enable programmers to easily employ hashing in applications.

This concept is profoundly important in our study of object-oriented programming. Classes encapsulate and hide complexity (i.e., implementation details) and offer user-friendly interfaces. Crafting classes to do this properly is one of the most valued skills in the field of object-oriented programming.

A *hash function* performs a calculation that determines where to place data in the hash table. The hash function is applied to the key in a key–value pair of objects. Class Hashtable can accept any object as a key. For this reason, class object defines method GetHashCode, which all objects inherit. Most classes that are candidates to be used as keys in a hash table override this method to provide one that performs efficient hash code calculations for a specific type. For example, a string has a hash code calculation that is based on the contents of the string. Figure 27.7 uses a Hashtable to count the number of occurrences of each word in a string.

```
1   // Fig. 27.7: HashtableTest.cs
2   // Application counts the number of occurrences of each word in a string
3   // and stores them in a hash table.
4   using System;
5   using System.Text.RegularExpressions;
6   using System.Collections;
7
8   public class HashtableTest
9   {
10     public static void Main( string[] args )
11     {
12        // create hash table based on user input
13        Hashtable table = CollectWords();
14
15        // display hash table content
16        DisplayHashtable( table );
17     } // end method Main
18
19     // create hash table from user input
20     private static Hashtable CollectWords()
21     {
22        Hashtable table = new Hashtable(); // create a new hash table
23
24        Console.WriteLine( "Enter a string: " ); // prompt for user input
25        string input = Console.ReadLine(); // get input
```

Fig. 27.7 | Application counts the number of occurrences of each word in a string and stores them in a hash table. (Part 1 of 2.)

```
26
27        // split input text into tokens
28        string[] words = Regex.Split( input, @"\s+" );
29
30        // processing input words
31        foreach ( string word in words )
32        {
33            string wordKey = word.ToLower(); // get word in lowercase
34
35            // if the hash table contains the word
36            if ( table.ContainsKey( wordKey ) )
37            {
38                table[ wordKey ] = ( ( int ) table[ wordKey ] ) + 1;
39            } // end if
40            else
41                // add new word with a count of 1 to hash table
42                table.Add( wordKey, 1 );
43        } // end foreach
44
45        return table;
46    } // end method CollectWords
47
48    // display hash table content
49    private static void DisplayHashtable( Hashtable table )
50    {
51        Console.WriteLine( "\nHashtable contains:\n{0,-12}{1,-12}",
52            "Key:", "Value:" );
53
54        // generate output for each key in hash table
55        // by iterating through the Keys property with a foreach statement
56        foreach ( object key in table.Keys )
57            Console.WriteLine( "{0,-12}{1,-12}", key, table[ key ] );
58
59        Console.WriteLine( "\nsize: {0}", table.Count );
60    } // end method DisplayHashtable
61 } // end class HashtableTest
```

```
Enter a string:
As idle as a painted ship upon a painted ocean

Hashtable contains:
Key:        Value:
painted     2
a           2
upon        1
as          2
ship        1
idle        1
ocean       1

size: 7
```

Fig. 27.7 | Application counts the number of occurrences of each word in a `string` and stores them in a hash table. (Part 2 of 2.)

Lines 4–6 contain using directives for namespaces System (for class Console), System.Text.RegularExpressions (for class Regex, discussed in Chapter 16, Strings, Characters and Regular Expressions) and System.Collections (for class Hashtable). Class HashtableTest declares three static methods. Method CollectWords (lines 20–46) inputs a string and returns a Hashtable in which each value stores the number of times that word appears in the string and the word is used for the key. Method Display-Hashtable (lines 49–60) displays the Hashtable passed to it in column format. The Main method (lines 10–17) simply invokes CollectWords (line 13), then passes the Hashtable returned by CollectWords to DisplayHashtable in line 16.

Method CollectWords (lines 20–46) begins by initializing local variable table with a new Hashtable (line 22) that has a default initial capacity of 0 elements and a default maximum load factor of 1.0. When the number of items in the Hashtable becomes greater than the number of cells times the load factor, the capacity is increased automatically. (This implementation detail is invisible to clients of the class.) Lines 24–25 prompt the user and input a string. We use static method Split of class Regex in line 28 to divide the string by its whitespace characters. This creates an array of "words," which we then store in local variable words.

The foreach statement in lines 31–43 loops over every element of array words. Each word is converted to lowercase with string method ***ToLower***, then stored in variable wordKey (line 33). Then line 36 calls Hashtable method ***ContainsKey*** to determine whether the word is in the hash table (and thus has occurred previously in the string). If the Hashtable does not contain an entry for the word, line 42 uses Hashtable method Add to create a new entry in the hash table, with the lowercase word as the key and an object containing 1 as the value. Note that autoboxing occurs when the application passes integer 1 to method Add, because the hash table stores both the key and value in references to type object.

Common Programming Error 27.4

Using the Add method to add a key that already exists in the hash table causes an ArgumentException.

If the word is already a key in the hash table, line 38 uses the Hashtable's indexer to obtain and set the key's associated value (the word count) in the hash table. We first down-cast the value obtained by the get accessor from an object to an int. This unboxes the value so that we can increment it by 1. Then, when we use the indexer's set accessor to assign the key's associated value, the incremented value is implicitly reboxed so that it can be stored in the hash table.

Notice that invoking the get accessor of a Hashtable indexer with a key that does not exist in the hash table obtains a null reference. Using the set accessor with a key that does not exist in the hash table creates a new entry, as if you had used the Add method.

Line 45 returns the hash table to the Main method, which then passes it to method DisplayHashtable (lines 49–60), which displays all the entries. This method uses read-only property ***Keys*** (line 56) to get an ICollection that contains all the keys. Because ICollection extends IEnumerable, we can use this collection in the foreach statement in lines 56–57 to iterate over the keys of the hash table. This loop accesses and outputs each key and its value in the hash table using the iteration variable and table's get accessor. Each key and its value is displayed in a field width of -12. The negative field width indicates that the output is left justified. Note that a hash table is not sorted, so the key–value pairs are not displayed in any particular order. Line 59 uses Hashtable property *Count* to get the number of key–value pairs in the Hashtable.

Lines 56–57 could have also used the foreach statement with the Hashtable object itself, instead of using the Keys property. If you use a foreach statement with a Hashtable object, the iteration variable will be of type *DictionaryEntry*. The enumerator of a Hashtable (or any other class that implements *IDictionary*) uses the DictionaryEntry structure to store key–value pairs. This structure provides properties Key and Value for retrieving the key and value of the current element. If you do not need the key, class Hashtable also provides a read-only *Values* property that gets an ICollection of all the values stored in the Hashtable. We can use this property to iterate through the values stored in the Hashtable without regard for where they are stored.

Problems with Non-Generic Collections

In the word-counting application of Fig. 27.7, our Hashtable stores its keys and data as object references, even though we store only string keys and int values by convention. This results in some awkward code. For example, line 38 was forced to unbox and box the int data stored in the Hashtable every time it incremented the count for a particular key. This is inefficient. A similar problem occurs in line 56—the iteration variable of the foreach statement is an object reference. If we need to use any of its string-specific methods, we need an explicit downcast.

This can cause subtle bugs. Suppose we decide to improve the readability of Fig. 27.7 by using the indexer's set accessor instead of the Add method to add a key/value pair in line 42, but accidentally type:

```
table[ wordKey ] = wordKey; // initialize to 1
```

This statement will create a new entry with a string key and string value instead of an int value of 1. Although the application will compile correctly, this is clearly incorrect. If a word appears twice, line 38 will try to downcast this string to an int, causing an InvalidCastException at execution time. The error that appears at execution time will indicate that the problem is at line 38, where the exception occurred, *not* at line 42. This makes the error more difficult to find and debug, especially in large software applications where the exception may occur in a different file—and even in a different assembly.

In Chapter 26, we introduced generics. In the next two sections, we demonstrate how to use generic collections.

27.5 Generic Collections

The System.Collections.Generic namespace in the FCL is a new addition for C# 2.0. This namespace contains generic classes that allow us to create collections of specific types. As you saw in Fig. 27.2, many of the classes are simply generic versions of non-generic collections. A couple classes implement new data structures. In this section, we demonstrate generic collections SortedDictionary and LinkedList.

27.5.1 Generic Class SortedDictionary

A *dictionary* is the general term for a collection of key–value pairs. A hash table is one way to implement a dictionary. The .NET Framework provides several implementations of dictionaries, both generic and non-generic (all of which implement the IDictionary interface in Fig. 27.1). The application in Fig. 27.8 is a modification of Fig. 27.7 that uses the generic class *SortedDictionary*. Generic class SortedDictionary does not use a hash table, but instead stores its key–value pairs in a binary search tree. (We discuss binary trees in depth in Section 25.5.) As the class name suggests, the entries in SortedDictionary are sorted in the tree by key. When the key implements generic interface IComparable, the SortedDictionary uses the results of IComparable method CompareTo to sort the keys. Notice that despite these implementation details, we use the same public methods, properties and indexers with classes Hashtable and SortedDictionary in the same ways. In fact, except for the generic-specific syntax, Fig. 27.8 looks remarkably similar to Fig. 27.7. This is the beauty of object-oriented programming.

Line 6 contains a using directive for the System.Collections.Generic namespace, which contains class SortedDictionary. The generic class SortedDictionary takes two type arguments—the first specifies the type of key (i.e., string), and the second specifies the type of value (i.e., int). We have simply replaced the word Hashtable in line 13 and lines 23–24 with SortedDictionary< string, int > to create a dictionary of int values keyed with strings. Now, the compiler can check and notify us if we attempt to store an object of the wrong type in the dictionary. Also, because the compiler now knows that the data structure contains int values, there is no longer any need for the downcast in line 40. This allows line 40 to use the much more concise prefix increment (++) notation. These are the only changes made to methods Main and CollectWords.

```
 1   // Fig. 27.8: SortedDictionaryTest.cs
 2   // Application counts the number of occurrences of each word in a string
 3   // and stores them in a generic sorted dictionary.
 4   using System;
 5   using System.Text.RegularExpressions;
 6   using System.Collections.Generic;
 7
 8   public class SortedDictionaryTest
 9   {
10      public static void Main( string[] args )
11      {
12         // create sorted dictionary based on user input
13         SortedDictionary< string, int > dictionary = CollectWords();
14
15         // display sorted dictionary content
16         DisplayDictionary( dictionary );
17      } // end method Main
18
19      // create sorted dictionary from user input
20      private static SortedDictionary< string, int > CollectWords()
21      {
22         // create a new sorted dictionary
23         SortedDictionary< string, int > dictionary =
24            new SortedDictionary< string, int >();
25
26         Console.WriteLine( "Enter a string: " ); // prompt for user input
27         string input = Console.ReadLine(); // get input
```

Fig. 27.8 | Application counts the number of occurrences of each word in a string and stores them in a generic sorted dictionary. (Part 1 of 2.)

```
28
29      // split input text into tokens
30      string[] words = Regex.Split( input, @"\s+" );
31
32      // processing input words
33      foreach ( string word in words )
34      {
35          string wordKey = word.ToLower(); // get word in lowercase
36
37          // if the dictionary contains the word
38          if ( dictionary.ContainsKey( wordKey ) )
39          {
40              ++dictionary[ wordKey ];
41          } // end if
42          else
43              // add new word with a count of 1 to the dictionary
44              dictionary.Add( wordKey, 1 );
45      } // end foreach
46
47      return dictionary;
48  } // end method CollectWords
49
50  // display dictionary content
51  private static void DisplayDictionary< K, V >(
52      SortedDictionary< K, V > dictionary )
53  {
54      Console.WriteLine( "\nSorted dictionary contains:\n{0,-12}{1,-12}",
55          "Key:", "Value:" );
56
57      // generate output for each key in the sorted dictionary
58      // by iterating through the Keys property with a foreach statement
59      foreach ( K key in dictionary.Keys )
60          Console.WriteLine( "{0,-12}{1,-12}", key, dictionary[ key ] );
61
62      Console.WriteLine( "\nsize: {0}", dictionary.Count );
63  } // end method DisplayDictionary
64  } // end class SortedDictionaryTest
```

```
Enter a string:
We few, we happy few, we band of brothers

Sorted dictionary contains:
Key:        Value:
band        1
brothers    1
few,        2
happy       1
of          1
we          3

size: 6
```

Fig. 27.8 | Application counts the number of occurrences of each word in a `string` and stores them in a generic sorted dictionary. (Part 2 of 2.)

Static method `DisplayDictionary` (lines 51–63) has been modified to be completely generic. It takes type parameters K and V. These parameters are used in line 52 to indicate that `DisplayDictionary` takes a `SortedDictionary` with keys of type K and values of type V. We use type parameter K again in line 59 as the type of the iteration key. This use of generics is a marvelous example of code reuse. If we decide to change the application to count the number of times each character appears in a string, method `DisplayDictionary` could receive an argument of type `SortedDictionary< char, int >` without modification. This is precisely what you will do in Exercise 27.12.

Performance Tip 27.7

Because class `SortedDictionary` keeps its elements sorted in a binary tree, obtaining or inserting a key–value pair takes O(*log* n) *time, which is fast compared to linear searching then inserting.*

Common Programming Error 27.5

Invoking the get accessor of a SortedDictionary indexer with a key that does not exist in the collection causes a KeyNotFoundException. This behavior is different from that of the Hash-table indexer's get accessor, which would return null.

27.5.2 Generic Class LinkedList

Chapter 25 began our discussion of data structures with the concept of a linked list. We end our discussion with the .NET Framework's generic **LinkedList** class. The LinkedList class is a doubly-linked list—we can navigate the list both backwards and forwards with nodes of generic class **LinkedListNode**. Each node contains property **Value** and read-only properties **Previous** and **Next**. The Value property's type matches LinkedList's single type parameter because it contains the data stored in the node. The Previous property gets a reference to the preceding node in the linked list (or null if the node is the first of the list). Similarly, the Next property gets a reference to the subsequent reference in the linked list (or null if the node is the last of the list). We demonstrate a few linked list manipulations in Fig. 27.9.

```
1   // Fig. 27.9: LinkedListTest.cs
2   // Using LinkedLists.
3   using System;
4   using System.Collections.Generic;
5
6   public class LinkedListTest
7   {
8      private static readonly string[] colors = { "black", "yellow",
9         "green", "blue", "violet", "silver" };
10     private static readonly string[] colors2 = { "gold", "white",
11        "brown", "blue", "gray" };
12
13     // set up and manipulate LinkedList objects
14     public static void Main( string[] args )
15     {
16        LinkedList< string > list1 = new LinkedList< string >();
17
```

Fig. 27.9 | Using LinkedLists. (Part 1 of 3.)

```
18          // add elements to first linked list
19          foreach ( string color in colors )
20             list1.AddLast( color );
21
22          // add elements to second linked list via constructor
23          LinkedList< string > list2 = new LinkedList< string >( colors2 );
24
25          Concatenate( list1, list2 ); // concatenate list2 onto list1
26          PrintList( list1 ); // print list1 elements
27
28          Console.WriteLine( "\nConverting strings in list1 to uppercase\n" );
29          ToUppercaseStrings( list1 ); // convert to uppercase string
30          PrintList( list1 ); // print list1 elements
31
32          Console.WriteLine( "\nDeleting strings between BLACK and BROWN\n" );
33          RemoveItemsBetween( list1, "BLACK", "BROWN" );
34
35          PrintList( list1 ); // print list1 elements
36          PrintReversedList( list1 ); // print list in reverse order
37       } // end method Main
38
39       // output list contents
40       private static void PrintList< E >( LinkedList< E > list )
41       {
42          Console.WriteLine( "Linked list: " );
43
44          foreach ( E value in list )
45             Console.Write( "{0} ", value );
46
47          Console.WriteLine();
48       } // end method PrintList
49
50       // concatenate the second list on the end of the first list
51       private static void Concatenate< E >( LinkedList< E > list1,
52          LinkedList< E > list2 )
53       {
54          // concatenate lists by copying element values
55          // in order from the second list to the first list
56          foreach ( E value in list2 )
57             list1.AddLast( value ); // add new node
58       } // end method Concatenate
59
60       // locate string objects and convert to uppercase
61       private static void ToUppercaseStrings( LinkedList< string > list )
62       {
63          // iterate over the list by using the nodes
64          LinkedListNode< string > currentNode = list.First;
65
66          while ( currentNode != null )
67          {
68             string color = currentNode.Value; // get value in node
69             currentNode.Value = color.ToUpper(); // convert to uppercase
70
```

Fig. 27.9 | Using LinkedLists. (Part 2 of 3.)

```
71                  currentNode = currentNode.Next; // get next node
72              } // end while
73      } // end method ToUppercaseStrings
74
75      // delete list items between two given items
76      private static void RemoveItemsBetween< E >( LinkedList< E > list,
77          E startItem, E endItem )
78      {
79          // get the nodes corresponding to the start and end item
80          LinkedListNode< E > currentNode = list.Find( startItem );
81          LinkedListNode< E > endNode = list.Find( endItem );
82
83          // remove items after the start item
84          // until we find the last item or the end of the linked list
85          while ( ( currentNode.Next != null ) &&
86              ( currentNode.Next != endNode ) )
87          {
88              list.Remove( currentNode.Next ); // remove next node
89          } // end while
90      } // end method RemoveItemsBetween
91
92      // print reversed list
93      private static void PrintReversedList< E >( LinkedList< E > list )
94      {
95          Console.WriteLine( "Reversed List:" );
96
97          // iterate over the list by using the nodes
98          LinkedListNode< E > currentNode = list.Last;
99
100         while ( currentNode != null )
101         {
102             Console.Write( "{0} ", currentNode.Value );
103             currentNode = currentNode.Previous; // get previous node
104         } // end while
105
106         Console.WriteLine();
107     } // end method PrintReversedList
108 } // end class LinkedListTest
```

```
Linked list:
black yellow green blue violet silver gold white brown blue gray

Converting strings in list1 to uppercase

Linked list:
BLACK YELLOW GREEN BLUE VIOLET SILVER GOLD WHITE BROWN BLUE GRAY

Deleting strings between BLACK and BROWN

Linked list:
BLACK BROWN BLUE GRAY
Reversed List:
GRAY BLUE BROWN BLACK
```

Fig. 27.9 | Using LinkedLists. (Part 3 of 3.)

The using directive in line 4 allows us to use the LinkedList class by its unqualified name. Lines 16–23 create LinkedLists list1 and list2 of strings and fill them with the contents of arrays colors and colors2, respectively. Note that LinkedList is a generic class that has one type parameter for which we specify the type argument string in this example (lines 16 and 23). We demonstrate two ways to fill the lists. In lines 19–20, we use the foreach statement and method *AddLast* to fill list1. The AddLast method creates a new LinkedListNode (with the given value available via the Value property), and appends this node to the end of the list. There is also an AddFirst method that inserts a node at the beginning of the list. Line 23 invokes the constructor that takes an IEnumerable< string > parameter. All arrays implicitly inherit from the generic interfaces IList and IEnumerable with the type of the array as the type argument, so the string array colors2 implements IEnumerable< string >. The type parameter of this generic IEnumerable matches the type parameter of the generic LinkedList object. This constructor call copies the contents of the array colors2 to list2.

Line 25 calls generic method Concatenate (lines 51–58) to append all elements of list2 to the end of list1. Line 26 calls method PrintList (lines 40–48) to output list1's contents. Line 29 calls method ToUppercaseStrings (lines 61–73) to convert each string element to uppercase, then line 30 calls PrintList again to display the modified strings. Line 33 calls method RemoveItemsBetween (lines 76–90) to remove the elements between "BLACK" and "BROWN", but not including either. Line 35 outputs the list again, then line 36 invokes method PrintReversedList (lines 93–107) to print the list in reverse order.

Generic method Concatenate (lines 51–58) iterates over list2 with a foreach statement and calls method AddLast to append each value to the end of list1. The LinkedList class's enumerator loops over the values of the nodes, not the nodes themselves, so the iteration variable has type E. Notice that this creates a new node in list1 for each node in list2. One LinkedListNode cannot be a member of more than one LinkedList. Any attempt to add a node from one LinkedList to another generates an InvalidOperationException. If you want the same data to belong to more than one LinkedList, you must make a copy of the node for each list.

Generic method PrintList (lines 40–48) similarly uses a foreach statement to iterate over the values in a LinkedList, and outputs them. Method ToUppercaseStrings (lines 61–73) takes a linked list of strings and converts each string value to uppercase. This method replaces the strings stored in the list, so we cannot use an enumerator (via a foreach statement) as in the previous two methods. Instead, we obtain the first LinkedListNode via the First property (line 64), and use a while statement to loop through the list (lines 66–72). Each iteration of the while statement obtains and updates the contents of currentNode via property Value, using string method *ToUpper* to create an uppercase version of string color. At the end of each iteration, we move the current node to the next node in the list by assigning currentNode to the node obtained by its own Next property (line 71). The Next property of the last node of the list gets null, so when the while statement iterates past the end of the list, the loop exits.

Notice that it does not make sense to declare ToUppercaseStrings as a generic method, because it uses the string-specific methods of the values in the nodes. Methods PrintList (lines 40–48) and Concatenate (lines 51–58) do not need to use any string-specific methods, so they can be declared with generic type parameters to promote maximal code reuse.

Generic method `RemoveItemsBetween` (lines 76–90) removes a range of items between two nodes. Lines 80–81 obtain the two "boundary" nodes of the range by using method *Find*. This method performs a linear search on the list, and returns the first node that contains a value equal to the passed argument. Method `Find` returns `null` if the value is not found. We store the node preceding the range in local variable `currentNode` and the node following the range in `endNode`.

The `while` statement in lines 85–89 removes all the elements between `currentNode` and `endNode`. On each iteration of the loop, we remove the node following `currentNode` by invoking method *Remove* (line 88). Method `Remove` takes a `LinkedListNode`, splices that node out of the `LinkedList`, and fixes the references of the surrounding nodes. After the `Remove` call, `currentNode`'s `Next` property now gets the node *following* the node just removed, and that node's `Previous` property now gets `currentNode`. The `while` statement continues to loop until there are no nodes left between `currentNode` and `endNode`, or until `currentNode` is the last node in the list. (Note that there is also an overloaded version of method `Remove` that performs a linear search for the specified value and removes the first node in the list that contains it.)

Method `PrintReversedList` (lines 93–107) prints the list backward by navigating the nodes manually. Line 98 obtains the last element of the list via the *Last* property and stores it in `currentNode`. The while statement in lines 100–104 iterates through the list backwards by moving the `currentNode` reference to the previous node at the end of each iteration, then exiting when we move past the beginning of the list. Note how similar this code is to lines 64–72, which iterated through the list from the beginning to the end.

27.6 Synchronized Collections

In Chapter 15, we discussed multithreading. Most of the non-generic collections are unsynchronized by default, so they can operate efficiently when multithreading is not required. Because they are unsynchronized, however, concurrent access to a collection by multiple threads could cause errors. To prevent potential threading problems, synchronization wrappers are used for many of the collections that might be accessed by multiple threads. A *wrapper* object receives method calls, adds thread synchronization (to prevent concurrent access to the collection) and passes the calls to the wrapped collection object. Most of the non-generic collection classes in the .NET Framework provide `static` method *Synchronized*, which returns a synchronized wrapping object for the specified object. For example, the following code creates a synchronized `ArrayList`:

```
ArrayList notSafeList = new ArrayList();
ArrayList threadSafeList = ArrayList.Synchronized( notSafeList );
```

The collections in the .NET Framework do not all provide wrappers for safe performance under multiple threads. Some guarantee no thread-safety at all. Many of the generic collections are inherently thread-safe for reading, but not for writing. To determine if a particular class is thread-safe, check that class's documentation in the .NET Framework class library reference.

Also recall that when a collection is modified, any enumerator returned previously by the `GetEnumerator` method becomes invalid and will throw an exception if its methods are invoked. Because other threads may change the collection, using an enumerator is not thread-safe—thus, the `foreach` statement is not thread-safe either. If you use an enumerator or `foreach` statement in a multithreaded application, you should use the `lock` keyword to prevent other threads from using the collection or use a `try` statement to catch the `InvalidOperationException`.

27.7 Wrap-Up

This chapter introduced the .NET Framework collection classes. You learned about the hierarchy of interfaces that many of the collection classes implement. You saw how to use class `Array` to perform array manipulations. You learned that the `System.Collections` and `System.Collections.Generic` namespaces contain many non-generic and generic collection classes, respectively. We presented the non-generic classes `ArrayList`, `Stack` and `Hashtable` as well as generic classes `SortedDictionary` and `LinkedList`. In doing so, we discussed data structures in greater depth. We discussed dynamically expanding collections, hashing schemes, and two implementations of a dictionary. You saw the advantages of generic collections over their non-generic counterparts.

You also learned how to use enumerators to traverse these data structures and obtain their contents. We demonstrated the `foreach` statement with many of the classes of the FCL, and explained that this works by using enumerators "behind-the-scenes" to traverse the collections. Finally, we discussed some of the issues that you should consider when using collections in multithreaded applications.

Summary

Section 27.1 Introduction

- The prepackaged data-structure classes provided by the .NET Framework are known as collection classes—they store collections of data.
- With collection classes, instead of creating data structures to store these sets of items, the programmer simply uses existing data structures, without concern for how they are implemented.

Section 27.2 Collections Overview

- The .NET Framework collections provide high-performance, high-quality implementations of common data structures and enable effective software reuse.
- In earlier versions of C#, the .NET Framework primarily provided the collection classes in the `System.Collections` namespace to store and manipulate object references.
- The .NET Framework 2.0 now includes the `System.Collections.Generic` namespace, which contains classes that take advantage of .NET's generics capabilities.

Section 27.3 Class **Array** and Enumerators

- All arrays implicitly inherit from abstract base class `Array` (namespace `System`).
- The `static` `Array` method `Sort` sorts an array.
- The `static` `Array` method `Copy` copies elements from one array to another.
- The `static` `Array` method `BinarySearch` performs binary searches on an array. This method assumes that it receives a sorted array.
- A collection's `GetEnumerator` method returns an enumerator that can iterate over the collection.
- All enumerators have methods `MoveNext` and `Reset` and property `Current`.

- `MoveNext` moves the enumerator to the next element in the collection. `MoveNext` returns `true` if there is at least one more element in the collection; otherwise, the method returns `false`.

- Read-only property `Current` returns the object at the current location in the collection.

- If a collection is modified after an enumerator is created for that collection, the enumerator immediately becomes invalid.

- The `foreach` statement implicitly obtains an enumerator via the `GetEnumerator` method and uses the enumerator's `MoveNext` method and `Current` property to traverse the collection. This can be done with any collection that implements the `IEnumerable` interface—not just arrays.

Section 27.4.1 Class *ArrayList*

- In most programming languages, conventional arrays have a fixed size.

- The .NET Framework's `ArrayList` collection class mimics the functionality of conventional arrays and provides dynamic resizing of the collection.

- If an `ArrayList` needs to grow, it doubles its current `Capacity` by default.

- `ArrayLists` store references to `objects`.

- `ArrayList` has a constructor that can initialize the contents of an `ArrayList` with the elements of any `ICollection` passed to it. Many of the collection classes have such a constructor.

- The `Count` and `Capacity` properties correspond respectively to the current number of elements in the `ArrayList` and the maximum number of elements that can be stored without allocating more memory to the `ArrayList`.

- Method `IndexOf` returns the position of a value in an `ArrayList`. `IndexOf` returns -1 if the element is not found.

- We can access an element of an `ArrayList` by following the `ArrayList` variable name with square brackets (`[]`) containing the desired index of the element.

- The `Remove` method removes the first occurrence of the specified object. All subsequent elements shift toward the beginning of the `ArrayList` to fill the emptied position.

Section 27.4.2 Class *Stack*

- Class `Stack` has methods `Push` and `Pop` to perform the basic stack operations.

- The non-generic `Stack` class can store only references to objects, so value-type items are implicitly boxed before they are added to the `Stack`.

- Method `Peek` returns the value of the top stack element, but does not remove the element from the `Stack`.

- Attempting to `Peek` or `Pop` an empty `Stack` causes an `InvalidOperationException`.

Section 27.4.3 Class *Hashtable*

- Many applications need a high-speed scheme for converting keys to unique array indices. One such scheme is called hashing, in which we store data in a data structure called a hash table. The .NET Framework provides class `Hashtable` to enable programmers to employ hashing.

- Class `Hashtable` can accept any `object` as a key.

- Method `ContainsKey` determines whether a key is in the hash table.

- `Hashtable` method `Add` creates a new entry in the hash table, with the first argument as the key and the second argument as the value.

- We can use the `Hashtable`'s indexer to obtain and set the key's associated value in the hash table.

- `Hashtable` property `Keys` gets an `ICollection` that contains all the keys.

- If you use a foreach statement with a Hashtable, the iteration variable is of type Dictionary-Entry, which has properties Key and Value for retrieving the key and value of the current element.

Section 27.5.1 Generic Class SortedDictionary

- A dictionary is the general term for a collection of key–value pairs. A hash table is one way to implement a dictionary.
- Generic class SortedDictionary does not use a hash table, but instead stores its key–value pairs in a binary search tree.
- Generic class SortedDictionary takes two type arguments—the first specifies the type of key, and the second specifies the type of value.
- When the compiler knows the type that the data structure contains, there is no need to downcast when we need to use the type-specific methods.
- Invoking the get accessor of a SortedDictionary indexer with a key that does not exist in the collection causes a KeyNotFoundException. This behavior is different from that of the Hashtable indexer's get accessor, which would return null.

Section 27.5.2 Generic Class LinkedList

- The LinkedList class is a doubly-linked list—we can navigate the list both backwards and forwards with nodes of generic class LinkedListNode.
- Each node contains property Value and read-only properties Previous and Next.
- The LinkedList class's enumerator loops over the values of the nodes, not the nodes themselves.
- One LinkedListNode cannot be a member of more than one LinkedList. Any attempt to add a node from one LinkedList to another generates an InvalidOperationException.
- Method Find performs a linear search on the list, and returns the first node that contains a value equal to the passed argument.
- Method Remove splices a node out of a LinkedList, then fixes the references of the surrounding nodes.

Section 27.6 Synchronized Collections

- Most of the non-generic collections are unsynchronized by default, so they can operate efficiently when multithreading is not required. Because they are unsynchronized, however, concurrent access to a collection by multiple threads could cause errors.
- Most of the non-generic collection classes in the .NET Framework provide static method Synchronized, which returns a synchronized wrapping object for the specified object.
- The collections in the .NET Framework do not all provide wrappers for safe performance under multiple threads.
- Because other threads may change the collection, using an enumerator is not thread-safe, and thus the foreach statement is not thread-safe either.

Terminology

Add method of class ArrayList	capacity
Add method of class Hashtable	Capacity property of class ArrayList
Addlist method of class LinkedList	Clear method of class Array
ArgumentException	Clear method of class ArrayList
Array class	collection
ArrayList class	collection class
BinarySearch method of class ArrayList	collision

Contains method of class `ArrayList`
Contains method of class `Stack`
ContainsKey method of class `Hashtable`
Copy method of interface `ICollection`
Count property of interface `ICollection`
CreatInstance method of class `Arrow`
Current property of interface `IEnumerator`
dictionary
DictionaryEntry variable of interface
    `IDictionary`
enumerator
Find method of class `LinkedList`
First property of class `LinkedList`
GetEnumerator method of interface
    `IEnumerable`
GetHashCode method of class `object`
hash function
hash table
hashing
`Hashtable` class
`ICollection` interface
`IDictionary` interface
`IEnumerable` interface
`IEnumerator` interface
`IList` interface
IndexOf method of class `Array`
IndexOf method of class `ArrayList`
int indexer of class `ArrayList`
`InvalidOperationException`
`KeyNotFoundException`
Keys property of interface `IDictionary`

Last property of class `LinkedList`
LastIndexOf method of class `Array`
`LinkedList` generic class
`LinkedListNode` generic class
load factor
MoveNext method of interface `IEnumerator`
Next property of class `LinkedListNode`
object indexer of class `Hashtable`
Peek method of class `Stack`
Pop method of class `Stack`
Previous property of class `LinkedListNode`
Push method of class `Stack`
`Queue` class
Remove method of class `ArrayList`
Remove method of class `LinkedList`
RemoveAt method of class `ArrayList`
RemoveRange method of class `ArrayList`
Reset method of interface `IEnumerator`
Sort method of class `Array`
Sort method of class `ArrayList`
`SortedDictionary` generic class
`SortedList` class
`Stack` class
Synchronized method
`System.Collections` namespace
`System.Collections.Generic` namespace
ToLower method of class `string`
ToUpper method of class `string`
TrimToSize method of class `ArrayList`
Value property of class `LinkedListNode`
Values property of interface `IDictionary`

Self-Review Exercises

27.1 Fill in the blanks in each of the following statements:

    a) A(n) _____ is used to walk through a collection but cannot remove elements from the collection during the iteration.

    b) Class _____ provides the capabilities of an array-like data structure that can resize itself dynamically.

    c) An element in an `ArrayList` can be accessed by using the `ArrayList`'s _____.

    d) If you do not specify a capacity increment, an `ArrayList` will (by default) _____ its size each time additional capacity is needed.

    e) Many collection classes offer a `static` method called _____ to create a collection wrapper that is safe in multithreaded applications.

    f) `IEnumerator` method _____ advances the enumerator to the next item.

    g) If the collection it references has been altered since the enumerator's creation, calling method `Reset` will cause a(n) _____ .

27.2 State whether each of the following is *true* or *false*. If *false*, explain why.

    a) Class `Stack` is in the `System.Collections` namespace.

    b) A class implementing interface `IEnumerator` must define only methods `MoveNext` and `Reset`, and no properties.

c) A hashtable stores key–value pairs.

d) Values of simple types may be stored directly in an ArrayList.

e) An ArrayList can contain duplicate values.

f) A Hashtable can contain duplicate keys.

g) A LinkedList can contain duplicate values.

h) Dictionary is an interface.

i) Enumerators can change the values of elements, but cannot remove them.

j) With hashing, as the load factor increases, the chance of collisions decreases.

Answers to Self-Review Exercises

27.1 a) enumerator (or foreach statement). b) ArrayList. c) indexer. d) double. e) Synchronized. f) MoveNext. g) InvalidOperationException.

27.2 a) True. b) False. The class must also implement property Current. c) True. d) False. An ArrayList stores only objects. Autoboxing occurs when adding a value type to the ArrayList. You can prevent boxing by instead using generic class List with a value type. e) True. f) False. A Hashtable cannot contain duplicate keys. g) True. h) False. Dictionary is a class; IDictionary is an interface. i) False. An enumerator cannot be used to change the values of elements. j) False. With hashing, as the load factor increases, there are fewer available slots relative to the total number of slots, so the chance of selecting an occupied slot (a collision) with a hashing operation increases.

Exercises

27.3 Define each of the following terms:
   a) ICollection
   b) Array
   c) IList
   d) load factor
   e) collision
   f) space–time trade-off in hashing
   g) Hashtable

27.4 Explain briefly the operation of each of the following methods of class ArrayList:
   a) Add
   b) Insert
   c) Remove
   d) Clear
   e) RemoveAt
   f) Contains
   g) IndexOf
   h) Count
   i) Capacity

27.5 Explain why inserting additional elements into an ArrayList object whose current size is less than its capacity is a relatively fast operation and why inserting additional elements into an ArrayList object whose current size is at capacity is a relatively slow operation.

27.6 In our implementation of a stack in Fig. 25.13, we were able to quickly extend a linked list to create class StackInheritance. The .NET Framework designers chose not to use inheritance to create their Stack class. What are the negative aspects of inheritance, particularly for class Stack?

27.7 Briefly answer the following questions:
   a) What happens when you add a simple type (e.g., double) value to a non-generic collection?

b) Can you print all the elements in an `IEnumerable` object without explicitly using an enumerator? If yes, how?

27.8 Explain briefly the operation of each of the following enumerator-related methods:
a) `GetEnumerator`
b) `Current`
c) `MoveNext`

27.9 Explain briefly the operation of each of the following methods and properties of class `Hashtable`:
a) `Add`
b) `Keys`
c) `Values`
d) `ContainsKey`

27.10 Determine whether each of the following statements is *true* or *false*. If *false*, explain why.
a) Elements in an array must be sorted in ascending order before a `BinarySearch` may be performed.
b) Method `First` gets the first node in a `LinkedList`.
c) Class `Array` provides `static` method `Sort` for sorting array elements.

27.11 Write an application that reads in a series of first names and stores them in a `LinkedList`. Do not store duplicate names. Allow the user to search for a first name.

27.12 Modify the application in Fig. 27.8 to count the number of occurrences of each letter rather than of each word. For example, the string `"HELLO THERE"` contains two Hs, three Es, two Ls, one O, one T and one R. Display the results.

27.13 Use a `SortedDictionary` to create a reusable class for choosing from some of the predefined colors in class `Color` (in the `System.Drawing` namespace). The names of the colors should be used as keys, and the predefined `Color` objects should be used as values. Place this class in a class library that can be referenced from any C# application. Use your new class in a Windows application that allows the user to select a color and then changes the background color of the `Form`.

27.14 Write an application that determines and prints the number of duplicate words in a sentence. Treat uppercase and lowercase letters the same. Ignore punctuation.

27.15 Recall from Fig. 27.2 that class `List` is the generic equivalent of class `ArrayList`. Write an application that inserts 25 random integers from 0 to 100 in order into an object of class `List`. The application should calculate the sum of the elements and the floating-point average of the elements.

27.16 Write an application that creates a `LinkedList` object of 10 characters, then creates a second list object containing a copy of the first list, but in reverse order.

27.17 Write an application that takes a whole-number input from a user and determines whether it is prime. If the number is not prime, display the unique prime factors of the number. Remember that a prime number's factors are only 1 and the prime number itself. Every number that is not prime has a unique prime factorization. For example, consider the number 54. The prime factors of 54 are 2, 3, 3 and 3. When the values are multiplied together, the result is 54. For the number 54, the prime factors output should be 2 and 3. Use generic `SortedDictionarys` as part of your solution by recording the factors as the keys and using the `Keys` property to enumerate the factors.

27.18 In Exercise 24.7, you performed a bucket sort of `ints` by using a two-dimensional array, where each row of the array represented a bucket. By instead using a dynamically expanding data structure to represent each bucket, you do not have to write code that keeps track of the number of `ints` in each bucket. Rewrite your solution to use a one-dimensional array of `LinkedList< int >` buckets.

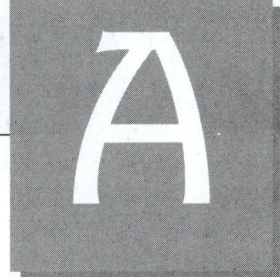

Operator Precedence Chart

Operators are shown in decreasing order of precedence from top to bottom with each level of precedence separated by a horizontal line. The associativity of the operators is shown in the right column.

Operator	Type	Associativity
.	member access	left-to-right
()	method call	
[]	element access	
++	postfix increment	
--	postfix decrement	
new	object creation	
typeof	get System.Type object for a type	
sizeof	get size in bytes of a type	
checked	checked evaluation	
unchecked	unchecked evaluation	
+	unary plus	right-to-left
-	unary minus	
!	logical negation	
~	bitwise complement	
++	prefix increment	

Fig. A.I | Operator precedence chart (Part I of 2.).

Operator	Type	Associativity
`--`	prefix decrement	
`(type)`	cast	
`*`	multiplication	left-to-right
`/`	division	
`%`	remainder	
`+`	addition	left-to-right
`-`	subtraction	
`>>`	right shift	left-to-right
`<<`	left shift	
`<`	less than	left-to-right
`>`	greater than	
`<=`	less than or equal to	
`>=`	greater than or equal to	
`is`	type comparison	
`as`	type conversion	
`!=`	is not equal to	left-to-right
`==`	is equal to	
`&`	logical AND	left-to-right
`^`	logical XOR	left-to-right
`|`	logical OR	left-to-right
`&&`	conditional AND	left-to-right
`||`	conditional OR	left-to-right
`??`	null coalescing	right-to-left
`?:`	conditional	right-to-left
`=`	assignment	right-to-left
`*=`	multiplication assignment	
`/=`	division assignment	
`%=`	remainder assignment	
`+=`	addition assignment	
`-=`	subtration assignment	
`<<=`	left shift assignment	
`>>=`	right shift assignment	
`&=`	logical AND assignment	
`^=`	logical XOR assignment	
`|=`	logical OR assignment	

Fig. A.1 | Operator precedence chart (Part 2 of 2.).

B

Number Systems

OBJECTIVES

In this appendix you will learn:

- To understand basic number systems concepts, such as base, positional value and symbol value.

- To understand how to work with numbers represented in the binary, octal and hexadecimal number systems.

- To abbreviate binary numbers as octal numbers or hexadecimal numbers.

- To convert octal numbers and hexadecimal numbers to binary numbers.

- To convert back and forth between decimal numbers and their binary, octal and hexadecimal equivalents.

- To understand binary arithmetic and how negative binary numbers are represented using two's complement notation.

B.1 Introduction

In this appendix, we introduce the key number systems that programmers use, especially when they are working on software projects that require close interaction with machine-level hardware. Projects like this include operating systems, computer networking software, compilers, database systems and applications requiring high performance.

When we write an integer such as 227 or –63 in a program, the number is assumed to be in the decimal (base 10) number system. The digits in the decimal number system are 0, 1, 2, 3, 4, 5, 6, 7, 8 and 9. The lowest digit is 0 and the highest digit is 9—one less than the base of 10. Internally, computers use the binary (base 2) number system. The binary number system has only two digits, namely 0 and 1. Its lowest digit is 0 and its highest digit is 1—one less than the base of 2.

As we will see, binary numbers tend to be much longer than their decimal equivalents. Programmers who work in assembly languages and in high-level languages like C# that enable programmers to reach down to the machine level, find it cumbersome to work with binary numbers. So two other number systems—the octal number system (base 8) and the hexadecimal number system (base 16)—are popular primarily because they make it convenient to abbreviate binary numbers.

In the octal number system, the digits range from 0 to 7. Because both the binary number system and the octal number system have fewer digits than the decimal number system, their digits are the same as the corresponding digits in decimal.

The hexadecimal number system poses a problem because it requires 16 digits—a lowest digit of 0 and a highest digit with a value equivalent to decimal 15 (one less than the base of 16). By convention, we use the letters A through F to represent the hexadecimal digits corresponding to decimal values 10 through 15. Thus in hexadecimal we can have numbers like 876 consisting solely of decimal-like digits, numbers like 8A55F consisting of digits and letters and numbers like FFE consisting solely of letters. Occasionally, a hexadecimal number spells a common word such as FACE or FEED—this can appear strange to programmers accustomed to working with numbers. The digits of the binary, octal, decimal and hexadecimal number systems are summarized in Fig. B.1–Fig. B.2.

Each of these number systems uses positional notation—each position in which a digit is written has a different positional value. For example, in the decimal number 937 (the 9, the 3 and the 7 are referred to as symbol values), we say that the 7 is written in the ones position, the 3 is written in the tens position and the 9 is written in the hundreds position. Note that each of these positions is a power of the base (base 10) and that these powers begin at 0 and increase by 1 as we move left in the number (Fig. B.3).

Binary digit	Octal digit	Decimal digit	Hexadecimal digit
0	0	0	0
1	1	1	1
	2	2	2
	3	3	3
	4	4	4
	5	5	5
	6	6	6
	7	7	7
		8	8
		9	9
			A (decimal value of 10)
			B (decimal value of 11)
			C (decimal value of 12)
			D (decimal value of 13)
			E (decimal value of 14)
			F (decimal value of 15)

Fig. B.1 | Digits of the binary, octal, decimal and hexadecimal number systems.

Attribute	Binary	Octal	Decimal	Hexadecimal
Base	2	8	10	16
Lowest digit	0	0	0	0
Highest digit	1	7	9	F

Fig. B.2 | Comparing the binary, octal, decimal and hexadecimal number systems.

Positional values in the decimal number system			
Decimal digit	9	3	7
Position name	Hundreds	Tens	Ones
Positional value	100	10	1
Positional value as a power of the base (10)	10^2	10^1	10^0

Fig. B.3 | Positional values in the decimal number system.

For longer decimal numbers, the next positions to the left would be the thousands position (10 to the 3rd power), the ten-thousands position (10 to the 4th power), the hundred-thousands position (10 to the 5th power), the millions position (10 to the 6th power), the ten-millions position (10 to the 7th power) and so on.

In the binary number 101, the rightmost 1 is written in the ones position, the 0 is written in the twos position and the leftmost 1 is written in the fours position. Each position is a power of the base (base 2) and that these powers begin at 0 and increase by 1 as we move left in the number (Fig. B.4). So, $101 = 1 * 2^2 + 0 * 2^1 + 1 * 2^0 = 4 + 0 + 1 = 5$.

For longer binary numbers, the next positions to the left would be the eights position (2 to the 3rd power), the sixteens position (2 to the 4th power), the thirty-twos position (2 to the 5th power), the sixty-fours position (2 to the 6th power) and so on.

In the octal number 425, we say that the 5 is written in the ones position, the 2 is written in the eights position and the 4 is written in the sixty-fours position. Note that each of these positions is a power of the base (base 8) and that these powers begin at 0 and increase by 1 as we move left in the number (Fig. B.5).

For longer octal numbers, the next positions to the left would be the five-hundred-and-twelves position (8 to the 3rd power), the four-thousand-and-ninety-sixes position (8 to the 4th power), the thirty-two-thousand-seven-hundred-and-sixty-eights position (8 to the 5th power) and so on.

In the hexadecimal number 3DA, we say that the A is written in the ones position, the D is written in the sixteens position and the 3 is written in the two-hundred-and-fifty-sixes position. Note that each of these positions is a power of the base (base 16) and that these powers begin at 0 and increase by 1 as we move left in the number (Fig. B.6).

For longer hexadecimal numbers, the next positions to the left would be the four-thousand-and-ninety-sixes position (16 to the 3rd power), the sixty-five-thousand-five-hundred-and-thirty-sixes position (16 to the 4th power) and so on.

Positional values in the binary number system			
Binary digit	1	0	1
Position name	Fours	Twos	Ones
Positional value	4	2	1
Positional value as a power of the base (2)	2^2	2^1	2^0

Fig. B.4 | Positional values in the binary number system.

Positional values in the octal number system			
Decimal digit	4	2	5
Position name	Sixty-fours	Eights	Ones
Positional value	64	8	1
Positional value as a power of the base (8)	8^2	8^1	8^0

Fig. B.5 | Positional values in the octal number system.

Positional values in the hexadecimal number system			
Decimal digit	3	D	A
Position name	Two-hundred-and-fifty-sixes	Sixteens	Ones
Positional value	256	16	1
Positional value as a power of the base (16)	16^2	16^1	16^0

Fig. B.6 | Positional values in the hexadecimal number system.

B.2 Abbreviating Binary Numbers as Octal and Hexadecimal Numbers

The main use for octal and hexadecimal numbers in computing is for abbreviating lengthy binary representations. Figure B.7 highlights the fact that lengthy binary numbers can be expressed concisely in number systems with higher bases than the binary number system.

Decimal number	Binary representation	Octal representation	Hexadecimal representation
0	0	0	0
1	1	1	1
2	10	2	2
3	11	3	3
4	100	4	4
5	101	5	5
6	110	6	6
7	111	7	7
8	1000	10	8
9	1001	11	9
10	1010	12	A
11	1011	13	B
12	1100	14	C
13	1101	15	D
14	1110	16	E
15	1111	17	F
16	10000	20	10

Fig. B.7 | Decimal, binary, octal and hexadecimal equivalents.

A particularly important relationship that both the octal number system and the hexadecimal number system have to the binary system is that the bases of octal and hexadecimal (8 and 16 respectively) are powers of the base of the binary number system (base 2). Consider the following 12-digit binary number and its octal and hexadecimal equivalents. See if you can determine how this relationship makes it convenient to abbreviate binary numbers in octal or hexadecimal. The answer follows the numbers.

Binary number	Octal equivalent	Hexadecimal equivalent
100011010001	4321	8D1

To see how the binary number converts easily to octal, simply break the 12-digit binary number into groups of three consecutive bits each and write those groups over the corresponding digits of the octal number as follows:

100	011	010	001
4	3	2	1

Note that the octal digit you have written under each group of three bits corresponds precisely to the octal equivalent of that 3-digit binary number, as shown in Fig. B.7.

The same kind of relationship can be observed in converting from binary to hexadecimal. Break the 12-digit binary number into groups of four consecutive bits each and write those groups over the corresponding digits of the hexadecimal number as follows:

1000	1101	0001
8	D	1

Notice that the hexadecimal digit you wrote under each group of four bits corresponds precisely to the hexadecimal equivalent of that 4-digit binary number as shown in Fig. B.7.

B.3 Converting Octal and Hexadecimal Numbers to Binary Numbers

In the previous section, we saw how to convert binary numbers to their octal and hexadecimal equivalents by forming groups of binary digits and simply rewriting them as their equivalent octal digit values or hexadecimal digit values. This process may be used in reverse to produce the binary equivalent of a given octal or hexadecimal number.

For example, the octal number 653 is converted to binary simply by writing the 6 as its 3-digit binary equivalent 110, the 5 as its 3-digit binary equivalent 101 and the 3 as its 3-digit binary equivalent 011 to form the 9-digit binary number 110101011.

The hexadecimal number FAD5 is converted to binary simply by writing the F as its 4-digit binary equivalent 1111, the A as its 4-digit binary equivalent 1010, the D as its 4-digit binary equivalent 1101 and the 5 as its 4-digit binary equivalent 0101 to form the 16-digit 1111101011010101.

B.4 Converting from Binary, Octal or Hexadecimal to Decimal

We are accustomed to working in decimal, and therefore it is often convenient to convert a binary, octal, or hexadecimal number to decimal to get a sense of what the number is "really" worth. Our diagrams in Section B.1 express the positional values in decimal. To convert a number to decimal from another base, multiply the decimal equivalent of each digit by its positional value and sum these products. For example, the binary number 110101 is converted to decimal 53, as shown in Fig. B.8.

To convert octal 7614 to decimal 3980, we use the same technique, this time using appropriate octal positional values, as shown in Fig. B.9.

To convert hexadecimal AD3B to decimal 44347, we use the same technique, this time using appropriate hexadecimal positional values, as shown in Fig. B.10.

B.5 Converting from Decimal to Binary, Octal or Hexadecimal

The conversions in Section B.4 follow naturally from the positional notation conventions. Converting from decimal to binary, octal, or hexadecimal also follows these conventions.

Converting a binary number to decimal					
Postional values:	32	16	8	4	2	1
Symbol values:	1	1	0	1	0	1
Products:	1*32=32	1*16=16	0*8=0	1*4=4	0*2=0	1*1=1
Sum:	= 32 + 16 + 0 + 4 + 0s + 1 = 53					

Fig. B.8 | Converting a binary number to decimal.

Converting an octal number to decimal				
Positional values:	512	64	8	1
Symbol values:	7	6	1	4
Products	7*512=3584	6*64=384	1*8=8	4*1=4
Sum:	= 3584 + 384 + 8 + 4 = 3980			

Fig. B.9 | Converting an octal number to decimal.

Converting a hexadecimal number to decimal				
Postional values:	4096	256	16	1
Symbol values:	A	D	3	B
Products	A*4096=40960	D*256=3328	3*16=48	B*1=11
Sum:	= 40960 + 3328 + 48 + 11 = 44347			

Fig. B.10 | Converting a hexadecimal number to decimal.

Suppose we wish to convert decimal 57 to binary. We begin by writing the positional values of the columns right to left until we reach a column whose positional value is greater than the decimal number. We do not need that column, so we discard it. Thus, we first write:

Positional values: 64   32   16   8   4   2   1

Then we discard the column with positional value 64, leaving:

Positional values: 32   16   8   4   2   1

Next we work from the leftmost column to the right. We divide 32 into 57 and observe that there is one 32 in 57 with a remainder of 25, so we write 1 in the 32 column. We divide 16 into 25 and observe that there is one 16 in 25 with a remainder of 9 and write 1 in the 16 column. We divide 8 into 9 and observe that there is one 8 in 9 with a remainder of 1. The next two columns each produce quotients of 0 when their positional values are divided into 1, so we write 0s in the 4 and 2 columns. Finally, 1 into 1 is 1, so we write 1 in the 1 column. This yields:

Positional values:	32	16	8	4	2	1
Symbol values:	1	1	1	0	0	1

and thus decimal 57 is equivalent to binary 111001.

To convert decimal 103 to octal, we begin by writing the positional values of the columns until we reach a column whose positional value is greater than the decimal number. We do not need that column, so we discard it. Thus, we first write:

Positional values: 512   64   8   1

Then we discard the column with positional value 512, yielding:

Positional values: 64   8   1

Next we work from the leftmost column to the right. We divide 64 into 103 and observe that there is one 64 in 103 with a remainder of 39, so we write 1 in the 64 column. We divide 8 into 39 and observe that there are four 8s in 39 with a remainder of 7 and write 4 in the 8 column. Finally, we divide 1 into 7 and observe that there are seven 1s in 7 with no remainder, so we write 7 in the 1 column. This yields:

Positional values:	64	8	1
Symbol values:	1	4	7

and thus decimal 103 is equivalent to octal 147.

To convert decimal 375 to hexadecimal, we begin by writing the positional values of the columns until we reach a column whose positional value is greater than the decimal number. We do not need that column, so we discard it. Thus, we first write:

Positional values: 4096   256   16   1

Then we discard the column with positional value 4096, yielding:

Positional values: 256   16   1

Next we work from the leftmost column to the right. We divide 256 into 375 and observe that there is one 256 in 375 with a remainder of 119, so we write 1 in the 256 column. We divide 16 into 119 and observe that there are seven 16s in 119 with a remainder of 7 and write 7 in the 16 column. Finally, we divide 1 into 7 and observe that there are seven 1s in 7 with no remainder, so we write 7 in the 1 column. This yields:

Positional values: 256   16   1
Symbol values: 1   7   7

and thus decimal 375 is equivalent to hexadecimal 177.

B.6 Negative Binary Numbers: Two's Complement Notation

The discussion so far in this appendix has focused on positive numbers. In this section, we explain how computers represent negative numbers using *two's complement notation*. First we explain how the two's complement of a binary number is formed, then we show why it represents the negative value of the given binary number.

Consider a machine with 32-bit integers. Suppose

```
int value = 13;
```

The 32-bit representation of value is

```
00000000 00000000 00000000 00001101
```

To form the negative of value we first form its *one's complement* by applying C#'s bitwise complement operator (~):

```
onesComplementOfValue = ~value;
```

Internally, ~value is now value with each of its bits reversed—ones become zeros and zeros become ones, as follows:

```
value:
00000000 00000000 00000000 00001101

~value  (i.e., value's ones complement):
11111111 11111111 11111111 11110010
```

To form the two's complement of value, we simply add 1 to value's one's complement. Thus

```
Two's complement of value:
11111111 11111111 11111111 11110011
```

Now if this is in fact equal to −13, we should be able to add it to binary 13 and obtain a result of 0. Let us try this:

```
 00000000 00000000 00000000 00001101
+11111111 11111111 11111111 11110011
-------------------------------------
 00000000 00000000 00000000 00000000
```

The carry bit coming out of the leftmost column is discarded and we indeed get 0 as a result. If we add the one's complement of a number to the number, the result would be all 1s. The key to getting a result of all zeros is that the twos complement is one more than the one's complement. The addition of 1 causes each column to add to 0 with a carry of 1. The carry keeps moving leftward until it is discarded from the leftmost bit, and thus the resulting number is all zeros.

Computers actually perform a subtraction, such as

```
x = a - value;
```

by adding the two's complement of `value` to a, as follows:

```
x = a + (~value + 1);
```

Suppose a is 27 and `value` is 13 as before. If the two's complement of `value` is actually the negative of `value`, then adding the two's complement of value to a should produce the result 14. Let us try this:

```
a (i.e., 27)        00000000 00000000 00000000 00011011
+(~value + 1)      +11111111 11111111 11111111 11110011
                   ------------------------------------
                    00000000 00000000 00000000 00001110
```

which is indeed equal to 14.

Summary

- An integer such as 19 or 227 or –63 in a program is assumed to be in the decimal (base 10) number system. The digits in the decimal number system are 0, 1, 2, 3, 4, 5, 6, 7, 8 and 9. The lowest digit is 0 and the highest digit is 9—one less than the base of 10.

- Internally, computers use the binary (base 2) number system. The binary number system has only two digits, namely 0 and 1. Its lowest digit is 0 and its highest digit is 1—one less than the base of 2.

- The octal number system (base 8) and the hexadecimal number system (base 16) are popular primarily because they make it convenient to abbreviate binary numbers.

- The digits of the octal number system range from 0 to 7.

- The hexadecimal number system poses a problem because it requires 16 digits—a lowest digit of 0 and a highest digit with a value equivalent to decimal 15 (one less than the base of 16). By convention, we use the letters A through F to represent the hexadecimal digits corresponding to decimal values 10 through 15.

- Each number system uses positional notation—each position in which a digit is written has a different positional value.

- A particularly important relationship of both the octal number system and the hexadecimal number system to the binary system is that the bases of octal and hexadecimal (8 and 16 respectively) are powers of the base of the binary number system (base 2).

- To convert an octal to a binary number, replace each octal digit with its three-digit binary equivalent.

- To convert a hexadecimal number to a binary number, simply replace each hexadecimal digit with its four-digit binary equivalent.

- Because we are accustomed to working in decimal, it is convenient to convert a binary, octal or hexadecimal number to decimal to get a sense of the number's "real" worth.

- To convert a number to decimal from another base, multiply the decimal equivalent of each digit by its positional value and sum the products.

- Computers represent negative numbers using two's complement notation.

- To form the negative of a value in binary, first form its one's complement by applying C#'s bitwise complement operator (~). This reverses the bits of the value. To form the two's complement of a value, simply add one to the value's one's complement.

Terminology

base	digit
base 2 number system	hexadecimal number system
base 8 number system	negative value
base 10 number system	octal number system
base 16 number system	one's complement notation
binary number system	positional notation
bitwise complement operator (~)	positional value
conversions	symbol value
decimal number system	two's complement notation

Self-Review Exercises

B.1 Fill in the blanks in each of the following statements:

a) The bases of the decimal, binary, octal and hexadecimal number systems are _____, _____, _____ and _____ respectively.

b) The positional value of the rightmost digit of any number in either binary, octal, decimal or hexadecimal is always _____.

c) The positional value of the digit to the left of the rightmost digit of any number in binary, octal, decimal or hexadecimal is always equal to _____.

B.2 State whether each of the following is *true* or *false*. If *false*, explain why.

a) A popular reason for using the decimal number system is that it forms a convenient notation for abbreviating binary numbers simply by substituting one decimal digit per group of four binary bits.

b) The highest digit in any base is one more than the base.

c) The lowest digit in any base is one less than the base.

B.3 In general, the decimal, octal and hexadecimal representations of a given binary number contain (more/fewer) digits than the binary number contains.

B.4 The (octal / hexadecimal / decimal) representation of a large binary value is the most concise (of the given alternatives).

B.5 Fill in the missing values in this chart of positional values for the rightmost four positions in each of the indicated number systems:

decimal	1000	100	10	1
hexadecimal	...	256	...	...
binary	...	...	...	...
octal	512	...	8	...

B.6 Convert binary 110101011000 to octal and to hexadecimal.

B.7 Convert hexadecimal FACE to binary.

B.8 Convert octal 7316 to binary.

B.9 Convert hexadecimal 4FEC to octal. [*Hint:* First convert 4FEC to binary, then convert that binary number to octal.]

B.10 Convert binary 1101110 to decimal.

B.11 Convert octal 317 to decimal.

B.12 Convert hexadecimal EFD4 to decimal.

B.13 Convert decimal 177 to binary, to octal and to hexadecimal.

B.14   Show the binary representation of decimal 417. Then show the one's complement of 417 and the two's complement of 417.

B.15   What is the result when a number and its two's complement are added to each other?

Answers to Self-Review Exercises

B.1   a) 10, 2, 8, 16. b) 1 (the base raised to the zero power). c) The base of the number system.

B.2   a) False. Hexadecimal does this. b) False. The highest digit in any base is one less than the base. c) False. The lowest digit in any base is zero.

B.3   Fewer.

B.4   Hexadecimal.

B.5   Fill in the missing values in this chart of positional values for the rightmost four positions in each of the indicated number systems:

decimal	1000	100	10	1
hexadecimal	4096	256	16	1
binary	8	4	2	1
octal	512	64	8	1

B.6   Octal 6530; Hexadecimal D58.

B.7   Binary 1111 1010 1100 1110.

B.8   Binary 111 011 001 110.

B.9   Binary 0 100 111 111 101 100; Octal 47754.

B.10   Decimal 2+4+8+32+64=110.

B.11   Decimal 7+1*8+3*64=7+8+192=207.

B.12   Decimal 4+13*16+15*256+14*4096=61396.

B.13   Decimal 177
to binary:

```
256 128 64 32 16 8 4 2 1
128 64 32 16 8 4 2 1
(1*128)+(0*64)+(1*32)+(1*16)+(0*8)+(0*4)+(0*2)+(1*1)
10110001
```

to octal:

```
512 64 8 1
64 8 1
(2*64)+(6*8)+(1*1)
261
```

to hexadecimal:

```
256 16 1
16 1
(11*16)+(1*1)
(B*16)+(1*1)
B1
```

B.14   Binary:

```
512 256 128 64 32 16 8 4 2 1
256 128 64 32 16 8 4 2 1
(1*256)+(1*128)+(0*64)+(1*32)+(0*16)+(0*8)+(0*4)+(0*2)+(1*1)
110100001
```

One's complement: 001011110
Two's complement: 001011111
Check: Original binary number + its two's complement

```
110100001
001011111
---------
000000000
```

B.15   Zero.

Exercises

B.16   Some people argue that many of our calculations would be easier in the base 12 number system because 12 is divisible by so many more numbers than 10 (for base 10). What is the lowest digit in base 12? What would be the highest symbol for the digit in base 12? What are the positional values of the rightmost four positions of any number in the base 12 number system?

B.17   Complete the following chart of positional values for the rightmost four positions in each of the indicated number systems:

decimal	1000	100	10	1
base 6	...	...	6	...
base 13	...	169	...	...
base 3	27	...	...	...

B.18   Convert binary 100101111010 to octal and to hexadecimal.

B.19   Convert hexadecimal 3A7D to binary.

B.20   Convert hexadecimal 765F to octal. (*Hint:* First convert 765F to binary, then convert that binary number to octal.)

B.21   Convert binary 1011110 to decimal.

B.22   Convert octal 426 to decimal.

B.23   Convert hexadecimal FFFF to decimal.

B.24   Convert decimal 299 to binary, to octal and to hexadecimal.

B.25   Show the binary representation of decimal 779. Then show the one's complement of 779 and the two's complement of 779.

B.26   Show the two's complement of integer value −1 on a machine with 32-bit integers.

C

Using the Visual Studio 2005 Debugger

We are built to make mistakes, coded for error.
—Lewis Thomas

What we anticipate seldom occurs; what we least expect generally happens.
—Benjamin Disraeli

It is one thing to show a man that he is in error, and another to put him in possession of truth.
—John Locke

He can run but he can't hide.
—Joe Louis

And so shall I catch the fly.
—William Shakespeare

OBJECTIVES

In this appendix you will learn:

- To use the debugger to locate and correct logic errors in a program.

- To use breakpoints to pause program execution and allow you to examine the values of variables.

- To set, disable and remove breakpoints.

- To use the **Continue** command to continue execution from a breakpoint.

- To use the **Locals** window to view and modify variable values.

- To use the **Watch** window to evaluate expressions.

- To use the **Step Into**, **Step Out** and **Step Over** commands to execute a program line-by-line.

- To use the new Visual Studio 2005 debugging features Edit and Continue and Just My Code™ debugging.

C.1 Introduction

In Chapter 3, you learned that there are two types of errors—compilation errors and logic errors—and you learned how to eliminate compilation errors from your code. Logic errors, also called *bugs*, do not prevent a program from compiling successfully, but can cause a program to produce erroneous results, or terminate prematurely, when it runs. Most compiler vendors, like Microsoft, provide a tool called a *debugger*, which allows you to monitor the execution of your programs to locate and remove logic errors. A program must successfully compile before it can be used in the debugger—the debugger helps you analyze a program while it is running. The debugger allows you to suspend program execution, examine and set variable values and much more. In this appendix, we introduce the Visual Studio debugger, several of its debugging tools and new features added for Visual Studio 2005.

C.2 Breakpoints and the **Continue** Command

We begin by investigating *breakpoints*, which are markers that can be set at any executable line of code. When a running program reaches a breakpoint, execution pauses, allowing you to examine the values of variables to help determine whether logic errors exist. For example, you can examine the value of a variable that stores the result of a calculation to determine whether the calculation was performed correctly. You can also examine the value of an expression.

To illustrate the features of the debugger, we use the program in Figs. C.1 and C.2, which creates and manipulates an object of class Account (Fig. C.1). This example is similar to an example you saw in Chapter 4 (Figs. 4.15–4.16). Therefore, it does not use features we present in later chapters like += and if...else. Execution begins in Main (lines 8–29 of Fig. C.2). Line 10 creates an Account object with an initial balance of $50.00. Account's constructor (lines 10–13 of Fig. C.1) accepts one argument, which specifies the Account's initial balance. Lines 13–14 of Fig. C.2 output the initial account balance using Account property Balance. Line 16 declares and initializes local variable depositAmount. Lines 19–20 prompt the user for and input the depositAmount. Line 23 adds the deposit to the Account's balance using its Credit method. Finally, lines 26–27 display the new balance.

```
1   // Fig. C.01: Account.cs
2   // Account class with a constructor to
3   // initialize instance variable balance.
4
5   public class Account
6   {
7      private decimal balance; // instance variable that stores the balance
8
9      // constructor
10     public Account( decimal initialBalance )
11     {
12        Balance = initialBalance; // set balance using property Balance
13     } // end Account constructor
14
15     // credit (add) an amount to the account
16     public void Credit( decimal amount )
17     {
18        Balance = Balance + amount; // add amount to Balance
19     } // end method Credit
20
21     // a property to get and set the account balance
22     public decimal Balance
23     {
24        get
25        {
26           return balance;
27        } // end get
28        set
29        {
30           // validate that value is greater than 0;
31           // if it is not, balance is set to the default value 0
32           if ( value > 0 )
33              balance = value;
34
35           if ( value <= 0 )
36              balance = 0;
37        } // end set
38     } // end property Balance
39  } // end class Account
```

Fig. C.1 | Account class with a constructor to initialize instance variable balance.

```
1   // Fig. C.02: AccountTest.cs
2   // Create and manipulate an Account object.
3   using System;
4
5   public class AccountTest
6   {
7      // Main method begins execution of C# application
8      public static void Main( string[] args )
9      {
10        Account account1 = new Account( 50.00M ); // create Account object
```

Fig. C.2 | Creating and manipulating an Account object. (Part 1 of 2.)

```
11
12          // display initial balance of each object using property Balance
13          Console.Write( "account1 balance: {0:C}\n",
14             account1.Balance ); // display Balance property
15
16          decimal depositAmount; // deposit amount read from user
17
18          // prompt and obtain user input
19          Console.Write( "Enter deposit amount for account1: " );
20          depositAmount = Convert.ToDecimal( Console.ReadLine() );
21          Console.Write( "adding {0:C} to account1 balance\n\n",
22             depositAmount );
23          account1.Credit( depositAmount ); // add to account1 balance
24
25          // display balance
26          Console.Write( "account1 balance: {0:C}\n",
27             account1.Balance );
28          Console.WriteLine();
29       } // end Main
30    } // end class AccountTest
```

```
account1 balance: $50.00

Enter deposit amount for account1: 49.99
adding $49.99 to account1 balance

account1 balance: $99.99
```

Fig. C.2 | Creating and manipulating an `Account` object. (Part 2 of 2.)

In the following steps, you will use breakpoints and various debugger commands to examine the value of the variable `depositAmount` (declared in Fig. C.2) while the program executes.

1. *Inserting breakpoints in Visual Studio.* First, ensure that `AccountTest.cs` is open in the IDE's code editor. To insert a breakpoint, left click inside the *margin indicator bar* (the gray margin at the left of the code window in Fig. C.3) next to the line of code at which you wish to break, or right click that line of code and select **Breakpoint > Insert Breakpoint**. You can set as many breakpoints as you like. Set breakpoints at lines 19, 23 and 28 of your code. A *solid circle* appears in the margin indicator bar where you clicked and the entire code statement is highlighted, indicating that breakpoints have been set (Fig. C.3). When the program runs, the debugger suspends execution at any line that contains a breakpoint. The program then enters *break mode*. Breakpoints can be set before running a program, in break mode and during execution.

2. *Beginning the debugging process.* After setting breakpoints in the code editor, select **Build > Build Solution** to compile the program, then select **Debug > Start Debugging** (or press the *F5* key) to begin the debugging process. While debugging a console application, the Command Prompt window appears (Fig. C.4), allowing program interaction (input and output).

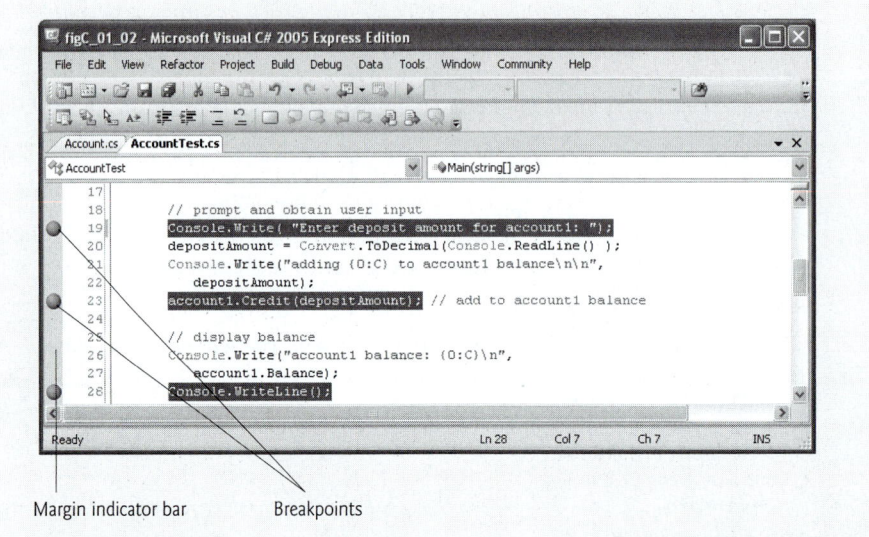

Fig. C.3 | Setting breakpoints.

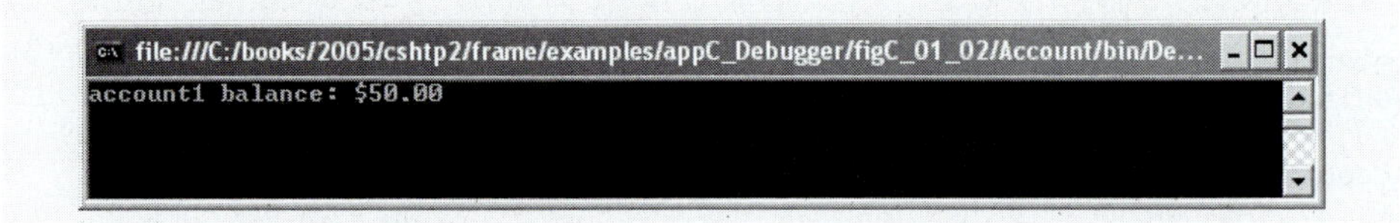

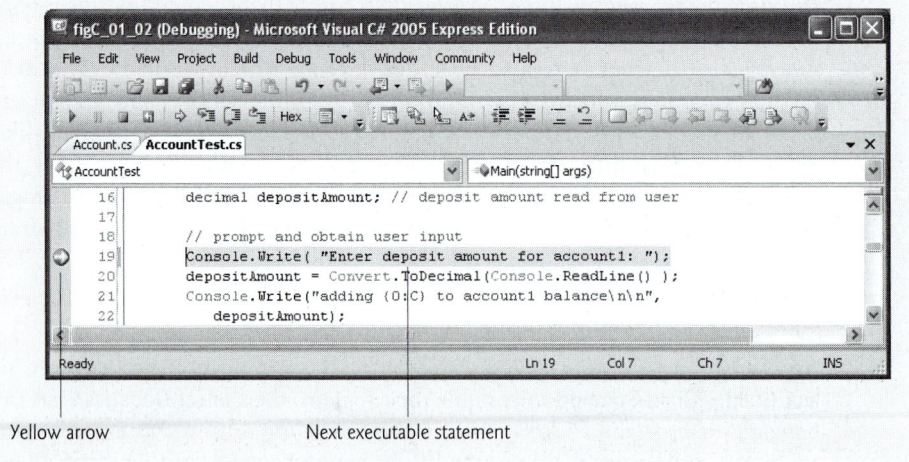

Fig. C.4 | Account program running.

3. *Examining program execution.* Program execution pauses at the first breakpoint (line 19), and the IDE becomes the active window (Fig. C.5). The *yellow arrow* to the left of line 19 indicates that this line contains the next statement to execute. The IDE also highlights the line as well.

Fig. C.5 | Program execution suspended at the first breakpoint.

4. *Using the Continue command to resume execution.* To resume execution, select **Debug > Continue** (or press the *F5* key). The ***Continue command*** will execute the statements from the current point in the program to the next breakpoint or the end of Main, whichever comes first. The program continues executing and pauses for input at line 20. Enter 49.99 in the Command Prompt window as the deposit amount. When you press *Enter*, the program executes until it stops at the next breakpoint (line 23). Notice that when you place the mouse pointer over the variable name depositAmount, its value is displayed in a ***Quick Info box*** (Fig. C.6). As you'll see, this can help you spot logic errors in your programs.

5. *Continuing program execution.* Use the **Debug > Continue** command to execute line 23. The program displays the result of its calculation (Fig. C.7).

6. *Disabling a breakpoint.* To *disable a breakpoint*, right click a line of code in which the breakpoint has been set and select **Breakpoint > Disable Breakpoint**. You can also right click the breakpoint itself and select **Disable Breakpoint**. The disabled breakpoint is indicated by a hollow circle (Fig. C.8)—the breakpoint can be re-enabled by clicking inside the hollow circle, or by right clicking the line marked by the hollow circle (or the circle itself) and selecting **Breakpoint > Enable Breakpoint**.

7. *Removing a breakpoint.* To remove a breakpoint that you no longer need, right click the line of code on which the breakpoint has been set and select **Breakpoint > Delete Breakpoint**. You also can remove a breakpoint by clicking the circle in the margin indicator bar.

8. *Finishing program execution.* Select **Debug > Continue** to execute the program to completion.

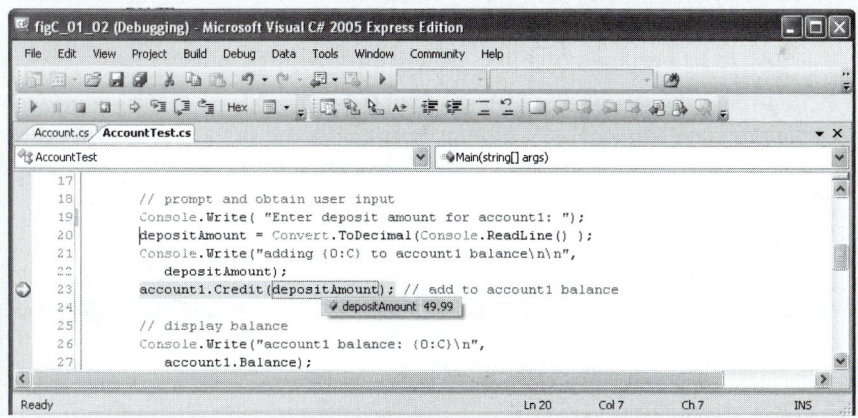

Fig. C.6 | *QuickInfo* box displays value of variable depositAmount.

Fig. C.7 | Program output.

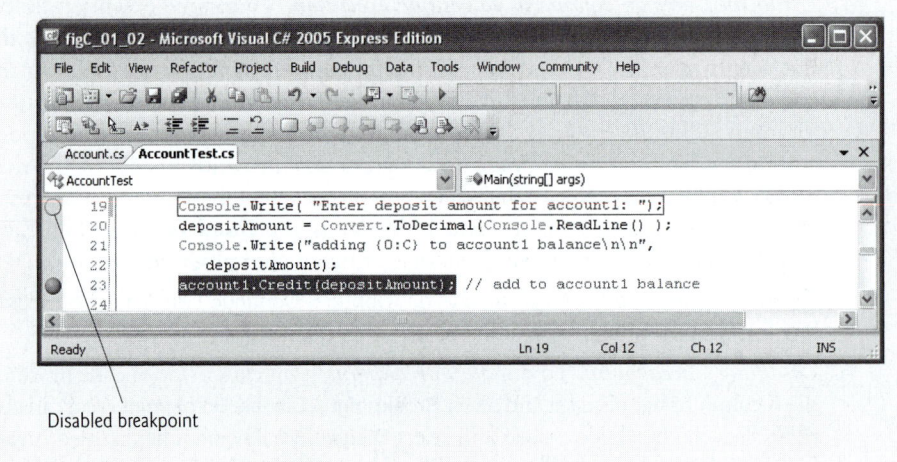

Fig. C.8 | Disabled breakpoint.

C.3 The Locals and Watch Windows

In the preceding section, you learned that the *Quick Info* feature allows you to examine the value of a variable. In this section, you will learn how to use the **Locals** *window* to assign new values to variables while your program is running. You will also use the **Watch** *window* to examine the values of expressions.

1. *Inserting breakpoints.* Set a breakpoint at line 23 (Fig. C.9) in the source code by left clicking in the margin indicator bar to the left of line 23. Use the same technique to set breakpoints at lines 26 and 28 as well.

2. *Starting debugging.* Select **Debug > Start Debugging**. Type 49.99 at the **Enter deposit amount for account1:** prompt (Fig. C.10) and press *Enter* so that the program reads the value you just entered. The program executes until the breakpoint at line 23.

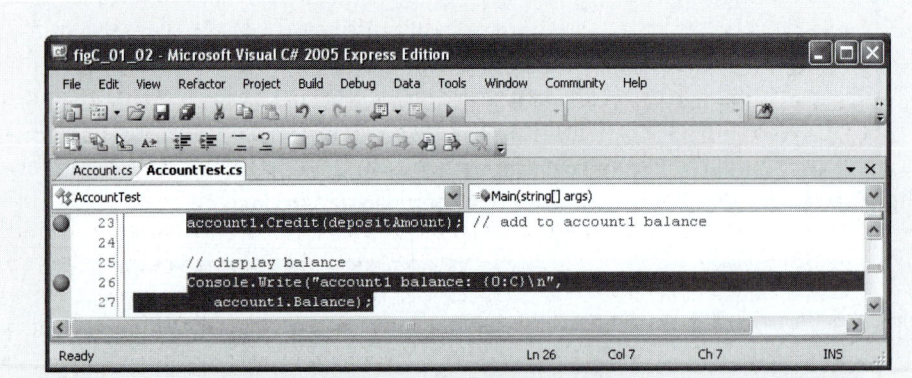

Fig. C.9 | Setting breakpoints at lines 23 and 26.

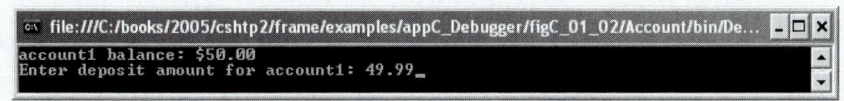

Fig. C.10 | Entering the deposit amount before the breakpoint is reached.

3. *Suspending program execution.* When the program reaches line 23, Visual Studio suspends program execution and switches the program into break mode (Fig. C.11). At this point, the statement in line 20 (Fig. C.2) has input the depositAmount that you entered (49.99), the statement in lines 21–22 has output that the program is adding that amount to the account1 balance and the statement in line 23 is the next statement that will execute.

4. *Examining data.* Once the program has entered break mode, you can explore the values of your local variables using the debugger's **Locals** window. To view the **Locals** window, select **Debug > Windows > Locals**. Click the plus box to the left of account1 in the **Name** column of the **Locals** window (Fig. C.12). This allows you to view each of account1's instance variable values individually, including the value for balance (50). Note that the **Locals** window displays properties of a class as data, which is why you see both the Balance property and the balance instance variable in the **Locals** window. In addition, the current value of local variable depositAmount (49.99) and the args parameter of Main are also displayed.

5. *Evaluating arithmetic and boolean expressions.* You can evaluate arithmetic and boolean expressions using the **Watch** window. Select **Debug > Windows > Watch** to display the window (Fig. C.13). In the first row of the **Name** column (which should be blank initially), type (depositAmount + 10) * 5, then press *Enter*. The value 299.95 is displayed (Fig. C.13). In the next row of the **Name** column in the **Watch** window, type depositAmount == 200, then press *Enter*. This expression determines whether the value contained in depositAmount is 200. Expressions containing the == symbol are bool expressions. The value returned is false (Fig. C.13), because depositAmount does not currently contain the value 200.

6. *Resuming execution.* Select **Debug > Continue** to resume execution. Line 23 executes, crediting the account with the deposit amount, and the program enters break mode again at line 26. Select **Debug > Windows > Locals**. The updated balance instance variable and Balance property value are now displayed (Fig. C.14).

7. *Modifying values.* Based on the value input by the user (49.99), the account balance output by the program should be $99.99. However, you can use the **Locals** window to change variable values during program execution. This can be valuable for experimenting with different values and for locating logic errors in programs. In the **Locals** window, click the **Value** field in the balance row to select the value 99.99. Type 66.99, then press *Enter*. The debugger changes the value of balance (and the Balance property as well), then displays its new value in red (Fig. C.15). Now select **Debug > Continue** to execute lines 26–27. Notice that the new value of balance is displayed in the Command Prompt window.

8. *Stopping the debugging session.* Select **Debug > Stop Debugging**. Delete all breakpoints.

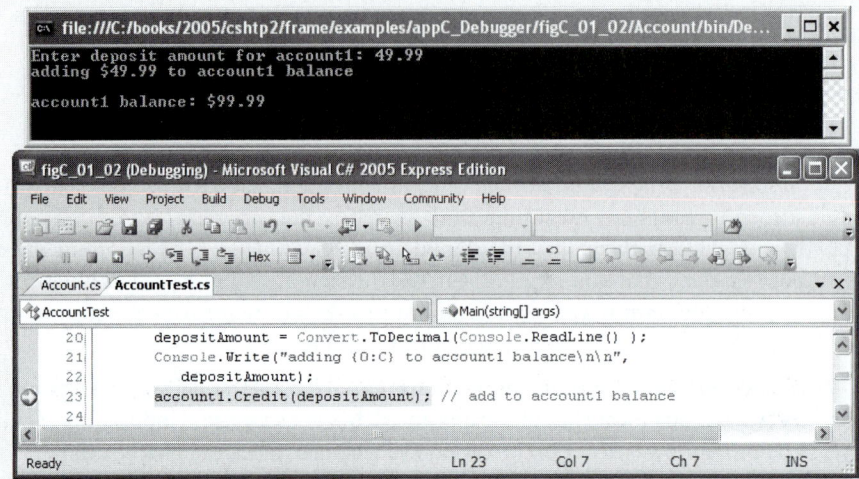

Fig. C.11 | Program execution pauses when debugger reaches the breakpoint at line 23.

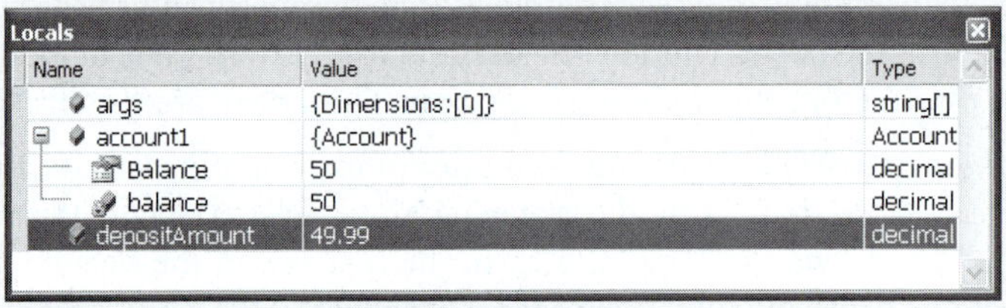

Fig. C.12 | Examining variable depositAmount.

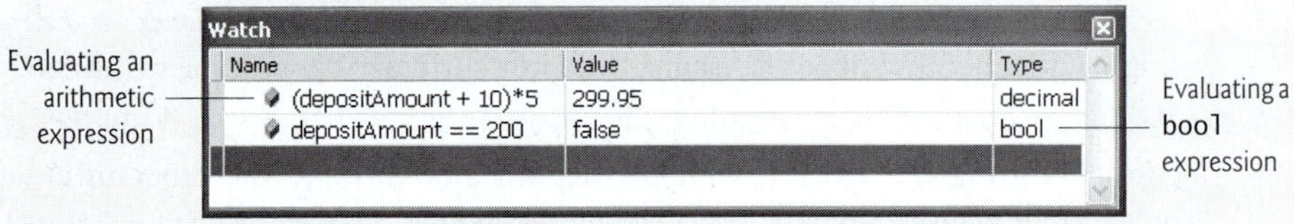

Evaluating an arithmetic expression

Evaluating a bool expression

Fig. C.13 | Examining the values of expressions.

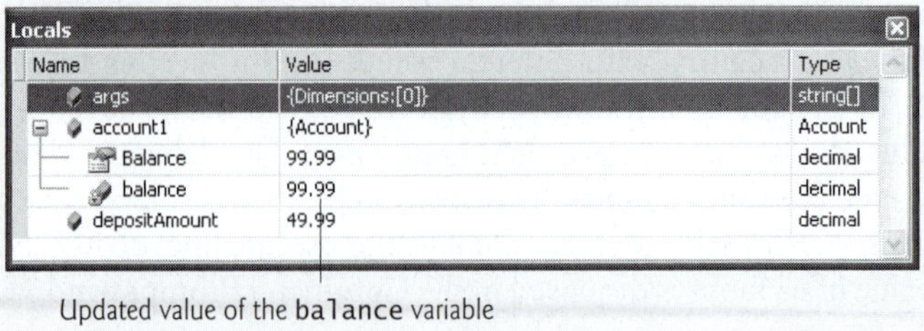

Updated value of the balance variable

Fig. C.14 | Displaying the value of local variables.

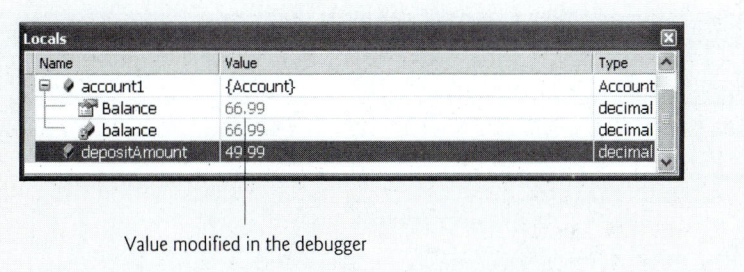

Value modified in the debugger

Fig. C.15 | Modifying the value of a variable.

C.4 Controlling Execution Using the Step Into, Step Over, Step Out and Continue Commands

Sometimes you will need to execute a program line-by-line to find and fix logic errors. Stepping through a portion of your program this way can help you verify that a method's code executes correctly. The commands you learn in this section allow you to execute a method line-by-line, execute all the statements of a method or execute only the remaining statements of a method (if you have already executed some statements within the method).

1. *Setting a breakpoint.* Set a breakpoint at line 23 by left clicking in the margin indicator bar (Fig. C.16).

2. *Starting the debugger.* Select **Debug > Start Debugging**. Enter the value 49.99 at the **Enter deposit amount for account1:** prompt. Program execution halts when the program reaches the breakpoint at line 23.

3. *Using the Step Into command.* The **Step Into** command executes the next statement in the program (the yellow highlighted line of Fig. C.17) and immediately halts. If the statement to execute is a method call, control transfers to the called method. The **Step Into** command allows you to follow execution into a method and confirm its execution by individually executing each statement inside the method. Select **Debug > Step Into** (or press *F11*) to enter the Credit method (Fig. C.18).

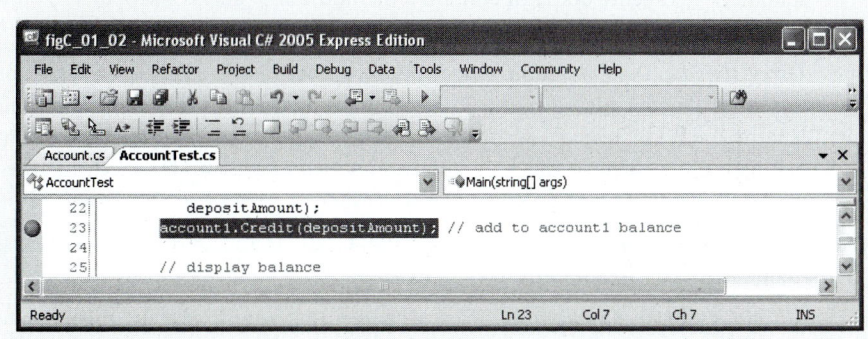

Fig. C.16 | Setting a breakpoint in the program.

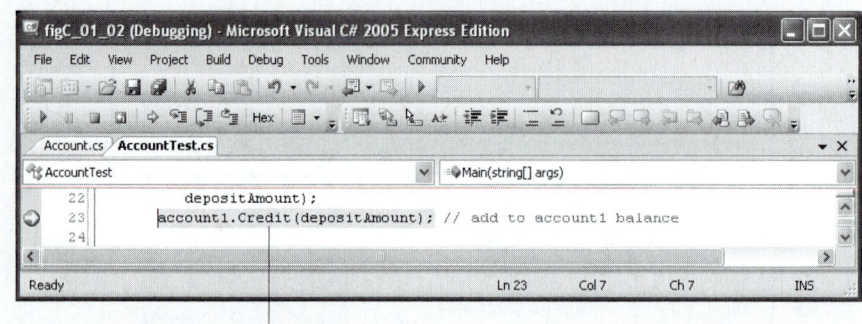

Next statement to execute is a method call

Fig. C.17 | Using the **Step Into** command to execute a statement.

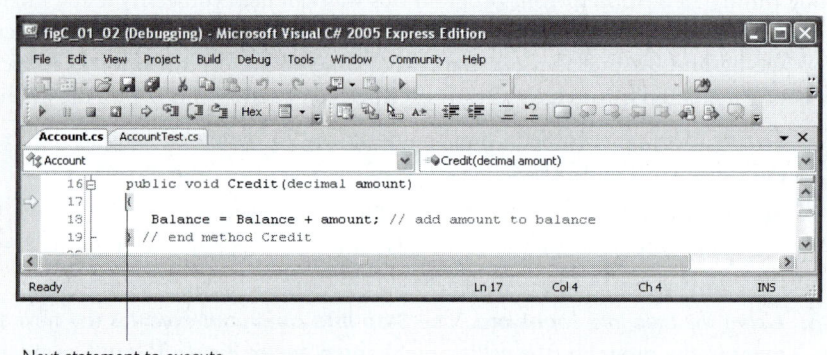

Next statement to execute

Fig. C.18 | Stepping into the Credit method.

4. *Using the Step Over command.* Select **Debug > Step Over** to enter the Credit method's body (line 17 in Fig. C.18) and transfer control to line 18 (Fig. C.19). The **Step Over** *command* behaves like the **Step Into** command when the next statement to execute does not contain a method call or access a property. You will see how the **Step Over** command differs from the **Step Into** command in *Step 10*.

5. *Using the Step Out command.* Select **Debug > Step Out** to execute the remaining statements in the method and return control to the calling method. Often, in lengthy methods, you will want to look at a few key lines of code, then continue debugging the caller's code. The **Step Out** *command* is useful for executing the remainder of a method and returning to the caller.

6. *Setting a breakpoint.* Set a breakpoint (Fig. C.20) at line 28 of Fig. C.2. You will make use of this breakpoint in the next step.

7. *Using the Continue command.* Select **Debug > Continue** to execute until the next breakpoint is reached at line 28. This feature saves time when you do not want to step line-by-line through many lines of code to reach the next breakpoint.

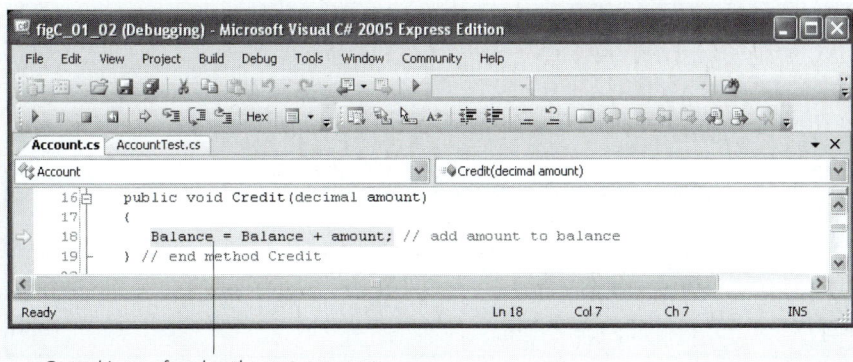

Control is transferred to the next statement

Fig. C.19 | Stepping over a statement in the Credit method.

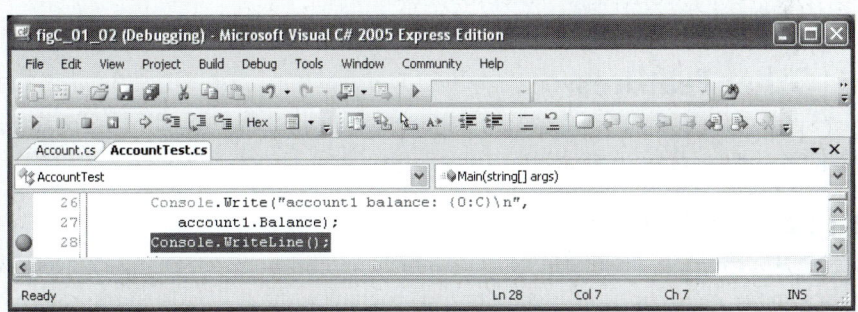

Fig. C.20 | Setting a second breakpoint in the program.

8. *Stopping the debugger.* Select **Debug > Stop Debugging** to end the debugging session.

9. *Starting the debugger.* Before we can demonstrate the next debugger feature, you must restart the debugger. Start it, as you did in *Step 2*, and enter the same value (49.99). The debugger pauses execution at line 23.

10. *Using the Step Over command.* Select **Debug > Step Over** (Fig. C.21). Recall that this command behaves like the **Step Into** command when the next statement to execute does not contain a method call. If the next statement to execute contains a method call, the called method executes in its entirety (without pausing execution at any statement inside the method—unless there is a breakpoint in the method), and the arrow advances to the next executable line (after the method call) in the current method. In this case, the debugger executes line 23, located in Main (Fig. C.2). Line 23 calls the Credit method. Then, the debugger pauses execution at line 26, the next executable statement.

11. *Stopping the debugger.* Select **Debug > Stop Debugging**. Remove all remaining breakpoints.

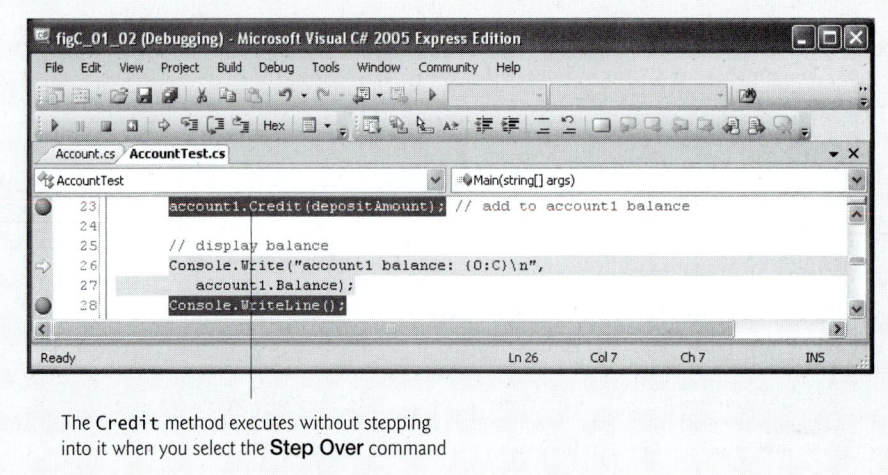

The **Credit** method executes without stepping
into it when you select the **Step Over** command

Fig. C.21 | Using the debugger's **Step Over** command.

C.5 Other Features

Visual Studio 2005 provides many new debugging features, that simplify the testing and debugging process. We discuss some of these features in this section.

C.5.1 Edit and Continue

The *Edit and Continue* feature allows you to make modifications or changes to your code in debug mode, then continue executing the program without having to recompile your code.

1. *Setting a breakpoint.* Set a breakpoint at line 19 in your example (Fig. C.22).

2. *Starting the debugger.* Select **Debug > Start Debugging**. When execution begins, the account1 balance is displayed. The debugger enters break mode when it reaches the breakpoint at line 19.

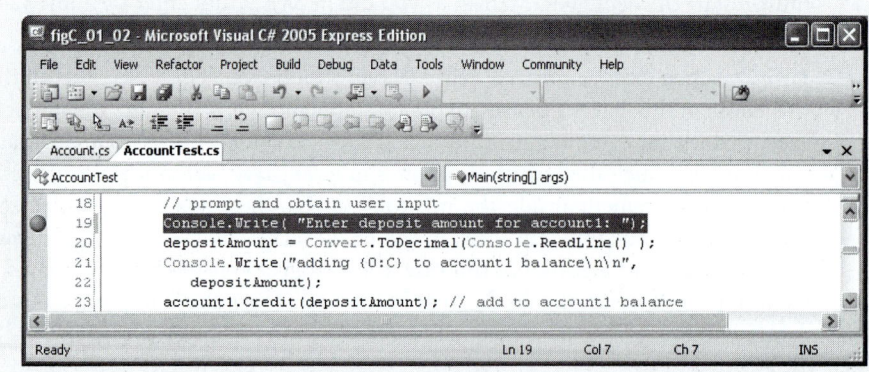

Fig. C.22 | Setting a breakpoint at line 19.

3. *Changing the input prompt text.* Suppose you wish to modify the input prompt text to provide the user with a range of values for variable depositAmount. Rather than stopping the debugging process, add the text "(from $1-500):" to the end of "Enter deposit amount for account1" at line 19 in the code view window (Fig. C.23). Select **Debug > Continue**. The application prompts you for input using the updated text (Fig. C.24).

In this example, we wanted to make a change in the text for our input prompt before line 19 executes. However, if you want to make a change to a line that already executed, you must select a prior statement in your code from which to continue execution.

1. *Setting a breakpoint.* Set a breakpoint at line 21 (Fig. C.25).

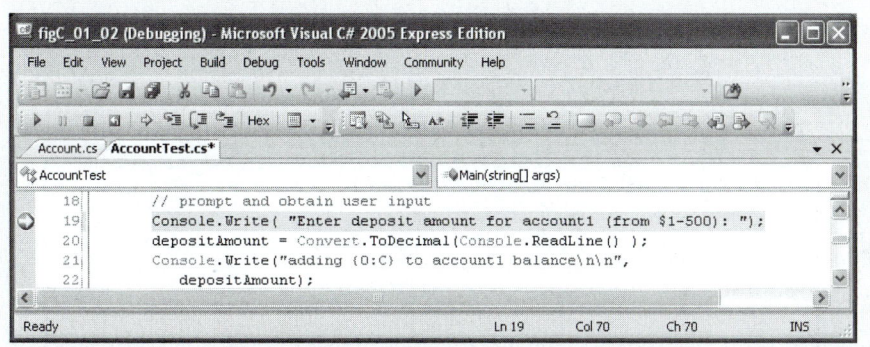

Fig. C.23 | Changing the text of the input prompt while the application is in **Debug** mode.

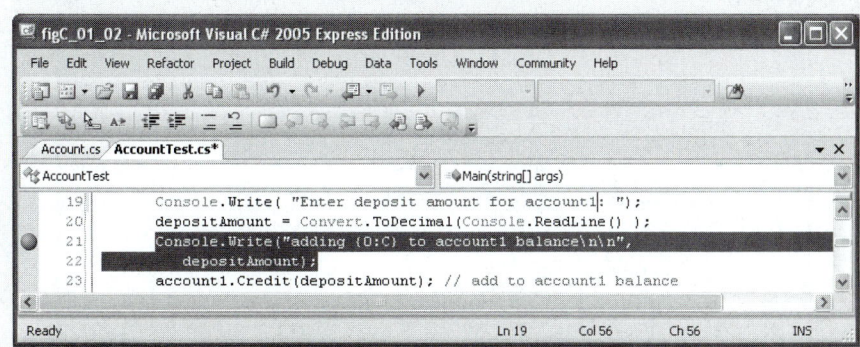

Fig. C.24 | Application prompt displaying the updated text.

Fig. C.25 | Setting a breakpoint at line 21.

2. *Starting the debugger.* Delete the "(from $1-500)" text you just added in the previous steps. Select **Debug > Start Debugging**. When execution begins, the prompt **Enter deposit amount for account1:** appears. Enter the value 650 at the prompt (Fig. C.26). The debugger enters break mode at line 21 (Fig. C.26).

3. *Changing the input prompt text.* Let's say that you once again wish to modify the input prompt text to provide the user with a range of values for variable depositAmount. Add the text "(from $1-500):" to the end of "Enter deposit amount for account1" in line 19 inside the code view window.

4. *Setting the next statement.* For the program to update the input prompt text correctly, you must set the execution point to a previous line of code. Right click in line 16 and select **Set Next Statement** from the menu that appears (Fig. C.27).

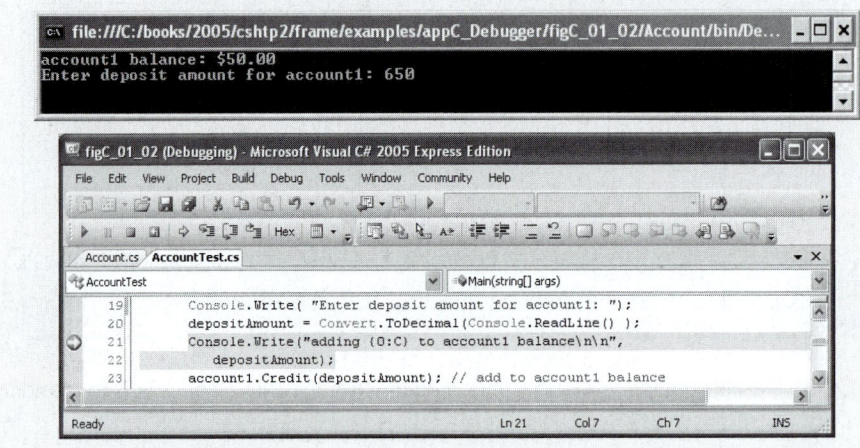

Fig. C.26 | Stopping execution at the breakpoint in line 21.

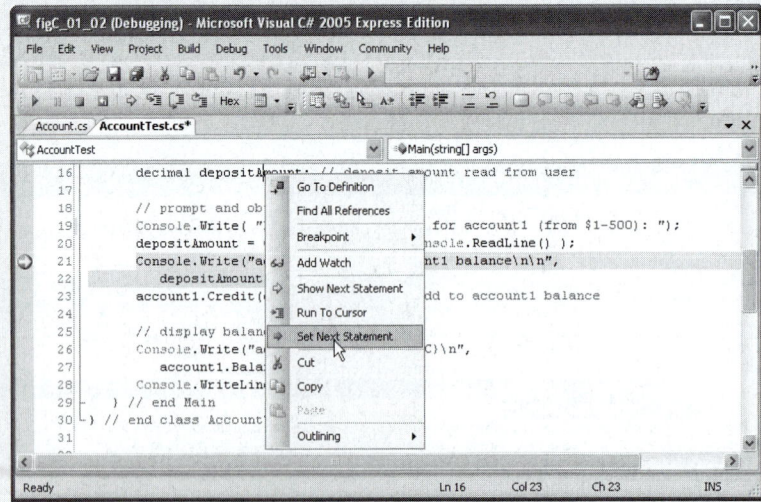

Fig. C.27 | Setting the next statement to execute.

5. Select **Debug > Continue**. The application prompts you again for input using the updated text (Fig. C.28).

6. *Stopping the debugger*. Select **Debug > Stop Debugging**.

Certain types of change are not allowed with the Edit and Continue feature once the program begins execution. These include changing class names, adding or removing method parameters, adding `public` fields to a class and adding or removing methods. If a particular change that you make to your program is not allowed during the debugging process, Visual Studio displays a dialog box as shown in Fig. C.29.

C.5.2 Exception Assistant

Another new feature in Visual Studio 2005 is the Exception Assistant. You can run a program by selecting either **Debug > Start Debugging** or **Debug > Start Without Debugging**. If you select the option **Debug > Start Debugging** and the runtime environment detects uncaught exceptions, the application pauses, and a window called the **Exception Assistant** appears indicating where the exception occurred, the type of the exception and links to helpful information on handling the exception. We discuss the Exception Assistant in detail in Section 12.4.3.

C.5.3 Just My Code™ Debugging

Throughout this book, we produce increasingly substantial programs that often include a combination of code written by the programmer and code generated by Visual Studio. The IDE-generated code can be difficult for novices (and even experienced programmers) to understand—fortunately, you rarely need to look at this code. Visual Studio 2005 provides a new debugging feature called *Just My Code™*, that allows programmers to test and debug only the portion of the code they have written. When this option is enabled, the debugger will always step over method calls to methods of classes that you did not write.

Fig. C.28 | Program execution continues with updated prompt text.

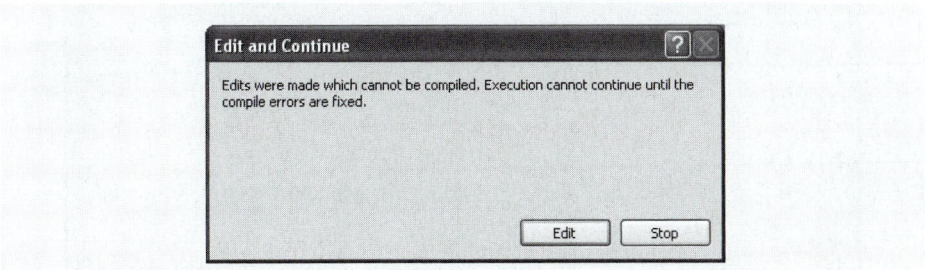

Fig. C.29 | Dialog box stating that certain program edits are not allowed during program execution.

You can change this setting in the debugger options. Select **Tools > Options**. In the **Options** dialog, select the **Debugging** category to view the available debugging tools and options. Then click the checkbox that appears next to the **Enable Just My Code (Managed only)** option (Fig. C.30) to enable or disable this feature.

C.5.4 Other New Debugger Features

All of the features discussed thus far in this section are available in all versions of Visual Studio, including Visual C# 2005 Express Edition. The Visual Studio 2005 debugger offers additional new features, such as visualizers, tracepoints and more, which you can learn about at `msdn.microsoft.com/vcsharp/2005/overview/debugger`.

C.6 Wrap-Up

In this appendix, you learned how to enable the debugger and set breakpoints so that you can examine your code and results while a program executes. This capability enables you to locate and fix logic errors in your programs. You also learned how to continue execution after a program suspends execution at a breakpoint and how to disable and remove breakpoints.

We showed how to use the debugger's **Watch** and **Locals** windows to evaluate arithmetic and boolean expressions. We also demonstrated how to modify a variable's value during program execution so that you can see how changes in values affect your results.

You learned how to use the debugger's **Step Into** command to debug methods called during your program's execution. You saw how the **Step Over** command can be used to execute a method call without stopping the called method. You used the **Step Out** command to continue execution until the end of the current method. You also learned that the **Continue** command continues execution until another breakpoint is found or the program terminates.

Finally, we discussed new features of the Visual Studio 2005 debugger, including Edit and Continue, the Exception Assistant and Just My Code™ debugging.

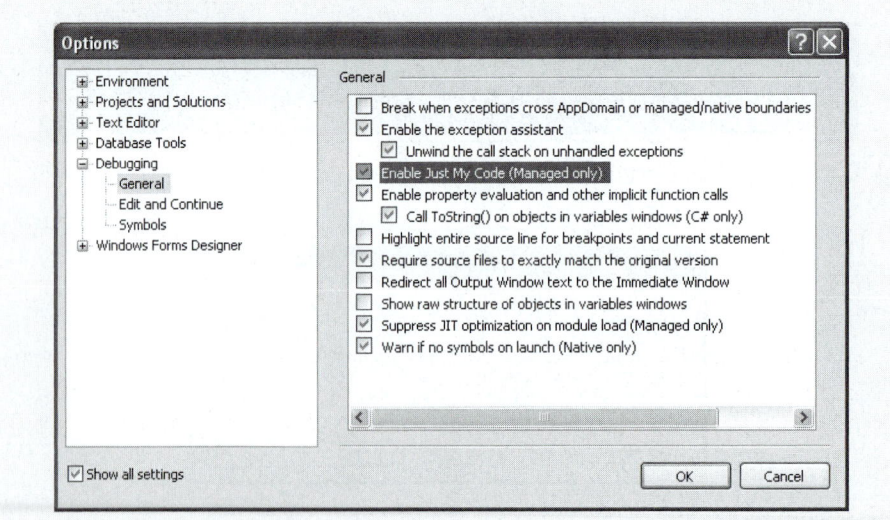

Fig. C.30 | Enabling the **Just My Code** debugging feature in Visual Studio.

Summary

Section C.1 Introduction

- Most compiler vendors, like Microsoft, provide software called a debugger, which allows you to monitor the execution of your programs to locate and remove logic errors.

- The debugger allows you to suspend program execution, examine and set variables, call methods without having to modify the program and much more.

Section C.2 Breakpoints and the Continue Command

- Breakpoints are markers that can be set at any executable line of code. When program execution reaches a breakpoint, execution pauses, allowing you to examine the values of variables to help you locate and correct logic errors.

- To insert a breakpoint in Visual Studio, left click inside the margin indicator bar next to the line of code at which you wish to break, or right click that line of code and select **Breakpoint > Insert Breakpoint**.

- A program is said to be in break mode when the debugger pauses the program's execution. Breakpoints can be set before running a program, in break mode or while a program is running.

- The **Continue** command will execute any statements between the next executable statement and the next breakpoint or the end of Main, whichever comes first.

- The value that the variable stores is displayed in a *Quick Info* box. In a sense, you are peeking inside the computer at the value of one of your variables.

- To disable a breakpoint, right click a line of code in which the breakpoint has been set and select **Breakpoint > Disable Breakpoint**. You can also right click the breakpoint itself and select **Disable Breakpoint**.

- To remove a breakpoint that you no longer need, right click the line of code on which the breakpoint has been set and select **Breakpoint > Delete Breakpoint**. You also can remove a breakpoint by clicking the solid circle in the margin indicator bar.

Section C.3 The Locals and Watch Windows

- The **Locals** window enables you to assign new values to variables while your program is running.

- The **Watch** window allows you to examine the value of arithmetic and Boolean expressions.

Section C.4 Controlling Execution Using the Step Into, Step Over, Step Out and Continue Commands

- You can step through a portion of your program line-by-line to find and fix logic errors and verify that a method's code executes correctly.

- The **Step Into** command executes the next statement in the program and immediately halts. If the statement to be executed as a result of the **Step Into** command is a method call, control is transferred to the called method. The **Step Into** command allows you to enter a method and confirm its execution by individually executing each statement in the method.

- The **Step Over** command behaves like the **Step Into** command when the next statement to execute does not contain a method call or access a property.

- The **Step Out** command is used for situations where you do not want to continue stepping through the entire method line-by-line.

Section C.5 Other Features

- The Edit and Continue feature allows you to make modifications or changes to your code as the debugger is running.

- If you want to make a change to a particular line that has been executed, you must select a prior statement in your code from which to continue execution. The **Set Next Statement** will allow you to do this

- Certain types of change are not allowed with the Edit and Continue feature once the program begins execution. These include changing the name of a class, adding or removing method parameters, adding public fields to a class and adding or removing methods.

- The Exception Assistant indicates where the exception occurred, the type of the exception and links to helpful information on handling the exception.

- The Just My Code™ feature allows programmers to test and debug only the portion of code which they have written.

Terminology

break mode	logic error
breakpoint	margin indicator bar
bug	*Quick Info* box
Continue command	solid breakpoint circle
debugger	**Step Into** command
disable a breakpoint	**Step Out** command
Edit and Continue	**Step Over** command
Exception Assistant	suspend program execution
insert a breakpoint	Visual Studio debugger
Just My Code™ debugging	**Watch** window
Locals window	yellow arrow in break mode

Self-Review Exercises

C.1   Fill in the blanks in each of the following statements:
   a) When the debugger suspends program execution at a breakpoint, the program is said to be in _____ mode.
   b) The _____ feature in Visual Studio .NET allows you to "peek into the computer" and look at the value of a variable.
   c) You can examine the value of an expression by using the debugger's _____ window.
   d) The _____ command behaves like the **Step Into** command when the next statement to execute does not contain a method call or access a property.

C.2   State whether each of the following is *true* or *false*. If *false*, explain why.
   a) When program execution suspends at a breakpoint, the next statement to be executed is the statement after the breakpoint.
   b) When a variable's value is changed, the value changes to yellow in the **Locals** windows.
   c) During debugging, the **Step Out** command executes the remaining statements in the current method and returns program control to the place where the method was called.

Answers to Self-Review Exercises

C.1   a) break. b) *Quick Info* box. c) **Watch**. d) **Step Over**.

C.2   a) False. When program execution suspends at a breakpoint, the next statement to be executed is the statement at the breakpoint. b) False. A variable's value turns red when it is changed. c) True.

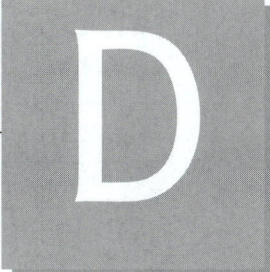

ASCII Character Set

	0	1	2	3	4	5	6	7	8	9
0	nul	soh	stx	etx	eot	enq	ack	bel	bs	ht
1	nl	vt	ff	cr	so	si	dle	dc1	dc2	dc3
2	dc4	nak	syn	etb	can	em	sub	esc	fs	gs
3	rs	us	sp	!	"	#	$	%	&	'
4	(	)	*	+	,	-	.	/	0	1
5	2	3	4	5	6	7	8	9	:	;
6	<	=	>	?	@	A	B	C	D	E
7	F	G	H	I	J	K	L	M	N	O
8	P	Q	R	S	T	U	V	W	X	Y
9	Z	[	\	]	^	_	'	a	b	c
10	d	e	f	g	h	i	j	k	l	m
11	n	o	p	q	r	s	t	u	v	w
12	x	y	z	{	|	}	~	del		

Fig. D.1 | ASCII Character Set.

The digits at the left of the table are the left digits of the decimal equivalent (0–127) of the character code, and the digits at the top of the table are the right digits of the character code. For example, the character code for "F" is 70, and the character code for "&" is 38.

Most users of this book are interested in the ASCII character set used to represent English characters on many computers. The ASCII character set is a subset of the Unicode character set used by C# to represent characters from most of the world's languages. For more information on the Unicode character set, see Appendix E.

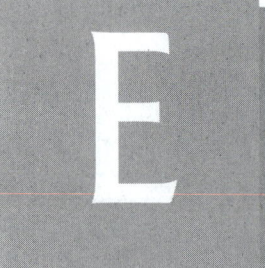

E

Unicode®

OBJECTIVES

In this appendix you will learn:

- Unicode fundamentals.

- The mission of the Unicode Consortium.

- The design basis of Unicode.

- The three Unicode encoding forms: UTF-8, UTF-16 and UTF-32.

- Characters and glyphs.

- The advantages and disadvantages of using Unicode.

E.1 Introduction

The use of inconsistent character *encodings* (i.e., numeric values associated with characters) in the developing of global software products causes serious problems, because computers process information as numbers. For instance, the character "a" is converted to a numeric value so that a computer can manipulate that piece of data. Many countries and corporations have developed their own encoding systems that are incompatible with the encoding systems of other countries and corporations. For example, the Microsoft Windows operating system assigns the value 0xC0 to the character "A with a grave accent"; the Apple Macintosh operating system assigns that same value to an upside-down question mark. This results in the misrepresentation and possible corruption of data when data is not processed as intended.

In the absence of a widely implemented universal character-encoding standard, global software developers had to localize their products extensively before distribution. *Localization* includes the language translation and cultural adaptation of content. The process of localization usually includes significant modifications to the source code (such as the conversion of numeric values and the underlying assumptions made by programmers), which results in increased costs and delays releasing the software. For example, some English-speaking programmers might design global software products assuming that a single character can be represented by one byte. However, when those products are localized for Asian markets, the programmer's assumptions are no longer valid; thus, the majority, if not the entirety, of the code needs to be rewritten. Localization is necessary with each release of a version. By the time a software product is localized for a particular market, a newer version, which needs to be localized as well, may be ready for distribution. As a result, it is cumbersome and costly to produce and distribute global software products in a market where there is no universal character-encoding standard.

In response to this situation, the *Unicode Standard*, an encoding standard that facilitates the production and distribution of software, was created. The Unicode Standard outlines a specification to produce consistent encoding of the world's characters and symbols. Software products that handle text encoded in the Unicode Standard need to be localized, but the localization process is simpler and more efficient because the numeric values need not be converted and the assumptions made by programmers about the character encoding are universal. The Unicode Standard is maintained by a nonprofit organization called the *Unicode Consortium*, whose members include Apple, IBM, Microsoft, Oracle, Sun Microsystems, Sybase and many others.

When the Consortium envisioned and developed the Unicode Standard, they wanted an encoding system that was universal, efficient, uniform and unambiguous. A universal encoding system encompasses all commonly used characters. An efficient encoding system allows text files to be parsed easily. A uniform encoding system assigns fixed values to all characters. An unambiguous encoding system represents a given character in a consistent manner. These four terms are referred to as the Unicode Standard *design basis*.

E.2 Unicode Transformation Formats

Although Unicode incorporates the limited ASCII character set (i.e., a collection of characters), it encompasses a more comprehensive character set. In ASCII each character is represented by a byte containing 0s and 1s. One byte is capable of storing the binary numbers from 0 to 255. Each character is assigned a number between 0 and 255; thus, ASCII-based systems can support only 256 characters, a tiny fraction of world's characters. Unicode extends the ASCII character set by encoding the vast majority of the world's characters. The Unicode Standard encodes all of those characters in a uniform numerical space from 0 to 10FFFF hexadecimal. An implementation will express these numbers in one of several transformation formats, choosing the one that best fits the particular application at hand.

Three such formats are in use, called *UTF-8*, *UTF-16* and *UTF-32*, depending on the size of the units—in bits—being used. UTF-8, a variable-width encoding form, requires one to four bytes to express each Unicode character. UTF-8 data consists of 8-bit bytes (sequences of one, two, three or four bytes depending on the character being encoded) and is well suited for ASCII-based systems, where there is a predominance of one-byte characters (ASCII represents characters as one byte). Currently, UTF-8 is widely implemented in UNIX systems and in databases.

The variable-width UTF-16 encoding form expresses Unicode characters in units of 16 bits (i.e., as two adjacent bytes, or a short integer in many machines). Most Unicode characters are expressed in a single 16-bit unit. However, characters with values above FFFF hexadecimal are expressed with an ordered pair of 16-bit units called *surrogates*. Surrogates are 16-bit integers in the range D800 through DFFF, which are used solely for the purpose of "escaping" into higher numbered characters. Approximately one million characters can be expressed in this manner. Although a surrogate pair requires 32 bits to represent characters, it is space-efficient to use these 16-bit units. Surrogates are rare characters in current implementations. Many string-handling implementations are written in terms of UTF-16. [*Note:* Details and sample code for UTF-16 handling are available on the Unicode Consortium Web site at `www.unicode.org`.]

Implementations that require significant use of rare characters or entire scripts encoded above FFFF hexadecimal should use UTF-32, a 32-bit, fixed-width encoding form that usually requires twice as much memory as UTF-16 encoded characters. The major advantage of the fixed-width UTF-32 encoding form is that it expresses all characters uniformly, so it is easy to handle in arrays.

Figure E.1 shows the different ways in which the three encoding forms handle character encoding. There are few guidelines that state when to use a particular encoding form. The best encoding form to use depends on computer systems and business protocols, not on the data itself. Typically, the UTF-8 encoding form should be used where computer systems and business protocols require data to be handled in 8-bit units, particularly in legacy systems being upgraded, because it often simplifies changes to existing programs. For this reason, UTF-8 has become the encoding form of choice on the Internet. Likewise, UTF-16 is the encoding form of choice on Microsoft Windows applications. UTF-32 is

Character	UTF-8	UTF-16	UTF-32
Latin capital letter A	0x41	0x0041	0x00000041
Greek capital letter ALPHA	0xCD 0x91	0x0391	0x00000391
CJK unified ideograph-4E95	0xE4 0xBA 0x95	0x4E95	0x00004E95
Old italic letter A	0xF0 0x80 0x83 0x80	0xDC00 0xDF00	0x00010300

Fig. E.1 | Correlation between the three encoding forms.

likely to become more widely used in the future as more characters are encoded with values above FFFF hexadecimal. Also, UTF-32 requires less sophisticated handling than UTF-16 in the presence of surrogate pairs.

E.3 Characters and Glyphs

The Unicode Standard consists of characters, written components (i.e., alphabetic letters, numerals, punctuation marks, accent marks, etc.) that can be represented by numeric values. Examples of characters include: U+0041 Latin capital letter A. In the first character representation, U+*yyyy* is a **code value**, in which U+ refers to Unicode code values, as opposed to other hexadecimal values. The *yyyy* represents a four-digit hexadecimal number of an encoded character. Code values are bit combinations that represent encoded characters. Characters are represented with **glyphs**, various shapes, fonts and sizes for displaying characters. There are no code values for glyphs in the Unicode Standard. Examples of glyphs are shown in Fig. E.2.

The Unicode Standard encompasses the alphabets, ideographs, syllabaries, punctuation marks, **diacritics**, mathematical operators, etc., that compose the written languages and scripts of the world. A diacritic is a special mark added to a character to distinguish it from another letter or to indicate an accent (e.g., in Spanish, the tilde "~" above the character "n"). Currently, Unicode provides code values for 94,140 character representations, with more than 880,000 code values reserved for future expansion.

E.4 Advantages/Disadvantages of Unicode

The Unicode Standard has several significant advantages that promote its use. One is the impact it has on the performance of the international economy. Unicode standardizes the characters for the world's writing systems to a uniform model that promotes transferring and sharing data. Programs developed using such a schema maintain their accuracy because each character has a single definition (i.e., *a* is always U+0061, % is always U+0025).

Fig. E.2 | Various glyphs of the character A.

This enables corporations to manage the high demands of international markets by processing different writing systems at the same time. Also, all characters can be managed in an identical manner, thus avoiding any confusion caused by different character-code architectures. Moreover, managing data in a consistent manner eliminates data corruption, because data can be sorted, searched and manipulated via a consistent process.

Another advantage of the Unicode Standard is portability (i.e., the ability to execute software on disparate computers or with disparate operating systems). Most operating systems, databases, programming languages and Web browsers currently support Unicode. Additionally, Unicode includes more characters than any other character set.

A disadvantage of the Unicode Standard is the amount of memory required by UTF-16 and UTF-32. ASCII character sets are 8 bits in length, so they require less storage than the default 16-bit Unicode character set. However, the ***double-byte character set (DBCS)*** and the ***multi-byte character set (MBCS)*** that encode Asian characters (ideographs) require two to four bytes, respectively. In such instances, the UTF-16 or the UTF-32 encoding forms may be used with little hindrance on memory and performance.

E.5 Using Unicode

Visual Studio uses Unicode UTF-16 encoding to represent all characters. Figure E.3 uses C# to display the text "Welcome to Unicode" in eight languages—English, French, German, Japanese, Portuguese, Russian, Spanish and Traditional Chinese. [*Note:* The Unicode Consortium's Web site contains a link to code charts that lists the 16-bit Unicode code values.]

```
1   // Fig. E.3: UnicodeForm.cs
2   // Unicode enconding demonstration.
3   using System;
4   using System.Windows.Forms;
5
6   namespace UnicodeDemo
7   {
8      public partial class UnicodeForm : Form
9      {
10         public UnicodeForm()
11         {
12            InitializeComponent();
13         }
14
15         // assign Unicode strings to each Label
16         private void UnicodeForm_Load( object sender, EventArgs e )
17         {
18            // English
19            char[] english = { '\u0057', '\u0065', '\u006C',
20               '\u0063', '\u006F', '\u006D', '\u0065', '\u0020',
21               '\u0074', '\u006F', '\u0020' };
22            englishLabel.Text = new string( english ) +
23               "Unicode" + '\u0021';
```

Fig. E.3 | Windows application demonstrating Unicode encoding. (Part 1 of 3.)

```
24
25          // French
26          char[] french = { '\u0042', '\u0069', '\u0065',
27             '\u006E', '\u0076', '\u0065', '\u006E', '\u0075',
28             '\u0065', '\u0020', '\u0061', '\u0075', '\u0020' };
29          frenchLabel.Text = new string( french ) +
30             "Unicode" + '\u0021';
31
32          // German
33          char[] german = { '\u0057', '\u0069', '\u006C',
34             '\u006B', '\u006F', '\u006D', '\u006D', '\u0065',
35             '\u006E', '\u0020', '\u007A', '\u0075', '\u0020' };
36          germanLabel.Text = new string( german ) +
37             "Unicode" + '\u0021';
38
39          // Japanese
40          char[] japanese = { '\u3078', '\u3087', '\u3045',
41             '\u3053', '\u305D', '\u0021' };
42          japaneseLabel.Text = "Unicode" + new string( japanese );
43
44          // Portuguese
45          char[] portuguese = { '\u0053', '\u0065', '\u006A',
46             '\u0061', '\u0020', '\u0062', '\u0065', '\u006D',
47             '\u0020', '\u0076', '\u0069', '\u006E', '\u0064',
48             '\u006F', '\u0020', '\u0061', '\u0020' };
49          portugueseLabel.Text = new string( portuguese ) +
50             "Unicode" + '\u0021';
51
52          // Russian
53          char[] russian = { '\u0414', '\u043E', '\u0431',
54             '\u0440', '\u043E', '\u0020', '\u043F', '\u043E',
55             '\u0436', '\u0430', '\u043B', '\u043E', '\u0432',
56             '\u0430', '\u0442', '\u044A', '\u0020', '\u0432', '\u0020' };
57          russianLabel.Text = new string( russian ) +
58             "Unicode" + '\u0021';
59
60          // Spanish
61          char[] spanish = { '\u0042', '\u0069', '\u0065',
62             '\u006E', '\u0076', '\u0065', '\u006E', '\u0069',
63             '\u0064', '\u006F', '\u0020', '\u0061', '\u0020' };
64          spanishLabel.Text = new string( spanish ) +
65             "Unicode" + '\u0021';
66
67          // Simplified Chinese
68          char[] chinese = { '\u6B22', '\u8FCE', '\u4F7F',
69             '\u7528', '\u0020' };
70          chineseLabel.Text = new string( chinese ) +
71             "Unicode" + '\u0021';
72       } // end method UnicodeForm_Load
73    } // end class UnicodeForm
74 } // end namespace UnicodeDemo
```

Fig. E.3 | Windows application demonstrating Unicode encoding. (Part 2 of 3.)

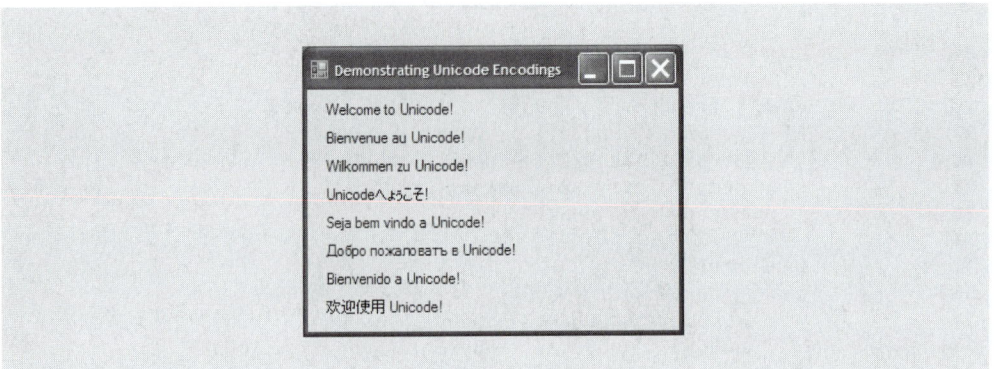

Fig. E.3 | Windows application demonstrating Unicode encoding. (Part 3 of 3.)

The first welcome message (lines 19–23) contains the hexadecimal codes for the English text. The **Code Charts** page on the Unicode Consortium Web site contains a document that lists the code values for the **Basic Latin** block (or category), which includes the English alphabet. The hexadecimal codes in lines 19–20 equate to "Welcome" and a space character (\u0020). Unicode characters in C# use the format \u*yyyy*, where *yyyy* represents the hexadecimal Unicode encoding. For example, the letter "W" (in "Welcome") is denoted by \u0057. The hexadecimal values for the word "to" and a space character appear on line 21 and the word "Unicode" is on line 23. "Unicode" is not encoded because it is a registered trademark and has no equivalent translation in most languages.

The remaining welcome messages (lines 26–71) contain the hexadecimal codes for the other seven languages. The code values used for the French, German, Portuguese and Spanish text are located in the **Basic Latin** block, the code values used for the Traditional Chinese text are located in the **CJK Unified Ideographs** block, the code values used for the Russian text are located in the **Cyrillic** block and the code values used for the Japanese text are located in the **Hiragana** block.

[*Note:* To render the Asian characters in a Windows application, you would need to install the proper language files on your computer. To do this, open the **Regional Options** dialog from the **Control Panel** (**Start > Settings > Control Panel**). At the bottom of the **General** tab is a list of languages. Check the **Japanese** and the **Traditional Chinese** checkboxes and press **Apply**. Follow the directions of the install wizard to install the languages. For additional assistance, visit www.unicode.org/help/display_problems.html.]

E.6 Character Ranges

The Unicode Standard assigns code values, which range from 0000 (**Basic Latin**) to E007F (*Tags*), to the written characters of the world. Currently, there are code values for 94,140 characters. To simplify the search for a character and its associated code value, the Unicode Standard generally groups code values by *script* and function (i.e., Latin characters are grouped in a block, mathematical operators are grouped in another block, etc.). As a rule, a script is a single writing system that is used for multiple languages (e.g., the Latin script is used for English, French, Spanish, etc.). The **Code Charts** page on the Unicode Consortium Web site lists all the defined blocks and their respective code values. Figure E.4 lists some blocks (scripts) from the Web site and their range of code values.

Script	Range of Code Values
Arabic	U+0600–U+06FF
Basic Latin	U+0000–U+007F
Bengali (India)	U+0980–U+09FF
Cherokee (Native America)	U+13A0–U+13FF
CJK Unified Ideographs (East Asia)	U+4E00–U+9FAF
Cyrillic (Russia and Eastern Europe)	U+0400–U+04FF
Ethiopic	U+1200–U+137F
Greek	U+0370–U+03FF
Hangul Jamo (Korea)	U+1100–U+11FF
Hebrew	U+0590–U+05FF
Hiragana (Japan)	U+3040–U+309F
Khmer (Cambodia)	U+1780–U+17FF
Lao (Laos)	U+0E80–U+0EFF
Mongolian	U+1800–U+18AF
Myanmar	U+1000–U+109F
Ogham (Ireland)	U+1680–U+169F
Runic (Germany and Scandinavia)	U+16A0–U+16FF
Sinhala (Sri Lanka)	U+0D80–U+0DFF
Telugu (India)	U+0C00–U+0C7F
Thai	U+0E00–U+0E7F

Fig. E.4 | Some character ranges.

Summary

Section E.1 Introduction

- Before Unicode, software developers were plagued by the use of inconsistent character encoding (i.e., numeric values for characters). Most countries and organizations had their own encoding systems, which were incompatible. A good example is the individual encoding systems on the Windows and Macintosh platforms.

- Computers process data by converting characters to numeric values. For instance, the character "a" is converted to a numeric value so that a computer can manipulate that piece of data.

- Without Unicode, localization of global software requires significant modifications to the source code, which results in increased cost and delays in releasing the product.

- Localization is necessary with each release of a version. By the time a software product is localized for a particular market, a newer version, which needs to be localized as well, is ready for distribution. As a result, it is cumbersome and costly to produce and distribute global software products in a market where there is no universal character-encoding standard.

- The Unicode Consortium developed the Unicode Standard in response to the serious problems created by multiple character encodings and the use of those encodings.

- The Unicode Standard facilitates the production and distribution of localized software. It outlines a specification for the consistent encoding of the world's characters and symbols.

- Software products that handle text encoded in the Unicode Standard need to be localized, but the localization process is simpler and more efficient because the numeric values need not be converted.

- The Unicode Standard is designed to be universal, efficient, uniform and unambiguous.

- A universal encoding system encompasses all commonly used characters; an efficient encoding system parses text files easily; a uniform encoding system assigns fixed values to all characters; and an unambiguous encoding system represents the same character for any given value.

Section E.2 Unicode Transformation Formats
- Unicode extends the limited ASCII character set to include all the major characters of the world.

- Unicode makes use of three Unicode Transformation Formats (UTF): UTF-8, UTF-16 and UTF-32, each of which may be appropriate for use in different contexts.

- UTF-8 data consists of 8-bit bytes (sequences of one, two, three or four bytes depending on the character being encoded) and is well suited for ASCII-based systems, where there is a predominance of one-byte characters (ASCII represents characters as one byte).

- UTF-8 is a variable-width encoding form that is more compact for text involving mostly Latin characters and ASCII punctuation.

- UTF-16 is the default encoding form of the Unicode Standard. It is a variable-width encoding form that uses 16-bit code units instead of bytes. Most characters are represented by a single unit, but some characters require surrogate pairs.

- Surrogates are 16-bit integers in the range D800 through DFFF, which are used solely for the purpose of "escaping" into higher numbered characters.

- Without surrogate pairs, the UTF-16 encoding form can only encompass 65,000 characters, but with the surrogate pairs, this is expanded to include over a million characters.

- UTF-32 is a 32-bit encoding form. The major advantage of the fixed-width encoding form is that it uniformly expresses all characters, so that they are easy to handle in arrays and so forth.

Section E.3 Characters and Glyphs
- The Unicode Standard consists of characters. A character is any written component that can be represented by a numeric value.

- Characters are represented with glyphs (various shapes, fonts and sizes for displaying characters).

- Code values are bit combinations that represent encoded characters. The Unicode notation for a code value is U+yyyy, in which U+ refers to the Unicode code values, as opposed to other hexadecimal values. The yyyy represents a four-digit hexadecimal number.

- Currently, the Unicode Standard provides code values for 94,140 character representations.

Section E.4 Advantages/Disadvantages of Unicode
- An advantage of the Unicode Standard is its impact on the overall performance of the international economy. Applications that conform to an encoding standard can be processed easily by computers anywhere.

- Another advantage of the Unicode Standard is its portability. Applications written in Unicode can be easily transferred to different operating systems, databases, Web browsers and so on. Most companies currently support, or are planning to support, Unicode.

Section E.5 Using Unicode

- To obtain more information about the Unicode Standard and the Unicode Consortium, visit www.unicode.org. It contains a link to the code charts, which contain the 16-bit code values for the currently encoded characters.
- In the marking up of C# documents, the entity reference \u*yyyy* is used, where *yyyy* represents the hexadecimal code value.

Terminology

\u*yyyy* notation	portability
ASCII	script
block	surrogate
character	symbol
character set	unambiguous (Unicode design basis)
code value	Unicode Consortium
diacritic	Unicode design basis
double-byte character set (DBCS)	Unicode Standard
efficient (Unicode design basis)	Unicode Transformation Format (UTF)
encode	uniform (Unicode design basis)
entity reference	universal (Unicode design basis)
glyph	UTF-8
hexadecimal notation	UTF-16
localization	UTF-32
multi-byte character set (MBCS)	

Self-Review Exercises

E.1 Fill in the blanks in each of the following.

a) Global software developers had to _____ their products to a specific market before distribution.

b) The Unicode Standard is a(n) _____ standard that facilitates the uniform production and distribution of software products.

c) The four design basis that constitute the Unicode Standard are: _____, _____, _____ and _____.

d) A(n) _____ is the smallest written component the can be represented with a numeric value.

e) Software that can execute on different operating systems is said to be _____.

f) Of the three encoding forms, _____ is currently supported by Internet Explorer 5.5 and Netscape Communicator 6.

E.2 State whether each of the following is *true* or *false*. If *false*, explain why.

a) The Unicode Standard encompasses all the world's characters.

b) A Unicode code value is represented as U+*yyyy*, where *yyyy* represents a number in binary notation.

c) A diacritic is a character with a special mark that emphasizes an accent.

d) Unicode is portable.

e) When designing C# programs, Unicode characters are denoted by #u*yyyy*.

Answers to Self-Review exercises

E.1 a) localize. b) encoding. c) universal, efficient, uniform, unambiguous. d) character. e) portable. f) UTF-8.

E.2 a) False. It encompasses the majority of the world's characters. b) False. The *yyyy* represents a hexadecimal number. c) False. A diacritic is a special mark added to a character to distinguish it from another letter or to indicate an accent. d) True. e) False. Unicode characters are denoted by \u*yyyy*.

Exercises

E.3 Navigate to the Unicode Consortium Web site (www.unicode.org) and write the hexadecimal code values for the following characters. In which block are they located?
  a) Latin letter "Z."
  b) Latin letter 'n' with the "tilde (~)."
  c) Greek letter "delta."
  d) Mathematical operator "less than or equal to."
  e) Punctuation symbol "open quote (")."

E.4 Describe the Unicode Standard design basis.

E.5 Define the following terms:
  a) code value.
  b) surrogates.
  c) Unicode Standard.
  d) UTF-8.
  e) UTF-16.
  f) UTF-32.

E.6 Describe a scenario where it is optimal to store your data in UTF-16 format.

E.7 Using the Unicode Standard code values, create a program that prints your first and last name. If you know other writing systems, print your first and last name in those as well. Use a Label to display your name.

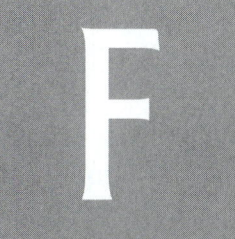

Introduction to XHTML: Part 1

To read between the lines was easier than to follow the text.

—Henry James

High thoughts must have high language.

—Aristophanes

OBJECTIVES

In this appendix, you will learn:

- To understand important components of XHTML documents.
- To use XHTML to create Web pages.
- To be able to add images to Web pages.
- To understand how to create and use hyperlinks to navigate Web pages.
- To be able to mark up lists of information.

F.1 Introduction

Welcome to the world of opportunity created by the World Wide Web. The Internet is now three decades old, but it was not until the Web became popular in the 1990s that the explosion of opportunity that we are still experiencing began. Exciting new developments occur almost daily—the pace of innovation is unprecedented by any other technology. In this chapter, you will develop your own Web pages. As the book proceeds, you will create increasingly appealing and powerful Web pages. In the later portion of the book, you will learn how to create complete Web-based applications.

This chapter begins unlocking the power of Web-based application development with *XHTML*—the *Extensible HyperText Markup Language*. In later chapters, we introduce more sophisticated XHTML techniques, such as *tables*, which are particularly useful for structuring information from *databases* (i.e., software that stores structured sets of data), and *Cascading Style Sheets* (*CSS*), which make Web pages more visually appealing.

Unlike procedural programming languages such as C, Fortran, Cobol and Pascal, XHTML is a *markup language* that specifies the format of the text that is displayed in a Web browser such as Microsoft's *Internet Explorer* or *Netscape*.

One key issue when using XHTML is the separation of the *presentation* of a document (i.e., the document's appearance when rendered by a browser) from the *structure* of the document's information. XHTML is based on HTML (HyperText Markup Language)—a legacy technology of the World Wide Web Consortium (W3C). In HTML, it was common to specify the document's content, structure and formatting. Formatting might specify where the browser placed an element in a Web page or the fonts and colors used to display an element. XHTML 1.1 (W3C's latest version of W3C XHTML Recommendation at the time of publication) allows only a document's content and structure to appear in a valid XHTML document, and not its formatting. Normally, such formatting is specified with Cascading Style Sheets (Chapter 6). All our examples in this chapter are based upon the XHTML 1.1 Recommendation.

F.2 Editing XHTML

In this chapter, we write XHTML in its *source-code form*. We create *XHTML documents* by typing them in a text editor (e.g., *Notepad, Wordpad, vi, emacs*) and saving them with either an *.html* or an *.htm* file-name extension.

Good Programming Practice F.1

Assign documents file names that describe their functionality. This practice can help you identify documents faster. It also helps people who want to link to a page, by giving them an easy-to-remember name. For example, if you are writing an XHTML document that contains product information, you might want to call it products.html.

Machines running specialized software called **Web servers** store XHTML documents. Clients (e.g., Web browsers) request specific **resources** such as the XHTML documents from the Web server. For example, typing www.deitel.com/books/downloads.html into a Web browser's address field requests downloads.html from the Web server running at www.deitel.com. This document is located on the server in a directory named books. For now, we simply place the XHTML documents on our machine and open them using Internet Explorer.

F.3 First XHTML Example

In this chapter and the next, we present XHTML markup and provide screen captures that show how Internet Explorer renders (i.e., displays) the XHTML.[1] Every XHTML document we show has line numbers for the reader's convenience. These line numbers are not part of the XHTML documents.

Our first example (Fig. F.1) is an XHTML document named main.html that displays the message "Welcome to XHTML!" in the browser.

The key line in the program is line 14, which tells the browser to display "Welcome to XHTML!" Now let us consider each line of the program.

Lines 1–3 are required in XHTML documents to conform with proper XHTML syntax. For now, copy and paste these lines into each XHTML document you create. The meaning of these lines is discussed in detail in Chapter 20, Extensible Markup Language (XML).

```
1   <?xml version = "1.0"?>
2   <!DOCTYPE html PUBLIC "-//W3C//DTD XHTML 1.1//EN"
3      "http://www.w3.org/TR/xhtml11/DTD/xhtml11.dtd">
4
5   <!-- Fig. F.1: main.html -->
6   <!-- Our first Web page   -->
7
8   <html xmlns = "http://www.w3.org/1999/xhtml">
9      <head>
10        <title>Internet and WWW How to Program - Welcome</title>
11     </head>
12
13     <body>
14        <p>Welcome to XHTML!</p>
15     </body>
16  </html>
```

Fig. F.1 | First XHTML example. (Part 1 of 2.)

---

1. All the examples presented in this book are available at www.deitel.com and on the CD-ROM that accompanies the book.

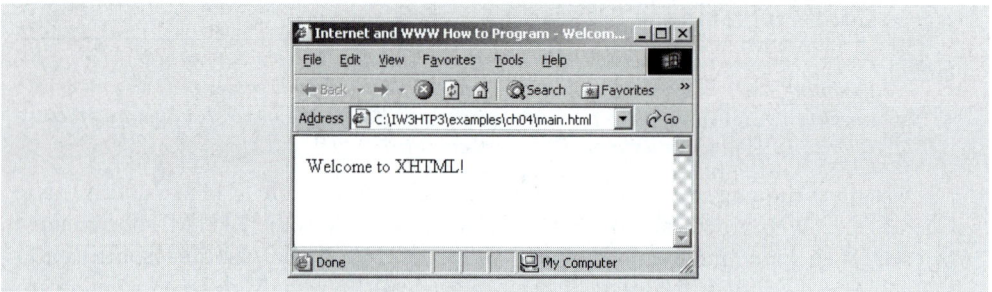

Fig. F.1 | First XHTML example. (Part 2 of 2.)

Lines 5–6 are **XHTML comments**. XHTML document creators insert comments to improve markup readability and describe the content of a document. Comments also help other people read and understand an XHTML document's markup and content. Comments do not cause the browser to perform any action when the user loads the XHTML document into the Web browser to view the document. XHTML comments always start with `<!--` and end with `-->`. Each of our XHTML examples includes comments that specify the figure number and file name, and provide a brief description of the example's purpose. Subsequent examples include comments in the markup, especially to highlight new features.

Good Programming Practice F.2

Place comments throughout your markup. Comments help other programmers understand the markup, assist in debugging and list useful information that you do not want the browser to render. Comments also help you understand your own markup when you revisit a document to modify or update it in the future.

XHTML markup contains text that represents the content of a document and *elements* that specify a document's structure. Some important elements of an XHTML document are the **html** element, the **head** element and the **body** element. The html element encloses the **head section** (represented by the head element) and the **body section** (represented by the body element). The head section contains information about the XHTML document, such as its *title*. The head section also can contain special document formatting instructions called *style sheets* and client-side programs called *scripts* for creating dynamic Web pages. (We introduce style sheets in Chapter 6 and scripting with JavaScript in Chapter 7.) The body section contains the page's content that the browser displays when the user visits the Web page.

XHTML documents delimit an element with *start* and *end* tags. A start tag consists of the element name in angle brackets (e.g., `<html>`). An end tag consists of the element name preceded by a / in angle brackets (e.g., `</html>`). In this example, lines 8 and 16 define the start and end of the html element. Note that the end tag in line 16 has the same name as the start tag, but is preceded by a / inside the angle brackets. Many start tags have *attributes* that provide additional information about an element. Browsers can use this additional information to determine how to process the element. Each attribute has a *name* and a *value* separated by an equals sign (=). Line 8 specifies a required attribute (xmlns) and value (`http://www.w3.org/1999/xhtml`) for the html element in an XHTML document. For now, simply copy and paste the html element start tag in line 8 into your

XHTML documents. We discuss the details of the `html` element's `xmlns` attribute in Chapter 20, Extensible Markup Language (XML).

Common Programming Error F.1

Not enclosing attribute values in either single or double quotes is a syntax error. However, some Web browsers may still render the element correctly.

Common Programming Error F.2

Using uppercase letters in an XHTML element or attribute name is a syntax error. However, some Web browsers may still render the element correctly.

An XHTML document divides the `html` element into two sections—head and body. Lines 9–11 define the Web page's head section with a `head` element. Line 10 specifies a `title` element. This is called a *nested element* because it is enclosed in the `head` element's start and end tags. The `head` element is also a nested element because it is enclosed in the `html` element's start and end tags. The `title` element describes the Web page. Titles usually appear in the *title bar* at the top of the browser window and also as the text identifying a page when users add the page to their list of **Favorites** or **Bookmarks** that enables them to return to their favorite sites. Search engines (i.e., sites that allow users to search the Web) also use the `title` for cataloging purposes.

Good Programming Practice F.3

Indenting nested elements emphasizes a document's structure and promotes readability.

Common Programming Error F.3

XHTML does not permit tags to overlap—a nested element's end tag must appear in the document before the enclosing element's end tag. For example, the nested XHTML tags `<head><title>hello</head></title>` cause a syntax error, because the enclosing head element's ending `</head>` tag appears before the nested title element's ending `</title>` tag.

Good Programming Practice F.4

Use a consistent `title`-naming convention for all pages on a site. For example, if a site is named "Bailey's Web Site," then the `title` of the links page might be "Bailey's Web Site—Links." This practice can help users better understand the Web site's structure.

Line 13 opens the document's `body` element. The body section of an XHTML document specifies the document's content, which may include text and tags.

Some tags, such as the *paragraph tags* (**`<p>`** and **`</p>`**) in line 14, mark up text for display in a browser. All the text placed between the `<p>` and `</p>` tags forms one paragraph. When the browser renders a paragraph, a blank line usually precedes and follows paragraph text.

This document ends with two end tags (lines 15–16). These tags close the `body` and `html` elements, respectively. The `</html>` tag in an XHTML document informs the browser that the XHTML markup is complete.

To view this example in Internet Explorer, perform the following steps:

1. Copy the Chapter 4 examples onto your machine from the CD that accompanies this book (or download the examples from `www.deitel.com`).

2. Launch Internet Explorer and select **Open...** from the **File** Menu. This displays the **Open** dialog.

3. Click the **Open** dialog's **Browse...** button to display the **Microsoft Internet Explorer** file dialog.

4. Navigate to the directory containing the Chapter 4 examples and select the file `main.html`, then click **Open**.

5. Click **OK** to have Internet Explorer render the document. Other examples are opened in a similar manner.

At this point your browser window should appear similar to the sample screen capture shown in Fig. F.1. (Note that we resized the browser window to save space in the book.)

F.4 W3C XHTML Validation Service

Programming Web-based applications can be complex, and XHTML documents must be written correctly to ensure that browsers process them properly. To promote correctly written documents, the World Wide Web Consortium (W3C) provides a *validation service* (`validator.w3.org`) for checking a document's syntax. Documents can be validated either from a URL that specifies the location of the file or by uploading a file to the site `validator.w3.org/file-upload.html`. Uploading a file copies the file from the user's computer to another computer on the Internet. Figure F.2 shows `main.html` (Fig. F.1) being uploaded for validation. The W3C's Web page indicates that the service name is **MarkUp Validation Service**, and the validation service is able to validate the syntax of XHTML documents. All the XHTML examples in this book have been validated successfully using `validator.w3.org`.

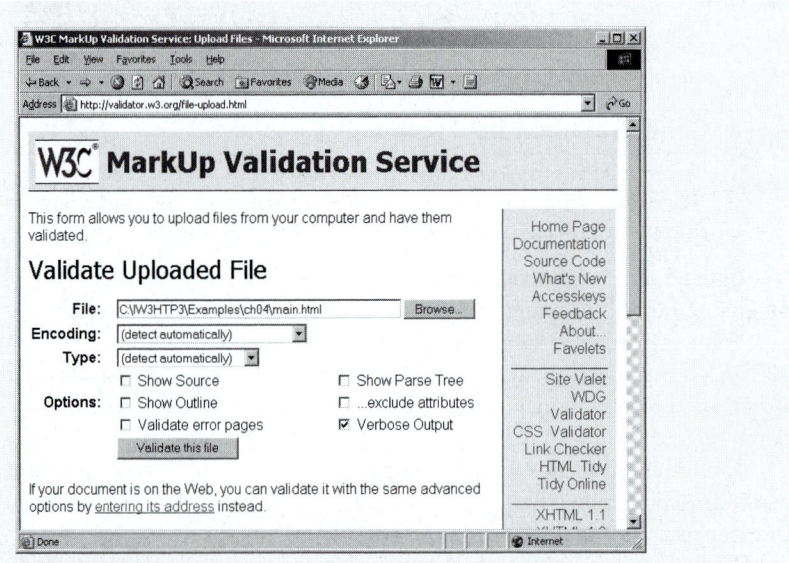

Fig. F.2 | Validating an XHTML document. (Courtesy of World Wide Web Consortium (W3C).)

By clicking **Browse...**, users can select files on their own computers for upload. After selecting a file, clicking the **Validate this file** button uploads and validates the file. Figure F.3 shows the results of validating main.html. This document does not contain any syntax errors. If a document does contain syntax errors, the validation service displays error messages describing the errors.

Error-Prevention Tip F.1

Most current browsers attempt to render XHTML documents even if they are invalid. This often leads to unexpected and possibly undesirable results. Use a validation service, such as the W3C MarkUp Validation Service, to confirm that an XHTML document is syntactically correct.

F.5 Headers

Some text in an XHTML document may be more important than other text. For example, the text in this section is considered more important than a footnote. XHTML provides six *headers*, called *header elements*, for specifying the relative importance of information. Figure F.4 demonstrates these elements (h1 through h6). Header element h1 (line 15) is considered the most significant header and is typically rendered in a larger font than the other five headers (lines 16–20). Each successive header element (i.e., h2, h3, etc.) is typically rendered in a progressively smaller font.

Portability Tip F.1

The text size used to display each header element can vary significantly between browsers. In Chapter 6, we discuss how to control the text size and other text properties.

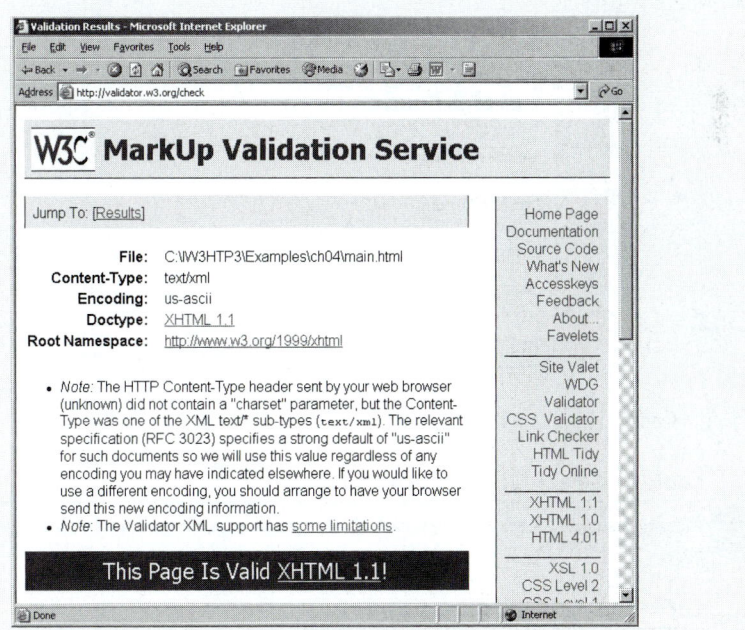

Fig. F.3 | XHTML validation results. (Courtesy of World Wide Web Consortium (W3C).)

```
 1    <?xml version = "1.0"?>
 2    <!DOCTYPE html PUBLIC "-//W3C//DTD XHTML 1.1//EN"
 3       "http://www.w3.org/TR/xhtml11/DTD/xhtml11.dtd">
 4
 5    <!-- Fig. F.4: header.html -->
 6    <!-- XHTML headers          -->
 7
 8    <html xmlns = "http://www.w3.org/1999/xhtml">
 9       <head>
10          <title>Internet and WWW How to Program - Headers</title>
11       </head>
12
13       <body>
14
15          <h1>Level 1 Header</h1>
16          <h2>Level 2 header</h2>
17          <h3>Level 3 header</h3>
18          <h4>Level 4 header</h4>
19          <h5>Level 5 header</h5>
20          <h6>Level 6 header</h6>
21
22       </body>
23    </html>
```

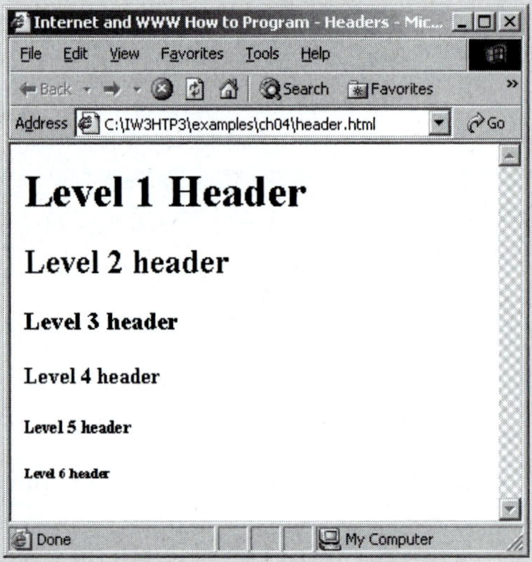

Fig. F.4 | Header elements h1 through h6.

Look-and-Feel Observation F.1

Placing a header at the top of every XHTML page helps viewers understand the purpose of each page.

Look-and-Feel Observation F.2

Use larger headers to emphasize more important sections of a Web page.

F.6 Linking

One of the most important XHTML features is the *hyperlink,* which references (or *links* to) other resources, such as XHTML documents and images. In XHTML, both text and images can act as hyperlinks. Web browsers typically underline text hyperlinks and color their text blue by default, so that users can distinguish hyperlinks from plain text. In Fig. F.5, we create text hyperlinks to four different Web sites.

Line 17 introduces the *strong* element. Browsers typically display such text in a bold font. Links are created using the *a* (*anchor*) *element.* Line 20 defines a hyperlink that links the text Deitel to the URL assigned to attribute *href*, which specifies the location of a linked resource, such as a Web page, a file or an e-mail address. This particular anchor element links to a Web page located at http://www.deitel.com. When a URL does not indicate a specific document on the Web site, the Web server returns a default Web page. This page is often called index.html; however, most Web servers can be configured to use any file as the default Web page for the site. (Open http://www.deitel.com in one browser window and http://www.deitel.com/index.html in a second browser window to confirm that they are identical.) If the Web server cannot locate a requested document, it returns an error indication to the Web browser, and the browser displays a Web page containing an error message to the user.

```
 1   <?xml version = "1.0"?>
 2   <!DOCTYPE html PUBLIC "-//W3C//DTD XHTML 1.1//EN"
 3      "http://www.w3.org/TR/xhtml11/DTD/xhtml11.dtd">
 4
 5   <!-- Fig. F.5: links.html        -->
 6   <!-- Introduction to hyperlinks -->
 7
 8   <html xmlns = "http://www.w3.org/1999/xhtml">
 9      <head>
10         <title>Internet and WWW How to Program - Links</title>
11      </head>
12
13      <body>
14
15         <h1>Here are my favorite sites</h1>
16
17         <p><strong>Click a name to go to that page.</strong></p>
18
19         <!-- Create four text hyperlinks -->
20         <p><a href = "http://www.deitel.com">Deitel</a></p>
21
22         <p><a href = "http://www.prenhall.com">Prentice Hall</a></p>
23
24         <p><a href = "http://www.yahoo.com">Yahoo!</a></p>
25
26         <p><a href = "http://www.usatoday.com">USA Today</a></p>
27
28      </body>
29   </html>
```

Fig. F.5 | Linking to other Web pages. (Part 1 of 2.)

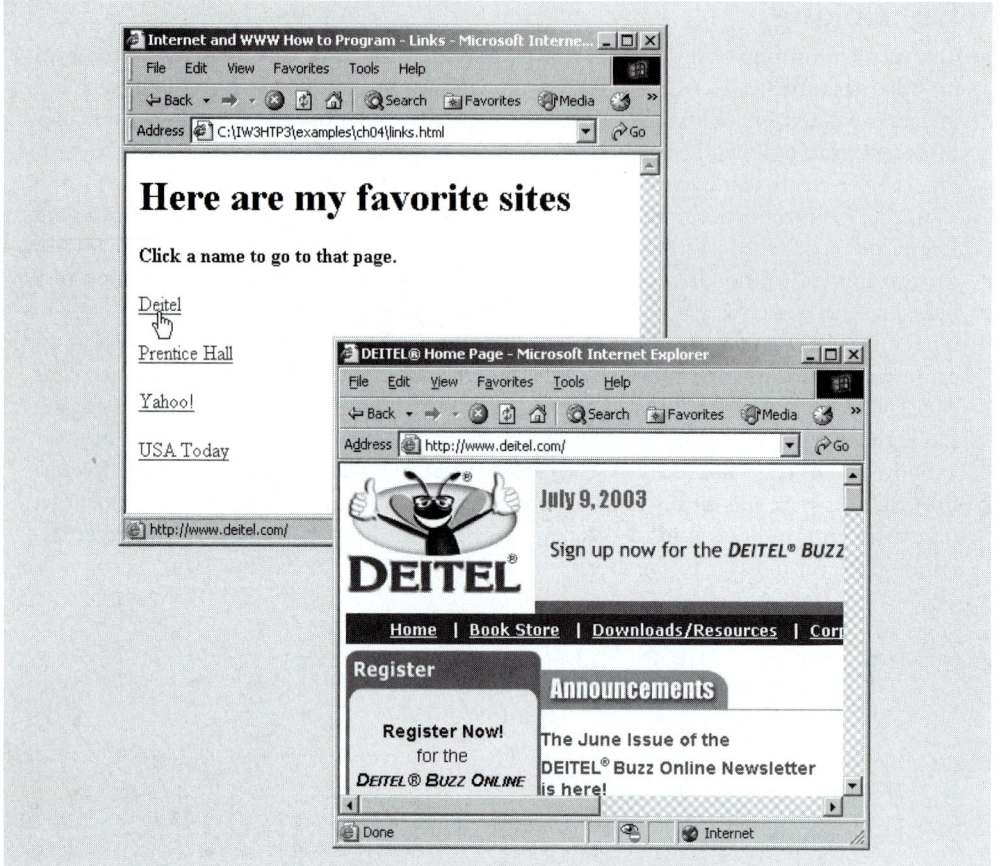

Fig. F.5 | Linking to other Web pages. (Part 2 of 2.)

Anchors can link to e-mail addresses using a *mailto:* URL. When someone clicks this type of anchored link, most browsers launch the default e-mail program (e.g., Outlook Express) to enable the user to write an e-mail message to the linked address. Figure F.6 demonstrates this type of anchor. Lines 17–19 contain an e-mail link. The form of an e-mail anchor is <a href = "mailto:*emailaddress*">...</a>. In this case, we link to the e-mail address deitel@deitel.com.

```
1   <?xml version = "1.0"?>
2   <!DOCTYPE html PUBLIC "-//W3C//DTD XHTML 1.1//EN"
3      "http://www.w3.org/TR/xhtml11/DTD/xhtml11.dtd">
4
5   <!-- Fig. F.6: contact.html  -->
6   <!-- Adding email hyperlinks -->
7
8   <html xmlns = "http://www.w3.org/1999/xhtml">
9      <head>
```

Fig. F.6 | Linking to an e-mail address. (Part 1 of 2.)

```
10          <title>Internet and WWW How to Program - Contact Page</title>
11      </head>
12
13      <body>
14
15         <p>
16            My e-mail address is
17            <a href = "mailto:deitel@deitel.com">
18               deitel@deitel.com
19            </a>
20            . Click the address and your browser will
21            open an e-mail message and address it to me.
22         </p>
23      </body>
24   </html>
```

Fig. F.6 | Linking to an e-mail address. (Part 2 of 2.)

F.7 Images

The examples discussed so far demonstrate how to mark up documents that contain only text. However, most Web pages contain both text and images. In fact, images are an equal, if not essential, part of Web-page design. The three most popular image formats used by Web developers are Graphics Interchange Format (GIF), Joint Photographic Experts Group (JPEG) and Portable Network Graphics (PNG) images. Users can create images using specialized pieces of software, such as Adobe Photoshop Elements 2.0 (discussed in Chapter 3), Macromedia Fireworks (www.macromedia.com) and Jasc Paint Shop Pro (www.jasc.com). Images may also be acquired from various Web sites, such as the Yahoo!

Picture Gallery (gallery.yahoo.com). Figure F.7 demonstrates how to incorporate images into Web pages.

Lines 16–17 use an *img* element to insert an image in the document. The image file's location is specified with the img element's **src** attribute. In this case, the image is located in the same directory as this XHTML document, so only the image's file name is required. Optional attributes **width** and **height** specify the image's width and height, respectively. The document author can scale an image by increasing or decreasing the values of the image width and height attributes. If these attributes are omitted, the browser uses the

```
 1   <?xml version = "1.0"?>
 2   <!DOCTYPE html PUBLIC "-//W3C//DTD XHTML 1.1//EN"
 3      "http://www.w3.org/TR/xhtml11/DTD/xhtml11.dtd">
 4
 5   <!-- Fig. F.7: picture.html    -->
 6   <!-- Adding images with XHTML -->
 7
 8   <html xmlns = "http://www.w3.org/1999/xhtml">
 9      <head>
10         <title>Internet and WWW How to Program - Welcome</title>
11      </head>
12
13      <body>
14
15         <p>
16            <img src = "xmlhtp.jpg" height = "238" width = "183"
17               alt = "XML How to Program book cover" />
18            <img src = "jhtp.jpg" height = "238" width = "183"
19               alt = "Java How to Program book cover" />
20         </p>
21      </body>
22   </html>
```

Fig. F.7 | Images in XHTML files.

image's actual width and height. Images are measured in *pixels* ("picture elements"), which represent dots of color on the screen. The image in Fig. F.7 is 183 pixels wide and 238 pixels high.

Good Programming Practice F.5

Always include the width and the height of an image inside the <img> tag. When the browser loads the XHTML file, it will know immediately from these attributes how much screen space to provide for the image and will lay out the page properly, even before it downloads the image.

Performance Tip F.1

Including the width and height attributes in an <img> tag can result in the browser loading and rendering pages faster.

Common Programming Error F.4

Entering new dimensions for an image that change its inherent width-to-height ratio distorts the appearance of the image. For example, if your image is 200 pixels wide and 100 pixels high, you should ensure that any new dimensions have a 2:1 width-to-height ratio.

Every img element in an XHTML document has an *alt* attribute. If a browser cannot render an image, the browser displays the alt attribute's value. A browser may not be able to render an image for several reasons. It may not support images—as is the case with a *text-based browser* (i.e., a browser that can display only text)—or the client may have disabled image viewing to reduce download time. Figure F.7 shows Internet Explorer 6 rendering the alt attribute's value when a document references a nonexistent image file (jhtp.jpg).

The alt attribute is important for creating *accessible* Web pages for users with disabilities, especially those with vision impairments who use text-based browsers. Specialized software called a *speech synthesizer* often is used by people with disabilities. This software application "speaks" the alt attribute's value so that the user knows what the browser is displaying. We discuss accessibility issues in detail in Chapter 29.

Some XHTML elements (called *empty elements*) contain only attributes and do not mark up text (i.e., text is not placed between the start and end tags). Empty elements (e.g., img) must be terminated, either by using the *forward slash character* (/) inside the closing right angle bracket (>) of the start tag or by explicitly including the end tag. When using the forward slash character, we add a space before the forward slash to improve readability (as shown at the ends of lines 17 and 19). Rather than using the forward slash character, lines 18–19 could be written with a closing </img> tag as follows:

```
<img src = "jhtp.jpg" height = "238" width = "183"
    alt = "Java How to Program book cover"></img>
```

By using images as hyperlinks, Web developers can create graphical Web pages that link to other resources. In Fig. F.8, we create six different image hyperlinks.

Lines 17–20 create an *image hyperlink* by nesting an img element in an anchor (a) element. The value of the img element's src attribute value specifies that this image (links.jpg) resides in a directory named buttons. The buttons directory and the XHTML document are in the same directory. Images from other Web documents also can be referenced (after obtaining permission from the document's owner) by setting the src attribute to the name and location of the image. Clicking an image hyperlink takes a user to the Web page specified by the surrounding anchor element's `href` attribute.

```
 1   <?xml version = "1.0"?>
 2   <!DOCTYPE html PUBLIC "-//W3C//DTD XHTML 1.1//EN"
 3       "http://www.w3.org/TR/xhtml11/DTD/xhtml11.dtd">
 4
 5   <!-- Fig. F.8: nav.html          -->
 6   <!-- Using images as link anchors -->
 7
 8   <html xmlns = "http://www.w3.org/1999/xhtml">
 9      <head>
10         <title>Internet and WWW How to Program - Navigation Bar
11         </title>
12      </head>
13
14      <body>
15
16         <p>
17            <a href = "links.html">
18               <img src = "buttons/links.jpg" width = "65"
19                  height = "50" alt = "Links Page" />
20            </a><br />
21
22            <a href = "list.html">
23               <img src = "buttons/list.jpg" width = "65"
24                  height = "50" alt = "List Example Page" />
25            </a><br />
26
27            <a href = "contact.html">
28               <img src = "buttons/contact.jpg" width = "65"
29                  height = "50" alt = "Contact Page" />
30            </a><br />
31
32            <a href = "header.html">
33               <img src = "buttons/header.jpg" width = "65"
34                  height = "50" alt = "Header Page" />
35            </a><br />
36
37            <a href = "table1.html">
38               <img src = "buttons/table.jpg" width = "65"
39                  height = "50" alt = "Table Page" />
40            </a><br />
41
42            <a href = "form.html">
43               <img src = "buttons/form.jpg" width = "65"
44                  height = "50" alt = "Feedback Form" />
45            </a><br />
46         </p>
47
48      </body>
49   </html>
```

Fig. F.8 | Images as link anchors. (Part 1 of 2.)

(called a *disc*). Each entry in an unordered list (element u1 in line 20) is an *li* (*list item*) element (lines 23, 25, 27 and 29). Most Web browsers render these elements with a line break and a bullet symbol indented from the beginning of the new line.

F.10 Nested and Ordered Lists

Lists may be nested to represent hierarchical relationships, as in an outline format. Figure F.11 demonstrates nested lists and *ordered lists*. The ordered list element *ol* creates a list in which each item begins with a number.

A Web browser indents each nested list to indicate a hierarchical relationship. The first ordered list begins at line 33. Items in an ordered list are enumerated one, two, three and so on. Nested ordered lists are enumerated in the same manner. The items in the outermost unordered list (line 18) are preceded by discs. List items nested inside the unordered list of line 18 are preceded by *circles*. Although not demonstrated in this example, subsequent nested list items are preceded by *squares*.

```
 1   <?xml version = "1.0"?>
 2   <!DOCTYPE html PUBLIC "-//W3C//DTD XHTML 1.1//EN"
 3      "http://www.w3.org/TR/xhtml11/DTD/xhtml11.dtd">
 4
 5   <!-- Fig. F.11: list.html              -->
 6   <!-- Advanced Lists: nested and ordered -->
 7
 8   <html xmlns = "http://www.w3.org/1999/xhtml">
 9      <head>
10         <title>Internet and WWW How to Program - Lists</title>
11      </head>
12
13      <body>
14
15         <h1>The Best Features of the Internet</h1>
16
17         <!-- create an unordered list -->
18         <ul>
19            <li>You can meet new people from countries around
20               the world.</li>
21            <li>
22               You have access to new media as it becomes public:
23
24               <!-- this starts a nested list, which uses a -->
25               <!-- modified bullet. The list ends when you -->
26               <!-- close the <ul> tag.                     -->
27               <ul>
28                  <li>New games</li>
29                  <li>
30                     New applications
31
32                     <!-- nested ordered list -->
33                     <ol>
34                        <li>For business</li>
```

Fig. F.11 | Nested and ordered lists in XHTML. (Part 1 of 2.)

```
35                    <li>For pleasure</li>
36                    </ol>
37            </li>
38
39            <li>Around the clock news</li>
40            <li>Search engines</li>
41            <li>Shopping</li>
42            <li>
43                Programming
44
45                <!-- another nested ordered list -->
46                <ol>
47                    <li>XML</li>
48                    <li>Java</li>
49                    <li>XHTML</li>
50                    <li>Scripts</li>
51                    <li>New languages</li>
52                </ol>
53
54            </li>
55
56        </ul> <!-- ends the nested list of line 27 -->
57        </li>
58
59        <li>Links</li>
60        <li>Keeping in touch with old friends</li>
61        <li>It is the technology of the future!</li>
62
63    </ul>    <!-- ends the unordered list of line 18 -->
64
65    </body>
66 </html>
```

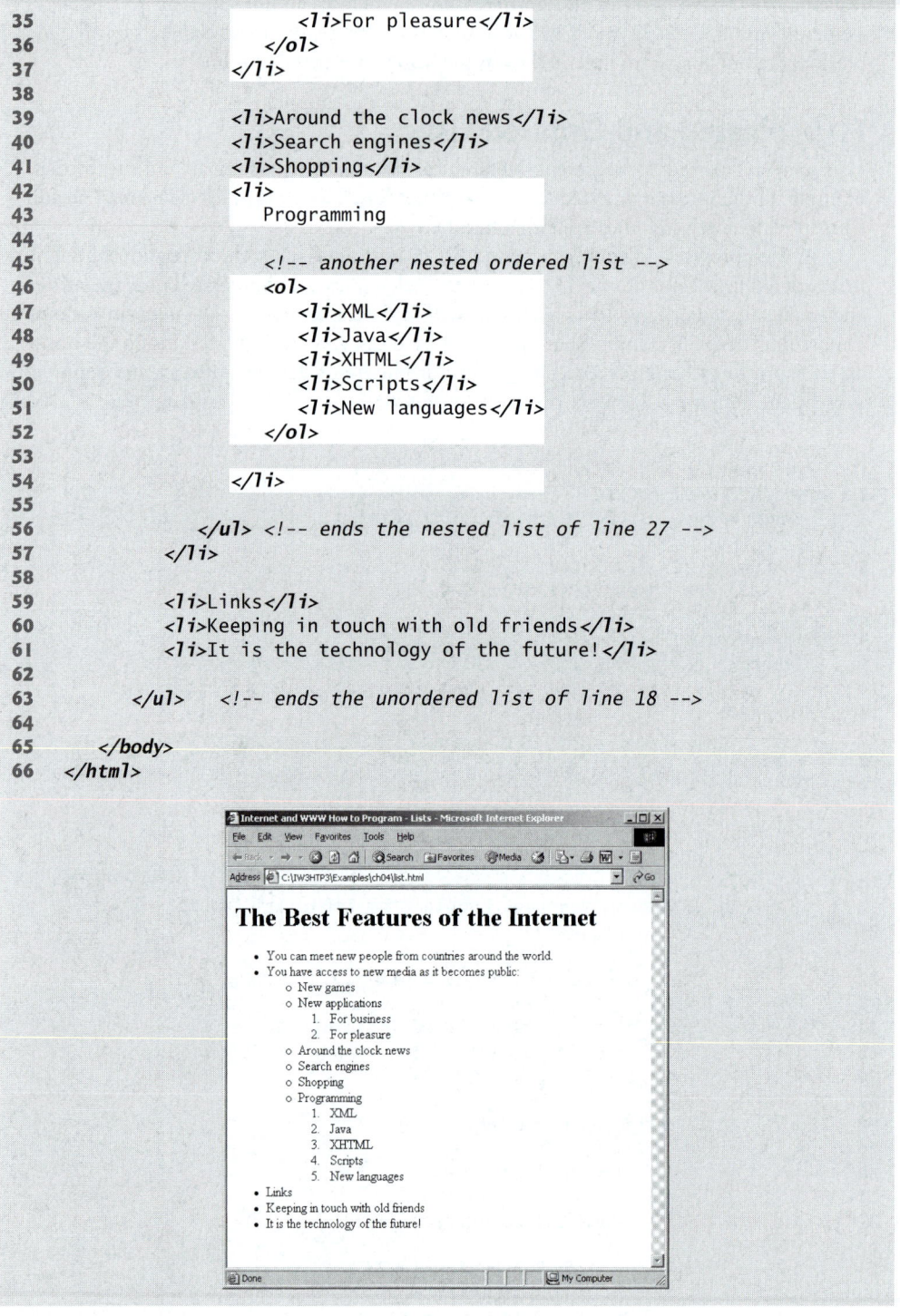

Fig. F.11 | Nested and ordered lists in XHTML. (Part 2 of 2.)

F.11 Web Resources

`www.w3.org/TR/xhtml11`

The *XHTML 1.1 Recommendation* contains XHTML 1.1 general information, compatibility issues, document type definition information, definitions, terminology and much more.

`www.xhtml.org`

XHTML.org provides XHTML development news and links to other XHTML resources, including books and articles.

`www.w3schools.com/xhtml/default.asp`

The *XHTML School* provides XHTML quizzes and references. This page also contains links to XHTML syntax, validation and document type definitions.

`validator.w3.org`

This is the W3C XHTML validation service site.

`hotwired.lycos.com/webmonkey/00/50/index2a.html`

This site provides an article about XHTML. Key sections of the article overview XHTML and discuss tags, attributes and anchors.

`wdvl.com/Authoring/Languages/XML/XHTML`

The *Web Developers Virtual Library* provides an introduction to XHTML. This site also contains articles, examples and links to other technologies.

`www.w3.org/TR/2001/REC-xhtml11-20010531`

The XHTML 1.1 DTD documentation site provides technical specifications of XHTML 1.1 syntax.

G

Introduction to XHTML: Part 2

Yea, from the table of my memory
I'll wipe away all trivial fond records.
—William Shakespeare

OBJECTIVES

In this appendix, you will learn:

- To be able to create tables with rows and columns of data.

- To be able to control table formatting.

- To be able to create and use forms.

- To be able to create and use image maps to aid in Web-page navigation.

- To be able to make Web pages accessible to search engines using `<meta>` tags.

- To be able to use the `frameset` element to display multiple Web pages in a single browser window.

G.1 Introduction

In the preceding appendix, we introduced XHTML. We built several complete Web pages featuring text, hyperlinks, images, horizontal rules and line breaks. In this appendix, we discuss more substantial XHTML features, including presentation of information in *tables* and incorporating *forms* for collecting information from a Web-page visitor. We also introduce *internal linking* and *image maps* for enhancing Web-page navigation, and *frames* for displaying multiple documents in the browser. By the end of this appendix, you will be familiar with the most commonly used XHTML features and will be able to create more complex Web documents.

G.2 Basic XHTML Tables

Tables are used to organize data in rows and columns. Our first example (Fig. G.1) creates a table with six rows and two columns to display price information for fruit.

Tables are defined with the **table** element (lines 16–66). Lines 16–18 specify the start tag for a table element that has several attributes. The **border** attribute specifies the table's border width in pixels. To create a table without a border, set border to "0". This example assigns attribute width the value "40%" to set the table's width to 40 percent of the browser's width. A developer can also set attribute width to a specified number of pixels. Try resizing the browser window to see how the width of the window affects the width of the table.

```
 1   <?xml version = "1.0"?>
 2   <!DOCTYPE html PUBLIC "-//W3C//DTD XHTML 1.1//EN"
 3      "http://www.w3.org/TR/xhtml11/DTD/xhtml11.dtd">
 4
 5   <!-- Fig. G.1: table1.html   -->
 6   <!-- Creating a basic table  -->
 7
 8   <html xmlns = "http://www.w3.org/1999/xhtml">
```

Fig. G.1 | XHTML table. (Part 1 of 3.)

```
 9    <head>
10       <title>A simple XHTML table</title>
11    </head>
12
13    <body>
14
15       <!-- the <table> tag opens a table -->
16       <table border = "1" width = "40%"
17          summary = "This table provides information about
18             the price of fruit">
19
20          <!-- the <caption> tag summarizes the table's    -->
21          <!-- contents (this helps the visually impaired) -->
22          <caption><strong>Price of Fruit</strong></caption>
23
24          <!-- the <thead> is the first section of a table -->
25          <!-- it formats the table header area            -->
26          <thead>
27             <tr>                    <!-- <tr> inserts a table row -->
28                <th>Fruit</th>  <!-- insert a heading cell -->
29                <th>Price</th>
30             </tr>
31          </thead>
32
33          <!-- the <tfoot> is the last section of a table -->
34          <!-- it formats the table footer                -->
35          <tfoot>
36             <tr>
37                <th>Total</th>
38                <th>$3.75</th>
39             </tr>
40          </tfoot>
41
42          <!-- all table content is enclosed   -->
43          <!-- within the <tbody>              -->
44          <tbody>
45             <tr>
46                <td>Apple</td>  <!-- insert a data cell -->
47                <td>$0.25</td>
48             </tr>
49
50             <tr>
51                <td>Orange</td>
52                <td>$0.50</td>
53             </tr>
54
55             <tr>
56                <td>Banana</td>
57                <td>$1.00</td>
58             </tr>
59
60             <tr>
61                <td>Pineapple</td>\
```

Fig. G.1 | XHTML table. (Part 2 of 3.)

```
62                    <td>$2.00</td>
63                </tr>
64            </tbody>
65
66        </table>
67
68    </body>
69 </html>
```

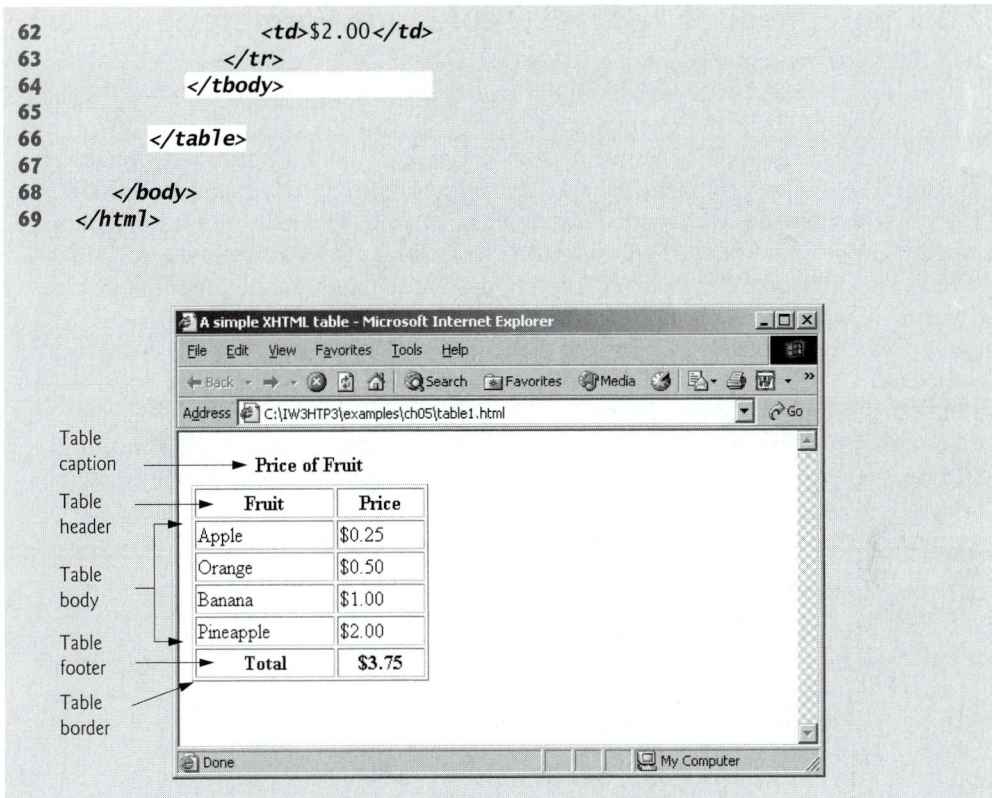

Fig. G.1 │ XHTML table. (Part 3 of 3.)

As its name implies, attribute **summary** (lines 17–18) describes the table's contents. Speech devices use this attribute to make the table more accessible to users with visual impairments. The **caption** element (line 22) describes the table's content and helps text-based browsers interpret the table data. Text inside the <caption> tag is rendered above the table by most browsers. Attribute summary and element caption are two of the many XHTML features that make Web pages more accessible to users with disabilities.

A table has three distinct sections—*head*, *body* and *foot*. The head section (or header cell) is defined with a **thead** element (lines 26–31), which contains header information such as column names. Each **tr** element (lines 27–30) defines an individual *table row*. The columns in the head section are defined with **th** elements. Most browsers center text formatted by th (table header column) elements and display them in bold. Table header elements are nested inside table row elements.

The foot section (lines 35–40) is defined with a **tfoot** (table foot) element. The text placed in the footer commonly includes calculation results and footnotes. Like other sections, the foot section can contain table rows, and each row can contain columns.

The body section, or *table body*, contains the table's primary data. The table body (lines 44–64) is defined in a **tbody** element. In the body, each **tr** element specifies one row. *Data cells* contain individual pieces of data and are defined with **td** (*table data*) elements within each row.

G.3 Intermediate XHTML Tables and Formatting

In the preceding section, we explored the structure of a basic table. In Fig. G.2, we enhance our discussion of tables by introducing elements and attributes that allow the document author to build more complex tables.

The table begins in line 17. Element **colgroup** (lines 22–27) groups and formats columns. The *col* element (line 26) specifies two attributes in this example. The *align* attribute determines the alignment of text in the column. The **span** attribute determines how many columns the col element formats. In this case, we set align's value to `"right"` and span's value to `"1"` to right align text in the first column (the column containing the picture of the camel in the sample screen capture).

Table cells are sized to fit the data they contain. Document authors can create larger data cells by using the attributes **rowspan** and **colspan**. The values assigned to these attributes specify the number of rows or columns occupied by a cell. The th element at lines 36–39 uses the attribute rowspan = `"2"` to allow the cell containing the picture of the camel to use two vertically adjacent cells (thus the cell *spans* two rows). The th element in lines 42–45 uses the attribute colspan = `"4"` to widen the header cell (containing `Camelid` comparison and `Approximate as of 9/2002`) to span four cells.

Common Programming Error G.1

When using colspan and rowspan to adjust the size of table data cells, keep in mind that the modified cells will occupy more than one column or row. Other rows or columns of the table must compensate for the extra rows or columns spanned by individual cells. If they do not, the formatting of your table will be distorted and you may inadvertently create more columns and rows than you originally intended.

```
 1   <?xml version = "1.0"?>
 2   <!DOCTYPE html PUBLIC "-//W3C//DTD XHTML 1.1//EN"
 3      "http://www.w3.org/TR/xhtml11/DTD/xhtml11.dtd">
 4
 5   <!-- Fig. G.2: table2.html      -->
 6   <!-- Intermediate table design -->
 7
 8   <html xmlns = "http://www.w3.org/1999/xhtml">
 9      <head>
10         <title>Internet and WWW How to Program - Tables</title>
11      </head>
12
13      <body>
14
15         <h1>Table Example Page</h1>
16
17         <table border = "1">
18            <caption>Here is a more complex sample table.</caption>
19
20            <!-- <colgroup> and <col> tags are used to -->
21            <!-- format entire columns                 -->
22            <colgroup>
23
```

Fig. G.2 | Complex XHTML table. (Part 1 of 3.)

```
24          <!-- span attribute determines how many columns -->
25          <!-- the <col> tag affects                       -->
26          <col align = "right" span = "1" />
27      </colgroup>
28
29      <thead>
30
31          <!-- rowspans and colspans merge the specified    -->
32          <!-- number of cells vertically or horizontally   -->
33          <tr>
34
35              <!-- merge two rows -->
36              <th rowspan = "2">
37                  <img src = "camel.gif" width = "205"
38                      height = "167" alt = "Picture of a camel" />
39              </th>
40
41              <!-- merge four columns -->
42              <th colspan = "4" valign = "top">
43                  <h1>Camelid comparison</h1><br />
44                  <p>Approximate as of 9/2002</p>
45              </th>
46          </tr>
47
48          <tr valign = "bottom">
49              <th># of Humps</th>
50              <th>Indigenous region</th>
51              <th>Spits?</th>
52              <th>Produces Wool?</th>
53          </tr>
54
55      </thead>
56
57      <tbody>
58
59          <tr>
60              <th>Camels (bactrian)</th>
61              <td>2</td>
62              <td>Africa/Asia</td>
63              <td>Yes</td>
64              <td>Yes</td>
65          </tr>
66
67          <tr>
68              <th>Llamas</th>
69              <td>1</td>
70              <td>Andes Mountains</td>
71              <td>Yes</td>
72              <td>Yes</td>
73          </tr>
74
75      </tbody>
76
```

Fig. G.2 | Complex XHTML table. (Part 2 of 3.)

```
77            </table>
78
79      </body>
80   </html>
```

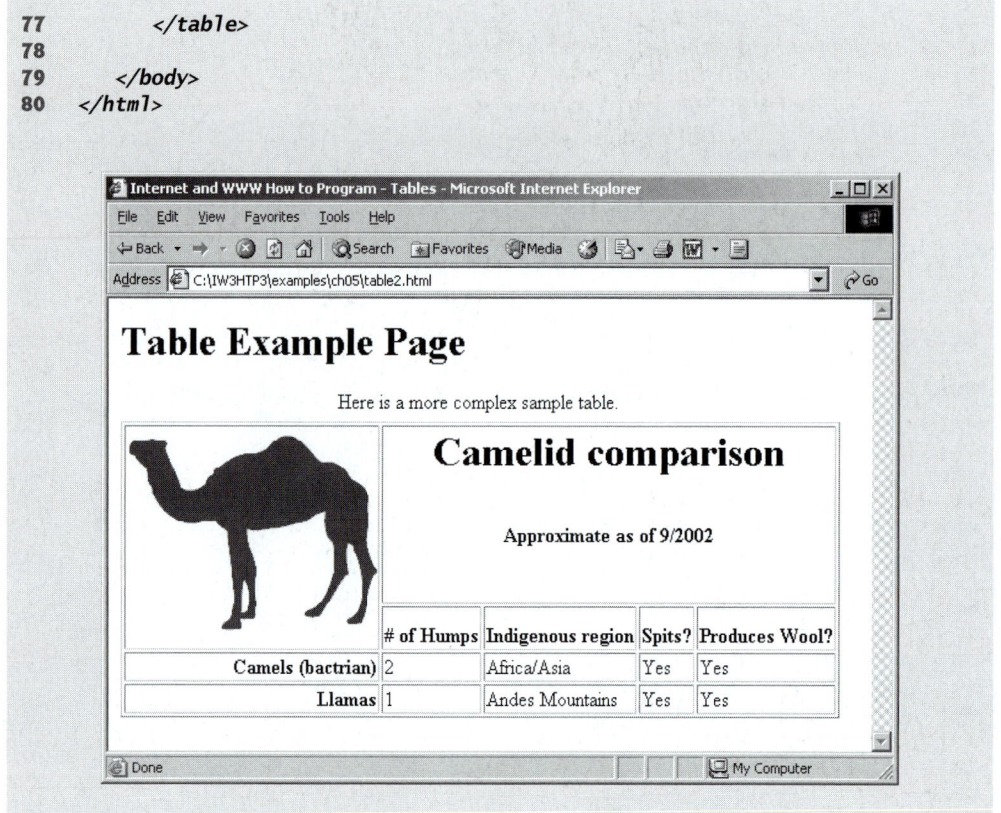

Fig. G.2 | Complex XHTML table. (Part 3 of 3.)

Line 42 introduces the attribute **valign**, which aligns data vertically and may be assigned one of four values—"top" aligns data with the top of the cell, "middle" vertically centers data (the default for all data and header cells), "bottom" aligns data with the bottom of the cell and "baseline" ignores the fonts used for the row data and sets the bottom of all text in the row on a common *baseline* (i.e., the horizontal line at which each character in a word is aligned).

G.4 Basic XHTML Forms

When browsing Web sites, users often need to provide such information as search keywords, e-mail addresses and zip codes. XHTML provides a mechanism, called a *form*, for collecting such data from a user.

Data that users enter on a Web page normally is sent to a Web server that provides access to a site's resources (e.g., XHTML documents, images). These resources are located either on the same machine as the Web server or on a machine that the Web server can access through the network. When a browser requests a Web page or file that is located on a server, the server processes the request and returns the requested resource. A request contains the name and path of the desired resource and the method of communication (called a *protocol*). XHTML documents use the Hypertext Transfer Protocol (HTTP).

Figure G.3 sends the form data to the Web server, which passes the form data to a *CGI* (*Common Gateway Interface*) script (i.e., a program) written in Perl, C or some other language. The script processes the data received from the Web server and typically returns information to the Web server. The Web server then sends the information as an XHTML document to the Web browser. [*Note*: This example demonstrates client-side functionality. If the form is submitted (by clicking **Submit Your Entries**) an error occurs because we have not yet configured the required server-side functionality.]

Forms can contain visual and nonvisual components. Visual components include clickable buttons and other graphical user interface components with which users interact. Nonvisual components, called *hidden inputs*, store any data that the document author specifies, such as e-mail addresses and XHTML document file names that act as links. The form is defined in lines 23–52 by a *form* element. Attribute *method* (line 23) specifies how the form's data is sent to the Web server.

```
 1    <?xml version = "1.0"?>
 2    <!DOCTYPE html PUBLIC "-//W3C//DTD XHTML 1.1//EN"
 3       "http://www.w3.org/TR/xhtml11/DTD/xhtml11.dtd">
 4
 5    <!-- Fig. G.3: form.html    -->
 6    <!-- Form Design Example 1 -->
 7
 8    <html xmlns = "http://www.w3.org/1999/xhtml">
 9       <head>
10          <title>Internet and WWW How to Program - Forms</title>
11       </head>
12
13       <body>
14
15          <h1>Feedback Form</h1>
16
17          <p>Please fill out this form to help
18             us improve our site.</p>
19
20          <!-- this tag starts the form, gives the    -->
21          <!-- method of sending information and the  -->
22          <!-- location of form scripts               -->
23          <form method = "post" action = "/cgi-bin/formmail">
24
25             <p>
26                <!-- hidden inputs contain non-visual -->
27                <!-- information                      -->
28                <input type = "hidden" name = "recipient"
29                   value = "deitel@deitel.com" />
30                <input type = "hidden" name = "subject"
31                   value = "Feedback Form" />
32                <input type = "hidden" name = "redirect"
33                   value = "main.html" />
34             </p>
35
```

Fig. G.3 | Form with hidden fields and a text box. (Part 1 of 2.)

```
36              <!-- <input type = "text"> inserts a text box -->
37              <p><label>Name:
38                  <input name = "name" type = "text" size = "25"
39                      maxlength = "30" />
40              </label></p>
41
42          <p>
43              <!-- input types "submit" and "reset" insert  -->
44              <!-- buttons for submitting and clearing the  -->
45              <!-- form's contents                          -->
46              <input type = "submit" value =
47                  "Submit Your Entries" />
48              <input type = "reset" value =
49                  "Clear Your Entries" />
50          </p>
51
52      </form>
53
54      </body>
55  </html>
```

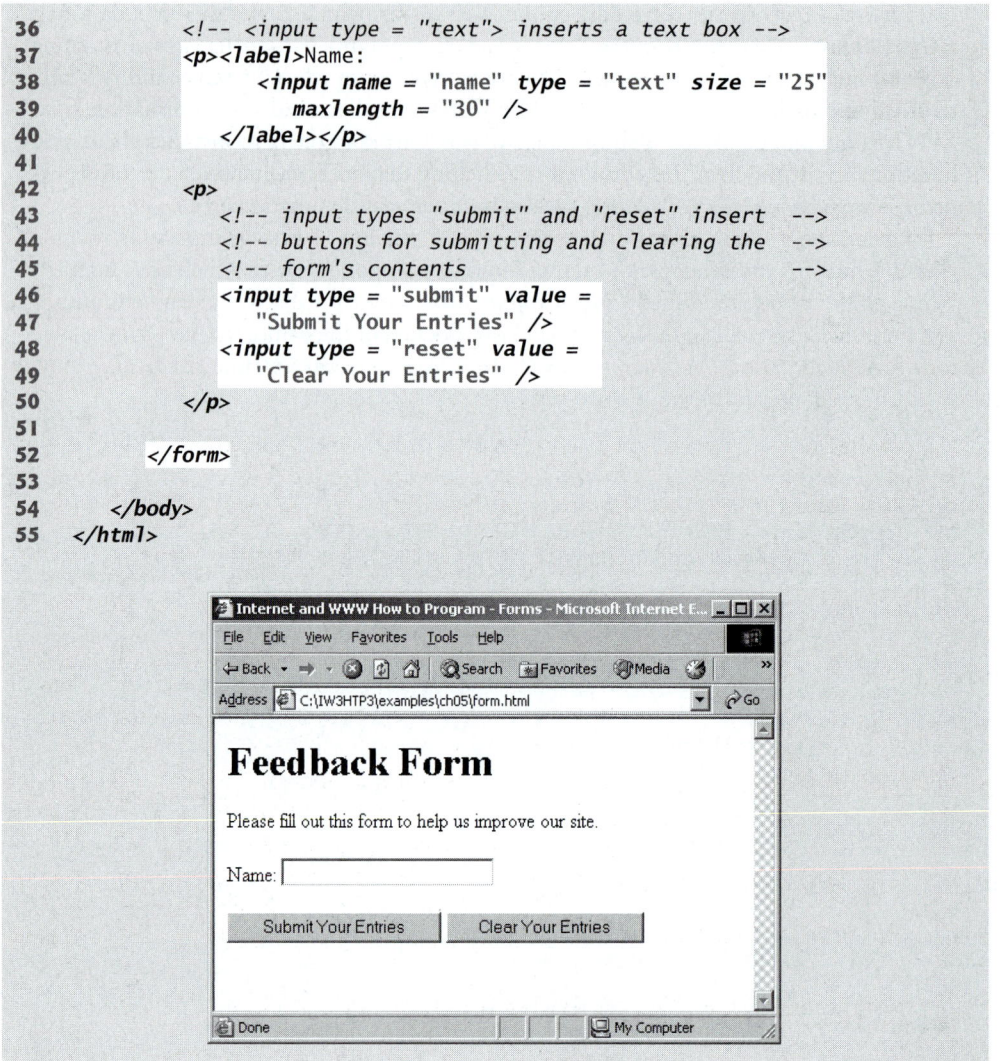

Fig. G.3 | Form with hidden fields and a text box. (Part 2 of 2.)

Using *method = "post"* appends form data to the browser request, which contains the protocol (i.e., HTTP) and the requested resource's URL. Scripts located on the Web server's computer (or on a computer accessible through the network) can access the form data sent as part of the request. For example, a script may take the form information and update an electronic mailing list. The other possible value, *method = "get"*, appends the form data directly to the end of the URL. For example, the URL /cgi-bin/formmail might have the form information name = bob appended to it.

The **action** attribute in the <form> tag specifies the URL of a script on the Web server; in this case, it specifies a script that e-mails form data to an address. Most Internet Service Providers (ISPs) have a script like this on their site; ask the Web site system administrator how to set up an XHTML document to use the script correctly.

Lines 28–33 define three **input** elements that specify data to provide to the script that processes the form (also called the *form handler*). These three input elements have the **type** attribute *"hidden"*, which allows the document author to send form data that is not input by a user.

The three hidden inputs are: an e-mail address to which the data will be sent, the e-mail's subject line and a URL where the browser will be redirected after submitting the form. Two other input attributes are *name*, which identifies the input element, and *value*, which provides the value that will be sent (or posted) to the Web server.

Good Programming Practice G.1

Place hidden input elements at the beginning of a form, immediately after the opening <form> tag. This placement allows document authors to locate hidden input elements quickly.

We introduce another type of input in lines 38–39. The *"text"* input inserts a *text box* into the form. Users can type data in text boxes. The **label** element (lines 37–40) provides users with information about the input element's purpose.

Look-and-Feel Observation G.1

Include a label element for each form element to help users determine the purpose of each form element.

The input element's **size** attribute specifies the number of characters visible in the text box. Optional attribute **maxlength** limits the number of characters input into the text box. In this case, the user is not permitted to type more than 30 characters into the text box.

There are two other types of input elements in lines 46–49. The *"submit"* input element is a button. When the user presses a *"submit"* button, the browser sends the data in the form to the Web server for processing. The **value** attribute sets the text displayed on the button (the default value is **Submit Query**). The *"reset"* input element allows a user to reset all form elements to their default values. The value attribute of the *"reset"* input element sets the text displayed on the button (the default value is **Reset**).

G.5 More Complex XHTML Forms

In the preceding section, we introduced basic forms. In this section, we introduce elements and attributes for creating more complex forms. Figure G.4 contains a form that solicits user feedback about a Web site.

```
1    <?xml version = "1.0"?>
2    <!DOCTYPE html PUBLIC "-//W3C//DTD XHTML 1.1//EN"
3       "http://www.w3.org/TR/xhtml11/DTD/xhtml11.dtd">
4
5    <!-- Fig. G.4: form2.html  -->
6    <!-- Form Design Example 2 -->
7
8    <html xmlns = "http://www.w3.org/1999/xhtml">
```

Fig. G.4 | Form with text areas, a password box and checkboxes. (Part 1 of 4.)

```
 9        <head>
10           <title>Internet and WWW How to Program - Forms</title>
11        </head>
12
13        <body>
14
15           <h1>Feedback Form</h1>
16
17           <p>Please fill out this form to help
18              us improve our site.</p>
19
20           <form method = "post" action = "/cgi-bin/formmail">
21
22              <p>
23                 <input type = "hidden" name = "recipient"
24                    value = "deitel@deitel.com" />
25                 <input type = "hidden" name = "subject"
26                    value = "Feedback Form" />
27                 <input type = "hidden" name = "redirect"
28                    value = "main.html" />
29              </p>
30
31              <p><label>Name:
32                 <input name = "name" type = "text" size = "25" />
33              </label></p>
34
35              <!-- <textarea> creates a multiline textbox -->
36              <p><label>Comments:<br />
37                 <textarea name = "comments" rows = "4" cols = "36">
38 Enter your comments here.
39                 </textarea>
40              </label></p>
41
42              <!-- <input type = "password"> inserts a    -->
43              <!-- textbox whose display is masked with   -->
44              <!-- asterisk characters                    -->
45              <p><label>E-mail Address:
46                 <input name = "email" type = "password"
47                    size = "25" />
48              </label></p>
49
50              <p>
51                 <strong>Things you liked:</strong><br />
52
53                 <label>Site design
54                 <input name = "thingsliked" type = "checkbox"
55                    value = "Design" /></label>
56
57                 <label>Links
58                 <input name = "thingsliked" type = "checkbox"
59                    value = "Links" /></label>
60
```

Fig. G.4 | Form with text areas, a password box and checkboxes. (Part 2 of 4.)

```
61              <label>Ease of use
62              <input name = "thingsliked" type = "checkbox"
63                  value = "Ease" /></label>
64
65              <label>Images
66              <input name = "thingsliked" type = "checkbox"
67                  value = "Images" /></label>
68
69              <label>Source code
70              <input name = "thingsliked" type = "checkbox"
71                  value = "Code" /></label>
72          </p>
73
74          <p>
75              <input type = "submit" value =
76                  "Submit Your Entries" />
77              <input type = "reset" value =
78                  "Clear Your Entries" />
79          </p>
80
81      </form>
82
83      </body>
84  </html>
```

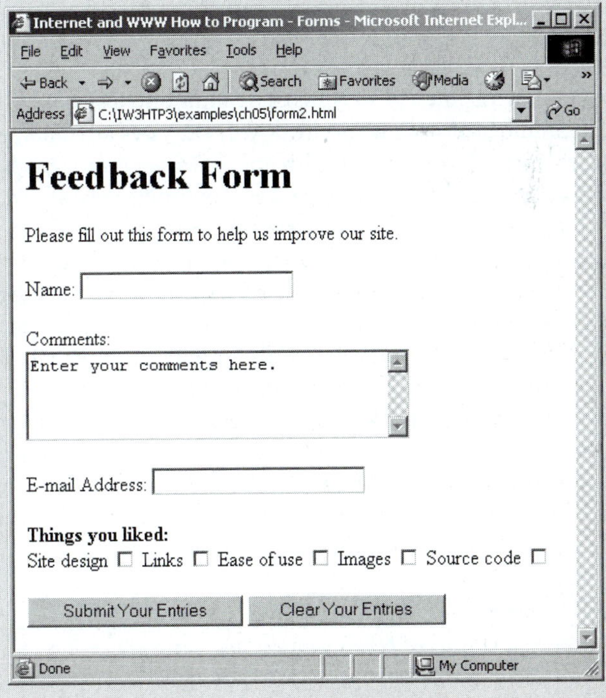

Fig. G.4 | Form with text areas, a password box and checkboxes. (Part 3 of 4.)

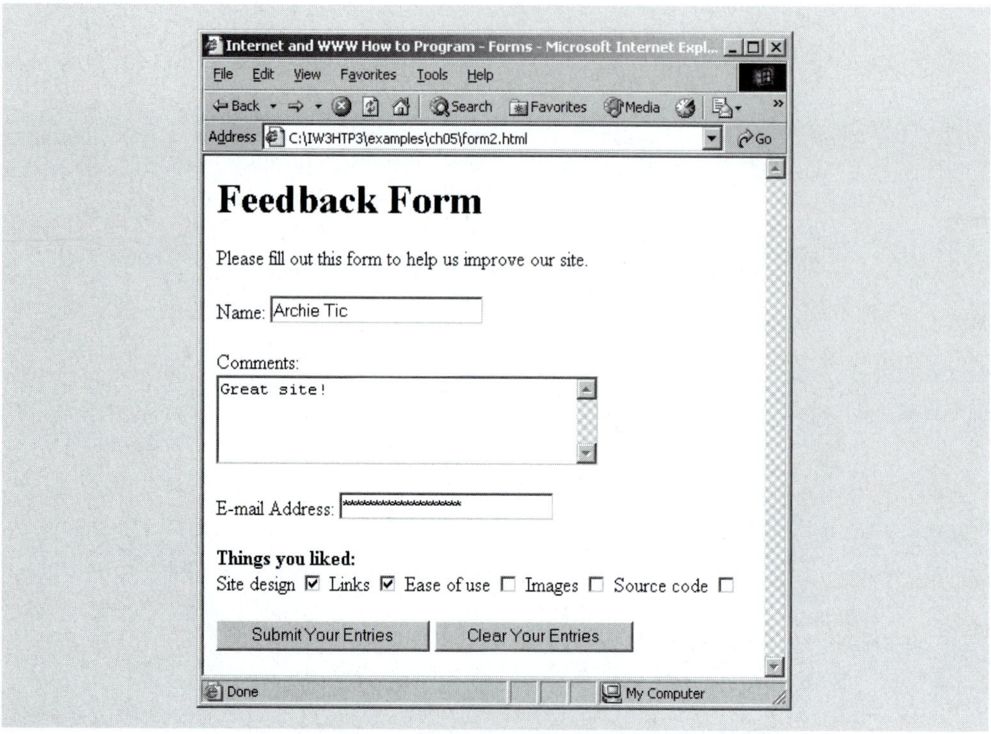

Fig. G.4 | Form with text areas, a password box and checkboxes. (Part 4 of 4.)

The ***textarea*** element (lines 37–39) inserts a multiline text box, called a ***text area***, into the form. The number of rows is specified with the ***rows*** attribute, and the number of columns (i.e., characters) is specified with the ***cols*** attribute. In this example, the textarea is four rows high and 36 characters wide. To display default text in the text area, place the text between the ***<textarea>*** and ***</textarea>*** tags. Default text can be specified in other input types, such as text boxes, by using the value attribute

The *"password"* input in lines 46–47 inserts a password box with the specified size. A password box allows users to enter sensitive information, such as credit card numbers and passwords, by "masking" the information input with asterisks (*). The actual value input is sent to the Web server, not the characters that mask the input.

Lines 54–71 introduce the ***checkbox*** form element. Checkboxes enable users to select from a set of options. When a user selects a checkbox, a check mark appears in the check box. Otherwise, the checkbox remains empty. Each *"checkbox"* input creates a new checkbox. Checkboxes can be used individually or in groups. Checkboxes that belong to a group are assigned the same name (in this case, "thingsliked").

Common Programming Error G.2

When your form has several checkboxes with the same name, you must make sure that they have different values, or the scripts running on the Web server will not be able to distinguish them.

We continue our discussion of forms by presenting a third example that introduces several additional form elements from which users can make selections (Fig. G.5). In this

```
 1   <?xml version = "1.0"?>
 2   <!DOCTYPE html PUBLIC "-//W3C//DTD XHTML 1.1//EN"
 3      "http://www.w3.org/TR/xhtml11/DTD/xhtml11.dtd">
 4
 5   <!-- Fig. G.5: form3.html  -->
 6   <!-- Form Design Example 3 -->
 7
 8   <html xmlns = "http://www.w3.org/1999/xhtml">
 9      <head>
10         <title>Internet and WWW How to Program - Forms</title>
11      </head>
12
13      <body>
14
15         <h1>Feedback Form</h1>
16
17         <p>Please fill out this form to help
18            us improve our site.</p>
19
20         <form method = "post" action = "/cgi-bin/formmail">
21
22            <p>
23               <input type = "hidden" name = "recipient"
24                  value = "deitel@deitel.com" />
25               <input type = "hidden" name = "subject"
26                  value = "Feedback Form" />
27               <input type = "hidden" name = "redirect"
28                  value = "main.html" />
29            </p>
30
31            <p><label>Name:
32               <input name = "name" type = "text" size = "25" />
33            </label></p>
34
35            <p><label>Comments:<br />
36               <textarea name = "comments" rows = "4"
37                  cols = "36"></textarea>
38            </label></p>
39
40            <p><label>E-mail Address:
41               <input name = "email" type = "password"
42                  size = "25" /></label></p>
43
44            <p>
45               <strong>Things you liked:</strong><br />
46
47               <label>Site design
48                  <input name = "thingsliked" type = "checkbox"
49                     value = "Design" /></label>
50
51               <label>Links
52                  <input name = "thingsliked" type = "checkbox"
53                     value = "Links" /></label>
```

Fig. G.5 | Form including radio buttons and a drop-down list. (Part 1 of 4.)

```
54
55            <label>Ease of use
56                <input name = "thingsliked" type = "checkbox"
57                    value = "Ease" /></label>
58
59            <label>Images
60                <input name = "thingsliked" type = "checkbox"
61                    value = "Images" /></label>
62
63            <label>Source code
64                <input name = "thingsliked" type = "checkbox"
65                    value = "Code" /></label>
66        </p>
67
68        <!-- <input type = "radio" /> creates a radio      -->
69        <!-- button. The difference between radio buttons -->
70        <!-- and checkboxes is that only one radio button -->
71        <!-- in a group can be selected.                  -->
72        <p>
73            <strong>How did you get to our site?:</strong><br />
74
75            <label>Search engine
76                <input name = "howtosite" type = "radio"
77                    value = "search engine" checked = "checked" />
78            </label>
79
80            <label>Links from another site
81                <input name = "howtosite" type = "radio"
82                    value = "link" /></label>
83
84            <label>Deitel.com Web site
85                <input name = "howtosite" type = "radio"
86                    value = "deitel.com" /></label>
87
88            <label>Reference in a book
89                <input name = "howtosite" type = "radio"
90                    value = "book" /></label>
91
92            <label>Other
93                <input name = "howtosite" type = "radio"
94                    value = "other" /></label>
95
96        </p>
97
98        <p>
99            <label>Rate our site:
100
101                <!-- the <select> tag presents a drop-down -->
102                <!-- list with choices indicated by the    -->
103                <!-- <option> tags                          -->
104            <select name = "rating">
105                <option selected = "selected">Amazing</option>
106                <option>10</option>
```

Fig. G.5 | Form including radio buttons and a drop-down list. (Part 2 of 4.)

```
107                         <option>9</option>
108                         <option>8</option>
109                         <option>7</option>
110                         <option>6</option>
111                         <option>5</option>
112                         <option>4</option>
113                         <option>3</option>
114                         <option>2</option>
115                         <option>1</option>
116                         <option>Awful</option>
117                     </select>
118
119                 </label>
120         </p>
121
122         <p>
123             <input type = "submit" value =
124                 "Submit Your Entries" />
125             <input type = "reset" value = "Clear Your Entries" />
126         </p>
127
128     </form>
129
130     </body>
131 </html>
```

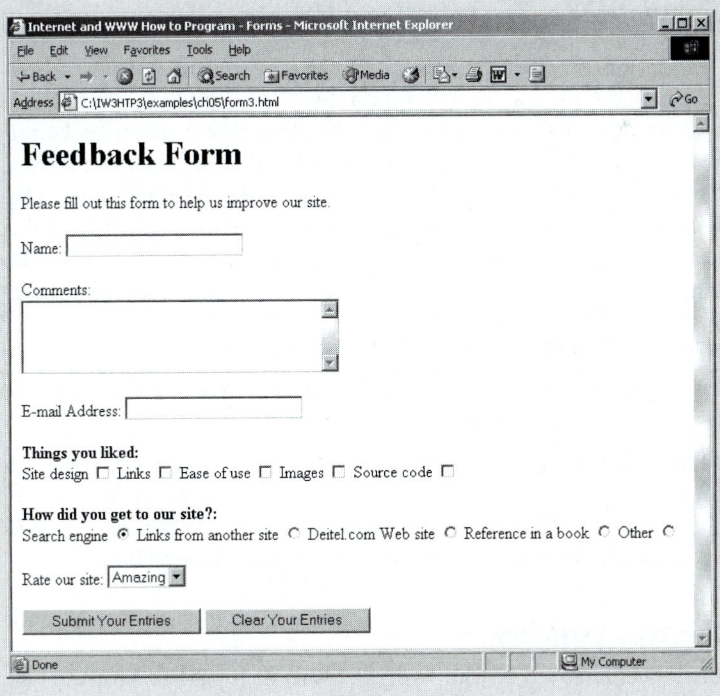

Fig. G.5 | Form including radio buttons and a drop-down list. (Part 3 of 4.)

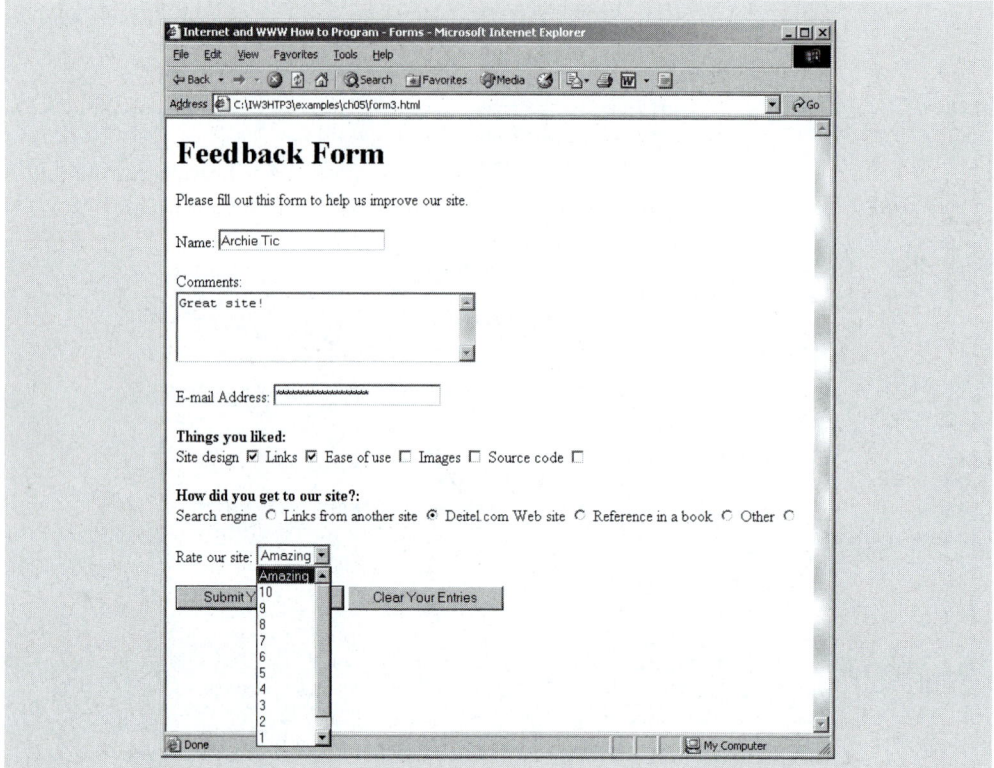

Fig. G.5 | Form including radio buttons and a drop-down list. (Part 4 of 4.)

example, we introduce two new input types. The first type is the *radio button* (lines 76–94) specified with type "radio". Radio buttons are similar to checkboxes, except that only one radio button in a group of radio buttons may be selected at any time. The radio buttons in a group all have the same name attributes and are distinguished by their different value attributes. The attribute-value pair checked = "checked" (line 77) indicates which radio button, if any, is selected initially. The checked attribute also applies to checkboxes.

 Common Programming Error G.3

Not setting the name attributes of the radio buttons in a form to the same name is a logic error because it lets the user select all of them at the same time.

The *select* element (lines 104–117) provides a drop-down list of items from which the user can select an item. The name attribute identifies the drop-down list. The *option* element (lines 105–116) adds items to the drop-down list. The option element's *selected attribute* specifies which item initially is displayed as the selected item.

G.6 Internal Linking

In Appendix F, we discussed how to hyperlink one Web page to another. Figure G.6 introduces *internal linking*—a mechanism that enables the user to jump between locations in the same document. Internal linking is useful for long documents that contain many sections. Clicking an internal link enables users to find a section without scrolling through the entire document.

Line 16 contains a tag with the *id* attribute (called "features") for an internal hyperlink. To link to a tag with this attribute inside the same Web page, the href attribute of an anchor element includes the id attribute value preceded by a pound sign (as in #features). Lines 61–62 contain a hyperlink with the id features as its target. Selecting this hyperlink in a Web browser scrolls the browser window to the h1 tag in line 16.

```
 1  <?xml version = "1.0"?>
 2  <!DOCTYPE html PUBLIC "-//W3C//DTD XHTML 1.1//EN"
 3     "http://www.w3.org/TR/xhtml11/DTD/xhtml11.dtd">
 4
 5  <!-- Fig. G.6: links.html -->
 6  <!-- Internal Linking      -->
 7
 8  <html xmlns = "http://www.w3.org/1999/xhtml">
 9     <head>
10        <title>Internet and WWW How to Program - List</title>
11     </head>
12
13     <body>
14
15        <!-- id attribute creates an internal hyperlink destination -->
16        <h1 id = "features">The Best Features of the Internet</h1>
17
18        <!-- an internal link's address is "#id" -->
19        <p><a href = "#bugs">Go to <em>Favorite Bugs</em></a></p>
20
21        <ul>
22           <li>You can meet people from countries
23              around the world.</li>
24
25           <li>You have access to new media as it becomes public:
26              <ul>
27                 <li>New games</li>
28                 <li>New applications
29                    <ul>
30                       <li>For Business</li>
31                       <li>For Pleasure</li>
32                    </ul>
33                 </li>
34
35                 <li>Around the clock news</li>
36                 <li>Search Engines</li>
37                 <li>Shopping</li>
38                 <li>Programming
39                    <ul>
40                       <li>XHTML</li>
41                       <li>Java</li>
42                       <li>Dynamic HTML</li>
43                       <li>Scripts</li>
```

Fig. G.6 | Internal hyperlinks to make pages more navigable. (Part 1 of 3.)

```
44                    <li>New languages</li>
45                 </ul>
46               </li>
47            </ul>
48         </li>
49
50         <li>Links</li>
51         <li>Keeping in touch with old friends</li>
52         <li>It is the technology of the future!</li>
53      </ul>
54
55      <!-- id attribute creates an internal hyperlink destination -->
56      <h1 id = "bugs">My 3 Favorite Bugs</h1>
57
58      <p>
59
60         <!-- internal hyperlink to features -->
61         <a href = "#features">Go to <em>Favorite Features</em>
62         </a></p>
63
64      <ol>
65         <li>Fire Fly</li>
66         <li>Gal Ant</li>
67         <li>Roman Tic</li>
68      </ol>
69
70   </body>
71 </html>
```

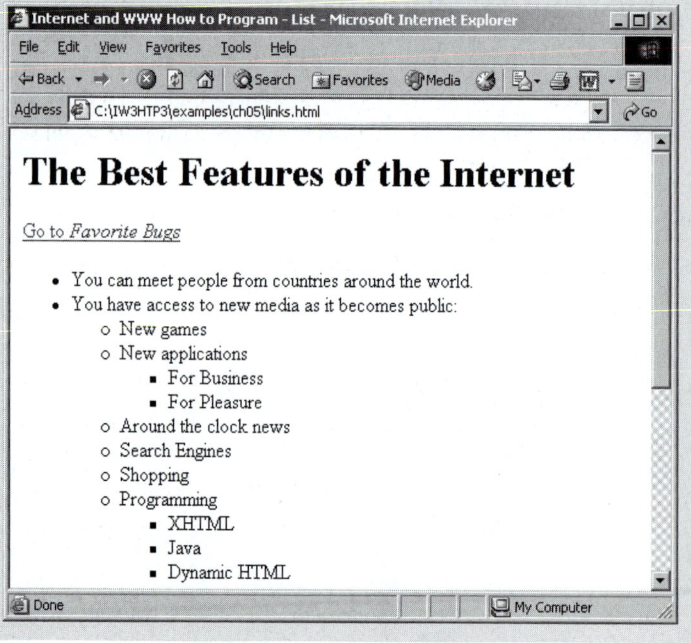

Fig. G.6 | Internal hyperlinks to make pages more navigable. (Part 2 of 3.)

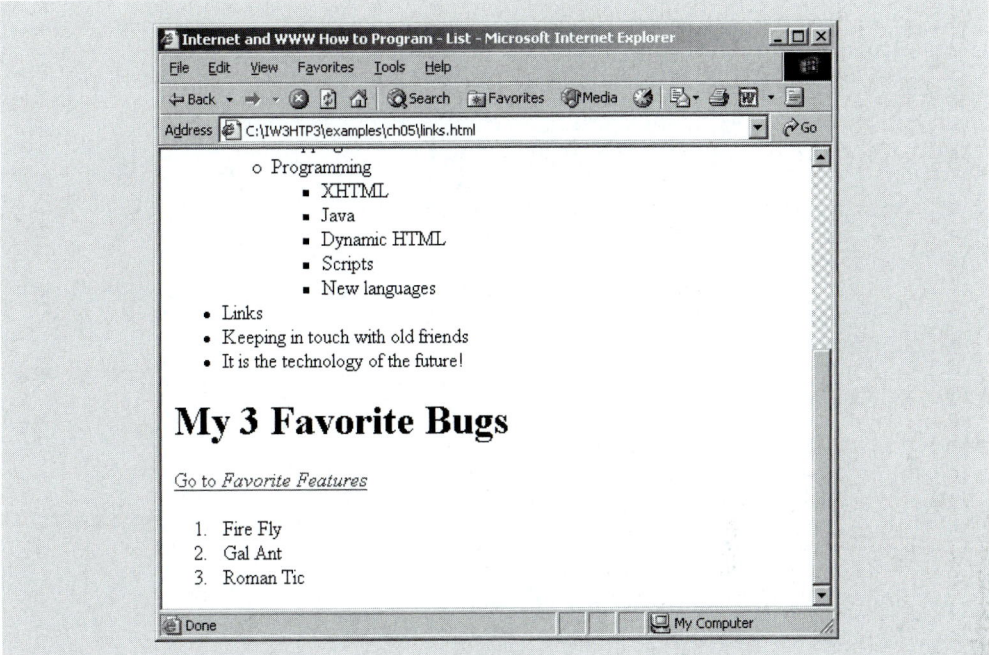

Fig. G.6 | Internal hyperlinks to make pages more navigable. (Part 3 of 3.)

Look-and-Feel Observation G.2

Internal hyperlinks are useful in XHTML documents that contain large amounts of information. Internal links to different parts of the page makes it easier for users to navigate the page. They do not have to scroll to find the section they want.

Although not demonstrated in this example, a hyperlink can specify an internal link in another document by specifying the document name followed by a pound sign and the id value, as in:

href = "*filename*.html#*id*"

For example, to link to a tag with the id attribute called booklist in books.html, href is assigned "books.html#booklist".

G.7 Creating and Using Image Maps

In Appendix F, we demonstrated how images can be used as hyperlinks to link to other resources on the Internet. In this section, we introduce another technique for image linking called *image maps*, which designates certain areas of an image (called *hotspots*) as links.[1] Figure G.7 introduces image maps and hotspots.

---

1. Current Web browsers do not support XHTML 1.1 image maps. For this reason we are using XHTML 1.0 Transitional, an earlier W3C version of XHTML. In order to validate the code in Figure G.7 as XHTML 1.1, remove the # from the usemap attribute of the img tag (line 53).

```
1   <?xml version = "1.0" ?>
2   <!DOCTYPE html PUBLIC "-//W3C//DTD XHTML 1.0 Transitional//EN"
3      "http://www.w3.org/TR/xhtml1/DTD/xhtml1-transitional.dtd">
4
5   <!-- Fig. G.7: picture.html         -->
6   <!-- Creating and Using Image Maps -->
7
8   <html xmlns = "http://www.w3.org/1999/xhtml">
9      <head>
10        <title>
11           Internet and WWW How to Program - Image Map
12        </title>
13     </head>
14
15     <body>
16
17        <p>
18
19           <!-- the <map> tag defines an image map -->
20           <map id = "picture">
21
22              <!-- shape = "rect" indicates a rectangular    -->
23              <!-- area, with coordinates for the upper-left  -->
24              <!-- and lower-right corners                    -->
25              <area href = "form.html" shape = "rect"
26                 coords = "2,123,54,143"
27                 alt = "Go to the feedback form" />
28              <area href = "contact.html" shape = "rect"
29                 coords = "126,122,198,143"
30                 alt = "Go to the contact page" />
31              <area href = "main.html" shape = "rect"
32                 coords = "3,7,61,25" alt = "Go to the homepage" />
33              <area href = "links.html" shape = "rect"
34                 coords = "168,5,197,25"
35                 alt = "Go to the links page" />
36
37              <!-- value "poly" creates a hotspot in the shape -->
38              <!-- of a polygon, defined by coords             -->
39              <area shape = "poly" alt = "E-mail the Deitels"
40                 coords = "162,25,154,39,158,54,169,51,183,39,161,26"
41                 href = "mailto:deitel@deitel.com" />
42
43              <!-- shape = "circle" indicates a circular -->
44              <!-- area with the given center and radius  -->
45              <area href = "mailto:deitel@deitel.com"
46                 shape = "circle" coords = "100,36,33"
47                 alt = "E-mail the Deitels" />
48           </map>
49
50           <!-- <img src =... usemap = "#id"> indicates that the -->
51           <!-- specified image map is used with this image       -->
52           <img src = "deitel.gif" width = "200" height = "144"
53              alt = "Deitel logo" usemap = "#picture" />
```

Fig. G.7 | Image with links anchored to an image map. (Part 1 of 2.)

```
54          </p>
55       </body>
56    </html>
```

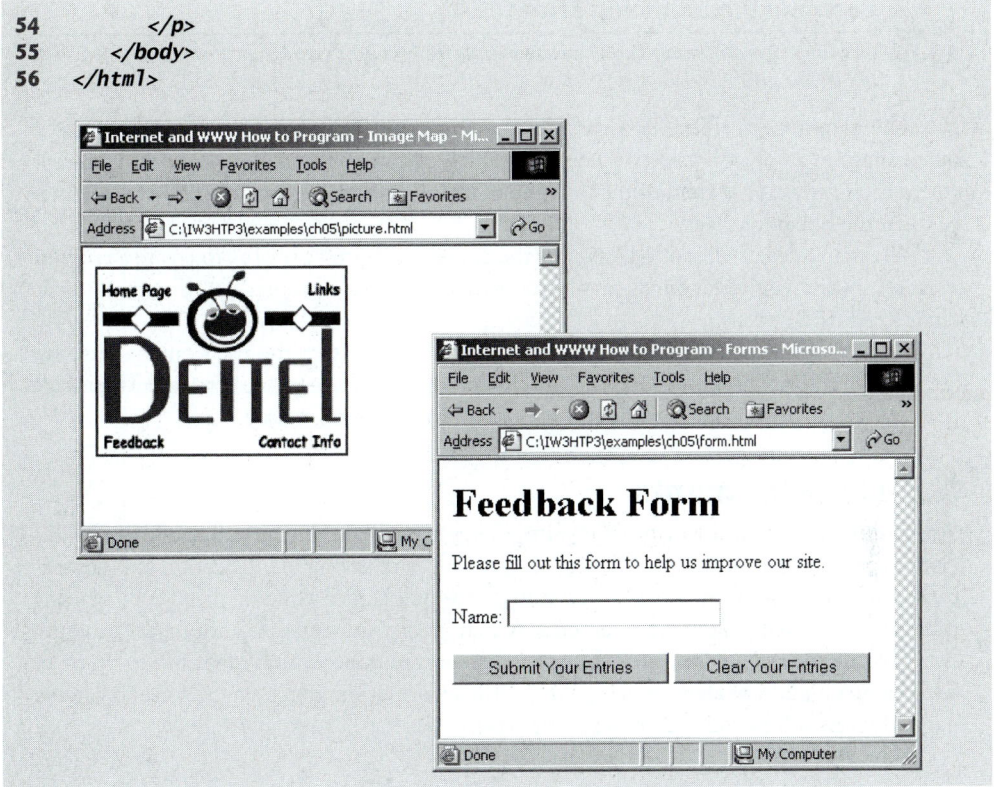

Fig. G.7 | Image with links anchored to an image map. (Part 2 of 2.)

Lines 20–48 define an image map by using a *map* element. Attribute *id* (line 20) identifies the image map. If id is omitted, the map cannot be referenced by an image (which we will see momentarily). Hotspots are defined with *area* elements (as shown in lines 25–27). Attribute href (line 25) specifies the link's target (i.e., the resource to which to link). Attributes *shape* (line 25) and *coords* (line 26) specify the hotspot's shape and coordinates, respectively. Attribute alt (line 27) provides alternative text for the link.

Common Programming Error G.4

Not specifying an id attribute for a map *element prevents an* img *element from using the* map's *area elements to define hotspots.*

The markup in lines 25–27 creates a *rectangular hotspot* (shape = "rect") for the *coordinates* specified in the coords attribute. A coordinate pair consists of two numbers representing the locations of a point on the *x*-axis and the *y*-axis, respectively. The *x*-axis extends horizontally and the *y*-axis extends vertically from the upper-left corner of the image. Every point on an image has a unique *x*-*y*-coordinate. For rectangular hotspots, the required coordinates are those of the upper-left and lower-right corners of the rectangle. In this case, the upper-left corner of the rectangle is located at 2 on the *x*-axis and 123 on the *y*-axis, annotated as *(2, 123)*. The lower-right corner of the rectangle is at *(54, 143)*. Coordinates are measured in pixels.

Common Programming Error G.5

Overlapping coordinates of an image map cause the browser to render the first hotspot it encounters for the area.

The map area at lines 39–41 assigns the shape attribute *"poly"* to create a hotspot in the shape of a polygon using the coordinates in attribute coords. These coordinates represent each *vertex*, or corner, of the polygon. The browser connects these points with lines to form the hotspot's area.

The map area at lines 45–47 assigns the shape attribute *"circle"* to create a *circular hotspot*. In this case, the coords attribute specifies the circle's center coordinates and the circle's radius, in pixels.

To use an image map with an img element, you must assign the img element's *usemap* attribute to the id of a map. Lines 52–53 reference the image map "#picture". The image map is located within the same document, so internal linking is used.

G.8 meta Elements

Search engines are used to find Web sites. They usually catalog sites by following links from page to page (known as spidering or crawling) and saving identification and classification information for each page. One way that search engines catalog pages is by reading the content in each page's *meta* elements, which specify information about a document.

Two important attributes of the meta element are *name*, which identifies the type of meta element, and *content*, which provides the information search engines use to catalog pages. Figure G.8 introduces the meta element.

```
 1   <?xml version = "1.0"?>
 2   <!DOCTYPE html PUBLIC "-//W3C//DTD XHTML 1.1//EN"
 3      "http://www.w3.org/TR/xhtml11/DTD/xhtml11.dtd">
 4
 5   <!-- Fig. G.8: main.html -->
 6   <!-- <meta> tag           -->
 7
 8   <html xmlns = "http://www.w3.org/1999/xhtml">
 9      <head>
10         <title>Internet and WWW How to Program - Welcome</title>
11
12         <!-- <meta> tags provide search engines with -->
13         <!-- information used to catalog a site       -->
14         <meta name = "keywords" content = "Web page, design,
15            XHTML, tutorial, personal, help, index, form,
16            contact, feedback, list, links, frame, deitel" />
17
18         <meta name = "description" content = "This Web site will
19            help you learn the basics of XHTML and Web page design
20            through the use of interactive examples and
21            instruction." />
22
23      </head>
```

Fig. G.8 | meta tags provide keywords and a description of a page. (Part 1 of 2.)

```
24
25      <body>
26
27          <h1>Welcome to Our Web Site!</h1>
28
29          <p>We have designed this site to teach about the wonders
30          of <strong><em>XHTML</em></strong>. <em>XHTML</em> is
31          better equipped than <em>HTML</em> to represent complex
32          data on the Internet. <em>XHTML</em> takes advantage of
33          XML's strict syntax to ensure well-formedness. Soon you
34          will know about many of the great new features of
35          <em>XHTML.</em></p>
36
37          <p>Have Fun With the Site!</p>
38
39      </body>
40  </html>
```

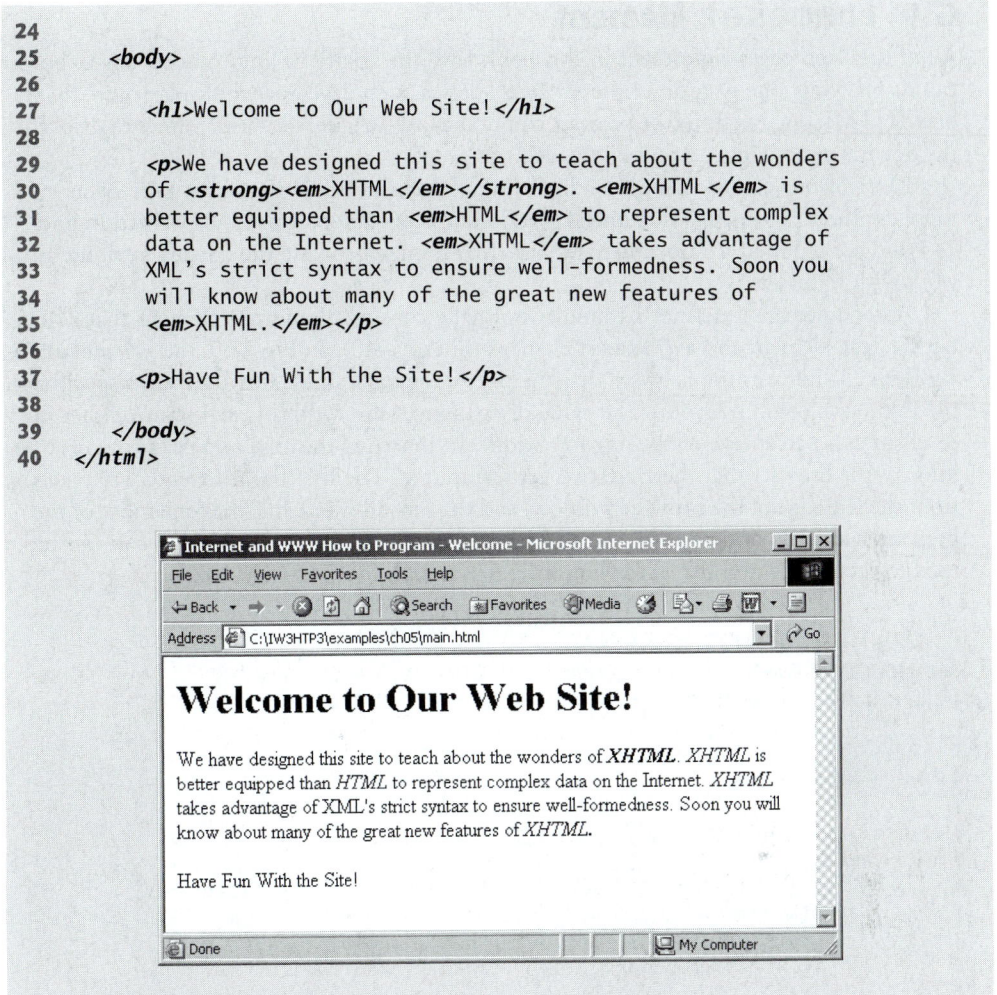

Fig. G.8 | meta tags provide keywords and a description of a page. (Part 2 of 2.)

Lines 14–16 demonstrate a *"keywords"* meta element. The content attribute of such a meta element provides search engines with a list of words that describe a page. These words are compared with words in search requests. Thus, including meta elements and their content information can draw more viewers to your site.

Lines 18–21 demonstrate a *"description"* meta element. The content attribute of such a meta element provides a three- to four-line description of a site, written in sentence form. Search engines also use this description to catalog your site and sometimes display this information as part of the search results.

Software Engineering Observation G.1

meta elements are not visible to users and must be placed inside the head section of your XHTML document. If meta elements are not placed in this section, they will not be read by search engines.

G.9 frameset Element

All of the Web pages we present in this book have the ability to link to other pages, but can display only one page at a time. *Frames* allow a Web developer to display more than one XHTML document in the browser simultaneously. Figure G.9 uses frames to display the documents in Fig. G.8 and Fig. G.10.

Most of our earlier examples adhere to the XHTML 1.1 document type, whereas these use the XHTML 1.0 document types.[1] These document types are specified in lines 2–3 and are required for documents that define framesets or use the target attribute to work with framesets.

A document that defines a frameset normally consists of an html element that contains a head element and a *frameset* element (lines 23–40). In Fig. G.9, the *<frameset>* tag (line 23) informs the browser that the page contains frames. Attribute *cols* specifies the frameset's column layout. The value of cols gives the width of each frame, either in pixels or as a percentage of the browser width. In this case, the attribute cols = "110,*" informs the browser that there are two vertical frames. The first frame extends 110 pixels from the left edge of the browser window, and the second frame fills the remainder of the browser width (as indicated by the asterisk). Similarly, frameset attribute *rows* can be used to specify the number of rows and the size of each row in a frameset.

```
 1   <?xml version = "1.0"?>
 2   <!DOCTYPE html PUBLIC "-//W3C//DTD XHTML 1.0 Frameset//EN"
 3      "http://www.w3.org/TR/xhtml1/DTD/xhtml1-frameset.dtd">
 4
 5   <!-- Fig. G.9: index.html -->
 6   <!-- XHTML Frames I       -->
 7
 8   <html xmlns = "http://www.w3.org/1999/xhtml">
 9      <head>
10         <title>Internet and WWW How to Program - Main</title>
11         <meta name = "keywords" content = "Webpage, design,
12            XHTML, tutorial, personal, help, index, form,
13            contact, feedback, list, links, frame, deitel" />
14
15         <meta name = "description" content = "This Web site will
16            help you learn the basics of XHTML and Web page design
17            through the use of interactive examples
18            and instruction." />
19
20      </head>
21
22      <!-- the <frameset> tag sets the frame dimensions      -->
23      <frameset cols = "110,*">
```

Fig. G.9 | XHTML frames document with navigation and content. (Part 1 of 3.)

---

1. XHTML 1.1 no longer supports the use of frames. The W3C recommends using Cascading Style Sheets to achieve the same effect. Frames are still widely used on the Internet and supported by most browsers, however. The frameset element and the target attribute are still supported in the XHTML 1.0 Frameset and the XHTML 1.0 Transitional document type definitions, respectively. Please refer to www.w3.org/TR/xhtml1/#dtds for more information.

```
24
25        <!-- frame elements specify which pages -->
26        <!-- are loaded into a given frame        -->
27        <frame name = "leftframe" src = "nav.html" />
28        <frame name = "main" src = "main.html" />
29
30     <noframes>
31        <body>
32           <p>This page uses frames, but your browser does not
33           support them.</p>
34
35           <p>Please, <a href = "nav.html">follow this link to
36           browse our site without frames</a>.</p>
37        </body>
38     </noframes>
39
40   </frameset>
41 </html>
```

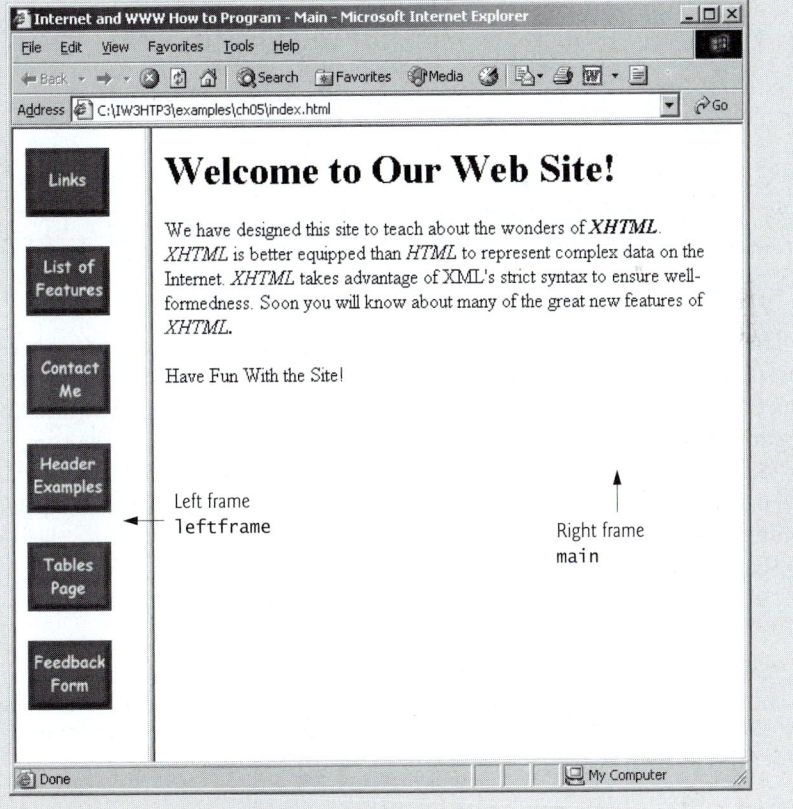

Fig. G.9 | XHTML frames document with navigation and content. (Part 2 of 3.)

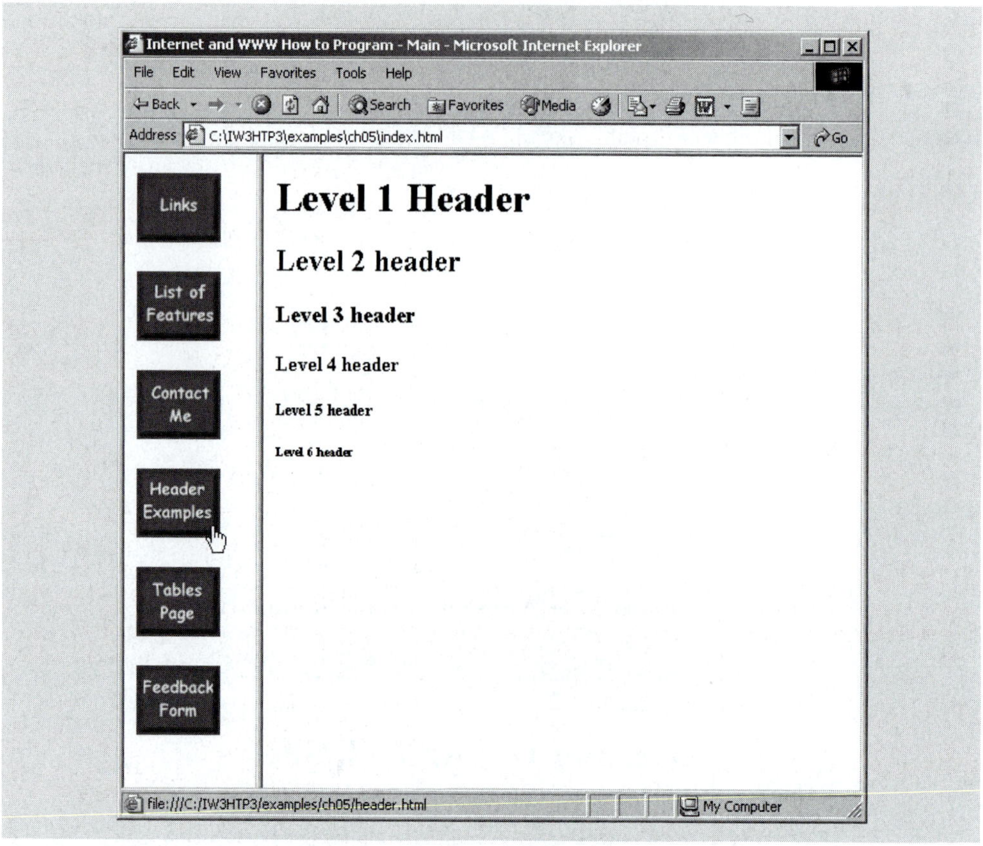

Fig. G.9 | XHTML frames document with navigation and content. (Part 3 of 3.)

The documents that will be loaded into the frameset are specified with **frame** elements (lines 27–28 in this example). Attribute src specifies the URL of the page to display in the frame. Each frame has name and src attributes. The first frame (which covers 110 pixels on the left side of the frameset), named leftframe, displays the page nav.html (Fig. G.10). The second frame, named main, displays the page main.html (Fig. G.8).

Attribute name identifies a frame, enabling hyperlinks in a frameset to specify the *target* frame in which a linked document should display when the user clicks the link. For example

```
<a href = "links.html" target = "main">
```

loads links.html in the frame whose name is "main".

Not all browsers support frames. XHTML provides the **noframes** element (lines 30–38) to enable XHTML document designers to specify alternative content for browsers that do not support frames.

Portability Tip G.1

Some browsers do not support frames. Use the noframes element inside a frameset to direct users to a nonframed version of your site.

Figure G.10 is the Web page displayed in the left frame of Fig. G.9. This XHTML document provides the navigation buttons that, when clicked, determine which document is displayed in the right frame.

Line 27 (Fig. G.9) displays the XHTML page in Fig. G.10. Anchor attribute `target` (line 18 in Fig. G.10) specifies that the linked documents are loaded in frame `main` (line 28 in Fig. G.9). A `target` can be set to a number of preset values: "_blank" loads the page into a new browser window, "_self" loads the page into the frame in which the anchor element appears and "_top" loads the page into the full browser window (i.e., removes the `frameset`).

```
1   <?xml version = "1.0"?>
2   <!DOCTYPE html PUBLIC "-//W3C//DTD XHTML 1.0 Transitional//EN"
3       "http://www.w3.org/TR/xhtml1/DTD/xhtml1-transitional.dtd">
4
5   <!-- Fig. G.10: nav.html          -->
6   <!-- Using images as link anchors -->
7
8   <html xmlns = "http://www.w3.org/1999/xhtml">
9
10     <head>
11        <title>Internet and WWW How to Program - Navigation Bar
12        </title>
13     </head>
14
15     <body>
16
17        <p>
18           <a href = "links.html" target = "main">
19              <img src = "buttons/links.jpg" width = "65"
20                 height = "50" alt = "Links Page" />
21           </a><br />
22
23           <a href = "list.html" target = "main">
24              <img src = "buttons/list.jpg" width = "65"
25                 height = "50" alt = "List Example Page" />
26           </a><br />
27
28           <a href = "contact.html" target = "main">
29              <img src = "buttons/contact.jpg" width = "65"
30                 height = "50" alt = "Contact Page" />
31           </a><br />
32
33           <a href = "header.html" target = "main">
34              <img src = "buttons/header.jpg" width = "65"
35                 height = "50" alt = "Header Page" />
36           </a><br />
37
38           <a href = "table1.html" target = "main">
39              <img src = "buttons/table.jpg" width = "65"
40                 height = "50" alt = "Table Page" />
41           </a><br />
```

Fig. G.10 | XHTML document displayed in the left frame of Fig. G.9. (Part 1 of 2.)

```
42
43                <a href = "form.html" target = "main">
44                    <img src = "buttons/form.jpg" width = "65"
45                        height = "50" alt = "Feedback Form" />
46                </a><br />
47            </p>
48
49        </body>
50    </html>
```

Fig. G.10 | XHTML document displayed in the left frame of Fig. G.9. (Part 2 of 2.)

G.10 Nested framesets

You can use the frameset element to create more complex layouts in a Web page by nesting framesets, as in Fig. G.11. The nested frameset in this example displays the XHTML documents in Fig. G.7, Fig. G.8 and Fig. G.10.

```
1    <?xml version = "1.0"?>
2    <!DOCTYPE html PUBLIC "-//W3C//DTD XHTML 1.0 Frameset//EN"
3        "http://www.w3.org/TR/xhtml1/DTD/xhtml1-frameset.dtd">
4
5    <!-- Fig. G.11: index2.html -->
6    <!-- XHTML Frames II          -->
7
8    <html xmlns = "http://www.w3.org/1999/xhtml">
9        <head>
10           <title>Internet and WWW How to Program - Main</title>
11
12           <meta name = "keywords" content = "Webpage, design,
13               XHTML, tutorial, personal, help, index, form,
14               contact, feedback, list, links, frame, deitel" />
15
16           <meta name = "description" content = "This Web site will
17               help you learn the basics of XHTML and Web page design
18               through the use of interactive examples
19               and instruction." />
20
21       </head>
22
23       <frameset cols = "110,*">
24           <frame name = "leftframe" src = "nav.html" />
25
26           <!-- nested framesets are used to change the -->
27           <!-- formatting and layout of the frameset   -->
28           <frameset rows = "175,*">
29               <frame name = "picture" src = "picture.html" />
30               <frame name = "main" src = "main.html" />
31           </frameset>
32
```

Fig. G.11 | Framed Web site with a nested frameset. (Part 1 of 2.)

```
33        <noframes>
34            <body>
35                <p>This page uses frames, but your browser does not
36                support them.</p>
37
38                <p>Please, <a href = "nav.html">follow this link to
39                browse our site without frames</a>.</p>
40            </body>
41        </noframes>
42
43    </frameset>
44 </html>
```

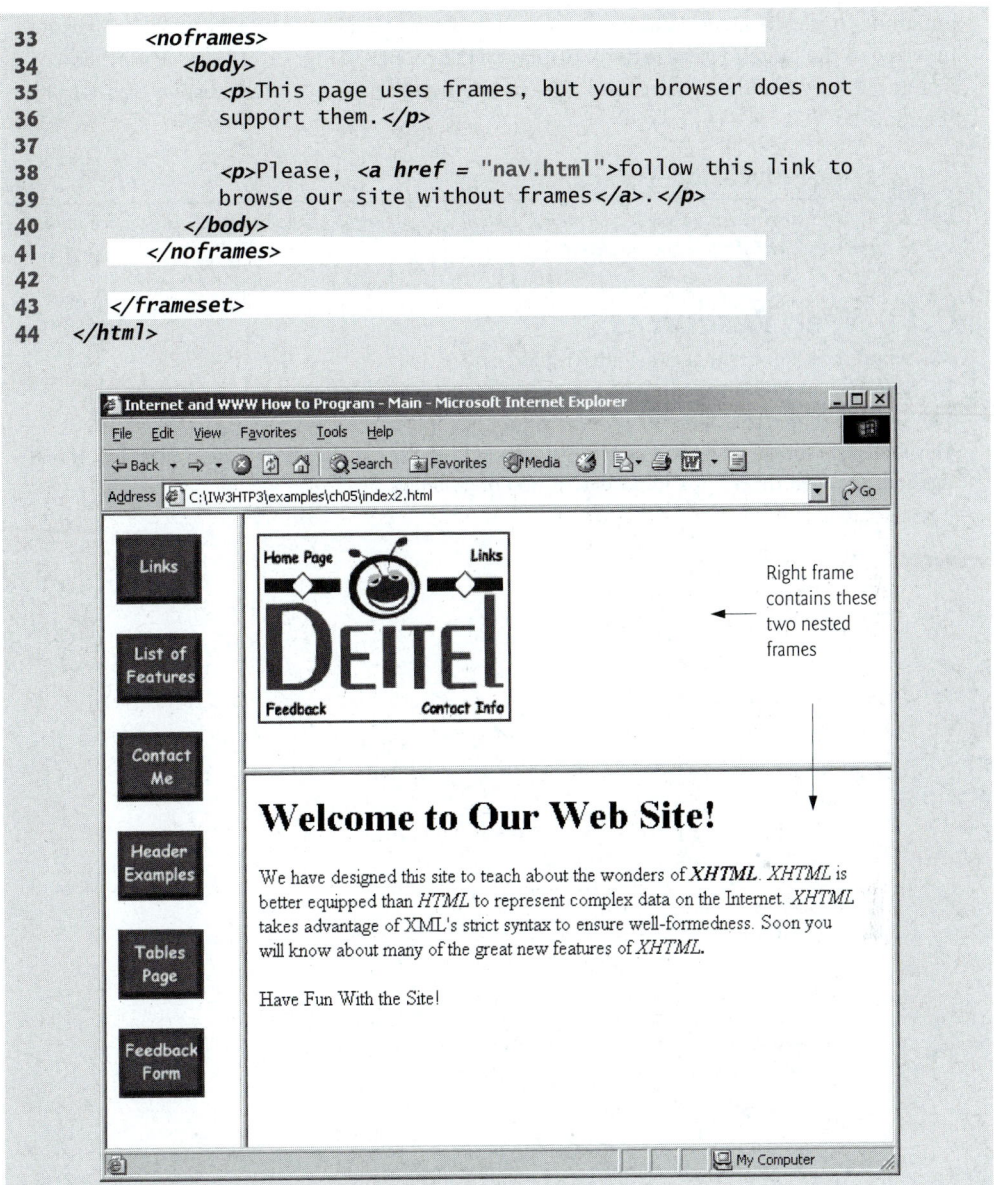

Fig. G.11 | Framed Web site with a nested frameset. (Part 2 of 2.)

The outer frameset element (lines 23–43) defines two columns. The left frame extends over the first 110 pixels from the left edge of the browser, and the right frame occupies the rest of the window's width. The frame element on line 24 specifies that the document nav.html (Fig. G.10) will be displayed in the left column.

Lines 28–31 define a nested frameset element for the second column of the outer frameset. This frameset defines two rows. The first row extends 175 pixels from the top of the browser window, as indicated by rows = "175,*". The second row occupies the remainder of the browser window's height. The frame element at line 29 specifies that the first row of the nested frameset will display picture.html (Fig. G.7). The frame element in line 30 specifies that the second row of the nested frameset will display main.html (Fig. G.8).

Error-Prevention Tip G.1

When using nested frameset elements, indent every level of <frame> tag. This practice makes the page clearer and easier to debug.

G.11 Web Resources

www.vbxml.com/xhtml/articles/xhtml_tables

The *VBXML.com* Web site contains a tutorial on creating XHTML tables.

www.webreference.com/xml/reference/xhtml.html

This Web page contains a list of frequently used XHTML tags, such as header tags, table tags, frame tags and form tags. It also provides a description of each tag.

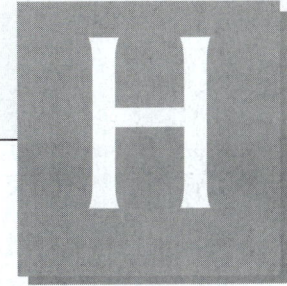

HTML/XHTML
Special Characters

The table of Fig. H.1 shows many commonly used HTML/XHTML special characters—called *character entity references* by the World Wide Web Consortium. For a complete list of character entity references, see the site

www.w3.org/TR/REC-html40/sgml/entities.html

Character	XHTML encoding	Character	XHTML encoding
non-breaking space		ê	&#234;
§	&#167;	ì	&#236;
©	&#169;	í	&#237;
®	&#174;	î	&#238;
π	&#188;	ñ	&#241;
∫	&#189;	ò	&#242;
Ω	&#190;	ó	&#243;
à	&#224;	ô	&#244;
á	&#225;	õ	&#245;
â	&#226;	÷	&#247;
ã	&#227;	ù	&#249;
å	&#229;	ú	&#250;
ç	&#231;	û	&#251;
è	&#232;	•	&#8226;
é	&#233;	™	&#8482;

Fig. H.1 | XHTML special characters.

I

HTML/XHTML Colors

Colors may be specified by using a standard name (such as aqua) or a hexadecimal RGB value (such as #00FFFF for aqua). Of the six hexadecimal digits in an RGB value, the first two represent the amount of red in the color, the middle two represent the amount of green in the color, and the last two represent the amount of blue in the color. For example, black is the absence of color and is defined by #000000, whereas white is the maximum amount of red, green and blue and is defined by #FFFFFF. Pure red is #FF0000, pure green (which is called lime) is #00FF00 and pure blue is #0000FF. Note that green in the standard is defined as #008000. Figure I.1 contains the HTML/XHTML standard color set. Figure I.2 contains the HTML/XHTML extended color set.

Color name	Value	Color name	Value
aqua	#00FFFF	navy	#000080
black	#000000	olive	#808000
blue	#0000FF	purple	#800080
fuchsia	#FF00FF	red	#FF0000
gray	#808080	silver	#C0C0C0
green	#008000	teal	#008080
lime	#00FF00	yellow	#FFFF00
maroon	#800000	white	#FFFFFF

Fig. I.1 | HTML/XHTML standard colors and hexadecimal RGB values.

Color name	Value	Color name	Value
aliceblue	#F0F8FF	deeppink	#FF1493
antiquewhite	#FAEBD7	deepskyblue	#00BFFF
aquamarine	#7FFFD4	dimgray	#696969
azure	#F0FFFF	dodgerblue	#1E90FF
beige	#F5F5DC	firebrick	#B22222
bisque	#FFE4C4	floralwhite	#FFFAF0
blanchedalmond	#FFEBCD	forestgreen	#228B22
blueviolet	#8A2BE2	gainsboro	#DCDCDC
brown	#A52A2A	ghostwhite	#F8F8FF
burlywood	#DEB887	gold	#FFD700
cadetblue	#5F9EA0	goldenrod	#DAA520
chartreuse	#7FFF00	greenyellow	#ADFF2F
chocolate	#D2691E	honeydew	#F0FFF0
coral	#FF7F50	hotpink	#FF69B4
cornflowerblue	#6495ED	indianred	#CD5C5C
cornsilk	#FFF8DC	indigo	#4B0082
crimson	#DC1436	ivory	#FFFFF0
cyan	#00FFFF	khaki	#F0E68C
darkblue	#00008B	lavender	#E6E6FA
darkcyan	#008B8B	lavenderblush	#FFF0F5
darkgoldenrod	#B8860B	lawngreen	#7CFC00
darkgray	#A9A9A9	lemonchiffon	#FFFACD
darkgreen	#006400	lightblue	#ADD8E6
darkkhaki	#BDB76B	lightcoral	#F08080
darkmagenta	#8B008B	lightcyan	#E0FFFF
darkolivegreen	#556B2F	lightgoldenrodyellow	#FAFAD2
darkorange	#FF8C00	lightgreen	#90EE90
darkorchid	#9932CC	lightgrey	#D3D3D3
darkred	#8B0000	lightpink	#FFB6C1
darksalmon	#E9967A	lightsalmon	#FFA07A
darkseagreen	#8FBC8F	lightseagreen	#20B2AA
darkslateblue	#483D8B	lightskyblue	#87CEFA
darkslategray	#2F4F4F	lightslategray	#778899
darkturquoise	#00CED1	lightsteelblue	#B0C4DE
darkviolet	#9400D3	lightyellow	#FFFFE0

Fig. I.2 | XHTML extended colors and hexadecimal RGB values (Part I of 2.).

Color name	Value	Color name	Value
limegreen	#32CD32	mediumblue	#0000CD
mediumpurple	#9370DB	mediumorchid	#BA55D3
mediumseagreen	#3CB371	plum	#DDA0DD
mediumslateblue	#7B68EE	powderblue	#B0E0E6
mediumspringgreen	#00FA9A	rosybrown	#BC8F8F
mediumturquoise	#48D1CC	royalblue	#4169E1
mediumvioletred	#C71585	saddlebrown	#8B4513
midnightblue	#191970	salmon	#FA8072
mintcream	#F5FFFA	sandybrown	#F4A460
mistyrose	#FFE4E1	seagreen	#2E8B57
moccasin	#FFE4B5	seashell	#FFF5EE
navajowhite	#FFDEAD	sienna	#A0522D
oldlace	#FDF5E6	skyblue	#87CEEB
olivedrab	#6B8E23	slateblue	#6A5ACD
orange	#FFA500	slategray	#708090
orangered	#FF4500	snow	#FFFAFA
orchid	#DA70D6	springgreen	#00FF7F
palegoldenrod	#EEE8AA	steelblue	#4682B4
palegreen	#98FB98	tan	#D2B48C
paleturquoise	#AFEEEE	thistle	#D8BFD8
palevioletred	#DB7093	tomato	#FF6347
papayawhip	#FFEFD5	turquoise	#40E0D0
peachpuff	#FFDAB9	violet	#EE82EE
peru	#CD853F	wheat	#F5DEB3
pink	#FFC0CB	whitesmoke	#F5F5F5
mediumaquamarine	#66CDAA	yellowgreen	#9ACD32

Fig. I.2 | XHTML extended colors and hexadecimal RGB values (Part 2 of 2.).

ATM Case Study Code

J.1 ATM Case Study Implementation

This appendix contains the complete working implementation of the ATM system that we designed in the nine "Software Engineering Case Study" sections in Chapters 1, 3–9 and 11. The implementation comprises 655 lines of C# code. We consider the 11 classes in the order in which we identified them in Section 4.11 (with the exception of Transaction, which was introduced in Chapter 11 as the base class of classes BalanceInquiry, Withdrawal and Deposit):

- ATM
- Screen
- Keypad
- CashDispenser
- DepositSlot
- Account
- BankDatabase
- Transaction
- BalanceInquiry
- Withdrawal
- Deposit

We apply the guidelines discussed in Section 9.17 and Section 11.9 to code these classes based on how we modeled them in the UML class diagrams of Fig. 11.21 and Fig. 11.22. To develop the bodies of class methods, we refer to the activity diagrams presented in Section 6.10 and the communication and sequence diagrams presented in Section 8.14. Note that our ATM design does not specify all the program logic and may not specify all the attributes and operations required to complete the ATM implementation. This is a normal part of the object-oriented design process. As we implement the system, we complete the program logic and add attributes and behaviors as necessary to construct the ATM system specified by the requirements document in Section 3.10.

We conclude the discussion by presenting a test harness (ATMCaseStudy in Section J.13) that creates an object of class ATM and starts it by calling its Run method. Recall that we are developing a first version of the ATM system that runs on a personal computer and uses the keyboard and monitor to approximate the ATM's keypad and screen. Also, we simulate the actions of the ATM's cash dispenser and deposit slot. We attempt to implement the system so that real hardware versions of these devices could be integrated without significant code changes. [*Note:* For the purpose of this simulation, we have provided two predefined accounts in class BankDatabase. The first account has the account number 12345 and the PIN 54321. The second account has the account number 98765 and the PIN 56789. You should use these accounts when testing the ATM.]

J.2 Class ATM

Class ATM (Fig. J.1) represents the ATM as a whole. Lines 5–11 implement the class's attributes. We determine all but one of these attributes from the UML class diagrams of Fig. 11.21 and Fig. 11.22. Line 5 declares the bool attribute userAuthenticated from Fig. 11.22. Line 6 declares an attribute not found in our UML design—int attribute currentAccountNumber, which keeps track of the account number of the current authenticated user. Lines 7–11 declare reference-type instance variables corresponding to the ATM class's associations modeled in the class diagram of Fig. 11.21. These attributes allow the ATM to access its parts (i.e., its Screen, Keypad, CashDispenser and DepositSlot) and interact with the bank's account information database (i.e., a BankDatabase object).

```
1   // ATM.cs
2   // Represents an automated teller machine.
3   public class ATM
4   {
5      private bool userAuthenticated; // true if user is authenticated
6      private int currentAccountNumber; // user's account number
7      private Screen screen; // reference to ATM's screen
8      private Keypad keypad; // reference to ATM's keypad
9      private CashDispenser cashDispenser; // ref to ATM's cash dispenser
10     private DepositSlot depositSlot; // reference to ATM's deposit slot
11     private BankDatabase bankDatabase; // ref to account info database
12
13     // enumeration that represents main menu options
14     private enum MenuOption
15     {
16        BALANCE_INQUIRY = 1,
17        WITHDRAWAL = 2,
18        DEPOSIT = 3,
19        EXIT_ATM = 4
20     } // end enum MenuOption
21
```

Fig. J.1 | Class ATM represents the ATM. (Part 1 of 4.)

```
22      // parameterless constructor initializes instance variables
23      public ATM()
24      {
25         userAuthenticated = false; // user is not authenticated to start
26         currentAccountNumber = 0; // no current account number to start
27         screen = new Screen(); // create screen
28         keypad = new Keypad(); // create keypad
29         cashDispenser = new CashDispenser(); // create cash dispenser
30         depositSlot = new DepositSlot(); // create deposit slot
31         bankDatabase = new BankDatabase(); // create account info database
32      } // end constructor
33
34      // start ATM
35      public void Run()
36      {
37         // welcome and authenticate users; perform transactions
38         while ( true ) // infinite loop
39         {
40            // loop while user is not yet authenticated
41            while ( !userAuthenticated )
42            {
43               screen.DisplayMessageLine( "\nWelcome!" );
44               AuthenticateUser(); // authenticate user
45            } // end while
46
47            PerformTransactions(); // for authenticated user
48            userAuthenticated = false; // reset before next ATM session
49            currentAccountNumber = 0; // reset before next ATM session
50            screen.DisplayMessageLine( "\nThank you! Goodbye!" );
51         } // end while
52      } // end method Run
53
54      // attempt to authenticate user against database
55      private void AuthenticateUser()
56      {
57         // prompt for account number and input it from user
58         screen.DisplayMessage( "\nPlease enter your account number: " );
59         int accountNumber = keypad.GetInput();
60
61         // prompt for PIN and input it from user
62         screen.DisplayMessage( "\nEnter your PIN: " );
63         int pin = keypad.GetInput();
64
65         // set userAuthenticated to boolean value returned by database
66         userAuthenticated =
67            bankDatabase.AuthenticateUser( accountNumber, pin );
68
69         // check whether authentication succeeded
70         if ( userAuthenticated )
71            currentAccountNumber = accountNumber; // save user's account #
```

Fig. J.1 | Class ATM represents the ATM. (Part 2 of 4.)

```
72            else
73                screen.DisplayMessageLine(
74                    "Invalid account number or PIN. Please try again." );
75        } // end method AuthenticateUser
76
77        // display the main menu and perform transactions
78        private void PerformTransactions()
79        {
80            Transaction currentTransaction; // transaction being processed
81            bool userExited = false; // user has not chosen to exit
82
83            // loop while user has not chosen exit option
84            while ( !userExited )
85            {
86                // show main menu and get user selection
87                int mainMenuSelection = DisplayMainMenu();
88
89                // decide how to proceed based on user's menu selection
90                switch ( ( MenuOption ) mainMenuSelection )
91                {
92                    // user chooses to perform one of three transaction types
93                    case MenuOption.BALANCE_INQUIRY:
94                    case MenuOption.WITHDRAWAL:
95                    case MenuOption.DEPOSIT:
96                        // initialize as new object of chosen type
97                        currentTransaction =
98                            CreateTransaction( mainMenuSelection );
99                        currentTransaction.Execute(); // execute transaction
100                       break;
101                   case MenuOption.EXIT_ATM: // user chose to terminate session
102                       screen.DisplayMessageLine( "\nExiting the system..." );
103                       userExited = true; // this ATM session should end
104                       break;
105                   default: // user did not enter an integer from 1-4
106                       screen.DisplayMessageLine(
107                           "\nYou did not enter a valid selection. Try again." );
108                       break;
109                } // end switch
110           } // end while
111       } // end method PerformTransactions
112
113       // display the main menu and return an input selection
114       private int DisplayMainMenu()
115       {
116           screen.DisplayMessageLine( "\nMain menu:" );
117           screen.DisplayMessageLine( "1 - View my balance" );
118           screen.DisplayMessageLine( "2 - Withdraw cash" );
119           screen.DisplayMessageLine( "3 - Deposit funds" );
120           screen.DisplayMessageLine( "4 - Exit\n" );
121           screen.DisplayMessage( "Enter a choice: " );
122           return keypad.GetInput(); // return user's selection
123       } // end method DisplayMainMenu
```

Fig. J.1 | Class ATM represents the ATM. (Part 3 of 4.)

```
124
125        // return object of specified Transaction derived class
126        private Transaction CreateTransaction( int type )
127        {
128           Transaction temp = null; // null Transaction reference
129
130           // determine which type of Transaction to create
131           switch ( ( MenuOption ) type )
132           {
133              // create new BalanceInquiry transaction
134              case MenuOption.BALANCE_INQUIRY:
135                 temp = new BalanceInquiry( currentAccountNumber,
136                    screen, bankDatabase);
137                 break;
138              case MenuOption.WITHDRAWAL: // create new Withdrawal transaction
139                 temp = new Withdrawal( currentAccountNumber, screen,
140                    bankDatabase, keypad, cashDispenser);
141                 break;
142              case MenuOption.DEPOSIT: // create new Deposit transaction
143                 temp = new Deposit( currentAccountNumber, screen,
144                    bankDatabase, keypad, depositSlot);
145                 break;
146           } // end switch
147
148           return temp;
149        } // end method CreateTransaction
150     } // end class ATM
```

Fig. J.1 | Class ATM represents the ATM. (Part 4 of 4.)

Lines 14–20 declare an enumeration that corresponds to the four options in the ATM's main menu (i.e., balance inquiry, withdrawal, deposit and exit). Lines 23–32 declare class ATM's constructor, which initializes the class's attributes. When an ATM object is first created, no user is authenticated, so line 25 initializes userAuthenticated to false. Line 26 initializes currentAccountNumber to 0 because there is no current user yet. Lines 27–30 instantiate new objects to represent the parts of the ATM. Recall that class ATM has composition relationships with classes Screen, Keypad, CashDispenser and DepositSlot, so class ATM is responsible for their creation. Line 31 creates a new BankDatabase. As you will soon see, the BankDatabase creates two Account objects that can be used to test the ATM. [*Note:* If this were a real ATM system, the ATM class would receive a reference to an existing database object created by the bank. However, in this implementation, we are only simulating the bank's database, so class ATM creates the BankDatabase object with which it interacts.]

Implementing the Operation

The class diagram of Fig. 11.22 does not list any operations for class ATM. We now implement one operation (i.e., public method) in class ATM that allows an external client of the class (i.e., class ATMCaseStudy; Section J.13) to tell the ATM to run. ATM method Run (lines 35–52) uses an infinite loop (lines 38–51) to repeatedly welcome a user, attempt to authenticate the user and, if authentication succeeds, allow the user to perform transactions.

After an authenticated user performs the desired transactions and exits, the ATM resets itself, displays a goodbye message and restarts the process for the next user. We use an infinite loop here to simulate the fact that an ATM appears to run continuously until the bank turns it off (an action beyond the user's control). An ATM user can exit the system, but cannot turn off the ATM completely.

Inside method Run's infinite loop, lines 41–45 cause the ATM to repeatedly welcome and attempt to authenticate the user as long as the user has not been authenticated (i.e., the condition !userAuthenticated is true). Line 43 invokes method Display-MessageLine of the ATM's screen to display a welcome message. Like Screen method DisplayMessage designed in the case study, method DisplayMessageLine (declared in lines 14–17 of Fig. J.2) displays a message to the user, but this method also outputs a newline after displaying the message. We add this method during implementation to give class Screen's clients more control over the placement of displayed messages. Line 44 invokes class ATM's private utility method AuthenticateUser (declared in lines 55–75) to attempt to authenticate the user.

Authenticating the User

We refer to the requirements document to determine the steps necessary to authenticate the user before allowing transactions to occur. Line 58 of method AuthenticateUser invokes method DisplayMessage of the ATM's screen to prompt the user to enter an account number. Line 59 invokes method GetInput of the ATM's keypad to obtain the user's input, then stores this integer in local variable accountNumber. Method AuthenticateUser next prompts the user to enter a PIN (line 62), and stores the PIN in local variable pin (line 63). Next, lines 66–67 attempt to authenticate the user by passing the accountNumber and pin entered by the user to the bankDatabase's AuthenticateUser method. Class ATM sets its userAuthenticated attribute to the bool value returned by this method—userAuthenticated becomes true if authentication succeeds (i.e., the accountNumber and pin match those of an existing Account in bankDatabase) and remains false otherwise. If userAuthenticated is true, line 71 saves the account number entered by the user (i.e., accountNumber) in the ATM attribute currentAccountNumber. The other methods of class ATM use this variable whenever an ATM session requires access to the user's account number. If userAuthenticated is false, lines 73–74 call the screen's DisplayMessage-Line method to indicate that an invalid account number and/or PIN was entered, so the user must try again. Note that we set currentAccountNumber only after authenticating the user's account number and the associated PIN—if the database cannot authenticate the user, currentAccountNumber remains 0.

After method Run attempts to authenticate the user (line 44), if userAuthenticated is still false (line 41), the while loop body (lines 41–45) executes again. If userAuthenticated is now true, the loop terminates, and control continues with line 47, which calls class ATM's private utility method PerformTransactions.

Performing Transactions

Method PerformTransactions (lines 78–111) carries out an ATM session for an authenticated user. Line 80 declares local variable Transaction, to which we assign a Balance-Inquiry, Withdrawal or Deposit object representing the ATM transaction currently being processed. Note that we use a Transaction variable here to allow us to take advantage of polymorphism. Also, note that we name this variable after the role name included in the class diagram of Fig. 4.21—currentTransaction. Line 81 declares another local variable—a bool called userExited that keeps track of whether the user has chosen to exit. This variable controls a while loop (lines 84–110) that allows the user to execute an unlimited number of transactions before choosing to exit. Within this loop, line 87 displays the main menu and obtains the user's menu selection by calling ATM utility method DisplayMainMenu (declared in lines 114–123). This method displays the main menu by invoking methods of the ATM's screen and returns a menu selection obtained from the user through the ATM's keypad. Line 87 stores the user's selection, returned by DisplayMainMenu, in local variable mainMenuSelection.

After obtaining a main menu selection, method PerformTransactions uses a switch statement (lines 90–109) to respond to the selection appropriately. If mainMenuSelection is equal to the underlying value of any of the three enum members representing transaction types (i.e., if the user chose to perform a transaction), lines 97–98 call utility method CreateTransaction (declared in lines 126–149) to return a newly instantiated object of the type that corresponds to the selected transaction. Variable currentTransaction is assigned the reference returned by method CreateTransaction, then line 99 invokes method Execute of this transaction to execute it. We discuss Transaction method Execute and the three Transaction derived classes shortly. Note that we assign to the Transaction variable currentTransaction an object of one of the three Transaction derived classes so that we can execute transactions. For example, if the user chooses to perform a balance inquiry, (MenuOption) mainMenuSelection (line 90) matches the case label MenuOption.BALANCE_INQUIRY, and CreateTransaction returns a BalanceInquiry object (lines 97–98). Thus, currentTransaction refers to a BalanceInquiry and invoking currentTransaction.Execute() (line 99) results in BalanceInquiry's version of Execute being called polymorphically.

Creating Transactions

Method CreateTransaction (lines 126–149) uses a switch statement (lines 131–146) to instantiate a new Transaction derived class object of the type indicated by the parameter type. Recall that method PerformTransactions passes mainMenuSelection to method CreateTransaction only when mainMenuSelection contains a value corresponding to one of the three transaction types. So parameter type (line 126) receives one of the values MenuOption.BALANCE_INQUIRY, MenuOption.WITHDRAWAL or MenuOption.DEPOSIT. Each case in the switch statement instantiates a new object by calling the appropriate Transaction derived class constructor. Note that each constructor has a unique parameter list, based on the specific data required to initialize the derived class object. A BalanceInquiry (lines 135–136) requires only the account number of the current user and references to the ATM's screen and the bankDatabase. In addition to these parameters, a Withdrawal (lines 139–140) requires references to the ATM's keypad and cashDispenser, and a Deposit (lines 143–144) requires references to the ATM's keypad and depositSlot. We discuss the transaction classes in detail in Sections J.9–J.12.

After executing a transaction (line 99 in method PerformTransactions), userExited remains false, and the while loop in lines 84–110 repeats, returning the user to the main menu. However, if a user does not perform a transaction and instead selects the main menu option to exit, line 103 sets userExited to true, causing the condition in line 84 of the while loop (!userExited) to become false. This while is the final statement of method PerformTransactions, so control returns to line 47 of the calling method Run. If the user enters an invalid main menu selection (i.e., not an integer in the range 1–4), lines 106–107 display an appropriate error message, userExited remains false (as set in line 81) and the user returns to the main menu to try again.

When method PerformTransactions returns control to method Run, the user has chosen to exit the system, so lines 48–49 reset the ATM's attributes userAuthenticated and currentAccountNumber to false and 0, respectively, to prepare for the next ATM user. Line 50 displays a goodbye message to the current user before the ATM welcomes the next user.

J.3 Class Screen

Class Screen (Fig. J.2) represents the screen of the ATM and encapsulates all aspects of displaying output to the user. Class Screen simulates a real ATM's screen with the computer monitor and outputs text messages using standard console output methods Console.Write and Console.WriteLine. In the design portion of this case study, we endowed class Screen with one operation—DisplayMessage. For greater flexibility in displaying messages to the Screen, we now declare three Screen methods—DisplayMessage, DisplayMessageLine and DisplayDollarAmount.

Method DisplayMessage (lines 8–11) takes a string as an argument and prints it to the screen using Console.Write. The cursor stays on the same line, making this method appropriate for displaying prompts to the user. Method DisplayMessageLine (lines 14–17) does the same using Console.WriteLine, which outputs a newline to move the cursor to the next line. Finally, method DisplayDollarAmount (lines 20–23) outputs a properly formatted dollar amount (e.g., $1,234.56). Line 22 uses method Console.Write to output a decimal value formatted as currency with a dollar sign, two decimal places and commas to increase the readability of large dollar amounts.

```csharp
1   // Screen.cs
2   // Represents the screen of the ATM
3   using System;
4
5   public class Screen
6   {
7      // displays a message without a terminating carriage return
8      public void DisplayMessage( string message )
9      {
10        Console.Write( message );
11     } // end method DisplayMessage
12
13     // display a message with a terminating carriage return
14     public void DisplayMessageLine( string message )
15     {
16        Console.WriteLine( message );
17     } // end method DisplayMessageLine
18
```

Fig. J.2 | Class Screen represents the screen of the ATM. (Part 1 of 2.)

```
19        // display a dollar amount
20        public void DisplayDollarAmount( decimal amount )
21        {
22           Console.Write( "{0:C}", amount );
23        } // end method DisplayDollarAmount
24     } // end class Screen
```

Fig. J.2 | Class Screen represents the screen of the ATM. (Part 2 of 2.)

J.4 Class Keypad

Class Keypad (Fig. J.3) represents the keypad of the ATM and is responsible for receiving all user input. Recall that we are simulating this hardware, so we use the computer's keyboard to approximate the keypad. We use method Console.ReadLine to obtain keyboard input from the user. A computer keyboard contains many keys not found on the ATM's keypad. We assume that the user presses only the keys on the computer keyboard that also appear on the keypad—the keys numbered 0–9 and the *Enter* key.

Method GetInput (lines 8–11) invokes Convert method ToInt32 to convert the input returned by Console.ReadLine (line 10) to an int value. [*Note:* Method ToInt32 can throw a FormatException if the user enters non-integer input. Because the real ATM's keypad permits only integer input, we simply assume that no exceptions will occur. See Chapter 12, Exception Handling, for information on catching and processing exceptions.] Recall that ReadLine obtains all the input used by the ATM. Class Keypad's GetInput method simply returns the integer input by the user. If a client of class Keypad requires input that satisfies some particular criteria (i.e., a number corresponding to a valid menu option), the client must perform the appropriate error checking.

J.5 Class CashDispenser

Class CashDispenser (Fig. J.4) represents the cash dispenser of the ATM. Line 6 declares constant INITIAL_COUNT, which indicates the number of $20 bills in the cash dispenser when the ATM starts (i.e., 500). Line 7 implements attribute billCount (modeled in Fig. 11.22), which keeps track of the number of bills remaining in the CashDispenser at any time. The constructor (lines 10–13) sets billCount to the initial count. [*Note:* We as-

```
 1    // Keypad.cs
 2    // Represents the keypad of the ATM.
 3    using System;
 4
 5    public class Keypad
 6    {
 7       // return an integer value entered by user
 8       public int GetInput()
 9       {
10          return Convert.ToInt32( Console.ReadLine() );
11       } // end method GetInput
12    } // end class Keypad
```

Fig. J.3 | Class Keypad represents the ATM's keypad.

sume that the process of adding more bills to the CashDispenser and updating the billCount occur outside the ATM system.] Class CashDispenser has two public methods—DispenseCash (lines 16–21) and IsSufficientCashAvailable (lines 24–31). The class trusts that a client (i.e., Withdrawal) calls method DispenseCash only after establishing that sufficient cash is available by calling method IsSufficientCashAvailable. Thus, DispenseCash simulates dispensing the requested amount of cash without checking whether sufficient cash is available.

Method IsSufficientCashAvailable (lines 24–31) has a parameter amount that specifies the amount of cash in question. Line 27 calculates the number of $20 bills required to dispense the specified amount. The ATM allows the user to choose only withdrawal amounts that are multiples of $20, so we convert amount to an integer value and divide it by 20 to obtain the number of billsRequired. Line 30 returns true if the CashDispenser's billCount is greater than or equal to billsRequired (i.e., enough bills are available) and false otherwise (i.e., not enough bills). For example, if a user wishes to withdraw $80 (i.e., billsRequired is 4), but only three bills remain (i.e., billCount is 3), the method returns false.

```csharp
1   // CashDispenser.cs
2   // Represents the cash dispenser of the ATM
3   public class CashDispenser
4   {
5      // the default initial number of bills in the cash dispenser
6      private const int INITIAL_COUNT = 500;
7      private int billCount; // number of $20 bills remaining
8
9      // parameterless constructor initializes billCount to INITIAL_COUNT
10     public CashDispenser()
11     {
12        billCount = INITIAL_COUNT; // set billCount to INITIAL_COUNT
13     } // end constructor
14
15     // simulates dispensing the specified amount of cash
16     public void DispenseCash( decimal amount )
17     {
18        // number of $20 bills required
19        int billsRequired = ( ( int ) amount ) / 20;
20        billCount -= billsRequired;
21     } // end method DispenseCash
22
23     // indicates whether cash dispenser can dispense desired amount
24     public bool IsSufficientCashAvailable( decimal amount )
25     {
26        // number of $20 bills required
27        int billsRequired = ( ( int ) amount ) / 20;
28
29        // return whether there are enough bills available
30        return ( billCount >= billsRequired );
31     } // end method IsSufficientCashAvailable
32   } // end class CashDispenser
```

Fig. J.4 | Class CashDispenser represents the ATM's cash dispenser.

Method DispenseCash (lines 16–21) simulates cash dispensing. If our system were hooked up to a real hardware cash dispenser, this method would interact with the hardware device to physically dispense the cash. Our simulated version of the method simply decreases the billCount of bills remaining by the number required to dispense the specified amount (line 20). Note that it is the responsibility of the client of the class (i.e., Withdrawal) to inform the user that cash has been dispensed—CashDispenser does not interact directly with Screen.

J.6 Class DepositSlot

Class DepositSlot (Fig. J.5) represents the deposit slot of the ATM. This class simulates the functionality of a real hardware deposit slot. DepositSlot has no attributes and only one method—IsDepositEnvelopeReceived (lines 7–10)—which indicates whether a deposit envelope was received.

Recall from the requirements document that the ATM allows the user up to two minutes to insert an envelope. The current version of method IsDepositEnvelopeReceived simply returns true immediately (line 9), because this is only a software simulation, so we assume that the user inserts an envelope within the required time frame. If an actual hardware deposit slot were connected to our system, method IsDepositEnvelopeReceived would be implemented to wait for a maximum of two minutes to receive a signal from the hardware deposit slot indicating that the user has indeed inserted a deposit envelope. If IsDepositEnvelopeReceived were to receive such a signal within two minutes, the method would return true. If two minutes were to elapse and the method still had not received a signal, then the method would return false.

J.7 Class Account

Class Account (Fig. J.6) represents a bank account. Each Account has four attributes (modeled in Fig. 11.22)—accountNumber, pin, availableBalance and totalBalance. Lines 5–8 implement these attributes as private instance variables. For each of the instance variables accountNumber, availableBalance and totalBalance, we provide a property with the same name as the attribute, but starting with a capital letter. For example, property AccountNumber corresponds to the accountNumber attribute modeled in Fig. 11.22. Clients of this class do not need to modify the accountNumber instance variable, so AccountNumber is declared as a read-only property (i.e., it provides only a get accessor).

```
1   // DepositSlot.cs
2   // Represents the deposit slot of the ATM
3   public class DepositSlot
4   {
5      // indicates whether envelope was received (always returns true,
6      // because this is only a software simulation of a real deposit slot)
7      public bool IsDepositEnvelopeReceived()
8      {
9         return true; // deposit envelope was received
10     } // end method IsDepositEnvelopeReceived
11  } // end class DepositSlot
```

Fig. J.5 | Class DepositSlot represents the ATM's deposit slot.

```csharp
1   // Account.cs
2   // Class Account represents a bank account.
3   public class Account
4   {
5      private int accountNumber; // account number
6      private int pin; // PIN for authentication
7      private decimal availableBalance; // available withdrawal amount
8      private decimal totalBalance; // funds available + pending deposit
9
10     // four-parameter constructor initializes attributes
11     public Account( int theAccountNumber, int thePIN,
12        decimal theAvailableBalance, decimal theTotalBalance )
13     {
14        accountNumber = theAccountNumber;
15        pin = thePIN;
16        availableBalance = theAvailableBalance;
17        totalBalance = theTotalBalance;
18     } // end constructor
19
20     // read-only property that gets the account number
21     public int AccountNumber
22     {
23        get
24        {
25           return accountNumber;
26        } // end get
27     } // end property AccountNumber
28
29     // read-only property that gets the available balance
30     public decimal AvailableBalance
31     {
32        get
33        {
34           return availableBalance;
35        } // end get
36     } // end property AvailableBalance
37
38     // read-only property that gets the total balance
39     public decimal TotalBalance
40     {
41        get
42        {
43           return totalBalance;
44        } // end get
45     } // end property TotalBalance
46
47     // determines whether a user-specified PIN matches PIN in Account
48     public bool ValidatePIN( int userPIN )
49     {
50        return ( userPIN == pin );
51     } // end method ValidatePIN
52
```

Fig. J.6 | Class Account represents a bank account. (Part I of 2.)

```
53        // credits the account (funds have not yet cleared)
54        public void Credit( decimal amount )
55        {
56           totalBalance += amount; // add to total balance
57        } // end method Credit
58
59        // debits the account
60        public void Debit( decimal amount )
61        {
62           availableBalance -= amount; // subtract from available balance
63           totalBalance -= amount; // subtract from total balance
64        } // end method Debit
65     } // end class Account
```

Fig. J.6 | Class Account represents a bank account. (Part 2 of 2.)

Class Account has a constructor (lines 11–18) that takes an account number, the PIN established for the account, the initial available balance and the initial total balance as arguments. Lines 14–17 assign these values to the class's attributes (i.e., instance variables). Note that Account objects would normally be created externally to the ATM system. However, in this simulation, the Account objects are created in the BankDatabase class (Fig. J.7).

public Read-Only Properties of Class Account

Read-only property AccountNumber (lines 21–27) provides access to an Account's accountNumber instance variable. We include this property in our implementation so that a client of the class (e.g., BankDatabase) can identify a particular Account. For example, BankDatabase contains many Account objects, and it can access this property on each of its Account objects to locate the one with a specific account number.

Read-only properties AvailableBalance (lines 30–36) and TotalBalance (lines 39–45) allow clients to retrieve the values of private decimal instance variables available-Balance and totalBalance, respectively. Property AvailableBalance represents the amount of funds available for withdrawal. Property TotalBalance represents the amount of funds available, plus the amount of deposited funds pending confirmation of cash in deposit envelopes or clearance of checks in deposit envelopes.

public Methods of Class Account

Method ValidatePIN (lines 48–51) determines whether a user-specified PIN (i.e., parameter userPIN) matches the PIN associated with the account (i.e., attribute pin). Recall that we modeled this method's parameter userPIN in the UML class diagram of Fig. 7.23. If the two PINs match, the method returns true; otherwise, it returns false.

Method Credit (lines 54–57) adds an amount of money (i.e., parameter amount) to an Account as part of a deposit transaction. Note that this method adds the amount only to instance variable totalBalance (line 56). The money credited to an account during a deposit does not become available immediately, so we modify only the total balance. We assume that the bank updates the available balance appropriately at a later time, when the amount of cash in the deposit envelope has be verified and the checks in the deposit envelope have cleared. Our implementation of class Account includes only methods required for carrying out ATM transactions. Therefore, we omit the methods that some other bank system would invoke to add to instance variable availableBalance to confirm a deposit or to subtract from attribute totalBalance to reject a deposit.

Method Debit (lines 60–64) subtracts an amount of money (i.e., parameter amount) from an Account as part of a withdrawal transaction. This method subtracts the amount from both instance variable availableBalance (line 62) and instance variable totalBalance (line 63), because a withdrawal affects both balances.

J.8 Class BankDatabase

Class BankDatabase (Fig. J.7) models the bank database with which the ATM interacts to access and modify a user's account information. We determine one reference-type attribute for class BankDatabase based on its composition relationship with class Account. Recall from Fig. 11.21 that a BankDatabase is composed of zero or more objects of class Account. Line 5 declares attribute accounts—an array that will store Account objects—to implement this composition relationship. Class BankDatabase has a parameterless constructor (lines 8–15) that initializes accounts with new Account objects (lines 13–14). Note that the Account constructor (Fig. J.6, lines 11–18) has four parameters—the account number, the PIN assigned to the account, the initial available balance and the initial total balance.

```
1   // BankDatabase.cs
2   // Represents the bank account information database
3   public class BankDatabase
4   {
5      private Account[] accounts; // array of the bank's Accounts
6
7      // parameterless constructor initializes accounts
8      public BankDatabase()
9      {
10        // create two Account objects for testing and
11        // place them in the accounts array
12        accounts = new Account[ 2 ]; // create accounts array
13        accounts[ 0 ] = new Account( 12345, 54321, 1000.00M, 1200.00M );
14        accounts[ 1 ] = new Account( 98765, 56789, 200.00M, 200.00M );
15     } // end constructor
16
17     // retrieve Account object containing specified account number
18     private Account GetAccount( int accountNumber )
19     {
20        // loop through accounts searching for matching account number
21        foreach ( Account currentAccount in accounts )
22        {
23           if ( currentAccount.AccountNumber == accountNumber )
24              return currentAccount;
25        } // end foreach
26
27        // account not found
28        return null;
29     } // end method GetAccount
```

Fig. J.7 | Class BankDatabase represents the bank's account information database. (Part 1 of 2.)

```
30
31        // determine whether user-specified account number and PIN match
32        // those of an account in the database
33        public bool AuthenticateUser( int userAccountNumber, int userPIN)
34        {
35           // attempt to retrieve the account with the account number
36           Account userAccount = GetAccount( userAccountNumber );
37
38           // if account exists, return result of Account function ValidatePIN
39           if ( userAccount != null )
40              return userAccount.ValidatePIN( userPIN ); // true if match
41           else
42              return false; // account number not found, so return false
43        } // end method AuthenticateUser
44
45        // return available balance of Account with specified account number
46        public decimal GetAvailableBalance( int userAccountNumber )
47        {
48           Account userAccount = GetAccount( userAccountNumber );
49           return userAccount.AvailableBalance;
50        } // end method GetAvailableBalance
51
52        // return total balance of Account with specified account number
53        public decimal GetTotalBalance( int userAccountNumber )
54        {
55           Account userAccount = GetAccount(userAccountNumber);
56           return userAccount.TotalBalance;
57        } // end method GetTotalBalance
58
59        // credit the Account with specified account number
60        public void Credit( int userAccountNumber, decimal amount )
61        {
62           Account userAccount = GetAccount( userAccountNumber );
63           userAccount.Credit( amount );
64        } // end method Credit
65
66        // debit the Account with specified account number
67        public void Debit( int userAccountNumber, decimal amount )
68        {
69           Account userAccount = GetAccount( userAccountNumber );
70           userAccount.Debit( amount );
71        } // end method Debit
72     } // end class BankDatabase
```

Fig. J.7 | Class BankDatabase represents the bank's account information database. (Part 2 of 2.)

Recall that class BankDatabase serves as an intermediary between class ATM and the actual Account objects that contain users' account information. Thus, methods of class BankDatabase invoke the corresponding methods and properties of the Account object belonging to the current ATM user.

private Utility Method GetAccount
We include private utility method GetAccount (lines 18–29) to allow the BankDatabase to obtain a reference to a particular Account within the accounts array. To locate the us-

er's Account, the BankDatabase compares the value returned by property AccountNumber for each element of accounts to a specified account number until it finds a match. Lines 21–25 traverse the accounts array. If currentAccount's account number equals the value of parameter accountNumber, the method returns currentAccount. If no account has the given account number, then line 28 returns null.

public *Methods*

Method AuthenticateUser (lines 33–43) proves or disproves the identity of an ATM user. This method takes a user-specified account number and a user-specified PIN as arguments and indicates whether they match the account number and PIN of an Account in the database. Line 36 calls method GetAccount, which returns either an Account with userAccountNumber as its account number or null to indicate that userAccountNumber is invalid. If GetAccount returns an Account object, line 40 returns the bool value returned by that object's ValidatePIN method. Note that BankDatabase's AuthenticateUser method does not perform the PIN comparison itself—rather, it forwards userPIN to the Account object's ValidatePIN method to do so. The value returned by Account method ValidatePIN (line 40) indicates whether the user-specified PIN matches the PIN of the user's Account, so method AuthenticateUser simply returns this value (line 40) to the client of the class (i.e., ATM).

The BankDatabase trusts the ATM to invoke method AuthenticateUser and receive a return value of true before allowing the user to perform transactions. BankDatabase also trusts that each Transaction object created by the ATM contains the valid account number of the current authenticated user and that this account number is passed to the remaining BankDatabase methods as argument userAccountNumber. Methods GetAvailableBalance (lines 46–50), GetTotalBalance (lines 53–57), Credit (lines 60–64) and Debit (lines 67–71) therefore simply retrieve the user's Account object with utility method GetAccount, then invoke the appropriate Account method on that object. We know that the calls to GetAccount within these methods will never return null, because userAccountNumber must refer to an existing Account. Note that GetAvailableBalance and GetTotalBalance return the values returned by the corresponding Account properties. Also, note that methods Credit and Debit simply redirect parameter amount to the Account methods they invoke.

J.9 Class Transaction

Class Transaction (Fig. J.8) is an abstract base class that represents the notion of an ATM transaction. It contains the common features of derived classes BalanceInquiry, Withdrawal and Deposit. This class expands on the "skeleton" code first developed in Section 11.9. Line 3 declares this class to be abstract. Lines 5–7 declare the class's private instance variables. Recall from the class diagram of Fig. 11.22 that class Transaction contains the property AccountNumber that indicates the account involved in the Transaction. Line 5 implements the instance variable accountNumber to maintain the AccountNumber property's data. We derive attributes screen (implemented as instance variable userScreen in line 6) and bankDatabase (implemented as instance variable database in line 7) from class Transaction's associations, modeled in Fig. 11.21. All transactions require access to the ATM's screen and the bank's database.

```
 1   // Transaction.cs
 2   // Abstract base class Transaction represents an ATM transaction.
 3   public abstract class Transaction
 4   {
 5      private int accountNumber; // account involved in the transaction
 6      private Screen userScreen; // reference to ATM's screen
 7      private BankDatabase database; // reference to account info database
 8
 9      // three-parameter constructor invoked by derived classes
10      public Transaction( int userAccount, Screen theScreen,
11         BankDatabase theDatabase )
12      {
13         accountNumber = userAccount;
14         userScreen = theScreen;
15         database = theDatabase;
16      } // end constructor
17
18      // read-only property that gets the account number
19      public int AccountNumber
20      {
21         get
22         {
23            return accountNumber;
24         } // end get
25      } // end property AccountNumber
26
27      // read-only property that gets the screen reference
28      public Screen UserScreen
29      {
30         get
31         {
32            return userScreen;
33         } // end get
34      } // end property UserScreen
35
36      // read-only property that gets the bank database reference
37      public BankDatabase Database
38      {
39         get
40         {
41            return database;
42         } // end get
43      } // end property Database
44
45      // perform the transaction (overridden by each derived class)
46      public abstract void Execute(); // no implementation here
47   } // end class Transaction
```

Fig. J.8 | abstract base class Transaction represents an ATM transaction.

Class Transaction has a constructor (lines 10–16) that takes the current user's account number and references to the ATM's screen and the bank's database as arguments. Because Transaction is an abstract class (line 3), this constructor is never called directly to instantiate Transaction objects. Instead, this constructor is invoked by the constructors of the Transaction derived classes via constructor initializers.

Class Transaction has three public read-only properties—AccountNumber (lines 19–25), UserScreen (lines 28–34) and Database (lines 37–43). Derived classes of Transaction inherit these properties and use them to gain access to class Transaction's private instance variables. Note that we chose the names of the UserScreen and Database properties for clarity—we wanted to avoid property names that are the same as the class names Screen and BankDatabase, which can be confusing.

Class Transaction also declares abstract method Execute (line 46). It does not make sense to provide an implementation for this method in class Transaction, because a generic transaction cannot be executed. Thus, we declare this method to be abstract, forcing each Transaction concrete derived class to provide its own implementation that executes the particular type of transaction.

J.10 Class BalanceInquiry

Class BalanceInquiry (Fig. J.9) inherits from Transaction and represents an ATM balance inquiry transaction (line 3). BalanceInquiry does not have any attributes of its own, but it inherits Transaction attributes accountNumber, screen and bankDatabase, which are accessible through Transaction's public read-only properties. The BalanceInquiry constructor (lines 6–8) takes arguments corresponding to these attributes and forwards them to Transaction's constructor by invoking the constructor initializer with keyword base (line 8). The body of the constructor is empty.

```csharp
1   // BalanceInquiry.cs
2   // Represents a balance inquiry ATM transaction
3   public class BalanceInquiry : Transaction
4   {
5      // five-parameter constructor initializes base class variables
6      public BalanceInquiry( int userAccountNumber,
7         Screen atmScreen, BankDatabase atmBankDatabase )
8         : base( userAccountNumber, atmScreen, atmBankDatabase ) {}
9
10     // performs transaction; overrides Transaction's abstract method
11     public override void Execute()
12     {
13        // get the available balance for the current user's Account
14        decimal availableBalance =
15           Database.GetAvailableBalance( AccountNumber );
16
17        // get the total balance for the current user's Account
18        decimal totalBalance = Database.GetTotalBalance( AccountNumber );
19
20        // display the balance information on the screen
21        UserScreen.DisplayMessageLine( "\nBalance Information:" );
22        UserScreen.DisplayMessage( " - Available balance: " );
23        UserScreen.DisplayDollarAmount( availableBalance );
24        UserScreen.DisplayMessage( "\n - Total balance: " );
```

Fig. J.9 | Class BalanceInquiry represents a balance inquiry ATM transaction. (Part 1 of 2.)

```
25          UserScreen.DisplayDollarAmount( totalBalance );
26          UserScreen.DisplayMessageLine( "" );
27       } // end method Execute
28    } // end class BalanceInquiry
```

Fig. J.9 | Class `BalanceInquiry` represents a balance inquiry ATM transaction. (Part 2 of 2.)

Class `BalanceInquiry` overrides `Transaction`'s abstract method `Execute` to provide a concrete implementation (lines 11–27) that performs the steps involved in a balance inquiry. Lines 14–15 obtain the specified `Account`'s available balance by invoking the `GetAvailableBalance` method of the inherited property `Database`. Note that line 15 uses the inherited property `AccountNumber` to get the account number of the current user. Line 18 retrieves the specified `Account`'s total balance. Lines 21–26 display the balance information on the ATM's screen using the inherited property `UserScreen`. Recall that `DisplayDollarAmount` takes a `decimal` argument and outputs it to the screen formatted as a dollar amount with a dollar sign. For example, if a user's available balance is `1000.50M`, line 23 outputs `$1,000.50`. Note that line 26 inserts a blank line of output to separate the balance information from subsequent output (i.e., the main menu repeated by class `ATM` after executing the `BalanceInquiry`).

J.11 Class `Withdrawal`

Class `Withdrawal` (Fig. J.10) extends `Transaction` and represents an ATM withdrawal transaction. This class expands on the "skeleton" code for this class developed in Fig. 11.24. Recall from the class diagram of Fig. 11.22 that class `Withdrawal` has one attribute, `amount`, which line 5 declares as a `decimal` instance variable. Fig. 11.21 models associations between class `Withdrawal` and classes `Keypad` and `CashDispenser`, for which lines 6–7 implement reference attributes `keypad` and `cashDispenser`, respectively. Line 10 declares a constant corresponding to the cancel menu option.

Class `Withdrawal`'s constructor (lines 13–21) has five parameters. It uses the constructor initializer to pass parameters `userAccountNumber`, `atmScreen` and `atmBankDatabase` to base class `Transaction`'s constructor to set the attributes that `Withdrawal` inherits from `Transaction`. The constructor also takes references `atmKeypad` and `atmCashDispenser` as parameters and assigns them to reference-type attributes `keypad` and `cashDispenser`, respectively.

```
 1   // Withdrawal.cs
 2   // Class Withdrawal represents an ATM withdrawal transaction.
 3   public class Withdrawal : Transaction
 4   {
 5      private decimal amount; // amount to withdraw
 6      private Keypad keypad; // reference to Keypad
 7      private CashDispenser cashDispenser; // reference to cash dispenser
 8
 9      // constant that corresponds to menu option to cancel
10      private const int CANCELED = 6;
```

Fig. J.10 | Class `Withdrawal` represents an ATM withdrawal transaction. (Part 1 of 4.)

```
11
12      // five-parameter constructor
13      public Withdrawal( int userAccountNumber, Screen atmScreen,
14         BankDatabase atmBankDatabase, Keypad atmKeypad,
15         CashDispenser atmCashDispenser )
16         : base( userAccountNumber, atmScreen, atmBankDatabase )
17      {
18         // initialize references to keypad and cash dispenser
19         keypad = atmKeypad;
20         cashDispenser = atmCashDispenser;
21      } // end constructor
22
23      // perform transaction, overrides Transaction's abstract method
24      public override void Execute()
25      {
26         bool cashDispensed = false; // cash was not dispensed yet
27
28         // transaction was not canceled yet
29         bool transactionCanceled = false;
30
31         // loop until cash is dispensed or the user cancels
32         do
33         {
34            // obtain the chosen withdrawal amount from the user
35            int selection = DisplayMenuOfAmounts();
36
37            // check whether user chose a withdrawal amount or canceled
38            if ( selection != CANCELED )
39            {
40               // set amount to the selected dollar amount
41               amount = selection;
42
43               // get available balance of account involved
44               decimal availableBalance =
45                  Database.GetAvailableBalance( AccountNumber );
46
47               // check whether the user has enough money in the account
48               if ( amount <= availableBalance )
49               {
50                  // check whether the cash dispenser has enough money
51                  if ( cashDispenser.IsSufficientCashAvailable( amount ) )
52                  {
53                     // debit the account to reflect the withdrawal
54                     Database.Debit( AccountNumber, amount );
55
56                     cashDispenser.DispenseCash( amount ); // dispense cash
57                     cashDispensed = true; // cash was dispensed
58
59                     // instruct user to take cash
60                     UserScreen.DisplayMessageLine(
61                        "\nPlease take your cash from the cash dispenser." );
62                  } // end innermost if
```

Fig. J.10 | Class `Withdrawal` represents an ATM withdrawal transaction. (Part 2 of 4.)

```
63              else // cash dispenser does not have enough cash
64                  UserScreen.DisplayMessageLine(
65                      "\nInsufficient cash available in the ATM." +
66                      "\n\nPlease choose a smaller amount." );
67          } // end middle if
68          else // not enough money available in user's account
69              UserScreen.DisplayMessageLine(
70                  "\nInsufficient cash available in your account." +
71                  "\n\nPlease choose a smaller amount." );
72      } // end outermost if
73      else
74      {
75          UserScreen.DisplayMessageLine( "\nCanceling transaction..." );
76          transactionCanceled = true; // user canceled the transaction
77      } // end else
78    } while ( ( !cashDispensed ) && ( !transactionCanceled ) );
79  } // end method Execute
80
81  // display a menu of withdrawal amounts and the option to cancel;
82  // return the chosen amount or 6 if the user chooses to cancel
83  private int DisplayMenuOfAmounts()
84  {
85      int userChoice = 0; // variable to store return value
86
87      // array of amounts to correspond to menu numbers
88      int[] amounts = { 0, 20, 40, 60, 100, 200 };
89
90      // loop while no valid choice has been made
91      while ( userChoice == 0 )
92      {
93          // display the menu
94          UserScreen.DisplayMessageLine( "\nWithdrawal options:" );
95          UserScreen.DisplayMessageLine( "1 - $20" );
96          UserScreen.DisplayMessageLine( "2 - $40" );
97          UserScreen.DisplayMessageLine( "3 - $60" );
98          UserScreen.DisplayMessageLine( "4 - $100" );
99          UserScreen.DisplayMessageLine( "5 - $200" );
100         UserScreen.DisplayMessageLine( "6 - Cancel transaction" );
101         UserScreen.DisplayMessage(
102             "\nChoose a withdrawal option (1-6): " );
103
104         // get user input through keypad
105         int input = keypad.GetInput();
106
107         // determine how to proceed based on the input value
108         switch ( input )
109         {
110             // if the user chose a withdrawal amount (i.e., option
111             // 1, 2, 3, 4, or 5), return the corresponding amount
112             // from the amounts array
113             case 1: case 2: case 3: case 4: case 5:
114                 userChoice = amounts[ input ]; // save user's choice
115                 break;
```

Fig. J.10 | Class Withdrawal represents an ATM withdrawal transaction. (Part 3 of 4.)

```
116                    case CANCELED: // the user chose to cancel
117                        userChoice = CANCELED; // save user's choice
118                        break;
119                    default:
120                        UserScreen.DisplayMessageLine(
121                            "\nInvalid selection. Try again." );
122                        break;
123                } // end switch
124            } // end while
125
126            return userChoice;
127        } // end method DisplayMenuOfAmounts
128    } // end class Withdrawal
```

Fig. J.10 | Class Withdrawal represents an ATM withdrawal transaction. (Part 4 of 4.)

Overriding abstract Method Execute

Class Withdrawal overrides Transaction's abstract method Execute with a concrete implementation (lines 24–79) that performs the steps involved in a withdrawal. Line 26 declares and initializes a local bool variable cashDispensed. This variable indicates whether cash has been dispensed (i.e., whether the transaction has completed successfully) and is initially false. Line 29 declares and initializes to false a bool variable transactionCanceled to indicate that the transaction has not yet been canceled by the user.

Lines 32–78 contain a do...while statement that executes its body until cash is dispensed (i.e., until cashDispensed becomes true) or until the user chooses to cancel (i.e., until transactionCanceled becomes true). We use this loop to continuously return the user to the start of the transaction if an error occurs (i.e., the requested withdrawal amount is greater than the user's available balance or greater than the amount of cash in the cash dispenser). Line 35 displays a menu of withdrawal amounts and obtains a user selection by calling private utility method DisplayMenuOfAmounts (declared in lines 83–127). This method displays the menu of amounts and returns either an int withdrawal amount or an int constant CANCELED to indicate that the user has chosen to cancel the transaction.

Displaying Options With private Utility Method DisplayMenuOfAmounts

Method DisplayMenuOfAmounts (lines 83–127) first declares local variable userChoice (initially 0) to store the value that the method will return (line 85). Line 88 declares an integer array of withdrawal amounts that correspond to the amounts displayed in the withdrawal menu. We ignore the first element in the array (index 0), because the menu has no option 0. The while statement at lines 91–124 repeats until userChoice takes on a value other than 0. We will see shortly that this occurs when the user makes a valid selection from the menu. Lines 94–102 display the withdrawal menu on the screen and prompt the user to enter a choice. Line 105 obtains integer input through the keypad. The switch statement at lines 108–123 determines how to proceed based on the user's input. If the user selects 1, 2, 3, 4 or 5, line 114 sets userChoice to the value of the element in the amounts array at index input. For example, if the user enters 3 to withdraw $60, line 114 sets userChoice to the value of amounts[3]—i.e., 60. Variable userChoice no longer equals 0, so the while at lines 91–124 terminates, and line 126 returns userChoice. If the user selects the cancel menu option, line 117 executes, setting userChoice to CANCELED and causing the method to return this value. If the user does not enter a valid menu selection, lines 120–121 display an error message, and the user is returned to the withdrawal menu.

The `if` statement at line 38 in method `Execute` determines whether the user has selected a withdrawal amount or chosen to cancel. If the user cancels, line 75 displays an appropriate message to the user before control is returned to the calling method—ATM method `PerformTransactions`. If the user has chosen a withdrawal amount, line 41 assigns local variable `selection` to instance variable `amount`. Lines 44–45 retrieve the available balance of the current user's `Account` and store it in a local `decimal` variable `availableBalance`. Next, the `if` statement at line 48 determines whether the selected amount is less than or equal to the user's available balance. If it is not, lines 69–71 display an error message. Control then continues to the end of the do...while statement, and the loop repeats because both `cashDispensed` and `transactionCanceled` are still `false`. If the user's balance is high enough, the `if` statement at line 51 determines whether the cash dispenser has enough money to satisfy the withdrawal request by invoking the `cashDispenser`'s `IsSufficientCashAvailable` method. If this method returns `false`, lines 64–66 display an error message, and the do...while statement repeats. If sufficient cash is available, the requirements for the withdrawal are satisfied, and line 54 debits the user's account in the database by `amount`. Lines 56–57 then instruct the cash dispenser to dispense the cash to the user and set `cashDispensed` to `true`. Finally, lines 60–61 display a message to the user to take the dispensed cash. Because `cashDispensed` is now `true`, control continues after the do...while statement. No additional statements appear below the loop, so the method returns control to class ATM.

J.12 Class `Deposit`

Class `Deposit` (Fig. J.11) inherits from `Transaction` and represents an ATM deposit transaction. Recall from the class diagram of Fig. 11.22 that class `Deposit` has one attribute, amount, which line 5 declares as a `decimal` instance variable. Lines 6–7 create reference attributes `keypad` and `depositSlot` that implement the associations between class `Deposit` and classes `Keypad` and `DepositSlot`, modeled in Fig. 11.21. Line 10 declares a constant `CANCELED` that corresponds to the value a user enters to cancel a deposit transaction.

Class `Deposit` contains a constructor (lines 13–21) that passes three parameters to base class `Transaction`'s constructor using a constructor initializer. The constructor also has parameters `atmKeypad` and `atmDepositSlot`, which it assigns to the corresponding reference instance variables (lines 19–20).

```
1   // Deposit.cs
2   // Represents a deposit ATM transaction.
3   public class Deposit : Transaction
4   {
5      private decimal amount; // amount to deposit
6      private Keypad keypad; // reference to the Keypad
7      private DepositSlot depositSlot; // reference to the deposit slot
8
```

Fig. J.11 | Class `Deposit` represents an ATM deposit transaction. (Part 1 of 3.)

```
 9      // constant representing cancel option
10      private const int CANCELED = 0;
11
12      // five-parameter constructor initializes class's instance variables
13      public Deposit( int userAccountNumber, Screen atmScreen,
14        BankDatabase atmBankDatabase, Keypad atmKeypad,
15        DepositSlot atmDepositSlot )
16        : base( userAccountNumber, atmScreen, atmBankDatabase )
17      {
18        // initialize references to keypad and deposit slot
19        keypad = atmKeypad;
20        depositSlot = atmDepositSlot;
21      } // end five-parameter constructor
22
23      // perform transaction; overrides Transaction's abstract method
24      public override void Execute()
25      {
26        amount = PromptForDepositAmount(); // get deposit amount from user
27
28        // check whether user entered a deposit amount or canceled
29        if ( amount != CANCELED )
30        {
31          // request deposit envelope containing specified amount
32          UserScreen.DisplayMessage(
33            "\nPlease insert a deposit envelope containing " );
34          UserScreen.DisplayDollarAmount( amount );
35          UserScreen.DisplayMessageLine( " in the deposit slot." );
36
37          // retrieve deposit envelope
38          bool envelopeReceived = depositSlot.IsDepositEnvelopeReceived();
39
40          // check whether deposit envelope was received
41          if ( envelopeReceived )
42          {
43            UserScreen.DisplayMessageLine(
44              "\nYour envelope has been received.\n" +
45              "The money just deposited will not be available " +
46              "until we \nverify the amount of any " +
47              "enclosed cash, and any enclosed checks clear." );
48
49            // credit account to reflect the deposit
50            Database.Credit( AccountNumber, amount );
51          } // end inner if
52          else
53            UserScreen.DisplayMessageLine(
54              "\nYou did not insert an envelope, so the ATM has " +
55              "canceled your transaction." );
56        } // end outer if
57        else
58          UserScreen.DisplayMessageLine( "\nCanceling transaction..." );
59      } // end method Execute
60
```

Fig. J.11 | Class Deposit represents an ATM deposit transaction. (Part 2 of 3.)

```
61         // prompt user to enter a deposit amount to credit
62         private decimal PromptForDepositAmount()
63         {
64            // display the prompt and receive input
65            UserScreen.DisplayMessage(
66               "\nPlease input a deposit amount in CENTS (or 0 to cancel): " );
67            int input = keypad.GetInput();
68
69            // check whether the user canceled or entered a valid amount
70            if ( input == CANCELED )
71               return CANCELED;
72            else
73               return input / 100.00M;
74         } // end method PromptForDepositAmount
75      } // end class Deposit
```

Fig. J.11 | Class Deposit represents an ATM deposit transaction. (Part 3 of 3.)

Overriding abstract Method Execute

Method Execute (lines 24–59) overrides abstract method Execute in base class Transaction with a concrete implementation that performs the steps required in a deposit transaction. Line 26 prompts the user to enter a deposit amount by invoking private utility method PromptForDepositAmount (declared in lines 62–74) and sets attribute amount to the value returned. Method PromptForDepositAmount asks the user to enter a deposit amount as an integer number of cents (because the ATM's keypad does not contain a decimal point; this is consistent with many real ATMs) and returns the decimal value representing the dollar amount to be deposited.

Getting Deposit Amount with private Utility Method PromptForDepositAmount

Lines 65–66 in method PromptForDepositAmount display a message asking the user to input a deposit amount as a number of cents or "0" to cancel the transaction. Line 67 receives the user's input from the keypad. The if statement at lines 70–73 determines whether the user has entered a deposit amount or chosen to cancel. If the user chooses to cancel, line 71 returns constant CANCELED. Otherwise, line 73 returns the deposit amount after converting the int number of cents to a dollar-and-cents amount by dividing by the decimal literal 100.00M. For example, if the user enters 125 as the number of cents, line 73 returns 125 divided by 100.00M, or 1.25—125 cents is $1.25.

The if statement at lines 29–58 in method Execute determines whether the user has chosen to cancel the transaction instead of entering a deposit amount. If the user cancels, line 58 displays an appropriate message, and the method returns. If the user enters a deposit amount, lines 32–35 instruct the user to insert a deposit envelope with the correct amount. Recall that Screen method DisplayDollarAmount outputs a decimal value formatted as a dollar amount (including the dollar sign).

Line 38 sets a local bool variable to the value returned by depositSlot's IsDepositEnvelopeReceived method, indicating whether a deposit envelope has been received. Recall that we coded method IsDepositEnvelopeReceived (lines 7–10 of Fig. J.5) to always return true, because we are simulating the functionality of the deposit slot and assume that the user always inserts an envelope in a timely fashion (i.e., within the two-minute time limit). However, we code method Execute of class Deposit to test for the possibility that the user does not insert an envelope—good software engineering demands that programs account for all possible return values. Thus, class Deposit is prepared for future versions of IsDepositEnvelopeReceived that could return false. Lines 43–50 execute if the deposit slot receives an envelope. Lines 43–47 display an appropriate message to the user. Line 50 credits the user's account in the database with the deposit amount. Lines 53–55 execute if the deposit slot does not receive a deposit envelope. In this case, we display a message stating that the ATM has canceled the transaction. The method then returns without crediting the user's account.

J.13 Class ATMCaseStudy

Class ATMCaseStudy (Fig. J.12) simply allows us to start, or "turn on," the ATM and test the implementation of our ATM system model. Class ATMCaseStudy's Main method (lines 6–10) simply instantiates a new ATM object named theATM (line 8) and invokes its Run method (line 9) to start the ATM.

J.14 Wrap-Up

Now that we have presented the complete ATM implementation, you can see that many issues arose during implementation for which we did not provide detailed UML diagrams. This is not uncommon in an object-oriented design and implementation experience. For example, many attributes listed in the class diagrams were implemented as C# properties so that clients of the classes could gain controlled access to the underlying private instance variables. We did not make all of these properties during our design process, because there was nothing in the requirements document or our design process to indicate that certain attributes would eventually need to be accessed outside of their classes.

We also encountered various issues with simulating hardware. A real-world ATM is a hardware device that does not have a complete computer keyboard. One problem with using a computer keyboard to simulate the keypad is that the user can enter non-digits as input. We did not spend much time dealing with such issues, because this problem is not possible in a real ATM, which has only a numeric keypad. However, having to think about issues like this is a good thing. Quite typically, software designs for complete systems involve simulating hardware devices like the cash dispenser and keypad. Despite the fact that some aspects of our ATM may seem contrived, in real-world systems, hardware design

```
 1   // ATMCaseStudy.cs
 2   // Application for testing the ATM case study.
 3   public class ATMCaseStudy
 4   {
 5      // Main method is the application's entry point
 6      public static void Main( string[] args )
 7      {
 8         ATM theATM = new ATM();
 9         theATM.Run();
10      } // end method Main
11   } // end class ATMCaseStudy
```

Fig. J.12 | Class ATMCaseStudy starts the ATM.

and implementation often occurs in parallel with software design and implementation. In such cases, the software cannot be implemented in final form because the hardware is not yet ready. So, software developers must simulate the hardware, as we have done in this case study.

Congratulations on completing the entire software engineering ATM case study! We hope you found this experience to be valuable and that it reinforced many of the concepts that you learned in Chapters 1–11. We would sincerely appreciate your comments, criticisms and suggestions. You can reach us at `deitel@deitel.com`. We will respond promptly.

UML 2: Additional Diagram Types

K.1 Introduction

If you read the optional Software Engineering Case Study sections in Chapters 3–9 and 11, you should now have a comfortable grasp of the UML diagram types that we use to model our ATM system. The case study is intended for use in first- or second-semester courses, so we limit our discussion to a concise subset of the UML. The UML 2 provides a total of 13 diagram types. The end of Section 3.10 summarizes the six diagram types that we use in the case study. This appendix lists and briefly defines the seven remaining diagram types.

K.2 Additional Diagram Types

The following are the seven diagram types that we have chosen not to use in our Software Engineering Case Study.

- *Object diagrams* model a "snapshot" of the system by modeling a system's objects and their relationships at a specific point in time. Each object represents an instance of a class from a class diagram, and several objects may be created from one class. For our ATM system, an object diagram could show several distinct Account objects side by side, illustrating that they are all part of the bank's account database.

- *Component diagrams* model the *artifacts* and *components*—resources (which include source files)—that make up the system.

- *Deployment diagrams* model the rsystem's runtime requirements (such as the computer or computers on which the system will reside), memory requirements, or other devices the system requires during execution.

- *Package diagrams* model the hierarchical structure of *packages* (which are groups of classes) in the system at compile time and the relationships that exist between the packages.

- *Composite structure diagrams* model the internal structure of a complex object at runtime. New in UML 2, they allow system designers to hierarchically decompose a complex object into smaller parts. Composite structure diagrams are beyond the scope of our case study. They are more appropriate for larger industrial applications, which exhibit complex groupings of objects at execution time.

- *Interaction overview diagrams*, new in UML 2, provide a summary of control flow in the system by combining elements of several types of behavioral diagrams (e.g., activity diagrams, sequence diagrams).

- *Timing diagrams*, also new in UML 2, model the timing constraints imposed on stage changes and interactions between objects in a system.

To learn more about these diagrams and advanced UML topics, please visit www.uml.org and the Web resources listed at the ends of Section 1.17 and Section 3.10.

L

Simple Types

Type	Size in bits	Value range	Standard
bool	8	true or false	
byte	8	0 to 255, inclusive	
sbyte	8	−128 to 127, inclusive	
char	16	'\u0000' to '\uFFFF' (0 to 65535), inclusive	Unicode
short	16	−32768 to 32767, inclusive	
ushort	16	0 to 65535, inclusive	
int	32	−2,147,483,648 to 2,147,483,647, inclusive	
uint	32	0 to 4,294,967,295, inclusive	
float	32	*Approximate negative range:* −3.4028234663852886E+38 to −1.40129846432481707E−45 *Approximate positive range:* 1.40129846432481707E−45 to 3.4028234663852886E+38 *Other supported values:* positive and negative zero positive and negative infinity not-a-number (NaN)	IEEE 754 IEC 60559
long	64	−9,223,372,036,854,775,808 to 9,223,372,036,854,775,807, inclusive	
ulong	64	0 to 18,446,744,073,709,551,615, inclusive	

Fig. L.1 | Simple types. (Part 1 of 2.)

Type	Size in bits	Value range	Standard
double	64	*Approximate negative range:* −1.7976931348623157E+308 to −4.94065645841246544E−324 *Approximate positive range:* 4.94065645841246544E−324 to 1.7976931348623157E+308 *Other supported values:* positive and negative zero positive and negative infinity not-a-number (NaN)	IEEE 754 IEC 60559
decimal	128	*Negative range:* −79,228,162,514,264,337,593,543,950,335 (−7.9E+28) to −1.0E−28 *Positive range:* 1.0E−28 to 79,228,162,514,264,337,593,543,950,335 (7.9E+28)	

Fig. L.1 | Simple types. (Part 2 of 2.)

Additional Simple Type Information

- This appendix is based on information from Sections 4.1.4–4.1.8 of Microsoft's version of the *C# Language Specification* and Sections 11.1.4–11.1.8 of the ECMA-334 (the ECMA version of the *C# Language Specification*). These documents are available from the following Web sites:

  msdn.microsoft.com/vcsharp/programming/language/
  www.ecma-international.org/publications/standards/Ecma-334.htm

- Values of type float have seven digits of precision.

- Values of type double have 15–16 digits of precision.

- Values of type decimal are represented as integer values that are scaled by a power of 10. Values between −1.0 and 1.0 are represented exactly to 28 digits.

- For more information on IEEE 754 visit grouper.ieee.org/groups/754/. For more information on Unicode, see Appendix E, Unicode®.

Index

[*Note:* Page references for defining occurrences of terms appear in **_bold italic._*]

The DEITEL® Suite of Products...

Visual Basic® 2005 How to Program Third Edition

©2006, 1500 pp., paper
(0-13-186900-0)

The complete authoritative DEITEL® LIVE-CODE introduction to Visual Basic programming. *Visual Basic® 2005 How to Program, Third Edition* is up-to-date with Microsoft's Visual Basic 2005. The text includes comprehensive coverage of the fundamentals of object-oriented programming in Visual Basic including a new early classes and objects approach and a new optional automated teller machine (ATM) case study that teaches the fundamentals of software engineering and object-oriented design with the UML 2.0 in Chapters 1, 3–9 and 11. Additional integrated case studies appear throughout the text, including the **Time** class (Chapter 9), the **Employee** class (Chapters 10 and 11) and the **Gradebook** class (Chapters 4–9). This book also includes discussions of more advanced topics such as XML, ASP.NET, ADO.NET and Web services. New Visual Basic 2005 topics covered include partial classes, generics, the **My** namespace and Visual Studio's updated debugger features.

Visual C#® 2005 How to Program Second Edition

©2006, 1400 pp., paper
(0-13-152523-9)

The complete authoritative DEITEL® LIVE-CODE introduction to C# programming. *Visual C#® 2005 How to Program, Second Edition* is up-to-date with Microsoft's Visual C# 2005. The text includes comprehensive coverage of the fundamentals of object-oriented programming in C#, including a new early classes and objects approach and a new optional automated teller machine (ATM) case study that teaches the fundamentals of software engineering and object-oriented design with the UML 2.0 in Chapters 1, 3–9 and 11. Additional integrated case studies appear throughout the text, including the **Time** class (Chapter 9), the **Employee** class (Chapters 10 and 11) and the **Gradebook** class (Chapters 4–9). This book also includes discussions of more advanced topics such as XML, ASP.NET, ADO.NET and Web services. New Visual C# 2005 topics covered include partial classes, generics, the **My** namespace, .NET remoting and Visual Studio's updated debugger features.

Visual C++ .NET® How To Program

©2004, 1400 pp., paper
(0-13-437377-4)

Written by the authors of the world's best-selling introductory/intermediate C and C++ textbooks, this comprehensive book thoroughly examines Visual C++® .NET. *Visual C++® .NET How to Program* begins with a strong foundation in the introductory and intermediate programming principles students will need in industry, including fundamental topics such as arrays, functions and control statements. Readers learn the concepts of object-oriented programming, then the text explores such essential topics as networking, databases, XML and multimedia. Graphical user interfaces are also extensively covered, giving students the tools to build compelling and fully interactive programs using the "drag-and-drop" techniques provided by Visual Studio .NET 2003.

C How to Program Fourth Edition

©2004, 1255 pp., paper
(0-13-142644-3)

C How to Program, Fourth Edition—the world's best-selling C text—is designed for introductory through intermediate courses as well as programming languages survey courses. This comprehensive text is aimed at readers with little or no programming experience through intermediate audiences. Highly practical in approach, it introduces fundamental notions of structured programming and software engineering and gets up to speed quickly.

A Student Solutions Manual is also available is for use with this text. Use ISBN 0-13-145245-2 to order the Student Solutions manual.

Advanced Java™ 2 Platform How to Program

BOOK / CD-ROM

*©2002, 1811 pp., paper
(0-13-089560-1)*

Expanding on the world's best-selling Java textbook—*Java™ How to Program*—*Advanced Java™ 2 Platform How To Program* presents advanced Java topics for developing sophisticated, user-friendly GUIs; significant, scalable enterprise applications; wireless applications and distributed systems. Primarily based on Java 2 Enterprise Edition (J2EE), this textbook integrates technologies such as XML, JavaBeans, security, JDBC™, JavaServer Pages (JSP™), servlets, Remote Method Invocation (RMI), Enterprise JavaBeans™ (EJB), design patterns, Swing, J2ME™, Java 2D and 3D, XML, design patterns, CORBA, Jini™, JavaSpaces™, Jiro™, Java Management Extensions (JMX) and Peer-to-Peer networking with an introduction to JXTA.

Internet & World Wide Web How to Program Third Edition

BOOK / CD-ROM

*©2004, 1250 pp., paper
(0-13-145091-3)*

This book introduces students with little or no programming experience to the exciting world of Web-based applications. This text provides in-depth coverage of introductory programming principles, various markup languages (XHTML, Dynamic HTML and XML), several scripting languages (JavaScript, JScript .NET, ColdFusion, Flash ActionScript, Perl, PHP, VBScript and Python), Web servers (IIS and Apache) and relational databases (MySQL)—all the skills and tools needed to create dynamic Web-based applications. The text contains a comprehensive introduction to ASP .NET and the Microsoft .NET Framework. A case study illustrating how to build an online message board using ASP .NET and XML is also included. New in this edition are chapters on Macromedia ColdFusion, Macromedia Dreamweaver and a much enhanced treatment of Flash, including a case study on building a video game in Flash. After mastering the material in this book, students will be well prepared to build real-world, industrial-strength, Web-based applications.

Wireless Internet & Mobile Business How to Program

*©2002, 1292 pp., paper
(0-13-062226-5)*

This book offers a thorough treatment of both the management and technical aspects of this growing area, including coverage of current practices and future trends. The first half explores the business issues surrounding wireless technology and mobile business. The book then turns to programming for the wireless Internet, exploring topics such as WAP (including 2.0), WML, WMLScript, XML, XHTML™, wireless Java programming (J2ME™) and more. Other topics covered include career resources, wireless marketing, accessibility, Palm™, PocketPC, Windows CE, i-mode, Bluetooth, MIDP, MIDlets, ASP, Microsoft .NET Mobile Framework, BREW™, multimedia, Flash™ and VBScript.

Python How to Program

BOOK / CD-ROM

*©2002, 1376 pp., paper
(0-13-092361-3)*

This exciting textbook provides a comprehensive introduction to Python—a powerful object-oriented programming language with clear syntax and the ability to bring together various technologies quickly and easily. This book covers introductory programming techniques and more advanced topics such as graphical user interfaces, databases, wireless Internet programming, networking, security, process management, multithreading, XHTML, CSS, PSP and multimedia. Readers will learn principles that are applicable to both systems development and Web programming.

XML How to Program

BOOK / CD-ROM

©2001, 934 pp., paper (0-13-028417-3)

This book is a comprehensive guide to programming in XML. It teaches how to use XML to create customized tags and includes chapters that address markup languages for science and technology, multimedia, commerce and many other fields. Concise introductions to Java, JavaServer Pages, VBScript, Active Server Pages and Perl/CGI provide readers with the essentials of these programming languages and server-side development technologies to enable them to work effectively with XML. The book also covers topics such as XSL, DOM™, SAX, a real-world e-commerce case study and a complete chapter on Web accessibility that addresses Voice XML. Other topics covered include XHTML, CSS, DTD, schema, parsers, XPath, XLink, namespaces, XBase, XInclude, XPointer, XSLT, XSL Formatting Objects, JavaServer Pages, XForms, topic maps, X3D, MathML, OpenMath, CML, BML, CDF, RDF, SVG, Cocoon, WML, XBRL and BizTalk™ and SOAP™ Web resources.

Perl How to Program

BOOK / CD-ROM

©2001, 1057 pp., paper (0-13-028418-1)

This comprehensive guide to Perl programming emphasizes the use of the Common Gateway Interface (CGI) with Perl to create powerful, dynamic multi-tier Web-based client/server applications. The book begins with a clear and careful introduction to programming concepts at a level suitable for beginners, and proceeds through advanced topics such as references and complex data structures. Key Perl topics such as regular expressions and string manipulation are covered in detail. The authors address important and topical issues such as object-oriented programming, the Perl database interface (DBI), graphics and security. Also included is a treatment of XML, a bonus chapter introducing the Python programming language, supplemental material on career resources and a complete chapter on Web accessibility.

e-Business & e-Commerce How to Program

BOOK / CD-ROM

©2001, 1254 pp., paper (0-13-028419-X)

This book explores programming technologies for developing Web-based e-business and e-commerce solutions, and covers e-business and e-commerce models and business issues. Readers learn a full range of options, from "build-your-own" to turnkey solutions. The book examines scores of the top e-businesses (examples include Amazon, eBay, Priceline, Travelocity, etc.), explaining the technical details of building successful e-business and e-commerce sites and their underlying business premises. Learn how to implement the dominant e-commerce models—shopping carts, auctions, name-your-own-price, comparison shopping and bots/intelligent agents—by using markup languages (HTML, Dynamic HTML and XML), scripting languages (JavaScript, VBScript and Perl), server-side technologies (Active Server Pages and Perl/CGI) and database (SQL and ADO), security and online payment technologies.

ORDER INFORMATION

For ordering information,
visit us on the Web at www.prenhall.com.

INTERNATIONAL ORDERING INFORMATION

CANADA:
Pearson Education Canada
26 Prince Andrew Place
PO Box 580
Don Mills, Ontario M3C 2T8 Canada
Tel.: 416-925-2249; Fax: 416-925-0068
e-mail: phcinfo.pubcanada@pearsoned.com

EUROPE, MIDDLE EAST, AND AFRICA:
Pearson Education
Edinburgh Gate
Harlow, Essex CM20 2JE UK
Tel: 01279 623928; Fax: 01279 414130
e-mail: enq.orders@pearsoned-ema.com

BENELUX REGION:
Pearson Education
Concertgebouwplein 25
1071 LM Amsterdam
The Netherlands
Tel: 31 20 5755 800; Fax: 31 20 664 5334
e-mail: amsterdam@pearsoned-ema.com

ASIA:
Pearson Education Asia Pte. Ltd.
23/25 First Lok Yang Road
Jurong, 629733 Singapore
Tel: 65 476 4688; Fax: 65 378 0370

JAPAN:
Pearson Education Japan
Ogikubo TM Bldg. 6F. 5-26-13 Ogikubo
Suginami-ku, Tokyo 167-0051 Japan
Tel: 81 3 3365 9001; Fax: 81 3 3365 9009

INDIA:
Pearson Education
Indian Branch
482 FIE, Patparganj
Delhi – 110092 India
Tel: 91 11 2059850 & 2059851
Fax: 91 11 2059852

AUSTRALIA:
Pearson Education Australia
Unit 4, Level 2, 14 Aquatic Drive
Frenchs Forest, NSW 2086, Australia
Tel: 61 2 9454 2200; Fax: 61 2 9453 0089
e-mail: marketing@pearsoned.com.au

NEW ZEALAND/FIJI:
Pearson Education
46 Hillside Road
Auckland 10, New Zealand
Tel: 649 444 4968; Fax: 649 444 4957
E-mail: sales@pearsoned.co.nz

SOUTH AFRICA:
Maskew Miller Longman
Central Park   Block H
16th Street   Midrand   1685
South Africa
Tel: 27 21 686 6356; Fax: 27 21 686 4590

LATIN AMERICA:
Pearson Education Latin America
Attn: Tina Sheldon
1 Lake Street
Upper Saddle River, NJ 07458

The SIMPLY SERIES!

The Deitels' *Simply Series* takes an engaging new approach to teaching programming languages from the ground up. The pedagogy of this series combines the DEITEL® signature *LIVE-CODE Approach* with an *APPLICATION-DRIVEN Tutorial Approach* to teach programming with outstanding pedagogical features that help students learn. We have merged the notion of a lab manual with that of a conventional textbook, creating a book in which readers build and execute complete applications from start to finish, while learning the fundamental concepts of programming!

Simply C++
An APPLICATION-DRIVEN Tutorial Approach

©2005, 800 pp., paper (0-13-142660-5)

Simply C++ An APPLICATION-DRIVEN Tutorial Approach guides readers through building real-world applications that incorporate C++ programming fundamentals. Learn methods, functions, data types, control statements, procedures, arrays, object-oriented programming, strings and characters, pointers, references, templates, operator overloading and more in this comprehensive introduction to C++.

Simply Java™ Programming
An APPLICATION-DRIVEN Tutorial Approach

©2004, 950 pp., paper (0-13-142648-6)

Simply Java™ Programming An APPLICATION-DRIVEN Tutorial Approach guides readers through building real-world applications that incorporate Java programming fundamentals. Learn GUI design, components, methods, event-handling, types, control statements, arrays, object-oriented programming, exception-handling, strings and characters, sequential files and more in this comprehensive introduction to Java. We also include higher-end topics such as database programming, multimedia, graphics and Web applications development.

Simply C#
An APPLICATION-DRIVEN Tutorial Approach

©2004, 850 pp., paper (0-13-142641-9)

Simply C# An APPLICATION-DRIVEN Tutorial Approach guides readers through building real-world applications that incorporate C# programming fundamentals. Learn GUI design, controls, methods, functions, data types, control statements, procedures, arrays, object-oriented programming, strings and characters, sequential files and more in this comprehensive introduction to C#. We also include higher-end topics such as database programming, multimedia and graphics and Web applications development.

Simply Visual Basic® .NET
An APPLICATION-DRIVEN Tutorial Approach

Visual Studio .NET 2002 Version:
©2003, 830 pp., paper (0-13-140553-5)

Visual Studio .NET 2003 Version:
©2004, 960 pp., paper (0-13-142640-0)

Simply Visual Basic® .NET An APPLICATION-DRIVEN Tutorial Approach guides readers through building real-world applications that incorporate Visual Basic .NET programming fundamentals. Learn GUI design, controls, methods, functions, data types, control statements, procedures, arrays, object-oriented programming, strings and characters, sequential files and more in this comprehensive introduction to Visual Basic .NET. We also include higher-end topics such as database programming, multimedia and graphics and Web applications development. If you're using Visual Studio® .NET 2002, choose *Simply Visual Basic .NET*; or, if you're using Visual Studio .NET 2003, you can use *Simply Visual Basic .NET 2003*, which includes updated screen captures and line numbers consistent with Visual Studio .NET 2003.

THE BUZZ ABOUT THE DEITEL® SUITE OF PRODUCTS!

Deitel & Associates garners worldwide praise for its best-selling *How to Program Series* of books and its signature *LIVE-CODE Approach*. See for yourself what our readers have to say:

"The examples and case studies are well thought out and keep the readers involved. As soon as I had a question about a topic it was answered in the next two paragraphs. You are writing from the reader's point of view and I'm sure that readers will appreciate that a lot."

— Amit Kalani, TechContent Corporation (pre-publication review)

"The book is comprehensive, correct and crystal clear. No other textbook comes close in carefully explaining the intricacies of this powerful language."

— James Huddleston, Independent Contractor

"This book is one of the best of its kind. It is an excellent 'objects first' coverage of C++ that remains accessible to beginners. The example-driven presentation is enriched by the optional OOD/UML ATM cases study that contextualizes the material in an ongoing software engineering project."

— Gavin Osborne, Saskatchewan Institute of Applied Science and Technology

"I am continually impressed with the Deitels' ability to clearly explain concepts and ideas, which allows the student to gain a well-rounded understanding of the language and software development."

— Karen Arlien, Bismarck State College

"Great early introduction to classes and objects. The combination of live-code examples and detailed figures provides a unique visualization of C++ concepts."

— Earl LaBatt, University of New Hampshire

"Probably the most complete coverage of learning through examples in published material today. This material is such high quality—it is unbelievable. The ATM is super."

— Anne Horton, AT&T Bell Laboratories

"Java How to Program, 6/e is an excellent book to learn how to program in Java. The book does an excellent job describing the new features included in the JDK 5.0, including generics and formatted output. The book is easy to read with numerous, simple-to-follow code examples."

— Doug Kohlert, Sun Microsystems

"An excellent combination of C#, UML and pseudocode that leads the reader to create good applications and well designed algorithms, using the best practices! Few books mix all of this so well. Great idea and great work!"

— Jose Antonio Seco, Adalucia's Parlament, Spain

"The writing style is comprehensive, systematic and clear. Nothing is either skipped or glossed over. Of particular note is the authors' attention to good software engineering concepts, and the wide selection of code examples provides excellent reinforcement for the practical application of developing Java skills."

— Dean Mellas, Computer and information Sciences, Cerritos College

"Good job! Introduces OOP without burying the reader in complexity. I think the level of conceptual detail is perfect. This will be a great help the next time I teach 101."

— Walt Bunch, Chapman University

"I think it is an excellent book for an introduction to the programming language C. The examples are well thought out ...concepts that are covered are explained concisely and ...in a manner that will allow a novice programmer to learn the concepts, both through the text and examples."

— John Benito, Convener of the ISO working group responsible for the C programming language

"The fundamental concepts are covered thoroughly, and the step-by-step tutorials are practical and well designed. This book provides an excellent springboard for the novice in preparation for the more advanced topics in Object-Oriented Programming."

— Gordon McNorton, Collin County Community College

wonderful learning experience! I have seen lots of programming books (Basic, C, C++) s, yours is number one on my list. Wow... it rk with. Thanks."

Thomas J. McGrail, Longs, SC

MULTIMEDIA CYBER CLASSROOMS

Premium content available FREE with *Java™* and *Small Java™ How to Program, Sixth Edition* and *C++* and *Small C++ How to Program, Fifth Edition!*

Java and *Small Java How to Program, 6/e* and *C++* and *Small C++ How to Program, 5/e* are now available with a **FREE** Web-based *Multimedia Cyber Classroom* for students who purchase new copies of these books! The *Cyber Classroom* is an interactive, multimedia, tutorial version of DEITEL textbooks. *Cyber Classrooms* are a great value, giving students additional hands-on experience and study aids.

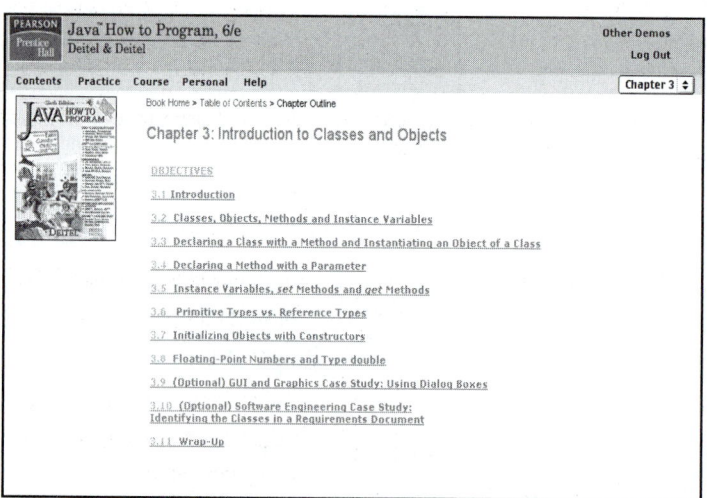

DEITEL® Multimedia Cyber Classrooms *feature an e-book with the complete text of their corresponding* How to Program *titles.*

Unique audio "walkthroughs" of code examples reinforce key concepts.

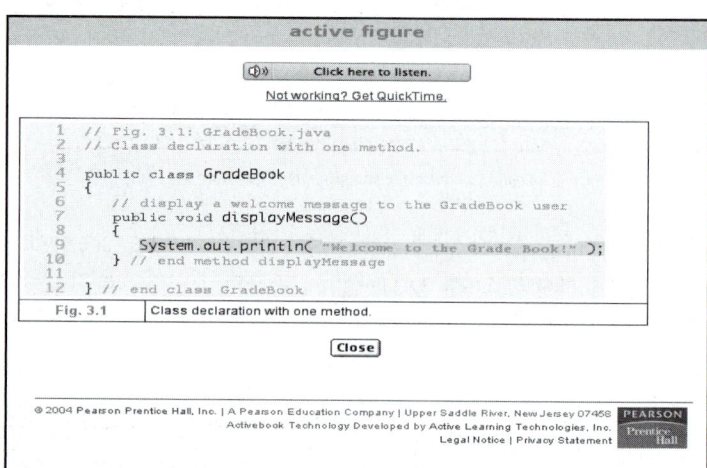

DEITEL® *Multimedia Cyber Classrooms* include:

- The full text, illustrations and program listings of its corresponding *How to Program* book.

- Hours of detailed, expert audio descriptions of hundreds of lines of code that help to reinforce important concepts.

- An abundance of self-assessment material, including practice exams, hundreds of programming exercises and self-review questions and answers.

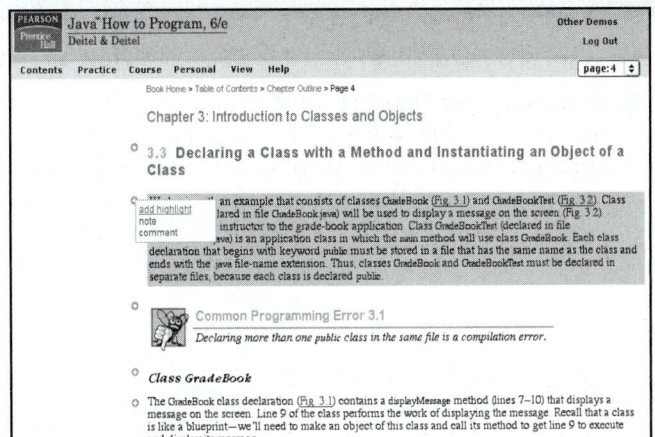

DEITEL® Multimedia Cyber Classrooms *offer a host of interactive features, such as highlighting of key sections of the text...*

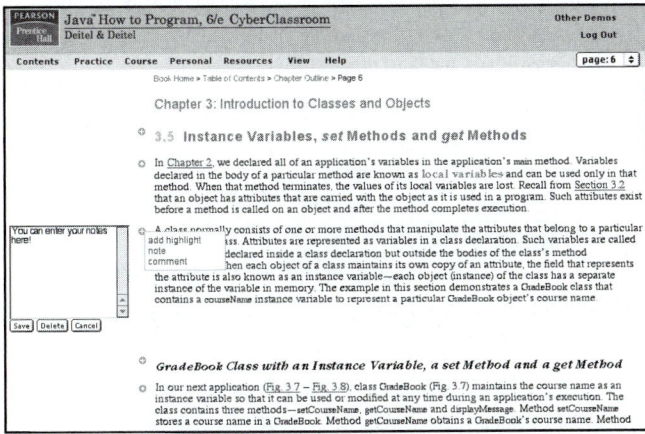

- Intuitive browser-based interface designed to be easy and accessible.

- A Lab Manual featuring lab exercises as well as pre- and post-lab activities.

- Student Solutions to approximately one-half of the exercises in the textbook.

...and the ability to write notes in the margin of a given page for future reference.

Students receive access to a protected Web site via access code cards packaged, for FREE, automatically with the purchase of a new textbook. (Simply tear the strip on the inside of the *Cyber Classroom* package to reveal access code.)

To redeem your access code or for more information, please visit:
www·prenhall·com/deitel/
cyberclassroom

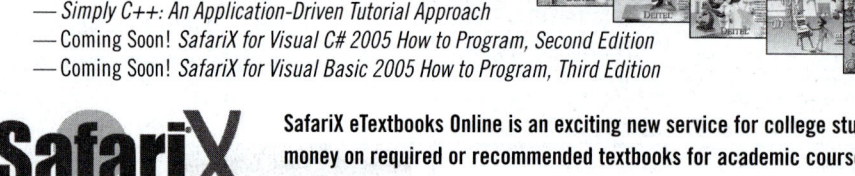

Deitel & Associates, Inc. provides intensive, lecture-and-laboratory courses to organizations worldwide. The programming courses use our signature *Live-Code Approach*, presenting complete working programs.

Deitel & Associates, Inc. has trained over one million students and professionals worldwide through Dive Into Series™ corporate training courses, public seminars, university teaching, *How to Program Series* textbooks, *Deitel® Developer Series* books, *Simply Series* textbooks, *Cyber Classroom Series* multimedia packages, *Complete Training Course Series* textbook and multimedia packages, broadcast-satellite courses and Web-based training.

Educational Consulting

Deitel & Associates, Inc. offers complete educational consulting services for corporate training programs and professional schools including:

- Curriculum design and development
- Preparation of Instructor Guides
- Customized courses and course materials
- Design and implementation of professional training certificate programs
- Instructor certification
- Train-the-trainers programs
- Delivery of software-related corporate training programs

Visit our Web site for more information on our Dive Into™ Series corporate training curriculum and to purchase our training products.

www.deitel.com/training

Would you like to review upcoming publications?

If you are a professor or senior industry professional interested in being a reviewer of our forthcoming publications, please contact us by email at **deitel@deitel.com**. Insert "Content Reviewer" in the subject heading.

Are you interested in a career in computer education, publishing and training?

We offer a limited number of full-time positions available for college graduates in computer science, information systems, information technology, management information systems and marketing. Please check our Web site for the latest job postings or contact us by email at **deitel@deitel.com**. Insert "Full-time Job" in the subject heading.

Are you a Boston-area college student looking for an internship?

We have a limited number of competitive summer positions and 20-hr./week school-year opportunities for computer science, IT/IS, MIS and marketing majors. Students work at our worldwide headquarters west of Boston. We also offer full-time internships for students taking a semester off from school. This is an excellent opportunity for students looking to gain industry experience and earn money to pay for school. Please contact us by email at **deitel@deitel.com**. Insert "Internship" in the subject heading.

Would you like to explore contract training opportunities with us?

Deitel & Associates, Inc. is looking for contract instructors to teach software-related topics at our clients' sites in the United States and worldwide. Applicants should be experienced professional trainers or college professors. For more information, please visit **www.deitel.com** and send your resume to Abbey Deitel at **abbey.deitel@deitel.com**.

Are you a training company in need of quality course materials?

Corporate training companies worldwide use our *How to Program Series* textbooks, *Complete Training Course Series* book and multimedia packages, *Simply Series* textbooks and our *Deitel® Developer Series* books in their classes. We have extensive ancillary instructor materials for many of our products. For more details, please visit **www.deitel.com** or contact us by email at **deitel@deitel.com**.

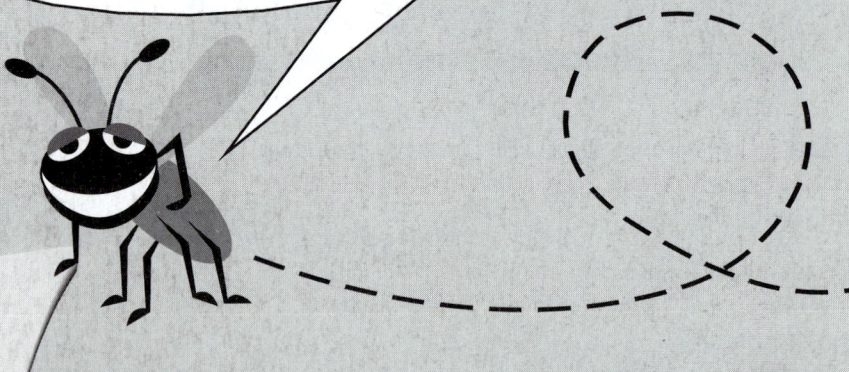